ENCYCLOPEDIA OF RELIGION

SECOND EDITION

ENCYCLOPEDIA OF RELIGION

11

SECOND EDITION

PIUS IX
•
RIVERS

LINDSAY JONES
EDITOR IN CHIEF

MACMILLAN REFERENCE USA
An imprint of Thomson Gale, a part of The Thomson Corporation

THOMSON
GALE

Detroit • New York • San Francisco • San Diego • New Haven, Conn. • Waterville, Maine • London • Munich

THOMSON
GALE

Encyclopedia of Religion, Second Edition

Lindsay Jones, Editor in Chief

For more information, contact
Macmillan Reference USA
An imprint of Thomson Gale
27500 Drake Rd.
Farmington, Hills, MI 48331-3535
Or you can visit our Internet site at
http://www.gale.com

LIBRARY OF CONGRESS CATALOGING-IN-PUBLICATION DATA

Encyclopedia of religion / Lindsay Jones, editor in chief.— 2nd ed.
p. cm.
Includes bibliographical references and index.
ISBN 0-02-865733-0 (SET HARDCOVER : ALK. PAPER) —
ISBN 0-02-865734-9 (V. 1) — ISBN 0-02-865735-7 (v. 2) —
ISBN 0-02-865736-5 (v. 3) — ISBN 0-02-865737-3 (v. 4) —
ISBN 0-02-865738-1 (v. 5) — ISBN 0-02-865739-X (v. 6) —
ISBN 0-02-865740-3 (v. 7) — ISBN 0-02-865741-1 (v. 8) —
ISBN 0-02-865742-X (v. 9) — ISBN 0-02-865743-8 (v. 10)
— ISBN 0-02-865980-5 (v. 11) — ISBN 0-02-865981-3 (v.
12) — ISBN 0-02-865982-1 (v. 13) — ISBN 0-02-865983-X
(v. 14) — ISBN 0-02-865984-8 (v. 15)
1. RELIGION—ENCYCLOPEDIAS. I. JONES, LINDSAY,
1954-

BL31.E46 2005
200'.3—dc22 2004017052

This title is also available as an e-book.
ISBN 0-02-865997-X
Contact your Thomson Gale representative for ordering information.

Printed in the United States of America
10 9 8 7 6 5 4 3 2 1

EDITORS AND CONSULTANTS

EDITOR IN CHIEF

LINDSAY JONES
Associate Professor, Department of Comparative Studies, Ohio State University

BOARD MEMBERS

DAVÍD CARRASCO
Neil Rudenstine Professor of Study of Latin America, Divinity School and Department of Anthropology, Harvard University

GIOVANNI CASADIO
Professor of History of Religions, Dipartimento di Scienze dell'Antichità, Università degli Studi di Salerno

WENDY DONIGER
Mircea Eliade Distinguished Service Professor of the History of Religions, University of Chicago

GARY L. EBERSOLE
Professor of History and Religious Studies, and Director, UMKC Center for Religious Studies, University of Missouri—Kansas City

JANET GYATSO
Hershey Professor of Buddhist Studies, The Divinity School, Harvard University

CHARLES HALLISEY
Associate Professor, Department of Languages and Cultures of Asia and Program in Religious Studies, University of Wisconsin—Madison

CHARLES H. LONG
Professor of History of Religions, Emeritus, and Former Director of Research Center for Black Studies, University of California, Santa Barbara

MARY N. MACDONALD
Professor, History of Religions, Le Moyne College (Syracuse, New York)

DALE B. MARTIN
Professor of Religious Studies, and Chair, Department of Religious Studies, Yale University

AZIM NANJI
Professor and Director, The Institute of Ismaili Studies, London

JACOB OLUPONA
Professor, African American and African Studies Program, University of California, Davis

MICHAEL SWARTZ
Professor of Hebrew and Religious Studies, Ohio State University

INÉS TALAMANTEZ
Associate Professor, Religious Studies Department, University of California, Santa Barbara

CONSULTANTS

GREGORY D. ALLES
Associate Professor of Religious Studies, McDaniel College
Study of Religion

SIGMA ANKRAVA
Professor, Department of Literary and Cultural Studies, Faculty of Modern Languages, University of Latvia
Baltic Religion and Slavic Religion

DIANE APOSTOLOS-CAPPADONA
Center for Muslim–Christian Understanding and Liberal Studies Program, Georgetown University
Art and Religion

DIANE BELL
Professor of Anthropology and Women's Studies, George Washington University
Australian Indigenous Religions

KEES W. BOLLE
Professor Emeritus of History, University of California, Los Angeles, and Fellow, Netherlands Institute for Advanced Studies in the Humanities and Social Sciences
History of Religions

MARK CSIKSZENTMIHALYI
Associate Professor in the Department of East Asian Languages and Literature and the Program in Religious Studies, University of Wisconsin—Madison
Chinese Religions

RICHARD A. GARDNER
Faculty of Comparative Culture, Sophia University
Humor and Religion

JOHN A. GRIM
Professor of Religion, Bucknell University and Co-Coordinator,

Harvard Forum on Religion and Ecology
Ecology and Religion

JOSEPH HARRIS
Francis Lee Higginson Professor of English Literature and Professor of Folklore, Harvard University
Germanic Religions

URSULA KING
Professor Emerita, Senior Research Fellow and Associate Member of the Institute for Advanced Studies, University of Bristol, England, and Professorial Research Associate, Centre for Gender and Religions Research, School of Oriental and African Studies, University of London
Gender and Religion

DAVID MORGAN
Duesenberg Professor of Christianity and the Arts, and Professor of Humanities and Art History, Valparaiso University
Color Inserts and Essays

JOSEPH F. NAGY
Professor, Department of English, University of California, Los Angeles
Celtic Religion

MATTHEW OJO
Obafemi Awolowo University
African Religions

JUHA PENTIKÄINEN
Professor of Comparative Religion, The University of Helsinki, Member of Academia Scientiarum Fennica, Finland
Arctic Religions and Uralic Religions

TED PETERS
Professor of Systematic Theology, Pacific Lutheran Theological Seminary and the Center for Theology and the Natural Sciences at the Graduate Theological Union, Berkeley, California
Science and Religion

FRANK E. REYNOLDS
Professor of the History of Religions and Buddhist Studies in the Divinity School and the Department of South Asian Languages and Civilizations, Emeritus, University of Chicago
History of Religions

GONZALO RUBIO
Assistant Professor, Department of Classics and Ancient Mediterranean Studies and Department of History and Religious Studies, Pennsylvania State University
Ancient Near Eastern Religions

SUSAN SERED
Director of Research, Religion, Health and Healing Initiative, Center for the Study of World Religions, Harvard University, and Senior Research Associate, Center for Women's Health and Human Rights, Suffolk University
Healing, Medicine, and Religion

LAWRENCE E. SULLIVAN
Professor, Department of Theology, University of Notre Dame
History of Religions

WINNIFRED FALLERS SULLIVAN
Dean of Students and Senior Lecturer in the Anthropology and Sociology of Religion, University of Chicago
Law and Religion

TOD SWANSON
Associate Professor of Religious Studies, and Director, Center for Latin American Studies, Arizona State University
South American Religions

MARY EVELYN TUCKER
Professor of Religion, Bucknell University, Founder and Coordinator, Harvard Forum on Religion and Ecology, Research Fellow, Harvard Yenching Institute, Research Associate, Harvard Reischauer Institute of Japanese Studies
Ecology and Religion

HUGH URBAN
Associate Professor, Department of Comparative Studies, Ohio State University
Politics and Religion

CATHERINE WESSINGER
Professor of the History of Religions and Women's Studies, Loyola University New Orleans
New Religious Movements

ROBERT A. YELLE
Mellon Postdoctoral Fellow, University of Toronto
Law and Religion

ERIC ZIOLKOWSKI
Charles A. Dana Professor of Religious Studies, Lafayette College
Literature and Religion

ABBREVIATIONS AND SYMBOLS USED IN THIS WORK

abbr. abbreviated; abbreviation
abr. abridged; abridgment
AD *anno Domini,* in the year of the (our) Lord
Afrik. Afrikaans
AH *anno Hegirae,* in the year of the Hijrah
Akk. Akkadian
Ala. Alabama
Alb. Albanian
Am. *Amos*
AM *ante meridiem,* before noon
amend. amended; amendment
annot. annotated; annotation
Ap. *Apocalypse*
Apn. *Apocryphon*
app. appendix
Arab. Arabic
ʿArakh. *ʿArakhin*
Aram. Aramaic
Ariz. Arizona
Ark. Arkansas
Arm. Armenian
art. article (pl., arts.)
AS Anglo-Saxon
Asm. Mos. *Assumption of Moses*
Assyr. Assyrian
A.S.S.R. Autonomous Soviet Socialist Republic
Av. Avestan
ʿA.Z. *ʿAvodah zarah*
b. born
Bab. Babylonian
Ban. Bantu
1 Bar. *1 Baruch*
2 Bar. *2 Baruch*
3 Bar. *3 Baruch*
4 Bar. *4 Baruch*
B.B. *Bavaʾ batraʾ*
BBC British Broadcasting Corporation
BC before Christ
BCE before the common era
B.D. Bachelor of Divinity
Beits. *Beitsah*
Bekh. *Bekhorot*
Beng. Bengali
Ber. *Berakhot*
Berb. Berber
Bik. *Bikkurim*
bk. book (pl., bks.)
B.M. *Bavaʾ metsiʿaʾ*
BP before the present
B.Q. *Bavaʾ qammaʾ*
Brāh. *Brāhmaṇa*
Bret. Breton
B.T. Babylonian Talmud
Bulg. Bulgarian
Burm. Burmese
c. *circa,* about, approximately
Calif. California
Can. Canaanite
Catal. Catalan
CE of the common era
Celt. Celtic
cf. *confer,* compare
Chald. Chaldean
chap. chapter (pl., chaps.)
Chin. Chinese
C.H.M. Community of the Holy Myrrhbearers
1 Chr. *1 Chronicles*
2 Chr. *2 Chronicles*
Ch. Slav. Church Slavic
cm centimeters
col. column (pl., cols.)
Col. *Colossians*
Colo. Colorado
comp. compiler (pl., comps.)
Conn. Connecticut
cont. continued
Copt. Coptic
1 Cor. *1 Corinthians*
2 Cor. *2 Corinthians*
corr. corrected
C.S.P. Congregatio Sancti Pauli, Congregation of Saint Paul (Paulists)
d. died
D Deuteronomic (source of the Pentateuch)
Dan. Danish
D.B. Divinitatis Baccalaureus, Bachelor of Divinity
D.C. District of Columbia
D.D. Divinitatis Doctor, Doctor of Divinity
Del. Delaware
Dem. *Demaʾi*
dim. diminutive
diss. dissertation
Dn. *Daniel*
D.Phil. Doctor of Philosophy
Dt. *Deuteronomy*
Du. Dutch
E Elohist (source of the Pentateuch)
Eccl. *Ecclesiastes*
ed. editor (pl., eds.); edition; edited by

'Eduy. *'Eduyyot*
e.g. *exempli gratia,* for example
Egyp. Egyptian
1 En. *1 Enoch*
2 En. *2 Enoch*
3 En. *3 Enoch*
Eng. English
enl. enlarged
Eph. *Ephesians*
'Eruv. *'Eruvin*
1 Esd. *1 Esdras*
2 Esd. *2 Esdras*
3 Esd. *3 Esdras*
4 Esd. *4 Esdras*
esp. especially
Est. Estonian
Est. *Esther*
et al. *et alii,* and others
etc. *et cetera,* and so forth
Eth. Ethiopic
EV English version
Ex. *Exodus*
exp. expanded
Ez. *Ezekiel*
Ezr. *Ezra*
2 Ezr. *2 Ezra*
4 Ezr. *4 Ezra*
f. feminine; and following (pl., ff.)
fasc. fascicle (pl., fascs.)
fig. figure (pl., figs.)
Finn. Finnish
fl. *floruit,* flourished
Fla. Florida
Fr. French
frag. fragment
ft. feet
Ga. Georgia
Gal. *Galatians*
Gaul. Gaulish
Ger. German
Giṭ. *Giṭṭin*
Gn. *Genesis*
Gr. Greek
Ḥag. *Ḥagigah*
Ḥal. *Ḥallah*
Hau. Hausa
Hb. *Habakkuk*
Heb. Hebrew
Heb. *Hebrews*
Hg. *Haggai*
Hitt. Hittite
Hor. *Horayot*
Hos. *Hosea*
Ḥul. *Ḥullin*
Hung. Hungarian
ibid. *ibidem,* in the same place (as the one immediately preceding)
Icel. Icelandic
i.e. *id est,* that is
IE Indo-European
Ill. Illinois
Ind. Indiana
intro. introduction
Ir. Gael. Irish Gaelic
Iran. Iranian
Is. *Isaiah*
Ital. Italian
J Yahvist (source of the Pentateuch)
Jas. *James*
Jav. Javanese
Jb. *Job*
Jdt. *Judith*
Jer. *Jeremiah*
Jgs. *Judges*
Jl. *Joel*
Jn. *John*
1 Jn. *1 John*
2 Jn. *2 John*
3 Jn. *3 John*
Jon. *Jonah*
Jos. *Joshua*
Jpn. Japanese
JPS Jewish Publication Society translation (1985) of the Hebrew Bible
J.T. Jerusalem Talmud
Jub. *Jubilees*
Kans. Kansas
Kel. *Kelim*
Ker. *Keritot*
Ket. *Ketubbot*
1 Kgs. *1 Kings*
2 Kgs. *2 Kings*
Khois. Khoisan
Kil. *Kil'ayim*
km kilometers
Kor. Korean
Ky. Kentucky
l. line (pl., ll.)
La. Louisiana
Lam. *Lamentations*
Lat. Latin
Latv. Latvian
L. en Th. Licencié en Théologie, Licentiate in Theology
L. ès L. Licencié ès Lettres, Licentiate in Literature
Let. Jer. *Letter of Jeremiah*
lit. literally
Lith. Lithuanian
Lk. *Luke*
LL Late Latin
LL.D. Legum Doctor, Doctor of Laws
Lv. *Leviticus*
m meters
m. masculine
M.A. Master of Arts
Ma 'as. *Ma'aserot*
Ma 'as. Sh. *Ma' aser sheni*
Mak. *Makkot*
Makh. *Makhshirin*
Mal. *Malachi*
Mar. Marathi
Mass. Massachusetts
1 Mc. *1 Maccabees*
2 Mc. *2 Maccabees*
3 Mc. *3 Maccabees*
4 Mc. *4 Maccabees*
Md. Maryland
M.D. Medicinae Doctor, Doctor of Medicine
ME Middle English
Meg. *Megillah*
Me 'il. *Me'ilah*
Men. *Menaḥot*
MHG Middle High German
mi. miles
Mi. *Micah*
Mich. Michigan
Mid. *Middot*
Minn. Minnesota
Miq. *Miqva'ot*
MIran. Middle Iranian
Miss. Mississippi
Mk. *Mark*
Mo. Missouri
Mo'ed Q. *Mo'ed qaṭan*
Mont. Montana
MPers. Middle Persian
MS. *manuscriptum,* manuscript (pl., MSS)
Mt. *Matthew*
MT Masoretic text
n. note
Na. *Nahum*
Nah. Nahuatl
Naz. *Nazir*
N.B. *nota bene,* take careful note
N.C. North Carolina
n.d. no date
N.Dak. North Dakota
NEB New English Bible
Nebr. Nebraska

Ned. *Nedarim*
Neg. *Nega'im*
Neh. *Nehemiah*
Nev. Nevada
N.H. New Hampshire
Nid. *Niddah*
N.J. New Jersey
Nm. *Numbers*
N.Mex. New Mexico
no. number (pl., nos.)
Nor. Norwegian
n.p. no place
n.s. new series
N.Y. New York
Ob. *Obadiah*
O.Cist. Ordo Cisterciencium, Order of Cîteaux (Cistercians)
OCS Old Church Slavonic
OE Old English
O.F.M. Ordo Fratrum Minorum, Order of Friars Minor (Franciscans)
OFr. Old French
Ohal. *Ohalot*
OHG Old High German
OIr. Old Irish
OIran. Old Iranian
Okla. Oklahoma
ON Old Norse
O.P. Ordo Praedicatorum, Order of Preachers (Dominicans)
OPers. Old Persian
op. cit. *opere citato,* in the work cited
OPrus. Old Prussian
Oreg. Oregon
'Orl. *'Orlah*
O.S.B. Ordo Sancti Benedicti, Order of Saint Benedict (Benedictines)
p. page (pl., pp.)
P Priestly (source of the Pentateuch)
Pa. Pennsylvania
Pahl. Pahlavi
Par. *Parah*
para. paragraph (pl., paras.)
Pers. Persian
Pes. *Pesahim*
Ph.D. Philosophiae Doctor, Doctor of Philosophy
Phil. *Philippians*
Phlm. *Philemon*
Phoen. Phoenician
pl. plural; plate (pl., pls.)
PM *post meridiem,* after noon
Pol. Polish
pop. population
Port. Portuguese
Prv. *Proverbs*
Ps. *Psalms*
Ps. 151 *Psalm 151*
Ps. Sol. *Psalms of Solomon*
pt. part (pl., pts.)
1Pt. *1 Peter*
2 Pt. *2 Peter*
Pth. Parthian
Q hypothetical source of the synoptic Gospels
Qid. *Qiddushin*
Qin. *Qinnim*
r. reigned; ruled
Rab. *Rabbah*
rev. revised
R. ha-Sh. *Ro'sh ha-shanah*
R.I. Rhode Island
Rom. Romanian
Rom. *Romans*
R.S.C.J. Societas Sacratissimi Cordis Jesu, Religious of the Sacred Heart
RSV Revised Standard Version of the Bible
Ru. *Ruth*
Rus. Russian
Rv. *Revelation*
Rv. Ezr. *Revelation of Ezra*
San. *Sanhedrin*
S.C. South Carolina
Scot. Gael. Scottish Gaelic
S.Dak. South Dakota
sec. section (pl., secs.)
Sem. Semitic
ser. series
sg. singular
Sg. *Song of Songs*
Sg. of 3 *Prayer of Azariah and the Song of the Three Young Men*
Shab. *Shabbat*
Shav. *Shavu'ot*
Sheq. *Sheqalim*
Sib. Or. *Sibylline Oracles*
Sind. Sindhi
Sinh. Sinhala
Sir. *Ben Sira*
S.J. Societas Jesu, Society of Jesus (Jesuits)
Skt. Sanskrit
1 Sm. *1 Samuel*
2 Sm. *2 Samuel*
Sogd. Sogdian
Soṭ. *Soṭah*
sp. species (pl., spp.)
Span. Spanish
sq. square
S.S.R. Soviet Socialist Republic
st. stanza (pl., ss.)
S.T.M. Sacrae Theologiae Magister, Master of Sacred Theology
Suk. *Sukkah*
Sum. Sumerian
supp. supplement; supplementary
Sus. *Susanna*
s.v. *sub verbo,* under the word (pl., s.v.v.)
Swed. Swedish
Syr. Syriac
Syr. Men. *Syriac Menander*
Ta' an. *Ta'anit*
Tam. Tamil
Tam. *Tamid*
Tb. *Tobit*
T.D. *Taishō shinshū daizōkyō,* edited by Takakusu Junjirō et al. (Tokyo,1922–1934)
Tem. *Temurah*
Tenn. Tennessee
Ter. Terumot
Ṭev. Y. *Ṭevul yom*
Tex. Texas
Th.D. Theologicae Doctor, Doctor of Theology
1 Thes. *1 Thessalonians*
2 Thes. *2 Thessalonians*
Thrac. Thracian
Ti. *Titus*
Tib. Tibetan
1 Tm. *1 Timothy*
2 Tm. *2 Timothy*
T. of 12 *Testaments of the Twelve Patriarchs*
Ṭoh. *ṭohorot*
Tong. Tongan
trans. translator, translators; translated by; translation
Turk. Turkish
Ukr. Ukrainian
Upan. *Upaniṣad*
U.S. United States
U.S.S.R. Union of Soviet Socialist Republics
Uqts. *Uqtsin*
v. verse (pl., vv.)
Va. Virginia
var. variant; variation
Viet. Vietnamese

viz. *videlicet,* namely
vol. volume (pl., vols.)
Vt. Vermont
Wash. Washington
Wel. Welsh
Wis. Wisconsin
Wis. *Wisdom of Solomon*
W.Va. West Virginia
Wyo. Wyoming

Yad. *Yadayim*
Yev. *Yevamot*
Yi. Yiddish
Yor. Yoruba
Zav. *Zavim*
Zec. *Zechariah*
Zep. *Zephaniah*
Zev. *Zevaḥim*

* hypothetical
? uncertain; possibly; perhaps
° degrees
+ plus
– minus
= equals; is equivalent to
× by; multiplied by
→ yields

P

CONTINUED

PIUS IX (Giovanni Maria Mastai-Ferretti, 1792–1878), pope of the Roman Catholic Church (1846–1878). Born on May 13 into a family belonging to the gentry of the Papal States, the future pope had his priestly formation delayed by an epilepsy-like illness. This left him with an excessively impulsive temperament for the rest of his life.

Mastai was ordained at Rome on April 10, 1815, and in an age when most young priests aimed at a successful career in the church, he stood out because of his piety and complete detachment from ecclesiastical honors. Serving as an assistant to the papal delegate to Chile (1823–1825) gave him an opportunity to see not only the difficulties that liberal governments with regalist tendencies could cause the church but also the new dimensions that missionary problems were acquiring. As bishop of Spoleto (1827), then of Imola (1832), in a region largely won over to the liberal and nationalist ideals of the Risorgimento, he won esteem not only for his pastoral zeal and sympathy for Italian patriotic aspirations, but also for his desire to improve the outmoded and repressive regime of the Papal States.

At the death of Gregory XVI, Mastai, a cardinal since 1840, became the preferred candidate of those conservatives who thought it necessary to make some concession to aspirations for a modernization of the administration of the pontifical state. He was elected pope on the second day of the conclave, June 16, 1846.

The first months of Pius IX's pontificate seemed to confirm the reputation of "liberal" that reactionary circles in Rome had pinned on this enlightened conservative. Disillusionment soon set in: first, in the area of internal reforms, because the new pope had no intention of transforming the Papal States into a modern constitutional state, and, second, when he refused to intervene in the war of independence against Austria because he thought such a step would be incompatible with his religious mission as common father of all the faithful. Economic difficulties and the pope's lack of political experience finally precipitated a crisis. The Roman uprisings of 1848–1849, crushed with the help of a French expeditionary force, left Pius IX more convinced than ever that there was an inher-

---

Clockwise from top left corner. Fifteenth-century woodcut depicting the burning of the Jews. *[©Bettmann/Corbis]*; Sixth-century BCE Laconian cup depicting Atlas and the punishment of Prometheus. Museo Gregoriano Etrusco, Vatican Museums. *[©Scala/Art Resource, N.Y.]*; The pyramids of Giza, Egypt: Menkaure (foreground), Khafre, and Khufu. *[©Yann Arthus-Bertrand/Corbis]*; The Temple of Poseidon in Sounion, Greece. *[©Jan Butchofsky-Houser/Corbis]*; Nineteenth-century carving of the Polynesian god Rongo, from the Gambier Islands. Museo Missionario Etnologico, Vatican Museums. *[©Scala/Art Resource, N.Y.]* .

ent connection between the principles of the French Revolution (1789) and the destruction of traditional social, moral, and religious values.

The reactionary restoration that followed upon the pope's return to Rome after his flight to Gaeta was to play into the hands of Cavour (Camillo Benso), who exploited the discontent of the middle classes and was able in 1860 to annex the greatest part of the Papal States. In 1870, the Italian army took advantage of the Franco-Prussian War to occupy Rome and its environs. Pius IX, who saw himself less as a dethroned ruler than as the owner of a property for which he was responsible to the entire Catholic world, felt he could not accept the unification of Italy and attempted, with little success, to organize Italian Catholic resistance.

Politically inexpert, Pius IX was advised mostly by men who judged affairs with the intransigence of theoreticians lacking any contact with the contemporary mind. He never understood that in the modern world the problem of the Holy See's spiritual independence could no longer be resolved by the anachronistic preservation of a papal political sovereignty. Thereafter, obsessed by what he called the "revolution," he identified himself increasingly with the conservative governments whose support seemed to provide the most effective guarantee for the maintenance and ultimate restoration of the Roman state. Moreover, seeing that the pope's temporal power had been challenged in the name of the liberal conception of the state and of the right of peoples to self-determination, he issued more and more protests against liberalism. The most spectacular of these were the encyclical *Quanta cura* (1864) and the *Syllabus of Errors* that accompanied it.

Pius IX was never able to distinguish between, on the one hand, what was of positive value in the confused aspirations of the age for a democratization of public life and was preparing in the long run for a greater spiritualization of the Catholic apostolate and, on the other hand, what represented a compromise with principles alien to the Christian spirit. He saw in liberalism only an ideology that denied the supernatural. He confused democracy with anarchy, and he could not grasp the historical impossibility of claiming for the Roman Catholic Church both protection from the state and the independence from it he valued so highly.

As a result, Pius IX was unable to adapt the Roman Catholic Church to the profound political and social developments of his time. Nor was he able to provide the impulse that Catholic thought needed if it was to respond effectively to the excesses of rationalism and materialistic positivism. By abandoning control of the church's intellectual life to narrow minds that could only condemn new tendencies as incompatible with traditional positions, he lost valuable time. The real roots of the modernist crisis may be traced back to his pontificate.

Central to the pope's zeal was a confused and clumsily expressed perception of the need to remind a society intoxicated by a scientistic conception of progress of the primacy of what theologians call the supernatural order: the biblical vision of humanity and salvation history, which is opposed to an interpretation of history as a progressive emancipation from religious values and to such a great confidence in human potentialities that there is no room for a redeemer. If we are to understand the inflexibility with which Pius IX fought his battle against liberalism, "the error of the century," as he called it, we must see this struggle as the center of his efforts to focus Christian thinking once again on the fundamental data of revelation. In his own mind, the First Vatican Council (1869–1870), which was interrupted by the entry of the Italians into Rome, was to be the crown upon these efforts.

Historians have for a long time judged the pontificate of Pius IX negatively because of his failures in the realm of diplomacy and his fruitless efforts to resist the advance of liberalism. More recently, however, scholars have come to see that matters were more complex and that Pius IX's activities were a notable help in strengthening the Roman Catholic Church in its religious sphere, whatever may be thought of certain debatable tendencies.

Missionary expansion advanced at an increasingly rapid pace on five continents during the thirty-two years of Pius IX's pontificate, and thriving churches were developed in Canada, Australia, and especially the United States as a result of Roman Catholic emigration from Europe, but his personal role in this expansion was secondary. On the other hand, he made an important contribution to the progress of the ultramontane movement, which caused guidance of the universal church to be concentrated increasingly in the pope's hands. This movement, given solemn approbation by Vatican I's definition of the pope's personal infallibility and his primacy of jurisdiction, did not go unresisted by those who saw the advantages of pluralism in the local churches and feared to see the episcopates come under the thumb of the Roman Curia. But Pius IX, whose very real virtues were idealized and who benefited from a special sympathy because of his repeated misfortunes, succeeded in rousing in the Roman Catholic world a real "devotion to the pope" which remarkably facilitated the enthusiastic adhesion of the masses and the lower clergy to the new conception of the pope's role in the church. While Pius IX did all he could to encourage this trend, he did so less from personal ambition or a liking for a theocracy than for essentially pastoral reasons: the movement seemed to him to be both a condition for the restoration of Catholic life wherever government interference in the local churches threatened to smother apostolic zeal and the best means of regrouping all the vital forces of Roman Catholicism for response to the mounting wave of "secularization."

No less important were the largely successful efforts of Pius IX to promote the renewal of the religious orders and congregations, encourage the raising of the spiritual level of the clergy, and improve the quality of ordinary Catholic life.

During his pontificate there developed an immense movement of eucharistic devotion, devotion to the Sacred Heart, and Marian devotion (the latter being encouraged by the definition in 1854 of the Immaculate Conception of the Virgin Mary). This movement has sometimes been faulted as superficial, but the multiplication of charitable works and pious associations and the immense development of the religious congregations give the lie to this simplistic judgment. Pius IX himself made a large contribution to these developments. First, he was an example of personal piety for the devotional movement. Second, and above all, he applied himself systematically to energizing, and at times even pushing, the development that had begun right after the great revolutionary crisis. It was precisely because he regarded an intransigent attitude as indispensable to this work of Christian restoration that he forced himself, despite his personal preference for conciliation and appeasement, to repeat unceasingly certain principles that he believed formed the basis for a Christian restoration of society.

Pius IX was handicapped by a superficial intellectual formation that often kept him from grasping the complexity of problems. In addition, the mystical confidence this deeply devout man had in Providence and the excessive importance he attached to prophecies and other manifestations of the extraordinary made him too ready to see in the political upheavals in which the church was involved only a new episode in the great conflict between God and Satan. But having said this we must not forget the very real qualities of the man—simplicity, refinement, serenity, and courage in adversity—and of the pastor, whose ruling concern was always to be first and foremost a churchman, responsible before God for the defense of threatened Christian values.

See Also Modernism, article on Christian Modernism; Ultramontanism; Vatican Councils, article on Vatican I.

Bibliography

Some of Pius IX's addresses can be found in Abbé Marcone's *La parole de Pie IX,* 2d ed. (Paris, 1868), and Pasquale de Franciscis's *Discorsi del sommo pontifice Pio IX,* 4 vols. (Rome, 1873–1882). Some letters are in Pietro Pirri's *Pio IX e Vittorio Emanuele II dal loro carteggio privato,* 5 vols. (Rome, 1944–1961).

The carefully written work of Carlo Falconi, *Il giovane Mastai* (Milan, 1981) covers only the first thirty-five years. The naively hagiographical work by Alberto Serafini, *Pio Nono* (Vatican City, 1958), stops at his election to the papacy. The excellent work by Giacomo Martina, *Pio IX,* 3 vols. (Rome, 1974–1990), is essential for a good understanding of the pope's personality. On the pontificate, see Joseph Schmidlin's *Papstgeschichte der neuesten Zeit,* vol. 2 (Munich, 1934) and my *Le pontificat de Pie IX, 1846–1878,* 2d ed., "Histoire de l'Église," vol. 21 (Paris, 1962). E. E. Y. Hales's *Pio IX: A Study in European Politics and Religion in the Nineteenth Century* (London, 1954) is superficial and focuses chiefly on the political aspects.

Roger Aubert (1987)
Translated from French by Matthew J. O'Connell

PLANTS

See VEGETATION

PLATO.

PLATO. Plato (c. 428–348 BCE), a Greek philosopher and founder of the Athenian Academy, was an Athenian citizen of high birth who grew up during the Peloponnesian War (431–404 BCE). He was a member of the circle of young men who surrounded the charismatic Socrates (469–399 BCE). After Socrates died, Plato withdrew from public life. He traveled to southern Italy and Sicily, where he not only met the tyrant Dionysius I and began a lifelong involvement with Dion of Syracuse, but also came in contact with the Pythagorean school that flourished in southern Italy. Soon after his return to Athens (c. 387 BCE) Plato began meeting with colleagues and pupils at his home near the grove of Academus outside the walls of Athens. The rest of his life—apart from two ill-starred visits to Syracuse at the behest of Dion—was devoted to teaching and inquiry in this community, where, in dialogue between teacher and pupils, the mathematical disciplines were pursued for the sake of their contribution to an understanding of the foundations of moral and political life (see *Republic* 526d–532c). Plato used the dialogue form in writing, not only to portray Socrates himself (in the so-called early dialogues, such as *Apology, Crito, Euthyphro,* and *Laches*), but also to present the outlines of his own growing and changing thought. In the great dialogues of the middle period—*Phaedo, Republic, Symposium, Phaedrus*—Plato develops the basic themes of his philosophical vision. In the late dialogues, he pursues a variety of insights and difficulties concerning the nature of knowledge and of being *(Theaetetus, Parmenides, Sophist),* produces a treatise on the structures of the visible cosmos *(Timaeus),* and offers reconsidered accounts of the best constitution for a city-state *(Statesman, Laws).*

Plato's Doctrine. The main feature that characterizes traditional Greek religion before Plato is the distinction between gods and human beings, or immortals and mortals. Inspired by minority religious beliefs, Plato reacted against this presupposition and assigned to human beings the goal of assimilating themselves to god. This radical reversal, to which the Platonic tradition was to lay claim throughout antiquity, was based on a twofold opposition: first, between intelligible realities and sensible things, which participate in the intelligible; and secondly, between soul and body. Soul accounts for the spontaneous movement of a living body, yet it can separate itself from its original body in order to transfer itself into another one.

Plato maintained the existence of "Forms" (*eide*) in order to explain how this world, where everything is in constant change, presents enough permanence and stability for human beings to be able to know it, act upon it, and talk about it. In the belief that such stability and permanence were not to be found in the sensible world, Plato therefore postulated the existence of a reality of another kind that would fulfill these requirements and explain why, within that which never stops changing, there is something that does not change. In the *Phaedo* (79b), Socrates admits "that there exist two species of beings: on the one hand, the visible species, and on the other the invisible species." In fact, these two species of beings are separate. Nevertheless, the separation between the "intelligible" and the "sensible" cannot be complete, simply because the existence of the "Forms" must contribute a solution to the paradoxes that "sensible" particulars never cease generating. "Sensible" realities receive their names from "intelligible" realities. Above all, "sensible" can be truly known only through the intermediary of the "intelligible."

Sensible things are bodies, which, as is explained in the *Timaeus*, are made up of the four elements—fire, air, water, and earth—and of them alone. Because the body (*soma*) has come into being, no body is indestructible in itself (*Timaeus* 28a3). Nevertheless, a distinction must be made between the bodies that receive their motion from outside and those that move spontaneously because they are endowed with a soul (*psyche*) that can be directed by a higher faculty: the intellect (*nous*). The intellect enables the perception of the intelligible realities in which sensible things participate.

The soul is defined as the self-moving principle of all motion, physical as well as psychic (*Laws* X, 896e–897a). The immediate consequence of this definition is as follows: we must attribute immortality (*Phaedrus* 245a–d) to the soul as a whole, which, by definition, can have no beginning or end. Particular souls, and namely those of mortal beings (those of human beings, which can transfer into other human bodies and even into the bodies of animals), are, as shall be seen, subject to cycles of ten thousand years, at the end of which they lose the features that characterize them. In the course of the following cycle, they acquire new characteristics.

WHAT PLATO UNDERSTANDS BY "GOD" (*THEOS*). If we wish to speak of religion in Plato, we must first ask ourselves what Plato understands by "god" (*theos*), that is, by "immortal." When, in the *Phaedrus* (246c–d), he tries to describe what a god is, Plato shows himself to be very prudent. He begins by situating his discourse not on the level of *logos,* which is based on argued knowledge that makes a claim to truth, but on that of *mythos,* or a story that remains likely; and he concludes by an appeal for benevolence on the part of the divinity, which takes the form of a prayer. There is, however, a definition that will not vary: a god is an immortal living being.

It follows that since the intelligible realities (including the Good) are defined as intelligible forms, they cannot be considered as gods. Since they are incorporeal, these intelligible forms cannot have a body, and since they are immutable, they can neither be nor have a soul, which, by definition, is a motion that moves itself. In addition, Plato never qualifies an intelligible form—even the highest one, that of the Good—as a god (*theos*), although it may happen that the intelligible is qualified as "divine" (*theion*) as it is in the *Phaedo* (81a3, 83e1, 84a1), the *Republic* (VI 500e3, VII 517d5, X 611e2), the *Statesman* (269d6), the *Theaetetus* (176e4), the *Parmenides* (134e4), and the *Philebus* (22c6, 62a8). Here, the adjective has a hyperbolic value, which implies opposition with regard to "human" (*anthropinon). Theion* designates what is perfect in its kind as a function of its relation with that which bestows this perfection: the intelligible, which is therefore also *theion.* The intelligible brings the god its nourishment and its very divinity (*Phaedrus* 247d). Thus, to imitate the god, who is wise (he is a *sophos*), human beings must seek to become wise themselves (*philosophoi*) and to tend toward that wisdom that is conferred by the contemplation of the intelligible.

For Plato, a living being is one endowed with a body and a soul. Among living beings, however, some are mortal and others are not. Since the soul is by definition immortal (*Phaedrus* 245a–d), a living being can therefore be declared to be "mortal" only as a function of its body. Those living beings whose body can be destroyed are mortal, and as a consequence the soul can separate itself from the body it moves (see *Timaeus* 85e). This is the case for mankind and all the beings that inhabit the air, the earth, and the waters (see *Timaeus* 90e–92c). However, there are living beings whose soul and body are united forever because their body cannot be destroyed. The body of these living bodies is not in itself indestructible, for, according to an axiom of Greek thought, all that is born is liable to perish (see *Timaeus* 28a and 38b). It is the goodness of he who has fabricated them that ensures that they will not be destroyed (*Timaeus* 41a–c).

In addition to being endowed with an indissoluble body, the gods possess a soul, whose higher faculty—intellect (*nous*)—is constantly active and seizes its object (that is, intelligible reality) immediately and without obstacles. Once his soul is incarnated, the human being can accede to the intelligible only through the intermediary of his senses, at the end of the complex process to which Plato gives the name of reminiscence (*anamnesis*), which enables the soul to remember the intelligible realities it contemplated when it was separated from all earthly bodies. Ultimately, it is the quality of this contemplation that makes a god a god. In brief, for Plato a god is a living being endowed with a body that is indestructible, not in itself but through the will of the demiurge, and with a soul that possesses a perfect intellect.

As compounds of a body and a soul, the gods form part of an extremely vast hierarchical structure. They are situated at the summit, together with the demons (see *Symposium* 202d), the most famous of whom is Eros. Then come human beings, men and women; then the animals that live in the air, on earth, and in the water, in which human beings may come to be incarnated by virtue of the quality of their intellectual activity; at the very bottom, we must range the plants (*Timaeus* 76e–77a). Two criteria enable the gods to be isolated from all the rest of living beings: their indestructibility and the quality of their intellect. This being the case, let us draw up an inventory of the beings that may be qualified as "gods."

Beings That May Qualify as "Gods." First, there is the universe, whose constitution is described in the *Timaeus.* The body of the world, which is unique, has the appearance of a vast sphere, bereft of organs and of members. This sphere includes within itself the totality of elements so that nothing can come to attack it from outside, and it is therefore exempt from illness and death. What is more, the demiurge, because of his goodness, does not wish the universe to be subject to corruption. Within this body he placed a soul, which is situated between the sensible and the intelligible and is endowed with a mathematical structure. In fact, its structure is twofold: motor, since it moves bodies as a whole, including the celestial bodies; and cognitive, insofar as it is Providence. The motion that animates the world is as simple as possible: that of a sphere rotating around its axis, from west to east, on the spot. This physical motion is associated in turn with a twofold cognitive faculty, which seems to deal with the intelligible and the sensible; this is a necessary condition if one admits that the world soul must rule over the universe. The world soul, associated with an indestructible body that it dominates, is in addition endowed with an intellect that is perfect and whose activity is incessant. How, then, can we avoid concluding that the universe is a blessed god (*Laws* VII 821a)?

The celestial bodies (made up of fire) and the earth (made up, above all, of earth) are qualified as "divine" because they meet the criteria stated above. They are indeed immortal living beings that consist of a body that cannot be destroyed, and of their own soul, endowed with an intellect. A hierarchy is established between the celestial bodies, associated with their motion, to which the passage mentioned bears witness. The fixed stars proceed from east to west in a perfectly uniform way, for the motion of their soul does not give rise to any interference. The soul governing the wandering stars introduces anomalies in the motion of their trajectories. The earth, for its part, remains at rest at the center of the universe simply because in it conflicting types of motion cancel each other out.

The traditional gods are mentioned in an enigmatic passage: "Thus, when all the gods, both those whose circular motions we observe, and those who show themselves only when they so wish, the begetter of this universe spoke to them" (*Timaeus* 41a). These are also living immortal beings, endowed with a soul and a body, although it is hard to know what the body of the traditional gods is made of. We can suppose it is fire, since we find in the *Timaeus* a passage where the different species of living beings are associated with an element: the gods with fire, the birds with air, the living beings that walk or crawl with earth, and fish with water (*Timaeus* 39e–40a). One might think that the association of the divinity with fire holds only for celestial bodies, but it is, it seems, permissible to extrapolate to the traditional gods for two reasons: (1) in the next paragraphs the celestial bodies are mentioned first (*Timaeus* 40a–d), then the traditional gods (*Timaeus* 40d–e); and (2) the demiurge then addresses the totality of these gods (*Timaeus* 41a–c).

The soul of the traditional gods is in every point similar in structure to that of human beings (see *Phaedrus* 246a–d); this is why the gods can be subject to aggressiveness and experience feelings and passions. Unlike that of human beings, the soul of the gods is always good because their soul is permanently guided by their intellect, which perfectly contemplates the intelligible (*Phaedrus* 247c–e). In this magnificent passage, we find a constant mixture between tradition and novelty, myth and philosophy, where myth is the object of a transposition. The gods, whom the poets describe as leading a life of banquets on Olympus, where they feed on special food, nectar and ambrosia, are described in the *Phaedrus* as nourishing their soul with the intelligible. We should also note their peculiar language, which is more correct than that of men, probably because of the quality of their contemplation.

This contemplation enables assimilation to the god: "Such is the life of the gods. Let us move on to the other souls. That which is the best, because it follows the god and seeks to resemble it . . ." (*Phaedrus* 247e–249a). This is the sense in which we must understand that the intelligible forms are qualified as "divine." However, the motion that animates the traditional gods is less uniform than that which animates the celestial bodies. In the central myth of the *Phaedrus,* they rise and fall, although many of the verbs that describe these movements feature the idea of circularity.

There remains the most controversial case: the *demiourgos* of the *Timaeus,* to whom we must assimilate the *phutourgos* of the *Republic.* He who fashions the universe in the *Timaeus* is explicitly qualified as a "god": "Thus, in conformity with an explanation which is merely probable, we must say that this world (*cosmos*), which is a living being provided with a soul that is endowed with an intellect, was truly engendered as a result of the reflective decision of a god" (*Timaeus* 30b–c). This god is, however, described as a worker who thinks, has feelings, speaks, and acts. At *Timaeus* 29e30b it becomes clear that the demiurge is a god endowed with an intellect: he "reasons" and "reflects"; he "takes things into consideration" and he "foresees," and he is author of acts of "will." His responsibility is engaged; he "speaks"; and when he contemplates his works, he "rejoices." In addition, the description of his activity is scarcely compatible with the absence of a body. Besides being qualified as a "father," the personage who causes the universe to appear is qualified as "demiurge," "maker," wax-modeller, and carpenter, and he is a builder whose most important function is assembling. Moreover, if one considers the verbs that metaphorically describe his action, one realizes that the demiurge carries out several activities that are typical of some arts and crafts.

However, nowhere is it said that the demiurge has a soul and a body simply because it is he who fashioned soul and body in their totality. This is probably the reason some commentators have maintained that the demiurge cannot be separated from the soul, of which he must, one way or another, be like the intellect. Yet it seems very difficult to accept this position, for this would amount to pulling up the ladder one has just used. In summary, Plato describes the demiurge, even if only metaphorically, as a god endowed with a body and a soul.

At the summit of the divine Platonic hierarchy, then, we find the demiurge, who fashions the other gods. He is thus considered as the god who always is, and he is in a paradoxical situation with regard to the soul and the body he is supposed to fashion. Then we find the universe, which comes into being as a result of the demiurge's action; this god takes on the appearance of the most perfect form in that he rotates on the spot. Then there come the fixed stars and the planets, whose body is also spherical: but the fixed stars take on a circular motion that is perfectly regular if we compare it to that of the planets, which feature certain irregularities. The status of the earth is also problematic; bereft of motion, it rests at the center of the universe and presents an imperfectly spherical form. The traditional gods, for their part, are subject to motions that are not only circular but also linear, for they can rise and descend in the heavens.

In brief, whether one looks at traditional mythology, at Plato, at Aristotle, at the Stoics or the Epicureans, the gods are always considered as living immortal beings, endowed with an indestructible body and a soul that possesses an intellect. The idea that there may be gods who do not possess either a soul or a body is, it seems, contemporary with the efforts made by the Middle Platonists to ensure the preeminence of the first god. In this divinity, they saw both the Demiurge of the *Timaeus,* and the Good of the *Republic,* which they considered as an intellect in actuality, whose intelligible forms were the thoughts. In addition, it bears the mark of the definitive assimilation carried out by Plotinus between the Intellect and the Intelligible that all the later Neoplatonists were to follow. Even in this context, however, there remained an important place for the lower gods, endowed with a soul and a body. The same holds true for the Neoplatonists.

Since the gods possess a soul whose highest faculty, the intellect (*nous*), is constantly active, and this intellect grasps its object, the Forms (*eide*), immediately and without obstacles, they are necessarily good (*agathoi*), since evil is equivalent to ignorance; hence the saying that "No one commits evil willingly." One can understand, then, why Plato condemns the poets who describe the gods indulging in unjust or indecent acts. Since every god is good, it follows that none can be responsible for any evil (*Republic* X 617e). Thus, in the myth of the *Statesman,* as in Book X of the *Laws,* the possibility of divinities opposing one another is rejected. This amounts to a condemnation of dualism.

MORTAL LIVING BEINGS. Beneath the gods in the hierarchy are souls that possess an intellect like the gods but are liable to be attached to a body that, unlike that of the gods, is destructible. These inferior souls are subject to temporality; their existence is marked by cycles of ten thousand years, imposed by destiny, which involve a system of retribution based on reincarnation.

In order to account for the soul's relations with an indestructible body, Plato, beginning with the *Republic,* distinguishes three powers within the soul, the first of which is in itself immortal, whereas the two others enjoy immortality only as long as the body over which they reign is indestructible. The immortal power of soul—that is, the intellect (*nous*)—contemplates the intelligible realities, of which sensible things are mere images. By its means, human beings are akin to a god, or rather to a *daimon.* The other two powers are: (1) the spirit (*thumos*) that enables mortal living beings to defend themselves, and (2) the desire (*epithumia*) that enables them to remain alive and reproduce. Whereas the intellect can be said to be immortal, these two powers are declared to be mortal because they are associated with functions that enable the survival of the sensible body to which the soul is attached, albeit only for a lifetime.

When applied to mortal living beings, and in particular to human beings, the psychic tripartition just mentioned is associated with one that is corporeal and even social. In the *Timaeus,* Plato associates each power of soul with a place in the body. The lowest or desiring power, which ensures the functions of survival (by provoking the desire for food) and of reproduction (by provoking sexual desire), is situated under the diaphragm, in the area of the liver. Above the diaphragm, in the area of the heart, is the spirited power, which enables human beings to remain alive by ensuring defensive functions, both within and without. This second power enables a mediation between the desiring power and reason, situated in the head, which is responsible for all the processes of knowledge that can be expressed in speech. In human beings, only reason is immortal, for the spirited power and the desiring power are restricted to ensuring the functions that enable destructible bodies to maintain themselves in good working order for a specific time. When this body is destroyed, the spirited power and the desiring power associated with it can only disappear, and this is why they are qualified as "mortal" (*Timaeus* 69d).

This psychic tripartition, associated with a corporeal one, is in addition related to a functional tripartition in a social context. At the end of Book II of the *Republic,* Plato proposes an organization in which individuals are distributed in *functional* groups in accordance with this hierarchy, based on the predominance in the human individual of one of three powers: intellect (*nous*), spirit (*thumos*), or desire (*epithumia*). The most numerous group, responsible for ensuring the production of food and of wealth, is made up of farmers and craftsmen. This group is protected by guardians, or warriors, responsible for ensuring the maintenance of order, both within and outside the city. Insofar as they can possess neither property nor money, the guardians are completely separated from the producers, who, in exchange for the protection they receive from the guardians, must feed them and ensure their upkeep. From these functional groups, a very small number of individuals are chosen, those who are intended for higher education and the government of the city.

Soul, as an incorporeal whole, is immortal; yet one individual soul can be attached to a particular body, which is, for its part, subject to destruction. However, the soul is recycled every ten thousand years; in this way, Plato's thought on soul is not so different from Asian (particularly Hindu) doctrines on reincarnation. We now turn to consider the soul's wanderings.

During the first millennium (*Phaedrus* 245d–248c), the soul is separated from all destructible bodies, whereas during the following nine millennia (*Phaedrus* 248c–e), it passes from body to body as a function of the moral value of its previous existence, which is determined by the quality of its intellectual activity. This intellectual activity is a reminiscence (*anamnesis*), or memory, of the soul's contemplation of intelligible realities when it was separated from all terrestrial bodies. At the end of this first millennium, all souls that are worthy of being associated with a sensible body inhabit the body of a man—that is, a male, even though the sexual organs are still missing; and this association remains valid for the following millennium. A man who loves knowledge or beauty and who has chosen an upright life for three consecutive millennia will be able to escape from the cycle of reincarnations and rise back up to the heavens. The others will voyage from one body to another, beginning with the third millennium (*Timaeus* 90e–92c). The first category of bodies in which these imperfect souls may be incarnated is that of women: whoever displays cowardice enters into the body of a woman, since virility is associated with war in ancient Greece. Only in the course of this millennium does the distinction of the sexes appear, thus allowing sexual reproduction. Then come incarnations in various kinds of what we call "animals," although there is no specific term in ancient Greek to designate this category of living beings. They are classified as a function of the elements (beginning with the air, since fire is reserved for the gods), in a vertical order. At the top, birds fly through the air. Then come the living beings that inhabit the surface of the earth; these are the quadrupeds, insects, and reptiles. Finally, there are the aquatic animals: fish, shellfish, and others, which are the most stupid.

In fact, Plato describes a psychic *continuum* in which one finds a hierarchical order of gods, demons, human beings, and the animals that live in the air, on the earth, and in the water—and even, as shall be seen, plants. Intellectual activity, conceived as the intuition of intelligible forms, constitutes the criterion that enables a distinction to be made between all these souls. Gods and demons contemplate the intelligible forms directly, and, as it were, incessantly. Human beings share this privilege only during a certain period of their existence, when their souls are separated from all bodies. Once human souls have been incarnated, their contemplation of the intelligible forms is mediate, since it must pass through the intermediary of the senses; above all, it is more or less uncertain. By contrast, animals use their intellect less and less as one goes down the scale of beings.

Within the psychic scale mentioned above, one notes two discontinuities: (1) a discontinuity between the souls of gods and of demons (which never fall into a body subject to destruction) and the souls of human beings and animals (which inhabit destructible bodies with diverse appearances); and (2) a discontinuity between the souls of human beings and animals (which are endowed with a rational power) and the souls of plants (which are reduced to the desiring power).

Let us consider one by one the consequences of these two discontinuities.

1. In this hierarchical system, only souls endowed with an intellect are subject to a retributive system, which makes them rise or fall on the scale of souls, incarnated according to the quality of their intellectual activity. Gods and demons are above this class, and plants are beneath it. Gods and plants thus always remain at their level, at the highest or the lowest extremity.
2. As a result, human beings, who are situated at the uppermost limit of the class of incarnate souls, must have as their goal assimilation to the gods and the demons by seeking contemplation of the intelligible forms. Hence the theme of the assimilation to the divinity by the philosopher, who tends toward the knowledge, that is, the contemplation of the intelligible forms, or true reality.
3. The hierarchy of human beings and animals, which is a function of the exercise of intellectual activity, is materialized by the body. The body, in which the soul is situated, illustrates the quality of that soul's intellectual activity; in short, the body is a "state of the soul."
4. Like human beings, whether men or women, the soul of animals is endowed with a rational power, and this is true even if animals are what they are because they make little or no use of their intellect. In any case, nothing prevents an animal, whatever it may be, from climbing back up the scale to become a human being.

It follows that changing the destiny of an animal may imply eating the soul of a former human being. How, in this case, can the survival of human beings, who need to feed themselves, be ensured without turning them into "anthropophagi"? By giving them as food a kind of living being that is not endowed with intellect—namely, vegetables. After mentioning the four types of living beings that populate the universe—the gods associated with fire; demons; human beings; and the birds, the animals, and the aquatic beasts—Timaeus rapidly mentions the origin of vegetables, which he associates with the third, or desiring power of soul. However, this call for vegetarianism enters into conflict with the traditional sacrifice (*thusia*) of the city, which implies slaughtering victims and consuming their flesh. Scarcely mentioned in the *Republic,* this kind of sacrifice seems to play an important role in the city of the *Laws.* Does Plato accept this contradiction, or does he give a wider meaning to *thusia*? It is impossible to say.

Transmigration of the Soul. Scholars usually consider that the transmigration of the soul was a dogma among the Orphics and the Pythagoreans and that Plato made it his own. The stakes here are important, insofar as the transmigration of the soul is the basis of the doctrine of reminiscence, which itself implies the notion of a separate intelligible form that can be contemplated by the soul even when separated from the body.

However, none of the testimonies advanced to prove that the Pythagoreans preached the doctrine of transmigration is decisive: whether it is that of Diogenes Laertios, who claims to cite verses by Xenophanes that he attributes to Pythagoras (Diogenes Laertios VIII 36 = Diels-Kranz 21B7); of Aristotle (*De anima* I 3, 407b20 = Diels-Kranz 59 B39; cf. also II 2, 414a22) on the soul's entry into the body; of Dicearchus on the dogmas that Pythagoras was the first to introduce into Greece (Dicearchus, fr. 33 Wehrli = Porphyry, *Vita Pythagorica* 19); or of Herodotus (IV 95–96), who affirms that the Greeks living in the region of the Black Sea attributed to Pythagoras the practices for obtaining immortality current among the Getae (*Getai athanatizontes*). There is every reason to believe that modern and contemporary historians of religions, following in the path of the Neopythagoreans, often project Plato's doctrine of the soul on the teachings of Pythagoras, about which, objectively, we know nothing.

In addition, no ancient testimony attributes explicitly the doctrine of transmigration to Orphism. All that is explicitly attributed to Orphism is the doctrine of the soul's preexistence (a preexistence that is not necessarily individual), and that of retribution in the next world. On this point as well, the testimonies of Plato (*Cratylus* 400b–c; *Phaedo* 62b; *Republic* II 364e–365a; *Laws* IX 870d-e) and that of Aristotle (*De anima* I5, 410b27) are insufficient to inspire persuasion.

The only way to affirm that Orphism maintains the transmigration of the soul would be to think that the priests and priestesses Plato mentions in the *Meno* (81a–e) are Orphic, or to slant in this direction the testimony of Herodotus (II 123), who refers the doctrine of transmigration to the Egyptians. It is presumptuous to supply names that Herodotus will not even reveal and say that the people in question are Orphics. In addition, the passage from the *Meno* (81b–c) in which are cited a few verses traditionally attributed to Pindar (fr. 133 Bergk = 126 Bowra) does indeed evoke the doctrine of transmigration but refers it to priests and priestesses intent on being able to account for the functions they fulfill; his goal is to make not only Pindar but also poets the spokesmen for this doctrine. The interpretation of this passage, where the names of Orpheus or of the Orphics never appear, remains debatable.

In the face of so many confusions and uncertainties, the only valid hypothesis at the present time is as follows: Pindar, Empedocles, Herodotus, and Plato were aware of the existence of religious movements that maintained the doctrine of transmigration. These movements seem to have had an influence on Pythagoreanism and on Orphism. In this perspective, the question of which group—Orphics or Pythagoreans—influenced the other is meaningless. Pythagoreanism and Orphism, like Plato, accepted and rejected some of the prohibitions and doctrinal points of these religious movements, which it is impossible to identify.

From this perspective, all human beings and animals that inhabit air, earth, and water constitute a vast system of symbols—symbols from the point of view of appearances, but also from the viewpoint of behavior, which justifies the recourse to a number of comparisons, images, and metaphors in which animals play a role. In the *Timaeus* these symbols refer to different types of soul, whose moral quality is ultimately determined by their contemplation of the intelligible, according to a number of details that may seem ironic or ridiculous but that can be interpreted only in this sense: birds are naive astronomers, who think that sight is the ultimate source of knowledge; quadrupeds need four feet in order to support their skull, which has been elongated by the deformations of the revolutions of the circles of its rational power. Stupid terrestrial animals crawl; fish are even more stupid, and the worst ignorance is that of shellfish.

Plato and Traditional Religion. Plato thus agrees with traditional mythology, particularly when he maintains that the gods have a body. However, even on this point he differs from his contemporaries. He can endure neither the idea that the gods have a corporeal aspect or a behavior that renders them akin to human beings (since the gods can only be good) nor the idea that the gods may change in corporeal appearance or in opinion. The violent criticisms that constitute Books II and III of the *Republic,* and the denunciation of the poets in Book X, are clear proof of this. Only a mythology fabricated by poets under the control of those who know—that is, the philosophers—is permitted. Myths of this kind can be used, together with a kind of rhetoric, as means of persuasion in the preambles to the laws for dissuading in advance those who might be thinking of breaking a law, as is explained by the Athenian Stranger in Book IV of the *Laws.*

A similar position can be observed in Book X of the *Laws,* where the goal is to demonstrate to young atheists that: (1) the gods exist, (2) they are interested in the fate of human beings, and (3) they are insensitive to all attempts to influence their judgment. This last point has the consequence of rendering traditional religion obsolete. In this context there can no longer be any question of making prayers or offering sacrifices in an attempt to sway any particular god. The only goal of the cult is to glorify the gods, with a view to assimilating oneself to them by one's contemplation.

In summary, although he takes up many ideas concerning the gods in ancient Greece, Plato appears as a revolutionary when he assigns to human beings the goal of assimilating themselves to god, seeks to submit the myths that narrate the deeds and exploits of the gods to the control of the philosopher, and attributes to cultic acts and ceremonies the original finality of the mere glorification of the gods.

See Also Dualism; Ficino, Marsilio; Gnosticism, article on Gnosticism from Its Origins to the Middle Ages; Hermetism; Neoplatonism; Platonism; Soul, article on Greek and Hellenistic Concepts.

Bibliography

Bianchi, Ugo. *La religione greca.* Turin, 1975.

Bianchi, Ugo. *The Greek Mysteries.* Leiden, 1976.

Brisson, Luc. *Plato the Myth Maker.* Translated by G. Naddaf. Chicago, 1998. Original edition, 1982.

Brisson, Luc. *Lectures de Platon.* Paris, 2000.

Brisson, Luc. *How the Myth Was Saved.* Translated by K. Tihanyi. Chicago, 2004.

Burkert, Walter. *Greek Religion. Archaic and Classical.* Translated by J. Raffan. Oxford, 1985. Original edition, 1977.

Burkert, Walter. *Ancient Mystery Cults.* Cambridge, Mass., 1987.

Casadio, Giovanni. "The *Politicus* Myth (268d–274c) and the History of Religions." *Kernos* 8 (1995): 85–95.

Despland, Michel. *The Education of Desire: Plato and the Philosophy of Religion.* Toronto, 1985.

Friedländer, Paul. *Plato: An Introduction,* 2nd ed. Translated by H. Meyerhoff. Princeton, 1969. Original edition, 1929–1930.

Garland, Robert. *Introducing New Gods: The Politics of Athenian Religion.* Ithaca, N.Y., 1992.

Gerson, Lloyd P. *God and Greek Philosophy: Studies in the Early History of Natural Theology.* London, 1990.

Goldschmidt, Victor. *La religion de Platon.* Paris, 1949; reprinted in *Platonisme et pensée contemporaine.* Paris, 1970 and 2000.

Laurent, Jérôme, ed. *Les dieux de Platon.* Caen, 2003.

Morgan, Michael L. *Platonic Piety: Philosophy and Ritual in Fourth-Century Athens.* New Haven, Conn., 1990.

Morgan, Michael L. "Plato and the Greek Religion." In *The Cambridge Companion to Plato,* pp. 227–247. Cambridge, 1991.

Pétrement, Simone. *Le dualisme chez Platon, les Gnostiques et les Manichéens.* Paris, 1947.

Reale, Giovanni. *Toward a New Interpretation of Plato.* Translated from the 10th edition by John R. Cactan and Richard Davies. Washington, D.C., 1997.

Reverdin, Olivier. *La religion de Platon.* Paris, 1945.

Rudhardt, Jean. *Notions fondamentales de la pensée religieuse et actes constitutifs du culte. Étude préliminaire pour aider à la compréhension de la piété athénienne au IVᵉ siècle.* Geneva, 1958.

Solmsen, Friedrich. *Plato's Theology.* Ithaca, N.Y., 1942.

Van Camp, Jean, and Paul Canart. *Le sens du mot theîos chez Platon.* Louvain, 1956.

Luc Brisson (2005)

PLATONISM.

PLATONISM. Taken in its broadest sense, Platonism refers to the influence of Plato in Western philosophical, religious, and political thinking. In the Hellenistic world, the vehicle of this influence was the Academy, but from the time of Athens' destruction by the Romans, accomplished by Sulla in 86 BCE, the Academy had ceased to exercise any real influence on Platonic thought. Thereafter, Platonic schools were founded in the most famous cities of the Roman Empire, including Pergamum, Athens, and Alexandria. A Platonic (i.e. Neoplatonic) school continued to exist in Athens until 529 CE, when it was dissolved by the emperor Justinian, but it cannot be called "Academy." Conveyed not only by the writings of Plato himself, but also by the works of later disciples and interpreters belonging to the so-called Middle Platonic and Neoplatonic schools, Platonism influenced Christian and Islamic philosophy in the late classical and medieval eras and underwent revivals not only at the time of the Renaissance but also in modern European philosophy.

The Old Academy. The immediate successors of Plato as heads of the Academy were his nephew Speusippus (410–339 BCE) and Xenocrates of Chalcedon (396–314 BCE), who carried on discussions held in the last period of Plato's life, when Aristotle was also a member of the Academy. Speusippus denied the existence of the Forms and the numerical Forms, and he reduced Plato's intelligible world to a complex of mathematical entities that represented the lowest level in Platonic metaphysics. He dismissed the opinion that reality depended on a First Principle (The One Which Is the Good), as taught by Plato in his "unwritten doctrines." Both Good and Beautiful exist as a derivation from the First Principle. Xenocrates, however, turned back to Plato, though not without distinguishing his thought from Plato's. He was the first to divide philosophy into physics (which included the so-called metaphysics), ethics, and logic, as later philosophers also did. Xenocrates abandoned Speusippus's mathematical metaphysics and re-proposed Plato's numerical Forms, together with other kinds of Forms. These various kinds of forms (numerical and other) constitute the intelligible world and are the production of the two basic Principles, the One and the indefinite Dyad. Xenocrates called the One "Zeus" (i.e., the highest male god, the father, and the ruler of universe). In contrast, the indefinite Dyad was the female goddess, the mother of All, the cosmic soul. Therefore Xenocrates interpreted in a religious way the highest ontological principles, and his interest in a religious philosophy is manifested also by his demonology. The *daimon* is an intermediate being between gods and humans. Active in shrines and oracles; he may be either good or bad, like humans, but he is immortal. Xenocrates' demonology and, as a whole, the ancient Academy's doctrines were taken up by second-century CE Platonism. Aristotle might well be added to this list of Plato's direct followers, even though he founded his own school, the Lyceum, in 335, after Xenocrates had succeeded Speusippus. Aristotle was notoriously critical of Plato's way of understanding Form and of his identification of Form with being. Further, he was contemptuous of Speusippus's devotion to Pythagorean number theory. Nevertheless, Aristotle's works pursued, in their own way, the agenda of Plato's Academy, and his account of the First Principle as self-thinking Intellect (*nous*) was early adopted in the Platonic tradition, and Pythagorean doctrines continued to be discussed in the Platonic school.

THE SKEPTICAL ACADEMY. With the succession of Arcesilaus (d. 241 BCE) as its head, the Academy took a fresh turn. The so-called New Academy—frequently labelled "sceptical"—maintained that neither Socrates nor Plato had taught any settled, dogmatic system but had pursued arguments on both sides of every question without seeking to reach definitive conclusions. Indeed, Arcesilaus's approach was not completely unsound, since Socrates had taught students to doubt traditional certainties. So, Arcesilaus maintained that the *epoche* (suspension of judgement) in which this procedure resulted represented the true philosophical position of Plato, but Arcesilaus's devotion to it was largely evoked by Stoic dogmatism, with its assertion of the existence of "indubitable perception" (*kataleptike phantasia*). Against this Stoic view the New Academy emphasized the doubtfulness and subjectivity of both perception and judgment. In response to the charge that such a stance left people without guidance for the conduct of life, Carneades (d. 129 BCE) developed his theory of *pithanon* (the "persuasive" or "probable"), holding, as Cicero sums it up (*Academica* 2.10), "that there is something which is probable and, so to speak, like the truth" and that this provides a "rule both for the conduct of life and for inquiry and discussion."

It was not, however, in scepticism that Platonism was to find its future. Even in the time of Carneades and his successor Philo of Larissa (d. about 80 BCE), Platonists were beginning, though solely in defense of their own position, to employ Stoic ideas and terminology; and at the same time, in the teaching of the Stoic Posidonius of Apamea (d. about 51 BCE) there are traces of Plato's influence. This incipient eclecticism became stronger in Antiochus of Ascalon (d. about 68 BCE), and with it came a repudiation of scepticism and a new, dogmatic Platonism—so-called Middle Platonism—that eventually set the stage for the work of Plotinus and his successors.

ANTIOCHUS OF ASCALON. The split between Antiochus and his teacher Philo of Larissa, a skeptic, had its basis in Antiochus's belief that the authentic tradition of Plato's teaching must be sought in the Old Academy and that this tradition embraced the contributions of Aristotle and the Stoics. Antiochus himself was substantially a Stoic in his assumption of Stoic *logos spermatikòs*, which he considered quite similar to the Platonic ideas and thus untypical of the later Middle Platonist tradition. Nevertheless his rebellion opened the way for the growth of a school of thought that treated the Platonic corpus as an authoritative text even while it brought other points of view—Pythagorean, Aristotelian, and Stoic—to the interpretation of that corpus. The influence of Antiochus was overestimated by critics of the nineteenth century and the first decades of the twentieth century who considered him the founder of Middle Platonism, but now it is thought more probable that Antiochus simply proposed a "return" to the Old Academy (including Aristotle) but was not able to give a new impulse to Platonism.

EUDORUS AND PHILO, THE MIDDLE PLATONISTS. According to most authoritative critics, Eudorus and the Jewish philosopher Philo, both active in Alexandria between the first century BCE and the first century CE, should be considered Middle Platonists. Eudorus influenced those who, during the first and second century, were interested in the theology of a First Principle, such as Plutarch of Chaeronea and Numenius of Apameia. Eudorus introduced the Pythagorean principle (the One), distinguishing between the absolutely transcendent One and the One that is correlated to the indefinite Dyad. This second One is the principle of limit (understood as form, "*eidos*") and is opposed to matter, from which disordered movement originates.

On the other side, Philo, whose imposing bulk of works was dedicated to a Greek exegesis of the Old Testament, employs many of the doctrines that were then considered Platonic, such as the "three principles theology" (*Dreiprinzipienlehre*, as it is called by German scholars). The first Principles, according to Philo, were not the first or the second One, but God, the Logos, who has in himself the ideas as his thoughts; and matter, out of which the Logos "created" the world, just as the platonic Demiurge "created" the world out of matter by contemplating the ideas. Philo also employed Stoic tenets, such as the doctrine of pathos.

The first and second centuries CE were the heyday of Middle Platonism. Once studied as preparation for Plotinus, the philosophers of the Middle Platonism are now considered worth studying in themselves, and their doctrines must be reconsidered as a more or less "organic building" (a coherent philosophical system). Therefore the word "eclectisism" must be excluded, since it means an assembly of doctrines from various schools, excluding the foundation of a coherent system of thought. On the contrary, the historical development of Platonism involved from its beginning confrontation with other philosophies, such as Pythagoreanism, Aristotelism, and, later, Stoicism, and it must appear neither an oddity nor a mark of eclecticism if Middle Platonists employed (and occasionally rejected) Stoic and Aristotelian doctrines. These philosophers did not by any means represent a uniform point of view but presented various interpretations of Platonic thought. Since the Academy had been dissolved long ago, they didn't represent a continuity, but only a loose "tradition." Platonic doctrines, in their new reassessment, were articulated by Areius Didymus, another scholar of the Augustan Age (like Eudorus and Philo), who was a doxographer more than a philosopher. His collection of Platonic doctrines took up many Antiochean tenets, which reappeared some decades later in the Stoic philosopher Seneca. For all their differences, however, these thinkers had much in common. In particular, they shared the corpus of Platonic dialogues, among which special attention was reserved for the Timaeus. Its interpretation, however, was not unanimous. Plutarch and Atticus took the view—which commended them to Christian readers—that the story of the Demiurge's "creation" of the cosmos was to be taken literally. Others, like Albinus and Calvenos Tauros, saw the story as a proper Platonic *muthos*, a tale intended not to explain how the cosmos came to be but to suggest how it is eternally structured.

In spite of such differences, however, all agreed (against traditional Stoicism) that the First Principle was transcendent and should be equated with the Good of Plato's *Republic*, the self-thinking Intellect of Aristotle's *Metaphysics*, or the One of Pythagorean cosmology. The Platonic realm of Forms appeared in Middle Platonism as the content of divine Intellect, and thus as the truth that actuated the World Soul in its work of ordering the visible cosmos. This scheme, in which the ultimate god was sometimes distinguished from a second "demiurgic" Intellect, foreshadowed the Neoplatonic hierarchy of three divine hypostases. At the same time, the human ideal became the contemplative life in which the soul achieves that "likeness to God" (*homoiosis theoi*) that Plato had commended in the *Theaetetus* (176b). Apart from the school philosophers, there are a number of individuals (e.g. the physician Galen, the mathematician Theon of Smyrna, and the rhetor Maximus of Tyre) who, while not quite philosophers themselves, give good evidence for contemporary Platonic schools.

The new form of Platonism appeared in an organic structure for the first time in Plutarch's (before 50–after 120 CE) works, and perhaps already in the doctrine of his teacher, Ammonius, who was an Egyptian like Eudorus and Philo. In physics, Plutarch was influenced by Pythagoreanism, whence he took the doctrine of the indefinite Dyad and number mysticism. In his interpretation of the *Timaeus* he insists on the temporal creation of the world as the result of God's intervention on matter, which is moved by a preexistent, disorderly, bad World Soul. He asserts the existence of the daemons, as Xenocrates had done, and he identifies them with the human soul, bad or good. In ethics, he abandoned Stoicism and, like Antiochus, returned to the peripatetic doctrines of the "moderation of affects." Apuleius (125–180), an important Sophist (i.e., orator) in the Latin-speaking West, is similar in some aspects to Plutarch. Apuleius was the author of a novel (*Metamorphoseon libri*) and of various orations (*Pro se de magia liber; Florida*) that show his interest in other problems, such as magic and literature, though without abandoning Platonic ideas (indeed, he was called *philosophus platonicus*). Apuleius followed the "doctrine of the three principles" and, in ethics, the Stoic *apatheia* and the Platonic "assimilation to god." More interesting is his practice of the Isiac cult, as it appears in the last book of the *Metamorphoses*, and of many other cults to which he adhered in his youth. So Apuleius's Platonism possesses a kind of henotheistic flavor; besides, he professed, like Plutarch, the Xenocratean daemonology.

Previously confused with Albinus, the author of a handbook of Platonic philosophy (*Didaskalikòs*), Alkinoos is not an original thinker, for his doctrines derive in great part from Areius Didymus's doxography.The three principles of Stoic origin (the *oikeiosis*, the innate ideas or *physikai ennoiai*, and the distinction between natural and perfected virtues) are also present in Apuleius (For this reason Alkinoos was supposed to be, like Apuleius, the pupil of the little-known Platonic philosopher Gaius). More than other Middle Platonists, Alkinoos represented the Aristotelian tradition, since his First principle is the *nous*.

As to the "rediscovered" Albinus, he wrote an *Introduction to Platonic Philosophy* (*Eisagoge*), which contains a discussion on nature, as well as characteristics of Platonic dialogues. In other works he was principally devoted to the *Timaeus* exegesis.

In contrast, Severus and Nicostratus fought against Aristotle and his doctrine of the *Categories*. Since, it seems, they had friends in Athens, scholars have proposed an "Athenian school," which John Dillon dismisses (like the school of Gaius) as "an empty name" (1977, p. 265). More important, Nicostratus's polemic against Aristotle fits very well with the philosophy of his contemporaries, Calvenus Taurus and Atticus. The first had some kind of school in Athens, and his ethics are akin to those of the Stoics in his doctrine of *oikeiosis* and his assumption that nothing is good unless virtuous. Taurus was interested in the interpretation of the cosmogony in the *Timaeus*, which he interpreted as an allegory and not according to the Aristotelian principle of the eternity of the world.

Atticus is distinguished by a lack of toleration, and his interpretation of Aristotle is substantially distorted. His polemic against Aristotle concentrated on cosmogony and ethics. He rejected the Aristotelian exegesis of the *Timaeus* and, following Plutarch, asserted the temporal creation of the world and the existence of an evil world soul. In ethics, he refused any peripateticism, considering it a moral weakness.

But the most interesting figure of Middle Platonism was surely the Syriac Numenius of Apameia. His doctrine shows an intermingling of Platonism and Pythagoreanism (and therefore he had often been considered as a Neopythagorean); but from Xenocrates and Eudorus onward, Platonic philosophy was often shadowed with Neopythagoreanism. Numenius was interested in Hermetism, Gnosticism, and Zoroastrian and Hebrew cultures. His Pythagorizing Platonism, perhaps through Ammonius Saccas, the master of Plotinus, exercised a powerful influence over Neoplatonism and Plotinus himself. Numenius is a radical dualist, taking the Pythagorean Dyad as the passive principle in opposition to One-god. The Dyad is the origin of matter, which is eternal and unorganized, like the evil Soul of Plutarch and Atticus, though put in an organized state by the Demiurge. As such, the Dyad was not produced by the Monad. Matter is fluid and without quality, but possesses an intrinsic evil force. The Demiurge is the second god. Above him is the first god, called "Father," and under him is the world. So the Demiurge is double, being both the first and the second god, and there is a triad of divine entities, perhaps corresponding to the triad of the second Platonic epistle (312e), which is now regarded a Pythagorean forgery.

The first and second centuries CE saw the growth and diffusion of Gnosticism and Hermetism. Middle Platonic doctrines are present to some degree in these philosophical-religious movements, mingled with and transformed by other doctrines of various origins. This is a large field, which Dillon has defined as "the underworld of Platonism" (1977, p. 384).

GNOSTICISM. The relationship between Gnosis and Platonism should begin with an examination of the concept of dualism, specifically, Platonic dualism. If by dualism we mean a doctrine of two principles, from which the whole universe derives and on which it depends, then Plato's *Timaeus,* with its doctrine of coeternal Demiurge (at a higher ontological level than ideas) and *chora* (interpreted as matter), is certainly dualist. However, such a dualism is pre-cosmic, since the created world is characterized by harmony and eternity, and *chora* is not a negative entity. Besides, Plato's anthropogony in *Timaeus* 42d and 69c, which describes the intervention of the inferior gods, who, obeying the Demiurge, create the human soul and body in order not to involve God in the responsibility for evil, foreshadows some Gnostic tenets. If the chief characteristic of Gnosticism is its negative depiction of world, Gnostic dualism, though of quite different origin, may be paralleled with Platonic dualism as it is expressed in Plutarch and Numenius. Among Gnostic schools, one of the most representative was that of Valentinus, who was a contemporary of Albinus and Numenius; Valentinus was considered *platonicus* by Christian writers. Some of his doctrines derive in part from certain forms of contemporary Platonism, where a relatively nondualistic position is present. For Valentinus, the creation of the world is not the result of the struggle between the principle of Good and the principle of Evil, as it is for Barbelognostics and Mani, but is rather the result of the corruption of a previously perfect system, just as for Neoplatonism the existence of evil is the corruption of perfection. Valentinus created an elaborate myth in order to explain the existence of the material world. The basic framework of his system is reminiscent of Pythagorean metaphysics, which had penetrated also into Middle Platonism. It has been supposed that Valentinus had interpreted the aeons of his metaphysics as a kind of Platonic idea. Tertullian was perhaps the first to interpret aeons as the thoughts and motions of the divine Being, whereas Ptolemaeus, one of Valentinus's followers, interpreted them as real persons. From the primordial reality new entities come out in a kind of "emanation" (*probole*). The new entities retain, in a depotentiated way, the essence of the original reality, just as in the Neoplatonic system. Initially there are a monadic and a dyadic figure, the latter being subordinated to the former. Their secondary, derived Principle has the titles of the Platonic supreme god, Father and First Principle, while the real supreme principle is called Forefather and Pre-first Principle. The name Ennoia, in the Valentinian system, is reminiscent of Philo's Sophia, which is the same as the Logos of God. Sophia, the aeon who originate last, was a female principle. Her sin is her desire to know her origin and the Forefather's nature, which leads her to try to bear a child without a *syzygos,* or partner. She has the function of the indefinite Dyad, which introduces evil at the highest level. Horos, the "limit" in the Valentinian myth, perhaps is akin to the Pythagorean *peras,* and his function is analogous to the regulating activity (for instance, in Philo) of divine Logos.

Before Valentinus lived Basilides (end of first century CE), who held views similar to those of Plotinus. He professed *apophatism* about divine Being as the natural consequence of the doctrine of divine transcendence. According to Basilides, both original Principles, light and darkness, originally were distinct, but when darkness saw the light, it longed for union with it, just as light desired to see darkness. In the beginning there was the absolute naught, which is perhaps identified with God (Hippolytus says that God was "not existing")—such is the conclusion of "negative theology," which was quite common in Platonic and Pythagorean schools. Basilides discussed, as Platonists did, the problem of the creation of the world, which, according to him, is created out of "seeds." These seeds are derived from the Stoic doctrine of *logos spermatikos,* which states that the cosmic Logos contains the *logoi spermatikoi,* and in this primordial seed is contained all that will be developed thereafter. Basilides' cosmic seeds also contain all that will happen. Like Plato (*Tim.* 73c), Basilides employs the word *panspermia.* God creates the world thanks to his free will, and cosmic seeds don't come out of preexistent matter. Middle Platonists, in contrast, considered God to be a craftsman. So, Basilides was the first Christian philosopher to consider the same problems as contemporary Middle Platonism. Valentinian cosmogony also took up some Middle Platonic doctrines, such as: Matter in itself is not body but possesses the fitness to become every kind of body.

HERMETISM. The treatises of the *Corpus hermeticum* were composed during the second and third century CE. Hermetism was influenced by Middle Platonism, which can be seen, for example, in the first and most important treatise of the *Corpus hermeticum,* the *Poemandres* (this name is perhaps a translation from Egyptian). Poemandres describes himself as the *nous* of the Supreme Power. It is open to interpretation whether the Supreme Power is above the *nous,* as God is above Mind, or whether *nous* possesses the Supreme Power. The description of the creation of the world owes something to the concept of the Platonic Demiurge. The Hermetic writer distinguishes between *nous* and *logos* in a manner similar to Philo of Alexandria. Like Philo, the Hermetic writer defines Logos as "son of God." The supreme *Nous* generates another *nous demiourgos,* who is the creator of fire and *pneuma,* the seven planetary gods, and other entities, such as the cosmic soul and *physis,* the archetypal man (borrowed perhaps from Philo). Also in ethic, the ideal of apatheia found its way into Hermetic doctrines.

CHRISTIAN MIDDLE PLATONISTS. Middle Platonism had a strong influence on Christian thought, beginning in the second century CE. Apologists such as Justin, Tatian, Athenagoras, and Theophilus of Antioch identified the Son of God with the Logos, or the second god of contemporary Middle Platonists, while the Father was considered the origin of the Logos and even superior to him, just as first *nous* is above second *nous.* Christian Middle Platonism was developed by much more representative thinkers, like Clement of Alexandria and Origen, who went deep into the question of the nature of God and of the relation between the Father and the Son, both being eternal and divine entities, but personally differentiated. In ethics, Clement of Alexandria and Origen recognized the Middle Platonic "assimilation to god" as the ideal implicit in the doctrine that God created Adam "in our image, after our likeness" (*Gn.* 1:26). The interpretation of *Genesis* 1:2 that the world was created out of shapeless matter is the Christian accommodation of Old Testament cosmogony to Middle Platonic philosophy. Philo of Alexandria had already proposed this, and it clearly appears in Athenagoras, Theophilus of Antioch, and Irenaeus of Lyon (second century CE). As soon as Apologists considered the biblical narration of the creation of the world, the problem of a philosophical interpretation became cogent, since the text of the Bible was not compatible with Platonic philosophy. The solution was a *creatio ex nihilo,* which developed at the end of second century CE, but Christian authors who were educated in the Middle Platonic philosophy, such as Justin, Athenagoras, and Clement of Alexandria, found it difficult to accept such a solution, and the contemporary heretic Hermogenes returned to the Middle Platonic doctrine of creation out of existing matter.

PLATONISM AND NEOPLATONISM. From the beginning of the Plotinian school in Rome (244 CE onward) and the research of Porphyry of Tyros (middle third century CE), we usually speak no more either of Middle Platonism or of Platonism, but of Neoplatonism. Of course, original Platonic doctrine mingled with Neoplatonic elaborations, and their influence can be traced in the writing of Christian and, later, Islamic theologians and philosophers. Plotinus (205–270) is normally considered the founder of Neoplatonism, though the evolution of Platonism is not so linear and direct as it was supposed in the nineteenth and twentieth century, such as in Eduard Zeller's strong Hegelian interpretation of the history of ancient philosophy. Plotinus wasn't the "schoolmaster of Neoplatonism," and Platonism from the third to sixth century had many peculiarities not derived from Plotinus. The essays Plotinus wrote for circulation among his pupils were collected by his disciple Porphyry (d. c. 305) in six sets of nine texts known collectively as the *Enneads.* In these terse and often difficult papers, Plotinus sets out a system according to which all reality issues spontaneously, coordinately, and timelessly from a single transcendent and inexpressible source called the One or the Good. This process of emanation produces a hierarchical world order in which each successive form of reality (*hypostasis*) images its superior at a lower level of unity. Thus Intellect—the unity of intuitive awareness with its intelligible objects (the Forms)—images the One. Soul, the third *hypostasis,* images Intellect, although its being and knowing are distended in time, and although, as "nature," it approaches division in space by giving rise to the corporeal, visible cosmos. The limit of this expansion of reality from the One is primal matter, which, Plotinus teaches, is in itself mere privation. To the emanation of reality from the One there corresponds a converse and simultaneous movement of "return" (*epistrophe*), by which each level of being seeks itself in its source and original. From this point of view, the structure of Plotinus's cosmos corresponds to the route that consciousness takes in contemplative activity as it moves from dispersion to integration. The highest normal level of consciousness is the unified awareness that belongs to Intellect, but in moments of mystical ecstasy the soul—as Plotinus records from his own experience—achieves a loss of particular selfhood in union with the One.

Porphyry was a commentator on Plato and Aristotle and the author of a lengthy treatise titled *Against the Christians.* In Porphyry's writings the scholastic tone and religious interests of later Neoplatonism are foreshadowed. He produced not only commentaries but also summary interpretations of Plotinian ontology and ethics, as in his *Sentences* and *Letter to His Wife Marcella.* Porphyry seems to be responsible for reviving the repute of a late-second-century collection of revelations known as the *Chaldaean Oracles.* Although sceptical of the claims that this collection made for the ritual-magical practice of theurgy, Porphyry apparently initiated the practice of interpreting the *Oracles* in the light of a Plotinian metaphysic.

Porphyry's disciple Iamblichus (d. c. 325 CE) wrote a commentary (now lost) on the *Chaldaean Oracles* and in his treatise *On the Mysteries* defended theurgy (against Porphyry) as necessary for the soul's union with the divine. He was also a speculative philosopher of great originality, and his system opened the way for the elaborate metaphysics that marked the thought of the later Platonic school at Athens. There, from about 400 until 529, a series of distinguished teachers developed both the philosophical and the religious positions that Iamblichus had defended. Most notable among these was Proclus (c. 412–485), whose *Elements of Theology* and *Commentary on the Timaeus* are monuments to the learning and dialectical skill of the Academy in its last days. Proclus saw his task as carrying Iamblichus's principles to their logical conclusion and filling any gaps he left in the metaphysical hierarchy. Therefore Proclus admitted within the First Hypostasis a series of Unities (*Henads*) in addition to the One itself. He establishes complete symmetry between that Hypostasis and lower orders by extending to it Iamblichus's distinction of Unparticipated and Participated Terms. The *Henads* thus constitute the Participated intermediaries linking lower realities to the One, which now becomes the First Hypostasis Unparticipated Monad. But the *Henads* are not simply aspects or attributes of the First Cause, but substantial, self-subsistent entities derived from the One and dependent on it. Hence arise their functions—one metaphysical, the other religious. The former function was that of bridging the gulf between Unity and Plurality. In particular, although the One is absolutely unknowable, the *Henads*, unknowable in themselves, can be known by analogy from their products. Fundamental is the basic Neoplatonic doctrine that the same attribute can exist under an appropriate mode on successive levels. Proclus emphasizes that such attributes are present perfectly only on the level of the *Henads*. Each order of reality, even the *Henads*, represents an appropriate combination of Limit and Infinity, whose cosmogonic roles can be traced back to early Pythagoreanism and to Plato's *Philebus*.

In the Latin West, Platonism and Neoplatonism were transmitted through Marius Victorinus (end of third century–360) and Augustine of Hippo (354–430). "Victorinus shows how lively, how original, how pulsating, how stimulating and, yea, how attractive was Platonism in the fourth century. Together with Augustine, Victorinus represents the best example that, for an intellectual, the reception of Christian doctrines was possible only through Neoplatonism, the dominating spiritual trend at the time" (Baltes, 2002, p.125). Victorinus's theology develops a rich metaphysical system, attributing to the Father the majority of the qualifications characterizing the Neoplatonic One, which are, of course, negative ones, according to apophatic trends widely developed by Greek philosophy and Christian culture (oneness, pureness, simpleness, invisibility, unutterability, motion, passions, corruption, and lack of body). Moreover, Victorinus's deep philosophical background shows in the majority of his doctrines. For example, his Trinitarian speculation is an attempt to join the triadic schemes already attested in Platonic texts, particularly in the *Enneads*. The relationship between the three Persons of the Trinity is in fact explained by means of Neoplatonic schemes, thus equating Father, Son, and Holy Spirit to the hypostatical moments of being-life-intellect (or being-intellect-life, in a reversed order), or introducing the more complex concept of predominance, according to which each Person of the Trinity is best characterized by the prevalence of one of these aspects (being-life-intellect), in order to preserve and reassert their mutual relationship. The Son's generative process is described in philosophical terms, such as stillness and movement, form and act, dynamis and activity, to which must be added the conversion, represented by the Spirit.

Augustine's conversion to Christianity accompanied his discovery of Neoplatonic thought, as represented by writings of Plotinus and Porphyry (writings probably translated into Latin by Marius Victorinus). His doctrine was permeated by Platonic themes, however revised and recast in the light of his Christian beliefs. Boethius (c. 480–c. 524), a Roman aristocrat in the service of the Ostrogothic king Theoderic, and an orthodox Christian, did as much as Augustine to transmit the heritage of Hellenic philosophy to the medieval West. Aiming to provide Latin versions of the major works of Aristotle and Plato, he succeeded, before his execution at the hands of Theodoric, in rendering certain of Aristotle's logical works as well as Porphyry's *Introduction to Aristotle's Categories*, the book that originally stimulated medieval philosophical debate. His *Consolation of Philosophy*, widely read during the Middle Ages, presented a simplified Neoplatonist outlook consistent with the structures of Christian doctrine.

It was largely through Augustine, whose influence is seen in thinkers as diverse as Anselm of Canterbury (c. 1033–1109), Hugh of Saint-Victor (c. 1096–1141), the School of Chartres, the Franciscan Bonaventure (c. 1217–1274), and the Dominicans Thomas Aquinas (c. 1225–1274) and Johannes Eckhart (c. 1260–1327?), that Platonist themes influenced medieval Latin philosophy and spirituality. Of the works of Plato, only the *Timaeus* was known (in the fourth-century Latin version of Calcidius). Plotinus and his successors were scarcely known at all, save through Boethius's translation of Porphyry's *Introduction to Aristotle's Categories*. What the Latin Middle Ages eventually harvested from the work of the late Platonists were the writings of Aristotle on natural philosophy, ethics, and metaphysics, which, during and after the thirteenth century, became standard texts in the liberal arts curricula of medieval universities.

MUSLIM NEOPLATONISM. Parallel to the Platonic tradition during the Middle Ages is the spread of Platonic thought among Muslims. Indeed, medieval Western interest in, and knowledge of Plato was stimulated and in part made possible by the labors of Islamic philosophers who worked on ninth- and tenth-century Arabic versions of the works of Aristotle, Plato, and their Neoplatonic commentators. But Neoplatonic thought didn't reach the Arabs only through translations from the Greek; Syriac translations of Greek texts were another major source. A major role was played by a remarkable forgery, the so-called *Theology of Aristotle*, which in fact consists of extracts from Plotinus's *Enneads* IV–VI augmented by supplementary or explanatory material perhaps derived from Porphyry's lost commentary. In 832 CE in Bagdad, Califf al-Mamoun founded the "House of Wisdom," whose direction was committed to famous and clever translaters, including Honayn ibn Ishaq (809–873 CE), who was famous for translating Greek books into Syriac and Arabic. Therefore the whole terminology of Arabic theology and philosophy was prepared during the ninth century, and the "hellenistic philosophers" (*falasifa* is the Arabic word for *philosophos*) could use the translation of Aristotle and his commentators, Plato and Galen. The "peripatetic reaction" by Averroes opposed the Neoplatonism of these thinkers. Al-Kindi (796–d. after 870) was interested not only in mathematics and geometry, but also in metaphysics, astronomy, and music. He tried to reconcile philosophy with prophetic revelation and distinguished between human science (which included logic, the arts of *quadrivium* and philosophy) and a divine science, which was the prophetic revelation. He accepted the *creatio ex nihilo*, which he interpreted as an act of God's will, not as an emanation. God creates the first Intelligence, from which the other are derived, as Neoplatonists taught. The structure of his worldview was essentially that of later Neoplatonism, and his thought derived from John Philoponus's works and the Neoplatonic school in Athens.

This Arab philosophical enterprise was continued by al-Fārābī (872–950), a great religious and mystical thinker. He wrote a work to demonstrate the agreement of Plato and Aristotle. In his opinion, wisdom began among the Chaldaeans in Mesopotamia and then spread to Egypt and Greece. According to his teaching, the cosmic Intelligences are derived from the One, but only through the first Intelligence, because *ex Uno non fit nisi unum.* The works of Ibn Sīnā (Avicenna, 980–1037), and al-Ghazālī (1058–1111) were also influenced by Neoplatonism.

PLATONISM IN THE RENAISSANCE. It was not until the fifteenth century and the work of Nicholas of Cusa (1401–1464), Marsilio Ficino (1433–1499), and others that Plato himself, read through the eyes of his Neoplatonic interpreters, was rediscovered. Nicholas, in *On Learned Ignorance,* presents a view of the world that owes much to Proclus, as well as to certain Platonic dialogues. Ficino translated Plato and Plotinus's *Enneads* into Latin and made a start on Porphyry and Iamblichus. Even Aristotle, in this new age, began to be read as the ancient Neoplatonists had read him. Platonic writings and ideas accompanied the spread of Renaissance humanism and went on to influence modern philosophy.

SEE ALSO Dualism; Fārābī, al-; Gnosticism, article on Gnosticism from Its Origins to the Middle Ages; Hellenistic Religions; Hermetism; Neoplatonism; Plato; Socrates.

BIBLIOGRAPHY

Andresen, Carl. *Logos und Nomos. Die Polemik des Kelsos wider das Christentum.* Berlin, 1955.

Armstrong, A. Hilary, ed. *The Cambridge History of Later Greek and Early Medieval Philosophy.* Cambridge, 1967.

Armstrong, A. Hilary. "Dualism: Platonic, Gnostic and Christian." In *Neoplatonism and Gnosticism,* edited by R.T. Wallis and J. Bregman, pp. 33–54. New York, 1992.

Baltes, Matthias. *Die Weltentstehung des platonischen Timaios nach den antiken Interpreten,* Leiden, 1976.

Baltes, Matthias. *Dianoemata. Kleine Schriften zum Platon und zum Platonismus.* Stuttgart and Leipzig, 1999.

Baltes, Matthias. *Marius Victorinus. Zur Philosophie in seinen Theologischen Schriften.* Munich, 2002.

Barnes, Jonathan. "Antiochus of Ascalon." In *Philosophia Togata I. Essays on Philosophy and Roman Society,* edited by Myriam Griffin and Jonathan Barnes, pp. 51-96. Oxford, 1989.

Bianchi, Ugo. *Selected Essays on Gnosticism, Dualism and Misteriosophy.* Leiden, 1978.

Bianchi, Ugo. *Il dualismo religioso. Saggio storico ed etnologico.* Rome, 1983.

Cherniss Harald. *Aristotle's Criticism of Plato and the Academy.* Baltimore, 1944.

Corbin, Henri. *Histoire de la philosophie islamique . . . avec la collaboration de Seyyed Hossein Nasr et Osman Yahya.* Paris, 1964.

Dillon, John. *The Middle Platonists. A Study of Platonism 80 BC to AD 220.* London, 1977.

Dillon, John. *The Golden Chain. Studies in the Development of Platonism and Christianity.* Aldershot, U.K., 1990.

Dörrie, Heinrich. *Platonica Minora.* Munich, 1976.

Dörrie, Heinrich, and Matthias Baltes. *Der Platonismus in der Antike.* Stuttgart and Bad Cannstatt, 1987–2001.

Donini, Pier Luigi. *Le scuole, l'anima, l'impero. La filosofia antica da Antioco a Plotino.* Turin, 1982.

Ferrari, Franco. *Dio, idee e materia. La struttura del cosmo in Plutarco di Cheronea.* Naples, 1995.

Festugière André-Jean. *La révélation d'Hermès Trismegiste.* Paris, 1944–1953.

Frede, Michael. "Numenius." In *Aufstieg und Niedergang der römischen Welt,* Volume II, 36,1, edited by Hildegard Temporini and Wolfgang Haase, pp. 1034–1075. New York and Berlin, 1987.

Gersh, Stephen. *Middle Platonism and Neoplatonism: The Latin Tradition,* I–II. Notre Dame, Ind., 1986.

Gersh, Stephen, and Charles Kannengiesser, eds., *Platonism in Late Antiquity.* Notre Dame, Ind., 1992.

Gioè, Adriano. *Filosofi medioplatonici del II secolo d.C.* Naples, 2002.

Glucker, John. *Antiochus and the Late Academy.* Göttingen, 1978.

Ivánka, Endre von. *Plato Christianus.* Einsiedeln, 1964.

Jonas, Hans. *The Gnostic Religion,* Boston, 1958.

Klibansky, Raymond. *The Continuity of the Platonic Tradition during the Middle Ages.* London, 1950; reprint, New York, 1982.

Krämer, Hans J., *Der Ursprung der Geistmetaphysik.* Amsterdam, 1964.

Lilla, Salvatore R.C., *Clement of Alexandria. A Study in Christian Platonism and Gnosticism.* Oxford, 1971.

Moreschini, Claudio. *Apuleio e il platonismo.* Florence, 1978.

Mansfeld, Jaap. *Heresiography in Context. Hippolytus' Elenchos as a Source for Greek Philosophy.* Leiden, New York, and Köln, 1992.

Merlan, Philip. *From Platonism to Neoplatonism.* The Hague, 1968.

Prächter, Karl. *Kleine Schriften.* Hildesheim, 1973.

Rist, John M. "Monism: Plotinus and Some Predecessors," *Harvard Studies in Classical Philology* 70 (1965): 329-344.

Runia, David T. *Philo of Alexandria and the Timaeus of Plato.* Leiden, 1986.

Tarrant, Harald. *Scepticism or Platonism? The Philosophy of the Fourth Academy.* New York, 1985.

Theiler, Willy. *Untersuchungen zur antiken Literatur.* Berlin, 1970.

Wallis, R.T., *Neoplatonism,* 2d ed. London, 1995.

Whittaker, John. *Studies in Platonism and Patristic Thought.* London, 1984.

Whittaker, John. "Platonic Philosophy in the Early Centuries of the Empire." In *Aufstieg und Niedergang der römischen Welt* Volume II, 36,1, edited by Hildegard Temporini and Wolfgang Haase, pp. 81–123. New York and Berlin, 1987.

CLAUDIO MORESCHINI (2005)

PLAY. The idea of play may be embedded in the very metaphysics of certain cosmologies (Handelman and Shulman 1997), as well as in particular ritual contexts. Although the idea of play has widespread currency in religions with differing epistemologies, the profundity of its presence corresponds to the level of premises at which it is lodged in a given religious system. The more abstract and encompassing the premises of a religion imbued with the ideation of play, the more pervasive and fateful are its systematic expressions in religious life.

ATTRIBUTES OF THE IDEA OF PLAY. The idea of play is universal among humankind, whether or not particular cultures have terms to denote such a conception. A first attribute of play is that its assumptions are preeminently conditional, for play is a medium through which the make-believe is brought into being and acquires the status of a reality.

Especially human is the capacity to imagine and, so, to create alternative realities. In question, however, are the truth values of such realities, that is, the extent to which, and under which conditions, they are accorded validity. In the logic of modern Western culture, the imaginary is not accorded any ultimate status of validity or truth. Gregory Bateson (1972) has argued that the messages that signify the existence of play are "untrue" in a sense, and that the reality that such messages denote is nonexistent. This, of course, holds in a culture whose religious cosmology is predicated in part upon a comparatively immutable boundary between the divine and the human, with the former accorded the status of absolute truth, while the latter is perceived in no small measure as sinful and as a profanation of the former. Given its imaginary character, the idea of play in much of modern Western thought often is rendered as pretense and is relegated to the domain of the culturally "unserious," like the world of fiction and that of leisure time activities, or to the realm of the "not yet fully human," like the play of little children. Yet to equate the imaginary universally with the frivolous is to render the essential powers of play impotent and to obscure their roles in religious thought and action, especially in cosmologies where a state of existence is also a condition of untruth.

A second attribute of play is the necessity of a form of reference that can be altered in systematic ways. Play changes the known signs of form into something else by altering the reified boundaries that define and characterize the phenomenon. What is changed still retains crucial similarities to its form of foundation and so remains intimately related to it. For example, the medieval European Feast of Fools, a rite of inversion, required the form of a traditional Christian Mass that could be altered. The play-mass would have no significance for participants were it not derived from and contrasted with its everyday analogue, the traditional Mass.

A third attribute of play is that any phenomenal form can be transformed through a sense of imagination that itself remains constrained to a degree by the composition of the "original" form. This attribute may be problematic for ontologies that strongly implicate the active presence of play in the acts of creation, as in Hinduism. For since the idea of play requires the existence of forms that can be differently modeled, how can this idea be present prior to the creation of form? Nonetheless, if the Hindu cosmos comes into being as the adumbrated dream of the all-encompassing universal principle, *brahman,* then this attribute of play is not obviated, since original form itself is imaginary and illusory.

A fourth attribute of play is that it brings into being something that had not existed before by changing the shape and positioning of boundaries that categorize phenomena and so altering their meaning. One may state simply that creation, destruction, and recreation occur and recur because those boundaries that demarcate the coherency of phenomena are altered. Therefore play is associated intimately with creativity and with creation, as Johan Huizinga (1938) and Arthur Koestler (1964) have maintained, as well as with its converse, destruction. In the most limited case of creation, that of the inversion of a phenomenally valid form, it is only the reflection of such form, still constrained by the original positioning of boundaries, that is brought into being. For example, the inversion of gender is constrained by finite permutations, as is the overturning of a clearly defined hierarchy, as long as gender and hierarchy remain the respective terms of reference of these inversions. On the other hand, cosmologies that strongly feature trickster figures also tend to be characterized by lengthier series of transformations of these types, so that it becomes difficult to state which form is the original and which the playful copy.

A fifth attribute of play is that it is an amoral medium, one that is marked by plasticity, by lability, and by flexibility in ideation—qualities closely related to those of imagination and creativity. In play, these qualities have the potential to meddle with and to disturb any form of stability and any conception of order.

A sixth attribute of play is a penchant for questioning the phenomenal stability of any form that purports to exist as a valid proposition and as a representation of "truth." The idea of play is amoral in its capacities to subvert the boundaries of any and all phenomena and so to rock the foundations of a given reality.

Whether, and to what degree, these qualities of play are integral to the metaphysics of a given religious system should illustrate how that system works. For example, whether the boundaries that divide the paranatural and human realms are quite absolute or are matters of continuous gradation and whether the character of a cosmology's population (deities, spirits, demons, tricksters, and so forth) is one of positional stability or of ongoing transformation should be illuminated by the relative presence of the attributes of play in a particular religious system.

THE IDEA OF PLAY AND PREMISES OF COSMOLOGY. The embeddedness of the idea of play does not appear to be associated, in particular, either with great religious traditions or with local ones, either with so-called tribal societies or with more complex ones. Hence the examples adduced here are of a tribal people and of Hinduism.

The Iatmul of the Sepik River area in New Guinea are a tribal people whose culture values monistic and yet dualistic conceptions of the cosmos. Both coexist, each continuously transforming into the other. For the monism of the Iatmul view of cosmic order fragments into a multitude of competing principles that explain that order. In turn, these recombine into an elementary synthesis, only to multiply once again and to flow together once more.

Thus the character of the Iatmul cosmos is one of immanent transmutability, of plays upon phenomenal form. This reverberates throughout the institutions of Iatmul society and parallels a conduciveness to paradox in Iatmul thought. This proclivity of paradox highlights ongoing disjunctions among phenomenal forms. Therefore strong tendencies toward fragmentation lurk within numerous cultural traditions that declare the validity of a coherent synthesis of differing principles in Iatmul society. Thus Iatmul men, in the heat of argument, were to display their most sacred ceremonial objects before the profaning gaze of women and uninitiated boys, thereby completely destroying for years to come the ritual efficacy of these collective representations. Superficially this behavior could appear simply as uncontrolled and destructive. Yet further consideration would reveal that such behavior was quite consistent with those premises of an Iatmul worldview that denied to boundaries a fixedness of form for lengthy durations.

In such cosmologies, as of course in others, boundaries of form are brought into being through change. Yet in such cosmologies both phenomenal form and the agencies of change are, in a sense, illusory: though they persuade that the solidity of reification is their state, this masks the more profound observation that impermanence is their condition. Here play, as illusion in action, is crucial. The ideation of play is processual: it can bring into being forms that signify the existence of the cosmos. Yet these forms themselves must be transcended through their own negation in order to reveal those deeper truths that are masked by the very force of illusion. Therefore the processuality of play, of imagination, also effaces its own creation.

Aspects of Hindu cosmology exemplify this abstract sense of play as cosmic process. The Hindu concept of *līla* commonly is translated as the "play" of forces and energies that are continually in motion. These spontaneously create and destroy the possibility of a phenomenal world in an unending process. *Līla,* as play, is a metaphor of flux, of movement, from which the cosmos emerges and into which it will eventually disappear. Any reification of form, implying inherent solidity and stability, denies this basic premise. Yet the premise itself cannot be realized without the creation of form, which is then the opposite of nonform, of flux. Momentarily (in cosmic terms) the premise of *līlā* must create phenomena in order to revalidate itself by then subverting and destroying them. The creation of phenomena is activated through the use of *māyā,* commonly translated as the force of illusion, that is, as another aspect of the idea of play as it is used here. All phenomena rest and shift on the premise of illusion. Their most abstract of purposes is to cease to exist as phenomena.

Among the products of *māyā* is the cosmos that gods and humans inhabit. This can be rendered as *saṃsāra,* a gloss for all phenomena that exist in the cosmos. *Saṃsāra,* too, is understood as flux, as the processual flow that shapes all forms, and not as phenomena whose reification is absolute in any sense. *Saṃsāra* is also related to the idea of play and refers to the cycle of birth and rebirth of all beings. One can attain salvation, and so escape *saṃsāra,* only by dissipating the forces of illusion that render deep flux as superficial form. For gods and humans, for renouncers and antigods, aspects of the ideation of play are both their confinement, through illusion, in the bounded phenomenal trap and their escape from it through the dissolution of fixed forms. As named beings, deities are not ultimate forms in and of themselves. Rather they are signposts on the way to salvation, just as other figures point in contrary directions. Without beginning to overcome the forces of illusion, thereby gaining insight into both creation and destruction, one is caught endlessly in the paradoxes of a world that appears stable but is in flux. Yet perceptions that are paradoxical on one level of abstraction become merely ironical on a higher one.

The logic of these ideas permeates numerous aspects of Hindu cosmology. Ideally, the creative role of the *saṃnyāsin,* the renouncer, which is dedicated to the penetration of illusion, is also built into the Hindu life cycle as the final stage of living in this reality. Therefore, in a theoretical sense, the desirability of piercing the force of illusion that makes the world possible is integral to living in that world.

Like humans, Hindu gods and antigods are not constructed culturally as unitary and homogeneous figures. Instead they are self-transforming types whose logic of composition depends on the alteration of hierarchical and lateral boundaries within and around themselves. In their transformations these figures bear witness to the ultimate impermanence of illusion and also to the necessity of this force upon which they, like humankind, depend for existence. The only final stability in the Hindu cosmos is that of motility; the only final coherence in classification is its mutation.

Such paranatural types, like other facets of Hinduism, often seem paradoxical to Western thinking, in which stability is believed to be truly real and flux is both a secondary and a deficient reality. In the South Indian Śaiva Tamil tradition, for example, Śiva is composed as a self-transforming figure. He is creator, protector, and destroyer. He is, in Wendy O'Flaherty's felicitous phrasing, the erotic ascetic. He transcends and contains the cosmos, yet also appears within it through synecdoche, the relationship of part to whole. He is trickster and tricked. He creates the antigods, the *asuras*, and, by the terms of their compact, is helpless before them as they wreak havoc. But he also transcends himself in creating his son, Murukan̲, who destroys the antigods. There are hints that Murukan̲ at once is greater than Śiva, is Śiva, and is reabsorbed into Śiva. In this example the power of imagination, intimately associated with illusion, has the capacity to expand upon, to extend, and to transform phenomenal reality beyond those boundaries that previously had contained it in an ongoing play of generative forces. This potential is actualized since reality and the fixedness that gives it definition are illusory.

Like the permutations of malleability in Iatmul cosmology, that of Hinduism, although operating in terms of a radically different epistemology, emphasizes the fragmentation of unitary principles that flow together in synthesis only to divide once again. In both of these cosmologies the idea of play would seem to inhere in their abstract conceptualizations of phenomenal reality that, on the one hand, perch and teeter precariously on the border between cosmos and chaos and, on the other, conceive of processuality as a condition of existence.

PREMISES OF PLAY IN RITUAL OCCASIONS. As the focus of play shifts to the positioning of this idea in religious or quasi-religious occasions, it becomes more constricted, since its presence threatens the validity and the stability of the occasion in which it is located. Nonetheless the idea of play does accomplish certain kinds of work in particular ritual contexts.

Within ritual contexts the notion of play has perhaps the most embracing mandate in that category of occasion termed *festival.* As the etymology of the English word denotes, a festival is an occasion of celebration, of joyous attitudes, and of rejoicing, marked by moods of cheer. In European tradition it has affinities with the carnivalesque and with certain liturgical periods in the Christian calendar. In the Hindu tradition it encompasses annual occasions that celebrate the powers of particular deities, and such times often are indistinguishable from pilgrimages to the deities in this culture.

Of especial significance here is that festival approximates a total collective performance, one that celebrates a holistic unity of cosmic and social order on the part of a relatively homogenized population of participants. This implies that many of the distinctions between social categories of persons—whether based on hierarchy, status, occupation, or age—may be temporarily subverted and dissolved in a playful spirit. Thus people, ordinarily separated by moral edicts and social rules, are brought together to experience the rediscovery of the significance of *sacra* that apply to all of them as a comparatively undifferentiated community of believers.

In part this may be done through inversions of social identity that reverse the relationships among everyday social distinctions, so that the high are made low and more peripheral positions become more central. This is the case in the North Indian holiday Krsnalila, or Feast of Love. Or, as in the European tradition of Carnival, the spirit of festive license and the erasure of social boundaries prepare the way for the ascetic restrictions of the days of Lent. In either instance the ideation of play is crucial to establish a comparative degree of social homogeneity among participants, permitting them to receive and to experience the power of *sacra,* individually and collectively. During carnivalesque occasions the indeterminacy of play serves as a mediating prelude to the transcendence of a social collective, preparing it to be recast as a religious community.

Still, the heyday of the European Carnival was during the medieval period, when the metaphysics of Christianity may have been quite different from their present-day counterparts. Then, the boundaries between the divine and the human were more mutable and interpenetrable, and the themes of the effervescent grotesque, itself a likely product of the mingling of domains, were pervasive. This more transformative cosmology was more similar in certain general respects to that of Hinduism than to its modern offsprings. And it is this kind of cosmology that encourages the genre of the religious festival. Here the playful celebration of the dissolution of boundaries creates the grounds for their reconstitution with renewed vigor.

The idea of play within ritual occasions, the boundaries of which are strongly and unequivocally reified, has a much narrower scope. Such occasions, unlike numerous festivals, tend to be organized as a clear-cut sequence of phases that follow one another in cumulative progression. Hierarchy is prominent; there are social distinctions among those who take part and between participants and others. Order is prevalent throughout, as is the measured progression to messages of the sacred. Where play is present, it rarely questions either the external boundaries that circumscribe the occasion or its internal distinctions. Instead, the mutability of play is bent to more specific purposes.

Across cultures the most characteristic of these operations is found in inversions that are featured in the commonly termed "rituals of reversal." These are not usually rituals in their own right but more often occur in a particular phase in a ritual sequence. Inversions are marked frequently by the mockery, the mimicry, and the ridiculing of one category of person or theme by another, or of a category in relation to itself. This tends to occur in a spirit of play, that is, through the subversion of one form and its substitution by another. Here the validity of existing social categories or roles is not questioned. These remain the same; only their valences change, so that access to them is temporarily altered. Moreover, the inversion of form often seems to carry connotations of an unnatural condition so that the morally correct version of form lies in the converse of what is inverted. Therefore, inversions revert to the foundation-for-form, from which the inverted image was derived. Furthermore, an inverted form remains a refraction of its usual image, and this suggests that inversion maintains the very domain of discourse that is defined initially by the original form. This effectively restricts the transformative force of play and strictly limits the possible permutations of its plays-upon-form.

Nonetheless such constricted mutability may perform significant work within ritual occasions. In the Booger Dance of the Cherokee Indians of the southeastern United States, as this was practiced during the first decades of this century, an alternative reality that was experienced as threatening by the community of believers was proposed in play and destroyed through it. The Booger Dance itself was preceded and succeeded by dances associated with the dead and the defunct. The Cherokee who were disguised as Boogers inverted their everyday identities and took on those of strangers with obscene names, exaggerated features, and strange speech. They burst noisily into the dwelling where the ritual-dance series was performed. Their behavior was aggressive and boisterous, and they were perceived as malignant and menacing creatures. As each Booger danced he was mocked, mimicked, and laughed at by the onlookers. Furthermore by their moral demeanor the onlookers quieted and tamed the Boogers and eventually ejected them from the ritual space. Outside, they unmasked, and then, as Cherokee, they rejoined the others in further ritual dances.

The Boogers, familiar men inverted as fearsome strangers, represented all that was frightful and evil beyond the boundaries of the moral community. Their intrusion underlined and reinforced these boundaries rather than threatening them. By their mockery and laughter, members of the moral community queried the valid presence of these characters within the community, expelled these symbols of evil from within, and so reasserted the correctness of the moral and social orders. In this example the alternative order proposed by the Boogers does not appear to have been entertained seriously by the other participants. The reality of the Boogers was inauthentic from the outset, and therefore the make-believe of play was contrasted throughout with the verities of ritual, reaffirming them.

In other orchestrations of ritual occasions, play is used to falsify alternative realities that are proposed as authentic and that deny sacred verities. In the following example, of Sinhala Buddhist exorcisms on the southern coast of Sri Lanka, the alternative reality is adumbrated in seriousness and falsified through play. This permits the correct order to reemerge with a sense of revelation and in sharp contradistinction to the illusory character of play. In the Sinhala cosmology demons are inferior to humankind, as is humankind to deities and to the Buddha. A person possessed by a demon is understood to invert the hierarchical superiority of the human in relation to the demonic: the possessed is thought to perceive reality as one dominated by demons and not by deities. The problem of the exorcists is to destroy the superordinate demonic reality of the possessed and to reestablish the moral superiority of deities and humans. To accomplish this, exorcists first reify the validity of a superior demonic reality. The demons then appear in the human realm, confident of their superiority there. However their assertion of authentic ascendancy is subverted and destroyed through comic episodes that show this status to be illusory. The demons are proved to be laughable savages who are ignorant of the very rudiments of correct human action, etiquette, and morality. The assertions of demonic reality are dissolved through play, and the demons are ejected from the human realm to reassume their inferior cosmological position. These tests of the validity of demonic reality, through the medium of play, prepare the grounds for the revelation of the reemergence of correct cosmic order and free the possessed from the demonic grip.

This brief survey of certain of the relationships among the idea of play and aspects of the organization of religion and ritual leads to a final point that is of widespread concern to religious experience. The presence of play induces and encourages reflection on the part of believers upon the elementary premises of their religious systems. Playing with boundaries and therefore with the coherency and verity of ideation and form emphasizes that every taken-for-granted proposition also contains its own potential negation. In turn, the experience of such challenges deepens and strengthens belief in the truths of cosmology and ritual once their validity is reestablished.

See Also Carnival; Chaos; Cosmology, overview article; Games; Līlā; Māyā; Performance and Ritual; Tricksters.

Bibliography

The classic work on the role of play in the evolution of society remains that of Johan Huizinga, *Homo Ludens: Versuch einer Bestimmung des Spielelements der Kultur* (Haarlem, 1938), translated by R. F. C. Hull as *Homo Ludens: A Study of the Play-Element in Culture* (London, 1949). The most comprehensive study of the role of play in modern philosophies is that of Mihai I. Spariosu, *Dionysus Reborn: Play and the Aesthetic Dimension in Modern Philosophical and Scientific Discourse* (Ithaca, 1989). Don Handelman and David Shulman, in *God Inside Out: Siva's Game of Dice* (New York, 1997) offer a radical perspective on the formative role of play in the constitution of Saiva cosmology. That play is integral to creativity is explored by, among others, Arthur Koestler in his *The Act of Creation* (London, 1964). Susanne Langer, in "The Great Dramatic Forms: The Comic Rhythm," included in her *Feeling and Form: A Theory of Art* (New York, 1953), argues for an intimate association of the spirit of comedy with that of life-renewing forces. In a contrasting vein, Henri Bergson's *Laughter: An Essay on the Meaning of the Comic* (New York, 1912), translated by Cloudesly Brereton and Fred Rothwell from three articles of Bergson's that appeared in *Revue de Paris,* persuades that the comic exposes the disjunction between the presumptions of rigidity of form and the vitality of human spirit. His work is best read in conjunction with a more semiological approach, like that of G. B. Milner, who, in "Homo Ridens: Towards a Semiotic Theory of Humour and Laughter," *Semiotica* 5 (1972): 1–30, discusses the shift to the ideation of play as a change in paradigm. Gilles Deleuze's *Logique du Sens* (Paris, 1969), translated by Mark Lester with Charles Stivale, as *The Logic of Sense* (New York, 1990), begins with an extended analysis of Lewis Carroll's *Alice in Wonderland* and seeks the shifting locations where sense and nonsense collide. The seminal essay on the paradoxical character of such a cognitive shift, at least in Western thought, is Gregory Bateson's "A Theory of Play and Fantasy," in his *Steps to an Ecology of Mind* (New York, 1972). Mary Douglas, in "The Social Control of Cognition: Some Factors in Joke Perception," *Man: The Journal of the Royal Anthropological Institute,* n. s. 3 (September 1968): 361–376, brings to the fore the plasticity of indeterminacy that the ideation of play introduces into social reality. The most comprehensive cross-cultural overview of theories of play, among both children and adults, is Helen B. Schwartzman's *Transformations: The Anthropology of Children's Play* (New York, 1978). This volume contains an excellent bibliography. *Game, Play, Literature,* Yale French Studies, no. 41 (New Haven, 1968), a special issue edited by Jacques Ehrmann, contains provocative studies on the assumptions of playful ideation. Brian Sutton-Smith, in his *The Ambiguity of Play* (Cambridge, Mass., 1997), uses an original and insightful approach in discussing theories of play in terms of the different varieties of rhetoric through which these theories are constituted. An explicit comparison of the idea of play with that of ritual is my "Play and Ritual: Complementary Frames of Meta-Communication"; in *It's a Funny Thing, Humour* (Oxford, 1977), edited by Anthony J. Chapman and Hugh C. Foot. My, *Models and Mirrors: Towards an Anthropology of Public Events* (New York, 1998, 2d ed.), discusses the constituting roles of play in a variety of rituals and proto-rituals. Galina Lindquist discusses the role of play in neo-shamanic ritual in, *Shamanic Performances on the Urban Scene: Neo-Shamanism in Contemporary Sweden* (Stockholm, 1997). A diverse collection on the relationships between religion and playful ideation is *Holy Laughter* (New York, 1969), edited by M. Conrad Hyers. His *Zen and the Comic Spirit* (London, 1974) is an in-depth study of such relationships in one Eastern religious tradition. Useful general considerations of festival are found in Roger Caillois's *Man and the Sacred* (Glencoe, Ill., 1959), pp. 97–127, and in René Girard's *Violence and the Sacred* (Baltimore, 1977). An insightful and varied collection on the relationships of play to power is the special issue of *Focaal: European Journal of Anthropology* 37 (2001): 7–156, entitled *Playful Power and Ludic Spaces: Studies in Games of Life,* edited by Galina Lindquist and Don Handelman. The most intensive, subtle, and nuanced study of socialization through play in a non-Western culture is that of Jean Briggs, *Inuit Morality Play: The Emotional Education of a Three-Year-Old* (New Haven, Conn., 1998). The North Indian Kṛṣṇa Līla is described most evocatively by McKim Marriott in "The Feast of Love," in *Krishna: Myths, Rites and Attitudes* (Honolulu, 1966), edited by Milton Singer. Medieval European worldview and the tradition of Carnival is discussed with imagination and insight, if with a modicum of exaggeration, in Mikhail Bakhtin's *Rabelais and His World* (Cambridge, Mass., 1968). Iatmul cosmology is analyzed by Gregory Bateson in *Naven,* 2d ed. (Stanford, Calif., 1958). The Booger Dance of the Cherokee is described by Frank G. Speck and Leonard Broom, with the assistance of Will West Long, in *Cherokee Dance and Drama* (Berkeley, Calif., 1951). The elements of play in Sinhala exorcism are analyzed richly by Bruce Kapferer in *A Celebration of Demons: Exorcism and the Aesthetics of Healing in Sri Lanka* (Bloomington, Ind., 1983). Among modern Christian theologians, Harvey Cox argues for the value to Christianity of a renewed interest in the spirit of play, in *The Feast of Fools: A Theological Essay on Festivity and Fantasy* (Cambridge, Mass., 1969); and Josef Pieper maintains that festivity without religious celebration is artifice, in his *In Tune with the World* (1965; Chicago, 1973). Brenda Danet has done pioneering work on playfulness in internet communication in *Cyberpl@y: Communicating Online* (Oxford, 2001).

DON HANDELMAN (1987 AND 2005)

PLOTINUS (205–270), founder of Neoplatonism. The *Life of Plotinus,* philosopher and mystic, was written by his pupil, Porphyry, who edited his master's lectures into six groups of nine treatises (*Enneads*). Completed in 309, the work comprises ethics, physics, the human and world souls, the Three Principal Hypostases (the One, the *Nous,* the Soul), and logical categories.

Plotinus was born in Lycopolis, now Asyut, in Upper Egypt. He studied in from 232 to 243 under Ammonius in Alexandria where a revival of interest in metaphysics and human non-bodily destiny had been influenced by Philo, the Middle Platonists, and the Neo-Pythagoreans in contrast to stoicism, epicureanism, and skepticism. Longing to study Persian and Indian thought, Plotinus joined an expedition of the Emperor Gordian against Persia. When the emperor was assassinated by his soldiers, Plotinus escaped to Antioch, then to Rome, where in 244 he began to teach what he learned from Ammonius. After ten years he was urged by students to write the treatises that have come down to the present. They are responses to students' questions and to teachings of Plato, Aristotle, their commentators, the Middle Platonists, Stoics, Epicureans, and Gnostics. Although he claimed to be merely an interpreter of Plato, the need to respond to the objections of non-Platonic philosophers, and his openness to whatever truth he found in their philosophy resulted in Plotinianism, called Neoplatonism in the modern period. Some main students were Amelius, Porphyry, the Emperor Gallienus, his wife, and Eustochious, a physician who was with him when he died and who reported his last words: "I am trying to bring back the divine in myself to the divine in the All."

Convinced of transcendent truth in Platonic Forms, Plotinus nevertheless agreed with Aristotle on the priority of thinking to the Forms, as well as with the Middle Platonic position that Forms are Ideas within the Divine Mind, adding his own conviction that Forms are living intelligences. Opposing Aristotle, he insisted that complexity of thinking must be preceded by a One, totally simple. Unity is needed for anything to exist, and the degrees of unity establish a hierarchy of ontological value. Influenced by Numenius, Plotinus departed from Plato's oral teaching on the forms arising from unity imposed on the Indefinite Dyad and adopted a radical metaphysical Monism.

The Plotinian First Principle, called the One or the Good, wills itself to be as it is. Thus it is from itself, and its goodness diffuses itself. Everything is a natural overflow from the One. The One is "all things and none of them" (V.2.1). Plotinus does not assume the existence of the One but argues for it.

From the One, actively self-contemplating, proceeds intelligible matter; converting and contemplating the One it becomes *Nous*, the Primal Intellect, and produces Essential Soul. According to its capacity this Hypostasis, Soul, contemplates the Forms, and there proceeds World Soul or Nature from which proceeds the most limited and faintest trace of the One, namely, matter. Unable to contemplate, matter is given forms by World Soul, and the physical world comes to be. Here Plotinus makes use of Aristotle's matter-form theory but only for sub-human things. The existence of the Three Principal Hypostases in the Intelligible World is eternal.

Whence human souls? They come from Essential Soul. Their individual archetypes are forms within *Nous* (V.9.12).The individual soul's descent into its body is both a fall and a necessity for carrying the governance of Essential Soul in parts of the world. But the soul does not wholly descend. Its intuitive intellect, its true self, aspiring for union with the One, remains in the intelligible world. It may become satisfied with living on its two earthly levels, discursive reason and perception, by over-occupation with the sensible world. The soul is a continuum of levels, the undescended Intellect intuiting the One the reason deliberating on earthly affairs, the perception of sense objects, the vegetative soul managing bodily appetites and emotions. The human soul can live on any level. Plotinus urges a return to one's true self by philosophical reflection, discipline, and a moral life leading to contemplation of one's transcendent Source, the One (V.3.3; VI.7.36). Living on this level means no return to an earthly body after death.

Contemplation, as productive, is the linchpin of the Intelligible World and of the sensible world, as well as of the return of the human soul to its true undescended self. This is made explicit in *Ennead* III.8.8.

Plotinus's views on the human body were influenced by Plato's *Phaedo* and *Timaeus*. Against the Gnostics (possible Sethians), he affirms the material world's goodness and beauty (*Enn.* II.9.8); yet he calls matter Absolute Evil (I.8.10) only because it lacks all form (*Timaeus* 48e–52d). But never existing alone, matter somehow is involved in physical evils and immoral human actions.

The Plotinian system is derived from the Classical Tradition, human reasoning, and everyday experience, not excluding religious experience. Through the Cappadocian fathers by way of the translations and writings of John Scottus Eriugena, Plotinus reached the medieval West. Augustine, freed from Manichaeism by reading treatises of Plotinus and Porphyry, also transmitted Plotinian concepts to Western philosophical theory. As founder of Neoplatonism, developed by Porphyry, Iamblichus, and Proclus, Plotinus became the source of negative theology and mystical theology, which through the works of the fifth century theologian Dionysius the Areopagite, influenced Thomas Aquinas and the Rhineland mystics, Eckhart, Suso, and Tauler. Direct knowledge of the *Enneads* in the modern world came through the Latin translations of Marsilio Ficino (1433–1499). By its refusal to confuse myths and rituals with religious philosophy, the work of Plotinus led intellectual Christians to recognize how far reason could go toward establishing divinely revealed truths, as well as how limited reason is with respect to a historically revealed and achieved salvation that requires faith in addition to reason.

See Also Neoplatonism.

Bibliography

Armstrong, A. Hilary, and Robert A. Markus. *Christian Faith and Greek Philosophy.* London, 1960. The tension and interplay of revealed doctrine and philosophical ideas, a dialogue that continues.

Armstrong, A. Hilary, ed. *The Cambridge History of Later Greek and Early Medieval Philosophy.* Cambridge, U.K., 1957, 1970.

Blumenthal, Henry J., and Robert A. Markus, eds. *Neoplatonism and Early Christian Thought: Essays in Honor of A. H. Armstrong.* London, 1981. Emphasis on Plotinus's dialogue with his contemporaries, the Neoplatonic background of Augustine, and the encounter between later Neoplatonism and the Christian tradition.

Dodds, E. R. *Pagan and Christian in an Age of Anxiety.* Cambridge, 1965. Two different responses to the breakdown of classical culture and imperial government.

Gersh, S. *Middle Platonism and Neoplatonism: The Latin Tradition.* 2 vols. Notre Dame, 1986.

Hadot, Pierre. *Porphyre et Victorinus.* Paris, 1970.

Harris, R. Baine, ed. *The Significance of Neoplatonism.* Albany, N.Y., 1976.

Harris, R. Baine, ed. *Neoplatonism and Indian Thought.* Albany, N.Y., 1982.

Lloyd, A. C. *The Anatomy of Neoplatonism.* Oxford, 1990.

O'Meara, Dominic J., ed. *Neoplatonism and Christian Thought.* Norfold, Va., 1981.

Smith, A. *Porphyry's Place in the Neoplatonic Tradition.* The Hague, 1974.

Wallis, Richard T. *Neoplatonism.* London, 1972. Discusses the interrelationships of all the Neoplatonic schools of thought.

Wallis, Richard T., and J. Bergman, eds. *Neoplatonism and Gnosticism.* Albany, N.Y., 1982.

Whittaker, Thomas. *The Neo-Platonists: A Study in the History of Hellenism.* 4th ed. Hildesheim, 1928, 1968. Before Wallis's book, this was the only survey of Neoplatonism.

Mary T. Clark (1987 and 2005)

PLUTARCH (L. Mestrios Ploutarchos, before 50–after 120 CE) was born at Chaironeia near Thebes. He spent much time at Athens but in later life seems to have resided mostly at Chaironeia and at Delphi, where he held a priesthood. He was a good friend of many eminent Greeks and Romans and accordingly had considerable political influence, advocating a partnership between Rome (the power) and Greece (the educator). Late authorities report that he received high distinctions from the emperors Trajan and Hadrian. The extant work of Plutarch, an extremely prolific writer, surpasses that of almost every classical author up to his time, while many nonauthentic works have survived under his name. The *Parallel Lives*, written in an idealistic but critical style, represents a vast and masterly achievement that has had enormous influence. Modern scholarship has also concentrated on his *Moralia*, treating Plutarch seriously as a creative thinker and writer whose views deserve respect and study.

LIFE, WORKS, AND RELIGIOUS OUTLOOK. Plutarch wrote on religious, ethical, philosophical, rhetorical, and antiquarian subjects called *Moralia* or *Moral Essays* (*Ethika* in Greek), but he is most famous for his *Parallel Lives of the Greeks and Romans*. As a youth he studied Platonism at Athens under an Alexandrian named Ammonios, and Plutarch's own works in general belong to philosophical and religious Platonism.

Plutarch traveled to Egypt, Asia Minor, and Rome (several times), but his religious knowledge and interpretations usually depend on standard works, such as those of the early Hellenistic authors Manethon and Hekataios of Abdera (Egyptian religion) and Varro (late Roman Republic). Plutarch's veiled criticism of imperial cult may reflect a distaste for the Roman emperors Nero and in particular Domitian. As a priest at Delphi and a devout believer in the "ancestral faith," Plutarch played a notable part in the revival of the shrine. This interest and his own role is reflected in his *Pythian Dialogues* (*The E at Delphi*, *The Oracles at Delphi*, and *The Obsolescence of the Oracles*), in the first of which he prefers *Apollo(n)* as the name to designate God.

Walter Burkert has noted in "Plutarco: Religiosità personale e teologia filosofica" (1996) the personal and optimistic dimension of Plutarch's attitude toward religion. In two essays, probably early, *On the Eating of Flesh I* and *II*, Plutarch attacked the killing of animals for food, but elsewhere he treats religious festivities, which included sacrifice, as joyous occasions. He believed in prophecy and, following the Platonic tradition, speaks of its transmission through intermediate spirits (daimones), especially in *The Sign [Daimonion] of Socrates*. However, in general Plutarch treats daimones as former or potential human souls. Though drawing inspiration from Plato's afterlife myths and the *Timaios*, Plutarch speaks in *The Face on the Moon* of a "second death," the separation of intellect (nous) from soul (psyche), on the moon. In his eschatological scenes and comments, he proposes that virtuous souls, apparently limited in number, after passing through the state of daimones and undergoing purification, become gods—that is, pure immortal intellects without passions or attachment to this world—and are rewarded with the blessed vision. Plutarch is a firm believer in divine providence and the basic goodness of the divine order, but he allows punishment for the sins of ancestors to be inflicted on their descendants (*The Delay of Divine Vengeance*).

Emphasis on Plutarch's demonology (better "daimonology") has been much exaggerated. His writings reflect the vast range of meaning carried by the words *daimon*, *daimones*, or *daimonion* (i.e., spirit, demon, lesser god, a god, the divinity, God) in Greek. His interest, however, may indicate the growing influence of Near Eastern and perhaps even New Testament–type demonology. In *The Obsolescence of the Oracles* and the *Lives of Dion and Brutus*, Plutarch introduces daimones similar to New Testament demons but without seeming to be aware of possession and exorcism.

Dualism. Scholars are divided over dualism in Plutarch. In *The Generation of the Soul in the Timaios*, Plutarch posits a "world soul," which existed in a precosmic state as a source of cosmic evil before this soul obtained an intellect (Logos). Elsewhere he suggests that Zoroastrian dualism may be responsible for the doctrine of daimones (415D), and he discourses on the struggle between good and evil forces in Zoroastrianism—for example, as a tentative explanation for the battle between Osiris and Seth in Egyptian myth (*Isis and Osiris* 369D–370C). But dualism in the strict sense (a world equally balanced between good and evil—that is, between equal spiritual beings, one good, one evil) is rarely in question and certainly inconsistent with his belief in a benevolent and providential God ruling a basically good world.

Eschatological myths. Some of Plutarch's afterlife myths (found in *The Sign of Socrates*, *The Face on the Moon*, and *The Delay of the Divine Vengeance*), while modeled on those of Plato, are more focused on the personal experience of the visionary, and a "blessed vision" seems more clearly to be the ultimate destiny of the soul. Horrors are more individually described and gripping, and at least at the end of *The Divine Vengeance*, where Nero appears, one finds an outstanding contemporary figure undergoing punishment. This is an exception but foreshadows Dante Alighieri's *Inferno* (fourteenth century). Moreover in some myths the moon becomes a place of transition for the souls, and in general the daimones (generally treated as former or potential human souls) have a much more important role than in Plato. In contrast to the pessimistic myth of eternal rebirth in Plato's *Republic* or the more optimistic version of recycling souls in the *Timaios*, Plutarch seems to envisage release and a blessed vision as the normal process for truly virtuous souls, though these are few in number.

Religious Platonism. Plutarch avoided more extreme positions, such as a first, second, or even third God (the world) or a God above being and knowledge. He identifies God with the highest Platonic entities—Being, One, the Form of the Good, Intellect—even though this is usually stated only indirectly. One of Plutarch's most important contributions is his literal interpretation of the Demiurge (craftsman, creator God) in Plato's *Timaios*. Another is his

Middle Platonic allegorical interpretation of "Egyptian" religion (*Isis and Osiris*). His intention probably was to domesticate and neutralize the Isis religion through Platonic exegesis. Against Herodotos, he champions the purity of Greek religion and its independence from the Egyptian. Plutarch thus affirms the superiority of Greek culture. However, the extensive explanation of the rites and myths, a sympathetic treatment, the importance given Osiris, and the addition of Greek eschatology probably gave more meaning to the "Egyptian" cult and helped popularize it.

Dying and rising gods. In *Isis and Osiris* (356B–359C) Plutarch treats at great length the death and resurrection, or resuscitation, of Osiris. Osiris is identified on occasion with Dionysos (e.g., 356B, 362B), who in turn is identified with Adonis (*Table Talk*, 671B–C). As Giovanni Casadio notes in "The Failing Male God" (2003), Plutarch prefers to treat the dying and rising Osiris as a daimon rather than a god (360E–361F). To fit Plutarch's allegorical interpretation, however, Osiris ends up not as king of the dead as in the traditional Egyptian religion but belonging to the ethereal regions.

Judaism and Christianity. Plutarch's knowledge of Jewish religion, some of it reporting Egyptian anti-Jewish propaganda from the Hellenistic period, is limited and superficial. His ignorance is surprising, considering that the Jewish revolts brought Jews to the attention of the Greek and Roman world. His knowledge is presumably derived from earlier non-Jewish authors and represents an outsider's view of the religion. For example, the use of wine, tents, and palm branches in the feast of the Tabernacles demonstrates that the Jewish god is Dionysos (*Table Talk* 4.4–4.6). Still in these *Table Talk* "questions," the only passages exclusively dedicated to Judaism, he treats it with respect and some sympathy. Thus he differs from Tacitus (e.g., *Histories* 5.6.4), who admired the Jews for not representing the divinity in images (something Plutarch ignores) but otherwise treats them with contempt. Plutarch's respectful attitude, though consistent with his general procedure, is noteworthy, considering the hostile climate toward Jews during his lifetime. Christianity is never mentioned in Plutarch's works. Since the Christian persecutions had started and Plutarch was acquainted with high Roman officials, its absence may represent a "conspiracy of silence."

Historian of religion. Plutarch, an extraordinary source for Greek religion, was probably its most outstanding historian and comparativist in his day. In the dialogues, which permit him to introduce often radical and contradictory opinions, his personal view is often difficult to assess. In other works, such as *Isis and Osiris* (a treatise) and *The Face on the Moon* (more a treatise than a dialogue), he presents several interpretations, usually moving from a less-probable opinion to a more-probable one, as, for example, when discussing dualism. As a scholar of comparative religion (especially in *Isis and Osiris*, *Greek Questions*, *Roman Questions*, and *Table Talk*), Plutarch treats religious practices with respect. He presumes there is a reasonable or edifying rationale for something, even if strange. Plutarch had an outstanding knowledge of Greek and a comprehensive knowledge of Roman religion, and he used excellent sources, such as Varro for the *Roman Question*.

Fritz Graf, however, in "Plutarco e la religione romana" (1996), notes both Plutarch's failure to see an essential difference between Roman and Greek religion and his tendency to give theological and moralistic explanations. A case is that of the *Flamen Dialis*, where modern scholars would see socio-religious taboos. The answers in the *Greek Questions* are authoritative and often short, like encyclopedia entries, normally without theoretical explanations. But the responses in the *Roman Questions*, frequently more than one, are actually open-ended questions. In these, often described as "Greek answers for Roman questions," though not always such, Plutarch seems unable to resist giving several theoretical answers. Apparently spun out of his own head, he sometimes introduces them with "Is it as Varro says, or . . .?" Moreover Rebecca Preston, in "Roman Questions, Greek Answers: Plutarch and the Construction of Identity" (2001), observes Plutarch's tendency to avoid explicit reference to contemporary religious practice, such as imperial cult.

Plutarch was surprisingly well-informed about Egyptian religion, making use of good, early Hellenistic sources, in particular the Egyptian priest Manethon. In general, as a religious historian he tries to let the reader into his decision-making process. He interprets other religions in Greek terms, deeming practices or beliefs worthy if they can be reconciled with Greek ideas. Typical in a sense is his derivation of the Egyptian or Greek transmission of the Egyptian name *Isis*, from the Greek word "to know." One of his guiding principles is *interpretatio graeca*, the identification of foreign gods with Greek gods, an identification often based on external resemblances in rites and attributes. Plutarch mostly used old sources, but because of the prominence given Osiris in them, his work harmonizes with the growing importance of Osiris in the early imperial period. In Plutarch's appropriation or domestication of the religion through shifting Platonic exegesis and the allegorical method, Osiris becomes Plato's Eros, or the Form of the Good, while Isis is the Platonic "receptacle," or the individual soul longing for the Form of the Good (or Beautiful).

PLUTARCH'S INFLUENCE. From his own age to modern times, Plutarch has been widely read for his religious views, partly because his ideas on creation and God could be reconciled with Christian thought. His influence can be seen in such Middle Platonists as Attikos and in the Neoplatonists, though the latter disliked his metaphysics. Christians such as Clement of Alexandria, Origen, Eusebios of Caesarea, Basil of Caesarea, Cyril of Alexandria, Theodoretos, Isidore of Pelousion, and Ioannes Philoponos read and admired Plutarch, in particular for his description of the unique creation of the world by God in time. *The Delay of the Divine Vengeance*—greatly admired throughout the ages, even if not necessarily for the best reasons—was transcribed and adapted in large part by the Neoplatonist Proklos, and it received many editions and translations, especially during the sixteenth to twentieth centuries.

Plutarch was overlooked by medieval scholars in the West, but in the early humanist period Greeks like Planudes and Ioannes Mauropos admired him. In the fifteenth century only Aristotle and Plato among prose writers were better represented in Italian libraries, but Plutarch's ethical writings were favored over his religious writings. Montaigne praised Plutarch's nondogmatic approach to religious questions. Though Erasmus translated several of the *Moralia*, once saying they were inferior only to the Bible in spirituality, and Plutarch was admired by Melanchthon, Martin Luther does not mention him. Already in the seventeenth century *Isis and Osiris* had become an important source for scholars of Egyptian religion; the work helped fuel the Egyptomania of the late eighteenth century and early nineteenth century, and it remains an important source for Egyptologists. Though Plutarch fell somewhat out of favor in the nineteenth century, his Platonism found a home among the New England transcendentalists (Ralph Waldo Emerson). He was a favorite of Johann Wolfgang von Goethe and Mary Shelley, while George Bernard Shaw oddly labeled his work "a revolutionists' handbook." In the twentieth and twenty-first centuries scholars have found Plutarch's works to be an indispensable source for the mentality of his time, a time that produced such profound changes in the religious history of the Western world.

SEE ALSO Delphi; Demons; Dualism; Hellenistic Religions; Isis; Orpheus; Osiris; Plato; Platonism.

BIBLIOGRAPHY

Babut, Daniel. *Plutarque: Oeuvres morales 72: Sur les notions communes, contre les Stoïciens.* Paris, 2002.

Baltes, Matthias. "Plutarchos [2] III: Philosophisches Werk." In *Der Neue Pauly: Enzyklopädie der Antike*, edited by Hubert Cancik and Helmuth Schneider, vol. 9, pp. 1166–1173. Stuttgart, 2000.

Betz, Hans-Dieter, ed. *Plutarch's Theological Writings and Early Christian Literature.* Leiden, Netherlands, 1975.

Bianchi, Ugo. "Plutarch und der Dualismus." In *Aufstieg und Niedergang der römischen Welt (ANRW)*, vol. 2, no. 36.1, pp. 111–120. Berlin and New York, 1987.

Boulogne, Jean. "Les 'Questions Romaines' de Plutarque." In *Aufstieg und Niedergang der römischen Welt (ANRW)*, vol. 2, no. 33.6, pp. 4682–4708. Berlin and New York, 1992.

Brenk, Frederick E. *In Mist Apparelled: Religious Themes in Plutarch's "Moralia" and "Lives."* Leiden, Netherlands, 1977.

Brenk, Frederick E. "An Imperial Heritage: The Religious Spirit of Plutarch of Chaironeia." In *Aufstieg und Niedergang der römischen Welt (ANRW)*, vol. 2, no. 36.1, pp. 248–349. Berlin and New York, 1987; Indices, vol. 2, no. 36.2, pp. 1300–1322. 1987.

Brenk, Frederick E. *Relighting the Souls: Studies in Plutarch, in Greek Literature, Religion, and Philosophy, and in the New Testament Background.* Stuttgart, 1998.

Burkert, Walter. "Plutarco: Religiosità personale e teologia filosofica." In *Plutarco e la religione*, edited by Italo Gallo, pp. 11–29. Naples, 1996.

Casadio, Giovanni. "The Failing Male God: Emasculation, Death, and Other Accidents in the Ancient Mediterranean World." *Numen* 50 (2003): 231–268.

Dillon, John. "Plutarch and God: Theodicy and Cosmogony in the Thought of Plutarch." In *Traditions of Theology: Studies in Hellenistic Theology, Its Background and Aftermath*, edited by Dorothea Frede and André Laks, pp. 223–237. Leiden, Netherlands, 2002.

Donini, Pierluigi. "L'eredità academica e i fondamenti del platonismo in Plutarco." In *Unione e Amicizia: Omaggio a Francesco Romano*, edited by Maria Barbanti, Giovanna Giardina, and Paolo Manganaro, pp. 247–273. Catania, Italy, 2003.

Ferrari, Franco. *Dio, idee e materia: La struttura del cosmo in Plutarco di Cheronea.* Naples, 1995.

Froidefond, Christian. "Plutarque et le platonisme." In *Aufstieg und Niedergang der römischen Welt (ANRW)*, vol. 2, no. 36.1, pp. 184–233. Berlin and New York, 1987.

García Valdés, Manuela, ed. *Estudios sobre Plutarco: Ideas religiosas.* Madrid, 1994.

Goldhill, Simon. "Why Save Plutarch?" In *Who Needs Greeks? Contests in the Cultural History of Hellenism*, pp. 246-293. Cambridge, U.K., 2002.

Graf, Fritz. "Plutarco e la religione romana." In *Plutarco e la religione*, edited by Italo Gallo, pp. 269–285. Naples, 1996.

Griffiths, John Gwyn, trans. and ed. *Plutarch's "De Iside et Osiride."* Cardiff, U.K., 1970.

Hani, Jean. *La religion égyptienne dans la pensée de Plutarque.* Paris, 1976.

Hirzel, Rudolf. *Plutarch.* Leipzig, Germany, 1912.

Klauck, Hans-Josef. *The Religious Context of Early Christianity: A Guide to Graeco-Roman Religions.* Translated by Brian McNeil. Edinburgh, 2000; reprint, Minneapolis, 2003.

Preston, Rebecca. "Roman Questions, Greek Answers: Plutarch and the Construction of Identity." In *Being Greek under Roman Rule: Cultural Identity, the Second Sophistic, and the Development of Empire*, edited by Simon Goldhill, pp. 86–122. New York and Cambridge, U.K., 2001.

Tsekourakis, Damianos. "Pythagoreanism or Platonism and Ancient Medicine? The Reason for Vegetarianism in Plutarch's *Moralia*." In *Aufstieg und Niedergang der römischen Welt (ANRW)*, vol. 2, no. 36.1, pp. 366–393. Berlin and New York, 1987.

Ziegler, Konrat. *Plutarchos von Chaironeia.* Stuttgart, 1964. Rev. and enl. version of *Paulys Realencyclopädie*, vol. 21, pp. 636–962. Stuttgart, 1951.

FREDERICK E. BRENK (2005)

PNEUMA SEE SOUL, *ARTICLE ON* GREEK AND HELLENISTIC CONCEPTS

POBEDONOSTSEV, KONSTANTIN

(1827–1907), procurator of the Holy Governing Synod of the Russian Orthodox church. Konstantin Petrovich Pobedonostsev was the last procurator effectively to control the administration of the church according to the stipulations of the Ecclesiastical Regulation of Peter the Great. Although this regulation remained on the statute books until the collapse of the tsarist regime in 1917, the upheavals of 1905–1906 in the church and the government necessitated adaptation in its application during the final decade of the old order.

Pobedonostsev served as procurator from 1880 to 1905, during which time he oversaw a major restructuring of ecclesiastical education and an impressive expansion of the parish school system. His purpose was twofold: to provide basic education to the Russian masses as they emerged from the shadow of serfdom and to ensure that that education firmly supported the tsarist political system. Within the seminaries and theological academies under his control he both raised the general level of education and tried to maintain control of its content. Unintentionally, he stimulated a major controversy over reform in the church and spent the later years of his career attempting to contain and stifle this controversy.

Among the forceful personalities Pobedonostsev dealt with in the controversy over church reform were Antonii Vadkovskii, metropolitan of Saint Petersburg (1898–1912), Sergei Witte, chairman of the Committee of Ministers (1903–1905) and prime minister (1905–1906), and Antonii Khrapovitskii, bishop and archbishop of Volhynia (1902–1914). The bishops were determined reformers, seeking to free the church from the bondage of the Ecclesiastical Regulation. During debates in the Committee of Ministers on proposed changes in legislation affecting non-Orthodox religious groups in the Russian empire, Witte was persuaded by Vadkovskii and others that termination of the Petrine regulation and restoration of autonomy of administration (possibly reviving the patriarchate of Moscow) were essential for good government of the church.

Pobedonostsev attempted to halt the momentum for reform and abolition of the Petrine system by having Tsar Nicholas II transfer deliberation of the question from the Committee of Ministers to the synod itself, where the procurator's agents would be able to control the debate. Vadkovskii, Khrapovitskii, and their allies outmaneuvered the synodal bureaucracy, however, and the synod itself declared for reform. As a result of the synod's decision, the procurator ordered the polling of all the bishops of the church in the hope that they would be opposed to a *sobor* (council) of the church and to the restoration of the patriarchate. But when the bishops had completed their replies, the overwhelming majority were found to favor a *sobor* and a sweeping reform.

During the months that the poll was being taken, Russia was wracked by violence and revolution. From the turmoil came the October Manifesto (1905), which granted a limited constitutional government. Pobedonostsev resigned as procurator, protesting against the manifesto, against Witte's having been appointed prime minister, and against the tsar's promise to summon an all-Russian *sobor*. He died within two years, convinced that his work of twenty-five years as procurator was being destroyed and that both the Russian church and the Russian state were doomed to collapse. He had been unyielding in his opposition to parliamentary forms of government, believing that they were the cause of the decadence of the West and that their introduction into Russia in any form would lead to corruption and disintegration.

Pobedonostsev's voluminous writings reflect his training as a lawyer. Among them are *Lectures on Civil Judicial Procedures* (Moscow, 1863), *History of the Orthodox Church until the Schism of the Churches* (Saint Petersburg, 1896), *Historical Juridical Acts of the Epoch of Transition of the Seventeenth and Eighteenth Centuries* (Moscow, 1887), *Course of Civil Law,* 3 vols. (Saint Petersburg, 1868–1880), *The Questions of Life* (Moscow, 1904), *Annual Report of the Over-Procurator of the Holy Synod concerning the Administration of the Orthodox Church* (Saint Petersburg, 1881–1909), and a number of articles published in journals during his public career.

BIBLIOGRAPHY

The definitive biography of Pobedonostsev in English is Robert F. Byrnes's *Pobedonostsev: His Life and Thought* (Bloomington, Ind., 1968). In German it is Gerhard Simon's *Konstantin Petrovic Pobedonoscev und die Kirchenpolitik des Heiligen Synod, 1880–1905* (Göttingen, 1969). Other useful books are John S. Curtiss's *Church and State in Russia: The Last Years of the Empire, 1900–1917* (1940; reprint, New York, 1965), Igor Smolitsch's *Geschichte der russischen Kirche, 1700–1917* (Leiden, 1964), *Russian Orthodoxy under the Old Regime,* edited by Robert Nichols and Theofanis Stavrou (Minneapolis, 1978), and my *Vanquished Hope: The Church in Russia on the Eve of the Revolution* (New York, 1981).

JAMES W. CUNNINGHAM (1987)

POETRY

This entry consists of the following articles:

POETRY: POETRY AND RELIGION

The language of religion, like the language of love, is persistently poetic, if by no means exclusively so. The reasons why religious expression is so often poetic are complex, however, and not always transparent. They can best be adduced by considering the principal ways in which poetry functions in different religious contexts and traditions. It will be useful, however, to begin by examining the overall features of poetry, and its corresponding religious potential.

POETRY AS PERFORMANCE AND EXPRESSION: BASIC ELEMENTS. Poetry has been described as heightened speech. Intensified and ordered through rhythm, sound, and image, such language is designed to be expressive or beautiful, and memorable. Poetic diction varies widely from style to style, and from culture to culture. Yet the language of poetry typically departs from both common sense and plain speech, being often figurative or metaphoric in the broad sense.

Poetry can be divided into three large genres: narrative, dramatic, and lyric. Narrative poetry includes epics, myths, sagas, fables, ballads, romances, and the like. Dramatic poetry includes verse forms of tragedy, comedy, and plays of an explicitly liturgical or ritual sort. As for the numerous kinds of lyric poetry, some of the more familiar are odes, hymns, elegies, laments, haiku, love sonnets, and meditative verse.

Many of the traits normally associated with poetry—meter, rhyme, alliteration, assonance, and consonance, for instance—become most vivid in oral expression. Religions have traditionally made much of the very orality of poetry. Thus the markedly poetic text of the Qur'ān (literally, "recitation"), which Muḥammad delivered orally, lends itself to beautiful modes of chanting out loud rather than to silent reading. Even in poetry that is unrhymed and irregularly metered, various salient features may come out more fully in oral performance. In the poetry of the Hebrew Bible, for example, oral rendition calls attention to a combined rhythm of meaning, syntax, and stress—something clearly audible in the celebrated parallelisms of the Psalms, a liturgical songbook.

Most of the poetry associated with religion and ritual is actually meant to be sung or chanted, taking the form of hymns, invocations, ritual incantations, and the like. Indeed, virtually all of the poetry in ancient Greece—not only epic and lyric poetry but also dramatic—was accompanied by instruments, and often by dance. The same can be said of traditional poetry in Africa, India, Bali, and elsewhere.

The connection between poetry and music was so intimate in Western antiquity that when Augustine of Hippo (354–430), the most influential of the Christian church fathers, wrote his only treatise on music, he approached the topic by dwelling at length on matters of number and meter associated with prosody. Unfortunately, no one knows for sure how the musical settings of ancient poetry sounded—even the hymns that Augustine confessed moved him to tears. The works of much later Christian hymn-writers—such as Paul Gerhardt (1606–1676), Isaac Watts (1674–1748), Charles Wesley (1707–1788), and Fanny Crosby (1820–1915)—were, of course, set to music that remains easily accessible; but such verse, however widely sung in churches, is rarely classified now as poetry.

In due course, religious poetry nonetheless came to exploit the possibilities of the written text. The epic narrative of the *Divine Comedy,* by Dante Alighieri (1265–1321), which traces the pilgrim Dante's progress from hell to heaven, employs an elaborate rhyme scheme (*terza rima*), complex allegory, and convoluted similes that are all savored better upon multiple readings than in a single oral performance. And though the English poet John Milton (1608–1674) was blind when he dictated the blank verse of his Christian epic *Paradise Lost,* the extended structure and density of the work's often Latinate syntax favors readers more than mere listeners. Again, the interlinked sequences of poetic stanzas in Japanese *renga* of the fifteenth and sixteenth century CE, which often touch lightly on Buddhist themes, allow poets to respond to one another in writing. There are even devotional poems by the Anglican priest George Herbert (1593–1633) that are arranged on the page in such a way as to create a two-dimensional visual image of the primary subject of the poem—as in "The Altar" and "Easter Wings."

Such features of poetry, even when seemingly of minor consequence in themselves, are reminders that the medium of poetry is never merely words in the abstract. Rather, poetry depends on imagination and a kind of embodiment. As with ritual and arts in general, the meaning of poetry registers on the whole self, appealing to head and heart, mind and body.

Despite that sort of immediacy, poetry distances itself from the merely mundane. In a variety of ways poetry estranges itself from the familiar and creates a measure of creative disorientation—something evident in modern poetry in particular. For instance, while *Four Quartets* by T. S. Eliot (1888–1965) is far removed from actual ritual practice or from prayer or other spiritual exercises in the usual sense, the structure of each of the quartets bears some resemblance to classic stages of the mystical path or, more particularly, of the spiritual progress of what Eliot elsewhere calls the "intellectual soul." The highly metaphoric language, the deferral from plain sense, and the attentiveness to sonic texture all contribute to the spiritual evocativeness of such poetry, influenced in part by the French symbolist tradition of the late nineteenth century. Again, the works of the Welsh poet Dylan Thomas (1914–1953), far more extroverted in character, have a virtually incantatory quality that is only heightened by the fact that the literal sense can be hard to fathom. It could be argued that creative dissonance likewise results from the often shocking lyrics of the highly rhythmic and rhyming popular music known as rap—originally an urban ghetto genre of African American musical verse but one that, since the late twentieth century, has begun to spread widely around the world and even to be employed in worship.

Poetry, Prophecy, and Revelation. In religious life, the means of poetry serve particular ends, beyond providing purely aesthetic delight. Two of the most important religious purposes of poetry can be termed prophecy and revelation. Two other religious purposes, which will be discussed subsequently, are devotion and mysticism.

Prophetic utterance is concerned with communicating divine messages, whether about the future or about conditions of self or society that need to be changed, possibly for the sake of justice and righteousness. Thus poetry in many parts of the world has been a medium of spiritual ecstasy or "madness" in the service of prophecy. Plato (c. 428–348 or 347 BCE) and many other ancient Greeks thought of poets not as knowledgeable artists in full control of their craft but rather as seers and prophets mediating mysterious truths and divine directives that the poets might not fully grasp themselves.

In Latin, one venerable term for poet is *vates,* or "prophet." Similarly, in Arabic, the word for poetry, *shi'r,* is derived from a verb denoting a special kind of knowledge associated with divination. Although the prophet Muḥammad's critics, in the seventh century CE, dismissed his recitations as mere poetry, Muslims themselves soon came to regard the supremacy of the Qur'ān as audible in that very poetry, with a truth and beauty beyond compare.

The aura of divine possession or prophetic inspiration has never completely departed from the role of poet, though in later times, especially in the West, it has become less visible. The prophet's call for righteousness and justice survives, for example, in poetry of protest, as exemplified by the war poems of England's Wilfred Owen (1893–1918) or the long poem *Babi Yar* by the Russian Yevgeny Yevtushenko (1933–), who, in mourning the Nazi massacre of thousands of Ukrainian Jews, also attacks Soviet anti-Semitism.

In addition to having a prophetic function, poetry serves as a medium of revelation—which, in the sense relevant here, is the inspired disclosure of deep wisdom or of holy presence. In a specifically religious sense, revelation can take place as epiphany or theophany: that which is divine or holy appears in an awe-inspiring form that is nonetheless accessible to human senses and awareness. Whereas prophecy employs exhortation and proclamation, revelation employs vision and manifestation, or sacramental embodiment. At a less lofty level, prophecy and revelation take the form of preaching and teaching, which likewise can employ poetry. Thus, in the sixth century CE, Romanos the Melodist, the most famous liturgical poet of the Orthodox Church, chanted his narrative verse sermons in a form known as *kontakia,* with the congregation joining in a repeated refrain.

In India, the most ancient sacred Hindu texts, revered as the original revelations, are the Vedas, the earliest portions of which became canonical by 1000 BCE. Those primary revelatory utterances are classified as *śruti*: that which is heard. Subsequent sacred texts (including the *Dharmaśāstras* and the epics) are classified as *smṛti*: that which is remembered. Both kinds of texts are, in many cases, composed in verse. Indian commentators have long spoken of *ṛṣhis* ("seers" and "poets") as in some sense the transmitters and composers of the Vedas—whose sacred hymns and largely non-narrative verses use vivid imagery and memorable sound and phrasing. The great epics are also attributed to poets—the *Mahābhārata* to Vyasa (a "collector") and the *Rāmāyaṇa* to Valmiki. The *Mahābhārata,* indeed, refers to itself as a *kāvya,* or great poem, and contains the *Bhagavadgītā,* which is acknowledged worldwide as a masterpiece of poetry.

Nevertheless, being regarded as revealed or inspired, those ancient texts of Hinduism were not received as poetic art or literature (*kāvya*) in the usual sense. Although, as time passed, one system of classification did recognize epics such as the *Mahābhārata* and the *Rāmāyaṇa* as *kāvya,* a second system maintained that the truthful story-telling of such epic poems or of the popular but nonetheless sacred *Purāṇas* should be distinguished from the mere fictions of literature. And none of the epics themselves were so self-consciously literary as the classical Sanskrit poetry that began to be composed around 200 CE, and that culminated in the work of the poet Kālīdasa in the fifth century.

Thus, as these examples indicate, when it comes to the revelatory quality of religious poetry, there is often a tension between a religious community's desire to recognize or acclaim the poetic art of sacred texts and the contrary desire to distance such elevated or supremely truthful texts from merely human poiesis, or poetic making, and from what otherwise might be seen as creative representation, or mimesis. Indeed, the difference between divine revelation and human expression can be interpreted at times in terms of a divine disregard for the lesser delights of mere poetry. While it is true that, in the West, Augustine and other church fathers were struck by the symbolism, figurative discourse, and rhetoric of the Bible, they were pleased to point out how frequently Scripture seems to disdain the lofty language and the polished poetry perfected by the pagans. Jerome (c. 342–420), for instance, thought that the language of the Scriptures was "harsh and barbaric" compared with the pagan classics. Christians of the patristic era saw the very roughness of scriptural language as serving a higher wisdom and (as Augustine would argue) a higher, invisible beauty not to be compared with human ornament and decorum.

At other times, sacred texts are valued by their devotees or believers as the very model of poetic excellence and most worthy of emulation. Thus, while an elevated view of the poetry of the Qur'ān has sometimes functioned to cast all other poetry in a comparatively negative light, the Qur'ān has also helped inspire the extensive repertoire of Islamic poetry, in Persian as well as Arabic. Similarly, in medieval Europe, biblical figurative language and the corresponding typological and allegorical approach to reading Scripture gave impetus to poetic allegory more broadly—and, eventually, to the poet Dante's adoption of the four commonly acknowledged levels of interpreting sacred texts, which he had the seeming audacity to apply to his own extra-biblical epic narrative, the *Divine Comedy.* Protestant Reformers of the sixteenth century, such as Martin Luther, engaged in tirades against medieval allegorizing; but Protestants themselves often looked on the figurative language of Scripture not only as exemplifying the Bible's poetic excellence but also as providing divine sanction for poetic simile, metaphor, metonymy, catechresis, and so forth.

Accordingly, in England, Philip Sidney (1554–1586) defended poetry not only by citing the Psalms of David as divine poems but also by claiming that the poet's imagination is analogous to the creativity of "the heavenly maker" who "made man to his owne likenes . . . which in nothing sheweth so much as in Poetry." The seventeenth-century Anglican poet and divine John Donne (c. 1572–1631) likewise found in scripture ample evidence that the Holy Spirit is the supreme poet. God is not only a "direct God," he said, but also a "figurative, a metaphorical God too." Such convictions inspired much Protestant lyrical poetry of the seventeenth century. And though the use of figurative language had as much to do with moving and delighting readers as with conveying higher truths, in the seventeenth century those functions of poetry were closely intertwined.

During the eighteenth century, by contrast, the increasing prevalence of empirical or scientific standards of truth in Western culture spawned, in many settings, a relatively rationalist approach to religion. Since the language of poetry conformed neither to the clear and distinct ideas of science nor to the kind of self-evident or revealed absolutes required in different ways by both deist and dogmatic religion, poetry lost some of its esteem as a serious medium of either truth or revelation, though it was still thought suitable for edifying instruction.

During this era, particularly under the influence of the philosopher Immanuel Kant (1724–1804), poetry and the other arts were granted a large degree of autonomy, apart from science, morality, or religion. Ironically, however, the price was that the beauty of poetry was often conceived of not as participating in divine beauty but as delighting in an ornamental way or as providing simply an appealing guise in which to clothe social commentary or instruction in matters of morality.

During the revolutionary age of European Romanticism, which commenced near the end of the eighteenth century and continued well into the nineteenth, poets and critics such as Friedrich Hölderlin (1770–1843), Samuel Taylor Coleridge (1772–1834), and Ralph Waldo Emerson (1803–1882) reacted against both scientific rationalism and religious dogmatism, partly by taking a very high view of works of poetic genius. Poetic imagination, according to many of the Romantics, transcends both scientific fact and religious dogma, becoming in a real sense revelatory of the highest truths available to human beings. William Wordsworth (1770–1850), for instance, could be found referring to the poet or bard as the "holiest of men." The Romantics, often enamored with the cult of the artist as genius, made the poetic Muse an ally of, or occasionally even substitute for, the Holy Spirit. "A Poet, a Painter, a Musician, and Architect: the Man or Woman who is not one of these is not a Christian," wrote the English poet and artist William Blake (1727–1857). Imagination, he said, "is the Divine Body of the Lord Jesus, blessed for ever."

In the Victorian era, when the creeds and prescribed rituals of religion further weakened under the assault of social change and scientific revolution, it began to appear to various shapers of culture that, if anything was going to remain of religion at all, it would be its "poetry." Now that fact and dogma were failing religion, wrote Matthew Arnold (1822–1888), people would increasingly need to turn for consolation to poetry, which he thought of as the "breath and finer spirit of knowledge" that could sustain humanity in the absence of secure creeds. At times, in the hands of theorists such as Walter Pater (1839–1894) and, later, Clive Bell (1881–1964), poetry—or art in general—became virtually a surrogate for religion.

Even the so-called New Critics of the mid-twentieth century, for all their preoccupation with the formal and self-reflexive features of poetic art, carried forward certain of these tendencies. For they viewed poetic language not simply as constitutive of its own world but also, paradoxically, as revelatory of a unique kind of knowledge unavailable to other modes of discourse.

Meanwhile, in the work of philosophers and theologians such as Martin Heidegger (1889–1976), Hans-Georg Gadamer (1900–2002), Paul Tillich (1886–1965), and Paul Ricoeur (1913–), truth and symbolic imagination were treated as intimately interrelated. Truth that is most important to human life and meaning, according to such thinkers, is not subject to propositional logic but appears in the simultaneous veiling and unveiling inherent in symbolic or poetic thought. In a related vein, the Roman Catholic theologian Karl Rahner (1904–1984) suggested that, ideally, the priest and poet should become one, though that fusion of roles is likely to remain an eschatological hope more than a present reality. To other theologians such as Hans Urs von Balthasar (1905–1988), that kind of hope would seem to transgress the necessary boundary between artistic inspiration and God's self-revelation. Yet Balthasar himself wanted to reclaim beauty as a transcendental, essential attribute of whatever is real and true, and he acknowledged that divine beauty can, by way of analogy, graciously manifest itself in artistic beauty as well.

All along, however, one whole line of modernist poetics, associated with formalism in particular, had resisted any attempt to think of poetry as concerned with truth at all, or with anything other than itself and the sheer play of language. In the latter part of the twentieth century, postmodern theorists such as the deconstructionist philosopher Jacques Derrida (1930–2004) took such skepticism about poetic truth and applied it to language as a whole, wherein they found all meaning to be in some degree deferred, and all representation to be artificial and unreliable to an indeterminate degree. But even then, Derrida appeared to leave room for something more—something still related to religion—to emerge from language and symbol and to entice belief. Truth might be elusive, but there was still something worth trusting in the darkness of unknowing, as Derrida would hint from time to time. Not surprisingly, this open-ended, postmodern approach, pushing to the limits of language and beyond, sounded to some students of theology and religion like a kind of negative theology—a *via negativa*—and sometimes almost like poetry, itself.

POETRY, DEVOTION, AND MYSTICISM. Religion has to do not only with prophecy and revelation, but also with devotion and spirituality: the response and expression of personal or corporate piety. In intense forms, that can entail mysticism—seeking and celebrating an experience of union (or intimate communion) with the divine or with ultimate reality transcending all imaginable qualities. Devotion that is corporate and public is usually termed worship. When private, devotion is known more often as personal prayer, meditation, or contemplation.

As noted earlier, the greater portion of poetry that has played a role in public worship has been accompanied by music. Some of that musical poetry is narrative in kind, reciting stories of the acts of deities, avatars, and exemplary human beings. Mostly, however, the poetry of worship is lyrical. Among the more complex and formal lyrics are odes praising or petitioning the divine, as occurs in cult hymns from the Alexandrian period in Greek literature (c. 300–30 BCE). In the Christian New Testament, the letters of Paul make reference to the singing of "hymns, psalms, and spiritual songs"—seemingly imprecise terms that nevertheless emphasize the lyrical mode, including canticles such as Mary's *Magnificat,* found in the book of Luke. Original lyric verse, once it has been set to music, has also been employed widely in public prayer, as one sees in the poems of the now-celebrated *Symphonia* of Hildegard of Bingen (1098–1179). The extra-biblical church hymns of the twelfth and thirteenth centuries, such as the *Stabat Mater* and the *Dies Irae,* are among the high marks of liturgical poetry. In Judaism, similarly, there is an extensive tradition of *piyyutim,* or liturgical poems and prayers, mostly composed between the early centuries of the Common Era and the eighteenth century.

While religious poetry that is not sung or chanted has not generally found a major place in liturgy or corporate worship, such poetry has served as a medium of private devotion and personal religious expression. The works of one of the greatest Hebrew poets of the medieval period, Judah ha-Levi (c. 1075–1141), generally fall into that category. In Christian circles, from the late sixteenth century through much of the seventeenth, meditative or metaphysical lyric poetry was in many instances deeply informed by the *Spiritual Exercises* of Ignatius of Loyola (1491–1556). Other lyric poetry of the same period, especially in Protestant England, was shaped—as already noted—by the poetry of the Bible itself, which at that time was thought to have been composed in regular meters.

Modern counterparts of such poetry can be found, but are seldom so openly devotional in character, and rarely so explicitly prayerful. Particularly notable examples in the West include lyrics composed by the American Emily Dickinson (1830–1886), the Russian Anna Akhmatova (1889–1966), the English Jesuit Gerard Manley Hopkins (1844–1889), Ireland's William Butler Yeats (1865–1939), the German Rainer Maria Rilke (1875–1926), and the Welsh Anglican priest R. S. Thomas (1913–2000). Americans such as Robinson Jeffers (1887–1962), Anne Sexton (1928–1974), Allen Ginsberg (1926–1997), and Gary Snyder (1930–) composed poetic exhortations and confessions, both lyric and narrative, that are still further removed from conventional Western religious norms—being panentheistic, feminist, "Beat," and Zen in their respective spiritualities. The works of the Jewish poet Paul Celan (1920–1970) constitute some of the most evocative and shattering uses of poetic language to have emerged in response to the Holocaust.

Outside the West, and many centuries earlier, in Shiʿa Islamic circles under the Sunni Umayyad dynasty (661–750), remarkable religious odes and laments were composed in order to praise and mourn martyrs. A very different form of lyric verse flourished during a golden age of poetry in the Tang dynasty of China (618–907). Many Tang lyrics, composed by civil servants and aristocrats for whom the making of poetry was often a daily exercise, manifest a Daoist interest in nature, especially the harmonies and quiet surprises of seasonal change. Other poems, like those of Wang Wei (c. 699–761), contemplate landscapes in such a way as to suggest an insubstantiality corresponding to the Buddhist metaphysical idea of "emptiness." In seventeenth-century Japan, Matsuo Bashō (1644–94) composed haiku that, in their extreme brevity, likewise observed nature with care, exhibiting Zen mindfulness and suggesting the interplay between the momentary and the timeless.

By contrast with such essentially quiet (though sometimes gently humorous) forms of verse, expressions of religious awe, affection, and ecstasy abound in the lyrical modes of Indian poets and singers associated with the popular movement known as *bhakti.* In the sixth century CE, South Indian poet-saints associated with this movement began to compose extensive Tamil hymns to Śiva or Viṣṇu; others oriented their poetry toward the ultimate reality *brahman,* regarded either as personal divinity with qualities, or as ultimately ineffable and beyond qualities. The movement spread to other parts of India. Later poets in the *bhakti* line include the female poets Akka Mahadevi (a twelfth-century devotee of Śiva) and Mīrā (a sixteenth-century devotee of Kṛṣṇa). The tradition continues, with modifications, into modern times, manifesting itself, for instance, in the poetry of Rabindranath Tagore (1861–1941), whose poetic art entails mystical self-realization and indeed joy, yet is not untouched by suffering.

In Islam as well, particularly in the Sūfī tradition, the more fervent forms of religious lyricism exhibit a recurrent tendency to become mystical, and often, in becoming mystical, to employ erotic metaphors to express intense longing for, or union with, the divine. Such poetic mysticism reaches a peak in the famous Persian Sūfī poet Jalāl al-Dīn Rūmī (1207–1273), whose narratives and lyrical couplets express a longing for God in both veiled and explicitly sexual imagery. Long before Rūmī's time, the Iraqi poet Rābiʿah al-ʾAdawīyah (d. 801) explored her love of God in terms of divine-human reciprocity, helping inspire a whole genre of Islamic mystical poetry in which God and the human self are imaged as beloved and lover.

The poetic traditions of Christianity and Judaism are generally less rapturous and mystical than those considered above, and are mostly inclined to seek communion with God, rather than union. But notable examples of the mystical poetic impulse can be found. The poems of the Spaniard John of the Cross (1542–1591) are classics of mysticism, known for tracing the path to God through the dark night of the soul. Many works of Jewish mystical poetry reflect the influence of medieval Qabbalah. Other Jewish poetry has been inspired by the Hasidic tradition of pietism and mysticism originating in the eighteenth century.

The mystical, and even the devotional, strands within religious poetry receive relatively little attention in the major Western theories of poetry. Although Western theories have sometimes related the poetic sense of the sublime to the religious experience of the holy, they have generally valued poetry as instruction and delight, as creative or beautiful making (poiesis) and artful representation (mimesis), and as self-expression. By contrast, Indian poetic theories have more frequently discerned a genuinely religious and potentially mystical purpose inherent within the experience of poetry itself. Thus various ancient theorists in India discuss eight or nine major aesthetic *rasas* (core sentiments or moods), one of which they commonly identify as profoundly peaceful (*santa*) and, as such, also religious. No later than the sixteenth century, a specifically devotional *rasa* is identified, which is called simply *bhakti*. Centuries before then, the great eleventh century theorist Abhinavagupta had said that a *rasa* produced by a drama (normally in verse and dance) can afford a kind of metaphysical bliss integral to, though not identical with, the experience of utmost spiritual liberation, or mokṣa.

The Larger Context: Religion, Poetry, and Society. As the preceding discussion has shown, poetry serves a variety of religious purposes, even as it heightens awareness of the power, beauty, and figurative play of language itself. Prior to the modern era, the poetry with the widest sphere of influence was mythical, epic, or quasi-historical, in the manner of the Babylonian epic Gilgamesh, the Indian *Rāmāyaṇa*, Dante's *Divine Comedy*, and Milton's *Paradise Lost*. Such poetry speaks for and to the wider community, in both religious and moral terms. Poetry in that public sense of establishing and exploring core communal values has largely been eclipsed in contemporary life, especially in the West. Some cultural critics have wondered whether theatre and prose fiction may also be fading from public significance in a phase of culture that seems preeminently visual and musical.

Nevertheless, if one includes song itself in the category of poetry—something for which there is historical precedent—then it can be said with some justification that the poetic medium, if less often poetry itself, still plays a role in public. Popular songwriters such as Bob Dylan (1941–), Paul Simon (1942–), Bob Marley (1944–1987), and the Indigo Girls (first recorded in 1989) have had a communal role with discernible moral and religious dimensions that go beyond entertainment per se. At a less popular level, but with a sizeable multinational audience, the morally engaging films of the Japanese director Akira Kurosawa (1910–1998) and the Polish director Krzysztof Kieslowski (1941–1996) are certainly not without poetic qualities. Meanwhile, in their widely acclaimed contemporary operas and large-scale choral works, composers such as John Adams (1947–), Philip Glass (1937–), and Tan Dun (1957–) employ poetic texts from Christian, Hindu, Buddhist, and Mayan traditions, partly in an attempt to recover a global sense, however mysterious, of purpose and hope.

In a postmodern culture, then, it appears that the larger social and communal dimension of moral and religious imagination is still being conveyed poetically, but more often by the poetic qualities of media such as music and film than by poetry.

See Also Bhagavadgītā; Dante Alighieri; Deconstruction; Film and Religion; John of the Cross; Mahābhārata; Qurʾān, overview article; Ramayana; Rumi, Jalal al-Din; Tagore, Rabindranath.

Bibliography

Two invaluable reference sources for the study of poetry and poetics, religious and otherwise, are *The New Princeton Encyclopedia of Poetry and Poetics,* edited by Alex Preminger and T. V. F. Brogan (Princeton, N.J., 1993), and *Encyclopedia of Contemporary Literary Theory: Approaches, Scholars, Terms,* edited by Irena R. Makaryk (Toronto, 1993).

The following studies, although centered on one particular period, genre, or text, provide insights into the overall relation between poetry and religion: M. H. Abrams, *Natural Supernaturalism: Tradition and Revolution in Romantic Literature* (New York, 1971), Robert Alter, *The Art of Biblical Poetry* (New York, 1985), Guy L. Beck, *Sonic Theology: Hinduism and Sacred Sound* (Columbia, S.C., 1993), Giles B. Gunn, *The Interpretation of Otherness: Literature, Religion, and the American Imagination* (New York, 1979), O. B. Hardison, Jr., *Christian Rite and Christian Drama in the Middle Ages* (Baltimore, 1965), David Lyle Jeffrey, ed., *Dictionary of Biblical Tradition in English Literature,* (Grand Rapids, Mich., 1992), Barbara Kiefer Lewalski, *Protestant Poetics and the Seventeenth-Century Religious Lyric* (Princeton, N.J., 1979), Louis L. Martz, *The Poetry of Meditation: A Study in English Religious Literature of the Seventeenth Century,* rev. edition (New Haven, Conn., 1962), Vijay Mishra, *Devotional Poetics and the Indian Sublime* (Albany, N.Y., 1998), Stephen Prickett, *Words and the Word: Language, Poetics, and Biblical Interpretation* (Cambridge, U.K., and New York, 1986), John Renard, *Seven Doors to Islam: Spirituality and the Religious Life of Muslims* (Berkeley, Calif., 1996), James H. Sanford, William R. LaFleur, and Masatoshi Nagatomi, eds., *Flowing Traces: Buddhism in the Literary and Visual Arts of Japan,* (Princeton, N.J., 1992), and Nathan A. Scott, Jr., *Visions of Presence in Modern American Poetry* (Baltimore, 1993).

These studies reflect more broadly on religious dimensions of poetry and poetics: Vincent Buckley, *Poetry and the Sacred* (London, 1968), Frank Burch Brown, *Transfiguration: Poetic Metaphor and the Languages of Religious Belief* (Chapel Hill, N.C., 1983), Giles B. Gunn, ed., *Literature and Religion* (New York, 1971), Hans Küng and Walter Jens, *Literature and Religion* (New York, 1991), Justus George Lawler, *Celestial Pantomime: Poetic Structures of Transcendence* (New Haven, Conn., 1979), Paul Mariani, *God and the Imagination: On Poets, Poetry, and the Ineffable* (Athens, Ga., 2002), William T. Noon, *Poetry and Prayer* (New Brunswick, N.J., 1967), Walter J. Ong, *Orality and Literacy* (New York, 1982), Nathan A. Scott, Jr., *The Poetics of Belief* (Chapel Hill, N.C., 1985), Gerardus van der Leeuw, *Sacred and Profane Beauty: The Holy in Art,* translated by David E. Green (New York, 1963), and Robert Wuthnow, *Creative Spirituality: The Way of the Artist* (Berkeley, Calif., 2001).

While there is no truly representative reader in the poetry of the world's religions, three collections that cross traditions are *Technicians of the Sacred: A Range of Poetries from Africa, America, Asia, and Oceania,* edited by Jerome Rothenberg (New York, 1968), *The Penguin Book of Religious Verse,* edited by R. S. Thomas (Harmondsworth, U.K., 1963), and *Modern Religious Poems: A Contemporary Anthology,* edited by Jacob Trapp (New York, 1964). A major, two-volume anthology in English combining Jewish and Christian poetry, along with poetry from the margins of those traditions, is *Chapters into Verse: Poetry in English Inspired by the Bible,* edited by Robert Atwan and Laurance Wieder (New York, 1993). Similar in nature, but focusing on modern poetry and the Hebrew Bible alone, is the anthology *Modern Poems on the Bible,* edited by David Curzon (Jerusalem, 1994). For what is possibly the most religiously diverse collection of poetry about any one religious figure, see *Divine Inspiration: The Life of Jesus in World Poetry,* edited by Robert Atwan, George Dardess, and Peggy Rosenthal (New York, 1998).

FRANK BURCH BROWN (2005)

POETRY: INDIAN RELIGIOUS POETRY

The most popular and influential devotional poetry in India is that associated with the *bhakti,* or popular devotional, movement—a wave of religious fervor that swept over India from South to North, beginning around the sixth century in the Tamil area and flourishing in the Hindi region between the fifteenth and seventeenth centuries. It was a grass roots movement, protesting against formalism and priestly domination; insisting on the direct accessibility of God to everyone; attacking purely external practices and hypocrisy; and stressing the importance of inner experience, which generally meant establishing a bond of fervent personal love with the deity. *Bhakti* is also associated with the rise of vernacular literature and with a group of poet-saints whose works are in many instances the classics of their respective languages. Much of this literature was composed orally, and all of it has been transmitted largely through singing. Written versions have typically been recorded and collected after the poets' lifetimes, though some poets did write down their own works. This article focuses mainly on short verse forms (lyrics and couplets) and on Hindu vernacular poetry, though there are brief sections on Sanskrit, Buddhist, and Jain materials as well.

HINDU POETRY IN SANSKRIT. The most ancient texts of Indian civilization, the Rgvedic hymns (1200–900 BCE), can be seen as remote first ancestors of the long tradition of devotional poetry in India. These poems include paeans to various Aryan gods, many of whom assumed places in the late Hindu pantheon.

The body of Sanskrit verse most relevant to this survey is the vast assortment of Hindu *stotras*—hymns of praise, adoration, and supplication—with examples ranging over two millennia, from before the common era to the present day. These poems are found imbedded in epics, Purāṇas, *māhātmyas*, Tantras, other sacred texts, and occasionally secular texts; or as independent works attributed to various devotees and teachers. The period in which *stotras* were most abundantly produced corresponds largely to that of the *bhakti* movement. Composed in all parts of India, the hymns are addressed chiefly to forms of Śiva, Viṣṇu, and Devī (the goddess), but they are also dedicated to other deities, such as Gaṇeśa and Sūrya. Their subjects extend further to sacred cities, rivers, shrines, plants; to *gurus* and ancestors; and to the impersonal Absolute. Many *stotras* are anonymous or of dubious attribution. Among numerous named composers, a few famous examples are the philosophers Śaṅkara and Rāmānuja, the Kashmiri Śaiva devotee Utpaladeva, the Bengali Caitanyite Rūpa Gosvāmin, and the South Indian poet Nīlakṇṭha Dīkṣita.

Sanskrit *stotras* are used widely in both temple and domestic worship. Their contents typically include detailed descriptions of a deity's form and accoutrements, praise of his or her attributes, references to mythological episodes, strings of names and epithets, prayers for grace and assistance, and testimonials to the devotee's grief, helplessness, love, and faith.

A. K. Rāmānujan (1981, p. 109) comments on the relation between Sanskrit and vernacular *bhakti* literature. "The imperial presence of Sanskrit," he writes, "was a presence against which *bhakti* in Tamil defines itself, though not always defiantly." While vernacular *bhakti* poets often defy Sanskritic norms, there is also a continuity between the two traditions. For example, in the *Rāmcaritmānas* of Tulsīdās there are many praise poems in highly Sanskritized Hindi, set apart in diction and form, obviously meant to echo the style of Sanskrit *stotras*. The *Saundaryalaharī*, a *stotra* popularly attributed to Śaṅkara, describes the experience of oneness with the divine in terms that later turn up almost identically in the Kabir tradition. An important transitional work between North Indian Sanskrit and vernacular *bhakti* literature is Jayadeva's *Gitagovinda,* composed in Bengal around 1200.

SOUTH INDIAN VERNACULAR POETRY. Partly in reaction to the strength of Buddhism and Jainism in the South, a great surge of faith in Viṣṇu and Śiva was touched off by poet-saints in the Tamil region between the sixth and ninth centuries. Śaiva and Vaiṣṇava saint-poets—at one level rivals, at a deeper level, collaborators in this awakening of faith—shared common themes and styles. They roamed the countryside reaching audiences of all classes and included among their number peasants, aristocrats, Untouchables, priests, women, and men. Tradition has preserved the names of sixty-three Śaiva poets, known as Nāyaṉārs, and twelve Vaiṣṇavas, or Āḻvārs. Nammāḻvār is often singled out as the greatest Āḻvār poet, Māṇikkāvacakar as the greatest Nāyaṉār. Around the tenth century Nāthamuni compiled the *Divya-prabhandam,* containing four thousand Āḻvār compositions for use in Śrī Vaiṣṇava worship. Similarly Nampi Āntār Nampi, at the request of a tenth-century king, is said to have compiled most of the *Tirumuṟai,* which includes eleven volumes of Nāyaṉār poetry (a twelfth volume, of hagiography, was added later). Śaivas often call the *Tirumuṟai,* as Vaiṣṇavas call Nammāḻvār's *Tiruvāymoḻi,* "the Tamil Veda."

The *siddhas* (Tam. *cittar*) are part of an ancient pan-Indian movement characterized by its use of yogic practices and Tantric symbols. Important *siddha* poets in Tamil range from the seventh to the eighteenth centuries and include Civavākkiyar, Pattirakiriyar, and Pāmpāttic Cittar. *Siddha* poetry is both linked to and distinguishable from mainstream *bhakti* poetry. Both tend to denigrate caste, mechanical ritual, and sterile intellectuality. But while the *bhaktas* continue to adore their images of Viṣṇu and Śiva, the *siddhas* favor an interior, impersonal Lord and unequivocally attack idol worship. Stylistically, too, the *siddhas* differ from the generally more refined devotional poets. Their verse, which often utilizes folksong forms and meters, is colloquial, forceful, and simple often to the point of being crude.

"Like a lit fuse, the passion of *bhakti* seems to spread from region to region, from century to century, quickening the religious impulse," says Rāmānujan (1973, p. 40). In the tenth to twelfth centuries the flame burned brightly in Karnataka with the Kannada verses of the Vīraśaiva saint-poets, the four greatest of whom were Basavaṇṇa, Dēvara Dāsimayya, Mahādēvīyakka, and Allama Prabhu. They composed *vacanas*, short free-verse utterances expressing intense personal experience and sometimes trenchant criticism of what the poets regarded as superstition and hypocrisy. A *vacana* by Allama Prabhu, for example, is a purely lyric outpouring:

Looking for your light,
I went out:
it was like the sudden dawn
of a million million suns,
a ganglion of lightnings
for my wonder.
O Lord of Caves,
if you are light,
there can be no metaphor. (trans. Rāmānujan, 1973, p. 168)

while the conclusion of a *vacana* by Basavaṇṇa has a note of biting criticism:

Gods, gods, there are so many
there's no place left
for a foot.
There is only
one god. He is our Lord
of the Meeting Rivers. (trans. Rāmānujan, 1973, p. 84)

Vaiṣṇava poetry emerges in the sixteenth century with Purandaradāsa Viṭṭhala, who is remembered as the founder of the southern (Karnatak) style of classical music. The greatest composer of Karnatak music, Tyāgarāja (1767–1847), acknowledges his debt to Purandaradasa. A devotee of Rām, Tyāgarāja composed many devotional songs in Telugu, often praising music as a pathway to God. Another well-known Telugu saint-poet is the seventeenth-century Rāmdās of Bhadrācalam, also a worshiper of Rām.

North Indian Vernacular Poetry. Four names stand out among a rich array of Maharashtrian singers between the thirteenth and seventeenth centuries: Jñāneśvar, also called Jñāndev (fl. late thirteenth century), Nāmdev (c. 1270–1350), Eknāth (1548–1600), and Tukārām (1598–1650). Jñāneśvar is best known for his long Marathi exposition of the *Bhagavadgītā,* the *Jñāneśvarī.* Nāmdev composed passionate devotional songs and consolidated the cult of the Vārkaris ("pilgrims") to the important pilgrimage center at Pandharpur. Eknāth translated and interpreted important Sanskrit works. He also poured out his own feelings in lyric poems and in a remarkable series of dramatic monologues, putting the most profound teachings of *bhakti* into the mouths of characters generally despised by society—Untouchables, prostitutes, ropedancers, demons, the blind, and the deaf. Tukārām, perhaps the most beloved of the four, was a *śūdra* (member of the lowest of the four broad categories of caste) pressed by misfortune to reject worldly values and devote himself to God. His lyrics run from harsh contempt of self-serving religious specialists ("the wretched pandit stewed in dialectics . . . a fool among fools / wagging a sage beard") to the most tender humility ("May I be, Lord, a small pebble, a large stone, or dust / on the road to Pandharpur / to be trampled by the feet of the saints").

Nasiṃha Mehta (fifteenth or sixteenth century), the major *bhakti* poet of Gujarat, composed songs that were incorporated into the rituals of the Vallabhācārya sect. The Kashmiri Lal Ded (fourteenth century) was a woman devotee of Śiva whose poetic utterances are famous throughout Kashmir and beyond. The earliest and still most important devotional poetry associated with the Punjab, that compiled in the Sikh *Ādi Granth* (1604), is largely in an old form of Hindi. True Panjabi literature, beginning in the seventeenth century, is almost entirely by Muslims.

The leading figures of Hindi *bhakti* poetry are Tulsīdās, Śūrdās, Kabīr, and Mīrā Baī, followed closely by Raidās, Nānak, and Dādū. Tulsīdās (1543–1623), who wrote in the

Avadhi dialect, is the author of the *Rāmcaritmānas,* a highly devotional version of the ancient *Rāmayāṇa* epic. Popularly known as the *Tulsī Rāmāyan,* it is probably the most influential single literary work in North India. Tulsīdās also wrote many lyrics.

Śūrdās (sixteenth century) is the most illustrious member of the *aṣṭacāp,* or eight Kṛṣṇaite poets associated with Vallabhācārya and the sect he founded in Vṛndāvana. He is most famous for his evocations of Kṛṣṇa's idyllic childhood, but recent scholarship suggests that Sūr's often emotionally harrowing personal supplications to God and his poems of grief-stricken separation may be closer to the authentic core of his work than the popular songs of the youthful deity. According to legend Sūr was blind, and "Śūrdās" is today widely used as a title for any blind singer of religious songs. Thousands of lyrics attributed to the poet are collected in the *Sūrsāgar* (Ocean of Sūr). He composed in Braj *bhāṣā,* the most important literary dialect of medieval Hindi.

Mīrā Baī was a Rajput princess who became a wandering saint. Although she is believed to have spent the later part of her life in Dwarka, Gujarat, and a considerable body of poetry ascribed to her exists in Gujarati, she is more closely linked to her native Rajasthan and to its regional form of Hindi.

The leading poet of the Sant (or *nirguṇa,* "without qualities") school in North India is Kabīr (c. 1398–1448). Born of a Muslim family in Banaras, Kabīr was influenced more by Hindu than by Muslim traditions and is popularly believed to have been a disciple of Rāmānanda. He is known particularly for his iconoclasm and for his rough, colloquial style. Kabīr called on the name of Rām as a sound that revealed ultimate reality, but he rejected the mythology of the popular *avatāra* Rām, insisting that God was beyond form.

Gurū Nānak (1469–1539), the founder of Sikhism, composed poems revering the formless God and criticizing superstitious practices. The same is true of Dādū (1544–1604), in whose name a sect was founded in Rajasthan. Raidās, an Untouchable leatherworker and Sant poet of the fifteenth century, is respected by all classes but has a particular following among his own caste, the *camārs*.

Mention should also be made of the poetry of the North Indian yogins called Nāth Paṇthis, who belong to the same broad tradition as the Tamil *siddhas*. The most significant collection is attributed to Gorakhnāth (eleventh century?), semilegendary founder of the Nāth Paṇth, whose teachings pervaded North Indian religious thought in the medieval period.

The story of Bengali *bhakti* poetry begins with a Sanskrit poet, Jayadeva, whose late twelfth-century masterpiece *Gītagovinda* sets the mood for the efflorescence of Kṛṣṇaite verse in the following four hundred years. In a series of subtle and sensuous lyrics, the *Gītagovinda* unfolds the drama of love between Kṛṣṇa and Rādhā, which became the major theme of devotion in medieval Bengal. In this poetry the strand of several traditions come together: secular erotic verse in Sanskrit, Tantrism, and orthodox Vaiṣṇavism.

The name *Caṇḍīdās* was used by at least two important Bengali poets whose dates can only be guessed (guesses range from the fourteenth to the sixteenth century). The enormously influential saint, Caitanya (1486–1533), though he composed very little himself, encouraged the development of Bengali song literature by establishing the widespread practice of *kīrtan,* or meeting for ardent group singing. Rāmprasād Sen (1718–1785) was a powerful poet of the Śākta (Goddess-worshiping) tradition. The Bauls, unique to Bengal, are iconoclastic wanderers who hover between Hindu and Ṣūfī mysticism and worship exclusively through singing.

Vidyāpati (c. 1352–1448) was one of the earliest poets to compose religious lyrics in Maithili—a border language between Bengali and Hindi. The outstanding figure of Assamese devotional literature is Śaṅkaradeva (c.1489–1568), who introduced a devotional dance drama form still widely used today. A unique *bhakti* institution in Assam is the *satra,* a religious center with a leader, lay members, and facilities for musical and dramatic performances. Another prominent poet of the same period is Mādhavadeva (1489?–1596). The best-known medieval *bhakti* poet in Oriya was a disciple of Caitanya named Jagannāthadāsa (fifteenth century).

BUDDHIST POETRY. Remarkable early examples of Buddhist poetry are found in the *Therīgāthā* and *Theragāthā* (Songs of the venerable women and Songs of the venerable men) of the Pali canon, recorded around 80 BCE. The women especially describe vivid personal experiences that led to their choice of a renunciant's life.

Two great Sanskrit poets appear in the second century of the common era. Aśvaghosa is most famous for the *Buddhacarita,* a biography of the Buddha in the form of a *mahākāvya* (lyric narrative). Mātṛceṭa, perhaps an older contemporary of Aśvaghosa, wrote beautiful Sanskrit hymns to the Buddha. The seventh-century Chinese pilgrim Yi Jing reported, "Throughout India everyone who becomes a monk is taught Mātṛceṭa's two hymns as soon as he can recite the . . . precepts."

Over the centuries Buddhist poets, such as the seventh-century monk Śāntideva, produced many *stotras* praising the Buddha and *bodhisattvas* and expressing fervent dedication to the Buddhist path. Like Hindu *stotras,* these are found incorporated into larger texts (such as *sūtras* and Jātaka tales) as well as in independent form with attribution to particular authors. In one such hymn Śāntideva expresses his vow to save all beings:

> I am medicine for the sick and
> weary may I be their physician and their nurse
> until disease appears no more . . .
> may I be a protector for the unprotected
> a guide for wanderers
> a bridge: a boat: a causeway

for those who desire the other shores. . . . (trans.
Stephan Beyer)

Finally mention must be made of Tibet's powerful and original contributions to Buddhist lyric poetry. Especially noteworthy are the many songs of the twelfth-century teacher Milaraspa (Milarepa).

JAIN POETRY. Like Hindus and Buddhists, the Jains have produced a large *stotra* literature. Their hymns, composed since at least the earliest centuries of the common era in Sanskrit and later in Prakrit, praise chiefly the twenty-four *jinas* as well as some ancient teachers of the Jain tradition. There also exists a body of vernacular Jain poetry, largely in Hindi and Gujarati. One of the most famous Jain hymns is the *Bhaktāmara Stotra* of Mānatuṅga, whose dates have been estimated to be as early as the third and as late as the ninth century. Several Jain authors composed both philosophical works and devotional poems. These include Siddhasena Divākara, Samantabhadra, Vidyānanda, and the great twelfth-century sage Hemacandra.

Many Jain *stotras* are organized around the sequential praise of all twenty-four *jinas*, the best known being the highly ornate *Śobhana Stuti* of the tenth-century poet Śobhana. As the repeated glorification of the *jinas* made for monotonously similar content, poets made great efforts to achieve originality of form, and thus the *stotras* contain the most ornate verse in Jain literature.

SEE ALSO Ādi Granth; Āḻvārs; Bhakti; Caitanya; Gorākhnāth; Jayadeva; Kabīr; Mahāsiddhas; Māṇikkavācakar; Mi la ras pa (Milarepa); Mīrā Bāī; Nānak; Rāmānuja; Śaivism, articles on Nāyāṉārs, Vīraśaivas; Śaṅkara; Śāntideva; Śūrdās; Tulsīdās.

BIBLIOGRAPHY

A good introduction to the *bhakti* movement is Eleanor Zelliot's "The Medieval Bhakti Movement in History: An Essay on the Literature in English," in *Hinduism: New Essays in the History of Religions*, edited by Bardwell L. Smith (Leiden, 1976), pp. 143–168. Zelliot provides accounts of the regional movements and bibliographies. Missing from her lists, however, are important recent translations.

Superb translations from Tamil and Kannada are given in A. K. Ramanujan's *Hymns for the Drowning: Poems for Viṣṇu by Nammālvār* (Princeton, N.J., 1981) and *Speaking of Śiva* (Harmondsworth, 1973). Kamil Zvelebil's survey of Tamil literature, *The Smile of Murugan* (Leiden, 1973), includes chapters on both *bhakti* and *siddha* poetry. Zvelebil has also written a book on the *siddhas*, *The Poets of the Powers* (London, 1973), which includes a number of translations.

Charlotte Vaudeville's numerous contributions in the Hindi field include her monumental *Kabīr,* vol. 1 (Oxford, 1974), which combines a 150-page introduction with extensive translations and painstaking scholarly apparatus. *The Bījak of Kabīr* (San Francisco, 1983), translated by Shukdev Singh and me, conveys a vivid sense of Kabīr's forceful style and includes essays on his style and use of symbols. Śūrdās is richly represented in Kenneth E. Bryant's *Poems to the Child-God: Structures and Strategies in the Poetry of Śūrdās* (Berkeley, Calif., 1978) and in John Stratton Hawley's *Sūr Dās: Poet, Singer, Saint* (Seattle, 1984). Tulsīdās's lyrics are available in reliable if not sparkling translations by F. R. Allchin in *Kavitāvalī* (London, 1964) and his *The Petition to Rām* (London, 1966).

An exceptionally lovely book of translations from Bengali is *In Praise of Krishna* (1967; Chicago, 1981), a collaborative effort of the scholar Edward C. Dimock, Jr., and the poet Denise Levertov. Lively translations of Ramprasad Sen are provided in *Grace and Mercy in Her Wild Hair: Selected Poems to the Mother Goddess* (Boulder, 1982) by another poet-scholar team, Leonard Nathan and Clinton Seely. Jayadeva's *Gītagovinda* is splendidly translated by Barbara Stoler Miller in *Love Song of the Dark Lord* (New York, 1977).

A good source for examples of Buddhist poetry is Stephan Beyer's *The Buddhist Experience: Sources and Interpretations* (Encino, Calif., 1974). On the *caryāgīti,* see Per Kvaerne's *An Anthology of Buddhist Tantric Songs* (Oslo, 1977; Bangkok, 1985).

A multivolume, English-language *History of Indian Literature,* edited by Jan Gonda (Wiesbaden, 1973–), is in progress. Individual volumes have been published on literature in Sanskrit and the vernacular languages as well as on the literatures of particular religious traditions. Maurice Winternitz's *A History of Indian Literature,* 2 vols. (Calcutta, 1927–1933) covers ground not covered elsewhere, particularly in volume 2, *Buddhist Literature and Jaina Literature.*

New Sources

Guptara, Prabhu S., ed. *The Lotus: An Anthology of Contemporary Indian Religious Poetry in English.* Calcutta, 1988.

Ramanujan, A. K., Velcheru Narayana Rao, and David Dean Shulman, ed. and trans. *When God Is a Customer: Telugu Courtesan Songs by Ksetrayya and Others.* Berkeley, Calif., 1994.

Rao, Velcheru Narayana, and David Dean Shulman, ed. and trans. *Classical Telugu Poetry: An Anthology.* New Delhi and New York, 2002.

Shulman, David Dean. *The Wisdom of Poets: Studies in Tamil, Telugu, and Sanskrit.* New Delhi and New York, 2001.

LINDA HESS (1987)
Revised Bibliography

POETRY: CHINESE RELIGIOUS POETRY

To speak of religious poetry in the Chinese context is to beg several questions. First, in classical Chinese there is no exact equivalent to the word *religion:* Confucianism, Daoism, and Buddhism are traditionally known as the Three Teachings (*sanjiao*). Second, it is debatable whether Confucianism is a religion and whether ancestral worship is a kind of religious ritual. (The latter question was the subject of the so-called Rites Controversy among Catholic missionaries to China in the early eighteenth century.) Finally, although Daoist and Buddhist liturgies both contain verses, these are generally not considered worthy of description as poetry. With these reservations in mind, we may nonetheless survey what may be called religious poetry in Chinese.

The earliest anthology of Chinese poetry, the *Shi jing* (The Book of Songs), consisting of three hundred and five poems dating from about 1100 to about 600 BCE, contains some hymns to royal ancestral spirits, eulogizing their virtues and praying for their blessing. These hymns are believed to have been sung to the accompaniment of dance. In these and some other poems in the anthology, references are made to a supreme supernatural being known sometimes as Di ("emperor") or Shangdi ("emperor above"), and at other times as Tian ("Heaven"). The first term, which is often translated as "God," appears to denote an earlier and more anthropomorphic concept than does Tian. For instance, in the poem *Shengmin* (The Birth of Our People), which recounts the myth of the miraculous birth of Hou Ji ("King Millet"), the reputed ancestor of the Zhou people, Hou Ji's mother, Jiang Yuan, is said to have conceived him after treading in the print of Di's big toe. By contrast, Heaven is generally depicted as a vague presence without specific physical attributes, sometimes wrathful but usually benevolent.

Some shamanistic songs from the kingdom of Chu, which flourished in the central Yangtze Valley from the seventh to the third century BCE, are preserved in the next oldest anthology of Chinese poetry, the *Chuci* (Songs of Chu), compiled in the second century CE. These songs are dedicated to various deities, such as the Lord of the East (the sun god), the Lord of Clouds, and the Lord of the Yellow River. In these songs, the relationship between the male shaman and the goddess or between the female shaman and the god is described in terms of erotic love. The sex of the speaker is not always clear: we cannot always be sure whether it is a male shaman addressing a goddess or a female shaman addressing a god. The shaman may also speak in the voice of the deity. Traditionally, these and other poems in the *Chuci* are attributed to Qu Yuan (343?–278 BCE), said to have been a loyal courtier of Chu who was unjustly banished and who committed suicide by drowning himself in the Milo River. He is generally believed to be the author of the longest poem in the anthology, the *Li-sao*, whose title is usually translated as "Encountering Sorrow," although the term may simply mean "complaints." In this poem the speaker sets out upon a journey through the cosmos, in a carriage drawn by dragons and heralded by phoenixes, attended by the gods of the winds and of thunder. He also courts certain goddesses without success, and finally resolves to "follow Peng Xian," an ancient shaman. Chinese commentators have generally taken this to mean a resolution to commit suicide but the modern scholar David Hawkes interprets it as a desire to study the occult. Although it is difficult to be sure how far the mythological figures in the poem are intended to be taken literally and how far allegorically, the poem certainly derives some of its imagery from a shamanistic cult; it has even been suggested that Qu Yuan was a shaman.

During the Han dynasty (206 BCE–220 CE), the court's Bureau of Music (Yuefu) composed ritual hymns to be used at the sacrifices made to imperial ancestral spirits. Similar hymns existed in later dynasties. They usually show a stilted style and have no great poetic merit. It was during the Han period that Daoism evolved from its early philosophic origins into an organized religion. At this time too, Buddhism was first introduced into China, although it did not become popular at once. Following the Han period, Chinese poets were mostly either eclectic or syncretic, and might express Confucian, Daoist, or Buddhist views in different poems or even all of them in the same poem. However, in the works of some poets, the propensity to one of the three major ideologies is fairly pronounced. The following are some of the most famous examples.

Cao Zhi (192–232 CE) wrote several poems about Daoist immortals, but it is difficult to say whether he really believed in them. The same may be said of Ruan Ji (210–263), who in some of his poems expressed a wish for immortality but in others showed frank skepticism. Scholars disagree about the religious and philosophical beliefs of Tao Qian (365?–427), whose withdrawal from officialdom was probably motivated by both Confucian ideals of integrity and Daoist wishes for simplicity and spontaneity. Although his poetry expresses both Confucian and Daoist views, his emphasis on following nature and his acceptance of death as a part of the eternal flux are more Daoist than Confucian. The landscape poetry of Xie Lingyun (385–433) evinces both Buddhist and Daoist influences. To him, natural scenery is a manifestation of spirituality, yet the self-conscious philosophizing in his poems suggests an inability to transcend worldly concerns.

During the Tang dynasty (618–907), the golden age of Chinese poetry, Daoism and Buddhism flourished, except during the reign of Emperor Wuzong (846–859), who persecuted the Buddhists. Many Tang poets were influenced by Daoism or Buddhism or both, although none openly rejected Confucianism. By coincidence, the three greatest Tang poets, Wang Wei (699?–761), Li Po (701–762), and Tu Fu (712–770), are considered to represent Buddhism, Daoism, and Confucianism respectively in their poetry, albeit not exclusively. Wang Wei, known as the Buddha of Poetry, wrote some explicitly Buddhist poems as well as others that embody a Buddhist vision of life without specific Buddhist references. In addition, he wrote court poems and social poems. His best poetry conveys a sense of tranquillity tinged with sadness as he quietly contemplates nature; the poems explicitly preaching Buddhism are less satisfactory as poetry. Li Po, the Immortal of Poetry, received a Daoist diploma and took "elixirs of life," which may have contributed to his death. Many of his poems express a yearning for the realm of the immortals and a wish to transcend this world, although they show him also to be far from indifferent to sensual pleasures such as wine, women, and song. Whether he succeeded in attaining Daoist transcendence or not, Li Po certainly found Daoist mythology a source of poetic inspiration and a stimulus to his exuberant imagination. Tu Fu, the Sage of Poetry, wrote mainly poetry with a Confucian outlook, although some of his poems refer to Daoist elixirs of life and others evince admiration for Buddhism. Perhaps, however, these are only signs of wishful thinking or polite expressions of respect for the beliefs of others.

Among late Tang poets, Han Yu (768–824), the self-appointed champion of Confucianism, attacked Buddhism and Daoism, yet befriended some Buddhist monks. Bo Jui (772–846) was strongly influenced by Buddhism and also experimented with Daoist alchemy. The calm and bland tone of his typical poems may result from Buddhist influence. Li Ho (791–817) wrote much about spirits, ghosts, and shamans, but it is difficult to ascertain whether he believed in these literally or used them figuratively. Li Shang-yin (813?–858) studied Daoism in his youth and was converted to Buddhism toward the end of his life. There are many allusions to Daoist mythology in his poetry, which is, however, seldom of a religious nature.

The best-known corpus of Chinese Buddhist poetry is that attributed to Han-shan ("cold mountain"), a legendary figure of whose historical existence we have little knowledge. Indeed, some scholars believe, on the basis of internal linguistic evidence, that the poems bearing Han-shan's name were by two or more hands and that they range in date from the late seventh to the ninth centuries. The best among these poems are quietly meditative with a touch of gentle melancholy, and the worst are short sermons in doggerel. Apart from Han-shan, some Chan masters wrote *gāthā* (a kind of hymn) in verse. These were intended as triggers to enlightenment, to be discarded as soon as enlightenment was attained, not as poetry to be read and cherished.

During the Song dynasty (960–1279), considered second only to the Tang in poetic achievements, such major poets as Wang Anshi (1021–1086), Su Shi (1037–1101), and Huang Tingjian (1045–1105) all wrote poetry chiefly expressing Buddhist views. In subsequent periods, the literati continued to write poetry reflecting Confucian, Daoist, and Buddhist attitudes, and Buddhist and Daoist priests continued to use verses in their respective rituals and sermons, even though such verses were not regarded as poetry. As for contemporary Chinese poetry, in the People's Republic of China there is hardly any poetry that can be called religious, whereas in Taiwan a few poets show Buddhist or Christian tendencies, but they are only a small minority.

Bibliography

Chen, Kenneth. *The Chinese Transformation of Buddhism.* Princeton, 1973. Contains a chapter on Buddhist influence on Chinese poets, especially Bo Jui.

Hawkes, David, ed. and trans. *Chuci, The Songs of the South* (1959). Reprint, Boston, 1962. Complete translation of the anthology of chiefly shamanistic songs.

Karlgren, Bernhard, ed. and trans. *The Book of Odes* (1950). Reprint, Stockholm, 1974. Literal translation of the *Shi jing.* See the ritual hymns to ancestral spirits.

Waley, Arthur. *The Poetry and Career of Li Po, 701–762 A. D.* New York, 1950. Contains discussions of Li Po's interest in Daoism.

Watson, Burton, trans. *Cold Mountain: 100 Poems by the Tang Poet Han-shan* (1962). Reprint, New York, 1970. Selected poems attributed to the monk Han-shan.

Yu, Pauline. *The Poetry of Wang Wei.* Bloomington, Ind., 1980. Contains translations and discussions of Wang's Buddhist poems.

James J. Y. Liu (1987)

POETRY: JAPANESE RELIGIOUS POETRY

Poetic language has long had a special prestige in Japan. The earliest extant written texts, including the *Kojiki* (Record of ancient matters; 712), *Nihonshoki* (Chronicle of Japan; 720), and *Man'yōshū* (Collection of Ten Thousand Years; late eighth century), all preserve examples of ancient oral poetry or song, as well as later written verse. The ancient inhabitants of the Japanese archipelago, like many traditional peoples, believed that ritual song or recitation had a magico-religious power. Special ritual and poetic language possessed the ability to move the deities or spirits to act in specific sorts of ways. The term *kotodama* (*koto,* "words"; and *tama,* "animating spirit") refers to this magico-religious power. *Man'yōshū* 1:27, for instance, is an example of incantational praise poetry. When recited by a ritual and political leader while surveying the land, the incantation was believed to assure the vitality and fertility of the land by praising and appealing to the local deities and ancestral spirits:

yoki hito no	The good ones [of the past]
yoshi to yoku mite	looked well and found it good,
yoshi to iishi	proclaimed it good.
Yoshino yoku miyo	Look well on Yoshino,
yoki hito yoku mi	O good ones, look well!

Man'yōshū 1:2 is another example of declarative ritual poetry. The emperor recited this verse, praising the land and its gods (*kami*) as he surveyed his realm from atop Kagu-yama. In myth, this is the hill to which the *kami* had originally descended from the high heavens. As was the case in China, the prosperity of the land (the verse uses *Yamato,* the ancient name of the country) was attributed to the emperor's role as ritual mediator between heaven and earth:

Sumeramikoto Kagu-yama ni noborite	Poem by the Sovereign when he
Kunimishi tamau toki no ōmi-uta	climbed Mount Kagu to view the land.
Yamato ni wa	Many are the mountains of Yamato,
murayama aredo	but I climb heavenly Mount Kagu,
toriyorou	cloaked in foliage,
ama no Kagu-yama	and stand on the summit
norboritachi	to view the land.
kunimi o sureba	On the plain of land,

kunihara wa	smoke from the hearths rises, rises.
keburi tachitatsu	On the plain of water,
umahara wa	gulls rise, rise.
kamame tachitatsu	A splendid land
umashi kuni so	is the dragonfly island,
akizushima	the land of Yamato.
Yamato no kuni wa	

(trans. Levy, 1981, p. 38, adapted)

Poetry served numerous other ritual functions as well. Funerary verses (*banka*) were recited by women to praise the deceased and to attract his or her *tama* back into the body. *Man'yōshū* 2:155 is an example of a ritual lament performed by women in the temporary burial palace for a deceased male member of the imperial family, in this case the Emperor Tenji (r.662–671):

Yamashina no mi-haka	Poem by Princess Nukata when
yori soki	the
arakuru toki, Nukata	mourners withdrew from the
no ōkimi no	
tsukuru uta isshu	Yamashina tomb and dispersed
yasumishishi	In awe we serve the tomb
wago ōkimi no	of our Lord, sovereign
kashikoki ya	of the earth's eight corners,
mi-haka tsukauru	on Kagami Mountain
Yamashina no	in Yamashina.
Kagami no yama ni	There through the night,
yoru wa mo	each night,
yoru mo kotogoto	through the day,
hiru wa mo	each day,
hi no kotogoto	we have stayed,
ne nomi o	weeping and crying aloud.
nakitsutsu tsukarite ya	Now have the courtiers
momoshiki no	of your great palace,
ōmiyabito wa	its ramparts thick with stone,
yuki-wakarenamu	left and gone apart?

(trans. Levy, 1981, p. 109)

Recitative poetry was also used in a ritual performed to pacify the spirit of the dead. In the case of grave illness or on undertaking a dangerous journey, ritual verse was used to call back the patient's vagrant spirit and to "tie" it to the patient's body (*tamamusubi*) or, alternatively, to "tie" the traveler's animating spirit in absentia into an object that was to be carefully guarded in order to guarantee the traveler's safe return. *Man'yōshū* 1:10, an example of this, also involves a critical moment of political intrigue. Reputedly, it was recited by the empress as her brother (later the Emperor Tenji) set off to initiate a coup d'état against the Emperor Kōtoku (r. 645–654):

Nakatsu sumeramikoto,	Poem by the August
Ki no ideyu	Intermediate
ni idemashishi no mi-uta	Sovereign Nakatsu when she went to the hot springs of Ki
kimi ga yo mo	The span of your life
waga yo mo shiru ya	and the span of my life, too,
Iwashiro no	are determined by the grass
Oka no kusane o	on Iwashiro Hill.
Iza musubitenu	Come, let us bind them together!

(trans. Levy, 1981, p.43, adapted)

The Shintō prayers of the imperial court (*norito*) include similar elements, such as rites and prayers to pacify the imperial *tama,* to reinvigorate it, and to guarantee its presence in the imperial body and shrine for another year (*tamashizume no matusuri* and *mi-tamashizumeno ihai-to no matsuri*). Magico-religious verse was also employed to control interpersonal relations (e.g., to attract or keep the attention of a loved one, to calm the anger of another human or divine being). Similar uses of recited verse or song were central to the ritual and cultural life of the Ainu, an "indigenous" people of northern Japan, down to the early twentieth century.

The belief in the magical efficacy of recitative verse survived long after the introduction of writing and literacy. Ki no Tsurayuki (884–946), an aristocratic poet, wrote the most famous statement on the magical power of Japanese poetry in his preface to the *Kokinshū*, the first imperially sponsored anthology of *waka,* the thirty-one syllable verse form: "*Waka* has its origins in the human heart and flourishes in the myriad leaves of words. . . .Without physical exertion, poetry moves heaven and earth, awakens the feelings of *kami* and invisible spirits, softens the relations between men and women, and calms the hearts of ferocious warriors."

Much of classical and medieval Japanese poetry was influenced by Buddhist ideals and values. Kūkai, or Kōbō Daishi (774–835), the founder of the esoteric Shingon school of Buddhism, wrote that the absolute truth of Buddhism was available only through the body, language, and thought, and this through three forms of esoteric practice—*mudrā* (hand gestures), *dhāraṇī* (*mantras*), and yoga (meditation), respectively. Numerous medieval poetic treatises identified *waka* poems with *mantras*; others, in an instance of mystical numerology, claimed that the thirty-one syllables of the *waka* form (5-7-5-7-7), plus one for the verse as a whole, were the same as the thirty-two marks of the Buddha. Thus, composing or reciting a *waka* could accrue the same religious merit as carving a statue of the Buddha or reciting a *mantra.*

Japanese religious poetry was not all composed in Japanese, however. Buddhist priests studied Chinese poetry and literature, as well as Buddhist sūtras and commentaries. Aristocratic males in the Nara and Heian periods also used Chinese in official matters, much as Latin functioned for centuries in Europe. Thus, from the seventh century on, one finds Buddhist poems being composed in Chinese by Japanese monks and other members of the educated elite. As one would expect, these poems were informed by Chinese aesthetics.

Even after writing had been introduced into Japan, however, oral forms of religious song and verse continued to flourish. In medieval Japan, numerous different types of popular religious figures sang or chanted religious verse around the country. For example, from the Heian period (794–1185) through the Kamakura period (1185–1333), *asobi* or *asobime* (itinerant female singers and dancers) performed songs called *imayō*. Some of these carried explicit Buddhist teachings; others portrayed the vicissitudes of life. *Imayō* served as vehicles to convey Mahāyāna Buddhist teachings to the masses, including the claim that all dualisms (e.g., high/low, sacred/profane, reality/illusion) were ultimately false. *Asobi* were often affiliated with specific temple-shrine complexes, and through their travels and songs they spread tales of the miracles associated with them. *Asobi* had a mixed reputation, however. Not unlike gypsy women in Europe, they were associated in the popular imagination with prostitution. Thus, Retired Emperor Go Shirakawa (1127–1192) scandalized some members of the aristocracy when he apprenticed himself for many years to an elderly *asobi* in order to master the religio-aesthetic art of *imayō*. He preserved many *imayō* in a work known as *Ryōjin hishō*, along with personal testimonies to their ritual power and efficacy. Go Shirakawa frequently engaged in all-night rituals of sūtra recitation, meditation, and the singing of *imayō* as a means of achieving religious insight.

Blind lay priests *(biwahōshi)* also performed religious songs and tales in the medieval period. *Biwahōshi* were organized into loose associations and were affiliated with temple-shrine complexes. They were found at many mountain passes and pilgrimage centers, where they played a lute (*biwa*) and chanted oral tales and verses about the ephemerality of life, the vicissitudes of fame and fortune, and so on. The famous oral epic, *Heike monogatari* (The tale of the Heike), which recounts the contestation and warfare between the Minamoto and Taira or Heike clans, was performed and transmitted by *biwahōshi* down through the centuries. Today only a few such reciters remain, and they preserve only parts of the *Heike monogatari* performative tradition.

Many of the best-known poets of medieval Japan were poet-monks. Of these, perhaps the most famous is Saigyō (1118–1190). He spent time in ritual retreat in the hills of Yoshino in a grass hut (*sōan*), yet he also actively participated in poetry contests and other aspects of the literary life of the capital. Saigyō became a major figure in the poplar imagination down to the modern period. Modern scholars have coined the phrase "grass hut literature" (*sōan bungaku*) to refer to the literary works produced by such "reclusive" poet-monks. Yet it must be understood that they were not completely separated from the mundane world. Rather, they sought to find the Buddhist truths that were to be found in the world as such. The cry of a cicada or the tolling of a temple bell at dusk equally spoke to the ephemerality at the heart of all existence (*mujō*). For those with eyes to see, ears to hear, and heart-minds (*kokoro*) cultivated to feel the pathos of the emptiness of all things in the material world (*mono no aware*), the phenomenal world itself revealed soteriological truths.

Still, as was the case in China, some Buddhists felt that the pursuit of poetry was incompatible with the religious life of a monk or nun. In general, however, poetry was embraced as an effective form of religio-aesthetic and meditative practice. Fujiwara no Shunzei (1114–1204), one of the leading poets of his age, was not alone in practicing a form of Tendai Buddhist meditation, known as *shikan* (concentration and insight), as a part of his poetic discipline. The way of poetry (*kadō*), like the way of tea and other arts, was first and foremost a discipline, in the old-fashioned religious sense of the term. The Chinese character *dō* in *kadō* is also read as *michi*—a path, way, or discipline.

Not all poets pursued the religio-aesthetic discipline of *kadō*, to be sure, but those who did undertook it as a rigorous form of self-discipline and ritual praxis. The works of the Chinese poet Bai Juyi (772–846) were extremely influential in medieval Japan and provided one model of practicing *kadō*. Comparing his own verse to the Buddhist sūtras, Bai Juyi called his poems little more than "wild phrases and flowery language" (Jap., *kyōgen kigo*), yet he offered them to Buddhist temples throughout his life. This practice of offering poems to temples and shrines has continued in Japan over the centuries.

Those who study the poems of medieval Japan as literature *tout court* risk missing the diverse religious functions that many of them served, as well as the religious practices out of which they were created. Although numerous medieval poetic treatises describe the poetic act as a spontaneous affective response on the part of the poet to the world around him, such rhetorical claims do not reflect historical reality. Rather than passively responding to the world or to events, Japanese poets often consciously sought to evoke specific mental and affective states that were deemed spiritually efficacious. That is, through acts of disciplined imagination or meditational techniques, they envisioned scenes and situations precisely in order to provoke specific stylized psychosomatic and affective states. Many medieval aesthetic terms, such as *mono no aware*, *yūgen*, *wabi*, and *sabi*, must be understood in these religio-aesthetic terms.

If the poetry of poet-monks has long been the object of study, the poetry composed by Buddhist nuns and Shintō shrine maidens has only recently begun to attract scholarly attention. With the recent release of archival materials long held out of sight by female religious institutions, however, we may anticipate that new perspectives on the religious lives of women will be opened. Similarly, these studies will help us to fill out more fully the religio-aesthetic milieu of medieval Japan.

Numerous other forms of religious poetry bear mention. The unique linked verse form (*renga*) flourished from the fifteenth century. *Renga* was performance art before it was a literary one—that is, the compositional or recitative act itself was originally the ritual art form. A *renga* sequence was composed by a group of poets, who "linked" verses of seventeen and fourteen syllables in sequences of thirty-six, one hundred, one thousand, ten thousand, or even one hundred thousand linked verses. (A single-poet form, *dokugin renga,* also existed, but was relatively rare). Although *renga* originated as a Buddhist ritual performative form, it was soon adopted and adapted as a parlor game in elite circles of the court and in samurai circles. *Renga* sequences were often performed on temple and shrine grounds, while the written records were presented as offerings to the buddhas and *kami.* Sequences were sometimes performed by priests and samurai soldiers before battles and on battlefields after an engagement in order to pacify the spirits of the dead. Renga sequences were also performed, like sūtra recitations, in order to restore the health of someone. Itinerant Buddhist priests sometimes performed *renga* under the blossoms of weeping cherry trees (known as *Saigyō zakura,* "Saigyō's cherry trees") in order to pacify the *kami* who caused the plague and, thus, to ward off the disease.

By the seventeenth century, *haikai no renga,* a more popular and democratic form of linked verse, emerged. This form was practiced by people across the social spectrum of Tokugawa Japan, including samurai, merchants, and traders. This was the genre practiced by Matsuo Bashō (1644–1694), perhaps the most translated Japanese poet in the West. Bashō is popularly known as a haiku poet, although this characterization is anachronistic. The opening seventeen-syllable verse of a sequence (*hokku*) only emerged as an independent verse form in the late nineteenth century. Bashō is an important transitional figure, however, with one foot in the medieval world and the other in the emerging modern world. He dressed in the garb of a lay Buddhist priest, styled himself in part on Saigyō, lived at times in a grass hut, and regularly went on religious pilgrimages. These pilgrimages doubled as business trips, though, for Bashō made his living by charging students for training in poetry. His travels both enabled him to visit notable religious and poetic sites and to meet with and compose linked verse with his students, or to gather additional ones. Like Saigyō before him, Bashō has become a significant figure in the popular, as well as the scholarly, imagination. The scholarly study of this popular imagery, even when inaccurate in terms of the historical Bashō, can provide important insight into the religious needs and nostalgias of later generations in Japan and the West.

Just as the central cultural role of religion has diminished in the modern world, explicitly religious poetry as a genre has also declined in importance. It has not disappeared, however. The founders and leaders of new religions sometimes use poems as a vehicle for spreading their teachings or proffer poems as revelatory statements, while some Buddhist temples and Shintō shrines continue to maintain their poetic traditions. In a recent "invented tradition," the emperor annually offers a New Year's verse—a *tanka* (once called *waka*)—that is reprinted in all the national newspapers. Moreover, hundreds of thousands of Japanese participate in haiku and other poetry clubs, millions of tourists visit historical sites associated with poets of the past, and offertory verses are still sometimes hung above the entranceway of new homes. If religious poetry plays a smaller role in the religious ritual lives of the Japanese today, concomitantly it plays a larger role in the collective remembered past as a national cultural heritage.

BIBLIOGRAPHY

Aoki, Takako. *Man'yō banka-ron.* Tokyo, 1984.

Aston, William G., trans. *Nihongi: Chronicles of Japan from the Earliest Times to 697* (1896). Rutland, Vt., and Tokyo, 1972.

Ebersole, Gary L. "The Buddhist Ritual Use of Linked Poetry in Medieval Japan." *The Eastern Buddhist* 16, no. 2 (1983): 50–71.

Ebersole, Gary L. *Ritual Poetry and the Politics of Death in Early Japan.* Princeton, 1989.

Ebersole, Gary L. "The *Dōka* of the Founder in Historical Perspective." In *Studies on Kurozumikyō,* edited by Willis M. Stoesz, pp. 156–171. Chambersburg, Pa., 1991.

Hoff, Frank, trans. *The Genial Seed: A Japanese Song Cycle.* Tokyo and New York, 1971.

Kamens, Edward. *The Buddhist Poetry of the Great Kamo Priestess: Daisaiin Senshi and Hosshin Wakashū.* Ann Arbor, Mich., 1990.

Kim, Yung-Hee. *Songs to Make the Dust Dance: The Ryōjin hishō of Twelfth-Century Japan.* Berkeley, 1994.

LaFleur, William R. "Saigyō and the Buddhist Value of Nature." *History of Religions* 13, no. 2 (1973): 93–128, and 13, no. 3 (1974): 266–274.

LaFleur, William R. "The Death and the 'Lives' of Saigyō: The Genesis of a Buddhist Sacred Biography." In *The Biographical Process: Studies in the History and Psychology of Religion,* edited by Frank E. Reynolds and Donald Capps, pp. 343–361. The Hague and Paris, 1976.

LaFleur, William R. *The Karma of Words: Buddhism and the Literary Arts in Medieval Japan.* Berkeley, 1983.

Levy, Ian Hideo, trans. *The Ten Thousand Leaves: A Translation of the Man'yōshū,* vol. 1. Princeton, 1981.

Matisoff, Susan. *The Legend of Semimaru: Blind Musician of Japan.* New York, 1978.

Morrell, Robert E. *Sand and Pebbles (Shasekishū): The Tales of Mujū Ichien, A Voice for Pluralism in Kamakura Buddhism.* Albany, N.Y., 1985.

Philippi, Donald L., trans. and ed. *Kojiki.* Tokyo, 1968.

Philippi, Donald L., trans. *Norito: A Translation of the Ancient Japanese Ritual Prayers.* Princeton, 1990.

Plutschow, Herbert E. *Chaos and Cosmos: Ritual in Early and Medieval Japanese Literature.* Leiden, 1990.

Rotermund, Hartmut O. *Majinai-uta: Grundlagen, Ihalte und Formelemente japonischer Majischer Gedichte des 17.–20. Jahrhunderts.* Tokyo and Hamburg, Germany, 1973.

Tsuchihashi, Yutaka. *Kodai kayō to girei no kenkyū.* Tokyo, 1965.

Watson, Burton. *Ryōkan: Zen Monk-Poet of Japan.* New York, 1977.

Watson, Burton, trans. *Grass Hill: Poems and Prose by the Japanese Monk Gensei.* New York, 1983.

Watson, Burton, trans. *Saigyō: Poems of a Mountain Home.* New York, 1991.

GARY L. EBERSOLE (2005)

POETRY: CHRISTIAN POETRY

Any consideration of the interplay between the predominant religion of European culture and the poetry that developed within its influence should properly begin with the textual legacy of sacred scripture. For in the Bible there is a fund of images, narrative reference, rhetorical formulas, and mythic patterns that for centuries has served as a powerful source for Western poetry, no matter whether a specific work is explicitly religious (or devotional) in nature or whether it is simply presumptive of a Christian interpretative context.

ORIGINS: THE HYMN. The earliest example of Christian poetry, the hymn, is also the most immediately expressive of doctrine and tradition. Its biblical precursors can be traced to the Hebrew psalms and the Lucan canticles (e.g., Magnificat and Nunc dimittis), in addition to fragments of apostolic hymns found both in the Pauline letters (e.g., *Eph.* 5:19, *2 Tm.* 2:15) and in the *Book of Revelation* (5:13–14). Like the Christian liturgy itself, Christian poetry was first composed in Greek. By the mid-fourteenth century, however, there existed compilations of Latin hymns by Hilary of Poitiers (d. 367) and Ambrose of Milan (d. 397), both of whom composed their texts for liturgical use. Prudentius (d. 410), best known for the allegorical poem that was to have such influence on medieval portrayals of the struggle between virtue and vice—the *Psychomachia*—also wrote many didactic hymns in a variety of meters not intended specifically for worship. The Latin hymnic tradition continued with works that were to have great influence on subsequent Christian literature: the *Vexilla regis* of Venantius Fortunatus (d. 610), the hymns of Peter Abelard (d. 1142) and Thomas Aquinas (d. 1274), and most important of all, the *Dies irae,* ascribed to Thomas of Celano (d. 1260). To the Franciscan Jacopone da Todi (d. 1306) is attributed not only the *Stabat mater dolorosa,* but also over one hundred hymns, or *laudes*, written in Italian. This tradition of vernacular poetry was nurtured in Franciscan circles and traditionally begins with Francis of Assisi (d. 1226) and his still renowned *Canticle of the Sun.*

MIDDLE AGES. In England Christian poetry in the vernacular was inaugurated by Cædmon (d. around 680), whose Anglo-Saxon hymn to God the Creator is also the first extant poem in the English language. Also attributed to him (if not to Cynewulf, a poet of the ninth century) is *The Dream of the Rood,* a visionary work in which the cross confronts the poet with an account of Christ's passion and resurrection, bidding him to follow the path of the rood thereafter in his own life. The culmination of Anglo-Saxon poetry, however, is the epic *Beowulf* (dated between 675 and 750), wherein pagan Germanic heroic traditions show signs of adaptation to the newer Christian sensibility.

The flowering of Christian medieval poetry in England occurs in the latter part of the fourteenth century. Both the *Pearl* and *Piers Plowman,* two anonymous Middle English poems, combine dream vision and allegory, a sense of spiritual crisis and the hope of victory in heaven. The most important work of this period, however, is Chaucer's *Canterbury Tales* (begun in 1386 and incomplete at the poet's death in 1400). Set within the popular medieval framework of a pilgrimage, this collection of Middle English poems represents a wide panorama of character types and narrative forms that draw heavily on French and Italian models. The work as a whole is an intriguing blend of sacred and profane, containing traditional saints' legends, as recounted by the Prioress and the Second Nun, as well as romances, as told by the Knight and the Squire, and bawdry, as employed by the Miller and the Wife of Bath. Contemporary criticism has argued over the extent to which the *Tales* should be given a Christian reading; D. W. Robertson, Jr.'s *Preface to Chaucer* (Princeton, 1962) offers the most eloquent case for doing so. Suffice it to say that whatever the case in this or that particular poem, Chaucer's work, as a whole, is unthinkable outside a Christian context.

The same might be said for the dominant form of early French vernacular poetry, the *chansons de geste,* which date from the eleventh and twelfth centuries and signal the beginning of French literature. Following the conclusions of Joseph Bédier's *Les légendes epiques* (1926–1929), most scholars consider that these narrative works, set in the ninth-century Age of Charlemagne, actually originated in churches and monasteries whose monks linked their own shrines to events, at once historical and legendary, that were associated with Charlemagne. The *Chanson de Roland,* set against the background of war with the Saracens for control of Spain and telling in particular of the battle of Roncevaux, presents characters who have become classics in Western literature: the impetuous warrior Roland (the "Orlando" of later romance-epic); the patriarchal monarch Charlemagne; the sage counselor Olivier; the priest-warrior Turpin; the traitor Ganelon. The twelfth-century Oxford manuscript of the poem, which is its earliest extant version (c. 1170), reflects a Christianization of materials coming from earlier, less religious sources. It extols Christianity, chivalry, and patriotism; for even though it portrays the folly of Roland's pursuit of personal fame and glory at the expense of Christian empire and the common cause, nonetheless, when Archbishop Turpin gives the fallen Roland his blessing and commends his soul to the safekeeping of Saint Gabriel, the errant hero is sufficiently absolved to become a kind of epic saint in subsequent handling of the legend, known as the *matière de France.*

The inaugural work of Spanish literature, the *Cantar de mio Cid* (c. 1140), shares with the *Chanson de Roland* not only certain literary models but the memory of feudal Germanic custom as well as a substratum of historical event. The poem, based on the life of an eleventh-century military leader, relates the misfortunes and ultimate triumph of Rodrigo Díaz de Vivar, who, although unjustly exiled by the sovereign of Castile, remains a faithful vassal, one who continuously sends back booty from battle with the Moors; when grossly misused by perfidious noblemen, he leaves the retribution of justice to King Alfonso, the monarch who has banished him. In the course of the poem (and subsequently in

Spanish mystique) Díaz, or "el Cid," becomes a paragon of justice and bravery. A pious deathbed scene, attributed by scholars to a later (and monastic) hand, attempts to bring the poem more resolutely within a Christian framework. And yet, like the *Chanson de Roland,* Spain's epic is more a celebration of battle against "the Infidel," as well as of loyalty to the anointed lord, than it is a seriously Christian poem.

A later development in narrative poetry, which turned its attention from battlefield to court, is the romance. Critics disagree over whether it arose as a sentimentalization of earlier epic materials such as the *chansons de geste* or whether, on the other hand, it represents a hearkening back to late classical models. In any event, it concerns itself with the characters and events of King Arthur's court (known as the *matière de Bretagne*) and has at its center an ideal of chivalry and a preoccupation with love, which it portrays as ennobling when sublimated in the chaste pursuit of excellence, but disastrous (both personally and socially) when acted out in adultery. Although Chrétien de Troyes (d. around 1180) was certainly not the originator of romance poetry, it is he who brought the genre to flower in French with his poems *Erec, Yvain, Lancelot,* and the unfinished *Perceval*—the story of a simple knight whose feudal service, transcending that owed to king or lady, is given to the pursuit of the Grail, a complex symbol of religious mystery associated with Christ's passion and resurrection.

A fuller and far more profound working of this material is offered by Wolfram von Eschenbach (d. around 1220), whose *Parzival,* written between 1200 and 1210, introduced the Grail theme into German literature and brought both epic and romance to a new level of spiritual profundity that places Wolfram in the same lofty sphere as Dante. Building on Chrétien's tale of the "guileless fool" who through innocence and faithful commitment attains a goal that evades those who are wise in the ways of the world, *Parzival* describes a quasi-allegorical pilgrimage through error, pride, despair, and repentance, undertaken in order to attain the most distinctive of Christian virtues, humility. In its possession, Parzival is able not only to be keeper of the Grail—a paradisiacal stone representing the love of God—but also to assume the role of king among a circle of knights whose ideals are set infinitely higher than the loves and adventures that characterize the traditional Arthurian court. The poem is notable for its inauguration of the *Bildungsroman,* which, along with the Grail story itself, has had such a powerful impact on subsequent German literature. *Parzival* also shares some of the essential qualities (though none of the superficial) that distinguish the greatest medieval poem of pilgrimage and vision, Dante's *Commedia.*

Written between the time of Dante's exile from Florence in 1302 and his death in 1321, the *Commedia* is an unparalleled synthesis of theological reflection and literary form, in which hymn and allegory, epic and romance, spiritual pilgrimage and personal *Bildungsroman* are all brought together in a narrative of enduring appeal, as well as of profound religious depth. Set against a typology of Exodus and Deliverance, which is enhanced by the story's unfolding between the evening of Good Friday and the Wednesday of Easter Week in the year 1300, the poem recounts Dante's exploration of the state of the soul after death in a journey that takes him from hell through purgatory to paradise, and culminates in the beatific vision (left undescribed, of course, at the close of the final canto). In the course of this experience, which unites the journeys of Aeneas and the apostle Paul even as it surpasses them with its own totality, he is guided first by Vergil, the paragon of poetry, natural reason, and the dream of empire, and then by Beatrice, the woman who in life represented for Dante the transforming love of God in Christ and on whose behalf the poet promised earlier in the *Vita nuova* (1295) to offer such praise as no other beloved had ever received. Critics have noted Dante's debt to classical poets (whom, indeed, he draws on extensively—especially Vergil, Ovid, Lucan, and Statius—at the same time that he transforms them for his own Christian purposes), as well as his connection to medieval accounts of earthly pilgrimage and heavenly vision. Theologically, he unites Thomistic clarity with the ardor of Augustinian and Franciscan traditions. And yet what remains astonishing is the sheer originality of the work, which mixes what the fourteenth century knew about the ancient world with a very contemporary appraisal of the poet's own time—all of it filtered through the personal experience of Dante Alighieri himself (who, like Augustine in the *Confessions,* is both the wise author and the developing subject of the same work). The sixteenth century was to call the *Commedia* "divine," an adjective that later centuries have continued to find appropriate. Indeed, in the intricately constructed plan of the hundred cantos of this epic, Christian poetry attains a scope of reference and a depth of resonance that are rivaled (if at all) only by John Milton's *Paradise Lost.*

THE RENAISSANCE. With the exception of the fourteenth-century English works noted above, the great religious movements and controversies of Europe did not after Dante produce poetry of major significance until the mid-sixteenth century. In the latter years of that century there is unmistakably evident a Christian poetic renaissance in the form of both long narrative works and meditational, or devotional, lyrics. Within the former category is found the Portuguese *Os Lusíadas* (1572), a Vergilian celebration of the voyage of Vasco da Gama to India and of his return via the Cape of Good Hope. This national epic, composed by Luis de Camões (d. 1580), tells its near-contemporary tale in mythic terms, mingling together history, Catholic religion, and the pagan Roman pantheon of the *Aeneid.* In this poem West meets East and attempts to conquer a paradise otherwise lost to Europe. Within its epic machinery, moreover, there is the working of Camões's own curious syncretism: his blending of Christianity with Neoplatonism and of pagan religion with Portuguese national (and religious) piety.

Writing at almost the same time, but closer to the censorious arm of the Counter-Reformation, Torquato Tasso

(d. 1595) published his *Gerusalemme liberata* in 1581. Although he was heir to the secular romances of Boiardo and Ariosto, with their reworking of the old Arthurian material, Tasso set out instead to produce a truly Christian epic, and for this purpose he chose the subject of Godfrey of Bouillon's retaking of Jerusalem from the Saracens during the First Crusade. Although replete with the requisite battle scenes and amatory interludes of the romance-epic, he intended the poem to be read allegorically as the struggle of the soul to overcome every sort of temptation (and perhaps especially those of the flesh) in order to achieve salvation. Whatever his noble intentions, the text caused him difficulties with the Inquisition; consequently he republished it in revised form under the title *Gerusalemme conquistata* (1593), thereby achieving the requisite piety, but only at the cost of poetic interest and integrity.

The epic poem (like the Renaissance itself) came relatively late to Protestant England, but found its belated poet in Edmund Spenser (d. 1599), whose *Faerie Queene* (published in parts between 1590 and 1609), although unfinished according to its original plan, nonetheless succeeded in realizing its partial goals: the incorporation of Vergilian epic into medieval (as well as Italian) romance, a multileveled allegory, an expression of the Reformed religious sensibility, and a celebration of Elizabethan England and its Virgin Queen (the model for that Gloriana who, while never seen in the poem's Faeryland, motivates all virtuous action). Book 1, the "Legend of Holiness," is the most explicitly theological of the six books that Spenser lived to complete. Its Red Cross Knight struggles against the various avatars of wickedness in order to champion Una, the true (English) church, and in so doing to realize his identity as England's patron, Saint George. The rest of the poem is preoccupied with the vicissitudes of the moral life and the cultivation of the virtues of temperance, chastity, friendship, justice, and courtesy, each of which is championed by a representative knight and exercised in a successful combat with evil. Pervading the entire work, however, is the sense of incomplete victory and of an unfulfilled longing, the desire for a vision of peace that can never be attained in this life, whether in the Faeryland of the poem or in the sixteenth-century world to which its "dark conceit" refers. In the end, in the fragmentary "Mutabilitie Cantos," the poet places his sole faith in a heavenly city built "upon the pillours of Eternitie."

SEVENTEENTH CENTURY. In the first half of the seventeenth century there is evident an enormous and rich outpouring of religious verse, lyric rather than epic, which is commonly characterized, after Samuel Johnson, as "metaphysical" or, since Louis Martz (1954), as "the poetry of meditation." It is distinguished by its delight in wit, learning, and paradox, and most especially by its cultivation of farfetched metaphors or "conceits." Examples can be drawn from the poetry of Italy, Spain, France, and Germany, but it is in England that the metaphysical poem found its fullest Christian expression; its foremost exponents were John Donne (d. 1631), George Herbert (d. 1633), Richard Crashaw (d. 1649), Thomas Traherne (d. 1674), and Henry Vaughan (d. 1695). With the exception of the Welsh doctor Vaughan, all were ordained priests in the Anglican church (but Crashaw later became a Roman cleric). To a greater or lesser extent, all drew upon the techniques of religious meditation that mingle a vivid reimagining of biblical scenes, intense self-scrutiny, and an orientation of the self toward God. In this group Crashaw is in every way the anomaly, drawing as he does on the more extravagantly Baroque continental sensibility typified by the convolution and artificiality of, for example, Giambattista Marino (d. 1625). But even among the more thoroughly English Anglicans, there is a wide range of feeling: the splendid self-absorption of Donne as he worries about his own salvation; the artful self-diminution of Herbert, with his exquisitely wrought lyrics of surrender to a loving Master; the mystically esoteric Traherne; the meditations of Henry Vaughan upon nature, a preoccupation that links him in anticipatory ways to William Wordsworth and the High Romantics.

John Milton (d. 1674) tried his hand at this sort of meditational poetry in the early ode entitled *On the Morning of Christ's Nativity.* But the religious lyric was never to engage his poetic imagination. To be sure, religious controversy and theological reflection preoccupied him his entire life and filled many volumes of prose as well. But it was not until his political hopes in Cromwell's Commonwealth had been frustrated and the monarchy subsequently restored in 1660 that the "sacred muse" returned—and then with an astonishing afflatus of poetry that took its "graver subject" from moments of scriptural history: the fall of Adam and Eve, the death of Samson, Christ's temptation in the wilderness. Following the example of the Huguenot Guillaume du Bartas (d. 1590) in the composition of a biblical epic, Milton made in *Paradise Lost* (1667) a deliberate decision to turn away from classical or romance themes, at the same time, of course, as he incurred openly a vast debt to Vergil on the one hand and Spenser on the other. (His later works, *Paradise Regained* and *Samson Agonistes,* both published in 1671, draw upon Greek dramatic form.) At the center of all three poems there stands an individual "sufficient to have stood, though free to fall," and in each case Milton undertakes an exploration of exactly what this sufficiency consists of: the exercise of right reason over against the appeal of lesser appetites. As in his prose writings against monarchy and episcopacy and as in those advocating freedom of speech and of divorce, the author of the poems assumes the role of prophet. This voice is especially audible in *Paradise Lost,* where again and again he claims the inspiration of the Holy Spirit in his articulation of what scripture has chosen to say little (or nothing) about. Dante too claimed enormous authority for his poetic undertaking, but while he dared to speak prophetically to his age, he did so as a Roman Catholic, as a loyal (if contentious) son of the "universal" church; Milton, by contrast, was in the composition of his great poems a denomination of one, a solitary church.

Milton's poetic enterprise is strangely Janus-faced. Late in the seventeenth century, almost as if he were resolutely looking backward, he chose unfashionable biblical subject matter and an epic genre so played out that by the end of the century it could only be mocked in satire. On the other hand, his portraits of divinity (and perhaps especially of God the Father in *Paradise Lost*) have an Enlightenment chill, as if they had passed over into a pantheon of deities no longer believed in. But perhaps the authentically religious note in Milton's poetry is rather to be found in his magnificent evocation of the physical beauties of heaven and earth as well as in the poignancy of his presentation of humanity itself—poised between innocence and experience and between obedience and rebellion, engaged in the process of choosing a self to become. It is in such emphases as these that one can anticipate the Romantic movement that was to follow upon Milton's death by a century, arriving at a time when poetry throughout Europe seems to have cut loose from the moorings of Christian tradition in order to explore new unorthodoxies of the spirit and imagination.

See Also Arthur; Dante Alighieri; Drama, articles on European Religious Drama, Modern Western Theater; Grail, The; Literature, article on Religious Dimensions of Modern Western Literature.

Bibliography

Christianity is so interwoven into the fabric of European poetry up through the seventeenth century that any worthwhile study of Dante, Chaucer, or Milton will of necessity explore the interconnection between poetry and belief. In *The Great Code: The Bible and Literature* (New York, 1982) Northrop Frye begins with the Christian ur-text and suggests the degree to which scripture informs literary culture in the West. Ernst Robert Curtius in his *European Literature in the Latin Middle Ages* (Princeton, N. J., 1953) and Erich Auerbach in his *Mimesis: The Representation of Reality in Western Literature* (Princeton, 1953) have produced classic studies of the foundations and development of European poetry, which also offer invaluable insight into the interaction of Christianity with its pagan inheritance. Helen Flanders Dunbar's *Symbolism in Medieval Thought and Its Consummation in the Divine Comedy* (New Haven, Conn., 1929) establishes a religious and cultural context not only for Dante but for medieval poetry in general. Sensitive study of the role of Christianity in the formation of European poetry is also offered in R. S. Loomis's *The Grail: From Celtic Myth to Christian Symbol* (New York, 1963), C. S. Lewis's *The Allegory of Love* (Oxford, 1936), Louis L. Martz's *The Poetry of Meditation* (New Haven, 1954), Helen Gardner's *Religion and Literature* (Oxford, 1971), and A. D. Nuttall's *Overheard by God: Fiction and Prayer in Herbert, Milton, Dante, and St. John* (New York, 1980).

New Sources

Atwan, Robert and Laurence Wieder, eds. *Chapters into Verse: Poetry in English Inspired by the Bible.* Oxford and New York, 1992.

Bradley, Ian C. *The Book of Hymns.* New York, 1989.

Curzon, David, ed. *The Gospels in Our Image.* New York, 1995.

Keyte, Hugh, and Andrew Parrott, with Clifford Bartlett. *The New Oxford Book of Carols.* Oxford, 1998.

Newman, Barbara. *God and the Goddesses: Visions, poetry, and Belief in the Middle Ages.* Philadelphia, 2003.

Troeger, Thomas H. *Borrowed Light: Hymn Texts, Prayers, and Poems.* New York, 1994.

Peter S. Hawkins (1987)
Revised Bibliography

POETRY: ISLAMIC POETRY

Since its emergence in the Middle East early in the seventh century, Islam has been practiced in many different cultural and linguistic areas throughout the world. As a result, Islamic religious poetry has been composed in a wide variety of languages. Among these, Arabic and Persian are distinctive for their transnational, or cosmopolitan, nature. Alongside these two classical languages, Islamic poets have employed a host of other languages, ranging from Bengali and Chinese to Swahili and Urdu. This article will summarize the development of Islamic poetry in Arabic and Persian, the important languages for classical Islamic literature, and will also commenti briefly on the nature and character of Islamic poetry in the regional vernacular traditions.

Arabic. Since the Qurʾān was revealed in a culture that prized the poetic arts and the beauty of oral expression, these values affected the role of poetry in many Muslim societies, both Arab and non-Arab. In pre-Islamic Arabian society, poets *(shaʾirs)* enjoyed a special status, along with soothsayers *(kahins)*; they were believed to be inspired in their utterances by their relationship with spirits and jinns. As a result, their words had a particularly powerful spiritual potency. Not surprisingly, when Muḥammad began to recite the particularly beautiful verses that eventually came to comprise the Qurʾān (which means literally "the Recitation"), his opponents accused him of being a poet. In response to such accusations, the Qurʾān (for example, in Chapter 26) clearly distinguishes between a poet, who is driven by egotistical desire, and a prophet, who utters the truth that is revealed to him or her by the one God. Although the Islamic scripture criticizes poets who compete with the Divine Word, the Qurʾān displays an acute sensibility to the spoken word, both for its aesthetic qualities and for the ethical values espoused in pre-Islamic Arabic poetry (such as generosity, valor, and hospitality), albeit in a new religious framework. Indeed, for the believer, the inimitability of Qurʾanic eloquence serves as proof of the scripture's divine origin.

Many poets ranked among Muḥammad's most dangerous opponents, including Kaʿb (d. c. 630). His father Zuhayr had composed one of the "Hanging Odes," the seven most celebrated poems of pre-Islamic Arabia. According to tradition, these odes, because of their polished eloquence, were embroidered in gold and hung from the walls of the Kaʿbah. When Kaʿb eventually decided to convert to Islam, he offered his allegiance to Muḥammad by presenting him a poem of praise. In response, the Prophet gave Kaʾb his cloak (*burda*); consequently, the poem came to be known as the

Burda, or Mantle Ode. This poem ushered in a new genre of panegyric poetry in praise of the Prophet that was to become ubiquitous in all Islamic literatures.

The transaction between the poet and prophet simultaneously rejects some pre-Islamic values and transforms other values in the new religious worldview that was heralded by the coming of Islam. As Michael Sells points out in *Approaching the Qur'ān,* instead of being draped with the Hanging Odes, the Kaʿbah, the most sacred site of Islam, was adorned with a black cloth embroidered with verses from the Qur'ān. Most importantly, poetry, which had once been shunned for representing the ideals of paganism, was brought into the service of Islam. Indeed, later Muslim poets proclaimed that their work was the "heritage of prophecy," referring to a tradition that calls the tongues of poets "the keys of the treasures beneath the Divine Throne."

The tradition that had begun with pre-Islamic poetry continued to develop throughout the history of Arabic and other Islamic literatures. Muslim poets adapted the pre-Islamic genre of the *qasida,* the monorhyme praise poem, for religious purposes. Instead of praising a ruler or a poet's patron, the *qasida* was now used to praise God, to eulogize the Prophet, or to laud and lament the martyr-heroes of Shīʿah Islam. In the ninth century, as the focus of Sufism or Islamic mysticism shifted from extreme asceticism to an emphasis on an intimate and loving relationship between devotees and God, mystics began composing exquisite mystical love poetry in Arabic. Drawing upon the *qasida*'s amatory prelude (the *nasib*), with its themes of remembering and longing for a lost beloved, this poetry depicted the many aspects and phases of love—the anguish of separation, blissful union, endless striving to be worthy and faithful, and longing for physical death and spiritual union with the Divine. Prominent poets included the Iraqi woman mystic Rab'ia al-ʿAdawiya (d. 801), the Egyptian Dhu al-Nun (d. 859), and the Baghdad natives Sumnun "the Lover," (d. c. 900), Shibli (d. 945), and the great "martyr of love" al-Hallaj, executed in 922.

After a period of decline in quality and quantity from the mid-tenth century onwards, Arabic mystical poetry experienced an efflorescence in the thirteenth century with the emergence of two great writers, the Egyptian Ibn al-Farid (d. 1235) and the Andalusian Ibn al-ʿArabi (d. 1240). Ibn al-Farid drew upon the heritage of the traditional *qasida* to compose exquisite odes on mystical love, including the *Khamriyya* (A Wine Poem) in praise of the primordial wine of divine love that intoxicates everything created, and the *Ta'iyya* (a *qasida* rhyming with the letter "t"), which recounts in high-flown imagery the soul's journey to God. Though more renowned in the history of Islamic mystical literature for his dense prose works, Ibn al-ʿArabi, inspired by his love for the daughter of a Persian Sufi, composed a collection of mystical poems entitled *Tarjuman al-Ashwaq* (The Interpreter of Ardent Longings), whose imagery recalls the pre-Islamic *qasida.* In order to prevent the work's amatory and erotic imagery from being read literally by opponents determined to accuse him of moral corruption, Ibn ʿArabi wrote a commentary highlighting the esoteric meaning of the work.

PERSIAN. By the time of its renaissance in the thirteenth century, however, Arabic mystical poetry had begun to be overshadowed by works composed in Persian, which was rapidly becoming the major language of religious poetry in many Muslim lands. The spread of Persian as a literary vehicle was facilitated by the rise of dynasties of Persianized Turks who, by the fifteenth century, controlled a vast territory, stretching from Anatolia in modern Turkey, through Iran and Central Asia to southern India.

Although Persian poets adopted the form of the Arabic *qasida* for the religious panegyric in Persian, their forte lay in the refinement of two other genres: the *masnawi* and the *ghazal.* A distinctively Persian form, the *masnawi,* a lengthy poem with rhymed couplets, was initially used to compose epics recounting the heroic deeds of Iranian rulers and champions. In a religious context, Persian Sufis favored the *masnawi* as a vehicle for explicating ethical and mystical concepts through anecdotes, tales, and romances. Among the early poets who employed this form was ʿAttar (d. c. 1221), the author of the *Mantiq at-Tayr* (The Bird's Conversation). Ostensibly a narrative concerning a group of birds on a quest for their mythical king, the *Mantiq at-Tayr* has come to be regarded as one of the classic Islamic expositions of the mystical journey and spiritual development of the soul. The most famous *masnawi* ever composed, however, was the *Mathnawi-yi ma'nawi* (Spiritual Couplets), by the most beloved of Persian mystic poets, Jalāl al-Dīn Rūmī (d. 1273). This monumental work, consisting of some thirty-five thousand couplets, has been called the "Qur'ān in the Persian tongue," since later generations have considered it to be an encapsulation of the spiritual and esoteric teachings of the Arabic scripture for Persian speakers.

In addition to the *Mathnawi,* Rūmī also composed a collection of ecstatic poems called the *Divan-i Shams-i Tabriz.* As its name indicates, this work was dedicated to the memory of his spiritual mentor and soul mate, the enigmatic Shams-i Tabriz. Tradition holds that Shams's mysterious disappearance caused Rūmīto become a poet, pouring out in the poems of the *Divan* his heartbreak at the loss of his beloved friend. For the *Divan,* Rūmī chose the most important form of lyric poetry in Persian—the *ghazal*—a short poem with loosely arranged couplets united by a single rhyme and common meter.

By convention, the *ghazal*'s central theme is unfulfilled love. The rules governing the *ghazal*'s prosody exercise such tight constraints on poets that they must resort to a vast stock of conventional images and motifs—wine and tavern, nightingales and roses, attractive young boys and veiled ladies, disheveled tresses and ruby lips—to draw analogies. Skillful *ghazal* poets effortlessly interweave these images together while engaging in intricate verbal acrobatics, making it difficult to grasp the real meaning of their poetry, as it subtly oscillates between the spiritual and the sensual. Is the lover drunk with wine, wild with passion for a handsome boy, or intoxicated with God? Although the meaning intended by the poet can be vague, audiences nevertheless delight in this ambiguity, thus accounting for the popularity of the *ghazal* in Persian and Persian-influenced cultures.

The supreme master of the *ghazal* in Persian was Hafiz (d. 1390). Generations of Persian speakers have regarded his collection of *ghazals*, known as the *Divan-i Hafiz*, as a source of wisdom to consult when making important life decisions. Like Rūmī's *Mathnawi*, the *Divan-i Hafiz* is believed to contain the wise voice of the mystic who has been fortunate enough to commune with the transcendent reality. And like Rūmī's poetry, the verse of Hafiz and other Persian mystics—such as Sanaʾi (d. 1131), ʿAttar, and Jami (d. 1492)—has inspired and informed seekers on the spiritual quest. As a result, Sufis have commonly regarded the incorporation of verses of poetry in rituals such as the *sama*ʾ (spiritual concert of music and poetry) as a means of triggering a mystical experience.

POETRY IN THE REGIONAL VERNACULARS. Arabic and Persian were the dominant languages for Islamic poetry until the fourteenth century; at that time, poets in other regions began adopting local languages for composing religious poetry. Many of these poets pioneered the development of literary traditions in these regional languages. In her book *As through a Veil*, Annemarie Schimmel compares the role of these Muslim poets, many of them Sufi, to that played by Christian mystics, nuns, and ascetics in the development of European vernaculars such as German, Dutch, and Italian.

To be sure, Muslim poets hesitated at first to experiment with composing religious verse in the vernacular. In some areas of South Asia, for example, anxiety about using a local language ran so deep that poets thought it necessary to apologize to readers. Many of these pioneer poets would have agreed with the Afghan poet Bayazid Ansari (d. 1585) when he commented: "God speaks in every language, be it Arabic, Persian, Hindi, or Afghani. He speaks in the language which the human heart can understand." Love for their mother-tongues, as well as the growing popularity of vernacular poetry among populations who could not access literature in the Arabic and Persian traditions, eventually resulted in a blossoming of regional vernacular poetic traditions from the eighteenth century onwards. Significantly, in the case of those languages which lacked a standard alphabet, poets used the Arabic script or adaptations of it to write their compositions.

Arabic and Persian poetry continued to exercise varying degrees of influence on the development of regional poetic traditions, however. Thus, Ottoman Turkish and Urdu poems are so heavily steeped in the Persianate tradition—from the appropriation of genres, such as the *ghazal* and *masnawi*, to the wholesale adoption of conventional Persian symbols and imagery—that it is impossible to truly appreciate poetry in these two languages without an awareness of the Persian background. The form of the Arabic *qasida* was adopted into a wide range of languages, often with adjustments in meter and imagery to suit local tastes. Indeed, in some instances, the *qasida* inspired the development of entirely new literary genres. For example, the *madah* is the religious praise poem in Sindhi, the *syair* is used in Malay for composing poems providing instruction on mystical themes, and the *qasidah moderen* in Indonesia is a genre of didactic religious poems set to popular music.

Islamic vernacular traditions also reflect an astounding array of poetic forms derived by various literary cultures around the world. Although these are too numerous to be discussed in detail, Muslim poets co-opted many forms of secular poetry, often in the form of songs, in order to compose different types of religious poetry. For instance, in the region around Bijapur in southern India, Sufi ideas were transmitted by songs sung in Dakhini Urdu by women as they performed daily tasks, such as spinning cotton or grinding grain, while in Tamilnadu, poets adopted the *kappiyam*, a long narrative poem that traditionally had related the stories of gods and the exploits of human heroes. In Senegal, odes retelling the history of prophets or praising Sufi masters employed forms traditional to Wolof praise-poetry. Hindi-speaking poets in North India used romantic ballads to create lengthy mystical allegories in verse; the most important example is the *Padmavat* of Malik Muḥammad Jaʾisi (d. after 1570). Along with vernacular forms, poets also adopted local literary conventions and adapted Islamic religious concepts and ideas to local cultural contexts. These adaptations helped Islam spread rapidly throughout many regions of the world.

Since vernacular poetry mediates between the community of believers and their religious tradition, much of this poetry tends to be didactic in character, addressing topics such as beliefs, fundamental rituals, ethics and morality, and the transitory nature of the world. Poems praising God, the prophets, and important religious personalities in Islamic history are also ubiquitous. Poetry composed under the influence of the Sufi tradition, particularly in Turkey and South Asia, tends to attack barren intellectualism and rote ritualism as paths that cannot lead to salvation. Instead, these poems laud the path of love, in which the believer develops a loving relationship with the Divine Beloved, as an interiorized form of religious practice that leads to the spiritual development of the soul. As expected, many Sufi poems also extol the virtues of the Sufi *shaykh* whose guidance helps the believer to traverse the spiritual path.

POETRY IN HONOR OF THE PROPHET. One subject common to all Islamic poetry, whether in the classical Arabic and Persian traditions or in the regional vernaculars, is praise and love for the Prophet Muḥammad. As devotion to the Prophet Muḥammad binds together Muslims from diverse cultural and national backgrounds, this subject provides an appropriate summation for this survey of Islamic religious poetry.

The tradition of composing poetry honoring the Prophet began in his lifetime, when his companions, Ka'b ibn Zuhayr and Hassan ibn Thabit, glorified him in verse. In subsequent centuries, innumerable poets have composed *na'ts*, or poems in praise of Muḥammad, in practically every language of the Islamic world. Since poets have employed a variety of styles, genres, and literary conventions, the figure of the Prophet is indigenized to different literary contexts. A Sindhi poet, for example, following the conventions of Sindhi mystical literature, may address him as a bridegroom and portray him in Sindhi garb, while a Tamil poet, influenced by the *pillaitamil* (baby poem), imagines him as a baby within a Tamil landscape. Notwithstanding these cultural differences, however, the poetry shares certain themes: extolling the Prophet's character, virtues, and beauty; recalling the events in his life, such as his birth and his ascension to heaven (the *Miʿrāj*), or describing the various miracles he performed; expressing hope for his intercession on the Day of Judgment and beseeching his assistance in difficult circumstances; and exalting the esoteric aspect of association with the light of prophethood. The leitmotif of this poetry, however, is love. Poets fervently express in different languages their powerful, all-consuming love for the Prophet, the Beloved of God as he is frequently called, using a range of symbols and ideas. The twentieth-century Urdu poet Muḥammad Iqbal hints of the theme's power and universality when he declares, "Love for the Prophet runs like blood in the veins of the community."

SEE ALSO Ḥallāj, al-; Ibn al-ʿArabī; Ibn al-Fāriḍ; Iqbal, Muḥammad; Literature, article on Literature and Religion; Rābiʿah al-ʿAdawīyah; Rūmī, Jalāl al-Dīn.

BIBLIOGRAPHY

Asani, Ali, and Kamal Abdelmalek. *Celebrating Muḥammad: Images of the Prophet in Popular Muslim Poetry.* Columbia, S.C., 1995.

Brown, Edward Granville. *A Literary History of Persia.* Cambridge, U.K., 1957.

De Bruijn, J. T. P. *Persian Sufi Poetry. An Introduction to the Mystical Use of Classical Poems.* Richmond, U.K., 1997.

Lewis, Franklin. *Rumi: Past and Present; East and West: The Life, Teaching and Poetryof Jalal ad-Din Rumi.* Oxford, 2000.

Renard, John. *Seven Doors to Islam: Spirituality and the Religious Life of Muslims.* Berkeley, Calif., 1996.

Schimmel, Annemarie. *As Through a Veil: Mystical Poetry in Islam.* New York, 1982.

Sells, Michael. *Early Islamic Mysticism: Sufi, Qur'ān, Miʿrāj, Poetic and Theological Writings.* Mahwah, N.J., 1996.

Sells, Michael. *Approaching the Qur'ān: The Early Revelations.* Ashland, Ore., 1999.

Sperl, Stefan, and Christopher Shackle, eds. *Qasida Poetry in Islamic Asia and Africa.* 2 vols. Leiden, 1996.

ALI S. ASANI (2005)

POETRY: NATIVE AMERICAN POETRY AND RELIGION

More than any other genre of Native American contemporary writing, poetry most closely reflects the Native American oral tradition. Traditional prayers, songs, and chants, first performed orally and later "preserved" by non-Natives who anticipated the demise of Native cultures in the nineteenth century, serve as a bridge between the oral tradition and the work of contemporary Native poets. This early poetics was an inherent part of ceremonial life for the tribes of North America, and it continues to inform contemporary American Indian poetry. Broadly defined, Native American poetry is "religious" in the sense that "[e]very factor of human experience is seen in a religious light as part of the meaning of life," as the Lakota author Vine Deloria Jr. explains in *God Is Red* (p. 195). Spirituality pervades the genre: poets incorporate mythic figures and stories, contemplate their relationships to sacred places, draw upon the rhythmic and performative aspects of the oral tradition, describe tribal ceremonies and healing rituals, and in some cases respond to experiences with Christian missionaries and conversion, as well as social justice issues related to colonization.

POETRY IN TRANSLATION. The first American Indian poetry in print consisted of ceremonial chants and songs collected by ethnographers and linguists in the late nineteenth and early twentieth centuries. These transcriptions were compiled in anthologies, including George W. Cronyn's *The Path on the Rainbow* (1918), Mary Austin's *The American Rhythm: Studies and Reëxpressions of Amerindian Songs* (1932), and Margot Astrov's *The Winged Serpent: An Anthology of American Indian Prose and Poetry* (1946). One must approach these texts with some caution. As the Anishinaabe poet and critic Kimberly M. Blaeser points out, "many early works were sifted from their cultural context, displayed in a textual and secular nakedness that ignored the performed quality or distorted the sacred layers of ceremonial poetry" (p. 413). Beginning in the 1960s, the new field of ethnopoetics revived interest in Native American songs and chants, attempting this time to present it in a more "authentic" form. Collections such as John Bierhorst's *In the Trail of the Wind* (1971), Jerome Rothenberg's *Shaking the Pumpkin* (1972), and Brian Swann's *Wearing the Morning Star* (1996) presented new translations of many of the same "texts" in an attempt to include Native perspectives in world poetics. Most of those connected to ethnopoetics did not know the language of these traditions, with the exception of the linguists. So again, content was often distorted.

THE NINETEENTH CENTURY. The first American Indian poets writing in English included the Ojibwa (or Chippewa) writer George Copway (*The Ojibway Conquest,* 1850), the Cherokee poet and novelist John Rollin Ridge (*Poems,* 1868), the Mohawk poet and performer E. Pauline Johnson (*The White Wampum,* 1895), and the Creek writer and activist Alexander Posey (*The Poems of Alexander Lawrence Posey,* 1910). These poets were educated in the Western tradition, and because the Catholic Church controlled a majority of the boarding schools they attended, much of their poetry is closely aligned with Christianity. The tenets of Manifest Destiny are likewise often apparent in the poetry of this era. Some writers adopted Western modes of thought and verse—often for the purpose of educating a white readership about their Native cultures. E. Pauline Johnson and Alexander Posey incorporate elements of Greek mythology in their work. In "The Flower of Tulledega," for example, Posey parallels two musicians, a Creek figure named Stechupco and the Greek god Pan. Ridge's poetry favors "progress" and thereby reflects the Christian principle of dominion over nature. Johnson's poem "A Cry from an Indian Wife" expresses a deep, ironic devotion to Christian beliefs, even as Indians lands are lost and Native people suffer. "What white-robed priest prays for your safety here[?]," Johnson asks.

Contemporary Poetry and the Oral Tradition. The first major anthology of Native American poetry, *Carriers of the Dream Wheel,* appeared in 1975. The Native American Renaissance, said to have begun in 1969 when N. Scott Momaday won the Pulitzer for *House Made of Dawn* (1968), saw a flourishing of Native poetry. The themes and stylistics of this poetry connect back to early poetic modes, to the oral tradition. In particular, poets of this era employ anaphora (repetition) and pay special attention to cadence, as well as to sound and language. For example, the Muskogee (or Creek) poet Joy Harjo uses repetition in a wide variety of poems. In "Woman Hanging from a Thirteenth Floor Window," for example, some form of the title phrase begins nearly every stanza, creating a sense of suspense and anxiety over the fate of the title character, whose life so precariously teeters on the edge. Her poem "She Had Some Horses" enacts a rhythmic chant of words and sounds, demonstrating the belief that language is creation.

Another way contemporary poets draw upon the oral tradition is by incorporating tribal cosmologies and stories. In "People from the Stars," the Osage poet Carter Revard recounts the creation story of the Wazhazhe or Osage people, who "come from the stars" and will "go back to the stars" at death. Other poets tell trickster stories in their poems. The figure of Coyote, the most common trickster in tribal stories, appears in a great number of contemporary poems. Simon Ortiz uses Coyote to recount the Acoma Pueblo origin story, in which the people emerged from the earth. In "The Creation, According to Coyote," Ortiz writes,

> My uncle told me all this, that time. Coyote told me too, but you know how he is, always talking to the gods, the mountains, the stone all around. And you know, I believe him.

Ortiz's affirmation of belief in the Acoma creation story reflects the renewal of traditional belief systems that occurred in late 1960s and early 70s. Leslie Marmon Silko (Laguna Pueblo) catalogs a number of Coyote tales in "Toe'osh: A Laguna Coyote Story," some of which tell of contemporary manifestations of the trickster, a powerful force in the Laguna creation story:

> Charlie Coyote wanted to be governor and he said that when he got elected he would run the other men off the reservation and keep all the women for himself.

Silko demonstrates how traditional stories are remembered and reconfigured to reflect modern-day concerns.

Remembering the Traditions. American Indian poets often describe tribally specific rituals and ceremonies in their work. In "The Gourd Dancer," the Kiowa author N. Scott Momaday relates the story of how his grandfather, Mammedaty, became a traditional dancer. Even though Momaday never met his grandfather, he highlights the importance of maintaining connections to the ancestors, via more immediate elders. The Mesquakie poet Ray A. Young Bear describes a male religious society in "Always Is He Criticized":

> There was this dance procession I was a part of, and we were all males following one another, demonstrating our place in Black Eagle Child society with flexed chest muscles and clenched fists.

Young Bear, too, places tradition in the present, as he goes on to reflect on the ironic position of warrior men, who would have traditionally supported their families but are now "perennially unemployed" and supported by their women.

Several Native poets have written "prayer poems" that reflect traditional religious beliefs. An example is Joy Harjo's "Eagle Poem," which begins,

> To pray you open your whole self To sky, to earth, to sun, to moon To one whole voice that is you.

Harjo likens the eagle's flight to the circle of life. One of Simon Ortiz's earliest poems, "This Preparation," describes the poet's preparation for prayer. He cuts prayer sticks in the traditional Acoma way and listens to the creek "speaking to the world." The poem ends with the affirmation that "prayers / make things possible." The Abenaki poet Joseph Bruchac's "Blessing the Waters" also describes the sacredness of water and the ancient ritual of blessing it and being blessed by it. He writes, "There is no blessing older / than the blessing of the waters." Bruchac's poem acts as both a reminder of the prayer and as the prayer itself.

The connection to nature in the prayer poems appears in other poems as well. Whereas Christianity purports dominion over the natural world, Native worldviews seek to maintain a spiritual connection between humans and their environment. Poets such as Linda Hogan (Chickasaw) have explored this connection. Her "Elk Song" begins,

> We give thanks to deer, otter, the great fish and birds
> that fly over and are our bones and skin.

Even though animals provide sustenance for humans, Hogan insists that we must never forget to give thanks for their sacrifice. She makes the connection between humans and other animals even clearer in "Morning: The World in the Lake." In this poem, the flight of a red-winged blackbird reminds the poet that we are "daughters, all of us." The Alaska Native poet Mary TallMountain takes this idea a step further in

"Coyotes' Desert Lament." The narrator lies on a hill listening to coyotes and wondering what their memories hold, when

> Suddenly I am coyote too, Nose a wet black tremble.
> Hound and I bunch together Among warm grey bodies
> Calling our brother home.

In exploring the possibility of actually becoming the coyote, TallMountain reinforces the view that all creatures are in some sense related.

Reverence for the environment extends to the landscape itself. Native poets speak of sacred places, which might include ancient homelands and reservation spaces. Leslie Marmon Silko's "Slim Man Canyon" is a contemplation of an awe-inspiring place on the territory of the Navajo Nation:

> 700 years ago people were living here water was running
> gently and the sun was warm on pumpkin flowers.

She describes "cliffs with stories and songs / painted on rock." Silko repeats the phrase "700 years" throughout the poem, giving reverence to the place and the long association between it and the Native peoples who have lived there for so long. Simon Ortiz's poem "A Story of How a Wall Stands" begins with a description of a four hundred-year-old wall at Acoma, "which supports hundreds of tons of dirt and bones." In the poem, Ortiz's father explains how the wall was made and why it continues to hold together, at the same time demonstrating how the people who built it have endured. In "This Is How They Were Placed for Us," the Navajo poet Luci Tapahonso reflects on four sacred mountains, now called Blanca Peak, Mount Taylor, the San Francisco Peaks, and Hesperus Peak, which correspond to the four directions, four seasons, four colors, and four cycles of Diné (Navajo) life. She writes, "These mountains and the land keep us strong. / From them, and because of them, we prosper." At the center is Huerfano Mountain: "This is where our prayers began," writes Tapahonso.

As Janice Gould (Maidu/Konkow) explains in the introduction to *Speak to Me Words,* "We respond to pain and suffering by seeking a healing, a healing that cannot be completed in the human world but must be completed by understanding our ties to the spirit world" (p. 11). Many poets focus on traditional healing practices in their work. For example, the Mohawk poet Peter Blue Cloud reflects on the conflict between traditional healing and Christianity in "Tota Ti-om (For an Aunt)." He writes,

> my aunt was an herb doctor, one-eyed with crooked
> yellow teeth the Christians called her pagan witch and
> their children taunted her or ran in fear of their bible
> lives at her approach

Blue Cloud's aunt is unaffected by their criticism, however, and she teaches the narrator how to collect and dry onanoron roots, "to preserve their sacred power." Another Mohawk poet, Maurice Kenny, recounts the story of a "Blackrobe" who is killed for his missionary activities in "Wolf 'Aunt.'" Kenny writes,

> I told him to stop mumbling over the sick children, that
> the duties of curing belonged to our doctors who have
> centuries of service and the herbs to heal.

Both poets resist conversion to Christianity, while expressing their faith in traditional healing practices.

CONTEMPORARY RESPONSES TO CHRISTIANITY. Numerous Native poets have responded similarly to forced conversion and missionization. In "Captivity," Louise Erdrich (Ojibwa, or Ojibwe) writes an imagined interior monologue of Mary Rowlandson, a Puritan woman taken captive during King Philip's War (1675–1676), who then wrote the first "captivity narrative." Erdrich questions the Puritan contempt for Natives as "savage" and "soulless" creatures, insinuating that perhaps Rowlandson felt an attraction toward her captor and wanted to become Indian herself. Erdrich grapples with Catholicism in a number of poems, including "Fooling God," "Saint Clare," and "Rez Litany." In the last, Erdrich parodies the availability of Christian saints to Native converts, creating such satirical figures as Saint Assimilus, "patron of residential and of government / boarding schools"; Saint Quantum, "Martyr of Blood / and Holy Protector of the Tribal Rolls"; and Saint Bingeous, "who fell asleep upside down on the cross / and rose on the third day without even knowing he had died."

The Blackfoot writer James Welch contemplates hypocrisy in the Catholic Church in "The Last Priest Didn't Even Say Goodbye." The narrator finds the priest's study empty, but smelling of "incense and bourbon." "The saints all / disapproved," Welch continues. Sherman Alexie (Coeur d'Alene/Spokane) expresses a cynical and sarcastic view of Catholicism in many of his poems. In "Rise," for example, he muses on the church's doctrine of transubstantiation, by which bread becomes the body of Christ, drawing a contrast to the worldview of the Spokanes, for whom "salmon is simply salmon." In other words, salmon is already sacred—no transformation is necessary. In "Drum as Love, Fear, and Prayer," Alexie asks, "how / do we say Indian prayers in English / and which God will answer? Is God red / or white?" And in "How to Remodel the Interior of a Catholic Church," he suggests, among other things, that the "priest's pockets are heavy with change." The Hopi/Miwok poet Wendy Rose takes her critique even further. Her poem "Excavation at Santa Barbara Mission" ends: "They built the mission with dead Indians." The line is repeated four times, as if the poet herself cannot fathom that such massacres occurred. Natives suffered at the hands of missionaries, allegedly men of God. Rose's use of the number four points to Pueblo ceremonial chants based on the cycles of life; she places it in opposition to the Christian sacred number, three, based on the Trinity. Poets like Erdrich, Welch, Alexie, and Rose weigh Christian beliefs against their respective tribal beliefs, and their poems act as reminders of both the effects of colonization and the endurance of traditional religions.

SEE ALSO Cosmology, article on Indigenous North and Mesoamerican Cosmologies; Ecology and Religion, overview article; Fiction, article on Native American Fiction and Religion; Native American Christianities; North American Indian Religions, article on Mythic Themes; Oral Tradition; Performance and Ritual; Politics and Religion, article on Politics and Native American Religious Traditions; Tricksters, articles on North American Tricksters.

BIBLIOGRAPHY

Primary Sources

Alexie, Sherman. *The Summer of Black Widows.* Brooklyn, N.Y., 1996.

Alexie, Sherman. *One Stick Song.* Brooklyn, N.Y., 2000.

Astrov, Margot. *The Winged Serpent: An Anthology of American Indian Prose and Poetry.* New York, 1946.

Austin, Mary. *The American Rhythm: Studies and Reëxpressions of Amerindian Songs.* New York, 1932.

Bierhorst, John, ed. *In the Trail of the Wind: American Indian Poems and Ritual Orations.* New York, 1971.

Blue Cloud, Peter. *Clans of Many Nations: Selected Poems 1969–1994.* Fredonia, N.Y., 1995.

Copway, George. *The Ojibway Conquest.* New York, 1850.

Cronyn, George W., ed. *The Path on the Rainbow: An Anthology of Songs and Chants from the Indians of North America.* New York, 1918.

Erdrich, Louise. *Jacklight.* New York, 1984.

Erdrich, Louise. *Baptism of Desire.* New York, 1989.

Erdrich, Louise. *Original Fire: Selected and New Poems.* New York, 2003.

Harjo, Joy. *She Had Some Horses.* New York, 1983.

Harjo, Joy. *In Mad Love and War.* Middletown, Conn., 1990.

Hogan, Linda. *Seeing Through the Sun.* Amherst, Mass., 1985.

Hogan, Linda. *Savings: Poems.* Minneapolis, 1988.

Johnson, E. Pauline. *The White Wampum.* London and Boston, 1895.

Johnson, E. Pauline. *Flint and Feather.* Toronto, 1917.

Milton, John R., ed. *The American Indian Speaks.* Vermillion, S.D., 1969. Contains poems by Simon Ortiz.

Momaday, N. Scott. *House Made of Dawn.* New York, 1968.

Momaday, N. Scott. *The Gourd Dancer.* New York, 1976.

Niatum, Duane, ed. *Carriers of the Dream Wheel: Contemporary Native American Poetry.* New York, 1975.

Niatum, Duane, ed. *Harper's Anthology of Twentieth-Century Native American Poetry.* New York, 1988. Contains poems by Maurice Kenny.

Ortiz, Simon J. *Going for the Rain.* New York, 1976.

Posey, Alexander Lawrence. *The Poems of Alexander Lawrence Posey.* Collected and arranged by Mrs. Minnie Posey. Topeka, Kans., 1910.

Purdy, John L., and James Ruppert, eds. *Nothing but the Truth: An Anthology of Native American Literature.* Upper Saddle River, N.J., 2001. Contains poems by Joseph Bruchac.

Revard, Carter. *Ponca War Dancers.* Norman, Okla., 1980.

Ridge, John Rollin. *Poems.* San Francisco, 1868.

Rose, Wendy. *Bone Dance: New and Selected Poems, 1965–1993.* Tucson, Ariz., 1994.

Rothenberg, Jerome, ed. *Shaking the Pumpkin: Traditional Poetry of the Indian North Americas.* Garden City, N.Y., 1972.

Silko, Leslie Marmon. *Laguna Woman: Poems.* Greenfield Center, N.Y., 1974.

Swann, Brian, ed. *Wearing the Morning Star: Native American Song-Poems.* New York, 1996.

TallMountain, Mary. *The Light on the Tent Wall: A Bridging.* Los Angeles, 1990.

Tapahonso, Luci. *Blue Horses Rush In: Poems and Stories.* Tucson, Ariz., 1997.

Welch, James. *Riding the Earthboy 40: Poems.* New York, 1971.

Young Bear, Ray A. *The Invisible Musician: Poems.* Duluth, Minn., 1990.

Secondary Sources

Blaeser, Kimberly. "The Possibilities of a Native Poetics." In *Nothing but the Truth: An Anthology of Native American Literature,* edited by John L. Purdy and James Ruppert, pp. 412–415. Upper Saddle River, N.J., 2001.

Bruchac, Joseph. "Many Tongues: Native American Poetry Today." *North Dakota Quarterly* 55, no. 4 (Fall 1987): 239–244.

Deloria, Vine, Jr. *God Is Red: A Native View of Religion.* Rev. ed. Golden, Colo., 2003.

Fast, Robin Riley. *The Heart as a Drum: Continuance and Resistance in American Indian Poetry.* Ann Arbor, Mich., 1999.

Hogan, Linda. "The Nineteenth Century Native American Poets." *Wassaja: The Indian Historian* 13, no. 4 (November 1980): 24–29.

Hymes, Dell H. *Now I Know Only So Far: Essays in Ethnopoetics.* Lincoln, Nebr., 2003.

Lincoln, Kenneth. *Sing with the Heart of a Bear: Fusions of Native and American Poetry, 1890–1999.* Berkeley, Calif., 2000.

Rader, Dean, and Janice Gould, eds. *Speak to Me Words: Essays on Contemporary American Indian Poetry.* Tucson, Ariz., 2003.

Swann, Brian. "Introduction: Only the Beginning." In *Harper's Anthology of 20th Century Native American Poetry,* edited by Duane Niatum, pp. vi–xxxii. San Francisco, 1988.

Wilson, Norma C. *The Nature of Native American Poetry.* Albuquerque, N.M., 2001.

Womack, Craig S. *Red on Red: Native American Literary Separatism.* Minneapolis, Minn., 1999.

LAURA FURLAN SZANTO (2005)

POINT LOMA THEOSOPHICAL COMMUNITY was an organization of American Theosophists that was based at Point Loma, California, from 1900 to 1942. The site for the Point Loma Theosophical Community was located on the western side of San Diego Bay, on the northern end of a peninsula also used by the U.S. military. Much of the site for the Point Loma Theosophical Community is now occupied by Point Loma Nazarene University.

The Point Loma Theosophical Community's origins can be found in the history of the American Theosophical movement. Helena P. Blavatsky (1831–1891) and Henry Steel Olcott (1832–1907), along with William Q. Judge (1851–1896) and several others interested in Spiritualism, comparative religions, and the occult, began the Theosophical Society in New York City in 1875. Until 1878 Blavatsky and Olcott supervised regular meetings in which participants heard lectures on and discussed various matters related to the occult, world religions, Spiritualism, and other topics of interest to urban middle-class individuals who gravitated away from traditional religions and toward the late-nineteenth-century alternatives available from a growing body of printed literature, as well as from leaders like Blavatsky. In 1878 Blavatsky and Olcott sailed for India to take up Theosophical work there. The movement in the United States experienced a period of decline. In 1883 Judge revived the Theosophical organization by conducting public meetings and publishing a monthly magazine, the *Path*, that appeared regularly from 1886 to 1896. Through Judge's efforts as a lecturer and a frequent contributor to the *Path*, an increasing number of middle-class Americans found Theosophy to be a viable alternative to the religious cultures in which they were raised.

Numerous conversion accounts printed in Theosophical magazines beginning in the late 1800s recount a similar story: the individual became dissatisfied with doctrines preached and taught in their churches, wandered among religious institutions and movements (often finding a temporary home among Spiritualists), then heard a lecture about Theosophy, read a Theosophical book or magazine, or was befriended by a Theosophist. Theosophy resolved their doubts and challenged their imaginations. It provided a satisfactory explanation for the structure of the universe, relying upon many of the scientific notions of the day, but still reserved a place for the religious teachings of the world.

Theosophy claims that humanity evolves through various stages across eons of time, reincarnating as waves of souls or sparks of divinity in progressively more advanced forms. The worlds on which these waves of evolution occur are themselves evolving, with each evolutionary cycle ultimately reaching a point of greatest material density and then slowly working toward heightened spiritual glory and maturity before the waves of human souls move on to other worlds. Watching, and to some extent overseeing, these grand cosmic developments are a class of beings called *masters* who have advanced intellectually and spiritually many levels beyond most souls. Theosophists claimed that Blavatsky frequently communicated with certain masters. The masters were supposedly responsible for much of the information contained in some of her most important published works, especially her magnum opus, *The Secret Doctrine* (1888). The Theosophical version of the universe, then, offered to late-nineteenth-century Americans a stimulating vision of the cosmos and their place in it. Those who embraced this vision sometimes cut off ties to family and friends. Theosophists reoriented their affiliations, associating with one another in local lodges that sprang up in dozens of American cities during the last two decades of the nineteenth century. In these lodges, members held regular meetings in which Theosophical topics were discussed, distributed literature, and instructed children in Theosophical Sunday schools called Lotus Circles. Judge was the president of the American Section of the Theosophical Society until 1895, when he led the Americans in convention to declare their independence from the rest of the Theosophical Society worldwide after a series of disputes involving Judge, noted British Theosophical leader Annie Besant (1847–1933), Olcott, and others.

Shortly before Judge's death, Katherine Tingley (1847–1929) assumed an increasingly important role in Judge's leadership circle in New York City. Her origins as a Theosophist are difficult to determine. She was a middle-class social reformer, like many women in her class at that time, who fed the poor and supported other charitable works. After Judge's death, many of those closest to him were convinced that Tingley should succeed him. This succession was ratified by a pro-Tingley convention of the American Theosophical Society in 1898, in which the organization adopted a new name, Universal Brotherhood and Theosophical Society. During this period, Tingley led Theosophists in New York City and other American cities to engage in activities consistent with the priorities of women reformers and the emerging political and cultural ethos of Progressivism, activities designed to improve the quality of life and living conditions of the urban poor (e.g., training and socializing children, feeding the hungry, offering job instruction, providing housing and support for prostitutes, and caring for orphans). During the Spanish-American War of 1898, Tingley and other Theosophists worked in a hospital camp on Long Island at one of the disembarkation points for returning American soldiers. Many of these soldiers were weak and ill from tropical diseases contracted while in Cuba, and they required food and medical treatment. Because the U.S. Army was slow to organize adequate facilities to receive the influx of returning troops, the care provided by the Theosophists—as well as by other organizations like the Red Cross—was crucial in saving many lives. In recognition of her organization's work, President William McKinley provided transport for Tingley and other Theosophists to journey to Cuba to establish relief work there. This led to the eventual foundation, during the first decade of the twentieth century, of four Theosophical schools in that island nation.

Meanwhile, Tingley and other leaders among her inner circle were increasingly interested in relocating to California. The reasons for this move are not entirely clear, but California was attractive to many Americans in the East and Midwest at the beginning of the twentieth century. It provided a mild climate, geographical diversity for agriculture and industry, and freedom from the cultural, social, and economic constraints characteristic of the more settled areas of the United States. During a worldwide tour of Theosophical lodges in 1896 called the Crusade, Tingley, with the assistance of Gottfried de Purucker (1874–1942), her eventual successor, learned of the exact location of available land on the Point Loma peninsula and directed her agents to purchase it.

When she returned to the United States in 1897, Tingley gathered American Theosophists for a dedication ceremony at the Point Loma site. But Theosophists did not take up residence in substantial numbers at Point Loma until 1900 and after. In the early days of the Point Loma Theosophical Community, several hundred adults lived in tents and other temporary structures that eventually gave way, over the years, to houses and bungalows, as well as buildings containing facilities for various activities supported by the community, including a printing press, medical clinic, classrooms. From the beginning, children were central to Point Loma's existence. Tingley and others justified the creation of Point Loma as a home for souls then entering the world as children who were morally and spiritually advanced. Given the proper environment and training, these children could become superior world citizens whose lives would be devoted to the service of humanity. Taking their cues from comments made by Blavatsky in print, Point Loma Theosophists believed that they lived at the beginning of a new cycle in human evolution. If they did not do everything possible to raise an exceptional generation of souls, they believed humanity might delay or even miss the opportunity to advance spiritually.

The educational approach at Point Loma was called Raja Yoga, a term borrowed from Hinduism that described the holistic educational philosophy held by Tingley and others. Under Raja Yoga, children were challenged to grow in all ways that mattered: intellectually, physically, culturally, spiritually, and emotionally. The curriculum of the Raja Yoga schools emphasized the fine arts and humanities, although instruction in business skills, engineering, mathematics, and the sciences was available, depending upon the expertise of Theosophical adults on the teaching staff. As children grew to adulthood at Point Loma, many of them became teachers and served in other capacities in the Point Loma Theosophical Community. One outstanding example was Judith Tyberg (1902–1980), who was born and raised at Point Loma. Tyberg taught young children when she became a young adult, and later, when the Theosophical University was founded at Point Loma in 1919, she took advanced degrees and ultimately became a teacher and administrator in that university.

At its largest, the Point Loma Theosophical Community numbered in the hundreds of adults and at least as many children. Many of the latter were the progeny of adult members, but they were not permitted to live with their parents on the Point Loma site. Instead, they were housed in collective homes, segregated according to age and sex. Other children were sent to Point Loma by their Theosophical parents or guardians, so that Point Loma served as a Theosophical boarding school. A few Cuban children were brought to Point Loma during the early years, but several of them presented discipline problems and were sent back to Cuba. Criticism of Raja Yoga education, raised by some Theosophical parents and echoed in the press, focused on the children's separation from their parents and strict control of eating habits, among other techniques used to control the children's living environment. Later in life, a number of these former Raja Yoga pupils would recall their childhood experiences with dismay. But others considered their upbringing to be beneficial, even inspirational. Although the quality of caregiving was uneven, those children who had loving adult caregivers generally had positive experiences and memories of their childhoods at Point Loma.

During the first three decades of the twentieth century, Tingley traveled across the United States and around the world many times. On most of these trips, she took selected Point Loma adults and adolescents with her. During a tour for world peace in 1913, she was accompanied by over twenty young men and women, who provided musical and dramatic entertainment at a Theosophical peace conference in Sweden. These young people, most of whom had grown up at Point Loma, embodied the ideals of Raja Yoga education. Many of them married one another, often due to Tingley's matchmaking choices, although some Point Loma youth married persons outside the Point Loma Theosophical Community. During the 1920s many young adults left Point Loma. The reasons for their departure varied. Some wanted to continue their education in colleges and universities elsewhere. Others wanted to live outside the protected, insular world of Point Loma and found employment in San Diego or other locations.

Tingley and others from her generation brought to Point Loma a Victorian decorum popular among their social classes in the late nineteenth century. This decorum was transmitted to the children of Point Loma. A moral and didactic tone infused the language and relationships at Point Loma during Tingley's tenure. By the 1930s the Raja Yoga school program had a higher percentage of paying students who lived in San Diego and attended during the daytime only than in earlier decades The older Victorian cultural sensibility among young people raised at Point Loma contrasted with the choices in music and other aspects of popular culture, as well as daily customs, of the students who did not live at Point Loma and were influenced by larger culture far more.

Tingley died as a result of an automobile accident in 1929. Her successor, de Purucker, was a self-taught polymath who specialized in ancient languages and religious texts. Over the years his duties as a community member at Point Loma permitted him to devote considerable attention to scholarly pursuits. By the time he assumed leadership responsibilities, his immersion in Theosophical literature and related areas of study enabled him to give numerous lectures that were later published as collections of essays. De Purucker's articulation of complex Theosophical ideas is known among Theosophists and students of the Theosophical movement as *technical Theosophy* because of his sophisticated presentation of Theosophical teaching going back to Blavatsky and carried forward, in the Point Loma Theosophical tradition, through Judge and Tingley. De Purucker altered the organization's name to the Theosophical Society, dropping the older appellation of the Universal Brotherhood and Theosophical Society. By the time of his death in 1942, the community had moved from Point Loma to Covina, near Los Angeles, to avoid the military activity occurring at Point Loma after the United States entered World War II. De Purucker's successor was not clearly identified. During the war years a group of leaders ran the organization. In 1945 a retired U.S. Army officer, Colonel Arthur L. Conger (1872–1951), was brought in as leader. Some lifelong Theosophists objected to Conger, but their party failed to carry the day. Many of these individuals left the Theosophical Society. Conger was succeeded by James A. Long (1898–1971) in 1951. He was succeeded in 1971 by Grace F. Knoche (b. 1909), who served as leader of the Theosophical Society, Pasadena, the organizational descendant of the Point Loma Theosophical Community. Their principal activities include the publication of *Sunrise*, a bimonthly magazine, as well as Theosophical classics by Blavatsky, Judge, Tingley, de Purucker, and others.

SEE ALSO Besant, Annie; Blavatsky, H. P.; Judge, William Q.; Olcott, Henry Steel; Theosophical Society; Tingley, Katherine.

BIBLIOGRAPHY

Ashcraft, W. Michael. *The Dawn of the New Cycle: Point Loma Theosophists and American Culture.* Knoxville, Tenn., 2002.

Blavatsky, Helena P. *The Secret Doctrine: The Synthesis of Science, Religion, and Philosophy.* 2 vols. London and New York, 1888; reprint, Pasadena, Calif., 1988.

Greenwalt, Emmett A. *California Utopia: Point Loma: 1897–1942.* Rev. ed., San Diego, Calif., 1978.

Judge, William Q. *The Ocean of Theosophy.* London and New York, 1893; reprint, Pasadena, Calif., 1973.

Knoche, Grace F. *To Light a Thousand Lamps: A Theosophic Vision.* Pasadena, Calif., 2002.

Purucker, Gottfried de. *Fountain-Source of Occultism.* Pasadena, Calif., 1974.

Tingley, Katherine. *The Gods Await.* Point Loma, Calif., 1926; rev. ed., Pasadena, Calif., 1992.

Waterstone, Penny. "Domesticating Universal Brotherhood: Feminine Values and the Construction of Utopia, Point Loma Homestead, 1897–1920." Ph.D. diss., University of Arizona, Tucson, 1995.

W. MICHAEL ASHCRAFT (2005)

POLEMICS

This entry consists of the following articles:

JEWISH-CHRISTIAN POLEMICS
MUSLIM-JEWISH POLEMICS
CHRISTIAN-MUSLIM POLEMICS

POLEMICS: JEWISH-CHRISTIAN POLEMICS

[*This article focuses primarily on Jewish polemics against Christianity.*]

The intensity, persistence, and significance of Jewish-Christian polemics are in large measure a function of the peculiar combination of intimacy and divergence that marks the relationship between the two faiths. It is not merely the fact that Christianity emerges out of Judaism; it is, further, the combination of the continuing centrality of the Hebrew Bible for Christians together with the profundity of the theological differences that separated Christians from Jews. In these respects, a comparison with Islam is particularly instructive. It too arose in large measure out of Judaism, but because it lacked the other crucial characteristics, polemic between Jews and Muslims, however important it may sometimes have been, never played the same role as did the Jewish-Christian debate. Muslims revered the Hebrew Bible; Muslims did not, however, elevate it to the position that it held in Christianity, and they expressed the most serious reservations about its textual accuracy. Moreover, Islamic monotheism left no room for the creative rancor that produced the philosophical dimension of Jewish-Christian discussions, which addressed such issues as trinitarianism and incarnation. Moses Maimonides (Mosheh ben Maimon, 1135/8–1204), who has sometimes been accused of inconsistency in his attitude toward the two other faiths, was accurately portraying a complex situation. On the one hand, he described Islam as a religion of "unblemished monotheism," an accolade he would not bestow upon Christianity; on the other hand, he maintained that teaching Torah to Christians can be a fruitful enterprise, while doing the same for Muslims is, from a Jewish point of view, an exercise in futility.

The dispute between Judaism and Christianity, then, revolved around both doctrine and exegesis. To Christians, Jesus was the Messiah, the ritual law was abrogated, and the church was the true Israel, not only because Christian scripture and tradition said so but because the Hebrew scriptures themselves supported such claims. Beginning with the New Testament and continuing with the earliest church fathers, Christian ingenuity was mobilized to uncover references to the full range of Christian beliefs in the Hebrew scriptures. The Jewish polemicist was required to undertake the onerous task of point-by-point, verse-by-verse refutation, and the sparse Talmudic references to debates with *minim* (a term for heretics that surely embraces many early Christians) describe precisely such conflicts in biblical interpretation.

The institutional separation of the two religions was furthered when a curse against the *minim* was inserted into the rabbinic prayer book, and doctrinal developments made it increasingly difficult even for "Jewish" as opposed to "gentile" Christians to remain a part of the Jewish people. The Jews, it was said, had been replaced by a new Israel, and their defeats at the hands of the Romans were a just punishment for their rejection of the Messiah; moreover, by the middle of the second century there were few Christians who did not believe in some form of Jesus' divinity, and this was a doctrine that remained beyond the pale of even the most flexible definition of Judaism.

In the wake of these developments, early Jewish sources record hostile perceptions not only of Christianity but of Jesus as well. In the Talmud itself, clear references to Jesus are exceedingly rare, but those that exist do include the assertion that he was a sorcerer who led his followers astray (cf. Goldstein, 1950). Outside the Talmudic corpus, there developed a more elaborate series of early Jewish folk tales that go by the name *Toledot Yeshu* and can probably best be described as a counter-Gospel. The various versions of *Toledot Yeshu* trace Jesus' life from his birth as a result of Mary's liaison with a Roman soldier through his checkered career as a sorcerer and on to his ignominious hanging between two thieves on a massive stalk of cabbage. Although such stories did not constitute binding Jewish doctrine, they colored Jewish views of Christianity and enraged Christians who became familiar with them in subsequent periods.

From the Jewish perspective, these early responses to Christianity remained episodic and peripheral. Before Christianity became the official religion of the Roman empire, there was little reason for Jews to confront its religious claims systematically; after that point, Jewish literary activity in the Christian world was on the wane, and before the high Middle Ages, Jewish arguments against Christianity were preserved primarily in Christian works. The only significant exceptions are a little book of eastern provenance called *Sefer Nestor ha-komer* (Book of Nestor the Priest), which was written by a convert to Judaism, and a handful of passages in Jewish philosophical works composed in the Muslim world.

In the second half of the twelfth century, this situation began to change. Partly because the inner dynamic of Christianity required a confrontation with Judaism, the "renaissance" of Christian literature and thought associated with the twelfth century included a renewal of anti-Jewish polemics. At this time Jewish literature too was in the midst of a vigorous revival, and Jews throughout western Europe began to engage in a literary polemic that was to remain active through the end of the Middle Ages.

Although this polemic extends to works of exegesis, philosophy, homiletics, and even liturgy and law, a list of explicitly polemical works through the fifteenth century can serve as a useful introduction to the scope and intensity of this activity.

- Twelfth century: Yosef Kimhi, *Sefer ha-berit* (Book of the Covenant), southern France; Yaʿaqov ben Reuʾven, *Milhamot ha-Shem* (The Wars of the Lord), southern France.
- Thirteenth century: *Vikkuah le-ha-Radaq* (The disputation of Rabbi David Kimhi), pseudonymous, provenance uncertain; Meʾir of Narbonne, *Milhemet mitsvah* (The obligatory war), southern France; Mordekhai of Avignon, *Mahaziq emunah* (Upholder of Faith), southern France; Shelomoh de Rossi, *ʿEdut ha-Shem neʾemanah* (The testimony of the Lord is perfect), Italy; *The Epistle of Rabbi Jacob of Venice,* Italy; *The Disputation of Rabbi Yehiʾel of Paris,* northern France; Yosef Official, *Sefer Yosef ha-meqanneʾ* (The book of Yosef the zealot), northern France; *The Disputation of Nahmanides,* Spain; *Sefer nitsahon yashan* (The old book of polemic), Germany.
- Fourteenth century: Moses ha-Kohen of Tordesillas, *ʿEzer ha-emunah* (Aid of faith), Spain; Yitshaq Polgar, *ʿEzer ha-dat* (Aid of religion), Spain; Hasdai Crescas, *Bittul ʿiqqrei ha-Notsrim* (Refutation of Christian doctrines), Spain; Shem Tov ibn Shaprut, *Even bohan* (Touchstone), Spain; Profiat Duran, *Al tehi ka-avotekha* (Do not be like your fathers) and *Kelimat ha-goyim* (The shame of the Gentiles), Spain.
- Fifteenth century: Yom Tov Lippman Mühlhausen, *Sefer ha-nitsahon* (The Book of polemic), Bohemia; Shimʿon Duran, *Qeshet umagen* (Bow and shield), Spain; the Tortosa Disputation, Spain; Shelomoh Duran, *Milhemet mitsvah* (The obligatory war), Spain; Hayyim ibn Musa, *Magen va-romah* (Shield and spear), Spain; Mattityahu ben Mosheh, *The Book of Ahituv and Zalmon,* Spain; Binyamin ben Mosheh, *Teshuvot ha-Notsrim* (Answers to the Christians), Italy; Eliyyahu Hayyim of Genezzano, *Vikkuah* (Disputation), Italy.

Polemics on Biblical and Philosophical Issues. Many of the issues addressed by the authors of the aforementioned works remained relatively unchanged from late antiquity through the end of the Middle Ages and beyond. To Jews, the fundamental Christian assertion that Jesus was the Messiah had been massively refuted by the evidence of history. Since the essential characteristic of the biblical Messiah involved the inauguration of an age of peace, virtually all Jewish polemicists pointed to the persistence of war and misery as a formidable refutation of Christianity. Moses Nahmanides (Mosheh ben Naḥman, c. 1194–1270), in fact, reports that he went so far as to tell James I of Aragon how difficult it would be for him and his knights if war were to be abolished.

Christians, of course, argued not only that scriptural evidence demonstrates that the Messiah had already come but also that it points to a first coming that would end in apparent failure. The key citations demonstrating these propositions were probably the most extensively debated biblical passages in the entire literature: *Genesis* 49:10 on the first point, and *Isaiah* 52:13–53:12 on the second.

"The scepter shall not pass away from Judah, nor shall a legislator pass away from among his descendants until Shiloh comes and to him shall the nations gather." This translation of *Genesis* 49:10, with *Shiloh* understood as *Messiah,* appeared to lend powerful support to the Christian position: since there was now no scepter in Judah, the Messiah must already have come. For this passage Jews did not have a particularly attractive alternative interpretation, but they did have a persuasive argument against the Christian position. That position, they said, cannot be valid because the scepter (understood by Christians as kingship) had passed from the Jews well before the time of Jesus; during the Babylonian exile there was no Jewish rule, and even during the second commonwealth there were no kings from the tribe of Judah. Although alternative explanations of this passage were beset by difficulties, they were nonetheless abundant: Shiloh indeed refers to the Messiah, but the verse is merely asserting that whenever there will be a Jewish king, he can legitimately come only from Judah; *scepter* and *legislator* refer not to kingship but to exil-archs and patriarchs or even to ongoing communal autonomy; Shiloh is not the Messiah but a place-name, and the verse refers to a past event, most likely the schism after Solomon's death.

With respect to *Isaiah* 53, which can be read as a description of an innocent servant of the Lord who will suffer and die for the sins of others, the situation of the Jewish polemicists was reversed: they had an excellent alternative interpretation, but some of them expressed disappointment at the absence of a crushing refutation of the christological exegesis. Despite a messianic understanding of this chapter in early rabbinic sources, medieval Jews overwhelmingly saw the servant as the exiled people of Israel, and strong arguments could be adduced for this identification. At the same time, Jews were sharply divided concerning the presence of a concept of vicarious atonement in the passage; to some exegetes and polemicists, such a concept was too Christian to be readily discerned in the Bible even if applied to Israel rather than the Messiah. Finally, specific refutations of the christological interpretation were proffered: aside from the inappropriateness of the term *servant* for a divine figure, this servant, unlike Jesus, "will see his seed and live a long life," will experience ongoing affliction and disease, and will suffer as a result of the sins of many rather than for the purpose of removing the original sin of Adam and Eve.

It has already been seen that Christians considered the Jewish rejection of the Messiah to have resulted in the suppression of "carnal Israel" and its replacement by the church. Initial Jewish bewilderment at this perception gave way to a charge of Christian arbitrariness in defining biblical references to Israel, and Jews pointed to a number of citations in which favorable eschatological references that Christians took as descriptions of the church seemed inextricably linked to pejorative passages that Christians referred to the Jews. By the thirteenth century, Jews had even begun to cite their own retention of the Hebrew language as evidence that they had not been exchanged by God for people who knew the Bible only in translation.

It was not only the Jewish people, however, who were supposed to have been superseded. The same was said about Jewish law, and here the issue of allegorical interpretation of the Bible became crucial. Christians argued that, at least in the postcrucifixion era, only a nonliteral meaning is to be assigned to the legal sections of the Pentateuch, and they buttressed their position by raising questions about the rationality and consistency of biblical law. This challenge added a polemical dimension to Jewish speculations about "the reasons for the commandments." While some Jews argued against any attempt to fathom the divine intent or even denied the very existence of rational explanations, others provided both hygienic and spiritual reasons that sometimes seemed so persuasive that they became the basis for questions about the Christian failure to observe such evidently beneficial injunctions. Christian allegorization did not stop with the law; consequently, Jewish insistence on literal, contextual reading of biblical verses is a central theme of polemical literature, and some scholars have even suspected an underlying apologetic motive for the radical insistence on straightforward exegesis advocated by several significant medieval commentators such as Rashbam (Rabbi Shemuʾel ben Meʾir, c. 1080–1158) who were not primarily polemicists.

While Christian questions about the rationality of the law were a minor theme in medieval polemics, Jewish questions about the rationality of Christian dogma were at center stage. Many Jews were unable or unwilling to see trinitarianism as anything but tritheism. Those who did come to grips with the full complexity of the doctrine maintained that it violates logic and that multiplicity in God inevitably implies corporeality in God himself (i.e., not just in the temporary form of the historical Jesus). Most important, sophisticated Jewish polemicists maintained that any truly monotheistic understanding of trinitarianism—in which three divine persons are identified with attributes of God or understood in light of the perception of God as thought, thinker, and object of thought—fails because of the second, crucial doctrine of incarnation. If only one of three divine persons took on flesh, then true unity was irretrievably compromised.

Jewish objections to incarnation were not confined to the troubling light that it shed on the Christian concept of a divine trinity. Not only did the attribution of divinity to a human being raise the ugly specter of idolatry; it also seemed vulnerable to definitive philosophical refutation. Jewish polemicists argued that since infinity and immutability are essential characteristics of God, incarnation could not take place even miraculously. Moreover, they said, it is equally impossible to unite a human and a divine nature in a single person with each nature retaining its distinctiveness. Finally, even if all this were possible, it is hard to imagine that God could find no way to redeem humanity without subjecting himself to the filth and indignity of spending nine months in a womb and then passing through all the stages of a life that culminated in a humiliating death.

Virginal conception, although denied by Jews, was not vulnerable to the charge of philosophical impossibility. However, the specific doctrine that Mary remained a virgin during childbirth did appear to violate the principle that two bodies cannot take up the same space simultaneously. More important, the miracle of transubstantiation also seemed impossible, partly because Jesus' body would have to have been in many places at the same time.

There was, of course, also a scriptural dimension to these philosophical issues. Christians attempted to demonstrate trinitarianism by citing verses that contain plural verbs in connection with God, as, for example, "Let us make man in our image" (*Gn.* 1:26); or a threefold repetition of a key word, as, for example, "Holy, holy, holy is the Lord of Hosts" (*Is.* 6:3); or a repetition of the names of God, as, for example, "Hear O Israel, the Lord [is] our God, the Lord is one" (*Dt.* 6:4). For the incarnation, they cited the eschatological king in *Jeremiah* 23:5, whose name they translated as "the Lord our Righteousness," and, most effectively, the child in *Isaiah* 9:5–6, whose name they translated as "Wondrous Counselor, Mighty God, Eternal Father, Prince of Peace." Jews had to respond by providing alternative explanations or, in some cases, alternative translations. Thus the plural verb in *Genesis* 1:26 is either a plural of majesty or God's statement to the earth, which would provide the body into which he would place a soul. The name in *Jeremiah,* they said, should be translated "the Lord *is* our Righteousness," and the child in *Isaiah,* at least according to most medieval Jews, was named only "Prince of Peace" by God, who is himself the "Wondrous Counselor, Mighty God, [and] Eternal Father."

The scriptural evidence for virgin birth gave Jews their best opportunity to use the argument from context. The evidence, Christians said, is to be found in *Isaiah* 7:14, in which the prophet promised King Ahaz the birth of a child from an *ʿalmah.* Jews not only argued that *ʿalmah* does not mean "virgin" but also pointed to Isaiah's promise to Ahaz that deliverance would come before the child would know how to distinguish good from evil as decisive refutation of any identification of the child with Jesus.

POLEMICS ON THE TALMUD. In its classic form, the Jewish-Christian debate centered on the Hebrew Bible. Beginning in the twelfth century, however, and especially in the thirteenth, Christians became intrigued with the possibility of utilizing the Talmud for polemical purposes, and Jews found themselves confronting two distinct but overlapping challenges from Christians quoting Talmud. Nicholas Donin, a Jewish convert to Christianity, began a campaign in the 1230s that led to a virtual trial in which Yeḥiʾel ben Yosef of Paris had to defend the Talmud against charges of blasphemy. Pointing to what would otherwise have been an anachronism in a Talmudic account of Jesus, Yeḥiʾel made the novel assertion that there were two Jesuses and that any pejorative Talmudic references are to the first, who had no connection whatever to Christianity. Potentially even more serious was Donin's assertion that the Talmud constituted "another law" that was entirely different from that of the Hebrew Bible. Since Jews were tolerated in part because they observed and authenticated the "Old Testament," the very existence of Jews in the Christian world could have been jeopardized by Christian acceptance of such an assertion. Yehiʾel argued that the Talmud was, rather, an indispensable interpretation of the Bible. Ultimately, although various Dominicans and Franciscans toyed with the delegitimation of Jews on grounds related to the "other law" argument, it was the accusation of blasphemy that predominated, and this could be satisfied by the censorship of a handful of Talmudic passages.

The second approach to the Talmud is usually associated with another convert to Christianity. In the third quarter of the thirteenth century, Pablo Christiani (Cristia) began to emphasize a very minor theme in some earlier Christian polemics: that the Talmud demonstrates the truth of Christianity. Pablo and his successors did not have a positive attitude toward the Talmud, but they believed that the rabbis had preserved evidence of Christian truth. One of the earliest examples of this sort of argument is one of the best. The Talmud says that the world will last six thousand years: two thousand years of chaos, two thousand of Torah, and two thousand of the messianic age (B. T., *San.* 97a). This, said Christian polemicists, proves two crucial Christian assertions—that the Messiah has already come, and that with his arrival the age of Torah has come to an end. When Nahmanides was forced to confront Pablo in the Barcelona disputation of 1263, he insisted, of course, on the implausibility of finding Christian doctrines in a work produced by unconverted Jews, but he also made the striking assertion that *midrash* is not dogmatically binding and that Jews are therefore free to reject certain rabbinic statements. This issue became a *cause célèbre* in the next two or three centuries, largely because of the popularity of Raymund Martini's monumental *Pugio Fidei,* and the rabbis at the Tortosa disputation had to confront it under particularly trying circumstances. Generally, Jewish polemicists attempted to refute each argument individually, and they fell back on Nahmanides' position reluctantly and only as a last resort.

JEWISH POLEMICAL USE OF THE NEW TESTAMENT. At about the same time that Christians began to examine the Talmud for polemical purposes, Jews began to scrutinize the New Testament. Here too the sacred text peculiar to the other faith could simply be attacked, and here too it could be used for more sophisticated polemical purposes. Jews pointed out contradictions in the New Testament, such as the differing genealogies in *Matthew* and *Luke,* but they also argued that the Gospels themselves support the Jewish position concerning the nondivinity of Jesus and the eternality of the law. The polemical usefulness of both approaches led to a sometimes ambivalent attitude toward Jesus himself. On the one hand, he was denounced for abrogating the Torah and turning himself into a divinity; on the other, his words were cited as testimony that later Christians distorted a message that was in large measure authentically Jewish. This last approach, which was to be particularly influential in the modern period, was developed most notably in Profiat Duran's impressive and sophisticated *Kelimat ha-goyim.*

The Issues of Jewish Exile and the Role of Christianity. The effect of increased Jewish familiarity with the New Testament and growing Christian awareness of the Talmud is but one example of the way in which a largely static debate could undergo dynamic transformation under the impact of historical change. Debates about interest taking, the blood libel, heresy, icons, worship of the saints, confession, priestly celibacy, the Crusades, and more all made their way into the polemical literature. Perhaps the most fundamental effect of the historical situation lay in the Jewish need to explain exile and suffering on grounds other than God's rejection of the Jews. Since Jewish polemicists insisted on the moral superiority of Jews to Christians, the standard explanation of exile as punishment was especially uncomfortable in this context. Consequently, there is found a whole array of efforts to turn the fact of suffering to polemical advantage: the Bible says that the truth would be hurled to the ground (*Dn.* 8:12); God is prolonging the exile so that the sin of the Christian oppressors should accumulate to a point where their utter destruction will be appropriate (cf. *Gn.* 15:16); God is punishing the Jews not for crucifying Jesus but for producing him. In a striking naturalistic argument, Yitshaq Polgar noted that Jewish suffering demonstrates that Christians and Jews stand in the same moral relationship as a bully and his victim.

Pressures ranging from the physical and economic to the moral and intellectual also led to transformations in the tone of Jewish polemics as well as to a reexamination of the role and religious standing of Christianity itself. This last development took place largely outside the context of medieval polemics, but its impact on later Jewish thought, including apologetic literature, was exceptionally significant. Medieval Jews generally regarded Christianity as an idolatrous religion. Nevertheless, in certain narrow legal contexts phrases such as "the gentiles among us do not worship idolatry" were used as an *ad hoc* justification for Jewish business dealings with Christians that were pursued despite injunctions against such interactions with idolaters. Menaḥem ha-Me'iri of Perpignan (1249–1316) created a new legal category that can roughly be characterized as "civilized people" in order to distinguish Christians from ancient idolaters. Without addressing the issue of idolatry in this context, Maimonides and other authorities had assigned to Christianity and Islam the positive role of spreading knowledge of Torah and thus preparing the world for the Messiah. By the sixteenth century, some major Jewish figures had begun to misread a statement of the medieval French tosafists to mean that Noahides are not forbidden to associate another divinity with the true God; hence, although Christianity is surely idolatry for Jews, it is not so regarded for gentiles.

Later Developments. Some polemical works of the sixteenth and seventeenth centuries reflect the aforementioned and other changes, while others remain true to standard medieval views. The major works of this period include the following.

- Sixteenth century: Avraham Farissol, *Magen Avraham* (Shield of Abraham), Italy; Ya'ir ben Shabbetai of Correggio, *Herev pifiyyot* (Double-edged sword), Italy; Meshullam ben Uri, *Zikhron sefer nitstsaḥon* (Commemoration of the Book of Polemic), provenance uncertain; *Kevod Elohim* (Glory of God), author and provenance uncertain; Yitshaq of Troki, *Ḥizzuq emunah* (Faith strengthened), Poland.
- Seventeenth century: ʿAzriʾel Petahiah Alatino, *Vikkuah* (Disputation), Italy; Yehudah Aryeh de Modena, *Magen va-herev* (Shield and sword), Italy; Yitsḥaq Lupis, *Kur matsref ha-emunot u-mar'eh ha-emet* (The crucible of beliefs and demonstrator of the truth), Syria.

Perhaps the most striking example of a more positive attitude toward Christianity is Avraham Farissol's remark that Jesus might well be regarded as a messiah for the Gentiles. Despite Maimonides' assessment of Christianity's place in the divine scheme, this assertion, highly unusual even around 1500, was virtually unimaginable in the high Middle Ages. In the sixteenth century, Shelomoh de Modena denied the idolatrous character of Christianity by equating incarnation with anthropomorphism and noting that the latter doctrine had been declared nonheretical (although also not true) by the twelfth-century authority Avraham ben David of Posquières. There was also a shift in the Jewish attitude with respect to certain moral questions. In the Middle Ages, for example, most Jews vigorously denied that there was anything unethical about taking interest on loans; in seventeenth-century Italy, both Simone Luzzatto and Yehudah Aryeh de Modena insisted that Jewish—and not just Christian—morality frowns on this activity, but that there is no avoiding cruel economic necessity. Closer Jewish-Christian contacts in Italy also led to greater Christian familiarity with Jewish literature, including the increasingly popular qabbalistic texts, and Jews now found themselves confronted with not only Talmudic but also qabbalistic passages that were supposed to demonstrate Christian doctrines.

Initially Jewish reactions to the Reformation were positive and hopeful. Aside from messianic hopes that were briefly kindled at the prospect of division in what Jews considered the biblical fourth kingdom (cf. *Dn.* 2:41), there was a feeling that many doctrinal points in the various forms of Protestantism seemed rather "Jewish": the rejection of papal authority, indulgences, transubstantiation, and clerical celibacy, as well as a return to the authority of the Bible. Moreover, there was the early work of Luther, *Dass Jesus ein geborener Jude Sei* (That Jesus Christ Was Born a Jew; 1523), which appeared to portend an amelioration of the Jewish condition under Protestant rule. When Luther later dashed these hopes, Jewish attitudes changed, and Jews living in Roman Catholic countries now looked to Catholic doctrines that could demonstrate the affinity of Judaism to Catholicism: the emphasis on works, the combination of scripture and tradition, the affirmation of free will and rejection of strict predestinarianism, and the retention of the traditional language of prayer. Needless to say, both Protestants and Catholics continued to affirm the central Christian beliefs that Judaism rejected, and when the Karaite Yitsḥaq of Troki wrote his *summa* of the traditional anti-Christian arguments the work became a standard reference even in the majority Rabbinite community.

The next, even more crucial turning point took place in the eighteenth century, when Jewish history moved into the modern period and Jewish-Christian relations underwent fundamental transformations. Even outside the orbit of the Jewish Enlightenment, Yaʿaqov Emden of Germany maintained that Jesus and even Paul were perfectly good Jews whose purpose was to spread the seven Noahic laws to the gentiles; like Farissol's stance, this is a highly idiosyncratic position that nonetheless reflected a broader phenomenon. The central figure, however, who both foreshadows and exemplifies modern Jewish attitudes to Christianity, is Moses Mendelssohn.

A Christian theologian named Johann Kaspar Lavater publicly challenged Mendelssohn to refute a defense of Christianity that Lavater had translated, or to do what Socrates would have done had he read the book and found it irrefutable. Mendelssohn, who for reasons of ideology, practicality, and temperament was not inclined to engage in polemic, responded reluctantly and cautiously. He had indeed expressed respect for Jesus in light of a conviction that the latter had made no claims to divinity. This did not mean that he was inclined to abandon Judaism, which is in perfect harmony with natural morality and religion, for a faith that contains irrational dogmas. Nevertheless, not all "prejudices" are equally harmful, and Judaism's teaching that righteous gentiles have a portion in the world to come renders missionary activity unnecessary and undesirable. This emphasis on Judaism's tolerance, rationality, morality, and respect for Christianity became the hallmark of modern Jewish discussions of Christianity, but these developments were not without ironic potential for reviving tension and polemic along new and unexpected lines.

Nineteenth-century Reform Judaism and liberal Protestantism arose out of the same environment and shared the fundamental conviction that the central message of religion is ethical. Reform Jews did away with much of the ritual component in Judaism, while liberal Protestants had grave misgivings about much of the dogmatic component of Christianity. What remained in each case was ethical monotheism. This sort of agreement, however, can lead to discord, since in the absence of a religious merger, each faith must claim that it is the quintessential bearer of the ethical message whose basic content is endorsed by both sides.

And precisely such discord developed. Christians complained about the "tasteless gibberish" spouted by Jews who claimed that theirs was the ethical religion *par excellence,* and they insisted that Jesus had introduced an advanced ethic into a Jewish society beset by dry, narrow legalism. This issue exploded into controversy after Adolf von Harnack propounded such views in his lecture series on the essence of Christianity in the winter of 1899–1900, but Jews were upset not only with Harnack but with a number of Christian historians whose scholarly work revealed the same sort of bias against Talmudic religion. The Jewish response was swift, vigorous, and international. In Germany, Leo Baeck's *Das Wesen des Judentums,* Joseph Eschelbacher's *Das Judentum und das Wesen des Christentums,* and Moritz Güdemann's *Jüdische Apologetik* denounced this Christian approach as motivated by considerations that had little to do with objective scholarship. In England, the articles of Israel Abrahams, Claude Montefiore, and Solomon Schechter pursued the same arguments. Somewhat later, Gerald Friedlander's *The Jewish Sources of the Sermon on the Mount* reflected a systematic apologetic effort to compare rabbinic morality with that of Jesus, and Joseph Bloch's *Israel und die Völker* was one of several efforts to counter Christian attacks on Talmudic morality.

This last work really addressed arguments of a more medieval sort, and it should not be assumed that such polemic simply disappeared in the modern period. Vigorous Christian missionary efforts in late eighteenth-century England inspired David Levi's rebuttals, *Letters to Dr. Priestly* and *Dissertations on the Prophecies of the Old Testament;* nineteenth-century challenges led Isaac Ber Levinsohn to write his *Ahiyyah ha-shiloni* and other apologetic works. As recently as the 1970s, the activities of the "Jews for Jesus" and similar groups led the Jewish Community Relations Council of New York to commission *Jews and "Jewish Christianity"* by myself and Michael Wyschogrod. The tone and occasionally the content of such works can reflect modern developments in scholarship, argumentation, and civility; some of them, however, deal with arguments that are largely unchanged since the Middle Ages.

In the wake of the Holocaust, and especially since the Second Vatican Council of the early 1960s, a concerted effort has been made to replace polemics with dialogue. Even in such discussions, however, there are subtle pressures that produce the sort of advocacy that is not altogether alien to polemics. Before Vatican II, Jules Isaac and other Jewish leaders asked Christian groups to reevaluate, on moral as well as on more narrowly theological grounds, the traditional ascription of ongoing guilt to Jews for their role in the crucifixion. This time Jewish arguments fell on receptive ears, and precisely such a reevaluation took place.

With the passage of time, however, some Christian participants in dialogue have begun to inquire about the possibilities of a Jewish reevaluation of the standing of Jesus and the role of Christianity. These inquiries are rooted in the awareness that twentieth-century Jewish scholars like Joseph Klausner, Claude Montefiore, David Flusser, and Pinchas Lapide have provided—with varying degrees of enthusiasm—a positive portrait of a fundamentally Jewish Jesus.

Moreover, Franz Rosenzweig spoke of Christianity as a manifestation of a divine covenant with the gentiles. Even Jewish ecumenists, however, are often wary of far-reaching revisions in their evaluation of Jesus, and it is unlikely that dialogue will produce a perception of Jesus as a quasi messiah or mitigate the historic Jewish distaste for the central dogmas of traditional Christianity.

Finally, a uniquely contemporary dimension has been injected into Jewish-Christian discussions by the establishment of the state of Israel. On the one hand, the establishment of Israel has undercut the old Christian argument based on the Jewish exile; on the other hand, it fits perfectly into some scenarios of the second coming of Jesus that are popular among Christian fundamentalists. In the context of dialogue, Jews have often attempted to explain the theological centrality of the Land of Israel in Judaism, and they have sometimes argued that Christian theology itself should lead to a recognition of the significance of the state of Israel in the divine plan. This delicate balance of politics and theology has produced both understanding and tension. It is but the most recent example of the effect of historical events on a relationship that reflects the unchanging disputes of two venerable traditions as well as the dynamic interplay of two communities acting and reacting in an ever changing world.

SEE ALSO Christianity; Jesus; Judaism; Paul the Apostle.

BIBLIOGRAPHY

There is no good survey of Jewish polemics from late antiquity to the present. A sketchy overview is provided in Hans Joachim Schoeps's *The Jewish-Christian Argument* (New York, 1963); and Morris Goldstein's *Jesus in the Jewish Tradition* (New York, 1950) surveys some Jewish discussions of Christianity through the Middle Ages. Frank Talmage's *Disputation and Dialogue: Readings in the Jewish-Christian Encounter* (New York, 1975) is a valuable collection of brief translated selections from the sources.

Judah Rosenthal provided a thorough bibliography of polemical works in his "Sifrut ha-vikkuaḥ ha-anṭi-Notsrit," *Areshet* 2 (1960): 130–179; 3 (1961): 433–439. The most comprehensive collection of such works remains J. D. Eisenstein's edited volume *Otsar vikkuḥim* (1928; reprint, New York, 1964), but the texts are unreliable and must always be checked against superior editions. For English translations of polemical texts, see Oliver S. Rankin's *Jewish Religious Polemic of Earlier and Later Centuries* (1956; reprint, New York, 1970); Hyam Maccoby's *Judaism on Trial: Jewish-Christian Disputations in the Middle Ages* (Rutherford, N.J., 1982); Yosef Kimḥi's *The Book of the Covenant,* translated by Frank Talmage (Toronto, 1972); and Yitsḥaq Troki's *Faith Strengthened,* translated by M. Mocatta (New York, 1970). See also my study, *The Jewish-Christian Debate in the High Middle Ages: A Critical Edition of the Nizzaḥon Vetus with an Introduction, Translation and Commentary* (Philadelphia, 1978); the introduction and commentary trace the major arguments through the thirteenth century. Other important studies of the medieval period include Daniel Lasker's *Jewish Philosophical Polemics against Christianity in the Middle Ages* (New York, 1977), Bernhard Blumenkranz's *Juifs et Chrétiens dans le monde occidental, 430–1096* (Paris, 1960), and Jacob Katz's *Exclusiveness and Tolerance* (New York, 1961). On *Toledot Yeshu,* see Samuel Krauss's *Das Leben Jesu nach jüdischen Quellen* (Berlin, 1902); on *Genesis* 49:10, Adolf Posnanski's *Schiloh: Ein Beitrag zur Geschichte der Messiaslehre* (Leipzig, 1904); on *Isaiah* 53, Adolf Neubauer and Samuel R. Driver's *The Fifty-Third Chapter of Isaiah According to the Jewish Interpreters,* 2 vols. (1876–1877; reprint, New York, 1969).

Jewish reactions to the Reformation are described in H. H. Ben-Sasson's *The Reformation in Contemporary Jewish Eyes* (Jerusalem, 1970). On the modern period, see Uriel Tal's *Christians and Jews in Germany in the Second Reich: Religion, Politics and Ideology, 1870–1914* (Ithaca, N.Y., 1975), Jacob Fleischmann's *Be'ayat ha-Natsrut ba-maḥshavah ha-Yehudit mi-Mendelssohn 'ad Rosenzweig* (Jerusalem, 1964), and A. Roy Eckardt's bibliography, "Recent Literature on Christian-Jewish Relations," *Journal of the American Academy of Religion* 49 (March 1981): 99–111.

New Sources

Abulafia, Anna Sapir, ed. *Religious Violence between Christians and Jews: Medieval Roots, Modern Perspectives.* Basingstoke and New York, 2002.

Aumann, Moshe. *Conflict and Connection: The Jewish-Christian-Israel Triangle.* Hewlett, N.Y., 2003.

Ben-Shalom, Ram. "Between Official and Private Dispute: The Case of Christian Spain and Provence in the Late Middle Ages." *AJS Review* 27 (2003): 23–71.

Braybrooke, Marcus. *Christian-Jewish Dialogue: The Next Steps.* [Concluding chapter by Tony Bayfield]. London, 2000.

Melnick, Ralph. *From Polemics to Apologetics: Jewish-Christian Rapprochement in 17th Century Amsterdam.* Assen, the Netherlands, 1981.

Nickelsburg, George W. E. *Ancient Judaism and Christian Origins: Diversity, Continuity, and Transformation.* Minneapolis, Minn., 2003.

Porter, Stanley E., and Brook W. R. Pearson, eds. *Christian-Jewish Relations through the Centuries.* Sheffield, U.K., 2000.

DAVID BERGER (1987)
Revised Bibliography

POLEMICS: MUSLIM-JEWISH POLEMICS

Down to the eighteenth century the majority of Jews lived in countries under Muslim rule, where they shared with Christians the status of "protected" minorities, tolerated on sufferance and subject at times and in certain areas to discrimination, ill will, abuse, and assault.

Arabic literature, the classical repository of theological lore in Islam, expresses and reflects the situation over centuries. While most of this lore is of Muslim origin, Jews and Christians have contributed to it upon occasion with Arabic writings added to their literary output in Hebrew and Syriac, respectively.

The vast Arabic literature that developed in the early centuries of Islam included works on religion, sectarianism, the treatment of the minorities, and so forth. Historians and travelers seeking to sketch the development of faiths, the rise of Islam, and its victorious march through countries and continents also threw light on the non-Muslims and their beliefs. Scholarly discussion concerning non-Muslims inevitably tended to indicate the miscreants' errors. Thus polemics appeared, and, as disputations took place, polemics gave rise to defensive apologetics.

MUSLIM POLEMICS. Indeed, Muslims knew from their own scripture that Islam is a continuation of earlier dispensations, and they were familiar with the Prophet's attitude toward their carriers—the Jews and Christians. According to the Qurʾān, the Jews (identified there as Yahūd or Banū Isrāʾīl, "Children of Israel") were an ancient people, descended from Abraham and later led out of Egypt by Moses. Favored by the Lord, who sent prophets to teach and guide them, they nonetheless became enmeshed in sin and disobedience, worshiping the golden calf, killing prophets, and rejecting Jesus, and were finally punished by destruction, exile, and dispersal. Further, the Qurʾān indicated that the Prophet had not only fought the pagan Arabs but also clashed with the Jews living in Arabia, especially those in Medina, and that the struggle had turned into a military clash when the Jews refused to accept the Prophet and his revelation.

These data were extended and embellished in the vast collections of traditions (*ḥadīth*) that arose in early Islam and were further enriched by an exegetical turn, as Qurʾanic allusions to biblical stories gave rise to commentaries on ancient Hebrew lore. Although the Jews had been instructed about the coming of Muḥammad, the Muslim commentators explained, they ignored these allusions or sought to interpret them away or to conceal them. They also fabricated stories among the *Isrāʾīlīyāt* (narratives set in the era of the Banū Isrāʾīl) that were apt to mislead true believers. Jewish converts to Islam also supplied information—albeit misleading—on Hebrew lore and the Jewish past. Kaʿb al-Aḥbār is the prototypical figure among them: a Jew from Yemen, he embraced Islam half a dozen years after the Prophet's death and was considered an expert on earlier scriptures. And presumably the anti-Jewish animus of the Near Eastern Christians percolated into Islamic circles following the Christians' conversion to Islam.

The earliest polemics, which can be traced to the eighth- and ninth-century disputations at the Abbasid court in Baghdad, are usually directed against both Jews and Christians. Only gradually does a polemical literature directed specifically against Jews emerge, beginning with special chapters on Jews and Judaism and with the writings of Jewish converts to Islam. Although such works are mentioned early on by Arab historians, the earliest surviving examples date only from the eleventh century.

Ibn Ḥazm. The earliest preserved substantial work of Islamic polemics against Jews and Judaism comes from the pen of Ibn Ḥazm (d. 1064), a leading figure of Islamic learning and Arabic literature in Spain. He dealt with the subject repeatedly and is the only major figure of Arabic letters to treat it.

Ibn Ḥazm apparently felt that his road to political success in the kingdom of Granada was blocked by the preeminence of the Jews, and in particular by their leader, Ibn Nagrela (known in the Jewish community as Shemu'el ha-Nagid, 993–1056), a successful administrator, diplomat, and military commander. Both Ibn Ḥazm and the Nagid wrote on theology, and both were poets, one writing in Arabic, the other in Hebrew. They met when they were in their early twenties, but the meeting was not conducive to mutual respect and appreciation.

In Ibn Ḥazm's major work, *Kitāb al-fiṣal wa-al-niḥal* (Book of groups and sects), a survey of theology, a section of nearly 130 pages is devoted to a critique of Jewish beliefs and texts. Passages from the Hebrew scriptures, quoted to reveal their deficiencies, are followed by counterparts from the Qurʾān, which are cited to demonstrate their excellence by comparison. Ibn Ḥazm displays a good knowledge of *Genesis*, but his knowledge of the rest of the Hebrew scriptures is weak, and he is unable to distinguish biblical data from later legends. It is possible that he used a list of suitable passages ("testimonies") culled for the purpose by others. He even cites a few items of Talmudic lore. He displays an interest in the origins of Hebrew words but here too falls prey to misinformation: quoting an informant, he explains, for example, that the name *Israel* was derived from *Asarʿel* ("he detained God," *Gn.* 32:25–31, where Jacob wrestles with divine beings and prevails), thus confusing the Hebrew roots *ʿsr* and *srh*.

In his view, the Hebrew scriptures are replete with contradictions, absurdities, anthropomorphisms, and objectionable and irrelevant matter. The Muslims should feel no reverence toward the scriptures of the Jews and Christians, he argues, and should reject these faulty, distorted remnants of the true scripture. Reverence is due only to the inimitable truth and beauty of the Qurʾān.

Ibn Ḥazm is particularly eager to point out discrepancies in the biblical text, especially where numbers are involved, as with varying statements on the length of the bondage in Egypt or the population of the Israelites during the wilderness period. Other contradictions he claims to find in the text include the report in *Exodus* 7:20–22 that after all the water in Egypt turned into blood, the native magicians repeated the deed: where, he asks, did they get the water to prove their skill? Likewise, citing *Exodus* 12:38, he asks where the Hebrews obtained the multitude of cattle in the desert, and further, if they had such cattle, why did they complain of lack of meat? Among the anthropomorphisms he cites are passages such as "The Lord is a man of war" (*Ex.* 15:3); "And they saw the God of Israel, and there was under his feet, as if it were a pavement of sapphire stone" (*Ex.* 24:10); and the Lord's various pronouncements in *Exodus* 33 where he "spoke unto Moses face to face. . . . And he said, 'You cannot see my face. . . . And I shall take away my hand and you shall see my back, but my face shall not be seen'" (vv. 11, 10, 22–23).

Unlike the Qurʾān, Ibn Ḥazm argues, the Hebrew scriptures are devoid of data on reward and punishment in the life to come. Yet the Qurʾān itself refers to biblical revelation, especially to that of Moses. How is this possible? Because, he claims, there was a true revelation of the divine word to Moses, but it was not preserved. The numerous civil strifes, wars, invasions, and defeats in ancient Israel destroyed not merely the Hebrew kingdoms but also their archives and with them, the scriptures, which went up in flames. There was no continuous tradition of learning. Indeed, there was merely one copy of the scriptures remaining in the hands of the priests, who knew only chapters, fractions of it. In Babylon, Ezra the priest concocted the Hebrew scriptures from remnants of the revelation as it was remembered by other priests and from his own additions.

Here Ezra is denounced as a master of deception lacking reason and conscience (as well as a knowledge of arithmetic). Yet, Ibn Ḥazm points out, it was Ezra who shaped the new religion during the Babylonian captivity by substituting the synagogue service for the ruined Temple of Solomon. Since the days of Moses, he says, *Deuteronomy* 32 (*Haʾazinu*, The Song of Moses) is the only chapter of the Hebrew scriptures that has been taught to the people, and even this chapter—which he quotes in full—is replete with passages that cannot be of divine origin, such as verses 20–22: "God is their father." Anyone who knows the Jews, continues our author, knows they are a filthy and witless rabble, repulsive, vile, perfidious, cowardly, despicable, mendacious. Hence Muslims should seek guidance about the children of Israel not from the Ezra-produced scripture but from the Qurʾān, which also includes data about the prophets (such as Hūd and Ṣāliḥ) who were unknown to the Jews.

Ibn Ḥazm maintains that the Jews reject abrogation of their scriptures and any suggestion of a post-Mosaic dispensation, to either Jesus or Muḥammad. For them the omniscient God's decree is immutable, and any change or caprice in divine will is not feasible. Without such a sudden change (*badāʾ*) in divine pleasure, however, a new dispensation would not be feasible and thus, they assert, would contradict divine omniscience. But this is wrong, Ibn Ḥazm counters. Precepts are commands to perform certain acts over a limited period, beyond which time they may turn into their opposites. Circumstances in space and time are known to God, and it is his pleasure to grant life, death, and resurrection, power, decline, restoration, virtue, and evil, belief and deviation. For the Jews, work is permissible on Friday, but prohibited on Saturday, only to become permissible again on Sunday.

Indeed, the Jews recognize that the law of Jacob differs from the law of Moses. Jacob married Leah and Rachel, who were sisters, yet the law of Moses (*Lv.* 18:18) proscribes such a marriage. The people of Gibeon escaped annihilation to become hewers of wood and drawers of water for the sanctuary after they fraudulently exacted a treaty from Joshua (*Jos.* 9). God's wrath was about to consume the Israelites, but Moses' fervent appeal made the Lord repent (*Ex.* 32:10–14). Abraham offered curd and milk and meat to the angels (*Gn.* 18), but this was not a kosher diet (as set forth in *Deuteronomy* 14:3–21 and elsewhere).

Ibn Ḥazm is quick to notice irregularities attested in the lineage of biblical figures and points with gusto to the extent of bastardization among them. The lineage of the patriarchs, prophets, and kings is sullied with incest and fornication: Abraham married Sarah, his sister; Lot was seduced by his daughters; Reuben had relations with Bilhah, his father's concubine; from Judah and his daughter-in-law Tamar sprang the line of David, Solomon, and the expected Messiah.

The few samples of postbiblical lore that he knew, possibly through the Karaites, horrified him as "old wives' tales": data for example, from the ancient treatise *Shiʿur qomah* on the measurement of the divine body; the Lord's grieving about the destruction of the Temple; reference to the angel Meṭaṭron as "the lesser Lord." He also recounts that, according to the Jews, Paul was sent to the disciples of Jesus in order to mislead them into the belief in Christ's divinity. Thus Ibn Ḥazm concludes that the Jews are liars and tricksters. This trait begins with Jacob filching Esau's birthright (*Gn.* 25:29–34) and Isaac's blessing (*Gn.* 27). Though I have seen many of them, he reports, I found only two who were devoted to truth.

Although he holds that the Hebrew scriptures are forgeries and harps on the necessity of rejecting them completely and relying instead on the Qurʾān, he cannot refrain from quoting some passages that seem to fit Muslim notions. Thus he accepts *Deuteronomy* 33:2 ("The Lord came from Sinai and rose from Seir unto them; he shined forth from Mount Paran") as an "annunciation" of the advent of Jesus (via Seir, in Edom, later identified with Christendom, while Paran was taken to be a reference to Mecca). Likewise he finds in *Deuteronomy* 18:18 ("I will raise them a prophet from among their brethren like unto thee") an annunciation of Muḥammad's ministry, since the Arabs, the progeny of Ismāʿīl (Ishmael), are the brethren among whom a prophet was to arise.

Ibn Ḥazm also wrote a treatise against a pamphlet alleged to have been composed by Ibn Nagrela (or his son) against the Qurʾān. Although he was unable to find a copy of this text and knew of it only from a Muslim author's refutations, he nonetheless proceeded to attack the Jewish leader and the rest of the infidels who had become so arrogant. In this treatise he also inveighs against the Muslim rulers, who enjoy their luxurious palaces and forget their duty to preserve strict Muslim domination over the infidels.

The impact of Ibn Ḥazm's polemical writings is unclear. He is not quoted by later writers, and it is possible that his adherence to the Ẓāhirī school of theology—a distinct minority within Sunnī Islam—may have limited the spread of his views. At least one brief Hebrew tract, Shelomoh ben Avraham Adret's thirteenth-century *Ma'amar 'al Yishma'e'l* (Treatise on Ishmael), reproduces and refutes passages of Ibn Ḥazm's argument on forgery, however. In any case, the full scope of the Muslim-Jewish controversy was given its first systematic exposition in Ibn Ḥazm's work: abrogation (*naskh*), distortion or forgery in the scripture (*taḥrīf*), anthropomorphism (*tajsīm*), the preserved annunciation of Islam and its prophet (*a'lām*).

Samau'al al-Maghribī. The pamphlet *Ifḥām al-Yahūd* (Silencing the Jews), written in 1163 in Marāgha (northern Iran), is the most important and influential work of Muslim polemics against Judaism. Its author was Samau'al al-Maghribī (c. 1125–1175), a Jew who converted to Islam and penned the pamphlet to mark his conversion. (It is not to be confused, however, with the Arabic pamphlet of Samuel Marrocanus, a convert to Christianity, which was translated into Latin and later into many Western languages.)

Samau'al's father was a minor Hebrew poet who had presumably fled Morocco during a wave of persecution, settled in Baghdad, and married a woman of a distinguished family. Samau'al, who studied under the eminent philosopher Abū al-Barakāt (also a Jewish convert to Islam), won fame as a mathematician and physician. His Jewish training seems to have been limited. In an autobiography added to his pamphlet in 1167, he claims that he was moved to convert by rational thinking along mathematical lines. Although he also describes visions of the prophets Samuel and Muḥammad, he still insists that purely logical arguments prevailed in his mind. A note of self-admiration is evident throughout:

> Then, after I had trained my mind on mathematical studies, especially geometry with its demonstrations, I asked myself about the differences in religious faiths and tenets. . . . I realized that reason is the supreme arbiter and that its rule should be established generally in . . . our world. . . . We realize that reason does not oblige us to accept ancestral tradition without examining it as to its soundness. . . . Mere reference to fathers and ancestry, however, is no proof. . . . I realize that the Jews had no proof . . . about . . . Moses other than the evidence of the chain of transmission, which is available for Jesus and Muḥammad just as it is for Moses . . . then all three are true prophets. . . . I have not seen Moses . . . nor have I witnessed his miracles, nor those of any other prophet. . . . A sensible person cannot believe one and disbelieve another of these prophets. . . . Rather, it is rationally incumbent either to believe all of them or to reject all of them. . . . As for disbelieving all, reason does not dictate that either. For we find that they all preached lofty morals, advocated the virtues and fought the vices, and regulated the world in a fashion beneficial to mankind.

In Samau'al's view, the record of the Jews in scientific advancement cannot compare with that of the Greeks and others; likewise, the literature of the Muslims is overwhelmingly superior.

The key issue of abrogation is demonstrated both logically and historically. Jewish legists, he says, offered discordant views on problems; how can they all be of divine origin? Indeed the law itself abounds in contradictions: in *Exodus*, for example, all the firstborn are consecrated to worship (13:2); in *Numbers*, only the Levites (8:18). As purification with the ashes of the red heifer (*Nm.* 19:11, 19:16, 19:17) is no longer available, he contends that the Jews must consider themselves impure. Prayers on exile, dispersion, and hope of restoration are clearly of late origin, yet they should not have been introduced at all in view of the injunction against adding to or diminishing from the divine word (*Dt.* 13:1).

An array of arguments is cited to prove that Jesus and Muḥammad were announced in the scriptures: *Deuteronomy* 18:15 announces a prophet from among their brethren; in *Genesis* 17:20, God promises to multiply Ishmael (here the letters of the Hebrew words for "exceedingly," *bi-m'od me'od*, numerically equal 92, which is the numerical value of the name *Muḥammad); Genesis* 21:21 deals with three revelations, the last in the abode of Ishmael, which is that of the Arabs.

The critique of the scripture follows. According to Samau'al, it perished long ago owing to the vicissitudes in the history of the Hebrews. King Saul (*1 Sm.* 22:16–20) massacred the line of Aaron. Centuries passed before Ezra, of the priestly Aaronids, reconstructed the scripture. As the priests begrudged authority to royalty, he added two stories derogatory to the lineage of David. One, that of the daughters of Lot (*Gn.* 19), establishes the origin of Moab and thus the illegitimacy of Ruth, the ancestor of the House of David, nay, of the expected messiah. The other story (*Gn.* 38) indicates that Boaz, husband of Ruth, was born of the union of Judah with Tamar.

Among other criticisms, Samau'al also charges that the law is oppressive and a burden (*iṣr*), as demonstrated by the dietary rules that separate Jews from non-Jews. Jews, he points out, call Muḥammad a fool and a raving madman (*meshugga'*, cf. *Hos.* 9:7) and also "unfit" (Heb., *pasul*, rhyming with *rasūl*, Arab., "messenger," a name for the Prophet as Messenger of God); likewise they refer to the Qur'ān as "dishonor" (*qalon*).

No doubt there is a similarity between the arguments of Ibn Ḥazm in the eleventh century and those of Samau'al in the twelfth. Here it is probable that both were reproducing older material concerning the scriptural passages and the theory that Ezra authored the Pentateuch (the hypothesis of Ezra's role in the history of the scripture goes back to late Hellenistic texts; see Edmund Stein's *Alttestamentliche Bibelkritik in der späthellenistischen Literatur*, Lwów, 1935).

Samau'al's tract in turn proved very influential as a quarry for Muslim authors over the centuries. His arguments reappear in *Al-ajwibah al-fākhirah* (The Perfect Replies), written by the Egyptian al-Qarāfī (d. 1285), and in works by Ibn Qayyim al-Jawzīyah (d. 1350). In copying Samauʿal's original pamphlet, which contained Hebrew passages in Hebrew characters followed by Arabic transliteration and translation, later scribes omitted the alien Hebrew characters. The tract was printed in Egypt in 1939 and again in the 1960s.

Al-Rāqilī. From somewhat different circumstances came Abū Zakarīyāʾ Yaḥyā al-Rāqilī's tract *Taʾyīd al-millah* (Support of the Faith), written in Huesca in 1360 and directed against Jews and Christians. Living in the Spanish kingdom of Aragon after the Christian reconquest, he expressed bitterness over the degradation of Islam, as Muslims fell from a position of domination to that of a tolerated minority, and especially over the treatment of Muslim peasants by Jewish officials and tax agents on behalf of the crown. Reading the biblical texts in translation, he "extracted from them passages and evidences with which to refute the Jews." God had chastised them, he observes, with permanent dispersion (*al-ghalūth al-dāʾim*) and humiliation. He mentions disputations and arguments (*al-munāẓarāt wa-al-iḥtijāj*) and hopes that God "may take us out of the country of polytheism to the lands of the Muslims."

The Hebrew scriptures, he says, show that the Jews were a rebellious, unfaithful, ungrateful, accursed breed. They transgressed against every one of the Ten Commandments. According to al-Rāqilī's historical reconstruction, Hagar, the mother of Ishmael, was Abraham's wife, not his concubine. She was not a mere slave but the daughter of an Egyptian prince, and in any case, even a slave could be a prophet, as with Joseph, who was Potiphar's slave. God ordered Abraham to sacrifice his son, then prevented the patriarch from doing so. This, al-Rāqilī concludes, is an evident case of abrogation. But even though the Jewish scriptures are not reliable, he cites *Isaiah* 21:7 ("a troop of asses, a troop of camels") as an annunciation of the prophethood of Jesus and Muḥammad, respectively.

Al-Rāqilī's pamphlet belongs to a lower level of disputation conducted between two oppressed communities under Christian domination. Also within this category of less sophisticated works, appealing more to the common Muslim reader, are two pamphlets by fourteenth-century Jewish converts to Islam. One came from the pen of Saʿīd ibn Ḥasan of Alexandria, who, in 1320, while living in the Great Mosque of Damascus, wrote an account of his conversion. Dangerously ill and expecting to die, he suddenly heard a voice urging him to read a surah of the Qurʾān. He complied and was miraculously saved. He became such a fervent believer that he turned against the Jewish and Christian unbelievers and in his tracts, which quote biblical texts, demonstrates no qualms about distortions and absurdities.

Such is also the case with ʿAbd al-Ḥaqq al-Islāmī from Ceuta, who wrote toward the end of the century. In addition to relying on *gimaṭriyyah,* the argument from the numerical value of names and words, he accused the Jews of fire worship, considered Ahab the transgressor (*1 Kgs.* 16–18) a righteous king, nay, a Muslim believer, and presented the Hebrew phrase "The gentile is like a dog" as an authentic text.

JEWISH APOLOGETICS. Jewish writings, in Arabic and in Hebrew, attempted to present a defense against Islamic attacks. They were apologetic replies to Muslim arguments and to an extent constituted an effort to reinterpret the Jewish cause in the light of the new intellectual atmosphere under Islam.

Maimonides. Although Moses Maimonides (Mosheh ben Maimon, d. 1204) warned against engaging in disputations with the Muslims, because they did not accept the Hebrew Bible as a revealed text and thus shared no common ground, his *Epistle to Yemen* is virtually a polemical treatise. Its purpose was to prepare the synagogue public to counter Muslim arguments: "Some hearts have gone astray . . . faith weakened," he tells his readers. "Ours is the true and authentic divine religion revealed to us through Moses. . . . In assaults upon us some use brute force; others, controversy. Christianity and Islam combine the two methods."

The Muslim polemicists, he continues, claim to have found Muḥammad's name and country in Hebrew scriptures (*Gn.* 17:20; *Dt.* 33:2, 18:15). Jewish converts to Islam (presumably Samauʿal) quoting these verses cannot really believe in them; their true purpose is to win favor in the eyes of the gentiles. Muslims, unable to indicate a single verse, accuse the Jews of having altered or concealed the text. In fact, he points out, the scriptures had been translated into Greek, Aramaic, and Latin centuries before Muḥammad appeared.

> On account of . . . our sins God has hurled us into the midst of this people, the Arabs, who have persecuted us severely and passed baneful and discriminatory legislation against us. . . . Never did a nation molest, degrade, debase, and hate us as much as they. . . . No matter how much we suffer and elect to remain at peace with them, they stir up strife and sedition, as David predicted (*Ps.* 120:7): "I am all peace, but when I speak, they are for war."

He concludes with a warning about the danger involved in reading his epistle, but he hopes that "the secret of the Lord may be entrusted to those who fear him (*Ps.* 23:14)."

Ibn Kammūnah. In a class by itself stands *Tanqīḥ al-abḥāth fī al-milal al-thalāth* (Critical Inquiry into the Three Faiths), written in Baghdad in 1280 by Saʿd ibn Manṣūr ibn Kammūnah. With the caliphate under Mongol rule, Islam could no longer be regarded as the faith of the ruler but remained the predominant faith of the masses. A review of Ibn Kammūnah's book in a sermon before a Friday mosque audience produced an angry mob assault, and the author had to be carried out of town hidden in a trunk.

The work begins with a brief discussion of religion in general, followed by chapters on the three monotheistic faiths. Two-thirds of the book is devoted to Islam and is based on Muslim texts; it is written in an unusually dispassionate spirit. Nonetheless, while Islam and its prophet receive a fair treatment, the cumulative impression is not favorable.

The chapter on Judaism contains a brief survey of biblical data and Jewish beliefs, followed by seven objections culled from Samauʿal al-Maghribī. These are rebutted in turn with arguments reflecting the views of Yehudah ha-Levi and Maimonides.

Ibn Kammūnah points out that communities may live side by side for centuries and yet know each other only slightly:

> But the contact of Muslims with Jews does not necessitate a Muslim inquiry into what the Jews assert, especially since the Jews are prevented from declaring their creed, and their [canonical] books are in a tongue the Muslims do not understand. The contact of a minority with a majority affects the majority and the minority differently. Thus, when a linguistic minority is in contact with a linguistic majority, the minority learns the language of the majority while the majority does not learn the language of the minority or, at best, learns it much later. Moreover, despite numerous contacts of the bulk of the Jews with the Muslims, many Jews still do not know the basic Islamic tenets known by the rank-and-file Muslims, let alone the elite. It is even more natural that a similar situation should obtain on the Muslim side, or, at the very least, that both sides should be equal [in mutual ignorance].

Moreover, the Muslims are split into various factions anathemizing one another. He lists the Christians' internal dissensions and remarks:

> I did not find most of these retorts in discussions by Christians; I supplied these retorts on behalf of the Christians, and in supplementation of the investigation into their belief.

This evoked the admiration of a Christian opponent.

In discussing the Muslims' factions and their respective claims, he notes:

> There is room for speculation in this matter. Namely, many a person will, for worldly goals and motives, do things for which, as he most assuredly knows, the founder of his respective religion has threatened severe punishment in the hereafter. This belief will not prevent a man from perpetrating that forbidden evil. Such is the case of the adulterer, wine-imbiber, and slanderer. In the quest for victory over opponents, human nature will urge the fabrication of reports favoring one's religion. Ignoring the prohibition against lying, a man will sometimes fabricate such a report in the [mistaken] belief that he will merit reward therefor. It may also be fabricated by one who joined a faith opportunistically—without inner conviction but rather in the quest for success, like many who nowadays join the faith of Islam in order to prevail over rivals, although they are not believers by conviction. If your assertion were true, no Muslim would ever have fabricated a false tradition; the contrary, however, is the case.

Summarizing the arguments for Muḥammad's prophethood, he contends that they remain unproven and remarks:

> That is why, to this day, we never see anyone converting to Islam unless in terror, or in quest of power, or to avoid heavy taxation, or to escape humiliation, or if taken prisoner, or because of infatuation with a Muslim woman, or for some similar reason. Nor do we see a respected, wealthy, and pious non-Muslim well versed in both his faith and that of Islam, going over to the Islamic faith without some of the aforementioned or similar motives.

Likewise, he rejects the argument that victory and power are proof of divine support:

> How, since the dominion of idol-worshipers and fire-worshipers continued for thousands of years in numberless countries throughout the world, can a multitude of followers be proof of a claim? I found they had no rebuttal to these arguments beyond the claim that the Islamic faith obviously excels over other faiths, and that it combines a maximum quantity and quality of perfection not attained by any other known faith. But he who, in rancor, makes this claim will never be able to present proof of it.

DECLINE OF THE GENRE. After 1400, Muslim polemics were largely reiterations of earlier arguments presented in insignificant pamphlets. One noteworthy exception is a disputation conducted in 1796 by a Persian scholar, Sayyid Muḥammad Mahdī Ṭabāṭabāʾī; known through an account in Arabic, this event appears to have been characterized by uncommon mildness and magnanimity. Within the Ottoman empire, probably from Christian circles, it was charged from time to time that the Jews used (Christian) blood to bake the unleavened bread for Passover. This "blood libel" emerged in Damascus in 1840 and resurfaced repeatedly thereafter.

In the nineteenth century, anti-Jewish moods and arguments began to penetrate the Muslim world from Western sources, at first especially through French anti-Semitism. In the twentieth century, the conflict in Palestine and the rise of Zionism were bound to rekindle the embers of the medieval controversy as a religious appendage to the conflict. But the literature of the religious aspect has proven extremely poor in content, confined to reiteration of arguments from the eleventh and twelfth centuries: passages from the Qurʾān and the traditions, a flood of epithets characterizing the Jews as eternally vicious fiends against the Muslims, against Muslims and Christians, and indeed, against all humanity, as enemies ever plotting against what is human and good, for the sake of world domination by Jewry and Israel.

All in all, Islamic polemics directed against Jews are an arid area of insubstantial writing, of minor interest to the Muslims themselves. For their part, the Jews kept a low profile and preferred not to retort. But many allusions to the Muslim arguments can be found in medieval prayers, as well as in exegetical and theological works.

BIBLIOGRAPHY

The classic compendium on Arabic-language polemics among Muslims, Christians, and Jews is Moritz Steinschneider's *Polemische und apologetische Literatur in arabischer Sprache, zwischen Muslimen, Christen und Juden* (1877; reprint, Hildesheim, 1965). Other early studies include several by Ignácz Goldziher in his *Gesammelte Schriften*, 3 vols. (Hildesheim, 1967–1970), and Martin Schreiner's "Zur Geschichte der Polemik zwischen Juden und Muhammedanern," *Zeitschrift der Deutschen Morgenländischen Gesellschaft* 42 (1888): 591–675.

Salo W. Baron addresses the subject, with extensive bibliography, in *A Social and Religious History of the Jews*, 2d ed., rev. & enl., vol. 5 (New York, 1957), pp. 82–108. I have also written a survey, "The Medieval Polemics between Islam and Judaism," in *Religion in a Religious Age*, edited by S. D. Goitein (Cambridge, Mass., 1974).

For specialized studies, see Jacob Mann's "An Early Theologico-Polemical Work," *Hebrew Union College Annual* 13/14 (1937–1938): 411–459; Emilio García Gomez's "Polémica religiosa entre Ibn Ḥazm e Ibn al-Nagrila," *Al-Andalus* 4 (1936): 1–28; Miguel Asín Palacios's "Un tratado morisco de polémica contra los Judios," in *Mélanges Hartwig Derenbourg* (Paris, 1909), pp. 343–366, reprinted in his *Obras escogidas*, vols. 2–3, *De historia y filogogia arabe* (Madrid, 1948); Joseph Perles's *R. Salomo ben Abraham ben Adereth: Sein Leben und seine Schriften* (Breslau, 1863); and ʿAfīf ʿAbd al-Fattāḥ Ṭabbārah's *Al-Yahūd fī al-Qurʾān* (Beirut, 1966). An Israeli view of modern developments is Yehoshafat Harkabi's *Arab Attitudes to Israel*, translated by Misha Louvish (New York, 1972).

A number of the original sources are also available in translation. Among the Muslim writers, Ibn Ḥazm's *Kitāb al-fiṣal wa-al-niḥal*, 5 vols. in 2 (1903; reprint, Baghdad, 1964), has been translated by Miguel Asín Palacios in volume 2 of his *Abenházam de Córdoba* (Madrid, 1927), and I have edited and translated Samauʿal al-Maghribī's *Ifḥām al-Yahūd: Silencing the Jews* (New York, 1964). The early formulations of the debate from the Jewish perspective are reflected in the third treatise of Sa'adyah Gaon's *The Book of Beliefs and Opinions*, translated by Samuel Rosenblatt (New Haven, 1948). Other Jewish texts include Moses Maimonides's *Epistle to Yemen*, edited by Abraham S. Halkin and translated by Boaz Cohen (New York, 1952), and *Ibn Kammūna's Examination of the Three Faiths: A Thirteenth Century Essay in the Comparative Study of Religion* (Berkeley, 1971), which I have edited and translated.

Moshe Perlmann (1987)

POLEMICS: CHRISTIAN-MUSLIM POLEMICS

The Qurʾān itself determines the polemic area between Muslims and Christians, because it states the terms and sets the limits of Christian error. The issues it defines have been disputed ever since: God is not three; Jesus is not the Son of God; he was not crucified (cf. surah 4:157, 171), and the Bible has been falsified and misinterpreted. This "corruption" (*taḥrīf*) includes suppressing forecasts of the Prophet. Christians have similarly sought to discredit the Qurʾān, but they have been under no comparable restraint in choosing their themes, and they have often attacked the reputation of the Prophet in order to argue that his revelation was contrived and fictitious.

Muslim Polemic. Christians long remained a majority under Muslim rule, but they began to attack Islam as soon as they realized that it had come to stay; however, it is convenient here to consider first the Muslim attack on *taḥrīf.* One of the first Muslims to argue that Christians had misunderstood rather than falsified their scriptures was a Zaydi Shīʿī from the Yemen, al-Qāsim ibn Ibrāhīm (d. AH 246/860 CE). Until the severe reaction against the colonialism of the last century, most Muslim polemic was purely doctrinal. In his *Book of Religion and Empire*, ʿAlī ibn Sahl al-Ṭabarī (ninth century), a former Nestorian, aims, perhaps to justify his conversion, to show that the Christian scriptures foretell Muḥammad and enjoin Islam, and his *Answer to Christians*, concerned with Christology, is again based on his knowledge of Christian sources. Supposedly earlier (c. 820) is the *Apology* of al-Hāshimī, but we know it in conjunction with its refutation by the pseudonymous ʿAbd al-Masīḥ ibn Isḥāq al-Kindī, attributed to Yaḥyā ibn ʿAdī (d. 974), and it is likely to be at most a revised and Christian-edited Muslim argument. Although it abuses Christianity, attacks the doctrine of the Trinity, despises the Cross, and deprecates Christian fasting, it plays into the hands of the refuter and has a contrived air. More typical is the writing of al-Jāḥiẓ (d. 869), who is aware of arguments actually used by Christians (e.g., that the Qurʾān misrepresents their beliefs), but his knowledge is superficial, and he is much put out by the existence of different Christian orthodoxies.

The Muslim critique of Christianity increased rapidly in knowledge and sophistication. The attack by Abū ʿĪsā al-Warrāq on the contradictions inherent in orthodox Christology seems to have made a considerable impact and was refuted at length by Yaḥyā ibn ʿAdī. Ibn Ḥazm (d. 1064) understands *taḥrīf* in the literal sense and devotes most of his *Discernment of the Confessions and Sects* to scriptural dispute and to the defects of the Gospels and other books of the Bible. Al-Ghazālī (d. 1111), in his *Excellent Refutation of the Divinity of Jesus Christ*, uses Christian scripture (known, says his Christian editor, from Muslim sources) to criticize in turn the christological positions of the Chalcedonian, non-Chalcedonian, and Nestorian churches. Muslims were now at grips with Christian apologists. Shihāb al-Dīn al-Qarāfī (d. 1285), answering the brief *Letter to a Muslim* by Paul (al-Rāhib, i.e., the Monk) of Antioch, Melkite bishop of Sidon (fl. 1160), shows a sound knowledge of Christian scripture and discusses such varied doctrines as the Eucharist and Qurʾanic abrogation (*nāsikh, mansūkh*). Ibn Taymīyah (d. 1328) also answered Paul, as a courteous address to the king of Cyprus, contrasting the Qurʾān and the Bible in authenticity and expounding long arguments against the Trinity. These disputes are quite inconclusive on both sides.

Toward the end of the European Middle Ages we begin to find Western writers converted from Christianity in the course of the Ottoman advance. ʿAbd Allāh al-Turjumān (early fourteenth century), a former Franciscan, discussed the authenticity of the holy books again in his *Intelligent Man's*

Gift in Reply to Christians. Murād Bay Turjumān, a Hungarian serving at the Porte, wrote a defense of Islam in Turkish and Latin (1556) and praises of the Prophet in Turkish, Latin, and Hungarian; he writes devotionally, often using the terminology of Western religious philosophy. The forged *Gospel of Barnabas,* in an unexplained sixteenth-century Italian manuscript, an *evangelium Muhammadanum* intended to accord with the Qurʾanic Jesus, has been conjectured to have a Morisco or convert background.

CHRISTIAN POLEMIC. Early polemic is at its best in the dialogue, notably that of the catholicos Timotheos I with the caliph al-Mahdī in about 781 and that of Timotheos's coreligionist Ilyās of Nisibis with the vizier Abū al-Qāsim al-Maghribī in 1026. These Nestorians naturally exploited a Christology that was at least superficially more understandable to Muslims. Such dialogue may not always have taken place as recorded, or even at all, but their conciliatory tone offers a Christian apologetic intended to be inoffensive to a Muslim audience. Timotheos's presentation of the Prophet as "in the way of the prophets" is effective, without conceding any Christian essential.

This was not the usual pattern, even in the form of dialogue. Muslim polemic was often contemptuous, but it was never as virulent as Christian abuse of Islam and the Prophet, and much matter that was largely ridiculous or irrelevant, and always offensive, cannot have been used to impress Muslims, unless imposed by force in regions reconquered by Christians. It may be assumed that polemic develops out of widespread previous discussion, and that much remains at a low level of oral culture. Even in intellectual criticism of the Qurʾanic text, writers forced it to mean what they chose, including, in some Byzantine cases, the worship of Aphrodite. The Byzantine tradition includes authors writing in Greek from within Islam or from outside, among them John of Damascus (d. 749), Theodore Abū Qurrah (eighth-ninth century), George Hamartolus ("the Monk"), Nicetas of Byzantium (both ninth century), and the pseudonymous author of the *Letter to the Emir of Damascus* (c. 920–940). Nicetas is hypercritical in his treatment of the Qurʾanic text; all these tend to attack the Prophet, especially his wars and his marriage to Zaynab bint Jaḥsh, the influence on him of a suppositious Arian adviser, and the doctrine of a material Paradise. The pseudo- Kindī (mentioned above), writing in Arabic, is the most consistently unscrupulous in distorting every episode of the Prophet's life as self-indulgence (mostly sexual) and aggression (banditry, assassination). He deliberately ignored the sense of the Prophet's holiness in the sources he must have used, and he supported the gratuitous notion that the Prophet expected the resurrection or ascension of his dead body.

These themes had already entered the West by the middle of the ninth century. The miniature polemic found in Pamplona by Eulogius of Cordova (d. 859), archbishop elect of Toledo, and encapsulated in his *Liber apologeticus martyrum,* contains nearly all the elements used by al-Kindī and by later Western polemicists: the Prophet is accused of aggression and libertinism; the Qurʾān is ridiculed; much is made of the disappointed resurrection; the Arabs of the Hejaz are described as brutish. Eulogius was the pupil of the abbot Speraindeo, who had written a short polemic, now lost, in which he attacked the Qurʾanic Paradise as a brothel (*lupanar*), but perhaps Eulogius derived from him his fairer knowledge of the Qurʾanic theology of Jesus. Eulogius's friend and fellow student Alvarus attacked Islam along the same general lines in almost hysterical rhetoric based on Old Testament parallels.

Except for this use of the Old Testament, all these attacks were renewed at the Spanish Reconquest. Most medieval polemic derived from Spanish sources, supplemented, but not extensively, from the literature of the Latin states in the East. Peter of Alfonso contributed Jewish folklore to the polemic pool, but the next important step was taken when Peter the Venerable, abbot of Cluny, visited Spain from 1142 to 1143 and commissioned translations from the Arabic, including a version of the Qurʾān (little better than a paraphrase) and one of the pseudo-Kindī. This Qurʾān circulated widely in manuscript until it was printed in the sixteenth century. Al-Kindī reinforced the libels on the Prophet with circumstantial detail of which the West had no other knowledge, and his work was circulated widely in the abbreviated form that appears in Vincent de Beauvais's encyclopedic *Speculum historiale.* Generally, the main polemic heads were *luxuriosus* (voluptuous) and *bellicosus* (aggressive), but Abbot Peter's own polemic, apparently never translated into Arabic, is consciously accommodating (on the information available to him) and much concerned with the authentication of scripture. The invalidation of the Qurʾān is a main theme of the mysterious *Contrarietas elpholica,* which Mark of Toledo translated early in the thirteenth century from an unknown Arabic original. He also made a much better translation of the Qurʾān, but it was generally ignored.

The Dominican Ricoldo da Monte Croce (c. 1243–1320) traveled to Baghdad (he was there about 1291), but the discussions he claims to have had with amiable Muslim divines left no mark on his polemic, derived from the *Contrarietas* and other inherited material. He attacks the Qurʾān as confused and obscure in ways equally applicable to the prophetic books of the Old Testament. The *Quadruplex reprobatio,* perhaps by another Dominican, Ramón Martí (c. 1220–1285), shows a detailed knowledge of genuine sources, such as al-Bukhārī and Muslim ibn al-Hajjāj, which he must have combed to find instances of Islamic jurisprudence objectionable to Christians as "contrary to reason" or "contrary to the public good," while ignoring the rest. Ramón Lull (1235–1315), "proving" the Trinity by "compelling reasons" in a number of works, had little impact, however. Peter Paschasius, a Mercedarian (c. 1227–1300), used authentic knowledge from the life of the Prophet by Ibn Isḥāq (d. 767) in a forlorn attempt to justify the more absurd of the Christian libels on the Prophet then circulating.

These, many of them originating in the East, enjoyed a great vogue, not only in two Latin poems and a French paraphrase but also in many fragments and in chronicles, annals, and various occasional works: an assortment of recurring legends of how a fraudulent holy book was "revealed" by a pigeon or a calf, of how Muḥammad was the dupe of a renegade Christian monk, or was even himself a frustrated cardinal. The *chansons de geste* describe a pantheon of Saracen gods, but it is doubtful if they were intended as more than a joke.

Thomas Aquinas (c. 1225–1274) advised against polemic that could not be based on shared premises. Nicolas of Cusa (1400–1464), although his polemic method shows no real advance, seems to be sincerely seeking conciliation in his *De pace fidei.* Gradually the refinement of scholarly method eliminated the worst absurdities. The greatest of the seventeenth-century Qurʾanic specialists, Ludovico Maracci (1612–1700), was scrupulously exact, but rigidly critical on traditional lines; his English imitator, George Sale (c. 1697–1736), was more sympathetic, although he is regarded by Muslims today as anti-Islamic. The old polemic lines were merely re-oriented toward the general critique of religion by the Enlightenment (e.g., Bayle's *Dictionnaire,* 1696–1697, s. v. *Mahomet*; Boulainvilliers's *Vie de Mahomed,* 1730; Gibbon; Voltaire).

The Modern Period. Polemic revived in the nineteenth century but was profoundly modified on both sides by the colonial experience. Orientalists and missionaries alike considered themselves the intellectual and social superiors of nations ruled by Europeans. Improved historical methods introduced a new precision without necessarily changing old prejudice. Protestant missions, from the polemicist Carl Pfander (1803–1865) to a culmination in the World Missionary Conference held in Edinburgh in 1910, never escaped intellectually from the medieval polemic, but they added some contemporary social criticism, especially of the status of women in Islam. On the Catholic side we may compare Cardinal Lavigerie (1825–1892), archbishop of Algiers, and his alliance with the *mission civilisatrice* of France. Political subordination forced Muslims to take the defensive.

A nineteenth-century *aggiornamento* led by Sayyid Ahmad Khan (1817–1898), Jamāl al-Dīn al-Afghānī (1838–1897), and Muḥammad ʿAbduh (1849–1905) was followed by a series of apologists rather than polemicists, modernists influenced in different degrees by Western Christian, and post-Christian attitudes; among these were Muhammad Iqbal (1876–1938), Ṭāhā Ḥusayn (1889–1973), Salāh al-Dīn Khudā Bakhsh (1877–1931), and Kāmal Ḥusayn (1901–1977). The use by ʿAbbās Maḥmūd al-ʿAqqād (1889–1964) of the historical techniques of the day to refute Western Orientalism has been very influential; he respected Christ as prophet, which Tawīq Ṣidqī (1881–1920), in violent reaction against the missionaries, did not. Widely read by an English-language public, Ameer Alī (1849–1928) skillfully reversed the Christian sociohistorical attack on Islam, notably in his *Spirit of Islam* (1891) and his *Short History of the Saracens* (1899).

The English annotations to editions of the Qurʾān by Mawlānā Muḥammad ʿAlī (Aḥmadī version, 1917) and by ʿAlī Yūsuf ʿAlī (Sunnī version, 1946) put forward arguments unfamiliar to Western readers; in a general way, Muslims felt that contemporary biblical criticism supported the accusation of *taḥrīf,* though Sayyid Ahmad Khan had minimized this. The Muslim Brotherhood saw itself as simply defending Islamic civilization. Rejected by most Muslim opinion at the time, ʿAbd al-ʿAzīz Jawīsh (1876–1929) attacked Coptic Christianity as colonialist, in his paper *Al-liwā,* but the militant Islam of the later twentieth century, preoccupied with the struggle against the moderates, has yet to produce major polemic against post-Christian neocolonialists; it may be expected, when it comes, to have large social content. The *jamāʿāt* (fundamentalist groups) already hark back to Ibn Taymīyah. On the Christian side, some fanatics remain, but the tendency among Western Christians (e.g., Louis Massignon, 1883–1962, and Kenneth Cragg, b. 1913) is to shake free of inherited bias.

See Also Modernism, article on Islamic Modernism.

Bibliography

For a conspectus of much of the field, Georges C. Anawati's "Polémique, apologie et dialogue islamo-chrétiens," *Euntes Docete* 22 (1969): 380–392, is invaluable, but it is short and does not cover all. For medieval Islamic polemic, see Erdmann Fritsch's *Islam und Christentum im Mittelalter* (Breslau, 1930). A short, useful account of Byzantine polemic is Alain Ducellier's *Le miroir de l'Islam: Musulmans et chrétiens d'Orient au Moyen Age, septième-onzième siècles* (Paris, 1971). For Arabic polemic, the writings of Armand Abel are crucial: *L'apologie d'al-Kindi et sa place dans la polémique islamo-chrétienne* "L'oriente christiano nella storia della civiltà," no. 62 (Rome, 1964), and many other monographs. For medieval Christian polemic, see Richard W. Southern's *Western Views of Islam in the Middle Ages* (Cambridge, Mass., 1962) and my own *Islam and the West: The Making of an Image,* 2d ed. (Edinburgh, 1980). For modern Christian polemic, Youakim Moubarac's *Recherches sur la pensée chrétienne de l'Islam: Dans les temps modernes et à l'époque contemporaine* (Beirut, 1977) spreads a fine net widely. For academic tendencies, see Jacques Waardenburg's *L'Islam dans le miroir de l'Occident,* 3d ed. (Paris, 1962), which studies five major scholars. There is no general survey of modern Muslim polemic against Christianity, but for India, see Aziz Ahmed's *Islamic Modernisation in India and Pakistan,* 1857–1964 (London, 1967).

Norman Daniel (1987)

POLITICAL THEOLOGY is one in a series of attempts made by Roman Catholic and Protestant theologians since the 1960s to come to grips with the foundations of Christianity in light of the twentieth-century crisis of culture. After World War I, theology had reached a kind of equilibrium wherein the Protestants were constellated about the three giants, Karl Barth (1886–1968), Rudolf Bultmann

(1884–1976), and Paul Tillich (1886–1965), and the Catholics were still operating under the auspices of the scholasticism evoked by Pope Leo XIII in 1879, when he called for a renewal of Thomism. By the close of the Second Vatican Council (1962–1965), however, these liberal and neoorthodox solutions to the mediation between Christianity and modern cultures had suddenly become irretrievably passé, for it was widely felt that none of the dominant theologies, estimable as they might be, had really come to terms with the crisis of modern culture in ways that were sufficiently profound or adequately differentiated.

These deficiencies were registered within the mainly academic context of European and North American theology through the increasing influence of the nineteenth-century "masters of suspicion," Karl Marx (1818–1883) and Friedrich Nietzsche (1844–1900). Nietzsche's critique of modernity had probed the enervating effects upon life in the West caused by the invasion of other cultures and the various forms of reflection upon culture by historical consciousness in terms of nihilism and the death of God. In his unforgettable image of the "last man," Nietzsche had limned the outcome of the liberal democratic and socialist solutions to the political problem. This radical crisis of meaning and value was explored during the mid-1960s in a variety of Christian theologies: the God-is-dead theologies of Thomas Altizer, Gabriel Vahanian, and Paul van Buren; the universal-historical theology of Wolfhart Pannenberg; the post-Bultmann hermeneutical theologies of Gerhard Ebeling, Ernst Fuchs, and Heinrich Ott; and the post-Heidegger theology of Karl Rahner. Philosopher Hans-Georg Gadamer, whose *Truth and Method* became required reading for theologians in the 1960s and 1970s, resumed the meditation of Martin Heidegger (1889–1976) upon the crisis indicated by Nietzsche and formulated the issue as follows: Since all normative traditions have been rendered radically questionable, hermeneutics (the auxiliary science of interpretation) has become a universal issue. However, the challenge of hermeneutics to theology is usually diffused in one of two ways. In academic theology hermeneutics is trimmed down to conventional scholarly dimensions, whereafter theology is subjected to subdisciplines that divide up the data on Christian religion for ever more minute and critical study. Alternatively, hermeneutics may be subsumed within a transcendental-metaphysical reflection (as in Rahner) or a wholly ontological reflection (as in process theology). These responses to the issue of a universal hermeneutic as formulated by Gadamer—fragmenting on the one hand, and totalizing on the other—bore the earmarks of that sort of interpretation that Marx, in his famous eleventh thesis on Feuerbach, said needed to be supplanted by practice. It became a real question whether theology was anything more than either a species of intellectual history or an academically domesticated speculation without any practical bearing or importance.

During the 1960s and 1970s this question became inescapable. At the same time a common awareness was starting to emerge of the spiritual impoverishment arising from what were cynically labeled state-controlled monopolies in the East and monopoly-controlled states in the West. In the developing nations, dissatisfaction spread at the popular, grassroots level in opposition to the dependence engendered by colonialist and imperialist policies of advanced industrial societies. In brief, the stage was set for theology to shift from hermeneutical methods of mediating Christianity with contemporary cultures to new approaches known as political or liberation theologies.

By 1970 it was already manifest that there were two distinct originating points for political theology: from within an academic context in advanced industrial societies, and from what have come to be called "basic communities" (from the Spanish *comunidades de base*) in developing nations. It is clear that both styles of theology are seeking to come to terms with the universal hermeneutic problem as portrayed by Nietzsche, Heidegger, Gadamer, and Paul Ricoeur. But it is no less evident that they mean to follow Marx's imperative of changing, rather than merely interpreting, history.

The leading exponents of political theology in Europe, the German Catholic J.-B. Metz and the German Protestant Jürgen Moltmann, might justly be characterized as asserting that interpretation of God is a practical and political issue. There is no split between change and interpretation: Human and even revolutionary change is at root interpretative; and, especially when it comes to the reality of God, interpretation is primarily a matter of practical reorientation (conversion) and concrete action (transformation of individual and collective life). Moltmann at first depended upon Ernst Bloch's philosophy of hope but later moved on, using motifs from the critical theory developed by the Frankfurt School to reinterpret Luther's theology of the cross in terms of its revolutionary social implications. Metz, ever a disciple of Rahner, was challenged by the experience of the Holocaust and by the writings of the enigmatic Jewish-Marxist satellite of the Frankfurt School, Walter Benjamin (1892–1940), to reformulate Rahner's theological anthropology in terms of less idealist and more concrete notions such as "dangerous memory," "religion as interruption," and "narrative theology." Both Metz and Moltmann have used the "dialectic of enlightenment" (that is, the secularist thesis that the progress achieved by modern science and technology and by the bourgeois and communist revolutions has been perverted by the dominance of instrumental reason and the "iron cage" of bureaucracy) as it was formulated by Max Horkheimer, Theodor W. Adorno, and Georg Lukács. Metz and Moltmann transpose that dialectic of progress and decline into the tension now being lived out between the pole of liberal democratic and Marxist "ideologies of winners" and the opposite pole of redemption with the radical evangelical challenge to solidarity with history's outcasts and victims.

Liberation theologies emanate less from the academic superstructure than from basic communities at the popular level. They reach public discourse in the writings of teachers like Gustavo Gutiérrez (Peru), Juan Segundo (Uruguay), José Miguez-Bonino (Argentina), Jon Sobrino (El Salvador), Leonardo and Clodovis Boff and Rubem Alves (Brazil), and so on. But they are also published in documents emanating from bishops' conferences as well as in the writings and political activity typified by the Nicaraguan priest-poet-revolutionary Ernesto Cardenal. In liberation theology the experiences of political and social oppression and of massive poverty have provoked a reading of the Bible and a celebration of ecclesial sacraments that are immediately political in the sense of being directly linked to the issue of emancipation from "structural" sin. Bourgeois social, political, and economic theories do not adequately explain the institutionalized schemes of recurrence that define the Latin American experience of oppression. Thus, liberation theology debunks bourgeois notions of "development" in favor of hypotheses like "dependency" and "national security state" in which Lenin's ideas about imperialism are applied anew. This is just one instance of the theology of liberation's penchant to have recourse to Marxism (especially the humanist strands) and Leninist or Maoist strategies in order to diagnose and remedy structural sin. This approach places liberation theologians under a double constraint since, on the one hand, genuine evangelical experience of God and faith in Jesus Christ Liberator is for them the wellspring and motive for social critique and action in a way that neither Marx nor Lenin could envisage, and, on the other hand, the theoretical weaknesses in Marxist analysis and practice sometimes threaten liberation theology with collapse back into the posture of the secularist dialectic of enlightenment. Added to this, liberal democratic and orthodox Christian misunderstanding and opposition perhaps unwittingly force the practitioners of liberation theology into increasing partisanship with secularist Marxist-Leninists.

Both European political theology and Latin American liberation theology have the Marxist orientation toward overcoming specifically bourgeois biases. In other advanced industrial countries like the United States and Canada, the Marxist analysis of structural sin in terms of class yields to three other emphases: racism (black and other ethnic theologies), sexism (feminist theologies), and issues of ecology. Like the liberation theologies of Latin America, each of these orientations struggles with the ambivalence between its roots in Christian religious experience and the terms of power and legitimacy as these terms were first formulated by secularist Enlightenment thinkers. Miscomprehension and unfavorable criticism force them, too, into stances ever more indistinguishable from their secularist counterparts. But then, reactions to such extremes among their cohorts have also led to recoveries and discoveries of Christian meanings and values.

Another increasingly prominent aspect of political theology is being explored by Ernest Fortin and James V. Schall, students of political philosopher Leo Strauss (1899–1973). Strauss took up the hermeneutic challenge laid down by Heidegger only to return to premodern authors (Xenophon, Plato, Maimonides, al-Fārābī) as an alternative to the mediations of the social sciences in the mold of Marx or Max Weber (1864–1920). Straussians bring out the tension between Christianity and liberal and socialist democracies. They tend to render Christianity as utterly apolitical; as a result, whereas liberation theology tends to flatten out into Marxism, Straussian political theory is perhaps too content with Platonic or Aristotelian reasons for espousing liberal democracy at the cost of solidarity with the poor.

The work of political scientist Eric Voegelin (1901–1985), as demonstrated by his multivolume *Order and History* (1956–), makes the tension of human existence—lived out in "the in-between" ("metaxy") as expressed paradigmatically in noetic and pneumatic differentiations of consciousness—normative for practical and political thought and action. Voegelin's ideas provide an antidote to the tendency of some political theologians to collapse that tension, and his ecumenical and transcultural comprehensiveness adds scope to conventional political theology. Nevertheless, by its very power and genericness, Voegelin's enterprise has a tendency to be too global to do justice to the particular problems of political practice.

Metz's American student Matthew Lamb has recently called attention to the relevance for political theology of the work of Bernard Lonergan (1904–1984). Lonergan, by demanding that the criteria of authentic performance in science, in scholarship, and in ordinary living be reconnected with the criteria for being authentically human (thematized in his notions of religious, moral, and intellectual conversion), has given political theologians a useful framework for the mediation of saving meaning and value in history. His stance toward the future in the light of the past, along with his germinal but still little-known work in economics, Lamb suggests, provides Christians with the first genuine alternative to either Marxist or liberal democratic political and economic theory. Whatever may be the fate of political theology as we know it, its reintegration of earlier forms of theology—emphasizing retrieval of past meaning and doctrinal and systematic restatement—into foundational, practical, and political questions about the right way to live can only be salutary for the practice of faith in society both now and in the future. Many contemporary theologians believe that political theology is, in fact, the chief symptom and response to the paradigm change theology is undergoing.

See Also Christianity, article on Christianity in Latin America; Heidegger, Martin; Lonergan, Bernard; Marx, Karl; Nietzsche, Friedrich; Rahner, Karl.

Bibliography

European Political Theology

Metz, J.-B. *Faith in History and Society: Toward a Practical Fundamental Theology.* Translated by David Smith. New York, 1980. A nuanced statement of Metz's mature position, with an account of the genesis and aims of political theology, his differences with Karl Rahner, and a basic elaboration of major concepts and themes.

Moltmann, Jürgen. *The Crucified God: The Cross of Christ as the Foundation and Criticism of Christian Theology.* Translated by Robert Wilson and John Bowden. New York, 1974. Uses themes from critical social theory as transposed into the perspective of the interaction between Father and Son in the crucifixion.

Latin American Liberation Theology

Freire, Paulo. *Pedagogy of the Oppressed.* Translated by Myra B. Ramos. New York, 1970. An extended commentary on the intrinsic nexus between language and life-form as the key to initiating a reflection upon and transformation of life-practice and to our becoming subjects instead of objects of history.

Gutiérrez, Gustavo. *A Theology of Liberation: History, Politics and Salvation.* Translated and edited by Caridad Inda and John Eagleson. Maryknoll, N.Y., 1973. Probably the classic text embodying the demarche of liberation hermeneutics, it correlates biblical texts on emancipation with the contemporary social situation as brought to light through Marxist social theory.

Feminist Liberation Theology

Plaskow, Judith, and Elisabeth Schüssler-Fiorenza, eds. *Journal of Feminist Studies in Religion.* Chico, Calif., 1985; Decatur, Ga., 1985–. A semiannual journal devoted to feminist research, discussion, and dialogue in all areas of religious studies, with articles regularly by all the leading theorists as well as newcomers.

Ruether, Rosemary Radford. *New Woman, New Earth.* New York, 1975. Here one of the most solid theorists not only retrieves many feminist motifs centrally important to secular feminism but goes on to use them to show how the concerns of feminist social critique are of intrinsic value to other emphases related to racism, ecology, and so forth.

Schüssler-Fiorenza, Elisabeth. *In Memory of Her: A Feminist Theological Reconstruction of Christian Origins.* New York, 1983. A superb critical historian and a tough-minded and sane thinker, Schüssler-Fiorenza is able to document clearly how patriarchalism is not integral to Christianity, how the Christian community got derailed from its own meanings and values, and how these meanings and values can be recovered in the present to the benefit of all Christians.

Black Political Theology

West, Cornel. *Prophesy Deliverance! An Afro-American Revolutionary Christianity.* Philadelphia, 1982. A brilliant work from the second generation of black theologians that brings the emancipatory thrust of black theology into dialogue with a large number of influential "discourses," including those of Jacques Derrida.

Wilmore, Gayraud S., and James H. Cone, eds. *Black Theology: A Documentary History, 1966–1979.* Maryknoll, N. Y., 1979. An excellent "backgrounder" with all the most influential statements and figures, along with bibliography.

Miscellaneous Works

Fiorenza, Francis S. "Political Theology as Foundational Theology: An Inquiry into Their Fundamental Meaning." *Proceedings of the Catholic Theological Society of America* 32 (1977): 142–177. Brief, lucid, and reliable, this is the best overview of the development of the notion of political/civil theology in the West from antiquity to the present.

Lamb, Matthew L. *Solidarity with Victims: Toward a Theology of Social Transformation.* New York, 1982. A difficult yet rewarding look at the possibilities of a comprehensive, differentiated, yet committed framework (for the tasks articulated by Metz, the Latin Americans, and the critical social theorists) to be found in the thought of Bernard J. F. Lonergan.

Lonergan, Bernard J. F. *Insight: A Study of Human Understanding* (1957). Reprint, San Francisco, 1978. An invitation and phenomenological maieutic toward an appropriation of one's rational self-consciousness and an intellectual conversion of the heart of concrete practice.

Lonergan, Bernard J. F. *Method in Theology.* New York, 1972. The best elucidation to date of the foundations of theology as practical and political in a differentiated society.

Strauss, Leo. *Natural Right and History.* Chicago, 1953. The best available account of the moral and political revolution from the classic tradition of natural right and natural law to the modern horizon of natural and human rights, along with its profound ambiguities.

Strauss, Leo. *Political Philosophy: Six Essays by Leo Strauss.* Edited by Hilail Gildin. Indianapolis, 1975. An expression of the core of Strauss's orientation, of which perhaps the most beneficial statement is the essay "The Three Waves of Modernity."

Voegelin, Eric. *Order and History,* vol. 4, *The Ecumenic Age.* Baton Rouge, La., 1974. An extended expression of Voegelin's most mature position, but especially pertinent reflections on the context of political theology in what he calls "historiogenesis."

New Sources

Cone, James H. *God of the Oppressed.* rev. ed. Maryknoll, N.Y., 1997.

Donovan, Oliver. *The Desire of Nations: Rediscovering the Roots of Political Theology.* Cambridge, U.K., 1996.

Ellis, Marc, and Otto Maduro, eds. *The Future of Liberation Theology; Essays in Honor of Gustavo Gutiérrez.* Maryknoll, N.Y., 1989.

Gottwald, Norman K., and Richard A. Horsely, eds. *The Bible and Liberation: Political and Social Hermeneutics.* Maryknoll, N.Y., 1993.

Hennelley, Alfred T., ed. *Liberation Theology: A Documentary History.* Maryknoll, N.Y., 1990.

Peterson, Anna L. *Martyrdom and the Politics of Religion: Progressive Catholicism in El Salvador's Civil War.* Albany, N.Y., 1997.

Smith, Christiana. *Disruptive Religion: The Forces of Faith in Social Movement Activism.* New York and London, 1996.

Tabb, William K., ed. *Churches in Struggle: Liberation Theologies and Social Change in North America.* New York, 1986.

Frederick G. Lawrence (1987)
Revised Bibliography

POLITICS AND RELIGION

This entry consists of the following articles:

POLITICS AND RELIGION: AN OVERVIEW

In his autobiographical account, Mohandas Gandhi (1869–1948) made the now famous observation that "those who say religion has nothing to do with politics do not know what religion is" (Gandhi, 1940, p. 371). The history of twentieth-century India—and, indeed, the entire modern world—would surely seem to have confirmed the mahatma's statement, as religion has clearly emerged as a powerful force inspiring nationalist identity, anti-colonial movements for independence, and revolutionary violence. While many sociologists had predicted that religion would gradually wane as a cultural force in the face of the increasing rationalization and "disenchantment" of the modern world, it would seem that quite the opposite has occurred. Since the mid-twentieth century, religion has re-emerged as a powerful, often violent and revolutionary force, with profound implications for global politics, social structure and transnational economics. The 1979 Shīʿī revolution in Iran, the rise of liberation theology in South America, the political success of Hindu fundamentalism in India, the conflicts in Bosnia and Kosovo, the ongoing violence in Israel and Palestine, the attacks on the World Trade Center Towers in 2001, and the rise of various forms of religious nationalism throughout the globe all offer ample evidence that religion has by no means become a minor force on the periphery of global political and economic issues. On the contrary, it is often at the heart of them.

One could, however, go a great deal further than Gandhi's assertion of the intimate relation between the religious and political realms. For the very idea of separating the terms *politics* and *religion* is itself a fairly recent invention, since these are both in a sense "imagined" categories that are largely the product of the European Enlightenment and the rise of modern Western nations. Just as European intellectuals of the seventeenth and eighteenth centuries began to "imagine religion" as a distinct and bounded category of human activity (Smith, 1982), so too, they began to imagine the separation between religious and political domains as a necessary condition for a rational, secular society. Rejecting the religious hegemony of the medieval Catholic Church, and recoiling from the wars of religion that tore Europe apart after the Protestant Reformation, many Enlightenment philosophers like John Locke insisted upon a separation of religious belief and political power as a necessary precondition for a rationally ordered civil society. Consequently, in the eyes of most European scholars of the eighteenth and nineteenth centuries, cultures that had not yet risen to this level of rational society were typically regarded as either "primitive" (i.e., most non-industrial indigenous traditions) or rooted in a despotic confusion of religion and political power (e.g. Islam).

Yet such a separation often makes little sense when examining non-Western and non-industrialized cultures in which the political and religious spheres are not only closely entwined, but typically indistinguishable. In fact, it is perhaps more accurate to say that the very act of defining religion, by demarcating it as a separate category distinct from social structure, art, economics and other aspects of human activity, is itself an inherently *political act.* It necessarily entails the questions of what counts as legitimate religion, as opposed to heresy, blasphemy, idolatry, savagery or "primitive" beliefs and practices.

Nowhere is this more apparent than in the expansion of European colonialism and the conquest of the Americas, India, Africa and other parts of the world. Just as Western nations were conquering new worlds, they were also categorizing and classifying newly discovered cultures in terms of their beliefs, superstitions and their distance from a rational, modern, "civilized" state. To cite just one of many examples, the rites of most Native American tribes were not initially recognized by U.S. government officials as legitimate religious forms on a par with Christianity or Judaism. Rather, their "primitive" and savage character was a symptom of the Native Americans' need to be governed, converted or simply removed. Many rites, such as the Sun Dance and Ghost Dance were banned altogether. Others, such as the use of peyote as a sacrament, had to be contested legally throughout the twentieth century, facing state prohibitions and congressional bills banning its use, before finally being recognized as a religious rite. Ironically, the use of peyote was only recognized as a legitimate form of religious expression once it was institutionalized in 1918 as the "Native American Church," dedicated "to teach the Christian religion with morality, sobriety, industry, kindly charity and right living"—in other words, with the appearance of something more recognizably "Church-like" in the eyes of the government.

Similar examples can be found throughout the history of the colonization of Africa, South America, and India, where the act of defining "religion" was often intimately bound to political conquest, colonial knowledge and control over indigenous populations. Increasingly since the nineteenth century, moreover, the act of defining religion has also become tied to explicitly political movements, such as religious nationalism (e.g. India, Sri Lanka) and revolutionary extremism (e.g. Egypt, Iran, Afghanistan).

It is therefore perhaps more helpful to use a term like "*religio-political power*" to refer to the complex ways in which this-worldly relations of power, domination and social control are inevitably intertwined with appeals to otherworldly, transcendent or supra-human sources of authority (Chidester, 1988, p. 2). Even in the contemporary United States—ostensibly founded on a "clear wall of separation between Church and State," and yet still committed to the ideals of "in God we trust" and "one nation under God"—it is not difficult to see complex intersections between the secular and the spiritual in the construction of a collective national identity.

This article will first suggest some basic ways of distinguishing between religious and political power in a practical or provisional way, and then examine seven modern theoretical approaches. Finally, it will outline eight basic modes of interaction between religion and politics, and conclude with some remarks on the role of religio-political power in the context of globalization and transnationalism.

HUMAN AND SUPRA-HUMAN SOURCES OF AUTHORITY. Despite the fact that the very idea of separating religion and politics is a relatively recent product of post-Enlightenment European discourse, it is arguably still useful to distinguish between them as a *heuristic device* or practical tool in order to understand how power works in particular cultures. Various authors have suggested ways of defining and distinguishing the two terms. Perhaps the most common way has been to identify religion and politics, respectively, with the sacred and profane aspects of human experience. Thus, according to historian George Armstrong Kelly, "politics is the ultimate control system of the profane, and religion is the ultimate control system of the sacred" (Douglas and Tipton, 1983, p. 208).

However, perhaps a more nuanced way to understand the distinction between religious and political phenomena lies in the sorts of authority to which they appeal in order to justify their power. In broadest terms, politics could be said to refer to the "network of power relations in society"; it consists of the "lines of authority, instruments of control, strategies of domination, and the enforcement of order that all contribute to a certain distribution of power within a set of social relations" (Chidester, 1988, p. 5). And a key part of political power is the right to exercise violence. Indeed, as Max Weber (1864–1920) observed, the State is simply a community that "claims the monopoly on the legitimate use of physical force" and the "'right' to use violence" within a given territory (1946: 78).

What most distinguishes specifically religious forms of discourse from political and other sorts of discourse, however, is their appeal to a particular kind of authority—namely, to a transcendent, supra-human or eternal source of authority believed to lie beyond the temporal, fallible, human realm. "Religion," Bruce Lincoln observes, ". . .is that discourse whose defining characteristic is its desire to speak of things eternal and transcendent with an authority equally transcendent and eternal" (Lincoln, 1996, p. 225). And this discursive appeal to a supra-human authority is in turn tied to a set of practices, to a community, and to an institution, all of which serve to reproduce and reaffirm this claim to transcendent authority (Lincoln, 2003, p. 6–7). Politics, history, economics, art, and other forms of cultural discourse, conversely, tend to speak in a fallible human voice about this-worldly, temporal and finite affairs; to the degree that they begin to speak with a more than human voice, we could say, they begin to move into the realm of religion.

In most cultures, the religious and political domains are bound in an intimate, symbiotic, but also tense and conflicted relationship. Religious discourse might be said to represent the ultimate motivator, that is, the most persuasive force used to mobilize individual and collective action. With its appeal to supra-human and transcendent authority, religious discourse can lend the ultimate legitimation to temporal political power. Indeed, even Niccolò Machiavelli, in his classic work on political pragmatism, recognized this legitimizing power. Thus he advised that the prince should "appear a man of compassion, a man of good faith, a man of integrity, a kind and a religious man," adding that the last quality is the most important (Machiavelli, 1999, p. 58). In turn, religious institutions typically rely upon the patronage, financial support and physical protection of political powers. Yet at the same time, the supra-human authority of religious discourse can also be invoked to critique, challenge, or subvert the dominant political order; and conversely, the "legitimate violence" of political power can be used to silence, suppress or crush dissident religious voices.

MODERN WESTERN THEORIES OF RELIGION AND POLITICS. Sophisticated reflection on the nature of spiritual and political power is not, of course, a modern phenomenon. Plato's *Republic* and Aristotle's *Politics* in classical Greece, Kauṭilya's's *Arthaśāstra* in ancient India, the works of Arab theologians in early Islam, the works of medieval theologians like Augustine, Aquinas, Maimonides, etc., all represent serious analyses of the ideal polity and its relation to the divine. Yet the idea of clearly defining religion and politics as two distinct spheres of human activity—spheres that should ideally have as little to with one another as possible—is a relatively modern idea with a history that is itself not free of political implications. Indeed, it was not until the Enlightenment that religion itself emerges as a distinct category in Western discourse and politics emerges as a category against which it is contrasted. The relationship between these two categories has, moreover, been theorized in many different ways over the last 300 years. For the sake of simplicity, six major models will be discussed that have emerged in Western discourse since the Enlightenment.

The European Enlightenment, from Locke to Kant. The European Enlightenment can be read as, among other things, a critique of the powerful religious hegemony held by the medieval Catholic Church, which had asserted the spiritual and temporal supremacy of the Papacy over all human domains, often including that of kings and emperors. By the end of the Middle Ages, and particularly after the Protestant Reformation and the ensuing violence of Europe's wars of religion, that religio-political hegemony had been seriously called into question and attacked on many sides.

Arguably the most influential modern author to argue for a clear separation of religious and political affairs was the English philosopher John Locke (1632–1704). In his "Letter Concerning Tolerance" (1667), Locke distinguishes religion and politics as two separate and legitimate spheres of human endeavor; the former primarily concerns individual belief and personal conviction, and the latter civil law and public action. As such, religious belief should not be restricted by political control, and conversely, political discourse should not be affected by religious conviction. Religion is for Locke an inward and private affair—indeed, "all the life and power of true religion consist in the inward and full persuasion of the mind"—which means that it cannot be governed by external political power: "the whole jurisdiction of the magistrate reaches only to these civil concernments. . . . [I]t neither can nor ought in any manner to be extended to the salvation of souls" (Cahn, p. 508). In the process, however, Locke also effectively reduced religion to a kind of disembodied, internal affair between the individual and God, something fundamentally removed from the political domain and thus of no practical importance for civil society.

By the late eighteenth century, philosophers like Immanuel Kant (1724–1804) would render judgment on the legitimate place of religion "within the limits of reason alone" (Kant, 1793). For Kant, religion was acknowledged to have a privileged place, engaged as it is in lofty metaphysical issues such as the existence of God or the immortality of the soul; but it was deemed inappropriate for all other more practical affairs, including polity and governance.

This intellectual definition of—and clear demarcation between—the appropriate domains of religion and politics set out by Locke, Kant and other Enlightenment philosophers would provide the theoretical basis for many modern Western nations, such as the early United States. Yet, as various scholars have observed, this definition of religion and politics as two separate domains of activity in rational, civilized society was itself part of a larger political agenda; it provided the basis for a hierarchical ranking of cultures from "primitive" to "modern," as well as the legitimation for ruling those who were incapable of distinguishing between proper rational governance and oppression of religious despotism.

Karl Marx and Neo-Marxism. If Locke and other Enlightenment intellectuals critiqued the dangerous mixture of religion and politics, many nineteenth century authors critiqued the very nature of religion itself as a mask or mystification of underlying economic and political interests. For Karl Marx, the criticism of religion is in fact the "prerequisite of all criticism"; for religion represents the most extreme form of ideology and "alienation." It involves the human being's own self-deception and mystification, which is the basis of all other sorts of alienation, including the more developed forms of modern capitalism. For Marx, God does not make human beings; rather, human beings make gods and then deny that they have done so, alienating themselves from the fruits of their own labor. This alienation is the spiritual analogue of the alienation suffered by the laborer in a capitalist economy, separated from the fruits of his own labor which becomes the profit of the boss or factory owner. As such, religion is itself the by-product of the social and political order; it is the "spiritual aroma" of the state, masking the domination of the powerful and the wealthy over the weak and the poor, and making oppressive social conditions appear at once agreeable and divinely ordained. Thus, "the criticism of heaven turns into the criticism of earth, the criticism of religion into the criticism of law, and the criticism of theology into the criticism of politics" (Raines, pp. 171–172).

Yet contrary to many popular interpretations, Marx is not entirely negative or dismissive in his evaluation of religion. Religion reflects a genuine need for meaning and consolation in the face of oppression, offering at once "the expression of real suffering and protest against suffering." Yet it is a protest that is misdirected, seeking imaginary ideals rather than real material happiness. In sum, the "abolition of religion as illusory happiness is necessary for real happiness" (Raines, p. 171).

Toward the end of his life, Marx would return to the question of religion as not simply a source of oppression, but also as a potential source of a kind of apocalyptic hope for radical transformation. The religious cry of protest could also perhaps articulate the voice of the oppressed seeking exodus toward a totally new world, as a kind of early, undeveloped prefiguration of genuine political revolution. This revolutionary potential of myth and religious ideology would later be taken up and developed by various later Marxists, from revolutionary nationalists in India to Liberation theologians in South America. As more recent authors like Bruce Lincoln have shown, religious discourse can indeed be used to buttress the existing political order and status quo. However, it can also be used to challenge, subvert and overthrow that same order by appealing to a transcendent source of authority that contests the status quo and provides the inspiration for rebellion or revolution.

If Marx sees the criticism of religion as necessary for a criticism of politics, he does not, however, hope for a simple replacement of religious authority by state power. On the contrary, the ultimate goal would be the "withering away of the state" altogether. In a truly egalitarian community, the specialized functions once held by political offices would be gradually turned over to the self-management of the proletariat, and finally class society itself would be transformed into a classless society in which hierarchical distinctions collapse altogether. In this sense, one might say that the criticism of religion and the abolition of its illusory promise are only the first steps toward the larger criticism of politics and the abolition of the illusory promises of the State. The great irony in the later history of Communist thought, of course, is that Marxism would itself be reinterpreted, transformed and used to create some of the most powerful state apparatuses, political ideologies, and some would say quasi-religious systems ever known, such as the former Soviet Union and Communist China.

Religion, society and politics: Émile Durkheim and Max Weber. While Marx saw religion primarily as a negative social force, imposing political conformity and resignation to suffering, other modern theorists like Émile Durkheim (1858–1917) had a more positive regard for religion's role in society. Durkheim's classic *Elementary Forms of the Religious Life* (1912) defines religion primarily as a system of beliefs and practices relative to sacred things which "unite into one single moral community . . . all those who adhere to them" (Durkheim, p. 62). Religion is primarily a source of social cohesion, binding individuals into a whole that seems to them larger than the sum of its parts—indeed, sacred. The sacred is, in sum, society writ large. Using as his primary example the system of "totemism" among Australian aboriginal communities, Durkheim suggests that the totem symbol is nothing less than the "flag" of the clan (Durkheim, p. 236). For the intense emotions generated by religious rites are attached to the totem, which then becomes a sacred object embodying the cohesion of individuals with the larger whole of the social group.

It is not difficult to see the relevance of Durkheim's analysis of religious totemism for modern politics and the "flag-totem" of the modern state. Indeed, Durkheim was concerned that the social cohesion once provided by traditional religious institutions like the Church were waning in the face of an increasingly complex and scientific modern world. The result of this loss of social unity was the growing sense of *anomie*, the isolation, fragmentation and suicidal despair felt by the modern individual. The decline of traditional religious institutions, did not, however, necessarily signal the dissolution of society altogether. Rather, Durkheim was hopeful that even as the "old gods are growing old or already dead," new kinds of rituals would emerge to affirm society's basic values, "keeping alive their memory by means of celebrations which regularly reproduce their fruits" (Durkheim, 1961, p. 475).

But clearly, religion is not only and always a source of social unity, cohesion and stability; rather, as Max Weber observed, religious ideas could act as forces of both the legitimation of established political structures and as forces of change and transformation. Religion was for Weber a separate institution inevitably involved in an ongoing process of interaction with other social institutions, assuming different meanings in specific social, economic and political contexts. Rejecting the historical materialism of orthodox Marxism, Weber saw religion not simply as a mask for underlying economic and political forces; rather, religious ideas could also transform the economic and political domains. In his best-known example of Protestant Christianity, the Calvinist ethics of hard work, thrift, and inner-worldly asceticism had a kind of elective affinity with the rise of modern capitalism and with the politics of modern European states. Other religious systems, such as Hinduism and Confucianism, instead impeded the growth of capitalist accumulation and supported very different political and economic systems.

In contrast to Durkheim, Weber was more interested in the role of individual agents, particularly extraordinary, charismatic agents such as prophets, reformers and founders who provide alternative sources of authority that shatter established patterns of traditional and legal authority. Indeed, charismatic religious power can erupt into a force of intense change, reform, even revolution against the established political order.

However, as he observed in his classic lecture on "Politics as a Vocation," the political realm also involves inherent ethical paradoxes that pose special problems for all religious traditions. Above all, politics demands the necessary use of force—indeed, "the decisive means for politics is violence"—which means that politics can never be the place for those who seek the salvation of souls or an "acosmic ethic of love" (1918, pp. 119, 121). The moral paradox of politics and violence is one with which every religion must struggle, yet always with limited success.

Mircea Eliade and the history of religions. In the middle of the twentieth century, a number of European and American scholars began to react against what they saw as the reduction of religion to various other, non-religious sorts of explanations, such as materialist critiques, social functionalism and Freudian psychoanalysis. Instead, they sought to reaffirm the independent, autonomous nature of religious experience prior to and beyond any other social, psychological or political phenomena.

The most influential figure in this regard—and indeed arguably the most influential historian of religions in the twentieth century—was the Romanian born émigré to the United States, Mircea Eliade (1907–1986). For Eliade, religious phenomena are fundamentally *sui generis* or "of their own origin"; in other words, they are irreducible to anything else. A religious phenomenon must be taken seriously "on its plane of reference," and not reduced to one of its "secondary aspects or its contexts," such as economic, social structure, psychology or politics. Even seemingly highly politicized phenomena such as the so-called cargo cults that emerged in Melanesia in the wake of western contact and colonization cannot be explained by their sociopolitical circumstances; rather they must be treated as genuine *"spiritual creations"* (Eliade, 1969, pp. 98–99). This respect for the autonomous value of religious phenomena, Eliade believed, could provide the basis for a kind of "new humanism" on a global scale. Unlike the social and political visions of Marx or Durkheim, Eliade's new humanism would demand an appreciation for the religious worldviews of all cultures, as legitimate encounters with the sacred that cannot be explained away as masks for political interests or mere products of social structure.

Although Eliade would become arguably the single most influential voice in the comparative study of religion in the latter twentieth century, he would also come under severe criticism—in part for his attempt to define religion as an autonomous *sui generis* phenomena distinct from history, society and politics. Thus he has been charged as the "leading anti-historian of religion" (Dudley, 1977:148) whose universalist approach does not so much interpret as it "manufactures" religion (McCutcheon, 1997). While many of these criticisms may be unfair, Eliade's attempt to avoid the pitfalls of reductionism did lead him to de-emphasize the political contexts, consequences and complications of religious phenomena in favor of their a-political or trans-political themes (see Wasserstom, 1998; Strenski, 1977).

Feminist critiques. If Marx made the criticism of religion the foundation for the criticism of all other forms of material oppression, many feminist theorists would also make the criticism of religion the foundation for a critique of gender politics and asymmetries of power between the sexes. The more extreme version of the feminist critique emerged out of the second wave and radical feminist movements of the 1960s, with theorists like Mary Daly. In Daly's view, the entire imagery of God the Father as divine judge and patriarch has served as the justification for a male-dominated hierarchy of power on the religious, social and political levels alike. For the past 2000 years mainstream western religious institutions have supported a fundamentally patriarchal social and political structure, built upon the oppression of female power. What is now needed, Daly suggests, is a kind of divine rage in order to deconstruct and move beyond the "biblical and popular image of God as a great patriarch in heaven;" indeed, they need to "castrate God," in order to free themselves from an icon that has for millennia justified a patriarchal political system, and to realize instead the inherent divinity of the female body (Daly, 1973, pp. 13–32).

Most later feminist theorists of religion distanced themselves considerably from the extreme rhetoric and essentialist gender politics of radical feminists like Daly. More moderate theorists have tried to find ways to apply a serious feminist critique of particular religious institutions, while still salvaging the meaningful dimensions of religious experience itself. Rita Gross, for example, suggests that it is possible to re-read religious history from a feminist perspective, critiquing oppressive gender relations, and so recovering women's religious voices and a feminine dimensions of the sacred. This requires a fundamental paradigm shift away form the current androcentric model of humanity to an androgynous or bisexual model of humanity (Gross, p. 20). As Wendy Doniger suggests, the frank recognition that religion is intimately tied to both political power and sexual oppression does not mean that one need jettison the spiritual baby with the patriarchal bathwater. That is, one can still recover the meaningfulness and value of religious narratives, while seriously critiquing their political and sexual implications (1998: 109–35).

Finally, in the wake of post-structuralism and French feminist thought, more nuanced critiques have been made by authors like Grace Jantzen in her work on medieval Christian mysticism. As Jantzen argues, the ways in which legitimate religious experience is defined—and also contrasted with heresy, delusion or demonic inspiration—is inherently tied to political interests and relations of power between the sexes. For it is inevitably bound to questions such as who has the authority to speak with divine sanction? Who has the legitimation to support or challenge existing religious and political institutions? Who, and which sex, is considered more naturally open to mystical experience, yet also more susceptible to delusion? In sum, mysticism—like the category of religion itself—is a constructed category that is inevitably tied to both gender and politics.

The micropolitics of power: post-structuralist approaches. It is perhaps worth noting at least one of the alternative approaches to the analysis of religion, politics and power that emerged in the second half of the twentieth century, particularly in the wake of movements like postmodernism and post-structuralism. Arguably the most influential figure for the theorizing of power in the latter twentieth century is the French historian, Michel Foucault (1926–1984). Contrary to most earlier analyses of power, which begin from the top down, viewing power primarily as an oppressive and dominating force wielded by the few, Foucault views power from the bottom up. Rather than viewing power on the "macro-political level" of nations and states, Foucault turns instead to the micro-politics or "capillary circuits" of power—the ways in which power operates in the lives of all individual members of a given social order, in the most mundane details of daily life such as dress, bodily comportment, physical practices, and diet (Foucault, 1978). Thus Foucault was particularly interested in a specifically embodied kind of power—bio-power or bio-politics—through which power is exercised upon individual human bodies and thereby human subjects. One of the most crucial fields for the operation of bio-power, for example, is sexuality; for sexuality lies at the pivot of two key axes: power over individual bodies and power over social bodies or the body politic (Gutting, 1994, p. 144). Control of individual sexual activity and reproduction, in other words, is the key to the larger control of populations and governance of society as a whole.

Religions, too, employ a variety of bodily and sexual techniques—such as chastity, penance, fasting, confession—in order to discipline the body and create certain kinds of subjects. The role of confession in the medieval Catholic church, for example, was a particularly effective form of "pastoral power," which gave the church intimate knowledge and individualized control over its subjects, while at the same time interiorizing a sense of sin, guilt and moral conscience within the individual believer.

However, Foucault sees an important shift in the operations of power in modern Western societies, particularly since the Enlightenment. Whereas the medieval Church exercised a kind of pastoral power, by monitoring and disciplining individuals through techniques like confession, modern European states developed ever more effective means of governing large populations through new sciences of the body, medicine and sexuality. Ultimately, Foucault sees modern forms of power as a fusion of the individualizing pastoral power once exercised by the Church and the modern totalizing power of the state: "This is government with the motto *ones et singulatum*—of all and of each. It represents the modern, biopolitical, and daemonic fusion of pastoral and polis. . . . It is a power that both individualizes and totalizes" (Fabion, 2001, p. xxviii).

Some have argued that Foucault's work offers an extremely useful new way to think about religion as a whole. Religion in this sense would be seen less as a matter of otherworldly faith than as a fundamentally embodied, corporal phenomenon concerned with physical practice and the disciplining of the self through bodily action. Finally, Foucault's model of power also forces us to view religion as an inherently political phenomenon, "taken out of its privileged realm and brought into the body politic and the heart of culture" (Carrette, 2000, p. xi). As Foucault put it in his comments on the Iranian revolution, this is a view of "religion which speaks less of a Beyond than of the transformations in this world" (Foucault, 1994, p. 716).

This brief overview of various theoretical approaches is surely not meant to be exhaustive. Yet it can be seen from these six models that the relationship between religion and politics can be construed in a variety of different, often contradictory ways, each of which is useful in understanding particular historical cases, but none of which is by itself complete. In the end, the attempt to construct a single grand theory that explains religion and politics on some universal scale is not a very fruitful endeavor. Rather, it is perhaps more useful to think of religious discourse, with its appeal to a transcendent source of authority, as a unique and powerful kind of cultural resource. This is a resource that can be deployed strategically for a wide range of political interests, at once to reinforce a given political formation and to contest it, to forge powerful nationalist bonds and to tear those bonds apart through revolutionary violence.

Strategic Relations between Religious and Political Power: Eight Patterns. As the sub-entries that follow this essay clearly demonstrate, the relations between religious and political power are remarkably varied, not simply between different traditions but even within the same tradition in different historical periods. These range from the complete fusion of religio-political power, to the suppression of religion by political power, to the violent revolt of the former against the latter.

Various authors have tried to make broad generalizations about the relations between religion and politics in particular traditions or families of traditions. Some, for example, have tried to contrast the "monotheistic" or Abrahamic religions with the "ontocratic" or "Oriental" and "primal religions." According to Max Stackhouse, the monotheistic traditions "distinguish between God and the world and reject political orders that are not in accord with God's will," while in the "ontocratic" religions of Asia, "the harmonious state is the supreme earthly embodiment of cosmic totality" (Stackhouse, 1986, p. 415). Others like William Scott Green have tried to distinguish and compare six major traditions, based on the core theological doctrines, which, he suggests, naturally lead to distinct relations between religion and politics in each case (Neusner, p. 5).

Yet all of these attempts to make sweeping comparisons based on Abrahamic vs. Oriental or core theological doctrines ultimately seem superficial. One need not look far into the history of any tradition to see that the relations between religious and political authority shift dramatically in different historical contexts. Buddhism, for example, begins with Siddhārtha Gautama's renunciation of his own royal status and a general withdrawal from the political realm. Yet from the time of Emperor Aśoka (r. c. 270–230 BCE) onward, Buddhism as an institution gained the patronage of kings throughout Asia, from China and Japan to Tibet and modern Thailand. Usually portrayed as a religion stressing peace, non-violence and compassion, Buddhism has also become a powerful force in modern nationalist movements and even religious violence in areas like Vietnam and Sri Lanka. Conversely, Islam begins with more or less complete fusion of religious and political power in the person of the Prophet and the early Caliphs. Yet in modern times, many Muslims have largely accepted a form of church-state separation in secular nations (e.g. Turkey, Bangladesh), while others have turned to extremist fervor and a revolutionary return to the ideal polity of early Islam.

There are no easy generalizations regarding the balance of religious and political power in different traditions. It may be true that one can identify certain kinds of elective affinities, to use Weber's phrase, between particular religious beliefs and particular socio-economic or political formations—such as the Protestant ethic and early modern capitalism, or certain forms of New Age spirituality and late capitalism. Yet even these examples show that every religious tradition has undergone radical change in different social and historical contexts, in some cases wedding religious and political authority, in other cases, turning religious appeals for transformation into a radical challenge to the existing political order.

In broadest terms, however, there are at least eight primary strategic relations between political and religious power. None of these is intended to represent a fixed or universal category, but simply a comparative pattern that recurs in various cultures and historical periods.

Religo-political synthesis: the religious as the political. One of the primary reasons modern Western scholars have had such difficulty understanding (and tolerating) Islam is its fusion of political and religious authority. For scholars raised in a post-Enlightenment separation of Church and State, the Prophet's skillful combination of military prowess, political leadership and spiritual authority has long been dismissed as a vulgar manipulation of religion for political ends. Yet this really misses the very point of Islam as a total worldview that does not separate the "religious" from other spheres of life, but rather embraces the social, political, economic and military realms in one total attitude of submission to God. The Islamic system of holy law and jurisprudence (*sharīʿah*) provides rules for the conduct of all aspects of life, including not only spiritual practice, but also family life, commerce, social activities, governance, and war. As John Esposito suggests, traditional Islam might be better described not as a theocracy but rather as a kind of nomocracy, that is, a community governed by divine law as the sovereign authority and embodiment of the Word of God.

Such fusion of religious and political power is by no means unique to Islam. Another particularly clear example is the rise of the Dalai Lama in Vajrayāna Buddhism, who served as the combined religious and political leader of Tibet from the fifteenth to the twentieth century. Embodying both the highest Buddhist ideals of infinite compassion and the center of the socio-political *maṇḍala*, the Dalai Lama survived as a powerful religio-political institution for 500 years until the Communist invasion of Tibet. Even into the twenty-first century, as a winner of the Noble Peace Prize and an outspoken commentator on global issues, the exiled Dalai Lama remains a potent religio-political symbol. He represents the spread of the once esoteric system of Tibetan Buddhism to all points of the globe and the hope of freedom for the Tibetan people.

Religious authority above political power. At least in its ideal form, the classical Hindu *varṇa* system provides one of the clearest examples of a hierarchical ordering of society in which the religious or priestly (*brahmana*) class is at once spiritually and metaphysically superior to the royal or warrior (*kṣatriya*) class. While the king is recognized for his physical power and political authority, the *brahmana* is recognized for his purity, which marks him as spiritually superior to all other classes. Since the time of the earliest Indian scriptures, the Vedas, this hierarchical model has been given both a mythological and a cosmological justification. According to the creation myth found in *Ṛgveda* X.90, the universe was born from the primal sacrifice of the first Person, *puruṣa*, whose body was dismembered and divided to create both the hierarchy of the universe (heaven, atmosphere, earth) and the hierarchy of the four social classes. Here the priest emerges from the head of the cosmic man, while the *kṣatriya* emerges from his torso. Although the king may be greater in terms of power and material capital, the *brahmana* is always superior in sacredness and spiritual capital. The two are bound in an intimate relationship of reciprocity. Thus the Vedic sacrificial ritual was, in many ways, an elaborate exchange between religious and political power, in which the *brahmana* received gifts and fees while the *kṣatriya* received status and legitimacy.

Of course, this superiority of the *brahmana* over the *kṣatriya* was probably always more an ideal than a practical reality. There would remain throughout Indian history a recurring tension between the religious and spiritual domains, with the constant threat that the superior strength of the king might break its bounds and reassert itself.

Religious and political power as separate (but interdependent or rival) forces. Medieval Christian Europe provides some instructive examples of the political and religious spheres in an ongoing relationship that was at once one of tension, rivalry, competition and symbiosis. Like the authors of the Vedas, medieval authors commonly imagined the social order as a hierarchical organism, usually a tripartite body comprised of clerics, nobles and serfs. Yet there was some disagreement as to which of the first two classes, priests or nobility, Pope or Holy Roman Emperor, was the true head of the social body. As Jacques Le Goff observes, "Christianity was bicephalous: its two heads were the pope and the emperor. . . [T]he relations between the two heads of Christianity displayed the competition at the top: the two dominant but rival orders, the clergy and the lay hierarchy—priests and warriors, magical power and military might" (Le Goff, pp. 264-265).

Since the time of Pope Gregory I (c. 540–604), the Papacy had proclaimed itself the supreme leader of both secular and religious domains; yet throughout the history the medieval Church, bishops and kings, Popes and Emperors existed in competitive and at times violent rivalry. Thus Pope Gregory VII would challenge the power of Emperor Henry IV in German lands, finally excommunicating him; in England, Archbishop of Canterbury Thomas à Becket defended the authority of the Church against King Henry II, leading to his own death in 1170. Perhaps the most remarkable conflict between religious and political authority was that between Pope Boniface VIII and Philip IV of France, which led to the Pope's arrest and death in prison in 1313, the "Babylonian exile" of the Church from Rome to Avignon (1378–1417), and finally the schism of the Church into a puppet Papacy in France and a series of rival Popes in Rome.

In modern times, one of the most striking examples of the interdependence of religious and political authority is the rise of the *Wahhābī* reformist movement in Saudi Arabia since the eighteenth century. The result of an alliance between the reformist theologian Muḥammad ibn Abd al-Wahhab (1702–1792) and a tribal chief, Muḥammad ibn Saud (d. 1765), the *Wahhābī* movement sought to unite the tribes of Arabia under the religious banner of Islam. Combining strict religious purification with military action to enforce religious precepts, the *Wahhābīs* used religious ideology to inform and guide political activity. This powerful alliance of religion and politics remains largely intact today in the kingdom of Saudi Arabia, while also powerfully influencing recent regimes such as the Taliban in Afghanistan.

Political power over religious authority. With its appeal to a transcendent supra-human and otherworldly source of authority, religious discourse always poses a potential threat to political power; as such, it is often tightly controlled, restricted, at times entirely suppressed by political regimes. Various Chinese emperors, for example, perceived Buddhism to be a subversive force within their domain; thus during the Huichang suppression under the Tang Emperor Wuzong (r. 840–846) purged monasteries, banned pilgrimages, and finally seized Buddhist property for the state.

Perhaps the most extreme example of the exertion of secular political power over religious institutions occurred in modern communist countries, such as China after the rise of the Communist Party and particularly during the Cultural Revolution (1966–1976). Targeting Buddhism, Daoism, and Confucianism as part of the "four olds" (old ideas, old culture, old customs, old habits), the Communist Party put an end to all public displays of religion, damaging temples and purging churches of religious symbols. Even more extreme state repressions of religion took place under other Marxist-inspired regimes, such as Albania under Enver Hoxha (1908–1985). Between 1947 and 1990, religion was not only stifled but simply abolished.

It is by no means only communist regimes that have been known to suppress religious movements. Already noted is the U.S. government's suppression of various Native American rituals such as the Sun Dance and Peyote religion. A more recent example is the assault on the Branch Davidian compound at Waco Texas by the BATF and FBI from February to April of 1993. In this case government agencies not only secretly infiltrated and monitored the movement, but mounted a large scale siege of the compound using heavily armed officers and tanks, resulting in the death of seventy-five people, including twenty-one children. If post-Enlightenment nations like the U.S. are founded on a separation of church and state, then cases like the Waco disaster make it clear that religious power is still, in the end, subordinate to the political power and military strength of the state.

Religious withdrawal from the political sphere. Particularly during periods of oppressive rule, many religious groups choose the option of general disengagement or withdrawal from the political realm. Turning to a supra-human, eternal source of authority, religious leaders can always claim to transcend any merely human government, and so ignore or treat as secondary the demands of worldly politics. The sayings of Jesus Christ and the life of the early church under Roman rule provide some of the clearest examples of this withdrawal from politics. Christ's assertion that his "kingdom is not of this world," while advising his disciples to "render unto Ceasar" what is owed to the Empire at once acknowledges the reality of alien political power and yet also denies it any ultimate significance. As an eschatological religion, early Christianity on the whole focused on the divine kingdom to come, not the world as it was; thus it delegitimized the latter with the promise of a more perfect rule in the heavenly kingdom.

A more recent and more disturbing example of this religious withdrawal from the political is the case of the Peoples Temple led by Jim Jones (1931–1978) in the 1970s. With a utopian vision of racial harmony between African Americans and whites, Jones preached a socialist brand of Christianity that fiercely attacked the United States government as the "antichrist" and American capitalism as the "antichrist system." After facing intense attacks from government agencies, the media, and white supremacist groups, Jones and his followers withdrew from the U.S. to Guyana in 1977. When the anti-cult group, Concerned Relatives, and Congressman Leo Ryan continued to pressure the movement, Jones decided it was time to withdraw from the world altogether. Over nine hundred of his followers drank or were forced to drink Kool-aid laced with cyanide, while Jones himself died of an apparently self-inflicted gunshot wound. As Jones put it in his farewell audio tape, "we didn't commit suicide, we committed an act of revolutionary suicide protesting the conditions of an inhumane world" (Wessinger, 2000, p. 51).

Religion in the service of political power: Religious nationalism in the modern state. Among the most striking features of the nineteenth and twentieth centuries is the rise of a new form of religious nationalism in more or less all parts of the colonial and post-colonial world. As new national "imagined communities" emerged out of the demise of European colonization (Anderson, 1983), a redefined and nationalized religious identity has often provided the foundation for this re-imagining of political communities. Indeed, it would seem that much of the world simply does not share the western ideal of a secular modern nation based on a clear separation of church and state. Instead, many national identities have been born out of deep religious roots, shaped by ritual performance and mythic narratives. A reformed religious and national identity has been an integral part of the rise of modern India, Sri Lanka, Israel, various parts of the Muslim world, Kosovo, Bosnia, and even the United States, as the rise of the new Christian right suggests. The modern state of Israel provides perhaps the clearest example of a new political entity emerging out of the collapse of European colonial power, and founded on a uniquely religious identity; thus the Balfour Declaration of 1917 promised European Zionists "a national home for Jewish people" (Farsoun and Zacharia, 1997). In the process of nationalization, however, these religious traditions have often been purged of their heterogeneous or divisive elements, re-packaged in a more homogenous form to attract the broadest number of devotees, and so used to define religious practice as a kind of patriotic duty.

The case of modern Hinduism is a particularly instructive example of the complex nature of religious nationalism. Indeed, the modern imagining of Hinduism itself —which is not an indigenous term but a construction of nineteenth century Indian elites and European scholars—went hand in hand with the rise of the Indian nation as an imagined community. For early religious nationalists like Swami Vivekananda (1863–1902), the young Aurobindo Ghose and many others, the revival of a strong and vigorous form of Hinduism was a crucial part of creating an autonomous Indian nation, free of the shackles of British rule. Thus Vivekananda called not just for the revival of his country but for the "conquest of the whole world by the Hindu race"; indeed, "we must conquer the world through our spirituality . . . The only condition of . . . awakened and vigorous national life is the conquest of the world by Indian thought" (Vivekananda, 1984: 276, 277).

This kind of Hindu nationalism is by no means a quaint relic of colonial India; rather, it has continued as a powerful force driving much of modern Indian politics. Thus, India's first nuclear missiles have been named after Agni, the Hindu god of fire, while Bharat Mata or "mother India" has emerged as a powerful civil religious deity, usually portrayed as a Goddess much like Durgā, riding a lion, circled with a halo of flames and superimposed on a map of India. At the same time, religious nationalism has also fueled a number of extremist groups such as the Rashtriya Svayamsevak Sangh (RSS)—a movement dedicated to the creation of a purely Hindu nation, with an open admiration for Nazi Germany. The RSS became the ideological backbone for the Bharatiya Janata Party (BJP), which rose to power in the 1980s in large part due to its ideal of Hindutva and the goal of building a temple to the god Rāma in the holy city of Ayodhya. One of the most striking examples of religio-political nationalist fervor exploded in Ayodhya on December 16, 1992, when mobs of Hindu extremists destroyed the Babri Masjid, a mosque that had allegedly been built on the site of Rama's birthplace. The destruction of the Babri Masjid in turn unleashed tremendous bloodshed between Hindus and Muslims throughout South Asia, and has since become a symbol of both Hindu nationalism and the alienation of non-Hindu communities in modern India. As seen in the ongoing violence in Kashmir and the slaughter of 2000 Muslims in Gujarat in 2002, the often horrific consequences of religious nationalism in India have by no means lessened in the years since Independence, but arguably grown more intense in a new age of nationalism and terror.

The political as the religious: civil religion. One of the more interesting and ironic consequences of the rise of modern secular nation states is the emergence of powerful new forms of civil symbolism, mythology and ritual practice. In a sense, the space opened up by the separation of religion and politics seems to have been filled in many cases by a modern state that now assumes a kind of quasi-religious power, invested with autonomy, disciplinary control and potential violence, for which citizens are called upon to make the ultimate sacrifice. In contrast to a form of religious nationalism, however, a civil religion does not support any one particular tradition, but instead advocates a sufficiently ambiguous sort of divine authority (such as God) and a sufficiently generic set of beliefs (a rational order to the universe, the immortality of the soul and judgment for good and evil actions) that can encompass many different faiths without alienating too many minority groups.

The idea of a civil faith was first suggested by Jean Jacques Rousseau in the second half of the eighteenth century. Rejecting traditional religious institutions like Christianity as divisive and in fact corrosive of social unity, Rousseau called instead for "a purely civil profession of faith whose articles the sovereign is competent to determine, not precisely as religious dogmas but as sentiments of sociability, without which it is impossible to be a good citizen or a faithful subject" (1762: Chidester, 1988, p. 82). The basis of Rousseau's civil faith was fairly minimal, asking only belief in an all-powerful deity, the survival of the soul after death, the reward of the good and punishment of wicked, and above all a commitment to the sanctity of the social contract.

Arguably one of the most powerful examples of civil religion in the modern era has emerged within the United States. As G. K. Chesterton observed, "America is the only nation in the world that is founded on a creed" (Chidester, 1988, p. 87). Despite its ostensible separation of the religious and political spheres, the U.S. has also developed its own set of creation myths (Exodus from British tyranny, the first Thanksgiving, etc.), its founding fathers, and a system of symbols and rituals. From the Annuit Coeptis ("God has smiled on our beginnings") and Novus Ordo Seclorum ("New Order for the Ages") on the dollar bill, the United States has been imagined in mythic terms as a nation formed under divine providence and guided toward a sacred destiny.

The United States also gave birth to an array of civil religious holy days, such as the Fourth of July and Thanksgiving (both ritual reenactments of national creation myths), Presidents' Day, Veterans Day, Flag Day, Memorial Day, among others. The celebration of Memorial Day in particular constitutes a kind of "cult of the dead which organizes and integrates the various faiths, ethnic and class groups into a sacred unity" (Warner, 1959, p. 249). This deeply ingrained civil religious faith only became more intense during the decades of the cold war, when the United States sought to distinguish itself as clearly as possible from the "godless communism" of the Soviet Union. Thus in the 1950s, the phrase "In God we Trust" was added to the dollar bill, while "One Nation under God" was added to the Pledge of Allegiance, a vow of faith mandatory in every public school. This American-style civil religion would find new, even more complicated expressions after the destruction of the World Trade Towers in 2001, as religious rhetoric was marshaled in a variety of ways to insure that God would "continue to bless America" against a new "axis of evil" (Lincoln, 2003, pp. 19–32).

Religion in conflict with political power: Resistance, rebellion, revolution and terrorism. Finally, as a form of discourse that makes an appeal to an ultimate, supra-human, transcendent or eternal source of authority, religious discourse can also be used to mount a profound challenge to political power. As the ultimate motivator, it can serve as the most powerful source of resistance, rebellion, and revolution against the dominant order.

This may take the form of a non-violent resistance against the dominant order, using religious authority as a means of rejecting the legitimacy of existing political power, yet without engaging in physical confrontation. Thus, even in the face of suppression by the U.S. government, Native American communities began to revive traditional rites like the Sun Dance during the late nineteenth and early twentieth century. In spite of—or perhaps in part because of—its suppression by the government, the Sun Dance would become one of the most powerful symbols of Native American identity, communal solidarity and personal power in the face of an alienating and oppressive political system. Religious resistance can have profound political consequences, such as Gandhi's *satyagraha* (cleaving to the truth) and *ahiṃsā* (non-harming) as non-violent struggle against the British Raj, or Martin Luther King's (1929–1968) use of Christian rhetoric and disobedience during the Civil Rights movement. Yet religious resistance may also take the form of more spectacular self-sacrifice like that of the Vietnamese monk, Thich Quang-Duc, who burned himself to death in 1963 in order to bring global attention to the suffering of the Vietnamese people.

When nonviolence and self-sacrifice appear futile, however, religious movements may turn to more aggressive forms of rebellion. Chinese history, for example, witnessed a number of religious rebellions against imperial power: the Daoist Yellow Turban rebellion at the end of the Han dynasty (206 BCE–220 CE), which was inspired by an apocalyptic vision of a Daoist utopia (second century); the White Lotus Societies at the end of the Yuan dynasty (1206–1368), which looked to the messianic prophecy of the coming of the future Buddha, Maitreya; and the Taiping rebellion (1851–1864), which used Christian messianic imagery and the hope for a Heavenly Kingdom to replace the Manchu regime.

In modern India, one of the most extreme examples of religious rebellion against the secular state is the rise of Sikh separatism in the Punjab region. In 1984, when militants under the lead of Jarnail Singh Bhindranwale took refuge in the Golden Temple complex in Amritsar, Prime Minister Indira Gandhi ordered a massive military assault (Operation Blue Star) that destroyed a large portion of the Temple and unleashed intense violence across the nation. Shortly after the operation, Gandhi was assassinated by her own Sikh body guards—clear evidence that, in some cases, the higher authority of religious conviction can indeed supercede secular political loyalty, even to the Prime Minister one has sworn to protect.

Ultimately, under the right conditions, religious rebellion and the appeal to a transcendent source of power can also lead to successful political revolution. The Iranian revolution led by Shīʿī Muslims against the Shah in 1979 was in many ways a surprise to the international community and to historians of religions alike. It offered perhaps the clearest evidence that religion had by no means waned in importance in the face of globalization and transnational capitalism, but had re-emerged as a powerful ideological alternative. Yet religious revolution is not limited to the Muslim world. Even the American Revolution, for example, was not without powerful elements of religious rhetoric. The Declaration of Independence itself could be said to express certain creedal statements of "sacred and undeniable" truths and divine rights, such as equality, life, liberty and the pursuit of happiness, the social contract, and even the legitimacy of revolution against oppression. As Jefferson famously put it, "Rebellion to Tyrants is Obedience to God" (Chidester, 1988, p. 61). Many revolutionaries would also describe their cause in almost millennial terms, with the vision of a new heaven and new earth created in America. As Thomas Paine wrote in 1776, "We have it in our power to begin the world over again . . . A situation similar to the present has not happened since the days of Noah until now" (Chidester, 1988, p. 61).

Terrorism has no doubt always been a tactic used in movements of resistance, rebellion, and revolution. Yet the twentieth and twenty-first centuries have witnessed arguably the most intense forms of religious terrorism ever known—indeed a global rise of religious violence. This in part due to the rise of religious extremism and nationalism, often setting themselves violently at odds with the forces of secularism and capitalism, and in part due to the widespread availability of inexpensive weapons, bombs, chemicals and other means of terror. More or less anyone can now concoct a fertilizer-bomb, as Timothy McVeigh did in the Oklahoma City bombing, or disseminate sarin gas, as the Aum Shinrikyō movement did in Tokyo subways. Perhaps the most disturbing form of terrorism in the modern era has come from extremist Palestinian groups such as Hamas, which have emerged since the first *intifada* against the Israeli occupation in 1987. Unable to contain their anger or find any other solution to an increasingly miserable situation, young Palestinian men and women have turned themselves into human bombs, killing thousands of ordinary people and injecting terror into daily life. Indeed, the charter document of Hamas is an overtly militant ideology, calling for violent self-sacrifice: "We will be its soldiers and the firewood of its fire, which will burn the enemies" (Farsoun and Zacharia, 1997, p. 339).

Similar kinds of revolutionary terrorist movements have emerged throughout the Middle East and now globally, inspired by radical leaders like Sayyid Quṭb (1906–1966) and the Muslim Brotherhood in Egypt. With an explicitly political agenda, Quṭb called for a violent revolution with the goal of overthrowing the Egyptian state. In Quṭb's view, the world is essentially divided into a party of God and a party of Satan, or those committed to God's rule and those opposed to it. As such, Quṭb was attacking both the secular modern West and those parts of the Arab world that did not support his vision of Islamic society. In Quṭb's interpretation, *jihād* is a call for immediate revolutionary struggle as the only way to implement a true Islamic order.

Although he was executed by the Egyptian government in 1966, Quṭb's radical vision and his revolutionary interpretation of *jihād* had a profound impact on many later Muslim extremists. Among others, he helped inspire the activities of Usāmah bin Lādin and the al-Qāʿidah network, who have similarly turned to extreme acts of violence as the means to restore a truly Islamic society in the face of Western imperialism. Indeed, al-Qāʿidah's attacks on the World Trade Towers—the supreme symbols and perhaps cathedrals of global capitalism—might be viewed as the ultimate use of religious authority as a revolutionary force of struggle against a secular economic and political power. As Lincoln suggests (2003, p. 18), their aim was to drop a kind of divine Hiroshima bomb upon what they regarded as a godless, materialist and inherently anti-Islamic power.

CONCLUSIONS. Although early sociologists and proponents of modernization theory had predicted a gradual waning of religious power amidst an increasingly rationalized, disenchanted modern world, it would seem that since the mid -twentieth century quite the opposite has happened. If anything, religious power and appeals to supra-human authority have been reasserted in emotionally intense, globally influential and spectacularly violent new ways. A striking number of political conflicts of the late twentieth century have involved religious identity as a central component: the nuclear standoff between India and Pakistan, the violence between Russia and Chechnya, Protestants and Catholics in Northern Ireland, bloody clashes between Christians and Muslims in Indonesia and Nigeria, and civil war in Sudan, Uganda and Sri Lanka. Indeed, some authors have expressed almost a nostalgia for the days of the Cold War, as we appear to be reverting to seventeenth century style wars of religion, but now fought with twenty-first century weapons.

Ironically, the relationship between religion and politics has not become clearer or simpler in the context of modernization and the emergence of a global economy. On the contrary, it has become infinitely more complex, as a wide array of religious movements adapt, transform or reject altogether the model of the modern secular nation and instead reassert the power of religion in the political sphere. Some authors have tried to analyze the post-Cold War global situation as a confrontation between major ideological forces—for example, Samuel Huntington's *Clash of Civilizations* (1996), or Benjamin Barber's *Jihad vs. McWorld* (1995), which describes a fundamental conflict between the forces of global capitalism and the reactionary "tribal" and religious forces who reject global monoculture and reassert local culture and identity.

Yet the post-Cold War situation would seem far more complex and multi-faceted than these simplistic ideological clashes or binary oppositions between secular political forces and religious extremism. One need only look to the case of the United States—with its powerful political forces on the religious right and its unique brand of civil religion—to see that religious authority can go hand in hand with political power, economic influence and military might. Even the most extreme "maximalist" religious movements such as al-Qāʿidah have no qualms about making sophisticated use of the networks of the global system, such as computers, telecommunications and international finance. Since the mid-twentieth century, moreover, a wide range of new international movements have emerged—such as Sōka Gakai Buddhism, the followings of gurus like Sathya Sai Baba, and various forms of transnational Islam—that are quite at home amidst the rapid flows of human beings and resources in a global era. Far from waning in significance, religions continue to provide a sense of meaning, value and collective identity that perhaps neither secular nations nor private corporations can offer. Calling as they do upon a transcendent source of authority, religious movements can also make demands upon their believers that supercede those of the nation or any other institution of merely human authority.

In sum, attempts to separate the imagined categories of religion and politics have not often resulted in the creation of rationally ordered secular nations, as imagined by Locke or America's founding fathers. On the contrary, they have given birth to even more complex kinds of religio-political power, in the form of civil religion, religious nationalism, extremism and terror. Gandhi himself could not have foreseen the role of religion in the post-colonial world, where it has had an even more dramatic impact on politics and national identity than he dared imagine.

SEE ALSO New Religious Movements, overview article.

BIBLIOGRAPHY

For good discussions of religion as a modern category and the problem of distinguishing it from politics, see Bruce Lincoln's, *Holy Terrors: Thinking about Religion after September 11* (Chicago, 2003), and "Theses on Method," *Method and Theory in the Study of Religion* 8, no.3 (1996): 225–28; Talal Asad, *Genealogies of Religion: Discipline and Reasons of Power in Christianity and Islam* (Baltimore, Md., 1993); Jonathan Z. Smith, *Imagining Religion: From Babylon to Jonestown* (Chicago, 1982); Russell McCutcheon, *Manufacturing Religion: The Discourse on Sui Generis Religion and the Politics of Nostalgia* (New York, 1997); Steven M. Wasserstrom, *Religion after Religion* (Princeton, N.J., 1999); David Chidester, *Patterns of Power: Religion and Politics in American Culture* (Englewood Cliffs, N.J., 1988); Derek R. Peterson and Darren R. Walhof, eds. *The Invention of Religion: Rethinking Belief in Politics and History* (New Brunswick, N.J., 2002); Richard King, *Orientalism and Religion: Postcolonial Theory, India and the Mystic East* (London, 1999).

More general works on religion and politics include Gustavo Benavides and M.W. Daly, eds. *Religion and Political Power* (Albany, N.Y., 1989); Jacob Neusner, ed. *God's Rule: The Politics of World Religions* (Washington, D.C., 2003); John L. Esposito and Michael Watson, eds. *Religion and Global Order* (Cardiff, 2000); Steven M. Cahn, ed., *Classics of Political and Moral Philosophy* (New York, 2002); Jeff Haynes, *Religion in Global Politics* (London, 1998); Max Stackhouse, "Politics and Religion," in *Encyclopedia of Religion*, Mircea Eliade, ed. (New York, 1987), v.11, pp. 408–422.

For modern approaches to religion and politics, see Niccolò Machiavelli, *The Prince*, George Bull, trans. (1513. Reprint,

New York, 1999); Maurice Cranston, ed., *John Locke on Politics, Religion and Education* (New York, 1965); Mark Goldie, ed., *Locke: Politics Essays* (Cambridge, U.K., 1997); Immanuel Kant, *Religion within the Limits of Reason Alone* (New York, 1960); Peter Gay, *The Enlightenment: An Interpretation* (New York, 1997); Karl Marx and Friedrich Engels, *The Communist Manifesto* (1847. Reprint, New York, 1980); "Die Revolution" (1852) in *Karl Marx, Friedrich Engels: Werke* (Berlin, 1960), vol. 8; John Raines, ed., *Marx on Religion* (Philadelphia, 2002); Émile Durkheim, *The Elementary Forms of the Religious Life* (1912. Reprint, New York, 1961); and *Moral Education* (New York, 1961); Max Weber, *Economy and Society*, 3 vols. (Berkeley, Calif., 1978), *The Protestant Ethic and the Spirit of Capitalism* (1905. Reprint New York, 2002); and "Politics as a Vocation" (1918) in H. H. Gerth and C. Wright Mills, trans., *From Max Weber: Essays in Sociology* (New York, 1946), pp. 296–450.

On Eliade's view of religion and his critics, see especially *The Quest: History and Meaning in Religion* (Chicago, 1969); John David Cave, *Mircea Eliade's Vision for a New Humanism* (New York, 1993); Bryan S. Rennie, *Reconstructing Eliade: Making Sense of Religion* (Albany, N.Y., 1996); Guilford Dudley III, *Religion on Trial: Mircea Eliade and His Critics* (Philadelphia, 1977); Ivan Strenski, *Four Theories of Myth in the Twentieth Century: Cassirer, Eliade, Lévi-Strauss and Malinowski* (Iowa City, 1977).

For feminist critiques, see Mary Daly, *Beyond God the Father: Toward a Philosophy of Women's Liberation* (Boston, 1973) and *Gyn/Ecology: The Metaethics of Radical Feminism* (Boston, 1978); Rita M. Gross, *Feminism and Religion: An Introduction* (Boston, 1996); Carol P. Christ and Judith Plashow, eds., *Womanspirit Rising* (New York, 1979); Grace M. Jantzen, *Power, Gender and Christian Mysticism* (Cambridge, U.K., 1995); Wendy Doniger, *The Implied Spider: Politics and Theology in Myth* (New York, 1998).

On Foucault's work, see *The History of Sexuality, Volume I: An Introduction* (New York, 1978), and "Le chef mythique de la revolte de l'Iran," in *Dits et ecrits 1948–1988*, vol. 3, edited by Daniel Defert and François Ewald (Paris, 1994); Jeremy R. Carrette, ed., *Religion and Culture* (New York, 1999) and *Foucault and Religion: Spiritual Corporality and Political Spirituality* (New York, 2000); Gary Gutting, ed. *The Cambridge Companion to Foucault* (Cambridge, U.K., 1994); James. D. Fabion, ed. *Power: Essential Works of Foucault, 1954–1984, volume 3* (New York, 2001).

Good studies of nationalism and religious nationalism include Peter van der Veer, *Religious Nationalism: Hindus and Muslims in India* (Berkeley, Calif., 1994); Mark Juergensmeyer, *The New Cold War* (Berkeley, Calif., 1993); Partha Chatterjee, *The Nation and its Fragments* (Princeton, N.J., 1993); Carlton Hayes, *Nationalism: A Religion* (New York, 1960); Benedict Anderson, *Imagined Communities: Reflections on the Origin and Spread of Nationalism* (London, 1983).

For studies of civil religion, see Robert Bellah, *The Broken Covenant: American Civil Religion in Time of Trial* (Chicago, 1992); Marcela Cristi, *From Civil to Political Religion: The Intersection of Culture, Religion and Politics* (Waterloo, Canada,2001); Christel Lane, *The Rise of Rulers: Ritual in Industrial Society—The Soviet Case* (Cambridge, U.K., 1981).

On the complex question of secularism and civil religion in the United States, see Carolyn Marvin and David W. Ingle, *Blood Sacrifice and the Nation: Totem Rituals and the American Flag* (New York, 1999); Mary Douglas and Steven M. Tipton, eds., *Religion in America: Spirituality in a Secular Age* (Boston, 1983); Ernest Tuveson, *Redeemer Nation: The Idea of America's Millennial Role* (Chicago, 1968); W. Lloyd Warner, *The Living and the Dead: A Study of the Symbolic Life of Americans* (New Haven, Conn., 1959).

On the role of religion in movements of resistance and revolution see Bruce Lincoln, ed., *Religion, Rebellion, Revolution* (New York, 1985); Mark Juergensmeyer, *Terror in the Mind of God: The Global Rise of Religious Violence* (Berkeley, Calif., 2003); Stanley J. Tambiah, *Leveling Crowds: Ethno-National Conflict and Collective Violence in South Asia* (Berkeley, Calif., 1997); Vittorio Lanternari, *The Religions of the Oppressed* (New York, 1963); Guenter Lewy, *Religion and Revolution* (New York, 1974); Samuel P. Huntington, *The Clash of Civilizations and the Remaking of the World Order* (New York, 1996); Benjamin Barber, *Jihad vs. McWorld: How Globalism and Tribalism are Reshaping the World* (New York, 1995).

For religion and politics in specific religious traditions, refer to the sub-articles below. Works cited in this article include, on Hinduism: Mohandas Gandhi, *Autobiography or the Story of My Experiments with Truth* (1927. Reprint, Ahmedabad, India, 1940); Romila Thapar, "Sacrifice, Surplus and the Soul," *History of Religions* 33 (1994): 305–324; Brian K. Smith, *Classifying the Universe: The Ancient Indian Varna System and the Origin of Caste* (New York, 1994); Lise McKean, *Divine Enterprise: Gurus and the Hindu Nationalist Movement* (Chicago, 1996); *The Complete Works of Swami Vivekananda* (Calcutta, 1984), vol. 3.

On Buddhism: Stanley J. Tambiah, *Buddhism Betrayed? Religion, Politics and Violence in Sri Lanka* (Chicago, 1992); John S. Strong, *The Legend of King Ashoka* (Princeton, N.J., 1983); Ian Harris, *Buddhism and Politics in Twentieth Century Asia* (London, 1999); Geoffrey Samuel, *Civilized Shamans: Buddhism in Tibetan Society* (Washington, D.C., 1993).

On Islam: John Esposito, *Islam and Politics* (Syracuse, N.Y., 1991) and *Unholy War: Terror in the Name of Islam* (New York, 2002); Peter G. Mandaville, *Transnational Muslim Politics: Re-imagining the Umma* (New York, 2001); Samih K. Farsoun and Christina E. Zacharia, *Palestine and the Palestinians* (Boulder, Colo., 1997).

On Christianity and Judaism: Jacques le Goff, *Medieval Civilization, 400–1500* (New York, 2000); Ernst Kantorowicz, *The King's Two Bodies* (Princeton, N.J., 1957); Ernst Troeltsch, *The Social Teaching of the Christian Churches* (Chicago, 1981); Alain Dieckhoff, *The Invention of a Nation: Zionist Thought and the Making of Modern Israel* (New York, 2002).

On Native American, African and other indigenous traditions: Joseph G. Jorgensen, *Sun Dance Religion: Power for the Powerless* (Chicago, 1986); James Mooney, *The Ghost Dance Religion and the Outbreak at Wounded Knee* (New York, 1973); Huston Smith and Reuben Snake, *One Nation under God* (Santa Fe, 1996); Omer C. Stewart, *The Peyote Religion: A History* (Lincoln, Neb., 1987); David Chidester, *Savage Systems: Colonialism and Comparative Religion in Southern Africa* (Charlottesville, Va., 1996).

On new religious movements: Catherine Wessinger, *How the Millennium Comes Violently: From Jonestown to Heaven's Gate*

(New York, 2000); James Tabor and Eugene Gallagher, *Why Waco? Cults and the Battle for Religious Freedom in America* (Berkeley, Calif., 1997); and Hugh B. Urban, *Tantra: Sex, Secrecy, Politics and Power in the Study of Religion* (Berkeley, Calif., 2003).

HUGH URBAN (2005)

POLITICS AND RELIGION: POLITICS AND BUDDHISM

In those parts of the Asian world where Buddhism is the religion of the majority, it continues to play a prominent role in many nations, not infrequently with consequences for national politics and destinies. Because Buddhism is so closely associated with cultural norms and worldviews, it cannot be isolated from politics, whether viewed historically or with regard to current events. Buddhism is a living organism, feeding off the political circumstances of a particular culture, time, or place. Its history reflects the strains of adolescence, maturity, and old age, and it has metamorphosed on occasion to accommodate changes in its environment. Buddhism's history of synthesis and adaptation led it to divide into three great branches (Theravāda, Mahāyāna, and Vajrayāna) and a myriad of schools and movements. This entry reviews the relationship between politics and Buddhism from four perspectives. It first asks how the Buddhist tradition understands and defines political life and faith and examines to what extent Buddhists see the two as separate spheres. Second, it isolates historical developments in religious and political power in the Buddhist tradition, showing the sometimes complementary, sometimes competitive interaction of the two forces. Third, the article considers how this interaction still resonates in the Buddhist world at the beginning of the twenty-first century. The article ends with a brief review of the impact of modernization and socioeconomic change on Buddhism's intersection with politics. Adapting to changing circumstances throughout history, Buddhism has sought to both protect and develop its place in the world to which it ministers—including the often polarizing and spiteful realm of politics.

DEFINING RELIGION AND POLITICS IN A BUDDHIST CONTEXT. This article will define politics as the science or art of government and the management of state affairs, with the state in turn defined as an organized political community. In many cases nationalism has played a significant role in politics; this slippery concept may be defined as a sometimes chauvinistic devotion to an ethnic, religious, or political community, with a concomitant impetus to advance its interests and traditions, often at the expense of other communities. Turning to religion, we may venture that Buddhism, in all its various forms, includes at least two features: in Pali, one of its traditional classical languages (the other being Sanskrit), these are the "church" (*sāsana*) and doctrine (*dhamma;* Sanskrit: *dharma*). A third, more contemporary characteristic is Buddhist "culture" (e.g., Sinhala: *bauddha sanskrutiya*). The aim of Buddhism is to help people find meaning in life. The religion has an institutional structure—for instance, the monastic *saṅgha* (Sanskrit: *saṃgha*) for monks and nuns, as well as various sects or Nikāyas)—but in essence it is a religion that teaches a state of mind, a way of being. Its doctrine is not primarily concerned with political systems or even social reform, which are considered to be irrelevant to salvation (Gombrich, p. 30). But history shows us that Buddhism has nonetheless been used to further political or sectarian goals, and some politicians have employed it as a vehicle to promote exclusivist, ethnically based nationalisms.

The relationship between Buddhism and politics, then, has been and continues to be a complex one, and it varies considerably among Asia's very diverse Buddhist communities. Politics in majority-Buddhist countries ranges from the relative freedom of expression enjoyed in Sri Lanka, Thailand, and Japan to the repressions imposed on the citizens of Myanmar, the People's Republic of China, and North Korea. Notwithstanding the apolitical nature of the teachings of Gautama Śākyamuni, the fifth-century- BCE Buddha, and despite the stereotype of a passivist, non-aggressive *dharma,* it can be argued that the seeds of a political worldview exist in the Pali Canon, a scripture composed of three "baskets" or collections, which all Buddhists acknowledge as a primary source. Later Mahāyāna texts also have political significance; the *Saddharmapundarīka Sūtra,* for example, served as the key text for the modern Japanese Sōka Gakkai (Value Creation Society), while the *Suvarnabhasottama Sūtra* expounded on the duties of a righteous king. Additionally, quasi-historical "chronicles" such as Sri Lanka's *Mahavamsa* or Myanmar's *Glass Palace Chronicle of the Kings of Burma,* which purport to give further insight into the Buddha's missionary travels, express an often deep religious conviction linking the *dharma* to a state.

Although Buddhism's primary scriptures do not set down a precise political philosophy, a polysemous reading of the Pali *Sutta Pitaka* reveals a political ideal that complements the soteriological teachings of the Buddha. This soteriology rests on the central problem of painfulness (*dukkha;* Sanskrit *duḥka*), to which Buddhism offers a practical solution, focused on life in the here and now. No eschatological dilemma or otherworldly goals preoccupy the Buddha; rather, his teachings rely primarily on seeing the facts of life as they are (*yathabhuta-dassana*) and eradicating superstition and useless social practices through reason (*takka*) and analysis (*vibhajja*). Beyond this epistemological basis, however, there is a definite social dimension to Buddhist teachings: The Buddha not only asks how and what we know, but also what we should do, not only for ourselves but for the common good.

The Buddha's message against coarse craving (*tanhā*) and the emotional cankers (*āsava*) of greed, hatred, and delusion applies not only to the individual, but also carries implications for the collective well-being of the community. Aggression (*patighanusaya*), indulgence (*kamasukhalikanuyoga*), and other spiritual hazards regularly upset the equilibrium of peoples, states, and the world at large. Several texts (e.g., the *Sigalovada Sutta* and *Dīgha-nikāya* 3.180) set down a layperson's code of conduct (*gihivinaya*) with regard to the society in which he or she lives. Two of the most significant sūtras dealing with what might loosely be described as political responsibility are the *Cakkavattisihanada-sutta* and the *Aggañña Suttas* (*Dīgha-nikāya* 3.58, 80). These texts treat the origin and development of the state and the rights and duties of both monarch and citizen. The model society and polity they present fosters ethical conduct and embodies a strong social ideal, which then guides the principal objectives of the state. *Dīgha-nikāya* 3.62 describes the ideal world-ruler, the "Celestial Wheel–turning king," who uses his civil authority to promote righteousness and security. In this and other canonical passages, the recommendations go beyond the caste-based worldview behind Hindu statecraft and law codes (*Arthaśāstra*). The *Aggañña Sutta* in particular urges equal rights and opportunities for all people simply as fellow members of humanity, irrespective of caste or race (see also *Majjihima Nikāya* 2. 85, 151, *Dīgha-nikāya* 1.99).

Based on these texts, one could argue that Buddhism charges the state and its citizens with the responsibility to maintain economic and social equality. Whether these texts can be seen as constituting a fully fledged political philosophy, however, is doubtful; nonetheless they do suggest that the state must not impede human freedom, and that both individual citizens and the polity as a whole should be allowed to evolve and mature. This is consistent with the Buddha's teaching that nothing is permanent, nor should anything rest on the basis of authority alone (*Aṅguttara-nikāya* 1. 189); both principles certainly apply to the state. More controversially, some scholars have tried to extrapolate from the Buddha's rule (*vinaya*) for his monastic order (*saṃgha*)—citing such practices as the pooling of resources—to arrive at a proto-socialistic interpretation of Buddhist political doctrine in general, in which similarly communal principles would guide the state as a whole. Others emphasize the *saṃgha's* democratic character and argue that its traditions spilled over into various forms of assembly and village administration (see Joshi, p. 33). Yet although the Vinaya Piṭaka undoubtedly gives us a picture of an early Indian community of mendicants organized along "socialist" and even "democratic" lines, this cannot be taken as a political model for lay society. In sum, whereas the traditional Buddhist *saṃgha* was not concerned with politics, the Pali Canon arguably contains a political philosophy of a sort, derived from the Buddha's advice to rulers and citizens. The ideal of harmonious coexistence between the two and among the latter lies at the core of this philosophy, which also emphasizes the individual's right to pursue his or her fortune, but not at the expense of others (*Anguttara Nikāya* 2.95).

Politics and Buddhism are acknowledged as distinct entities in the canonical scripture, but with the rise of the Mauryan empire under Aśoka (c. 250 BCE), the association between religion and state shifted subtly toward state leadership in religious affairs. A. L. Basham indicates this when he writes: "In place of the traditional policy of territorial expansion [Aśoka] substituted conquest by Righteousness (as we here inadequately translate by the very pregnant word *dharma*)" (1954, p. 54). The monarch's conversion to Buddhism and the subsequent widespread propagation of its values, including respectful veneration and oversight of the *saṃgha*, produced an important model of a Buddhist state and its relationship with Buddhist monastic orders. In due course, the *saṃgha* sought to assume a position to grant legitimacy to the state. And much later, a new three-fold "refuge" arose in parts of the Buddhist world to complement the traditional refuges (*śārańa*) of the Buddha, *dhamma* and *saṃgha*. This new, inescapably political "refuge" consisted of country, national identity, and religion—or as expressed in the state motto adopted by Cambodia's 1993 Constitution, "nation, religion, king."

HISTORICAL DEVELOPMENT. Historically, Buddhism is considered to have developed more in concert than in conflict with political power. In fact, Trevor Ling has coined the term "royal Buddhism"to describe the increasingly symbiotic relationship between *saṃgha* and monarchy in the medieval period (though it was of course not wholly devoid of antagonism; see p. 133). By extension, the relationship between *saṃgha* and laity has been described as leading to a "mass politicization" of the Buddhist population (see Bechert, 1978, p. 16). The Theravāda polities of South and Southeast Asia provide good examples of this symbiosis of Buddhism and political authority. In addition to the well-developed Mon kingdoms of southern Burma and the central plain of the Chao Phraya (e.g., Dvaravati), Sri Lanka serves as an excellent example, with its celebrated story of the early Buddhist ideal "warrior-king" Dutthagamini (c. 150 BCE). According to the story, he requested five hundred monks to accompany him as a "blessing and protection" or "merit-field" in his efforts to repel Tamil invaders; he is also said to have carried a relic of the Buddha on his own spear as an amulet (see Alice Greenwald in Bardwell Smith, 1978, p. 13). The Khmer court in ninth- through thirteenth-century Cambodia extravagantly endorsed a cult of Hindu-Buddhist divine kingship, which reached its apogee during the reign of Jayavarman VII (1181–c. 1215), who modeled his image of the Buddha in the Angkor temple of Bayon after himself. At his death in 1218 he received the title Mahaparamasaugata, or "the great and supreme Buddhist" (see Coedès, p. 172). Burma's Pagan period (c. 800–1200 CE) was a golden age of the Buddhist monarchical ideal, represented by the Ananda temple (*zedi*) built by King Kyanzittha (r. 1084–1113). Writing about this kingdom, which was centered around the upper Irrawaddy, Michael Aung Thwin observes

> [T]he protective capacity of the state in twelfth and thirteenth-century Burma was a strong one; it was not a violent or chaotic society but an ordered and hierarchical one, concerned not with individual political freedom as a measure of happiness, but with social and political order, ruled not by independent lords and armies,

> but by a sovereign and his officials, and pacified by a [Buddhist] primate and his monks. (p. 96)

In the fourteenth- through eighteenth-century Lao kingdom (Lan Xang), the *saṅgha* legitimized what was perceived as a karmically justified kingly rule; in return they expected the king to meet their standards of just rule (*dhammaraja*). In Sukhothai (middle Thailand, 1230–1378 CE), the respected king Rama Kamheng was a precursor of the royal Buddhism associated with the great Ratnakosin dynasty (1782–present), in which the monarchs are not only the foremost sponsors of the Buddhist faith, but also symbols of national unity.

The function of the monarch. One feature common to most of these examples is the function of the monarch (clearly a "political" figure) as purifier and unifier of the Buddhist monastic order, as exemplified by the amalgamation of the Sinhalese *saṅgha* under Parakamabahu I (1153–1186 CE). In Mahāyāna Buddhist Asia, by contrast, Japan experienced the rise of powerful Buddhist temples and even armies of "priest-warriors" *(sohei)* from the time of Prince Regent Taishi Shōtoku (c. 600 CE). The Buddhist monk Nichiren's reforms (c. 1270 CE) and his promotion of the *Saddharmapuṇḍarīka Sūtra* (*Lotus Sūtra*) as an intrinsic aspect of national identity—and of himself as something of a messiah—resulted in a unique situation where "much religio-political capital was made of his inheritance in subsequent centuries" (see Harris, p. 15). In Tibet, the concept of the Buddhist monk (lama) as a political ruler originated with Sa skya Paṇḍita, who was made vice-regent to the Mongol khan Godan (1246 CE). This concept was reinforced when the head of the Dge lugs pa sect, the lama Sodnams Gyamtsho, received the honorific Dalai Lama from the Altan khan in 1578.

The Himalayan region. The traditional Himalayan Buddhist kingdoms of Tibet, Nepal, Sikkim, and Bhutan are further interesting examples of the merging of religion with political order over a period of many centuries. In this regard, Nepal's polity has been dominated by a strong connection between the royal house and Hinduism for centuries. As recently as 1962, the Constitution referred to "the Hindu kingdom of Nepal," and although the 1990 Constitution no longer uses this language, the king (traditionally revered as an incarnation of Viṣṇu) is still identified as the "symbol of the nation." The majority of Nepal's diverse population being Hindu notwithstanding, Buddhism has also had a prominent place in Nepal's unique culture and sociology for over a millennium. Rose and Fisher (1970, p. 9) reflect on the many migrations that have affected Nepal over the centuries, their combined impact "encrusted with mythological lore." For example, the great Buddhist saint Milarepa (c. 1050 CE) is associated with several holy sites in Nepal. Tibetan Buddhism has clearly dominated entire communities, notably the high mountain peoples, Sherpas and Tamangs, and the Newar in the Valley of Nepal. What is remarkable is the close theological connection (including yogic practices and iconography) between Buddhism and Hinduism, something remarked on as far back as the seventh century CE by Hsüan Tsang. A sense of the contribution of Buddhism to Nepal's cultural and spiritual identity is everywhere apparent either in great historic structures (e.g., the Swayambhunath Stupa outside of Kathmandu), or in some of its contemporary leading personalities, such as the role of Dilgo Khyentse Rinpoche, the Nyingmapa *terton*, "discoverer of holy treasure" and founder of the Shechen temple.

Nonetheless, despite self-evident respect for Buddhism, the government of Nepal is careful not to permit politicization of the faith. Given the dominance of Tibetan forms of Buddhism in Nepal (other sects are present but of modest significance), and the always-sensitive proximity to China, no promotion of Tibetan political rights, or public veneration of the Dalai Lama for that matter, is permitted. Any suggestion of a pan-Himalayan Buddhist renaissance is alarming to the dominant Hindu communities and the regional super powers. Apart from the occasional anomaly (e.g., a Tibetan Buddhist exile guerrilla presence in Mustang), Buddhism has no political role to play in contemporary Nepal.

Neighboring Sikkim is the smallest of the traditional Himalayan Buddhist polities, ruled in recent centuries by an absolute Buddhist monarchy associated with the Namgyal family, which in turn traced its roots to the ninth-century Minvang dynasty of eastern Tibet's Chumbi Valley. Nyingmapa Buddhism was the faith of the early Tibetan migrants to Sikkim, the Bhutia people, and became the state religion. In the seventeenth century, a Minvang prince, Phuntsok Namgyal, became Sikkim's king *(chogyal)*. The last of his lineage was the twelfth *chogyal*, Palden Thondup Namgyal, who died in 1982. In time, other indigenous communities (e.g., Lepcha, Gurung, Rai) accepted both Namgyal dynastic rule and Buddhism. After years of interfering with its affairs, and alarmed by continuing border problems with China, in 1975 India annexed Sikkim. Even before Sikkim became India's twenty-second state, the era of Buddhist cultural dominance was already compromised by a longstanding migration of Hindu Nepalis, which began in the British period and has continued unabated. But Indian sovereignty has not crushed Sikkim's Buddhist spirit or cultural identity, and New Delhi conscientiously supports the maintenance of *chortens* (stupas) and sites of Sikkimese historical and spiritual importance. Sikkim's monarchial collapse has left Bhutan as the last Himalayan Buddhist kingdom and, in a sense, curator of a once widespread religio-political world view and civilization.

Tradition claims that Bhutan (Druk Yul) was converted to Buddhism by the storied Indian saint Padmasambhava in the eighth century CE. The faith was reinforced by the arrival of the great Nyingmapa teacher, Guru Rinpoche, from Tibet. A specific Buddhist polity emerged only in the seventeenth century when a Tibetan Kagyupa monk, Ngawang Namgyal, took on the title Shadrung ("at whose feet one submits"). Apart from centralizing authority, he set down a legal system and promoted the building of religious structures.

Thus began a Buddhist state that functioned for 270 years based on a shared rule between a religious leader thought to be the Shandung's reincarnation (*je khenpo*) and a secular authority (the Deb Raja). A British presence from 1864 was unobtrusive and the country essentially escaped an interfering colonial experience. In 1907, in response to the perceived political needs of the time by both religious and civil leaders, a monarchial system was introduced. Hereditary kings from the Wangchuck family formed the basis of an erastian Buddhist polity which is still in place. The kings have been capable rulers, and although an advisory national assembly (*tshoghu*) was introduced in 1951, when the prime minister was assassinated in 1964, his office was never replaced. The present king, the fourth Druk Gyalpo, Jigme Singye Wangchuck, was consecrated monarch by the *je khenpo* in 1972. As his predecessors, the king wears as part of his regal garments a saffron scarf (*kabne*), the mark of a Buddhist ruler, and an item shared only with the *je khenpo*.

Unlike the destabilized Nepal monarchy (ruinously cut down in 2001 by a deranged crown prince), the Bhutan royal house appears educated, and realistic about the pressures of modernity. Bhutan isolated itself in the mid-twentieth century from the backpackers, counter-culture visitors, and other effects of globalization. It kept India at arm's length through prudent foreign policy, and has independently and forcefully attacked various Indian secessionist organizations that periodically seek refuge in Bhutan's borders. Many challenges remain, notably widespread illegal immigration and imported political notions contrary to a traditional Buddhist monarchy, no matter how progressive. Bhutan has shown the benefits of this kind of rule. King Jigme Singye Wangchuck has, as one commentator notes, "enlightened but constrained attitudes towards progress and development" (Crossette, 1995, p. 182). This, along with a *saṅgha* active in welfare and development activities, suggests an ultimately successful and enduring Buddhist state.

Colonial experience. Another essential feature of this formative historical period is Buddhist nationalism in the context of the colonial experience. Although nationalism is often associated with political events in eighteenth- and nineteenth-century Europe, Buddhist nationalism in Asia arose very early. "In this way," writes Heinz Bechert, "a form of nationalism originated in ancient Ceylon which was rather close to modern nationalism with its conceptions of a united nation with common linguistic, cultural and religious traditions" (1978, p. 8). Steven Kemper (p. 17) shows that a "full-fledged set of identities" was in place in Sri Lanka a thousand years before the colonial era, and that some of the same conditions applied as well to the "theater states" and "galactic polities" of premodern South and Southeast Asia. In virtually all of these instances, Buddhism played a prominent role in nurturing national identity and was thus implicated in the political repercussions of the rise of nationalism.

With the advent of colonialism the autonomous Buddhist world faced increasing confusion and doubt. The eighteenth century brought British incursions into the subcontinent, while the next century saw the establishment of French hegemony in Indochina. Japanese colonial expansion into Korea, Manchuria, and Formosa (1895–1945) brought different forms of Buddhism into these countries. A takeover by Buddhist Japan created much less of a culture shock, though, than did Victorian Christian imperialism, which attacked the emerging sense of national uniqueness and purpose in British-occupied Asian countries, and thereby also disrupted the intimate and still developing connection between Buddhism and political identity. In many cases religious identity fuelled political reactions to imperialism (see Pye, p. 91). In general, the faith retained its hold over the majority of believers, contributing to a religious revival that nurtured struggles for independence. Siam (Thailand) alone escaped foreign subjugation, largely through the capable statecraft of three perceptive monarchs who ruled the country between 1851 and 1925: Mongkut (later Rama IV), Chulalongkorn, and Vajiravudh. These monarchs were realists who acknowledged the need to modernize their country, to that end accepting those foreign values and technologies they deemed useful. At the same time, however, they centralized both the polity and the *saṅgha*, bringing the religion directly under the control of what was quickly becoming a modern nation state (see Ishii, p. 47).

By contrast, the government of Burma, long isolationist and introverted, was completely unprepared to meet the ideological and intellectual challenges of colonialism and modernization. Burma-centrism, supported by a mythological cosmology, had given the Burmese "a disproportionate overestimation of their own power" (Sarkisyanz, p. 99). Buddhism emerged as the only foundation upon which to build a Burmese national consciousness, as various nationalist groups, including "heritage protection" (*wuthanu athin*), and monks such as U Wissera and U Ottama assumed quasi-political leadership roles. Buddhist millenarian expectations—centered around the *set kya min* or Restorer of the Golden Age, the future Buddha who would reestablish the perfect society—accompanied Burmese nationalism, as did elements of magic and sorcery such as the notion of *yadaya chay*, or "outwitting fate by prompt action." (In fact, these ideas have persisted into the twenty-first century, and they still resound in the corridors of political power in Myanmar). In Ceylon (later Sri Lanka), the British initially found it politically expedient to grant state protection to Buddhism, but Christian missionary agitation led the crown to withdraw this protection in 1853. This created an immediate vacuum, with which the *saṅgha* was unable to cope. Only in the latter part of the nineteenth century did Sinhalese Buddhism assume a proactive posture, under such individuals as Anagārika Dharmapāla (1864–1933) and the American convert Col. Henry Steel Olcott (1832–1907), who inspired a Buddhist political renaissance.

BUDDHISM AND POLITICS IN THE POSTCOLONIAL ERA. The political position of Buddhism at the end of the colonial era created institutional arrangements and led to events that still resonated decades later. After Sri Lanka gained its independence in 1948, its *saṅgha* directly entered into political life, issuing a declaration of intent via Vidyālankara, a leading Buddhist seminary. The declaration broadly defined the expectations for the *saṅgha*'s activity beyond the monastery, and the Ven. Walpola Rahula's still much-cited work *Bhiksuvage Urumaya* (Heritage of the Bhikkhu, 1946) offered further guidance. Both maintained that the modern monk, alert to the decline of Buddhist influence in national affairs, should see political engagement as a responsibility. The initiative also promoted a doctrine of Sinhalese distinctiveness, leading to what Tessa Bartholomeusz has called a "marriage of religion and ethnicity" (p. 78). This marriage spurred the creation of a number of politicized Sinhala Buddhist societies and nationalist (*deshapremi*) groups, which at times have had significant influence over state affairs. No Sri Lankan head of state could afford to marginalize Buddhism without jeopardizing his or her power. Some couched their political aims in grandiose religio-political language, as did President J. R. Jayawardene in his 1978 *dharmishta,* or righteous policy objectives. Others, such as Ranasinghe Premadasa (1989), used Sri Lanka's royal past to legitimate their authority, symbolically standing on the once-royal dais at Kandy's Temple of the Tooth.

Religio-cultural issues also run deep in Myanmar, where in 1962 a rogue military junta seized power from the pro-Buddhist government of Prime Minister U Nu, who had styled himself as the Mahathammada or true leader of Buddhism. The new dictatorship forced the long-autonomous *saṅgha* to conform to strict government control. As elsewhere in Buddhist Asia, Burmese political rulers rewarded cooperative monks, and the ruling junta frequently "makes merit" through major public demonstrations of institutional support for the faith, seeking to justify its rule to a skeptical and downtrodden society. Widespread but usually unvoiced sympathy among the *saṅgha* for the dissident leader Aung San Suu Kyi periodically erupts into public demonstrations. For a month in 1990, for instance, monks "turned over the begging bowl" (*patta ni kauz za na kan*) to military personnel in political protest, an extraordinary manifestation of Buddhism's quiet influence, even under military tyranny. In Vietnam, where French colonialism led to a society divided between Buddhists and Roman Catholics, the 1930s saw a Buddhist renaissance that accelerated with the struggle for independence, particularly after the defeat of the French at Dien Bien Phu in May 1954. President Ngo Dinh Diem's overt partiality to Catholicism at a time of intense nationalist fervor alienated Buddhists, who were refused a public voice. Vietnam's *saṅgha* never demanded a "Buddhist" government, but through their actions they sought to awaken a humanitarian and nationalist consciousness in their country. Most famously, in June 1963 Ven. Thich Quang-Du'c burned himself to death in Saigon to call attention to the sufferings of the Vietnamese people. Other monks followed with similar ritual deaths, which devotees characterize as acts of heroism.

As Thich Nhat Hanh has noted, "in every Buddhist the ideas of Buddhism and nationalism are intertwined and cannot be easily separated" (p. 45, 107). In Vietnam, however, Ho Chi Minh's victorious Communist Party sought to harness Vietnamese nationalism to support its own ideology. Their claim to a monopoly on both politics and Vietnamese consciousness robbed Buddhism of any critical social or political voice. Indeed, the government sought to bring Buddhism under its control by establishing a single, state-sponsored Vietnamese national Buddhist *saṅgha* (Giao Hoi Phat Giao Viet Nam). Although communist governments in Vietnam, China, and North Korea continue to tolerate Buddhism, they never invite it to play a role either in political power or in defining official national ideology. Non-communist countries such as Thailand and Sri Lanka have often enshrined Buddhism in their constitutions, but only to patronize or protect it or to secure its place in what Bartholomeusz calls "Buddhist secularism" (p. 5). Here, as in the communist countries, the state does not envision an active political role for Buddhism or its clergy.

Effects of Modernization and Globalization. As R. N. Bellah points out, modernization is not simply a matter of adopting new technologies; it also involves a "modernization of the soul" (1965, p. 196). In early-twentieth-century Asia, Buddhists often adopted concepts imported from the West, such as social welfare or socialism, and adapted them to their own countries' circumstances, endowing them with a distinctive, indigenous vigor. In Japan, the Sōka Gakkai lay sect of Nichiren Buddhism exemplifies this process; through its influential leftist Clean Government Party (Kōmeitō, founded 1964), it pushes for the establishment of a welfare state to secure the health and material well-being of lower social classes. What is now referred to as "engaged Buddhism" has its roots in the late nineteenth century; in the late twentieth and early twenty-first centuries, "engaged" Buddhist thinkers and activists such as Burma's Aung San Suu Kyi, Tibet's Dalai Lama, Thailand's Sulak Sivaraksa, and Sri Lanka's A. T. Ariyaratna have used the faith to respond to a host of issues brought on by modernization and globalization. In a unique response to the devastation of their country's environment, some Thai monks have "ordained" trees otherwise doomed to be cut down. Among the other issues Buddhism must grapple with are rampant consumerism, the deluge of Western popular culture, and political tyranny, often supported or simply ignored by the international community. It is no exaggeration to claim that "Buddhism in contemporary Asia means energetic engagement with social and political issues and crises at least as much as it means monastic or meditative withdrawal" (Queen, p. ix).

Referring to Buddhism's long association with a wide array of cultures, regimes, and governments, Thich Nhat Hanh is surely correct when he writes that "the forms of Buddhism must change so that the essence of Buddhism remains unchanged" (p. 94). In principle, the religion remains ready to offer political guidance and criticism, without seeking theocratic power or adherence to any type of dogmatic fundamentalism.

SEE ALSO Colonialism and Postcolonialism.

BIBLIOGRAPHY

Aris, Michael. *Bhutan: The Early History of a Himalayan Kingdom.* Warminster, U.K., 1979.

Aung-Thwin, Michael. *Pagan: The Origins of Modern Burma.* Honolulu, 1985.

Bartholomeusz, Tessa. *In Defense of Dharma: Just-War Ideology in Buddhist Sri Lanka.* London and New York, 2002.

Basham, Arthur L. *The Wonder that Was India.* New York, 1954.

Bechert, Heinz. *Buddhismus, Staat und Gesellschaft in der Ländern des Theravāda-Buddhismus.* Frankfurt, 1966. This remains a foremost source for the history and infrastructure of the Buddhist monastic order and its role in society and state in South and Southeast Asia.

Bechert, Heinz. *Buddhism and Society.* Kandy, Sri Lanka, 1978.

Coedès, George. *The Indianized States of Southeast Asia.* Edited by Walter F. Vella. Translated by Susan Brown Cowing. Canberra, 1968. A classic text by a great scholar on the Hindu-Buddhist background of early Southeast Asian polities.

Collins, Steven. *Nirvana and Other Buddhist Felicities: Utopias of the Pali Imaginaire.* Cambridge and New York, 1998.

Crossette, Barbara. *So Close to Heaven: The Vanishing Buddhist Kingdoms of the Himalayas.* New York, 1995.

Davidson, Ronald M. *Indian Esoteric Buddhism: A Social History of the Tantric Movement.* New York, 2002.

Goldstein, Melvyn C., and Matthew T. Kapstein. *Buddhism in Contemporary Tibet: Religious Revival and Cultural Identity.* Berkeley, Calif., 1998.

Gombrich, Richard, and Gananath Obeysekere. *Buddhism Transformed: Religious Change in Sri Lanka.* Princeton, N.J., 1988.

Harris, Ian, ed. *Buddhism and Politics in Twentieth-Century Asia.* London and New York, 1999. The best single-volume source on politics and Buddhism at the millennium, with contributions by ten experts on specific modern nations.

Heine-Geldern, Robert. *Conceptions of State and Kingship in Southeast Asia.* Ithaca, N.Y., 1956.

Houtman, Gustaaf. *Mental Culture in Burmese Crisis Politics: Aung San Suu Kyi and the National League for Democracy.* Tokyo, 1999. A perceptive study of certain Buddhist dimensions underlying the politics of modern Myanmar.

Ishii, Yoneo. *Sangha, State, and Society: Thai Buddhism in History.* Translated by Peter Hawkes. Honolulu, 1986.

Jones, Charles Brewer. *Buddhism in Taiwan: Religion and the State 1660–1990.* Honolulu, 1999.

Joshi, L. M. *Aspects of Buddhism in Indian History.* Kandy, Sri Lanka, 1973.

Kemper, Steven. *The Presence of the Past: Chronicles, Politics, and Culture in Sinhala Life.* Ithaca, N.Y., 1991.

Keyes, Charles F. *The Golden Peninsula: Culture and Adaptation in Mainland Southeast Asia.* Honolulu, 1995. A dependable analysis of Theravāda civilization in Southeast Asia and Mahāyāna Buddhist culture and indigenous traditions in Vietnam.

Ling, Trevor. *Buddhism, Imperialism, and War: Burma and Thailand in Modern History.* London, 1979. A study of how Buddhism in Southeast Asia has helped strengthen the political aims of national rulers.

Lopez, Donald S., Jr. *Prisoners of Shangri-La: Tibetan Buddhism and the West.* Chicago, 1998.

Mendelson, E. Michael. *Sangha and State in Burma: A Study of Monastic Sectarianism and Leadership.* Edited by John P. Ferguson. Ithaca, N.Y., 1975.

Metraux, Daniel. *The History and Theology of Soka Gakkai: A Japanese New Religion.* Lewiston, N.Y., 1988.

Mus, Paul. *Viet Nam: Sociologie d'une Guerrre.* Paris, 1952. The historical and cultural background to Vietnamese patriotism in the late colonial period.

Nhat Hanh, Thich. *Vietnam: Lotus in a Sea of Fire.* New York, 1967. The best single study of the role of Buddhism in the history of Vietnamese nationalism.

Pye, Lucien W., with Mary W. Pye. *Asian Power and Politics: The Cultural Dimensions of Authority.* Cambridge, Mass., 1985.

Queen, Christopher S., and Sallie B. King, eds. *Engaged Buddhism: Buddhist Liberation Movements in Asia.* Albany, N.Y., 1996.

Rahula, Walpola. *The Heritage of the Buddha.* New York, 1974. A foremost text by a leading Buddhist monk, originally published in Sinhalese in 1946, urging a politicized monastic order.

Rose, Leo, and Margaret Fisher. *The Politics of Nepal.* Ithaca, N.Y., 1970.

Sarkisyanz, Manuel. *Buddhist Backgrounds of the Burmese Revolution.* The Hague, 1965.

Schecter, Jerrold L. *The New Face of Buddha: Buddhism and Political Power in Southeast Asia.* New York, 1967. An account of politics and Buddhism in the mid-twentieth century by a foremost journalist.

Seneviratne, H. L. *The Work of Kings: the New Buddhism in Sri Lanka.* Chicago, 1999. An informative and well-argued study of contemporary Buddhist social and political activism.

Smith, Bardwell L. *Religion and Legitimation of Power in Sri Lanka.* Chambersburg, Pa., 1978.

Smith, Bardwell L. *Religion and the Legitimation of Power in Thailand, Laos, and Burma.* Chambersburg, Pa., 1978. A reliable series of essays on various aspects of Buddhism and politics in Southeast Asia.

Smith, Donald Eugene. *Religion and Politics in Burma.* Princeton, N.J., 1965. A good historical account of the turbulent pre–military government era in Burma (Myanmar).

Snellgrove, David. *Himalayan Pilgrimage.* Boston, 1989.

Spiro, Melford E. *Buddhism and Society: A Great Tradition and its Burmese Vicissitudes.* Berkeley, Calif., 1982.

Suksamran, Somboon. *Political Buddhism in Southeast Asia: The Role of the Sangha in the Modernization of Thailand.* London, 1977.

Swearer, Donald K. *Buddhism in Transition.* 2d, exp. ed. Philadelphia, 1970. An overview of Buddhism's adaptation to change in South and Southeast Asia.

Tambiah, Stanley. *World Conqueror and World Renouncer: A Study of Buddhism and Polity in Thailand against a Historical Background.* Cambridge, U.K., and New York, 1976.

BRUCE MATTHEWS (2005)

POLITICS AND RELIGION: POLITICS AND CHINESE RELIGION

Few would deny that politics has played an important role in the development of Chinese religion, yet the terms *religion* (*zhengzhi*) and *politics* (*zongjiao*) were not used in premodern China. Both of these words only entered into Chinese usage in the last century, as Japanese neologisms for modern Western concepts. Prior to the twentieth century, it is often difficult to distinguish between politics and religion: the imperial court drew upon religious symbolism in its displays of political authority, and religious leaders often claimed authority usually reserved for the state.

While the following discussion will use the terms *politics* and *religion* in describing the complex interactions of the secular and the sacred in Chinese history, it is worth bearing in mind how modern analytical categories do not always fit premodern conceptual landscapes. This article will address six main topics: (1) the politics of religion in China, (2) the development of the imperial cults, (3) religious conceptions of sovereignty and political power, (4) the analogy of the bureaucracy, (5) religious persecutions and rebellions, and (6) religious advisors and state patronage.

THE POLITICS OF RELIGION IN CHINA. Following Western models of the secular, modernized state, both the Nationalist (Guomindang, or GMD) and the Communist governments of China legislated the institutional separation of state and religion. Yet governmental policies that require the registration and monitoring of civic religious activities have complicated this claim. The constitution of the People's Republic of China (PRC) officially protects religious freedoms, but the government nevertheless monitors and controls all religious activities through the State Bureau of Religious Affairs (SBRA). All major religions in China (Buddhism, Daoism, Islam, and Christianity) are required to affirm their support of the Communist Party and leadership, to register with the SBRA, and to sever ties with foreign networks or organizations (including parent organizations such as the Roman Catholic Church). In return, religious organizations receive official state recognition and protection.

Yet as Stephan Feuchtwang has noted, religious organizations that maintain foreign ties, do not publicly support the leadership, or do not register with the SBRA are considered purveyors of superstition (*mixin*) rather than religion. Practitioners of this so-called superstition are often seen as deceiving the people, and they may be punished for a number of economic crimes, such as fraud. Here, what is noteworthy is how the state arrogates the power to define the categories of religion and superstition—that is, the religious forms protected by the state and those punishable by the state.

The religious policies of the PRC reflect a longstanding ambivalence between governing bodies and religious groups throughout Chinese history. Simply put, religion poses a counter-authority to that of the state, and as a result the state must seek means of controlling or neutralizing the potential threat of religious authority. The modern Communist government has chosen to do so by claiming the right to delimit the religious sphere. Yet the PRC's appropriation of religious authority is not a new phenomenon; Chinese governments of earlier periods have consistently sought to align, if not unify, political and religious concerns. Further, traditional Chinese concepts of sovereign power were founded on religious grounds or elaborated through religious language and imagery.

THE IMPERIAL CULTS. One sees this most clearly in the long history of imperial cults and state rituals that date from the earliest historical period to the fall of imperial China in 1911. In general, imperial cults consisted of devotions and rituals that had to be performed by the ruler, or by an official surrogate, to ensure the continued well-being and prosperity of the empire. These included the sacrifices to the Altars of Soil and Grain and at the Hall of Light, as well as ritual observances for the cults of Laozi (fl. 6th century BCE) and Confucius (Kongzi, 551–479 BCE). The most important of the imperial cults were those with the most ancient provenance: (1) the imperial ancestral cult, and (2) the worship of a supreme god known as variously as "Heaven" (Tian), "God" (Di), or the "High God" (Shangdi).

The imperial ancestral cult was related to other forms of ancestor worship in China. Yet whereas ordinary ancestral spirits concerned themselves only with their own descendents, the imperial ancestors watched over the dynastic house and, by extension, the entire empire. Scholars have noticed that the imperial ancestral cult often held a relatively low rank among the great sacrifices of state. Nevertheless, the ruler's ancestors possessed a significance that greatly exceeded the actual status of the sacrifice. Victor Xiong has noted how the placement of the ruler's ancestral spirit tablets within the capital city transformed mere urban space into the sacred center of the empire.

The imperial cult of Heaven provided the other crucial source of political authority. Early political theory had constructed the analogy between Heaven and the human ruler: just as Heaven asserted sovereignty over the pantheon of spirits, so the human ruler asserted sovereignty over the empire and its people. Yet at the same time, the ruler derived his (and, in the single exception, her) authority directly from Heaven. He was referred to as the "Son of Heaven" (*Tianzi*), the one person charged by the "Mandate of Heaven" (*Tianming*) to rule over all things. The idea of a Heaven-bestowed mandate complicated the authority of the emperor, since Heaven did not unwaveringly favor one dynastic house above all others. In fact, a dynasty that had become morally bankrupt would lose the mandate to rule. The Zhou dynasty (c. 1150–256 BCE) first introduced the Mandate of Heaven as justification for overthrowing the Shang (sixteenth to eleventh centuries BCE), and later dynasties continued to invoke the doctrine in political rhetoric and discourse.

OTHER RELIGIOUS CONCEPTIONS OF SOVEREIGNTY. The imperial cults provided the most visible means by which rulers laid claim to sacred authority. Other religious traditions, however, played important roles in the imagination and construction of political sovereignty. The following section will discuss three traditions: (1) early immortality quests, (2) Daoist models of kingship, and (3) Buddhist models of kingship. Of course, not all Chinese emperors were equally interested in alternative sources of sacred authority to the imperial cults. Rather, these reflected the personal inclinations or aspirations of particular rulers, as well as larger trends in Chinese religious history.

The most famous of the early immortality quests are those undertaken by Qin Shihuangdi (r. 221–210 BCE), the First Emperor of the Qin dynasty (221–207 BCE). The Qin succeeded in unifying China through its superior military efficiency and rigid code of laws. The First Emperor was fascinated with the possibility of becoming an immortal in the flesh, and so he traveled throughout the empire in search of spirits or gods who might give him their secrets. He also paid vast sums of money to magicians (*fangshi*) to seek out the mythical island of Penglai, upon which magical herbs of longevity were rumored to grow. The First Emperor even performed the Feng and Shan sacrifices on altars at Mount Tai (the sacred Eastern Marchmount) and Liangfu, in the hopes of achieving self-deification. For Confucian intellectuals, this was a distortion of the great sacrifices, which were supposed to announce the establishment of the age of great peace to Heaven and Earth. In the end, not only did the First Emperor fail to achieve personal immortality, but his dynasty only survived him by about four years.

The Han dynasty (206 BCE–220 CE) succeeded the short-lived Qin. The sixth ruler, Han Wudi (r. 141/140–87/86 BCE), presided over one of the longest reigns in Chinese history. Wudi oversaw the political, economic, and military stabilization of the empire, as well as the establishment of "state Confucianism" (the cultural ideology that later came to encompass a sacred canon, state academies, and the examination system). At the same time, however, Wudi imitated Qin Shihuangdi in seeking the secrets of immortality throughout the empire; he even re-performed the Feng and Shan sacrifices at Mount Tai.

Both the First Emperor and Han Wudi were heavily criticized by the Han historian Sima Qian (c. 145–c. 85 BCE), who saw the rulers' desire for immortality as a combination of despotism and gullibility. Sima Qian's critique did not prevent later rulers from seeking immortality, some of whom perished from ingesting large amounts of cinnabar (mercury sulfide), following the instructions of their Daoist advisors.

Generally speaking, however, the adoption of Daoist models of kingship often served more politically conventional goals. In the medieval Daoist tradition, the deified Laozi became the model of the perfect ruler. Rulers that drew upon the image and rhetoric of Laozi could secure the support of Daoist factions within the court, as well as of Daoist believers throughout the empire. This was the case for Cao Pi (r. 220–226 CE), also known as Wei Wendi. As Howard Goodman has shown, Cao Pi made use of a Celestial Masters prophecy to legitimate his establishment of the Wei dynasty (220–265). Daoism also played a prominent role in the legitimation of the Tang dynasty (618–907 CE). Because the Tang imperial house shared the same surname (Li) as Laozi, the members of the Tang royal house could make the claim that they descended from the Daoist sage. Actual interest in Daoism varied among the twenty-one Tang emperors. The seventh emperor, Tang Xuanzong (Li Longji, r. 712–756), was fascinated by Daoism and was initiated by a Highest Purity (Shangqing) Daoist master as an adept of the sect. In the Song dynasty (960–1279), Emperor Huizong (Zhao Ji, r. 1101–1125) was even more involved in Daoist study and training, to the extent that he was deified as "The Great Emperor of Long Life." In one of the most striking examples of religious sovereignty, Huizong received cult worship as a god in his own lifetime.

The adoption of Buddhist models of kingship could serve similar political ends. The perfect ruler of Buddhism was the cakravartin or "wheel-turning king." Buddhism spoke of the inevitable decline of Buddhist law (*mofa*), but it also maintained that the cakravartin could arrest or even reverse the decline. Therefore, the title of cakravartin was often used to honor rulers who had been generous in their patronage of Buddhist monasteries and their activities. Exemplary Buddhist monarchs included Emperor Wu of the Liang dynasty (Xiao Yan, r. 501–549), who received the title "Imperial Bodhisattva" for his intense devotion to Buddhist learning. Emperor Wu famously ransomed himself on several occasions to monasteries in order to channel funds to the Buddhist community. On the other hand, there is the example of the Tang Empress Wu Zetian (r. 684–704). Empress Wu had her monk-lover fabricate the spurious *Scripture of the Great Cloud*, which prophesied the imminent appearance of Maitreya, the Buddha of the Future, in the form of a female deity—that is, Wu Zetian herself.

THE BUREAUCRATIC ANALOGY. A hallmark of Chinese religion is the way in which the world of the gods parallels the human realm of officialdom: the supernatural realm, like this one, is ordered by bureaucracy. As Peter Nickerson has shown, a fifth-century Daoist text of the Celestial Master tradition describes the registers kept by each Daoist household, so that the gods would have accurate records when supernatural intervention was required. By the seventh century, the Buddhist afterlife likewise was represented as a bureaucracy. After death, one's soul would travel through the ten courts of the underworld, each ruled by a king who sat in judgment over the deceased.

Also, documents and papers akin to those necessary for moving through government bureaucracy facilitated communication with the gods. Like the government of this world, the bureaucracy of the gods has roles and hierarchy; in contemporary practice, those seeking help from the gods should first locate the god with the appropriate jurisdiction. But the bureaucratic analogy does have its limits. As Emily Ahern notes, it is possible to appeal directly to the highest deities in a way that is not possible within government bureaucracy. Moreover, people do not relate to the gods solely on the model of supplicant and official; for believers, rank within the supernatural hierarchy may be a consideration secondary to the efficaciousness of a given deity.

While throughout much of China's history the government occasionally granted deities honorary titles, this practice increased sharply during the late eleventh century. Local elites recommended deities associated with their region and with proven records of responsiveness. The granting of titles allowed the central government to extend its reach into each locality and simultaneously to share the accomplishments of these regional supernatural powers. However, as Robert Hymes argues, the titles granted to local gods were purely honorific and based on archaic feudal titles; the government honored the gods but did not grant them functional positions or assign them specific duties. In a related way, the government throughout history also issued ordination certificates to monks and nuns and granted temples plaques that established imperial recognition. Over time, these activities served to create a national, centralized religious network administered by the state.

SUPPRESSION AND REBELLION. As discussed above, religion frequently has been an alternate source of authority to that of the state. From time to time, this has led to religiously influenced rebellions and to the proscription and persecution of religion by the state. For example, Buddhism often has been perceived as a corrupting influence in times of political or cultural crisis because of its foreign origins, and it thus was a frequent target of state suppression. Anti-Buddhist attitudes among officials were exacerbated by the perceived negative economic impact of Buddhist monasteries: monks and nuns were not taxed, and monasteries also owned large tracts of untaxed land. Occasionally, these tensions resulted in attempts to limit or eliminate Buddhist institutions. Emperor Wu of the Northern Wei (Tuoba Tao, r. 423–452) ordered one such large-scale suppression of Buddhism. Most monks survived in hiding, but many temples, scriptures, and works of art were destroyed.

The Buddhist persecution of the Tang Emperor Wuzong (Li Yan, r. 840–846) was perhaps the most far-reaching. This suppression is usually called the "Huichang Suppression," after Wuzong's reign title. First, monasteries were ordered to purge their ranks of unregistered monks, along with those monks who failed to keep their vows, had been convicts, practiced magic, or were otherwise questionable. The government then banned pilgrimages and eliminated smaller Buddhist establishments, relocating monks to larger temples. Shortly thereafter, all Buddhist property was seized by the state. Buddhist statuary and ritual implements made of metal were melted down and made into currency or agricultural tools. The monastic population further declined as the state laicized monks and nuns under forty and set strict limits on the number of monasteries and clergy. The Huichang suppression of Buddhism was part of a larger xenophobic trend; other religions were also purged or suppressed. In 843, Uighur Manichaean priests in Chang'an and Luoyang, as well as Nestorian and Zoroastrian priests, were laicized, and their temple property was confiscated. Two months later the government ordered the execution of all Manichaean priests. The situation eased only after Wuzong's death in 846.

Subsequent dynasties never employed such drastic measures, but modernizing movements in the twentieth century led to efforts to weed out religion as a negative force. When the Communist Party came to power, Buddhist monastic holdings were decimated by land reform, and monks were expected to become productive citizens. In the Cultural Revolution (1966–1976), virtually all public displays of religion came to a halt; Buddhism, Daoism, and Confucianism were attacked part of the "Four Olds" (old ideas, old culture, old customs, old habits). Temples were damaged, closed, or converted to other uses. Muslims were made to eat pork, and Christian churches were purged of their religious symbols. Much religious activity went underground during this time, reemerging only after the Cultural Revolution ended and the political mood shifted.

The state was capable of acting against religion in the kinds of suppressions discussed above, but religion often motivated or guided rebellions against the state. Perhaps the earliest such example is that of the Daoist Yellow Turban revolt at the end of the Han dynasty. Apocalyptic ideology and the desire to establish a Daoist utopia motivated this revolt, which began in 184 CE. Similarly, at the end of the Yuan dynasty (1264–1368), Red Turban armies grew out of millenarian White Lotus societies, drawing inspiration from their belief in messianic prophecies that Maitreya, the Buddha of the Future, would soon be reborn. The founder of the subsequent Ming dynasty (1368–1644), Zhu Yuanzhang, was affiliated with this movement early in his rise to power.

Toward the end of the Qing dynasty, rebellions that incorporated religious elements became more frequent. The Taiping Rebellion (1851–1864) was one of the most destructive. Its founder, Hong Xiuquan, was a convert to Christianity who had a vision in which he was identified as God's son and charged with driving the devils (i.e., the foreign Manchu regime) out of China. He was then to establish the Heavenly Kingdom of Great Peace (Taiping Tianguo). Taiping forces managed to take a major city, Nanjing, which they declared the capital of their new kingdom. Around the same time, Muslim rebellions broke out in both Yunnan province and in northwest China, lasting until the mid-1870s. Key background causes included Qing discriminatory laws and tension between minority and majority communities. Ethnic and cultural identities were as much an issue as religion in these insurgencies. To varying degrees, religion also played a role in other late Qing rebellions, such as the 1813 Eight Trigram Revolt and the Boxer Rebellion of 1899 to 1901.

Religious Advisors and State Sponsorship. Religious figures often served as official and unofficial advisors to emperors, in which capacity they provided rulers with another source of personal or political power. Buddhist or Daoist adepts advised emperors on the protection of the state and personal cultivation. For example, in the Yuan dynasty, Khubilai Khan (r. 1279–1294) employed the Tibetan lama Phags pa (Phagpa; 1235–1280) as his liaison to Tibet and Buddhists; Phags pa in turn provided the emperor with religious legitimacy. The Mongol Yuan government made wide use of Muslim officials, but their employment perhaps had more to do with ethnicity than belief. During the late sixteenth and seventeenth centuries, Jesuit missionaries worked in the service of the emperor, providing guidance on Western science and culture. While their work at court was not religious in nature, their collaboration eased the way for the continued presence of Western missionaries.

Throughout history, imperial patronage has also included the building and restoration of temples and the commission of religious art. Scriptural compilation projects were also examples of major collaborations between religious orders and the state. In both the Tang and Song dynasties, the state sponsored large-scale projects to translate Buddhist sūtras into Chinese. The Song dynasty sponsored the first printing of the entire Buddhist canon, and later dynasties commissioned reprintings. Early Song emperors ordered the collection of Daoist texts, which were then published in an early form of the Daoist canon (*Daozang*); in the Ming, the Yongle emperor (r. 1402–1424) ordered the compilation of the present version of the *Daozang*.

Politics and Religion in Modern China. Such examples demonstrate that the relationship between the state and religious groups was often a trade-off: the transactions, whether intellectual or material, were most successful when both parties benefited, but the religious group did not overtly challenge secular authority. However, the negotiations between religious and political claims to authority have been considerably more difficult in the late twentieth and early twenty-first century China. For example, the state-recognized Chinese Catholic Church (officially known as the Chinese Catholic Patriotic Association) has severed its relationship with the Vatican, bowing to pressure from the state which has frowned upon foreign influence inside China. The Roman Catholic Church does survive in China, but it has been forced underground.

The government likewise has asserted the right to administrate Tibetan Buddhism as a corollary to its claim of political sovereignty over Tibet. In 1950, the newly formed Communist government ordered the military invasion of Tibet, and in the following year, coerced Tibetan representatives to sign the "Agreement on the Peaceful Liberation of Tibet." As a consequence, central Tibet became an autonomous region within China, while other Tibetan territories were incorporated into neighboring Chinese provinces. Under this agreement, Tibetans could continue to govern according to their own traditions, leaving in place the theocracy led by the fourteenth Dalai Lama. However, land reform and other modernizations introduced by the PRC in the 1950s were met with resistance, and tensions escalated to the point of military clashes. With concern growing that Chinese forces would harm the Dalai Lama, he fled to India with an entourage of government leaders and religious followers. A Tibetan government-in-exile was established at Dharamsala, while in Tibet the Communists replaced traditional institutions with socialist ones.

As was true throughout China, the 1980s brought a more relaxed governmental stance toward religious and political expression. Seeking to capitalize on this change in official attitude, the Dalai Lama brought the issue of Tibet and its desire for autonomy to the global stage. Limited attempts at negotiations between the two sides took place in the early 1990s. The Chinese government also attempted to modernize Tibet, which had lagged behind the rest of China in terms of economic and social development. Part of this new approach included increased state patronage of religion, usually in the form of restoring temples; the government also hoped these efforts would attract tourists. But religious revival also needed to be kept in check, and the Communist government stepped up its efforts to control religious leaders. The contrast between traditional notions of religious leadership and Communist expectations clearly manifested itself in the controversy over the reincarnation of the Panchen Lama, whose tenth incarnation had died in 1989. When the eleventh Panchen Lama was identified and approved by the Dalai Lama in 1995, Beijing not only rejected this choice, but also removed the young boy from Tibet. Beijing then installed their own candidate for Panchen Lama through a process controlled by the government. Because the Panchen Lama traditionally plays an important role in identifying and sanctioning the next incarnation of the Dalai Lama, this decision will have long-ranging effects.

In the government's stance toward both the Roman Catholic Church and Tibetan Buddhism, the Chinese state has acted from concern over alternative sources to political authority. This concern also manifests itself in the state's aggressive repression of the Falun Gong movement, also known as Falun Dafa. The group was founded by Li Hongzhi (b. 1952) in 1992. Li's teachings incorporate elements of Buddhism, Daoism, and *qigong* practice, though he also claims that his teachings are superior to both Buddhism and Daoism. There are three components to religious cultivation within Falun Gong: (1) members practice a simplified form of *qigong*; (2) they study Falun Gong teachings; (3) they seek to develop the key moral qualities of truthfulness (*zhen*), goodness (*shan*), and forebearance (*ren*). The goal of such cultivation is to cleanse oneself of bad *karma,* purify one's body, and eventually become a god or buddha.

The case of Falun Gong demonstrates the problem of defining religion in modern China. The government only recognizes five religions (Buddhism, Daoism, Catholicism, Protestantism, and Islam) and thus there is no option for new religious groups to register as such. Moreover, Falun Gong has asserted that it is not a religion, but rather a scientific, rational movement based on a deep understanding of the structure of the universe. Also related to the group's claims are its promises of the health benefits of breathing exercises; these benefits may have attracted people inadequately served by the socialist healthcare system in China. Yet the government has used Falun Gong's claims of health benefits to prove the danger posed by the group, arguing that its "superstitious" practices have prevented people from seeking medical care. In the late 1990s, critics of the group began to air their concerns, causing the state to ban several Falun Gong publications. Falun Gong members began to stage demonstrations, objecting to the label of "superstition" and to state persecution. In April 1999, ten thousand Falun Gong adherents protested in Beijing's Tiananmen Square; in July 1999, the government banned the group. The state has called Falun Gong a dangerous sect that defrauds the populace, and it has used arrests, forced institutionalization, and other forms of pressure to weaken the group. For its part, Falun Gong has availed itself of new technologies, using the internet, cell phones, and pagers to organize its resistance to government pressure. While the most dramatic example of government treatment of new religious groups, Falun Gong is not an isolated case. Scores of religious groups, drawing on a range of traditions, have been banned and members subjected to harsh treatment by the government.

CONCLUSION. Throughout the history of China, religious elements have been integral to the development of Chinese political thought and discourse. Moreover, the multireligious nature of China has meant that different traditions have helped shape the sociocultural landscape. In the above discussion of the relationship between politics and religion in China, three broad positions can be identified. First, those holding political authority used religious claims to provide moral or cosmological legitimation to their rule. Second, politics and religion often existed in a state of balance or compromise, in which each side recognized advantages to cooperation or tolerance. Finally, politics and religion at times failed to recognize the legitimacy of one another's claims to authority, leading to conflict, rebellion, or suppression.

SEE ALSO Buddhism, article on Buddhism in China; Buddhism, Schools of, article on Chinese Buddhism; Chinese Religion, overview article; Confucianism, overview article; Daoism; Emperor's Cult.

BIBLIOGRAPHY

Ahern, Emily Martin. *Chinese Ritual and Politics.* Cambridge, U.K., 1981.

Chang, Maria Hsia. *Falun Gong: The End of Days.* New Haven, Conn., 2004.

Duara, Prasenjit. "Knowledge and Power in the Discourse of Modernity: The Campaigns against Popular Religion in Early Twentieth-Century China." *The Journal of Asian Studies* 50, no. 1 (February 1991): 67–83.

Feuchtwang, Stephan. *Popular Religion in China: The Imperial Metaphor.* Richmond, U.K., 2001.

Goldstein, Mervyn C. *The Snow Lion and the Dragon: China, Tibet, and the Dalai Lama.* Berkeley, Calif., and Los Angeles: University of California, 1997.

Goodman, Howard L. *Ts'ao P'i Transcendent: The Political Culture of Dynasty-Founding in China at the End of the Han.* Seattle, Wash., and Richmond, U.K., 1998.

Hansen, Valerie. *Changing Gods in Medieval China, 1127–1276.* Princeton, N.J., 1990.

Hymes, Robert. *Way and Byway: Taoism, Local Religion, and Models of Divinity in Sung and Modern China.* Berkeley, Calif., and Los Angeles, 2002.

Janousch, Andreas. "The Emperor as Bodhisattva: The Bodhisattva Ordination and Ritual Assemblies of Emperor Wu of the Liang Dynasty." In *State and Court Ritual in China,* edited by Joseph P. McDermott, pp. 112–149. Cambridge, U.K., and New York, 1999.

Lipman, Jonathan N. *Familiar Strangers: A History of Muslims in Northwest China.* Seattle, and London, 1997.

Nickerson, Peter. "Abridged Codes of Master Lu for the Daoist Community." In *Religions of China in Practice,* edited by Donald S. Lopez, Jr., pp. 347–359. Princeton, N.J., 1996.

Orzech, Charles D. *Politics and Transcendent Wisdom:* The Scripture for Humane Kings *in the Creation of Chinese Buddhism.* University Park, Pa., 1998.

Puett, Michael J. *To Become a God: Cosmology, Sacrifice, and Self-Divination in Early China.* Cambridge, Mass., 2002.

Rawski, Evelyn S. *The Last Emperors: A Social History of Qing Imperial Institutions.* Berkeley, Calif., and Los Angeles, 1998.

Seidel, Anna. "The Image of the Perfect Ruler in Early Taoist Messianism." *History of Religions* 9 (1969–1970): 216–247.

ter Haar, Barend. "Falun Gong: Evaluation and Further References." June 2002. Universiteit Leiden. <http://www.let.leidenuniv.nl/bth/falun.htm>.

Weinstein, Stanley. *Buddhism under the T'ang.* Cambridge, U.K., and New York, 1987.

Welch, Holmes. *Buddhism Under Mao.* Cambridge, Mass., 1972.

Xiong, Victor Cunrui. *Sui-Tang Chang'an: A Study in the Urban History of Medieval China.* Ann Arbor, Mich., 2000.

Yang, C. K. *Religion in Chinese Society.* Berkeley, Calif., and Los Angeles, 1961.

JACK W. CHEN (2005)
NATASHA HELLER (2005)

POLITICS AND RELIGION: POLITICS AND JAPANESE RELIGIONS

One of the most striking photographs of the twentieth century—a kamikaze plane crashing headlong into an Allied ship during the last year of the Pacific war—illustrates dramatically an extreme version of the collusion of religion and politics in Japan. The ideal of dying valiantly to defend or preserve one's sacred homeland is of course found in societies all over the world. However, few societies have combined diverse religious traditions, political will, educational curricula, and coercive social controls to elevate and sustain an ideology of personal self-sacrifice to the extent once found in Japan. Moreover all of these twentieth-century characteristics can be traced to earlier precedents within Japanese social and political history.

The practice of using religious traditions to enhance political power in Japan has a momentum of over eighteen hundred years. And yet the concepts of religion and politics have only recently begun to acquire in Japan some of the same semantic and legalistic meanings with which they are regarded in Europe or North America. The Japanese Supreme Court ruled in 1997 on a case that for the first time clearly upheld a 1947 constitutional distinction between religious and political activities.

The term for religion in Japanese, *shukyō*, consists of two characters: *shu*, meaning "sect," and *kyō*, or "teaching." Originally used in Chinese Buddhism, it was first employed in a treaty in 1869 to translate the German word *Religionsübung* (religious exercise). This conception of the word is adequate for religions such as Buddhism or Confucianism—both with thousands of texts, teachings, and commentaries—but less appropriate for Japan's premodern oral traditions that venerate local deities connected with healing, agriculture, fertility, defense, and control of the weather.

FORMATIVE PERIOD. The earliest recorded period in Japanese history shows clearly a symbiotic interaction of religion and politics. Starting around the sixth century CE, correct governmental administration was based upon the principle of *saisei-itchi* (a Chinese reading of the Japanese term *matsurigoto*), or "unity of ritual and government." Any ruler wanting his or her realm to prosper was obligated to formulate policies reflecting the will of the deities *(kami)*, delivered through oracles at certain ancient, powerful shrines (such as Mount Miwa in the central region or at Usa Hachiman on the island of Kyushu) and manifest also through omens and natural phenomena. There is considerable but not conclusive evidence that powerful women shamans, one identified in Chinese chronicles as Himiko, channeled the will of the *kami* as the basis of their rule in the second and third centuries CE.

When Buddhism first arrived in Japan in 538, it too became a valuable resource in building a stable political and social order. The emperor Kinmei received a Buddha statue and several volumes of scriptures from King Songmyong of Paekche (Korean Peninsula), who advised him that not only did great people of the past have full knowledge of the Buddhist doctrine but also it had benefited those who built strong states. Some of Kinmei's vassals, who had been displaced and then immigrated from the Korean Peninsula some two to three centuries earlier, were supportive of this new religion, whereas native clans warned that its adoption would anger local *kami.*

Soon, with religious differences serving to focus other conflicts over title and territory, these two opposing forces met in battle in 587 CE. After the immigrant Soga clan defeated the native Mononobe, religious and political development centered on Buddhism flourished during the seventh century. Some of the patterns established at that time have continued throughout Japanese history: the emperor system, the idea of Japan as a sacred country, state support of Buddhism (and vice versa), regional temples and shrines (as well as the rituals conducted there) designed to protect the state, and venerating (in order to pacify and control) the spirits of the dead.

Shortly after the temporary setback for the native clans mentioned earlier, court nobles were commanded in 593 CE by Suiko, the first of a series of powerful empresses, to support Buddhism. Two important precedents associated with the religion in China and Korea were now to be established in Japan. The first was the *Golden Light Sūtra* (*Suvarnaprabhasa*) and its message of protection for kings, their families, and countries. The other sūtra was the *Benevolent Kings' Sūtra* (*Kārunikā-rāja-prajñāpāramitā*), which in a similar vein assured rulers that by reading and explaining the sūtra they would enact the "Rite of Protecting the Country." Thus the reign of Buddhist law and that of a local king were seen to coincide, benefit, and legitimate each other.

At the same time the regional deities and myths of conquered clans from the recent past were being consolidated into a systematic account, the *Kojiki* (712 CE), to legitimate what has since become the world's oldest extant imperial system. King Tenmu (r. 673–686 CE) bolstered his imperial position as emperor by co-opting the kind of authority traditionally reserved for clan priests. A four-layered system of *kami* worship developed: imperial *kami* were superior to all others, the emperor as a "manifest *kami*" (*akitsukami*) directly descended from the sun deity (Amaterasu) outranked clan chiefs, the most important rituals were conducted by the emperor, and finally the imperial shrine at Ise stood above all other shrines. Tenmu also stationed an imperial princess at Ise to worship on his behalf and created the Council of Kami Affairs to supervise ritual activities of benefit to the state at shrines. The concept of Japan as a "divine nation" (*shinkoku*) first appeared in a subsequent chronicle of 720 CE (the *Nihonshoki*) and then, as will be evident in a moment, emerges again at various critical moments in Japan's history.

Tenmu's grandson Shōmu further developed Buddhism as a tool of the state. In 741 CE he issued an edict requiring every province to build both a monastery and a nunnery, where rituals aimed at protecting the regime (*chingo kokka*) could be held on a regular basis, conducted by priests and nuns certified by the state. "Protect the country [through Buddhism] against all calamity, prevent sorrow and pestilence, and cause the hearts of believers to be filled with joy"

(Kōjiro, 1993, p. 255). At the center of power in what is now Nara in central Japan, Shōmu first consulted a *kami* oracle (at Usa Hachiman in Kyushu) for approval, then constructed the Tōdaiji temple, housing what was at that time the largest seated Buddha in the largest wooden building in the world, dedicated to the peace and prosperity of the state.

In many ways this early period of interactive religious and political development created institutional precedents for subsequent eras. Although the political power of emperors was soon usurped by regional clan chiefs, the structure of the imperial system, though buffeted by centuries of political wrangling, would remain essentially unchanged until 1868. When the capital moved from Nara to nearby Kyoto in 793 CE (in part to escape the meddling influence of powerful Buddhist priests in Nara), its placement followed established "religious" designs strongly influenced by Chinese Daoist principles that now are identified (with varying accuracy) as *feng-shui*, or geomancy. Before moving into the Kyoto Plain, the court had to negotiate with powerful local shrines (such as Matsuo, Fushimi, and Kamo) and gain the protection of their deities for the stability of the realm. It also established temples (Tōji, Saiji, Enryakuji) located at key directional quadrants of the capital (east, west, northeast, respectively) that would further enhance the court's spiritual defenses.

It would be safe to say that those in power during this time saw political and social change as well as calamities as originating from the willful agency of meddlesome spirits, divine beings, and transhuman forces. For example, a belief in the power of departed spirits *(goryō)* gained considerable influence during the Heian period (794–1192). These spirits were thought to be responsible for everything from epidemics to earthquakes, as droughts, famines, stillbirths, pestilence, ominous dreams, and so on were "imbued with a strong political coloration: disasters of all kinds were a barometer of political injustices" (McMullin, 1988, p. 272).

When the Fujiwara clan rose to power through intrigue, assassinations, and exile, these moves left in their wake a number of departed and potentially vengeful spirits. The first rite to propitiate six of these spirits in particular, believed responsible for an epidemic of tuberculosis, was held in 863 CE, later developing into one of the nation's three most famous festivals, Kyoto's midsummer Gion Festival. Likewise a court official exiled to Kyushu around this same time, Sugawara Michizane (845–903 CE), was later believed to have returned as a vengeful spirit to wreak havoc via lightning, flooding, and fires upon the city and court. Shrines dedicated to his spirit, known as Tenjin or Tenmangū shrines, are still prevalent in Japan and are thought to be propitious for academic success. Another vivid example of *goryō* belief will be encountered in the contemporary period.

MIDDLE PERIOD. Following a major battle between supporters of the court (Taira) and a rival faction (Minamoto) in 1185, political power again shifted both to a new clan and location. Not only had the infant emperor drowned in the climactic sea battle at Dan-no-ura, but also one of three imperial regalia—a sword supposedly plucked from the tail of a dragon and given by the *kami* to the imperial lineage—had also been lost at sea. Although the court held fast to the other two relics (a mirror and a magical jewel) and remained in Kyoto with a newly installed emperor, political power moved to Kamakura, far to the north. New and innovative alignments between religion and politics also ensued.

The turmoil of clan warfare as well as the instability of establishing military and administrative control provided an opening for radically different and highly popular religious movements—Pure Land, True Pure Land, Nichiren—to develop centers of political power during what was considered a time of "degeneration of the Buddhist doctrine" *(mappō)*. Though differing in religious emphasis (Amida's Pure Land paradise versus the magical effects of chanting the *Lotus Sūtra*), all three movements were founded by charismatic monks (Hōnen, Shinran, and Nichiren, respectively) whose methods to reach salvation through chanting special prayers appealed to all social classes.

Nichiren in particular promoted his version of the *Lotus Sūtra* as an exclusive truth that, if adopted by the government, would save the nation from threats he predicted were immanent. Soon after this warning came the first Mongol invasion of 1274. Even though vastly outmanned by the Mongol and Korean forces, a typhoon wrecked their fleet and forced a withdrawal in the first "divine wind" (*kamikaze*) intervention, attributed to the deity Hachiman. Incredibly the second Mongol attack in 1281 also met the same fate, but this was not enough to convince the state that Nichiren's theocracy was correct.

Although the new rulers of Japan were from the warrior class, many of their religious affiliations followed established patterns. They rebuilt the clan shrine, Tsurugaoka Hachiman, dedicated to the *kami* of military power and swift intervention. Also just as King Tenmu had done in the Nara period, the next generation of rulers, the Hōjō, established a ranking system of regional temples as well as "temples for the peace of the nation" *(ankokuji)*. An influential text by Kitabatake (1293–1354) titled *Chronicle of the Direct Descent of Gods and Sovereigns* argued that Japan is a "divine country" (*shinkoku*) and helped to develop further a national consciousness among ruling elites.

The Kamakura government promoted and patronized both Zen and Pure Land Buddhism as favored institutions. Major Zen temples, many of which had head abbots from China or who had studied in China, were organized by the state into the *gozan* or "five mountain temple" system around 1298. Samurai warriors and their feudal lords found in Zen Buddhism the discipline, self-negation, and nonostentatious aesthetics amenable to their code of loyalty and service *(bushidō)*. Should samurai die in service to their lord, the saints of Pure Land Buddhism (particularly one noted for compassion, Kannon) were ready to usher their souls into the western paradise of the Amida Buddha.

The regional nation-protecting temples established earlier had become centers of enormous wealth and territory, some of which rivaled the central government before and during the Kamakura period. Because of ongoing political conflict, these religious estates (*shōen*) became even more autonomous and powerful. Fearful of losing territory to rival estates, *shōen* administrators began a practice of turning low-ranking monks into security personnel to defend their territorial interests and policies. Over time, these "priest soldiers" (*sōhei*) developed into fierce fighting units dressed in the garb of mountain monks.

In Kyoto *sōhei* monks at Enryakuji temple atop Mount Hiei, home to the Tendai sect of Buddhism, were notorious for descending into the city with sacred regalia at the front of their procession and intimidating the imperial court or battling rival factions. They fought with and burned to the ground at least six times a temple (Mii-dera) north of Mount Hiei whose founder had split from Enryakuji in the tenth century. They clashed with the great Nara temples (in particular Kōfukuji), battled against new Pure Land sects (including destroying the tomb of the founder of Pure Land Buddhism in Japan, Hōnen), burned the headquarters of the Higashi Honganji Pure Land sect in 1465, and destroyed twenty-one Nichiren temples in Kyoto in 1536.

For nearly five hundred years neither the military government in faraway Kamakura, nor the imperial court in Kyoto, nor fragile alliances of regional warlords could control the Enryakuji militias. But in 1571 they finally met their match. Having angered Oda Nobunaga (who was soon to become Japan's first leader of a centralized state after nearly three hundred years of internal wars) by siding with his opponents, he led twenty-five thousand samurai against the mountain monks. His forces not only killed over three thousand priests and monks of all ranks but burned to ashes one of the most sacred religious sites in Japan. After all, the temple was established in 788 CE first as a hermitage and later was reconsecrated for protecting the city from malevolent spirit forces issuing from the northeast. Shortly after Nobunaga was assassinated in 1582, the Enryakuji complex was slowly rebuilt in the same location.

THE MODERN PERIOD. Despite Nobunaga's razing of the Mount Hiei temples, he was not antireligious and contributed to many important temples and shrines during his short rule. He also permitted contact with foreign Jesuit Catholic missionaries who had first appeared in southern Japan in 1549. They followed three Portuguese adventurers who had traveled aboard a Chinese ship and landed in 1543, making a favorable impression with their matchlock rifles, a technology that would revolutionize clan warfare in Japan. Trade ensued over the next decade, although it was closely linked to the missionaries as translators and middlemen. Through these relations, Christianity established a foundation in western Japan for roughly sixty years, bringing with it European-born missionaries who also conveyed to Japanese scholars ideas about science, engineering, cartography, anatomy, and medicine.

Nobunaga's successor, Toyotomi Hideyoshi, was still quelling rebellions against his rule and so had less tolerance for a faith thought to shift allegiance away from the shogun toward a foreign notion of transcendent divinity. What had been a system of lucrative trade (as "Black Ships" traveled from Europe to Asia and back again) and a permissive attitude (allowing the building of churches in local fiefs) was now curtailed in 1587 as Hideyoshi accused the missionaries of preaching a "devilish law in the land of the *kami*," again evoking the sacred nation concept. Throughout the coming decades and after the Tokugawa clan seized firm control of the country in 1600 after Hideyoshi's death, Christianity was both tolerated and reviled, with a final persecution and expulsion of missionaries occurring in 1639. The military government then closed itself off from Western trade and diplomacy for over two hundred years.

The rise of the Tokugawa was credited to the cunning brilliance of its founder, Ieyasu, but he (as well as subsequent Tokugawa leaders) was ably assisted by several Buddhist priests (such as Hayashi Raizan and the abbot of Nanzenji temple, Sūden) as well as by neo-Confucian scholars. After his death in 1615, he was deified (as had been all previous military leaders) and later enshrined in the mountains at Nikkō in a temple-shrine complex (the Tōshōgū) unsurpassed for its ostentatious extravagance.

As their predecessors had done, the Tokugawa used Buddhist temples throughout the land to promote the stability of their regime. Not only were rituals held, but the temples themselves were organized into the *terauke* system to serve as extensions of state administration: all those residing within a temple's traditional precincts had to register as members of that temple. By doing so the populace entered into a system of religiously based surveillance and monitoring.

Shrines were also part of the Tokugawa government's system of control. Fearing a resurgence of Christian sentiments in the major port city of Nagasaki, the military government sponsored a revitalization of *kami*-based rites and institutions. The city's main Shintō shrine, Suwa Jinja, dates from 1614 and enshrines a deity known for its military prowess and vigilance. Like many others, the shrine also hosts on its grounds a subsidiary of the main shrine to the deified Tokugawa founder.

Beginning around 1825, more than two centuries after the Tokugawa clan gained control of the state, serious fissures in their administrative competence were becoming apparent. Critics of the inward-looking and increasingly corrupt feudal system feared Japan would be invaded and colonized by more technologically advanced European and American powers. To avoid a fate shared by China and India, samurai scholars and administrators began a discourse on reform, often at the cost of their careers and sometimes their lives. Klaus Antoni noted in *Religion and National Identity in the Japanese Context* (2003) that this ideology of a national polity, or *kokutai*, began to emerge among scholars of "national" (rather than foreign) learning (*kokugaku*) who promoted a reexamination and revitalization of Japan's ancient myths and the imperial system they legitimized. National learning scholars developed a "postulated common ethnicity" that promoted a strong and unified imagined community under the emperor's rule.

In ways similar to the formative period of civilization in the early fourth and fifth centuries, Japan was once again exalted as a "land of the *kami*" whose emperor provided a direct link to the nation's founding deities. By extension the Japanese people, like one big extended family, were also privileged to have something termed the "soul of Japan" *(yamato-damashi)* running through their blood. Sharing so many commonalities—language, race, culture, ethnicity, respect for *kami* and buddhas, veneration of ancestors—and with the emperor as both father figure and "deity visible as a human being" *(arahitogami),* the national learning scholars attempted to influence political policy toward the establishment of a state that could defend itself against colonizing predators.

Over a decade after American gunboat diplomacy forced open Japan's ports beginning in 1853, troops allied with samurai reformers (who wanted a modern state based on European parliamentary models but headed by an emperor) clashed with those of the feudal Tokugawa government, with the former emerging victorious in 1868. This major transition in Japanese history ushered in an age of radical change and innovation in many areas but none more striking than the interaction of religion and politics. One of Japan's founding fathers, Fukuzawa Yukichi, observed, "There is only a government in Japan, but still no nation." It would take a new and oftentimes coercive alignment of religion and politics to produce the national consciousness he sought.

First, the new government legitimated the *kokutai* ideology described earlier as central to their agendas of modernization, industrialization, education, and socialization. Similar to King Tenmu in the seventh century, the emperor's divinity was emphasized even as the country embarked on an ambitious race to catch up with other industrialized world powers. Because of its association with the feudal regime, Buddhism suffered through a brief but destructive persecution in the 1870s and 1880s but recovered state patronage and influence in the early twentieth century. As in the past Buddhist leaders once again promoted the "unity of royal law and the Buddha-*dharma*" (*ōbō Buppō furi*) and actively participated in Japan's territorial and militaristic expansion.

Of far more utility to the state was the ancient religious and ritual tradition of venerating local and regional *kami*, known to scholars as Shintō (way of the *kami*). Every village had at least one Shintō shrine that could be linked to the state cult of the emperor and the sun goddess. Since Shintō had no sacred texts or a centralized, organizational structure, the Meiji government used shrines in much the same way the Tokugawa had used local Buddhist temples: to register and monitor residents but also to involve them with festivals and rituals that promoted state ideologies. Only two years after the revolution ended, an 1870 attempt to create a codified national religion based on *kami* worship failed. Nonetheless schools began teaching imperial and national mythology as if it were history, effectively sidestepping the contentious issue of freedom of religion. Domestic and foreign critics of this policy were told that Shintō was not a religion but a matter of social etiquette and long-established custom.

By the late 1880s the Japanese state had the necessary ideologies, laws, and infrastructure to establish itself as a modern nation—which meant in part exploiting political weakness in surrounding countries (China, Formosa, and Korea) in order to appropriate their natural and human resources. With a war almost every ten years, soldiers killed in service to the nation were honored at a special Shintō shrine built by the government—Yasukuni—where their spirits could be propitiated, calmed, and then employed as guardians of the empire. Like the *goryō* belief established in the tenth century, the "peaceful nation shrine" incorporated potentially vengeful spirits and transformed them via pacifying rituals. Outside Tokyo large upright stones (*chukonhi*) served as memorials to the military dead after the Russo-Japanese War (1906–1907) and were likewise sanctified through both Shintō and Buddhist rituals. Community officials, school administrators, and citizen leaders were constantly engaged in these and other plans to promote national ideologies and agendas. Helen Hardacre has shown in her important work *Shintō and the State, 1868–1988* (1989) that alternate versions, espoused by new religious movements such as Tenrikyō, Kurozumikyo, Konkōkyō, Sōka Gakkai, and Ōmotokyō, were seen as subversive "pseudo-religions," with some headquarters destroyed and founders harassed and imprisoned.

Even after the Pacific war ended with Japan's defeat in 1945, Yasukuni shrine (and the regional "nation-protecting" shrines established in 1939) were permitted to continue venerating over 2.466 million spirits of the military dead, including (after 1978) officers deemed "class-A" war criminals by the Tokyo War Crimes tribunal. Although the Japanese constitution's Article 20 specifically prohibits any governmental sponsorship of religious activity or institutions, several postwar prime ministers (Miki, Nakasone, Hashimoto, Koizumi) have made official visits to the shrine to pay their respects and to appease political supporters. As might be expected after these visits, both public and diplomatic protests erupt in countries once occupied and ravaged by Japan's military. In 2000 a prime minister used the phrase "*kami no kuni*," or "land of the *kami*," to describe Japan and set off a similar furor because of prewar associations fusing religion and politics as the ideology of a nation fighting a divinely sanctioned war.

There is less ambiguity regarding the government's attitude toward religious organizations, especially after the Aum Shinrikyō group's sarin gas attack on Tokyo subways in

1995. With twelve deaths and over five thousand injuries, the Japanese government moved quickly to revise laws on religious organizations. Increased reporting requirements and monitoring, more financial transparency, and greater governmental powers to restrict activities were the result. Taking this case and state reaction as a precedent, one can surmise that the coming years will increasingly reflect worldwide standards among highly industrialized nations in treating religious activity as a private, civil right but that religious organizations must be carefully monitored for antistate activities. At the same time one should not underestimate the historic appeal of religious movements in Japan that promote within a rhetoric of democracy and peace both state stability and a veneration of the imperial household.

See Also Aum Shinrikyō; New Religious Movements, article on New Religious Movements in Japan; Sōka Gakkai.

Bibliography

Adolphson, Mikael S. *Gates of Power: Monks, Courtiers, and Warriors in Premodern Japan.* Honolulu, 2000.

Antoni, Klaus, et al., eds. *Religion and National Identity in the Japanese Context.* Münster, 2003.

Brown, Delmer, ed. *The Cambridge History of Japan: Ancient Japan.* New York, 1993.

Collcutt, Martin. *Five Mountains: The Rinzai Zen Monastic Institution in Medieval Japan.* Cambridge, Mass., 1984.

Ebersole, Gary L. *Ritual Poetry and the Politics of Death in Early Japan.* Princeton, N.J., 1989.

Friday, Karl. *Samurai, Warfare, and the State in Early Medieval Japan.* New York, 2004.

Hardacre, Helen. *Shintō and the State, 1868–1988.* Princeton, N.J., 1989.

Hardacre, Helen. *Religion and Society in Nineteenth-Century Japan.* Ann Arbor, Mich., 2002.

Heisig, James, and John Maraldo. *Rude Awakenings: Zen, the Kyoto School, and the Question of Nationalism.* Honolulu, 1994.

Ketelaar, James. *Of Heretics and Martyrs in Meiji Japan.* Princeton, N.J., 1990.

Kisala, Robert, and Mark Mulllins. *Religion and Social Crisis in Japan.* New York, 2001.

Kōjiro, Naoki. "The Nara State." Translated by Felicia Bock. In *The Cambridge History of Japan: Ancient Japan,* edited by Delmer Brown, pp. 222–267. New York, 1993.

McMullin, Neil. "On Placating the Gods and Pacifying the Populace: The Case of the Gion Goryo Cult." *History of Religions* 27 (1988): 270–293.

Nakano, T., T. Iida, and H. Yamanaka, eds. *Shūkyō to Nationalism (Religion and Nationalism).* Kyoto, Japan, 1997.

Nelson, John. *A Year in the Life of a Shintō Shrine.* Seattle, Wash., 1996.

Nelson, John. *Enduring Identities: The Guise of Shintō in Contemporary Japan.* Honolulu, 2000.

Nelson, John. "Social Memory as Ritual Practice: Commemorating Spirits of the Military Dead at Yasukuni Shinto Shrine." *Journal of Asian Studies* 62 (2003): 443–468.

Ohnuki-Tierney, Emiko. *Kamikaze, Cherry Blossoms, and Nationalisms.* Chicago, 2002.

Reader, Ian. *Religious Violence in Contemporary Japan: The Case of Aum Shinrikyō.* Honolulu, 2000.

Shimazono, Susumu. *Posuto-modan no Shin Shūkyō (Post-Modern New Religions).* Tokyo, 2001.

Stone, Jacqueline. *Original Enlightenment and the Transformation of Medieval Japanese Buddhism.* Honolulu, 1999.

Stronach, Bruce. *Beyond the Rising Sun: Nationalism in Contemporary Japan.* Westport, Conn., 1995.

John K. Nelson (2005)

POLITICS AND RELIGION: POLITICS AND ANCIENT MEDITERRANEAN RELIGIONS

A discussion of religion and politics in the ancient Mediterranean faces two large obstacles: the geographical and cultural diversity of the traditions encompassed by this rubric and the very difficulty of defining the terms *religion* and *politics* in each culture. None of the societies of Mesopotamia, Egypt, Greece, and Rome possessed a word for religion in the modern sense of a system of faith in and worship of a transcendent power. Certainly all of these societies feared the power wielded by higher beings, but *religio* in Rome, for instance, does not have the same meaning as the modern word *religion;* it conveys rather the sense of a binding obligation between two parties. To define religion in these societies, one might apply the definition offered by Christiane Sourvinou-Inwood ("What Is *Polis* Religion?," 2000, but cf. the critique by Woolf, "*Polis*-Religion and Its Alternatives," 2004) of Greek *polis*-religion: religion provided a means of structuring chaos and making it intelligible by articulating a cosmic order that was guaranteed by a divine order, which then grounded human order. That order in turn was incarnated in a properly ordered state, so the state served as the institutional authority responsible for articulating a pantheon of divinities and a system of rituals and sanctuaries that would organize the universe and the divine world in a religious system. The system so constructed concerned itself with the proper performance of ritual actions to maintain the cosmic order rather than with issues of belief or ethics—orthopraxy rather than orthodoxy. In this type of system, religion and the state were fundamentally intertwined.

The interrelationship of religion and politics in these societies led naturally to a high degree of integration between religious authority and political authority. Indeed, even to use the categories of religious authority and political authority with regard to the ancient world is anachronistic, for authority was not divided along these lines. Often the persons whom most people would categorize as priests acted more as administrators, responsible for the upkeep of the sanctuary and its possessions and for the performance of rites. This is well illustrated by the Greek term conventionally translated as priest, *hiereus,* which literally means "the one in charge of the sacred things" (cf. the Latin *sacerdos,* "giver of the sacred"). None of these traditions possessed sacred texts or revelations that might dictate human behavior, so priests never formed a branch with specialized training completely separate from the institutions of the state. It fell to the state to develop mechanisms designed to appease the power of the transcendent beings, and the role of the priests was not to explicate the system, but to perform the proper rituals. Though it will become clear below that priests functioned differently in each of these societies, the selection of priests in each society and the manner in which they fulfilled their duties mirrored the political structure and developments within that structure to a remarkable degree.

Part of the explanation for the close links between religion and politics in the ancient Mediterranean lies in the fact that, unlike in most modern traditions, the very purpose of these systems was to safeguard and improve the welfare of the state. The very notion of separating religion and state would have astonished these societies; religion and politics could not be considered separate spheres of human activity because both were directed toward the prosperity of the community. Each city had its own tutelary divinity, and with the rise of centralized states, the tutelary deities of the leading city often became state deities. The success of the state was felt to depend on the favor of these deities, and its failure was interpreted as a sign that the deities had abandoned the state. Thus one of the primary functions of the state authorities was to maintain the favor of the divine through the proper performance of rituals, as noted above. Given the connection between religion and state, political relationships and diplomacy between states might be expressed through religious actions. Such actions are not evidence of the manipulation of religion for political purposes; they bespeak rather the deep interpenetration of religion within the life of these ancient Mediterranean societies. Functions that many modern traditions consider to be the province of religion, such as the enforcement of ethical standards, were the responsibility of the community, while the well-being of the community and its members, which most people tend to imagine as the purpose of politics, was the primary purpose of religion. In these circumstances, religion was inherently a part of political life: every communal action had a religious aspect and every religious action had a communal aspect.

Late-twentieth-century scholarship, perhaps driven by an increasing focus on individualism in the modern world, paid significant attention to the role of the individual citizen within these traditions. On the one hand, this research emphasized that the presence of ritual formalism did not mean that ancient Mediterranean religion was devoid of spirituality and that its coldness left individuals unsatisfied. By participating in civic rituals individuals affirmed their membership in the community, while the lack of an official dogma left individuals free to conceive of the gods and the world as they saw fit. Scholars have also noted the many religious actions performed by individuals, in addition to their participation as spectators in large state rituals. These actions, however "private" they may seem to moderns, still fall within the realm of public religion as defined in the ancient world. "Private" religious actions did not focus on eschatological salvation but involved different subsets of the larger community, and in this way continued to be public; indeed this behavior highlights the inadequacy of the terms "public" and "private" when used with regard to the ancient world. *Polis*-religion made room for individual behavior—and welcomed it—because such behavior was mediated through the state, which had approved the deities or cults to whom these "private" offerings were made or had incorporated cults that involved personal behavior into its religious structure. "Private" religion may have provided opportunities for the individual to perform rituals rather than to be an observer at a state festival, but it cannot be seen as an activity completely separable from political life. Despite the individual differences between the societies of the ancient Mediterranean, there is no clear demarcation between the spheres of religion and politics—or between religious and political authority—in any of them, down to the end of the Western Roman Empire and beyond.

MESOPOTAMIA. Because of their similarities and their influence upon one another, the religions of the ancient Tigris and Euphrates River valley will be treated together here, though of course Assyrian and Babylonian religions differed in some respects. For the ancient Mesopotamian, the divinities were responsible for creating order out of the chaos that existed before creation. The king, considered the earthly representative of the gods, was entrusted with maintaining order on earth, and in this way the religious beliefs of ancient Mesopotamia buttressed the political system that developed in the region. The interlocking nature of the political and religious authorities can be seen most clearly in the Assyrian Akitu ceremony, where the king's right to rule for the next year was granted to him by the divine beings, while the princes and the nobility renewed their oaths of loyalty. That religion was important to Assyrian kings throughout the year and not just at this ceremony can be seen from letters of the Sargonid period, many of which discuss the numerous religious obligations of the king. While temples in the Near East tended to have their own hierarchies of personnel and to own significant amounts of property, the kings still wielded significant authority over the priests. The head of the temple was responsible to the king as the representative of the gods, and many of these temple estates also derived income from royal benefits as well as from their own property holdings. To the extent that the temples became dependent on royal grants rather than on their own holdings, they came under more direct control of the kings, further eradicating the distinction between religious and political authority.

The "rise and fall" of individual Mesopotamian divinities also provides a very clear example of the interdependence of politics and religion at the level of city or state relations. The history of Babylonia demonstrates how the rise of individual cities to prominence brought their tutelary deities to the level of national gods; Marduk, the primary god of Babylon, became the national deity of the Babylonian empire and with the decline of Babylonian power saw a concomitant loss of worshipers. The process could also work in the opposite direction; the neo-Assyrian empire from the ninth to the seventh centuries BCE destroyed temples and carried cult statues into captivity to emphasize the weakness of those gods and goddesses and of the peoples whom they were supposed to protect. In keeping with this ideology, shrines to Ashur, the eponymous god of the traditional first capital of the Assyrian empire, might be placed in some cities, but the Assyrians also rebuilt temples or restored images as a means of conducting imperial policy. Religion thus provided one means of taking political action and marking political developments in both Assyria and Babylonia.

EGYPT. The relationship between religion and politics in Egypt has many striking affinities with the situation in Mesopotamia, despite some major theological differences. Because the Nile River, the lifeblood of ancient Egypt, operated on a much more regular cycle of flood and retreat than the Tigris and Euphrates, Egyptian divinities were considered guarantors of a stable cosmic order rather than forces that might unleash chaos at any moment. The outstanding feature of Egyptian society during its long history as an independent polity, from roughly 3000 BCE until the capture of Alexandria by the Romans in 30 BCE, was that the king was considered to be of divine essence, a god incarnate. Egyptians identified the king as Horus, king of the gods, and each successive king took a Horus-name upon his succession. In the Egyptian conception, the primary responsibility of the gods, and thus of the king as Horus, was to maintain the cosmic and timeless order of the Egyptian world, and in this way Egyptian religious belief supported the institution of kingship.

In practice the existence of numerous local cults throughout Egypt complicated the situation. Each cult possessed its own temple and cult structures, as in Mesopotamia, and was served by its own local priesthood, and each priesthood aimed at advancing the claims of its divinity toward primacy. Egyptian ruling dynasties when they came to power tended to raise their local cult to the status of supreme royal god, and the shifting importance of Ptah, Re, and Amun in Egyptian history owes much to the changes in Egyptian dynasties. But as in Mesopotamia, the relationship between kings and priests was not a one-way street; as Egyptian dynasties sought to raise individual cults to supremacy by granting their priesthoods special favors, they ceded power to those priesthoods as well. The supremacy of the kings may have been felt most strongly in the Old Kingdom, from roughly 2700 to 2200 BCE, the period in which the great Pyramids of Giza were constructed. By the end of this period, however, the kings had adopted the title "Son of Re," perhaps implying that they no longer held a status equal to the sun-god. That fact, and the disappearance of the king's relatives from the higher ranks of priests, may indicate that the kings had lost much of their power to the priesthoods, a trend that repeated itself throughout Egyptian history.

The Theban princes of the Middle Kingdom (c. 2000–1800 BCE) raised Amun to a position of primacy, whereas the rulers of the New Kingdom (c. 1550–1100 BCE) joined Amun with Re and made the new deity the supreme god of Egypt. During the latter period especially, the priesthood of Amun-Ra amassed great wealth due to royal generosity, and thus wielded significant political power, to the point of having influence on the selection of a new king. The celebrated reforms of Akhenaton (c. 1350–1336 BCE), who attempted to install the sun-disk Aton as the sole god of Egypt and erected a new palace and temple complex for this purpose, may have been intended in part to break the power of the priesthood of Amun-Ra. The attempt ultimately failed, and when the centralized power of the New Kingdom gave way at the end of the Twentieth dynasty, the priests of Amun-Ra found themselves the effective rulers of southern Egypt. As in Mesopotamia, political and religious authority were interlocked and developed to the point where distinctions between the two are difficult to make.

GREECE. The situation in ancient Greece presents some marked differences to that in the Near Eastern kingdoms, though some similarities can be observed. Considering that in Greece one does not find a unified polity ruled by a single king, but a plethora of independent polities usually governed by aristocracies, it should not be surprising to find differences in the relationship between religious and political authorities. In Greece there was no separate class of priests, but rather religious personnel were drawn from the citizen body just as were civic officials, and indeed they were often selected and served in the same manner. For instance at Athens, priests and priestesses were frequently chosen by lot and served a term of a single year; the number of hereditary and lifelong positions was always small and diminished over time. This similarity underscores the fact that in ancient Greece civic and religious authority were really two aspects of the same power; both were charged to protect the well-being of the state.

The fact that religion was so embedded in the life of every Greek city meant that considerations which most people would label religious often played a major role in both internal and external affairs. Public spaces, such as the agora in Athens, were in fact consecrated religious spaces, and cities might display their civic pride through religion. The temples of the Acropolis in Athens, built in the second half of the fifth century BCE, are the best-known example of a city's self-promotion through religion, but other cities used religious spaces in similar ways. Less significant states such as Sicyon or Siphnos erected elaborately decorated buildings, filled with dedications, at Panhellenic sites such as Delphi in order to boost their image among the other Greeks. While each city might promote its tutelary divinity, the fragmentation of political authority throughout Greece meant that the temporary predominance of one state, such as Athens, did not lead to the promotion of that state's deity (in this case Athena) at the expense of others, as it did in the Near East.

Despite their political fragmentation, the Greeks recognized that they shared a common bond. Religion, especially in the form of shared practices and sanctuaries, served as one of the primary markers of Greek identity. Of the Panhellenic sanctuaries, the oracle at Delphi was one religious authority in Greece that made itself felt in all of the Greek city-states. Delphi was customarily consulted prior to the foundation of a new colony, a declaration of war, and other momentous decisions; the Spartans' decision to aid in the overthrow of the tyranny at Athens in 510 BCE, which ultimately led to the establishment of Athenian democracy, was driven in part by a series of responses they had received from the oracle. But even here the authority of the Delphic oracle was limited, for her ambiguous utterances needed interpretation, and this left sufficient room for politicians to pursue their chosen paths by interpreting the oracle in a manner favorable to their policies. For example, during the Persian Wars, Themistocles famously interpreted an ambiguous, but largely negative, oracle to mean that the Athenians should pursue his policy of staking their all on a naval campaign at Salamis (480 BCE). The fact that Greeks from many city-states consulted the oracle at Delphi should therefore not be considered as evidence of religious authority external to the state; rather, the oracle formed a part of the entire system of religion embedded with civic authority.

The high degree of correlation between civic and religious authority in ancient Greece aids in understanding one of the dominant religious trends in Greece during the Hellenistic period (323–30 BCE): the development of ruler cult. The rise of Macedon brought the inhabitants of Greece under the rule of kings, and the religious system naturally changed to accommodate the altered political landscape. Unlike their Near Eastern counterparts, Hellenistic kings were not worshiped as representatives of the divine on earth, but as divinities themselves. Scholars following the seminal work of Simon Price (*Rituals and Power*, 1984) have moved beyond asking whether rulers were really considered to be gods or whether this was simply a means of expressing their transcendent political power. Rather, the two kinds of power were inseparable—the locus of political power was the locus of religious power as well, whether that be a corporate body of citizens or an individual. The absence of sharp distinctions between the religious and the political in earlier periods of Greek history meant that ruler cult could be grafted onto the religious systems of the Hellenistic period without serious difficulty.

ROME. The study of Roman religion has perhaps been most affected by the recognition that the entanglement of religion with politics signifies the health of the system, not its decay. Indeed it is scarcely possible to imagine a public action at Rome that could be undertaken without religious approval: declarations of war, decisions of when to offer battle, elections, judicial proceedings—all took place literally under the auspices of the divine. In these circumstances, it should be expected that political developments, both external and internal, would be reflected in religion. The Romans themselves were quite aware of this connection; indeed Roman ideology ascribed their imperial success to their piety. Since the Roman religious system was quite open to the incorporation of foreign religious traditions, including even the adoption of cults of defeated enemies, the imperial expansion of Rome can be read in the expansion of her pantheon, as elements first from other cities on the Italian peninsula, then from Sicily, Greece, Africa, and the Levant found homes within the Roman state religion. Roman religious imperialism is scarcely separable from her territorial imperialism.

In similar fashion the organization of political power and religious power at Rome proceeds from the same sources. The same principles guided the selection of both civic and religious authorities: during the Republic (c. 509–31 BCE), the intent was to keep power in the hands of the aristocracy while at the same time not allowing any one member of the aristocracy to accumulate too much power. So while the records of membership in the religious colleges at Rome are filled with the same prominent names of Rome's political history, tradition dictated that no person should serve in more than one college. Furthermore, these colleges in essence were advisory only: the civic magistrates themselves carried out the necessary religious rituals, with the aid of a priestly advisor, while the Senate needed to approve decisions pertaining to the state religious system. As in other Mediterranean societies, religious authority had no separate existence in Rome.

Just as Roman expansion can be seen in the expansion of the Roman pantheon, internal political change can be read in religious developments. For instance, as the non-aristocratic residents of Rome began to muscle their way into the political arena, the method of selection for the priestly colleges changed from co-option to election by secret ballot. On the other side, as individual Romans began to accrue greater power and amass a series of unprecedented offices, their religious behavior reflected their changed status. Individuals such as Lucius Cornelius Sulla (138–78 BCE) or Pompey the Great (Gnaeus Pompeius Magnus, 106–48 BCE) increasingly used religious actions or religious offices to further their careers or attempted to claim divine sanction for their activities. Though precedents existed in Rome for this type of behavior, it occurred more frequently and on a larger scale in the Late Republic and thus presented a challenge to the traditional Roman form of religion, just as these newly powerful individuals challenged the Roman political structure. Julius Caesar (100–44 BCE), whose actions ultimately resulted in the end of the republican system of government, first drew attention to himself by unexpectedly winning (in 63 BCE) the election for *pontifex maximus*, the most important priestly office in Rome, even though it had limited authority even over religious affairs. Caesar also promoted himself by claiming a connection to the goddess Venus as his special divine patron. Rather than a sign of decay, as scholars looking to explain the emergence of Christianity long argued, these developments are a natural outgrowth of a society with a high degree of integration between politics and religion. As the political structure underwent revolutionary changes, religious changes paralleled the political.

The actions of Augustus (63 BCE–14 CE), as he effected the transformation in Rome from a Republic to an imperial system, clearly reflect these changes. During the struggle for power, Augustus made effective use not only of claims to a special connection with Venus, but also, following the deification of Caesar in 42 BCE, of his status as the son of a god. In this regard he followed the pattern already laid down by Caesar and others, but he also inaugurated a pattern of ruler cult that closely approximated the Hellenistic model, even if most Roman emperors were careful not to be openly worshiped in Rome itself. The priesthoods provide perhaps the best view of the revolution in Roman society: Augustus was the first to serve on all the religious colleges at once, and after scrupulously waiting for the death of the previous *pontifex maximus* he assumed that position as well. As he consolidated political authority under his control, it was natural for him also to consolidate religious authority. Subsequent emperors followed his lead, so that henceforth when the titular head of Roman religion spoke, the head of the Roman Empire spoke at the same time. Ultimately, this combination of religious and political authority in the figure of the *pontifex maximus* outlived the Roman Empire in the West, as it came to be embodied in the Pope, who continues to reside in Rome.

BIBLIOGRAPHY

Beard, Mary, and John North, eds. *Pagan Priests: Religion and Power in the Ancient World.* Ithaca, N.Y., 1990. An outstanding comparative collection, including essays on both Mycenean and Classical Greece, Republican and Imperial Rome, Ptolemaic Egypt, and sixth-century Babylonia.

Beard, Mary, John North, and Simon Price. *Religions of Rome.* 2 vols. Cambridge, U.K., and New York, 1998.

Dandamaev, M. A. "State Gods and Private Religion in the Near East in the First Millennium BCE." In *Religion and Politics in the Ancient Near East,* edited by Adele Berlin, pp. 35–45. Bethesda, Md., 1996.

David, Rosalie A. *The Ancient Egyptians: Beliefs and Practices.* 2d ed., rev. and exp. Portland, Ore., 1998.

Frankfort, Henri. *Kingship and the Gods: A Study of Ancient Near Eastern Religion as the Integration of Society and Nature.* Chicago, 1948.

Garland, Robert. *Introducing New Gods: The Politics of Athenian Religion.* Ithaca, N.Y., 1992.

Holloway, Steven W. *Assur Is King! Assur Is King!: Religion in the Exercise of Power in the Neo-Assyrian Empire.* Leiden and Boston, 2001.

MacBain, Bruce. *Prodigy and Expiation: A Study in Religion and Politics in Republican Rome.* Brussels, 1982.

North, John A. "Conservatism and Change in Roman Religion." *Papers of the British School at Rome* 44 (1976): 1–12. One of the critical articles that revolutionized the approach to religion and its connection to politics in Rome.

Price, Simon. *Rituals and Power: The Roman Imperial Cult in Asia Minor.* Cambridge, U.K., and New York, 1984.

Shafer, Byron E., ed. *Religion in Ancient Egypt: Gods, Myths and Personal Practice.* Ithaca, N.Y., 1991.

Sourvinou-Inwood, Christiane. "What Is *Polis* Religion?" In *Oxford Readings in Greek Religion,* edited by Richard Buxton, pp. 13–37. Oxford, and New York, 2000. The *Oxford Readings* collection includes several other essays of interest, including another discussion of *polis* religion by Sourvinou-Inwood, as well as one by Robert Parker on Greek states and oracles.

Woolf, Greg. "*Polis*-Religion and Its Alternatives in the Roman Provinces." In *Roman Religion,* edited by Clifford Ando, pp. 39–54. Edinburgh, 2004.

ERIC M. ORLIN (2005)

POLITICS AND RELIGION: POLITICS AND CHRISTIANITY

Although the relation of Christians to their governing political power usually follows Jesus's teaching, "Give to Caesar what is Caesar's, and to God what is God's," interpretations of this command vary with different historical circumstances and traditions. In Jesus's time, the relation of the Jews to their Roman conquerors was different from the relation a thousand years later of Christians to Christian emperors. Another thousand years later the relationship has become, for the most part and particularly in democracies, one of separation of church and state.

THE PRE-CONSTANTINIAN CHURCH. The first followers of Jesus were Jews gathered in Jerusalem at the time of his crucifixion, death, and—according to the *Gospel of Luke* and the *Book of Acts*—his resurrection and ascension to the right hand of God. But the belief that Jesus was the long-awaited and now risen Messiah resulted in the expulsion of his followers from Jewish synagogues. As a conquered people under the rule of the Roman Empire, Jews nevertheless enjoyed a special exemption from the otherwise required worship of Roman gods. Once the followers of Jesus gained a distinct identity, they were no longer protected from Roman persecution. Though sporadically persecuted from the time of Emperor Nero (r. 54 CE–68 CE) until Emperor Constantine (r. 312–337) legitimized Christianity in 313, Christians generally were good citizens who disobeyed only in the matter of religion.

FROM CONSTANTINE TO THE REFORMATION. When Christianity became the favored religion of the empire, Christians affirmed one God but disputed the way in which Jesus Christ, the Son of God, was also divine. Constantine called a council of Christian bishops and theologians that met in Nicaea in 325 and condemned one interpretation, known as Arianism. The right of the emperor to call councils and command bishops continued in the Byzantine Empire, established in 330 when Constantine moved from Rome to Byzantium, an ancient city on the Bosporus, which he rebuilt and renamed Constantinople. Constantine's successors ruled over this eastern empire, while the western half of the empire languished under poor political leadership. Barbarians northeast of Byzantium swept into eastern and then western Europe, destroying towns and cities. In these devastated lands, bishops were often the only effective authorities. In northern

Gaul, Clovis, the ruler of the Franks, converted to Christianity in 496 CE. The Franks became fierce defenders of their Christian faith and lands. Another Frank, Charles the Hammer (Charles Martel, c. 688–741), halted the advance of Islam into Europe by defeating the Muslim army at Poitiers in 732. His grandson was Charles the Great (Charlemagne), who ruled from 768 to 814 and by 800 had conquered most of central Europe, from the Pyrenees to the Rhine River.

Charlemagne imposed as uniform a Christianity as his fine organizational skills could manage. He brought the scholar Alcuin (c. 735–804) from Britain to Gaul and in other ways fostered learning, leading to what is known as the Carolingian Renaissance. Under Charlemagne monasteries adopted the Benedictine Rule and became repositories of learning; monks copied manuscripts, sometimes in the new, flowing "Carolingian minuscule." When rebellion threatened Pope Leo III, he appealed to Charlemagne, who thenceforth became the papal champion. On Christmas Day, 800, Leo crowned Charlemagne emperor of the Romans. Latin Christianity now had a strong emperor whose very success emphasized a latent problem: the relation of the pope to the emperor.

As a Christian Charlemagne was subject to the pope, but Leo depended upon Charlemagne for military protection. So who was the more powerful, the pope who crowned Charlemagne or the emperor whose army stood at the gates of Rome during the coronation? The tug-of-war between pope and emperor continued until the Reformation of the sixteenth century split Western Christianity and established a new political-religious dynamic. A few salient encounters will clarify the nature of the continuing conflict. After Pope Gregory VII (r. 1073–1085) stripped the secular power of the right to invest bishops with the insignia of their pastoral office, Emperor Henry IV summoned a synod of bishops, who in 1075 voted to depose Gregory. Gregory retaliated by excommunicating Henry. Since excommunication dissolved the feudal bond between rulers and their subjects, Henry repented, kneeling in the snow outside the papal residence at Canossa. Gregory thus established a principle of papal freedom from secular control. In 1208 Pope Innocent III placed England under interdict and the next year excommunicated its king. The consequent weakening of King John made room for the revolt of the barons, who managed to force John to sign the Magna Carta, "The Great Charter of English liberty granted (under considerable duress) by King John at Runnymede on June 15, 1215." The rights obtained in Magna Carta constituted a significant legal step toward democracy.

In 1303 Philip IV of France captured Pope Boniface VIII, thereby reversing the power dynamic between sovereign secular and ecclesiastic authority. Philip moved the papacy to Avignon, a move that eventually led to schism (1378–1417) and scandal, as three popes claimed to be St. Peter's successors. The Council of Constance (1414–1418) resolved the schism, but only through the action of "conciliarists," a group of clergy and philosophers who wanted to reform the church by decentralizing it and convening councils every five years. They argued that the church should return to the methods of the first four centuries, when the people elected their bishops. The pope's role, they argued, should be that of an executive secretary carrying out the decisions of a representative council consisting not only of clergy but of laymen and, according to Marsilius of Padua and William of Ockham, of laywomen as well—a remarkable idea in a time of male dominance. Although Pope Eugene IV (r. 1431–1447) succeeded in defeating conciliarism, the conciliarists had brought the West another step toward democracy.

At the council, Eugene disappointed a delegation from the Byzantine emperor, John VIII Palaeologus (r. 1425–1448), who sought military aid against the Turks. From Constantine on, the Byzantine emperor or empress ruled the Eastern church, whose patriarchs never gained the kind of power exercised by the Roman popes. When Constantinople, the "second Rome," fell to the Turks in 1453, the Russian Orthodox church assumed leadership of Eastern Christianity, and its main seat in Moscow became the "third Rome." Similar liturgies and hierarchies, barely changed since the days of Constantine, united the Orthodox churches. Relative to the Latin church of the West, state-control Orthodox churches offered fewer opportunities for rebellion by nobles, clergy, or philosophers. The lands of Eastern Christianity thus had no counterparts to the Magna Carta or the conciliarist movement, and they experienced nothing like the splintering the Western church underwent in the sixteenth-century.

From the Reformation to the Enlightenment. Martin Luther began the Protestant Reformation in 1517, insisting on the doctrine of justification by faith alone and the right of individual Christians to read the Bible in their own languages and to interpret its meaning themselves. This move toward individualism was another step toward the doctrines of human rights that developed during the subsequent two centuries. Luther survived papal condemnation and the ire of Emperor Charles V (r. 1519–1556) only because he was protected by his own suzerain, Frederick the Wise, ruler of Saxony from 1486 to 1525 and one of the Holy Roman Empire's seven electors. The empire, consisting mainly of German-speaking lands, comprised myriad territories whose lords, while jealous of their power in their own lands, were sworn in fealty to the emperor. By 1529 three of the seven electors had become "Lutherans," and that year at the Diet of Speyer they protested for their right to chose preachers in their own districts (hence the term "Protestant"). Charles V, fighting the Turks at Vienna, needed the support of all his lords and so yielded to their demands. Because Protestant preachers required the protection of their lords, the latter exercised considerable power over the churches in their territories.

In Zurich, one of the cantons of the Swiss confederation, Huldrych Zwingli in 1518 began another phase of the

Reformation. By 1525 the town's council had accepted Zwingli's reforms, voting against Catholic objections. Other republics and "free cities" within the empire that enjoyed the chartered right to elect their own municipal governments followed suit. In a sense, the Reformation's success—through the actions of locally elected magistrates and an elected emperor—stemmed from political systems developed in the Middle Ages; the liberties guaranteed by medieval town charters took on new relevance in the context of religious reform and thus made possible another step toward democracy in the West.

Luther's principle of private interpretation of the Scriptures was carried further by the so-called Anabaptists, or "rebaptizers." Originating in Zurich in 1520, the sect had spread to the empire by 1525. An imperial edict read at the Diet of Speyer in 1529 condemned them on the grounds that "no man, having once been baptized according to Christian order (as an infant), shall let himself be baptized again or for the second time." With the activities of the "rebaptizers" declared "forbidden on pain of death," Protestants and Catholics alike made martyrs of Anabaptists well into the next century.

Politics played a major part in England's revolt against the papacy, which occurred through a series of legislative acts by Parliament. The new laws paved the way for King Henry VIII (r. 1509–1547) to divorce Catherine of Aragon (1485–1536), who had borne him a daughter, Mary Tudor (1516–1558), but no sons. In 1531 Parliament declared Henry to be "their only and supreme lord and, as far as the law of Christ allows, even supreme head." After his divorce from Catherine and from Rome, Henry married the pregnant Anne Boleyn (1507–1536) in 1533. That same year, Anne bore a daughter, later Elizabeth I (r. 1558–1603), one of England's greatest sovereigns. After the miscarriage of a son, Anne fell from favor and was beheaded in 1536. In 1537 Henry married Jane Seymour, who five years later gave him his long-desired son and heir, Edward VI (r. 1547–1553).

Edward succeeded his father under the regency of Edward Seymour, Duke of Somerset. Through Somerset and Thomas Cranmer, the archbishop of Canterbury and author of *The Book of Common Prayer* (1549), England became Protestant in theology and liturgy. In 1553 Edward died and Mary Tudor, devoutly Roman Catholic, inherited England's throne. Through Parliament she reversed much of the Edwardian legislation. She had Cranmer executed for treason, while other Protestant leaders fled abroad to form a powerful group of "Marian exiles," who returned when Mary's half-sister Elizabeth ascended to the throne in 1558. England's people suffered from the changing religious legislation, which led to bitter divisions between Protestants and Catholics. In 1559 Parliament passed a new Act of Supremacy that required an oath affirming Elizabeth as the Supreme Head of the Church of England. In the same year, the Act of Uniformity introduced a system of penalties ranging from fines for not attending Sunday services as mandated by the restored *Book of Common Prayer* to death for attending a Catholic Mass. This "Elizabethan Settlement" was reached only after bitter debates between Henrician Anglicans and Edwardian Protestants, many of whom had learned their theology in the Reformed states of Zurich and Geneva. The latter's discontent over the retention of the office of bishop and the sanctioning of elaborate liturgical practices led to rebellion in the next century.

Among the Marian exiles who took refuge in Geneva during the reign of Mary Tudor was the Reformed preacher John Knox (c. 1514–1572). Upon his return to Scotland, Knox persuaded its great barons and other nobles to sign the First Covenant in 1557. In 1560 the Scottish Parliament abolished the jurisdiction of the Roman Catholic Church in Scotland, adopted a Reformed confession of faith, and organized the Scottish church along Presbyterian lines. In 1707 the Treaty of Union required the English sovereign to swear to protect the Church of Scotland, but merely as a member, not as its Supreme Governor. Church and state in Scotland continue to be thus divided; each year the General Assembly of the Church of Scotland chooses its own head, the Moderator.

In the tiny republic of Geneva, which granted refuge to English Protestants fleeing Mary Tudor's Catholic regime, Guillaume Farel (1489–1565) began the Reformation in 1532. In 1536 Geneva's General Council swore "to live according to the Word of God." Two months later Farel prevailed upon a young Frenchman, John Calvin (1509–1564), to assist him. Earlier that year Calvin had published the first edition of his *Institutes of the Christian Religion,* the definitive Latin edition of which appeared in 1559, followed by a French edition in 1560. The work presented a powerful, consistent theology that, together with the Genevan Confession of Faith and the articles of church organization, both introduced in 1537, formed the pillars of the Genevan Reformation. Calvin's Geneva was ruled by a Council of Sixty and a Council of Two Hundred. These councils annually elected twelve lay elders to serve in the Consistory along with five pastors, whose position was more or less permanent. The Consistory therefore represented both state and church in matters of church discipline. While it could neither judge nor punish civil offenses, it could admonish or, in the worst cases, excommunicate offenders. Genevan citizens had to sign the Genevan Confession of Faith, which created a marriage of church and state emulated by the settlers of the Massachusetts Bay Colony, founded in 1630.

From the Reformation to the Enlightenment. From the Reformation on, the developing nations of Western Europe had official state churches, a situation that led to bloody and bitter religious wars. Rulers determined the religion of their subjects, who had to convert or move to another territory to avoid dire consequences, including death. Territorial wars were ipso facto religious wars—Catholics fought Lutherans and Calvinists, Lutherans and Calvinists fought each other, and all three persecuted Anabaptists. To bolster armies, warring factions hired mercenaries, sometimes including Muslim Turks. The intermittent but frequent bloody chaos of the Thirty Years' War (begun in 1618) ended only with the Treaty of Westphalia in 1648.

In the meantime, Christians living under Muslim rule in southern Spain, southern Italy, and along the shores of the eastern Mediterranean enjoyed religious liberty; even though their faith relegated them to second-class citizenship, they certainly fared much better than Muslims and Jews under Christian rule. When Ferdinand and Isabella defeated the Moors in the battle of the Alhambra in January 1492, they declared all Spain a Christian country. Muslims and Jews had either to convert to Christianity or to leave Spain. Some Jews signed onto the ships of Christopher Columbus, who set sail in August 1492. Columbus welcomed Jewish crewmembers, thinking that he might meet one of the lost tribes of Israel during his voyage and thus require Hebrew speakers.

In the Americas, native populations learned painfully what it was to be "discovered" by white Europeans. Spanish conquistadors killed and enslaved Aztecs, Mayas, and Incas, contrary to orders of both the Spanish king and the Holy Roman Emperor. But the conquistadors were a law unto themselves; distance made royal and imperial mandates from Europe ineffective. Missionaries either colluded with the conquistadors or fought for the rights of the natives. Even as Christian converts, the natives of Mexico and Central and South America had few rights, although the Spaniards allowed intermarriage and did not confine natives to reservations.

Natives of North America fared worse. Like those of Central and South America, they made friendly overtures and agreed to treaties, which the colonists then broke. The governments of the United States and Canada forced natives from their homelands onto reservations with inadequate space and resources for tribes to support themselves. Decimated by starvation and disease and robbed of their dignity and rights, Native Americans on reservations were given over to the influence of Protestant and Catholic missionaries. Missionaries took Indian children from their families and confined them in boarding schools, barring them from speaking their own languages. Native American religious rituals that expressed and supported traditional life-ways were forbidden. Not until 1978 did a joint resolution of Congress—the American Indian Religious Freedom Resolution—assure that the U.S. government would "protect and preserve for American Indians their inherent right of freedom to believe, express, and exercise the traditional religions of the American Indian, Eskimo, Aleut, and Native Hawaiians, including but not limited to access to sites, use and possession of sacred objects, and the freedom to worship through ceremonials and traditional rites."

Thinkers and jurists in the United States and Europe in the seventeenth and eighteenth centuries prepared the way for the unique experiment enshrined in the U. S. Constitution and its First Amendment, which guarantees freedom of religion by preventing any federal or state agency to officially sanction any one religion to the exclusion of others. As the wars of religion made clear, the Reformation itself did not result in religious freedom. In one of the most influential treatises on toleration, Sebastian Castellio (1515–1563) developed a consistent argument for freedom of conscience, arguing against the execution as a heretic of Michael Servetus by the Genevan magistrates, at Calvin's urging. Castellio said simply and forcefully that "to kill a man is not to defend a doctrine; it is to kill a man." Doctrine, he argued, could be defended by argument, by the pen and not by the sword. But his was a lonely position. Calvin's stance derived from the teachings of Luther and indeed of the medieval church back to St. Augustine, which saw unrepentant heretics as a threat to the spiritual health of the community. Castellio's position began to gain a following only a century later, in a Europe exhausted by religious wars. The Treaty of Westphalia between the Holy Roman Empire and all adjacent nations cracked the age-old armor of intolerance, affirming "Liberty of the Exercise of Religion" (paragraphs XXVIII, XLIX. A practical necessity to assure peace, religious liberty was not, however, considered a matter of ethical principle.

The uninspired scholasticism of the confessional churches in place by the early seventeenth century bored thinking minds and discouraged individuals looking for spiritual enlightenment. Two movements, both based primarily in France, emerged from this restlessness. The first was a remarkable spiritual resurgence, the "devout movement." The second, gathering strength from the systematic doubt of the otherwise pious Catholic René Descartes (1596–1650), intellectually prepared the way for the next century's Enlightenment. With Descartes' rational dualism, reason increasingly asserted its independence from theology.

Among Descartes' readers was John Locke (1632–1704), one of the strongest influences on the development of English and American democracy. Locke, a highly educated Puritan, lived through some of England's most tumultuous years, from the beheading of Charles I in 1649, through Oliver Cromwell's Puritan Commonwealth and the subsequent Restoration of the Stuart monarchy in 1560, to the Glorious Revolution of 1688, which sent James II into exile and brought William and Mary (r. 1689–1702) to England from Holland. (William and Mary, both Stuarts and grandchildren of Charles I, nonetheless countered the Catholicizing tendencies of Charles II or James II.) Locke therefore had ample material for his reflections on the relationship between religion and state. Initially defending the right of a ruler to require religious obedience, he only later came around to support religious tolerance. By 1689, returning to England after five years of exile in Holland, he published three major works: the classic philosophical treatise *An Essay on Human Understanding*, *Two Treatises on Government,* which defended the English Revolution; and *A Letter concerning Toleration,* written in Holland in 1685. He argued that faith went beyond reason and so was not available to reason's arguments in a conclusive fashion. Faith, therefore, could not be coerced. Because love and good will were marks of a true Christian, tolerance should be the chief mark of the true church. Further, argued Locke, there must be a distinction between the business of religion, concerned with individual salvation, and the public business of the commonwealth. He thus separated the responsibilities and legal obligations of the church and the state.

Locke read not only Descartes, but also Castellio; nonconformists like Hugo Grotius of Holland (1583–1645) and William Penn (1644–1718), founder of Pennsylvania; the pantheistic Dutch-Jewish philosopher Barukh Spinoza (1632–1677); and the French Huguenot and skeptic Pierre Bayle (1647–1706). Bayle, fleeing persecution in France following the revocation of the Edict of Nantes in 1685, settled in Rotterdam, where he published his influential *Dictionnaire historique et critique* (Historical and critical dictionary, 1697) and met Locke. Both philosophers, raised as Calvinists, argued that no one should try to coerce the individual conscience. The argument for religious liberty from this time forward became intertwined with the concept of individual rights, especially the right to follow one's own conscience. No longer did shapers of public thought and policy argue that the common good required the removal of unrepentant heretics from society. Rather, wrote Bayle, individuals must be left to God, who gave them a conscience that was "the natural and true light of reason" and a "clear and distinct conception."

FROM THE ENLIGHTENMENT TO POST-MODERNITY. The works of Locke and Bayle influenced both the American (1776) and the French (1789) revolutions. Some of the American colonies had established churches; all had citizens who had fled state-established churches in Europe. It was not difficult for the leaders of the American Revolution and the framers of the U.S. Constitution (1787) to see that tolerance did not go far enough, as it implied that a state could maintain an established church and merely tolerate, or bear with, other denominations. Disestablishment was therefore their goal, accomplished through the First Amendment to the Constitution (1791), which protected the colonists' most cherished freedoms, beginning with freedom of religion: "Congress shall make no law respecting an establishment of religion, or prohibiting the free exercise thereof. . . ." In a letter dated January 1, 1802, Thomas Jefferson allayed the fears of a Connecticut minority, the Danbury Baptists, stating that the First Amendment's declaration of religious freedom amounted to "building a wall of separation between Church & State." According to some interpreters, the intent of Congress and of Jefferson's letter was to assure the free exercise of different religions, which could not be inhibited by any contravening law or the establishment of a particular religion: the state must remain neutral. Others understand Jefferson's letter as interpreting the establishment clause of the First Amendment as a protection of citizens from the demands of any organized religion.

In both the First Amendment and Jefferson's letter, the word "religion" included only forms of Christianity or deism. Challenges to this narrow conception of religion began to arise as the United States expanded. On April 30, 1803, Jefferson signed the Louisiana Purchase, for the sum of 15 million dollars in exchange for more than 800,000 square miles of land. Extending from the Mississippi River to the Rocky Mountains, this territory included the port of New Orleans, at the mouth of the Mississippi, and St. Louis, the "gateway to the west" at the confluence of the Mississippi and Missouri rivers. English was a foreign language along the Mississippi, where francophone Haitians and Canadians mingled with various Native Americans and English-speaking Americans from the east.

Throughout the eighteenth and nineteenth centuries the spread of Christianity continued, both in the western United States and elsewhere around the world, as missionaries followed conquering flags. The labors of these missionaries, in many cases, resulted in religious beliefs and practices far removed from the conceptions of Christianity they attempted to inculcate. At the beginning of the twenty-first century, many native peoples practice Christianity in tandem with their indigenous religions. In some areas, the two are so mixed that it is difficult to extract particular strands. And in the United States, the influx of people belonging to all the world's religions and the very belated recognition of Native American religions has brought new pressures to bear on the First Amendment and the interpretation of the word "religion."

Throughout history and around the globe, religion has been used and abused as politicians cited scripture to justify war, slavery, and male domination of women. Pacifists, abolitionists, and the Woman Suffrage Movement, however, have likewise used Christianity to advance their causes. Women obtained the vote in most of Europe, New Zealand, Australia, and North America between the end of the nineteenth century and the middle of the twentieth. Some Swiss cantons, however, enfranchised women only in the 1970s, and religious arguments are still used to deny women the right to vote in some parts of the world. The relation between church and state remains relevant in the social and cultural battles of the early twenty-first century In the United States, the controversy over same-sex marriage tests how thoroughly the country remains culturally "Christian" (and what Christianity means to its very diverse practitioners); it also reflects the wide spectrum of views regarding the desirability of both religious influence on state policy and state involvement in religious matters. Organized conservative Christians from various denominations use political means to oppose same-sex marriage, seeking to amend both state and federal constitutions to define marriage exclusively as a union between a man and a woman. "Secularists," too, continue their own fight against the privileged position of Christianity in their states. Beginning with Constantine, Christian governments awarded churches tax-exempt status and offered their clergy exemption from compulsory military service. Both exemptions have been challenged in the United States as contrary to the establishment clause of the First Amendment. In France, the government's strict secularism (especially, critics argued, vis-à-vis religious displays by non-Christian, and above all Muslim, immigrants) led to a 2004 law forbidding schoolchildren from wearing religious symbols, including Muslim headscarves, Sikh turbans, large crosses, or Stars of David.

Twentieth-century pundits predicted that science and rational skepticism, the legacies of the Enlightenment, would result in the triumph of secularism and a world in which the pursuit of goods and power was balanced by a political concern for democratic values and human rights, without reference to any religious belief or practice. Except in Europe, however, religion appeared to be gaining in influence at the beginning of the twenty-first century, both culturally and politically. While the European Union argued over whether its constitution should reference Europe's Christian past, its nations have become increasingly diverse in the wake of decolonization and globalization, with respect to both ethnicity and religion. Europe's residents are Christian and Muslim, Hindu and Buddhist. Governments based on a Christian European culture struggle to maintain their identity and at the same time to understand that Christian hegemony is a thing of the past. In the United States, too, immigrants demand an equal share in the liberties promised by the Constitution and the Bill of Rights. Muslims ask to sound the call to prayer in towns that previously heard only church bells, whereas Christians must recognize that, for their neighbors, Sunday is an ordinary day. In the face of globalization and its complex political realities, Christians will have to negotiate their place in the world.

SEE ALSO Anabaptism; Arianism; Liberation Theology; Reformation; Religious Diversity; Secularization.

BIBLIOGRAPHY

American Indian Religious Freedom Resolution. Public Law 95–341. 95th Cong., August 11, 1978.

Ariew, Roger, and Marjorie Grene, eds. *Descartes and His Contemporaries Meditations, Objections, and Replies.* Chicago, 1995.

Bouwsma, William J. *The Waning of the Renaissance, 1550–1640.* New Haven, Conn., 2000.

Chidester, David. *Christianity, A Global History.* San Francisco, 2000.

Driesbach, Daniel L. *Thomas Jefferson and the Wall of Separation Between Church and State.* New York, 2002.

Dunn, Richard S. *The Age of Religious Wars, 1559–1715.* 2d ed. New York, 1979.

Dyson, R.W., ed. *The Pilgrim City: Social and Political Ideas in the Writings of St. Augustine of Hippo.* Woodbridge, U.K., and Rochester, N.Y., 2001.

Fogel, Robert William. *The Fourth Great Awakening and the Future of Egalitarianism.* Chicago, 2000.

Fortin, Ernest L. *Classical Christianity and the Political Order: Reflections on the Theologico-Political Problem.* Edited by J. Brian Benestad. Lanham, Md., 1996.

Gutiérrez, Gustavo. *We Drink from Our Own Wells: The Spiritual Journey of a People.* Translated by Matthew J. O'Connell. Maryknoll, N.Y., 1984.

Hamburger, Philip. *Separation of Church and State.* Cambridge, Mass., 2002. A clear and learned exposition of the history and meanings of the First Amendment and Thomas Jefferson's sometimes abused phrase.

Hastings, Adrian, ed. *A World History of Christianity.* London, 1999.

Hatch, Nathan O. *Democratization of American Christianity,* New Haven, Conn., 1989.

Hollenbach, David. *The Common Good and Christian Ethics.* Cambridge, U.K., and New York, 2002.

Inter-Parliamentary Union. For a list of countries and dates of women's enfranchisement see http://www.ipu.org/wmn-e/suffrage.htm.

Johnson, Douglas, and Cynthia Sampson, eds. *Religion, The Missing Dimension of Statecraft.* New York, 1994.

Kaufman, Peter Iver. *Redeeming Politics.* Princeton, N.J., 1990.

Kingdon, Robert M. *Adultery and Divorce in Calvin's Geneva.* Cambridge, Mass., 1995.

O'Donovan, Oliver, and Joan Lockwood O'Donovan. *Bonds of Imperfection: Christian Politics, Past and Present.* Grand Rapids, Mich., 2004.

Thiemann, Ronald F. *Religion in Public Life: A Dilemma for Democracy.* Washington, D.C., 1996.

Witte, John, Jr. *Religion and the American Constitutional Experiment: Essential Rights and Liberties.* Boulder, Colo., 2000.

Witte, John, Jr., ed. *Christianity and Democracy in Global Context.* Boulder, Colo., 1993.

Yoder, John Howard. *The Politics of Jesus: Vicit Agnus Noster.* Grand Rapids, Mich., 1994.

Zagorin, Perez. *How the Idea of Religious Toleration Came to the West.* Princeton, N.J., 2003.

JILL RAITT (2005)

POLITICS AND RELIGION: POLITICS AND ISLAM

Muslims have both an individual and a corporate religious identity and responsibility. Thus to be a Muslim, to follow Islam ("submission" to God), entails both an individual and a communal responsibility as members of a worldwide community (*ummah*) to obey and implement God's will on earth in both the private and public spheres. The Qur'ān and the example of the prophet Muḥammad teach that Muslims have a universal mission to spread the religion of Islam and to establish a just society on earth, based on recognition of God (Allāh) as the source of all authority, law, and order. Historically politics have often been a central vehicle by which Islam was implemented in state and society.

RELIGION AND POLITICS IN EARLY ISLAM. How and under what form and institutions an Islamic society is to be established has been subject to many interpretations across time and space. The Qur'ān and *ḥadīth* do not provide any specific format for an "Islamic state" or even prescribe one as necessary. Instead, they contain general prescriptions or norms about the function of the state as well as ethical considerations. Early Islamic empires and sultanates developed systems that combined elements adopted from conquered societies with religious prescriptions and institutions. During this time period most states, non-Muslim as well as Muslim, controlled or used religion as a source of legitimacy or to mobilize popular support.

Historically Islam's role in the state reinforced a sense of common identity for Muslims as well as a sense of continuity in Muslim rule. The existence of an Islamic ideology and system, however imperfectly implemented, both validated and reinforced a sense of a divinely mandated and guided community with a unifying purpose and mission, giving the Islamic state a divine raison d'être.

Belief in the divine mandate of the Muslim community gave Muslim rulers the rationale for spreading their rule and empire over the entire Middle East and major portions of Africa and South, Southeast, and Central Asia as well as into Spain and southern Italy on the European Continent. Islam served as the religious ideology for the foundation of a variety of Muslim states, including great Islamic empires: Umayyad (661–750 CE), Abbasid (750–1258 CE), Ottoman (1281–1924 CE), Safavid (1501–1722 CE), and Mughal (1526–1857 CE). In each of these empires and other sultanate states from the seventh to the eighteenth centuries, Islam was used by rulers to legitimate their governance, and it informed the state's legal, political, educational, and social institutions.

Sunnī Muslims (85 percent of the Muslim community, in contrast to Shīʿī, a 15 percent minority) see the success and expansion of Islam as religion and empire as evidence of God's favor upon Muslims when they fulfill their divine mandate to spread God's word, guidance, and governance, whereas the increasing decline and powerlessness from the eighteenth century through the early twenty-first century are understood to reflect their failure to adhere to God's will. It is this worldview that has in part given rise to the Islamic revival that began in the eighteenth century and experienced a major resurgence and reformulation in the twentieth century.

GOVERNMENT: THE SUNNĪ CALIPHATE. Sunnī Muslims believe that Muḥammad died without designating a specific successor (caliph) and that the most qualified person should become the head of the Muslim community. The caliph succeeded Muḥammad as political leader, not as prophet. Because Muḥammad was the last of the prophets, leadership of the Muslim community following Muḥammad's death ceased to be a religio-political position and became strictly political instead. Thus Sunnīs believe that the leader (caliph) of the Muslim community possesses human and worldly, rather than divine, authority. They look to the rule of Muḥammad (610–632 CE) and of the Four Rightly-Guided Caliphs (632–661 CE) as a special normative period in which God's favor was clearly upon the Muslims.

One of the most contentious questions faced by religious scholars throughout Muslim history has been whether the character of the ruler was a decisive factor in determining that the state was truly Islamic. That is, if the ruler is known to be immoral, did this necessarily render the state un-Islamic, so that its citizens were obligated to overthrow the ruler? The majority of religious scholars, or ʿulamaʾ, determined that maintaining social order and avoiding anarchy were more important than the character of the ruler. The decisive factor rendering a state or society "Islamic," they concluded, is its governance by Islamic law.

However, a minority of ʿulamaʾ, most notably the thirteenth-century scholar Taqi al-Din Ibn Taymīyah, ruled that the character of the ruler was in fact decisive. If a ruler was unjust or immoral, Muslims were bound to overthrow him. Ibn Taymīyah's enduring influence, direct and indirect, on contemporary political thought and politics is also reflected in several other doctrines: the necessary synthesis between religion and state (that Islam is *din wa-dawlah*, or religion and state); insistence that one who claims to be a Muslim but does not act like one cannot be considered a true Muslim; a bipolar view of the world in which only two choices or sides existed, Muslim and non-Muslim, belief and unbelief. These viewpoints have been appropriated in particular by extremist movements, past and present.

THE SHĪʿĪ IMAMATE. In contrast to Sunnī Islam, Shīʿī Islam teaches that Muḥammad decreed that succession or leadership (the *imām* or leader) of the Muslim community belonged to the family of the Prophet, beginning with Alī, his cousin and son-in-law. However, ʿAlī's caliphate began only after three other caliphs had ruled; ʿAlī was assassinated by opponents and the caliphate was seized by his enemy, Muʿāwiya. Shīʿī regard the caliphs, in particular Muʿāwiya, as usurpers and believe ʿAlī's son, Ḥusayn, was ʿAlī's rightful successor. Ḥusayn was persuaded by some of ʿAlī's followers to lead a rebellion against Yazīd, Muʿāwiya's son, in 680 CE. Ḥusayn and his army were slaughtered in battle at Karbala (in modern-day Iraq). The tragic death of Ḥusayn and his followers, commemorated by Shīʿīs every year during ʿĀshūrā, shaped the Shīʿī worldview and its view of history as one of disinheritance and oppression, suffering, protest, and struggle against injustice and discrimination under Sunnī Muslim governments.

In contrast to the Sunnī caliphate, Shīʿī believe that leadership of the Muslim community belongs to the leader, or *imām,* a direct descendant of Muḥammad who serves in a religious as well as political-military capacity. Although the *imām* is not considered a prophet, since the Qur'ān states that Muḥammad was the last of the prophets, the *imām* is nevertheless considered divinely inspired, infallible, sinless, and the final and authoritative interpreter of God's will as formulated in Islamic law. After decades of rebellion against early Sunnī rulers, Shīʿī found a formula for coexistence, a means to recognize de facto Sunnī rule and participation in Sunnī majority territories without acknowledging the legitimacy of the Sunnī caliphate.

Because Shīʿī existed as a disinherited and oppressed minority among the Sunnī, they understood history to be a test of the righteous community's perseverance in the struggle to restore God's rule on earth. Realization of a just social order led by the *imām* became the dream of Shīʿī throughout the centuries. Whereas Sunnī history looked to the glorious and victorious history of the Four Rightly-Guided Caliphs and then the development of imperial Islam, Shīʿī history traced the often tragic history of the descendants of ʿAlī and Fāṭimah. Thus whereas Sunnīs can claim a golden age when they were a great world power and civilization, evidence, they believe, of God's will and favor and historic validation of Islam, Shīʿī see these same developments as an illegitimate usurpation of power by Sunnī rulers at the expense of a just society.

Shīʿī view history more as a paradigm of the suffering, disinheritance, and oppression of a righteous minority community who must constantly struggle to restore God's rule on earth under his divinely appointed *imām.* In the twentieth century this history was reinterpreted as a paradigm providing inspiration and mobilization to actively fight against injustice rather than passively accept it. This reinterpretation had a significant impact during the Islamic Revolution of 1978–1979 in Iran, where the shah was equated with Yazīd and Ayatollah Khomeini and his followers with Ḥusayn. Thus the victory of the Islamic Revolution was declared the victory of the righteous against illegitimate usurpers of power.

VISIONS OF POLITICS AND THE STATE IN MODERN ISLAM. Classical definitions of the role of Islam and the state have undergone substantial revision in modern times. Up until the nineteenth century Muslims generally thought of politics in terms of the Muslim *ummah* (the universal Islamic community) and either a universal caliphate (in which its religious character was emphasized) or diverse sultanates (in which its political character was emphasized). Politics was more a matter of dynasties and rulers (referred to as *dawlah*) than of popular participation.

The proposition that Islam is both a religion and a state (*din wa-dawlah*) dates to the early twentieth century, when Muslims were confronted with both the abolition of the Ottoman (Turkish) Caliphate and the territorial division of Muslim communities under the impact of European colonialism. Although the caliphate had in fact come to a forcible end with the fall of the Abbasid dynasty to the Mongols in 1258, it remained a powerful religious symbol of political legitimacy. The Ottoman sultans had adopted the title of caliph in order to lend religious legitimacy to their rule; their claim to the caliphate was abolished in 1924. Desire to restore the caliphate provided an alternative to fragmentation, reasserting the unity of the Muslim *ummah.* It also provided an alternative political vision to the territorial nationalism of Europe. Those who supported the continued existence of the caliphate defined it as a combination of political and religious authority in its ideal form. Since then there have been occasional calls among Islamic revivalists for a revival of the caliphate as a means of maintaining unity of the broader Muslim community, but such calls have not garnered significant popular support.

POLITICAL ISLAM. Twentieth-century visions of the relationship of religion to the modern nation-state varied. At one end of the spectrum was the "self-described" Islamic state of Saudi Arabia and at the other modern Turkey's secular state. Most Muslim countries were states whose majority population was Muslim and had some Islamic provisions, such as the requirement that the head of state be a Muslim, but that adopted Western political, legal, and educational models of development. However, the mid-twentieth century also brought the creation of modern Islamic movements, in particular the Jamāʿat-i-Islāmī in Pakistan and the Muslim Brotherhood in Egypt. Both called for the foundation of a specifically Islamic state, a God-centered one run only by true believers with the Qurʾān and *sunnah* as guides. They believed Islam should inform all spheres of the state—political, economic, and legislative as well as moral—and called for the Islamization of society and state.

In the late twentieth century political Islam, often referred to as "Islamic fundamentalism," became a dominant factor in Muslim politics, the primary language of political discourse and mobilization. New Islamic republics were created in Sudan, Iran, and Afghanistan. Muslim rulers as well as mainstream opposition leaders and movements appealed to Islam to legitimate their rule or policies. Islamists have been elected president, prime minister, or deputy prime minister and to parliament, and they have served in cabinets in countries as diverse as Sudan, Egypt, Algeria, Jordan, Lebanon, Kuwait, Bahrain, Yemen, Pakistan, Afghanistan, Malaysia, and Indonesia. At the same time extremist organizations have used violence and terrorism in the name of Islam to threaten and destabilize governments, attacking government officials, institutions, and ordinary citizens in Muslim countries and in the West. Usāmah bin Lādin and al-Qāʿidah have become a symbol of the threat of international terrorism, driven home by the September 11, 2001, attacks against New York's World Trade Center and the Pentagon.

ISLAMIC FUNDAMENTALISM OR POLITICAL ISLAM? Though convenient, the use of the term *fundamentalism,* which originated in Christianity, can be misleading when applied to a diverse group of governments, individuals, and organizations. The conservative monarchy of Saudi Arabia, the radical socialist state of Libya, clerically governed Iran, the Taliban's Afghanistan, and the Islamic Republic of Pakistan have all been called "fundamentalist." The term obscures significant differences in the nature of the governments (monarchy, military, and clerical rule) as well as their relations with the West. For example, Libya and Iran have in the past been regarded as anti-Western and enemies of the United States, while Saudi Arabia and Pakistan have often been close allies of the United States. Similarly Islamic activists are not monolithic; they represent a broad spectrum: mainstream and extremist, progressive and conservative. Therefore *political Islam* or *Islamism* are more useful terms than fundamentalism when referring to the role of Islam in politics and society and the diversity of Islamic political and social movements.

ORIGINS AND NATURE OF POLITICAL ISLAM. The reassertion of Islam in politics is rooted in a contemporary religious revival or resurgence affecting both personal and public life that began in the late 1960s and 1970s. On the one hand, many Muslims became more religiously observant (emphasizing prayer, fasting, dress, family values, and a revitalization of Islamic mysticism or Sufism). On the other, Islam reemerged as an alternative religio-political ideology to the perceived failures of more secular forms of nationalism, capitalism, and socialism. Islamic symbols, rhetoric, actors, and organizations became major sources of legitimacy and mobilization, informing political and social activism. Governments and Islamic movements spanned both the religious and political spectrums from moderate to extremist, using religion to enhance their legitimacy and to mobilize popular support for programs and policies.

The causes of the Islamic resurgence have been many: religio-cultural, political, and socioeconomic. More often than not, faith and politics have been intertwined causes or catalysts. Issues of political and social injustice (authoritarianism, repression, unemployment, inadequate housing and social services, maldistribution of wealth, and corruption) combined with concerns about the preservation of religious and cultural identity and values.

Among the more visible crises or failures that proved to be catalytic events in the rise of political Islam were:

1. the 1967 Arab-Israeli War (Six-Day War) in which Israel decisively defeated the combined Arab armies of Egypt, Syria, and Jordan, occupied Sinai, the West Bank and Gaza, and East Jerusalem, transforming the liberation of Jerusalem and Palestine into a transnational Islamic issue;
2. the 1969 Malay-Chinese riots in Kuala Lumpur reflecting the growing tension between the Malay Muslim majority and a significant Chinese minority;
3. the Pakistan-Bangladesh civil war of 1971–1972, heralding the failure of Muslim nationalism;
4. the Lebanese civil war (1975–1990), among whose causes were the inequitable distribution of political and economic power between Christians and Muslims, which led to the emergence of major Shīʿah groups: AMAL and the Iranian-inspired and backed Hizbollah;
5. the Iranian Revolution of 1978–1979, a pivotal event with long-term global impact and implications for the Muslim world and the West;
6. the continued conflict in Palestine-Israel, which grew in strength during the 1980s and spawned its own Islamist movements, among them HAMAS and Islamic Jihad.

The failures of the West (both its models of development and its role as an Arab and Muslim ally) and fear of the threat of westernization and its political, economic, and cultural dominance were pervasive themes of the resurgence. Many blamed the ills of their societies on the excessive influence of and dependence upon the West, in particular the superpowers the United States and the Soviet Union. Modernization, as a process of progressive westernization and secularization and increasingly globalization, have been regarded as forms of neocolonialism exported by the West and imposed by local Western-oriented elites, undermining religious and cultural identity and values.

While most Islamic movements developed in response to domestic conditions, international issues and actors increasingly played important roles in Muslim politics: the Soviet-Afghan War; the Arab-Israeli conflict; sanctions against Ṣaddām Ḥusayn's Iraq; the "liberation" of Bosnia, Kashmir, and Chechnya; and Usāmah bin Lādin and al-Qāʿidah. Countries like Saudi Arabia, Iran, and Libya as well as individuals used their petrodollars and wealth to extend their influence internationally, promoting their religious-ideological worldviews and politics and supporting government Islamization programs as well as Islamist movements, mainstream and extremist.

ISLAMIC MOVEMENTS: LEADERSHIP AND IDEOLOGY. Political Islam is in many ways the successor of failed nationalist ideologies and projects in the mid-twentieth century, from the Arab nationalism and socialism of North Africa and the Middle East to the Muslim nationalism of postindependence Pakistan. The founders of many Islamic movements were formerly participants in nationalist movements: the Egyptian Muslim Brotherhood's founder, Ḥasan al-Banna; Tunisia's Rashid Ghannoushi of the Renaissance Party; Algeria's Abbasi Madani of the Islamic Salvation Front (the FIS, or Front Islamique du Salut); and Turkey's Ecmettin Erbakan, founder of the Welfare (Refah) Party.

Islamic political and social movements proved particularly strong among the younger generation, university graduates, and young professionals recruited from the mosques and universities. Contrary to popular expectations, the membership of movements, especially in Sunnī Islam, has not come from religious faculties and the humanities so much as from the fields of science, engineering, education, law, and medicine. Thus the senior leadership of many movements includes judges, lawyers, teachers, engineers, physicians, journalists, and prosperous businesspeople. At the same time leaders of militant movements like Egypt's Islamic Jihad and Usāmah bin Lādin, al-Qāʿidah, and those specifically responsible for the attacks of September 11, 2001, also included many university graduates.

IDEOLOGICAL WORLDVIEW. Islamists believe the Muslim world's state of decline is the result of corrupt authoritarian regimes and excessive political, economic, and cultural dependence on the West. The cure is a return to the faith and values of Islam. Islam, they assert, is a comprehensive ideology or framework for Muslim society. It embraces public as well as personal life. They believe the renewal and revitalization of Muslim governments and societies require the restoration or reimplementation of Islamic law, the blueprint for an Islamically guided and socially just state and society. While westernization and secularization of society are condemned, modernization as such is not. Science and technology are accepted; but the pace, direction, and extent of change are subordinated to Islamic belief and values in order to guard against excessive influence and dependence on the West.

The majority of Islamists have worked to bring about change through social and political activism within their societies, participating in electoral politics and civil society where permitted. However, a significant and dangerous minority of extremists, *jihād* groups from Egypt to Indonesia, al-Qāʿidah, and other terrorists, believe that they have a mandate from God to make changes and that the rulers in the Muslim world and their societies are anti-Islamic. For these extremists, those who remain apolitical or resist—individuals and governments—are no longer regarded as Muslims but rather as atheists or unbelievers, enemies of God, against whom all true Muslims must wage holy war (*jihād*).

Extremists also believe Islam and the West are locked in an ongoing battle that stretches back to the early days of Islam, is heavily influenced by the legacy of the Crusades and European colonialism, and is the product in the twenty-first century of a Judeo-Christian conspiracy. This conspiracy, they charge, is the result of superpower neocolonialism and the power of Zionism. The West (Britain, France, and especially the United States) is blamed for its support of un-Islamic or unjust regimes and biased support for Israel in the face of Palestinian occupation and displacement. Violence against such governments, their representatives, and citizens (Jews, Christians, and other Muslims, noncombatants as well as combatants) is regarded as legitimate self-defense.

The Quiet Revolution. In contrast to the 1980s, when political Islam was simply equated with revolutionary Iran or clandestine groups with names like Islamic Jihad or the Army of God, the Muslim world in the 1990s saw Islamists participate in the electoral process. A quiet revolution had taken place. While a minority of religious extremists sought to impose change from above through terror and holy wars, many others pursued a bottom-up approach, seeking a gradual transformation or Islamization of society through words and example, preaching, and social and political activism.

Islamic organizations and associations emerged as part and parcel of mainstream society and institutional forces in civil society, active in social reform and providing educational, medical, dental, legal, and social welfare services. The number of Islamic banks, insurance companies, and publishing houses mushroomed. Social activism was accompanied by increased political participation. In the late 1980s and the 1990s failed economies and discredited governmental development policies led to political crises and mass demonstrations, resulting in limited political liberalization. Islamic candidates or leaders were elected as mayors and parliamentarians in countries as diverse as Morocco, Egypt, Turkey, Lebanon, Kuwait, Bahrain, Pakistan, Malaysia, and Indonesia. They served in cabinet-level positions and as speakers of national assemblies, prime ministers (Turkey, Iran, and Pakistan), a deputy prime minister (Malaysia), and Indonesia's first democratically elected president. The general response of many governments to this political power of Islam was to retreat from open elections, identifying their Islamic opposition as extremist or simply canceling or manipulating elections, as in Tunisia, Algeria, Egypt, and Jordan.

Usāmah bin Lādin and Global Terrorism. September 11, 2001, was a watershed in the history of political Islam and of the world. Its terror and carnage signaled the magnitude of the threat of Usāmah bin Lādin and al-Qāʿidah. The multimillionaire, seemingly devout, well-educated, wealthy son of a prominent Saudi family had fought against the Soviets in Afghanistan, a struggle that allied him with a cause supported by the United States, Saudi Arabia, Pakistan, and many others. However, after the war he became radicalized when faced with the prospect of an American-led coalition in the Gulf War of 1991 to oust Ṣaddām Ḥusayn from his occupation of Kuwait and the prospect of the presence and increased influence of the United States in Saudi Arabia and the Persian Gulf. Usāmah bin Lādin was regarded as the major godfather of global terrorism, a major funder of terrorist groups suspected in the bombing of the World Trade Center in 1993, the slaughter of eighteen American soldiers in Somalia, bombings in Riyadh in 1995 and in Dhahran in 1996, the killing of fifty-eight tourists at Luxor, Egypt, in 1997 as well as the bombings in Tanzania and Kenya. He threatened attacks against Americans who remained on Saudi soil and promised retaliation internationally for cruise missile attacks.

In February 1998 bin Lādin and other militant leaders announced the creation of a transnational coalition of extremist groups, the Islamic Front for Jihad against Jews and Crusaders. Al-Qāʿidah was linked to a series of acts of terrorism: the truck bombing of U.S. embassies in Kenya and Tanzania on August 7, 1998, that killed 263 people and injured more than 5,000, followed on October 12, 2000, by a suicide bombing attack against the USS *Cole,* which killed 17 American sailors.

Usāmah bin Lādin's message appealed to the feelings of many in the Arab and Muslim world. A sharp critic of American foreign policy toward the Muslim world, he denounced its support for Israel, sanctions against Iraq that resulted in the deaths of hundreds of thousands of civilians, and the substantial American (military and economic) presence and involvement in Saudi Arabia that he dismissed as the "new crusades." To these were added other populist causes like Bosnia, Kosovo, Chechnya, and Kashmir.

Usāmah bin Lādin and al-Qā'idah represented a new international brand of Sunnī militancy associated with the Afghan Arabs, those who had come from the Arab and Muslim world to fight alongside the Afghan Mujāhidīn against the Soviets. It was also reflected in the growth of extremism and acts of terrorism in Central, South, and Southeast Asia (where it has often been referred to as Wahabism because of its reported Saudi financial backing). Islam's norms and values about good governance, social justice, and the requirement to defend Islam when under siege are transformed into a call to arms in order to legitimate the use of violence, warfare, and terrorism. Their theology of hate sees the modern world in mutually exclusive, black-and-white categories, the world of belief and unbelief, the land of Islam and of warfare, the forces of good against the forces of evil. Those who are not with them, whether Muslim or non-Muslims, are the enemy and are to be fought and destroyed in a war with no limits, no proportionality of goal or means.

Sayyid Quṭb: Godfather and Martyr of Islamic Radicalism. It would be difficult to overestimate the role played by Sayyid Quṭb (1906–1966) in the reassertion of militant *jihād.* He was both a respected intellectual and religious writer whose works included an influential commentary on the Qur'ān and a godfather to Muslim extremist movements around the globe. In many ways his journey from educated intellectual, government official, and admirer of the West to militant activist who condemned both the Egyptian and the American governments and defended the legitimacy of militant *jihād* has influenced and inspired many militants, from the assassins of Anwar al-Sadat to the followers of Usāmah bin Lādin and al-Qā'idah.

Quṭb had a modern education and was a great admirer of the West and Western literature. After graduation he became an official in the Ministry of Public Instruction as well as a poet and literary critic. Quṭb's visit to the United States in the late 1940s proved a turning point in his life, transforming him from an admirer into a severe critic of the West. His experiences in the United States produced a culture shock that made him more religious and convinced him of the moral decadence of the West.

Shortly after he returned to Egypt, Quṭb joined the Muslim Brotherhood. Quṭb quickly emerged as a major voice in the brotherhood and its most influential ideologue amid the growing confrontation with the Egyptian regime. Imprisoned and tortured for alleged involvement in a failed attempt to assassinate Nasser, he became increasingly militant and radicalized, convinced that the Egyptian government was un-Islamic and must be overthrown. Quṭb's revolutionary vision is set forth in his most influential tract, *Milestones.* His ideas have reverberated in the radical rhetoric of revolutionaries from Ayatollah Khomeini to Usāmah bin Lādin.

Quṭb sharply divided Muslim societies into two diametrically opposed camps, the forces of good and of evil, those committed to the rule of God and those opposed, the party of God and the party of Satan. There was no middle ground. He emphasized the need to develop a special group, a vanguard, of true Muslims within this corrupt and faithless society. Since the creation of an Islamic government was a divine commandment, he argued, it was not an alternative to be worked toward. Rather it was an imperative that Muslims must strive to implement or impose immediately.

Given the authoritarian and repressive nature of the Egyptian government and many other governments in the Muslim world, Quṭb concluded that *jihād* as armed struggle was the only way to implement the new Islamic order. For Quṭb, *jihād,* as armed struggle in the defense of Islam against the injustice and oppression of anti-Islamic governments and the neocolonialism of the West and the East (the Soviet Union), was incumbent upon all Muslims. Muslims who refused to participate were to be counted among the enemies of God, apostates who were excommunicated (*takfir*) and who should be fought and killed along with the other enemies of God. Sayyid Quṭb's radicalized worldview became a source for ideologues from the founders of Egypt's Islamic Jihad to Usāmah bin Lādin and al-Qā'idah's call for a global *jihād.*

Globalization of the *Jihād*. In the late twentieth century and early twenty-first century the word *jihād* gained remarkable currency, becoming more global in its usage. On the one hand, *jihād's* primary religious and spiritual meanings, the "struggle" or effort to follow God's path, to lead a good life, became more widespread. It is applied, for example, to individual struggles to be religiously observant as well as improve one's society through educational and social welfare projects.

The Soviet-Afghan War marked a new turning point as *jihād* went global to a degree never seen in the past. The Mujāhidīn holy war drew Muslims from many parts of the world and support from Muslim and non-Muslim countries and sources. In its aftermath *jihād* became the common term for all armed struggles, used for resistance, liberation, and terrorist movements alike in their holy and unholy wars. Most major Muslim struggles were declared a *jihād,* from Palestine to Kashmir, Chechnya, Daghestan, and the southern Philippines. Those who fought in Afghanistan, called Afghan Arabs, moved on to fight other *jihāds* in their home countries and in Bosnia, Kosovo, and Central Asia. Others stayed on or were trained and recruited in the new *jihādi madrasahs* (religious schools) and training camps, joining in Usāmah bin Lādin and al-Qā'idah's global *jihād* against Muslim governments and the West.

Although the distinction is often made between Qur'anic prescriptions about just war versus unjust war, many and conflicting interpretations of the verses have been made over time. At issue are the meaning of terms like *aggression* and *defense,* questions about when the command to sacrifice life and property to defend Islam is appropriate, and how to define the "enemies" of Islam. For example, the Qur'ān speaks repeatedly of the "enemies of God" and the "enemies of Islam," often defining them as "unbelievers." Although other Qurʾanic verses appear to make it clear that such people should be physically fought against only if they behave aggressively toward Muslims, some Muslims have interpreted the call to "struggle" or "strive" against such enemies to be a permanent engagement required of all Muslims of every time and place until the entire world is converted to Islam.

Terrorists like bin Lādin and others have gone beyond classical Islam's criteria for a just *jihād* and recognize no limits but their own, employing any weapons or means. Adopting Sayyid Quṭb's militant worldview of an Islam under siege, they ignore or reject Islamic law's regulations regarding the goals and means of a valid *jihād* (that violence must be proportional and that only the necessary amount of force should be used to repel the enemy), that innocent civilians should not be targeted, and that *jihād* must be declared by the ruler or head of state. As the Islamic scholars of the Islamic Research Council at al-Azhar University, regarded by many as the highest moral authority in Islam, forcefully stated in condemning bin Lādin's calls for *jihād* and terrorism: "Islam provides clear rules and ethical norms that forbid the killing of non-combatants, as well as women, children, and the elderly, and also forbids the pursuit of the enemy in defeat, the execution of those who surrender, the infliction of harm on prisoners of war, and the destruction of property that is not being used in the hostilities" (*Al-Hayat,* November 5, 2001).

POLITICAL ISLAM AND THE DEMOCRACY DEBATE. In the late twentieth century and early twenty-first century the call for greater liberalization and democratization has become widespread in the Muslim world, as diverse sectors of society, secular and religious, leftist and rightist, educated and uneducated, increasingly use democratization as the litmus test by which to judge the legitimacy of governments and political movements alike.

A diversity of voices exists in debates over political participation and democratization. Secularists argue for secular forms of democracy, the separation of religion and the state. Rejectionists maintain that Islam has it own forms of governance and that it is incompatible with democracy. Accommodationists, or Islamic reformers, believe that traditional concepts and institutions can be utilized to develop Islamically acceptable forms of popular political participation and democratization. Maintaining that Islam is capable of reinterpretation (*ittiḥād*), traditional concepts of consultation (*shura*), consensus (*ijmāʿ*), and public welfare (*maslaha*) are reinterpreted to provide the bases for the development of modern Muslim notions of democracy, parliamentary government, and the like. While some would reinterpret traditional beliefs to essentially legitimate Western-generated forms of democracy, others wish to develop forms of political participation and democracy appropriate to Islamic values and realities.

BIBLIOGRAPHY

Ayubi, N. *Political Islam: Religion and Politics in the Arab World.* London, 1991.

Baker, R. W. "Invidious Comparisons: Realism, Postmodernism, and Centrist Islamic Movements in Egypt." In *Political Islam: Revolution, Radicalism, or Reform?* edited by John L. Esposito. Boulder, Colo., 1997.

Burgat, F. *The Islamic Movement in North Africa.* 2d ed. Austin, Tex., 1997.

Cooley, J. K. *Unholy Wars: Afghanistan, America, and International Terrorism.* London, 2000.

Esposito, John L. *Islam and Politics.* 4th ed. Syracuse, N.Y., 1998.

Esposito, John L. *The Islamic Threat: Myth or Reality?* 3d ed. New York, 1999.

Esposito, John L. *Unholy War: Terror in the Name of Islam.* New York, 2002.

Esposito, John L., and J. O. Voll. *Islam and Democracy.* New York, 1996.

Fuller, Graham. *The Future of Political Islam.* New York, 2003.

Haddad, Y. Y., and John L. Esposito, eds. *Contemporary Islamic Revival since 1988: A Critical Survey and Bibliography.* Westport, Conn., 1997.

Huntington, S. P. *The Clash of Civilizations and the Remaking of World Order.* New York, 1997.

Kramer, M. "Islam vs. Democracy." *Commentary,* January 1993, pp. 35–42.

Lewis, B. "Islam and Liberal Democracy." *Atlantic Monthly,* February 1993, p. 89. Available from http://www.theatlantic.com/issues/93feb/lewis.htm.

Milani, M. M. "Political Participation in Revolutionary Iran." In *Political Islam: Revolution, Radicalism, or Reform?* edited by John L. Esposito, pp. 77–94. Boulder, Colo., 1997.

Norton, A. R. "Hizballah: From Radicalism to Pragmatism?" *Middle East Policy* 5 (January 1998). Available from http://www.mepc.org/public_asp/journal_vol5/9801_norton.asp.

Piscatori, J. P., and D. F. Eickelman. *Muslim Politics.* Princeton, N.J., 1997.

Rashid, A. *Taliban: Militant Islam, Oil, and Fundamentalism in Central Asia.* New Haven, Conn., 2000.

Shahin, E. *Political Ascent: Contemporary Islamic Movements in North Africa: State, Culture, and Society in Arab North Africa.* Boulder, Colo., 1996.

Voll, J. O., and John L. Esposito. "Islam's Democratic Essence." *Middle East Quarterly,* September 1994, pp. 3–11, with ripostes, pp. 12–19. Voll and Esposito reply, *Middle East Quarterly,* December 1994, pp. 71–72.

JOHN L. ESPOSITO (2005)

POLITICS AND RELIGION: POLITICS AND AFRICAN RELIGIOUS TRADITIONS

Africa is home to nearly 600 million people. Christianity and Islam are leading religious traditions—each has in excess of 250 million followers in Africa. As a result, there are declining numbers of followers of traditional indigenous religions and very few atheists or agnostics. Both Islam and Christianity were imported into Africa in the historical past. Islam gradually spread over the last thousand years, whereas Christianity was imported by and intimately associated with European—especially British and French—colonialism beginning in the late nineteenth century.

SOCIAL DYNAMICS. The main analytical problem involving an understanding of the relation between religion and politics in Africa is the region's astonishing multifariousness of religious beliefs, ethnic divisions, cultural distinctions, and political modes. Africa is marked by a high degree of political and religious heterogeneity, making a study of politics and religion in the region complex but rewarding. To ascertain the nature of the contemporary relation between religion and politics in Africa, it is necessary to take into account the impact of European colonialism, especially from the 1880s, as it was the primary modernizing force throughout the region. One of its key impacts was—theoretically, officially, and ostensibly—to divide Africa's religious world from its secular and, hence, political sphere.

Within Western social sciences, theoretical dividing lines between politics and other social actions are relatively clear cut. Such disciplinary divisions between, for example, political science, sociology, and economics frequently lead to assumptions that a complex reality can be neatly compartmentalized. However, the relation between politics and religion in Africa cannot be so easily compartmentalized. Not least of the problems is the difficulty in deciding where religion ends and politics begins. For example, during the colonial period, religious movements were often simultaneously anticolonial political movements and fundamentally concerned with both sociocultural and religio-spiritual reform. As such, in looking at Africa's colonial period it is difficult to be clear whether individual religious, political, or social objectives—or a mixture of all three—were paramount when seeking to account for the motivations of certain groups and organizations. Overall, it is more analytically satisfactory to perceive such movements as involving a combination of motivations that often defy easy or precise pigeonholing.

Generally, religion relates to politics in Africa in ways that are themselves linked to the particular historical and developmental trajectories of individual societies, whether traditional or modern. In traditional (i.e., precolonial) African societies, the relationship between religion and politics was always a close one, for religious beliefs and practices underpinned political power, while political concerns permeated to the heart of the religious sphere. Rulers were not only political heads but also religious leaders whose well-being was closely linked to their people's health and welfare. The modernization that accompanied European colonialism led to a secularization of public life and a practical separation of politics and religion at the state level. As a result, the notion of politics not only involves general relations of power but also relates to the workings of formal political institutions (e.g., legislatures, executives, presidents), as well as focusing attention more generally on issues of authority, legitimacy, power, and equity.

In seeking to peel away the layers of interaction between religion and politics, it becomes clear that each issue has several dimensions in Africa. However, attempts to arrive at an analytically precise definition of the term *religion* is fraught with difficulties because no consensus exists as to the proper understanding of what religion in Africa is. Theologians are interested primarily in understanding the nature of its individual or collective spiritual significance. Anthropologists see religion as one, albeit an important, component of the cultural aspects of Africans' social life. Sociologists seek to identify and examine religion's general and specific social imports in the countries of the region. Political scientists look for signs of political activity associated with religion, as they are keen to assess religion's political roles, especially in relation to specific groups and organizations. For example, they may question to what extent a certain religious group also serves as a vehicle of sociopolitical change. Such differing assessments of the nature of religion in Africa suggest that it would be most constructive to note its combined spiritual and material dimensions. This involves both personal belief systems as well as group ideologies, which together help to motivate individuals and groups to behave in a variety of ways. Clearly, most Africans would regard themselves as religious people, believing in a God (or gods) who looks over them and helps guide what they do. In addition, many believe that religious worship, or involvement with religious organizations, is an important means to try to improve their current earthly positions. In other words, it can be difficult to discern whether an African's individual religious motivations are primarily religious, political, or social.

Social dynamics in Africa may best be viewed as an entwined triple-stranded helix of state, class, and ethnicity. The metaphor of the triple strand is useful in understanding the political and social role of religion in Africa, with the three strands of the helix comprising religion, ethnicity, and politics. Each appears to be a facet of most Africans' individual worldviews, and in certain situations and at certain times, one element may, as least temporarily, dominate the others. For example, sometimes religious beliefs or solidarity will serve to form the main context for political action, with political concerns imbued with religious notions that help determine the nature of a particular group's collective response. Examples in this regard include recent political developments in both Nigeria and Sudan, where interreligious conflict—in both cases between Muslims and non-Muslims—reflects an array of both spiritual and material concerns that interact within very fluid boundaries.

COLONIALIZATION. This points to how religious and political power have developed historically in and between African religious traditions. The nature and characteristics of the contemporary African state are in large part a function of the legacy of the colonial era, a period of time that ended in most cases, in the 1960s. During the main period of European colonization in Africa (1880s–1914), the two main colonizing countries, France and Britain, were themselves evolving their own democratic political systems. However, the political institutions both countries created in Africa during colonialism were little, if anything, more than naked instruments of domination. With administrative networks often grafted on to preexisting institutions, European hegemony and security were very closely linked.

Colonial administrations attempted to employ religion as a tactic in their pursuit of political domination. Yet religious interaction between ordinary Africans and the colonial authorities was by no means a straightforward relationship between dominance and dependence. Africans often used their religious beliefs as a means to adjust the relationship between themselves and colonial authorities in their favor (as far as possible). Whether through the founding of independent churches or via Africanized modes of Islam, religious leaders sought to create and develop socially and communally relevant and popular religious organizations. Such religious organizations tended to function well during the colonial period because they served as appropriate focal points for ordinary people's attempts to come to terms with and to adapt to the forces of change (summarized as modernization), that were a result of the intrusion of European rule. In other words, such religious organizations functioned as statements of social, political, and economic interaction as well as important foci of community aims and strategy.

European mission churches, on the other hand, were an important facet of attempted colonial cultural domination. They had both repressive and liberating functions as agents of European superiority and political domination. However, they were also purveyors of modernization, especially Western education, the acquisition of which was quickly noted by many Christian Africans as the key route to advancement in colonial society. Preexisting Muslim communities, however, reacted to European-inspired modernization by attempting to deal with its impact without compromising Islamic ideals. Other Muslim groups adopted armed struggle against the Europeans, especially during the period from the 1880s to 1914, when they were soundly defeated by the superiority of the Europeans' military technology.

The consequences of the colonial period for the relation between religion and politics in Africa were profound. Consequently, it is appropriate to regard the nature and characteristics of religion's role in politics in contemporary Africa as a result of the multiple changes occasioned by European colonialism. The few territories that did not undergo entrenched and formal foreign control (Liberia, Ethiopia, and several others) nevertheless absorbed European-led modernizing influences almost as though they had. Colonies, where a majority of the population were neither Christian nor Muslim during the period of colonial rule (e.g., Guinea-Bissau, Upper Volta [now Burkina Faso], and Sierra Leone, where traditional African religions were followed by the great majority of local populations), were nevertheless ruled by Christian Europeans. As a result, the various traditional religious activities had to function within the Europeans' legal jurisdiction. In addition, throughout much of Africa, Muslims had to coexist with and be bound by European power, as they were ultimately under the latter's control.

It is important to note that the role of mission Christianity as an institutional force during the colonial period was not simply one of undifferentiated support of temporal political power. Whether or not the colony was settler-dominated was significant for an understanding of the relationship between Christian missionaries and colonial authorities. If large numbers of settlers were present (e.g., Kenya, Algeria, and South Africa), then there was a complex relationship that developed between the white settler community, Christian missionaries, and colonial authorities. On the other hand, where substantive numbers of white settlers were absent (as in most of West and west-central Africa, as well as Uganda), then Christian missionaries and the colonial authorities tended to develop clearly mutually supportive relationships.

Yet because various Christian churches (Roman Catholic, as well as a variety of Protestant denominations) were in direct competition for converts, there was rivalry between them. Sometimes, however, a truce would be declared in face of the common enemy of Islam. When Islam appeared as a key threat to Christian dominance and well-being, steps were taken to try to undermine its attraction by offering Western education to putative converts. However, where Islam was already religiously and culturally dominant, as in vast swathes of North, northwest, and East Africa, then the temptation of Western-style education and its attendant material rewards was usually insufficient in the face of cultural and community solidarity to win many, if any, converts to Christianity. However, sometimes after serious opposition (e.g., in the West African empire of El Hadj Oumar against the French, the Hausa-Fulani empire against the British, and in much of Muslim Somalia prior to World War I) Muslim leaders were generally pragmatic enough to reach a *modus vivendi* with the colonial authorities. It is noteworthy that a particular form of transnational Islam, or pan-Islamism, was of great concern for colonial rulers in the early years of the twentieth century. Especially around the time of World War I, many European colonial administrations were worried that both Germany and the Turkish Ottoman Empire were in tandem politically, seeking out and cultivating African Muslim leaders to be allies in their strategic rivalries with Britain and France. But in fact there was virtually no realistic chance of a pan-Islamic movement developing in Africa at that time because African Muslims were—and still are—often fundamentally divided, whether by ethnicity, nationality, area of domicile (urban or rural located), their view of the role of Islam in both private and public spheres, or a combination of these factors.

Modernization and Christianity. As in the early twentieth century period in Africa, contemporary trends relating to the relation between religion and politics in Africa often reflect not only what occurs locally, but are also connected to what takes place outside the region. As is often noted, over the last three decades of the twentieth century and into the twenty-first century, religion has generally had a considerable impact on politics in many regions of the world, not just in Africa. One common explanation points to a resurgence of religion in the face of failed or flawed modernization. That is, the earlier widespread affirmation that modernization (i.e., the growth and spread of urbanization, industrialization, mass education, economic development, scientific rationality, and social mobility) would combine to diminish significantly the social position of religion in the region has not been substantiated.

In Africa, what are widely perceived as unwelcome symptoms of modernization, such as a perceived breakdown of moral behavior (especially among the young), educational overliberalization, and generally worsening social habits, are frequently linked to persistent governmental failures throughout the region to push through and consolidate appropriate programs of social improvement. Reactions in many African countries not only to failed modernization but also to ideas such as democracy spread by globalization were often focused in vociferous demands for incumbent governments to resign. In such protests, religious leaders were frequently well represented. In many African countries in the 1990s, mass protests occurred in which millions of ordinary people took to the streets to protest at their venal and corrupt governments.

A consequence of such protests was that, in the 1990s, many African countries underwent at least a degree of democratization. This involved a series of widespread political upheavals, focusing on demands for qualitative political change as well as more and better economic and human rights. This development reflected a reawakening of civil society's political voice, with trade union officials, higher-education students, businesspeople, civil servants, and, in many African countries, Christian leaders coordinating and leading protest efforts. Such demands were later focused by professional politicians as integral parts of political programs. The hope was that following democratization elected leaders would tackle—with energy, resourcefulness, and imagination—the pressing economic, political, and social problems of the continent.

African demands for both democratization and economic change were the result of a rediscovery of political voice by long quiescent interest groups who were encouraged by international developments, most notably the shift away from Communism in the former Soviet Union. Concerns were exacerbated by years of popular frustration and disappointment, for the promises of independence had turned out, almost everywhere, to be hollow. Frequently, senior Christian figures were instrumental in the clamor for political and economic changes—for example, in South Africa, Kenya, and various francophone West African countries. Christian, especially Roman Catholic, leaders were often prominent in prodemocracy campaigns opposing, denouncing, and frustrating authoritarian regimes and, in several cases, these campaigns were successful in removing entrenched governments from power.

It is significant that such Christian leaders were not, on the whole, in the forefront of demands for similar political reforms during the twilight of colonial rule in the 1950s and 1960s. Why was this? The simple answer is that in the 1950s and 1960s senior Christian leaders in Africa were almost always Europeans. Such people tended overwhelmingly to support the concept—if not always every aspect of the practice—of colonial rule for three main reasons. First, they shared racial bonds with colonial administrators. Second, they believed that colonial rule had provided much-needed law, order, and European civilization to Africa. Third, both religious leaders and secular rulers were members of the same socioeconomic elite, with a class stake in the status quo. In short, class, racial, and institutional bonds bound Christian leaders to the colonial regimes.

During the 1960s and 1970s, mainline Christian churches swiftly Africanized, with control shifting from Europeans to Africans. Later, in the 1980s and 1990s, leaders of mainline African Christian churches were significantly involved in demands for democracy. For example, senior Christian figures were involved in national democratization conferences in seven francophone African countries in the early 1990s; these were events held to ascertain the best ways to deliver appropriate political reforms, notably democratization. At times, Christian leaders were very prominent in the fight to oust nondemocratic governments. Such people tended to have prodemocracy convictions for three main reasons: (1) because of personal conviction, (2) because their Christian beliefs encouraged this notion, and (3) because many among their followers were palpably suffering from the effects of poor governments, especially economically and in terms of human rights abuses. Given their perceptions of their Christian leaders as spiritual guides, and in the customary absence of independent and effective political parties, ordinary Christians quite naturally turned to their religious leaders as appropriate figures to take action on their behalf. In short, Africa's recent democratization was linked to the individual and collective efforts of many Christian leaders and was a testimony to their tenacity, clear-sightedness, and lack of fear of the consequences of their actions in leading popular protests.

Such leaders were in a privileged position to head such protests because of the general, although not uniform, Christian institutional independence and integrity throughout much of Africa. In the postcolonial period, African political leaders have generally accorded a high level of respect to leaders of the main religious institutions, both Christian and Muslim. Because most mainstream expressions of both Christianity and Islam tended to be unidentified with the main interest groups, whether ethnic or class, their leaders stood on relatively neutral ground and thus could serve as a mediating element when social or political conflict occurred. Consequently, leaders of both religious traditions were often key interlocutors between state and society. Many were highly respected figures whose own personal desires and preferences were believed to be subsumed by their concern to mediate disinterestedly between followers and the state.

ISLAM AND THE STATE. Regarding the relation between Islam and temporal power in contemporary Africa, it is often suggested that Muslims are less concerned with or interested in democracy than are many Christians. Certainly, African Muslim leaders were not, on the whole, in the forefront of demands for political changes in the 1990s. It should be noted, however, that two of the seven francophone countries—Mali and Niger, which held national conferences on new political arrangements in the 1990s—are both strongly Muslim countries. On the other hand, Islam is often regarded by Western analysis as an authoritarian, even totalitarian, religion whose proponents sometimes seek to impose fundamentalist visions as a putative means of purifying society. What such fundamentalists are said to want, namely Muslim (*sharī ʿah*) law, is regarded as anathema by non-Muslims.

Three issues contextualize a contemporary discussion of the political role of Islam in Africa. First, there are a number of versions of Islam in the region. Many Africans belong to Ṣūfī brotherhoods. In addition, many ethnic groups, especially in West and East Africa, converted historically to Islam en masse, some of whom are also members of Ṣūfī brotherhoods, so these Ṣūfī groups may also have an ethnic dimension. Orthodox conceptions of Islam—nearly always Sunnī in Africa—are the province of the religious elite, the *ʿulamāʾ* (religio-legal scholars). Thus, in Africa, Islam is a multifaceted term covering a number of Muslim interpretations of the faith.

Islam in Africa can be divided into at least three distinct categories, corresponding to extant social, cultural, and historical divisions. The first includes the dominant sociopolitical and cultural position of Islam found in the emirates of northern Nigeria, the *lamidates* of northern Cameroon, and the shiekdoms of northern Chad. In each area, not only is religious and political power typically fused in the hands of a few individuals, but, over time, class structures developed based on extant religious differentiation. Second, there are the areas where Ṣūfī brotherhoods predominate—generally in West and East Africa, and especially in Senegal, the Gambia, Niger, Mali, Guinea, Kenya, and Tanzania. Finally, in a number of African states, Muslims, fragmented by ethnic and regional concerns, are politically marginalized into a minority bloc, as in, for example, Benin, Côte d'Ivoire, Ghana, and Togo.

The second factor is that Islamic fundamentalism is rare, although not unknown, in tropical Africa. Ṣūfī Islam—the faith of many African Muslims—is actually a frequent target for Islamic fundamentalists found within the *ʿulamāʾ* and their secular allies because it is regarded as a primitive or degraded form of Islam that must be reformed or purified. Such fundamentalist interpretations of Islam are of particular political importance in Sudan (where it is the ruling ideology) and in parts of northern Nigeria, where conflict (with thousands of deaths since the late 1990s) between Muslims and Christians has long been an important politico-religious issue.

Third, there is ambivalence in the way that many Muslims regard the concept of liberal democracy itself. Many Muslims oppose Western interpretations of democracy, in which sovereignty is said to reside with the people because it is seen as a secularized system negating God's own sovereignty. The *ʿulamāʾ* are typically strong supporters of the status quo, not least because it allows them integral involvement in running the affairs of Muslims in their state. They exert influence by controlling national Muslim organizations. As a result, a partnership with state-level politicians is of crucial importance.

SEE ALSO African Religions, overview article; Christianity, articles on Christianity in North Africa and Christianity in Sub-Saharan Africa; Islam, article on Islam in North Africa.

BIBLIOGRAPHY

Allen, Tim. "Understanding Alice: Uganda's Holy Spirit Movement in Context." *Africa* 51, no. 3 (1991): 370–399. An account of the emergence and development of a politicized religious movement in contemporary Uganda.

Birai, U. M. "Islamic Tajdid and the Political Process in Nigeria." In *Fundamentalisms and the State: Remaking Politics, Economics and Militance,* edited by Michael Marty and R. Scott Appleby, pp. 184–243. Chicago, 1993. Discusses the political roles of Islam in Nigeria.

Dijk, Rijk van. "Young Puritan Preachers in Post-independent Malawi." *Africa* 61, no. 2 (1992): 159–181. Examines the emergence of a particular stratum of young puritan preachers in Malawi and traces their sociopolitical and spiritual significance.

Etherington, Norman. "Missionaries and the Intellectual History of Africa: A Historical Survey." *Itinerario* 7, no. 2 (1983): 116–143. Traces the variable responses of Christian missionaries to temporal power in Africa during colonial times.

Fields, Karen. *Revival and Rebellion in Colonial Central Africa.* Princeton, N.J., 1985. A comprehensive account of the development of religio-political anticolonial movements in colonial Central Africa.

Gifford, Paul. "'Africa Shall Be Saved.' An Appraisal of Reinhard Bonnke's Pan-African Crusade." *Journal of Religion in Africa* 17, no. 1 (1987): 63–92. A discussion of the infiltration of foreign fundamentalist churches in contemporary Africa, with particular emphasis on the pastor Reinhard Bonnke.

Gifford, Paul. "Some Recent Developments in African Christianity." *African Affairs* 93, no. 4 (1994): 513–34. A survey of the spiritual and political roles of contemporary Christianity in Africa.

Gray, Richard. "Popular Theologies in Africa." *African Affairs* 85 no. 4 (1986): 49–54. Surveys the contemporary spiritual positions and sociopolitical thrust of popular religion in Africa.

Hastings, Adrian. *A History of African Christianity, 1950–75.* Cambridge, U.K., 1979. Traces the development of African Christianity during a crucially important period and emphasizes the faith's political involvement.

Haynes, Jeff. *Religion and Politics in Africa.* London, 1996. Outlines the interaction of religion and politics in Africa from colonial to the turn of the twenty-first century.

Haynes, Jeff. "Religion, Secularization and Politics: A Postmodern Conspectus." *Third World Quarterly* 18, no. 4 (1997): 709–728. A comprehensive discussion of the impact of secularization and modernization on religion in Africa and elsewhere in the developing world.

Haynes, Jeff. "Religious Fundamentalism and Politics." In *Major Religions of the World: Past, Present and Post-Modern,* edited by Lloyd Ridgeon, pp. 321–375. London, 2003. A comprehensive discussion of religious fundamentalisms, including a focus on Africa.

Lan, David. *Guns and Rain.* London, 1985. This is a case study of neotraditional religion's political involvement in Rhodesia and Zimbabwe.

Lapidus, Ira. *A History of Islamic Societies.* Cambridge, U.K., 1988. Outlines the development of Islam in Africa from precolonial to present times.

Mayer, Anne. "The Fundamentalist Impact on Law, Politics, and Constitutions in Iran, Pakistan, and the Sudan." In *Fundamentalism and the State: Remaking Polities, Economies, and Militance,* edited by Michael Marty and R. Scott Appleby, pp. 110–151. Chicago, 1993. Comparative examination of the political role of Islam in three countries.

Mbembe, Achille. *Afriques Indociles. Christianisme, Pouvoir et Etat en Societé Postcoloniale.* Paris, 1988. Traces the emergence of popular religion in Africa and outlines its socio-political roles.

Oliver, Ronald. *The African Experience.* London, 1991. Locates the role of religion in Africans' anticolonial struggles.

Ranger, Terence. *Peasant Consciousness and Guerrilla War in Zimbabwe.* Berkeley, Calif., 1985. A comprehensive overview of neotraditional religion's political involvement in Rhodesia and Zimbabwe during the anticolonial struggle.

Stewart, C. C. "Islam." In *The Cambridge History of Africa,* vol. 7, *From 1905 to 1940,* edited by A. Roberts, pp. 191–222. Cambridge, U.K., 1986. Historical account of the development of Islam in Africa during the first four decades of the twentieth century, as the faith came into competition with Christianity.

Walshe, Peter. "South Africa Prophetic Christianity and the Liberation Movement." *Journal of Modern African Studies* 29, no. 1 (1992): 27–60. Examines the role of various Christian churches in the antiapartheid and prodemocracy movement in South Africa.

JEFFREY HAYNES (2005)

POLITICS AND RELIGION: POLITICS AND OCEANIC RELIGIONS

In the late eighteenth century, at the beginning of extensive European intervention in the region, Oceanic peoples spoke more than twelve hundred languages and lived out their lives in tens of thousands of mostly highly localized political units. Religious beliefs and activities were correspondingly diverse, although one can detect very broad regional patterns. In traditional Oceanic societies, people lived in intimate relationship to spiritual forces and entities. Notions of the spiritual reinforced the social order that governed community relationships, informed understandings of leadership, and underlay the external politics of warfare and alliance-building. In the past two centuries, the region has moved from intermittent encounters between Pacific Islanders and Europeans through colonization to the emergence of independent nations. At the beginning of the twenty-first century, the overwhelming majority of the indigenous citizens of the twenty-eight states and dependencies in the region are Christians living in circumstances markedly more secular than those experienced by their ancestors. All the same, religion remains a very strong and politically potent force in most places.

For convenience, it is useful to divide the consideration of Oceanic religions and their relationship to politics into three rough historical phases: indigenous societies as they were before extensive European contact; the colonial period, marked by intensified missionary efforts and a loss of local political autonomy; and the postcolonial period, in which religion, like much of politics in the region, is increasingly shaped by global forces. A caveat is in order. With the exception of the last period, these phases do not correspond neatly with calendar years. Some isolated groups in the interior of New Guinea did not look upon a white face until the 1960s, and a good number of islanders continue to live under colonial regimes. Many aspects of indigenous religions and political arrangements have survived or been revived in all areas, but especially those with relatively shallow histories of interactions with the outside world. Indeed, it is still possible today to observe all three of the phases described here, sometimes in the same place.

THE POLITICAL FUNCTIONS OF INDIGENOUS RELIGIONS. Oceanic languages possess no words corresponding to the concepts of "politics" or "religion." Most cultures recognized at least a degree of religious specialization in the forms of part-time magicians, healers, sorcerers, and priests; a much smaller subset developed distinct places of worship and sacrifice and supported full-time priests. The elaboration of religious functionaries and institutions reached its apogee in Hawai'i, where a priestly class periodically contested the influence of the high chiefs. But even in this case one cannot speak of a separation of religion and politics, as the chiefs, like the priests, were regarded as direct descendents of the gods and themselves possessed godlike powers of life and death over commoners. Religious assumptions infused all aspects of life in Oceanic societies, not least those concerned with the exercise of political power.

Across the region, the vast majority of people lived in small political entities made up of several hundred to a few thousand members bound by ties of kinship (real and fictitious) and territory on the one hand, and hostility to neighboring groups on the other. The daily round for most people comprised subsistence activities, usually directed by households, and reciprocal exchanges of food, labor, and wealth items that cemented relationships with kin and neighbors. Virtually everywhere, people assumed that the recent and distant dead continued to take an interest in the community. People also generally assumed the existence of impersonal spiritual forces possessing tremendous powers of transformation and destruction. The specific conception of these two notions of the spiritual and their elaboration varied tremendously from place to place—from the rather simple, vague religious notions found in many Melanesian societies to the extremely complex religions of some parts of Polynesia, with their detailed mythologies, dedicated temples, and elaborate ritual codes. All the same, Oceanic people conceptualized the implications of divine intervention in the human world in essentially similar ways. First, spiritual power was a necessary component, often along with human skill, for success, whether as a gardener or a lover or in making the transition from child to adult or from life into death. Ancestors could intervene of their own accord, but everywhere people attempted to capture and channel spiritual forces to their own advantage through the practice of magic or by offering prayers and sacrifices. Second, spiritual entities were conceptualized as extremely powerful, dangerous, and ultimately autonomous. They had to be approached with great caution and often elaborate ritual preparation. Even so, they had the potential of wreaking havoc upon the people if mishandled or angered—or simply because they could. Third, those who interacted with the divine took on divine attributes themselves.

In Oceania, as elsewhere, the spiritual could provide a source of revolutionary change but for the most part served to maintain the existing order, first by making that order appear to members to be natural and inevitable, and, second, by punishing those who deviated from the social norm. In one particularly striking example, the deepest secret of many of the elaborate male initiation cults that developed in parts of Melanesia was that the power monopolized by men was originally stolen from women. The cults served, in the men's eyes at least, to assert their domination over women, who were barred from most rituals and cult houses under pain of death. In many other places, supernaturally sanctioned food taboos, fears of pollution, and purification rituals served to distinguish men and women and to assign them distinct roles in society, usually with the men on top. By the same token, understandings of the workings of the supernatural tended to reinforce social conventions and morality. In many places, for instance, ancestors or sorcerers were assumed to attack those who failed to live up to their social obligations by making them or their loved ones sick or by destroying their gardens. To this day, parents in many parts of rural Papua New Guinea commonly explain the death of a beloved aunt or uncle to their children as the result of sorcery attacks brought on by some apparently trivial breach of the rules of sharing or respect toward others. This strongly sanctions conformity.

The political aspects of Oceanic religion become more visible when one turns to patterns of leadership. Most societies in Melanesia lacked formal offices of leadership. While powerful leaders did emerge, they largely gained influence by demonstrating their own abilities as warriors, managers of exchanges, and orators. In several areas, men rose to prominence in the course of organizing initiation and mortuary rituals, often involving years of careful coordination and spectacular forms of artistic expression. Melanesian leaders could also gain influence by gaining command over various forms of esoteric knowledge, such as garden and war magic or sorcery. Chiefs in the more hierarchical societies stretching from eastern Melanesia through Polynesia and Micronesia, by way of contrast, were considered to be inherently sacred. In the larger societies, chiefs were ranked according to their genealogical closeness to a founding ancestral god, following a principle of primogeniture. Chiefs at different ranks possessed equivalent degrees of *mana* (spiritual potency), with the highest chiefs approaching the level of the gods themselves. Polynesians often pictured their chiefs as the "fathers" and, less frequently, "mothers" of their communities. The chief was often also the highest priest, receiving first fruits from commoners in various rituals meant to assure success and fertility. The visible splendor and wealth of a chief corresponded to level of his *mana* and, by extension, the success of the community he represented. By virtue of their *mana*, chiefs demanded tribute from commoners and proclaimed *tabu* (ritual prohibitions) over economic resources. As sacred beings themselves, chiefs were often surrounded by a variety of ritual restrictions and *tabu*. These were extremely elaborated in the most hierarchical Polynesian societies. The sanctity of the high chiefs of Tahiti was such, for instance, that they would not enter houses except those dedicated to their own use or allow their feet to touch the ground outside of their own hereditary district. Violations of chiefly *tabus* in Tahiti, Tonga, and Hawai'i often resulted in execution of the offender.

Contrary to romantic stereotypes of a South Seas paradise, most areas of Oceania were subject to endemic warfare. Religious ideas both reflected and propelled the violence. The ghosts of the dead in many Melanesian societies could only be satisfied by a revenge killing, and in areas of southern New Guinea a boy's initiation into manhood depended on the acquisition of a human head. In Polynesia, success in warfare provided perhaps the main venue within which a chief could demonstrate his *mana* in the face of challenges from rivals. Continuing success in warfare required the proper rituals and sacrifices to the ancestral gods. Aspiring chiefs cultivated new gods with spectacular rituals, including human sacrifices in some of the cults that developed in Tahiti and Hawai'i.

The Colonial Era. Although Ferdinand Magellan crossed the Pacific Ocean in 1521, centuries passed before most islanders were disturbed by European intruders. Roman Catholic priests accompanied Spanish forces in the northwest reaches of Micronesia, forcibly converting the Chamorros in the 1680s. The next wave of missionary activity did not get under way until 1797, when poorly equipped parties of English Protestants landed at Tahiti, Tonga, and the Marquesas. Far from outside support, pioneer missionaries to Polynesia and many parts of Micronesia were forced to rely upon alliances with local chiefs in order to survive. Conversions, when they came, tended to follow the baptism of chiefs, who in turn ordered their followers to enter the churches. The early missions entered the islands during a period of considerable social turmoil caused in part by the increasing presence of European whalers and traders, who introduced devastating diseases, alcohol, and guns. Whatever their understanding of the missionaries' teachings, some aspiring chiefs evidently saw many advantages in forming alliances with the powerful new god of the white man. In Tahiti, Tonga, and Fiji, chiefs allied with the missions managed to conquer their enemies and to establish themselves as Christian kings. White missionaries, in turn, became councilors to the new rulers, helping them establish codes of law, courts, and new customs based on a mix of traditional chiefly privilege and the Ten Commandments. The association between chiefly rule and Christianity remains strong in many islands to this day, marked by the exalted social status of pastors in Samoa, for instance, and the strict Sabbatarianism of Tonga.

By the time European powers took an interest in the South Pacific, missionary regimes were well established on the larger islands in Polynesia, and armies of Native evangelists were taking the Word to smaller islands and into Melanesia. Missionaries and indigenous clergy wielded considerable power for a time in southern Vanuatu, Mangareva, Tuvalu, and elsewhere. By the end of the 1900s, however, colonial rule had been established over the entire region, with missionaries relegated to mostly nonpolitical roles. Still, colonial administrations everywhere depended very heavily upon them for the provision of educational and medical services and, in Papua New Guinea, as a bulwark against tribal fighting. Through such operations, as well as the networks they established, the missions played a fundamental role in easing the integration of small autonomous communities, often no larger than a village, into emerging states. In the extremely diverse linguistic context of Papua New Guinea, for instance, mission schools introduced students to the idea of a multicultural country as well as providing the tools to participate in it, through the teaching of a common language and literacy and by familiarizing students with European concepts of time, work, and authority. The most senior graduates of the mission school system, when they did not become missionaries themselves, entered the nascent bureaucracies of the colonial states and formed the seed of the elite classes that would eventually rule the new countries.

Christian ideas spread remarkably quickly, even in areas where people resented the presence of Europeans. From a very early date, prophets won followings with powerful combinations of Christian and indigenous themes that challenged white power. In New Zealand, for instance, the prophet Te Ua Haumene taught that the Maori were the true chosen people of Jehovah, whose *mana* would grant them immunity from European diseases and guns (a teaching that had disastrous consequences in the Maori wars of 1864–1865). The leaders of the so-called cargo cults of Melanesia skillfully wove together local mythology, prophetic visions, and borrowed elements of Christianity in ways that helped explain to followers the reasons for their apparent inferiority in the face of white power and wealth. The forms these movements took often struck observers as bizarre, but they are best understood as attempts to gain a moral equivalence with whites through rituals meant variously to raise the stature of indigenous followers or expel the whites while claiming their power. Colonial regimes regarded indigenous religious movements with suspicion and often brutally suppressed them. Most of the movements did not last long, brought down as much by disappointment in the lack of results as by state suppression. At their height, however, they temporarily brought together disparate communities in aspirations for a better life, leading some scholars to consider them "proto-nationalist movements."

The Present. With the exception of the Indonesian province of West Papua, which recognizes only the world religions present at the time of the country's independence and closely monitors the activities of churches and missions, residents of the Pacific islands today formally enjoy the right of free religious association. Since all but a tiny minority are affiliated with a Christian church, religious freedom has meant, in effect, competition between established groups and the mostly unfettered influx since the 1960s of a wide range of primarily evangelical Protestant sects. The domains of politics and religion are more distinct than in the past, but still overlap far more than in most Western countries. The constitutions of Papua New Guinea and Vanuatu, for instance, formally recognize Christianity and indigenous traditions as the twin foundations of the nation. Many of the most prominent politicians, including the first prime minister of Vanuatu, Father Walter Lini (1942–1999), have come from the ranks of the clergy. In Papua New Guinea, as in several other former colonies, the state shares administration of the school system with the churches.

As in earlier times, many ordinary people in the islands tend to perceive their world through a spiritual lens. Some election campaigns in Papua New Guinea resemble revival meetings, punctuated by prayers and appeals to God and posters in which Jesus appears as a politician's effective running mate. From Samoa to the Solomon Islands, chiefs legitimate their authority to followers by merging traditional statuses and customs with strong public declarations of Christian faith. Many Pacific Islanders take this conception one step further, viewing Christianity and ancestral traditions as one and the same, merely different faces of a single religious identity. In one of the uglier twists on this powerful synthesis, members of the Tukai ("land") movement in Fiji appealed to Christian nationalism and traditional land rights in attacking the rights of Indo-Fijians in the wake of government coups in 1987 and 2000.

All but the most remote areas of Oceania are experiencing rapid change in response to improved communications, increasing migration, and the influx of commodities, all of which work to undermine the former autonomy of local communities. Increasingly, people have choice in their religious affiliation as in other areas of life, and even the most established churches are gradually becoming more individualistic and democratic in response to global influences. For some, the newer Fundamentalist and Pentecostal sects sweeping through the region provide a refuge from the confusing changes undermining old certainties. But for others, the churches and faith have provided a platform and venue to challenge given orders, including political arrangements. Thus, churches have provided spiritual and organizational support to the pro-democracy movement in Tonga, protesting the autocratic power of the king, as well as to protests against continuing French colonial rule in New Caledonia and French Polynesia. In Papua New Guinea and elsewhere, church leaders and activists have spoken up, often at risk to their lives, against rampant political corruption, the rape of precious natural resources for short-term profits, and the impoverishment of local peoples. The churches have been especially important for women, as one of the few venues in which they can organize to improve the economic conditions for their families and to urge action against alcoholism, drug abuse, and associated domestic violence. Finally, the churches have provided a center of community life and a link to home for the vast and quickly expanding numbers of islanders from places like Samoa or much of Micronesia who now make their home in distant places like New Zealand or the United States.

It seems likely at the beginning of the twenty-first century that increasing globalization will continue to diversify and fracture the religious choices and identities available to Pacific Islanders. If so, the political potency of religion is likely to decline, because it depends to a high degree on a sense of shared community. Increasing numbers of Pacific Islanders are also likely to abandon religious affiliation entirely, particularly in urban areas. Still, one cannot help but be struck by the centrality of a spiritual outlook in the lives of most Pacific Islanders, a face they share with much of the so-called Third World peoples. As long as this is the case, religion and politics will form a potent mix in Oceania.

See Also Afterlife, article on Oceanic Concepts; Cargo Cults; Colonialism and Postcolonialism; Cosmology, article on Oceanic Cosmologies; Gender and Religion, article on Gender and Oceanic Religions; Globalization and Religion; Mana; Maori Religion; Melanesian Religions; Micronesian Religions; Missions; Oceanic Religions; Polynesian Religions; Revenge and Retribution; Rites of Passage, article on Oceanic Rites; Taboo.

Bibliography

Studies Bearing on the Political Aspects of Indigenous Religious Traditions

Firth, Raymond. *Rank and Religion in Tikopia: A Study in Polynesian Paganism and Conversion to Christianity.* London, 1970. A rare analysis of a traditional Polynesian chieftainship as observed in action by an anthropologist.

Goldman, I. *Ancient Polynesian Society.* Chicago, 1970. An excellent comparative survey of eighteen traditional Polynesian cultures. Contains a great deal of information on variant notions of sanctity and their relationship to political hierarchies.

Lawrence, Peter, and Mervyn J. Meggitt, eds. *Gods, Ghosts, and Men in Melanesia: Some Religions of Australian New Guinea and the New Hebrides.* Melbourne, Australia, and New York, 1965. A classic collection of articles on Melanesian religious conceptions and experiences. K.O.L. Burridge's contribution on the Tangu of New Guinea is exceptionally good in teasing out the religious, moral, and political dimensions of big-man leadership.

Trompf, G. W. *Payback: The Logic of Retribution in Melanesian Religions.* Cambridge, U.K., and New York, 1994. More compendium than analysis, this massive work documents the presence of the logic of revenge in traditional local religions, regional cargo cults, and modern circumstances across Melanesia.

Tuzin, Donald F. *The Voice of the Tambaran: Truth and Illusion in Ilahita Arapesh Religion.* Berkeley, Calif., 1980. One of the most detailed and sophisticated treatments of a Melanesian male initiation cult available, with a provocative reading of the implications of such cults in the politics of gender.

Valeri, Valerio. *Kingship and Sacrifice: Ritual and Society in Ancient Hawaii.* Translated by Paula Wissing. Chicago, 1985. A challenging but fascinating ethnohistorical reconstruction of a sacrificial cult that buttressed chiefly power in precontact Hawai'i.

Studies Concerning Missionaries, Conversion, Cargo Cults, and Colonialism

Gunson, Niel. *Messengers of Grace: Evangelical Missionaries in the South Seas, 1797–1860.* Melbourne, Australia, and New York, 1978. The best account of early evangelical missionaries to the South Pacific, with a sophisticated treatment of their political views and interactions with chiefs.

Howe, K.R. *Where the Waves Fall: A New South Sea Islands History from First Settlement to Colonial Rule.* Honolulu, Hawaii, 1984. This lively history of the early contact period provides detailed information on the political and cultural impact of Christian missions in several Pacific societies.

Jolly, Margaret, and Martha Macintyre, eds. *Family and Gender in the Pacific: Domestic Contradictions and the Colonial Impact.* Cambridge, U.K., and New York, 1989. Includes case studies examining the reconstruction of local political space and notions of gender after conversion to Christianity in various Oceanic societies.

Kaplan, Martha. *Neither Cargo Nor Cult: Ritual Politics and the Colonial Imagination in Fiji.* Durham, N.C., 1995. An important study of creative tensions between indigenous religious assumptions and the expansion of colonial institutions in Fiji.

Latukefu, Sione. *Church and State in Tonga: The Wesleyan Methodist Missionaries and Political Development, 1822–1875.* Canberra, Australia, 1974. Studies the mutual reinforcement of chiefly authority and missionary progress in Tonga, which culminated in the creation of the Tongan kingdom and the first independent church in Oceania.

Robbins, Joel. *Becoming Sinners: Christianity and Moral Torment in a Papua New Guinea Society.* Berkeley, 2004. This richly detailed anthropological study investigates the implications of conversion on an indigenous group's conception of community, personal morality and leadership.

Siikala, Jukka. *Culture and Conflict in Tropical Polynesia: A Study of Traditional Religion, Christianity, and Nativistic Movements.* Helsinki, Finland, 1982. An exceptionally detailed account of early syncretic religious movements in Polynesia.

Worsley, Peter. *The Trumpet Shall Sound: A Study of "Cargo" Cults in Melanesia.* New York, 1968. A classic survey of cargo cults from a neo-Marxist perspective, emphasizing their political implications.

Studies on Religion and Politics in Contemporary Oceania

Barker, John, ed. *Christianity in Oceania: Ethnographic Perspectives.* Lanham, N.Y., 1990. Examines contemporary Christianity, including its political dimensions, from the perspective of local indigenous societies.

Ernst, Manfred. *Winds of Change: Rapidly Growing Religious Groups in the Pacific Islands.* Suva, Fiji, 1994. The most comprehensive review of the contemporary religious scene in Oceania, with a great deal of information on the interface between politics and the churches, new and old.

Garrett, John. *Where Nets Were Cast: Christianity in Oceania Since World War II.* Suva, Fiji, and Geneva, 1997. A regional survey that provides information on politics within as well as without Christian denominations across Oceania.

Gibbs, Philip. "The Religious Factor in Contemporary Papua New Guinea Politics." *Catalyst* 28, no. 1 (1998): 27–51. A rare treatment of the prominent role of religious rhetoric in contemporary political campaigns.

Keesing, Roger M., and Robert Tonkinson, eds. "Reinventing Traditional Culture: The Politics of Kastom in Island Melanesia." *Mankind* 13, no. 4 (1982). A stimulating and controversial collection of studies on political manipulations of tradition, including traditional religion, in postcolonial Oceanic societies.

Marshall, Mac, and Leslie B. Marshall. *Silent Voices Speak: Women and Prohibition in Truk.* Belmont, Calif., 1990. One of the few studies available detailing the political role of women's church groups.

Robbins, Joel, Pamela J. Stewart, and Andrew Strathern, eds. "Charismatic and Pentecostal Christianity in Oceania." *Journal of Ritual Studies* 15, no. 2 (2001). Several of the studies in this collection examine the growing influence of Pentecostal churches on local political perspectives and activities.

White, Geoffrey M. *Identity Through History: Living Stories in a Solomon Islands Society.* Cambridge, U.K., and New York, 1991. An engaging study of the melding of tradition and Christianity in the contemporary construction of Oceanic chieftainship.

John Barker (2005)

POLITICS AND RELIGION: POLITICS AND NATIVE AMERICAN RELIGIOUS TRADITIONS

The problem of determining the relationship between church and state, so prevalent in Western European history, is notably absent in the traditions and practices of American Indian tribes. Although tribal traditions lack church and state concepts, we can nevertheless find in tribal cultures practices suggesting separate realms. American Indian religion was characterized by rituals enabling individuals to attain a measure of extraordinary power bestowed by spirits in visions or dreams. Political leadership, meanwhile, demanded a reputation for courage and a man's continued good fortune in warfare. But no formal vesting of religious or political power in an institutional setting occurred. If an individual had personal charisma, projected spiritual gifts or courage in fighting, he became a leader and attracted a following.

Religion. For most Indian societies no mediating structure existed between the individual and the higher powers. Through vision quests, puberty rituals, sweat lodges, dances, and ceremonies welcoming the change of seasons or responding to personal crises, people had unusual experiences that could be called "religious" or "mystical." Most rituals were designed to remind people of the existence of higher spiritual powers from which they might seek help. People remembered clearly an unusual event, they listened carefully when they heard unusual voices, and they heeded the content of their dreams. Sometimes it was not necessary to approach the higher powers. They came in dreams or startling daytime events, identified themselves, and gave instructions to the person on how he or she should live thereafter. Almost always the individual received a song from the spirit and sang it whenever he needed the assistance of the spirit.

The spiritual message in American Indian religion was culturally and geographically specific. There was little of the general feeling of universal acceptance reported by mystics of both East and West. People did not feel they were merging with a timeless universal essence. Spiritual gifts were always practical and specific. No one felt compelled to convince others of the validity of his or her experience or to defend the knowledge received. Usually the person was given an herb or plant or taught a song to be used for specific purposes and situations. With the gift came the warning that the use of this power had limits.

A vision might impart prohibitions against killing certain creatures who assisted humans, although American Indian people generally already recognized such prohibitions. A man having a relationship with a particular creature would buy or trade goods so that he might obtain skins and feathers of his particular bird or animal. Thus members of the Fox society could not kill foxes but could trade with those who were permitted to kill them. People were sometimes told to avoid certain foods. The food might be a part of a particular animal, and the prohibition might have nothing to do with an assisting spirit animal. The Cheyennes, for example, were forbidden to eat a little piece of meat found in the chest area of the buffalo, because it represented the flesh of humans that the giant carnivorous buffalo had eaten in the previous world. Roman Nose (1830–1868), the great Cheyenne warrior, was prohibited from eating food that had been touched by metal, because the metal would remain in his body and attract bullets. He violated this prohibition at the battle of Beecher's Island and was mortally wounded. In general, special powers were meant to be used on behalf of community members, and witchcraft was forbidden and punished wherever it was identified.

Young people sought the advice of several spiritual elders before they engaged in rituals, so that they would know how to respond to the spirits when they came. Elders supervising a vision quest or other ritual seemed to have the power to monitor their protégé's progress and knew what the initiate was experiencing. Stories abound that describe how elders intervened when they saw the initiate endangered by a predator or an enemy. Following the ritual the initiate would be cleansed in a sweat lodge and asked to share what he or she could discuss about the experience. No one revealed the whole experience, because to do so would reveal the limitations of the person and thus make him or her vulnerable to the powers of hostile people. As a protection against fakery, though, the Plains tribes required the person performing the ritual or having a dream to demonstrate the powers they had been given in front of the community.

In each generation a tribe had a number of people able to perform amazing feats with the powers granted them by the spirits. One man might be able to foretell the future and would always be consulted when people prepared for a hunt or went to war. Another man might have the power to care for horses and dogs with special medicines, in order to enhance their abilities; in the case of the Appaloosa horse, such medicines might actually change the coloring of a colt. Some people could break fevers or set bones. The Ponca leader Luther Standing Bear (1829?–1908) said that he had never seen anyone with amputated limbs until the wars with the whites, indicating that healing powers had served the people well. An unusual gift was the ability to use remote seeing to locate missing people and find lost things.

The Lummi Indians, who live in the far northwestern United States near the Canadian border, had a person who could perform a rain ceremony, which they needed despite living in a very rainy climate. The rainmaker used his power when a heavy snowfall threatened to trap people in their longhouses. His power would change the snow to rain and prevent large drifts from trapping people inside their houses. This gift was restricted to a particular family, and everyone knew that each generation of that family would have the power to perform the ritual.

Spiritual leaders, without fear of retribution, could pass on—or sometimes sell—the powers given to them. In the Plains it was common to loan or give away small stones that performed many functions for tribal elders. A primary loyalty nonetheless existed between the stones and their original owners. A sale was thus actually a loan, because the second owner did not have complete control over the stone. Women had the primary knowledge of medicinal plants, and they passed this information down to their daughters and granddaughters, so that a family could become noted for its medicinal knowledge. Prohibitions against misuse of a sacred object also carried over through the generations. Even if people might no longer use the powers of a stone or pipe, it still kept its potency and so had to be respected long after its original owner had died.

Young people often served under a medicine man or spiritual leader in order to gain the knowledge and experience necessary to become practitioners of certain rituals. Their learning in some cases bound them to certain restrictions; for instance, initiates learning star knowledge could not use this knowledge until their teacher had passed on. Some scholars have described this apprenticeship as a priesthood of elders, but closer examination reveals no formal institutional practice comparable to the priesthood of Western religions. With the development of the Native American Church in the twentieth century, however, the Roadman (or ceremonial leader) played a role comparable to that of a priest. In general, however, people simply deferred to certain individuals known to have power to perform certain rituals.

POLITICS. When Europeans initially encountered Indian tribes, they looked for familiar political institutions. Thus they dubbed Indian leaders "kings"; accordingly, the daughters of these "kings" became princesses. Throughout American history, whites attempted to force the Indians to adopt Western political institutions. The period of initial contact occasioned many bitter lessons; for instance, a group of chiefs asked to cede lands might encounter opposition from another group, which would deny the sale and demand return of the land. Such incidents quickly gave rise to the custom of having both the chiefs and the headmen of smaller bands sign treaties. The U.S. government thereby hoped to reduce the chance that a dissident group would later challenge the legality of the transaction. Soon corrupted, however, the treaty system turned into a means of forcing land sales from weak peoples with no legitimate representation. Presidential peace medals or certificates were given at treaty negotiations as a way of identifying Indians who were subject to the treaty; Indians then had to present these tokens or documents at the next gathering, in order to confirm their status.

The traditional ways of organizing a community politically differed significantly from Western forms. The Six Nations—which after 1722 comprised the Iroquois, the Mohawks, the Oneidas, the Onondagas, the Cayugas, the Senecas, and the Tuscaroras—had a formal council of over fifty chiefs who conducted the affairs of the Confederacy. Chieftain positions were distributed unevenly over the six Nations, but none complained about the manner of their allocation. The Clan Mothers chose the chiefs, so that anyone holding an office in the Confederacy had to respond to the concerns of the heads of families. The Red Lake Chippewa

(Ojibwa) had a council of seven chiefs who conducted business on behalf of everyone in their tribe. The Pueblos had a formal council with specific responsibilities assigned to each member. When they came under Spanish domination the Pueblos simply created additional offices to deal specifically with the Spanish. The Sioux had a general council consisting of the important chiefs, but they also designated four outstanding younger leaders to represent the whole nation in dealing with the incursions of the white man.

According to custom and tradition, no formal political organizations existed, although there were some exceptions. Most Indian settlements and bands were small. Even the settlements of the Five Civilized Tribes (the Creeks, the Chickasaws, the Cherokees, the Choctaws, and the Seminoles) were tiny in comparison with most rural communities. Longhouses, used the by eastern woodland and Pacific Northwest peoples, often represented the basic political entity. The task of governing relied heavily on cultural kinship customs and the consensus of the community. Heads of families represented their relatives in informal meetings of the group. If a person showed strong leadership qualities, the community might designate him as the primary spokesman in encounters with other groups.

American Indian institutions became more formal as dangers from the outside escalated. In the 1820s the Cherokees, Creeks, and Choctaws modified their traditional councils to resemble more closely the government of the United States, eventually adopting written constitutions. After tribes were confined to reservations in the 1870s, Indian agents tried to appoint reservation governments, including courts, so that the people could control their own civil and criminal jurisdiction. Generally tribal communities maintained their allegiance to the old chief- or headman-based form of government, and the traditional chiefs quite often became representatives of the new governments.

COLONIAL DAYS. From the first decades of colonization, representatives of various Christian denominations, with the aid of colonial governments, worked to convert the natives. French colonial policy sought not only to convert Indian, but also to intermarry with them, in effect seeking to create a new society composed of a mixture of French and Indian genes and culture. The fortunes of the various French monastic orders shifted back and forth, subjecting the Indians to different interpretations of the Christian religion. Thus the Jesuit and Recollect orders had varying success with the different eastern tribes. So pervasive was the effort of the French that many tribes became strongly Roman Catholic and insisted on securing funds and lands for their priests when the United States began making treaties with them.

English settlement was quite different. The British sought to displace the Indians in favor of their own colonists, and they discouraged mixed marriages. Various denominations sent missionaries to the tribes of New England; the emphasis, typically Protestant, was to win individual converts from local tribes or from people living on the frontier. Education was regarded as a magic wand to change the Indians from hunters and farmers into staid English merchants. The British therefore established schools to educate Indian youth, so that they might appreciate the benefits of "civilization." Thus Dartmouth, Princeton, William and Mary, and other universities began as schools for Indian youth. With the increasing prosperity of the colonists, however, these institutions increasingly served middle- and upper-class whites rather than Indians. By the time Americans began to settle the Illinois country, there was no pretense of founding colleges to educate the Indians; instead, treaty moneys designated for Indian education were often sent to churches to build schools at Indian agencies. The Choctaw Academy in Kentucky was established in the 1820s for the leading families of that tribe and later for children from the Five Civilized Tribes. The academy closed after an epidemic killed a large portion of its students.

In mid-seventeenth-century New England, Puritan missionaries—having deemed a sufficient number of Indians ready to live a "civilized" and Christian life—gathered the converts together and resettled them in villages known as "Praying Towns." These settlements consisted of Indians from several different tribes who had in common only their conversion to Christianity. The towns had the same status as other political subdivisions, with landholdings equal to those of the colonists' townships. As land became more valuable, however, the colonists assigned white trustees to the Praying Towns. These trustees gradually dissipated the Indian estates. Over the years white settlers attempted similar experiments with different tribes, but, as with the New England Praying Towns, the white man's greed for land undermined any initial religious or educational intentions. In one of the bloodier examples, a group of converted Delawares, convinced to move to western Pennsylvania before the Revolutionary War, established their own town, Gnadenhütten. When frontier violence flared up in the Ohio country, a white militia invaded this peaceful town and on March 8, 1782 slaughtered the converts. During the Removal period—after the passage of the Removal Act in 1830—the missionary Isaac McCoy attempted to set up an Indian state west of the Mississippi, and in the 1850s missionaries founded the short-lived Hazelwood Republic of the Minnesota Sioux. But neither conversion to Christianity nor the adoption of Western-style forms of government proved sufficient to save American Indians from destruction.

Just prior to the passage of the Removal Act, rumors of fantastic gold deposits on the Cherokee lands within its borders led the state of Georgia to encourage its white residents to invade these lands. The conflict led to the two most famous Indian-related U.S. Supreme Court cases—*Cherokee Nation* v. *Georgia* and *Worcester* v. *Georgia.* In the latter case Baptist missionaries insisted that their adherence to federal treaties gave them immunity from state penalties. Although the Supreme Court decided in their favor, they were nonetheless convicted under state law and sentenced to years of hard labor. Thereafter missionaries ensured that they had federal authorization to seek converts before investing in Indian missions.

Reservation Period. In 1869 the newly elected president, Ulysses S. Grant (1869–1877), sought the advice and support of Christian churches in formulating policy toward Indians on the western frontier. Popularly called the Peace Policy, the result of this church-state collaboration allowed Christian denominations to nominate Indian agents for reservations, gave churches primary responsibility for Indian education, and in many cases also granted them exclusive rights to establish missions on reservations. Here American hypocrisy reached its zenith. No white American questioned the idea that a "full blood Christian" was most fit to impart religion and civilization to a full-blooded Indian. With a few exceptions, however, church-appointed agents exploited the Indians and established dictatorial rule on the reservations. The Bureau of Indian Affairs, created in 1824, ordered that Indians who did not work or who failed to send their children to school be denied rations. The use of tribal languages was permitted only if they had written forms, and the only materials available for reading were Christian religious writings. On all counts the Peace Policy brought only turmoil and despair to the tribes.

Because they lacked the complex bureaucratic organization of the Roman Catholic Church, Protestant churches found it difficult to bear the financial burden of operating schools. The Bureau of Indian Affairs therefore allowed them to use secular tribal annuity funds for support of their schools. The Supreme Court upheld this practice in *Quick Bear v. Leupp* (1908), on the transparently spurious ground of providing religious freedom to the Indians. Eventually, however, the practice was discontinued. With no government funds coming to the Protestants, only the Catholic Church could afford to operate schools, which it continued to establish on Indian reservations until the 1960s.

Federal and state governments prohibited Sun Dances and ceremonies beginning in the 1880s, and the Courts of Indian Affairs on the reservations rigorously enforced these regulations. Some tribes skirted this oppression by pretending their dances celebrated American holidays such as the Fourth of July or presidents' birthdays. As late as the 1920s the government deliberately worked to isolate traditional religious practitioners and began to punish participation in Indian dances with fines. Only when the Pueblos allowed some visitors to view some of their more secular dances did they find some relief from government interference. One can also perhaps credit the Fred Harvey restaurants, which sprang up on the route of the Santa Fe Railroad beginning in the late nineteenth century, with helping to ease the rigor of government prohibition of dances—Indian dances provided spectacular entertainment, and thus a source of profits, at the major stations along the line.

The 1880s also saw the spread of peyote use in religious practices. Originating with the southwestern tribes, the practice spread to Oklahoma and eventually to the northern plains and Great Lakes areas. Practitioners held night-long singing ceremonies in which they ingested the peyote cactus button, a bitter herb (and hallucinogen), in order to aid in the seeing of visions. They employed some elements of the Christian ritual to explain the place of peyote in their religious practice, making it roughly equivalent to the bread and wine of the Christian mass. The attraction of peyote lay in its origins in traditional practices and in the idea that it could serve as the center of a new religion designed for Indians by the Creator. The famous Comanche chief Quanah Parker (1845?–1911) was one of the more prominent adherents to this new religion; his prestige made it acceptable to tribes that had not practiced the ritual before.

Some tribes welcomed the new religion, while others bitterly opposed it, favoring either the old religion or Christianity. Missionaries condemned peyote rituals as the work of the devil, and religious conflict in some communities escalated so much so as to disrupt families. In 1919 the U.S. Congress held hearings on the subject and considered a bill to ban peyote use. Prohibitions against peyote had previously been justified with reference to alcohol laws, but it was not clear that these laws in fact applied. In spite of intense pressure from the Christian churches, the congressional committee considering the matter refused to send the bill to the floor. Secular social scientists sided with the Indians in the hearings, arguing that peyote use was an integral part of traditional Indian culture. On the reservation level the struggle continued, and since Indians regarded the practice as authentically theirs, the hearings only served to publicize and spread the religion. But practitioners realized that they would not be protected unless their religion could mimic the institutional organization of the Christian churches. They therefore incorporated "Native American Churches" in several states.

The Reform Era. President Franklin D. Roosevelt's New Deal (1933–1939) brought about radical changes in Indian religious life. The new Indian Commissioner John Collier (1933–1945), a strong supporter of traditional Indian customs and practices, changed the directives of the Bureau of Indian Affairs to support rather than suppress dances and peyote use. The Wheeler-Howard Act (or Indian Reorganization Act) of 1934, which authorized the creation of tribal governments, allowed the tribes themselves to regulate religious practice on their own reservations. A few prohibited the Native American Church. Whereas the Pueblos generally struggled to convince their members not to join the new church, the Navajos formally passed a tribal ordinance banning the use of peyote. The federal district court upheld the ban on the basis that Indian tribes were sovereign nations "higher" in political status than states and therefore not subject to the Bill of Rights in religious matters.

The Protest Period. By the mid-1950s traditional dances were held openly on most reservations. Other ceremonies, however, had been neglected and could no longer be performed, and in some cases religious practitioners continued to mistrust the government and kept their rituals hidden. As the Indian protest movement began to grow in the early 1970s, traditional spiritual leaders supported the activists and often attended their rallies and gatherings. During the occupation of the Bureau of Indian Affairs headquarters in the fall of 1972 and the subsequent protest at Wounded Knee, South Dakota, during the winter of 1973, Sioux medicine men were prominent participants, giving a sense of legitimacy to the protest. During the trials following the occupation of Wounded Knee, some Indian defendants insisted on swearing oaths on the sacred pipe rather than the Bible, thereby alarming white Christian juries.

The watershed event in raising the status of tribal religions, however, was the restoration of the sacred Blue Lake to Taos Pueblo in 1970. The Pueblo had refused money for this mountain area of forty-four thousand acres after it sued the United States in the Indian Claims Commission, preferring to work toward restoration of lands through legislative action. With the backing of a strong bipartisan coalition in Congress, the land was returned. Not only did this legislation represent a major reversal of federal policy toward Indian lands, but it also placed the issue of sacred lands on the national agenda.

MODERN ACHIEVEMENTS. In 1978 Congress passed the American Indian Religious Freedom Resolution, which ordered federal agencies to make special efforts to cooperate with tribes needing to use certain locations on federal lands for ceremonial purposes. Although the resolution contained no enforcement provisions, it did alert federal agencies, state governments, and museums that traditional Indian religions deserved respect. The more elevated legal status of traditional religion led to further reforms.

The lack of enforcement provisions in the Religious Freedom resolution created great uncertainty in Indian country. Litigation to stop various construction projects on the basis of the resolution were usually turned aside by rhetorical court decisions that failed to establish a clear interpretation of the resolution. In 1988 the Supreme Court heard *Lyng v. Northwest Indian Cemetery Protective Association,* a case involving the construction of a logging road in northern California that compromised the performance of certain rituals. In spite of factual findings by lower courts in favor of the Indians, the justices ruled that Indian religious freedom could not stand in the way of the routine bureaucratic activities of the federal government. This decision was a major setback, because it meant that any activity by the federal government, no matter how trivial, had priority over Indian religious practices.

Indians turned to Congress to change this situation, and in 1990 President George H. W. Bush signed into law the Native American Graves Protection and Repatriation Act. The initial demand for such a law had been triggered by the discovery by Senator Daniel Inouye of Hawai'i that the Smithsonian Institution held nearly twenty-five thousand human skeletons—a substantial portion of which belonged to American Indians—that had been stolen from graves or gathered as trophies after battles with the U.S. cavalry. Hearings leading up to the bill revealed widespread wrongdoing by most U.S. museums, most of which had skeletal materials and in some cases also sacred objects obtained through less than ethical means. The law had three basic purposes: First, to protect against further grave desecration, second, to repatriate thousands of dead relatives housed in museum display cases and vaults, and finally, to restore stolen or improperly acquired religious and cultural property to their rightful owners.

Archaeologists and museums curators were at first appalled by the scope of the bill and its broad and somewhat confusing language. Eventually, however, they found their position morally untenable and cooperated to help secure final passage of the bill. Not surprisingly, the institution most reluctant to engage in the process of repatriation was the Smithsonian, whose staff was doctrinally bound to outmoded studies of human skulls to determine race, intelligence, and moral character. During the 1990s a significant number of objects and skeletons were returned for reburial and continued ceremonial use. Some tribes, abhorring the idea of receiving skeletal matter for fear that it might affect their fortunes, asked the museums to preserve the materials until a time when their people might feel differently about repatriation.

CONTEMPORARY ISSUES. The problem of ensuring American Indian religious freedom in modern times has been twofold. Because Indians had been forced onto small tracts of land to make way for white settlers, many shrines and holy places were no longer accessible, as they now lay on federal land. Traditional practitioners seeking entrance to certain locations, such as the Bear's Lodge (Devil's Tower) in Wyoming, Zuni Heaven in Arizona, or Mount Shasta in California were subject to strict regulation under multiple-use doctrines on federal lands. The trend at the beginning of the twenty-first century has been to open more national lands to industry, changing forever the landscape of the American West and destroying many shrines. Although the Religious Freedom Resolution directs agencies to work with American Indians to avoid conflicts, rumors emanating from Washington indicated that some federal agencies had "war rooms" to prepare for conflict with Indians over possible claims.

The use of peyote off the reservations and in the cities became an issue in 1990, when *Employment Division, Department of Human Resources of the State of Oregon v. Smith* came before the Supreme Court. Alfred Smith and Galen Black, two Indians, were fired from their jobs at a private drug rehabilitation program because they ingested peyote in private religious ceremonies. When they applied for unemployment compensation from the state of Oregon, they were refused on the grounds that they had been discharged for work-related misconduct. On appeal they cited a well-grounded constitutional doctrine that the government must have a "compelling" interest in the enforcement of a law before it can be invoked to infringe on or restrict freedoms guaranteed by the First Amendment. Sadly, the court overturned this test of constitutionality, leaving all religious practitioners in a legal limbo regarding the application of general statutes to religious activities.

Following the Smith case, a coalition of religious bodies sought clarification of the decision in Congress. Unfortunately this coalition refused to allow Indians to participate in the reform movement, arguing out of ignorance that peyote was merely a drug. Indians instead fought for the passage of amendments to the Religious Freedom Resolution, and they succeeded in 1994. The amendments clarified much of the confusion that the Smith case had engendered and offered increased protection for the practices of the Native American Church. Since 1994 these new protections have been tested in a number of cases, the outcomes of which have not diluted the rights of Indians. These cases, however, raised novel questions regarding the manner in which the Native American Church authorizes, appoints, or anoints its ceremonial leader, the Roadman. Some non-Indians sought to become Roadmen, forecasting a major case some time in the future. The main problem faced by the Native American Church at the beginning of the twenty-first century was one of self-definition: whether it was to be a church with no missionary responsibilities, which it certainly was on reservations, or whether it should be a more universal church that can accept non-Indian members.

To understand the historical journey of American Indians and their religious traditions one must place the developments of the modern era within a broader context. Christianity, primarily through its involvement in Indian education, made tremendous inroads into tribal cultures. As education became a function of the secular federal government and state educational institutions, religious instruction faded and Indian children received the same tepid, occasional religious instruction as non-Indians. Improved roads and modern communications reduced the distance between reservation villages and outside society. With increased mobility, people no longer felt tied to the old ways and looked for more meaningful religious experiences. Traditional tribal religions and Pentecostal neighborhood churches became more attractive.

At the beginning of the twenty-first century, Indian membership in the mainstream Christian churches declined precipitously, as compared to the previous generation. Many reservation churches and chapels closed or consolidated. Membership was primarily made up of the elderly, who had grown up with church traditions. Some denominations have discussed merging their missionary activities for lack of clergy and active members. The vast majority of Indians simply lived secular lives or substituted secular cultural activities for religious commitment. Traditional religions gathered more followers, but practice of the old ceremonies, for the most part, lost its supernatural capability; as with contemporary Christian ceremonies, the feeling of mystery faded. Whether this experience can be restored in the world in which we live is yet to be determined.

See Also Anthropology, Ethnology, and Religion; Conversion; Cosmology, article on Indigenous North and Mesoamerican Cosmologies; Drama, article on North American Indian Dance and Drama; Ecology and Religion; Gender and Religion, article on Gender and Native American Religious Tradition; Missions; Native American Christianities; Native American Church; North American Indian Religions; North American Indians; Performance and Ritual; Poetry, article on Native American Poetry and Religion; Rites of Passage, article on North American Indian Rites.

Bibliography

Deloria, Vine, Jr., and Clifford Lytle. *The Nations Within: The Past and Future of American Indian Sovereignty.* New York, 1984.

Fritz, Henry E. *The Movement for Indian Assimilation: 1860–1890.* Westport, Conn., 1981.

Irwin, Lee. *The Dream Seekers: Native American Visionary Traditions of the Great Plains.* Norman, Okla., 1994.

Keller, Robert H., Jr. *American Protestantism and United States Indian Policy, 1869–82.* Lincoln, Neb., 1983.

Smith, Huston, and Reuben Snake, comp. and eds. *One Nation under God: The Triumph of the Native American Church.* Santa Fe, N. Mex., 1996.

Thomas, David Hurst. *Skull Wars: Kennewick Man, Archaeology, and the Battle for Native American Identity.* New York, 2000.

Walker, James R. *Lakota Belief and Ritual.* Edited by Raymond J. DeMallie and Elaine A. Jahner. Lincoln, Neb., 1980.

Vine Deloria, Jr. (2005)

POLLUTION See PURIFICATION; TABOO

POLYNESIAN RELIGIONS

This entry consists of the following articles:

POLYNESIAN RELIGIONS: AN OVERVIEW

Polynesia consists of several thousand islands contained within an immense triangle in the central Pacific with its corners at Hawai'i, New Zealand, and Easter Island. Polynesian peoples also inhabit a few "outliers" to the west of the triangle, such as Tikopia and Ontong Java in the Solomon Islands. Polynesian islands range from the huge, continental North and South Islands of New Zealand through the high, volcanic islands found in the Hawaiian, Samoan, and Society (Tahitian) chains, to the tiny, low atolls of the Tuamotu archipelago. Although a good deal of cultural diversity does exist within Polynesia, even more noteworthy—given the vast distances between island groups and the striking ecological differences between the continental, volcanic, and coral islands—are the cultural consistencies that hold throughout the region. These include closely linked languages, related forms of social and political organization, and similar religious beliefs and ceremonies.

While numerous isolated beliefs and practices from the pre-European period survive on many islands, the native Polynesian religion described in this essay no longer exists in a pure state. Conversion to Christianity began in Tahiti at the beginning of the nineteenth century. The process was essentially completed on most major islands by the middle of the century, although some remote islands, such as Tikopia, were not fully Christian until a hundred years later.

A CASE STUDY: KAPINGAMARANGI. Discussion begins with a description of some religious practices on one island—as it happens, an island of little significance by most measures. But it will serve as an introduction to Polynesian religion generally, because it is possible to detect in the religious practices of that island patterns that are basic to religion throughout Polynesia.

Kapingamarangi is a tiny, isolated atoll located to the south of the Caroline Islands in the western Pacific. It consists of an oval coral reef surrounding a lagoon six to eight miles in diameter, along the eastern edge of which are about thirty islets. The total land area more than five feet above sea level is less than one-half of a square mile; this is the living space for about five hundred inhabitants. Although it is an outlier, located well outside the Polynesian triangle, the culture and people of Kapingamarangi are distinctly Polynesian.

Every day, according to traditional beliefs, the gods would visit Kapingamarangi. They came from the sea, emerging in mid afternoon off the southeastern portion of the atoll and making their way northward along the outer reef toward an islet called Touhou. Shortly before sunset a priest would call out an invitation to the gods. They would come ashore at Touhou and proceed to a special cult house. They entered the seaward end of the house, which a pair of priestesses had just opened for them by taking down the wall screens. The high priest stood outside the opposite (lagoon) end of the cult house and delivered evening prayers, after which the priestesses replaced the wall screens. The following morning, just before sunrise, the high priest came again to the house. This time he went to the seaward end, took down the wall screens, delivered morning prayers, and then replaced the screens. The gods, who had spent the night in the house, departed after the prayers had been addressed to them, retraced their path along the outer reef to the southeastern part of the atoll, and, about mid-morning, returned to the sea. Several hours later they appeared again, and the entire process was repeated.

These daily events on Kapingamarangi encapsulate, in microcosm, many of the basic elements of religion throughout Polynesia. Although numerous variations may be found in different islands, Polynesians are unanimous in these beliefs: that the gods inhabit a realm distinct from the physical world populated by human beings; that they are frequent visitors to the physical world; that the gods are responsible for a great deal of what happens in the physical world, including events both beneficial and detrimental to human beings; that humans may exercise, through properly executed ritual, some control over the visits of the gods to the physical world and what they do here; and (what is one of the most distinctive features of Polynesian religion) that the gods may be ritually induced to withdraw from the physical world in circumstances where their influence is not, or is no longer, desirable. At bottom, Polynesian religion is a story of gods who are immensely active in this world and of people who attempt to control the activities of the gods by directing their influence into places where it is desired and expelling it from places where it is not. The essence of Kapingamarangi's daily cycle—the entrance of the gods into the human world, ushering them into a place of human choosing, requesting their assistance in matters of human needs, and then dismissing them to their own spiritual realm—was enacted in a thousand ways throughout Polynesia.

COSMOS. The universe, with its spiritual and physical realms, its myriads of gods, human beings, plants, and animals, was established by a series of creative acts. Myths from Samoa and the Society Islands tell of an uncreated creator god—Tangaloa or Taʾaroa (elsewhere Tangaroa, Kanaloa, etc.)—who was stirred to create the beginnings of a world. In other myths the first spark of creation is a series of abstract mental qualities and urges, existing and evolving in themselves: thought, remembrance, consciousness, and desire. In most Polynesian accounts of creation, existence was soon differentiated into a male sky and a female earth. These were joined together in copulation. The earth gave birth to a number of sons, the major gods of the Polynesian pantheon. Their numbers and identities differ among the various islands, but frequently the names Tane, Tu, and Rongo appear in one linguistic form or another among them. Tangaroa, the creator already mentioned for certain myths from Samoa and Tahiti, often appears in other myths as another of the sons of the earth and sky.

With the sky pressed so closely to his terrestrial mate, the living space between them was dark and cramped, and their sons could scarcely stand upright. They resolved to separate their parents. After numerous fruitless efforts, one of the sons succeeded in wrenching the lovers apart and raising the sky to the position it now occupies. Perhaps this is a mythological source for the notion that existence is divided into a spiritual and a physical realm, because on many islands the gods were thought to dwell in the heavens. (The spiritual realm normally includes more than just the heavens, however. As described already, the gods of Kapingamarangi came from the open sea. The underworld, as the home of the dead, was also widely considered to be part of the spiritual realm.)

Further stages of creation are usually expressed in genealogical terms. In a Samoan myth, various sorts of rocks and plant and animal species are born and mate to produce still other furnishings of the earth through many generations following the initial union of celestial and terrestrial rocks. In the ninth generation, Pili, a lizard, mates with a tropical bird, and their three sons and daughter are the first human beings. In the mythology of the Maori of New Zealand, the progenitor is the god Tane. Unable to create alone, he sought an *uha,* or female partner. He found a great many of them, and from his unions with them were born water and the various species of insects, birds, and trees and other plants. Through all this, however, Tane was frustrated in his abiding desire to create humankind. Finally he and his brothers, the sons of the sky and the earth, shaped a woman from the earth. Tane breathed life into her nostrils, mouth and ears. Unsure of himself, he then copulated with the various orifices and crevices of her body. This was the origin of the bodily excretions, for the places fertilized by Tane gave birth to saliva, mucus, earwax, excrement, and perspiration. Finally Tane tried her genitalia, and she bore a daughter, whom they named Hinetitama. Later Tane incestuously took his daughter as his mate, and she gave birth to the first human beings.

It fell to a number of heroes, of whom the most famous throughout Polynesia was named Maui, to put the finishing touches on creation. In those earliest days the sun moved rapidly across the sky, making night much longer than day. People found it difficult to accomplish their work in the brief span of daylight. Māui (or, on some islands, a hero of another name) journeyed to the place where the sun emerges from the underworld at dawn, and there he laid a snare. When the sun appeared Maui caught it and gave it a drubbing with his club (made, in some versions of the story, from the jawbone of one of his female ancestors). Thenceforth it could move only slowly and painfully across the heavens, and thus was the day lengthened to equal the span of the night. Mythic heroes are also credited with fishing up many islands from the depths of the sea. The North Island of New Zealand is known as Te-Ika-a-Māui, or Māui's fish, because he caught it with a fishhook (also made from the same jawbone), which he baited by smearing it with his own blood.

GODS. The spiritual realm was thought to be populated by an indefinitely large number of beings, known in most islands by some variant of the term *atua.* The term may be translated as "god," although it should be borne in mind that in Polynesia this is a remarkably broad category. Some gods have never lived as humans (for example, the sons of the earth and sky), while others are spirits of deceased ancestors or of quasi-human entities such as stillborn babies and menstrual clots. Some gods are benevolent, others are mischievous or downright malicious, and still others have no particular moral qualities at all. The gods have a diverse range of occupations and interests. Their number includes creator gods; gods responsible for various "departments" of existence (such as the sea, the forests, cultivated plants, and so on); gods that concern themselves with particular places, particular tribes, or particular families; gods of warfare, fishing, carpentry, and various other occupations; even gods that specialize in bringing on certain diseases or ravishing people whose hair was a certain color. All in all, they are an extremely numerous and varied lot.

While the gods properly belong to the spiritual realm, it was thought throughout Polynesia that (as with the daily visits of the gods to Kapingamarangi) they would frequently enter the human world. Indeed, so extensive was their influence deemed to be that Polynesians tended to attribute any condition or event for which a physical cause was not immediately apparent to the work of the gods. Among a great many other things, this included thunder and lightning, shifts in the wind, and the growth of plants, animals, and people. The gods were authors of dreams and human artistic accomplishments; they underwrote the rank and power of chiefs and success in love or war; and they generated courage and cowardice, illness and accidents, and even involuntary twitches in the muscles.

An indication of the variety of events that Polynesians would attribute to the gods is recorded by the traveler and artist Augustus Earle. When he sailed from New Zealand to Australia in 1828, several Maoris also made the trip. Earle writes in his *Narrative of a Residence in New Zealand* (Oxford, 1966):

> The second day after we were at sea, I saw a group of savages lying round the binnacle, all intently occupied in observing the phenomenon of the magnetic attraction; they seemed at once to comprehend the purpose to which it was applied, and I listened with eager curiosity to their remarks upon it. "This," said they, "is the white man's God, who directs them safely to different countries, and then can guide them home again. . . ." Nothing could exceed the delight manifested by our New Zealanders as we sailed into Port Jackson [Sydney] harbour; but above all, the windmills most astonished them. After dancing and screaming with joy at beholding them, they came running and asking me "if they were not gods." (pp. 196–197)

Polynesians took great stock in omens. Belief in godly instigation of events of all sorts, and that the gods had knowledge superior to that of humans—knowledge of what was happening far away, or would happen in the future, for example—led Polynesians to think that many events could be read as messages from the gods about matters of importance to humans. Dreams were a particularly rich source of information from the world of the gods. One's own spirit or soul could leave the body in sleep, traveling great distances as the gods do, and gathering all sorts of intelligence while out of the body. Sometimes the message of dreams was straightforward, as when a Maori woman's dream that raiders were gathering in the hills to attack her village was confirmed when scouts found that raiders were indeed in the hills. Other dreams needed expert interpretation to reveal their meanings. If a Maori man dreamed of skulls lying on the ground, and decorated with feathers, it was a sign that his wife was pregnant; moreover, the color of the feathers foretold the sex of the baby.

Diviner priests in Hawai'i and Tahiti would read the outcome of a proposed battle in the entrails of sacrificial animals. The configurations of rainbows, clouds, and other heavenly phenomena were everywhere understood as omens. Should a Maori war party see the moon situated above the evening star, for example, they would abandon plans to attack a fortified village because the battle would go against them. The moon situated below the evening star, on the other hand, was a sign that their attack would be crowned with success.

An important way in which Polynesian gods were thought to make their influence felt in the physical world was literally to enter and possess human beings. Often this was an unwelcome situation, for the intruding god might be malicious and proceed to bite, twist, or pinch the individual's internal organs—a common explanation for disease. On the other hand, certain persons were particularly prone to spirit possession by which a deceased chief, ancestor, or some other god would communicate with human beings. The medium would go into a trance, during which his or her tone of voice might change drastically. That was thought to be the voice of the possessing god, conveying information about the cause of some disease, the identity of a thief, the outcome of a military expedition, or some other matter of importance to the human community.

The gods also frequented animals of various species: sharks, herons, lizards, owls, and so on. Because the indwelling gods were often malicious, and in any event had power enough to make them dangerous to ordinary people, such animals were regarded with fear, or, at least, with a great deal of circumspection. Lizards were thought in many islands to be favorite earthly vehicles for particularly malevolent gods, rendering these animals objects of terror to people. In his *Journal of a Ten Months Residence in New Zealand* (London, 1823), the early visitor Richard Cruise reported that when a visiting ship's officer in the early nineteenth century brought a lizard to a Maori women in order to ascertain the local word for it, "She shrunk from him in a state of terror that exceeded description, and conjured him not to approach her, as it was in the shape of the animal he held in his hand, that the Atua [god] was wont to take possession of the dying, and to devour their bowels" (p. 320).

MANA AND TAPU. Persons, places, and things that were possessed by or were otherwise under the influence of the gods were often referred to by one or the other of the two most well-known concepts in Polynesian religion: *mana* and *tapu.* While these terms have usually been understood by Western observers to function as nouns—so that one might have a certain amount of *mana,* infringe a *tapu,* or put *tapu* on or remove it from something—some scholars think that they properly describe states of being rather than things. From this perspective, *mana* or *tapu* are similar to fame: One may "have" fame, but that is not like having a concrete thing such as a computer.

Mana (a form used in many Polynesian languages) refers to the state of being that is enjoyed by those objects, places, or persons that benefit permanently (or at least for an extended period) from the strengthening influence of the gods. A primary mark of *mana* is outstanding effectiveness in action. Hence the term was applied to certain weapons (many of which had proper names and unique qualities, as did the swords Excalibur and Nothung in European lore) that were thought to be invincible in and of themselves.

Individuals who had distinguished themselves by outstanding accomplishments as warriors, navigators, priests, or artists were thought to have *mana.* At least as important, *mana* characterized certain families and descent lines. Polynesian society on many islands (particularly on Tahiti and the other Society Islands, and on Samoa, Tonga, and Hawai'i) was highly stratified, with great gulfs of rank separating the chiefs and other nobles from the commoners. The rank of the nobility passed from generation to generation, reaching its culmination in the line of firstborn children. These lines traced their descent back to the high gods and existed under their special protection. Their rank and position was validated precisely by this relationship to the gods, which was the source of their intense *mana.* In many respects the relationship was so close that those of exalted rank were considered to be very like gods themselves. In Tahiti high chiefs were carried on the backs of servants whenever they ventured out, because if their feet had touched the ground, that spot would have been made so sacred that it could no longer be used for ordinary purposes. All persons along the chief's path had to bare their bodies to the waist as a sign of deference. In Hawai'i the concern that nobles not marry spouses of standing lower than their own resulted in the approval of brother-sister marriage for chiefs of the highest rank. The offspring of such unions were considered to be divine, and all persons were required to prostrate themselves in their presence.

Tapu, a form used in the Maori and Tahitian languages, is a term taken into English as "taboo," and is close in meaning to *mana.* It too is concerned primarily with the influence that the gods exercise over people, places, and things of the physical world. *Tapu* is often defined with reference to restrictions or prohibitions, it being *tapu* to enter a certain place, eat certain food, touch certain objects, or undertake various other activities. The word, however, refers not so much to the sheer fact of restriction as to the reason for it: that the place, person, or object in question was possessed by or under the influence of the gods and therefore had to be treated with extreme care.

It is tempting to translate *tapu* as "sacred," but that term has a consistently positive connotation that is by no means always the case with the Polynesian concept. As has been noted already, to be under the influence of a Polynesian god is not necessarily a desirable condition, for it may entail physical or mental illness, loss of courage, or any number of other unwelcome states. All of these may be described in terms of *tapu.* This points up one distinction between *tapu* and *mana.* While both terms refer to states brought on by the influence of gods, *mana* was limited to conditions characterized by outstanding effectiveness of action or elevated rank. *Tapu* might also be used in those circumstances, but it describes detrimental or debilitating states as well.

Again, both *mana* and *tapu* may refer to states of long duration, but these were perhaps more commonly described in terms of *mana.* On the other hand, only *tapu* was used to describe conditions in which the influence of the gods was experienced for relatively brief or defined periods—such as during festivals or religious ceremonies, seasons for growing crops, expeditions for hunting, fishing, or raiding, or times of tattooing or building a canoe or house. Because Polynesian rituals dealt primarily with such temporary influence of the gods, channeling it into areas of life where it was desired at the moment and away from areas where it was not, they were much more concerned with *tapu* than *mana.*

One reason that the *tapu* state tended to be of relatively short duration was because it was easily transmitted. *Mana* could be diminished or lost by defilement of some sort, but it was not easily communicated from one person or thing to another, except from parent to child by descent. To the contrary, *tapu* was considered to be a highly volatile state that was readily transmitted. This, indeed, is the primary reason why the term is so often translated as "forbidden" or as having to do with prohibitions: because it was necessary to hedge someone or something in the state of *tapu* with all sorts of restrictions in order to prevent its unintentional communication to other persons or things to which it might be detrimental. At this point it is well to recall that *tapu* refers not to a thing but to a state of being under the influence of gods. Should that influence pass from one person or thing to another, as Polynesians thought it commonly did, then the person or thing newly brought under godly influence would enter a state of *tapu.* If the godly influence should completely leave the "donor" in this situation, then that person or thing would be released from the *tapu* state.

Transmission of *tapu* was normally by direct or indirect contact. In many parts of Polynesia menstrual blood was thought to be dangerously *tapu,* and great precautions were taken to avoid contact with it. The Marquesan belief was that such contact produced leprosy. Throughout Polynesia food was considered to be an excellent conductor of *tapu.* Today women of Rapa, in the Austral chain, avoid preparing anyone's food but their own while they are menstruating. In ancient Tahiti and Hawai'i men and women ate separately on a regular basis in order to insulate the male from the dangerous influences connected with the female.

An intriguing example of how *tapu* may spread involves an unfortunate dog at Ruatoki, New Zealand. The dog contracted the extremely dangerous *tapu* associated with the dead because it rooted in a grave and began to chew on the corpse of a recently deceased person. The situation deteriorated when the dog, chased by numerous enraged Maoris, tried to escape by swimming across the Whakatane River. It was caught and killed in midstream, but by then the entire river had become *tapu* because the dog had been swimming in it. After that its water could not be used for any purpose until a priest had performed a special ceremony to release the river from *tapu.*

RITUAL. Polynesian ritual covered an extensive field of activity. It could be destructive, as in witchcraft rites that directed gods to injure or kill their victims. Maori legend, for example, tells how a sorcerer bewitched a New Zealand tribe called Maruiwi by calling upon the god Ira-kewa to confuse their minds so that they began to wander about in the night, walked over a high cliff, and fell to their deaths. Other rites were performed for the more constructive purposes of securing fertility of crops or success in voyaging, hunting, or fishing. Some rites consisted of no more than conventional incantations that an individual might mutter to secure the gods' approval or avoid their wrath when crossing a forest or a stream; others were elaborate festivals demanding immense preparations and lasting for days, or even, as in the case of the Hawaiian festival called Makahiki, for months. In all cases, however, Polynesian ritual had the same purpose as the daily rites on Kapingamarangi, that is, to move and focus godly influence in accordance with human wishes.

Understood in this way, it is possible to distinguish three phases in Polynesian ritual. The first is an invitation to the gods to come to the place where the ritual is taking place. The second is an attempt to induce the gods to lend their influence or support to whatever goal (fertility of crops, victory in battle, success in an interisland voyage, and so on) the rite is designed to promote. While these two phases are found in the ritual process of many religions, a third phase receives particular elaboration in Polynesia. In this phase, after the purpose of the rite has been achieved, the gods are dismissed and their influence is terminated.

Invitations. Polynesian gods were conceptualized as behaving very much like human beings, so ritual invitations to them were similar in kind to the way one might invite human guests. In Tahiti this included preparing an attactive place for them. Tahitian rituals normally took place in rectangular enclosures called *marae.* Between rituals very little attention was paid to the *marae.* The gods were not present, so there was no danger, no particular *tapu* associated with the *marae* at such times. When a ceremony was about to take place, however, a necessary prelude was to clear weeds and sweep the courtyard, to repair and scrape moss from the stone altar, to set up perches upon which the gods might settle, and in general to make the *marae* as attractive as possible for the gods who were to be summoned to it. Before lineage gods were invoked in Tonga, special mats would be spread out as places for them to sit.

Rituals normally began with an invitation to the gods to attend. In Tahiti lesser gods might be dispatched as messengers to invite the greater gods, and priests would intone long chants that described how each emissary had located the god it had been sent to fetch and was leading it to the *marae.* Other Tahitian chants inaugurating rituals were designed to awaken the gods from sleep. Hawai'ians would sometimes appeal to the gods' sexuality, attracting them to a ritual with an erotic hula dance.

New Zealand Maori invited the gods to certain places by setting out material objects in which they could take up residence. Rudely carved stone images, called "resting places for the gods," would be placed in fields after sweet potatoes had been planted. The intention was for gods to enter the images, whence they would establish a state of *tapu* over the crop by lending their growth-stimulating power to it. Other special objects, either natural or human-made, were placed in forests, near the sea, or in fortified villages. These constituted domiciles for the gods who ensured an abundance of birds and rats in the forest, fish of various species in the sea, or protection for the village. It was important to conceal these objects carefully, lest they fall into the hands of some malefactor who would perform certain spells causing the god to depart and bringing disaster on the forest or village.

Priests in certain parts of New Zealand carried "godsticks": small, carved wooden pegs that, when wrapped in a certain way and stuck in the ground, would be entered by gods. Idols or images were thought to provide housing for the gods in many parts of Polynesia. In the early nineteenth century the several chiefs who were competing to become king of a centralized Tahiti went to great lengths to secure the image of the war god Oro. Where the image was, so the belief went, there Oro himself would come, bringing with him success in war and politics.

New Zealand Maori were particularly conscious of boundaries between the human and the spiritual worlds. Frequently their rituals would be held at such places, where the gods could readily pass from the spiritual realm into this one. One of the most intriguing of these boundaries had to do with the village latrine. This was commonly built on the outskirts of a village, often on the brow of a cliff or steep hill, over which excreta would fall. The latrine consisted of a pair of carved posts that supported a low horizontal beam where the feet would be placed while squatting. Handgrips to assist in preserving one's balance were planted in the ground in front of the beam. The beam was thought to be a boundary between the realms of existence: The physical world was on the village side of the beam, with all its human hustle and bustle, while the region behind the beam, where excrement fell and where people never went, was the spiritual world. Of the numerous rituals the Maori performed at the latrine, none presents a clearer view of it as a point of emergence of the gods into the physical world than the consecration of the Takitumu canoe. According to Maori lore, this was one of the canoes that brought their ancestors to New Zealand. The tradition relates how Takitumu was placed in a state of *tapu,* so as to enjoy the gods' protection during the long and dangerous voyage, by literally hauling the canoe up to the latrine and inviting the gods to embark.

Propitiations. Once the gods had arrived at the site of the ritual, the next phase was to carry out the purpose for which they had been invited. This might be to convince them to do something for the human community, or to thank them for services already rendered. A common means of accomplishing either of these ends was to give the gods gifts. In many places in Polynesia the gods were thanked for their assistance by offering them the first crops harvested, the first birds snared, or the first fish caught. War gods might be given the first enemy killed; often a hook would be placed in his mouth and he would be announced as the first fish. Human sacrifices were offered in many parts of Polynesia including Hawai'i, Tahiti, Tonga, the Marquesas, Mangaia (in the Cook Islands), and New Zealand. Human lives were sacrificed for a variety of purposes, including the commemoration of significant events in the lives of high chiefs, the launching of important new canoes, or the opening of major houses. People in Tonga would strike off joints of their little fingers as sacrificial supplications to the gods to restore relatives to health.

Another common means of influencing the gods on ritual occasions was by incantations. After a Maori priest had induced a god to enter his godstick by wrapping it in the proper way and sticking it in the ground, he would step back a few paces and intone his requests. Often the priest held a bit of string that was tied to the stick and that he would jerk occasionally to prevent the god's attention from wandering.

The efficacy of an incantation, and, indeed, of a ritual observance in its entirety, was thought to depend on the perfection with which it was accomplished. This mispronunciation of a word, a breath drawn in the wrong place, or any disturbance of the general atmosphere surrounding the rite, was thought to abort the whole ceremony. On many islands, during a religious ceremony the people who were not participating in the rite were constrained to remain in their houses, lighting no fires and making no noise. Cocks must not crow, nor dogs bark; absolutely nothing was allowed to disrupt the highly *tapu* atmosphere of the rite. In the Society Islands, should a woman or child wander near the place where a ritual was occurring, the intruder would be killed immediately (perhaps by the husband or father) and offered to the gods as a sacrifice to amend for the disturbance. Perhaps such rules and practices, although far more severe, were not different in intent from a Maori priest tugging at the string tied to his godstick in order to prevent the attention of the gods from being distracted by matters other than those addressed in the ceremony.

The emphasis on perfection of delivery of incantations and performance of ceremonies indicates that Polynesians believed their gods to be concerned with the outer form of worship. Inner feelings and convictions were not relevant issues in Polynesian religion. New Zealand provides the most striking bit of evidence for this proposition. An imaginative chief there arranged for the necessary incantations that accompanied the planting of crops to be delivered by a talking bird!

Dismissals. The final phase of Polynesian ritual was the departure of the gods and, with them, the termination of the state of *tapu.* Occasionally this constituted not a phase but the rite in its entirety. This would apply to rituals designed to cure illness or to counteract witchcraft, where the god involved was malevolently inclined and the sole purpose of the rite was to exorcise it. In other cases, as in the departure of the gods from Kapingamarangi's cult house each day at dawn, the gods were excused in the final stage of ritual, after prayers or thanks had been addressed to them or when the beneficial results for which they had been summoned had been realized. Many Polynesians believed, for example, that crops could grow, battles be won, or houses and canoes be successfully built only with the assistance of the gods. Only, that is, when the field, warriors, weapons, builders, tools, and raw materials were in a state of *tapu.* But that very *tapu,* together with the numerous restrictions designed to control its unintended spread, rendered it impossible for the crops to be eaten once they were harvested, for warriors to take up normal activities after battle, for people to live in the house or to travel in the canoe when built. Therefore it was necessary to excuse the gods once their contribution had been achieved—to release the crop, the warriors, the house, or the canoe from the state of *tapu.*

A person, place, or thing that had been released from *tapu* entered a state of being known on many Polynesian islands as *noa.* Often translated as "common" or "profane" (in contrast to views of *tapu* as "sacred"), *noa* may be understood simply as the opposite of *tapu*—as the state of not being under the influence of the gods. Rituals or segments of rituals designed to provide a release from *tapu* were often designated by words such as *fa'anoa* (in the Society Islands) or *whakanoa* (in New Zealand), meaning "to make *noa.*"

Normally the dismissal of the gods was, as in Kapingamarangi, a temporary situation. They would be invited back the next time their assistance was needed. Occasionally, however, the lifting of the *tapu* state was intended to be permanent. This of course applied to disease-dealing or otherwise malicious gods. People wanted to escape their influence forever. But it might also be the case with a god from whom assistance had been expected, if it became clear that the god was not performing satisfactorily. Tahitians had a special ceremony for casting off a god. If a family found that it was receiving few benefits from the god it venerated, the family priest would address a special incantation to the god. He would berate it roundly for its feeble support, and inform it that the family would have nothing more to do with it. Then they would select another god that promised to be more helpful.

A variety of means were available to terminate the state of *tapu.* One was simply to get away from the god. Many gods were restricted in their spheres of influence, so if a person were suffering from a disorder known to be caused by a certain god, the healer's prescription might be for the patient to leave the area frequented by that god.

The more common tactic, however, was to send the gods or their influence away. One of the most common ritual agents used for this purpose throughout Polynesia was water. By sprinkling or immersion in salt or fresh water, Polynesians of Samoa, the Marquesas, New Zealand, the Society Islands, and Hawai'i would return to the *noa* state after participating in war, rituals, funeral observances, and other activities. The rationale was doubtless that the water washed away the godly influence responsible for the *tapu.*

Fire was another agent for releasing persons and things from *tapu,* because of its capacity to consume or drive out indwelling gods. In the Society Islands sickness or insanity might be caused by a malicious spirit that dwelt in a stone buried by a witch near the victim's residence. Should a diviner ascertain where the stone was concealed, he would unearth it and throw it into the fire to destroy or expel the infecting spirit.

Probably the *tapu*-eradicating properties of fire account for the fact that, in New Zealand, cooked food (that is, food that has been exposed to high heat or fire) was one of the most common agents used in rituals concerned with the expulsion or transfer of godly influence. Some scholars claim the Maori view to have been that cooked food repelled the gods, others that it attracted them. In any event, it was very commonly a part of *whakanoa* rituals, such as that in which the hands of someone who had been cultivating a garden, curing an illness, or cutting the hair of a chief were released from *tapu* by passing a bit of cooked sweet potato or fernroot over them.

The Maori were extremely careful in their direct or indirect association with cooked food when they were in a state of *tapu* that they wished to preserve. They were most reluctant to enter European hospitals, where water to wash patients might be heated in pots previously used for cooking. The same reasoning explains why some Maoris who had embraced Christianity and wished to purge themselves of the influence of the pagan gods would purposely wash their heads in water heated in cooking pots. One European trader engendered the wrath of a Maori chief when he joked that a cooking pot that he had for sale would make a fine helmet for the chief, and made as if to put it on his head.

The Maori concern with thresholds between the spiritual and physical realms, discussed above in connection with ritual means of bringing the gods into this world, is also important in rituals designed to send them out of it. One cure for illness was to bite the latrine beam, presumably with the intention of repatriating the affecting god to the spirit realm by sending it over the threshold between the worlds. After a session of training in sacred lore, which required that students be in a state of *tapu* if the learning process were to take place successfully, the students would bite the latrine beam in order to return to the *noa* state. Finally, a warrior who was afraid before battle might fortify himself by biting the beam, although it is not entirely clear in this case whether the purpose was to be rid of a fear-producing god, or to take on the influence of a courage-producing one.

Unquestionably one of the most intriguing agents for the ritual release from *tapu* was the female. In New Zealand

and the Marquesas Islands new houses would be made free of *tapu* by having a woman enter them. Women participated in the *tapu*-dispelling phase of the war ritual known as Luakini in Hawai'i. In New Zealand women would eat the first tubers and thereby render a newly harvested crop of sweet potatoes *noa.* Maoris would rid themselves of the malicious spirit that might be lurking in a lizard by killing the animal and then having a woman step over it. Marquesans would exorcise the demon afflicting a sick person by having a naked woman leap over or sit on the affected part of the patient's body. Women were not permitted to assist at major rites in the Society Islands, for fear that their presence would expel the gods. For the same reason women were not allowed to go near sites of canoe or house construction in New Zealand or, in the Marquesas, to have any contact with men who had been made *tapu* prior to turtle fishing or battle.

The usual interpretation is that the gods found women to be repugnant, particularly because of their connection with menstrual blood (a substance thought, on this interpretation, to be more polluting than any other). Hence the gods would withdraw upon the appearance of a woman, taking their *tapu* with them. An alternative view is that the gods were attracted to women rather than repelled by them, and that women therefore terminated *tapu* by absorbing the godly influence into themselves. On this interpretation the female is understood, as is the Maori latrine, to represent a passageway between the godly and human realms of existence. The rites in which women acted to dispel *tapu* would of course be examples of the movement of godly influence through the female from the human to the spiritual world. Certain practices in New Zealand can be interpreted as the movement of godly influence in the opposite direction, as when students about to be instructed in sacred lore would enter the state of *tapu* by eating a piece of cooked food that had first been passed under the thigh of a woman.

The view of the female as a passage between the two realms leads to some possible insights into the Polynesian view of birth and death. In New Zealand and the Society Islands incantations addressed to newborn infants of rank welcomed them into the physical world from the world of the gods. An infant, that is, was apparently viewed as an embodied spirit that had passed from the spiritual realm to the human realm. And, of course, the infant accomplished the transit by being born of a woman.

Polynesians understood death as the passage of the soul from the physical world to the spiritual realm, where it continued to exist as a god or spirit of some sort. Most interesting is that, in New Zealand at least, this passage too was thought to be made through the female. This is evident in the intriguing story of the death of the culture hero Māui. Having fished up islands and slowed the sun, Māui resolved to bestow upon humankind the ultimate gift of eternal life. He intended to accomplish this by killing Hine-nui-te-po, the female personification of death. Accompanied by his friends, the birds, Māui came upon her while she was asleep. His plan was to kill her by entering her vagina, passing through her body, and emerging at the mouth. He cautioned his friends not to laugh if they found the sight amusing, for fear of waking her. Then he stripped naked and, binding the thong of his club tightly about his wrist, he proceeded to enter the sleeping woman. But predictably the birds found the sight hilarious and they burst out in raucous laughter. That awakened Hine-nui-te-po who, discovering Maui attempting to enter her, clenched her thighs tightly together and crushed him to death. And such, opined a Maori commentator, is the fate of all humans: to be drawn at death into the genitals of Hine-nui-te-po.

Hence the female seems to constitute a two-way passage between the spiritual and physical realms of existence, for humans as well as for the gods. Moreover, the very distinction between human beings and the gods now begins to collapse. Humans, arriving at birth from the supernatural realm, apparently were thought to have a spiritual existence before birth, and they definitely were thought to return to the spiritual realm as ghosts and ancestral gods after death.

For a final bit of evidence of a Polynesian belief that human beings exist as spirits in the godly realm prior to birth, this article will return to where it began—the tiny atoll of Kapingamarangi. After a woman had given birth, she and her infant would go for a set of birth ceremonies to the islet of Touhou. That is the place, it will be recalled, where the gods would come ashore every day. Therefore, while it might actually have been born on another islet, the infant was ritually introduced into Kapingamarangi on the islet of Touhou, just as the gods were. After a period of ceremonies on Touhou, mother and child participated in a ritual that took place on Werua islet, located just to the north of Touhou. After that, they would return to their home islet and to normal life.

Interpreting this, it is seen that the child, like the gods, has come from the spiritual realm of Touhou. But whereas the gods remain gods by leaving Touhou and traveling south, the same direction from which they came, the child becomes human by leaving Touhou to the north. From that point forward the child becomes a full member of human society. In essence this is not unlike ceremonies that release one from *tapu* in other parts of Polynesia, rites in which the removal of godly influence enables a person to participate without restriction in normal human existence.

BIBLIOGRAPHY

Two general books are E. S. Craighill Handy's *Polynesian Religion* (Honolulu, 1927) and *Anthropology and Religion* (1959; reprint, Hamden, Conn., 1970) by Peter H. Buck (Te Rangi Hiroa). Both are written by acknowledged experts in the field, although, as their dates imply, neither benefits from contemporary methods of anthropological analysis. The same may be said for the larger but less influential compendia by Robert W. Williamson, *Religious and Cosmic Beliefs of Central Polynesia,* 2 vols. (1933; reprint, New York, 1977), and *Religion and Social Organization in Central Polynesia*

(Cambridge, 1937). Katharine Luomala's *Maui-of-a-Thousand-Tricks* (Honolulu, 1949) is an interesting study of myths, dealing with a single culture hero, drawn from all parts of Polynesia. The most thoroughly documented of traditional Polynesian cultures is New Zealand's. George Grey's *Polynesian Mythology* (London, 1922) is a widely read collection of Maori myths. Despite its forbidding title, J. Prytz Johansen's *The Maori and His Religion in Its Non-Ritualistic Aspects* (Copenhagen, 1954) is a rich and fascinating analysis, as is his companion book, *Studies in Maori Rites and Myths* (Copenhagen, 1958). More recent Maori studies are Jean Smith's *Tapu Removal in Maori Religion* (Wellington, 1974), and F. Allan Hanson and Louise Hanson's *Counterpoint in Maori Culture* (London, 1983). For the Society Islands, the most useful works are Teuira Henry's *Ancient Tahiti* (Honolulu, 1928) and, by Douglas L. Oliver, a three-volume compilation of information from the sources plus analysis of his own, *Ancient Tahitian Society* (Honolulu, 1974). A good deal on religion may be found in E. S. Craighill Handy's *The Native Culture in the Marquesas* (1923; reprint, New York, 1971); William Mariner's *An Account of the Natives of the Tonga Islands,* 3d ed., 2 vols. (Edinburgh, 1827); Edward Winslow Gifford's *Tongan Society* (Honolulu, 1929); and John B. Stair's *Old Samoa* (1897; reprint, Papakura, New Zealand, 1983). Books with useful information on Hawaiian religion are Martha Warren Beckwith's *Hawaiian Mythology* (1940; reprint, Honolulu, 1970) and David Malo's *Hawaiian Antiquities,* 2d ed. (Honolulu, 1951). Religion of the Polynesian outliers has been well analyzed in Torben Monberg's *The Religion of Bellona Island* (Copenhagen, 1966); Raymond Firth's *The Work of the Gods in Tikopia,* 2d ed., and *Tikopia Ritual and Belief* (both, London, 1967); and finally, the source from which the information on Kapingamarangi in this essay is taken, Kenneth P. Emory's *Kapingamarangi: Social and Religious Life of a Polynesian Atoll* (Honolulu, 1965).

New Sources

Charlot, John. "Towards a Dialogue between Christianity and Polynesian Religions." *Studies in Religion/Sciences religieuses* 15, no. 4 (1986): 443–450.

Howard, Alan. "Cannibal Chiefs and the Charter for Rebellion in Rotuman Myth." *Pacific Studies* 10 (1986): 1–27.

Mageo, Jeannette Marie, and Alan Howard. *Spirits in Culture, History, and Mind.* New York, 1996.

McLean, Mervyn. *Weavers of Song: Polynesian Music and Dance.* Honolulu, 1999.

Ralston, Caroline, and Nicholas Thomas, eds. "Sanctity and Power: Gender in Polynesian History." *Journal of Pacific History* 22 (July–October 1987): 115–227.

Ritchie, James E. *Sacred Chiefs and Secular Gods: The Polynesian View of the World.* Hamilton, N.Z., 1998.

Wallin, Paul. *The Symbolism of Polynesian Temple Rituals.* Oslo, Norway, 1998.

F. ALLAN HANSON (1987)
Revised Bibliography

POLYNESIAN RELIGIONS: MYTHIC THEMES

Although one might argue whether the gods created the Polynesians in godlike form or the Polynesians created the gods in their own image, it is a truism that in Polynesia gods and people are aspects of the same reality and form a continuum of the sacred and the profane. Even as, in relative terms, the gods are sacred and the people profane, so also are the chiefs sacred and the commoners profane. This axiom underlay the sociocultural organization of the Polynesians and gave religious justification to ranked social and kinship structures. The mythological threads of Polynesian religions developed an intimate association among gods, chiefs, priests, and people. High gods, demigods, ancestral gods, culture heroes, spirits, elves, and people were intertwined in different ways in each island group to create separate religions that were particularized and parochial while at the same time part of a homogenous religious fabric that was spread over a vast expanse of ocean containing hundreds of large and small Polynesian islands.

Polynesia can be conveniently divided into western Polynesia (including Tonga, Samoa, Tuvalu, the Tokelau Islands, Niue, the Futuna Islands, and Uvéa) and eastern Polynesia (Hawaii, the Society Islands including Tahiti, the Marquesas, the Cooks, the Australs, Mangareva, the Tuamotus, Easter Island, and New Zealand). A number of small islands lie outside the Oceanic region commonly designated as Polynesia, but they have Polynesian religious and cultural traditions (Rennell, Bellona, Tikopia, Anuta, Ontong Java, Kapingamarangi, Takuu, Sikiana, and others). These "outliers" are closely related to western Polynesia. Fiji, Lau, and Rotuma, on the western fringe of Polynesia, are in some ways closely related to western Polynesia, although religiously Fiji is probably more closely related to the Melanesian islands to the west. The religion of each of these groups and its mythological basis formed a coherent whole with the social organization. The connections between gods, ancestors, and humans were often made visually apparent and ritually maintained through religious architecture and works of art including songs, dances, sculptured images, and, most fundamental of all, oral literature. Although it is difficult to separate sacred and secular in Polynesia, the emphasis in this article will be on the mythological themes that help to explain the religious element of the society with its emphasis on *mana* and *tapu,* rather than on the mythological basis of secular storytelling. From a Polynesian point of view, the terms *mythic* and *mythological* are not entirely appropriate because these sacred traditions are considered historical and unquestionable in much the same sense as is *Genesis* by many Christians.

COSMOGONY. One of the most important and widespread mythic themes in Polynesia deals with the origins of the universe, the gods, and various aspects of nature. From the primary void or chaos came heaven and earth, which lay close together. The Sky Father (variously, Langi, Rangi, or Atea) and the Earth Mother (Papa or Fakahotu) clung together in a warm embrace and, in the cosmogonic myths of many of the islands, were the progenitors of the gods, the land and sea, the elements, and of plants, animals, and people. Rangi and Papa were usually forcefully separated by gods or demigods.

In western Polynesia the most important agent in this separation was usually some form of the high god Tangaroa (Tangaloa) or the demigod trickster, Māui. In Tonga, for example, Māui-motua (the senior Māui) pushed up the sky; this let in the light and permitted humans, who had previously crawled as crabs, to stand.

Our land was created
Shrouded from above
And we crawled as crabs.
The first and second skies
Tell to Māui-motua
To push them high
So the breeze can come in, for it is hot
And bring light to the land
And then we stood up
And walked about proudly.

In Rotuma, Lagi and Otfiti ("heaven" and "earth") were joined together. The male and female principles of heaven and earth, Lagatea and Papatea, were the progenitors of the high god Tangaloa. When Tangaloa was born he rose to a kneeling position and pushed Heaven and Earth apart; he did not rise to his full height, however, because of the distress of his parents who did not want to be completely separated.

In eastern Polynesia, especially among the Maori of New Zealand, cosmogonic origins were more detailed. While Rangi and Papa clung together, they produced offspring; the four great gods Tane, Tangaroa, Tu, and Rongo, known throughout Polynesia, as well as two specialized gods Haumia and Tawhiri. These offspring felt cramped with their dark close quarters and debated if and how they should separate from their father and mother. Except for Tawhiri, who disagreed, each son attempted to separate the parents. Rongo, god of cultivated foods, tried; Tangaroa, god of fish and reptiles, tried; and Tu, god of destruction, tried. Tane, god of the forests, found that he was strong enough but that his arms were too short; so he placed his head against his mother and pushed his father up with his feet. Tawhiri, god of the winds, rose with his father. Upset by Tane's success, Tawhiri sent his own offspring—the four great winds, smaller but more violent winds, clouds of various kinds, and hurricanes—against him. Tawhiri's brothers and their offspring were terrified. Tangaroa's fish offspring plunged deep into the sea, but the reptiles sought safety in the forests of Tane, even though many of Tane's trees were snapped and destroyed. Rongo and Haumia hid themselves in Mother Earth. Only Tu withstood Tawhiri's wrath and finally defeated him. During the long storm Tawhiri's progeny multiplied to include rains of various kinds, mist, and dew. Finally, light increased and the progeny of the other brothers increased. Rangi and Papa have never been reconciled to their separation; and, to this day, Papa's sighs rise to Rangi as mist, and Rangi's tears fall to Papa as dewdrops.

This cosmogonic story explains not only Tawhiri's periodic outbursts, but also the reasons for disagreements among the other brothers. Tangaroa was upset that some of his progeny deserted him for the forests of Tane, and Tu took revenge on his brothers for deserting him in battle against Tawhiri. Tane gives wood for canoes, spears, and fishhooks to the children of Tu in order to destroy the offspring of Tangaroa. The latter, however, overwhelms canoes, land, and trees with his relentless waves. Tu also traps the birds of Tane's forest, enmeshes the children of Tangaroa in fishnets, uproots the children of Haumia and Rongo, consumes all his brothers' offspring as food and controls his brothers with incantations.

Variations of this theme, especially the belief in a primal pair and their existence in a void or darkness (often called *pō*), exist in other eastern Polynesian areas. In some locales, Tangaroa was thought to be the originator of all things in the universe; in others his place was taken by Tane; while in others Tangaroa and Tane together serve this function. In the Society Islands, for example, a great octopus held the sky and earth together in his great arms. Ta'aroa (Tangaroa) existed in the darkness of contemplation, and from this darkness he called the other gods into being. When Ta'aroa shook himself, feathers fell and turned into trees, plantains, and other green plants. Ta'aroa then called the artisans to fashion him into something beautiful—a carved wooden image in most versions. Rua (the Abyss) killed the octopus by conjuring, but it did not release its hold, and, still in darkness, the demigods Ru, Hina, and Māui were born. Ru raised the sky as high as the coral tree, but ruptured himself so that his intestines floated away to become the clouds that usually hang over the island of Bora-Bora. Māui, the trickster, then used wedges to support the sky and went to enlist the help of Tane, who lived in highest heaven. Tane drilled into the sky with a shell until light came through. The arms of the octopus fell away and became the island of Tubuai. Tane then decorated the sky with stars and set the sun and moon on their courses. The fish and sea creatures were given places and duties, and the god Tohu was given the job of painting the beautiful color on the fish and shells of the deep. In Tahiti, Tane was symbolized by a piece of finely braided coconut-fiber sennit, while in the Cook Islands, Tane the artisan was symbolized by beautifully made basalt adzes lashed to carved handles with braided coconut fiber.

In Hawaii, Kāne (Tane) and Kanaloa (Tangaroa) were not usually represented in tangible form. Kāne, the ultimate ancestor of the other gods, was usually associated with the upper atmosphere, while Kanaloa, in paired opposition, was associated with the sea and its creatures. Lono (Rongo) and Kū (Tu) were less distant and abstract and were concerned with agriculture, plants, rain, pigs, peace and war, forests, canoes, houses, and crafts. Many attributes of Lono and Kū were interrelated; they depended on each other both as necessary opposites and as aspects of each other. Various attributes of Lono, Kū, Kāne, and Kanaloa might be considered as separate gods. There were hundreds of these gods, each known by a compound name that coupled the god's name with a specific attribute, such as Kāne-hekili (Kāne of the thunder) or Kūkā'ilimoku (Kū the snatcher of land, that is, the war god).

In addition to the four major gods of eastern Polynesia, other gods were often associated with specific aspects of nature. Sometimes separate gods, such as Haumia and Tawhiri in New Zealand, were given the care of particular natural phenomena, such as uncultivated food and the winds, that were elsewhere part of the domains of the four great gods. Special gods appeared to meet special requirements of different natural environments, as did Pele the goddess of volcanos and Poli'ahu the snow goddess in Hawaii. In short, the four great gods, especially in eastern Polynesia, were usually concerned with the creation of the universe, of most of the elements of nature, of the rest of the gods, and, ultimately, of human beings. Most of these cosmogonic stories begin in the *pō,* or primal darkness, and tell how one of the gods alone (often Tangaroa) or the Sky Father and Earth Mother together created the other gods and, eventually, all their progeny, each of which was a personification of a selected aspect of nature. Each island or island group had a slightly different cast of characters and emphasized different plants, animals, and natural phenomena. Whereas in the Cook Islands the creation of the universe was involved with a coconut shell that was organized in layers with Vari or chaotic mud at the bottom, in Hawaii a gourd and its association with Lono was more important. To maintain a connection with Lono, an *ipu o Lono* ("gourd of Lono") was kept in a sacred area of each household to receive offerings and prayers, which were usually concerned with fertility and protection against sorcery. In other areas a local deity sometimes replaced or elaborated one or more of the four great gods. Thus, in New Zealand the existence of two gods of food, Haumia and Rongo, indicates the importance of uncultivated food to the Maori, which was not the case in other Polynesian areas; and in Hawaii the existence of Pele and Kū, both gods of destruction, suggests a philosophical distinction between destruction by nature and destruction by humans.

Origin of the Islands and People. In western Polynesian creation myths more emphasis was given to the creation, genealogies, and interrelationships of human beings than to the creation, genealogies, and interrelationships of the gods from whom human beings descended. In Tonga, for example, the god Tangaloa 'Eitumatupu'a climbed down from the sky on a great casuarina tree and cohabited with a woman of the earlier Tongan population, which had descended from a worm. The child of this union was 'Aho'eitu. When 'Aho'eitu was old enough he went to the sky to visit his father and returned with several celestial inhabitants who became his ceremonial attendants. Half man and half god, 'Aho'eitu became the first Tu'i Tonga ("paramount chief"). The succeeding Tu'i Tonga descended from 'Aho'eitu and were born of the daughters of the highest chiefs in the land. Several Tu'i Tonga were assassinated, and in about the fifteenth century the incumbent twenty-fourth Tu'i Tonga appointed his younger brother as a subsidiary ruler, the Tu'i Ha'a Takalaua. The Tu'i Ha'a Takalaua was given only temporal power, while the Tu'i Tonga retained for himself high rank and spiritual status. The sixth Tu'i Ha'a Takalaua created a similar split in authority, reserving for himself high rank and giving to one of his sons the title of Tu'i Kanokupolu and the tasks of ruling and collecting tribute. All three lines descended from 'Aho'eitu and were further linked by marriage. The origins of Tangaloa, the sky, the island of Tonga, or the other elements of nature, however, are often not detailed. The gods were less important than was the way that the chiefs traced their genealogies to them. Tangaloa (Tangaroa) and Māui were the important male gods in western Polynesia, while the female god Hikule'o was in charge of Pulotu, the underworld (a concept undeveloped in eastern Polynesia). Tangaloa was often considered the sole creator god, whose universe was the sky and a vast expanse of ocean. According to a Samoan story, Tangaloa threw a rock into the ocean, and it became Manu'a, one of the Samoan group of islands. Tonga was said to have been created when the gods threw down chips of wood from their workshops. In Tonga, the first occupants were worms, a female of which cohabited with Tangaloa to start the first ruling dynasty. Samoans believed Samoa had been created when Tangaloa threw down a rock as a place for his bird-daughter to live. He also sent vines to the island; the vines developed maggots, which in turn generated humans. Rather than being thrown down from the sky, or sometimes in addition to this type of creation, a widespread mythic theme of island origin recounts that the islands were fished up from the sea bottom by Māui or, occasionally, by Tangaloa or Tiki. In some areas of eastern Polynesia humans originated when the god Tane, or a separate character in the creation story, Tiki (Ti'i), impregnated a female form that had been shaped by the god from sand and that held the essence of the female principle, Mother Earth. In other areas Tangaloa created Ti'i, the first man, for Hina, who was thought of as a goddess in some locales and as the first woman in others. In Tahiti the chiefs traced their genealogies to Ti'i and Hina. Along with the creation of human life came the creation of death. According to the Maori, Hina-titama, an offspring of Tane and Hina the Earth-Formed, mated with her father and had several children. Her realization that this union was incestuous drove her to the underworld; from there she snared their children one by one. This was the origin of death. The origin of human life is usually associated with the Sky Father and the male principle, while the origin of death is usually associated with the female principle. In some areas there are quite different accounts of the origins of humankind. On Easter Island the most important god was the local deity Makemake, who was not only the patron of the rituals of the bird cult but was also the creator of humans. In Tuvalu the male parent was the sun, the female parent a stone, altering the more generalized sky and earth into more specific aspects of the upper and lower atmospheres. Although the origin of individual plants or animals may not be specified, items of local importance are often given stories of their own. For example, in Tahiti one of the lovers of the demigoddess Hina was an eel named Tuna from whom the coconut plant originated after he was buried. Hina, who embodies the essence of femininity, is also credited with the origin of the banyan tree, which grew on earth after she dropped a branch of such a tree from her abode in the moon. Similarly, in Tonga *kava* and sugarcane originated from the head and body of a dead child who was killed as food for a visiting high chief. This child was not eaten but buried, and the two plants grew from her grave. A rat that had eaten from the *kava* plant staggered but regained its balance after eating from the sugarcane plant. This was the origin of the ritual drinking of *kava* and of the ritual eating of sugarcane that accompanies *kava*-drinking. In Hawaii an extremely complicated mythology reveals the intimate relationships among gods, humans, and elements of the natural environment. The order of the islands' origins is given in great detail—starting in the east with the island of Hawaii, moving west through the major islands of the Hawaiian chain, and ending at Niihau (an afterbirth), Lehua, Kaula, and finally the low reef islands. The parents of the islands were primarily Wakea (Sky Father) with Papa (Earth Mother). Wakea's secondary mates were Kaula and Hina while Papa's secondary mate was Lua. In addition, the Kumulipo chant sets out the origin and order of all plants and animals in the universe as well as the origin of gods and men. Kane and Kanaloa were the first gods to be born, La'ila'i was the first woman and Ki'i the first man. Some generations later the goddess Haumea bore children to Kanaloa and then took a husband among men and became the goddess of childbirth. In many forms, nature, gods, and people interacted—not only to create, but also to change and destroy.

MĀUI. The demigod Māui was the trickster who upset the status quo. Maui has been immortalized by Katharine Luomala in her study, *Māui-of-a-Thousand-Tricks* (Honolulu, 1949). Māui's most important deeds included fishing up islands on his magic fishhook (taking the place of Tangaloa in other areas), snaring the sun, and stealing fire from the gods. He also had specialties in the traditions of some areas, such as pushing up the sky in Tonga and Uvéa (taking the place of Tane, who often performed this feat in eastern Polynesia), trying to overcome death in New Zealand, and in Tokelau taking the place of the original male parent. Māui was often considered a magician, but his most admired characteristic was trickery against authority. In classic tales Māui usually does not create, for this was the domain of the gods. Instead, as half man and half god, he transformed what had already been created into something useful to man. Thus, he slowed down the sun, which previously had raced across the sky, so that days would be long enough to beat out and dry bark cloth, grow and prepare food, and build temples to the gods. Māui stole conveniences of the gods (such as fire to cook food) for the comfort of men. Māui was the archetypal culture hero who could deal with both gods and humans. The mythic themes of Polynesian religion are complex social metaphors that helped to justify rank and social stratification to a people concerned with genealogy, respect and disrespect, and aspects of nature that needed to be explained and appeased. The gods and mythical heros were blamed for, and became part of, human vanity. Polynesian religion was an outgrowth of Polynesian social structure that focused on genealogical connections and the integration of the gods with nature and the human condition.

SEE ALSO Māui; Oceanic Religions, overview article.

BIBLIOGRAPHY

Bibliographies on Polynesian mythology are very extensive, but they usually focus on specific islands or island groups. The best bibliography, of more than three hundred entries, can be found in Katharine Luomala's *Māui-of-a-Thousand-Tricks: His Oceanic and European Biographers* (Honolulu, 1949). As sources of first resort, the following works are recommended.

Alpers, Anthony. *Legends of the South Sea.* London, 1970.

Beckwith, Martha Warren. *Hawaiian Mythology* (1940). Reprint, Honolulu, 1970.

Best, Elsdon. *Maori Religion and Mythology.* Wellington, New Zealand, 1924.

Burrows, Edwin G. *Western Polynesia: A Study in Cultural Differentiation.* Göteberg, 1938.

Craig, Robert D. *Dictionary of Polynesian Mythology.* New York, 1989.

Dixon, Roland B. *The Mythology of All Races,* vol. 9, *Oceanic* (1916). Reprint, New York, 1964.

Emory, Kenneth P. "Tuamotuan Concepts of Creation." *Journal of the Polynesian Society* 49 (1940): 69–136.

Firth, Raymond. *Rank and Religion in Tikopia: A Study of Polynesian Paganism and Conversion to Christianity.* London, 1970.

Fornander, Abraham. *Fornander Collection of Hawaiian Antiquities and Folklore.* 3 vols. Bishop Museum Memoirs, vols. 4–6. Honolulu, 1916–1920.

Gifford, Edward W., comp. *Tongan Myths and Tales.* Honolulu, 1924.

Grey, George. *Polynesian Mythology and Ancient Traditional History of the New Zealanders.* London, 1922.

Luomala, Katharine. "Polynesian Mythology." In *Encyclopedia of Literature,* edited by Joseph T. Shipley. New York, 1946.

Luomala, Katherine. *Māui-of-a-Thousand-Tricks.* Honolulu, 1949.

Luomala, Katharine. *Voices on the Wind: Polynesian Myths and Chants.* Honolulu, 1955.

Poignant, Roslyn. *Oceanic Mythology: The Myths of Polynesia, Micronesia, Melanesia, Australia.* London, 1967.

Subramani. *South Pacific Literature: From Myth to Fabulation.* Suva, 1985.

ADRIENNE L. KAEPPLER (1987 AND 2005)

POLYTHEISM.

The term polytheism, derived from the Greek *polus* ("many") and *theos* ("god") and hence denoting "recognition and worship of many gods," is used mainly in contrast with *monotheism,* denoting "belief in one god." The latter concept is considered by theological apologists and nineteenth-century cultural evolutionists alike as a "higher" form of belief, to be superseded (at best) by modern, scientific atheism. To understand polytheism, one must look at the base component *theism,* meaning the belief in "gods" as distinct from other types of powerful or supernatural beings (ghosts, ancestor spirits, etc.). Unfortunately, no discussion of polytheism can ignore the connotations implied by the Greek word *theos,* especially as it is the Greek term that has influenced most Western discourse on the subject. Clearly Japanese *kami* (whose number according to Shintō tradition is 800,000) and Greek *theos* are not quite the same; nevertheless this article shall, at the risk of oversimplification, stay with traditional Western usage.

Historical (or rather, pseudo-historical) theories concerning the origin of polytheism were closely related to the evolutionist views that characterized early *Religionswissenschaft.* Primitive humanity was aware of its dependence on a variety of powers that were often conceived as individual nonmaterial ("spiritual") beings—for instance, the spirits of departed humans, especially ancestors—or as supernatural entities. One of the many modes of contact with this world of spirits was shamanism, a level of primitive beliefs and ritual behavior that has also been referred to as "polydaemonism." Sometimes more important figures emerge in these systems, especially in connection with accounts of the origins and beginnings of all things (first ancestors, culture heroes, originator gods), but such figures are not always central in the actual cultic life of the community. Even originator gods often remove themselves subsequently to the highest heavens and remain inactive. Although no longer generally accepted, this account of things has been reproduced here because for some time scholars have viewed it as a kind of initial stage in religious development, the last and final stage being monotheism. In this view, animism and polydaemonism become polytheism, and the latter evolves (how and why, nobody seems to know) into monotheism.

An opposing view known as the "Ur-monotheism school" (associated with Wilhelm Schmidt and the so-called Vienna School that defended also the *Kulturkreiselehre*) asserted that monotheism was the original creed of humankind and that polydaemonism and polytheism developed as humans degenerated from a more innocent state. The element of theological apologetic in this theory is evident (though by itself that fact constitutes no argument either for or against its validity). In fact, it is an anthropological refurbishing of the traditional theological doctrine that Adam and his descendants were obviously monotheists, but that at some time between Adam and Noah, and then again after Noah, a process of corruption set in. The medieval Jewish version of this process is spelled out in detail by Moses Maimonides (Mosheh ben Maimon). Polytheistic humanity was then reintroduced to monotheism by divine revelation or by more mature philosophical reflection. There is an element of truth in the latter assertion, for although there is no evidence whatsoever of an evolution from polytheism to monotheism, it seems true to say that monotheism appears either as a sudden, revolutionary development (for example, no really polytheistic stage can be demonstrated in ancient Israelite religion) or else as a monistic tendency (as in late Roman antiquity or in certain forms of Indian religion), as a result of which the multiplicity of gods (divine powers or manifestations) are subsumed under one superior, all-embracing principle ("the One," "the All," *brahman,* and so on.).

The Nature of Polytheism. Turning from speculative historical guesswork to the phenomenology or morphology of polytheism, one is struck by the curious fact that polytheism, while it is one of the major and most widespread phenomena in the history of religions, has attracted less than the attention it deserves. It seems to have fallen, as it were, between the two stools of "primitive religions" and monotheism. Or perhaps one should say three stools, if nontheistic religions such as Buddhism are also taken into account. Like all phenomenological ideal types (to borrow Max Weber's term), polytheism does not exist as a pure type. The historical variety is not easily reducible to a common denominator. Greek polytheism is different from Japanese Shintō, and the latter is different again from Maya religion. Nevertheless some basic and characteristic features are discernible, even though not all of them may be present in each and every case.

Perhaps the most striking fact about polytheism is its appearance in more advanced cultures only. (This may, incidentally, be one of the reasons why the evolutionists saw it as a post-primitive phenomenon.) In most cases, at least for the purposes of this article, the phrase "advanced cultures" means literate cultures (e.g., China, India, the ancient Near East, Greece, and Rome), though polytheism is occasionally also found in nonliterate cultures (e.g., in Mesoamerican and South American pre-Conquest religions, among the Yoruba people of West Africa, or in Polynesia). Usually such cultures also practice a more sophisticated type of agriculture (for example, one in which the plow supersedes the hoe), although, once again, this is not necessarily the case everywhere. In the case of Polynesia it could be argued that the bountiful earth itself produced the surplus that rendered possible the social and cultural background of polytheism (social stratification, division of labor, authority structures, and so forth), which elsewhere depended on more advanced types of food production. "More advanced" cultures are those whose economy in some way provides sufficient surplus to create a certain distance between humankind and nature. Society no longer lives with its nose to the grindstone, as it were. The result is increased division of labor (including bureaucracies and a priesthood), social stratification (including warrior castes, chieftains, royalty), and political structures (cities, city-states, temple establishments, empires). Greek polytheism flourished in city-states; Mesopotamia (Sumer, Assyria, Babylonia) and Egypt were kingdoms and at times empires, and the same holds true of pre-Conquest Mesoamerica and Peru.

The Indo-Aryan and pre-Zoroastrian Iranian religions certainly were not primitive. Similarly, the Yoruba kingdoms of Ọyọ and Ifẹ (present-day Nigeria), for example, clearly represent a high though nonliterate culture, as does early Japan with its *kami* worship, practiced long before the infiltration of Chinese culture and literacy.

The above considerations are not meant to explain or otherwise account for the appearance of polytheism. They merely suggest the cultural and spiritual background against which the emergence of polytheism becomes intelligible. In every religion, society attempts to articulate its understanding of the cosmos and of the powers that govern it, and to structure its relationship with these powers in appropriate symbolic systems. In the societies under discussion here, humankind already faces the cosmos: closely linked to it but no longer inextricably interwoven in it. There is a sense of (at least minimal) distance from nature and even more distance from the powers above that now are "gods," that is, beings that are superhuman, different, powerful (though not omnipotent) and hence beneficent or dangerous—at any rate their goodwill should be secured—and to be worshiped by cultic actions such as sacrifices. These divine beings are personal but not material (although they can assume bodily shape temporarily and for specific reasons); above all, their behavior and motivations are similar to those of humans. Their relevance to human life is due to the fact that, unlike the primitive high gods (originator gods of the *deus otiosus* type), they intervene in human affairs, either on their own initiative or because called upon to do so in prayer, sacrifice, or ritual.

One of the most distinctive characteristics of gods, as compared to human beings, is their immortality. Though not eternal in the abstract, philosophical sense, the gods, as the worshiper knows them, are the "immortals." Herein lies the main distinction, not (as in monotheistic religions) in a fundamental difference of essence that then, on the philosophical level, becomes transcendence. Even when the difference is emphasized, it is not a contrast between creator and creature, but one of levels of power and permanence. The relation is one of bipolarity; humans and the gods, though different, are related. Hesiod (*Works and Days* 108) relates "how the gods and mortal men sprang from one source." Even so, "one is the race of men, one is the race of gods, and [i. e., although] from one mother [i. e., Gaia] do we both derive our breath. Yet a power that is wholly separated parteth us: In the one there is nought, while for the other the brazen heaven endureth as an abode unshaken forever" (Pindar, *Nemean Odes* 6.1–5).

Yet although the gods to whom humanity is related are durable and permanent, this does not mean that they do not have origins or a history. Unlike the biblical God who makes history but himself has no history, let alone a family history, their history is the subject of mythological tales, including accounts of their family relations, love affairs, offspring, and so on. Hence the mythological genealogies, stories of the gods that preceded the ones ruling at present (e.g., Greek Ouranos-Gaia; followed by Kronos, followed by Zeus; or, in later Indian religion, the replacement of originally principal gods like Indra, Varuṇa, and Mitra by Śiva, Viṣṇu, and other deities). These gods are personal (in fact, this personal character is also one of the main features and constitutes one of the main philosophical problems of monotheism), and herein resides their religious significance: They are accessible.

Such a generalization must, of course, be somewhat qualified in view of the phenomenon of "dying and rising" gods such as Adonis, Attis, Osiris, Dumuzi, also in polytheistic myths and rituals.

Most polytheistic religions possess, as has been indicated in the preceding paragraph, a highly developed mythology that is not restricted to theogony and cosmogony though it is often used, or deliberately manipulated, to account for things as they are and to legitimate the cosmic, social, political, and ritual order. But such is not always or necessarily the case. Perhaps the best example of a highly developed polytheism with an elaborate ritual system but almost totally lacking a mythology is ancient Rome. In this respect the contrast with ancient Greece is striking. Yet even when there exists a rich body of mythology, its imagery reaches the present in comparatively late literary elaborations. Thus the mythology of ancient (pre-Buddhist) Japan is accessible only in literary works composed after the absorption of Chinese (i. e., also Buddhist) influences.

Without implying commitment to any simplistic theory about the divine order always and necessarily being a mirror of the human and social order, one cannot deny that the two are correlated. The polytheistic divine world is more differentiated, more structured, and often extremely hierarchized, because the human view of the cosmos is similarly differentiated, structured, and hierarchized. There are many gods because humans experience the world in its variety and manifoldness. Hence there is also specialization among the gods, of a nature that is either local and tribal-ethnic (gods of specific localities, cities, countries, families) or functional (gods of specific arts, gods of illness, cure, fertility, rains, hunting, fishing, etc.). The highly developed Roman sense of order could take things to extremes, and the early Christian fathers in their antipagan polemics made fun of the Roman *indigitamenta,* or invocations of highly specialized gods. Each householder had his *genius;* women had their Junos; children were protected when going in, going out, or performing their natural functions by Educa, Abeone, Potin. In fact, there was a goddess responsible for the toilet and sewage system: Cloacina. (The Roman example illustrates another important principle. Deities can be mythological beings of symbolic immediacy, to be subsequently "interpreted" or rationally allegorized; they can also be the personifications of abstract concepts.)

To cite another example of parallel hierarchy, few divine worlds were as hierarchical as the Chinese; in fact, these realms seem to be exact replicas of the administrative bureaucracy of imperial China. Just as the illustrious departed could be deified by imperial decree, so gods too could be promoted to higher rank. (Japan subsequently adopted this Chinese model, as it did so many others.) As late as the nineteenth century, these imperial promotions were announced in the *Beijing Gazette.*

The possibility of elevation to divine rank of living or departed humans (in the Western world such was the case with Hellenistic kings and Roman emperors) calls for a qualification of an earlier statement that polytheism displays an unbridgeable difference (though not quite as radical as that of monotheism) between humans and gods. For, much as humans can occasionally attain to divinity, the gods can assume human shape (as in the example of the Hindu *avatāras*) or exist in human manifestation (as in the Japanese concept of *ikigami*).

An important corollary of polytheism is that, though the major deities can be very powerful, no god can be omnipotent. Only a monotheistic god, being *monos,* can also be all-powerful. With growing moral differentiation, originally ambivalent gods split into positive (good) and negative (bad, evil, or demonic) divinities. Thus the original Indo-Aryan *asuras* (deities) became, in Vedic and post-Vedic India, demonic antigods, in opposition to the *devas*. The multiplicity of gods of necessity produced a hierarchy of major and minor gods and a pantheon, or overall framework in which they were all combined. The more important gods have names and a distinct personality; others form the *plebs deorum,* a body often indistinguishable from the nameless spirits of animism. Many gods are experienced as real though unidentified, and hence a Roman might invoke the deity *si deus si dea* or distinguish between *dei certi* and *dei incerti* (rather like addressing a prayer "to whom it may concern"). There even is a reference to *aius locutus* "[the god] who has spoken [on a certain occasion, whoever he may be]."

When polytheism is superseded by monotheism, the host of deities is either abolished (theoretically), or bedeviled (i. e., turned into demons), or downgraded to the rank of angels and ministering spirits. This means that an officially monotheistic system can harbor a functional *de facto* polytheism. No doubt for the urban masses in fourth-century Rome, the cult of the Christian martyrs was merely a kind of transformation of the earlier polytheistic cults, and the same is probably still true of much Roman Catholic Christianity, especially in rural areas.

Some scholars consider henotheism (the exclusive worship of one god only without denying the existence of other gods) as an intermediary stage between polytheism and monotheism, the latter being defined as the theoretical recognition of the existence of one god only, all the others being (in the language of the Old Testament) sheer "vanity and nothingness." The terminology seems somewhat artificial (both *hen* and *monos* signify "one" in Greek), but it attempts to express a real distinction. Thus it has been claimed that henotheistic vestiges can still be detected even in the monotheistic Old Testament (e.g., *Exodus* 15:11, "Who is like unto thee among the gods, O Yahveh," or *Micah* 4:5, "For all nations will walk each in the name of its god" while Israel walks in the name of Yahveh, their god for evermore). The fact that the most frequent Old Testament name for God, *Elohim,* is an originally plural form is often mentioned in this connection, but the arguments are doubtful and perhaps influenced by lingering evolutionist patterns of thought. Henotheist tendencies are also evident in Vedic religion and, to a lesser degree, in the *bhakti* ("devotion") directed toward a variety of later Hindu deities.

One problem that cannot be ignored is the disappearance (with a few exceptions) of polytheism as a result of either monotheistic "revolutions" (e.g., ancient Israel, Islam) or unifying tendencies. Indeed, too little scholarly attention has been paid to the strange fact that polytheism has gradually disappeared except in some East Asian religions. In most contemporary philosophical discussions the alternatives considered as available to society seem to be monotheism or atheism; polytheism is treated as an important phenomenon or stage in the history of religions but hardly ever, philosophically or theologically, as a live option.

The quest of an overarching unity (one universe in spite of the multiplicity of forms of existence; one natural law under which all other laws can be subsumed) is clearly one factor that led to a view of the divine as one. By using impersonal language, it is relatively easy to speak of "the divine" in the singular. A personal god is a more difficult matter. But at any rate unifying tendencies are discernible everywhere, even in antiquity. The Greek dramatist Aeschylus speaks of "the one with many names," and the *Ṛgveda* says of the evidently one god that "men call him Indra, Mitra, Varuṇa, Agni." The polytheistic paganism of the late Roman empire was syncretistic in the sense of evincing a tendency to identify the individual gods of the various (Greek, Roman, Oriental, Germanic) cultures. Hence it becomes possible to speak of a "pseudo-polytheism," a religious system that preserves the traditional polytheistic terminology but considers the many gods mere manifestations of what is ultimately one divine principle. This tendency is especially noticeable in many modern types of Neo-Hinduism. For some Hellenistic writers (e.g., Marcus Aurelius) the grammatical distinction between *theos* (singular) and *theoi* (plural) has become practically meaningless.

All monistic—even nontheistic—views on the higher and more sophisticated doctrinal levels notwithstanding, a *de facto* functional polytheism can continue to exist among the masses of devout believers. This is not the place for a psychological and sociological analysis of the role of the cult of saints among many Roman Catholics. In India, no matter what monist or nondualist doctrines are theoretically held, the religious life of the mass of believers is a de facto polytheistic one. The case of Mahāyāna Buddhism is even more striking. On the doctrinal and scholastic level, as well as on the level of higher mystical experience, there may be no god or divine being, and the key terms are emptiness, nothingness, and the like. Yet the ordinary Buddhist (and even the Buddhist monk) relates to the many Buddhas and boddhisattvas that in fact constitute the Buddhist pantheon like a polytheist to his gods.

SEE ALSO Anthropomorphism; Apotheosis; Deus Otiosus; Dying and Rising Gods; Gods and Goddesses; Henotheism; Incarnation.

BIBLIOGRAPHY

There is little, if any, systematic literature on the subject. Discussions of polytheism can be found in articles on monotheism in the older, standard encyclopedias (the *Encyclopaedia of Religion and Ethics,* edited by James Hastings, *Die Religion in Geschichte und Gegenwart,* and so on) as well as in accounts of specific polytheistic religions (for example, Germanic and Celtic; ancient Near Eastern; Greek and Roman; Indian, Chinese, and Japanese; Mesoamerican and South American). Perhaps the first modern discussion of polytheism, in the Western sense, is David Hume's *The Natural History of Religion* (1757), though Hume's account is obviously shaped by eighteenth-century European Enlightenment attitudes. Systematic considerations can be found in Gerardus van der Leeuw's *Religion in Essence and Manifestation,* 2 vols. (1938; Gloucester, Mass., 1967); E. O. James's *The Concept of Deity* (New York, 1950); and Angelo Brelich's "Der Polytheismus," *Numen* 7 (December 1960): 123–136. On the relationship of polytheism to more highly developed political organization (e.g., the Greek polis), see Walter Burkert's "Polis and Polytheism," in his *Greek Religion* (Cambridge, Mass., 1985), pp. 216–275.

R. J. ZWI WERBLOWSKY (1987)

PONTIFEX.

The Latin noun *pontifex,* designating certain Roman high priests, is thought of as deriving from *pons* ("bridge") and *facere* ("to make"). This etymology, held by Varro (*De lingua Latina* 5.83), is accepted by the majority of modern scholars. Yet the discrepancy between this definition of "bridge maker" and the broad extent of the pontifical function has aroused some resistance among scholars both ancient and modern. At the beginning of the first century BCE the *pontifex maximus* Q. Mucius Scaevola (cited by Varro, ibid.) preferred to see in the word *pontifices* a corruption of the word *potifices* (from *posse,* "to be able," and *facere,* "to do," undoubtedly in the sense of "to sacrifice"). Today, there are those who think that *pons* originally meant "path," even "obstacle path," by reason of its likeness to the Vedic *pānthāh.*

Commentators since antiquity have been struck by the contrast between the apparent specialization of the titleholder (Varro referred to the construction and restorations of the bridge of Sublicius by the pontiffs) and the importance of the role. The contrast is transparent in Festus: In one and the same paragraph he points out the attribution to the *pontifex maximus* of the fifth and last rank in the hierarchy of priests, even while defining him as the "judge and arbiter of things divine and human" (Festus, ed. Lindsay, 1913, p. 198 L.). Indeed, the *pontifex maximus* (aided by the pontifical college, which successively numbered three, nine, fifteen, and sixteen members) had become, from simple adviser to the king, the true head of Roman religion. Under the republic, it was he who sat in the Regia, which had become the *domus publica* of the pontifical college. He was the one who named—more precisely, it was said that he "seizes" (*capit;* Gallius, 1.12.15)—the *rex sacrorum* ("king of the sacrifices"), the *flamines,* and the Vestals whenever a vacancy occurred, and he had the right of supervision over all of them. He convoked and presided over the Comitia Calata, the assembly that witnessed the inauguration of the *rex sacrorum* and the *flamines maiores* ("greater priests"). During that same assembly there also took place each month on the nones the proclamation by the *rex* of the month's holidays (*feriae primae menstruae;* Varro, *De lingua Latina* 5.83).

For a long time the pontiffs were the true regulators of time, in that the calendar was not published until 304 BCE, when this was finally done at the instigation of the *aedilis curulis,* G. Flavius (Cicero, *Pro Murena* 25). In their archives the high priests kept all documents concerning the *sacra publica,* the public religion: lists of divinities to invoke (*indigitamenta*); prayer formulas (*carmina*) for the fulfillment of vows, dedications, and consecrations; cultic rules (*leges templorum*); and prescriptions for expiatory sacrifices (*piacula*).

Fundamentally, pontifical activity was carried out on two levels. On the liturgical level the high priests participated actively in public ceremonies, as for instance the anniversaries of temples. (The sacrificial utensils, the knife, *secespita,* and the ax, *sacena,* are among the pontifical symbols; Festus, op. cit., p. 422 L.) On the theological level the high priests provided decisions and responses (*decreta* and *responsa*), which came to constitute the *ius pontificium* ("pontifical law"). The authority acquired by the *pontifex maximus* explains why, following the example of Julius Caesar, Augustus chose to add this dignity to his set of titles in 12 BCE. Thereafter it remained attached to the imperial function.

BIBLIOGRAPHY

Bleicken, Jochen. "Oberpontifex und Pontifikalkollegium." *Hermes* 85 (November 1957): 345–366.

Bouché-Leclercq, Auguste. *Les pontifes de l'ancienne Rome.* Paris, 1871.

Dumézil, Georges. *La religion romaine archaïque.* 2d ed. Paris, 1974. See pages 573–576. This work has been translated from the first edition by Philip Krapp as *Archaic Roman Religion,* 2 vols. (Chicago, 1970).

Hallett, Judith P. "Over Troubled Waters: The Meaning of the Title Pontifex." *Translations and Proceedings of the American Philological Association* 101 (1970): 219–227. A reconciliation of *pons* with the Vedic *pānthāh.*

Rhode, Georg. *Die Kultsatzungen der römischen Pontifices.* Berlin, 1936.

Szemler, G. J. "Pontifex." In *Real-encyclopädie die Altertumwissenschaft,* vol. 15. Munich, 1978.

Wissowa, Georg. *Religion und kultus der Römer.* 2d ed. Munich, 1912. See pages 501–521.

New Sources

Campanile, Enrico. "Sulla preistoria di lat. pontifex." *Studi Classici e Orientali* 32 (1982): 291–297.

Champeaux, Jacqueline. "Pontifes, haruspices et decemvirs. L'espiation des prodiges des 207." *Revue des Études Latines* 74 (1996): 67–91.

Desnier, Jean-Louis. "Les débordements du Fleuve." *Latomus* 57 (1998): 513–522.

Draper, Richard D. *The Role of the Pontifex Maximus and Its Influence in Roman Religion and Politics.* Ann Arbor, 1988.

Dupuis, Xavier. "Pontifes et augures dans les cités d'Afrique: modèle romain et specificités locales." In *Idéologies et valeurs civiques dans le monde romain. Hommages à Claude Lepelley,* ed. by Hervé Ingelbert, pp. 215–219. Paris, 2002.

Seguin, Roger. "Remarques sur les origines des pontifes romains. Pontifex maximus et Rex sacrorum." In *Hommage a Henry Le Bonniec. Res sacrae,* edited by Danielle Porte et Jean Pierre Néraudau, pp. 405–418. Brussels, 1988.

ROBERT SCHILLING (1987)
Translated from French by Paul C. Duggan
Revised Bibliography

POOR CLARES SEE FRANCISCANS; SOUL, *ARTICLE ON* CHRISTIAN CONCEPTS

POPULAR CULTURE.

The study of popular culture brings together three different yet related concerns: culture, the popular, and mass culture. *Culture* is the term used to denote a particular way of life for a specific group of people during a certain period in history. It also references the artifacts, narratives, images, habits, and products that give style and substance to that particular way of life. *Mass culture* is a term that highlights the profit motive that directs the production of certain products made available for commercial sale. It refers to both these mass-produced products and the consumer demand for them that justifies their widespread production and distribution. *The popular* makes reference to "the people," and as such there are in some discussions overlaps between "folk" and "popular" culture. What usually distinguishes the two in the common use of these terms is that whereas "folk" culture is presumed to refer to cultural products and practices that emerge from the people, often having a historical connection to a certain racial, ethnic, or geographically located group, popular culture usually refers to those commercially produced items specifically associated with leisure, the mass media, and lifestyle choices. Whereas there is therefore a great deal of overlap between mass and popular culture, the latter retains its populist impulse and thus tends to be less pejorative in tone than references to mass culture. In this sense elements of popular culture are presumed to be popular in that they are well liked by many people and they hold special meaning for certain groups of consumers at certain points in history.

Items of popular culture become important markers for identity construction in the context of a society increasingly defined by differentiated lifestyle segments or taste cultures. As such popular culture includes elements produced for consumption: (1) by the mass media industries, including products such as reading materials, music, visual images, photos, film, television, advertising, video games, celebrity culture, professional sports, talk radio, comics, and the World Wide Web; (2) by artistic and creative realms, such as live and performance theater, art, musical arrangements and performances, and museum installations designed for popular consumption; and (3) by manufacturers and other players within global capitalism who seek to link certain taste cultures with commercially available products. This latter category includes a seemingly endless variety of goods, including modes of transportation, fashion, toys, sporting goods, and even food—in short, anything that can be successfully packaged for consumers in response to their desire for a means to both identify with some people, ideas, or movements and to distinguish themselves from others.

The phrase popular culture first came into use in the English language in the early nineteenth century, when for the first time it was possible to manufacture and widely distribute cultural products with relative ease and speed. Prior to the emergence of a capitalist market economy with industrialization, the popular was a term with legal and political meaning that derived from the Latin *popularis,* or "belonging to the people." The term was used as a way to draw distinctions between the views of "the people" and those who wielded power over them. In the past therefore the term popular culture was used to reference the folk traditions created and maintained by the people outside of the purview of cultural authorities and away from the demands of labor. The term is still used in this way among historians who examine practices and products that were in existence prior to a commercially dominated marketplace.

By the late nineteenth century, however, the term popular culture had come to have a rather specific meaning in relation to presumed distinctions between the elite and the people that echoed presumed distinctions between superior and inferior culture, between the artistic and the vulgar, or between the sophisticated and the banal. These distinctions gained political importance as the industrial era progressed.

THEORY, CRITICISM, AND THE STUDY OF POPULAR CULTURE. As the working class that staffed the industrial landscape continued to grow in the late nineteenth century, concerns about both the influx of people in urban areas and the popular culture they favored came to be closely entwined. The bourgeoisie in industrialized Europe tended to view the shared artifacts of working-class culture as evidence of both their unity and their inferiority. Fearing an uprising similar to that of the French Revolution, early criticism of popular culture, known in the twenty-first century as the "culture and civilization" tradition, linked the growth of what critics viewed as inferior popular culture with concerns over the weakening of a social order that had been based on power and privilege. This tradition had its beginnings in the writings of Matthew Arnold. In his book *Culture and Anarchy* (1882), Arnold contrasted "culture" (now "high culture") with what he viewed as the anarchic and disruptive nature of working-class or popular culture.

Arnold believed that much of the problem of his generation lay in the emergent working class and its seeming refusal to adopt a position of subordination and deference to the elite. Part of the problem, in Arnold's view, was illustrated in the refusal of the working class to adhere to the suggestions of the elite in terms of which elements of "culture" to consume. This presumed problem was echoed in the writings and sermons of ministers and other religious leaders, who were particularly animated in their concerns about fiction, as will be discussed in a subsequent section.

The "culture and civilization" tradition of popular cultural critiques found renewed expression in the writings of F. R. Leavis and Q. D. Leavis, who began writing about popular culture in the 1930s in England. Believing that popular culture provided a dangerous distraction to responsible participation in democracy, they advocated that public schools engage in education about the ill effects of popular culture on young people. The Leavises promoted the idea of a mythic "golden age" of England's rural past, in which they believed a "common culture" (or "folk" culture) had flourished. Their many treatises aimed to keep the expansion of popular culture's influence under control so as to maintain what they believed were the truly valuable aspects of England's cultural tradition.

A similar strand of thought has long been a part of U.S. approaches to popular culture. In 1957 Bernard Rosenberg and David Manning White published *Mass Culture: The Popular Arts in America,* a collection of essays that bemoaned the supposed dehumanizing impact of popular culture. Other popular culture critics, such as Dwight Macdonald (who contributed to the Rosenberg and White volume) and later Daniel Boorstin, Stuart Ewen, and Neil Postman, voiced similar concerns about popular culture's ill effects on society. In the shadow of the cold war, the contributors to the Rosenberg and White volume feared that a passive audience in the sway of popular culture could be easily brought under the influence of a totalitarian government.

A fear of totalitarianism animated the writings of scholars such as Theodor Adorno, Max Horkheimer, Leo Lowenthal, and Herbert Marcuse of the Frankfurt school as well, although their intellectual roots were in Marxism rather than in the Romanticism that often informed the nostalgia-tinged desire for a culture untrammeled by popular culture. Expatriates from Adolf Hitler's Germany, the scholars in the Frankfurt school feared the manipulative potential of popular culture through the workings of what they called the "culture industries." Bringing to their work a perspective informed by Hegelian philosophy, they articulated a critique of popular culture known as critical theory. Although often dismissed as overly pessimistic in that these scholars saw little potential for change in the relations between the privileged and the disadvantaged in society, the critical school inaugurated several important streams of thought regarding popular culture. Particularly influential have been the ideas of the critical theorist Walter Benjamin, whose attention to both the mass production and ideological role of images in contemporary society has been influential in debates of art, politics, and postmodernism. Equally important, the critical school spawned the scholarly tradition of cultural imperialism, which came to prominence in the 1970s as it explored the flow of mass media across transnational borders.

Critiques of popular culture that grew out of cultural imperialism tended to assume a central role for the media in the creation of popular culture. Similar to their predecessors in the critical school, popular culture was approached methodologically through an analysis of political and economic structures, with specific attention to the relations among governments, policy makers, and development efforts as they played out in relation to media. The theory was articulated among Latin American scholars of media and popular culture, such as Antonio Pasquali, Luis Ramiro Beltran, Fernandez Reyes Matta, and Mario Kaplun. These scholars, as well as Herb Schiller in the United States and Dallas Smythe in Canada, were concerned about the ways multinational media corporations were, through the organization of profit and commerce, able to dominate the development of media and by extension popular culture in smaller and less-wealthy nations.

By the 1980s, however, a new school of thought regarding popular culture had taken root in the United States and Europe. There were several reasons for the emergence of a critique that challenged the "high culture–low culture" and cultural imperialist assumptions of the time. In the mid-1960s "pop art" had called into question the very definition of art and high culture, foregrounding meanings made by the viewer of art rather than by the creator or the art critic. A similar revolution had begun with the emergence of reader-response theory in literary criticism, as theorists posited that what made for "classic" texts were assumptions often based in race, gender, and economic privilege and that literary criticism would benefit from an examination of meanings readers made of differing texts. With the advent of pop art and reader-response theory, along with the rising prominence of feminism, black, and cross-cultural perspectives and the emergence of social analysis informed by cultural anthropology, the cultural studies approach to popular culture coalesced in Great Britain, Australia, the United States, and Latin America.

Much of the early scholarship in cultural studies approaches to popular culture was motivated by a desire to demonstrate that audiences were not passive consumers of the products produced for them by the culture industries. Drawing upon the earlier scholarship of British cultural theorists, notably Raymond Williams, cultural studies scholars such as Stuart Hall, David Morley, Charlotte Brundsen, John Fiske, Ien Ang, Meghan Morris, Jesus Martin-Barbero, Nestor Garcia Canclini, Lawrence Grossberg, and a host of others set out to demonstrate that the reception of popular culture was much less predictable than previously thought. Pointing to such factors as the vast numbers of heavily promoted popular cultural artifacts that failed to find a positive reception in the marketplace, they argued that popular cultural artifacts must meet the emotional needs of their audiences in order to succeed in the cultural economy. Methodologies differed, although many embraced textual criticism, semiotics, audience reception research, and cultural history. In the increased recognition of the need for multiple voices contributing to analysis, feminists in the United States and Europe looked at how particular popular cultural artifacts speak to and in some cases offer symbolic resolution for the real tensions in women's lives, Latin American scholars explored the role of *telenovelas* in the creation of a collective identity that may be at some distance from national identity as it has been defined within a dictatorial government, and Asian scholars explored the intersection of cultural policy and popular cultural creation and consumption.

Within the context of an affluent United States in the 1990s and the rise of interest in postmodern theory, some cultural studies critiques of popular culture tended toward a populist celebration of popular culture. A reinvigoration of neo-Marxism through the emergence of postcolonial perspectives and critiques in anthropological methods, combined with a renewed interest in cultural history, everyday life, and issues of visual representation, have redirected cultural studies toward its central concern with the ways in which specific narratives and representations contribute to maintaining power relations as they are. Multiple methodologies are now applauded in the effort to provide analyses of the nuanced relations between power and agency, creation and consumption, consciousness and control, and individual and society in understanding the relations between popular culture and its audiences.

EARLY POPULAR CULTURE AND RELIGION. Religious popular cultural artifacts have roots in the particular popular religious practices of every culture in the world. By the mid-nineteenth century the industrial market revolution of the United States and northern Europe, and later in Asia, Latin America, and Africa, had resulted in the increased availability of religious products in various forms. Some popular cultural items had distinct roles to play in relation to practices of piety that were embraced at the time. In the United States and in Europe popular art for the home and church featured biblical scenes as well as Christ's visage along with mass-produced statues of saints, angels, Mary, and Jesus and of course the family Bible. In China, although the nineteenth-century elite viewed Daoist practices as debased "folk" traditions, religious popular cultural practices endured through ritual theater, music, incense, chanting, and dance, all of which were designed to attract the attention of the gods and to communicate to them the human needs they were asked to address. Analyses of festivals and celebrations of China as well as those related to Hindu deities point to the difficulties of distinguishing between popular religion and popular culture, as it is impossible to consider these events apart from the locations in which they are held.

There is increasing evidence that items related to religious practices in other parts of the world were influenced by the colonial encounters of the nineteenth century. With the awareness of colonial British attitudes toward feminine bodies and modesty, for example, saris worn by women for ceremonial and religious festivals (as well as for daily wear) became longer in the nineteenth century, an influence found in styles of dress in India, Bangladesh, Pakistan, Indonesia, and Sri Lanka among other places. In Nepal a change in traditional Buddhist meditation paintings also reflected this encounter, as the Rajesthani style gave way to European-style portraiture. Scholars of nineteenth-century Islamic, Hindu, and Buddhist popular and "high" art similarly contend that it is virtually impossible to understand religious art and popular religious artifacts of the period without taking the colonial encounter into consideration.

In the early-twentieth-century Victorian society of the United States and the United Kingdom, sentimentalized and domesticized Christian art and objects became popular decor items among the well-heeled and middlebrow alike, making piety but one reason to own such products. Tea was served from tea sets depicting scenes from the Bible, and angel statuary and artwork decorated walls and furniture. By the early twentieth century people who embarked on leisurely travel purchased and sent home postcards embossed with biblical figures and scriptural messages. Each of these signaled an identification with Christianity but also with a distinctive worldview that underscored elite and middlebrow tastes. Not surprisingly therefore many of these products were made available to consumers not through official religious sources but through mail-order catalogs and department stores.

A significant increase in the rates of literacy among the general population at this time meant that commercial publishing expanded as well, making available new genres of reading materials, notably those written specifically for entertainment purposes. Fiction quickly became an immensely popular commodity, illustrated in the often-told story of how Charles Dickens was mobbed by fans when he toured the United States in 1848. Many religious leaders were skeptical, believing that practices such as fiction reading could rouse inappropriate passions and distract from a moral, faith-centered life.

Their skepticism about fiction did not prevent some religious leaders from seeking to harness what they believed to be the powers of the new medium, however. Some saw in the nascent publishing industry the opportunity to further their cause for Christian witness and education. With the rise of wood engraving, lithography, and later photography, religious leaders employed mass-produced images both for advertising and for didactic purposes. These visionaries produced some of the earliest best-selling printed popular cultural items in the form of devotional materials, magazines of missionary societies, readers for Christian schools, and fictional novels that purportedly advanced Christian moral messages. Members of evangelical voluntary societies, who in the mid-nineteenth century traveled from town to town distributing literature such as the *Family Christian Almanac* or other materials from the American Tract Society and the American Sunday School Union, offered many people in the United States their first exposure to modern mass media and its popular cultural artifacts.

Fiction writers of the late nineteenth century and early twentieth century often relied upon religious themes for inspiration as well yet produced less didactically oriented materials for commercial consumption, forming an enduring intersection of popular culture and religion in Western cultures and beyond. Louisa May Alcott's *Little Women* (1868) emphasized compassion and even Christian pity for the disadvantaged, whereas the novelist L. Frank Baum wrote *The Wonderful Wizard of Oz* (1900) as a means of reinforcing the importance of inner resources, such as courage and love, considered of spiritual significance among the Theosophical Society of which he was a part.

TWENTIETH-CENTURY POPULAR CULTURE AND RELIGION. "Christian kitsch," a derogatory term used to refer to sentimental material cultural products, is generally believed to have appeared less frequently among elite households in the United States and Europe after the decline of Victorian styles in the 1930s. Yet popular culture of the middlebrow and of other taste cultures continues to incorporate religious references within it. Precious Moments figurines, cross necklaces and angel lapel pins, Bible covers (or "cozies"), posters with God's "footprints," *santos* and votive candles, dashboard statues of the Madonna, items purchased in relation to religious pilgrimages, as well as the more ubiquitous bumper stickers, T-shirts, hats, and key chains with a variety of messages all comprise some of the materials that can be purchased to signify identification with religion in its various forms. Elite culture in the United States and Europe, rather than being devoid of religious popular cultural items, prefers the esoteric and Eastern, as found in such items as small indoor fountains, crystals, yoga mats and accoutrements, and African, Asian, and Latin American religious artwork. Research on the contemporary religious popular cultures of Judaism, Islam, Hinduism, Buddhism, Daoism, and other traditions has much to contribute to understandings of how these religions have been encoded and commodified in the realm of items for sale in various contexts around the world. Existing work suggests that contemporary religious festivals and material objects associated with them extend an association with various religious, racial-ethnic, and taste cultures.

Throughout the twentieth century U.S. filmmakers incorporated religious themes and imagery into their stories, looking to sources such as the German passion play at Oberammergau to produce religiously themed epics. Many early films centered on Christ's life and death, such as Sidney Olcock's *From the Manger to the Cross* (1912) and Cecil B. DeMille's epic *The King of Kings* (1927). The pattern of borrowing from religious stories continued in the 1940s and 1950s. Films such as *Samson and Delilah, David and Bathsheba, Quo Vadis?, The Robe,* and *The Ten Commandments* were successful both at the box office and with critics. The religious epic *Ben-Hur* set an unsurpassed record of receiving eleven Academy Awards. The 1960s and 1970s saw the successful return of Jesus films with the 1961 remake of *King of Kings, The Gospel according to Matthew, The Greatest Story Ever Told, Godspell, Jesus Christ Superstar,* and *Jesus of Nazareth.* New genres such as satire and the art film influenced the production of religiously themed films of the 1980s and 1990s, such as *Monty Python's Life of Brian, Jesus of Montreal,* and *The Last Temptation of Christ.* Mel Gibson's widely publicized film *The Passion* (2004) reinvigorated the genre of biblical epic at the beginning of the twenty-first century. Various television interests have retained the broadcast rights for these films over the years, thus domesticating them from large-screen spectacle to small-screen rituals, airing frequently in conjunction with the U.S. holiday calendar.

Many less-celebrated films and television programs of the twentieth century have referenced Christianity in more popular ways through themes and characters such as angels, heaven and hell, and "the Big Guy upstairs." Stateside audiences during World War II frequented *A Guy Named Joe, The Bishop's Wife,* and *Carousel,* each of which featured a person who came from the realm beyond to provide heavenly assistance to those on earth. The guardian angel theme gained renewed interest near the close of the millennium. Film audiences of the 1990s saw *Always* and *The Preacher's Wife* (both remakes of World War II films) as well as *Michael, City of Angels,* and the satiric *Dogma,* while the CBS television program *Touched by an Angel* demonstrated the small-screen appeal of angelic helpers and haloed backlight. In the early years of the new millennium the popular CBS drama *Joan of Arcadia* posited a God who appeared in varying forms to a typically nonreligious teenage girl, while PAX television audiences enjoyed *It's a Miracle!* and even *Pet Psychic.* Before that spate of films and television programs, *Oh, God!* had garnered box office success in the 1970s, and the Catholic Church had been dubiously featured in relation to demon possession and devils in such horror films as *Rosemary's Baby, The Exorcist,* and *The Omen.*

The link of religion's dark side and horror remained throughout the 1980s and 1990s, with such entries as *Stigmata, Priest, Seven, The Devil's Advocate,* and many others in addition to the ironic references of the popular teen television series *Buffy the Vampire Slayer, Angel,* and *Charmed.* The increase in cultural and religious pluralism in the latter part of the twentieth century was reflected in films, as reincarnation was popularly depicted in Hollywood films in the 1970s, 1980s, and 1990s as well as in such entries as *Heaven Can Wait, All of Me, Switch, Chances Are, Made in Heaven,* and *Hearts and Souls.*

While these and other films were popular at the box office, religiously themed popular books remained on the best-seller list throughout the twentieth century. Charles Sheldon's *In His Steps;* Ralph Connor's (Charles Gordon) *Black Rock;* and Harold Bell Wright's *The Shepherd of the Hills* and *The Calling of Dan Matthews* were widely read and indeed outsold almost every other book in the period before World War I. The 1965 publication of *The Gospel according to Peanuts* sold ten million copies and served as a prototype for a series of popular books that emerged nearly four decades later, including *The Gospel according to Harry Potter* (2002), *The Gospel according to the Simpsons* (2001), *The Gospel according to the Lord of the Rings,* and even *The Gospel according to the Sopranos.* In the 1990s and 2000s books about angels, the Apocalypse, and the Holy Grail topped the best-seller charts, with the fictional *Left Behind* thriller series, penned by the fundamentalist writers Tim LaHaye and Jerry Jenkins, and less didactically motivated books such as the thriller *The Da Vinci Code* (2003) by Dan Brown and *The Five People You Meet in Heaven* (2003) by Mitch Albom. Meanwhile the Bible remained a best seller, including the fashion magazine format New Testament edition aimed at teenage girls, titled *Revolve.*

CONCLUSION. Religious groups of all backgrounds have long held what seem to be contradictory views on popular culture. On the one hand, they have been wary of entertainment, believing that it can rouse inappropriate passions and distract people from leading a moral, God-centered or ritually organized life. Yet on the other hand, throughout their history religious leaders, especially those within Christianity, have sought to harness the power of entertainment in their efforts to introduce their beliefs to nonbelievers. The twentieth-century development of the dramatic television and film industries in the United States provided new avenues for proselytization efforts while enlarging the reasons for concern. In the United States and Europe religious leaders continue to worry about popular culture's ill effects on morality and consumption practices, whereas religious leaders elsewhere in the world express grave concerns about the influence of U.S. culture's secular and materialistic representations. Despite the varied viewpoints on religion and popular culture, a revolution in the relationship between popular culture and religious leadership was begun in the earliest part of the nineteenth century and continues to play out.

The twentieth century ushered in an era of unprecedented popular culture materials, not only in written form but in oral and visual media as well. The sheer quantity of materials that have entered the commercial marketplace has made it virtually impossible to ignore the fact that popular culture and popular religiosity are now forever entwined. Religion has found a solid footing in commodified popular culture.

SEE ALSO Art and Religion; Popular Religion; Visual Culture and Religion.

BIBLIOGRAPHY

Arnold, Matthew. *Culture and Anarchy.* New York, 1882.

Clark, Lynn Schofield. *From Angels to Aliens: Teenagers, the Media, and the Supernatural.* New York, 2003.

Danto, Arthur C. *After the End of Art: Contemporary Art and the Pale of History.* Princeton, N.J., 1997.

Journal of Religion and Popular Culture. Available at: http://www.usask.ca/relst/jrpc/.

Lippy, Charles H. *Being Religious, American Style: A History of Popular Religiosity in the United States.* Westport, Conn., 1994.

McDannell, Colleen. *Material Christianity: Religion and Popular Culture in America.* New Haven, Conn., 1995.

Morgan, David. *Protestants and Pictures: Religion, Visual Culture, and the Age of American Mass Production.* New York, 1999.

Rosenberg, Bernard, and David Manning White. *Mass Culture: The Popular Arts in America.* Glencoe, Ill., 1957.

Schiller, Herbert. *Communication and Cultural Domination.* White Plains, N.Y., 1976.

Storey, John. *An Introductory Guide to Cultural Theory and Popular Culture.* Athens, Ga., 1993.

Williams, Raymond. *Keywords: A Vocabulary of Culture and Society.* London, 1976.

Zelizer, Barbie. "Popular Communication in the Contemporary Age." *Communication Yearbook* 24 (2000): 297–316.

LYNN SCHOFIELD CLARK (2005)

POPULAR RELIGION.

Every society exhibits divisions and segmentations based upon the classification of its members and their activities, functions, and relationships (e.g., sex, work, knowledge, etc.). However, it was long a universally common assumption that the meaning of any institution within the society, or the meaning of the society as a whole, was the privileged province of the upper, or elite, levels of the society. Indeed, the idea that social meaning could be gained from any other level, especially the lower levels of the social structure, is a relatively new notion. The setting forth of the notion that a positive and necessary knowledge of society could be gained from its lower levels defined this strata as a locus of interpretation, meaning, and value.

The idea that the positive meaning of a society is represented by the "common people," "the folk," or the peasants may be seen as an expression of "cultural primitivism," the dissatisfaction of the civilized with the quality and style of civilization and the expression of a desire to return for orientation to the archaic roots of the culture. This "discovery of the people," to use Peter Burke's apt phrase, began in the late eighteenth and early nineteenth centuries in Europe. The philosophical justification for this orientation can be seen in the writings of Giovanni Battista Vico (1668–1744) and Johann Gottfried Herder (1744–1803). Probably more than any others, these two thinkers represented new theoretical approaches to the nature of history, religion, and society. They distinguished the notions of the *"populari"* and "the *volk*" as the basis for an alternate and new meaning of humanism apart from the rationalizing and civilizing processes set in motion by the European Enlightenment.

The discovery of two new and different forms of societal orders—one outside Europe (the so-called primitives), the other internal to European cultures (the peasants and the folk)—was prompted, in fact, by a search for origins. The search was in some senses antithetical, and in other senses supplementary, to the meaning of the origins of the West in the biblical and Greek cultures. The discovery that the archaic levels of human culture and society had an empirical locus in existing Western cultures became the philosophical, theological, and ideological basis for the legitimation of these new structures of order in modern and contemporary societies.

The notion of popular religion has to do with the discovery of archaic forms, whether within or outside Western cultures. It is at this level that the meaning of popular religion forms a continuum with both primitive religions and peasant and folk cultures in all parts of the world. This continuum is based upon structural similarities defined by the organic nature of all of these types of societies rather than upon historical or genetic causation.

Primitive and peasant-folk societies are, relatively speaking, demographically small. The relationships among people in these societies were thought to be personal in nature. Underlying all modes of communication is an intuitive or empathetic understanding of the ultimate nature and purpose of life.

This is what Herder meant by "the organic mode of life," an idea given methodological precision by the social philosopher Ferdinand Tönnies, who made a typological distinction between communities ordered in terms of *Gemeinschaft* and those expressing a *Gesellschaft* orientation to life and the world. *Gemeinschaft* represents community as organic form; *Gesellschaft* is society as a mechanical aggregate and artifact. A similar distinction is made by the anthropologist Robert Redfield when he describes pre-urban cultures as those in which the moral order predominates over the technical order. The moral order, in this interpretation, is the common understanding of the ultimate nature and purpose of life within the community. The notions of the organic nature of community (*Gemeinschaft*) and the primacy of the moral order lead to different meanings of the religious life in primitive and folk or peasant cultures as compared to societies in urban *Gesellschaft* orientations. Furthermore, the relationship or the distinction between the religious and the cognitive within the two kinds of societies differ.

While it can be said that religion is present when a distinction is made between the sacred and the profane, the locus of this distinction in primitive and folk-peasant cultures is a commonly shared one. There is a unified sense of those objects, actions, and sentiments that are sacred, and those that are profane. The religious and the moral orders tend to be synonymous; thus, the expression of religious faith on the ordinary and extraordinary levels of these cultures form a continuum. The extraordinary expressions are those that commemorate important punctuations of the temporal and social cycles (e.g., a new year, the harvest and first fruits, birth, marriage, and death). The ordinary modes are expressed in the customs, traditions, and mundane activities that maintain and sustain the culture on a daily basis.

One of the goals of the early studies of folk, peasant, and popular cultures was to come to an understanding of the qualitative meaning of religion in human cultures of this kind. Attention was focused on the meaning of custom and tradition, on the one hand, and upon the qualitative meaning and mode of transmission of the traditional values in cultures that were not predominantly literate.

The two early innovators, Herder and, especially, Vico, had already emphasized the modes and genres of language of the nonliterate. Vico based his entire philosophical corpus on the origin and development of language, or, to be more exact, of rhetoric. By the term *rhetoric* Vico made reference to the manner in which language is produced as a mode of constituting bonds between human beings, the world, and other beings outside the community. Closely related to Herder's philosophy of culture and history is the work of the Grimm brothers in their philological studies of the Germanic languages. Their collection of fairy tales, *Märchen,* and folktales represents the beginning of serious scholarly study of oral traditions. In the work of the Grimms, the first articulation of the relationship between genres of oral literature and modes of transmission are raised. This relationship is important, for, given the presupposed organic form of nonliterate societies, the genres of transmission of ultimate meaning, whether ordinary or extraordinary, defined a locus of the religious. The romantic notion (present in Herder and in the theologians Friedrich Schleiermacher and Paul Tillich), namely, that religion is the ultimate ground and substance of culture, underlies the importance given to transmission, manifestation, and expression of this form of culture as religion. Religion is thus understood to be pervasive in society and culture, finding its expression not only in religious institutions, but in all the dimensions of cultural life.

The genres of the folktale, folk song, art, and myth became the expressive forms of popular religion. The investigation of poetic meaning and wisdom, and of metaphorical, symbolic expressions, emerged as sources of the religious sentiment in the traditions of popular religion. The initial "discovery of the people" as a approach to the interpretation of culture and society and as a new form of human value was made under the aegis of intuitive methods within literary studies and from the perspective of a speculative philosophy of history. Once serious scholarly attention was given to the data of the popular, certain ambiguities were noted. The original discovery of the people was based, by and large, on a contrast between the popular and the urban, or the artificiality of the urban mode as a form of civilization. In this sense, the popular represented the archaic and original forms of culture; it was its roots. However, the meaning of the popular could not be limited to the conservative, value-retaining, residual, self-contained unit of a society or culture. One of the basic elements in the meaning of a popular cultural tradition was the mode of its transmission, and it was precisely this element that allowed the meaning of such a tradition to be extended beyond that of the nonliterate strata of society—the rural peasants and the folk.

Varieties and Dimensions. Critical investigations of the meaning of popular culture and religion from the disciplinary orientations of the anthropology and history of religion, and from the sociology of knowledge, revealed a wide variety of the forms of popular religion. From the anthropological and historical perspectives, one is able to delineate and describe the characteristic modes of experience and expression of religion at the various levels of the cultural strata, and to show the dynamics of the interrelationships of the popular forms with other cultural strata. The sociology of knowledge provides an understanding of the genesis, contents, and mode of thought and imagination present in popular religion, and demonstrates how various strata within a social order participate in the values, meanings, and structures of popular religion.

Though scholarly, disciplinary approaches led to a more precise definition of the popular and to a critique of the original meaning of the popular and popular religion, such studies also brought about a proliferation of different meanings and interpretations of popular religion. Of these, the following seven are the most significant.

1. *Popular religion is identical with the organic (usually rural and peasant) form of a society. The religious and moral orders are also identical; in this sense, popular religion is closely related to the meanings of primitive and folk religion.* This is the original meaning of popular religion as the religion of folk and peasant culture. Though the distinction between the folk and peasant religion and the religion of the urban areas is clear-cut in the industrial periods of all cultures, such a distinction does not rest simply on this basis. In the feudal periods of various cultures, this distinction is more pronounced in relationship to certain practices and in the hierarchical structures of the society. Within feudal structures, the upper classes participated in and controlled a form of literacy that was confined within this group. In various cultures, this meant access to an orientation of religious meaning revolving around sacred texts. In China, for example, there appeared Confucian classics; in India, the Sanskritic literary tradition; in Christianity, the Bible, and so on.

The limitation of the modes of literacy suggest that though there are authoritative sacred texts, they are situated in a context that is often dominated by illiteracy and oral traditions. The line of demarcation between the culture of literacy and that of the oral traditions is seldom clear-cut. In many cases, the traditions of literacy embody a great deal of the content, form, and style of the oral traditions of the peasants and the folk. Prior to the universalization of the modes of literacy in many cultures, the prestige of literacy was to be found in the belief in, and regard for, the sacred text, which itself was believed to have a magical, authoritative meaning in addition to the content of its the particular writings. The written words of the god or gods (the authoritative text) resided with, and was under the control of, elites within the culture.

Another characteristic of folk-peasant societies is that they define the lives of their members within the context of a certain ecological niche (agricultural, pastoral, etc.), and the modes and genres of their existence are attached to this context by ties of tradition and sentiment. The group and the ecological structure thus define a continuity of relationships. The sentiment and the moral order of communities of this kind are synonymous with the meaning of their religion. In agricultural peasant and folk cultures, the rhythms of the agricultural seasons are woven into the patterns of human relationships and sociability. The symbols and archetypes of religion are expressions of the alternation and integration of the human community, the techniques of production, and the reality of the natural world. In most cultures this type of popular religion carries the connotation of religion as *ab origine* and archaic. Robert Redfield has suggested that the folk-peasant mode of life is an enduring structure of human community found in every part of the world. As such it is not only an empirical datum of a type of human community, but may also represent an enduring source of religious and moral values.

2. *Popular religion as the religion of the laity in a religious community in contrast to that of the clergy. The clergy is the bearer of a learned tradition usually based upon the prestige of literacy.* Another type of popular religion is notable in religious communities where literacy is by and large limited to the clergy. The clergy carries out the authority of the tradition through the use of religious texts. The laity may memorize and repeat certain of these texts in worship and rituals, but they are not in possession of the instruments and institutional authority of sacred literacy. Both clergy and laity may participate in and honor other traditions that arise from the life of the laity. Such traditions are those related to the sacralization of agricultural seasons and worship centered around the cults of relics and saints, holy persons, pilgrimages, and so on.

Another meaning of this kind of popular religion stems from a society in which literacy is not confined to the clergy or elite. The laity may have access to certain authoritative or quasi-authoritative texts without being in possession of the power of normative interpretation and sanction of these texts. They therefore interpret these texts in their own manner, according to their own needs and sensibilities. A notable case of this kind of popular religion is the account given in *The Cheese and the Worms* (1980) by Carlo Ginzburg of the Italian miller Domenico Sandella (nicknamed Menochhio), a literate peasant who created and thought through an entire cosmology radically different from that of the church authorities. In other cases the clergy may create for the laity popular religious literature of a devotional or catechismal nature that takes on the forms of a more pervasive popular culture of the laity. This can be seen in the adaptation of archetypes from the authoritative tradition to a popular structure: for example, the popularization of Guanyin in Buddhist literatures, and the local and popular traditions concerning Kṛṣṇa among Hindus. In another example, Christmas (the celebration of the birth of Jesus Christ), which developed from older, popular (pagan) traditions, has been adapted to the popular cultures and economies of modern societies.

3. *Popular religion as the pervasive beliefs, rituals, and values of a society. Popular religion of this type is a kind of civil religion or religion of the public. It forms the general and wide context for the discussion of anything of a religious nature within the society.* Two studies of Greek religion may be used to illustrate this point. Martin P. Nilsson, in his *Greek Folk Religion,* described the religion of the countryside, the folk-peasant religion of ancient Greece. Jon D. Mikalson, in his *Athenian Popular Religion,* treats Greek religion not in terms of class structures, nor through a distinction between the rural and the urban, but rather concentrates on the views and beliefs that were a part of the common cultural experience of the majority of Athenians during the late fourth and fifth centuries CE. Mikalson goes on to point out that one of the most important sources for this type of popular religion was the orations presented in law courts, where the orators addressed juries that numbered from five hundred to twenty-five hundred or more Athenian male citizens.

Similar forms of popular religion are found in all cultures where the religious substratum of the culture radiates into, and finds explicit expression—or vague nuances and derivations—in the formation and processes of public institutions other than those dedicated to specific religious ceremonials. As such, this form of popular religion provides a generalized rhetoric and norm for the meaning and discussion of religion within the context of the culture in which it is found. In most cases the meaning of this kind of popular religion is expressed in terms of a dominant religious tradition that has had a profound and pervasive influence upon the culture. For example, in the Western world, one could speak of Christendom or biblical orientations; in India, of the Sanskritic language and cultural traditions; in China and other parts of the Far East, of the Confucian and Buddhist traditions; and, in Islamic countries, of the Islamic tradition. In each case a specific religious orientation has so informed the cultural life that it has become the "natural" and normative language of religion in general, and the secular forms of cultural life as well give expression to their origins in that religious tradition.

Of particular interest in this regard is the discussion surrounding the issue of "civil religion" in the United States since the end of World War II. This discussion has come to the fore in many democratic societies due to the growing democratization and secularization of the processes and institutions within societies of this kind. The case of the American republic is an extreme example of this problem because, as a nation-state, it is not philosophically based upon an explicit or implicit meaning derived from either an archaic or aboriginal religion, nor upon any meaning of a named, empirical religion. Neither did the nation's founders find it necessary to come to terms with the religion of the original inhabitants of the land as the Spanish did in Mesoamerica and South America. The notion of "God" or "Nature's God" is used as an analogue for an archaic principle of founding, but its connotations remain vague; thus, specific religious groups interpret this principle in their own manner in accord with the principle of religious freedom in the United States. However, this same meaning is not limited to its interpretation by specific religious groups; it is also evoked and given extensive interpretation in the speeches of prominent political, judicial, and public figures, and in documents of the nation's history. Sidney E. Mead (1963) and Robert N. Bellah (1967) have shown how the symbolic interpretations of the meaning of the "God of the Republic" in the rhetoric of American presidents have attempted to define—and persuade the citizenry of the United States of—the public religious and moral meanings and implications of the American Republic.

4. *Popular religion as an amalgam of esoteric beliefs and practices differing from the common or civil religion, but usually located in the lower strata of a society.* Popular religion in this form more often than not exists alongside other forms of religion in a society. Reference is made here to the religious valuation of esoteric forms of healing, predictions of events not based on logical reasoning, and therapeutic practices that have an esoteric origin and may imply a different cosmology than the one prevalent within the society as a whole. In most cases the practitioners and clients have not eschewed the ordinary modes of healing and therapy; the esoteric beliefs and practices are supplementary, representing a mild critique of the normative forms of this kind of knowledge and practice in the society at large. This form of popular religion is present in industrial societies in practices such as phrenology, palm reading, astrology, and in the accompanying esoteric, "metaphysical" beliefs. The pervasive nature of this kind of popular religion may be noted by the fact that in almost all of the larger cities of industrialized countries, every major newspaper and magazine finds it necessary to carry astrological forecasts or some other symbolic mode that appeals to an alternate interpretation of the world.

5. *Popular religion as the religion of a subclass or minority group in a culture.* Particular classes defined by their ethnicity or by an ideology or mythology associated with their work (e.g., miners, blacksmiths, butchers, soldiers, etc.), form another mode of popular religion. In most cases such groups do not represent foreign communities residing in another culture, but pose the problem of "otherness" or strangeness for people outside their communities due to their racial type or occupation. These groups are, nevertheless, integrated into the social structure as a necessary ingredient of a common cultural ideology and its functioning; they constitute "a part of the society by not being a part of it." In most traditional cultures of the world, certain occupations, such as mining or blacksmithing, represent this meaning. They are restricted to certain places of residence within the villages and they in turn have their own rituals and alternate understandings of the nature of the cosmos. While the role and function of such occupations is understood by the rest of society, and is felt to have a place in its general cosmology, they nevertheless form the basis for an alternate understanding of the nature of society. Examples of the ethnic and racial meaning of this form of popular religion may be seen in the history of the Jews within Christendom or the religions of African Americans in the New World.

6. *Popular religion as the religion of the masses in opposition to the religion of the sophisticated, discriminating, and learned within a society.* This is a variation on the difference between the laity and the clergy in hierarchical and traditional societies. Reference is made in this form of popular religion to a meaning of the masses that is the product of democratic polities and industrialism. Whereas in the older, traditional, hierarchical societies, the clergy and the laity both possessed traditions, the modern definition of "the masses" implies the loss of tradition and canons of value and taste, which are now defined in terms of a privileged class order of the elite who have had the benefit of special education. Alexis de Tocqueville's comments on the meaning of democracy in America imply that democracy and mass culture are synonymous. The form of popular religion will tend to express the existential and ephemeral concerns of the mass population at any moment of its history.

7. *Popular religion as the creation of an ideology of religion by the elite levels of a society.* From the very beginning of the study of popular culture and religion, the discovery, meaning, and valuation of "the popular" was undertaken by elites within the society. Especially with the coming of industrialization and the rise of the nation-state, the provincial traditions of the peasant and rural folk within a culture had to fall under the political and ideological meanings of larger generalizing and centralizing orders of the state and its bureaucracy. To the extent that the ideological meaning of the rural and peasant cultures served the aims of the state, it was promoted as the older, traditional meaning of the state deriving from its archaic forms. Popular culture and religion in this mode was invented and promoted by the state through folklore societies, museums, and by the promotion of historical research into the past of the society. On the basis of a genuine and authentic folk and peasant tradition of culture and religion, a new meaning of the popular forms is now embraced and supported by the state.

Given this variety of forms and meanings of popular religion, it is appropriate to ask what is the common element in all of them. There are two common elements. First of all, "the popular" in any of its varieties is concerned with a mode of transmission of culture. Whether the group be large or small, or whether the content of the religion be sustaining or ephemeral, "the popular" designates the universalization of its mode of transmission. In peasant and folk situations, this mode of transmission is traditionally embodied in symbols and archetypes tht tend to be long-lasting and integrative. In modern industrial societies, the modes of transmission are several, including literacy, electronic media, newspapers, chapbooks, and so on. Such modes of communication bring into being a popular culture that is different from, but may overlap with, other social strata within the culture. Due to the intensity of these forms of communication, the content of the forms of popular culture is able to change quickly. It is not, however, the content that is at the fore here, but the type of cognition afforded by the modes of transmission. Given the intensification of transmission and the ephemerality of content, this form of popular religion and culture is semiotic—it is embedded in a system of signs rather than in symbols and archetypes.

The Nature of Culture. The meaning of popular religion presupposes an understanding of the nature of culture that is capable of making sense of differences and divisions within the totality of any culture. Furthermore, the notion of culture must allow room for the meaning of religion as one of the primary modes of transmission of the cultural tradition.

Clifford Geertz's description (1965) of religion as a cultural system is one of the most adequate understandings of culture as a mode of transmission. His definition is as follows: Religion is (1) a system of symbols that acts to (2) establish powerful, pervasive, and long-lasting moods and motivations in people by (3) formulating conceptions of a general order of existence and (4) clothing these conceptions with an aura of factuality so that (5) the moods and motivations seem uniquely realistic. This notion of religion as a cultural system enables one to understand how religion is the expression and transmission of a conception of the reality of the world, and it is clear that such a powerful and pervasive notion must of necessity imply a mode of transmission.

If this notion of religion as a cultural system is seen in relationship to Robert Redfield's analysis of the divisions and distinctions within a cultural system, a basis for the meaning of popular religion within a cultural milieu is established (Redfield, 1955). Redfield makes a broad distinction within a culture between what he calls the "great tradition" and the "little tradition." The great tradition is that of the learned elite and often the ruling class, while the little tradition is that of the large classes and groups of the lower classes. His combination of these two theories provides an understanding of the meaning of popular religion from the point of view of culture as a whole. However, in all parts of the world, due to industrialization and modernization, it is becoming increasingly difficult to define the meaning of culture in these terms. Whereas political power may continue to reside in an elite ruling class that has hegemony over many forms of cultural expression, the modes of transmission, through literacy and electronic media are so intense that the distinction between the elite and the lower class as well as between the urban and rural milieus fail to mark a line of demarcation that is true to social reality. From this point of view, the modes of communication and transmission have as much or more to do with the integration and wholeness of the culture as the content of symbolic clusters or ideological meaning.

Considerations of this sort raise issues regarding the locus and meaning of religion in contemporary industrialized societies. Because of the intensity of transmission, the content of what is transmitted tends to be ephemeral; thus, the notion of religion as establishing powerful, pervasive, and long-lasting moods and motivations is shifted away from content and substance to modes of experience. Popular religion is thus no longer defined in terms of sustaining traditions, but in the qualitative meaning of the nature of experience. Thus, in attempting to describe popular religion in modern societies, the investigator may undertake research in a wide variety of media where members of the culture express their experiences, such as television, radio, and newspapers; and in occurrences such as sports and recreational events, political activities, and so on. Seen from this point of view, the popular approximates some aspects of the older and original notion of "popular" as the peasant-folk and organic meaning in a society. In the peasant-folk, organic society, the mode of transmission were relatively slow, and thus the content of the transmission predominated, allowing for the comprehension of the symbolic content to consciously and unconsciously inform the life of society. In modern industrial societies, transmission is almost universal throughout the society, but the content is no longer the bearer of organic and integrative form.

SOCIAL CHANGE. The notion of an organic social order, whether defined as a primitive, peasant, or folk culture, often implies complete equilibrium, integration, and stasis in a society. This is hardly ever true: All societies exhibit divisions and segmentations of various kinds, and these are often expressed in religious terms. They may be seen in the religious meanings defined by gender as well as in the gradations of the types of religious knowledge wherein certain types of esoteric or secret knowledge is held by an elite, and a more public and general religious meaning is present in the society at large. A good example of this is given in Marcel Griaule's account of the knowledge of Ogotemmêli, the old Dogon sage. The knowledge held by Ogotemmêli has a correspondence to the public meaning and symbols of Dogon religion, but his knowledge is more profound and possesses a metaphysical dimension. This type of knowledge and these types of human beings are found in many traditional societies.

A similar situation is present in societies where shamans possess a different and superior knowledge to that of ordinary persons. Where differences of thought and social structure exist, there is always the possibility for a tension among and between social divisions and/or modes of thought; these tensions at any moment may lead to the expression of novelty, thus causing changes in the society as a whole.

In addition to internally induced changes in organic societies based on differences of thought or social divisions, change may also arise from certain pervasive rituals. The rite of initiation is especially conducive to the influx of new religious orientations and changes in the social order. Initiation is that ritual concerned with the creation of new human beings. It introduces the initiand into the human community through the religious experience of the world of sacred beings in mythic times. Often in initiation rituals, the candidate is made to experience a regression to a time before creation and then to ritually imitate the archetypal stages of the first creation. The ability to imitate, re-create, or renew the cosmos is a possibility present in every initiation ritual, and this experience may become the basis for social change within the society. The notion that there can be a new mode of being is the basis for radical change in this religious ritual.

There is hardly any knowledge available on the expression of initiation leading to broad societal change in non-European societies prior to the coming of the Europeans; however, initiation cults of this kind in pre-Christian European cultures attest to their implications for changes in the societal order. The Greco-Oriental mystery religions posed an extreme tension between the public religious cults of the Hellenistic period in their expression of a deeper and more personal experience of sacred realities.

The preponderance of the data regarding the relationship between popular religion and social change has come primarily from religious traditions defined by their geographical extension in time and space, where the religious tradition has become synonymous with a cultural tradition (e.g., Hinduism, Islam, Christianity). These traditions cover a wide variety of forms of social divisions and thought. As such, the tensions among and between them are many, and are much more intense. It is in such traditions that the distinctions between the organic structure of society and the elite ruling class is most pronounced. Exchanges of thought and experience between these two major structures of society may occur in ritualized forms such as the festival, carnival, and pilgrimage. These ritual forms allow for a lessening of the social divisions, and for the communication and integration of modes and styles of life that are not governed by the everyday power defined by the political and social differences between the two groups. Not only do such rituals permit the relaxation of social differences, they allow for the interchange of vital knowledge between the two groups. M. Bahktin shows how these particular ritual forms have led to the creation of specific literary genres among the elite and literate members of the culture, especially as this is related to the carnival and the festival. Literary critics have long attested to the effect of the ritual pilgrimage on the literary imagination. E. Le Roy Ladurie, in his work *Carnival in Romans* (1979), has shown how the carnival provided the setting for revolutionary activities of the peasants and townspeople. Daniel L. Overmyer has described a similar situation in the White Lotus sect and the school of Luo Qing (1443–1527) in China in the sixteenth century (Overmyer, 1976).

Movements and actions of this kind from the popular strata of the society have been called "pre-political" by Eric J. Hobsbawm (1959). By this he means that the people have not found a specific form of political ideology in which to express their aspirations about the world. While this may be true in most cases, such aspirations expressed in religious terms, and it is on this level of expression that unique dimensions of the meaning of popular religion emerge. In a manner reminiscent of the initiation structure of primitive societies, peasant and folk societies express a new self-consciousness of their solidarity through archaic symbols drawn from the genres of their lives and from a reinterpretation of the traditional religion. In many cases, symbols and teachings of the traditional religion are understood in a more literal manner, expecially as these symbols and teachings express renewal and change, the end of one order and the beginning of a new one. Banditry, outlawry, and other actions that violate the social order are permitted in the revolutionary milieu, for they are sanctioned by what Victor Turner has called the liminal state, which forms the context of the revolutionary activity. This state is a regression to chaos on the level of society.

Two major types of religious personages appear in popular religious movements of this kind: the prophetic figure and the outlaw. The prophet as a religious personage is not unique to the situation of popular religion. In most cases, figures of this sort are a part of the traditional teaching of the culture. From the stratum of popular religion, the meaning and role of the prophet is enhanced as the critical and condemnatory voice of the people against the abuses and injustices of the ruling and elite class. It is the prophet who relates the existential situation of the people to primordial religious depths forged from the life of the people and a new interpretation of the religious tradition.

The outlaw is the heroic religious figure in popular revolutionary religious movements. The archetypal outlaw is the one whose banditry establishes justice within the society; the outlaw takes from the rich to give to the poor. Myths and legends of the outlaw, such as Robin Hood in England, Janosik in Poland, Corrientes in Andalusia, or Finn in Irish and Scottish tales, abound.

The religious meaning of renewal of the world is a prominent theme of popular revolutionary movements. Within Western religious traditions, this theme is derivative of the religious symbol of the Messiah, whose coming announces the destruction of the old world or the radical renewal of the world. The world will be reversed—turned upside down—thus there will be a redress of all wrongs. These millennial expectations are not only goals of a movement; they pervade all the activities of its followers, allowing for a reordering of psychic structures as well as opening up the possibility of a new social religious order on the level of popular religion.

GLOBAL STRUCTURES. With increasing rapidity and intensity since the late fifteenth century, the Western world—through exploration, conquest, and military and economic exploitation—brought the non-European world under its modes of communication through the structures of the modern industrial system. The Western systems of economics and communications were the bearer of Western forms of religious mythology and ideology, often characterized by millennial hopes. From this point of view, the West became the center of the world; the other areas, the peripheries. In other words, the West took over the role and function of the ruling elite, with other parts of the world playing the role of the older peasant or folk societies.

There has been a religious response to this hegemony of the West in almost all parts of the world. In many cases, a new elite comes into being in the colonized countries, imitating the structures and forms of the Western center. This, in turn, creates a new form of the popular—the traditional religion of the indigenous culture becomes a popular religion and must reorder itself in relationship to the power and authority of the new, indigenous elite. The situation does not simply create a tension of opposition. The religious and ideological meaning of the West will inform, in varying degrees, the whole of the society, and the reordering of the indigenous tradition will represent an amalgam of the older indigenous forms and a reinterpreted Western religious tradition. New meanings of popular religion will emerge in this context. Making use of the communication systems of the Western colonizers, many of these movements will move beyond the provincial confines of their local culture in one of their modes. A notable example is the universal influence and acceptance of African American music in almost all parts of the world. Walter J. Hollenweger has argued in his work *The Pentecostals* (1972) that this form and style of religion represents a global phenomenon, an alternate and critical response binding together religious communities in all parts of the world.

SEE ALSO Folklore; Folk Religion; Implicit Religion; Invisible Religion; Popular Culture.

BIBLIOGRAPHY

While religious institutions exist on the popular, folk, and peasant levels of culture, the meaning of religion is not centered in the segmented religious institution. Because of the nature of these kinds of societies, religion is more often diffused throughout the forms of societal life. Given the various forms and modes of popular, folk, and peasant societies and communities, it is too much to say that religion is identical with the totality of the community. However, almost all aspects of the communal life are capable of expressing the religious life. This bibliography thus covers those works dealing specifically with popular religion as well as the wider range of the forms of popular, folk, and peasant communities.

History of the Study of Popular Religion

For interpretations of the philosophical impact of Giambattista Vico and J. G. Herder, Isaiah Berlin's *Vico and Herder* (London, 1976) is the best introduction. See also *The New Science of Giambattista Vico,* translated by Thomas Goddard Bergin and Max Harold Fisch (Ithaca, N.Y., 1948). Commentaries on the writings of Vico are found in Donald Phillip Verene's *Vico's Science of Imagination* (Ithaca, N.Y., 1981) and in *Vico: Selected Writings,* translated and edited by Leon Pompa (Cambridge, U.K., 1982). For Herder, see Frank E. Manuel's abridged edition of his *Reflections on the Philosophy of the History of Mankind* (Chicago, 1968). Interpretive studies of Herder are H. B. Nisbet's *Herder and the Philosophy and History of Science* (Cambridge, U.K., 1970), G. A. Wells's *Herder and After* (The Hague, 1959), and Frederick M. Barnard's *Herder on Social and Political Culture* (1969). For a short and illuminating essay on the impact of the Grimm brothers on the study of modern literature, see William Paton Ker's *Jacob Grimm,* Publications of the Philological Society, vol. 7 (Oxford, 1915). A highly critical study of the Grimm brothers' method and scholarship is found in John M. Ellis's *One Fairy Story Too Many* (Chicago, 1983).

The best history of the study of folklore in Europe is Giuseppe Cocchiara's *The History of Folklore in Europe,* translated by John N. McDaniel (Philadelphia, 1981). Peter Burke's *Popular Culture in Early Modern Europe* (New York, 1978) is historically oriented but is more systematic than historical. Older works such as Stith Thompson's *The Folktale* (1946; reprint, New York, 1979) and Alexander H. Krappe's *The Science of Folklore* (1930; New York, 1962) are still valuable. They should be supplemented by Alan Dundes's *The Study of Folklore* (Englewood Cliffs, N. J., 1965) and Richard Dorson's *Folklore and Folklife* (Chicago, 1972).

Some of Max Weber's works bear on certain problems of popular religion; see especially *The Protestant Ethic and the Spirit of Capitalism,* translated by Talcott Parsons (London, 1930); *The Sociology of Religion,* translated by Ephraim Fischoff (Boston, 1963); *The City,* translated and edited by Don Martindale and Gertrud Neuwirth (Glencoe, Ill., 1958); and *From Max Weber: Essays in Sociology,* translated and edited by Hans H. Gerth and C. Wright Mills (Oxford, 1946). From an earlier sociological school there are the works of Ferdinand Tönnies, *Community and Association,* translated and edited by Charles P. Loomis (London, 1955), and William Graham Sumner's *Folkways* (Boston, 1907). Much can still be learned from Ernst Troeltsch's *The Social Teaching of the Christian Church,* 2 vols., translated by Olive Wyon (1931; Chicago, 1981), as well as from Joachim Wach's *Sociology of Religion* (Chicago, 1944). Wach's work remains the only sociology of religion written by a historian of religions and is thus valuable for that reason. Clifford Geertz's informative essay "Religion as a Cultural System" can be found in *Anthropological Approaches to the Study of Religion,* edited by Michael Banton (New York, 1966), and in *Reader in Comparative Religion,* edited by William A. Lessa and Evon Z. Vogt (New York, 1965).

Regional Studies of Popular Religion

Numerous publications have been devoted to popular, folk, and peasant religions around the world. Without attempting to cover all areas of the globe, I offer here a sampling of works that are valuable for their contribution to theory as well as for their descriptive detail.

Africa

African Folklore, edited by Richard M. Dorson (New York, 1972), covers most of the genres of folklore in Africa. Two sections, "Traditional Narrative" and "Traditional Ritual," are especially relevant to the notion of popular religion. Ruth Finnegan's *Oral Literature in Africa* (London, 1970) is a highly controversial work. She makes a strong argument for the literary nature of oral literature and finds many interpretations by anthropologists and folklorists wanting because they fail to appreciate the literary character of this form of literature. She devotes a chapter to religious poetry, but she confines the meaning of religion to a very conventional usage. Jan Vansina's *Oral Tradition,* translated by H. M. Wright (Chicago, 1965), is a thorough working out of the problems and methods involved in using oral testimony as historical data. The data for his work are the traditions of the Kuba. This work has bearing on the relationship between the modes of transmission and the nature and meaning of the knowledge that is transmitted.

Japan

Cornelis Ouwehand's *Namazu-e and Their Themes* (Leiden, 1964) is important for the light it sheds on the reception and alternate interpretations of events on the folkloric levels of Japanese society. Especially in the case of catastrophic event, on the folkloric levels there is the appearance of a kind of savior figure as a motif of the understanding of these events. Ichori Hori's *Folk Religion in Japan,* edited by Joseph M. Kitagawa and Alan L. Miller (Chicago, 1968), is the best general study of the forms and structures of folk religion in Japan. *Studies in Japanese Folklore,* edited by Richard M. Dorson (Port Washington, N.Y., 1963), covers the folk traditions of various classes of workers and is one of the best studies of the traditions of workers. Michael Czaja's *Gods of Myth and Stone* (New York, 1974) is a thorough study of the mythic and religious significance of certain forms of fertility symbols and rituals in Japan; it is informed by sophisticated methodology.

Ancient Greece

Of the many works in Greek religion, I mention only three, the classic study of N. D. Fustel de Coulanges, *The Ancient City,* new ed. (Baltimore, 1980), Martin P. Nilsson's *Greek Folk Religion* (New York, 1961), and Jon D. Mikalson's *Athenian Popular Religion* (Chapel Hill, N. C., 1983).

Europe

Most studies of popular religion in Europe are to be valued as much for their detailed content as for their theoretical approach and methodological contributions. Marc Bloch's *Feudal Society,* 2 vols., translated by L. A. Manyon (Chicago, 1961), is a pioneer work in focusing on the entire range of the cultural reality of the feudal period. Two representative works dealing with the amalgam of religious traditions in Europe are Albert B. Lord's *The Singer of Tales* (Cambridge, Mass., 1960) and Gail Kligman's *Calus: Symbolic Transformation in Romanian Ritual* (Chicago, 1981).

Norbert Elias's *The Civilizing Process* (New York, 1978), *Power and Civility* (New York, 1982), and *The Court Society* (New York, 1983), all translated by Edmund Jephcott, demonstrate the social behavior patterns and psychological attitudes that define the processes that create the class and value orientation of the ideology of civilization. Similar processes, but directed from a centralized governmental center, are described in Eugen Weber's *Peasants into Frenchmen* (Stanford, Calif., 1976). A detailed account of popular culture in France is found in Robert Muchembled's *Popular Culture and Elite Culture in France, 1400–1750,* translated by Lydia Cochrane (Baton Rouge, 1985). One of the most prolific and brilliant scholars of popular religion and culture in France is the Annales historian Emmanuel Le Roy Ladurie. His works include *Montaillou: The Promised Land of Error,* translated by Barbara Bray (New York, 1978); *Carnival in Romans,* translated by Mary Feeney (New York, 1979); and *The Peasants of Languedoc,* translated by John Day (Urbana, 1974). *Religion and the People, 800–1700,* edited by James Obelkevich (Chapel Hill, N.C., 1979) is a good survey of some important themes in the study of popular European religion. One of the essays in this volume, Lionel Rothkrug's "Popular Religion and Holy Shrines," has been followed up in Rothkrug's *Religious Practices and Collective Perceptions: Hidden Homologies in the Renaissance and Reformation* (Waterloo, Ont., 1980). The importance of this work lies not only in the detailed description of such phenomena as the cult of Mary on the popular level but equally in the way it raises the issue of the forms of perception and knowledge that stem from certain modes of religious apprehension. Concrete historical detail is given to issues of the sociology of religious knowledge that are discussed more abstractly by Georges Gurvitch in *The Social Frameworks of Knowledge,* translated by Margaret A. Thompson and Kenneth A. Thompson (Oxford, 1971). Carlo Ginzburg's *The Cheese and the Worms,* translated by John Tedeschi and Anne Tedeschi (Baltimore, 1980), an account of the cosmology of a sixteenth-century Italian miller, is fast becoming a classic of popular religion. Miriam Usher Chrisman's *Lay Culture, Learned Culture: Books and Social Change in Strasbourg,* 1480–1599 (New Haven, Conn., 1982), shows the impact of printing and literacy on the various cultural layers of this period. William A Christian's *Local Religion in Sixteenth Century Spain* (Princeton, N. J., 1981), examines the spirituality of several towns in New Castile. A. N. Galpern's *The Religions of the People in Sixteenth-Century Champagne* (Cambridge, Mass., 1976), undertakes a similar investigation of this area. *The Pursuit of Holiness in Late Medieval and Renaissance Religion,* edited by Charles Trinkaus and Heiko A. Oberman (Leiden, 1974), contains essays covering almost all aspects of late medieval and Renaissance religion. Of particular interest is part 2, "Lay Piety and the Cult of Youth." James Obelkevich's *Religion and Rural Society: South Lindsey, 1825–1875* (Oxford, 1976), deals with the churching of agrarian laborers by the Methodist Church. It goes far in showing the interaction of the lower classes and the middle and upper classes as this is related to the form and structure of the religious institution. There is, finally, a beautifully written book by the folklorist Henry Glassie, *Passing the Time in Ballymenone* (Philadelphia, 1982). In this study of a rural community in Ireland, the author demonstrates in his research the moral meaning of this kind of community. While there is no one chapter or section devoted to religion, the entire work reflects the religious orientation of a small Irish village. The closest one comes to an explicit meaning of religion is in part 8, "A Place on the Holy Land."

Modern America

There are few general and systematic studies of American popular religion. For orientation to the issues of the meaning of "the people," "culture," "religion," and the national state in the American democracy, Alexis de Tocqueville's classic *Democracy in America,* 2 vols. in 1, translated by George Lawrence and edited by J. P. Mayer (Garden City, N.Y., 1969), is still a very good orientation. H. Richard Niebuhr's *The Social Sources of Denominationalism* (1929; New York, 1957) is one of the few works that raises the issue of the relationship of popular lower-class-strata religion to the founding of religious institutions in the United States. W. Lloyd Warner's *The Living and the Dead* (New Haven, Conn., 1959) is an anthropological interpretation of the major sacred and secular symbols in American society. The methodological point of view lends itself to the meaning of American religion from the perspective of popular religion. Sidney E. Mead's *The Lively Experiment* (New York, 1963) is a group of essays that touch upon the broader religious symbolic values of American cultural reality as the context for religious understanding.

Catherine L. Albanese's *America: Religions and Religion* (Belmont, Calif., 1981) is the first systematic attempt to deal with all the religious traditions in the United States in an integrated manner. As such it eschews the normativity of the mainline traditions as the basis for American religion, thus allowing for the meaning of popular religion to become an empirical and methodological ingredient in the study of American religion. See also Albanese's *Sons of the Fathers* (Philadelphia, 1976) for a discussion of the manner in which popular religion instituted and responded to the apotheosis of George Washington as the founding father of the nation.

Will Herberg's *Protestant, Catholic, Jew* (Garden City, N.Y., 1955) shows how denominational designations were used to define cultural modes of popular American religiosity. For a discussion of civil religion in the United States, see Robert N. Bellah's "Civil Religion in America," *Daedalus* 96 (Winter 1967): 1–21. Peter W. Williams's *Popular Religion in America* (Englewood Cliffs, N.J., 1980) is excellent for data but lacks methodological sophistication. The later two works contain the best bibliographical sources for the many forms of popular religion in the United States.

China

Daniel L. Overmyer's *Folk Buddhist Religion* (Cambridge, Mass., 1976) is one of the few thoroughgoing discussions of folk Buddhism in China and is distinguished by its methodological astuteness. *Popular Culture in Late Imperial China,* edited by David Johnson, Andrew J. Nathan, and Evelyn S. Rawski (Berkeley, Calif., 1985), brings together several essays on popular culture of this period. Of special note are "Religion and Popular Culture: The Management of Moral Capital in the Romance of the Three Teachings" by Judith Berling, "Values in Chinese Sectarian Literature: Ming and Qing Baozhuan" by Daniel L. Overmyer, and "Language and Ideology in the Written Popularizations of the Sacred Edict" by Victor H. Mair.

Theoretical Studies

Almost all of the works cited above discuss theoretical issues, but there are, in addition, a number of valuable works written from a purely theoretical orientation. Among them are three books by anthropologist Robert Redfield that have had great influence on the study of popular culture and religion: *The Primitive World and Its Transformations* (Ithaca, N.Y., 1953), *The Little Community* (Chicago, 1955), and *Peasant Society and Culture* (Chicago, 1956). Two works by Milton Singer are also recommended; although devoted to the Hindu tradition, they have much broader implications for many of the issues of popular religion and its relationship to urbanism and the great traditions: *Traditional India: Structure and Change* (Philadelphia, 1959) and *When a Great Tradition Modernizes* (New York, 1972).

Approaches to Popular Culture, edited by C. W. E. Bigsby (Bowling Green, Ohio, 1976), is an illuminating group of essays that demonstrate the ambiguity and difficulty of clear definition of the meaning of popular culture. Of particular interest are "Popular Culture: A Sociological Approach" by Zev Barbu, "Oblique Approaches to the History of Popular Culture" by Peter Burke, and "The Politics of Popular Culture" by C. W. E. Bigsby. The political and ideological meaning of popular culture is also explored in Herbert J. Gans's *Popular Culture and High Culture* (New York, 1974).

Finally, for a group of essays discussing the meaning of social history in various historical contexts, see *Reliving the Past,* edited by Olivier Zunz (Chapel Hill, N. C., 1985).

New Sources

Berlinerblau, Jacques. "Max Weber's Useful Ambiguities and the Problem of Defining 'Popular Religion.'" *Journal of the American Academy of Religion* 69 (September 2001): 605–626.

Feuchtwang, Stephan. *Popular Religion in China: The Imperial Metaphor.* Richmond, U.K., 2001.

Marsh, Christopher. *Popular Religion in 16th-Century England.* New York, 1998.

Mikalson, Jon. *Honor Thy Gods: Popular Religion in Greek Tragedy.* Durham, 1992.

Samuel, Geoffrey, Hamish Gregor, and Elisabeth Stutchbury, eds. *Tantra and Popular Religion in Tibet.* Columbia, Mo., 1994.

Scribner, Robert, and Trevor Johnson, eds. *Popular Religion in Germany and Central Europe, 1400–1800.* New York, 1996.

Sharot, Stephen. *A Comparative Sociology of World Religions: Virtuosos, Priests, and Popular Religion.* New York, 2001.

Stahl, William A. "The Village Enlightenment in America: Popular Religion and Science in the Nineteenth Century." *Sociology of Religion* 62 (Fall 2001): 407–408.

CHARLES H. LONG (1987)
Revised Bibliography

PORTALS. A portal is any gateway or doorway, insofar as it elicits ritual actions or becomes a locus of concentrated architectural symbolism. It is a space framed to call attention to spatial transition; thus it has characteristics of both a path and a place. Because a portal often separates a sacred precinct from a profane one, or a regulated from an unregulated zone, it is both a termination and a beginning. As a structure that is both inside and outside the same zone, and one that attracts dangerous as well as beneficent forces, it is a site of considerable ambivalence.

The most rudimentary forms of a portal are the cave entrance, the stone heap, the upright post, and two uprights supporting a lintel. More elaborate ones add not only familiar features such as a threshold, doors, knobs, and hinges, but also figures, inscriptions, porches, domical towers, cupolas, niches for statues, and crowning arcades. In some eras portals have been so emphasized as to become freestanding monuments separated from buildings, bridges, or city walls. No longer only markers of paths, they become places in their own right. Three famous examples are the Great Gateway (1630–1653 CE) at the Taj Mahal in India, the *bailou* ("entrance") leading to the Temple of the Sleeping Buddha (eighteenth century) near Beijing, and the Gates of Paradise (1403–1424 CE), designed by Lorenzo Ghiberti for the Florence Baptistry (c. eleventh century CE). In cases where a road originates or terminates at a gate—for instance, the Ishtar Gate of Babylon (c. 575 BCE) and its grand procession way, or the Lion's Gate (rebuilt by Sultan Süleyman in 1538–1539 CE) leading to the Via Dolorosa in Jerusalem—it seems that the portal usually sanctifies the path rather than vice versa. It is not uncommon for a pilgrim to have to pass through several preliminary gateways on a road leading to a major portal.

FUNCTIONS. The widespread, cross-cultural separation, elaboration, and multiplication of portals suggests that their importance far exceeds their two most obvious functions, namely regulating traffic and providing military defense. Other functions are to commemorate noteworthy events, memorialize cultural heroes and royalty, instruct the faithful, propagandize strangers and outsiders, advertise the nature or use of a building, and dramatize the status of inhabitants.

The bronze doors (1015 CE) of the cathedral at Hildesheim in Germany, for example, teach Christian believers to consider Jesus' crucifixion and resurrection as both a parallel and a reversal of the disobedience of Adam and Eve by presenting the two stories on opposing door leaves as a visual *concordantia* of the Old and New Testaments. The best-known examples of Roman triumphal arches, such as the arches of Titus (82 CE), Trajan (114 CE), and Constantine (312 CE), commemorate the victories and accomplishments of generals and emperors. Portals such as the Stonehenge monuments in Wiltshire, England, and the Gates of the Sun (c. 1000–1200 CE) at Tiahuanaco, Peru, probably had astrological and initiatory uses.

In both East and West, portals have been the object of intense syncretism. Consequently, historians of art and religion are able to trace a remarkable continuity of style and consistency of symbolism connecting Indian *toraṇa* with Chinese *bailou* and Japanese *torii* (of which there are twenty different styles). Egyptian pylons and *heb-sed* tents (under which a pharaoh appeared as the god Horus or Re during a jubilee festival) are historically linked with Greek *propulaia,*

Roman triumphal arches, the entrances of synagogues, and the cupolas of mosques and churches.

SYMBOLISM. In most cases portal symbolism is distinctly celestial. Besides decorative stars, rosettes, and solar discs, birds and wings appear over portals with considerable frequency; the Japanese characters for *torii* mean "bird" and "to be." Among ancient Hittites and Egyptians a winged solar disc formed the lintel, which was supported by two pillars often personified as guardian spirits. The identification of a lintel with a deity or royalty, and of columns with protector spirits or intermediaries, is widespread.

In theocratic societies royal dwellings, like the divine kings who inhabited them, were sacred. Portals, because they were one of the architectural features most obvious to commoners, stood for the entire palace, which itself stood for the king, who in turn incarnated the divine. The Ottoman court in Istanbul, for example, was referred to as "the divine portal." As a result of this tendency, a single pillar or the imprint of a façade on a coin could stand (especially in sixth-century Thrace) for the entirety of royal/divine power. The ability of an image of a portal to evoke such authority was probably enhanced by the practice of administering justice at city gates. Only the throne rivals the gateway in embodying the convergence of heavenly and imperial authority. Jesus' claim to be the "door of the sheep" (*Jn.* 10:7) reaches back to a Mesopotamian sensibility typified by a hymn to King Ur-Nammu (2113–2096 BCE) addressing him as "Thy gate, thy God." The name "Babylon" itself means "the gate of the gods." The guardian-like pillars of fire and cloud (*Ex.* 13:21) that led the Israelites in the desert could be interpreted in relation to the personified doorposts, Boaz and Jachin (*1 Kgs.* 7:21), that flanked Solomon's Temple. Pillars in both freestanding and supporting forms frequently undergo stylization as trees or mountains, thus serving as symbolic links between heaven and earth.

RITES. Evidence testifying to the importance and meaning of portals is not only architectural but also ritualistic. Large-scale portal rites in the West have been intensely royal. Examples include the Babylonian New Year processions, the Hellenistic epiphany (a cultic action in the mysteries at Eleusis), the Roman Adventus, and the Great Entrance (of the Byzantine rite)—all ceremonies for greeting royalty or divinity. The intentions of participants seem to have been to purify and protect as well as celebrate and elevate. Also, testing and humiliation at gateways is a ritual practice, one with evidence extending from Ishtar's tests at each of the seven portals of the underworld to modern border crossings.

Small-scale ritual practices at portals are still an active part of folklore. Making offerings, smearing blood on doorposts, burying the dead beneath thresholds, removing shoes, touching pillars, and either jumping, crawling, or being carried over thresholds are common. Lustrations and baths are widespread preparatory rites for passing through portals. Jews touch *mezuzot* on the doorposts of their houses; Catholics dip their fingers in holy water and make the sign of the cross upon entering churches. From the tradition of carrying brides across thresholds to the shrinking doors of *Alice in Wonderland*, and from popular old idioms like "gates of hell" to recent ones like "gates of the dream," popular religion, folklore, and fairy tales are replete with threshold customs and with dangerous doors that miraculously open or that one must not (but surely will) enter.

MOTIFS. Not only do portals become freestanding structures and objects of veneration, but the portal as a motif becomes metaphorically extended beyond its monumental form. Tombstones are carved in the shape of a doorway, and ossuaries have doorways etched on them, thus associating the dead with the divine. Altars incorporate architectural features of portals; by analogy, both the tabletop and the lintel are cathedras (Gk., *kathedrae,* "divine seats"). Virtually any vessel of transition, such as a mother's body, becomes a doorway. The church itself in the Carolingian era (eighth to tenth centuries CE) was regarded as a *porta coeli* ("heavenly portal"). And in modern times the threshold (*limen*) has provided the key metaphor for the widely utilized theory of ritual developed by Arnold van Gennep in *The Rites of Passage* (Chicago, 1960).

Finally, there is suggestive evidence that the shaman's experience of a difficult passage across a bridge or through a narrow pass may be a variation on the theme of smiting doors and clashing rocks (for example, the Symplegades through which Jason and his argonauts had to pass). The image of the *vagina dentata* ("toothed vagina") may be another variant. But the portal, unlike the bridge and symbolic vagina, emphasizes royally authorized security rather than shamanistically induced risk.

SEE ALSO Caves; Pilgrimage; Procession; Tombs; Towers.

BIBLIOGRAPHY

Bernard Goldman's *The Sacred Portal: A Primary Symbol in Ancient Judaic Art* (Detroit, 1966) is a careful art-historical analysis of the portal symbolism of the fifth-century synagogue at Beth Alpha. Because he sets his study so fully in its context, the book is probably the best single volume on the gateways and door symbolism of the ancient Near East. An excellent companion to it is E. Baldwin Smith's *Architectural Symbolism of Imperial Rome and the Middle Ages* (1956; reprint, New York, 1978), a tightly argued study of the imperial city-gate concept and its appropriation by Christianity and Islam. John Summerson's chapter on "An Interpretation of Gothic" in his *Heavenly Mansions* (New York, 1963) traces the development of the *aedicula* ("little house") from its ceremonial function as a miniature shrine within a shrine to its role in inspiring the shape of Gothic arches and finally to its demise as mere decoration on Georgian door castings.

J. A. MacCullough's article, "Door," in the *Encyclopaedia of Religion and Ethics,* edited by James Hastings, vol. 4 (Edinburgh, 1911), is dated but remarkably useful. The classic work on which both this article and van Gennep's theory depend is H. Clay Trumbull's *The Threshold Covenant: Or the Beginning of Religious Rites,* 2d ed. (New York, 1906). Gertrude R. Levy's *The Gate of Horn: A Study of the Religious Concep-*

tions of the Stone Age (London, 1948) is a valuable source of information on primitive gates, especially those bearing horns, at megalithic sites in Malta and Paleolithic caves in southwestern France. *Romanesque Bronzes: Church Portals in Medieval Europe* (London, 1958), by Hermann Leisinger, shows the richness of myth and art to be found on church doors.

A reliable compendium of pictures and line drawings, as well as a general source of comparative materials on gates, is Banister Fletcher's *A History of Architecture,* 18th ed., revised by J. C. Palmes (New York, 1975). On the relation of portals to the shaman's narrow pass and the *vagina dentata,* see Mircea Eliade's *Myths, Rites, Symbols,* 2 vols., edited by Wendell C. Beane and William G. Doty (New York, 1975); Stephen Larsen's *The Shaman's Doorway* (New York, 1976); and Jill Raitt's "The *Vagina Dentata* and the *Immaculatus Uterus Divini Fontis,*" *Journal of the American Academy of Religion* 48 (1980): 415–431.

New Sources

Glass, Dorothy F. *Portals, Pilgrimage, and Crusade in Western Tuscany.* Princeton, 1997.

Goldman, Bernard. *The Sacred Portal: A Primary Symbol in Ancient Judaic Art* (1966). Lanham, 1986.

Goto, Seiko. *The Japanese Garden: Gateway to the Human Spirit.* New York, 2003.

Kowalski, Jeff Karl, ed. *Mesoamerican Architecture as a Cultural Symbol.* New York, 1999.

Langdon, E. Jean Matteson, and Gerhard Baer. *Portals of Power: Shamanism in South America.* Albuquerque, 1992.

Morant, Roland W. *The Monastic Gatehouse and Other Types of Portals in Medieval Religious Houses.* Sussex, U.K., 1995.

RONALD L. GRIMES (1987)
Revised Bibliography

PORTENTS AND PRODIGIES are signs that, if understood or interpreted correctly, can reveal personal destinies and the will of the gods. They may be observed and interpreted either by the person who witnessed them or, more usually, by a priest specializing in the science required.

Portents and prodigies are one of the sources of the art of divination (*divinatio* in Latin, *mantikē technē* in Greek). The diviner, who is capable of predicting the future, could have recourse either to the exegesis of observed signs or to prophetic inspiration, a kind of delirium (*mania*) deriving from his possession by some divinity who comes into contact with diviners, sibyls, or Pythian priestesses.

Some of the words designating portent or prodigy in the languages of classical antiquity (Greek, Latin, and also Etruscan, which remains largely obscure to us) have a clear origin and significance; others have an original meaning that eludes us.

Sēmeion in Greek and *signum* in Latin correspond closely to the word *sign.* The ancients lived in a world where signs were ever present and were to be found in the most diverse parts of the universe: heaven, earth, and underworld. Portents and prodigies often appeared in everyday observation. Even today, popular belief often attributes favorable or unfavorable meanings to apparitions, no matter how natural: to animals of certain breeds, aspects, or colors, or to certain ecclesial phenomena such as a flash of lightning or a thunderclap in a peaceful sky.

OMENS. The most universal portent is the word or phrase heard by chance. Although it is not intended for the listener, it is perceived to have some bearing on one's daily life. In antiquity, as today, people imagined that utterances spoken or heard fortuitously could foretell a dark future or a bright and happy one. The listener, of course, might fail to recognize the omen for what it was, and remain deaf to its warning.

The Roman had the right to accept a portent—an *omen*—by declaring it in a loud and clear voice. This was the meaning of the expression *omen accipere* ("to accept the omen"). But the Roman could just as easily strip the omen of its value and efficacy by declaring in a loud and clear voice that he or she refused to take it into account: *omen exsecrari, abominari* ("omen execrated, abominated"). The ancients also knew how to transform the omen's value and meaning by adroit wording that modified or transformed its scope. Celebrated narratives from Latin writers illustrate the efficacy of human speech in this regard, as in Ovid's *Fasti* (3.330ff.), in which the legendary king of Rome, the pious Numa Pompilius, avoided by clever replies Jupiter's cruel demand for human lives to expiate the stain left on the soil by a bolt of lightning.

AUSPICES. As with all peoples of Indo-European origin, the most important and frequent portents for the Greeks and Romans were furnished by the flights, cries, and behavior of birds. The importance of birds as portents is clear in Aristophanes' comedy *The Birds,* which was performed at the festival of the Great Dionysia in Athens in 414 BCE. In this play, in which distant memories are muted by the satiric medium, the birds proudly bestow upon themselves leading roles as true guides, not mere advisers of human beings. Although this might simply be poetic fancy, it must reflect the memory of a very ancient reality whose origins are lost in the mists of protohistory.

In the vast domain of portents conveyed by birds, ancient Italy deserves attention. From its origins, Rome had a very important priestly college, the augurs, whose responsibility was to preserve scrupulously and apply methodically the religious regulations pertaining to signs given by birds, that is, auspices. By their presence, advice, and collaboration, the augurs could ensure the propriety of the actions of the magistrates. They possessed the compilations of sacred precepts, the *Libri augurales,* which preserved in full detail the rules of auspication and the precise record of controversies over procedure.

Numerous Greek and Latin texts describe minutely the ritual capture of the auspices, a ceremony dating from the beginnings of Rome. The fratricidal rivalry of the twins Romulus and Remus was adjudicated and the founder of the city selected through precise augural interrogation of the divine will. Romulus's *lituus,* a curved stick, which he used to take the portents, became the characteristic emblem of the augural *sacerdotia.*

The object of augury was to obtain signs testifying to the agreement of the gods with the city in any political, religious, or military actions it wanted to undertake. The juridical and pragmatic Roman mind knew how to organize the ritual needed to obtain this assent in the most efficacious way possible. A sacred formula, which served as a veritable pact between humans and gods, was read in a loud and clear voice by the priest who was to perform the augury. The formula specified both the time and place in which the signs were to be observed. The augurs thus received certified, enabling signs that had legal force and value in themselves. But the ceremony could be marked also by accidental, unforeseen phenomena that had to be taken into account.

The Romans were not, to be sure, the only people in Italy who possessed such an augural law. The longest religious inscription left by classical antiquity, the Eugubine tablets, attest to the existence of augural law among other Italic peoples, especially the Umbrians. According to this well-known text, a sacerdotal college called the Attiedii Brotherhood practiced a system of explication very similar to that used by the Roman augers. In both cases, the observation and interpretation of portents was carried out with the same formalism and attention to minute detail in the ritual procedures. The question put to the gods was the same among both peoples: Were they in agreement with the proposed enterprise or not?

HARUSPICES. Among the series of portents that lent themselves to observation, those furnished by a sacrificial victim consecrated on the altar of a divinity held a major importance in classical antiquity and in other civilizations. The reason is clear. By virtue of its consecration, the sacrificial animal passes from the domain of the human to that of the god. The gods express their disposition by means of the victim itself in the moments preceding, accompanying, and following the sacrifice. It was important, then, to observe everything in the victim's behavior with the greatest attention: When it was led to the altar and when it received the mortal blow, the crackling of flesh on the brazier, the colors of the flame, and the speed of the smoke's ascent into the sky.

But the clearest and most decisive indications were provided by the examination of the entrails of the sacrificial animal by experienced specialists: in Greece, the Iamides, diviners at Olympia; in Etruria and Rome, the haruspices. The haruspices, according to the ancients, enjoyed an immense reputation and seemed to practice a science that was infallible. They can be compared only with the *baru,* Babylonian priests who in the second millennium BCE had a veritable library of clay tablets at their disposal. These tablets detailed a complex doctrine based on minute observation of the organs of victims that was transmitted from one generation to the next.

For the haruspex, as for the *baru,* each fact noted at the sacrifice—i.e., form, color, presence or absence of specific parts of the viscera—unfailingly foretold the approach of specific events, favorable or foreboding, in human society. Rome received its haruspicinal science primarily from Etruria, which, long before it was conquered, had entrusted its best diviners to Rome. But did Etruria develop this discipline independently, or did it borrow elements from the Greek world or even from regions of the Near East? The latter is more likely, although the paths such influences followed are difficult to determine.

In various lands of the Near East, numerous terra-cotta models have been discovered. These models represent organs of sacrificed sheep and bear inscriptions clearly indicating the portents foretold by anomalies in the organs. Etruria is the source of the famous bronze liver found in the Po plain in 1877 near the city of Piacenza. The convex surface of the Piacenza Liver is divided into two lobes bearing the names of the sun (Usil) and the moon (Tiur). The concave surface, admirably sculptured and engraved, is divided into a large number of compartments, on which can be read forty-two inscriptions and twenty-seven names of divinities. This is a graphic illustration of the haruspex's fundamental belief: that the gods actually occupy different parts of the sacrificed animal, and their places there correspond to those they occupy in the sky.

OTHER PORTENTS. The sky, in antiquity, was the home of reigning gods and the place from which they launched comets, falling stars, lightning, and thunder (sources of joy or, more often, terror), considered in some places portents, in other places prodigies. Lightning and thunder were major phenomena, intended to warn humans, who noted with the keenest attention the path of meteorites and deep claps of thunder, foretelling, according to Cicero, the most serious perils for the city and state.

The Etruscans developed most fully the so-called science of interpretation of major celestial portents. Indeed, the master of thunder and lightning, the Etruscan Tinia, was the homologue of the Hellenic Zeus, undisputed master of meteorological phenomena, and of the Roman Jupiter, who hurled thunderbolts during the day (Summanus was master during the night). The Etruscans developed a complete methodology for the interpretation of thunderbolts, including directions for expiation if the portents were unfavorable.

The Greek historian Diodorus was not exaggerating when he wrote, "Etruscan keraunoscopia [*keraunos* was the Greek word for thunder and lightning] was renowned throughout nearly the whole earth" (5.40.2). Seneca, in *Natural Questions* (2.32ff.), discourses knowingly on the differences between Roman and Etruscan approaches to portents, and on the importance the Etruscans placed on thunder portents. He wrote, "Since the Etruscans relate everything to divinity, they are persuaded not that thunderclaps foretell the future because they have been formed, but that they take form because they must foretell the future."

If portents are taken to include inanimate objects and the earth itself, they are even more numerous in the Greek, Roman, and Etruscan traditions. The importance of portents furnished by waters, especially the waters of springs, is attested by texts and archaeological data. These portents depended on the way the water spurted out from the depths of the earth, and also on the way that objects thrown into them were carried along or sank. They were attributed to nymphs reigning over these streams and to various female divinities who were objects of popular devotions in different parts of the ancient world.

Like the surface of water, the mirror was thought to present future events in its reflected images. Drawing lots by choosing among similar objects also appeared to translate either the will of the gods or the will of destiny. Thus, as a response to a question, the white bean drawn by the Greek diviner represented a positive answer, the black bean a negative answer. At Delphi, the center of divination in the ancient world, Apollo spoke through the mouth of his priestess, the Pythia, but she, too, in certain cases, had recourse to drawing lots.

In inspired divination, the priest or prophetess, after attaining the necessary precondition, entered into direct contact with the deity. The god then spoke through their voices and permitted them to prophesy the future, albeit in obscure terms that required professional exegesis.

The premonitory dream is the object of one of the most widespread human beliefs, and in antiquity it was connected with rituals of incubation. The believer, after carrying out certain rituals before induced sleep, sees in a dream what the priests interpret upon awakening.

THE WORLD OF PRODIGIES. To move from portents to the world of prodigies is not really to change domains, because the prodigy, like the portent, is a sign, a warning the gods transmit to humans. Nevertheless, there is a serious difference between the two, which lies in the importance and gravity of the sign. The prodigy, wherever it appears, is a truly exceptional phenomenon that disrupts the normal course of things for a time.

The Greeks could call the prodigy *sēmeion,* but the proper term is *teras,* whose semantic field is the same as that of the archaic term *pelōr.* Both words lack an Indo-European etymology and undoubtedly represent loanwords derived perhaps from one of the Near Eastern civilizations. Despite their importance in Etruscan divination, the Etruscan word or words designating prodigies are not known. Although the word *teras* is found in one of two Etruscan inscriptions, the exact meaning of the word in this context cannot be confirmed.

In Latin, the numerous names for the prodigy reveal the importance the notion possessed in the Roman mind. It is called *prodigium, monstrum, miraculum, ostentum,* and *portentum.* It is not easy to distinguish among the usages of these different words. *Prodigium* is the most often used; its etymology is unclear. *Monstrum* and *miraculum* are applied to something unexplainable in a living creature, human or animal. *Ostentum* and *portentum,* properly speaking, designate what the gods present to humans. None of these terms implied, however, the idea of portent, in the sense of warning about the future. Finally it should be noted that the Roman term *miraculum* became specialized in modern languages to designate all events that ignored natural laws, particularly those associated with Christ. In the shift from paganism to Christianity, the word remained very much alive.

In Etruria, as well as in Rome and the rest of the Italic world, prodigies appeared in various forms. In Greece, as in many other countries, the prodigy could occur in any aspect of nature: earth, sea, sky, underground, in the realms of humans, animals, vegetables, and inanimate objects. The prodigy was attributed to one or another of the gods. The most diverse chthonian phenomena—subterranean rumbles, volcanic displays, earthquakes, and tidal waves—terribly feared in themselves, were also considered forewarnings of the most dire events. Sources of terror for the ancients, these phenomena required expiatory ceremonies intended to pacify the gods.

PRODIGIES IN ETRUSCAN LIFE. Etruria devoted a part of its sacred books to *ostentaria,* collections of rules for observing, explicating, and expiating prodigies. For this function, Rome called on the knowledge of the haruspices. For these priests, as for the Greeks, a prodigy could have a favorable or an evil and disastrous meaning. Presumably it was different in Rome, at least at the beginning of its history.The world of Etruscan prodigies is rather well known because Roman writings accord them considerable importance and familiarize researchers with the haruspices' behavior vis-à-vis the most extraordinary phenomena. The exegeses were often subtle, but usually based on a rather clear symbolism. A comet, a meteor, or a ringing that seemed to burst out of a serene sky could mark the end of a *saeculum,* one of those centuries that formed the history of Etruria. As in Greece, seismic activity on Tuscan soil foretold the most serious events. Conversely, however, certain prodigies could foretell the high destiny of humans, often divining in certain individuals the charisma necessary for kingship. Before the first two Etruscan kings of Rome, Tarquinius Priscus and Servius Tullius, acceded to the throne, they had been marked by prodigies announcing their elevated destiny. The former, upon arriving in Rome had his hat removed by an eagle, which then replaced it, uttering loud cries. Divine favor distinguished Servius Tullius during his childhood, for flames would surround his head for long periods, frightening those around him, and then flicker out.

It is clear that haruspices did not need uncommon wisdom to interpret correctly miraculous phenomena by means of transparent symbolism. But the priests were also masters of ritual as well as of the propitiatory expiations rendered necessary by any prodigy that they thought defiled the land or the city. The priests purified places that had been struck by lightning by interring all objects that it had touched. Compelled by a deep sense of cosmic order, they pitilessly eliminated abnormal creatures as products of the cruelty of nature. The appearance of monsters in the animal or human realm was a tangible sign of divine wrath, representing a disturbance of the rhythm and laws of the universe. Thus, the haruspices made monsters disappear from the face of the earth by fire or drowning, but without laying hands on them, lest they suffer contagion from the contamination.

PRODIGIES IN ROMAN LIFE. In Rome, the prodigy went through a perceptible evolution; its characteristics were modified during the course of history. In the beginning, according to Greek and Roman historians, the prodigy was not a divinatory sign, not a simple presaging of an important event. An unforeseen event that appeared in some form of nature broke the course of natural laws and indicated the wrath of the gods, a rupture of the peace the gods maintained with Rome. A sudden disruption of the *pax deum* represented a terrible threat. Such a situation most often came about through the failure of either citizens or the state to fulfill religious duties. To obtain the reestablishment of the crucial *pax deum,* high authorities had at their disposal an arsenal of expiatory measures. They addressed the keepers of whatever religious traditions were indicated—the pontiffs, the guardians of the Sibylline Books, or even the haruspices—to act without delay in restoring calm to a world momentarily threatened. This was known as *procuratio prodigiorum* ("prodigy management"), and it influenced greatly the evolution of Roman religion.

In the crises that characterized Roman religious history from the time of the Second Punic War, an anxious public felt new divinatory needs. Portents and prodigies became nearly indistinguishable, except for the force of the meaning they signified. To be sure, the expiation of contamination continued, but the search for divinatory meaning now intervened. At the end of the republic and the beginning of the empire, Hellenic mystery religions and religions of the Near East increased in popularity, and Christian monotheism made gradual inroads. The person of the emperor, now the center of religious life, was surrounded by an entire series of charismatic signs, portents, or prodigies. The belief in traditional prodigies, however, gave way gradually to other more complex and increasingly widespread beliefs that came from Greece and the East. Astrology and magic became more important, and it was only in great crises that the haruspices, the most ancient priests in Italy, dared to show their strength by calling attention to the prodigies whose secrets they had jealously guarded.

SEE ALSO Divination; Etruscan Religion; Oracles; Sky.

BIBLIOGRAPHY

Works on Portents

Bouché-Leclercq, Auguste. *L'astrologie grecque.* Paris, 1899.

Catalano, Pierangelo. *Contributi allo studio del diritto augurale,* vol. 1. Turin, 1960.

Nougayrol, Jean. "Les rapports des haruspicines étrusque et assyro-babylonienne, et le foie d'argile de *Falerii veteres.*" In *Comptes rendus, Académie des Inscriptions et Belles Lettres,* pp. 509–519. Paris, 1955.

Thulin, Carl O. *Die etruskische Disciplin* (1906–1909). 3 vols. Reprint, Darmstadt, 1968.

Works on Prodigies

Aumüller, Ernst. "Das Prodigium bei Tacitus." Ph.D. diss., University of Frankfurt, 1948.

Bloch, Raymond. *Les prodiges dans l'Antiquité classique: Grèce, Etrurie et Rome.* Paris, 1963.

Brassmann-Fischer, Brigitte. *Die Prodigien in Vergils Aeneis.* Munich, 1966.

Macbain, Bruce. *Prodigy and Expiation: A Study in Religion and Politics in Republican Rome.* Brussels, 1982.

Weinstock, Stefan. "Libri Fulgurales." *Papers of the British School at Rome* 19 (1951): 122–153.

RAYMOND BLOCH (1987)

Translated from French by Marilyn Gaddis Rose

POSEIDON

POSEIDON is the ancient Greek god who embodies primitive power—the power of the untamed, the brutal, the wild. His name, which has not yet been convincingly explained, occurs on clay tablets from Pylos dating from the period preceding the destruction of Mycenaean civilization (1200 BCE). The god thus belongs to the older strata of Greek religion. His exact place in the Mycenaean pantheon is unknown, but he seems to have been more important that Zeus, who was the most prominent Greek god in the Classical period. The tablets of Pylos also mention the Posidaion (a sanctuary most probably located within the city of Pylos) and a goddess Posidaeja (possibly Poseidon's wife, though she is not heard of in later times).

In the Classical period, Poseidon was mainly connected with the sea, earthquakes, the horse, and men's associations. In Homer's *Iliad,* most commonly dated from the eighth century BCE, Poseidon is pictured as the ruler of the sea. When he drives over the waves, his chariot remains dry and the monsters of the deep play beneath him: "They know their lord" (*Iliad* 12.28). In the post-Homeric period, he was not so much the god of the sailors as of the fisherman, whose tool, the trident, became his symbol.

Besides the sea, Poseidon was also connected with the earth. His anger was considered the cause of the earthquakes that hit Greece regularly (Homer refers to him as *gaiēochos,* "earthshaking"), but the god was also invoked to end them; in many cities (especially on the western coast of Asia Minor) Poseidon was worshiped with the epithet *asphaleios* ("the immovable one"). When volcanic activity in 198 BCE caused the emergence of a new, small island, the inhabitants of neighboring Thera, as was typical, dedicated a temple to Poseidon Asphaleios on it.

Poseidon was also widely associated with horse breeding and racing; Greek myth even made him the father of the first horse, and the father or grandfather of the famous horses Pegasus and Areion. Whereas the goddess Athena was considered to be responsible for the technique of horse racing, Poseidon was connected with the wild, nervous, and powerful nature of the horse. Consequently, Athena was invoked during the race, but Poseidon before or after.

Finally, Poseidon was connected with men's associations. His temples were the meeting places of the pan-Ionic league and of the early amphictyony that comprised Athens and its neighbors. Various epithets of the god connect him with specific clans and tribes. Elsewhere Poseidon was worshiped with the epithet *phutalmios* ("the fostering one"), which points to an association with rites of initiation. Indeed, myth relates that the god's love turned the girl Kaineus into an adult man; her sex change is a mythical reflection of the ritual transvestism of the initiands. At a festival for Poseidon in Ephesus, boys acting as wine pourers were called "bulls," just as the god himself was sometimes called "Bull." All this evidence seems to point to a onetime connection of the god with Archaic men's associations (*Männerbünde*) and their ecstatic bull-warriors, which also could be found among the early Germanic peoples.

The Greeks experienced the power of Poseidon as both numinous and untamed. His sanctuaries were usually located outside city walls. Although his power was inescapable, the god was given no place within the ordered society of the Greek city-state.

SEE ALSO Berserkers.

BIBLIOGRAPHY

The best collection of sources for Poseidon's cult is still the reliable discussion in Lewis R. Farnell's *The Cults of the Greek States,* vol. 4, *Poseidon, Apollo* (Oxford, 1907), pp. 1–97. The epigraphical material presented by Farnell on a number of epithets is now supplemented by Fritz Graf's *Nordionische Kulte* (Rome, 1985), pp. 171–2, 175, and 207–8; see now also Joannis Mylonopoulos, *Heiligtümer und Kulte des Poseidon auf der Peloponnes* (Liège, 2003). Marcel Detienne and Jean-Pierre Vernant subtly discuss Poseidon's relationship with the horse in *Cunning Intelligence in Greek Culture and Society,* translated by Janet Lloyd (Atlantic Highlands, N.J., 1978), pp. 187–213. For a new synthesis see my "'Effigies Dei' in Ancient Greece: Poseidon," in D. van der Plas (ed.), *Effigies Dei: Essays on the History of Religions* (Leiden, 1987), pp. 35–41.

JAN N. BREMMER (1987 AND 2005)

POSITIVISM. The terms *positivisme* and *positiviste* were coined by Auguste Comte (1798–1857), who first employed them in his *Discours sur l'ensemble du positivisme* (1848) and his *Catéchisme positiviste* (1852).Comte's neologisms were accepted by the Academie Française in 1878. Equivalent English terms were employed by John Stuart Mill in his *Auguste Comte and Positivism* (1865).

For Comte, "positive philosophy" means real, certain, organic, relational philosophy, and positivism is a philosophical system founded on positive facts and observable phenomena. Because positive facts are not isolated but comprehended by the positive sciences, positivism is a philosophy drawn from the whole of those sciences, and the scientific method determines positivist doctrine. But positivism, as developed by Comte, is both a philosophical system and a religious system that develops from that philosophy.

POSITIVISM AND THE THREE-STATE LAW. In his *Cours de philosophie positive* (1830–1842), Comte explains the relation of positive philosophy to the positive sciences: "The proper study of generalities of the several sciences conceived as submitted to a single method and as forming the several parts of a general research plan." He compares positive philosophy to what is called in English "natural philosophy." However, this latter does not include social phenomena, as does positive philosophy.

Comte contrasted positive philosophy to theological philosophy and metaphysical philosophy. These three philosophies are distinguished according to a three-state law of human knowledge, first presented in *Plan des travaux scientifiques nécessaires pour réorganiser la société* (Plan of the scientific tasks necessary for the reorganization of society, 1822) and developed in the Cours de philosophie positive. The first lesson of the course sketches the progressive march of the human mind and the whole development of human understanding through three methods, or states, of philosophizing: theological, or fictitious; metaphysical, or abstract; and scientific, or positive.

Before the positive method was developed, philosophers, using the metaphysical method, had recourse to abstract forces to explain all natural phenomena; before the metaphysical method, they had recourse to theological modes of explanation—to supernatural entities, to first and final causes—in the search for absolute truth. Though the positive way of philosophizing is, according to Comte, the highest accomplishment of the human mind, the most fundamental of the three methods remains the theological, which is itself divided into three substates: the fetishistic, the polytheistic, and the monotheistic. Comte appreciates the role of each of these substates in the development of the human mind and in the "intellectual history of all our societies"; they ground the possibility of three logics within positive logic: a feeling logic, a picture logic, and a sign logic. The "fetishistic thinker" is the founder of human language and of the fine arts; he is nearer to reality and to scientific truth than is the "dreamy theologist." Theologism, identified with polytheism, is thus opposed to both fetishism and positivism. Monotheism, the third of the theological substates, is "basically metaphysical theology, which reduces fiction by means of reasoning." The metaphysical state is always presented by Comte as a transitional state between theology and positive science, but it also operates as a principle of transformation in the movement from fetishism to polytheism, and from polytheism to monotheism. Beyond this, the metaphysical continues its mediation in the "anthropological revolution" that begins with Comte's own synthesis.

Time, Progress, History. Comte did not create the idea of positivism; it was created by the scientific progress of his century. Emphasis on the relation between the concept of positivism and the concept of progress helps to avoid misconstruing positivism as a nondialectical position based on the mere assertion that scientific data exist. The three-state law introduced to the system of the sciences the notion of time as threefold, dialectical, and progressive.

The predecessors of positivism can be identified among the founders of positive science. Comte often invoked the names of Francis Bacon (1561–1626), Galileo Galilei (1564–1642), and René Descartes (1596–1650); nor did he forget Roger Bacon (1220–1292), pioneer of the experimental method and among the finest medieval thinkers engaged in natural philosophy.

Roger Bacon's *scientia experimentalis* ("experimental science") was the first form of positive science and as such was conceived in correlation with the idea of progress. The idea of progress arises from the dialogue between humans and nature—between the questions of humans and the answers of nature. Along with experience, experiment is the foundation of the human-nature dialogue, which has been expressed in mathematical formulas; an example is Galileo's *De motu* (On motion).

From the thirteenth to the seventeenth century, a developing critical attitude effected a transition from the common religious beliefs of the theological period. During this transition, authority was rejected in favor of evidence and observation. Roger Bacon, in his *Opus maius* (Great work), and Francis Bacon, in his *Novum organum* (New instrument), discuss authority as a cause of error. By circumventing such error, progress in the sciences and the advancement of learning became possible: the concept of progress emerges with the birth of positive science.

Giordano Bruno (1548–1600), in *La cena de le ceneri* (The Ash Wednesday supper), writes that truth is in progress: "Time is the father of truth, its mother is our mind." A concept of time was thus introduced into the scientific method. It was further developed by subsequent philosophers. Galileo's *Discorso del flusso e riflusso del mare* (Discourse on flood and ebb) demonstrates that nature does not concern itself with the human capacity to understand natural laws: Humans must create a method to understand nature. In *Discours de la méthode* (Discourse on method), Descartes introduces a method of reasoning that requires time, as opposed to evidence (which reveals itself in the present). Bernard Le Bovier de Fontenelle (1657–1757) emphasizes the history of scientific progress in his *Entretiens sur la pluralité des mondes* (Talks on the plurality of worlds).

The notion of history, implied by the concept of progress, was further developed by Anne-Robert-Jacques Turgot (1727–1781) in *Les progrès successifs de l'esprit humain* (The successive developments of the human spirit) and by Condorcet (1743–1794) in *Esquisse d'un tableau historique des progrès de l'esprit humain* (Sketch of a historical picture of the successive developments of the human spirit). The progress of enlightenment becomes the motor of history, a movement beyond the progress of virtue emphasized by the three monotheistic religions: Judaism, Islam, and Christianity. A manifold time is therefore necessary to Comte's conception of science: the time for discovering the truth, or method; the time of scientific progress, or the history of discoveries; the time for the awakening of consciousness from simple sensation.

Science and Sociology. The three-state law reiterates and condenses observations of Turgot and Condorcet on the human mind in a formula that belongs to a new science of the system of sciences: sociology or anthropology. The law must be understood in correlation with the system of the sciences presented in the course on positive philosophy, in which Comte demonstrates the three-state law in each of the several sciences, from mathematics to biology to sociology. The aim of the course is realized with the coordination of all scientific conceptions and the birth of a new science: social science. Here, the social scientific discovery of social history reveals the intimate interrelation of scientific and social development. Moreover, mind and history play upon one another. Thus, Comte's philosophy of mind is also a philosophy of history and, hence, positivistic.

The paradigm of the three-state law organizes the classification of the sciences, and the relation between law and classification may be expressed in the definition of positivism as *scientia scientiarum,* or science of sciences. Robert Flint (1838–1910), in *Philosophy as Scientia Scientiarum* and a *History or Classifications of the Sciences* (Edinburgh, 1904), writes:

> Philosophy as *scientia scientiarum* may have more functions than one, but it has at least one. It has to show how science is related to science, where one science is in contact with another; in what way each fits into each, so that all may compose the symmetrical and glorious edifice of human knowledge, which has been built up by the labours of all past generations, and which all future generations must contribute to perfect and adorn. (p. 4)

For Comte, historical practice itself implies the social theory of the three-state law, which implies the logical and historical necessity of social science, which implies positivism, positive philosophy, or the system of positive knowledge. In its turn, positivism implies a practice of social reorganization, advocated by Comte both at the beginning and at the end of his own intellectual history.

RELIGION AND POSITIVISM. That the question raised by positivism with regard to religion was the most important problem for believers at the end of the nineteenth century can be observed in such studies as *Science et religion dans la philosophie contemporaine* (Science and religion in contemporary philosophy) by Émile Boutroux (1845–1921) and *The Varieties of Religious Experience* by William James (1842–1910). Boutroux gives a positivist account of the relation of science to religion and recognizes their common components of solidarity, continuity, love, and altruism, but he does not see a relation of these components to the positivist starting point in the observation of concrete things. Thus, Boutroux is unable to admit the principles of religion as he conceived them: God and immortality of the soul. The positivist philosophers Richard Avenarius (1843–1896) and Ernst Mach (1838–1916), on the other hand, rejected all absolute entities. In a letter dated July 14, 1845, Comte himself wrote to John Stuart Mill:

> Actually, the qualification of *atheists* suits me, going strictly by etymology, which is almost always a wrong way to explain frequently used terms, because we have in common with those who are so called nothing but disbelief in God, without sharing in any way with them their vain metaphysical dreams about the origin of the world or humankind, still less their narrow and dangerous attempts to systematize morals.

Nevertheless, in another letter to Mill, Comte did not reject praying. "For a real positivist, to pray is to love and to think, first to think by praying, then to pray by thinking, in order to develop subjective life toward those whose objective life is accomplished" (October 28, 1850). To the claim of Emil Du Bois-Reymond (1818–1896)—"Ignorabimus" ("We shall ignore [nonnatural events]"), such positivists as Alfred Fouillée (1820–1912) replied "Sperabimus" ("We shall hope"). Fouillée assented in some spiritualist claims; like Herbert Spencer (1820–1903), he admitted an unknowable.

THE IMPULSE OF POSITIVISM. Positivism is characterized by the will to realize a synthesis that takes into account all human concerns. Some positivists, like Émile Littré (1801–1881) and Abel Rey (1873–1940), reduce philosophy to a mere history of scientific thought. Nevertheless, Littré concluded that beyond the positivist object of thought there is a reality unattainable yet within the human range of clear vision. Instead of God or the unknowable, Comte proposed humanity as the focus of his synthesis, and his "religion of humanity" attracted many followers in France and abroad, especially in Brazil.

SEE ALSO Comte, Auguste.

BIBLIOGRAPHY

For discussion of the birth and development of positivism, see Henri Gouhier's *La jeunesse d'Auguste Comte et la formation du positivisme,* 3 vols. (Paris, 1933–1941). Exegesis of the entire philosophical and scientific enterprise of Comte and the positivists can be found in my *Entre le signe et l'histoire: L'anthropologie positiviste d'Auguste Comte* (Paris, 1982), *Le positivisme* (Paris, 1982), and *Le concept de science positive: Ses tenant et ses aboutissants dans structures anthropologiques du positivisme* (Paris, 1983). For a study of religious positivism, see Walter Dussauze's *Essai sur la religion d'après Auguste Comte* (Paris, 1901) and Paul Arbousse-Bastide's "Le positivisme politique et religieux au Brésil" (Ph.D. diss., Sorbonne, 1953). Paul Arbousse-Bastide treats Comte's philosophy of education in *La doctrine de l'éducation universelle dans la philosophie d'Auguste Comte,* 2 vols. (Paris, 1957). Pierre Arnaud's *"Le Nouveau Dieu"* (Paris, 1973) examines positive politics.

New Sources

Cashdollar, Charles. *The Transformation of Theology, 1830–1890: Positivism and Protestant Thought in Britain and America.* Princeton, N.J., 1989.

Friedman, Michael. *Reconsidering Logical Positivism.* New York, 1999.

Groff, Ruth. *Critical Realism, Post-Positivism, and the Possibility of Knowledge.* New York, 2004.

Guest, Steven, ed. *Positivism Today.* Issues in Law and Society series. Aldershot, U.K., 1996.

Scharff, Robert. *Comte after Positivism.* New York, 2002.

ANGÈLE KREMER-MARIETTI (1987)
Revised Bibliography

POSSESSION, SPIRIT SEE SPIRIT POSSESSION

POSTURES AND GESTURES are primal aspects of religious belief and behavior and as such have emerged, with other elements of culturally symbolic expression and communication, at the threshold of human existence. Their use is not, of course, restricted to the human species; nonhuman animals display a wide variety of postures and gestures that serve to demarcate species from each other and to signify territorial dominance, propagation procedures, and social hierarchy. However, culturally generated and transmitted postures and gestures, which may retain elements of phylogenetically evolved ones, nevertheless transcend these in their specific configurations of learned and intentional patterns, significations, and symbolizations.

Every religious tradition recognizes an intimate relationship between inward dispositions and external postures and gestures of the human body, which is capable of expressing and celebrating a great range of attitudes, moods, motivations, and intentions, whether sacred or profane. The study of postures and gestures has not progressed as far as the study of other aspects of religion or as far as the study of social science as a whole; but such study—especially the emerging disciplines of kinesics, ethology, and semiotics—deserves close attention.

ISLAM: A CASE FOR PRELIMINARY OBSERVATION AND ANALYSIS. Among the Abrahamic religions, Islam contains in its ritual observances a rich and varied repertory of postures and gestures that are mastered by every adherent. Christianity also has many body movements and gestures of deep significance, but they are neither universally performed within the tradition nor permitted across all classes of believers. All Muslims perform the *rakʿahs* (bowing cycles) of each *ṣalāt,* or prayer service, with a combination of standing, bowing, prostration, and sitting postures accompanied by coordinated head, hand, arm, and foot gestures. By contrast, the postures and gestures of Christian worship, for example in the Roman Catholic tradition, are assigned to laity or clergy in a carefully regulated manner; although certain basic forms, such as kneeling and making the sign of the cross, are shared, the laity nevertheless do not raise the sacramental elements, nor serve them, nor bless—these are gestures reserved for ordained priests.

A Muslim, or a knowledgeable outside observer, can tell at a glance and from a distance when a Muslim is at formal prayer (*ṣalāt*), and moreover at what point in the ritual, just from observing postures and gestures. If the worshiper is standing, with the hands placed slightly in front and to the sides of the head, with the thumbs aligned with the earlobes, then the observer knows that the prayer has just begun with the utterance "Allāhu akbar" ("God is most great!"). But the worshiper seated with knees on the floor and buttocks resting on the ankles is either at the midpoint of the cycle or near the end, depending on the precise placement of feet and hands. If the right hand is resting on the right thigh, and gathered into a fist, with the index finger waving slowly back and forth, and if the left foot has been placed beneath the right ankle, under the buttocks, then the cycle is nearly finished. If it is the final cycle in the series—and each daily *ṣalāt* has a set number of required *rakʿahs*—then the observer will know that the prayer is nearly over by the worshiper's turning of the head to the right and the left, uttering a blessing in each direction. This is the only point in any *ṣalāt* service at which the worshiper turns aside in any manner from the *qiblah,* or direction of Mecca. Other important parts of the *rakʿah,* which itself means "bowing," are actual bowing and, most important, a full prostration with the forehead touching the floor or ground; this gesture, called in Arabic *sajda,* is the climax of Islamic worship, when the slave of God symbolizes his total submission and obedience. If the worshiper is seen in the sitting posture, but with hands extended in front, palms upward, he or she is not engaged in the formal *ṣalāt,* probably, but is performing *duʿāʾ,* the voluntary prayer of personal petition frequently uttered after formal worship and at other auspicious times, such as at the close of a Qurʾān recitation, especially of the entire text. Or a prostration may be enacted in conjunction with the recitation of a special Qurʾān verse—whose hearing renders meritorious an immediate *sajda*—but omitting the other postures and gestures of the full *rakʿah.*

SOCIAL FUNCTIONS OF RELIGIOUS POSTURES AND GESTURES. Religious postures and gestures serve not only to symbolize and regulate devotion; they also demarcate religious communities and subcommunities. If one sees, for example, in a Middle Eastern or Southeast Asian context, where the vast majority of people are Muslim, a person kneeling in an attitude of devotion, with hands folded or palms pressed together, with head bowed and eyes closed, one is seeing a member of the Christian tradition or possibly a Buddhist. Muslims do not kneel at prayer, fold their hands, or bow their heads with closed eyes like the Christians. Moreover, within Christianity itself there are significant variations that identify specific churches, denominations, and sects and, in some cases—as evident from art and iconography—distinct historical periods. Kneeling, for example, is a biblically warranted posture of piety that has been adopted at some time or other by most Christian communities. But in formal worship, Christians from different traditions do not necessarily all kneel at the same point, or for the same reason. Some Christians kneel in adoration, whereas others reserve that posture for penitence, which is often done in private. Some Christians stand while receiving Communion, whereas others kneel.

Likewise, there are varying ways of making the sign of the cross, two of which distinguish Roman Catholics from Eastern Orthodox: the former move the hand from the left to the right shoulder, whereas the latter move the hand from right to left. Both gestures are unambiguously Christian, yet the slight difference symbolizes also a great historical and communal separation. Similarly, particular Islamic subcommunities may exhibit variations of gesture: for example, in the standing position of formal worship some allow the hands to hang loosely at the sides, whereas others fold them gently in front of the body. By contrast, as already noted, the Islamic cultus of posture and gesture is remarkably uniform throughout the world and has been so since its early formalization. A Baptist of narrow experience who visits a high church Episcopal service would be at sea about what to do next in the liturgy: stand, kneel, or sit? But every Muslim with minimal religious upbringing would be at home in Islamic worship anywhere in the world. Even a Muslim who does not understand a word of Arabic—though most do know a few religious phrases—probably knows the postures and gestures of worship in every detail.

SYMBOLIC RANGE OF RELIGIOUS POSTURES AND GESTURES. Religious postures and gestures are cultural products and are transmitted in various ways and with different understandings. Consequently, the question of whether there is an intrinsic relationship between inward dispositions and outward manifestations is difficult to resolve. It would seem that in most cases these manifestations are intentional signs that serve to reinforce as well as express doctrines and attitudes. Nevertheless, they are similar in many cultures; there is a high correlation between certain postures and gestures and a wide range of emotions and purposes that are usually if not exclusively religious or magical. Among these are adoration, affirmation, blessing, consecration, curse, gratitude, greeting, humility, invocation, meditation, mourning, oath taking, penitence, pleading, praise, prayer, protection, remorse, reverence, sorrow, and submission.

Kneeling is often associated with adoration, blessing, confession, humility, penitence, pleading, petition, remorse, and submission, especially in Christianity. Prostration is a dramatic posture expressing submission, penitence, consecration, and humiliation. It is especially closely associated with Islamic worship, but known also in the Bible and other religious contexts.

The sitting posture sometimes symbolizes religious attitudes, particularly in the Buddhist attitude of concentration wherein the legs are crossed, right over left, with soles facing upward, hands resting on the thighs, with thumbs touching. This "Lotus Position" is basic to Buddhist meditation as well as to Hindu yoga. Muslims commonly sit in a posture similar to the Lotus Position when in a mosque or adopt it as a normal posture anywhere. Egyptian Muslims like to rock back and forth in this position when listening to Qurʾān recitation, which can be highly rhythmic. A similar practice is found among Jews. Sitting is also understood as a royal and a divine posture, as evidenced by thrones and mounts, from whence commands and judgments descend.

Standing is a posture that in religious tradition signifies respect, as evidenced when Christians stand for the reading aloud of the gospel lesson. Early Christians stood for congregational prayer, and standing throughout the service is still practiced in Eastern Orthodoxy. Muslims stand at the beginning of the *ṣalāt* when making their *nīyah,* or "intention," and uttering the first *takbīr,* "God is most great!" The Islamic funeral service may be performed only in a standing position, and it is recommended that Muslims stand in respect when a funeral procession passes, because a soul is being transported to its place of repose until the Resurrection. The most profound point of the Islamic pilgrimage to Mecca *(ḥajj)* is the *wuqūf,* or "standing" ceremony, when the pilgrims stand for hours in repentance and hope for mercy from God. So important is this ritual standing to the Muslim that its omission for any reason invalidates the individual's pilgrimage; unlike certain other elements of the pilgrimage, the *wuqūf* must be performed beginning on a set day and at noon.

Dance as practiced in religious contexts combines many postures and gestures in complex configurations. The American Indians, for example, developed dance for religious and magical purposes in pursuit of healing, hunting success, rain, good crops, and victory over enemies, as well as for critical and calendrical rites having to do with matters such as puberty, initiation, seasons, harvests, and natural calamities. Dance has been of central importance in the religious life of peoples in all regions, and it extends far back into prehistory. The Mevlevīs, members of the Ṣūfī order of "dancing" or "whirling" dervishes founded by Jalāl al-Dīn Rūmī (d. 1273), spin around their leader like heavenly bodies rotating about the sun. The twentieth century has seen a renewed interest in both Roman Catholic and Protestant worship in sacred dance, in the conviction that the body and its movements are repositories of holiness and a fundamental means for communing with God and celebrating the mysteries of salvation. Likewise, celebration of the whole person, soul and body, was a basic dimension in the worship of the Jews of biblical times, who danced and clapped their hands in joy in the presence of God.

Hands, which express the broadest range of religious and magical meanings and are major instruments of gesture in all traditions, are used in such motions and configurations as are necessary for blessing, praying, consecrating, healing, anointing, protecting, welcoming, ordaining, and other purposes.

Mudrā, a Sanskrit word meaning "sign, gesture," denotes a highly ramified and conceptually sophisticated symbolic hand language developed by the closely related Indian religions Hinduism and Buddhism; it interpenetrates and connects various levels of their belief, behavior, aesthetic sensitivity, and communal life. *Mudrās* take many forms, each of which symbolizes a doctrine or truth or realization or experience. In Buddhism, for example, a fundamental event in the founder's career may be symbolized by means of *mudrā. Mudrās* are used extensively in ritual, iconography, dance, drama, and teaching in Hindu and Buddhist regions. Without an understanding of *mudrā,* one could not interpret and thus fully appreciate the hundreds of stone reliefs concerning the Buddha's cosmic evolution that adorn the magnificent stupa of Borobudur in Central Java.

Not only the hands, but also the arms have been important in religious gesture. Extending the arms out to the sides has been practiced as a gesture of solar adoration. Coptic Christians spread out their arms in the form of a cross at baptism. Ancient Egyptian, Sumerian, Babylonian, and Etruscan worshipers spread their arms in prayer. Ancient Egyptians, Buddhists, and Romans prayed with arms crossed on the chest. Present-day extending of the arms by Armenian Christians is symbolic of the Trinity; in this position the neophyte turns toward the west and spits at the Devil, then turns east with spread arms and faces heaven in acknowledgment of Father, Son, and Holy Spirit.

Mouth and lips, too, have been prominent in sacred gesture among very diverse peoples. Magical practices have included spitting three times into the folds of one's garment to avoid the evil eye (ancient Greece), spitting on children for the same reason (ancient Rome), spitting into the eye of a close relative to prove the absence of evil-eye intentions (ancient and modern Greece), and other spitting gestures, such as the Shintō and Buddhist practice in Japan of spitting at healing deities. The Qurʾān instructs one to take refuge from the "evil of the women who blow on knots," meaning the witches who cast harmful spells by ritual spitting on knots tied in a cord (113:5).

Kissing particularly is often used in ritual gesture. Women kissed Christ's feet (*Lk.* 7:38). The thresholds of churches have traditionally been kissed, as have been relics, burial sites, and other powerful repositories of the holy. Muslim folk practices include the kissing of saint shrine enclosures for *barakah* ("blessing"). Christians have been known to kiss the Bible when taking an oath. Shīʿī Muslims sometimes kiss copies of the Qurʾān. Jews kiss the *mezuzah* when leaving or entering the home. Mecca pilgrims try to kiss the holy Black Stone embedded in the Kaʿbah, in imitation of Muhammad's custom. Ancient Greeks kissed the sacred oak of Zeus at Aegina. Catholics kiss the crucifix. Many ancient Near Eastern peoples kissed the hands, feet, and clothing of sacred images. Pope John Paul II kisses the ground of the countries he visits. Muslim youth kiss the hand of their Qurʾān teacher as a gesture of deep respect not only for the teacher as a person but for the treasure that the teacher carries and imparts.

In addition to postures adopted by the living are those imposed upon the deceased by others acting on their behalf. Burial in a fetal position, for example, has been known for prehistoric archaeology and ethnography. This unusual practice may have come about to prevent the spirit of the deceased from wandering about after death, especially in cases wherein the body has been tightly bound. An alternative interpretation is that the position imitates the state in the womb, with burial representing a sort of return. Most peoples lay the body on the back for burial, sometimes with particular orientations. Muslims sometimes bury their dead lying on the right side, with the face pointing toward Mecca; even if the body is supine, the face is oriented in that direction. Al-Ghazālī, the great Muslim theologian (d. 1111), advised the pious to go to bed at night lying on the right side, facing Mecca, because sleep in the Islamic view is a "little death," from which an individual might not wake. Again, Christian baptism by immersion imitates a posthumous position, in which the initiate submits passively as the officiant symbolically buries the old person who is presently to be cleansed and resurrected in the new life in Christ.

SOCIAL, MAGICAL, AVOIDANCE, AND SELF-DESTRUCTIVE GESTURES. Perhaps the most extensively studied, if not the most richly developed, social gestures among civilized peoples are those found in Mediterranean societies, such as Italy, France, Spain, Greece, Egypt, Lebanon, Turkey, Syria, and the Maghreb. Most of the postures and gestures cannot be interpreted as religious; in fact, many are utterly profane, even obscene, and have been so since antiquity. An example is the sign of the fig, made with the thumb protruding from between the index and middle fingers. This is a sexual insult, usually, and in the Middle Ages was declared illegal if directed at religious images and symbols. The sign of the horns, made by extending the index and little fingers from a closed fist, and directing it toward the eyes of a threatening person, has long been an apotropaic gesture. Among Muslims, for example in North Africa, a gesture called the Hand of Fāṭimah is made by extending the fingers toward a supposed enemy in order to neutralize the evil eye. If uncertain whether harm is actually intended, the gesturer may make the gesture under a cloak or other covering, particularly when the danger is not perceived to be grave. The "horns" are also sometimes thus covered.

Social postures and gestures sometimes involve ritual avoidances. Among Muslims, especially in the Middle East and Southeast Asia, a strong distinction is made between the right and left sides of the body. Only the right hand is considered clean and fit for gesturing, giving, receiving, blessing, greeting, eating, and touching. The left hand is considered as unclean because it is used for humble tasks only, such as the toilet. It is a great breach of propriety to use the left hand for what is properly a right-hand function. The right foot leads when entering a mosque, but one leaves a holy place left foot first. The toilet room is entered left foot first and exited with the right foot leading. The soles of the feet are considered, by Muslims and other Eastern peoples, to be unclean, and so it is essential to avoid directing them toward anyone (as an American may inadvertently do when resting the feet on a desk top). In Java it is considered arrogant and disrespectful for a boy or man to cross his legs or ankles in the presence of a superior, especially while sitting in a chair. Although that is a cultural taboo, the observance of it is especially noticeable in pious Muslim contexts, where proper physical deportment is a mark of the religious person. Social postures and gestures in highly stratified traditional societies, like Java, provide valuable clues about religious worldview.

In religious practice certain self-destructive gestures exist that express powerful emotion. One is the ritual flagellation practiced by Christian ascetics, especially during Passion Week. A structurally similar practice is the self-flagellation, often with chains, of Shīʿī men in processions associated with the Tenth of Muharram, the anniversary of the martyrdom of Imam Ḥusayn ibn ʿAlī at Karbala, Iraq, in 680. The ancient Israelites mourned by putting ashes on their heads (*2 Sm.* 13:19) or tearing their hair and beards (*Ezr.* 9:3). Modern Palestinian women beat their breasts, tear their hair, scratch their cheeks, and throw soot on their heads in mourning, gestures that can be traced back to ancient times.

SEE ALSO Dance; Hands; Haṭhayoga; Human Body; Knees; Mudrā; Ṣalāt; Spittle and Spitting; Touching.

BIBLIOGRAPHY

For an excellent collection of sources and an extensive bibliography, see Betty J. Bäuml and Franz H. Bäuml's *A Dictionary of Gestures* (Metuchen, N.J., 1975). Religious postures and gestures have yet to be given much attention by students of religion, at least as a comprehensive subfield. However, a comprehensive literature on ritual and devotional practices, including detailed analysis and interpretation of postures and gestures, exists within numerous religious traditions. In addition to ritual, liturgical, and scriptural sources, a variety of other sources, for example, works on law, ethnography, and art history, provide information on the subject.

The relatively new sciences of ethology, kinesics, and semiotics give great promise of increasing the understanding of posture and gesture. Konrad Lorenz's studies, for example, offer some provocative ideas concerning the relationship between phylogenetically transmitted and culturally transmitted gestures in animals and humans; see his *Behind the Mirror: A Search for a Natural History of Human Knowledge* (New York, 1977).

FREDERICK MATHEWSON DENNY (1987)

POTLATCH is any of a disparate variety of complex ceremonies among the Indians of the Pacific Northwest Coast of North America, associated with the legitimization of the transfer or inheritance of hereditary aristocratic titles and their associated rights, privileges, and obligations. Potlatches are characterized by the reenactment of the sacred family histories that document the legitimacy of the claimant to the rank, by ritual feasting, and by the formal distribution of gifts by the host group to its guests, each according to his rank. Though the wealth distributed at a potlatch may be quite substantial, the amount distributed is much less important than the requirement that it be distributed according to the correct social protocols and moral prescriptions.

Potlatches have traditionally occurred at points of social stress accompanying any part of the process of ascension or succession to rank: investiture into a new name; the building of a house; erecting of a totem pole or other emblem of hereditary prerogative, such as a marriage or a child's coming of age; or alternatively as a mortuary feast for a previous rankholder, as a means of acquiring prestige; and sometimes even as a means of discrediting rival claimants. The legitimacy of the rankholder's claims is proven by his dual ability to command the allegiance of his family group in putting together such a complicated ceremony and to perform correctly the formal display of his family's origin myths and ceremonial objects. The acceptance of gifts by the guests signals their acceptance of the validity of his claim.

Anthropologists have focused on the secular, social aspects and functions of the potlatch—on the way in which potlatches maintain social equilibrium, consolidate chiefly power over commoners, provide for the orderly transfer of wealth and power, provide a measure of group identity and solidarity, redistribute surplus wealth and level economic imbalances, provide outlets for competition without recourse to violence, and provide an occasion for aesthetic expression and dramatic entertainment. Irving Goldman has suggested in his *The Mouth of Heaven* (1975) that, since in Northwest Coast philosophy all status, power, and wealth are considered to be a gift from the beneficent supernatural beings who provide the materials that humans need to survive, the potlatch is inherently a religious institution, fundamentally endowed with a sacramental quality. Each of the family origin myths, whose retelling is such an important part of the potlatch, tells of how one of a particular family's ancestors was able to make a covenant with a supernatural being. In return for the right to collect food of a specific type at a specific location, to possess an aristocratic name, to impersonate (and thus become) the supernatural being in ceremonies, and to invoke the aid of that being in times of distress, the ancestor accepted the responsibility of performing the rituals that would ensure the reincarnation of that supernatural being. This covenant expresses the mutual dependency of human and supernatural, and the potlatch is the ceremony through which the aristocrat fulfills his responsibilities to the supernatural being.

The chief is the representative of his house to the spirits and in his person are brought together all the historical, social, and spiritual aspects of his group's identity. He is the being who links the spiritual world to the social world, and his costume and behavior at potlatches clearly state the duality of his role as spirit in human form. Indeed, since chiefs are the representatives of particular supernatural beings, the distribution of wealth to other chiefs at potlatches can be seen as a metaphorical distribution by one supernatural being to others, and as such it represents the flow of substance throughout the entire universe.

The potlatch, obviously a rite of passage for human beings, a death of an old identity and a rebirth into a new one, is also a rite of passage for the supernaturals. The supernatural beings sustain human beings not only by giving them power and knowledge, but by being their food—when supernatural beings come to the human world, they put on costumes that transform them into animals. The objects displayed, transferred, or distributed in potlatches are manifestations of the bodies of supernatural beings: the flesh and skins of animals (which, since they are thought to be the animals' ceremonial costumes, imply that humans survive by ingesting the ceremonial, spiritual essence of their prey); the coppers (large, ceremonial plaques that represent repositories of captured souls awaiting reincarnation); and the feast dishes (which are the coffins for the animal substance before the humans who partake of that substance begin the process of its reincarnation). Potlatches, in a sense, are funerals for the supernaturals and inherently involve the reaffirmation of the eternal moral covenants between humankind and the other inhabitants of the universe. As animals sacrifice their flesh that humans may eat it and live, so humans must sacrifice themselves or their wealth, which is a symbol of themselves, that the dead may be reborn.

In Northwest Coast thought, moral order and spiritual purity are achieved through acts of self-sacrifice, and the giving away of possessions places humans in harmony with the moral order of the universe. The universe is imagined to have been originally a place of self-interest and possessiveness, that is, until culture heroes started the process of distribution. Northwest Coast peoples believe that the universe will collapse back into the primordial chaos of selfishness unless humans continually reaffirm their willingness to disburse their possessions, to pass out wealth to their fellow men, and to pass on rank to their children. The potlatch provides the ceremonial realization of that commitment to the cosmic moral order and is a reaffirmation by all its participants—hosts, guests, ancestors, the unborn, and supernatural beings—of the system of moral covenants and mutual dependencies that lie at the basis of Northwest Coast society. The potlatch reenacts myth, and then, through redistribution, recreates its processual nature, thereby becoming a graphic representation of the continuing reality and salience of those myths, linking the past to the present, the dead to the living, the sacred to the mundane, the human to the supernatural, the local to the cosmic, and the momentary to the eternal.

It should be noted that the potlatch underwent substantial change during the nineteenth century. Heavy governmental and missionary pressures contributed to the abandonment or secularization of many Northwest Coast Indian rituals. Potlatches and all other native ceremonies were illegal in Canada between 1876 and 1951, and though some ceremonies were carried out in secret, Northwest Coast religion was irreparably altered. The potlatch and other ceremonies have played an important role in the native renaissance of the 1960s, 1970s, and 1980s, but few studies of the potlatch in contemporary Indian life have been conducted, and very little can be said of the particulars of its role in Indian society today.

BIBLIOGRAPHY

Philip Drucker and Robert F. Heizer provide a lucid review of the literature and a discussion of the potlatch as a social institution in *To Make My Name Good* (Berkeley, Calif., 1967); Helen Codere's *Fighting with Property: A Study of Kwakiutl Potlatching and Warfare, 1792–1930* (New York, 1950) deals with the issue of historical changes in the potlatches of the Kwakiutl; Irving Goldman's *The Mouth of Heaven* (New York, 1975) reexamines many of the Kwakiutl materials collected by Franz Boas and argues for a new religio-philosophical interpretation of Northwest Coast culture.

STANLEY WALENS (1987)

POWER. The term *kratophany* literally rendered is "the appearance of power." Mircea Eliade, however, who made this a technical term in English, used it to indicate an appearance of the sacred in which the experience of power dominates. Thus, that every kratophany must be, at the same time, a hierophany ("appearance of the sacred") is certain by definition, while the converse is less clear; indeed, assent to it will hinge upon the degree to which one regards the concept or experience of power to be an irreducible part of the concept or experience of the sacred.

That the idea of power is central to much religious experience can be seen by means of a simple mental exercise: try to imagine hierophany without the elements of awesomeness, authority, or effectiveness. Most will agree that it is possible to imagine intellectual constructs such as truth or value without power, but hierophany seems to require more. Here is one difference between philosophy and religion, between the intellectual grasp of an idea and the experience of a sacred reality: the religious experience involves the whole personality and not merely the intellect. It includes the emotions as well as less obvious aspects of human awareness such as the kinesthetic sense and deep instinctual and symbolic structures. Finally, it may be that the sense of reality and the sensing of power are inextricably combined into what is experienced as a unity that might be labeled "real presence." As a category of modern physics, power can be described as a potentiality, or a potential ability to do "work," which in turn implies the expenditure of energy to change the distribution of energy in a given system, just as water piled up behind a hydroelectric dam has great potential for generating electricity because of its advantageous location with respect to the direction of gravitational forces. Unlike water, however, the sacred always remains potential even after awesome power has been expended, and it is this mysterious characteristic of being an inexhaustible source of power that in part gives to hierophany its paradoxical tendency both to attract and to repulse.

The normal reactions to sacred power within a given culture can conveniently be classified under the rubrics of *mana* and *taboo*. *Mana* implies a positive attitude toward power within an object or symbol or person—power that can be appropriated for useful purposes. *Taboo* implies the opposite, namely, power in an object or symbol or person that must be avoided for safety's sake or at least hedged about with special "insulating" rites before it can be made useful. Examples are amulets and charms, holy books, saints' relics, and living sacred persons. Infraction of such governing rules constitutes sacrilege and usually brings down cultural or cultic sanctions upon the guilty, or even the direct intervention of sacred power itself.

Perhaps the most important, because clearest, example of the role played by power in religion can be seen by examination of the meaning of cosmogonic myths and of what appears to be the psychological reality that informs them, namely, the universal experience of the prestige of origins. Here, above all, is demonstrated the positive side of sacred power in its intrinsic creativity. Here is the power to bring a world into being, to shape reality, and thereby to found human cults and cultures. It is literally true that within cosmogonic myths everything that happens is a unique demonstration of creative power, since everything that happens does so for the first time. Examples abound, but consider only the Dreaming adventures of many sacred beings in Australian tribal religions, where the seemingly trivial acts performed while traveling around the countryside actually create the landscape and populate it with sacred places gravid with meaning. Or consider the Shinto myths in which with nearly every gesture of the gods—whether by sexual contact, by breaking or cutting something, or by uttering special words—new deities came into existence, deities whose intimate relationship with nature and culture made them constitutive of the world.

More dramatic examples may be found in the Hebrew scriptures, in the *Book of Job*, for example, where frequent references are made to God's creative power in ordering the world and controlling the awesome forces of the cosmic ocean. As the text comes down to us, Job's response is one of terror and repentance without understanding. The Hindu classic *Bhagavadgītā* provides another forceful revelation of the sacred as power in Arjuna's trembling witness to Lord Kṛṣṇa's true nature: nothing less than the world process is portrayed in the deity's simultaneous destructive function as death and his creative function as the womb of all beings.

POWER AND THEORIES OF THE ORIGINS OF RELIGION. Although scattered speculations can be found in the classical civilizations of China, India, and Greece, theoretical reconstructions of the possible origins of religion stem in their modern forms from the European encounter with those cultures that, from about the time of the Enlightenment until a few decades ago, were known collectively as "the savages." Knowledge of these so-called primitive (or archaic, or nonliterate) peoples made a strong impression on the Western imagination. Among other things, it played an important role in the foundation during the nineteenth century of such academic disciplines as psychology, sociology, and anthropology. Perhaps because many of the more detailed accounts of such cultures came from religious professionals and perhaps also because it was an age in the West of great religious ferment, the discovery of primitive cultures was both a discovery of exotic social customs and of strange and disquieting systems of belief and ritual. The most significant systematic attempt of this period to reconstruct a "natural history" of religion was E. B. Tylor's *Primitive Culture* (1871). There the theory of animism was first propounded.

Tylor defined *animism* as belief, or a tendency toward belief, that all nature was endowed with a spiritual, animating essence, or soul. Thus, by anthropomorphizing analogy, every natural power or object was directed by a personality possessing intellect and will. According to this theory, all things were supposed by humans' primitive ancestors to be humanlike—if not in outward appearance, then in their inner being. Power was implied in this view in that the power of being of every thing, its uniqueness and its efficacy, was assumed to be potentially greater than what one would call its mere physical possibilities. Yet the experiences that lay behind this animistic worldview were not, in Tylor's view, fundamentally of power, with its exciting, often daunting emotional concomitants, but were instead of a different and more coolly logical kind. He reasoned that primitives must have been perplexed by their own dreams and thoughts, in which they themselves as well as other people, both living and dead, and not present in the usual sense, appeared. Adding this to their own natural experience of themselves as thinking, willing, self-moving beings, primitives must have concluded that a soul, or animating principle, must inhere in all things and that it could sometimes be separated from the body. In this way, Tylor sought not only to explain primitive beliefs but also to define a proto-religious stage of cultural evolution. Religion, or more strictly the prerequisite for religion, he went on to define as "a belief in spiritual beings." Animism, then, is but one type of religion, namely, the belief that all things have souls, or, as it were, both a material and a spiritual "body" or aspect.

Tylor's theory of animism, and indeed his view of religion as a phenomenon that properly encompasses both primitive and so-called higher forms in a unified theory, provided the *locus classicus* of most anthropological work, including the formation of new theories, until well past the turn of the century. The main thrust of theorizing in this period was to reconstruct the origins of religious behavior itself, that is, to isolate the most elementary impulse, feeling, or experience that constituted the *sine qua non* of religion, and to place all forms of religious behavior on an evolutionary scale of development from this point of origin. It should be noted here that a shift in emphasis in anthropological studies occurred in an early reaction to what was deemed by many to be Tylor's excessively intellectualist view of human nature, at least as it was displayed regarding primitives. Increasingly anthropologists viewed human beings primarily as active creatures whose thought processes are subordinated to action: thought "rationalizes" action to the degree that ideas are formed only in reaction to deeds and to provide a more or less emotionally satisfying intellectual justification for them. It is here that the idea of power, in a variety of forms, began to play its part in the great quest for origins.

Animatism is the name given to a theory, formulated by R. R. Marett, that sought to build upon the work of Tylor. Although he accepted animism as a higher stage in religious development, Marett rejected the "intellectualist fallacy" inherent in the theory of animism insofar as it claimed to represent the first stage of religion. He suggested instead that primitives experience the world as fundamentally divided into the familiar and the unfamiliar. The unfamiliar object is so because it exhibits some sort of strangeness suggestive of hidden power. This he called variously "occult power" and "the sacred." To the compound of unusual and hidden power he added the notion of life in much the same sense that Tylor had used animus, that is, life or soul, except that he believed that, at the stage of animatism, the primitive mind had not yet made the leap from life or life force to separable soul. This meant that animatism could also properly be understood as "preanimism."

The full articulation of this theory was published in 1909 in Marett's *The Threshold of Religion*, but as early as 1900 he had made the first steps toward it in his establishment of the Oceanic word *mana* as a general category of religious experience. He based his usage primarily upon the work of R. H. Codrington (see *The Melanesians*, 1891), who reported that for many South Pacific island cultures, the religious system was based upon a single concept, which they called *mana*. Among the Melanesians, *mana*, the power that inhered in all things, had special significance for their religious and social system, because it could be concentrated in some objects and because it inhered in a concentrated form in some people. Indeed, the hierarchical structure of their society was justified upon the basis of the aristocrats' inborn great *mana.* Everything possessed some mana, and, in this respect, the term might be translated "the power of being." Since so much was made of its concentratability, however, in many cases the term is better rendered as "sacred." But for many scholars, particularly in the nineteenth century, this usage permitted an unacceptable broadening of the meaning of *sacred,* since mana could be transferred from one object or person to another. Many tended to classify this notion not as religious but as pertaining to magic. The fluidity of *mana* made it a kind of physical energy, or at least analogous to such an energy: the transfer could be affected by touching one mana-charged object with another with less *mana*; in particular, a person of high *mana* could infuse an object with some of his or her *mana* by handling it.

It was not long after the publication of Codrington's findings that similar discoveries began to be made in other parts of the world. American anthropologists were especially active at this time, and the Huron *orenda,* the Lakota *wakan,* and the Algonquin *manitou* were soon added to the list of *mana*-like concepts. Later the Arabic *barakah* and East Asian terms such as the Chinese *ling-pao* and the Japanese *kami* were suggested as counterparts to the Melanesian idea of *mana.* From such evidence, Marett then posited a general psychological tendency of human beings to experience the world as well as themselves under the guise of a controlling religious concept: sacred or occult power. This view has had great influence among scholars. However, contemporary anthropology does not generally accept Marett's insistence that even the most elementary religious experience engrafts to the notion of power the assumption of personality—or, to put it another way, that *mana* and animatism are necessarily combined. It may, of course, be true in certain cultures, as he argued, that because mana most powerfully manifested itself in certain types of persons, it was treated as if it were the willpower of a human being, but it is not true in all cultures. And the value of the term mana is just in its use as a general descriptive category denoting a sacred power that is not in itself personal. Thus, in fact, the modern usage implies a psychological, if not necessarily chronological, priority to the idea of *mana* over even Marett's animatism.

POWER AND THE NATURE OF RELIGION. In 1909, with the publication of *Les rites de passage,* Arnold van Gennep applied the label dynamistic to the theories of the origin of religion put forth by Marett (1900) and by J. N. B. Hewitt (1902), based upon the experience of the sacred as power. But van Gennep drew a sharp line between what he called dynamism, or the conceptual framework that assumed impersonal sacred power, and animism, which assumed that sacred power was personal. Since his goal was to classify rituals, and to a large extent to understand by means of classification, he did not enter into the theoretical debate concerning the origins of religion. Yet, because of the obvious value of his way of discussing ritual activities, his work did influence the theoretical debate, if only by showing that it was possible to make significant contributions to the study of religion without choosing a position concerning the question of origins.

No less implicit in van Gennep's work was the assumption of the centrality of the idea of power in religion, not so much in its own theorizing or attempts at self-understanding, but in its actual behavior. Thus he coined the term *magico-religious* to emphasize the practical side of human interaction with sacred power. All ritual activity he labeled as magical because it was in the realm of technique; that is, it sought to implement a practical goal, namely, to influence or even to manipulate the sacred power for useful purposes. It was, therefore, the efficacy of the sacred, its potentiality to effect change or to prevent change—in short, its power—that van Gennep emphasized in his basic insight that ritual, or, at any rate, many rituals, seek to effect transitions from one state or situation to another.

At about the same time that Marett and van Gennep were formulating their views of religion, other theories about the nature and, to some extent, the origin of religion were being formulated outside the conceptual circle of the new discipline of anthropology. Influenced by anthropological and ethnological studies, but operating in a very different intellectual framework, was Rudolf Otto, a theologian who took as his spiritual mentor Friedrich Schleiermacher. In *Das Heilige* (1917), Otto presented what might be called a phenomenological psychology of religion, in that he sought to describe the structure of human reaction to what is experienced as "the holy." Otto's work as a religious theorist, because of his attitude toward human nature and in his introspective approach to religion, may be considered a late flowering of the Romantic movement. He exhibits a qualified anti-intellectualist stance toward religious psychology: religion is an ineradicable part of human nature, present from the beginning, but, while religion itself admits of historical development, the psychological makeup of human beings, which makes religion possible, does not. Therefore, any religious experience, however far removed in time and space, can be understood by the modern student, because it shares a fundamental unity with all religion. Further, Otto appeals in a famous passage to the reader's own experience, rather than to his rational faculties, as the guarantor of the accuracy and usefulness of his descriptions:

> The reader is invited to direct his mind to a moment of deeply-felt religious experience, as little as possible qualified by other forms of consciousness. Whoever cannot do this, whoever knows no such moments in his experience, is requested to read no farther; for it is not easy to discuss questions of religious psychology with one who can recollect the emotions of his adolescence, the discomforts of indigestion, or, say, social feelings, but cannot recall any intrinsically religious feelings. (Otto, [1917] 1923, p. 8)

The fundamental religious experience Otto termed as the feeling of the presence of "the numinous." In this, his theory closely approximates that of Marett's "occult power" (or mysterious power or the sacred). But Otto sought in a systematic way to show that this feeling existed psychologically prior to any conceptualization of a god or spirit or soul and, at the same time, was the religious *sine qua non* behind these concepts. As he put it, the "ideogram" of the numinous must be present in the "concept" of god, since the former is the nonrational, feeling component of the rational concept. The mental process by which ideograms become concepts he called "schematization."

Implicit in his argument is a tension between experience or feeling, on the one hand, and *a priori* ideas, on the other, since he wished to affirm both the priority of religious experience and the truth of certain religious concepts. Indeed, it is his strong allegiance to a belief in the superiority of Christian theological formulations that has been largely responsible for Otto's lack of influence in anthropology and in related disciplines concerned with the study of religion. Added to this was his insistence upon the *sui generis* character of religious experience, which tended to isolate religion from other psychological realms, such as the experience of beauty, sexual pleasure, or terror.

The heart of Otto's system is his description of the feelings that, to a greater or lesser extent and in varying mixtures, all religious experiences evoke. These *are mysterium tremendum* and *mysterium fascinans.* The ambivalence in the human response to the object of religion that has already been encountered in the dichotomy of mana and taboo, the positive and negative aspects of sacred power. In Otto's schema, van Gennep's work focused primarily upon the *fascinans* aspect, since the efficacy of sacred power is necessary for ritual goals to be realized, although of course van Gennep also discussed rituals of avoidance. It is particularly in the analysis of the negative side of the dichotomy that Otto's unique contribution to the understanding of religious experience can be seen. Choosing as his illustrative data primarily the canonical literature of Christianity, but supplementing it with references to such famous Christian virtuosi as Martin Luther as well as to Islamic and Hindu mystics, he documents minutely the daunting presence of the numinous in the more complex or "higher" religions. For purposes of exposition, he divides his first category into two. The first is *mysterium,* which he explains as having its closest analogy in the feeling of uncanniness that irrationally can seize one when, for example, one is listening to ghost stories or passing graveyards. This feeling emphasizes the radical otherness (*das ganz Andere*) of the numinous and results in a uniquely religious dread. If, according to Otto, this feeling is allowed to predominate in the religious experience, aberrations such as demon worship can result. To this is inextricably joined the element of *tremendum,* the overpoweringness of the numinous, whose ideogram in Christianity is God's wrath. Moving from experience (*der Moment*) to ideogram to developed theological concept, *tremendum* becomes divine omnipotence.

Tremendum, therefore, is the place in Otto's schema where the experience of sacred power has its proper location. He further elaborates its effects by the ideogram of "creature consciousness," the elementary feeling articulated by the thought of having been created, assembled, as it were, as a kind of contingent and therefore somewhat arbitrary and temporary configuration with no intrinsic merit or value or power. To sense this is to feel that one is nothing over against the infinite power and presence of the Other. Out of it come the relatively sophisticated ideas of creation and of sin. Notice that sin is now partly derived not only from the memory of having contravened a law or broken a taboo; it is also intrinsic to the religious encounter itself, particularly from the encounter with power in its overwhelming immensity. Of course it is here referred to the joining or schematization of *tremendum* and the doctrine of sin, especially of original sin, which Otto argues finally makes the Christian concept of sin credible and intellectually satisfying.

It could be argued that the element of *fascinans,* or attraction, in the numinous experience also implies a tacit recognition of kratophany, but in Otto's own handling of it, *fascinans* is expressed in such terms as love, duty, and the motivation to pursue the religious life. It is an elementary recognition or experience of value rather than a perception of utility or status, which seem to predominate in the idea of mana.

MIRCEA ELIADE AND THE HISTORY OF RELIGIONS. Mircea Eliade linked his own work in the phenomenology of religion with that of Otto when in *The Sacred and the Profane* (1957) he expressed admiration for Otto's descriptions of religious experience. Yet he sought to establish, at the same time, a different perspective, one that took as its starting point the categories of the sacred/profane dichotomy first given prominence by the French sociologist Émile Durkheim. Eliade was concerned with what might be called collective psychology, rather than a psychology of individual, particular experiences. His work has sought to catalog and explain (as in *Patterns in Comparative Religion,* 1958) the great collective representations, that is, symbols, by which religious meaning is mediated in a variety of cultural contexts. In accepting Otto's description of the "irrational" aspect of encounters with the sacred, Eliade infuses his use of the term sacred with specific meaning that includes power as a central element. Thus the encounter with sacred power is seen in the structure of the symbols of the sacred, while power is one of the necessary attributes of the sacred.

Eliade is perhaps most like Otto when he discusses archaic techniques of ecstasy, as he does at length in his *Shamanism* (1951). Here he shows that the shaman often unwillingly encounters, and is possessed by, sacred power in an unequal test of strength that leaves the human personality transformed. The result is the ability ritually to achieve ecstasis, or a projection of self out of self, in order to tap the power of sacred realities as a religious specialist serving the community. But the interpretation of shamanism is not restricted to psychological aspects: the symbols, for example, of drum and "flying costume," by which shamanic rituals are accomplished, are also presented, as well as myths that both buttress and explain the worldview of shamanism.

Throughout his works dealing with archaic religion, Eliade has emphasized the creative power of myth and of the sacred beings whose stories myths are (see *Myth and Reality,* 1963). Of course, this power is understood by those for whom myths still live as the power of the sacred itself, made knowable and thus usable through myth. For Eliade, cosmogonic myth is perforce the most important type, since it taps into the ubiquitous psychological tendency that he has termed the assumption of the "prestige of origins." Here, knowledge of the origin of a thing is equivalent to having power over that thing. Thus knowledge of the origin of the world as contained in the cosmogonic myth gives human beings power over their entire environment. Rituals that celebrate this knowledge by reiterating the myth, or, more dramatically, by reenacting it, are at least very useful to the scholar in attempting to grasp the meaning of a religious worldview. Eliade has also noted that the prestige of origins and the supposed power of origins continue to function psychologically, often unconsciously, in modern secular contexts.

The sacred has power, in Eliade's view, both to make the world meaningful by providing a religious worldview and to provide a means of escape from a desacralized and therefore meaningless world (*Cosmos and History,* 1949). His work on yoga (*Yoga: Immortality and Freedom,* 1954) details this latter function of sacred power in Hinduism and Buddhism. In *samadhi,* the yogin achieves the final stage in the personal journey by which the true self realizes its identity with the sacred. This state brings with it not only the bliss of a superconsciousness but also a number of sacred powers: knowledge and sensitivity beyond the ordinary as well as psychophysical powers (*siddhis*) that mark the accomplished practitioner of yoga.

In his discussion of yoga, Eliade also touches upon an especially revealing concept of Hinduism, namely, *tapas.* This idea, which is very old in the Indian subcontinent, can be rendered as "the power of asceticism," or "the sacred power by which the world was created." Sometimes, indeed, in later popular folk tales and myths, *tapas* becomes the power of desire and of sexual potency, which both creates all beings and threatens all with dissolution. Yoga as an ascetic discipline is thought to tap the power of *tapas,* for it is sometimes understood that *tapas* is the power by which the extraordinary accomplishment of final liberation is won. Among the devotional cults of modern Hinduism, the Śaivas honor Śiva, the phallic creator god who is also the prototype of all yogins.

Belief in the power of sacred models to raise individuals to new states of being (see *Rites and Symbols of Initiation,* 1958), especially as this power is brought to bear in rituals, is documented in Eliade's work on "initiation scenarios," which are so widespread even in secular literature and fantasy. These survivals of living symbol systems continue to haunt modern people's dreams and imaginative creations. In archaic societies, these symbols of death and rebirth—of being swallowed by a monster, for example—are especially significant ways by which the power of the sacred can bring about the transition from childhood to adulthood, from ordinary living human being to powerful ancestor, from ordinary human to powerful shaman. In salvation religions, these same techniques and symbols are employed in the crucial transition from a state of damnation to that of salvation and beatitude.

The amazing ability of symbols to endure through the ages and despite profound cultural changes, as Eliade has documented in the historical portions of his work, testifies to the power that symbols wield in human life. These powerful symbols appear to possess almost a life of their own, inasmuch as they are constitutive of the human personality. To possess sacred power is at the same time to be possessed by it, a view that Rudolf Otto would heartily support and one that the psychologist C. G. Jung emphasized with his theory of archetypes.

Phenomenologically, it is impossible to determine the source of symbols either within or without the self that experiences them. Indeed, Jung regarded religion as a traditional response to especially powerful symbols that arose from the hidden energy- and meaning-centers of the psyche, that is, the archetypes. What a symbol in a dream of myth masked or partially revealed of an archetype could be determined from the human reaction to it. Archetypal symbols engender great fear, awe, and longing: they are the mainsprings of the deepest and strongest emotions, and are experienced as numinous centers of power:

> When an archetype appears in a dream, in a fantasy, or in life, it always brings with it a certain influence or power by virtue of which it either exercises a numinous or fascinating effect, or impels to action. . . . Owing to their specific energy—for they behave like highly charged autonomous centres of power—they exert a fascinating and possessive influence upon the conscious mind and can thus produce extensive alterations in the subject. (Jung, 1953, p. 80)

The very process of maturation, both culturally and individually, which Jung believed to be the main focus of religious behavior, is a process of the ever-deepening experience of archetypal images and of the progressive transformation of archetypally generated symbols.

Thus, in Jung's thought the ideas of power and of religious experience were strongly associated. Religion was one way of dealing with these internal structures although by no means the only way. On the other hand, religious behavior was derived from these structures as the driving force of both thought and action.

Van der Leeuw and the Phenomenology of Religion. One major work on the nature of religion requires special mention, because it uses the idea of power as its central organizing principle. This is Gerardus van der Leeuw's *Phänomenologie der Religion* (1933), translated into English as *Religion in Essence and Manifestation* (1938). Van der Leeuw begins his ambitious work with a discussion of the experience of power as the founding impetus of religion:

> The religious man perceives that with which his religion deals as primal, as originative or causal; and only to reflective thought does this become the Object of the experience that is contemplated. . . . Theory, and even the slightest degree of generalization, are still far remote; man remains quite content with the purely practical recognition that this Object is a departure from all that is usual and familiar; and this again is the consequence of the *Power* it generates. (van der Leeuw, 1938, p. 23)

He thus describes a pretheoretical mode of perception in which the experience of power and otherness are combined, and in which the notion of efficacy dominates. This power originates and causes events; it is thus fundamentally creative.

Van der Leeuw quickly finds the traditional language of scholarship to be misleading, since it improperly distinguishes religion and magic at this elemental level:

> It is precisely a characteristic of the earliest thinking that it does not exactly distinguish the magical, and all that borders on the supernatural, from the powerful; to the primitive mind, in fact, all marked "efficiency" is *per se* magical, and "sorcery" *eo ipso* mighty. . . . Magic is certainly manifested by power; to employ power, however, is not in itself to act magically, although every extraordinary action of primitive man possesses a tinge of the magical. (ibid., pp. 24-25)

Although he often calls this elemental level of religiosity "primitive," he rejects the hypothesis that it exists as a stage in religious evolution. For him, the term designates a level of thought and experience that is found, to a degree, in all religions at all times. Further, van der Leeuw considers the notion of an ordering power, or sacred order, as in the Sanskrit *ṛta* or the Chinese *dao,* to be theories about power as advanced as the notion of an individual soul as a personal center of power.

Van der Leeuw interprets taboo as perhaps the most elemental reaction to the experience of sacred power: one is characteristically fearful in the face of the disparity of power, and taboo is an attempt to mount some defense against it. Indeed, he derives the Roman *religio* from an experience of dread. Thus religion for the Romans was a system of taboos set up in response to the awesome appearance of sacred power. "Observance," he writes, "is just benumbed awe which, at any moment, can be revived" (ibid., p. 50).

The entire first part of *Religion in Essence and Manifestation* is a long essay demonstrating that the notion of power is the key to understanding a wide variety of religious phenomena. For example, celestial symbols are an important part of many religions because they manifest cosmic power in such a way that humans can model their behavior upon the orderly motions of heavenly bodies, thus tapping their great power. Again, animal cults and totemism van der Leeuw explains as an attempt by humans to obtain for themselves the powers that animals control by virtue of their superior strength and skills, such as the ability to fly. The totem animal is especially significant in this regard because it "is a sort of reservoir for the potency of the tribe or clan" (ibid., p. 79). Angels represent a projection or emanation (they are "messengers") of specific powers of gods; sacred kingship is a recognition that the power of the most powerful person is, in part, sacred power, while belief in salvation implies faith in an extraordinary power of transformation.

Part 2 of this work takes up the reaction to sacred power as apprehended within: that is, the effect of the experience of power on human lives. Here religious functionaries, such as priest or shaman, are discussed, as well as the transformed life of the saint. Finally, religious organization, the social reaction to power, is sketched out.

Further description of van der Leeuw's work must founder because of his own interpretation of the phenomenological task: he eschewed any conscious hermeneutic or theory of religion as false to the data. Thus his work cannot be neatly summed up by reference to a relatively simple theoretical model. But in much of his work, the basic experience of power functions as much as a heuristic device as a basic insight into the nature of religion.

Another scholar who has influenced the notion of religious power held by students of religion in recent years is Georges Dumézil, who sought to develop some structural tools for dealing not with all religions but with that large class of religions known to have been derived from Indo-European cultures. His fundamental thesis is that the gods of Indo-European peoples reflect, and in turn are reflected in, the social structure of a given culture. This structure, in three main divisions, can be described in terms of the functions, or typical activities, performed by the gods or social classes in question. Although this thesis has far-reaching implications, most important for present purposes is the fact that in many cultures, most clearly in ancient India in the Vedic literature, these functions, in turn, seem to be based upon different concepts of power. Thus, because the concerns of the third-function gods are fecundity and productivity in the terrestrial sphere, they possess a special power or energy that controls and thus either promotes or inhibits the growth of herds or the abundance of harvests. This power was often thought of as sexual in nature.

But it is in the second and first functions, as Dumézil defined them, that differences in the basic nature of power become most apparent. Here he distinguishes sharply between the mysterious, hidden, even magical, power of the first-function gods and the merely physical power wielded by the gods of the second function. The second function belongs to the warrior, in India especially to Indra, who slew the cosmic demon Vrtra, and who was the protector of the Aryan tribes and the leader of the human warriors. Indeed, so important did this physical power become that there is evidence in the *Ṛgveda* that Indra to some extent replaced Varuna, the primary first-function god. Varuna and Mitra together are the representative of the function of sovereignty, whose position at the apex of the hierarchy of gods and humans was, originally at least, assured by the power they wielded. The first function Dumézil characterizes in general as celestial, priestly, and concerned with the exercise of magical and juridical sovereignty. Varuna especially is "a great sorcerer, disposed more than any other on the level of sovereignty to *maya,* magic which creates forms either temporary or permanent, disposed also to the knots in which he binds the guilty, a capture both immediate and irresistible" (Dumézil, 1968–1973, vol. 1, p. 148).

Coupled both to the characteristic celestial symbolism and to the idea of mysterious power is the association of Varuna and Mitra with the cosmic order, *ṛta.* Increasingly subservient to this impersonal order, the first-function gods nonetheless reflect and to a degree wield the very power by which the cosmos moves. This dynamism was especially impressive because the means of its motion was unseen: just as the stars or the sun followed their preordained courses; just as the seasons followed their patterns and other events such as disease occurred as punishments whose agents or mechanism, so to speak, could not be discovered by means of the ordinary senses; just so did the sovereign gods control the very power by which the world was ordered and by which its order was maintained. Physical power, the power of Indra and of war, could be understood, if not always defended against. Even the enormous physical power of a god was still physical and palpable, and therefore of a fundamentally different nature than was *maya,* the unseen and all the more frightening power of Varuna.

In the human realm, according to Dumézil's thesis, the social structure also reflected these different types of power. Of course it is the brahman caste, the hereditary priests, who wield Varuna's power, to some degree, because of their knowledge of the rites of sacrifice. In the cult, the priests function as mediators of sovereign sacred power: the words and actions of the rituals place in the priestly hands this same mysterious power, which is the power to influence cosmic forces for the benefit of humans.

Although Dumézil's point of departure is the Vedic texts of India, he applies this schema also to later Indian epics as well as to Persian, Greek, and other European religious literature. Beyond this, other scholars have sought to extend the three function theory to non-Indo-European cultures as well. Most notable of these, perhaps, is Atsuhiko Yoshida, whose "La mythologie japonaise: Essai d'interpretation structurale" (1961–1963) is the most thorough attempt to apply these categories not so much in order to show Indo-European influences upon Japanese mythology but as a useful interpretive tool.

POWER, MAGIC, AND CHARISMA. The use of the term *magic* has had a checkered career, both within Christian theological circles and within the realm of comparative religion or history of religions (*Religionswissenschaft*). On the one hand, it has shared the pejorative connotations of such terms as *superstition* and *idolatry* in its emic or confessional evaluation; on the other hand, as evidenced by such compounds as *magico-religious,* from the etic viewpoint the term has been used in a purely descriptive way, as, for example, in the work of Arnold van Gennep, noted above. From this latter perspective, magic denotes simply sacred power experienced as impersonal and, to a degree, manipulatable: it is power in its most useful mode, since it can be turned to one's advantage with what might be called a minimum of harmful side effects. Providing only that the formulae and rituals are properly followed, results are predictable, even automatic. For many theologically inclined thinkers, this notion, and even more the attitude toward the sacred that it implies, must necessarily be a "lower" form of religion, or degenerate religion—or perhaps not religion at all. This is because it is felt to be incompatible with the proper sense of reverence and dependence due to a personal god as in Christianity or Judaism. From this perspective, to treat God as an object of magic is to blaspheme since this tends to reduce the majesty and freedom of the deity.

The lack of consensus among scholars as to the proper definition and use of the term *magic* reflects not so much differences in perception as differences in the purposes to which the data are put. From the purely descriptive point of view, a distinction between magic and religion, or between magical religion and pure religion, has proved practically impossible to make. But from the normative, theological point of view, the term *magic* has proved too useful a term to be easily given up, since it delineates what is felt to be a theologically unacceptable attitude toward the power of God. Thus, even when a pejorative sense is not intended in descriptive works, it is often improperly assumed by many readers.

Examples of the difficulties that lie in wait for those who would distinguish between a manipulative approach to the sacred and a properly humble and propitiatory approach are easily produced. Subtle psychological distinctions must be made, since the existential concern of all religious people for their own welfare makes a totally unselfserving approach to sacred power improbable, if not impossible, for ordinary human beings. Put another way, one may ask how often Christians pray for forgiveness of sins out of nothing more than a pure and unselfish love of their god? Or again, rites of passage, which are ubiquitous, seek always a more or less definite personal or communal gain—but who can assess with complete certainty the motivation of the participants? Discounting "manipulativeness" can lead to a restriction of the term *religion* to such an extent that it is lost as a useful descriptive term.

Another conceptual tool relating to religious power is *charisma,* a term made popular by the sociologist of religion Max Weber (in *Religionssoziologie,* 1922), who defined it as the authority by which individuals were accorded status and power over others or, related to that, by which the functions or offices themselves—regardless of the officeholder—were felt to be worthy of respect. Indeed, Weber expressly linked charisma both to *mana* and to the Iranian *maga* (Skt., *maya*), from which the word *magic* is derived. Looked at closely, it may be seen that the notion of charisma, at least from the limited horizon of sociology, is rather mysterious. That is to say, the reason or means whereby one person is accorded this respect, or is seen as having a special inner power of attraction, is not explained or well understood. Certainly such things as character, unusual skills, great stature or strength, or force of mien or manner all seem to contribute, but, finally, *charisma* remains a relational term that classifies the reaction of others to the person whom scholars then label as charismatic.

The Chinese religious tradition offers a concrete example of belief in charisma, and even of theorizing about it within two ancient systems of thought, namely, Confucianism and Daoism. These two religions, although often antagonistic, nonetheless share a common origin and a number of common ideas. Two are especially relevant here: *dao,* or cosmic order, and *de,* variously translated as "virtue," "character," "power," or "charisma." It is possible to view these two concepts not only as closely associated in Chinese thought but as two aspects of a single reality: sacred power. *Dao* is in many ways similar to the Sanskrit *ṛta,* in that it is not only order but also the power that drives a dynamic universe. All things ultimately derive from *dao* (Laozu appropriately calls it "the mother of all things"), and all things move and change according to its "laws." To be sure, it is not entirely knowable, although Confucianism is more optimistic on this point, with its emphasis on study of the way of the ancients and its belief that *dao* is perfectly embodied in *li* (ritual or decorum).

When *dao* is perfectly embodied in a person, then he is called a sage. Such a one is as perfect an exemplar of the universal *dao* as a human being can be. To be a sage is to be perfectly in harmony with *dao.* But taken from the point of view of the individual, such a one has great *de* or personal power. This power, like *dao,* although it may be embodied in a person, is not in itself personal: it is without consciousness, or will, or emotion; it has no purpose. The intrinsic power of a sage is expressed, both in Confucianism and in Daoism, in the image of the sage-king Shun, who "acted without action"—yet all things were accomplished, and the empire was at peace. Shun is also likened to the pole star, which merely sits facing south, while all things revolve around it in a kind of cosmic ballet.

This *de* or charisma is brought down to earth, as it were, in the Confucian ideal of the *junzi* the "superior man" or "true gentleman," who also brings about by example, by ritual, and by the power of his presence the longed-for proper ordering of human society. It is not, of course, that he does nothing; rather, he is so well attuned to *dao* (or to "heaven," *tian*) that whatever he chooses to do will be the correct thing in the circumstances. When such a person is a ruler, or, one might say after Weber, when charisma of person is combined with charisma of office, one has an especially powerful force for harmony. Interestingly, however, even here, at least in the more mystical Daoist writings, a sage does not will the right, does not arrive by careful thought or logical deduction at the right course of action; rather, because he is a sage, such action will spontaneously occur, sometimes with the sage as direct agent, but sometimes at the hands of others mysteriously influenced by him.

This mysteriously acting power, action at a distance and without conscious will, sounds in many ways like the Vedic *maya.* It is sacred power, at work in the human world, that reflects and ultimately is one with the sacred power that underlies all activity in the world of nature.

Is such a belief crude magic, or perhaps mere superstition? Some would answer in the affirmative. Certainly it insists upon the impersonal nature of the sacred and of the workings of sacred power. And the will to manipulate this power to benefit self, or the society as a whole, is strong, especially in Confucianism. Yet there is also awe and reverence for the power: it is difficult to gain, and it has its own ways. Others would claim that this example shows the impossibility of separating magic and religion, that they are inextricably merged into the idea of sacred power and into the active responses of human beings as they have perceived that power over the millennia of religious history.

In religions having a central concern for extra-worldly salvation, the way in which the power by which such a transformation can be effected has been understood has resulted in unresolved and perhaps unresolvable controversies. The early fifth century struggle between the Christian thinkers Pelagius and Augustine of Hippo concerned two very different assessments of that most elusive form of power known as human freedom. Did human beings, as Pelagius argued, have the power within themselves to live sinless lives and thus achieve salvation through their own efforts? Or, as Augustine argued, did the Fall that occurred in the Garden of Eden taint all humans descended from Adam and Eve to such an extent that they were incapable of perfection without divine aid, or grace? Roman Catholic orthodoxy eventually declared for Augustine's position, although the issue has continued to this day to exercise Christian theologians, and it played a major role in the Protestant Reformation. Strikingly similar was the controversy that raged in the thirteenth century in Japan with the rise of the Pure Land movement in Buddhism. Shinran witnessed to the all-encompassing "other-power" (*ta-riki*) offered by the Buddha Amitabha that was available through faith to ordinary believers; this he juxtaposed to the use of "self-power" (*ji-riki*) by the traditional monastic forms of Buddhism, by which *nirvana* itself could be achieved. By contrast Augustine saw the fall into sin, and thus also relative powerlessness, to be positioned at the beginning of time with its effects pervading all human existence until the end of history; whereas Shinran's "fall" occurred within history. Shinran believed that the degenerate age (*mappo*), characterized by humans' decreased powers, had arrived, but it had come long after the founding of the path to salvation by the historical Buddha. Such parallel developments so far separated in time and space strongly suggest that there exists a universal deep structure of meaning to the conceptualization of power as it relates to salvation.

To be sure, many religions know of powers associated with the persons of religious elites, especially perhaps the power of healing. This power may be understood to be ultimately from God or the gods, the practitioner merely acting as a channel for it, as in western monotheism, or it may be seen as the product of the practitioner's own spiritual accomplishments. In the latter category may be placed the many forms of Buddhism that know the powers (*siddhi*) that often accompany yogic meditative accomplishments, a tradition that is also reflected in the pan-Indian idea of *tapas*, depicted in many Hindu tales of the puranic period as a power generated by yoga that is potentially so strong as to threaten the very sovereignty of the gods. The relationship between such forms of power and the ultimate goal of salvation is sometimes ambiguous.

SEE ALSO Animism and Animatism; Archetypes; Hierophany; Magic; Sacred and the Profane, The.

BIBLIOGRAPHY

Codrington, R. H. *The Melanesians: Studies in Their Anthropology and Folklore* (1891). New Haven, 1957.

Dumézil, Georges. *L'ideologie tripartie des Indo-Européens.* Brussels, 1958.

Dumézil, Georges. *Mythe et epopée.* 3 vols. Paris, 1968–1973.

Eliade, Mircea. *Cosmos and History: The Myth of the Eternal Return* (1949). New York, 1959.

Eliade, Mircea. *Shamanism: Archaic Techniques of Ecstasy* (1951). Rev. & enl. ed. New York, 1964.

Eliade, Mircea. *Yoga: Immortality and Freedom* (1954). 2d ed., rev. & enl. Princeton, 1969.

Eliade, Mircea. *The Sacred and the Profane* (1957). New York, 1959.

Eliade, Mircea. *Patterns in Comparative Religion.* New York, 1958.

Eliade, Mircea. *Rites and Symbols of Initiation: The Mysteries of Birth and Rebirth* (1958). New York, 1975.

Gennep, Arnold van. *The Rites of Passage* (1909). Chicago, 1960.

Hewitt, J. N. B. "Orenda and a Definition of Religion." *American Anthropologist* 4 (1902): 33–46.

Jensen, Adolf E. *Myth and Cult among Primitive Peoples* (1951). Chicago, 1963.

Jung, C. G. "The Psychology of the Unconscious" (1943). In *The Collected Works of C. G. Jung,* vol. 7. Princeton, 1953.

Leeuw, Gerardus van der. *Phänomenologie der Religion.* Tübingen, 1933. Translated by J. E. Turner as *Religion in Essence and Manifestation,* 2 vols. (1938; reprint, Gloucester, Mass., 1967).

Marett, R. R. "Pre-animistic Religion." *Folklore* 11 (1900): 162–182.

Marett, R. R. *The Threshold of Religion.* London, 1909.

Otto, Rudolf. *Das Heilige.* Breslau, 1917. Translated by John W. Harvey as *The Idea of the Holy* (1923; 2nd ed., London, 1960).

Tylor, E. B. *Primitive Culture* (1871). 2 vols. New York, 1970.

Vries, Jan de. *The Study of Religion.* New York, 1967.

Wach, Joachim. *Sociology of Religion* (1944). Chicago, 1962.

Weber, Max. *Religionssoziologie.* Tübingen, 1922. Translated by Ephraim Fischoff as *The Sociology of Religion* (Boston, 1963).

Yoshida, Atsuhiko. "La mythologie japonaise: Essai d'interpretation structural." *Revue de l'histoire des religions* 160 (1961): 47–66; 161 (1962): 25–44; and 163 (1963): 225–248.

Yoshido, Atsuhiko. "Nihon shinwa to In-o shinwa." In *Nihon shinwa no hikaku kenkyu,* edited by Obayashi Taryo. Tokyo, 1974.

ALAN L. MILLER (1987 AND 2005)

PRABHUPADA, A. C. BHAKTIVEDANTA.

A. C. Bhaktivedanta Prabhupada (1896–1977) was the founder of the International Society for Krishna Consciousness (ISKCON), more commonly known as the Hare Krishna movement.

On September 19, 1965, the steamship *Jaladuta* sailed into New York harbor from Calcutta and docked at a Brooklyn pier. Seventy-year-old A.C. Bhaktivedanta Swami emerged from the ship to fulfill the instructions of his spiritual master to teach the spiritual message of the Caitanya cult in the West. Caitanya, the founder of *bhakti-yoga,* preached that all people regardless of their station in life, could reach spiritual realization through love and devotion to Kṛṣṇa (God). Bhaktivedanta Swami was dressed in traditional garb: he wore *kaṇṭhī-mālā* (neck beads), a plain cotton *dhotī* around his body, a *cādar* (shawl), and he carried *jāpā-mālā* chanting beads). His head was shaven except for the *sikhā* (tuft of hair) in the back, and his forehead was marked with *tilaka* (sacred clay). Carrying only forty Indian rupees (about seven U.S. dollars), Bhaktivedanta set out to bring the message of "Kṛṣṇa Consciousness" to the United States, and ultimately to the world.

Prabhupada was born Abhay Charan De into a Gauḍīya-Vaiṣṇava family in Calcutta, India, on September 1, 1896. His father was Gour Mohan De, a cloth merchant, and his mother was Rajani. Across the street from the Des's residence in north Calcutta was a Rādhā-Govinda temple where the family worshipped. Prabhupada's father raised his son to be Kṛṣṇa conscious. At night, Gour Mohan read from the *Caitanya-caritāmṛta* and the *Śrīmad Bhāgavatam* (the principle scriptures of Bengali Vaiṣṇavas), chanted on his *jāpā* beads, and worshiped the deity of Kṛṣṇa. He wanted his son to become a preacher of the *Bhāgavatam* and to grow up singing *bhajans* (religious songs), and playing the *mṛdaṅga* (a drum used to accompany congregational chanting).

In 1916 Prabhupada began studies at Calcutta's Scottish Churches' College, where he majored in English, philosophy, and economics. Yet after completing his fourth year and passing the exams for his degree, Prabhupada refused to accept his diploma. He did this to register his protest against British rule of India, for he had become sympathetic to Mahatma Gandhi's Indian independence movement. During his college years Prabhupada's father arranged for his marriage to Radharani Datta. After marrying, Prabhupada gained employment as a manager in a pharmaceutical firm in Calcutta to support his wife and family.

In 1922 Prabhupada met his spiritual master, Srila Bhaktisiddhanta Sarasvati Thakura (1874–1936). Prabhupada was impressed by Srila Bhaktisiddhanta's boldness after, upon meeting Prabhupada for the first time, he commented, "You are educated. . . .Why don't you preach Lord Caitanya's message throughout the whole world?" (Goswami, 1980a, p. 39). Later he would tell Prabhupada, "If you ever get money, print books" to help spread the mission of Lord Caitanya (Goswami, 1980a, p. 91). Although Prabhupada had accepted Bhaktisiddhanta as his spiritual master after their first meeting, he became formally initiated as his disciple in 1932. Thereafter, Prabhupada assisted in the work of his spiritual master's organization, the Gauḍḍīya Maṭh. Following Bhaktisiddhanta's death, the Gauḍīya Maṭh suffered years of infighting and schism, and Prabhupada decided to create his own movement, the League of Devotees, in 1953 in Jhansi, India. After only two years, however, the organization collapsed, having made no full-time members. In 1944 Prabhupada began publishing *Back to Godhead* magazine, which he distributed in India—and then worldwide after he began ISKCON in 1966.

In recognition of his philosophical learning and devotion, the Gauḍīya Vaiṣṇava Society bestowed the title of "Bhaktivedanta" on Prabhupada in 1947. In 1950, at the age of fifty-four, Prabhupada retired from family life and four years later adopted the *vānaprastha* (retired) order to devote himself completely to study and writing. Thereafter he took up residence in Vrindaban, India, where he lived and worked at the Rādhā-Damodara temple. On September 17, 1959, Prabhupada accepted the renounced order of life (*sannyāsa*), whereupon he was given the name Abhay Caranaravinda Bhaktivedanta Swami. While living alone at the Rādhā-Damodara temple, Prabhupada began translating and providing commentaries on the *Śrīmad Bhāgavatam* (*Bhāgavata Purāna*).

After publishing three volumes of the *Bhāgavatam* in India, Prabhupada decided to fulfill the instructions of his spiritual master by traveling to the United States. Having received free passage aboard the freighter the *S.S. Jaladuta*, Prabhupada left his Indian homeland for the United States as a poor Indian *sādhu* (saintly person). After six months of hardship, Prabhupada established his International Society for Krishna Consciousness in July of 1966. His first temple was a rented store front at 26 Second Avenue in New York's Lower East Side. In that year he also initiated his first American disciples. In 1967, Prabhupada traveled to the emerging hippie community in the Haight-Ashbury district of San Francisco. There, amid the drug culture, Prabhupada taught that the chanting of "Hare Krishna" was a "high" superior to LSD. In San Francisco, Prabhupada attracted 150 to 200 converts to his movement within two years. From San Francisco, Prabhupada sent disciples to Montreal, Los Angeles, Boston, London, and other major cities to begin ISKCON temples.

Prabhupada established over one hundred temples worldwide, wrote more than sixty volumes, including *Bhagavad-Gītā As It Is (1972)*, the multivolume *Śrīmad Bhāgavatam (1972–1977)* and *Caitanya-caritāmṛta (1974–1975)*, *The Nectar of Devotion (1970*, and many other books on the Vedic scriptures. These volumes included translations of the original Sanskrit and Bengali texts, along with Prabhupada's commentaries. His writings have been translated into more than fifty languages by the Bhaktivedanta Book Trust, established in Los Angeles in 1972 to publish Prabhupada's works. Between 1973 and 1977 several million books and other pieces of Kṛṣṇa Consciousness literature were distributed yearly by ISKCON members in shopping malls, airports, and other public locations in the United States and worldwide. As Prabhupada commented, "If one percent of the readers become devotees. . .that will change the world" (Goswami, 1983b, p. 5).

A. C. Bhaktivedanta Swami Prabhupada died on November 14, 1977, in Vrindaban, India. In just twelve years from the time he arrived in North America, Prabhupada initiated nearly five thousand disciples worldwide, circled the globe eight times lecturing on Kṛṣṇa Consciousness, began and oversaw a worldwide movement, and established himself as a scholar of Vedic philosophy and religion.

SEE ALSO International Society for Krishna Consciousness.

BIBLIOGRAPHY

Goswami, Satsvarupa dasa. *Srila Prabhupada-lilamrta: A Biography of His Divine Grace A. C. Bhaktivedanta Swami Prabhupada.* Los Angeles, 1980–1983; 2d ed, 1993. Vol. 1: *A Lifetime in Preparation: India, 1896–1965* (1980a). Vol. 2: *Planting the Seed: New York City, 1965–1966* (1980b). Vol. 3: *Only He Could Lead Them: San Francisco, India, 1967* (1981). Vol 4: *In Every Town and Village: Around the World, 1968–1971* (1982). Vol. 5: *Let There Be a Temple: India, Around the World, 1971–1975* (1983a). Vol. 6: *Uniting Two Worlds: Around the World, Return to Vṛndāvana, 1975–1977* (1983b).

Goswami, Tamal Krishna. "His Divine Grace A.C. Bhaktivedanta Swami Prabhupada: Founder, Prophet, and Priest." In *A Hare Krishna at Southern Methodist University: Collected Essays 1995–1997,* pp. 247–265. Dallas, Tex.

International Society for Krishna Consciousness. "A. C. Bhaktivedanta Swami Prabhupada." Available from http://www.iskcon.com.

Selengut, Charles. "Charisma and Religious Innovation: Prabhupada and the Founding of ISKCON." *ISKCON Communications Journal* 4, no. 2: 51-63.

E. BURKE ROCHFORD JR. (2005)

PRAJĀPATI belongs to the powerful ritual center of Vedic traditions and their discourses known as the Brāhmaṇas, where he is the supreme being and father of the gods. He is the link between the ancient Puruṣa mythology that instituted sacrifice, on the one hand, and the late Vedic bifurcation into a metaphysics of the impersonal Absolute (*brahman*) and the personal god Brahmā, on the other. In the religious history of South Asia, cosmogony, sacrifice, the soma cult, asceticism and self-mortification, the concept of salvation, the ritualization of procreation, and the advisory role of the grandfather of the gods are all dependent to a significant degree on the various guises of Prajāpati.

As lord *(pati)* of creatures *(prajā)*, Prajāpati is best known in the tenth book of the *Ṛgveda* through speculations about the creation of the world. Identified there with several cosmogonic motifs, he is later associated in the Brāhmaṇas more precisely with Puruṣa, thereby assuring his preeminence in the sacrificial drama of creative transformations through self-sacrifice. Like Puruṣa projecting himself sacrificially into world being (*Ṛgveda* 10.90), Prajāpati is said in the Brāhmaṇas to have sacrificed himself in the exhausting fervor of ascetic and erotic heat (*tapas*), the cosmic result being, first, *brahman,* the sacred verbal power, and then the various components of creation, including gods and humans (see, e.g., *Śatapatha Brāhmaṇa* 6.1.1.8ff.). Elsewhere, he himself is regarded as the result of *tapas.* A constant theme in these discourses is the human necessity of repeating the exemplary primordial event by reintegrating all the space, time, and being that the Puruṣa-Prajāpati sacrificial victim, dispersed into manifestation, represents. The Vedic *śrauta* ritual known aa the Agnicayana became one of the major expressions of this Brahmanic doctrine of sacrifice: By identifying Agni as Prajāpati, the ceremonial installation of fire *(agni)* was advanced to a soteriology. A yearlong procedure systematically reconstituted the world as a five-layered altar, its fire-center-heart being the recovered *ātman* ("self") not only of Prajāpati but also of his human correspondent, the sacrificer (*yajamāna*). Another great *śrauta* ritual was the Vājapeya, the "drink of strength," a soma ceremony in which the mystical totality of Prajāpati and the power of the number seventeen were realized. By entering such ritually produced correspondences as these, the sacrificer was able to avoid repeated death (*punarmṛtyu*). This ideology prefigured the later Upaniṣadic notion of *ātman-brahman* equivalence and of spiritual liberation obtained not by ritual but by intuitive knowledge.

Prajāpati's control over human and animal reproductive energies assured him the same prominence in the domestic ritual, mythology, and folklore that he gained in the texts for the great cosmic ceremonies. *Ṛgveda* 10.121, a hymn of creation addressed to the "golden germ" (*hiraṇyagarbha*), identified Prajāpati as the "fiery seed" within the cosmic waters. The images of seed, egg, embryo, and parturition continued into the *Atharvaveda* and the Gṛhyasutras that became manuals for such life-cycle rites (*saṃskāras*) as marriage, impregnation, production of a male, safe delivery, first feeding, and first tonsure. Prajāpati was also included as one of certain male figures surrounded by four feminine powers in gestation symbolism.

Prajāpati has numerous zoomorphic expressions, some of them evidently archaic. The boar, Emūṣa, is identified with him in the mythology of the cosmic earth diver, the creature that descends to procure a fragment or prototype of earth-world, as are two creatures prominent in the Agnicayana, the bird and the tortoise (all three perpetuated in later Hindu Vaiṣṇava myths). The goat, bull, cow, horse, stag, ant, and other animals are also drawn into Prajāpati's orbit of symbols. Vedic deities linked with Prajāpati include Vāyu, Varuṇa, Dakṣa, Vāc, and, in an incestuous theme, his daughter Uṣas. In the post-Vedic texts, Brahmā absorbs his character as Hiraṇyagarbha, and the Prajāpatis are, variously, the ten or seven spiritual sons of Brahmā.

SEE ALSO Agni.

BIBLIOGRAPHY

The clearest, most concise explication of Prajāpati in the myth-ritual speculation of the Brāhmaṇas is Mircea Eliade's *A History of Religious Ideas,* vol. 1 (Chicago, 1978), pp. 223–235. On Prajāpati in the Agnicayana ritual and theology, see Frits Staal's *Agni: The Vedic Ritual of the Fire Altar,* vol. 1 (Berkeley, Calif., 1983), chapters 4 and 5, especially pages 65ff. (on Śāṇḍilya's teaching in the *Śatapatha Brāhmaṇa*), 115ff., and 159ff. The popular (i.e., nonpriestly) traditions of Prajāpati outside the sacrificial cult are illuminated in Jan Gonda's "The Popular Prajāpati," *History of Religions* 22 (1982): 129–149. All three authors point to the archaic rather than the late Ṛgvedic character of Prajāpati; only Staal suggests an indigenous Indian origin.

New Source

Gonda, Jan. *Prajāpati's Relations with Brahman, Bṛhaspati and Brahmā.* Amsterdam and New York, 1989.

DAVID M. KNIPE (1987)
Revised Bibliography

PRAJÑĀ. The Sanskrit term *prajñā* (Pali, *paññā;* Tib., *shes rab*), variously translated as "wisdom, gnosis, insight," or "intuitive knowledge," is central to all Buddhist traditions, imparting unity to them as well as serving to distinguish them from other philosophical and religious systems. *Prajñā* is primarily understood as a complete comprehension of the nature and aspects of phenomenal existence (*saṃsāra*), the forces that govern it, the method of becoming free from it, and the reality that stands beyond it. Although the notion has been expounded in a variety of ways by Buddhist thinkers, it serves for them all as an intellectual and spiritual faculty that imparts a correct grasp of Buddhist teachings, guides and perfects the spiritual life, imbues it with a sense of direction, and brings it to maturation.

Early Buddhist scriptures record that Śākyamuni Buddha frequently explained to his followers how, during his striving toward enlightenment, he mastered the four consecutive stages of mental concentration (*dhyāna*) and gained knowledge of his previous lives, knowledge of the past and future lives of other people, and knowledge of the destruction of the depravities (*āsrava*). Awakening to this threefold knowledge was considered by early Buddhist thinkers as the factor fundamental to the transformation of the practitioner into an arhat. One becomes an arhat by mastering these three kinds of knowledge, but it is the knowledge of the destruction and elimination of the depravities that possesses the decisive and essential power to bring final deliverance.

The standard code of religious training for the early disciples (*śrāvakas*) comprised a trilogy of morality (*śīla*), meditation (*samādhi*), and wisdom (*prajñā*). Through the practice of morality, it was held, one becomes purified, perceptive, and mindful, and thus prepares and develops the ground for meditation. Being mindful, one is able to control the senses, thus conducing to the practice of meditation, through which the mind becomes purged of the five "hindrances" (*nīvaraṇa*). In the course of well-developed meditational techniques one becomes able to pursue the four consecutive stages of mental concentration (*dhyāna*). Skill in practicing these concentrations leads to gaining and perfecting the threefold knowledge. That is, one first applies one's thought to the knowledge of one's own former lives; second, one directs the mind to the knowledge of the demise and rebirth of other people; and third, one gains the knowledge of the destruction of the depravities. The third knowledge is the most important, for it contains the penetrating and comprehensive insight into phenomenal existence and thus brings final deliverance. Once this knowledge is acquired, an intrinsic understanding of the sorrow and impermanence of *saṃsāra,* its cause, the means of pacifying it, and the path that leads to its elimination is intuitively gained. Being endowed with such knowledge, one's mind becomes free from the four depravities—sensual desire, attachment to life, wrong views and opinions, and ignorance. One understands perfectly that birth is destroyed, that religious aspirations are accomplished, and that there remains nothing more to be strived for or achieved. One has thus reached the state of *prajñā,* which endows arhat status on the practitioner.

The threefold knowledge comprised within *prajñā* is often grouped together with three other kinds of knowledge, that of magical feats, intuitive hearing, and clairvoyance. Within this set of six knowledges, jointly known as the six "superknowings" (*ṣaḍabhijñā*), the first five are regarded as spiritual and psychic endowments and the sixth, the knowledge of the destruction of the depravities, as an inherent function of the mind in its purified state. *Prajñā* stands both at the beginning of the path of spiritual purification and at its final stage. The practice of morality and meditation alone, although indispensable, cannot bring about the realization of the final goal. It is *prajñā* that imparts unity, perfects virtues, and provides the guidance toward the goal, thus bringing its realization. Its presence at the initial stages of religious striving is not fully apparent or understood, but in spite of its being obscured by impurities and imperfections, *prajñā* is active as the controlling factor throughout the religious career of the practitioner. It grows and unfolds with the gradual purification and perfection of human personality. In Buddhaghosa's *Visuddhimagga* there is an excellent exposition of the gradual stages in which *prajñā* unfolds itself: The roots of *prajñā* are purity of morality and purity of the mind. Purity of morality is achieved through the observance of monastic rules, through correct living, and through control of the senses; purity of the mind is attained through meditational practices. The foundation of *prajñā* lies in correct comprehension of, and acquaintance with, the aggregates (*skandhas*), the elements of existence (*dharmas*), the twenty-two faculties (*indriyas*), the causal nexus of dependent origination (*pratītya-samutpāda*), and the four noble truths (*āryasatya*). The inherent quality of *prajñā* consists of a perfect and thorough comprehension of the various categories and aspects of phenomenal existence and the comprehension of the correct path of liberation.

In Vasubandhu's *Abhidharmakośa* the attainment of the immaculate and perfect *prajñā* is said to be a process of gradual purification of impure *prajñās* that are inborn and natural to the human personality. The accumulation of *prajñā* can be achieved in three ways: through listening to Buddhist teachings, through mental reflection, and through contemplation. The elements (*dharmas*) of existence are here divided into two groups, conditioned (*saṃskṛta*) and unconditioned (*asaṃskṛta*); the unconditioned elements are further divided into space (*ākāśa*), emancipation through discerning knowledge (*pratisaṃkhyānirodha*), and emancipation through nondiscerning knowledge (*apratisaṃkhyānirodha*). These three elements are considered to be unchanging, pure, and timeless. Discerning knowledge (*pratisaṃkhyā*) refers to a pure *prajñā* of transcendental order that brings the destruction of all desire and imperfection and that is thus viewed as synonymous with *nirvāṇa.* Within the division of the elements into the twenty-two faculties (*indriyas*), *prajñā* is listed among the five moral faculties, along with faith, vigor, mindfulness, and meditation. These five faculties, together with the last three faculties of the group as a whole—namely, the knowledge of the unknown (*ajñātam ajñāsyāmi*), the faculty of perfect knowledge (*ajñā*), and the faculty of the "one who knows" (*ajñātāvī*)—are considered the predominant factors in the purification from worldly entanglements. These three faculties are unified by the common factor of *ajñā,* or perfect knowledge, which leads to the realization of the truths that are unrealized, uncomprehended, unknown, and unattainable.

One section of the *Abhidharmakośa* deals with an exposition of the ten kinds of correct knowledge (*jñāna*). Within this group of ten, four relate to the four noble truths (the knowledge of suffering, the knowledge of its origin, the knowledge of its cessation, and the knowledge of the Eightfold Path), further analyzed into sixteen characteristics as enumerated here: The truth of suffering is the knowledge of impermanence, pain, sorrow, and nonexistence of self (*anātmya*). The second truth is the knowledge that understands the cause, origin, successive evolvements, and terminal effects of the causal nexus that is the empirical person. The third truth is the knowledge of the abolition of the impure *skandhas*, of calming the three poisons (ignorance, hatred, and desire), of the absence of pain, and of the presence of freedom. The fourth truth is the knowledge characterized by the correct path, the requisite resources, the potential attainment of *nirvāṇa,* and the departure into it. The notion of *prajñā* comprehends all these sixteen characteristics of the four knowledges.

Many Mahāyāna Buddhist texts, in particular the Prajñāpāramitā Sūtras and the important commentaries on them, deal in great detail with the exposition of *prajñā. Prajñāpāramitā,* or "perfection of wisdom," is seen as the essence of all wisdom and knowledge. It is explained from various angles and approaches, often through the use of figurative descriptions, dialogues, and similes. Perfection of wisdom, expounded and praised as the highest value and goal of human aspirations, is proclaimed as the mother of all the Buddhas and becomes personified as the goddess Prajñāpāramitā. Within the newly construed concepts of cosmic Buddhahood, the theory of the three Buddha bodies (*trikāya*), and the philosophical exposition of "emptiness" (*śūnyatā*) as an identity or nonduality of conditioned existence (*saṃsāra*) and unconditioned reality (*nirvāṇa*), *prajñā* receives a much broader and deeper interpretation than it did in the early stages of Buddhist thought. There, its role and function, although fully recognized, were somewhat overshadowed, insofar as *prajñā* was viewed almost exclusively as a tool for gaining individual deliverance, as exemplified in the idea of arhatship.

In the Mahāyāna one strives for supreme wisdom and perfect enlightenment in order to share these gifts with all living beings by guiding them on the path toward this state. Acquisition of, and abode within, perfect wisdom becomes the primary goal. The focus of the Prajñāpāramitā teachings is on the penetration into the true sense of things by metaphysical discernment and by appropriate moral conduct, as advocated by the *bodhisattva* ideal. A *bodhisattva,* out of compassion (*karuṇā*) for all living beings, pursues the path of the *pāramitās* ("perfections") in order to gain the supreme enlightenment, which he wishes to impart to others. The philosophical tenets of the Prajñāpāramitā teachings are a further development of the earlier teachings. First, one must acquire the wisdom of understanding the nonexistence, or emptiness, of self and of the elements of existence. By making the distinction between the conditioned and unconditioned elements—and through the comprehension of the conditioned elements as empty, impermanent, and as repositories of unhappiness—one acquires the wisdom of knowing that they are not worth pursuing, adhering to, or striving for. The next step leads to considering the unconditioned elements characteristic of *nirvāṇa* as also being empty insofar as they are devoid of any identification with the conditioned elements of existence and with anything that concerns one's life. Having reached this stage of wisdom, the perception of the emptiness of both the conditioned and unconditioned elements, one advances to the next stage of perfect wisdom, through which one is able to identify the conditioned (*saṃsāra*) and the unconditioned (*nirvāṇa*) with the aim of transcending both their common identity, characterized by emptiness, and their inherent differences. Once one considers them as being without any real distinction one reaches a state of transcendent nonduality in which all opposites—negation and affirmation, *saṃsāra* and *nirvāṇa*—are identified and comprised within the notion of emptiness.

This speculative process, realized through meditation and moral purification, brings about the realization of supreme and perfect wisdom. The path toward that realization is demonstrated by the *bodhisattva*'s career. A *bodhisattva*'s striving for supreme enlightenment follows the unique course of practicing six or ten "perfections." He also practices the thirty-seven principles conducive to enlightenment (*bodhipakṣā dharma*) practiced by an arhat, but it is the practice of the perfections that dominates all his activities and occupies the central position in his spiritual journey. By means of perfect wisdom he gains the correct understanding of the true nature of reality and of the very means (*upāya*) that he can employ for the benefit of others; concurrently, he surpasses and transcends the categories of *saṃsāra* through his wisdom. Thus, through his compassion he remains in *saṃsāra* and pursues the cause of living beings; through his perfect wisdom he abides in the sphere of *nirvāṇa.*

There is an inherent relationship between perfect wisdom and all the other perfections. The other perfections bring spiritual purification and progress and provide the ground for perfect wisdom to grow and to reach its fullness. Without them, perfect wisdom can neither be fully developed nor attained. On the other hand, perfect wisdom accompanies, guides, and elevates the other perfections to the status of being truly perfections. On their own the other perfections can bring positive results within the world of *saṃsāra,* but they cannot lead beyond it. Thus, their elevation from the sphere of *saṃsāra,* within which they are practiced, is facilitated by perfect wisdom. The harmonious growth and development of all the perfections leads to spiritual maturation and to the acquisition of perfect wisdom, which coincides with enlightenment.

Using his dialectical method, Nāgārjuna (c. 150–250), the chief exponent of the Mādhyamika philosophy, demonstrated that through conceptual constructions (*vikalpa*) reality is perceived as phenomenal existence. By stripping away all thought constructions one arrives at the perception of absolute reality, which Nāgārjuna defined in a negative way as "emptiness" (*śūnyatā*). According to him, conceptual constructions are motivated by ignorance (*avidyā*), and the process of unveiling the true reality is activated by *prajñā* and compassion. He applied the term *emptiness* to both phenomenal existence and absolute reality. Phenomenal existence is emptiness as it does not possess a true nature of its own (*niḥsvabhāva*); absolute reality is also emptiness in that it is devoid of all conceptual distinctions, because the comprehension and realization of absolute reality escapes and transcends all intellectual categories. Its realization can only be achieved through the intellectual and spiritual intuition represented by *prajñā*. *Prajñā* as free of all concepts and speculations coincides with the absolute reality as defined by emptiness. As an intuition of the absolute reality, where all knowledge and the absolute coincide, *prajñā* penetrates into the absolute and views it without making distinctions or differentiations that conceptual thinking entails. It simply views the absolute just as it is. *Prajñā* is not the same as an intuition resulting from empirical perception or from discursive thinking; it is an intuitive insight into total reality and thus is described as infinite, inexpressible, universal, and unfathomable.

In the Vijñānavāda school, *prajñā* coincides with supreme truth (*paramārtha*); as unobstructed and lucid knowledge it comprises everything that can be known (*sarvajñeyānāvaraṇajñāna*). It implies the correct comprehension of Buddhist teachings, the correct vision of the path, and the knowledge of all intellectual categories and appropriate conduct. It is neither thought nor lack of thought; it does not think but springs naturally from thought. Its object is the inexpressible and indescribable nature of things. It is free of any characteristics, as it is inherent and manifest in its object of cognition. As an unconstrued knowledge (*nirvikalpajñāna*), it stands beyond all mental categories and constructions. It does not make up the description of reality or the destruction of consciousness. It is nonconceptual and free of reflection. It is intuitive, born spontaneously, and surpasses all kinds of ordinary and mundane knowledge. *Prajñā* as the perfect wisdom in all its aspects is the knowledge of the absolute reality *(tathatā).*

The Tantras, following the philosophical assumptions of the Mādhyamika school, assert the basic unity of *nirvāṇa* and *saṃsāra.* The purpose of different kinds of Tantric practices is to eliminate the apparent duality of these two entities, which are wrongly conceived as dual because of defilements and lack of knowledge. The sphere of knowledge and understanding of nonduality between these two is perceived in *nirvāṇa,* the chief force and attribute of which is constituted by wisdom (*prajñā*). In Tantric meditation and ritual performances wisdom is explicitly identified with *nirvāṇa* and means (*upāya*) with *saṃsāra.* The highest truth as mystical experience is described in the Tantras as the union or mingling of wisdom and means. In ritual and meditational practices, wisdom is symbolized by a bell, a lotus, or a sun, as well as by the vowels. In yogic practices involving a female partner, wisdom is identified with a *yoginī.* In the union of wisdom and means, it is wisdom that plays a dominant role, for although it is unattainable without means, it embraces the highest truth of emptiness. In Tantric texts wisdom is frequently named Nairātmyā ("absence of selfhood"), and it is with her that a Tantric practitioner, as means, attempts to become united. Wisdom is mostly characterized as having a female aspect, but it also appears under a masculine aspect, symbolized by a *vajra,* an epitome of the perfect and indestructible truth. Buddha Vairocana and any other Buddha of the Tantras comprehend within them the whole truth and wisdom just as much as does the goddess Prajñāpāramitā or Nairātmyā. In such cases, the Tantric goddess is made to transmute into the male deity. In yogic practices with a female partner, it is the yogin who is absorbed into wisdom.

Comparing *prajñā* with *jñāna,* one can make the following observations. *Prajñā* is a religious term that at once encompasses both knowledge and deliverance. Within the context of worldly existence permeated by ignorance, *prajñā* comprehends false notions and leads away from everything that binds one to this world. *Prajñā* is a spiritual realization gained through correct knowledge and moral purification. Buddhist thinkers of all times refrained from categorizing *prajñā* in the same way as they did *jñāna. Prajñā* was always seen as being beyond the categories of knowledge and as being born naturally within a fully perfected practitioner; *jñāna,* on the other hand, was categorized and graded from that of ordinary empirical knowledge to the level of the highest and transcendent knowledge. From the scholarly approach it is possible to make clear distinctions between the highest levels of knowledge, often described as being intuitive, and *prajñā;* doing so is difficult, though, because these notions very often overlap and coincide. The correct assessment of their relationship should be sought, perhaps, in seeing the acquisition of knowledge as an important and necessary factor that, along with meditation, induces the presence of *prajñā.*

In the early phases of the Mahāyāna, compassion and wisdom are given equal status. However, at some stage in the Buddhist writings wisdom assumed a dominant role. Mañjuśrī, as a manifestation of wisdom, became frequently invoked and praised. The glorification of wisdom reached its climax in the Prajñāpāramitā and Mādhyamika literature, in which *prajñā* is constantly praised and extolled while *karuṇā* is seldom mentioned. During the later phase of the Mahāyāna a reverse process occurred. Compassion became more emphasized, and Avalokiteśvara, as its manifestation, assumed a predominant position, overshadowing other *bodhisattvas* and even the Buddhas. Despite extreme tendencies in literary works, in iconography, and in practice, the tradition has always recognized that proper balance between compassion and wisdom must be retained, for it is the practice of both that brings enlightenment. Compassion as the basis for enlightenment is not a simple feeling of pity but an application of appropriate practical means (*upāya*) that lead toward the realization of the final goal. The employment of different means (such as the practice of the Perfections—giving, morality, etc.) and *prajñā* always go together. *Prajñā* cannot be fully realized without *upāya;* in turn, *upāya* cannot ascend beyond the worldly existence without *prajñā.*

SEE ALSO Arhat; Bodhisattva Path; Buddhism, Schools of, article on Early Doctrinal Schools of Buddhism; Buddhist Philosophy; Dharma, article on Buddhist Dharma and Dharmas; Four Noble Truths; Indian Philosophies; Jñāna; Karuṇā; Nirvāṇa; Pāramitās; Śūnyam and Śūnyatā; Tathatā; Upāya; Wisdom.

BIBLIOGRAPHY

In the early Buddhist scriptures *prajñā* is dealt with in many passages in the four Nikāyas, but the most comprehensive and condensed expositions are found in later writings, namely in Buddhaghosa's *Visuddhimagga,* translated by Pe Maung Tin under the title *The Path of Purity* (London, 1971), and in Vasubandhu's *Abhidharmakośa,* translated by Louis de La Vallée Poussin under the title *L'Abhidharmakośa de Vasubandhu,* 6 vols. (1923–1931; reprint, Brussels, 1971). Much reliable information and many references to the original sources can be found in I. B. Horner's *The Early Buddhist Theory of Man Perfected* (1936; reprint, London, 1975) and also in K. N. Jayatilleke's *Early Buddhist Theory of Knowledge* (London, 1963).

All the necessary information relevant to the Prajñāpāramitā literature is contained in Edward Conze's *The Prajñāpāramitā Literature* (The Hague, 1960; reprint, Tokyo, 1978). The most succinct exposition of *prajñāpāramitā* is contained in the shorter sūtras, and a translation of nineteen of them, including the *Vajracchedikā,* can be found in Conze's *The Short Prajñāpāramitā Texts* (London, 1973).

The *Mahāprajñāpāramitāśāstra,* which contains a detailed exposition of *prajñā,* was translated into French from the Chinese translation of Kumārajīva by Étienne Lamotte as *Le traité de la grande vertu de sagesse,* 5 vols. (Louvain, 1944–1980). Asaṅga's *Mahāyānasaṃgraha,* which expounds the Yogācāra position, was also translated by Lamotte as *La somme du Grand Véhicule d'Asaṅga,* 2 vols. (Louvain, 1938–1939).

Other recommended works include T. R. V. Murti's *The Central Philosophy of Buddhism,* 2d ed. (London, 1955; reprint, London, 1970); Étienne Lamotte's *The Teaching of Vimalakīrti,* translated by Sara Boin (London, 1976), a translation of the *Vimalakīrtinirdeśa Sūtra;* Marion L. Matics's *Entering the Path of Enlightenment: The Bodhicaryāvatāra of the Buddhist Poet Śāntideva* (New York, 1970); Har Dayal's *The Bodhisattva Doctrine in Buddhist Sanskrit Literature* (London, 1932; reprint, Delhi, 1975); and David L. Snellgrove's *The Hevajra Tantra,* 2 vols. (London, 1959).

New Sources

Asaṇga, L. M. Joshi, and Kendriya-Tibbati-Ucca-Siksa-Samsthanam. *Vajracchedika Prajñāpāramitāsūtra; Tatha, Acaryā Asangakṛta Trisatikakarikasaptati.* Varanasi, 1997.

Cheetham, Eric. "The Pāramitās of Dhyāna and Prajna." *Middle Way* 70 (1995): 111–120.

Conze, E. *Perfect Wisdom: The Short Prajñāpāramitā Texts.* Devon, U.K., 1993.

Ichimura, S. *Buddhist Critical Spirituality: Prajñā and Śūnyatā.* Delhi, 2001.

Kuiji, H.-c. Shih, and D. Lusthaus. *A Comprehensive Commentary on the Heart Sūtra (Prajñāpāramitā-Hrdaya-Sūtra).* Berkeley, Calif., 2001.

Obermiller, E., and H. S. Sobati. *Prajñāpāramitā in Tibetan Buddhism.* New Delhi, 1999.

Skorupski, T. *The Six Perfections: An Abridged Version of E. Lamotte's French Translation of Nāgārjuna's Mahāprajñāpāramitāśāstra, Chapters 16–30.* Tring, U.K., 2002.

Tivari, M. *Śīla, Samādhi, and Prajñā: The Buddha's Path of Purification.* Patna, 1987.

TADEUSZ SKORUPSKI (1987)
Revised Bibliography

PRAKṚTI is a Sanskrit word meaning "nature, origin, progress." As a philosophical concept it refers to one of the two basic principles of the Sāṃkhya school, material stuff, or materiality. Materiality, according to the Sāṃkhya school, is manifest and unmanifest. There are other specific terms for the designation of unmanifest materiality, such as *mūlaprakṛti* ("original materiality") or *pradhāna* ("main principle"). *Prakṛti* is a term designating materiality in both its manifest and its unmanifest forms. The use of this term dates back to the middle group of Upaniṣads, composed in the last centuries BCE.

The concept of materiality can be traced to the Vedic creation myths. Although these myths vary, they all take as their starting point the existence of an original being, such as the "first man" (see, e.g., *Ṛgveda* 10.90). The subsequent development of the concept of *prakṛti* can be divided into two periods, a creative-formative period and a classical period.

The creative-formative period is well reflected in the Upaniṣads (from c. 600 BCE to the first centuries CE) and the *Mahābhārata* (compiled in the period between the last centuries BCE and the first centuries CE). "The first being was alone, and it desired to be many." Such descriptions are numerous in the Upaniṣads. The being that wishes to multiply itself is known by several names: *puruṣa,* Prajāpati, *ātman,* and a term of particular note *mahān ātman.* This "large self" is unborn and yet it exists, as described in, for example, the *Bṛhadāraṇyaka Upaniṣad* 4.4.22. The *mahān ātman* next embodies itself in creation. This creation is an expansion of the self, and in its embodiment as creation the self is complete.

The self is aware of itself, as expressed in the phrases "I am!" or "I myself am this creation." This awareness initiates such processes as cognizing, perceiving, and so forth. The self cognizes as if it had different sense faculties. For example, it hears, although it does not have ears. The various processes that the awareness initiates gave ground to the distinction of the different principles (*tattvas*) as a result of an analysis that required a single function for a single principle.

The *Mokṣadharma,* the twelfth book of the *Mahābhārata,* calls the first-born the "large one." The "large one" is born on account of its knowledge. But the "large one" is not the only one to whom this function is ascribed. Similarly, here the *buddhi* (usually translated as "intellect") is considered the creator of the universe. The "large one" and the *buddhi* are two concepts that overlap from this time.

Such overlapping is prominent in the theory of the evolution of the universe as described in the *Mokṣadharma.* Here two cosmogonic patterns are presented. In one pattern, as typified by *Mokṣadharma* 187, the intellect (*buddhi*) exists in three *bhāvas,* later usually known as *guṇas* (constituents of materiality). In this pattern of evolution the sequence runs: intellect, then mind, then senses, and so on. The other pattern adds ego and places it between the intellect and the mind, whereby the sequence of evolution becomes intellect, then ego, then mind, and so forth. There is also a difference in how the three *bhāvas* relate to the intellect. In the first pattern, the three *bhāvas* are not inherent in the intellect; in the second pattern, the three *bhāvas* are "psychological" qualities of the individual beings.

The second period in the development of the concept of *prakṛti* is the classical period. The *Sāṃkhyakārikā* of Īśvarakṛṣṇa (c. 500 CE) is a product of the classical period. Both patterns of evolution are recorded in the *Sāṃkhyakārikā* (vv. 24–25). The first pattern involves a diversification of ego into three distinct qualifications which are also ascribed to the *guṇas.* In the early descriptions of the evolution theory, they are the three *bhāvas.*

A version of the second pattern, on the other hand, became the established pattern for the theory of evolution in the Sāṃkhya school (cf. *Sāṃkhyakārikā* 3 and 22). In this pattern, all principles (intellect, ego, etc.) emerge from the original unmanifest materiality. Evolution starts when intellect emerges from the original unmanifest materiality; this intellect produces ego. From ego several principles emerge: mind, the ten faculties (the five sense faculties and the five action faculties), and the subtle elements. From these subtle elements, the material elements emerge. Hence there are twenty-four principles of materiality. According to the Sāṃkhya school, materiality together with consciousness form the twenty-five principles that comprise the universe.

In both patterns of production, the transformation of the original materiality into twenty-three developed principles is explained by a relation of cause and effect. Since the various principles, which are simply different forms of the original unmanifest materiality, emerge from materiality, the original unmanifest materiality is understood as the cause of the produced principles that become its effects. Since the original materiality is unmanifest, it can be known only through its effects. This theory of causality relies on an effect that is already preexistent in the cause (*satkāryavāda*), just as yogurt is latent in milk.

Materiality is distinctly described in two ways, the original unmanifest and the manifest. The Sāṃkhya school postulates a pulsating universe, which means that creation and reabsorption follow one another; at the time of reabsorption, materiality is in a dormant and unmanifest state. During this time, the three *guṇas* are in a state of equilibrium. Upon the disturbance of the equilibrium, materiality starts to emerge in varying combinations of the three constituents.

The manifest materiality is characterized as being the opposite of consciousness in the *Sāṃkhyakārikā* 11. For example, materiality is caused, finite, spatial, active, composite, dependent, undifferentiated, productive, has a substratum, and is formed of three constituents. Although multiple in its transformations, it is only one. Since materiality is nonconscious, it is dependent on consciousness to make the experience of materiality conscious.

Prakṛti, in short, is one of the dual principles of the Sāṃkhya school that finds its origin in Vedic creation myths. Originally the creation began with the first being, which eventually gave up its procreative function, bequeathing it to *prakṛti.* Thus *prakṛti* is always connected with the theory of the evolution of the universe.

SEE ALSO Guṇas; Puruṣa; Sāṃkhya.

BIBLIOGRAPHY

A detailed exploration of the origins of the concept *prakṛti* can be found in J. A. B. van Buitenen's three-part article "Studies in Sāṃkhya," *Journal of the American Oriental Society* 76 (July–September 1956); 153–157, 77 (January–March 1957): 15–25, and 77 (April–June 1957): 88–107. For a succinct study of the development of the concept *prakṛti* see J. A. B. van Buitenen's "The Large *Ātman,*" *History of Religions* 4 (1964): 103–114. The most up to date detailed study of the Sāṃkhya school is *Samkhya: A Dualist Tradition in Indian Philosophy* by Gerald James Larson and Ram Shankar Bhattacharya, the third volume of the *Encyclopedia of Indian Philosophies,* edited by Karl H. Potter (Princeton and Delhi, 1987). See also Knut A. Jacobsen, *Prakṛti in Samkhya-Yoga: Material Principle, Religious Experience, Ethical Implications.* (Delhi, 2002).

EDELTRAUD HARZER (1987 AND 2005)

PRALAYA, or doomsday in the Hindu eschatological scheme, comes at the end of the fourth and worst of the four ages, or *yugas*, at the end of each *kalpa,* or day of Brahmā. The Purāṇas, which describe this process in great detail, differ as to the precise length of time that this process requires, but the scale is always astronomical, involving hundreds of thousands of years. At the end of the *kalpa,* the heat of the sun becomes so intense that it dries up the whole earth and sets the three worlds (heaven, earth, and the underworld) on fire; when they have been entirely consumed, enormous clouds appear and rain falls for hundreds of years, deluging the whole world until the waters inundate heaven and all is reduced to the primeval ocean of chaos. In anthropomorphic terms, this is the moment when Brahmā, whose waking moments or whose dream has been the source of the "emission" of the universe from his mind, falls into a deep, dreamless sleep inside the cosmic waters. And at the end of that sleep, at the end of the period of quiescence, the universe, or the consciousness of the god, is reborn once more out of the waters of chaos.

This circular pattern contains within it an infinite number of linear segments. For India, like Greece, developed a theory of four ages of declining goodness. Whereas the Greeks named these ages after metals, the Indians called them after throws of the dice, the first and best being the *kṛtayuga,* which is followed by the *tretā,* the *dvāpara,* and finally the present age, or the *kaliyuga.* The importance of the metaphor of dice is also manifest in the fact that the royal ceremony of consecration included a ritual dice game; in the second book of the *Mahābhārata,* King Yudhiṣṭhira loses his entire kingdom in a game of dice against an opponent whom he knows to be a cheat, thus inaugurating a period of exile that is also a part of the ritual of consecration. Moreover, as Madeleine Biardeau has convincingly argued, the catastrophic battle that ends the *Mahābhārata,* an Armageddon in which all the heroes as well as all the villains are killed, is a reenactment on the human level of the cosmic doomsday that is constantly alluded to in the epic. This human doomsday, like the big dice game in the sky, begins with Yudhiṣṭhira's unlucky loss and ends, inevitably, with the losing throw for humankind.

Yet the "end" that comes after the *kaliyuga* is not the end at all, but a new beginning; a new *kṛtayuga* will follow after the fallow interval. Moreover, there is a "seed" of humanity that survives doomsday to form the stock of the new race of humans. Sometimes this seminal group is said to be the Seven Sages, whom Viṣṇu in the form of a fish saves from the cosmic flood; sometimes it is Manu, the ancestor of all humankind, and his family; sometimes it is an unspecified group of "good men" who resist the corruption that overtakes everyone else at the end of the *kaliyuga,* a group that retires to the forest to live in innocence while the cities of the plain drown in their own depravity. This "seed" functions on the macrocosmic level as a metaphor for the transmigrating soul on the microcosmic level, the *ātman* that leaps across the barrier between individual human death and rebirth, just as the good "seed" leaps across the barrier between one *pralaya* and the next cosmic emission, or *prasarga.* In the Vedantic mythology of the late Purāṇas, and in Indian literature in general, recurrent images of doomsday serve to emphasize the insubstantiality of the world; the things that people think of as permanent are constantly destroyed and recreated.

BIBLIOGRAPHY

A good introduction in English is provided by Hermann Jacobi's article on the "Ages of the World," in the *Encyclopaedia of Religion and Ethics,* edited by James Hastings, vol. 1 (Edinburgh, 1908). Details of the Sanskrit texts are cited in Willibald Kirfel's *Das Purāṇa Pañcalakṣaṇa* (Bonn, 1927), though without any useful interpretation. The classic discussion remains Mircea Eliade's "Time and Eternity in Indian Thought," in *Papers from the Eranos Yearbooks,* vol. 3, *Man and Time,* edited by Joseph Campbell (New York, 1957), pp. 173–200. A thoughtful and complex interpretation of the *pralaya* may be found in Madeleine Biardeau's *Études de mythologie hindoue* published in the *Bulletin de l'École Française d'Extrême Orient* (Paris, 1968, 1969, 1971, and 1976).

WENDY DONIGER (1987)

PRĀṆA.

The Sanskrit term *prāṇa* (from the conjunction of *pra* and *ana,* "breathing forth") can signify (1) the Absolute (*brahman*) as the transcendental source of all life, (2) life in general, (3) the life force or "breath" of life in particular, (4) respiration, (5) air (in secular contexts only), and (6) the life organs (i.e., the five cognitive senses, the five conative senses, and the sense-related mind, or *manas*).

The third connotation is of special interest to the historian of religion, because it conveys a vibrant psychophysical reality (visible to the yogin) similar to the Greek *pneuma* and the Melanesian *mana.* In this sense, *prāṇa* is a creative force, defined in the *Yogavāsiṣṭha* (3.13.31 et passim) as the "vibratory energy" (*spandaśakti*) that is responsible for all manifestation. Most metaphysical schools of India—one of the exceptions being Hīnayāna Buddhism—subscribe to this notion, although the details of interpretations differ.

In archaic Vedic thought, *prāṇa* is considered to be the "breath" of the macranthropos, the cosmic Puruṣa (e.g., *Ṛgveda* 10.90.13; *Atharvaveda* 11.4.15), and the breath or life force of the human body is regarded as a form of that all-pervading *prāṇa.* Later writers make a terminological distinction between the life force that interpenetrates the entire universe as a sort of subtle energy—called *mukhyaprāṇa* or "principal breath"—and the life force that sustains and animates the individual body-minds. *Prāṇa* in this latter sense has from earliest times been classified into five individualized breaths. These speculations, dating back to the *Atharvaveda* (see esp. chap. 15), betray a culture of intense introspection and acute sensitivity to bodily processes.

The five individualized breaths, sometimes known collectively as *vāyu* ("wind"), are the following:

(1) *prāṇa,* the ascending breath issuing from the navel or the heart and including both inhalation and exhalation;

(2) *apāna,* the breath associated with the lower half of the trunk;

(3) *vyāna,* the diffuse breath circulating in all the limbs;

(4) *udāna,* the "up-breath" held responsible for belching, speech, and the spontaneous focusing of attention in the esoteric "centers" (*cakras*) of the brain, as realized in or associated with higher states of consciousness;

(5) *samāna,* the breath localized in the abdominal region, where it is chiefly associated with the digestive process.

The soteriological literature of the post-Śaṅkara period often adds to this classical pentad a further set of five secondary breaths (*upaprāṇa*), about whose locations and functions, however, there is no unanimity. These are the following:

(1) *nāga* ("serpent"), generally held responsible for belching and vomiting;

(2) *kūrma* ("tortoise"), associated with the opening and closing of the eyelids;

(3) *kṛkara* ("*kṛ*-maker"), thought to cause hunger, hiccups, or blinking;

(4) *devadatta* ("God-given"), associated with the processes of sleep, especially yawning;

(5) *dhanaṃjaya* ("conquest of wealth"), responsible for the decomposition of the corpse; also sometimes said to be connected with the production of phlegm.

These ten types of breaths are generally conceived of as circulating in a complex lattice of bioenergetic pathways called *nāḍīs* ("ducts"). They are widely thought to constitute an experiential field or bodily "sheath," the *prāṇāmaya-kośa* (*Taittirīya Upaniṣad* 2). In the *Chāndogya Upaniṣad* (2.13.6), the five principal breaths are styled "the gatekeepers to the heavenly world," which hints at an esoteric understanding of the close relationship between breathing and consciousness. This connection was later explored in the various soteriological schools, notably in *haṭhayoga.*

Sometimes *prāṇa* and *apāna* simply represent inhalation and exhalation, but in yogic contexts both terms are used in the technical sense noted above. Particularly in *haṭhayoga,* both breaths play an important role in the technique of breath control (*prāṇāyāma*) as a means of curbing, through sensory inhibition, the rise and fall of attention.

SEE ALSO Breath and Breathing; Cakras; Haṭhayoga; Yoga.

BIBLIOGRAPHY

Brown, George William. "Prāṇa and Apāna." *Journal of the American Oriental Society* 39 (1919): 104–112.

Ewing, Arthur H. "The Hindu Conception of the Functions of Breath." *Journal of the American Oriental Society* 22 (1901): 249–308.

Wikander, Stig. *Vāyu: Texte und Untersuchungen zur indo-iranischen Religionsgeschichte.* Uppsala, 1941.

New Sources

Connolly, Peter. *Vitalistic Thought in India: A Study of the "Prāṇa" Concept in Vedic Literature and Its Development in the Vedānta, Sāṃkhya and Pañcarātra Traditions.* Delhi, 1992.

GEORG FEUERSTEIN (1987)
Revised Bibliography

PRATĪTYA-SAMUTPĀDA.

The term *pratītya-samutpāda* (Pali, *paṭicca-samuppāda*), "dependent origination" or "dependent arising," was first used by the Buddha to characterize the understanding of the nature of human existence that he had attained at his enlightenment. Essentially a doctrine of causality, this notion is so central to Buddhist thought that a proper understanding of *pratītya-samutpāda* is often declared tantamount to enlightenment itself. In it, an entire complex of notions about moral responsibility, human freedom, the process of rebirth, and the path to liberation coalesce.

Pratītya-samutpāda was promulgated against a background of four contemporary theories of causality. These were (1) self-causation (*svayaṃ kṛta*), advocated by the traditional Brahmanic philosophers; (2) external causation (*parakṛta*), upheld by the materialist thinkers; (3) a combination of self-causation and external causation, advocated by the Jains; and (4) a denial of both self and external causation, probably championed by certain skeptical thinkers who refused to recognize any form of causation. While all four of these theories were explicitly rejected by the Buddha, the brunt of his analysis was directed against the former two.

According to the Buddha, a theory of self-causation leads to the belief in permanence (*śāśvata*), that is, the recognition of a permanent and eternal "self" (*ātman*), which the Buddha found to be an unverifiable entity. External causation, on the other hand, implies the existence of an inexorable physical law of nature (*svabhāva*) that would render the human being a mere automaton with no power to determine the nature of his own existence. Ultimately, such a position divests beings of all bases for personal continuity and hence, moral responsibility. This he referred to as the theory of annihilation (*uccheda*). *Pratītya-samutpāda,* on the other hand, is presented as the "middle (*madhyama*) position" between these two extremes. This middle position is explained in great detail in the *Discourse to Kātyāyana,* which serves as the *locus classicus* of all subsequent interpretations of the Buddha's "middle path." Following is the text of the discourse in the Pali version:

> Thus have I heard. The Blessed One was once living in Savatthi. . . . At that time the venerable Kaccāyana of that clan came to visit him, and saluting him, sat down at one side. So seated, he questioned the Exalted One: "Sir, [people] speak of 'right view, right view.' To what extent is there right view?" This world, Kaccāyana, is generally inclined toward two [views]: existence and nonexistence. For him who perceives, with right knowledge, the uprising of the world as it has come to be, whatever view there is in the world about nonexistence will not be acceptable. Kaccāyana, for him who perceives, with right knowledge, the ceasing of the world as it has come to be, whatever view there is in the world about existence will not be acceptable. "The world, for the most part, Kaccāyana, is bound by approach, grasping and inclination. Yet, a person who does not follow that approach and grasping, that determination of mind, the inclination and disposition, who does not cling to or adhere to a view: 'This is my self,' who thinks [instead]: 'suffering that is subject to arising arises; suffering that is subject to ceasing ceases,' such a person does not doubt, is not perplexed. Herein, his knowledge is not other-dependent. Thus far, Kaccāyana, there is 'right view.'

> 'Everything exists'—this, Kaccāyana, is one extreme.
>
> 'Everything does not exist'—this, Kaccāyana, is the second extreme. Kaccāyana, without approaching either extreme, the Tathāgata teaches you a doctrine in the middle.
>
> Dependent upon ignorance [*avidyā*] arise dispositions [*saṃskāra*]; dependent upon dispositions arises consciousness [*vijñāna*]; dependent upon consciousness arises the psychophysical personality [*nāma-rūpa*]; dependent upon the psychophysical personality arise the six senses [*ṣaḍāyatana*]; dependent upon the six senses arises contact [*sparśa*]; dependent upon contact arises feeling [*vedanā*]; dependent upon feeling arises craving [*tṛṣṇā*]; dependent upon craving arises grasping [*upādāna*]; dependent upon grasping arises becoming [*bhava*]; dependent upon becoming arises birth [*jāti*]; dependent upon birth arises old age and death, grief, lamentation, suffering, dejection and despair. Thus arises this entire mass of suffering. However, from the utter fading away and ceasing of ignorance, there is cessation of dispositions . . . from the ceasing of birth, there is ceasing of old age and death, grief, lamentation, suffering, dejection and despair." (*Saṃyutta Nikāya* 2.16–17)

Existence (*atthitā;* Skt., *astitva*) and nonexistence (*n'atthitā;* Skt., *nāstitva*) referred to here are not simple notions of empirical existence or nonexistence. In the Indian context, existence implies permanence; hence the Buddha's appeal to the empirical fact of cessation of phenomena to reject the notion of existence. Nonexistence refers to complete annihilation without any form of continuity, hence the Buddha's appeal to the empirical fact of arising of phenomena. Thus, the fundamental philosophical problem involved here is how to account for continuity in human experience without either having to posit permanence of some sort or accept absolute discontinuity.

Linguistic conventions of his day did not provide the Buddha with a term to express his ideas, hence it was necessary to coin an entirely different compound term: *pratītya-samutpāda. Samutpāda* literally means "arising in combination," or "co-arising." But when compounded with the term *pratītya* (a gerund from the root *i,* "to move," with prefix *prati* meaning "toward"), implying "moving" or "leaning toward," the term means "dependence." *Pratītya-samutpāda* may, therefore, be translated as "dependent arising." Formulating his experience in this way, the Buddha was able to avoid several metaphysical issues that have plagued most discussions of the principle of causation in the East as well as in the West.

Attempts to understand how a cause produces an effect have led philosophers to adopt a reductionist perspective and look for an "essence," or "substance" in the cause that gives rise to the effect. Such a perspective is also motivated by a desire to predict with absolute certainty the manner of the emergence of the effect from the cause. By speaking of the *dependence* of the effect on the cause, which is what the term *pratītya-samutpāda* is intended to express, both the reductionist or essentialist perspective and the impossible task of predicting an event with absolute certainty are avoided.

Thus, the Buddha spoke not of self-sufficient things or substances but of "dependently arisen phenomena" (*pratītyasamutpanna-dharma*). These refer to phenomena that have already occurred. There is no implication here that individual and discrete phenomena (*dharma*) are experienced and that their "dependence" upon one another is imagined (as was understood by the Humeans) or is the result of transcendental categories of understanding (as the Kantians believed). On the contrary, both phenomena and the manner of their dependence are part of human experience. However, this "dependence" is then stretched out, by means of an inductive inference, to explain the events of the dim past as well as of the future. This is the manner in which the Buddha arrived at the uniformity of the principle of dependence. When he claimed that this "dependent arising" has remained as such despite either the arising of the Tathāgatas or the nonarising of the Tathāgatas he was hinting at the universality of that experience. The uniform and universal principle of dependence is expressed in a most abstract way in the oft-recurring statement: "When that exists, this comes to be; on the arising of that, this arises. When that does not exist, this does not come to be; on the cessation of that, this ceases" (*Majjhima Nikāya* 1.262–264).

In the *Discourse to Kātyāyana* this principle of dependence is utilized to explain the processes of human bondage as well as of freedom. The positive statement of the twelve-fold formula, beginning with the statement "Depending upon ignorance arise dispositions," explains the human personality in bondage, avoiding both eternalistic and nihilistic views. The human person is here referred to as *nāma-rūpa* (the psychophysical personality). The nature of that person is conditioned mostly by his or her consciousness (*vijñāna*), which, in its turn, is determined by the person's understanding (and in the case of the person in bondage, by his or her lack of understanding—*avidyā*) and the dispositions (*saṃskāra*) formed on the basis of that understanding. Conditioned by such understanding and dispositions, a person comes to experience (*sparśa, vedanā*) the world through the six sense faculties (*ṣaḍāyatana*) and to respond by being attracted to it (*tṛṣṇā*). Thus, the person's behavior (*karman*) comes to be dominated not only by the world he or she experiences but also by the way in which the person experiences it. If one is attracted by that world one tends to cling to it (*upādāna*). One's whole personality, what he or she wants to be or achieve, will be determined by that craving and grasping. Such would be this person's becoming (*bhava*), not only in this life, but also in a future life (*jāti*). Involved in such a process of becoming (*bhava*), the person will be pleased and satisfied when obtaining what is craved and unhappy and frustrated when he or she does not. Yet even these satisfactions, which are temporary at best, turn out to be dissatisfactions as the craving and grasping continue to increase. Such is the mass of suffering the person will experience through successive stages of life and in subsequent births.

A proper understanding of phenomena as impermanent (*anitya*) and nonsubstantial (*anātman*) would enable a person to pacify his or her dispositional tendencies (*saṃskāropasama*). Pacification of dispositions leads to a better understanding of one's own personality as well as the world of experience. Perceiving phenomena as being nonsubstantial, one will neither assume the existence of an inexorable law nor believe in complete lawlessness. When one responds to that world of experience with an understanding of conditionality one's responses will not be rigidly predetermined (*asamskṛta*). Abandoning passion or craving (*tṛṣṇā*), one's actions will be dominated by dispassion (*vairāgya*), and more positively, by compassion (*karuṇā*) for one's self as well as others. Thirsting for nothing, with few wants, the person will be freed from most of the "constraints" and lead a happy and contented life until death. With no grasping, there will be no more becoming (*bhava*) and hence the cessation of any possible future births (*jātikṣaya*). The recognition of the possibility of replacing ignorance (*avidyā*) with wisdom (*jñāna, vidyā*) and craving and grasping with dispassion and compassion leaves the individual with the capacity to attain freedom. Thus, the principle of dependent arising avoids both strict determinism and absolute indeterminism; it is neither an absolutely inviolable law nor a chaotic lawlessness.

The explanation of the human personality, both in bondage and in freedom, was of paramount importance for the Buddha. Hence the discussion of the principle of dependence is confined to these two aspects in the *Discourse to Kātyāyana.* Elsewhere, however, he applies this principle to explain most other aspects of human existence. For example, without positing a first cause or any primordial substance he applied the principle of dependence to explain the evolution and dissolution of the world process. This principle is also utilized in the explanation of the process by which one comes to have knowledge of the world through sensory as well as extrasensory means. Moral behavior, social life, and religious and spiritual phenomena are given causal explanations as well. For this reason, the Buddha did not hesitate to declare, "He who sees dependent arising sees the doctrine (*dharma*)" (*Majjhima Nikāya* 1.190–191).

The Abhidharma period was the most active and highly vibrant epoch of scholastic activity in Buddhist history. During this period the contents of the discourses were carefully analyzed and presented in nondiscursive form. In the process, the "dependently arisen phenomena" referred to by the Buddha came to be listed and classified, together with an analysis of the various types of causal relations (*pratyaya*) that obtain among them. However, a few centuries later, metaphysical speculations began to emerge in the Buddhist tradition. Two schools of Buddhism, the Sarvāstivāda and Sautrāntika, speculating on the concepts of time and space, produced theories of momentariness and atomism, thereby engendering insoluble problems such as the metaphysical notions of absolute identity and absolute difference. Contradicting the Buddha's notion of nonsubstantiality, the Sarvāstivādins accepted an underlying "substance" (*svabhāva*) in phenomena, while the Sautrāntikas surreptitiously introduced a metaphysical notion of a transmigrating personality (*pudgala*).

The Pali Abhidharma work *Kathāvatthu* criticized and rejected these views. In spite of this criticism, these views continued to survive. The early Mahāyāna *sūtras* represent another attempt to get rid of the substantialist metaphysics of these two schools by emphasizing a negative approach to the problem of reality, one based upon the notion of "emptiness" (*śūnyatā*). For example, one of the early Mahāyāna *sūtras*—the *Kāśyapaparivarta*—continued to describe the "middle path" in negative terms, while at the same time retaining the positive version discussed in the *Discourse to Kātyāyana.*

Nāgārjuna's famous treatise, the *Mūlamadhyamakakārikā,* considered by many as the most sophisticated philosophical justification of Mahāyāna, is a determined attempt to return to the original message of the Buddha by criticizing the substantialist views of the Sarvāstivādins and the Sautrāntikas. Restatement of the principle of "dependent arising" without having to posit a substantial connection (*svabhāva*) between a cause and an effect (as the Sarvāstivādins did), or to emphasize their difference (as the Sautrāntikas did), seems to be the foremost concern of Nāgārjuna. "Emptiness" here becomes a synonym for "nonsubstantiality" (*anātman*).

The Buddha's conception of karmic continuity and moral responsibility also had to be rescued from the substantialist interpretations of the Buddhist metaphysicians. Nāgārjuna seems to have been aware of a statement popular among the Buddhists relating to the doctrine of *karman* that read: "*Karmas* do not perish (*na praṇaśyanti*) even after a hundred myriads of aeons. Having attained the harmony of conditions (*sāmagrī*) and the proper time (*kāla*), they bear fruit for the human beings" (La Vallée Poussin, 1903, p. 324). Inspired probably by this verse, Nāgārjuna (*Mūlamadhyamakakārikā* 17.14) upheld the notion of a nonperishable (*avipraṇaśa*) *karman,* comparing it with the unacceptable interpretations offered by the substantialists. After denying a "self" (*ātman*), he proceeded to compile chapters on the "harmony of conditions" (*sāmagrī*) and on time (*kāla*), giving a nonsubstantialist interpretation of these.

Having devoted twenty-five chapters to recasting the full range of Buddhist ideas in terms of the doctrine of "emptiness," Nāgārjuna returns to the conclusion of the *Discourse to Kātyāyana* in chapter 26, where he analyzes the twelvefold factors describing the human personality in bondage as well as freedom. Thus, Nāgārjuna's treatise should more appropriately be considered a grand commentary on the *Discourse to Kātyāyana,* this being the only discourse referred to by name in the text.

Nāgārjuna's exposition of the twelvefold formula in chapter 26 (which incidentally consists of twelve verses) focuses on the positive statement of the Buddha regarding the human life process, that is, how a human being conditioned by ignorance suffers in bondage. The negative statement of the Buddha explaining freedom is briefly outlined in the last two verses of this chapter.

Nāgārjuna begins the chapter explaining how the destiny (*gati*) of a human being, as he continues with his life-process, is determined by ignorance and dispositions. Taking a cue from the *Mahānidāna Suttanta,* where the Buddha speaks about consciousness (*viññāṇa;* Skt., *vijñāna*) entering the mother's womb in order to influence the psychophysical personality formed therein, Nāgārjuna explains the psychophysical personality (*nāma-rūpa*) as being infused (*niṣicyate*) by consciousness that is dispositionally conditioned. The most interesting addition to the formula appears in the explanation of the three links: the psychophysical personality (*nāma-rūpa*), the six spheres of sense (*ṣaḍāyatana*) and contact (*sparśa*). At this point Nāgārjuna introduces the contents of a passage explaining the process of sense experience occurring in the *Mahāhatthipadopama Sutta* that, though implied, is not specifically stated in the twelvefold formula. This passage refers to the various conditions needed for sense experience, namely, the existence of the unimpaired sense organ, the object that has come into focus, and the availability of attention arising in such a context. The rest of the formula is then briefly presented without explanations. Verse 10 introduces the idea of the perception of truth (*tattva-darśana*) in place of the cessation of ignorance (*avidyā-nirodha*). Nāgārjuna did not have to specify what this conception of truth is, for he has already compiled twenty-five chapters in its explanation. It is the perception that all (experienced) phenomena are empty (*sarvam idam sunyam*) of substance (*svabhavato*).

BIBLIOGRAPHY

For a detailed study of *pratītya-samutpāda,* see my *Causality: The Central Philosophy of Buddhism* (Honolulu, 1975). My translation and annotation of the *Mūlamadhyamakakārikā* of Nāgārjuna, *Nāgārjuna, the Philosophy of the Middle Way* (Albany, N.Y., 1986) gives further elaboration to the view that Nāgārjuna's *Mūlamadhyamakakārikā* is in essence a commentary on the *Discourse to Kātyāyana.* See also Alex Wayman's detailed treatment, "Buddhist Dependent Origination," *History of Religions* 10 (1971): 185–203. The passage on the imperishability of karmas quoted above can be found in Louis de La Vallée Poussin's *Mūlamadhyamakakārikās de Nāgārjuna avec la Prasannapadā commentaire de Candrakirti* (Saint Petersburg, 1903), p. 324.

New Sources

Basso, Pierre. "Language for a Causal Conditional Logic Foundations and Objectives: Is It Possible to Formalize Dependent Origination?" *Journal of Indian Philosophy* 16, no. 2 (1988): 123–166.

Bielefeldt, Carl. "The Four Levels of Pratitya-samutpada According to the Fa-hua hsuan i." *Journal of the International Association of Buddhist Studies* 11, no. 1 (1988): 7–29.

Boucher, Daniel. "The Pratīyasamutpādagātha and Its Role in the Medieval Cult of the Relics." *Journal of the International Association of Buddhist Studies* 14 (1991): 1–27.

Cox, Collett. "Dependent Origination: Its Elaboration in Early Sarvastivadin Abhidharma Texts." In *Researches in Indian and Buddhist Philosophy: Essays in Honour of Professor Alex Wayman,* edited by Ram Karan Sharma, pp. 119–143. Delhi, 1993.

Lamotte, Étienne. *Karmasiddhiprakarana: The Treatise on Action by Vasubandhu.* Translated by Leo M. Pruden. Berkeley, 1988.

Potter, Karl, Robert Buswell, Padmanabh Jaini, and Noble Reat, eds. *Encyclopedia of Indian Philosophies: Volume VII: Abhidharma Buddhism to 150 A.D.* Delhi, 1996.

Wayman, Alex. "The Secret of Nagarjuna's Position on Dependent Origination and Sunyata." In *Indo-Tibetan Mādhyamika Studies,* pp. 82–109. New Delhi, 1996.

DAVID J. KALUPAHANA (1987)
Revised Bibliography

PRATT, JAMES B. (1875–1944) was an American philosopher and psychologist of religion. Born James Bissett Pratt in Elmira, New York, and raised in the Presbyterian tradition, Pratt graduated from Williams College in 1898. He returned to the school in 1905 to teach, a post he held until 1943. From 1899 to 1905 Pratt studied philosophy at Harvard, primarily with William James (1842–1910) and Josiah Royce (1855–1916). From 1902 to 1903 Pratt studied in Berlin, valuing especially his work with the philosopher of religion Otto Pfleiderer. Pratt also visited eastern Europe and the Middle East, establishing a habit of travel that informed his comparative religion work. In 1911 Pratt married the Italian-born Catherine Mariotti. That devoted relationship was fundamental in expanding Pratt's Protestant sensibility to a sympathetic approach to Catholicism. Pratt's significance lies in three areas: the psychology of religion, comparative religion, and the philosophy of religion.

Philosophically Pratt was a firm critic of James's pragmatism as in *What Is Pragmatism?* (1909). Nevertheless he was a follower of James's psychology of religion, as can be seen by his doctoral thesis, *The Psychology of Religious Belief* (1907). This is an important reminder that the psychology of religion was not dependent on pragmatism for its foundation. Pratt's most significant work, *The Religious Consciousness* (1920), is second only to James's *Varieties of Religious Experience* as the hallmark of that movement. Both attempt to take religious experiences seriously and sympathetically. There are also interesting differences in their approaches. Pratt draws on a much wider range of religious phenomena and represents generally what James would have called the position of the "healthy minded." He speaks from a rich and deep but not anguished religious faith. This leads him to put less emphasis on the drama of involuntary conversion experiences than James did and to critique the evangelical theology that privileges this type. The more frequent type of conversion for Pratt was the product of the deliberate acts taken by individuals who knew their goals, were not satisfied with "any sort of merely emotional state," and were rewarded with "a new sense of calm and satisfaction" (Pratt, 1920, p. 140).

As Pratt moved from privileging extreme forms of conversion, he also distinguished mild and extreme forms of mysticism, insisting that the more mild type had been overlooked and that the extreme forms of mysticism, many of which had pathological features, had received too much attention. Pratt's work also showed a much greater sensitivity to the role of cult and worship in religious life than James and a developing sense of the religious developments through the life cycle. *The Religious Consciousness* remains the most balanced synthetic statement of the issues and approaches of the American-born movement of psychology of religion. In its attempt to hold together the social and the psychological and to take religious consciousness as an irreducible phenomenon, it did not survive the onslaught of the European trends of Durkheimian sociology and Freudian psychology. Pratt was familiar with both of these currents but could not fully embrace either.

Pratt's wide acquaintance with comparative religion was evident in his psychology works but also in two landmark titles, *India and Its Faiths: A Traveler's Record* (1915) and *The Pilgrimage of Buddhism and a Buddhist Pilgrimage* (1928). Both works are sensitive mixtures of textual study, done in translation, and rich impressions from travel. They seek to give the reader a sense for how it feels to be a Hindu or a Buddhist. Although informed by the questions of the psychologist of religion, they focus more on the worldviews and histories of the traditions under examination and therefore stand independent of Pratt's psychology of religion work.

The remainder of Pratt's writing falls into two types. First, he articulated his realist philosophical stance, which affirmed the reality of both material world and mind in such works as *Matter and Spirit* (1922), *Personal Realism* (1937), and *Naturalism* (1939). Second, his work in the philosophy of religion, *Adventures in Philosophy and Religion* (1931), *Can We Keep the Faith?* (1941), *Eternal Values in Religion* (1950), and his unpublished *God and the War,* articulated a defense of liberal religion against any overemphasis on supernaturalism. In these writings Pratt called for a return to the centrality of symbol and ritual for the nourishment of the religious imagination and for the restored vitality of religion in the modern world.

SEE ALSO Comparative Religion; James, William; Philosophy, article on Philosophy of Religion; Psychology, article on Psychology of Religion.

BIBLIOGRAPHY

The memorial volume Gerald E. Meyers, ed., *Self, Religion, and Metaphysics: Essays in Memory of James Bissett Pratt* (New York, 1961), deals mainly with philosophy. The fullest assessment of Pratt's psychology of religion is in David W. Wulff, *Psychology of Religion: Classic and Contemporary* (New York, 1997), pp. 507–523. Eric J. Sharpe, *Comparative Religion: A History,* 2d ed. (La Salle, Ill., 1986), pp. 114–117, gives brief attention to the comparative-religion aspects of Pratt's work.

WILLIAM R. DARROW (2005)

PRAYER, understood as the human communication with divine and spiritual entities, has been present in most of the religions in human history. Viewed from most religious perspectives, prayer is a necessity of the human condition. When the human material world is accounted for in an act of creation resulting in a cleavage or separation from the divine or spiritual world, prayer is one means by which this gap of createdness is overcome, if but momentarily.

Abundant texts of such communications exist as well as extensive literatures about them. Still, the general study of prayer is undeveloped and naive. The question of the universality of prayer has yet to be seriously addressed to the relevant materials. A careful comparative and etymological study of just the terminology that designates acts of human-spiritual communication has yet to be done among even the widespread and best-known religious traditions. Studies of prayer in terms of modern communications theories and semiotics are limited and rare. The theories, as well as the intuitive understandings, of prayer have been heavily influenced by Western religious traditions.

A general schema will be used in the following consideration of the typologies, theories, and interpretive issues of prayer phenomena. First, prayer will be considered as *text,* that is, as a collection of words that cohere as a human communication directed toward a spiritual entity. Second, prayer will be considered as *act,* that is, as the human act of communicating with deities including not only or exclusively language but especially the elements of performance that constitute the act. Finally, prayer will be considered as *subject,* that is, as a dimension or aspect of religion, the articulation of whose nature constitutes a statement of belief, doctrine, instruction, philosophy, or theology.

PRAYER AS TEXT. Prayer is thought of most commonly as the specific words of the human-spiritual communication, that is, as the text of this communication, such as the Lord's Prayer (Christian), the Qaddish (Jewish), and the prayers of *ṣalāt* (Muslim). Scores of prayers appear in books of prayer, books of worship, descriptions of rituals and liturgies, ethnographies of exclusively oral peoples, and biographies of religious persons.

A common basic typology of prayer has been formulated by discerning what distinguishes the character and intent expressed by the words of prayer texts. This kind of typology includes a number of classes, all easily distinguished by their descriptive designations. It includes petition, invocation, thanksgiving (praise or adoration), dedication, supplication, intercession, confession, penitence, and benediction. Such types may constitute whole prayers or they may be strung together to form a structurally more complex prayer.

This kind of typology serves to demonstrate the extent of prayer phenomena. It may be used as a device for the comparative study of religion. It suggests that prayer is widespread and has a commonality as well as diversity. The most extensive use of this kind of typology was made in studies, done mostly in the nineteenth and early twentieth centuries, of the development of religion over time. Petitionary prayers were thought to be most widespread and thus the oldest form of prayer. The presence of ethical, moral, and spiritual concerns in petitionary prayers was believed to have come later as a development beyond purely personal and material needs. While these developmental aspects are no longer considered valid nor are they of much interest in the study of religion, this content typology has continued to provide the basic descriptive language of prayer.

In his classic early anthropological study *Primitive Culture* (1873), E. B. Tylor attributed a psychological and spiritual character to prayer. He called prayer "the soul's sincere desire, uttered or unexpressed" and "the address of personal spirit to personal spirit." In perhaps the most extensive comparative study of prayer, *Prayer: A Study in the History and Psychology of Religion* (1932), Friedrich Heiler understood prayer in much the same terms, describing it, using Hebrew scriptural imagery, as a pouring out of the heart before God. Thus, in both of these classic descriptions, prayer is characterized as free and spontaneous, that is, heartfelt. Such characterization is still broadly held and is, for most, so obvious that critical discussion is unnecessary. However, when the understanding of prayer as a free and spontaneous "living communion of man with God" (Heiler) is conjoined with the general restriction of prayer to the text form, incongruency, confusion, and dilemma arise. Prayer texts, almost without exception and to a degree as part of their nature, are formulaic, repetitive, and static in character, much in contrast with the expected free and spontaneous character of prayer. In the case of Tylor, whose study of culture and religion was directed to the documentation of the evolution of culture, this was particularly confounding. His theory called for religion to follow magic and thus for prayer to follow magical spells and formulas. Yet the abundance of liturgical and meditational prayer forms in the cultures he considered the most fully developed confounded his thesis. Tylor could resolve this dilemma only by holding that prayer "from being at first utterances as free and flexible as requests to a living patriarch or chief, stiffened into traditional formulas whose repetition required verbal accuracy, and whose nature practically assimilated more or less to that of charms" (Tylor, vol. 2, p. 371). Thus, the structural characteristics of prayer that contradicted the expectations of prayer were held to be a product of civilization and evolution.

Heiler was also confounded by this incongruity. He held that prayer texts were, in fact, not true prayers, but were rather artificially composed for the purpose of edifying, instructing, and influencing people in the matters of dogma, belief, and tradition. Heiler's study of prayer, therefore, was a failed effort from the outset in the respect that he denigrated his primary source of data for his study of prayer, leaving him wistfully awaiting the rare occasion to eavesdrop on one pouring out his or her heart to God. Heiler's predisposition for the psychological nature of prayer, conjoined with his failure to make any clear or useful distinction between prayer as text and prayer as act, placed his consideration of prayer in a nonproductive position, one that has generally discouraged the academic study of prayer, especially beyond particular prayer traditions.

Due to the nature of the materials available, prayers must often be considered primarily, if not solely, as texts, whose study is limited to the semantic, informational, and literary aspects of the language that constitutes them. Despite such limitations, the texts of prayers reflect theological, doctrinal, cultural, historical, aesthetic, and creedal dimensions of a religious culture.

PRAYER AS ACT. Intuitively prayer is an act of communication. In its most common performance, prayer is an act of speech. Prayer has been considered as act, including not only the words uttered but some of the performance elements of the speech act, in order to classify and describe prayers in terms of the identities of those praying, the occasions of prayer, the motivations for praying, and such physically descriptive matters as body and hand attitudes. These classifications have been primarily descriptive with institutional and psychological aspects in the foreground.

The distinction between personal and ritual prayer has often been made when viewing prayer as act. Personal prayer, regarded as the act of persons pouring forth their hearts to God, has been considered by many as the truest form, even the only true form, of prayer. Yet, the data available for the study of personal prayer are scant. Still, the record of personal prayers found in letters, biographies, and diaries suggests a strong correlation and interdependence of personal prayer with ritual and liturgical prayer in language, form, style, and physical attitude. A person praying privately is invariably a person who is part of a religious and cultural tradition in which ritual or public prayer is practiced.

Ritual prayer, by not conforming to the naive notions of the spontaneity and free form of prayer, has often been set aside. It was not incorrect of Heiler to understand ritual prayer as being composed for the purpose of edifying, instructing, and influencing people in the matters of dogma, belief, and tradition, although this is but a partial understanding. But Heiler radically truncated his, and consequently many others', understanding of prayer by denigrating these important functions. Such aspects of prayer must be recognized as important and often essential to the continuity and communication of tradition and culture. In its capacity of performing these important functions, the formulaic, repetitive, and standardized characteristics of prayer are effective pedagogically and to enculturate.

Furthermore, and importantly, it can be shown that prayer when formulaic, repetitive, and redundant in message can be a true act of communication, even heartfelt. In recent years a range of studies has developed showing the performative power of language and speech acts. Simply put, these studies show that language and other forms of human action not only say things, that is, impart information, they also do things. Ordinary language acts may persuade, name, commit, promise, declare, affirm, and so on; and these functions are often more primary than that of transmitting information.

The study of prayer has yet to be extensively influenced by this understanding of the performative power of language, but it is clearly relevant. From this perspective, the many dimensions of the act of prayer apart from the heartfelt communication with God can be appreciated more fully. For example, a prayer of invocation, through its form as well as its content, when uttered in the appropriate ritual context, serves to transform the mood of the worshipers. It sets the tone and attitude of worship. It effects the presence of the spiritual in the minds of worshipers. Likewise, a prayer of benediction releases worshipers from a ritual domain. It serves to extend the reorientation achieved in ritual to the world beyond while releasing people from the restrictions imposed by ritual. Prayers of praise direct the attention of those praying to positive divine attributes, they effect and reflect a doctrine of God, while prayers of confession and penitence direct the attention of those praying to negative human elements, they effect and reflect a doctrine of sin and humankind. Even when formulaic and without a motivation arising directly from individual felt needs, the emotive experience and affective qualities of these prayers differs markedly according to their type. Prayers of praise or thanksgiving are joyous, uplifting, and outgoing, while prayers of confession and penitence are introspective and somber. The formulaic character of liturgical prayers invites participation by establishing a frame of expectation, a pattern that becomes familiar.

Studies of the performative power of language suggest that such enactment capabilities of speech are conventionalized, formalized, and ordinarily involve physical action as well as the utterance of words in order to be felicitious. In other words, a prayer act, to have effect, to be true and empowered includes not only the utterance of words, but the active engagement of elements of the historical, cultural, and personal setting in which it is offered. It may include certain body postures and orientations, ritual actions and objects, designated architectural structures or physical environments, particular times of the day or calendar dates, specified moods, attitudes, or intentions. For example, a Muslim does not enact *ṣalāt* (daily ritual prayer) by simply uttering the words "Allahu akbar." Rather, *ṣalāt* is a performance that requires proper timing, dress, directional orientation, a sequence of bodily actions that includes standing, prostration, proper attitudes—all of these, as well as the proper recitation of a sequence of words.

When prayer is considered as act, the unresponsive and noncreative dimensions that seem inseparable from the rigidity of words tend to dissolve, for a prayer act always involves one praying in a historical, cultural, social, and psychological setting. These ever-changing contextual elements are necessarily a part of the act. In some prayer traditions, the Navajo of North America for example, it has been shown that highly formulaic constituents of prayer are ordered in patterns and conjoined with familiar ritual elements in combinations that express very specifically the heartfelt needs and motivations of a single person for whom the prayer is uttered. Analogous to ordinary language where familiar words can be ordered according to a single set of grammatical principles in infinite ways to be creative and expressive, prayer passages may be ordered in conjunction with ritual elements to achieve the same communicative capabilities.

The importance of the performative power of prayer acts is attested within many religious traditions by the expressed view that the most important prayers are those spoken in a special language, those mumbled, or those uttered silently, even those that are accomplished without words. Other nonspeech forms are also commonly recognized as essentially prayer, such as song, dance, sacrifice, and food offerings. These nonspeech forms may be understood as heartfelt and spontaneous human acts directed toward the spiritual world, but they may also be understood as religious forms whose enactment strengthens emotion, sustains courage, and excites hope.

When prayer is considered as act, a whole range of powerful characteristics and religious functions may be discerned. Here the issue is not primarily to show that prayer is communication with the spiritual or divine, or even necessarily to discern what is communicated, but rather to direct attention to the comprehension and appreciation of the power and effectiveness of communication acts that are human-divine communications. Likewise, when seen as act, the distinction between prayer and other religious speech acts—chant, spell, and formula—is less significant than it often is when distinguished and evaluated within particular religious traditions or theories of religion.

Various traditions of Buddhism present a test case in the consideration of prayer as they do many categories and dimensions of religion. For those traditions that are not theistic, like Theravāda Buddhism, prayer understood as human-divine communication is not possible. However, a number of kinds of Buddhist speech acts, such as meditational recitations, scriptural recitations, *mantras*, and *bodhisattva* vows, have certain resemblances to prayer, especially in terms of many of its functions. Commonly the distinction between prayer and these Buddhist speech forms has simply been ignored and they are considered as forms of Buddhist prayer. It would be more valuable to comprehend specifically the similarities and differences of the various forms and functions of these Buddhist speech acts compared with prayer acts of theistic traditions. In their similarities lies the nature of religion, in their differences lies the distinctiveness of Buddhism among religious traditions.

Prayer as Subject. In religious traditions, prayer is not only words recited, prayer is not only an action enacted, prayer is also a subject that is much written and talked about. It is the subject of theory, of theology, of sermons, of doctrine, of devotional guides, of prescribed ways of worship and ways of life, and of descriptions of methods of prayer. In the style and interest of a number of academic fields that consider human communication processes and the language forms that take these communications as their subject, we propose to term this dimension of prayer "metaprayer," signifying thereby the communications in religious traditions about prayer. The extent of literature in religious traditions about prayer is massive and ranges from personal meditations on the "way of prayer" to formal theologies and philosophies of prayer. In these writings, prayer becomes the subject by which to articulate the principles and character of a religious tradition or a strain within a tradition.

There are countless memorable and distinctive metaprayers. The following examples illustrate the range and character of these statements. In Plato's *Timaeus* (27b-c), Socrates and Timaeus discuss the necessity of prayer:

> *Socrates:* And now, Timaeus, you, I suppose, should speak next, after duly calling upon the gods. *Timaeus:* All men, Socrates, who have any degree of right feeling, at the beginning of every enterprise, whether small or great, always call upon God. And we, too, who are going to discourse of the nature of the universe, how created or how existing without creation, if we be not altogether out of our wits, must invoke the aid of gods and goddesses and pray that our words may be above all acceptable to them and in consequence to ourselves.

On the Lord's Prayer, Immanuel Kant in 1793 wrote in *Religion within the Limits of Reason Alone* that "one finds in it nothing but the resolution to good life—conduct which, taken with the consciousness of our frailty, carries with it the persistent desire to be a worthy member in the kingdom of God. Hence it contains no actual request for something which God in His wisdom might well refuse us" (trans. Greene and Hudson, New York, 1960, p. 183).

Friederich Schleiermacher, in a sermon entitled "The Power of Prayer" (*Selected Sermons*, London, 1890, p. 38), describes prayer in familiar, sweeping terms: "To be a religious man and to pray are really one and the same thing."

Powerful and provocative are the many statements on prayer of Abraham Joshua Heschel. In *Man's Quest for God* (New York, 1954) he wrote, "The issue of prayer is not prayer; the issue of prayer is God" (p. 87). In an essay entitled "On Prayer" he wrote, "We pray in order to pray. . . . I pray because I am unable to pray. . . . We utter the words of the *Kaddish: Magnified and sanctified by His great name in the world which He has created according to His will.* Our hope is to enact, to make real the sanctification of this name here and now" (*Conservative Judaism*, Fall 1970, pp. 3–4). And finally, in *The Insecurity of Freedom* (New York, 1966) Heschel wrote, "Different are the languages of prayer, but the tears are the same. We have a vision in common of Him in whose compassion all men's prayers meet" (p. 180).

In Western religious traditions, prayer has raised classic issues, the resolution of which corresponds to interpretive traditions. One notable issue is whether or not prayer, particularly petitionary prayer, is necessary or useful, since God is understood as all-knowing and all-caring. The explanation of this issue is an articulation of a theology and an anthropology, and it constitutes a statement of faith. Another classic issue has been whether prayer is monologue, dialogue, or neither. If one holds that prayer is monologue, one must explain how prayer is prayer at all rather than meditation or personal reflection. If one holds that prayer is dialogue, one must describe how God participates in the communication act. Theologies and philosophies of Western traditions no longer give much attention to prayer, but it has nonetheless been a significant topic in many of the classic theological and philosophical systems.

In *Varieties of Religious Experience* (New York, 1902), William James, upon considering a number of statements about prayer, concluded that "the fundamental religious point is that in prayer, spiritual energy, which otherwise would slumber, does become active, and spiritual work of some kind is effected really."

> In *Young India*, on 24 September 1925, Mohandas K. Gandhi wrote: Prayers are a confession of our unworthiness, or our weakness. God has a thousand, which means countless, names, or say rather that He has no name. We may sing hymns to Him or pray to Him, using any name we prefer. Some know Him by the name Rama, some know Him as Krishna, others call Him Rahim, and yet others call Him God. All these worship the same spiritual being. However, just as everyone does not like the same food so all these names do not find acceptance with everyone. . . . This is to say that one can pray, sing devotional songs not with the lips but with the heart. That is why even the dumb, the stammerer and the brainless can pray.

And on June 10, 1926, he wrote in *Young India:* "It seems to me that it [prayer] is a yearning of the heart to be one with the Maker, an invocation for his blessing. It is in this case the attitude that matters, not words uttered or muttered."

A final example taken from American fiction not only illustrates that metaprayer appears in a variety of forms of literature, but that metaprayer may even be used to disavow the use and efficacy of prayer. In the following passage from Mark Twain's *Adventures of Huckleberry Finn*, Huck distinguishes his own religiousness from that of old Miss Watson:

> Miss Watson she took me in the closet and prayed, but nothing come of it. She told me to pray every day, and

whatever I asked for I would get it. But it warn't so. I tried it. Once I got a fishline, but no hooks. It warn't any good to me without hooks. I tried for the hooks three or four times, but some how I couldn't make it work. By and by, one day, I asked Miss Watson to try for me, but she said I was a fool. She never told me why, and I couldn't make it out no way.

CONCLUSION. In the general study of prayer, the term *prayer* has been used loosely to designate a variety of human acts, principally speech acts associated with the practice of religion, especially those that are communications with a divine or spiritual entity. There can be no precise definition given the word when used in this way, for it serves as but a general focusing device for more precise comparative and historical study. The term gains definitional precision when seen as any of dozens of terms used in specific religious traditions as articulated in practice or in doctrine.

What can be articulated to facilitate the general study of prayer is the significance of the tripartite distinctions of prayer as text, as act, and as subject.

SEE ALSO Language; Lords Prayer; Mantra; Meditation; Ṣalāt; Siddur and Mahzor.

BIBLIOGRAPHY

Prayer as a general religious phenomenon has received scant attention by students of religion. There are no recent global or extensive studies. The discussions of prayer that continue to be the standard, while obviously inadequate, are E. B. Tylor's *Primitive Culture: Researches into the Development of Mythology, Philosophy, Religion, Language, Art, and Custom*, 2 vols., 4th ed. (London, 1903), and Friedrich Heiler's *Prayer: A Study in the History and Psychology of Religion*, edited and translated by Samuel McComb (Oxford, 1932). Most of the general studies of prayer are strongly psychological in character. Prayer was a topic of extensive consideration by William James in *The Varieties of Religious Experience: A Study in Human Nature* (1902; New York, 1961), pp. 359–371. Prayer and related religious speech acts are of interest in phenomenologies of religion; see, for example, Gerardus van der Leeuw's *Religion in Essence and Manifestation*, 2 vols., translated by J. E. Turner (London, 1938), pp. 403–446.

Statements of a comparative nature are found scattered throughout the literature, especially comparing specific prayers among Western religious traditions. However, broader and detailed comparative studies of prayer do not exist. Extensive studies of prayer that have attempted to see prayer in more general and universal terms may still be of interest, even though they have a dominantly Christian perspective. Such studies include Alexander J. Hodge's *Prayer and Its Psychology* (New York, 1931) and R. H. Coats's *The Realm of Prayer* (London, 1920).

An exemplary study of prayer that makes a clear distinction between prayer as a text, act, and subject is Tzvee Zahavy's "A New Approach to Early Jewish Prayer," in *History of Judaism: The Next Ten Years*, edited by Baruch M. Bokser (Chico, Calif., 1980), pp. 45–60.

Sources for prayer within specific religious traditions can be found under the heading "Prayer" in the *Encyclopaedia of Religion and Ethics*, edited by James Hastings, vol. 10 (Edinburgh, 1918), which includes a number of articles, some now outdated, on various religious traditions. See also *The Oxford Book of Prayer*, edited by George Appleton and others (New York, 1985).

There are numerous studies that demonstrate the importance of considering prayer as act. Harold A. Carter's *The Prayer Tradition of Black People* (Valley Forge, Pa., 1976) is a fine study of the American black prayer tradition; it traces the African heritage, describes the theological influences, discerns the major functions, and demonstrates the remarkable power of this prayer tradition in the context of black movements in American history. Gary Goosen's "Language as a Ritual Substance," in *Language in Religious Practice*, edited by William J. Samarin (Rowley, Mass., 1976), pp. 40–62, considers Chamul prayers as encoding messages interpreted in terms of Victor Turner's method of considering symbols.

On the performative power of Navajo prayer, see my "Prayer as Person: The Performative Force in Navajo Prayer Acts," *History of Religions* 17 (November 1979): 143–157. On the centrality of prayer to the whole system of Navajo religion, see my *Sacred Words: A Study of Navajo Religion and Prayer* (Westport, Conn., 1981). A notable study of prayer as a tradition of creative acts of oratory, focusing on the inhabitants of sea islands along the Atlantic Coast of the southern United States, is Patricia Jones-Jackson's "Oral Traditions in Gullah," *Journal of Religious Thought* 39 (Spring-Summer 1982): 21–33.

An examplary study of nonspeech acts considered as communication acts similar to prayer is Gabriella Eichinger Ferro-Luzzi's "Ritual as Language: The Case of South Indian Food Offerings," *Current Anthropology* 18 (September 1977): 507–514.

The performative power of speech acts, relevant to the study of prayer as act, has been shown in many essays. See, for example, Benjamin C. Ray's " 'Performative Utterances' in African Rituals," *History of Religions* 13 (August 1973): 16–35; Stanley J. Tambiah's "The Magical Power of Words," *Man*, n. s. 3 (June 1968): 175–208; and Tambiah's *Buddhism and the Spirit Cults in North-East Thailand* (Cambridge, 1970).

While folklore studies have become interested in the performance of many speech forms, especially among exclusively oral peoples, prayer is a form that has received little attention despite its abundant resources and importance within the traditions studied.

On the consideration of second-order language acts (metalanguages), see Alan Dundes's "Metafolklore and Oral Literary Criticism," *The Monist* 50 (October 1966): 505–516, and Barbara A. Babcock's "The Story in the Story: Metanarration in Folk Narrative," in her and Richard Bauman's *Verbal Art as Performance* (Rowley, Mass., 1977). Sources for prayer as subject are coincident with the second-order interpretative and critical literary traditions of all religions. In the contemporary religions and popular literature of the Western traditions, prayer is a constant topic. It has also been a consideration of major theologies and philosophies, as shown for modern Western thought in a summary treatment by Perry Le Fevre, *Understandings of Prayer* (Philadelphia, 1981). In *Prayer: An Analysis of Theological Terminology* (Helsinki, 1973), Antti Alhonsaari considers the theological issue of whether prayer is monologue or dialogue, discerning systematically the forms of prayer that correspond to the combinations of the variable on which this metaprayer discussion turns. While the rubric "Prayer" is not so dominant among non-Western religious traditions, there are nonetheless abundant comparable statements about prayer and prayerlike phenomena found among the writings of the interpreters and believers in these many traditions.

Sam D. Gill (1987)

PREANIMISM. In the years around 1900, the scholarly debate about the origins and evolution of religion was still in large measure dominated by the theories put forward by E. B. Tylor thirty years previously, notably in his *Primitive Culture* (London, 1871). The key concept was *animism,* which denoted both a primitive belief in spiritual beings and a belief in the "animation" of nonhuman beings—from the higher mammals down to trees, plants, and stones—by spirits or spirit forces. By 1900, however, Tylor's theory had been challenged by two of his Oxford disciples, both of whom were and remained his personal friends. In his *Cock Lane and Common Sense* (London, 1894) and definitively in his celebrated *The Making of Religion* (London, 1898), Andrew Lang had questioned the animistic hypothesis from one direction, suggesting that "perhaps there is no savage race so lowly endowed, that it does not possess, in addition to a world of 'spirits,' something that answers to the conception of God" (*Cock Lane and Common Sense,* p. 334). At a meeting of the British Association in 1899, the animistic theory was questioned from another direction, this time by the philosopher-anthropologist R. R. Marett. Whereas Lang was saying that adherents of the animistic theory had been prevented by their presuppositions from even noticing the evidence in favor of what he called "high gods" among peoples on a low level of material development, Marett claimed that the term *animism* was ambiguous and that the mental processes it assumed were too sophisticated to have been present at the lowest level of human evolution.

Marett's paper "Pre-Animistic Religion" was first published in the journal *Folk-Lore* (June 1900, pp. 162–182); it subsequently formed the first chapter of his book *The Threshold of Religion* (London, 1909; 2d exp. ed., London, 1914). Although brief, its argument was revolutionary. On the one hand, it suggested that in view of the double meaning of the word *animism* in Tylor's *Primitive Culture,* a distinction might be drawn between animism proper, as a belief in spiritual beings, and the belief in the "animation" of animals, plants, and natural objects, which he proposed to call "animatism." This of course had nothing to do with any theory of the origin of religion as such, but was merely a plea for greater terminological precision. On the other hand—and this appeared to be an outright challenge to the Tylorian hypothesis—Marett also ventured the opinion that animism was simply not "primitive" enough to represent the earliest form of religion. Beneath (though not necessarily chronologically prior to) the belief in spirits, he argued, there is a more amorphous sense of the world as being filled with the manifestations of supernatural power. This notion was unlikely to have been reasoned out in the first instance; rather it involved a "basic feeling of awe, which drives a man, ere he can think or theorize upon it, into personal relations with the supernatural" (Marett, 1914, p. 15). In search of a word to characterize this power, Marett settled finally upon the Melanesian word *mana,* as described by the missionary R. H. Codrington in his book *The Melanesians* (Oxford, 1891). Mentioned only in passing in his 1899 paper, alongside other "power-words," over the next few years *mana* came to eclipse the others as a *terminus technicus* to describe what lay at the root of preanimism.

Mana, however, was by no means an exclusively Melanesian concept. It was common to the whole of the Pacific, to Polynesia as well as Melanesia. It had been first noted by Captain James Cook in 1777 and long before Codrington's time had been fairly fully discussed in relation to the Maori of New Zealand. F. E. Maning in his book *Old New Zealand* (Auckland, 1863) had stressed, for instance, that *mana* had no single meaning but was associated with such diverse ideas as "virtue, prestige, authority, good fortune, influence, sanctity, luck" (Maning, [1863] 1927, pp. 239–240). However, the early preanimists remained generally unaware of the New Zealand material and were content to rely for the most part on Codrington's evidence as transmitted first by Marett and subsequently by the German and French sociologists.

Marett himself was most unwilling to "dogmatize" about religious origins and always expressed himself with great caution. Thus although in his 1899 paper he went so far as to suggest that what he there called "supernaturalism" might be "not only logically but also in some sense chronologically prior to animism" (Marett, 1914, p. 11), he did not say in what sense. Again—and this is important in view of the direction subsequently taken by the debate—he did not categorize *mana* as unambiguously impersonal. In a later paper, in fact, he stated explicitly that *mana* "leaves in solution the distinction between personal and impersonal" (1915, p. 119) and noted that although it may in some circumstances be used in a somewhat impersonal way, it is always necessary to take account of "the ambiguity that lies sleeping in *mana*" (p. 121). Other writers on the subject found this degree of ambiguity unmanageable and unwelcome.

In the wake of Marett's work, the first decade of the twentieth century saw the appearance of a great deal of writing on the subject of preanimism and on *mana* and its various equivalents. In Germany, Wilhelm Wundt of Leipzig wrote extensively in his *Völkerpsychologie* (1900) about "die präanimistische Hypothese," followed by K. T. Preuss in a series of articles in the journal *Globus* (1904–1905). Both, however, seem to have assumed Marett's theory to have been conceived in direct and complete opposition to Tylor—a charge that Marett, who admired Tylor greatly, strenuously denied. In France, the *Année sociologique* school (which included Durkheim, Hubert, and Mauss) produced a theory very similar to Marett's, perhaps independently, though Hubert and Mauss's article "Esquisse d'une théorie générale de la Magie" appeared in *Année sociologique* only in 1904, and Durkheim's magnum opus did not appear until 1912.

By this time, however, *mana* had been coupled with a bewildering variety of terms drawn from primal cultures in various parts of the world, all of which, it was claimed, conveyed the same basic sense of that supernatural power that had inspired an initial human response of awe. A proportion of these words had been culled from the vocabularies of various Amerindian peoples: From the Iroquois came *orenda* (as in Hewitt's "*Orenda* and a Definition of Religion," *American Anthropologist,* n.s. 4, 1902), from the Algonquin *manitou,* and from the Lakota *wakan* and *wakanda.* The Australian Aranda (Arunta) term *arungquiltha/arúnkulta,* the Malagasy *andriamanitra,* the Fijian *kalou,* and even the Old Norse *hamingja* and the Hindu *brahman* were added to the list, which by 1914 had assumed considerable proportions. *Mana,* however, continued to serve as the flagship of the preanimistic fleet.

It is important to remember that Marett had stated (not in his original article but at the Oxford Congress of the Science of Religion in 1908) that it was by now his express intention to endow *mana* with "classificatory authority to some extent at the expense of the older notion [i.e., animism]" (Marett, 1915, p. 102). Every new science had to create its own specialist terminology; this being so, Marett was proposing the use of *mana* whenever and wherever circumstances appeared to warrant it as a technical term expressive of preanimistic religions and virtually independent of the etymological meaning of the word in its original Pacific context. In the light of Marett's express intention, it is slightly embarrassing to note the solemnity with which some scholars have subsequently believed themselves to be demolishing Marett's argument by pointing out that the etymology of *mana* is not altogether what he supposed it to be.

Another critical point concerns the supposed impersonality of the power of *mana.* As has been seen, Marett was initially insistent that *mana* is an ambiguous concept, even as he knew perfectly well that his chief informant Codrington had stated that it was always associated with and derived from persons, spirits, or ghosts. On at least one later occasion, however, in his article "Mana" in Hastings's *Encyclopaedia of Religion and Ethics* (vol. 8, Edinburgh, 1915), he was prepared to state that *mana* was "in itself impersonal" while always associated with personal beings. (Often in such contexts he used the analogy of electricity, which remains latent until tapped and channeled.) The ambiguity between personal and impersonal remained in force nonetheless. But just as Marett read *mana* through the prism of Codrington, one feels that almost all later debaters have read Marett through the prism of the greater international celebrity Émile Durkheim.

To Durkheim, writing in *The Elementary Forms of the Religious Life,* first published in French in 1912 and in English in 1915, there were no ambiguities. Caution was replaced by assertion. According to Durkheim, Marett had shown "the existence of a religious phase which he called *preanimistic,* in which the rites are addressed to impersonal forces like the Melanesian mana and the wakan of the Omaha and Dakota" (1968 edition, p. 201). Durkheim categorically stated that *mana* was "an impersonal religious force" (pp. 192, 198), "an anonymous and diffused force" (p. 194); because it was not, according to Codrington, a supreme being, Durkheim concludes that it must possess "impersonality" (p. 194). One need look no further for the later impression that preanimism must of necessity involve belief in impersonal forces; it comes not from Marett but from Durkheim.

The preanimistic theory of the origin of religion (as it had developed between 1900 and 1914) first began to be called in question in the years following World War I. In 1914 Nathan Söderblom (who had been a professor in Leipzig from 1912 to 1914) published in the *Archiv für Religionswissenschaft* an article, "Über den Zusammenhang höherer Gottesideen mit primitiven Vorstellungen," in which the customary preanimistic points were discussed (see also Söderblom, *Gudstrons uppkomst,* Stockholm, 1914, pp. 30–108). One of his students, F. R. Lehmann, was inspired by this article to take up the question of *mana* and in 1915 presented his dissertation on the subject, in which he penetrated beyond Durkheim and Marett to Codrington, and beyond Codrington to the etymology and implications of the common Polynesian/Melanesian word *mana* itself.

Lehmann's researches had the effect of discrediting altogether the notion that the term *mana* had ever been used in the Pacific region to denote an impersonal force. Even when trees, stones, or other inanimate objects were declared to possess *mana,* this was because spirits had associated themselves with those objects, and not by virtue of their having an impersonal force of their own. Paul Radin had made substantially the same point in 1914, when he asked, "What warrant have we for thinking of the god as a deity plus power, and not merely as a powerful deity? Are we not committing the old error of confusing an adjective with a noun?" (*Journal of American Folklore* 27, 1914, p. 347). Following Lehmann, and in the increasingly antievolutionary atmosphere of the interwar years and beyond, more and more frequent criticisms were leveled against the preanimistic hypothesis, the interpretation of *mana* that had supported it, and against those who had written in these terms. A powerful broadside against the theory was produced by the Germanist Walter Baetke, in his book *Das Heilige im Germanischen* (Tübingen, 1942), and another by Geo Widengren, in a polemical article, "Evolutionism and the Problem of the Origin of Religion" (*Ethnos* 10, 1945, pp. 57–96). Widengren, incidentally, admired Baetke's work; and it was in the Baetke festschrift that Lehmann described the course of his research in the area of *mana,* in an article called "Versuche, die Bedeutung des Wortes 'Mana'. . . festzustellen" (pp. 215–240). Widengren summed up: "The best experts in the field of Melanesian religion have explicitly stated that *mana* is actually never an impersonal power"; it is "in reality a quality. It goes without saying that not *mana* in itself but persons and things possessing *mana* are the objects of worship" (p. 84). One last critic may be quoted. In his 1958 *Patterns in Comparative Religion* and in virtually identical terms in his 1968 *Myths, Dreams and Mysteries,* Mircea Eliade denies the existence of any such "impersonal and universal force" as *mana* was once thought to represent, not least because "impersonality" is "without meaning within the archaic spiritual horizon" (Eliade, 1968, p. 129). All these critics, however, have tended to attribute to Marett extreme opinions that were actually those of Durkheim.

It remains to be noted that Rudolf Otto, in his celebrated book *Das Heilige,* produced a theory of the origin of religion in an ineffable *sensus numinis,* in the course of which he praised Marett for coming "within a hair's breadth" of his own views. Otto, too, was criticized by Baetke and Widengren, who used arguments very similar to those they had used against Marett and the preanimists. Otto's *numen* could hardly be called "impersonal," however.

Preanimism and the debate about preanimistic religion belong less to the world of religion as such (and hardly, it would seem, to the area of primal religion at all) than to the intellectual history of the early twentieth century in the West. Possibly the popularity of the concept was not unrelated to the West's growing estrangement from fixed forms of religious belief and doctrine and its simultaneous maintenance of a sense that there might be "something" (rather than "someone") in charge of the world's destiny. It involved the evolutionists' conviction that religion had emerged out of something other than, and simpler than, religion. It also made assumptions about personality and (at least after Durkheim) impersonality that later critics found it all too easy to demolish. The critics, however, may have gone too far in the opposite direction. In their desire to disassociate themselves from the evolutionists, they have frequently misrepresented and misinterpreted them, without realizing that the evolutionists themselves were quite capable of raising objections—often the same objections—to their own work. Preanimism as such can be neither proved nor disproved as a rudimentary stage in the evolution of religion. There may, however, remain an area of religion within which supernatural (or at least uncontrollable) power is sensed, while remaining inchoate and unconnected with any firm notion of deity. This need not be a stage out of which more precise notions emerge. It is just as likely to be found at the end of a long process of decline, and thus to be as much posttheist as preanimist. There is no word that can be used as a technical term to describe this. *Preanimism* clearly will not do, because of the implicit sequence involved. Some use might however still be found for the term *mana* in this connection. In 1907 Marett wrote that "the last word about *mana* has not been said" (p. 219). By 1965, *mana* had almost been dismissed from the technical vocabulary of the study of religion. It may be high time for its reexamination.

SEE ALSO Animism and Animatism; Evolution, article on Evolutionism; Marett, R. R.; Power.

BIBLIOGRAPHY

References to the "preanimistic hypothesis" will be found scattered throughout the anthropological literature of the first half of the twentieth century. The seminal articles are gathered in R. R. Marett's *The Threshold of Religion,* 3d ed. (London, 1915), and Émile Durkheim's application of the theory is found in *The Elementary Forms of the Religious Life,* translated by Joseph Ward Swain (1915; reprint, New York, 1965), in which see especially pages 191–204. For the subsequent attempted demolition of the theory, reference must be made to the German works of F. R. Lehmann, beginning with *Mana: Der begriff des "ausserordentlich wirkungsvollen" bei Südseevölkern* (Leipzig, 1922) and ending with his essay "Versuche, die Bedeutung des Wortes 'Mana' . . . festzustellen," in *Festschrift Walter Baetke,* edited by Kurt Rudolph et al. (Weimar, 1966), pp. 215–240; and Walter Baetke's *Das Heilige im Germanischen* (Tübingen, 1942). See also Geo Widengren's "Evolutionism and the Problem of the Origin of Religion," *Ethnos* 10 (1945): 57–96, which follows substantially the same line.

ERIC J. SHARPE (1987)

PRE-COLUMBIAN RELIGIONS

SEE CARIBBEAN RELIGIONS; MESOAMERICAN RELIGIONS

PREDESTINATION

SEE FREE WILL AND PREDESTINATION

PREHISTORIC RELIGIONS

This entry consists of the following articles:

AN OVERVIEW
OLD EUROPE
THE EURASIAN STEPPES AND INNER ASIA

PREHISTORIC RELIGIONS: AN OVERVIEW

The term *prehistory* refers to the vast period of time between the appearance of humanity's early hominid ancestors and the beginning of the historical period. Since the invention of writing is used to mark the transition between prehistory and history, the date of this boundary varies greatly from region to region. The study of prehistoric religion, therefore, can refer to religious beliefs and practices from as early as 60,000 BCE to almost the present day. Generally, however, the term *prehistory* is defined by its European application and hence refers to the period from the Paleolithic period, which occurred during the Pleistocene epoch, to the protohistoric Neolithic period and the Bronze and Iron ages.

The biases of a literate culture are apparent in the term. Clearly, a people's literacy bespeaks their accessibility by a literate culture, but it is not, as has often been assumed, an adequate criterion for determining intellectual or cultural depth and complexity. To divide human cultures by the single invention of writing suggests that literacy somehow marks a specific stage of mental development or a radical turning point within the development of human culture conceived of according to an evolutionary scheme. Neither such a radical break nor such an inevitable evolutionary development can, however, be demonstrated.

This division notwithstanding, it should be noted that prehistory is understood to be singularly human. In his *Philosophical Investigations,* Wittgenstein quips, "If a lion could talk, we could not understand him." Wittgenstein is suggesting that language would not enable us to understand a "world," or perspective, that was so radically distinct in kind from our own. In contrast to Wittgenstein's lion, prehistoric humanity is regarded as understandable: a psychic unity between prehistorical and historical humanity is assumed. We believe that with sufficient evidence the prehistoric "world" can be grasped. The problem is accessibility, not difference in kind.

Access to a prehistoric culture, however, is highly problematic. And when one attempts to understand a phenomenon such as religion, the problem becomes acute. We understand religion primarily in terms of "language," that is, its principal characteristics are its interpretive meanings and valuations. The wordless archaeological remains of prehistoric religion—cultic or ceremonial artifacts and sites, pictures and symbols, sacrifices—have provided limited access to the religious "language" of prehistoric cultures. For example, knowledge of how corpses were disposed during the Neolithic period does not reveal why they were so disposed. Consequently, even when there is clear evidence of a prehistoric religious practice, interpretation of the nature of prehistoric religions remains highly speculative and disproportionately dependent upon analogies to contemporary "primitive" cultures.

Our knowledge of prehistoric religion is therefore the product of reconstructing a "language" from its silent material accessories. Among the oldest material forms of cultic practice are burial sites, dating from the Middle Paleolithic. One can trace, from the Upper Paleolithic on, a growing richness and diversity of grave goods that reach extravagant proportions during the Iron Age. The practices of second burials, the burning of bodies, and the ritual disposition of skulls are also common. Megalithic graves date back to the Neolithic period. Despite the cultic implications of these massive stone constructions (e.g., ancestor cults), a uniform religious meaning remains undemonstrated.

Evidences of sacrifices from the Middle Paleolithic period in the form of varied quantities of animal bones near burial sites suggest offerings to the dead. Sacrificial traditions that were associated with game (e.g., bear ceremonialism) date back to the Upper Paleolithic. There is no evidence of human sacrifice prior to the Neolithic period, and hence this practice is associated with the transition from a hunter-gatherer culture to an agrarian culture and, consequently, with the domestication of plants and animals.

Prehistoric works of art dating back to the Paleolithic period—paintings, drawings, engravings, and sculpture—are the richest form of access to prehistoric religion. The primary subjects of these earliest examples of graphic art were animals; humans, rarely depicted, were often drawn with animal attributes. The intimate and unique role of animals in the physical and mental lives of these early hunter-gatherers is clearly demonstrated. (This role is also evidenced in the sacrificial traditions.) Though some form of animalism is suggested, the religious significance of these animal figures is difficult to interpret.

Shamanistic practices are also reflected in this art, especially in the paintings of birds and of animals that have projectiles drawn through their bodies. Common in prehistoric sculpture is the female statuette. Although frequently related to fertility, these figurines are open to numerous interpretations of equal plausibility (e.g., spirit abodes, ancestor representations, house gods, as well as spirit rulers over animals, lands and other physical or spiritual regions, hunting practices, and natural forces).

It is unlikely that we shall ever be able adequately to interpret the "language" of prehistoric religion. The material evidence is too scarce and the nature of religious phenomena too complex. There is, however, a meaning in these wordless fragments that is itself significant for any study of religion. The power and depth of these silent archaeological remains cause one to recognize the limitation of written language as a purveyor of religious meaning. The connections one is able, however tenuously, to draw between the evidences of religious life among prehistoric peoples and the beliefs and practices of their descendants address the conditions that have inspired human beings, from our beginnings, to express our deepest selves in art and ritual.

See Also Animals; Funeral Rites; Lord of the Animals; Neolithic Religion; Paleolithic Religion; Sacrifice.

Bibliography

Breuil, Henri, and Raymond Lantier. *The Men of the Old Stone Age: Palaeolithic and Mesolithic* (1965). Translated by B. B. Rafter. Reprint, Westport, Conn., 1980.

James, E. O. *The Beginnings of Religions: An Introductory and Scientific Study* (1948). Reprint, Westport, Conn., 1973.

Jensen, Adolf E. *Myth and Cult among Primitive Peoples.* Translated by Marianna T. Choldin and Wolfgang Weissleder. Chicago, 1963.

Levy, Gertrude R. *The Gate of Horn: A Study of the Religious Conceptions of the Old Stone Age* (1948). Reprint, New York, 1963.

Maringer, Johannes. *The Gods of Prehistoric Man.* Translated and edited by Mary Ilford. New York, 1960.

Ucko, Peter J. *Anthropomorphic Figurines of Predynastic Egypt and Neolithic Crete.* London, 1968.

MARY EDWARDSEN (1987)
JAMES WALLER (1987)

PREHISTORIC RELIGIONS: OLD EUROPE

The term *Old Europe* is used here to describe Europe during the Neolithic and Copper ages, before it was infiltrated by Indo-European speakers from the Eurasian steppes (c. 4500–2500 BCE). The Indo-Europeans superimposed their patriarchal social structure, pastoral economy, and male-dominated pantheon of gods upon the gynecocentric Old Europeans, whose millennial traditions were officially disintegrated. Nonetheless, these traditions formed a powerful substratum that profoundly affected the religious life of European cultures that arose during the Bronze Age. Western Europe remained untouched by the Indo-Europeans for one millennium longer; Crete, Thera, and other Aegean and Mediterranean islands maintained Old European patterns of life until about 1500 BCE.

The agricultural revolution spread gradually to southeastern Europe about 7000 to 6500 BCE. A full-fledged Neolithic culture was flourishing in the Aegean and Adriatic regions by 6500 BCE. The Danubian basin and central Europe were converted to a food-producing economy circa 6000 to 5500 BCE. Around 5500, copper artifacts first appeared, leading to the creation of a fully developed copper culture in the fifth millennium BCE. The rise of agrarian cultures in western and northern Europe occurred about two millennia later.

The Old European religion of southeastern Europe and the Danubian basin persisted through three millennia, 6500–3500 BCE; the Neolithic period extended from 6500 to 5500 BCE, the Copper Age from 5500 to 3500 BCE. In northern Europe, the Neolithic period continued to about 2000 BCE. (Dates given here are calibrated radiocarbon dates.)

Old European beliefs and practices have been reconstructed primarily through analysis of the archaeological record. The evidence examined includes temples, temple models, altars, frescoes, rock carvings and paintings, caves and tombs, figurines, masks, and cult vessels, as well as the symbols and signs engraved or painted on all of these.

Cult objects, particularly figurines, provide some clues to the types of rituals performed by Old Europeans and the deities they worshiped. The richest finds have been unearthed in southeastern and Danubian Europe, as far north as the Carpathian Mountains. This region encompasses present-day Greece, Italy, Yugoslavia, Bulgaria, Romania, the western Ukraine, Hungary, and Czechoslovakia, as well as the Aegean and Mediterranean islands. The second region yielding cult relics is western Europe (present-day Spain, Portugal, France, and the British Isles). The best-preserved monuments are megalithic tomb walls engraved with symbols and images of deities, stone stelae, and figurines associated with burials.

Despite the multitude of culture groups in Old Europe and the diverse styles of their artworks, the pantheon of deities was the same throughout the vast landmass. Old European religious beliefs stemmed from the gynecocentric Paleolithic and early agricultural world, created by a birth giver, mother, root gatherer, and seed planter and concerned with feminine cycles, lunar phases, and seasonal changes. Skylight and stars, prominent in Indo-European mythology, hardly figure in Old European symbolism.

The images of Old Europe are those of the earth's vitality and richness. The transformative processes of nature are symbolically manifested in sprouting seeds, eggs, caterpillars and butterflies, and in such "life columns" (symbols of rising and spontaneous life) as trees, springs, and serpents, which seem to emerge from the earth's womb. Sacred images represent both the miracle of birth—human, animal, and plant—and the awe and mystery surrounding the cyclic destruction and regeneration of life.

Most Old European sacred images symbolize the ever-changing nature of life on earth: the constant and rhythmic interplay between creation and destruction, birth and death. For example, the moon's three phases—new, waxing, and old—are repeated in trinities of deities: maiden, nymph, and crone; life-giving, death-giving, and transformational deities; rising, dying, and self-renewing deities. Similarly, life-giving deities are also death wielders. Male vegetation spirits also express life's transitional nature: they are born, come to maturity, and die, as do plants.

GODDESSES AND GODS. The Old European evidence reveals clear-cut stereotypes of divinities that appear repeatedly throughout time and geography in sculptural art. The stereotypes include anthropomorphic deities and innumerable epiphanies in the form of birds, animals, insects, amphibians, stones, and hills.

Goddesses. The principal goddesses are composite images, encompassing an accumulation of traits from the preagricultural era.

The water-bird goddess appears with a beak or a pinched nose, a long neck, a beautiful head of hair or crown, breasts, wings or winglike projections, and protruding female buttocks outlined in the shape of a duck, goose, or swan. Her epiphany is a water bird, most frequently a duck. There is an association between this divinity and divine moisture from the oceans, rivers, lakes, bogs, and the skies. Meanders, streams, V's, and chevrons are her principal symbols. (The V sign, duplicated or triplicated in the chevron, probably derives from the shape of the pubic triangle.) They can be found on objects that are associated with her and also as decorations on her images. She is associated with the number three (triple source, totality) and with the ram, her sacred animal. The symbols give a clue to her function as a giver of life, wealth, and nourishment. She is of Paleolithic origin.

Since the early Neolithic she also was a weaver and spinner of human fate and giver of crafts and was worshiped in house shrines and temples.

A related image of the life-giving goddess appears in the shape of a water container (large pithos), decorated with M's, nets, brushes, meanders, and running spirals. She also appears in figurines marked with net-patterned pubic triangles and squares, symbolic of life-giving water.

The snake goddess has snakelike hands and feet and a long mouth and wears a crown. The snake spirals and snake coil are her emblems. She is life energy incarnate. As a symbol of fertility and well-being of the family she is worshiped in house shrines. Her crown very likely was a symbol of wisdom as it still is in European folklore. The horns of a snake, resembling a crescent moon, link this deity with lunar cycles. In megalithic tomb-shrines of western Europe, the winding snake figures as a symbol of regeneration. In symbolism, the snake coil is a source of energy comparable to the sun; and both are metaphors of the regenerating eyes of the goddess.

The birth-giving goddess is portrayed in a naturalistic pose of giving birth. She is well evidenced in Paleolithic art in France (Tursac, c. 21,000 BCE) and in all periods of Old Europe (from the seventh millennium onward). The vulva, depicted alone (known from the Aurignacian period, circa 30,000 BCE, and throughout the Upper Paleolithic and Old Europe), may have served as *pars pro toto* of this goddess. Her epiphanies were the doe (both deer and elk) and the bear, stemming from an early belief in a zoomorphic birth-giver, the primeval mother.

The nurse or mother holding or carrying a child is portrayed in hunchbacked figurines or, in more articulate examples, as a bear-masked madonna carrying a pouch for a baby and as a bird, snake, and bear-masked mother holding a child. Images of her date from the early Neolithic and appeared throughout the Copper Age and into historical times.

The vulture or owl goddess, a maleficent twin of the birth-giving goddess, appears as Death in the guise of a vulture, owl, or other predatory bird or carrion eater, yet has qualities of regeneration. A vulva, umbilical cord, or labyrinth is painted or engraved on her images. Hooks and axes—symbols of energy and life stimulation—are engraved on western European stone stelae and on passage-grave slabs representing the owl goddess. In one of the Çatal Hüyük shrines of central Anatolia (seventh millennium BCE), the beaks of griffins emerge from the open nipples of female breasts. The owl goddess's breasts, depicted in relief on slabs of megalithic gallery graves in Brittany, also suggest that regeneration is in her power.

The snowy owl appears in a number of engravings on the Upper Paleolithic (Magdalenian) cave walls of France, probably already as an epiphany of Death. There is rich evidence of the owl goddess throughout the Neolithic, Copper, and Early Bronze ages. During the last period, the owl form became the usual shape of urns. Burials of birds of prey as sacrifices to this goddess are known from the Paleolithic (Ksar Akil, Lebanon, mid-Paleolithic; Malta, c. 15,000 BCE), earliest Neolithic (Zawi Chemi Shanidar, northern Iraq, more than 10,000 years before our time), the Neolithic, and the Bronze Age (Isbister, Scotland). It is clear that large wings had enormous symbolic importance for millennia.

The White Lady, or Death, is portrayed with folded arms tightly pressed to her bosom and with closed or tapering legs. She is masked and sometimes has a polos on her head. Her abnormally large pubic triangle is the center of attention. A reduced image of her is a bone. Her images are made of bone or of such bone-colored materials as marble, alabaster, and light-colored stone. She dates back to the Upper Paleolithic, has been found throughout Old Europe, and appears in the Aegean Bronze Age as the Cycladic marble figurines. Most of the White Ladies were recovered from graves and found singly, in threes, or in groups of six or nine.

The goddess of regeneration appears in myriad forms, the most prominent of which are fish, toad, frog, hedgehog, triangle, hourglass, bee, and butterfly. All these appear in art as amphibians, animals, insects, and hybrids: fishwoman, frog-woman, hedgehog-woman, hourglass with bird's feet or claws, bee and butterfly with a human head.

The peculiar relationship, even equation, of the fish, frog, and toad with the uterus of the regenerating goddess accounts for their prominent role in European symbolism. The importance of the hedgehog probably derives from its equation with a wart-covered animal uterus. As life and funerary symbols, hedgehogs continued to appear throughout later prehistory and history. When manifested as a bee, butterfly, or moth, the goddess is thought to symbolize reborn life. Frequently, these images emerge from a bucranium, also the symbol of the female uterus as evidenced from the earliest Neolithic. The key to understanding the equation of the female uterus with the bucranium lies in the extraordinary likeness of the female uterus and fallopian tubes to the head and horns of a bull (Cameron, 1981, pp. 4ff.).

The Pregnant Goddess (*Mother Earth*) is portrayed naturalistically as a nude with hands placed on her enlarged belly. The abdominal part of her body is always emphasized. She is also depicted as a bulging mound and oven. In the infancy of agriculture, her pregnant belly was apparently likened to the fertility of the fields. Her image was associated with lozenges, triangles, snakes, and two or four lines. Her sacred animal is the sow. She is the Mother of the Dead: her uterus or entire body is the grave (hypogea of Malta and Sardinia, passage graves of western Europe, and court tombs of Ireland) or temple (Malta).

Although evidence of her exists from the Upper Paleolithic, it was probably not until the Neolithic that she became the earth mother and bread giver, appearing enthroned and crowned. She is the dominant figure in the early phases of the Neolithic. Her figurines are found on oven platforms (as at Achilleion, Thessaly, c. 6000 BCE; author's excavation,

1973), never on altars in house shrines, which were used exclusively for bird and snake goddesses.

Pairs of larger and smaller figurines known from all periods of Old Europe represent both the major and minor aspects of the goddess, sometimes as a mother-daughter pair (an analogy to Demeter and Persephone). Furthermore, the major temples of Malta consist of two constructions, one larger and the other slightly smaller, both in the anthropomorphic shape. This suggests again the dual or cyclical nature of the goddess as both summer and winter, old and young.

Gods. There are only two certain stereotypes of male gods: (1) the Sorrowful Ancient and (2) the mature male holding a crosier.

The Sorrowful Ancient is portrayed as a peaceful man sitting on a stool, hands resting on knees or supporting his face. Since the Sorrowful Ancient appears together with seated pregnant figurines that probably represent harvest goddesses, it can be assumed that he represents a dying vegetation god.

The bull with a human mask and the goat-masked male sculptures of the Vinca culture (fifth millennium BCE) may portray an early form of Dionysos in the guise of a bull or a he-goat—the god of annual renewal in full strength. However, lack of documentation from other culture groups warrants his preclusion as a stereotype.

The mature male holding a crosier and seated on a throne, from Szegvár-Tüzköves (Tisza culture, Hungary), may be a relation to Silvanus, Faunus, and Pan, historical era forest spirits and protectors of forest animals and hunters who also are depicted with a crosier. This image, as well as representations of bearded men, is probably of Upper Paleolithic origin (cf. bison men and other half-man, half-animal figures from the French caves of Les Trois Frères, Le Gabillou, and others). The type is poorly documented; only single examples of sculptures are known. The majestic posture of the Szegvár-Tüzköves god, however, suggests its importance in the pantheon.

Other images of the masculine principle, such as nude men with bird masks in leaping or dancing posture, were probably portrayals of participants in rituals, worshipers of the goddess. Male images are rare among the Old European figurines; usually they constitute only 2 to 3 percent of the total number recovered in settlements.

Summary. The concept of a divine feminine principle is manifested in human, animal, and abstract symbolic form: woman, water bird, bird of prey, doe, bear, snake, bee, butterfly, fish, toad, hedgehog, triangle, and hourglass form. Her manifestations are everywhere; her worship is attuned to the infinite round of life, death, and renewal.

Judging by the stereotypes that recur in figurines over the millennia, the religion of Old Europe was polytheistic and dominated by female deities. The primary goddess inherited from the Paleolithic was the Great Goddess, whose functions included the gift of life and increase of material goods, death-wielding and decrease, and regeneration. She was the absolute ruler of human, animal, and plant life and the controller of lunar cycles and seasons. As giver of all, death wielder, and regeneratrix, she is one and the same goddess in spite of the multiplicity of forms in which she manifests herself.

The prehistoric Great Goddess survives still in folklore. She appears as Fate (or sometimes as the three Fates), who attends the birth of a child and foretells the length of its life. She appears as White Lady (Death) with her white dog. Sometimes she is recognized in the toad or frog that brings death and regeneration, in the water birds and snakes that bring well-being and fertility, or in the crowned snake, whose crown grants the power of seeing all things and understanding the language of animals.

Although degraded to the status of a witch, the Old European Vulture (or Owl) Goddess lives on in fairy tales as an old hag with a hooked nose who flies through the air on a broom. She can slice the moon in half, cause cows to go dry, tie blossoms into knots, destroy human happiness, and inflict illness.

In European folklore as well as in prehistory, witches and fairies most often appear in groups with one the most important, the queen or "lady." This pattern reflects an ancient gynecocentric and matrilinear social structure.

As a consequence of the new agrarian economy, the Pregnant Goddess of the Paleolithic was transformed into an earth fertility deity in the Neolithic. The fecundity of humans and animals, the fertility of crops and thriving of plants, and the processes of growing and fattening became of enormous concern during this period. The drama of seasonal changes intensified, which is manifested in the emergence of a mother-daughter image and of a male god as spirit of rising and dying vegetation.

Let us note here that fertility is only one of the goddess's many functions. It is inaccurate to call Paleolithic and Neolithic goddesses fertility goddesses, as the fertility of the earth became a prominent concern only during the food-producing era. Hence, fertility is not a primary function of the goddess and has nothing to do with sexuality. The goddesses were primarily creatresses of life; they were not Venus figures or beauties and most definitely not wives of male gods. It is also inaccurate to call these prehistoric goddesses mother goddesses, a misconception found often in the archaeological literature. It is true that there are mother images and protectresses of young life, as well as a Mother Earth and Mother of the Dead, but the other female images cannot be categorized as mother goddesses. The bird goddess and the snake goddess, for example, are not mothers, nor are many other images of regeneration and transformation, such as the frog, fish, and hedgehog. They personify life, death, and regeneration; they represent more than fertility and motherhood.

SHRINES AND SANCTUARIES. Much of the corpus of information about the Old European religion comes from shrines, which have been found as models, within homes, or standing free. They demonstrate the close connections between secular and sacred life, especially in relation to functions performed by women.

Temples. The fifty or more clay models of temples discovered so far allow us to see the workings of Old Europe's shrines in striking detail. Usually found in front of or near the site of a former altar, these miniature shrines, generally small enough to be held in a person's hand, were probably gifts to the goddess of the temple. They are doubly revealing: in addition to reproducing the temple's configuration, the models are often elaborately decorated with symbolic designs and inscribed with religious symbols. Frequently a divine image in relief adorns the gables, rooftops, or roof corners of the temple.

Among the earliest models discovered are several from the Neolithic Sesklo culture of Thessaly in Greece. Dating from about 6000 BCE, they portray rectangular buildings that have pitched or saddle roofs, painted checkerboards or striated rectangles on their walls, and decorated gables. Noteworthy openings in their roofs and sometimes in their sides make them look, perhaps not coincidentally, like tiny birdhouses. A group of clay models from a slightly later date was found in a mound of the Porodin settlement near Bitola in Macedonia, southwestern Yugoslavia. Produced by the Starcevo culture of the central Balkans, dating from about 5800 to 5600 BCE, these models are capped with unusual features. Cylindrical "chimneys," located in the center of their roofs, bear the mask of a goddess; a necklace spreads down over the roof. The temple building below seems to have been constructed as the literal "body" of the deity; the structure, with the cylinder head on top, seems to be essentially a deified portrait bust. Perhaps for a mythologically related reason, a number of these shrine models have mysteriously shaped entrances, either inverted T's or triangulars.

Other temple models from the Vinca culture of the central Balkans (late sixth millennium BCE) and from the Tisza culture (around 5000 BCE) in present-day eastern Hungary are often distinctly bird shaped and have numerous incisions on their sides to indicate plumage. Their entrances have a round hole on their top half—again, like those found in birdhouses. Motifs of a bird goddess are found throughout the Vinca culture and Old Europe in general, and it seems likely that these openings were fashioned as symbolic entrances for the visiting goddess in the epiphany of a bird.

An exquisite, unusually large model of a temple with numerous large, round openings was discovered in the settlement on the island of Cascioarele on the Danube River in southern Romania. Dating from about 4500, this model has dramatically enhanced knowledge of Copper Age architectural and cult practices. The shrine model itself consists of a large substructure supporting four individual temples, each of which has a wide, arched portal crowned with horns. The facade is pierced by ten round apertures and is decorated with irregular, horizontally incised lines. This detailing suggests wood construction. The top surface of the substructure probably constituted a terrace that could hold a large congregation. Presumably—if this was, as it seems to be, a model of an actual structure—the whole temple complex was at least ten meters tall, with the individual roof temples measuring about three meters in height. The structure is clearly of European tradition, and no close parallels to this configuration exist.

Other models of two-story temples have been found at Old European settlements at Ruse on the lower Danube River in Bulgaria, Izvoarele in Romania, and Azmak in central Bulgaria. Still another model, this time from the Ros River Valley at Rozsokhuvatka in the western Ukraine, depicts a two-story sanctuary standing on four legs, with the second floor constituting a two-room temple. This model is from the Cucuteni culture, dating from about 4300 to 4000, the farthest outpost of Old European civilization in the northeast. This culture has been made famous through systematic excavations of entire villages, whose spacious, two- to four-room houses include altars and platforms, as well as by its magnificent ceramic art. The model has wide entrances on both floors and a platform, adorned with bull horns and perhaps used for worship, in front of the large portal on the second floor. A round window appears in the rear, and horizontal beams that support the roof are indicated in relief.

The walls of many models of temples were painted and decorated with incisions, excisions, and encrustations in symbolic motifs. Often these were arranged into panels in the same manner as on cult vases. The parallels between these forms are often particularly revealing. One dominant Old European motif, for example, found repeatedly on the models, cult vases, and other votive objects, is the meander, or the figurative representation of a snake; sometimes an abstract derivative of this image, in the form of single or pairs of spiraling lines, will appear.

A model of a Vinca temple unearthed in Gradesnica in northwestern Bulgaria, dating from about 5000 BCE, is a good example of the use of these symbolic decorations. Each wall and roof of this model constitutes a separate panel, each marked with a different design of meanders or sinuous lines, chevrons, and dotted bands. The vertical panels on either side of the entrance are inscribed with signs in a configuration that may comprise some sort of formula associated with the temple's goddess. Above the entrance to the temple are bands of dots and zigzags—snakeskin designs—further suggesting that the shrine belongs to a deity, perhaps the Snake Goddess. Above the facade, a schematic head in the center probably represents the actual goddess, and the masked heads on the corners may symbolize her divine associates.

Still other models, although otherwise complete, are roofless, so it is possible to peer into the scene of the cult activities. Such open models have a dais along the back wall and a bread oven on the side wall. A model of a roofless temple from Popudnia, a late Cucuteni settlement north of Uman in the western Ukraine, sits on four cylindrical legs and consists of a main room and vestibule; between them is a rectangular entrance with a threshold. On the right side of the large central chamber are benches and a large rectangular oven on a raised platform. To the right of the oven sits a female figurine with her hands on her breasts; near the outer wall another female figurine is grinding grain, and close by is a depression for storing flour. Almost in the center of the shrine stands a raised platform in the shape of a cross.

Among the actual temples is a two-story temple uncovered in Radingrad, near Razgrad in northeastern Bulgaria, by Totju Ivanov of the Archaeological Museum, Razgrad, from 1974 to 1978. Probably similar to the four-legged Rozsokhuvatka model from the Ukraine, this Karanovo culture temple dates from about 5000 BCE. Its first floor had a ceramic workshop with a large oven to one side; on the other side was a clay platform with tools for making, polishing, and decorating pots. Flat stone containers for crushing ocher stood nearby. Exquisite finished vases and unbaked ones were also found in the room. The second floor, like that of the Rozsokhuvatka model, comprised the temple proper. Inside was a large rectangular clay altar seventy-five centimeters high, and to its left stood a vertical loom and many figurines and temple models. A number of the vases near the altar were filled with clay beads.

One important discovery was that of a pillar temple, unearthed in the village of Cascioarele. Excavated by Hortensia and Vladimir Dumitrescu of the Institute of Archaeology, Bucharest, from 1962 to 1969, this Karanovo culture sanctuary, found just below the model of the edifice, dates from the early part of the fifth millennium BCE. Rectangular in plan, the sixteen- by ten-meter temple was divided into two rooms by six rows of posts. The interior walls of one room are painted red with bands of cream-colored curvilinear designs; above the entrance is a striking terracotta medallion with a red snake-coil outlined by a thin line of cream. This room contains also two hollow pillars, both measuring about two meters in height, that were originally modeled around two tree trunks. The thicker one was encircled by posts and, like the walls, had been painted three times with different designs. Near it lay an adult skeleton in a crouched position. The thinner pillar, measuring about ten centimeters in diameter, stood close to the interior wall and was painted with cream ribbons on a reddish brown background. Next to it was a terracotta bench or dais about forty centimeters high with painted curvilinear ribbons of cream color. Nearby lay numerous fragments of painted vases and of large vessels decorated with excised motifs. Rituals or mysteries performed here were probably connected with the idea of regeneration and the invocation of the vital source of life. The pillars, decorated with the running angularized spiral or snake motif, can be interpreted as life columns. The tradition of the life column motif can be traced as far back as the seventh millennium BCE, when it appeared in Çatal Hüyük frescoes, and in the Sesklo temples of Thessaly around 6000 BCE. In representations on Old European vases, life columns are usually shown flanked with horns, whirls, spirals, male animals, and uterus symbols.

The remains of an early Cucuteni shrine in Sabatinivka in the southern Bug River Valley of the Ukraine present an even more dramatic picture. A rectangular building of about seventy square meters, this temple has a clay-plastered floor and an entrance area paved with flat stones. The center of the room contains a large oven with a female figurine at its base. Nearby stood an incense burner and a group of vessels; these included a dish containing the burned bones of an ox and a channel-decorated pot with a small cup inside, once used for libations. Also nearby was a group of five concave grinding stones and five seated terracotta figurines with their bodies leaning backward. Along the rear wall, sixteen other female figurines were seated in low, horned-back chairs on a six-meter-long altar. In the corner adjacent to the altar stood a clay throne with a horned back and a meter-wide seat that had originally been covered with split planks. Altogether, thirty-two of these nearly identical, armless figurines with massive thighs and snake-shaped heads were found in this sanctuary. Oddly, several of them had been perforated through the shoulders, and one held a baby snake.

The Sabatinivka sanctuary demonstrates that bread ovens, grinding stones, and storage vessels played a fundamental role in the cult rites performed at Old European shrines. The seated figurines strongly suggest that temple worshipers participated in a ritual grinding of grain and baking of sacred bread and that these ceremonies were supervised from a throne, at least at Sabatinivka, by an overseer, probably a priestess. It seems likely that sacred cakes were dedicated to the goddess at the conclusion of the rites. Also the clay figurines on the altar may have been presented as votive offerings to the goddess or used as effigies to celebrate her presence.

These images of cult practices are further illuminated by a site near Trgoviste in northeastern Bulgaria, excavated by Henrieta Todorova of the Institute of Archaeology, Sofia, in 1971. This house shrine site at Ovcarovo, a product of the Karanovo culture, dates from about 4500–4200 BCE. The site yielded remains of twenty-six miniature cult objects, including four figurines with upraised arms, three temple facades or possible altar screens, decorated with chevrons, triple lines, and spirals around a central motif of concentric circles—nine chairs, three miniature tables, three vessels with lids, several large dishes, and three drums. It seems possible that this large collection of objects may have been used in different groupings at various times according to the required tableau of each particular ceremony.

The four figurines were painted with meanders and parallel lines. But most interesting was the presence of drums, which suggests the ritual use of music and dance in Old Europe. Other cult objects include miniature vessels with lids, found on small tables where they may have been used as sacrificial containers. Slightly larger than the figurines, these dishes or basins may have been used in some form of lustration or spiritual cleansing during the ceremony. The nine chairs, finally, may have been used to seat three of the figurines—the fourth is larger than the others—alternatively at the three altars, three tables, or the three drums. These miniature replicas are particularly important because lifesize Old European altars and tables holding sacrificial equipment have rarely been preserved.

A very interesting cache of twenty-one figurines, probably used for the reenactment of earth fertility rites, came to light in an early Cucuteni shrine at Poduri-Dealul Ghindaru, Moldavia, northeastern Romania. The figurines were stored in a large vase. In addition, there were fifteen chairs or thrones on which larger figurines could sit. The figurines are from six to twelve centimeters in height. The different proportions, workmanship, and symbols painted on the figurines suggest a clear hierarchy in this tableau. The three largest ones are painted in red ocher with symbols that are typical of Mother Earth: antithetic snakes coiling over the abdomen, lozenges on the back, and dotted triangles and lozenges over the ample thighs and legs. The medium-sized figurines have a striated band across the abdomen and stripes across their thighs and legs. The small figurines were rather carelessly produced and are not painted with symbols. Such differences may reflect different cult roles ranging from dominant personages (goddesses or priestesses) to assistants and attendants.

Although merely a selection in themselves, these Old European temple sites demonstrate that a long and varied list of cult paraphernalia—sacrificial containers, lamps, altar tables and plaques, libation vases, ladles, incense burners, and figurines—could have been employed in worship rituals. While the sacred rite of breadmaking appears to have been among the most consecrated and pervasive practices, there may well have been many additional distinct categories of religious ceremonies.

Caves. In the tradition of their Upper Paleolithic ancestors, the people of Old Europe used caves as sanctuaries. An excellent example of an Old European sanctuary is the cave of Scaloria in southeastern Italy, which dates from the mid-sixth millennium BCE. It consists of a large cave that is connected by a narrow tunnel to a lower-level cave containing a pool of water. The upper cave, which shows signs of seasonal occupation, contains a mass grave of 137 skeletons. The cave yielded stalagmites, stalactites, and pottery decorated with crescents, snakes, plant motifs, and egg or uterus shapes. These decorative symbols indicate that the cave was a sanctuary where funerary and/or initiation rites of mysteries took place, associated with the idea of regeneration and renewal. Many as yet unexplored cave sanctuaries have been discovered along the Adriatic coast and Greece's Peloponnese Peninsula.

Tomb-shrines. In central Europe, a sacred place of tombs and shrines has been discovered at Lepenski Vir in the Iron Gate region, northern Yugoslavia, during the excavation of 1965–1968 (Srejovic, 1972). The trapeze-shaped (i.e., triangular with the narrow end cut off) structures with red lime plaster floors of Lepenski Vir, dating from the late seventh to the early sixth millennium BCE, are dug into an amphitheater-like recess in the bank of the Danube. The essential feature of the shrine is the rectangular altar built of stones, which has an entrance in the shape of the open legs of a goddess, similar to that found in Irish court tombs. At the end of the altar stood one or two sculptures representing the fish goddess and a round, or egg-shaped, stone engraved with a labyrinthine design.

Fifty-four red sandstone sculptures were found. The dead were buried in similar triangular structures; they were placed on the red floor with their heads in the narrow end and positioned so that their navels were in the very center of the structure.

The main activities at Lepenski Vir were ritual sacrifice and the carving and engraving of sacred sculptures and cult objects. Paleozoologists were astonished to find a very high proportion of dog bones in the early phases of the site, when there were yet no herds to be watched by dogs. The bones were not broken up, indicating that dogs were not used for meat, and the often intact skeletons lay in anatomical order. Large fish bones (carp, catfish, sturgeon, pike) were identified in almost all structures; one exceptionally large catfish may have weighed from 140 to 180 kilograms! Twenty shrines contained a red deer skull or shoulder blade, which often was associated with the bones of dogs and boars. In three cases human bones were found in hearths. It can be seen from the above that the sacrificial animals at Lepenski Vir were fish, deer, dogs, and boars—the animals known from prehistory and early history to be associated with the life-giving aspect of the goddess (deer, fish) and with her death aspect (dog and boar).

Summary. That the preponderance of figurines found in Old European shrines are female suggests that religious activities during this period were largely, if not exclusively, in the hands of women. Although men participated in religious ceremonies—for instance, as bird- or animal-masked dancers—it is women who are portrayed in the overwhelming majority of figurines as engaged in cult activities or as supervising these events from thrones. Furthermore, the rituals mirror daily secular tasks associated with women, most importantly, preparation of bread from grains, manufacture of ceramics, and weaving.

In the process of sacralizing their creative lives, women in Old Europe developed many religious practices whose occurence in later periods is taken for granted. For instance, the four elements so central to ritual historically—air (incense), earth (bread and clay objects), fire (lamps and ovens), and water (liquid contents of vessels)—were represented in Old Europe. Also integrated into rites were music and dance, the use of masks, sacrificial offerings, lustration, and rites involving bread and drink.

SEE ALSO Birds; Caves; Goddess Worship; Megalithic Religion, article on Prehistoric Evidence.

BIBLIOGRAPHY

d'Anna, A. *Les statues-menhirs et stèles anthropomorphes du midi méditerranéen.* Paris, 1977.

Atzeni, Enrico. *La Dea Madre: Nelle culture prenuragiche.* Sassari, 1978.

Cameron, D. O. *Symbols of Birth and of Death in the Neolithic Era.* London, 1981.

Delporte, Henri. *L'image de femme dans l'art préhistorique.* Paris, 1979.

Dumitrescu, Vladimir. *Arta preistorica in România.* Bucharest, 1974.

Gimbutas, Marija. "The Temples of Old Europe." *Archaeology* 33 (November-December 1980): 41–50.

Gimbutas, Marija. "The 'Monstrous Venus' of Prehistory or Goddess Creatrix." *Comparative Civilizations Review* 7 (Fall 1981): 1–26.

Gimbutas, Marija. *The Goddesses and Gods of Old Europe, 6500–3500 B.C.: Myths and Cult Images.* Berkeley, 1982.

Kalicz, Nándor. *Clay Gods: The Neolithic Period and Copper Age in Hungary.* Translated by Barna Balogh. Budapest, 1970.

Marshack, Alexander. *The Roots of Civilization: The Cognitive Beginnings of Man's First Art, Symbol, and Notation.* New York, 1972.

Mellaart, James. "Earliest of Neolithic Cities: Delving Deep into the Neolithic Religion of Anatolian Chatal Huyuk," pt. 2, "Shrines of the Vultures and the Veiled Goddess." *Illustrated London News* 244 (1964): 194–197.

Mellaart, James. *Çatal Huyuk: A Neolithic Town in Anatolia.* New York, 1967.

Srejovic, Dragoslav. *Europe's First Monumental Sculpture: New Discoveries at Lepenski Vir.* London, 1972.

Thimme, Jürgen, ed. *Art and Culture of the Cyclades.* Translated and edited by Pat Getz-Preziosi. Chicago, 1977.

Twohig, Elizabeth Shee. *The Megalithic Art of Western Europe.* Oxford, 1981.

MARIJA GIMBUTAS (1987)

PREHISTORIC RELIGIONS: THE EURASIAN STEPPES AND INNER ASIA

During the Aeneolithic epoch of the fifth to the third millennium BCE two types of cultures developed in the steppe zone of Eurasia. One was a sedentary culture of primitive agriculturists and livestock breeders. They lived in clay-walled dwellings that were grouped in fortified settlements. To this type belong the Anau (Jeytun) culture of southern Turkmenia, whose scientific study was inaugurated with the excavations made by Raphael Pumpelly's American expedition to the Anau mounds near Ashkhabad, and the Tripolye-Cucuteni culture between the Dnieper River and the eastern Carpathian Mountains. (The Tripolye-type remains were identified by the prerevolutionary Russian scholar V. V. Khvoiko.) These cultures are known in detail today primarily through the work of Soviet scholars.

The Aeneolithic cultures were closely connected with the oldest centers of agricultural civilization in the Near East—the Anau culture directly so, and the Tripolye-Cucuteni through the medium of the archaeological cultures of the Balkans. Adjoining the Aeneolithic cultures were those of livestock-breeding steppe tribes. In the steppe areas around the Caspian and Black seas, from the Urals to the Crimea, was the Pit-Grave cultural community; in the south of Siberia, in the Minusinsk Basin, was the Afanas'evo culture. The tribes of these two groups of cultures were closely related.

TRIPOLYE-CUCUTENI RELIGION. The religious concepts of the Tripolye-Cucuteni tribes are revealed by analysis of amulets, paintings on pottery, anthropomorphic and zoomorphic statuettes, models of dwellings and utensils, altars, and so on. The clay models of dwellings are in the form of two-storied houses with an accentuated rounded or quadrangular upper story. Inside is a representation of a bread-baking oven, with an anthropomorphic idol next to it. Excavations of the settlements have revealed that some houses contained clay altars in the form of a female figure, sometimes with a bird's head or a head in the shape of a chalice or cylinder. There were also ritual clay dippers. Sanctuaries adjoined the dwellings and were entirely separate from them, and the cult they housed was evidently a fertility cult. In the sanctuaries were distinctive clay "horned thrones" whose backs imitated bulls' horns.

The most abundant source for understanding the Tripolye ideology are the pottery with its paintings and moldings, and the statuettes. The paintings on Tripolye vessels are divided into three vertical zones that evidently represent a tripartite concept of the universe. In mythological depictions the sun is associated with the bull, and also, at times, with the female principle (the female breast). This apparently symbolizes a cosmogonic configuration of the world that combined the male and female principles. The snake as well occupied a high position in the mythological hierarchy. The world was thought to have the form of a square or a circle, and a female deity may have taken part in the process of creation, as suggested by a vessel with a female figure in relief embracing it, as it were, with both arms. A parallel is the Sumerian goddess Ninhursaga, who gives form as "mistress creator" or "mistress potter." Religious customs included ritual dances; dancing female figures are depicted on several vessels. The dances may be Dadolaic ceremonies for bringing rain, or magic fertility rites.

Anthropomorphic plastic art, especially statuettes, is combined with ornamental designs and portrayals. There are several types of female statuettes, some with signs of pregnancy. One group of statuettes has designs with a diamond shape—a sexual symbol. In this way, the female principle and the idea of fertility were emphasized, as also seen in depictions of a snake on the stomachs of clay female statuettes that were clearly pregnant. The snake is a frequent motif in the oldest European art, and this motif often has a cosmogonic meaning. But on these statuettes the snake, as in Crete, appears as an attribute of a female deity; everywhere in the ancient East the snake symbolized fertility. Direct evidence of this is given by a group of statuettes in which the clay is mixed with flour or grains, and by another group with depictions of plants or animals. Thus, the cult of fertility and the deity (deities?) of fertility were prominent in the religion of the Tripolye-Cucuteni tribes.

ANAU RELIGION. A complex system of religious beliefs existed among the Anau tribes. Both dwellings and cultic structures expressed spatial concepts, with squarish and rectangular buildings predominating. Structures at the center of a group of buildings had a special type of hearth, in which a fire was lit for cultic ceremonies. At Karadepe two sanctuaries, side by side, have squarish hearths. Adjoining are auxiliary structures. This cult center may be regarded as a prototemple, although it also served as a granary. Together with large sanctuaries there were domestic ones, with traces of large fires inside, raising the hypothesis that they were deliberately burned down.

Vessel paintings show clear-cut spatial and geometric concepts and relationships. Goat and tree (vegetation) motifs testify to a fertility cult; sometimes the goat is next to the tree. Unquestionably, there was a cycle of beliefs associated with the reproductive power of the goat, which in general serves as a symbol of the fructifying powers of nature and which may function as an attribute or embodiment of a corresponding deity. The goat motif is one of the most widespread in ancient Eastern glyptics; association of the goat with vegetation (the tree) also signifies a connection with the earth. Another mythologem reflected in the designs is a bird with the sun disk.

Equally important for revealing religious concepts are the earthenware statuettes. Most are of sitting women with arms schematically raised at the sides, with well-defined facial features, and with markedly emphasized breasts, pelvis, and buttocks. The sitting pose itself was evidently evoked by fertility concepts and an association with the chthonic principle. It symbolized birth and, more generally, the birth and organization of the cosmos. The marks and depictions on the statuettes confirm and develop this symbolism. Some of the statuettes are holding a child and perhaps a goat. The back and bosom of one statuette are covered with numerous female breasts; other statuettes are covered with schematic depictions of trees, and sometimes of snakes. It is not possible to formulate concretely the religio-mythological cycles reflected by these statuettes, but one may surmise that they were connected with communal cults. The feminine protectors of earthly births and the ancestors of communal groups were worshiped. These female deities had created an orderly world out of chaos and had established cosmic and terrestrial law and order. On them, then, depended the continuation of humankind, the reproduction of wild and domestic animals, and the fertility of fields.

CULT CENTERS. In the Late Bronze Age (end of the third through the second millennium BCE), large cult centers with monumental edifices appeared in the agricultural and livestock-breeding communities of southern Central Asia. One such center, at Altyn-tepe in southern Turkmenia, consisted of a stepped towerlike edifice, a burial complex, dwellings ("the house of the priest"?), and household buildings. Most grandiose was a four-stepped towerlike edifice with a facade 26 meters in length and an estimated height of 12 meters. In configuration it resembled a Mesopotamian ziggurat. In one of the buildings of the burial complex was an altar, together with a gold bull's head, a wolf's head, and a plaque with astral symbols. The bull's head is akin to analogous but earlier Mesopotamian depictions, although it is more schematic. Characteristically, the Altyn-tepe bull has on its forehead a moon-shaped lapis lazuli laid-plate. The cult and image of the bull were widespread among early agricultural cultures (such as Çatal Hüyük), especially in Mesopotamia. A "heavenly bull" or a moon deity may have been worshiped at Altyn-tepe. Much later, in Zoroastrianism, the moon was called *gao čithra* ("having bull semen"). It was from this semen that all animals had been born, whereas from the semen falling on the ground domesticated plants had arisen. The mythic First Man had stood on one side of the Mythic River, and on the other side was the First Bull (*Greater Bundahishn* 1a.12–13, 6e.1–3; *Yashts* 7.3–6).

Another, later, cult center, Dashly 3 (second half of the second millennium BCE), has an entirely different structure. In the center of a square enclosure (roughly 150 meters on each side) is a round edifice in the form of a circumambulatory gallery, its interior divided into compartments and its exterior having nine salient towers. Three passageways lead into this gallery, whose interior includes chambers with fire-bearing altars. Parallel to the central edifice and outside it are two concentric walls that divide the space into three circles. All the enclosing walls are very thin and were clearly not used as fortifications.

This cultic ceremonial center mirrors in its structure a cosmogram of a ritual universe (Indic *maṇḍala*), as well as a sociocosmic model of society with its tripartite division. The central part is the spiritual center of the universe, and the three outer rings must correlate with a tripartite universe. The tripartite division of Indo-European (in this case, proto-Indo-Iranian) communities was clearly reflected in this plan. In the center—the focus of the entire composition—are reflected again the sacred triads (three gates, nine small towers). During rituals the sacred altars were lit and animals were sacrificed. This group of tribes evidently combined the idea of a tripartite world with a concept of the four sides of the world joined in a square. There is a certain correspondence with the ancient Iranian concept of *vara* and the divine fortress of the Kafirs.

BURIAL GROUNDS AND RITES. A significant migration of tribes took place in the Eurasian steppes during the second millennium BCE. Indo-Iranian tribes left the area of the Timber-Grave culture (the steppes between the Urals, the Volga, and the northern Black Sea region) and the western area of settlement of the Andronovo tribes (western Kazakhstan). They migrated south to Central Asia, spreading through that region in several waves and bringing in Indo-Iranian language, social institutions, and beliefs.

The rites performed at the Sintashta burial ground (in the southern Ural region, northeast of Magnitogorsk) had a pronounced Indo-Iranian character. The tribes that used this and related burial grounds from the eighteenth to the sixteenth century BCE carried out both individual and group interments. The wooden burial cover was held up by wooden posts; the most ancient of Indian scriptures, the *Ṛgveda,* makes reference to a similar practice. In the graves are massive finds of the bones of sacrificial animals. For example, in Pit I five horse skulls were in a row along a wall; along the opposite wall were four skulls of hornless oxen and a horse skull. In another grave were seventeen skulls of cows, rams, and horses. There were also dog bones. In a number of graves horse skulls and leg bones were laid at one end of the burial chamber, and a chariot, complete with wheels and spokes, stood at the other end. Horse skeletons were generally laid either behind each other or with skulls and legs facing each other. Many of the buried were warriors. On the earth-covered tombs, long-burning fires had been built. The chariots and steeds reflect the beliefs that the soul departs for the world beyond on a chariot and that the steed is the fire deity's companion. The same may be said of the dog. The sacrifice of animals is reminiscent of another ancient Indian sacrificial custom, the Agnicayana.

The Sintashta burial ground reflects a stage of ancient Indian beliefs earlier than that found in the *Ṛgveda.* Moreover, elements of the funeral rites have parallels to those in a wider area. For example, many steppe tribes of western Europe used burial covers on posts and cremated the deceased. In the Bronze Age, cremation and the corresponding cycle of beliefs existed in a vast area of the Eurasian steppes, particularly among the Fedorovo tribes of Kazakhstan and the Timber-Grave tribes of the Volga and northern Black Sea areas.

These Bronze Age beliefs were also widespread in Central Asia. In the Tigrovaia Balka burial ground, one central *kurgan* (burial mound) was surrounded by a ring of twenty, and another by forty-one, small mounds under which hearths were found. During the burial ritual, a ring of fire was lit around the entombed persons. This fiery barrier bore witness simultaneously to a belief in a circular universe (isomorphic with the ancient Indian belief) and to its fiery essence. This group of beliefs was further developed in the religion of the Saka peoples of the Eurasian steppes.

SAKA RELIGION. The vast area of the steppe and mountain-steppe zones, from the Aral Sea in the west to the Minusinsk Basin in the east and including Mongolia, Sinkiang, and Central Asia, was inhabited by tribes related culturally, and probably ethnically, to the East Iranians—the Saka group, mentioned in Old Persian and Greek sources. They spoke an East Iranian language. The tribes of Central Asia and of southern, western, and central Kazakhstan are termed Saka; those farther to the east are called Saka-Siberian.

In the Greco-Roman sources, references to the Saka beliefs are very scant. They may be supplemented by material from the ancient sacred works of the Indo-Iranians, especially the Avesta and the Vedas; from Middle Persian Zoroastrian works; and from the religious concepts of contemporary East Iranian and Indo-Aryan peoples. On the other hand, the archaeological materials of the Saka tribes, dating from the seventh century BCE to the beginning of the common era, are unusually abundant, especially the burial grounds and works of art. They are the main source for an assessment of the Saka religion, which had an overall similarity to that of the Scythians, although the two were by no means identical.

Divine gifts. An important mythological isogloss uniting the religious beliefs of the European Scythians and the Asian Saka is the motif of divine gifts. According to the account of Quintus Cortius Rufus, a Latin biographer of Alexander the Great, the Saka received from the gods the yoke, plow, spear, arrow, and chalice (7.8.17–18). The first two are associated with obtaining the fruits of the earth; the spear and arrow, with the defeat of enemies; and the chalice, with libations to the gods. The three-layered social condition emerges here with absolute clarity.

Sun cult. In the *Histories* of Herodotos, Queen Tomyris of the Massagetae pronounces the formula "I swear by the sun, the lord of the Massagetae" (1.212). Oaths by the sun and by fire were widespread among Iranians in antiquity and in medieval times. But even until recently the inhabitants of the Pamir, who formerly called the sun "great," swore by the "sun's head" as their strongest oath. They perceived the sun as an anthropomorphic being. The ancient Iranians had the same anthropomorphic concept of the great luminary. To them the sun was the visible form of the supreme deity, Ahura Mazdā—his child or his eye. The fact that these concepts were those of the Saka as well is made evident by the word for "sun" in the medieval language of Khotan, which is, as in the Pamir dialects, *urmaysde* (cf. Old Iranian *Ahura Mazdāh*).

Concerning the beliefs of the Massagetae, Herodotos wrote: "The only god they worship is the sun, to whom they sacrifice horses. The idea behind this is to offer the swiftest animal to the swiftest of the gods" (1.216). According to the Avesta, the ancient Iranians repeated: "We worship the shining sun, the immortal, the rich, [who owns] swift steeds (*aurvaṭ-aspem*)." They conceived of the sun's movement across the sky as that of a gleaming carriage to which heavenly steeds were harnessed. In the *Ṛgveda* as well, that is, among the ancient Hindus, the theme of white heavenly steeds in connection with the sun god (Sūrya) is elaborated in great detail. Thus, in the *Ṛgveda* the sun repeatedly appears in the form of a horse, Dadhikrā (Dadhikrāvan).

After the beginning of the common era, the solar cult in India greatly increased in importance because of the arrival there of the Central Asian Saka and the related Yüeh-chih. By the first millennium CE there were temples honoring the sun in various places in Central Asia, particularly Merv and Ferghana. Nothing is known about their structure. Some edifices in the south of Siberia give us an idea of the cult places associated with the sun and with steeds, the sun's attribute.

The Arzhan *kurgan* (in Tuva), a very ancient monument of Scytho-Siberian culture (eighth and seventh centuries BCE), had a round stone platform mound about 110 meters in diameter and 3 to 4 meters high. Under the mound was an enormous wood edifice, in whose center was a square (8 by 8 meters) wooden frame. In the middle of this structure was a smaller one with a king and a queen interred in coffins, surrounded by six wooden coffins and two small enclosures in which the king's courtiers were interred. Here too were the king's personal horses. Lines of logs, like spokes of a gigantic wheel, came radially out of the central structure. The entire surface was divided into seventy trapezoidal compartments by cross-pieces forming concentric lines. Some of these compartments had additional divisions. In nine of the compartments there were mass burials of horses; burials of humans and horses were found in a number of other compartments. The king was dressed in a rich garment of wool and one of sable; both he and his female companion had numerous gold ornaments. The ground in the royal compartment was covered with horse tails and manes. The courtiers too were clothed in costly garments and had gold ornaments. The mass horse-burials included groups of fifteen or thirty old stallions, evidently gifts to the king from tribal units subordinate to him.

The Arzhan *kurgan* clearly testifies to a developed cult of the sun. The king is at the center of a gigantic wheel, which symbolized the solar chariot or, rather, the sun itself. The concept of the "solar wheel" is widespread in Indo-European thought. Not only is the king equated with the sun, at the center, but the steeds accompanying the sun are placed, both individually and as a body, in strictly defined groups within the construction. This clearly indicates that they are immediate participants of the myth depicted by the Arzhan *kurgan*. The horses of the *kurgan* enter, as it were, the inner essence of the sun on the one hand, and on the other they indicate the way by which souls may reach this luminary.

Such sepulchral "temples of the sun" were not isolated instances. Another, simpler, variant is the Ulug-Khorum *kurgan* (also in Tuva), in whose center is a semi-spherical stone mound 22 meters in diameter. Thirty-three meters from the mound's center is a stone wall. The ring between the foundation of the mound and the wall is divided into sections by thirty-two radial spokes made of stone. On the stone are incised depictions of horses.

Cult of the horse. Throughout the entire Scythian, Saka, and Saka-Siberian areas there are burials of horses, both individual and collective, and either with or without human burials. In Central Asia and Kazakhstan there were until recent times a number of variants of the custom of dedicating a horse to the deceased. The Kafir of Nuristan retained the practice of setting up on the grave a wooden statue of a horseman, and in Central Asia, dolls on a wooden horse were set up. All this reflects a perception of the chthonic nature of the horse and, on the other hand, of its functions as an intermediary between worlds—an animal hastening to the upper worlds and conveying the soul of the deceased there.

The cult of the horse was associated with its otherwordly nature, and this cult was reflected in numerous depictions of horses. Very frequently these were made on cliffs and mountains, as the Oglakhta pictograph in the Yenisei region, and the pictograph on the Aravan cliff in Ferghana. In Chinese sources, Central Asian, and especially Ferghana, horses are termed "heavenly," evidently reflecting local concepts. A "heavenly steed" was said to live in a mountain cave in Tokharistan. Wherever there were many horse depictions in mountainous areas, as at Oglakhta, there were sanctuaries dedicated to the heavenly steed.

In ancient Central Asian legends, sacred horses dwell in a lake, a motif that may be traced back to ancient Iranian beliefs. In the Avesta, the deity of water and river streams, Aredvi, was drawn by four horses, whereas the rain deity, Tistrya, appeared in the form of a white horse with golden ears and muscles who received rainwater from the celestial lake, Vourukasa. It is possible, however, that the concept of the horse as a water steed has an even older, Indo-Iranian, foundation.

Thus, the Saka tribes had a cult of a supreme deity with pronounced solar coloration. Originating in the ancient Iranian pantheon, which is known from Zoroastrian works, this deity may have been Ahura Mazda, Mithra, or perhaps Mithra Ahura; moreover, different hypostases of this deity may have had primary significance among different Saka tribes. The cult of the horse and the cult of fire in its various manifestations (see below) were associated with the worship of this deity.

Cult of fire. The cult of fire played a large role in funerary ritual. In the Uigarak and Tagisken burial grounds (Aral Sea region); in those of Besshatyr (the Semirech'e region of Kazakhstan), Kokuibel (the Pamirs), and Tashkurgan (Sinkiang); and in the Sauromatian burial grounds of the North Caucasus the funerary structure was sometimes burned, either with total or partial cremation of the deceased, or without such cremation. Funerary pyres were sometimes burned over the deceased or around the funerary platform, and sometimes the deceased was covered with coals from a pyre that had been lit to one side of him.

In the Pamirs, the Aral Sea area, and among the Sauromatians the deceased was colored red or red paint was placed in the grave. The color red functions as a symbol and substitute for fire. Perhaps this was based on a deeper stratum of beliefs with a universal cosmological dichotomy, in which red denoted the world of the beyond, and painting the deceased red led him from the world of the living and joined him to the world of the dead. All these customs are echoes of Indo-European beliefs in the necessity of cremation. A number of Saka tribes believed that burning the deceased and his property was a sacrifice to the gods. For the deceased himself it was a "blessing," since the tongues of the flames, like horses, would perforce carry him off to heaven.

The Saka world had other manifestations of the cult of fire, differing among the groupings of the Saka tribes. The tribes of the Semirech'e and adjoining regions of Sinkiang had censers and sacrificial altars with depictions of animals, processions of beasts, and scenes of battle between beasts. The censers reflected the mytheme of the "tree of the world" and the tripartite division of the universe. They constituted a sacred cosmogram whose functions, realized in the ritual of the fire cult, were denoted by animals and their groupings.

Myths. The available data confirm that the Saka had a well-developed (although less complex than among the ancient Hindus) system of myths. It united deities and their animal incarnations with the cosmological concept of the triadic nature of the universe (and of all that existed) and that of the "tree of the world." These deities and concepts were united with the sacred act isomorphic to the Hindu *yajña* (lit., "worship of the god"; later, any sacred act). In these beliefs, in complex oblique ways, the earthly and the divine, the profane and the sacred, were interwoven. Through sacrifices associated with fire and animals, a socially defined human being became a participant in a series of transformations. When the small sacred area of the sacrificial altar extended to the limits of the entire universe, the person making the sacrifice was embodied in the altar itself (an emanation of the deity), in the sacred fire, and in the animals associated with the deity or deities. In this way he merged with the infinite.

On a felt rug from Pazyryk *kurgan* V (Altai), there is a frequently repeated scene: a goddess with the appearance of a man sits on a throne, wearing a long-sleeved garment covering her to the feet. On her head is a spiked crown. Her left hand is raised to her mouth, and in her extended right hand is a flowering sacred tree. Before her is a mounted archer with a quiver. This is one of the feminine deities of the Saka pantheon. If she originates in the Scythian pantheon, she is most likely Tabiti or, perhaps, Api. The scene is a divine wedding, with the king acquiring divine status.

Cult of gold. According to Ctesias (see Diodorus 2.34.1), the Saka built a sepulcher above the grave of their queen, Zarina, in the form of a huge pyramid. On top of it "they set up a colossal gold statue, to which they rendered heroic homage." Archaeological excavations have not unearthed the gold statue, but "golden burials" have been found. At the Issyk *kurgan,* not far from Alma-Ata, a princely burial dating from the fourth or third century BCE has been discovered. The deceased wore a headdress richly decorated with gold clasps and plaques; his clothing and footgear were almost solidly covered with gold plaques. More than four thousand gold objects, as well as two silver vessels, were found at this burial. In northern Afghanistan, at the Tillya-tepe mound, princely graves of the first century BCE to the first century CE were found. The deceased wore gold-embroidered clothing decorated with small gold plaques. Each grave contained from twenty-five hundred to four thousand of these plaques. The deceased were indeed clad in gold; they also wore gold crowns, and under their heads gold or silver chalices had been placed.

In ancient Iran, in Parthia, only the king could sleep on a golden couch. The Achaemenid kings, including Cyrus II, were buried in gold sarcophagi. Gold symbolized royal power in ancient India (*Śatapatha Brāhmana* 13.2.2.17). In Kazakhstan and Afghan "golden" burials the idea that gold is the symbol of the king—of his power, his fate, and his good fortune (*farn*)—was the dominant one in decorating royal corpses with an enormous quantity of gold, a literal "wrapping" in gold.

These concepts are underlain by deeper ones, according to which gold is the inner content and the outer environment of divinities, for example, Agni and other gods of ancient Indian mythology. In the Hindu epics there are "golden-eyed" and "golden-skinned" gods. The newly born Buddha Śākyamuni's body was radiant like the sun and shone with gold (Aśvaghoṣa, Buddhacarita 1.1.14, 1.1.45). The ancient Iranian god Vainu wore red clothing decorated in gold, and in medieval Iran a person whose skin had a golden hue was thought to be divine. The wrapping of a corpse in clothing covered with gold distinguished it from ordinary corpses, making it a divine being from another world, for the deceased ruler was like the setting sun. The same beliefs gave rise to the custom of setting up gold statues on the graves of the Saka kings or covering their corpses with gold.

The Issyk royal headdress. Knowledge of the religious beliefs of the Saka tribes facilitates analysis of the complex spiked headdress of the Issyk prince. Above the diadem are two horse's heads turned in different directions but with a single body. In back are two more horse heads, as well as vertical arrow shafts and bent plates that imitate birds' wings. The decorations on the sides have a distinct zonal character, with mountains, trees with small birds on them, mountains with snow leopards, and medallions with depictions of goats and snow leopards. On top of the headdress is a figurine of a snow leopard. This cosmogram is the Saka variant of the sacred macrocosm and also a depiction of the "tree of the world." It is undoubtedly associated with the texts of rituals, invocations, and myths, and was an iconographic embodiment of some of these.

The Saka king undoubtedly functioned also as a priest. He was believed to know and to personify the cosmological structure of the world; it was he who correlated it with the social structure of the tribe or tribes. The *axis mundi* went through the king, as embodied in his head and crown. This was the most sacred point in space, corresponding with the sacred space and axis of the sacrificial altar.

Still more concrete conclusions may be made. Double horse heads with a single body may reflect beliefs in divine twins that are akin to beliefs widespread among different Indo-European traditions. Their contrast with depictions of ordinary earthly horses laid out side by side sets off and emphasizes the former's unearthly power. The facial part of the headdress is associated with symbols of royal power in the form of birds' wings with feathers. This may stand for the ancient Iranian god of victory, Verethragna, who was symbolized by the bird of prey *vāregna.* An amulet made of feathers from this bird gave *khvarenah,* in this case "royal good fortune." For the ancient Hindus, the eagle was the personification of Indra, and Agni the "eagle of the heavens." The symbolism of royal power is reinforced by the vertical arrows and by the figurine, atop the headdress, of a ram—the symbol of Farn, the Iranian deity of royal destiny and good fortune.

The depictions on the sides of the headdress are in three tiers, which reflect the concept of a tripartite model of the world. The bottom layer, in turn, is in three parts, recalling the ancient Indian belief that there are three worlds, this one and two beyond. The idea of triplicity permeated the Saka cosmogony and was its essence; however, each of the component elements was not homogeneous. The concept of a tripartite universe corresponded to the tripartite structure of Saka society.

Thus, the depictions on the Issyk royal headdress linked together the king's earthly and sacred power (as portrayed on the frontal part) and his cosmic essence (as portrayed on the sides). All this is united with the diadem below and the figurine of the ram above—the pole toward which everything strives and which embodies the divine attribution of the king.

Burial customs. Mircea Eliade has established that after a mythic, cosmic catastrophe only devout people, shamans, and so on may ascend to the heavens, with the help of a "sacred cord" (tree, cliff, etc.). To facilitate their ascent, at the interment of these persons wooden stakes are set up in the burial pits, or stone columns are placed on the burial mounds (as in the Pamir).

Burial rituals and customs varied considerably among the different Saka tribes. Among the large kurgans of the Pazyryk group, a chamber made of logs was sometimes set on top of the stone foundation of the burial pit, which was about 4 meters deep. On top of the chamber, the pit was packed with logs and stones. Its surface was covered with rounded earth, topped with a stone mound that had a diameter of 36 to 46 meters. The burial pit was quadrangular, oriented to the cardinal directions. The largest *kurgans* had a double log chamber, protected from pressure by a wooden covering resting on posts. In the northern third of the burial pit, horses (up to ten) were buried and carts were placed. In the largest *kurgans*, human burials were in log coffins with covers. One such sarcophagus was decorated with roosters cut out of leather, another with reindeer cutouts. The chamber walls were draped with felt rugs. The burial chambers and rites of the Bashadyr and Tuekta kurgans, also in the Altai, were similar. Although the *kurgans* were robbed in antiquity, the objects were so diverse and their remains so amazingly well preserved, owing to permafrost, that they give a clear impression of the ancient inhabitants' appearance, their material culture, and, in part, their beliefs.

In Scythian times in the Altai region, deceased persons of outstanding importance were embalmed, by rather complex methods. Evidently, these deceased were believed to play a special role in the world beyond. The Scythians, for example, embalmed the corpses of their kings (Herodotus 4.71).

Some of the Altai princely burials have preserved traces of the removal of muscle tissue. Hecataeus of Miletus (fl. 500 BCE) wrote of the Massagetae: "They consider it the best kind of death, when they are old, to be chopped up with the flesh of cattle and eaten mixed up with that flesh" (Strabo, Geography 11.8.6). Similar evidence is found in Herodotus (1.216). Classical sources and the Avesta hint at the ritual killing, among a number of Iranian-speaking peoples, of aged men. In the Altai, small pieces of the deceased's flesh were apparently eaten; in this way his spiritual and physical qualities and his social rank were acquired. If a woman consumed one of these pieces of flesh, her subsequent children would inherit the outstanding qualities of the deceased. A deeper stratum of these animistic beliefs is the totemic one. Also associated with animistic beliefs was the custom of placing in the grave nail parings from the deceased and small sacks containing his hair. The burial was accompanied by purifying and ecstatic rites, particularly the smoking of hemp.

The religious worldview of the Saka was reflected in the artworks of the animal style. Analysis of these works and of the materials associated with funerary rituals confirms the existence of shamanistic beliefs and practices, especially in Siberia. The origins of the heroic epos of the Inner Asian and Siberian peoples date to Saka times. The greatest Iranian epic hero, Rotastahm (Rustam), had the epithet *Sagčīk,* "from among the Saka." His name is a symbol of the hero.

SEE ALSO Ahura Mazdā and Angra Mainyu; Fire; Horses; Indo-European Religions, overview article; Indus Valley Religion; Iranian Religions; Sarmatian Religion; Scythian Religion; Sheep and Goats; Snakes; Sun; Vedism and Brahmanism.

BIBLIOGRAPHY

Books covering the overall subject of this article do not exist. A general review of the Aeneolithic sites of the Eurasian steppes is *Arkheologiia SSSR: Eneolit SSSR,* edited by V. M. Masson and N. Ia. Merpert (Moscow, 1982). The first work on the Aeneolithic and Bronze ages of Central Asia to contain information on religious beliefs was *Explorations in Turkestan: Expedition of 1904; Prehistoric Civilizations of Anau,* 2 vols., edited by Raphael Pumpelly (Washington, D.C., 1908). The most recent review and analysis is Philip L. Kohl's *Central Asia: Palaeolithic Beginnings to the Iron Age* (Paris, 1984), which has an outstanding bibliography and only a few serious omissions.

Two excellent monographs by Elena V. Antonova are devoted to the religion of the Aeneolithic and Bronze Age tribes: *Antropomorfnaia skul'ptura drevnikh zemledel'tsev Perednei i Srednei Azii* (Moscow, 1977) and *Ocherki kul'tury drevnikh zemledel'tsev Perednei i Srednei Azii: Opyt rekonstruktsii i mirovospriiatiia* (Moscow, 1984). The latter is a fundamental work that investigates in depth the religions of the ancient agriculturist tribes of the entire East, from Anatolia to Central Asia.

For extensive material on the beliefs of the Tripolye tribes, see S. M. Bibikov's *Rannetripol'skoe poselenie Luka-Vrublevetskaia na Dnestre* (Moscow, 1953). See also Aina P. Pogozheva's *Antropomorfnaia plastika Tripol'ia* (Novosibirsk, 1983). The beliefs of the Tripolye-Cucuteni tribes are examined in the context of other European beliefs in Marija Gimbutas's *The Goddesses and Gods of Old Europe, 6500–3500 B.C.* (Berkeley, Calif., 1982); her interpretations, however, are sometimes unjustifiably bold.

For the religion of the proto-Iranians, Iranians, and, in particular, the Saka, see Mary Boyce's *A History of Zoroastrianism,* 2 vols. (Leiden, 1975–1982). It is an excellent investigation of the origins and early history of Iranian religions. An outstanding overall review of these religions, especially that of the Saka, is Geo Widengren's *Die Religionen Irans* (Stuttgart, 1965), based on nonarchaeological materials. On the Saka, see also Julius Junge's *Saka-studien: Der Ferne Nordosten in Weltbild der Antike* (Leipzig, 1939) and my own archaeologically based study *Kangiuisko-sarmatskii farn* (Dushanbe, 1968), translated as "Das K'ang-chü-sarmatische Farnah," *Central Asiatic Journal* 16 (1972): 241–289 and 20 (1976): 47–74.

Comprehensive descriptions and valuable analyses of the materials from the Saka archaeological complexes can be found in M. I. Artamonov's *Sokrovishcha sakov* (Moscow, 1973) and in Karl Jettmar's *Die frühen Steppenvolker* (Baden-Baden, 1964), translated as *The Art of the Steppes* (New York, 1967). For a general survey of all the Saka materials in Central Asia, see my book *Eisenzeitliche Kurgane zwischen Pamir und Aral-See* (Munich, 1984).

Monographs devoted to recent discoveries at individual complexes usually include a chapter on religious beliefs. Among them are K. A. Akishev's *Kurgan Issyk: Iskusstvo sakov Kazakhstana* (Moscow, 1978), K. A. Akishev and G. A. Kushaev's *Drevniaia kul'tura sakov i usunei reki Ili* (Alma-Ata, 1963), O. A. Vishnevskaia's *Kul'tura sakskikh plemen nizov'ev Syrdar'a v VII–V vv. do n. e.: Po materialam Uigaraka* (Moscow, 1973), M. P. Griaznov's *Arzhan: Tsarskii kurgan ranneskifskogo vremeni* (Leningrad, 1980), S. I. Rudenko's *Kul'tura naseleniia Gornogo Altaia v skifskoe vremia* (Moscow, 1953) and *Kul'tura nasaleniia Tsentral'nogo Altaia v skifskoe vremia* (Moscow, 1960), V. I. Sarianidi's Bactrian *Gold: From the Excavations of the Tillya-Tepe Necropolis in Northern Afghanistan* (Leningrad, 1984), and my *Drevnie kochevniki "Kryshi mira"* (Moscow, 1972). Considerable attention is devoted to the Saka religion in two outstanding works by D. S. Raevskii: *Ocherki ideologii skifo-sakskikh plemen: Opyt rekonstruktsii skifskoi mifologii* (Moscow, 1977) and *Model' mira skifskoi kul'tury* (Moscow, 1985).

New Sources

Dandamaev, Muhammad A. and Vladimir G. Lukonin. *The Culture and Social Institutions of Ancient Iran.* Translated by Philip L. Kohl with the assistance of D.J. Dadson. New York, 1989.

Dexter, Miriam Robbins. and Edgar C. Polomé, eds. *Varia on the Indo-European Past: Papers in Memory of Marija Gimbutas.* Washington, D.C., 1997.

Hiebert, Fredrik T. *Origins of the Bronze Age Oasis Civilization in Central Asia.* Cambridge, 1994.

Ionesov, Vladimir I. *The Struggle Between Life and Death in Proto-Bactrian Culture: Ritual and Conflict.* Lewiston, N.Y., 2002.

Kenoyer, Jonathan Mark. *Ancient Cities of the Indus Valley Civilization.* New York, 1998.

Mair, Victor H. *The Bronze Age and Early Iron Age Peoples of Eastern Central Asia.* Washington, D.C., 1998.

Mallory, J. P. *In Search of the Indo-Europeans: Language, Archaeology and Myth.* London, 1989.

Zbenovich, V. G. "Tripolye Culture: Centenary of Research." *Journal of World Prehistory* 10, no. 2 (1996): 199–241.

B. A. Litvinskii (1987)
Translated from Russian by Demitri B. Shimkin
Revised Bibliography

PRESBYTERIANISM, REFORMED.

The word *presbyterian* refers both to a particular form of church government and, more generally, to churches that are governed by presbyters (elders or priests) but have many other characteristics. The word *reformed* defines a theological perspective. The two words usually but not always belong together. Most Reformed churches are presbyterian, but they may also be congregational and occasionally episcopal in governance.

Historical Origins of Presbyterianism. Presbyterians are catholic in their affirmation of the triune God and of the creeds of the ancient catholic church: the Apostles' Creed, the Nicene Creed, and the Chalcedonian definition. They are Protestant in the sense of Martin Luther's treatises of 1520. Their Reformed roots are in the Reformation at Zurich, under the leadership of Ulrich Zwingli (1484–1531) and Heinrich Bullinger (1504–1575); at Strasbourg, under Martin Bucer (1491–1551); and at Geneva, with the work of John Calvin (1509–1564).

Reformed theology at the time of the Reformation. Reformed theology was a type of Protestantism—as distinct from Lutheranism, Anglicanism, and the theology of the radical Reformation—that originated in Switzerland, the upper Rhineland, and France. Most of the early Reformed theologians had a background in Christian humanism. They were more energetic and radical in their reform of medieval Catholicism than were the Lutherans. The Lutherans' practice was guided by the principle that everything in church life contrary to the word of God should be eliminated. The Reformed church insisted upon positive scriptural warrant for all church practice.

Reformed theology was characterized by its emphasis upon the doctrine of God, who was conceived not so much as beauty or truth but as energy, activity, power, intentionality, and moral purpose. Reformed theologians believed that all of life and history is rooted in the decrees or purposes of God. They emphasized the lordship of God in history and in the salvation of the Christian as emphasized in the doctrine of predestination. They shared the Lutheran doctrine that no one ever merits salvation and that salvation is always grace, always forgiveness. Yet they understood the Christian life as obedience to the law of God and as the embodiment of the purposes of God. As far as the relation of Christian faith to society was concerned, they neither withdrew from society nor identified Christian faith with culture. They were converters of culture and transformers of history, at least in intention.

A central theme of Reformed theology was the glory of God. The salvation of souls and concern for one's own condition was subordinate to giving God the praise, acknowledging his grace, and fulfilling his purpose in personal life and history. The Reformed churches were also characterized by an emphasis on the life of the mind as proper service of God. John Calvin, the most influential of Reformed theologians, was not a speculative thinker. While rejecting curiosity as destructive of faith, Calvin insisted that Christians should know what they believed; the way a person thinks determines action. Calvin also placed high value upon verbal expressions of faith. The sermon became the focus of Reformed worship. Through its example of disciplined, logical thinking, the sermon became a factor in influencing culture in Reformed communities.

The major theological works that shaped Reformed theology in Presbyterian churches were Calvin's *The Institutes of the Christian Religion* (1536), *Institutio Theologiae Elencticae* (1688) of Francis Turretin, and *Systematic Theology* (1871–1873) of Charles Hodge. The most influential creeds have been the Scots Confession of 1560 and the Westminster Confession and Catechisms.

Reformed liturgy. In liturgy the Reformed churches placed a premium upon intelligibility and edification. As with life generally, Calvin insisted that worship should be simple, free from theatrical trifles. The sacraments were limited to the Lord's Supper and baptism, which were believed to have been instituted by Jesus Christ. Within the Reformed tradition some emphasized a preaching service, intending only an occasional celebration of the Lord's Supper. Others believed that the normative service united preaching and the Lord's Supper. Among the more prominent documents of the liturgical tradition are Huldrych Zwingli's *Liturgy of the Word*, Guillaume Farel's *The Order Observed in Preaching*, Calvin's *The Form of Church Prayers*, John Knox's *The Form of Prayers*, *The Westminster Directory of Worship*, the *Book of Common Order* (Church of Scotland), and the *Book of Common Worship* (Presbyterian Church in the U.S.A.).

Presbyterian polity. The word *presbyterian*—a graded system of representative ecclesiastical bodies—has its primary reference not to theology or liturgy but to church government. The prominence of the word in the names of churches has two sources. First, the Reformed churches all believed that the way a church is ordered is important. This was especially the case with Calvin, who devoted long sections of the *Institutes* as well as a major part of his active life to questions of church governance and order. He believed that order is determined by theology and, in its turn, shapes life. Second, English-speaking Presbyterians were involved in lengthy and at times bitter struggles over the order of the church, sometimes with those who shared their theology. This was true in the sixteenth- and seventeenth-century Church of England, which included in its membership Congregationalists and Presbyterians as well as Episcopalians and in which many Episcopalians were also Reformed in theology. The Congregationalists and Presbyterians formed dissenting churches in England. Presbyterians in Britain and Northern Ireland never forgot these controversies, especially the attempts to impose episcopacy by governmental authority in Scotland and Ulster. The word *presbyterian* first began to be used in Scotland in the first half of the seventeenth century. Since then it has been the designation of English-speaking, Reformed Christians who maintain a presbyterian polity. Reformed churches on the European continent with presbyterian polities are called Reformed after their theology.

Presbyterianism is not a fixed pattern of church life but a developing pattern that has both continuity and diversity. Many features of the system vary from time to time and from place to place. In the United States, for example, Presbyterianism developed from the congregation to the presbytery, to the synod, to the General Assembly. In Scotland, Presbyterianism grew out of a gradually evolving notion of how the church should be governed, out of conflict with episcopacy, and from the General Assembly down to the congregation.

Presbyterians find the roots of their polity in the reforming activity of Calvin. With the reform of doctrine, the city council in Geneva had also driven out the bishop and the whole clerical establishment. This gave the reformers greater freedom in shaping the order of the church than in places where so much of the traditional structure remained intact. Calvin gave special attention to the organized life of the church partly because of his personal inclinations as a trained lawyer and also out of the theological conviction that proper order was necessary for both the piety and the purity of the church.

In his doctrine of the church, Calvin's primary emphasis was on the action of the Holy Spirit, who created the church through word and sacrament. Jesus Christ is the only head of the church, and under him all are equal. In addition, Calvin struggled all his life for a church that was independent of state control. He held to the notion of a Christian society with a magistrate whose work in the civil order is a vocation from God, but ideally Calvin wanted church and state to work together under God yet in independence of each other organizationally. Calvin placed great emphasis on the minister, who interprets and applies the word of God. On occasion Calvin refers to the preacher as the mouth of God. The importance of the minister in leading worship, in preaching, in teaching, and in pastoral care is one of function not of status. Calvin insisted that the government of the church should be in the hands of a consistory (council) composed of ministers and elders chosen from the congregation. (In Geneva the choice was limited to members of the city council.) He was opposed on theological grounds to government by individuals who were neither good nor wise enough for such responsibility, and he was likewise opposed to rule by the masses, who were not sufficiently qualified to govern. In both church and state, Calvin advocated government by an aristocracy, in the Aristotelian sense of the qualified, tempered by democracy. In representative government the will of God was more likely to be done. With few exceptions (Hungary, for example), Reformed churches that looked to Geneva for leadership were governed by a council.

Calvin also worked for a disciplined church. Discipline was the primary responsibility of the consistory. Calvin located the exercise of discipline at admission to the Lord's Table. The consistory examined communicants on knowledge based on catechetical instruction and on manner of life. Another of Calvin's achievements was the restoration of the office of deacon as exercising the church's ministry of compassion to the sick and needy.

Calvin developed a polity only for Geneva and the surrounding countryside; hence, in his own work he left the full development of church structure open-ended. Some have argued that Calvin's polity is compatible with episcopacy, but the most that can be established is that Calvin did not oppose existing administrative and judicial episcopal structures.

Although some Calvinists became Congregationalists, Calvin's successor in Geneva, Theodore Beza, was an ardent Presbyterian. Beza guided the Reformed church in France as it worked out the first presbyterian church government on a national scale, with local, district, provincial, and national assemblies composed of ministers and elders. Presbyterianism also became the form of church government in the Netherlands and other Reformed churches on the continent. It received its great emphasis, however, in Scotland, where the controversy about the structure of the church, whether it should be congregational, presbyterian, or episcopal, was vigorously contested and received an importance not given to questions of polity elsewhere.

There are four basic principles of presbyterian polity. The first is the authority of scripture. Some Presbyterians, such as Thomas Cartwright in Puritan England and James Henley Thornwell in American Presbyterianism, contended that presbyterianism was the biblical form of church government. Most Presbyterians have argued that presbyterianism is agreeable to scripture. Traditionally, Presbyterians have wanted to test government as well as doctrine by scripture. They have always subordinated church government to the gospel and have never made the form of government a test of the reality of the church.

The other three principles of presbyterian polity relate to form of governance and relations among clergy and between clergy and laity. Presbyterians have emphasized the unity of the church governed by a graded series of church courts. These assemblies are composed of ministers and elders elected by the people. The word *church* applies both to the local congregation and to the whole body of believers. There is no local congregation without its participation in the whole body of believers, and no church without local congregations. It is in the governance of the church through assemblies that presbyterianism most clearly differs from episcopacy and congregationalism. A third principle is the parity of ministers, who have the same and equal authority under the one head of the church, Jesus Christ. Finally, the fourth principle is the right of the people to call their pastors and to elect those who govern them. Sometimes this right has been limited by circumstance to approval or consent, but the demand to exercise the right of the people has continually reasserted itself.

Among the primary documents of Presbyterian polity are book four of the *Institutes*; *Ecclesiastical Ordinances of Geneva*; the *First Book of Discipline* and the *Second Book of Discipline* of the Church of Scotland; the *Book of Discipline of the Elizabethan Presbyterians.* Also primary are the Westminster Assembly's *Form of Presbyterian Government* and *The Form of Government* of American Presbyterian churches.

The Presbyterian Churches. The Church of Scotland continues the tradition in which English-speaking Presbyterianism was first established. The Congregational church in England and Wales and the Presbyterian Church of England became the United Reformed Church in 1972. By the beginning of the twenty-first century, the United Reformed Church, the Church of Scotland, and the Presbyterian churches of Ireland and Wales had approximately 1.5 million members.

The Presbyterian churches in the United States have their origin in emigration from Scotland and Northern Ireland. Puritan influences were also strong. The Presbyterian Church at Hempstead and later Jamaica, Long Island, was composed largely of Puritans and is probably the oldest continuing Presbyterian Church in the United States, dating from 1644. The first presbytery was organized under the leadership of Francis Makemie, who had come from Ulster, at Philadelphia in 1706. The organization of a synod followed in 1717, and the adoption of the Westminster Confession and Catechisms as theological standards occurred in 1729. The General Assembly held its first meeting in 1789. American Presbyterians have divided on three occasions. The

Old Side–New Side division (1741–1768) had to do with the accommodation of the church to the American frontier; the New School–Old School division (1837–1864 and 1869) was concerned with doctrinal and ecclesiastical issues; the Presbyterian Church in the U.S.A. and the Presbyterian Church in the Confederate States (later the Presbyterian Church in the U.S.A.) split in 1861 and reunited in 1983. The Presbyterian Church in the U.S.A. had a uniting membership of approximately 2.5 million in 2004.

The Cumberland Presbyterian Church originated in a split from the main body of Presbyterians during the revivals in the first decades of the nineteenth century. A major portion of the Cumberland Church reunited with the Presbyterian Church in the U.S.A. in 1903. The Second Cumberland Church, with a predominantly black membership and numbers of 15,500 in 1993, exists independently but in close cooperation with the main body of Cumberland Presbyterians.

The Associate and the Reformed Presbyterians, who originated in secessions from the Church of Scotland, continued their existence in the immigration to the United States. The major body of Associate and Reformed Presbyterians, having become the United Presbyterian Church (1858), merged with the mainstream of Presbyterians in 1958, becoming the United Presbyterian Church in the U.S.A. The Associate Reformed Presbyterian Church, located largely in the South, and the Reformed Presbyterian Church of North America continue the traditions of the Scottish secession Presbyterians.

Other Presbyterian churches originated out of the controversies generated by the conservative and liberal theologies of the twentieth century. The Orthodox Presbyterian Church, a withdrawal from the Presbyterian Church in the U.S.A. in 1936, the Bible Presbyterian Church, a split from the Orthodox in 1938, and the Presbyterian Church of America, organized in 1973 in a pullout from the Presbyterian Church in the U.S.A., have their origins in these controversies.

Presbyterianism came to Canada chiefly through emigration from Scotland and represented all the divisions of Presbyterianism there. In 1875 they united in one church. The majority combined in 1925 with Congregationalists and Methodists to form the United Church of Canada. The Presbyterian Church in Canada had a membership of 129,684 in 2004.

Presbyterian churches in Australia and New Zealand were also established by Scottish immigrants. In the 1961 census, 9.3 percent of Australians declared themselves to be Presbyterian, and in the 1996 census, this percentage dropped to 3.8. In 1977 the Presbyterians, Methodists, and Congregational churches formed the Uniting Church in Australia (300,000 members in 2001, with 1.3 million claiming an association). The (continuing) Presbyterian Church of Australia in 1996 had 675,534 members. Scottish immigration and the Church of Scotland's support of immigrants are the basis of the Presbyterian Church of New Zealand (54,000 members in 1999).

Presbyterian churches have been established throughout the world by the missionary movement of the nineteenth and twentieth centuries. Strong Presbyterian churches exist especially in Korea and also in Brazil, Mexico, and Africa. The World Alliance of Reformed Churches, which is now organized on the basis of theology rather than polity, reported a worldwide membership of 75 million in 2003. This includes younger churches in Africa, South America, and Asia with Reformed theologies but not necessarily presbyterian polities.

See Also Beza, Theodore; Calvin, John; Church, article on Church Polity; Farel, Guillaume; Humanism; Knox, John; Zwingli, Huldrych.

Bibliography

Bolam, C. Gordon, et al. *The English Presbyterians: From Elizabethan Puritanism to Modern Unitarianism.* London, 1968.

Henderson, George D. *Presbyterianism.* Aberdeen, Scotland, 1955. A comprehensive introduction to the origin and development of presbyterian polity.

Leith, John H. *Introduction to the Reformed Tradition: A Way of Being the Christian Community.* Rev. ed. Atlanta, 1981. Chapters on the ethos, theology, polity, worship, and the cultural expression of the Reformed community.

Loetscher, Lefferts A. *A Brief History of the Presbyterians.* 4th ed. Philadelphia, 1984. Brief but reliable.

McNeil, John Thomas. *The History and Character of Calvinism.* New York, 1954. Comprehensive, reliable, judicious. The work of a distinguished historian who cherished the tradition.

New Sources

Hart, D. G., and Mark A. Noll, eds. *Dictionary of the Presbyterian and Reformed Tradition in America.* Downers Grove, Ill., 1999.

John H. Leith (1987)
Revised Bibliography

PREUSS, KONRAD T. (1869–1938), was a German ethnologist and historian of religions. Konrad Theodor Preuss was born on June 2, 1869, in the Prussian city of Eylau (present-day Bagrationovsk, Russia). Shortly after completing school in Königsberg in 1887, he began studying history and geography at the university there and in 1894 received his doctorate from these departments. In 1895 he took a position at the Berlin Ethnological Museum; during his career there he first became head of the North and Middle America department and, eventually (in 1920), director of the museum. He received a professorship from the University of Berlin in 1912, and from that time on he conducted lectures and seminars in North and South American ethnology and archaeology. He also conducted an interdisciplinary colloquium in religious history. In accordance with regulations, Preuss retired from his positions in 1934; his retirement did not, however, hinder his scientific work. Preuss's publications, which appeared on a regular basis throughout his career, concentrated on American ethnology and linguistics.

Within the anthropological study of primal religious traditions, Preuss became known as the foremost German exponent of the "preanimist" theory of magic. Preuss, along with those who followed his theoretical course, held that there had been a stage in human religious development prior to the stage named "animism" by evolutionist anthropologists. During this "preanimist" stage, human beings had construed causality in nature in accordance with belief in the efficacy of magical practices in influencing the environment. In this connection, Preuss spoke of the "primal ignorance" of humankind.

The preanimist hypothesis was quickly disputed and has since been thoroughly rejected (see, e.g., Adolf E. Jensen's *Myth and Cult among Primitive People,* 2d ed., 1969). Deities of later religious eras, even after the existence of an impersonal power came to be accepted, were attended with the same magical methods that Preuss had indicated had been employed by people of an earlier age. But Preuss had already recorded his theoretical construct in a series of articles titled "Der Ursprung der Religion und Kunst" (*Globus* 86 and 87, 1904–1905), and he retained these principles throughout his life.

The experience Preuss gained on two field-research expeditions furnished additional information. The first of these expeditions (1905–1907) brought him into contact with the Cora, Huichol, and Mexicanos tribes of the Sierra Madre of Mexico's Pacific coast. The second journey (1913–1915) was devoted to the study of the Witóto in the lowlands and the Cágaba in the highlands of Colombia. In the religion and mythology of the Witóto, especially, Preuss was able not only to recognize correspondences between various myths and the particular cults that enact them but also to see the roots of these correspondences in an ancient period (see *Religion und Mythologie der Uitoto,* 2 vols., 1921–1923; cf. *Der religiöse Gehalt der Mythen,* 1933). The cultic religions that followed the preanimistic stage were the direct result of these deep-rooted sentiments; they were later superseded by religions in which prayers, not magical practices, were employed.

These later religions were built around a central supreme deity. The form taken by this deity became a major concern for Preuss in his work *Glauben und Mystik im Schatten des Höchten Wesens* (1926). In contrast with Wilhelm Schmidt's view that there has been a universal *Urmonotheismus* ("primitive monotheism") at the earliest stage of human religious evolution, Preuss did not believe that the supreme being was a predominant element during the initial stage of religious development.

According to Preuss's view, religion is more than the "expressive repetition of prayers of thanksgiving and humble obedience to a supreme deity" (see "Fortschritt und Rückschritt in der Religion," *Zeitschrift für Missionskunde und Religionswissenschaft* 47, 1932, p. 241). Like that of other gods, the supreme deity's origin can ultimately be traced. Preuss thought, to perceptual impressions of nature. Beside the theoretical problems surrounding the question of the origin of the idea of God, Preuss devoted the remainder of his career to the study of ancient Mexican religion and history.

Bibliography

For further information, see F. R. Lehmann's article, "K. Th. Preusz," in *Zeitschrift für Ethnologie* 71 (1939): 145–150.

New Sources

Preuss, Konrad Theodor, Jesús Jáuregui, and Johannes Neurath. *Fiesta, literatura y magia en el Nayarit: ensayos sobre Coras, Huicholes y mexicaneros.* México, D.F., 1998.

Otto Zerries (1987)
Translated from German by John Maressa
Revised Bibliography

PRIAPUS was an ithyphallic deity of ancient Greece and Rome. He is known mainly as the god of Roman gardens, where images of him, usually holding up his fruit-laden garment to exhibit his outsize sexual organ, were often placed. However, from the time of his appearance at the dawn of the Hellenistic age well into the Christian Middle Ages, Priapus (Gr., Priapos) may have a basis in some very different realities. From Ptolemy II Philadelphus (Athenaeus, 5.201c), for whom Priapus occupies a mythico-political position, to the epigrams in the *Greek Anthology* or to the kitchen gardens of Priapea in the *Corpus Priapeorum,* this god—whom Horace makes into an obscene scarecrow (*Satires* 1.8)—finds no place among the theological definitions proposed by the ancients. Neither do they seem to have assigned him his own place in their pantheon, even though he was traditionally considered to be the son of Dionysos and Aphrodite and could have been part of the Dionysian *thiaseii* ("revels"). There is, however, one notorious exception: in the system of Justin the Gnostic, the ithyphallic Priapus becomes central to cosmogony; indeed, he is the supreme being, "the one who made creation, even though nothing existed before" (*Elenchos* 5.26.33).

The fate that history has dealt this *divus minor* ("minor god"; *Corpus Priapeorum* 53) is therefore surprising, for both ancient and modern authors have ceaselessly confused him with other figures of sexuality: Pan, the satyrs, and Hermaphroditus, as well as his own father, Dionysos. This confusion is perhaps due to the fact that Priapus's congenital feature is his oversize and perpetually erect penis, so that authors have often tended to identify everything hypersexual with him. It is as if his excessive sexuality has confused the erudite mythographers. Also, when Diodorus Siculus (4.64) and Strabo (13.1.12) try to describe Priapus, they can do so only by mentioning his "resemblance" to the Attic gods Ithyphallos, Orthnes, Konisalos, and Tychon, all ithyphallic powers about whom almost nothing is known except the priapic resemblance that defines them.

However, in spite of these frequent confusions, the ancient sources give this divinity a specific character. Unlike his phallic colleagues, Pan and the satyrs, who are hybrids, Priapus is fully anthropomorphic. He has neither horns nor hoofs nor a tail. His sole anomaly and unique pathology is the immense sexual organ that defines him from birth. Fragments of myths tell how the newborn Priapus was rejected by his mother, the beautiful Aphrodite, for no other reason than his deformed ugliness (*amorphos*) and his disproportionate virile member. It is this oversize organ, described by the Latin texts as "terribilis" (Columella, *De re rustica* 10.33), that allows Priapus to be recognized in images and that identifies him in writings by giving him the form necessary to one of his major functions, that of protecting small-scale cultivations against the evil eye or against thieves by threatening sexual violence to all who pass near the domain he guards (*Planudean Anthology* 241; *Corpus Priapeorum* 11, 28, 44, 59, 71).

In both Greek and Latin epigrams, it is the ithyphallic effigy of the god, often carved from the ordinary wood of a fig tree and daubed with red, who is the speaker pronouncing obscene threats. But Priapus is all talk and no action. In guarding his little gardens, as well as in his amorous adventures, he is often ineffectual. Ovid (*Fasti* 1.391-440, 6.319–348) relates how Priapus failed in his courtship of the beautiful Lotis (or Vesta in another version) and found himself empty-handed every time, his sex up in the air, derided by an assembly laughing at the obscene spectacle of the god frustrated and obliged to flee, his heart and his member heavy.

But it is perhaps the ancient physicians who, in their nosology, best illustrate certain aspects of this impotent phallocrat. *Priapism* is the term they use to name an incurable disease in which the male organ persistently remains painfully erect. The medical texts of Galen (8.439, 19.426) and Caelius Aurelianus (3.18.175) also insist on an important point: Priapism must not be confused with satyriasis, a comparable disease in which the pathological erection does not exclude either seminal emission or erotic pleasure, which is not the case in priapism.

This difference between the ithyphallism of Priapus and that of the satyrs may indicate still another division: Priapus, the citizen of Lampsacus, whose representations are always anthropomorphic, can be classified close to humans, whereas the satyrs, who are hybrids between men and beasts, belong with demons and the wild. It is as if immeasurable sexuality, which is impossible for a human, is viable for beasts and half-humans.

Aristotle specifies in his biological writings that nature has endowed the virile member with the capacity to be or not to be erect, and he wryly notes that "if this organ were always in the same state, it would be an annoyance" (*De partibus animalium* 689a). This, however, is precisely the case of Priapus, who, always ithyphallic, never knows the slightest sexual relief. The ancients considered such phallic excess to be a kind of deformity. The same kind of ugliness characterizes the functional aspects of apotropaic objects that, like Priapus, evoke laughter (Aristotle, *Poetics* 5.1449a) in order to distance evil. This also holds for those amulets that, as Plutarch noted, "draw the bewitcher's gaze" with their strange aspect (*atopia*).

Given his laughable ugliness, which turns people away, and the Dionysian milieu he belonged to, Priapus remained for a long time a vulgarized figure of ancient fertility. Yet, the appeal of this little god of gardens has endured across the centuries. In the late Middle Ages he was known even to the Cistercians (*Chronique de Lanercost*, 1268); he was rediscovered by the artists and craftsmen of the European Renaissance; and his image has continued in use as guardian of gardens down to the present day.

Bibliography

Herter, Hans. *De Priapo.* Giessen, 1932.

Morel Philippe. "Priape à la Renaissance: Les guirlandes de Giovanni da Udine à la Farnésine." *Revue de l'art* 69 (1985): 13–28.

Olender, Maurice. "Éléments pour une analyze de Priape chez Justin le Gnostique." In *Hommages à Maarten J. Vermaseren*, edited by Margreet B. de Boer and T. A. Eldridge, vol. 2. Leiden, 1978.

Olender, Maurice. "L'enfant Priape et son phallus." In *Souffrance, plaisir et pensé*, edited by Alain de Mijolla. Paris, 1983.

Richlin, Amy. *The Garden of Priapus: Sexuality and Aggression in Roman Humor.* New Haven, 1983.

New Sources

Bérard, Claude. "Le satyr casseur." *Metis* 5 (1990): 75–92.

Boardman, John. "The phallos-bird in archaic and classic Greek art." *Revue archéologique* 2 (1992): 227–242.

Carabelli, Giancarlo. *In the Image of Priapus.* London, 1996.

Csapo, Eric. "Riding the Phallus for Dionysus: Iconology, Ritual and Gender-Role Deconstruction." *Phoenix* 51 (1997): 253–295.

Gassner, Jutta. *Phallos: Fruchtbarkeitssymbol oder Abwehrzauber? Ein ethnologischer Beitrag zu humanethologischen Überlegungen der apotropäischen Bedeutung phallischer und ithyphallischer Darstellungen.* Wien, 1993.

Goldberg, Christiane. *Carmina Priapea. Einleitung, Übersetzung, Interpretation und Kommentar.* Heidelberg, 1992.

Habash, Martha. "Priapus." *Classical Journal* 4.3 (1998–1999): 285–297

Ian, Marcia. *Remembering the Phallic Mother: Psychoanalysis, Modernism and the Fetish.* Ithaca, 1993.

Keuls, Eva. *The Reign of the Phallus: Sexual Politics in Ancient Athens.* New York, 1985.

O'Connor, Eugene M. *Symbolum Salacitatis: A Study of the God Priapus as a Literary Character.* Frankfurt am Main, 1989.

Olender, Maurice. "Priape à tort et de travers." *Nouvelle revue de psychanalyse* 43 (1992): 59–82.

Olender, Maurice. "Priape le mal taillé." *Le temps de la réflexion* 7 (1986): 373–388.

Olender, Maurice. *Priape et Baubô.* Paris, 1995.

Parker, W.H. *Priapea: Poems for a Phallic God.* London, 1988.

Turcan, Robert. "Priapea." *Mélanges École Française de Rome* 72 (1960): 167–189.

Vanggaard, Thorkil. *Phallós: A Symbol and Its History in the Male World.* London 1972.

MAURICE OLENDER (1987)
Translated from French by Claude Conyers
Revised Bibliography

PRIESTHOOD

This entry consists of the following articles:

AN OVERVIEW
JEWISH PRIESTHOOD
CHRISTIAN PRIESTHOOD
HINDU PRIESTHOOD
BUDDHIST PRIESTHOOD
SHINTŌ PRIESTHOOD
DAOIST PRIESTHOOD

PRIESTHOOD: AN OVERVIEW

Cross-cultural use of the terms *priest* and *priesthood* is an example of a familiar pattern in modern description of religion. Frequently, terms with European meanings and linguistic derivations are pressed into service for the description of a range of phenomena worldwide. If we pay attention to this fact, we can often enhance our appreciation not only of the terminology itself but of the material to which it is applied.

USAGE IN THE WEST. In the case of *priest,* we can discern a "core" meaning in the Western use of the term. At this core, one may argue, are two identifying factors. The priest, first, performs a sacrificial ritual, usually at a fixed location such as an altar. Second, the priest does so as a specialist on behalf of a community or congregation. When both of these factors are present, we have priesthood in a strict or narrow sense.

In fact, the strict sense of the meaning of *priest* prevailed prior to modern times, while looser and more inclusive applications of the term have come into use more recently. This development has to do with religious and conceptual horizons of the Christian West, in which the vocabulary of Latin and its derivatives has been dominant. In the traditions of the Judeo-Christian West, our point will become clear when we consider circumstances in which the term *priest* has not been used. The two principal cases are the Jewish and the Protestant.

For Judaism, priesthood is a well-defined and central role in the biblical tradition. The performance of sacrifices was one of its essential characteristics. The priests carried out the sacrificial ritual at altars, and from the seventh century BCE onward such ceremony was centralized at the temple in Jerusalem. When, however, the Jerusalem temple was destroyed, the sacrificial practices lapsed, and there were no longer active priests, even if there were hereditary priestly families. Religious leadership in the synagogue, which replaced the temple, passed to the rabbis in their role as teachers. The only continuation of ancient Israel's animal sacrifice is among the small community of the Samaritans, whose officiants to this day are referred to as priests. As far as the Hebraic context is concerned, the terms we translate by *priest* regularly imply the performance of sacrifice, and in the absence of the sacrifice the concept has been considered inapplicable.

Protestants do not generally refer to their clergy as "priests" either. (In this context, the Anglican communion's usage is closer to a Roman Catholic than to a Protestant understanding of things.) But Protestants do have a conception of priesthood, referred to as "the priesthood of all believers." Each member of the community, in this view, is his or her own priest, with direct access to God. The salient feature of priesthood which this Protestant understanding illustrates, then, has not so much to do with sacrifice as such but with the priest's role as an officiating intermediary. In avoiding the term *priest* as a designation of their own clergy, most Protestants have implied a repudiation of the notion that priestly ordination should elevate any man above his fellow human beings or confer on him any access to the divine that is denied others. Protestants did differ from Rome on the senses in which the Lord's Supper, the eucharistic meal of the Mass, might be considered in itself a sacrifice, for they held that Jesus' self-sacrifice was commemorated rather than repeated. But the truly sore point was the privileged, controlling status enjoyed by the officiating Roman clergy. In the Reformation context, then, an essential characteristic of priesthood was its privileged role of mediating benefits and requests between the divine and the human community.

Before we leave the historical meanings of priesthood we may take note of the derivation of the term *priest* itself. Etymologically, the word in English comes from the French *prêtre* and ultimately from the Greek *presbutēs.* In Greek, however, that term means "elder"; hence in the course of Christian usage the semantics of the term shifted from the ordained person's place in ecclesiastical polity to his role as a cultic celebrant. Semantically, on the other hand, the chief words whose meaning corresponds to "priest" are *hiereus* in Greek, *sacerdos* in Latin, and *kohen* in Hebrew.

DESCRIPTION OF PRIESTHOOD IN NON-WESTERN RELIGION. A great many other activities and attributes of priests in the European Christian tradition have built up a range of connotations of the term and role extending far beyond the two critical factors we have reviewed so far. Priests in the West generally wear ceremonial robes while officiating and have distinctive details of street clothing; hence, Western visitors to Japan, for instance, termed the robed personnel of temples "priests," whether Shintō or Buddhist. Priests in the Latin Christian tradition are unmarried; hence the disposition of visitors to Sri Lanka, Burma, or Thailand sometimes to refer to Buddhist monks as "priests," even if the status of their ritual as a sacrifice is debatable. Priests are inducted into their office through ordination; hence the tendency to view tribal societies' ritually initiated specialists in divination, exorcism, healing, and the like as priests. Priests deliver sermons and moral injuctions; hence, presumably, occasional references to the *'ulamā'*, or religious scholars of traditional Islamic lands, as priests, despite the fact that they are neither ordained nor do they perform ritual sacrifice.

In the extended, cross-cultural uses of the term *priest*, then, a priest is any religious specialist acting ritually for or on behalf of a community. With a term used in so broad and flexible a general sense, one excludes little from the category. Ritual activities as such, however, do not make the laypeople who perform them priests; a priest, in any useful sense of the term, is characteristically an intermediary set apart by a recognized induction into office and functioning on behalf of others. Nor does religious specialization or professionalism on behalf of a lay clientele necessarily constitute someone as a priest; there are healers, teachers, and the like who function as professionals but whose activity is not tied to the ritual of a sanctuary.

ELIGIBILITY FOR PRIESTHOOD. The world's priests in various traditions can be divided into what one might term *hereditary* priesthoods and *vocational* priesthoods. In the first case, the priestly prerogatives and duties are the special heritage of particular family or tribal lineages. The ancient Hebrew priesthood, for example, was reserved to the Levites, or descendants of Levi. Levi does not figure in the list of Israelite tribes in *Numbers* 1 (where Ephraim and Manasseh as sons of Joseph each have a place on the list of twelve), but the Levites appear to have gained tribal status in the tradition of *Genesis* 49 (also a list of twelve, including Levi and Joseph but not Ephraim or Manasseh).

Similarly, hereditary is the priesthood in Zoroastrianism, the national religion of pre-Islamic Iran, which today still claims a hundred thousand Iranian and Indian adherents. Traditionally, fathers who were practicing priests trained their sons in the proper recitation of the prayers. More recently, *madrasah*s (schools) for the training of priests have been established. A priest's son may exercise the option to become a priest, and even if he does not do so, the grandson may; but after two or three generations of inactivity the eligibility of the line lapses.

The *brahman* class of India constitutes another important example of priests whose eligibility is hereditary. The traditional Indian social scale known as the caste system places the priests in the highest rank in terms of prestige and respect, ahead of the warrior-rulers. Not surprisingly, the warrior class had already gained greater practical power by the time documented by extant historical records. The other strata continued nonetheless to behave in the apparent confidence that their own positions might be legitimated, confirmed, or blessed by the *brahmans,* however impoverished the *brahmans* might become.

It is generally expected that the clergy in hereditary priesthoods will marry, so that the line may be perpetuated. Indeed, the genealogical awareness of hereditary priesthoods is often as carefully documented as is that of royalty, and for similar reasons. Families claiming the right to officiate in a particular location are known to record their descent back a number of centuries in order to substantiate their legitimacy. Hereditary control of certain temples, whether in Japan or India or elsewhere, can imply some financial advantage, such as access to housing on the premises or to the temple's revenues as income.

Many professions and lines of work are reflected in people's surnames, and a family association with priesthood is no exception. The Jewish surname *Cohen* is an example, as is also *Katz* (an acronym for "righteous priest"), even though the temple sacrifice has not been performed for nineteen centuries. Among Lebanese and other Arabic-speaking Christians a common surname is *Khoury*, an Arabic word for "priest," and another is *Kissis*. Common among the Parsis, the Zoroastrian community of India, is the family name *Dastur*, meaning "high priest."

What one may call a vocational priesthood, on the other hand, recruits its members from the pool of promising young people in the community. It has the potential advantage of selectivity for devotional, intellectual, or moral qualities. All branches of Christianity recruit their personnel on a vocational basis, often promising challenge rather than comfort as the reward of the priestly life. Celibacy is something that a tradition of vocational priesthood can require, as does the Roman Catholic Church, but many vocational priesthoods still permit marriage, such as those of the Greek Orthodox, Russian Orthodox, and other Eastern Christian churches.

Even in the case of vocational priesthoods, the notion of lineage is not absent, but it is expressed in terms of the transmission of legitimacy from teacher to pupil or from ordaining authority to ordained, as, for example, in Tibetan Buddhist lineages or the Christian notion of apostolic succession.

In the vast majority of the world's religious traditions, eligibility for priesthood has been restricted to males. The Hindu, Buddhist, Daoist, Zoroastrian, and Christian traditions have had exclusively male clergy until modern times. Judaism likewise restricted the rabbinate (its equivalent to the more inclusive current sense of the term *priest*) to males. In today's world various branches of both Christianity and Judaism have begun to ordain women to serve as the ritual and spiritual leaders of congregations. To the extent that Islam has leadership analogous to priests, it too has been exclusively male. Only in some "primitive" tribal traditions such as in Africa and some "archaic" traditions such as Shintō and the religions of ancient Greece, Rome, and pagan northern Europe do we find much evidence of priestesses. In most of the world religions there are analogous but supporting roles for women as nuns, deacons, or other assistants. Contemporary initiatives calling for equality for women have raised serious questions concerning the subordination that these roles imply.

Another feature of eligibility for priesthood is a sound physical and mental condition. Apart from practical considerations of community leadership, this requirement is frequently supported by a notion of perfection as appropriate to the sacrificial ritual. Just as a sacrificial animal is expected to be whole and without blemish, so should the sacrificer himself be. Traditional Roman Catholic custom has required in particular that the hands of a priest, which perform the sacrament, be without deformity.

TRAINING AND ORDINATION. A wide variety of instruction, training, and initiation for work as a priest exists among the world's religious traditions. The content of the training is generally a blend of three components that one could term the practical, the theoretical, and the disciplinary.

The practical side of a priest's training includes most saliently the skills the community expects for correct performance of ritual. In a great many traditional settings the efficacy of a prayer or incantation has been held to depend on the acoustic correctness of its utterance. To tap divine power, the formula may need to be invoked in the right language, in the right words, with the right pronunciation, and even with a precise musical intonation. The Hindu concept of *mantra* as a verbal formula entails such training on the part of those who will pronounce *mantra*s, and in the view of many Zoroastrians the exactness of the priests' pronunciation of the liturgical prayers in the Avestan language is what makes the prayers effective.

Consequently the appropriate priestly training amounts to rote memorization of the text of the Vedas in the Hindu case and of the Avesta in the Zoroastrian. This may be begun at a quite early age, and the course is sometimes completed before the candidate reaches puberty. It is knowledge of the text, rather than understanding, that is cultivated. Achievements of memorization in premodern societies can be quite impressive; the Hindu surname *Trivedi*, for example, etymologically means "one who has committed to memory three of the Vedas."

Besides the formulas of the ritual text itself there is much else for a priest to learn: where the ceremonial objects and the officiant should be placed; how the right time for an observance is to be determined; and so on. Where the celebration of a ritual has depended for its timing on direct observation of the sun, moon, or stars, the training of a priest has necessitated mastering a certain amount of practical astronomy. Where the means of divination have included the bones or entrails of animals, the priest has of necessity had to be a practical veterinary surgeon. Indeed, it is instructive to observe in the history of cultures that many professions that became independent specializations have had their origin as branches of priestly learning. But this should not distract us from the fact that priestly training that is merely rote in nature, and oriented only toward ritual performance, may not be sufficient for the demands of the modern world.

What can be termed theoretical training stands at the other end of the spectrum. The world's major religious traditions have all at one time or another undergone challenges of critical inquiry, often philosophical in character. Their scholars have wrestled with the epistemological and metaphysical implications of religious cosmologies, and the ethical and psychological assumptions entailed by religious views of human nature and personality. Some of these traditions have come to expect of their officiating clergy that they not only perform rituals but also minister to the intellectual life of their congregations. Training for priesthood thus may contain a substantial component of historical and philosophical study, in which the prospective congregational leader is given at least a rudimentary exposure to the results of scriptural and doctrinal scholarship.

The perceived need for competence in theoretical matters has generally led religious communities to develop courses of formal academic instruction for their priests (or comparable personnel) in theological studies. Throughout the Islamic world, religious scholarship flourished in a type of school known as a *madrasah*, meaning etymologically "place of study." In small towns these institutions might be modest, but many of the *madrasah*s in the chief cities of medieval Islam were substantially endowed, and to this day certain of their buildings are numbered among the finest monuments of traditional Islamic architecture. In medieval Europe, the origin of universities as institutions was frequently closely tied to the need to educate the Christian clergy, and in a number of northern European countries since the Protestant Reformation both Protestant and Roman Catholic theological faculties have continued to be integral parts of the older universities.

In eighteenth- and nineteenth-century America, the founding of many of the older colleges and universities was based on a similar desire to insure that there would be an educated clergy. The American principle of separation of church and state, however, contributed to the emergence, in the state universities, of curricula in which Christian theology played no part. Religious denominations trained their clergy in separate seminaries, but mainline Protestant bodies by the late nineteenth century were presuming a university bachelor's degree as a prerequisite for entry into them. The normal ordination course emerged as three years following the B.A., roughly from the age of twenty-one to twenty-four. The development of comparable three-year post-B.A. rabbinical curricula from the late nineteenth century onward is one of the marks of Jewish acculturation to the American environment. And the entry of Roman Catholic institutions into close ecumenical cooperation from the 1960s onward made the three-year post-B.A. theology degree standard for Catholic priests as well. The creation of cluster arrangements among Protestant and Catholic theological seminaries has resulted in a significant sharing of resources and experiences in the educational preparation of Christian clergy.

Under the heading of "discipline" can be considered a third kind of preparation for priesthood. In various cultures, from tribal to modern, the priest-to-be is expected to undertake regimes of physical or spiritual self-cultivation—the better to be worthy of, or effective in, the practice of his role.

The concept of purity seems to be associated with a great number of these disciplinary practices and is expressed in a variety of forms. Bodily cleanliness is a frequent requirement, so that the candidate before ordination, or the celebrant before a ritual, may need to undergo a bath in water, or the ablution of some parts of the body, to remove any polluting substances of a physical nature. Or the washing of the body may be a symbolic act, in which magical, mental, or spiritual pollutants are contained or eliminated. Among some peoples, semen, as a product of sexual desire or activity, is held to be polluting. For instance, a certain preparation of a Zoroastrian priest for the conduct of cermonies involves a ritual extending over several days, which is invalidated and must be started over if the candidate shows signs of sexual excitement.

Celibacy for priests is a discipline for which a number of rationales have been offered. There is, of course, the just-mentioned notion of sexual activity as a physical pollution. Beyond this may lie a cosmological or metaphysical view most characteristic of Gnostic and Manichaean thinking, that the very perpetuation of physical existence in this world hinders the eventual release of pure spirit from its imprisonment in inherently evil matter. The early Christian rejection of Gnostic teachings made procreation a positive good and an obligation—but for the laity. Other rationales for priestly celibacy have had to do with eliminating contenders for one's allegiance: the celibate priest, it is held, can give all his time to his ecclesiastical duties, can move whenever and wherever the need arises, and can take personal risks in the cause of his community which a husband or parent might feel constrained to avoid. Finally there is the justification of discipline for discipline's sake: the very confronting of a challenge, even if that challenge itself be arbitrary, makes one a stronger or more worthy individual who can hope to be found worthy and acceptable by God.

The most nearly universal discipline among the world's priesthoods is probably the discipline of meditation. To speak of this, we must deal with the question of whether a common "core" or set of identifiable characteristics of meditation exists such that we can speak of it cross-culturally. Leading candidates for such characteristics are three: some formal physical posture (such as sitting or kneeling), a suspension of conversation with other individuals (though one may be expected to chant or pray aloud), and a concentration of the awareness on divine or transcendent power (sometimes aided by facing an image or symbol). The priest in his exercise of his role may be expected to lead others in meditation; in his training, he is prepared by its practice. A general feeling of well-being or decisiveness can be a personal benefit of meditation to those who practice it; but as a spiritual discipline, meditation needs to serve an unselfish goal, the control of the self and dedication of the priest's personal identity to a power or cause beyond himself.

Upon completion of his training, the priest is ceremonially inducted into the exercise of his role, a process to which Westerners often apply the Christian term *ordination.* Essential here is an ordaining authority such as a senior priest or a religious council. What results over time is a succession of priests, transmitting the role from generation to generation and basing its authority on the legitimacy of the founder of the line. Thus, among Christians, the notion of "apostolic succession" implies that each priest has a pedigree of ordination going back to the apostles, the first generation of Jesus' followers. Buddhist lineages are similar in that monks or pupils trace their ordination back for centuries to earlier teachers.

The process of ordination generally involves some sort of examination or ritual test to ascertain that the candidate is properly prepared. Where formal schools and curricula exist, it is seldom the diploma of the school as such that certifies the candidate, for the school may be distant or its curriculum or methods the subject of dispute. Rather, the local religious jurisdiction conducts its own examination, satisfying itself as to the candidate's dedication and competency.

The actual ceremony of ordination may involve the first wearing of clothing or an ornament or emblem which sets priests apart from others in the society. It generally includes some symbolization of the transfer of power; notable in Christian ordination is "the laying on of hands," in which clergy place their hands on the head of the new ordinand. Another common feature of the ordination process is the ordinand's first performance of a ritual act reserved to priests, such as celebrating a sacrifice or invoking divine pardon or blessing on the worshipers.

PRIESTHOOD AND THE STATE. Any consideration of the relationship of priesthood to the political governance of society must encompass a diversity of cultures. In this context, variation from one time and place to another is so great that the distinctiveness of individual cases probably outweighs in importance the generalizations that can be ventured. Nonetheless, certain types of patterns can be observed that are reflected in more than one historical and social context. For schematic purposes, we shall designate them as follows: the priest as chaplain, the king as priest, the priest as king, and the priest as critic.

By "the priest as chaplain" we mean the many cases in which the priest is a functionary attached to the ruling circles. In tribal societies this may take the form of the frequent presence or attendance of the sacrificer, dancer, diviner, or healer at the hut of the tribal chieftain. In such situations, the priest is on call in supporting roles in the conduct of the affairs of the tribe, and he receives contributions in return from the chieftain or from the tribe as a whole. Essentially the same professionalization is manifested in many of the great ancient empires. Priests were kept as part of the palace retinue, serving both to maintain the ritual worship attended by the court personnel and to deliver omens or otherwise to pronounce auspicious the acts of the royal house. Royal patronage could establish one religious tradition in preference to another, as in the case of Iran in the third century CE, when an ambitious Zoroastrian high priest, Karter, eliminated rivals such as the Manichaeans. Established religion implies a subsidized priesthood, as is evident in the chapels of European palaces and castles dating from medieval to modern times. It suggests a divine sanctioning of a nation's institutions, even in relatively secularized contexts. Although the Christian tradition maintains a theoretical distinction between what one is to render to God and what to Caesar, Christian priests have frequently asked God to bless the Caesar of the day. An instructive contemporary example is found in the prayers of invocation offered by clergy on behalf of religiously diverse public constituencies—state functions such as the opening of a legislative session or the graduation ceremonies of a tax-supported university.

Under the heading "the king as priest" may be grouped those situations in which the chief ruler himself performs ceremonial acts of a religious nature. Some of these may be directed toward his own benefit as an individual, but in far more cases the purpose of the ritual is the welfare of the community as a whole. When this is so, the king's priestly role is demonstrably that of a cultic intermediary between the divine and the community. The New Year observances in ancient Babylonia are an example. In them, the king participated in an annual reenactment of the divine creation of the world, recalling the narrative in which the chief god slays the primordial watery chaos-monster and, by splitting its carcass, structures the world into water-surrounded heavens above and water-surrounded earth below. The drama served as a charter of rights and responsibilities for the king as the god's representative or intermediary, maintaining an order in society consonant with the divinely established order of the physical universe. Not very different in its function was the ritual practiced in ancient China, at the sanctuary in Beijing known as the Temple of Heaven. In this, the king performed the annual sacrifices on an open-air altar, symbolically mediating the unity of the cosmic order with that of society.

There are few instances of "the priest as king" that are not in some way debatable. In some cases, leaders have come to political power through having gained a spiritual following first. Muḥammad's career as a prophet is one example; but his leadership as an intertribal negotiator or as a military commander can hardly be called priestly. The American black civil rights movement of the 1960s and the Iranian revolution of 1979 offer two cases in which the professional religious leaders were the principal leadership possessed by people who were excluded from the ruling establishment; but once having gained power, each of these movements relied on other bases than the cultus for its maintenance and extension. Among the Jews in the Hellenistic era, the Hasmoneans were kings from a priestly lineage; but as a dynasty, they behaved as kings rather than as priests. On the whole, indeed, priests in the exercise of their cultic role seem to have become chaplains more often than kings, losing real political power and economic status rather than gaining it, as in the case of the *brahmans* of India. Perhaps the notion that priests might gain power to become kings is an elusive dream of priestly writers in much the way that the ideal of the philosopher-king is the philosopher's wishful thinking.

To speak of "the priest as critic" is to locate situations in which the priest's voice is one calling for penance or reform. To consider reform part of the vocation of a priest is in keeping with much current Christian discussion. It does, however, raise a semantic issue that calls for a historical answer. For were not the ancient Hebrew reformist critics characteristically referred to as prophets, while the priests were more the cultic chaplains of the establishment? This is indeed true for the period of Israel's religion before the sixth-century BCE Babylonian exile. Thereafter, however, prophecy tended to lapse as an institution, and it consequently became the mandate of others, particularly the clergy, to be "prophetic" in the moral sense. However much prophets and priests may have had clearly differentiated functions in antiquity, the role of the prophet as the voice of conscience in the community has become part of the portfolio of the priest in the centuries since. Struggles for justice and protests for peace throughout the Christian world today bring us constant reports of priests who summon up the courage to defy the current regime, as part of their calling as priests. Activist priests in other communities, such as the Buddhist, have sometimes made a similar contribution.

The Future of Priesthood. The challenge of maintaining an ancient ritual tradition in a modern secular and technological age is a major one. In most of the modern world's religious communities, recruitment of priests is a pressing problem. The celibate life, for instance, surely deters many Roman Catholic males from opting for a priestly vocation, and the desire to marry is clearly a major impetus in the case of many who leave the priesthood. Economic considerations are also a factor: the offerings of the faithful sometimes no longer support a priest in the comfort, compared with other lines of work, that they once afforded. Priests have been reduced to mendicant roles even in those communities which have not characteristically expected priests to be poor. Among the Zoroastrian Parsis of India, most priests are paid on a piecework basis for prayers said, as opposed to being salaried; this fact has contributed to a certain distaste for priests as peddlers of their ritual services, though the community has left them little alternative.

Even more serious than this is a widespread decline in intellectual respect for priests throughout the contemporary world. The factors operative here are probably both philosophical and sociological. Philosophically, modern secularist criticism of traditional religous affirmations has to a certain extent called the content of the priest's affirmations into question, and the response from the pulpit has unfortunately sometimes been pietistic obscurantism. But at least as important has been the sociological fact of the growth of other skills and professions around the world. Formerly, priests often enjoyed status as the only educated, or the most educated, persons in small communities. Formerly, as we have suggested, skills and institutions associated with priesthood were the basis from which other professions and institutions were launched. Today, however, it is not unusual for the spiritual leader of a congregation to count among his flock scientists, engineers, or other professionals whose training is much more highly focused than his own. Some commentators suggest that priesthood as a vocation is in a vicious circle of decline in status, in that the caliber of personnel now being attracted is hardly such as to serve as models for recruiting the best minds of the next generation to a priestly vocation. The challenge of life's ultimate questions, however, persists. Priesthood will probably attract able personnel in significant and perhaps sufficient numbers for many generations to come.

SEE ALSO Ministry; Ordination; Spiritual Discipline; Vocation.

BIBLIOGRAPHY

General studies of priesthood are relatively few. Two that can be recommended are E. O. James's *The Nature and Function of Priesthood* (London, 1955) and Leopold Sabourin's *Priesthood: A Comparative Study* (Leiden, 1973).

WILLARD G. OXTOBY (1987)

PRIESTHOOD: JEWISH PRIESTHOOD

[*This article discusses the nature of ancient Israelite priesthood.*]

The most common biblical term for "priest" is the Hebrew word *kohen* (pl., *kohanim*). It is a West Semitic term known in other ancient societies, and although it is a primitive noun, not derived from any verbal root, its meaning can be established from context. The term *levi* (pl., *leviyyim*), on the other hand, often used to designate certain types of priests, has eluded precise definition, but is translated as "Levite." It seems to be a North Israelite term for "priest" in its earliest biblical occurrences.

The problem that has faced historians in reconstructing the history of Israelite priesthood is the character of the biblical literary evidence, itself, which confronts us with two alternative traditions of Israelite history. In the first, that of the Torah in general, and the Priestly tradition in particular, priests are the tribe of Levi, one of the twelve tribes of Israel, descended from and named after one of Jacob's twelve sons, though usually represented as being different from the other tribes in certain respects. The Levites had no territory of their own, were counted separately in the census, and relied on cultic emoluments, most notably the tithe, for their support. According to some biblical traditions, the Levites became collectively consecrated, or were collectively chosen for sacred tasks because of their loyalty to the God of Israel when others were wayward. In this set of traditions, the Levites were at one point demoted, relegated to maintenance functions and the like. Only one family of priests—the Zadokites according to *Ezekiel* 44, and the Aaronites according to *Leviticus* 8–10 and other priestly texts—were retained as proper priests, fit to officiate in the cult. Another set of biblical traditions, less systematically presented but apparently authentic, portrays priestly groups as professional associations in their initial stages, which became consolidated along family and clan lines through the usual tendency of families to inhabit the same towns and locales and to transmit esoteric skills within the family or clan. Clans, however, were not exclusively ancestral; they admitted outsiders to the study of their skills and eventually to full membership. These processes eventually led to the emergence of identifiable priestly, or Levitical, families, inhabiting towns throughout the land. Biblical writers could thus speak of "Levites" as a tribe, albeit a tribe different from other tribes.

Throughout the period of the northern Israelite and southern Judahite monarchies and even prior to that time, priests were appointed by heads of families, military commanders, kings, and other leaders, and served in their employ. During the period of the Second Temple, when Judaea and Jerusalem were under the domination of foreign empires, the priesthood of Jerusalem played an important political role, the priests serving also as leaders of the Jewish communities.

This is one dimension of priestly status. In religious terms, priests were consecrated persons, subject to laws of purity and restricted in all matters, including marriage and the performance of funerary functions. Priests also wore distinctive vestments.

Common to both dimensions is the factor of skilled training. Priests were taught from *torot* (sg., *torah*), "instruction" manuals for cultic officiation, instruction of the people, adjudication, and oracular and therapeutic functions. Priests also administered temple business and maintained temple facilities. In the postexilic period of the Second Temple of Jerusalem, after the status of the city had changed from a national capital ruled by native kings to a temple city under foreign imperial domination, the priests of Jerusalem assumed quasi-political functions as well. They managed community affairs, while leading priests represented the Judean community to the imperial authorities, first Persian, then Ptolemaic and Seleucid.

Preexilic biblical sources refer to chief priests (sg., *kohen ha-ro'sh, Jer.* 52:24) and their deputies (sg., *kohen ha-mishneh, 2 Kgs.* 23:4), whereas the Priestly tradition provides the title "the high priest" (*ha-kohen ha-gadol, Lv.* 21:10) which was more widely used in the postexilic period. The internal organization of the priesthood is gleaned from later biblical literature and from the writings of Josephus Flavius (fl. first century CE), as well as from the Mishnah (second-third centuries CE). Priests were assigned to tours of duty called *mishmarot,* "watches," usually of one week's duration, during which they lived in the Temple complex. The Mishnah mentions priestly officials, such as *ha-segan* ("the director") and *ha-memunneh* ("the priest designate"), who were in charge of specific temple functions in offices of the day.

Priests were supported by levies and donations to the Temple (or temples, in the earlier period) and were required to partake of sacred meals within the Temple precincts. There are indications that, especially in the postexilic period, but perhaps earlier as well, priestly families amassed independent wealth and owned large estates.

Priestly functions may be summarized in the following five categories: (1) cultic functions, (2) oracular functions, (3) therapeutic functions, (4) instructional and juridical functions, and (5) administrative and political functions.

1. *Cultic functions.* The indispensable role of the priest was to officiate in the public sacrificial cult, a role for which only priests were fit. In addition to officiating, priests were involved in the preparation of sacrificial materials and the examination of sacrificial animals and their assignment to specific rites.

2. *Oracular functions.* Both early sources on priestly activity and the subsequent Priestly codification of priestly functions lend prominence to oracular inquiry. The only permitted type of divination was by means of casting lots to secure a binary, or yes or no, response. Often mentioned in this connection is the *efod,* a finely embroidered vestment with a pouch in which the two stones called Urim and Tummim were most likely kept (*Ex.* 28:6, *Lv.* 8:7). Although it is the general view that such oracular inquiry was more characteristic of the earlier periods, their inclusion in the Priestly codes of law, and in certain postexilic references to priestly activity suggests that their utilization persisted (*Ezr.* 2:63). The Urim and Tummim could determine innocence or guilt, and lots are recorded in the Priestly tradition as the means for assigning territories to the tribes.

3. *Therapeutic functions. Leviticus* 13–15 prescribes a quasi-medical role for the Israelite priest relevant to the treatment of certain skin diseases, which also appeared as blight on leather and cloth and on plaster-covered building stones. The purificatory priest combined medical procedures such as symptomatic diagnosis, quarantine, and observation, with magical and sacrificial rites dealing with the threat of these afflictions. Although nothing is said of this role elsewhere in the Bible, comparative evidence of similar functions in Mesopotamia and Egypt suggests that this was a realistic function of priests.

4. *Instructional and juridical functions.* The priest was brought into contact with the people through his role as one who taught the people the *torah* ("instruction"), the correct procedures in religious and legal matters. Priests usually served as judges, and the high courts were traditionally located in the Temple complex of Jerusalem at certain periods. This was true of the Sanhedrin of Hellenistic and Roman times. The key verb often used in characterizing this priestly activity is the Hebrew *horah* ("to teach").

5. *Administrative and political functions.* Priests managed the business of the Temple, which involved accounting, assessing the value of donations in various forms, maintaining the Temple plant, and carrying out periodic inspections and purifications. At times, especially in the postexilic period, but perhaps earlier as well, priests did double duty as tax collectors in royal outposts and later as traveling collectors.

In the postexilic period Levites, as distinct from priests, performed nonsacral tasks in maintaining the Temple, and the later biblical books speak of them as gatekeepers and temple singers or musicians (e.g., *Neh.* 7:1). This latter role is also suggested by the captions attached to many psalms, attributing them to Levitical clans.

The various biblical traditions, including the Priestly traditions themselves, agree on the view that not ritual but rather obedience to God's command in all things, especially in relations "between man and man," is the ultimate goal of religious life. And yet it was the priesthood that made it possible for the individual Israelite and the community as a whole to experience the nearness and presence of God.

SEE ALSO Levites; Rabbinate.

BIBLIOGRAPHY

Cody, Aelred. *A History of Old Testament Priesthood.* Rome, 1969.

Gray, G. B. *Sacrifice in the Old Testament.* Reissued with an introduction by Baruch A. Levine. New York, 1971. See pages 179–270.

Kaufman, Yehezkel. *The Religion of Israel.* Translated and abridged by Moshe Greenberg. Chicago, 1956.

McCross, Frank, Jr. "A Reconstruction of the Judean Restoration." *Journal of Biblical Literature* 94 (1975): 4–18.

Milgrom, Jacob. *Studies in Levitical Terminology I.* Los Angeles, 1970.

Milgrom, Jacob. *Studies in Levitical Terminology II.* Berkeley, Calif., 1974.

New Sources

Bamberger, Henry. "Aaron: Changing Perceptions." *Judaism* 42 (1993): 199–213.

Fleming, Daniel E. "The Biblical Tradition of Anointing Priests." *JBL* 117 (1998): 401–414.

Leithart, Peter J. "Attendants of Yahweh's House: Priesthood in the Old Testament." *JSOT* 85 (1999): 3–24.

Nurmela, Risto. *The Levites: Their Emergence as a Second-class Priesthood.* South Florida Studies in the History of Judaism, no. 193. Atlanta, 1998.

Rooke, Deborah W. *Zadok's Heirs: The Role and Development of the High Priesthood in Ancient Israel.* Oxford and New York, 2000.

BARUCH A. LEVINE (1987)
Revised Bibliography

PRIESTHOOD: CHRISTIAN PRIESTHOOD

The Roman Catholic, Orthodox, and Anglican Churches apply the term *priesthood* both to the ministry of bishops and presbyters and, more fundamentally, to the baptized members of those communions. Despite historical and theological differences among these churches, there are strong commonalities in the meaning and function of priesthood. To understand these commonalities and differences, it is necessary to consider the origins of Christian priesthood in its historical and religious contexts, major divergences, and continuing developments and controversies. Because it is the early centuries that these churches have in common, they require particular attention here.

The idea and practice of Christian priesthood in early Christianity formed around two poles: the nascent communities' understanding of themselves and of Jesus Christ in light of the Jewish traditions of priesthood with which he and they were familiar. Civic and religious priesthoods in the Greco-Roman world were also significant features of the contexts within which the Christian movement grew, hence a further source of influence as Christian priesthood evolved in the early centuries.

New Testament Period. In the first century, the followers of Jesus used the terminology and imagery of the Hebrew Bible to interpret his ministry, death, and resurrection, seeing in him the high priest (*archiereus*) who offers sacrifice for the sins of the people. But in Jesus they also saw the perfecting or completion of priesthood and sacrifice, one who intercedes eternally for them at God's right hand (*Heb.* 5:1–10; 6:23–28; 10:10–12). Early Christians understood themselves in terms of the Israelites chosen and covenanted as a priestly people (*Ex.* 19:5-6), now constituted as a holy priesthood and God's own people (1*Pt.* 2:5, 9-10; *Rv.* 1:6; 5:10; 20:6). The two concepts are so closely intertwined that it is difficult to assign temporal or logical priority to either one. Over time the focus would come to be fixed on the priesthood of Jesus Christ and his ministers. Starting in the latter part of the twentieth century, largely as the result of growing consensus in biblical studies and ecumenical dialogue, the priesthood of all the Christian people has garnered renewed attention and importance in churches that regard their bishops and presbyters as priests.

Differences over priesthood, temple sacrifice, and communal identity moved from an intra-Jewish question to a site of conflict between Christians (including now Gentile Christians) and Jews by the end of the first century CE. Christian literature of the early second century reflects the growing estrangement between these two groups; the so-called *Letter of Barnabas* is notable for its appropriation of identity as the spiritual temple and God's new Israel at the same time as it excoriates the priesthood and cult of Judaism (13–16).

The New Testament does not apply the term *priest* to any Christian ministry or function other than the role it ascribes to Jesus Christ as eternal high priest. Paul, however, does use the metaphor of "priestly service" (*Rom.* 15:16) to describe his preaching of the gospel but does not expound on its meaning. Leadership roles, offices or ministries, and an array of charismatic gifts were exercised by many believers in service of mission and community life. Nowhere in the New Testament is there any indication of who presided at the Lord's Supper (the Eucharist, as it was later called), but in accord with general social practice of the period, it is likely that the head of the household (male or female) in which the community met was the host or presider at the meal.

Over the course of the second and third centuries, Christian practice and writings increasingly associated the terms priest and priesthood with ministerial office—at first that of bishop, later that of presbyter as well. Two developments fostered this association: articulation of more formal structures of ministry within the churches, and interpretation of the Lord's Supper not simply as a memorial meal but as a representation of the death of Jesus understood as a sacrificial offering to God.

Ordered ministerial offices were beginning to evolve by the late first or early second century, as the Pastoral Epistles (1 and 2 *Tm.*; *Ti.*) witness. The qualifications and to some extent the functions of bishops (*episkopoi*) and deacons (*diakonoi*) were set forth in these letters; the office of elders or presbyters (*presbyteroi*) received briefer mention. The distinction between bishops and presbyters-elders was not well defined, but the bishop may have been a senior member or leader among the elders; the deacon served the bishop and was his representative in the church community. Over the course of the second century, these offices became more firmly established and the distinctive functions of bishops and presbyters more clearly defined.

The bishop served as leader of a local church, which was more like a parish in these early centuries than a diocese, and by the end of the second century he was the regular presider at the Eucharist. In large cities where there were multiple churches, and for outlying churches and rural areas, the bishop would delegate the role of presider to presbyters. By the early third century, the threefold structure of ministry was widespread among the churches. The offices were restricted to men, thus narrowing the ministerial roles of women to widows, who engaged in a ministry of prayer, and deaconesses, who exercised a liturgical ministry chiefly in regard to the baptism of woman, and increasingly marginalizing their leadership.

Second and third centuries. The so-called *First Letter of Clement* (written from the Roman church, c. 96) compares in a general way the ministers of the church to the high priest, priests, and Levites of Israel. Around 200 in Carthage, Tertullian applied the term *sacerdos* (priest) to bishops, only once using the term *high priest* (*summus sacerdos*) for them. Third-century texts known as church orders—the *Apostolic Tradition* (c. 212) ascribed to Hippolytus of Rome and the *Didascalia* (or *Teachings of the Apostles*) from Syria or Palestine (c. 230)—are more specific about the analogy. The *Apostolic Tradition* designates the bishop as presider at the Eucharist. The ordination prayer names him as high priest, propitiating God by his ministry and his offering of the church's gifts to God (I.iii); presbyters are compared to the elders chosen by Moses (I.viii). The *Didascalia* requires that the bishop, like the levitical priests, be unblemished in body and conduct (IV). He is due the first offerings of the community because he is priest, prophet, king, and mediator for the people, imitating Christ in bearing their sins (VIII). The use of priestly language remains largely metaphorical, however, and Christian priesthood never became a hereditary office restricted to specific families, as it did in ancient Israel.

Supported by these developments, a theology of priesthood, Eucharist, and sacrifice began to take form in the third century, particularly in the West. Cyprian, bishop of Carthage (c. 248–258), articulated this emerging nexus for the Latin churches. He considers Melchizedek a figure of Jesus Christ and the eucharistic bread and wine a sacrifice (*Eph.* 63.4–5) offered by the priest (bishop). By association, presbyters share in the priestly role of the bishop (*Ep.*61.3; 72.2). Augustine, bishop of Hippo (396–430), used the term *sacerdos* for bishops and presbyters, but was sparing in its application in order to emphasize the unique priesthood of Jesus Christ, which the ministry of bishops and priests serves. His caution was intended to counter Donatist schismatics who held that sacramental efficacy depended on the worthiness of the minister. Augustine regarded Jesus' death and the Eucharist as sacrificial, contrasting Christian spiritual sacrifice with the ineffective material sacrifices of pagan cult (*City of God* X.5, 6). But he also had a strong conception of the priesthood of the Christian people, the church (*City of God* XVII.5). In the East, the language of sacrifice was applied to the Eucharist and priesthood but was modulated somewhat by an emphasis on overcoming sin and death rather than a preoccupation with propitiating God (as in Origen, Athanasius, Cyril of Alexandria).

Constantinian era. With the growing interest of Emperor Constantine (r. 306–337) in Christianity after his surprise victory at the Milvian Bridge in 312, the church entered a new era of toleration that allowed for expansion of membership and a rapid rise in its social and political status that culminated in its establishment as the religion of the Roman Empire during the reign of Theodosius I (r. 379–395). Prior to the fourth century, the practice and conception of Christian priesthood had evolved largely in relation to the levitical priesthood of the Hebrew Bible. Given the shifts set in motion by Constantine, subsequent developments in Christian priesthood inevitably referred to and drew on Roman civic and religious priesthoods as well as the ceremony of the imperial court.

As imperial largesse transformed the church's major public spaces in Rome, Constantinople, and Jerusalem, the scale and style of Christian liturgy changed to meet the grandeur of these new environments. The use of incense, candles, processions, and vestments reflected imperial ceremony, creating an atmosphere of awe from the subtle overlay of divine and imperial presence. As presider at the eucharistic liturgy in its newly enlarged form, the bishop (and, by extension, his presbyters) began to acquire a sacral aura. John Chrysostom, the "golden-mouthed" preacher and later bishop of Constantinople (r. 398–404), gives fullest expression to these developments in his treatise *On Priesthood* (c. 386), written as an apologia for declining priestly ordination. Chrysostom describes the burdens of pastoral care (II), preaching (IV.12), and teaching (V.13) and highlights the immense honor that attends the priest (bishop) who calls down the Holy Spirit, making present the body and blood of Jesus Christ at the eucharistic sacrifice (III.7). He repeatedly takes issue with those who seek episcopal office as a means of self-promotion (III.7, 9), a concern that reflects the changed status of the church and suggests that Christian priesthood had assumed the political prestige of the old Roman priesthoods.

By recognizing bishops and priests as a legal and social class, Constantine had incorporated them into the political structures of the empire in which those holding public offices constituted distinct ranks or orders (*ordines*). The process of assimilation increased when Constantine granted bishops judicial powers to hear civil cases. Use of the political term *ordo* for priestly office reached back to Tertullian and Cyprian in the West, but its significance increased as the Christian church took its place solidly within the social and political life of the Roman Empire. The distinction between clergy (those in the priestly *ordo*) and laity (*laici, plebs*) arose clearly in the third century; distance between the two widened considerably in the fourth and continued to increase in subsequent centuries.

LATER DEVELOPMENTS AND DIFFERENCES. The decline of the Roman Empire in the West in the fifth century and its gradual retraction in the East served to solidify the ecclesiastical and political status of Christian priesthood. Institutional structures once derived from their Roman historical context acquired a kind of ontological status when incorporated into the platonic thought-world of late antiquity. Pseudo-Dionysius the Areopagite (sixth century, Syria) crystallized this process in his treatises, the *Celestial Hierarchy* and the *Ecclesiastical Hierarchy*, which saw church structures as reflecting and participating in the eternal structures of the angelic hierarchies in heaven. Within the hierarchy of the church there were two orders: the clerical hierarchy and the lay hierarchy. The picture of intricately ordered and interlocking hierarchies was influential in later medieval social and political thought.

Medieval period. The economic and political structures of feudalism that developed in the West from 500 to 800 were likewise hierarchical and congenial to the kind of church order envisioned by Pseudo-Dionysius. Theological developments in this period furthered a conception of priesthood as hierarchical and sacral, rooted in the priesthood of Christ (e.g., Thomas Aquinas, *Summa Theologiae* III.q.22), and removed from the masses of laity. Scholastic theologians articulated a sacramental theology that defined clerical ordination as the sacrament of orders. For bishops and priests, the sacrament of orders was understood to confer an indelible character on the recipient, conveying to him the spiritual capacity for ministry, especially for administering the sacraments (e.g., *ST* III. q. 63, on sacramental character and participation in Christ's priesthood; III. q. 83, a. 4, on the priest's consecratory role in the Eucharist). Episcopal ordination also conferred the authority of jurisdiction (e.g., *ST, Suppl.,* q. I, aa. 5,7). Focus on the Eucharist as the central cultic work of the priest, who acted in the person of Christ (*in persona Christi*), further sacralized the understanding and practice of priesthood. Concentration on the real presence of Christ in the Eucharist and formulation of a philosophical-theological explanation of the nature and causality of that presence (transubstantiation, as defined at the Fourth Lateran Council, 1215) reinforced the sense of cultic awe attaching to priesthood and sacrament. Devotions to the Blessed Sacrament, adored but not received, increased the distance and deference granted to priesthood.

Serious efforts to require and enforce celibacy of the clergy in the West date to the wide-ranging reform program of Pope Gregory VII (r. 1073–1085). The local Spanish synod of Elvira (c. 306) had directed bishops, priests, and deacons to observe marital continence, and the first ecumenical Council of Nicaea (306) had forbidden marriage after ordination to the diaconate, but neither had lasting effect. In both the Greek and Latin churches, the promotion of clerical celibacy owed much to the influence of the ascetic-monastic movement that predated Constantine and spread rapidly during the fourth century as the church became increasingly acculturated. The metaphor of eucharistic sacrifice was taken more literally as arguments for clerical celibacy appealed to levitical laws of ritual purity.

Marriage and concubinage of the clergy were common in the West through the Middle Ages, even after the Gregorian reforms and the imposition of celibacy as a requirement for ordination at the First Lateran Council in 1123. In the East the practice of requiring celibacy of bishops but not of priests had become the norm, with the result that most bishops were drawn from the ranks of monks. Weekly eucharistic services (rather than the Western practice of daily masses) made it possible for priests to observe ritual purity without having to be celibate. Differences over clerical celibacy were one factor in the increasing estrangement of the Latin and Greek churches in this period. Both the requirement of celibacy and the failures in its observance added fuel to the growing calls for reform of the Western church's life and teaching from the thirteenth century onward.

Reformation period. Integral to Martin Luther's critique of the Catholic sacramental system and its abuses was a rejection of the theology of transubstantiation and eucharistic sacrifice, as well as of the notion of priesthood that accompanied it (*The Babylonian Captivity of the Church,* 1520). Luther held that the only Christian priest was Jesus Christ. The minister does not represent Christ in a way different from other believers; every Christian is to be an *alter Christus* (another Christ) to his or her neighbor. The central task of Christian ministry is the preaching of the Word. Although Luther's conception of church, sacraments, and ministry was formulated as a critique of medieval Catholicism, he nevertheless maintained the importance of an ordained (ordered) ministry and the evangelical practice of the two sacraments of Christian faith, baptism and Eucharist. Equally important, however, was his rediscovery of the New Testament understanding of the priesthood of the whole Christian body, taken now as the priesthood of all believers. All baptized Christians, not simply the ordained, participate in the priesthood and kingship of Christ (*On the Freedom of a Christian,* 1520).

John Calvin, too, held that the preaching of the gospel was the heart of ordained ministry and that priesthood belonged to Christ alone (*Institutes of the Christian Religion* IV.19). He further developed an understanding of the threefold offices of Christ as prophet, priest, and king, and the participation of all believers in his priesthood (*Institutes* II.15). Calvin rejected as well the theology of eucharistic sacrifice and any sort of material presence of Christ in the Eucharist, but held a strong doctrine of real spiritual presence (*Institutes* IV.17-18). Ulrich Zwingli agreed with Luther and Calvin in recognizing that Jesus Christ was the only Christian priest. He also rejected a sacramental or sacrificial interpretation of the Eucharist, but in sharp contrast with Luther or Calvin he rejected any notion of eucharistic presence of Christ and taught that the Eucharist was simply a memorial observance (*On the Lord's Supper*).

The so-called middle way (*via media*) taken by the English reformation and brought to a settlement by Elizabeth I (1558-1603) charted a broad course between continental Protestantism as represented particularly by Calvin on the one hand, and Roman Catholicism on the other. Successive editions of the *Book of Common Prayer* reflected these and other influences as it became the norm for the "one use" throughout the English church ("Of Ceremonies," 1559 BCP). The sixteenth-century English reformers largely rejected the idea of eucharistic sacrifice and a clerical priesthood that served the altar. They affirmed the common priesthood of all Christians. Unlike their continental counterparts, they retained the offices of bishop, priest (presbyter), and deacon, but did not define these offices with any specificity. The ordination services were included in Archbishop Thomas Cranmer's 1552 prayer book and retained in later editions; more radically Puritan or presbyterian understandings were excluded in the 1662 book published after the restoration of the monarchy and the episcopacy. Elizabeth's religious policy of "comprehension" (to include within the English church a broad middle range of perspectives) had set a course that allowed for considerable diversity of interpretation and practice in the Anglican communion during subsequent centuries. In regard to priesthood and related matters, the resulting spectrum of positions encompassed the language of both priesthood and ministry, sacrifice and memorial, transubstantiation and spiritual presence, as well as a wide variety of liturgical sensibilities and styles.

In response to the Protestant reformers and by way of its own internal process of reform, the Council of Trent (1545–1563) pursued a dual agenda of doctrinal decrees and pastoral reforms. Doctrinally the council did nothing new, reasserting traditional Catholic positions regarding priesthood, Eucharist, and sacrifice (*Decree on the Sacrifice of the Mass; Decree on the Sacrament of Order; Decree on the Eucharist*). In particular it affirmed transubstantiation, the Eucharist as sacrifice, the priest acting *in persona Christi,* and the indelible sacramental character of ordination that distinguished the ordained from the laity. In the area of pastoral reforms, the council required that bishops be resident in their dioceses and priests in their parishes, reaffirmed the necessity of clerical celibacy, and returned preaching to the center of the bishop's pastoral responsibilities.

CONTEMPORARY ISSUES. Matters related to the theology and practice of priesthood in the early twenty-first century can be noted briefly in three categories: ecumenical and liturgical developments; matters of gender and sexuality; and the growing importance of lay ministry.

The liturgical movement of the twentieth century drew attention back to sources from the early church, finding in these texts common principles for liturgical renewal in the Western churches, especially the Anglican, Roman Catholic, and Lutheran. The entrance of the Roman Catholic Church into the ecumenical arena after the Second Vatican Council (1963–1965) and the rapid growth of bilateral ecumenical dialogues furthered common study of divisive issues surrounding ministry and sacraments. Agreed statements from these dialogues and the World Council of Churches' 1982 document, *Baptism, Eucharist, and Ministry,* are pointing the way toward mutual recognition of ministry, members, and sacraments. At the same time, contemporary biblical scholarship has contributed to a growing consensus on the origins of church and ministry.

Issues related to gender and sexuality in connection with ordained ministry and priesthood have become a critical topic within the churches as well as in ecumenical relations between and among churches. The 1974 ordination of eleven women to the priesthood in Philadelphia sparked a crisis within the Episcopal Church in the United States and, more broadly, in the Anglican Communion. The ordinations were regularized in 1977, though recognition of women priests was not imposed on dioceses or provinces that could not in conscience accept them. Since then Anglican churches in many parts of the world have ordained women priests; the first woman bishop of the Episcopal Church was consecrated in Boston in 1989. More recently, in 2004 the first openly gay bishop was consecrated for the Diocese of New Hampshire, with worldwide repercussions among Anglicans; it remains to be seen what effects this will have on the unity of Anglicanism.

The ordination of women to the priesthood and episcopacy and the consecration of a gay bishop have raised strong questions and objections from the Roman Catholic and Orthodox Churches, both of which restrict priestly ordination to men and consider women's ordination a serious impediment to ecumenical progress. The Roman Catholic Church explicitly condemns homosexuality as intrinsically disordered, while the Orthodox churches have objected vigorously to the new Episcopal bishop's election and consecration. The chief arguments advanced against ordaining women to the priesthood are that tradition does not permit it and that the essence of priesthood makes it impossible: Jesus was male and chose only males to be his apostles (understood as the first ordained priests or bishops); the priest acts *in persona Christi* (Roman Catholics) and is an icon of Christ (Orthodox), but women cannot represent Christ in their bodies.

Within the Roman Catholic Church, a movement for women's ordination to the priesthood has been growing since the late 1970s, particularly in the United States and Europe. Several Vatican documents since 1977 have reiterated the prohibition of women's ordination, including a 1995 statement that declared the question closed. Nevertheless, the discussion continues. Within the Orthodox churches, too, there is a movement to permit ordination to the diaconate for women, with proponents pointing to the history of deaconesses in these churches. Addressing these questions of gender and sexuality increases pressure in the Roman Catholic Church to reexamine the requirement of clerical celibacy, a matter explicitly debated since Vatican II and made more urgent by the shortage of priests in western Europe and North America.

Finally, in each of these churches there is ongoing growth of involvement in many kinds of lay ministry, both professional and volunteer, formal and informal. This movement is related to a renewed appreciation of the common ministry of all Christians that is rooted in the priesthood of Christ and the sacrament of baptism. As it continues to grow and mature, lay ministry will gradually reshape the theology and practice of ordained ministry and priesthood.

BIBLIOGRAPHY

Allen, Joseph J., ed. *Vested in Grace: Priesthood and Marriage in the Christian East.* Brookline, Mass., 2001.

Bartlett, David. *Ministry in the New Testament.* Minneapolis, 1993.

Beard, Mary, and John North, eds. *Pagan Priests: Religion and Power in the Ancient World.* London, 1990.

Brown, Raymond. *Priest and Bishop: Biblical Reflections.* Paramus, N.J., 1970.

Cooke, Bernard. *Ministry to Word and Sacrament: History and Theology.* Philadelphia, 1976.

Daly, Robert J. *The Origins of the Christian Doctrine of Sacrifice.* Philadelphia, 1978.

Eisen, Ute E. *Women Officeholders in Early Christianity: Epigraphical and Literary Studies.* Trans. Linda M. Maloney. Collegeville, Minn., 2000.

Ferguson, Everett, ed. *Church, Ministry, and Organization in the Early Church Era.* New York and London, 1993.

Gryson, Roger. *Les origines du célibat ecclésiastique du premier au septième siècle.* Gembloux, France, 1970.

Gryson, Roger. *The Ministry of Women in the Early Church.* Trans. Jean Laporte and Mary Louise Hall. Collegeville, Minn., 1976.

Hanson, R. P. C. *Christian Priesthood Examined.* London, 1979.

Hopko, Thomas, ed. *Women and the Priesthood.* Crestwood, N.Y., 1983.

Jones, Cheslyn, Geoffrey Wainwright, Edward Yarnold, and Paul Bradshaw, eds. *The Study of Liturgy.* Rev. ed. New York and London, 1992.

Mitchell, Nathan. *Mission and Ministry: History and Theology in the Sacrament of Order.* Message of the Sacraments 6. Wilmington, Del., 1982.

Noll, Ray Robert. *Christian Ministerial Priesthood: A Search for Its Beginnings in the Primary Documents of the Apostolic Fathers.* San Francisco, 1993.

Osborne, Kenan B. *Priesthood: A History of the Ordained Ministry in the Roman Catholic Church.* New York, 1988.

Osborne, Kenan B. *Ministry: Lay Ministry in the Roman Catholic Church: Its History and Theology.* New York, 1993.

Power, David N. *The Sacrifice We Offer: The Tridentine Dogma and Its Reinterpretation.* New York, 1986.

Sabourin, Leopold. *Priesthood: A Comparative Study.* Leiden, 1973.

The Sacrament of Holy Orders: Some Papers and Discussions concerning Holy Orders at a Session of the Centre de Pastoral Liturgique, 1955. Collegeville, Minn., 1962.

FRANCINE CARDMAN (2005)

PRIESTHOOD: HINDU PRIESTHOOD

Hindu priesthood has its origins primarily in the Vedic religion, in which the primary focus was the ritual tradition. The Indo-Aryan-speaking invaders of northwestern India in the middle and late second millennium BCE were apparently divided into a threefold hierarchy of social classes with religious as well as economic functions, the priestly class being uppermost and distinct from the warrior, and both of these relatively small echelons ranking above the masses, the pastoral, artisan, and agricultural producers. Kings and chieftains were evidently drawn from the warrior tradition, but the function of sovereignty itself involved divine-human relationships perceived as sacrificial exchanges and therefore the sacred work (*karman*) of an elite priesthood, whose members came from the priestly social class (*brāhmaṇa*). That this sacerdotal elite was diversified according to long tradition, being responsible not only for a wide range of cultic functions but also for the composition and preservation of the sacred traditions of oral poetry, is documented from comparative study of the *Ṛgveda,* the oldest of the Vedic texts, composed c. 1200 BCE, and the Avesta of ancient Iran. Similarities in the functions not only of Vedic brahmans and Iranian magi but also of Celtic druids and Roman flamens have led some scholars to discuss a proto-Indo-European priestly tradition. In the absence of interpretable literary records from the Indus Valley, it remains undetermined what contribution a hypothetical Harappan priesthood may have made to subsequent South Asian religions.

VEDIC PRIESTHOOD. The expansion of the priesthood during the period of composition of Rgvedic hymns and subsequent texts has a complicated history. The initial verse of the *Ṛgveda* identifies Agni, god of fire, as divine priest and *hotṛ,* or invoking priest, originally the "pourer" of libations (his Avestan counterpart in name and function being the *zaotar*). The *Ṛgveda* itself came to serve as the handbook of this essential priest, who called the gods to the sacrifices. *Ṛgveda* 2.1.2 honors Agni not only with the *hotṛ*'s office but also with those of the *adhvaryu,* or administrative priest, and the *brahmán* (possibly indicating *brāhmaṇācchaṃsin*), *potṛ, neṣṭṛ, agnīdh,* and *praśāstṛ,* with the householder, *gṛhapati,* as eighth priest. In several respects this staff corresponds to ancient Iranian sets of seven or eight priests. But the fully developed Vedic staff for the great *soma* rituals consisted of four major officiants, or *ṛtvij* (a number including the *udgātṛ* with the *hotṛ, adhvaryu,* and *brahmán* from the above group), and allowed each to employ three assistants for a total of sixteen, occasionally seventeen if an additional priest was required. Just as the *Ṛgveda* was the manual from which the *hotṛ* recited, so the three subsidiary Samhitas eventually came to be specific texts for the other principal *ṛtvij* and their assistants, the *adhvaryu* instructing and proclaiming from the *Yajurveda,* the *udgātṛ* and his acolytes singing as a quartet from the *Sāmaveda,* and the *brahmán* serving as proctor or monitor for the rituals, silently observing and listening for errors in need of expiation, his relationship to the *Atharvaveda* being only nominal because his training necessarily included coverage of all three primary Vedas. *Ṛgveda* 10.71.11 alludes to the tasks of the four major priests, that of the *brahmán* being the relating of knowledge (*vidyā*), a significant clue to the nature of this important figure who, as transcendent fourth, represents the totality of priesthood. As *brahmán* (masculine) he is one who knows *bráhman* (neuter), the cosmic word in poetic formula. He "knows" and applies to the human world this *vidyā* of cosmic correspondences, his efforts being simultaneously ritual, speculative, intuitive, even magical. The *bráhman* as cosmic revelation is thus the sacred responsibility of the *brahmán* priest, and by extension, of the entire social class (*varṇa*) of *brāhmaṇa*s.

In the early centuries of the first millennium BCE, Vedic civilization expanded across North India, and sacerdotal literature explored new genres beyond the four Vedic Samhitas, including Brāhmaṇas, or theological and ritual discourses, and *sūtra*s, treatises for both levels of rituals, the great public (*śrauta*) ceremonies requiring three fires and a staff of priests, and the domestic (*gṛhya*) ceremonies dependent upon a single fire and priest. There developed an interactive system of schools (*śākhā*s) to safeguard and transmit oral traditions, each linked to one of the Vedas just as priests claimed descent from one of the traditional seven *ṛṣi*s. Partly competitive but largely cooperative, these schools produced a specialized, highly skilled priesthood that was eventually to be found throughout the Indian subcontinent, and fragments of which exist in marginal areas, particularly in South India, still today. *Prayoga*s and *paddhati*s developed as combinative handbooks for specific rituals, as, for example, in detailing the procedures for the morning and evening milk-offering known as the Agnihotra, or for funerary and ancestral rites.

In ancient and classical India the sacrificer (*yajamāna*), belonging to any one of the three high *varṇas*, engaged one or more priests for the performance of his rites. His family priest was the *purohita,* an office known already in the *Ṛgveda.* The *purohita*'s spiritual guidance as *guru* or *ācārya* came to be regarded as highly as his textual skill as *śrotriya* or his ritual expertise for life-cycle rites (*saṃskāras*). The *purohita* linked to a king could become a powerful state figure, as illustrated by Kauṭilya, court chaplain to the emperor Candragupta Maurya (late fourth century BCE) and author of the influential political treatise known as the *Arthaśāstra.*

HINDU PRIESTHOOD FROM THE CLASSICAL TO THE MODERN PERIOD. From the middle of the first millennium BCE, the Vedic sacrificial structure and its priestly custodians had faced competition from renunciant movements (including the Jains and Buddhists), Upaniṣadic speculation, and yogic techniques, all dispensing with or "interiorizing" the sacrifice. Then emergent Hindu theistic movements promoted devotion *(bhakti)* and worship *(pūjā)* above *yajña,* the Vedic sacrifice. The great *śrauta* system enjoyed a revival in the classical Gupta period, but began to disappear as an institution after the fifth century CE, while the Vedic domestic ritual system was absorbed into Hindu faith and practice, as indeed was its priesthood; the brahmans were now divided into temple officiants in villages, towns, and cities, or linked as *purohitas* in traditional hereditary exchanges of services with twice-born classes, known as the *jajmāni* relationship (in the vernacular, from Vedic *yajamāna,* "sacrificer-patron"). Increasingly, brahman priests found themselves to be one category among specialists of the sacred as "Hinduism" slowly broadened its base to accommodate virtually every religious expression of the multicultural subcontinent. Still the most versatile of priests by virtue of their paramount social position and range of linkages across classes and caste groups (*jātis*), brahmans nevertheless gave significantly more space to nonbrahman religious specialists, who doubtless had long been part and parcel of religious life but had been accorded neither prominence nor legitimation in Vedic and Sanskrit Brahmanic literatures.

By the early medieval period the "priesthood" of Hinduism could be said to have included at least three distinct groups, each with its own interior hierarchy: a remnant of Vedic brahmans (Vaidikas) whose textual and ritual locus remained one or another Vedic school; a larger segment of brahmans whose textual and ritual base was not the Vedas but largely the Sanskrit epics, Purāṇas, and Āgamas, and whose recourse was increasingly toward regional vernacular renditions of these in Tamil, Konkani, Bengali, Hindi, and so forth; and a far larger representation of nontextual priests, unlettered but not unlearned, drawn largely but not exclusively from the lower castes and marginally Hindu tribal peoples, connected with an inexhaustible variety of localized shrines and cult phenomena, and more likely than their brahman counterparts to be concerned with village boundary, hero and goddess cults, spirit possession, exorcism, divination, healing, sorcery, astrology, and shamanic calls to office. Villages afforded priestly roles within virtually every caste or even subcaste. Temples in urban areas displayed wide latitude in the range of priests, including (to cite one eleventh-century example) some fifty priests among a staff of hundreds, all ranked in office and salary from the brahman *pandita* down through lesser priests appointed to serve acolyte deities in the temple or perform animal sacrifices, and even listing as part-time priests specialists in the *Ṛgveda, Sāmaveda,* and *Yajurveda.*

Hindu priesthood in the twentieth century retains many features of the past, including the hereditary *jajmāni* relationship, the location of brahman priestly subcastes near the top of the *jāti* hierarchy (although, interestingly, not as high as most nonpriestly brahman subcastes), a strong emphasis on purity and consecrated ritual status, a hierarchical organization as well as a sectarian one, and a bewildering range of specialization from every caste group, from the incongruously high-caste but low-ranking brahman funeral priest of North India (the *mahāpātra*) to the low-caste barber who performs the same function in parts of South India, to the priests from a wide range of brahman and nonbrahman castes who frequent the great holy centers and engage as patrons the incoming pilgrims. The village or urban brahman *purohita* and his nonbrahman counterpart may find themselves jacks-of-all-trades, called upon to recite *mantras*, perform or advise on life-cycle rites, inaugurate a new house, provide horoscopes, sanction marital arrangements, advise on illnesses, counteract the evil eye, arbitrate disputes, perform accounting, or administer the age-old ritual attentions to the images in the household shrine. The urban brahman priest of a famous Vaiṣṇava or Śaiva temple, like the nonbrahman *pūjāri* of the crudest roadside rock shrine, will find his role more circumscribed than that of the domestic priest, yet still fixed in the same office of mediation between the human and divine worlds.

SEE ALSO Brahman; Druids; Flamen; Magi; Vedism and Brahmanism.

BIBLIOGRAPHY

There is no detailed study of the Vedic priesthood and its history. *Agni: The Vedic Ritual of the Fire Altar,* 2 vols., edited by Frits Staal (Berkeley, Calif., 1983), presents the *śrauta* staff of priests in the context of the Agnicayana ritual (vol. 1, pp. 40–54); numerous color plates from the 1975 Kerala Agnicayana and an excellent bibliography make this an indispensable work. Volume 2 contains a catalog of living and recently deceased Vedic sacrificers with brief regional histories, "Śrauta Traditions of Recent Times," compiled by C. G. Kashikar and Asko Parpola (pp. 199–251). The Indo-Iranian background to Vedic priesthood is summarized by Bruce Lincoln in his *Priests, Warriors and Cattle* (Berkeley, Calif., 1981); see especially pages 60–63, with references. Henk W.

Bodewitz's "The Fourth Priest (the *Brahmán*) in Vedic Ritual," in *Selected Studies on Ritual in Indian Religions: Essays to D. J. Hoens,* edited by Ria Kloppenborg (Leiden, 1983), has summarized and contributed to interpretations of the fourth *śrauta* priest. An innovative and influential discussion of the relationship among Vedic priests, their sacrificer patrons, and renunciation is Jan C. Heesterman's "Brahmin, Ritual and Renouncer," *Wiener Zeitschrift für die Kunde Süd- und Ostasiens* 8 (1964): 1–31. Still useful for both Vedic and later Hindu priesthood is the overview by Arthur Berriedale Keith, "Priest, Priesthood (Hindu)," in the *Encyclopaedia of Religion and Ethics,* edited by James Hastings, vol. 10 (Edinburgh, 1918).

The best single book on Hindu temple priests is the field study by C. J. Fuller, *Servants of the Goddess: The Priests of a South Indian Temple* (New York, 1984), with details on the hierarchy of priests in the Mīnākṣī temple of Madurai, Tamil Nadu. L. P. Vidyārthi, B. N. Saraswati, and Makhan Jha's *The Sacred Complex of Kashi* (Delhi, 1979) includes a dozen types of sacred specialists active in Banaras. Among the best anthropological field studies to include sustained and informed discussion of priestly activities in villages are Lawrence A. Babb's *The Divine Hierarchy: Popular Hinduism in Central India* (New York, 1975), especially chapter 6, a comparative study of brahman priests and the *baiga* (nonbrahman priest-exorcist) of Chhattisgarh, Madhya Pradesh; and David F. Pocock's *Mind, Body and Wealth* (Totowa, N.J., 1973), especially chapter 3 on goddess cults in central Gujarat, in which the *bhuvo* (nonbrahman priest) is possessed by a particular *mātā,* or goddess.

DAVID M. KNIPE (1987)

PRIESTHOOD: BUDDHIST PRIESTHOOD

The English word *priest* is frequently used by both Buddhists and non-Buddhists alike to refer to the Buddhist holy men of various Asian cultures. The use of the term is due more to the concomitant presence of Roman Catholic priests in Asia during the early periods of colonial history than to Buddhistic understandings of the religious vocation per se.

Normatively, Buddhist holy men are fundamentally more concerned with cultivating wisdom (*prajñā*), mental concentration (*samādhi*), and ethical virtue *(śīla)* in pursuit of personal spiritual attainment than with the performance of mediating ritual acts for the religious or material benefit of the laity. Moreover, it is clear from studies of the early Buddhist scriptures that early Buddhism was originally antagonistic to the performance of rites as a means for spiritual advancement. In one sūtra *(Saṃyuttanikāya,* 4.218–220), for example, the Buddha ridicules ritualistic practices of Brahman priests who, by the recitation of *mantras* (magical incantations), believe that they are assisting the dead by empowering their progress through a heavenly afterlife sojourn. In contrast to this practice, the Buddha specifically identifies the power of performing moral actions in this lifetime to determine the quality of life in the next.

Furthermore, clear distinctions between Buddhist holy men and priestly ritual specialists are found in the religious vocabularies of most Buddhist peoples. In Tibet, Buddhist holy men are known as *blamas*, while local priests involved in the manipulation of occult powers are known as Bonpos, or adherents of the indigenous Bon religion. In Sri Lanka, *kapuralas* (priests) officiate at *devalayas* (shrines to gods) where they chant their *yatika* (entreaties) to the *devas* (gods) on behalf of lay petitioners. This practice is in contrast to that of Buddhist *bhikkhus* (monks), who formally do not become involved with the supernatural powers attributed to deities.

Thus, in virtually every Buddhist culture, Buddhist holy men have been more clearly associated with the cultivation of spiritual qualities within than with the orchestration of divine powers operative at various levels of the external cosmos. Indeed, the Sanskrit and Pali terms used for Buddhist clerics are, respectively, *bhikṣu* and *bhikkhu,* which literally mean "beggar" or "mendicant," and do not connote a priestly role as such.

ORIGIN OF MINISTERIAL ASPECTS OF BUDDHIST PRIESTHOOD. In early Buddhist literature, however, the Buddha is depicted as a compassionate teacher who foresaw the need for a priestly or ministerial dimension of Buddhist mendicancy. While this priestly dimension was not expressed through the clerical performance of rites, it is nevertheless evident in the Buddha's injunctions to "wander for the benefit of the many," to become a "field of merit" *(puṇyaksetra)* for the laity, and to preach *dharma* (law, order, truth) to those seeking understanding. When these injunctions are understood in relation to the altruistic ethic of *dāna* (the perfection of giving) and the metaphysical centrality of *anātman* (non-self, selflessness), the basis for a mediating priestly role of service within the context of the Buddhist religious vocation becomes evident.

The priestly dimension of the Buddhist religious vocation assumed greater degrees of importance and specificity as the tradition spread beyond India to East and Southeast Asia. In the process of acculturation, Buddhist holy men actually assumed many of the responsibilities and functions of ritual specialists indigenous to those areas. Today, it is not uncommon to find Buddhist holy men in Tibet who are experts in exorcism, or monks in Sri Lanka who are highly proficient in astrology, or Buddhists in China who played roles similar to Daoist priests in performing funeral rites for the dead. In both Theravāda (Way of the Elders) and Mahāyāna (Great Vehicle) traditions, Buddhist holy men have become ritual specialists who serve the laity through popular ritual practices whenever specific needs arise. They also minister to the needs of the laity in nonritualized ways.

THE BUDDHIST PRIEST IN CHINA, JAPAN, AND THE THERAVĀDA COUNTRIES. Chinese religion has been characterized from ancient times to the present by an exceedingly deep reverence for ancestors. It is the duty of the living to remember and venerate their deceased kin. In light of the fact that renunciation of social and family ties is incumbent upon Buddhist holy men, Buddhism came under severe criticism, especially from Confucian quarters, during its early history in China. To mollify critical Chinese, Buddhists quite consciously popularized the legend of Mulien (Maudgalyāyana), one of the Buddha's closest disciples, who, according to tradition, dramatically and heroically attempted to save his deceased mother, who had been reborn in hell due to her inadvertent consumption of meat. Buddhist apologists stressed that Mulien endured many forms of torture and in the process suffered vicariously for his mother in a variety of miserable hells. At the moment of his greatest need, however, he was succored by the Buddha, who announced the happy news that his mother could be saved if a body of monks would come together and perform a mass for her soul. This legend became the basis for the widespread practice of Buddhist monks offering masses for the dead of their lay supporters.

These masses were also popularized by disseminating the mythologies of two *bodhisattvas* (enlightened ones): Kṣitigarbha (Chin., Dizang; Jpn., Jizō), who vowed to delay his own entry into *nirvāṇa* until he saved all suffering souls dwelling in the many hells; and Avalokiteśvara (Chin., Guanyin; Jpn., Kannon), who wandered through the hells of the damned preaching *dharma* for their eternal benefit. Masses for the dead were held to transfer to Kṣitigarbha the positive karmic power derived from sacrificial and moral actions in order to assist him in his salvific endeavors, and/or to call upon Avalokiteśvara to bring the suffering of the damned to an end.

In modern Japan, the chanting of scriptures on behalf of the dead remains one of the preeminent responsibilities of the Buddhist holy man. In this manner, Buddhist clerics share priestly duties regarding primary rites of passage with Shintō priests, who are generally called upon to officiate at birth or naming ceremonies and weddings. When priestly duties are seen in this fashion, it is apparent that Buddhist clerics share a complementary role with priests of other religious traditions. In Japan, the ritual responsibility of caring for the dead has fallen to Buddhist clerics, while their Shintō counterparts ritually assist the living during occasions of social transition.

The ritual care of the dead also forms an important part of the priestly role of Buddhist monks in the Theravāda countries of Burma, Thailand, and Sri Lanka. Following the death of kin, families assemble for commemoration rites on the seventh day, after three months, and after one year. At these times monks are invited by the family to receive alms *(dāṇa),* to preach *(baṇa),* or to chant sacred scriptures (Pali, *paritta;* Sinh., *pirit*). Karmic merit derived from these religious acts is then transferred to the departed. The subsequent anniversary dates of family deaths are annually commemorated in this manner, and it is not unusual for a given family to undertake a *dāṇa* (almsgiving) on the behalf of various departed family members several times a year. Accordingly, all departed family members of the preceding generation are continuously "assisted."

The basic religious reason for the continued care of the departed is rooted in the fundamental concept of karmic retribution and rebirth. In traditional Buddhist cultures, the ultimate path to *nirvāṇa* is one that spans many lifetimes, and it is incumbent upon family members to assist their departed kin in progressing to this ultimate goal. The specific role of the Buddhist monk in these rites is pivotal. On the one hand, his presence constitutes a worthy object for the performance of meritorious actions, inasmuch as he symbolizes the virtues of the Buddha, the *dharma,* and the *saṃgha* (or *sangha*; the Buddhist order). On the other hand, his sermons invariably focus on the central reality for Buddhists that all conditioned life in *saṃsāra* (repeated cycles of birth, suffering, and death) is temporary, subject to change, and compounded; that whatever is subject to uprising is also subject to decay and whatever is subject to birth is also subject to death. It is the monk's calling to make known this message.

Aside from rites pertaining to the dead, the most evident priestly role in the lives of Theravāda Buddhist monks involves the performance of *paritta,* the chanting of specially selected Buddhist *suttas* in Pali, which when recited are believed to be infused with protective sacral power. The chanting of these *suttas* usually lasts for the duration of a night but in some cases may last for as long as a week or a month, depending upon the specific purpose. The chanting is performed by a number of monks seated under a *mandapa,* a specially constructed canopy. During the chants each monk holds a sacred thread that has been placed in a water vessel. The specific texts are believed to be *buddhavacana* (words of the Buddha), and chanting them therefore charges the sacred thread with power that protects and sanctifies one and that cultivates prosperity and peace. At the conclusion of the chanting the thread is tied around the wrists of all who are present, monks and laity alike, an action symbolizing the distribution of sacral power.

Paritta ceremonies may be held on any occasion that signifies a new beginning or that needs to be considered auspicious. In Sri Lanka, the chanting of *pirit* precedes the opening of parliament, the building of personal residences, campaigns for an end to political strife, or the *Kaṭhina* ceremony, in which new robes are given to members of the *saṃgha* (a monastic Buddhist community) at the end of the *vassa,* the rain-retreat season. Studies of *paritta* indicate that its chief purpose is to establish conditions under which the individual, family, village, or state can carry out required duties favorably. Of all the priestly roles performed by Buddhist monks, the chanting of *paritta* best epitomizes sacerdotal responsibilities, for it is within this ritual context that the monk most dramatically performs the task of mediating sacred power. By articulating the words of the Buddha through chant, he magically diffuses sacred power for the benefit of the faithful.

Buddhist Priests and the Laity. Buddhist monks have also traditionally filled the roles of spiritual advisers and teachers of the laity. In ancient times eminent monks in traditional Asian cultures were selected by the royalty to educate the elite youth. In medieval Southeast Asia, virtually all adolescent males donned the yellow robes of the *bhikkhu* for at least one rain-retreat season to be taught the essentials of Buddhist life. This practice still continues in Thailand and Burma. In modern Sri Lanka, monks spend most of their *poya* (full moon) days educating the laity about Buddhist precepts and meditation. It is also not uncommon for monks and "nuns" (strictly speaking, the *bhikkhunī saṃgha* has been defunct since the tenth century CE) to counsel laity regarding personal or family problems.

The *saṃgha* is a refuge not only for the laity but for its own members as well. An especially poignant petition made by aspiring monks during the process of their ordination rite *(upasampadā)* illustrates how Buddhist monks serve as priests for one another: "I ask the *saṅgha,* reverend sirs, for the *upasampadā* ordination: Might the *saṅgha,* reverend sirs, draw me out of compassion for me" (Vinaya Piṭaka, 4.122). The life of the Buddhist holy man has normatively been characterized by compassion, and it is out of compassion that he offers his own services to the wider community of faithful adherents.

It is precisely this ethic of compassion that serves as the motivating force for new forms of priestly expression now emerging in Buddhist societies. In more traditional societies, the Buddhist holy man performed a variety of ritual tasks for the benefit of the laity in addition to cultivating the spirituality necessary for advancing along the path to eventual *nirvāṇa.* However, modernization and the influence of other religious traditions, especially Christianity, have affected the Buddhist clergy in significant ways. It is now not uncommon to find *saṃgha* social services in Therāvada countries like Thailand and Sri Lanka. In Japan, weekend meditation retreats take place in the center of bustling commercial metropolises and are advertised in local papers as therapeutically worthwhile within the high-intensity pace of the Japanese lifestyle. In virtually all Buddhist countries, temples and monasteries organize pilgrimages to famous historical shrines and sacred places. While these new forms of Buddhist priesthood have yet to endure the test of tradition, they bear witness to the vitality of Buddhist clerics endeavoring to work for the welfare of the many.

While it is clear that Buddhist monks have performed important priestly duties within the context of most Buddhist communities throughout those regions of Asia where Buddhism has become culturally and socially dominant, it is also the case that many Buddhist laymen and laywomen have assumed professional priestly vocations as well. Moreover, these lay priests and priestesses understand the purpose of their ritual perfomances within the context of a prevailing Buddhist worldview, so they do not see themselves in competition with the sacerdotal work of Buddhist monks. Rather, as in the case with Japanese Shintō or Chinese Daoist priests, their ritual transactions are regarded as complementary to the work of monks, a kind of division of spiritual labor.

In Sinhala regions of Buddhist Sri Lanka, for example, Buddhist laymen known as *kapuralas*, ritual specialists tending to the shrines of various of gods (many of whom are of Hindu origins, such as Viṣṇu, Skanda, the goddess Pattini), assert that the efficacious nature of their ritual observances performed on behalf of lay petitioners is fully consonant with the teachings of the Buddha. When *kapuralas* ritually facilitate entreaties of devotees for this-worldly help in order to help assuage existential conditions of suffering (*dukkha*), they are quite aware that the first of the Buddha's four noble truths is that human existence is characterized by the experience of *dukkha.* Therefore, from their perspectives, any divine help that can be enlisted from supernatural sources to alleviate the fundamental condition of suffering in the world is, perforce, a contribution to the basic aims of the Buddhist religion.

The gods ritually served by *kapuralas* are also deemed to be aspiring *bodhisattvas*, relatively advanced on their own paths to buddhahood. According to popular conceptions rooted in medieval Sinhala Buddhist poetry and folk ballads, the gods are said to have received their warrants to exercise their divine powers in the world as a result of the Buddha's own sanction. Gods have gained their powerful positions, it is believed, because throughout their own long careers of rebirth in *saṃsāra* they have cultivated a morally wholesome consciousness that has been expressed through altruistic and compassionate actions, actions that are karmicly fortuitous. They are not understood as saviors who can assist devotees with the ultimate attainment of *nirvāṇa,* but rather as powerful sources of potential this-worldly assistance who may intercede on behalf of devotees when called upon in times of suffering or trouble.

It is not uncommon for devotees to petition a deity's help through priestly intermediaries in matters of family planning, health, marriage prospects, business and political matters, and, in some cases, exorcism. A growing number of priestesses in Sri Lanka, who attribute their powers to their ecstatic encounters with various gods, function as mediums for their clients to communicate with the recently deceased. Other priests and priestesses, who claim special affinities with lesser deities deemed not as fully advanced on the path to becoming *bodhisattvas*, may engage in sorcery.

The ability of these lay Buddhist priestly intermediaries to function successfully on behalf of devotees is dependent upon the perfomance and observance of their own regimens of purity, including dietary prohibitions and ritual ablutions, designed to resist the contagion of pollution (*kili*). Priests and priestesses are also forbidden from performing rituals if a death has occurred within their immediate families or if a priestess is experiencing menstruation. Many priests and priestesses also assert that their continuing powers to function as effective intermediaries are dependent upon the living of a moral life that is deemed pleasing to the gods.

SEE ALSO Buddhist Books and Texts, article on Ritual Uses of Books.

BIBLIOGRAPHY

Bailey, Greg, and Ian Mabbett. *The Sociology of Early Buddhism.* Cambridge, U.K., 2004.

Bareau, André. *Les sectes bouddhiques du petit véhicule.* Saigon, 1955.

Batholomeusz, Tessa J. *Women Under the Bo Tree.* New York, 1994.

Bunnag, Jane. *Buddhist Monk, Buddhist Layman.* Cambridge, U.K., 1973.

Buswell, Robert. *The Zen Monastic Experience.* Princeton, N.J., 1992.

Dreyfus, Georges. *The Sound of Two Hands Clapping: The Education of a Tibetan Buddhist Monk.* Berkeley, Calif., 2003.

Dutt, Sukumar. *Buddhist Monks and Monasteries of India.* London, 1962.

Gitschow, Kim. *Being a Buddhist Nun.* Cambridge, Mass., 2004.

Holt, John C. *Discipline: The Canonical Buddhism of the Vinayapitaka.* Delhi, India, 1981.

Holt, John C. *The Buddhist Visnu: Religious Assimilation, Politics, and Culture.* New York, 2004.

Joseph, Marietta B. "The Viharas of the Kathmandu Valley." *Oriental Art* 18 (1971): 121–144.

Kariyawasam, A. G. S. "Bhikkhu." In *Encyclopaedia of Buddhism,* edited by G. P. Malalasekera, vol. 3, pp. 36–43. Colombo, Sri Lanka, 1961.

Kieschnick, John. *The Eminent Monk: Buddhist Ideals in Medieval Chinese Hagiography.* Honolulu, 1997.

Kitagawa, Joseph M. *Religion in Japanese History.* New York, 1966.

Leclère, Adhémard. *Le buddhisme au Cambodge.* Paris, 1899.

Mendelson, E. Michael. *Sangha and State in Burma: A Study of Monastic Sectarianism and Leadership.* Edited by John P. Ferguson. Ithaca, N.Y., 1975.

Miller, Robert J. *Monasteries and Culture Change in Inner Mongolia.* Wiesbaden, Germany, 1959.

Pathoumxad, Krough. "Organization of the Sangha." In *Kingdom of Laos: The Land of the Million Elephants and of the White Parasol,* edited by René de Berval. Saigon, Vietnam, 1959.

Prip-Møller, Johannes. *Chinese Buddhist Monasteries.* London, 1937.

Rahula, Walpola. *The Heritage of the Bhikkhu.* New York, 1974.

Ray, Reginald. *The Buddhist Saints in India: A Study in Buddhist Values and Orientations.* New York, 1994.

Saha, Kshanika. *Buddhism and Buddhist Literature in Central Asia.* Calcutta, 1970.

Seneviratne, H. L. *The Work of Kings: The New Buddhism in Sri Lanka.* Chicago, 1999.

Sok, Do-ryun. "Son Buddhism in Korea." *Korea Journal* 4, no. 1(1964): 34–40; no. 3: 41–47; no. 4: 32–37; no. 5: 31–36; and no. 6: 28–31.

Suzuki, D. T. *The Training of the Zen Buddhist Monk* (1934). New York, 1965.

Tambiah, Stanley J. *Buddhism and the Spirit Cults in North-East Thailand.* Cambridge, U.K., 1970.

Tiyavanich, Kamala. *The Buddha in the Jungle.* Seattle, 2003.

Tucci, Giuseppe. *Tibet: Land of Snows.* Translated by J. E. Stapleton Driver. New York, 1967.

Visser, Marinus W. de. *Ancient Buddhism in Japan.* 2 vols. Leiden, 1935.

Waddell, Laurence Austine. *The Buddhism of Tibet* (1895). Reprint, New York, 1972.

Welch, Holmes. "Dharma Scrolls and the Succession of Abbots in Chinese Monasteries." *T'oung pao* 50 (1963): 93–149.

Welch, Holmes. *The Practice of Chinese Buddhism.* Cambridge, Mass., 1967.

JOHN CLIFFORD HOLT (1987 AND 2005)

PRIESTHOOD: SHINTŌ PRIESTHOOD

The term *shinshoku* ("Shintō priesthood") is used in modern Japan to refer to those persons serving at shrines in the performance of various religious duties. Prior to the Meiji period (1868–1912) no uniform organization existed within the Shintō priesthood, with the result that clerical titles and functions varied widely depending on the period and shrine involved.

CLERICAL TITLES. Religious titles in use since premodern times include the following:

1. *Saishu* (supreme priest/priestess). The *saishu* is highest-ranking priest at the Grand Shrine of Ise, in charge of all ceremonials and administration relating to the shrine. In the early historical period, the post was filled by a member of the Nakatomi family from the central government's Bureau of Kami (*jingikan*), but after the mid-sixteenth century, the post became a hereditary office of the Fujinami branch of the Nakatomi family. From the Meiji Restoration (1868) to the end of World War II, the post was held by a male member of the imperial family, and by a female member thereafter.

2. *Kuni no miyatsuko* (provincial governor). Originally holding joing political and relgious office, these persons were restricted primarily to ritual functions following the Taika Reforms (645).

3. *Gūji* (chief priest). Originally, *gūji* was an admistrative official with a status superior to other clerical ranks who held responsibility for construction and finance at the largest of shrines. Depending on the status of the shrine, a supreme chief priest (*daigūji*) might have placed under him a junior chief priest (*shōgūji*) or associate chief priest (*gongūji*). At present, the *gūji* holds joint responsibility for all administrative and ceremonial functions within a shrine.

4. *Kannushi* (master of divinities). This title refers to the priest holding chief responsibility for a shrine and the role of central officiant in divine ritual. In later times, the term came to be used as an overall synonym for members of the Shintō priesthood.

5. *Negi* (senior priest). Deriving from the old Japanese word for "entreat" (*negai*), the title *negi* referred to priests primarily engaged in addressing prayers and general worship to the deities. The term later came to indicate a post directly subordinate in rank to the *kannushi* of a shrine, and was also used as a general synonym for members of the priesthood. At present, it refers to a clerical rank subordinate to *gūji.*

6. *Hafuri* or *hafuribe* (liturgist). One of the oldest titles within the Shintō priesthood, this term was used variously to refer to a specific priestly office next in rank to *kannushi* and *negi,* or as a general application for members of the priesthood, a usage it retains today among the common people.

7. *Tayū.* Formerly an honorific title given to middle-grade government officials, this term later came to be used as a general title for Shintō priests, in particular those *religiosi* serving the Grand Shrine of Ise. It is still used among the common people as a general name for Shintō clerics.

8. *Jinin* (divine attendant). Formerly, *jinin* were low-ranking functionaries of shrines, entrusted with miscellaneous duties.

9. *Tōya.* A lay member of a local parish organization (*miyaza*), selected from qualified parish members to serve for a specific period as ritualist for the parish shrine. Still widely seen in villages around the Kyoto-Osaka area, the custom of selecting a shrine *tōya* from the lay community on a rotating yearly basis was apparently a general practice for shrine organizations in premodern periods. With the development of a specialized priesthood, the post has changed in many areas into that of a lower-ranking, part-time priest, or a lay role requiring its incumbent to serve only on certain ceremonial occasions.

10. *Shasō.* The *shasō* were Buddhist clerics serving at shrines as part of the historical phenomenon known as the harmonization of Shintō and Buddhism (*shinbutsu shūgō*). Depending on the shrine, such priests were given a wide variety of titles, but the practice ceased after 1868 with the governmental policy enforcing the separation of Shintō and Buddhism.

Women held high ceremonial positions within early Shintō, but they were gradually relegated to roles assisting the male members of the priesthood. The following are representative of roles for females serving at shrines in the premodern period:

1. *Saigū* or *saiō* (supreme priestess). A *saigū* was an unmarried imperial princess sent as the emperor's representative to the Grand Shrine of Ise. The practice continued until the early fourteenth century.

2. *Saiin* (high priestess). A *saiin* was an unmarried imperial princess sent to serve at the Kamo Shrine in Kyoto, following the custom practiced at Ise. The practice continued until the twelfth century.

3. *Mikannagi* (priestess). This was a general term for young girls aged seven to eight, selected from the daughters of *kuni no miyatsuko* to attend the deities served by priests from the government Bureau of Kami.

4. *Monoimi* (abstainer). *Monoimi* were young girls selected from among daughters of the shrine clergy to lead lives of exceptional ritual purity. Incumbents could be found at many of the great shrines under various titles.

5. *Miko.* The term *miko* is a general title designating female attendants serving at shrines. Formerly ranking below *kannushi, negi,* and *hafuri* as regular members of the priesthood, *miko* at present serve exclusively in supplementary roles, often as sacred dancers.

In addition to the foregoing, numerous other terms have been used as general referents for the Shintō clergy, including *shake, shanin, shashi,* and *shikan.* Individual shrines might also make use of a variety of special titles to refer to specific clerical ranks, such as *uchibito, tone, tanamori, gyōji, azukari,* and *oshi.* In the ancient period, political administrators simultaneously served as ceremonial officiants; there was no independent, professional clergy. For example, the leader of a clan (*uji no kami*) would lead his kinship group in ritual worship of the clan deity. With time, these two roles became specialized, and as professional clerics became more numerous the tendency was strong for such individuals to pass their religious profession on to their descendants.

THE SHINTŌ PRIESTHOOD FROM 1868 TO 1945. Following the collapse of the Tokugawa regime in 1868, the authorities of the new Meiji government revived the ancient concept of *saisei-itchi* (unity of worship and rule), thus placing all shrines and members of the Shintō priesthood under direct government control. Because shrines and priests were thus considered to belong within the public domain, a comprehensive national ordering of shrines and priests was instituted to replace the non-unified ranks, duties, numbers of staff, statuses, and remuneration that had previously existed independently from shrine to shrine.

Under this system, priests of the Grand Shrine of Ise were given the outright status of national officials, with the special title *shinkan* (divine official); the titles and complement of clergy at Ise included one *saishu,* one *daigūji,* one *shōgūji,* eleven *negi,* twenty *gonnegi* (associate *negi*), forty *kujō* (lower-ranking priests), and others. Because the *saishu* was to offer worship in place of the emperor, a member of the imperial family was appointed to the post. The *daigūji* was under the direction and supervision of the Minister of Home Affairs, assisting the *saishu* in matters of ceremonial, and exercising overall control and management of other priests. The *shōgūji* allotted administrative duties and acted as a ceremonial assistant to the *daigūji.* Together, these three priests directed the activities of *negi* and other lower-ranking priests in the various ceremonies and administrative responsibilities of the shrine.

Imperial shrines (*kanpeisha*), and national shrines (*kokuheisha*) were divided respectively into three classifications based on size, and the priests of these shrines were treated as quasi-government employees (*junkanri*) appointed under the jurisdiction of the Minister of Home Affairs and local magistrates. (The only exception was the Yasukuni Shrine in Tokyo; the ministers of the army and navy had the power of appointment for the priests of this shrine.)

These shrines were allotted one *gūji,* one *gongūji* (limited to six major shrines including the Atsuta Jingū), in addition to one *negi,* one or two *shuten* (lower-ranking priests), and (at Atsuta only) up to thirteen *kujō;* these priests were responsible for all ceremonial and administrative functions at their respective shrines.

Smaller shrines at the level of *fu* (urban prefecture), *ken* (prefecture) and *gō* (district) were allotted one *shashi* and several *shasho,* while village shrines (*sonsha*) and unranked shrines (*mukakusha*) were staffed by several *shashō,* who were responsible for all ceremonial and administrative functions. *Shashi* and *shashō* were priests of low rank, selected by local magistrates from among candidates recommended by lay leaders of the parish. These priests were also treated as quasi officials of the national government.

Individuals selected for these various priestly ranks were required to be males over the age of twenty who had either passed a qualifying examination or had received an education preparing them for the priesthood at an approved educational institution. No provisions were made for female members of the clergy.

THE PRIESTHOOD SINCE 1945. Following Japan's defeat in World War II, the Occupation authorities abolished the system of national shrine control and disestablished priests from their previous status as public officials. Shrines were given the same treatment as other religious bodies; their chief priests were allowed to exist as religious judicial persons. In February 1946 the Jinja Honchō (Association of Shintō Shrines) was established in Tokyo as an administrative organ to oversee the activities of shrines; with the exception of a few choosing independent status, the majority of Shintō shrines in Japan became members of the association. As a result, the majority of priests at present are appointed in accordance with the regulations of the Jinja Honchō. As of December 31,1983, the number of priests included within the association was 19,810, including 1,306 (6.6 percent) women.

Depending on the size and status of the shrine, the complement of priests may include a *gūji, gongūji* (generally one only), a *negi* (usually one), and several *gonnegi.* With a status equivalent to chief director for a religious judicial person, the *gūji* must be above twenty years of age and is appointed by the president of the Jinja Honchō on the basis of recommendations from lay representatives of the organization. While the *gūji* has authority to set the number of *negi* at his shrine, the approval of the president of the association is required for the appointment of a shrine's *gongūji.*

Requirements for individuals appointed as priests include a specialized education, general learning, and training at shrines. Qualifications are divided into five levels and are acquired by passing a qualifying examination or by graduating from an accredited Shintō institution with training for the priesthood. Once appointed, priests are ranked in six grades, based on their qualifications, performance, and years of service, and these grades are reflected in the formal costume worn on ceremonial occasions. With a uniquely revered position among Shintō shrines, the Grand Shrine of Ise maintains an independent system of clergy, based on the tradition followed previous to World War II.

Members of the Shintō priesthood not only serve in the performance of formal shrine rituals but also bear responsibility for such administrative tasks as the upkeep and management of shrine facilities and finances. While Shintō ceremonial places heavy emphasis on ritual purification (*saikai*), priests are also expected to display a personal culture and character in their everyday lives consonant with their traditional role as protectors of the faith and leaders in community worship. Since the end of World War II, a strong need has been felt for the active involvement of priests in proselytizing activities among the parish and community of believers, and great expectations are placed on them as well for activities in the areas of social welfare and education.

SEE ALSO Shintō.

BIBLIOGRAPHY

Few references specifically relating to the Shintō priesthood are available in English, although some information may be gleaned from the articles included within *Basic Terms of Shintō* (Tokyo, 1958), compiled by the Shintō Committee for the Ninth International Congress for the History of Religions. Among works in the Japanese language, the *Shintō daijiten,* 3 vols. (Tokyo, 1937–1940), represents the most comprehensive dictionary of Shintō yet printed and includes several articles relating to the Shintō priesthood. Quotations from historical sources regarding the titles, functions, and qualifications of Shintō priests can be found listed topically in the section "Shinshoku" ("Jingi-bu": 45–46) of the *Koji ruien* (1898; reprint, Tokyo, 1967). Basic issues relating to the Shintō priesthood are treated by Ono Motonori (Sokyō) in his *Shintō no kiso chishiki to kiso mondai* (Tokyo, 1964), pp. 472–553, while the historical development of the priesthood is particularly emphasized by Umeda Yoshihiko and Okada Yoneo in their article "Shinshoku," in *Shintō yōgoshū, saishi-hen,* vol. 2 (Tokyo, 1976), compiled by the Institute for Japanese Culture and Classics at Kokugakuin University.

New Sources

Breen, John, and Mark Teeuwen, eds. *Shinto in History: Ways of the Kami.* Honolulu, 2000.

Hardacre, Helen. *Shinto and the State, 1868–1988.* Princeton, N.J., 1989.

Kurozumi, Tadaaki. *The Opening Way: Kurozumi Munetada, Founder of Kurozumikyo.* Lanham, Md., 1994.

Kurozumi, Tadaaki. *Kyososama no Goitsuwa: The Living Way, Stories of Kurozumi Munetada, a Shinto Follower.* Walnut Creek, Calif, 2000.

Littleton, S. Scott. *Shinto: Origins, Rituals, Festivals, Spirits, Sacred Places.* New York, 2002.

Toki Masanori (1987)
Translated from Japanese by Norman Havens
Revised Bibliography

PRIESTHOOD: DAOIST PRIESTHOOD

The Daoist priesthood began with the establishment of the first organized Daoist community among the Celestial Masters in the second century CE. The sources suggest that all followers were hierarchically ranked on the basis of ritual attainments, with the so-called libationers (*jijiu*) at the top of the priesthood. They served as leaders of the twenty-four districts and reported directly to the Celestial Master himself. Beneath them were the demon soldiers (*guizu*), meritorious leaders of households who represented smaller units in the organization.

All leadership positions could be filled by either men or women, Han Chinese or ethnic minorities. At the bottom were the common followers, again organized and counted according to households. Each of these had to pay the rice tax or its equivalent in silk, paper, brushes, ceramics, or handicrafts. In addition, each member, from children on up, underwent formal initiations at regular intervals and was equipped with a list of spirit generals for protection against demons—75 for an unmarried person and 150 for a married couple. The list of spirit generals was called a register (*lu*) and was carried, together with protective talismans, in a piece of silk around the waist.

The world of the Celestial Masters was created by the Dao in its personification as the Highest Lord Lao (Taishang Laojun) and governed by the Three Bureaus (*san guan*) of Heaven, Earth, and Water. Led by the senior priests, these three were celebrated at the major festivals of the year, known as the Three Primes (*sanyuan*), held on the fifteenth day of the first, seventh, and tenth months. They were also the occasion of general assemblies and tax management: in the first month, the tax was set according to the number of people in the household; in the seventh and tenth months, it was collected as the harvest was brought in.

Beyond that, the priests throughout the year practiced the recitation of Laozi's *Dao de jing* and were encouraged to follow a set of three-times-nine precepts based on it, which survives in a later text associated with the Xiang'er commentary. The precepts emphasize austerity and moral discipline and instill a sense of being special and separate from ordinary folk in the community leaders. Some scholars suspect that both the mantric, magic recitation of the *Dao de jing* and the impulse to develop a formal priesthood were inspired by Buddhist monks. The monks first appeared in China around this time and may well have had contact with the new religious groups, but the issue remains unresolved.

This changed with the fourth-century code *Laojun yibai bashi jie* (The 180 precepts of Lord Lao), which was definitely inspired by early Buddhist community rules known as the *prātimokṣa.* Directed at the higher priests of the religion, it provides many detailed rules on practical living and emphasizes personal honesty and community life. The text strongly prohibits theft, adultery, killing, abortion, intoxication, destruction of natural resources, and waste of food, and regulates the proper behavior toward community members and outsiders. It prohibits fraternization with brigands and soldiers, punishes cruelty to slaves and animals, and insists upon polite distance when encountering outsiders and officials. Many details of daily life are regulated, and pettiness and rudeness are discouraged as much as the accumulation of personal wealth.

While ordinary life was governed by discipline and simplicity, the Three Primes and other major community events were celebrated in style with banquets known as kitchen-feasts (*chu*). Wine would flow, animals were slaughtered, and everyone had a good time, leading certain critics of the movement to condemn their practices as "orgiastic." The same criticism was made of an initiatory practice known as the "harmonization of *qi" (heqi),* which involved formally choreographed intercourse between selected nonmarried couples in an elaborate ritual. Practitioners underwent this rite when they were promoted from one level of ritual standing to another (and gained more generals in their registers), enacting the matching of yin and yang in their bodies and thus contributing to greater cosmic harmony.

A reform movement in the fifth century, led by the so-called New Celestial Master Kou Qianzhi (365–448), brought the Daoist priesthood into the imperial government. Having received several revelations from Lord Lao in 415 and 423, Kou set up a system of religious activity based on longevity techniques and bolstered by a set of thirty-six community rules as handed down by the deity. In due course he became the head of a state-sponsored Daoism, geared to bring peace and harmony to the northern Toba Wei empire. This involved setting himself up in a palace cum monastery in the capital together with key followers and administrators said to have numbered 120, and establishing Daoist institutions—temples, priests, moral rules, and rituals—throughout the country.

As described in the *Laojun yinsong xinke jiejing* (Scripture of Lord Lao's new code of precepts chanted to the *Clouds Melody*), the surviving remnant of Kou's instructions, all people had to be loyal to the ruler, obedient to their parents and elders, and subservient to the Dao. To express their proper attitude, they had to observe daily, monthly, and special festival rites throughout the year. Such festivals were led by lay priests working throughout the empire and could last three, five, or seven days. As among the Celestial Masters of old, they involved community assemblies and formal kitchen-feasts. Daily and monthly rites were performed by the priests through a series of bows and prostrations, as well as by the burning of incense and offering of a prayer or petition. Strictly forbidden were popular practices such as shamanic séances and blood sacrifices, as well as traditional Celestial Masters rites of sexual initiation.

In the sixth century, under the political urge to unify the country, the Daoist religion too strove for integration and unity. As a result, a comprehensive system was created, the so-called Three Caverns (*sandong*). Originally a bibliographic classification by the fifth-century master Lu Xiujing (406–477), this was influenced by the Buddhist notion of the three vehicles (*triyāna*) and included the three major schools at the time, Highest Clarity (Shangqing), Numinous Treasure (Lingbao), and Three Sovereigns (Sanhuang), with the Celestial Masters placed at the foundation of the entire pyramid—not counted as one of the Three Caverns, yet essential to them all.

Based on this scheme, Daoist texts were arranged into three main categories, each school associated with a special "Cavern" and a "Supplement." The latter contained technical and hagiographic materials and served as a home for texts of nonmainstream schools. The overall system, still used in the Daoist canon today, is as follows:

Cavern	*School*	*Supplement*
Perfection (Dongzhen)	Shangqing	Great Mystery (Taixuan)
Mystery (Dongxuan)	Lingbao	Great Peace (Taiping)
Spirit (Dongshen)	Sanhuang	Great Clarity (Taiqing)
Orthodox Unity (Zhengyin)		

In ritual practice, the system of the Three Caverns led to the establishment of a formal integrated priesthood and ordination hierarchy, first described in the *Fengdao kejie* (Rules and precepts for worshiping the Dao) of about the year 620. It consisted of a total of seven ranks:

School	*Rank*
Zhengyin (Celestial Masters)	Register Disciple
Taixuan (Great Mystery)	Disciple of Good Faith
Dongyuan (Cavern Abyss)	Disciple of Cavern Abyss
Laozi (*Dao de jing*)	Disciple of Eminent Mystery
Sanhuang (Three Sovereigns)	Disciple of Cavern Spirit
Lingbao (Numinous Treasure)	Preceptor of Highest Mystery
Shangqing (Highest Clarity)	Preceptor of Highest Perfection

The first three ranks were those of lay masters, while the last three were monastic, and the middle rank (Disciple of Eminent Mystery) signified a transitional stage that could be held either by a householder or a recluse.

Ordinations into these ranks began very early, with children being initiated first into the Celestial Masters level and receiving registers of protective generals. After that, each level required extended periods of training, the guidance of an ordination master, and several sponsors from the community. Ordination into any rank of the priesthood involved the transmission of precepts (*jie*), scriptures (*jing*), and ritual methods (*fa*), as well as the endowment of the candidate with various cosmic writs and talismans. In return ordinands had to surrender completely to the Dao and make a pledge to the organization. This pledge involved the presentation of lavish gifts of gold, silk, and precious objects to the master and the institution, as well as the formal oath to follow the rules and work toward the goals of the religion. Higher ranks had as many as three hundred precepts, focusing on social behavior, interaction with community members, and forms of cosmic consciousness, but most ranks involved the observation of ten precepts first formulated by the Lingbao school. These ten consist of five prohibitions, imitating the five precepts of Buddhism, and five resolutions that reflect Daoist priorities. They are:

1. Do not kill, but be always considerate to all living beings.
2. Do not commit immoral deeds or think depraved thoughts.
3. Do not steal or receive unrighteous goods.
4. Do not lie or misrepresent good and evil.
5. Do not intoxicate yourself, but be always mindful of pure conduct.
6. I will maintain harmony with my ancestors and kin and never do anything that harms my family.
7. When I see someone do good, I will support him with joy and happiness in my heart.
8. When I see someone unfortunate, I will help him with my strength to recover good fortune.
9. When someone comes to do me harm, I will not harbor thoughts of revenge.
10. As long as all beings have not attained Dao, I will not expect to do so myself.

(*Fengdao kejie*, chap. 6)

Ordinands were then equipped with the insignia of their new status: religious names, as well as the titles, robes, and headdresses appropriate for their new rank. To show their new affiliation, they would tie their hair into a topknot, unlike Buddhists who shaved theirs. Also unlike Buddhism, where nuns had to observe many more rules than monks and were given a lower status, women in Daoism were treated equally. They underwent the same ceremonies and wore the same garb as men, distinguished only by their elaborate headdress, the so-called female hat (*nüguan*), a term also used for "Daoist priestess."

The complex structure of the Daoist priesthood as it developed in the middle ages and flourished during the Tang dynasty (618–907 CE) collapsed during the Tang-Song transition. Institutions ceased to function, lineages were interrupted, and ordinations were no longer held. Instead, individual seekers emerged, wandering from one sacred mountain to the next, connecting with isolated hermits, perchance finding a stash of old texts, or discovering certain efficacious techniques by trial and error. Occasionally they even secured the support of a local ruler—who was usually more interested in alchemical ways of making gold than in spiritual pursuits—and proceeded to reconstruct one or another temple center of old.

These practitioners had no financial cushion to fall back on, and thus had to find ways of serving communities for a fee so they could continue their quest. As a result—and coinciding fortuitously with the needs of the growing merchant class—Daoists, in competition with wandering Buddhists, Tantric ritualists, and local shamans, began to offer practical rites of healing, exorcism, and protection. They issued spells and talismans for concrete goals, and undertook funerals and communication with ancestors to set people's minds at rest. Daoists of this type became very common in the Song and were known as ritual masters *(fashi)*. They were at the roots of the new schools that soon developed. However, the ritual ranks remained haphazard.

A new orthodoxy only arose with the school of Complete Perfection (Quanzhen), which dates back to the twelfth century, and its founder Wang Chongyang (1112–1170), an official in the military administration of the Jurchen-Jin dynasty who became an eccentric hermit and had several revelatory encounters with Daoist immortals. Organizing his teaching, he left his ascetic life in 1167 and moved to Shandong in eastern China, where he preached his visions and began to win followers. He founded five religious communities, all located in northern Shandong, and continued to spread his teaching until his death in 1170.

His work was continued by seven disciples, six men and one woman, known collectively as the Seven Perfected (*qizhen*), who founded various communities that later developed into separate branches or lineages *(bai)*. The most important among these disciples is Qiu Chuji (1148–1227), better known as Master Changchun, the founder of the leading Longmen lineage, which is still the main Daoist organization in mainland China today.

The ordination system of the Complete Perfection priesthood was formalized in the seventeenth century under its leader Wang Kunyang (1622–1680), abbot of the Longmen branch's headquarters in Beijing, the Baiyun Guan (White Cloud Temple). In this role, he reorganized the religious precepts and ordination system of the school in accordance with neo-Confucian ethics as supported by the Qing court at the time. He outlined three major ranks, each associated with specific sets of precepts, considered an indispensable means to enlightenment and an important element in the education of the Daoist clergy. The three ranks and major precepts texts were:

Master of Wondrous Practice (Miao xingshi)—Precepts of Initial Perfection (*Chu zhenjie*)

Master of Wondrous Virtue (Miao deshi)—Precepts of Medium Ultimate (*Zhongjie jie*)

Master of Wondrous Dao (Miao daoshi)—Great Precepts for Celestial Immortals (*Tianxian dajie*)

Ordination into these ranks involved, as in the earlier, medieval model, the presence of several masters as well as witnesses. Like their Tang predecessors, ordinands of Complete Perfection would take refuge in the Dao, the scriptures, and the masters, provide pledges to the institution, and take formal vows. Unlike their earlier counterparts, they would then live a strictly controlled monastic life with a strong emphasis on discipline and ascetic practices. They would, however, also function as priests, tending to local temples and performing rituals for the public. There is also an order of nuns in Complete Perfection with similar ranks as for monks, but the tendency is that they function mainly in a monastic setting and less as priests for the general public. However, nuns can also be quite influential in the organization and reach high rank as abbots and teachers.

The monastic-based priests of Complete Perfection are the dominant form the Daoist priesthood takes in mainland China today. They are more common than the lay-based priesthood of the Celestial Masters, which has survived from the very beginning of the religion and is today the main form of Daoist organization in Taiwan, with a growing impact in southeast China. These lay priests—who are all male—are specialists in the service of the communal religion. Called Daoists *(daoshi)*, they share responsibilities also with mediums or "divining lads" *(jitong)* and exorcists or "ritual masters" *(fashi)*. All three serve to bring the power of the gods to bear on local problems. What distinguishes them is basically the number of gods whose power they can bring to bear—the medium is the mouthpiece of a single local god; the exorcist is familiar with all the local gods; and the Daoist knows how to invite the gods of the entire universe.

The medium is someone who simply "lends his body to the gods." The exorcist is the medium's master, because his technical knowledge of the system of forces that ordinary people refer to as "gods" and "ghosts" enables him to direct the medium's trance to a useful end. The Daoist is completely self-possessed: the forces he uses in the war against evil are not those of a medium but his own. His chief function is that of a civil official in the celestial administration, in the court of the Dao. By means of formal rituals, accompanied by visualizations, he transforms his own body into the body of the Dao and conducts things back to their original purity and primordial state. His rituals are accordingly complex scenarios for the symbolization of the process and combine all the various arts: painting, music, song, dance, gesture, recitation, and visualization.

Lay Daoist priests are trained carefully and often come from generations of Daoist families. A typical priest usually grows up surrounded by all the arts of Daoist ritual and inherits a veritable family treasure of texts and traditions. In addition, he often completes what he has learned from his father by studying with one of his father's colleagues. The rituals he performs divide into two major categories, offerings (*jiao*) for the renewal and enhancement of the living, and rituals of merit or requiem services (*gongde*) for saving the dead from the punishments of hell, but he also engages in internal cultivation practices, refinement of his *qi* or vital energy, and the concentrated visualization of otherworldly forces.

The Daoist priesthood has been limited to China until very recently. Besides several Daoist scholars who trained in Taiwan and became fully ordained, there is now also an American branch of the Celestial Masters, called Orthodox Daoism of America. Its leader, Liu Ming, was originally Charles Belyea from Boston. Training in Taiwan, he attained high Daoist rank and was formally adopted into the Liu family, which claims a 2,000-year history of Daoist practice and works with scriptures that have only partially made it into official collections—undertaken by the Complete Perfection school in the Ming dynasty. Liu Ming is passing the teaching on to Western students along with Chinese, and he helps create a new dimension of the age-old priestly organization of Daoism.

SEE ALSO Daoism, overview article; Worship and Devotional Life, article on Daoist Devotional Life; Zhenren.

BIBLIOGRAPHY

Benn, Charles D. "Daoist Ordination and *Zhai* Rituals." In *Daoism Handbook*, edited by Livia Kohn, pp. 309–338. Leiden, 2000. A brilliant, well-researched survey of the medieval ordination system.

Davis, Edward L. *Society and the Supernatural in Song China.* Honolulu, 2001. An exemplary study of the role of Daoist priests and their interaction with mediums and exorcists in the Song dynasty.

Despeux, Catherine, and Livia Kohn. *Women in Daoism.* Cambridge, Mass., 2003. A detailed survey of the different roles, functions, and practices of women in the Daoist tradition, including chapters on ancient immortals, medieval priestesses, and abbots of Complete Perfection.

Hendrischke, Barbara, and Benjamin Penny. "*The 180 Precepts Spoken by Lord Lao:* A Translation and Textual Study." *Taoist Resources* 6, no. 2 (1996): 17–29. A good analysis of the priestly rules of the early Celestial Masters.

Kleeman, Terry. *Great Perfection: Religion and Ethnicity in a Chinese Millenarian Kingdom.* Honolulu, 1998. An outline and historical description of the organization of the early Celestial Masters.

Kohn, Livia. "Monastic Rules in Quanzhen Daoism: As Collected by Heinrich Hackmann." *Monumenta Serica* 51 (2003): 367–397. A discussion of the monastic organization of Complete Perfection.

Kohn, Livia. *The Daoist Monastic Manual: A Translation of the Fengdao kejie.* New York, 2004. A translation of the main source for ordination ranks and priestly behavior in medieval China.

Kohn, Livia. *Cosmos and Community: The Ethical Dimension of Daoism.* Cambridge, Mass., 2004. A study of Daoist precepts and ordination patterns through the ages, with translations of multiple documents.

Lagerwey, John. *Taoist Ritual in Chinese Society and History.* New York, 1987. A detailed analysis of the activities and ritual practices of Celestial Masters priests in contemporary Taiwan.

Schipper, Kristofer M. "Taoist Ordination Ranks in the Tunhuang Manuscripts." In *Religion und Philosophie in Ostasien: Festschrift für Hans Steininger*, edited by Gert Naundorf, Karl-Heinz Pohl, and Hans-Hermann Schmidt, pp. 127–148. Würzburg, Germany, 1985. A study of Tang-dynasty manuscripts that describe ordination ranks and practices.

JOHN LAGERWEY (1987)
LIVIA KOHN (2005)

PRIMITIVE MONOTHEISM

SEE SCHMIDT, WILHELM; SUPREME BEINGS

PROCESSION

PROCESSION is the linearly ordered, solemn movement of a group through chartered space to a known destination to give witness, bear an esteemed object, perform a rite, fulfill a vow, gain merit, or visit a shrine.

Some processions, such as the Via Dolorosa procession in modern Jerusalem, constitute major rituals in their own right. Others, such as the "Little Entrance" of Christian Orthodox tradition (in which the Gospels are carried to the front of the sanctuary) or the procession of a bridal party down a church aisle, are only facilitating gestures—formalized comings and goings. The most familiar settings for processions are civil ceremonies (such as coronations, military fanfares, and enthronements), weddings, funerals, initiations, and fertility rites. Major processions seem most widespread in agricultural or urban cultures or those in transition from the one to the other. In hunting, nomadic, and industrial cultures, processions are likely to decline in frequency or significance and thereafter function only as minor gestural tributaries to other rituals.

The ritual space of a procession is linear. When it is completed by a subsequent recession, one might speak of it as "bilinear." By virtue of its linearity, procession differs from circumambulation. Processual action is not movement *around* a sacred object but *to* a special place. Even when a procession returns to its beginning point, its circuit is not generally continuous. The movement is oriented toward a destination rather than a center. Processants do not occupy centralized sacred space. Instead, they carry their "center" with them. The usual places of honor in hierarchically ordered processions are at the head or end of the line. Whereas circumambulation usually sanctifies or protects the place bounded by its circumference, a procession normally links different spatial orders, for instance, civic and sacred or urban and rural space. The rhythms of processing and recessing establish a corridor between a nucleus of sacred space and adjacent, nonsacred zones, or satellite shrines beyond these zones. Distances traversed in processions are usually moderate. One of the longer ones, held during the Greek Eleusinian festival, was fourteen miles. Others, such as the chorus's entrance (*parados*) and exit (*exodos*) to ancient Greek theater, were only a few yards long. Robigalia, the ancient Roman procession intended to avert blight and later adapted by early Christianity into its Rogation processions, was five miles, a more typical distance.

Walking meditation in Zen Buddhism is called *kinhin.* This practice falls between procession and circumambulation. *Kinhin* is not directed *to* any place, so it is not strictly a procession. And although its course is usually around a meditation hall, there is no centralized object of attention. Instead, practitioners' eyes are on the floor, and their attention is directed to the way of walking itself.

The solemn or meditative tone of a procession differentiates it from the expansive, celebrative ethos of a parade or the martial, aggressive one of military marches, picketing, or conquests (such as Don Diego de Vargas's *entrada* into Santa Fe, New Mexico, in 1692). When Joshua brings down Jericho's walls, he is not processing so much as circumambulating in the service of conquest. Unlike mere invasion, conquest, now an obsolete military tactic, is akin to ritual because of its obvious stylization and emphasis on symbolic, rather than strategic, ordering. Examples of ritual elements that might distinguish conquest from invasion include carrying flags, playing drums, wearing uniforms, singing, chanting, and marching in columns. These activities sometimes retain their symbolic value long after their practical military values are lost.

The usual distinction between processions and parades identifies the former as sacred, the latter as profane. The distinction is minimally useful because processions often try to link these or other classificatory domains. Perhaps parades and processions should be considered as celebrative and solemn versions, respectively, of the same basic type of action. Consequently, speaking of a "religious parade" or an "academic procession" is no contradiction in terms. The pace of a procession is typically slower than that of a parade, and its rhythms are more deliberate than that of ordinary walking (or driving if, say, chariots, pageants, floats, or automobiles are employed to transport participants).

Participation in processions is more restricted than in parades. There seems to be a persistent tendency for every procession gradually to relax its exclusivity and become a popular parade in which bystanders can join. Because processing is group movement, it contrasts with running races, which is ritualized, for example, in the Olympic Games and among some modern-day Pueblos. A race is agonistic, setting one person in competition with another. The object of a race is to arrive ordinally (first place, second, third, and so on), not corporately or simultaneously. Perhaps the best term to appropriate for applying to an "individual procession" is *quest.* "Quest," however, is probably better treated as individualized pilgrimage.

Because a procession's destination is known, it is distinct from ritualized hunting, divination-directed migration, religious wandering (of the Hebrews in the desert, for example), and wayfaring (a common practice in medieval China and Japan). Whereas essential elements of these perambulatory rituals include becoming disoriented, abiding in unprotected places, and having to invent or discover one's destination, in processions there is no doubt where to begin and end, and little need for concern about personal safety.

Dancing has no destination; processing does. Processional dances such as the medieval European Dance of Death or the Hasidic dance with the Torah, are borderline instances. Dance presupposes not only rhythm but, typically, music. When dancing arises in a procession, as it does in Rio's Carnival, perhaps the event should be spoken of as a parade. And when dancing shifts from circularity and symmetry to linearity and asymmetry, the religious climate is likely to shift from prophetic criticism to priestly conservatism.

The space through which a pilgrim passes may be mapped, but, unlike a procession path, it is not chartered. Pilgrims pass through what Victor Turner calls liminal ("threshold") zones as they go from near to far. Whereas pilgrims tread ways they may not recognize or cross borders that make them subject to foreign authority, processants pass down ways specially cleared, decorated, and authorized for their arrival. Toward the end of certain pilgrimages—for instance, to the shrine of Guadalupe in Mexico City—one may sometimes join a procession. The chartered quality of procession paths is usually emphasized by the use of stations along the *via sacra;* at these, processants stop, rest, and oftentimes perform ancillary rites.

Even priestly processants may have little to say about the intentions of their actions. Processions, unlike initiation rites or sacrifices, evoke little codified commentary, so scholars usually have to infer intentions. The most obvious one is to display what Erving Goffman might have called a "with": These people "go with" that god. By walking with a god, processants gain merit by association and give witness that sacredness is not geographically restricted to one spot but capable of annexing, even if temporarily, other places. Both a territorial imperative and a hierarchy of gods or sacred places is implied in most processions. Being seen, particularly in postures of homage before elevated, but proximate, sacred objects, legitimizes bonds and often establishes these *sacra* as a group's own. Far from having an inversion effect, as a Mardi Gras parade might, public processions confirm established hierarchies and sacralize ownership and order. For example, one of the oldest known processions was part of the

Great Akitu festival held in Babylon in honor of Marduk. The first day of the new year was set aside for a solemn procession in which Nabu and other gods (carried in boats), kings, and subjects were seen visiting and paying homage to Marduk in his "chamber of fates." Royalty was allowed to take the hand of the god, as if inviting him down an elaborately paved procession way, in order to confirm and renew the divine kingship. At an earlier time Marduk may have been obligated to go in procession to Nabu. Whichever deity was made the goal of a procession was by implication at the pinnacle of the pantheon.

The display of venerated objects, such as the Host during Christian Corpus Christi processions, or symbols of power, such as weapons in Roman triumphal entries, is a common motive for processing. Lustrations, or gestures of purification, are sometimes enacted to ensure that such objects do not come to be contaminated or regarded as common because of overexposure.

The ritual form most akin to procession is pilgrimage. Though both are styles of symbolic journeying, they differ in essential respects. While pilgrimage is more goal-oriented (the return is usually anticlimactic), processions may be more focused on a carried object than a goal, and recessing may be as significant as processing. In contrast to pilgrims, processants do not usually eat, sleep, or suffer together, nor do they endure long periods of solitude. Furthermore, processants are usually the objects of spectating, while such is not the case with pilgrims. For these reasons processions tend more strongly toward social conservatism. Ironically, however, the more popularly successful a procession becomes, the more likely it is to become a ritual of inversion.

See Also Circumambulation; Pilgrimage, overview article.

Bibliography

In the 1910s A. E. Crawley wrote—in his article "Processions and Dances" in the *Encyclopaedia of Religion and Ethics,* edited by James Hastings, vol. 10 (Edinburgh, 1918)—that no comprehensive or scientific work on processions had yet been written. His observation is still largely true. His article, like B. I. Mullahy's in the *New Catholic Encyclopedia* (New York, 1967) and Lawrence J. Madden's in the *Encyclopaedia Britannica* (Chicago, 1973), draws from scant comparative data and depends largely on Christian, specifically Roman Catholic, categories (functional, ordinary, and extraordinary processions) for its analyses and definitions. Rare is the book that includes a chapter, section, or even an index entry on processions.

Presently, data on processions are still largely to be found in works on the religion and ritual of a particular area or tradition or, more specifically, their festivals and pilgrimages. Such works are Herbert William Parke's *Festivals of the Athenians* (Ithaca, N.Y., 1977) and J. M. C. Toynbee's *Death and Burial in the Roman World* (Ithaca, N.Y., 1971).

In *Symbol and Conquest: Public Ritual and Drama in Santa Fe, New Mexico* (Ithaca, N.Y., 1976), pp. 62–74, I have written more fully on the distinctions among processions, pilgrimages, and parades.

Because processing and dancing are so often linked, Eugène Louis Backman's *Religious Dances in the Christian Church and in Popular Medicine,* translated by E. Classen (London, 1952), is still helpful, as is Lillian B. Lawler's *The Dance in Ancient Greece* (London, 1964).

New Sources

Ashley, Kathleen, and Wim Hüsken, eds. *Moving Subjects: Processional Performance in the Middle Ages and the Renaissance.* Amsterdam and Atlanta, 2001.

Billows, Richard. "The Religious Procession of the Ara Pacis Augustae: Augustus' Supplicatio in 13 B.C." *Journal of Roman Archaeology* 6 (1993): 80–92.

Higgins, Sidney, and Fiorella Paino, eds. *European Medieval Drama, 1999.* Papers from the Fourth International Conference on Aspects of European Medieval Drama, Camerino, August 5–8, 1999. Camerino, Italy, 2000.

Hockings, Paul. *Mortuary Ritual of the Badagas of Southern India.* Chicago, 2001.

Reis, João José. *Death Is a Festival: Funeral Rites and Rebellion in Nineteenth-Century Brazil.* Chapel Hill, N.C., 2003.

Ronald L. Grimes (1987)
Revised Bibliography

PRODIGIES

See PORTENTS AND PRODIGIES

PROKOPOVICH, FEOFAN

PROKOPOVICH, FEOFAN (1681–1736) was a Russian Orthodox archbishop who collaborated with Peter the Great to subordinate the administration of the Russian Orthodox church to the imperial government. The instrument of subordination was the Dukhovnyi Reglament (Ecclesiastical Regulation), Prokopovich's most famous writing, which Peter had proclaimed on January 25, 1721.

The Ecclesiastical Regulation achieved the subordination of the church's administration to the tsarist state until the tsardom collapsed in 1917. It abolished the patriarchate of Moscow, replacing it with an Ecclesiastical College modeled on the collegial system that had just been introduced into the civilian administration of the Russian empire. The Ecclesiastical College immediately and successfully sought to rename itself the Most Holy Governing Synod. The change in name symbolized the beginning of a nearly two-hundred-year struggle by churchmen and supporters of the church to regain administrative autonomy for the church.

One of the more burdensome features of the Ecclesiastical Regulation was the subjugation of the clergy to police supervision. Priests were obliged to witness against their penitents or face severe legal sanctions. The regulation had the immediate effect of strengthening the Old Believer schism and the long-term effect of alienating the clergy from their flocks.

Prokopovich's career signified a secularizing and protestantizing development within the Russian church. Like

Peter, Prokopovich believed that the concept of *symphonia,* which defined church and state as two autonomous but interrelated phenomena, served to weaken political authority, to encourage Old Believer intransigence, and to foster political disloyalty.

Raised by his uncle, Prokopovich studied in Jesuit colleges in the Polish Ukraine and in Rome, where, of necessity, he converted to (Uniate) Catholicism. In Kiev, he reconverted to Orthodoxy; he was appointed rector of the Kiev Theological Academy (1711), bishop of Pskov (1718), and archbishop of Novgorod (1720).

When the tsar died in 1725, Prokopovich came under attack from traditionalist churchmen determined to restore canonical equilibrium between church and state. Prokopovich counterattacked. He was a key supporter of the candidacy to the Russian throne of Anna Ivanovna of Kurland (r. 1730–1740), thereby becoming instrumental in bringing upon the Russian church the so-called German yoke.

Prokopovich's final years found him in the anomalous situation of defending the traditional hierarchical organization and the apostolic succession of the Orthodox church against further reforms of the Kurlander administration. A collection of Prokopovich's religious and political works titled *Words and Speeches* (Saint Petersburg, 1765) appeared posthumously.

BIBLIOGRAPHY

Cracraft, James. *The Church Reform of Peter the Great.* Stanford, Calif., 1971.

Curtiss, John S., ed. *Essays in Russian and Soviet History in Honor of Geroid Tanquary Robinson.* New York, 1963.

Muller, Alexander V., ed. *The Spiritual Regulation of Peter the Great.* Seattle, 1972.

Smolitsch, Igor. *Geschichte der russischen Kirche, 1700–1917.* Leiden, 1964.

Wittram, Reinhard. *Peter I, Czar und Kaiser: Zur Geschichte Peters des Grossen in seiner Zeit.* 2 vols. Göttingen, 1964.

JAMES W. CUNNINGHAM (1987)

PROMETHEUS was one of the Titans of the generation of gods prior to the Olympian Zeus. According to the eighth-century BCE Greek poet Hesiod, he became the major benefactor of the human race by introducing them to crafts, fire, and sacrifice. The ambiguous position that he occupied during the rule of the Olympians around Zeus is hinted at in his name of "forethinking one" and the presence of a twin brother, Epimetheus, the "one who thinks too late." Together they seem to form one personality, as Károly Kerényi (1956) has pointed out.

ORIGINS OF MYTH. Prometheus is the major mediator between the world of the gods and that of humankind. If one takes Hesiod as starting point, his original encounter with the Olympian Zeus shows his ambivalence as benefactor and bringer of evil to the human race, evils in the form of limitations to human existence when compared to the eternal lives of the gods. He challenges Zeus to a duel of wits, as Zeus had similarly challenged Kronos, his father, and Kronos still earlier had challenged his own father, Ouranos, for sovereignty. As Jean-Pierre Vernant (1980) shows in a meticulous structural analysis of the existing mythical texts of Hesiod, the contest with Zeus also contains the paradigmatic mythical prototype of sacrificial rites for the Greek city-states. Prometheus divides an ox into two parts, one of which Zeus is to choose; one part hides the bones under an appetizing layer of fat, whereas the other part hides the meat under the unappetizing layer of the animal's stomach. Zeus, despite his all-encompassing foreknowledge (obtained by swallowing the goddess Metis, or Wisdom), fulfils Prometheus's expectations by choosing for himself the heap of bones, implying that humankind is to live on meat from then onwards (having partaken previously in divine nectar or "ambrosia," i.e. that which belongs to the "immortals," *ambrotoi).*

The outcome of the contest thus establishes paradigmatically the division between divinity and humanity while leaving a ritual channel of communication open through sacrifices. Here the ambiguities of the mythical structure are most pronounced. Both Prometheus and Zeus play a duplicitous game, as Zeus pretends in his choice that he does not see through the wiliness of Prometheus. Since he possesses ultimate foresight, however, his pretense at being angry at the deception through Prometheus becomes an arbitrary legitimization for punishing humankind with the withdrawal of fire, throwing humanity back to the stage of animality. Prometheus must then steal the fire to enable humankind to lead a civilized life, for which cooked food as well as sacrifices are basic preconditions. For this second "trickery" by Prometheus, the Olympians punish humankind with the gift of the first woman, Pandora, as fashioned by Hephaistos and endowed with sexual desirability by Aphrodite. Pandora, in spite of her inviting allure, brings humankind a box filled with all evils but also containing hope. Ultimately, she is the indicator of the lost immortality of humankind in the original state of living with the gods, though it is a state without mind or care, and linked to the acceptance of biological immortality through sexual procreation.

The structural opposition between surface appearance and true meaning or essence, between good that is hidden under evil, and evil that comes from well-intentioned deeds, is paradigmatically depicted in this myth of Prometheus who, like all the Titans, seems to straddle divine and human nature through his mediatory position: his thinking is called *ankulomeitas* ("crooked of counsel," "wily"); he is the one who "snares himself in his own trickery" (Kerényi, 1963). While trying to challenge Zeus for sovereignty through sacrificial partition, he establishes one of the main features of civilized life—namely, those sacrifices that while opening a channel of communication to the divine world fix forever the separation of the human and the divine spheres: humans have to eat cooked meat, whereas the gods sustain themselves on the mere vapors of burned bones and fat. While Prometheus wants to benefit humankind by introducing fire, an element indispensable for sacrifices and civilization, he also brings about mortality for humankind, for Pandora is the gods' poisoned countergift to humans for a gift to the gods—sacrifice—that hid its true nature—bones—under an appealing exterior. Since receiving this countergift from the gods, humankind has had to labor in the fields for sustenance, plant seeds in the earth and in womankind, and tend the fire to perform such tasks as smithery, pottery, cooking, and sacrifice (Detienne and Vernant, 1989, pp. 21–86).

PROMETHEUS AS TRICKSTER. When combining the philological analysis of Kerényi, which stresses the craftiness of the Titanic culture hero, with the structural reading of Detienne and Vernant—who rely on the logic of sacrificial practices as seen through the theoretical combination with the logic of gift-exchanges as proposed by Marcel Mauss (1872–1950)—Prometheus becomes the archetype of the ambivalent and ambiguous trickster-god, who through the themes of theft and deception is structurally equivalent to such figures as Loki in Germanic mythology. In this respect Prometheus is also akin to figures such as Athena, Hermes, and Hephaistos, deities of crafts and craftiness. He removes humankind from the state of innocence as well as from barbarism (the eating of raw meat) by introducing knowledge and crafts, but he brings mortality as well.

While this structuralist reading of the myth follows closely the text of Hesiod and generally seems to fit the sacrificial practices of Greek city-states, it does not solve entirely all interpretative problems of the sacrificial logic in Greek ritual practices. A concentration on Homer instead of the reliance on Hesiod brings about a quite different theoretical conclusion about the message of the story, as Walter Burkert shows in his stressing of those aspects which have to do with the act of killing (1987, p. 3). Besides, the apportioning of bones and meat seems to have been a variable ritual practice in different Greek regions and furthermore dependent upon the purpose of the specific sacrifice (Henrichs, 1997, pp. 42–44, on specific local practices, and Bremmer, 1997, pp. 29–31, on the scarcity of Greek sources regarding the notion and practices of ritual performances).

THE BRINGER OF FIRE. In Athenian perception at least the ritual activities connected with the figure of Prometheus are elusive and scarce. Prometheus seems predominantly to have been honored as the bringer of fire. Thus, a torch procession or run took place at a still-unknown date during the so-called Promethia which proceeded from an altar in the Academy via the Kerameikos to an unknown destination. Literary fragments refer to Prometheus in the main as the protector of pottery and smithing crafts, thus putting him close to Hephaistos and Athena.

In contrast to the scarcity of references to ritual practices, the allegorical allusions to Prometheus as bringer of fire (as important ingredient of major crafts) connect him in most literary sources, from Plato to Publius Ovidius Naso and Apollodor, to the fashioning of the first human figures from earth and water. Yet, from Hesiod to Apollodor the emphasis of the creation of the first couple shows the gods as stringent, withholding knowledge or wisdom ("craftiness") from humanity, allowing them just to exist like other created animals. This pure "animality" of life leaves humankind as deficient, except if they would gain knowledge for developing those crafts which make civilized life possible and to attain the basis of that, foreknowledge or cognitive faculties for strategic planning in the first instance. It is here that the role of Prometheus as bringer of fire becomes as pronounced as the structuralist analysis tries to show. Most ancient philosophical and literary sources refer to the stealing of fire as allegorically connected to the gaining of "a fire within," either as cognitive faculty or as life-inducing force (the soul as animating force). In this respect, the stressing of Prometheus as the bringer of civilizational skills accords well with that generalized structuralist position elaborated by Claude Lévi-Strauss in all major publications that myths—in particular creation myths—problematize everywhere: the opposition between nature and culture, pure life and civilizational achievements.

Thus the variations on the story as told by Hesiod seem all to point in the direction of a Greek (and later also Roman) perception of the ambiguities arising from the discrepancies between humankind's animality and reliance on means to surpass its deficiencies. These means are the crafty application of culture as extensions of a faculty of the mind, connected with the fire which Prometheus has to steal from the gods. Humans are then seen in the same hybrid condition, sharing traces of both categorizing domains of reality and imagination, the divine and the animal kingdom, much as their benefactor, the Titanic culture hero Prometheus is neither completely divine nor completely human.

LEGACY. At least since the Aeschylean tragedy, the image of the rebellious nature of the culture hero as allegory to self-created humanity through their invention of civilizational skills or crafts has permeated European literary consciousness. The figure of Prometheus is punished through being bound to the Kaukasos mountains and tormented by an eagle that eats daily at his liver, yet he is unable to die—after all, he is immortal. His character becomes a challenger of arbitrary and authoritarian divine rule as well as mediating benefactor of humanity, combined into the image of a culture hero who even in suffering does not renounce his deeds, but riles at the ruling gods and predicts their demise. Besides the use of the difference between planning foresight and rash unthinking action as human traits (Prometheus versus Epimetheus) which pervades the writings from Plato to the neo-Platonists like Marsilio Ficino (1433–1499), the notions of the rebelliousness combined with the power of self-fashioning (the pottery image of the creation of humankind from clay through Prometheus) appeal in particular to the age of the classics and of Romanticism, from Goethe to Hölderlin and Nietzsche.

Greek vase paintings as well as sculptures are not clear about the position of the Promethean figure: he is often either juxtaposed with Atlas (the Titan holding up the earth at the Western end of the ancient mythical geography) or shown with Herakles, who finally releases him from his sufferings by killing the eagle; Herakles is himself a distant descendant of Io, whose punishment by Hera for her illicit union with Zeus is likened by Aeschylus to the fate of Prometheus, as Io is eternally tormented by a hornet and driven to madness. The notion of Prometheus as indirect bringer of the evil of mortality may make sense of interpretations which identify his figure in the circle of deities of the underworld in the combination of Dionysos and the earth goddess Demeter, as Aeschylus hints at the descent of Prometheus from Gaia-Themis.

SEE ALSO Culture Heroes; Fire; Gods and Goddesses; Hesiod; Tricksters, overview article; Zeus.

BIBLIOGRAPHY

Bianchi, Ugo. "Prometheus, der titanische Trickster." *Paideuma* 7–8 (1961): 414–437. Reprinted in *Selected Essays on Gnosticism, Dualism and Mysteriosophy.* Leiden, 1978.

Brelich, Angelo. "La corona di Prometheus." In *Hommages à Marie Delcourt,* pp. 234–242. Brussels, 1970.

Bremmer, Jan N. "Religion, Ritual, and the Opposition of Sacred vs. Profane." In *Ansichten Griechischer Rituale,* edited by Fritz Graf, pp. 9–32. Stuttgart, 1998.

Burkert, Walter. *Homo Necans: The Anthropology of Ancient Greek Sacrificial Ritual and Myth.* Berkeley, 1983.

Detienne, Marcel, and Jean-Pierre Vernant, eds. *The Cuisine of Sacrifice among the Greeks.* Chicago, 1989. A collection of superb contributions, all from a strongly structuralist perspective, to Greek sacrificial notions through analysis of myths and pictorial representations, with emphasis on the equivalence of sacrificial and culinary practices.

Duchemin, Jacqueline. *Prométhée: Histoire du mythe, de ses origins orientales à ses incarnations modernes.* Paris, 1974.

Dumézil, Georges. *Loki.* Paris, 1948. An extension of the Indo-European parallels with concentration on one divinity of the Germanic pantheon. Dumézil stresses the impulsive intelligence of the trickster figure through comparison with Syrdon of the Ossetes and thus indirectly with Prometheus.

Henrichs, Albert. "Dromena and Legomena." In *Ansichten griechischer Rituale,* edited by Fritz Graf, pp. 33–71. Stuttgart, 1998.

Kerényi, Károly. "The Trickster in Relation to Greek Mythology." In *The Trickster,* by Paul Radin, with commentaries by Károly Kerényi and C. G. Jung, pp. 173–191. New York, 1956. Kerényi's most incisive treatment of Prometheus, supported by a comparison to tribal myths from North America. It stresses the trickster-like qualities of the mediator and the crooked thinking of the Titans.

Kerényi, Károly. *Prometheus: Archtypal Image of Human Existence.* New York, 1963.

Köpping, Klaus-Peter. "Absurdity and Hidden Truth: Cunning Intelligence and Grotesque Body Images as Manifestations of the Trickster." *History of Religions* 24 (February 1985): 191–214. A treatment of Prometheus from a comparative perspective, emphasizing the theme of the trickster as deceived deceiver. Prometheus is shown to be one instance of the ambiguity and ambivalence of the mediator as culture hero, a theme that continues in the European literary tradition, as seen in the dialectic between the wisdom and folly of the picaro, or rogue.

Pisi, Paola. *Prometeo nel culto attico.* Rome, 1990.

Séchan, Louis. *Le mythe de Prométhée.* Paris, 1951.

Turcan, Robert. "Note sur les sarcophages au Prométhée." *Latomus* 27 (1968): 630–634.

Vernant, Jean-Pierre. *Myth and Society in Ancient Greece.* Atlantic Highlands, N. J., 1980. See the chapter titled "The Myth of Prometheus in Hesiod." An exemplary and controversial analysis of Hesiod's account through philological and semantic investigation, leading to a demonstration of the structural logic of the myth, with no hint of the trickster qualities.

KLAUS-PETER KÖPPING (1987 AND 2005)

PROOFS FOR THE EXISTENCE OF GOD.

Early generations of Christian thinkers accepted God's existence as a given that needed no proof and was surmised on the basis of immediate evidence in an act that did not clearly distinguish faith from reason. The dominant exponent of this approach was Augustine (d. 430), who posited, for instance, an awareness of God as "first truth" in the intuition of truth as such that occurs in the depths of human consciousness. Bonaventure (d. 1274) was a legitimate heir of Augustine in the medieval period, as was Blaise Pascal (d. 1662) in the modern era. Nicolas Malebranche (d. 1715), by contrast, promoted an ontologism, in which "God" is made the first innate idea implanted in the human mind, of which all other ideas are modifications.

THE ONTOLOGICAL ARGUMENT. Those who have sought God's existence by deploying the processes of reasoning have done so in one of two ways: either *a priori* or *a posteriori.* The first approach derives God's existence from an idea of him in the consciousness of the knower. The original formulation of this argument is that of Anselm of Canterbury (d. 1109); it describes God as "that than which a greater cannot be conceived." Such a notion demands, for Anselm, God's real existence (*Proslogion* 2), and indeed entails it as something necessary (*Proslogion* 3). Various versions of this argument appear in the works of René Descartes (d. 1650), who argues that God cannot be conceived as nonexisting (*Third Meditation*), and Gottfried Wilhelm Leibniz (d. 1716), who, echoing John Duns Scotus (d. 1308), declares that if God is possible, he exists (*New Essays concerning Human Understanding* 4.10). Among the contemporary defenders of the ontological argument are Norman Malcolm, Alvin Plantinga, and Charles Hartshorne. Its two most trenchant critics are Thomas Aquinas (d. 1274), who views it as making an unfounded move from the ideal to the real order (*Summa theologiae* 1.2.1–2), taking Anselm's idea of God to include the concept of real existence but not the actual exercise thereof; and Immanuel Kant (d. 1804), who insists that existence is not a predicate included in any concept and so can only be encountered empirically ("Of the Impossibility of a Cosmological Proof of the Existence of God," *Critique of Pure Reason* A592/B620 ff.).

THE COSMOLOGICAL AND TELEOLOGICAL ARGUMENTS. An alternative position repudiates any a priori approach on the ground that nothing antecedes or explains God's beingness. Finite entities of the world, however, are not the explanation of their own reality but rather are the effects of a transcendent creative cause. This explains a posteriori the mere existence at least of a primal cause, which Christians have identified materially with God. In the language of Thomas Aquinas, arguments of this kind are not designated "proofs," but five "approaches" or "ways" (*viae*) to God that function as "prerequisites to faith" (*praeambula fidei*) in the God of revelation. The starting points of all such arguments are facts readily observable in the world of ordinary experience: motion, causality, contingency of existence, grades of ontological perfection, and intrinsic finality. The nerve of the thought process is causality: efficient, exemplary, and final. An infinite regress in any series of such causes is deemed unintelligible as long as the ordering is an essential and not merely an accidental one. The rational intelligence is thus led to postulate the existence of God as primal or ultimate cause—not as the first member of the series but as the analogical cause of the series as such. The lineaments of such a procedure were not original with Christian thinkers but were already to be found in Plato, Aristotle, Ibn Sīnā (Avicenna), Ibn Rushd (Averroës), and Moses Maimonides. Significantly, Thomas himself never refers to these movements of thought as establishing God's existence, only as justifying the judgment that "God is"; all that is claimed, then, is the legitimacy of using the copula "is" of God in a transsubjective sense.

THE MORAL ARGUMENT. This conviction within Christian thought, of an intrinsic intelligibility at the heart of reality bespeaking a transcendent ground to the real order, reached its clearest expression in the thirteenth century but began to erode into skepticism with the rise of nominalist theology in the fourteenth century, especially with William of Ockham (d. 1349). Immanuel Kant, in the late eighteenth century, insisted in his *Critique of Pure Reason* that human understanding has no access whatsoever to any possible realm of meaning beyond the phenomenal, which is given immediately to consciousness and structured further by categories innate to the subjectivity of the knower. God is thus, for Kant, a regulative idea formed by the mind to legitimate the ethical order. Thus, ethics becomes the grounding principle for postulating God's existence, rather than vice versa, as had been the case in the past. Moral imperatives mean, simply, postulating one who imperates; any question of a real referent to that concept outside consciousness lies beyond the competency of human reason.

JUDAISM AND ISLAM. Jewish thought eschews all efforts to prove God's existence, seeing this as established beyond dispute in the prophets, whose concern is God's moral governance. Philo Judaeus (d. circa 50 CE), however, under the stimulus of Greek and Arabic thought during the Hellenistic period, integrated rational reflection on the world with what the scriptures teach. Maimonides (d. 1204), in the medieval period, advanced two forms of the cosmological argument: one from motion and one from the contingency of existence. Among moderns, Moses Mendelssohn (d. 1786) stresses the role of reason in those areas in which revelation appears unnecessary, while Franz Rosenzweig (d. 1929) argues that the existential encounter dispenses with rational inquiry and itself constitutes revelation. This position accords with Martin Buber's (d. 1965) way to God as the eternal Thou in humanity's dialogue with every finite thou.

Islamic thought did not employ reason on things divine that were taught in the Qurʾān until medieval times, when Ibn Sīnā (d. 1037), distinguishing essence from existence, argued for God as the necessary existent. Ibn Rushd (d. 1198), integrating Islamic tradition with his understanding of Aristotle, maintained that the metaphysician can demonstrate the revealed truth about God available to believers in metaphorical language. Ibn Rushd's influence, in the form of Latin Averroism, extended to the University of Paris in the thirteenth century and to the universities of Bologna and Padua until the mid-seventeenth century.

MODERN ATHEISM. G. W. F. Hegel (d. 1831) returned to the ontological argument; he maintained that finite consciousness was a "moment" in the self-enactment of Absolute Spirit, which thus assumed prerogatives formerly ascribed to divinity. Ludwig Feuerbach (d. 1872) explicitly launched atheism against Christian thought by inverting Hegel's thinking and reducing all references to the infinite to mere projections of finite spirit confronted with its own seemingly inexhaustible resources and aspirations. This tendency soon manifested itself as psychological atheism with Sigmund Freud (d. 1939), as socioeconomic atheism with Karl Marx (d. 1883), as ethical atheism with Jean-Paul Sartre (d. 1980) and Albert Camus (d. 1960), and as anthropological atheism with Maurice Merleau-Ponty (d. 1961), thereby pervading much of modern Western thought.

THE POST-ATHEISTIC AGE. Reactions against this denial of any accessible signs of God's existence began with Friedrich Schleiermacher (d. 1834), who postulated, below the level of either reason or will, a feeling *(Gefühl)* or immediate awareness of the utter dependence of consciousness upon the sustaining reality of the transcendent whole, amounting to a God-consciousness within humankind. Roman Catholic thought, for its part, in the constitution *Dei filius* approved by the First Vatican Council in 1870, repudiated a "traditionalism" on the one hand and a "semirationalism" (in which, after a revelation from God, reason is able on its own to understand the pure mysteries of God that form the content of such revelation) on the other, opting instead for the possibility of a natural knowledge of at least God's existence. Paul Tillich (d. 1965) set a new tone in analyzing existential encounter, as opposed to metaphysical reflection; what he called disclosure experiences enable humankind to posit questions of ultimacy that are then answered in correlation to the revelatory act of a self-manifesting God. Wolfhart Pannenberg has recently argued, in reaction to Karl Barth's neoorthodoxy, which makes all acknowledgment of the true God a matter of religious faith, that history in its universality, open to human reason, offers hypothetical grounds for the reality of God. The available "proofs," then, are simply anthropological ways of formulating the question with precision and urgency—the question that humanity itself is. Because history has not yet run its course, all answers are provisional in kind, based upon anticipating the consummation of history in the resurrection of Christ.

Karl Rahner (d. 1984) and Bernard Lonergan (d. 1984) have attempted a rehabilitation of Thomas Aquinas's five "ways," viewing them as reflective and logical formulations of a prereflective, unthematic dynamism of finite spirit. This transcendental structure of human consciousness, which actualizes itself in the historical and categorical order, is described by Rahner as a pregrasp *(Vorgriff)* of God himself under the formality of holy mystery. In a radically different vein, Alfred North Whitehead (d. 1947), originating a movement loosely called process thought, views God as a coprinciple with the world in a universe ultimately not of being but of creative becoming. This argument for the existence of God arises from the need to explain novelty in a self-creative universe without making God an exception to, rather than the prime instantiation of, the metaphysical schema. Here God "lures" the world forward, even as it in turn supplies data for God's own creative advance into novelty (*Process and Reality,* 1929, 5.2).

PRESENT STATUS OF THE PROOFS. Much of modern thought, especially that indebted to analytic philosophy, tends to dismiss all talk about proofs for God's existence as meaningless, because no verifiable content can be given to the very idea of God. De facto, neither theism nor atheism is considered to be either demonstrable or refutable by reason. The affirmation of God is taken to be a matter of faith (religious or otherwise) rather than of reason—but one which, once made, may manifest itself as entirely reasonable.

SEE ALSO Atheism; Attributes of God; Doubt and Belief; Enlightenment, The; God; Nominalism; Philosophy, article on Philosophy of Religion; Scholasticism.

BIBLIOGRAPHY

Cobb, John B., Jr. *A Christian Natural Theology.* Philadelphia, 1965. Chapters 4 and 5 contain an exposition of the argument from Alfred North Whitehead by one committed to its validity.

Dupré, Louis. *A Dubious Heritage.* New York, 1977. Incisive studies of the ontological, cosmological, and teleological arguments in the light of post-Kantian thought.

Gardet, Louis, and M. M. Anawati. *Introduction à la théologie musulmane.* Paris, 1948. A basic survey from a Christian perspective.

Goichon, Amélie-Marie. *La philosophie d'Avicenne et son influence en Europe mediévale.* Paris, 1944.

Guttmann, Julius. *Philosophies of Judaism: The History of Jewish Philosophy from Biblical Times to Franz Rosenzweig.* New York, 1964.

Hick, John, ed. *The Existence of God.* New York, 1964. Critical appraisals including the moral and religious arguments in light of present discussions.

Kenny, Anthony. *The Five Ways.* New York, 1969. A rejection, scholarly and moderate in tone, of each of the "five ways" as based ultimately on an outmoded cosmology.

Küng, Hans. *Does God Exist?* Garden City, N.Y., 1980. Contemporary argument against atheism and nihilism based on experiencing the trustworthiness of human existence.

Mackie, J. L. *The Miracle of Theism: Arguments for and against the Existence of God.* Oxford, 1982. Largely rejections of the traditional and contemporary arguments, with emphasis on the negating power of evil in the world.

Maritain, Jacques. *Approaches to God.* New York, 1954. Detailed defense of the "five ways" of Thomas Aquinas, plus a prephilosophic approach and one based on the dynamism of the intellect.

Mascall, E. L. *The Openness of Being: Natural Theology Today.* London, 1971. A survey of arguments including those of transcendental Thomism, of process thought, and of empiricism; basically a defense of a metaphysical approach to the question of God against Anglo-Saxon positivism.

Plantinga, Alvin, ed. *The Ontological Argument, from St. Anselm in Contemporary Philosophers* (1940). New York, 1965. An expository and critical exploration of the argument in its varied forms; does not include Plantinga's own ingenious formulation of the argument he presents later in chapter 10 of *The Nature of Necessity* (Oxford, 1974).

Smith, John E. *Experience and God.* New York, 1968. Critical assessments of the ontological, cosmological, and teleological arguments from a pragmatist's point of view. See especially chapter 5.

WILLIAM J. HILL (1987)

PROPHECY

This entry consists of the following articles:

PROPHECY: AN OVERVIEW

The term *prophecy* refers to a wide range of religious phenomena that have been manifested from ancient to modern times. The Greek term *prophētēs* is the etymological ancestor of the English word *prophet,* and it has cognates in most European languages. The indigenous Greek *prophētēs* was a cultic functionary who "spoke for" a god; that is, the *prophētēs* delivered divine messages in association with a sanctuary where the god had made its presence known. However, the word *prophētēs* influenced European languages primarily because early Jewish and Christian writers used the term in translations of the Hebrew Bible and in the New Testament to refer to religious specialists in Israelite, Jewish, and Christian traditions. Today comparativists use *prophecy* to describe religious phenomena in various contexts on analogy with the activity of ancient Hebrew prophets and other figures who had a similarly pivotal role in founding world religions in Southwest Asia.

ANCIENT PROPHECY. In antiquity it was commonly believed that gods controlled events in the world and made their intentions known to human beings in various ways. The earliest written records tell of religious functionaries whose responsibility it was to interpret signs or deliver messages from the gods in order to supply information useful in the conduct of human affairs. In early tribal societies the clan leader often carried out these duties, or perhaps some other individual who used a variety of divinatory and visionary techniques to gain access to special knowledge about divine intentions. These activities usually included intercessory functions, whereby the leader or "prophet" petitioned spirits or a god or gods for special favors for their group.

However, this picture of such figures (such as the *kāhin* of pre-Muslim Arabia or the *kohen* of patriarchal, presettlement Israel) is only inferential. They were active in nonliterate societies that left no linguistic records of themselves except by the transmission of oral traditions that eventually were written down by later, literate generations. The groups that did leave written records had more complex forms of religious and political organization, suggesting that adepts in religious knowledge had correspondingly more specialized functions.

From the records of ancient cultures in Mesopotamia and the Mediterranean region there is knowledge of a large number of religious specialists who sought out and interpreted messages from the gods. Their access to the world of the gods came through two different means. In the first place, there were diviners who practiced a variety of studied techniques to interpret symbolic messages in the natural world. Some techniques were manipulative (such as the casting of lots, the incubation of dreams, and the examination of the entrails of sacrificial animals); others were more purely observational (such as the interpretation of animal movement and the cataloguing of auspicious, often horrible, events). Second, the gods were also believed to communicate their will through oracles, that is, in human language through the mouth of an inspired person. The behavior of these divine spokesmen is often thought to have been ecstatic, frenzied, or abnormal in some way, which reflected their possession by the deity (and the absence of personal ego) at the time of transmission. Some groups used divination to test the accuracy of oral prophecies (e.g., prophecies at Mari), while others gave priority to oral prophecy, with only marginal appeal to divination (e.g., in Israelite religion).

Within general categories the nature and function of divine intermediation was diverse. Oracles and signs could appear without request; but more commonly, especially in the Greco-Roman world, cultic officials provided answers to specific questions asked to the sanctuary's god. Ecstatic oracular behavior seems to have been the most common form of intermediation among figures not connected with recognized sanctuaries (e.g., the Akkadian *muhhu*), but it was also acceptable among those who did have such official legitimacy (e.g., the Akkadian *apilu* and various Greek mantic figures). The terminology applied to intermediaries is often ambiguous or vague, as with the Greek term *prophētēs,* which at times denotes the oracular mouthpiece for divine speech and at others refers to the official interpreter of divinatory signs within a sanctuary. The diversity is immense. But it is clear from the complexity that the need for knowledge about divine activity was perceived at various social levels; ancient societies often maintained a large and varied staff of religious functionaries to keep such knowledge alive.

PROPHETIC FOUNDERS OF RELIGIOUS TRADITION. Throughout ancient Israel's history as an independent state (c. 1000–586 BCE), the religious orientation of a large segment of its population was polytheistic, and as such, it shared in the general worldview of its neighbors. But even in the monotheistic elements of Israelite culture, there were different functionaries who transmitted the will of the same god, Yahveh, to the people. During the earliest part of this history, it appears that the Yahvists relied on at least three different figures for divine communication: (1) cultic officers who performed certain techniques (like casting lots), maintained cultic implements (like the Ark), and occupied sacred space; (2) seers (Heb., *ro'eh* and *ḥozeh*), whose function is rather unclear, but may be designations from different periods of visionaries and diviners (cf. *1 Samuel* 9:9); and (3) ecstatics (Heb., *navi',* commonly translated as "prophet"), whose unusual behavior was stimulated when Yahveh's spirit came upon them. As Yahvism evolved, the *navi'* came to be its predominant intermediary, though as this occurred the activity of the *navi'* came to include functions that were previously within the province of the other two specialists. Accordingly, the *nevi'im* depended less exclusively on ecstatic oracles for their identity, and many came to be (in some cases) cultic functionaries and inspired interpreters of ancient tradition. The evidence indicates, however, that prophetic legitimacy depended primarily on their acceptance within a given group as oracular vehicles for the communication of Yahveh's word, regardless of whether the *navi'* was an ecstatic, a cultic official, an independent critic, or some combination of these roles.

By at least the eighth century BCE the Hebrew prophets or their scribes commonly wrote down their oracles, and the prophetic writings of the Hebrew Bible (Old Testament) contain, in part, a modest literary residue of this extensive oracular activity. Historians have reached no consensus about why this development took place, nor about how these writings in particular came to be accepted among later generations as eternally authoritative. Yet, that oracular revelation came to be regarded as having an enduring value, and that followers of prophets could disseminate their written oracles among various groups with whom the prophets originally had no connection, was a major change in the history of religions. Within the religious worldview that permeated the time of the first Hebrew prophets, messages from the gods were seen as portentous for only the particular audience, time, and place attendant to the moment when they had been revealed on earth. Thus, it was necessary to maintain a retinue of religious specialists to prophesy anew and interpret messages that regularly came from the gods. As certain specified written oracles came to be accepted in Israel as the repository of normative divine instruction, the nature of prophecy itself began to change, as did the character of religious tradition.

What happened among the Hebrew prophets occurred more generally within several religious traditions in Southwest Asia. The following figures can be classed with the Hebrew prophets as intermediaries whose oracles became, at least in part, the revelational basis of a major world religion. Zarathushtra (Zoroaster), a Persian prophet of the late second millennium BCE, was the founder of Zoroastrianism (Boyce, 1975). Jesus appears in many respects as a prophet, even though Christianity has traditionally portrayed him as a unique messiah. Mani, a Babylonian born in 216 CE, founded Manichaeism, which gained a large following in countries from India to the western Mediterranean. Finally, Muḥammad, like no other, established a believing community around himself as divine messenger, and succeeding generations of Muslims have accepted the oracles written down in the Qurʾān as the unparalleled expression of divine communication.

Defining precisely what these individual prophets share in common is not a simple matter. The social location of their activity differs in each case, and the success of each prophet in gaining a following during his lifetime varied widely, from Muhammad, who led armies and established a moderate-sized empire by the time of his death, to Jesus, who died an ignominious death on a cross. Moreover the message of each prophet, if examined in detail, depends more on the particular traditions to which it was heir and the historical-cultural setting of the prophet's activity than upon a transcendent ideal that applies to every member of the group. Nonetheless, five features are common to all.

1. *They all conceived of their activity as the result of a personal divine commission.* They thought that their supreme deity had appointed them individually to bear a specific revealed message to the human (or some more narrowly defined) community, and this message usually consisted of oracular speech and writing. Even Jesus, who frequently did not use traditional forms of prophetic speech, seems to have regarded his words and actions as communicating the message he was commissioned to bear.

2. *Religious traditions arose that regarded some oracles of these prophets as uniquely heaven-sent, sacred, and binding upon people in perpetuity.* In such cases, the prophets' words became part (or the substance) of a scriptural canon that was regarded as the repository of revealed knowledge; each sacred canon became, in turn, the standard by which the tradition judged all later religious pronouncements and activity. For prophets whose speech or writing was formally oracular (e.g. the Hebrew prophets and Muḥammad), the scripture became, at least in part, a collection of those oracles. Stories about the symbolic activities and miraculous deeds performed by these prophets also found their way into the canons (note particularly the Gospels and the prophetic narratives in the Hebrew Bible), and the members of each tradition regarded this material as having paradigmatic importance.

Whether these prophets were themselves the founders of traditions is not a question to be answered easily. Both Muḥammad and Mani organized the early Muslim and Manichaean communities, respectively, and they promoted their own writings as perpetually relevant revelation. But in the other three cases (Zoroastrianism, Judaism, and Christianity), the historical prophets had little or no influence on the organization of the later religious tradition, and others determined the content and organization of the sacred scripture. In fact, the authors and compilers of the Hebrew Bible shaped the words and actions of Moses to such a degree that his biblical portrait probably has little in common with the historical person. Nonetheless, because these prophets all had an important role in founding religious tradition, and especially because later generations revered them as the fountainheads of divine revelation, this group shall be called the "founding prophets."

3. Though the content of their messages differs significantly from one prophet to the next, depending on historical circumstance and inherited tradition, *all of the founding prophets proclaimed what their later tradition regarded as universal truths.* The theological development of these prophetic, revealed religions tended toward conceptions of a deity or deities (Zoroastrianism and Manichaeism) that transcended tribal, geographical, national, and cultic boundaries. While it would be too ambitious to attribute to these prophetic figures alone the creation of universal religious claims, the writings of such prophets as Amos, so-called Second Isaiah, and Muhammad are among the most radical innovations in the history of religious thought.

4. *The founding prophets were, in their own individual ways, social critics,* even though their ideas about society were quite different from one another. Muhammad, for example, seems to have been a great deal more concerned with the structures of society on this earth than Mani, who addressed social issues primarily in order to help promote gnosis (the salvific knowledge of ultimate things). Still, all of them considered moral behavior to be central in complying with the wishes of their supreme deity. Particularly in the Judeo-Christian and Muslim traditions, prophetic teachings have been seen as attempts to denounce injustices practiced against the weak and powerless. In the prophetic writings of these traditions questions of social morality have such prominence that scholars have often characterized the religion of the prophets as "ethical monotheism."

5. Finally, *the founding prophets helped both to maintain and to reform religious tradition.* They regarded their demands for change as having a basis in ancient tradition, but they insisted that their contemporary religious situation be reshaped in accordance with that tradition. Naturally, these demands met stiff resistance from those contemporaries of the prophets who wanted to maintain other traditions or the status quo. As a result each of the founding prophets suffered indignities, sometimes even torture and death. Typically, prophets who met with resistance saw popular rejection as proof of their legitimacy, since earlier prophets had been similarly despised.

Just as these prophets constitute a group because of their mutual similarites, they are also distinct from other figures in the history of religions. They are different from the various intermediaries who preceded them in that the revelation they communicated has an enduring relevance in religious tradition and remained intimately connected with their individual personalities. Revelation had previously been relevant only for a limited time, and, with a few minor exceptions, the personality of the prophet had been of relatively little significance in the mediation of divine messages. The roles of these prophets often stood in sharp contrast with priestly functions. The innovative and reforming messages of the prophets were accepted within the religious community and tradition on the basis of their personal charisma. Priests, however, are typically those who maintained the dominant, received tradition by virtue of their position within an established religious institution.

Finally, the founding prophets are distinct from others who founded major religious traditions (such as Buddhism, Jainism, Confucianism, and Taoism). The founders of these traditions originating in India and China were not divinely chosen messengers bearing a revealed message to humankind, but rather teachers and sages who had developed new philosophic insight and practical discipline as a way of addressing religious problems. These teachers, like the prophets, were often missionaries and social critics, but the basis of their words was the perfection of their own intellectual, spiritual, and moral talents, rather than their election by a deity to bear a specific message.

PROPHECY UNDER THE INFLUENCE OF CANON. One of the most outstanding features of the founding prophets was the special importance that their personal communication of revelation had for succeeding generations of their religious communities. Just as the Hebrew prophets and Zarathushtra were influenced by the traditions that preceded them, so too were the prophets who came later. But for Jesus, Mani, and Muhammad the traditional inheritance included the message of the Hebrew prophets (and Zarathushtra), as well as the model they had established as prophets whose messages were canonized within scripture.

It was rarely easy for a person bearing revelation to effect basic reforms in the structure of religious life. Among the biblical prophets themselves, the active mediation of fresh revelation had been an accepted part of religious life. However, once prophecy became written and canonical, the revelation of these same prophets attained a special status that inevitably lessened the importance and limited the scope of active mediation generally. The guardianship and transmission of prophecy—now newly conceived as the substance of prophetic oracles within the canon—moved from the ecstatics and visionaries who originally created it to the inspired sages, priests, and scribes who maintained and passed along the scriptures.

The evolution of Hebrew prophecy into received written tradition became the cornerstone upon which all subsequent prophetic constructions were built. By 350 BCE the last of the canonical prophetic writings to find acceptance in the Hebrew Bible had been written. And by the time of Jesus' ministry (c. 25–30 CE) the preeminence of these canonical prophets was generally accepted within Judaism, even among prophets such as Jesus. Within the context of this religious tradition it became necessary for contemporary prophets who did not consider their calling subordinate to any earlier prophet to claim a special status for themselves. Therefore, Jesus on occasion appears as an eschatological prophet who proclaimed the imminent arrival of the "kingdom of God." In this way his message and character could fit the traditional conception of prophets in early Judaism, where it was believed—in certain quarters, at least—that God would send prophets (who would be of equal stature with their canonical predecesors) to announce the end of the world.

By the time of Mani (216–276) and Muḥammad (580–632), several canonical religions had come to prominence. Both these prophets understood themselves explicitly as successors to a line of prophets that included (though variously) Abraham, Moses, Elijah, other Hebrew prophets, Zarathushtra, Jesus, and even the Buddha. Moreover, they each wrote down their oracles as a self-conscious attempt to form a canon that would be authoritative for their own communities. Indeed, early Muslims distinguished between two terms for prophet: *nabi,* a generic Arabic term denoting anyone who has a vision or audition of God, and *rasū,* the Arabic word referring only to those special "messengers" (such as Moses, Jesus, and Muḥammad) who founded a religious community and transmitted their messages with a sacred book. In Islam "religions of the Book" are the highest form of religious expression.

As the words of these historical prophets attained reverential status within scriptural canons, the book replaced the living religious specialist as the primary agent of revelational mediation. The history of surviving religious traditions with a prophetic scripture (now Judaism, Christianity, and Islam) has depended in no small measure upon this development. Exegetes of various sorts replaced prophets as the maintainers of the revelational tradition, and often those who safeguarded the sanctity and purity of the written scriptures were suspicious of, even hostile to, those who claimed to have visions not mediated through the scripture. Since textual interpretation has gained the dominant socio-political position within all three traditions (probably because this mode of religious inquiry responded better to the increasingly complex social organization within which the traditions flourished), the ecstatic elements common to the earliest prophetic activity played a diminished role in later tradition. Since Muḥammad there has been no prophet to form a religious tradition with a stature equaling that of Judaism, Christianity, or Islam.

Even so, while contemporary prophetic inspiration lost influence at the center of religious authority, it was never eliminated entirely. Throughout history, in pre-Christian Judaism, in early Christianity, and in pre-Muslim and early-Muslim Arabia, prophetic figures were active alongside (though often in competition with) the rationalized institutions of canonical religion. Within the exegetical tradition itself inspirational interpretation has been a perennial source of innovation in theological thinking. In early Judaism, some of those who collected and arranged sacred writings within the Hebrew Bible conceived themselves to be prophets, for example, the levitical priests Korah and Asaph, who claimed prophetic inspiration for their hymnology and arranged the psalter in a structure that gives special prominence to a prophetic interpretation of psalms. And later, during the medieval period, qabbalist interpretation of the Bible elevated not only the revelational experiences of the biblical authors, but also the necessity for inspiration among exegetes. Similar attitudes are present among Christian (e.g., Jerome and Bonaventura) and Muslim (e.g., al-Ḥallāj) interpreters.

More generally one can speak of mysticism within Judaism, Christianity, and Islam as being analogous with prophecy in earlier tradition. Insofar as mystics define religious knowledge as the immediate (i.e., unmediated) perception of the divine, the nature of their experience and epistemology is similar to earlier prophets. However, their activity is to be distinguished sharply from earlier prophecy, since the canonical traditions had no recognized need for specialists in mediating divine revelation. Each tradition accommodated spontaneous outbreaks of inspirational, ecstatic, visionary behavior, but each also maintained strict controls, lest the ultimate authority of canonical revelation be undercut.

Sufism (Muslim mysticism) first appeared within one hundred years of Muhammad's death. While some Ṣūfīs who quietly made claim to personal revelation or mystical vision could coexist peaceably with those nearer the center of religious power, others met violent repression when they threatened the structure and cohesion of the Muslim community. So, while Abū Yazīd al-Bisṭāmī, a Persian Ṣūfī (d. 875), encountered some opposition for his claims of achieving unity with God, it amounted to his being labeled an eccentric. He died peaceably, and afterward his tomb became the object of some veneration. However, al-Ḥallāj was executed (in 922) when he translated his visions and miracles into a political following that threatened the dominant order.

Within European Christianity (from the time of Constantine, at least, until well into the modern period) the orthodox were closely connected with the ruling political groups. Christian mystics, like their Muslim counterparts, were accepted by the orthodox as long as their revelational claims were subordinated to the authority of the church and Bible (e.g., Francis of Assisi and Teresa of Ávila). Yet, wherever claims of fresh revelation threatened the ecclesiastical and political power structure, the authorities responded—and violently, as with Joan of Arc, whom the English burned for heresy when she transformed her revelational claims into a potent military force. It is easy to understand why few Christians claimed to be prophets, and why, at the same time, accusations of false prophecy were leveled at those whose voices one wanted to silence.

Since fairly early in the common era, Jews have been outside the dominant power structure in cultures where they lived. Only if the prophetic claims of a messianic hopeful threatened the dominant social order of the host society was there any likelihood of political repression. Such was the case with Shabbetai Tsevi (1626–1676), whose messianic movement was perceived as a threat by his Turkish (Muslim) overlords. Tsevi recanted under threat of death. Otherwise, tensions between the more rationalist orthodoxy and mystical visionaries was something to be settled among Jews. Since Jewish orthodoxy had no power greater than rational persuasion, its ability to control mystical elements was minimal. Hence the Besht (Yisraʾel ben Eliʿezer, 1700–1760) was able to generate a massive following despite the detraction of his orthodox opponents.

In no case, however, could visionaries or mystics claim for themselves a mediational status equal with the founding prophets without subverting revealed canons and the traditions that rested upon them. Those who made such claims founded new traditions (i.e., Jesus, Mani, and Muḥammad) or failed in the attempt. Otherwise prophetic and mystical vision was subordinated to the revelation that had already been canonized. In all three traditions the canonical revelation, once defined, resisted internal challenges and remained the touchstone of religious truth for well over a thousand years.

PROPHECY IN MODERN TIMES. During the modern period in Europe public recognition of biblical prophecy has dwindled along with certain other aspects of European religion that had supported its primacy. The importance of prophets as the mediators of revealed truth declined sharply as the Enlightenment demolished confidence in the truth of revelation generally and enshrined a new standard of knowledge arrived at on the basis of observation and critical reasoning. At first these changes affected only the intellectual elite who had considered the impact of philosophical developments upon conceptions of God, religious truth, and divine mediation. Some philosophers (such as Hume) denied altogether the importance of revelation (and, therefore, prophetic mediation) as a source of knowledge. Others tried to accommodate revelational truths within a philosophical framework (e.g., Descartes and Kierkegaard). But others, such as Blake and Nietzsche, considered themselves to be prophets, though in their writings it is clear that they had redefined concepts related to inspiration, revelation, and truth to suit the needs of people living in post-Enlightenment civilization.

The discussion of such ideas among philosophers, scientists, and literati was contained within a minuscule portion of European culture, and the effects of their writings upon the general population materialized only very slowly. Of greater significance for popular religious culture was the diminished authority of the church. In some cases the reduction in ecclesiastical power was a direct outgrowth of Enlightenment thinking, as in the United States, where religion was consciously and explicitly separated from the centers of political power. But for the most part it seems that reductions in the power of the church to enforce its dogmas allowed for greater religious diversity (as during the Reformation), so that Enlightenment thinkers, and others, could express their religious views openly. Within this religious environment a new set of prophets arose to proclaim themselves as messengers bearing the divine word, and some have found success in founding new sects that revere their writings as sacred canon. Joseph Smith (1805–1844), for example, established the Church of Latter-Day Saints upon the claim that he had received revelations from Jesus Christ and from an angel who entrusted him with the *Book of Mormon.* Those who profess Christian Science regard the writings of Mary Baker Eddy (1821–1910) as sacred and inviolable. Others, notably the members of the international Pentecostal or the later charismatic movements, are modern ecstatics who consider themselves capable of receiving the spirit and speaking as divine agents.

As Europe exported culture during its colonialist expansions, it came to affect and discover religious traditions elsewhere. Among Muslims, for example, critical thinking about the status of Muḥammad has had some impact under the influence of and on analogy with Western reflections about religious origins. However, more important for the study of prophecy has been the impact of imperialism and modern Western culture on the indigenous tribal societies of the Americas, Africa, and maritime colonies (see bibliography, especially the entries on the ghost dance among Native Americans and cargo cults in Melanesia). As colonists encroached on territory inhabited by tribal peoples, they often found among the native religious specialists figures who showed a marked similarity to the traditional image of prophets within the major Western canonical religions. Anthropologists and comparative religionists have studied such modern prophets and their religious environment, where truths revealed through the mouths of inspired speakers remain a dominant influence in all aspects of social and personal life. Through direct observation of such religious systems scholars now understand the dynamics of prophecy with some specificity, and detailed research has dispelled various myths about its nature. It is known, for example, that ecstatic behavior among religious specialists can help maintain the structure of society, whereas scholars had long thought that ecstasy destabilized social order through its irrational influence. Likewise, the widespread opinion that ancient prophets were individualists crying to deaf ears from the loneliness of the desert now seems to be a romantic ideal. Rather, groups tend to support prophets who express their interests, while prophets acting entirely on their own rarely find a significant audience.

CONCLUSION. Though comparative theorists working with modern evidence have not yet established a single dominant interpretation of prophecy, a variety of complementary approaches now challenges the exclusivistic confessional interpretations that characterized the earlier period. Some scholars (e.g., I. M. Lewis—see bibliography) consider ecstatic religious behavior a means of expression used by disenfranchised groups who find standard channels of communication closed to them. Those studying religious behavior among shamans, Pentecostals, and other modern prophetic figures have found "deprivation theory" useful in showing how ecstatic persons support the position and structure of groups whose position in society is outside the normal channels of power and influence. Others (e.g., Victor Turner—see bibliography) interpret prochecy within a framework of social evolution. These scholars see prophets as appearing in periods of transition between societies organized along lines of kinship and clan affiliation and those structured according to more highly complex groupings that accompany the rise of states, class stratification and institutional religion. Either interpretive model applies consistent evaluative criteria to both the ancient evidence and the modern anthropological data without elevating the status of any one religious tradition over another. In this they are distinctively modern interpretations of prophecy, in contrast with canonical views, which persist in granting special recognition to the prophet(s) of a single confessional tradition.

SEE ALSO Canon; Divination; Oracles.

BIBLIOGRAPHY

For the background of mediation between gods and human beings within world religions, Mircea Eliade's *Shamanism: Archaic Techniques of Ecstasy,* rev. & enl. ed. (New York, 1964), remains unsurpassed for its breadth. Works about the founding prophets normally contain a general discussion and bibliography concerning their specific precursors. Such are Robert R. Wilson's *Prophecy and Society in Ancient Israel* (Philadelphia, 1980); David L. Petersen's *The Roles of Israel's Prophets (Journal for the Study of the Old Testament,* supp. 17; Sheffield, 1981, which surveys the evidence for Israelite intermediation in the ancient Near East, and David E. Aune's *Prophecy in Early Christianity and the Ancient Mediterranean World* (Grand Rapids, Mich., 1983), which gives a thorough discussion of Greco-Roman prophecy as well as its forms among the first Christians. Many critical works on Hebrew prophecy approach the subject from within the confessional community of Jews (e.g., Martin Buber's *The Prophetic Faith,* New York, 1949, and Abraham Joshua Heschel's *The Prophets,* New York, 1962 or Christians (e.g., Gerhard von Rad's *The Message of the Prophets,* London, 1968. Most treatments of prophecy ignore the significance of Zarathushtra and Mani, since they both have few, if any, modern followers to proclaim their value. Mary Boyce's *A History of Zoroastrianism,* 2 vols. (Leiden, 1975–1982), and Kurt Rudolph's *Gnosis* (San Francisco, 1983) provide useful bibliographies and discussions of the life and time of these prophets, respectively. The books on Muḥammad are many; the most readable and intelligent is Maxime Rodinson's *Mohammed* (New York, 1971), which contains a critical evaluation of the works that preceded it. Toufic Fahd's "Kāhin," in *The Encyclopaedia of Islam,* new ed., vol. 4 (Leiden, 1978), pp. 420–422, is a short peculiarly lucid account of the difficulties inherent in reconstructing Arab divination during the pre-Islamic period.

Regrettably, no book discusses prophecy within a framework as broad as that suggested in this article. Hence, we suggest that the reader consult other articles within this encyclopedia for detailed bibliographies on such topics as mysticism, ecstasy, canon, scripture, and the Enlightenment, as well as on individuals that we have mentioned in the text.

Among works that may not be listed in other articles is the anthropological literature on prophecy. Max Weber's work has had a seminal influence on the field; see both *Ancient Judaism* (1922; Glencoe, Ill., 1952) and *The Sociology of Religion* (1922; Boston, 1963). I. M. Lewis's *Ecstatic Religion* (Harmondsworth, 1971) is a sociology of ecstatic behavior based on a broad range of comparative evidence, and though it does not address prophecy per se, it has influenced others (viz. Wilson, cited above) that do. Victor Turner's "Religious Specialists: Anthropological Study," in the *International Encyclopedia of the Social Sciences,* edited by David L. Sills (New York, 1968), vol. 13, pp. 437–444, offers analytical categories useful in distinguishing prophets from other religious personnel. A number of books describe the activity of prophets in modern cultures: Peter Worsley's *The Trumpet Shall Sound: A Study of "Cargo" Cults in Melanesia* (1957; New York, 1968); E. E. Evans-Pritchard's *Nuer Religion* (Oxford, 1956) and *The Sanusi of Cyrenaica* (Oxford, 1949); James Mooney's *The Ghost-Dance Religion and the Sioux Outbreak of 1890* (1896; abr. ed., Chicago, 1965); and Vittorio Lanternari's *The Religions of the Oppressed: A Study of Modern Messianic Cults* (New York, 1963).

Finally, Kenneth Cragg's *Muhammad and the Christian: A Question of Response* (New York, 1984) is a valuable beginning for the dialogue between Muslim and Christian conceptions of prophetic revelation.

Gerald T. Sheppard (1987)
William E. Herbrechtsmeier (1987)

PROPHECY: BIBLICAL PROPHECY

Throughout much of the history of Western thought, the biblical prophets have been understood as unique figures whose sudden appearance in ancient Israel had a profound impact on the development of Judaism and Christianity. They have been considered ethical and moral innovators whose views decisively shaped later Jewish and Christian theology. Particularly in Christian tradition, they have been seen as revealers of the future whose oracles predicted the coming of Jesus and whose words may still contain unrecognized clues to the course of world history.

This understanding of the biblical prophets continues to exist today. However, during the past century the traditional view has come under increasing attack from biblical scholars, who have reexamined the biblical evidence and then proposed a number of alternative and often conflicting theories about the nature and functions of Israelite prophecy. Rejecting the common notion that prophecy is concerned only with the future, scholars have portrayed the prophets variously as creators of a highly intellectual form of ethical monotheism, as ecstatics scarcely in control of their own actions, as religious officials with regular duties in the Israelite cult, as shrewd political advisers, as isolated mystics, and as guardians of Israel's religious traditions. The Hebrew Bible contains evidence to support all of these interpretations, and for this reason the scholarly debate on the nature of prophecy continues with no sign of an emerging consensus.

However, scholars have increasingly recognized that an adequate understanding of Israelite prophecy can be achieved only by using extrabiblical evidence to supplement the narratives about prophetic activity and the words of the prophets that have been preserved in the Bible. The most important extrabiblical evidence comes from two different sources. The first source provides additional documentary evidence on the nature of prophecy in antiquity. During the past century archaeologists have uncovered a number of ancient Near Eastern texts that challenge the traditional notion that the Israelite prophets were unique religious figures in antiquity. In the Mesopotamian city of Mari on the Euphrates, excavators have found letters from the eighteenth century BCE describing the activities and messages of several different types of oracle givers who bear some resemblance to the later Israelite prophets. The Mari oracles come from various gods and do not seem to have been solicited by the person to whom they are addressed. Some of the oracle givers described in the letters are ordinary individuals, but others have special titles, which indicates that these figures exhibited characteristic behavior and filled a recognized religious role in the society of Mari. Among the specialists mentioned are the "answerer" (*apilu*), the "ecstatic" (*muhhu*), the "speaker" (*qabbatum*), and a member of the cultic personnel of the goddess Ishtar, the meaning of whose title (*assinnu*) is uncertain. Later texts from the time of the Assyrian kings Esarhaddon (r. 680–669 BCE) and Ashurbanipal (r. 668–627 BCE) record the oracles of Assyrian contemporaries of some of the Israelite prophets. In addition to the ecstatic, the texts mention the "shouter" (*raggimu*), the "revealer" (*shabru*), and the "votary" (*shelutu*).

Religious specialists resembling the biblical prophets also existed outside of Israelite territory in other areas of Palestine. Inscriptions from the eighth and ninth centuries BCE refer to a "message giver" (*ʿdd*) and a "visionary" (*ḥzh*), a title also given to some of the biblical prophets. This evidence suggests that prophetic activity was going on elsewhere in the ancient Near East before and during the time when prophets were active in Israel. Furthermore, the apparent diversity of these non-Israelite specialists suggests that prophecy in Israel may have been a more complex phenomenon than scholars have previously thought.

This suggestion is reinforced by extrabiblical evidence from the second source, the studies that sociologists and anthropologists have made of contemporary oracle givers. These specialists form a highly diverse group that includes various types of mediums, diviners, priests, and shamans, but like the biblical prophets they all see themselves as intermediaries between the human and divine worlds. In spite of obvious differences, these figures often exhibit similar behavioral characteristics and interact with their societies in much the same way. This interaction has been analyzed extensively by anthropologists and shown to be highly complex. By delivering messages from the divine realm, oracle givers are capable of bringing about changes in their societies, but at the same time societies play a direct role in accrediting oracle givers and shaping their behavior.

The modern anthropological evidence indicates that the phenomenon of prophecy can be adequately understood only when the dynamic relationship between prophet and society is fully explored. This means that any account of prophecy in ancient Israel (c. 1200–200 BCE) must see the prophets in particular social contexts rather than treating them as ideal figures abstracted from their historical settings. For this reason it is necessary to avoid making too many statements about biblical prophecy in general. Each prophet occupied a unique place in the history of Israel and was part of a complex interaction between prophecy and society in a particular time and place. The history of Israelite prophecy is the history of a series of such interactions. However, once the uniqueness of each prophet is recognized, it is possible to outline some general features that characterized Israelite prophecy as a whole and to isolate some characteristics that were peculiar to particular groups of prophets.

The Prophetic Experience. Direct information about Israelite prophecy comes from two sources: the oracles of the prophets themselves, now preserved primarily in the fifteen prophetic books of the Hebrew Bible, and the narratives describing prophetic activity, found mainly in the books of the Deuteronomic history (*Joshua, Judges, 1* and *2 Samuel, 1* and *2 Kings*). Both of these sources are difficult to interpret because of their unusual character. At least until the exile (587/6 BCE), the prophets seem to have composed and delivered their oracles orally. Only later were their words collected, written down, and finally arranged in small collections, or books. This work was done either by the prophets themselves or by their disciples. Some of the written collections were then further edited by later generations of writers and editors, who were interested in preserving and above all interpreting the prophets' original pronouncements. As a result of this long process of transmission and composition, it is often difficult to separate genuine prophetic material from the interpretive work of later editors. A similar sort of problem exists in the case of the prophetic narratives of the Deuteronomic history. Some of the stories, such as those concerning Elijah and Elisha (*1 Kgs.* 17–2 *Kgs.* 9), probably circulated individually or as collections in oral tradition before being incorporated in the written work of the historian. As part of the incorporation process, the stories were edited at least once, and perhaps several times, in order to express the political, social, and religious views of the writers. For this reason, it is sometimes difficult to use the narratives for historiographic purposes.

Because of the nature of the sources from which a description of prophecy must be derived, any attempt to reconstruct a picture of prophetic activity must necessarily involve a great deal of interpretation, and the results will often be incomplete and tentative. This is particularly true of attempts to describe the prophets' supernatural experiences, which by their very nature were private and not open to public scrutiny. The prophets say very little about their experiences and even in recounting their "calls" to prophesy rarely describe more than the initial vision that they saw (*Is.* 6, *Ez.* 1–3) or the words that they heard (Jer. 1:4–10; *Am.* 7:15). Instead, the texts concentrate on the messages that the prophets received during their encounters with God. However, enough clues exist to suggest that Israel conceived of the prophetic experience as one that occurred when individuals were possessed by the spirit of God. "The hand of the Lord" fell upon them (*1 Kgs.* 18:46; *2 Kgs.* 3:15; *Jer.* 15:17; *Ez.* 1:3), or the spirit of God "rested on them" (*Nm.* 11:25–26) or "clothed itself" with them (*Jgs.* 6:34) so that they were no longer in control of their own speech and actions. As is typical in cases of spirit possession in a number of cultures, Israel interpreted the words that the prophets spoke during possession not as human words but as the words of God. The prophets were simply the channels through which the divine word came to the world. Once the prophets were possessed by God, they felt compelled to deliver the message that God wanted to communicate (*Am.* 3:8). The divine word was perceived as a "burning fire" that gnawed at them until it was delivered (*Jer.* 20:9).

Because of the loss of personal autonomy associated with divine possession, the prophets did not usually view the experience positively. In the accounts of their initial call, they sometimes speak of trying to avoid becoming prophets (*Jer.* 1:6), and some of them report that they repeatedly sought release from their prophetic roles (*Jer.* 11:18–12:6, 15:15–21; cf. *Ez.* 2:1–3:15). However, such attempts at resistance were always futile, and in the end the compulsion to prophesy could not be thwarted.

Although the prophets themselves were apparently reluctant to describe the process through which they received their oracles, additional information on the nature of the prophetic experience can be deduced from the various titles given to these individuals and from the descriptions of their characteristic behavior. This evidence suggests that the prophetic experience was not the same for all prophets and that the prophets' characteristic behavior and social functions varied enough to require more than one title or role label.

Prophetic titles. The English word *prophet* is ultimately derived from the Greek *prophētēs,* a noun that means both "one who speaks forth" or "one who proclaims" and "one who speaks before" or "one who speaks of the future." The Greek translators of the Hebrew Bible used this word to render several Hebrew titles and apparently understood it to be a general term capable of being applied to various types of religious specialists. However, in ancient Israel the different types of prophetic figures bore distinctive titles, although the understanding and usage of these titles varied with the group that used them and the time in which they were used.

The most common prophetic title used in the Hebrew Bible is *navi'*. Extrabiblical occurrences of the word are extremely rare, and its etymology is uncertain, although scholars normally relate it to the Akkadian verb *nabu,* "to call, to announce, to name." The title may thus mean either "one who calls" or "one who is called," but this etymology sheds little light on the precise characteristics of the figure so designated. In preexilic times the label *navi'* was particularly common in northern Israel (Ephraim), where it was a general term for any prophetic figure and was the only title given to legitimate prophets. In Israelite literature produced in the north or influenced by traditions originating there (the Deuteronomic history, *Hosea, Jeremiah*), the *navi'* played a central role in religious life and was associated with the preservation of ancient theological traditions. To the south, in Judah and particularly in Jerusalem, the title was also in use as a general role label, but it appears much less frequently in Judahite literature and is often used in negative contexts. After the exile navi' was used by all biblical writers as a general prophetic title and seems to have no longer been recognized as a distinctive role label.

While *navi'* was the most common prophetic title in the north, in Judah and particularly in Jerusalem the term "visionary" (*ḥozeh*) was the preferred designation. This role label appears primarily in texts originating in the south (*Amos, Micah, Isaiah, 1* and *2 Chronicles*), and when it does not, it refers to figures located there. Judahite historical traditions suggest that visionaries were particularly active during the period of the early monarchy (during the reigns of David, Solomon, and Rehoboam), when some of them were part of the royal court in Jerusalem, but references to them in the writing prophets indicate that they persisted at least until the exile (1 *Chr.* 21:9, 25:5, 29:29; 2 *Chr.* 9:29, 12:15, 19:2, 29:25, 30; cf. 2 *Sm.* 24:11). The title "visionary" clearly refers to the distinctive means by which these figures received their revelations, and indeed three of the Judahite prophetic books explicitly speak of the visionary origin of their oracles (*Am.* 1:1; *Mi.* 1:1; *Is.* 1:1), while a fourth (*Ez.*) contains numerous descriptions of revelatory visions. This particular mode of divine-human communication was apparently not well regarded in the north, where prophets preferred to speak of their oracles as the words that they heard rather than the visions that they saw (*Hos.* 1:1, *Jer.* 1:1–4). In some circles outside of Judah, visions may have been considered an inferior form of revelation (Nm. 12:6–9; cf. *Dt.* 13:1–6), a fact that may help to explain the northern priest Amaziah's derisive characterization of the Judahite prophet Amos as a professional visionary (*Am.* 7:12–15).

In addition to the *navi'* and the *ḥozeh,* the biblical writers mention three other prophetic titles, which were apparently not widely used. In *1 Samuel* 9:9 Samuel is called a "seer" (*ro'eh;* lit., "one who sees"), a title that the writer affirms was already archaic. If the old story in this chapter is historically accurate, then the seer was a specialist in communicating with the divine world, presumably through visions, dreams, or divination. People who wanted to request information from a deity could go to the seer, who in exchange for a fee would transmit the petitioner's request and return an answer. In the north this particular function was later asigned to the *navi',* while elsewhere various diviners and priests were the agents of intercession (*1 Sm.* 9:9, *Dt.* 18:9–22). Late references to the seer may be archaisms (*2 Ch.* 16:7, 16:10), and it is probable that the title ceased to be used in the early monarchical period.

Better attested is the title "man of God" (*ish ha-Elohim*), which appears in northern sources, particularly in the old prophetic legends of the Elijah-Elisha cycle in the Deuteronomic history (1 Kgs. 17–2 Kgs. 10). This label may have originally been applied to people who were thought able to control divine power and use it in various miraculous ways, but its usage was eventually broadened to include anyone who had a special relationship to God. When the designation "man of God" became an honorific title, any specifically prophetic connotations that it may have had were presumably muted or lost.

In addition to titles normally applied to a single individual, the biblical writers also apply the label "sons of the prophets" (*benei ha-nevi'i*m) to members of prophetic groups. The title is attested only in the Elijah-Elisha stories and seems to have been used for a relatively brief period in northern Israel (c. 869–842 BCE). The sons of the prophets were clearly members of a prophetic guild that had a hierarchical structure headed by a leader with the title "father." On the death of the leader, the title was transferred to another prophet (*2 Kgs.* 2:12, 6:21, 13:14). Members of the group sometimes lived together and shared common meals (*2 Kgs.* 4:1, 4:38–41, 6:1). It has been suggested that the sons of the prophets were ecstatics, but there is no evidence of such behavior in the narratives about them.

Prophetic behavior. In ancient Israel, as in every society, the behavior of divinely possessed individuals followed certain stereotypical patterns, although these patterns varied somewhat depending on the historical, geographical, and social setting of the prophets' activities. There are two reasons for the existence of this behavior. First, Israelite society set definite limits on the kinds of behavior that its prophets could exhibit. In most social situations violent or uncontrolled actions were not tolerated, and when they occurred, they were considered a sign of mental illness or possession by evil powers. Prophets who wished to be considered genuine therefore had to keep their behavior within recognized boundaries or risk being considered insane. Second, members of social groups in which prophets operated had to face the problem of determining when divine possession was actually present. They needed to have some grounds for assigning a prophetic title to a particular individual. One of the ways in which they solved this problem was to examine the behavior of people in the past who were known to have been genuine prophets of God. Individuals who wished to be accredited as prophets were thus subtly pressed to conform to the group's picture of genuine prophetic behavior.

Prophetic actions. Biblical writers rarely describe behavior indicative of possession, but the existence of stereotypical prophetic actions can be inferred from the Bible's occasional use of the verb *hitnabbe'*, which seems to mean "to act like a prophet, to exhibit the behavior characteristic of a *navi'*." This verb refers to both prophetic words and deeds, but the texts give it no specific definition. It is clear, however, that the prophet's characteristic behavior was evaluated positively by some groups but negatively by others. In some cases it was seen a a sign of divine legitimation and favor (*Nm.* 11:11–29, *1 Sm.* 10:1–13), while on other occasions it was considered an indication of madness or possession by an evil spirit (*1 Sm.* 18:10–11, 19:18–24; *1 Kgs.* 18:26–29; *Jer.* 29:24–28).

It is likely that some of Israel's prophets were ecstatics. The word *ecstasy* is usually understood to refer to a type of trance behavior marked by psychological and physiological symptoms such as a reduction of sensitivity to outside stimuli, hallucinations or visions, a garbled perception of surrounding events, and an apparent loss of conscious control over speech and actions. The intensity of ecstasy and its specific characteristics vary depending on the individual being possessed and the group in which possession occurs. The actions of an ecstatic prophet may range from apparently uncontrolled physical activity to completely normal physical activity, and his speech may range from unintelligible nonsense syllables to perfectly coherent discourse. Sometimes ecstatic behavior in Israel was incapacitating or dangerous (*1 Sm.* 19:18–24, *1 Kgs.* 18:26–29), but at least in the case of those prophets who wrote, ecstasy appears to have involved controlled actions and intelligible speech (*Jer.* 4:19, 23:9; *Ez.* 1:1–3:15, 8:1–11:25).

As part of their characteristic behavior, some of Israel's prophets accompanied their oracles with symbolic acts, although this practice was by no means common even among the prophets who employed it. In most cases these acts seem to have been designed to provide the background for an oracle or to dramatize the prophet's words. Thus Hosea and Isaiah gave their children symbolic names that foretold the fate of the nation (*Hos.* 1:4–9; *Is.* 7:3, 8:1–4). Isaiah reportedly walked naked through the streets of Jerusalem for three years to drive home the point that the Assyrians would lead the Egyptians into captivity (*Is.* 20). Jeremiah smashed a pot before his listeners to dramatize the destruction what would soon occur in Jerusalem, and he later wore a wooden yoke before the king to reinforce an oracle counseling surrender to the Babylonians (*Jer.* 19:1–15, 27:1–28:17). A few of these acts seem to move beyond symbolism into the realm of magic. When Elisha commanded the Israelite king Joash to strike the ground with his arrows, the number of times that the king struck the ground determined the number of victories that Israel would have over Syria (*2 Kgs.* 13:14–19). Similarly, Ezekiel's elaborate drawing of the besieged Jerusalem actually seems to bring the siege into existence (*Ez.* 4:1–8). However, in spite of these examples of sympathetic magic, the working of miracles was not normally a component of prophetic behavior in Israel.

In addition to performing certain characteristic actions, some of Israel's prophets wore distinctive clothing and bore a special mark that identified them as prophets or as members of a prophetic guild (*1 Kgs.* 20:35–41, *2 Kgs.* 1:8, *Zec.* 13:4). However, this practice does not seem to have been widespread.

Prophetic speech. As part of their characteristic behavior, some prophets may have used stereotypical speech patterns and shaped their oracles in certain traditional ways. The existence of a distinctive northern oracle pattern is suggested by the fact that the Deuteronomic history and the prophetic literature dependent on it (*Jeremiah*) often quote prophetic oracles that have a tripartite structure. The oracle begins with the commissioning of the prophetic messenger and then moves to an accusation against an individual who has violated Israel's covenantal law. Following the accusation, an announcement of judgment is addressed directly to the accused. The announcement is usually introduced by a stereotypical "messenger formula," such as the following: "Thus says the Lord"; "Therefore, thus says the Lord"; or "For thus says the Lord" (*1 Sm.* 2:27–36, 13:11–14, 15:10–31; *2 Sam.* 12; 1 *Kgs.* 11:29–40, 13:1–3, 14:7–14, 17:1, 20:35–43, 21:17–22, 22:13–23; *2 Kgs.* 1:3–4, 1:6, 20:14–19, 21:10–15; *Jer.* 20:1–6, 22:10–12, 22:13–19, 22:24–27,

28:12–16, 29:24–32, 36:29–30, 37:17). If this pattern is not simply a literary convention of the Deuteronomic authors, then what is often called the "announcement of disaster to individuals" may have been a characteristic feature of the speech of Ephraimite prophets. Other Israelite prophets also announced disaster to individuals and to the nation as a whole, but their oracles did not conform to rigid patterns.

Judahite prophets may have once used stereotypical forms of speech, but if so, the patterns had broken down by the time the oracles were recorded in writing. Early Judahite writing prophets such as Amos, Micah, and Isaiah seem to have favored distinctive judgment oracles beginning with the cry "alas" (Heb., *hoy*) and followed by one or more participles describing the addressee and specifying his crime. This introduction was followed by an announcement of disaster in various forms (*Am.* 5:18–20, 6:1–7; *Is.* 5:8–10, 5:11–14, 5:18–19, 5:20, 5:21, 5:22–24, 10:1–3, 28:1–4, 29:1–4, 29:15, 30:1–3, 31:1–4; *Mi.* 2:1–4). However, even if the "alas oracles" were once characteristic of southern prophetic speech, they were later used by prophets outside of that tradition.

The Hebrew word massaʾ, traditionally translated "burden," may have once designated a specialized type of Judahite oracle against foreign nations (*Is.* 13:1, 14:28, 15:1, 17:1, 19:1, 21:1, 21:11, 21:13, 22:1, 23:1, 30:6; *Na.* 1:1; *Hb.* 1:1; *Zec.* 9:1, 12:1; *Mal.* 1:1). However, if so, the original characteristic form of the oracle has not been preserved, and its distinctive function has been lost.

In addition to using speech patterns that seem to be primarily prophetic, Israel's prophets employed specialized language drawn from various spheres of Israelite life. For example, from the courts they took legal language and formed trial speeches that mirrored judicial proceedings (*Is.* 1; *Mi.* 6; *Jer.* 2; *Is.* 41:1–5, 41:21–29, 42:18–25, 43:8–15, 43:22–28, 44:6–8, 50:1–3). From the Temple they took priestly instruction and liturgical fragments and incorporated them into prophetic oracles. However, scholars have not usually succeeded in uncovering widespread structural patterns in oracles of this sort, and it is probably best not to understand them as characteristic of the behavior of prophetic possession in general.

PROPHECY AND SOCIETY. In the past there has been a tendency to portray the Israelite prophets as isolated individuals who appeared suddenly before a particular group, delivered an uncompromising divine message, and then disappeared as quickly as they had come. It was assumed that this individualism set them at odds with their society and inevitably brought them into conflict with rival religious professionals, particularly the priests. However, more recently scholars have recognized that the prophets were integrally related to the societies in which they lived. These individuals played many social roles, not all of which were related to their prophetic activities. Because in ancient Israel there were apparently no restrictions on the type of person who could be possessed by God's spirit, and because possession was not a constant experience for any given person, many of the prophets participated fully in other areas of communal life. Thus, for example, Jeremiah and Ezekiel were both priests who were possessed and transformed into prophets (*Jer.* 1:1, *Ez.* 1:3). Some priests may have delivered prophetic oracles as part of their regular cultic activities, while in the postexilic period Levitical singers in the Temple also had prophetic functions (*1 Chr.* 25:1–8; *2 Chr.* 20:1–23, 34:30). Some prophets, like Gad, seem to have earned their living through prophecy and were members of the royal court (*1 Sm.* 22:1–5, *2 Sm.* 24:1–25), while others, like Amos, engaged in other occupations and prophesied only occasionally (*Am.* 1:1, 7:14–15).

Prophetic authority. Discussions of prophetic authority normally focus on the prophetic-call narratives (*Is.* 6, *Jer.* 1, *Ez.* 1–3) and on the "charisma" that these extraordinary individuals are thought to have possessed. It is assumed that because the prophets were endowed with supernatural power, they were automatically accorded authority and viewed as divinely chosen leaders. To be sure, the prophets did sometimes cite their initial experiences of possession in order to gain support for their message, and they may be accurately described as charismatics, although they were certainly not the only ones in Israelite society. However, these two factors must not be stressed at the expense of recognizing the role that Israelite society played in creating and sustaining prophets.

The process by which ancient Israel recognized and accepted the authority of genuine prophets was subtle and complex, but at least some of its elements can be identified. One element concerned a prophet's conformity to certain standards of behavior. At least those Israelites who created and carried the biblical traditions recognized as authoritative only those prophets who stood in a recognizably Israelite prophetic tradition. This meant above all that the only legitimate prophets were those who were possessed by Yahveh, the God of Israel. Prophets possessed by other deities were not to be taken seriously, and the Deuteronomic writers went so far as to decree the death penalty for prophets who spoke in the name of other gods (*Dt.* 18:20). However, outside of these circles, possession by other gods was accepted, and for a brief time prophets of Baal and Asherah were part of the religious establishment in the northern kingdom of Israel (Ephraim) (*1 Kgs.* 18:19–40).

Prophets who wished to be considered legitimate also were pressed to make their behavior conform to what various Israelite groups recognized as traditional prophetic behavior. Canons of acceptable behavior varied from group to group within Israel, and for this reason prophets who were considered legitimate by one group might not be considered legitimate by other groups. Thus, for example, shortly before the fall of Jerusalem to the Babylonians, Jeremiah and the group that supported him condemned those prophets who predicted the salvation of the city, even though they were accepted as legitimate prophets by powerful groups within the royal court. In the eyes of Jeremiah and his supporters, these prophets were illegitimate because the form and content of their oracles and the means by which they received them did not conform to the patterns that Jeremiah's community accepted (*Jer.* 23:9–40). Isaiah and his disciples, too, had rejected the authority of some of the prophets in Jerusalem because of their aberrant behavior (*Is.* 28:7–10), and in Babylonia the exilic community of Ezekiel denied legitimacy to those prophets who were still active in the Temple in Jerusalem (*Ez.* 13:1–23).

A second element involved in the process of prophetic authentication was the degree to which the prophet fitted into a recognized Israelite theological tradition. This did not mean that the prophet was not free to innovate or criticize the tradition, but he had to remain rooted in it. Thus, for example, in Deuteronomic tradition any prophet who advocated the worship of other gods was considered to have placed himself outside of the tradition by violating its overarching monotheistic principle, and the prophet not only was considered unauthentic but, like the prophet who spoke in the name of another god, was to be put to death (*Dt.* 13:1–5).

Because Israel's theological traditions were not always in agreement with each other at every point, what was acceptable prophetic behavior in one tradition might not be acceptable in another. When such theological disagreements occurred, a particular prophet might be an authoritative figure in his own tradition but would not be taken seriously elsewhere. Clear cases of this phenomenon can be seen in some of the writing prophets. The prophet Amos, a native of Judah and presumably standing in the tradition of the theology developed by the royal theologians in Jerusalem (which saw the establishment of the northern kingdom of Israel as a revolt against the Davidic dynasty), prophesied against the north and predicted the destruction of the Ephraimite royal sanctuary at Bethel. Such behavior was not acceptable in the north, and Amaziah, the priest of Bethel, accused Amos of treason and refused to recognize his prophetic authority (*Am.* 7:10–13). A later case is that of the prophet Jeremiah, who was influenced by Deuteronomic tradition that saw as conditional the election of Jerusalem as the dwelling place of God. He delivered oracles in the Jerusalem Temple that predicted the destruction of the city and the Temple unless the people reformed their conduct and obeyed God's covenantal law. To the officials of the royal court and the Temple, who believed that God had chosen Jerusalem as an eternal dwelling place, such words were treasonous and deserved the death penalty (*Jer.* 26). Although Jeremiah was not killed, many of the officials of Jerusalem refused to recognize his prophetic authority and considered him to be insane (*Jer.* 29:24–28).

A final element involved in the process of accrediting prophets can be seen most clearly in the Deuteronomic literature, which held that authentic prophets were those whose words always came to pass. This was particularly true of prophets said to be "like Moses," a special class of prophets in Deuteronomic theology. These prophets had more direct communication with God than did ordinary prophets and for this reason were more effective intercessors and gave more reliable oracles. The words of a Mosaic prophet would inevitably come true, according to the Deuteronomists, and when these figures appear in the Deuteronomic history, the fulfillment of their oracles is always noted (*Nm.* 12:1–8; *Dt.* 18:15–22; *1 Kgs.* 11:30–39, 12:15, 14:7–11, 15:27–30, 16:1–4, 16:9–13; *2 Kgs.* 1:15–17). This criterion for recognizing authentic prophets was not always useful, for oracles might only later be fulfilled, in the distant future, and the reliability of a particular prophet's predictions could not always be determined.

Once a prophet was considered authentic by a particular group in Israel, he seems to have been at least tolerated by the rest of the society. Some of the prophets had free access to the king, the royal court, and the Temple and could carry out their activities without being harassed. Prophets were generally not held responsible for their words or actions because they spoke a divine word and not their own (*Jer.* 26:12–16). However, there were some limits to this freedom, particularly when the prophet criticized the king and the priesthood, and some of the prophets were killed because of their oracles (*Jer.* 26).

Because of the way in which prophetic authority was assigned, prophetic conflicts were common. When a prophet supported by one group gave oracles that conflicted with those of a prophet supported by another group, the conflict was often resolved only when one group simply refused to recognize the authority of one of the other group's prophets. Thus, for example, Jeremiah fought his prophetic opponents not by attacking their theological position but by accusing them of being false prophets (*Jer.* 23:9–32, 28:1–17, 29:15–32; cf. *Ez.* 13:1–23). When false prophecy led to the imposition of the death penalty, as was the case in Deuteronomic law, such accusations were effective tools for social control, whether they were used by the prophets themselves or by a government seeking to suppress troublesome critics.

Social locations and functions. In ancient Israel prophets carried out their activities in all parts of the society. However, because the prophets' functions to a certain extent depended on their social location, it is useful to identify prophets according to their relationship to the society's centers of social, political, and religious power. At the center of the social structure were prophets who may be identified as "central prophets." They carried out their activities in the context of the royal court or the central sanctuary, and individually or as part of a prophetic group they performed the functions considered necessary by the establishment. Because of their central social location, they enjoyed a certain amount of prestige and were considered authoritative by Israelite leaders. At the other end of the social spectrum were prophets who were located away from the centers of power and carried out their activities on the fringes of society. They were considered authoritative only by the small groups of supporters who shared their social location and theological views. Peripheral prophets were usually dispossessed individuals who were tolerated by the religious establishment but enjoyed little social status or political power. In Israel prophets were located at various points on the continuum that stretched between the society's center and its periphery, and some prophets changed their position on the continuum when there were alterations in the social structure.

Locating a particular prophet in the social spectrum was sometimes a subjective process, particularly in the case of peripheral prophets. Because prophets with small support groups and little status had minimal power, they could easily be classified as peripheral by the establishment, and their messages could be ignored. However, to the members of the prophets' support groups they played the crucial role of articulating group values and concerns. For this reason the prophets could be considered central by the groups that supported them. Biblical views on the social location of prophets thus often depended on the social location of the people articulating those views.

All Israelite prophets shared a single basic task. They were to deliver to individuals and groups the divine messages that had been transmitted during their possession experiences. In addition, Deuteronomic prophets served as intercessors who were responsible for communicating the people's questions and requests to God. Beyond these primary tasks, however, the prophets' social functions varied somewhat depending on their social location. Central prophets were normally concerned with the orderly functioning of the society. If they were active in the cult, they were responsible for providing oracles whenever the religious, political, or social occasion required them. They also represented God in state affairs and in general helped to preserve public morality. Such prophets were interested in maintaining and preserving the existing social order. They felt free to criticize existing conditions and structures, but they were generally opposed to radical changes that might make the society unstable.

In contrast, peripheral prophets by definition represented positions that were at odds with the majority views and practices of the society. Being possessed by God and becoming prophets gave marginal individuals an authority that they did not previously have and allowed them to bring their messages to the attention of the political and religious establishment. Peripheral prophets normally advocated basic reforms in the social structure and thus served as agents of rapid social change. Their reform programs often aimed at restoring older religious and social values and practices that the society as a whole had rejected. At the same time, the prophets were concerned with improving their marginal social position and moving their support groups closer to the centers of power. However, there were limits on the degree to which they could advocate major social changes. Up to a point, their views were tolerated, but if they became too vocal in their demands, then they ran the risk of being considered enemies of the society and having their activities brought to a halt through accusations of false prophecy or legal sanctions that would physically remove them.

Prophecy in Israelite History. Because most of Israel's prophets were active during the monarchical period (c. 1020–587/6 BCE), it is sometimes argued that prophecy and monarchy were coeval and interdependent. However, biblical traditions coming from northern Israel speak of the existence of prophets well before the rise of the monarchy, and there is no reason to doubt their accuracy. Similarly, prophets played a role in Israel's restoration after the exile (c. 538–400), so it is probably safe to suppose that prophecy played a role in Israelite society from its origins to about 400 when, according to orthodox Jewish tradition, prophecy ceased. Prophets certainly existed in Israelite society in later times and played a minor role in early Christian communities, but they do not seem to have had major social functions and have left few traces in the biblical record.

Although prophecy existed in Israel for a fairly long period of time, it is impossible to trace a comprehensive history of the phenomenon. Earlier attempts to trace an evolutionary development from "primitive" ecstatic prophecy to the high ethical principles of the writing prophets are now generally discredited. However, it is possible to describe the complex roles that prophets played at various points in Israel's political and religious development.

Premonarchical period. The Elohist traditions of the Pentateuch and the Deuteronomic history suggest that prophets were at work in Israel before the rise of the monarchy (c. 1020). Although the narratives describing the activities of these early figures have certainly been colored by later prophetic ideology, there is no reason to deny the existence of prophecy in early Israel. Prophetic phenomena are attested elsewhere in the ancient Near East in the second millennium in roughly the same areas as those thought to have been occupied by Israel's ancestors. There is no evidence to suggest that early Israelites borrowed prophecy from elsewhere, but it may well have appeared spontaneously in some of the tribes that later joined together to form Israel.

The nature and functions of these early prophets are unclear. Biblical references to the prophetic activities of Abraham and Moses are probably retrojections from later times, and certainly the Moses stories were used by Deuteronomists to support their distinctive views of prophecy (*Gn.* 20:7, *Nm.* 12, *Dt.* 18:9–22). In addition to these traditional figures, Miriam and Deborah are both said to have been prophetesses (*Ex.* 15:20–21, *Jg.* 4:4–10), and an unnamed prophet is said to have been sent during the period of the judges to explain why the people were oppressed (*Jg.* 6:1–10). If these references are in any way indicative of the role that prophets actually played in early Israel, then it would appear that prophets had a position in the central social structure and had important functions in the conduct of warfare.

It is more certain that prophecy was well established in northern Israel in the period shortly before the rise of the monarchy. A band of prophets was part of the cultic personnel at the sanctuary at Gibeah (*1 Sm.* 10:9–13), and there are numerous traditions about the prophetic activities of Samuel. He had prophetic, priestly, and governmental roles at several northern sanctuaries and was clearly a central prophet of major importance (*1 Sm.* 3:1–21, 7:1–12:25). People came to him in order to obtain information from God (*1 Sm.* 9:6–10), and he represented God among the people. Although traditions differ about Samuel's role in the rise of the monarchy, the Deuteronomists saw him as the religious official responsible for anointing and legitimating Saul as Israel's first king (*1 Sm.* 9:15–10:8).

Monarchical period. Throughout the history of the Israelite monarchy, prophets played important religious roles both inside the royal court and on its periphery. The tradition of prophetic participation in government began with Samuel, who continued to advise Saul on cultic matters during his reign. However, Saul's disagreements with Samuel and Samuel's northern support groups over the extent of royal authority eventually broke into open warfare, and Samuel stripped the kingship from Saul and anointed David as the new king (*1 Sm.* 13:1–16:13). The presence of prophets in the royal court continued during David's reign. The court prophet Nathan delivered to David an oracle promising the king an eternal dynasty in Jerusalem and designating Jerusalem as the divine dwelling place forever (*2 Sm.* 7). This oracle became the cornerstone of the Jerusalem royal theology, and it was cited as authoritative by later royal sources (*Ps.* 89, 132). Later in David's reign his royal visionary, Gad, legitimated the building of a temple in Jerusalem (*2 Sam.* 24). David is also said to have installed prophets as religious officials in the central sanctuary (*1 Chr.* 24). Although this report undoubtedly reflects the Temple administration of the Chronicler's own time, it may well be that prophets had central cultic functions in Jerusalem during the monarchical period.

Prophecy does not seem to have been prominent during Solomon's reign, but it emerged in a new form in the time of his successor, Rehoboam. In response to general Ephraimite dissatisfaction with the growing power of the Jerusalem monarchy, the prophet Ahijah, from the old northern sanctuary at Shiloh, established the dissident northern tribes as an independent kingdom by delivering an oracle legitimating Jeroboam as king of Ephraim (*1 Kgs.* 11:29–40). Ahijah was clearly a peripheral prophet representing interests that were not connected with the royal court in Jerusalem, and his newly created state may have been intended to restore his supporters to positions of power. If so, his intentions were thwarted when Jeroboam created in Ephraim a syncretist religious establishment that horrified the Deuteronomic historians. According to the Deuteronomists, Ahijah was the first of a series of peripheral prophets who attempted to reform the northern political and religious establishments (*1 Kgs.* 13–16).

Prophetic opposition in the north reached its height during the time of Elijah and Elisha (c. 869–815), when groups of peripheral prophets appeared to denounce the Ephraimite kings and the heterodox worship that they permitted in the land. This inevitably brought the peripheral prophets into conflict with the prophets of Yahveh, Baal, and Asherah, who were part of the religious establishment in the north (*1 Kgs.* 18, 22). The peripheral prophets finally prevailed and succeeded in overthrowing the northern dynasty and bringing about cultic reforms (*1 Kgs.* 17–*2 Kgs.* 10). However, by the time of the prophets Amos and Hosea (c. 760–746), Baal worship had been firmly reestablished in Ephraim. Both of these prophets, from Judah and Ephraim respectively, continued the activities of their predecessors and predicted the destruction of the evil kingdom. The prophecies were finally fulfilled with the destruction of the northern capital, Samaria, in 721, an event that the Deuteronomic historians traced to the failure of the kings and the people to listen to the warnings that God had sent through the prophets (*2 Kgs.* 17:7–18).

Little is known of prophecy in Judah during the period of the divided monarchy until the very end of that period, when the prophets Isaiah and Micah began their activities. Both reflect an acceptance of elements of the royal theology of Jerusalem and both may be examples of prophets who were more central than periphral. Isaiah in particular seems to have had access to the court (*Is.* 7:3, 8:2, 22:15–16), and he may have played an official role in resolving the crisis caused by the Assyrian invasion of 701 (*Is.* 36–39). However, he was certainly capable of criticizing the abuses of the royal theology and advocated judicious social change to preserve traditional religious values.

Most of the remaining preexilic prophets in Jerusalem were much more supportive of the government than were Isaiah and Micah. Nahum and Habakkuk have both been linked with the Jerusalem cult, and both may have had an official part in it. Both deliver oracles against Israel's enemies and in general behave like typical central prophets.

Toward the end of the monarchical period, peripheral prophecy reappeared in a mild way with the writings of Zephaniah, but it did not become a major force until the work of Jeremiah and Ezekiel (c. 627–571). Jeremiah, a priest who seems to have been heavily influenced by the Deuteronomic movement, launched a series of increasingly harsh attacks on the king and the people, urging them to repent in order to avoid the punishment that God had decreed against Jerusalem. In the final days before the destruction of the city in 587/6, he advocated surrender to the Babylonians, a policy that brought him into conflict with the royal court and the central prophets, who still advocated the old theology of the eternal election of Jerusalem. Jeremiah narrowly escaped with his life, but when the city fell, his prophecies were vindicated. At about the same time, Ezekiel, a priest who had been exiled to Babylon in 597, advocated major modifications of the Jerusalem royal theology held by most of his fellow exiles, but his words had little effect.

Exile and its aftermath. The fall of Jerusalem and the destruction of the Temple in 587/6 created serious authority problems for Israel's prophets. The political and religious institutions that sheltered the central prophets disappeared with the conquest, and those prophets who supported the traditional Jerusalem theology were tragically wrong in their predictions. Peripheral prophets, such as Jeremiah and Ezekiel, gained new credibility because of the fall; but in their latter days they also gave oracles of promise, and as the exile continued, these oracles too seemed to be false.

The prophets of the exilic and postexilic periods faced this problem of authority in several ways. First, they turned away from oral prophecy and adopted writing as the means of circulating their words. Written prophecies were apparently thought to have more authority because of their concreteness. Second, they often attached their prophecies to those of preexilic prophets in an attempt to borrow the authority of their predecessors. Finally, these last representatives of Israelite prophecy turned increasingly toward the divine world for solutions to Israel's overwhelming problems, a move that brought prophecy closer to apocalyptic. Instead of advocating the reform of human behavior in order to cure Israel's religious and social ills, as earlier prophets had done, the postexilic prophets often looked instead to God's direct intervention in history on behalf of those who waited faithfully for God's plan for Israel's salvation to be realized. Some of these postexilic solutions to the problem of prophetic authority can be seen in the postexilic books of Zechariah, Haggai, Joel, and Malachi, and all of them are visible in the writings of the anonymous prophets ("Second Isaiah" and "Third Isaiah") responsible for the last part of the *Book of Isaiah.*

After the exile, central prophecy was briefly restored in the reconstructed Judahite state, and Zechariah and Haggai in particular had roles in shaping the restored community. However, after Ezra's mission to Jerusalem toward the end of the fifth century, officially recognized prophecy was restricted to Levites with specific duties in the cult of the Second Temple (*1 Chr.* 25). After this point, other types of prophecy disappear from the biblical record.

See Also Amos; Ecstasy; Ezekiel; Hosea; Isaiah; Israelite Religion; Jeremiah; Levites; Micah.

Bibliography

The most thorough general treatment of ancient Israelite prophecy is still Johannes Lindblom's *Prophecy in Ancient Israel* (Philadelphia, 1962), although the comparative evidence and the scholarly bibliography on which the book is based are now out of date. A good, nontechnical introduction is provided by Klaus Koch's *The Prophets,* 2 vols., translated by Margaret Kohl (Philadelphia, 1982–1984). Koch gives an overview of biblical prophecy and then treats the major prophets individually. Some of the older literature still contains valuable observations, although many of the points of view expressed in these works have been rejected or modified by modern scholars. See in particular Theodore H. Robinson's *Prophecy and the Prophets in Ancient Israel* (London, 1923) and A. B. Davidson's *Old Testament Prophecy* (Edinburgh, 1903).

A specialized study of the difficult area of postexilic prophecy may be found in David L. Petersen's *Late Israelite Prophecy* (Missoula, Mont., 1977). Aubrey R. Johnson has mounted a strong case for the cultic involvement of most of Israel's prophets. Although few scholars would accept all of Johnson's conclusions, he has produced a valuable survey of the available evidence. See in particular his *The Cultic Prophet in Ancient Israel* (Cadiff, 1962) and *The Cultic Prophet and Israel's Psalmody* (Cardiff, 1979). The fundamental study of the literary patterns in the prophets' oracles is Claus Westermann's *Basic Forms of Prophetic Speech,* translated by Hugh Clayton White (Philadelphia, 1967), although Westermann's work needs to be set in a broader perspective, such as the one provided by W. Eugene March's article "Prophecy," in *Old Testament Form Criticism,* edited by John H. Hayes (San Antonio, 1974), pp. 141–177.

The sociological dimensions of biblical prophecy have been treated comprehensively in my *Prophecy and Society in Ancient Israel* (Philadelphia, 1980). Note also the more specialized study of David L. Petersen, *The Roles of Israel's Prophets* (Sheffield, 1981). A useful synthesis of anthropological evidence on spirit possession is provided by *I. M. Lewis's Ecstatic Religion* (Harmondsworth, 1971). Several illuminating case studies have been collected in *Spirit Mediumship and Society in Africa,* edited by John Beattie and John Middleton (New York, 1969).

A detailed study of the theology of the prophetic traditions has been made by Gerhard von Rad in the second volume of his *Old Testament Theology,* translated by D. M. G. Stalker (New York, 1965). A popular treatment of the same subject may be found in Walter Brueggemann's *The Prophetic Imagination* (Philadelphia, 1978). For two classic studies of prophetic thought, see also Martin Buber's *The Prophetic Faith,* translated by Carlyle Witton-Davies (New York, 1949), and Abraham Joshua Heschel's *The Prophets* (New York, 1962).

New Sources

Aberbach, David. *Imperialism and Biblical Prophecy, 750–500 BCE.* London; New York, 1993.

Arthur, David. *A Smooth Stone: Biblical Prophecy in Historical Perspective.* Lanham, Md., 2001.

Blenkinsopp, Joseph. *A History of Prophecy in Israel.* Rev. and enl. ed. Louisville, Ky., 1996.

Bronner, Leila Leah. "Biblical Prophetesses through Rabbinic Lenses." *Judaism* 40 (1991): 171–183.

Glazov, Gregory Yuri. *The Bridling of the Tongue and the Opening of the Mouth in Biblical Prophecy.* Sheffield, U.K., 2001.

Kaiser, Walter C. *Back toward the Future: Hints for Interpreting Biblical Prophecy.* Grand Rapids, Mich., 1989.

Lieb, Michael. *The Visionary Mode: Biblical Prophecy, Hermeneutics, and Cultural Change.* Ithaca, 1991.

Orton, David E., ed. *Prophecy in the Hebrew Bible: Selected Studies from Vetus Testamentum.* Leiden; Boston, Mass., 2000.

Sandy, D. Brent. *Plowshares and Pruning Hooks: Rethinking the Language of Biblical Prophecy and Apocalyptic.* Downers Grove, Ill., 2002.

Sawyer, John F. A. *Prophecy and the Biblical Prophets.* Rev. ed. Oxford Bible Series. Oxford; New York, 1993.

ROBERT R. WILSON (1987)
Revised Bibliography

PROPHECY: PROPHECY IN POST-BIBLICAL JUDAISM

Rabbinic literature presents no detailed account of prophecy. Approaches to this phenomenon must be gleaned from scattered statements and tales. Moreover, rabbinic literature contains the views of numerous sages, living in different times and places, who were subject to diverse cultural influences and who formulated their views in response to different challenges. As is to be expected, they do not speak with a single voice on this issue. Nevertheless, a number of dominant trends of thought relating to this topic can be discerned.

The prevailing view of the rabbinic sages is that the period of classical prophecy ended with the destruction of the First Temple (586 BCE), and certainly no later than the beginning of the Second Temple (538 BCE). The establishment of the canon of the Hebrew Bible, although an informal process, reflects the feeling that the period of prophecy has come to a close. This view may be attributed in part to the introduction of Hellenism in the Near East in the wake of the conquests of Alexander the Great (356–523 BCE). The major social and cultural-intellectual changes brought about by this event led to a general feeling that a new era has begun. The view that the period of prophecy has ended gained further dominance in rabbinic thought in response to competing sects within Judaism (including the followers of Jesus) who claimed revelation as the basis for their teachings. Yet the general agreement among the sages that classical forms of prophecy belong to the past and to the messianic future did not eradicate a contrary trend that was also very popular. Many continued to view revelation as an ongoing phenomenon that existed in their era in different forms, such as that of a heavenly voice. One can also find in the Talmud a tradition that views the proper understanding of Ezekiel's account of the celestial domain ("Account of the Chariot") as leading to a revelatory experience. Other sages, although acknowledging these types of phenomenon, are adamant in negating revelation's role in determining law after the revelation of the Torah to Moses. Authority in this matter belongs to the sages and their institutions. The sages see themselves as the true heirs of the prophets and in some way even superior to them. Furthermore, the prophets themselves are viewed as having been sages. In keeping with Moses's role in the transmission of the divine law, his prophecy alone is accorded a unique status.

Other issues related to prophecy also find expression in rabbinic literature. Some sages posit necessary conditions for attaining prophecy, such as wisdom, valor, and wealth. This view may also have served to combat popular approaches to revelation that viewed it as an ongoing phenomenon available to everyone. Other sages regard prophecy as depended solely on the divine will. One view goes so far as to accord the wicked Balaam a status that is at least equal to that of Moses. In the Middle Ages Jewish thinkers were to draw from these diverse views in developing and defending their approaches to prophecy.

SAʿADYAH GAON'S APPROACH TO PROPHECY. The first comprehensive attempt to understand prophecy in medieval Jewish thought is presented by Saʿadyah Gaon (882–942) in his theological treatise *Book of Beliefs and Opinions* (933 CE). Of particular concern to him is the problem of how to interpret the texts of divine revelation in a manner that negates divine corporeality. Agreeing with the rational proofs for the incorporeality of God presented in Islamic theology (*kalām*), Saʿadyah interprets figuratively all corporeal descriptions of God in the Bible. He rejects their literal meaning entirely. Saʿadyah is not oblivious to the problems this approach poses to the authority of Scripture once one dismisses its literal truth. He insists that the literal meaning should be maintained in all instances in which it is not blatantly contradicted by knowledge attained by a different reliable source, such as rational demonstration or sense perception. Even in the cases in which the literal meaning is rejected, the figurative interpretation should be in harmony with Hebrew usage. Saʿadyah's approach to biblical exegesis paved the way for reconciling the truths of revelation with the fruits of rational enquiry. It also enabled him to continue to uphold the authority of Scripture as a source of truth in theoretical matters. This approach has a sharp impact on subsequent Jewish thought.

An incorporeal deity possesses no organs of speech nor has any physical form that can be seen. This poses a severe challenge to the veracity of the biblical accounts of God addressing the prophet. Saʿadyah solves this difficulty by maintaining that the divine speech heard by the prophets was audible speech created by God in the air and conveyed to their hearing. The visions of God seen by the prophets were not actually of God but of a special luminous being, termed God's Glory (*kavod*) or Indwelling (*shekhina*), which assumed different forms in accordance with the divine will. Moses's request to behold God (*Ex.* 33: 18–20) is interpreted by Saʿadyah as a request to see the front part of the Glory. This request is denied him because the intensity of the light would inevitably destroy him; instead he is allowed to attain a close-up view of the back of the Glory. One can detect in some of Saʿadyah's descriptions of the Glory a hint of the idea of the divine Logos, an idea known to him by way of Jewish sources and Moslem theological ones. By accepting the existence of such a being and treating it as composed of a special form of light, Saʿadyah is able to interpret the prophetic visions of God in as literal manner as possible without treating God as corporeal. His approach also enables him to treat the visions seen by the prophets, as well as the words they heard, as empirically verifiable by them—the senses being a source of reliable knowledge in his view. Given his perception of the danger that the idea of a divine intermediary poses to strict monotheism, he at the same time stresses that the Glory is created and not coeternal with God, and he sharply curtails its providential role in the world. Its primary function is to verify to the prophet the truth of the message attained.

Saʿadyah continues the dominant rabbinic trend in not viewing prophecy as a living phenomenon. It existed in the biblical period and will be reintroduced only in messianic times. It served primarily as a mission for conveying divine commands as well as theoretical truths and knowledge of the future. The truth of the prophetic message was verified to the people by means of miracles. God was directly involved in the choice of each prophet, the particular mission bestowed and the miracles performed. In Saʿadyah's view, God's incorporeality and unity do not preclude God's immediate relation with the material world and its inhabitants.

Prophecy in the Philosophy of Maimonides. Already in the period of Saʿadyah a number of Jewish philosophers begin to view prophecy more in terms of a naturally attained perfection than a supernaturally bestowed mission. This followed developments taking place in Islamic philosophy. Two distinct, but not mutually exclusive, models of prophecy emerge based on earlier Greek philosophic approaches. In the first model, prophecy is consequent on the perfection of the intellect resulting in a form of ontological conjunction with the supernal Intellect and the attainment of intellectual illumination or revelation. In addition to the higher level knowledge of theoretical truths attained in this state the individual experiences an immense spiritual pleasure. In the second model, prophecy is consequent on a perfect imagination, enabling the individual to attain knowledge of the future in accordance with the matters that preoccupy the individual's thought. This form of prophecy occurs most frequently in individuals lacking a well-developed intellect, and it generally assumes the form of veridical dreams. Both models can be found in the writings of the tenth century Islamic philosopher Alfarabi, who combines them in the case of one possessing both a perfect intellect and perfect imagination. He regards the one attaining revelation as the ideal ruler, thereby transforming Plato's (c. 428–347/8 BCE) philosopher-king to the prophet-lawgiver. God's role is confined to being the first cause of all that happens in the world. God does not personally choose each prophet or bestow on the individual a specific message. Alfarabi's approach strongly influenced that of Moses Maimonides (1135/8–1204), writing in the twelfth century.

No approach to prophecy in Jewish thought is as multifaceted as the one presented by Maimonides. In the *Guide of the Perplexed* (2.36) Maimonides defines prophecy as an emanation from God through the intermediation of the Active Intellect to the rational faculty and then to the imagination. To attain this emanation the individual must possess a perfect intellect that has mastered all the sciences, a perfect imagination, and a strong moral character. Anyone who fails to meet any of these conditions cannot become a prophet. As a result of the prophetic emanation, the individual attains knowledge of profound theoretical matters, rules for the governance of others, and knowledge of the future. Maimonides leaves little doubt that he regards prophecy as a natural phenomenon. He equates it with the highest level of human perfection, which lies primarily in the perfection of the intellect. The prophetic visions, consisting of sights or words, are the product of the prophet's own imaginative faculty and they have no physical reality.

Maimonides implies that the emanation resulting in prophecy is a force from the Active Intellect that strengthens the individual's perfect faculties and enables the individual to reach new heights of knowledge. God plays no immediate role in what the prophet learns as a result of this experience. A superior imagination enables the prophet to translate conceptual knowledge into figurative form, in addition to attaining knowledge of the future. This is important for the prophet's role in educating the masses, who are incapable of grasping profound theoretical truths in a purely conceptual manner. It may also aid the prophet to grasp better these highly abstract matters.

Maimonides' discussions alternate between stressing the imaginative aspect of prophecy and the intellectual one. In some passages he also alludes to the nature of the experience itself. At the end of *Guide* (3.51) he describes the death of the perfect individual, in which the human intellect, having conjoined with the Active Intellect, permanently leaves the body and remains eternally in a state of ultimate spiritual pleasure. This description is reminiscent of accounts of ecstatic death found in mystical literature and can be traced to the common Neoplatonic roots of medieval philosophy and mysticism.

Prophecy in itself does not entail a mission in Maimonides' view and may remain an entirely private attainment. Moreover, no one who has attained this illumination is eager to undertake a public role rather than continue to enjoy this most pleasurable of states. The prophetic mission results from the emanating perfection characterizing superior prophets, which drives them to perfect those around them and not rest satisfied with their own perfection. Maimonides compares this to the emanating perfection of the greatest philosophers that lead them to write books and teach others the truths they have attained. As is the case of the individual who has seen the light of the sun but nevertheless is made to return to the cave in Plato's famous myth, the public prophet must return to society and assume a leadership role. Yet for Maimonides it is not any external pressure that compels the prophet to do so. The vision in which God commands the prophet to go to the people is a figurative representation in the soul of the prophet of the feeling of compulsion to act in this manner after experiencing illumination. The mission itself in this case is part of the prophetic experience and reflects the workings of divine providence within the natural order.

Although Maimonides follows Alfarabi in regarding the prophets as philosopher-kings, he stops short of ascribing to them any legislative role. The laying down of the divine law is confined to Moses alone. He treats Mosaic prophecy and the revelation at Sinai as supernatural events, both involving audible speech whose author was God. In this manner he preserves the traditional foundations of Judaism. Yet one can read Maimonides's discussions as subtly indicating that he has a naturalistic understanding of these phenomena as well. Moses attained the highest level of perfection possible resulting in a purely intellectual illumination that did not involve the imagination at all in the apprehension of the most profound theoretical truths. This illumination enabled him to lay down a perfect law that directed society to its utmost perfection, one in which its citizens reach the highest perfection of which each is capable. Only this law deserves the label "divine." This notion is to be hidden from the masses, whose faith in Judaism is contingent on belief that God personally revealed the Law.

When dealing with prophecy in his legal works, Maimonides sharply curtails any role the prophet has in deciding legal matters notwithstanding the ideal leadership qualities they possess in his view. He is very concerned about the threat to Judaism posed by those whom he regards as false prophets, particularly charismatic individuals who seek to introduce major modifications in Mosaic Law on the basis of revelation. Maimonides seeks to insulate the Law from any changes that are not brought about by the formal institutions in Judaism entrusted with the power to determine legal matters. The leadership role of the prophets is be exercised primarily as members of those institutions and not by virtue of their claim to revelation. For the same reason he also posits near impossible tests for any latter-day claimant to public prophecy.

Although Maimonides at times expresses the traditional sentiment that prophecy has ceased to exist and will only reemerge at the advent of the messianic period, his naturalistic approach to prophecy allows for the possibility at least that individuals in any generation may satisfy the requisite conditions for its attainment. It could hardly be otherwise given the integral connection he draws between prophecy and human perfection. There are a number of allusions in his writings to the fact that he regards prophecy as a living phenomenon, one that was attained by some of the great sages of the past after the biblical period, such as R. Judah the Prince and R. Akiva, although they made no claim to public prophecy. There are even hints that Maimonides himself felt he had experienced revelation.

Maimonides's approach to prophecy bridges what appears to be an unfathomable chasm between Aristotelian philosophy and Jewish tradition. The texts of the Bible are completely true. The prophets were great philosophers who presented the truths they had attained in figurative form. Yet the reader who wishes to understand these truths must turn to Greek philosophy to unlock the meaning of the prophetic texts.

Generations of Jewish philosophers after Maimonides differ on the extent the Bible taught theoretical truths not attained in philosophy. The early fourteenth century philosopher Gersonides (1288–1344; *Wars of the Lord)*, for example, essentially negates the view that the prophets grasped truths not available to the philosophers. Later philosophers such as Hasdai Crescas (1340–1410; *Light of the Lord)*, Joseph Albo (1380–1444; *Book of Principles*) and Isaac Abrabanel (1437–1508; *Commentary on the Guide of the Perplexed*), on the other hand, argue the contrary position. They accord the prophets the attainment of truths beyond the realm of the discursive reasoning of the philosophers. They also challenge the completely naturalistic foundation underlying Maimonides' approach and seek to ascribe to God a more immediate involvement in the choice of prophets and the content of their revelation. Yet for all the differences between the medieval philosophic approaches, they share the view that underlying the figurative language and the parables of the Bible are to be found the most profound conceptual truths.

SPINOZA ON PROPHECY. Baruch Spinoza (1632–1677), writing in the seventeenth century, sets out to negate this view in his *Tractaus Thologico-Politicus.* He thereby attempts to undermine the authority of the Bible (i.e., the Hebrew Scriptures, or Old Testament) as a source of truth, let alone the ultimate source. Ironically he utilizes the authority of the Bible to accomplish this task. A literal understanding of the Bible, he argues, leads to the conclusion that it in no way touches on conceptual matters belonging to the domain of philosophy, not even in figurative form.

Spinoza rejects any supernatural conception of divine activity. Everything must be understood in accordance with the eternal laws of nature. In his approach to revelation he builds on the two naturalistic models of prophecy found in the medieval sources. Yet, instead of combining them, he treats them as completely distinct. Against Maimonides and his followers, Spinoza argues that the biblical prophets possessed solely a perfect imagination and lacked intellectual perfection (i.e., the mastery of science and philosophy). As one can discern from the Bible itself, they were simple individuals who addressed other simple people. Hence the revelation they attained involved only the workings of the imagination.

Spinoza accords the prophets a strong moral sense but no true speculative knowledge, including a philosophic understanding of morality. This was no less true of Moses who lacked a proper understanding of the nature of his own prophetic experience. Hence, the divine law Moses legislated as a result of his imaginative prophecy does not lead to perfection and ultimate felicity, only to a society well ordered for its time. The second type of prophecy, purely intellectual illumination, is ascribed by Spinoza to Jesus. The nature of this illumination is treated in greater detail towards the end of his *Ethics*, in which he labels it "the third kind of knowledge." It is the final stage in the quest for intellectual perfection. The conclusion to which the reader is drawn is that only the truths attained in a natural manner by the human intellect should be labeled divine and the prophetic texts contain no divine truths at all. Hence the medieval Jewish philosophic enterprise that treats philosophy and the Bible as teaching essentially the same truths is without foundation. Spinoza's approach to biblical revelation and human reason plays a critical role in the development of modern Jewish thought, even among those philosophers who stopped far short of his radical conclusions or who challenged them.

Prophecy in Qabbalistic Thought. Alongside medieval Jewish philosophic treatments of prophecy, there also developed mystical approaches. It may be argued that inherent in the turn to mystical study is the attempt to attain conjunction (termed *devequt*) with the higher realms (if not with God) and the illumination of the intellect. This in essence is identical with what the mystics perceive as the prophetic experience. Some of the early mystical texts written after the Talmud, termed *heikhalot* literature, present the road to illumination as a journey of the soul through the celestial palaces. The texts convey knowledge of the secret names of the angels (and of God) that allows the mystic to continue the ascent until he or she reaches the final palace in which he or she beholds God in all the divine glory, together with myriads of angels. Most of the subsequent qabbalistic texts do not present the road to mystical illumination or the nature of the experience so explicitly. They tend to be theosophical in character, describing the world of the Godhead, at times by way of mystical homilies on biblical verses. This is true particularly of the most important texts in the Jewish mystical tradition, those that constitute the Zohar. Yet it appears that some of the stories found there dealing with the experience of enlightenment that the authors ascribe to the rabbinic sages hint to their own experience of revelation. The proper study of the Bible, particularly the Torah, from the perspective of the system of the ten divine sefirot (emanations) the text embodies, is the path to this experience.

An important exception to the reticence on the part of Qabbalists to talk explicitly about mystical illumination and the path to its attainment is the school of prophetic Qabbalah belonging to Abraham Abulafia (thirteenth century). Abulafia laid claim to revelation and wrote a number of works, including prophetic manuals, describing the state of mystical ecstasy as well as indicating how to attain this state. His mystical approach combines older forms of Jewish mysticism focusing on the divine sefirot and the divine names with techniques involving Hebrew letter combinations. It also shares some striking similarities with Sufi and Eastern mysticisms.

Qabbalistic approaches to conjunction with the divine realm and the attainment of mystical illumination, particularly those approaches focusing on the study of the Zohar, gave rise to a good number of mystical movements within Judaism, such as Hasidism, that continue to attract followers.

Approaches to Prophecy in Modern Jewish Philosophy. The idea of revelation occupies a central position in the thought of many of the most prominent modern Jewish philosophers. As in the case with the medieval Jewish philosophers, their approaches to revelation are integrally related to their overall philosophy and tend to combine ideas found in Jewish sources with contemporary philosophical developments. Immanuel Kant's (1724–1804) philosophy, in its stress on the inherent limitations of reason in attaining speculative theological truths yet its ability to attain moral truths that are to serve as the basis for theology, sets the stage for many modern Jewish philosophical approaches to revelation. Far different thinkers in the nineteenth century, such as Samson Raphael Hirsch (1808–1888; *Horeb*) and Salomon Steinheim (1789–1866; *Revelation according to the Doctrine of the Synagogue*), utilize Kant's strictures on reason to defend the idea of supernatural revelation. Hirsch sees the transmitted text of the Torah in its entirety as a product of divine revelation and hence the basis for understanding God's thoughts. Revelation for Steinheim, on the other hand, is in essence synonymous with faith. He identifies the content of revelation with the doctrines of the freely willed creation of the world *ex nihilo* (out of nothing) on the part of the one God, the human being's moral freedom and the immortality of the soul. These doctrines in his view are closed to reason. It is revelation, and not autonomous ethical reason, that makes ethical activity possible.

Abraham Geiger (1810–1874), a leading theologian in the early Reform movement and a pioneering scholar of the academic study of Judaism, is also influenced by Kant as well as by G. W. F. Hegel (1770–1831), in developing his approach to prophecy. Geiger sees Judaism as a living organism developing in history as it assumes different forms. At its heart lies the prophetic idea of God and morality. By means of a careful study of Jewish history Geiger sought to reform Judaism to best express this idea in his own day without breaking completely with its past.

In the early twentieth century, Hermann Cohen (1842–1918) developed his philosophy of Judaism (*Religion of Reason out of the Sources of Judaism*) on a Kantian foundation while breaking with Kant on fundamental points of his philosophy. Revelation for Cohen is the bridge between God's Being and the human being in the state of becoming. Revelation addresses itself to reason, indeed it is the creator of reason, which culminates in the idea of ethical monotheism. Cohen does not think of revelation as an event but as an attribute of relation that expresses itself primarily in ethical activity. This relation is expressed in the message of the biblical prophets.

Cohen's philosophy of religion on one hand and the approaches of different existential philosophers—particularly Søren Kierkegaard (1813–1855) and Martin Heidegger (1889–1976)—on the other exert a profound influence on the approach to revelation in the religious existential-dialogical philosophy developed by the twentieth-century philosophers Martin Buber (1878–1965; *I and Thou*) and Franz Rosenzweig (1886–1929; *Star of Redemption*). True human existence for them does not begin with one's awareness of individuality, but with the next step—the encounter with the other not as an object but as a subject. God is the Absolute Other. Revelation is neither the result of union with God (the individual always remains an independent subject in their view), nor is it concerned with attaining conceptual truths about the Godhead. It is the name given to the encounter in which the individual experiences God's love, listens to God's "speech," and is drawn into a dialogue with God by returning love. By means of this relation one is redeemed from one's isolation. Moreover, divine love or speech always makes demands on the listener in the form of ethical activity. Love must be extended to others also drawing them into the dialogue. The Law heard by Moses and the divine speech heard by the prophets are to be read as historical reflections of this existential dialogue.

Buber's and Rosenzweig's philosophy heavily influenced Abraham Joshua Heschel (1907–1972), most of whose philosophy and scholarship focuses on prophecy. In developing his own philosophy, he is particularly concerned with understanding the existential confrontation between the prophet and God on one hand, and between the prophet and society on the other. In his book *The Prophets,* Heschel defines prophecy as "exegesis of existence from a divine perspective. Understanding prophecy is an understanding of understanding rather than an understanding of knowledge. It is exegesis of exegesis. It involves sharing the perspective from which the original understanding is done" (Heschel, 1962, p. xviii). The writings of other modern Jewish philosophers, such as Joseph B. Soloveitchik (19903–1993) and Emmanuel Lévinas (1906–1995), also reflect the influence of the religious existential-dialogic philosophy of Buber and Rosenzweig, whose thought continues to attract new generations of students.

BIBLIOGRAPHY

For rabbinic views on prophecy see Ephraim Urbach, *The Sages: Their Concepts and Beliefs,* translated by Israel Abrahams (Jerusalem, 1975). The most comprehensive treatment of this phenomenon in medieval Jewish philosophy is to be found in Howard Kreisel, *Prophecy: The History of an Idea in Medieval Jewish Philosophy* (Dordrecht, Netherlands, 2001). For qabbalistic thought, see Elliot Wolfson, *Through a Speculum that Shines* (Princeton, N.J., 1994), as well as the works of Moshe Idel, particularly *Studies in Ecstatic Kabbalah* (Albany, N.Y., 1988). No comprehensive treatment of prophecy in modern Jewish thought has yet been written in the English language (Eliezer Scweid has written in Hebrew a book on this subject), and one must turn to studies of the individual thinkers. Noteworthy is the fact that some of the most important modern Jewish thinkers also produced studies exploring the biblical phenomenon of prophecy, which allow readers at the same time to attain a further glimpse of their own thought on the subject. See for example Martin Buber, *The Prophetic Faith,* translated by Carlyle Witton-Davies (New York, 1949) and Abraham Joshua Heschel, *The Prophets* (New York, 1962). Mention deserves to be made also of the studies of Leo Strauss focusing on medieval political approaches to prophecy. See for example his *Philosophy and Law,* translated by Eve Adler (Albany, N.Y., 1995).

HOWARD KREISEL (2005)

PROPHECY: AFRICAN PROPHETISM

Studies of African religious leaders provide many descriptions of priests, diviners, healers, and witch finders, although relatively few have focused on the role of prophets within African religions. Although historians of religion debate about what constitutes a prophet, it is possible to distinguish two distinct visions: (1) the Greeks envisioned a prophet as a cultic figure who spoke on behalf of a god, and (2) ancient Israelite religion translated the term *prophet* from the Hebrew word *navi,* thereby defining prophets as spokespersons only for a supreme being. The role of these prophets was eventually narrowed to those leaders who played an oppositional role within the society in which they taught. It was this image of the prophet that captured the imaginations of scholars of religion.

Given Western commentators' assumptions that the supreme being played a relatively unimportant role in African religions, this category of prophets was rarely applied to African religions. Those who have used the term remain divided about its breadth. Some apply it to more institutionalized and hereditary forms of religious leadership, such as the office of the Mugwe among the Meru of Kenya. They served as religiously sanctioned chiefs, healers, and judges but did not necessarily receive privileged communication either from the supreme being or lesser spirits. Most commentators, however, insist on a more dramatic prophetic calling involving a direct experience of an extraordinary communication. Some apply it only to those who claim revelation from a supreme being (i.e., the Abrahamic model); others apply it to such communication from lesser deities or ancestors (i.e., the Greek model). Herein the usage of the term refers to the broader category and, as has been the practice in most studies of African prophets, includes people claiming revelation from lesser deities.

MEDIUMS, DIVINERS, AND PROPHETS. There are distinctions among mediums, diviners, and prophets. Spirit mediums are extremely common in African religious experience. These are individuals who receive messages from the supreme being or a lesser spirit, which are then interpreted by a priest to the community of adherents. It is the priest, rather than the medium, who controls community understanding of the revelation. Shona and Igbo religions, for example, have important mediums of the supreme being. In each case, a woman becomes possessed by and speaks in the voice of the supreme being, usually in a language other than her own. A male ritual specialist then interprets the message for those in attendance. Spirit mediums for lesser spirits are common to most African religions. In sharp contrast, however, prophets—whether they enter into an ecstatic state to receive communications—control the interpretation of their message and present it directly to the community. Both prophets and mediums, however, are considered to be speaking with the authority of the spiritual being who revealed the message to them. Prophets are more closely associated with specific periods of social stress and collective instability. Mediums are more closely associated with individual problems and disturbances. Both must be distinguished from diviners, who either examine signs or omens in nature or have developed mechanical techniques for ascertaining the will of deities or other spiritual forces. These religious specialists are extremely common in African religion but are understood as interpreters of signs rather than recipients of messages from spiritual beings.

Finally, distinctions must also be made between prophets within indigenous African religions and prophets within African independent churches, who situate themselves explicitly within a Judeo-Christian tradition of prophetic authority. Figures such as Simon Kimbangu (1889–1951) of Congo, John Maranke and Alice Lenshina (c. 1924–1978) of Zambia, and Isaiah Shembe (c. 1870–1935) of South Africa all claimed prophetic revelations, which led them to create independent African churches. Ecstatic visionaries associated with African Ṣūfī orders, such as Cheikh Ahmadou Bamba (1853–1927) of Senegal and Usuman dan Fodio (1754–1817) of Nigeria, are not considered prophets by African Muslims, but they share many characteristics with African Christian prophetic figures.

EAST AFRICAN TRADITIONS. Most of the religious leaders in East Africa identified as prophets tend to be individuals claiming privileged communication from lesser spirits rather than the supreme being. In some Nilotic religious traditions, however, lesser spirits are often seen as emanations of the supreme being. Through his field research on the Nuer people of southern Sudan, the British anthropologist Edward E. Evans-Pritchard was the first to describe an African prophetic tradition. The term *guk*, which earlier commentators had translated as *witch doctors*, Evans-Pritchard understood as *prophet*. He defined *guk* as a "man possessed by a spirit of some kind. . . . They are mouthpieces of the Gods" (cited in Anderson and Johnson, 1995, p. 2). He also emphasized their role in the development of oppositional politics in the wake of Mahdist and British intervention in the southern Sudan. These Nuer prophets claimed direct revelation from spirits of the above or sky deities, which Evans-Pritchard described as emanations of the supreme being Kwoth Nhial. These prophets, who also served as healers in the Nuer society, became prominent during the period of political instability and warfare as Egyptian forces penetrated the southern Sudan and began slaving in the area during the mid–nineteenth century.

Many of the most prominent prophets, such as Ngundeng and his son Gwek, claimed to speak with the authority of a spirit known as Deng. Both would spend long periods in the bush, either in ecstatic states or in the quiet repose of meditation. Ngundeng created a massive mound of brush, earth, and ivory tusks, where he conducted sacrifices and disseminated his teachings. He ritually removed evil substances and powers from the community and buried them within the mound. He also led his Nuer followers to a military victory over a neighboring Dinka community of southern Sudan before eventually being challenged by the British. He died in 1906. In the 1920s his son Gwek claimed to be a prophet of Deng, but his career was short-lived. He was killed by the British, who also destroyed the ritual center established by his father. Since the 1950s other Nuer prophets have become involved in the Sudanese civil war. The most famous of these, Wutnyang Gatakek, who claimed his authority from Kwoth Nhial and Deng, became well known in the 1990s while working for an independent southern Sudan and peace between Nuer and their Dinka neighbors.

Similar to the Nuer, the neighboring Dinka had religious leaders inspired by clan and free divinities. They were known as *ran nhialic* (men of divinity). Like Nuer prophets, Dinka prophets served as peacemakers in disputes between clans but were also capable of cursing malcontents and leading war parties. Other Nilotic groups, like the Meban of Ethiopia, had prophets who claimed they had direct contact with a divinity and allegedly could control life and death through both word and thought. The Kalenjin of Kenya and the Maasai of Kenya and Tanzania also had prophets. Among the Maasai these prophets, known as *laibon*, were associated with rainmaking and were thought to be either of foreign or celestial origin. During the period of resistance to British and German occupations, the *laibon* played an important role in the preparation of war medicines to ensure the safety of Maasai warriors and to enhance the possibility of victory. These later roles earned them the enmity of colonial authorities and often led to their arrest and detention. In central Kenya in the early twentieth century missionaries described Embu and Kikuyu men who had dreams or visions of God and who taught what was revealed to them.

By far the most famous of the East African prophets was Kinjikitile of the Matumbi hills area of southeastern Tanganyika. Claiming that he was possessed by a divinatory spirit known as Lilungu and by a more widely worshipped spirit known as Hongo, he organized a movement that led to the unsuccessful Maji-Maji revolt of 1905–1907. His initial contact with Hongo came as a result of a shamanic journey in which he was said to have entered a river and to have emerged a considerable time later, wearing dry clothes and teaching about the imminent return of the ancestors and the departure of the Europeans. Word spread that he was planning to organize resistance and that people needed to wash with a sacred *maji*, Swahili and Arabic for water, which would protect them against European weapons. The actual revolt, however, began prematurely and was brutally suppressed. Warfare and famine brought on by German destruction of local farms and granaries led to the death of over seventy-five thousand people, including Kinjikitile himself. His multiethnic movement, however, was later hailed as a first war for independence and the beginning of a Tanganyikan national movement.

Xhosa Tradition. In southern Africa a prophetic tradition developed among the Xhosa in the wake of a series of military defeats and land losses in the late eighteenth century and early nineteenth century that led to the European occupation of the Western Cape Province. By 1816 Nxele began to teach of an African god he called Mdalidephu and of Thixo, the god of Europeans. Having lived on a settler farm for a number of years, Nxele became familiar with basic Christian teachings, which he placed within a Xhosa context. He claimed that Europeans murdered Thixo's son Tayi and were punished by being thrown in the sea. They emerged from the ocean on Xhosa lands, where they threatened Xhosa independence and control of their land. Nxele, who claimed to teach in the name of the "Chief of heaven and earth," proclaimed that they must abandon witchcraft to purify themselves and to rid the land of the whites. Then the ancestors would return from the dead. British officials arrested Nxele and imprisoned him at Robben Island; he died trying to swim to freedom.

In 1850 another Xhosa prophet, Mlanjeni, gathered a substantial following. He was a young man, about eighteen years old, when he began to teach. He fasted frequently, remained for long periods of purification in the wilderness, and kept celibate to preserve his powers from what he regarded as dangerous contact with women. Initially his teachings were not taken seriously, because he began to teach before he had been initiated in a circumcision school. He prayed to the supreme being whom he identified with the sun. Mlanjeni linked the drought of 1850 and the loss of cattle and land to a pervasive evil substance (*ubuthi*), which was associated with witchcraft. He became a witch finder and purged the witchcraft from those he found had practiced it. He also ordered people to destroy all charms, amulets, and medicines. Furthermore Mlanjeni provided his followers with a root that he said would protect them against European guns. In 1850 his followers went to war but met a decisive defeat after several years. In 1855 five prophets claimed to be in touch with the Russians, a black nation across the sea that was also battling the British in the Crimean War, and taught the Xhosa that they should expect Russian assistance.

In April 1856 a teenage girl named Nongqawuse heard her name called by a couple of strangers standing in the scrubland near the gardens she was watching over. They told her to tell her uncle Mhlakaza that all the ancestors would rise from the dead and that the Europeans would be expelled if the Xhosa slaughtered all their cattle and destroyed their grain, both of which had been contaminated by witchcraft. Her uncle, a major chief, decided that the strangers included his brother, Nongqawuse's father, who had died many years before. With Mhlakaza's support, what became known as the Xhosa Cattle Killing spread rapidly, leading to the destruction of thousands of cattle and granaries. Yet the prophecy did not come true. Some attributed this to the refusal of some Xhosa to make the sacrifice; others questioned the prophetic teaching itself. In either case, however, the severe famine that resulted from the sacrifice forced many Xhosa to accept British authority, and it effectively ended Xhosa resistance in South Africa.

Diola Tradition. The Diola of Senegal, Gambia, and Guinea-Bissau have a continuous tradition of prophetic revelation from their supreme being, Emitai, dating back to the founding of major Diola communities, described by their oldest oral traditions. The epithet *Emitai dabognol* (God had sent him or her) was applied to those individuals who claimed a prophetic calling. Most of these prophets focused their attention on the procurement of rain from Emitai. *Emitai ehlahl* is the word for rain and indicates that rain is something that falls from the supreme being. Oral traditions concerning the precolonial era describe eleven men who claimed that Emitai communicated with them. Many of the traditions concerning the earliest prophets resemble accounts of cultural heroes, who establish communities and introduce a variety of spirit shrines (*ukine*) for prayers to Emitai to obtain rain. Since the effective establishment of colonial rule in the late nineteenth century, more than forty people have claimed prophetic revelation, two-thirds of whom are women. Sixteen of these prophets were active in the closing years of the twentieth century. Thus colonization seemed to play a causal role in the intensification and transformation of this prophetic tradition into one in which women played a central role.

Alinesitoué Diatta was the most famous of these prophets. In 1942 she introduced a major new spirit shrine (*boekine*) that she claimed Emitai gave her in an auditory revelation. Her rituals stressed the importance of neighborhood-wide celebrations that focused on the sacrifice of a black bull and six days and nights of feasting and celebrations in the public square. She insisted that women and children as well as men could be priests of her shrine and that the ritual knowledge should be shared publicly. She also taught that Emitai looked with disapproval on those who violated a Diola Sabbath for the land by working in the rice paddies, on those who neglected to plant African varieties of rice in favor of Asiatic forms introduced by Europeans, and on those men who abandoned rice farming for the cultivation of peanuts as a cash crop.

As a result of these actions and the neglect of ritual obligations by converts to Christianity and Islam, Emitai withheld life-giving rain. Her ritual of *Kasila* reaffirmed the community of indigenous Diola religion and stressed the importance of local crops as well as the role of Emitai in protecting Diola communities. In 1943 Vichy French officials arrested her, tried her under a native law code for obstructing colonial initiatives, and exiled her to Tombouctou in French Soudan. She died a year later, but news of her death was kept as a state secret until 1987. Since her death, others have come forward, claiming that Emitai had sent them in the tradition of Alinesitoué Diatta.

SEE ALSO African Religions, overview article; Alinesitoué; East African Religions, overview article; God, article on African Supreme Beings; Politics and Religion, article on Politics and African Religious Traditions.

BIBLIOGRAPHY

Anderson, David M., and Douglas H. Johnson, ed. *Revealing Prophets: Prophecy in East African History.* London, 1995.

Baum, Robert M. *Shrines of the Slave Trade: Diola Religion and Society in Precolonial Senegambia.* New York, 1999.

Baum, Robert M. "Alinesitoué: A West African Woman Prophet." In *Unspoken Worlds: Women's Religious Lives,* edited by Nancy A. Falk and Rita M. Gross. Belmont, Calif., 2001.

Bernardi, Bernardo. *The Mugwe: A Failing Prophet.* London, 1959.

Evans-Pritchard, Edward E. *Nuer Religion.* New York, 1956; reprint, 1974.

Johnson, Douglas H. *Nuer Prophets: A History of Prophecy from the Upper Nile in the Nineteenth and Twentieth Centuries.* Oxford, 1994.

Lienhardt, Godfrey. *Divinity and Experience: The Religion of the Dinka.* Oxford, 1961; reprint, 1978.

Peires, Jeffrey B. *The Dead Will Arise: Nongqawuse and the Great Xhosa Cattle-Killing Movement of 1856–7.* Johannesburg, 1989.

Ray, Benjamin. *African Religions: Symbol, Ritual, and Community.* Upper Saddle River, N.J., 2000.

ROBERT M. BAUM (2005)

PROPHET, MARK AND ELIZABETH CLARE.

Mark (1918–1973) and Elizabeth Clare (b. 1939) Prophet (and the movements they founded, the Summit Lighthouse and Church Universal and Triumphant) are key figures in the emergence of American New Age apocalypticism during the second half of the twentieth century. The Prophets combined charismatic authority, Gnostic spirituality, patriotism, and esotericism to construct an influential system of alternative spirituality in America's New Age subculture.

Mark L. Prophet was born in Chippewa Falls, Wisconsin, on December 24, 1918. His devout mother reared him in the Methodist tradition, but also exposed him to the teachings of the Unity School of Christianity. Later publications of Church Universal and Triumphant claim that Prophet met the Ascended Master El Morya when he was seventeen years old and working as a railroad employee. "Ascended master" is a concept borrowed from the I AM Religious Activity, and refers to a spiritual hierarchy of advanced entities ("masters") who are responsible for the evolution of humankind. During World War II, Prophet served in the Army Air Corps and began to immerse himself in the alternative spiritual teachings of the Rosicrucians and the Self-Realization Fellowship. By the 1950s, the now-married Prophet was publishing "dictations" from El Morya anonymously for an I AM-offshoot organization, the Lighthouse of Freedom.

In 1958, Prophet moved to Washington, D.C., and founded his own organization, the Summit Lighthouse, whose mission was to publish the periodical teachings he received from the ascended masters. An inner core of followers, the Keepers of the Flame Fraternity, received advanced teachings from Prophet on such topics as decreeing, ascension, the ascended masters, reincarnation, and the coming Golden Age of spiritual illumination. Central to Prophet's eclectic version of Theosophical and I AM Activity teachings was his own role as the sole messenger for the ascended masters in the dawning Aquarian Age. Also central to his teachings was his conviction that the coming Golden Age was destined to appear first in the United States, where a race of "lightbearers" would be born. This appearance was endangered, however, by supernatural forces of evil that worked through world communism and the elite leaders of international finance and "one-world" political movements.

The purpose of humanity, according to Prophet, was to attain "ascension," a state of divinelike existence in which the human soul was united to its divine self. Before this could occur, a soul must "balance its karma," the accumulated negative energies of its past lives, and dedicate itself to the path of the ascended masters. The basic spiritual practice taught by Prophet was "decreeing," in which disciples vocalized dynamic affirmations that included the biblical name of God, "I Am." Prophet claimed that this practice gave students the power to overcome negative conditions in their lives and to create a proper relationship with their God-self. Prophet's fusion of esoteric spirituality, conspiracy theories, and right-wing political ideology would provide the catalyst for a dangerous period of apocalyptic urgency in the group during the late 1980s and early 1990s.

Prophet met Elizabeth Clare Wulf (b. 1939 in Red Bank, New Jersey) at a public lecture in 1961. Wulf, a student of Russian politics at Boston University, was the daughter of a Swiss governess and a German naval officer. By 1963, Mark Prophet and Elizabeth Wulf had divorced their respective spouses, married, and moved to Fairfax, Virginia. In 1964, Elizabeth Clare Prophet was "anointed" as co-messenger for the ascended masters by Saint Germain, the ascended master responsible for the destiny of the United States.

Between 1964 and 1972, the Prophets had four children and moved Summit Lighthouse to Colorado Springs. It was during this period that the group began attracting the youth counterculture and expanding in significant numbers in the United States. The Prophets bought a mansion that became the movement's international headquarters, publishing center, and residence for themselves and their most dedicated students. They also established Montessori International, a children's school based on the teachings of Maria Montessori and the ascended masters, and Ascended Master (now Summit) University to provide advanced students with an intensive immersion in the group's system of esoteric spirituality.

Mark Prophet died suddenly on February 26, 1973. Elizabeth Clare Prophet proclaimed that her late husband's soul was now the Ascended Master Lanello. The group was able to maintain continuity of leadership during this crisis through periodic dictations from Lanello to Keepers of the Flame gatherings. In 1974, Elizabeth Clare Prophet renamed the group Church Universal and Triumphant and founded teaching centers in major cities throughout the United States. Summit Lighthouse continued as the movement's publishing arm. Prophet moved the church's headquarters to the Los Angeles area in 1976, where it remained for ten years before relocating to the Royal Teton Ranch in Corwin Springs, Montana. Prophet appeared regularly in both print and electronic media during the late 1970s and toured the United States, "stumping for higher consciousness" and preaching against the evils of abortion and communism.

The move to Montana occurred as a result of growing opposition to Church Universal and Triumphant in California and the church's increasingly apocalyptic ideology. Prophet organized seminars during the mid-1980s for her followers that featured nationally known conspiracy theorists who issued dark warnings concerning alien civilizations, AIDS, and nuclear holocaust. Beginning in 1986, in response to apocalyptic warnings from Saint Germain, the church built a series of fallout shelters on its ranch property that were designed to protect staff members from the fallout of a global thermonuclear war. By late 1989, apocalyptic fears had reached a fever pitch, and members from around the world began moving en masse to Paradise Valley, Montana. After two predicted nuclear exchanges between the Soviet Union and the United States failed to occur in 1990, disillusioned members began leaving the valley and the church became the brunt of sensational negative media stories.

In response to the organizational upheavals caused by this cycle of apocalyptic urgency, the church began a public relations offensive in 1991 to combat its media image as a doomsday cult. Prophet published a new book, *The Astrology of the Four Horsemen* (1991), which envisioned a more hopeful future in which it was possible to mitigate the earth's "returning karma" through dynamic decreeing. During the early 1990s, she also distanced her church from the Branch Davidians and the Montana Freemen, claiming on national television programs such as *Larry King Live* and *Nightline* that her followers were law-abiding Americans who were working peacefully for a better world. In 1995, Prophet hired a Belgian corporate consultant, Gilbert Cleirbault, to begin a radical reorganization of the church. Under Cleirbault's leadership, Church Universal and Triumphant refocused its efforts on the publication and dissemination of the Prophets' teachings and on the creation of spiritual communities throughout the world.

In 1999, Prophet disclosed that she was suffering from Alzheimer's disease and turned over both temporal and spiritual authority to a leadership team that includes a president, a board of directors, and a twenty-four-member council of elders. She remains a revered figure to church loyalists but is no longer involved in the church's daily affairs.

See Also Church Universal and Triumphant.

Bibliography

Prophet, Elizabeth Clare. *The Great White Brotherhood in the Culture, History and Religion of America.* Colorado Springs, Colo., 1976.

Prophet, Elizabeth Clare. *The Lost Years of Jesus: Documentary Evidence of Jesus' 17-Year Journey to the East.* Livingston, Mont., 1984.

Prophet, Elizabeth Clare. *The Astrology of the Four Horsemen: How You Can Heal Yourself and Planet Earth.* Livingston, Mont., 1991.

Prophet, Mark L., and Elizabeth Clare Prophet. *Climb the Highest Mountain: The Everlasting Gospel.* Colorado Springs, Colo., 1972.

Prophet, Mark L., and Elizabeth Clare Prophet. *Science of the Spoken Word.* Colorado Springs, Colo., 1974.

Whitsel, Bradley C. *The Church Universal and Triumphant: Elizabeth Clare Prophet's Apocalyptic Movement.* Syracuse, N.Y., 2003.

Phillip Charles Lucas (2005)

PROPHETHOOD, ISLAMIC See NUBŪWAH

PROSELYTISM See CONVERSION; MISSIONS, *ARTICLE ON* MISSIONARY ACTIVITY

PROSTITUTION See HIERODOULEIA

PROTESTANTISM.

[*This article provides an overview of the Protestant branch of Christian religion. The historical origins of Protestantism are examined in* Reformation. *Particular manifestations of Protestantism are discussed in* Denominationalism *and in numerous articles on Protestant churches and biographies of Protestant leaders.*]

Protestantism is a worldwide movement that derives from sixteenth-century reforms of Western Christianity. As a movement it is both a set of church bodies and a less well defined ethos, spirit, and cultural achievement. Thus, one speaks of Reformed or Methodist churches as being Protestant, just as one may speak of a "Protestant ethic" or a "Protestant nation."

Through the years different needs have occasioned a variety of attempts to determine the definitional boundaries of

Protestantism. Sometimes there may be theological or liturgical motives for restricting these boundaries. Some Anglicans, or members of the Church of England, for example, who stress how closely they are identified with the ancient catholic tradition, often resent being classified as Protestant at all. So do Lutherans of similar outlook, even though the term *Protestant* was first applied in 1529 on Lutheran soil. At another extreme, many Protestants refuse to include movements like the Jehovah's Witnesses or Mormons in their ranks, even though these new nineteenth-century religious traditions flourished on Protestant soil and kept something of the Protestant impulse in their church life.

FOUR PROTESTANT CLUSTERS. For demographic purposes, David B. Barrett in his *World Christian Encyclopedia* (1982) tries to bring some order to definitional chaos by classifying the non-Roman Catholic and non-Orthodox part of the Christian world into five families, or blocs, which he calls "Protestant," "nonwhite indigenous," "Anglican," "marginal Protestant," and "Catholic (non-Roman)." All but the last of these have some sort of Protestant ties. The mainstream Protestant category includes long-established Northern Hemisphere churches such as the Congregationalist and Baptist. The Anglican family includes plural, low church, high church, evangelical, Anglo-Catholic, and central (or Broad church) traditions. The category of marginal Protestants includes Jehovah's Witnesses, Mormons, Religious Science, and Unitarian, Spiritualist, and British-Israelite churches.

The existence of the fourth category, nonwhite indigenous Christianity, "a whole new bloc of global Christendom," Barrett speaks of as "one of the more startling findings" documented in his survey. Its existence has been long known, but few, says Barrett, realized that by 1980 it numbered eighty-two million. For all their independent rise and growth, however, nonwhite indigenous forms of Christianity still derive from missionary efforts by classic Protestants. They share many of the doctrines and practices of the Western parentages. In almost all cases they also share the familiar names Baptist, Lutheran, Anglican, and the like. Therefore, while attention to them may be secondary, these younger churches do belong in any encyclopedic coverage of the longer Protestant tradition.

LOCATION OF OLD AND NEW PROTESTANTISM. After more than 450 years, worldwide Protestantism is entering a new phase, because of this shift of power to nonwhite indigenous versions. Classically the movement was strongly identified with northwestern Europe and Anglo-America. Philosopher Alfred North Whitehead once spoke of the Reformation itself as a family quarrel of northwestern European peoples. From the early sixteenth century until well into the nineteenth, the vast majority of the heirs of this Reformation did remain in Europe and its North American colonies. The Latin American nations were almost entirely Roman Catholic in makeup. Around the turn of the nineteenth century, this older Protestantism underwent vast expansion through missionary efforts to convert people in all nations and to establish churches everywhere. It was in the mid-twentieth century that the inventive and often autochthonous character of the nonwhite indigenous groups became evident, particularly in sub-Saharan Africa, parts of Latin America, and the Pacific island world.

The power shift from northwestern Europe, where established Protestantism consistently lost power in the face of secularizing forces, to the vibrant world of the Southern Hemisphere portended great changes in the Protestant ethos as well. For centuries Protestant religion had been seen as an impetus toward capitalist economies, yet the new growth came in portions of the world where capitalism had little chance and few promoters. This religious emphasis in Europe had characteristically been established in coordination with the state. However, in the new nations of Africa or in Latin America, where Catholicism was first established but where anticlerical revolutions later barred privilege to any Christian bodies, nonwhite indigenous Protestantism had to make its way as a movement independent of state establishment or privilege.

Other changes came with the shift. Historically the Protestantism of Europe relied on thought patterns that depended upon and connected with older Catholic philosophies. The Protestant reformers of the sixteenth century protested against some uses Catholics made of, for example, Platonic or Aristotelian philosophies through the centuries. Yet soon they were themselves developing theologies that relied on the mainline Western philosophical synthesis. In the new area of growth, however, leaders of nonwhite indigenous flowerings of Protestantism did not have the luxury of exploring these philosophical schools. They saw no need to relate to them and often explicitly rebelled against them.

All these changes make generalizing about Protestantism far more difficult at the beginning of the twenty-first century than at the end of the nineteenth. Often one must fall back on definitions from the classic period, the first three or four centuries, keeping in mind the exceptional new developments as a subtheme. In any case, much of the plot of Protestantism after its period of expansion has revealed the dialectic of adaptation and resistance on the part of both missionary agents and the missionized. The agents of the West often arrived along with merchants or military forces, and they had to choose between being openly identified with their purposes or establishing an, at least, subtle detachment from them. Inevitably they were bearers of Western national values, but they could choose to keep their distance from uncritical embrace of these values. On the other hand, those who accepted Christianity at the hands of the missioners also had the choice of adopting as much of Western culture as possible or picking and choosing those elements of Protestantism that they could most easily or advantageously graft onto their old culture and ways.

PROTESTANT DIVERSITY AND COHERENCE. The first perception of both old and new Protestantism has always been its diversity. Barrett claims that the one billion and more practicing Christians of the world belong to 20,780 distinct denominations. While more than half the Christians are Catholic, the vast majority of these 20,780 denominations would be classed as part of the Protestant movement. Thus, in classic Protestantism, in 1980 there were almost 345 million people in 7,889 of these distinct bodies in 212 nations. The nonwhite indigenous versions, almost all of them Protestant, were located in 10,065 distinct bodies. There were also 225 Anglican denominations and 1,345 "marginal Protestant" groups. Indeed, this diversity and this fertility at creating new, unrelated bodies were long used as a criticism of Protestantism by Roman Catholicism, which united under the Roman pope, and by Orthodoxy, which was divided more into national jurisdictions but saw itself as united in holy tradition.

It is possible to move behind this first perception of the chaos of unrelated bodies to see some forms of coherence. Great numbers of Protestant bodies, along with many Orthodox ones, are members of the World Council of Churches, established in 1948, which has a uniting confessional theme around the lordship of Jesus Christ. In many nations there are national councils or federations of cooperating churches, which allow for positive interaction even where there is not organic unity. World confessional families of Lutherans, Reformed, Baptists, and others throughout the twentieth century brought into some concord these churches that have family resemblances. Finally, there have been significant mergers of Protestant churches both within families, such as Lutheran with Lutheran, Presbyterian with Presbyterian, and across family lines, as in America's United Church of Christ, which blended a New England Congregationalist tradition with a German Reformed heritage.

Whoever chronicles Protestant diversities and coherences also has to recognize that significant differences appear within each group and that important elements of concord transect the groups. Liberal Episcopalians and Methodists may have more in common with each other on many issues and in numbers of practices than either of them has with conservative members of their own communion. It is probably the better part of discretion not to seek rigid categories in classifying Protestant bodies; the concept of something like "zones" is more fruitful. Thus across the Protestant spectrum one may begin with "high church" Anglican zones, where many formal practices of Catholicism prevail, the liturgy is extremely complex, and worship is highly adorned (with icons, incense, and artifacts or gestures). At the opposite end of the spectrum and at least as securely in the orbit of sociological Protestantism is a "low church" zone, where groups may have rejected as much as possible from the Catholic past; for example, the Quakers seek utter simplicity and silence in worship and make no use of the sacraments of Catholic Christianity at all.

Some Protestant Elements Held in Common. To accent only Protestant diversity, as demographers or critics may be tempted to do, does not take into account the fact that the word *Protestant* arose to cover a distinct set of phenomena. In the minds of those who use the term, it may denote something fairly specific. The easiest way to put a boundary around Protestantism is to deal with it negatively and say that it is the form of Western Christianity that rejects obedience to the Roman papacy. Such an approach is an immense clarifier, since Protestants do reject the papacy. The only remaining element of confusion in this negative definition comes from the fact that Western (non-Roman) Catholic Christians also reject the papacy. In 1980 this group, including the Catholic Apostolic, Reformed Catholic, Old Catholic, and Conservative Catholic churches, numbered 3,439,375, as against 344,336,319 old- and new-style Protestants.

While the resistance to papal claims is a uniting factor, it is not likely that many people ever choose to remain loyal to Protestantism on such marginal and confining grounds alone. One is Protestant for many reasons; one *then* differentiates one's faith and practice from Roman Catholicism in nonpapal-versus-papal terms. That issue was strong in the sixteenth century at the time of the Protestant break with Rome, and it became a subject of intense controversy late in the nineteenth century, when papal infallibility was declared. The controversy remains to plague Catholic-Protestant ecumenical relations. But in the daily life of believers, the rejection of the papacy has little to do with churchly commitments. One must seek elsewhere for the positive elements and accents of Protestantism, even if it shares many of these with Catholicism.

The first common mark of Protestantism is historically clear and clean; virtually all Protestant groups derive from movements that began in the sixteenth century. When later groups were formed, as were the Disciples of Christ in nineteenth-century America, they may not have seen themselves as working out the logic of earlier Protestantism; yet historians at once traced the roots of this typical new group to various older Presbyterian and Baptist forms, among others.

A very few Protestant groups can also trace their lineage back to pre-Reformation times. Modern Waldensians, for example, are heirs of a movement begun under Pierre Valdès (Peter Waldo) in the twelfth century, and some modern Czech churches are heirs of traditions that go back to the Hussite Jednota Bratrská (Society of Brethren, known in Latin as Unitas Fratrum) of the fifteenth century. Yet the Waldensians, the Czech groups, and others began to be recognized as something other than illicit sects on Roman Catholic soil as a result of the Protestant breakthrough. At another point on the spectrum is the Church of England, or Anglicanism. Most of its articulators stress that they remain the church Catholic as it has been on English soil since the Christianization of England. Although it has kept faith in the apostolic succession of bishops and has retained many pre-Reformation practices, the Anglican communion as it has existed since the break with Rome under Henry VIII in the sixteenth century is vastly different from the Catholic church under Roman papal obedience in England before and since the Reformation. In short, the Waldensians, the Czech groups, and the Anglicans alike were, and were seen to be, part of the Protestant revolt from both the viewpoints of Roman Catholic leadership and historical scholarship ever since.

To have undergone formal separation from the papally controlled church or to have been transformed by the fact that one's tradition changes through such separation are the major historical marks of Protestantism. Individual groups may have parentage in the Middle Ages or may have sprung up late in the twentieth century, yet the sixteenth-century breach in Christendom is the event by which Protestant existence is somehow measured. Beyond the normativeness of that breach, Protestants begin to share elements of Catholicism. That certain elements are shared in no way diminishes their importance in Protestant definition. They tend to acquire a special color when viewed through the prism of Protestant experiences.

God in Protestantism. All Christian movements, unlike some other religions, focus finally on their witness to God. Protestantism is theistic. There have been momentary expressions by theological elites of a "Christian atheism," but these have been dismissed by the Protestant public as idiosyncratic, personal forms of witness or philosophical expression. Then, too, some prophets and observers have pointed to a "practical atheism" among Protestants who in their ways of life seem to ignore the claims of God upon them. Yet such practical atheism is unself-conscious, reflexive. When called to their attention, it is usually vigorously dismissed by the people to whom it is applied, a sign that they regard theistic belief to be focal.

At the left wing of marginal Protestantism, as Barrett clarifies it, stand some former Protestant groups that have retained certain elements of the Protestant tradition. Among these are Unitarianisms of humanistic sorts and Ethical Culture movements, which grew up on Jewish soil in America but acquired some Protestant traits. It is significant that such groups are dismissed by the vast cohort of Protestants precisely because they are humanistic, or because they exclude themselves from Protestantism, usually on grounds of theism.

If Protestants are not humanistic or atheistic, they also are not pantheistic. Individual pantheists may exist as mystics, and there have been pantheistic Protestant heresies, so regarded both by those who have innovated with them and by those who have excluded their advocates. In some formal theological circles, one sometimes hears advocated teachings that seem to verge on pantheism, the proposition that the world and God are coextensive, identical. Yet articulators of such teachings usually take pains to distance themselves from pure pantheism, for example, through panentheisms, which speak both of identity and distance. Marginal Protestants such as the Mormons teach doctrines that look pantheist to mainstream Protestantisms. Here, as so often, it is their departure from theism that is at issue in the principles of exclusion.

Protestantism on occasion has had deistic proponents, agents of a natural religion that made no room for a personal God, special revelation, or reasons to pray to an unresponsive, divine, originating, but now absentee force. In eighteenth-century England there were Anglican Deists, and in the continental Enlightenment one heard of equivalents. In practice, many Protestant believers may act as though they are deistic in their prayer life, which means that they somehow believe in a divine force but see no reason for prayerful intercourse with it. Yet deism has consistently in due course been seen as a deviation from, not a part of, the Protestant impulse.

The God of the Bible and Trinitarianism. The freedom that belongs to the Protestant ethos has made room for the enterprising and innovating philosopher of religion, but the determining element in Protestant concepts of God has been some form of adherence to the biblical witness. The God of Protestants is the God of Abraham, Isaac, and Jacob. Along with Catholics, Protestants believe in the God revealed in the Hebrew scriptures, which Protestantism has taken over intact from Judaism and made its own. This God, Yahveh, is the God of Israel and the God of the prophets. Protestantism thus relies on God as creator and sustainer of the universe, existent though hidden, being and not nonbeing, somehow an agent in history. Although not all Protestants speak of a "personal" God, most conceive of God as personal and thus addressable.

Protestant theologians spoke of the Protestant intention as one directed to what H. Richard Niebuhr called "radical monotheism." This intention has meant that Protestants share the concern of Hebrew prophecy to distance believers from "many gods" and false gods alike. The Protestant impulse, sometimes directed even against itself by its own prophets, has been iconoclastic. Pioneers of the movement such as John Calvin saw the natural human mind as an instinctive idol maker, always busy serving either the true God or gods of its own making, who must be smashed. It would be impossible to say that Protestant believers have been more successful at being radical monotheists than have others; yet reflective Protestantism has been so nervous about icons or images that might be construed as having identity with the divine or divinized figure they represent that the iconoclast always has a privileged place in Protestant arguments.

The battle against icon and idol in Protestantism may sometimes continue on the abstract planes of philosophical discourse or theological definition, but the iconoclastic position is usually stated most forcefully when Protestants explain the biblical account of Israel's witness to Yahveh, the one God. The God to whom Protestants point is one who, although hidden, exists, acts, and speaks through a divine word. This God is in every case a God of judgment and mercy, wrath and love, holiness and forgiveness.

While some Protestants have been unsure about the meaning of the covenant with Israel in the Old Testament, few have doubted the witness to God in the New Testament. The God of Israel is present in a special way in Jesus of Nazareth. Some forms of liberal Protestantism were reluctant to speak of Jesus as partaking uniquely in the divine nature associated with the one he called Father. When they showed this reluctance, this was in the interest of radical monotheism. When most other forms of Protestantism remained content with or became emphatic about classic creeds that associated Jesus Christ with God, they did so in conscious reference to the fact that this in no way detracted from monotheistic faith. Protestant interpretation of philosophies of history have always seen this God of Israel as somehow active in history.

At the same time, Protestantism is a Christ-focused faith. Here again one may speak in the language of H. Richard Niebuhr about a tendency that he saw as less compatible with true Protestantism and that, indeed, was a heresy on any terms. Some forms of evangelical, Christ-centered Protestantism, he charged, were guilty of a "Unitarianism of the Second Person" of the Trinity. This meant that just as earlier theistic Unitarians believed only in the divinity of the one God whom Jesus called Father, at the expense of the Son and the Holy Spirit, these gospel-minded people, without usually meaning to, identified Jesus almost exclusively with God and had little to say or do about God apart from witness to Jesus.

Not all Protestants have been ready to use the inherited language of the preexistent Logos, or Word, that became incarnate in the historical Jesus. They have, however, found ways to witness to the bond between Jesus and God. In his best-known hymn, "A Mighty Fortress," Protestant pioneer Martin Luther spoke of Jesus Christ as "the Lord of hosts" and then burst forth with the assertion "And there's no other God." There is no other God than the one revealed in Jesus Christ. Such witness led to radical expressions that verge on the ancient heresy of patripassionism, the claim that God the Father suffered with the Son on the cross. In this spirit Martin Rinkhart offered a line in a Good Friday hymn to the effect that in the death of Jesus "our God is dead." Nineteenth-century critics, especially left-wing Hegelians, seized on incautious lines like these to claim that the death of Jesus meant the death of God, even on orthodox soil. Rinkhart and the Protestants were not ready for such consequences or corollaries, but they left themselves open to this claim, so eager were they to proclaim the divinity of Jesus Christ. Protestants in the main have been so Jesus- or Christ-centered that they are more willing to take such risks than to side with humanistic or minority liberal Protestants who broke up notions of the Trinity and saw Jesus as a distinctive but not unique human.

As for what the creeds describe as the Third Person of the Trinity, the Holy Spirit, one despairs of pointing to a distinctive witness held by almost all Protestants. Negatively, again as a corollary to the nonpapal witness, Protestants have refused to identify the Holy Spirit with the tradition, the magisterium or official teaching, or the papal authority of the Roman Catholic Church. Most have been more at home seeing the Holy Spirit connected with revelation and authority as the inspirer of the text of the Bible. Some left-wing reformers of the sixteenth century and their heirs down to twenty-first-century Pentecostal Protestants have been ready to speak of revelation from the Holy Spirit direct to the individual, apart from scripture. Yet it is significant that in their minds, this revelation occurs alongside and not in antagonism toward or independent of what is heard in the inspired Bible.

This witness to God in three persons, historically as Father, Son (Jesus Christ), and Holy Spirit, has added up to a Protestant trinitarianism. Once the term *Trinity* is introduced, it is difficult to see what distinctions remain. True, a few Protestants, especially among the Pentecostals and others who resist Catholic creeds and dogma, reject the trinitarian approach because the word does not appear in the Bible and because it points to human formulations. Yet without using the term, they tend to reproduce the substance of trinitarian faith even while rejecting its formulations.

In sum, the distinctive characteristics of Protestantism emerge from the variety of models that Protestants endorse in forming their churches. Because of their diversity, Protestant churches have been less likely or less able to converge on the basis of each other's witness than have churches in the more homogeneous Eastern Orthodox and Roman Catholic traditions. As a result, Protestants are thrown back more on story than on dogma, more on biblical narrative than on creedal formulation, yet for the most part without rejecting dogma or creed. And they have been pressed to develop special ways of understanding how God is mediated and present in human affairs and, specifically, in the circle of believers and the church. Urgent on its agenda for centuries, then, has been the concept of mediation in formal authority and structure.

Authority and Structure: The Scriptures. If the believer on Protestant soil is to be responsive to God as creator (or, sometimes, Father), Son, and Holy Spirit, questions arise. Who says so? How is this God to be known? What are the boundaries of witness to such a God? Eastern Orthodoxy and Roman Catholicism stress the authority of tradition, magisterium, apostolic succession of bishops (as do Anglicans and some Lutherans), and, uniquely to Catholicism, the Roman papal office. They also testify to God's revelation in scripture, but Protestantism is thrown almost wholly on scripture. Since the end of the nineteenth century, however, more and more Protestants have been willing to see a relationship between the Bible and tradition. They have become contextual thinkers who see that the Bible reiterates the tradition it grows out of. Yet for their ancestors in faith the Bible held a special status, and tradition or papal authority could never match it. So emphatic was this Protestant emphasis that critics from within, such as the Enlightenment-era Protestant Gotthold Ephraim Lessing, complained that Luther substituted the Bible as a "paper pope" for Protestants to match the authority of Catholicism's human pope.

The Bible of Protestantism is the canon of the Old and New Testaments, and almost never the Apocrypha, which has special status in the Orthodox and Catholic traditions. The canon is theoretically open; it is conceivable that a book could still be added to it. So teach most Protestants. It is difficult to imagine the circumstance in which the many Protestant church bodies could agree on a later-discovered and apparently canonical-level writing, yet, for thoughtful Protestants, the openness of the canon is a partial safeguard against making an icon or idol of the Bible.

While the Bible has become the only document used and useful for uniting Protestant witness or helping determine Protestant theological argument—it provides at least something of the genetic programming of Protestantism, or the ground rules for their games—there is here as so often a very broad spectrum of approaches to its authority. Most Protestants have accepted the Luthern mark *sola scriptura,* that the Bible alone is the authority; but this formula tells all too little about how to regard the book.

At one extreme, conservative Protestants who have resisted modern historical criticism of biblical texts stress that the Bible is somehow not only inspired but infallible and inerrant. The inerrancy applies not only to revelation in matters of faith but also in all details of history, geography, and science, at least as would apply to the original autographs. Some of the originators of Protestantism often used language of biblical authority that was so confident of biblical truth that it gave reasons for later theologians to build elaborate theories of this inerrancy. In later centuries, some dogmatic teachers went so far as to propound mechanical or dictation theories, in which the author of a biblical writing was a kind of conduit or secretary for God, at the expense of personal inspiration and independent style. Most proponents of inerrancy, however, have been less extreme. They have tended to build on the basis of various Aristotelian or Baconian philosophies, stressing syllogisms in which a perfect, hence inerrant, God chooses to engage lovingly in revelation, hence taking care to assure that readers receive no error or ambiguity. These inerrantists have engaged in heated polemics against all, no matter how high their view of biblical authority, who have not found inerrancy to be a biblical or theologically defensible concept.

At the other end of the spectrum are a minority of Protestants, chiefly in academic centers, who have completely adopted post-Enlightenment views of biblical criticism. They have thus treated the biblical text as they would any other ancient literary text. They grant no special status to the inspiration of biblical authors. For them the Bible still has authority as a document that both reflects and promotes the norms of the Christian community. Many schools of interpretation, even among those who have immersed themselves in historical and literary criticism, find that the Bible "discloses," or potentially discloses, what God would reveal. This disclosure or revelation, it is contended, can occur even if the Bible includes grammatical inaccuracies, historical misstatements, and scientific concepts long proven wrong and rendered obsolete. The polemic of these contenders is against the inerrantists, who, they claim, do make the Bible into a quasi-papal authority or turn it into an icon at the expense of radical monotheism.

The spectrum is visible in another way when one considers how different Protestants regard the reader of the Bible. At one end, there are those who contend that "the right of private judgment" is the Christian mark of distinctiveness. Thus Martin Luther was said to have challenged the emperor in 1521 to convince him that he, Luther, was wrong on the basis of the Bible and reason. One cannot go against conscience for the sake of authority. In a sense, the conscience and intelligence of the individual in such a case take priority over claims of the community. At the other end of the spectrum, there is as much concern as in any other part of Christianity for Christian community and the nurturing of the word in the context of congregation or church. In these cases, the church is credited with preserving the Bible, seeing that it is embodied in people who effectively display its power in their lives, and calling people to belief on the basis of biblical texts that are turned into calls of faith by living people. In all cases, it is fair to speak of Protestants as being especially "people of the Book."

The Authority of the Church. Lacking paper authority as they do, and unwilling as they are for the most part to yield to bishops as having a determinative role in dispensing tradition, how do Protestants see the authority of the church? The vast majority of Protestants in all ages, though they be churched and faithful, have rendered secondary to the Bible all other church authority, creeds, confessions, and forms of polity. When they are serious and are seriously confronted, most Protestants characteristically will say that they get authority for teaching and practice from the Bible alone.

Despite this claim, reflective Protestants will also admit that over the centuries they have spilled much ink in treatises on churchly authority. As much as Catholics, they may have exacted sweat and blood from people who ran afoul of church authorities, who tested the bounds of orthodoxy, or who came under ecclesiastical discipline. Protestantism, in other words, may seem chaotic to the outsider who sees its many groupings and varieties, but to most confessors and members the chaos is minimized, because they are ordinarily touched only by the authority system of which they are a part, that of their own church.

Once one insists on making churchly authority secondary, other values come to be dominant in association with the church. The church on Protestant soil is a fellowship, a congregation of people who have like minds or similar purposes. The church may be seen as "the body of Christ" or "the communion of saints" before it is an authority to compel conformity in teaching or practice. Yet once one assigns values to the group, even in forms of Protestantism that accent the right of private judgment or go to extremes of individualism, there must be and in practice have been many subtle ways to assert authority and to effect discipline. A small congregation's authority on Baptist or Congregational soil can be felt more immediately, for instance, than might Catholic authority asserted from the distance between Rome and India by a not always efficient and always pluralistic church. Democracies can turn authoritarian. Ambiguity about authority can often lead to expressions of arbitrary discipline. So polity and authority have been nagging questions in Protestantism.

First, there has been ambiguity about the lay-clerical distinction. Theologian Hendrik Kraemer, in *A Theology of the Laity* (1958), accurately pointed out that Protestantism was a revolt against authoritarian and overly hierarchical clericalism. Yet almost all Protestantism retained a professional and ordained clergy, somehow setting it aside with sacred sanctions and for special functions. The "somehow," however, became problematic. Protestantism wanted to engage in a leveling of ranks by insisting that all believers were priests, that they could all intercede for one another at the altar, symbolically before the throne of God. Then what were these ordained "priests," or whatever Protestants called their ministry or clergy, and how did they hold power?

Kraemer, historian Wilhelm Pauck, and others have shown that authority (in all but Anglicanism, the Lutheran Church of Sweden, and other "high" episcopal bodies) resides chiefly in the word of God and in the responsive congregation. The minister has tended to become the person called and set aside to be the more expert preacher and expounder of the word. Yet Protestantism was unwilling to say that the laity could not be expert at speaking the word, which was accessible to all. It was also easy to demonstrate that the succession of faith in congregations that were responsive to the word was vulnerable to faithlessness and error or heresy. To claim that ministry consisted in the clergy's unique right to administer the sacraments or holy ordinances was something that not all Protestants were eager to do. They did not want the sacramental life to seem in any way magical. As a result, in almost all cases they retained a specially sanctioned clergy, ascribed great authority also to the laity, and left the status of both ambiguous and thus problematic.

CONFESSIONS AND CREEDS. Church authority is not only an issue of clergy and laity. It must also concentrate on the substance or content of the faith that holds people together and finds them members of one Protestant confession and not another. Of course, heredity, accident of birth, and many casual factors based on aesthetics, personal choice, or marriage across denominational lines have played their parts. But thoughtful Protestantism has also insisted that its members are not only "believers" but "believers in" and in some ways, necessarily, "believers that" something or other is true. Whether or not they call these creeds or confessions, and whether these statements are formal or informal, there tend to be some common expressions that give clarity to faith and that establish boundaries between one set of beliefs and others.

Most Protestant bodies display their distinctiveness by resorting to documents from the times of their origins. In their first or second generation, leaders of groups were called upon or felt impelled to define themselves and to witness to their truths. For Lutherans the instrument was chiefly the Augsburg Confession; for the Reformed, the Heidelberg Catechism; for Presbyterians, the Westminster Confession; and for Anglicans the Thirty-nine Articles. Even loose bodies such as seventeenth- and eighteenth-century New England Congregationalism in America produced enough creeds and confessions to make up large anthologies. These documents have attracted various levels of respect and authority. Some came to be neglected or even rejected by huge parties. Yet the ecumenical movement, in which these churches had to find out who they and their counterparts were, exposed to view these ancient documents and showed their enduring power.

By some Protestants their originating confessions were believed *quia* ("because"), that is, because they were held to be simply and perfectly congruent with biblical witness. Others held to them *quatenus* ("insofar"), that is, insofar as they witnessed to biblical truth in later times and special circumstances. At times the claim was much more informal than either of these, and in some cases it is not possible to point to a church confession at all. For many Protestants a confession says "This we believe" as a hearty declaration to the world; for others it comes across as "This you must believe" and is used to rule out heresy or to provide a basis for polemics.

PROTESTANT CHURCH POLITIES. As with confession, so with structure, or polity: Protestantism presents a broad spectrum of often mutually incompatible polities. Again, they can be inclusively categorized according to what they negate. They all resist the notion that the Roman papacy is the best, or only, conduit of divine revelation and that the guardianship of the Christian church must rest in the hands of the pope as the vicar or representative of Christ on earth. Beyond that, most Protestant churches have preserved elements of the polity that came with their birth, transformed by exigencies of local, contemporary demands and, in the modern world, adjustments to the managerial and bureaucratic impulse. Yet even in the last and most practical case, the Protestant impulse is to see some legitimation for polity in the Bible and in the experience of the early Christian church.

On one end of this spectrum are churches like the Anglican church or the Lutheran church in Sweden, which insist on apostolic succession in an episcopacy that is of the essence (displays the *esse*) of the church. Elsewhere, as in Methodism and much of Lutheranism, bishops belong to the *bene esse* of the church; they are beneficial for its order but theoretically could be replaced in a different polity. Many Reformed churches rely on synodical or connectional and associational patterns under the rule of presbyters or elders. From the days of the radical reformation in the sixteenth century through various later Baptist and Congregational witnesses into modern times, and especially in burgeoning nonwhite indigenous Protestantism, the authority and even the autonomy of the local congregation is asserted.

Those Protestants at the "catholic" end of the spectrum, who regard bishops as of the *esse* of the church, have been least ready to see their polity as negotiable in an ecumenical age. Presbyterian, synodical, and congregational bodies, while emphatically cherishing and defending their polities, have shown more signs of flexibility. A safe generalization suggests that even Baptist and Congregationalist groups, who find biblical rootage for congregationalism, have adopted enough bureaucratic instruments that they have functional polities that transcend mere congregationalism. Yet they would find it a part of their Protestantism to be suspicious of bishops.

Civil Government. Alongside church confession and internal polity has been the issue of the authority of the church or religious realm in or alongside the state or governmental and civil realms. Here one can speak of a long trend, based on Protestant latencies, to move from church establishment toward disestablishment and a celebration of voluntarism.

It is historically inaccurate to say, based on the record of American celebration of "separation of church and state" with Protestant concurrence, that Protestantism has always been voluntaristic. It would be more fair to say that the sixteenth-century Reformation carried with it some potential for voluntarism—seeds that broke open, sprouted, and grew from two to four centuries later.

In the late twentieth century, most of the new nations in which nonwhite indigenous Protestantism prospered had undergone experiences of modernization that, whatever else these meant, provided no room for fusion of church and state or an interwoven pattern of religious and civil authority. Similarly, it was on the soil of largely Protestant nations such as the United States that the greatest degree of constitutional separation between the two authorities first occurred. Yet political philosopher Hannah Arendt is correct to chide Protestants for claiming that modern democracy with its religious freedom is simply a Christian invention. Some Christians have found it easy to reach into their repository of options to find impetus for supporting republicanism based on Enlightenment principles and practical support of equity and civil peace whenever pluralism has been strong.

Historical Protestantism in almost all its mainstream and dominant forms first simply carried over authority patterns from medieval Catholicism. In the Church of England, the Presbyterian church in Scotland, the Lutheran churches of Scandinavia, the Lutheran and Reformed churches of Germany, Switzerland, and the Netherlands, and wherever else leaders had the power to do so, they naturally clung to establishment. They simply broke from Roman Catholic establishment to form Protestant versions. Martin Luther supported a "territorial church" with princes as bishops. Elsewhere, monarchy and legislative bodies gave establishment power or privilege to the favored church and forced disabilities on others.

Only the left-wing, or Anabaptist, churches of the first generations were independent of the state, and they tended to be harassed as much by Protestant establishments as by Catholic establishments. Where they became powerful, as did the Puritans from England who founded New England, they reversed themselves and became the new established monopoly church. Even in much later republics, where no form of Protestantism ever came to dominance, Protestants were tempted to reassert power by looking for legal privilege.

Despite all these establishmentarian dimensions, it is also fair to say that Protestantism did contain the seed that helped disestablishment and separation of church and state develop. A religion of the word, Protestantism called for that word to separate people from attachment to the culture as it evoked decision. So the boundaries of the church and the state could not be coextensive, as they aspired then to be in Catholicism. Whatever "the priesthood of all believers," "the right of private judgment," and the call to conscience in biblical interpretation meant theologically, they had as their practical consequence an honoring of individualism and personal profession of faith. Both of these would become confined were there an official and authoritative church.

Another way to describe this individualism is in terms of modern theologian Paul Tillich's famed "protestant principle" of prophetic protest. This principle calls believers to question all structures and institutions, also and especially those of their own state and church. Naturally, Protestants have not found it any easier to do this than have others, since seldom does one wish to give up ease and privilege and to share power voluntarily. Yet, in contrast to much Orthodox and Roman Catholic theology, Protestant theology at least had a legitimating principle for criticizing church structure and its bond with human governmental authority. Protestantism, then, has lived with a heightened dialectic. On the one hand, it called for support of government, in the terms of Paul's biblical letter to the Romans, chapter 13, as God's instrument. On the other hand, it was critical, along the lines of *Revelation* 13, of civil and ecclesiastical government as being especially subtle and potent concentrations of power, symbols, and capacities for self-idolization and the oppression of others.

Personal Experience as Authority. A word should be said about personal experience as authority in Protestantism. From the first its "spiritualists," "mystics," and "enthusiasts," who claimed that God spoke directly to and through them, have been both recognized and under suspicion. Those who carry these claims to extremes, as did many of the Quakers, or Friends, the seventeenth-century Puritan sect, and some modern Pentecostals, know that they are "on the margin," out of step with mainstream Protestantism. Their own protests and the way the rest of Protestantism unites against them reveal this.

At the same time, few Protestants have been willing to resist going further than Orthodox and Catholic teachers in granting much authority to individual assent in the grasp of faith. Calvin spoke of the inner testimony of the Holy Spirit in the heart and mind of the believer who hears the word of God or reads the Bible. Luther's possibly apocryphal cry at the Diet of Worms in 1521, a cry against emperor and pope, state and church, "Here I stand!" has acquired mythical dimensions as an act of Protestant heroism. There is always at least the theoretical possibility that the individual may be right and the church wrong, a possibility that both nagged and inspired Luther and other reformers.

In the end, most Protestantism asks the Christian who claims to have had an experience of God or a direct revelation and a call to individual conscience to subject these claims to the responsibilities of the congregation or church at large. There may be great suspicion by fellow believers of such claims, and the individuals who make them may suffer liabilities and persecution. Yet on the other hand, Protestantism honors "heart religion," insists on heartfelt response to the word and the claims of God upon the mind, and thus it sees experience as an authority alongside the Bible and the church.

PROTESTANT SUBSTANCE. Original or classic Protestantism was more ready to see itself as distinctive in the content of faith than is modern pluralist Protestantism. In the sixteenth century, late medieval Catholicism presented what to Protestant eyes was an egregious violation of God's system of approach to human beings. Catholicism had generated, or degenerated into, a system that progressively depended more and more upon human achievement. Key words were human *merit* or humanly gained *righteousness*. Elaborate schemes, for example, the sale of indulgences to help make up the required number of merits to assure salvation, had been devised. These led to abuses, which contemporary Catholic reformers and later historians have agreed made Protestant revolt plausible.

Protestantism across the board held to generally extreme views of human finitude, limits, "fallenness," and need. Mainstream and marginal reformers alike were not convinced by claims that human beings retained enough of the image of God upon which to build so that their own works or merits would suffice to appease a wrathful God. They exaggerated the way Catholicism had diminished the role of Jesus Christ as giver of a gift or imparter of grace upon the wholly undeserving. Once again Paul Tillich from the twentieth century can be called in as witness to what Protestantism affirmed: that God "accepts the unacceptable." Because of the sacrifice of Jesus Christ, God does not wait for sinners to become acceptable through their efforts.

In the sixteenth century, there were many variations on this theme, and Martin Luther's proclamation of "justification by grace through faith," while at home in all of Protestantism, was not necessarily the chosen formula for all Protestants. Yet all did accent divine initiative, human limits, the gifts of God in Jesus Christ, and the new condition of humanity as a result of divine forgiveness. The variations from the first included some new Protestant ways of propping up the moral quest. Not all were as sure as Luther was that the law of God, as revealed in the Ten Commandments or the sermon on the mount, played no positive guiding role in salvation. They often feared "antinomianism" or lawlessness. The grace-proclaimers protected themselves against this by insisting that faith must be active in love, that works must follow grace, that "sanctification" is an inevitable consequence and correlate of "justification."

Where such resorts to human claims and achievements were not part of original Protestantism, they did develop later. An example of this was a revision on Dutch and then English soil in a movement named after one Jacobus Arminius and called Arminianism. This system proclaimed the benevolence of a God who gave humans more capacity for benevolence on their own. In some Unitarianism this teaching became a kind of philosophical or moral system that moved to the edges of Protestantism. In Wesleyan Methodism it remained "evangelical," gospel-centered, but picked up on the themes of sanctification and the quest for perfection. In the latter case, it did not make the sacrifice of Christ or the imparting of grace as a gift unnecessary or even secondary. Somehow, then, Protestants have concentrated on faith and grace in distinctive ways. Modern Catholicism, however, has undergone such a revitalizing of faith in similar approaches to grace that the distinctively Protestant note has become compromised—a trend that most Protestants profess to welcome enthusiastically. Protestantism has considered the church always to be reforming, never reformed; Catholicism and Protestantism alike, many would say, stand in need of being reformed, and from time to time they move past rigid, older identities and formulas. Such moves are not incongruent with the Protestant ethos and spirit.

THE PROTESTANT RESPONSE TO GOD. To speak of Protestant creeds and a Protestant substance or content does justice to the cognitive dimensions of its faith. At the same time, one can easily exaggerate these elements. In the lives of most people called Protestant, behavioral factors are at least as vivid and more easily grasped, if defined with more difficulty. One can readily consult a dogmatics text to see what Protestants believe or are supposed to believe. It takes more subtle observation, more willingness to risk generalization, to observe their response in practice.

Protestantism has honored the rites of passage through life. Few Protestants would call their ordinances "rites of passage," yet most can easily be led to see that their sacraments and ceremonies do relate the individual to cosmos and community in patterns that match those observed on other soil by historians of religion. They may not see themselves classified with "the primitives" with respect to initiation, fertility, or funerary rites, but there are parallels.

Thus, almost all Protestants—Quakers chiefly excepted—see the need for a rite of initiation. With so few exceptions that they do not merit pointing to, this rite is "water baptism," something shared with the rest of Christianity. Most Protestants retained infant baptism, as either an instrument of grace (as in Lutheranism) or an expression of covenantal life (as in most of Reformed Protestantism). Yet Protestants, when called to reflect, also resisted what they saw to be Catholic notions of *ex opere operato,* which Protestants regarded as a "magical" application of human elements in sacramental life. This left those who baptized infants with the burden of showing how faith can be active among children who can have no rational conception of what is going on. How to explain the decision that was still called for in response to gifts of grace in faith, or the expectation that some disciplined life must follow?

Many mainstream Protestants compensated by accenting reaffirmation of baptism in some version of a rite of confirmation. Others saw each act of repentance and each day's conscious Christian affirmation as a new death of "the old Adam" and a "being born again" as a new being in Christ. These ideas have held the imagination of millions and made it possible for the rite of initiation to occur very early in human life.

At the same time, the logic of Protestantism and the impulse to connect rites of initiation with conscious response to the word of God led many Protestant branches to grow restless about infant baptism and to move closer to locating initiation in or after adolescence, as so many other religions have it. This meant a further move from seeing water baptism as an instrument of grace to seeing it as a human response based on decision. The new evangelizers or converters, then, called for a decision that issued in repentance and faith and then initiation. "Adult baptism" as a sign of response, usually dramatized in baptism by immersion, better exemplified the sense of ordeal and the passage across a "liminal" or threshold stage to new community. As a result, whole church bodies became "Baptist," and the baptist forms of Protestantism came to prevail progressively in the modern world, where the demand for choice and identity grew more intense. Most of fast-growing nonwhite indigenous Protestantism stressed this form of passage.

Marriage, regarded on Orthodox and Roman Catholic soil as a sacrament with an imparting of grace, distinctively stopped being that on most Protestant soil. The reformers tended to regard it as essentially a civil act, with the church serving merely as an agent to bless the couple and to hear their vows. The church was the custodian and recordkeeper of the state's work until the modern secular state took over the recording functions. One could, at least in theory, be validly married without the blessing of the church and clergy. In practice, however, the impulse of people to see their acts of bonding and fertility sacralized has won out. On most Protestant soil, whatever the theology of the marriage ceremony and act, people have seen to the development of elaborate churchly rites at times of nuptials. Yet it is distinctively Protestant to prevent notions of grace-giving or sacramental character from developing in most places.

Protestantism has not encouraged distinctive funeral traditions, but almost everywhere its churches have been participants in memorial or mourning rites. Again there occurred the negation of the Catholic notion that a sacrament was involved at the point of passage to a life to come. Some Protestants use oils for symbolic purposes associated with prayer for healing but assign them no sacramental or instrumental significance. When death comes, there is much reflection upon the event and its meaning. Almost always a cleric holds rites of the word that accent the gospel of what God has done in and for the deceased person and assure that God's love is stronger than death. These rites may occur in the sanctuary of a church or in a mortuary, and burial (whether of a body or ashes) can occur on church cemetery grounds or in public burial places. Here Protestantism offers few consistent words except that one sees the life of the believer wrapped up in divine beneficence despite human frailty.

Alongside baptism, then, the only act seen as sacramental in the vast majority of Protestantism is the sacred meal. Such meals are common in religions, and Protestants often have failed to see theirs in a larger context. Yet they have almost unanimously—the Salvation Army and the Quakers being the nearly sole exceptions—taken over the Catholic sacrament of this meal and put their stamp on it. For centuries the Mass, in which the laity received bread and the clergy partook of bread and wine, was the repeated event in which Jesus Christ was made really present through priestly act, the word of God, and faith.

Lutheranism, as an expression of a conservative Reformation, came closest to keeping the sacramental worldview with its implications for the bread and wine *as* body and blood of Christ. But even Lutheranism rebelled against *ex opere operato* concepts and did not want to see a change in the visible elements, a transubstantiation, of any sort. This could lead to what Lutherans saw to be superstitious or magical reverence. Most other Protestants sided with the Reformed tradition. They did not see the Lord's Supper or Holy Communion as an occasion for seeing God in Christ as present or for regarding Christ as sacramentally experienced in assemblies. Instead they located the Lord's Supper in a system of grace as a human response, to which people brought their faith and their intentions in response to a command of God.

Whatever their doctrinal attitude toward the rite, these Protestants took the meal seriously. For example, the nineteenth-century Protestant movements associated with the Disciples of Christ, which were attempts to restore primitive Christianity, rejected Catholic and Lutheran sacramental views. Yet, more than most Protestants, they kept the frequent, indeed weekly, practice of sharing the sacred meal, which usually takes place during the formal Sunday observance of congregations, although usually with less frequency than in the sacramental and Catholic churches. Communicants receive both bread and wine (or, in some temperance-minded bodies, unfermented grape juice) from a central table, either at that table or in the pew. The event occurs in a spirit of great solemnity, after there have been preaching and examination of hearts.

The Role of the Word. While baptism and the Lord's Supper as sacraments, and marriage, confirmation, and funeral rites as practices, receive much attention, Protestantism is supremely a religion of the word. By this most believers mean not simply the word of the Bible but the Logos of God, the expression of God. God creates the universe by a word, pronounces sinners forgiven by a word, speaks the word to heal them, builds community through the word.

This has necessarily meant dissemination of the word. Protestantism was born early in the age of Johann Gutenberg during a revolution in printing that made literacy necessary and the spread of words possible. Some modern critics have seen Protestantism as so identified with Gutenberg's invention of movable type and a great impulse to use it that they predict its demise as print gives way to the competition from electronic and visual disseminations. However, Protestantism also makes much of the oral word and sees voice as a summons for belief. Its leaders have long quoted the Pauline notion that "faith comes by hearing" and hearing by the word of God. This has meant that most Protestant revitalizations have occurred as theologies of the word or, for the people, as enhanced preaching.

Protestantism came on the scene after the great tradition of Catholic preaching was over, and there was little new attention being given to homiletics. For Protestants, the preached word or sermon, expounding the word and applying it to the needs of people in a new day, became a challenge to the Mass as the focal act of worship. This vast majority of Protestants measure the effectiveness of worship by reference to the preaching. It is the scriptural word that gives power to baptism and the Lord's Supper, whether as instruments of grace or as human response. The word shapes prayer; people use the word in teaching and conversation. In times of crisis, it is the word that inspires intercessory prayer. Most Protestant healing involves no herbs, potions, or exercises—only spiritual direction under the word. There are as many theories about why faith comes from hearing and believing the word as there have been theologies, Protestant bodies, or movements and ages in Protestantism. Given the complexity of human psychology, the variety of social contexts, and the pluralism of philosophical options, it is difficult to picture a final definition. Despite the lack of a unitary position on the power of the word, Protestants are united in believing that somehow theirs is a religion of the word.

Protestant Worship. In describing baptism (whether sprinkling of infants or immersion of adults), the Lord's Supper, and the act of preaching and the uses of the word, the outlines of Protestant worship become generally clear. To these should be added that Protestants characteristically have gathered for worship in buildings set aside for that purpose. While they believe that the gathered community may effectively baptize, eat and drink, hear and pray under the sky or in secular buildings, they have had an impulse to set aside and consecrate a sacred space, which symbolically, not actually, becomes a house of God.

The building may be of almost any architectural style. Original Protestant churches tended to be slightly stripped-down Catholic churches that had been taken over by Protestants. In general, the concept of being "stripped down" is appropriate; when Protestants build churches, they tend to be somewhat simpler than Orthodox or Catholic churches. Rejecting icons and minimizing the sacral role of statues and painting, Protestants have tended to use pictorial art for purposes of teaching, reminder, or inspiration. This approach has led to direct and simple expressions, with the exception of a very few periods in which Protestants did revert to ornate Gothic expressions.

The sacred space usually accents a place for preaching, a baptismal font or pool, and a table or altar for the Lord's Supper. Around these the people gather, in pews or on chairs. The gathering occurs to recognize the presence of God, to follow divine commands to congregate for purposes of praise, to build the morale of the group for purposes outside the sanctuary, and to celebrate the seasons of the church year, the events of the week, and the passages of life.

With few exceptions, Protestantism is also a singing religion. It took the act of praising in song, which had become largely a preserve of clergy and choir, and enlarged it to include the congregation. There may be chorally apathetic Protestantism, but in practice Protestants honor the word of God in song. Most of their revivals—Luther's and Charles Wesley's are but two examples—have been promoted through distinctive song.

Except in Seventh-day Adventism, Protestant worship almost always occurs on Sunday, the Lord's Day, the Day of Resurrection, although believers are urged to worship at any time or place. Most Protestants observe the inherited Catholic church year but have purged it of many of its occasions. That is, they annually follow the life of Christ from Advent and Christmas, with its birth rites, through another season of repentance and preparation, Lent, on the way to a climax at Good Friday and Easter weekend, and then a festival of the Holy Spirit at Pentecost. The more Puritan forms of Protestantism, however, saw something "papist" in these seasonal observances and did away with almost all of them, sometimes including Christmas itself. The rest of Protestantism, which kept the church year of observances, also honored biblical saints like Paul and John on special days but rejected most postbiblical saints. It was believed that honor directed to them distracted from worship of God in Christ. In many places a new church year tied to national and cultural events has emerged. Thus in the United States many observe a Thanksgiving Day, Mother's Day and Father's Day, Stewardship Sunday, Lay Sunday, and the like. The impulse to ritualize life is strong even on the purging, purifying, and simplifying soil of Protestantism.

The Way of Life. How, it may be asked, can one speak of a Protestant way of life when the ways are so varied? What do a wealthy American high church Anglican executive, a Latin American Pentecostal, and a black under oppression in South Africa have in common as a "way of life"? It would be foolish to impose a single ideal, force a straitjacket, or overgeneralize a vision, but something can and must be said about Protestant styles of behavior. Sometimes activities are so obvious that no one bothers to note them, and this is the case with some Protestant commonalities.

First, most overlooked and yet obvious on a second glance, is the widespread assumption that the life of grace to which Protestants witness by faith must issue in some form of personal ethic. This seems unremarkable, but by no means have all religions of the world made much of this moral notion. Many have centered themselves more on matters of rites and mores than on matters of conscience and morals. Protestantism has almost always been stereotyped as moralistic in intention and outlook. Catholic Christians have dismissed some of their own heresies, such as Jansenism, as being like "grim Calvinism" or dour Protestantism. Others have rebelled against the Protestant impulse to reform the world, to rearrange by law or example or injunction the lives of others, or to convert the experience of grace into severe new legalisms. While these rejections of Protestantism may be based on exaggerations or partial misperceptions, there is enough consistency in Protestantism to warrant elaboration of the theme.

Catholic Christianity has stressed personal ethics and produced people of impressive moral conviction and achievement. Yet often it has implied that participation in the Mass and the act of having a soul saved are paramount, and that the faithful as a group are the moral agents. Protestantism, through its tendency toward individualism, expects more of an internalization and personal application of the message of the church.

Protestantism has often been impelled to be critical of the sexual mores of its day and to ask its people for restraint in expressions of sexuality. Partly under the impetus of sixteenth-century reformers who, as clerics, had been celibate but who later married, established families, and lived in "parsonages," Protestants chose to affirm sexuality in familial contexts. Scorning monasticism most of the time, and speaking of the vocation to propagate where that was possible, Protestants became champions of the family. Their critics see Protestantism as being so familial that it tends to adopt the norms of bourgeois families wherever these appear, without sorting out what is temporary cultural expression from what is integral to the faith or biblically based. Sometimes, despite Protestant individualism, the individual who is not vividly involved in family life has felt left out by the norms of preaching and teaching that see the family as a basic unit of revelation, nurture, and discipline.

It is not easy to strain all the Protestant impulses for personal ethics and morals into a single mold. In general, Protestantism has called not just for applying the faith within the Christian community but for taking it into the world as well. The line between the sacred and the secular calling and sphere was supposed to be a fine one, whether it turned out to be so in practice or not. Some Protestant ethics have been legalistic, a somber response to the commands of God in the divine law. Yet more frequently reformers have insisted that Protestantism is an issuing of faith in forms of love that seek to serve as conduits of God's *agapē,* which is a spontaneous, unmotivated love. This understanding, it has been claimed, is more liberating than those Catholic forms that stress almsgiving or doing good to obtain merit and thus would be partly self-serving. Similarly, Protestant ethicists have often criticized Catholics for using models of human desire and friendship or natural love, not the *agapē* that exemplifies the initiative of divine love.

Protestant response often generates an ethic of attention to the life of the church. Lacking the appeal of the sacramental presence of Christ in the reserved communion Host, or bread, or the understanding that something happens uniquely in the sanctuary, Protestants have often had to work strenuously to provide reasons for attending worship regularly. "Go to church" becomes a large part of the ethic, and the quality of Christian life is often measured by faithfulness in participation on church premises.

Public Life. As for social ethics, Protestantism includes several strains. There has been a denial of the world of a sort that, in H. Richard Niebuhr's terms, pits Christ *against* culture or sees Christ to be too pure and lofty to be stained in society and thus sees Christ *above* culture. There have been constant temptations for Protestantism, where it prevails, simply to baptize the surrounding culture in forms of a Christ *of* culture. Then all lines between the Christian and the world on some terms or other are obscured.

Two other types have tended to dominate wherever Protestants have been reflective and self-critical. One of these would be called by observers and critics a form that keeps transforming culture with a millennial or utopian tinge. In this version, Protestants pick up biblical witness to the always-coming kingdom of God. Proclaiming this coming kingdom involves a prophetic denouncing of the world as it is, the vision of a better world, and some sort of program for reaching it. This transforming strain of Protestantism tends to prevail in times when progressivism is plausible in the culture and calls forth a buoyant, activistic kind of response. On its soil there have been genuine efforts to change the structures of society, to promote more justice. Many Reformed and especially Puritan and later moderate evangelicalisms have been dedicated to such models.

This form of approach tends to call forth common action by the church. Either through movements, demonstrations, or the issuance of teaching and prophetic proclamations, church bodies ask for corporate wrestling with issues. The church as church takes some stand in society and tries to work for change that will make the empirical world look like or realize some dimension of life in the kingdom of God. Then the accent on personal morality is not secondary, but it becomes specialized. It works in some aspects of life but not in others.

The other main Protestant stream also asks for engagement with culture, but it is more individualistic and relies less on progressivist models. Although the kingdom of God may be wholly eschatological, coming or to come only after human history as now known is exhausted, the individual Christian is not relieved of responsibilities of citizenship. But he or she is now a more isolated representative who does not wait for and may not agree with joint Christian efforts. In this school there is more accent on the perduring element of the demonic in human history. People are seen as more intransigent, as less malleable to change. The task of the church is more otherworldly, and salvation is seen in individualistic and spiritualizing terms. There are instincts to be more conservative, to support the status quo at its best, to honor the government and the authorities or powers that be as ordained of God.

In either case, Protestantism has been culturally productive. Whether on corporate or individual terms, this movement, in the eyes of many social thinkers, including Max Weber, took advantage of new economic opportunities that arose during and after the Reformation era in western Europe and Anglo-America. By turning its ascetic and self-denying powers from the search for salvation, as in the monastery, to the search for productive life in the secular setting, Protestants produced new motives and energies. They were ready to work hard and long. They wanted to be stewards of the earth and its resources. They would not waste and wished to save. Consequently, as they took risks with capital and invested, they developed a "Protestant ethic," which spread wherever Protestantism did.

More recent sociologists have questioned Weber's thesis. There seems to have been capitalism, as in fifteenth-century Venice, before there were Protestants. There is an equivalent to the Protestant ethic in nations such as Japan, where there have never been many Protestants. Motivations for capitalist venture were too broad to be clustered under a "this-worldly ascetic" motif. Yet the Protestants, for the most part, in Europe and now in nonwhite indigenous circles, have been great promoters of individual work and responsibility. The use of leisure, the concept of siesta and fiesta, is not dealt with so consistently where Protestants dominate. They would live out a divine-human drama in the workaday world, one that calls for them to be productive and busy.

THEOLOGY. Only with broadest brush strokes need one show how Protestantism issues in a variety of thought patterns. It goes almost without saying that as a religion of the word it must connect with other patterns of word use, other systems of thought. While it could inherit much of Catholic theology and convert it to embody the new or renewed Protestant concepts, Protestantism also placed on individuals more burden for formulation than did Catholicism, where more was inherited through the tradition. Since Protestantism also induced variety and pluralism, it became important for each group or profound thinker to formulate what was special about his or her locale, context, public, and program. The freedom that Protestantism professed to bring was a mandate and a license to be enterprising in theological form-building.

By contrast, in reaction to the Reformation, Roman Catholicism through the Council of Trent tended to freeze theological development. Experiment was downgraded, and innovation was a subject that induced suspicion. The theologian became the reformulator, the custodian of assured truths. Developmental or modernist thought was formally condemned, and the papacy came to elevate Thomistic scholasticism to privileged—indeed, virtually monopolistic—status. Protestantism also engendered scholasticisms and orthodoxies but was unable to suppress the experimental tendencies it had opened up.

Protestant theology saw the Bible as its basic set of texts and, often, the only norm and source for theology. Many thinkers, with their churches, were ready also to accept the main themes and modes of early Christian orthodoxy from the creed-making period. To these they added the statements of faith from the first or second generation of each Protestant expression. Finally, there was room for individual witness and ingenuity dependent upon available philosophy and urgent cultural necessity. Protestantism was born not in episcopal residences or monasteries but, for the most part, in universities and academies. This meant that the new formulators were uncommonly exposed to rival and alien—but also sometimes alluring—patterns of thought.

Protestant thought has moved through a number of epochs. The first generation tended to be open, explosive, rich in dialectic, ready for ambiguity, indulgent with paradox. A second period led to reaction and scholastic impulses to nail everything down, to be secure and neat, to defend propositions of faith. Later, in most of the older Protestantism, new movements of the heart, new Pietisms, forced changes in thought patterns. These were quickly supplanted by the rationalisms of the Enlightenment, which colored Protestantism almost everywhere. Then came a crisis of historical consciousness, a readiness to see everything in the Christian scheme colored by accident and contingency in history. In the twentieth century, among the explosion of options, there was some embrace of existentialist and personalist outlooks. To the non-Protestant Christian, this meant individualist irresponsibility. To the churched forms of Protestantism it became both a challenge and a threat, as theologians applied Protestant witness in varied thought patterns in changing cultures. In nonwhite indigenous Protestantisms new patterns are still emerging.

Protestant Expression. That Protestants chose preaching, hymnody, architecture, and the like for cultural expression and economics or reform for social expression can be inferred from preceding passages. In general, Protestantism has been less fertile than Catholic Christianity in affirming the literary and artistic worlds. Sometimes this has resulted from a certain suspicion about the validity of the earthly venture for the sake of salvation. Tillich balanced his "protestant principle" with "Catholic substance," the ability to relish and invest in the sights and sounds of human endeavor, which was often lacking in Protestantism. Sometimes moralism has prevented Protestants from literary expression, since literature often pushes at the edges of moral convention. The tinge of iconoclasm in much of Protestantism has kept it from being free for artistic expression.

All this has meant that Protestantism seemed most productive in the field of music, perhaps because the kinetic character of music seemed to be congruent with a word-centered, iconoclastic tradition. One thinks here of the musical poets of Protestantism, most notably the composer Johann Sebastian Bach. In literature there have been John Milton and John Bunyan, but in the contemporary world Protestantism has seldom helped produce anything approaching modern classics. In the visual arts geniuses like Lucas Cranach or, supremely, Rembrandt, have given expression to their evangelical sympathies and Protestant outlook. But this artistic tradition is no match for Catholic versions. The Protestant movement, then, has concentrated on other fields and still awaits substantial aesthetic articulation.

The Future. Protestantism has been in decline in its heartland, western Europe and the British Isles. The old establishments there survive, but languidly, and churches are nearly empty in much of secular western Europe. In North America the picture is more complex, varied, and promising. While mainstream Protestantism as an heir of establishment has been languishing, revitalized conservative movements, more worldly than their antecedents, prosper. The greatest growth is in nonwhite indigenous Protestantism, especially in sub-Saharan Africa. Following present trends in the Southern Hemisphere, Christianity, and Protestantism with it, is on the way toward becoming numerically dominant. What it will choose to retain from the missionary forms of Protestantism and where it will choose to innovate are not yet determined. As the two clusters come together, the result will help determine the future of Protestantism wherever that form of Christianity propagates itself.

See Also Anabaptism; Anglicanism; Baptism; Baptist Churches; Basilica, Cathedral, and Church; Biblical Exegesis, article on Christian Views; Christianity; Christian Liturgical Year; Christian Science; Christian Social Movements; Church; Creeds, article on Christian Creeds; Deism; Ecumenical Movement; Ethical Culture; Eucharist; Evangelical and Fundamental Christianity; Funeral Rites; God, article on God in Postbiblical Christianity; Hus, Jan; Hutterian Brethren; Iconography, article on Christian Iconography; Initiation; Jesus; Literature, article on Religious Dimensions of Modern Western Literature; Lutheranism; Marriage; Mennonites; Methodist Churches; Ministry; Modernism, article on Christian Modernism; Moravians; Mormonism; Music, article on Religious Music in the West; Neoorthodoxy; Pentecostal and Charismatic Christianity; Pietism; Poetry, article on Christian Poetry; Presbyterianism, Reformed; Priesthood, article on Christian Priesthood; Puritanism; Quakers; Rites of Passage; Sacrament, article on Christian Sacraments; Salvation Army; Seventh-day Adventism; Shakers; Theology, article on Christian Theology; Trinity; Unitarian Universalist Association; Waldensians; Worship and Devotional Life, article on Christian Worship.

Bibliography

One of the more ambitious histories of Protestantism is Émile G. Léonard's *Historie générale du protestantisme,* 3 vols. (Paris, 1961–1964), translated as *A History of Protestantism* (London, 1965–1968). Most Protestant history is simply incorporated as half of the latter third of general church histories, such as Kenneth Scott Latourette's *A History of Christianity* (New York, 1953). The most extensive easily accessible bibliography is in my own *Protestantism* (New York, 1972). One way to approach Protestantism is through its root experience in the Reformation era; on the thought of the period, see Wilhelm Pauck's *The Heritage of the Reformation,* rev. ed. (Oxford, 1968); Harold J. Grimm's *The Reformation Era, 1500–1650,* 2d ed. (New York, 1973), is especially useful for its bibliographies.

Louis Bouyer's *The Spirit and Forms of Protestantism* (London, 1956) is an informed view by a Calvinist turned Catholic. Einar Molland's *Christendom: The Christian Churches, Their Doctrines, Constitutional Forms, and Ways of Worship* (New York, 1959) is especially interesting for its comparison between Protestant and other forms of Christianity. Few scholars have attempted to discern the genius of Protestantism as a whole, but there are good reasons to consult an imaginative attempt by Robert McAfee Brown, *The Spirit of Protestantism* (Oxford, 1961), or George W. Forell's *The Protestant Faith* (Englewood Cliffs, N.J., 1960); for a European view, see Karl Heim's *The Nature of Protestantism* (Philadelphia, 1963). John B. Cobb, Jr., in *Varieties of Protestantism* (Philadelphia, 1960), treats modern theology.

New Sources

Asselt, William J. van, and Eef Dekker, eds. *Reformation and Scholasticism: An Ecumenical Enterprise.* Grand Rapids, Mich., 2001.

Berg, Johannes van Den. *Religious Currents and Cross-Currents: Essays on Early Modern Protestantism and the Protestant Enlightenment.* Leiden and Boston, 1999.

Dillenberger, John, and Claude Welch. *Protestant Christianity: Interpreted through Its Development.* 2d ed. New York, 1988.

Marty, Martin E. *Protestantism in the United States: Righteous Empire.* 2d ed. New York, 1986.

Marty, Martin E., ed. *Theological Themes in the American Protestant World.* Munich and New York, 1992.

Marty, Martin E., ed. *Varieties of Religious Expression.* New York, 1993.

Martin E. Marty (1987)
Revised Bibliography

PROVIDENCE SEE CHANCE; FATE; FREE WILL AND PREDESTINATION; HISTORY

PRZYLUSKI, JEAN. Of Polish ancestry and French nationality, Jean Przyluski (1885–1944) was a linguist, Buddhologist, and historian of religions His wide-ranging interests led him to publish prolifically on topics as varied as the structure of the Vietnamese language, the development of Buddhist myths and legends, and Indo-European folk traditions (e.g., werewolf cults), and to theorize about the general evolution of human religiosity.

Przyluski began his career as a colonial civil servant in Indochina, where he perfected his competency in Vietnamese, as well as Chinese and Sanskrit, and became a correspondent for the École Française d'Extrême-Orient. In 1913 he returned to France where he soon took a post as professor of Annamese at the École des Hautes Études. He was eventually elected as an officer of the first Congress of Linguists and was chosen to write the entries on virtually all the languages of Southeast Asia in the first edition of Antoine Meillet's encyclopedic *Les Langues du Monde* (1934).

But Przyluski's most important and lasting contribution was to the field of Buddhist studies. His book-length presentations of traditions associated with the *parinirvāṇa* and funeral of the Buddha, with the first Buddhist Council, with the legend of King Aśoka, and with the expansion of Buddhism to Northwest India, remain landmark contributions to our understanding of the development of Buddhism in India. Przyluski was also influential as editor of the series *Buddhica* (begun in 1925) and of the periodically published *Bibliographie bouddhique* (1928–1958).

Przyluski has sometimes been criticized for his tendency to view changes in the Buddhist tradition as the result of influences coming from other religious traditions, often outside India. For example, he looked to Iranian and even Babylonian sources to explain the development of the cults of the cakravartin king, of the *bodhisattva* Maitreya, and of the buddha Amitābha. But he was also likely to trace certain traditions (e.g., the cult of the arhat Gavāṃpati and certain features of the Buddha's funeral) to indigenous Indian or "austro-asiatic" traditions, often invoking etymological connections to make his points. At the same time, he sought to identify different stages in the evolution of traditions (e.g., in the legend of King Aśoka) by identifying cycles of stories that he associated with different geographic locales and hypothetical stages in the development of Buddhism. Przyluski's often speculative and always forcefully made interpretations are not generally followed by Buddhologists today, but his insights remain interesting and stimulating, and the many translations he made—especially of Chinese Buddhist sources—are still valued and used.

More short-lived was the influence of the trilogy of works of a general philosophical nature that he wrote during the war—*Participation* (1940), *L'évolution humaine* (1943), and *Créer* (1943)—as well as his posthumously published *La grande déesse: Introduction à l'étude comparative des religions* (Paris, 1950). In the latter, Przyluski presents his own grand evolutionary scheme tracing humanity's development through economic, social, and spiritual stages, which he associates with belief in *mana,* magical ritualism, and the emergence of dogma, three phases that he claims also parallel a general evolution from the worship of a mother goddess ("mistress of animals") to the cult of a father god. Such a scheme, reminiscent of an earlier generation of scholars, was dismissed by reviewers almost as soon as it appeared.

BIBLIOGRAPHY

On Przyluski's life and work, see Charles Picard, "Jean Przyluski (1885–1944)," *Revue archéologique* 35 (1950): 101–102; and A. W. Macdonald and Marcelle Lalou, *L'oeuvre de Jean Przyluski* (Paris, 1970). Among his nearly fifty substantive publications, special mention should be made of the following: "Le Nord-ouest de l'Inde dans le Vinaya des Mūlasarvāstivādin et les textes apparentés," *Journal asiatique* 4 (1914): 493–568; *Le parinirvāṇa et les funérailles du Buddha* (Paris, 1920); *La légende de l'empereur Açoka (Açokāvadāna) dans les textes indiens et chinois* (Paris, 1923); "La princesse à l'odeur de poisson et la nāgī dans les traditions de l'Asie orientale," *Études asiatiques* 2 (1925): 265–284; *Le concile de Rājagṛha* (Paris, 1926); and "La ville du cakravartin: Influences babyloniennes sur la civilisation de l'Inde," *Rocznik Orjentalistyczny* 5 (1927): 165–185.

JOHN S. STRONG (2005)

PSALMS are ancient Hebrew songs addressed to or invoking the deity; the Hebrew Bible, or the Old Testament in the Christian scriptures, includes a book of 150 of these religious songs. In ancient and later Jewish tradition, the book is known in Hebrew as *Tehillim* ("Praises"), although only one of the songs (Psalm 145) is so designated within the biblical text. The English title *Psalms* derives from the Greek rendering of the Hebrew *mizmor* (a song accompanied by string plucking), a label that introduces fifty-seven of the Hebrew psalms. In Christian circles, the *Book of Psalms* is often referred to as the Psalter, a name taken from the psaltery, a stringed instrument that accompanied the singing of many of the psalms. Use of the word *psalter* also implies that the *Book of Psalms* has been used as a hymnal, an official collection of religious songs, since ancient times.

In the Jewish canon, *Psalms* is the first book in the third section of the Hebrew Bible, the Writings. In the Christian canon, *Psalms* appears among the so-called wisdom books, between *Job* and *Proverbs.*

Apart from the canonical psalms, which seem to have been accorded official status in the second century BCE, there are many other ancient Hebrew songs of the psalm type. Within the Hebrew Bible are the song of triumph in *Exodus* (15:1-18), the prayer of Hannah in *1 Samuel* (2:1–10), the song of thanksgiving in *2 Samuel* 22 (which is nearly identical with Psalm 18), the prayer of Hezekiah in *Isaiah* (38:10–20), the thanksgiving psalm in *Jonah* (2:3–10), and the prayer of *Habakkuk.* The *Psalms of Solomon* in the pseudepigrapha, dated to the first century BCE, comprises eighteen hymns, personal pleas for salvation in particular, which resemble certain biblical psalms. Although only versions in Greek and Syriac are extant, the pseudepigraphical psalms clearly reflect Hebrew originals.

In addition, seven noncanonical psalms have been recovered among the Dead Sea Scrolls. They appear interspersed with a number of canonical psalms in the large manuscript of psalms from Qumran cave 11. Of these seven, one is included as Psalm 151 in the Septuagint (the ancient Greek translation of the Hebrew Bible), one is contained in the apocryphal *Book of Ben Sira,* and two have been preserved in ancient translations. A fifth appears in another Dead Sea Scroll, so that only two of the seven compositions are "new." As many as four Dead Sea psalters, dating from no later than the first century CE, include noncanonical psalms; this suggests that ancient hymnals were not restricted to the biblical *Book of Psalms.* A lengthy Dead Sea composition, the *Hodayot* (Songs of praise and thanksgiving), contained over forty hymns patterned after and drawing phrases from the *Book of Psalms.* The canonical psalms, then, served as models for ancient Jewish hymnody. At least two psalms within the New Testament, the Magnificat of Mary (*Lk.* 1:46–55) and the Benedictus of Zechariah (*Lk.* 1:68–79), similarly drew upon and emulated canonical prototypes.

FORMATION OF THE PSALTER. In its canonical form, *Psalms* comprises five sections or "books": Psalms 1–41, 42–72, 73–89, 90–106, and 107–150. The fivefold structure may have been patterned after the Pentateuch. The first four books end with a doxology, or call to praise the Lord, and the fifth ends with an entire psalm (Psalm 150) that constitutes a doxology. It has been noted that books 1, 4, and 5 tend to employ the unvocalized personal name of God in the Hebrew Bible, YHVH (traditionally and in this article rendered as "the Lord"), while books 2 and 3 refer to God as Elohim, suggesting that divergent theological traditions, or schools, may have compiled the different books.

There are a number of indications that the psalms had formerly been organized differently. Psalm 135 concludes with a doxology, and Psalm 72 ends with an attribution to a special collection of "David." These two, then, may have once designated the close of earlier collections. A number of psalms are attributed in their titles or openings to various types or collections: the psalms of David (*Ps.* 3–9, 11–32, 34–41, 51–65, 68–70, 86, 101, 103, 108–110, 124, 133, 138–145—a total of seventy-two); the psalms of the sons of Koraḥ (*Ps.* 42, 44–49, 84, 85, 87, 88); the psalms of Asaph (*Ps.* 50, 73–83); the psalms of *ma'alot,* usually rendered "ascents" (*Ps.* 120–134); and the "hallelujah" psalms (*Ps.* 104–106, 111–113, 115–117, 135, 146–150). Because psalms of similar attribution generally occur in blocks, because very similar psalms appear in more than one collection (*Ps.* 14 and 53; parts of 40 and 70; 57 and 60 and 108), and because the attributions seem to refer to liturgical compilations (Koraḥ and Asaph were eponymous names of priestly guilds) or functions ("ascents" and "hallelujah" psalms), it is likely that the canonical books were formed from earlier groups of psalms, with psalms from one group interpolated into sets of psalms from other groups.

Evidence from the Dead Sea psalters suggests that books 1 and 2 were standardized by the second century BCE but that the order of psalms in the last three books remained flexible as late as the first century CE. At that time, the canonical Psalter was fixed within the Jewish community of ancient Judaea.

ATTRIBUTION OF THE PSALMS. Most psalms bear headings that serve either to attribute them to certain authors or collections (David, Koraḥ, Asaph, Moses, Solomon), to describe their type (accompanied song, chant, prayer), to prescribe their liturgical use (Psalm 92 is assigned for Sabbath worship), or to direct their musical performance.

Nearly half the canonical psalms are attributed to David, king of the Israelite empire in the tenth century BCE. Few of the psalms, however, are dated by scholars to so early a period. The attributions to David are generally held to stem from a later attempt to enhance the authority of the psalms by ascribing their origin to Israel's most famed singer and psalmist, David. David is represented as a musician in *1 Samuel* 16, and within the narrative of *2 Samuel* he is credited with three songs: an elegy for Saul and Jonathan (*2 Sm.* 1:17–27), a psalm of thanksgiving for his having been delivered from enemies (*2 Sm.* 22), and a reflection on the covenant between YHVH and David (*2 Sm.* 23:1–7). Some of the psalm headings place the following psalm in a specific situation in the life of David. For example, Psalm 34 begins: "Of David, when he feigned madness before Abimelech, and he chased him out, and he went." (This ascription is clearly inauthentic, however, for it was Achish of Gath, not Abimelech, who chased out David; see *1 Sm.* 21:10–16.) The attribution of psalms to David manifests a later interest; in fact, the ancient Greek translation inserts references to the life of David where the Hebrew has none.

Large groups of psalms are attributed to Koraḥ and Asaph. According to *Chronicles, Ezra,* and *Nehemiah,* they were the ancestral heads of the priestly functionaries in the Second Temple in Jerusalem (c. 515 BCE–70 CE), the Levites. *Chronicles* further credits David with establishing the Levitical functions in the Temple (see *1 Chr.* 15–16). It would seem, then, that the attributions to David, Koraḥ, and Asaph refer historically to collections of psalms among Second Temple personnel. The fact that *1 Chronicles* 16 incorporates a psalm virtually identical with Psalm 105 supports this conclusion.

Beginning in the second century BCE with the apocryphal *2 Maccabees* (2:13), Christian and Jewish sources (e.g., *Heb.* 4:7; B.T., *B.B.* 14b) attribute the entire *Book of Psalms* to David. A noncanonical composition toward the end of the large Psalms Scroll from Qumran cave 11 credits David not only with the 150 canonical psalms, but with a total of 4,050 (150 x 3^3) psalms and songs. Jewish and early Christian tradition ascribe all the laws to the classic biblical lawgiver, Moses; the wisdom books, *Proverbs, Ecclesiastes,* and *Song of Songs,* to Solomon, a king celebrated for his sagacity; and, accordingly, the sacred songs to David. Although certain Christian and Jewish savants in the Middle Ages questioned the Davidic authorship of all the psalms, it was not until the writing of Barukh Spinoza in the seventeenth century and that of critical scholars in the nineteenth century that David was no longer held to have composed even those psalms ascribed to him in the Bible. Fundamentalists continue to believe in the Davidic authorship.

DATE AND PROVENANCE OF THE PSALMS. Although modern scholarship has abandoned the belief that David authored all the psalms, their date and provenance has been variously determined. Nineteenth-century scholars tended to date the composition of the psalms to the period in which their use was first explicitly attested, following the return of Judahites from the Babylonian exile in the fifth century BCE and later. Similarities between the psalms and the prophetic literature were explained as the influence of the prophets on the psalmists. A number of factors led twentieth-century scholars to conceive earlier datings. One was the discovery of hymns and prayers from ancient Egypt, Hatti (in Asia Minor), and Mesopotamia, which often display themes, motifs, and formulas similar to those of the biblical psalms. Likewise, the recovery of Ugaritic (northern Canaanite) texts shows that they exhibit a language and prosodic style similar to that of the psalms. Since psalmody is attested in the ancient Near East as early as the third millennium BCE, there is no reason to think Israel did not develop it until a late stage in its history. A second factor is thematic. If most psalms are postexilic or from the period of the Second Temple, it is surprising that they are not preoccupied with the return from the exile and the restoration of a Davidic king. A third factor is cultic or liturgical. If, as most scholars believe, many psalms functioned in the Temple cult, it is likely that a large number had already served such a function in the First, preexilic, Temple (see further below).

Because the psalms contain within them few historical references, the most scientific method for establishing the date and provenance of the individual psalms is linguistic. Psalms, like liturgical literature generally, tend to archaize. Even taking this into account, texts such as Psalms 18, 29, 68, 132, and others appear, by dint of their somewhat primitive content, affinities to Canaanite literature, and outmoded linguistic features, not merely to archaize but to be old. On the other hand, Psalms 103, 117, 119, 124, 125, 133, 144, 145, and, perhaps, others betray distinctively postexilic linguistic characteristics, making their Second Temple dating reasonably certain. Psalm 137 relates directly to the experience of exile, but most others cannot with certainty be dated before or after the sixth-century BCE exile. As regards provenance, as will be suggested below, certain psalms manifest clear origins in the ritual cult, some appear to have been commissioned by the monarchy, and others probably derive from scribal or unofficial circles.

TYPES OF PSALMS. Before discussing the ancient and later uses of the psalms, it will be helpful to describe their types. The prosodic form of the psalms, their language, and their motifs are for the most part highly conventional, suggesting they were composed according to typical patterns.

Their predominant form is comprised of parallelism—the formation of couplets and, occasionally, triplets of lines, through the repetition of syntactic structure and/or semantic content. For example, *Psalms* 92:2–3:

> Good it is to give thanks to the Lord,
> and to make song to your name, O one on high:
>
> To tell in the morning of your devotion,
> and of your faithfulness in the nights.

Several phrases and lines, such as "Give thanks to the Lord, for his devotion is eternal," "Chant to the Lord a new chant," "Do not in your wrath reprove me," "He has saved me from the enemy," and the like, abound in *Psalms*, such that most psalms appear contrived of common vocabulary and images. A number of psalms are arranged by artificial devices such as the alphabetic acrostic (Psalms 25, 34, 119, 145, and, more or less, others).

Many of the most common themes in the psalms also appear in the hymns and prayers of other ancient Near Eastern cultures. Psalm 104, for example, in which the deity's all-encompassing wisdom is compared to the sun and manifested in creation, bears sriking similarities to the fourteenth-century BCE Egyptian hymn to Aton (the sun disk) as well as to a Babylonian hymn to Shamash, the sun god. The Israelite victory hymn in *Exodus* 15 shares a number of motifs with the thirteenth-century Egyptian song of the pharaoh Merneptah. Both exalt the deity among the other gods; both describe the submission of other peoples witnessing the triumph. Prayers of Egypt, Hatti, and Mesopotamia praise the gods, as the Hebrew psalms praise YHVH, for protecting and upholding the poor, the feeble, the widow, and the orphan. All fear the god turning away his (or her) compassionate face; all ask undeserved forgiveness for the suppliant's sins; all assert that the righteous will prevail, that evildoers will stumble; all ask vengeance on enemies. As in *Psalms* 27:4, an Egyptian prayer seeks acceptance by the deity, the opportunity to gaze upon the image, or presence, of the god. The Hebrew psalms even share the typical outcry, "How long, O Lord," with Babylonian supplications. Although very few ancient Canaanite hymns or prayers have yet been discovered, the biblical psalms attest divine titles, such as "rider of the clouds" (*Ps.* 68:5), and entire verses, such as *Psalms* 92:10 and 145:13, which vary little from mid-second-millennium BCE Canaanite (Ugaritic) lines of epic. Considering these and many other parallels, and the Phoenician locale and archaic Canaanite style of Psalm 29, it would seem that

Israelite psalmists drew upon, perhaps even borrowed, common Canaanite material and patterns for their own hymns and prayers.

The conventional nature of so many biblical psalms and their relations to ancient Near Eastern hymnody in general have led scholars to delineate specific types of psalms and to associate those types with specific social or cultic circumstances in which they were presumably used in ancient Israel. In the early twentieth century, Hermann Gunkel isolated five major, as well as some minor, psalm types:

1. *Hymns,* liturgical songs of praise to the deity, sometimes beatifying God's power in nature (e.g., *Ps.* 29, 33, 34, 92, 100, 104, 105, 111, 114, 134–136, 145, 146)
2. *Personal songs of praise or thanksgiving,* similar to hymns but ostensibly offered by individuals (e.g., *Ps.* 18, 30, 32, 34, 41, 56, 116, 118, 138)
3. *Communal laments* (e.g., *Ps.* 28, 86, 106, 115)
4. *Individual laments or supplications* (e.g., *Ps.* 6, 25, 26, 38, 41, 91)
5. *Songs for the king* (e.g., *Ps.* 2, 20, 21, 45, 72, 101, 110, 132)

Several psalms mix different types; Psalm 18, for example, is both a royal song and an individual thanksgiving. Some psalms recount God's redemptive acts in Israelite history in the context of a hymn or other psalm type (e.g., *Ps.* 78, 105, 106, 136). Among the minor psalm types are didactic songs which teach piety and divinely favored conduct (e.g., *Ps.* 1, 19, 37, 49, 73, 112, 119, 127, 128, 133); meditations (e.g., *Ps.* 23, 27, 90); and communal thanksgivings (e.g., *Ps.* 67, 124).

Each of the psalm types exhibits certain characteristic traits. Within the most common type of psalm, the individual supplication, for example, in both the biblical and the extrabiblical specimens we find most of the following features: a description of the suppliant's ailment; a characterization of the suppliant as somehow disadvantaged in society; a plea for divine succor, often accompanied by a vow to the deity; and praise for the deity and/or an expression of trust that the deity will heed the plea. It is also widespread in this type for the suppliant to refer both to a physical distress and to mortal foes, on whom the suppliant seeks retribution. Note, for example, these excerpts from Psalm 6 (vv. 3, 6, 8, and 9):

> Show grace, O Lord, for languishing am I,
> Heal me, O Lord, for my limbs have been trembling. . . .
>
> For in death there is no mind of you.
> In She'ol [the netherworld] who will praise you? . . .
>
> My eye from vexation has grown sore,
> It has pined from all my adversaries.
>
> Turn away from me, all evildoers!
> For the Lord hears my crying voice.

The stereotyped nature of so many psalms suggests they may have been composed to fit into a particular, probably liturgical, function.

The Settings of the Psalms. Some of the psalms cannot readily be associated with any specific historical or cultic setting. This is especially so for didactic and meditative compositions. In many other cases, the content of the psalm suggests a likely usage. Psalm 24, for example, does seem like an appropriate text for a ceremony in which the ark was conveyed to Jerusalem. Psalm 45 sounds like an ode to be chanted at the wedding of a king. Psalms 114 and 136 pertain to the Exodus from Egypt and would have served well as texts for the spring festival of Pesaḥ (Passover), which celebrates Israelite freedom from Egyptian bondage.

There are a number of reasons for thinking that many, if not most, of the biblical psalms functioned within the daily and special occasional rituals of the Israelite Temple cult. It is likely that the later use of psalms in Jewish and Christian worship continued ancient practice. Ritual literature from ancient Near Eastern societies outside Israel, such as Babylon, prescribe the recitation of prayers and hymns similar to those of the Bible within various cultic ceremonies. One may infer that the biblical psalms served a similar function.

Indeed, references and statements within *Psalms* and elsewhere in the Bible suggest a liturgical usage. This is clear in Second Temple times, as *Ezra* (3:10–11) and *Chronicles* (*1 Chr.* 16:8–36) cite the singing of Psalms 117, 96, 105, and 106. Some psalms speak of chanting psalms in the sanctuary (*Ps.* 11:4, 134:2, 150:1), and several allude to worship in the sanctuary (e.g., *Ps.* 17:15, 18:7, 23:6, 26:8, 27:4). Psalms 66 and 135 display a liturgical nature, and the numerous references to singing and musical accompaniment in *Psalms* bespeak a liturgical usage.

Preexilic biblical texts such as *Isaiah* 30:29 and *Amos* 5:23 link music to worship. Not only do many psalms describe instrumental accompaniment (e.g., *Ps.* 43:4, 71:22, 81:2–4, 92:3, 150:3–5), but several psalm headings also appear to direct the method of chanting or playing the psalm. Several psalms are introduced by the ascription *la-menatseaḥ,* which, on the basis of *1 Chronicles* 15:21, refers to the conductor of stringed instruments in the liturgy. Psalms 57, 58, 59, and 75 were to be chanted to the tune of a popular song, "Destroy Not"; Psalms 45 and 80, to the tune of "Roses"; Psalm 22, to "Gazelle of Dawn"; and Psalm 56, to "Dove of the Distant Terebinths." A number of the headings appear to prescribe the manner of, or instruments for, playing a psalm, although the precise meaning of the terms cannot be defined: *neginot* (stringed instruments?); *sheminit* (on the octave?, eight-stringed instrument?); *ʿalamot* (soprano?); *neḥilot* (reed pipe?); and *gittit* (vintner song?).

Psalms 42–43 (which comprise a single piece) and 107 feature refrains that may well have served as responses for a chorus, and Psalm 136 presents the same phrase after each new line, suggesting a choral or congregational response. The fact that the refrain "Blessed is the Lord and blessed is his name forever and ever" follows each verse of Psalm 145 in the Dead Sea Scroll from cave 11 supports the view that at least some, if not most, of the psalms played a role in the Temple liturgy.

What role they played in First Temple times can only be surmised. It is often assumed that, as in the postexilic period, psalms were chanted in conjunction with the daily cult of animal offerings and on Sabbaths and festivals. Individuals may have recited psalms privately, as *1 Samuel* 2 represents of Hannah and *Jonah* 2 of Jonah. Many psalms are indeed spoken by a first-person singular "I." Such psalms, however, frequently refer to the speaker's enemies as "the nations" (e.g., *Ps.* 44, 60, 66, 74, 89, 94, 102, 118), which suggests that the "I" of these psalms is not an individual but the entire people of Israel. How many psalms served as texts for private prayer is, therefore, unclear.

In general, the psalms deal with broad themes of human anguish and need, the deity's grandeur and pathos, and the virtues and pleasures of piety. Many psalms touch on an array of themes. The nonspecific nature of so many psalms makes them, theoretically, applicable to a variety of occasions without limit to a particular time and place. For this reason, it is difficult, and perhaps inconsistent, to define the historical setting or function of any psalm in narrow fashion. Nevertheless, the presence of striking motifs in various series or groups of psalms has led some scholars to try to find for them a common ancient setting.

A number of psalms (e.g., *Ps.* 47, 93, 95–100) speak of the kingship of the biblical god, YHVH. On the basis of festivals in Egypt (Min) and Babylonia (Akitu) in which the chief god is celebrated for vanquishing the god(s) of chaos and establishing order and is then enthroned and acclaimed as king, Sigmund Mowinckel and other twentieth-century scholars have hypothesized that ancient Israel acclaimed YHVH as king at the fall New Year, on Sukkot (Tabernacles, Feast of Booths). As many as forty psalms have been presumed to have been recited as part of this "enthronement" festival. During this festival, the primeval triumph of YHVH over the forces of chaos and his creation of the world would be recounted, YHVH would be declared king, his defeat of Israel's historical enemies would be anticipated, and he would be ensconced in his temple and adulated. Psalm 103, for example, ends with an exaltation of YHVH as king over all (v. 19), and it is followed by Psalm 104, which beatifies YHVH's majestic dominion over the entire world of nature. It has been held that such juxtapositions of theme are appropriate to an enthronement festival.

The hypothesis that ancient Israel had a fall New Year celebration of YHVH's kingship may be supported by the fact that early Judaism made the acknowledgment of the Lord as king an integral part of its New Year (Ro'sh ha-Shanah) liturgy. Without an explicit textual reference to such an enthronement festival, the use of psalms on such an occasion will remain conjectural. The wide use of psalms in later Jewish and Christian worship, however, does make their earlier liturgical use fairly assured.

USE OF PSALMS IN JEWISH LITURGY. In addition to the few, above-mentioned references in the later books of the Hebrew Bible, the use of psalms in Second Temple worship is attested in the Dead Sea and early rabbinic literature. At least thirty psalters have been discovered among the Dead Sea Scrolls—more than any other text, which suggests that a collection of psalms served the Jewish sectarians as a hymnal. The late second-century CE rabbinic code, the Mishnah, states that a specific psalm was chanted in the Temple each day (*Tam.* 7.4). According to Jewish tradition, the psalms corresponded to the order of creation as delineated in *Genesis* 1. On Sunday, the first weekday, the psalm commonly known as Psalm 24 was chosen, as it praises God's command of all creation; on the second day, Psalm 48, which exalts God for dividing the waters; on the third, Psalm 82, which refers to God's sitting as judge over the land; on the fourth, on which the sun, moon, and stars were created, Psalm 94, for it seeks vengeance on Israel's star-worshiping persecutors; on the fifth, Psalm 81, in which the marvels of creation evoke praise; on the sixth, Psalm 93, in which the wondrous creation of humankind elicits awe at God's majesty; and on the Sabbath, Psalm 92, which is assigned to that day by its title. Traditional Jewish liturgy to this day includes the recitation of these daily psalms.

On the basis of their content, Psalm 135 was prescribed for Pesaḥ; Psalm 81, for Ro'sh Ḥodesh (the New Moon); and Psalms 120–134, songs of "ascent," or pilgrim songs, for Sukkot, the joyous pilgrimage of the fall harvest. Psalm 136, the so-called Hallel ha-Gadol ("the great praise"), was recited on festive days, and Psalms 113–118 comprised a varied series of hallelujah-songs for all festivals. The juxtaposition of these psalms in the Psalter may reflect their joint liturgical function. A number of other psalms form part of the daily morning service, Psalm 145 opens the afternoon service, and certain psalms are recited for penitence and in mourning. Altogether, some eighty-four of the biblical psalms form a regular part of the Jewish liturgy. Owing to their blending of praise and petition, the psalms are also traditionally recited on behalf of the seriously ill and dying.

USE OF PSALMS IN CHRISTIAN WORSHIP. Since ancient times, the psalms have held a prominent place in Christian hymnals. Early churches inherited the regular recitation and chanting of psalms from the Jewish synagogue. The ancient church fathers, however, pointed to Jesus' quotation of *Psalms* 22:2 when he was crucified (e.g., *Mt.* 27:46) and assumed as a matter of course that Jesus recited psalms. Christian practice would accordingly emulate Jesus by making *Psalms* central to its liturgy. Jerome, for example, in the late fourth century attests to the chanting of psalms in Latin, Greek, and Syriac at funeral processions.

In the Middle Ages, *Psalms* formed the larger part of all regular worship. Psalm 119, the longest in the canon, was recited daily by clerics, who were required to memorize the entire Psalter; over the course of a week all the psalms were systematically recited. The psalms functioned both as devotion and as guides to piety and inspiration.

Various Christian churches and denominations utilize different texts of the Psalter, most of them adapted for public worship from the Latin of Jerome. Many English versions today stem from revisions of the Great Bible produced in 1539–1541. In addition to public worship, modern Christians have recited psalms in school and at home for meditation and for insight into God's ways.

The Psalms as Revelation. Although the psalms have been understood in Jewish and Christian tradition to embody the reflection and devotion of David, that is, as the expression of human spirit, they have also been taken to contain divine revelation of the future of the pious, on the one hand, and of the wicked, on the other.

An early rabbinic *midrash* on *Psalms* says: "Rabbi Yudan states in the name of Rabbi Yehudah: All that David said in his book [i.e., *Psalms*], he said with respect to himself, with respect to all Israel, and with respect to all times" (*Midrash Tehillim* 18.1). The fact that *Psalms* speaks in very general terms of the righteous and pious, who are favored by God, and of their enemies, the wicked, whom God will ultimately destroy, facilitates the traditional interpretation of *Psalms* as predictive of the respective fates of the good and the bad. Thus the Dead Sea sectarians, in their commentaries on *Psalms*, see themselves as the righteous and their personal opponents as the wicked; the Gentile nations that God will overturn, they, like the early rabbis, identify as the Romans. Christians see themselves as the true Israel, as the devotees of the Lord in the psalms. *Acts* 4:23–28, for example, interprets *Psalms* 2:1–2 to refer to the Romans and Jews as enemies of Jesus. Jesus is said, according to *Luke* 24:44, to have told his disciples: "Everything written about me in the Law of Moses and the Prophets and the Psalms must be fulfilled."

Jews and Christians have found in a number of psalms (e.g., *Ps.* 2, 18, 67, 72, 75, 100) predictions of an eschatological age at which the legitimate, anointed king (the Messiah) would be reinstated or vindicated. Church fathers and rabbis adduced verses from *Psalms* in support of various doctrines, and in the Middle Ages Jewish and Christian clerics disputed doctrines, such as the authenticity of Jesus as the Messiah and the trinitarian character of the deity, on the basis of the psalms and other canonical texts. While Christians would seek in the psalms clues to the coming of the eschaton, Jews would more often find consolation in the assurances that the righteous would be saved and the Jewish Diaspora ended.

Theology of the Psalms. Historically, various psalms date from diverse periods and provenance, so that one finds in them a variety of perceptions of God and religious concerns. In Psalm 18, for example, the Israelite God responds to the outcry of his worshiper by flying down from the sky amid wind and cloud, casting out lightning bolts, and bellowing thunder. In Psalm 104, God as controller of all nature spreads the sky out as his tent, wraps himself in celestial light, and makes a chariot of the clouds. He dispatches the winds to push the waters back from covering the entire land. These bold naturalistic images contrast sharply with the more abstract God of Psalms 1 and 119, the source of wisdom and moral guidance.

In the Psalter as a whole, one encounters a deity who is here transcendent and awesome, there immanent and caring. Ultimately, the conception of God one will find in any given psalm depends upon the type and function of that psalm. In psalms of praise and thanksgiving, for example, one is apt to find a powerful creator god whose marvelous dominion even the phenomena of nature adore (e.g., *Ps.* 19:2). In psalms of supplication, however, the petitioner must express his confidence in a compassionate deity who listens to the prayers of his devotees. The worshiper may adduce a traditional doctrine of God's pathos (*Exodus* 34:6 is quoted in *Psalms* 86:15, 103:8, and 145:8), and he may allude to his God's saving acts for his people in the past. He may, as in Psalm 77, invoke the deity's prehistoric show of power by vanquishing the primordial forces of chaos and setting the world as we know it in order.

It is everywhere posited that God is just and, accordingly, shows special concern for the just and righteous. The occasional successes of the wicked, therefore, dismay the pious, but psalms such as Psalm 37 repeatedly affirm that God will confound the wicked:

> The wicked plots against the righteous,
> and he gnashes his teeth against him;
>
> But my Lord smiles at him,
> for he sees his day [of doom] is coming. (37:12–13)

The pious trusts that God will "repay a man according to what he does" (*Ps.* 62:13). Nevertheless, out of an apparent impatience with the prosperity of the wicked and the foes of Israel, psalms often appeal to the deity to take vengeance on the enemies of Israel and its pious (e.g., *Ps.* 5:11, 31:18, 35:4, 40:15, 58:7, 104:35, 139:19). Such imprecations, which have disturbed many Christian theologians in particular, evince a frustration with God's temporary inaction:

> O God of vengeance, Lord,
> O God of vengeance, appear!
>
> Raise yourself up, O judge of the earth,
> Turn retribution on the arrogant!
>
> How long will the wicked, O Lord,
> How long will the wicked celebrate? (*Ps.* 94:1–3)

The psalmists hope that the deity's care for the world and its creatures, and the indigent and weak especially, will redound to them, that God will want them to live so as to acknowledge and praise their creator. The psalms present not a systematic theological picture but a confluence of themes and interests, of which Psalm 146 is an example:

> Let me praise the Lord as I live,
> let me make song to my God while I am.
>
> Trust not in princes,
> in a human who has not saving.
>
> When his spirit leaves, he returns to the land,
> on that day his deliberations vanish.

Happy is he whose aid is the God of Jacob,
whose succor is the Lord his God,

Maker of heaven and earth,
of the sea and of all that is in it,
faithful guardian forever;

Doing justice for the oppressed,
giving bread to the hungry . . .

The Lord loves the righteous . . .
but the path of the wicked he will pervert.

Let the Lord reign forever,
your God, O Zion, in every generation.

Halleluyah! (146:2–10)

The interplay of the individual and the people Israel, on the one hand, and of the transcendent and immanent deity, on the other, is fairly typical of many psalms, and of the Psalter in general.

Psalms as Literature. Owing to their liturgical origins and functions, many psalms display the sorts of stereotyped forms and wording, as well as the frequent refrains and repetitions, that characterize formal hymn singing and prayer. Their conventionality makes them easy to join; their repetitive rhythms and phrases can, when chanted, produce a *mantra*-like drive and intensity. When read as poems rather than prayers, many psalms do not feature the sophisticated configurations of words and deployment of tropes that are usually associated with poetry. The liturgical power of *Psalms* has, however, often been praised by readers, and certain of the psalms do exhibit artful arrangements of language and memorable images. A celebrated example is Psalm 23:

The Lord is my shepherd;
I shall not lack.

In pastures of grass he has me lie down
along waters of stillness he leads me.

My spirit he revives.

He guides me on just courses
for his name's sake.

Even when I walk in a vale of darkness
I fear no evil,
for you are with me.

Your rod and your staff—
they comfort me.

You set before me a table
opposite my adversaries.

You anoint with oil my head;
my cup overruns.

Aye, good and love will pursue me
all the days of my life;

And I shall dwell in the house of the Lord
for a length of days.

The recurrent rhythm of short, asymmetrically balanced couplets, the contrast of the idyllic pasture and the confrontation of enemies, the fear of danger mitigated by the support of the divine shepherd—these and the psalm's various tropes have made this poem a classic statement of confidence.

See Also Biblical Literature, article on Hebrew Scriptures; Music, article on Music and Religion in the Middle East.

Bibliography

For a detailed summary of modern scholarship on the psalms, with attention to the individual psalms as well, see Leopold Sabourin's *The Psalms: Their Origin and Meaning,* rev. ed. (New York, 1974). Recent approaches are surveyed in detail by David M. Howard, Jr., in "Recent Trends in Psalms Study," in *The Face of Old Testament Studies: A Survey of Contemporary Approaches,* edited by David W. Baker and Bill T. Arnold (Grand Rapids, Mich., 1999), pp. 329–368. The literary history of the canonical Psalter has been thoroughly analyzed in Gerald H. Wilson's *The Editing of the Hebrew Psalter* (Chico, Calif., 1985). The canonical shape of the Psalter is discussed in Brevard S. Childs's *Introduction to the Old Testament as Scripture* (Philadelphia, 1979), pp. 504–525. The classic study of types of Psalms is Hermann Gunkel, *Introduction to the Psalms: The Genres of the Religious Lyric of Israel,* completed by Joachim Begrich and translated by J. D. Nogalski, Jr. (Macon, Ga., 1998; first published in German in 1933). The ancient cultic functions of the Psalms are pressed by Sigmund Mowinckel's *The Psalms in Israel's Worship,* 2 vols., translated by D. R. Thomas (Oxford, 1962). For psalm by psalm commentary and bibliography see, for example, Erhard S. Gerstenberger's *Psalms, Part 1, with an Introduction to Cultic Poetry* (Grand Rapids, Mich., 1988); *Psalms, Part 2, and Lamentations* (Grand Rapids, Mich., 2001). The development of prayers and hymns in postbiblical and especially Qumran literature is treated in detail by Bilhah Nitzan in *Qumran Prayer and Religious Poetry,* translated by Jonathan Chipman (Leiden, 1994). The liturgical uses of Psalms are discussed in W. O. E. Oesterley's *A Fresh Approach to the Psalms* (New York, 1937). On the literary incorporation of poetic songs and prayers within the narrative prose of the Bible, see Steven Weitzman, *Song and Story in Biblical Narrative: The History of a Literary Convention in Ancient Israel* (Bloomington, 1997). For a fairly comprehensive analysis of the religion and spirituality of the Psalms, with attention to their Near Eastern setting as well, see Patrick D. Miller, Jr.'s *They Cried to the Lord: The Form and Theology of Biblical Prayer* (Minneapolis, 1994). Near Eastern parallels to the Psalms, as well as specimens of liturgical texts, are found in *Ancient Near Eastern Texts relating to the Old Testament,* 3d ed., edited by James B. Pritchard (Princeton, 1969).

Edward L. Greenstein (1987 and 2005)

PSELLUS, MICHAEL

PSELLUS, MICHAEL (1018–1078?) was a Byzantine statesman, philosopher, theologian, and historian. Born in Constantinople, Psellus's talents, broad learning, and eloquence soon made him the favorite in the emperor's court, in which he served simultaneously as head of the chair of rhetoric and philosophy (at the University of Constantinople) and as grand chamberlain. He subsequently served as secretary of state, prime minister, and diplomat. As a patriot and philosopher in an often corrupt political setting, he may justly be compared to Francis and Roger Bacon, who had similar political roles and literary careers. His extensive knowledge in philosophy and rhetoric earned him the coveted title "consul of the philosophers." After thirty years, however, Psellus abruptly abandoned the court, frustrated by the incompetence of his favorite student, the emperor Michael VII Ducas. He died a poor and forgotten man. Psellus's most important works are commentaries on the Greek philosophers and theologians. He also wrote poetry, funeral orations, historical treatises, and works on ancient Greek topography, alchemy, and astrology. In addition, five hundred of Psellus's letters are known.

Psellus's task was to interpret the Greek spirit in a conspicuously Christian setting. He soon became controversial and was almost excommunicated from the church. Nevertheless, he insisted in his teaching and writings that philosophy and theology ought not be seen as two different disciplines but as one. The former lays the intellectual foundations upon which the latter builds its spiritual mansions—philosophy is not a handmaiden of Christian theology, but a collaborator. Psellus was convinced that philosophy and theology, or science and faith, in unison could give humanity the answer to its perennial questions.

By reviving the pursuit of philosophy and learning in Constantinople, Psellus single-handedly renewed the spirit of excellence patterned on that of ancient Athens. This revival of classical study had longstanding effects, for Psellus is considered the forerunner of the Italian Renaissance. Two examples suffice to show the influence he had, not only among his own, but abroad: Giovanni Pico della Mirandola and Marsilio Ficino were two of Psellus's spiritual heirs.

Bibliography

The works of Psellus are available in *Patrologia Graeca,* edited by J.-P. Migne, vol. 122 (Paris, 1864). Two works on Psellus are Christos Zervos's *Un philosophe néoplatonicien de l'onzième siècle: Michael Psellos* (Paris, 1920) and my doctoral dissertation "The Philosophical Trilogy of Michael Psellos, God-Cosmos-Man" (University of Heidelberg, 1970), written in English. I also recommend Joan M. Hussey's *Church and Learning in the Byzantine Empire, 867–1185* (Oxford, 1937) and *The Byzantine World,* 3d ed. (London, 1967); and Petros Perikles Ioannou's *Christliche Metaphysik in Byzanz: Die Illuminationslehre des Michael Psellos und Johannes Italos* (Ettal, Germany, 1956).

George Karahalios (1987)

PSEUDEPIGRAPHA See BIBLICAL LITERATURE, *ARTICLE ON* APOCRYPHA AND PSEUDEPIGRAPHA

PSEUDO-DIONYSIUS See DIONYSIUS THE AREOPAGITE

PSYCHEDELIC DRUGS.

PSYCHEDELIC DRUGS. Psychedelic substances, derived from plants—and more recently, from chemical syntheses—have been used by human beings for thousands of years, mainly as facilitators for religious ecstasy and firsthand contact with spirit or divinity. In this essay, the term *mysticism* is used interchangeably with *spiritual experience* to refer to any person's direct, subjective communion with a deity, spirit, or ultimate reality. Anthropologists often make a distinction between mysticism, which they see as an individual's firsthand, direct encounter with deities or spirits, and religious experiences that are mediated through a church, temple or some type of formal ecclesiastic structure. In discussing psychedelics and religion, Houston Smith reports that while psychedelics have been said to provoke religious experiences, they are not necessarily able to promote religious lives.

Overall, religious behavior universally makes efforts to induce an ecstatic spiritual state by crudely and directly manipulating physiological processes. These include drugs as well as sensory deprivation, mortification of the flesh by pain, sleeplessness and fatigue, and deprivation of food and water. Wallace (1966) argued that the physiological manipulation of the human body by any means available to produce euphoria, dissociation or hallucination is one of the nearly universal characteristics of religion. The ecstatic experience is a goal of religious effort, and whatever means are found to help the communicant achieve it will be employed.

Mystical-religious experience, enhanced by psychedelic drug or plant ingestion, has as one of its most arresting aspects, a sense of unity or awe. This has been termed "absolute unitary of being" by D'Aquili and Newberg (2001, p. 79). In this state, individuals directly apprehend absolute unity with themselves, others and the universe. Subject and object merge and boundaries to the self are weakened. Reality itself is perceived as oneness. Attached to this experience is a profound and intrinsic sense of underlying beauty and goodness. The universe is perceived as whole, good and purposeful. When people leave this state, they do not perceive it as having been an illusion, hallucination, or delusion. Rather, they see it as the fundamental reality that underlies all reality. In this model, rational consciousness is merely one type of consciousness, equally valid with that induced spiritually or by LSD-like substances. Science arises from our rational baseline state of consciousness, which perceives reality as an amalgam of multiple discrete beings in emotionally neutral subject-object relationships. The absolute unitary state, on the other hand, arises from discrete altered states of consciousness. The trance stage progressively becomes intense with a blurring of the boundaries of individuals until they perceive no spatial or temporal boundaries at all and experience absolute unity, devoid of content. The individual ultimately experiences a movement from a baseline orientation in external reality to a more intense sense of unity with the rest of the world and an increasing loss of a sense of self and other. The person can now lose his or her individuality and experience a sense of absorption into the object of focus or the universe in general.

The unitary state is experienced and interpreted as the presence of the Absolute, or union with God. In Buddhism it is seen as a void. Often there is an experience of freedom from fear of death. While these experiences may be rare and individualized, those who have them universally interpret them as being absolutely transcendent or beyond ordinary experience. They are remarkable and worth investigating.

For most of human prehistory, psychedelics were associated with nomadic hunter-gatherer societies, where male hunters used psychedelics in shamanistic religious rituals to divine the future and the location of the animals they hunted. In shamanic cultures, there are no salvational goals to achieve by using psychedelics, and the chief focus is on power and its exercise by religious practitioners who seek out and often achieve ecstatic states of consciousness. One finds a multiplicity of spirit forces, often named and mythic, rather than any concept of a high or solitary god.

We note that psychedelics have always been viewed in human cultures as a two-edged sword. On the one hand they have been utilized because of their perceived ability to access spiritual realms. If we change our body chemistry, we may be able to ascertain realms of being that are not ordinarily available to most human beings. The obverse of this is simply a faulty-wiring hypothesis, which argues that the plant chemicals deceive and trick. In a Euro-American rational world, there is no spirit realm to access, so we are merely left with tricks of the mind. On the other hand, such substances have always had a potential for abuse, even when well-controlled in traditional settings. Plant psychedelics as a psychotechnology allow tribal elders to manage the altered states of consciousness of their adolescents through hypersuggestibility. They utilize the properties of the plant psychedelics to decondition youth and heighten religious experiences deemed important for social survival.

Anthropologists and archaeologists, who work within a paradigm of cultural evolution, look at the vast array of human societies in terms of the historic changes from simple to complex structures and they view culture as adaptation to distinctive ecological niches. Over time, societies tend to move in the direction of more complexity.

Table 1 is a model of hunter-gatherers, incipient agriculturists, intensive agriculturist and pristine state societies. The division is made according to economic, social, and ideological or spiritual practices. Anthropologists often view four basic types of religious behavior across time and space: namely shamanism, the religion of hunters and gatherers, with a focus on personal ecstasy and awe, and direct knowledge of the preternatural; communal cults where lay people participate in rituals to enhance economic gains such as hunting and fishing magic and where different segments of nature are named and sacralized; in Olympian religions where a hierarchy of spiritual forces is known and respected; and in monotheistic institutions where there is a supremacy of one spiritual entity or god. A class of social science specialists, called neuroanthropologists, would argue that human beings are wired for ecstasy and the ability to have nonordinary experiences in order to apprehend the divine. It is the facile ease with which human beings enter into what psychiatrists called "dissociative states," frequently within a cultural context. Psychedelic ingestion for purposes of religious ecstasy has been reported in all segments of human societies as presented in Table 1.

As societies became more complex, access to drug-induced altered states of consciousness became part of sumptuary laws, as fewer individuals were permitted entry to these states. This contrasts with societies of hunter-gatherers, for example, where a study found that in a community of eighty Peruvian hunters and gatherers, as many as twenty-five adult men might use the plant hallucinogen *ayahusca* (various *Banisteriopsis* species) twice a week or more in ritual ceremonies for spiritual purposes. With the rise of ancient civilizations where psychedelics were employed, abrogation of such drug access was no doubt related to the supposed power of the psychedelic state and the power believed to be conferred upon the user to control or harm others through magical means or witchcraft. A movement occurred from exoteric rituals, open and accessible to all adults, to esoteric rituals, much like the Eleusinian mysteries in ancient Greece. Unauthorized drug use under these circumstances may have become a crime against the commonwealth.

Illustration of some of these different societies' use of plant psychedelics in religious practice exemplifies general principles.

Australian Aborigines. Contemporary examples of hunter/gatherers include the Australian Aborigines, who utilized the plant hallucinogen *pituri*, taken within a ritualized, sacrosanct, socially sanctioned context with the intent to contribute to group cohesiveness and survival. The unique ability of the biochemical properties of the *pituri* plant (various *Duboisia* spp.) to evoke suggestibility in those who ingested them made these plants ideal catalysts. The elders provided their adolescents with a fast-paced educational experience and inculcated values, beliefs, and religious tenets. Using the suggestible states created by such substances, particularly in pubertal initiatory rituals that marked the transition to manhood, this contributed to cultural cohesiveness and survival. The hallucinogen was used by shamans—technicians of ecstasy—to obtain power and perquisites and to act as seers. The use of the plant was shrouded in secrecy and there are no first-hand descriptions of the plant use in male initiation rituals at puberty, only various early commentaries. The plant was most probably used to provide revelations, which allowed the youth to view the world and themselves as sacred.

Characteristics of Culture

	Egalitarian Hunters & Gatherers	Ranked Incipient Agriculture	Stratified Intensive Agriculture	State Agriculture
Economic Features	Small, Face-to Face; Food Sharing; Nomadic	Horticulture, Dense Population; Villages; No Work Specialization;	Eco. Redistribution; Surpluses; Complex Division of Labor; Work Specialization;	Differential Access to Basic Means of Livelihood;
Social Organiz. Features	Band Is Basic Social Unit; No Leadership; Kinship As Govt Functions;	Descent Principles; Leadership W/O Authority;	Social Classes; Status Differences; Federations; Militarism; Role of Chief;	Use of Military to Maintain Control; Diverse Populations Within State; Formal Government;
Religion & Ideology	Shamanism; No Religious Specialists; Shaman/Client.	Community Cults; Lay Participation; Congregation;	Olympian Religions; Named Deities; Hierarchy of Dieties; Ecclesiastic Institutions;	Monotheistic Institutions;

TABLE 1. *Table courtesy of the author.*

The initiation rituals for adolescents included separation, liminality, and reintegration. The boys went into special isolated camps, were educated about sacred matters from the elders, and had circumcision and subincision sexual operations performed on their body. The meanings of ritual objects presented to them were disclosed in secret ceremonies and there was a ritual cleaning of all traces of the sacred world, followed by a ceremonial return to ordinary life.

The theme of death and rebirth is often found among psychedelic plant drug users in traditional society. The youth returned to social life as a new person, with a new name, responsibilities and knowledge of the supernatural world. The psychedelic states heightened the learning of sacred knowledge and created a bonding among members of the cohort group such that individual psychic needs were subsumed to the needs of the group.

A key feature of these rituals was the cultural utilization of the hypersuggestibility, induced by the use of the plant hallucinogen. In the altered state of consciousness managed by adult tutors, adolescent behavior patterns were framed, and religious and secular values were internalized. The plants were one way that their society had available to them to inculcate conformity in young people to patterns, mostly sacred, which would contribute to group survival and harmony. Like many other tribal societies, the Australian aborigines incorporated plant psychedelics into group initiation rites. The drugs were accepted to be of sacred origin and were treated with awe and reverence. The plants were in limited supply and protected from abuse and profanation by deviants by remaining under adult control and administration.

THE FANG OF EQUATORIAL AFRICA. With the domestication of plants and animals about ten to twelve thousand years ago, changes occurred in the spiritual use of psychedelics. In northwestern equatorial Africa, the Fang peoples are village farmers of peanuts, corn, manioc, and plantains. They use the psychedelic plant *tabernanthe iboga* as part of their adaptation to cultural upheaval caused by European domination of their society. The plant has been incorporated into a religious revitalization movement known as the Bwiti, dated to the end of the nineteenth century. Large doses bring on fantastic visions, and smaller doses of *iboga* produce marginal hallucinatory effects, possibly a dreamy or floating sensation. The plant is used as an adjunct to initiation into the Bwiti cult and the superior Bwiti divinity is revealed to the initiate. The term *Bwiti* also refers to the ancestors and the supernatural realm of the dead.

Men who drink the *iboga* participate in a cult which blends elements of traditional Fang beliefs with Christian symbols. The Bwiti cult operates to honor particular ancestors, to conduct rites linked to fertility and to help cement feelings of cohesion and solidarity. The cult presents its members with a cosmogony of religious thoughts centered on the idea of fecundity and death as well as a defense against the dangers of sorcery. In this society with a strong linkage to ancestor worship, the plant hallucinogen is believed to enable the individual to accompany a phantasm to a special place—a city of the dead, full of cadavers and skeletons. Such visionary experience is valued by the Fang, whose traditional cultural focus has been to worship ancestors who are believed to play an important role in directing the lives of those still on earth. The Fang take *iboga* because of a need to see, know, and communicate with greater powers hidden in and known through the plant. Aside from heavy ingestion in the initial session, the religious use of the substance achieves a state of one-heartedness after night-long rituals during which the Fang consume moderate amounts of *iboga* to achieve ecstatic states. Ancestors are called upon for advice.

The initiated candidate is told of the great honor he receives by knowing about the things of the earth. Most festivities are linked to initiation rites. The religion has reference not only to a person's immediate clan ancestors, but to all the ancestors of the community. The Bwiti cult gives different kinship groups—alienated by fragmentation and atomization as the result of culture contact and domination by European society—sanctified character by using the *iboga* plant since it permits direct communication with the valued ghosts of the past.

In Western culture *iboga* has a medical use, although it is still experimental. In Western clinics with drug-addicted participants, huge doses give rise to lucid visions. Clinical reports on essential loss of opiate craving and the absence of withdrawal suggests a mechanism for the substitution, which is a placebo effect enhanced by suggestibility. From a religious/metaphysical perspective, the psychedelic experience causes a sense of death and subsequent rebirth, allowing the user to return to a new beginning. The physical effects of vomiting also provide a sense of cleanliness and renewal to the individual.

THE ANCIENT MAYA. Analysis of the art of the ancient Maya led to a discovery of the presence of a psychedelic plant, *Nymphaea ampla,* the water lily. Historically it appears that high-ranking segments of society usurped the use of psychedelics. With culture change in the form of conquest and colonialism, esoteric knowledge did not diffuse to the folk level again from where it surely originated. Many of the beliefs connected to such drug use were coded in the religious art of these societies. With social change, these belief systems, as among the ancient Maya, disappeared and could only be retrieved in contemporary times through an analysis of their art.

The common water lily, *Nymphaea ampla* and *N. caerulea,* were depicted in Maya art, suggesting that esoteric drug rituals were practiced. The presence of aporphine, an opiate similar in structure to apomorphine, was found in the water lily plant. The psychoactive properties of the water lily seemed to merge well with the high value placed by the Maya on ecstatic states as a vehicle to communicate with supernatural forces. Among the ancient Maya, there are various mythic associations connected with the water lily, which include death symbols and mythic beings as the source of the plant, including a long-nosed serpent or rain god. Other associations include the jaguar, and anatomical sources associated with the water lily are the top of the head, ears, eyes, mouth, hands, and neck regions, suggestive of the psychoactive effects on sensory modalities. Shape shifting or morphing—the transformation of human beings (in this case, religious practitioners) into animals is also found associated with this plant drug. This may symbolize the power source of the individual who calls upon animal familiars to do his bidding.

UNIAO DO VEGETAL. Adherents of the contemporary Brazilian *ayahuasca* church Uniao do Vegetal (UDV), who number more than 8,000, utilize the plant hallucinogen containing *Banisteriopsis caapi* and *Psychotria viridis* in religious rituals blended with elements of Christianity. The *ayahuasca* drink is made by boiling the stems of the *Banisteriopsis caapi* vine together with the leaves of *Psychotria viridis.* Widely used in the Amazon, *ayahuasca* was taken up by mestizos living near tribal peoples who adapted it for their own needs. There are a number of different movements that have incorporated *ayahuasca* into their doctrines and activities with several *ayahuasca* churches such as the UDVand Santo Daime that combine traditional African and Christian elements in their pattern of use. There are sixty *nuclos,* or centers of church activity, among the UDV. Since 1987 the Brazilian government has allowed the use of *ayahuasca* within the context of a religious ritual.

The *ayahuasca* drink is imbibed in a ritual setting, with church elders and advisors present. Members ingest about 100 milliliters of a tea made from the two plants twice a month. New members and participants are carefully screened. There is congregational and community involvement in social activities and prayer. *Hoasca,* as *ayahuasca* is termed in Portuguese, is a consecrated sacrament of the church, a material expression of divinity, much as for Roman Catholics the consecrated wafer is the Holy Eucharist embodying the Holy Spirit.

The UDV is a Christian religion with syncretic elements that arose from the interaction between Christianity and indigenous beliefs and practices regarding *ayahuasca* in South America. The UDV was founded and is headquartered in Brazil and is recognized officially by the government of Brazil. The tea is considered sacred and indispensable, and the UDV carefully controls the cultivation and harvesting of the plants contained in it. The quantity ingested at any particular ceremony is effectively limited by the ceremonial components. Studies have shown redemptive features of the psychedelic experience among the UDV. This consists of elimination of neurotic and antisocial behavior by members of the religious community as well as their abstinence from alcohol and drugs of abuse.

PEYOTISM: THE NATIVE AMERICAN CHURCH AND THE HUICHOL INDIANS. The modern use of peyote (*Lophophora williamsii*), a psychedelic cactus, originated in central Mexico and spread to southern Texas by the 1870s. Archaeological finds from Texas show remnants of peyote that date back 7,000 years. The Spanish, when first invading Mexico, labeled peyote the "diabolic root" and tried to stamp out its use.

More than a century ago the use of peyote eventually led to the foundation of the Native American Church (NAC), which is the largest pan-Native America religion in North America. Peyote has been used ritually since its inception. It is estimated that a quarter of a million Native Americans have been involved with this church, with the strongest representation in the southwest and midwestern United States. The peyote religion combines elements of the vision quest, a belief in general supernatural power and the Christian Trinity. Its doctrine teaches that God is a great spirit and Jesus is a guardian spirit. Morality and ethics are also derived from the Judeo-Christian tradition. Some scholars see the church as a response to cultural/community dislocation and its attendant problems. The plant was legalized in 1994 in the United States for members of certain American Indian religions after a long legal battle.

Generally the Native American Church focuses on holistic health and harmony with nature. There is a redemptive feature in response to severity of alcoholism among Native Americans whereby the church prohibits alcohol use and promotes the sacrament of peyote ingestion as a powerful treatment for that disorder.

Within the NAC, peyotism provides a spiritual approach to facilitating a sense of identity, groundedness, connection and belonging. The plant is a spineless cactus with a rounded top surface that appears above the soil. It is cut off and dried and becomes a peyote button which is ingested during church rituals. Church members believe that their medicine functions sacramentally by allowing them to see the truth about their lives and connects them to the peyote spirit, who will give them guidance and direction. Peyote meetings are organized for those in need of healing from alcohol and drug addiction and who are personally motivated to change. During the peyote rituals, individual introspection, group interaction and healing are promoted. There is a powerful leader or guide, and benefit is derived from the actual group marathon session in the form of strengthening social networks. Healing benefits are derived from the psychotropic substance that is used as a nonspecific facilitator.

During peyote rituals, one commonly hears testimonial accounts of various psychological, physical, and emotional maladies being lifted by the healing powers of the ceremony. Members report altered states of consciousness that provide a fast-paced educational and redemptive experience. Youth learn community values, beliefs, and their religious traditions. Often paraphrased is a peyotist comment about how the white man goes into his church and prays to God, whereas the Indian goes into his church and talks directly to God. The shamanic value of direct and personal communication with deity is enhanced by the psychedelic properties of the peyote plant. A complex hierarchy of church positions in the NAC allows Native Americans to have a parallel status structure for sincere and hard-working church members in the community.

Huichol Indians who live in western Mexico have been using peyote to communicate with their gods for thousands of years. As practitioners of shamanic religion, they utilize psychedelics or other mind-altering techniques to communicate with their gods, their underworld and in order to understand the meaning of life. These agricultural peoples utilize peyote as the focus of their religious and emotional life. There is an annual cycle of communal and extended family ceremonial and religious activity. Schaefer (1998) wrote that peyote for the Huichol

> serves as an enculturating force which echoes religious tenets and re-occurring themes that are transcended to visions, the spoken word, through myths and songs, actions and rituals and ceremonies and beliefs that permeate all levels of individual and collective consciousness. In their sacred peyote rituals, the ordinary boundaries between the past and present vanish and the gods, ancestors and events of Huichol mythic history become a physical and emotional reality (p. 274).

The use of peyote appears to be pivotal in the continuing profound pride that the Huichol maintain in their culture despite Mexican governmental attempts at cultural annihilation. A Huichol artform, known as yarn painting, depicts complex arrays of dancing deer, snakes and other figures as native artists try to evoke the peyote visions. Each year, small bands of Huichol travel 300 miles to a desolate spot deep in the Chihuahuan desert to hunt for the squat, round peyote cactus.

Psychedelics, Spirituality, and the 1960s. No discussion of psychedelics and religion would be complete without reference to widespread runaway use of such substances in European and American society, generally focused on the decade of the 1960s and thereafter. Flower children, cultic groups in the 1960s, utilized synthetic drugs. The founders of the cult were white Americans—including physicians and psychologists, and many had scientific as well as religious interest in the phenomena.

Drugs such as LSD, psilocybin, mescaline, and marijuana were widely used, and Timothy Leary was generally acknowledged to be the spokesperson for "tuning in, turning on and dropping out," a more aggressive segment of the psychedelic cult. He had an extraordinary capacity to stir up paranoid tendencies of the then titled "establishment." Leary and colleagues gave LSD and related substances to prison inmates, neurotics, psychotics and alcoholics as well as to those who were dying of cancer. The focus was as much a search for meaning as for religious activity, although it was frequently reported that Leary would read segments from the Tibetan *Book of the Dead* to those tripping on psychedelics, in order to create a mystical setting for drug ingestion.

Leary and others were certain that psychedelics produced true religious experience, and the Marsh Chapel experiment, conducted by Walter Pahnke, is often referenced. In this experiment, twenty theology students virgin to the use of psychedelic drugs were given 30 milligrams of psilocibin on Good Friday in a religious setting in Marsh Chapel, Boston. The effects were compared to a matched group who were given a placebo containing nicotinic acid, which produced a tingling, but not a psychedelic effect. Nine of the subjects who received psilocybin had what they called "a religious experience," whereas only one in the control group did.

Leary, a professor at Harvard, was forced to resign after giving psychedelics to his students. His studies indicated that when the setting for the drug ingestion was supportive but not spiritual, between 40 and 75 percent of his psychedelic subjects reported intense, life-changing religious experiences. The percentages were much higher when the set and setting were supportive and spiritual, with revelatory and mystico-religious experiences.

PSYCHEDELICS, DRUG TOURISM, AND THE GLOBAL VILLAGE. Since the 1980s there has been an upsurge in the postmodern phenomenon of drug tourism. Individuals who are on a never-ending search for self-actualization and growth demand to find drug experiences abroad. Post-World War II has been described as the empty self period, where individuals are soothed and filled up by consuming food, consumer products and experiences. Resultant psychological states such as low self-esteem, values confusion, and drug abuse (the compulsion to fill the emptiness with chemically induced emotional experiences) is expressed. Today, knowledgeable men and women travel to distant exotic places such as the Peruvian or Brazilian Amazon where they participate in drug rituals among so-called native shamans or witchdoctors.

Charlatan psychiatry is a term applied to a long tradition in Latin America of non-authentic folk healers with malicious and fraudulent intention who provide psychedelic plant drugs in ritual settings for personal gain. Unscrupulous practitioners exploit their victims and are conscious of the farce in which they are involved. In California and elsewhere today, there are zealots who devote their life to a new age of drug use, and they urgently proselytize others to immerse themselves in drugs, "to make more, to use more, to sell more." Many are irresponsible and unconscionable individuals. In Peruvian and Brazilian Amazonian cities and large towns, there are mestizo men who become instant traditional healers without undergoing any apprenticeship period, without having any teachers and without control. They provide American and European tourists mixtures of ten or more different psychedelic plants to help them become embedded in the universe and to provide them with mystical experiences. The psychedelic plants in question have never been used traditionally in the way that the self-styled healers use them and there are numerous psychological casualties.

Drug tourism is found on a smaller scale than international mass tourism. This phenomenon is shrouded in a special rhetoric, and travel literature includes terms such as "advanced shamanic training," which is coupled with descriptions of a specific healer who has explored inner space, or other terminology to cue the tourist as to the real meaning. The drug tourist perceives the natives as timeless and ahistoric. They do not recognize the vast worlds of change between the tribal native, the civilized Indian, and the lower-class laborer, the striving middle-class individual or managerial elites of the Amazon region's major industries. Nor do the tourist guides have any interest in filling in all the shades of gray for them. The drug tourist is desperate to find the vanishing primitive. They cannot or will not see the urban and civilizing influences in these Amazon cities, including 400 years of Catholic and Protestant proselytization. They miss out on the movies, radio, TV, schools, libraries, and other Western-type infrastructures found everywhere. The westerner is not involved in a native ritual of spiritual dimensions as he has been led to expect, but rather in a staged drama to turn him on and extract his cash.

There is an evil, exploitive aspect of this drug tourism that is impossible to ignore. These so-called native healers are common drug dealers, dressed for deception. They provide the exotic setting and prep the tourist to have an authentic personal experience. Theater is based on illusion and facade. The Amazon drug tourism does not dismantle the illusion nor destroy the sense of the exotic. But it can on occasion leave psychotic depression and confusion in its wake.

LSD AND SPIRITUALITY IN THE 1950S: JANIGER'S EXPERIMENT. In the tribal and industrialized societies that are examined in this essay where psychedelics are used, we see that access to supernatural power and the unitive experience were highly valued. Psychedelic plants were used to enhance perception and intuition. Recent published research on an early psychiatric study with more than 950 American subjects who were given LSD from 1954 to 1962 show some interesting insights occurring regarding psychedelics and religious experience. This was at a time when there was little prior knowledge about LSD. Oscar Janiger, a psychiatrist, made a real effort to avoid any religious prompts over the eight years of the study, but nonetheless, 24 percent, or some 228 men and women in Janiger's sample reported spontaneous spiritual/religious experiences. In the tribal societies under scrutiny and throughout studies of traditional societies of the world that utilize psychedelics, plant psychedelics provided little if any abuse potential. Most of the plants were of limited availability, were given in religious ritual settings in natural environments with all the senses engaged, had elders and religious leaders present to ensure a smooth interior voyage, and were laden with educational and didactic contact to reassure the individual.

Not discussed in this essay are the general findings on cultural patterning of the hallucinatory experience in tribal society, which gives us a fascinating glimpse into the extent to which the human psyche is subject to cultural conditioning. In such traditional societies of the world, drug-induced stereotypic visions are eagerly sought after to indicate that contact with the realm of the sacred has occurred. Psychedelics have been used in a magical-religious context, with ceremony, to celebrate or contact the realm of the supernatural and to divine the future. Psychedelic plants have been used as sacraments and have had redemptive effects on participants. In human history, the power of mind-altering plants was acknowledged to belong to special realms constrained with taboos and rituals. Anyone who entered those portals had to be properly prepared for the journey.

BIBLIOGRAPHY

Balandier, G. *Ambiguous Africa: Cultures in Collision.* Paris, 1957.

Callaway, J. C. "Phytochemistry and Neuopharmacology of Ayahuasca." In *Ayahuasca: Psychedelics, Consciousness, and the Spirits of Nature,* edited by Ralph Metzner. New York, 2002.

Cushman, Philip. "Why the Self is Empty: Toward a Historically Situated Psychology." *American Psychology* 45, no. 5 (1990): 599–611.

D'Aquili, Eugene, and Andrew Newberg. *The Mystical Mind: Probing the Biology of Religious Experience.* Minneapolis, 2001.

De Rios, Marlene Dobkin. "The Influence of Psychotropic Flora and Fauna on Maya Religion." *Current Anthroplogy* 154, no. 2 (1974): 147–165.

De Rios, Marlene Dobkin. *Psychedelics: Cross-Cultural Perspective.* Albuquerque, 1984.

De Rios, Marlene Dobkin. "Twenty-Five Years of Psychedelic Studies in Cross-Cultural Perspective." *Anthropology of Consciousness* 4, no. 1 (1993): 1–8.

De Rios, Marlene Dobkin. "On Human Pharmacology of Hoasca: A Medical Anthropology Perspective." *Journal of Nervous and Mental Disease* 184, no. 2 (1996): 95–98.

De Rios, Marlene Dobkin, and Charles S. Grob. "Psychedelics, Suggestibility, and Adolescence." In *Yearbook for Ethnomedicine and the Study of Consciousness,* edited by Christian Ratsch and John R. Baker. Berlin, 1994.

De Rios, Marlene Dobkin, Charles S. Grob, and John Baker. "Psychedelics and Redemption." *Journal of Psychoactive Drugs* 34, no. 3 (2002): 239–248.

De Rios, Marlene Dobkin, and Oscar Janiger. *LSD, Spirituality, and the Creative Process.* Rochester, Vt., 2003.

De Rios, Marlene Dobkin, and David E. Smith. "Drug Use and Abuse in Cross-Cultural Perspective." *Human Organization* 36, no. 1 (1977): 14–21.

Doblin, Rick. "Pahnke's Good Friday Experiment: A Long-Term Followup and Methodological Critique." *Journal of Transpersonal Psychology* 23, no. 1 (1991).

Garbarino, M. S., and R. F. Sasso. *Native American Heritage.* 3d ed. Prospect Heights, Ill., 1994.

Grob, Charles S., et al. "Human Pharmacology of Hoasca." *Journal of Nervous and Mental Diseases* 184, no. 2 (1996): 85–94.

Grob, Charles S., and Marlene Dobkin de Rios. "Adolescent Drug Use in Cross-Cultural Perspective." *Journal of Drug Issues* 22, no. 1 (1992): 121–138.

Luciano, D. "Observations on Treatment with Ibogaine." *American Journal on Addictions* 7, no. 1 (1998): 89–90.

Mash, Deborah. "Ibogaine: Development as an Anti-Addictive Drug." *MAPS* 6, no. 1 (1995): 29.

Mash, Deborah. "Phase I Clinical Trial of Ibogaine in Human Patient Volunteers." *MAPS* 6, no. 3 (1996): 3.

Schaeffer, Stacey, and Peter Furst, eds. *People of the Peyote: Huichol Indian History, Religion, and Survival.* Albuquerque, N.M., 1998.

Seguin, Carlos Alberto. *Psiquiatria folklórica.* Lima, Peru, 1979.

Siskind, Janet. *To Hunt in the Morning.* New York, 1977.

Tart, Charles. *Transpersonal Psychologies.* New York, 1975.

Wallace, Anthony F. C. *Religion: An Anthropological View.* New York, 1966.

Wasson, R. Gordon, et al. *The Road to Eleusis: Unveiling the Secret of the Mysteries.* Los Angeles, 1998.

MARLENE DOBKIN DE RIOS (2005)

PSYCHOLOGY

This entry consists of the following articles:

PSYCHOLOGY OF RELIGION
PSYCHOTHERAPY AND RELIGION
SCHIZOANALYSIS AND RELIGION

PSYCHOLOGY: PSYCHOLOGY OF RELIGION

In its most basic sense, the field of the psychology of religion is composed of a variety of studies that have utilized a broad spectrum of theoretical frameworks to interpret the psychological meaning and patterns of collective and individual religious contents, ideation, and practice. Certainly, precursors to the introspective and empirical investigations found in the psychology of religion can be discerned in the mystical, existential, philosophical, theological, and poetic texts of religious traditions both East and West. However, by the late nineteenth century, numerous factors (e.g., the rise of science, the cultural ascendancy of religious pluralism, a liberal theological atmosphere, the stress on authentic personal experience, the growing disillusionment with dogmatic forms of religious expression) gave rise to widespread attempts at more systematic, social-scientific approaches to religious phenomena. This survey will proceed by detailing the central figures, theoretical models, issues, and themes that have animated the field of the psychology of religion. The history of the field can be divided into three periods: (1) 1880 to World War II; (2) the postwar period through the 1960s; and (3) 1970 to 2005.

1880 TO WORLD WAR II. The era from 1880 to World War II was the formative period of the psychology of religion, with pathbreaking contributions from a number of researchers. Although the most influential scholarship came from Europe and North America, it is important to stress that the contributors exerted mutual influence and that collaboration was international in scope. This is well illustrated by the famous photograph of, among others, Sigmund Freud (1856–1939), G. Stanley Hall (1844–1924), William James (1842–1910), and Carl Jung (1875–1961) at the legendary conference at Clark University (Worcester, Massachusetts) in 1909. Several journals were inaugurated by these scholars, including *Archiv für Religionspsychologie, Zeitschrift für Religionspsychologie*, and the *American Journal of Religious Psychology and Education.* Topics investigated varied from prayer, conversion, mysticism, religious emotion, the paranormal, revival movements, and religious growth to the wide assortment of issues linked to the comparative study of religion and the psychosocial dynamic between religion, culture, and society.

EUROPEAN CONTRIBUTIONS. In Europe, seminal contributions came from several countries. In Germany, one cannot ignore the figure of Wilhelm Wundt (1832–1920), known as the founder of experimental psychology, who established the first laboratory for the study of psychological phenomena. Wundt bequeathed to later generations a psychophysical approach to human experience and consciousness that stressed the importance of analysis and the classification of data. Wundt eschewed collecting individual instances of religious faith in favor of a historical, ethnographical, and folk psychological approach to religion that highlighted its evolving cultural structure and expression. The analysis of individual religious experience was left to Wundt's successors. His student Oswald Külpe (1862–1915), the head of the Würzburg School of psychology, modified Wundt's advances to create an approach in experimental introspection that could be applied to religion. Külpe's student Karl Girgensohn (1875–1925), famous for his Dorpat School of religious psychology, introduced questionnaires and religious stimuli of various kinds into the laboratory setting, concluding that religious experience was a complex phenomenon composed of cognitive, emotional, and existential elements. As David Wulff notes in his *Psychology of Religion: Classic and Contemporary* (1997), members of the Dorpat School, in relying on the laboratory setting yet attending to descriptive detail, championed elements of the phenomenological approach to the psychology of religion (which was carried on most decisively in this era by William James and evident in the works of later humanistic and existential theorists), as well as the empirical approach (which was also apparent in the North American researchers and multiple theorists in subsequent periods of history in the field).

In France, a distinctly psychopathological approach to religion emerged, centering on the creative theoretical advances of Jean Martin Charcot (1825–1893) and his student Pierre Janet (1859–1947). Through their work, which eventuated in the articulation of pyschopathological processes based on the theory of the subconscious, the development of hypnosis, and the analysis of a number of case histories involving unusual religious states, this school laid claim to demonstrating the complicity of diseased mental states (notably hysteria), in individual religious faith and its expression. The most famous product of this school was the Viennese-based (and later, London-based) based founder of psychoanalysis, Sigmund Freud.

Freud was one of the three most influential psychologists of religion of this era (the other two being William James and Carl Jung). In abandoning hypnosis in favor of the free associative technique to gain insight into the psychological dynamics of his patients, Freud went well beyond Charcot and Janet in developing a radically new theory of the mind. This theory was essentially a conflict model which divided the psyche into three parts: the unconscious, or id (seen as the repository of repressed wishes and ruled by primary instinctual processes); the ego (seen as cognizant of the exigencies of external reality and ruled by the light of reason); and the superego (the internalized voice of conscience). In addition, Freud posited a psychosexual developmental line, the central dynamic of which was ruled by the existence of childhood sexual impulses and the Oedipus complex, and a theory of the instincts (the biologically based instinctual forces of Eros [life and sexual drives] and Thanatos [aggressive and death drives]) that impacted development and the relations between the id, ego, and superego. Freud applied his theory to cultural products, particularly religion, in works such as *Totem and Taboo* (1913) and *Future of an Illusion* (1927). Freud was convinced of the superiority of science and the fact of secularization, and he endeavored to create a social space for psychoanalysis as a secular cure of souls. To that end, Freud proclaimed religion to be a historical vestige, a collective universal obsessional neurosis whose various accoutrements were composed of projected, regressive, and defensive Oedipal and related unconscious elements. His analysis deeply influenced subsequent ego-psychological and object-relational approaches (about which more shall be said below). As an architect of modernity, he is still the foremost figure of a depth-psychological approach to religion that champions, as the philosopher Paul Ricoeur once said, the hermeneutics of suspicion.

Other proponents of a subconscious, subliminal, or unconscious dimension of the personality were not wholly antithetical towards religious phenomena. In France the Catholic thinkers Henri Delacroix (1873–1937) and Joseph Maréchal (1878–1944) utilized theories of subliminal, subconscious states to enrich theological understandings of mystical states, whereas F. W. H. Myers (1843–1901), operating out of Great Britain, exercised an enormous influence on North American researchers, especially William James, by writing about how conceptions of such states could help to explain paranormal phenomena. In particular, Switzerland proved to be a most hospitable home to a methodological approach sympathetic to religion. Theodore Flournoy (1854–1820), who held a position in experimental psychology at the University of Geneva, wrote several essays and books composed of analyses of case histories and autobiographical material. Flournoy advocated a nonpathological approach that bracketed the ontological reality of the divine and, in cautioning that religious experience is complex, promoted the integration of physiological, developmental, and comparative perspectives in coming to an understanding of exceptional religious states. A good friend of William James, Flournoy also influenced Georges Berguer (1873–1945), a professor of the psychology of religion who argued that the methodological framework of psychology was necessarily limited, thus creating a dialogical intellectual space for theological perspectives. Flournoy was also a force in the development of the Jean-Jacques Rousseau Institute, where Jean Piaget (1896–1980), a subsequent director of the institute known primarily for his theories of cognitive development, also wrote about religion. Piaget distinguished between an immature, socially determined form of faith that engendered negative emotions and a more humanistic faith championing autonomy and equality. However, without question, the most important figure associated with the Swiss tradition is Carl Jung.

Jung, who studied with Janet, was deeply influenced by Flournoy and James, and was heir apparent to Freud before their complete break, is known as the founder of analytical psychology. In contrast to Freud's tripartite structural theory of the psyche, reliance on the developmental determinism of childhood, and negative evaluation of religion, Jung's valorization of the transformative potential of religion was based on the related concepts of the collective unconscious and individuation. Beneath Freud's personal unconscious, thought Jung, lay a collective unconscious housing universal archetypes, conceived of as forms (without specific content) known only by their cultural and religious expressions and effects on the individual psyche. The task of psychological growth, which Jung termed *individuation*, was to acknowledge and therapeutically work through the contents of the personal and collective unconscious, gradually heightening the feeling of wholeness, harmony, and the totality of the self. Although Jung posited many archetypes, he thought those of the persona, shadow, anima/animus, the wise man, the child, the great mother, and the self were particularly evident in religious ideation. Jung's psychology of religion, while establishing a theoretical framework for analyzing the therapeutic and healing nature of religion (including Eastern religions, which Jung promoted with greater success than any other psychologist of his era), also tended to blur the line between a psychology "of" religion and a religious psychology. In positing a generic, religious dimension to the unconscious, Jung is in part responsible for establishing the unchurched, mystical form of self-actualization prevalent in the modern era.

North American Contributions. The originative contributions to the psychology of religion from North America stemmed primarily from two major figures, G. Stanley Hall and William James, and their students. These contributors as a group were sympathetic towards religion, many having been drawn initially to theological education, the ministry, and the value of a progressive social worldview. Hall, who founded the Clark School of the Psychology of Religion (at Clark University), was initially influenced by Wundt and set up a laboratory for the empirical investigation of religion. Particularly interested in conversion, religious growth, mysticism, and education, Hall and two of his best-known students, E. D. Starbuck (1866–1917) and James Leuba (1868–1946), were instrumental in developing questionnaires, interviews, and a statistical approach to the psychology of religion. Hall developed the view that religion was socially adaptive and, in books such as *Jesus, the Christ, in the Light of Psychology* (1917), that religious figures embodied higher forms of morality. Psychology, argued Hall, could help mankind to actualize those ethical ideals. Starbuck followed suit, publishing a landmark study, aptly titled *The Psychology of Religion* (1899), which centered on the relation between adolescence and conversion. However, Leuba, in works such as *The Psychology of Religious Mysticism* (1925), evinced a marked sympathy towards the methods of psychophysiology, remaining unconvinced of the ontological reality of the divine. Yet even Leuba, the most reductionistic of the group, also argued for the potential of religion to morally transform individuals and society. Leuba also studied with James, as did James Bisset Pratt (1875–1944), whose work on Buddhism and Hinduism, like that of Jung's, was instrumental in heightening awareness of the value of Eastern religious traditions. W. E. Hocking (1873–1966), James's successor at Harvard University, argued for a psychologically pragmatic, democratic, and socially activist form of mysticism. James also had a long correspondence with R. C. Bucke (1837–1902), the Canadian psychologist and author of the classic book *Cosmic Consciousness* (1901), who became an important figure for later humanistic and transpersonal psychologists. Bucke's major contribution proceeded as a result of an epiphany he later conceptualized as an instance of "cosmic consciousness." He was an early advocate of perennialism, arguing that cosmic consciousness lay at the heart of all religion, that mankind was evolving towards a utopian socialist and mystical society, and that all outward religious forms would disappear as mankind actualized its inherent ability to achieve cosmic consciousness.

Despite the fact that during this era it was Hall and his students who were perceived as the main instigators of the psychology of religion, it is James, author of the classic work *The Varieties of Religious Experience* (1902), who continues to exert influence on the field. Although James never developed a therapeutic system like Freud and Jung, he was the most prolific and philosophically astute of the American contributors. A product of the modern worldview, James proclaimed experience as more primary than religious dogma, theology, or church accoutrements. Adopting the descriptive, phenomenological method, he compiled the most diverse, substantial, and compelling anthology of personal religious experience of his day, offering typologies such as the sick soul, the healthy-minded, and the divided self, as well as parameters for understanding religious phenomena such as mysticism and conversion. James was a thoroughgoing pragmatist who posited a radical form of empiricism (which allowed for personal religious experience as a source for ascertaining the nature of reality), and he offered the possibility of a pluralistic universe (which threw into doubt the ascertainable existence of one, underlying absolute truth). In bracketing the divine, or "More," on the further side of the individual psyche, his interpretative evaluation of religious experiences aimed at providing *existential* judgements (classification schemes and an examination of the subconscious dynamic involved) and *spiritual* judgements (an assessment of their "fruits," or pragmatic value for one's life).

By 1930 there was a general decline of interest in colleges and culture at large in the psychology of religion. Benjamin Beit-Hallahmi (1974) has adduced several factors for this, including the rise of National Socialism, the threat of war, the Great Depression, the rise of behaviorism (which eschewed introspection and subjectivity) and theological neo-orthodoxy (a conservative theological movement which challenged the ability of psychology to apprehend religious truth), and the perception that the methods of psychology were less than competent, objective, and value-neutral. Nevertheless, one can discern the beginnings of theoretical models (depth-psychological, humanistic, phenomenological-existential, empirical) and dialogical enterprises (with humanistic, theological, and social-scientific methods) that would become the foundation upon which advances could be built.

The Postwar Period Through the 1960s. The aftermath of the Second World War brought new resources into the psychology of religion. Immigration brought European, Asian, and North American intellectuals representing a variety of religious traditions into greater dialogue. With respect to theory, there were substantial developments in psychoanalysis, analytical psychology, empirical studies, and humanistic-existential forms of therapy. Perhaps as important, the effect of psychology on many sectors of society was impressive enough that many culture theorists began to take note. The sociologist Philip Rieff (b. 1922), in his classic work *The Triumph of the Therapeutic* (1966), wrote that previously, all societies were "positive" in nature, by which he meant guided by a religious symbol system that facilitated repression, insured the allegiance of individuals to the communal whole, and offered religious forms of healing to ward off anomie. However, with the impact of psychology, particularly the depth-psychology of Freud and Jung, a new controlling symbolism displaced the reigning religious one. The key to the rise of the therapeutic culture (or "negative" communities) was the valorization of the individual over the communal whole and the creation of a cultural space for the working through of previously repressed unconscious contents. Given the enormous impact of this new science, philosophers, theologians, and comparativists were eager to dialogue with proponents of the psychology of religion, not simply on the grounds of the field's intellectual merits, but also due to their (correct) perception that psychology was becoming the preferred, even dominant cultural mode of introspection. This period saw both an extension and a creative rebirthing of the efforts of the prewar era. The major developments of the 1950s and 1960s were ego psychology; analytic psychology; humanistic, phenomenological, and existential psychology; empirical and behavioral studies; and pastoral psychology.

Ego psychology. Classic psychoanalysis as developed by Freud rendered the ego weak, beset by the more powerful forces of the id and superego. The next generation of psychoanalysts, headed by his daughter Anna Freud (1895–1982) and including Heinz Hartmann (1894–1970), Ernst Kris, David Rapaport (1911–1960), and Erik Erikson (1902–1994), formulated a much more positive understanding of the ego. They granted it independent energy, more sophisticated defenses, increased ability for adaptation and play, and a central role in an epigenetic, developmental process whose multiple stages of growth spanned the life cycle. These theoretical advances allowed for the resolution of infantile fixations and conflicts, eventuating in virtues such as trust, integrity, identity, generational care, and generativity. Erikson, the best known of this group, was instrumental in using such advances to reverse Freud's negative evaluation of religion. Utilizing the genre of psychobiography, Erikson analyzed religious figures such as Martin Luther (*Young Man Luther*, 1958) and Gandhi (*Gandhi's Truth*, 1969) to show how ego psychology could illuminate the healing, transformative power of religion. In the 1960s Erich Fromm (1900–1980), in his *Zen Buddhism and Psychoanalysis* (1960), and Herbert Fingarette (b. 1921), in his *The Self in Transformation* (1965), similarly used the insights of ego psychology to frame Buddhism as a healing enterprise commensurate with the best aims of psychoanalysis.

Analytic psychology. Jung's psychology was increasingly influential during the 1950s and 1960s, not simply due to the efforts of Jung, who wrote many of his most influential books on religion during this time (e.g., *Answer to Job* [1952]), but also due to subsequent interpreters such as Erich Neumann (1905–1960) and, later, James Hillman (b. 1926). During this period Jung's psychology was also made accessible to empirical, correlational testing through the creation of the Meyers-Briggs Type Indicator (MBTI), a personality test based on Jung's description of personality types. It is still a popular tool utilized to measure religious orientation. Jung's psychology also had considerable impact on the comparative study of religion. Mircea Eliade (1907–1986), one of the leading comparativists of his generation, used Jung's notion that the collective unconscious housed a generic religious dimension to facilitate his project of trying to recover the sacred (see *Myths, Dreams, and Mysteries*, 1960). Additionally, Joseph Campbell (1904–1987) in works such as *The Hero with a Thousand Faces* (1949), established a considerable oeuvre on myths which drew heavily on Jungian archetypal thought to demonstrate their universal significance and meaning.

Humanistic, phenomenological, and existential psychology. The extension of previous attempts at developing phenomenological, existential, and humanistic elements in the psychology of religion received impetus from a variety of figures, of which three should be singled out. Gordon Allport's (1897–1967) central contribution, found in his *The Individual and His Religion* (1950), was the distinction between mature, intrinsic forms of religious orientation and more immature forms of extrinsic religious orientation. In the former case, individuals treated religion as an end in itself. Allport listed the guiding characteristics of such an orientation as being differentiated, dynamic, directive, integral, heuristic, and comprehensive. In extrinsic forms of religious orientation, Allport thought that individuals treated religion as a means, often exhibiting egoistic, wish-fulfilling forms of behavior. Allport's typology led to an immensely influential empirical, correlational scale, the Religious Orientation Scale, which measured extrinsic and intrinsic forms of religious behavior. Victor Frankl (b. 1905), influenced by phenomenological philosophy, existentialism, and his own experiences in Nazi concentration camps, was the founder of the therapeutic system known as logotherapy (see *Man's Search* *for Meaning,* 1962). Deeply religious, eschewing the total determinism of childhood development, and stressing the uniqueness of every individual and the intimate relation of the self to a personal God, Frankl highlighted issues pertaining to individual freedom, responsibility, self-transcendence, conscience, and will to meaning. Abraham Maslow (1908–1970) spent his life articulating a psychology which, over and against classical psychoanalysis and behaviorism, detailed the development of higher forms of consciousness. Maslow distinguished between basic needs for physiological sustenance, safety, belonging, and self-esteem, and the higher need for self-actualization. The latter, a general designation for experiences of joy, completeness, and unity, reached their culmination in *peak-experiences,* Maslow's most famous term and one crucial to his understanding of religion. In his *Religions, Values, and Peak-Experiences* (1964) Maslow espoused a perennialism based on peak-experiences, distinguishing between "legalists" (nonpeakers and curators of a bureaucratic understanding of religion) and "mystics" (peakers who experientially grasped the essence of religion). Mystical states and peak-experiences, now understood as the psychological core uniting all religions, could be accessed through scientific, technical means. Maslow thus advocated a naturalistic, unchurched religion that was commensurate with the scientific, psychological enterprise.

Empirical and behavioral studies. B. F. Skinner, the central theorist of behaviorism, viewed religion in generally negative terms. Skinner thought religion was a determined form of social behavior whose continued existence can be attributed to "operant conditioning" (that is, because religious behavior is reinforced) and the need of religious authorities to maintain power and control. Although behaviorism, at least at the outset, was the most powerful new form of psychological theory during this period, it met with multiple competitors. As mentioned above, the theories of Allport and Jung impacted empirical studies through the development of the Religious Orientation Scale (Allport) and the MBTI (Jung). In addition, the meteoric rise of interest in Eastern religions gave creative impetus to laboratory science. Experimental studies of meditation measured the physiological effects of practices such as Zen and yoga on respiration, heart rate, skin resistance, and cerebral activity. Similarly, the interest in altered states of consciousness accessed through psychedelics (or *entheogens,* a word which means "containing God") such as lysergic acid diethylamide (LSD), peyote, and mescaline resulted in numerous studies measuring their effect on faith and religiousness. Insofar as these studies occurred during a volatile cultural atmosphere in the 1960s, it should be noted that many of these empirical studies were conducted and advanced by figures and psychologists associated with the human potential movement. As a group, the movement championed the values of receptivity, spontaneity, nowness, and the cultivation of an essentially unchurched, mystical-experiential form of religiousness.

Pastoral psychology. In the prewar period, pastoral psychology had been practiced by figures such as Oskar Pfister (1873–1956), the Swiss pastor, lay analyst, and confidant of Freud, and Anton Boisen (1876–1965), a minister who parlayed his own bout with schizophrenia into establishing a form of clinical pastoral psychology. However, it was not until the postwar period that pastoral psychology became a powerful social institution. As ably detailed by Peter Homans in his *The Dialogue between Theology and Psychology* (1968), its aim was to formulate a mature, psychologically sophisticated form of faith by investigating the relation between developmental determinants, existential issues (such as freedom, choice, and responsibility) and theological issues (such as faith, sin, morality, and redemption). Many of its proponents (e.g., Albert Outler, Seward Hiltner, David Roberts) engaged in dialogue with proponents of existential, humanistic, psychoanalytic, and analytical psychology. Several noted philosophers and theologians entered this debate, including Reinhold Niebuhr (1892–1971), who utilized psychological insights to nuance the Christian distinction between nature and spirit, and Paul Ricouer (b. 1913), who, in respecting the depth-psychological "hermeneutics of suspicion," argued for a more mature form of faith he called a second naiveté. Of the theologians, however, none was more important than Paul Tillich (1886–1965). As his "correlational method" made abundantly clear, psychology was American culture's mode of formulating the central existential questions about the nature of the human condition. Any theological system, then, could not dispense with active dialogue with psychology. In over two dozen essays, later published in *The Meaning of Health* (1984) and in major works such as *The Courage to Be* (1952), Tillich proceeded to integrate the insights of numerous therapeutic frameworks to show how pastoral psychology could help overcome the "heteronomous" God; reveal the universal, structural anxieties of guilt, death, and meaninglessness; and mediate the only God (who he called the God "above" the God of "theological theism") who could truly heal the plight of the modern person. In many ways Tillich was the central architect of pastoral psychology and, as is so evident in his essays, the religious intellectual most responsible for fermenting a bona fide dialogue between theologians and psychologists of all stripes.

1970 TO 2005. As may be evident from the foregoing, the developments of the 1950s and 1960s began a process of blurring the understanding of psychology as a value-neutral methodological tool independent of and objective with respect to its subject (in this case the contents, practices, and ideation of religious traditions). Although the value-neutral, objective stance of psychology vis-à-vis religion remains a desired end, ongoing developments in culture studies and the postmodern deconstruction of any perspective claiming to possess objective, absolute truth has further necessitated an analysis of the relativity, selectivity, and implicit scale of values harbored within psychological theories of all kinds. The net effect has been the opening of the tent of the psychology "of" religion to include "religious psychology" and studies whose orientation consists of a dialogical enterprise between psychology and various humanistic and social scientific perspectives (e.g., philosophy, theology, comparative/cultural studies). The introduction of new terms that reflect this inclusion (e.g., *religion and the human sciences; religion, person, and culture; psychology "and" religion*) have become, for many, accepted parts of the nomenclature when designating the field. Although it is fair to say that debates over designation and inclusion still rage (some would like to narrowly circumscribe what constitutes the psychology "of" religion, omitting religious psychology and dialogical enterprises), it is also fair, in detailing the contours of this period, to mention not only developments in the psychology "of" religion but also those developments signaling the move towards a wider, more inclusive understanding of the field. Although the framework and typology utilized to conceptualize the latter can be debated, the use of alternate categorization schemes cannot safely neglect object-relations theory, transpersonal psychology, empirical and behavioral studies, practical theology, the psychology–comparativist dialogue, and psychology of religion and culture studies.

Object-relations theory. Although Freud's own emphasis was on the Oedipus complex, he also offered a preliminary framework for considering the pre-Oedipal, narcissistic (used as a descriptive, not pejorative term) phase of development. Several subsequent theorists, including Melanie Klein, D. W. Winnicott, Ronald Fairbairn, and Heinz Kohut (founder of "Self psychology"), added clinical and theoretical contributions that have increased our knowledge of the developmental line of narcissism. In contrast to Freud's emphasis on instinct and conflict, these theorists emphasized relational issues of separation and merger, the processes of idealization and identification/internalization, and the development of a cohesive self, self-esteem, and creativity. Although studies of this genre proliferate, particularly successful is Ana-Maria Rizzuto's *The Birth of the Living God* (1979), which, in utilizing Winnicott's notion of a "transitional object," elaborated a clinically based understanding of belief in a "God Representation." This is created by individuals from a variety of representational objects (the pre-Oedipal mother, the Oedipal father, siblings, relatives, and significant others), is capable of evolving with changes in the life cycle, and functions to insure adaptation to life's exigencies. With respect to Eastern religions, Sudhir Kakar, in books such as *The Inner World* (1981) and *The Analyst and the Mystic* (1991), illuminates how Hindu forms of religious ideation and practice are especially conducive to a pre-oedipal theoretical analysis. On the whole, object-relations theory allows for a marked sympathy towards religion that is absent in Freud. Several originative theorists in this tradition come close to Jung in their metapsychological conceptualization of a religious dimension to the personality (e.g., Kohut's "cosmic narcissism," Wilfred Bion's "O," Jacques Lacan's "The Real"). In this respect it is noteworthy, as is evident in Peter Homans's *Jung in Context* (1979), which sees Jung as anticipating Kohut's Self psychology, that theories concerning the developmental line of narcissism have become for many the long-awaited bridge linking the often contentious battle between Jungians and Freudians.

Transpersonal psychology. Late in his life, Abraham Maslow took his formulations on humanistic psychology and peak-experience one step further by initiating the formation of a full-blown religious psychology. Called transpersonal psychology, its proponents frame it as part of a tradition in the psychology of religion which includes the researches of James, Jung, and R. M. Bucke. Influenced by Eastern religions, its essence is devoted to the study of all higher forms of psychological and religious consciousness, including peak experiences, unitive forms of mystical consciousness, and feelings of bliss, awe, and wonder. Starting in the late 1960s, advocates of transpersonal psychology created professional, academic outlets for their work, including programs for transpersonal psychotherapy and a journal, the *Journal of Transpersonal Psychology.* A number of scholars during this period, including Charles Tart, Ken Wilber, Stanislav Grof, and Michael Washburn, have utilized a variety of psychological approaches to advocate the scientific study of mystical and paranormal phenomena. Tart has written extensively on paranormal phenomena, and Grof is known for his work on entheogens and their ability to illumine structural elements of religious consciousness, including Jungian archetypes. Wilber has articulated a version of the perennial philosophy, drawing from maps of consciousness found in Western psychotherapies and the world's mystical traditions. He argues for a "spectrum of consciousness" ranging from the lower egoistic forms to the dissolution of self characteristic of various forms of Buddhism and the Hindu Vedanta tradition. Each level can be addressed, both metapsychologically and therapeutically, by various kinds of Western psychologies. Washburn, also drawing on a variety of psychotherapeutic frameworks, argues that spiritual development has a spiral path, and his work has concentrated on elucidating characteristic forms of experience which unfold during the course of this spiraling upwards.

Empirical and behavioral studies. Arrays of studies in the empirical and behavioral category have appeared since 1970. Utilizing Allport's distinction between intrinsic and extrinsic religious orientations, several theorists have added developments to empirical analysis, including the following: the Quest Scale (a more nuanced view of intrinsic forms of religious orientation); the Religious Viewpoints Scale (which distinguishes between committed [personal religious style] and consensual [socially generated forms] of religiousness); general attribution theory (which links religion with matters of self-esteem, meaning, and control); attachment theory (which examines the strong relational bonds religion fosters); and coping theory (which seeks to analyze religion as a means of coping with the existential and social exigencies of life). Social role theory has proved useful in analyzing how motivation, behavior, and learning proceed through identification with religious role models. Sociobiology, relying on the researches of physiology, ethology, and evolutionary biology, looks at the biological basis for all social behaviors, concentrating in particular on the relationship between religion, society, and altruistic forms of relating. The continued interest in Eastern religious practices has spawned a vast assortment of laboratory analysis. Particularly significant are those researchers who have used the findings of work in bihemispheric studies to show how the myths, symbols, and practices of religious traditions signify the working of the right (devoted to spatial orientation, art, and holistic mentation) and left (involved with analytic reasoning, language, and math) hemispheres of the brain. Additionally, with the advent of brain imaging, and drawing on the researches of evolutionary psychology and biology, many in cognitive neuroscience have endeavored to locate with greater precision which areas of the brain are responsible for specific forms of religious experience and behavior.

Practical theology. The dialogue between psychology and theology and the development of pastoral psychology has continued in practical theology. Indeed, programs in pastoral education and counseling have thrived since the 1970s in many seminaries and universities. Building on the efforts of theologians and religious intellectuals of the previous period, practical theology continues to involve proponents of Christianity and Judaism, evincing a marked theoretical sophistication over previous attempts at dialogue. A noted example is James Fowler, who, in his *Stages of Faith* (1981), offers a stage approach to the maturation of faith based on the ego psychology of Erikson, the cognitive developmental framework of Piaget, and the developmental theory of morality found in the works of Lawrence Kohlberg. Don Browning, whose substantial oeuvre in this area includes *Religious Thought and the Modern Psychologies* (1987), has utilized a revised version of Tillich's method of correlation to tease out the religious and ethical horizons of various psychological theories. Having established that psychology is not simply a neutral science but, with respect to its effects on culture and individuals, has implications for religion and ethical theory, Browning brings the results of such an analysis into dialogue with Protestant cultural values and attendant notions of virtue and selfhood.

The psychology-comparativist dialogue. The continued influx and popularity of Eastern religions, scholarly advances in the exegesis of non-Western religions, and the rise of academics familiar with both psychological and indigenous religious psychophysiological techniques has given rise to a "psychology-comparativist dialogue" (see Jonte-Pace and Parsons, 2001). Germinal elements of this dialogue can be found in previous eras, although to speak of a true dialogue is problematic. The well-intended researches of Jung, James, and Pratt did much to elevate the status of Eastern religions in the eyes of psychologists in the early 1900s. However, they were marked by orientalism and marred by faulty translations, reductionism, and the lack of engagement with scholars within Eastern traditions. Studies of the 1950s and 1960s, intent on creating dialogue and tolerance, were too often inclined to level differences, succumbing to a naive perennialism. After 1970 there was more accurate exegesis of alternate understandings of self, world, and other found in Eastern religions. Although there is some overlap with humanistic, empirical, and transpersonal approaches, the psychology-comparativist dialogue is marked by a synthesis of interdisciplinary methods (i.e., psychological, cultural, philosophical, comparative) in arriving at an appreciation of real differences and attempts at respectful dialogue. Examples can be found in Luis Gomez's careful evaluation of a Jungian approach to the texts of Indian Buddhism in *Curators of the Buddha* (1995) and Jeffrey Kripal's *Kali's Child* (1995), which performs a classic Freudian interpretation by seeing symptoms of repressed homoeroticism in the visions and acts of Ramakrishna (1836–1886), but then, in exemplifying the interdisciplinary approach of this dialogue, legitimates Ramakrishna's religious visions by situating psychoanalytic discourse in a wider Tantric worldview. Jack Engler, another theorist in this category, draws on his expertise as a psychologist and meditation teacher in arguing that Western psychotherapy and Buddhist *abhidharma* each have different, legitimate aims if viewed in their proper cultural contexts (see *Transformations of Consciousness* [1986]). According to Engler, psychotherapy aims at helping to grow a cohesive, healthy sense of self; Buddhist meditation, presupposing a healthy self, aims at "losing" it. Jeffrey Rubin, in his *Psychotherapy and Buddhism* (1996), includes a careful consideration of culture in his attempt to steer a middle path between "Orientocentrism" (the privileging of Asian thought and practice) and Eurocentrism. In the period under consideration, this dialogue is also marked by an increasing number of interdisciplinary studies critiquing Western psychological attempts at creating dialogue with Eastern religions, notably J. J. Clarke's analysis of Jung and comparative studies (*Jung and Eastern Thought*, 1994) and William B. Parsons's evaluation of psychoanalytic interpretations of comparative mysticism (*The Enigma of the Oceanic Feeling*, 1999).

Psychology of religion and culture studies. Although many of the above-cited studies deal in some way with culture studies, there are several types of studies that can be directly subsumed under the category psychology of religion and culture studies. Among the most important is psychology, religion, and gender studies. As Diane Jonte-Pace (in Jonte-Pace and Parsons, 2001) has carefully pointed out, the feminist critique of psychological studies of religion is an ongoing enterprise that has incorporated three kinds of scholarship: (1) feminist critics have sought to uncover the androcentric biases of theory; (2) feminist analysts have exposed the gender imbalance and prejudice constructed by culture; and (3) feminist inclusivists have proposed creative new ways of reframing women's experiences.

Another important subcategory is psychology, religion, and the social sciences. There is a growing trend to include the psychology of religion as part of a more inclusive social scientific approach to religion. From this perspective psychology is a cultural science that cannot afford to dispense with the findings of sociology and anthropology in analyzing religious phenomena. In addition, such collaboration helps to actualize a self-reflective movement through which those that utilize psychological theory may become more aware of the ethnocentric assumptions and values embodied in psychological metapsychology. Cases in point are the work of sociologist Michael Carroll, whose *The Cult of the Virgin Mary* (1986) weds social theory with psychoanalysis; the work of anthropologist Gananath Obeysekere, who, in works such as *Medusa's Hair* (1981) and *The Work of Culture* (1990), uses culturally sensitive psychological, anthropological, and philosophical theory to interpret Hindu ideation and practice; and the work of social scientist Peter Homans, who, in *The Ability to Mourn* (1989), has fashioned an integration of social-scientific disciplines, focusing on the psychodynamics of individual biography in the context of social change in an attempt to understand the emergence of creative theorizing about religion in figures such as Jung, Freud, and Max Weber.

Another group of studies that can be categorized as psychology of religion and culture studies deals with psychology "as" religion. The term *psychology as religion* is understandably anathema to many scholars in the psychology of religion, given that it undermines the seemingly objective character of psychology as a method for the analysis "of" religion. Nevertheless, since the time of Philip Rieff's *The Triumph of the Therapeutic* (1966), culture theorists have increasingly written about the ways in which psychology not only analyzes religion but also, culturally speaking, has acted "like a religion." As is evident in the case of Jung and the transpersonal psychologists, psychological theory is often utilized for purposes of organizing and expressing the existential search for wholeness, numinous experiences, and individuation. Ostensibly a method for the analysis of religion, psychology has its own scale of values, and it not only seeks to interpret religious phenomena but also offers itself, at times quite intentionally, as a modern, nontraditional way to map one's religiosity. With respect to popular culture, this is illustrated by the success of books that rely on Jungian theory and its derivatives in promoting a version of unchurched, psychological spirituality (e.g., M. Scott Peck's *The Road Less Traveled* [1978]).

SEE ALSO Freud, Sigmund; Hall, G. Stanley; James, William; Jung, C. G.

BIBLIOGRAPHY

The below bibliography is divided into two sections: (1) general, which lists textbooks, annotated bibliographies, and other general surveys of the field; and (2) specific, which catalogs studies treating individual authors and central debates in the field.

General

Argyle, Michael. *Psychology and Religion: An Introduction.* New York, 2000.

Beit-Hallahmi, Benjamin. "Psychology and Religion: 1880–1930: The Rise and Fall of a Psychological Movement." *Journal of the History of the Behavioral Sciences* 10 (1974): 84–90.

Beit-Hallahmi, Benjamin. *Psychoanalytic Studies of Religion: A Critical Assessment and Annotated Bibliography.* Westport, Conn., 1996.

Capps, Donald, Lewis Rambo, and Paul Ransohoff. *Psychology of Religion: A Guide to Information Sources.* Detroit, Mich., 1976.

Crapps, Robert W. *An Introduction to the Psychology of Religion.* Macon, Ga., 1986.

Dyer, Donald R. *Cross-Currents of Jungian Thought: An Annotated Bibliography.* Boston, 1991.

Fuller, Andrew R. *Psychology and Religion: Eight Points of View.* Lanham, Md., 1994.

Hood, Ralph W., Jr.; Bernard Spilka; Bruce Hunsberger; and Richard L. Gorsuch, eds., *The Psychology of Religion: An Empirical Approach.* New York, 1996.

Jonte-Pace, Diane, and William B. Parsons, eds. *Religion and Psychology: Mapping the Terrain.* New York, 2001. A selection of essays summarizing recent dialogical trends, including the intersection of psychology, religion, and gender studies; the psychology-comparativist dialogue; the dialogue between theology and psychology; and psychology "as" religion.

Murphy, Michael, and Steven Donovan. *The Physical and Psychological Effects of Meditation: A Review of Contemporary Research with a Comprehensive Bibliography, 1931–1996.* 2d ed. Sausalito, Calif., 1997.

Spilka, Bernard, and Daniel M. McIntosh, eds. *The Psychology of Religion: Theoretical Approaches.* Boulder, Colo., 1997.

Wulff, David. *The Psychology of Religion: Classic and Contemporary.* 2d ed. New York, 1997. The most complete and definitive survey of the field.

Specific

Allport, Gordon. *The Individual and His Religion.* New York, 1950.

Barnard, G. William. *Exploring Unseen Worlds.* Albany, N.Y., 1997. A constructive analysis of the views of William James.

Barnard, G. William. "Diving into the Depths: Reflections on Psychology as a Religion." In *Religion and Psychology: Mapping the Terrain,* edited by Diane Jonte-Pace and William B. Parsons, pp. 297–318. New York, 2001.

Browning, Don. *Religious Thought and the Modern Psychologies.* Philadelphia, 1987.

Bucke, R.C. *Cosmic Consciousness.* Philadelphia, 1901.

Campbell, Joseph. *The Hero with a Thousand Faces.* Princeton, N.J., 1949.

Carroll, Michael. *The Cult of the Virgin Mary.* Princeton, N.J., 1986.

Clarke, J. J. *Jung and Eastern Thought.* London, 1994.

Eliade, Mircea. *Myths, Dreams, and Mysteries.* New York, 1960.

Engler, Jack. *Transformations of Consciousness.* Boston, 1986.

Erikson, Erik. *Young Man Luther.* New York, 1958.

Erikson, Erik. *Gandhi's Truth: On the Origins of Militant Nonviolence.* New York, 1969.

Ferrer, Jorge. *Revisioning Transpersonal Theory.* Albany, N.Y., 2002.

Fingarrette, Herbert. *The Self in Transformation.* New York, 1965.

Fowler, James. *Stages of Faith.* New York, 1981.

Frankl, Victor. *Man's Search for Meaning.* New York, 1962.

Freud, Sigmund. *Totem and Taboo.* New York, 1913.

Freud, Sigmund. *Future of an Illusion.* New York, 1927.

Fromm, Erich. *Zen Buddhism and Psychoanalysis.* New York, 1960.

Gomez, Luis. *Curators of the Buddha.* Chicago, 1995.

Hall, G. Stanley. *Jesus, the Christ, in the Light of Psychology.* Garden City, N.Y., 1917.

Heisig, James W. *Imago Dei: A Study of C. G. Jung's Psychology of Religion.* Lewisburg, Pa., 1979.

Homans, Peter. *The Dialogue between Theology and Psychology.* Chicago, 1968.

Homans, Peter. *Jung in Context.* Chicago, 1979.

Homans, Peter. *The Ability to Mourn.* Chicago, 1989.

James, William. *The Varieties of Religious Experience.* New York, 1902.

Jones, James. *Contemporary Psychoanalysis and Religion.* New Haven, Conn., 1991.

Jonte-Pace, Diane. "Analysts, Critics, and Inclusivists: Feminist Voices in the Psychology of Religion." In *Religion and Psychology: Mapping the Terrain,* edited by Diane Jonte-Pace and William B. Parsons, pp. 129–146. New York, 2001.

Jonte-Pace, Diane. *Speaking the Unspeakable: Religion, Misogyny, and the Uncanny Mother in Freud's Cultural Texts.* Berkeley, Calif., 2002.

Jung, Carl. *Answer to Job.* London, 1952.

Kakar, Sudhir. *The Inner World.* Delhi and New York, 1981.

Kakar, Sudhir. *The Analyst and the Mystic.* Chicago, 1991.

Kripal, Jeffrey J. *Kali's Child: The Mystical and the Erotic in the Life and Teachings of Ramakrishna.* Chicago, 1995.

Kripal, Jeffrey J., and T. G. Vaidyanathan. *Vishnu on Freud's Desk: A Reader in Psychoanalysis and Hinduism.* Delhi, 1999.

Leuba, James. *The Psychology of Religious Mysticism.* London and New York, 1925.

Maslow, Abraham. *Religions, Values, and Peak-Experiences.* New York, 1964.

McDargh, John. *Psychoanalytic Object-Relations Theory and the Study of Religion: On Faith and the Imaging of God.* Lanham, Md., 1983.

Molino, Anthony, ed. *The Couch and the Tree: Dialogues in Psychoanalysis and Buddhism.* New York, 1998.

Newberg, Andrew, Eugene D'Aquili, and Vince Rause. *Why God Won't Go Away: Brain Science and the Biology of Belief.* New York, 2001.

Obeysekere, Gananath. *Medusa's Hair.* Chicago, 1981.

Obeysekere, Gananath. *The Work of Culture: Symbolic Transformation in Psychoanalysis and Anthropology.* Chicago, 1990.

Ornstein, Robert. *The Psychology of Consciousness.* New York, 1986. A classic work utilizing bihemispheric studies to analyze religious phenomena.

Parsons, William B. *The Enigma of the Oceanic Feeling: Revisioning the Psychoanalytic Theory of Mysticism.* New York, 1999.

Peck, M. Scott. *The Road Less Traveled.* New York, 1978.

Rieff, Philip. *The Triumph of the Therapeutic: Uses of Faith After Freud.* New York, 1966.

Rieff, Philip. *Freud: The Mind of the Moralist.* Chicago, 1979. A substantial and still useful study of Freud's psychology of religion.

Rizzuto, Ana-Maria. *The Birth of the Living God.* Chicago, 1979.

Rubin, Jeffrey. *Psychotherapy and Buddhism.* New York, 1996.

Starbuck, E. D. *The Psychology of Religion.* London, 1899.

Stein, Murray. *Jung's Treatment of Christianity.* Wilmette, Ill., 1986.

Tillich, Paul. *The Courage to Be.* New Haven, Conn., 1952.

Tillich, Paul. *The Meaning of Health.* Chicago, 1984.

Vitz, Paul C. *Psychology as Religion: The Cult of Self-Worship.* 2d ed. Grand Rapids, Mich., 1991.

Zock, Heddy. *A Psychology of Ultimate Concern: Erik H. Erikson's Contribution to the Psychology of Religion.* Amsterdam, 1990.

WILLIAM B. PARSONS (2005)

PSYCHOLOGY: PSYCHOTHERAPY AND RELIGION

Historically, the relationship between psychotherapy and religion has been strained, because until recently it has been dominated by psychoanalytic theory and has turned on that field's conceptualization of *illusion.* Influenced as it is by the psychobiological origins of psychoanalytic theory, psychotherapy traditionally has considered religion an illusion in a strictly pejorative sense. Only relatively recently have many psychotherapists come to understand that illusion is a psychological need and that, as such, it can be healthily enjoyed in a socially beneficial way or distorted into pathology, just as any need can be. Religion has defensively reacted to psychoanalysis's largely negative consideration of it by campaigning against psychoanalysis, ignoring it altogether, or prematurely incorporating its theory. Understandably, religion has bridled at being considered merely illusory, for this consideration inherently denies the reality of religious experience. Often the psychoanalytic consideration of religious material has used a methodology based in nineteenth-century physical science that, because of its own assumptions, makes study of religious experience impossible. The scientific origins (some would say aspirations) of psychoanalysis have enabled the field to lay claim to a position of objectivity, which must then see religion experience as illusory. Fortunately there have been positive developments in the relationship between psychotherapy and religion: Psychotherapy has begun to appreciate the psychological and cultural role of religion, and religion has begun to utilize psychotherapy more appropriately and less defensively. This article examines the main features of this developing relationship.

PSYCHOANALYTIC THEORY. Any consideration of the relationship between psychotherapy and religion must start, of course, with the work of Sigmund Freud (1856–1939). And there the difficulties also begin.

Freud and illusion. It is a testament to Freud's greatness that readers are frustrated with him for his shortcomings, which are clearly evident in his consideration of religion. (His shortcomings in his attempts to understand women and female experience, another glaring area of difficulty, are beyond the purview of this article.) Regardless of his greatness, the limitations of his era's scientific methodology—especially its psychobiology—and his own personal prejudice against and ambivalence toward religion combined to make it impossible for him to study religion objectively (i.e., in a way which would grant credence to others' subjectivity). Freud was able to see clearly the religious pathology in individual cases of neurosis and the social hypocrisy that probably has always been a feature of organized religion, but it is a deep irony that the man who cleared the way for the recognition of the developmental interrelation of pathology and health was not able to apply his own discovery to religious experience.

In numerous works, but nowhere as clearly as in *The Future of an Illusion* (1927), Freud considers religion as illusion. He contends that religion originated in early humanity's (and continues to originate in the child's) primordial fears and need for help. The idea of God is the psyche's projection onto the cosmos of infantile, unconscious wishes for omnipotence and protection, an effort to control the cosmos's impersonal harshness by personalizing it as a father-god. God is therefore only a psychic phenomenon, the product of wishful thinking—in short, an illusion. For Freud, then, illusion is a pejorative concept, an adaptation that, if possible, should be overcome in favor of facing reality without illusion. Although Freud does distinguish between delusion and illusion (the former definitely a false belief and the latter a belief that, whether true or false, is arrived at independently of rational means), it is nonetheless the case that by the strictures of the nineteenth-century scientific paradigm that Freud employed, religion is false because it is not real.

Psychoanalysts and other psychotherapists whose practice has been influenced by Freud, then, have little use for religion, seeing it as a defense the maladapted ego has formulated against the harsh realities of the world. In all likelihood, given a patient with a strong enough ego, such a therapist would work to encourage the patient to see that this defense is not needed. There would be some latitude here, because psychoanalytic theory has adherents at all stages of its development. There are Freudian psychoanalysts and also psychoanalytic institutes that represent the full range of Freudian thought from psychobiology to pre-ego psychology. Typically, however, the faculties of these institutes come from backgrounds in psychiatry or clinical psychology (and, more recently, social work) and therefore are little influenced by religious perspectives.

Transitional figures. Few psychoanalysts after Freud were as concerned as he was with religion. Freud's pronouncements on religion receded from controversy and became the status quo in psychoanalysis until theoretical developments necessitated their being questioned. Psychoanalytic theory developed into two broad, interrelated categories, one continuing Freud's psychobiological interests and focusing on mechanistic descriptions of psychodynamics and the other pursuing the more holistic study of the experiential psychic life of the person. In the first group, Anna Freud (1885–1982) and others contributed to the shift in psychoanalysis (a shift that had actually already been begun by Freud himself) toward the study of the ego and its defense mechanisms. In this way, the older view of the adaptation to reality at all costs began to be modified by this school, which came to be known as ego psychology. In the second group, Melanie Klein (1882–1960) and others began to study the earliest development of the person in terms of what have come to be called object relations theory. In psychoanalytic theory, an object is the psychological representation of a person in the most elementary terms—as a good object, one which is nurturing, or as a bad object, one which is persecutory. (Klein thus laid the groundwork for D. W. Winnicott's study of transitional phenomena, as well as for self psychology and the study of narcissism.) Both theoretical groups unwittingly undermined Freud's attitude toward religion: The first came to appreciate less stringent adaptation to reality than had been advocated by earlier analysis, and the second prepared the way for examining the methods—including illusion itself—that the psyche necessarily uses to come to grips with reality.

Three other psychoanalytic theorists who should be mentioned in a discussion of psychotherapy and religion are Eric Fromm (1900–1980), Victor Frankl (1905–1997), and Erik H. Erikson (1903–1987). The first two are included not so much because they contributed in a fundamental way to the development of psychoanalytic theory, nor even because they advanced the psychoanalytic understanding of illusion, but because they took religion seriously on its own terms and thus began to break away from Freud's reductionistic methodology in studying religion. Fromm, as a representative of the first group of psychoanalytic theorists previously mentioned, saw religion's value from a broad cultural perspective, whereas Frankl, as a representative of the second group, appreciated religion's psychological function in assisting the individual's search for meaning. The work of Erikson must also be considered in the psychoanalytic examination of religion. Erikson, popularly known for his study of the "identity crisis," pioneered the discipline of psychohistory. With *Young Man Luther* (1958) and *Gandhi's Truth* (1969), Erikson studied what he called *homo religiosus,* that is, the person whose nature and historical circumstance demand a religious existence—a kind of life that, Erikson insisted, can be psychologically healthy. Erikson treats the religious quests of both Luther and Gandhi with dignity, humaneness, and compassion. Even two decades before, it would have been unheard of for an analyst of Erikson's stature to psychoanalytically examine a religious figure without reducing him to a case study in psychopathology.

Winnicott and transitional phenomena. As the first pediatrician to be trained as a psychoanalyst, the Englishman D. W. Winnicott (1896–1971) was in a unique position to study the psychological development of infants and children, as well as the relationship between parents (particularly mothers) and their children. Winnicott's primary theoretical interest was the psychological emergence of the infant into the social world. In Winnicott's view, the bridging of these two worlds is accomplished through the presence of *good enough mothering* and the child's use of transitional objects. For Winnicott, a good-enough mother is concerned about her child and sensitive to his or her needs, but she does not err either by psychologically impinging on the child or by traumatizing him or her with inconsistent care. She sees her child as progressively separate from herself; psychologically as well as physically, she weans her child carefully. In weaning, she often allows the child transitional objects: physical objects such as teddy bears and blankets that, through their association with the mother, help to ensure the infant's own psychological continuity. As such, they ward off insanity, which Winnicott saw as psychological discontinuity.

Winnicott's central theoretical breakthrough is his study of how transitional objects are used by the child as a bridge from the child's inner reality to the outer reality of the adult world. By studying these phenomena, he became the first psychoanalyst to study illusion systematically and, thus also, to study the psychoanalytic correlate of religion. In his 1951 paper "Transitional Objects and Transitional Phenomena," Winnicott placed the antecedent of religious development in the period of transitional phenomena and, in this way, illustrated the object-related nature of religious experience. (He did not, however, trace the development of the representation of God.) For Winnicott, transitional phenomena are located in the psychological space he calls *intermediate space* or *potential space.* In successful psychological cultural development, this space becomes the location of all cultural experience, including religion, which he also ties to good enough mothering: "Here where there is trust and reliability is a potential space, one that can become an infinite area of separation, which the baby, child, adolescent, adult may creatively fill with playing, which in time becomes the enjoyment of the cultural heritage" (Winnicott, 1971, p. 108).

What was pejorative illusion for Freud becomes for Winnicott positive potential space or the location of cultural experience. Winnicott redeems the idea of illusion in psychoanalytic theory and thereby redeems the psychoanalytic study of religion. Whereas Winnicott fully recognizes pathological illusion, he contends that illusion per se is by no means pathological. For Winnicott, although illusion is not real, it is not untrue. The psychologically healthy person is one who can use the transitional phenomenon of illusion in a healthy way. He writes, "We are poor indeed if we are only sane" (1958, p. 150).

As excellent example of the application of object relations theory to religion can be found in Ana-Maria Rizzuto's *The Birth of the Living God: A Psychoanalytic Study* (1979). Rizzuto develops Winnicott's idea of transitional objects and applies it to religion in a systematic way by focusing on the development within the individual psyche of what she calls the *God-image.* (In this way, she avoids the argument about the reality of religious experience.) Rizzuto argues that the God-image is a necessary and inevitable part of the human psyche (whether it is used for belief or not), and she traces its origins from the infant's earliest object-relations. The God-image is a specific object, she states, because it is formed not through experience or reality-testing, but instead is created out of imaginary materials. Further, she argues that even though the God-image may be subject to repression, it can never be fully repressed. Instead, it is evoked at crucial times of life, such as the transitions between major stages of development. Rizzuto's contribution is especially important in two ways. First, departing from Freud and aligning herself with Winnicott's positive appreciation of illusion, she comes to the conclusion that religious belief is not a sign of immaturity, let alone pathology. Rather, she asserts it is simply a part of the psyche's development. Second, by tracing the personal development of the God-image, she points up the differences between the official God of religious doctrine and the living God of personal experience. She implies that for religion to continue to be a living force the personal, living God must be recognized and incorporated into organized religion.

The profound influence of Winnicott's work has also led psychoanalysts from outside objects relations theory to employ his theory in the integration of psychotherapy and religion. Ann Belford Ulanov, a Jungian psychoanalyst and a theologian, applies Winnicott's idea of potential space to what she sees as the space between the human and the divine. In *Finding Space: Winnicott, God, and Psychic Reality* (2001), she suggests that Winnicott's focus on the experience of being real can help counter the sense many have of contemporary religion as passionless.

In general, psychoanalysts and psychotherapists influenced by the work of Winnicott—and their number is likely to increase as the profound importance of his work continues to be recognized—appreciate the importance of transitional objects of all kinds, including religion and religious beliefs. The aim of such a therapist would be to provide a *good enough* therapeutic environment (through the therapeutic relationship) and not simply to interpret unconscious conflicts, so that clients' natural ability to develop transitional objects emerges and they can become their own resource for bridging the psychological and social worlds. In part, this bridging can result from playing, an activity Winnicott devoted considerable theoretical effort to understanding and an activity (such as the arts and religious ritual and experience) that is in the intermediate area between inner and outer realities. The correlation of play and religious practice may well be an area explored in future applications to religion of psychoanalytic thought as influenced by Winnicott.

Self psychology and relational psychoanalysis. As they have in the past, those who seek to integrate psychotherapy and religion look to new developments in psychoanalytic theory, not only to justify religion against the historical onslaught fueled in part by psychoanalysis itself but also to deepen understanding of these facets of human experience. Self psychology, a school of psychoanalysis developed in the 1970s by Heinz Kohut (1913–1981), and relational psychoanalysis, a second school developed in the 1980s primarily by Stephen Mitchell (1946–2001), are late twentieth-century developments in psychoanalytic theory used in this way.

Like Winnicott, Kohut was not directly concerned with religion. He worked with patients suffering from narcissistic personality or behavior disorders, conditions classical psychoanalytic theory considered unable to be analyzed because such patients were so self-preoccupied that they could not sustain meaningful relationships with others, including analysts. Kohut was able to analyze the narcissistically arrested because he saw that parental misattunement (and not only overindulgence) created narcissistic disturbances in children. He reasoned that if these patients were responded to empathically (i.e., from within the perspective of their own developmental needs), their development would proceed. In contrast to traditional psychoanalytic theory, Kohut held that narcissism has an independent line of development, so that the extreme self-love of primitive narcissism is not transformed by maturation into object-love but develops instead into mature forms of narcissism (e.g., personally or professionally advocating for one's self). In the course of his writing, Kohut shifted his focus away from narcissism itself and came to recognize that these patients suffered from what amounted to disorders of the self (thus, self psychology in contrast to ego psychology).

In contrast to Kohut's developmental arrest model, relational psychoanalysis argues that "the pursuit and maintenance of human relatedness is the basic maturational thrust in human experience," as Mitchell writes in *Relational Concepts in Psychoanalysis, An Integration* (1988, p. 289). Relational psychoanalysis, then, emphasizes the social over the individual. Although it is a very influential perspective in psychoanalysis, it is not a unified school of thought that represents a single point of view. Rather, it is inclusive of the many psychoanalysts who have become disenchanted particularly with classical psychoanalysis. Still, there are some points on which these analysts agree. For example, Mitchell portrays the analytic process as the analyst's struggle to disentangle from the patient's preset relational configurations. Further, in one tie to the classical psychoanalysis of Freud as well as Klein's object relations theory, relational psychoanalysis sees aggression as inborn and thus part of every relationship (including the analyst–patient relationship).

Although psychoanalysts of both self psychology and relational psychoanalysis have occasionally written on religion and pastoral counselors have occasionally utilized both psychoanalytic schools, no single voice has yet emerged from either discipline uniquely employing the insights these theories might provide in the understanding of psychotherapy and religion. Even mainstream psychoanalysis, then, has moved from considering illusion in a pejorative to a positive light. Many other disciplines, including those considered in this article, start from the experiential basis of illusion.

ANALYTICAL PSYCHOLOGY (JUNG). In a consideration of the relationship between psychotherapy and religion from the perspective of the concept of illusion, a unique position is held by analytical psychology (popularly called Jungian psychology or theory, after its founder, Carl Jung, 1875–1961). Jung and the Jungians have been outside the mainstream of psychoanalytic theory since the early decades of the twentieth century—a divorce that has impoverished both mainstream psychoanalysis and the Jungians themselves. The isolation of the Jungians has slowed the humanization of classical psychoanalytic theory, narrowing its field of study by excluding the consideration of many common human phenomena, and it has isolated the Jungians to the extent that, with a few exceptions, their vocabulary and model of the psyche has little relation to the rest of psychoanalytic theory. Moreover, the separation of the Jungians from classical psychoanalysis has had the effect of further divorcing the disciplines that make use of these two schools of psychoanalytic theory. Freud has been used primarily by the social sciences, whereas Jung has been employed by the arts and humanities, especially theology and religious studies.

Theology's kinship with Jungian theory can be explained by Jung's refutation of the classical psychoanalytic correlation of religion and illusion. The Jungian position on illusion is represented by Jung's concept of the *psychological fact:* Jung states that all psychic products, including visions, dreams, and hallucinations, are facts that should be considered as having the same basis in reality as other facts, including physical facts. There is, therefore, almost no such thing as illusion in Jungian psychological theory. It is almost an illusionless psychology. Jung could be reductionistic, but his reductionism was unlike Freud's reduction of religion. Jung was able to see religion more clearly on its own terms as a human activity that, although it could often be contaminated by social hypocrisy or personal pathology, could nonetheless be based on a reality of experience irreducible by psychological method to other unconscious motives. Here Jung makes an important methodological point: It is not the business of psychology to prove or disprove the existence of God. He held that psychology can discuss the psychic effects of the God-image and its mythic antecedents, but it cannot discuss the existence of God apart from the human psyche. The insistence on the reality and importance of religious experience was a position Jung held to the end of his life.

The religious was deeply important to Jung. In part, this was the result of his own personal history. His father was a clergyman, as were a number of his uncles. But it was also a consequence of his experience as a psychoanalyst. In fact, in "Psychotherapy or the Clergy" he went so far as to state, "Among all my patients in the second half of life—that is to say, over thirty-five—there has not been one whose problem in the last resort was not that of finding a religious outlook on life." He went on to add, "This of course has nothing whatever to do with a particular creed or membership of a church" (Jung, 1967, vol. 11, p. 334). Jung's experience as a psychoanalyst informed and was informed by his work as an analytic theorist. It was his theory that the psyche is comprised of archetypes in a collective unconscious. That is, Jung held there was an unconscious aside from the personal unconscious of the individual's unremembered or repressed past, and this was the collective unconscious whose contents are archetypes (i.e., typical images and patterns of human behavior, but not predestined behavior itself, that endlessly recur and are found in the psyche precisely because it is human). The most important and central archetype is the self (similar to, but not the same as, the self in Kohut's self psychology). Jung thought the psychological purpose of the second half of life was for the personal ego to come to terms with the self, the apersonal center of the collective unconscious. Jung has often been criticized by less religiously inclined psychoanalysts for projecting religious meaning onto the self and thus, his critics claim, for advocating a religious psychology. He believed he was simply an empirical scientist.

Developments within Jungian theory have expanded the dialogue between psychotherapy and religion outside traditional boundaries. One somewhat formally organized schism of Jungian theory is called archetypal psychology. Led by James Hillman, it has an almost exclusive concentration on the archetypes of the collective unconscious. Polytheism is studied by this group. A second movement is marked by the rise of interest in the goddess among some Jungians. They argue that modern consciousness, including more specifically modern religion, has a patriarchal bias. A number of Jungian analysts and writers have focused on studies on the historical goddess religions and sometimes have urged a return to religious focus on the goddess in the lives of modern individuals. Two phenomena of popular culture reflect these ideas, although neither is strictly about the goddess. In 1992, Jungian analyst Clarrisa Pinkola Estes published *Women Who Run with the Wolves* in which she argued that women's wholeness depends on reengaging their repressed instinctual nature, and in 2003 Dan Brown wrote *The Da Vinci Code*, which suggested that the sacred feminine is on the rise.

The psychoanalyst or psychotherapist who has been influenced by Jung and by developments in Jungian theory is necessarily respectful of a client's religious issues. From the beginning, in contrast to other psychoanalytic institutes, Jungian institutes have accepted candidates with theological degrees. The reality of religious experience is therefore appreciated in a way that is unusual among psychoanalytic institutes. Jungians are also trained to differentiate psychologically healthy from psychologically unhealthy religion. Yet an often-heard criticism of Jungian psychology applies here: Usually a client is not encouraged to reintegrate their religious experience back into already established religious groups. Individuality is prized in the Jungian system in a way that can impoverish the individual, as it unwittingly demeans group experiences.

SPIRITUALITY IN PSYCHOTHERAPY. A consideration of psychotherapy and religion must include the remarkable growth of a number of new movements that can be gathered under the rubric of spirituality. A number of social movements and developments in science have combined to influence the development of spirituality. In the United States, the counterculture movement in the 1960s, which arose in part in protest of the Vietnam War, exposed great numbers to Eastern cultural practices for the first time, especially to Indian gurus who promoted a variety of spiritual practices. Transcendental meditation was adopted from these sources and became increasingly legitimate as scientific studies showed its effectiveness in promoting psychological and physical health. In academic psychology, humanistic psychology as the foundation for treatment gained influence. Especially important were Carl Rogers's (1902–1987) client-centered therapy, which featured the therapist's "unconditional positive regard" of the client, and Abraham Maslow's (1908–1970) theory of hierarchy of needs, which begins with the physical needs of the body and culminates in self-actualization. Humanistic psychology arose to counter psychoanalysis, particularly the classical (Freudian) psychoanalytic theory of the previous decades, and laid the groundwork for incorporating other, seemingly nonrational needs into psychotherapy. Even modern physics, especially relativity theory and quantum mechanics, can be thought to contribute to the development of spirituality, as they describe physical reality in profoundly counterintuitive ways.

Several common themes underlie these disparate developments. Both the new physics and the mystical thought of centuries hold that everything is interconnected and that order follows from chaos. Older ways of thought are seen as linear, and these newer ways are held to be nonlinear. Critics of older, established religions see them as dualistic in that typically the self is separate from a deity. Traditional Christian concepts such as original sin, a concept that emphasizes the separation of the individual from the holy, are sharply criticized. Those who embrace these newer ways of thinking hold that any religion that produces separatism is antispiritual; the concepts of joining and union are considered spiritual to them. In religion, for these people, there has been a shift away from monotheism toward polytheism and especially toward nontheism.

Many have observed there is a basic conflict in organized religion. To maintain itself, an organized religion needs to continue to promote its own doctrines, and this is often in conflict with individual religious experiences. Thus it follows that the mystic tradition in many religions is marginalized. Yet individual experience is also at the heart of religion (as contrasted to religious organization). This discrepancy has reached the point that many have come to feel that organized religions are stifling and rigid. However, this perception is not without paradox. Interestingly, at least in the United States, established religions such as Roman Catholicism and mainline Protestantism, which judge individual religious experience with external standards, are losing members, yet newer religious organizations, especially fundamentalism, which also emphasize external judgment, are thriving.

Some of those who are disenchanted with organized religion have begun to practice or develop spiritual practices on their own; others have turned to nontraditional sources, including psychotherapists who include spirituality in their practices. These practitioners span a wide spectrum of theoretical backgrounds and include a wide variety of techniques in their psychotherapeutic practices, including meditation, yoga, and chanting—none of which would have been considered appropriate in psychotherapy (not to say psychoanalysis) even fifteen years ago. Although spirituality in psychotherapy is not widespread, there is reason to believe that it will continue to expand its foothold and perhaps even transform the discipline.

RELIGIOUS COUNSELING. In the relationship between psychotherapy and religion, religious counseling, in contrast to psychoanalytic theory, takes as its foundation the legitimacy of religious experience. Organized religious counseling has been influenced by three factors that have interacted with each other over time: seminary education, clinical pastoral education, and pastoral counseling itself as a discipline.

Seminary education. Two interrelated factors have influenced the development of religious counseling in seminary education: the need for seminarians to be taught counseling and the development of the discipline of pastoral counseling. The first factor is important because, according to polls, more people in the United States will consult clergy before other professionals for help with personal problems. Yet an already-crowded seminary curriculum does not typically allow for in-depth training in counseling (let alone psychotherapy), and when it does, the counseling tends to be based not on psychological insight but on biblical precepts, which are culturally bound and can be punitive. As religious conservatism continues to grow and to become institutionalized, psychology and psychoanalysis are likely to become even less influential in pastoral counseling. Despite these possible developments, two classics in the field remain valuable: Paul W. Pruyser's *The Minister as Diagnostician* (1976) and Wayne E. Oates's *When Religion Gets Sick* (1970).

Very broadly, the character of a seminary education is formed by the denominational affiliation of the seminary, by the intellectual climate of its geographic locale, and in part by whether it is associated with a university. In the northeastern United States, psychology programs in seminaries traditionally reflect the psychoanalytic and history of religions approaches of the area. In the Midwest, scholars have been working toward a methodology of pastoral care. In the West, the influence of humanistic psychology and the psychologies arising from the counterculture of the late 1960s and early 1970s influenced the writing of those at the consortium of seminaries near San Francisco.

Clinical pastoral education (CPE). Although first organized in 1925, CPE—a formalized system to clinically train seminarians and clergy to work with persons in hospitals, mental institutions, and prisons—had a number of antecedents. These movements had in common the urge to study spirituality scientifically, as well as a discontent with the theological education of the time, which was perceived as too concerned with theological doctrine and not concerned enough with the reality of the emotional life of the person. (This was the time of the first impact of psychoanalysis in the United States.)

The development of CPE is usually attributed to Anton T. Boisen (1876–1965), a Congregational minister. Boisen had suffered a breakdown with psychotic features in the early 1920s and was consequently institutionalized. He graphically depicted his efforts to find meaning in his experience in *Out of the Depths* (1960), a book that still makes interesting reading. Slowly he and others were able to establish an ongoing, organized ministry with its own training program. A powerful speaker who used his own experiences, Boisen was able as a chaplain to engage in therapeutic relationships with the most disturbed patients at the Worcester (Massachusetts) State Hospital, the same hospital in which he had been institutionalized. The amusing and chaotic experiences of the seminarians who comprised the first group of CPE trainees are recorded by Doris Webster Havice in *Roadmap for Rebel* (1980). The growing influence of CPE, as well as closer cooperation between CPE and various denominations, led to the formation in 1967 of the Association for Clinical Pastoral Education from several smaller organizations.

A psychotherapeutic practitioner influenced by CPE essentially functions as a pastoral counselor, balancing a clinical perspective on psychodynamics with his or her own religious belief and, typically, with the client's religious belief as well. It is possible that CPE will need to change its focus, as there are now fewer mental institutions and hospital stays have been reduced by insurance policies and advances in medical technology.

Pastoral counseling. As a response the development of CPE in the mid-1920s, in the 1930s seminaries began to lay the groundwork for the continuing integration of religion and psychology. Following World War II, due to what would now be recognized as the trauma of the war, attendance at religious services reached record levels. Psychotherapy also burgeoned during World War II as it had in World War I (in fact, almost every major figure in American and English psychoanalysis was directly involved in the war effort), largely in an effort to treat traumatized soldiers so that they could be returned to battle in the best condition. One response by seminaries to the cultural needs of the time was to create chairs and departments of pastoral care (although the titles varied considerably). Four theologians emerged as leaders of the theory and practice of pastoral care: Seward Hiltner, author of one of the first books in the field, *Pastoral Counseling*, who was originally at the University of Chicago and later at Princeton; Paul Johnson at Boston University; Carroll Wise at Garret Seminary at Northwestern University; and Wayne Oates, a Southern Baptist physician affiliated with the Louisville, Kentucky, School of Medicine.

Graduate programs integrating theology and psychology began to be developed at this time, also (again, the titles of these programs varied considerably). These programs began in Protestant seminaries; only later did Catholic and Jewish seminaries develop them. Professional organizations began to develop, as well, the most prominent being the American Association of Pastoral Counseling (AAPC), which was founded in 1963. Aside from the cultural forces outlined, AAPC was established in part by Protestant ministers who in their ministries had become burned out and who had gone into their own therapy to deal with their professional exhaustion and sometimes estrangement from the church. Consequently, there was a theoretical focus on the individual, reflected in the influence of leading contemporary psychological humanistic theory, such as Rogers' client-centered therapy or Fritz Perls's gestalt therapy.

As so often happens in therapeutic movements and psychoanalysis, the theory goes faddishly in one direction; in this case, pastoral psychology started to disregard its own theological resources, forgetting nineteen hundred years of rich history. The focus was so much on individual psychology that those outside the field started to make legitimate critiques of the loss of a theological perspective, and in response psychiatrist Karl Menninger wrote *Whatever Became of Sin?* (1973). These critics encouraged pastors to recognize the universe of concepts from their own field at their disposal that could be helpful to those in their care. A contemporary theoretician who has made a similar convincing argument is Deborah Van Duesen Hunsinger in *Theology and Pastoral Counseling, a New Interdisciplinary Approach* (1995), in which she argues that theology and depth psychology are two different frames of reference and demonstrates how these two ways of thinking relate to each other in an inter-disciplinary approach that maintains the integrity of both disciplines.

More recently, AAPC has made attempts to be more truly interfaith and to move away from focusing solely on the individual, trying to overcome its basically liberal, anti-evangelical Protestantism. In AAPC, an appreciation has developed of the social dimension of faith, from the familial, community, and societal problems (such as domestic abuse, power problems in congregations, and clergy sexually acting-out). Another aspect of including a social dimension is an evaluation of what social systems and faith communities have to offer in terms of individual health. In this regard, it is important to note that considerable empirical research has demonstrated that spiritual belief has a markedly positive effect on physical health and psychological well-being. For example, in *Spirituality and Patient Care* (2002), Harold Koenig, an associate professor of psychiatry and medicine at Duke University in North Carolina, demonstrates that people who go to church are better off by almost every measure.

Social Work. In considering the relationship between psychology and religion, social work is especially important. In the United States, social workers provided more psychotherapy than members of any other profession. The historical development of social work is intimately tied both to psychoanalytic theory and to religion and thus might be expected to be caught in the middle of the conflict between the two. This is not at all the case, however. With few exceptions, insofar as they still emphasize clinical training (albeit a declining focus) social work schools have opted to align themselves with psychoanalytic theory as academically and professionally the more powerful of the two approaches and to eschew any religious connections.

Social work developed in urban areas in the United States from the recognition on the part of many clergy that, following the Judeo-Christian obligation to be charitable, there was a dire need for social services and that these services required organization to be effective. The religious innovators of social work projects included individual clergymen such as Joseph Tucker, a Unitarian minister who organized charity for the poor in early nineteenth-century Boston; Stephen Humphreys Gurteen whose Charity Organization Society in Rochester, New York, gave rise to community welfare councils and to agencies serving families; and Charles Loring Brace whose "orphan trains" relocated large numbers of poor urban children—not always orphans—to the midwestern and western United States. Religious organizations also emerged, including the Young Men's Christian Association and the Salvation Army. Despite these historical associations, however, the three major religious traditions involved in social work in the United States have not directly tied religion into their social services. They have varied in how they relate religion to the services they deliver. Historically, Protestantism's decentralized structure has led to the secularization of the social services it delivers. Roman Catholicism, on the other hand, with its hierarchical structure, has tended to develop social agencies that are under church auspices. Jewish social services fall between these two extremes, offering services with a religious affiliation but without direct religious supervision. In part, this lack of a direct link between religion and the delivery of services has been mandated: These agencies have been prohibited from proselytizing because their programs often receive federal government funding. However, political changes in the United States may eventually alter this historic tradition.

The training that social workers receive also increases the separation between religion and the delivery of services, especially psychotherapy. This is true even though a growing number of graduate schools of social work award joint degrees with seminaries. (In part, this movement toward joint degree programs is motivated by economic and not just intellectual concerns: Both seminaries and schools of social work have seen a steady decline in enrollments for the past three decades.)

CONCLUSION. This article has traced the history of the relationship between psychotherapy and religion from its development in psychoanalysis as pejorative illusion in Freud, to the positive potential space in Winnicott, through Jung's defense of religious experience as a psychic fact, to the emergence of spirituality in psychotherapy, to the religiously based disciplines of pastoral counseling and CPE, and ending with the studiously nonreligious discipline of social work. It is only to be hoped that the modern disciplines springing from psychoanalytic theory will mature to the point of accommodating themselves to the powerful and lasting influence of religion on human life. This accommodation is well under way, as almost all writers in the integration of psychotherapy and religion recognize that religion is inherent in human life.

SEE ALSO Freud, Sigmund; Jung, C. G.

BIBLIOGRAPHY

An excellent short conceptual introduction to the development of psychoanalytic theory from Freud to Winnicott is Harry J. S. Guntrip's *Psychoanalytic Theory, Therapy, and the Self* (New York, 1971). Jay R. Greenberg and Stephen A. Mitchell's *Object Relations in Psychoanalytic Theory* (Cambridge, Mass., 1983) provides a good introduction, although the reader is cautioned that their readings of the development of psychoanalytic is biased toward object relations theory, as is to be expected (and as is indicated by the title.) The interrelation between religion and the work of numerous psychoanalysts is discussed in Ann Belford Ulanov and Barry Ulanov, *Religion and the Unconscious* (Philadelphia, 1975). The best study of Erikson's work is Lawrence Freidman's *Identity's Architect: A Biography of Erik H. Erikson* (New York, 1999). F. Robert Rodman's *Winnicott: His Life and Work* (Cambridge, Mass., 2003) is an excellent biographical introduction to the life and work of this seminal psychoanalyst. For original source information, see D. W. Winnicott, *Collected Papers* (London, 1958) and *Playing and Reality* (London, 1971), which includes a reprint of his paper "Transitional Objects and Transitional Phenomena." For a treatment of object relations theory, see Ana-Maria Rizzuto's *The Birth of the Living God: A Psychoanalytic Study* (Chicago, 1979). For an application of Winnicott's theory of potential space, see Ann Belford Ulanov, *Finding Space: Winnicott, God, and Psychic Reality* (Louisville, Ky., 2001). Stephen Mitchell's *Relational Concepts in Psychoanalysis, An Integration* (Cambridge, Mass., 1988) outlines his understanding of relational psychoanalysis.

Michael Palmer, *Freud and Jung on Religion* (London, 1997) is the best introduction to this topic. Two noteworthy books on Jung and religion are Murray Stein's *Jung's Map of the Soul* (Chicago, 1998) and *Jung's Treatment of Christianity* (Wilmette, Ill., 1985). Ann Belford Ulanov's *The Feminine in Jungian Psychology and in Christian Theology* (Evanston, Ill., 1971) has several chapters that pertain specifically to religion. For primary source information, see Carl Jung, *The Collected Works*, edited by Sir Herbert Read, Michael Fordham, and Gerhard Adler (Princeton, N.J., 1969); for his understanding of *psychological fact,* see volume 11, pp. 3–105. For a feminist approach to Jung, see Clarrisa Pinkola Estes, *Women Who Run With the Wolves* (New York, 1992). Three books are recommended as an introduction to spirituality and psychotherapy: Henry Grayson's *Mindful Loving* (New York, 2003) redefines the concept of the self from the psychoanalytic to the spiritual perspective, its relation to the new physics and includes an introduction to spiritual practices; Tara Brach's *Radical Acceptance: Embracing Life with the Heart of a Buddha* (New York, 2003) emphasizes practicality and personal openness, using Buddha for personal growth; and Mark Epstein's *Thoughts without a Thinker* (New York, 1995), which relates Buddhism to psychotherapy through focusing on meditation.

The best initial introduction to pastoral counseling is John Patton's *Pastoral Counseling: A Ministry of the Church* (Nashville, Tenn., 1983). Margaret Kornfeld's *Cultivating Wholeness: A Guide for Care and Counseling in Faith Communities* (New York, 1998) emphasizes basic skills for clergy and has an excellent annotated bibliography. Brooks Holifield's *A History of Pastoral Care: From Salvation to Self-Realization* (Nashville, Tenn., 1983) is an excellent history of the field. Paul W. Pruyser's *The Minister as Diagnostician* (Philadelphia, 1976) and Wayne E. Oates's *When Religion Gets Sick* (Philadelphia, 1970) are considered classic studies in the role of the seminary-trained pastoral counselor. Also see Seward Hiltner, *Pastoral Counseling* (Nashville, Tenn., 1949), one of the first books in the field. For an early accounting of CPE, see Anton T. Boisen's *Out of the Depths* (New York, 1960) and Doris Webster Havice, *Roadmap for Rebel* (New York, 1980). For a critique of pastoral counseling, see Karl Menninger, *Whatever Became of Sin?* (New York, 1973) and Deborah Van Duesen Hunsinger, *Theology and Pastoral Counseling: A New Interdisciplinary Approach* (Grand Rapids, Mich., 1995). For religion's effect on personal well-being, see Harold Koenig, *Spirituality and Patient Care* (Radnor, Pa., 2002).

MICHAEL D. CLIFFORD (1987 AND 2005)

PSYCHOLOGY: SCHIZOANALYSIS AND RELIGION

Although Gilles Deleuze and Félix Guattari explicitly define the approach they develop in *Anti-Oedipus* (1972) as a "materialist psychiatry" and insist repeatedly that the unconscious be thought of as an "orphan and an atheist," schizoanalysis turns out to have important ramifications for the study of religion. That religion plays such an important role in a book of materialist psychiatry may be less surprising given the centrality of Baruch Spinoza to Deleuze's thought; but then again, Deleuze reads Spinoza through the lenses of Karl Marx and Friedrich Nietzsche. An evaluation of religion is thus both crucial to the development of schizoanalysis and quite complex, even ambivalent.

Schizoanalysis is, first and foremost, a world-historical, Marxian critique of Freudian psychoanalysis. While it is true that schizoanalysis combines insights from all three of the great high-modern materialists (Marx, Nietzsche, and Sigmund Freud), each of whom is used to critique the others, Freud—and particularly his theory of the Oedipus complex—receives the brunt of the critique, as the book's title itself proclaims. Just as Marx understands capitalism and the bourgeois political economy of writers such as Adam Smith and David Ricardo in relation to a theory of modes of production spanning all of known history and anthropology, Deleuze and Guattari situate the nuclear family and the "bourgeois psychiatry" of Freud in relation to an equally broad theory of modes of libidinal production, based largely on Marx, but also in part on the anthropological typology of Lewis Morgan. Through comparisons with "savagery" and "barbarism" (terms drawn from Morgan's typology), Deleuze and Guattari conclude that the nuclear family itself, as well as the Freudian version of psychoanalysis that does so much to illegitimately universalize, and hence reinforce, the nuclear family and its Oedipus complex, are strictly capitalist institutions, with little validity outside capitalist society (and only a detrimental or symptomatic role to play within it).

Modernity represents a key turning point in this view of world history, for a crucial discovery is made in a number of different fields: first by Martin Luther, then by Adam Smith and David Ricardo, and somewhat later by Freud. The key discovery, according to Deleuze and Guattari, is that value does not inhere in objects but rather gets invested in them by human activity, whether that activity be religious devotion, physical labor, or libidinal desire. In this fundamental reversal of perspective, objects turn out to be merely the support for subjective value-giving activity. Yet in each of the three fields—religion, economics, psychology—the discovery of the internal, subjective nature of value-giving activity is accompanied by a re-subordination of that activity to another external determination: In the case of Luther, subjective faith freed from subordination to the Catholic Church is nevertheless re-subordinated to the authority of Scripture; in Smith and Ricardo, labor-power freed from feudal obligations is re-subordinated to private capital accumulation; in Freud, polymorphous libido is re-subordinated to heterosexual reproduction in the privatized nuclear family. To free human activity from these last external determinations is the task of world-historical critique: Marx provides the critique of political economy to free wage-labor from private capital, just as Deleuze and Guattari provide the critique of psychoanalysis to free libido from the private nuclear family and the Oedipus complex. Can schizoanalysis provide a point of departure for a similar, world-historical critique of religion? Probably not, for reasons that will be considered below. But one thing is clear: if schizoanalysis insists that the unconscious be considered an orphan, this is in order to free it from the repressive confines of the nuclear family and the psychoanalytic Oedipus complex. Why must the unconscious also be considered an atheist?

There would be two key turning points in a schizoanalytic world history of religion, the second of which has already been broached in the allusion to Martin Luther. The first involves the transition from "savagery" to "barbarism"—or, roughly translated, from polytheism to monotheism. Under savagery, social relations comprise a patchwork of reciprocal and temporary debts and obligations, sponsored by a plethora of spirits or gods, that link everyone in society more or less indirectly with everyone else. Such a "horizontal" pattern of social relations contrasts sharply with the "vertical" relation characteristic of barbarism, which links everyone directly with a despot and his god; equally important, the patchwork of temporary and reciprocal debts gets replaced by one unidirectional debt that everyone owes to the despot and his god, an infinite debt that can never be discharged. Whereas the earth had been the focal point (or what Deleuze and Guattari call the "natural presupposition" or "quasi-cause") of social life under savagery, it is God that appears as the divine presupposition or quasi-cause of social life under barbarism, and it is ultimately on God that barbaric social relations converge and to God that the infinite debt is owed.

In this context, the emergence of (mercantile and then industrial) capitalism and the Protestant Reformation represent a second key turning point, occurring within monotheism, because Protestantism and capitalism subordinate the secular institutions of the despot (The Church) to a more abstract God (a *deus absconditus*)—the divine but absent Voice of Scripture and capital, respectively. This is Deleuze and Guattari's adaptation of Max Weber's *Protestant Ethic and the Spirit of Capitalism* (1904–1905) thesis, as it were: liberal-democratic capitalism and psychoanalysis pick up where Protestantism left off, as they replace waning external social authority with forms of internalized, subjective authority or self-discipline. The infinite debt once owed to the despot now transfers to the equally infinite debt owed to capital, the new god or divine presupposition of modern social life; society is henceforth governed by economic forces rather than moral principles. And as the cash nexus of capitalism subverts all religious and social authority in society at large, all that remains is the internalized authority of private conscience—first in the form of an individualized Protestant conscience nonetheless still supported by the external authority of Scripture and the congregation, then as a liberal-civic conscience with no support except the fainter and fainter echoes of the Father's Voice in the superego. But in a society governed only by the imperative to accumulate capital, the Father ultimately has no social imperative to impose on privatized conscience other than to work in order to pay the infinite debt. Capital invents secular institutions to invest with authority—most notably the nation-state, along with the nuclear family—but ultimately these too succumb to the primacy of private accumulation (through the combined forces of globalization and mediatization).

The unconscious, then, is an orphan at home and an atheist in society at large. But this atheism is not only or primarily a specifically religious disbelief, but a general disbelief in despotism of any kind—monotheistic god, absolute monarchy, private capital—that attributes the productive activity of society to itself as its "quasi-cause." This rather bleak assessment of the anachronism of belief and of the role of monotheism and despotism in world history is tempered, however, by another current of schizoanalysis derived from Nietzsche (though here again, the figure of Spinoza is important, too). Nietzsche's virulent critique in *The Genealogy of Morals* (1887) and elsewhere of Christian "slave morality" in the name of personal self-transformation (the "overman") is well known; less well-known and more important to schizoanalysis is his insistence in the same work (Essay 2, especially section 11) on the increase in power obtained by assembling human beings into larger groups. Inasmuch as Nietzsche posits will-to-power as the basic human motivation, the formation of human groups should be of major interest to him; but for the most part he disdains groups for their all-too-human "herd instinct" and focuses instead on superhuman individuals and their heroic "transvaluation of values."

Here, the schizoanalytic amalgamation of Nietzsche and Marx proves salutary and illuminating. For unlike Nietzsche, Marx is indeed focused on the formation of human groups, and he pays particular attention to the increase in human power obtained through the socialization of production, especially under capitalism. The centralization of capital; the extension of the market to now global proportions; the development of factories, assembly-line production, and, more recently, out-sourcing and computer-coordinated production—all lead to increases in human capacities through what Marx called the productive force of cooperation. Yet Marx, unlike Nietzsche (and Freud), pays insufficient attention to the unconscious, which is the very hero of schizoanalysis and the primary agent of its version of world history. This neglect has engaged Marx and Marxism in a mostly unproductive attempt to persuade people to act in accord with their own interests. Following Nietzsche and Freud, Deleuze and Guattari's response to this predicament is categorical: people are not motivated to act by interest, but by desire—much of which is unconscious; and what desire wants is power and the increase of power. Moreover, socialized production is not the only source of such power. Any binding together of human beings in larger groups will have the same effect: an increase of power. And as Émile Durkheim perhaps most famously observed, religion (from the Latin *ligare*, to bind together) has been and continues to be one of the most pervasive and effective forms of human grouping for that very reason: it increases the power of the group in and of itself (regardless of whether material productivity in the narrow sense is thereby increased or not). Far from being an "opiate," as Marx notoriously said, religion (according to the principles of schizoanalysis) is something human beings desire precisely because it represents an increase in their power. This is why schizoanalysis does not offer a world-historical critique of religion: as with capitalism and psychoanalysis, schizoanalysis considers the phenomenon of religion to be ambivalent, and therefore in need of careful evaluation.

This explanation of the appeal of religion (in this fundamental etymological sense) to human will-to-power raises a number questions for schizoanalysis, however. For one thing, can one be sure that religious groups are still viable under current market conditions, if the cash nexus and capital accumulation rule society and effectively preclude any belief? (Among others, Giorgio Agamben argues in *The Coming Community* (1990) specifically for the formation of human communities that are not held together by shared beliefs.) More important, can desire want power and at the same time want to exercise power freely? To what extent are power and freedom compatible? And most important, how can the power attained specifically through group formation be exercised free from external determination? Can group coherence remain immanent to group activity, or does it require something transcending the group itself (such as a "God above") to act as its center or ground, to which productive group activity may then become subordinate? These are some of the questions that schizoanalysis would want to ask about religion in general, as a species of group formation among others.

But a schizoanalysis of religion would be even better suited to the examination of specific instances of religious group-formation, since the answers to general questions like those above will never be black and white, but a matter of degrees. In Deleuze and Guattari's view, the unity of a human group is never simply given or naturally ordained; it is always produced and maintained by the group itself. That is why it is crucial for them to identify, in connection with the large-scale typology of social formations they derive from Morgan, the "natural" or "divine" presupposition or quasi-cause around which each type of social formation organizes itself: the earth, God, capital. Much the same would apply to human groups on smaller scales: here, too, schizoanalysis would want to discover the quasi-cause around which a group organizes itself, whether that be a totem animal (as in Durkheim), or a team mascot, a book of scripture and a prophet, a flag and a constitution, or whatever. Then the task would be to assess whether the power associated with a given quasi-cause takes on a life of its own and turns against the group—or, on the contrary, remains in consonance with group activity and enables the group to flourish—and to evaluate in each particular case the degree to which a specific mode of group-formation enhances or curtails the power of the group and of members of the group.

SEE ALSO Marxism.

BIBLIOGRAPHY

Agamben, Giorgio. *The Coming Community.* Translated by Michael Hardt. Minneapolis, 1993. Proposes that the coming community be organized around "whatever," rather than a specific set of shared beliefs or a common project.

Bataille, Georges. *The Accursed Share: An Essay on General Economy.* Translated by Robert Hurley. New York, 1988. Demonstrates with several examples that all societies except capitalism are centered on expenditure rather than accumulation.

Bryden, Mary, ed. *Deleuze and Religion.* London and New York, 2001. Examines the intersection of Deleuze's thought with religious matters, from a variety of angles.

Deleuze, Gilles. *Expressionism in Philosophy: Spinoza.* Translated by Martin Joughin. New York, 1990. The more important of Deleuze's two studies of Spinoza, whose insistence on immanence becomes a central features of Deleuze's own thought.

Deleuze, Gilles, and Félix Guattari. *Anti-Oedipus: Capitalism and Schizophrenia.* Translated by Robert Hurley, Mark Seem, and Helen R. Lane. New York, 1977. Originally published in French as *L'anti-Œdipe* in 1972. Presents the theory of schizoanalysis based on a critique of the psychoanalytic oedipus complex.

Deleuze, Gilles, and Felix Guattari. *A Thousand Plateaus: Capitalism and Schizophrenia.* Translated by Brian Massumi. Minneapolis, 1987. Extends the approach developed in *Anti-Oedipus* to a wide range of phenomena, from geology to bird songs to postmodern capitalism.

Durkheim, Émile. *Elementary Forms of Religious Life.* Translated by Karen E. Fields. New York, 1995. Proposes that the basis of religion is the augmentation of power inherent in assembling people in larger groups.

Foucault, Michel. *The Order of Things: An Archaeology of the Human Sciences.* New York, 1970. Analyzes the emergence of modernity and confirms Deleuze and Guattari's conclusion that "Freud is the Luther and the Adam Smith of psychiatry."

Holland, Eugene W. *Deleuze and Guattari's Anti-Oedipus: Introduction to Schizoanalysis.* London and New York, 1999. Explains the theory of schizoanalysis in light of its derivation from Freud, Kant, Marx, and Nietzsche.

Marx, Karl. *Capital: A Critique of Political Economy.* 3 vols. New York, 1967. The classic analysis and critique of capitalist exploitation.

Morgan, Lewis H. *Ancient Society: or, Researches in the Line of Human Progress from Savagery through Barbarism to Civilization.* Chicago, 1877. Early anthropological typology of social forms from which Deleuze and Guattari borrow the names for their typology of libidinal modes of production.

Negri, Antonio. *The Savage Anomaly: The Power of Spinoza's Metaphysics and Politics.* Translated by Michael Hardt. Minneapolis, Minn., 1991. Innovative reading of Spinoza's ethics (contemporary with Deleuze's own) that stresses its relevance for present-day political and philosophical concerns.

Nietzsche, Friedrich. *On the Genealogy of Morality.* Translated by Carol Diethe. New York, 1994. The classic analysis of moral theories in terms of will-to-power.

Spinoza, Baruch. *Ethics.* Translated by G. H. R. Parkinson. New York, 2000. Arguably the first work of immanent materialism, and the inspiration for Deleuze's re-reading of Marx.

Weber, Max. *The Protestant Ethic and the Spirit of Capitalism.* New York, 1958. The classic analysis of the relation between Protestant asceticism and capital accumulation.

EUGENE W. HOLLAND (2005)

PSYCHOPOMP SEE SPIRITUAL GUIDE

PTAH was the creator god of Memphis who conceived a thought in his mind (heart) and brought it forth by speaking it with his tongue. Because the founding of Memphis and the erection of a temple to Ptah at that site were accomplishments of the first king of a united Egypt, Menes, the cult of Ptah must date at least to the beginning of Egyptian history. The text that best describes the Memphite theology, however, is preserved in a very late copy dating from the twenty-fifth dynasty (c. 700 BCE). The original text may not have been much older, but it is a very interesting document, not only for its description of the creation, but also for its handling of the other two major creation myths. In this text Ptah is identified with the last pair of the Hermopolitan ogdoad—that is, Nun and Naunet, who represent the watery abyss from which the creator god comes forth. The creator god who is thus created by Ptah is Atum, who proceeds to create the other gods of the Heliopolitan ennead and all else. In this way the theologies are all connected, and Ptah as an anthropomorphic creator god is given precedence by being placed between the chthonic, precreation cosmic aspects known as the ogdoad and the old creator god, Atum.

Almost nothing remains of the temple of Ptah at Memphis, even though it was one of the three largest and best endowed of ancient Egypt. Smaller temples (such as those at Gerf Hussein and Karnak) were dedicated to Ptah in many locations, and statues of him are plentiful. His image is that of a tightly cloaked man holding a composite scepter before him. Ptah became identified, at least to some extent, with the local mortuary god of Memphis, Sokar, and also with Osiris. His consort was Sekhmet, the powerful lioness, who was the mother of his son, Nefertem, the lotus god.

BIBLIOGRAPHY

The most extensive study available is *The God Ptah* (Lund, 1946) by Maj Sandman-Holmberg.

LEONARD H. LESKO (1987)

PTOLEMY (c. 100–170), Alexandrian astronomer, geographer, and mathematician. The last of the great astronomers of antiquity, Claudius Ptolemaeus (Ptolemy) compiled works that remained the standard astronomical textbooks until the Copernican revolution in astronomy in the sixteenth century. Almost nothing is known of the details of Ptolemy's life. His *Hē mathēmatikē syntaxis* (Mathematical Compilation) was written about 150 CE; the title by which this work is better known, the *Almagest,* is a medieval Latin derivation from an Arabic corruption of the Greek title under which the work came to be known in later antiquity, *Ho megale syntaxis* (The Great Compilation). The *Almagest* sums up the mathematical astronomy of the ancient world; it became the basis of Latin and Arabic astronomy.

Ptolemy's work follows in the Greek philosophical tradition, in which the sacred nature of the heavens is expressed by the incorruptibility of the celestial realm, the divinity of the heavenly bodies, and the perfection of their motions (uniformly circular, because the circle was considered the most perfect of figures and motion around a circle was eternal). The fact that the motions of the sun, moon, and planets are evidently not circular provided a formidable challenge to thinkers within this tradition; especially challenging were the planets' periodic reverses, or retrograde motions. Drawing upon the work of his Greek predecessors, Ptolemy was able to "save the appearances" of celestial motion by using circles in his geometry of the heavens. By employing Greek and Babylonian observational data, he was able to adjust his theoretical solutions to observed celestial positions and to predict them with a precision unmatched until the work of Johannes Kepler in the seventeenth century. The geometrical devices that Ptolemy used—the eccentric, the epicycle, and the equant—were never thought to possess a physical reality, as he makes clear in the preface to the *Almagest.* But it was just for this reason that astronomy had a religious value. Astronomy developed the correspondence between the order of divine celestial things and the order of mathematical propositions.

Its science Aristotelian and its format Euclidean, the *Almagest* describes a stationary, spherical earth surrounded by concentric spheres carrying the sun, moon, planets, and stars. Motion is described geometrically by arrangements of several kinds of circles: (1) *eccentrics,* which are not centered on the earth; (2) *epicycles,* which orbit other circles that are centered on the earth; and (3) *equants,* in which the motion of the body on the circle is variable in relation to the center of the circle but uniform in relation to some noncentral point within the circle. The *Almagest* includes a star catalog and a table of observations later revised and expanded in Ptolemy's *Prokheiroi kanones* (Handy Tables).

Ptolemy's work on geometry, the *Planisphaerium,* of which only a distorted Greek title survives, *Exaplōsis epiphaneias sphairas* (Unfolding of a Spherical Surface), details the theory of the astrolabe, the chief astronomical instrument of antiquity and the Middle Ages. Ptolemy's *Hypotheseis tōn planōmenon* (Planetary Hypotheses) suggests that the spheres of the planets nestle within one another. The astrological complement to Ptolemy's astronomy is his *Tetrabiblios.* Ptolemy also wrote works on optics and music, as well as a *Geography* (Gr., *Geographikē hyphēgēsis*), which gives directions on how to map the spherical earth on a flat surface and provides tables of longitude and latitude for generating maps. Because of a lack of precise longitude, Ptolemy's map of the known world was severely distorted, even where descriptive information abounded.

Ptolemy's works present an interrelated whole dominated by the successful application of mathematics to complex technical problems. For example, the determination of terrestrial latitude in the *Geography* is achieved through calculations based on astronomy. This in turn specifies the astrological character of the inhabitants of various parts of the earth. His cartography employs the mathematics of his optics and of the *Planisphaerium.* Ptolemy's authority in applied mathematics was undisputed for more than a millennium.

Ptolemy went to great lengths in his texts to provide procedures whereby his technical achievements could be reproduced. He thus laid the foundation for other civilizations to assimilate his work, become expert at it, and progress beyond it. Such cultural innovation is invariably associated with religious creativity, though not in a predictable fashion. For example, though Ptolemy's astronomy was used to corroborate the religious view that the earth was at the center of the universe, no one was ever convinced of this view *because* of the astronomy of eccentrics, epicycles, and equants. However, becoming technically expert in these devices did allow the accurate prediction of religious feasts. Although the Jewish philosopher Maimonides (Mosheh ben Maimon, 1135/8–1204) criticized Ptolemy, he did incorporate some of the astronomer's techniques for determining the date of Passover.

The translation of Ptolemy's work into Arabic in the ninth century was a catalyst for the flowering of Islamic culture. Refined astronomical tables were created, such as the *Toledan Tables* of al-Zarḳālla (c. 1080). This served as the basis for the *Alfonsine Tables,* which was compiled circa 1252 by some fifty astronomers assembled for that purpose by Alfonso X of Castile, and which predicted the dates of the Easter moon. New theories of optics were proposed by the Arab heritors of Ptolemy; new geographical values were established. The Islamic appropriation of Hellenistic natural philosophy inspired the Christian Middle Ages. A desire for the *Almagest* brought the greatest of medieval translators of Arabic, Gerard of Cremona (1114–1187), to Toledo. The merits of a true physical astronomy and of "saving the appearances" by geometry were argued in medieval universities, where Ptolemaic astronomy became part of the curriculum. Although the celestial bodies were no longer thought of as gods by medieval Europeans, their movement was believed to exhibit God's will (and their order his wisdom), and hence Ptolemy's astronomy continued to provide for the intellectual contemplation of the divine celestial order. Dante drew upon Ptolemy for the cosmology of his *Commedia* (1321).

When the *Geography,* with its techniques of projection, was first translated into Latin in fifteenth-century Florence, it contributed to the rediscovery of linear perspective and to the development of cartography during the voyages of exploration. Because the distortions of Ptolemy's map of the globe bore the prestige of his mathematics, Columbus and others were convinced that it would be quite easy to reach Asia by sailing west. When Renaissance astronomers finally became truly competent in Ptolemy's astronomy, their dissatisfaction with his accuracy and methods culminated in the Copernican revolution that established modern cosmology. The Jesuit mission to China in the seventeenth century used the predictive precision of Ptolemaic astronomy to enhance the value of their religious teaching at the emperor's court. Thus it was ironic that Ptolemy's science and technology were helping to introduce Christianity to the Far East at the same time that Copernican astronomy was making Ptolemaic astronomy obsolete in the West. And well after Ptolemy's cosmos was superseded by the physical universe as defined by Copernicus, Newton, and others, the *Tetrabiblios* remained an astrological standard. It was translated into English and published in 1701, the second edition in 1786.

BIBLIOGRAPHY

A translation of Ptolemy's *Almagest* was done by R. Catesby Taliaferro in *Ptolemy, Copernicus, Kepler,* vol. 16 of the "Great Books of the Western World," edited by Robert Maynard Hutchins (Chicago, 1952). The inclusion of the *De revolutionibus* by Copernicus in the same text facilitates the comparison of these two all-important works in the history of astronomy. A scrupulous new translation of the *Almagest* is provided in G. J. Toomer's *Ptolemy's Almagest* (London, 1984). Frank E. Robbins translated the *Tetrabiblios* for the "Loeb Classical Library" (Cambridge, Mass., 1940). An English translation of the Latin *Geographia* is found in Edward Luther Stevenson's *Geography of Claudius Ptolemy* (New York, 1933). An exhaustive technical account of the *Almagest* and its historical antecedents is provided in Otto Neugebauer's *A History of Ancient Mathematical Astronomy,* vol. 1 (New York, 1975). G. J. Toomer, in his article "Ptolemy, Claudius," in the *Dictionary of Scientific Biography* (New York, 1970–1980), gives a concise description of Ptolemy's science with an up-to-date bibliography. A very readable discussion of the problems posed by observational astronomy and the Greek solutions to them, as well as of their cultural context, is provided in Thomas Kuhn's *The Copernican Revolution: Planetary Astronomy in the Development of Western Thought,* rev. ed. (New York, 1959).

MICHAEL A. KERZE (1987)

PUER AETERNUS SEE CHILD

PŪJĀ

This entry consists of the following articles:

PŪJĀ: HINDU PŪJĀ

From ancient times, Hinduism has known two preeminent methods of approaching divinity in ritual: (1) the method of *yajña,* which conveys offerings to a distant god by consigning them to an intermediary fire, and (2) the method of *pūjā,* which extends offerings to a present divinity by placing them before, or applying them to, the god's symbol or image. The *yajña* appears in the earlier records; it was the principal ritual method of the ancient Aryan peoples whose priests produced the collection of texts known as the Veda. The *pūjā* is first mentioned in texts supplementary to the Veda that are known as *sūtras* (composed around 600–400 BCE). It first became prominent in India as a result of the god-centered devotional movements that spread throughout India during the early centuries of the common era. The method of *pūjā* now predominates in Hindu practice, although the *yajña* remains important to priestly and domestic ritual.

ORIGINS AND ETYMOLOGY. Scholarly opinion is divided regarding the origins and etymology of *pūjā.* Many scholars have argued that *pūjā* was initially a Dravidian practice native to India and point to the sharp distinction traditionally drawn between *pūjā* and *yajña,* the refusal of the strictest Vedic priests to participate in *puja,* the long-standing prevalence of *pūjā* in village cults, and the long role of low-caste (and hence non-Aryan) hereditary priests in village *pūjās.* But no clear-cut Dravidian derivation has been established for the term *pūjā;* the best-known attempt at a Dravidian etymology is that of Jarl Charpentier (1927), who proposed to derive *pūjā* from Tamil *pūcu* or Kannada *pūsu,* "to smear," a reference to the applications of sandalwood, turmeric, or vermilion pastes that are common in *pūjā* offerings.

Alternatively, the Sanskritist Paul Thieme proposed in 1939 that the term *pūjā* is derived from the Sanskrit (and hence Aryan) *pṛc,* "to mix," a reference to the *madhuparka,* or mixture of honey and water that was commonly offered to guests in ancient Indian times. Analyzing the uses of the term *pūjā* in *sūtra* and epic literature, Thieme concluded that it had once referred primarily to a ritual of guest worship. The offerings and gestures characteristic of *pūjā* are in fact still utilized in India to honor distinguished guests, as well as other meritorious persons, sacred plants and animals, and occasionally also weapons or tools. Furthermore, elements from ancient guest ritual such as offering a seat and washing the feet still play a significant role in conventional *pūjās.* However, traces of guest ritual are rarer in village practice and in *pūjās* of heterodox (i.e., Buddhist and Jain) traditions; hence the question of the term's origin remains open.

TYPES. *Deva- pūjās* (i.e., *pūjās* for the gods) are offered in four sorts of settings: (1) at shrines maintained for family (*kula*) and/or "chosen" (*iṣṭta*) divinities within the Hindu home; (2) at temples devoted to pan-Indian deities such as Śiva and Viṣṇu; (3) during the course of festivals, which may be sponsored either by temples or by local communities; (4) at shrines or temples of localized village divinities. *Pūjās* in any of these contexts may be quite freely structured, consisting of little more than gestures of reverence (*namas*) and minimal offerings. Or they may follow conventional patterns, which vary only slightly according to the devotional sect of the performer and the deity who is honored.

Pūjā at the home shrine. Most Hindus maintain a home shrine for one or more divinities honored within the household. Ideally, the home shrine is located in a small room of the house that is set aside solely for worship (*pūjāśālā*). The shrine itself may consist of pictures of gods set up on a table or low platform, or images may be housed in a wooden shrine-cabinet, whose doors are opened only during the service. Images housed in such shrines may be Śiva-*liṅgas*, small cast-metal statues of various gods, or the stones sacred to Viṣṇu that are known as *śālagrāma*. A single family representative generally offers the *pūjā*; other household members enter at the close of the rite to offer prostrations and/or sip the water in which the image has been bathed. Worshipers of Viṣṇu will also eat the food (*prasāda*) that the god has sanctified by his taste, and may append to their *pūjā* special offerings of homage for the family's *ācārya*, or religious teacher. An ambitious household *pūjā*may incorporate all or several of sixteen traditional *upacāras*, "attendances," which also form the core of traditional temple services. (The following list varies slightly in different textual sources.)

1. *Āvahāna* ("invocation"). The god is invited to be present at the ceremony.
2. *Āsana.* The god is offered a seat.
3. *Svāgata* ("greeting"). The worshiper asks the god if the journey has gone well.
4. *Pādya.* The worshiper symbolically washes the god's feet.
5. *Arghya.* Water is extended so that the god may cleanse his or her face and teeth.
6. *Ācamanīya.* Water is offered for sipping.
7. *Madhuparka.* The god is offered the water-and-honey drink.
8. *Snāna* or *abhiṣekha.* Water is offered for symbolic bathing; if submersible, the image may literally be bathed and then toweled dry.
9. *Vastra* ("clothing"). Here a cloth may be wrapped around the image and ornaments affixed to it.
10. *Anulepana* or *gandha.* Perfumes and/or ointments are applied to the image.
11. *Puṣpa.* Flowers are laid before the image, or garlands are draped around it.
12. *Dhūpa.* Incense is burned before the image.
13. *Dīpa* or *ārati.* A burning lamp is waved in front of the god.
14. *Naivedya* or *prasāda.* Foods such as cooked rice, fruit, clarified butter, sugar, and betel leaf are offered.
15. *Namaskāra* or *pranāma.* The worshiper and family bow or prostrate themselves before the image to offer homage.
16. *Visarjana* or *udvāsana.* The god is dismissed.

Temple pūjās. A full *pūjā* of sixteen *upacāras* is in effect a miniaturized temple ritual; the daily worship, or *nitya pūjā*, in a major temple differs from it principally in scale and in the number of times that the *pūjā* is repeated (three to six times daily for the temple ritual). Temple officiants are usually brahmans; however, brahmans who are temple priests enjoy lesser status than those who perform Vedic rituals. In non-Śaiva temples *pūjās* are usually addressed to anthropomorphic images, but in temples of Śiva the central "image" is always the nonanthropomorphic *linga.* A sequence of temple *pūjās* may actually involve two images, for a moveable image stands in for the permanently fixed central symbol when it becomes necessary to manipulate or transport the divinity.

The god of a major temple is more of a resident than a guest. Segments of the daily *pūjā* will vary accordingly; hence the god is "awakened" rather than "invoked" in the morning, and may quite literally be aroused from a bed where his or her moveable image was laid the night before. Furthermore, the temple god is royal; the temple is his or her palace, and its priests are palace servants. Hence the god's "seat" is a throne, and ornaments affixed to the image may include a crown; furthermore, the "ruler," in the form of the moveable image, is carried each day in procession around the temple grounds, much as local rulers in India formerly processed through their territories. Temple *pūjās* differ slightly according to sect and region. Thus temples of Śiva in South India once featured performances by dancing girls (*devadāsīs*) maintained as part of the temple staff. Śaiva *pūjā* s also incorporate many Tantric elements; for example, an officiating priest begins his *pūjā* by summoning Lord Śiva into his own body. Devotional hymns are often sung during *pūjās* at Vaiṣṇava temples; while images of Vaiṣṇava saints are honored as well as images of Viṣṇu.

Daily temple *pūjās* are not communal performances; as in the home, one person (here, the temple priest) acts for the benefit of all. Individuals may, however, make special requests of the gods by means of special offerings. This practice is known as *kāmya pūjā*, "the *pūjā* undertaken by choice." Such optional *pūjās* are most often performed at the small shrines that dot a major temple's grounds. The intended worshiper commissions a priest to place his or her offerings before or onto the image.

Festivals. All major temples sponsor festivals. A frequent type is the *ratha yātrā*, or "car festival," in which the moveable image is mounted on a large (sometimes multistoried) cart and pulled through the town on a set processional path. The devotee thus receives an opportunity for *darśana*, or "sight," of the god; he or she may toss flowers, break coconuts, or sprinkle the image with water as the cart progresses. Communities may also sponsor festivals in which public display and celebration of images is a central feature. Community associations or families may commission elaborate and expensive clay images for such festal *pūjās*. The images are feted with music and entertainments, then paraded to a river and left to dissolve in its waters. *Pūjā* festivals of this type are especially popular in the state of Bengal, in northeastern India.

Village pūjās. Animal sacrifice has fallen out of favor among Hindus in the early twenty-first century. It was once, and sometimes remains, a standard feature of the worship of fierce goddesses such as Kālī. Animal sacrifice was also common in *pūjās* of village divinities (*gramādevatā*), which differ in several respects from *pūjās* of the urban-based pan-Indian deities. Such divinities associated with specific locales have been reported from ancient times, not only in Hindu, but also Buddhist and Jain writings. The cult of village gods is now most prominent in South India, where the village divinity is often a goddess whose name is a compound of *amma,* "mother." Although temples for *ammas* have become increasingly popular, an *amma's* shrine may be quite minimal. Sometimes it is just a bare enclosure outside the bounds of the village proper *amma's* shrine may be minimal; sometimes it is just a bare enclosure outside the boundaries of the village proper. The "image," if any permanent image exists, may be a rock or an earthen pot or lamp. The hereditary shrine priest, or *pūjāri,* is of low caste, often a potter. Village *pūjās* are not necessarily maintained on a regular basis, nor do they commonly follow the *upacāra* model; coconuts, bananas, margosa or betel leaves, turmeric, and cooked rice are the most common nonbloody offerings. Village gods may possess their *pūjāri* s or other mediums during the course of *pūjās*; festivals feature such possession experiences, as well as processions, sometimes fire walking, and sometimes sacrifices of sheep, goats, fowls, or buffalo.

SEE ALSO Domestic Observances, article on Hindu Practices; Rites of Passage, article on Hindu Rites; Worship and Devotional Life, article on Hindu Devotional Life.

BIBLIOGRAPHY

Sources cited for proposed etymologies of the word *pūjā* are Jarl Charpentier's "Über den Begriff und die Etymologie von pūjā," *Beiträge zur Literaturwissenschaft und Geistesgeschichte Indiens: Festgabe Hermann Jacobi,* edited by Willibald Kirfel (Bonn, 1926), pp. 276–297; also Paul Thieme's "Pūjā," *Journal of Oriental Research* 27 (1957–1958): 1–16. For a summary of precepts governing *pūjā* s in classical Sanskrit literature, see Pandura Vaman Kane's *History of Dharmaśāstra: Ancient and Medieval Religious and Civil Law in India,* vol. 2, pt.1 (Poona, 1941), pp. 705–740. Temple *pūjās* vary somewhat in different locales and sectarian traditions. Good resources for scholars exploring these variations are: Gudrun Bèuhnemann's *Pūjā: A Study in Smārta Ritual* (Vienna, 1988), examining Vedic *pūjās* of Maharashtra; Carl Gustav Diehl's old but still useful *Instrument and Purpose: Studies in Rites and Rituals in South India* (Lund, 1956), reflecting southern *āgama*-based traditions; and Hillary Peter Rodrigues, *The Liturgy of the Durgā Pūjā with Interpretations,* comparing Banaras and Bengal-based versions of *pūjās* for the great goddess festival. For non-specialists, fine you-are-there portrayals of *pūjā* in practice are found in Stephen P. Huyler's *Meeting God: Elements of Hindu Devotion* (New Haven, Conn., 1999) and Elizabeth U. Harding's *Kali: The Black Goddess of Dakshineswar* (Delhi, 1998). Huyler includes many superb photographs.

NANCY AUER FALK (1987 AND 2005)

PŪJĀ: BUDDHIST PŪJĀ

According to Buddhist texts, the gods worshipped Śākyamuni Buddha during his lifetime, as did humans. Gods and humans began the heartfelt ritual veneration of the Buddha's material remains as soon as he abandoned his mortal body. The term *pūjā* refers to such acts of ritualized worship. Relics, trees, mortuary monuments, and eventually images and texts associated with the three jewels (the Buddha, the teachings, and the community of Buddhists) as well as a wide range of pacific or ferocious buddhas and bodhisattvas were made the objects of worship. Yet conflicting interpretations of Śākyamuni's instructions, together with the philosophically subtle condition of possibility that the Buddha was both absent and immanent for such veneration, yielded a creative tension in the intellectual understanding of *pūjā* within the developing Buddhist traditions. Moreover, as the tradition developed local forms, which in turn took over the cults of local deities, the worship of deities who were neither buddhas nor bodhisattvas became part of the ritual calendar. Elite debates do not seem to have restrained the popular perception of ferocious dharma-protecting deities as very real agents, different only in efficacy from the great bodhisattvas and buddhas. Thus the form and interpretation of Buddhist *pūjā* varies widely, depending on the cultural context and social register of the worshipper, although the fundamental devotional impulse has never been denied.

ORIGINS AND EARLY EVIDENCE. The verbal root *pūj* in early Buddhist sources, as with other early Indic material, refers to ritual worship generally. The *Mahāparinirvāṇa-sūtra* (MPNS), an early text that exists in Sanskrit, Pali, and Chinese versions, is particularly rich in descriptions of various kinds of worship: the gods worship Śākyamuni with showers of celestial blossoms, music and sandalwood powder; Mahākāśyapa, who races across India to be present for the cremation of his teacher's body, seizes the feet of his dead teacher and presses them onto his head; and Śākyamuni himself gives instructions for the construction of mortuary monuments (stūpas or caityas) and their proper worship. The earliest known Buddhist sites, the stūpas at Vaiśālī and Piprāwhā, give evidence for pre-Mauryan relic veneration. Aśoka is said to have redistributed the relics contained in the original eight stèpas into 84,000 stūpas across the Mauryan empire; and indeed, several sites that exist to this day, such as the four stūpas that surround the Newar city of Lalitpur in the Kathmandu Valley, are said to have been established by Aśoka. At the Aśokan stūpa complexes of Bharhut and Sañchi in central India, there are carvings of trees and stūpas being worshipped, as well as numerous inscriptions documenting relic worship by renunciant and lay Buddhists.

PRACTICING *PŪJĀ*. In the fifth chapter of the MPNS, Śākyamuni makes several overlapping statements about what, and how, to worship. It is taken for granted that the appropriate object of worship is a tathāgata, either directly or through mediating symbols. In other sūtras, the worship of deities is criticized; deities rather should worship the Tathāgata. When the gods do arrange a spontaneous rain of heavenly flowers and sandalwood, Śākyamuni takes the opportunity to distinguish between offering material things such as flowers and the offering of abiding in the *dharma.* Good practice, according to Śākyamuni, is the highest form of worship of a tathāgata by the four sections of the Buddhist community (nuns, monks, and female and male lay Buddhists), all of whom are clearly expected to be interested in performing *pūjās*.

Pūjā offerings can be as simple as a handful of flowers offered by an unexpected visitor or a vast array of incense, lamps, garlands, sandalwood paste, delicious foods, water for washing and drinking, musical sounds ranging from the single peal of a bell up to a whole orchestra, dance, scatterings of unbroken rice, parasols, prayer flags and banners, circumambulations, and sculptures made from butter or flour.

Later in the same chapter of the MPNS, Śākyamuni recommends pilgrimage to the four sacred sites (that is, Lumbini, Bodhgayā, Sarnath, and Kapilvastu) and the creation and veneration of stūpas as appropriate forms of religious devotion. Morevoer, he instructs that his remains be enshrined in a stūpa. When, however, Ānanda asks the dying Śākyamuni, "What should we do about the Tathāgata's body?" he is told that the *saṃgha* ought not trouble themselves, as it will be dealt with by three sorts of paṇḍit, and he then receives instructions on funerary practices. Although this passage was taken by many Western scholars and some conservative reformists to mean that relic worship is only appropriate for lay Buddhists, it has become clear that the discussion in the MPNS is more to do with who should perform cremation rituals.

The ritual management of stūpas, as well as images and other material bases for the performance of *pūjā*, makes it clear that they are understood to be infused with a presence that makes their worship efficacious. The empowering of stūpas and images by the insertion of relics is a specially potent form of a general precondition for any Buddhist worship that takes a material item, such as a sculpture, painting, or manuscript, as its immediate object. The object must be ritually quickened before it can be worshipped. In Theravāda countries, the ritual of empowering a Buddha image is often referred to as "opening the eyes" of the image while Vajrayānists visualize, invoke, and install the appropriate deity. For certain deities, such as the ancient Newar Avalokiteśvara known as Būgadyaḥ, there is an annual cycle of deconsecrating the image by removing its essence into a separate container, renovating the image, and then reconsecrating and re-empowering it.

DEVELOPMENTS. The fundamental declaration for Buddhists is taking refuge in the Three Jewels: the Buddhas, the truth that they understand and teach, and the community that preserves that teaching. Nonetheless, the original object of worship for the earliest Buddhists was the Tathāgatha himself, continuing to be present in the physical relics of his body, the implements he had carried, and the tree under which he attained enlightenment. The relic cult was not confined to Śākyamuni. At the passing of great teachers, whether in Thailand or Tibet, the cremated remains often yield tiny relic fragments. Among Tibetans, the most powerful of these relics can, when held in the hand of another great lama, spontaneously multiply. For all Buddhists, relics are treasured possessions; and when a new monastery is founded, such relics are often gathered or donated in order to be incorporated into its new statues and stūpas. The finding of such relics in the remains of a great teacher is a confirmation of her or his holiness, and the incorporation of such relics into an image or monastic site is one way of asserting membership in the lineage of such a teacher. In Theravāda countries, *pūjā* has come to be considered a popular affair; everyone participates, and the most precious objects of worship are relics. The Śrī Laṅkan Tooth Relic is still the center of an elaborate priestly ritual cycle that reminds us of the Indic heritage that Theravāda shares with Newar and Tibetan Buddhism.

In the highest Vajrayāna tantras, it is sometimes said that the material requisites for *pūjā* can be dispensed with and the entire ritual performed as a visualization. Regardless of whether the offerings are actually present, the practitioner identifies herself with the main deity of the maṇḍala and performs subsequent ritual actions as the deity. Within the Zen school, the question of just what is present within an external image is informed by the doctrine of buddha-nature, which is thought to be present in all beings. Therefore, when a Zen practitioner bows to an image of Śākyamuni, she is not bowing to something outside herself, but as a buddha aware of her own buddha-nature.

Indic patterns. Buddhism in South Asia and, later, Southeast Asia developed along with other Indic religions. From the perspective of the present, Indic Buddhist worship looks a great deal like Hindu worship, but in fact the mutual historical influence is so complex as to make such statements vacuous. From an elite perspective, Buddhist *pūjā* depends on a sophisticated understanding of emptiness and impermanence that is pointedly opposed to the sense of divine presence that drives devotional Hinduism *bhakti.* However, much of the language and theory is held in common, including the terms for many tools and elements of the offering and the distinction between daily (*nityā*), required *(naimittikā)*, and optional *(kāmyā) pūjā*; and at a popular level, the efficacy of the *pūjā* is far more interesting to the participants than its ontology. Vajrayāna Buddhists developed their own version of the Vedic fire sacrifice *(homa)* and this remains a common element among all surviving strands of Vajrayāna in Nepal, Tibet, Mongolia, Japan, and Indonesia.

The Seven-Part Worship. With the rise of the Mahāyāna came a new understanding of *pūjā*. Behind almost all Mahāyāna and Vajrayāna *pūjās* is the Seven-Part Worship *(saptāṅgapūjā)*, a framework for worship that is presaged in the second century *Ajātaśatru-kaukṛtya-vinodanā* and crystallized in the *Bhadracaryā-praṇidhāna*, the vows of Samāntabhadra. This is an undated poem, still recited by Newar priests today, and it became the final chapter of the much larger fourth century text *Gandhavyūha.* Here, the structure of the Seven-Part Worship is as follows:

1. Praise (*vandanā*).
2. Worship (*pūjā*).
3. Confession of misdeeds (*pāpadeśanā*).
4. Taking delight in the good deeds of others (*anumodanā*).
5. Requesting the buddhas (and their successors) to teach (*adhyeṣaṇā*).
6. Begging the buddhas (and their successors) to remain in the world (*yācana*).
7. Dedicating the merit arising from this *pūjā* (*pariṇāmaṇā*).

The elements of the Seven-Part Worship can vary in number as well as order. Arousing the mind of awakening *(bodhicitotpāda)* is part of the ritual in both the earlier *Ajātaśatru-kaukṛtya-vinodanā* and in the later *Bodhicaryāvatāra* of Śāntideva, who also inserts going for refuge to the Three Jewels *(śaraṇagāmanā).* However flexible, the Seven-Part Worship forms a basic liturgy for the subsequent tradition.

Further rituals in Indic Buddhism. In high Indic Mahāyāna/Vajrayāna, such as is found among the Newar and Tibetan schools, Buddhist *pūjās* have developed a modularity reminiscent of Vedic ritual. For Newar Vajrayāna priests, the most basic *pūjā* is the Guru Maṇḍala *Pūjā,* and indeed the successful performance of this *pūjā* is part of the initiation of a Vajrcārya priest. Larger rituals, such as marriages, initiations, or guiding clients through the worship of the Bodhisattva Amoghapāśa all begin with the Guru Maṇḍala *Pūjā* but add more complex visualizations and the worship of other maṇḍalas. Medieval Indic visualization compendia such as the *Sādhanamālā* and the indigenous Tibetan or Newar works that follow them often begin with an abbreviated reference to the Seven-Part Worship and perhaps a suggestion of prior rituals to be completed before the main work of the visualization. Finally, mention should be made of the *gcod* offering, a development of the *pūjā* ritual influenced by Tibetan funerary practices. Here the practitioner, through a terrifying meditation in which she offers up her own body, senses, and life, uses *pūjā* as a means to sacrifice attachment to the self.

SEE ALSO Relics; Stupa Worship; Worship and Devotional Life, articles on Buddhist Devotional Life in East Asia, Buddhist Devotional Life in Southeast Asia, and Buddhist Devotional Life in Tibet.

BIBLIOGRAPHY

Gellner, David N. "Ritualized Altruism, Devotion and Meditation: The Offering of the Guru Maṇḍala in Newar Buddhism." *Indo-Iranian Journal* 34 (1991): 161–197.

Śāntideva. *The Bodhicaryāvatāra.* Translated by Kate Crosby and Andrew Skilton. Oxford, 1996.

Suzuki, D. T., and Hokei Idzumi. *Gaṇḍavyūha.* Kyoto, Japan, 1934.

Trainor, Kevin. *Relics, Ritual and Representation in Buddhism: Rematerializing the Sri Lankan Theravada Tradition.* Cambridge, U.K., 1997.

Tuladhar-Douglas, William. *Remaking Buddhism for Medieval Nepal.* London, 2005.

Walshe, Maurice. *The Long Discourses of the Buddha.* Boston, 1995.

WILLIAM TULADHAR-DOUGLAS (2005)

PUNISHMENT SEE HEAVEN AND HELL; JUDGMENT OF THE DEAD; REVENGE AND RETRIBUTION

PURĀṆAS are extensive compendiums of the mythohistory of Bhāratvarṣa (the earlier name of the Indian subcontinent). They participate in the same mythological milieu as epic (*itihāsa*) and poetic (*kāvya*) works, but they are structured as exhaustive amalgams of epic lore seen through particular (some would say sectarian) perspectives. The Purāṇas may be thought of as core texts of Hindu religiosity; some have become cornerstones of particular devotional traditions, and others have served as templates for institutions, social observances, and traditions of secular knowledge.

The word *purāṇa* itself means "ancient," and a good deal of Purāṇic lore may have coexisted with the Vedas themselves. *Purāṇa* appears in the *Ṛgveda* (where it means "ancient") and is used in a sacrificial context in the *Atharvaveda* and the *Śatapatha Brāhmaṇa,* leading scholars such as R. C. Hazra (1940) to suggest that the Purāṇas originated as narrative portions of the Vedic sacrifice. In early Upaniṣads, Purāṇas are spoken of along with the Vedas as texts of divine origin and are also referred to (with the epic narratives) as a type of fifth Veda. Along with the epics, they gradually came to form a vast textual base of sacred cultural memory.

On a textual-critical level, the enormity and diversity of these narratives, the extensive oral tradition from which they derive, the layering of variant materials through time, and the sectarian claims made on specific works have made the Purāṇic materials difficult to fully catalog or comprehend. The effort by the All-India Kashiraj Trust to publish critical editions of the eighteen principal Purāṇas has proven daunting. Issues of textual criticism are further complicated by the lack of agreement as to what a Purāṇa actually is, because numerous works bear the said name, and none of the conventional classifications of these texts can be called definitive. An early datable definition is found in the sixth-century lexicon *Amarakośa,* which identifies *purāṇa* as that which has five characteristics (*pañcalakṣaṇa*): *sarga* (creation); *pratisarga* (recreation of the universe after its dissolution); *vaṃśa* (genealogies of gods, sages, kings, and patriarchs); *manvantara* (cyclic ages of humanity presided over by Manu, the father of humanity); and *vaṃśānucaritam* (royal dynastic histories). Although the Purāṇas all contain variations on these themes, none of them literally follows this definition, because the *pañcalakṣaṇa* materials only make up a small percentage of their volume. Other topics covered include the *puruṣārthas* or "aims of humanity" (*dharma,* "sacred duty"; *artha* "material power"; *kāma,* "pleasure"; and *mokṣa,* "ultimate freedom"), religious observances, pilgrimage, charitable offerings, rites for the dead, the glorification of various divinities, descriptions of cycles of time, cosmographies of space (including graphic images of heavens and hells), philosophy and doctrinal expositions, sacraments, and social duties as well as treatises on yoga, sacrifice, and other spiritual practices.

A list of eighteen Mahāpurāṇas (Great Purāṇas) existed in the time of the Arabian traveler al-Bīrūnī (973–1048), who cites two somewhat different versions of it. The traditionally accepted list, often named after the principal narrator of the work, is as follows:

1. *Brahma* (or *Ādi,* first)
2. *Padma* (Lotus)
3. *Viṣṇu* ("all-pervading" deity)
4. *Vāyu* (deity of the wind)
5. *Bhāgavata* (Kṛṣṇa)
6. *Nārada* (sage son of Brahmā)
7. *Mārkaṇḍeya* (great sage)
8. *Agni* (Vedic fire deity)
9. *Bhaviṣya* (future)
10. *Brahmavaivarta* (transformation of Brahmā)
11. *Liṅga* (symbol of Śiva)
12. *Varāha* (Viṣṇu as a boar)
13. *Skanda* (god of war and son of Śiva)
14. *Vāmana* (Viṣṇu as a *brahman* dwarf)
15. *Kūrma* (Viṣṇu as a tortoise)
16. *Matsya* (Viṣṇu as a fish)
17. *Garuḍa* (Viṣṇu's bird carrier)
18. *Brahmāṇḍa* (the egg of Brahmā)

These eighteen Mahāpurāṇas, said to contain a total of 400,000 verses, are attributed to the divine sage Vyāsa, who is said have arranged the revealed material (along with the Vedas and epics) and transmitted them to disciples who further elaborated upon them.

This narrative of authorship, the occurrence of the word *purāṇa* in the singular in a number of early works, and the scholarly tradition of a search for origins led a number of scholars to promote the notion of there being an original *purāṇa* that gradually was expanded and elaborated upon. The Purāṇas themselves, however, contain numerous and variant versions of their authorship (divine and human) and seem to accommodate multiperspectives of origin and meaning. This would be consistent with their derivation from a vast oral tradition and would suggest that the very idea of their being "books," as Ludo Rocher (1986) has argued, may be more a product of manuscript codification between the fourth and tenth centuries and later textual critical traditions than Purāṇic ones.

Various traditions have classified and continue to classify Purāṇas in a number of ways: devotionally, according to the main deity they glorify; qualitatively, according to the said quality (*guṇa*) of nature they participate in (*sattva,* "purity-being"; *rajas,* "passion"; *tamas,* "dark inertia"); chronologically; by subject; and by the number of major revisions, particularly from different doctrinal standpoints.

Along with various lists of Mahāpurāṇas, there are Upapurāṇas, or shorter Purāṇas of supposedly later composition and more particular focus. Another Purāṇic literature is called a Māhātmya, which is a text (usually attached to a Purāṇa) that glorifies a divinity, a place of pilgrimage, or a ritual offering. There are also works known as Sthalapurāṇas, which are connected with specific localities, giving rise to the idea that every place may have had a Purāṇa of its own, rich with legendary history, and which may or may not be written down. Vaṃśapurāṇas (sometimes called Caste Purāṇas) devote themselves to the history of a lineage or particular social group. And finally, an enormous number of Purāṇic translations and derivative works exist in regional languages. These too are Purāṇas, especially when one considers how the regional traditions, local legends, and sensibilities of one area can become absorbed, "brahamanized," and reconstituted as part of a Mahāpurāṇa.

PURĀṆIC NARRATIVE. The Sanskrit of the Purāṇas is similar to epic Sanskrit, but it shows a *Prakrit* influence and frequent grammatical irregularities, leading some scholars to speculate on their local origins and subsequent brahmanical appropriation. The *Bhāgavata,* as the most Sanskritized and literary-conscious Purāṇa, may be an exception here, or it may be the most obvious example of the above process.

Within the major Purāṇic literatures there is a significant diversity of style: *Agni, Garuḍa,* and *Nārada* are primarily encyclopedic compendiums; *Padma, Skanda,* and *Bhaviṣya* deal largely with places of pilgrimage; *Vāmana* and *Mārkaṇḍeya* pay a good deal of attention to doctrinal concerns; and *Vāyu* and *Brahmāṇḍa* are concerned with history. Within this great variety, however, certain common narrative styles and sensibilities can be observed.

What kinds of stories do the Purāṇas tell? Not original ones, or ones set down by a single author; they are collections that have been passed down through the ages. These narratives often begin with a scene at the celebrated snake sacrifice of King Janamejaya, where sages have gathered in the Naimiṣa forest. The sages ask a *sūta* or bard, who is spoken of as a "holder of knowledge of the ancient lore," to narrate what he has heard, and so begins a series of dialogues within dialogues, in which narrators refer to other narrations that took place in other times and places. This technique of multinarrative frames is significant in its free-associative mythopoetic sensibility. Information is always contextualized within a particular situation. Hence whereas a Purāṇa is an admittedly collaborative retelling of the epic past, it may be filled with variants, with different versions of a particular tale appearing in the same text. Looked at historically, one sees a developing tradition quite unlike that of the fixed Vedic *mantras*. Looked at through its own narrative logic, one may see this style as a most authentic mode of mythmaking, not "myth" in the sense of something false but as a sacred narrative that imaginatively transmits that which is most dear to a culture.

SIGNIFICANCE OF THE PURĀṆAS. Whether or not the Purāṇas can ultimately claim the same revelatory power or priestly status as the Vedas or whether they were arranged by Vyāsa or edited by priests in order to absorb local cults and practices under a normative brahmanical fold, their widespread influence and importance is undeniable. The *Devībhāgavata* puts it thus: "*Śruti* and *smṛti* are the two eyes of *dharma* but the Purāṇa is its heart" (XI.1.21).

This heart, however, was often ignored or debunked by nineteenth-century ideologues who saw them as a corruption of Vedic religion and by Western scholarship that devalued them as "pseudo-histories" displaying masses of superstitious contradictions. With the emergence of scholarship acknowledging the important psychological and cultural value of myth, however, the Purāṇic world is seen not only as a storehouse of information about the emergence of Hindu India but as the imagistic and narrative revelation of a profoundly imaginative and sophisticated worldview.

The importance of this body of discourse is thus manifold. In devotional religious terms, Purāṇas often champion the superiority of a particular divinity (although their devotion to one god does not necessarily exclude others). Moreover their eclectic and all-encompassing characters have allowed them to serve as a major medium for the transmission of customs and traditions, for long-held ideas around geography, politics, and social organization, and for the subjects of astronomy, medicine, grammar, metrics, architecture, poetics, divination, and a host of others. They are indispensable for understanding popular Hindu traditions and their formation and for the grand narratives that have shaped Indian religious sensibilities.

PURĀṆIC HISTORY. Dating Purāṇas and seeking their origins have been preoccupations of Western orientalist scholarship, although their composite nature resists chronological specificity. Moreover the fluid Purāṇic notion of "textuality" presents problems, because texts were transmitted orally, frequently elaborated upon, and often changed. There have been numerous speculations about the existence of an original Purāṇa, which expanded into the others. One hypothesis attempted to chronologically date the Purāṇas in terms of increasing complexity, seeing their various layers of discourse like the rings of a tree, but the reverse hypothesis has also been offered. The *Prākrit* aspect of their language has caused some scholars to see them as originally non-*brahman* works, reappropriated in reaction to the heterodox schools of the Buddhists and Jains. Others have suggested that the Purāṇas appeared as a result of an effort to provide each Vedic school with a text of its own, whereas another view sees them as developing from many local works within specific parts of India.

The Purāṇic vision of narrating events that occurred in "the distant past" often takes the form of dynastic histories (*Vāyu*, *Matsya*, *Viṣṇu*, *Brahma*), and although their history has been disparaged by many, some European scholars (Hermann Jacobi, for example) found a "genuine and valuable historical tradition" in the Purāṇas. F. E. Pargiter (1922) championed their historicity and attempted to reconstruct what he considered the "ancient Indian historical tradition" from Purāṇic sources. The issue as to whether or not such sources can be used to reconstruct ancient history is almost impossible to answer. What one can do, however, is work to understand the intrinsic sensibility of the Purāṇic "past" as a paradigm for the present that can provide cultural visions and ideals. Long-standing narratives, such as the churning of the milky ocean, the childhood pranks of Kṛṣṇa, the great Bhārata War, the exploits of the *avatāras* of Viṣṇu, the awesome influence of great places of pilgrimage, and the divinities, saintly kings, and sages whose lives shine through eons of time, are very much alive and well in the Hindu religious imagination.

TIME AND SPACE. In contrast to Western teleological sensibilities, Indian thinking as exemplified in the Purāṇas envisions time as cyclical. The four ages or *yugas* (*kṛta* or *satya*, *treta*, *dvāpara*, and *kali*), whose names are the same as those of the throws of dice, are said to repeat themselves in declining order. The *Bhāgavata Purāṇa* speaks of the sacred law (*dharma*) as a cow possessed of four feet (austerity, cleanliness, mercy, and truthfulness), losing one after another in each declining age. The duration of the *yugas* is said to be 4,800, 3,600, 2,400, and 1,200 years of the *devas* (gods), with a dawn and twilight preceding and following each age. These 12,000 divine years are converted into human years when multiplied by 360, so the *kaliyuga*, for example, would last for 432,000 earth years. While some texts speak of world dissolutions at the end of a cycle of four ages, the majority of Purāṇas depict a thousand successive *yuga* cycles composing a day of Brahmā, or a *kalpa*, followed by the dissolution of the world, and a night of Brahmā, which is as long as his day. This entire system of days and nights is repeated for the lifetime of Brahmā, which endures for a hundred years, followed by another dissolution and the beginning of a new cycle.

Alongside of this cyclic system is one of fourteen *manvantaras*, each presided over by a different Manu, who is the progenitor of humanity. Most Purāṇas set the length of a *manvantara* as seventy-one *yugas*, which leaves unaccounted for time and hence the speculation that two separate traditions were grafted together. The present age is said to be that of the seventh Manu and is described in all the Purāṇas as one of chaos and confusion.

Purāṇas offer vast spatial as well as temporal cosmologies, such as the one of infinite universes expanding and contracting from the pores of the great breathing Viṣṇu, who rests upon Anantaśeṣa, the endless world serpent. In some texts a world egg is said to be at the center of a greater universe, surrounded by the five elements (earth, water, fire, air, and space), containing seven continents and oceans (including oceans of milk, sugarcane juice, and wine), seven higher planetary systems, and seven lower ones arranged around a central axis, Mount Meru, along with a series of heavens and hells. This Purāṇic universe is populated by a vast array of beings, including animals, humans, demons of the netherworlds, and a variety of divine and semidivine beings, including tree spirits (*yakṣas*), celestial musicians (*gandharvas*), nymphs (*āpsaras*), and subterranean serpents (*nāgas*) with luminous jewels on their heads.

THE RELIGION OF THE PURĀṆAS. There is no single religion of the Purāṇas, just as there is no one religious tradition of India, but religiosity is a primary characteristic of Purāṇic tradition. The complex religious narratives and discussions in the Purāṇas serve as the basis for a large variety of rituals, devotional liturgies, sacred dramas and poems, and *sādhanas* or spiritual practices. Again there is no one philosophical position that the texts take, but they combine theistic and nontheistic perspectives, *saṁkhya* cosmologies in which the world is seen as a challenging combination of matter and consciousness, yogic and meditative practices, and *bhakti* or loving devotion toward a personal divinity.

While one finds devotion to a number of deities, including Brahmā, whose cults have disappeared, Viṣṇu, Śiva, and Devī dominate the tradition. Yoga and ascetic traditions are generally associated with Śaivism, whereas *bhakti* or devotional ones are associated with Vaiṣṇavism. Śākta traditions that worship the Goddess in a number of forms, as well as Tantric traditions of immanent awareness and working with the elements of the phenomenal world, are also found in the Purāṇas.

Śiva. Śiva, known as Mahādeva, the "Great God," is described as the one with a thousand forms, whose breath causes creation, preservation, and destruction. In other texts Śiva is identified as the cause of all causes and as the one appearing in many forms, including one that is half male and half female (*ardhanarīśvara*), and as manifest in twenty-eight specific forms. As the Lord of Yoga, Śiva sits forever rapt in meditation. He also maintains a household relationship with his consort, the goddess Pārvartī. This tension between his ascetic and erotic natures, as noted by Wendy Doniger (1993), is the subject of numerous narratives, as is the relatively antisocial nature of Śiva, who is covered in ash and draped with serpents. Many Purāṇas recount narratives of the births and activities of the divine children of Śiva and Pārvartī, Skanda, the god of war, and the elephant-headed Gaṇeśa, the lord of obstacles. Śiva's great sign is the *liṅga*, a primordial phallic-looking form that signifies potency and divine power. The *Liṅga Purāṇa*, a most important text for the workshop of Śiva, discusses the *liṅga* as a supreme symbol of absolute reality.

Devī. Śakti, the divine feminine force, invoked under 1,008 names in the *Kūrma Purāṇa* (1.11) is often associated with Śiva. In other texts (*Devībhāgavata, Devīmāhātmya, Mārkaṇḍeya Purāṇa*), however, the Great Goddess is worshipped as the Supreme Being.

The supremacy of the Goddess, who is created from the combined potency of all the gods, is portrayed in the celebrated story of the defeat of the Buffalo Demon, Mahiṣa. The *Devīmāhātmya*, the first full-scale Sanskrit account of this narrative, which extends through various modalities throughout India, is part of the *Mārkaṇḍeya Purāṇa*. Although the Goddess is one, she is known by many names that indicate her different aspects and qualities, including Caṇḍikā ("Angry"), Ambikā ("Mother"), Nārāyaṇī ("Resting Place of Men"), Kālī ("Dark"), Bhagavatī ("Beneficent"), Durgā ("Protectress"), Vaiṣṇavī ("Related to Viṣṇu"), Gaurī ("Golden"), Lakṣmī ("Fortune"), and Śakti ("Potency").

The *Devībhāgavata* propounds the Śākta polemic that unlike other *mārgas*, or spiritual paths that demand renunciation as a prerequisite for spiritual attainment, the goddess offers worldly enjoyment (*bhukti*) along with liberation (*mukti*). As the mother of all beings, the Goddess sees no reason to deprive her devotees of anything. Hence, through her grace, she offers both to devotees, who simply need to acknowledge her as the source of all.

Viṣṇu. Glorified as the Supreme Being and as Creator but usually as the preserver and sustainer of the universe, Viṣṇu is envisioned as the all-pervading spirit and is worshipped with devotion. One of the most striking features of the Purāṇas devoted to Viṣṇu is the notion of *avatāras*, incarnations of Viṣṇu who descended into the world to accomplish particular missions. The lists of the *avatāras* are many, as are the variant concepts about them. There is a generally accepted list of ten principal avatars. Matsya (fish) appeared to rescue Manu, the seven sages, and the seeds of all existing beings from the rising waters and in the *Bhāgavata Purāṇa* is said to have saved the Vedas after they had sunk into the ocean of dissolution. This particular story has attracted a good deal of scholarly attention due to similarities with flood narratives from other cultures.

The appearance of Kūrma, the tortoise incarnation, revolves around the major Purāṇic legend of the churning of the milky ocean in which *devas* and *auras*, gods and demons, use the serpent Vāsuki as a rope for a tug-of-war in which the great Mount Mandara is churned on the tortoise's back. As the ocean is churned, deadly poison emerges and is drunk by the god Śiva (who is hence called Nīlakaṇṭa or "the blue throated one"). A series of treasures then emerges from the ocean, culminating in an elixir of immortality, which is spirited away from the *auras* by Mohinī ("the beguiling one"), a female incarnation of Viṣṇu.

Varāha, the boar incarnation, appears to save the earth, which had been thrown down to the muddy bottom of the universe by the demon Hiraṇyākṣa. The notion of Viṣṇu appearing in animal forms is believed by some scholars to indicate the incorporation of earlier cults, while others see this phenomenon as an evolutive progression, mirroring the development of an embryo in the womb.

Narasiṁha ("man-lion") delivers the world from the powerful demon Hiraṇyakaśipu, who sought immortality by receiving boons from the gods to be neither killed indoors nor outdoors, by human nor beast, by day nor night, nor by any weapon. Viṣṇu, appearing in a man-lion form, kills the demon at twilight, on a porch and with his long nails, and rescues his devotee, Prahlāda, as Hiraṇyakaśipu's son. As in many Purāṇic narratives, the demonic mentality is portrayed as being desirous of immortality through egotism and power, a project that ultimately fails.

The above incarnations are said to appear in the *kṛta yuga.* In the next age (*treta*), Viṣṇu appears as the *brahman* dwarf, Vāmana, before the demon king Bali, who had acquired dominion over the three worlds, and asks Bali for a boon of three steps. Assuming a huge form, Vāmana covers the entire universe and deprives Bali of his sovereignty while restoring order to the world.

Paraśurāma (Rāma with an ax), a brutal avatar, rids the world of the errant *kṣatriya* race twenty-one times over. Rāma, the epitome of righteousness, appears in Purāṇic narratives not as a human king but as a divine incarnation of Viṣṇu. The *avatāra* of Kṛṣṇa is celebrated in the *Viṣṇu Purāṇa* and *Bhāgavata Purāṇa* as the supreme cause of all causes. His eternal consort, Rādha, perhaps hinted at in the *Bhāgavata,* is present in the *Brahmaivrta Purāṇa.* The celebrated tenth book of the *Bhāgavata Purāṇa* recounts the childhood and youth of Kṛṣṇa in stories that have been canonized by *bhakti* traditions, serving as the bases for poems, plays, and stories in regional languages throughout the subcontinent.

The *kali* age is said to begin with Kṛṣṇa's disappearance. Buddha appears later in this period as an *avatāra* of Viṣṇu preaching "heresy" to delude atheists and end the slaughter of animals. The addition of Buddha, whose doctrines pitted him against the *brahman* class, to this list marks a process known as *Sanskritization,* through which various deities and regional traditions are absorbed into the normative one. The final avatar of Viṣṇu, Kalki, will appear on a horse, bearing a sword, and will destroy all the demonic elements that have taken over the earth at the end of the *kali* age.

Within the variety of Purāṇic narratives of the various forms of the divine is the idea that the entire physical manifestation is an illusion, an appearance that is ultimately unreal, for the one reality, the *brahman* alone, is real. This supreme *brahman* is identified with different gods (usually Śiva, Viṣṇu, or Devī) as well as with the self (*ātman*) in all beings in different Purāṇic texts. In some Purāṇas *brahman* is envisioned in a more dualistic sense as substantively alike but qualitatively different from the individual self. Hence to say that the Purāṇas are monistic or dualistic are partial visions, leading a number of theologians to put forth the idea of "inconceivably one and many." Nevertheless the Purāṇas are not always tolerant of the "many," with Vaiṣṇava- and Śaivaite-based Purāṇas frequently criticizing one another in the most severe terms.

Along with discussions of yoga and meditative *sādhanas,* Purāṇic devotional tracts contain chapters discussing images of worship or *mūrtis.* The word *mūrti* means "embodiment," and the worship, consecration, and installation of divine images involve specific rules and procedures. The worship of images, hymns of praise to various gods, and the practices of hearing and remembering the *līlās,* or plays of gods on earth, are all aspects of the *bhakti* tradition that comes to the fore in the Purāṇas. *Bhakti,* or "loving devotion," develops strongly in the Purāṇas and may well reflect cultural and social changes in Hindu traditions that were reconfigurating their relationship with brahmanical ceremony and ritual.

FUTURE OF THE PURĀṆAS. Purāṇas continue to emerge through contemporary translations in regional languages, including English, through ritual recitations and public performances, and through new innovative forms that continue to shape Hindu traditions. Cultures evolve and change by reconsidering their pasts. And indeed this is what a Purāṇa is, in its largest sense. Rather than seeing Purāṇas only as relics of medieval culture, one can understand them as the matrix of myth that people return to again and again to find new meaning through stories that draw contemporary attention even as they speak of what happened long ago.

SEE ALSO Avatāra; Indian Religions, article on Mythic Themes.

BIBLIOGRAPHY

Critically edited texts of the Mahāpurāṇas are available through the All-India Kashiraj Trust, including the *Garuḍa, Kurma, Vāmana,* and *Varāha.* Many texts and translations are also available through Motilal Banarsidass Indological Publishers in Delhi, including the *Agni, Bhāgavata, Brahmāṇḍa, Brahmavaivarta, Liṅga,* and *Nārada.* The *Bhaviṣya, Brahmā, Mārkaṇḍeya, Matsya, Padma, Skanda, Vāyu,* and *Viṣṇu* are all translated and available in older versions.

There are a number of valuable secondary sources and studies of Purāṇas available. These include Cheever Mackenzie Brown, *The Triumph of the Goddess: The Canonical Models and Theological Visions of the Devī Bhāgavata Purāṇa* (Albany, N.Y., 1990); Thomas Coburn, *The Devī Māhātmya: The Crystallization of the Goddess Tradition* (Delhi, 1988); V. R. Ramachandra Dikshitar, *The Purana Index* (Delhi, 1995); Cornelia Dimmitt and J. A. B. Van Buitenen, eds. and trans.,

Classical Hindu Mythology: A Reader in the Sanskrit Purāṇas (Philadelphia, 1978; reprint, Delhi, 1988); Wendy Doniger, ed., *Purāṇa Perennis: Reciprocity and Transformation in Hindu and Jain texts* (Albany, N.Y., 1993); R. C. Hazra, *Studies in the Purāṇic Records on Hindu Rites and Customs* (Dhaka, Bangladesh, 1940; reprint, Delhi, 1987); E. H. Rick Jarow, *Tales for the Dying: The Death Narrative of the Bhāgavata-Purāṇa* (Albany, N.Y., 2003); Willibald Kirfel, *Das Purāṇa Pañcalakṣaṇa: Versuch einer Textgeschichte* (Bonn, Germany, 1927); F. E. Pargiter, *Ancient Indian Historical Tradition* (London, 1922; reprint, Delhi, 1969); Ludo Rocher, *The Purāṇas: A History of Indian Literature,* vol. 2., fasc. 3 (Weisbaden, Germany, 1986); and P. Flam et al., eds., and Heinrich von Stietencrom et al., comps., *Epic and Purāṇic Bibliography (up to 1985): Annotated and with Indexes* (Weisbaden, Germany, 1992).

E. H. RICK JAROW (2005)

PURE AND IMPURE LANDS. In Mahāyāna Buddhism, a "Pure Land" is a purified land where buddhas and *bodhisattvas*, the future buddhas, dwell. In contrast, the realms inhabited by ordinary sentient beings are called "Impure Lands," for they are tainted by blind passion.

In Chinese Buddhism, two technical terms, *jingtu* and *huitu*, are used to refer to Pure and Impure Lands, respectively. The concept behind these terms, however, is attested to in Indian Buddhist texts by such terms as *buddhakṣetra-pariśuddhi* ("the purification of the buddha land") or *pariśuddhaṃ buddhakṣetram* ("purified buddha land"), as in the *Aṣṭasāhasrikā-prajñāpāramitā Sūtra* (edited by Rajendralala Mitra, Calcutta, 1888, pp. 362–363), and *apariśuddhaṃ buddhakṣetram* ("unpurified buddha land") or *kliṣṭaṃ buddhakṣetram* ("tainted buddha land"), as in the *Karuṇāpuṇḍarīka Sūtra* (edited by Yamada Isshi, London, 1968; vol. 2, pp. 52, 81). It was in accordance with such usage that *jingtu* and *huitu* were established in Chinese as technical terms.

The notion of a "buddha land" (Skt., *buddhakṣetra*; Pali, *buddhakkhetta*) derives from the period of early Buddhism. According to the Theravāda interpretation, the *buddhakṣetra* is the realm in which the teachings of Śākyamuni Buddha prevail. However, in Mahāyāna Buddhism numerous buddha lands are said to exist in order to accommodate the numerous *bodhisattvas* who become buddhas; or rather, the merit accumulated by these *bodhisattvas* through their long spiritual careers goes toward creating a purified realm responsive to their influence. In other words, because of the basic Buddhist premise that no two buddhas can preside over the same Buddha land, the "new" buddhas are forced to emerge, as it were, in lands far distant from that of Śākyamuni, which is called the Sahā Land. These are located variously in the ten directions (the eight points of the compass, the zenith, and the nadir) of the cosmos. It is among these "distant" Pure Lands, described as "numberless as the sands of the River Ganges," that we find Amitābha (Amitāyus) Buddha's Sukhāvatī (to the west), Akṣobhya's Abhirati (to the east), and Bhaiṣajyaguruvaiḍūryaprabha's Vaiḍūryanirbhāsā (also to the east).

The best-known of these Pure Lands is Sukhāvatī. This Pure Land is described in detail in three sūtras, the *Larger Sukhāvatīvyuha Sūtra,* the *Smaller Sukhāvatīvyuha Sūtra,* and the *Guan Wuliangshou jing.* Of these, the first two *Sūtras* are believed to have been compiled in northwest India around 100 CE. Modern scholarship is in general agreement, however, that the main body of the *Kuan ching* was compiled in Central Asia, and that accretions were made during the course of its translation into Chinese. But while the conditions surrounding the compilation of these sūtras differ, all three texts share in depicting the splendor of the Pure Land and the majestic appearances of Amitābha (Amitāyus) and his disciples and attending *bodhisattvas*. These depictions undoubtedly reflect ideal perceptions of the buddha land, buddhas, and *bodhisattvas* of the period when each of the sūtras was compiled. The ideal depiction of Sukhāvatī can be viewed as a symbolic and hypostatized representation of Mahāyāna Buddhist enlightenment. A Pure Land is a "purified land," that is, a realm that came into existence by "purifying the land." To "purify the land" means that the Mahāyāna *bodhisattvas* purify everything in the land in which they will appear upon becoming buddhas; this "purification" includes leading all sentient beings to buddhahood. Of course, such acts entail nothing less than the fulfillment both of the *bodhisattvas*' cultivation of the *pāramitās* ("perfections") and of his vow to benefit all beings. As such, the Pure Land can be regarded as hypostatized representation of the Buddha's enlightenment. For example, even though Sukhāvatī is described as a realm that exists to the west, it is in reality a realm that transcends space. While it is said to exist beyond billions of buddha lands, this is actually nothing but a symbolic expression for infinite distance; what is originally beyond space was expressed in the context of space.

By means of such descriptions, the Pure Land sūtras succeeded in capturing the imagination of ordinary people. Consequently, the practice of contemplating the Buddha (*buddhānusmṛti*; Chin., *nianfo*), a relatively easy form of religious practice leading to birth in the Pure Land and eventual enlightenment (buddhahood) there, gained wide popularity among Buddhists. In the same vein, the name Sukhāvatī ("realm of bliss"), which originally denoted a realm of absolute religious bliss, also acquired connotations of relative, this-worldly happiness. Given its popular appeal, Sukhāvatī quickly became the object of the most dominant form of Buddhist devotion in East Asia. Hence, "Pure Land" in Chinese Buddhism came to be regarded as synonymous with Amitābha's Pure Land. In following this practice, the Japanese Buddhist sects that are based on the worship of Amitābha (Jpn., Amida) Buddha are called Jōdoshū (the Pure Land sect) and Jōdo Shinshū (the True Pure Land sect).

In Mahāyāna Buddhism there are also other kinds of Pure Lands different in nature from the "distant" Pure Lands discussed earlier. The *Vimalakīrtinirdeśa Sūtra* espouses the idea that when *bodhisattvas* purify their mind this Sahā world itself becomes a Pure Land. This view of Pure Land was advocated in China and Japan by the Chan and Zen sects respectively and led to the development of the concept of the "mind-only Pure Land." The *Lotus Sūtra* contains elements that lead some to regard Gṛdhrakūṭa—the Vulture's Peak where Śākyamuni Buddha preached the *Lotus Sūtra*—as a Pure Land. The Japanese Nichiren sect later came to view this mountain as an ideal realm and espoused the notion of "Vulture's Peak Pure Land." The *Avataṃsaka Sūtra* speaks of Vairocana's Padmagarbha, a Pure Land in which the entire world is enveloped in a lotus flower, a notion that the Chinese Huayan and Japanese Kegon sects have made an integral part of their doctrine. Finally, the *Ghandhavyūha Sūtra* speaks of a Ghandhavyūha realm. Later, the Japanese Shingon sect came to regard this realm as the Pure Land of Mahāvairocana Buddha and to identify it with our present Sahā world. In Chinese and Japanese Buddhism the Tuṣita Heaven, where the *bodhisattva* Maitreya now dwells, and the Potalaka Mountain, where the *bodhisattva* Avalokiteśvara dwells, are both sometimes referred to as Pure Lands and have been the objects of large devotional followings.

In response to such views, the *Karuṇāpuṇḍarīka Sūtra* emphasized the great compassion of Śākyamuni Buddha, who appeared in this Impure Land, rather than the buddhas of the "distant" Pure Lands such as Amitābha and Akṣobhya. This text developed in opposition to the notion of "extra-worldly" Pure Lands but never wielded much influence. The same sūtra explains that our Impure Land is characterized by the "five corruptions" (*pañca kaṣāyāḥ*: the corruptions of the times, of views, of blind passion, of sentient beings, and of life). However in later periods, especially in Japan, it became customary to explain the Impure Land as coextensive with the "six destinies" (*ṣaḍ gatayaḥ*: the destinies of hell, of hungry spirits, of beasts, of *asuras*, of humans, and of heavenly beings) as seen, for example, in Genshin's *Ōjōyōshū*. In this case also, the Impure Land was posited in contradistinction to Amida's Pure Land. Here the Impure Land was characterized as something that one grows weary of and wishes to leave behind in favor of birth in Sukhāvatī.

SEE ALSO Amitābha; Jingtu; Jōdo Shinshū; Jōdoshū.

BIBLIOGRAPHY

Fujita Kōtatsu. *Genshi jōdo shisō no kenkyū*. Tokyo, 1970. A comprehensive examination of the formation of Pure Land texts and doctrines. Contains a brief summary in English.

Suzuki, D. T. "The Development of the Pure Land Doctrine in Buddhism." *Eastern Buddhist* 3 (1925): 285–326. Reprinted in *Collected Writings on Shin Buddhism*, edited by the Eastern Buddhist Society (Kyoto, 1973), pages 3–31. Although limited in focus to Japanese Buddhism, this work provides an excellent introduction to the Pure Land tradition.

New Sources

Blum, M. L., and Gyonen. *The Origins and Development of Pure Land Buddhism: A Study and Translation of Gyonen's Jodo Homon Genrusho*. New York, 2002.

Hirota, D. *Toward a Contemporary Understanding of Pure Land Buddhism: Creating a Shin Buddhist Theology in a Religiously Plural World*. Albany, N.Y., 2000.

Nattier, Jan. "The Realm of Aksobhya: A Missing Piece in the History of Pure Land Buddhism." *Journal of the International Association of Buddhist Studies* 23, no. 1 (2000): 71–102.

Payne, R. K., and K. K. Tanaka. *Approaching the Land of Bliss: Religious Praxis in the Cult of Amitabha*. Honolulu, 2004.

Wong, D. C. *Four Sichuan Buddhist Steles and the Beginnings of Pure Land Imagery in China*. New York, 1999.

Won, U.-b., and B. H. Lim. *A History of Korean Buddhist Culture and Some Essays: The Buddhist Pure Land & the Christian Kingdom of Heaven*. Seoul, 1992.

FUJITA KŌTATSU (1987)
Translated from Japanese by Kenneth K. Tanaka
Revised Bibliography

PURIFICATION

This entry consists of the following articles:

PURIFICATION: AN OVERVIEW

Concepts of pollution and purity are found in virtually all the religions of the world. While some religions recognize subtle distinctions of relative pollution, others place less emphasis upon the social and religious categories that determine pollution. The range extends from cultures like that of the Pygmies, who place almost no emphasis on concepts of pollution and purity, to hierarchical systems like Hinduism, with its highly developed mechanisms for transforming impurity from a dangerous category to a meaningful structuring principle of the Indian cultural system.

It is impossible to understand religious pollution and purification as separate phenomena; these two inseparable categories of religious experience are locked into a dynamic complementarity. Rules governing religious pollution imply a corollary code for ameliorating the condition. The purification of religious pollution is a major religious theme because it forges a path of expiation, healing, renewal, transcendence, and reintegration, establishing harmonious triangular links among the individual, the cosmos, and the social structure.

The range of activities or events considered to be polluting is vast, and there is an equally impressive range of purification rituals. In Tibetan Buddhism, for instance, pollution may be associated with trivial situations, such as crowds where polluted persons may lurk (this deters no one from being in a crowd); or it may lead to very serious conditions of impurity, as in the case of big game hunting, when pollution can cause famine or drought (Keyes and Daniel, 1983).

While some pollution may be due to deliberate acts that violate social or religious norms, pollution may be accidental or unintended by the agent, as in the case of menstrual or death pollution. This distinction is important because the specific corrective rite of purification may differ depending on whether the state of pollution was attained deliberately or accidentally. Shintō, for instance, is permeated with purification rites that can be traced back to origin myths according to which the god Susano-o committed offenses against the divine order through ignorance and error. Consequently, in the Shintō religion general rites of purification must be performed periodically to resacralize the world. This contrasts with more specific occasions for purification rites, which are associated with the deliberate breaking of taboos by individuals.

Virtually all aspects of life may be surrounded by notions of pollution and purity. Not only must sins and devils be purged in annual purification ceremonies celebrated as rites of renewal; pollution rules are also applied to the ordinary products of human physiology, regulating human behavior in relation to contact with blood, vomit, excreta, cooked foods, hair clippings, and so on. The critical rites of passage associated with major transitions in life (birth, adolescence, marriage, and death) are usually governed by rules of pollution and purity, since these are times when humans are most vulnerable to attacks by evil spirits. There is no clear pattern of cross-cultural uniformity in these concepts of pollution and purity; in some societies menstruation or death may be considered especially dangerous and surrounded with elaborate rites of purification, while other cultures particularly fear pollution from eating certain foods or from contact with members of lower classes. Yet, despite this cultural diversity, there remain a number of consistent patterns that yield important insights about the nature of religious experience.

The literature on religion is replete with concern about the symbolism of purification. Nineteenth-century figures like James G. Frazer, Robertson Smith, Émile Durkheim, and Lucien Lévy-Bruhl attempted in various ways to explain principles of defilement and purification in primitive religions. Anthropologists of religion in the early twentieth century paid little attention to the subject. However, field work among African cultures and in South Asia during the 1960s challenged anthropologists to develop theoretical explanations for the increasingly complex data associated with concepts of pollution and purity in the cognitive structures of different religions. In 1966 Mary Douglas presented her extensive analysis of the topic in the classic volume *Purity and Danger.* That same year Louis Dumont published his controversial treatment of pollution and purity norms in Hinduism under the title *Homo Hierarchicus.* Since that time, symbolic anthropologists, structuralists, and religion specialists have elaborated on this theme in many different religions and cultures.

Purity and Danger is a landmark in the study of religious symbolism because it systematizes divergent information in an elegant analytical framework. For Mary Douglas, religious pollution is a property of the "betwixt and between" in human cultures; whatever falls between the social categories developed by human religious systems to comprehend and impute a sense of order and reality is considered to be impure (Parker, 1983). The concepts of pollution and purity in a particular religion make no sense without reference to a total structure of thought. Thus, along with other scholars, Douglas emphasizes the analysis of rituals and sacred texts in order to reveal semantic categories that determine mechanisms by which different peoples divide the world into domains of relative pollution or purity. Fortunately, this more systematic approach to purification has restored the concept as a major theme in the study of world religions.

Forms of Religious Pollution. The range of human activities related to religious pollution is immense. However, it is possible to isolate three general categories of pollution associated with (1) bodily functions, (2) social bonding, and (3) the maintenance of boundaries of the "holy" or "sacred." The categories of pollution presented here are artificial devices developed to facilitate analysis; they are not meant as descriptive categories to characterize the phenomenon. It should be remembered that these categories overlap and form a continuum, and that emphasis on different sorts of pollution varies greatly from one religio-cultural context to another.

Pollution associated with bodily functions. Ideas about dirt are linked into complex symbolic systems in virtually every society. One of the most widespread concepts of pollution is associated with emissions from the human body. Urine and feces are particularly impure, partly because of their odor, but also due to their more general association with putrefaction and death. In India, the left hand, used for cleansing after defecation, is forbidden to be used when touching other people or sacred objects. Other bodily secretions, such as saliva, vomit, menstrual blood, and afterbirth, are also considered to have polluting qualities. In some traditions, even sperm is polluting outside the sanctified context of marriage. All of these bodily excretions have social significance; they are usually surrounded with heavy ritualization to ensure that they will be contained within a specific religious, cultural, temporal, or spatial context. Since they are natural physiological functions, the resulting pollution is focused not on preventing their occurrence but rather on providing boundaries for control and purification.

Anything that enters the human body may be a source of pollution. Thus, air, liquid, and food are potentially polluting agents that must be carefully controlled. Contamination by polluted food is a widespread danger, involving elaborate rules of avoidance. In some religions, dietary laws are very strict. Orthodox Judaism, with its emphasis on kosher foods, carefully articulated in the Hebrew scriptures, sets the Jews apart as a holy people who are considered to be clean and consequently prepared to receive the blessings of God, along with the heavy responsibilities that accompany this covenant. Hindus are also known for their strict dietary laws. The ascendent principle operative in Hinduism is the concept of *ahiṃsā* ("nonviolence"). Hindu dietary laws stress pure vegetarianism as an ideal. Pollution from food intake, particularly meat, has serious consequences. Thus, the highest castes strive to be strict vegetarians, while meat is allowable only to lower castes and untouchables.

In many parts of the world, food is carefully preserved to avoid putrefaction. Food must be protected from contact with impure persons who can transmit their contamination to it. Thus, in many societies menstruating women, sick people, and the lower classes are prohibited from involvement in the preparation of foods. Nobles, priests, and other persons of high status are particularly vulnerable to food pollution. Due to their magnified social visibility and influence, they must be especially vigilant to avoid pollution through careful control of food intake. While most food in rural Greece is prepared by women, men cook meals to be consumed on ceremonial occasions because they are not tainted by women's general pollution. India has an extensive system of strict rules of avoidance about interdining between different castes; the leftovers of higher castes may be consumed by lower castes, but the reverse results in contamination.

Bodily pollution, in its most extreme form, results in illness or even death. Before the emergence of the germ theory to account for biotic disorders, illnesses were universally explained as the invasion of evil spirits, the curse of the evil eye, or the result of broken taboos. Even in modern societies, illnesses may be attributed to spiritual causes. Elaborate rituals to ward off pollution from evil spirits that cause human sickness are found throughout the world. Among the Inuit (Eskimo), illness was attributed to pollution associated with breaking taboos. The shaman entered a trance, then took a spiritual journey to the abode of the goddess Sedna under the sea; there he would ask her to forgive the sins of his people. This ritual act involved confessions by community members, resulting in the possibility of a cure. The Indian goddess of smallpox, Sitala, could be angered easily and subsequently needed to be "cooled" through various rituals of purification. The innocent, the vulnerable, the aged, and those individuals who have transgressed religious and social norms are all potential victims of illness. It is widely believed that the human body can best be equipped to fight illnesses by avoiding pollution, such as the ingestion of unclean foods, contact with menstrual blood, the performance of prohibited sexual relations, neglect of proper rituals to placate deities, and lack of bodily cleanliness.

Pollution and social bonding. The intense socialization of natural bodily functions is another aspect of purification. Birth, adolescence, marriage, and death are linked to physiological stages that are highly controlled and ritualized to ensure protection from the dangers of pollution. These life crisis events demarcate major points of transition, critical both for individuals and the community. Failure to attain these transitions would threaten the survival of human culture.

The danger of childbirth is often accompanied by rigorous rituals designed to bring about a healthy outcome for both mother and child. Consequently, the whole process of birth, in some cases including pregnancy, requires special rites of purification. The pregnant woman may be expected to observe food taboos, take daily baths, and perform only a few restricted household chores. Impurities connected with childbirth are usually associated with the afterbirth; these impurities extend to the fragile bond between mother and child and to other family members. Pollution is attributed to the invasion of evil spirits that thrive on vulnerable individuals during crisis events. Often mother and child are placed in seclusion for a period of time, then ritually welcomed into the larger community after rituals of cleansing have taken place.

The transition to adulthood is considered the proper time for prophylactic rites of purification. These rites protect the initiate from pollution during his state of liminality. In some societies uncircumcised males are considered intrinsically polluted. Among the Ndembu people of northwestern Zambia, an uncircumcised boy lacks "whiteness" or "purity" and is permanently polluting; his presence can threaten the luck of hunters. An uncircumcised Ndembu man is polluted because of the dirt beneath his foreskin. He is considered "white" or "pure" only when the glans of his penis is exposed through circumcision (Turner, 1967).

Menstruation is one of the functions most widely seen as polluting, second only to death. Menstrual impurity may apply only during menses, or it may be more generalized as a kind of gender pollution, rendering women permanently impure due to their sexuality. Menstrual pollution is usually controlled by dietary restrictions, isolation in separate huts or parts of the household, and avoidance of either cooking or the performance of ordinary household tasks. Also, women are debarred from participation in religious ceremonies during menstruation. Gender pollution appears to be related, at least partially, to male dominance and the demarcation of clear male spheres of influence; thus, the very presence of women causes dangerous pollution (Douglas, 1975). In many tribal societies, women, under the threat of death, are kept away from men's houses where sacred masks are carved and the secrets of the ancestors are kept. Some Mediterranean and Near Eastern cultures elaborate gender pollution to the point of associating women with all kinds of dark forces (such as the evil eye, the world of ghosts, and magical occult powers). Unattached women in these societies must be watched carefully because they are a great source of pollution: Women are believed to be shameful creatures who can upset the entire social order by threatening the lines of distinction between separate gender domains.

Marriage and human sexuality are surrounded by elaborate pollution/purity norms in many parts of the world. Sexual relations outside culturally prescribed rules are generally treated as potential sources of pollution. These rules vary greatly from one society to another. Premarital sexual relations, for instance, are not considered to be polluting in some societies. In other parts of the world, women, in particular, who engage in premarital sex are considered to be polluted by their loss of virginity. While pollution norms surrounding sex and marriage vary, many societies consider adultery a source of defilement. Incest is a more serious offense and is universally taboo. Incestuous activities are so thoroughly polluting as to pose serious threats to the community as a whole. Consequently, persons who have committed incest are either killed or permanently banished.

The most widespread source of pollution is death and the putrefaction of bodily decay. Death breaks fragile social bonds, and the bonds that remain must be rearranged so that death pollution can be prevented from becoming a generalized condition of social disorder or chaos. The corpse and the possessions of the deceased are highly dangerous. Even though death is the most polluting social event, not all religions treat it uniformly. In some religions, as in Christianity, dead human bodies are allowed into sacred shrines or even buried there. This contrasts dramatically with Hinduism, where corpses are never allowed near a sacred shrine; even an accidental death that occurs inside a Hindu temple requires the performance of elaborate purification rites.

Funeral rituals have three general purposes: (1) the transformation of dead spirits into ancestors; (2) the placement of the ancestors in the proper realm of the afterlife (heaven, hell, or a new life via reincarnation); and (3) a restoration of both social and cosmic order from the disorder caused by death pollution (Nielsen et al., 1983). Thus, funerals are designed to accomplish a number of important tasks necessitated by the wound of death. Not only do they provide a ritual context for disposing of the pollution linked with the dead body, they also activate, contain, and assist in the resolution of grief.

Since death represents a rending of the social fabric, its pollution has far-reaching effects. In India, death pollutes the whole family, requiring strict rites of purification during prescribed periods of mourning, the length of which is determined according to the degree of kinship to the deceased. In Japan, death is believed to result in harmful and contagious pollution that can be transmitted through social contact. The idea that death pollution is communicable can be found throughout the world. The Polynesians abandoned any house where death had occurred. After the death of a Samoan chief, his house could not be entered and fishing in the lagoon was prohibited (Steiner, 1956). However, not all ceremonies surrounding death are designed to prevent the contagion of pollution; some of these rites help mourners to participate in the condition of death itself. According to Robert Parker, in ancient Greek religion death pollution was a kind of temporary participation in the condition of the dead man, who was, through the decay of the corpse, "foul" (*miaros*). "Pollution is a transposition of this sympathetic befoulment to the metaphysical plane. 'Being polluted' is a kind of metaphysical suit of mourning" (Parker, 1983, p. 64). In the Parsi religion, contact with dead bodies pollutes family, community, and even the natural elements of air, fire, water, and earth. Consequently, earth burial and cremation are forbidden among the Parsis. They resolve the problem of contaminating the natural elements by exposing the deceased on a *dakhma* ("tower of silence") to be devoured by vultures. In this extreme case, death pollution is so highly contagious that unless contained it extends to all nature.

Violent death is the most polluting of all, for both the victim and the perpetrator of the crime. The pollution generated by violent death is exceedingly dangerous because it may activate a revenge cycle. Among headhunters in New Guinea and other parts of the world, the ghost of an individual who has been murdered is considered extremely dangerous unless it is appeased by taking another head. In some societies both the murderer and the victim of violent death are refused ordinary funeral rites; in some cases these corpses are denied burial in community cemeteries.

Pollution and purity norms are related to social rank, particularly in complex societies with strong social boundaries established by ascription. People who break conventional rules of behavior in hierarchically oriented societies by crossing lines of class or caste are considered polluted by their transgression. In Polynesia the person of the chief was highly charged with *mana*, a kind of sacred energy that could be lost through touching people of lower rank. The Hindu social system, with its strict endogamous tradition for establishing social status, is even more rigid about the link between rank and pollution; Hindu castes involve strict rules requiring marriage within subcastes, prohibiting caste interdining, and restricting physical contact between members of lower and upper castes. While these rules are less rigid than in the past, they continue to thrive in contemporary India. The degree of intrinsic pollution of each caste depends on its rank in the overall system. The lowest castes are more polluted than higher ones because of their traditional occupations; the highest brahman castes are least polluted, due to their priestly duties, and the lowest castes are most contaminated because of their contact with polluting items in the environment. Untouchables, who are outside the caste system, are most polluted because they come in contact with such highly polluting substances as leather and dead bodies. Physical contact with untouchables by caste Hindus requires strong purification rites. In the past untouchables, due to their intrinsic pollution, were prevented from entering temples; this custom was banned legally by the Indian constitution (November 26, 1949).

Pollution and the maintenance of sacred boundaries. The definition of religious pollution cannot be limited to social, psychological, or physiological domains alone. The definition of the "sacred" also involves issues of spiritual pollution. This is clear to individuals who have dedicated themselves to the religious life. Rules governing pollution are more stringent for the religious because they come in contact with the supernatural more directly than the laity. Anyone who approaches the divinity, either as an intermediary or in a state of deep reverence, is required to perform extensive rites of purification.

As the religious are more vulnerable to pollution, they also may be singled out to suffer its consequences more than others. The idea of being set apart for a holy purpose is exemplified by Judaism, Christianity, and Islam. Particularly in Judaism, the idea of a sanctified, priestly people becomes highly elaborated, to the point that Yahveh's chosen may become impure by worshiping other gods, consulting fortune-tellers, or coming in contact with foreigners. The same notion is expressed throughout the world in varying degrees, as people attempt to define a relationship to divinity.

The polar tension between pollution and purity is activated in pilgrimage: pilgrims enter a dialectic where pollution is dissolved by the journey to a sacred place. Thus, in the great pilgrimage traditions of Islam, Hinduism, Shintō, or Christianity, one not only attains merit, community status, and indulgences for the afterlife; one also undergoes a "spiritual bathing" that opens the eyes, transforms consciousness, and centers human focus on the sacred. Pilgrimage is often prescribed to resolve conditions of spiritual pollution. In the classical pilgrimages, the devotee's journey returned him to a place of great sacrality and prepared him to cross boundaries and to enter more deeply into the realm of the sacred.

The definition of any sacred place is contingent on its opposite, namely, the removal of polluting elements that contaminate the "holy." In Hinduism, whenever a particular place is selected for worshiping a deity, it is sanctified through elaborate purification rites so that demons, evil spirits, and the dark forces of ignorance are excluded and conditions for invoking the presence of divinity are most favorable. Thus, the locus of the holy of holies in any religion embodies that religion's ideal of purity. This is not to imply that pollution has no place in sacred centers; on the contrary, it is through the very process of purifying the impure that human life is transformed and integrated into the religious sphere.

RITES OF PURIFICATION. Religious pollution always calls for specific rites of purification, which can range from the ingestion of sacraments to painful acts of purgation. There are five types of rites, involving the use of (1) fire, (2) water, (3) detergents, (4) purgation, and (5) scapegoats. Usually several purificatory mechanisms are employed together, as parts of a sacred technology, to eliminate pollution and restore wholeness to both individual and community.

Fire. Both fire and smoke are considered sources of purification. In some parts of the world, stepping over a fire is a rite demarcating a transition from defilement. The Hindu god Agni is the personification of fire, and purified butter is poured into fire as an offering to the god. At certain times of the year, sacrifices to Agni are performed to purify the whole world. Hindus attain sacramental benefit by passing their hands over fire. The eternal fire that burns day and night in Parsi fire temples is a source of purity for worshipers, who offer bread and milk while portions of the sacred text, the Avesta, are read before it.

Incense and fumigation are employed widely in the world's religions for purificatory purposes. Typically, both sacred objects and the assembled worshipers are purified with incense during the recitation of prayers. According to Parker, the ancient Greeks saw fire as an important source of purity: "Torches were an indispensable part of many ceremonies, and swung vigorously, they could purify a room or a person. Normally, however, sharp-smelling substances were added to the fire when purification was needed" (Parker, 1983, p. 227). The Greeks exposed polluted objects to the pungent odor of sulphur; by contrast, sweet-smelling burnt offerings were selected to please the gods.

Water. Water, the universal cleanser, is the most widely employed means of ritual purification. Often water is used with other elements, such as fire, salt, or herbs. It is a particularly potent source of purification when obtained from holy springs, wells, or other sacred bodies of water. The many holy wells of Ireland are special places of purification. A bath in the sacred Ganges river is accompanied by such a high level of purification that it is an object of pilgrimage for millions of devotees from all over India.

A widespread requirement before worship is the custom of ritual bathing, either of the whole body or parts of the body most exposed to pollution, especially the feet. In most religions the deity must not be approached unless the devotee is ritually clean. The Hindu is expected to bathe early in the morning, recite special prayers, and consecrate his day to the service of God. Water has purificatory qualities in Hinduism, not because of its intrinsic purity, but because it absorbs pollution and carries it away (Babb, 1975). Thus, the flow of water determines its purificatory efficacy.

Water also makes the sacred more accessible to devotees. Muslims clean their mouths and ears with water to sanctify their prayers and open their hearing to the will of God. Most life crisis events, such as childbirth, marriage, or death, involve the use of water to create a state of purification in which the transaction between humans and divinity is encouraged and the danger of pollution is minimized. The best-known instance of ritual purification with water is Christian baptism, which washes away sin and prepares the devotee to lead a religious life. In this case, water both washes away the pollution of sin and acts as a sign that the individual belongs to an initiated group who share a common state of purified grace. The statues of deities are ritually cleansed with water in preparation for religious ceremonies. The water that supports life is a sacred source of renewal. It is the "mother of being" in opposition to the accumulation of filth, evil, defilement, and decay associated with death.

Detergents. Aside from fire and water, a variety of agents are utilized in ritual purification. These various detergents include salt water, liquid concoctions made from propitious herbs and spices, and various other sacramental substances applied to the polluted individual or space. In Africa and the Middle East, sand or dry dirt is used as a detergent when water is not available. Charcoal, mud, and clay from special sacred places are also employed to remove religious pollution. These clinging substances are daubed on a person's body to absorb defilement, then washed away. In India, ash from cow dung is widely employed as a cleansing agent. Among the Nuba of Sudan, the ash from burnt branches of the acacia tree has purificatory qualities. In this society, sacred ash is linked to success in wrestling contests, fertility of the earth, rites of initiation, death, and the afterlife. Young Nuba men, at various critical points in their lives, cover their bodies with sacred ash as a symbol of purification.

Throughout the world, cow dung is used as fuel and as mortar to build shelters. Thus, it represents an important resource for human communities. It is not surprising, therefore, that in some cultures cow dung is used as a detergent with purificatory qualities. Since cows are sacred in India, cow dung and other bovine products are considered to be extremely pure. In the case of Indian death pollution, for example, when an individual has died in a house or temple, or whenever there is a need for special acts of purification, five products of the cow (dung, milk, ghee, curds, and urine) are mixed together and applied as a detergent to clean walls or apply to human beings. In Hinduism the sacredness of the cow, mother of life, makes this mixture almost sacramental in its efficacy.

Purgation. This category subsumes a large variety of purificatory rites. The common thread is either a physical or psychological purging to eliminate pollution, often involving self-sacrifice, pain, and suffering by the devotee. Purificatory purgation, found in one form or another throughout the world, always involves a metaphysics of cleansing transformation, as natural bodily or psychic pollution is purified through rituals that alter the human condition.

One means of cleansing the human body from defilement is to shave the head, eyebrows, and other body hair. In Hinduism, the hair and beard must not be cut until the end of the mourning period. At that time the head is shaved to demarcate the end of death pollution. Novices in some monastic traditions are shaved to signify the termination of their worldly life and their dedication to holy orders. Even the rite of circumcision, with its removal of the foreskin, is an act of purification as well as a rite of passage designed to integrate the individual into a new level of community.

Throughout the world special clothing is used in the context of sacred ceremonies; the hair may be covered, shoes removed, or new clothes required. In the case of death pollution, old clothes of the deceased may be burned. This change of clothing signifies a termination of uncleanliness. Deities in Hinduism must be approached by devotees wearing the purest possible garments. According to Lawrence A. Babb,

> as a general rule . . . the principal actor or actors in ritual must be in a purified condition before approaching or making offerings to the deity. This usually means that the worshippers will be freshly bathed and will be wearing garments appropriate to a condition of purity: a minimum of cotton, which is quite vulnerable to pollution; silk, if possible, which is more resistant to accidental pollution. (Babb, 1975, p. 47)

Throughout the world, fasting is an act of purgation, a sacrifice to honor the divinity, and a mechanism for cleansing the body. In Islam, the whole month of Ramadan is a time for fasting. Until recently, Roman Catholics fasted on Fridays to recall the passion of Christ. The season of Lent is a more protracted period of fasting commemorating the passion. Intense fasting as a form of purgation is widely associated with states of visionary ecstasy. Typically, the religious specialist prepares himself to receive visions by abstaining from food and drink for long periods of time; he may become emaciated, undergo symbolic death, then experience intense spiritual illumination.

Both Judaism and Islam forbid the eating of pork. No religion has a more strict set of dietary laws than Orthodox Judaism, where eating is a sacramental act. The Jewish dietary laws were a sign of the holiness of God's people; they served to preserve monotheism and to set the Jews apart from surrounding pagan societies. Dietary laws are found in the books of *Deuteronomy, Genesis,* and *Exodus,* but they are most widely articulated in *Leviticus.* Animals that have true hoofs and chew their cud, including oxen, sheep, harts, and gazelles, may be eaten. Only a few birds are considered clean: chickens, ducks, geese, and turkeys. Fish must have fins and scales to be considered clean; thus, all shellfish are excluded. Also classified as unclean are those animals that creep, crawl, or swarm upon the earth. Animals permitted in the Mosaic dietary laws may be eaten only under certain conditions: they must be slaughtered by a man trained in Jewish law, using a sharp knife and severing the animal's throat with one continuous stroke. Even then, the meat is not kosher unless it has been properly drained of blood, prepared with salt, then washed clean (Trepp, 1982, pp. 281–284). According to Mary Douglas, Jewish dietary laws act as signs to inspire meditation on the "oneness, purity and completeness of God" (Douglas, 1966, p. 57). Observance of these laws helps the Jewish people to express their holiness at every meal and to prepare for the sacrifice in the temple.

The body may be purged of pollution by various emetics that induce vomiting or diarrhea. The peyote ritual found among Indians of Mexico and the American Southwest involves a phase of vomiting, considered to have both physical and spiritual purifying effects (Malefijt, 1968). Purgatives such as castor oil are used as purifying agents in African religions. Emetics of various kinds are prescribed by shamans to flush out evil spirits and purify the human body. Among North American Indians, the sweat bath is widely employed to cure illnesses and remove impurities.

Psychological forms of purgation are connected to the condition of the human body. Various forms of physical torture have been employed in the world's religions to bring about a psychological state of penance and humility in the presence of the supernatural. Mortification of the flesh includes various forms of flagellation, walking on nails, lacerations, suspension on hooks driven through the skin, the wearing of hair shirts, and sleeping on rough surfaces. These painful acts of self-sacrifice are not reserved only for religious specialists; in many religions with strong pilgrimage traditions, self-denial is an act of purification for laypeople. At the great pilgrimage shrine of Our Lady of Guadalupe in Mexico City and at numerous Marian devotions in Europe, pilgrims may be seen crawling on their bleeding knees toward the sanctuaries. Pilgrimages to Mecca, the medieval shrines of Europe, and the great pilgrim centers of Hinduism are associated with danger, hardship, and self-denial, which are believed to be purificatory. The ultimate form of purgation occurs when the pilgrim dies along the journey; in Hinduism it is considered highly auspicious to die on pilgrimage, an act equivalent to dying near the sacred Ganges River.

Another form of physical and psychological purification is sexual abstinence or celibacy. In some religions, the highest spiritual experiences can occur only for individuals who have given up all worldly pleasures. Sexual abstinence is believed to place the individual in a state of grace where he can concentrate on the supernatural. In some respects, strong marriage vows prohibiting extramarital sexual activity are designed to ensure the purity of sex within the marriage contract. The transgression of sexual boundaries is an act of pollution that may require intense rites of purification.

Confession of misdeeds appears in one form or another in most religions. The public or private recitation of transgressions purges the individual of guilt and acts as an antidote to both the personal and the collective pollution resulting from the breaking of taboos. The Inuit custom of group confession, particularly practiced during times when seal hunting is unsuccessful, is an example of corporate purgation through confession. It is believed that when the hair of the great goddess Sedna, who lives under the sea, has become dirty because of human sins (like secret miscarriages and various breaches of taboos) she angrily holds back the sea animals. During a trance, the shaman appeases Sedna, then calls for a group confession so that hunting may be plentiful (Eliade, 1964). Confession often results in a flood of tears, self-mortification, or other acts intended to express sorrow for transgressions. Thus, confession removes the stain of sin through a psychological act of expiation and purification.

Contact with holy items, such as relics of saints, sacraments, and statues of deities, is an important source of purification. The utterance of prayers also has cleansing value. In Hinduism, mantras may be used either as agents to combat evil or as foci for concentration leading to spiritual awakening. Rituals of purification in Buddhism are metaphors for inner transformations and mystical enlightenment. Prayer and meditation, particularly by ascetics, purify the soul, rendering it a fitting receptacle for God-consciousness and the spiritual life. Here purgation is followed by the contemplation of sublime spiritual visions.

Substitution and catharsis. The use of substitutions to remove pollution is a widespread purificatory custom. The sick human body may be rubbed with sticks, stones, or other objects to which the pollution is transferred. A means of curing mental disorders in Nigeria is to remove the person's clothes and rub his body with a sacrificed dove, which absorbs the evil spirits. In the American Indian peyote cult, individuals are purified by being rubbed with sagebrush. The institution of kingship is widely accompanied by the purificatory anointing of the king's body. The annual Qingming ceremony in China involves a tradition of sweeping clean the graves of the ancestors. This rite of purification renews the whole community. Shintō priests transfer their pollution to a special wand, which is then thrown away so that they may perform sacred ceremonies in a state of ritual purity.

There are numerous instances of transferring pollution to either human or animal scapegoats. Specially selected individuals may be whipped, beaten, and then expelled from a community to rid it of pollution. In Fiji, the polluted person is washed in a stream; he or she then wipes their hand on a pig or turtle to remove pollution. At one time among the Maori of New Zealand, when an epidemic disease raged in the community, a man was selected as a temporary scapegoat; a fern stalk was attached to his body, he was submerged in a river, and the fern stalk was allowed to float downstream. The epidemic was transferred to the scapegoat (the fern stalk), then washed away by the river. Sometimes scapegoats are institutionalized corporately, so that a whole social class takes on the burden of pollution. Thus, Indian untouchables have been singled out to bear the suffering associated with pollution; consequently the other social castes may be at least relatively free of pollution.

Community catharsis, through substitution and the use of scapegoats, is most widely practiced in the form of ritual sacrifice, where the animal's head is exchanged for that of a human who is spiritually polluted (Preston, 1980). Sacrifice is a widespread custom in the world's religions; although it is performed for many different purposes, one major reason is to purify both the individual and community of defilement. Consequently, the dramatic shedding of blood is typically surrounded with a milieu of powerful ritual catharsis. Among the cattle-keeping Nuer tribe of the Sudan, sacrifices are performed as atonements for breaking taboos. The ancient Greeks employed blood sacrifices as rites of absorptive purification, transferring defilement to despised animals (Parker, 1983). Cattle, sheep, goats, chickens, and pigs are the animals most widely employed as scapegoats in ritual sacrifices. While human sacrifice occurred widely in the past, this form of expiation has mostly disappeared. However, in its symbolic form cathartic human sacrifice has been retained in the passion of Christ, where Jesus of Nazareth takes on the "sins of the world," becoming the "perfect offering" to cleanse the world of its collective pollution.

Secular forms. The symbolism of purification is not confined to the religious sphere. Modern secular societies continue to utilize powerful symbols of pollution and purity. Even though the religious content has been removed from much of this symbolism in technological societies, some of it lingers. The wide array of soaps and other chemicals used for cleansing the bodies and living habitats of modern peoples cannot be understood merely as extensions of scientific insights about health stemming from germ theory. Much of the preoccupation of American hospitals with white walls, antiseptics, and unstained clothing is suspiciously reminiscent of Puritan notions of religious cleanliness.

Fire, water, detergents, purgation, and substitutions remain important sources of both religious and secular purification rites in the modern world. However, the most noteworthy addition would be an array of chemicals added to this set of purificatory devices for removing pollution. Also significant is the tendency to perceive both pollution and purity in materialistic terms. Even though religious pollution is not an extinct concept in modern societies, it has often been isolated and compartmentalized away from the material world. Thus, today diseases such as smallpox are not usually thought to be related to sin or the breaking of taboos; nor are the cures of these diseases sought by performing religious purification rites. Still, some illnesses and critical life crisis events that have escaped the control of the rational scientific method remain, in many quarters, mysterious enough to require both religious and secular rites of purification. This is particularly true for some types of cancer, which remain mysterious and defy ingenious medical technologies born of the modernist world view.

Religious Meaning. Rites of purification are rarely isolated or discrete events. Usually they are linked together as sequences of rites within the larger semantic network of purity symbolism in a particular religious or cultural context. Among the Ndembu of northwestern Zambia the unifying symbol is the color white. This compound image of purity permeates every aspect of Ndembu religion. Water is regarded as white because it cleanses the body of dirt. After a funeral the widower is anointed with oil, shaved, washed, given new white cloth, and adorned with white beads. According to Victor Turner, "Behind the symbolism of whiteness, then, lie the notions of harmony, continuity, purity, the manifest, the public, the appropriate, and the legitimate" (1967, p. 77). Rites and symbols of purification have no meaning unless they are interpreted as part of a larger religious language.

This article has not exhausted the range of purificatory rites available in the world religions; other mechanisms of purification that could be added to this list include the application of sandalwood paste to the skin, bleeding the little finger, chewing hot chiles, touching sacred relics, eating or drinking sacraments, and making loud noises (as in the Chinese custom of setting off firecrackers). The important question is what all this means in terms of human religion. What is the relationship of the social categories of pollution and purity to the religious impulse itself?

Pollution/purity norms serve clear sociological and psychological purposes, reinforcing the boundaries of the community, ensuring the survival of the group, reinforcing principles of health, and assisting individuals to cope ritually with life crises. Still, the relationship of people to the supernatural remains the focal point of purification rites throughout the world. In Confucianism, a state of purity is necessary to establish a channel of communication between living persons and the spiritual world. The Hindu performs yoga only after purification; higher levels of consciousness may be blocked by painful impurities unless the devotee manages to overcome them. The loving God of Christianity helps his people to transcend impurities by sending his son and offering salvation through the Eucharist. In all these cases, channels of communication with the divinity are made possible through the establishment of boundaries between domains of pollution and purity, the identification of a situation of defilement, the performance of appropriate purificatory rites, and the experience of a new encounter with the ultimate supreme being.

Mary Douglas and other structuralists have noted correctly that pollution/purity norms impose order on the untidiness of life experiences: "Reflection on dirt involves reflection on the relation of order to disorder, being to non-being, form to formlessness, life to death" (Douglas, 1966, p. 5). Yet categories of pollution and purity represent more than ideological or social systems. Defilement represents human failure to attain perfection, to realize a godlike nature, while purification is the human expression of divine aspirations.

See Also Ablutions; Celibacy; Confession of Sins; Fasting; Fire; Hair; Incense; Kashrut; Mortification; Rites of Passage; Scapegoat; Water.

Bibliography

Babb, Lawrence A. *The Divine Hierarchy: Popular Hinduism in Central India.* New York, 1975.

Douglas, Mary. *Purity and Danger.* New York, 1966. This landmark volume has had a profound effect on the understanding of religion. Pollution and purity are analyzed in different religious systems to reveal underlying structural similarities. The author stresses the need to understand concepts of pollution and purity in the context of a total structure of thought.

Douglas, Mary. "Deciphering a Meal." *Daedalus* 101 (Winter 1972): 61–81. An elegant structural analysis of the meaning of the sacred meal with particular reference to Jewish laws regarding purification and diet.

Douglas, Mary. *Implicit Meanings: Essays in Anthropology.* Boston, 1975. A collection of excellent essays, some of which expand on the author's earlier structural analysis of purity norms.

Dumont, Louis. *Homo Hierarchicus.* Translated by Mark Sainsbury. Rev. ed. Chicago, 1980. A classic study of Hinduism, with particular emphasis on structural oppositions, including notions of pollution and purity as manifested in the caste system.

Eliade, Mircea. *Shamanism: Archaic Techniques of Ecstasy.* Rev. & enl. ed. New York, 1964.

Lichter, David, and Lawrence Epstein. "Irony in Tibetan Notions of the Good Life." In *Karma: An Anthropological Inquiry,* edited by Charles F. Keyes and E. Valentine Daniel. Berkeley, Calif., 1983.

Malefijt, Annemarie De Waal. *Religion and Culture.* New York, 1968.

Nielsen, Niels C., et al. *Religions of the World.* New York, 1982.

Parker, Robert. *Miasma: Pollution and Purification in Early Greek Religion.* Oxford, 1983. An excellent, thorough analysis of pervasive purity norms in ancient Greek religion.

Preston, James J. *Cult of the Goddess: Social and Religious Change in a Hindu Temple.* New Delhi, 1980.

Steiner, Franz. *Taboo.* New York, 1956.

Trepp, Leo. *Judaism: Development and Life.* Belmont, Calif., 1982.

Turner, Victor. *The Forest of Symbols: Aspects of Ndembu Ritual.* Ithaca, N. Y., 1967.

JAMES J. PRESTON (1987)

PURIFICATION: PURIFICATION IN JUDAISM

The concept of purity represents one of the cornerstones of Jewish religiosity from its earliest articulation in biblical literature. Indeed, the ideal of attaining purity by purification from the various kinds of impurities enumerated in the Book of Leviticus forms an integral part of the notion of holiness in that book, as well as in later Jewish sources. At the same time, purity is not a uniform concept. On the contrary, the idea of purity is mobilized in numerous thematic, literary, and chronological contexts, ranging from ritual to purely metaphysical or spiritual. It plays a fundamental role in constructions of gender identity in Jewish culture, just as gender is a structural element of the various manifestations of the conceptualization of purity. Not so much a linear development of a uniform idea, from ritual to spiritual, purity is rather a concept which acquires different layers of meanings and can be variously drawn on.

RITUAL IMPURITY AND PURIFICATION IN BIBLICAL AND JEWISH LAW. The primary context in which the idea of purity plays a fundamental role is in the so-called priestly source of the Book of Leviticus and its concern for the ritual life of the sanctuary. Purity (*taharah*) and impurity (*tum'ah*) are primarily functional concepts and connote the status of a person or an object with respect to the Temple. A person needs to be in a status of ritual purity in order to enter the Temple area. If the person or an object has been affected by a source of impurity they need to undergo a process of ritual purification before they can again enter the Temple or be put to use for work related to the Temple.

Primary sources of impurity are the carcasses of various animals deemed to be impure (*Lv.* 11:1–47) and human corpses (*Nm.* 19:10–22). Further, certain physical or physiological conditions will render a person impure, namely childbirth (*Lv.* 12:1–8); scale disease, traditionally translated as leprosy, even though this is most likely not the condition described in the text (*Lv.* 13:1 – 14:32); and genital discharges (*Lv.* 15:1–33). These conditions affect first and foremost the people suffering from them. However, the priestly thinking about impurity further understands the state of impurity to be transferable from one person to another, or from a person to an object, and vice versa. Such transference can occur in numerous ways, such as by direct and indirect touch, by spittle, through sexual means, or in the case of corpse impurity, even by simply being under the same roof as the corpse.

Corresponding to these primary and secondary states of impurity, the priestly source defines different degrees of severity of impurity by legislating different durations of states of impurity, as well as different procedures of purification. For example, a woman who menstruates is in a status of impurity for seven days, but the one who touches her for the remainder of the day only (*Lv.* 15:19). A man or a woman who have irregular discharges (*zav/zavah*) are in a status of impurity as long as their discharge lasts and then have to count out seven days without a discharge before they can undergo purification (*Lv.* 15:13 and *Lv.* 15:28), while again the person who touches them remains in a status of impurity for the remainder of the day (*Lv.* 15:7 and *Lv.* 15:27). A person who has been affected by corpse impurity remains in a status of impurity for seven days (*Nm.* 19:11).

Purification is effected by various aspects: (1) by time, or by simply waiting a set amount of time free of the physiological condition that caused the status of impurity to begin with; (2) by water, that is, by washing one's clothes if one has touched an impure person or object, or washing the object such a person touched (e.g., *Lv.* 15:12); and by bathing (*Lv.* 15:13, 15:5–11, *Lv.* 15:21–22); (3) finally, the process of purification is completed by variously prescribed sacrificial offerings (e.g., *Lv.* 12:6–7, *Lv.* 15:14, *Lv.* 15:29). Surprisingly, the biblical text noticeably omits the practice of washing or immersion in all cases of women's impurity, after birthing as well as after menstruating and after suffering from an abnormal genital discharge. Finally, a further and less obvious means of purification is constituted by the ritual of the red heifer which is burned and whose ashes are mixed with fresh ("living") water to be sprinkled on the objects and people affected by corpse impurity (*Nm.* 19).

These priestly regulations concerning ritual impurity and the process of purification avoid any suggestion that they should be understood as punitive measures. Contracting a ritual status of impurity does not constitute a transgression in any way, neither of a legal nor a moral kind. On the contrary, in most cases impurity is the result of a natural occurrence in a person's life, such as birth, ejaculation, menstruation, and death. Also, ritual impurity is a temporary status, which can easily be ameliorated. In this context, the legal rhetoric merely suggests that if ritual impurity is contracted, a process of purification specified in the text should be undergone. Surprisingly, this applies even to the man who has sexual relations with a menstruating woman (*Lv.* 15:24). The actual prohibition of menstrual sex (*Lv.* 18:19 and 20:18) stems from a different source of biblical law, the *Holiness Code*, which removes it from the ritual context and places it in the lists of prohibited sexual relations. Here, contrary to *Leviticus* 15:24, the man and the woman are threatened with *karet* (commonly translated as "cutting off from their people", *Lv.* 20:18) in case of transgression. This tension between sources of biblical law makes the case of menstrual impurity unique, since here two different discourses overlap, the discourse of ritual impurity and the discourse of regulations of sex. The priestly source, however, generally lacks warnings of transgression in the context of defining the process of contracting a status of impurity. It merely warns people to avoid bringing impurity in touch with the sanctuary: "Thus you shall keep the people of Israel separate from their impurity, so that they do not die in their impurity by impurifying my tabernacle that is in their midst" (*Lv.* 15:31; cf. 7:20–21 and 22:3–9). Finally, especially in the context of corpse impurity, the priestly law enjoins people to purify themselves, or else (*Nm.* 19:13 and 19:20). Hence, the Israelites are enjoined to be aware of their ritual status, rather than being told to avoid impurity altogether, notes Jonathan Klawans in *Impurity and Sin in Ancient Judaism.* This applies especially to the priests (*Lv.* 7:20–21; cf. 22:3–9), with the exception of their prohibition to contract corpse impurity (*Lv.* 21:1–3).

It is the priestly notion of ritual purity that is subsequently encoded in Jewish law since rabbinic law draws predominantly on this concept of purity. The earliest rabbinic legal code of the end of the second century CE, the Mishnah, devotes one of its six orders to "Purities" (a euphemism for what should be "Impurities"), subdivided into twelve tractates, in order to further develop the laws of ritual purity. Individual tractates are devoted to the impurity of a corpse, of vessels, of the menstruating woman, of the man with an abnormal genital discharge, and others. Early rabbinic law aims to systematize the degrees of impurity into originary and derivative sources. Further, the rabbis also specify in the greatest detail what a normative pool of immersion (*mikveh*) for purification as an actual built structure should look like. While biblical law merely speaks of "living water" as a means of immersion (*Lv.* 15:13), rabbinic law thus institutionalizes the practice of immersion. Significantly, rabbinic law accepts it as a given that women immerse in the *mikveh* at the end of their period of impurity (e.g., Mishnah, *Mikva'ot* 8:1 and 5).

Theoretically, therefore, rabbinic law remains wedded to the functional aspect of ritual purity with the Temple as the implied point of reference. The great medieval scholar of Jewish law Moses Maimonides (Mosheh ben Maimon, 1135/8–1204) thus writes: "Whatever is written in the Torah and in traditional teaching about the laws relating to things impure and pure is relevant only to the Temple and its hallowed things and to heave-offering and second tithe, for it warns those impure against entering the Temple or eating anything hallowed, or heave-offering, or tithe. However, no such prohibition applies to common food, and it is permitted to eat common food that is impure and to drink impure liquids." (Mishnah *Torah,* Mishnah *Okhelim* 16:8). However, already at the time of the Mishnah, the Temple in Jerusalem no longer existed. With the destruction of the Temple (70 CE) the laws of ritual purity lost their point of reference and, therefore, their context of applicability. This is often cited as the reason for the lack of a talmudic discussion of the mishnaic "Order of Purities," with the notable exception of the tractate dealing with menstrual impurity. Regulations of menstruation remain applicable due to the prohibition of menstrual sex in the *Holiness Code*, which, according to the rabbis, applies independent of any historical context, whether pertaining to the existence of the Temple or conditions of exile.

Generally, the entire system of purification has been rendered inoperable in the post-Temple era, since sacrifices form an integral part of the purification process. Furthermore, since medieval times all Jews are considered to be in a status of corpse impurity, due to the cessation of the ritual of the red heifer and its function of purification from corpse impurity. Consequently, the codification of the purity laws in Jewish law by and large remains a theoretical issue.

Various scholars have attempted to explain the rationale of the priestly system of ritual purity in biblical and, by implication, later Jewish law. The priestly writers themselves do, of course, not provide any explanations for either the origins or the reasons for any of their purity regulations. In describing the "priestly theology" of impurity, the biblical scholar Jacob Milgrom, in his work *Leviticus 1–16: A New Translation with Introduction and Commentary,* takes a history-of-religion approach which posits "Israel's victory over pagan beliefs" in almost each one of its rituals of purification (Milgrom, 1991, pp. 42–51). He thinks of this process in terms of a monotheistic reworking of pagan conceptions of demonic impurity. Accordingly, Milgrom traces the ostensible background of pagan (Mesopotamian) religion to the priestly writers, in which the deities are dependent on a metadivine realm that spawns a multitude of malevolent and benevolent entities. The malevolent metadivine entities were perceived to be the source of human pollution, a threat both to humans and gods, and purification entailed a process of exorcism.

According to Milgrom, in his *Leviticus 1–16,* the biblical writers partially adopt, with significant changes, this mythical imagination, but they thoroughly eviscerate the pagan demonic force, which finds its expression in their concept of impurity. God can still be driven out of the sanctuary, but it is now humans who do so by polluting it with their moral and ritual transgressions. And now it is exclusively the sanctuary. Hence, in the priestly writings "impurity" has become harmless, since it retained potency only with regard to the sancta, not to other people (Milgrom, 1991, p. 43). This process of reducing the power of impurity takes places in various stages within the priestly materials of the Bible and reaches its completion in the rabbinic stage which limits its "malefic effects to actual contact with sancta," while it is no longer sinful to remain otherwise impure (Milgrom, 1991, p. 317). The biblical and rabbinic ages are to be considered a single historical continuum as far as the religious concept of impurity is concerned. Other biblical scholars, however, argue that monotheism could not have effected such a radical break with ancient Near Eastern culture. In contrast to Milgrom, Baruch Levine argues that biblical writers perceived impurity as the "actualized form of evil forces operative in the human environment" (Levine, 1974, p. 78).

As an anthropologist, Mary Douglas takes a different approach altogether to make sense of the biblical notion of ritual purity. In her now famous early work on *Leviticus, Purity and Danger* (1966), she eschews the question of conceptual origins of the biblical notion and instead focuses on the ritual legislation as it presents itself. Accordingly, she argued first of all for the systemic nature of any given culture's conceptions of impurity, and especially in the biblical case. Secondly, she demands that such systems of impurity have to be understood symbolically. It is prominently body symbolism she regards as central to any understanding of systems of impurity, since the body symbolizes society and attitudes to bodily boundaries correspond to attitudes to societal boundaries. Hence, closed societies such as that which supposedly produces the biblical priestly writings will, for instance, articulate more anxiety about bodily fluids. Finally, beliefs of impurity have to be interrogated as to their function as tools of social control. They therefore have a primarily oppressive function and serve to marginalize certain groups of people, prominently women. In her more recent work, however, Douglas revises her earlier approach somewhat, even though she still adheres to the fundamental tenets of her approach of structural symbolism. However, rather than regarding the system of impurities as static, she now focuses more on the opportunity of purification provided by the priestly writers to everybody, not just the priests: "In so far as the Levitical rules for purity apply universally they are useless for internal disciplining. They maintain absolutely not social demarcation . . . the book insists over and over again that the poor and the stranger are to be included in the requirements of the laws; no one is excluded from the benefits of purification" (Douglas, 1993–94, pp. 112–113). This emphasis undermines her earlier assessment of the oppressive social function of the system, even though she still recognizes the exclusive powers of the priests within the system.

In his *Leviticus 1–16,* Milgrom equally determines the rationale of the ritual complexes of *Leviticus* 1–16 by treating them as aspects of a symbolic system that is governed by a comprehensive theory. He argues that death is the common denominator in the three major sources of impurity: scale disease, where the wasting of the body symbolizes the death process; genital discharges, which represent the life force and their loss the opposite; and corpse impurity. Since impurity and holiness are antonyms in the priestly system, impurity is to be equated with death and holiness with life. The symbolic system enjoins the Israelites to separate impurity from God and his sanctuary as the quintessential source of holiness. Thus, according to Milgrom, it serves as a reminder of the divine imperative to reject death and choose life.

IMPURITY OF TRANSGRESSIVE BEHAVIOR. However, aside from the concept of ritual purity, biblical law elsewhere and prophetic literature—most prominently *Ezekiel*—draw on the concept of purity in ways that extend beyond the functional, ritual context. In a number of prophetic and poetic passages, it has a clearly metaphoric function (e.g., *Ps.* 51, *Lam.* 1:8, *Is.* 1:15–17). But elsewhere certain human transgressive behavior is labeled as "impurity" (*tum'ah*). Such behavior includes the sexual transgressions listed in the *Holiness Code* (*Lv.* 18:24–30), idolatry (*Lv.* 19:31, 20:1–3), and murder (*Nm.* 35:33–34). The reference point for these "impurities" is not merely the Temple. Rather, such acts impose impurity upon the perpetrator (*Lv.* 18:24), the land of Israel (*Lv.* 18:25, *Ez.* 36:17), and the sanctuary (*Lv.* 20:3, *Ez.* 5:11). However, neither the land nor the sanctuary is rendered impure by direct or indirect contact. Rather, their impurity is the cumulative, spiritual consequence of the behavior deemed to be reprehensible. In these legal contexts and in the prophetic reproach, the rhetoric is clearly punitive: the individual perpetrator(s) will be "cut off" from their people (*Lv.* 18:29), while the cumulative, collective consequence of such acts is the expulsion of the people from the land of Israel: "Do not render yourselves impure with any of these things (sexual transgressions), for with all these the nations were rendered impure which I cast out before you, and the land was rendered impure. Therefore I do punish its iniquity upon it, and the land vomits out her inhabitants" (*Lv.* 18:24–25). Finally, none of these texts provide any overt process of purification. Only *Ezekiel* envisions the future ingathering of the exiles in the terms of a divine purification of the people (*Ezek.* 36:24) that will allow them to re-inhabit the land.

The tension between the conception of impurity in the priestly source and the *Holiness Code* and *Ezekiel* has caused considerable debate, particularly in biblical scholarship on the ritual purity system, since any analysis of the nature of the ritual purity system depends on the way the relationship between the ritual purity system and those other uses of purity terminology are defined. At the same time, it has provided a fertile ground for the adaptation of the language and conceptualization of purity and purification in post-biblical Jewish literature and later Jewish religiosity. For the sake of conceptual clarity we will briefly review the former, before describing the latter.

Jacob Neusner's approach in *The Idea of Purity in Ancient Judaism* can be found on one end of the scale in that he considers the two to have a metaphorical relationship. Purity and impurity are primarily "cultic matters," but can serve as metaphors for moral religious behavior, even though in some post-biblical Jewish formations (Qumran, rabbis) transgressive behavior may serve as a source for actual pollution. Milgrom, however, recognizes the defiling force of sinful behavior and develops a specific description of the process by which various types of transgressions render the sanctuary impure. To Milgrom, in *Leviticus 1–16*, the defiling force on transgression is concentrated on the sanctuary, and the reference point for purification remains to be the sanctuary ("Israel's Sanctuary"). His lasting contribution is to have recognized that what has commonly been translated as a "sin-offering" (*hatta't*) should actually be translated and understood as a "purification-offering," whose main function is to purify the Temple from the cumulative effects of people's transgressive behavior (Milgrom, 1991, pp. 253–261). While individuals have to bring purification-offerings during the course of the year for inadvertent transgressions (*Lv.* 4), the climax of this process of purification is the ritual of the Day of Atonement (also known as Purgation Day), when the entire sacred area or all that is most sacred is purged with the blood of the purification offering.

Early in the twenty-first century, Klawans has taken issue with these prevailing theories in biblical and rabbinic scholarship. He insists on a categorical distinction between "ritual" and "moral" impurity which each have their distinct defiling forces. These two categories can be correlated to the different approaches the priestly source and the *Holiness Code* (and related texts) take in biblical law. Contra Neusner, moral impurity is not merely a metaphorical concept, and contra Milgrom, he focuses on those transgressive behaviors deemed to cause impurity to the land and not merely the sanctuary. Klawans emphatically rejects the idea that the concept of the defilement of the land (*Lv.* 18:24–30) is only metaphorical. Rather, the performance of sexual transgressions defiles the sinner and the land upon which the sins are committed. This defilement is understood to be moral, and what is conveyed is a permanent degradation of status. In *Impurity and Sin in Ancient Judaism,* Klawans views moral and ritual impurity as two analogous, but distinct, perceptions of contagion, each of which brings about effects of legal and social consequence.

It should be added that Christine E. Hayes builds on Klawans and introduces one additional category of impurity in the biblical and post-biblical literature in her work *Gentile Impurities and Jewish Identities: Intermarriage and Conversion from the Bible to the Talmud.* Taking a similar history-of-idea approach, she traces the notion of genealogical purity in biblical and post-biblical literature. The innovative moment with regard to this category lies with *Ezra* and *Nehemiah* who extend the requirement of genealogical purity to all Israelites, beyond the priestly groups as in the Pentateuch and *Ezekiel.* A terminological shift occurs in these books according to which priestly exogamy is no longer described as profanation but as defilement (*Neh.* 13:28–30; *Ezr.* 2:61–62/*Neh.* 7:62; cf. *Lv.* 21:15). In this genealogical context, the term "pure" comes to mean unalloyed or free of admixture, notes Hayes, and *Nehemiah* accomplishes purification by separating the Israelites from the foreign wives. She notes that while moral impurity defiles the land, the sanctuary, and the sinner, it is not said to impair ones seed in any way, as in the case of exogamy. Hayes argues therefore that these differences should caution against adopting the view that Ezra's concern for the holy seed of Israel as simply an extension of the concept of moral impurity. Both Klawans and Hayes argue that different views of their respective categories of impurity are at the root of Jewish sectarianism during the period of the Second Temple.

Post-Biblical Judaism. Various Jewish groups during the last two centuries BCE and first century CE draw on the conceptualization of purity for boundary making purposes, among them prominently the sectarians who produced the Dead Sea Scrolls. On the one hand, these sectarians make use of ritual purity laws to differentiate themselves from other Jews, by adding more laws and interpreting some laws differently as for instance in the scroll *Miqsat Ma'ase Hatorah* (4 QMMT). But furthermore, they also conflate the differences between what were different types of discourse in biblical law. In the sectarian literature of the Dead Sea Scrolls moral transgressions are considered to have a polluting force and the technical ritual language in the priestly source of biblical law is applied to moral transgressions. Even more significantly, repentance and atonement require actual ritual purification, as reflected for instance in the *Rule of the Community.* One can also speak of a literalization of what in biblical literature appeared to operate as a metaphor, when prophetic and poetic passages draw on the terminology of purity and purification to illustrate their notion of atonement.

Early Rabbinic Judaism, on the other hand, by and large adheres to the conceptualization of purity reflected in the priestly source of the Bible. To be sure, it does champion the concept of the cumulative polluting effect of moral transgressions on the land and the punitive theological consequences. But this appears as a trope mostly in homiletic contexts and in the context of biblical interpretation, while it does play no role in the context of legal discussions. However, the legal development and talmudic discussions of purity laws atrophy, and the codification of the laws of ritual impurity as reflected in later legal codes (e.g., Mishneh *Torah*) remains a theoretical issue in post-Temple times, with the one notable exception of the discussion of menstrual impurity (*niddah*). As mentioned above, this is the only subject of the mishnaic "Order of Purities" to receive a talmudic discussion. The ongoing interest of the rabbinic scholars in the subject is warranted by the continuous applicability of at least some of its aspects, prominently the unconditional prohibition of menstrual sex in the *Holiness Code.* It is this prohibition that perpetuates the interest in the legal discussions of menstrual impurity. At the same time, even in this context most of the impurity rules have become irrelevant and therefore inapplicable in the absence of the Temple, according to Charlotte Elisheva Fonrobert in *Menstrual Purity: Rabbinic and Christian Reconstructions of Biblical Gender.* The focus of the practice is no longer the possible transference of a status of ritual impurity to other people by the menstruating woman. Nor does the synagogue legally function as a Temple substitute to prevent women from going there or from touching sancta, a practice that has nonetheless been customary in various Jewish communities over the centuries. Still, observant married women to this day still immerse monthly in the *mikveh*, while men no longer do, other than for spiritual purposes in some pious circles, such as spiritual purification before the Sabbath or a holiday. In fact, in the contemporary popular didactic literature instructing young couples on the abstention from menstrual sex, the set of practices is often called "the laws of family purity" (*taharat ha-mishpahah*). This term is technically a misnomer in that the actual practice is no longer concerned with ritual purification (*taharah*), nor is it concerned with the family as a whole, rather than the married couple itself. It entered Jewish legal discourse in the late nineteenth and early twentieth century before it was popularized in the market of handbooks for married couples. One of its main functions is rooted in its polemical force, vis a vis liberal, non-observant Jews, which is captured by Kalman Kahana, the author of one of the most popular of these handbooks, *Daughter of Israel*: "Daughter of Israel! The time has arrived to throw off alien garments, to cast away the product of strange cultures. With head erect, and with pride, remember! You are a daughter of Israel, the sacred people. Remember your forefathers, who sacrificed their lives for the sanctity of the Jewish nation. You too, bear faithful fruit, and carry forth the illustrious tradition of Jewish purity," (Kahana, 1977, p. 35).

As far as the context of the legal and ritual discourse in Judaism is concerned, one could speak of a channeling of the concerns about impurity into the discussions of the menstruating women. Time and again, Jewish legal literature reflects disputes over incorrect immersion practices by women. This process has been accompanied over the centuries by extra-normative literature in which the so-called *Baraita de-Niddah* assumes an early and prominent role. Presumably a post-talmudic text from approximately the seventh century CE, but posing as an early talmudic text, it lists a number of extremist strictures concerning the menstruating woman, including her exclusion from the synagogue or any house filled with books (1:2, p. 3; cf.2:2, p.10; Koren, 1999, p. 18), as well as prohibiting her to light the Sabbath candles (2:5, p. 17) and threatening her offspring with leprosy into the hundredth generation should she have sex with her husband. Here, the menstruating woman is all but demonized, and the fact that she can undergo purification is almost irrelevant in light of her threatening impurity. In spite of its extremism, this text has a vital afterlife, in that it is quoted in biblical commentaries by prominent medieval scholars (Moses Nahmanides on *Gn.* 31:35, *Lv.* 12:4, and 18:19, cf. Cohen, "Menstruants and the Sacred," p. 295 n. 30) and may even have influenced legal discussions in some parts of the Jewish world. This discourse of demonizing menstrual impurity continues throughout the medieval period, especially in the literature of Jewish mysticism where the concept of impurity takes on a metaphysical force of mythic proportion. In the *Zohar*, the canonical text of Jewish mysticism from the thirteenth century CE, it is menstruation that is the most prominent type of impurity. At the same time, the mystery of the laws of menstrual impurity are so deep that it cannot be disclosed to the unworthy (*Zohar* 3:79a). These texts, even though they represent extra-normative voices in Judaism, are enormously influential and add layers of meaning to the prevalent legal definitions. Thus, they still inform the Jewish imagination at least to a certain degree.

If one treats the ongoing discourse of menstrual impurity as a left-over of the priestly purity system, one can speak also of a progressive feminization of ritual impurity in recent history of Jewish culture. Ultimately, these discussions and their concomitant ritualization of women's bodies inform women's self-understanding in Judaism considerably. It is because of this that contemporary Jewish feminist literatures focuses prominently on critiquing, readapting, and reshaping the discussions of menstrual impurity.

SEE ALSO Israelite Religion; Miqveh; Rabbinic Judaism in Late Antiquity.

BIBLIOGRAPHY

Cohen, Shaye. "Menstruants and the Sacred in Judaism and Christianity." In *Women's History and Ancient History*, edited by Sarah B. Pomeroy, pp. 273–299. Chapel Hill, N.C., 1991.

Cohen, Shaye. "Purity and Piety: The Separation of Menstruants from the Sancta." In *Daughters of the King: Women and the Synagogue*, edited by Susan Grossman and Rivka Haut, pp. 103–117. Philadelphia and Jerusalem, 1992.

Cohen, Shaye. "Purity, Piety, and Polemic: Medieval Rabbinic Denunciations of 'Incorrect' Purification Practices." In *Women and Water: Menstruation in Jewish Life and Law*, edited by Rahel R. Wasserfall, pp. 82–101. Hanover, N.H., and London, 1999.

Douglas, Mary. "Atonement in Leviticus." *Jewish Studies Quarterly* 1:3 (1993–94): 109–130.

Douglas, Mary. *Purity and Danger: An Analysis of Concept of Pollution and Taboo.* London and New York, 1996; reprint, 2002.

Douglas, Mary. *Natural Symbols: Explorations in Cosmology.* 2d ed. London and New York, 2003.

Fonrobert, Charlotte Elisheva. *Menstrual Purity: Rabbinic and Christian Reconstructions of Biblical Gender.* Stanford, Calif., 2000.

Frymer-Kensky, Tikva. "Pollution, Purification, and Purgation in Biblical Israel." In *The Word of the Lord Shall Go Forth: Essays in Honor of David Noel Freedman in Celebration of His Sixtieth Birthday*, edited by Carol L. Meyers and M. O'Connor, pp. 399–410. Winona Lake, Ind., 1983.

Harrington, Hannah K. *The Impurity Systems of Qumran and the Rabbis: Biblical Foundations.* Atlanta, Ga., 1993.

Hayes, Christine E. *Gentile Impurities and Jewish Identities: Intermarriage and Conversion from the Bible to the Talmud.* Oxford and New York, 2002.

Kahana, Kalman. *Daughter of Israel.* New York, 1977.

Klawans, Jonathan. *Impurity and Sin in Ancient Judaism.* New York, 2000.

Koren, Sharon. "'The Woman from Whom God Wanders';: The Menstruant in Medieval Jewish Mysticism." Ph.D. diss., Yale University, New Haven, Conn., 1999.

Levine, Baruch. *In the Presence of the Lord.* Leiden, the Netherlands, 1974.

Levine, Baruch. *The JPS Torah Commentary: Leviticus.* Philadelphia, 1989.

Milgrom, Jacob. "Israel's Sanctuary: The Priestly 'Picture of Dorian Gray'." *Revue Biblique* 83, no. 3 (1976): 390–399.

Milgrom, Jacob. *Leviticus 1–16: A New Translation with Introduction and Commentary.* New York and London, 1991.

Neusner, Jacob. *The Idea of Purity in Ancient Judaism.* Leiden, the Netherlands, 1973.

Neusner, Jacob. *A History of the Mishnaic Law of Purities,* 22 vols. Leiden, the Netherlands, 1974–1977.

Neusner, Jacob. *Purity in Rabbinic Judaism, A Systemic Account: The Sources, Media, Effects, and Removal of Uncleanness.* Atlanta, Ga., 1989.

Swartz, Michael D. "'Like Ministering Angels': Ritual and Purity in Early Jewish Mysticism and Magic." *AJS Review* 19 (1994): 135–167.

CHARLOTTE ELISHEVA FONROBERT (2005)

PURIM ("lots") is a minor Jewish festival (one in which work is not prohibited) that falls on the fourteenth day of Adar. It celebrates the deliverance, as told in the *Book of Esther,* of the Jews from the designs of Haman, who cast lots to determine the date of their destruction. According to some historians, the events recorded in *Esther* are fictitious, the festival probably having its origin in a Babylonian festival. But there is evidence that Purim was celebrated as a Jewish festival from the first century BCE. Purim was observed also as a reminder to Jews that God often works "behind the scenes" in order to protect his people. Medieval thinkers found a basis for this idea in the absence of God's name in *Esther,* the only book in the Hebrew Bible in which the divine name does not appear.

The central feature of Purim is the reading of the Megillah (scroll), as the *Book of Esther* is called, in the form of a parchment scroll, written by hand and occasionally profusely illustrated. This public reading takes place on the night of Purim and again during the morning service in the synagogue. During this service the passage in the Torah concerning the blotting out of the name of Amalek (*Ex.* 17:8–16) is read because Haman was a descendant of Amalek. Based on this is the practice, frowned upon by some Jews, of making loud noises with rattles and the like whenever the name of Haman is mentioned during the reading of the Megillah.

Esther 9:22 speaks of sending portions to friends and giving alms to the poor. Hence the rabbinic rule is that each person must send a gift of at least two items of food to a friend and give at least one donation to two poor men. From the reference in *Esther* 9:17 to "days of feasting and joy," the rabbis further established the Purim festive meal, at which there is much imbibing of wine. A Talmudic statement has it that a man must drink until he is incapable of telling whether he is blessing Mordechai or cursing Haman.

As part of the Purim jollity, undoubtedly influenced by the Italian Carnival, people dress up, and children, especially, produce Purim plays in which they assume the characters mentioned in the Megillah. Rabbis objected to men dressing up as women and vice versa since this offends against the law in *Deuteronomy* 22:5, but Meir of Padua in the sixteenth century defended the practice as a harmless masquerade. In some communities it is the practice to appoint a "Purim rabbi" whose duty it is frivolously to manipulate even the most sacred texts.

The Jews of Shushan (*Est.* 9:18) celebrated Purim on the fifteenth day of Adar. To pay honor to Jerusalem, it was ordained that cities that, like Jerusalem, had walls around them in the days of Joshua should celebrate Purim on the fifteenth. Consequently, the citizens of Jerusalem today keep the festival and read the Megillah on Shushan Purim, the fifteenth of Adar, while for other Jews Purim is on the fourteenth of the month.

SEE ALSO Purim Plays.

BIBLIOGRAPHY

N. S. Doniach's *Purim* (Philadelphia, 1933) is a competent survey in English of the origins, rites, and ceremonies of Purim in which both the critical and the traditional views are fairly stated.

New Sources

Polish, Daniel F. "Aspects of Esther: A Phenomenological Exploration of the 'Megillah' of Esther and the Origins of Purim." *JSOT* 85 (1999): 85–106.

LOUIS JACOBS (1987)
Revised Bibliography

PURIM PLAYS. Known in standard Yiddish as *purimshpiln* (sg., *purimshpil),* the Purim plays, presented during the holiday of Purim, were the most common form of folk drama among eastern and western Jews up until the Holocaust. The earliest written accounts of such plays are from the middle of the sixteenth century. They describe single-actor performances in Yiddish of *purimshpiln* based on non-biblical themes that took place in Venice, Italy, and Brest (in Belarus). In the eighteenth century, more full-fledged plays with troupe performances were produced in various communities by *yeshivah* students, musicians, artisans, and apprentices; they were enacted in synagogues and in the homes of the well-to-do, where the actors received small sums of money. Examples of especially popular biblical stories that were performed were those of Esther and Ahasuerus (main characters in the *Book of Esther)*, Joseph and his brothers, the binding of Isaac, and David and Goliath—all these plots emphasized redemption from impending destruction.

Today, most well-known traditions of *purimshpiln* occur in several Hasidic communities, of which the best known are the Reb Arele Ḥasidim (known also as Toledot Aharon), who came to Jerusalem from Hungary during World War I; the Vizhnitzer Ḥasidim, who came to Bene Beraq (in Israel) from Romania during World War II, and the surviving members of the Bobover Ḥasidim of Poland, who established themselves in Brooklyn, New York, after World War II.

In addition to the religious events of the common Jewish calendar, the Ḥasidim have established their own traditions; to a great extent these were inspired by the sixteenth- and seventeenth-century qabbalists of Safad. The qabbalists elevated the status of Purim to that of a major festival. Playing on the Hebrew word *kippurim* ("atonements," an alternate name of Yom Kippur), reading it to mean "like Purim" (*ki-Purim*), the Purim holiday thus placed in importance alongside Yom Kippur, the most solemn of all Jewish holidays.

Like their forefathers, contemporary Ḥasidim draw on the message of Purim, particularly as it is dramatically presented through the *purimshpil,* as a means of strengthening their ideology and tradition. On both Yom Kippur and Purim, a central theme is that repentance is requested and granted; the Ḥasidim believe that God is more attentive to supplication on these days.

The *purimshpil* has assumed the role of sacred work; the *rebe* (spiritual leader of the community) uses it to bring members of the community closer to God. The first evidence of the *purimshpil* as an element in Hasidic ritual is attributed to Aryeh Leib (1725–1813) of Shpola, a city in Russia. He believed that the performance of a play on Purim could influence the course of events, a phenomenon known to anthropologists as "sympathetic magic." Folk belief has it that when a decree was issued against Jews, Aryeh Leib suggested to his followers that they act in a play, the plot of which described a reversal of such a feared situation. Other stories are told of how these *purimshpiln* were instrumental in offsetting specific disasters. The quality of inversion is inherent in the original Purim text, the *Book of Esther.* A central idea underlying the *Book of Esther* is *ve-nahafokh hu'* (Heb., "and it was reversed," *Est.* 9:11). Accordingly, Haman, the king's vizier who wanted to hang Mordecai, is hanged himself, and Mordecai becomes a minister of the court. The Jewish community is avenged of its enemies rather than harmed by them.

Themes nowadays are also drawn from biblical sources, East European folklore, and issues of day-to-day life. In the Bobover repertoire, for example, the *Book of Daniel* serves as the background for the *Play of Nebuchadnezzar.* Similarly, a Hasidic legend retelling the wonder of a pious Hasid has been dramatized as the *Three Revenges.* Consistent with the *Purim-Kippurim* notion, the plays are always serious and didactic despite the comic overlay, depicting central themes in Jewish experience—survival, martyrdom, and redemption.

The production of the *purimshpil* by the community replaces the sermon the *rebe* would otherwise deliver. The *purimshpil* is incorporated into the *rebe's tish* (table) on the midnight of Purim. The *tish* is a central ritual in the life of Hasidic men, who assemble around their *rebe's* table in their prayer hall on festivals to share a communal meal, dance, and sing together. The *purimshpil* may last all night, and women may be part of the audience. The production of the play is considered sacred work rather than "entertainment," and the manner in which it is performed is as carefully monitored by those involved in the production as the content since the performance itself and the texts used may appear to be in contradiction to Jewish law. Making fun of God and misquoting biblical phrases, for example, are forbidden and could result in God punishing the actors. Therefore, it is important that the themes of Jewish belief are accurately followed.

Usually the spiritual elite of the community, the married male students and teachers, take part in the production, writing, selection of music and costume, and painting of backdrops. The comic elements are incorporated into the play during both rehearsals and the performance itself. The actors suggest jokes, which may be accepted or rejected for particular scenes. The time allocated for the preparation of the production is limited because it is viewed as taking the men away from their primary function, studying Torah.

The *purimshpil* more than any other event in the Hasidic festival calendar engages the members of the community in ludicrous, playful behavior antithetical to everyday conditions. During the performance, men become actors, wear costumes and makeup, and assume both male and female roles. In the audience, the division between male and female is also relaxed; women speak with men across the *mehitsah* (the separation between the women's and the men's sections in the synagogue, a division mandated by religious law), which has been drawn aside. Thus, the prayer hall is converted from a house of study and prayer into a theater. In fact, the Purim play is one of the rare occasions during the year for the community to view theater: The Hasidic way of life prohibits the participation in, and viewing of, movies or plays.

Inspired by the male production of *purimshpiln,* Hasidic women have started to perform their own versions of the Purim plays for mainly female audiences during the week of Purim. Referred to by the women as "Purim musicals," the texts have sources similar to those of the male *purimshpiln* but are more influenced by musicals and modern stage effects.

World War II for the most part brought an end to the folkways of Ashkenazic Jewry. Traditions of Yiddish song, music, literature, and drama, which were integral parts of Jewish life in Europe, were brutally destroyed. The revitalization of the *purimshpil* in the latter half of the twentieth century exemplifies how traditional art forms may survive physical and spiritual catastrophes. The annual performance of the *purimshpil,* once an all-encompassing Ashkenazic Jewish tradition, has evolved among Hasidim into a continuation ritual, dramatizing their need to remember the past, thereby connecting that past to the present.

SEE ALSO Hasidism, overview article.

BIBLIOGRAPHY

Almost all the literature on the Purim plays is in Hebrew. Among works in English are Philip Goodman's *The Purim Anthology* (1949; reprint, Philadelphia, 1960), which has a musical supplement, and my doctoral dissertation, "The Celebration of a Contemporary Purim in the Bobover Hassidic Community" (University of Texas, 1979). A videotape of the play described in my work is available at the YIVO Institute in New York (*Purimshpil,* R-70-54-11 and R-80-54-29). The Purim play is also discussed in the context of Hebrew drama in Israel Abraham's *Jewish Life in the Middle Ages* (1896; reprint, New York, 1969), pp. 260–272. Following is a list of a few of the works available in Hebrew.

Moskowitz, Zvi. *Kol ha-kattuv le- Ḥayyim.* Jerusalem, 1961/2. This volume discusses "everything attributed to Ḥayyim," who is Ḥayyim Halberstam (1793–1876), of the city of Nowy Zanz (southeastern Poland), the originator of the Bobover Ḥasidim. See especially pages 84–87.

Rosenberg, Yehudah. *Tiferet MaHaR'el: Mi-shpi'lei ha-niqra' "der shpaler zayde."* Peyetrekow, 1912; reprint, 1975. A selection of the miraculous deeds of Rebe Aryeh Leib of Shpola. See especially pages 38–53.

Shmeruk, Chone. *Mahazot miqra'iyyim be-Yiddish, 1697–1750.* Jerusalem, 1979. This is one of the best reference books in Hebrew available on the history and origin of the *purimshpil.* Also included are early texts of plays as well as a bibliography of manuscripts and printed books.

New Sources

Baumgarten, Jean. "Un 'Purim-shpil' à Kyriat Vizhnitz de Bnei Braq (1996)." *Perspectives* 10 (2003): 127–142.

Belkin, Ahuva. "Joyous Disputation around the Gallows: A Rediscovered Purim Play from Amsterdam." *JTD* 1 (1995): 31–59.

Belkin, Ahuva. "Clowns et mendiants: les costumes de 'Purim-shpil'." *Cahiers du Judaïsme* 6 (1999–2000): 105–112.

Epstein, Shifra. *"Daniyel-shpil" be-hasidut Bobov: mi-mahazeh 'amami le-tekes Purimi.* Jerusalem, 1998.

Rozik, Eli. "The Adoption of Theater by Judaism despite Ritual: A Study in the Purimshpil." *European Legacy* 1 (1996): 1231–1235.

SHIFRA EPSTEIN (1987)
Revised Bibliography

PURITANISM. In its most common historical usage *Puritanism* refers to a movement within English Protestantism in both the British Isles and colonial America. Some historians, identifying the essence of Puritanism as a reaction to the tardy pace of the English Reformation, date it from the activities of William Tyndale (1495–1536) and John Hooper (d. 1555) in the formative years of the Church of England. But its major impact was felt during the century between the coming of Elizabeth I to the throne in 1558 and the death of Oliver Cromwell in 1658. For most of that period Puritanism had no institutional identity of its own. Puritans sought to purge the existing English church of its Catholic remnants rather than to set up a rival church. Because their goal was reform, the line that separated them from their non-Puritan brethren was often unclear, a situation to the advantage of those clergy and laity who wished to use the institutions of the church to effect an ultimate change in the ecclesiastical structure and beliefs of the nation.

The first stirrings of Puritan reform came in the reign of Elizabeth from a group of former Marian exiles, clergy and laity who had fled to Protestant centers on the continent to escape the persecutions of the Catholic queen Mary I (1553–1558). These believers had been radicalized by their experience at Geneva and elsewhere and were dissatisfied with the conservative nature of the Elizabethan settlement. That settlement was a *via media* between the demands of Catholicism and those of extreme reform. A compromise that many returning exiles could and did accept, it was unpalatable to many who saw no grace in an accommodation with sin. Initial protests focused on outward signs and ceremonies of the church such as the wearing of vestments, the physical position of church furnishings, and matters of nomenclature. The usage of the establishment, in the view of its critics, symbolized belief in a sacrificial priesthood, a real presence of Christ in the Eucharist, and other elements of Roman Catholic faith and practice.

Clerical opposition to the dictates of the queen and her archbishop of Canterbury, Matthew Parker (1559–1575), caught the public's attention. But while the position of the clergy forced them to make public displays of their conformity or nonconformity, the movement they represented was not simply a clerical protest. Puritanism drew the support of laity as distinguished as members of the queen's Privy Council and tapped deep wells of popular support in town and village, so much so that in some cases of the nonuse of vestments it was lay pressure that strengthened the will of a Puritan clergyman rather than pressure from a clergyman stirring up popular discontent.

Puritan hopes for early reform were bolstered when Edmund Grindal (1519–1583) succeeded Parker as archbishop of Canterbury in 1575. A progressive bishop, although not a Puritan, Grindal was less concerned than Parker with enforcing practices that had caused friction in the church. He promoted efforts to upgrade the education of the clergy and to reform ecclesiastical abuses, positions strongly supported by Puritans but advocated by progressive members of the establishment as well. When Grindal refused to carry out the queen's desire to suppress prophesyings (clerical conferences designed to promote the continuing education of the participants), Elizabeth suspended him, and the division within the church widened.

Frustrated throughout Elizabeth's reign by the resistance of the episcopal hierarchy, Puritans sought other methods of reforming English religion. *An Admonition to Parliament* (1572) urged the Parliament of 1572 to take responsibility for the church. While some members of that body showed sympathy, the queen was able to block their efforts. Other clergy and laity began to discuss and advocate an alternative system of church government. Presbyterianism, first advocated by Thomas Cartwright (1535–1603), was not universally popular among Puritan reformers, most of whom were able to work with the church hierarchy on a wide range of issues. Some Puritans, however, began to despair of reforming the church. Under the leadership of men such as Robert Browne (c. 1550–1633), Henry Barrow (1550–1593), and John Greenwood (d. 1593), they broke apart from the church and organized Separatist congregations.

In the last years of Elizabeth's reign and during the rule of James I (1603–1625), a new generation of religious thinkers began to articulate their theologies. One group, which would eventually rise within and then dominate the episcopal hierarchy, was represented by Richard Hooker (1554–1600), Richard Neile (1562–1640), and William Laud (1573–1645). This strain in Anglican thought reflected an accommodation to the views of the Dutch theologian Jacobus Arminius (1559–1609), who had sought to temper the rigidity of Calvinistic predestinarianism. The Arminians in the church also stressed the authority of king and bishops, the efficacy of the sacraments in the process of salvation, and the return to a more elaborate use of liturgical ceremony. In contrast to this evolving "new orthodoxy," John Preston (1587–1628), William Perkins (1558–1602), and William Ames (1576–1633) spelled out the essentials of Puritan belief that would characterize the seventeenth-century history of the movement in England and in the New England in America. The lines of demarcation between "orthodox" and Puritan members of the church became more sharply defined, and compromise became less likely.

The starting point for Puritan theology was an emphasis on the majesty, righteousness, and sovereignty of God. God created and maintained the universe by exercise of his will and directed all things to an intelligent end. The awe-inspiring Puritan image of the Father drew heavily on the Old Testament. In contrast was the Puritan concept of man. Scripture, their social surroundings, and an intense personal introspection all persuaded the Puritans that human beings were depraved sinners incapable of earning merit in the eyes of God. But although Adam's sin had led to this fallen state and thus precluded humankind from using the Adamic covenant of works to earn its way to heaven, a benevolent and loving God predestined some of his fallen creatures for the gift of salvation included in the covenant of grace. In emphasizing humankind's sin-diminished faculties and inability to bridge the gap separating humans from the creator, the Puritan stood in increasing contrast to the orthodox Anglican point of view.

In their speculation about the means whereby God reached out to elect certain souls for the gift of salvation, the Puritans developed elements of traditional Calvinism. Puritan theologians, William Perkins in particular, made concepts of the covenant central to their evangelism and moralism. Believing in predestination, they explained that all human beings were pledged by the covenant of works to adhere to the divine law and were justly condemned for failure to adhere to it. They also wrote and preached an evangelical message of hope centering on the free gift of saving grace to the elect. For those saved from the consequences of their actions by this gift, the law still remained the standard of behavior according to which they tried to live lives expressive of gratitude to their savior.

The covenant of works depended on human action, while the covenant of grace required a faith that God himself enabled the elect to grasp. This emphasis on contractual relationships became a controlling metaphor for Puritans in their social as well as their religious thought.

If the idea of the covenant was to be found in the Reformed roots of Puritanism, so was the language of conditionality that the Puritans employed in their discussion of the doctrine. While, in the words of a foremost student of covenant theology, the ministers "from the standpoint of high Calvinism . . . were solid on election but soft on perseverance," they were still within the main current of that tradition. This nuance in their thought was revealed most clearly in their tracing of the normal path of the elect to salvation.

Most Puritan preachers developed a complex morphology of conversion, identifying stages in that process such as election, vocation, justification, sanctification, and glorification. Election signified God's choosing of those to whom the grace of salvation was to be offered. Vocation was the Holy Spirit's offer to humankind of the grace enabling it to seek contrition, faith, and cooperation with that grace. Puritans developed an extensive literature on humanity's preparation with God's help for the next and pivotal stage, justification. God provided natural means such as the scripture, the sacraments, and the sermons of godly preachers to facilitate the process of salvation. By grasping hold of these means sinners could not save themselves, but the elect could cooperate with the Spirit's transforming work on their souls.

For the blessed, justification—the soul-wrenching, born-again experience of conversion—represented a passage from sinner to saint, from a vile and loathsome creature to a being embraced by God. Justification placed the stamp of election on the saint and rehabilitated, though it did not perfect, human faculties. Sanctification was the life of grace lived by the saint, a life of endeavoring to show gratitude to the divine author of one's salvation by living as God's law prescribed. Because of human frailty, assurance of one's state was sometimes in doubt. Glorification was the unification of the soul with God after death, the final resolution of doubt, and the gathering of the elect into the communion of saints.

In his pilgrim's progress to the celestial kingdom the Puritan constantly encountered the moral law. Perhaps the simplest explanation of the rule by which the Puritan sought to live is the statement by Richard Baxter (1615–1691) that "*Overdoing* is the most ordinary way of *undoing*." The Puritan life was a life of vigorous involvement in the world without excessive or abusive use of the natural order. Some later commentators and contemporary critics have sought to blame Puritans for all that they themselves perceive as repressive in Protestant culture. But contrary to the image painted by their detractors, Puritans were not killjoys or prudes. They dressed as befitted their social class, participated in lotteries, drank alcoholic beverages, and approached sex as more than a mere obligation.

Puritans did, however, scorn what they viewed as the libertine excesses of many of their peers, condemning not the drink but the drunkard, not the expression of sexual love between husband and wife but extramarital sex. They felt called to vocations that were social, economic, and civic as well as religious. They rejected the monastic ideal of separation from the world and embraced a vision of total Christian involvement in the creation. As one of the elect the Puritan was called to use fully all the talents God provided without overstressing any one call; in early Massachusetts the civil magistrates had occasion to gently remind the clergy that even sermonizing could be overdone when the number of lecture days began to interfere with the task of community building. While some Puritans such as Michael Wigglesworth (1631–1705) allowed their fears of sin to become obsessions that made them walking parodies of Puritanism, the ideal of the Puritan moral life was one of sober moderation.

The Puritans' moral stance and belief that their role in history was that of a chosen people called to create a New Jerusalem and usher in the millennium made Puritans, on both sides of the Atlantic, culturally distinct from their peers. The elect envisioned themselves as a group apart, a saved and saving remnant. Their lifestyle was different enough to symbolize their uniqueness. Their effort to give God his due by spending the Sabbath reading the scriptures rather than indulging in sport or dance, their rejection of set prayers for spontaneous expressions, their disdain for the ritualization of the liturgy, their coming together in New England on designated fast days and days of thanksgiving—all of these reinforced the Puritans' sense of being apart from yet responsible for saving their native land.

The task of redeeming England seemed more difficult than ever as the reign of James I gave way to that of Charles I (1625–1649). Puritans had wielded considerable influence at Oxford and Cambridge and from those universities a brotherhood of reformed preachers had spread the Puritan message throughout the realm. The patronage of sympathetic gentry and of some borough officials secured pulpits for the Puritans. A group of lay and clerical leaders called the Feofees for Impropriation solicited donations to fund the purchase of numerous church livings that would be controlled by the movement. But the rise of William Laud symbolized the growing determination of the king and his chief counselors to root out dissent. Puritan clergymen were haled before ecclesiastical courts, deprived of their livings, and harried out of the land.

Having failed to reform England by their written or spoken word, some Puritan leaders conceived the idea of persuading their countrymen by the example of a model Puritan community. This was the goal of many who joined in the Great Migration to New England in the 1630s. As John Winthrop (1588–1649), the first governor of Massachusetts, expressed it: "We shall be as a City upon a Hill." Massachusetts and her sister commonwealths of Connecticut (founded in 1636) and New Haven (1637) and the moderate Separatist colony of Plymouth represented an orthodoxy that was designated the New England Way. Their social and political fabric was knit from ideas of Christian organicism owing much to English rural traditions as well as to the corporate strain in Puritan thought. In matters of religion the orthodox developed a congregational church structure with all residents required to attend service but with full membership and its privileges reserved for those who could persuade their peers that they had experienced saving grace.

The achievement of this orthodoxy was not without struggle. Puritans who migrated from England left the status of dissenting minority within the structure of the state church to cope with the challenge of translating their general principles into institutional practice and statements of faith. Various individuals offered their perspectives, and through the efforts of clergymen such as John Cotton (1584–1652), Richard Mather (1596–1669), Thomas Hooker (1586–1647), John Davenport (1597–1670), and Thomas Shepard (1605–1649) a consensus emerged that would be articulated in the Cambridge Platform (1648). Some Puritans found themselves outside these emerging boundaries of acceptable belief. Many responded by conforming, but Roger Williams (1603–1683), Anne Hutchinson (1591–1643), and others who would not bend were excluded; some, including Williams and Hutchinson, took up residence in Rhode Island, forming a society that rapidly achieved notoriety as a haven of radicalism.

In England Puritans who had stayed at home were at the forefront of the coalition that formed in opposition to the king's foreign policy, religious innovations, forced loans, and use of prerogative courts. The civil wars that erupted (1642–1648) pitted Parliament against the king, and so heavily was the House of Commons dominated by the reformers that the struggle also earned the name of the Puritan Revolution. During the course of the conflict Puritan reformers sought to construct a new Church of England. The same tensions that had threatened Puritan uniformity in New England appeared and the circumstances of the war made controlling them impossible.

Although most Puritans could agree on the doctrines contained in the Westminster Assembly's Confession of Faith (1647), many rejected the Presbyterian ecclesiastical structure that that reform convocation recommended to Parliament. Presbyterians, Congregationalists, and Baptists became distinct groups within the movement, while hosts of radical sects found sustenance in the excitement of the times. While political stability was provided by the rise of Oliver Cromwell (1599–1658) as lord protector in 1649, religious diversity did not come to an end. Cromwell did, however, make progress toward the establishment of a Puritan state church uniting moderate Congregationalists such as Thomas Goodwin (1600–1680) and John Owen (1616–1683), moderate Presbyterians such as Stephen Marshall (1594–1655), and moderate Baptists such as Henry Jessey (1601–1663).

The return of the Stuart monarchy with the Restoration of Charles II (1660–1685) in 1660 saw the casting out of Puritanism from the Church of England. What had been a reform movement within Anglicanism became nonconformity in the shape of Presbyterian, Congregational, and Baptist denominations. Across the Atlantic, Puritan values still dominated, but the institutional separation from the Church of England that had always been a fact of colonial life was accepted in theory as well, and New Englanders adopted the denominational badges of their brethren in England.

The story of Puritanism merges into the story of the denominations it spawned, but as a cultural movement it continued to have relevance. In England the poems of John Milton (1608–1674), the devotional writings of Richard Baxter, and the *Pilgrim's Progress* of John Bunyan (1628–1688) were fruits of the Puritan outlook. In America the literary offerings of Anne Bradstreet (1612–1672), Michael Wigglesworth, and Edward Taylor (1662–1729) and the range of writings of Cotton Mather (1663–1728) betokened the vitality of Puritanism. When Jonathan Edwards (1703–1758) spoke to the people of the Connecticut valley in the 1730s, there was sparked a great awakening not only of religious enthusiasm in general but of a distinctively Puritan outlook on the universe, its creator, and the sinners who inhabit it.

See Also Browne, Robert; Bunyan, John; Edwards, Jonathan; Hooker, Richard; Hooker, Thomas; Hutchinson, Anne; Mather Family; Williams, Roger.

Bibliography

My book *The Puritan Experiment: New England Society from Bradford to Edwards* (New York, 1976) is an introductory survey to the English origins and American development of Puritan ideas and practice. *The Puritan Tradition in America, 1620–1730,* edited by Alden T. Vaughan (New York, 1972), is the best single-volume anthology of Puritan writings. For those interested in the origins of the movement, the works of Patrick Collinson, especially *The Elizabethan Puritan Movement* (Berkeley, 1967), are indispensable. Barrington R. White's *The English Separatist Tradition: From the Marian Martyrs to the Pilgrim Fathers* (Oxford, 1971) is an excellent analysis of that important offshoot from mainstream Puritanism. The seventeenth-century evolution of Puritanism in England is well surveyed in Michael R. Watts's *The Dissenters: From the Reformation to the French Revolution* (Oxford, 1978). The starting point for an understanding of the faith of New England Puritans remains the classic studies by Perry Miller, especially *The New England Mind: The Seventeenth Century* (New York, 1939). Puritan polity is skillfully examined by Edmund S. Morgan in *Visible Saints: The History of a Puritan Idea* (New York, 1963). Many key facets of Puritan theology are unraveled in E. Brooks Holifield's *The Covenant Sealed: The Development of Puritan Sacramental Theology in Old and New England, 1570–1720* (New Haven, Conn., 1974). The devotional aspects of Puritan life are the subject of Charles E. Hambrick-Stowe's *The Practice of Piety* (Chapel Hill, N.C., 1982).

New Sources

Brockway, Robert W. *Wonderful Work of God: Puritans and the Great Awakening.* Bethlehem, Pa., 2003.

Como, David R. *Blown by the Spirit: Puritanism and the Emergence of An Antinomian Underground in Pre-Civil War England.* Stanford, Calif., 2004.

Danner, Dan G. *Pilgrimage to Puritanism: History and Theology of the Marian Exiles at Geneva.* New York, 1999.

Davies, Horton. *The Worship of the American Puritans, 1629–1730.* New York, 1990.

Durston, Christopher, and Jacqueline Eales. *The Culture of English Puritanism, 1560–1700.* New York, 1996.

Knight, Janice. *Orthodoxies in Massachusetts.* Cambridge, Mass., 1994.

Sasek, Lawrence A., ed. *Images of English Puritanism.* Baton Rouge, La., 1989.

Wood, Ellen Meiksins, and Noal Wood. *A Trumpet of Sedition: Political Theory and the Rise of Capitalism 1509–1688.* New York, 1997.

Francis J. Bremer (1987)
Revised Bibliography

PURUṢA is a Sanskrit word meaning "person" or "a man." Throughout Indian intellectual history the term has acquired the independent meanings of "the first man, self," and "consciousness." The development of the concept of *puruṣa* therefore overlaps with the development of the concepts of *ātman* ("self"), *brahman* ("universal self"), and *kṣetrajña* ("knower"). The interrelationships among these concepts can be traced through the literature of the Upaniṣads and the epics, in the work of the Buddhist writer Aśvaghoṣa, in the medical work of Caraka, and in the texts of the Sāṃkhya school.

Puruṣa first occurs in the oldest extant book of Vedic hymns, the *Ṛgveda* (c. 1200 BCE). Hymn 10.90 refers to the first man from whose bodily parts sprang the different groups of society (*varṇas*) based on the division of labor. In the oldest Upaniṣads (600–300 BCE), the term still refers to the first man, whose essence is entirely self (*ātman*): "In the beginning this world was just a single self (*ātman*) in the form of a man (*puruṣa*)" (*Bṛhadāraṇyaka Upaniṣad* 1.4.1). When *puruṣa* first came into existence he became aware of himself and exclaimed, "Here I am" (1.4.1).

Both *ātman* and *brahman* inherited the function of creation from the original *puruṣa,* the first man. Such examples in the case of *ātman* are found in *Bṛhadāraṇyaka Upaniṣad* 1.4.1–10, and in the case of *brahman* in *Bṛhadāraṇyaka Upaniṣad* 1.4.11–16. Various creation myths described how the "one," desiring to be many, multiplied itself, forming a new creation.

The concepts of *ātman* and *puruṣa* as the original entities are first replaced by *brahman* in a verse of the *Bṛhadāraṇyaka Upaniṣad:* "In the beginning this world was *brahman,* one only" (1.4.11). The fully articulated concept of *brahman,* according to the Upaniṣads, refers to the cosmic entity, an omnipresent self that holds the whole universe within itself. It is this universal self (*brahman*) that is a counterpart to the individual self (*ātman*). The aim of many of the Upaniṣadic teachings was to realize the identity of these two principles through mystical experience.

The concept of *puruṣa* cannot be uniformly understood as self or consciousness. In its development it underwent such functional transformations that at times it took on opposing functions. This development can be seen, for example, in the description of *brahman* as having two aspects: "There are, indeed, two forms of *brahman:* the tangible (*mūrta*) and the formless, the mortal and the immortal, the moving and the motionless" (*Bṛhadāraṇyaka Upaniṣad* 2.3.1).

Change and creation were not the primary functions of the concept of *puruṣa;* eventually *puruṣa* took on other functions, while that of creation came to be associated with *prakṛti* (materiality). Thus, although *puruṣa* served at one time as the foundation of the whole universe it was also instrumental in establishing materiality, an opposing concept set forth by the Sāṃkhya school. Together, *puruṣa* and *prakṛti* constituted the essential entities of Sāṃkhya. This separation of *prakṛti* from *puruṣa* is reflected in the term *kṣetrajña.*

Kṣetrajña ("knower of the field," i.e., knower of materiality) is a term used to describe *puruṣa* as consciousness (cf. *Maitri Upaniṣad* 2.5). A section of the twelfth book of the *Mahābhārata* called the *Moksadharma* employs *kṣetrajña* as a synonym for *puruṣa,* while the *Buddhacarita* of Aśvaghoṣa uses *kṣetrajña* for consciousness in its descriptions of Sāṃkhya teachings (e.g., *Buddhacarita* 12.20).

The *Sāṃkhyakārikā* (c. 500 CE) of Īśvarakṛṣṇa, the first extant complete work of the Sāṃkhya school, is regarded as the classic statement on Sāṃkhya thought. According to this work, *puruṣa* is a contentless consciousness distinct in every respect from materiality. Consciousness (*puruṣa*) is, in fact, said to be the exact opposite of materiality or *prakṛti* (*Sāṃkhyakārikā* 19). For example, consciousness is uncaused and is not itself a cause; it is eternal, without space, without motion, without complexity, without substratum, without parts, independent, differentiated, and unproductive. The purpose of consciousness is to lend, so to speak, consciousness to materiality at the time of knowledge and thus to justify the existence of materiality.

By its mere presence, consciousness is the "passive witness" (*sākṣin*) of materiality. Consciousness is also the beneficiary of the activities of materiality, and finally, because it is different from all ordinary experience, *puruṣa* makes this ordinary experience meaningful by being different from it, by being conscious, and by making the experience a *conscious* experience.

Originally, *puruṣa* was spoken of as one, just as *brahman* and *kṣetrajña* are one. Yet in classical Sāṃhkya *puruṣa* came, like *ātman,* to be considered plural or many. This plurality of consciousnesses served to explain differences in existence, such as different births and different deaths. If, according to classical Sāṃkhya, there were only one consciousness, it would follow that when any one person attained liberation all individuals would attain liberation at the same time.

Under the influence of the dominant philosophical school of Advaita Vedānta, the Sāṃkhya-Yoga teacher Vijñānabhikṣu (sixteenth century) attempted to reconcile the plurality of consciousnesses with the one universal self of Vedantic thought. Vijñānabhikṣu claimed that it is possible for consciousness to be many under certain conditions. This was not to be considered a contradiction to the claim that there is only one consciousness, since, he maintained, the plurality of *puruṣa* is ultimately only a matter of convenience for the purposes of discourse. He thereby effected a conflation of the Sāṃkhya with Advaita Vedānta.

Sāṃkhya shares in pursuing the highest aim, liberation, with most other philosophical and religious traditions. Unlike these, liberation in Sāṃkhya comes from that knowledge whereby one distinguishes between two entities, contentless consciousness (*puruṣa*) and materiality (*prakṛti*), as essentially different things. Isolating (*kaivalya*) the two entities from each other is the recognition of this distinction. This is the truth that grants liberation.

SEE ALSO Brahman; Prakṛti; Sāṃkhya.

BIBLIOGRAPHY

A minute analysis of the formative stages of the concept of *puruṣa* is found in Erhardt Hanefeld's *Philosophische Haupttexte der älteren Upaniṣaden* (Wiesbaden, 1976). For the beginnings of the development of the concept, see E. H. Johnston's *Early Sāṃkhya: An Essay on Its Historical Development according to the Texts* (1937; reprint, Delhi, 1974). A detailed study of the Sāṃkhya school is provided in *Sāṃkhya: A Dualist Tradition in Indian Philosophy* by Gerald James Larson and

Ram Shankar Bhattacharya, the third volume of the *Encyclopedia of Indian Philosophies,* edited by Karl H. Potter (Princeton and Delhi, 1987). See also Patrick Olivelle, *Upaniṣads.* (World's Classics. Oxford, 1996).

EDELTRAUD HARZER (1987 AND 2005)

PUSEY, EDWARD BOUVERIE (1800–1882), along with John Keble and John Henry (later Cardinal) Newman, a leader of the Oxford Movement (sometimes called Tractarianism), a high church development in the Church of England that flourished between 1833 and 1845. Pusey was educated at Eton and at Christ Church, Oxford, and was a fellow at Oriel before becoming regius professor of Hebrew and canon of Christ Church. Newman said of Pusey, "He at once gave us a position and a name." With Newman's defection to Roman Catholicism, Pusey became the primary leader of the movement until his death.

Pusey was among the first English scholars to become acquainted with the modern critical approach to scripture emerging in Germany, but throughout this exposure he maintained a quite conservative posture. His influence on the religious life of England can be seen in several areas: his tracts and sermons gave popular impetus to a revival of medieval piety in England, he was a friend and mentor of the nineteenth-century monastic revival, and the practice of private confession to a priest in modern Anglicanism can be traced to his sermon on the subject in 1846.

Extreme rigor characterized his personal piety, and his theology left little room for the forgiveness of sins after baptism. His long and diligent work on the subject of baptismal regeneration suffered from his failure to define the meaning of the term. As a whole, his scholarship lacked the subtle, seminal, and lasting quality of Newman's, or the poetic warmth of Keble's.

Pusey's life seemed characterized by defeats or disappointments: the appointment as regius professor of divinity of the liberal theologian Renn Hampden over Tractarian protests; the promulgation of the doctrine of papal infallibility; his censure by the university for his sermon on the real presence in the Eucharist; the departure from Anglicanism of Newman and others; and the Privy Council's overruling of the Ecclesiastical Courts on the Gorham case, and others like it, which seemed to Pusey to be an unwarranted intrusion of the state into the affairs of the church. However, his prestige, loyalty, and steadying influence within the Oxford Movement and subsequent Anglo-Catholicism marked a permanent change in direction within Anglicanism.

SEE ALSO Newman, John Henry.

BIBLIOGRAPHY

Good collections of Pusey's writings are *Spiritual Letters,* edited by J. O. Johnston and W. C. E. Newbolt (New York, 1901), and *The Mind of the Oxford Movement,* edited by Owen Chadwick (Stanford, Calif., 1960). Useful biographical matter can be found in *Life of Pusey,* 4 vols., edited by Henry P. Liddon (London, 1884–1887), which includes an extensive bibliography of Pusey's published works in volume 4.

C. FITZSIMONS ALLISON (1987)

PYGMY RELIGIONS. African Pygmies comprise a variety of ethnic groups who dwell as hunter-gatherers in the rain forest of central Africa. Because they live as nomads in a demanding and inaccessible environment, few serious studies have been done on them. Most studies of Pygmy life have been concerned with how they relate to the history of religions. According to Wilhelm Schmidt (1868–1954), an ordained priest and ethnologist interested in the origin of religion, the Pygmy peoples represented humanity in its childhood; they were a living equivalent of one of the earliest stages of human culture. Since early evidence seemed to indicate the existence of monotheistic belief in primitive societies, Schmidt engaged his colleagues to explore Pygmy religious life. Hence, for years the Pygmies were studied by Catholic missionaries seeking to support the idea that monotheism (rather than animism or fetishism) was the earliest form of religion.

This article discusses three Pygmy groups that are better known through fieldwork: the Aka, located in the southern region of the Central African Republic; the Baka of eastern Cameroon; and the Mbuti of the Ituri rain forest of Zaire. Other more sedentary and less documented groups such as the Gyeli of western Cameroon and the Twa of central Zaire and Rwanda are not included.

AKA PYGMIES. According to Aka cosmology, a creator god named Bembe made the world, including the sky, earth, forest, and animals. He then fashioned the first male and female couple, Tole and Ngolobanzo. He later added a younger brother, Tonzanga. Bembe gave all worldly knowledge and goods to Tonzanga, but Tole subsequently stole them from his brother to ensure the survival of the family as a totality. Because of this theft, Bembe withdrew into the sky where he now lives without paying further attention to the world he created.

The primary twin couple, Tole and Ngolobanzo, gave birth to two children whose union later engendered the rest of humanity. Since that time, the three original beings created by Bembe have continued to live in a parallel world that represents the ideal to which human society should conform. The ghosts of human beings (*edio*) live in the forest where they lead an endless existence under the rule of humanity's two ancestral spirits, Ezengi and Ziakpokpo. Ghosts are neutral toward human beings and act either benevolently or malevolently depending on how well humans treat one another and whether they show respect for the ghosts themselves. However, it is believed that those areas outside the forest (forest edge, villages, and rivers) are inhabited by foreign malign spirits. In Aka thought, the village is a nonhuman (bad) world, the forest a realm of ghosts, and the campsite the only fully human realm.

The forest is impregnated with vital principles; from these, either by initiation or by inheritance, an individual may appropriate the spiritual power (*kulu*) that will assist him by blessing his various endeavors. However, malign spirits (*kose*) are attracted by malevolence and slander among human beings. The evil that individuals may wish upon each other is the cause of human misfortune because it provokes the wrath of the spirits.

Aka religious rituals fall into two types: large festivals that concern the entire community and small rites undertaken for more private purposes. All Aka rituals relate to three fundamental functions: propitiation of supernatural powers (ghosts or the forest god Ezengi) so as to bring about abundance and fertility; divination of the cause of disorder or the likely result of a prospective action; and the propitiation of irritated spirits, whether they are ancestor ghosts during a period of social conflict or shortage or animal spirits after a murder (the death of an animal during a hunt).

Rituals are performed before undertaking a journey. In Aka thought (which relies upon the juxtaposition of camp, village, and forest with all their other associated values), any passage from one world to the next is potentially dangerous and requires ritual action. While every adult male may be in contact with certain familiar spirits, it is the function of various specialists (an elder, chief hunter, or diviner-healer) to meet major spirits such as Ezengi or the elephant spirit.

The Aka obtain most of their food by hunting, and insofar as it is a highly dangerous activity with unpredictable results, it is surrounded by rites of various natures: rites of individual and collective propitiation, rites of divination, rites thanking the ghosts with offerings, and a rite of collective expiation vis-à-vis the game spirit. A period of successive hunting failures calls for a divination and propitiation ceremony that includes the appearance of ghosts in the form of leaf masks. When men are absent on extended hunting forays, women perform particular songs and dances asking not only that the men come back with large amounts of game but also explicitly asking for the resumption of sexual relations.

The value the Aka place on human fertility and human life in general is even more apparent in the Mokondi ceremony, a large festival devoted to Ezengi. During Mokondi, a figure wearing a raffia-cloth mask dances inside a throng of people who are segregated by sex into concentric circles. The ceremony is performed every night for an entire month to mark the settlement of a new camp after the death of a community member. It is intended to restore the welfare of the community by obtaining the benevolence and protection of the supreme being.

The last salient Aka ritual is connected with honey gathering. Mobandi, an annual rite linked to the flowering of a particular tree, is a collective purification ritual that involves flagellation; by gently beating their bodies with leafy boughs, the Aka hope to expel malign forces (*kose*) from the community. Moreover, as honey stands as a sexual symbol for the Aka, the Mobandi ritual corresponds to the periodic regeneration of the world.

BAKA PYGMIES. Certain religious conceptions held by the Baka are similar to those of the Aka. Several terms are also employed by both groups but are used to designate different aspects of their religious life. According to Baka cosmology, the god Komba created the world and all its creatures. He is part of a divine family that includes his sisters, a culture hero named Waito, and various offspring. In this complicated mythology, all of these creatures function as a many-faceted hermaphroditic entity that is self-engendering and productive of all humanity, including Pygmies as well as tall Africans.

Waito, who stole from Komba such goods as game and fire for the benefit of humanity, is the figure who introduced women and sexuality into human culture. Komba, on the other hand, brought death into the world. While Komba remains distant in the sky, it is his spirit, Ezengi, who gives Baka youths knowledge of the world and of social existence during initiation ceremonies. Ezengi protects humans and rules over their death and rebirth as ghosts in the forest. Communication with either the forest god Ezengi or the ghosts is the concern of a specialist (the diviner-healer), or of initiated adult males during the collective dances, and is achieved by means of songs, charms, offerings, or at times, with a fire.

The function of ritual among the Baka is akin to that of the Aka: prediction of the future, propitiation of the spirits so as to ensure a successful hunt, restoration of normal life after times of trouble, and procurement of Ezengi's continued benevolence toward the community. Before beginning on a spear hunt for large game, a divination session will be performed, followed by a women's ritual that includes yodeling and dances to entice the animals. A death requires two ceremonies. The night the death occurs, a masked spirit (symbol of life against death) performs a dance, insulting the audience and making obscene jokes. Following the burial, the deceased soul dances in the camp but is then chased off with firebrands and driven into the forest. Once the campsite is deserted, a large festival begins in order to restore the normal existence of the community. At this point, Ezengi appears in the form of a raffia mask. Because women are not allowed to participate, each family is represented in the ritual by an adult male. The ceremony, involving a large number of people, is also the culmination of the initiation of pubescent boys that generally lasts for several weeks. Through such pervasive participation, this ritual, which is marked by the collective singing of polyphonic songs, provides an occasion to reaffirm group unity after a serious crisis.

MBUTI PYGMIES. The Mbuti Pygmies of the Ituri rain forest are the most well known of the various Pygmy ethnic groups. According to Paul Schebesta, the Mbuti believe that God created the universe (that is, the forest) and all its creatures and forces. God then retired into the sky, ending his participation in earthly affairs. The first human, a culture hero named Tore, became god of the forest; he gave the Mbuti both fire and death and is seen as the source of game, honey, and protection. Essentially a benevolent god, Tore is thought to be particularly offended by evil. According to this version of the story, both humans and animals are endowed with vital forces (*megbe*). Furthermore, it is believed that the shadow of a deceased human becomes a forest spirit, part of an invisible people who mediate between humans and the forest god Tore.

Colin Turnbull (1965) disagrees with this account of Mbuti cosmology. According to him, there is no creator god; instead, the Mbuti worship God as a living benevolent being personified by the forest. To them, God is the forest. Turnbull also diverges from Schebesta's account of the mediating forest spirits, for he views the Mbuti as a practical people who have a direct relationship with the forest as sacred being.

The Mbuti Pygmies lack both ritual specialists and divination practices. Communication with the forest is achieved through fire and smoke, offerings, whistles, wooden trumpets, and polyphonic songs. As with the Aka and the Baka, rituals surround hunting, honey gathering, food shortages, puberty, and death.

The onset of puberty in women is celebrated by an initiation festival known as Elima. At the time of the first menstruation, a girl goes into seclusion together with all her young friends. Staying in the Elima hut for several weeks, the girls receive instruction concerning motherhood and various ritual responsibilities from a respected older female relative. They are also taught how to sing the songs of adult women. Elima also functions as a means for choosing a mate.

Although Elima functions as an initiation into adult life for both girls and boys, there is a separate initiation rite, known as Nkumbi, exclusively for males. During Nkumbi, the Mbuti boys are circumcised together with the young males of the neighboring peoples who live in fixed agricultural settlements outside the forest. Nkumbi is primarily a way for the Mbuti boys to gain status in village society, but it also works to cement ties between the Mbuti and their village neighbors.

The first killing of game marks a further initiation rite for young Mbuti men. Until he has accomplished this, a young man is not allowed to participate in the most important Mbuti ritual, Molimo, which takes place after a crisis in the community (usually a death) and lasts for an entire month. The Mbuti believe that because God is benevolent, death or similiar misfortunes cannot occur unless the forest has fallen asleep. Hence, the purpose of the Molimo is to wake up the forest with songs and to thereby restore the normal life of the community. During this rite God sings through a wooden trumpet with the whole community. The Molimo fire is kindled each day by taking embers from the hearth of each family, emphasizing the collective nature of the celebration. As a reaction to crisis and a means of seeking the regeneration of the world through polyphonic song, Molimo represents a perfect form of communication with the spiritual world.

SEE ALSO Schmidt, Wilhelm.

BIBLIOGRAPHY

On the Aka, the basic reference is the *Encyclopédie des Pygmées Aka: Techniques, langage et société des chasseurs-cueilleurs de la forêt centrafricaine,* edited by Serge Bahuchet and Jacqueline M. C. Thomas (Paris, 1981–). Volume 1, *Les Pygmées Aka* (1983), and volume 2, *Dictionnaire Aka-Français* (1981), of the projected fifteen volumes have already appeared. See also Bahuchet's *Les Pygmées Aka et la forêt centrafricaine* (Paris, 1985), which presents detailed chapters on the Aka worldview and Aka rituals. On the Baka, see Robert Brisson and Daniel Boursier's *Petit dictionnaire Baka-français* (Douala, Cameroon, 1979) and Brisson's *Contes des Pygmées Baka du Sud-Cameroun,* 4 vols. (Douala, Cameroon, 1981–1984). On the Mbuti, see Paul Schebesta's *Die Bambuti-Pygmäen vom Ituri,* vol. 3, *Die Religion* (Brussels, Belgium, 1938), and his *Les Pygmées du Congo Belge* (Brussels, Belgium, 1957); the documentation in these two works is rich but is notably difficult to use because data from various sources are mixed. Colin Turnbull's *The Forest People: A Study of the Pygmies of the Congo* (New York, 1961) is an intimate account of daily life and ritual among the Mbuti. Two other works by Turnbull deserve attention: *The Mbuti Pygmies: An Ethnographic Survey* (New York, 1965) and *Wayward Servants: The Two Worlds of the African Pygmies* (New York, 1965). The first is a valuable synthesis of previous work, including that of Schebesta, and the second, despite its materialistic emphasis, is a classic study of the Ituri peoples.

In the study of the history of religions, Wilhelm Schmidt's *Die Stellung der Pygmäenvölker in der Entwicklungsgeschichte des Menschen* (Stuttgart, Germany, 1910) remains useful. Although dated, Schmidt's work provides interesting insights into the evolutionary school of religious analysis.

For ritual music, the following recordings can be recommended: Simha Arom's *Anthologie de la musique des Pygmées Aka* (Paris, 1978), Simha Arom and Patrick Renaud's *Baka Pygmy Music (Cameroon)* (Paris, 1977), and Colin Turnbull and Francis S. Chapman's *The Pygmies of the Ituri Forest* (New York, 1958).

New Sources

Abega, Severin Cecile. *Pygmess Baka: Le droit à la difference.* Yaounde, Cameroon, 1998.

Bailey, Robert Converse. *The Behavioral Ecology of Efe Pygmy Men in the Ituri Forest, Zaire.* Ann Arbor, Mich., 1991.

Ballif, Noël. *Les Pygmées de la grande forêt.* Paris, 1992.

Biesbrouck, Karen, Stefan Elders, and Gerda Rossel. *Central African Hunter-Gatherers in a Multidisciplinary Perspective: Challenging Elusiveness.* Leiden, Netherlands, 1999.

Brisson, Robert. *Mythologie des Pygmées Baka (Sud Cameroun): Mythologie et contes.* Paris, 1999.

Duffy, Kevin. *Children of the Forest.* New York, 1984.

Hewlett, Barry S. *Intimate Fathers: The Nature and Context of Aka Pygmy Paternal Infant Care.* Ann Arbor, Mich., 1991.

Kent, Susan, ed. *Cultural Diversity among Twentieth-Century Foragers: An African Perspective.* New York, 1996.

Mark, Joan T. *The King of the World in the Land of the Pygmies.* Lincoln, Neb., 1995.

Meurant, Georges, and Robert Farris Thompson. *Mbuti Design: Paintings by Pygmy Women of the Ituri Forest.* New York, 1996.

Turnbull, Colin M. *The Mbuti Pygmies: Change and Adaptation.* New York, 1983.

SERGE BAHUCHET (1987)
JACQUELINE M. C. THOMAS (1987)
Revised Bibliography

PYRAMIDS

This entry consists of the following articles:

PYRAMIDS: AN OVERVIEW

The structure of the pyramid may unite the two religious monuments of the burial mound and the elevated altar. Because these functions are not mutually exclusive but rather are in many cases complementary and combined with yet other functions, modern archaeologists often face serious difficulties of interpretation. This problem becomes especially evident when they attempt to situate the monuments in their original contexts.

On the one hand, the pyramid can be a logical derivation of the burial mound, with the primary function of concealing the tomb of a prominent ruler while exalting his often-deified memory. The Egyptian pyramid, with its wonderfully refined form, is the perfect embodiment of this initial phase. It is, in addition, the only monument that can be considered a true pyramid in the geometric sense of the word (excluding, of course, the oldest example, in Saqqara, built with trunk-pyramidal elements).

On the other hand, the pyramid can constitute the monumental culmination of the elevated altar, an extreme manifestation of the "cult of height." Overwhelmed by the sacred, the simple mortal tends to place everything that relates to that sphere at a higher level, whether they be effigies, images, or altars, whether visible or invisible. The most outstanding forms of this genre are the ziggurats in Mesopotamia and the temple-pyramids of pre-Columbian America (particularly those of Mesoamerica and, on a lesser scale, those of the Andean region).

Chronologically, the Mesopotamian buildings are older; they date from the fourth millennium BCE. The temples, such as those of Uruk (modern Warka, Iraq), are placed on high, artificial platforms accessible by staircases or ramps. From the third millennium BCE these develop into massive ziggurats, which were usually composed of terraced blocks on a square foundation. The terraced blocks, perpendicular or parallel to the foundation, ascend in broken patterns, either directly or in spans. Archaeologists believe that a sanctuary usually crowned the last platform, but total destruction of the upper parts of the monuments makes confirmation of this thesis difficult. In profile such monuments present a terraced succession of vertical or near-vertical shapes. Their cubical appearance is often counterbalanced by great flutings that alternate rhythmically with the buttresses to animate the exterior facings and cast elongated shadows accentuating the vertical over the horizontal.

Even more versatile than the Mesopotamian pyramid is that of Mesoamerica, which originated between 1200 and 900 BCE among the Olmec of San Lorenzo and La Venta on the Gulf Coast of Mexico and continued to develop until the sixteenth century CE. The Mesopotamian pyramid often has a quadrangular foundation, but occasionally it is circular, as in the main pyramid at La Venta or that of Cuicuilco; it can also be semicircular, as in some of the *yácatas* ("mounds," "pyramids") in Michoacán or the temples dedicated to the wind god Quetzalcoatl-Ehécatl that were part of the Aztec political expansion just before the Spanish conquest.

Conceived as a single truncated block—or, more commonly, formed by a series of terraced blocks—and generally having one staircase, the Mesoamerican pyramid almost invariably presents ornamentation in talus form, an intuitive adaptation of the natural sloping angle of its solid earth fill. A formal element that works to define the principal volumes and to differentiate regional, local, and other styles is the talus panel (*tablero-talud* or *talud-tablero*) with its salient moldings that produce well-marked shadows. The pyramid, usually crowned by a temple (single or, in certain cases, twin), tends to be complemented by plazas, esplanades, and other open spaces. These, together with stairways and altar-platforms, make up a nearly inseparable whole. This type of pyramid was conceived to satisfy the needs of a form of worship that, in its community aspects, took place outdoors.

BIBLIOGRAPHY

For a general approach to the pyramids of Egypt and Mesopotamia see *World Architecture,* edited by Trewin Copplestone (New York, 1963) and *Le grand atlas de l'architecture mondiale* (Paris, 1982). For information on the pyramid in pre-Columbian America, George Kubler's *The Art and Architecture of Ancient America* (New York, 1982) can also be consulted.

PAUL GENDROP (1987)
Translated from Spanish by Gabriela Mahn

PYRAMIDS: EGYPTIAN PYRAMIDS

Egyptian pyramids are essentially royal tombs. Throughout the centuries their great size and architectural excellence have led to several alternative explanations for their existence, such as the medieval notion that they were granaries built by Joseph during the seven good years mentioned in the Bible

(*Gn.* 41), but such theories are quite fanciful. There is a connection, however, between the origin of pyramid building and the idea of a staircase; one such stairway, which must be symbolic, was found incorporated in a mud-brick bench-shaped tomb dating from the end of the first dynasty (c. 2900 BCE) at Saqqara, south of modern Cairo, but it is far from certain that this was a royal monument. The first pyramid, however, is the Step Pyramid, also at Saqqara, consisting of six such bench tombs arranged on top of one another in the form of a stairway. This is the earliest known monumental stone building (2700 BCE), and it has earned its architect, Imhotep, a place in history which was recognized by the ancient Egyptians themselves. Subsequent step pyramids, although unfinished, show increasing confidence in the use of stone, and they developed rapidly, replacing the step structure with something closer to a true pyramid.

THE AGE OF THE GREAT PYRAMIDS. The apogee of pyramid building was reached at the beginning of the fourth dynasty, with the two massive pyramids at Dahshur built by Snefru and the Great Pyramid at Giza, the work of his son Cheops (2600 BCE). Each successive king seems to have at least planned a pyramid for himself (over eighty are known), down to the end of the Middle Kingdom (1600 BCE), when the concept was abandoned in favor of a less conspicuous burial place. Later royal pyramids are known from the Sudan, and smaller imitations are common in private tombs of the New Kingdom (c. 1569–1085 BCE) at Thebes. One such example was discovered at Memphis in 1980. Here the idea seems to have been borrowed directly from the royal prototype. The earliest pyramids show frequent changes of plan in their interior corridors, either for religious or architectural reasons or a combination of both. Pyramids of the fifth and sixth dynasties show a regular plan and are effectively standardized. Middle Kingdom pyramids have labyrinthine passages within them to provide for greater security from tomb robbers.

THE PYRAMID TEXTS. Beginning with the reign of Unas, the last king of the fifth dynasty (2350 BCE), the sarcophagus, burial chamber, antechamber, and parts of the descending corridor were inscribed with hieroglyphic texts in vertical columns. These so-called Pyramid Texts are undoubtedly the major source on the religious ideas underlying the architecture. The Pyramid Texts make it clear that the dead king, himself a god, was thought to ascend to heaven, either by a staircase or via the sun's rays; the form of the pyramid itself clearly embodies both concepts. Some texts also hint at a primeval mound, the site of the original creation, and it is possible that a pyramid also symbolizes this idea. Other notions of the next world are explored in the Pyramid Texts as well. The most common is that of a fusion with the sun god—joining in his voyage through the night, repelling his enemies, assuming his identity; this idea is so pervasive that pyramids were in effect solar symbols to the ancient Egyptians. An alternative concept is a stellar one: the king's soul or *bai* joins the "imperishable ones," the circumpolar stars which never set in the northern sky. The king's death is seen as an event of the night, ideally taking place at the end of a season in the year, and his rebirth to new life is epitomized in the sunrise. The orientation of pyramids reflects these astronomical ideas: they were built to face the points of the compass, usually with remarkable accuracy, and the entrance was invariably placed in the middle of the northern face, at least before the Middle Kingdom; the descending passage of the Great Pyramid was oriented toward the celestial north pole. In the southern sky, the constellation of Orion was explicitly identified with the resurrected king.

A very interesting analysis sees in the position of the texts within the pyramid a clue to the organization of the funeral ceremonies and in the use of walls and ceilings a symbolic "map" of the netherworld. While this is not unlikely, it is important to remember that the texts themselves were published in an arbitrary order, and that only one pyramid has in fact been treated as a coherent whole.

PYRAMID COMPLEXES. It is a mistake to imagine pyramids in isolation. Even the Step Pyramid was designed as the center of a stone palace, intended for the spirit of the dead king. This idea was soon abandoned, but a classic later pyramid would have a mortuary temple at its eastern side for the daily cult of the dead king and a valley temple at the edge of the floodplain where rites of embalming were carried out and cult regalia stored. Both temples would be richly decorated. The two were connected by a covered causeway, also decorated, which could be up to seven hundred meters long. Subsidiary pyramids and a series of solar or funerary boats also adorned the complex. The three pyramids at Abusir, south of Giza, dating from the fifth dynasty (c. 2400 BCE), show these features well. As much work could have gone into this part of the architecture as into the pyramid itself; the mere size of a pyramid tells us little about the power or ambition of its owner. The existence of a population relatively idle during the months of the Nile flood made such building projects easier; it may even have made them necessary, as a means of gratifying popular expectations.

OTHER PYRAMIDAL STRUCTURES. Pyramid-like structures also exist in Mesopotamia; these are better known as ziggurats. They were not funerary at all but seem to have been exclusively religious, and they were the objects of a cult. In two cases temples have been found on their summits, and it is tempting to believe that the ziggurats represented either heavenly mountains or celestial stairways between gods and humans, but their function is surprisingly obscure. It is possible that Egyptian pyramids were influenced vaguely by ziggurats, or vice versa, but their purposes were markedly different. The same is even more true of the pyramid structures of Central America, which were quite different in design and function, being more like gigantic sacrificial altars. There is no reason to assume any link with Egypt, especially as the Central American "pyramids" were built two or three thousand years later. An underlying feeling that the world of the gods is elevated from that of humans and that this gap needs bridging is probably enough to explain the similarities.

SEE ALSO Egyptian Religion, article on The Literature.

BIBLIOGRAPHY

Most of the essential information on Egyptian pyramids is contained in the series of articles written by Dieter Arnold and Hartwig Altenmüller in *Lexikon der Ägyptologie,* vols. 4 and 5 (Wiesbaden, 1982–1983). Walter B. Emery's *Archaic Egypt* (Baltimore, 1967) is essential for the origins of royal tombs. Ahmed Fakhry's *The Pyramids,* 2d ed. (Chicago, 1969), is clear and well illustrated; Eiddon Edwards's *The Pyramids of Egypt* (1961; reprint, Harmondsworth, 1980) is informative, and Kurt Mendelssohn's *The Riddle of the Pyramids* (London, 1974) challenges some accepted notions. The best edition of the Pyramid Texts is by Raymond O. Faulkner, *The Ancient Egyptian Pyramid Texts* (Oxford, 1969), but the reconstructed order is best seen in the light of Jean Leclant's "Les textes des pyramides," in *Textes et langages de l'Égypte pharaonique,* vol. 2 (Cairo, 1972), pp. 37–52. Texts from a single pyramid are collected in *The Pyramid of Unas,* edited by Alexandre Piankoff (Princeton, 1968). Essential studies on the interpretation of these texts are those of Winfried Barta, *Die Bedeutung der Pyramidentexte für den verstorbenen König* (Munich, 1981), and Herbert W. Fairman in *Myth, Ritual, and Kingship,* edited by S. H. Hooke (Oxford, 1958). Babylonian ziggurats are dealt with by André Parrot in his *Ziggurats et Tour de Babel* (Paris, 1949).

J. D. RAY (1987)

PYTHAGORAS. The ancient tradition presents different images of Pythagoras (c. 570 BCE–c. 500 BCE) that hardly square with one another: philosopher and initiator of rational inquiry, scientist and mathematician, politician and lawgiver, and religious wonderworker and leader of a sect of initiates. Surely he was an extraordinary personality and a charismatic chief, venerated by his followers and desecrated by his opponents. Soon he became a legend, whose historical nucleus is difficult to ascertain. The very nature of the association he founded is consequently controversial: it is mainly described as a philosophical school where scientific inquiries were practiced, as a political party, or as a religious confraternity.

The main sources on Pythagoras, while plentiful, are late and rarely impartial; for the most part they are cast in the distorting light of hostile polemic or religious veneration. Whether Pythagoras left any writing was in ancient times already controversial and is still debatable. Original works by him, if there were any, were soon lost. In addition, there are no extant writings from ancient Pythagoreans. Pythagorean material is mainly constituted by reports whose reliability is uncertain and by apocryphal writings, which were composed beginning in the Hellenistic age and gradually increased until a remarkable amount existed.

Few details of Pythagoras's life are definitively known. He was born to Pythais and Mnemarchos (or Mnesarchos), a gem-engraver or merchant, on the Ionian island of Samos in 571 or 570 BCE. He lived there until 532 or 531, when he migrated, perhaps to escape the tyranny of Policrates, to the Achaean city of Croton in Magna Graecia (southern Italy), soon after the defeat of the city by its neighbors, the Locrians. By his teaching, which Pythagoras gave to citizens through public speeches, he is said to have converted the city from luxury to temperance. In Croton he founded an association, some of whose members came to exercise a leading role in the government of the city. During this period Croton extended its power over many cities of southern Italy, defeating the rival Sibaris in 510. There followed a period of internal struggle; anti-Pythagorean movements culminated in a burning of the houses of some Pythagoreans, where Pythagoras himself perished. Other sources have him dying, probably at about the age of eighty, in Metapontum, where he had retired having predicted the events.

Pythagoras's image as wonderworker is variously attested. His followers, who avoided pronouncing his name, considered him a god, or at least a semidivine person ("among rational beings one is god, another one man, the third like Pythagoras"), while some of his detractors depicted him as "chief of swindlers" and a charlatan. The ancient sources connect him with the Orient and its wisdom. He journeyed in Egypt, where he was told the secret lore of the priests; he also had contacts with the Phoenicians, the Chaldeans, and the Magi in Babylonia, and was initiated into their mysteries. Among his teachers were Pherecydes of Syros and Zaratas (Zoroaster), by whom he is said to have been purified and instructed in cosmology. The connections of Pythagoras with Apollo are basic; he was called the Hyperborean Apollo by the Crotoniates, and he revealed his golden thigh to the Hyperborean Abaris, a priest of Apollo, who identified him as the god. According to other reports Pythagoras was born from Apollo and Pythais and was the god's prophet among humans.

Pythagoras was credited with supernatural faculties and extraordinary mental powers, as is shown by miraculous tales that attribute to him the capacity of predicting future events, healing diseases, being simultaneously in different places, and taming animals. Still more impressive than his magical relationship with the natural world are his connections to the underworld and the afterlife—he could remember his past lives and journeyed to Hades. Hence the much discussed interpretation that sees him mainly as a sort of shaman.

The sources unanimously ascribe to Pythagoras the belief in transmigration and reincarnation of the soul (metempsychosis), whose origin can be traced back to Indo-Iranian cultures. Though most details remain unknown, it is safe to assume that for Pythagoras the soul (*psyche*) was immortal, being not merely the life or spirit of the body, but independent, and in many ways an opposing force to the physical self; it enters other human bodies and certain species of animals, thereby experiencing the cycle of punishments and rewards that stems from one's conduct in life. The metempsychosis was in fact connected with an eschatology, whose traces survive in the so-called *akousmata* (things heard) or in symbols.

It seems certain that Pythagoras developed a practical way of life (*bios*) based upon such oral maxims and instructions. Perhaps Aristotle originated a threefold distinction of them: *what is* ("what is the oracle of Delphi? the *tetractys*, that is, the harmony in which the Sirens sing"); *what most* ("what is the wisest thing? number"); and *what should or should not be done* (e.g., one should not travel by the main roads). Some symbols seem bizarre and difficult to explain: do not stir the fire with a knife; do not wear the image of a god on a ring; do not urinate towards the sun. For this reason, in the fourth century BCE some authors provided an allegorical interpretation, which purported to explain their hidden meaning (e.g., do not stir the fire would mean "do not excite an angry man"; abstinence from beans would mean "the prohibition of sexual intercourse"). The original connection is, however, with sacrificial ritual and related purity: do not eat the heart, do not sacrifice the white cock, do not dip the hand into holy water. Some of the symbols are undoubtedly related to mystery cults, including those that command silence and fasting; prescribe the practices of sacrifice, entering the temple barefoot, and wearing a linen garment; or forbid picking up food that has fallen to the earth. Other symbols exhibit connections to an eschatology whose details are little known: what, for example, are the isles of the blest? sun and moon. Bread is not to be broken, because it contributes to the judgment of Hades. Symbols are also passwords for recognition of the initiates by their fellows and by the gods.

Reports about dietetic instructions are also variegated and sometimes self-contradictory. A logical corollary of metempsychosis was total abstinence from meat (including some fishes). Such a radical prohibition clearly contrasted with official cults of Greek religion, where animal sacrifice was central, and was thus incompatible with political offices. The original prohibition may have come to be restricted to animals into which the souls of human beings were supposed to enter, and members of the society may have been allowed to eat animals that could be sacrificed. Other reports limit the prohibition against eating meat to particular parts of the animal, such as the heart or womb. Some sources have Pythagoras making only inanimate offerings and worshiping at Delos at the altar of Apollo *genetor*, where sacrificing animals was forbidden. Most notorious is the beans taboo (*vicia faba*), which has been variously explained, though the main connection is, once again, with metempsychosis: beans represent the gates of Hades, and through beans souls return to earth for reincarnation. Some explanations point to supposed similarities between humans and beans.

The connections with Orphism are important with regard to eschatology. Some traditions made Pythagoras a direct disciple of Orpheus, attributing to him similar powers, such as mastery over animals. Both movements were concerned with salvation of the soul and the afterlife; yet, while Orphism seemingly assured salvation by simple offerings and vows, Pythagoreanism, as a sort of puritanism, was centered on an irreprehensible conduct of life. It is highly probable that Pythagoras and Pythagoreans composed or commented on Orphic literature, where theogonies and cosmogonies were interpreted and further developed.

Ancient reports describe the internal organization of the association in terms of a monastic brotherhood, whose adherents shared their goods and followed strict rules of community life. New disciples underwent a rigid process of admission with a probationary period of five years of silence before final initiation. Close fraternal ties bound the members to each other ("common are the things of friends"). Much discussed is the distinction made by later sources between *acusmatics* (members who received only basic, undemonstrated tenets) and *mathematics* (truly philosophizing members). The distinction points not to different degrees of membership but to a deepened interest in scientific inquiry by later groups compared to the former, prescientific wisdom based upon the *akousmata*. Many of these tracts, as with the community of gods, are possibly later projections of a monastic ideal of life.

Nevertheless, it is undeniable that the Pythagorean society was something more than an ordinary political club (*hetairia*) or a philosophical group; it was rather an association whose adherents were tied to the way of life expressed by the symbols. Being a Pythagorean meant not so much professing a definite philosophical doctrine or practicing scientific inquiry as following a certain sort of life. This will also explain Pythagoras's image as a lawgiver and reformer, a founder of a politically oriented educational program, and a promoter of social concord and moral authority, which had a strong influence on the political life of many cities in southern Italy. Pythagoras's actions in Croton, in fact, seem to have consisted in political advice rather than in direct involvement in the government; his supposed activity as a lawgiver has left no concrete traces, though his influence on politics is undeniable.

According to Diogenes Laertios (third century CE) Pythagoras was the originator of Italian philosophy, the first to use the term *philosophy*, and the first to call himself a *philosopher*, although these are probably later projections of the ideal of contemplative life. More questionable is whether Pythagoras can be considered a philosopher at all. Plato's Academy played a fundamental role in the transmission of Pythagorean philosophy, though in a profoundly transfigured form. Academics attributed to ancient Pythagoreanism doctrines they themselves had worked out, as that of two principles (one and indefinite dyad). The most reliable source for Pythagorean philosophy remains therefore, despite possible distortions, Aristotle, who strives to avoid confusion between Platonism and Pythagoreanism. Based on a written source, Aristotle sketches the philosophy of the "so-called Pythagoreans" (he dealt with Pythagoras's mirabilia in the lost works), which is a later development, maybe due to Philolaos. In any case, it cannot be ruled out that Pythagoras himself had worked out some general philosophical ideas about number as principle and cosmic harmony. Plato alludes to him, recalling a novel Prometheus that gave to humankind a divine doctrine: all things consist of oneness and multiplicity, limitedness and unlimitedness, in close analogy with the system described by Aristotle.

Both Plato and the Pythagoreans regard number as the principle of reality; for the latter, however, numbers are not separate entities, but the things themselves. Having applied mathematics, they discovered affinities between numbers and existing things and assumed that the elements of numbers were the elements of the things; heaven itself is harmony and number. Elements of the number are the even (unlimited) and the odd (limited). Limited and unlimited are then the ultimate principles; from them rises the odd-even "one," which is a principle of number. Here cosmogony and arithmogony are intermingled: once the "one" came into being, the unlimited, which was outside, was breathed in as void by the limited, thereby separating things from one another. The Pythagorean cosmos includes, along with fire at the center, the invisible "counter-earth," the earth, the moon, the sun, the five planets, and the fixed stars. Cosmic harmony is explained by numerical relations that determine the concordant intervals of the scale (2:1, the octave; 3:2, the fifth; 4:3, the fourth). Of paramount importance is, among other "sacred" numbers, the *tetraktys*, or decad, containing the basic ratios (1+2+3+4=10). Other Pythagoreans listed ten basic principles in a table of oppositions (limited/unlimited, oneness/multiplicity, odd/even, square/oblong, good/bad, male/female, right/left, at rest/moving, straight/crooked, light/darkness). The representation of numbers by arrangements of pebbles was based on the correspondence of odd and limited.

Pythagoras emerges from many reports as a mathematician and a scientist. He is credited with the discovery of the celebrated theorem of musical harmony and its basic intervals, together with the construction of musical instruments. Testimonies that attribute to him the theoretical study of geometry or the discovery of irrational magnitudes are not reliable and are deeply influenced by the tradition of Platonism. Yet it is reasonable that, having come of age in the Ionia of the sixth century BCE, Pythagoras could not ignore the major scientific achievements of his time, which possibly are mirrored in his doctrines.

Pythagoreanism soon spread outside Croton. Iamblichus's catalogue, which may date back to Aristoxenos in the fourth century BCE, lists 235 Pythagoreans from different cities, with Croton, Metaponto, Locri, and Tarent playing prominent roles. After the anti-Pythagorean strife the only center in Magna Graecia where Pythagoreanism survived was Tarent, where Archytas held the office of *strategos*. After its extinction in the fourth century BCE, Pythagoreanism survived as a philosophy, inspiring individual personalities who continued to lead a Pythagorean way of life. Beggars-Pythagorists appear in the Middle Comedy (fourth century BCE); they live ascetically, practicing silence and following such dietetic rules as meat abstinence or intensive fasting. However, the existence of Pythagorean groups in Greece cannot be clearly documented.

Much debated is whether Pythagorean communities survived elsewhere during the Hellenistic age. An interest in Pythagoreanism of a literary or antiquarian nature is well attested, which explains the production in the third to second centuries BCE of apocryphal writings attributed to Pythagoras (the *Golden Verses* being the best known) or ancient Pythagoreans, whose place of origin remains controversial (candidates are Rome, Alexandria, and southern Italy). A revival of Pythagoreanism is attested in the first century BCE in Rome, where Nigidius Figulus attempted to revive the *antica disciplina*. There is also somewhat questionable evidence in Rome of the existence of circles and religious sects that referred to Pythagoreanism. In addition, a renewed philosophical interest became visible in Alexandria of Egypt, where the circle of the Pythagorean Platonic Eudoros possibly contributed to the production of *apocrypha*. Between the first century BCE and the second century CE, a number of authors arose who explicitly defined themselves or came to be defined as Pythagoreans. They include Moderatus, Nicomachus, and Numenius, all of whom profess doctrines that are substantially Platonic, and some of whom are supposed to have adopted a Pythagorean *bios*. At this point, boundaries between Platonism and Pythagoreanism become very unclear. More clear is the case of Apollonios of Tiana, a wonderworker who explicitly purported to revive the Pythagorean life and presented himself as *Pythagoras redivivus*. Such Neoplatonic writers as Iamblichus and Porphyry accomplished in their biographies the apotheosis of Pythagoras, until Pythagoreanism completely merged into Neoplatonism.

SEE ALSO Neoplatonism; Orpheus; Plato; Platonism.

BIBLIOGRAPHY

The best sourcebook in English containing texts and fragments related to Pythagoras is Cornelia J. de Vogel's *Greek Philosophy: A Collection of Texts,* vol. 1, *Thales to Plato* (Leiden, 1950). The most complete collection of testimonies is M. Timpanaro Cardini, *I Pitagorici: Testimonianze e frammenti*, 3 vols. (Florence, Italy, 1958–1964). Two excellent background works, which place Pythagoras within the context of Greek religious thought, are E. R. Dodds's *The Greeks and the Irrational* (Berkeley, Calif., 1951) and Walter Burkert's *Greek Religion* (Cambridge, Mass., 1985). Edwin L. Minar's *Early Pythagorean Politics in Practice and Theory* (Baltimore, 1942) offers a summary of the Pythagorean *hetaireia.* Francis M. Cornford's "Mysticism and Science in the Pythagorean Tradition," *Classical Quarterly* 16 (1922): 137–150, is very good on defining the religious vision of Pythagoras, less so on Pythagorean atomism. J. E. Raven gives a controversial account of the development of Pythagorean thought in the fifth century in *Pythagoreans and Eleatics* (Cambridge, U.K., 1948). W. K. C. Guthrie's account of Pythagoras in *A History of Greek Philosophy,* vol. 1, *The Earlier Presocratics and Pythagoreans* (Cambridge, U.K., 1962), can be considered the standard general assessment on the subject.

Other important works on Pythagoras are James A. Philip's *Pythagoras and Early Pythagoreanism* (Toronto, 1966) and above all Walter Burkert's *Lore and Science in Ancient Pythagoreanism* (Cambridge, Mass., 1972). Philip sees little evidence for a religious organization in early Pythagoreanism. Burkert, conversely, offers the most detailed analysis of the Pythagorean religious understanding and practices. Charles H. Kahn's "Pythagorean Philosophy before Plato," in *The Pre-Socratics,* edited by Alexander P. D. Mourelatos (Garden City, N.Y., 1974), pp. 161–185, provides a balanced overview of Pythagoras's religious and scientific holdings. Leonid Zhmud, *Wissenschaft, Philosophie, und Religion im frühen Pythagoreismus* (Berlin, 1997), while reappraising the image of Pythagoras as scientist and philosopher, is a strong critic of the "shamanistic" interpretation. Critical surveys of the whole phenomenon of Pythagoreanism are Bruno Centrone, *Introduzione ai Pitagorici* (Rome, 1996) and Christoph Riedweg, *Pythagoras: Leben, Lehre, Nachwirkung* (Munich, 2002). A complete collection of *pseudopythagorica* is Holger Thesleff, ed., *The Pythagorean Texts of the Hellenistic Period* (Åbo, Finland, 1965). See also Thesleff's *An Introduction to the Pythagorean Writings of the Hellenistic Period* (Åbo, Finland, 1961). Constantinos Macris's "Pythagore, un maître de sagesse charismatique de la fin de la période archaïque," in *Carisma profetico: Fattore di innovazione religiosa,* edited by Giovanni Filoramo (Brescia, Italy, 2003), pp. 243–289, uses the tools of the sociology of religion with historical and philological accuracy to interpret Pythagoras as a charismatic "master of wisdom" (a rich and well-chosen bibliography is included).

BRUNO CENTRONE (2005)

Q–R

QABBALAH. The term *Qabbalah* is derived from the Hebrew root *qbl,* which means "to receive"; in early medieval texts, *qabbalah* commonly signified "reception," namely a received tradition, mainly concerning halakhic matters. Since the early thirteenth century it has become the main term for Jewish mystical traditions, which deal almost exclusively with (1) a theosophical understanding of God combined with a symbolic view of reality and the theurgical conception of religious life, and (2) the way to attain a mystical experience of God through the invocation of divine names. These two traditions had much earlier roots, but the term *Qabbalah* refers in general to Jewish mysticism from the twelfth century onward. The following presentation will discuss the history of Qabbalah and its phenomenological aspects.

Historical Survey. The first written evidence of the existence of theosophical and theurgical thought in Judaism comes from Provence, in southern France, in the second half of the twelfth century. A series of well-known halakhic authorities, beginning with Avraham ben David of Posquières and Ya'aqov the Nazirite and later including Moses Nahmanides and his principal student, Shelomoh ben Avraham Adret, were full-fledged qabbalists, though their literary output in Qabbalah was minimal compared to their voluminous halakhic writings. Doubtless this situation is the result of a deliberate policy to keep Qabbalah an esoteric lore limited to a very small elite. However, at the beginning of the thirteenth century, the veil of esotericism began to disappear. Yitsḥaq Sagi Nahor (Yitsḥaq the Blind), Avraham ben David of Posquières's son, is known as the teacher of several qabbalists, of whom the best known are Yitsḥaq's nephew Asher ben David and 'Ezra' of Gerona. They committed to writing the first qabbalistic documents, which consist of commentaries on the cosmogonical treatise *Sefer yetsirah* and on *ma'aseh bere'shit* (the biblical account of creation), and explanations of the rationale for the commandments. During the same period, an important treatise called *Sefer ha-bahir* (The book of brightness), falsely ascribed to Ne unya' ben ha-Qanah, a second-century mystic, began to circulate among Yitsḥaq's students. Although the qabbalistic doctrines incorporated

Clockwise from top left corner. Qur'ān written in Nashki script. *[The Art Archive/Private Collection/Eileen Tweedy]*; Pre-Toltec Quetzalcoatl in the form of the morning star. Ethnologisches Museum, Staatliche Museen zu Berlin. *[©Werner Forman/Art Resource, N.Y.]*; Etruscan bronze capitoline she-wolf, c. fifth century BCE, with twins added later by Antonio Pollaiuolo. Musei Capitolini, Rome. *[©Timothy McCarthy/Art Resource, N.Y.]*; Cathedral of Saint Basil in Moscow. *[©Corbis]*; Fifteenth-century illustration by Marco dell'Avogadro of Ruth at work during the harvest, from the *Bible of Borso d'Este.* Biblioteca Estense, Modena. *[©Scala/Art Resource, N.Y.]* .

into these works are presented in a fragmentary and obscure manner, it seems highly reasonable that they reflect more complex systems whose sources predated them by decades and even centuries.

In the middle of the thirteenth century, more extensive works were produced by Spanish qabbalists, who continued the major trends of their predecessors; the most important among them were ʿAzriʾel of Gerona and Yaʿaqov ben Sheshet. After flourishing briefly in Catalonia, the center of qabbalistic creativity passed to Castile, where it underwent a renaissance. In Castile a circle of anonymous qabbalists produced a series of short treatises, known as the *ʿIyyun* (speculation) literature, that combined ancient Merkavah literature (commentaries on the chariot vision in *Ezekiel*) with a Neoplatonic mysticism of light. Another group became interested in the theosophy of evil and described in detail the structure of the "other side," the demonic world. This circle included the brothers Yaʿaqov and Yitsḥaq, the sons of Yaʿaqov ha-Kohen; Mosheh of Burgos; and Ṭodros Abulafia. The quintessential ideas of these qabbalistic schools appear in the most important work of Qabbalah, the *Zohar,* a collection of mystical writings that was circulated among the Castilian qabbalists beginning in 1280. Subsequently, between 1285 and 1335, the qabbalists produced many translations, commentaries, and imitations of the *Zohar,* mainly extant in manuscript, that contributed to the eventual acceptance of the *Zohar* as a canonic book.

Because of fierce controversy between the representative of the more conservative form of Qabbalah that preserved and transmitted older traditions, Shelomoh ben Avraham Adret, and Avraham Abulafia, the most important exponent of ecstatic Qabbalah, the creative and anarchic elements peculiar to the latter were rejected by adherents of Spanish Qabbalah, a fact that contributed to its overt stagnation in the latter part of the fourteenth century and most of the fifteenth century.

The expulsion of the Jews from Spain and Portugal in 1492 and 1497 respectively caused an exodus of important qabbalists from the Iberian peninsula to North Africa, Italy, and the Levant, thereby contributing to the dissemination of Qabbalah in those regions. Fifteenth-century Spanish Qabbalah, with the *Zohar* as its nucleus, became more and more influential in the new communities that were established by the expelled Jews and gradually developed into an important spiritual factor in Jewish life by the middle of the sixteenth century. The literary output of the first generation after the expulsion is remarkable, and several outstanding qabbalistic works were composed before the middle of the sixteenth century, including Yehudah Hayyat's *Minḥat Yehudah* in Italy and Meʾir ibn Gabbai's *ʿAvodat ha-qodesh* in the Ottoman empire. This generation of qabbalists was interested in preserving the esoteric traditions they had inherited in Spain; hence the eclectic nature of their writings. However, there were efforts to build up comprehensive speculative schemes in which the whole theosophic and cosmic chain of being was described. This work was undertaken by some Spanish qabbalists who systematically arranged older esoteric traditions, and by Italians such as Yoḥanan Alemanno, who combined philosophy, magic, and Qabbalah.

After the expulsion, a growing stream of qabbalists began arriving in Palestine. At the very beginning of the sixteenth century, Jerusalem became an important center of qabbalistic studies; its most famous members were Yehudah Albotini, Yosef ibn Saiaḥ, and Avraham ben Eliʿezer ha-Levi. Beginning in the 1540s, the small Galilean village of Safad rapidly acquired a dominant place in qabbalistic activity. For half a century, Safad was the arena of crucial developments in the history of Qabbalah. The arrival of two central figures from Turkey, Yosef Karo and Shelomoh ha-Levi Alkabets, prompted the establishment of mystical groups that formed the nuclei of intensive qabbalistic activities. Karo, the major halakhist of his time, produced a mystical diary dictated by a *maggid,* an angelic messenger who spoke from Karo's throat. Karo represents a Spanish qabbalistic trend that was primarily interested in incubational techniques to induce revelations in dreams. Alkabets, who had been close to Karo before their arrival, was aware of the philosophical perceptions of Qabbalah presented in David Messer Leon's work *Magen David* and seems to have been one of the major channels of the infiltration into Safad of Qabbalah developed by the Jews of the Italian Renaissance. However, the first towering qabbalist in Palestine was Mosheh Cordovero (1522–1570), the author of the *Pardes rimmonim* (1548), the most comprehensive exposition of all previous types of Qabbalah. He combined Spanish Qabbalah with ecstatic Qabbalah that was already flowering in Jerusalem. His clear and systematic presentation of all the major qabbalistic doctrines contributed to the immediate dissemination of his views, which remained influential for centuries, both in the Qabbalah of Isaac Luria and in Hasidism. Cordovero's main disciples, famous qabbalists themselves, were Ḥayyim Vital, Eliyyahu de Vidas, and Elʿazar Azikri. Through their literary activities—especially their moralistic works, which were intended for the public at large—they contributed to the further propagation of their master's doctrines.

A crucial development in qabbalistic theosophy occurred after Cordovero's death when one of his former students, Isaac Luria, rapidly moved to the center of the qabbalist community in Safad, where he became a profound influence through his saintly behavior, occult powers, and exposition of a novel type of theosophy. Luria's doctrines, commonly delivered orally to his disciples, elaborated upon some elements that had previously played a rather marginal role in the qabbalistic system. According to Luria, the initial movement in the process of creation consisted of the withdrawal of the all-pervading godhead into itself, leaving a point in which the world would come to exist. This withdrawal, or contraction (*tsimtsum*), made possible the elimination of "evil" elements inherent in the godhead. (The evil elements that left the godhead during *tsimtsum* formed the "material domain.") This cathartic event was followed by a series of emanations from the godhead that were intended to constitute the created world. As the emanations proceeded from their divine source, a catastrophic event occurred—the breaking of the vessels that carried them. Sparks of the divine light fell into the material domain where they were imprisoned in shells of matter. The task of the qabbalist was to liberate the sparks in order to reconstitute the divine configuration, the primordial man (*adam qadmon*), a goal with eschatological overtones.

The success of Luria's thought was instantaneous; his theosophy was accepted unanimously by the former disciples of Cordovero, and his Qabbalah was regarded as superior to the Cordoverian system. With the premature death of Luria in 1572 his disciple, Ḥayyim Vital, committed Luria's views to writing, but Vital limited their dissemination to the small circle of qabbalists who recognized his leadership. In comparison to other authentic disciples of Luria, notably Yosef ibn Tabūl and Mosheh Yonah, Vital was highly prolific; his best-known work was *ʿEts ayyim* (Tree of life). A rather different version of Luria's Qabbalah was brought to Italy during the 1590s by Yisraʾel Sarug, a qabbalist who considered himself a disciple of Luria. He disseminated it through intensive oral and written activity, recruiting disciples from among former Cordoverian qabbalists. The most important exponent of the Sarugian version of Lurianism was Menaḥem ʿAzaryah of Fano. Sarug's success was partly due to the speculative interpretations given by Sarug himself and by his disciple Avraham Herrera, who used Neoplatonic philosophy in his *Shaʿar ha-Shamayim* and *Beit Elohim.* Both Neoplatonic and atomistic views of Lurianic Qabbalah appeared in the work of Yosef Shelomoh Delmedigo of Kandia, another of Sarug's disciples.

During the seventeenth century, there was a clash between adherents of Vital's version of Lurianic Qabbalah and adherents of Sarug's version. Among the qabbalists, Vital's views prevailed in the compilations of Shemuʾel Vital, Meʾir Poppers, and Yaʿaqov Tsemaḥ.

The following centuries saw the development of various mixtures of Cordoverian and Lurianic doctrines. The theosophy of the followers of the seventeenth-century mystic and false messiah Shabbetai Tsevi was influenced mainly by Sarug's trend of thought; the theologies of eighteenth-century Polish Hasidism represented a revival of some of Cordovero's views, such as his view of prayer, at a period when Lurianic Qabbalah failed to supply appropriate answers.

Some central figures of the eighteenth century, were known as qabbalists; the most important among them were Eliyyahu ben Shelomoh Zalman, known as the *gaon* of Vilna (Vilnius) (1720–1797) and Yaʿaqov Emden (1697–1776), who continued the Lurianic tradition, though not without some reservations. In the nineteenth century, major systematic presentations of Lurianism were composed by Yitsḥaq Eiziq Haver and Shelomoh Elyashar.

The dominant brand of Qabbalah in the modern qabbalistic *yeshivot* (traditional Jewish academies) is the Lurianic system. It is studied according to the interpretations offered by Mosheh Ḥayyim Luzzatto, by Eliyyahu ben Shelomoh Zalman, by Habad, the Lubavitch Hasidic movement, and by the Sefardic qabbalists of the Beit El Academy in Jerusalem. Avraham Yitsḥaq Kook (1865–1935) offered a pantheistic and mystical version of Qabbalah that tried to explain the secularism of many modern Jews as part of a larger scheme of religious evolution; his views had great influence. After the establishment of the state of Israel, and especially after 1967, the messianic overtones in Kook's thought were stressed by his son Yehudah Kook. David ha-Kohen the Ascetic (ha-Nazir), the most important figure in Kook's entourage, developed a peculiar type of mysticism in his *Qol ha-nevuʾah* that leaned heavily on the oral aspects of Jewish tradition. Some interest in Avraham Abulafia's ecstatic Qabbalah has been recently discerned in Hasidic circles.

CHRISTIAN QABBALAH. Although Qabbalah was considered to be an esoteric lore that dealt with the secrets of the law (*Sitre Torah*) and was therefore peculiar to the Jewish people, it found its way into Christian thought. The first steps in the infiltration of Qabbalah were accomplished by converts to Christianity, of whom the most important were Abner of Burgos (Alfonso de Valladolid), who lived at the beginning of the fourteenth century; Paulus de Heredia, who lived in the second half of the fifteenth century; and Flavius Mithridates, who had by far the greatest impact. A teacher of the fifteenth-century Italian Christian humanist Giovanni Pico della Mirandola, Flavius translated a voluminous body of qabbalistic literature into Latin. His translations, which he intentionally distorted, represented the most important source for Pico's *Theses,* the first qabbalistic composition written by a Christian. Although he was the initiator of this new current of Christian thought, Pico did not write lengthy treatises on Qabbalah, but presented it as an ancient Jewish theology that foreshadowed, in a veiled manner, Christian tenets. He divided Qabbalah into a high form of legal magical lore and a low form of demonic magic. Besides these Christian and magical interpretations of Qabbalah, which owe much to the distorted translations of Mithridates, Pico interpreted Qabbalah philosophically, mainly using Neoplatonic sources previously translated into Latin by his friend Marsilio Ficino, as well as hermetic Zoroastrian or Chaldean sources. These three perceptions of Qabbalah had a profound impact on the views that were developed by Pico's followers. Johannes Reuchlin, who studied Qabbalah under Pico's influence, produced in his *De arte cabalistica* the first systematic descriptions of Christian Qabbalah to be presented to the European public. In the early sixteenth century, theologians such as Egidio da Viterbo and Francesco Giorgio expanded the philosophical and Christological views of Qabbalah in influential treatises. The magical interpretation of Qabbalah reached its peak in Heinrich Cornelius Agrippa of Nettesheim's *De occulta philosophia.* Through the writings of these Italian and German authors, as well as artwork of

Dürer, Qabbalah entered French and English literature and art in the second half of the sixteenth century. In the seventeenth century, Christian Knorr von Rosenroth's *Cabbala denudata,* a compendium of translations of important qabbalistic texts, was widely read by the European intelligentsia and it remained for a long time, together with John Pistorius's earlier *Artis cabalisticae,* the main source of the influence of Jewish esotericism on European thought. Philosophers like G. W. Leibniz and the Cambridge Neoplatonists in the seventeenth century, and writers like G. E. Lessing, Emanuel Swedenborg, and William Blake in the following century, absorbed qabbalistic ideas. The occult groups that flourished in eighteenth century central Europe were influenced by qabbalistic and Shabbatean thought. The impact of Zoharic Qabbalah is especially evident in the works of the nineteenth-century Theosophist H. P. Blavatsky. In the twentieth century, traces of Qabbalah can be found in the fiction and poetry of Franz Kafka, Yvan Goll, and Jorge Luis Borges, and in the cultural criticism of Walter Benjamin and the literary criticism of Harold Bloom and Jacques Derrida.

PHENOMENOLOGICAL SURVEY. During the long history of Qabbalah, its adherents developed a variety of theosophical doctrine, symbolic systems, and methods of textual interpretation, some of them contradictory and paradoxical.

Qabbalistic theosophy. The Talmud and Midrash speak of two crucial attributes, the attribute of mercy (*middat ha-raḥamim*) and the attribute of stern judgment (*middat ha-din*). These divine qualities are believed to exist in a dynamic balance and to have been instrumental in the creation of the world and in its governance. In other texts, ten creative *logoi* or creative words (Heb., *ma'amarot*) are mentioned in this context; in *Sefer yetsirah,* the ten *sefirot* have a similar function. Pleromatic entities are also evident in the Merkavah literature. However, no detailed and systematic Jewish theosophy is extant before the composition of qabbalistic works at the beginning of the thirteenth century. Most qabbalists viewed the divinity as consisting of two layers: (1) the innermost, supreme godhead, Ein Sof (literally "the endless"), which is sometimes described in terms borrowed from Neoplatonic negative theology and sometimes described in explicitly anthropomorphic terminology; and (2) the sefirotic realm emanating from within the godhead as a pleromatic structure, that was said to be comprised of ten aspects, known variously as attributes (*middot*), potencies (*koḥot*), degrees (*ma'alot*), or, most frequently, *sefirot* (literally "numbers"). These divine powers were conceived of as forming a supernatural man, or tree, that represents the revealed as well as the creative God. Figure 1 shows the commonly accepted set of names for the *sefirot,* although slight differences are known among qabbalists.

In some post-Lurianic texts, an additional *sefirah* was discussed, Da'at ("knowledge"), which is situated between the second and the third *sefirot,* and which plays a role similar to that of Tif'eret or Yesod, namely, a balance between two higher poles.

There were two main ideas of the nature of the *sefirot* among the qabbalists. The view expressed in the main body of the *Zohar* and by important qabbalists was that the *sefirot* constitute the essence of God and therefore are purely divine manifestations. Since the beginning of the fourteenth century, some qabbalists viewed the *sefirot* as vessels created by God to contain the divine efflux; according to a proximate view they are the instruments by which God created and governs the world. Mosheh Cordovero combined these two views, speaking of divine *sefirot* that are inherent in the external *sefirot,* with the latter functioning as vessels for the former. This approach became prevalent in later Qabbalah. Lurianic Qabbalah also developed a representation of the divine realm according to five anthropomorphic configurations (*partsufim*), each composed of ten *sefirot.* Attempts were made in the Middle Ages to interpret the *sefirot* as symbols of human spiritual powers, and this tendency was adopted and strengthened by eighteenth-century Hasidic masters.

Qabbalistic cosmogony recognized the existence of four worlds or realms of existence: the *sefirot,* called the world of emanation (*'olam ha-atsilut*); the world of creation (*'olam ha-beri'ah*), consisting of the divine chariot and higher angels; the world of formation (*'olam ha-yetsirah*), in which the angels are found; and the world of action (*'olam ha-'asiyyah*), the celestial and terrestrial material world. Under the impact of Sufism, some qabbalists mentioned a fivefold division that includes the world of images (*'olam ha-demut*).

Qabbalistic theurgy. One of the most important tenets of mainstream Qabbalah is the view that humanity can influence the inner structure of the godhead. By performing the commandments with the proper qabbalistic intention, humankind is capable of restoring the lost harmony between the lesser *sefirot,* Tif'eret and Malkhut, making possible the transmission of the divine efflux from the higher *sefirot* to the human world. Moreover, humans can draw this efflux from Ein Sof, the hidden divinity, downward to the *sefirot.* According to some early qabbalists, the very existence of the revealed divinity in the *sefirot* is the result of human observance of the commandments, which, by drawing the efflux downward, counteracts the "natural" movement of the *sefirot* upward in their desire to return to their primordial status within the godhead. Qabbalistic observance of the commandments constitutes a theurgic activity, since its aim is the restructuring of God.

This view of the commandments represents a sophisticated presentation of an ancient trend in Jewish thought that found its earliest expression in Talmudic and Midrashic literature, in which God is sometimes presented as requesting Moses' blessing, desiring the prayer of the righteous, and even increasing or decreasing his power in accordance with the fulfillment or nonfulfillment of the commandments by Israel. With the emergence of Lurianic Qabbalah, the emphasis was transferred to the extraction of the divine sparks (*nitsotsot*) from the material, demonic world as a progressive eschatological activity whose ultimate aim is to restore the primeval anthropomorphic configuration of the divinity. This theurgy has obvious affinities to Manichaean theology and is phenomenologically different from Neoplatonic theurgy, which was focused mainly upon the performance of rituals intended to attract the gods to descend into statues from which they could deliver divinatory messages. In the same manner, qabbalistic theurgy differed from magical ceremony in both its means and its aims. The Qabbalah used biblical commandments to effect its goals rather than magical devices; and whereas magic is chiefly directed toward attaining material results needed by certain persons, qabbalistic activity was primarily intended to restore the divine harmony, and only secondarily to ensure the abundance of the supernatural efflux in this world.

These phenomenological differences notwithstanding, Neoplatonic types of theurgy, as well as various types of magic, infiltrated into qabbalistic systems at different stages of their development, although their influence never became dominant. An interesting blend of qabbalistic and Neoplatonic theurgies with magical practices was evident in late-fifteenth-century Spain where Yosef della Reina, a Faustian figure, attempted to facilitate the arrival of the messianic eon by means of theurgico-magical activities.

Mystical techniques in Qabbalah. After the middle of the thirteenth century, qabbalists produced a series of treatises that discussed techniques for reaching ecstatic experiences and described such experiences. The most important representative of this trend was Avraham Abulafia (1240–c. 1291). In his numerous works, almost all of them still in manuscript form, he focused on complex devices for uniting with the Agent Intellect, or God, through the recitation of divine names, together with breathing techniques and cathartic practices. Some of Abulafia's mystic ways were adapted from the Ashkenazic Hasidic masters; Abulafia may also have been influenced by Yoga and Sufism. Taking as his framework the metaphysical and psychological system of Moses Maimonides (Mosheh ben Maimon, 1135/8–1204), Abulafia strove for spiritual experience, which he viewed as a prophetic state similar to or even identical with that of the ancient Jewish prophets. Furthermore, he perceived his attainment of such a state as an eschatological event, because he thought of himself as the messiah. This spiritual and highly individualistic conception of salvation adumbrated the later Hasidic view of spiritual messianism. Abulafia's messianic pretensions led him to undertake such exploits as his unsuccessful attempt to discuss the true nature of Judaism with the pope.

Abulafia's prophetic and messianic pretensions prompted a sharp reaction on the part of Shelomoh ben Avraham Adret, a famous legal authority who succeeded in annihilating the influence of Abulafia's ecstatic Qabbalah in Spain. In Italy, however, his works were translated into Latin and contributed substantially to the formation of Christian Qabbalah. In the Middle East, ecstatic Qabbalah was accepted without reservation. Clear traces of Abulafian doctrine are

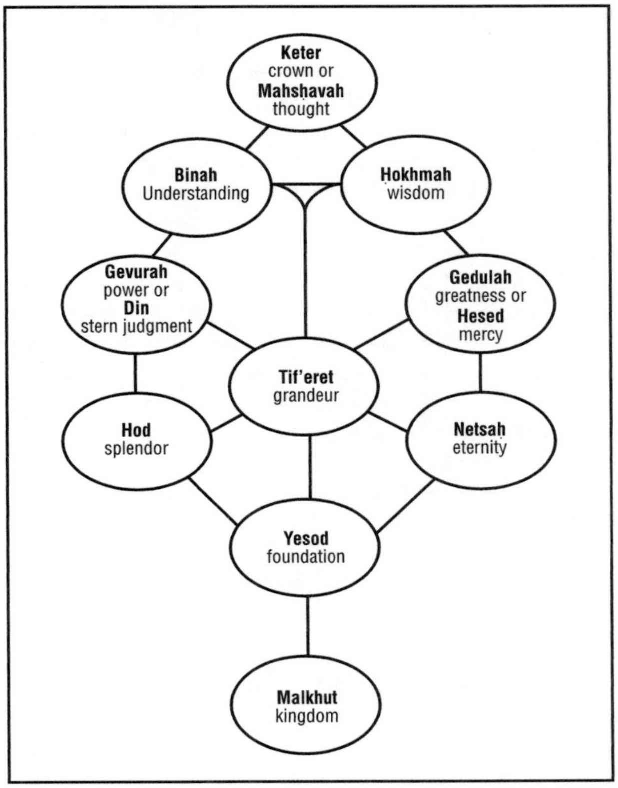

FIGURE 1. The ten divine aspects, or *sefirot,* in their symbolic configuration.

evident in the works of Yitsḥaq ben Shemu'el of Acre and Yehudah Albotini. In Palestine, Abulafia's ideas were combined with Ṣūfī elements, apparently stemming from the school of Ibn Arabi; thus Ṣūfī views were introduced into European Qabbalah. After the expulsion of the Jews from Spain, Spanish theurgical Qabbalah, which had developed without any significant impact from ecstatic Qabbalah, was integrated with the latter; this combination became, through the book *Pardes rimmonim* by Mosheh Cordovero, part of mainstream Qabbalah. Ḥayyim Vital brought Abulafian views into his *Sha'arei qedushah,* and the eighteenth-century qabbalists of the Beit El Academy in Jerusalem perused Abulafia's mystical manuals. Later on, mystical and psychological conceptions of Qabbalah found their way directly and indirectly to the Polish Hasidic masters. The influence of ecstatic Qabbalah is to be seen in isolated groups today, and traces of it can be found in modern literature (e.g., the poetry of Yvan Goll), mainly since the publication of Gershom Scholem's researches.

Unio mystica. Theurgical Qabbalah assumes an independent and forceful human existence whose ritual activity can influence the sphere of divinity, though humans and God remain, in principle, distinct and apart. However, even among the theurgical qabbalists the idea of a mystical union between humankind and God was known—as, for example, in the writings of ʿEzraʾ of Gerona—although it never came to the forefront. In the writings of Nahmanides and his followers, a distinction was made between the preliminary cleaving of reason to God (*devequt ha-daʿat*) and the final cleaving of the soul to God. In contrast, nontheurgical Qabbalah of Avraham Abulafia focused upon the fusion of the human and the divine intellects as the supreme goal of the mystic; extreme literary expressions of this ideal used Hebrew forms of the Ṣūfī formula Huwa Huwa (he is he) or even *anokhi anokhi* ("I I"), which symbolized the complete union of God and humanity. Sometimes the qabbalists referred to mystical union with the Active Intellect, thereby giving a mystical interpretation to the psychology developed by the Islamic philosopher Ibn Rushd. They also borrowed Aristotelian concepts of intellect, intellection, and intelligibles (which form a unity during the act of thinking) to describe mystical union. Explicit unitive phenomena were reported in the writings of Yitsḥaq of Acre, and under the latter's influence and that of Abulafia expressions of *unio mystica* were included in Safadian texts, which turned out to be one of the most important sources for the eighteenth-century Hasidic masters in their search for union with God.

Eschatology. Qabbalah developed eschatological themes considerably. Traditional messianic views contributed only marginally to qabbalistic eschatology. Under the influence of Neoplatonic or Aristotelian psychologies, the qabbalists regarded individual salvation as the ultimate spiritual achievement. Under the influence of Islamic sources, they developed the idea that cosmic processes operate in cycles of seven thousand (*shemiṭṭah*) and forty-nine thousand *(yovel)* years, with each cycle culminating in a thousand years of total rest; each millennium—or, according to other sources, seven millennia—is governed by a separate *sefirah* that influences the processes taking place during this span of time. These qabbalistic views were integrated into the well-known work *Dialoghi d'amore* by Judah Abravanel (Leone Ebreo), through which they entered general European culture. Lengthy discussions on various types of metempsychosis *(gilgul)*, or the transmigration of souls, are found in Qabbalah from the very beginning. Metempsychosis was regarded mainly as an opportunity given to a sinner to amend his former sins and rarely as a purgative period.

Qabbalistic hermeneutics. Two major methods of interpretation used in Qabbalah are the symbolic and the mathematical. The former is paramount in theurgical and theosophical Qabbalah, which considered the scriptures, the phenomena of nature, and the events of history to be symbols for the dynamic and continuous changes taking place within God. The symbolization of the whole of reality enabled the qabbalists to give theosophical significance to virtually every event and, through the "intentional" performance of the commandments, to participate mystically in the divine life. The various possibilities of symbolic interpretation changed the scriptures into an "open text" pregnant with infinite meanings. With the appearance of the *Zohar,* symbols referring to the erotic union of Tifʾeret and Malkhut, and those pointing to the demonic world (the *siṭraʾ aḥraʾ*), became more central. Since the late thirteenth century, a fourfold division of interpretation has been accepted by qabbalists.

Under the influence of Ashkenazic Hasidism of the thirteenth century, the ecstatic Qabbalah used such hermeneutical devices as *gimaṭriyyah,* the calculation of the numerical value of letters; *notariqon,* the use of letters as abbreviations for whole words; and *temurah,* the interchanging of letters. Abulafia developed a sevenfold system of hermeneutics that culminated in an ecstatic experience.

LITERARY GENRES. Qabbalah, like other bodies of Jewish literature, produced exegetical genres. Qabbalists tended to comment upon the traditional canonic texts, although they chose to discuss issues peculiar to the Qabbalah.

The qabbalists produced more than 150 commentaries on the *sefirot* containing lists of symbols that referred to each of the ten divine potencies. These commentaries were handbooks intended to instruct novices in the relations between all the elements of reality—canonic texts, human life, and the supernatural forces. This genre flourished from the thirteenth to the sixteenth centuries. Qabbalistic commentaries on the Pentateuch had a great impact on the propagation of Qabbalah. Tens of these commentaries are extant. The most important are those of Nahmanides, Baḥye ben Asher, Menaḥem Recanati, Avraham Saba, and Ḥayyim ben Attar. Almost every important qabbalistic school produced its own commentary on the daily liturgy, thereby introducing novel theoretical elements into the common religious activity. This vast body of literature, which is partly extant in manuscripts, still requires an extensive critical analysis.

Since its beginning, Qabbalah expressed itself through numerous commentaries on the rationale for the commandments, the most important of which are still unpublished. The qabbalists also produced commentaries on *Sefer yetsirah,* commentaries on the *Zohar,* and works of moralistic literature that were deeply influenced by Cordovero's views and that contributed to the infiltration of the qabbalistic *via mystica* among the Jewish masses. The greater part of the extant qabbalistic literature, including thousands of folios, has not been examined in detail and has not been the subject of critical analysis.

EXTERNAL INFLUENCES. Some modern scholars, such as Naḥman Krochmal in the early nineteenth century and Gershom Scholem in the twentieth, viewed Qabbalah as having been influenced by Gnostic concepts, although no hard evidence has been adduced to substantiate this assumption. The influence of Islamic and Christian Neoplatonism on early Qabbalah is indeed evident and was recognized by such opponents of Qabbalah as Eliyyahu Delmedigo and Yehudah Aryeh Modena (Leone da Modena) as early as the Renaissance period. The thesis proposed by Shulamit Shahar about the influence of Catharism on *Sefer ha-bahir* and Avraham Abulafia has not been confirmed by further studies. The qabbalistic view of evil seems to stem from older texts whose ultimate source was probably Iranian, perhaps Zurvanian. Renaissance Neoplatonism influenced the philosophical interpretation of Qabbalah in the early seventeenth century, but that trend remained without major influence on Jewish Qabbalah.

Although Qabbalah was flexible enough to enrich itself through the acceptance of external ideas, the latter never became dominant factors in its spiritual physiognomy. Through the process of absorption, the alien elements were adapted to the peculiar need of the comprehensive ideological system.

PHILOSOPHICAL INTERPRETATION OF QABBALAH. An important tendency in some qabbalistic writings is the philosophical interpretation of its theosophical and theurgical concepts. This tendency is evident from the middle of the thirteenth century in the works of ʿAzriʾel of Gerona and Yitsḥaq ibn Latif. It came to the forefront in the middle of the fourteenth century, when an array of Spanish authors formed a rather homogenous intellectual current into which Qabbalah was blended by means of concepts derived from the Islamic philosophers Ibn Rushd and Ibn Sīnā. The most important figures of this trend were Yosef ibn Vaqar and Shemuʾel ibn Motot. However, from the beginning of the fifteenth century this philosophical Qabbalah was rejected by the Spanish qabbalists, who now focused their interest on the "pure" theurgical views of the *Zohar.* In the last decades of that century, the philosophical interpretation of Qabbalah became prominent in northern Italy, mostly in the writings of Yo anan Alemanno, David Messer Leon, Yitsḥaq of Pisa, and Isaac Abravanel and his son Judah. The influence of this philosophical interpretation can be discerned in the Ottoman empire, Safad, central Europe, and eastern Europe. At the end of the sixteenth century and early in the seventeenth, important authors such as Avraham Herrera, Avraham Yagel, Yosef Delmedigo, and Menasseh ben Israel made extensive use of ancient texts translated during the Renaissance in order to interpret Cordoverian and Lurianic Qabbalah. Through the works of Menasseh ben Israel and the Latin translation of Avraham Herrera's *Shaʿar ha-shamayim,* this qabbalistic trend found its way into Christian Qabbalah and thus influenced European philosophy. The latest important repercussions of this trend are to be found in the period of the Enlightenment, in the writings of Salomon Maimon and Isaac Satanov, and later on in the works of modern Jewish theologians such as Franz Rosenzweig.

This type of Qabbalah commonly mitigated or even totally nullified the mythical elements that are paramount in mainstream Qabbalah, including the theurgical nature of the commandments, processes by which God's internal life unfolds, and messianic eschatology. For this reason, representatives of philosophical Qabbalah never became influential in Jewish theology.

SEE ALSO Ashkenazic Hasidism; Hasidism; Messianism, article on Jewish Messianism; Scholem, Gershom; Sefer Yetsirah; Shabbetai Tsevi; Zohar.

BIBLIOGRAPHY

Altmann, Alexander. *Studies in Religious Philosophy and Mysticism.* Ithaca, N.Y., 1969. Pioneering studies in qabbalistic history of ideas.

Altmann, Alexander. *Panim shel Yahadut.* Tel Aviv, 1983. Contains a major contribution to the phenomenology of Qabbalah.

Ben-Shlomo, Joseph. *Torat ha-elohut shel R. Mosheh Cordovero.* Jerusalem, 1965. The most extensive analysis of the thought of an important qabbalist.

Dan, Joseph, and Frank Talmage, eds. *Studies in Jewish Mysticism.* Cambridge, Mass., 1982.

Gottlieb, Efraim. *Meḥqarim be-sifrut ha-Qabbalah.* Edited by Joseph Hacker. Tel Aviv, 1976. On the history and phenomenology of early Qabbalah.

Idel, Moshe. "Kitvei R. Avraham Abulafia u-mishnato." 2 vols. Ph. D. diss., Hebrew University of Jerusalem, 1976. A study of ecstatic Qabbalah.

Scholem, Gershom. *Major Trends in Jewish Mysticism.* 3d ed. New York, 1961. Includes chapters on the various phases of Jewish mysticism and Qabbalah, with an extensive bibliography.

Scholem, Gershom. *On the Kabbalah and Its Symbolism.* New York, 1965. Indispensable for understanding qabbalistic phenomenology.

Scholem, Gershom. *Les origines de la Kabbale.* Paris, 1966. Discusses the first manifestations of Qabbalah in Europe.

Scholem, Gershom. *The Messianic Idea in Judaism.* New York, 1971. Important for the history of messianism.

Scholem, Gershom. *Kabbalah.* New York, 1974. Summary of Scholem's numerous studies, with a full bibliography.

Tishby, Isaiah. *Torat ha-raʿ ve-ha-qelippah be-qabbalat ha-Ari* (1942). Jerusalem, 1984. Most important for understanding Lurianism.

Tishby, Isaiah. *Netivei emunah u-minut.* Tel Aviv, 1964. Studies in later Qabbalah and its phenomenology.

Tishby, Isaiah. *Ḥiqrei Qabbalah ve-shiluḥoteyah: meḥqarim umeqorot,* vol. 1. Jerusalem, 1982. Studies in central events of early and later Qabbalah.

Vajda, Georges. *Recherches sur la philosophie et la Kabbale dans la pensée juive du Moyen Age.* Paris, 1962. Major contribution to the analysis of neglected material.

Vajda, Georges, ed. and trans. *Le commentarie de Ezra de Gérone sur le Cantique des Cantiques.* Paris, 1969. Important for understanding of early Qabbalah.

Werblowsky, R. J. Zwi. *Joseph Karo: Lawyer and Mystic.* London, 1962. Analysis of the mystical component of a central figure of Jewish culture.

Wirszubski, Chaim. *Sheloshah peraqim be-toledot ha-Qabbalah ha-notsrit* and *Mequbbal notsri qoreʾ be-Torah.* Jerusalem, 1975 and 1977. Two booklets that include pioneering researches into Pico della Mirandola's Qabbalah.

MOSHE IDEL (1987)

QĀḌĪ. A *qāḍī* is a judge responsible for the application of Islamic positive law (*fiqh*). The office originated under the rule of the first Umayyad caliphs (AH 40–85/661–705 CE), when the provincial governers of the newly created Islamic empire, unable to adjudicate the many disputes that arose among Muslims living within their territories, began to delegate this function to others. In this early period of Islamic history, no body of Islamic positive law had yet come into existence, and the first *qāḍī*s therefore decided cases on the basis of the only guidelines available to them: Arab customary law, the laws of the conquered territories, the general precepts of the Qurʾān, and their own sense of equity. During the later Umayyad period (705–750 CE), a growing class of Muslim legal scholars, distinct from the *qāḍī*s, busied themselves with the task of supplying the needed body of law, and by the time of the accession to power of the Abbasid dynasty in 750 their work could be said to have been essentially completed. In constructing their legal doctrine, these legal scholars took as their point of departure the precedents already established by the *qāḍī*s, some of which they rejected as inconsistent with Islamic principles as these were coming to be understood, but most of which they adopted, with or without modification. Thus the first *qāḍī*s in effect laid the foundations of Islamic positive law. Once this law had been formed, however, the role of the *qāḍī* underwent a profound change. No longer free to follow the guidelines mentioned above, a *qāḍī* was now expected to adhere solely to the new Islamic law, and this adherence has characterized the office ever since.

A *qāḍī* continued, however, to be a delegate of a higher authority, ultimately the caliph or, after the demise of the caliphate, the supreme ruler in a given territory. This delegate status implies the absence of a separation of powers; both judicial and executive powers were concentrated in the person of the supreme ruler (caliph or otherwise). On the other hand, a certain degree of autonomy was enjoyed by a *qāḍī* in that the law that he applied was not the creation of the supreme ruler or the expression of his will. What a *qāḍī* owed to the supreme ruler was solely the power to apply the law, for which sanctions were necessary that only the supreme ruler as head of the state could guarantee.

The qualifications that a *qāḍī* must possess are stated in the law, although the law is not uniform on this subject. The minimal requirement upon which all the jurists agree is that a *qāḍī* possess the same qualifications as a witness in court, that is, that he be free, sane, adult, trustworthy, and a Muslim. Some require that he also possess the qualifications of a jurist, that is, that he be well versed in the law, while others regard those qualifications as simply preferable, implying that a person may effectively discharge the duties of the office without being well versed in the law. This latter position presupposed that a *qāḍī* who is not learned in matters of law would consult those who are before reaching a decision. Indeed, consultation was urged upon the learned *qāḍī* as well, since even the learned are fallible and can profit from the views of others. Those consulted did not, however, have a voice in the final decision making. The Islamic court was a strictly one-judge court and the final decision rested upon the shoulders of a single *qāḍī.*

The jurisdiction of a *qāḍī* was theoretically coextensive with the scope of the law that he applied. That law was fundamentally a law for Muslims, and the internal affairs of the non-Muslim, or *dhimmī*, communities living within the Islamic state were left under the jurisdictions of those communities. Islamic law governed *dhimmī*s only with respect to their relations to Muslims and to the Islamic state. In actual practice, however, the jurisdiction of a *qāḍī* was hemmed in by what must be regarded as rival jurisdictions, particularly that of the *maẓālim* court and that of the *shurṭah.* The former was a court (presided over by the supreme ruler himself or his governor) that heard complaints addressed to it by virtually any offended party. Since Islamic law did not provide for any appellate jurisdiction but regarded the decision of a *qāḍī* as final and irrevocable, the *maẓālim* court could function as a kind of court of appeals in cases where parties complained of unfair decisions from *qāḍī*s. The *maẓālim* judge was not bound to the rules of Islamic law (*fiqh*), nor for that matter was he bound to any body of positive law, but was free to make decisions entirely on the basis of considerations of equity. The *maẓālim* court thus provided a remedy for the inability of a *qāḍī* to take equity freely into account. It also made up for certain shortcomings of Islamic law, for example, the lack of a highly developed law of torts, which was largely due to the preoccupation of the law with breaches of contracts. In addition, it heard complaints against state officials. The *shurṭah,* on the other hand, was the state apparatus responsible for criminal justice. It too provided a remedy for a deficiency in the law, namely the incompleteness and procedural rigidity of its criminal code. Although in theory a *qāḍī* exercised a criminal jurisdiction, in practice this jurisdiction was removed from his sphere of competence and turned over entirely to the *shurṭah,* which developed its own penalties and procedures. What was left to the *qāḍī* was a jurisdiction concerned mainly with cases having to do with inheritance, personal status, property, and commercial transactions. Even within this jurisdiction, a particular *qāḍī*'s jurisdiction could be further restricted to particular cases or types of cases at the behest of the appointing superior.

The principle of delegation of judicial powers not only allowed the supreme ruler to delegate these powers to a *qāḍī*; it also allowed *qāḍī*s to further delegate them to others, and there was in principle no limit to this chain of delegation. All persons in the chain, except for the supreme ruler or his governor, bore the title *qāḍī.* Although in theory the appointment of a *qāḍī* could be effected by a simple verbal declaration on the part of the appointing superior, normally it was accomplished by means of a written certificate of investiture, which obviated the need for the appointee to appear in the presence of the superior. The appointment was essentially unilateral rather than contractual and did not require acceptance on the part of the appointee in order to be effective. It could be revoked at any time.

The Abbasids created the office of chief *qāḍī* (*qāḍī al-quḍāh*), whose holder acted primarily as adviser to the caliph in the appointment and dismissal of *qāḍī*s. Later Islamic states generally retained this office, while granting to its holder the authority to issue appointments and dismissals in his own name. The Mamluk state, which ruled Egypt and Syria from 1250 to 1516 CE, introduced the practice of appointing four chief *qāḍī*s, one for each of the Sunni legal schools (*madhhabs*).

Although the primary responsibility of a *qāḍī* was a judicial one, he was generally charged with certain nonjudicial responsibilities as well, such as the administration of religious endowments (*waqf*s), the legitimization of the accession or deposition of a ruler, the execution of wills, the accreditation of witnesses, guardianship over orphans and others in need of protection, and supervision of the enforcement of public morals (*ḥisbah*).

See Also Islamic Law.

Bibliography

Schacht, Joseph. *An Introduction to Islamic Law.* Oxford, 1964.

Tyan, Emile. "Judicial Organization." In *Law in the Middle East,* vol. 1, edited by Majid Khadduri and Herbert J. Liebesny, pp. 236–278. Washington, D. C., 1955.

Tyan, Emile. *Histoire de l'organization judiciaire en pays d'Islam.* 2d ed. Leiden, 1960.

Bernard G. Weiss (1987)

QĀḌĪ AL-NUʿMĀN

QĀḌĪ AL-NUʿMĀN. Abū Ḥanīfah al-Nuʿmān ibn Muḥammad ibn Manṣūr ibn Aḥmad ibn Ḥayyūn al-Tamīmī (d. AH 363/974 CE), generally called al-Qāḍī al-Nuʿmān, was the most eminent exponent of Fāṭimid jurisprudence and an official historian of the Fāṭimids. His works, all written in Arabic, cover various other subjects, including Qurʾanic exegesis *(taʾwīl)* and religious etiquette. He entered the service of the first Fāṭimid caliph, al-Mahdī (r. 909–934), in about 924 in Ifrīqiyah (present-day Tunisia and eastern Algeria) and served the first four caliphs of the Fāṭimid dynasty in various capacities for almost fifty years until his death.

On the eve of the advent of the Fāṭimids, Ismāʿīlī jurisprudence had not yet developed, while the Muslim population of Ifrīqiyah mostly belonged to two recognized Sunnī schools of jurisprudence: the school of Mālik ibn Anas (d. 796), followed by the popular majority, and the school of Abū Ḥanīfah (d. 767), which was usually favored by the deposed Aghlabid dynasty. The new rulers introduced the application of Ismāʿīlī ritual and law in some specific matters, and sought to win adherents. Among those who readily joined the Ismāʿīlī cause were members of old established Shīʿī families, who were not a recognized community in Ifrīqiyah, as well as Ḥanafī scholars deprived of patronage. Among the few Mālikī scholars of al-Qayrawān (Kairouan) to embrace the Ismāʿīlī faith was al-Nuʿmān's father, and it is most likely that al-Nuʿmān was brought up as an Ismāʿīlī. Already in his youth he was assiduous in collecting and transcribing books. At al-Mahdī's suggestion, al-Nuʿmān undertook the collection and classification of a vast number of legal traditions (*ḥadīth*s) narrated on the authority of the family of the Prophet (*ahl al-bayt*). This endeavor resulted in his voluminous first work, entitled *Kitāb al-Īḍāḥ* (The book of elucidation), of which only a small fragment has survived. Fortunately, some of his several abridgments of the work, including an easy-to-memorize versified version composed during the reign of the second Fāṭimid caliph, al-Qāʾim (r. 934–946), have survived. These, as well as his subsequent works on jurisprudence, represent a development of his thought towards consolidating the legal practices with a view to the codification of Ismāʿīlī jurisprudence.

In his several polemical works refuting the principles and methods adopted by the Sunnī schools of jurisprudence and their founders, al-Nuʿmān established as authorities of jurisprudence, apart from the Qurʾān and the *sunnah,* the rulings of the *imām*s from the family of the Prophet, including the reigning *imām.* In one of the earliest Fāṭimid treatises on the imamate, entitled *al-Urjūzah al-mukhtārah* (The exquisite poem), composed during the reign al-Qāʾim, he defended the rights of the Fāṭimids to the imamate, supreme leadership of the Muslim community. This legitimist doctrine was seriously challenged by the Khārijīs, who comprised the indigenous Berbers. Their rebellion challenged the Fāṭimid state during the last two years of al-Qāʾim's reign and the early part of the reign of his successor, al-Manṣūr (r. 946–953). After crushing the rebellion, al-Manṣūr founded, near al-Qayrawān, his new residential town al-Manṣūrīyah to mark his victory. The caliph summoned al-Nuʿmān from Tripoli, where he had appointed him as a judge shortly after his accession to the caliphate, and invested him with the judgeship of al-Manṣūrīyah, al-Mahdīyah, al-Qayrawān, as well as all the other towns and provinces of Ifrīqiyah.

Al-Nuʿmān reached the height of his career during the reign of al-Muʿizz (r. 953–975), when he was invested with absolute judicial authority to investigate complaints brought before him from the subjects. He was also authorized to hold sessions of wisdom (*majālis al-ḥikma*) in the royal palace to instruct the congregation in the Ismāʿīlī religious doctrines. Under the close supervision of the caliph he composed his *Daʿāʾim al-Islām (The Pillars of Islam),* which represents a culmination of more than thirty years of effort to codify Fāṭimid jurisprudence. It was proclaimed as the official code of the Fāṭimid state, and continues to be the greatest source of authority on medieval Ismāʿīlī law up to the present day.

Al-Nuʿmān is also rightly regarded as the founder of Fāṭimid historiography. His major historical work, *Iftitāḥ al-daʿwah* (The commencement of the mission), completed during the reign of al-Muʿizz, relates in detail the exploits of the Ismāʿīlī mission (*daʿwah*), first in Yemen and then in Ifrīqiyah among the Kutāma Berbers, which eventually succeeded in establishing a long-awaited Shīʿī state under the supreme authority of a hereditary *imām* from the *ahl al-bayt*. It remains the most important primary source for the history of that period and was used by subsequent chroniclers as a reference.

When al-Muʿizz moved to Egypt in 973 after the Fāṭimid conquest of that country, al-Nuʿmān, together with members of his family, accompanied the caliph. Fāṭimid law, as codified by al-Nuʿmān, began to be applied and taught in Egypt. He continued to serve al-Muʿizz and died in Cairo on March 27 of the following year. His sons and grandsons continued to teach his works and serve the Fāṭimids in the judiciary for nearly half a century.

BIBLIOGRAPHY

Madelung, Wilferd. "The Sources of Ismāʿīlī Law." *Journal of Near Eastern Studies* 35 (1976): 29–40. Reprinted in his *Religious Schools and Sects in Medieval Islam*. London, 1985. Article XVIII.

Nanji, Azim. "An Ismāʿīlī Theory of *Walāyah* in the *Daʿāʾim al-Islam* of Qāḍī al-Nuʿmān." In *Essays on Islamic Civilization Presented to Niyazi Berkes*, edited by Donald P. Little, pp. 260–273. Leiden, 1976.

al-Nuʿmān ibn Muḥammad, al-Qāḍī Abū Ḥanīfah. *Daʿāʾim al-Islām*. Translated by Asaf A. A. Fyzee. Completely revised and annotated by Ismail Kurban Husein Poonawala as *The Pillars of Islam*. New Delhi, 2002.

Poonawala, Ismail K. *Biobibliography of Ismāʿīlī Literature*. Malibu, Calif., 1977. On pages 51–68, Poonawala gives a complete list of al-Nuʿmān's works, including those attributed to him, numbering sixty-two works.

Poonawala, Ismail K. "Al-Qāḍī al-Nuʿmān and Ismaʿili Jurisprudence." In *Mediaeval Ismaʿili History and Thought*, edited by Farhad Daftary, pp. 117–143. Cambridge, U.K., 1996.

HAMID HAJI (2005)

QARĀMIṬAH (sg., Qarmaṭī) is the name applied to a dissident Muslim group that broke away from the parent Ismāʿīlī movement. At first, this name referred to the followers of Ḥamdān al-Qarmaṭ, an Ismāʿīlī *dāʿī* (missionary) in the rural district of Kufa, who was given the surname Qarmaṭ (meaning either that he was short-legged or red-eyed). Later the term was used in a wider and derogatory sense to include all the Ismāʿīlīyah.

BACKGROUND. The missionary activities of Ḥamdān, who was converted to the Ismāʿīlī cause by the *dāʿī* Ahwazi, began around 873. He was assisted by his deputy and brother-in-law, ʿAbdān. In 899, because of change in the central leadership of the Ismāʿīlī movement and the doctrinal issue involved in this change, Ḥamdān severed his relations with the leadership. Shortly thereafter he disappeared, and ʿAbdān was murdered by his subordinate *dāʿī* Zikrawayh, who at first showed loyalty to the central leadership. When Zikrawayh was threatened with revenge by ʿAbdān's followers he went into hiding. In 902 Zikrawayh's son succeeded in winning the support of tribes in the Syrian desert and attacked and pillaged several cities in Syria. Two years later he was captured and executed. After several unsuccessful attempts at organizing revolts, Zikrawayh himself came out of hiding in 906 and defeated the Abbasid army, but the following year he was routed and killed, and the Qarmaṭī revolts in Syria came to an end.

The split of the Ismāʿīlīyah into two factions profoundly affected the loyalty of the various *daʿwah* (mission) groups to the central leadership. The *daʿwah* in Syria-Mesopotamia and western Persia refused to recognize the Fatimid claims to the imamate and instead supported the Qarāmiṭah. The *daʿwah* in Yemen at first remained loyal to the central leadership, but in 913 ʿAlī ibn al-Faḍl renounced his allegiance to the Fatimids and began waging war against his companion Manṣūr al-Yaman, who had remained loyal to them. Because of internal strife the political power of the Qarāmiṭah disintegrated rapidly. The *dāʿīs* in Rayy, who were successful in gaining the support of the Daylamis and some rulers of the Musafirid dynasty, maintained their contacts with the Qarāmiṭah.

QARĀMIṬAH OF BAHREIN. Abū Saʿid al-Jannābī, the founder of the Qarmaṭī state in Bahrein (the coastal area of eastern Arabia between Basra and Oman, embracing the oases of al-Qaṭīf and Hajar/al-Ḥasā), who was sent by Ḥamdān al-Qarmaṭ and ʿAbdān, began his missionary activity in 886/7. Following the murder of ʿAbdān, he sided with the rebels against the central leadership and plotted the murder of the *dāʿī* Ẓamāmī, who had been sent to Bahrein before him by Manṣūr al-Yaman from Yemen and who had remained loyal to the central leadership. He himself was murdered in 913. In 923, under the leadership of Abū Ṭāhir, the son of Abū Saʿīd, the Qarāmiṭah launched devastating attacks on southern Iraq and raided pilgrim caravans. Then, interpreting the conjunction of Jupiter and Saturn in 928 as a sign indicating the end of the Islamic era and the beginning of the final era, Abū Ṭāhir predicted the appearance of the Mahdi (messiah) in the near future. In 927–929 he led new attacks on southern Iraq and threatened the Abbasid capital of Baghdad itself. In 930 he attacked the holy city of Mecca during the pilgrimage season, committed slaughter, and carried away the Black Stone of the Kaʿbah, thus demonstrating the end of the Islamic era. The following year he handed over his reign to a Persian youth from Isfahan in whom he recognized the expected Mahdi, but events took an entirely unexpected turn when the Persian ordered the cursing of all the prophets and instituted the worship of fire. When the Persian encouraged certain extravagant abominations and executed prominent Qarmaṭī leaders, Abū Ṭāhir plotted his murder and admitted that he had been duped by the youth. This episode demoralized his followers. Consequently, the Iraqi Qarāmiṭah, who had escaped from the Abbasid army and had joined Abū Ṭāhir, left Bahrein. Many apostatized, disclosing their secrets, and some tribal leaders joined the army of the Sunnī rulers. Abū Ṭāhir nevertheless continued to raid southern Iraq until his death in 944.

After the death of Abū Ṭāhir his brothers ruled jointly, and in 951 they returned the Black Stone for a high sum paid by the Abbasids. The Fatimid caliph al-Muʿizz li-Dīn Allāh (953–975) failed in an effort to bring the Qarāmiṭah of Bahrein back to the Ismāʿīlī/Fatimid fold. Open hostilities broke out after the Fatimid conquest of Egypt, when their army advanced to northern Syria, provoking the Qarāmiṭah, who had their own interests in Syria. Temporary alliances were formed when the Qarāmiṭah were aided by the Buyids of Baghdad and the Ḥamdānids of Syria against the common enemy, the Fatimids. Subsequently, the Qarāmiṭah threatened the Fatimid capital of Cairo, but they were defeated both times. As their relations with Baghdad became strained they renewed their attacks on southern Iraq. In 988 the Abbasid army inflicted a crushing defeat on the Qarāmiṭah; their capital, al-Ḥasā, was besieged; and al-Qaṭīf was pillaged. When they were defeated and reduced to local power they renewed their nominal allegiance to the Fatimids in return for a tribute, but these relations did not last long. Gradually, the Qarmaṭī communities outside of Bahrein were either absorbed by the Ismāʿīlīyah or disintegrated. In 1067 they lost the island of Uwāl, and soon thereafter al-Qaṭīf was lost. Finally, in 1077–1078, after a long siege al-Ḥasā was lost to an emerging local tribe that was aided by the Seljuks of Baghdad, thus ending the Qarmaṭī rule of almost two centuries.

TEACHINGS. The basic tenet of Qarmaṭī doctrine was the appearance of Muḥammad ibn Ismāʿīl as the seventh *nāṭiq* ("apostle" of God), the Mahdi, al-Qāʾim (the Redeemer), who would abrogate the *sharīʿah* (Muslim canon law) and promulgate the *bāṭin* (inner truth of religion). The doctrine carries an antinomian tendency. The reports of historians that the Qarāmiṭah dispensed with Islamic ritual and law are therefore correct, but other accusations, of licentiousness and libertinism, are not true. Abū Hātim al-Rāzī (d. 934/5), Abū al-Ḥasan al-Nasafī (d. 943), and Abū Yaʿqūb al-Sijistānī (d. after 971) are some of the illustrious *dāʿīs* who have elaborated Qarmaṭī doctrine.

The Qarāmiṭah drew a fundamental distinction between the *ẓāhir* ("exoteric") and the *bāṭin* ("esoteric"), the two aspects of religion. The former consists of external aspects of religion as laid down in the religious law and explains the apparent meaning of the Qurʾān. The *ẓāhir* changes, therefore, with each prophet in accordance with time and circumstance. The *bāṭin* is comprised of the inner, true meaning of the law and the Qurʾān. It remains unchanged.

The Qarāmiṭah formulated a new synthesis of reason and revelation based on Neoplatonic cosmology and Shīʿī doctrine. Thus, they offered a new world order under the imam, who resembles Plato's philosopher-king. The classic formulation of this synthesis is found in the well-known encyclopedic work entitled *Ras āʾil Ikhwān al-Safāʾ* (Epistles of the Brethren of Purity). The Qarāmiṭah viewed history as a developmental process that progresses through seven major cycles, each containing seven minor cycles. The length of these cycles varies. In conjunction with the cyclical view of the Qarāmiṭah history also had a notion of different epochs, according to which the seven major cycles progress through three different epochs: *dawr al-kashf* ("epoch of unveiling"), *dawr al-fatrah* ("epoch of langor"), and *dawr al-satr* ("epoch of occultation"). During the first epoch good prevails, hence there is no need for external law, and the *bāṭin* is promulgated openly. This is followed by the second epoch, during which goodness loses its hold over the people and religion becomes corrupted. At the end of this period begins the third epoch, when the prophet receives the revelation and lays down the law. The prophet then appoints his successor, known as *waṣī* ("plenipotentiary"), who promulgates the *bāṭin*. The imams during this epoch remain hidden. At the end, when the people are ready, al-Qāʾim appears and abrogates the law; he thus becomes the first imam of the following epoch of unveiling. These cycles are repeated until all souls are emancipated from matter and return to the Universal Soul.

HISTORICAL AND SOCIAL SIGNIFICANCE. The Qarāmiṭah were a powerful movement that shook Sunnī Islam, threatened the Abbasid caliphate, and terrorized southern Iraq. They had such an enormous influence in the region that during the Buyid supremacy in Baghdad the Qarāmiṭah had their own customhouse in the port of Basra alongside that of the Abbasid government. Their representatives resided in Baghdad, Kufa, and Jaʿfarīyah and wielded considerable influence. Sunnī Muslim authors considered them a heretic group led by people of the faiths superseded by Islam in order to undermine the latter from within. The general accusation against them that they practiced communism of goods and women is false; however, the shift in their opponents' arguments from theological issues to economic ones does indicate that they were perceived as a social threat.

The Qarāmiṭah constituted a messianic movement promising a better future with the rule of justice and equity; hence the social character of their preaching is undeniable. The famous historian al-Ṭabarī (d. 923) observes that the Qarāmiṭah consisted mainly of peasants and tillers. Their support came from rural areas and from the bedouin. Although the backbone of the army consisted of able-bodied Qarāmiṭah who were trained militarily, bedouin tribesmen joined them regularly for military campaigns. Some tribes, such as Banū Kilāb and Banū ʿUqayl, were integrated into the Qarmaṭī community. They did experiment with communal ownership of property, but those experiments remained peripheral. Their concern for the welfare of their community produced a unique experiment in the state of Bahrein. Its order and justice even evoked the admiration of non-Qarmaṭī travelers. Ibn Ḥawqal, who visited Bahrein in the latter half of the tenth century, makes interesting observations on its political structure. According to his account, the Qarmaṭī state was very much like an oligarchic republic. The ruler was not absolute and ruled with the aid of a ruling council comprised of important government officials and his own close associates. Following Abū Ṭāhir's death, the leadership was held collectively by his brothers.

Ibn Ḥawqal also describes the various taxes and tolls by which the state raised its revenue, and the distribution of these revenues among the ruling council. Income from grain and fruit estates was assigned to the Qarmaṭī community, while the revenues from customs on the island of Uwāl were allocated to Abū Saʿīd and his descendants. All other revenues from taxes, tribute, protection fees paid by the pilgrim caravans, and booty from military campaigns were disposed of in agreement with the ruling council after setting aside one-fifth for the Mahdi.

Nāsir-i Khusraw, a Persian Ismāʿīlī who visited Bahrein in the eleventh century, makes the following observations. There were in al-Ḥasā more than twenty thousand inhabitants capable of bearing arms. Though the inhabitants acknowledged the prophethood of Muḥammad, they observed neither fasts nor prayers. The ruling council ruled with equity and justice; it owned thirty thousand black slaves who did agricultural labor. No taxes were paid by the inhabitants, and any impoverished person could obtain a loan without interest. New artisans arriving there were given loans to establish themselves. Repairs for poor homeowners were done by the state. Grain was ground free of charge in the mills owned by the state. There were no mosques, but a foreign merchant was allowed to build a mosque for the use of Muslim visitors. People did not drink wine.

The fourth century of Islamic history, known for the flowering of Islamic civilization, witnessed a dramatic Shīʿī ascendancy to power, with the Fatimids in North Africa and Egypt and the Buyids in Baghdad. It was during this period that the Qarāmiṭah, representing a powerful, radical revolutionary movement, also succeeded in establishing their state in Bahrein. This state exemplifies their rule of justice and equity.

SEE ALSO Shiism, article on Ismāʿīlīyah.

BIBLIOGRAPHY

The surviving fragments of Qarmaṭī writings from early historical works are collected, along with extracts from later works, in *Taʾrīkh akhbār al-Qarāmiṭah,* edited by Souhayl Zakkar (Beirut, 1971). The best modern studies are by Wilferd Madelung, S. M. Stern, and Vladimir A. Ivanov. Madelung's article "Ḳarmaṭī" in the new edition of *The Encyclopaedia of Islam* (Leiden, 1960–) contains an excellent bibliography.

ISMAIL K. POONAWALA (1987)

QI is one of the most complex and multifaceted terms in all of Chinese philosophy, religion, and science. No single word can translate it adequately. Its root meaning is "moist emanation." Steam, clouds, and mist are *qi,* and the word appears frequently in compounds that refer to meteorological phenomena. Another basic meaning is "breath." Later, these meanings were sometimes amalgamated; the Daoist philosopher Zhuangzi (fourth century BCE) wrote, "When the Great Clod [the Earth] exhales breath, it is called wind."

During the Warring States period (481–221 BCE), the classical age of Chinese philosophy, the word *qi* began to be employed in an expanded variety of meanings. The concept of breath gave rise to the meaning "vital spirit," that is, the life force of all creatures. "Nourishing the vital spirit" (*yang qi*) by means of diet, yogic exercises, breath control, or sexual yoga became an important part of the Daoist quest for immortality from the late Warring States period onward. A true adept could dispense with food and even with the physical body itself; immortal spirits nourished themselves on *qi. Qi* could also be thought of as a flow of energy within the body. To control this flow of *qi,* traditional Chinese medicine employed acupuncture, therapeutic massage, and other techniques. The East Asian martial arts, which have a strong spiritual component, emphasize the need to regulate one's *qi* in order to achieve absolute physical mastery of the body.

Drawing on such earlier concepts as *yinyang* and the Five Phases (*wuxing,* sometimes misleadingly called "five elements"), Zou Yan (fourth century BCE) and his followers employed the idea of *qi* as the key to a systematic organic natural philosophy. For them, *qi* had two sets of meanings. First, it was an extension of the idea of "vital spirit," whereby all things, animate or not, are what they are. Things with similar *qi,* as determined by such classificatory criteria as *yinyang* and the Five Phases, were similar in nature and could interact organically without a demonstrable mechanical cause-and-effect relationship. A typical summation is that found in the second-century BCE *Huainanzi*: "All things are the same as their *qi*; all things respond within their own class." Second, *qi* was a sort of ethereal resonating medium through which such interactions took place. Both concepts entered the mainstream of Chinese philosophy during the early Han period (206 BCE–7 CE), especially in the work of the Confucian syncretist Dong Zhongshu (179?–104? BCE). During this period *qi* also came to mean something like "power"; thus, character traits and psychological states such as vigor, rage, or fortitude could be described with reference to a person's *qi.* This sense survives in the modern vernacular Chinese term meaning "to become angry": *shengqi,* literally, "to engender *qi.*"

In the Neo-Confucian revival of the Northern Song period (960–1127) the term *qi* acquired a radically new meaning. Cheng Yi (1033–1108) and especially Zhu Xi (1130–1200) developed a Neo-Confucian metaphysics according to which all phenomena are manifestations of preexisting ideal principles. *Qi* was what gave physical substance to metaphysical ideals *(li).* From the time of Zhu Xi, this sense of *qi* tended to be dominant in Chinese philosophy and religion, although the earlier senses persisted as well.

Neo-Confucian metaphysics provided indigenous (non-Buddhist) Chinese philosophy and religion with a comprehensive explanation of the phenomenon of evil. Confucianism had always held that the world and everything in it is by nature good; yet evil undeniably exists. For the Neo-Confucians, the resolution of this enigma involved the concept of *qi*. All metaphysical principles *(li)* are inherently good, but their physical manifestations may be good or not, according to the quality of *qi*. The *qi* that gives physical substance to *li* may be pure, clear, and good, or it may be turbid and flawed. A person whose *qi* is "muddy" will exhibit a flawed moral nature and will be capable of acting in evil ways, despite the fundamental goodness of man.

Fortunately, such flaws could be overcome; and the quest to do so was what gave Neo-Confucianism some of the qualities of a personal religion as well as a moral and ethical social philosophy. Sagehood—human perfection—was to be sought through the "investigation of things"; one should, through study and self-cultivation, inquire exhaustively into the perfect and enduring principles of things, and, by imitating them, purge oneself of all that is impure and inharmonious.

However, for later generations of Neo-Confucians, the "investigation of things" too often became the investigation of books. Received authority rather than active inquiry guided attempts at self-cultivation. Partly in response to this tendency, the Ming dynasty philosopher Wang Yangming (1472–1529) emphasized instead introspection and meditation. Yet in both cases the goal was the same: the purification of *qi*, leading to enlightenment and the perfect unity of consciousness and action.

Used continuously and pervasively in a variety of technical and vernacular senses, the term *qi* over the centuries has repeatedly acquired new meanings and connotations while retaining older ones. Any occurrence of the term, therefore, will be correctly understood only through careful attention to its context.

See Also Confucianism.

BIBLIOGRAPHY

A good explanation of the concept of *qi* and its role in Chinese natural philosophy can be found in Joseph Needham's *Science and Civilisation in China*, vol. 2, *History of Scientific Thought* (Cambridge, 1956). Fung Yu-lan's standard *A History of Chinese Philosophy*, 2d ed., 2 vols., translated by Derk Bodde (Princeton, 1952–1953), deals extensively with the term in its various religious and philosophical contexts.

John S. Major (1987)

QIYĀS ("analogy") is a method of reasoning that entails the extension of a precedent to an essentially similar situation. One of the four principal sources of law among *Sunnī* Muslims, *qiyās* was the last to gain explicit recognition, and then only after a fierce controversy that has left its mark on the history of Islam. The expansion of the territorial domains of Islam after the great conquests raised an increasing variety of issues not covered by the Qurʾān or the *sunnah* (tradition of the prophet Muḥammad). Islamic jurists, therefore, felt the need to have recourse to reason, logic, and opinion. Their freedom was, however, limited. In a society committed to the authority of the revelation, the use of personal opinion *(raʾy)* in religious and legal matters evoked opposition. In theory, the Qurʾān contained a complete revelation and, supplemented by the *sunnah*, was considered to respond to all eventualities. To admit any source of law other than the Qurʾān and the *sunnah* meant the renunciation of the ideal of founding the individual and collective life of Muslims exclusively on divine revelation. To overcome this difficulty, the theory of *qiyās* was elaborated with a view to restricting and setting formal limits on the use of *raʾy*.

The argument in favor of *qiyās* is based on the juristic premise that divine prescriptions follow certain objectives and have effective causes that can be ascertained and applied to similar cases. The opponents of *qiyās*, however, challenged this view by emphasizing that divine prescriptions have no causes except when these are specifically indicated. Besides, distinguishing the effective cause of a ruling involves doubt, and legal rules must not be based on doubt. In the view of the challengers, the proper conduct in response to the divine prescriptions is to accept them with devotion and without attempting to determine causes. It was on the strength of these arguments that the Ẓāhirīyah and the Akhbārī branch of the Twelver Shīʿah rejected *qiyās* altogether, and the Ḥanābilah permitted its use only in cases of dire necessity.

Neither the Qurʾān nor the *sunnah* refers directly to *qiyās*. The jurists have resorted to both, however, in supporting their arguments for or against *qiyās*. Its opponents argued that *qiyās* is alien to the Qurʾān, which says "We have sent to you the Book as an explanation for everything" (16:89) and "In whatever you differ, the verdict therein belongs to God" (42:10). They also contended that analogy is a conjecture and that "surely conjecture avails not aught against truth" (53:28). They concluded that *qiyās* is not legal evidence and that action upon it is null and void.

The defenders of *qiyās* argued that the Qurʾān stipulates "As for these similitudes, we cite them for mankind, but none will grasp their meaning save the wise" (29:43) and "Learn a lesson, O you who have vision to see" (59:2). They held the view that *qiyās* is essential to appreciate and evaluate the similitudes. Furthermore, on two occasions, when Muḥammad sent Muʿādh ibn Jabal and Abū Mūsā al-Ashʿārī as judges to the Yemen, the Prophet is reported to have sanctioned the exercise of *raʾy* in the absence of guidance in the Qurʾān and the *sunnah*.

Although *qiyās* as a technical formula was elaborated in the second century AH (eighth century CE), evidence suggests that the companions of the Prophet approved of it in principle. For example, the caliph ʿUmar's directive to Abū Mūsā al-Ashʿārī reads "Know the similitudes and weigh the cases against them." Again, when ʿUmar consulted the companions on the penalty for the wine drinker (*shārib*), ʿAlī drew an analogy between the *shārib* and the slanderer *(qādhif)* and suggested the same penalty (of eighty lashes) for both. ʿAlī reasoned thus: "When a person drinks he becomes intoxicated; when he is intoxicated he raves; and when he raves he accuses falsely."

During the second and third centuries AH, *raʾy* and *qiyās* became the focus of a controversy between the party of tradition *(ahl al-ḥadīth)* and the party of opinion (*ahl al-raʾy*). Mālik and Ibn Ḥanbal, the leading jurists of Medina and Mecca, the original seat of Islam, laid particular emphasis on tradition, which they adopted as their standard in deciding legal issues. The situation was different in the conquered territories. Iraqi jurists, for example, who were farther removed from the birthplace of tradition, had used *raʾy* and *qiyās* extensively. The leading figure in this controversy was Abū Ḥanīfah, who openly declared *qiyās* to be a valid source of law. But the person credited with ending the controversy is al-Shāfiʿī, who came out squarely in favor of *qiyās* by including it among the four roots of law, though he was very careful to state that *qiyās* must be based strictly on the revealed sources and on consensus (*ijmaʿ*).

In its technical sense, *qiyās* is the extension of the value of an original case (*aṣl*) to a subsidiary case (*farʿ*) by reason of an effective cause (*ʿillah*) that is common to both. For example, when a legatee slays a testator, the former is precluded from the latter's will. This prohibition is based on the tradition that "the killer does not inherit" *(lā yarith al-qātil)*. Although this ruling refers to intestate succession only, through analogy it is extended to bequests by reason of a common effective cause, namely the prohibition on hastening the realization of a right before it is due.

The cause in analogy must be intelligible to the human mind and it must be clearly identifiable. *Qiyās* is thus not applicable in matters of worship *(ʿibādāt)*, such as the number of daily prayers, where the mind cannot understand the value in question (the command to pray five times a day rather than twenty times has no identifiable cause). A further restriction in the use of *qiyās* concerns the exercise of caution in the application of penalties. Thus, under Ḥanafī law, prescribed penalties *(ḥudūd)* may not be analogically extended to similar offences. The Shāfiʿīs and some jurists from other schools are in disagreement on this point, for they consider that the basic rationale of the *ḥudūd* is ascertainable with a reasonable degree of certainty in the Qurʾān and the *sunnah*. A total ban on the use of analogy concerning the *ḥudūd* is, therefore, not warranted. But the Ḥanafī ruling, which favors caution in the enforcement of penalties, has wider support among jurists.

There are three other conditions governing the validity of *qiyās:*

(1) The value extended to a new case should be established in the Qurʾān, *sunnah,* or consensus but not in another *qiyās.*

(2) *Qiyās* should not result in the altering of a prescription (*naṣṣ*). For instance, the Qurʾān (24:4) renders false accusation *(qadhf)* a permanent bar to the acceptance of one's testimony. Al-Shāfiʿī, however, compares the false accuser to the perpetrator of other grave sins (*kabāʾir*) and argues that since punishment and repentance absolve the latter and entitle him to be a witness, this exemption should also apply to the false accuser. The Ḥanafīyah have replied that this conclusion would amount to altering the divine prescription on the basis of personal judgment.

(3) The value in question should not be expressly limited to the original case. Thus, while the Prophet exceptionally accepted the testimony of Khuzaymah as legal proof (the standard being two witnesses), *qiyās* may not be used to justify accepting the testimony of another single individual as legal proof.

SEE ALSO Uṣūl al-Fiqh.

BIBLIOGRAPHY

Textbooks on Islamic jurisprudence *(uṣūl al-fiqh),* which are mainly in Arabic, normally devote a section to *qiyās*. There is a wide selection of both classical and modern works in Arabic. Among the best are Sayf al-Dīn al-Āmidī's *Al-iḥkām fī uṣūl al-aḥkām* (Cairo, 1914) and Muḥammad al-Khuḍārī's *Kitab uṣūl al-fiqh,* 3d ed. (Cairo, 1938). Comprehensive information on Shīʿī law can be found in Sayyid Muḥammad Asghari's *Qiyās va sayr-i takvīn-i ān dar ḥoqūq-i Islām* (Tehran, 1982). The best single book in English that devotes a section to *qiyās* remains Nicolas P. Aghnides's *Muhammadan Theories of Finance* (New York, 1916). A more condensed but accurate summary of *qiyās* can be found in S. R. Mahmassani's *The Philosophy of Jurisprudence in Islam,* translated by Farhat Ziadeh (Leiden, 1961), which also contains a very useful bibliography. Interesting information on *qiyās* can also be found in Joseph Schacht's *The Origins of Muhammadan Jurisprudence* (London, 1950) and Noel J. Coulson's *A History of Islamic Law* (1964; reprint, Edinburgh, 1971).

M. HASHIM KAMALI (1987)

QUAKERS. The Quakers, or the Religious Society of Friends, arose in seventeenth-century England and America out of a shared experience of the Light and Spirit of God within each person. This source of worship, insight, and power they identify as the Spirit of Christ that also guided the biblical prophets and apostles. Quakers also affirm each person's ability to recognize and respond to truth and to obey the Light perfectly through the leading of an inner witness, or "Seed," called by some Quakers "Christ reborn in us" and by others "that of God in every [hu]man," out of which transformed personalities can grow. They therefore ask of each other, and of human society, uncompromising honesty, simplicity of life, nonviolence, and justice. Quakers have often been sensitive to new forms of social evil and creative in their programs to overcome them. Their worship has been based on silent waiting upon God without outward ritual.

The early Friends, as Quakers were named (from *John* 15:5) by their first leader George Fox, arose in England during the Puritan Commonwealth under Oliver Cromwell, manifesting an inward intensification of radical and spiritual forms of Puritanism; they were influenced by uncompromising Baptists, quietist Seekers, antinomian Ranters, and theocratic militants; and these were in turn influenced by English Lollards, by European Anabaptist Mennonites who rejected both the state and class inequality, and by mystics like Jakob Boehme and the Familists. Unlike their predecessors, Quakers held distinctive ideas on the purely inward nature of true baptism and Communion, on the ministry of all laymen and women, on God's power judging and working within hearts and history, and on the need for biblical events to be fulfilled within each person's life-story; but many of these ideas simply carried further those trends, already active in the mainstream of Protestant doctrine, that had turned English Christians from Catholics into Anglicans, and then into Presbyterians or radical Puritans. Indeed, many Quakers had fought in the Puritan armies of the English Civil War and had turned back from the futility of merely military millennia.

A regional mass awakening in the English Northwest, which had not been strongly reached by Puritanism or any other vital religious movement, sprang up in 1652 around George Fox and the Quaker preachers inspired by him. From open-air meetings on the Yorkshire, Westmorland, and Cumberland moors, groups were gathered who were convinced to sit under the Light, largely in silence, for months of anguished self-searching of their motives and habits. The name *Quaker* reflected the physical impact of their inner struggles to yield all self-will to the judgments and guidance of the Light until they could live purely and speak entirely by its "leadings." Only then would joy and love come.

The early Quaker mission throughout England, in 1654–1656, was presented as the "Day of Visitation" by the Lord to each town or region; newly transformed Friends spoke in markets and parish churches despite mobbing and arrests. In New England, Quakers challenging the "biblical commonwealth" were banished on pain of death, and Mary Dyer and three men were hanged in Boston. The pope and the sultan of Turkey had been visited but not converted. To Quakers, Puritan apocalyptic hopes for God's cosmic victory over evil seemed fulfilled as through their work the spirit of Christ conquered the world nonviolently in "the Lamb's war" (*Rev.* 19:11–15). Outward violence they saw as only the devil's distraction, injuring God's good physical creation. All early Quaker ethical standards were part of the crucial inward war of truth against human pride and, thus, were sure to arouse anger; among them were the use of "thee" and "thou" to individuals, the making of true statements without oaths, the refusal of titles such as sir, doctor, and my lady, and the refusal of hat honor and of tithe taxes to state churches.

To persecution for these offenses under the Puritans was added, after the restoration of Charles II, mass arrests—due to the Anglicans' Conventicle Acts of 1664 and 1670. Out of fifty thousand Friends, five hundred died in jail. Quaker courage won over to Quakerism such leaders as William Penn, the mystic Isaac Penington, and the theologian Robert Barclay. Quaker ethical testimonies of speech and dress and the continuing of silent Meetings for worship were increasingly stressed as badges of loyalty and as the fruits of the Spirit guiding "the sense of the Meeting."

The formal network of Quaker Meetings for Business, held monthly for a town, quarterly for a county, or yearly for a state or nation, was set up to replace reliance on individual leaders. The duties of these Meetings were to register births, marriages, and burials and to aid prisoners, widows, and poor Friends. Fox insisted after 1670 on independent Women's Meetings for Business throughout Quakerism. The monthly Meeting for Sufferings in London and local Meetings recorded imprisonments, oversaw publication of Quaker books, and disowned actions untrue to Quaker norms, disavowing those who so acted until they renounced their acts. Later, Yearly Meeting Epistles and Queries became regular parts of Quaker books of discipline.

Quaker theological writings began with 461 wordy debate tracts poured out by Fox and all other major Quaker leaders to answer the charges made by anti-Quaker writings; Penn wrote more systematically on the universality of the saving Light; Robert Barclay's 1678 *Apology* became the most-read statement of Quaker beliefs and worship, presenting the Bible as testimony to authentically inspired experience, parallel to that of the Friends. In Barclay's words, the death of Jesus atones for past sins, but the power of the Spirit can purify from sinning in the present. The cross stands for self-renunciation. The essence of the sacraments is inner washing, nurture, and Christ's real presence in worship; outward water, bread, and wine are needless. Ministry and even prayer must wait for and result from direct divine leading.

Toleration was always a concern for Friends: their arguments early turned from protests against persecution of God's messengers to moral, rational, and pragmatic appeals. Penn spoke for increasing groups of Englishmen convinced of the need to allow dissenting or nonconformist worship outside the national Anglican church, which led both to the Toleration Act of 1689 and the tradition of liberal Protestant reformers; he made moral appeals to all consciences, advising nonviolence and loyal opposition to government policies and people in power.

Quaker governments were set up in 1675 and 1682 by Edward Billing and Penn in their new colonies of West New Jersey and Pennsylvania; the charters of these governments mandated toleration and political and legal rights for all including the Delaware Indians. Yet even after Quakers had become a minority in these colonies, all citizens' consciences were expected to concur with the Quakers' in rejecting forts and arms, oaths, most capital punishment, and the slave trade. England's wars with France forced increasingly unacceptable compromises on Pennsylvania Quaker legislators, most of whom resigned in 1755–1758. By tender persuasion, John Woolman and others led Quakers also to make collectively the harder decision to liberate their slaves and disown Quaker slave owners. Friends were jailed and fined throughout America in the wars of 1755–1763 and 1812 and during the Revolution; the few Friends who joined or paid for the militias were disowned by their Meetings.

Friendship with the American Indians was a Quaker policy: a Quaker committee shared in peace negotiations in 1756–1758 and 1763–1768, and others set up schools and mediation for the New York Senecas and for the Shawnees and other tribes evicted from Ohio and sent to Oklahoma after 1830. In the 1870s, President Grant asked Friends to administer the Indian Agencies of Kansas-Nebraska.

The antislavery work of British and American Quakers and their allies helped to end legal slave trade in both countries in 1807, but tension piled up against Quakers such as the poet John Greenleaf Whittier, Lucretia Mott, and the Grimke sisters (pioneers also in the women's rights movement) who advocated immediate national abolition of slaveowning. Many Quakers felt driven for the first time to break laws secretly in order to protect fugitive slaves through the Underground Railroad. During the American Civil War, southern Quakers suffered much; northern Friends were inwardly torn; some enlisted to fight. In England, John Bright sacrificed his parliamentary career to oppose both England's entry into the Crimean War and cotton mill owners' support for the American Confederacy.

Change and growth characterized Quaker activities during the eighteenth and nineteenth centuries. Eighteenth-century English industry, banking, and science were increasingly led by the interbred Quaker families of Darbys, Barclays, Lloyds, and Gurneys, who (notably Elizabeth Fry) also pioneered in reforming prisons, mental hospitals, and education for Quaker youth and the poor. Philadelphia Friends emulated them. Quaker worship, watchful against self-will, rationalism, and emotionalism had turned quietist. Among non-Quaker partners in trade or philanthropy, an evangelical orthodoxy that returned to the Bible and Christ's atonement was resurgent and began after 1800 to shape the experience of urban Quakers such as banker Joseph John Gurney, who wrote theology and traveled in America. Community revivals and regional awakenings further stimulated evangelicalism in both the creed and the experience of fifty thousand Friends who between 1795 and 1828 had been drawn to the American frontier in Ohio and Indiana from Virginia, the Carolinas, New England, and Pennsylvania by the promise of open land and freedom from slave-owning neighbors.

The 1827–1828 separation was initiated by the preaching of quietism and the urging of a boycott of slave-made products by Elias Hicks, the patriarchal farmer from New York State. The breach was widened by the influence of evangelical English Quakers traveling in America and disciplinary acts of evangelical urban elders. Friends from older close-knit rural Meetings who withdrew in protest from the Philadelphia Yearly Meeting did not foresee that the split would extend to Yearly Meetings and most Monthly Meetings, as well as to schools and committees in New York, Baltimore, Ohio, and Indiana, and that it would continue permanently.

New methods of revivalism begun after 1830 by Charles G. Finney in midwestern America seemed to the Rhode Island Quaker John Wilbur to be reflected in Gurney's Bible study methods. Rural Wilburite Friends, evangelical in doctrine but rejecting evangelism, were driven in 1846 into a second split, followed by like-minded Friends in Ohio and Canada and later in Iowa and Carolina.

The word *holiness*, in midwestern revivals and Bible conferences after 1858, came to mean a sudden second work of grace totally purifying the hearts of already-converted Christians. This experience predominated in Quaker Holiness revivals in Ohio, Indiana, and Iowa after 1867 led by John Henry Douglas and David Updegraff and others close to non-Quaker revivalists. Simultaneously, evangelical Friends were aroused to foreign mission projects in India, Japan, China, Jamaica, Cuba, Mexico, Kenya, Guatemala, Bolivia, and among both Indians and Inuit in Alaska.

Quaker organization and worship, not greatly changed since 1690, were now centered in the American Midwest on revivals and hymns and hence on pastors and superintendents, led by Douglas in Iowa and Oregon. By 1898 half the Meetings, even in Indiana, supported pastors and programmed worship with sermons and hymns and biblical Sunday schools. The Richmond Conference of 1887 gathered all orthodox Friends to look at these new patterns and to restrain Updegraff's advocacy of water baptism. The Richmond Declaration of Faith reaffirmed evangelical orthodoxy. Concern for unity led in 1902 to a formally gathered Five Years Meeting, which since 1960 has been called Friends United Meeting, and is still centered in Richmond, Indiana; it currently includes seven Orthodox (evangelical) American Yearly Meetings (mostly midwestern); the reunited Baltimore, Canadian, New England, New York, and Southeastern Yearly Meetings; three Yearly Meetings in Kenya; and one each in Cuba, Jamaica, and Palestine arising from missions. Their total 2002 membership was 34,863 in North America and about 100,000 overseas. The year 1902 also saw the gathering of Hicksite Yearly Meetings into the Friends General Conference, centered in Philadelphia, with a 2002 membership of 34,557, including Yearly Meetings of "silent Meeting Friends" in western and midwestern cities and colleges. The three Wilburite or Conservative Yearly Meetings had shrunk by 1981 to a membership of 1,832. Intensifying of the biblical and Holiness concentration, however, drove evangelical Yearly Meetings of Ohio, Kansas, and Oregon out of the Richmond network and led in 1961 to their forming the Evangelical Friends Alliance, to which were added other Friends Churches, some begun by Quaker missions in Asia and Latin America. In 1998, there remained 20,000 Friends in England and Scotland, 1,750 in Ireland as of 1985, approximately 3,000 in Australia, New Zealand, and South Africa as of 1996, and 20 to 400 each in eight post-1918 Yearly Meetings in nations of continental Europe.

Quaker universalism and mysticism were replacing quietism as the central religious experience of many Hicksite and British Friends even before Rufus Jones, student and teacher at Haverford College, Pennsylvania, drew on Emerson and European mystics to make normative for their language "positive" or "ethical mysticism" and the experience of the soul's unity with "the divine in every [hu]man." Quaker education and service programs became linked to these humanitarian or humanist ideas. Rufus Jones channeled the service of Quaker conscientious objectors in World War I by helping to found the American Friends Service Committee, which then joined with the older British War Victims Relief and Friends Service Council in feeding two million German children and many victims of the 1922 Russian famine. The 1929–1939 Depression and World War II prompted Quaker interest in their own nations' unemployed and then in issues of world peace. In 1943 the Friends Committee on National Legislation was formed to coordinate and lobby for Quaker ideals in American policy. Quaker schools of all levels moved away from the guarded education of a purist sect toward a humanism aimed at developing the whole person. American colleges of Quaker origin (Haverford, Guilford, Earlham, Swarthmore, Bryn Mawr, and others) and the famous Quaker secondary boarding schools on both continents increasingly draw brilliant students of all faiths and none. Graduate study centers have been set up at Woodbrooke by the Cadbury family and at Pendle Hill near Philadelphia. The Earlham School of Religion trains all branches of Friends for ministry of all kinds.

New patterns of unity and division have emerged since the 1960s. Conferences, international visits, and sharing of theological concerns are sponsored by the Friends World Committee for Consultation. Increasingly periodicals such as *Friends Quarterly* and *The Friend* in England and *Quaker Life*, *Friends Journal*, and *The Evangelical Friend* in America transcend Quaker divisions. Reunion of Yearly Meetings and local Meetings from the Hicksite separations have occurred in Philadelphia, Canada, New York, and Baltimore. Young Friends, who have often led Quakers into new ways, are concerned now with nuclear arms, communes, and new foundations in theology.

SEE ALSO Fox, George; Penn, William; Puritanism; Quietism.

BIBLIOGRAPHY

The *Journal* of George Fox, edited by Thomas Ellwood (1694; reprint, Richmond, Ind., 1983); John Woolman's *Journal* (1774; reprint, New York, 1971); Robert Barclay's *Apology* (1676; reprint, Newport, R.I., 1729); and William Penn's *No Cross, No Crown* (London, 1669) remain the central classics of the Friends. *The Papers of William Penn* (Philadelphia, 1987) photocopies of *The Works of George Fox*, 3 vols. (1831; New York, 1975), and *A Collection of the Works of William Penn*, 2 vols. (1727; New York, 1974), are in print. Other primary sources are in *Early Quaker Writings, 1650–1700*, edited by Hugh Barbour and Arthur O. Roberts (Grand Rapids, Mich., 1973).

Joseph Smith's *Descriptive Catalogue of Friends Books*, 2 vols. (London, 1867), remains the most complete bibliography, but see also Donald Wing's *Short-Title Catalogue of Books . . . 1641–1700*, 3 vols. (New York, 1945–1951). Leonard Hodgson's *Christian Faith and Practice* (Grand Rapids, Mich., 1950), with topical selections from all periods, and *Church Government*, rev. ed. (London, 1951), together make up the London Yearly Meeting's *Book of Discipline*; those of other Yearly Meetings are less complete.

William C. Braithwaite's *The Beginnings of Quakerism* (1912; 2d ed., Cambridge, U.K., 1955) and *The Second Period of Quakerism* (1919; reprint, Cambridge, U.K., 1961), together with Rufus M. Jones's studies titled *The Later Periods of Quakerism*, 2 vols. (1921; reprint, Westport, Conn., 1970), and *The Quakers in the American Colonies* (1911; reprint, New York, 1962) were designed to form the normative "Rowntree Series," based on documentary work by Norman Penney. A. Neave Brayshaw's *The Quakers* (London, 1921) combines history and ideas, as do Howard Brinton's study of Quaker mysticism titled *Friends for Three Hundred Years* (New York, 1952) and John Punshon's *Portrait in Grey* (London, 1984). Each is an outstanding interpretation. Elbert Russell's *The History of Quakerism* (1945; reprint, Richmond, Ind., 1980), centered on America, with Efrida Vipont Foulds's *The Story of Quakerism* (London, 1954). Both are good one-volume histories.

Each Yearly Meeting has a printed history, and biographies have been written of most key Quakers. On early Quaker history, see various works by Edwin Bronner and Frederick Tolles; on the eighteenth century, by Sydney James and Arthur Raistrick; and on the nineteenth, by J. Ormerod Greenwood, Elizabeth Isichei, and Philip Benjamin. On Quaker ethical outlooks and doctrines, especially for the early periods, Richard Bauman's *Let Your Words Be Few: Symbolism of Speaking and Silence among Seventeenth Century Quakers* (Cambridge, U.K., 1983), Melvin B. Endy, Jr.'s *William Penn and Early Quakerism* (Princeton, N.J., 1973), J. William Frost's *The Quaker Family in Colonial America* (New York, 1973), and works by Hugh Barbour, Lewis Benson, Maurice Creasey, Christopher Hill, and Geoffrey Nuttall give solid data and a variety of insights. Thomas R. Kelly's *A Testament of Devotion*, 6th ed. (New York, 1941), remains beloved as inspiration.

New Sources

Benefiel, M., and R. D. Phipps. "Practical Mysticism: Quakers and Social Transformation." In *Mysticism and Social Transformation*, edited by Janet Ruffing, pp. 129–142. Syracuse, N.Y., 2001.

Steinkraus, W. E. "Quaker Mysticism." In *Mysticism and the Mystical Experience: East and West,* edited by Donald H. Bishop, pp. 110–132. Selinsgrove, Pa., 1995.

HUGH BARBOUR (1987)
Revised Bibliography

QUATERNITY, or a fourfold structure (together with its multiples—eightfold, twelvefold, etc.), expresses symbolically the nature of the divine and, by extension, describes the structure of the world that mirrors that divinity. Like the other great numerical symbols in its class, quaternity is impersonal; it may stand alone, or it may be associated with the attributes of a personal god. God is one, says Plotinus, and so is the truth of this world. The divine is dual, say the Zoroastrians, and thus one must choose between truth and falseness. Christians say that God is a trinity, a perception that explains for Augustine the threefold nature of human love. Yet others have experienced the divine mystery as a quaternity, and its reality can be dimly perceived in the world's four cardinal directions, the four seasons, the four elements, and the four temperaments of classical thought.

Something of this symbol's power can be seen in the boyhood vision of Black Elk, the Oglala visionary. He heard voices: "Behold him, the being with four legs!" The divine quadruped was a horse that turned in the four directions to reveal four sets of twelve horses of four different colors. These forty-eight beings went into formation, four abreast, and introduced the boy to the four Grandfathers, who were the powers of the four quarters of the world. Two other Grandfathers, the dual powers of sky and earth, were also present. This experience lasted twelve days, and for twelve days thereafter Black Elk felt homesick for his extraordinary "other world" (described in John G. Neihardt's *Black Elk Speaks,* Lincoln, Neb., 1979). In this vision, the fourfold structure orders the religious experience and provides an image for the order of divine things.

It is, therefore, something of a surprise to learn that this North American medicine man disparages the square, a fourfold geometrical figure—especially in light of the fact that the Navajo Indians use squares, and quaternities generally, in the healing pictures called sand paintings. But Black Elk contrasts the square with the circle, which he finds more natural and thus more compatible with deity. The Navajos integrate the image of the circle with its geometrical "opposite," the square. The same is true for Tantric Buddhists, who make meditative use of an image called a *maṇḍala.* Tantric devotees imagine that the gods—often numbering a multiple of four, such as the thirty-two deities of the *Guhyasamaja Tantra*—reside in a square "palace" with four gates in the four directions; their residence, however, is surrounded by a "circle" (i. e., a *maṇḍala*). Confucius, in his *Analects* (7.8), describes the proper way to teach a religious truth through an image that appears to be a square: "If I hold up one corner and a man cannot come back with the other three, I do not continue the lesson." Here, a whole truth is symbolically fourfold; further, there lies inside the fourfold structure of truth a distinction between three of its parts and a fourth. Navajo sand paintings are often bordered on three sides only; the eastern fourth side is left open, because evil cannot enter there.

Ezekiel's vision of God's chariot in the Hebrew scriptures contains a fourfold image that inspired Judeo-Christian symbolism. The prophet saw Yahveh—the four consonants of whose name, incidentally, comprise the mystical tetragrammaton of Judaism—supported by "four living creatures." They had four wings and also four faces, three of which were those of animals (the ox, lion, and eagle) and the fourth the face of a man. Their "spirits" were in the chariot's four wheels, which seem to have been intersected by four other wheels permitting them to move in four directions (*Ez.* 1). In the apocalyptic vision of the New Testament, God's throne is encircled at a distance by twenty-four other thrones; "round the throne, on each side of the throne, are four living creatures"—like an ox, a lion, an eagle, but also like a man (*Rv.* 4). Irenaeus stated in defense of Christianity (*Against Heresies* 3.11.7–9): "The Gospels could not possibly be either more or less in number than they are," namely, four. He argued that the *Gospel of Matthew* is like a "man" while the other three are like an "ox," a "lion," and an "eagle." Perhaps it should be noted that, symbolism aside, these four fundamental documents of the Christian religion naturally divide themselves into a set of three—the so-called Synoptic Gospels—and the very different *Gospel of John,* which became the favorite of Gnostic heretics. Structurally, something similar can be said for the fundamental teaching of Buddhism called the four noble truths, the fourth of which is the Eightfold Path. Three of these truths describe conditions in the phenomenal realm of *saṃsāra,* but the "truth of cessation" alone describes the goal of *nirvāṇa.*

When Vedic seers of ancient India perceived the divine as an enormous person (Puruṣa), he was a quaternity: "All creatures are but one-fourth of him, three-fourths have eternal life in heaven" (*Ṛgveda* 10.90). Their vision lay behind the later and more impersonal view of the ultimate expressed by Upaniṣadic sages as *ātman* or *brahman.* According to the *Chāndogya Upaniṣad* (3.18.2), the divine has "four feet" or quarters—speech, breath, eye, and ear. But the *Māṇḍūkya Upaniṣad* develops the point psychologically and describes the *ātman* or self as comprised of four states of mind, three of which are waking, dreaming, and dreamless sleep; the mysterious "fourth" (*turīya*) state is the unity of the other three. When these matters are expressed in later Hinduism by anthropomorphic deities such as Brahmā and Śiva, the gods often have four heads as an optimum number. It is said that Brahmā once had a single stag's head when he lusted for his daughter; he was properly punished and lost his head, but then he was given the four heads one often sees in art. Or, he once had five heads but was too proud, so the number was reduced to four (*Skanda Purāṇa* 3.40.1–59; *Śiva Purāṇa*

Sacred gaze

SACRED GAZE

Sacred images engage viewers in acts of seeing that are themselves forms of religious experience. When human beings "see," they do so by means of an extensive apparatus of vision that may be designated by the term gaze. The gaze is not simply an optical event, the physiological act of looking at something, but the constellation of numerous events and aspects of vision: the engagement of the body of the viewer, the regimentation of time, the application of an epistemology of seeing that makes things intelligible, the eclipse of spaces and orders outside the boundaries of the gaze, and the focus of memory and consciousness on certain matters. The act of vision orchestrates all of these as a culture of thought, feeling, and sensation shared by members of a group. Glimpsing, glancing, glaring, gleaming, gorging, and other discrete visual operations, such as blinking—all are to apprehend images in various ways and construct very different relationships between viewer and image and whatever is evoked or represented by the image. Even the destruction or privation of imagery creates an experience that can be profoundly meaningful.

Visitors to labyrinths **(a)** experience a form of gaze turned inward. The body is submitted to a simple and repetitive routine of movement that allows regular breathing and mental focus on bodily rhythm. This deflection from competing forms of attention delivers the mind from distraction and aligns body, mind, and sensation. "Performing" the material image of a labyrinth is often reported to be very refreshing and enabling to focused contemplation. For practitioners of Tantric Buddhism, imagery plays an explicit role in meditation. *Maṇḍalas* **(b** and

(a) An outdoor labyrinth near Michigan City, Indiana. *[Photograph by David Morgan]*

c) are highly detailed schematic images that organize levels of imagery around a central figure, a tutelary deity or buddha with whom the meditator ultimately seeks identity in mediation. The *maṇḍala* is a mnemonic device and an instructional aid in preparing for meditation, visualizing the many stages of meditation and helping one to remember them.

Seeing the deity or gazing upon the image of the saint or savior is an important aspect of many different religious traditions. *Visual piety* is a term that designates acts of veneration or adoration that engage the viewer in a powerful relationship with the sacred. Hindus perform *darśan* as a visual engagement in which the believer's vision of the deity is reciprocated as the deity's visual contact with the believer **(d)**. Some Christians contemplate the suffering

(b) LEFT. Seventeenth-century painting of the meditational deity Hevajra with Skati, the female embodiment of energy, gouache on silk, Tibet. *[The Art Archive/Musé Guimet Paris/Dagli Orti]* **(c)** BELOW. Novice monks from Simtokha, a Buddhist *dzong* near Thimphu, Bhutan, contribute to a sand *maṇḍala*. *[©Jeremy Horner/Corbis]*

of Jesus or the saints as a way of participating empathetically in their passion and thereby experiencing pain and suffering as transfigured into a likeness or kinship with the sacred figure. An especially theatrical performance of empathy is enabled by Gian Lorenzo Bernini's well known sculpture and architectural installation, the Cornaro Chapel **(e)**, in which the viewer is invited to gaze on the sensuous vision of Saint Teresa of Ávila, who receives an ecstatic visitation of pain in the form of a golden arrow administered by an angel. In her autobiographical account of the mystical life, *The Interior Castle*, Saint Teresa describes the experience visualized by Bernini's sculpture: "I know that this distress seems to penetrate to [the soul's] very bowels; and that, when He that has wounded [the soul] draws out the arrow, the bowels seem to come with

(d) RIGHT. An Indian couple prays before a domestic shrine to the goddess Lakṣmī, wife of Viṣṇu, during the Dīvalī festival. *[©Arvind Garg/Corbis]* **(e)** BELOW. An eighteenth-century painting of Gian Lorenzo Bernini's sculpture (1645–1652) of the ecstacy of Saint Teresa of Ávila in the Cornaro Chapel of the church of Santa Maria della Vittoria in Rome. *[©Eric Lessing/Art Resource, N.Y.]*

(f) El Greco, *The Burial of Count Orgaz*, 1586, in the church of Santo Tomé, Toledo, Spain. *[©Scala/Art Resource, N.Y.]*

it, so deeply does it feel this love" (Sixth Mansion, chap. 2). Bernini has included opera boxes on either side of the event, in which members of the Cornaro family devoutly witness the mystic spectacle. Above, the heavens open in a dazzling epiphany and illuminate the central event below. The artist's intention is not to craft a lurid spectacle, but to create a compelling image of the saint's embodied spirituality, in which pain was not explicitly erotic, but the register of divine presence.

The intermingling of heavenly and earthly domains was treated by another important artist. Vision is carefully parsed as a system of visual relays in El Greco's masterwork, *The Burial of Count Orgaz* **(f)**. The viewer's gaze is met by the young boy in the lower left and directed by his gesture to the body of the dead count, who is embraced by Saint Augustine. Another level of gestures and gazes directs the viewer upward to the angel ushering the soul of the count (the body of an infant) through a luminous conduit into the celestial domain where it is received first by the Madonna, who receives the homage of John the Baptist, who looks upward to the enthroned Christ. This succession of relays forms a vertical hierarchy that structures the ascent of the soul and maps the ontology of iconic devotion. Venerating the images of the saints means directing one's worship of God in and through Christ.

Jews, Muslims, and Protestant Christians often insist that they do not practice an iconic piety, but their traditions are not without visual forms of devotion. *The Way to Happiness* **(g)** is a good example of a Protestant configuration of the gaze. Instead of looking at an icon of Jesus, the young woman portrayed in this print by Nathaniel Currier looks longingly, with gleaming eyes, to the memory of her parents' devotional reading of scripture as she meditates prayerfully on the Bible. The print deftly interweaves reading, seeing, and remembering as corresponding acts of piety. For Chinese literati and artists such as Ma Yuan, who practiced an erudite and aesthetically refined Daoism, images of sages contemplating nature **(h)** were wistfully poetic ways of evoking a mindfulness of simplicity and a rustic transcendence of urban complexities and life at court during the Song dynasty. Modern viewers might

(g) ABOVE. Nathaniel Currier, *The Way to Happiness*, c. 1860–1870, lithograph. ***[Courtesy of the Billy Graham Center Museum, Wheaton, Ill.]*** **(h)** BELOW. Ma Yuan, (active 1190–1225) *Bare Willows and Distant Mountains*, ink on mounted silk fan, China. ***[©Burstein Collection/Corbis]***

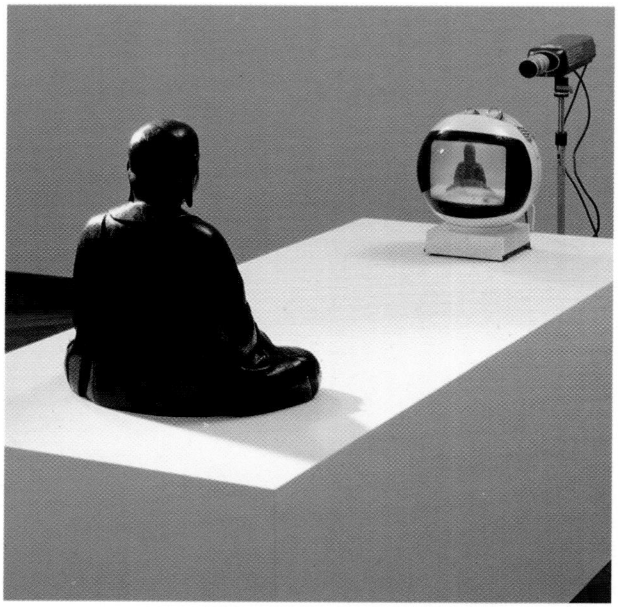

(i) TOP. Tobi Kahn, *Ya-Ir XX,* 1999, oil on canvas. *[©1999 Tobi Kahn]* (j) ABOVE. Nam June Paik, *TV Buddha,* 1974. *[Stedelijk Museum Amsterdam]*

find something of an equivalent refuge in Tobi Kahn's paintings of marine horizons **(i)**, in which the portentous contact of water and sky suggests something mythical, a moment of revelation about to occur. Like Ma Yuan's painting, the viewer is urged to regard the natural world as pregnant with meaning that cannot be spoken, only glimpsed.

Painters such as Ma Yuan and Tobi Kahn focus the viewer's attention on the material qualities of paint and canvas, while other image makers direct our attention to new media that rely on streams of electronic signals. Nam June Paik's *TV Buddha* **(j)** explores the relevance of videography for Buddhist meditation. One wonders who the real Buddha is: the statue of the seated figure or the image on the video monitor? The two seem inextricably and perpetually engaged in a single loop, mediating one another. By equating meditation and mediation, this work demonstrates strikingly how the sacred gaze constructs religious experience: to see the other is to think it and to provide thereby the medium for contemplating the self. A variation of this contemplative use of new media is the web user's devotional exercises at goddess sites. Coursing down a seamless electronic scroll, the viewer consumes the site in glancing movements of the eye, beholding not a discrete image, but an ever-shifting screen of pixels.

The destruction of imagery is actually a fundamental part of religious visual culture. The erasure of Buddhist and Navaho sand *maṇḍalas* **(c)** is a necessary part of their ritual significance. The histories of Judaism, Christianity, and Islam offer countless instances of the ritual destruction of images. For example, the Taliban in Afghanistan destroyed ancient carvings of the Buddha at Bamiyan **(k)** in the face of widespread objections. They did so in order to broadcast the militancy of their version of Islam, knowing that the act would elicit an unambivalent response through the instantaneous loop of global media, but also because the images may genuinely have offended their religious sensibility. Prompted by the rhetoric of iconoclastic audacity, the viewer glares at the broken image, either to celebrate its destruction or to loathe its destroyers in paroxysms of disgust. In yet another manner of iconoclasm, the Russian artist Kasimir Malevich both negated and reaffirmed the long Russian history of icon painting and veneration in his image *Black Cross* **(l)**. Whereas icon painting necessarily focused on the face and body of the saints, whose veneration was a fundamental aspect of Orthodox liturgy and devotion, Malevich's painting cancels the presence of the face with a bold geometry that both denies presence and reasserts it in the austere

(k) ABOVE. Colossal standing Buddha in Bamiyan, Afghanistan, contructed no later than the sixth century CE, and destroyed 2001 by the Taliban. *[©Reuters/Corbis]* **(l) LEFT.** Kasimir Malevich, *Black Cross*, 1915, oil on canvas. ***[CNAC/MNAM/Dist. Réunion des Musées Nationaux/Art Resource, N.Y.]***

(m) René Magritte, *Le Rossignol* (The nightingale), 1955, gouache on paper. *[©Herscovici/Art Resource, N.Y.]*

abstraction of the cross. If the sacramental materiality of the human body is gone, the robust darkness of the cross replaces it with a new and foreboding presence. The shape of absence is the symbol of hope.

René Magritte's *Le Rossignol* (The nightingale) **(m)** may appear irreligious by causing the viewer to blink at the absurd juxtaposition of God in heaven and a roaring locomotive. The two images belie one another, though God comes off the worse. Thwarting the sacred hierarchy of El Greco's painting **(f)**, Magritte's image suggests that the same universe is not big enough to contain the world-view of industrial technology and the traditional deity perched on a cloudy throne above. Yet Magritte may use this iconoclastic device to suggest that the traditional conception of God is limited. An effective way to transcend the constraints of an idea is to violate its sanctity.

BIBLIOGRAPHY

Eck, Diana L. *Darśan: Seeing the Divine Image in India,* 3d ed. New York, 1998.

Latour, Bruno, and Peter Weibel, eds. *Iconoclash: Beyond the Image Wars in Science, Religion, and Art.* Karlsruhe, Germany, and Cambridge, Mass., 2002.

Morgan, David. *Visual Piety: A History and Theory of Popular Religious Images.* Berkeley, 1998.

Teresa of Ávila. *Interior Castle.* Translated by E. Allison Peers. Garden City, 1961.

Wu Hung. *The Double Screen: Medium and Representation in Chinese Painting.* Chicago, 1996.

DAVID MORGAN (2005)

3.8.36–66). Śiva, on the other hand, was not punished when he lusted after a celestial nymph who danced seductively; he had one head but, in order to see more, he increased the number to four (*Mahābhārata* 1.203.15–26). Perhaps the nymph's dance was the "dance of *māyā*," or phenomenal life, which the Indian Buddhists say must be seen fully if one is to become emancipated. For that to happen, say the Mahāyānists, one has to experience the "twelve acts" of a Buddha, which include the critical "four visions" (of a sick man, an old man, and a dead man; but also of a monk). Then, on the night of one's enlightenment, one must have a dream that four birds of four different colors fly from the four directions, fall at one's feet, and turn completely white (*Mahāvastu* 2.136).

SEE ALSO Architecture; Calendars, article on South American Calendars; Cosmology; Geometry; Maṇḍalas.

BIBLIOGRAPHY

The quaternity image is so important to Carl Jung's *Collected Works,* 2d ed., edited by Herbert Read, Michael Fordham, and Gerhard Adler (Princeton, N.J., 1968–), that one should consult them for materials and also for a psychological interpretation. On the problem of "three and four," however, Edward F. Edinger's essay on the Trinity in *Ego and Archetype* (New York, 1972) is exceptional. Wendy Doniger O'Flaherty's *Śiva: The Erotic Ascetic* (Oxford, 1981) relates the head symbolism in Hinduism to phallic symbolism. Alex Wayman's neat essay "Buddhism," in *Historia Religionum,* edited by C. Jouco Bleeker and Geo Widengren, vol. 2, *Religions of the Present* (Leiden, 1971), gives ample evidence of quaternities in the Buddhist religion.

New Sources

Berner, Robert. *The Rule of Four: Four Essays on the Principle of Quaternity.* Studies on Themes and Motifs in Literature series. New York, 1996.

Oxford-Carpenter, Rebecca. "Gender and the Trinity." *Theology Today* 41 (April 1984): 7–25.

von Franz, Marie-Louise. *Archetypal Dimensions of the Psyche.* Boston, 1999.

von Franz, Marie-Louise. *The Golden Ass of Apuleius: The Liberation of the Feminine in Man.* Boston, 2001.

GEORGE R. ELDER (1987)
Revised Bibliography

QUESTS.

The Ojibwa Indians tell the story of the boy Wunzh and his vision quest. Having reached the appropriate age for the ritual search for totem spirits, Wunzh is left alone in the great forest. After several days of fasting, he retires exhausted to the lonely hut provided for him and waits for the dreams he hopes his guardian spirits will send. There he prays for advice on how his family and tribe might more efficiently obtain food. Wunzh takes to his mat and soon has a vision of a strange young man dressed in yellow and green with feathers on his head. As he descends from the sky, the young man announces that he comes from the Great Spirit to answer Wunzh's prayer. "I will teach you to help your people," he says, "but first you must wrestle with me." Weak from fasting, the boy nevertheless does as he is told and holds his own in the match. "Enough!" cries the spirit. "I will return tomorrow." On the next day the spirit returns. The boy is of course weaker than before but feels that he has gained an inner strength, and he fights well. Again the spirit cries, "Enough! I will return tomorrow." On the third day the boy is weaker still, but his inner strength has grown proportionately. He fights so well that the spirit concedes defeat and begins to instruct him. "Tomorrow, because it will be the seventh day of your fast, your father will come and offer you food. You must not eat until you have wrestled with me one more time. Then, if you defeat me, strip me and bury me in the ground after clearing a spot and loosening the earth. In the weeks that follow, you must remove the weeds from my grave and keep the earth soft. If you do exactly as I say, you will learn something of great value to your people." Wunzh's father does bring food and begs the boy to eat. The boy asks his father to leave him and promises to return home by sundown. The spirit appears at the usual hour, and the boy, now full of supernatural power, easily defeats his adversary, kills, strips, and buries him as instructed, and returns to his father's lodge to eat. During the spring Wunzh visits the grave of the spirit regularly and tends it with care. Soon the green plumes of the sky visitor's headgear begin to push through the ground. In late summer, the boy asks his father to accompany him to the spot of his fasting, and there he reveals the grave from which has sprung a fine plant with great yellow tassels. "This is my sky friend Mondawmin, the spirit of maize. If we do as the spirit has taught, we can have food from the ground. The Great Spirit has answered my prayer; my fast has been rewarded."

The story of Wunzh and Mondawmin is but one mask of a basic pattern to be found in the stories of any number of culture heroes and in the rituals of various cults. The story would not be foreign to the young San or Australian Aborigine initiate. The newly confirmed Christian, the Jew who has just become bar mitzvah, or the newly circumcised Muslim might feel inklings of familiarity with it. The process by which inner strength grows at the expense of physical strength during a period of self-denial and searching is as familiar to the reader of Hindu, Buddhist, Christian, Islamic, or Jewish Scripture as it is to the American Indian on his vision quest.

STRUCTURE OF THE QUEST. At its most basic level the quest is a phenomenon inherent in existence itself. In a universe in which all things must ultimately be defined in terms of their relation to the dominant pull toward energy dispersal or entropy, simply to exist is to be part of the great quest for survival. For the human being another dimension is added by virtue of the existence in humans of consciousness, specifically, consciousness of linear time. To see a beginning, a middle, and an end is to see a "road of life," and to see such a road is to see a potential quest. One cannot in fact be human without being to some degree questers, and this fact is the source of the power of the quest story to speak to humans wherever and whoever they are.

Not surprisingly then the quest myth is inexorably associated with the figure of the hero, the human metaphor for the all-encompassing chaos-to-cosmos creation process by which entropy is held at bay. The quest of course takes many forms. The hero's nature, motives, and goals derive from the particular legend of which he or she is a part and the society he or she represents. The hero might be a knight, a sage, or a prince and the goal a golden fleece, a princess, or a pot of gold. The earliest quest stories, like the earliest religious systems, must have reflected a society concerned primarily with fertility and physical survival in the face of a hostile environment. One senses the vestiges of this in the many tales in which a prince seeks and finds a princess and through union with her brings prosperity to a kingdom.

One of the best known of the European quests is that of the Holy Grail. It was Jessie Weston in her classic *From Ritual to Romance: An Account of the Holy Grail from Ancient Ritual to Christian Symbol* (1957) who pointed out that, although the grail legend was an outgrowth of medieval Christianity and chivalry, it had deeper roots in ancient fertility cults. The ostensible quest of the grail knights is for the cup used by Christ at the last supper. A less conscious but more profound objective is the renewal of a society represented not only by the infertile kingdom of the Fisher King but by the somewhat complaisant order of the Round Table. The quest of the knights for the Holy Grail is analogous to—and a metaphor for—the Christian's quest for the kingdom of God in life and in the ritual of the holy elements. Life renewal is always the ultimate goal of the quest, and life renewal is both a spiritual and a physical process.

For example, one of the world's greatest quest stories, one that influenced nearly all narratives that followed it, is Homer's *Odyssey.* Whereas Odysseus's goal seems to be a purely secular one—he wishes to return to his wife and his child—it is also true that his adventures depict a process by which a "lost soul" is reconciled with the cosmos, which is represented by the gods. The trials he undergoes, culminating in a visit to the land of the dead, are the means by which, with Athena's help, he is able to regain his proper place in the gods' order of things. Odysseus's quest is not altogether unlike that of another famous Greek, Oedipus, who can release Thebes from the bondage of infertility only by discovering himself, by finding an answer to the ultimate spiritual question: who am I?

The spiritual aspect of the quest is perhaps most obvious in those traditions that stress mystical values. The image of the Buddha under the bodhi tree or that of the Hindu ascetic in deep contemplation are as much true masks of the quest as is the story of the Holy Grail, the myth of Jason and the Golden Fleece, or the account of the magi seeking the Christ child. Literal movement from one place to the other is not necessary to the quest; the point is that the Buddha under the bodhi tree seeks enlightenment as actively in his own way as Gawain seeks the Holy Grail. Whether the hero gallops off to faraway lands or sits under a tree, the quest involves a journey to and often beyond the boundaries of human experience and knowledge. In this sense the story of the quest is always what the Hindu might call a search for the Self or what the psychiatrist Carl Jung (1875–1961) called the process of individuation. In short, the quest is a metaphor for the spiritual journey, one's own potential spiritual journey represented by that of the hero.

The ur-hero and the ur-myth that emerge from a comparison of the world's many quest stories then reveal what can be called a universal ritual of re-creation. The ritual requires certain steps. First, like the priest in any ritual, the hero must be properly vested, made clearly recognizable and ordained for the task, a task—the realization of one's humanity—that is a matter of life and death for all. So it is that the quester's heroism has been preliminarily established by a miraculous conception or birth, a divine sign of some sort, or by an extraordinary childhood deed. Before his ordeal, Oedipus is recognized as a savior-hero by virtue of his defeat of the Sphinx that had plagued Thebes. His abandonment in the wilderness as a child marks him as well, placing him in a sacred order as it were—one that includes Moses, Siegfried, and the Indian Karna as well as the Phrygian Cybele (the Great Mother) and Attis. Herakles and the *avatāra* Kṛṣṇa are marked by their defeat of evil monsters while still in infancy. Jesus' nature is indicated by the circumstances of his conception and birth and by his extraordinary intelligence, as demonstrated in the Temple when he is twelve. He also receives a sign from God at his baptism. The Buddha, as a white elephant, is the agent of his own conception and, like the Toltec-Aztec Quetzalcoatl, further proves his nature by possessing adult qualities at birth. Sir Gawain and the other Arthurian questers are eligible for the Grail search by virtue of past "adventures" and because of their association with Arthur as knights in the sacred society of the Round Table.

The hero, having been proclaimed, is ritually called to the quest. The call might come through a natural object: Moses is called by Yahveh in the burning bush; the magi are called by the star; and the Grail knights by the Holy Grail itself, appearing in their midst at Pentecost. Angels or other supernatural heralds are common, and often the herald remains as a guide. The Buddha is called when, driven about by his charioteer, he is made to witness several forms of suffering humanity "fashioned" magically by the gods. Another important charioteer-herald or guide is found in the *Bhagavadgītā,* part of one of the great Indian epics, the *Mahābhārata.* In this work the god Kṛṣṇa in the guise of a charioteer urges Prince Arjuna on to battle and to higher values.

However the call is made, it signals the necessity of an awakening to destiny in the face of an individual or societal malaise. A renewal is called for, and the hero either responds to the call immediately or at first refuses it. A natural enough reaction of any individual faced with a serious psychological, spiritual, or physical task is to withdraw from the field. Prince Arjuna at first refuses the call to battle; Kṛṣṇa must convince him to fight. Even the most "religious" of heroes express their common humanity by their reluctance. "No, Lord, send whom thou wilt," is Moses' answer to God's call. And Jesus, in the garden of Gethsemane on the eve of his Crucifixion, prays to God, saying, "My Father, if it is possible, let this cup pass me by." A particularly dramatic example of this category is the story of Jonah, whose refusal results in an unwanted voyage in the belly of a whale. The Buddha's father might be said to have attempted to refuse the call for his son when he so desperately tried to isolate him from the real world. Occasionally the call itself is a test and the refusal one of omission rather than commission. For instance, Parzival fails to ask certain ritual questions while being entertained at the castle of the Fisher King and misses his chance to free the king and his land of the ancient curse.

In ultimately accepting the call, however, the hero undertakes a series of trials; these adventures reflect the agonies involved in confronting the inner realities that one glimpses in dreams or periods of disorientation. In the context of the spiritual journey, the monsters, demons, and impossible tasks that confront the hero are all those factors that would imprison one in the barren world of egocentricity. They would prevent one from attaining renewal—the spiritual vitality represented by the attainment of the Golden Fleece, the elixirs of life, the Holy Grail, and the rescued princesses toward which the heroic adventures lead.

So it is that in the Hindu epic the *Rāmāyaṇa*, the demon king Rāvaṇa kidnaps Rāma's wife Sītā, setting up a quest that is a struggle between the forces of love and union and those of violence and disintegration. And the figures that stand between Odysseus and his reunion with the faithful Penelope are such nightmarish beings as the one-eyed Cyclops; the witch Circe, who turns men into beasts; and the bewitching Sirens. The Babylonian-Sumerian epic hero Gilgamesh must overcome Huwawa, the monster of death, and Inanna-Ishtar in her form as seductress. Jesus is tempted in the wilderness by the devil, who offers tangible worldly achievements as a substitute for the intangible ones inherent in the quest for the kingdom of heaven. The Buddha is tempted similarly by Māra the fiend, who attempts to dislodge the Great One from his position under the tree by reminding him of the more ordinary values of human life. Māra assumes the form of a messenger who informs Siddhārtha that his father's kingdom has been usurped and his wife taken and that he must return home. When this approach fails, he resorts to violence, to theological argument, and finally to sexual temptation, all to prevent the renewal of life that is the hero's goal.

The penultimate test of the hero is the descent into the underworld and confrontation with death itself. Only by, in some sense, dying to the world can the hero be resurrected as "eternal man" renewed. Only by going down can the sun hope to arise. Odysseus, Theseus, Herakles, Jesus, the Egyptian Osiris, Dionysos, and the goddess-heroine Hainuwele in Ceram all journey to the land of the dead. And the more mystical questers such as John of the Cross (the Spanish poet-monk of the sixteenth century) and Julian of Norwich (an English mystic of the fourteenth century) or "psychological" ones such as Carl Jung take equivalent journeys, "night journeys" or "dark nights of the soul," which are characterized by agonies and fears that necessarily mark a journey into the spiritual or psychic underworld. In such journeys as these, one senses the real purpose of the descent in general as one having to do with the retrieval of a lost self. Odysseus and Aeneas seek their destinies among the dead. Jesus, the "second Adam," descends to retrieve the "lost" Adam. The sun king Gilgamesh descends to find eternal life but also hopes to retrieve his friend and double Enkidu. In one of the oldest quest stories—if not the oldest—known, the Sumerian goddess Inanna takes the hero's role by descending into the underworld to find her lost lover Dumuzi; the lost lover of course is the other half without which significant wholeness—what the Chinese would call the oneness of yin and yang—is not possible.

PERSONAL ENACTMENTS. It should be pointed out that what heroes do in the old quest stories, flesh and blood human beings act out or in some sense imitate through the medium of religious ritual and related disciplines. The Muslim who journeys to Mecca is given the special title of *ḥājj* for having followed in the steps of the Prophet. The shaman, whether American Indian or Siberian, journeys ritually and psychically to the "other world" to confront the spirits who would deprive an individual or tribe of health or life. And tribal initiation at puberty often involves a quest, as the story of Wunzh and Mondawmin indicates. Even the ordinary worshiper becomes a real quester in the physical realm. A Hindu, Buddhist, or Christian who enters a place of worship undertakes a re-creative journey in microcosm from the chaos of the world to the cosmos of ultimate reality or primal cause. Reminders of the hero journey are frequently in evidence in these temples of worship. Gargoyle monsters guard the doorways—the thresholds—as if to say, "Enter here at risk." Indeed the true religious quest, like the shaman's descent, can be a dangerous affair.

The symbolism of the quest sometimes literally determines the place of worship. Such is the case with the traditional church building. Having passed by the monsters over the doorway, the Christian voyager in the great medieval cathedral confronts the font that represents baptism, the spiritual rebirth that is now reaffirmed by the making of the sign of the cross with holy water. The initiate enters the church proper to participate in the Mass, itself a complex representation of the journey of Christ through death, descent, and resurrection—a journey that the worshiper shares and literally acts out by moving eventually to the altar at the far end of the church in order to experience the Eucharistic sacrifice before reentering the world as a renewed being. A secular modern version of this spiritual journey takes place on the psychiatrist's couch, where renewal involves a quest of self-discovery by means of a process of recalling—literally remembering.

The most obvious expression of the quest is in literature. As has been suggested, anything that has a beginning, a middle, and an end, in the manner that plot does, is likely to be in some sense a quest. Gilgamesh seeks eternal life, Rāma goes in search of the abducted Sītā, Odysseus seeks reunion with Penelope, Aeneas looks for a new Troy, Dante Alighieri's and John Bunyan's pilgrims journey toward the kingdom of God, Tom Jones hopes to become worthy of his Sophia, and Anton Chekhov's three sisters long for Moscow.

Geoffrey Chaucer's great work *The Canterbury Tales* (fourteenth century) is among the finest examples of quest literature in the West. In their pilgrimage to Canterbury the pilgrims seek something spiritual that will carry them beyond their mundane and often corrupt lives. In the East the most famous of pilgrimage tales is probably the sixteenth-century *Xiyouji* (The journey to the west), the ancient Chinese story of the journey of a monkey, a pig, a white dragon horse, and a monk who travel from China to India in search of Buddhist sūtras. This fantasy tale has a strong historical basis in the actual Silk Road journeys to India of monks, such as the seventh-century BCE monk Xuanzang (Hsüan-Tsang), who brought back sacred manuscripts to China.

A type of literature in which the quest motif is particularly unveiled and therefore particularly open to observation is the fairy tale. A good example is one that appears in many parts of the world and takes its most familiar form as *The Water of Life* in the Grimm brothers' collection. As the title indicates, it is a story in which the spiritual goal of life renewal is only barely masked. "Once upon a time, there lived a king who was desperately ill"; the beginning of this tale—and of most fairy tales—involves the ritual placing of a situation in time. It is one-half of a framework that will be completed in the "happily ever after" ending, releasing the hero of the tale from his or her temporal trials by placing him or her in a state of wholeness that is eternal. In the first image of *The Water of Life*, the king, like nearly all kings, represents the kingdom of humans on earth brought into conflict by the universal nemesis, mortality. That which was once whole—in harmony with the absolute—is now unwhole. The king's mythical and literary relatives are such figures as the Fisher King of the Grail romance and Shakespeare's Lear. The sick old king constellates the theme of salvation or renewal, which is the religious essence of the quest.

The king has three sons, who weep in the palace garden at their father's plight. As potential saviors, the children must remind us of the knights of the Round Table. The symbolic nature of numbers in fairy tales, as in religious ritual and theology, is such that the presence here of three children is significant. The number four represents the quaternity, which symbolizes balance and wholeness, and four brothers would mean a common effort. Three, on the other hand, tends to suggest the discord of two against one.

In the garden an old man appears to the sons to tell them that their father might be cured by the water of life: "One drink of it and he will be well, but the water is difficult to find." As shown above, the guide is a familiar figure in quest tales. His function is to point to the solution of the insoluble problem, to establish the means of salvation by interjecting the "other" into the limited world of time and space. His way invariably involves a difficult quest.

The oldest son goes to his father to request permission to attempt the search for the water of life. Refused at first, he perseveres so that the king finally agrees, the prince thinking all the while, "If I find the water, my father will give me his kingdom." Soon after setting off, the prince meets a dwarf, who inquires as to his destination. When he answers back in an insulting manner, the dwarf imprisons him on horseback between two mountains that magically converge upon him. When the first son fails to return, the second son makes the same request of his father, is answered in the same way, and like his brother, dreams of inheriting the kingdom. Upon meeting the same dwarf, he is asked where he is going, and he gives the same insulting answer. Needless to say his punishment is the same as his brother's. The identical formula used in connection with the first two sons suggests a ritual purpose: the two older sons act out the negative aspect of a pattern in which the son who is an honest and unsullied quester for Self contrasts with the sons who embody a corrupt unreceptiveness to the call.

When his brothers fail to return, the youngest son begs for and obtains his father's reluctant permission to set out on the same quest. But unlike his brothers, he thinks only of the welfare of his father. Where the others are motivated by hope for material gain—by egotism—and are appropriately punished by their imprisonment in a narrow ravine, the young son is motivated by love, which is the proper attitude on the path to salvation. His meeting with the dwarf is therefore different from that of his brothers.

"Where are you going?" asks the dwarf, following the ritual pattern. "I am seeking the water of life to cure my ailing father" is the humble reply. The dwarf, pleased, instructs the boy on how to achieve his goal: "The water runs from a fountain in an enchanted castle. Take this iron wand, and knock three times to open the castle door. And take these two loaves of bread to quiet the lions who guard the door. Only be sure that you obtain the water and leave the castle before the clock strikes twelve, or you will be imprisoned there for life."

The dwarf, like the old man in the garden, is a personification of the spiritual guide. Here he takes the form of the shaman-teacher, who trains the good prince in magic and provides the paraphernalia necessary to release the healing forces—the water of life. The instructions he gives make no rational sense but, as in the case of all rituals, must be performed on faith, just as the ugly little dwarf himself must be accepted on faith. Only the young son has such faith; only he passes the test. The old dwarf is to him what the fairy godmother is to Cinderella or Athena to Odysseus. As an agent of the other world, the dwarf is not subject to mere physical law; for this reason, he possesses the magic that can lead to wholeness.

Arriving at the castle, the young prince follows the ritual instructions. The iron doors are overcome by the iron rod; the lions are quieted with the bread. Inside the castle, the prince finds a sword and a loaf of bread and several enchanted princes. A beautiful princess greets him as her liberator and promises to give herself to him in marriage if he will return in a year. The princess now leads the prince to the water of life and reminds him to be sure to leave the castle before the clock strikes twelve.

Many of the elements of the hero's descent into the underworld and of the psychological and spiritual process it represents are operative in these events. The prince embodies, as do all heroes of the quest, the potential journey into the unknown, which is the locked and enchanted castle. The hero always descends to redeem those imprisoned by the darkness. Jesus brings back Adam and Eve; Orpheus almost liberates Eurydice. In this case the retrieved one is the princess, who, like the enchanted Sleeping Beauty, is the deeper, lost half of the unredeemed Self longing to be released, an embodiment of the divine wisdom, or Sophia, apart from whom the Logos cannot be made flesh. The lions, overcome by the magic of supernatural power, are the bestial deterrents to the journey within.

In the princess's promise of marriage there is no question of realistic love. The relationship is ritualistic; the hero and heroine act in a way that is archetypal and symbolic rather than sentimental. The marriage of the future is established as the prince's ultimate goal after the curing of his father. The sword and the bread, symbols of power and nourishment and potential good deeds, are to be magical aids to that goal. It is the princess who leads the prince to the magical water, because, as Divine Wisdom, she is the proper guardian of the symbol of eternal life to be gained from the eventual emergence of the Self. Her repetition of the dwarf's interdiction concerning the hour of the prince's departure from the castle is an indication that she and the dwarf are of one and the same power, the universal creative impulse by which the continuing evolution symbolized by the quest itself is made feasible. In terms of the Christian culture in which the Grimms discovered this tale, the princess takes on meaning in the context of the Virgin cult. The Virgin is the earthly form of the mother of God, but as the church—the castle freed from enchantment—she is also God's bride. In this role as both mother-guide and wife, she reaches back to the most ancient traditions of the Great Goddess herself.

When the princess leaves him, the prince comes upon a fine bed that he finds irresistible, and he lies down to sleep. In so doing he conveys ritually his brotherhood with all the offspring of the primordial fallen parents. Like Christ in the garden of Gethsemane, he demonstrates his human nature. Only the sound of the clock striking midnight awakens him. He quickly draws water from the fountain and escapes through the closing doors, losing only a piece of his heel, which signifies his having almost ignored the interdictions of the dwarf and the princess. In this incident one is reminded not only of Cinderella and her glass slipper but of the fact that the journey is fraught with many temptations and dangers, any of which could prevent success. Perhaps the loss of a part of the body also ties the prince to the many dismembered man-gods of the Middle Eastern fertility cults. It seems evident, as the prince's mishap is never mentioned again in the story, that this is a ritual event with symbolic rather than narrative significance.

The prince is now ready for the trials that, if accomplished, will lead him back to a final reunion with the princess. Journeying homeward, he again meets the dwarf, who informs him of the magical powers contained in the sword and the loaf of bread found in the castle. The sword can be used to defeat whole armies; the bread can feed the hungry indefinitely. The religious significance of the sword as God's righteous justice and of the bread as the bread of life is clear. Much of this symbolism is traceable to the Christian tradition, in which much is made of the Christ's coming with both bread and the sword. But the ultimate source of the symbolism very likely lies in much older traditions.

The young prince now emerges more clearly as a savior figure when he begs the dwarf to release his sinful brothers. The dwarf, in his ancient wisdom, warns the boy of the danger in this course but to no avail. The attempt to redeem them must be made; the road to reunion with the Self must involve direct dealings with the dark forces represented by the brothers. And when the brothers are released, the prince—foolishly from a practical point of view—tells them of his quest and of his prospects for the future. The three brothers travel on together, and three kingdoms are saved by the sword and the bread. It is not surprising that the older sons betray their brother at the earliest possible opportunity. One night as he sleeps, they steal the magic fluid and substitute saltwater for it. The betrayal by siblings is an ancient and recurring motif found, for example, in the biblical story of Cain and Abel, the Egyptian story of Seth and Osiris, and any number of familiar fairy tales. Goodness in its mercy is by nature vulnerable to evil, which is itself by nature aggressive. It is as if the hero must, as a part of his trials, allow himself to be placed in the position of the ritual sacrificial victim.

The king is given the false water by the young prince, and his health worsens. The older sons accuse their brother of attempting to murder the king and produce the real water, claiming that it is they who have found it. The father is immediately cured. The young son, remaining silent—again as if this were necessary for the inevitable ritual process—is exiled, and an old hunter is given instructions to slay him in the forest. The hunter, like the one in the story of Snow White, cannot bear to carry out his orders: the simple man can recognize innocence where the king cannot. He releases the prince to wander in the woods. Mythically this period points to the hero's withdrawal into the wilderness, a symbolic death during which he must undergo the ultimate separation that will render him transcendent. It is the period of preparation for the final step in the discovery of Self—an initiation rite that will transfer him from a state of mortality to one of immortality, from immaturity to wisdom.

During this period several things happen. Three cartloads of treasure arrive at the king's palace from the three kings saved by the sword and bread of the good prince. The king begins to suspect that his son might be innocent: "How I wish he were not dead," he laments. Then comes the ritual cry from the huntsman: "He lives! He lives!" Meanwhile the princess of the castle has prepared one final test. A path of gold is laid before her door, and her servants are told to admit only the knight who rides to the castle upon this path. The two evil brothers, remembering what their brother has told them, approach the castle but will not allow their horses to ride over the gold path, for they value the precious metal more than the object of the quest. Hence they are turned away: evil is unable to attain to divine wisdom. Only those whose priorities extend beyond material gain can enter into the absolute. The young prince, his mind only on the princess, rides on the path without even noticing it and is greeted again by the sacred maiden. The ritual separation is ended; the goddess receives the reborn son.

Like the ascent to paradise in myth, the ritual marriage that ends this and many quest tales expresses the achieved goal of wholeness. The masculine principle is joined to the feminine, and in that union of yin and yang the Self is discovered, at which time the present becomes eternity; life can be lived "happily ever after." The joy one feels at the end of the fairy tale and other quest stories is more than a sentimental one. It results from one having gained a vision of the achieved goal of individual growth and human evolution. One glimpses oneself literally awakening into the permanent consciousness that is self-knowledge. In this sense, the quest tale is always a creation story in which the hero emerges from chaos as re-created God in man.

SEE ALSO Heroes; Otherworld; Pilgrimage, overview article.

BIBLIOGRAPHY

The most lively analysis of the hero's quest is still Joseph Campbell's classic study *The Hero with a Thousand Faces* (New York, 1949; reprint, Princeton, N.J., 1968). C. M. Bowra's "The Hero," in *The Hero in Literature*, edited by Victor Brombert (New York, 1969), is an important essay on the subject. A collection of mythic stories illustrating and representing the heroic mono-myth is in David Adams Leeming's *Mythology: The Voyage of the Hero*, 3d ed. (New York, 1998).

The best treatments of the quest motif in literature, particularly in romance, and of the motif's overall importance for literary criticism are Northrop Frye's *The Anatomy of Criticism* (Princeton, N.J., 1957) and Frye's "The Archetypes of Literature" and "Quest and Cycle in *Finnegans Wake*," in *Fables of Identity: Studies in Poetic Mythology* (New York, 1963). One of the best and most accessible versions of the Arthurian story is *King Arthur and His Knights: Selected Tales by Sir Thomas Malory*, edited by Eugene Vinaver (Oxford, U.K., 1975). On the Grail myth, see Henry Kahane and Renée Kahane's *The Krater and the Grail: Hermetic Sources of Parzival* (Urbana, Ill., 1965; reprint, 1984). The Grail myth is one important source for what is perhaps the most famous twentieth-century quest poem, T. S. Eliot, *The Waste Land* (1922). Eliot's *Four Quartets* (New York, 1943) is also a poetic quest, one that owes much to both Occidental and Oriental quest mythology.

For a psychological approach to the quest as a search for self in the modern world, see C. G. Jung's *Modern Man in Search of a Soul* (New York and London, 1933). For the best study of the shamanic quest, see Mircea Eliade's *Shamanism: Archaic Techniques of Ecstasy* (New York, 1964). Versions of the Buddhist and Hindu quest stories are in Ananda K. Coomaraswamy and Sister Nive-dita (Margaret E. Noble), *Myths of the Hindus and Buddhists* (London, 1913; reprint, New York, 1967), and in Ananda K. Coomaraswamy, *Buddha and the Gospel of Buddhism* (New York and London, 1916). Any work by Coomaraswamy on the religions of the East is likely to contain useful information on the quest as a mystical spiritual journey. Thomas Merton's writings offer a moving record of a Christian's mystical quest. See, for example, *A Thomas Merton Reader*, rev. ed., edited by Thomas P. McDonnell (Garden City, N.Y., 1974).

The pilgrimage of Xuanzang is treated in Sally Hovey Wriggens's *Xuanzang: A Buddhist Pilgrim on the Silk Road* (Boulder, Colo., 1996). Several works devoted to secular versions of the quest myth are Jon Krakauer's *Into the Wild* (New York, 1996); Rowland A. Sherrill's *Road-Book America: Contemporary Culture and the New Picaresque* (Champaign, Ill., 2000); and David Adams Leeming's *Myth: A Biography of Belief* (Oxford, U.K., and New York, 2002).

DAVID ADAMS LEEMING (1987 AND 2005)

QUETZALCOATL was one of the most powerful and multifaceted gods in Mesoamerican religions. The cult of Quetzalcoatl, the "quetzal-feathered serpent," was prominent in central Mexico from at least the time of Teotihuacán (100–750 CE) to the collapse of the Aztec capital of Tenochtitlán in 1521. He was called Kukulcan in the postclassic Maya culture that developed from 1000 to 1521, and he played a prominent role in the organizing of the capitals of Chichén Itzá and Mayapan. In the more than seventy painted, written, and archaeological sources that carry the elements of the Quetzalcoatl tradition, he appears both as a major celestial creator god and as intimately identified with the paradigmatic priest-king Topiltzin Ce Acatl Quetzalcoatl, whose great kingdom of Tula, or Tollan, flourished between 900 and 1100, and who is remembered as a primary source of culture, political order, and religious authority in Mesoamerica. The archaeological and ethnographic records show that Quetzalcoatl was the symbol of effective organization and sacred authority in a series of capital cities that dominated the history of Mesoamerican religions for almost fifteen hundred years.

In the cosmogonic episodes of the early sources known as *Historia de los Mexicanos por sus pinturas,* the *Anales de Cuauhtitlán,* and the *Leyenda de los soles,* Quetzalcoatl, one of the four sons of the androgynous creator god Ometeotl, plays a number of creative roles: He generates the universe (together with his brother, Tezcatlipoca), rules over various cosmogonic eras, assists in the discovery of maize and pulque, creates fire, participates in the great sacrifice of the gods that leads to the creation of the fifth cosmic age, or Fifth Sun, and becomes transformed into the morning-and-evening star, Venus.

In a number of instances, this creative activity reflects the symbolic design of the Mesoamerican universe as a world divided into five major parts (four cardinal sections around a central space). For instance, in the elaborate cosmology of the *Historia de los Mexicanos por sus pinturas,* Quetzalcoatl and Tezcatlipoca, Lord of the Smoking Mirror, revive the broken universe and set the stage for the fifth age by dispersing the water of chaos and restoring dry land by carving four roads to the center of the earth, from which they raise the sky to create a living space for human beings. Coincidentally, in a number of primary sources that depict the capital city of Tollan, the ceremonial centers are shown divided into five sections with four temples and mountains surrounding the central mountain or temple where the priest-king Quetzalcoatl ruled.

In another series of sources Quetzalcoatl is depicted as the inventor of agriculture, the arts, and the calendar and the restorer of human life through a cosmic dive into the underworld, Mictlan, where he outwits the lord of the dead, Mictlantecuhtli, to recover the bones of the ancestors. In this story, Mictlantecuhtli prepares a death trap for Quetzalcoatl. Quetzalcoatl falls to his death, but then he revives himself to escape Mictlan, meanwhile revitalizing the bones of the dead.

Quetzalcoatl also took the form of Ehécatl, the wind god. As depicted in Fray Bernardino de Sahagún's *Historia general de las cosas de la Nueva España* (compiled 1569–1582; also known as the Florentine Codex), Ehécatl announces the coming of the fertilizing rains and, in one episode, blows the sun into its cosmic orbit, thereby starting the fifth age. Furthermore, a number of sources reveal Quetzalcoatl's close association with the cycles and hierophany of Venus (Tlahuizcalpantecuhtli), one of the major astronomical bodies influencing ritual, architecture, and the calendar in Mesoamerica. The cycles of Venus were a central part of Quetzalcoatl's cult in the city of Chollolan (100–1521 CE), and the *Leyenda de los soles* depicts the self-sacrifice of Ce Acatl Quetzalcoatl following the fall of the kingdom of Tollan, which ends with his heart rising into the sky to become the Morning Star.

Historically, the god Quetzalcoatl was the patron deity of the Toltec empire centered in Tula-Xicocotitlán, also called Tollan. Some scholars, such as H. B. Nicholson, have identified in the primary sources a sacred history of Tollan that relates the seven stages of the priest-king Topiltzin Quetzalcoatl's exemplary human career, including his miraculous birth after his mother swallowed a precious green stone, his teenage revenge of his father's murder, his training for the priesthood, his years as a warrior, his ascension to the throne, the fall of his capital, his flight from Tollan, and his promise to return one day in the future to restore the kingdom. The Tollan of the primary sources is a kingdom secure in agricultural resources, rich in artwork, ritual innovation, and technological excellence, and the birthplace of astronomy and of cardinally oriented ceremonial structures. This world of stability and creativity collapsed through the magical attacks of the magician, Tezcatlipoca, whose cult in some sources was said to depend on human sacrifice. The long-range significance of Quetzalcoatl's Tollan in Mesoamerican history is attested to by the identification of five other capitals—Teotihuacán, Xochicalco, Chichén Itzá, Chollolan, and Tenochtitlán—as places replicating Tollan and the cult of Quetzalcoatl.

In Aztec Mexico, Quetzalcoatl was the patron god of the schools of higher learning, the *calmecacs*, and the model for the office of the high priesthood at the Templo Mayor in Tenochtitlán, in front of which his round temple was apparently located.

When Cortés arrived and began his assault on Tenochtitlán, a number of sources state unequivocally that Moctezuma Xocoytzin (Moctezuma II) identified him as Quetzalcoatl returning to reestablish his kingdom in Mexico.

BIBLIOGRAPHY

Carrasco, Davíd. *Quetzalcoatl and the Irony of Empire: Myths and Prophecies in the Aztec Tradition.* Chicago, 1982. This study places the evidence of Quetzalcoatl's multivalence within the context of urban structure and history in central Mesoamerica. It utilizes the history-of-religions approach to interpret the paradigmatic sacred authority of Quetzalcoatl and Tollan as the sources for empire and destruction in the Aztec capital.

López Austin, Alfredo. *Hombre Dios: Religion y política en el mundo nahuatl.* Mexico City, 1973. The best Spanish-language interpretation of the historical development in pre-Hispanic times of the mythic structure of Quetzalcoatl and its impact on paradigmatic leadership and political ideology in pre-Aztec and Aztec Mexico.

New Sources

Anaya, Rudolf A. *Lords of the Dawn: The Legend of Quetzacoatl.* Albuquerque, 1987.

Elzey, Wayne. "A Hill on a Land Surrounded by Water: An Aztec Story of Origin and Destiny." *History of Religions* 31 (1991): 105–149.

Ritchlin, Sheri. "The Myth of Quetzacoatl." *Parabola* 26, no. 4 (2001): 65–69.

DAVÍD CARRASCO (1987)
Revised Bibliography

QUIETISM.

QUIETISM. Although some of the important insights of Quietism—a movement distinguished from the generic sense of the word *quietistic*, which implies withdrawal or passivity with regard to politics or ethics—can be found in medieval devotion, in sixteenth-century Spanish spirituality, and in various mystical sources, both Christian and Buddhist, the usual meaning of the word is restricted to the late seventeenth-century devotional movement in the Catholic Church in Italy and France. The main figure in the history of Quietism was Miguel de Molinos (1628–1696), a Spanish priest who settled in Rome at the end of 1663. He became an enormously popular spiritual adviser, especially among nuns and women of high society. His new contemplative way of Christian perfection was summed up (without some of its esoteric aspects) in a book he published simultaneously in Spanish and Italian: *Guida Spirituale, che disinvolge l'anima e la conduce per il interior camino all'acquisito della perfetta contemplatione e del ricco tesoro della pace interiore* (1685), often referred to as his *Spiritual Guide.*

Though supported by a number of theologians and, for a time, probably by Innocent XI, the *Guide* was soon attacked by the Jesuits for its total disregard of meditation, spiritual asceticism, vocal prayers, and, implicitly, the cults of Jesus and of the Virgin. The criticism ended with the arrest of Molinos on the order of the Holy Office, a long trial, and his condemnation in May 1687. He spent the rest of his life in prison. On November 20, 1687, the papal bull *Coelestis pastor* anathematized sixty-eight of his statements. The material of the condemnation was taken not only, and not mainly, from his published works, but also from about twelve thousand of his letters and from his oral teaching; in addition to the enumerated theological errors, it included the charge of sexual licentiousness—something Molinos inferred from his own doctrines and apparently frequently practiced with his penitent women.

The new devotion (the word *Quietists* had been used since the early 1680s by the enemies of Molinos) was based on the belief that any Christian can achieve an entirely disinterested insight into God; this insight is permanent, internally undifferentiated, and free from images and affects, and it involves a previous destruction of one's own will and consciousness; it is the work of divine grace, which, after the self has emptied itself, totally fills the void and becomes the sovereign owner of the higher part of the soul; as a result, the animal part of the soul as well as the body are no longer the responsibility of the person. This state of perfectly passive contemplation is not only the highest form of religious life, but makes other, more specific forms of worship—the cults of Jesus and of the saints, the acts of repentance and hope, confession, mortifications, prayers, and even concern about one's own salvation—either useless or even harmful insofar as they divert the soul from union with God. And although contemplation is at the beginning inspired by the love of God, it eventually abolishes love, desires, will, and all separate affects. What remains is not an affect, but God himself present in the soul. While it is God's gift, this contemplation is in fact given to everybody who makes a sufficient self-destructive effort, and it does not depend on education, sex, or status. Once acquired, it is effectively permanent. Since it involves a total separation of the soul from the body, the acts of the latter do not disturb it; in fact the devil often inflicts violence on the body of a contemplative and compels it to perform externally sinful acts, in particular, of a sexual character, but those acts cannot break the union with God, as they do not affect the soul. Sexual permissiveness is thus justified. The contemplative, being absolutely devoid of his will and transformed into God, cannot do good works on his own initiative or have any intention to help his neighbors; he can perform such works only on a direct order from God.

Molinos's doctrine was obviously unacceptable to the church not only because of its suspect moral consequences, but because it practically abrogated the entire external cult, along with discipline, intellectual effort, and the variety of virtues, merits, and religious acts. It reduced the religious life to one habitual act for which the mystic no longer needs the church and which is proclaimed to be the only genuine way of union with God. Further, although Molinos did not consider himself a rebel, but rather a reformer within the church, his devotional program, especially since it was not confined to monasteries but was also propagated among the laity, undermined the role of the church as a mediator between God and humans.

Molinos had a few less well-known predecessors, such as the Spanish mystic Jean Falconi (1596–1638), the blind theologian from Marseilles, François Malaval (1627–1719), and the bishop of Jesi, Pier Matto Petrucci (1636–1701), all of whom preached the superiority of passive and unreflective contemplation over meditations and vocal prayers, none of whom, however, extended the theory of mystical kenosis (kenosis meaning the relinquishment of the form of God by Jesus in becoming a man and suffering death) to the acceptance of "diabolic violence" or to the point of advising that we should not fight against temptations.

The more philosophically elaborated variety of Quietism arose on French soil, thanks to the works of Jeanne-Marie de la Motte Guyon (1648–1717) and François Salignac de Fénelon. Guyon had already been trained in mystical devotion when she met, in 1680, the Barnabite father François La Combe, who had been converted in Rome to Molinos's way of perfection. She lived in Paris after 1686, having previously organized small conventicles of mystics in various places. Among her many works, amounting to over forty volumes in the collected writings, the most popular were *Moyen court et très facile de faire oraison* and *Les torrens spirituels.* With highly developed prophetic claims, Guyon believed that God had entrusted her with the mission of a total renewal of Christianity. The contemplative devotion in her description involves all the previous Quietist tenets except for the theory of diabolic violence, but adds some metaphysical ideas. A totally passive contemplation, implying the absolute annihilation of the self, is said to be the only proper way of Christian life. At the highest stage the soul loses everything that is personal or human *(laisser agir Dieu)* and is transformed into God, like a river after reaching the ocean. The self, indeed the very fact of separate existence, is the source of evil, or rather is evil itself, and, after the annihilation, the soul attains the status of God before the act of creation. The soul returns to the original source of being where no place is left for differentiation: "At the very beginning one has to die to everything by which we are something." And this form of being cannot be lost; the deification is inalienable. Indifference to everything other than God, to sin, to the past and to the future, to life and death, to one's own and others' salvation, indeed to divine grace, all this naturally accompanies the blessed state of *theōsis.* The entire variety of religious worship, both external and internal, is done away with once the soul reaches perfection. Priests and the visible church are nothing but obstacles.

Accused of spreading heretical doctrines, Guyon was imprisoned at the beginning of 1688, but she was released after a few months. She then experienced a period of celebrity, during which she enjoyed the friendship of Fénelon and Mme. de Maintenon. The attacks did not stop, however, and a special committee headed by the influential prelate Jacques Bossuet organized a campaign against the Quietist doctrine. Although both Fénelon and Guyon signed the articles confirming the church's traditional doctrine in points where it seemed to be incompatible with the Quietists' devotion, the debates, accusations, pamphlets, and intrigues continued. They ended with the formal condemnation, in a breve (1699) of Innocent XI, on twenty-three erroneous statements on contemplation and *caritas pura* (disinterested love of God, with no regard to one's salvation) taken from Fénelon's book *Explication des maximes des saints sur la vie intérieure.* Fénelon immediately bowed to the verdict. Guyon was imprisoned from 1695 to 1702.

The Quietist mysticism was certainly incompatible with the teaching and educational system of the Roman church; implicitly, and sometimes explicitly, it questioned the very need of the visible church. The condemnation of Molinos and Fénelon, however, had a negative impact for many decades on the development of mystical spirituality in the Catholic world.

See Also Fénelon, François.

Bibliography

Brémond, Henri. *Apologie pour Fénelon.* Paris, 1910.

Cognet, Louis. *Crépuscule des mystiques: Bossuet, Fénelon.* Tournai, Belgium, 1958.

Dudon, Paul. *Le quiétiste espagnol, Michel Molinos, 1628–1696.* Paris, 1921.

Guerrier, Louis. *Madame Guyon: Sa vie, sa doctrine, et son influence.* Orléans, France, 1881.

Knox, Ronald A. *Enthusiasm: A Chapter in the History of Religion, with Special Reference to the XVII and XVIII Centuries.* New York, 1950.

Kolakowski, Leszek. *Chrétiens sans église.* Paris, 1969.

Petrocchi, Massimo. *Il quietismo italiano del seicento.* Rome, 1948.

Schmittlein, Raymond. *L'aspect politique du différend Bossuet-Fénelon.* Baden-Baden, Germany, 1954.

Leszek Kolakowski (1987)

QUIRINUS.

The god Quirinus was originally one of the main Roman divinities. The priest responsible for his cult was one of the three major flamines, along with the flamines of Jupiter and Mars, who outranked him in the *ordo sacerdotum,* the order of precedence of the most important priests (Festus 299 L). These three gods (Jupiter, Mars, and Quirinus) made up the early triad that Georg Wissowa (1912, p. 23) has reconstructed from various features of ancient Roman life, such as the invocation of these three deities in the practice of *devotio,* in which a leading Roman offered his life to ensure victory against the enemy (Livy, 8.9.6); the law, attributed to the king Numa Pompilius, which differentiated between three kinds of booty according to the rank of the person who seized the booty from the enemy leader and who allocated it in different amounts to each of the three gods (Festus 204 L); and the fact that the *ancilia,* shields which the Salian priests wielded in their armed dances, were under the joint protection of these three gods (Festus, commentary on Virgil, *Aeneid,* 8.663).

Romans of the later Classical period, however, wondered about Quirinus, who was certainly not, from their point of view, as important a god as the other two gods who were formerly part of the triad, Jupiter and Mars. Naturally he had his own temple on the Quirinal, the hill of Rome which owed its name to him, and his feast day, the *Quirinalia* (February 17th), fell on the last day of the festival of *Fornacalia,* a festival dedicated to the goddess of the furnace, Fornax, who presided over the roasting of the corn. Quirinus's flamen intervened rarely, however; besides the cult which the three flamines jointly controlled, once a year, in honor of the personification of good faith, Fides (Livy, 1.21.4), the Quirinal flamen officiated at the cult of Robigo, the goddess of corn blight (Ovid, *Fastes,* 4.910-942), and of Consus, the god of cereal storage (Tertullian, *De spectaculis,* 5). As a result, ancient writers offered various interpretations of Quirinus. Given the link between Quirinus and Mars, which meant that Quirinus was patron of the twelve Quirinal Salian priests and Mars of the twelve Palatine ones (Dionysius of Halicarnassus, 2.70.7, 3.32.4), and that he appeared as *Mars tranquillus* (Mars in his peaceful aspect), *qui praest paci* (who presides over peace) according to Servius (commentary on Virgil, *Aeneid,* 1.292 and 6.859 respectively), Quirinus was portrayed as a war god, hence his identification with the Greek Enyalios, an epithet of Ares. Since there was a convenient link between Quirinus's name and the Sabine town of Cures, considered the home of the Sabines who, by joining with the Romans of Romulus, had allowed Rome to be founded, Quirinus was regarded as a Sabine god, introduced by their king, Titus Tatius. An alternative explanation, incompatible with the Sabine explanation, has Quirinus as the founder of Rome—as Romulus himself—deified under the name Quirinus after his mysterious disappearance. This absorption must predate our first source, Cicero (*De re publica,* 1.64).

Such confusion over the identity and origins of Quirinus explains why modern scholars have had very different ideas concerning this god. Because of his position in relation to Mars (and beneath Jupiter) in the triad, Quirinus has been viewed with Mars as representing only a part of the city. He has often been seen as the god of the Sabine part of the original population of Rome, linked to the Capitol, the Sabine Hill. More recently, André Magdelain has taken him to be the god of the city, as opposed to Mars, who would thus be the god of land outside the city itself, the *ager Romanus.* Georges Dumézil has applied to the Jupiter/Mars/Quirinus triad the trifunctional system which he sees as a conceptual framework shared by various Indo-European peoples. He regards Quirinus as patron of third-function values (fertility and related values), with Mars governing the second (war) and Jupiter the first (sovereignty). This may be admitted, as long as Quirinus is not considered an agricultural god (something that Angelo Brelich takes furthest). In Brelich's view, Quirinus is a god of the kind known ethnographically as *dema,* or the first leader of a community who, after his death, became a chthonic deity ensuring the nourishment of his people. In this regard, the etymology of Quirinus's name, the most certain aspect of this ancient god, is especially significant. Despite an attempt by Gerhard Radke to explain Quirinus's name as deriving from a Sanskrit verb meaning "to plough" and of linking it with the *sulcus primigenius,* the furrow dug by Romulus to mark out the city perimeter when Rome was founded, the name must in fact be made up of the prefix *co(m),* "with," and of the Latin word for man, *vir.* Quirinus, **co-wir-inos,* is thus the god of men assembled together. However, as Danielle Porte (1981) and Dario Sabbatucci (1988, pp. 63–70) have emphasized, this gathering of people brings together individuals who are citizens within their particular social and political framework.

Ancient writers (Varro, *De lingua Latina* 5.73; Ovid, *Fastes* 2.479; Plutarch, *Life of Romulus* 29.1) had identified the name Quirinus as being associated with the old term *Quirites,* indicating Roman citizens, and the name is also linked with that of the *curiae* (**co-wir-ia*), which represented, in terms of the earliest organization of the city, the thirty units, grouped in three tribes, into which these *Quirites* were divided. Quirinus is thus the god of citizens. If, in Dumézil's terms, he is also patron of third-function values, this is as a result of his link with the masses, with the populace, but in Rome such a connection was considered within a social and political perspective (Briquel). In other words, if Quirinus is involved in matters concerning the food supply of the citizenry (the link with the *Fornacalia,* the cult of Robigo, things which are a normal part of the third function), he does not desert his *Quirites* when they are soldiers (second function), even taking on an official or religious role (first function). This sociopolitical factor is in evidence even in those of his functions that are most clearly related to agriculture: the *Quirinalia* falls on the last day of *Fornacalia,* called *stultorum dies,* "the day of fools," since it allowed those Romans who no longer knew to which *curia* they belonged to sacrifice to the goddess Fornax on that particular day. Her cult had been performed on the preceding days, *curia* by *curia,* presided over by the *curio,* the priest of the *curia.* Quirinus's being the patron of citizens explains his relation with the god Mars. Despite the contemptuous use Caesar makes of the term *Quirites* (Suetonius, *Life of Caesar,* 70) to berate soldiers who had revolted, Roman citizens who were called to serve in the army, *cives* who had become *milites,* remained *Quirites* (the ancient formula used to mobilize the army quoted by Varro [*De lingua Latina* 6.88] refers to *Quirites pedites armatos,* or *Quirites* footsoldiers) and thus remained linked to Quirinus. It is also possible to understand how Quirinus can be identified with Romulus, who founded the city with its political and social structure, the *curiae* who constituted the *Quirites.*

SEE ALSO Flamen; Roman Religion, article on The Early Period.

BIBLIOGRAPHY

Alföldi, Andreas. *Die Struktur des voretruskischen Römerstaates.* Heidelberg, 1974.

Brelich, Angelo. "Quirinus, una divinità romana alla luce della comparazione storica." *Studi e Materiali di Storia delle Religioni,* 31 (1960): 63-119.

Briquel, Dominique. "Remarques sur Quirinus," *Revue belge de philologie et d'histoire,* 74 (1996): 99–120.

Briquel, Dominique. "Canonical Representative of the Third Function in Rome." *Theoretical Frameworks for the Study of Graeco-Roman Religions, Adjunct Proceedings of the XVIIIth Congress of the International Association for the History of Religions, Durban, South Africa.* Edited by Luther H. Martin and Panayotis Pachis, pp. 43–52. Thessaloniki, 2003.

Coarelli, Filippo. *s.v. Quirini aedes, s.v. Quirini sacellum. Lexicon Topographicum Urbis Romae,* 4. Rome, 1999, pp. 185–187.

Dumézil, Georges. *La religion romaine archaïque.* Paris, 1966; 2d edition, 1974.

Magdelain, André. *De la royauté et du droit, de Romulus à Sabinus.* Rome, 1995.

Porte, Danielle. "Romulus-Quirinus, prince et dieu, dieu des princes." *Aufstieg und Niedergang der römischen Welt* 16, no. 1 (1981): 300–342.

Radke, Gerhard. "Eine kritische Überprüfung der Überlieferung und ein Versuch." *Aufstieg und Niedergang der römischen Welt,* 16, no. 1 (1981): 276–299.

Rosivach, Vincent J. "Mars, the Lustral God." *Latomus,* 42 (1983): 509–522.

Sabbatucci, Dario. *La religione di Roma antica, dal calendario festivo all'ordine cosmico.* Milan, 1988.

Varro, Marcus. *De lingua Latina (On the Latin language).* With an English translation by Roland G. Kent. 2 vol. London and Cambridge, Mass., 1938–1958.

Wissowa, Georg. *Religion und Kultus des Römer.* 2nd edition. Munich, 1912.

Ziolkowski, Adam. *The Temples of Mid-Republican Rome and their Historical and Topographical Context.* Rome, 1992.

Dominique Briquel (2005)

QUMRAN See DEAD SEA SCROLLS

QUR'ĀN

This entry consists of the following articles:

TRADITION OF SCHOLARSHIP AND INTERPRETATION
ITS ROLE IN MUSLIM PRACTICE AND LIFE

QUR'ĀN: TRADITION OF SCHOLARSHIP AND INTERPRETATION

The Qur'ān is, for Muslims, the revealed word of God. Hence, the interpretation of the Qur'ān (*tafsīr*) has emerged as one of the most revered disciplines in Islam. Given that the life of the early Muslims revolved around the Qur'ān from the beginning, one of their earliest concerns was to understand the message of the sacred text. The Prophet Muḥammad (d. 632) and his immediate followers (known as the *companions*) used the Qur'ān for day-to-day guidance, prayer, and spiritual enrichment, and for liturgical and congregational use. Although interpretation of the Qur'ān as a discipline developed over time, Muslims engaged with it from the beginning in less formal ways: reflecting on it, reciting it, discussing it, and attempting to explain it to each other. It was such activities that gradually led to the development of the exegetical tradition in Islam.

The standard traditional Muslim view, both Sunnī and Shīʿī, of the revelation attributes the composition of the Qur'ān to God alone, and denies any human role in its production. According to this view, the Prophet faithfully communicated what had been "dictated" to him by God in the Arabic language through the angel of revelation, usually identified as Gabriel, without addition or alteration. Muslims also view the language of the Qur'ān, Arabic, as an essential aspect of the revelation. Similarly, when the Qur'ān says that God "says," "speaks" or "commands," these words were understood by most Muslims literally, not metaphorically. Thus, the revelations the Prophet "received" were transmitted verbatim to his followers, who passed them on to succeeding generations. On the whole, this understanding of the revelation has been maintained throughout Islamic history and is still the basis of most Islamic exegetical work. By and large, Muslim scholars, even of the modern period, adhere to this doctrine of revelation (Saeed, 1999).

***Tafsīr* and *Ta'wīl*.** There are two key terms for Qur'anic exegesis: *tafsīr* and *ta'wīl.* The term *tafsīr* occurs in the Qur'ān once in the sense of "explanation" (25:33), not in a technical sense, and its meaning may be related to the uncovering or revealing of something that is hidden. Linguistically, *ta'wīl* is derived from the root *a.w.l,* which means to go back to the origin of something. Edward Lane lists *ta'wīl* as "the discovering, detecting, revealing, developing or disclosing, or the explaining, expounding or interpreting, that to which a thing is, or may be, reduced. . . ." (1955–1956, p. 126). In the Qur'ān, *ta'wīl* is used to mean explanation, discovery, and clarification (Zurqānī, 1988, vol. 2, p. 6) and therefore is virtually synonymous with *tafsīr.* It seems to have been used in this way by the early generations of Muslims, as is shown in the Prophet's reported invocation to God to bestow upon Ibn ʿAbbās (d. 652), his cousin, the understanding of religion and to teach him the *ta'wīl* (interpretation of the Qur'ān) (Ibn Saʿd, 1957, vol. 2, p. 365). A number of early exegetes, such as Mujāhid (d. 722), and even some relatively later ones, such as Ṭabarī (d. 923), used *ta'wīl* in this sense (Zurqānī, 1988, vol. 2, p. 7).

There are, however, some scholars who argue that *tafsīr* is different from *ta'wīl.* For some, *tafsīr* deals with the "literal" meaning of the text, whereas *ta'wīl* deals with the "deeper" meaning. For others, *tafsīr* is associated with narration, tradition, and text (*riwāyah*), while *ta'wīl* is associated with understanding and interpretation (*dirāyah*) (Suyūṭī, 1974–1975, vol. 4, p. 193). *Tafsīr* is thus closely related to the knowledge handed down from the early generations (tradition), whereas *ta'wīl* may involve giving preference to one meaning over another, supported or unsupported by evidence, or attributing allegorical meanings to the text. In its more controversial sense, *ta'wīl* may be used for purely personal interpretation of the text, without linguistic or textual evidence and driven by one's theological or religio-political beliefs and doctrines, as well as for interpretation based on "esoteric" meanings, or to avoid anthropomorphism. In Shīʿī, Ṣūfī, and Ismāʿīlī exegesis, the term *ta'wīl* acquired a more technical meaning.

Early development of *tafsīr*. Contradictory opinions are held by Muslims (and Western scholars) on early attitudes toward interpreting the Qur'ān (Gilliot, 2002, p. 101). There are reports that senior companions, such as ʿUmar I (d. 644), discouraged Muslims from engaging in interpretation and in fact punished some for doing so. Equally, there are traditions from ʿUmar himself encouraging Muslims to explore the meanings of the Qur'ān. If there was general opposition to interpretation in the very early period, it is difficult to explain why a companion like Ibn ʿAbbās (d. 687) managed to engage in exegetical activity apparently on a large scale, and why other companions appear to have had no difficulty in doing the same, examples being ʿAbd Allāh ibn Masʿūd (d. 653) and Ubayy ibn Kaʿb (d. c. 656). This suggests that it may have been only a particular form of exegetical activity that was discouraged, perhaps exegesis that relied solely on personal opinion or that attempted to elaborate on verses that were considered ambiguous (*mutashābihāt*); however it must be acknowledged that Muslim scholars did not agree on which verses of the Qur'ān were ambiguous (Rippin, 1988).

A rudimentary *tafsīr* tradition began during the Prophet Muḥammad's time. On numerous occasions, the Qurʾān refers to itself as being in "clear Arabic" and as a book that is "clear" (26:195). At other times, it says that one of the functions of the Prophet is to explain the Qurʾān (16:44). There is debate among Muslims as to whether the Prophet ever provided explanations for the whole Qurʾān. Those who say he did rely on the Qurʾanic verse, "And We have sent down unto thee [also] the Message; that thou mayest explain clearly to people what is sent for them" (16:44). Others believe that the Prophet only explained very small portions of the Qurʾān, arguing that his followers were already familiar with it because it was in their own language, Arabic. Despite this general familiarity with the language of the Qurʾān among the first generation of Muslims, the need for explanation and interpretation must have existed from the very beginning, most importantly because the Qurʾān introduced new concepts and used many pre-Islamic terms in new ways. Examples include *ṣalāt* (prayer), *zakāt* (alms tax), *ḥājj* (pilgrimage), *ṣawm* (fasting), *allāh* (God), *malak* (angel), *yawm al-ʾākhirah* (the Last Day). In particular, converts to Islam from other religious traditions might have had very different understandings of many or some of these terms.

Little of the Prophet's own interpretation of the Qurʾān is recorded, and much of it exists only in the form of what we may call *practical exegesis*, but this should not be considered insignificant. Practical exegesis exists where the Qurʾān used a particular term or concept that the Prophet then illustrated by his actions, notnecessarily explained in the form of a *ḥadīth*.. From the substantial body of information encompassed in the *ḥadīth*, one may argue that the time of the Prophet should be considered the richest period of exegetical activity through practice. The emerging "established practice" (for example, descriptions of how the Prophet performed the *ṣalāt*) thus became the foundation of later exegesis. With the death of the Prophet, the Qurʾān was ipso facto in its final and complete form. Muslim tradition holds that it was compiled ("collected") during the caliphate of the third caliph, ʿUthmān (r. 644–656).

Even though the Prophet had hundreds of followers (companions) at the time of his death, only a few reportedly contributed directly to Qurʾanic exegesis. They included the first four caliphs, Abū Bakr (d. 634), ʿUmar (d. 644), ʿUthmān (d. 656) and ʿAlī (d. 661), as well as ʿĀʾishah (d. 678), the Prophet's wife. Others included ʿAbd Allāh ibn Masʿūd, who settled in Iraq, Ubayy ibn Kaʿb (in Medina), ʿAbd Allāh ibn ʿAbbās (in Mecca), and Zayd ibn Thābit (in Medina). Of these, the most celebrated are ʿAbd Allāh ibn ʿAbbās, who reportedly had a large number of students in Mecca and who is known as the "Interpreter of the Qurʾān," ʿAlī ibn Abī Ṭālib, and ʿAbd Allāh ibn Masʿūd, to whom many exegetical traditions are attributed. However, the small number of sound exegetical *ḥadīth* coming from most of the companions, even those listed here, suggests that there was no pressing need to embark on a large scale "explanatory drive" during their time.

With the Prophet's death and the conquests that followed from 634 onwards, many companions decided to settle in the newly emerging "Muslim" towns outside Arabia, such as Kufa and Basra in Iraq, while others remained in Medina and Mecca. Thus Ibn Masʿūd became the teacher of the Qurʾān in Iraq, Ibn ʿAbbās in Mecca, and Ubayy ibn Kaʿb in Medina. The *tafsīr* tradition that developed during the course of the first AH (seventh CE) and second AH (eighth CE) centuries often traces its material to these teachers.

The companions who engaged in exegesis had several sources for understanding and interpreting the Qurʾān: parts of the text itself that explained other parts; information received from the Prophet, both oral and praxis; and their own understanding of what the Qurʾanic text meant. They were also familiar with the language of the Qurʾān, the context of the revelation, the Prophet's ways of thinking, and the norms, values, and customs of the Arabs, all of which provided them with a unique basis for making sense of the Qurʾanic text within the overall framework of the emerging "established practice" of the community (living *sunnah*). The final source was the traditions of the People of the Book (the Jews and Christians, or *ahl al-kitāb*), particularly in relation to the narratives in the Qurʾān about past prophets, peoples, and events. Since the Qurʾān in many cases alluded only briefly to these narratives, many companions referred to accounts by converts to Islam, particularly ʿAbd Allāh ibn Sallām (d. 663) and Kaʿb al-Aḥbār (d. 653)), both formerly Jews (Dhahabi, 1976, vol. 1, pp. 42–67).

The need for interpretation increased with the second generation of Muslims, known as "successors" (*tābiʿūn*), who were a more heterogeneous group. They included children of the Arab companions brought up within the new religious (Islamic) environment, Arabic-speaking converts to Islam from other religions, mainly Christianity, and non-Arabic-speaking converts, mainly from Christianity and Zoroastrianism. Their different backgrounds meant that they had to approach the Qurʾān in different ways. Also, the wider the gap between their era and the time of the Prophet, the stronger the need was to address questions of exegesis. With the successors based in key locations such as Medina, Mecca, and the area now known as Iraq, these locations began to develop proto-traditions of local exegesis around the teachings of their respective companions.

It was during the seventh century CE that the domain of Islam expanded dramatically to include all of Arabia and a large part of the Middle East and North Africa, lands previously under the Sassanid and Byzantine empires. Muslims thus came into contact with other civilizations, peoples, and traditions. In due course, many of the peoples of the "conquered" regions professed Islam as their religion. In this new environment, answers to new problems that were primarily legal in nature caused by the expansion had to be found. It was the companions who provided a basis for solving these emerging problems, based on the established practice of the community. The companions had been flexible in relating the text (Qur'ān) and their experiences with the Prophet to the new conditions. In this, they appear to have relied on key objectives of the Qur'anic message, such as "establishing justice." An instance of this was the Caliph ʿUmar's rationale for not distributing the lands (in present-day Iraq) that were conquered during his caliphate (634–644). Unlike the Prophet, ʿUmar refused to distribute the land as booty to warriors, arguing that the relevant Qur'anic verses on the distribution of booty in general did not favor such a division of land. In his view, the land should be retained as public property from which the whole community would benefit, not just the warriors (Maḥmaṣṣāni, 1984, pp. 576–577). In his interpretation of the relevant Qur'anic texts, he was relying on the general Qur'anic principle of justice and of sharing wealth with the wider community.

Also during the seventh century CE, material from both the Jewish and Christian traditions (later to be known as *isrā'īliyyāt*) began to enter the discourse of exegesis via converts to Islam. These converts found an eager audience in exegetes, storytellers, and popular preachers who wanted to fill out details that were often only alluded to in the Qur'anic narratives such as those related to Joseph, Moses, and Jesus. Significant divisions along religio-political and theological lines among Muslims began to emerge in this period too, for example on the definition of concepts such as "believer," "free will" and "predestination." This resulted in substantial differences in opinion among the successors on a range of issues to interpretation of several Qur'anic texts (Dhahabī, 1976, vol. 1, pp. 140–141). Differences of opinion arose concerning who was right and who was wrong, and who was a true Muslim and who was not. Questions such as these contributed to the formation of theological discourse during the seventh century.

Several factors and events thus led to the further development of exegesis apart from the obvious religious reasons: (1) the political conflicts and their associated theological debates that raged after the death of the Prophet and in the wake of the assassination of ʿUthmān, the third caliph, in 656; (2) the conversion of a large number of non-Arabs to Islam; (3) the interest of popular preachers and storytellers in the Qur'anic narratives; and (4) the development of *ḥadīth* and Arabic linguistics and literature as new disciplines. A number of other disciplines also began to develop during the late Umayyad and early Abbasid periods (eighth century CE) and provided further support to the emerging tradition of *tafsīr.* These included *qirā'āt* (readings/recitations of the Qur'ān), which explored the variety of ways in which the Qur'ān could be recited, the legitimate recitations, their sources, and their chains of transmission. Much of this academic activity took place in Iraq (in Kufa and Basra). Another discipline was Arabic grammar in particular and linguistics in general, which began with figures such as al-Khalīl ibn Aḥmad (d. c. 786) and Sībawayh (d. c. 796). Early linguists contributed to the tradition of exegesis directly or indirectly by documenting Arabic dialects and their associated vocabulary and grammar. Formal study of the language of the Qur'ān encouraged a more formal approach to understanding its meaning.

EARLY EXEGESIS. There is debate in the literature on the existence of written exegesis in the seventh century CE (first century AH). While Muslim tradition holds that some written works indeed existed from the mid-seventh century, the evidence of recent research indicates that they had begun to emerge at least by the early part of the eighth century (Gilliot, 2002, p. 104). The earliest exegesis (going back to the time of the Prophet and the companions) was primarily oral and depended on oral transmission; written exegesis developed later. Ibn Khaldūn (d. 1406) suggests that the explanations of the Qur'ān "continued to be transmitted among the early Muslims until knowledge became organized in scholarly disciplines and systematic scholarly works began to be written. At that time, most of these explanations were committed to writing" (Peters, 1990, vol. 2, p. 142). The exegetical writings from this early period, where they exist, are not necessarily complete commentaries; rather, they should be seen as the beginning of the documentation of teachings related to exegesis from the seventh century that continued into the eighth century.

It was perhaps natural for the *tafsīr* to begin with brief explanatory comments on specific words or phrases of the Qur'ān that appeared unclear, difficult, or ambiguous. Much of the very early exegesis falls into this category. No attempt is made to justify the explanatory comments, nor is grammatical or linguistic analysis systematically provided. An example of such a *tafsīr* work is that of Mujāhid ibn Jabr (d. 722), who belongs to the Meccan tradition of *tafsīr* going back to Ibn ʿAbbās. There is also *tafsīr* attributed to Ḥasan al-Baṣrī (d. 728), probably compiled later; Sufyān al-Thawrī (d. 778), a Kufan jurist and traditionalist; and Sufyān ibn ʿUyaynah (d. 811) (Gilliot, 2002). The Shīʿah also attribute the development of this exegetical tradition to ʿAlī and his immediate circle of followers.

Another form of early *tafsīr* was related to the community's interest in legal and ritual matters. Given that a number of Qur'anic verses deal with law and ritual, this must have been an important part of the Prophet's explanatory task. For example, the Qur'ān commands the payment of *zakāt* and the performance of *ṣalāt* but does not give detailed instruction on how this is to be done. It was the Prophet who provided the explanation and demonstration. Attempts to collate, identify, and classify verses related to legal and ritual matters were probably among the earliest *tafsīr* works. An example of this early *tafsīr* is by Muqātil ibn Sulaymān (d. 767). In his *Tafsīr khams mi'at āyah*, Muqātil dealt with several legal topics: prayer, *zakāt*, fasting and pilgrimage; marriage and contracts; and punishments related to theft, adultery, and consumption of wine (Rippin, 1988).

The third most common form of *tafsīr* in this early period was where the exegete focused on certain Qur'anic narratives, particularly about past prophets and their communities. One of the characteristics of Qur'anic narratives is that they are brief, lacking in detail and often without references to time or place. These Qur'anic narratives were elaborated upon and were used by the storytellers (*quṣṣāṣ*) and popular preachers for entertainment or propagation of religion. Much of this extra-Qur'anic material came from Jewish and Christian sources and from the folklore of the region (Rippin, 1988). Using such material, an elaborate narrative was constructed, and even if *ḥadīth* were used in elaborating the narrative there was no emphasis on the precautions taken in *ḥadīth* transmission by the scholars of *ḥadīth* such as scrutinizing the chain of transmission. It was perhaps for this reason that a number of *ḥadīth* scholars were highly skeptical about the value of the material used in this form of exegesis, and were openly critical of the material, which they considered as lacking in authenticity. In the later development of the *tafsīr* tradition, such material came to be known as *isrā'īliyyāt* (Judeo-Christian materials), and highly suspect. But this attitude does not seem to have existed in the early development of the *tafsīr* tradition. In fact, Muslim tradition holds that even companions such as Ibn ʿAbbās approached a number of Jewish and Christian converts to Islam seeking information about the Qur'anic narratives. Those who later contributed to this genre included al-Daḥḥhāk ibn Muzāḥim (d. 723) and al-Suddiyy (d. 746).

The early period of *tafsīr* continued into the eighth century. By the end of the eighth century, the stage was set for exegetical works that covered the entire Qur'ān, from beginning to end. Perhaps the most important figure that emerges in the late eighth and early ninth century is Ṭabarī (d. 923), whose *tafsīr* is extensive and systematic and covered the entire Qur'ān. By this time, *tafsīr* had become a fully established discipline and several scholars were writing complete *tafsīr* works. After this period, the body of work becomes large and varied and includes theological, legal, religio-political, and mystical exegetical works. Authors of *tafsīr* works often responded to and emphasized issues important to their communities, either historically or in a contemporary sense.

TAFSĪR: BETWEEN TRADITION AND REASON. *Tafsīr* is often divided into two broad categories: *tafsīr bi-al-ma'thūr*, exegesis that relies on tradition; and *tafsīr bi-al-ra'y*, exegesis that is based on reason. In Sunnī Islam, *tafsīr bi-al-ma'thūr* is considered the most authoritative form of *tafsīr* because it is based on one of the most important sources of religious authority: the Prophet and his companions who were able to elaborate on the meaning of the Qur'ān based on the Prophet's instructions (*ḥadīth*). Even *tafsīr* whose sources are the successors (the second generation of Muslims) is considered as deriving its authority from the Prophet himself either directly or indirectly.

Some Muslims see *tafsīr bi-al-ra'y* as unacceptable in Islam, based, in their view, on a prohibition of such *tafsīr* in the Qur'ān (Calder, 1993, pp. 131–134) It is also said that the Prophet Muḥammad prohibited interpretation based on *ra'y* on the authority of the *ḥadīth*: "Whoever explains the Qur'ān without knowledge [*ʿilm*] let him take his place in hell" (Qurṭubī, 1993, vol. 1, p. 25). There are also several reports of the companions expressing their fear of interpreting the Qur'ān based on *ra'y*.

However, proponents of *tafsīr bi-al-ra'y* argue that there is nothing wrong with this form of interpretation and that the Qur'ān urges Muslims to reflect upon the text in that way (Calder, 1993, pp. 132–133). They maintain that if *tafsīr* based on *ra'y* is not allowed, then even arriving at Islamic laws from the Qur'anic text is impossible. They also rebut the claim that the companions and successors did not engage in interpretation based on *ra'y*. Some of the proponents of *tafsīr bi-al-ra'y* differentiate between *tafsīr* based on *ra'y* that is acceptable and *tafsīr* based on *ra'y* that is not acceptable. Acceptable *tafsīr bi-al-ra'y* is that supported by linguistic and/or textual evidence while unacceptable *tafsīr bi-al-ra'y* is that which has no such support.

Despite the claims and counter claims, it is clear that *tafsīr* based on *ra'y* occurred in Qur'anic exegesis from its inception. While it may be difficult for some Muslims to suggest that the Prophet Muḥammad based his interpretation of the Qur'ān simply on his own "personal opinion," it could be argued that the origins of the *tafsīr* tradition are strongly grounded in *ra'y*. Comments by companions and successors on the Qur'ān, as recorded in sources like Ṭabarī, indicate that the *tafsīr* of the very early period consisted of three things, all of which were largely related to personal opinion or reason and were not necessarily based on the Prophet's instructions and advice. They include: (1) ad hoc exploration of the meaning of a word or phrase, often through its usage in pre-Islamic times; (2) exploration of Qur'anic narratives on the basis of Judeo-Christian material (*isrā'īliyyāt*); and (3) ad hoc comments or remarks on Qur'anic verses by the earliest Muslims simply on the basis of their personal opinion. On the whole, early understandings of the Qur'ān were characterized by a high degree of subjectivity, fluidity, flexibility, and absence of absolute dogmatism in interpretation.

TRENDS IN TAFSĪR: FROM THE NINTH CENTURY. The ninth century saw the maturing of distinct groups, schools, or trends within Islam, following heated debates among Muslims on religio-political, legal, and theological issues. While the germ of many of these trends lay in the early to mid-seventh century, it took approximately one to two centuries for the trends to form and distinguish themselves from one another. While one may not speak about Sunnī *tafsīr* or Shīʿī or Khārijī *tafsīr* in the seventh century, one can certainly use those terms in the ninth century, by which time the trends were established, with each one supported, inter alia, by a body of *tafsīr* tradition. The vast majority of Muslims (mainstream in terms of numbers) came to be known as Sunnīs. Others were Khārijīs and Shīʿah who were further subdivided into Zaydīs, Twelvers (or Imāmīs), and Ismāʿīlīs. Apart from these groups, there were also the Ṣūfīs (mystics), the theologians (*mutakallimūn*), and the legists, who usually belonged to one of the three key groups: Sunnīs, Shīʿah, and Khārijīs.

Sunnī exegesis. Sunnism developed in the seventh and eighth centuries in the religio-political, theological, and intellectual context that emerged during this period. Early debates on religio-political and theological issues ranging from the imamate, freewill and predestination, God's attributes or the definition of a "believer" or "unbeliever," or the status of grave sinners, that existed among Muslims gave way to the adoption of certain positions by the majority of Muslims in relation to these and other similar matters, which in turn came to be known as *Sunnism.* In the ninth and tenth centuries, Sunnism accepted a set of creeds and legal schools (*madhāhib*). With this came the consolidation of Islamic disciplines that provided the intellectual basis for Sunnism: *tafsīr, ḥadīth, fiqh,* and early Islamic biographical history (*sīrah*). Given that Sunnism reflected the position of the majority of Muslims, it also came to be considered the "orthodoxy." Other groups that did not adhere to the Sunnī positions on theological, religio-political, or legal matters continued to exist and develop in their own ways, however.

Ṭabarī's (d. 923) exegetical work represents the most important early "Sunnī" *tafsīr.* He was born in Tabaristan and studied Qur'ān, *ḥadīth, fiqh,* history, grammar, lexicography, and poetry. While Ṭabarī's writings are enormous and varied, our interest is primarily in his thirty-volume *tafsīr* called *Jāmiʿ al-bayān ʿan taʾwīl āy al-Qurʾān.* Ṭabarī brought together in this massive work much of the *tafsīr*-related material of his time. He commented on each verse of the Qur'ān from beginning to end, brought together *ḥadīth* and other reports attributed to early authorities in relation to each verse, provided grammatical and linguistic analyses, noted systemically the various meanings of each text attributed to early authorities, and finally offered his own interpretation and the reasons for choosing that interpretation. Ṭabarī's *Tafsīr* is usually identified with the tradition of *tafsīr bi-al-maʾthūr* even though in some respects it can be associated with *tafsīr bi-al-raʾy* too. His mastery of the variety of Islamic disciplines and his encyclopedic knowledge make his *tafsīr* unrivalled in Sunnī tradition. Given that he compiled very early material, and that many of those early works are lost, Ṭabarī's *tafsīr* remains to this day the most important single primary source of information about the early period of the *tafsīr* tradition.

From the time of Ṭabarī, a large number of multivolume *tafsīr* works emerged that fall into the broad category of Sunnī *tafsīr,* for example, Ibn Abī Hātim al-Rāzī's (d. 938), *Tafsīr al-Qurʾān al-ʿazīm;* al-Thaʿālabī's (d. 1035) *Kashf al-bayān ʿan tafsīr al-Qurʾān;* Ibn ʿAtiyyah's (d. 1147) *al-Muḥarrar al-wajīz;* al-Nasafī's (d. 1310) *Madārik al-tanzīl wa ḥaqāʾiq al-taʾwīl;* and al-Suyūṭī's (d. 1505) *al-Durr al-manthūr.* Another example is that of Ibn Kathīr (d. 1373), who was a student of the Ḥanbalī theologian Ibn Taymiyah (d. 1328). Ibn Kathīr took Sunnī *tafsīr* to its extreme by rejecting reason-based interpretation of the Qur'ān, insisting on the rejection of *isrāʾīliyyāt,* emphasizing "tradition" to explain the meaning of the text, and indirectly rejecting the intellectual tradition of *tafsīr* (Calder, 1993) It could be argued that the vibrancy, creativity, and innovation that existed in *tafsīr* (as in other disciplines) began to wane from around the thirteenth century. The work of Ibn Kathīr may be seen as representing this phase.

Key characteristics of Sunnī *tafsīr* are emphasis on literal interpretation of the Qur'ān wherever possible, strongly justified by linguistic evidence; reliance on tradition (*ḥadīth/athar*) in explaining the text; use of reason (*raʾy*) within limits; rejection of the idea of esoteric meanings as unjustifiable speculation; respect for the companions of the Prophet collectively as the most important source of religious authority after the Prophet; acceptance of a set of theological positions on God's attributes, eschatology, prophecy and revelation, the definition of a believer (*muʾmin*), and sources of authority in law; and rejection of positions held by rationalist theologians known as Muʿtazilah.

Shīʿī exegesis. The Shīʿah, the second most important religio-political group of Muslims, is subdivided into a number of groups, most importantly, the Zaydīs, the Imāmīs, and the Ismāʿīlīs. Among the most important differences between the Shīʿah in general and the Sunnī Muslims are the Shīʿah doctrine of the *imām* and their view of the companions.

The Zaydīs are the closest to the Sunnī Muslims on these key issues. Several *tafsīr* works by Zaydī scholars have been lost, while many extant works remain in manuscript form. Zaydī *tafsīr* is heavily influenced by Muʿtazilī theology: many Zaydīs rely on the Muʿtazilī exegete Zamakhsharī's (d. 1144) *al-Kashshāf* as a primary source given the similarity between their theological positions and those of the Muʿtazilah (Dhahabi, 1976, vol. 2, p. 308). In many other respects, the exegetical works of Zaydīs come very close to those of the Sunnīs. A Zaydī scholar of the modern period is al-Shawkānī (d. 1834) from Yemen, who wrote *Fatḥ al-qadīr,* a 5-volume *tafsīr* that is largely tradition-based (*al-maʾthūr*) and is widely available. The perceived closeness of the Zaydīs to Sunnism perhaps explains why Shawkānī's *Fatḥ* is widely used in Sunnī circles.

The Imāmīs (also known as Twelvers) are the largest subgroup among Shīʿah. The early Imāmīs strongly criticized the mode of compilation of the Qur'anic text during the caliphate of ʿUthmān. They accused the compilers of the text of omitting and adding verses. However, many later Imāmī scholars toned down the criticism and argued that the existing Qur'anic text did not contain falsifications (Bar-Asher, 1999, p. 16). For Imāmīs, the *imāms* are divinely inspired, endowed with a special *ʿilm* (knowledge). The *imām* should also be nominated as heir by his predecessor through an explicit designation (Bar-Asher, 1999, p. 12). Thus, ʿAli was the first *imām* designated as such by the Prophet himself, and any who befriended him are considered friends of the Shīʿah, but any who opposed him are seen as enemies, an example of an enemy being the Prophet's wife ʿĀʾishah because of her political opposition to ʿAli. Imāmīs were also heavily influenced theologically by the Muʿtazilah. Moreover, they believe in differences between the "inner" and "outer" meanings of the Qurʾān. This allows them to read into the Qurʾanic text their own theological and religio-political views, a characteristic that is not confined to Imāmīs, however, but cuts across almost all groups within Islam. Among the key *tafsīr* works of the Imāmīs are: al-Qummī (early tenth century), *Tafsīr al-Qummī;* al-Ṭūsī (d. 1067), *al-Tibyān fī tafsīr al-Qurʾān;* and al-Ṭabarsī (d. 1153), *Majmaʿ al-bayān fī tafsīr al-Qurʾān.*

On extant evidence, Ismāʿīlīs have not produced any *tafsīr* of the whole of the Qurʾān. Their exegetical works are interpretations of selected verses or groups of verses. According to Gilliot (2002, p. 118), "the science of *tafsīr* (exoteric exegesis) is absent from their literature." Ismāʿīlīs distinguish between the exterior (*ẓāhir*) and interior (*bātin*), related to exoteric and esoteric meanings respectively. For the Ismāʿīlīs, the true meaning of the Qurʾān can be arrived at only through *taʾwīl* (esoteric interpretation), which had its origin in the legitimate *imām* (Gilliot, 2002, p. 118). However, more recent studies suggest that there was a well-developed tradition of Qurʾanic interpretation among Ismāʿīlī thinkers of the Fatimid period.

Khārijī exegesis. Within Muslim tradition, Khārijīs have not contributed to *tafsīr* and other Islamic disciplines as extensively as have other groups. This is most likely because of the relatively small number of Khārijīs who were widely dispersed in North Africa, the Arabian Gulf, and East Africa. Most Khārijī *tafsīr* works were written by Ibāḍīs, a "moderate" Khārijī group, from a Sunnī point of view. Some of the Khārijī works have been lost, such as the *tafsīr* of ʿAbd al-Raḥmān ibn Rustum al-Fārisi (ninth century). Among the best known Khārijī *tafsīr* works are the *Tafsīr* of Hūd ibn Muḥakkam al-Hawwāri (d. c. 893) from North Africa and *Himyān al-zād ilā dār al-maʿād* (13 vols.) of Muḥammad ibn Yūsuf al-Itfish (d. 1913), also from North Africa.

Khārijī *tafsīr* relies heavily on the literal meaning of the text and often does not delve into deeper meanings. More recent research suggests a revision of the notion of a "wooden literalism" as associated with Khārijī exegetical thinking. Like other groups in Islam, Khārijīs interpret the text in line with their theological positions, an example being that the grave sinner (*murtakib al-kabīrah*) is an unbeliever (*kāfir*) and will remain in Hell forever (Dhahabī, 1976, vol. 2, pp. 329–344).

***Kalām*-based exegesis.** *Kalām* is the discipline of dialectical theology in Islam. Debates on the definition of "believer" (*muʾmin*), God's predetermination of events, human freedom versus God's power, the unity of God, God's attributes, God's justice, and the status of categories of human beings in the hereafter continued in intellectual circles in the seventh and eighth centuries. Theologians who wrote *tafsīr* works, who belonged to various groupings in Islam such as Sunnīs, Shīʿah, or Khārijīs, had to deal with these debates in their works. Among theologians, the Muʿtazilīs and Ashʿarīs have been the most prominent in their contribution to *tafsīr.*

Many theologians who wrote exegetical works were from a Muʿtazilī background. Many of these works have not survived, and those that have, while they may not be strictly speaking *tafsīrs,* give a sense of *kalām*-based exegetical work. Qādi ʿAbd al-Jabbār (d. 1025) made great contributions to this field in his *al-Mughnī* (a juridical and theological encyclopedia) (Gilliot, 2002, p. 114). The Shīʿī scholar al-Ṭabarsī's *Majmaʿ al-bayān fī tafsīr al-Qurʾān* is heavily influenced by Muʿtazilī doctrines. The most famous of Muʿtazilī *tafsīrs* is al-Zamakhsharī's *al-Kashshāf ʿan ḥaqāʾiq al-tanzīl.* However, Zamakhsharī's "reputation for exegesis rests not so much on his Muʿtazilism as on his qualities as a grammarian, philologist, and master of rhetorical and literary criticism" (Gilliot, 2002, p. 115).

Kalām-based *tafsīr* of the Muʿtazilīs emphasize interpretation of the Qurʾān in line with what reason demands, especially in relation to theological matters, rejection of "traditions" that conflicted with their theological positions, the use of linguistic evidence to support interpretation (particularly when literal meanings contradicted their theological positions), and an emphasis on the metaphorical meanings of the Qurʾān.

Ṣūfī exegesis. Ṣūfī exegesis was associated with the development of the Ṣūfī movement, *taṣawwuf,* which in part grew out of the early religious and political tensions within the Muslim community. It also arose from intense interest in the spiritual dimension of Islam, distaste for the materialism that developed as a result of the great wealth generated by the conquests (*futūḥāt*) of the seventh century, and the legalism that came to dominate Islam from the ninth century. For many Ṣūfīs, the theological, legal, and religio-political debates of the seventh and eighth centuries drew believers away from the purpose of the Qurʾān towards legalism and other irrelevancies. For Ṣūfīs it was the language of the Qurʾān that held the answers to deeper questions, such as the nature of human existence and its relation to the divine. The inner dimension of the Qurʾān was paramount, and one could not arrive at those inner meanings by superficial reading and argument over points of law or theology. For Ṣūfīs, it was the allusions in the Qurʾanic text that were most closely related to the human spiritual condition.

Ṣūfī *tafsīr* is often traced back to figures like Ḥasan al-Baṣrī (d. 728), some of whose teachings are scattered in various *tafsīr* works, including that of Ṭabarī. Among the most influential Ṣūfī *tafsīr* works (or related works) are those of Ibn ʿArabī (d. 1240), as well as of other great Ṣūfīs, such as al-Qāshānī (d. 1329), al-Sulamī (d. 1021) in his *Haqāʾiq al-tafsīr,* and ʿAbd al-Karīm al-Qushayrī (d. 1072) in his *Laṭāʾif al-ishārāt.* Ṣūfī *tafsīr* also continued right up to the modern period and includes al-Maybūdī's *Kashf al-asrār wa*

ʿuddat al-abrār (written in Persian), al-Brusāwī's (d. 1725) *Rūh al-bayān*, and al-Alūsī's (d. 1854?) *Rūh al-maʿānī.*

Some Ṣūfī *tafsīrs* are primarily "theoretical," while others are chiefly "intuitive" (Chaudhary, 2002, p. 1484). Ibn ʿArabī's (d. 1240) works are considered to belong to the theoretical tradition. He did not compose a *tafsīr* himself; the work usually attributed to him, *Tafsīr ibn al-ʿArabī*, was written by al-Qāshānī, but it does reflect the thought of Ibn ʿArabī. From a Sunnī perspective, the intuitive Ṣūfī *tafsīrs* were more moderate in their claims and interpretations. Examples of such *tafsīrs* include al-Sulamī's *Haqāʾiq al-tafsīr*, one of the most important works in Ṣūfī *tafsīr.*

TAFSĪR IN THE MODERN PERIOD: FROM THE MID-NINETEENTH CENTURY. *Tafsīr* of the modern period begins with the mid-nineteenth century and follows several trends. Many writers, however, adopted traditionalist patterns and approaches; in fact, many traditionalist Muslims of the modern period have written Qurʾanic commentaries that differ little from premodern works. This applies to the Sunnīs, as well as to other groups within Islam. Examples include al-Shawkānī's (d. 1839) *Fatḥ al-qadīr;* al-Alūsī's (d. 1853) *Rūḥ al-maʿānī*, and al-Marāghī's (d. 1945) *Tafsīr al-Marāghī.*

Modernist exegesis. Despite this, a significantly richer environment has emerged for exegetical work in which writers make a conscious effort to relate the Qurʾān to issues in the modern world. For many Muslims, particularly of a non-traditionalist orientation, this is the key problem for exegesis today, and it was in this light that Sayyid Ahmad Khan (d. 1898) of India and Muḥammad ʿAbduh (d. 1905) of Egypt, two modernist Muslims, embarked on their exegetical work.

Although from different parts of the Muslim world, both knew life for Muslims under British colonial rule. Furthermore, although they approached the Qurʾān differently in many respects, their works had much in common (Gilliot, 2002, pp. 126–129). Both stressed the importance of moving away from imitation of the past towards a responsive approach compatible with modern life. Both believed that the Qurʾān could guide Muslims towards becoming part of the modern world. Both had an affinity with rationalist thinkers in early Islam, such as the Muʿtazilah, and saw the need for interpretation of the Qurʾān with a scientific worldview in mind. In line with this, both, each in his own way, wanted to reinterpret what appeared to be "miracles" in the Qurʾanic text in line with modern science and reason. Both believed that the contemporary exegete should make the Qurʾān familiar to the modern mind, and realized that the exegetical procedures and jargon of previous generations had made the text obscure. In their works and teaching they argued for the rethinking of approaches to the Qurʾān in the modern period and attempted to demonstrate how this could be undertaken. Both these scholars were highly influential, particularly until the middle of the twentieth century.

Muḥammad ʿAbduh's treatment of the issue of polygamy is an example of modernist *tafsīr.* The problem is whether men should continue to be allowed four wives in an era of greater gender equality and in the light of changed economic, social, political, and economic conditions. ʿAbduh's solution to this problem was to interpret some of the phrases in the relevant Qurʾanic text. ʿAbduh argued that, by Qurʾanic logic, a man should be married to only one woman because permission to marry more than one is conditional upon "justice," which, according to the Qurʾān itself, must be strived for but is impossible to achieve. According to ʿAbduh, Qurʾanic logic states that the only form of marriage ideally should be monogamy (Riḍā, n.d., vol. 4, pp. 369–370). This example highlights the problems associated with the interpretative efforts of many modernist Muslims. At times the interpretation is forced upon the text when changed norms and values are taken as the basis for a fresh understanding.

"Scientific" exegesis. Another distinctly modern approach involves examining the Qurʾān in the light of modern science. There are two ways in which "scientific" exegesis could be understood. First, the approach taken by the Egyptian Ṭanṭāwī Jawharī (d. 1940), who wrote *al-Jawāhir fī tafsīr al-Qurʾān al-karīm.* Although referred to as a *tafsīr*, it is not a *tafsīr* in the strict classical sense. Rather, it is an encyclopedia that enables Muslims to link the text of the Qurʾān to a modern scientific worldview (Gilliot, 2002, p. 130). Although his treatment of the Qurʾān is also called "*al-tafsīr al-ʿilmī*" (scientific exegesis), Ṭanṭāwī Jawharī was not interested in what in the mid to late twentieth century came to be known as the "scientific miraculous nature of the Qurʾān" (*al-iʿjāz al-ʿilmī*). His main interest was to encourage Muslims to learn and understand the sciences, which he saw as the main factor driving modern societies.

The second use of "scientific exegesis" is, in contrast, the use of science to highlight the so-called "scientific miraculous nature of the Qurʾān," which is essentially apologetic and attempts to demonstrate that modern scientific achievements were somehow foreseen in the Qurʾān fourteen centuries ago. It is also used as evidence that the Qurʾān had to have been composed by God, as the unlettered Prophet could not have possessed such knowledge. Its practitioners read what they consider scientific interpretations into the Qurʾān. The popular nature of this discourse is demonstrated by the large number of conferences, seminars, and publications devoted to it. Many Muslim thinkers, however, criticize it as ignoring the open-ended nature of scientific discovery and as misreading the Qurʾān, ignoring how the texts were understood by the earliest Muslims and also by the succeeding generations. Notwithstanding these criticisms, this latter form of scientific exegesis has become one of the most popular forms of exegesis in the modern period.

Sociopolitical exegesis. Sayyid Quṭb (d. 1966) wrote his *Fī Ẓilāl al-Qurʾān* essentially to provide a new perspective on the relevance of the Qurʾān to modern Muslims. Quṭb's particular style of writing, his uncompromising commitment to his view of Islam, and his portrayal of many of the institutions of modern society as *jāhiliyyah* (akin to pre-Islamic institutions, that is, un-Islamic), ensure him an important place among those whose primary aim is to establish Islam as the dominant sociopolitical force in Muslim societies. Quṭb's work, a good example of a *tafsīr* of a personal reflective nature, is somewhat divorced from standard exegetical tradition in its more free-floating ideas: it draws in the modern world and its challenges, and refuses to follow dogmatically early approaches to *tafsīr*. It is, as the title suggests, "in the shade" of the Qurʾān, and attempts to find relevance and meaning at a personal and collective level for Muslims of the modern period. This perhaps explains its wide acceptability among Muslim youth. It lies at the heart of an understanding of Islam as an ideology and a system. In many ways it is the most inspiring and powerful *tafsīr* in the contemporary world for many young Muslims influenced by the thought of Muslim Brotherhood.

Literary-historical exegesis. Studying the Qurʾān from a literary perspective is not new but the approaches adopted and the modern emphasis on the Qurʾanic narratives and whether these stories represent any historical reality are new. Tāhā Ḥusayn (d. 1973) caused a stir in Egypt when he argued for analyzing the Qurʾān as a literary text and suggested that the biblical stories mentioned in the Qurʾān may not necessarily be historical. Amīin al-Khūlī of Egypt (d. 1967) also argued for a study of the Qurʾān from a literary perspective, keeping in mind how this text was received by the first recipients (the Prophet and the companions) because this first reception and understanding are crucial to such a project.

This emphasis on the study of the Qurʾān from a literary perspective was taken up by a number of scholars who benefited from al-Khūlī's methodological insights. Muḥammad Khalafallah, also from Egypt, applied these ideas into his doctoral dissertation (in 1947), *al-Fann al-qasasī fī al-Qurʾān al-karīm*, which again caused a stir among the religious establishment of Egypt, leading to significant personal hardship for Khalafallah. Given the sensitivities associated with such studies, particularly if they question the "truth" (historical truth) of any aspect of the Qurʾān, not many Muslims attempt such studies.

Thematic exegesis. In the mid-twentieth century, another popular approach emerged called thematic exegesis. This approach emphasizes the unity of the Qurʾanic text over the interpretation of verses in isolation. Verse by verse treatment in exegesis is seen as distorting the Qurʾanic message, and as not giving sufficient emphasis to related verses on a particular theme across the Qurʾān. This form of exegesis also goes back to the ideas developed by Amīn al-Khulī, who emphasized that it is more beneficial to interpret the Qurʾān by focusing on specific themes. In this way, one can explore in depth such concepts as "justice" and "unity of God" by looking at all aspects of the concept as dealt with in the Qurʾān in different *sūrahs*. Such an approach, besides enabling an in-depth look at relevant issues, facilitates a more "objective" treatment of the issues at hand. While these observations may be true about the thematic exegesis to a large extent, practitioners of thematic exegesis often advocate quite different views about how it should be undertaken, the benefits of such an exercise, and the reasons for engaging in it. Practitioners argue that this approach can be useful today in dealing with questions such as women's rights, human rights, and ethical problems, to give a few examples. Thematic exegesis has become very popular and influential in many parts of the Muslim world, including Egypt and Indonesia.

Feminist exegesis. Muslim feminism brings cultural politics into exegetical scholarship. Several Muslim feminist exegetes have recently argued that it is important today to re-read the Qurʾān because the "male-oriented" readings of early and modern exegetes and theologians are biased against women. Historical injustices against women are thus seen to have been perpetuated in these readings. Feminist interpreters argue that if one half of the Muslim population is to enjoy equality with men, the Qurʾanic rules and values concerning women must be understood in the light of the sociohistorical context of the revelation. The argument continues that if the context in which the event occurs changes, so can the interpretations and rulings derived therefrom. Although it is accepted that the Qurʾān improved the position of women, the argument of these feminists is that the cultural and historical context of the revelation has remained a barrier to realizing the Qurʾanic ideals regarding women (Wadud-Muhsin, 1988; Barlas, 2002).

Unlike some so-called "radical feminists," mainstream Muslim feminists are not interested in casting religion and scripture aside in order to gain the rights they are seeking. Muslim feminists use the Qurʾān to assert their rights as women. Their weapon is the Qurʾān itself and how it should be read. Fatima Mernissi (1991) developed a critical approach to Islamic tradition and ventured into hitherto "sacred" areas. In a number of her works, she has examined the Qurʾanic text in the light of the *ḥadīth*, focusing on the biases of some of the companions who narrated these *ḥadīth*, particularly those concerning women. Amina Wadud-Muhsin and Asma Barlas have argued for a return to the message of the original text but with an emphasis on relating the Qurʾān to its historical and contemporary contexts as argued by Fazlur Rahman, in the light of the "spirit of the Qurʾān" (Wadud-Muhsin, 1988, p. 129).

***Tafsīr* and the Question of the Relevance of the Qurʾān Today.** The literature on Qurʾān interpretation in the modern period shows that there is a strong desire on the part of Muslims, scholars and laity alike, to find the relevance of the Qurʾanic text to contemporary issues without compromising the Qurʾanic value system and its essential and core beliefs and practices. It is seen as particularly urgent in relation to the ethico-legal content of the Qurʾān (Saeed, 2004). There are, broadly speaking, three trends among those who believe that the ethico-legal content of the Qur'ān is relevant to Muslims in the modern period: textualists, semitextualists, and contextualists.

Textualists seek to maintain the interpretation of the ethico-legal content of the Qur'ān as handed down in the tradition and argue for a strict following of the text (as well as the "authorized" interpretations within the tradition, be they Sunnī or Shī'ī). Where possible, they prefer to be faithful to the literal reading of the ethico-legal texts. For many textualists, there is no need at all for the scripture or its understanding to change. For them, it is the Qur'ān that should guide Muslims, not any so-called modern "needs." The Qur'ān (both in its text and meaning) is permanent and universal. For instance, if the Qur'ān says that a man may marry four wives, then that should remain so forever. Textualists may be found today among those referred to as Salafīs, neo-Salafīs, and traditionalists.

Semitextualists essentially follow the textualists, but attempt to present the Qur'ān's ethico-legal content in a modern garb. They do not ask fundamental questions about the relationship the ethico-legal content may have to the sociohistorical context of the Qur'ān or about interpretations of that ethico-legal content in the following generations. They package the ethico-legal content in a somewhat "modern" idiom, often within an apologetic discourse. Semitextualists can be sympathizers or members of modern neo-revivalist movements, such as the Muslim Brotherhood and Jamā'at-i-Islāmī, as well as some traditionalists and some modernists.

In contrast, the contextualists emphasize the sociohistorical context of the ethico-legal content of the Qur'ān, as well as its subsequent interpretations. They argue for understanding the ethico-legal content in the light of the political, social, historical, religious, and economic contexts in which this content was revealed, understood, interpreted, and applied. Thus they argue for a high degree of freedom for the modern Muslim scholar in arriving at what is mutable (changeable) and immutable (unchangeable) in the area of ethico-legal content. Contextualists are found among what Fazlur Rahman called neo-modernists and among more "liberal" Muslim thinkers today.

The methodological innovations introduced in Qur'anic exegesis by important figures such as Fazlur Rahman to resolve this problem are highly relevant (Saeed, 2004, pp. 37–66). They represent an important step in relating the Qur'anic text to the contemporary needs of Muslim societies. Rahman relies heavily on understanding the historical context of the revelation at the macro level, and then relating it to a particular need of the modern period. In this, he draws on the idea of the "prophetic spirit" or, in other words, how the Prophet might act were he living in these times. Thus one could argue that many modern-era Muslim scholars, like Rahman, are preoccupied with a correct method of interpreting the Qur'ān that will show its relevance to the contemporary needs of Muslims (Rahman, 1982). They emphasize the thematic and spiritual unity of the Qur'ān, and that the revelation was not a "book" given at one time but a process over a twenty-two-year period, reflecting, throughout the mission's vicissitudes and the needs of the first community. The Qur'ān's guidance, in their view, was directly connected with, and organically related to, the linguistic, cultural, political, economic, and religious life of the people of Hijaz and, more broadly, of Arabia.

More radical approaches to the interpretation of the Qur'ān are also entertained by a number of Muslim thinkers today, including Muḥammad Arkoun and Nasr Ḥāmid Abū Zayd. While these approaches are not yet widely accepted, it seems likely that we will be seeing a more intense debate on the rethinking of approaches to the Qur'ān, and perhaps a more creative period in the area of *tafsīr*.

See Also Tafsīr.

Bibliography

Alūsī, Maḥmūd ibn 'Abd Allāh al-. *Rūḥ al-ma'ānī fī tafsīr al-Qur'ān al-'aẓīm wa-l-sab' al-mathānī.* 30 vols. in 15. Cairo, 1926; reprint, Beirut, n.d.

Arkoun, Mohammed. *Rethinking Islam: Common Questions, Uncommon Answers.* Translated by Robert D. Lee. Boulder, Colo., 1994.

'Ayyāshī, Muḥammad ibn Mas'ūd al-. *Tafsīr.* 2 vols. Tehran, 1961.

Baljon, J. M. S. *Modern Muslim Koran Interpretation (1880–1960).* Leiden, 1968.

Balkhī, Muqātil ibn Sulaymān al-. *Tafsīr al-khams mi'at āyah min al-Qur'ān.* Edited by I. Goldfeld. Shfaram, Israel, 1980.

Barlas, Asma. "Believing Women" in *Islam: Unreading Patriarchal Interpretations of the Qur'an.* Austin, Tex., 2002.

Bayḍāwī, 'Abd Allāh ibn 'Umar al-. *Anwār al-tanzīl wa-asrār al-ta'wīl.* Edited by H. O. Fleischer. 2 vols. Leipzig, 1846; Beirut, 1988.

Calder, Norman. "*Tafsir* from Tabari to Ibn Kathir: Problems in the Description of a Genre, Illustrated with References to the Story of Abraham." In *Approaches to the Qur'an,* edited by G. R. Hawting and Abdul-Kader A. Shareef. London and New York, 1993.

Chaudhary, Tahir. "Tafsir Literature: its Origins and Development." In *Encyclopaedia of the Holy Qur'ān,* edited by N.K. Singh and A.R. Agwan, pp. 1473–1488. 5 vols. Dehli, 2000.

Dhahabī, Muḥammad Ḥusayn al-. *Al-Tafsīr wa-l-mufassirūn.* 2 vols. Cairo, 1976.

Esack, Farid. *Qur'ān: Liberation and Pluralism.* Oxford, 1988.

Gharnāṭī, Abū Ḥayyān al-. *Tafsīr al-baḥr al-muḥīṭ.* 8 vols. Cairo, 1911. Edited by 'Ādil Aḥmad 'Abd al-Mawjūd and 'Alī Muḥammad Mu'awwaḍ. Beirut, 1993.

Gibb, H. A. R., and J. H. Kramers, eds. *Shorter Encyclopaedia of Islam.* Leiden, Netherlands, 1961.

Gilliot, Claude. "Exegesis of the Qur'ān: Classical and Medieval." In *Encyclopaedia of the Qur'ān,* edited by Jane Dammen McAuliffe, pp. 99–124. Leiden, Netherlands, 2002.

Gilliot, Claude. "Exegesis of the Qur'ān: Early Modern and Contemporary." In *Encyclopaedia of the Qur'ān,* edited by Jane

Dammen McAuliffe, pp. 124–142. Leiden, Netherlands, 2002.

Hawting, G. R., and Abdul-Kader A. Shareef, eds. *Approaches to the Qur'ān.* London, 1993.

Hūd ibn Muḥakkam (Muhkim al-Huwwārī). *Tafsīr.* Edited by Balḥājj Sa'īd Shariff. 4 vols. Beirut, 1990.

Ibn Kathīr, 'Imād al-Dīn Ismā'īl ibn 'Umar. *Tafsīr al-Qur'ān al-Azīm.* Beirut, 1987.

Ibn Khaldūn, 'Abd al-Raḥmān. *The Muqaddimah: An Introduction to History.* Translated by Franz Rosenthal. 3 vols. New York, 1958; 2d rev. ed., Princeton, N.J., 1967.

Ibn Sa'd, *al-Tabaqāt al-kubrā,* 8 vols. Beirut, 1957.

Jansen, J. J. G. *The Interpretation of the Koran in Modern Egypt.* Leiden, 1974.

Lane, Edward William. *Arabic-English Lexicon,* VIII. New York, 1955–1956.

Maḥmaṣṣānī, Ṣubhī, *Turāth al-khulafā' al-rāshidīn fi al-fiqh wa al-qadā',* Beirut, 1984.

Mernissi, Fatima. *Women and Islam: an Historical and Theological Enquiry,* Translated by Mary Jo Lakeland. Oxford, U.K., 1991.

Mujāhid ibn Jabr. *Al-Tafsīr.* Edited Muḥammad 'Abd al-Salām Abū al-Nīl. Cairo, 1989.

Nasafī, 'Abd Allāh ibn Aḥmad ibn Maḥmūd al-. *Madārik al-tanzīl wa-ḥaqā'iq al-ta'wīl.* Edited by Zakariyyā 'Umayrāt. 2 vols. Beirut, 1995.

Peters, F. E. *Judaism, Christianity, and Islam: The Classical Texts and Their Interpretation,* vol. 2: *The Word and the Law and the People of God.* Princeton, N.J., 1990.

Poonawala, Ismail K. "Muḥammad Darwaza's Principles of Modern Exegesis." In *Approaches to the Qur'ān,* edited by G. R. Hawting and Abdul-Kader A Shareef. London and New York, 1993.

Qummī, Abū al-Ḥasan 'Alī ibn Ibrāhīm al-. *Tafsīr.* Edited by Tayyib al-Mūsawī al-Jazā'irī. 2 vols. Najaf, 1967; Beirut, 1991.

Qurṭubī, Muḥammad ibn Aḥmad al-Anṣārī al-, *Al-Jāmi' li aḥkām al-Qur'ān,* 10 vols. Beirut, 1993.

Quṭb, Sayyid. *Fī Zilāl al-Qur'ān.* Beirut, 1992.

Rahman, Fazlur. *Islam and Modernity: Transformation of an Intellectual Tradition.* Chicago, 1982.

Rahman, Fazlur. *Major Themes of the Qur'ān.* 2d ed. Minneapolis, 1989.

Rāzī, Abū al-Futūḥ Ḥusayn ibn 'Alī. *Rawḥ al-jinān wa-rūḥ al-janān.* 12 vols. Tehran, 1962–1965.

Rāzī, Fakhr al-Dīn al-. *Al-Tafsīr al-kabīr (Mafātīḥ al-ghayb).* Edited by Muḥammad Muḥyi al-Dīn Abd al-Ḥamīd. 32 vols. in 16. Cairo, 1933; Beirut, 1981.

Riḍā, Muḥammad Rashīd, and Muḥammad 'Abduh. *Tafsīr al-Qur'ān al-ḥakim al-shahir bi-tafsīr al-Manār.* 12 vols. Beirut, n.d.

Rippin, Andrew, ed. *Approaches to the History of the Interpretation of the Qur'ān.* Oxford, 1988.

Saeed, Abdullah, "Fazlur Rahman: a Framework for Interpreting the Ethico-Legal Content of the Qur'an." In *Modern Muslim Intellectuals and the Qur'ān,* edited by Suha Taji-Farouki, pp. 37–66. Oxford, 2004.

Saeed, Abdullah. "Rethinking 'Revelation' as a Precondition for Reinterpreting the Qur'ān: A Qur'anic Perspective." *Journal of Qur'anic Studies* 1, no. 1 (1999): 93–114.

Sells, Michael. *Approaching the Qur'ān: The Early Revelations.* Ashland, Ore., 1999.

Shawkānī, Muḥammad ibn 'Alī al-. *Fatḥ al-qadīr al-jāmi' bayna fannay al-riwāyah waal-dirāyah fī 'ilm al-tafsīr.* 5 vols. Cairo, 1930; reprint, Beirut, 1973.

Sufyān al-Thawrī. *Al-Tafsīr.* Edited by Imtiyāz 'Alī 'Arshī. Beirut, 1983.

Sulamī, Abu 'Abd al-Raḥmān Muḥammad ibn al-Ḥusayn al-. *Ziyādāt ḥaqā'iq al-tafsīr.* Edited by Gerhard Böwering. Beirut, 1995.

Suyūṭī, Jalāl al-Dīn al-. *Al-Durr al-manthūr fī l-tafsīr bi-l-ma'thūr.* 6 vols. Beirut, 1990.

Suyūṭī, Jalāl al-Dīn al-. *Al-Itqān fī 'ulūm al-Qur'ān.* Cairo, 1974–1975.

Ṭabarī, Abū Ja'far Muḥammad ibn Jarīr al-. *Jāmi' al-bayān 'an ta'wīl āy al-Qur'ān.* Edited by Maḥmūd Muḥammad Shākir and Aḥmad Muḥammad Shākir. 16 vols. Cairo, 1954–1968.

Tabarsī, Abū 'Alī al-Faḍl ibn al-Ḥasan al-. *Majma' al-bayān fī tafsīr al-Qur'ān.* 30 vols. in 6. Beirut, 1961.

Taji-Farouki, Suha, ed. *Modern Muslim Intellectuals and the Qur'ān.* Oxford, 2004.

Troll, Christian. *Sayyid Ahmad Khan: A Reinterpretation of Muslim Theology.* New Delhi, 1978.

Tustarī, Sahl ibn 'Abd Allāh al-. *Tafsīr al-Qur'ān al-'azīm.* Cairo, 1911.

Wadud-Muhsin, Amina. "Qur'ān and Woman." In *Liberal Islam: A Source Book,* edited by Charles Kurzman, pp. 127–138. New York, 1998.

Wansbrough, John. *Quranic Studies: Sources and Methods of Scriptural Interpretation.* Oxford, 1977; reprint, Amherst, N.Y., 2004.

Wild, Stefan, ed. *The Qur'ān as Text.* Leiden, 1996.

Zamakhsharī, Maḥmūd ibn 'Umar al-. *Al-Kashshāf 'an ḥaqā'iq ghawāmid al-tanzīl wa-'uyūn al-aqāwīl fi wujūh al-ta'wīl.* 4 vols. Beirut, 1947; edited by Muḥammad 'Abd al-Salām Shāhīn. 4 vols. Beirut, 1995.

Zarkashī, Muḥammad ibn 'Abd Allāh al-. *Al-Burhān fī 'ulūm al-Qur'ān.* Beirut, 1988.

Zurqānī, Muḥammad 'Abd al-'Aẓīm al-. *Manāhil al-'irfān fī 'ulūm al-Qur'ān.* Beirut, 1988.

ABDULLAH SAEED (2005)

QUR'ĀN: ITS ROLE IN MUSLIM PRACTICE AND LIFE

The Qur'ān is the primary source of theological and religious knowledge in Islam. Its significance goes beyond the concept of a mere written document, for it is seen by Muslims as a paradigm for God's communication with human beings and as a token of divine presence in the world. Reflecting its paradigmatic nature, the Qur'ān calls itself *Umm al-Kitab* (literally "Mother of the Book" or "Sourcebook," *sūrah* 13:39). It is made up of "signs" (*ayah,* pl. *ayat*) whose semantic messages replicate all of the "languages" that are to be found in the world of human experience. As a form of divine expression, the Qur'ān acts as a spiritual touchstone and code of conduct, detailing the main themes of the message of Islam as revealed to the Prophet Muḥammad. As a theological statement, it is a criterion of discernment (*furqan*), which demonstrates the existence and nature of Allāh, the One God. As a form of literature, it is regarded by both Muslims and Arab Christians as the source of the Classical Arabic language. As a work of meta-history, it imparts meaning to human affairs by detailing God's plan for the world in the rise and fall of civilizations and in the creation and end of the universe.

As the written text declares, the original form of the Qur'ān is with God, "a Glorious Qur'ān preserved in a well-guarded tablet" (85:21–22). Although it takes on the character and logic of human language, the Qur'ān remains in essence a transcendent medium of communication, free from the limitations of purely human expression. This essential Qur'ān was communicated to the Prophet Muḥammad through the mediation of Gabriel, the angel of revelation, in words that were written down and memorized by the pious and later codified into an official document *(mushaf)*. However, the Prophet claimed that he also received the Qur'ān in humanly unintelligible sounds like the ringing of bells: apparently, at least part of the revelation came to him as an inspiration directly from God. This bestowal of divine knowledge, which according to the Qur'ān was sent down directly onto Muḥammad's heart (26:94) on the Night of Power (*laylat al-qadr,* 96:1), enabled the Prophet to become not only the mouthpiece, but also the prime interpreter of the divine word.

For more than fourteen centuries, Muslims of all sects and schools of thought have internalized the Qur'ān as the transcendent word of God, which is relevant for all times and places. Because its divine origin makes the Qur'ān a sacred, and therefore unique, form of communication, its significance depends on a worldview that accepts its authenticity. Consequently, its significance for the pious Muslim is entirely different from that of the non-Muslim or agnostic. Because each and every written word or recited sound of the Qur'ān is revered as divine in origin, any attempt to create a critical or historicist interpretation of its text can only do violence to the revelation in terms of its meaning to its audience. One who wishes to understand the resonance of the Qur'ān in the heart of the Muslim believer must not overlook the surplus of meaning in a text that is considered so sacred that it is often recited in a baby's ears as soon as it emerges from the womb. As the sixth Shīʿī *imām,* Ja'far al-Sadiq, declared, "Whoever recites the Qur'ān while yet a youth and has faith, the Qur'ān becomes intermingled with his flesh and blood" (Ayoub, vol. 1, p. 12).

SACRED CHARACTER. As a revelation directly from God, the Qur'ān is the main theophany of Islam. Although it was revealed to the prophet Muḥammad in the Arabic language (12:2), its text is believed to consist of divine rather than human speech (9:6). Thus, its significance for Muslims is similar to that of the Logos (divine speech) in Christianity. However, unlike the Christian view of scripture as a divinely inspired discourse, the words of the Qur'ān are regarded by Muslims as divine in and of themselves. In Islam, the divine word does not become flesh, but the words and letters of the Qur'ān retain a profound sense of power and mystery. Muslims show their reverence for the Qur'ān by approaching it in a state of ritual purity or ablution (*ṭahārah*). At times, it may also be treated as a prized artifact, as demonstrated by the production of hand-decorated, calligraphic copies and the popularity of medieval Qur'ān manuscripts in collections of Islamic art. Ṣūfīs, Muslim mystics, have long regarded the Qur'ān as a paradigm for divine knowledge and inspiration. In the thirteenth century, the great Andalusian Ṣūfī Ibn ʿArabi organized the entirety of *al-Futuhat al-Makkiyah* (The Meccan inspirations), his magnum opus, to conform to the order and meaning of the discourses and signs of the divine text.

POWER AND PROTECTION. Because the word of God resonates continually in sacred scripture, the divine text and even the calligraphic text of the Qur'ān are believed to possess awesome powers. In a well known verse the Qur'ān states: "Were we to cause this Qur'ān to descend on a mountain you would see it humbled and torn asunder in awe of God" (59:21). A tradition reports that when the fifth *sūrah* was sent down to the prophet Muḥammad while he was traveling on a she-camel, the animal fell to the ground, unable to support the divine words. However, this divine Qur'ān, which even the mountains cannot sustain, is also a source of tranquility and peace for the hearts of those with faith. Muslims consider this quality a divine gift of mercy; as the commentator al-Qurtubi asserts, "Had God not fortified the hearts of his servants with the ability to bear [the Qur'ān], . . . they would have been too feeble and distraught before its great weight" (al-Qurtubi, vol. 1, p. 4).

The powers of the Qur'ān are reputed in Muslim folklore to heal the sick, to cause strange natural occurrences, and even to charm snakes and find lost objects. When placed in a locket, a verse of the Qur'ān may protect a child from the evil eye, and strengthen, or break the bond of love between two people. Qur'anic verses are often inscribed on vehicles, shops, and entrances to homes or public buildings to provide protection against evil and to express gratitude for God's bounties. In medieval Islam, Qur'anic words, phrases, or even entire verses were often written or uttered in combination with ancient Aramaic words or symbols as formulas against magic. Today, Muslims of all beliefs, from literalistic *Wahhābīs* in Saudi Arabia to mystical Ṣūfīs and rationalist Pakistani engineers, often recite selected short *sūrahs* of the Qur'ān as a protection against evil or ill fortune. *Sūrahs* that are especially popular for such purposes include *al-Kahf* (The cave, 18), *Ya-Sin* (36) and *al-Waqi'ah* (The event, 56). In modern Egypt, these and other protective *sūrahs* are compiled in small booklets that police officers carry in their shirt-pockets as a protection against the dangers of their job.

In times of sickness and adversity, believers turn to the Qur'ān as a source of "healing and mercy for the people of faith" (17:82). The first *sūrah* of the Qur'ān, *al-Fatihah* (The opening) is sometimes called *Al-Shafiyah* (The healer). It is often recommended that a sick person drink the water in which a parchment inscribed with Qur'anic verses has been soaked; this custom has persisted to the present day in many areas of the Muslim world. In some countries, Qur'anic verses are written on incantation bowls with a special type of ink. When the bowl is rinsed with water and the water is drunk, the power of the Qur'anic verses in the ink mixes with the water and enters the body of the believer as a charm. The commentator al-Qurtubi cautions that when using the Qur'ān for such purposes, a person seeking a cure must invoke the name of God in every breath he or she takes while drinking the potion, and must be sincere in prayerful attention, because his or her reward depends upon that sincerity. In the text of the Qur'ān itself, the medicinal power of the Qur'ān to heal is often linked to its rhetorical power to persuade, as in the following passage: "Oh humankind! An exhortation has come to you from your Lord, a healing for what is in your breasts, and a guidance and mercy for those who believe" (10:57).

COMFORT AND NEED. The Qur'ān also serves as a source of strength and reassurance in the face of the unknown. For pious Muslims, the Qur'ān provides a means of controlling future events or mitigating their outcome through *istikharah,* seeking guidance or a good omen in the text. Istikharah represents the choice of what God has chosen. It is carried out by averting the face, opening the book, pointing to a randomly chosen verse, and letting the verse speak directly to one's need or condition. This action is often accompanied by specific prayers or rituals. According to the famous Ṣūfī and theologian Abū Ḥāmid al-Ghazālī (1058–1111) companions said that the Prophet emphasized the practice of istikharah as much as he emphasized memorizing the Qur'ān itself. Al-Ghazālī recommends reciting the Fatihah, the *Sūrah* of the Unbelievers (109), and the *Sūrah* of Sincerity (111) when practicing istikharah. Then the following supplication is to be made:

> Oh God! I seek goodness from you through your knowledge, I seek power from you through your power, and I beseech you through your great favor. For you are powerful and I am powerless, you are knowledgeable and I am ignorant, and you are the Knower of the Unseen. If you know that this matter will be good for me in my spiritual and material life and at the end of my life whether it tarries or hastens, then make it possible for me, and bless me and ease my life through it. But if you know that it will harm me in my spiritual and material life and at the end of my life whether it tarries or hastens, then avert me from it and avert it from me and empower me with good wherever I may be, for you are powerful over all things. (al-Ghazālī, vol. 1, p. 206)

The good bestowed by the text of the Qur'ān is a mercy for believers both in life and after death. In his discussion of *ṣalāt al-Hajah* (The prayer of need), al-Ghazālī states that petitioners to God should perform twelve prostrations, each of which is to be preceded by recitations of the Fatihah, the Verse of the Throne (2:255), and the *Sūrah* of Sincerity (al-Ghazālī, pp. 206–207). Often, before a Muslim dies, he or she stipulates that the Qur'ān be recited at the grave for three days to ensure the repose of the soul. Sometimes, at the tombs of rulers or great Ṣūfī saints, teams of readers would be employed to recite the sacred text around the clock. Whenever a deceased person is remembered by friends or family, the Fatihah is recited; it is considered a gift to the dead, a fragrant breeze from Paradise to lighten the hardship of the grave. However, the verses of the Qur'ān that are learned in this world will bring believers the greatest merit in the Hereafter. The Prophet Muḥammad said, "It shall be said to the bearer of the Qur'ān [after death], 'Recite and rise [to a higher station]. Chant now as you did in the world, for your final station shall be the last verse you recite'" (al-Qurtubi, vol. 1, p. 9).

RECITATION AND MEMORIZATION. Because the Qur'ān contains the word of God, its text stipulates that no one should touch it but the purified (56:79), nor should anyone recite it that is not in a state of ritual purity. Before beginning to recite the Qur'ān, the Muslim is encouraged to clean her teeth and purify her mouth, because the body will become the "path" of the Qur'ān. The Qur'ān reciter must also put on her best attire, as she would when standing before a king, for she is in fact speaking with God, in God's own language. Likewise, because the Qur'ān is the essence of Islamic prayer, the reciter should face the *qiblah,* the direction of prayer toward Mecca. Muslims believe that anyone who yawns while reciting the Qur'ān is obliged to stop, because yawning is caused by Satan. Normally, the recitation of the Qur'ān begins with the formula of refuge (*al-ta'wiz*): "I take refuge in God from Satan the accursed." It is therefore necessary that the reciter seclude herself whenever possible so that she not be interrupted. If the word of God were to become mixed with profane speech, the reciter would lose the power of the formula of refuge with which she began her recitation.

According to a well-known tradition, those who have memorized the Qur'ān (the "Bearers of the Qur'ān") were described by the Prophet Muḥammad as being specially favored with the mercy of God because they are the teachers of his word. The tradition goes on to assert that God protects those who listen to the Qur'ān from the afflictions of this world and protects its reciters from the trials of the world to come. The Prophet is said to have further asserted that God would not torment a heart in which he had caused the Qur'ān to dwell. All obligations of worship are believed to cease with death except the recitation of the Qur'ān; it will continue to be performed forever as a delight for the people of Paradise.

TEACHING AND INTERPRETATION. According to Muslim convention, the Qur'ān is not a book with a beginning, middle, and end. Every portion, even every verse, is a "Qur'ān," a divine lecture, just as the entire book is the Qur'ān, properly speaking. In the history of Qur'anic exegesis, this belief has led to an unfortunate tendency to take Qur'anic verses out of context. However, this decontextualization of the Qur'ān has a spiritual benefit, in that the study of the Qur'ān is a journey through an infinite world of meaning, a journey to God through God's own words. The outward purpose of this journey is to shape one's character and life according to the word of God, and thus to attain God-consciousness (*taqwa*). The inner purpose of the journey, the path often followed in the Shīʿī and Ṣūfī traditions, is to travel toward God through the practice of deep hermeneutics *(ta'wīl),* and thus to attain a direct knowledge of God (*ma'rifah*) by repeatedly going back (*ta'awwala*) to the divine speech that is the basis of all creativity. A man is reported to have asked the Prophet Muḥammad, "What is the most excellent deed?" He was told, "Be a sojourning traveler." The man then asked, "Who is the sojourning traveler?" The Prophet replied, "It is the man of the Qur'ān, he who journeys from its beginning to its end, and then returns again to its beginning. Thus, he stops for a brief sojourn and then departs" (al-Qurtubi, vol. 1, p. 36).

Muslims believe that the Qur'ān guides its bearers to the eternal bliss of Paradise. It will pray on their behalf, and God will bestow upon them the crown of glory and will be pleased with them. Those who have internalized the sacred text through memorizing its verses and who recite it and teach others the art of recitation are described in a famous prophetic tradition as the people of God and his elect. According to another tradition, the best person is the one who studies the Qur'ān and teaches it to others. This is why people who teach the Qur'ān to children are highly respected throughout the Islamic world. The prophet Muḥammad declared that the highest merit for which a person can hope in the world to come is that of engaging with others in the study of the Qur'ān: "There is no people assembled in one of the houses of God to recite the book of God and study it together but that divine tranquility descends upon them. Mercy covers them, angels draw near to them, and God remembers them in the company of those who are with him" (Ayoub, vol. 1, pp. 8–9). The Qur'ān states that divine light descends upon houses in which God's name is remembered (24:36). All of God's ninety-nine "beautiful names" (7:180) are to be found in the Qur'ān. For this reason, the text of the Qur'ān is considered the truest approach to knowledge of God.

However, blindly reciting verses that are not understood, whether linguistically, intellectually, or spiritually, is not the best way to approach the Qur'ān, according to the majority of Islamic scholars. A person has not truly read the Qur'ān if both the heart and the mind are not fully engaged in understanding it. Approaching the Qur'ān has an outer, ritual dimension, and an inner, conceptual dimension, of which both are necessary for a full appreciation of the text. For al-, the "inner practice" of approaching the Qur'ān consists of ten levels of understanding that must be cultivated by the informed reader:

1. The reader of the Qur'ān must have a basic understanding of theology, so that he or she can appreciate the divine origin of its words.
2. The reader must fully understand the exalted nature of the divine speaker and the difference between Qur'anic discourse and human speech.
3. The reader must cultivate the faculties of the heart and suppress mind-chatter so that the spiritual nature of the divine discourse may be revealed.
4. The reader must practice disciplined concentration when reading or reciting the sacred text.
5. The reader must concentrate on the attributes, actions, and states of God revealed in the text in order to understand how God works in the world.
6. The reader must eliminate all intellectual impediments that may block his or her understanding the spiritual message of the Qur'ān.
7. The reader must understand the contextual nature of the divine commands and prohibitions in the Qur'ān and be aware of the limitations to be applied when following its rules.
8. The reader must allow the discourse of the Qur'ān to influence the attitudes of the heart in its emotional states.
9. The reader's understanding of the text must "ascend" such that one hears the word of God speaking in the Qur'ān and not one's own ego.
10. The reader must attain "freedom" through understanding the Qur'ān from the limitations of personal effort and initiative in seeking the blessings and favor of God. (al-Ghazālī, vol. 1, pp. 280–288)

True reverence of the Qur'ān and awareness of God's will for humankind demands an approach that favors intellectual and spiritual inquiry over the mere memorization of the text and its explanatory traditions. Refuting a tradition in which the Prophet Muḥammad supposedly stated, "Whoever interprets the Qur'ān with his own opinion will find his seat in Hell," al-Ghazālī asks, "How can one possibly understand the Qur'ān without studying its interpretation?" Anyone who believes that the only way to understand the Qur'ān is through its superficial meaning has in fact limited the meaning of the word of God to the limitations of one's own understanding. Such a person is trapped in what modern scholars would call the "hermeneutical circle" of traditional knowledge *(ʿilm al-naql),* which literally "transports" text but not meaning. On the contrary, says al-Ghazālī, a complete and balanced knowledge of tradition would reveal that the ways to interpret the Qur'ān are wide for those who understand (al-Ghazālī, p. 289).

INFLUENCE. Every verse of the Qur'ān contains seventy thousand potential ways of understanding its text, because each Arabic word of the Qurʾān bears multiple, legitimate levels of meaning. Understanding this truism of Arabic hermeneutics is key to understanding the importance of the Qurʾān to Muslims. Even beyond the creedal confines of Islam, the Qurʾān has set the standard for Arabic language and literature as the highest expression and model for literary Arabic. Its style of storytelling, its similes, and its metaphors have shaped classical Arabic literature and have even influenced modern writers. It was the demand for absolute correctness in studying, writing, and reciting the Qurʾān that provided the basis for Arabic grammar and other linguistic sciences. Qurʾanic maxims and phrases have permeated all the languages of the Muslim world, and beautifully rendered Qurʾanic calligraphy graces the walls of mosques, schools, and the homes of the pious.

The Qurʾān is one of the most important bases of unity in a highly diverse Islamic civilization. Its impact on the life of Muslims may be summed up in a prayer attributed to ʿAli and intended to be offered at the completion of a Qurʾān recitation: "Oh God, relieve with the Qurʾān my breast; occupy with the Qurʾān my entire body; illumine with the Qurʾān my sight, and loosen the Qurʾān with my tongue. Grant me strength for this, so long as you allow me to remain alive, for there is neither strength nor power except in you" (Majlisi, vol. 89, p. 209).

BIBLIOGRAPHY

The role of the Qurʾān in Muslim piety, although crucial to Islamic spirituality, has until recently been neglected in Western scholarship. More surprisingly, it has also been neglected in contemporary Muslim scholarship, where moral and political approaches to Islam have been considered more important. Since the late 1980s, however, the subject has begun to appear in the writings of Muslims, many of them converts to Islam, who live in Europe and the United States. Several recent introductions to Islam contain important discussions of the spiritual importance of the Qurʾān. Exegetical works that combine scholarly and personal approaches also have appeared, which include readings of the Qurʾān from the newly relevant perspectives of gender and social justice.

Premodern discussions of the importance of the Qurʾān in Muslim spiritual life are typically found in "Virtues of the Qurʾān" (*fadaʾil al-Qurʾan*) literature. Such discussions are included in many works of Qurʾanic exegesis; see, for example the work by Ibn Kathir (d. 1373) titled *Fadaʾil al-Qurʾan* and appended to volume 7 of his Qurʾān commentary *Tafsir al-Qurʾan al-ʿazim,* Beirut, 1966. This literature also forms a part of major collections of tradition. See, for example, the chapter on *fadaʾil al-ʾan* in *Sahih Bukhari,* translated by Muḥammad Muhsin Khan, *Translation of the Meanings of Sahih al-Bukhari,* Beirut, 1979, volume 6.

The sources used for the present article are representative of these literary traditions. Muḥammad al-Qurtubi (d. 1273) was a noted Qurʾān commentator and jurist who lived and wrote in Egypt. Abū ʿAli ibn al-Hasan al-Tabarsi (d. 1153) was an important jurist of the Imāmī Shīʿī tradition, whose commentary is considered foundational to Shīʿī thought. Mulla Muḥammad Baqir al-Majlisi (d. 1699) was one of the most prolific Shīʿī traditionists. Abū Ḥāmid al-Ghazālī was one of the most important theologians of Sunnī Islam. He was uniquely influential in setting the standards for Sunnī thought and practice in late medieval Islam.

Ayoub, Mahmoud M. *The Qurʾan and its Interpreters,* 2 vols. Albany, N.Y., 1984.

Chodkiewicz, Michel. *An Ocean Without Shore: Ibn ʿArabi, the Book, and the Law.* Albany, N.Y., 1993. This work discusses the meaning of the Qurʾān to the Spanish Ṣūfī and mystic Muhyiʾ al-Din Muḥammad ibn ʿArabi (d. 1240).

Eaton, Charles Le Gai. *Islam and the Destiny of Man.* Cambridge, U.K., 1994. See especially Chapter 4, "The World of the Book."

Esack, Farid. *Qurʾan, Liberation, and Pluralism: An Islamic Perspective of Interreligious Solidarity Against Oppression.* Oxford, 2002.

Ghazālī, Abū Ḥāmid al-. *Ihyaʾ ʿulum al-din,* 5 vols. Beirut, n.d. The material used in this article comes from *Kitab adab tilawat al-* Qurʾ*an,* which is found in volume 1. Al-Ghazālī's approach to the Qurʾān is strongly influenced by Ṣūfī notions of piety.

Isutzu, Toshihiko. *God and Man in the Koran: Semantics of the Koranic Weltanschauung.* New York, 1980. This is a uniquely valuable study of the meaning of the Qurʾān to Muslims. It was written by a Buddhist scholar who was a pioneer of the academic tradition of Islamic Studies in Japan.

Majlisi, Mulla Muḥammad Baqir al-. *Bihar al-anwar.* 110 volumes. Beirut, 1983. See especially, volume 89, which discusses the Qurʾān and its virtues.

Nasr, Seyyed Hossein. *Ideals and Realities of Islam.* Chicago, 2000.

Qurtubi, Abu ʿAbd Allah Muḥammad al-. *Al-Jamiʾ li ahkam al-*Qurʾ*an.* Cairo, 1966. See especially al-Qurtubi's introduction to this work.

Schuon, Frithjof. *Understanding Islam.* Bloomington, Ind., 1994. See especially the chapters entitled "Islam" and "The Qurʾān."

Tabarsi, Abu ʿAli al-Fadl ibn al-Hasan al-. *Majmaʾ al-bayan fi tafsir al-* Qurʾ*an.* Cairo, 1958.

Wadud, Amina. *Qurʾan and Woman: Rereading the Sacred Text from a Woman's Perspective.* Oxford and New York, 1999.

MAHMOUD M. AYOUB (1987)
VINCENT J. CORNELL (2005)

QURRAT AL-ʿAYN ṬĀHIRAH

QURRAT AL-ʿAYN ṬĀHIRAH (c. 1818–1852), was a Bābī preacher and poet, and their first woman martyr. Both *Qurrat al-ʿAyn* ("solace of the eyes") and *Ṭāhirah* ("the pure") were given as honorifics, and her original name has fallen into oblivion.

The daughter of a prominent Shīʿī mullah in Qazvin, she was married to her first cousin, the son of another important mullah. She was a highly intelligent woman and early studied the works of Shaykh Aḥmad Aḥsāʾī, who spoke of the imminent coming of the Bāb. After corresponding with Aḥsāʾī's disciple, Sayyid Kāẓim-i Rashtī, she took the decisive step of leaving her husband and children in order to join his circle in Karbala; but he died shortly before she performed the pilgrimage there in 1843. During her three years' stay in Karbala, Ṭāhirah preached the new doctrine with fervor and success and was accepted by the Bāb (whom she never met) as one of his eighteen disciples known as Ḥurūf-i Ḥayy ("the letters of the living," i. e., the letters that make up the word *ḥayy*). It was from the Bāb's description of her as Janab-i Ṭāhirah ("her excellency, the pure") that she became known as Ṭāhirah or, among Bahā'īs, Ṭāhirih.

Her preaching made the authorities suspicious, and in 1847 she was put under surveillance in Baghdad. After the shah's Jewish physician became a convert to Babism during a visit there, Ṭāhirah and her followers were expelled from Iraq. Upon her return to Qazin, she was divorced from her husband, who opposed the new teachings of the Bāb. The assassination of her uncle (her former father-in-law), also an adversary of the Bābīs, resulted in the first persecution of the adherents of the new faith, and she went to Tehran and stayed as a guest of Bahā' Allāh, whom she hailed as the awaited leader of the community. During a Bābī conference in Badasht in 1848, the beautiful young woman is said to have preached without a veil, an action that is taken as the first attempt to win freedom for Persian women. When Nāṣir al-Dīn Shāh ascended the throne later that year, Ṭāhirah was placed under arrest. After a Bābī attempt to assasinate the shah, she was executed, probably by strangulation, in August 1852.

Ṭāhirah is considered the first Iranian woman to preach equality of the sexes and religious freedom; E. G. Browne called her appearance in Iran "a prodigy—nay, almost a miracle." Her Persian poems are of great beauty; one of them is included in Muhammad Iqbal's *Javīd-nāmah* (1932), where the Bābī heroine appears as one of the "martyrs of love."

Bibliography

The only biography of Qurrat al-ʿAyn is Martha L. Root's brief *Tahirih the Pure, Iran's Greatest Woman* (1938; reprint, Los Angeles, 1980). See also Edward G. Browne's sympathetic accounts in his *Materials for the Study of the Babi Religion* (Cambridge, 1918) and his *A Traveller's Narrative Written to Illustrate the Episode of the Bāb,* 2 vols. (Cambridge, 1891), which is the translation of a memoir by Abbas Effendi, Bahā' Allāh's son.

ANNEMARIE SCHIMMEL (1987)

QUTB, SAYYID. Sayyid Qutb (1906–1966), among the most influential Islamist thinkers of the twentieth century, was born on October 9, 1906, in the village of Musha (Upper Egypt). His father was a supporter of Mustafa Kamil's al-Hizb al-Watani (Nationalist Party). Studying at the village *kuttab* (religious school) and government school, he reportedly memorized the Qur'ān by the age of 10. In 1921 he left Musha for Cairo to stay with his uncle, a journalist; migration offered an escape from the limited socioeconomic opportunities of rural village life. Having decided to become a schoolteacher, Qutb attended preparatory schools in Cairo, then formally enrolled in Dar al-ʿUlum (established to train instructors for government schools) in 1929 to 1930, completing his modern-style, largely Western-shaped education in the shadow of British control of Egypt. After graduating in 1933, he taught in provincial towns and was later employed by the Ministry of Education as inspector of primary schools, and he continued thus until his resignation in 1951 or 1952 due to disagreement with government policies. In 1948 the ministry sent him to the United States to investigate educational methods. He enrolled at colleges of education in New York and Colorado and traveled widely, returning to Cairo through Europe. In 1951 or 1952 he joined the Society of the Muslim Brothers (Ikhwān al Muslimūn) and was appointed director of its Section for Propagation of the Call and Publication. There is a perception that Qutb enjoyed a close relationship with the Free Officers who overthrew the monarchy in 1952 (including ʿAbd al-Nasir), serving as liaison between them and the Brothers. Thus, he is believed to have been the only civilian to attend the Revolutionary Command Council's meetings. Although the Brotherhood was at first optimistic about Egypt's future after the coup, tensions with the new regime mounted as its aim to steer the country towards secular republicanism became clear. In 1954 ʿAbd al-Nasir banned the Brotherhood following a failed assassination attempt on his life, in which Brothers were implicated. Qutb was arrested along with other Brotherhood leaders, some of whom were later executed) and sentenced in 1955 to fifteen years hard labor for subversive activity against the state. His poor health led to his transfer to the prison hospital, from where he was able to write and publish. His release in 1964, ostensibly on grounds of ill health (possibly thanks to intervention by Iraqi president ʿAbd al-Salam ʿArif), proved to be short-lived. In 1965, having become closely associated with reconstituted Brotherhood circles, he was re-arrested with other Brotherhood members and sympathizers. His trial by special military tribunal focused on the implications of his work *Milestones* (the thesis of which was later refuted by the mainstream Brotherhood) as the basis of the state's case against him. It ended with the charge of attempting forcible overthrow of the government. Sentenced to death, Qutb was executed on August 29, 1966.

Qutb's career as a writer spanned an earlier, secular-oriented phase and a later Islamist one, itself encompassing two phases. From his student days, he was involved in literary circles in Cairo as a second-rank poet, literary critic, and essayist. He also engaged in the cultural politics of the day, contributing articles to the Egyptian press. Welcoming the modernizing impulse and receptive to the postwar nationalist current, Qutb nevertheless seems from the outset to have resisted the Western values upheld by the liberal-oriented establishment and its intellectual voices. This position possibly reflected his traditional background; as the 1930s progressed, it found common ground with the growing trend of dissident voices disenchanted with the liberals' view of Egypt, emphasizing instead the indigenous Muslim dimensions of Egyptian cultural and national identity. The 1940s saw Qutb gravitate from a position of cultural nationalism to one deeply engaged with the Qur'ān as a potential blueprint for change, in the context of a postwar opposition seeking a viable ideological alternative to the liberal parliamentary monarchical system. From around 1948, Qutb indeed appears to have turned from a cultural understanding of the role of Islam in society to one that saw in it a system that could respond to the political and economic needs of his context. His early works in the first phase of this explicitly Islamist vein had a modernist outlook compatible with the Brotherhood's reformist discourse, with its characteristically apologetic argumentation. The first such substantial work, *al-ʿAdala al-Ijtimaʿiyya fi al-Islam* (Social justice in Islam), appeared in 1949; this was followed by *Maʿrakat al-Islam wa'l-Raʿsmaliyya* (The struggle between Islam and capitalism, 1951) and *al-Salam al-ʿAlami wa'l-Islam* (Islam and world peace, 1951). However, Qutb's most significant work is a multivolume Qur'anic exegesis entitled *Fi Zilal al-Qur'ān* (In the shade of the Qur'ān), written and repeatedly revised during his incarceration. Extracts from this were published in 1964 as *Maʿalim fi al-Tariq* (*Milestones,* 1978), summarizing his theory concerning God's sovereignty and the role of *jihad* in a non-Islamic society. This marked a change in his Islamist writing. Also published in the early 1960s and belonging to this second Islamist phase were *al-Islam wa Mushkilat al-Hadara* (Islam and the problem of civilization) and *Khasa'is al-Tasawwur al-Islami* (The characteristics of Islamic theory). *Muqawwimat al-Tasawwur al-Islami* (Fundamentals of Islamic theory) appeared posthumously.

His second Islamist phase is responsible for Qutb's main intellectual and political legacy, consisting in the inauguration of a new Islamic discourse and radical activism. This discourse introduced interrelated concepts and propositions intended to reestablish Islam on firm foundations. They have since become an integral part of the vocabulary of most radical Islamist groups and, as such, represent more than a merely theoretical innovation. Qutb's scheme stressed the twin concepts of *jahiliyya* (paganism) and *hakimiyya* (sovereignty) on the one hand, and on the other called for the adoption of *jihad* as the ultimate means for delivering political power to a new generation of Islamist revolutionaries. The term *jahiliyya* (developed from writings of the Indian Abu al-Aʿla al-Mawdudi) functioned as a shorthand descriptive for the present condition of all societies, Muslim and non-Muslim. Qutb declared that all human societies had entered a new cycle of paganism by excluding "true religion" from their daily life and transactions. This state of affairs demanded the restitution of Islam as the only legitimate system capable of guiding humanity in all its endeavors. To enable such a restitution it was imperative to reassert God's sovereignty as the linchpin of a solid structure erected to lead mankind to material prosperity, moral rectitude, and salvation. God's sovereignty was thus put forward to indicate the exclusion of all systems of thought and government not derived from divine injunctions embodied in the Qur'ān. Moreover, the affirmation of God's sovereignty requires the creation of a "vanguard" of dedicated revolutionaries able to conduct a tightly coordinated program of ideological inculcation and political activity. Hence, Islam is both a doctrine and a method. The doctrine takes priority and thus constitutes the essence of Islam (particularly God's attributes of unicity, lordship, divinity, and absolute authority) that must first be firmly embraced by members of the vanguard prior to its implementation. The method is the most efficient means of initiating the second stage, of building a new Islamic order. Qutb warned that the struggle to restore Islam is long and arduous and involves adherence to a strict code by a cohort of professional revolutionaries. This code entails total dissociation from non-Islamic societies and the creation of alternative forms of organization, leadership, and loyalty. Separation inevitably leads to the division of society into two irreconcilable warring camps: this confrontation, spanning ideological, cultural, financial, and political fields, finds its culmination in armed struggle, or the highest stage of *jihad. Jihad* may thus be conducted through various forms, peaceful and violent, but its ultimate aim is to disarm the enemy so that Islam will be allowed to develop freely, by removing the obstacle of idolatrous tyrannies.

Translated into several languages, Qutb's writings are read by Muslims and Islamists of many hues, Sunnī and Shīʿī, across the Muslim world: *Fi Zilal al-Qur'ān* is considered to be among the most widely read modern Islamic works of the twentieth century. The apparent justification for direct (including violent) action aimed at overthrowing un-Islamic regimes and fighting Islam's enemies that is elaborated in Qutb's later works inspired radical Egyptian Islamist groups such as Jamaʿat al-Muslimin (1970s), al-Jihad al-Islami (responsible for Egyptian president Anwar al-Sadat's assassination in 1981), and al-Jamaʿat al-Islamiyya. Since 2001, attention has been drawn to Qutb as the intellectual inspiration behind currents that coalesced to form the terrorist network al-Qāʿidah: described as the major influence on Usāmah bin Lādin, Qutb has been dubbed the "philosopher of Islamic terror." Any proper assessment of his legacy must consider the possibility, suggested by some close to him, that his purpose has been misconstrued by such trends. It must pay due attention to other dimensions of his *oeuvre,* including his underlying near-mystical approach to Islam and his appreciation of Qur'anic aesthetics.

SEE ALSO Modernism, article on Islamic Modernism; Wahhabiyah.

BIBLIOGRAPHY

Calvert, John "The Individual and the Nation: Sayyid Qutb's *Tifl min al-Qarya* (*Child from the Village*)." *Muslim World* 90, nos. 1–2 (2000): 107–132. Analysis of Qutb's partial autobiography, published 1946, exploring his views on the question of Egyptian national identity during the final years of the monarchy.

Calvert, John. "'The World Is an Undutiful Boy!': Sayyid Qutb's American Experience." *Islam and Christian-Muslim Relations* 11, no. 1 (2000): 87–103. Study of this little-examined episode in Qutb's career.

Choueiri, Youssef M. "Islam and Islamic Fundamentalism." In *Contemporary Political Ideologies*, edited by Roger Eatwell and Anthony Wright, pp. 255–278. London, 1999. Nuanced discussion of Qutb's contribution to modern Islamic thought, and his association with other radical Islamists.

Choueiri, Youssef M. *Islamic Fundamentalism*. Revised ed. Washington, D.C., and London, 2002. Comprehensive overview of Qutb's philosophical and political approach, based on a close reading of his Qur'ānic commentary.

Kepel, Gilles. *The Prophet and Pharaoh: Muslim Extremism in Egypt*. Berkeley, Calif., 1985. Informative discussion of the influence of Qutb's ideas on the Brotherhood members in prison (among them the founder of Jamaʿat al-Muslimin).

Khalidi, Salah ʿAbd al-Fattah. *Sayyid Qutb: al-Shahid al-Hayy* (*Sayyid Qutb: Living Martyr*). Amman, Jordan, 1981. Generally reliable biographical source (in Arabic).

Moussali, Ahmad S. *Radical Islamic Fundamentalism: The Ideological and Political Discourse of Sayyid Qutb*. Beirut, Lebanon, 1992. Theoretical interpretation of Qutb's political project as an ideology that seeks to link knowledge and action.

Nettler, Ronald L. "A Modern Islamic Confession of Faith and Conception of Religion: Sayyid Qutb's Introduction to the *Tafsir, Fi Zilal al-Qur'ān*." *British Journal of Middle East Studies* 21, no. 1 (1994): 102–114. Discussion of the introduction to Qutb's Qur'ānic exegesis, indicating the broader contours of his thought in this important work and his direct experience of the revelation.

Qutb, John. "Qur'ānic Aesthetics in the Thought of Sayyid Qutb." *Religious Studies and Theology*. 15, nos. 2–3 (1996): 61–76. Comprehensive analysis of Qutb's understanding of Qur'ānic aesthetics and its role in the evolution of his career, adopting a helpful contextual approach.

Qutb, Sayyid. *Milestones*. Beirut, 1978. Clear summary of Qutb's principal ideas in the radical phase of his career as an Islamist writer (in translation).

Shepard, William E. "Sayyid Qutb's Doctrine of *Jahiliyya*." *International Journal of Middle Eastern Studies* 35 (2003): 521–545. Analysis of this pivotal concept in Qutb's later thought.

Tripp, Charles. "Sayyid Qutb: The Political Vision." In *Pioneers of Islamic Revival*, edited by Ali Rahnema, pp. 154–183. London, 1994. Overview of Qutb's career and thinking, discussing the evolution of his political vision and his influence.

SUHA TAJI-FAROUKI (2005)
YOUSSEF M. CHOUEIRI (2005)

RA SEE RE

RABBAH BAR NAHMANI (d. around 330 CE), a third-generation Babylonian amora, rabbinical colleague of Yosef bar Ḥiyya' and Ḥisda'. Rabbah studied with Huna' and several other Babylonians, including Yehudah bar Yeḥezqe'l and, some modern scholars argue, with Yoḥanan bar Nappaḥa' in Palestine. After Yehudah's death, Rabbah began a twenty-two-year career as the head of a circle of students and a court in the city of Pumbedita. Serving as a judge, he had authority to impose rabbinic law in the marketplace and in various civil, property, and communal matters (B.T., *Ḥul.* 43b; Neusner, 1969).

Rabbah taught his disciples Torah, including everyday practical advice, lectured to them in the *kallah* gatherings (B.T., *B.M.* 86a), and, in his court, trained them as apprentice judges. His support for rabbinical privileges such as a tax exemption apparently brought him into conflict with the exilarch (lay leader considered to be of Davidic descent) (Neusner, 1969). His devotion to Torah study (see, e.g., B.T., *ʿEruv.* 22a) and his sinless character reportedly gave him special access to the divine—the ability to call upon God to revive the dead (B.T., *Meg.* 7b), to receive teachings from Elijah, and to be protected from demons (B.T., *Ḥul.* 105b). Perceived as a strict follower of the law who reproved the community, he was reportedly disliked in certain circles (B.T., *Shab.* 153a).

Some stories regarding Rabbah's life apparently served to counter less flattering accounts. For example, one text describing Rabbah's death after government agents had pursued him for inciting mass tax evasion justifies his early death: Miraculously protected from malicious humans, Rabbah died early in life only because he was needed in the heavenly study session to resolve a dispute (B.T., *B.M.* 86a).

Rabbah was noted for the dialectical sharpness with which he analyzed and supplemented received teachings (B.T., *Ber.* 64a). To render the Mishnah smoothly, he emended it or read in elliptical language (Epstein, 1964). Similarly, on the basis of his own views, he revised *baraitot* (texts purporting to represent extra-Mishnaic tannaitic teachings) and other earlier traditions that students cited before him. Although he treated numerous halakhic (legal) topics from ritual, civil, and even purity laws no longer in effect, few of his preserved dicta deal with aggadic (non-halakhic) matters.

SEE ALSO Amoraim.

BIBLIOGRAPHY

A comprehensive treatment and bibliography of Rabbah and his teachings can be found in Jacob Neusner's *A House of the Jews in Babylinia*, 5 vols. (Leiden, 1966–1970), esp. vol. 4. Noteworthy, too, are Jacob N. Epstein's *Mavo' le-nusaḥ ha-Mishnah*, 2 vols. (1948; reprint, Jerusalem, 1964), pp. 363–368, and David M. Goodblatt's *Rabbinic Instruction in Sasanian Babylonia* (Leiden, 1975).

New Sources

Faur, José. "Of Cultural Intimidation and Other 'miscellanea': Bar-Sheshakh vs. Raba." *Review of Rabbinic Judaism* 5 (2002): 34–50.

BARUCH M. BOKSER (1987)
Revised Bibliography

RABBINATE

This entry consists of the following articles:

RABBINATE: THE RABBINATE IN PRE-MODERN JUDAISM

The rabbinate as an institution of intellectual, spiritual, and religious leadership developed relatively late in the history of the Jewish people. It is found neither in the Bible nor in other Jewish literature from the biblical period. In Mishnaic parlance, the term *rav* (which means "great" or "distinguished" in biblical Hebrew) connotes a teacher of students, and this is its primary usage during the Talmudic period in Babylonia. The derivative term *rabbi* (*rebbe*, my master) is an honorific used originally to address sages in the Land of Israel following the destruction of the Second Temple. The title "Rabban" was used at this time to designate singularly important scholar-leaders of the generation, such as the patriarch (*Nasi*). The term *rabbinate* is perhaps derived from this title, if not from a form of the titles *rav* or rabbi. Prior to the destruction, even the greatest sages (such as Hillel and Shammai) were referred to without any honorific title.

The references in the Gospels to Jesus as rabbi (which occur for the most part in John, and not at all in Luke) have been explained in different ways. Some have suggested that this is an anachronism that was applied after the destruction of the Second Temple. Others have argued that it was an unofficial title for a personal teacher or spiritual leader, a usage that was to be found in the pre-destruction period. Within Talmudic literature, the title "rabbi" sometimes referred to those with high standing in the community who were not religious authorities, such as individuals of great wealth or lay leaders.

Rabbinic ordination (*semikhah* or *minnui*) had its origins in the biblical account of Moses placing his hands on Joshua. Ordination was conferred by sages in the Land of Israel (according to tradition, in an unbroken chain) through the period of the Second Temple, as a means of allowing or authorizing a worthy student to issue judicial rulings or to otherwise decide matters of Jewish law. After the destruction of the Temple, ordination was still conferred (despite attempts by the Roman Emperor Hadrian to prohibit it) at least until the suppression of the patriarchate in 425 CE.

The rabbis of the Talmudic period in both Israel and Babylonia were best known and venerated for their mastery of the Torah and for their devotion to its study and observance. They conducted themselves modestly and concerned themselves with communal mores and needs such as the proper burial of the dead, the support of widows and orphans, and the ability of the people to pursue livelihoods that were consonant with Jewish law. Some rabbis were appointed as *parnasim*, an office that charged them with various charity functions or more general communal leadership. Rabbis were approached with all kinds of religious, economic, and personal questions and requests, ranging from the nullification of oaths to the laws of inheritance, and from Sabbath observance to permitted contact with Gentiles, to note but a few.

There was a degree of tension between the rabbis and the less learned (*'ammei ha-aretz*), and religious laxity led to rebuke. Certain rabbis were well known and quite adept as preachers, although the extent of public sermons varied widely. At the same time, the tax exemptions and other privileges to which Torah scholars and rabbinic figures were entitled during this period could sometimes arouse the ire of the communities. Rabbinic arrogance, borne for the most part of a rabbi's superior knowledge of Torah scholarship, also manifested itself on occasion. Nonetheless, the strong and sustained influence of the rabbinate during the Talmudic period was directly linked to the fact that the majority of the larger Jewish community accepted its authority.

Established rabbis served their teachers in both the educational and personal spheres, and expected their students to do likewise. Rabbinic teachers encouraged the practice of praising their able disciples and attempted to moderate academic and personal disagreements. Debates in the academies of the Tannaim and Amoraim were often conducted in a spirited manner. Although deep intellectual clashes and sharp words sometimes ensued, students and teachers alike were bidden to conduct themselves with mutual friendship and respect.

Until medieval times, rabbis received no salaries for their religious and judicial services and leadership, in accordance with a Mishnaic dictum which prohibited the deriving of any income or benefit from the Torah. Rabbis typically had other occupations. Talmudic literature does endorse the concept of *sekhar batalah*, whereby a rabbi or judge was permitted to receive monetary compensation for his rabbinic services in lieu of the money that he could have earned had he been able to devote that time to his regular occupation.

At some point in the post-Talmudic period, the original chain of rabbinic ordination was broken. Moses Maimonides (Mosheh ben Maimon, 1135/8–1204) writes that this form of *semikhah* may possibly be restored just prior to the coming of the Messiah. Nonetheless, other means of licensing judges, masters, and religious heads of the communities were developed in both Palestine and Babylonia during the Geonic period. The scope of these forms of (quasi-) ordination was considered to be more limited than the original *semikhah*, and there were differing views about who had the right to grant them.

In the medieval Muslim world, the synagogue, study hall, and rabbinic court (*beit din*) shared the same space and were interconnected. As such, the rabbis who served as the judges at the court and as the heads of the study halls also regulated synagogue life and ritual. Rabbis were involved with maintaining and disbursing the assets of the communities for charitable and other purposes, and even with quality of life issues. Throughout the Geonic period, the relationship between the local rabbinic authorities and the academies of the Geonim was governed by a series of understandings or regulations. In some instances rabbinic judges were appointed by the head of the Geonic academy, while in others they were appointed by the local community in which they served. Local rabbinic judges often reviewed their cases with the students who studied in their *beit midrash* and sought the counsel of the Geonim when they were unsure of the ruling at hand. Ordination in the Orient during the period of the Cairo geniza was viewed as a license to issue authoritative legal rulings and to act as a judge. The title *haver* was used to signify that a rabbinic scholar was ordained.

Rabbinic judges and courts did not only hear cases that involved litigation of economic matters and transactions. They also drafted legal documents for various kinds of transactions as well as bills of divorce, and they regulated and supervised ritual slaughter (*shehitah*). Judges typically received a yearly fee from all the members of the community, although some of the services that they provided required additional payments. There was extensive discussion among medieval rabbinic authorities about whether litigants had to appear before the rabbinic court in their own area or whether one litigant could compel the other to have their case heard before a rabbinic court of greater repute in another locale.

In medieval Spain, ordination was regarded as a sign of rabbinic authority, based on the Talmudic tradition. Rabbi Judah ben Barzillai of Barcelona (c. 1100) describes the procedure of ordination in his day. The direct result of ordination (which is characterized by Judah as a mere vestige, *zekher*, of the earlier institution) was that its incumbent would henceforth bear the title Rabbi and that he would be initiated into the ranks of the scholars. In addition, individual rabbinic masters in Spain at this time ordained their outstanding disciples. The duties of the communal rabbi, however, were not always clearly defined, and there were regional differences. In Aragon, for example, rabbis served as preachers, teachers, cantors, ritual slaughterers, scribes, and judges, in addition to providing general religious guidance to the community.

A formulation of Rabbi Isaac ben Sheshet Perfet (1326–1408; Ribash [the leading Spanish rabbinic authority of his day]) suggests that the traditional *semikhah* was unknown in Spain by his day, though it was still in vogue (since at least the early twelfth century) in Franco-Germany. The communal rabbinate in medieval Spain had begun to become professionalized and salaried as early as the eleventh century, and it remained so, despite Maimonides' strong objections concerning direct payment for any rabbinic services (in accordance with his understanding of what had been practiced during the Talmudic period). Communal appointments of salaried academy heads, judges, and masters, based on the recommendation of established authorities, were regarded *ipso facto* as a form of rabbinic authorization.

In Ashkenazic communities, on the other hand, the formation of a professionalized rabbinate did not occur until at least the end of the thirteenth century (in the face of a spate of persecutions), due to the relative weakness of communal organization in these matters. This state of affairs was predicated on the ready availability of capable rabbinic scholars in Ashkenaz who could respond to a broad range of queries and halakic problems, and who could voluntarily undertake various regular rabbinic functions, such as supervision of ritual slaughter and the ritual bath (*miqveh*) and the establishment of communal *ʿeruvin.* In any case, the delay in establishing a professionalized rabbinate in Ashkenaz meant that there was still a need for individual masters to give their students *semikhah*, as a means of testifying to the student's worthiness to serve as master and rabbi, a need that was not felt as keenly in Spain.

A protracted controversy erupted in the late fourteenth century (1386–1387), between Rabbi Yoḥanan Treves and Rabbi Meir ben Barukh of Vienna about the nature and extent of Ashkenazic *semikhah* (occasioning the formulation of Ribash just mentioned). A certain Rabbi Isaiah (who had been ordained by Rabbi Matatyah, father of Yoḥanan Treves and the *de facto* chief rabbi of northern France), arrogated for himself the right to appoint all rabbis in France, invalidating the bills of divorce (and *halizah*) ceremonies executed by anyone who did not accept this condition. Rabbi Isaiah was supported in his action by Rabbi Meir ben Barukh of Vienna, an important rabbinic leader of the day. Yoḥanan of Treves, as the successor to his father's office, appealed to the rabbis of Catalonia (and especially to Ribash) for help.

Rabbi Meir of Vienna's apparent desire to oust Rabbi Yoḥanan, and to replace him from afar with a less-qualified scholar (Rabbi Isaiah), has been understood by some as a reaction to the intervention of the king of France, who had confirmed Rabbi Yoḥanan's appointment as his father's successor. In fact, however, royal confirmation (and interference) in rabbinic appointments was already common in Spain. It is more likely that this controversy centered on Rabbi Meir's plan to introduce a rabbinic diploma that would regulate the rabbinic office and its functions (in light of the deteriorating conditions following the Black Death), an innovation that Rabbi Yoḥanan resisted. As opposed to the prevalent practice in which a community appointed an able rabbinic figure to serve as its rabbi, Rabbi Meir held that the certification of ability granted by a teacher to his student should also regulate all commercial appointments. References to appointments of rabbis in Germany and Austria by leading rabbinic figures (without any discussion of the role of the community in the appointment) are found in the responsa of two fifteenth-century authorities, Jacob Weil and Israel Bruna.

The formalizing of *semikhah* in Ashkenaz from the late fourteenth century onward is marked by the exclusive use of the title *Morenu ha-Rav* (our teacher and rabbi) for one who had been ordained. This title gave the candidate the right to teach and to decide matters of Jewish law (*heter hora'ah*). Writs of this ordination were issued in the middle of the fifteenth century by Israel Bruna and Israel Isserlein. These documents conveyed the formal title and status indicated, and also included the rights to open a *yeshivah*, to teach and to judge, and to deal with all matters of marriage, divorce, and *halizah*. As this form of *semikhah* spread, it became common for a candidate to receive such writs from more than one authority. Eventually, communal acceptance of a rabbi depended on his presenting a formal writ of *semikhah*. At the same time, both younger and more mature students and scholars in Germany and Austria who did not earn or receive documents of ordination were often called *haverim* (or even simply *lomdim*) to signify that they were learned and accomplished to some degree, even though they did not hold the title of *Morenu*.

In the aftermath of the controversy between Rabbi Yoḥanan Treves and Rabbi Meir of Vienna, Rabbi Moses Mintz was moved to characterize the ordination of his day as a direct continuation of the original (Palestinian) institution of old. The controversy replayed itself in several respects in Valona, Italy, in the period following the expulsion of the Jews from Spain. Rabbi David Messer Leon's overarching authority, which was based on his Ashkenazic *semikhah*, was called into question by Spanish exiles. Messer Leon was supported in his position by Rabbi David ha-Kohen of Corfu. In Safed during the 1530s, Rabbi Jacob Berab ordained four of his most outstanding students (including Rabbi Joseph Caro, author of the *Shulhan Arukh*) with the aim of reestablishing the original *semikhah* as it had been granted by leading Torah scholars in the land of Israel. This development might have allowed for the reconstitution of the Sanhedrin as well, but Berab could not convince the rabbis of Jerusalem to support his initiative, and it ultimately failed.

First in Spain—and later in France, Germany, Italy, and eastern Europe—rabbinic elections or appointments had to be confirmed by kings or other rulers, who often designated certain rabbinic figures as chief rabbis. These rabbis typically collected taxes on behalf of the crown and, at the same time, were granted by the crown to rule in both civil and criminal matters. In instances where lawsuits and other disputes remained unsettled by the local *dayyanim*, the crown itself sometimes reached out to leading scholars with whom it had a relationship. Thus, King Pedro III of Aragon (1276–1285), consulted several of the most outstanding Catalan halakhists including Rabbi Solomon ibn Adret (1235–1310; Rashba), and Rabbi Yom Tov Ashivili (Ritba). The well-known Polish rabbinic scholar and commentator Samuel Edels (1555–1631; Maharsha) wrote that "It would be fitting that the scholars and rabbis themselves elect a chief," but this was never achieved.

There were more than a few instances in which a candidate for rabbi or *dayyan* supported by the king was deemed unacceptable by the community. As in earlier periods, however, the rabbinate existed and functioned in many Jewish communities irrespective of any formal communal or external appointments. Questions in matters such as prayer customs, laws of *kashrut*, economic interactions, and marriage law received authoritative answers from rabbinic decisors, formally appointed or not. In eastern Europe, on the other hand, communities paid specially appointed *yeshivah* heads handsome salaries so that they could faithfully discharge their instructional duties and spend their remaining time completely immersed in Torah study.

Recorded decisions taken by Italian Jewish communities to appoint a communal rabbi are extant for Verona in 1539, and subsequently for Cremona and Padua. Nonetheless, a communal ordinance in Ferrara dated 1554 distinguishes (with respect to promulgating edicts) between "a rabbi of the city" (i.e., a rabbi who simply lived in that city) and "a rabbi appointed by the community." The earliest extant rabbinic contract (*ketav rabbanut*), dated 1575, was established between Rabbi Todros (Theodorus) and the Jewish community of Friedberg (Hessen, Germany). One copy of the contract was given to the rabbi, the other was incorporated into the communal ledger (*pinkas*). The contract specified the length of the appointment, the salary, and other financial benefits that were to be extended (including a fee for performing weddings and for executing marriage contracts and bills of divorce), as well as support for the students who studied with the rabbi, and other responsibilities and prerogatives. In addition to overseeing the procedures for marriage and divorce, and for appointing and supervising the ritual slaughterers, the rabbi directed the rabbinic court in the city that adjudicated all kinds of disputes. Although the rabbi was granted the power to issue various kinds of warnings (and bans) to members of the community, these had to be authorized by the communal board.

The salary specified in Rabbi Todros' contract appears rather inadequate, although it was supplemented by the fees indicated for other rabbinic services. The same held true for Italy in the late sixteenth century. Certain *yeshivah* heads were well paid, but many communal rabbis had other sources of income. Some Italian rabbis engaged in private tutoring in the homes of wealthy benefactors or in the writing of rabbinic works in honor of their patrons.

The rabbinic contract of Rabbi Asher Loeb (known as *Sha'agat Aryeh*, the title of his best-known work), who was appointed rabbi of Metz in 1765, provides a window into the nature of the rabbinate in Europe at the end of the early modern period. Rabbis were typically appointed (and reappointed) for fixed periods of time (between three and six years) and were not granted tenure. The community provided suitable housing for the rabbi and his family, exempted the rabbi from taxes, indemnified him from suits that might result from the performance of his duties, and provided for housing and support of his widow in the event that the rabbi passed away. The rabbi was the only one who could preach publicly, although he served primarily as the chief judge (*av beit din*) of the community, and as the "judge of the widows and the keeper of the orphans," monitoring their needs and protecting their interests. The rabbi would also teach local *yeshivah* students (whom the community supported), as well as members of the community. The rabbi was to be honored by being called to the Torah on special Sabbaths throughout the year. In the case of Rabbi Asher Loeb, at least, the salary level appears to be rather satisfactory.

The rabbinate in the pre-modern period was characterized by an ill-defined hierarchy that culminated (at least in theory), with the leading scholars of the generation (*gedolei ha-dor*). This lack of formal structure contributed to tensions between different groups of rabbinic figures (e.g., heads of academies and communal rabbis) and between rabbis and the lay leadership of the communities. At the same time, it enabled the rabbinate to overcome numerous challenges and obstacles in providing ritual, judicial, and educational services, as well as spiritual and intellectual leadership, for an ever-changing array of communities throughout the Jewish world.

SEE ALSO Conservative Judaism; Hasidism; Orthodox Judaism; Reconstructionist Judaism; Reform Judaism; Synagogue; Yeshivah.

BIBLIOGRAPHY

Alon, Gedaliah. *The Jews in Their Land in the Talmudic Age.* Jerusalem, 1980.

Assis, Yom Tov. *The Golden Age of Aragonese Jewry.* London, 1997.

Bonfil, Robert. *Rabbis and Jewish Communities in Renaissance Italy.* Oxford, 1990.

Breuer, Mordechai. *Assif* (in Hebrew). Jerusalem, 1999. A collection of articles on the history and nature of the rabbinate.

Gafni, Isaiah. *The Jews of Babylonia in the Talmudic Period* (in Hebrew). Jerusalem, 1990.

Goitein, S. D. *A Mediterranean Society,* vol. 2. Berkeley, Calif., 1999.

Kanarfogel, Ephraim. *Jewish Education and Society in the High Middle Ages.* Detroit, Mich., 1992.

Katz, Jacob. "Rabbinical Authority and Authorization in the Middle Ages." In *Studies in Medieval Jewish History and Literature,* edited by I. Twersky, pp. 41–56. Cambridge, Mass., 1979.

Levine, Lee. *The Rabbinic Class of Roman Palestine in Late Antiquity.* Jerusalem, 1989.

Schwartzfuchs, Simon. *A Concise History of the Rabbinate.* Oxford and Cambridge, U.K., 1993.

Shatzmiller, Joseph. "Rabbi Isaac ha-Kohen of Manosque and his Son Rabbi Peretz: The Rabbinate and its Professionalization in the Fourteenth Century." In *Jewish History: Essays in Honour of Chimen Abramsky,* edited by Ada Rapoport-Albert and Steven J. Zipperstein, pp. 61–83. London, 1988.

Urbach, Ephraim. *The Sages,* Cambridge, Mass., 1979.

Yuval, Israel. *Scholars in Their Time: The Religious Leadership of German Jewry in the Late Middle Ages* (in Hebrew). Jerusalem, 1998.

EPHRAIM KANARFOGEL (2005)

RABBINATE: THE RABBINATE IN MODERN JUDAISM

The modern rabbinate is a product of the Enlightenment and of the political emancipation of the Jews in western and central Europe. Under the influence of such Enlightenment ideas as natural human rights and the concept of the nation-state, Jews in those areas were gradually emancipated from their medieval status in the late eighteenth century and the nineteenth century and became the political equals of their Christian neighbors.

The emancipation process was slow, however; it varied from place to place in some particulars but was regarded as a two-way effort everywhere in western Europe. For their parts, the governments of these countries recognized Jews as the political equals of their fellow citizens. On the other hand, Jewish communities no longer constituted a "state within a state" as they had in medieval times, and rabbis no longer possessed legal authority and judicial power. In addition European rulers expected the Jews to transform themselves into modern citizens by giving up traditional garb, learning to speak the vernacular, abandoning the Yiddish language, and familiarizing themselves with modern European culture. Under the leadership of such individuals as Moses Mendelssohn (1729–1786), Naphtali Herz Wessely (1725–1805), and Israel Jacobson (1768–1828), Jews began to accept the educational and social standards of Western modernity; as a result, the need for a progressive rabbinate educated in secular universities soon became apparent to all.

To fill this need, rabbinical seminaries were created throughout Europe, first in Padua in 1829 and later in Metz (subsequently transferred to Paris), Amsterdam, London, and other large cities. In Germany, where the movement for religious reform was strongest and was led by such rabbis as Abraham Geiger (1810–1874), there were ultimately three such seminaries: the Jewish Theological Seminary in Breslau, espousing what would now be called a Conservative theology; the Berlin *Hochschule für die Wissenschaft des Judentums,* which served primarily a Reform or liberal constituency; and the Orthodox Hildesheimer Seminary, also in Berlin. The curricula of these institutions were quite different from those of traditional *yeshivot,* in which the Talmud and the Jewish legal codes constituted almost the entire object of study. The new seminaries naturally saw the Talmud as paramount but also taught the Hebrew Bible, midrash, history, homiletics, pedagogy, and other subjects relevant to the modern rabbinate. In addition the seminaries usually required their students to enroll in secular universities at the same time that they were in rabbinical school. Most of these seminaries were disbanded or destroyed during the Holocaust (1933–1945). Contemporary European rabbis are generally are trained in England, France, or Hungary, where seminaries still exist, as well as in the United States and Israel.

The United States. Although the American Jewish community traces its origins to the year 1654, there were no ordained rabbis in the United States until the 1840s. In colonial America, where all the synagogues followed the Sephardic (Spanish and Portuguese) ritual, religious services were led by a *hazzan* (cantor), who had generally been trained in London, Amsterdam, or the West Indies—the exception being the well-known Gershom Mendes Seixas (1745–1816), who was born and educated in New York City. With the large-scale immigration of Jews from central Europe in the three decades before the Civil War, however, there was a growing need for ordained rabbinic leadership. The first ordained rabbi to come to America was Abraham Rice (1802–1862), who arrived in Baltimore, Maryland, from Bavaria in 1840. Throughout the nineteenth century the American Jewish community was served by spiritual leaders who often lacked formal rabbinical ordination. The outstanding leaders in this period were Isaac Leeser (1806–1868), a traditionalist who served at Congregation Mikveh Israel in Philadelphia from 1829 to 1850, and Isaac Mayer Wise (1819–1900), a reformer who came from Europe in 1846 and served congregations in Albany and Cincinnati down to 1900. These men worked tirelessly to promote the practice of Judaism in the United States through their translations of Jewish texts, composition of educational materials for children, and establishment of newspapers with nationwide circulation.

In 1875 Wise and his supporters founded the Hebrew Union College in Cincinnati, which continues to train Reform rabbis in the early 2000s. In response the traditionalists, led by Sabato Morais of Philadelphia, Isaac Leeser's successor, established the Jewish Theological Seminary in New York City in 1886. The seminary still serves the Conservative movement of the twenty-first century. The more traditional Orthodox, whose numbers were soaring as a result of the immigration of Jews from eastern Europe, established the Rabbi Isaac Elchanan Theological Seminary, also in New York, in 1897. The seminary is the rabbinical school of Yeshiva University as of the early 2000s. To complete the picture the Reconstructionist movement established the Reconstructionist Rabbinical College outside of Philadelphia in Wyncote, Pennsylvania, in 1968. Together with a number of smaller rabbinical seminaries, some of which are nondenominational, these schools train the great majority of pulpit rabbis in the United States. In addition there are many traditional Orthodox *yeshivot*, such as the Beth Medrash Govoha in Lakewood, New Jersey, that also provide rabbinical training; however, the graduates of these institutions generally do not serve congregations.

With the push for gender equality that began in the 1960s, the more liberal branches of American Judaism began to call for the ordination of women as rabbis. The idea was not a new one, going back at least to the 1880s; indeed Regina Jonas (1902–1944), who had graduated from the Berlin *Hochschule*, was privately ordained in Germany in 1935. The first American woman to be ordained was Sally Priesand, who graduated from the Hebrew Union College in 1972. Two years later Sandy Eisenberg Sasso was ordained by the Reconstructionist Rabbinate College. After a prolonged and often bitter debate, the Conservative Jewish Theological Seminary opened its doors to women rabbinical students in 1984. Amy Eilberg became the first woman ordained at the seminary in 1985.

Prior to the emancipation era, rabbis generally served entire communities rather than individual synagogues. In the modern world, however, rabbis are hired by individual congregations. Although such European nations as England and France have chief rabbis, attempts to introduce a rabbinical hierarchy in the United States proved unsuccessful. In the nineteenth century rabbis were generally poorly paid and subject to the whims of congregational officers, who often had little respect for the rabbinical office.

Throughout the twentieth century, however, the rabbinate came to be regarded as a learned profession: rabbinical salaries were increased, benefits and vacations became the norm, and national rabbinical organizations were created, which helped to raise the prestige and status of their members. The modern American rabbi is called upon to fulfill many roles that premodern rabbis never envisioned: he or she is often a marriage and family counselor, a provider of adult religious education, an administrator, a school principal, and a participant in ecumenical or interfaith activities. In small communities the rabbi is sometimes the only Jewish religious professional, and rabbis in small synagogues are often called upon to serve as the cantor, Torah reader, and bar and bat mitzvah instructor as well. Many rabbis do not serve in pulpits but rather work as educators, chaplains, directors of Hillel Foundations on college campuses, or in other positions of service in the Jewish community. In general American Jews regard their rabbis as role models of faithfulness to the Torah in the congregation or other constituency.

Israel. In Israel the situation of the rabbi is generally different from that of the rabbi in the United States; in many ways it resembles that of the premodern era. In Israel religious affairs are controlled by the office of the chief rabbinate. There are two chief rabbis, one Ashkenazic (for people of central eastern European origin) and one Sephardic. Rabbis in Israel, with the exception of the traditional Orthodox and the rather small number of Reform and Conservative rabbis, are all employees of the state. Most Israeli rabbis are products of the traditional *yeshivot*; few have attended rabbinical seminaries. Some serve as judges in the rabbinical courts, which have legal jurisdiction over such matters of personal status as marriage and divorce, whereas others serve as supervisors of *kashrut* (maintaining the dietary laws), ritual baths, and other public institutions. Israeli synagogues are financed by the government; members do not join by paying dues as they do in North America. Consequently Israeli rabbis tend to have fewer pastoral duties than do rabbis in Europe and North America, and their relationship with the people who worship in their synagogues is often far less personal. On the other hand, non-Orthodox synagogues in Israel are generally patterned after those in North America, with members paying dues and usually having close relationships with the rabbi.

THE HASIDIM. In the Hasidic world the spiritual leader of the community is known as the *rebbe*. Hasidism traces its origins back to Rabbi Israel, the Baʿal Shem Tov (Master of the Good Name), who lived in Podolia in the southwestern Ukraine in the eighteenth century. He was a charismatic leader credited with performing a number of miracles. The modern Hasidic *rebbe*, always male, also is a charismatic individual, whose influence over his followers comes from the sheer force of his personality and aura of holiness. Although the *rebbe* is generally a learned rabbi, his position, which is often inherited from his father, does not depend upon his interpretations of Jewish law, for there are traditional rabbis in the Hasidic community who deal with such matters. Rather, the *rebbe* is often thought to be a person of keen human understanding whose closeness to God enables him to provide leadership, guidance, and advice to his followers. In some cases, his powers of intuition are thought to verge on the supernatural. The most influential Hasidic leader of the twentieth century was Rabbi Menachem Mendel Schneerson (1902–1994), known as the Lubavitcher Rebbe, who initiated a global Jewish outreach program that was especially successful on college campuses.

SEE ALSO Baʿal Shem Tov; Hasidism, overview article; Leeser, Isaac; Mendelssohn, Moses; Schneerson, Menachem M.; Wise, Isaac M.

BIBLIOGRAPHY

For a general view of the rabbinate, the reader is referred to Simon Schwarzfuchs, *A Concise History of the Rabbinate* (Cambridge, Mass., 1993). The emancipation era is thoroughly described by Jacob Katz in *Out of the Ghetto: The Social Background of Jewish Emancipation, 1770–1870* (New York, 1978). On the American rabbinate, see the entire issue of *American Jewish Archives* 35, no. 2 (November, 1983): 100-341, specifically Jeffrey S. Gurock, pp. 100–187; Abraham J. Karp, pp. 187–262; David Polish, pp. 263–341,for lengthy articles dealing with Orthodox, Conservative, and Reform rabbis in the United States. Also see Jonathan D. Sarna, *American Judaism: A History* (New Haven, Conn., 2004). The issue of women's ordination is the subject of Pamela S. Nadell's *Women Who Would Be Rabbis: A History of Women's Ordination, 1889–1985* (Boston, 1998). The modern Israeli rabbinate is described in Schwarzfuchs, *Concise History*, and in M. Hacohen and Y. Alfassi, "Rabbinate of Israel," in *New Encyclopedia of Zionism and Israel*, edited by Geoffrey Wigoder (Madison, N.J., and Cranbury, N.J., 1994), vol. 2, pp. 1081–1084. On the Hasidic *rebbe*, see Jerome R. Mintz, *Legends of the Hasidim: An Introduction to Hasidic Culture and Oral Tradition in the New World* (Chicago, 1974).

ROBERT E. FIERSTIEN (2005)

RABBINIC JUDAISM IN LATE ANTIQUITY.

In its formative period, 70–640 CE, rabbinic Judaism forged a synthesis between two antithetical phenomena in the religion of Israel: first, the messianic movement, with its stress on history's meaning and end, and second, the priestly component, with its interest in enduring and ahistorical natural life, celebrated in the cult. Starting with the Mishnah, the systematic expression of the priestly viewpoint, composed in the aftermath of the two great messianic wars against Rome (66–73 and 132–135), the rabbis of late antiquity so reconstructed the Mishnah's system of law and theology as to join to that system the long-standing messianic and historical emphases. Rabbinic Judaism thus presents a way of life of order and regularity, lived out beyond the disturbances of one-time events of history, but in which Jews looked forward to the end of time and the coming of the Messiah. That is, as a result of their adhering to that same, permanent, holy way of life, the Messiah would come. The thesis of historical and teleological messianism generated its antithesis, the Mishnaic system of the everyday celebration of eternal things, which then fused into the rabbinic synthesis, legal-messianic Judaism as it has been known from late antiquity to the present time.

DEFINITIONS. By *Judaism* is meant a worldview and way of life held by a group of Jews, defining the holiness of their people. Any kind of Judaism will draw upon the Hebrew scriptures (the "Old Testament"), usually called Tanakh, an acronym standing for *Torah* (Law), *Neviʾim* (Prophets), and *Ketuvim* (Writings). Every kind selects and interprets a particular part of the Hebrew scriptures.

Late antiquity refers to the first six centuries of the common era, from the destruction of the Jerusalem Temple in 70 CE to the Muslim conquest of the Near and Middle East about 640 CE. The countries in which rabbinic Judaism took shape and flourished were the Land of Israel (Erets Yisraʾel, i.e., "Palestine") under Roman, then Byzantine, rule (from before the first century CE to the Muslim conquest nearly seven centuries later) and Babylonia, part of the western satrapies of the Iranian empire (to about 225 under the Parthians, an Iranian people of the northeast; from about 225 to the Muslim conquest, under the Sasanids, an Iranian dynasty from the province of Fars).

As to sources, rabbinic Judaism is known from documents created in the period under discussion: the Mishnah (c. 200 CE) and the two Talmuds (one produced in Babylonia about 500 CE, the other in the Land of Israel a century earlier), which in form constitute commentaries to the Mishnah. Other important rabbinic documents of the time include commentaries on parts of the Hebrew scriptures—in particular *Mekhilta'*, for *Exodus; Sifra'*, for *Leviticus;* and *Sifrei,* for *Numbers* and *Deuteronomy*—and *Bere'shit Rabbah* and *Vayiqra' Rabbah,* compilations of exegeses on *Genesis* and *Leviticus.* The Jewish prayer book (*siddur*) and certain mystical writings come down from this same period. They clearly relate to the larger rabbinic form of Judaism. But the precise definition of that relationship has not been fully clarified.

The adjective *rabbinic* before the noun *Judaism* signifies a kind of Judaism named after its principal kind of leader, a rabbi, a supernatural sage. The definition of *rabbi* shifts in ancient times. The title itself was originally quite neutral, and not unique to Jews. It means simply "My lord," and hence no more than *Monsieur* or *Mein Herr.* When Jesus was called "rabbi," the term was equivalent to *teacher* or *master, Sir.* Rabbis in the Mishnah, figures of the first and second centuries, generally give opinions about trivial legal matters; they were considered sages but were never represented as wonder-workers. Representations of rabbis in documents from the third century onward, including discussion of first- and second-century figures in those later documents, by contrast present the rabbi as a supernatural figure. The rabbi then emerges as a lawyer-magician, or supernatural judge-sage-mystic. Accordingly, through the centuries the title *rabbi* has come to refer solely to a distinctive amalgam, within the Jewish nation, of learning, piety, and holiness or supernatural power, associated with the sages of the Talmud and related writings.

"Rabbinic Judaism," then, is the worldview and way of life applied to the Jewish nation by rabbis. The Judaism under discussion also is called "Talmudic," after its principal literary documents. It may be called "classical" or "normative" in reference to its definitive character from its own day to today. In Talmudic times, however, the conception of a systematic *-ism,* a Judaism, is not attested in the rabbinical literature. Outsiders, coming after the fact, identify and name a religion. That an abstract system was perceived and named is not likely. One cannot isolate a word, or a concept to be presented by a single word, for "Judaism." The closest verbal symbol for this kind of Judaism is *Torah.* A sage became a rabbi because he knew Torah in the right way, having learned under proper auspices and having given ample evidence of accurate mastery and correct interpretation of the Torah.

It follows that the definitive trait of rabbinic Judaism is stress upon Torah. In fact, one may define the character of this kind of Judaism within three elements: holy faith, holy man, holy way of life. Thus, first is emphasis upon the doctrine of the dual revelation to Moses at Sinai, a written Torah (the Pentateuch) and an oral Torah. Second comes belief in the leadership of the sage, or rabbi (in context, "My lord"). Third is stress upon doing the will of God through study of Torah under the guidance of sages and upon living the holy way of life laid down in the Torah as interpreted by rabbis.

THE MYTH. This article will now consider in detail the definitive symbolic structure of rabbinic Judaism, as it emerges from late antiquity. The central myth of classical Judaism is the belief that the ancient scriptures constituted divine revelation, but only a part of it. At Sinai God had handed down a dual revelation: the written part known to one and all, but also the oral part preserved by the great scriptural heroes, passed on by prophets to various ancestors in the obscure past and finally, and most openly and publicly, handed down to the rabbis who created the Talmuds. The "whole Torah" thus consisted of both written and oral parts. The rabbis taught that the "whole Torah" was studied by sages of every period in Israelite history from Moses to the present. It is a singular, linear conception of a revelation preserved only by the few but pertaining to the many, and in time capable of bringing salvation to all.

The Torah myth further regards Moses as "our rabbi." It holds that whoever embodies the teachings of "Moses, our rabbi," thereby conforms to the will of God, and not to God's will alone but also to his *way.* In heaven God and the angels study Torah just as rabbis do on earth. God dons phylacteries like a Jew. He prays in the rabbinic mode. He carries out the acts of compassion called for by Judaic ethics. He guides the affairs of the world according to the rules of Torah, just as he does the rabbi in his court. One exegesis of the creation legend taught that God had looked into the Torah and therefrom had created the world.

The myth of Torah is multidimensional. It includes the striking detail that whatever the most recent rabbi is destined to discover through proper exegesis of the tradition is as much a part of the way revealed to Moses as is a sentence of scripture itself. It therefore is possible to participate even in the giving of the law by appropriate, logical inquiry into the law. God himself, studying and living by Torah, is believed to subject himself to these same rules of logical inquiry. If an earthly court overrules the testimony, delivered through miracles, of the heavenly one, God would rejoice, crying out, "My sons have conquered me! My sons have conquered me."

This is a mythical-religious system in which earth and heaven correspond to one another, with Torah as the nexus and model of both. The heavenly paradigm is embodied upon earth. Moses "our rabbi" is the pattern for the ordinary sage. And God himself participates in the system, for it is his image that, in the end, forms that cosmic paradigm. The faithful Jew constitutes the projection of the divine on earth. Honor is due to the learned rabbi more than to the scroll of the Torah, for through his learning and logic he may alter the very content of Mosaic revelation. He is Torah, not merely because he lives by it but because at his best he forms as compelling an embodiment of the heavenly model as does a Torah scroll itself.

The final and generative element in the rabbinic Torah myth concerns salvation. It takes many forms. One salvific teaching holds that had Israel not sinned—that is, disobeyed the Torah—the scriptures would have closed with the story of the conquest of Palestine. From that eschatological time, the sacred community would have lived in eternal peace under the divine law. Keeping the Torah was therefore the veritable guarantee of salvation. The opposite is said in many forms as well. Israel had sinned; therefore, God had called the Assyrians, Babylonians, and Romans to destroy the Temple of Jerusalem; but in his mercy he would be equally faithful to restore the fortunes of the people when they, through their suffering and repentance, had expiated the result and the cause of their sin.

So, in both negative and positive forms, the Torah myth tells of a necessary connection between the salvation of the people and of the world and the state of Torah among them. For example, if all Israel would properly keep two Sabbaths, the Messiah would come. Of special interest here is the rabbinic saying that the rule of the pagans depends upon the sin of Israel. If Israel would constitute a full and complete replication of "Torah"—that is, of heaven—then pagan rule would come to an end. When Israel makes itself worthy through its embodiment of Torah—that is, through its perfect replication of the heavenly way of living—then the end will come.

THE MISHNAH'S LAYER OF RABBINIC JUDAISM. The history of the Judaism expressed in this Torah myth is obscured by the superficially uniform character of the rabbinic compilations of late antiquity. All of them, early and late, appear to wish to say pretty much the same thing. It goes without saying that each rabbinic document finds in scripture ample precedent for its own viewpoint. That is why they all look alike. The documents, moreover, are collective, bearing the names of many authorities in common. Accordingly, when turning to the sources for the viewpoint just now outlined, one finds it everywhere. So it is difficult to trace the history of the ideas shared in common by them. Yet that is not entirely the case, for there is one rabbinic document of late antiquity, the Mishnah, that stands apart from the rest. It ignores scripture and the need for proof-texts, on the one side, and it omits reference to the Torah myth as the critical symbolic element, on the other.

The Mishnah is the first document of rabbinic Judaism, and it constitutes the foundation for the two Talmuds and the law of Judaism thereafter. The Mishnah rarely cites a scriptural proof-text for any of its propositions, even when the laws simply rephrase in the Mishnah's own language the facts supplied by scripture. Except for the tractate *Avot,* distinct in language and character, the Mishnah finds no room in its definitive construction—that is, in the formation of its principal divisions, let alone in its subdivisions (tractates) and their chapters—for extended discussion on the matter of the study of Torah, the place of the sage in the heavenly-earthly continuum, and those other propositions definitive of the Judaism that rests upon the Mishnah.

That is not to say the Mishnah knows nothing of the priority of learning. On the contrary, here and there are found explicit statements that the sage takes precedence. But the issue is this-worldly, not a matter of supernatural consequence, as is the case in equivalent allegations in Talmudic and later writings. An instance of the Mishnah's phrasing of the matter is in *Horayot* 3.5, followed by the Tosefta's gloss of the passage:

> A priest takes precedence over a Levite, a Levite over an Israelite, an Israelite over a *mamzer,* a *mamzer* over a *natin,* a *natin* over a proselyte, a proselyte over a freed slave. Under what circumstances? When all of them are equivalent [in other regards]. But if the *mamzer* was a disciple of a sage, and a high priest was an ignoramus, the *mamzer* who is a disciple of a sage takes precedence over a high priest who is an ignoramus. The Tosefta adds: A sage takes precedence over a king. [For if] a sage dies, we have none who is like him. [If] a king dies any Israelite is suitable to mount the throne. (Tosefta, *Horayot* 2.8)

Here is the first stage in the process by which the sage is moved from a merely earthly status as a principal authority to the supernatural position described above. Accordingly, the notion that Torah-learning enjoys priority is not alien to the Mishnah, and indeed begins there. But the Mishnah contains no hint of the view of the sage as a supernatural figure. Furthermore, the Mishnah distinguishes wonder-workers, such as Honi the Circle Maker (*Taʿan.* 3.8), from the sages, expressing disapproval of the former.

A still more striking trait of the Mishnah's kind of Judaism is the stress, within the Mishnah's system, upon enduring things and the omission of reference to one-time, historical events. The Mishnah presents a world in stasis, in which regularities and orderly patterns govern. It scarcely alludes to the coming of a messiah, the end of days, the meaning of Israel's suffering. The Mishnah offers no explanation or interpretation of Israel's history. If, therefore, one may characterize the first literary evidence of rabbinic Judaism in late antiquity, as of about 200 CE, this Judaism is described as focused upon the ongoing life of nature, the priesthood, and the Temple, with the sage telling the priests what to do. The Mishnah's simple, descriptive laws indicate how Israelite society, revolving about the cult, is maintained in stasis.

THE TALMUDIC RABBIS' RETURN TO SCRIPTURE AND HISTORY. Now at the other end of the period at hand, about 600 CE, that is not the Judaism that emerges. On the contrary, as has been seen, rabbinic Judaism fully revealed focused upon the meaning of Israel's history, its end in the coming of the Messiah. It was deeply engaged by one-time events and their meaning. Torah was defined by the sage as a supernatural figure who was qualified by constant reference to scripture. The contrast between the Mishnah's statements, divorced from scripture even where repeating scripture's own facts, and the later reception of the Mishnah, is seen in one fact. Both Talmuds systematically supply to Mishnah's laws precisely those proof-texts omitted by the Mishnah's framers. Accordingly, the Talmudic authorities will cite Mishnah's passage and immediately ask, "How do we know these things?" What follows will be scriptural proof-texts.

There is further indication that, in the two centuries after the closure of the Mishnah, about 200 CE, a massive reaction against the Mishnah's formulation of an ahistorical Judaism of eternal return took place. The character of other writings produced by the rabbis of those centuries provides important evidence of a renewed interest in history and its meaning. Beyond the two Talmuds and Tosefta, centered upon the Mishnah, is the formation of compilations of exegetical remarks, systematically laid forth for the Pentateuchal books of *Genesis* and *Leviticus.* These are generally supposed to have come into existence in the fifth century, that is, just as the Talmud of the Land of Israel had come to conclusion and the Talmud of Babylonia was coming to closure. Even more striking is the character of *Sifra',* a systematic essay on the *Book of Leviticus.* One basic literary form of that exegetical document is the citation of a passage of the Mishnah, or of Tosefta, verbatim or nearly so. The anonymous voice of the document then asks, "Is this not a matter of [mere] logic?" The argument then will unfold to prove that logic alone cannot prove with certainty the proposition of the Mishnah that has been cited. To the contrary, the only foundation of certainty is in a cited scripture, sometimes then subjected to exegetical work to prove the proposition of the Mishnah that stands at the head of the passage. The polemic is unmistakable. The Mishnah's laws, standing by themselves, cannot endure. Only provision of exegetical bases for them will suffice.

MESSIANISM. Beyond the emphasis upon the sage as a supernatural figure and upon scripture as the sole sound basis of truth, the third pillar of rabbinic Judaism as it emerged from late antiquity was its emphasis upon Torah as the means of reaching the messianic fulfillment and resolution of Israel's history. The authoritative expression of the messianic expectation is in the *siddur* (prayer book), emerging from late antiquity and enduring to the present day:

> Sound the great shofar to herald man's freedom;
> Raise high the banner to gather all exiles;
> Restore our judges as in days of old;
> Restore our counselors as in former times;
> Remove from us sorrow and anguish.
> Reign over us alone with loving kindness;
> With justice and mercy sustain our cause.
> Praised are You, O Lord, King who loves justice.

The restoration of the exiles to Zion and the gathering of the dispersed followed naturally by the prayer for good government, government under God's law. Then comes the concrete reference to the Messiah:

> Have mercy, O Lord, and return to Jerusalem, Your city;
> May Your presence dwell there as You promised.
> Rebuild it now, in our days and for all time;
> Reestablish there the majesty of David, Your servant.
> Praised are You, O Lord, who rebuilds Jerusalem.
> Bring to flower the shoot of Your servant David.
> Hasten the advent of the messianic redemption;
> Each and every day we hope for Your deliverance.
> Praised are You, O Lord, who assures our deliverance.

The link between the messianic hope for salvation and the religion of Torah and of rabbinic authority is expressed time and again in rabbinic writings. One example is as follows:

> Rabbah [a fourth-century rabbi] said, "When a man is brought in for judgment in the world to come, he is asked, 'Did you deal in good faith? Did you set aside time for study of Torah? Did you engage in procreation? Did you look forward to salvation? Did you engage in the dialectics of wisdom? Did you look deeply into matters?'" (B.T., *Shab.* 31a)

Rabbah's interpretation of the scripture "And there shall be faith in thy times, strength, salvation, wisdom and knowledge" (*Is.* 33:6) provides one glimpse into the cogent life of rabbinic Judaism. The first consideration was ethical: Did the man conduct himself faithfully? The second was study of Torah, not at random but every day, systematically, as a discipline of life. Third came the raising of a family. Celibacy and abstinence from sexual life were regarded as sinful. The full use of human creative powers for the procreation of life was a commandment. But, fourth, merely living day by day according to an upright ethic was not sufficient. It is true that people must live by a holy discipline, but the discipline itself was only a means. The end was salvation, daily expected in consequence of everyday deeds.

When one reflects upon the Talmudic teaching, already cited, that if all Israel only twice will properly keep the Sabbath (as the rabbis instruct), the Messiah will come, one sees the true state of affairs. The heirs of the Mishnah took over the messianic hope, so deep in the consciousness of the Jewish nation from biblical times onward, and harnessed its power to the system now known as rabbinic Judaism, a holy way of life taught by masters of Torah. Accordingly, as stated at the outset, in late antiquity is witnessed the formation on the disparate foundations of, first, the Mishnah, a law code lacking reference to history, on the one side, and, second, hope for the end of history and the coming of the Messiah, on the other, the kind of Judaism called rabbinic.

INSTITUTIONS. The institutional forms of rabbinic Judaism as known in particular from the Talmuds, are two. The first, not surprisingly, is the figure of the rabbi. The second is the court-school, that is, the place in which the rabbi ruled on certain matters affecting the Jewish community and also taught his apprentices, that is, disciples. First considered will be the figure of the rabbi as known in the third through the seventh century in the Babylonian Talmud.

The rabbi. The rabbis of that period conceived that on earth they studied Torah just as God, the angels, and "Moses, our rabbi," did in heaven. The heavenly schoolmen were even aware of Babylonian scholastic discussions. This conception must be interpreted by reference to the belief that the man truly made in the divine image was the rabbi; he embodied revelation, both oral and written, and all his actions constituted paradigms that were not merely correct but actually heavenly. Rabbis could create and destroy people because they were righteous, free of sin, or otherwise holy, and so enjoyed exceptional grace from heaven. It follows that Torah was held to be a source of supernatural power. The rabbis controlled the power of Torah because of their mastery of its contents. They furthermore used their own mastery of Torah quite independently of heavenly action. They were masters of witchcraft, incantations, and amulets. They could issue blessings and curses, create men and animals, and communicate with heaven. Their Torah was sufficiently effective to thwart the action of demons. However much they disapproved of other people's magic, they themselves were expected to do the things magicians did.

The rabbi was the authority on theology, including the structure and order of the supernatural world. He knew the secret names of God and the secrets of the divine "chariot"—the heavens—and of creation. If extraordinarily pious, he might even see the face of the Shekhinah, the presence of God; in any event, the Shekhinah was present in the rabbinical schools. The rabbi overcame the evil impulse that dominated ordinary men and was consequently less liable to suffering, misfortune, and sickness. He was able to pray effectively because he knew the proper times and forms of prayer. Moreover, the efficacy of his prayers was heightened by his purity, holiness, and other merits, which in turn derived from his knowledge of the secrets of Torah and his consequent particular observances. He could bring rain or cause drought. His blessings brought fertility, and his curse, death. He was apt to be visited by angels and to receive messages from them. He could see and talk with demons and could also communicate with the dead. He was an authority on interpretation of omens and dreams, on means of averting witchcraft, on incantations for cures, on knot tying (for phylacteries), and on the manufacture and use of amulets.

A central conception set rabbinic Judaism apart from Manichaeism, Mazdaism, Christianity, and other contemporary cults. It was not expected that the masses would assume the obligations of or attain to the supernatural skills of the Manichaean elect, Mazdean magi, Christian nuns and monks, or the religious virtuosi and cultic specialists of other groups. All male Jews, however, were expected to become rabbis. The rabbis wanted to transform the entire Jewish community into an academy where the whole Torah was studied and kept.

These beliefs aid in understanding the rabbis' view that Israel would be redeemed, the Messiah brought, through Torah. Because Israel had sinned, it was punished by being given over into the hands of earthly empires; when it atoned, it would be removed from their power. The means of this atonement or reconciliation were study of Torah, practice of commandments, and doing good deeds. These would transform each male Jew into a rabbi, hence into a saint. When all Jews had become rabbis, they then would no longer lie within the power of history. The Messiah would come. So redemption depended upon the "rabbinization" of all Israel, that is, upon the attainment by all Jewry of a full and complete embodiment of revelation or Torah, thus achieving a perfect replica of heaven. When Israel on earth became such a replica, it would be able, as a righteous, holy, saintly community, to exercise the supernatural power of Torah, just as some rabbis were already doing. With access to the consequent theurgical capacities, redemption would naturally follow.

The school. Study of Torah was just that: primarily an intellectual enterprise whose supernatural effects were decidedly secondary. The resources of the schools were knowledge of the laws and traditions that for the rabbis constituted the Torah of Moses. The actual method of learning used by the academies had nothing whatever to do with magic. The "Torah" of the rabbis was essentially no more than a legal tradition that had to be studied by the classical legal methods. The rabbis were expected to act as did other holy men, but they themselves respected legal learning and the capacity to reason about cases. Not everyone would achieve such skills of reasoning any more than everyone could make rain, and the academies doubtless attracted many who could only memorize and repeat what they knew. The whole process of learning, not merely its creative and innovative aspects, was, however, regarded as sacred, for the words themselves were holy.

The following exposition from the school of Rabbi ʿAnan exemplifies this process:

> What is the meaning of the Scripture *You that ride on* white asses, that sit on rich cloths, and that walk by the way, tell of it (*Judges* 5:10)? Those *that ride on asses* are the sages who go from city to city and from province to province to study Torah. *White* means that they make it clear as the noon hour. *Sitting on cloths* means that they judge a case truly. *And that walk* refers to masters of Scripture. *On the way,* these are masters of Mishnah. *Tell of it* refers to masters of Talmud, all of whose conversation concerns matters of Torah. (B.T., *Eruv.* 54b)

Found in the Song of Deborah, this verse about the victory of Israel over the Canaanites was explained by the rabbis as a description of the triumph of the Lord in the "wars of the Torah," a frequent image of rabbinic Judaism, and the consequent celebration by the people of the Lord. That people included many whose talents were limited but who, added all together, constituted, and celebrated, the Lord's triumph. Some, like itinerant philosophers, would wander in search of teachings. Others had great skill at clarification. Others were able and selfless judges. Still others merely knew scripture, or Mishnah, or Talmud, but spoke of nothing else. Here is the integrated, mature vision of the academies: a whole people devoted to revelation, each in his own way and according to his talent.

RABBIS AND ORDINARY FOLK. What average Jews ordinarily did not know and the rabbis always did know was the one thing that made a common man into a rabbi: *"Torah" learned through discipleship.* It begs the question to speak of the ordinary people as "ignorant of Judaism." One does not have to exaggerate the educational attainments of the community as a whole to recognize that learning in the rabbinic traditions did not by itself separate the rabbi from other people. It would, accordingly, be a gross error to overestimate the differences separating the way of life of the ordinary Jews from that of the rabbinical estate.

In general the rabbis' merely conventional social manners or customs were deepened into spiritual conceptions and magnified by their deeply mythic ways of thinking. In the villages ordinary people regarded the rabbi as another holy man, but still as a man, heart and soul at one in community with other Jews. The rabbinical ideal was antidualistic; the rabbis believed that all Israel, not just saints, prophets, and sages, stood at Sinai. All bore common responsibilities. No one conceived of two ways of living a holy life—two virtues or two salvations—but of only one Torah to be studied and observed by all, and thus the cutting edge of rabbinical separateness was blunted. The inevitable gap between the holy man and the layperson was further reduced by the deep concern felt by rabbis for the conduct of the masses. This concern led them to involve themselves in the everyday affairs of ordinary people, and it produced considerable impact upon daily life.

A review of the primary distinctive characteristics of the rabbinical school will show that the rabbis could not have created unscalable walls of social or religious difference. The sages spent a good part of their years in these schools; ordinary Jews, obviously, did not. Yet the schools were not monasteries. Disciples who left but who remained loyal to the school's way of life did not engage in ascetic disciplines of an outlandish sort, calculated to utterly divide the sages' way of living from that of normal men. They married. They ate regularly and chose edible food, not wormwood or locusts or refuse. They lived in villages, not in the wilderness. They did not make their livelihood through holy vagrancy. Their clothes were not supposed to be tattered or in rags. These differences between rabbis and other types of holy men, such as the Christian monks and the Manichaean elect, are obvious and therefore all the more important. The sages sought the society of ordinary Jews, so they lived in the villages rather than in the countryside ("wilderness"). Not engaged in begging ("holy vagrancy"), they owned property and were glad of it. They occupied important and permanent positions in the administration of communal life, and so came into constant and intimate contact with the common people. Access to rabbinical schools remained open to all, and the rabbis actively proselytized within the community to gain new candidates for their schools. Advantages of birth were minimal. In no way did the rabbis form a caste or a clan; the right marriage counted for little.

What, therefore, did the peculiarities of the rabbinical way of living amount to? A rabbi could eat with any other Jew in Babylonia because the biblical taboos about food were widely observed. Differences between the rabbis' interpretation of taboos about food and those advanced by others gradually diminished, as in time the rabbis' growing domination made their learned exegeses seem more commonplace. For example, although the rabbis said grace at meals and offered intelligible blessings for food, they were willing to teach others just what those blessings and prayers meant. Nothing in the rabbinical ritual of eating was to be kept secret. A person showed himself "ignorant" if he violated the rituals. His remedy was to go to a sage to study and learn, and this was explicitly recommended by the rabbis.

The Rabbi as Judge. What did a rabbi actually do as a community administrator? The following account gives a helpful portrait of the workday function of Rabbi Huna', head of the Sura academy about 300 CE:

> Every cloudy day they would carry him out in a golden palanquin, and he would survey the whole town. Every wall which looked unsafe he would order torn down. If the owner could rebuild it, he did so, but if not, he [Rabbi Huna] would rebuild it of his own funds. On the eve of every Sabbath, he would send a messenger to the market, and all the vegetables that remained to the market-gardeners, he would buy and throw into the river. Whenever he discovered a medicine, he would fill a jug with it, and suspend it above the doorstep and announce, "Whoever wants to, let him come and take." Some say, he knew from tradition a medicine for [a certain disease caused by eating with unwashed hands], and he would suspend a jug of water and proclaim, "Whoever needs it, let him come so that he may save his life from danger." When he ate bread, he would open his door wide, and declare, "Whoever is in need, let him come and eat." (B.T., *Ta'an.* 20b–21a)

The variety of public responsibilities carried out by the rabbi is striking. He had to prevent the collapse of mud buildings during a rainstorm. He had to ensure a constant market by encouraging truck gardeners to provide a steady supply of fresh vegetables. He had to give out medical information, to preserve public health, and to make certain that poor people could benefit from the available remedies. And he had to provide for the poor, so that no one would starve in his town.

These responsibilities reflected the different roles played by the rabbi. Only the first and second duties listed depended upon his political function. As judge he could order the destruction of dangerous property; as administrator he had to supervise the marketplace and use his funds to control supply and prices. But these roles had nothing to do with medical and eleemosynary activities. The former was contingent upon his reputation as a man of learning who had mastered the occult sciences, which then included medicine; the latter was based upon his possession of great wealth, accruing from his positions in politics, administration, and academic life.

Litigations coming before the Jewish courts were not particularly important in the evidence covering 200–500 CE.

On the whole they corresponded to those likely to come before a small-claims court in modern society. Thefts involved a book or a few rams. Betrothal cases concerned the exchange of property, such as a few *zuz,* a willow branch, some onions, or a piece of silk. Settlements of marriage contracts required division of a robe of fine wool, a silver cup. A few cases of alleged adultery were recorded, all of sufficient innocence for the court to rule that no adultery had taken place. The preparation and delivery of proper divorce documents hardly amounted to weighty matters of state. Divorce litigations in any event were provoked by peculiar and exceptional circumstances; normally a man could divorce his wife without court intervention, merely with the help of a scribe who wrote out the writ of divorce in accordance with the law.

The settlement of estates entailed somewhat larger sums of money. A woman's marriage contract stipulated that if she were divorced, she would be given an alimony of four hundred *zuz,* a round number that probably represented approximately enough capital for two years' maintenance. Provisions by the court for widows (food, wine, clothing) were humble and more typical matters. Even most estate cases pertained to rather small claims, such as a few trees, a slave, or a choice plot of ground. Settlement of debts, collections of mortgages and bonds, and the like did require rulings on somewhat more substantial sums, but the real issues were still relatively inconsequential—a hundred *zuz,* or whether a pledged spoon or knife had to be returned.

Some commercial litigations were brought before the courts. Questions of contract involved a few ferrymen and sharecroppers, or devolved upon a hired ass, a purchase of wine or poppy seed, a flooded field. Some commercial disputes demanded that the courts decide about a few *zuz* worth of silk beads, some sour wine, the sale of a wine press or a field. Others concerned a damaged jar or utensil, a dead goat, a stolen purse, a broken ax or wine barrel. Property cases similarly involved alleged fraud in a relatively small plot, the claim of an option to purchase a field, the use of canal water, and, very frequently, squatter's rights over a house or field and the eviction of tenant farmers.

Cases such as these clearly reveal the real substance of issues left in the rabbis' hands. With a few exceptions, strikingly petty sums of money or barely consequential pieces of property were all that the lower classes of society brought to litigation. And it was those classes that were primarily subject to rulings by the rabbinical courts. Large commercial transactions for many thousands of *zuz* worth of silk or pearls, wine or beer; enormous property transactions involving a whole village or town; claims of a considerable number of workers against a single employer, or vice versa; the affairs of large estates, rich landowners, big businessmen, important officials—none of these appears with any frequency, if at all, in extant reports.

The rabbis surely could not have agreed, however, that the humble and petty issues before them were of no consequence. It was their view—a very old one in Judaism—that the least and humblest affairs, as much as the largest and most weighty ones, testified to heaven about the moral state of society. If the prophet Amos had condemned Israel of old because a poor man was cheated of his shoes, then one can hardly be surprised that a later rabbi insisted upon the return of a cooking utensil given in pledge. What was important to the rabbis was that justice should prevail. They knew that if justice did not characterize the street, the trading market, the small farms and shops, then great affairs of commerce and the state would not likely be morally superior. They knew that the ethics of daily life, the life concerned with exchanges of onions and the use of water in a small canal, determined the destiny of Israel.

SUMMARY. The history of Judaism in late antiquity can be summarized very simply. First came the Mishnah, shaped over the first and second centuries CE. Then, second, followed four hundred years in which the legal and theological system of the Mishnah was drastically reshaped into something new. Since the Mishnah's system constituted a reaction against the messianic wars of the time in which it came into being, one sees a process by which the messianic "thesis" generated the Mishnah as its antimessianic antithesis, so producing the rabbinic synthesis in the Talmuds. That is to say, the messianic "thesis" rested on prophetic, historical, and apocalyptic passages of scripture. The Mishnah's "antithesis" constructed a system based on priestly and ahistorical legal passages. The Mishnah's system stood aloof both from biblical proof-texts and from the messianic interest in the meaning and end of history characteristic of its own day. Over the next four hundred years the rabbinic heirs of both the Mishnah and the scripture brought the two back into relationship. They forged them into a messianic and legal synthesis, the one "whole Torah" of "Moses, our rabbi," just as their Torah myth alleged.

SEE ALSO Amoraim; Judaism, overview article; Midrash and Aggadah; Mishnah and Tosefta; Pharisees; Talmud; Tannaim.

BIBLIOGRAPHY

The best systematic account of the theology of rabbinic Judaism is George Foot Moore's *Judaism in the First Centuries of the Christian Era: The Age of the Tannaim,* 3 vols. (Cambridge, U.K., 1954). The same categories of historical theology are addressed by E. E. Urbach in *The Sages: Their Concepts and Beliefs,* 2 vols. (Jerusalem, 1975), translated from the Hebrew by Israel Abrahams; by Solomon Schechter in *Some Aspects of Rabbinic Theology* (1909; reprint, New York, 1936); and by E. P. Sanders in *Paul and Palestinian Judaism: A Comparison of Patterns of Religion* (Philadelphia, 1977). These three works present a categorically similar picture of rabbinic Judaism's theology. An important anthology of sources is C. G. Montefiore and Herbert Loewe's *A Rabbinic Anthology* (New York, 1974). Two collections of essays on special topics provide guidance into the principal scholarly approaches of the last generation: Jacob Z. Lauterbach's *Rabbinic Essays* (Cincinnati, 1951) and Louis Ginzberg's *On Jewish Law and Lore* (Philadelphia, 1955). A different approach to the description of rabbinic Judaism is provided in my book *Judaism: The Evidence of the Mishnah* (Chicago, 1981). On the mysticism of rabbinic Judaism the most important book is Gershom Scholem's *Major Trends in Jewish Mysticism* (New York, 1954); on messianism, Scholem's *The Messianic Idea in Judaism* (New York, 1971). On the liturgy of Judaism in this period, the two definitive books are Joseph Heinemann's *Prayer in the Talmud* (Berlin and New York, 1977) and Lawrence A. Hoffman's *The Canonization of the Synagogue Service* (Notre Dame, Ind., 1979). On the archaeology of Judaism in this period one should consult, as a start, Eric M. Meyers and James F. Strange's *Archaeology, the Rabbis, and Early Christianity* (Nashville, 1981) and Lee I. Levine's edition of *Ancient Synagogues Revealed* (Jerusalem, 1981). On rabbinic Judaism viewed historically, there is my own *History of the Jews in Babylonia,* 5 vols. (Leiden, 1965–1969).

New Sources

Avery-Peck, Alan J., ed. *The Mishnah in Contemporary Perspective.* Leiden and Boston, 2002.

Baskin, Judith Reesa. *Midrashic Women: Formations of the Feminine in Rabbinic Literature.* Hanover, N.H., 2002.

Boccaccini, Gabriele. *Roots of Rabbinic Judaism: An Intellectual History, from Ezekiel to Daniel.* Grand Rapids, Mich., 2002.

Cohen, Shaye J. D., ed. *The Synoptic Problem in Rabbinic Literature.* Providence, R.I., 2000.

Freeman, Gordon M. *The Heavenly Kingdom: Aspects of Political Thought in the Talmud and Midrash.* Lanham, Md., Jerusalem and Philadelphia, 1986.

Harrington, Hannah K. *Holiness: Rabbinic Judaism and the Graeco-Roman World.* London and New York, 2001.

Hoffman, Lawrence A. *Covenant of Blood: Circumcision and Gender in Rabbinic Judaism.* Chicago, 1996.

Jacobs, Irving. *The Midrashic Process: Tradition and Interpretation in Rabbinic Judaism.* Cambridge and New York, 1995.

Neusner, Jacob. *The Four Stages of Rabbinic Judaism.* New York, 1999.

Zlotnick, Helena. *Dinah's Daughters: Gender and Judaism from the Hebrew Bible to Late Antiquity.* Philadelphia, 2002.

JACOB NEUSNER (1987)
Revised Bibliography

RABBITS. The belief that a rabbit dwells in the moon is widely attested not only in Inner Asia, South Asia, and East Asia but also in North America, Mesoamerica, and southern Africa. Among the Turco-Mongol peoples of Inner Asia, the shaman hunts a rabbit in the moon during his ecstatic journey to the heavenly world. In China, as early as the Han period, the rabbit is represented on bronze mirrors as inhabiting the moon, pounding the drug of immortality with a pestle and mortar. The Japanese depict him as pounding rice cakes in the moon spots.

The Khoi and the San of the Kalahari in southern Africa also tell of a rabbit in the moon. In Khoi myths of the origin of death, the hare is presented as the careless messenger. Charged by the moon with bringing a message of immortality to humankind, he mistransmitted the good tidings as a message of death. The San have similar stories.

In North America, a rabbit is at the center of the creation myth of the ancient Algonquin. At the mythical time of beginning, the Great Hare appeared on earth and laid the foundation of the world. He instructed people in the medicine dance and other forms of life; he fought the oceanic monsters; he reconstructed the earth after the deluge, and on his departure he left it as it is today. The rabbit, as well as the hare, appears as a trickster in the Indian tales of the southeastern United States.

In ancient Mesopotamia and Syria, about the beginning of the second millennium BCE, the hare was imbued with the symbolism of death and rebirth. In Egypt it was probably associated with Osiris, the god of rebirth and immortality. The hare appears in Islam, for example, in Rūmī's poetry, as one of the animals symbolizing the base human soul.

In the Greco-Roman world, the hare was multivalent: It was widely recognized for its lubricity, it was thought to be androgynous, and its flesh was used as an aphrodisiac. It was most pleasing to Aphrodite and sacred also to Eros, who hunted the animal. However, it was especially associated with Dionysos, the god not only of love, fertility, and life but also of death and immortality. The hare was hunted, torn to pieces and eaten, and used as a love gift. It was considered a most appropriate symbol for a grave stele, because in humanity's basic dreams it represents the love that will conquer death. As belief in immortality became more popular, the hare was increasingly used in funerary art. Early Christians accepted this rabbit symbolism and depicted rabbits on gravestones. In modern times, the Easter Bunny, whose eggs represent the source of life, seems to be a continuation of archaic religious values associated with both the rabbit and the egg.

BIBLIOGRAPHY

On the symbolism of the rabbit in the Mediterranean world, see Erwin R. Goodenough's excellent study in *Pagan Symbols in Judaism,* volume 8 of his *Jewish Symbols in the Greco-Roman Period* (New York, 1958), pp. 85–95. See also Johannes Maringer's "Der Hase in Kunst und Mythe der vor- und frühge- schichtlichen Menschen," *Zeitschrift für Religions- und Geistesgeschichte* 30 (1978): 219–228, and Ananda K. Coomaraswamy's review of John Layard's *The Lady of the Hare: A Study in the Healing Power of Dreams* (London, 1945) in *Psychiatry* 8 (1945): 507–513. Coomaraswamy's review was also published under the title "On Hares and Dreams" in the *Quarterly Journal of the Mythic Society* (Bangalore) 37 (1946): 1–14.

New Sources

Birchfield, D. L. *Rabbit: American Indian Legends.* New York, 1996.

Davis, Susan, and Margo Demello. *Stories Rabbits Tell: A Natural and Cultural History of a Misunderstood Creature.* New York, 2003.

Ross, Gayle. *How Rabbit Tricked Otter and Other Cherokee Trickster Stories.* New York, 1994.

MANABU WAIDA (1987)
Revised Bibliography

RĀBIʿAH AL-ʿADAWĪYAH (d. AH 185/801 CE), was an Arab mystic, poet, and Muslim saint. Even though she attained great age and fame, little is known of Rābiʿah's personal life. Her name indicates that she was a fourth (*rābiʿah*) daughter, probably of a poor family. For some time she was a house servant in Basra, but, thanks to her amazing piety, her master released her from bondage. Her life thereafter, marked by austerity and otherworldliness, was spent largely in retirement, although her sanctity attracted many who sought her prayers and teachings. Rābiʿah of Basra is regarded as the person who introduced the concept of pure love of God into the ascetic way of life prevalent among God-seeking Muslims during the second century AH.

It seems probable that Rābiʿah met some of the well-known ascetics of her time, among them Ibrahim ibn Adham of Balkh (d. 770?). However, the stories that connect her with the ascetic preacher Ḥasan al-Baṣrī, and even claim that he proposed marriage to her, are pure invention, for Ḥasan (whose constant call to renunciation and fear of God certainly colored the spiritual atmosphere in Basra) died in 728, when Rābiʿah was only about ten years old.

Many legends have been woven around her. When she performed the pilgrimage, the Kaʿbah is said to have moved forward to greet her, and her donkey, which had died on the road, was miraculously revived. But Rābiʿah, faithful to the ascetic tradition, and extremely afraid of hellfire, rejected the common belief that she was capable of performing miracles. Rather, she considered such miracles as satanic temptations.

Rābiʿah's greatest contribution to the development of Sufism lay in her insistence upon pure love of God, emphasizing the Qurʾanic verse "He loves them and they love him" (surah 5:59). She expressed her feelings sometimes in short, artless poems, sometimes in beautiful prayers, for she spent long nights in intimate conversation with her beloved Lord. In daily life, she experienced remorse when her thoughts strayed from him. Her heart was filled with love of God, with no room left even for a special love of the Prophet. Asked whether she hoped for Paradise, she answered with the Arabic proverb "Al-jār thumma al-dār" ("First the neighbor, then the house"), meaning that she thought only of him who had created Paradise and Hell.

Thus arose the best-known legend about her: having been seen carrying a flaming torch in one hand and a pitcher of water in the other, she explained that this symbolic act meant that she would set Paradise on fire and pour water into Hell, "so that these two veils may disappear and nobody may worship God out of fear of Hell or hope for Paradise, but solely for his own beauty." This tale, which reached Europe in the early fourteenth century, is the basis of several short stories, mystical and otherwise, in Western literature. Other accounts, too, eventually became known in the West, at least in nineteenth-century England, as Richard Monckton Milnes's poems *The Sayings of Rabiah* prove.

In the Islamic world, Rābiʿah was highly praised by ʿAṭṭār (d. 1221) in his *Tadhkirat al-awliyāʾ* (Biographies of the Saints), where he states that a woman who walks in the path of God cannot be called merely (i. e., deprecatively) "woman." Some centuries later, however, Jāmī (d. 1492) reminded his readers that the fact that the sun is feminine in Arabic does not distract from its grandeur. Certainly, her gender never clouded Rābiʿah's renown. The legend that she refused to go out to admire nature on a radiant spring day, preferring to contemplate the beauty of the Creator in the darkness of her house, has been retold for centuries, often without mentioning her name, and her life has even served as scenario for at least one Arab movie. Her name is still used to praise exceptionally pious women.

SEE ALSO Sufism.

BIBLIOGRAPHY

Modern Arabic scholars, among them ʿAbd al-Raḥmān Badawī, have devoted studies to Rābiʿah, but the only comprehensive study in a Western language is Margaret Smith's *Rābiʿah the Mystic, and Her Fellow Saints in Islam* (1928; reprint, Cambridge, 1984).

ANNEMARIE SCHIMMEL (1987)

RABINDRĀNATHA THAKŪR SEE TAGORE, RABINDRANATH

RACHEL AND LEAH, or in Hebrew, Raḥel and Leʾah, were wives of Jacob and daughters of Laban. According to *Genesis,* Rachel, who was the great-granddaughter of Abraham's brother Nahor, met Jacob at a well after he had fled Canaan to escape his brother Esau. Jacob worked for Laban for seven years so that he might marry Rachel, but he was deceived into marrying her older sister Leah and had to work another seven years to earn Rachel's hand.

Both women have animal names: *Raḥel* means "ewe" and *Leʾah* means "cow." Although Rachel was beautiful, Leah was more fertile. They thus embody the two aspects of femininity that are emphasized in the Bible, and their conflict demonstrates the importance attached to male attention and appreciation. At one point Leah gave Rachel mandrakes to improve her fertility in exchange for Rachel's turn to spend the night with Jacob. In so doing the sisters exerted some control over where their shared husband spent his time.

Ultimately Leah produced seven children (Reuben, Simeon, Levi, Judah, Issachar, Zebulun, and Dinah); two more (Gad and Asher) were born to her slave girl Zilpah. Rachel's slave girl Bilhah bore Dan and Naphtali; later Rachel produced two sons of her own, Joseph and Benjamin.

When Jacob fled from Laban, Rachel took the family idols, sitting on them when her father came and claiming she could not rise "because the way of women has come upon me" (*Gn.* 31:35). She died after giving birth to Benjamin and was buried at the spot, between Bethel and Ephrath. Her purported tomb is venerated to this day and may have been similarly regarded in biblical times (*Gn.* 35:20, *1 Sm.* 10:2, *Jer.* 31:15). Leah apparently died in Canaan and was buried in the cave of Machpelah (*Gn.* 39:31).

Most scholars agree that these stories include personifications of Israelite tribal history. The Leah tribes may have formed an early confederation. The monarchy and the priesthood are ascribed to tribes descended from her sons Judah and Levi. Rachel is the mother of the Joseph tribes, which were dominant in northern Israel, and of the adjoining Benjamin tribe, from which came the first king, Saul.

See Also Jacob; Joseph; Saul.

Bibliography

A thorough survey of the patriarchal narratives is in Nahum M. Sarna's *Understanding Genesis* (New York, 1966). The historical material is discussed in great detail in Roland de Vaux's *The Early History of Israel,* translated by David Smith (Philadelphia, 1978). Postbiblical traditions pertaining to biblical events are collected in Louis Ginzberg's *The Legends of the Jews,* 2d ed., 2 vols., translated by Henrietta Szold and Paul Radin (Philadelphia, 2003).

Frederick E. Greenspahn (1987 and 2005)

RADCLIFFE-BROWN, A. R. (1881–1955) was an English social anthropologist. Alfred Reginald Radcliffe-Brown, as he was known formally after changing his name in 1926 (Radcliffe having been his mother's original surname), was born in Sparkbrook, Birmingham. He was educated at King Edward's School in Birmingham, at Birmingham University (where he spent a year as a premedical student), and at Trinity College, Cambridge University, from which he graduated with a bachelor's degree in mental and moral science. Among those who taught him as an undergraduate were C. H. Myers and W. H. R. Rivers (both medical psychologists who had participated in Cambridge's pioneering anthropological expedition to the Torres Strait off the northeastern tip of Australia). After graduation in 1904 Radcliffe-Brown went on to study anthropology under Rivers and A. C. Haddon (who had also been on the expedition of 1898–1899) and was sent by them in 1906 to study the people of the Andaman Islands, southwest of Burma, for two years.

Radcliffe-Brown's initial report on this expedition, "The Religion of the Andaman Islanders," published in *Folk-Lore* in 1909 (his book *The Andaman Islanders* was not published until 1922), led Trinity College to offer him a fellowship, the tenure of which (from 1908 to 1914) was for a brief period combined with a teaching position at the London School of Economics. It was in those years that he first encountered and became permanently influenced by the sociological orientation of Émile Durkheim. Radcliffe-Brown quickly became part of the rapidly developing, distinctively sociological approach to the study of primal societies, and by the 1920s he was probably this movement's most influential figure. Until well into the twentieth century this field was dominated by the ethnological approach, the practitioners of which were particularly interested in the detailed history of particular societies and the patterns of diffusion and transmission of their cultures. That style of analysis was itself still influenced by the evolutionist approach that had been strongly in evidence in the later part of the nineteenth century and had largely regarded religion as a primitive form of science. While the ethnologists of the early part of the twentieth century did not cling strongly to the latter view, they stood in contrast to the emphasis that Radcliffe-Brown, under Durkheim's influence, increasingly placed on the idea that primitive societies should be analyzed synchronically rather than diachronically. In other words, Radcliffe-Brown's work increasingly involved the claim that in order to comprehend scientifically the main features of a society one should regard it as a functioning whole; its different parts were explainable in terms of their interrelatedness and their contribution to its maintenance.

Radcliffe-Brown's impact, which grew intermittently but strongly in the 1920s and 1930s through his teaching and writing in various countries, was based primarily on his advocacy and practice of what he came to call a natural science of society, with particular reference to social structure. His attention to religion was largely confined to the study of ritual and ceremony—which was particularly evident in the book that he published on the Andaman Islanders in 1922—and the related phenomenon of totemism. In his work on ritual, Radcliffe-Brown was greatly influenced by Durkheim's argument that the primary significance of ritual is its expression and promotion of collective sentiments and social solidarity.

In his first major essay on totemism, "The Sociological Theory of Totemism," published in the *Proceedings of the Fourth Pacific Science Congress* in 1929, Radcliffe-Brown maintained that Durkheim, by arguing that a totemic object acquires its significance via its sacredness, had begged the crucial question as to why totemism in primal societies typically involves plants or animals, even though Durkheim had pointed cogently to the ways in which ritualized collective conduct in connection with totems was intimately related to social structure and social integration. Radcliffe-Brown argued that plants and animals should not be regarded simply as emblems of social groups, but rather that they are selected as representatives of groups because objects and events that deeply affect the material and spiritual well-being of a society (or any phenomenon that represents such an object or event) are likely to become what he called objects of the ritual attitude. Although there has been disagreement as to the extent to which Radcliffe-Brown's second essay on this subject ("The Comparative Method in Social Anthropology," *Journal of the Royal Anthropological Institute,* 1952) involved a substantial change of position, there can be no doubt that it exhibits a very explicit interest in a theme that was not conspicuous in the essay of 1929—namely, the various relationships between totemic objects and between these objects and the structures of the groups that maintain ritual attitudes toward them.

Some have regarded Radcliffe-Brown's work at this point as embracing a form of cognitive structuralism, which is committed to the view that while animals and plants are good to eat they are even better to "think" (that is, they constitute a highly suitable and accessible symbolic means for "talking about" central features of a society's social structure and its relationship with its environment). Others have insisted that Radcliffe-Brown did not move so far beyond his original position of maintaining that the selection of totems is based primarily upon the tangible effects that particular plants or animals are perceived to have in a society. For discussion of the debate see Milton Singer's book, *Man's Glassy Essence: Explorations in Semiotic Anthropology* (1984).

BIBLIOGRAPHY

Radcliffe-Brown's major writings on religion are to be found in *The Andaman Islanders,* 3d ed. (Glencoe, Ill., 1948), *Structure and Function in Primitive Society* (London, 1952), and *The Social Anthropology of Radcliffe-Brown,* edited by Adam Kuyper (London, 1977). Illuminating discussion of his work can be found in Adam Kuyper's *Anthropology and Anthropologists,* rev. ed. (Boston, 1983).

New Sources

Câmara, J. L. Bettencourt da. *Radcliffe-Brown and Lévi-Strauss: A Reappraisal.* Lisbon, 1995.

Maddock, Kenneth. "Affinities and Missed Opportunities: John Anderson and A. R. Radcliffe-Brown in Sydney." *Australian Journal of Anthropology* 3 issue 1/2 (1992): 3–19.

Singer, Milton. "On the Semiotics of Ritual: Radcliffe-Brown's Legacy." In *Theory and Method: Evaluation of the Work of M.N. Srinivas.* New Delhi, 1996.

ROLAND ROBERTSON (1987)
Revised Bibliography

RĀDHĀ.

RĀDHĀ. The cowherd woman *(gopī)* whose passionate love for the god Kṛṣṇa has been celebrated in song and story throughout the Indian subcontinent since medieval times, Rādhā has been revered by Vaiṣṇava devotees not only as Kṛṣṇa's earthly beloved but also as his eternal consort, as one half of the divine duality. Her name may be a feminine form of the Vedic *rādhās* ("desired object"). Epitomizing the ideal of *prema bhakti* ("loving devotion"), she has herself been an object of Vaiṣṇava worship, sometimes as a mediator but often as the highest reality, surpassing even Kṛṣṇa.

ORIGINS AND HISTORY. Despite the considerable scholarly attention that has been devoted to Rādhā's origins, the matter remains veiled in obscurity. Available evidence points to possible literary beginnings, perhaps in the songs of the Ābhīrs, a cattle-herding community of North India. From the earliest source material—a succession of stray verses in Sanskrit, Prakrit, and Apabhraṃṣa from roughly the third century CE that celebrate the love of Rādhā and Kṛṣṇa—it is clear that her association with him was established throughout much of the subcontinent by the close of the first millennium.

The transfiguration of Rādhā from literary heroine to object of religious devotion was a complex and gradual process. The *Gītagovinda* of Jayadeva gives evidence that already in the twelfth century she was viewed as Kṛṣṇa's eternal consort. In the succeeding centuries, especially in eastern India, she continued to appropriate designations earlier applied to such goddess figures as Devī or Durgā, notably, *śakti* (strength, power), *prakṛti* (nature), and *māyā* (the creative energy of illusion). Recent studies have revealed her kinship with Ekānaṃśā-Durgā, whose complexion is also fair, and suggested that she may be in part a transformation of Durgā. Her counterpart and possible precursor in the South, Pinnai, who is portrayed as Kṛṣṇa's consort and wife among the cowherds, likewise appears to have had connections with Ekānaṃśā-Durgā. Both Rādhā and Piṉṉai have also assimilated aspects of Viṣṇu's consort Śrī-Lakṣmī, especially her role as mediator between God and human souls.

Although there are references to Rādhā in the Purāṇas, the most characteristic and important arena of her development is not narrative myth but poetry, or, more strictly, song, for Hindu poetry is composed to be sung. Building on the literary tradition of the courts, the poets of eastern India (and, to a lesser extent, of the North) sensitively and feelingly portrayed every phase and mood of her love with Kṛṣṇa: her shyness and ambivalence at its first dawning, her fulfillment in union with him and her subsequent hurt and jealous anger (*māna*) when he betrays her, and her final agony of separation when he leaves the cowherd village to fulfill his destiny by slaying the demon-king Kaṃsa. Most of the poets and dramatists who developed this theme appear to have presupposed that Rādhā was already married, leaving to the theologians the awkward task of reconciling her status as a *parakīyā* heroine—one who belongs to another—with her role as consort of Kṛṣṇa, who as lord of the universe is the upholder of the moral order (dharma). In one such resolution, the Bengali Vaiṣṇava Rūpa Gosvāmī (sixteenth century) explains that Rādhā and the other *gopīs* belong eternally to Kṛṣṇa; their marriage to earthly cowherds is thus an expedient designed to enhance the intrigue of Kṛṣṇa's *līlā.*

THEOLOGY AND WORSHIP. Although the *gopīs* have been depicted with Kṛṣṇa in images dating from the seventh century or even earlier, it is not known whether they were at that time themselves objects of worship. It is only much later, from approximately the time of Caitanya (1486–1533), that one finds clear evidence for the worship specifically of Rādhā with Kṛṣṇa, often in the characteristic *yugala-mūrti* ("paired image," the two side by side) that can still be seen in temples in Bengal and Vṛndāvana. Rādhā's worship, however, is not confined to those communities that place her image next to his; in the main Rādhāvallabha temple in Vṛndāvana, for example, she is represented simply by a throne cushion over which hangs a golden leaf that bears the inscription of her name. Nor need her presence be marked even to that degree: Members of the Nimbārka and Vallabha communities regard Rādhā and Kṛṣṇa as indistinguishable from one another, and hence a devotee worshiping Kṛṣṇa is considered to be worshiping Rādhā as well. The Nimbārkīs in fact interpret the honorific element "Śrī" in "Śrīkṛṣṇa," a title of Kṛṣṇa used throughout India, as explicitly designating Rādhā; thus, "Śrī-Kṛṣṇa." Her paramount importance for residents of Vṛndāvana is also reflected in their use of the vocative form of her name, "Rādhe," as a standard mode of greeting. Members of the Rādhāvallabha community further honor her name by writing it on vines, stones, and pieces of wood placed in certain sacred spots. Like Kṛṣṇa's name, then, Rādhā's functions as a mantra, a group of syllables embodying sacred power.

In addition to worshiping Rādhā through her images and her name, devotees attend performances in which episodes from the love story of Rādhā and Kṛṣṇa are sung and enacted by professional and amateur performers. In Bengal, for example, where she has always been especially popular, the medieval verses celebrating her love for Kṛṣṇa are sung in a semidramatic musical form known as *padāvalī-kīrtan.* In a typical performance, the lead singer, assisted by several other singers and two or three drummers, spins out a single episode in the divine love story over the course of three or four hours, interspersing narrative and dialogue with the lyrical verses describing and reflecting on Rādhā's feelings. These songs play on the central juxtaposition of the physical and the metaphysical as well as the paradox of the human-divine encounter. Devotees respond with expressions of wonder at the intensity, depth, and steadfastness of Rādhā's love, which, while representing the heights of human passion, also symbolizes the religious ideal of selfless, unswerving devotion to God. Her unexpected triumph over the lord of the universe, which is indicated, for example, by his abject submission as he begs for her forgiveness, invariably evokes exclamations of astonishment and delight.

The chief basis for the worship of Rādhā is thus the transcendent quality of her love for Kṛṣṇa; even when the theological designation *śakti* is applied to her, its meaning shifts from its usual Tantric sense of strength and activity to one of love. That she is the personification of love is indicated by a common designation for her: *mahābhāva* ("great emotion"). So exalted has this love rendered her that many Vaiṣṇavas since the time of Caitanya have felt that one should not imitate her directly; they have chosen rather to assume in their devotion the role of a humble maidservant of hers, a *mañjarī,* who is privileged to assist her and thereby enjoy vicariously the bliss of her union with Kṛṣṇa.

Rādhā's nature contrasts with that of all other major Hindu goddesses. She is neither mother goddess nor fertility deity, neither angry and destructive goddess nor social paradigm. Worshiped solely in relation to Kṛṣṇa, she has never become an independent deity. Yet her importance for Vaiṣṇava devotion since the sixteenth century can scarcely be overestimated. In the intensity and steadfastness of her love for Kṛṣṇa, especially in her separation from him, she serves as the highest inspiration to the devotee. The strength of Rādhā and her friends and the superiority of their devotion provide a valorization of the religious capacities of women that has had social implications as well. Finally, as the embodiment of supreme love, Rādhā in her eternal relation to Kṛṣṇa represents ultimate reality, for love (*prema*) itself, in the Vaiṣṇava vision, is the highest principle in the universe.

SEE ALSO Kṛṣṇa; Līlā; Nimbārka; Vallabha; Vṛndāvana.

BIBLIOGRAPHY

Two books serve as major sources for the study of Rādhā. The most comprehensive treatment of her, a work in Bengali by S. B. Dasgupta, *Śrīrādhār kramabikās darśane o sāhitye* (Calcutta, 1952), is a judicious, well-documented account of her origins and development that traces her relations to other goddesses and to Indian conceptions of *śakti.* A more recent volume, *The Divine Consort: Rādhā and the Goddesses of India,* edited by John Stratton Hawley and me (Berkeley, Calif., 1982), contains articles on the religious significance of Rādhā in various texts and traditions, together with an extensive annotated bibliography.

Two other articles, as well as portions of two books, treat particular aspects of Rādhā. In "A Note on the Development of the Rādhā Cult," *Annals of the Bhandarkar Oriental Research Institute* 36 (1955): 231–257, A. K. Majumdar surveys evidence for the worship of Rādhā. Bimanbehari Majumdar's *Kṛṣṇa in History and Legend* (Calcutta, 1969) includes two chapters documenting her importance in religious literature. In a more recent article, "Rādhā: Consort of Kṛṣṇa's Vernal Passion," *Journal of the American Oriental Society* 95 (October-December 1975): 655–671, Barbara Stoler Miller surveys early verses in Sanskrit, Prakrit, and Apabhraṃśa on the Rādhā-Kṛṣṇa theme. Finally, Friedhelm Hardy's *Viraha-bhakti: The Early History of Kṛṣṇa Devotion in South India* (Delhi, 1983) distinguishes the primarily secular early poetic traditions of the love of Kṛṣṇa and Rādhā from the epic and Puranic traditions of Kṛṣṇa and the *gopīs.*

Four studies contain portraits of Rādhā as she is presented in particular literary works and performance traditions. In her *Love Song of the Dark Lord: Jayadeva's Gitagovinda* (New York, 1977), Barbara Miller includes a chapter on the figure of Rādhā. My own *Drama as a Mode of Religious Realization: The Vidagdhamādhava of Rūpa Gosvāmī* (Chico, Calif., 1984) discusses and illustrates through summary and translation the treatment of Rādhā by the Bengali Vaiṣṇava theologian and playwright Rupa Gosvami. Finally, two works of John Hawley throw new light on the interpretation of Rādhā in the Braj region of North India. The introductions and translations in his *At Play with Krishna: Pilgrimage Dramas from Brindavan* (Princeton, N.J., 1981) present Rādhā as she is portrayed in the *rās līlās,* and a chapter of his *Sur Das: Poet, Singer, Saint* (Seattle, 1984) traces the conception of Rādhā through the successive layers of the *Sūr Sāgar,* the collection of poetry attributed to the sixteenth-century poet Sūr Dās.

New Sources

Banerjee, Sumanta. *Appropriation of a Folk-Heroine: Radha in Medieval Bengali Vaishnavite Culture.* Shimla, 1993.

Hawley, John S., and Donna M. Wulff, eds. *Deva: Goddesses of India.* Berkeley, 1996.

DONNA MARIE WULFF (1987)
Revised Bibliography

RADHAKRISHNAN, SARVEPALLI (1888–1975), Indian philosopher, statesman, and president of India (1962–1967). Born in Tirutani, a small town south of Madras noted as a pilgrimage center, Radhakrishnan attended Christian missionary schools for twelve years, until his graduation from Madras Christian College in 1908. The tension between the Hindu piety he learned at home and the Christian doctrine he was taught at school generated an interest in comparative philosophy, religion, and ethics that occupied him for the remainder of his life. Both of his major works, *An Idealist View of Life* (published in 1932 on the basis of his 1929 Hibbert Lectures) and *Eastern Religions and Western Thought* (lectures delivered at Oxford University, 1939), show the interplay of Indian and Western religious thought characteristic of his entire life's work.

The scant information that Radhakrishnan disclosed concerning his personal life is contained in a brief essay, "My Search for Truth" (1937). A seventy-five-page essay, "The Religion of the Spirit and the World's Need: Fragments of a Confession" (1952), intended as an autobiographical writing, offers one of the clearest summaries of his thought but treats his personal life in a few unrevealing pages. In refusing an editor's request for a brief autobiography, Radhakrishnan insisted, in "Fragments of a Confession," that discretion prevented him from doing so, and further, that his writings were worth more than his personal life.

In 1908, at the age of twenty, Radhakrishnan published his master's thesis, "The Ethics of the Vedānta and Its Metaphysical Presuppositions," and continued publishing one or more works almost every year for the next five decades. His first full-length work, *The Philosophy of Rabindranath Tagore* (1918), reveals most of the themes that would occupy him throughout his career: the Indian sources, varieties, and ethical implications of religious and philosophical intuition. With the exception of his first original work, *The Reign of Religion in Contemporary Philosophy,* wherein he criticizes the influence of religion on philosophy, Radhakrishnan's writings are characterized by the intimate relationship between religious experience (particularly the Hindu mystical tradition) and philosophy (particularly modern Western idealism). With the publication of his next major works, *Indian Philosophy* (vol. 1, 1923; vol. 2, 1927), *The Hindu View of Life* (1926), and *An Idealist View of Life* (1932), Radhakrishnan established his case for the positive relationship between idealist philosophy and a universalist religious attitude that he later termed "religion of the spirit."

In various ways, all of Radhakrishnan's mature writings focus on three closely related concerns: his presentation and positive interpretation of classical Indian religious thought, or Vedanta, especially as found in its three fundamental scriptures, the Upaniṣads, the *Bhagavadgītā,* and the *Brahma Sūtra;* his defense of philosophical idealism, both in its Indian expression and as found in Western philosophers from Plato to Hegel and F. H. Bradley; and his critique of contemporary (and especially Western) materialist and scientific thinking insofar as it excludes religious and spiritual values. On behalf of each of these three concerns, Radhakrishnan sought to show that although *brahman* (the Absolute) is the ultimate self-sufficient reality, the world is nevertheless valuable and worthy of humanity's deepest commitment and dedication.

Radhakrishnan's own dedication to the affairs of the world could not have been more convincing: in addition to his positions as professor of philosophy (University of Mysore, 1918-1921; University of Calcutta, 1921–1931 and 1937–1941) and university administrator (vice-chancellor of Andhra University, 1931–1936; vice-chancellor of Banaras Hindu University, 1938–1948; chancellor, University of Delhi, 1953–1962), he served in many demanding diplomatic positions, including head of the Indian delegation to UNESCO (1946–1952) and Indian ambassador to the Soviet Union (1949–1952). He was vice-president of India from 1952 to 1962, and president from 1962 to 1967.

BIBLIOGRAPHY

In addition to *An Idealist View of Life* (1932; 2d ed., London, 1957) and *Eastern Religions and Western Thought* (Oxford, 1959), which represent Radhakrishnan's major works in philosophy and in comparative religion and ethics, respectively, three other of his works are especially to be recommended. For the Indian expression of Radhakrishnan's religious and philosophic position, the fullest account is his 240-page introduction to the *Brahma Sūtra, The Philosophy of Spiritual Life* (New York, 1960). The best introduction to his understanding of contemporary religious life and thought is *Recovery of Faith* (New York, 1955). *The Philosophy of Sarvepalli Radhakrishnan,* edited by Paul Arthur Schilpp (New York, 1952), contains twenty-three essays covering all aspects of Radhakrishnan's thought, as well as his "Replies to Critics," his semiautobiographical essay "Fragments of a Confession," and a complete bibliography of his writings through the year 1952.

New Sources

Banerji, Anjan Kumar, ed. *Sarvepalli Radhakrishnan, A Centenary Tribute.* Varanasi, 1991–1992.

Brookman, David M. *Sarvepalli Radhakrishnan, in the Commentarial Tradition of India.* Bhubaneswar, 1990.

Gopal, Sarvepalli. *Radhakrishnan, A Biography.* Delhi and New York, 1989.

Kulangara, Thomas. *Absolutism and Theism: A Philosophical Study of S. Radhakrishnan's Attempt to Reconcile Sankara's Absolutism and Ramanuja's Theism.* Trivandrum, 1996.

Murty, K. *Satchidananda Radhakrishnan: His Life and Ideas.* Delhi, 1989.

Nandakumar, Prema S. *Radhakrishnan. Makers of Indian Literature.* New Delhi, 1992.

Parthasarathi, G., and D. P. Chattopadhyaya, eds. *Radhakrishnan: Centenary Volume.* Delhi; New York, 1989.

ROBERT A. MCDERMOTT (1987)
Revised Bibliography

RADIN, PAUL (1883–1959) was an American anthropologist. Born in Lódź, Poland, Radin was brought to the United States by his parents while he was still an infant, in 1884. Upon completing his studies in anthropology at Columbia University, he spent his life as a vagabond scholar, teaching at numerous colleges and universities in the United States and lecturing at most of the major universities of western Europe. Among them were the University of California at Berkeley, Cambridge University, Fisk University, the University of Chicago, Kenyon College, Black Mountain College, and Brandeis University. He was never offered, nor did he seek, tenure anywhere; devoted to his studies of the cultures of primitive societies, he was content to be institutionally rootless.

Radin was perhaps the most cultivated anthropologist in the history of the discipline. He was a man of paradox: a skeptic with a strong sense of the sacred, an agnostic who was fascinated by all religious phenomena, a Jew who disclaimed the uniqueness of the revelation contained in the Hebrew scriptures. In deconstructing the specificity of Old Testament claims, Radin's work follows that of Andrew Lang and others on the ubiquity of high gods among primitive—that is, pre-class, or stateless—peoples.

Radin was always equivocal about primitive religions. In *Primitive Religion* (1937) he argues for a Freudian explanation of religious concepts, and a "Marxist" awareness of the potential for domination in religious establishments, but he does not thereby deny the authenticity of a given faith stripped down to its core. In his arguments, Radin clearly indicates a belief in the irreducible universality of religious faith, which universality is an essentially phenomenological matter. On the other hand, he was fully aware of the exploitative potential of all significant religious figures and movements. These include the primitive shaman who could conceivably dominate others through his peculiar capacity to evoke religious states. Nonetheless, as he makes clear in *Primitive Man as Philosopher* (1927), Radin did not imagine that structures of domination, as normally understood, could be found in primitive societies. In fact, Radin's sense of the comparative deficiencies of civilization is evident throughout his work.

Radin brought to the study of religion a powerful sense of human fatality and historical contingency. It is probable that his own personality, continuously shaped by a very broad understanding of human experience, led him to focus on the ambivalent figure of the trickster, which is given free reign in primitive societies but is repressed in more advance civilization. More than any other aspect of his work, this concern—presented in *The Trickster: A Study in American Indian Mythology* (1956)—commended him to philosophers and psychologists alike. For Radin, the trickster reflected the double image of God: an androgynous figure, bursting with energy, without values, both creator and destroyer, the cosmic villain, and, at the same time, a bumbling fool. This definition of the trickster, which has become a classic, probably represents Radin's most striking contribution to the development of anthropological thinking.

Radin's interest in primitive religion covered a wide range of subjects. *The Autobiography of a Winnebago Indian* by Sam Blowsnake (1920), which Radin edited and translated, is a pioneer work that represents, presumably in the protagonist's own words, the cultistic efforts to compensate for a lost culture, and the conflicts that ensue. Radin had a particular concern for people caught between faiths.

However, it is not Radin's focus on religious matters that commands attention, but rather the great sweep of his thinking and his powerful, indirect critique of modern secularism (see *The World of Primitive Man,* 1953) and the depths of his humanity that bound him to the primitive peoples and sacred societies he studied. If Paul Radin was the most cultivated anthropologist in the history of the discipline, he was also the most faithful, in every sense of the word.

BIBLIOGRAPHY

Besides the works cited above, most of which are available in reprint editions, the following books represent important contributions made by Radin to anthropological studies: *The Genetic Relationship of the North American Indian Languages* (Berkeley, Calif., 1919) and *The Method and Theory of Ethnology: An Essay in Criticism* (New York, 1933).

STANLEY DIAMOND (1987)

RAËLIANS. The International Raëlian Movement is the world's largest and best-known UFO religion. Headquartered in Geneva, Switzerland, the organization claims a membership of approximately sixty-thousand in ninety countries. As of 2004, Japan was home to the most Raëlians, followed by France and Canada. The Raëlians achieved fame (or notoriety) following the 2002 announcement of the birth of the world's first human clone—a claim that was never proven.

The International Raëlian Movement is an atheistic organization that demands recognition as a religion. Raëlians are atheists in that they deny the existence of God and of the human soul, but they are religious in that they worship godlike extraterrestrials, and they participate in rituals designed to link humans to their creators and to infinity. Raëlians call these extraterrestrials *Elohim,* viewing them as loving creators who will return to earth on or before the year 2035 to endow the human race with advanced technology. The movement's two aims are to spread the message of humanity's extraterrestrial origins and to build an embassy, landing field, and hotel that will be used to welcome the Elohim upon their return to earth.

Raël, the founder and charismatic leader of this movement, is French journalist and racecar driver Claude Vorilhon, who was born in September 1946, near Vichy. Vorilhon has reported that he experienced a close encounter of the third kind on December 13, 1973, in the crater of an extinct volcano called Puy de Lassolas near Clermont-Ferrand in France. He claims a UFO descended through the mist, and that a childlike being emerged and invited him to come aboard. Over the next three days he was taught the true meaning of the Bible, a "scientific" interpretation that he outlines in his 1974 book, *Le livre qui dit la vérité* (The book that tells the truth).

According to the Raëlians, all life on Earth, including human beings, was created scientifically through the manipulation of DNA. This was accomplished by extraterrestrial beings, called the Elohim (singular, Eloha) in the original Hebrew Bible, who were masters in genetic engineering. The Raëlians believe the term *Elohim* was erroneously translated as *God*, and that it actually means "those who came from the sky." Throughout the ages, the Elohim have sent thirty-nine prophets to the earth, among them Moses, Muḥammad, Buddha, and Joseph Smith. These prophets are born through unions between an Eloha and a mortal woman chosen for her "virgin DNA." One of the prophets, Jesus, foretold an epoch when truth would be revealed—the Age of Apocalypse, from the Greek *apocalypsis*, meaning *revelation*. The Raëlians believe that this epoch started on August 6, 1945, with the explosion of the atomic bomb over Hiroshima, Japan. The Elohim decided that it was time to contact a final messenger, Vorilhon, whom they renamed Raël (from Israël). The Elohim gave Raël the mission of spreading their message worldwide. He was also responsible for building an embassy, preferably in Israel, where the Elohim will descend in a mass landing with the thirty-nine prophets and will officially meet with representatives of the world's nations.

Raël founded Madech (Mouvement pour l'Accueil des Elohim, Créateurs de l'Humanité; Movement for Welcoming the Elohim, Creators of Humanity) in 1974, which was actually more of a UFO club than a religious organization. Raël claims to have encountered the extraterrestrials again on October 7, 1975. This meeting is described in his second book, *Les extra-terrestres m'ont ammené sur leur planête* (Extraterrestrials took me to their planet; 1975), in which Raël reports that he was given the keys needed to enable humans to fully blossom. He was also introduced to the mysteries of cloning and watched his own double being formed in a vat. The Elohim further taught him about their system of government, called *geniocracy*, an oligarchic meritocracy in which geniuses rule.

During his trip to the Elohim's planet, Raël was instructed in a meditation awareness technique intended to activate one's brain potential and develop one's sensuality in order to gain the capacity to feel connected to the infinite, and to feel infinite oneself. This technique is outlined in Raël's *Sensual Meditation* (1980), and it became a group meditation practice during the Raëlians' monthly meetings. On returning to earth, Raël established a political party in France called La Geniocratie, whose aim was to create a one-world government in which leadership was based on intelligence tests. This, coupled with the Raëlian symbol (a swastika inside a Star of David), led to fears that the Raëlians were preaching a form of fascism, and many of the Raëlian leaders were arrested, held for questioning, and had their documents seized. Raël responded by abandoning the group's political project.

In 1976, dissatisfied with the direction of Madech's executive, Raël orchestrated a schism, from whence emerged the new Raëlian Movement, to which Raël added all the building blocks of a viable religious movement: baptism, clergy, a system of values, annual festivals, and a meditation ritual that induces altered states of consciousness.

In August 1998 the movement's name was changed to the "Raëlian Religion" in the United States, where they achieved legal recognition as a religion. A subsequent application to Canada's Supreme Court for recognition as the "Raëlian Church" was denied. According to the legal definition of a religion in Canada, Raëlianism did not qualify because its "gods" were material beings with no transcendental status.

ORGANIZATIONAL STRUCTURE. Raëlian membership is divided into two levels. The committed core group, made up of a hierarchy of *guides*, is called the *Structure*. More loosely affiliated members are called simply *Raëlians*; they must pay an annual membership fee ($100 in Canada) and receive the Raëlian newsletter, *Apocalypse*. New members must sign an "act of apostasy," which stipulates a renunciation of one's former religious beliefs, before they are eligible for initiation or baptism. Raëlian baptism, also called "the transmission of the cellular plan," is a formal act whereby initiates recognize the Elohim as their scientific, loving creators. Only adults can become Raëlians; the movement strongly discourages inducting children into any religion until they are old enough to understand it. New initiates are encouraged to sign a contract giving a local mortuary permission, upon their death, to remove one square centimeter of their frontal bone. This is done in hope of eventual re-creation through the cloning process. Thus, all Raëlians aspire to achieve physical immortality. These pieces of bone are stored in a bank vault in Geneva, Switzerland.

The International Raëlian Movement, as well as affiliated national organizations, are nonprofit and voluntary. Members are encouraged, but not required, to pay a 10 percent tithe. The national membership tithe is 3 percent after tax per annum, and the international membership tithe is 7 percent of net income.

The six levels in the Structure represent different stages of responsibility: assistant animator, animator, assistant guide, priest guide, bishop guide, and guide of guides (Raël himself). The bishop guides have the power to reelect the guide of guides every seven years. A "council of the wise," composed of bishops, controls heresy and sanctions rule breakers. A "council of discipline" sanctions rule breakers and promotes loyalty to the guides and allegiance to the chain of command. The ethics committee handles the movement's business affairs. All members of the Structure are required to abstain from recreational drugs, alcohol, nicotine, coffee, and tea out of concern for protecting the purity of the genetic code. Every summer Raël reviews the performance of the members of the Structure and promotes or demotes them based on their level of harmony in three areas of life: philosophical, professional, and sensual.

PRACTICES AND BELIEFS. The Raëlians are often portrayed as libertines due to an apparent antinomian streak in their ritual nudity and sexual practices. However, Raël has forged a distinct ethical system that is strictly enforced, at least among the members of the Structure. Raëlian values include absolute respect for life, self-respect and self-love, respecting and tolerating differences (whether racial, ethnic, or philosophical), nonviolence, pacifism, equal distribution and sharing of resources, strict birth control, democracy, and responsibility. The Raëlian Revolution (an alternative name for the group) aims to contribute to the conscience of humanity, mobilizing individuals and groups to action for positive changes—anything that improves human freedom, rights, and justice among individuals, minorities, or majorities.

Raëlians celebrate four festivals during the year, occasions where baptisms are performed. The Raëlian calendar begins on August 6, 1945, in commemoration of the Hiroshima bombing. Raël's two close encounters are celebrated annually on October 7 and December 13. In addition, the Elohim's scientific creation of the first humans (Adam and Eve) in a lab on earth is commemorated on the first Sunday in April.

Members also participate in Awakening seminars held every year on every continent. These seminars present the teaching of the instruction manual given by the Elohim on how to awaken one's potential, open one's mind, and lead a happy and fulfilled life. Seminars feature daily lectures, sensual meditation, one-day fasting, nonmandatory nudity, sensory awareness exercises, and an evening cabaret featuring artists from all over the world. A second seminar follows for those who wish to become part of the Structure and earn a level of responsibility within the organization.

Raëlians believe that there are infinite levels of life. The infinitely "large matter" of which humans are a part (the planets, stars, and galaxies) is similar to the infinitely "small matter" (atoms, quarks) that people are made of. The Elohim explained that the earth is just one particle of a gigantic being that itself is watching another sky. The particles that compose atoms are themselves universes in which there are galaxies, stars, and planets with others living beings, ad infinitum.

Raëlians believe that during this age of scientific revelation, humanity will come to understand its true origin. Raël's theology holds that, with the Elohim's guidance and humanity's right choice, this age holds marvelous potentials: liberation, power and immortality once the Elohim arrive (before 2035) and bequeath to their creation scientific knowledge that will enable humans to travel through space and colonize virgin planets in their image. Raël also argues that:

> Ethics is simply a last-gasp attempt by deist conservatives and orthodox dogmatics to keep humanity in ignorance and obscurantism, through the well tried fermentation of fear, the fear of science and new technologies. On the contrary, let us embrace Science and the new technologies, for it is these which will liberate mankind from the myth of god, and free us from our age old fears, from disease, death and the sweat of labor. (Rael 1987, p. 81)

According to Raël, gender is an artificial construct because the Elohim designed men and women as biological robots programmed to give each other pleasure, and only incidentally to procreate. Raël emphasizes the essential androgyny of the human being and the fluidity of gender as a result of different combinations of X and Y chromosomes. Men and women are considered equal and indistinguishable in their intelligence, abilities, and emotional makeup. Raël condemns the marriage contract as a proclamation of ownership of a person, and he argues that "when one has signed a contract one feels like a prisoner, forced to love and sooner or later each one begins to hate the other" (Rael 1978, p.285).

Raëlians favor short-term, spontaneous sexual relationships, although free choice is strongly emphasized. Homosexual relationships are respected, and homosexual experimentation is encouraged. Raël advises members to postpone parenthood, and for those who aspire to be cloned, to forgo reproduction altogether. It is rare to find new parents among the members of the Structure. Women can attain the high ranks of priests and bishops, although women are generally outnumbered by men at the higher echelons of the Structure. Still, Raël announced in January 2003 that his successor will be a woman—Dr. Brigitte Boisselier, a Raëlian bishop.

The status of women within the organization changed profoundly in July 1998 when Raël announced his latest revelation at the Raëlian summer camp, held that year at Valcourt in Quebec. Raël reported that the Elohim had asked him to create an "Order of Raël's Angels," a cadre of beautiful women, trained by Raël to act as hostesses to the Elohim and the thirty-nine prophets, in preparation for their landing. Two ranks of Angels were created, Pink Angels and White Angels, distinguishable by pink or white feathers on their necklaces. Pink Angels reserved their sexuality for the

Elohim, although they could have sex with Raël and with each other. White Angels were permitted to have other lovers, and their role was to act as missionaries to bring more women into the movement.

Unlike many new religious movements, the Raëlian Movement has always courted the attention of the media. The Raëlians even established a "Planetary Week," to be held every April, to publicize what Raëlianism stands for. Raëlians have demonstrated against nuclear testing and in support of such issues as gay rights and genetically modified foods. Raëlians have also long supported genetic engineering. But by far the Raëlians' best-known platform has been their support of efforts to clone human beings.

CLONING EFFORTS. On March 9, 1997, shortly after the successful cloning of a sheep by Ian Wilmut in Scotland, Raël announced the creation of Valiant Venture, through which the Raëlians hoped to mobilize potential investors, customers, and scientists interested in cloning projects. Later that year, Raël announced his creation of a company called Clonaid at the Las Vegas Hilton. Pope John Paul II had issued a statement condemning cloning as against the will of God, and in defiance of the pope, Raël set up a company to promote cloning and facilitate access to this technology when it became available. Clonaid hired a team of geneticists, biologists and in vitro fertilization specialists, whose main goal was to offer reproductive human cloning on a worldwide basis to infertile couples, homosexual couples, people infected with the HIV virus, and families who had lost a beloved family member. Clonaid also offered a range of cloning-related services with such names as Insureaclone, Ovulaid, and Clonapet, and proposed to cultivate personal stem cells for customers. Raël handed directorship of the Clonaid project to Boisselier, who holds doctoral degrees in both physical chemistry and analytical chemistry.

In March 2001, Raël and Boisselier testified at a hearing on human cloning held by the United States House Energy and Commerce Committee. In December 2002 Boisselier announced at a televised press conference in Hollywood, Florida, that the first cloned human baby girl was born; her name was Eve. Boisselier later announced the births of four other cloned babies and claimed that twenty more were on the way. The journalist Michael Guillen was prepared to oversee an international team of scientists who would test the newborn Eve, but ultimately Boisselier claimed that the parents had moved to Israel and wished to maintain the baby's anonymity. Bernard Siegel, a Miami attorney, filed a suit to place the child under the protection of the state so that her health could be safeguarded. At a subsequent hearing, Clonaid vice president Thomas Kaenzig admitted that Clonaid was not registered as a company and that he knew only what Boisselier told him about the baby. Boisselier then admitted that she had only seen a videotape of the baby. Although the media and scientific establishment have dismissed Clonaid's claim to have cloned a human as a hoax, Raëlians continue to believe that there are clones in our midst. Raël asked Boisselier to build a "babytron," in which cloned babies can be placed to undergo accelerated growth, a technology he claimed was developed by the Elohim thousands of years ago.

THE EMBASSY. Raël receives ongoing revelations from the Elohim, which he experiences as voices or as dictated messages that he receives through his hand. In October 1991 the Raëlian Movement sent out letters to every Israeli embassy in the world demanding that a plot of land in Jerusalem be provided for the construction of the "embassy," otherwise the Elohim would withdraw their protection of the Jewish people. In a stern warning to the State of Israel, Raël claimed that "the Age of Apocalypse has arrived. The long-awaited messiah has come. The fate of Israel is in your hands." According to Raëlianism, the sole purpose of Israel is to recognize the messiah (Raël) and build an embassy (the third temple) to welcome the Elohim and all the prophets of old. The letter claimed that if the people of Israel do not abide by the Elohim's request, Israel will disappear.

In 1990 Raël received permission from the Elohim to change the swastika in the movement's symbol to a more ambiguous, swirling, daisylike form. This was an expression of respect for the victims of the Holocaust and an attempt to improve the prospect of obtaining land in Israel. Since 1991, the Raëlian Movement has repeatedly asked the Israeli government and the chief rabbis in Jerusalem to grant them international neutral territory upon which to build the embassy, but as of 2004 there had been no positive response. In December 1997 the Elohim told Raël that he could address his request of extraterritoriality to other countries.

SEE ALSO UFO Religions.

BIBLIOGRAPHY

Vorilhon, Claude. *Le livre qui dit la vérité.* Vaduz, Liechtenstein, 1974.

Vorilhon, Claude. *Les extra-terrestres m'ont amené sur leur planête.* Vaduz, Liechtenstein, 1975.

Vorilhon, Claude. *La géniocratie.* Brantome, France, 1977.

Vorilhon, Claude. *Accueiller les ectar-terrestres.* Vaduz, Liechtenstein, 1979.

Vorilhon, Claude. *La méditation sensuelle.* Montreal, Quebec, 1980.

Vorilhon, Claude. *Oui au clonage humain: La vie eternelle grâce à la science.* Montreal, Quebec, 2001.

Secondary Sources

Palmer, Susan J. "Woman as Playmate in the Raelian Movement: Power and Pantagamy in a New Religion." *Syzygy: Journal of Alternative Religion and Culture* 1, no. 3 (1992): 227–245.

Palmer, Susan J. "Women in the Raelian Movement: New Religious Experiments in Gender and Authority." In *The Gods Have Landed,* edited by James Lewis, pp. 105–136. New York, 1995.

Palmer, Susan J. "The Raelian Movement International." In *New Religions in the New Europe,* edited by Robert Towler, pp. 194–210. Aarhus, Denmark, 1995.

Palmer, Susan J. "The Raelians Are Coming: The Future of a UFO Religion." In *Religion in a Changing World,* edited by Madeleine Cousineau, pp.139–146. Westport, Conn., 1998.

Palmer, Susan J. "I Raeliani." In *Collana religioni e movimenti,* edited by Massimo Introvigne. Torino, Italy, 2000.

SUSAN J. PALMER (2005)

RAHNER, KARL (1904–1984) was the most prolific and influential Catholic theologian of the twentieth century. Rahner's bibliography comprises more than four thousand entries. Writing primarily as a dogmatic theologian, he also addressed philosophical, historical, pastoral, and spiritual questions. His work as a whole may be summarized as theological anthropology, correlating human experience and God's self-communication. His method is most often described as transcendental, inasmuch as it seeks to discover the conditions of possibility for divine salvific action, but it also has an inseparable historical dimension, inasmuch as the humanity addressed by God's word and presence is understood as always situated in a temporal world. Indeed, it may be even more accurate to see Rahner as a Catholic dialectical theologian whose career was marked not only by personal response to the religious issues of his day but also by an enduring effort to conceive human history as destined for eternal communion with God, achieved through the course of time.

Born and raised in Freiburg im Breisgau, Rahner entered the Society of Jesus in 1922. During his education in the Jesuit order he developed an Ignatian spirituality of "seeking God in all things." His formal philosophical (1924–1927) and theological (1929–1933) studies were shaped largely by the neoscholastic revival; but through the writings of the Belgian Jesuit Joseph Maréchal he entered into philosophical conversation with Immanuel Kant and later with G. W. F. Hegel and German Idealism. To these general influences on his thought must be added his intensive reading in patristic sources and in medieval mysticism. Ordained a priest in 1932, Rahner concluded his basic theological program the following year and then pursued a further year of pastoral and ascetic studies (the Jesuit tertianship).

In 1934 Rahner began a doctoral program in philosophy at the University of Freiburg, where he attended Martin Heidegger's seminars. His doctoral dissertation, a modern retrieval of Thomas Aquinas's theory of knowledge, centered on the theme of *conversio ad phantasma* (conversion to the phantasm) as the ground of all human knowledge, and it conceived human existence fundamentally as "spirit in world." When his director rejected the thesis as insufficiently traditional (it was published in 1939 as *Geist in Welt*), Rahner left for Innsbruck. After quickly completing a theological doctorate and habilitation, he began in 1937 to teach dogmatic theology. From those first years came an eloquent book of meditations, *Worte ins Schweigen* (1938), and also the publication of his Salzburg summer lectures on human history as the place where God's self-revelation must be sought, *Hörer des Wortes* (1941).

When the Nazis closed the Innsbruck faculty in 1938, Rahner moved to Vienna and served at the Pastoral Institute until 1944. From 1945 to 1948 he taught theology under straitened circumstances at Pullach bei München. Returning to Innsbruck in 1949, he was responsible for courses on grace and the sacrament of penance, topics that shaped his thought for the rest of his life. Rooted in the experience of grace as God's mysterious self-communication, Rahner's thought broke new ground in a whole range of areas: for example, the biblical understanding of God; current problems in Christology, nature, and grace; the human condition after original sin; human dignity and freedom; the meaning of church membership; existential ethics; and the pastoral situation of the church. His major essays were collected from this time on in a multivolume collection, *Schriften zur Theologie* (1954–1984).

Already in *Hörer des Wortes* it was clear that Rahner was developing a philosophy of religion on the assumption that Christian revelation had occurred, and in order to make plausible how that was possible. A theologian of grace and reconciliation, he engaged in extensive positive research, as is made abundantly clear in *Schriften,* vol. 11 (1973), with his historical essays on penance in the early church. But the special creativity of his writing showed itself in his efforts to correlate the circumstances of particular experience with the permanent "existentials" of the human condition. This interrelation of historical and transcendental moments was evident as well in the prodigious editorial labors that began in his early Innsbruck years and continued with the publication of four editions of Denzinger's *Enchiridion Symbolorum* (1952–1957) and seven editions of *Der Glaube der Kirche in den Urkunden der Lehrverkündigung* (1948–1965).

Building on the early Innsbruck period came a second phase of Rahner's thought, during which he was coeditor of the second edition of the *Lexikon für Theologie und Kirche* (1957–1965) and a leading figure in the preparation and course of the Second Vatican Council (despite efforts to disqualify his participation). His retrieval and renewal of tradition in light of contemporary perspectives had previously been achieved largely through pressing particular questions against the background of School Theology. Now he drew out the consequences of these studies and began to speak more programmatically of a theological anthropology encompassing the history of a world whose call to union with God (the "supernatural existential") evokes transcendental reflection on the structural possibilities for such salvation. In powerful essays on mystery, incarnation, theology of symbol, and hermeneutics of eschatological assertions, collected in *Schriften,* vol. 4 (1960), Rahner developed his analogy of transcendence. Facing questions posed by evolutionary science, the great world religions, and utopian views of the future, other major essays in *Schriften,* vol. 5 (1962), present the scope of the divine salvific will in more comprehensive terms and argue for the coextension of salvation history and the history of the world. Corresponding to the council's ecclesiological focus, *Schriften,* vol. 6 (1966), collects papers that present a dialogue with secularized, pluralistic society and seek to express the Christian church's new self-understanding in it. Earlier, Rahner had published a large collection of essays in pastoral theology (*Sendung und Gnade,* 1959). He gathered a new collection of essays in spirituality (*Schriften,* vol. 7, 1967), and in 1962 he cooperated in drafting a plan for the *Handbuch der Pastoraltheologie,* which subsequently appeared in five volumes between 1964 and 1972, with Rahner as one of its editors.

In 1964 Rahner succeeded Romano Guardini in the chair of Christian *Weltanschauung* at the University of Munich. As it became apparent that he would not be allowed to direct doctoral students in theology, he accepted in 1967 a call to the University of Münster, where he taught until his retirement in 1971. In these first years of Vatican II's reception within Catholicism, criticism of Rahner's thought grew in various quarters. Concerned with fidelity to the tradition and to Christian symbolism, some writers, for example, Hans Urs von Balthasar, accused him of anthropological reductionism. Others, especially his former student J.-B. Metz, drew back from what they considered an individualistic, idealistic existentialism. Rahner took the second critique more seriously and gave new emphasis to the historical concreteness of Christianity and its social responsibility. Renewing the dialectic of unity in difference with which he had from the beginning sought to understand time in its openness to eternity, he addressed basic conciliar themes with a deepened sense of faith's constructive participation in its secular context. *Schriften,* vols. 8, 9, and 10 (1967, 1970, 1972), calls for a new understanding of Jesus of Nazareth as the human way to God ("Christology from below") and reform of the church in the direction of a declericalized, more democratic, and socially critical community of service. Meanwhile Rahner had undertaken additional editorial responsibilities for the four volumes of *Sacramentum Mundi* (1967–1969) and for *Concilium* (1965–).

During the first years of Rahner's retirement in Munich, his major project was the preparation of his *Grundkurs des Glaubens* (1976), an introduction to the idea of Christianity. While not intended as a complete systematic theology, the book does present many of his basic positions on the central topics of Christian doctrine and has commonly been seen as a summation of his thought.

In the last years of his life Rahner continued to lecture and write vigorously. Four further volumes of the *Schriften* were published (vols. 13–16: 1978, 1980, 1983, 1984), two while he was still living in Munich, two more after his final retirement to Innsbruck in 1981. They were accompanied by numerous smaller works and several anthologies, one of which, *Praxis des Glaubens* (1982), may also serve as a general introduction to its author's thought. These later years are again of a piece with the whole career and include familiar themes as well as considerable repetition. Nevertheless, some significant developments occur here too: in the consolidation of a historical Christology, in the proposal of a "universal pneumatology" that might precede Christology, in pleas for ecumenical seriousness, and in arguments for a truly world church.

In these last years of his life Rahner was newly concerned with addressing the mounting relativism and skepticism he saw about him. In addition, the writings of this last phase show how thoroughly dialectical his thought was, as it sought to mediate between opposed positions in either doctrine or morals, to speak of the fruitful tension between permanent polarities of historical existence, and, above all, to understand the relation between continuity and discontinuity through the passage of time.

Rahner's future influence will depend largely on how effectively his students and readers will be able to draw on his thinking for a continuing dialogue with scientific and technological culture, the social sciences, and narrative and symbolic modes of discourse. It remains to be seen how a more biblically imagined, historically diverse, and socially responsible theology will appropriate his legacy. Many who knew him would insist that the personal witness of his life will surely endure alongside the remarkably elastic architecture of his thought.

BIBLIOGRAPHY

For a complete, chronological listing of Rahner's publications, see *Bibliographie Karl Rahner: 1924–1969,* edited by Roman Bleistein and Elmar Klinger (Freiburg, 1969); *Bibliographie Karl Rahner: 1969–1974,* edited by Roman Bleistein (Freiburg, 1974); "Bibliographie Karl Rahner: 1974–1979," compiled by P. Imhof and H. Treziak, in *Wagnis Theologie,* edited by Herbert Vorgrimler (Freiburg, 1979), pp. 579–97; and "Bibliographie Karl Rahner: 1979–1984," compiled by P. Imhof and E. Meuser, in *Glaube im Prozess,* 2d ed., edited by Elmar Klinger and Klaus Wittelstadt (Freiburg, 1984), pp. 854–871.

The core of Rahner's work is in his *Schriften zur Theologie,* 16 vols. (Einsiedeln and Zurich, 1954–1984), of which fourteen volumes have been published in English as *Theological Investigations,* 20 vols. to date (New York, 1961–). Outstanding examples of his spiritual writing can be found in *Worte ins Schweigen* (Leipzig, 1938), translated as *Encounters with Silence* (Westminster, Md., 1960), and in *Von der Not und dem Segen des Gebetes,* 4th ed. (Innsbruck, 1949), translated as *On Prayer* (New York, 1958). Key essays on charismatic gifts and existential decision are in *Das Dynamische in der Kirche* (Freiburg, 1958), translated as *The Dynamic Element in the Church* (New York, 1964). The major late work is *Grundkurs des Glaubens: Einführung in den Begriff des Christentums* (Freiburg, 1976), translated as *Foundations of Christian Faith: An Introduction to the Idea of Christianity* (New York, 1978). Karl Lehmann and Albert Raffelt have edited a fine anthology of Rahner's spiritual writings in *Praxis des Glaubens* (Freiburg, 1982), translated as *The Practice of Faith* (New York, 1983).

For further biographical information and commentary, see Herbert Vorgrimler's *Karl Rahner: His Life, Thought and Works* (London, 1966) and my collection of studies entitled *A*

World of Grace: An Introduction to the Themes and Foundations of Karl Rahner's Theology (New York, 1980).

LEO J. O'DONOVAN (1987)

RAIN. The symbolism of rain derives from its correlation with the sacred substance water, a universal metaphor for the origin and renewal of life. The primacy and awesome mystery of natural phenomena for early humans, and his vital dependence on their manifestations, are reflected in the human exaltation of rain as a supreme creative power and intermediary between heaven and earth. In the seasonal revival of nature and the infusion of new life, rain was seen as the dispenser of divine grace and plenty, the promise of survival; in the periodic destruction wrought by storms and floods, as the agent of divine retribution and disaster, the threat of annihilation. Rain signified the descent of heavenly influences upon the earth; at times the gods themselves descended in rain or spoke in the thunder. Like the sun's rays, "the rain from heaven" (*Gn.* 8:2) was cognate to light, illumination.

The sacrality of sky and the supremacy of rain deities are fundamental elements in the structure of the myths and religions of archaic peoples. As the "most high," sky gods were assimilated to transcendence, their very names often connoting elevation. The Mesopotamian hieroglyph for "height" or "transcendence of space" also meant "rainy sky," and thus linguistically linked rain to divinity. Baal, the chief god of the Syro-Palestinian nomads, was called "rider of the clouds" and was worshiped as the dispenser of fertility. When the Israelites reached Canaan and their prophets condemned the widespread cult of fertility gods, a conflict arose between the worshipers of Baal and those faithful to Yahveh. The ancient Hebrews conceived of rain as a reservoir of treasure in heaven, a benison bestowed in return for loving God and obeying his law, and withheld as retribution for sin. In times of abundance, the Israelites were drawn to the fertility gods, and the Lord's promise to Moses, "Behold, I will rain bread from heaven for you" (*Ex.* 16:4), was forgotten. In the New Testament, rain is the symbol of joy and fruition, the answer to prayer from a loving Father in heaven who sends rain on the just and the unjust alike.

The life-renewing, life-sustaining powers of rain have been personified in the pantheons of both primitive and higher religions. Worship of rain gods as symbols of fertility prevailed in the East, among the main branches of Aryan stock in early Europe, and in parts of Africa, Oceania, and the Americas; and many, like the Maya god Chac, were believed to be the creator of all things. The Mesoamerican moon god whose name meant "I am the dew of the heavens, I am the dew of the clouds" was the father of gods as well as of humans, and represented death and resurrection.

The perennial, universal aspiration for rain is reflected in all traditions in the divine promises recorded in their sacred texts. Every Egyptian god was in some way related to water. In the *Ṛgveda,* the god Varuṇa proclaims, "I made to flow the moisture-shedding waters"; in the *Vendidad,* Ahura Mazdā pledges to "rain down upon the earth to bring food to the faithful and fodder to the beneficent cow"; in the Qurʾān, Allāh is described as "he who created the heavens and earth and sent down for you out of heaven water." The Persians conceived the tree of life as rising from a lake of rain, its seeds mingling with the water to maintain the earth's fertility. A common saying among the ancient Greeks when rain fell was "The Father [heaven] is pressing grapes." Both tribal rain gods and a national rain spirit were propitiated by the Burmese.

A dominant theme in universal mythology is the celestial marriage between Heaven and Earth, or between the fructifying sky god and fecund earth goddess. Rites and festivals of the seasonal fertilization of the earth by the penetrating rains have been celebrated since Neolithic times, when the correlations of rain and serpent, woman and vegetation, and death and rebirth were integrated into the complex of lunar symbolism. The union of the divine couple was the archetypal image of fruitfulness. Speaking in the storm, the Sumerian high god called himself the "fecund seed." Homer described the conjugal couch where Zeus lay with his spouse on Mount Ida as covered with a cloud from which rain fell, and Aeschylus wrote, "Rain impregnates the earth so that she gives birth to plants and grains." Birth and its attendant dangers are symbolized by a great storm in Vergil's *Aeneid.* In many of the prayers and tribal myths of North American Indians, the gentle rain is called "female" and the pelting rain "male."

Rites to ensure rain and fertility had their origin in remote antiquity and have been observed throughout the world. At the lower stages of civilization, sorcery and magical charms related to imitative or sympathetic magic were employed by shamans to evoke rain; later, prayer and sacrifice were combined with magico-religious rituals. A rain sacrifice rock painting from the Rusape district of Zimbabwe, now in the Frobenius Institut in Frankfurt, depicts a man standing with hands uplifted as if conjuring heaven, a female figure lying under a tree, and another bending forward above falling rain. Rainmakers were the most important members of the community and exerted enormous authority over the group. There is reason to believe that both chieftainship and kingship stemmed from the powerful position of the shaman. Ramses II of Egypt was credited with the faculty of rainmaking. The Zand Avesta, the Pahlavi translation of the Avesta with added commentaries, states that Ahura Mazdā (Pahl., Ōhrmazd) would raise the dead on the first day of the New Year with libations and purifications by water to ensure rain. Saints, especially in desert lands, were often reputed to be rainmakers, and the lives of Muslim saints abound with such miracles. The offices of the rainmaker are recorded among the Vedic rites of remote antiquity, where the sacred drink soma is called "son of the rain god." Water libations were celebrated by ancient Jewry as a so-called rain charm.

At the Feast of Tabernacles in Jerusalem, the priest performed the ritual mixture of wine with water from the Pool of Siloam to induce rain. At a later period, Orthodox Jews practiced a rain charm that may have had its origin in fertility rites: As they recited the names of the Ten Plagues of Egypt at the Seder on Passover eve, a few drops of water were poured into a jar of wine and the mixture was cast upon the ground in front of the house. In Greece, after the participants in the Eleusinian mysteries had been purified by water, they cried out, "Let there be rain! Be fruitful!"

According to the Chinese doctrine of "like to like," similar things summon one another, which implies that the dragon, traditionally associated with rain, generates rain. Evidence of rainmaking magic on oracle bones attests to the antiquity of such beliefs. The *Li ji* (Record of rites) from the first century BCE chronicles the practice of ritual nakedness, a magic formula continued into late Chinese history in which even Confucian officials participated in time of drought. Buddhist priests poured water into little holes in the temple floor to symbolize rain going into the earth. Rainmaking spells are mentioned in sūtras of 230 BCE.

In many parts of the East, the custom of immersing the fertility goddess, and in Europe the rite of drenching the Corn Mother, reflect earlier practices of sacrificing human victims to induce rain. In Mesoamerica, small children and birds were sacrificed to propitiate rain gods, and on the occasion of the Itzamna festival in March the hearts of certain species of wild animals were immolated. A custom among the Arabs of North Africa was to throw a holy man into a spring to end a drought, and in Russia to drench a priest or the figure of a saint for the same purpose. In societies where blood was assimilated to water, as in Abyssinia (ancient Ethiopia), human blood was the oblation offered to rain spirits. In Java, men whipped one another to draw blood, the symbolic equivalent of rain.

A milder form of rain magic was the sprinkling or scattering of water. In Lithuania, when rain was needed, people sprinkled themselves with water as they stood facing the sun at their morning prayers. The Celtic priests, the druids, bearing the image of a saint, led a procession to a sacred spring or well where water was sprinkled over special stones, which were then tossed into the air to fall to earth like rain. Pausanius left a description of the priests of Lycaean Zeus sacrificing an oak branch to a spring in time of drought, and the wizards of New Guinea and Siberia dipped branches into water and scattered the drops. Northern Dravidian tribes held an "umbrella feast" at the critical period of transplanting the rice crop, and Australian tribes performed ceremonial dances and songs around a pool to call down rain.

Rain dances figured prominently among American Indian tribes. The Omaha, members of a sacred buffalo society, filled vessels with water before they danced. Buffalo-head rituals were performed by the Plains and Woodland tribes when rain was lacking, and the Shawnee dipped a buffalo tail in water and shook it to bring rain. The Hopi and Zuni tribes depicted aquatic animals and symbolic rain clouds on their sand altars, half circles from which vertical lines depended as rain. An important feature of these rites was the bull-roarer, a sacred instrument that simulated the sound of thunder and was originally used in primitive initiations and Greek mystery ceremonies to represent the voice of God. Many of the peoples of Africa and Oceania believed that their gods spoke in the thunder. In the rites of the Oglala Lakota Indians, the water in the sweat lodge represented the thunder beings, fearsome powers that tested the warriors' strength and endurance and brought them the blessings of purification.

Rain accompanied by a thunderbolt symbolizes power or energy. In the form of a double trident, the thunderbolt is prominent in representations of the gods of ancient Sumer, Babylonia, Assyria, and Akkad. The Etruscan doctrine of thunderbolts related eleven different kinds of thunder to the powers of eleven gods. The synthesis of a sun god and a storm god connotes the energy of the pairs of opposites. An Assyrian sun god with a thunderbolt, believed to be the national deity Assur, is depicted on an alabaster wall panel from the palace of Ashurnasirpal II (c. 850 BCE), now in the British Museum. The Hebrew god Yahveh unites traits of both storm and solar god, as does Zeus, who destroyed the Titans with his thunderbolt. His Roman counterpart was believed to descend in the form of a thunderbolt and is represented on the Antonine column as the rain god Jupiter Pluvius hovering over the Roman legions with outspread wings and raining down his power upon them. This same synthesis pertains to the prehistoric Peruvian deity Viracocha, universal father and creator of all things, who as a rain god is depicted with a thunderbolt in each hand, his head surrounded by a rayed solar disk and his eyes shedding tears of life-renewing rain. The names of the Teutonic and Scandinavian war gods (Óðinn, Þórr, Donar, etc.) all mean "thunder."

Lightning symbolizes the action of the higher realm upon the lower, and in every culture has been assimilated either to a god, his weapon, or the manifestation of his sovereignty. At times, lightning has been construed as the salutary arrow of a god bringing deliverance or illumination to humankind, as when Mithra, the Persian god of light, pierced a rock with his arrow to end a drought by freeing the waters; at others, as the portent of his wrath or retribution. The lightning of the Vedic god Indra split the head of the dragon Vṛtra, demon of drought, to release the waters obstructed by him and regenerate the world, which had been made a wasteland. The storm god Rudra and his sons the Maruts, who shared the dual powers of their benign and destructive father, wielded their lightning bolts both to slay and to heal. The lightning god of the Indonesians was venerated as a supreme deity.

In the Hindu-Buddhist notion of the forms of divine manifestation, the *vajra,* lightning or thunderbolt, symbolizes the mystic, divine energy and the adamantine weapon of truth. As the invincible force in the sphere of transcendental reality, the *vajra* is the illusion-shattering light of spiritual illumination, which links the grace flowing into the world from the sun with the energy of the lightning bolt. In Buddhist iconography, the *vajra* is an emblem of the spiritual power of Buddhahood, an image of which is the solar Buddha, Vairocana, encircled by the halo of his emanations. The double trident wand carried by Buddhist monks is a form of the *vajra.* In early Tantrism, in which magic and science were inseparable, the Vajrayāna, doctrine of the "way of the thunderbolt," related to a form of electric energy.

Rain clouds and thunderstorms symbolized celestial activity in ancient China, and lightning was regarded with the same awe as were the thunderbolts of rain gods in other cultures. *Shen,* the pictogram for lightning, signifies divinity and the operation of the expansive forces. When the thunder ceases and rain ends, it is the work of demons and the contractive forces. These opposing forces symbolize two facets of the human spirit, the one ascending in life, the other descending in death. In the *Book of Changes,* the trigram *zhen,* the Arousing, is the image of thunder and signifies tension resolved after the cloudburst, nature refreshed, deliverance. According to the *Li ji,* only when the two opposing forces of yin and yang are in proper harmony will the beneficent rains fall, and when they fail to come, yin must be activated.

As a symbol of purification and redemption, rain is associated with the dissolving and washing away of sin, followed by rebirth and renewal. Every torrential rainfall bears the implication of the archetypal flood, the creation destroyed by its creator, and humankind submerged in an initiatory ordeal or cosmic baptism preliminary to redemption and regeneration. The concept of a cataclysmic inundation of the world is found in myths of every part of the world except Egypt and Japan, and only rarely in Africa. The two major interpretations of the Deluge reflect two ways of relating to the universe. The first, for which the early Mesopotamian *Epic of Gilgamesh* is the model, characterizes humanity's identity with a wholly impersonal universe controlled by the cosmic rhythm or recurrent cycle of the manifestation and disappearance of the world at the turn of every aeon. Engulfing rains alternate with a world drought in the Hindu myth in which Viṣṇu rescues humanity by becoming first the sun, then wind, then fire, and finally a great cloud from which fall the restorative rains. The second concept, exemplified in the biblical story of Noah, represents the flood sent by God as a punishment for humanity's sins and expresses the Semitic dissociation from, and guilt toward, God, with the implication of free will.

No other natural phenomenon has been so universally associated with the Holy Spirit as the rainbow, which on every continent has been the emblem of some aspect of human spiritual life, or some stage in the development of human consciousness. From the myths of Paleolithic and Neolithic peoples to the aborigines of Oceania and the Americas, the rainbow has been equated with the celestial serpent, the Great Father, the creator, or fertility god. The Egyptian sky mother Nut is depicted on coffins and papyri arced over the earth like a rainbow to signify the creation of the world. A representation of this figure is in the Egyptian Museum in Turin. A rainbow goddess in the identical posture appears in Navajo Indian sand paintings made to effect cures.

Like all sky phenomena, rainbows possess an ominous aspect, but for the most part have been regarded as an auspicious omen. An arc of light between earth and sky, the rainbow is a perennial symbol of the bridge linking the material world to Paradise and making possible communication between them. The rainbow was the path to the gods for the Mesopotamian, Indian, Japanese, and Hebrew peoples; for the Nordic peoples, it was the Bifrost, the "tremulous way" to Ásgarðr; in the Greco-Roman world, it was a sign from Zeus. To the Pygmies of equatorial Africa, the rainbow was a sign of the god's desire to communicate with them, and to the American Indian, it was the ladder affording access to the other world. The heroes of Polynesian and Hawaiian myths ascend the rainbow in order to deliver the souls of the dead to Paradise. Often construed as a prophetic sign or portent of blessings when appearing in the sky after a storm or flood, rainbows denote God's appeasement and reconciliation to humankind. Sealing his bond with Noah, God declared, "I do set my bow in the cloud, and it shall be for a token of a covenant between me and the earth" (*Gn.* 9:13). As a symbol of transfiguration and heavenly glory, rainbows are associated with the nimbus, aureole, halo, and mandorla surrounding the body of a god or saint. In Buddhism, the rainbow symbolizes the highest state attainable in the realm of *saṃsāra* before attaining to the clear light of *nirvāṇa,* and in Hinduism, the "rainbow body" is the highest yoga state. The rainbow is depicted in Christian art as the Lord's throne, and in scenes of the Last Judgment, Christ is frequently portrayed seated on a rainbow. In the *Revelation to John* in the New Testament, when the door opened in Heaven, "there was a rainbow round about the throne" (*Rv.* 4:3).

SEE ALSO Meteorological Beings; Water.

BIBLIOGRAPHY

Allen, Don Cameron. *Mysteriously Meant: The Rediscovery of Pagan Symbolism and Allegorical Interpretation in the Renaissance.* Baltimore, 1970. An exhaustive conspectus of interpretations by Renaissance authors of symbol, myth, and allegory in ancient Egypt and in pagan writers of classical antiquity. Includes an extensive bibliography.

Morley, Sylvanus Griswold. *The Ancient Maya.* 3d ed. Revised by George W. Brainerd. Stanford, Calif., 1956. A comprehensive account of the benevolent and malevolent rain gods and their personification of the struggle between good and evil in the dualistic Maya religion.

Needham, Joseph. *Science and Civilisation in China,* vol. 2, *History of Scientific Thought.* Cambridge, 1956. A fully documented account of the correlations in Chinese thought of the symbolic forms in Daoism and Tantrism as they relate to the positive and negative aspects of rain and the balance of energy in the yin-yang system.

Pettazzoni, Rafaele. *Dio: L'essere celeste nelle credenze dei popoli primitivi.* Rome, 1922. A history of the symbolism of rain, and of the sky and storm gods, in the belief systems of early peoples of Africa and Australia.

Reichard, Gladys A. *Navajo Religion: A Study of Symbolism.* 2 vols. New York, 1950. Both volumes are relevant: vol. 1, *An Investigation of Symbolism in Navajo Rain Ceremonies;* vol. 2, *Symbols in the Sandpaintings of the Rainbow Guardians.*

Sébillot, Paul. *Le folklore de France,* vol. 2. Paris, 1905. A valuable survey of rainmaking rites in southern France from pagan to modern times.

ANN DUNNIGAN (1987)

RAINBOW SNAKE (Rainbow Serpent) is an almost ubiquitous but elusive mythological figure throughout the Australian continent. To A. R. Radcliffe-Brown (1930), the Rainbow Snake was "perhaps the most important nature-deity, . . . the most important representation of the creative and destructive power of nature, principally in connection with rain and water." Writing about southeastern Australia, he notes the Rainbow Snake's association with waterfalls, as well as with smallpox, and he mentions the belief that ordinary people who approached the Snake's home site were in danger of being eaten. He adds that paraphernalia prepared for young men's initiation sequences in the Bora rites included a snakelike earth mound up to forty feet long. Although Radcliffe-Brown concludes that the *bunyip* in Victoria was not a Rainbow Snake, Charles P. Mountford (1978) includes *bunyips*, as well as other Snake-like characters, in this category of beings. Even among traditionally oriented Aborigines, the name Rainbow Snake can apply to snakes with no obvious rainbow connections. They may have quasi-crocodile shapes or just "something" about them that is dangerous or not normally visible.

HUMAN CONTACT WITH RAINBOW SNAKE POWER. Because of the aura of danger surrounding the *idea* of Rainbow Snakes and other similar beings, certain places are taboo to ordinary people but not to Aboriginal "doctors," the men or, less often, women whose experience goes beyond cases of illness or injury to include the supernatural dimension, usually through special initiation rites involving the Rainbow Snake and perhaps spirits of the dead. According to some Kimberley and Western Desert beliefs recorded by A. P. Elkin (1945), the novice was taken up into the sky, where he underwent a ritual death and had inserted into his body quartz crystals and perhaps *maban* (sometimes called "pearl shell"), both associated with the Rainbow Snake. The crystals or shells are invisible and confer particular powers on the recipient; or he might be given "little rainbow-snakes . . . from a water-hole at the foot of the rainbow" (Elkin, 1945, pp. 32–33). A person with such powers can see Rainbow Snakes and other beings and perhaps have a personal Rainbow Snake as a spirit familiar. He can use the rainbow as a vehicle in which to travel great distances through the sky.

Actual pearl shells from the northwest coast of Western Australia, some engraved with water and rain designs, were also associated with Rainbow Snakes. Used in initiation and in rainmaking rites, they were (and are) passed on along recognized trade routes, eastward well beyond the Victoria River district and south to the Great Australian Bight.

During the wet season (the cyclone season), the northwest coast is subject to monsoon storms that deluge the whole north coast across to northern and eastern Queensland. Rainbow Snake and other Snake stories are especially common throughout these potential flood areas. The Rainbow Snake of arid zones, known as Wonambi, Wanambi, and other names, is dangerous and powerful, but less dramatically so than his northern counterparts. Even inland, however, dry sandy creek beds can suddenly become raging torrents that flood the surrounding country (for example, the Tod River in Alice Springs and other rivers in northern South Australia or the usually dry Lake Eyre, which floods less often).

Along the northwestern Australian coast, for instance, summer cyclones threaten coastal towns—sometimes extending even into the southwest. For the non-Aboriginal population, the urgent questions have to do with whether a given cyclone will cross the coast, where and when it will do so, how destructive it will be, and, if it moves inland, whether it will become a rain-bearing low-pressure system, bringing water to areas that depend on the monsoon. Weather officials still regard cyclone movements as unpredictable. For traditional Aborigines, however, the matter is plain: mythic characters control the seasonal weather and tidal patterns, including cyclones, and the decisions are theirs.

Among the most important mythic characters are the *wandjina* (*wondjina*), well known to the outside world through cave and bark paintings. In Ungarinyin territory, these spirits, which can be manifestations of Rainbow Snake, are also sometimes called Ungud. Ungud "brings down spirit babies in the rain to the waterholes" (Elkin, 1930, p. 351). Elkin adds, "The rainbow-serpent is associated with the coming of rain, the increase of natural species and the continuance of mankind." According to Phyllis M. Kaberry, in northeastern Kimberley, the Rainbow Snake known as Galeru (Kaleru) is also a life saver and sustainer, the embodiment of fertility, "the most sacred of the totemic ancestors and . . . revered as such." He is a lawgiver, responsible for such features of social organization as marriage rules and subsections, and he is "the source of magical power not only in the past but also in the present" (Kaberry, 1937, pp. 194, 200–201; see also pp. 193, 196n). Pearl shells come from him, and in some circumstances it is dangerous to dream of them (p. 206); in the creative era of the Dreaming (the *ngarunggani),* he carried inside him certain foods now subject to life-crisis or age-linked taboos; white stones used for rainmaking also belong to him (p. 207).

Here, as in many cases, the main emphasis is on the Rainbow Snake as a male being: for example, as husband to

Kunapipi. In north-central Arnhem Land, Yulunggul is more often thought to be male. His Rainbow Snake identification there, less positive than it is in northeastern Arnhem Land, may have been influenced by the strong Rainbow Snake presence in western Arnhem Land. The Rainbow Snake in the west has several names—Ambidj, for instance, among the Maung of Goulburn Islands and the adjacent mainland, and Ngalyod among Gunwinggu speakers farther inland. Numereji, noted by Baldwin Spencer in 1912 as the Kakadu (Gagadju) name, has not been in use for at least forty years.

Gunwinggu speakers, especially, prefer to speak of the Rainbow Snake only obliquely, not directly by name. One everyday word for "creature(s)," edible or otherwise, is *mai*—provided it is included in the noun class that takes the prefix *na-* (which can be a masculine prefix). When *mai* is used with the indicator *ngal-*, which can be a feminine prefix, it usually refers to the Rainbow Snake. If Gunwinggu speakers had traditionally used written language, they would surely have written *Mai.* As it is, the context and the *ngal-* indicators differentiate it quite plainly. Among other such oblique names, one that depends partly on intonation and context for its maximum effect is Ngaldargid: here the prefix *ngal-* is attached to a word in ordinary use, *dargid,* meaning "living," or "alive." It could be taken in more than its ordinary sense, as in "the living one" or even, perhaps, as "the life-charged one." In other instances, such as in Ngaldargidni, it means that the Rainbow Snake is still there, still living, at a particular site. Hundreds of myths recount the events of the creative era in which the landscape was formed, and the Rainbow Snake plays an active role in the majority of them.

In one traditional western Arnhem Land view the Rainbow Snake is a creator, the first mother. She travels under the sea from the northwest, and on the mainland she eventually gives birth to the people she is carrying inside her. She vomits them out, licking them with her tongue to make them grow and scraping them with mussel shells to make their skin smooth and lighter in color. Some Gunwinggu women have told this author,

> No matter what our [social affiliations], we all call her *gagag,* "mother's mother." We live on the ground, she lives underneath, inside the ground and in the water[s]. She urinated fresh water for us to drink, otherwise we would all have died of thirst. She showed us what foods to collect. She vomited the first people, the Dreaming people, who prepared the country for us, and she made us, so that we have minds and sense to understand. She gave us our [social categories and] language, she made our tongues and teeth and throats and breath: she shared her breath with us, she gave us breath, from when we first sat inside our mothers' wombs. . . . She looks a bit like a woman, a bit like a snake.

In myth, and in recent and even present belief, the Rainbow Snake, Ngalyod, can be aroused by too much noise, such as that of a crying child, or by too much shouting, too much interference with the ground, the breaking of a taboo-rock, or a person's failure to take precautions at times when he or she is especially vulnerable (by going near water during pregnancy or menstruation or too soon after childbirth or by allowing a young baby to do so). Gunwinggu women at Oenpelli summed up the expected consequences:

> Far away, she lifts up her head and listens, and she makes straight for that place. A cold wind blows, there is a red glow like a bush fire, a great roaring sound, the ground cracks and moves and becomes soft and wet, water flows rushing, a flood covers the rocks, stones are falling, she comes up like a dream and swallows all those people. She carries them about for a while. Then she vomits their bones, and they turn into stone. They are still there today, as *djang,* eternally present: their spirits remain at [that place]. Let nobody go near [that place], where they came into Dreaming!

There are many variations of this account just as there are many distinctive rock formations in the Arnhem Land escarpment. Most of the named sites throughout the region have their specific *djang* spirits, and in almost all cases the Rainbow Snake was an agent in their transformation (see Berndt and Berndt, 1970).

On the coastal islands and nearby mainland, the Rainbow Snake is more often specifically categorized as male; the inland classification, however, is sometimes acknowledged to be partly a matter of grammatical gender, and the Rainbow Snake is occasionally described as either male or ambisexual. Moreover, in coastal and island contexts, myths often tell of parties of men who track down and kill the Rainbow Snake, cut her (him) open, and try to save the people inside. In one version they cook and eat the Snake to give them strength in the long task of pulling out the living and burying the great numbers of dead. But the Rainbow Snake is timeless, indestructible, and not limited to any one locality. Rainbow Snake manifestations can be almost everywhere or anywhere. For all the people of western Arnhem Land, the Rainbow Snake is traditionally a symbol of monsoon storms, rain, floods, *and* of danger; her (his) formal links with the sphere of the sacred are epitomized in the secret-sacred rites of the Ubar.

THE RAINBOW SNAKE AS CATALYST AND SYMBOL. Not only healers and law keepers can draw on the Rainbow Snake's power. In one western Arnhem Land myth, a man with a grievance deliberately smashes a taboo rock, knowing that when the Snake comes rushing to swallow (drown) everyone at that site he himself will die along with the people he wants to kill. Some sorcerers were believed to send their own Rainbow Snake familiars on vengeance missions.

In other areas a sorcerer could also supposedly draw on that power, for personal reasons or on someone else's behalf, to avenge a perceived wrong. When sorcery is identified as the cause of death, it is likely to be condemned as a misuse of the powers obtained from the Rainbow Snake and from spirits of the dead (e.g., Kaberry, 1937, p. 211). The argument is that such powers are directed toward selfish ends that are not socially approved, whereas directing them outside the community to avenge the death of one of its own members is assumed to have the community's approval.

Nevertheless, in many respects the Rainbow Snake is a guardian of the status quo as well as a source of power. The terror and dismay of victims in myth are sometimes a consequence of their own carelessness, sometimes a matter of fate or destiny (particularly in western Arnhem Land) or of seemingly harsh treatment for their own ultimate good. The Rainbow Snake is not necessarily a destroyer, to go back to Radcliffe-Brown's comment, but rather a symbol and a reminder of the potentially destructive and overpowering, as well as revitalizing, forces of nature, which can be fearsome as well as splendid. This constellation of cosmic imagery attracts within its orbit a host of other figures not necessarily categorized as Rainbow Snakes. Thus, according to Ursula H. McConnel, in North Queensland the deadly taipan snake is identified with the Rainbow Snake by virtue of its assumed "power . . . as arbiter of life and death" (McConnel, 1957, p. 111).

The Rainbow Snake is Our Mother, but there are other mythic mothers. In some accounts he is Our Father, but there are other mythic fathers (although fewer, perhaps, than mothers). There are other phallic symbols, as well as other storm, flood, cyclone, lightning, thunder, wind, rain, and fertility symbols. Other Snakes and other beings are associated with deep pools, waterfalls, whirlwinds, and rivers. But the rainbow in the sky and the Rainbow Snake on the ground and in the waters are somehow—directly or indirectly, explicitly or potentially—linked to any or all of these from the very beginning of time. Very few elaborate ritual sequences are devoted to the Rainbow Snake alone as a central personage, and he or she has not one localized site but rather many actual or potential sites in all parts of the continent. These are pointers to a frame of beliefs that, though partly open, has as its central core image a wide-ranging, powerful deity of cosmic proportions, never wholly visible at any one time or place.

See Also Gadjeri; Ungarinyin Religion; Wandjina; Yulunggul Snake.

Bibliography

Berndt, Ronald M. *Kunapipi: A Study of an Australian Aboriginal Religious Cult.* Melbourne, 1951. Discusses the Rainbow Snake in the context of rituals and associated myths.

Berndt, Ronald M., and Catherine H. Berndt. *Man, Land and Myth in North Australia: The Gunwinggu People.* Sydney, 1970. Includes discussion of myths and ritual relating to the Rainbow Snake in western Arnhem Land, including the Snake as an agent of destiny or fate in the transformation of the "First People."

Berndt, Ronald M. and Catherine H. Berndt. *The World of the First Australians* (1964). Rev. ed., Adelaide, 1985. Includes a number of references to Rainbow Snakes in the contexts of myth and ritual and of seasonal fertility.

Eliade, Mircea. *Australian Religions: An Introduction.* Ithaca, N.Y., 1973. Includes an overview and discussion of Rainbow Snake material from various parts of the continent, with critical comments and comparisons, see the sections on "The Wondjina and The Rainbow Serpent" (pp. 76–80) and "The Rainbow Serpent," pp. 113–116. Footnotes to the text cover a large range of published items on this topic.

Elkin, A. P. *Aboriginal Men of High Degree* (1945). 2d ed. New York, 1977. The John Murtagh Macrossan Memorial Lectures for 1944. Summarizes material available to that date, including his own earlier field notes and published material, on the initiation of Aboriginal "native doctors" or "clever men" in various parts of Australia.

Kaberry, Phyllis M. *Aboriginal Woman, Sacred and Profane.* London, 1939. Includes useful references to the Rainbow Snake in its (his) sociocultural context, in the Kimberley region of Western Australia, where her field research covered several different "tribal" groups. The book would have a stronger impact on present-day readers if she could have revised and updated it, compacting and reframing her data and her arguments. Unfortunately, she did not live to do that.

Mountford, Charles P. "The Rainbow Serpent Myth of Australia." In *The Rainbow Serpent,* edited by Ira R. Buchler and Kenneth Maddock, pp. 23–97. The Hague, 1978. Includes some interesting items, but needs to be read with caution. It is most useful for the quite lavish illustrations.

Radcliffe-Brown, A. R. "The Rainbow Serpent Myth in South-East Australia." *Oceania* 7 (October–December 1930): 342–347. In addition to Radcliffe-Brown's essay, this issue of *Oceania* includes articles by Ursula H. McConnel on the Rainbow Serpent in North Queensland, by A. P. Elkin on the Rainbow Serpent in northwestern Australia, and by Ralph Piddington on the Water Serpent in Karadjeri mythology. They are short, tentative statements based on some field research, and mostly expanded in later publications. Radcliffe-Brown had an earlier article on the Rainbow Serpent in the *Journal of the Royal Anthropological Institute* 56 (1926): 19–25. McConnel later included the story of "Taipan, the 'Rainbow Serpent'" in *Myths of the Mungkan* (Melbourne, 1957), pp. 111–116. She added that "the most dangerous snakes, and the water-snakes, are associated with the rainbow, and of these Taipan, the deadly brown snake of North Queensland, is the most destructive. It is therefore Taipan who goes up in the rainbow, with his sisters, and causes all these troubles"—storms and cyclonic disturbances that bring "terrors and discomforts," floods and high tides "in the low-lying Gulf Country."

Stanner, W. E. H. "On Aboriginal Religion: IV, The Design-Plan of a Riteless Myth." *Oceania* 31 (June 1961): 233–258. One part of Stanner's larger study of Australian Aboriginal religion, this concentrates on a particular myth in the sociocultural setting of the Murinbata and neighboring groups in the Port Keats region, in the northwest of the Northern Territory. He analyzes various versions in some detail, exploring issues of interpretation and explanation in his usual carefully thought-out prose style and includes Aboriginal comments and differences of opinion in his assessment.

New Sources

Chippindale, Christopher, Meredith Wilson, and Paul S. C. Tacon. "Birth of the Rainbow Serpent in the Arnhem Land Rock Art and Oral History." *Archaeology in Oceania* 60, no. 3 (1996): 103–124.

Gardner, Robert L. *The Rainbow Serpent: Bridge to Consciousness.* Toronto, 1990.

Hulley, Charles E. *The Rainbow Serpent.* Sydney, 2000.

McKnight, David. *People, Countries, and the Rainbow Serpent: Systems of Classification among the Lardil of Mornington Island.* New York, 1999.

Noonuccal, Oodgeroo, and Kabul Oodgeroo Noonuccal. *The Rainbow Serpent.* Canberra, 1988.

Taylor, Luke. "The Rainbow Serpent as Visual Metaphor in Western Arnhem Land." *Oceania* 60 (June 1990): 329–344.

CATHERINE H. BERNDT (1987)
Revised Bibliography

RAJNEESH, Bhagwan Shree (1931–1990), later known as Osho, was a controversial spiritual teacher from India whose disciples at the start of the twenty-first century include thousands of Americans, Europeans, and Asians, who are called *sannyasins.* The spiritual movement is centered at the Osho Commune International in Pune, India, at 17 Koregaon Park, where it was first established in the early 1970s.

There are Osho centers in more than fifty nations. In the United States, the largest are Osho Academy in Sedona, Arizona; Viha Meditation Center in Mill Valley, California; and Osho Padma Meditation Center in New York City. Centers are independent, with some tensions developing because of different emphases, but they share common bonds through Osho's meditations and teachings.

Osho Meditation Resort in Pune began as the Shree Rajneesh Ashram and continues as the movement's heart, housing a multiversity offering myriad courses on spiritual growth, healing, creative arts, and intimate relationships. There are also meditation workshops and programs emphasizing meditative aspects of sport.

From 1958 to 1966, Osho, then known as Rajneesh and holding a master of arts degree in philosophy, taught that subject primarily at the University of Jabalpur in the city of Jabalpur. He resigned his post in 1966 to travel throughout India as an independent religious teacher, also offering meditation camps during summer months. In the early 1970s he shifted headquarters from his Bombay apartment to the Shree Rajneesh Ashram in Pune.

Osho's synthesis of spirituality with personal-growth psychology attracted significant numbers of Westerners, many in midlife transition. *Sannyasins* often received new names signifying their spiritual rebirth. These *sannyasins* were known as new or neo-*sannyasins;* they renounced living in either the past or the future, but emphatically did not renounce material or sexual indulgence. He developed unique meditations, many involving intense, emotionally cleansing activity preceding stillness. Before his death, he shifted his emphasis to meditative therapies encouraging individuals' responsibility for their own personal and spiritual growth.

Meditation remains central to the movement, and Osho meditations have been taught in schools, corporations, and other venues. Osho's philosophical approach blends Western and Eastern traditions, with special emphasis on Zen Buddhism. Important themes include dropping the ego and its conditioned beliefs and integrating the material and the spiritual. The ideal human is Zorba the Buddha, a consummate being combining Buddha's spiritual focus with Zorba's life-embracing traits.

A major reason that Osho was controversial in India was his advocacy of sexual freedom and exploration. However, the greatest international controversy developed in the United States when he settled at the Big Muddy Ranch in central Oregon. From the summer of 1981 until the late fall of 1985, several thousand *sannyasins* labored to create the communal city of Rajneeshpuram and a model agricultural collective. Their dream disintegrated because of financial, legal, and political conflicts, and Rajneesh embarked on a world tour before returning to Pune in 1987. Two years later he took the name Osho, which means dissolving into the totality of existence, or merging with all life. Osho died on January 19, 1990.

Osho Meditation Resort is an international center where a core staff hosts thousands of visitors annually. Both *sannyasins* and other seekers visit the resort center in Pune, read some of the more than six hundred books that have been transcribed from Osho's lectures or have been written about him, communicate on the internet, gather to meditate throughout the world, or enroll in Osho-based counseling and personal growth training.

At the beginning of the twenty-first century, there is discord within the movement between those who regard Osho's general teachings and methods as of primary importance and those who put primary emphasis on Osho himself as an embiodied charismatic individual. This is a major dispute that could lead to a segmentation in which new centers, without connection to the Pune headquarters, incorporate and spread Osho's teachings. Such schism may result in either continued growth and spread of the belief system or attenuation of the movement and its teachings.

BIBLIOGRAPHY

Carter, Lewis. *Charisma and Control in Rajneeshpuram.* New York, 1990. A thorough, balanced look at the Rajneesh organizational structure, history, and the politics of the communal city, Rajneeshpuram.

Friends of Osho. http://www.sannyas.net.

Goldman, Marion S. *Passionate Journeys: Why Successful Women Joined a Cult.* Ann Arbor, Mich., 1999. A book about the high-achieving women who gave up families and careers to follow Rajneesh to central Oregon.

Osho. *Osho: Autobiography of a Spiritually Incorrect Mystic.* New York, 2000. Osho's own words about his philosophies and personal experiences.

Palmer, Susan J., and Arvind Sharma, eds. *The Rajneesh Papers: Studies in a New Religious Movement.* Delhi, 1993. A collection of chapters written about Osho by both his devotees and also by academics.

MARION S. GOLDMAN (2005)

RALBAG (ACRONYM FOR RABBI LEVI BEN GERSHOM) SEE GERSONIDES

RĀMA, the hero of the *Rāmāyaṇa,* an epic of ancient India, is the figure most celebrated in literature, music, and art throughout India and Southeast Asia. Vālmīki's *Rāmāyaṇa* is the earliest known source of Rāma's heroic biography. Many modern scholars agree that in the central part of Vālmīki's epic Rāma is depicted as a secular hero. The first and the sixth books of the Vālmīki text, however, depict Rāma as an incarnation of Viṣṇu, who comes down to the earth as a human warrior to kill the menacing demon Rāvaṇa. Medieval devotional *Rāmāyaṇas* developed this theme, making Rāma the god himself. In this view, Rāma's wife, Sītā, is the goddess Śrī, and his brother Lakṣmaṇa is perceived as the human incarnation of the snake Ādiśeṣa, on top of whom Viṣṇu sleeps. Rāma and Lakṣmaṇa are perceived as inseparable brothers, identical even in physical appearance except for their skin color: Rāma is blue, Lakṣmaṇa is golden yellow.

Rāma is described as perfect: He is self-controlled, eloquent, majestic, and capable of annihilating all his enemies. Above all, he is truthful and totally devoted to only one wife. Similarly, Sītā is described as the ideal in chastity, devoted to Rāma in thought, word, and deed.

The idealizations of Rāma and Sītā are not totally free of problems, particularly for the authors of *bhakti* texts. Several events described in Vālmīki's text tarnish Rāma's character. For instance, after his wife is abducted by Rāvaṇa, Rāma makes a pact with the monkey king Sugrīva to kill the latter's brother Valin in return for Sugrīva's help in finding Sītā. To keep his part of the contract, Rāma, hiding behind a tree, kills Vālin. This act violates all norms of justice and valor. A second such incident occurs later, when Rāma wages a battle against Rāvaṇa. Rāma succeeds in killing the demon king, but refuses to take Sītā back because she has lived in another man's house. To prove her innocence, Sītā has to go through the fire ordeal. Later, Rāma again abandons Sītā (who is now pregnant) when the people of Ayodhyā spread vicious talk about her stay in Rāvaṇa's house.

Buddhist texts transform Rāma from a martial hero into a spiritually elevated person. In the *Dāśaratha Jātaka,* Rāma is depicted as a *bodhisattva* figure. In this version there is no mention of Rāvaṇa, and Sītā is not abducted. Indeed, Sītā is depicted as Rāma's sister. The intrigues of their stepmother make their father, Daśaratha, send Rāma, Sītā, and Lakṣmaṇa into the forest for twelve years. At the end of twelve years Rāma returns and is crowned king. He rules with Sītā for sixteen thousand years. Other Jātaka stories also incorporate the Rāma theme, with some variations.

If Buddhists made Rāma a *bodhisattva,* Jains transformed him into one of their sixty-three *śalākāpuruṣas.* In Jain retellings, prominent among which is Vimalasūri's *Paumacariya* (written in Prakrit in the early centuries of the common era), Rāma eats no meat, performs no sacrifices involving animals, and wins his battle by wit rather than by violence. Jain *Rāmāyaṇas* include the story of Rāma up to the birth of his twin sons. Other *Rāmāyaṇa* texts of the Jain community include Hemacandra's *Jaina Rāmāyaṇa* and Nāgacandra's *Rāmacandracarita Purāṇa,* both of the twelfth century. In these versions Rāma eventually enters the Jain order as a monk and finally achieves liberation through heroic mortifications.

Rāma's story is mentioned in a number of Purāṇas. The Śaiva Purāṇas, such as the *Liṅga Purāṇa* and *Śiva Purāṇa,* make Rāma a devotee of Śiva, while the *Bhāgavata Purāṇa* and other Vaiṣṇava Purāṇas describe him as an incarnation of Viṣṇu.

In about the twelfth century, the Vaiṣṇava theology, particularly that of Rāmānuja, gave rise to a cult of Rāma. Numerous Vaiṣṇava commentators on the *Rāmāyaṇa* interpret Rāma as the manifestation of the divine among human beings. In keeping with Vaiṣṇava influences, the *bhakti* Rāmāyaṇas make Rāma the god (Viṣṇu) incarnate exercising his *līlā* ("divine play") with his consort, Sītā.

A late fourteenth-century text, *Adhyātma Rāmāyaṇa,* uses the narrative form to provide an *advaita* (nondualist) philosophical orientation to the teachings of the Rāma cult. In this book, presented as a conversation between Śiva and Pārvatī, Rāma is *brahman,* the Absolute itself, which takes a human shape as a pretext to accomplish his divine purposes. Sītā, in this text, is the eternal consort of the Lord. In keeping with this logic, the events leading to the abduction of Sītā, her later abandonment, the birth of her two sons Lava and Kuśa, and the final separation of Sītā and Rāma are significantly altered to represent the reuniting of the couple in Vaikuṇṭha, Viṣṇu's heavenly abode.

Tulsidas's *Ramcaritmanas* (composed around 1574) adopts ingenious themes to free Rāma's biography of its problems. In this text all the characters of the *Rāmāyaṇa,* including Rāvaṇa and all the demons whom Rāma kills, are described as Rāma's devotees. According to the devotional theory presented here, even an enmity to God is one of the means of reaching God. For human beings, however, the model of devotion is said to be set by Hanumān, the monkey servant of Rāma, who attends upon his master with intense devotion. *Bhakti* Rāmayanists also borrow elements of stories about Kṛṣṇa, especially relating to the god's childhood, to describe the child Rāma.

The figure of Rāma remains prominent in many *bhakti* cults. There, devotees believe that chanting Rāma's name and reflecting upon the main incidents of his biography ultimately lead them to reach God.

See Also Līlā; Rāmāyaṇa; Tulsidas.

Bibliography

Bulcke, Camille. *Rāma-katha* (1950). 2d ed. Allahabad, 1962.

Goldman, Robert P., trans. *The Rāmāyaṇa of Valmiki,* vol. 1, *Balakanda.* Princeton, N. J., 1984.

Hill, W. Douglas P., trans. *The Holy Lake of the Acts of Rāma* (1952). Reprint, Oxford, 1971.

Smith, H. Daniel. *Reading the Rāmāyaṇa: A Bibliographic Guide for Students and College Teachers.* Syracuse, N.Y., 1983.

New Sources

Blank, Jonah. *Arrow of the Blue-Skinned God: Retracing the Ramayana through India.* Boston, 1992.

Buck, Harry Merwyn. *The Figure of Rama in Buddhist Cultures.* Bhubaneswar, 1995.

Velcheru Narayana Rao (1987)
Revised Bibliography

RAMABAI, PANDITA. Ramabai (1858–1922) was an extraordinary woman of her time—an educator, scholar, feminist, and social reformer, whose life was an example of how womanhood and religious identity were negotiated against the backdrop of Brahmanical culture, Christianity, and colonialism. For Hindus and Christians, her life and work, including her intellectual probings and hermeneutical clashes with Hindu social reformers and Christian missionaries, seemed to signal contradictory and confusing messages. As a learned scholar of her own tradition, she vigorously questioned the status of women within Hinduism. Later, when she became a Christian, she challenged institutionalized Christianity with its creeds, which she felt stifled the power of the gospel, and she subsequently quarreled with Bible translators for their unwitting use of Vedāntic terms in the Marathi version of the Bible. She seems to have lived and worked out her life on the margins of traditions, constructing her own independent agency.

Ramabai was born into a Chitpavan Brahman family in Karnataka. She was the youngest child of Anant Shastri Dongre, a devout Hindu and erudite Sanskrit pundit, and his much younger wife, Lakshmibai. Contrary to the prevailing mood of the time, Anant Shastri believed in women's education and he opposed outdated customs like child marriage, having witnessed the sad fate of his daughter Krishnabai's child marriage. Ramabai had an unconventional upbringing in that she was taught at home, receiving Sanskrit education mainly from her mother, who herself was taught by her husband despite fierce opposition from their community. From an early age, Ramabai was exposed to a life of never-ending pilgrimage and the reciting of the Purāṇas in various locations, a traditional religious vocation, which her family undertook in order to earn a modest living. While this kind of precarious living brought untold hardship later, it freed Ramabai from domesticity and any form of patriarchal control.

Ramabai's life was marked by a series of unfortunate deaths in her family. She lost her parents, elder sister, elder brother, husband, and finally her daughter shortly before her own death. Her travels around India with her brother after her parents' demise not only offered her the opportunity to visit several important Hindu holy places, but it also enabled her to witness the plight of women, which led her to champion their cause.

It was Ramabai's visit to Calcutta in 1878 that brought a dramatic turn of events. Her knowledge of the Sanskrit language and literary and religious texts came to be widely known and appreciated, and in recognition of her Sanskrit learning the honorific title *paṇḍita* (learned) was conferred on her. She defied traditional caste norms by accepting an offer of marriage from a non-Brahman Brahmo Bengali lawyer, Bipin Behari Das, but he died within two years of their marriage, leaving her with an infant daughter, Manorama.

While her early widowhood deepened her concern for women in a similar predicament, her faith in the kind of Purāṇic and ritualistic Hinduism in which she was raised was beginning to wear off. When she later became acquainted with other Hindu texts, such as the *Dharmaśāstras,* with a pronounced patriarchal bias, she was not convinced that Hinduism as such had any hope for women. She found, however, that her early forays into reform movements, such as the Brāhmo Samāj and Prarthana Samāj, were fruitless as alternatives to Hinduism because in her view these movements focused more on philosophical aspects than on the plight of women. She came into contact with Christian missionaries but had no intention of becoming a Christian until much later in 1883 while she was in England, much to the dismay of Hindus back home. She was not wholly accepting of Christianity at this stage. She was not willing to substitute one form of patriarchy with another. She proved to be a thorn in the flesh of Anglicans when she questioned such basic tenets as the Trinity, miracles, the divinity of Christ, and the resurrection.

What is extraordinary is that Ramabai was able to make an impression in the strongly male-dominated public discourse of her time. Her highly persuasive books, both in the vernacular and in English, established her as one of the important voices of the era. The fact that she wrote *Stri Dharma Niti* (Morals for women, 1882) in order to finance her trip to England (where her hope of studying medicine never materialized) testifies that her reforming zeal preceded her attraction to Christianity. In this book she urges women to educate themselves and transform their lives, citing mythological examples of Hindu womanhood. *The High Caste Hindu Woman* (1887) is a trenchant feminist critique of a Brahmanical patriarchy that accords its women a low position. *United Stateschi Lokasthiti ani Pravasavritta* (The Peoples of the United States, 1889) is an account of her visit to the United States, and it reflects her feminist concerns whilst contrasting freedoms in the United States and colonial India. *A Testimony of Our Inexhaustible Treasure* (1907), her last public discourse, was a pamphlet narrating a spiritual odyssey that culminated in her final acceptance of the Christian faith.

The last decade of her life was spent translating the Bible into Marathi and producing Greek-Marathi and Greek-Hebrew lexicons.

Ramabai put teaching into practice. It was her early disappointment with her own community that made her turn to England and the United States to solicit help for her work among women. Realizing the importance of education for empowering women, she ran a number of vocational programs. Sharada Sadan (Home of Learning), initially a home for high-caste child widows but later for destitute women and children of all castes, provided training and education. Although the school was initially secular in orientation, it gradually became explicitly Christian. There were allegations of conversions at Sharada Sadan, which caused a major rift between Ramabai and Hindu social reformers; although Ramabai was exonerated, the rift remained.

The fact that Ramabai's commitment to Christianity coexisted with her conscious attempt to declare herself a Hindu and Indian in public discourses, continues to puzzle Hindus and Christians who would like to categorize her neatly.

Bibliography

For Ramabai's own writings in English, see *The High Caste Hindu Woman* (New York, 1887) and *A Testimony of Our Inexhaustible Treasure* (Pune, India, 1907). For *United Stateschi Lokasthiti ani Pravasavritta* (1889), see two acclaimed translations: *Pandita Ramabai's American Encounter: The Peoples of the United States* by Meera Kosambi (New York, 2003) and *Pandita Ramabai's America*, edited by R. E. Frykenberg (Grand Rapids, Mich., 2003). For a comprehensive contextualized introduction to a selection of Ramabai's writings, both in original English and translations from Marathi, see *Pandita Ramabai Through Her Own Words: Selected Works* (Oxford, 2000). For a helpful biography, see *Pandita Ramabai* by Nicol MacNicol (Calcutta, 1926), later published under the title *What Liberates a Woman? The Story of Pandita Ramabai, a Builder of Modern India* by Nicol MacNicol and Vishal Mangalwadi (Delhi, 1996). See also S. M. Adhav's *Pandita Ramabai* (Madras, India, 1979). For the historical and cultural background to Ramabai's life and work, see Uma Chakravarti's *Rewriting History: The Life and Times of Pandita Ramabai* (Delhi, 1998). For hermeneutical issues related to Ramabai's conversion, see Gauri Viswanathan, *Outside the Fold: Conversion, Modernity, and Belief* (Princeton, N.J., 1998). For a detailed chapter on the numerous Ramabai Associations that functioned in her support in the United States, see Kumaria Jayawardena, "Going for the Jugular of Hindu Patriarchy: American Fund-Raisers for Ramabai" in *The White Woman's Other Burden: Western Women and South-Asia During British Rule* (New York and London, 1995); this article also addresses Ramabai's complex and difficult relationship to Vivekananda, Annie Besant, and Sister Nivedita.

Sharada Sugirtharajah (2005)

RAMADĀN See ISLAMIC RELIGIOUS YEAR; ṢAWM

RAMAKRISHNA

RAMAKRISHNA (1834/6–1886) was a Hindu ecstatic and mystic, and to many Hindus a "supremely realized self" (*paramahaṃsa*) and an *avatāra*, or incarnation of the divine. Through his disciple, Swami Vivekananda, his gospel of the truth of all religions became a source of inspiration for modern Hindu universalism.

Life. Born Gadādhar Chatterjee in an isolated village in Bengal, Ramakrishna belonged to a Vaiṣṇava *brahman* family whose primary deity was the *avatāra* of Viṣṇu, Rāma, although the family also worshiped other deities, such as Śiva and Durgā. As a boy, Gadādhar was gifted with immense emotional and aesthetic sensitivity, which was nurtured by norms of ecstatic devotion (*bhakti*) common within the Bengali Vaiṣṇava tradition. Often, when overwhelmed by beauty and emotion, the boy would lose consciousness in an ecstatic trance.

His father's death in 1843 increased Ramakrishna's dependence upon his mother, while the role of father figure was assumed by his eldest brother, Rāmkumār, whom he followed to Calcutta in 1852. Rāmkumār became adviser to a wealthy widow, herself a Śākta, or devotee of *śakti* (the divine power symbolized as the Goddess), who was building a temple to the Divine Mother Kālī at Dakshineshwar, just north of the city. Though dedicated to Kālī, the temple also included shrines to Śiva and to Rādhā-Kṛṣṇa, thus combining the major strands of Hindu devotional religion. Rāmkumār was appointed the temple's chief priest and Ramakrishna became priest to Rādhā-Kṛṣṇa.

When Rāmkumār died in 1856, Ramakrishna became priest to the Divine Mother. Bereft and overwhelmed by the pain of separation, Ramakrishna developed a frenzied longing for Kālī. Eating and sleeping little, his anguish over being separated from the Mother drove him to seize a sword in her temple, determined to end his life. Instead, he lost consciousness in a bliss-filled vision of Kālī. After this he desperately sought continual awareness of the Mother, seeking to become her instrument. As he later attested, he was nearly driven insane, spending several years in a state of divine madness in which visions of various deities came to him repeatedly, while he was unable even to close his eyes.

By 1858 concerns about Ramakrishna's mental health were mounting. His family arranged for him to return to their village, where he was married to a local girl, Sāradāmaṇi Devī, then age six. Sāradā remained in her parents' home for several more years, only visiting Ramakrishna at Dakshineshwar for the first time in 1872. By this time Ramakrishna was practicing strict celibacy, his ascetic inclinations routinely summed up in his professed aversion to *kāminī-kañcan*, "women and gold." His marriage to Sāradā was never consummated, but she served him as helpmate until his death.

In 1861 a middle-aged female Tantric practitioner *(bhairavī)* named Yogeśvarī arrived at Dakshineshwar. She became Ramakrishna's first *guru,* guiding him through a remarkable transformation, teaching him a panoply of Tantric rituals. Tantric practice seeks to overcome all socially based distinctions, enabling one to realize in a direct, experiential manner that all aspects of existence are manifestations of the Divine Mother, the *śakti,* the divine productive power. This discipline, which Ramakrishna underwent over a three- or four-year period, had a decisive impact upon his development, helping him to overcome his sense of separation and transforming his self-destructive frenzies into the joyful play *(līlā)* of a child in his Mother's "mansion of mirth," as he came to call the physical universe. This Tantric transformation also provided a theological framework into which he integrated all of his religious experiences, helping him to realize all divinities as forms of the Mother and inspiring him to participate fully in all aspects of her divine play. Thus he was able to re-experience his Vaiṣṇava heritage, playing with and realizing the divine child Rāma and, in the guise of Rādhā, longing for the divine lover Kṛṣṇa. It was such training that also led Ramakrishna to worship Sāradā as the Divine Mother in 1872, an event that would in later years serve to support her deification.

In 1864 or 1865, Ramakrishna took instruction from another renunciant, this time a naked ascetic named Ishwara Totāpurī, a master of the absolute nondualism of Advaita Vedānta taught by the eighth-century philosopher Śaṅkara. Advaita teaches the sole reality of the impersonal absolute (*nirguṇa brahman*), which is realized in a state of consciousness devoid of all conceptual forms (*nirvikalpa samādhi*). Under Totāpurī's forceful tutelage, Ramakrishna wrenched his mind from the beloved form of Kālī in order to plunge into this trancelike state; for more than a year he was so preoccupied with it and so neglectful of his body that he came near to death. According to his canonical biographers, Ramakrishna returned from this state only at the Mother's command and for the welfare of the world.

After this experiment, Ramakrishna returned to enjoy life as a child at play within his Mother's world. During this period he expanded his religious experience beyond Hindu religion, first devoting three days to the worship of Allah and then, some years later, four days to Christ. In both cases, he had visionary realizations that he held to be the same as those he had had of the various Hindu divinities. These brief but intense visions became the experiential basis for his claim that all religions can lead to the same realization of the divine.

In the mid-1870s he began to attract wider notice, especially among a generation of educated, middle-class urbanites. Surprisingly, the rustic and untutored mystic was soon entertaining some of the brightest young minds of Calcutta, including the likes of Keshab Chandra Sen (1838–1884), the fiery apostle of the Brāhmo Samāj, and Narendranath Datta (1863-1902), who first met Ramakrishna in 1881 and who would emerge as his favorite. These were men who were educated in a colonial curriculum that stressed the norms of reason, learning, and social progress, but Ramakrishna's disdain for book learning and his scorn for the workaday world of the clerk, challenged them to question their commitments. And while many of the youth had internalized the colonizer's disdain for so-called Hindu superstition, the authenticity of Ramakrishna's spiritual experiences forced his visitors to reevaluate the dignity of their spiritual heritage. Ramakrishna's final years were spent teaching such visitors and a gathering circle of disciples.

After his death in 1886, a small band of Ramakrishna's young disciples took formal vows of renunciation (*saṃnyāsa*), inspired by the example of Narendranath Datta, who later took the monastic name, Swami Vivekananda. These disciples became the swamis or "masters" who would form the core of a monastic order known as the Ramakrishna Math (Skt., *maṭha,* "monastery"). Out of this order grew the Ramakrishna Mission, a movement to spread Ramakrishna's teachings throughout India and the world. Leadership again came from Swami Vivekananda, who made a dramatic appearance at the World's Parliament of Religions in Chicago in 1893, where he spoke on the dignity of Hinduism. Before his premature death in 1902, Vivekananda traveled widely in India and the West, promoting what he called "Practical Vedānta," a religious vision that supported not just spiritual progress, but interreligious understanding, social uplift, and Indian national pride. As for Sāradā Devī, after Ramakrishna's death she was elevated to the status of Sāradā Mā, the Holy Mother, a complex status that reflects not simply her devoted service of Ramakrishna, but more importantly the power of the Divine Mother. Sāradā died in 1920. In official iconography she is depicted alongside Ramakrishna and Vivekananda, while popular images often show Ramakrishna accompanied by Sāradā and Kālī; as Gwilym Beckerlegge points out, in such images the Bengali word *Mā* "could refer equally to Kali or Sarada Devi" as mother (2000, p. 137).

TEACHINGS. Ramakrishna left no written work, but his conversations from 1882 to 1886 were recorded in Bengali by Mahendranath Gupta, writing under the pseudonym "M," and published as *Śrī Śrī Rāmakṛṣṇa Kathāmṛta* (Holy nectar of Sri Ramakrishna's teachings). The five-volume Bengali text is widely read in Bengal. Elsewhere, readers discover the *Kathāmṛta* through Swami Nikhilananda's translation, *The Gospel of Sri Ramakrishna.*

Ramakrishna's followers maintain that his realization of the nondual absolute under Totāpurī was the culmination of his spiritual quest and provides the basis for his teaching of the truth of all religions as paths leading to this ultimate goal. In his teachings, however, he stressed that withdrawal from the world as advocated by Advaita produces a "knower," or *jñānī,* who is negative and self-centered. Ramakrishna contrasted the *jñānī* with the *vijñānī,* the "complete knower" who does not reject the world as an illusory distraction from the absolute but who sees it as the play (*līlā*) of the Divine Mother. Ramakrishna saw merit in both positions. The formless absolute is real, but so is the Divine Mother, or *śakti,* who is ever at play in the world of form. Viewing *brahman* and *śakti* as two sides of the same reality, Ramakrishna affirmed the reality of the goal sought by the followers of Śaṅkara, while also making clear that his own ideal was a complete knowledge that realizes the reality of the One who is both beyond change and playfully active.

The global appeal of Ramakrishna's teachings stems from his articulation of an inclusive worldview that promises to integrate the diverse and often conflicting aspects of Hinduism and that seems to provide the basis for a more harmonious relationship among the world's religions. As he was fond of saying, *yato mat, tato path,* "there are as many paths as there are points of view."

However, Ramakrishna's gospel of the truth within all religions is not based simply on the belief that they all lead to the realization of the same formless absolute, in which all difference is transcended and negated. Rather, it is based upon his own experience of the truth and reality of the divine power at work in all manifest forms. While aware that human ignorance, lust, and greed can obscure this divine presence, he had confidence that a sincere and ardent devotee of any religion would discover the Divine Mother at work, or rather at play, ever leading her child back to herself.

INTERPRETATIONS OF RAMAKRISHNA. Ramakrishna was, in Walter Neevel's words, both "multifaceted and mystifying" (1976, p. 53). The challenge of understanding his life and teachings is compounded by the need to disentangle Ramakrishna's spiritual experience from the hagiography and canonical accounts promulgated by the Ramakrishna Mission. We may consider three areas of debate within the literature on Ramakrishna, each reflecting tensions between insider and outsider views.

The first area of debate centers on the question of what philosophical framework best represents Ramakrishna's thought. As we have seen, the official position is that Ramakrishna's spiritual experience is epitomized by the teachings of Advaita Vedānta. While official sources record details of Ramakrishna's transformation under the tutelage of Yogeśvarī, this experience is relativized by the putative supremacy of Totāpurī's teachings. However, in the 1950s Heinrich Zimmer called attention to the specifically Tantric aspects of Ramakrishna's devotion to, and awareness of, the Divine Mother. In 1976, Neevel built upon Zimmer's interpretation to argue that Ramakrishna's view of the ultimate was best understood as a form of Tantric nondualism, not a Vedāntic one. Among other things, this allowed Neevel to interpret Ramakrishna's concern with worldly activity as arising from his understanding of the Mother's playful *śakti.* This, in turn, seemed to accord better with the ideals of service that are so characteristic of the Ramakrishna Mission, since the renunciatory ethic of Advaita Vedānta less readily supports the value of worldly activity.

The problem remains vexing, however, precisely because Ramakrishna's commitment to asceticism sits somewhat uncomfortably with the later ethic of social engagement promulgated by the Ramakrishna Mission. The *Kathāmṛta* provides numerous examples of Ramakrishna's outspoken impatience with those who spend their time trying to improve the world. Consequently, a second area of debate centers on tracing the exact inspiration for the movement's guiding ethic. Is it in direct continuity with Ramakrishna's teaching or does it reflect a departure? Official sources present the service-based monastic movement as grounded in Ramakrishna's embodiment of Vedāntic truth. While they recognize the creative contribution of Vivekananda, they do not raise the question of innovation. Scholars outside the movement have explored a variety of theories that might explain alternate inspirations for Vivekananda's Practical Vedānta, be it his early exposure to Western morality, his travels in the West, or his appropriation of Western reconstructions of Vedānta as found in the writings of Arnold Schopenhauer and Paul Deussen. Finally, if Ramakrishna's worldview was fundamentally Tantric, the question remains as to why this aspect of his thought has been played down in the official literature.

This suggests one final area of debate, which centers on the question of how best to account for the particulars of Ramakrishna's experience of Tantra. Postcolonial scholarship has made us aware of the stigma attached to Tantra in late Victorian discourse about India. The very mention of Tantra in the late nineteenth and early twentieth centuries would have conjured up visions of antinomian religious practices—most threateningly, ritualized sexual intercourse. Seen in this light, it is understandable that Vivekananda and the early disciples would have been sensitive about foregrounding the importance of Tantra for Ramakrishna. But beyond this, there were the sometimes scandalous particulars of Ramakrishna's own psychosexual development, be it his fondness for wearing women's clothing, his aversion to heterosexual relations, or the possible homoerotic dimensions of his spiritual life. Bourgeois prudery regarding Tantra and sexuality, on the part of both devotees and Western interpreters, has meant that these aspects of Ramakrishna's life were often denied or interpreted away.

Open discussion of such matters remained scandalous for most of the twentieth century, as is evident from the uproar surrounding the publication of Jeffrey J. Kripal's book *Kālī's Child* in 1995. Although scholars like Zimmer and Neevel had previously brought the Tantric side of Ramakrishna to light, Kripal attempted to put the ritual and theology of Tantra in conversation with Ramakrishna's psychosexual development. Kripal's search for a cross-cultural hermeneutic of Ramakrishna's experience that could do justice to the mystical and the erotic earned the indignation of devotees and of Hindus more generally, some of whom sought to have the book banned in India. To understand why, one need not only appreciate the fears of devotees who mistook Kripal's book for an attack on Ramakrishna, but also the sensibilities of postcolonial Hindus for whom such scholarship appeared to be yet another attempt to assert Western superiority. In the furor over the book two things were overlooked. First, far from trying to stigmatize Ramakrishna's sexuality, Kripal sought to recognize it as one dimension of a profoundly spiritual life; second, Kripal explicitly rejected any simplistic psychologism that reduced Ramakrishna's spirituality to a matter of pathology. Unflattering psycho-biographies of Ramakrishna exist, but they seem to have attracted far less attention than *Kālī's Child*, which suggests the degree to which the task of interpreting Ramakrishna must include reflection upon the place of Hinduism, Tantra, and the erotic in modern discourse about India. Without a doubt, the "multifaceted and mystifying" Ramakrishna will continue to generate fascinating discussions of mysticism and ethics, Tantra and Vedānta, and the dynamic relationship between modern Hindu apologetics and postcolonial identity.

SEE ALSO Līlā; Vivekananda.

BIBLIOGRAPHY

The official translation of the *Śrī Śrī Rāmakṛṣṇa Kathāmṛta* is Swami Nikhilananda's *The Gospel of Sri Ramakrishna* (New York, 1952). The *Kathāmṛta* is discussed in Sumit Sarkar, "The Kathamrita as Text," in *Occasional Papers on History and Society*, vol. 12 (New Delhi, 1985), and Jeffrey J. Kripal, *Kālī's Child: The Mystical and the Erotic in the Life and Teachings of Ramakrishna*, 2d ed. (Chicago, 1998). Swami Saradanada's *Sri Ramakrishna: The Great Master*, 3d ed., translated by Swami Jagadananda (Madras, India, 1963), provides a canonical biography, as does the *Life of Sri Ramakrishna Compiled from Various Authentic Sources*, 2d ed. (Calcutta, 1964). F. Max Müller's *Ramakrishna* (1899; reprint, New York, 1975), is an early account by a westerner, while Romain Rolland's biography, *The Life of Ramakrishna* (reprint, Calcutta, 1970), helped promote Ramakrishna's mystical experiences in the West. For a Western devotee's perspective, read Christopher Isherwood's *Ramakrishna and His Disciples* (New York, 1965). Sāradā Devī is the subject of Narasingha P. Sil's *Divine Dowager: The Life and Teachings of Saradamani, the Holy Mother* (Selinsgrove, Pa., 2003). Swami Gambhirana's *History of the Ramakrishna Math and Mission* (Calcutta, 1957) provides a standard history of the movement. For the movement in the West, see Carl. T. Jackson, *Vedanta for the West* (Bloomington, Ind., 1994). Heinrich Zimmer discusses Ramakrishna and Tantra in his *Philosophies of India*, edited by Joseph Campbell (1951; reprint, Princeton, 1969), pp. 560–602, a theme explored by Walter Neevel in his essay, "The Transformation of Sri Ramakrishna," in *Hinduism: New Essays in the History of Religions*, edited by Bardwell L. Smith (Leiden, 1976), pp. 53–97. On Ramakrishna and Kālī, see Carl Olson, *Mysterious Play of Kālī: An Interpretive Study of Ramakrishna* (Atlanta, 1989). On the mystical and the erotic, see Kripal mentioned above, which may be contrasted with Narasingha P. Sil's psychological interpretation in *Ramakrisna Paramahamsa* (Leiden, 1991). On this, see William Parsons, "Psychoanalysis and Mysticism: The Case of Ramakrishna," in *Religious Studies Review* 23, no. 4 (1997): 355–361, and Brian A. Hatcher, "Kali's Problem Child: Another Look at Jeffrey Kripal's Study of Sri Ramakrishna," in *International Journal of Hindu Studies* 3, no. 2 (1999): 165–182. Part 1 of Gwilym Beckerlegge, *The Ramakrishna Mission: The Making of a Modern Hindu Movement* (New York, 2000) provides a useful overview of interpretive debates. For Marxian and subalternist interpretations, see Sumit Sarkar, "Kaliyuga, Chakri, and Bhakti: Ramakrishna and His Times," in his *Writing Social History* (Delhi, 1997), pp. 282–357, and Partha Chatterjee, *The Nation and its Fragments: Colonial and Postcolonial Histories* (Princeton, 1993). Hans Torwesten explores the theme of incarnation in *Ramakrishna and Christ, or, The Paradox of the Incarnation* (Calcutta, 1999), while Sudhir Kakar's novel *Ecstasy* (New York, 2002), is loosely based on the lives of Ramakrishna and Vivekananda.

WALTER G. NEEVEL, JR. (1987)
BRIAN A. HATCHER (2005)

RĀMĀNUJA

RĀMĀNUJA (1017–1137), Hindu philosopher-theologian and the most influential exponent of a theistic interpretation of Vedantic philosophy that opposed the earlier monistic teaching of Śaṅkara. Within the Śrī Vaiṣṇava community Rāmānuja's importance comes from his authoritative exposition of the Vedānta, his leadership of the community in a period of formative growth that brought Tamil devotion together with Sanskrit philosophy and ritual, and, above all, his decisive mediation of divine grace to Śrī Vaiṣṇavas of all subsequent generations.

Accounts of Rāmānuja's life figure prominently in many Tamil and Sanskrit hagiographies. Two purport to be by contemporaries of Rāmānuja, but the earliest that can be dated with certainty was written more than a century after his death. Rāmānuja is presented as the last of the three great *ācāryas*, the first of whom was Nāthamuni, and second, his grandson Yāmuna. Rāmānuja just failed to meet Yāmuna before the latter's death, but during his own lifetime he was able to carry out Yamuna's unfulfilled wishes for establishing the community on a firm footing. Yāmuna's extant writings do in fact anticipate major tenets of Rāmānuja's philosophy; they also provide a spirited defense of the Pāñcarātra system of ritual, and express in Sanskrit verse some of the sentiments of the earlier Tamil hymns of the Ālvārs.

Rāmānuja had to be instructed in five aspects of Yāmuna's teachings by five of the latter's disciples. The one who was to teach Rāmānuja the secret meaning of the fundamental ritual formula (mantra) of the community made Rāmānuja come to see him eighteen times before he swore the bright young convert to silence and disclosed the secret. The very next day, however, Rāmānuja went up onto the temple balcony and shouted down the secret to the Śrī Vaiṣṇavas below. Cheerfully acknowledging that for disobeying his teacher he would go to hell, he added, "But because of their connection with you these souls will be saved!" The teacher was so impressed with Rāmānuja's concern for the welfare of others that he recognized him as Yāmuna's successor and the new leader of the community. This well-known story, along with many other stories in the hagiographies, suggests a gradual shift in emphasis from a secret yoga passed on to a small number of disciples to a more open teaching shared with a community jointly worshiping Lord Viṣṇu and his consorts, incarnate in temple images.

Rāmānuja is responsible for many innovations in the Śrī Vaiṣṇava community. He reorganized the central Śrī Vaiṣṇava temple at Śrīrangam to accommodate his growing band of disciples, traveled widely to other temples to try to persuade them to adopt a more strictly Vaiṣṇava liturgy, and went all the way to Kashmir to consult ancient commentaries. He then composed new commentaries intended to convince brahman scholars all over India of the theistic Vaiṣṇava interpretation of the Sanskrit scriptures.

Much of the latter part of Rāmānuja's life was spent in the Hoysala kingdom to the north where he fled to escape the persecution of the Śaiva-oriented Cōḻa king. Indeed, the earliest "hard evidence" for Rāmānuja's historical reality is a stone carving and inscription showing him with the Hoysala king he is said to have converted from Jainism.

In general, the hagiographers put less emphasis on Rāmānuja's intellectual prowess than on his fervent devotion to Lord Viṣṇu, his lifelong efforts to establish Yāmuna's teaching, and his skill in awakening the loyalty and utilizing the distinctive talents of his disciples and scholarly converts. The success of his efforts to persuade many of his own relatives and other brahmans to join the multicaste community of Viṣṇu worshipers had a double effect: The leadership of the community passed still more completely into brahman hands, while Brahmanic Hinduism itself was transformed so that forever after caste ranking, in principle if not always in practice, has been subordinated to the quality of devotion. The story about Rāmānuja's renouncing his wife and becoming an ascetic does not imply that it is necessary in general for devotees to leave their life in society, but in this particular case Rāmānuja's wife stood in the way of his spiritual progress. She was unwilling to subordinate caste ranking to spiritual preeminence and therefore thwarted Rāmānuja's desire to honor his lower-caste teacher.

Nine writings have consistently been attributed to Rāmānuja since the earliest hagiographies and biographical compendia. Three are commentaries on the *Vedānta Sūtra*: the famous *Śrībhāṣya* and the briefer *Vedāntadīpa* and *Vedāntasāra.* One, perhaps his earliest work, is an independent summary of his philosophical position, called the *Vedārthasaṃgraha.* A fifth is his commentary on the *Bhagavadgītā,* in which his mood is at least as devotional as polemical. The remaining four works are very much in the devotional mood and are sufficiently different from the major works that their authenticity has recently been challenged. One is a manual of daily worship called the *Nityagrantha.* The other three are hymns in prose, the *Śaraṇāgatigadya, Śrīrangagadya,* and *Vaikuṇṭhagadya.* The first of these has been interpreted as Rāmānuja's own conversation with the Lord during the solemn ceremony of "taking refuge" *(śaraṇāgati),* and is taken by the tradition to provide a clear warrant for replacing the path of disciplined meditation with the path of "humble approach" or "surrender" *(prapatti).* (The text itself seems not to diverge so radically from the philosophical works as either the renowned teacher Vedānta Deśika or modern critics maintain. In this author's opinion all these minor works are genuine.)

Rāmānuja's epistemology is hyperrealistic. The first two sources of knowledge are perception and inference, and they are trustworthy notwithstanding general human subjection to "beginningless ignorance." Knowledge is always of the real, even in dreams, and error is a disordered perception or faulty inference concerning what is really there. The third source of knowledge is the testimony of scripture, or more strictly, *śabda* ("eternal sound"), which helps to establish much that is uncertain on the basis of sense perception and inference, notably the existence and nature of the ultimate reality (*brahman*), who is also the Supreme Person and personal Lord. In explicit contrast to Śaṅkara's doctrine of two levels of truth in scripture, Rāmānuja maintains that scriptural texts are all at the same level; apparent discrepancies or contradictions must therefore be resolved without placing one side or the other on a lower level. The emphasis on unity in some texts and duality or plurality in others is resolved by noting the synthetic principle in a third group of texts: radical distinction and inseparable connection coexist in the relation between the self (whether finite or infinite) and the body that it ensouls, and likewise in the relation between a substance and its mode.

Scripture testifies to a supreme self who is the inner self of finite selves. Thus the finite self is to the supreme self as the material body is to the finite self. This is Rāmānuja's celebrated doctrine of *śarīra-śarīri-bhāva*: the relation of the self to the body, which corresponds to the relation between grammatical subject and predicate adjective, or substance and mode. It is the special characteristic of finite selves to be a mode in relation to God and substance in relation to material things, which are their bodies or instruments. The entire finite universe of souls and material bodies is also the body of God. Thus God is the only ultimately substantial reality, and reality may be viewed as *viśiṣṭādvaita* (the later philosophical label for this school of Vedānta, not used by Rāmānuja): the nondual reality of that which is (internally) distinguished.

Rāmānuja defines the self-body relation in terms of three subordinate relations, those between the support and the supported, the controller and the controlled, and the owner *(śeṣī)* and the owned *(śeṣa).* It is the third relation that is most distinctive, for ownership is understood to include the obligation of the slave to serve the master and the confident expectation that the master will look after the slave. In each case it is the Supreme Self who provides the defining instance; the finite self's relation to its body is only a limited approximation of complete supporting, controlling, and owning its body.

Rāmānuja assumes that there are three kinds of reality: nonsentient matter (*acit*), sentient but finite selves (*cit*), and the Lord (Īśvara), who is the Supreme Self. The world consists of material bodies controlled by finite selves. While the particular bodies are temporary, the basic matter of which they consist and the finite selves that they embody have no beginning in time. The bondage of many finite selves to "beginningless *karman*" causes their repeated return to the world in new bodies, but the entire world of material bodies and embodied souls is intended to glorify God, that is, to express in the finite realm his power and goodness. Those who escape the ignorance induced by *karman* can see that the finite world is *now,* along with God's infinite world, a realm of glory (*vibhūti*). Despite his horror of linking God with anything defiling in the material world, Rāmānuja insists that the entire finite universe is the body of God.

Finite selves and the Supreme Self are similar but not identical in their essential natures: both have consciousness and bliss as their essential characteristics, but the finite self is limited in its power and extent whereas the Supreme Self is all-powerful and all-pervasive. Moreover, finite selves still "bound" to the material world have their secondary consciousness (that which they *possess* rather than *are*) obscured by the ignorance produced by "beginningless *karman.*"

The Vedānta is concerned with the proper knowledge of reality in order to find liberation from this bondage. In Rāmānuja's interpretation of Vedānta both performance of social and ritual duties and knowledge of reality are auxiliary means in seeking liberation, but the chief means is *bhakti* (devotion), a calling to mind of God's attributes with an attitude that should become as constant as the flow of oil, as vivid and immediate as sense perception, and so emotionally gripping that the devotee feels unable to live without the pervading presence of God.

The ultimate reality thus "remembered" in devotion is not an abstract principle but that most concrete and substantial reality who is the personal Lord, the Lord who escapes all self-confident seeking by finite selves but who chooses to become available to those who acknowledge their dependence. The Lord descends and condescends out of his great compassion to save, but those who most deeply feel their need for God's presence learn the deepest secret: the Lord also needs them. This emphasis on God's initiative along with the surprising secret that the Lord who owns everything needs his devotees' love leads to a second way of talking about the salvific process that is quite different from the first. Instead of loving devotion being the means to attaining the Lord's presence, the Lord is the means to enabling devotion that is a mutual participation of infinite and finite selves. The end has become the means, and the means has become the end. Rāmānuja seems to be able to move back and forth between the older concept of devotion as means and the implications of a radical doctrine of grace.

A century after his death, Rāmānuja was understood by his followers to have taught surrender (*prapatti*) as a preferable alternative to the path of devotion, and they were beginning to differ as to whether some human response to grace was part of this surrender. That difference would gradually split the community in two, but for both groups it was Rāmānuja's own act of surrender that gave the assurance of divine grace for all his followers, a grace then mediated through the generations by a succession of teachers. It is as if they continue to say to Rāmānuja what he is purported to have said to the teacher whose secret he made public: "Because of their [our] connection with you their [our] souls will be saved."

See Also Śrī Vaiṣṇavas; Vaiṣṇavism, article on Pāñcarātras; Vedānta; Yāmuna.

Bibliography

Buitenen, J. A. B. van., trans. *Rāmānuja's Vedarthasamgraha.* Poona, 1956.

Buitenen, J. A. B. van. *Rāmānuja on the Bhagavadgita* (1953). Reprint, Delhi, 1968.

Carman, John B. *The Theology of Rāmānuja.* New Haven, Conn., 1974.

Lester, Robert C. *Rāmānuja on the Yoga.* Madras, 1976.

Lott, Eric J. *God and the Universe in the Vedantic Theology of Rāmānuja.* Madras, 1976.

Raghavachar, S. S. *Introduction to the Vedarthasangraha of Sree Rāmānujacharya.* Mangalore, 1957.

Raghavachar, S. S. *Śrī Rāmānuja on the Gita.* Mangalore, 1969.

Yamunacharya, M. *Rāmānuja's Teachings in His Own Words.* Bombay, 1963.

New Sources

Veliath, Cyril. *The Mysticism of Ramanuja.* New Delhi, 1993.

John B. Carman (1987)
Revised Bibliography

RĀMĀYAṆA. Along with the *Mahābhārata,* the *Rāmāyaṇa* is the most influential epic of India. Attributed to the sage Vālmīki, it is a poem of about fifty thousand lines narrating in Sanskrit the tale of Rāma and his wife, Sītā. The core of the epic is the story surrounding Rama's birth, his marriage to Sītā, his exile, Sītā's abduction by the demon king Rāvaṇa, the battle leading to the killing of the demon, and the recovery of Sītā.

The origins of the epic are obscure and beyond definitive recovery. The epic is available in three recensions—the Northeastern, the Northwestern, and the Southern. The recensions vary considerably; approximately a third of the text of each is not common to the other two. However, the variations, substantial as they are, do not alter the main theme of the epic.

The *Rāmāyaṇa* consists of seven books called *kāṇḍas.* The story contained in these seven books is divided into two unequal parts, the first part consisting of the first six books and the second part covered by the seventh book. The content of these books is too complicated to capture in a summary, but the main storyline is recounted here.

Daśaratha, the king of Ayodhyā, is childless. He performs a sacrifice to obtain sons. At that time the gods, who are disturbed by the atrocities of the ten-headed demon Rāvaṇa, pray to the god Viṣṇu for protection. Viṣṇu responds to their prayers and decides to incarnate himself as a human being. He will be born as Rāma, son of Daśaratha. At the end of the sacrifice Daśaratha's three wives give birth to four sons, Queen Kausalyā to Rāma, Queen Kaikeyī to Bharata, Queen Sumitrā to Lakṣmaṇa and Śatrughna. Rāma is the favorite son of the king, and Lakṣmaṇa is devoted to his elder brother Rāma. While the boys are still young, the sage Viśvāmitra takes Rāma and Lakṣmaṇa to the forest and instructs them in the use of magic weapons.

King Janaka of Videha, who has the mighty bow of Śiva in his possession, declares that the prince who can wield the weapon will be eligible to marry his beautiful daughter Sītā. Rāma wields the weapon and with his superior strength breaks it, then marries Sītā.

In Ayodhyā King Daśaratha decides to have Rāma installed as prince regent. The decision, which was made while Kaikeyī's son Bharata was away, causes Kaikeyī, on the advice of her maidservant, to rebel against the king. Kaikeyī insists that Bharata should be declared prince regent and that Rāma should be exiled to the forest for fourteen years. The king, who owes Kaikeyī two wishes, is compelled to obey her desire. Obeying his father's command, Rāma leaves the capital city accompanied by his wife, Sītā, and his brother Lakṣmaṇa. Daśaratha dies from the pain of separation from his most beloved son.

In the forest a demoness, Śurpaṇakhā, the sister of Rāvaṇa, attempts to seduce Rāma. Frustrated in her efforts, she attempts to kill Sītā. Rāma punishes Śurpaṇakhā by having her ears and nose mutilated. Śurpaṇakhā complains to her mighty brother. Enraged by Rāma's action and attracted by Sītā's beauty, Rāvaṇa decides to abduct Sītā. Rāvaṇa sends his subject Mārīca to lure Rāma away. Mārīca assumes the form of a golden deer and attracts the attention of Sītā. Consenting to her request, Rāma chases the deer, leaving Lakṣmaṇa to guard Sītā. Sītā persuades Lakṣmaṇa to go in protection of his brother. Once Sītā is alone, the demon Rāvaṇa appears at her doorstep dressed as an ascetic and carries her off by force.

When Rāma learns that Rāvaṇa has abducted Sītā, he secures the friendship of the monkey king Sugrīva. Sugrīva's minister Hanumān flies across the ocean to the island of Laṅkā and locates Sītā in a forest grove. Rāma, aided by the monkey army, besieges Laṅkā, defeats Rāvaṇa's armies, kills Rāvaṇa, and brings Sītā back.

The seventh book of the *Rāmāyaṇa* describes how Rāma abandons Sītā, this time by his own choice. The inhabitants of Ayodhyā doubt the purity of Sītā's character because she has lived in another man's house. Sītā, now pregnant, is given shelter by the sage Vālmīki. In the sage's hermitage, Sītā gives birth to two sons, Lava and Kuśa. Vālmīki composes the story of Rāma and teaches the boys to sing the story.

In Ayodhyā, Rāma begins a sacrifice that Vālmīki attends with the twin boys. The boys sing the epic for Rāma, who then discovers that the boys are his own sons and that Sītā is alive. Vālmīki announces before the assembled crowd that Sītā is pure and without fault. Rāma accepts Lava and Kuśa as his sons. Sītā appears before the guests and prays that her mother, the earth, receive her as a proof of her purity. The earth breaks open, and Sītā is received on a golden throne. Rāma, saddened by the loss of his queen, gives the kingdom to his sons and returns to the world of the gods.

According to tradition, the *Rāmāyaṇa* is believed to belong to the legendary *tretayuga*, the second of the four mythic ages. Historically, the date of the epic is a matter of considerable controversy and nearly impossible to fix with certainty. Extensive scholarly work on the linguistic, stylistic, sociological, geographical, and political data narrows down the possible dates of the epic in is current form to the period between 750 and 500 BCE.

Western scholarly opinion is fairly unanimous in agreement with Hermann Jacobi's finding that substantial parts of the first and seventh books of Vālmīki's version are later additions to the core of the five books. In the Hindu scholarly tradition, however, it is believed that the epic is the first poem (*ādikāvya*) and is composed by a single poet, Vālmīki, who is called the first poet (*ādikavi*). Thus it is believed to predate the other Indian epic, the *Mahābhārata.* Comparative dating of these two epics is a tangled issue because both the epics evolved together, borrowing extensively from each other. Although no evidence is available to establish Vālmīki as a historical personage, the stylistic evidence suggests that the central core of the five books of the *Rāmāyaṇa* are most likely to be the work of a single author.

The origins of the Vālmīki text are most likely to be folk oral narratives of the hero Rāma, a prince of the eastern Indian state of Kosala. Vālmīki's version itself has been sung orally for centuries by bards, known as *kusilavas*, before being set down in writing. Secular and heroic in quality, the Vālmīki version depicts the story of a perfect hero, steadfast in virtues and devoted to the control of his passions. The secular, heroic, and tragic messages of the *Rāmāyaṇa* have continued to influence generations of poets like Bhasa, Kalidasa, and Bhavabhuti, as well as a number of poets from the regional languages of India.

A major shift in the interpretation of the *Rāmāyaṇa* took place during the Middle Ages. Rāma was then identified as an *avatara* (incarnation) of Viṣṇu. The story of Rāma was read as an allegory of the conflict between good and evil in which the good always succeeds under the leadership of God.

Prominent among such devotional *(bhakti) Rāmāyaṇas* is Kamban's *Iramavataram* (twelfth century), in Tamil. A further development in the devotionalization of the *Rāmāyaṇa* becomes popular with Tulsidas's *Ramcaritmanas,* in the sixteenth century. In Tulsidas all the characters of the *Rāmāyaṇa,* including the demon Rāvaṇa, are Rāma's devotees. All the conflicts of the story and its tragedy are eliminated to produce a harmonious, balanced, lyrical world of God and his devotees.

In addition to literary *Rāmāyaṇas,* there are a number of folk/oral versions all over India with significant variations in emphasis and messages. Folk versions of the *Rāmāyaṇa* sung by women emphasize the role of Sītā and portray her as more independent than she is in the literary versions.

SEE ALSO Mahābhārata; Rāma; Tulsidas; Vālmīki.

BIBLIOGRAPHY

Bulcke, Camille. *Rāma-kathā* (1950). 2d ed. Allahabad, 1962.

Goldman, Robert P., trans. *The Rāmāyaṇa of Vālmīki,* vol. 1, *Bālakāṇḍa.* Princeton, N.J., 1984.

Jacobi, Hermann. *Das Rāmāyaṇa: Geschichte und Inhalt nebst Concordanz der gedruckten Recensionen.* Bonn, 1893.

Raghavan, V., ed. *The Rāmāyaṇa Tradition in Asia.* New Delhi, 1980.

Shastri, Hari Prasad, trans. *The Rāmāyaṇa of Vālmīki.* 3 vols. London, 1962.

Smith, H. Daniel. *Reading the Rāmāyaṇa: A Bibliographic Guide for Students and College Teachers.* Syracuse, N.Y., 1983.

New Sources

Richman, Paula, ed. *Many Ramayanas: The Diversity of a Narrative Tradition in South Asia.* Berkeley, 1991.

Richman, Paula, ed. *Questioning Ramayanas: A South Asian Tradition.* Berkeley, 2001.

VELCHERU NARAYANA RAO (1987)
Revised Bibliography

RAMBAM SEE MAIMONIDES, MOSES

RAMBAN SEE NAHMANIDES, MOSES

RAM MOHAN ROY SEE ROY, RAM MOHAN

RAPPAPORT, ROY A. (1926–1997). The American anthropologist Roy A. Rappaport's writings, which span ecology, systems theory, and religion, address the large issues of ritual and religious logos in human survival and evolution. After helping to conceptualize the field of anthropological human ecology in the 1960s, Rappaport did fieldwork among the Maring of highland New Guinea and crafted a truly innovative "systems" ethnography, in what became the classic *Pigs for the Ancestors: Ritual in the Ecology of a New Guinea People* (1968), which explores the ritual regulation of environmental relations in their local ecosystems. Rappaport followed up on his analysis of what religion does by probing—through cybernetic studies of the sacred and in essays that link adaptation, the structure of human communication, and ritual life—*why* ritual should order ecosystems and human life. While conducting his religion research, he also consulted with government agencies on the notion of human impacts, arguing for a more public- and policy-engaged anthropology. From beginning to end, he saw anthropology as a holistic discipline that could provide value-based moral and intellectual foundations for both the sciences and the humanities and that could help bridge their divide.

Rappaport, a New Yorker and credentialed innkeeper, was already close to forty when he began his graduate anthropology studies at Columbia University in the politically turbulent 1960s, a time of heightened public debate on ecology, civil rights, the Vietnam War, and the threat of nuclear war. At Columbia he contended with Marvin Harris's cultural materialism; Harold Conklin's ethnoscience; Conrad Arensberg's political anthropology; Andrew Vayda's, Fredrik Barth's, and Harold Conklin's interpretations of anthropological ecology, and Leslie White's theory of general evolution as presented by Morton Fried. Building on Arensberg and White, he developed his own ideas of ordered general systems; and he transformed the ethnoscience and ecologies of Conklin, Vayda, and Barth into his own notions of "cognized" and "operational" environments that introduced ideas of structure in adaptive systems. He also departed from Conklin and Barth by intentionally introducing clearly specified units of analysis, such as "human population," not only "culture," and by tracing energy and nutrient flows, not only ideas. He also bypassed the vague social structural-functional formulations and simple functionalist or materialist arguments of Harris to explore not ritual's function but its adaptive value in maintaining empirical ("reference") values, as in the numbers of humans, plants, and animals living in peace or in conflict within a given territory over a specified unit of time.

The identification of ritual as an important mechanism regulating peace and warfare, distribution of regional population, and humans' sustainable use of environmental resources was innovative, as was the ritual analysis that did not try to specify whether local models of the natural world (which included the superhuman) were true but only whether they were appropriate to maintain the ecosystem.

Despite Rappaport's personal ambivalence toward religion, his research then turned to understanding ritual's internal structure, the principles of sanctity that govern it, and how these principles connect individuals, societies, and ecosystems. Influenced by the ideas of Gregory Bateson (1904–1980) in cybernetics and adaptation, Charles Peirce (1839–

1914) in semiotics, and J. L. Austin (1911–1960) in performatives, he sought the etiology, structure, and attributes of logos (transcendent or higher truths) that bind human beings into meaningful and enduring social orders and enable the trustworthy communication necessary for a shared social and cultural life. A key to his arguments centers on the ambivalent role of language in human evolution, which introduces new content and flexibility into human ideas of desirable, creative, moral, and imaginary orders, but also permits lies. Ritual, he concluded, is the universal basis for establishing trust, given the possibility of linguistic dissembling and falsification. His concept of "the holy" weds discursive liturgical order both to nondiscursive religious experience, which allows human beings to commit themselves to orderly rules that organize their collective lives, and to cultural conventions that help maintain ecological balance. To reach these conclusions, Rappaport continued to ground his abstract theory in Maring ethnography and his ideas of ultimate sacred postulates, logos, and resilience in his understandings of Judaism, his ancestral religion.

Rappaport's main interest in ritual was in adaptive, not maladaptive, structure. Regarding the clash between science and religion, he critiqued the role of science in the modern world—where science seeks to usurp the place of religion ("the holy")—as a dangerous systemic "inversion," because while science questions the value of ritual acts, it offers nothing to replace them. Although science offers up new realms of thought, with calculations based on facts organized under theories, all scientific knowledge can be questioned, and so it fragments and precludes certainty. But humanity needs certainty and wholeness to survive. This certainty is provided by the sacred, which adds cultural structures of meaning to observations and analysis based on accordance with natural (scientific) law.

Rappaport joined the department of anthropology at the University of Michigan in Ann Arbor in 1965, then served as chair of the department (1975–1980), was elected a senior fellow of the Michigan Society of Fellows (1975), and in 1991 became director of the university's program on studies in religion. He served as president of the American Anthropological Association from 1987 to 1989.

See Also Anthropology, Ethnology, and Religion; Ritual Studies.

Bibliography

Messer, Ellen, and Michael Lambek, eds. *Ecology and the Sacred: Engaging the Anthropology of Roy A. Rappaport.* Ann Arbor, Mich., 2001.

Rappaport, Roy A. *Pigs for the Ancestors: Ritual in the Ecology of a New Guinea People.* New Haven, Conn., 1968. A second edition, with new preface, appendix, and epilogue, was published in 1984.

Rappaport, Roy A. *Ecology, Meaning, and Religion.* Richmond, Calif., 1979.

Rappaport, Roy A. "The Anthropology of Trouble." *American Anthropologist* 95, no. 2 (1993): 295–303.

Rappaport, Roy A. "Humanity's Evolution and Anthropology's Future." In *Assessing Cultural Anthropology,* edited by Robert Borofsky, pp. 153–167. New York, 1994.

Rappaport, Roy A. *Ritual and Religion in the Making of Humanity.* Cambridge, U.K., 1999.

Ellen Messer (2005)

RASHI, acronym (RaSHI) of Rabbi Shelomoh ben Yitsḥaq of Troyes (1040–1105) was the most influential Jewish commentator on the Bible and the Babylonian Talmud. Nine hundred years after his death, Rashi's writings remain the standard commentaries for any serious student of the Hebrew Bible or the Babylonian Talmud, and new scholarly studies of his achievement continue to be published.

Rashi was born in Troyes, the political center of the county of Champagne, in northeastern France, but outside the close-knit rabbinical circles of the founding families of German Jewry. After pursuing his preliminary studies in Troyes, including studies with his father, he married and around 1060 traveled to the *yeshivot* of the Rhineland, then the most advanced in northwestern Europe. He studied there with the two heads of the Mainz academy, Yaʿaqov ben Yaqar, whom he considered his most important teacher of Talmud and Bible, and after the master's death in 1064, his successor, Yitsḥaq ben Yehudah, for a short time. Almost immediately, he went to Worms to study with Yitsḥaq ha-Levi, whose academy was superseding the Mainz school in advanced Talmud instruction. By the end of the decade he was back home, but he continued to correspond with Yitsḥaq ben Yehudah and Yitsḥaq ha-Levi.

Rashi attracted his own students in Troyes, and he served as the local rabbinical authority there. Though he wrote answers (*responsa*) to hundreds of questions sent to him, he was not a professional rabbi. He made a living some other way; however, the often repeated assertion that he was a vintner has been disputed.

Rashi had no sons. His well-educated daughters married learned men; their sons became eminent rabbinical authorities. Yokheved married Meʾir ben Shemuʾel, and among their four sons were Shemuʾel ben Meʾir (known by the acronym Rashbam), one of the most important commentators on the Hebrew Bible and developer of the literal method of interpretation, and Yaʿaqov ben Meʾir (known as Rabbenu Tam), who dominated the new scholastic method of Talmud study in the form of additions (*tosafot*) of questions and answers to his grandfather's running gloss. Rashi's daughter Miryam married Yehudah ben Natan, whose commentary to the end of *Makkot* is printed in the standard editions of the Babylonian Talmud. In this way, Rashi created his own French rabbinical family elite.

Rashi lived through the devastation of Jewish rabbinical leadership in the Rhenish academies of Mainz and Worms caused by the First Crusade riots of 1096, and some traces of early anti-Crusade polemic have been detected in his writings. Thus he says that the Bible begins with the creation of the world and not with the first law given to the Jewish people (*Ex.* 12:1), in order to teach that the Land of Israel belongs to the Jewish people, and not to the Christians or Muslims who were fighting over it in the First Crusade. Why? Since God created the world, the entire earth belongs to him, including the Land of Israel, which he first gave to the nations of Canaan and then gave to Israel (Rashi on *Gn.* 1:1).

Rashi's major achievement was his composition of comprehensive running commentaries to most of the Hebrew Bible and Babylonian Talmud. Of the biblical commentaries attributed to him, those to *Job* from 40:25, *Ezra, Nehemiah,* and *Chronicles* are not his but may be based on his approach. Of the Talmudic commentaries, those to *Ta'anit, Mo'ed Qaṭan, Nedarim, Nazir,* and *Horayot* are not his. The gloss he began to *Bava' Batra'* was finished by his grandson Shemu'el ben Me'ir, and the one to *Makkot* was completed by his student and son-in-law Yehudah ben Natan.

In his Talmud commentary, Rashi focused on each difficult term or passage in sequence and supplied punctuation or logical transitions that were not clear from the text itself. He used his profound knowledge of the Talmud and Jewish law to help the student by briefly introducing the general topic that the text is about to discuss in detail, and he provided reasons for particular laws and mentioned historical conditions in ancient times. At times, he indicated that he preferred a particular version of a passage, and later copyists corrected the text so that there is no difference between the Talmud and Rashi's correction. His commentary became widely used from the beginning of the thirteenth century and has been printed with the Talmud from the first editions to this day.

Although Rashi based about three fourths of his commentary to the Pentateuch on earlier Midrashic works, he integrated into his work a newer method of Jewish biblical exegesis that focused on the plain meaning of the text. When an ambiguity in the text created the possibility of different interpretations, Rashi explicitly contrasted a straightforward textual interpretation (*pe-shuto shel miqra'*)—which could be arrived at through (1) a literal reading of the text, (2) a contextual approach, or (3) the use of a *midrash* that explains the plain meaning of the words as written—to an interpretation which he paraphrased from a Midrashic source. This dual method of interpretation is Rashi's most characteristic innovation, but it has sometimes been misunderstood. Whereas later twelfth-century French commentators like Shemu'el ben Me'ir and Yosef ben Yitsḥaq (Bekhor Shor) developed a method of interpretation based on the systematic inquiry into the literal meaning of the text (*peshaṭ*) in preference to one based on earlier rabbinical homilies (*derash*), Rashi himself did not explicitly distinguish between the two methods of reading; he did not use the terms *peshaṭ* and *derash* and so certainly did not prefer the former. In his glosses to the other books of the Bible, such as *Isaiah* and *Psalms,* scholars have detected explicit or implied anti-Christian polemics. While there is no evidence that Rashi read Latin, he could have heard many Christological arguments and arguments derived from scriptural proof texts from Christian neighbors and introduced counterinterpretations for the benefit of his students.

From Rashi's commentaries and *responsa,* it is obvious that Jews and Christians lived in the same towns, walked the same streets, bought their household goods in the same markets, and paid for them with the same coinage. Although the medieval fairs at Troyes began only in the twelfth century, the town was already a manufacturing center and commercial depot in Rashi's day, and many travelers passed through. His commentaries include remarks about the city of Venice and about German currency. He observed firsthand in Troyes embroidery of silk with gold, soldering and engraving techniques, and the manufacture of parchment. He also comments about popular customs and street life: some women pierced their ears; butchers sometimes used their hands for scales, putting the meat in one hand and a weight in the other; the well-to-do slept in four-poster beds or else had rods constructed to support a tentlike curtain to keep flies away when they slept.

In addition to noting hundreds of such concrete references to everyday life, Rashi uses approximately a thousand medieval French terms or phrases to explain or illustrate Hebrew or Aramaic terms; these lexical items, written in phonetic Hebrew characters, have preserved important evidence about linguistic characteristics of eleventh-century French.

Apart from its value as a source for Jewish intellectual history and early French, Rashi's biblical commentary also influenced Christian biblical exegesis. Already in the twelfth century, Hugh of Saint-Victor and other Victorine scholars in Paris were interested in the Hebrew text and reflect familiarity with Rashi. But it was especially the Franciscan Nicholas of Lyra (c. 1270–1349), writing in Paris at the very time that a chair in Hebrew had been established in accordance with the Council of Vienne (1312), who made systematic use of Rashi's biblical commentary in his own running gloss on the whole Bible, the *Postilla litteralis.*

The immense influence of Rashi's commentaries in shaping the religious culture of European Judaism still awaits proper historical treatment. As a bridge between the Rhenish center of Jewish learning in Mainz and Worms and the newer dialectical methods of Bible and Talmud study that were developed in the twelfth century based on Rashi's own commentaries, his place in Jewish cultural history is secure. Through Nicholas of Lyra, Rashi also influenced subsequent Christian Hebraists down to Martin Luther and beyond.

SEE ALSO Biblical Exegesis, article on Jewish Views; Tosafot.

BIBLIOGRAPHY

Rashi's commentary to the Pentateuch has been translated into English by Morris Rosenbaum and Abraham M. Silbermann as *Pentateuch with Targum Onkelos, Haphtaroth and Prayers for the Sabbath, and Rashi's Commentary,* 5 vols. (London, 1929–1934).

An important interpretive sketch about him is Alexander Marx's "Rashi," in his *Essays in Jewish Biography* (Philadelphia, 1947) and the most comprehensive, if dated, biography is still Maurice Liber's *Rashi,* translated by Adele Szold (Philadelphia, 1906).

Rashi's influence on Christian Bible commentaries in the early Middle Ages is discussed in Beryl Smalley's *The Study of the Bible in the Middle Ages,* 2d ed. (1951; Notre Dame, 1964) and for the later period in Herman Hailperin's *Rashi and the Christian Scholars* (Pittsburgh, 1963). An illustration of Rashi as anti-Christian polemicist is Michael A. Signer's "King/Messiah: Rashi's Exegesis of Psalm 2," *Prooftexts* 3 (September 1983): 273–278.

Esra Shereshevsky's *Rashi: The Man and His World* (New York, 1982) is of particular interest for his compilation of data from Rashi's oeuvre about everyday life.

Rashi's methodology as Bible exegete is discussed in Benjamin J. Gelles's *Peshat and Derash in the Exegesis of Rashi* (Leiden, 1981) and assessed in a review essay by Sarah Kamin in the *Journal of Jewish Studies* 36 (Spring 1985): 126–130, based on her own sophisticated study of this tricky problem which she has summarized in "Rashi's Exegetical Categorization with Respect to the Distinction between Peshat and Derash," *Immanuel* 11 (1980): 16–32.

New Sources

Banitt, Menahem. *Rashi, Interpreter of the Biblical Letter.* [Tel Aviv], Israel, 1985.

Berman, Scot A. *Learning Talmud: A Guide to Talmud Terminology and Rashi Commentary.* Northvale, N.J., 1997.

Bonchek, Avigdor. *What's Bothering Rashi? A Guide to In-depth Analysis of His Torah Commentary.* Jerusalem and New York, 1997–2002.

Doron, Pinhas. *Rashi's Torah Commentary: Religious, Philosophical, Ethical, and Educational Insights.* Northvale, N.J., 2000.

IVAN G. MARCUS (1987)
Revised Bibliography

RASHĪD RIḌĀ, MUḤAMMAD. (1865–1935),

Arab Muslim theologian and journalist. Born in a village near Tripoli, Lebanon, Riḍā had a traditional religious education. The writings of the pan-Islamic thinker Jamāl al-Dīn al-Afghānī and the Egyptian theologian Muḥammand ʿAbduh opened his mind to the need to reform Islam. In 1897 he settled in Cairo and from then until his death published a periodical, *Al-manār* (The Lighthouse), devoted to explaining the problems of Islam in the modern world.

His starting point was that of ʿAbduh, whom he regarded as his master: the need for Muslims to live virtuously in the light of a reformed understanding of Islam. That understanding involved drawing a distinction between the doctrines of Islam and its social morality. Doctrines and forms of worship were unchanging, laid down by the Qurʾān and the practice of the prophet Muḥammad and the first generation of his followers (the *salaf,* hence the name *salafīyah,* often used for this type of thought). He opposed what he regarded as innovations, in particular the beliefs and practice of later Ṣūfīs, and in his later years drew close to the Wahhābī point of view.

Riḍā believed that, apart from some specific injunctions, the Qurʾān and the practice of the Prophet gave only general principles of social morality and law; their implications had to be drawn out by competent Muslims in the light of circumstances. Blind imitation of past teaching led to stagnation and weakness; the changed circumstances of the present age made a new interpretation necessary, and its guiding principle should be *maṣlaḥah* (interest), a concept accepted in traditional legal theory but broadened by Riḍā so as to mean social utility. By using this principle, his aim was to create a body of modern Islamic law on which the different legal schools could agree; to this end he published a large number of rulings on hypothetical cases raising important questions of law.

Riḍā was much concerned with the question of political authority. He believed it should be delegated by the community to a combination of just rulers and men of religious learning, trained to deal with the problems of the modern world; there was a need for a caliph, not as universal temporal ruler but as the final and generally accepted authority on law. He emphasized the central position of the Arabs in the Muslim world; Arabic was the language of the Qurʾān and the religious sciences, and without the Arabs Islam could not be healthy. He played some part in the Arab nationalist movement, but the influence of *Al-manār* spread far beyond the Arab world, and some of its ideas were adopted by later movements aiming to restore Islam as the moral norm of modern society.

BIBLIOGRAPHY

General summaries of Riḍā's ideas can be found in my work, *Arabic Thought in the Liberal Age, 1798–1939,* 2d ed. (Cambridge, 1983), chaps. 9 and 11, and in Hamid Enayat's *Modern Islamic Political Thought* (London, 1982). A fuller treatment is that of Malcolm H. Kerr in his *Islamic Reform: The Political and Legal Theories of Muḥammad ʿAbduh and Rashīd Riḍā* (Berkeley, 1966). Jacques Jomier's *Le commentaire coranique du Manâr: Tendances modernes de l'exégèse coranique en Egypte* (Paris, 1954) studies the commentary on the Qurʾān which ʿAbduh and Riḍā published jointly in *Al-manār.* Riḍā's treatise on the caliphate has been translated into French and annotated by Henri Laoust in *Le califat dans la doctrine de Rašīd Riḍā* (Beirut, 1938). Of his other works, the biography of ʿAbduh, *Taʾrīkh al-ustādh al-imām al-shaykh Muḥammad ʿAbduh,* vol. 1 (Cairo, 1931), is full of information about the Islamic reformers. His legal rulings have been collected by Ṣalāḥ al-Dīn al-Munajjid and Yūsuf Q. Khūrī in *Fatāwā al-imām Muḥammad Rashīd Riḍā,* 5 vols. (Beirut, 1970–1971).

New Sources

Dallal, Ahmad. "Appropriating the Past: Twentieth-Century Reconstruction of Pre-modern Islamic Thought." *Islamic Law and Society* 7 (October 2000): 325–359.

Haddad, Mahmoud. "Arab Religious Nationalism in the Colonial Era: Rereading Rashid Rida's Ideas on the Caliphate." *Journal of the American Oriental Society* 117 (April-June 1997): 253–278.

Sirriyeh, Elizabeth. "Rashid Rida's Autobiography of the Syrian Years, 1865–1897." *Arabic and Middle Eastern Literatures* 3 (July 2000): 179–195.

ALBERT HOURANI (1987)
Revised Bibliography

RASTAFARIANISM. Rastafari (the preferred name for Rastafarianism) was once categorized simply as a syncretic Afro-Caribbean religio-political cult. The reality is much more complex. It might be meaningfully described as a Jamaica-spawned global spiritual movement that is rooted in returning to, retrieving, or reinventing African heritage and identity (and occasionally other historically disparaged or submerged identities). Rastafari includes a variety of specific manifestations, traversing a broad spectrum of religious, political, and cultural forms. The name Rastafari derives from the title and given name (Ras, translated as "prince," and Tafari, "he who must be feared," from the Amharic language of Ethiopia) of Haile Selassie (Amharic for "power of the Trinity"; 1892–1975), the former Ethiopian emperor, whom most Rastafari worship as a god-king or messiah. Yet Rastafari as a whole cannot be defined simply by reference to beliefs about the messiah, common practices, or common organizational forms. Instead, one should approach Rastafari holistically.

RASTAFARI AS A SPIRITUAL MOVEMENT. Rastafari can be considered foremost an expression of retrieved African spirituality. If all concerns about the sacred can be seen as ranging along a continuum between the ideal-typical poles of "religion" and "spirituality," then Rastafari tends toward the latter. Indeed it is important to note that most Rastas (individual participants in the movement) typically eschew the category religion because of what they consider to be the term's colonial, imperialistic, and organizational connotations. In this negative sense religion signifies an essentially dogmatic relationship to the sacred, grounded in the notion that a particular tradition is the only gateway to the Truth. Spirituality, on the other hand, represents a relationship to the sacred that allows for many different gateways and acknowledges that one path may be stronger in certain areas while weaker in others. Whereas religion tends to draw firm lines to distinguish the sacred and the secular, spirituality provides scope for fluidity between sacred and secular, promoting mutual exchange and borrowing among people with different senses of the sacred. Spirituality is also a useful descriptor because, for Rastafari, it evokes an African relationship to the sacred (cf. Mbiti, 1969; Blakely, van Beek, and Thompson, 1994), which is crucial because the movement seeks to break with its Western colonial past and retrieve and revive its African heritage.

It is nevertheless important to note that Rastafari remains intertwined with biblical, Judeo-Euro-Christian values and doctrines and has always included select notions borrowed historically from the Hinduism of the East Indian indentured workers in Jamaica (see Mansingh and Mansingh, 1985). All of these influences were part of the multicultural Caribbean world of early Rastafari patriarchs and matriarchs, and they continue to shape successive generations. As it expands Rastafari continues to borrow from a variety of other cultural expressions.

Rastafari can be considered a "movement" in three senses. First, in its early years and continuing in some circles in the early twenty-first century, movement-relocation to Africa has been a major articulated aim of Rastas. (Relocation to Africa is generally called *repatriation*, a theme explored in its fuller theological sense of redemption later in this article.)

Second, even when physical relocation is not a goal of Rastas, Rastafari represents a conscious cognitive move away from a Western colonial consciousness and toward a recovered, reconceived, or reinvented consciousness. Most typically this consciousness is intentionally oriented toward Africa, though in select cases it has also involved similar orientations to other ancestral consciousnesses (e.g., among Rastafari Maori in Aotearoa/New Zealand). This new consciousness can also be characterized as a cognitive turn inward to a more powerful and authentic sense of self. Rastafari emphasizes the interior location of deity, often referred to as the *I*—an overdetermined symbol that includes both a sense of the self as divinity residing internally and the notion that the spirit and power of Haile Selassie I dwell within individual Rastafari. In terms of the collective, Rastas tend to speak of "InI" (I&I), as opposed to "you" and "me." This urges Rastafari to identify human value universally, communally, and from a viewpoint independent of the value projected on people by a corrupted society.

Third, Rastas themselves and Rastafari ideas and symbols have increasingly expanded geographically, moving beyond their original Jamaican context into different parts of the world. In less than a century Rastafari has taken on global proportions, adapting its contours in creative ways to fit sociocultural contexts ranging from Aotearoa to Poland, from South Africa to Japan, and throughout the world.

The spread of Rastafari has been due in part to the movement's association with popular culture, especially reggae music, from the late 1960s onward. Consequently Rastafari manifests itself not only as an expression of spirituality but also as a secular style. It is not clear among either scholars or the Rastafari themselves where the division of style, politics, and spirituality-religion should reside. Thus different branches of the Rastafari movement reflect the differing degrees to which religious, spiritual, or secular features are ascendant. The historical root of the movement in Jamaica—the Order of Nyahbinghi—is arguably the most traditionally "religious" (including its populous offshoot, the Bobo Dreads of the Ethiopia Africa Black International Congress). These are the most churchical groups, the *houses* (or denominations) of Rastafari that are the most biblically based (especially attending to the Hebrew Scriptures), the most fervently black nationalist in orientation, as well as the most tightly structured around ceremonial worship. Although there is no universally recognized Rastafari orthodoxy at this point, Carol D. Yawney and John P. Homiak (2001) have pointed to an important trend within the House of Nyahbinghi to assume responsibility for upholding traditional Rastafari doctrine, especially in its overseas missions. At the other extreme, those who enter the movement via its broad cultural appeal and who may not belong to any particular house tend to be more open to other dimensions of spirituality and may not relate significantly to the Bible, worship with any special congregation, or even have any commitment to relocate to the continent of Africa. There are also clusters of Rastas who link with more directly political organizations, like the Rastafari Centralization Organization in Jamaica, which attempts to coordinate the different houses and focus them on political issues (for example, challenging the ganja [marijuana] laws or setting up a practical program for relocation to Africa).

Doctrines, organizational patterns, and ritual practices vary widely within the Rastafari movement. It is difficult to define Rastafari according to doctrine, for Rastafari groups do not require allegiance to a single creed from those wishing to join or participate, and doctrine continues to progress semiautonomously in the spirit of a dynamic ethos of theological inquiry and dialogue (a practice called *reasoning*). At the same time in the more churchical houses of Rastafari one is likely to find fairly widespread theological cohesion. Similarly Rastafari groups vary in how they are organized: with some notable exceptions (such as the Bobo Dreads, who maintain a distinction of prophet, priest, and king), authority in the movement is not vested in particular religious offices. Among the Nyahbinghi a collective authority flows from the de facto leadership and seniority (in terms of years in the movement) of various elders in the group. The authority structure among Twelve Tribes and Ethiopian World Federation groupings involves more conventional positions, such as an executive, president, secretary, treasurer, and others. Rastafari organization has been characterized as acephalic, but in reality the organization of the movement varies tremendously.

Finally, there is no formal ritual, practice, or symbol sine qua non that conclusively denotes Rastafari. But the more churchical the group, the more likely one is to find common practices (ranging from common ways of passing the communion chalice [water pipe] to common clothing, such as the Bobo Dreads' distinctive turbans, and common psalms and prayers). Though some practices, such as smoking ganja, are virtually ubiquitous among the Rastafari and other practices, such as wearing the long matted hair known as *dreadlocks*, are now universal in the movement, historically they have not always been so and are increasingly adopted as a style by people not associated with Rastafari. Reasoning might be considered a universal practice in the movement, but it is similar to types of dialogue and conversation outside of Rastafari, and it is too informal and unstructured (outside of the formal Nyahbinghi ceremony of worship—a more structured drumming, chanting, dancing, and prophesying ritual) to be an identifying marker of Rastafari.

With such a fluid range of characteristics, it is impracticable as an outsider to the movement to define conclusively who is part of the movement and who is not. In any case, most Rastas themselves will say that one does not become a Rasta, "believe in Rastafarianism," or join Rastafari as a choice or identity. Rastafari, in their view, is an "inborn conception"—one is a Rasta from birth. The only question is whether or not one knows it and lives it. Indeed the brethren and sistren often refer to their movement as a "way of life," or "*livity*," thereby emphasizing its holistic qualities.

History of Rastafari. The roots from which Rastafari sprang were present in Jamaica long before Rastafari emerged as a movement. In his early treatment of Rastafari, Leonard Barrett (1988/1977) laid great emphasis on Rastafari as a continuation of Jamaica's traditional Ethiopianism. Ethiopia held a prominent place in the imagination of black Jamaicans; it was a meronym of Africa as a whole, and because of Ethiopia's importance in the Bible, it stood not only as a representation of homeland but also as a symbol of eschatological redemption. Barrett and other scholars have also linked Rastafari's roots to other indigenous Jamaican religions and traditions. Perhaps most comprehensively, Barry Chevannes (1994) explores Rastafari's continuity with the Jamaican Revival tradition, which itself has roots both in colonial and indigenous Christianity and in a Pan-African religion, myalism (a communal healing and anti-witchcraft tradition). Thus Rastafari reflects a continuation of indigenous religious resistance in Jamaica (Besson, 1995).

Most scholars agree that the Rastafari movement per se began in Jamaica at the time of the emperor's grand coronation in 1930, when several early leaders arrived independently at similar ideas regarding Haile Selassie I as a black messiah. Included among these early Rastafari were Leonard Howell (1898–1981), Joseph Hibbert, Robert Hinds, Archibald Dunkley, and Altamont Reed. Howell is typically regarded as the earliest, a "catalyst" for the movement (Hill, 1981), especially insofar as he sought to establish a community of believers (Chevannes, 1994, p. 122).

But the international context was also critical to the emergence of Rastafari, playing an important part in the lives of the early leaders themselves. Howell, for example, had worked as a laborer and resided in the United States, Panama, and according to some accounts, Africa. And virtually all of the founding fathers were influenced by Marcus Garvey's (1887–1940) internationalist vision of Pan-African unity. Garvey (though not a Rasta himself) directed black people's attention toward Africa (best seen in his prophecy—now lost to the written record but preserved in Rastafari oral tradition—"Look to Africa for the crowning of a black king") and raised black awareness concerning Africa and things African both on the continent and in its diaspora. To a significant extent Garvey was responsible for revalorizing Africa in the diaspora, a process the Rastafari continued.

Perhaps the most important galvanizing events for these early Bible-reading leaders were the crowning on November 2, 1930, of Ras Tafari Makonnen as Emperor Haile Selassie I, King of Kings, Conquering Lion of the Tribe of Judah (fulfilling the prophecies of *Rv.* 5:5 and *Rv.* 19:11–16 in the Rastas' biblical exegesis) and the Italian invasion of Ethiopia in 1935–1936. The latter event ignited angry protests in Africa and evoked an unprecedented wave of solidarity and racial consciousness at the grassroots across the African diaspora. Leaders such as Garvey, George Padmore, Kwame Nkrumah, Jomo Kenyatta, and C. L. R. James all came together at this time in England, where Haile Selassie had been forced into exile, in effect giving birth to the modern Pan-African movement.

This early stage in the formation of Rastafari also coincided with widespread political upheaval throughout the West Indies. A number of scholars (e.g., Hill, 1981; Post, 1978; Waters, 1985) have argued that Rastafari ideology played an active part in sparking the labor uprisings of 1938 in Jamaica. Not surprisingly government authorities immediately branded the movement as seditious. By 1940 Howell and his group had established Pinnacle, a community of believers in the rural parish of St. Catherine, Jamaica. In what would become a persistent pattern for the next fifty years, police persecuted the group, and it was under this intense harassment that several contemporary features of Rastafari developed on a mass scale, including dreadlocks (uncombed hair), collective worship, the centrality of the "shepherd figure" as leader in the more churchical houses, along with the practice of living in a self-enclosed agriculturally based community and planting marijuana as a cash crop.

Throughout this period the Rastafari movement also grew under the leadership of other founding figures and independent followers. Moreover as migration from the Caribbean region to the United Kingdom increased in the 1950s, subcultural styles linked to Rastafari became important markers of identity for Caribbean immigrants and started to diffuse through British popular culture (see Hebdige, 1991/1979). Rastafari thus developed not only in Jamaica but also as a subcultural style responding to the double alienation of black West Indians excluded from full participation in British life yet separated from the changes occurring back home. Some three decades later the development of Rastafari motifs in popular culture grew to exert a semiautonomous influence on the global spread of the movement.

In 1947 a number of Rastafari brethren, including most notably Ras Boanerges (1925–2000), formed the Youth Black Faith (YBF) in Trench Town, West Kingston. Other Rastafari groups also existed, but the YBF is of decisive importance for its seminal influence on the movement. Chevannes characterizes it as a militant reformist group "born out of [younger leaders'] contempt for the waywardness of the older leaders" (Chevannes, 1994, p. 154). What was distinctive about the YBF was its zeal to purge Rastafari of the elements of the Revival tradition that could still be found in it such as ritual activity that invoked the spirit world or appeared to Rastafari as magical. This is a seminal point of formative influence, with deep implications for the crisis of "religion" verses "spirituality" currently resonating in the movement. When viewed through the lens of Biblical literalism the Revival use of magical ritual, incantations, potions and other activities appeared to the Rastafari of the YBF as bordering on necromancy. The YBF ultimately was also important for institutionalizing dreadlocks, the heartbeat rhythm of drumming and chanting, ritual use of ganja, vegetarian diet, the importance of words and sounds in Rastafari (including a distinctive Rasta idiom), and the predominance of men in the movement. The YBF developed these elements into a composite whole, the Order of Nyahbinghi, at once a guideline for living and a ceremony of worship centered around a ritual of music, dancing, prayer, and prophesying that remains an important basis of churchical gathering for many Rastas. The Nyahbinghi is based on a radical reinterpretation (through the prism of the Bible) of the rituals of a traditional, anticolonial, late-nineteenth-century religious cult by the same name in Uganda. It should be noted that although the Nyahbinghi had an explicit political message calling for "death to black and white oppressors," most Rastafari did not overtly participate in conventional politics at this time.

Two general developments were especially important for Rastafari in the 1950s and 1960s. First, relations between Rastafari and the police further polarized, owing largely to the inherently radical political message of Rastafari, the militancy of the YBF and other reform groups, and the association of these groups with certain illegal activities (e.g., ganja production). Police finally destroyed Howell's Pinnacle commune in 1954, and there were several infamous conflicts between Rases (males in the movement; females are often called Empresses) and police as the decade progressed (i.e., the Coronation Market riot [1959], the Claudius Henry affair [1960], and most importantly the Coral Gardens massacre [1963]). Ironically two of these incidents were not in fact triggered by Rastas.

Second, as a consequence of this polarization and at the invitation of Rastafari, the University of the West Indies (UWI) produced a report (Smith, Augier, and Nettleford, 1960) that detailed the history, social conditions, and doctrines of Rastafari. The report also made a series of concrete recommendations as to how to broker relations between

Rastafari and the larger community. The UWI report had several consequences that were pivotal for the movement. Crucially the academic credentials of the scholars who produced it and their calls for tolerance of the movement sewed the seeds of the Rastafari's subsequent public legitimacy. Though persecution of Rastafari did not by any means end with the UWI report, the report initiated a positive trend in social perceptions of Rastafari that continues in the twenty-first century. The report further recommended that the Jamaican government send a mission, including Rases, to select African countries to explore possibilities for relocation of Rastafari to Africa. Such international missions were not common in the movement for over a decade, but with the historic 1961 delegation that visited five African states, including Ethiopia, a vital precedent was set.

Changes in the scope and nature of the Rastafari movement since the 1960s are too numerous to catalog comprehensively, but nonetheless a few key trends are noteworthy. Most important of all was the tremendous impact of Haile Selassie's watershed visit to Jamaica in April 1966, ushering in a new cycle in the movement that was characterized by greater levels of formal organization among the brethren and sistren, particularly through the channels of the Ethiopian World Federation (EWF) and organization founded in 1937 (first Jamaican branch founded in 1938) to garner support worldwide for Ethiopia's struggle against Italian imperialism. (The EWF became an important vehicle for pan-African consciousness and brought important elements of formal structure to the Rastafari movement, especially from the late 1930s into the 1970s. It also became the major early instrument for the repatriation to Ethiopia of hundreds of Rastafari who have settled on Haile Selassie's land grant at Shashamane). Other important trends were the entry of a sizable number of persons, especially the youth, from the educated class into the movement and increasing social acceptance of the Rastafari.

The 1970s saw the incorporation of Rastafari symbols into wider Jamaican culture, for example, in the 1972 election campaign of Michael Manley and in the hugely popular film *The Harder They Come* (1973). Among other things, this public recognition marked the beginning of Rastas' transition "from outcasts to culture bearers" (Edmonds, 2003). But the transition has been ambivalent, making Rastafari more acceptable to a broader segment of society while also co-opting Rastafari's prophetic voice (e.g., by appropriating uncritical portions of the reggae icon Bob Marley's [1945–1981] song "One Love" as the anthem for the Jamaican Tourist Board). However, the trend to co-opt Rastafari has not been lost on the Rastas, and several prominent Rastas have denounced the dilution of Rastafari by popular culture. Moreover in the 1990s a more radical stream of young musicians such as Sizzla (Miguel Collins), Luciano (Jepther McClymont), and Capelton (Clifton George Baily III) reignited Rastafari's musical critique of status quo culture by increasingly calling down fire on Babylon in their lyrics.

The 1970s also witnessed the growth of the Twelve Tribes of Israel, a Rastafari organization founded in 1968 by the Prophet Gad. The Twelve Tribes were less stringent in the renunciation of contemporary society and embraced more openly Rastafari's links to Christianity. Because of their less-severe critique of the status quo, the Twelve Tribes started to draw more middle-class Jamaicans into the movement, further contributing to Rastafari's increasing level of acceptance. The emergence of Twelve Tribes was also linked to the charismatic black Marxist historian at the UWI, Walter Rodney (1941–1980), whose political activism among the grassroots in Jamaica before he was deported in October 1968 radicalized a number of students and ghetto youths, most of whom gravitated to the organization. With the continued rise of black power in the Caribbean and increasing scholarship on the movement during this period, Rastafari found a new cadre among UWI students from the eastern Caribbean islands. They carried Rastafari and reggae with them when they returned home, where the movement continued to develop. Some of the most radical cultural manifestations and political conflicts involving Rastafari in the 1970s were in the eastern Caribbean, such as Dominica's notorious Dread Act (an act that made Rastafari illegal by prohibiting dreadlocks, suspending standard arrest and trial procedures, increasing without limit police capacity to use deadly force in apprehending those with dreadlocks, and giving *de facto* power to citizens to shoot someone with dreadlocks on sight if he or she was caught entering their property; see Salter, 2000), the attempted Rasta takeover in 1979 of St. Vincent's Union Island, and early Rasta participation in and critique of the Grenadian revolution that same year (see Campbell, 1987; Salter, 2000; Tafari, 2001).

In terms of Rastafari's global spread, the most important development of the late 1960s and the 1970s was the association of Rastafari with reggae and the popular Jamaican music's worldwide growth as a result of new, affordable transistor radios and cassette players as well as the popularity of international reggae superstars, such as Bob Marley, Peter Tosh, and Burning Spear. Reggae at that time emphasized themes of justice, liberation, racial equity, and love, which resonated with alienated youth globally. Regardless of whether the specific artist considered himself or herself Rastafari, popular culture linked reggae music and Rastafari ideals.

Finally, in 1975 a formal mission set out to spread word of Rastafari outside of Jamaica. In April 1975 Ras Boanerges, Jah Prof, Ras Nedley Seymour, and Ras Ikael Tafari visited Barbados to spread the faith and culture of Rastafari and Nyahbinghi. From Barbados this group launched a series of divine missions through the region that marked the first self-conscious attempt by Rastafari to spread the movement. If any particular trend characterizes Rastafari since the start of the 1980s, it is the increasing efforts by Rastafari to spread knowledge of the movement and to organize. These efforts include an explosion of Rasta-authored books, newspapers, and pamphlets, including excellent monographs by Rastafari scholars, and an incredible array of Web pages devoted to Rastafari in all of its various manifestations. There has also been an exponential growth in missions outside of Jamaica to teach and inform about the movement. The House of Nyahbinghi has been especially active in missions, but other organizations, such as the EWF and the Twelve Tribes, have also established themselves in different locations around the globe. At the same time Rastafari has continued to spread independently of these organizations (e.g., through popular culture).

RASTAFARI SYMBOLS. Rastafari is an iconographically rich movement. It also manifests itself as a subcultural style, hence the various symbols associated with it accumulate both spiritual and secular meanings over time. Four elements continue to reflect central components of Rastafari spirituality: Haile Selassie I, marijuana, dreadlocks, and repatriation.

Rastafari views on Haile Selassie I range widely. The most crucial variable concerning the status of Haile Selassie is arguably the divide between Rastafari in Jamaica and the rest of the movement. But of course generation, political consciousness, the particular Rasta organization one is affiliated to, and even gender all account significantly for different viewpoints. In the absence of empirical data, the overall impression is that a clear majority of Rastafari view Haile Selassie in some degree of messianic or divine light, whether as the creator, god-king, Christ, or some more vague concept of divinity. This majority status becomes more overwhelming when one turns to Jamaica. In examining the way the figure of Haile Selassie is constructed among Rastafari, once again the contradictions are as great as they are seminal to the contours of the movement. Perhaps the overriding factor is the limited knowledge among many Rastafari of Haile Selassie's actual life, his policies, and even his statements. Consequently many of the classic doctrinal positions of, for instance, the Nyahbinghi—the roots from which most of the other branches of the movement willy-nilly sprang—are in diametric opposition to the stand taken by the emperor. Thus wide divergence separates the emperor from many Rasta brothers and sisters on key topics, such as education, democracy, race, gender, politics, modernization, and even the significance of Jesus Christ.

While the above polarity may well be dialectical and admittedly has to do with the radically different contexts within which the Rastafari and Haile Selassie found themselves, it still reflects a fundamental lack of synchronicity in certain vital areas between a movement and the leader they proclaim themselves to be following. Similar contradictions exist between the Rastafari and their other main cultural icon, Garvey. Nevertheless in their overlapping, essentially Pan-African vision, their uncompromising commitment to the mother continent, and their shared exaltation of spirituality, the Rastafari, their god-king, and their prophet-avatar are one. The comment of Hans Wilhelm Lockot, possibly the emperor's most insightful biographer, is worth noting in this regard: "The uncritical admiration of the Rastafarians offended people of sophisticated views, *but they none the less did greater justice to Haile Selassie for what he was and what he stood for than did most of his contemporaries*" (Lockot, 1989, 40, emphasis added).

Central to their movement is the Rastafari use of the psychotropic herb variously called ganja or marijuana, particularly as a sacrament in their communion ritual. Because controversy continues to accompany the marijuana question, given its illegal status in most countries, the Rastafari advocacy of this substance has been the major basis of persecution of the movement as well as the source of much of the dismissive attitude often directed at the brethren and sistren. For the Rastafari traditions, as with so many other spiritual traditions, the herb acts as a mediator between a person's surface consciousness and the deeper layers of awareness—the divinity that lies within. It is also a crucial medium for the energy connecting the divine consciousness in one human vessel to that of another via the smoking ritual that involves passing the pipe (chalice of communion) among the circle of worshippers (usually brethren). Various authors (Yawney, 1978; Forsythe, 1996) have argued that the use of marijuana is integral to the movement's visionary ethos. The multipurpose herb also has tremendous healing potency, the range and depth of which has only just begun to be appreciated by modern medical science but which the Rastafari make full use of. Of course, like any other substance, it can be abused, and most Rastas stress the distinction between "use" and "abuse" of the herb. On the whole the herb has been the catalyst for an incredible creativity and imaginative renaissance in the arts among the Rastafari, especially in Jamaica.

With regard to the dreadlocks, if from the vantage point of another hundred years down the corridor of history one were to look back at the indescribable force and contribution of the Rastafari and to ask what set the movement apart from its own time and circumstance, it would not be first and foremost the emphasis on love and natural living (other movements have championed these before), nor the unrepentant focus on African culture (there are other Afrocentric expressions of cultural resistance), nor the idea of a return to an Edenic Africa (the Garveyites raised that cry earlier), nor even the smoking of the herb (the hippie and jazz movements also celebrated this). The force and power of Rastafari would, in the final analysis, be seen to lie in the magnetic iconoclastic power of their flashing dreadlocks, making so many subliminal statements that sum up the points listed above all at once (natural roots, cosmic antenna, lion's mane, judge's wool, priestly garment, ancient crown, or just simply black man's or woman's hair, once despised as "hard" and ugly, now affirmed as rich and beautiful). It is perhaps inconceivable that the Rastafari could have broken the mental-spiritual-psychological chains of four hundred years of slavery, colonialism, neocolonialism, and racism without the shattering symbolism of the dreadlocks, projected globally through their charismatic music icons.

Justified by scriptural reference to the Nazarite Vow (*Nm.* 6) and confirmed by the fact that members of the militant anticolonial Land and Freedom Party in Kenya in the early 1950s expressed their nationalist zeal in the wearing of dreadlocks, the image of the dreadlocks has invested the Rastafari with an aura of black dignity and self-love at the same time that it has been the visible source of their social marginalization. Moreover because anyone can wear hair in this style, the locks have been the main means whereby the movement has been on occasion infiltrated and tarnished by criminals and other negative elements.

The Rastafari (from Howell and Hibbert through Claudius Henry to Ras Boanerges and the Nyahbinghi) always conceived of repatriation in biblical, Black Zionist, Garveyite terms. Their prophetic concept is apocalyptic (liberally strewn with verses from *Rv.*) and on a grand scale. The classic scriptural reference on repatriation is from *Isaiah*: "Bring my sons from far and my daughters from the ends of the earth" (*Is.* 43:3–7). As Ras Boanerges once spelled out its contours, the repatriation vision is not about migration. "I&I are not dealing upon migration. I&I are dealing upon the ransom of Israel by the moral laws of Almighty God—Jah Rastafari" (Barrett, 1968, 139). Ras Boanerges and the elders accordingly viewed the Twelve Tribes and EWF programs as merely land settlement and emigration initiatives. For the former, then, repatriation involved a long-term moral process of black redemption as well as the ensuing large-scale removal of African people (predominantly Rastafari) en masse from the West and their return to their "own vine and fig-tree," Ethiopia (a Biblical reference meaning all of Africa), their ancestral homeland.

In the elders' conception, repatriation was either to be immediately preceded or followed by what the Rastafari foresee as the pending destruction of the Western world via the long-prophesied military conflagration of world war III and its biblical climax—Armageddon—spreading out from its epicenter in Palestine. Such a historical retribution for the horrors of four hundred years of chattel slavery, colonialism, and neocolonialism would inevitably be accompanied by massive reparations along the lines spelled out in *Exodus* 12. Thus the Rastafari are the harbingers of the virtually global movement for black reparations, though not perhaps in the way they anticipated.

Not all Rastas are committed to repatriation, however, and those so committed hold different conceptions of the process. The Twelve Tribes' ultimate destiny does not lie in Ethiopia but in Jerusalem. Nevertheless the Tribes have a major resettlement program at Shashamane just outside Addis Ababa, Ethiopia. So too do the Bobo Dreads, the Nyahbinghi, and the EWF. About six hundred to seven hundred persons live there in the early twenty-first century, and the community includes a school, a bakery, a tabernacle, and some other communal facilities. Much smaller groups of Rastafari from the West have migrated individually or collectively to South Africa, Ghana, Burkina Faso, Benin, and other parts of the continent. Despite severe financial constraints, the Rastafari are upgrading the level of organization involved in their repatriation program, shifting the focus more toward a developmental Pan-Africanist enterprise rather than mere land settlement and emigration initiatives. This is in keeping with the ongoing transition in the Rasta movement in general from an originally millenarian emphasis, in which the brethren and sistren tended to look to the emperor to bring in the covenanted kingdom, to an emancipatory mode, in which the Rastafari are intensifying their organizational efforts to transform their vision of African redemption into a praxis of liberation (Tafari, 2001). This internal development in turn has led the Rastafari to a greater awareness of and participation in the political and economic dimensions of the wider Pan-African struggle, of which their quest for repatriation remains a crucial spearhead.

CONTROVERSIES WITHIN RASTAFARI. Unity is a supremely important political and ethical concern for many Rasta brethren and sistren. Thus raising controversial questions about the differences among Rastafari may be perceived as sewing disunity. Nevertheless, setting aside theological differences over the status of Haile Selassie and disputes over issues like vegetarianism, whether Rastas should be involved in politics, or how completely to separate oneself from society, there remains one area that causes more controversy among Rastafari than anything else: the question of how closely to adhere to the Bible. At stake is the fundamental issue of how committed the Rastafari are to elements of the Euro-Christian worldview they inherited. Literal readings of the Bible provide a foundation for some of Rastafari's most intransigent positions (e.g., the condemnation of homosexuality as an abomination) and continue to define traditional gender roles in the movement.

Though Rastafari is in many senses a liberation movement, it can also subordinate women (Lake, 1998). Some groups prohibit the sistren from speaking or drumming at Nyahbinghi rituals or reduce their role to support for men. Strict interpretations of the Bible can impose harsh restrictions on women. For example, the Bobo Dreads maintain a long period of separation for menstruating women (twenty-one days). On the other hand, there is a growing spectrum of opinions in Rastafari concerning women, and increasingly (especially as Rastafari leaves its Jamaican context) women have been playing important roles in the movement. Among other things, women have started to play essential roles in spreading and organizing Rastafari, in producing Rastafari literature and art, and in challenging the patriarchal assumptions of the earlier leaders.

One explanation for Rastafari's ambivalent treatment of women is the historical legacy of chattel slavery in the New World. Some scholars argue that the nature of the ancestral black culture predisposed the black woman in the New World to play a central, dominant role in the family structure. At the same time the economic reality of the lower strata black male tended to marginalize him. Given the heavy matrifocal pull within Jamaican grassroots family life, the patriarchal concepts the early Rases evolved would have been a vital buffer to their manhood, which was always under heavy siege from the time of slavery. The early Rastafari patriarchs (and to a lesser extent most of the subsequent leaders in the movement) were raised on the Bible and internalized the pervasive patriarchal teachings (and interpretations) of that book, which they understood as part of the natural divine order of things. In fact the Rastafari movement is notably distinct from most, if not all, of the other African revivalist religions in the Caribbean (Vodou, Santeria, Revival, Pocomania, Kumina, even the Spiritual Baptists), which tend to celebrate leading matriarchal figures, such as the priestess, shepherdess, or mother-queen.

Over time this early model of masculinity and femininity in Rastafari has been eroded. Much of Rastafari has shifted away from its early Euro-Christian influences (some groups more than others), and in the process space has opened for women to play central roles and to refigure their place in the movement in ways that make sense to them. The Twelve Tribes allow the sisters to speak at their meetings and even have a night when twelve of them collectively preside over the gathering. Among other things working to change gender relations in Rastafari, the theological emphasis on the I as divinity within is genderless, providing groundwork for equality among men and women.

Controversies in the Study of Rastafari. Controversies surrounding research on Rastafari fall into three categories: ethical considerations, methodological concerns, and practical considerations of where to do research on Rastafari. Most important is the ethical consideration that there are growing numbers of Rasta researchers who are able to represent the movement to the academic community. In the past there were few Rastafari trained in the academy, so information about the movement came from outside researchers. In theory the fact of both "inside" and "outside" viewpoints focusing on the movement represents the possibility of arriving at a more complete understanding. But whereas the "insider" is generally assumed to be subjective, as Tafari (2001) has pointed out, there is an entrenched "myth of objectivity" in the literature on Rastafari that allows ideological and even epistemological biases on the part of the "outsider" to lurk beneath the cloak of "objectivity." In the view of Richard Salter (2000), the academy should recognize the legitimacy of Rasta scholars of Rastafari and create a voice for them in the academy in the same way that it has, for example, recognized the legitimacy of Christian theologians. Only then will research on Rastafari continue to reflect the dynamism of the movement.

There is also an ongoing methodological debate between scholars who seek to research Rastafari through ethnographic fieldwork and hands-on experience and those who seek to research Rastafari primarily through representations of the movement in the arts. The former type of research is limited by all of the constraints that any ethnography faces. Ethnography is limited in scope and duration, and one can never be entirely sure of the degree to which the researcher is projecting himself or herself into the research (for a summary of this critique in early studies of Rastafari, see Johnson-Hill, 1995). For example, an ethnographic study like *Dread* (1976) by Joseph Owens, for all its sympathetic views of the Rastafari, distorted the overall picture of the movement by dwelling only on the religious brethren mainly from the Nyahbinghi, thus reproducing a kind of inverse reflection of Catholic doctrinal orthodoxy among the Rastas that is inaccurate.

Typically the scholars who work with the arts focus on music lyrics or poetry, though they may also base some of what they say on interviews with the musicians or poets. The problem with this approach is that most Rases are not musicians or poets, and the search for Rastafari exclusively through music or poetry misses less-studied aspects of the movement, such as Rasta political organizations. Moreover this approach runs the risk of misunderstanding the dynamic nature of the movement (which has resisted routinization to a large extent and thus is not fixed in the written form of lyrics or poetry). At the same time it has been argued that the resistance of Rastafari to routinization owes a great deal precisely to the influence of artists in the movement rather than to the religious brethren and sistren, who can be rigid and dogmatic.

Finally, there is the practical controversy concerning where studies of Rastafari are located. As Rastafari spreads globally it is important that scholars of Rastafari recognize that the movement differs from place to place and can no longer be represented as a whole based solely on studies in any one location.

Rastafari Past and Future. African culture. Biblical narratives of redemption. Grassroots practices of healing, talking, and connecting to the divine. Prophecies of divine justice and divine wrath poured out on a corrupted world. The intrepid sign of liberation reflected in untamed locks. Drawing on treasures buried deep within the soil of slavery, colonialism, and poverty, Rastafari make meaning in a barren world. That they have done so for so many, in so many places, and in such a short time is living testament to the movement's irrepressible vitality.

For two-thirds of the twentieth century the Rastafari revitalized awareness of the pristine glory of black civilization and threw up mythical heroes and heroines of the likes of Brother Bob Marley, his queen Rita, and the wailing Wailers, who through the intense rhythmic language of reggae music provided a new canopy of Africanity under which a whole generation of black youth as well as youth from other nations sheltered from the ravages of a Western world devoid of dreams, mystery, and dread.

It is the fulfillment of a vision the children of Jah (God) have shared with the rest of humanity for most of the twentieth century and into the twenty-first, and it leaves a positive omen that suggests that the Rastafari, with their fiery black love, pulsating rhythms, and bright rainbow hues of ites, gold and green, will be around for countless generations to come.

SEE ALSO African American Religions; African Religions; Caribbean Religions; Christianity; New Religious Movements.

BIBLIOGRAPHY

Barrett, Leonard E. *The Rastafarians: A Study in Messianic Cultism in Jamaica.* Rio Piedras, Puerto Rico, 1968.

Barrett, Leonard E., Sr. *The Rastafarians: Sounds of Cultural Dissonance* (1977). Rev. and updated ed. Boston, Mass., 1988.

Besson, Jean. "Religion as Resistance in Jamaican Peasant Life: The Baptist Church, Revival Worldview, and Rastafari Movement." In *Rastafari and Other African-Caribbean Worldviews,* edited by Barry Chevannes. Bassingstoke, U.K., and the Hague, 1995.

Blakely, Thomas D., Walter E. A. van Beek, and Dennis L. Thompson. *Religion in Africa: Experience and Expression.* Portsmouth, N.H., 1994.

Campbell, Horace. *Rasta and Resistance: From Marcus Garvey to Walter Rodney.* Trenton, N.J., 1987.

Chevannes, Barry. *Rastafari: Roots and Ideology.* Syracuse, N.Y., 1994.

Edmonds, Ennis Barrington. *Rastafari: From Outcasts to Culture Bearers.* Oxford, 2003.

Forsythe, Dennis. *Rastafari: For the Healing of the Nations.* New York, 1996.

Hebdige, Dick. *Subculture: The Meaning of Style* (1979). New York, 1991.

Hill, Robert. "Dread History: Leonard P. Howell and Millenarian Visions in Early Rastafari Religions in Jamaica." *Epoché* 9 (1981): 31–70.

Johnson-Hill, Jack A. *I-Sight, the World of Rastafari: An Interpretive Sociological Account of Rastafarian Ethics.* ATLA Monograph Series no. 35. Metuchen, N.J., 1995.

Lake, Obiagele. *Rastafari Women: Subordination in the Midst of Liberation Theology.* Durham, N.C., 1998.

Lockot, Hans Wilhelm. *The Mission: The Life, Reign, and Character of Haile Sellassie I.* New York, 1989.

Mansingh, Ajai, and Laxmi Mansingh. "Hindu Influences on Rastafarianism." *Caribbean Quarterly Monograph.* Mona, Jamaica, 1985.

Mbiti, John S. *African Religions and Philosophy.* New York, 1969.

Owens, Joseph. *Dread: The Rastafarians of Jamaica.* Kingston, Jamaica, 1976.

Post, Ken. *Arise Ye Starvelings: The Jamaica Labour Rebellion of 1938 and Its Aftermath.* The Hague, 1978.

Salter, Richard. "Shooting Dreads on Sight: Violence, Persecution, and Dominica's Dread Act." In *Millennialism, Persecution, and Violence: Historical Cases,* edited by Catherine Wessinger. Syracuse, N.Y., 2000.

Smith, M.G., Roy Augier, and Rex Nettleford. *The Ras Tafari Movement in Kingston, Jamaica.* Mona, Jamaica, 1960.

Tafari, Ikael L. *Rastafari in Transition: The Politics of Cultural Confrontation in Africa and the Caribbean (1966–1988).* Chicago, 2001.

Waters, Anita M. *Race, Class, and Political Symbols: Rastafari and Reggae in Jamaican Politics.* New Brunswick, N.J., 1985.

Yawney, Carole D. "Lions in Babylon: The Rastafarians of Jamaica as a Visionary Movement." Ph.D. diss., McGill University, 1978.

Yawney, Carol D., and John P. Homiak. "Rastafari." In *Encyclopedia of African and African American Religions,* edited by Steven D. Glazier, pp. 256–266. New York, 2001.

RICHARD C. SALTER (2005)
IKAEL TAFARI (2005)

RASTAFARIANS SEE CARIBBEAN RELIGIONS, *ARTICLE ON* AFRO-CARIBBEAN RELIGIONS

RAUSCHENBUSCH, WALTER (1861–1918),

Baptist clergyman and intellectual leader of the Social Gospel movement in American Protestantism. Rauschenbusch was born in Rochester, New York, received most of his schooling there, and taught at the Rochester Theological Seminary from 1897 to 1918. His father, August, a highly educated Westphalian Lutheran pastor, had gone to Missouri in 1846 as a missionary to German immigrants. After becoming a Baptist, August Rauschenbusch headed the Rochester seminary's program for German-speaking clergy. He bequeathed to his son an enduring appreciation of both evangelical piety and the Western cultural tradition.

Following his graduation from the Rochester Theological Seminary in 1886, young Rauschenbusch became pastor of the Second German Baptist Church in a tenement section of New York City. Here he was stirred by the hardships of the people: "I saw how men toiled all their life . . . and at the end had almost nothing to show for it; how strong men begged for work and could not get it in the hard times; how little children died" (*The Social Gospel in America, 1870–1920,* p. 265). He realized that his training had not equipped him to understand the powerful social, economic, and intellectual currents sweeping through American life; nor had his conservative seminary professors offered him a religious perspective adequate to cope with those currents. During his eleven-year pastorate in New York City he undertook an intense schedule of reading, discussion, and writing, much of it in collaboration with colleagues in two new organizations he helped to direct, the Baptist Congress and the Brotherhood of the Kingdom. Rauschenbusch received intellectual stimulation from a variety of authors, notably the American economist Henry George, the English theologians Frederick D. Maurice and Frederick W. Robertson, the Russian novelist Leo Tolstoi, the Italian patriot Giuseppe Mazzini, and the German sociologist Albert Schäffle.

Rauschenbusch returned to the Rochester Theological Seminary in 1897 as professor of New Testament; from

1902 until his death he was professor of church history. More than any other person in the United States, he provided a theological undergirding for the growing numbers of laity and clergy who sought to mold social and economic institutions according to Christian principles. His chief books were *Christianity and the Social Crisis* (1907), *Prayers of the Social Awakening* (1910), *Christianizing the Social Order* (1912), *The Social Principles of Jesus* (1916), and *A Theology for the Social Gospel* (1917).

Central in Rauschenbusch's message were the affirmations that the churches must recognize afresh that the kingdom of God had been Jesus' key teaching, that God intends this kingdom to reach into every realm of life, and that the competitiveness and selfishness fostered by capitalism must be opposed by persons committed to fulfilling God's beneficent will for humanity.

In the decades following Rauschenbusch's death many churches continued to address the tasks of social criticism and reconstruction, albeit not with the single-mindedness and effect for which he and other Social Gospel leaders had wished. Some influential religious thinkers in the middle third of the twentieth century judged Rauschenbusch's theological perspective to have been colored excessively by the optimism of his era. Recently, his thought has been viewed more appreciatively by persons who find richly provocative such Rauschenbuschian themes as the centering of Christianity in Jesus' proclamation of God's reign, the historical and social character of sin and salvation, and the complementarity of personal piety and social activism.

BIBLIOGRAPHY

The information contained in Dores R. Sharpe's *Walter Rauschenbusch* (New York, 1942) makes this an indispensable volume. However, it offers little historical and theological perspective, and significant gaps exist in Sharpe's presentation of Rauschenbusch's life. A more recent biography is Paul M. Minus, *Walter Rauschenbusch: American Reformer* (New York, 1988). Perceptive analyses and important portions of Rauschenbusch's writings can be found in *The Social Gospel in America, 1870–1920*, edited by Robert T. Handy (New York, 1966); "Sources of American Spirituality," in *Walter Rauschenbusch: Selected Writings*, edited by Winthrop S. Hudson (Mahwah, N. J., 1984); and Walter Rauschenbusch, *A Theology for the Social Gospel* (New York, 1917), "Library of Theological Ethics" (Louisville, 1997), with introduction by Donald W. Shriver, Jr.

PAUL M. MINUS (1987 AND 2005)

RAV (lit., "rabbi"), epithet of Abba' bar Ayyvu (c. 155–c. 247), a first-generation Babylonian amora. Rav helped lay the foundations for rabbinic Judaism in Babylonia. He studied in Palestine with his uncle Ḥiyya' and with Yehuda ha-Nasi', from whom he reportedly received authorization to render decisions in many areas. These contacts gave him a rich reservoir of teachings, self-reliance, and the freedom to go beyond tannaitic traditions.

Later Talmudic circles considered his resettlement in Babylonia, conventionally dated to 217, a turning point in Jewish history, one presaged by natural omens (B. T., *Shab.* 108a). First dwelling in Nehardea, a city on the Euphrates River, he assisted other rabbis and served as a market administrator (J.T., *B.B.* 5.11[5]; 15a–b). He later moved to Sura, a town hitherto said to lack a rabbinical presence. There he gathered a circle of students but probably did not head an academy, as was anachronistically claimed by some post-Talmudic chronicles (Goodblatt, 1975).

Rav's prestige was enhanced by a claim of Davidic descent and by his daughter's marriage into the exilarchic family. He was perceived as a master of wisdom and practical advice (B.T., *Pes.* 113a), able to read natural signs and endowed with the power to hurl curses to maintain respect (B.T., *Meg.* 5b).

In explaining the Mishnah, he drew on Palestinian sources and patterned his teachings after the Mishnah's style and phraseology even where he disputed it (Epstein, 1964). Though later Talmudic circles considered Rav especially authoritative in ritual matters, his dicta affected the way amoraim approached issues in general. Indeed, his comments, with those of Shemu'el the amora, were subsequently reworked to form a structure around which later teachings were organized; thereby they eventually became the literary rubric for the *gemara'* (Bokser, 1980).

Rav stands out for his wide-ranging theological interests. He emphasized that God rules with supremacy and that he benevolently and with knowledge created the world (B.T., *Ḥag.* 12a). The latter belief was expressed in a Ro'sh ha-Shanah prayer, *teqi'ata' devei Rav,* selected or edited by Rav, which stresses creation (J.T., *'A.Z.* 1.2; Neusner, 1966). Describing the future, Rav distinctively suggested that the righteous will experience as a reward a spiritual nourishing analogous to what the mystic visionaries of God experience in their lifetime (Chernus, 1982). He often emphasized the importance of Torah study and the respect due to Torah students (B.T., *Ta'an.* 24a, *San.* 93b). Rav made the fulfillment of messianic hopes dependent on human repentance and good deeds (B.T., *San.* 97b). He reportedly asserted that the commandments were designed to purify (*tsaref*) people, in the sense of refining or improving (*Gn. Rab.* 44.1). His ideas, teachings, and activities thus started the process of transforming tannaitic Judaism in Babylonia into a wider social movement.

SEE ALSO Amoraim.

BIBLIOGRAPHY

A comprehensive treatment and bibliography of Rav and his teachings can be found in Jacob Neusner's *A History of the Jews in Babylonia,* 5 vols. (Leiden, 1966–1970), esp. vol. 2, passim. Valuable works in Hebrew are Jacob Samuel Zuri's *Rav* (Jerusalem, 1925); Jacob N. Epstein's *Mavo' le-nusaḥ ha-Mishnah,* 2 vols. (1948; reprint, Jerusalem, 1964), pp. 166–211, on Rav's attitude to tannaitic traditions and the Mishnah; and E. S. Rosenthal's "Rav," in *Sefer Hanokh Yalon* (Jerusalem, 1963), pp. 281–337, on Rav's lineage and background. Works in English that include discussion of Rav are David M. Goodblatt's *Rabbinic Instruction in Sasanian Babylonia* (Leiden, 1975), my own *Post Mishnaic Judaism in Transition* (Chico, Calif., 1980), and Ira Chernus's *Mysticism in Rabbinic Judaism* (Berlin, 1982), esp. pp. 74–87.

New Sources

Kalmin, Richard Lee. "Changing Amoraic Attitudes toward the Authority and Statements of Rav and Shmuel: A Study of the Talmud as a Historical Source." *HUCA* 63 (1992): 83–106.

BARUCH M. BOKSER (1987)
Revised Bibliography

RAVAʾ (d. circa 352 CE) was a leading fourth-generation Babylonian amora, based in the city of Mahoza. The son of Yosef bar Ḥamaʾ and a student of Ḥisdaʾ, Nahman, and Yosef bar Ḥiyyaʾ, Ravaʾ gathered students in Mahoza after the deaths of Yosef bar Ḥiyyaʾ (c. 323) and Abbaye (c. 338). In his work he attempts to analyze and further disseminate earlier rabbinic teachings.

Through his function as a *dayyan* (judge) and market supervisor, Ravaʾ imposed rabbinic norms on Babylonian Jewry (B.T., *Ket.* 67a, *San.* 99b–100a). He lectured in the *pirqaʾ* gatherings, where aggadic and halakhic topics were discussed. These were convened on sabbaths and special occasions especially for the general public, although students were also expected to attend (B.T., *Pes.* 50a). He instructed many students who attended the *kallot* (sg., *kallah*), academic conventions that lasted several days. He trained disciples as well in his court and had them observe and emulate his personal practices (B.T., *Ber.* 6a; Goodblatt, 1975). Stories depict the students' deep involvement in learning and the insistence of Ravaʾ that they maintain family and community ties (B.T., *Ket.* 62b).

Ravaʾ also played an important part in transmitting earlier Babylonian teachings and possibly the third-century Palestinian traditions of Yoḥanan bar Nappahaʾ (Dor, 1971). With Abbaye, his fellow student and older colleague, he led in critically analyzing the logic of both sides of issues. Conventionally these discussions have been considered key building blocks of the Talmud, though recent research (by David Weiss Halivni and others) suggests they may have been shaped and especially preserved by postamoraic circles. Ravaʾ in particular recognized that to construe the Mishnah, one might have to emend the text or posit an ellipsis (Epstein, 1964). He particularly sought the biblical basis for various Mishnaic laws and practices (B.T., *Sot.* 17a, *B.Q.* 92a–b)

Ravaʾ taught the full range of halakhic, aggadic, and exegetical topics as well as practical advice. In comments such as "a person when distraught cannot be held accountable" (B.T., *B.B.* 16b), he recognized the significance of a person's mental or psychological state. He spoke of God's place in the world and, in stressing public and private study, he claimed that Torah study, even more than good deeds, can counter demons (B.T., *Sot.* 21a). In emphasizing the respect and privileges due to Torah students, he asserted that rabbis, like the priests and Levites of Ezra's day (*Ezr.* 7:24), should be exempt from poll taxes (B.T., *Ned.*)

Ravaʾ stands out in his generation not only for a judicial role with extensive jurisdiction, his reportedly large number of students, and his unusual methods of teaching but also, with Abbaye, for the large number of supernatural stories told about him (B.T., *Taʿan.* 21b–22a). People believed that Torah study and good deeds brought Ravaʾ divine blessings, protection against evil and demons, and divine communications in omens and dreams (B.T., *Ber.* 56a–b). His great prestige is reflected in the Talmudic stories describing the gifts he received from the mother of King Shapur II and in the subsequent principle that his legal opinions should be followed in all but six cases (B.T., *B.M.* 22b).

SEE ALSO Abbaye; Amoraim.

BIBLIOGRAPHY

A comprehensive treatment and biblography of Ravaʾ and his teachings can be found in Jacob Neusner's *A History of the Jews in Babylonia,* 5 vols. (Leiden, 1966–1970), esp. vol. 4, passim. Noteworthy, too, is Jacob N. Epstein's *Mavoʾ le-nusaḥ ha-Mishnah,* 2 vols. (1948; reprint, Jerusalem, 1964), pp. 381–391, on the attitude of Ravaʾ to tannaitic traditions and the Mishnah. Other informative works are Zwi Moshe Dor's *Torat Erets-Yisraʾel be-Bavel* (Tel Aviv, 1971); David M. Goodblatt's *Rabbinic Instruction in Sasanian Babylonia* (Leiden, 1975) and his "The Babylonian Talmud," in *Aufstieg und Niedergang der römischen Welt,* vol. 2.19.2 (Berlin and New York, 1979), reprinted in *The Study of the Ancient Judaisim,* edited by Jacob Neusner, vol. 2, *The Palestinian and Babylonian Talmuds* (New York, 1981); and David Weiss Halivni's *Midrash, Mishnan, and Gemara* (Cambridge, Mass., 1986).

New Sources

Hayman, Pinchas. "Disputation Terminology and Editorial Activity in the Academy of Rava Bar Yosef Bar Hama." *HUCA* 72 (2001): 61–83.

Margolies, Morris B. *Twenty/Twenty: Jewish Visionaries through Two Thousand Years.* Northvale, N.J., 2000.

BARUCH M. BOKSER (1987)
Revised Bibliography

RĀWẒAH-KHVĀNĪ is the Persian ritual of public lamentation over the suffering of Imam Ḥusayn and other Shīʿī martyrs. Together with the *taʿziyah* (passion play) and the Muḥarrm mourning procession, known in Iran as *dastah,* it forms a part of the trilogy of the mourning observances that determines the basic popular ritual orientation in Shīʿī Islam. Similar rituals are known by different names in other countries with Shīʿī populations.

The recitation and chanting of eulogies for the Shīʿī martyrs, which has flourished in the Muslim world during the last thirteen centuries, produced a literary genre known as *maqtal* (pl., *maqātil*). It was precisely at the beginning of the Safavid period (1501), when Shīʿī Islam became the state religion of Persia, that the major Persian *maqtal* masterpiece was composed. This was the work of Ḥusayn Vāʿiẓ Kāshifī, titled in Arabic *Rawḍat al-shuhadāʾ* (The Garden of the Martyrs), from which *rāwẕah-khvānī* takes its name: The second word of the Arabic title was replaced with the Persian *khvāni* ("chanting" or "recitation") to yield *rāwẕah-khvānī,* or "garden recitation."

The public lamentation of *rāwẕah-khvānī* is performed most often during the first two months of the Muslim calendar, Muḥarrm and Ṣafar, in commemoration of the murder of Imam Ḥusayn on the tenth of Muḥarrm in AH 61/680 CE. As the son of ʿAli and the grandson of the prophet Muḥammad, Ḥusayn was the third imam of the Shīʿah, who consider his death at the hands of the caliph's troops the treacherous murder of the just and rightful ruler at the hands of an evil usurper. Mourning for Ḥusayn thus combines grief over his death with a strong condemnation of tyranny and injustice.

All classes of society participate in the *rāwẕah-khvānī*s (popularly called *rawẕah*s), which can be held in black tents set up for the occasion in the public square of a town or village, in mosques, or in the courtyards of private houses. During the late eighteenth and the nineteenth century, special edifices known as *Ḥusaynīyah*s or *takīyah*s were also built for the performance, often by official patrons. Richly decorated and carpeted, they displayed black standards and flags, as well as a variety of weapons intended to recall the Battle of Karbala.

The *rawẕah* usually begins with the performance of a *māddaḥ* ("panegyrist") reciting and singing in praise of the Prophet and the saints. He is followed by the *rawẕah khvān* (also known as a *vāʿiẓ,* "preacher"), who offers storytelling and songs about Ḥusayn and the other martyrs. His rapid chanting in a high-pitched voice alternates with sobbing and crying to arouse the audience to intense emotion. The *rāwẕah-khvānī* ends with congregational singing of dirges called *nawḥah*s. The performances last anywhere from several hours to an entire day and well into the night, and the emotional atmosphere that is generated can result in weeping, breast-beating, and body flagellation, as in the Muḥarrm parades. Through the choice of episodes and the modulation of their voices, a succession of chanters are able to excite and manipulate the emotions of their audiences so that they identify with the suffering of the martyrs, who will serve in turn as their intercessors on the Day of Judgment. At the same time, the *rawẕah khvān*s frequently make digressions into contemporary political, moral, and social issues, creating the kind of social and religious climate that is ripe for political action. There is no doubt that the religious symbolism of the just Imam Ḥusayn, martyred at the hands of a tyrannical ruler, played a major role in the Iranian Revolution of 1978–1979.

Outside of Iran, it is only in Bahrein that public lamentations for Ḥusayn and other Shīʿī martyrs follow the Persian model of *rāwẕah-khvānī.* The Shīʿah of India, Pakistan, Iraq, and Lebanon, along with smaller Shīʿī communities in Turkey and the Caucasus, observe the mourning months of Muḥarrm and Ṣafar according to various local traditions, although the intensity of the feelings is the same.

SEE ALSO ʿĀshūrāʾ; Taʿziyah.

BIBLIOGRAPHY

Mahmoud Ayoub's *Redemptive Suffering in Islam* (The Hague, 1978) is an important discussion of the philosophical concept of redemption. For discussions of rituals, see my *Taʿziyeh: Ritual and Drama in Iran* (New York, 1979); B. K. Roy Burman's *Moharram in Two Cities: Lucknow and Delhi* (New Delhi, 1966); G. E. von Grunebaum's *Muhammadan Festivals* (New York and London, 1958); and Gustav Thaiss's "Religious Symbolism and Social Change: The Drama of Husain," in *Scholars, Saints and Sufis,* edited by Nikki R. Keddie (Berkeley, Calif., 1972).

PETER CHELKOWSKI (1987)

RĀZĪ, FAKHR AL-DĪN AL-, Muḥammad ibn ʿUmar (AH 543–606/1149–1209 CE), was a celebrated twelfth-century Muslim theologian and a prolific scholar. The period in which Rāzī flourished is marked by a cautious reassessment of some of the basic principles of Neoplatonic philosophy, after a period in which this tradition had suffered strong criticism, primarily in the writings of the famous Muslim theologian al-Ghazālī (d. 1111). Rāzī was the principal protagonist of this reassessment of the philosophical tradition, particularly as it had been expounded and established by Ibn Sīnā (d. 1037). Although he was not a philosopher in the strict sense, Rāzī's mature theological works manifest an unquestionable Avicennian influence. But what he perceived as being the excesses of the Neoplatonic tradition he sought to moderate, in order to accommodate its fundamental theories within the traditional framework of Muslim rational discourse. Thus his works arguably represent the most successful synthesis of the conflicting traditions of Muslim philosophy (*falsafa*) and Muslim speculative theology (*kalām*).

LIFE. Rāzī was born in Rayy, near modern-day Tehran, in 1149. Not much is known of his early years, but most Muslim biographers agree that it was Rāzī's father, Ḍiyāʾ al-Dīn, the city's main preacher (*khaṭīb*), who was responsible for the education of his son in the two principal Muslim sciences of jurisprudence (*fiqh*) and theology (*kalām*). In accordance with the scholastic tradition to which his father belonged, Rāzī received his training in the Shāfiʿī branch of jurisprudence and in the Ashʿarī school of theology, both of which were classical Sunnī affiliations. His formation in philosophy took place in Marāgha (Azerbaijan) at the hands of Majd al-Dīn al-Jīlī, who also happened to be the teacher of the famous illuminationist philosopher, Shihāb al-Dīn al-Suhrawardī. It should also be noted that al-Jīlī's teacher had been a student of al-Ghazālī himself.

Having completed his formative studies in Rayy, Rāzī set off for Khwārazm. There he engaged in serious disputations with the Muʿtazila (upholders of the kind of rationalism to which Sunnī Islam, as championed by Rāzī, was vehemently opposed). Khwārazm was at that time the only remaining Muʿtazilī stronghold, after the decline of the movement in Baghdad, and the opposition stirred up by Rāzī was such that he was soon forced to leave the town and return to Rayy. From there he traveled on to the major towns of Transoxiana, and reportedly even as far as the Indian frontier, before finally returning to settle in Herāt. He died there in 1209.

During his early years Rāzī was of very modest means. But his fortunes quickly changed after he entered into a series of high-profile relationships, most notably with the Ghūrid rulers of Ghazna, Ghiyāth al-Dīn and his brother Shihāb al-Dīn. Later on, Rāzī's travels took him to Khurasan, where he was welcomed by the Khwārazm-Shāh ʿAlāʾ al-Dīn Tekesh, whose generous patronage he enjoyed. Ibn al-Athīr, a medieval Muslim historian, informs us that these relationships brought Rāzī enormous wealth. The legal schools (*madrasah*) set up in his name in various towns added considerably to his fame. Throughout these various sojourns, however, he was never quite free of controversy. Rāzī was undoubtedly an impressive speaker and his proselytizing sermons—as well his ruthless public criticisms of doctrines associated with various Muslim groups, among them Ḥanbalīs, the Karrāmiyya, and Ismaʿīlīs—won him many dangerous enemies. On one notorious occasion his scurrilous attack against the head of the Karrāmiyya (an extreme anthropomorphist sect active in Ghūr) led to serious public disturbances, and to Rāzī's subsequent expulsion from the town.

WORKS. By any standard, Rāzī was a prolific scholar. Close to a hundred works can be attributed to him with near certainty, although some biographers have suggested twice this number. The range of subjects covered by Rāzī is indeed encyclopedic: he wrote works on history, exegesis, theology, jurisprudence, philosophy, rhetoric, medicine, ethics, geometry, astrology, and physiognomy. He composed a well-known treatise on the theory and practice of magic, but it seems that he abandoned the field after his research did not meet with any real success. Of the range of subjects that Rāzī covered, his principal contributions to Muslim intellectual thought are to be found in his theological writings; his two commentaries (*sharḥs*) on Ibn Sīnā's work (one on the latter's *Kitāb al-Ishārāt waʾl-Tanbīhāt*, another on his *ʿUyūn al-Ḥikma*); and his voluminous commentary on the Qurʾān, the *Mafātīḥ al-Ghayb* (The keys to the unseen).

Though Rāzī wavered on certain Ashʿarī doctrines (viz., atomism, God's attributes, and the theory of human "acquisition" of acts), he was generally a staunch defender of this school of *kalām*, as can be seen in his major theological works (*al-Muḥaṣṣal, Lawāmiʿ al-Bayyināt, al-Arbaʿīn*). Rāzī, however, would devote the large part of his theological writings to the development of what may be termed a Muslim "philosophical" theology (almost a third school of *kalām*, after Muʿtazilism and Ashʿarism). One of his earliest efforts in this respect is a work entitled *al-Mabāḥith al-Mashriqiyya* (Oriental investigations). Here, as elsewhere, Rāzī's debt to two philosophers is obvious: Abūʾl-Barakāt al-Baghdādī (d. after 1164/5) in physics, and Ibn Sīnā in metaphysics (especially Ibn Sīnā's *al-Shifāʾ* and *al-Najāt*).

Rāzī took exception, however, to certain Avicennian fundamentals, most notably the emanationist principle that from the "one" can only issue one, the notion of God's knowledge being limited to universals, and the eternity of the universe. Rāzī refuted these concepts at length, and further refined Ibn Sīnā's proof for God as the "necessary being" by drawing a subtle distinction between *essence* and *being*. Rāzī's *al-Maṭālib al-ʿāliya min al-ʿilm al-ilāhī* (The noble pursuits of the science of divinity) possibly represents the best example of his synthetic approach to theology, since in this work Rāzī makes use, somewhat eclectically, of the methods of Muslim *kalām* and those of Avicennian philosophy. Rāzī's magnum opus, however, on account of its sheer breadth and sophistication, remains his commentary on the Qurʾān. Here, dogmatic principles are affirmed through a combination of philosophical and theological arguments interwoven in such a way that one cannot discern the traditional separation between the two. Finally, Rāzī's contribution to the field of Islamic ethics has been neglected, although it has recently been shown to be quite significant.

A deeply religious individual, Rāzī believed that he could reassert the fundamental principles of the Muslim faith through a synthesis of arguments drawing on traditional *kalām* and Neoplatonic philosophy. Notwithstanding his famous deathbed renunciation of the methods of rational discourse, Rāzī's contribution to Muslim intellectual thought remains considerable.

BIBLIOGRAPHY

Anawati, Georges C. "Fakhr al-Dīn al-Rāzī." In *Encyclopaedia of Islam.* 2d ed. Edited by H. A. R. Gibb et al., vol. 2, pp. 751–755. Leiden and London, 1960. A necessary follow-up article, in which the main aspects of Rāzī's life are put into perspective, together with a summary of the contents of each of Rāzī's main works.

Ceylan, Yasin. *Theology and Tafsīr in the Major Works of Fakhr al-Dīn al-Rāzī.* Kuala Lumpur, 1996. Surveys key philosophical and theological issues examined by Rāzī in his Qurʾanic commentary and major *kalām* works.

Cooper, John. "Al-Razi, Fakhr al-Din." In *The Routledge Encyclopaedia of Philosophy,* edited by Edward Craig, vol. 8, pp. 112–115. London and New York, 1998. A brief but useful synopsis of Rāzī's main objections to Ashʿarism and Ibn Sīnā's theories.

Fakhry, Majid. *A History of Islamic Philosophy.* 2d ed. New York, 1983. Chapter 11, "Theological Reaction and Reconstruction," pp. 312–332, deals with Rāzī's place within the overall framework and development of Muslim philosophy.

Iskenderoğlu, Muammer. *Fakhr al-Dīn al-Rāzī and Thomas Aquinas on the Question of the Eternity of the World.* Leiden, 2002.

Kholeif, Fathalla. *A Study of Fakhr al-Dīn al-Rāzī and his Controversies in Transoxiana.* Beirut, 1966. A critical edition and translation of Rāzī's autobiographical account of his famous disputations in Transoxiana, with a good biographical introduction and follow-up analysis of the topics of these disputations.

Shihadeh, Ayman. "Fakhr al-Dīn al-Rāzī on Ethics and Virtue." Ph.D. diss., Oxford University, 2002. The only in-depth study of Rāzī's ethics; constitutes an original contribution to studies on Rāzī and provides a comprehensive bibliography of Rāzī's published and unpublished works.

Street, Tony. "Concerning the Life and Works of Fakhr al-Din al-Razi." In *Islam: Essays on Scripture, Thought, and Society, a Festschrift in Honour of Anthony H. Johns*, edited by Peter G. Riddell and Tony Street, pp. 135–146. Leiden, 1997.

FERAS Q. HAMZA (2005)

RE, the ancient Egyptian sun god, was, for most of the pharaonic period, the chief god or at least among the chief gods. His cult center was at Heliopolis, where he seems to have displaced Atum as universal god during the fifth dynasty, and at the same time he also achieved some supremacy over Horus. In the Pyramid Texts the deceased king, who becomes identified with Osiris, joins Re in the solar bark and serves as a guide on the voyage through the day and night skies. By the First Intermediate Period (c. 2181 BCE), local monarchs and other nobles were having these same texts copied on the interior of their coffins, and thus the right to become Osiris (or join him) and the right to join Re was extended. The theology of the Re religion is known not only from mortuary literature but also from the tenth-dynasty *Instruction for King Merikare* and the later solar hymns.

Re is combined with the old Heliopolitan creator god, Atum, as Re-Atum, the supreme god of the later Old Kingdom, and he is assimilated to the Theban god Amun as Amun-Re, "king of the gods," in the Middle and New kingdoms. Representations of Re in his combined forms are very common, but Re does occur individually on Memphite stelae as a human with hawk head surmounted by a sun disk. This is also his regular appearance in the late New Kingdom, when as Pre-Ha-rakhty (the Re-Horus of the Horizon) he is universal lord. The sun disk itself is known as Aton, and in the eighteenth dynasty this became the object of Akhenaton's devotion at the expense of Amun-Re's cult temple at Karnak. The old Heliopolitan priesthood may have persuaded Akhenaton to transfer his allegiance, but his movement failed and he was later regarded as a heretic.

Hathor is the consort of Re and personification of the entire ennead of gods, and in this way she is also mother of Horus, the king. "Son of Re" was one of the major titles of the king beginning in the fourth dynasty. The great temple of Re at Heliopolis has not survived, but there are separate chapels to the sun god in New Kingdom mortuary temples. The great rock-cut temple of Ramses II at Abu Simbel was dedicated to the sun god in his two aspects, Re-Harakhty and Amun-Re. Re's central position in the early mortuary literature continued in the New Kingdom, when papyri of the *Book of Going Forth by Day* were available to anyone who could afford them and kings used new books that described the underworld of Sokar of Memphis, through which the deceased ruler was to guide the solar bark. The solar hymns acknowledge Re's involvement with creation and with sustaining and overseeing what he created. Other gods are described as coming from his sweat, and humankind from the weeping of his eye.

BIBLIOGRAPHY

The best single source of further information is Hans Bonnet's article "Re" in the *Reallexikon der ägyptischen Religionsgeschichte* (Berlin, 1952), pp. 626–630.

LEONARD H. LESKO (1987)

REBBE SEE TSADDIQ

REBECCA, or in Hebrew, Rivqah, was the wife of Isaac and the second of the biblical matriarchs. The name *Rivqah* is usually taken to be an animal name, like those of Rachel and Leah; it is derived from a hypothetical form (**biqrah*) meaning "cow." According to *Genesis,* Rebecca was the granddaughter of Abraham's brother Nahor.

Abraham sent his servant to find a wife for Isaac in Mesopotamia, where he encountered Rebecca drawing water from a well, a meeting place often indicative of divine providence in the Bible. God's involvement is further evidenced by Rebecca's offer of hospitality, fulfilling the servant's stipulated sign. Rebecca subsequently consented to make the journey back to Canaan, where she met and married Isaac. Like his father Abraham, Isaac once claimed that his wife was his sister so that Abimelech, king of Gerar, would not have him killed in order to possess her. The ruse was discovered, however, when the king observed an amorous encounter between them.

After twenty years of infertility, Rebecca bore twins. According to a divine oracle, they were to become two nations, with the descendants of the older serving those of the younger. Rebecca ensured the fulfillment of this prophecy by helping Jacob, her younger son, deceive his blind father while the elder son, Esau, was away. As a result Isaac gave Jacob the blessing intended for Esau. According to rabbinic tradition, Rebecca instigated this deception because she recognized from her sons' behavior that Jacob would make the better leader. She later helped Jacob flee Canaan to escape Esau's anger. Her earlier reassurance to Jacob that the "curse [for this deception] will be on me" (*Gn.* 27:13) came to be fulfilled when she never again saw her favorite son.

The Bible presents Rebecca as a strong and incisive figure, complementing the relatively weak Isaac. She is the only woman whose birth is noted in the Bible (*Gn.* 22:20–23). Her judgment as to the better son corresponds with God's, and her actions not only control the transmission of authority within the family but also ensure the fulfillment of God's will.

SEE ALSO Isaac; Jacob.

BIBLIOGRAPHY

Nahum M. Sarna's *Understanding Genesis* (New York, 1966) contains a thorough treatment of all the patriarchal narratives from a modern scholarly perspective. Rabbinic traditions pertaining to these figures are collected in Louis Ginzberg's *Legends of the Jews,* 2d ed., 2 vols., translated by Henrietta Szold and Paul Radin (Philadelphia, 2003). An evaluation of the biblical depiction of Rebecca is in Christine Garside Allen's essay "Who Was Rebekah? 'On Me Be the Curse, My Son!'" in *Beyond Androcentrism: New Essays on Women and Religion,* edited by Rita M. Gross (Missoula, Mont., 1977).

FREDERICK E. GREENSPAHN (1987 AND 2005)

REBIRTH SEE REINCARNATION; TRANSMIGRATION

RECITATION SEE CHANTING; TILĀWAH

RECLUSES SEE EREMITISM

RECONSTRUCTIONIST JUDAISM.

Reconstructionist Judaism originated in the philosophy of Mordecai Kaplan (1881–1983) and is widely considered the fourth religious denomination of American Jewry, along with Reform, Conservative, and Orthodox. Kaplan coined the term *Reconstructionism* in his major work, *Judaism as a Civilization* (1934), to define his intentions for making Judaism in the United States meet the needs of the generation of the children of eastern European immigrants who arrived in the United States in the early twentieth century and those who were born in the country subsequently. He believed Judaism as practiced in Europe would not be viable in the American environment, and he sought to create a blueprint for a new way of being Jewish that would combine the best features of traditional Judaism with the American way of life. He chose the term *reconstruct* because it indicated both a respect for Jewish tradition and an awareness that Judaism needed to be remodeled to fit the conditions of life in the United States. He saw his plan in contrast to reform, which lacked a connection to Jewish traditional practice because it focused on theology rather than customs. He also rejected the idea of more traditionally oriented Jews that Judaism needed to be conserved without change.

THE CIVILIZATIONAL APPROACH. Kaplan's most influential idea, which was central to his platform of reconstruction, was that the Jews were neither solely a religious group nor a nation, as they were constituted in prior eras, but a people. He suggested that belonging to the Jewish people was what bound Jews together, even if they disagreed about belief and practice.

Kaplan's blueprint entailed a redefinition of the terms of Jewish life. Judaism was the evolving religious civilization of the Jewish people. Influenced by the ideas of modern sociology, Kaplan retold the story of Jewish history through the conceptual framework of evolution, arguing that change was central to Jewish development over time. Just as Judaism in the past had changed from the times of the Bible through the rabbinic period and into modernity, the Jews in each era in the future would have a responsibility to reconstruct Judaism to meet the needs of the times. The key to this process in early-twentieth-century America was for Jews to understand Judaism as a civilization parallel to other ancient civilizations, like Greece or Rome, or modern ones, like France or England. While religion was central to Judaism, Kaplan viewed Judaism as more than a religion. Jewish civilization should be understood to have the same characteristics of those of other groups, including language, law, literature, customs, art, food, and music. Judaism was not simply a religion or a nation, as others claimed, but a fully developed way of life. This perspective supported those who were alienated from Jewish religious practice but were interested in remaining Jewish through their connections to literature or the culinary arts, for example.

Kaplan dealt with the problem of being both Jewish and American by claiming that Jews could live in two civilizations, the American and the Jewish, taking the best from each. He saw these two civilizations as perfectly compatible. The idea of living in two civilizations was an antidote to the melting-pot ideal that suggested that immigrants shed their ethnic backgrounds. Kaplan's idea that one could be both Jewish and American without experiencing conflict between those identities prefigured the ethnic and racial identity politics that became popular in the 1960s.

What Kaplan wanted Jews to take from the American framework was a connection to what he called the sancta of American civilization: the holidays, myths, and customs of America. To this end Kaplan created liturgies for holidays like Thanksgiving and the Fourth of July. He also was a passionate believer in democracy and sought to transform Jewish institutions into the democratic patterns of American life. An intellectual disciple of Émile Durkheim and John Dewey, Kaplan wanted to reorganize American Jewish institutions to function in a democratic way. Instead of organizing Jewish life into synagogues and denominations, Kaplan envisioned the creation of organic Jewish communities where democratically elected leaders would reconstruct Jewish political, social, and religious life in concert. Kaplan was also an avid cultural Zionist and believed that a Jewish state in what was then Palestine would be the center that would hold these organic communities together in a worldwide, democratic Jewish structure of governance. Although this dimension of Kaplan's social vision was utopian and never was achieved, his ideas were influential in the movement to create synagogue centers and communal structures, like the Federation of Jewish Philanthropies, and in Zionist and other organizations that sought worldwide connections among Jews.

KAPLAN'S THEOLOGY. To Kaplan, religion was the most important contribution of Jewish civilization to the world. Kaplan's own religious vision was controversial and achieved much attention but little support. In 1937 Kaplan published a theological treatise, *The Meaning of God in Modern Jewish Religion.* Espousing a theology of religious naturalism, Kaplan defined God as "the Power that makes for salvation" and rejected anthropomorphic and supernatural views of God, instead defining God as an impersonal force that acts through and not beyond the natural world and inspires human beings to aspire to do good in the world. Influenced also by pragmatism, Kaplan's main concern was on how this Power functioned in people's lives to encourage them to seek out a meaningful and moral life. Although many have considered Kaplan's position atheistic, he was a passionate believer in the existence of this impersonal force.

Another controversial dimension of Kaplan's religious philosophy was his elimination of the notion that the Jews were the chosen people. A God that did not act in history could not single out one people for any special role. Kaplan taught that all peoples had a unique function to fulfill in the world and that each group could, through what he called "ethical nationhood," serve a divine purpose.

THE PAST HAS A VOTE, NOT A VETO. Kaplan defined the traditional practices of the Jews as folkways rather than law. The idea that "the past has a vote but not a veto" became an important slogan for Reconstructionism. While the past needed to be respected, it could not be the final factor determining Jewish practice. Kaplan did encourage people to observe the Sabbath and other holy days and keep kosher, not because they were commanded to do so by God but because these observances were still meaningful to bind them together as a people and connect them to Jews in the past and the future. He encouraged Jewish groups to take Jewish folkways seriously and think about ways to reconstruct them. If customs in their ancient forms still had meaning, Jews should continue to observe them as they had been practiced. Other practices that no longer conformed to the ethical vision of modernity, such as the inequality of the sexes in ancient Jewish teaching, should be abandoned, however. Many customs that no longer were meaningful, Kaplan argued, should be reconstructed, given new meanings, and observed.

One of Kaplan's great contributions was to publish prayer books that illustrated his intention to reconstruct Judaism. He published a Haggadah in 1941 that told the Passover story as a tale of the triumphs of Moses and the people of Israel rather than God. *Sabbath Prayer Book,* published in 1945, changed the wording of key prayers to eliminate the concept of chosenness, reward, and punishment, as well as references to Temple sacrifice. The prayer book also removed special status for the ancestors of the priests and Levites, as Kaplan saw that practice as not in keeping with democratic principles and therefore in need of reconstruction. *Sabbath Prayer Book* was publicly burned by Orthodox rabbis in 1945, and Kaplan was excommunicated. Unlike his other works, *The New Haggadah* achieved great popularity and brought Kaplan great attention in American Jewish life in the mid-1940s.

THE SPREAD OF RECONSTRUCTIONISM. Kaplan's ideas were most influential with the leadership of Reform and Conservative Judaism from the 1920s, when *Judaism as a Civilization* was published, through the late 1940s. His magazine, the *Reconstructionist,* was a leading forum for discussion and debate about critical Jewish issues, from Zionism to economic justice. Kaplan was interested in influencing the leadership of the American Jewish community to follow his ideas. He was not interested in starting a movement based on those ideas. He was a rabbi of a synagogue he founded in 1922, the Society for the Advancement of Judaism (SAJ). The SAJ was a place to carry out his experiments in liturgy. The services conducted at SAJ were based largely on the traditional Hebrew liturgy but also included English readings in keeping with the themes of the service and provided ample opportunity for discussion of the Torah portion and its relationship to issues of the day. The SAJ is also famous as the location of the first modern bat mitzvah, held rather unceremoniously for Kaplan's eldest daughter, Judith, in 1922.

Kaplan's primary vocation was as professor of homiletics at the Jewish Theological Seminary, a position he held from 1909 to 1963. During Kaplan's years at the seminary, Reconstructionism was seen primarily as the left wing of the Conservative movement. Kaplan's greatest influence was on the several generations of rabbis he taught, many of whom became his ardent followers. His followers were among those most dissatisfied with the way Conservative Judaism was developing, and they urged Kaplan to separate from the institutional structure of Conservative Judaism and embark on the creation of a Reconstructionist movement. He gave tacit permission and support to these rabbis but never embraced the idea of creating a separate movement based on his ideology. He refused opportunities to start his own seminary or to teach at other Jewish institutions.

But Kaplan's ardent followers were intent on creating a movement based on his philosophy. The task of movement building fell to Kaplan's son-in-law, Ira Eisenstein (1906–2001). Eisenstein was one of the many young men who became followers of Kaplan while training for the rabbinate at the Jewish Theological Seminary. Eisenstein slowly built an organizational structure that began with the Reconstructionist Foundation in 1940. The foundation was a membership organization that coordinated the publications produced by the nascent movement, including the magazine, the works of liturgy, and pamphlets explaining the Reconstructionist program.

Assuming that the future of a movement depended on attracting synagogues in addition to building an individual membership base, Eisenstein in the early 1950s took a position as rabbi of Anshe Emet, a large Conservative synagogue in Chicago thought to be sympathetic to the Reconstructionist program. Unsuccessful in the effort to make Anshe Emet a Reconstructionist synagogue, Eisenstein returned to New York in 1959. He and his colleagues organized their own synagogues and small study groups, which they called havurot, to further the work of the movement. With the cooperation of several rabbis who revered Kaplan as their teacher and who encouraged their congregations to affiliate with both the Reconstructionist and Conservative movements, the Reconstructionist movement began to grow. In 1954 they organized the Reconstructionist Federation of Congregations, which consisted of the SAJ and two other groups. As more affiliates joined the movement, the federation was reorganized as the Federation of Reconstructionist Congregations and Havurot (FRCH) in 1960, and it later was renamed the Jewish Reconstructionist Federation (JRF). Through the next few decades the organization grew gradually, adding a few dozen or more Reconstructionist groups around the United States and Canada. Some of Kaplan's followers were also instrumental in creating a Reconstructionist presence in Israel, founding a synagogue, Mevaqshe Derekh, in 1962.

The slow growth of the movement can be attributed to several other factors in addition to Kaplan's own reticence. Many rabbis who were his followers were also institutionally loyal to the Reform and Conservative movements and did not want to build new institutions. And Kaplan's ideology was intellectually challenging and rigorous, and consequently attractive to only a small number of Jews who were dissatisfied with traditional synagogue life. As the sociologist Charles Liebman pointed out in an influential study in the 1970s, Reconstructionism functioned as the folk religion of American Jewry. Kaplan's work described what American Jews actually believed and practiced but not the way Jews wanted their religious institutions to represent Judaism in America. While Reconstructionist ideology may have described the actual theology and behavior of American Jewry, most Jews preferred that their synagogues hold up an ideal that was not necessarily reflected in their own belief or practice.

FOUNDING A RABBINICAL COLLEGE. Although the Reconstructionist movement did not attract large numbers, congregations did form, and they sought leadership. Many Conservative rabbis were taught by Kaplan, but they were, like Kaplan, loyal to their institutional homes and were not willing to serve these new congregations. For Reconstructionism to grow as a movement, it was necessary to start a school to train its own rabbis. The Reconstructionist Rabbinical College (RRC) was founded in 1968 in Philadelphia by Ira Eisenstein who became the first president. While Kaplan generally opposed to the institutionalization of the Reconstructionist philosophy and was not involved directly in the school's creation, he did travel from New York to Philadelphia to teach a class once a week, and continued to do so until 1972 when he moved to Israel. The establishment of this school put Reconstructionism on the map as an independent denomination in the American Jewish community.

The timing for the creation of such an institution was excellent. Young men fleeing the draft considered this new kind of theological training. Young women influenced by women's liberation were another source of students for the new school. (Although the Reform seminary, the Hebrew Union College, ordained its first woman candidate a year before Sandy Eisenberg Sasso, the first woman RRC graduate, completed her training; when RRC admitted Sasso, no woman had yet been ordained.)

Eisenstein sought to provide a training program and curriculum that reflected the Reconstructionist ideology. The ordination of women followed Kaplan's principled belief in women's equality. Living in two civilizations meant that graduates of the RRC would also obtain doctoral degrees in religious studies from a secular institution. To that end the RRC was located in Philadelphia based on an arrangement for rabbinical candidates to take doctoral studies at the Department of Religion at Temple University. The curriculum at RRC was constructed around seminars that focused on the evolving history and culture of the Jewish people. The first year was devoted to the Bible, the second to the Talmud, the third to medieval studies, the fourth to modern studies, and the fifth to the contemporary world. Text study was considered ancillary to the history seminar. This distinguished studies at RRC from those at the Jewish Theological Seminary, where learning Talmud text was central. It also distinguished the program from Hebrew Union College, which focused more on practical rabbinical training. At RRC practical rabbinical training was limited. The ideal was that RRC graduates would be teacher-scholars who worked with small congregations on weekends while they pursued their academic studies as their primary occupation.

Whereas some of the early students were interested in pursuing academic careers, others were more interested in traditional careers as synagogue rabbis. The Reconstructionist congregations were also seeking leadership. During the first decade, the Ph.D. requirement was reduced to a master's degree, and students began pursuing master's degrees in education and social work to support their vocational interests. Some of the graduates began to assume leadership in Reconstructionist congregations, whereas others served Reform and Conservative congregations or took positions as Jewish communal service directors, institutional chaplains, principals of day schools, or chaplains on college campuses.

Slow growth continued through the 1970s. The first graduates organized the Reconstructionist Rabbinical Association (RRA) in 1974. The RRA welcomed not only graduates of the RRC but rabbis who were supportive of the Reconstructionist philosophy and movement. The addition of an organization of Reconstructionist rabbis enabled the Reconstructionist movement to mirror the tripartite organizational structure of the Reform and Conservative movements and gain legitimacy on the national level.

The Next Generation of Leadership. For many years Eisenstein served as editor of the *Reconstructionist* magazine, the head of the Reconstructionist Foundation, and the president of the RRC. In the early 1980s he began the process of retiring from these posts, having accomplished his goal of establishing the institutions of the Reconstructionist movement. Eisenstein's retirement in 1981 was soon followed by the death of Mordecai Kaplan, and a new era of leadership and change ensued.

In 1981 Ira Silverman succeeded Eisenstein as president of the RRC, and David Teutsch became the head of the Federation of Reconstructionist Congregations and Havurot. Neither man had a prior association with the Reconstructionist movement. Silverman had been the executive director of the American Jewish Committee, and Teutsch was a recently ordained Reform rabbi. Both had been strongly influenced by the newly developing Ḥavurah movement in Judaism. Although Reconstructionists had formed *ḥavurot* (small fellowships for study and celebration) as early as the 1950s, the Ḥavurah movement envisioned these small groups quite differently.

Ḥavurah Jews formed their groups as an alternative to synagogue membership. The groups usually consisted of young people in their twenties and thirties who came of age in the 1960s, singles and couples, some with small children. Many were educated in the Conservative movement's youth and summer programs and as a result were quite knowledgeable about Jewish texts and practice. While they were generally comfortable with traditional theology, they were critical of Jewish institutional life and uninterested in synagogues and rabbis, preferring intimate, participatory gatherings where the participants could alternate leadership roles. With the exception of an annual conference and newsletter, they opposed the creation of new institutions. They preferred celebrating and studying together in these small groups, and most such groups had no need for Jewish communal institutions. Teutsch and Silverman, on the other hand, saw the potential of the institutions of the Reconstructionist movement as a structure within which to harness the energy of Ḥavurah Judaism.

Important elements of the ideological orientation of Reconstructionism are compatible with Ḥavurah Judaism. Reconstructionism and Ḥavurah Judaism share an emphasis on peoplehood, community, and democracy; a passionate embrace of women's equality; an interest in developing new rituals and practices; and an informal and emotive worship style. However, Kaplan's theology and his unbridled enthusiasm for America were not of importance to the Ḥavurah orientation and would no longer be emphasized. This rejection of Kaplan's ideas was a source of tension between those who came to be defined as classical Reconstructionists and the next generation.

Silverman made many changes at RRC. He moved the campus from its small, urban home near Temple University to a much larger building in a northern suburb, and he added the nationally recognized scholars Hershel Matt, Arthur Green, Arthur Waskow, and Zalman Schachter-Shalomi to the faculty. The presence of Waskow and Schachter-Shalomi in particular created problems for the small movement. These men were the key leaders in what later became known as the movement for Jewish Renewal.

Like Reconstructionism and Ḥavurah Judaism, the Renewal movement emphasizes community, equality for women, and ritual innovation. But Renewal Judaism, particularly as defined by Schachter-Shalomi, is also neo-Hasidic with an emphasis on charismatic leadership and mystical union with God. Schachter-Shalomi taught that Jewish life is enriched by borrowing practices from other religious traditions, like Sufism, Yoga, and Native American spirituality. This emphasis created enormous tension and debate among Reconstructionists, who did not appreciate his mystical orientation. Waskow was controversial within the organized Jewish community for his outspoken political views, including his criticisms of the government of Israel. The Reconstructionist movement endured much censure for keeping him on the faculty during Silverman's presidency.

When Silverman resigned in 1986, Arthur Green became the president of RRC. Green was a scholar of Hasidism and a critic of Kaplanian theology. He shifted the curricular focus of the rabbinical program, ending the requirement for outside study. He replaced the requirement with an emphasis on traditional textual study, shifting the curricular focus away from historical critical study. He added a mandatory year of study in Israel and increased Hebrew language requirements in the curriculum. Green left in 1993 to resume his career as a university professor.

Teutsch resigned as the director of the Federation of Reconstructionist Congregations and Havurot to serve RRC as dean of admissions and then as executive vice president. He was chosen to follow Green as RRC president in 1993. Teutsch embarked on a program to fulfill the institutional mandate of the original Reconstructionist leaders, to make Reconstructionism a legitimate fourth denomination on the American Jewish scene. In his years as president, Teutsch initiated capital improvements, began master's degree and cantorial training programs, and solidified the financial base of the Reconstructionist Rabbinical College. But his most important contribution was as the editor of the five-volume prayer book series *Kol Ha-neshamah*, published over a ten-year period, 1989–1999.

This prayer book series replaced the old Reconstructionist prayer books that had been so controversial and popular in their time. *Kol Ha-neshamah* includes the classical Reconstructionist formulation of the prayers alongside traditional prayers and more contemporary innovations. By making these options available, the prayer books provided room for Reconstructionists of different theological orientations to feel welcome within the Reconstructionist community. The prayer books made a definitive statement that the Reconstructionist movement had a distinctive worship style and a contribution to make to Jewish religious life. For Reconstructionist congregations, *Kol Ha-neshamah* created a perception that even if congregations make different choices about which prayers to use, they are all part of one Reconstructionist community, reflecting Teutsch's emphasis on consensus building. The number of Reconstructionist congregations also expanded during this era, growing in number from several dozen to over one hundred as the movement placed greater emphasis on supporting congregational life.

BEYOND CLASSICAL RECONSTRUCTIONISM. The emphasis on creating liturgy linked the new era to the Reconstructionist past but also highlighted how spirituality became a dominant feature of contemporary Reconstructionism. Reconstructionist congregations welcome Jews who embrace Kaplan's theology of religious naturalism, or a cultural rather than religious orientation to Jewish life. But Reconstructionist Judaism has followed the contemporary Jewish trend toward a focus on the human-divine encounter that is predicated on a more traditional view of God as a partner in conversation. Reconstructionist Jews are not likely to believe that God responds directly to prayer or acts to reward or punish them in their lives. But they are likely to seek a relationship with God through prayer and meditation. Rabbinical students at RRC have mentors for their spiritual direction, and Reconstructionist synagogues sponsor healing groups, prayer circles, and Jewish meditation.

The emphasis on community, and in particular on inclusive community, became the other hallmark of Reconstructionist Judaism under Teutsch. Kaplan was a maverick, often at odds with the faculty at the Jewish Theological Seminary, espousing a theology that many perceived as heretical. Eisenstein also propounded an antiestablishment orientation, founding an upstart movement and school in an era when few new institutions were being developed in American Judaism. Following that pattern, contemporary Reconstructionist philosophy emphasizes welcoming Jews who see themselves as unwelcome in the rest of the Jewish community, particularly gay men, lesbians, and the intermarried. The Reform movement has also reached out to these groups, but the Reconstructionist movement has taken bold steps to welcome them without the institutional strength of the Reform movement. The RRA adopted patrilineal descent (accepting the child of a Jewish father and a non-Jewish mother as a Jew) and developed guidelines for welcoming intermarried couples in 1978, supporting a position taken by the Jewish Reconstructionist Foundation in 1968. The RRC under Silverman was the first seminary to admit openly gay and lesbian students, in 1984. The emphasis on inclusive community reinforced the classical Reconstructionist orientation toward acceptance of those who were alienated from Jewish life but took the idea in a new direction.

In 2002 Teutsch stepped down as president to direct the Center for Jewish Ethics at RRC. He was succeeded in the presidency by Dan Ehrenkrantz, the first RRC graduate to hold the position. With an alumnus of the rabbinical college in the highest leadership position for the first time and with the stabilization of its institutions, Reconstructionist Judaism claimed a place in the mainstream of Jewish life.

SEE ALSO Kaplan, Mordecai.

BIBLIOGRAPHY

Alpert, Rebecca T., and Jacob J. Staub. *Exploring Judaism: A Reconstructionist Approach.* New York, 1985. 2d ed. Wyncote, Pa., 1997. A basic introduction to the ideas of Reconstructionism.

Eisenstein, Ira, and Eugene Kohn. *Mordecai M. Kaplan: An Evaluation.* New York, 1952. Essays by the early leaders of the movement, including a brief autobiographical essay by Kaplan.

Goldsmith, Emanuel S., Mel Scult, and Robert M. Seltzer. *The American Judaism of Mordecai M. Kaplan.* New York, 1990. Essays chronicling Kaplan's contributions to Jewish life and the development of the Reconstructionist movement.

Kaplan, Mordecai M. *Judaism as a Civilization.* Rev. ed. Philadelphia, 1994. Kaplan's most influential work, this book describes his program for the reconstruction of American Judaism.

Kaplan, Mordecai M. *The Meaning of God in Modern Jewish Religion.* Rev. ed. Detroit, Mich., 1994. Kaplan's most accessible work, this book illustrates his theology through the cycle of the Jewish year.

Kaplan, Mordecai M., and Eugene Kohn, eds. *Sabbath Prayer Book.* Jewish Reconstructionist Foundation. New York, 1945. The prayer book that was burned by Orthodox rabbis for its iconoclastic prayers.

Kaplan, Mordecai M., Eugene Kohn, and Ira Eisenstein, eds. *The New Haggadah for the Pesah Seder.* Jewish Reconstructionist Foundation. New York, 1941. The original Reconstructionist Haggadah that focuses on the story of the people of Israel and not on God's liberatory intervention.

Levitt, Joy, and Michael Strassfeld, eds. *A Night of Questions: A Passover Haggadah.* Elkins Park, Pa., 2000. The new Reconstructionist Haggadah.

Liebman, Charles S. *Aspects of the Religious Behavior of American Jews.* New York, 1974. The first critical academic study of the Reconstructionist movement.

Scult, Mel. *Judaism Faces the Twentieth Century: A Biography of Mordecai M. Kaplan.* American Jewish Civilization Series. Detroit, Mich., 1993. A definitive Kaplan biography.

Teutsch, David A., ed. *Kol Ha-neshamah: Shabat Ve-hagim.* Translated by Joel Rosenberg. Wyncote, Pa., 1995. The Reconstructionist prayer book for the Sabbath and holy days.

Teutsch, David A., ed. *Kol Ha-neshamah: Mahzor Leyamim Nora'Im.* Translated by Joel Rosenberg. Wyncote, Pa.,

2000. The Reconstructionist prayer book for the high holy days.

Rebecca T. Alpert (2005)

REDEMPTION (from Lat. *redemptio,* derived from *redemere,* "to buy back") literally means liberation by payment of a price or ransom. The term is used metaphorically and by extension in a number of religions to signify the salvation from doom or perdition that is wrought by a savior or by the individual himself. Like the concepts of salvation, sacrifice, and justification, the concept of redemption belongs to a cluster of religious notions that converge upon the meanings of making good, new, or free, or delivering from sickness, famine, death, mortality, life itself, rebirth, war, one's own self, sin and guilt, anguish, even boredom and nausea. Redemption bears the closest conceptual kinship to salvation, sharing with it the intentionality of the need or desire to suppress an essential lack in human existence and to be delivered from all its disabling circumstances. This deliverance requires various forms of divine help, succor, or intervention to be achieved, which often secures for the believer an access to the *dunamis* of the spirit and to its outpourings, thereby leading to charismatic gifts. Redemption may be of God's or of humanity's doing. In a certain sense, redemption makes possible a recovery of paradise lost, of a primordial blissful state. In another sense, it points to new creation or ontological newness in the future. Creation is in many religions a highly sacrificial act that requires prior destruction, as in the dismemberment of Prajāpati's body in Hinduism or the thorough destruction of the shaman's body in northern Asian religions. These acts signify reconstruction-participation in divine fecundity or, respectively, multi-fecundation by the god Prajāpati, equivalent to partnership in the world. To be redeemed may mean to be divinized, either by the reenactment of the primordial creative act (preceded by a descent) or through the theandric, sacrificial action of a savior (*sōtēr*). In both cases, grace plays an important role; forgiveness also may be redemptive to the extent that it is provoked by, or calls for, repentance.

In Judaism, the psalmist's "God of my salvation" (Heb. *Go'el,* "redeemer," from the verb *ga'al,* used to refer to the redeeming of relatives from slavery, of property from foreign possessions, etc.) is a savior from distress and disaster, yet sometimes is himself in need of salvation (*salvator salvandus*). Says Job: "I know that my Redeemer liveth, and that he will at last stand forth upon the dust" (*Jb.* 19:25). And the Psalm: "Truly no man can redeem himself!" (*Ps.* 49:7). "Israel, hope in the Lord. He will redeem you from all your sins" (*Ps.* 130:7–8). In Judaism the concept of redemption is closely associated with repentance.

Liberation from exile (*Dt.* 15:15), restoration of freedom (*Is.* 62:12, 63:4), and the vision of a just society have always been signs of divine redemption for the people of Israel. Messianic Judaism projected the new heaven and the new earth, the final restoration and reintegration in peace and harmony of the people of Israel into a remote, utopian future, an ultimate event that, however, was to be preceded by apocalyptic, catastrophical changes; in this respect, the liberation of Israel from slavery in Egypt and the Sinai covenant are complementary to each other. Yet there are in the Old Testament elements of realized eschatology, of "redemption here and now," beliefs that were carried over by various sects (the Ebionites, Essenes, Nazarenes) into Christianity. While having an indubitable eschatological dimension, redemption cannot be reduced to it. And, the extent that it is involved with sacrifice, redemption shares with sacrifice either an active or a passive character. Redemption points to both liberation and repurchase.

This mystery of redemption is best illustrated in Christianity: Christ suffered on the cross in order to satisfy retributive justice. The meaning of redemption in the New Testament is chiefly that of the deliverance of humanity from sin, death, and God's anger, through the death and resurrection of Christ. A certain Greek influence makes itself felt through Paul, who took in the notion of ransom (*lutron,* from *luō,* "to loose") and thus pointed to the Greek custom of emancipating slaves through payment. "Jesus Christ gave himself for us, to ransom us from all our guilt, a people set apart for himself." (*Ti.* 2:14); and "that flock he won for himself at the price of his own blood" (*Acts* 20:28). Also in *1 Corinthians:* "A great price was paid to ransom you; glorify God by making your bodies shrines of his presence" (6:20); and "A price was paid to redeem you" (7:23).

Yet *lutron* must not be taken literally, as denoting a particular commercial price, a barter; it may mean any instrument of deliverance without there being a question of paying a ransom. (One must exercise prudence, as Thomas Aquinas did, and use the word *price* as that which is payable to God, not to the devil.) Going beyond the juridical notion of punishment and ransom, Paul emphasized the gratuitous aspect of redemption as an act of love: Christ's passion and death take on their supreme redemptive value due to the voluntary nature of the sacrifice, the free acceptance of suffering. Obedience to the divine Father's decree is the proof of love; *price* here equals liberating satisfaction, deliverance from the double slavery of sin and punishment. The exaltation of Christ and the sending of the Holy Spirit signify the decisive act of salvation history (*Heilsgeschichte*), which ushers in the new age proclaimed by the prophets (*Is.* 65:17). Works of satisfaction for sin—fasting, almsgiving, prayer, and works of mercy—all have redemptive value, not only for Christianity, but for other religions as well. Functional equivalents of the Judeo-Christian notion of redemption can be found in many other religions, especially in ethically oriented ones that stress the virtues of action. Salvation is of course the primary and essential goal. But to gain it many primitive cults devised severe and sometimes complicated rituals and ceremonies of redemption.

The Egyptian Pyramid Texts of 2400 BCE looked upon salvation as both a mystery and a technique. Osiris, slain by his brother Seth, is rescued by Isis and brought back to life by means of a secret and complicated ritual; he becomes the one savior from death and from its consequences. The redeeming efficacy of the mortuary ritual of embalming, in which the devotee is identified with the god, was believed to stem from Osiris' primordial experience, which, by being reenacted, made salvation possible.

The primitive vegetation-gods were redeemer gods who required the sacrifice of a symbolic part of the crop to save the whole and allow its use by humans. The agrarian sacrifices of the Romans were meant to appease the wrath of the gods and bring about plentiful crops. The sacrifice of an animal instead of a human was believed to cure illness. According to Ovid, the Romans sacrificed to the *manes,* or spirits of the ancestors. In Babylon, as in ancient Israel, the sacrifice of the firstborn or vicarious forms of it played an important role in the process of redemption by transmitting the tension and effecting the link between primordial time (*Urzeit*) and the eschaton (*Endzeit*). The idea that the sins of the fathers are visited upon the sons appears in the *Ṛgveda,* even before the notion of *karman* was unfolded. To be cleansed of paternal sin, the son has to break violently away from his past; this is viewed as a split between the ascetic and erotic parts of man, located respectively in a mental seed (above the navel), and a lower seed (below the navel). The alchemic function of yoga tends to transform animal instinct into soma, the mental type of seed. Blood functions here as mediator between semen and *soma.* The sacrifice of wild beasts as well as the taming of the cows are symbolic of this sought-for individual regeneration.

The Vedic sacrifice is more beneficial to the gods than to the individual; indeed, it strengthens the gods, but their prosperity in turn reverberates on humans; thus it is said that the gods nourish you if you nourish them. Agni, the god of fire and sacrifice, behaves like a demon and tries to burn everything down, but placated by sacrifice, he resurrects humankind from ashes. Hence sacrificial food is a bribe to the gods. In the post-Vedic, ascetic mythology, sacrifice becomes a two-edged sword, for Hindu mythology, even demons can be redeemed. The *bhakti* spirit generates entire cycles of its own, in which even apparently malevolent acts of God are regarded as being of ultimate benefit to humanity; hence the practice of a magic of friendship or of friendliness as means of redemption.

In Zoroastrianism, the redemption of humankind, viewed as both individual and universal eschatology, is linked with the hope of seeing that Ohrmazd, having been released from his entanglement with darkness and evil, emerges victorious from the war over Ahriman. The *haoma* ritual, a central act of worship, actualizes such a god-centered redemption. The theological trend in Sasanid Zoroastrianism exhibits a belief in the redemption of the world through the individual's efforts to make the gods dwell in his body while chasing the demons out of it. Mazdaism admits of a cosmical redemption besides individual deliverance, which is supposed to occur at the end of time at the hand of Saoshyant, the savior.

Buddism is a religion fully bent on salvation. In Mahāyāna Buddism the doctrine of the Buddha and the *bodhisattva* shows the great vows required by the spiritual discipline of enlightenment to be a devotion to the principle that the merit and knowledge acquired by the individual on this path be wholly transferred upon all beings, high and low, and not jealously accumulated for one's self. This "activity without attachment" involves a free restraint from entering upon *nirvāṇa,* exercised for the sake of one's fellow beings. In Japanese Buddhism the principle of salvation by self-power (*jiriki*) is contrasted by salvation through "another" (*tariki*), that is, through the power of the Buddha Amida. In Zen, devotion, fervor, and depth are all equally redeeming inner attitudes. Some types of mysticism have been categorized as redemptive: for instance, true gnosticisms rely on the dispelling of ignorance, as, for example, the gnosticism of *al-insanal-kamil* ("the perfect human being") and the dispensers of the individual's proper spirituality in Hinduism. Some others cannot be so categorized; Hasidic mysticism, for example, is self-redemptive, noneschatological, and nonmessianic.

There are three main ways of redemption in mystical religions: through illumination, as in Zen Buddhism, or through a dispelling of ignorance of the gnostic type, as in Islam; through membership and participation in the community (the Buddhist *saṃgha,* the Christian *ekklēsia,* the Muslim *ummah*); or, in secular types of religiosity by a redirection of the libido, a reordering of the soul's powers in a harmonious use of the personality, which may mean either a widening or a narrowing of consciousness.

Ancient Mexican religions knew a variety of redemptive types, among which was a form of plain self-redemption from diseases such as leprosy, cancer, buboes, or bubonic plague, and from spiritual sins such as falsehood, adultery, or drunkenness. The Aztec religion favors redemption from existence itself during one's very lifetime, the highest aim being identification with divinity. One example of such a "perfect redemption" (Joachim Wach) is the return of the high priest Quetzalcoatl after his beatification achieved by encounter with the divinity.

In African traditional religions, the need for redemption is expressed in myths of the Baganda peoples: terms such as *kununula* ("to buy back, to ransom, to redeem") and *kulokola* ("to save, to rescue") point to deadly misfortunes from which the spirits of the departed (*lubaale,* "deity of the below") may rescue one. Redemption is far more directed toward the reintegration of the cosmic, social, and political order in the present moment of the community than toward the afterlife, in spite of the general belief in immortality.

SEE ALSO Soteriology.

BIBLIOGRAPHY

Brandon, S. G. F., ed. *The Savior God.* Manchester, 1963.

Florovskii, Georgii Vasilevitch. *Creation and Redemption.* Belmont, Mass., 1976.

Knudson, Albert C. *The Doctrine of Redemption.* New York, 1933.

O'Flaherty, Wendy Doniger. *The Origins of Evil in Hindu Mythology.* Berkeley, Calif., 1976.

Przyluski, Jean. "Erlösung im Buddhismus." *Eranos-Jahrbuch* (Zurich) (1937): 93–136.

Schär, Hans. *Erlösungsvorstellungen und ihre psychologischen Aspekte.* Zurich, 1950.

Toutain, Jules. "L'idée religieuse de la rédemption." In *Annuaires de l'École des Hautes Études* (Sciences Religieuses), Section 5. Paris, 1916–1917.

Trinité, Philippe de la. *What Is Redemption?* New York, 1961.

Werblowsky, R. J. Zwi. *Types of Redemption.* Leiden, 1970.

New Sources

Arnault, Lynne. "Cruelty, Horror, and the Will to Redemption." *Hypatia* 18 (spring 2003): 155–189.

Ferdinando, Keith. *The Triumph of Christ in African Perspective: A Study of Demonology and Redemption in the African Context.* Carlisle, U.K., 1999.

Gorringe, Timothy. *A Theology of the Built Environment: Justice, Empowerment, Redemption.* New York, 2002.

Koenig, John. *The Feast of World's Redemption: Eucharistic Origins and Christian Mission.* Harrisburg, Pa., 2000.

Ruether, Rosemary Radford. *Women and Redemption: A Theological Study.* Minneapolis, Minn., 1998.

ILEANA MARCOULESCO (1987)
Revised Bibliography

REFERENCE WORKS

REFERENCE WORKS in the field of religion are extensive and of many types. A specific work may cover religion broadly or be limited to a particular religion or area in the study of religion. The titles listed in this article are primary reference works chosen to provide the reader with resources for definitions, background information, and bibliographies of basic works. Technical works such as concordances and lexicons utilized for translation and exegesis of specific religious texts are not included. The titles, with annotations, are arranged under two main sections: "General Religion" and "Specific Religions."

The General Religion section includes works that provide a broad view of religion or a concentration on at least two specific religions. The listed titles are arranged under five genres: "Atlases," "Bibliographies," "Dictionaries," "Encyclopedias," and "Websites."

Atlases present history and geography via a collection of maps and text. The titles found under this heading cover the biblical world as well as history and growth of the world's religions.

Bibliographies are works that provide the basic titles in a field. Hundreds of bibliographies have been published on specific areas of religion. Many are published as part of two primary bibliography series: the *ATLA Bibliography Series* (Metuchen, N.J.) and *Bibliographies and Indexes in Religious Studies* (Westport, Conn.). The books listed here offer broader coverage of multiple religions.

Dictionaries and Encyclopedias are two genres for which the distinctive lines are very often blurred. Typically, a dictionary is one volume long, contains short definitions of terms or proper names, and includes no, or only brief, bibliographies. Encyclopedias are thought of as comprehensive, multivolume sets including lengthy articles with bibliographies and cross-references. There are, however, many works which fit the description of one genre but carry the title of the other; examples are the one-volume *Encyclopedia of Cults, Sects, and New Religions* (Amherst, N.Y., 2002) and the six-volume encyclopedic work *The Anchor Bible Dictionary* (New York, 1992). For the purposes of this section of the article, irrespective of their titles, one-volume works are found under the heading of Dictionaries and multivolume works under Encyclopedias. Websites represent a fairly new but growing genre. Religious websites may function as bibliographies or guides pointing to other resources on the internet, or they may contain substantive content.

Websites represent a fairly new but growing genre. Religious websites may function as bibliographies or guides pointing to other resources on the internet, or they may contain substantive content. The websites listed are considered to be among the most stable and provide the best starting points for religious studies.

The Specific Religions section lists resources under the headings of five religions: Buddhism, Christianity, Hinduism, Islam, and Judaism. The titles included are primary works in the genres of the earlier section. The inclusion of these five particular religious traditions over others reflects the number of major reference works available rather than number of adherents to a particular group. There are many important religious groups and movements for which unique reference works are scant (e.g., Sikhism, Asian new religions), and information on them may be found more readily in the general resources.

Readers interested in additional resources listing reference works in religion will find numerous guides available. The following titles are basic starting points: *Critical Guide to Catholic Reference Books* by James Patrick McCabe, 3rd ed. (Englewood, Colo., 1989); the religion section of *Guide to Reference Books,* edited by Robert Balay, 11th ed. (Chicago, 1996); *Judaica Reference Sources: A Selective, Annotated Bibliographic Guide* by Charles Cutter, 3rd rev. and expanded ed. (Westport, Conn., 2004); *Recent Reference Books in Religion: A Guide for Students, Scholars, Researchers, Buyers, and Readers* by William M. Johnston, 2d ed. (Chicago, 1998); and *Theological and Religious Reference Materials* by G. E. and Lyn Gorman, 3 vols. (Westport, Conn., 1984–1986).

SEE ALSO Festschriften; Periodical Literature.

Bibliography

General Religion

Atlases

Aharoni, Yohanan, et al., eds. *The Carta Bible Atlas.* 4th ed. Jerusalem, 2002. Updates *The Macmillan Bible Atlas* (New York, 1993). Includes indexes to persons (new in this edition) and place names; key to maps arranged by books of the Bible; and chronological table (2800 BCE to 140 CE).

Baly, Denis, and A. D. Tushingham. *Atlas of the Biblical World.* New York, 1971. The best atlas for the geology and geography of Palestine in the context of the Middle East. Includes both Judaic and Christian perspectives on the biblical world, with some references to the beginnings of Islam. Chronologies span 3000 BCE to 700 CE. Excellent maps and color plates.

Fārūqī, Isma'īl Rāgī al, ed. *Historical Atlas of the Religions of the World.* Maps edited by David E. Sopher. New York, 1974. Text divided into religions of the past, ethnic religions, and the world religions of Buddhism, Christianity, and Islam. Each religion is presented in written text accompanied by photographs, maps showing its history and present distribution, diagrams, and chronologies.

Pritchard, James B., ed. *The Harper Atlas of the Bible.* New York, 1987. Extensive text and illustrations accompany the detailed color relief maps; covers time period of prehistory (150,000 BCE) to 135 CE. Editorial board comprised of outstanding biblical scholars.

Smart, Ninian, ed. *Atlas of the World's Religions.* New York, 1999. Provides geographical as well as historical understanding of the birth, growth, expansion, and interconnections of the world's religious groups. Generous array of color relief maps, photographs, and charts.

Survey of Israel (Tel Aviv), ed. *Atlas of Israel: Cartography, Physical and Human Geography.* 3d ed. New York, 1985. 40 sheets (maps). The land of Israel considered historically, sociologically, religiously, ethnographically, and economically. For more current information, compare the maps and numbers of this atlas with *Atlas Yisra'el he-hadash* (New York, 1995). Although nearly all of the text of this latter work is in Hebrew, it is similar in its arrangement to the 1985 work, so maps and numbers can easily be compared. The 1995 work also includes satellite photos.

Bibliographies

Barrow, John Graves. *A Bibliography of Bibliographies in Religion.* Ann Arbor, Mich., 1955. Comprehensive listing of separately published bibliographies from approximately 1500 to 1955. Arranged chronologically by date published; includes extensive index. Although dated, contains information not found elsewhere.

International Association for the History of Religions. *International Bibliography of the History of Religions.* 23 vols. Leiden, 1952–1973. Published annually. Index of scholarly studies of religion in general and the history of specific religions, exclusive of biblical studies and folklore. Articles listed were published in English, several European languages, and, to a small degree, other languages, and arranged by religious group. Continued by the *Science of Religion Bulletin,* quarterly (1976–1979), and *Science of Religion,* semiannual (1980–).

Melton, J. Gordon. *Religious Information Sources: A Worldwide Guide.* New York, 1992. Provides an overview of the field of religion and religions. Eight sections list resources on religion from general and theoretical considerations; religions of the world; issues in comparative religion; Christianity; and esoteric, New Age, and occult religion.

Turner, Harold W. *Bibliography of New Religious Movements in Primal Societies.* 6 vols. Boston, 1977–1992. Covers religious movements in primal societies, defined by the author as "those which arise in the interaction of a primal society with another society where there is great disparity of power or sophistication" (p. vii). Each volume covers a different geographic area: volume 1, Black Africa; volume 2, North America; volume 3, Oceania; volume 4, Europe and Asia; volume 5, Latin America; volume 6, the Caribbean.

Dictionaries

Brandon, S.G.F., ed. *A Dictionary of Comparative Religion.* New York, 1970. Short, initialed articles by British scholars include brief bibliographic references. Designed to discuss religions in proportion to their significance in human cultural history. Contains synoptic index of fifteen major religions as well as a general index. Important first reference tool.

Douglas, J.D., ed. *New Twentieth-Century Encyclopedia of Religious Knowledge.* Grand Rapids, Mich., 1991. An updated edition of the *Twentieth-Century Encyclopedia of Religious Knowledge* (1955). The 2,100 historical, biographical, geographical, and topical entries attempt to "present a retrospective view of one period in church and world history" (p. v). Related to the *New Schaff-Herzog Encyclopedia of Religious Knowledge* (see under Encyclopedias).

Ferguson, John. *Illustrated Encyclopedia of Mysticism and the Mystery Religions.* London, 1976. Brief articles on names, movements, and terminology of mysticism in its various forms. Extensive bibliography.

Fischer-Schreiber, Ingrid, et al. *The Encyclopedia of Eastern Philosophy and Religion: Buddhism, Hinduism, Taoism, Zen.* Edited by Stephan Schuhmacher and Gert Woerner. Boston, 1988. Introduction for the general reader to the terminology and doctrinal systems of Buddhism, Hinduism, Daoism, and Zen. Some illustrations.

Grim, Keith, ed. *Abingdon Dictionary of Living Religions.* Nashville, Tenn., 1981. Guide to the historical development, beliefs, and peculiarities of the variety of religions in the world today. Comprehensive, signed articles on the major religions; some include brief bibliographies. Well illustrated.

Hinnells, John R., ed. *A New Dictionary of Religions.* Oxford, and Cambridge, Mass., 1995. Brief entries on terms related to living religions; also includes information on ancient religions, astrology, magic, the occult, new religious movements, and secular alternatives to religion. Includes extensive bibliography.

Lewis, James R. *The Encyclopedia of Cults, Sects, and New Religions.* 2d ed. Amherst, N.Y., 2002. Brief entries on approximately 1,000 non-mainstream religious groups. Bibliographies included in some articles, as well as extensive general bibliography. Includes photographs of leaders of many of the groups.

MacGregor, Geddes. *Dictionary of Religion and Philosophy.* New York, 1989. Brief entries of basic terms, movements, and persons related primarily to the Judeo-Christian traditions. Bibliography.

Melton, J. Gordon. *Encyclopedic Handbook of Cults in America.* Rev. ed. New York, 1992. Begins with essay exploring the term *cult.* Entries on individual groups include basic information on the history, beliefs, practices, organization, controversies, membership, and primary and secondary bibliographic sources.

Melton, J. Gordon. *Encyclopedia of American Religions.* 7th ed. Farmington Hills, Mich., 2003. Introductory and historical essays trace the growth and development of religion in the United States and Canada, followed by 2,630 descriptive entries on religious bodies located primarily in North America. Includes bibliographies.

Parrinder, Edward Geoffrey. *Dictionary of Non-Christian Religions.* Philadelphia, 1973. Short entries, many with black and white photos and line drawings. Strongest on Hinduism, Buddhism, and Islam; Christianity and the Bible not treated. Basic general bibliography.

Rice, Edward. *Eastern Definitions: A Short Encyclopedia of Religions of the Orient.* Garden City, N.Y., 1978. Dictionary of terminology of major and minor Eastern religions. Some illustrations; no bibliographies.

Smith, Jonathan Z., ed. *The HarperCollins Dictionary of Religion.* San Francisco, 1995. Published in conjunction with the American Academy of Religion. Longer articles on major religious groups by area editors. Numerous illustrations.

Encyclopedias

Betz, Hans Dieter, ed. *Religion in Geschichte und Gegenwart: Handwörterbuch für Theologie und Religionswissenschaft.* 4th ed. Tübingen, Germany, 1998–. Six volumes (A–Q) as of 2004 (eight volumes projected). A major authoritative resource for the history of the study of religions in the West. Lengthy signed articles written from a liberal Protestant viewpoint. Includes maps, some in color. The earlier three editions remain useful as they reflect the changes in theological climate over time.

Cancik, Hubert, and Helmut Schneider, eds. *Brill's New Pauly: Encyclopedia of the Ancient World.* Leiden, 2002–. Three volumes (A–Cyp) as of 2004 (twenty volumes, with index, projected). Translation of *Der neue Pauly: Enzyklopädie der Antike* (Stuttgart, Germany, 1996–2003; 15 vols. plus index), an updated and expanded version of *Paulys Real-Encyclopaedie der Classischen Altertumswissenschaft* (1894–1980; 24 vols. plus supplements). Basic resource for Greco-Roman religion.

Doniger, Wendy, ed. *Mythologies.* 2 vols. Chicago, 1991. Translated and restructured edition of *Dictionnaire des Mythologies et des Religions des Sociétés Traditionnelles et du Monde Antique* (Paris, 1981). Organized by geographic or cultural area. Signed articles, many with bibliographies. Numerous black and white photographs.

Freedman, David Noel, ed. *The Anchor Bible Dictionary.* 6 vols. New York, 1992. Nearly 1,000 contributors prepared the 6,200 signed entries, many with bibliographies. Attempts to treat all biblical subjects and topics. Scriptural references based on the Revised Standard Version. Also available on CD-ROM.

Hauck, Albert, ed. *The New Schaff-Herzog Encyclopedia of Religious Knowledge.* 13 vols. New York, 1908–1912. Signed articles, usually brief. Based on Herzog and Hauck's *Realencyklopädie für Protestantische Theologie und Kirche* (Leipzig, Germany, 1896–1913); major revision and expansion to introduce later and non-Germanic materials. Most useful for entries on persons, ancient religions, and extensive bibliographies. Comprehensive index. Available on the internet at http://www.ccel.org/s/schaff/encyc/. Supplemented by the *Twentieth Century Encyclopedia of Religious Knowledge* (Grand Rapids, Mich., 1955; 2 vols.) and *New Twentieth-Century Encyclopedia of Religious Knowledge* (Grand Rapids, Mich., 1991).

Hillerbrand, Hans J., ed. *The Oxford Encyclopedia of the Reformation.* 4 vols. New York, 1996. Covers the religious life and "related societal phenomena" of sixteenth-century Europe. Four hundred and fifty scholars contributed 1,200 signed articles, many with bibliographies. Numerous biographical entries. Includes maps and synoptic outline.

Melton, J. Gordon, and Martin Baumann, eds. *Religions of the World: A Comprehensive Encyclopedia of Beliefs and Practices.* 4 vols. Santa Barbara, Calif., 2002. Includes approximately 200 essays on the major religious traditions and the religious history and environment in each country of the world, plus 2,000 shorter articles on religious groups and communities throughout the world. Arranged alphabetically by topic and includes a comprehensive index.

Van Huyssteen, J. Wentzel Vrede, ed. *Encyclopedia of Science and Religion.* 2 vols. New York, 2003. Contains more than 400 signed entries with bibliographies on topics that highlight the intersections and interrelationships between science and religion. Includes synoptic outline and annotated bibliography of significant resources.

Vigouroux, Fulcran. *Dictionnaire de la Bible.* 5 vols. Paris, 1899–1928. Supplement, 1928–. Thirteen volumes as of 2004. Lengthy signed articles by French biblical scholars writing from a Roman Catholic perspective. The supplement has extensive, signed articles on the religion of the Bible and the ancient world. Includes bibliographies.

Young, Serinity, ed. *Encyclopedia of Women and World Religion.* 2 vols. New York, 1999. A helpful reference work for first orientation and rich bibliographic sources on the fast-growing field of women's and feminist studies in religion. At present no comparable reference work on gender studies or men's studies in religion has been produced.

Websites

Cowan, Douglas E., ed. "Religious Movements Home Page." Available from http://religiousmovements.lib.virginia.edu/. Begun in 1996 as a project by a religious studies professor at the University of Virginia, now developed by an editor-in-chief and monitored by an advisory board. Contains profiles of religious movement groups, cult group controversies, course materials, and links to religious freedom and religious broadcasting sites. "Each profile offers basic demographic and background information, a summary of beliefs, discussion of controversial issues (when appropriate), links to important websites about each group, and select print bibliographies" (homepage).

Gresham, John L. "Finding God in Cyberspace: A Guide to Religious Studies Resources on the Internet." Available from http://sim74.kenrickparish.com/contents.htm. Begun in 1994 and continually updated, this was one of the first guides to religious resources on the internet. Categorizes religion sites on the internet by type (print, people, digital, and teaching resources) and content (academic disciplines, religious traditions, and religion and cyberspace).

"Ontario Consultants on Religious Tolerance." Available from http://www.religioustolerance.org/. Organized in 1995. Includes essays, historical information, belief statements, definitions, statistics, news feeds, and reading lists on various belief groups, particularly those that have been targeted for discrimination.

Thursby, Gene L. "Religion Religions Religious Studies: Information and Links for Study and Interpretation of Religions." Available from http://www.clas.ufl.edu/users/gthursby/rel/. Resources arranged under major headings: Religious Traditions (historical as well as alternative/new religions); Religion—Modernity—Beyond (Freedom *of* Religion, Freedom *from* Religion, etc.); Religious Experience (Cultural Diversity, Mysticism, Psychology, Transpersonal); Religious Studies Programs; Research and Teaching Resources. Includes news sources and additional reference sources.

"Virtual Religion Index." Available from http://religion.rutgers.edu/vri/index.html. Developed and maintained by the Religion Department of Rutgers University. Organized by general topics, including the major religious traditions and general topics such as "Academic Sites," "Anthropology and Sociology," "Ethics and Moral Values," and "Philosophy and Theology."

Specific Religions

Buddhism

Buddha Dharma Education Association. "BuddhaNet: Buddhist Information and Education Network." Available from http://www.buddhanet.net/. Created and maintained by the Buddha Dharma Education Association of Sydney, Australia. Contains listings of study guides, e-books, image files, meditations, and activities for children; historical and biographical information; a worldwide directory of Buddhist sites and masters; and links to other web resources.

Buswell, Robert E., Jr., ed. *Encyclopedia of Buddhism.* 2 vols. New York, 2004. Aims to serve as the definitive reference work on Buddhism and Buddhist perspectives on religious issues. More than 250 international scholars contributed signed articles, which include short bibliographies. Numerous illustrations, some in color.

Chitkara, M.G., ed. *Encyclopaedia of Buddhism.* New Delhi, India, 1961–. Six volumes (A–Minayett) as of 2004 (ten volumes projected). Massive work on all aspects of Buddhism: names, literature, history, and religious and moral aspects and concepts. Most articles signed; some include bibliographies.

Ciolek, T. Matthew, et al. "Buddhist Studies WWW Virtual Library: The Internet Guide to Buddhism and Buddhist Studies." Available from http://www.ciolek.com/WWWVL-Buddhism.html. Edited by Dr. T. Matthew Ciolek, Australian National University, Canberra, and others. Clear table of contents directs users to numerous internet resources, including websites, electronic texts, maps, and bibliographies.

Keown, Damien. *A Dictionary of Buddhism.* Oxford, 2003. Succinct entries on concepts, practices, persons, places, schools, and texts. Appendices include maps, a pronunciation guide, a guide to Buddhist scriptures, and a chronology.

Prebish, Charles S. *Historical Dictionary of Buddhism.* Metuchen, N.J., 1993. Introductory materials include an essay on history and doctrine, introduction to Buddhist scriptures, and a chronology of Buddhist history. Entries provide short definitions of biographical, geographical, and topical subjects. Offers a 98-page bibliography. Also published as *The A to Z of Buddhism* (2001), which does not include the bibliography.

Christianity

Cross, F. L., ed. *The Oxford Dictionary of the Christian Church.* 3d ed. New York, 1997. The 6,000 entries (most with bibliographies) cover history, doctrines, persons, and ecclesiastical terms. The latest edition reflects the many changes in the Christian church due to Vatican Council II, feminist theology, liberation theology, and the globalization of Christianity.

Di Berardino, Angelo, ed. *Encyclopedia of the Early Church.* 2 vols. New York, 1992. Translated from the Italian *Dizionario Patristico e di Antichità Cristiane* (Rome, 1990). Covers archaeological, philosophical, linguistic, theological, historical and geographical topics related to Christianity of the first to the eighth centuries. Nearly half of volume 2 is composed of a synoptic table, maps, photographs, and line drawings. A French translation, *Dictionnaire Encyclopédique du Christianisme Ancien* (Paris, 1990), is also available.

"Ecole Initiative." Available from http://www2.evansville.edu/ecoleweb/. Rich content related to church history: translations of Judeo-Christian and Islamic primary sources to 1500; short essays on significant persons and topics, from Peter Abelard to Zosimus; longer essays on major topics and figures; images of iconography and religious art; and a timeline with geographic cross-index (limited entries). Sections are hyperlinked to each other. Also contains a bibliography of sources used in the articles on the page, a list of contributors with short listings of credentials and links to their contributions to the site, and a list of web pages related to church history.

Ente Per L'Enciclopedia Cattolica. *Enciclopedia Cattolica.* 12 vols. Città del Vaticano, 1948–1954. Major pre-Vatican Council II encyclopedia treating the life, thought, history, and general relationship of the Catholic Church to other religions and systems of thought. Numerous biographical entries and illustrations.

Fahlbusch, Erwin, et al., eds. *The Encyclopedia of Christianity.* Grand Rapids, Mich., 1999–. Three volumes (A–O) as of 2004 (five volumes projected). Updated and augmented translation of the third edition of *Evangelisches Kirchenlexikon* (Göttingen, Germany, 1986–1997), a standard German Protestant work on the teaching of the Christian churches. Endeavors to reflect global, ecumenical, sociocultural, and historical contexts of Christianity at the opening of the twenty-first century. Includes demographic and religious statistics for the six major geographic areas as well as individual countries. Signed articles include bibliographies. No illustrations.

Ferguson, Everett, ed. *Encyclopedia of Early Christianity.* 2d ed. 2 vols. New York, 1997. Over 1,200 signed articles include bibliographies and cover persons, places, doctrines, and movements of the early church—from the life of Christ to the seventh century. Includes photographs, line drawings, maps, and chronologies.

Ganzer, Klaus, and Bruno Steimer, eds. *Lexikon für Theologie und Kirche.* 3d ed. 11 vols. Freiburg, Germany, 1993–2001. The standard German encyclopedia, written from a Roman Catholic viewpoint; covers a variety of religions, faiths, and practices. Authoritative signed articles, with extensive bibliographies.

Hillerbrand, Hans J., ed. *Encyclopedia of Protestantism.* 4 vols. New York, 2004. Provides latest scholarship on the historical and theological dimensions of Protestantism. Articles on persons, movements and events, creeds, denominations, theological and social issues are signed and include brief bibliographies. Also includes an appendix of statistical tables.

"Internet Christian Library." Available from http://www.iclnet.org/. Provides links to Christian mission organizations and resources; general Christian resources, including Christian internet tools, mail-based services, Christian college sites, alphabetical and subject listings of Christian websites, electronic newsletters and journals, electronic bulletin boards, and usenet groups; online Christian texts; and directories of Christian organizations.

Jedin, Hubert, ed. *Atlas zur Kirchengeschichte.* 3d ed. Freiburg [im Breisgau] and New York, 1987. The best atlas for church history. Outstanding worldwide coverage in numerous clear maps and charts; seventy pages of textual commentary includes bibliographies. A French edition, *Atlas d'histoire de l'eglise: les eglises chrétiennes hier et aujourd'hui* (Paris, 1990), and Italian edition, *Atlante Universale di Storia della Chiesa: le Chiese Cristiane Ieri e Oggi: 257 Carte e Schemi a Colori* (Rome, 1991), are also available.

Klauser, Theodor, ed. *Reallexikon für Antike und Christentum.* Stuttgart, Germany, 1950–. Twenty volumes (A–K) as of 2004 (forty volumes projected). Lengthy authoritative articles by leading scholars on all aspects of antiquity and Christianity; extensive bibliographies.

Krause, Gerhard, and Gerhard Müller, eds. *Theologische Realenzyklopädie [TRE].* 36 vols. plus Abkürzungsverzeichnis (glossary and abbreviations of periodicals indexed) and index. Berlin, 1976–2003. Major reference work interpreting theology broadly. Signed articles, often monographic in length; extensive international bibliographies. Includes maps (some fold-out) and illustrations.

Marthaler, Berard, ed. *New Catholic Encyclopedia.* 2d ed. 15 vols. Farmington Hills, Mich., and Washington, D.C., 2003. Includes short, signed articles with bibliographies and numerous photographs, maps, and tables. Treats not only traditional Catholic topics, but also movements, institutions, religions, philosophies, and scientific trends that impinge on Catholic thought and life. Numerous biographical entries (excludes living persons, except for Pope John Paul II). Electronic version available through the *netLibrary* collection.

Piepkorn, Arthur Carl. *Profiles in Belief: The Religious Bodies of the United States and Canada.* 4 vols. New York, 1977–1979. Extensive articles on the history, polity, and thought of the major Christian bodies. Massive documentation; lengthy bibliographies. Covers Roman Catholic, Old Catholic, and Eastern Orthodox (vol. 1); Protestant Denominations (vol. 2); Holiness and Pentecostal (vol. 3); and Evangelical, Fundamentalist, and Other Christian Bodies (vol. 4).

Van Der Meer, F., and Christine Mohrmann. *Atlas of the Early Christian World.* London, 1958. Covers the early church from circa 30 BC to 700 AD in pictures, text, and color maps.

Hinduism

Global Hindu Electronic Network. "Hindu Universe." Available from http://www.hindunet.org/home.shtml. Developed by Global Hindu Electronic Networks(GHEN), a project of the Hindu Students Council, Boston, Massachusetts. Includes lists of Hindu resources, electronic texts, tourism information (India), glossary, and links to some commercial sites for products related to Hinduism.

Himalayan Academy, Hawaii "Hindu Resources Online." Available from http://www.hindu.org/. Public service portal site.

Klostermaier, Klaus K. *A Concise Encyclopedia of Hinduism.* Oxford, 1998. Designed to provide balanced information on the "people and places, scriptures and philosophical systems, art and architecture, mythology and history" (p. vii). Appendices on the philosophical schools, Hindu scriptures, principal schools of Vedānta, and the eightfold practice of Yoga.

Sullivan, Bruce M. *Historical Dictionary of Hinduism.* Lanham, Md., 1997. Short entries that cover the significant terms, doctrines, events, persons, places, and texts related to the various aspects of Hinduism. The introductory pages include a chronology of the history of Hinduism and a survey essay on its history, doctrines, and community life. Includes an extensive bibliography, mostly of English works. Electronic version available through the *netLibrary* collection. Also issued as *The A to Z of Hinduism* (2001), which does not include the bibliography.

Smart, Ninian, ed. *Hindu World.* 2 vols. New York, 1968. Dictionary of Hinduism; content drawn from secondary sources. Includes bibliographies.

Islam

Ahlul Bayt Digital Islamic Library Project. "al-Islam.org." Available from http://www.al-islam.org/. Maintained by the Ahlul Bayt Digital Islamic Library Project, an internet-based group with members from throughout the world. Includes electronic books, texts, and multimedia resources, with particular emphasis on the Twelver Shīʿah Islamic school of thought. Arabic and Kiswahili interfaces are available to link to resources on the site specific to those languages.

Al Fārūqī, Ismaʿil R., and Lois Lamyāʾ al Fārūqī. *The Cultural Atlas of Islam.* New York, 1986. Describes Islamic culture and civilization in text, maps, photographs, chronologies, tables, and line art.

Esposito, John L., ed. *The Oxford Encyclopedia of the Modern Islamic World.* 4 vols. New York, 1995. Includes 750 signed articles, written by over 450 authors, arranged by category: Islamic thought and practice, Islam and politics, Muslim communities and societies, Islam and society, Islamic studies. Each article includes a bibliography. Synoptic outline of contents in last volume.

Gibb, H. A. R., et al., eds. *The Encyclopaedia of Islam.* New ed. 11 vols. plus supplement. Leiden, Netherlands, 1960–2003. Signed articles by authorities on every aspect of Islam: history, religion, science, geography, and so on. Excellent bibliographies; comprehensive cross-referencing. Separate volumes for glossary, proper names, subjects, and indexes. Also available on CD-ROM.

Godlas, Alan. "Islam, Islamic Studies, Arabic, and Religion." Available from http://www.uga.edu/islam/. Created and maintained by Professor Alan Godlas, Department of Religion, University of Georgia, and administered by the University of Georgia Virtual Center for Interdisciplinary Studies of the Islamic World. Contains "information for the study of Islam, religion, Qur'ān, hadith, the Sunnah, Shi'ism, Sufism, Islam in the modern world, Muslim women, Islamic art, architecture, music, history, and Arabic."

Joseph, Suad, ed. *Encyclopedia of Women and Islamic Cultures.* Leiden, 2004. One volume (on "Methodologies, Paradigms, and Sources") as of 2004 (five volumes projected). Described by the publisher as "an essential reference work for students and researchers in the fields of gender studies and Middle Eastern and Islamic Studies, as well as scholars of religion, history, politics, anthropology, geography, and related disciplines." Each volume covers specific topics: "Methodologies," "Paradigms and Sources," "Family, Law, and Politics," "Family, Body, Sexuality, and Health," "Economics, Education, Mobility, and Space," and "Practices, Interpretations, and Representations."

Kennedy, Hugh. *Historical Atlas of Islam.* Leiden, Netherlands, 2002. Parallel text in English and French, map legends in English. Includes eighty-five color relief maps which document pre-Islamic Arabia through the mid-twentieth-century presence of Islam throughout the world. CD-ROM version contains pdf files of maps from the printed edition.

Martin, Richard C., ed. *Encyclopedia of Islam and the Muslim World.* 2 vols. New York, 2004. Articles of varying length written by 500 scholars, arranged alphabetically by topic; thematic outline included in front matter. Includes approximately 170 photographs, drawings, maps, and charts, with glossary of commonly used terms. Written for the general reader.

McAuliffe, Jane Dammen, ed. *Encyclopaedia of the Qur'an.* Leiden, Netherlands, 2001–. Three volumes (A–O) as of 2004 (five volumes projected). Projected to have nearly 1,000 signed articles with bibliographies. Attempts to treat important figures, concepts, places, values, actions, and events within or related to the Qur'ān. Includes black and white illustrations.

Judaism

Barnavi, Eli, ed. *A Historical Atlas of the Jewish People.* New York, 1992. Historical essays, arranged chronologically beginning with the twentieth to sixteenth centuries BCE, which put the history of the Jewish people in "spatial context" (preface). Contents page is at the back of the book, preceded by index and glossary. Color maps and photographs.

Hebrew College Online. "Shamash, The Jewish Network." Available from http://www.shamash.org/. Project of Hebrew College (Newton Centre, Mass.) Online. Highly rated network of Jewish information and services; hosts the portal "Judaism and Jewish Resources," created and maintained by Andrew Tannenbaum.

Neusner, Jacob, Alan J. Avery-Peck, and William Scott Green, eds. *The Encyclopedia of Judaism.* 3 vols. Supplement, 2002–. New York, 1999. Published in collaboration with the Museum of Jewish Heritage, New York. Comparative approach to Judaism. Most articles are signed and include bibliographies and notes. Includes maps, numerous sections of photographs, and other illustrations. Volume 3 includes a general index and an index of textual references. Also issued as *Encyclopaedia of Judaism* (Leiden, 2000). Supplements includes additional articles on related topics on Judaism.

"Princeton University Library Jewish Studies Resources." Available from http://www.princeton.edu/~pressman/jewish.html. Provides links to databases (e.g., *Rambi*), libraries/archives/research centers, websites, Israel sites, news sources, and listservs.

Roth, Cecil. *Encyclopaedia Judaica.* 16 vols. Jerusalem, 1974. Comprehensive, standard reference work for the area of Jewish studies. Updated by yearbooks through events of 1992. Entries are initialed and include bibliographies. Includes 8,000 photographs, plus maps, charts, diagrams. CD-ROM version (Shaker Heights, Ohio, 1997) includes updated articles, text of the yearbooks, audio and video recordings, and special collections of images and photographs.

Werblowsky, R. J. Zwi, and Geoffrey Wigoder, eds. *The Oxford Dictionary of the Jewish Religion.* New York, 1997. An updated and expanded work based on the *Encyclopedia of the Jewish Religion* (New York, 1966), also edited by Werblowsky and Wigoder. The short, scholarly entries cover the history, persons, practices, and beliefs related to the Jewish religion; most are signed and include brief bibliographies. Serves as a companion to *The Oxford Dictionary of the Christian Church* (Oxford, 1997).

Wigoder, Geoffrey, ed. *The New Encyclopedia of Judaism.* New York, 2002. Revised and expanded edition of Wigoder's *The Encyclopedia of Judaism* (New York, 1989). Concise, scholarly articles (unsigned) on aspects of Jewish religious life and development, with special attention given in this edition to liturgical aspects of Judaism and the place of women. Includes an annotated bibliography of basic works on Judaism; numerous illustrations, some in color; and index. Aimed at the general reader.

Edgar Krentz (1987)
Martha S. Alt (2005)
Roberta A. Schaafsma (2005)

REFLEXIVITY is a potent and popular concept; it is also a problematic and paradoxical one. The term is problematic because it is so popular today; it is used in several different disciplines to refer to a wide variety of mental, verbal, and performative phenomena that nonetheless share a family resemblance. Reflexivity is a paradoxical concept because the type of self-referential activity—consciousness of self-consciousness—that it denotes involves the epistemological paradox so well discussed by Gregory Bateson (1972, pp. 177–193) and Rosalie L. Colie (1966, pp. 6–8), in which the mind by its own operation attempts to say something about its operation—an activity difficult both to contemplate and to describe without conceptual vertigo and verbal entanglements.

In the most general sense, the terms *reflexive, reflexivity,* and *reflexiveness* "describe the capacity of language and of thought—of any system of signification—to turn or bend back upon itself, to become an object to itself, and to refer to itself" (Babcock, 1980, p. 4). This is anything but the rarefied activity it might at first seem, for reflexivity has come to be regarded as a *sine qua non* of human communication.

When, for example, Kenneth Burke defines humanity in the first chapter of *Language as Symbolic Action* (1966), he describes as "characteristically human" this "'second-level' aspect of symbolicity or 'reflexive' capacity to develop highly complex symbol systems about symbol systems, the pattern of which is indicated in Aristotle's definition of God as 'thought of thought,' or in Hegel's dialectics of 'self-consciousness'" (p. 24).

The adjective *reflexive* first appeared in English in 1588; it was used as early as 1640 to refer to the capacity of mental operations to be "turned or directed back upon the mind itself." Regarding things grammatical, *reflexive* has been used since 1837 to describe pronouns, verbs, and their significations that are, as the *Oxford English Dictionary* says, "characterized by, or denote, a reflex action on the subject of the clause or sentence." With reference to mental operations, the adjective is frequently confused and used interchangeably with its near synonym, *reflective.* To be reflexive is to be reflective; but one is not necessarily reflexive when one is reflective, for to reflect is simply to think about something, but to be reflexive is to think about the process of thinking itself. In its present usage, *reflection* does not possess the self-referential and second-level characteristics of reflexivity. Such was not always the case, and the terminological confusion arises because Locke, Spinoza, and Leibniz, as well as subsequent philosophers, used the term *reflection* to denote the knowledge that the mind has of itself and its operations, in contrast to mere "thinking" about matters external to the mind itself.

A related confusion occurs with the term *self-consciousness,* which denotes primary awareness of self rather than the consciousness of self-consciousness characteristic of reflexivity—what Fichte described as the "ability to raise oneself above oneself," in contrast to "vain self-reflection." The latter phrase raises yet another terminological tangle and, in this instance, a negative connotation that must needs be dispensed with: the association of reflexivity with narcissism and solipsism. By definition, both involve self-reference and self-consciousness, but both are forms of "vain self-reflection" without any second-level awareness of that self-absorption. Unlike reflexivity, neither narcissism nor solipsism partakes of epistemological paradox, ironic detachment, or, hence, the ability to laugh at oneself. Reflexivity involves what Maurice Natanson defines as "methodological solipsism," that is, the examination of all experience from the perspective of the self-aware ego, in contrast to "metaphysical solipsism," which claims that the individual is the sole reality (1974b, pp. 241–243). As Merleau-Ponty pointed out in a discussion of modern painting in *Signs* (Evanston, 1964), reflexivity "presents a problem completely different from that of the return to the individual." Rather, like Husserl's concept of the transcendental ego, it involves the problem of knowing how one thinks and communicates, of "knowing how we are grafted to the universal by that which is most our own" (p. 52).

In Western philosophy, reflexivity has been recognized at least since Socrates as an inevitable if not always welcome companion of thought. A human being is not only an animal who thinks, but who also—certainly if a philosopher—thinks about thinking, and thinks of him or her self as a thinker: "to be a questioner in reality is to locate oneself as part of the questionable and also as the source of questions" (Natanson, 1974a, p. 233). Philosophers have tended to explain this paradoxical state of affairs in two related ways. The first and most familiar is "the two-in-one that Socrates discovered as the essence of thought and Plato translated into conceptual language as the soundless dialogue *eme emauto*—between me and myself" (Arendt, 1977, p. 185). While the participants in this dialogue have been variously named—me and myself, I and me, self and other, self and soul, "naked self" and "selfsame," I and Thou—philosophers from Socrates to Arendt have similarly described the dynamics of thinking as an exchange between an experiential or perceiving self and a reflexive or conceptual self. In all cases, the viewpoint of the latter is regarded as a higher form of consciousness, and it is frequently regarded as transcendent, if not explicitly divine. Hence, the second mode of explaining reflexivity and its seeming transcendence of human symbol systems—its thought-trains by which one could take one's way out of the world—is to equate it with the divine. To give but a few examples: In Platonic dialectic, a movement toward the abstract was equated with a movement toward the divine; Aristotle similarly defined God as "thought of thought"; Augustine's reflexive or "selfsame" self is the mind illuminated by God; and, for Kant and Hegel, ultimate meaning, if not divine, is nonetheless described respectively as "transcendental reflection" and "absolute knowledge." While acknowledging this affinity between reflexivity and the higher forms of consciousness in religion, philosophers since Hegel have argued that reflexivity is beyond any particular system of belief, that "thinking is equally dangerous to all creeds" (Arendt, 1977, p. 176).

More recently, phenomenological philosophers such as Schutz and Merleau-Ponty have "grounded" reflexivity by conceiving of it as embodied institution tied to temporality and situation, rather than as transcendental constitution. Far from being a philosopher's prerogative, reflexivity so conceived is nothing more nor less than the process of rendering experience meaningful— the inevitable and necessary "framing" that everyone engages in. Phenomenological discussions of reflexivity as a series of exchanges between subject and object, or between individual consciousness and social reality, recall not only the Socratic conception of thought as internal dialogue but also the conception of the self as reciprocal, dialogical, and reflexive as formulated by American pragmatic philosophers and psychologists, notably Peirce, James, Mead, and Cooley.

In *Mind, Self, and Society* (1962), social psychologist George Herbert Mead defines reflexiveness as "the turning back of experience of the individual upon himself," asserting that "it is by means of reflexiveness that the whole social process is brought into the experience of the individuals involved in it" and that "reflexiveness, then, is the essential condition, within the social process, for the development of mind" (p. 134). Mead's concept of "reflexiveness" as a dialogue between a personal "I" and a social "me" is closely related to Cooley's formulation of the "looking-glass self" and to Jacques Lacan's more recent description of "le stade du miroir," for Mead indicates that the achievement of identity involves mirroring, or the assumption of a specular image; the individual "becomes a self in so far as he can take the attitude of others and act toward himself as others act" (p. 171). The self, therefore, "as that which can be an object to itself, is essentially a social structure" (p. 140); or, in Charles Sanders Peirce's terms, it is a semiotic construct: "When we think, then, we ourselves, as we are at that moment, appear as a sign" (*Philosophical Writings of Peirce,* New York, 1955, p. 233). Thus described, the self, like the world, is a text embedded in and constituted by (as well as constitutive of) interconnected systems of signs, of which the most important and most representative is language.

While Peirce asserts that reflexivity is perforce semiotic, subsequent semioticians, linguists, and philosophers have argued that *all* systems of signification are inherently and necessarily reflexive. As Fredric Jameson summarizes in *The Prison House of Language* (Princeton, 1972), "Every enunciation involves a kind of lateral statement about language, about itself, and includes a kind of self-designation within its very structure" (p. 202). Because of its descriptive usefulness, the metalinguistic or metacommunicative model has become pervasive in discussions of all forms of reflexivity. It would be wrong, however, to regard linguistic self-reference as either the cause or the explanation of reflexivity. As Robert Nozick has recently pointed out, reflexive self-knowledge is a basic phenomenon without which neither cognition nor communication is possible, and it is pointless to argue which comes first (1981, p. 82).

Both the idea that reflexivity consists of the self representing itself to itself and the notion that all forms of representation involve self-reference or reflexivity are present in the plural in the concepts of collective representations and cultural performances, as defined and discussed by sociologists and anthropologists since Durkheim. In *The Elementary Forms of the Religious Life* (1915), Durkheim defined collective representations, such as a clan's mythic ancestor, as forms in which the group "represents itself to itself," implying that the collective symbolization process as expressed in myths and rituals includes within its operations consciousness of itself. In recent decades, Claude Lévi-Strauss has argued not only that myths are sociocultural metacommentaries but that all myth is "meta-" insofar as its implicit if not explicit subject is the emergence of language or communication. In his earlier work on ritual and ritual symbols, Victor Turner (1974) suggested that liminal periods are reflexive moments when society "takes cognizance of itself" and reflects on the order of things through symbolic disordering, through the "analysis and recombination of the factors of culture into any and every possible pattern" (p. 255). In later works (1979, 1982, 1984), Turner argued that *all* genres of cultural performance (ritual, myth, theater, narrative, games, etc.) are instances of plural reflexivity because they are self-critiques and reflections *upon,* rather than simply reflections *of,* the structures and strictures of the everyday world. Clifford Geertz (1973) has similarly asserted not only that religion is a reflexive cultural system that provides "models of" and "models for" self and society but that illicit, secular cultural performances such as Balinese cockfights are stories that a group "tells itself about itself" (pp. 93, 448). While not all collective representations—verbal, visual, and performative—are religious, it is no surprise that many of them are, for as Robert Bellah states in *Beyond Belief* (New York, 1970), religion has been "the traditional mode by which men interpreted their world to themselves" (p. 246)—the "pattern of patterns" or epitome of plural reflexivity.

If, as has already been implied, it is difficult to discuss reflexivity without discussing religion, the reverse is equally true. Regardless of whether one considers religion as a system of belief and body of texts or as praxis and experience, one is concerned with the interpretation of the moral complexities and paradoxes of human social and individual life—thus, with signs about signs, with reflexive self-reference. In myths, humans not only render an account of themselves and their world, they testify to the power of language to make a world and to create gods. In rituals and sacred symbols, humans embody and reenact these comprehensive ideas of order, and every time sacred words and deeds are retold and represented, these primal interpretations are interpreted and criticized yet again.

Quite apart from the metadiscourse about religion—explicit reflexivity—that has developed in the great religious traditions in the form of systematic theology, religious history, and textual hermeneutics, every religious system is implicitly reflexive. The communication of the highest truths and the most sacred order of things is invariably accompanied by the subversive self-commentary of *aporiae* (liminal disorder in such diverse forms as Ndembu monsters, Sinhala demons, Zen *koans*, Pueblo clowns, Midrash tales, and Christ's parables). Such ambiguous and paradoxical elements generate reflexive processes that redirect thoughtful attention to the faulty or limited structures not only of thought, language, and society but of religion itself (cf. Colie, 1966, p. 7).

In addition to this ineluctable reflexivity of religion's collective representations and plural expressions, many singular religious practices are explicitly reflexive. Contemplation, meditation, prayer, and confession all have in common a withdrawal from the world and a bending back toward the self. Frequently, the reflexive character of such practices is marked by their literal or figurative association with mirrors, with *specula,* reminding us not only that mirrors reflect the essence of things and are crucial to the achievement of identity (Fernandez, 1980, pp. 34–35) but that "as in mirror images, self-reference begins an endless oscillation between the thing itself and the thing reflected, begins an infinite regress [or progress]" (Colie, 1966, p. 355). Such mirroring frequently occurs as well in language itself, for careful analysis of sacred discourse reveals a markedly higher proportion of metalinguistic verbs in contrast to everyday speech.

In sum, reflexivity is not a consequence of social complexity or the degree of religious articulateness; it is an essential and inevitable dimension of all religious experience. The power of religious consciousness that humans keep trying to explain is probably not its prescriptive, descriptive, or explanatory force but its reflexiveness—religion offers a system of interpretation of existence that is itself subject to interpretation, and that is infinitely compelling.

Bibliography

Arendt, Hannah. *The Life of the Mind,* vol. 1, *Thinking.* New York, 1978. Arendt's final work is a rich, challenging analysis of humanity's mental activity; it brings together and reflects upon the major insights of the Western philosophical tradition into the nature of thought and its reflexive and dialogic structure.

Babcock, Barbara A., ed. *Signs about Signs: The Semiotics of Self-Reference.* Special issue of *Semiotica* 30 (1980). An interdisciplinary collection of essays that examine reflexive forms and processes in a variety of genres and cultural traditions, with an introduction that summarizes the meanings and uses of reflexivity.

Bateson, Gregory. "A Theory of Play and Fantasy." In *Steps to an Ecology of Mind.* New York, 1972. This seminal formulation of the paradoxical metacommunicative or reflexive frame essential to all forms of play has inspired much subsequent work on metacommunication and framing, notably Erving Goffman's *Frame Analysis* (New York, 1974).

Colie, Rosalie Littell. *Paradoxia Epidemica: The Renaissance Tradition of Paradox.* Princeton, 1966. This stunning and comprehensive study of paradox is especially important for illuminating both the reflexive self-reference of paradoxes and the paradoxical nature of self-referential operations.

Fernandez, James W. "Reflections on Looking into Mirrors." *Signs about Signs,* special issue of *Semiotica* 30 (1980): 27–40. An especially important discussion of the African use of mirrors and a speculation on the ritual and symbolic significance of this magical object cross-culturally.

Geertz, Clifford. *The Interpretation of Cultures.* New York, 1973. A selection of this interpretive anthropologist's most important essays on the concept of culture, which are notable for their analysis of cultural systems, institutions, symbols, and performances as reflexive forms and processes.

Hofstadter, Douglas R. *Gödel, Escher, Bach: An Eternal Golden Braid.* New York, 1979.

Hofstadter, Douglas R., and Daniel C. Dennett. *The Mind's I: Fantasies and Reflections on Self and Soul.* New York, 1981. Like Hofstadter's *Gödel, Escher, Bach,* this is an important and unconventional meditation on the paradoxical and reflexive nature of thought processes and on the problem of self and self-consciousness.

Mead, George Herbert. *Mind, Self, and Society* (1934). Edited by Charles W. Morris. Reprint, Chicago, 1963. This edition of Mead's lectures presents the outlines of his system of social psychology and his classic formulation of the self as reflexive, as a social construct.

Natanson, Maurice. *Phenomenology, Role, and Reason: Essays on the Coherence and Deformation of Social Reality.* Springfield, Ill., 1974. (Cited in text as Natanson, 1974a.) This book and Natanson's article cited below are summaries of the major issues in social phenomenology, including the central conception of reflexivity.

Natanson, Maurice. "Solipsism and Sociality." *New Literary History* 5 (1974): 237–244. (Cited in text as Natanson, 1974b.)

Nozick, Robert. *Philosophical Explanations.* Cambridge, Mass., 1981. This speculation on philosophical issues contains a superb chapter, "The Identity of the Self," and the best single, summary discussion available of reflexivity.

Singer, Milton. "Signs of the Self: An Exploration in Semiotic Anthropology." *American Anthropologist* 82 (September 1980): 485–507. The single most important discussion of Peirce's conception of the self as semiotic and reflexive.

Turner, Victor. *Dramas, Fields, and Metaphors: Symbolic Action in Human Society.* Ithaca, N.Y., 1974. This collection contains several essays that summarize Turner's view of liminality and liminal symbols and their implicit reflexivity.

Turner, Victor. *Process, Performance, and Pilgrimage: A Study in Comparative Symbology.* New Delhi, 1979. Contains several essays that extend the notion of liminality beyond tribal ritual and examine the public and plural reflexivity of cultural performances.

Turner, Victor. "Dramatic Ritual/Ritual Drama: Performative and Reflexive Anthropology." In *A Crack in the Mirror: Reflexive Perspectives in Anthropology,* edited by Jay Ruby, pp. 83–98. Philadelphia, 1982.

Turner, Victor. "Liminality and the Performative Genres." In *Rite, Drama, Festival, Spectacle: Rehearsals toward a Theory of Cultural Performance,* edited by John J. MacAloon, pp. 19–41. Philadelphia, 1984. Like Turner's "Dramatic Ritual/Ritual Drama," this essay expands upon the concepts of liminality and reflexivity and examines a variety of genres of cultural performance as instances of and occasions for metasocial commentary, for public and plural reflexivity.

Turner, Victor, ed. *Celebration: Studies in Festivity and Ritual.* Washington, D.C., 1982. An interdisciplinary collection of essays that explore the reflexivity of human celebrations through the medium of ceremonial objects.

New Sources

Adams, Matthew. "The Reflexive Self and Culture: A Critique." *British Journal of Sociology* 54 (June 2003): 221–239.

Gumperz, John, and Stephen Levinson. *Rethinking Linguistic Relativity.* New York, 1996.

Kripal, Jeffrey John. *Roads of Excess, Palaces of Wisdom: Eroticism and Reflexivity in the Study of Mysticism.* Chicago, 2001.

Lockie, Robert. "Relativism and Reflexivity." *International Journal of Philosophical Studies* 11 (Sept. 2003): 319–340.

Schirato, Tony. "Bourdieu's Concept of Reflexivity as Metaliteracy." *Cultural Studies* 17 (May 2003): 539–554.

Smart, Barry. *Facing Modernity: Ambivalence, Reflexivity, and Morality.* Thousand Oaks, Calif., 1999.

BARBARA A. BABCOCK (1987)
Revised Bibliography

REFORM. In everyday usage, the term *reform* generally connotes advance, progress, modernization. In discussions within religious groups, the use of this word is not so limited. It occurs in the most varied contexts, with reference to a wide range of individual and social questions, as well as with regard to specifically religious matters. Proposals for reform may be directed at the actions, or even the attitudes, of a relatively few persons within a particular faith-community. In this case, unless the change that is advocated would entail either a conflict with the law of the entire community or a violation of public decency—as might, for example, a restoration of animal sacrifices—the change at issue should be of no concern to those persons outside the particular group involved. On the other hand, the reform that is urged may pertain to the entire society. In many modern situations, however, the larger society encompasses members of other religious groups and persons of no religious attachment for whom the proposed reform may seem totally undesirable and unwarranted. If this is the case, and if the reform would affect the lives of persons other than those who propose it, as would, for example, the recriminalization of abortion in the United States, then the proposed reform should become a matter of public concern, properly to be decided by public procedures.

The examples just touched on may seem to suggest that, as applied to religion, the term *reform* is always used to refer to a return to older, more traditional ways of acting. In some cases, this is so, but far more often the reform that is advocated is seen as a step forward. Its acceptance would further progress toward the realization of an ideal future; rather than signal a return to the past, it would usher in ways that never were, in actual time and place. Every world religion has called often for the moral reform of individuals, both among its own followers and among those others too unregenerate to heed its saving message. The content of the morality thus imagined has deepened with the complications of human culture and will, no doubt, change even further as the social order changes. Often, too, the political and economic conditions of a particular time and place affect the customary morality and evoke a religiously grounded demand for reform. Less often, perhaps, but with reasonable frequency, a call from within has demanded that the religion set its own house in order.

RELIGIOUS CONCERN FOR MORAL REFORM. Religious sanctions designed to enforce the morality of a particular tribe or other small group almost certainly preceded the religious proclamation of a universal morality. But once the idea of universal morality had been broached, some time during the first millennium before the common era (the "axial age"), it was inevitable that the sovereignty claimed for a moral ideal would become as universal as the ideal itself. Just as tribal cults had maintained their own tribal moralities as sacrosanct, so the universal religions all proclaimed the sacred, and often the revealed, character of their own versions of universal morality. The Ten Commandments of Judaism and Christianity enshrine one version of such a religiously sanctioned universal moral code. Other forms, some even older, are to be found in China, in India, in Iran, in Mesopotamia, and in Egypt. These codes differ in detail but are alike in their claim to universality.

The most important issue is not which of these codes came first, nor even whether the codes had their origin in religious belief or were merely adopted by the various religious groups. The point is that, once they were accepted as partial statements of the religiously sanctioned rules of behavior, one aspect of the proper function of religion was to try to assure that these rules of moral behavior were observed, and to call attention to any failure to observe them. In this way universal morality added an important accent to the universality of religious ideas, while the emphasis on morality tended to become, increasingly, the raison d'être of religious life. This transformation of tribal religion into universal moral religion had what might be termed its apotheosis in the Zoroastrian tradition of Iran. There, the divine forces of good in the universe, led by the god Ahura Mazdā (Pahl., Ōhrmazd), are in eternal conflict with the comparably divine forces of evil in the universe, under the rule of Angra Mainyu (Pahl., Ahriman). The moral life of each person, if good, helps the cause of Ahura Mazdā; if evil, it aids Angra Mainyu and his cohorts. Thus individual reform has not only a moral but also a metaphysical or transcendental part to play in the age-old struggle between good and evil. In the end, during the final era of the universe, Zoroastrians believe that Ahura Mazdā will triumph. Thus, although Zoroastrianism has dualistic strains, it is not formally a theological dualism. Through its offshoot, the religion of the solar deity Mithra, Zoroastrianism's theology of moral strife reached the Occident and, through the adherents of Mithraism in the Roman legions, had some influence on both Judaism and Christianity.

In some religions, as in the tradition of Confucianism in China, the moral emphasis has been so dominant as to virtually eliminate concern for the theistic aspects of religious life. This is true also of the classical (Theravāda, or Hīnayāna) schools of Buddhism, which, although they arose in India, have remained especially vital in Southeast Asia (Sri Lanka and Myanmar). A like emphasis on the moral and social aspects of Christianity appears from time to time; it has given rise to such predominantly sectarian groups as the Society of Friends (Quakers) and to "religious humanist" offshoots such as Unitarian Universalism. In some aspects of liberal Judaism (Reform Judaism) a similar moral emphasis has been manifest. In their major developments, however, both Christianity and Judaism have remained too theocentric to permit moral concern to become the autonomous core of religious belief and practice. Relations among people, the central theme of the moral life, have in Western religious thought been considered for the most part as relations mediated through the presence of divinity.

Consequently, the reform of the moral lives of individuals has been treated in Western religions as a means toward entering into a right relation with God, rather than as an end in itself or as a matter of right relations with one's fellow humans. This indirectness of moral consciousness does not imply greater or lesser morality in the Western world than in the Eastern. It indicates only that moral reform has been preached in Western religions on ulterior grounds. As the prophet Micah insisted, God demands of his human creations that they act justly, love mercy, and walk in ways of humility, not before priests, kings, or presidents, but only with their God (*Mi.* 6:8). Micah, like his predecessor Amos, his contemporary Isaiah, and many of his successors among the prophets, including Jesus, affirmed the centrality of moral reform among religious values over against the priestly emphasis on cultic ritual. Prophetic reform called for the moral regeneration of relations among people as the sovereign road to a revivified relation with God.

In more recent times, as a consequence especially of development in the social sciences of psychology, sociology, and anthropology, religious leaders in many faiths have come to realize that an absolute, universal moral code is by itself not enough to ensure higher levels of morality. Principles like the Golden Rule, whether in its negative ("Do not do unto others . . .") or affirmative ("Do unto others . . .") version; codified sets of rules, like the Ten Commandments; even the Kantian categorical imperative ("Act as if the maxim from which you act were to become through your will a universal law") all are far too general to give guidance for the majority of specific moral problems. In addition, their very form of expression as rules or laws is foreign to the moral context in which they are proposed as guides.

The reform of individual morality that is sought in current advanced religious thought is one grounded not in a formal rule but in a concern for one's fellows that takes into account all the individual and cultural factors that arise in each moral situation. General rules and laws are the business not of morality but of legislatures and courts of law. In ethical discourse, "right" and "wrong" must yield place to "good" and "bad." As Henry Thoreau wrote, in the mid-nineteenth century: "Absolutely speaking, Do unto others as you would that they should do unto you is by no means a golden rule, but the best of current silver. An honest man would have but little occasion for it. It is golden not to have any rule at all in such a case" ("Sunday," in *A Week on the Concord and Merrimack Rivers*). To be good is to be "good for" somebody or something other than oneself.

Thus the reform of morality is not to be achieved by the passage of more laws, by the criminalization of more acts. Making more laws only makes more lawbreakers. Criminalizing more acts only makes more criminals. A truly religious understanding of morality would recognize that the causes of immorality are rooted in the home and family, in the educational experiences of the streets as well as the schools, in the popular entertainments, in the world of work and of play, indeed in all the social world that is the matrix within which a child grows to an adult. As these roots differ from child to child, so the development of child into adult will differ. If healthy shoots are to develop, if society is to harvest healthy fruits, then society must care for the roots. This recognition is the reason for religious reform's more recent tendency to place greatest emphasis on social change, so that the soil may be prepared for the growth of a better humanity in the future.

RELIGIOUS CONCERN FOR SOCIAL REFORM. When the universal religions are in complete accord with the social orders in which they are embedded, they are clearly not serving their proper function within society. They are then functioning as tribal, not as universal, religions. An important part of the obligation and of the value of any religion to society is its ability to make critical judgments of the social order from a larger and more transcendent perspective than the society can adopt in judging itself. The religious view of society and its institutions should properly be *sub specie aeternitatis* (from the point of view of eternity). In immediate, local, and temporal terms, any social order may seem to be doing very well; viewed, however, from the perspective of the larger religious demand, the demand for righteousness, it may be in very bad condition. It has been noted many times that some of the kings of ancient Israel who had the longest and, from the secular point of view, the most successful reigns are dismissed in the biblical books of *Kings* with the terse judgment that they "did evil in the sight of the Lord." Religion does not exist to glorify the current social order but as a spur to its reform.

In many periods of history, in many parts of the world, those who spoke for the religion of the place and time have been keenly aware of their obligation to criticize the social status quo and to promote its reform. The modes in which they have carried out this obligation have varied greatly. Some, especially in the Buddhist and the medieval Christian world, have done so by setting up communities of monastics whose "discipline" exemplified an approximation to the envisaged ideal form of social life. It is a measure of the humanness of human beings that these ideal communities themselves frequently needed to be reformed.

Even within these monastic communities there were differences in the degree of separation from the evils of the surrounding social world. Some monasteries were a base from which the monks made sorties into the secular world to teach, to preach, and, most importantly, to exemplify, as nearly as possible, the ideal they represented. Other monastic communities were content with complete withdrawal; this type of community served as a retreat from the evils of the social world, a passive exemplar rather than an active witness. A beautiful example of this type is described by Philo Judaeus of Alexandria in his treatise *On the Contemplative Life.* In the Buddhist tradition, in its early form, the ideal of the arhat, or saint, although available to anyone was thought most readily achievable by those who pursued the monastic life, that is, by those who exemplified a reformed society rather than those who preached it. On the other hand, among Protestant Christians, the impulse to social reform has tended to be expressed in many different forms of worldly intervention; the most usual, other than charitable relief, has been the formation of special bodies established for the promotion of specific reforms of great urgency, as, for example, antislavery groups in the eighteenth and nineteenth centuries, temperance groups in the nineteenth and twentieth, and "honest government" groups in every time and place.

The methods pursued by dedicated religious adherents of social-reform causes have ranged from prayer services dedicated to enlisting divine aid to the most militant forms of civil disobedience. Men and women of all religious groups have not hesitated to risk imprisonment, even execution, in their struggle to achieve social reforms that they conceived as sanctioned by their religious commitments. It must be noted, of course, that such social reforms are not always "liberal." Highly conservative and even reactionary positions are frequently defended ardently on religious grounds. Examples of such retrograde "reforms" are commonplace: the retention of the caste system in India; the persistent maintenance of an all-male priesthood in Roman Catholicism; the agitation, in many parts of the United States, for so-called voluntary prayer in public schools. Because it is of the essence of a religious position that it be a strong commitment, religiously motivated advocates of a social reform tend to become, for better or for worse, dominated by a single issue.

If religiously motivated social reform is to have a significant impact upon society in the late twentieth century, it cannot concentrate on a limited range of such matters. In the process of bearing witness to the changes that are necessary in the complexly woven fabric of modern life, many of the older simplicities must be abandoned, however reluctantly. For example, just one twentieth-century development, that of air travel, has wrought great change, bringing all the parts of the earth into relatively close proximity. Long-distance travel and its resultant interactions have become commonplace, not only between residents of one country or one continent, but between people of very different backgrounds and customs from all over the globe. The number of cross-cultural contacts has increased phenomenally within less than half a century. The more mobile of American men and women, as well as a great many American youths, have the opportunity to experience life and to meet people in countries where prevailing customs are different from those in the United States. Similar groups from other countries can now visit the United States and get to know some of its people.

It is inevitable that these multitudes of travelers will soon begin to make critical comparisons of their countries' social orders and institutions with those of countries they have visited. They will not at first be considering larger theoretical questions of politics or economics. They will look at the actual day-to-day lives of people. Their consciousness in such matters will rapidly become a world consciousness. Religious reformists must be prepared to adapt their visions of directions and goals to the concerns of this new kind of "international" public mind. Even as individual churches have had to expand the horizons of their awareness to include the concerns of a denomination, so denominations must broaden their thought to the interlocked concerns of the human world.

Religious Concern for Religious Reform. Religions are not only faiths; they are also churches. That is, they not only express a deep feeling for the mutual interrelation of humankind and the universe but are also organized groups of people who come together on specified occasions for specific purposes, groups of people who relate to the transcendent, to each other, to outsiders, to animals, and to nature in traditional, ritualized ways. In addition to those members who come together periodically for celebratory or ceremonial purposes, most of these organized groups have a professional corps of leaders with specialized educational (sometimes merely vocational) preparation and qualifications. These leadership corps go under various names (priests, ministers, rabbis, etc.). In some cases, they constitute a separate class within the larger society, such as the *brahman* caste in Hinduism, and they may have still, though in a reduced form in modern times, certain privileges or prerogatives, sometimes called "benefit of clergy."

While some internal reforms in religious life have been inaugurated by members of the nonprofessional group, the "laity," in most cases both the need for reform and the program for putting the reform into practice have been first recognized and then expressed by members of the professional class, the "clergy." It is scarcely to be wondered at that this should be so—that those whose lives and careers are centered in the institution, the "church," and who are, as a general rule, more fully trained for the understanding of matters of religion, should be those who see that old words, old ways, or old rules no longer serve the faith as they presumably did at an earlier time. What does surprise is that so many of the clergy, seeing this, have called loudly for reform of their institution, placing its future and its purposes above their own convenience and comfort. On the one hand, the clergy as a body is composed of those who have most to gain from not troubling the waters, from not disturbing institutional stability; on the other hand, most of the prophetic calls have come from members of the clergy and have pointed emphatically to the need for reform, for change, and, by implication, for instability.

Because there are these two internal strains in each major religious tradition, and perhaps also in the thinking of many individual members of the clergy, religions do change—although, as a rule, slowly and very cautiously. The heretic of one age is gradually transformed into the saint of a later time; the philosophy of Thomas Aquinas was forbidden reading to Franciscans for many years after his death, and some of his ideas were officially regarded as dubious even at the end of his life. But within a century he was proclaimed a saint, and his philosophy became the dominant intellectual system within the Roman Catholic church. Similarly, the roundness of the earth was acknowledged in practice long before it was accepted in religious cosmology. Step by cautious and hesitant step, reluctant at every move, religious bodies ultimately accept new moral and social ideas and are even led, in the end, to *novellae* (new theological formulations) and to revised religious practices derived from the new ideas. Characteristically, however, these novelties, on first proposal, are greeted with dismay, even with horror. The earliest formulators of the novelties may be silenced, denounced, unfrocked and expelled from their orders, even excommunicated, as were the founders of many of the more extreme Christian sects of the Middle Ages and as was so well-known a figure as Martin Luther in the early modern period. During the Protestant Reformation itself John Calvin's Geneva burned Michael Servetus at the stake for his antitrinitarian views.

Both Christianity and Judaism, in earlier times, tended to be more akin to tribal religions than to universal religions, and therefore harsher in their treatment of dissenters. In the modern Western world, most religious leaders are more ready to recognize that silencing the thinker does not silence the thought. Toleration of religious reform and religious reformers has come to be the norm in the Western world in the past two centuries. Intolerance, however, has again begun to flourish in the Middle East, in the form of religio-political strife. The resurgence of such conflicts raises doubts whether the message of religious toleration has roots as deep as they seem to be, whether in fact mutual toleration has become as widespread as was once believed. It is surely evident that there is a need for the reform of interreligious relations, as well as for maintaining within each religion a climate hospitable to the idea of reform.

Religious Reform and Traditional Practice. There is no aspect of religion that is more important to the members of any religious group than the traditional practices to which they adhere. Truly, religious practice is the context in which the child that is latent in every adult comes closest to self-revelation. Psychologists maintain that what people learn in early life persists longest in their memories, and the traditional practices associated with every religion are a large part of what holds the attention of young children. Some traditional practices are peculiar to a particular family and remain in use within that family for many generations. Others are traditions of a national group and are carried with the members of that group wherever they may migrate. The most persistent practices are those handed down from the founders of a religious movement or from its great leaders. Some may even be held over from the religious tradition that preceded the one by whose members it is now practiced, as some pre-Buddhist traditions have persisted in the Tibetan form of Buddhism, or as earlier Arab pagan practices were preserved in Islam. Even today, despite its explicit prohibition by the hierarchy of the Orthodox Greek church, a pre-Christian fertility rite (now called Pyrovasia), in which young men jump through a fire as a magical way to ensure good crops, is still performed in Thrace, usually with the connivance of local priests. A very similar practice is associated with the Holi, a spring festival in popular Hinduism. This festival, too, is thought to antedate the Hindu religion, which would explain why it is found only in popular Hinduism and not in the formal religion. Thus rituals and other religious practices precede, in many cases, the religions in which they are preserved; theology comes to people later in their lives and is accepted with little questioning because it comes wrapped in the haze of familiar, traditional rites and practices.

Because these rituals are so deeply embedded in people's consciousness at the most impressionable period of their lives, it would be most desirable if the advocates of religious reform could consistently retain the ancient ritual traditions. In some instances it is possible to do so without being false to the reforms advocated. There is no great virtue in withholding the experience of Christmas celebration from a Christian child on the grounds of the historical falsity of the date, or because snow in the vicinity of Bethlehem is impossible, or because there is no astronomical report of so bright a star as that in the Christmas story. Christmas is itself often reinterpreted today as the Christmas version of a far more ancient festival of the winter solstice, developed by Roman Christians as an alternative to the Mithraic Birthday of the Invincible Sun (Dies Natalis Solis Invicti), celebrated on the day in the Roman calendar equivalent to December 25. To the Roman Christian rites of celebration there were added, as Christianity spread into northern Europe, a variety of elements more suitable to the climate of that region. Easter, too, must be recognized as a christianized and spiritualized version of the widespread festivals celebrating the arrival of spring. To acknowledge the earlier ancestry of these Christian festivals adds a universal dimension to their significance; it does not diminish their Christian poetic and symbolic value. Similarly, it is possible to take many of the festivals of other religions and, while retaining all or most of their attractive ceremonial, to refine their traditional basis. Reforming religion does not necessarily imply destroying its poetry or its myth; it requires only recognizing the difference between myth and actuality, between poetry and history.

There are other instances, however, in which ancient traditions have already had to yield to later and higher ideals, and still others in which the advocates of reform must continue the struggle to change traditional practice. The age-old Hindu practice of *satī*, immolating widows on the funeral pyres of their husbands, was forbidden by British rulers as early as 1829 in those parts of India that they controlled. In the "native states," enclaves ruled by native princes, the traditional *satī* was maintained for a time but was gradually eliminated. The theological rationale (perhaps originally an economic rationale) could not be maintained against the higher sense of women's personhood that has developed in modern Indian society. Hindu scholar-priests found no difficulty in reinterpreting the Vedic texts by which the old practice had been justified. Similarly, the Bible, the basic text of Judaism and Christianity, still presents animal sacrifice as a ritual practice divinely commanded and to be routinely carried out by the priests. Both religions have long since given up the practice literally commanded and have replaced actual sacrifice with the symbolic sacrifice of almsgiving. Other biblical injunctions, too, such as the "levirate" obligation, in which the brother of a man who died childless married the widow of his deceased brother in order to sire a son to perpetuate the dead brother's name (*Dt.* 25:5-10), have been either totally abandoned or replaced by a merely symbolic substitute.

Reform is a process that is never finished. Those who carried forward the reforms that have been mentioned, and others like them, may have thought that they had made all the changes that were necessary. But because human knowledge is always increasing, there is no point at which people can say that there is nothing left for them to learn and that all their beliefs are final. It is a continuing part of the religious reformers' obligation to carry on in their own time the unending struggle to renew tradition by bringing features of the religious systems into line with the most advanced knowledge and the most modern sensibilities of their time. There is no reason, for example, why the struggle to achieve parity for women should not, in the present age, be pursued in every religion, even though the achievement of this goal would require the overthrow of certain traditional practices and beliefs. In any area of life in which traditional religious practice comes into conflict with modern sensibility there is a frontier for religious reform. It might well be extremely difficult to eliminate the exclusively masculine language that has become traditional in speaking of God in the monotheistic faiths. But as the role of women in the formal services of these religions is increased, and as certain ritual formulas, such as ". . . who hast not made me a woman," are forced out of the prayer books by insistent and repetitive agitation, the development of a gender-neutral language for religious practice should be possible.

These examples suggest that there are two directions to follow in achieving reform of traditional religious practice. The easier of the two, for all concerned, is to reinterpret, in the light of modern understanding, the theoretical doctrine or historical principle upon which a practice is based, and thus to modify the meaning that the practice has for people today without forcing them to give up the practice itself. Wherever it is possible to do so, the goal of religious reform should be to change meaning without eliminating well-loved practice. Where this is impossible, however, where the practice itself involves a kind of behavior unacceptable in the modern world, reform must be total; the practice and the principle on which it rests must be uprooted, not merely reinterpreted. To be modern, religions must not require either practices that fail to conform to the present-day moral ideas of their environing cultures or beliefs that contradict the best knowledge available. If religions fail in either of these respects, they require reform.

SEE ALSO Morality and Religion; Revival and Renewal; Tradition.

BIBLIOGRAPHY

Most general discussions of religion concentrate on antiquity rather than modernity, on tradition rather than reform. An exception worthy of mention is a collection of essays, *Religious Movements in Contemporary America,* edited by Irving I. Zaretsky and Mark P. Leone (Princeton, 1974). Although limited in geographic scope, these articles present interesting theoretical material on marginal sectarian groups, chiefly among minorities. For our purposes, it is more useful to look at works that view particular major religious traditions in their modern development.

Hinduism

In addition to the useful collection of essays by Hindu scholars, *The Religion of the Hindus,* edited by Kenneth W. Morgan (New York, 1953), Philip H. Ashby's perceptive discussion in *Modern Trends in Hinduism* (New York, 1974) looks at recent trends with a discriminating eye. More recent, and more of a textbook, is *Hinduism: A Cultural Perspective* (Englewood Cliffs, N.J., 1982) by David R. Kinsley, an excellent resource for the reader with little previous knowledge of Hindu religion.

Buddhism

Buddhism, in its many forms, has received a great deal of attention; perhaps the most useful starting point is a collection of essays, *Buddhism in the Modern World,* edited by Heinrich Dumoulin and John C. Marald (New York, 1976). *The Buddhist Religion,* 3d ed. (Belmont, Calif., 1982), by Richard H. Robinson and Willard L. Johnson, is an extremely informative work, valuable for its broad perspective. *Buddhism: The Light of Asia* (Woodbury, N.Y., 1968) by Kenneth Chen is especially valuable for its material on Buddhism in China. Similarly valuable for Southeast Asia is Kenneth Perry Landon's *Southeast Asia: Crossroads of Religion* (Chicago, 1969). Buddhism and other religions in China are the subject matter of Wingtsit Chan's *Religious Trends in Modern China* (New York, 1969). Comparable concerns in relation to the religions of Japan are presented by Joseph M. Kitagawa in *Religion in Japanese History* (New York, 1966).

Islam

Wilfred Cantwell Smith's *Islam in Modern History* (1957; Princeton, N. J., 1966) presents a sensitive and sympathetic study by a Western scholar. Unfortunately, it was published too early to take into account contemporary Islamic fundamentalism, which must still find its historian. Smith's *Modern Islam in India* (London, 1946) is a useful supplement to the work mentioned above. For those who know little of Islam, an older work by Henri Lammens, *Islam: Beliefs and Institutions* (London, 1968), provides good background material; so, too, does *Islam: A Concise Introduction* (San Francisco, 1982) by Dennis S. Roberts.

Judaism

My own work, *Modern Varieties of Judaism* (New York, 1966), deals briefly with both the Reform and the Reconstructionist movements in Judaism, as does *American Judaism: Adventure in Modernity* (Englewood Cliffs, N.J., 1972) by Jacob Neusner. The best studies of the Reform movement, however, are *The Rise of Reform Judaism* (New York, 1963) and *The Growth of Reform Judaism* (New York, 1965), both edited by W. Gunther Plaut. For Reconstructionism, consult two works by the founder of the movement, Mordecai M. Kaplan: *The Purpose and Meaning of Jewish Existence* (Philadelphia, 1964) and *Judaism without Supernaturalism* (New York, 1958).

Christianity

The literature of reform movements in Christianity is far too extensive to be listed here. For the period of the Reformation, a convenient summary with a good bibliography is provided by Roland H. Bainton in *The Reformation of the Sixteenth Century* (Boston, 1952). For the modern period in America, as good a brief exposition as one can hope for is found in the last three sections of Sydney E. Ahlstrom's magisterial *A Religious History of the American People* (New Haven, Conn.,1972).

New Sources

Akbarzadeh, Shahram, and Abdullah Saeed. *Islam and Political Legitimacy.* London and New York, 2003.

Browers, Michaelle. *An Islamic Reformation?* Lanham, Md., 2004.

Copley, A. R. H. *Gurus and Their Followers: New Religious Reform Movements in Colonial India.* Delhi, 2000.

Esposito, John L. *Political Islam: Revolution, Radicalism, or Reform?* Boulder, Colo., 1997.

Mor, Menahem. *Jewish Assimilation, Acculturation, and Accommodation: Past Traditions, Current Issues, and Future Prospects.* Lanham, Md., 1992.

Phongphit, Seri. *Religion in a Changing Society: Buddhism, Reform and the Role of Monks in Community Development in Thailand.* Hong Kong, 1988.

Robinson, Catherine A. *Tradition and Liberation: The Hindu Tradition in the Indian Women's Movement.* New York, 1999.

Sen, Amiya. *Social and Religious Reform: The Hindus of British India.* Delhi, 2003.

JOSEPH L. BLAU (1987)
Revised Bibliography

REFORMATION.

[*This entry discusses the sixteenth-century movement within Western Christendom that led to the emergence of the several Protestant churches.*]

The term *reformatio* (from the Latin *reformare,* "to renew") was employed in the Middle Ages to denote attempts to reform church and society; the use of the term *Reformation* in the sixteenth century indicates a sense of continuity with earlier efforts. While the term expressed the notion of turning the church from alleged worldliness and lack of proper theological emphasis, it did not, either conceptually or pragmatically, entail the notion of separation from the one church.

When it became evident in the sixteenth-century controversy over the proper interpretation of the Christian faith that the Protestant reformers in fact believed the Roman Catholic Church to be in theological error rather than merely to have mistaken emphases, a major step in the direction of separation had been taken. The Catholic Church, in turn, viewed the Reformation movement as rebellion and revolution. The term *Protestant,* applied to the adherents of the Reformation, stemmed from the "protest" voiced at the Diet of Speyer (1529) by the Lutheran estates against the revocation of the policy of toleration decreed at the Diet of Speyer three years earlier.

Reformation scholarship has tended to be dominated by confessional perspectives. Catholic scholars have viewed the Reformation as a religious and theological aberration and (as regards its historical significance) the cause of modern secularism. Protestant historiography, in turn, has depicted the Reformation as the restoration of authentic Christianity, with different emphases placed, according to the orientation of particular scholars, on the particular branch (Lutheran, Calvinist-Reformed, Anabaptist, Anglican) of the Reformation. Protestant Reformation historiography has generally focused on theological foci, stressing the distinctive emphases of the respective Protestant churches.

BACKGROUND. The traditional view, from the Protestant perspective, has been that in the early sixteenth century, church and society were in a state of crisis. The church was seen as suffering from various moral and theological abuses and the Reformation as a necessary reaction against that state of affairs. Recent research has drawn a different picture, holding that in the early sixteenth century, church and society were essentially stable, although not without problems. Therefore, the explanation for the outbreak of the Reformation is sought elsewhere, namely in a complex interplay of an essentially stable society and powerful new forces.

The foremost political reality of the time, the "Holy Roman Empire of the German Nation," was characterized by uncertainties about its boundaries and the respective roles of the emperor and the territorial rulers. A demand for greater effectiveness in governance had begun to surface in the late fifteenth century, particularly among the territorial rulers. A call for imperial reform was variously voiced and diets (parliamentary assemblies) in 1495 and 1500 went far in reorganizing the formal institutional structures of the empire.

The territories of the empire were in a state of transition in the late fifteenth century. The territorial rulers sought to enhance their own power at the expense of the emperor, while striving for a balance with the nobility in their territories. Because of his need for increased financial resources to support more extensive governmental activities and the flourishing bureaucracies, the emperor had to rely for support on the territorial rulers, who in turn depended on the nobility. The towns, many of which, as free imperial cities, were politically autonomous, presented a similar picture of superficial power relationships. Important centers of commerce and finance were emerging, the political power of which remained restricted. Tensions between the towns and the territories in which they were located were real, since the territories depended on the fiscal resources of the towns but sought to curb their political aspirations.

The Catholic Church stood in the center of society. It had extensive land holdings. It controlled education. It possessed its own legal system. It provided the ethical principles on which society was based and which were meant to guide it. Above all, the church, as the guardian of eternal truth, mediated salvation. There is no doubt that, on the eve of the Reformation, the church possessed a great vitality, especially in Germany, and that it commanded considerable loyalty and devotion. Heresy had virtually disappeared. Ecclesiastical benefactions increased in the late fifteenth and early sixteenth centuries. Pilgrimages were popular. Preaching positions in churches were established, and the newly invented printing press provided a host of devotional materials for a growing reading public.

Along with these manifestations of vitality, there were also problems. The hierarchy seemed distant and too cumbersome to deal with the spiritual needs of the people. The higher clergy, notably the bishops, were mainly recruited from the nobility and viewed their office as a source of prestige and power. This was particularly true in Germany, where many bishops were political rulers as well as spiritual rulers. The condition of the lower clergy, the parish priests, was often deplorable. Their theological learning was fragmentary and their economic circumstances marginal. Many parishes had absentee priests; as a result, clerical responsibilities were assumed by the less qualified curates.

In this setting many voices pleaded for church reform. The argument was that the church was too worldly, the papacy too far removed, the clergy too greedy, the religion of the people too vulgar. The humanists, notably Erasmus of Rotterdam, were outspoken in their opposition to scholastic theology. They argued that the simple religion of Christ should be restored. They objected to the scholastic concern over trivia, to the vulgar popular preoccupation with such matters as pilgrimages and relics, and to the pomp and worldliness of the hierarchy. The dominant theological influence emanated from Gabriel Biel, whose Ockhamism seemed a balanced treatment of the themes of human effort and divine action. An overall assessment of the theological situation on the eve of the Reformation must stress the presence of harmonious consistency.

The decades before the Reformation brought the growth of "territorial church government." Political authority became increasingly involved in ecclesiastical affairs, while, quite consistently, the role of the church in society—politically, fiscally, and legally—was challenged. In the towns the municipal councils became concerned with responsibility for education, the supervision of morality, and the care of the poor, all of which previously had been the prerogative and function of the church.

When all is said, however, a survey of church and state on the eve of the Reformation fails to reveal extensive symptoms of a profound crisis. Tensions existed but were hardly fundamental, and sundry efforts were being made to alleviate them. Despite criticism and anticlericalism, the call was for change and reform, not for disruption and revolution.

Controversy over Indulgences. The Reformation originated in a controversy over indulgences precipitated by Martin Luther's Ninety-five Theses of October 31, 1517. Indulgences, originally remissions of certain ecclesiastical penalties, had by the early sixteenth century come to be understood as offering forgiveness of sins in exchange for certain payments. Luther's misgivings about a singularly vulgar sale of indulgences by the Dominican monk Johann Tetzel found expression in a probing of the theology of indulgences. In a letter to Archbishop Albert of Hohenzollern, Luther pleaded for the discontinuance of the sale. What was meant as an academic and pastoral matter quickly became a public one, however, primarily because Luther sent out several copies of the theses, and the positive response of the recipients helped to propagate them. Moreover, Luther had inadvertently touched upon a politically sensitive matter. By attacking the sale of indulgences, he had infringed upon the fiscal interests of both the papacy and Archbishop Albert.

The subsequent course of events that turned Luther's expression of concern into a public controversy finds its explanation primarily in the astonishing intensity and swiftness of the official reaction: By early 1518 Luther had been cited as a suspected heretic. Undoubtedly, the church still had a vivid memory of the Hussite troubles of the previous century, and its strategy was to squelch the controversy as quickly as possible. The next three years were characterized by dogged pursuit of the official ecclesiastical proceedings against Luther, culminating, in January 1521, in his formal excommunication. After much deliberation and amid unresolved legal uncertainties, a rump diet issued the Edict of Worms in May 1521, whereby Luther was declared a political outlaw.

Events between 1517 and 1521 were dominated not only by the official ecclesiastical proceedings against Luther but also by the concurrent unfolding of his public presence and the increasing echo thereof. Luther's public message was a combination of cautious anticlericalism and a call to a deepened spirituality. This message explains at once the popular response: people responded precisely because they were not called upon to break with the church or to embrace a new theology.

Beginning of the Reformation. At Luther's formal condemnation in 1521 the nature of events changed. With Luther removed from the scene (many thought him dead), the message of reform was spread by an increasing number of comrades-in-arms and supporters. By that time consequences of the new message and its call for reform were beginning to emerge. What would be the practical consequences of Luther's call for a deepened spirituality? If, as Luther had argued, monasticism was unbiblical, what was to be done about the monks and the monasteries? If clerical celibacy was wrong, should priests marry? As these questions were asked and practical answers were offered and implemented, the Reformation in the real sense of the word can be said to have begun.

The Edict of Worms proved but a scrap of paper. Most territorial states plainly ignored it in view of the widespread support for Luther, the dubious legality of the edict, and the rulers' concerns for their legal prerogatives. In the Imperial Council, which exercised the emperor's function during his absence from Germany for the remainder of the decade, the debates about the execution of the edict were lengthy and inconclusive. Nor did diets meeting in Nuremberg in 1523 and 1524 have any greater success, other than issuing plaintive pleas for the convening of a general or at least a German council.

The message that evoked such widespread support is evident in the multitude of pamphlets published between 1517 and 1525. Their themes were simple. They were concerned more with personal piety than with theological propositions. Their message was that of a religion of substance rather than form, of inner integrity rather than outward conformity, of freedom rather than rules. It was also a message of utter dependence on God's grace. At the same time, certain key slogans made their appearance: "human traditions," "works righteousness," "the pure word of God," and, once the battle lines were drawn, the fateful declaration that the papacy was the seat of the antichrist.

The impact of the reformers was so strong because they deliberately took their arguments to the people whom they knew to be interested in the issues discussed. Abandoning Latin as the language of religious discourse, the reformers used the vernacular in their writings and preferred the brief tract, the pamphlet, to the weighty tome. The genres used for disseminating the message of the Reformation were extensive and varied—straightforward expositions, satires, dialogues, plays, even cartoons. The quantitative output was enormous. Within the first decade of the controversy, over a million copies of Reformation tracts were disseminated in Germany, with its population of roughly ten million. Many tracts were reprinted more than fifteen times.

At this point in its development, the movement was diverse and imprecise in its theological focus. The common denominator was the vague notion of the need for change and reform. Everything else was up in the air, so to speak; the only certainty was that Luther clearly occupied a position of central eminence. The issues propounded were not merely religious ones; they encompassed a wide variety of social and political concerns that made for an intertwining of religious and nonreligious motifs.

The further course of events brought a variety of issues to the fore that defined and divided the Reformation movement. Luther became engaged in controversy with several fellow reformers—among them Ulrich Zwingli, Andreas Karlstadt, and Thomas Müntzer—who challenged both his perspective and his eminence. The controversy with Zwingli, about the Lord's Supper, dominated the remainder of the decade of the 1520s.

By the end of the 1520s the reform movement had firmly established itself, especially in southern and central Germany, so much so that the Diet of Speyer in 1526 concluded the impossibility of enforcing the Edict of Worms. Accordingly, the diet allowed the territorial rulers for the time being the freedom to proceed with the edict according to the dictates of their consciences and their sense of responsibility to the emperor.

Two themes were dominant in the years between the Diet of Speyer (1526) and the Peace of Augsburg (1555): the expansion of the Reformation and the pursuit of reconciliation (or coexistence) between the two sides. The theme of Protestant expansion found striking expression in the spread throughout Europe and, in Germany, of the acceptance of the Reformation by a majority of the imperial cities. The convergence of societal concerns and religious goals, characteristic of the Reformation as a whole, is clearly discernible in the cities. The cities were centers of economic power and literacy, and in many were manifest a pronounced anticlericalism and a conflict between the church and those who held political power.

Three patterns of ecclesiastical change in the cities emerged. In some, the agitation for change came from the councils, which sought to bring their quest for full control of all areas of municipal life to a consistent conclusion. In others, the Reformation became part of the political conflict between the council, the ruling oligarchy, and the guilds. The attempt to introduce the Reformation paralleled the effort to democratize. In the third pattern, the quest for ecclesiastical change came from a group of intellectuals who forced the city council to embrace the Reformation.

The second Reformation theme between 1526 and 1555, the pursuit of reconciliation between Catholics and Protestants, had both its political and constitutional aspects. At the Diet of Speyer (1529) the Catholic estates mustered a majority, which insisted on enforcement of the Edict of Worms. But this move had no discernible consequences, and Charles V convened a diet at Augsburg in 1530 to resolve the controversy. The Lutheran estates were invited to submit a confessional statement; the Zurich reformer Zwingli was deemed politically insignificant; the theologically extreme were ignored.

The Lutheran declaration of faith, known as the Augsburg Confession, argued that there was agreement in major matters and that the disagreements pertained only to minor issues, notably the married clergy and episcopal jurisdiction. The issues that had dominated the controversy—the sacraments, authority, and justification—were treated in a broad and most general fashion. This approach of stressing conciliation may have been an astute propaganda move, since there was reason to believe that the Catholics would be rigid. In fact, however, the papacy had also decided on a conciliatory policy, and the eventual failure of the discussions was in part attributable to the failure of each side to understand the other.

At the adjournment of the diet, the Protestants were given six months to rescind their ecclesiastical changes. When the deadline came, however, nothing happened. The emperor, preoccupied militarily with the Turks, was dependent on the support of all the estates, including the Protestants. Moreover, the important Protestant territories had formed the Smalcaldic League to resist any attempt to resolve the religious controversy by force. Accordingly, Charles V had to agree to the Peace of Nuremberg (1532), which afforded the Protestants legal recognition until the convening of a general council.

The 1530s brought continued Protestant expansion in Germany. At the end of the decade new attempts were made to explore the possibility of theological agreement. At the Colloquy of Worms (1539), agreement was reached concerning justification, which had been the main point of controversy between the two sides. In the end, however, disagreement prevailed, and the attempt to resolve the controversy by theological conciliation failed.

Charles V was now determined to use force. Upon concluding peace with France in 1544, he was ready to face the Protestants. War broke out in 1546 and despite a good deal of blundering, Charles emerged successful, winning the decisive Battle of Muhlberg in 1547. The victorious emperor convened a diet at Augsburg in 1548 to impose his religious settlement on the Protestants. The result was the Augsburg Interim, which afforded the Protestants two temporary concessions—use of the communion cup and the married clergy—but left little doubt about the emperor's determination to restore Catholicism fully in the end. At the same time, Charles V sought also, through an ambitious constitutional reform project, to enhance imperial power in Germany. The pairing of these two objectives proved his undoing, for once his political objectives had become clear, his military coalition promptly disintegrated. A conspiracy of territorial rulers, headed by Maurice of Saxony, almost succeeded in imprisoning the emperor.

Charles faced increasingly formidable opposition from the territorial rulers, Protestant and Catholic alike, and he had to acknowledge that Protestantism was firmly entrenched in Germany. The formal recognition of Protestantism could no longer be avoided. Lengthy negotiations conducted by his brother, Ferdinand, culminated in the Peace of Augsburg in 1555. While both sides affirmed the ideal of eventual reconciliation, the realities intimated a permanent division. The foremost provision of the peace was "Cuius regio, eius religio," by which territorial rulers were given the freedom to choose Lutheranism or Catholicism as the official religion in their territory. The emerging distribution of political power in Germany provided the framework for the settlement of the controversy. Even as political power shifted from the emperor to the territorial rulers, so was the religious countenance of Germany formed by the territories rather than the empire.

Differentiation of Reformation Views. As the Reformation movement spread, it became evident that the reformers' common opposition to the Catholic church did not entail a common theological position. Differences of views emerged, pertaining both to the timing and to the scope of reform.

The first incidence of differentiation came in 1522, when Andreas Karlstadt, a colleague of Luther's at the University of Wittenberg, publicly disagreed with Luther. Two years later Thomas Müntzer, minister at Allstedt, not far from Wittenberg, published two pamphlets in which he dramatically indicted Luther's notion of reform. He accused Luther of selling out to the political authorities by preaching a "honey-sweet Christ." In the spring of 1525, Müntzer joined the rebellious peasants in central Germany and became their spiritual leader. The pamphlets that issued from his pen were vitriolic and categorical: the true church would be realized only through suffering and by a resolute opposition to the godless rulers.

While the most famous of the peasant programs, the Twelve Articles, astutely linked peasant aspirations with the Lutheran proclamation, the connection between the reform movement and the peasants was tenuous at best. It must remain doubtful whether, given their illiteracy, the peasants were extensively touched by the Reformation. But Luther felt sufficiently implicated to publish two pamphlets against the peasants in which he expressed sympathy for their plight yet categorically declared that the gospel did not provide the justification for its amelioration and that rebellion was against the gospel. These tracts heralded a fundamental divorce of the Reformation from a major social issue of the time.

Huldrych Zwingli. The major division within the ranks of the reformers is associated with the Swiss reformer Huldrych (Ulrich) Zwingli, of Zurich. Unlike Luther, whose theological development occurred in the setting of monastery and university, Zwingli matured as a parish priest and as a theologian greatly influenced by Erasmus. In 1522, he publicly defended eating meat during the Lenten fast and in so doing precipitated a lively controversy about the propriety of the prescribed ecclesiastical practices. The Zurich city council ordered a disputation to resolve the contested issues. It took place in January 1523 and resulted in the public declaration of support for Zwingli by the council, a declaration that had the noteworthy underlying assumption that a community could itself determine the faith, regardless of established ecclesiastical authority. A new norm of religious authority was evident here.

A second disputation, in October 1523, dealt with the issues of the use of images in churches and the interpretation of the Mass. Agreement was quickly reached that both were unbiblical, but opinion differed as to the most propitious time for their abolition. From the ranks of some of Zwingli's followers came the same kind of impatience with the course of ecclesiastical change that Luther had witnessed in Wittenberg in 1522. Eventually some of these followers broke openly with Zwingli; thus was launched the Anabaptist movement.

The specific issue that was to divide the Reformation was the interpretation of the Lord's Supper. Luther, while rejecting the Catholic doctrine of transubstantiation, affirmed the real presence of Christ in the elements of bread and wine, while Zwingli affirmed a spiritual presence. The controversy between the two men erupted in 1525 and continued, with increasing vehemence, for years to come. By 1529 political overtones to the theological disagreement had surfaced. Since military action against the Protestants was a possibility, the internal disagreement weakened the Protestant position. It became clear that the future of the Reformation lay in political strength. Landgrave Philipp of Hesse, the driving force behind such notions, arranged for a colloquy between Luther and Zwingli at Marburg in October 1529. Luther was a reluctant participant, not only because he had little empathy for Zwingli's theology but also because he reflected a different political perspective. Any rapprochement with Zwingli, who was seen as both anti-Habsburg and a theological radical, would make conciliation with the Habsburg emperor Charles V more difficult.

The Marburg colloquy, therefore, manifested both political and theological issues. No agreement was reached in the lengthy discussions, even though the document signed by those present skillfully buried the disagreement concerning communion in an inconspicuous sentence. The Reformation movement remained divided. Zwingli's influence was strong in Zurich, Switzerland, and even southwestern Germany even though the second of two military engagements between Swiss Catholics and Protestants in 1529 and 1531 ended with Protestant defeat and the curtailment of further Protestant expansion. Zwingli himself died on the battlefield of Kappel in 1531.

The Anabaptists. A second major division within the ranks of the Reformation pertained to a heterogeneous group whom contemporaries called "Anabaptists." This term, derived from a Greek word meaning "rebaptizer," indicated the Anabaptists' most prominent assertion: that baptism should be performed in adulthood as the outgrowth of an individual's decision. More important was the Anabaptist conviction, which echoed Thomas Müntzer, that the major reformers had been neither serious nor comprehensive in their effort to restore biblical Christianity. The Anabaptists thus placed great emphasis on the personal commitment to follow Christ (exemplified by the desire to be baptized), viewed the church as a voluntary group of believers, and held for complete aloofness from the political structures.

Anabaptism originated formally in Zurich among young humanist associates of Zwingli who, influenced by Müntzer and Karlstadt, were disenchanted with the slow progress of reform. Their attempt to impose their own vision of speedier and more comprehensive reform on the course of events proved unsuccessful. They broke with Zwingli, administered believer's baptism early in 1525, and found themselves promptly persecuted, since the authorities were unwilling to tolerate diverse forms of religion in their midst. Impatience and dissatisfaction with the course of ecclesiastical change were widespread in the mid-1520s, so that it is not possible to speak of a single point of origin for Anabaptism. Events were moving too slowly for many, and the theological atmosphere at the time was so diverse as to suggest a multiplicity of mentors and sources.

The Anabaptist movement expanded throughout Austria and Germany, chiefly through itinerant lay preachers. Small congregations developed as a result of their preaching. Both ecclesiastical and secular authorities declared the Anabaptists to be revolutionaries and pursued a harsh policy of persecution. This caused Anabaptism to become an underground movement. Its literature was sparse, since it had to be clandestinely printed and disseminated. It had no trained clergy. Despite such handicaps Anabaptism enjoyed a widespread, if modest, expansion.

The catastrophe of Anabaptism at the northwestern German town of Münster, in the early 1530s, proved to be a turning point in the history of the movement. The coming of the Reformation to Münster had prompted the town's leading minister, Bernd Rothmann, to embrace Lutheran notions and successfully secure the appointment of other reform-minded Lutheran clergy. Elections to the city council in 1533 resulted in a Lutheran majority. Subsequently, Rothmann came under Anabaptist influence, and Münster underwent a second Reformation in embracing Anabaptism. Early in 1534 representatives of the Dutch Anabaptist leader Melchior Hofmann arrived to administer adult baptism. Euphoria set in, since Hofmann had earlier prophesied that the imminent end would be preceded by the victory of the elect over the godless. The events at Münster seemed to vindicate his prophecy of the glorious things to come.

Extensive changes occurred in the city. In 1534 Jan van Leyden, who had assumed leadership, declared himself king of the New Jerusalem. Communism and polygamy were introduced, both measures forced upon the Münster Anabaptists as much by external pressures as by biblical reflection; these changes prompted Catholic and Protestant authorities to lay siege to the city. Food and other supplies were at a premium, and women vastly outnumbered men.

After Münster was captured in the spring of 1535, and this New Jerusalem came to its end, the consequences for Anabaptists proved catastrophic. The authorities concluded that their fears had been vindicated: religious dissent had indeed, as they had predicted, escalated into political revolution. The persecution of Anabaptists intensified, and their very credibility suffered disastrously.

In northern Germany and Holland, Anabaptism was significantly aided by the leadership of a former Dutch priest, Menno Simons. With sensitive theological reflection and organizational skill, he succeeded in directing the perplexed Anabaptists to the ideal of a quiet, otherworldly Christianity that removed itself from any involvement in the political structures of society and acknowledged that existing authorities could not be replaced. While the themes of nonviolence and withdrawal from society had been voiced by earlier Anabaptist leaders, Simons emphasized them as hallmarks of Anabaptism. The Netherlands became, with Switzerland, the center of the movement.

The Antitrinitarians. Although some of the intellectual roots of Antitrinitarianism can be traced to the late Middle Ages, the catalytic influence of the Reformation was paramount in the movement. The atmosphere of challenge of established opinion and the stress on the Bible as sole authority seemed to call for the repudiation of the doctrine of the Trinity. A most dramatic event, in the early 1530s, was the publication of two staunchly antitrinitarian tracts by a Spanish lay theologian and physician, Michael Servetus. Servetus's later *Restitution* of 1553 offered a detailed critique of traditional dogma. However, it was not until the second half of the sixteenth century that a new ecclesiastical tradition embracing such notions emerged, notably in Poland. In an atmosphere of toleration, a part of the Calvinist church in Poland became antitrinitarian, greatly influenced by the Italian reformers Laelius and Fausto Sozzini.

John Calvin. An urbane French lawyer and humanist by background, John Calvin was the embodiment of both the differentiation of Reformation views and of its European dimension. Calvin had left his native country for Switzerland to arrange for the publication of his brief summary statement of Reformation theology, *Institutes of the Christian Religion.* Passing by chance through Geneva in 1536, the twenty-seven-year-old scholar was pressured into staying to take part in the reform there. His first attempt to implement reform led to conflict with the city authorities and to his expulsion in 1538. Three years later, however, he was invited to return and he remained there until his death in 1564.

Institutes of the Christian Religion, an originally slender volume that was many times revised and enlarged, stands as the monumental systematic delineation of reformed religion. Its basic motif, echoed in many variations, is the majesty of God, from which humanity's eternal destiny—predestination to salvation or to damnation—is reasoned. While Calvin always wished to emphasize God's majesty as the overarching theme of biblical religion, the concept of predestination emerged as the characteristic feature of Calvin's thought.

Calvin's notion of election to salvation made the elect the warriors for God. At the same time, Calvin consciously sought to implement the societal implications of the Christian religion. Following notions of Zwingli and the Strasbourg reformer Martin Bucer, he undertook to reform not merely the church but all of society. Thus Geneva, Calvin's seat of action, was to become the most famous of the towns of the Reformation.

Calvin's instrument of reform was the *Ecclesiastical Ordinances* of 1541, a comprehensive summary of the structure of the church and its place in society. The most important administrative institution in Geneva (and wherever Calvin's version of the Reformation gained a foothold) was the consistory, a body composed of both clergy and laity whose task was to supervise the maintenance of true faith and pure morals. Thus, it was not an ecclesiastical (or clerical) body, turning Geneva into an ecclesiastical tyranny. The political authorities participated fully in it in pursuit of an orderly and moral community.

Calvin's determination to implement his vision of God's law brought him into conflict with influential Genevans. There were several serious confrontations, and matters remained at an uneasy stalemate until 1553, when the trial of Michael Servetus forced the issue. Calvin, who despised Servetus for his heretical views, regarded his appearance in Geneva as part of a larger plot to undo Calvinist reforms in the city. Servetus's condemnation and execution consolidated Calvin's role. Elsewhere in Europe, notably in Poland, the Low Countries, Scotland, and especially France, Calvinism emerged as the major form of the Reformation. Lutheranism at the time was rife with internal theological controversy, leaving to Calvin and his followers the role of the dynamic force of the Reformation in the second half of the sixteenth century.

EUROPEAN DIMENSION OF THE REFORMATION. In light of the European dimension of the Reformation the question has been asked whether to view this dimension as the result of the transmission of ideas from Germany or as the emergence of simultaneous reform movements in a number of European countries. There has been support for both views, although there seems little doubt that the Lutheran controversy in Germany affected theologians and laity throughout Europe. Travelers and the printed word carried forth the message from Germany. To this German influence the native reformers added their own emphases.

The European theological themes were also uniform; they were determined by a common opposition to Roman Catholicism and a common stance concerning the authority of scripture. Moreover, the essential course of development of the Reformation in Europe hardly differed from one country to another, in that theological discussion was always accompanied by a quest for legal recognition. In each country the period of the Reformation ended with a legal pronouncement: in France with the Edict of Nantes (1598); in Poland with the Confederation of Warsaw (1573); and in Scotland with an act of Parliament (1560).

The spread of the Reformation movement was uniformly related to local political issues and to the concomitant ability of the Protestants to demonstrate that their religion could have relevance for these issues. The success of the Reformation hinged on its ability to convert king or nobility, whichever was crucial in the struggle. As events turned out, in England, Sweden, Norway, Denmark, Finland, and Scotland, the Protestants were on the winning side.

At the time the Reformation movement broke out in Germany, reform notions were already strong in France. Although Jacques Lefèvre d'Étaples had anticipated some of Luther's notions and had translated the New Testament into French, one may see the first phase of the Reformation in France as the dissemination of Lutheran ideas and pamphlets. The official reaction was that of suppression. While Francis I was himself a humanist by disposition, political prudence led him to take a Catholic and papal course. The *placard* affair of 1534, in which a Protestant poster was affixed to the door of the king's bedroom, symbolized Protestant strength in the country. Francis responded with persecution and a stern censorship of books. His successor, Henry II, continued this policy, which found embodiment in the Edict of Chateaubriand (1551).

Henry's unexpected death in 1559 precipitated a constitutional crisis over the exercise of regency during the minority of the new king, Francis II. Cardinal Guise summarily assumed the regency, but his move was opposed by the prestigious Bourbon family, which argued for a council of regency. The constitutional issue had religious overtones, since the Guises were staunch Catholics, while the Bourbons had Protestant leanings. To side with the Bourbons seemed to promise toleration for the Protestants. The constitutional uncertainty prompted the question whether royal authority was being properly exercised. This crisis saw the emergence of the issue of political resistance among French Protestants. Calvin's doctrine of the right of resistance to rulers who did not fulfill their duty served as sanction for the contention that the higher nobility had the right to oppose the king when he violated the law.

The Wars of Religion, which began in 1562, sought to resolve the issue of political power in France and saw the French Protestants (Huguenots) combine political concerns with their religious cause. The Edict of Nantes (1598) ended the struggle and brought the French Reformation to an end. It resembled the Peace of Augsburg in that the Protestants failed in their effort to win acceptance of their religion by France. They were recognized legally, however, and were given freedom of worship. In Germany only the territorial rulers possessed freedom of religious choice; in France this freedom was extended to all.

The Reformation in England. In the 1520s England underwent a period of lively agitation against the Roman Catholic Church. Although this agitation was influenced by events on the continent, there were indigenous forces at work as well: anticlericalism, the tradition of the Lollard heresy, and Erasmian humanism. Henry VIII had himself participated in the initial Reformation controversy with a defense of the traditional Catholic teaching on the sacraments, for which Pope Leo X granted him the title "Defender of the Faith." The king's conservative temperament was thus on record.

This atmosphere of religious agitation was complicated by Henry's sudden desire for an annulment of his marriage to Catherine of Aragon (his deceased brother's widow) on the grounds that the marriage violated canon law. Extensive efforts to obtain a favorable papal decision proved unsuccessful, and Henry eventually chose, on the advice of Thomas Cromwell, the parliamentary route to provide legal justification for his intention. In 1533 Parliament passed the Act in Restraint of Appeals to Rome, which declared England an "empire" whose sovereign could adjudge all spiritual and temporal matters in his realm. This act kept the judicial resolution over Henry's "divorce" in England. The king had broken with the papal church.

The doctrinal statement of the religion imposed by Henry came with the Six Articles of 1539. These articles were Catholic in orientation—as, for example, in espousing transubstantiation and clerical celibacy. Thomas Cranmer, archbishop of Canterbury, who was married, had to send his wife abroad. Although the legal situation was restrictive, the actual situation was relatively free. The penalties imposed by the articles were rarely applied, and antipapal propaganda flowed openly. Protestant sentiment, except of the ardent kind, could be easily disseminated. Adamant Catholics were persecuted no less than adamant Protestants. The influence of Erasmian religion made itself felt in England, a religion relatively open, yet essentially Catholic in orientation.

When Henry died in 1547 religious affairs were thus in a precarious balance, neither strongly Protestant nor strongly Catholic. He had intended this state of affairs for his minor son, Edward VI, but the Council of Regency was dominated by men of Protestant sympathies. The official religion of the land veered in the direction of Protestantism. Under the aegis of Archbishop Cranmer, a new order for worship *(The Book of Common Prayer)* was promulgated in 1549. Drawing on the rich liturgical heritage of the medieval church, this order for worship, with the beauty of its language and its structure of the divine office, proved to be an immensely enriching contribution to English Christendom. The theological tone of the prayer book was conservative in that it espoused a Lutheran view of Communion. A revision of the book, three years later, embraced a Zwinglian view.

Mary, Henry's daughter by Catherine of Aragon, who succeeded her half brother in 1553, attempted to restore Catholicism, with an increasingly heavy hand and, in the end, with a ruthless persecution of all avowed Protestants. In so doing, she overlooked the fact that England's ties with the Catholic Church had been severed for almost a quarter of a century; what is more important, she failed to understand the danger of creating martyrs. After her reign (1553–1558), John Foxe wrote his *Book of Martyrs,* a gripping, often melodramatic description of Protestant suffering, torture, and martyrdom. Put into the context of the martyrs of the faith of all times, the book helped make Catholicism impossible in England.

The Elizabethan settlement. With the succession of Mary's half sister, Elizabeth I, in 1558, the English situation changed dramatically. Elizabeth was predisposed to Protestantism and promptly set out to effect a religious settlement in that direction. She wished only for a limited restoration of Protestantism, aiming for the initial reestablishment of royal supremacy and the possibility of further religious change later. But Parliament, convening in 1559, was determined to move in a more Protestant direction. Elizabeth yielded to a settlement that restored religion as it had existed at the end of Edward's reign. An important change, however, made the section on Communion in *The Book of Common Prayer* less precise. By juxtaposing language of the 1549 and 1552 editions of *The Book of Common Prayer* with respect to Communion, it was left uncertain if Christ was bodily present in the Communion bread and wine.

In 1563 the Convocation adopted a theological statement for the Church of England. With Thomas Cranmer's Forty-two Articles of 1551 serving as the point of departure, various revisions resulted in the Thirty-nine Articles, a theologically moderate statement.

Puritanism. Before long the settlement of 1559 began to evoke opposition from those for whom it was not sufficiently Protestant. Its critics argued that too many vestiges of Catholicism remained in the English church. They wanted a "pure" church, and before long they came to be called "Puritans." The Puritans were to be a major element in English history until the second half of the seventeenth century. Puritanism underwent significant changes in the course of its lengthy history. Toward the end of the sixteenth century it became increasingly diverse and sectarian, some strands determined to break with the established church. It also became increasingly political.

Until the end of the sixteenth century, England witnessed successive waves of Puritan dissent. Clerical vestments and the episcopal form of church government soon became the subject of controversy. By the 1580s some Puritans had concluded the impossibility of effecting change from within. Robert Browne's *A Treatise of Reformation without Tarrying for Any* argued for the establishment of separate congregations because the Church of England was unable to reform. In response, Richard Hooker's monumental *Laws of Ecclesiastical Polity* stated the case for Anglicanism as the perfect middle way, arguing with an impressive command of the principles of natural law and the early church.

On the continent the Reformation controversies had virtually subsided by the end of the sixteenth century. In England, however, the separatist sentiment came to fruition during that time with the emergence of different groupings, of which several—Congregationalists, Baptists, and Quakers—were to become ecclesiastical traditions in Anglo-Saxon Christendom.

THE CATHOLIC REACTION. The initial reaction of the Catholic church to Luther was astoundingly swift and categorical. Undoubtedly, it was influenced by the apprehension that, if not properly handled, the conflagration would lead to another Hussite debacle. By 1520 the position of the church had been delineated: Luther's understanding of the Christian faith was declared heretical and his notion of reform rejected. It was to be of profound import for subsequent events that despite this condemnation, the Catholic Church possessed neither a comprehensive policy for reform nor a clear perception of how to execute the judgment against Luther or halt the increasing defections. Moreover, the papacy had its own priorities, which were slow to focus on the Lutheran affair and the Protestant Reformation, even though there was no dearth of voices predicting disaster unless a solution was found.

The disadvantages facing the defenders of the Catholic Church were obvious. They had to defend the status quo with all its shortcomings, while the reformers were able to delineate a splendid vision of an ideal church. Many of those who attacked the church did so for other than religious reasons, thus introducing an element of power politics into what purported to be a religious matter. Pope and emperor, whose concerted efforts would have been able to stem the Protestant tide, frequently were at odds with each other, working at cross-purposes, and thereby aiding the Reformation.

The question of whether a general council should be convened was undoubtedly the overriding issue during the first two decades of the Reformation. With striking unanimity Christians throughout Europe saw a council as the panacea not only for the ills of the church but also for those of society. To be sure, notions differed as to what the function of a council should be, and perhaps not much would have been accomplished had a council actually convened. But the negative stance of Pope Clement VII, who feared a resurgence of conciliarism, precluded a council in the early years of the Reformation.

When a council eventually convened at Trent in 1545, it was clear that it could have no other function than to sharpen the true Catholic position on a wide variety of issues. Thus the council, which met intermittently until 1563, possessed significance only for the Catholic Church. Its canons and decrees were consciously anti-Protestant and offered conciliatory views only with respect to issues contested within Catholicism. Thus the council served to revitalize the Catholic Church, formulating the principles and policies that characterized an invigorated Catholicism for the century to come.

The Council of Trent gathered together the sundry strands of renewal within the Catholic Church, some of which had been discernible even before 1517. The revival of monasticism, for example, antedated the Reformation. Renewal continued in the 1520s and 1530s, in many instances not influenced by the Reformation. The foremost expression of this renewal was the work of Ignatius Loyola and the Society of Jesus, which he founded. The manifestation of Catholic renewal became an instrument of reaction against the Reformation, and in one of its central forms, namely, monastic spirituality, it reiterated the traditional vehicle of Catholic reform.

SIGNIFICANCE OF THE REFORMATION. Perceptions of the significance of the Reformation have differed markedly since the sixteenth century. Generally it is the ecclesiastical persuasion of the observer that has provided the cue for the interpretation.

Protestants saw the Reformation as the restoration of biblical Christianity against a worldly and perverted church. In turn, Catholics saw the Reformation as rebellion against truth and, concomitantly, as a triumph of subjectivism. Nineteenth- and twentieth-century Catholics have argued that, because the Reformation repudiated authority, it was a direct forerunner of the French Revolution. Such stereotypes as these have largely disappeared. Catholic scholars have been willing to acknowledge the religious depth and significance of Luther, while Protestants have revised their negative assessment of the pre-Reformation church and are prepared to see greater continuity between the late Middle Ages and the Reformation. Recent scholarship has also made clear that there was great misunderstanding among the protagonists on both sides of the sixteenth-century controversy. The theological differences are nowadays seen to have consisted in divergent notions of authority and salvation: authority of the Bible and the church or of the Bible alone; salvation by works and grace or by grace alone.

Although the divergence between Catholic and Protestant historiography of the Reformation has largely disappeared, the resurgence of the interpretation first delineated by Friedrich Engels has perpetuated the tradition of divergent assessments of the Reformation. Marxist historians view the Reformation and the German Peasants' War collectively as "early bourgeois revolution." In their view the rising class of townspeople engaged in commerce and trade and holding increasing economic power, found itself in conflict with the holders of political power. In opposing this political power, the new class had to reject the ideological undergirding of medieval society, the Catholic Church. Luther was the religious spokesman for economic power and a new, bourgeois mentality.

The foremost consequence of the Reformation was the division of Western Christendom into several churches. The centrality of the Catholic Church was irretrievably destroyed, and the universal church gave way to national churches. While the political authorities precluded the formal recognition of more than one church, the existence of several religious perspectives (bitterly opposing one another) surely diminished the public as well as private significance of religion in Europe. This disintegrated the notion that had characterized medieval society—the oneness of this world and the next. The existence of diverse religious options did not, however, entail a sense of toleration or religious liberty. All parties clung to the notion of objective truth and the impossibility of allowing the public expression of religious error.

The masses, illiterate and living in isolation in rural areas, remained untouched by the controversies of the Reformation. In other words, the sixteenth century is not to be viewed as a time of intense popular preoccupation with religion. Evidence abounds of outright disinterest in religion, despite countless governmental mandates stipulating church attendance or religious instruction. Popular religion was a simple folk religion, little influenced by the sophisticated theological arguments that characterized Reformation controversies.

The role of the political authorities in these religious controversies has already been noted. Throughout Europe the rulers had the last word about the success or failure of the Reformation. They rarely hesitated to exercise that power, at times for religious reasons and at other times for political reasons. In exercising their power, they enhanced their political stature and enlarged the scope of their authority.

Clearly, the role of political authority in religion was more firmly established at the end of the sixteenth century than it had been at the beginning. If the Reformation thus conformed harmoniously with the new self-understanding of the political rulers, it also proved exceptionally congenial to the mentality of a new type of person, very much in evidence in the late fifteenth century—literate, self-confident, and energetic. The Reformation, after all, affirmed the priesthood of all believers, the freedom of the Christian individual, and the sanctity of the common life. The autonomy of the individual was asserted not with respect to transcendental concerns but with respect to the role and place of the church in society.

In such a setting, the Reformation provided a host of stimuli for all areas of life. The notion of vocation declared all jobs to be spiritually meaningful. This sanctity of the common life must not be defined merely by an individual sense of liberation, enabling men and women to go about their daily rounds with confidence, but also by a societal sense, embodied by statute no less than by ethos, that society did not need to be dominated by the church. All facets of life, both individual and societal, became subject to new formulations. Conceptual and practical problems of education, law, commerce, and behavior were approached with eagerness and enthusiasm. The common denominator was the notion of a lay culture, where the laity rather than the clergy played the incisive role. This did not entail the secularization of society: religion continued to be very much in the center of things, if for no other reason than that a divine order was generally agreed to govern all of life. If the genius of the medieval world had been its notion of the oneness of society under the aegis of the church, the Reformation stipulated a oneness that entailed the equality of church and society.

SEE ALSO Anabaptism; Anglicanism; Browne, Robert; Bucer, Martin; Calvin, John; Christianity, article on Christianity in Western Europe; Church; Denominationalism; Eucharist; Free Will and Predestination, article on Christian Concepts; Grace; Hooker, Richard; Humanism; Ignatius Loyola; Justification; Luther, Martin; Monasticism, article on Christian Monasticism; Müntzer, Thomas; Papacy; Protestantism; Puritanism; Reform; Revival and Renewal; Sacrament, article on Christian Sacraments; Servetus, Michael; Simons, Menno; Sozzini, Fausto Pavolo; Theology, article on Christian Theology; Trent, Council of; Zwingli, Ulrich.

BIBLIOGRAPHY

General Surveys

The best general introductions to the history of the Reformation are G. R. Elton's *Reformation Europe, 1517–1559* (New York, 1963); *The Reformation, 1520–1559,* edited by G. R. Elton, "The New Cambridge Modern History," vol. 2 (Cambridge, 1958); Lewis W. Spitz's *The Renaissance and Reformation Movements,* 2d ed., 2 vols. (Saint Louis, 1980); and my *The World of the Reformation* (New York, 1973). The Literature Survey of the Archiv für Reformationsgeschichte (Leipzig and Berlin, 1903–) provides an annual annotated survey of all literature pertaining to the Reformation. Useful also is *Bibliography of the Continental Reformation: Materials Available in English,* 2d ed., rev. & enl., edited by Roland H. Bainton and Eric W. Gritsch (Hamden, Conn., 1972). A survey of current research emphases is *Reformation Europe: A Guide to Research,* edited by Steven E. Ozment (St. Louis, 1982).

Specialized Studies

Blickle, Peter. *The Revolution of 1525.* Baltimore, 1982.

Brady, Thomas A. *Ruling Class, Regime and Reformation at Strasbourg, 1520–1555.* Leiden, 1978.

Clasen, Claus-Peter. *Anabaptism: A Social History, 1525–1618.* Ithaca, N.Y., 1972.

Edwards, Mark U., Jr. *Luther's Last Battles.* Ithaca, N.Y., 1983.

Elton, G. R. *Policy and Police.* Cambridge, U.K., 1972.

Goertz, Hans, ed. *Profiles of Radical Reformers.* Scottdale, Pa., 1982.

Hendrix, Scott H. *Luther and the Papacy.* Philadelphia, 1981.

Lienhard, Marc, ed. *The Origins and Characteristics of Anabaptism.* The Hague, 1977.

Lortz, Joseph. *The Reformation in Germany.* New York, 1968.

Moeller, Bernd. "Piety in Germany around 1500." In *The Reformation in Medieval Perspective,* edited by Steven E. Ozment, pp. 50–75. Chicago, 1971.

Moeller, Bernd. *Imperial Cities and the Reformation.* Philadelphia, 1972.

Ozment, Steven E. *The Reformation in the Cities.* New Haven, Conn., 1975.

Stayer, James M. *Anabaptism and the Sword.* Lawrence, Kans., 1972.

Walton, Robert C. *Zwingli's Theocracy.* Toronto, 1967.

Williams, George H. *The Radical Reformation.* Philadelphia, 1962.

New Sources

Aston, Margaret. *England's Iconoclasts.* Oxford and New York, 1988.

Greengrass, M. *The French Reformation.* Oxford and New York, 1987.

Oberman, Heiko. *The Dawn of the Reformation.* Edinburgh, 1992.

Oberman, Heiko. *The Two Reformations: The Journey from the Last Days to the New World.* New Haven, Conn., 2003.

Olin, John C. *Catholic Reform from Cardinal Ximenes to the Council of Trent 1495–1563.* New York, 1990.

Olin, John C. *The Catholic Reformation from Savanarola to Ignatius Loyola.* New York, 2001.

Williams, George H. *The Radical Reformation.* 3d ed. Kirksville, Mo., 1992.

HANS J. HILLERBRAND (1987)
Revised Bibliography

REFORMED PRESBYTERIAN CHURCH

SEE PRESBYTERIANISM, REFORMED

REFORM JUDAISM is the branch of the Jewish faith that has been most adaptive, in belief and practice, to the norms of modern thought and society. It is also sometimes called Liberal Judaism or Progressive Judaism. By *Reform* is meant not a single reformation but an ongoing process of development. Well over one million Reform Jews live in the United States and Canada, with about another 100,000 in Europe, Latin America, South Africa, Australia, and Israel. Internationally, all Reform congregations are united in the World Union for Progressive Judaism, which holds biennial conferences, usually in Europe or Israel. In the United States some nine hundred independent congregations constitute the Union of American Hebrew Congregations (UAHC), and more than seventeen hundred rabbis—some of them serving abroad—make up the Central Conference of American Rabbis (CCAR). Rabbis, as well as scholars, educators, community workers, and cantors, are trained at the Hebrew Union College–Jewish Institute of Religion (HUC–JIR), which has branches in Cincinnati, New York, Los Angeles, and Jerusalem. The most influential role of organizational leadership in Reform Judaism is the presidency of the UAHC, since the late twentieth century a professional position held by a rabbi.

BELIEFS AND PRACTICES. Unlike more traditional forms of the Jewish faith, Reform Judaism does not hold that either the written law (Torah) or the oral law (Talmud) was revealed literally by God to Moses at Sinai. It accepts biblical and other historical criticism as legitimate, understanding Scripture and tradition as a human reflection of revelation rather than its literal embodiment. Whereas theologies among Reform Jews vary greatly, from the traditional to the humanistic, concepts of God strike a balance between universal and particular elements, with somewhat more stress upon the former than among other religious Jews. Like other branches of Judaism, Reform recognizes the close connection between religion and ethics. It especially emphasizes the prophetic message of social justice and seeks to act upon it both congregationally and as a united movement. Judaism is seen to exist for a higher universal purpose, which aims messianically at the biblical vision of world peace. Traditionally, in Reform Judaism, this sense of purpose has been known as the "mission of Israel."

The doctrine that most significantly sets Reform Judaism apart from more traditional currents is the conception of progressive revelation. Reform Jews hold that revelation is ongoing with the progress of human knowledge and moral sensitivity. This represents a reversal of the Orthodox belief whereby the theophany at Sinai, as interpreted by the rabbis, constitutes the authoritative, permanent expression of God's will, which must therefore remain normative for all time. The Reform conception of progress in understanding of the divine does not necessarily imply an unbroken moral advance of the Jews or of Western civilization, although Reform Judaism before the Holocaust was prone to draw that conclusion.

The freedom of the individual Jew to be selective, to draw from Jewish tradition those elements of belief and practice that he or she finds the most personally meaningful, is far greater among Reform Jews than among either Orthodox or Conservative. Religious anarchy, while always a danger, is restrained by a common though theologically diverse liturgy, general agreement on basic commitments, and a well-structured organizational framework. Reform Jews do not accept the Jewish legal tradition as binding but have always—and especially since the late twentieth century—turned to it for guidance in ritual matters. The CCAR has issued guides for Sabbath and holiday observance and for the Jewish life cycle.

At most Reform congregations in America the main religious service of the week is held after dinner on Friday evenings, though a service before the meal has gained increasing popularity; men and women sit together, participating equally in the service. In the last two decades of the twentieth century, many rabbis, some male congregants, and a much smaller number of women began to wear the ritual head covering (*kippah,* or yarmulke) during worship. In nearly all Reform synagogues (or temples, as they are often called) the liturgy is accompanied by an organ, while musical responses are led or performed by a choir or a cantor. Most of the prayers are spoken in English, except for those of central significance, which are rendered in Hebrew; the ratio varies from congregation to congregation. Especially under the impact of the state of Israel, the relative amount of Hebrew in the service has generally increased, and its pronunciation has been altered from the Ashkenazic (central and eastern European) to the Sefardic (Spanish and Near Eastern) accent used in the Jewish state. Formality and decorum have been hallmarks of the Reform temple, but a growing number of congregations have sought to regain some of the informality and emotion of the traditional synagogue through greater congregational involvement in the service and experimentation with alternative musical instruments, such as the guitar. The influence of worship services conducted in the summer camps of the National Federation of Temple Youth has been an appreciable factor in this regard.

Outside the synagogue, Reform Jews practice their faith by attempting to guide their lives according to the moral precepts of Judaism. A large percentage practices some Jewish rituals in the home, especially the lighting of the Sabbath candles on Friday evening; the sharing of the Passover eve ceremony, or seder; and the celebration of Ḥanukkah. Once especially aware of their religious differences from traditional Jews, Reform Jews emphasize to a greater extent their common ethnic identity and the faith shared by all religious Jews, limiting the significance of denominational differences.

Reform Jews remain more favorably inclined to proselytism than other branches of religious Judaism. The largest portion of converts to Judaism become Reform Jews, often as the result of marriage with a Jewish partner. Such "Jews by choice" comprise a small but growing percentage of the membership of most Reform congregations. Reform Judaism has given much attention to issues concerning procedures for conversion as well as the Jewish legal status of children born from mixed marriages in which the father is Jewish but not the mother. According to the *halakhah* (traditional Jewish law), such children are not Jewish unless formally converted; however, Reform Judaism recognizes them as Jewish if they are being brought up as Jews. About one-half of Reform rabbis will conduct weddings for mixed couples in which the non-Jewish partner does not intend to convert to Judaism. In such instances, however, the couple usually promises to raise its children as Jews.

The Movement in Europe. Reform Jews have often pointed out that religious reform was inherent in Judaism from its beginnings. They have noted that the prophets were critics of contemporary religious practices, that the Talmud includes reforms of earlier biblical legislation, and that even later legal scholars were willing to alter received beliefs and practices. Such willingness to adjust to historical change waned only under the pressure of persecution and the isolation of the ghetto. Latter-day Jews seeking religious reform thus sought, and to a degree found, precedent for their programs in earlier layers of Jewish tradition. However, they soon became aware that most of their fellow Jews, and especially the established rabbinical leadership, did not share such views. The result was a movement for reform originally intended to harmonize all aspects of Jewish life with the modern world into which European Jews increasingly entered beginning in the eighteenth century. Only gradually did the movement come to focus specifically on the religious realm, and only after a generation did it separate itself as a differentiable religious current with a more or less fixed religious philosophy. In discussing origins, it is therefore more accurate to speak of the "Reform movement in Judaism" than of Reform Judaism. Even this terminology, however, requires the qualification that self-conscious awareness of being a movement with definite goals came only gradually with the coalescence of various elements of belief and practice.

Beginnings. The background for the emergence of the Reform movement is the changing political and cultural situation of central and western European Jewry in the last decades of the eighteenth century and the beginning of the nineteenth. For numerous generations Jews had been physically and intellectually excluded from the surrounding, largely Christian civilization. With occasional exceptions, they lived within their own spiritual world. Their communities possessed corporate status; they were allowed to conduct their internal affairs according to Jewish law. The curriculum of their schools was confined almost exclusively to study of traditional Jewish texts. Secular knowledge was gained only informally and only to the extent necessary for the conduct of daily affairs. This medieval situation of the Jews was undermined by two novel elements: political centralization and the universalism of the Enlightenment. As European states sought greater concentration of power, they found it necessary to remove the divisive elements of medieval corporatism. Jews were brought more directly under state control; their autonomous jurisdiction and the coercive power of their rabbis were curtailed. Hopes were raised among Jews that political integration would lead to the abolition of political, economic, and social disabilities. At the same time a more friendly attitude toward Jews, which regarded them foremost as creatures of the same God rather than as Christ killers, began to pervade enlightened circles, drawing Jews to respond with their own broader, more universal identifications. In increasing numbers they now began to learn modern European languages, to read contemporary literature, to absorb the prevalent aesthetic sensibilities, and to regard themselves culturally as Europeans no less than religiously as Jews.

Gradually, a gap was created between Jewish traditions, harmonious with medieval realities, and the new economic, social, and cultural status of a portion of Western Jewry. To be sure, this modernizing process did not affect all Jews at once or to the same degree. Well into the nineteenth century most Jews in eastern Europe remained virtually untouched by the norms of modern civilization, whereas even in western Europe modernization among Jews was a slow process, more so in the religious than in the cultural sphere. However, as early as the beginning of the nineteenth century there began, especially in Germany, a pronounced falling away from Jewish belief and observance on the part of those Jews most exposed to the currents of modernity. Fears arose that, unless Jewish traditions could be brought into harmony with the intellectual canons and the social norms of the surrounding society, Judaism might find itself relegated to the dustbin of medievalism. The Reform movement arose as an attempt to reconcile Jewish religious tradition with cultural and social integration, to stem the rising tide of religious apathy—and even conversion—in certain circles, and to reshape Judaism in such a way as would make it viable under radically novel circumstances.

The first religious issue to arouse major controversy was burial on the very day of assumed death, as required by Jewish law. The famed Jewish philosopher of the Enlightenment, Moses Mendelssohn (1729–1786), who remained an Orthodox Jew, broke with established practice in 1772 when he advocated temporary "burial" above the ground and a graveyard vigil until actual death could be determined with certainty. Mendelssohn based his view both on the precedent of an ancient custom and on current medical experience. For decades thereafter, this question served as a touchstone separating traditionalists from modernists, those who held that all customary practice was sacred and inviolable from those who believed that, at least in some instances, criteria external to the Jewish tradition should be invoked to determine religious obligation.

A new theoretical religious position, which thereafter was largely if not directly absorbed by the Reform movement, first appears in a work titled *Leviathan* (1792) by Saul Ascher (1767–1822), a Jewish book dealer living in Berlin. Ascher rejected the Mendelssohnian dichotomy between natural religion (that shared by all rational human beings) and revealed law (that given exclusively to the Jews and the basis for their separation as a religious community). For Ascher the distinguishing feature of Judaism was not its legal corpus but its unique religious faith. Thus, Judaism was not dependent on political or judicial autonomy; it could take its place alongside Protestantism and Roman Catholicism, differentiated from them as one faith from another. In contrast to Mendelssohn, Ascher held that Judaism does indeed possess specific dogmas that set it apart from natural religion. These include belief in the God of love, who revealed himself to the patriarchs, who rewards and punishes, and who guides the world through divine providence. Likewise essential to Judaism are certain practices—including circumcision, observance of Sabbaths and holidays, and atonement—as a way of seeking God's favor. Ascher's arbitrary selectivity marks a sharp departure from traditional Jewish thought. In the fashion of non-Jewish thinkers of the eighteenth century, it makes religion largely a means to the end of personal spiritual happiness *(Glückseligkeit)* rather than, as in Judaism, the fulfillment of God's will as expressed in divinely ordained commandments. Though Ascher's specific program remained idiosyncratic, his subjectivization of the Jewish faith and its confessionalization soon became characteristic of the Reform movement. In later literature the differentiation is repeatedly made between what is essential to Judaism and what has been added by historical accident—"the kernel and the husk." In Jewish education the concomitant to this endeavor to isolate the basic tenets and distinctive practices of the faith was the catechism, increasingly introduced in place of, or supplementary to, traditional texts.

The reform of synagogue ritual under modern cultural influence was undertaken for the first time by the Adath Jeshurun congregation of Amsterdam in 1797. This synagogue was established in separation from the general community following the grant of emancipation to Dutch Jewry by the French-controlled Batavian Republic the previous year. The congregation buried its dead only on the third day, shortened its liturgy, made aesthetic "improvements" in the worship service, introduced a regular sermon on a moral theme, and eliminated a prayer that asked for vengeance against those who had martyred Jews at the time of the Crusades. The congregation had existed for only about a decade when the new king of Holland, Louis Bonaparte, required it to rejoin the general Jewish community.

Although France preceded other European states in giving its Jews complete political equality (at the time of the French Revolution), its Jewish community did not lead the movement for religious reform. The Assembly of Jewish Notables (1806) and the Sanhedrin (1807), called by Napoleon, committed French Jewry to the fulfillment of all civic obligations and to the official acceptance of the superiority of the law of the state over Jewish law. However, the delegates were not required to undertake liturgical reforms, give up any religious practices, or alter their theological conceptions. The centralized Jewish consistory system, which emerged in France shortly thereafter, militated against individual initiative in religious matters, favoring a superficially modernized official orthodoxy.

A program of religious reforms for an entire Jewish community was first undertaken by an officially constituted body enjoying government support in the kingdom of Westphalia. Under the leadership of the wealthy and influential financier Israel Jacobson (1768–1828), a Jewish consistory composed of three rabbis and two laymen was created there in 1808. The consistory introduced the confirmation ceremony (which it borrowed from Christianity) removed secular elements from the sacred space of the synagogue, and generally sought to impose a more dignified and decorous mode of worship. One of the rabbinical members of the consistory, Menachem Mendel Steinhardt (1768–1825), attempted to justify some of its reforms by reference to Jewish law and tradition as well as to the variant customs of Sefardic Jewry.

Jacobson moved to Berlin following the demise of the Westphalian kingdom and its Jewish consistory in 1813, and some months later he established regular weekly worship in his home for those members of the community who desired a service modeled on that of Westphalia. Like the services that Jacobson had instituted at the chapel of a school that he sponsored in the small Westphalian town of Seesen, the worship here was enhanced by the use of an organ and by a boys' choir. Later moved to larger quarters, these services attracted as many as four hundred worshipers. There were hymns and regular edifying sermons in the German language. However, the liturgy—for which a special prayer book was published—remained mostly traditional in content if not in form. As long as the prayer gatherings remained a private venture, the Orthodox faction of the community was willing to tolerate them. However, once it seemed that some of these reforms would be introduced into the community synagogue, traditionalist opposition, combined with Prussian government hostility to religious innovations, led to a royal edict in 1823 prohibiting any and all Jewish religious reform. This was the first of many disputes and polemical exchanges between reformers and traditionalists that thereafter punctuated the history of the Reform movement.

In 1817 the New Temple Association was formed in the independent city of Hamburg. Its members, who represented a broad economic and social cross section of the city's Jewry, succeeded in establishing and maintaining their own synagogue, despite Orthodox opposition, on account of the more indulgent attitude of the city's senate. The Hamburg temple, which lasted until the Holocaust, remained for a generation the model for the movement. In 1819 it issued a prayer book that, for the first time, made substantial changes in the liturgy. Intensely particularist passages were removed or altered. While references to Zion were not wholly excised, the prayer book reflected the members' abandonment of the desire to return to the Land of Israel and reestablish the ancient sacrificial service. Two lay preachers gave regular German sermons on the Christian model and prepared both boys and girls for the confirmation ceremony.

Ideologists. The next two decades may be described as a period of latency in the history of the Reform movement. The climate of political reaction in Europe was not conducive to religious innovation. Orthodox opposition, moreover, had proven to be pervasive and united. No new Reform prayer books were published between 1819 and 1840, and no new congregations were established. Aside from the Hamburg temple, Reform of any more than a minimal variety flourished only in those modern Jewish schools that, as in Berlin and Frankfurt am Main, offered a modified worship service for the children and their parents.

However, during this same period a new generation of rabbis came to maturity, some of them eager to institute religious reforms. Schooled not only in traditional Jewish texts but also at German universities, this younger rabbinical generation was able to provide spiritual leadership for what heretofore had been basically a lay movement. Gradually these men received rabbinical positions, first in the smaller Jewish communities and then in the larger ones. A number of them possessed considerable scholarly abilities and applied themselves to the task of creating a historical theology for the Reform movement. The most prominent was Abraham Geiger (1810–1874), who rapidly became the leading ideologist of the movement in Europe. Employing the new critical approach to Jewish texts, an approach known as *Wissenschaft des Judentums,* Geiger wrote scholarly studies and delivered lectures that presented Judaism as an evolving entity subject to the forces of history. The essence of Judaism, Geiger argued, was not its legal system but its religious spirit, reflected and symbolized in its rituals. This Jewish spirit was the product of revelation and created, in turn, the great literary monuments of Judaism. Geiger stressed the universal message of Judaism, setting its rational ethical monotheism into sharp contrast with Christian trinitarian dogma and pagan materialism. Under the influence of the early Romantic thinker Johann Gottfried Herder (1744–1803), who conceived spiritual epochs succeeding one another in nondialectical fashion, Geiger saw Judaism as a spiritual historical entity that in the modern world was entering a new epoch in its history. It bore within it the combined heritage of previous stages of its development and was moving toward yet undetermined forms of historical existence. For Geiger it was the task of the Reform rabbi to press the wheel of history forward with a program of modernizing and rationalizing reforms.

Geiger's colleague Zacharias Frankel (1801–1875), the rabbi of Dresden, took a more conservative position. Frankel recognized the historical development of Jewish law, but also its centrality, and he believed that the rabbinical leadership should be responsive to the present collective will and spiritual situation of the community, rather than attempt to direct and hasten its course of development. In 1845 Frankel broke with fellow reformers on the issue of Hebrew in the worship service, and in 1854 he became the head of the new conservatively oriented rabbinical seminary in Breslau. The most prominent radical reformer in this period was Samuel Holdheim (1806–1860), who believed the revolutionary new situation of Western Jewry demanded a thoroughgoing transformation of Judaism. Holdheim favored transfer of the Jewish Sabbath to Sunday and the abolition of all legal elements in Judaism. He regarded his own age as representing a clearly higher level of religious evolution, and he then argued that contemporary Jews had the right to reshape Judaism in messianic, universal terms without overmuch regard for preserving continuity with the past. Holdheim eventually became the rabbi of a separatist Reform congregation in Berlin that radically abbreviated and altered the traditional liturgy, retained only a minimum of Hebrew, and conducted its principal weekly service on Sunday.

Collective activity and diffusion. In the 1840s the Reform movement in Germany underwent a major revival. After considerable opposition, Geiger was able in 1840 to assume his tasks as one of the rabbis in the influential Breslau community. A year later the Hamburg temple issued a new version of its prayer book on the occasion of its move to more spacious quarters. Lay societies seeking more radical reforms sprang up in Frankfurt am Main, Berlin, and Breslau. Led for the most part by university-educated, highly acculturated German Jews, these societies proposed elimination of national symbols and ritual prescriptions from Judaism in favor of a highly spiritualized and universalized faith, anchored in a humanistic understanding of the Hebrew Bible and virtually excluding later rabbinic tradition. In their religious radicalism they paralleled similar contemporary movements in German Protestantism and Catholicism.

The rabbis inclined to religious reform now undertook a collective initiative for the first time. A total of forty-two rabbis, most still in their thirties and holding doctorates, participated in three conferences in the years 1844 to 1846. Although the rabbis represented a spectrum of opinion, the tenor of these conferences reflected a middle position among German reformers, dissatisfying both conservatives like Frankel, who favored only the slightest revisions in existing law and custom, and radicals like Holdheim, who urged strict conformity to the demands of the zeitgeist. Among the conclusions reached were that the use of Hebrew in the service was a subjective but not an objective necessity, that prayers for the return to Zion and the reinstitution of the sacrificial service should be eliminated from the prayer book, and that it was permissible to accompany the service with an organ even on the Sabbath. Plans for a new common liturgy and a committee report favoring the lay religious equality of women were not acted upon when the annual conferences ceased after the third year, in part because of the agitated political situation preceding the revolution of 1848.

In the second half of the nineteenth century, the Reform movement in Germany continued to make inroads in the Jewish communities, though generally with less éclat and polemic than heretofore. Increasingly, the larger Jewish communities provided for modified services (with organ accompaniment and a modified liturgy) as well as traditional ones. Religious reform became institutionalized in Germany as Liberal Judaism, one of two religious currents or trends *(Richtungen)* within the general community, and it soon won over the majority of German Jews. Synods, including laity as well as rabbis, were held to discuss further reforms in 1869 and 1871. At the end of the century a permanent union of Liberal rabbis was established, and a similar national organization for all Liberal Jews came into existence in 1908. However, a common prayer book for the German Liberal congregations—quite traditional in character—was not issued until 1929.

While the Reform movement in Europe remained centered in Germany, which had the largest Jewish population west of the czarist empire, it spread to other countries as well. As early as 1826 the Vienna community adopted a number of aesthetic reforms, as did some congregations in Hungary, Galicia, Holland, and Denmark. Even in Russia certain circles of *maskilim* ("enlightened" Jews) or immigrants from the West introduced decorum, choirs, and vernacular sermons. In the 1860s some Russian Jewish intellectuals argued, as did reformers in the West, that religious reform was indigenous to Jewish tradition from ancient times and that Orthodoxy in fact reflected stagnation.

In England a Reform congregation, called the West London Synagogue of British Jews, was founded in 1840. Generally conservative in character, its most pronounced reform was the abolition of the second days of certain holidays that were celebrated only according to rabbinic, not biblical, precept. Similar congregations were established elsewhere in

England. After the beginning of the nineteenth century, a more radical religious movement emerged that soon adopted the term *Liberal* to differentiate itself from the earlier Reform. British Liberal Judaism, which was patterned closely upon the American Reform Judaism of the time, sought to win back to the synagogue the large mass of English Jews who had become alienated from all religious Judaism. Its liturgy was largely in English, and men and women sat together.

In France the centralized consistory long militated against religious division. Some reforms, mostly cosmetic, were undertaken by the chief rabbis, and proposals for more radical change were aired with some regularity in the Jewish press. However, a viable, independent Reform congregation, the Union Libérale Israélite, was established only after the separation of church and state in France in 1905.

European Liberal Judaism—together with its counterpart in America—finally achieved international organizational unity with the establishment of the World Union for Progressive Judaism in London in 1926. Until World War II, the work of the Union, and of Reform Judaism in Europe generally, was particularly influenced by Leo Baeck (1873–1956), a Liberal rabbi in Berlin and a teacher at the seminary of the movement, the Hochschule für die Wissenschaft des Judentums, which had been established there in 1872. As a religious thinker, Baeck elaborated an antiromantic theology, greatly indebted to Immanuel Kant (1724–1804), which stressed the revealed moral commandment that emerges out of the mystery of revelation. Under the influence of Rudolf Otto (1869–1937), Baeck's theology later became less rationalistic, whereas his perspective grew more particularistic as he came to focus his attention on the unique religious history of the people of Israel.

AMERICANIZATION. Reform Judaism has enjoyed its greatest success in the United States. In Europe it was repeatedly forced to assert itself against an entrenched Orthodoxy, sometimes supported by the government; in the New World it faced no such established institutions. The United States lacked officially recognized Jewish communities, like the German *Gemeinde* with its powers of taxation and centralized control over Jewish affairs. The complete separation of church and state, the numerous Christian denominations existing side by side, and the prevalent notion that religious activity was strictly a matter of free choice created an atmosphere most conducive to Jewish religious fragmentation. Moreover, it was difficult for an immigrant Jew in nineteenth-century America to make a living while still observing all the inherited traditions. Given the large influx of Jews from Germany in the second third of the nineteenth century—among them some who had had experience with religious reform, as well as a number of Reform rabbis—it is understandable that, until the massive Jewish immigration from eastern Europe in the last decades of the century, Reform Judaism should play the dominant role in American Jewry. In the freer atmosphere of America, Reform soon took on a considerably more radical character than its counterpart in Europe.

Classical American Reform. With the exception of an isolated and short-lived attempt in 1824 to create a Reform congregation in Charleston, South Carolina, somewhat on the model of the Hamburg temple, Reform Judaism took hold in the United States only toward the middle of the nineteenth century. Beginning in 1842 with Har Sinai in Baltimore, liturgical reforms were gradually introduced into existing synagogues or new Reform congregations founded in New York City, Albany, Cincinnati, Philadelphia, and Chicago during the next twenty years. Jewish periodicals favoring religious reform appeared, as did new prayer books embodying various degrees of liturgical revision. When a rabbinical conference held in Cleveland in 1855 reaffirmed the authority of the Talmud, it aroused protests from the more thoroughgoing reformers, whose influence increased in the following decades.

During the second half of the nineteenth century, American Reform was dominated by two immigrant rabbis representing, respectively, a consistent, separatist ideological position and a pragmatic, relatively more conservative stance, which sought to make Reform Judaism broadly acceptable. David Einhorn (1809–1879), a rabbi in Baltimore and later in New York, stressed the priestly mission of the Jewish people and vigorously opposed mixed marriages, but he saw little value in most Jewish ceremonials and was a firm believer in the progress of Judaism beyond its ancient sacred texts. His influence was dominant at a meeting of Reform rabbis held in Philadelphia in 1869. Following debate in the German language, this conference declared that the dispersion of Israel providentially served its universal messianic aim. It also rejected the traditional dogma of bodily resurrection in favor of belief only in the immortality of the soul.

Isaac Mayer Wise (1819–1900) was the founding father of organized Reform Judaism in the United States. Unlike Einhorn, whose intellectual stature he did not rival, but whom he far excelled in practical energy, Wise sought to create an Americanized Judaism that could appeal to the widest spectrum of Jewry in the United States. Eschewing consistency, Wise sometimes took one position on religious issues, sometimes another, being concerned more with momentary effect than with crystallized ideology. However, unlike the radicals, he consistently rejected pentateuchal criticism as undermining the foundations of Judaism. As a rabbi in Cincinnati, Wise came to represent the more moderate midwestern wing of Reform Judaism, which differentiated itself from the more thoroughgoing Reform of the East Coast. It was largely due to Wise's efforts that the national organizations of Reform Judaism were created: the UAHC in 1873, Hebrew Union College (HUC) in 1875, and the CCAR in 1889.

In 1885 Wise served as president of a rabbinical conference that formulated the Pittsburgh Platform, a document that represented the ideological position of American Reform Judaism for the next half-century. The key figure at the conference, however, was not Wise but Kaufmann Kohler (1843–1926), a son-in-law and spiritual heir of David Einhorn, who became the movement's leading theologian and, after a short interval, succeeded Wise as president of Hebrew Union College. Under Kohler's influence the Pittsburgh conference declared that "Judaism presents the highest conception of the God-idea as taught in our holy Scriptures and developed and spiritualized by the Jewish teachers in accordance with the moral and philosophical progress of their respective ages." It recognized in the Bible "the record of the consecration of the Jewish people to its mission as priest of the One God," but found only the moral laws of the Pentateuch to be binding, while ritual precepts were to be subjected to the criterion of their continuing capacity to sanctify life and to be harmonizable with modern civilization. Jews were defined as a religious community, not a nation, their religion as progressive, "ever striving to be in accord with the postulates of reason." A final paragraph expressed a commitment to seek social justice in American society by reducing the "contrasts and evils" in its present organization (Meyer and Plaut, 2001, pp. 197–199). For the next fifty years, Reform Judaism adhered to the Pittsburgh Platform. During this period the movement increased in numbers, reaching a high point of about 60,000 families in 285 congregations before the Great Depression temporarily halted its growth. In 1892 the CCAR published the first edition of the *Union Prayer Book,* which, with only relatively minor revisions, remained standard in Reform Judaism until 1975. However, during this same half-century the movement was forced to give up its hopes of becoming the norm for American Jewry. It was increasingly associated specifically with the German Jewish immigrants and their descendants. Eastern Europeans, concentrated in New York, either remained Orthodox, dissociated themselves from religion entirely, or in the second generation were attracted by the more ethnic and nostalgic appeal of Conservative Judaism. Until the late 1930s most Reform Jews were opposed to Jewish nationalism, seeing in Zionism a retreat from the universal mission of Judaism. Nonetheless, a small percentage, especially among the rabbis, played active roles in Zionist affairs from the beginning of the century.

Reorientation. Only in the late 1930s did Reform Judaism in the United States began to lose its identification with the German immigrants. Reform rabbis, and then increasingly the laity as well, were now coming from eastern European backgrounds. During this same decade, awareness of the lot of Jews in Nazi Germany created stronger national ties among all Jews. Gradually, Reform Judaism began a process of transformation from which it emerged with a much more significant ethnic and ceremonial component than heretofore. Eventually the earlier period came to be designated Classical Reform Judaism, and whereas its particular emphases continued to be represented in a small number of congregations, even down to the early twenty-first century, a reoriented Reform Judaism began to displace or modify it at an increasing pace.

The first major indication of this shift in position was the Columbus Platform, adopted by the CCAR in 1937. This document was largely the work of Samuel Cohon (1888–1959), an eastern European Jew who served for many years as professor of Jewish theology at Hebrew Union College. The Columbus Platform spoke of a "living God" rather than a "God idea"; described Torah, in its broad sense as both written and oral law, as enshrining Israel's "ever-growing consciousness of God"; and declared that it was the task of all Jews to rebuild Palestine as a Jewish homeland, both as a "refuge for the oppressed and a center of Jewish culture and spiritual life" (Meyer and Plaut, 2001, pp. 199–203). In contrast to the Pittsburgh Platform, it stressed the use of Hebrew in worship and the importance of customs, symbols, and ceremonies. Like its predecessor, the platform declared the movement's commitment to social justice, a dominant concern of Reform Judaism during those years of economic distress in the United States.

Developments after World War II. In the immediate postwar years, Reform Judaism in the United States enjoyed remarkable growth. New congregations were established in the suburbs of major cities as increased Jewish affluence made possible higher levels of support for religious institutions both locally and nationally. The Christian religious revival of the 1950s produced renewed interest in Jewish theology. In 1951 the UAHC moved its offices from Cincinnati to New York, the center of Jewish life in the United States. From 1943 to 1973 the congregational union was headed by Rabbi Maurice Eisendrath (1902–1973), a talented organizer and impressive public speaker. The well-known biblical archaeologist Nelson Glueck (1900–1972), as president of Hebrew Union College from 1947 to his death in 1971, was able to achieve a merger with the Jewish Institute of Religion, founded by the Zionist Reform rabbi Stephen S. Wise (1874–1949) in 1922, and to bring about considerable expansion of the combined institution.

Reform Judaism now engaged vigorously with the moral issues troubling American society. Rabbis and laity participated actively in the civil rights movement and later in the organized opposition to the Vietnam War. In 1961 the UAHC established the Religious Action Center in Washington, D.C., with the intent of making a direct impact on legislation of Jewish and general religious or moral concern as well as educating the Reform constituency with regard to questions under current legislative consideration. In the spirit of ecumenism the UAHC developed a department dealing with interfaith activities, supplementing the long-standing work of individual congregations and of the National Federation of Temple Brotherhoods in this area.

Reform theology in this period grew increasingly diverse. A group of Reform rabbis, who became known as "covenant theologians," favored a more personalist and existential grounding of their faith. Influenced by the twentieth-century European Jewish thinkers Franz Rosenzweig (1886–1929) and Martin Buber (1878–1965), they eschewed the earlier idealist theology based on progressive revelation in favor of the notion of divine-human encounter as represented both by the testimony of the Torah and by contemporary religious experience. At the same time, however, there arose a significant rationalist and even humanist faction within the movement. Its members stressed the impact of biblical criticism and psychoanalysis upon religion, as well as the difficult theological questions that the Holocaust had raised for Jewish theism.

Whereas theological positions in Reform Judaism generally moved apart, religious practice, for the most part, became more traditional. The postwar period witnessed a renewal of interest in Jewish law not as authoritative in the Orthodox sense but as a guide for the religious life. Over three decades Solomon Freehof (1892–1990) of Pittsburgh, one of the most influential Reform rabbis, published half a dozen collections of Reform responsa on issues ranging from aspects of synagogue ritual to matters of individual observance. The publication of these responsa, as well as guides for religious observance, was due in part to the feelings of most of the religious leadership that Reform Judaism needed to reengage with traditional symbols and practices if it was not to dissipate in the absorptive social climate of postwar America. It was also prompted by a heightened ethnicism and personalism in Reform Judaism. The individual *bar mitsvah* ceremony for boys reaching the age of thirteen, and later the equivalent *bat mitsvah* ceremony for girls, were increasingly adopted by Reform congregations, preceding the group ceremony of confirmation. The rabbinical role, which in Reform Judaism had principally been that of prophetic preacher, now became more priestly, as congregants especially sought rabbis whose personal warmth would enhance life-cycle ceremonies. Reform synagogues introduced more Hebrew into the liturgy and encouraged greater congregational participation.

Jewish education among Reform Jews became more comprehensive in the 1970s. In place of the customary two hours per week of Sunday school instruction, most temples now offered twice-weekly classes supplemented by weekends or summer sessions at a camp. A handful of Reform day schools came into existence for those children whose parents desired them to obtain more extensive Jewish knowledge and depth of Jewish commitment. The National Federation of Temple Youth introduced study programs for Reform teenagers beyond religious-school age, and rabbinical education was extended to women. The first woman, Sally Priesand, was ordained by HUC–JIR in 1972. In 1981 the UAHC published its own Torah commentary, encouraging lay study of the Pentateuch according to the liberal approach of Reform.

The commitment of Reform Judaism to Zionism deepened in the postwar period. Reform Jews welcomed the establishment of the state of Israel in 1948, shared feelings of crisis and relief during its Six-Day War, and increasingly appropriated its cultural impact. Israeli melodies entered the synagogues, religious schools, and summer camps. The CCAR declared Israeli Independence Day a religious holiday, and beginning in 1970 HUC–JIR required all entering rabbinical students to spend the first year of their study at its campus in Jerusalem. Reform Jews organized the Association of Reform Zionists of America (ARZA) to give Reform Judaism an individual voice in the world Zionist movement.

In the state of Israel, the first successful Progressive congregation was established, mostly by German Jewish immigrants, in Jerusalem in 1958. Congregations in the other major cities followed, and attendance reached about five thousand for the High Holy Days. The congregations and their rabbis united as the Movement for Progressive Judaism in Israel, a regular constituent of the World Union for Progressive Judaism. The latter moved its headquarters to Jerusalem in 1974. In the 1970s, Israeli Reform also established its first *kibbuts* (collective agricultural settlement) in the southern desert and a youth movement with groups in various cities. In 1980 HUC–JIR for the first time ordained an Israeli Reform rabbi in Jerusalem. However, Reform Judaism (and also Conservative Judaism) remained unrecognized by the Israeli rabbinate and was forced to wage a continuous, and by the early twenty-first century incompletely successful, struggle for equal rights with Orthodoxy. In general, Israeli Reform emerged as considerably more traditional than its counterpart in the United States, finding the positions taken by the American radical wing on such matters as rabbinical officiation at mixed marriages and conversion procedures embarrassing in the Israeli milieu.

The centrality of Jewish peoplehood, symbolized by the state of Israel, found clear expression in a new platform of Reform Judaism. Called "A Centenary Perspective" because it was composed about one hundred years after the creation of the first national institutions of American Reform Judaism, it was adopted by the CCAR in 1976. The statement was the work of a committee chaired by Rabbi Eugene Borowitz, a professor at the New York school of HUC–JIR and one of the most influential contemporary theologians of the movement. Unlike previous platforms, it did not seek to define Judaism as a whole dogmatically, but only to give a brief historical account of Reform Judaism—what it has taught and what it has learned—and to describe its present spiritual convictions. Recognizing and affirming the diversity of theology and practice in contemporary Reform, it pointed to those broad conceptions and values shared by most Reform Jews. In the wake of the Holocaust, and recognizing the physically precarious situation of Israeli Jewry and the assimilatory forces operative on American Judaism, the statement gave prominence to the value of ethnic survival, an element not highlighted in earlier platforms. It affirmed the reality of God without setting forth any specific theology and defined the people of Israel as inseparable from its religion. Torah was seen as the product of "meetings between God and the Jewish people" (Meyer and Plaut, 2001, pp. 203–207), especially, but not only, in ancient times. Rejecting the optimism of nineteenth-century Reform Judaism, the statement nonetheless reaffirmed the religious significance of human history and the moral obligations of Jews, both particularly in Jewish matters and in the pursuit of universal messianic goals.

LATE-TWENTIETH-CENTURY TRENDS. During the last two decades of the twentieth century, Reform Judaism continued to assume a more traditional character. Religious services incorporated a higher proportion of Hebrew; ritual practice became as important as social action. In other respects, however, Reform Judaism took radical positions that separated it from both Conservative Judaism and Orthodoxy. Unlike the latter, and in contradiction to Jewish law, Reform Judaism accepted children of mixed marriages whose fathers but not mothers are Jewish and gave full equality in religious leadership to gays and lesbians. It sought to make non-Jews married to Jews feel welcome in the synagogue.

Whereas a generation earlier the Reform movement, like American Judaism in general, was largely focused upon Jewish peoplehood, the Holocaust, and the state of Israel, it increasingly emphasized the religious life of the individual, introducing prayers for healing into its services and stressing spirituality. Its rabbinate, perhaps under the influence of an increasing number of women within its ranks, came to place less emphasis upon the sermon and more upon pastoral counseling. Finally, the leadership of the movement stressed Jewish literacy, resulting in enhanced Jewish education for both children and adults. Most of these new trends were reflected in the platform of the movement adopted in Pittsburgh in 1999.

SEE ALSO Baeck, Leo; Buber, Martin; Frankel, Zacharias; Geiger, Abraham; Herder, Johann Gottfried; Holdheim, Samuel; Judaism, article on Judaism in Northern and Eastern Europe since 1500; Kohler, Kaufmann; Mendelssohn, Moses; Otto, Rudolf; Rosenzweig, Franz; Wise, Isaac M.; Wise, Stephen S.

BIBLIOGRAPHY

The most comprehensive historical work on Reform Judaism is Michael A. Meyer, *Response to Modernity: A History of the Reform Movement in Judaism* (New York, 1988), which replaced David Philipson, *The Reform Movement in Judaism*, 2d ed. (New York, 1931), reissued with a new introduction by Solomon Freehof (New York, 1967). Earlier, W. Gunther Plaut brought together a copious selection of primary sources, abbreviating the lengthier ones and translating into English those in other languages. The material in two volumes edited by Plaut, *The Rise of Reform Judaism* (New York, 1963) and *The Growth of Reform Judaism* (New York 1965), extends to 1948. Still of value is Max Wiener's *Jüdische Religion im Zeitalter der Emanzipation* (Berlin, 1933), translated into Hebrew (Jerusalem, 1974) but not, regrettably, into English. The specific matter of liturgical change is comprehensively treated, with extensive quotation from primary sources, in Jakob J. Petuchowski's *Prayerbook Reform in Europe* (New York, 1968). The initial phases of Reform Judaism in the United States are well understood from Leon A. Jick's study, *The Americanization of the Synagogue, 1820–1870* (Hanover, N.H., 1976), and the story of the movement's seminary from Samuel E. Karff, ed., *Hebrew Union College–Jewish Institute of Religion at One Hundred Years* (Cincinnati, 1976).

The more significant speeches delivered at meetings of the Central Conference of American Rabbis have been collected in Joseph L. Blau, *Reform Judaism: A Historical Perspective* (New York, 1973), and some of the more thoughtful members of the CCAR reflect on various aspects of the history of their organization in Bertram Wallace Korn, ed., *Retrospect and Prospect: Essays in Commemoration of the Seventy-Fifth Anniversary of the Founding of the Central Conference of American Rabbis, 1889–1964* (New York, 1965). The variety in Reform Jewish theology after World War II is well reflected in Bernard Martin, ed., *Contemporary Reform Jewish Thought* (Chicago, 1968). Two sociological analyses based on surveys taken in the early 1970s present the state of belief and practice among Reform rabbis and laity at that time: Theodore I. Lenn, *Rabbi and Synagogue in Reform Judaism* (New York,1972), and Leonard J. Fein et al., *Reform Is a Verb: Notes on Reform and Reforming Jews* (New York, 1972).

Principal sources and the texts of the platforms of American Reform Judaism are in Michael A. Meyer and W. Gunther Plaut, eds., *The Reform Judaism Reader: North American Documents* (New York, 2001). Dana Evan Kaplan has edited two volumes of reflections on the American Reform movement, *Contemporary Debates in American Reform Judaism* (New York, 2001) and *Platforms and Prayer Books: Theological and Liturgical Perspectives on Reform Judaism* (Lanham, Md., 2002). Contemporary American Reform Judaism is best followed through its major periodicals: *Reform Judaism* is a popular UAHC magazine circulated to all members four times a year; the *CCAR Journal*, a quarterly, is the official organ of the Reform rabbis. Current information on Reform Judaism is available on the websites of its major institutions.

MICHAEL A. MEYER (1987 AND 2005)

REGULY, ANTAL

REGULY, ANTAL (1819–1858) was a Hungarian traveler, linguist, and ethnographer and one of the founding fathers of Finno-Ugric studies. A typical romantic hero of his time, he was an extremely talented, persuasive, melancholic, and uneven person. As a talented nobleman he started to study law in Hungary, then he left for a "grand tour" to the North, and in Stockholm he met the Finnish-Swedish poet and politician A. I. Arwidsson (then in exile from his homeland), who called Reguly's attention to the national awakening in Finland (then a grand duchy in the Russian Empire). Reguly, who knew about the affinities of Hungarian, Finnish, and other Finno-Ugric languages, went to Finland, where between 1839 and 1841 he learned the Finnish language and made his first ethnographic and linguistic fieldwork trips (also among the Lapps, then in Estonia and Ingermanland, and among the Votes).

In Finland, Reguly was one of the first to follow Elias Lönnrot's footsteps as a folklore collector in Finland, and he even started to translate the "old" *Kalevala* into Hungarian. He met all the important intellectuals (including the mythologist and initiator of the "awakening movement" of the Lapps, L. L. Laestadius), and from 1841 on he met the intellectuals in Saint Petersburg (including K. E. von Baer and Peter von Köppen) and Swedish Lapland. Beginning in 1843, to some extent supported by the Czarist Academy and by the Hungarian Academy of Sciences, Reguly traveled to West Siberia to describe the peoples, akin to the Hungarians. Reguly traveled alone and visited several groups of the Voguls and Ostiaks. In 1844 in Tobolsk he met the famous Finnish linguist Matthias Alexander Castrén (1813–1852), who was in Siberia collecting material for his comparative studies of Uralic languages and mythologies. Reguly, on his way from Siberia (during the winter of 1845–1846) in the central area by the River Volga, collected some material of language and lore of the Finno-Ugric Cheremis and Mordvins and also the Turkic people, the Chuvash. Exhausted by the hardship of the climate and having serious financial troubles, he nevertheless was able to collect important linguistic, anthropological, and folklore material, including epic songs and other genres. After his return to Saint Petersburg in 1846, he engaged in drawing the first detailed map of the Ural Mountains.

Due to his failing health and hidden intrigues among Finnish and Russian scholarly circles in Saint Petersburg, Reguly had to return to Hungary, where in 1848 he was appointed first librarian of the university. In that time of reforms and a war of liberation in Hungary, the whole society wanted to find "noble relatives" for the Hungarians with elaborate mythology and majestic heroic songs, like the Finnish *Kalevala*. Reguly's trips did not fulfill such expectations. He could not find the ancient homeland (*Urheimat*) of the Hungarians, and the "mythology" in his Vogul and Ostiak texts seemed to be little and uninteresting. Moreover Reguly was unable to decipher and translate most of his fieldwork notes. Despite his nonsystematic training in linguistics, he could master foreign languages with ease. But he collected too much material in a hasty way. After suffering a nervous breakdown, he recovered slowly. In 1857 he conducted anthropological research among the *palóc* group in Hungary, but he died suddenly, without publishing the texts he collected.

Generations of Finno-Ugric linguists in Hungary (such as Pál Hunfalvy, Bernát Munkácsi, József Pápai, Miklós Zsirai, Dávid Fokos Fuchs, and Béla Kálmán) undertook the painstaking task of editing Reguly's manuscripts. From the end of the nineteenth century they organized several fieldwork trips to western Siberia, and with the help of native informants, they have tried to translate Reguly's texts. Of course they have collected new material as well. In the early twenty-first century practically a complete, bilingual edition of Reguly's Vogul and Ostiak texts exists, with scholarly notes. The notes describe several genres of folk literature of the Ob-Ugrians and give detailed summaries on bear ceremonialism and personal and epic songs.

Reguly was not specialized in collecting mythology or in grammar. In this respect his contemporary, the Finnish scholar Castrén surpassed him. But Reguly's folklore texts are of unparalleled importance. He registered perhaps at the last moment the traditional texts, and he had the anthropologist's view on the life of the people. Moreover the later Hungarian expeditions collected good comparative material, often from the same village, but from informants two or three generations later. The poetic genres and religious ceremonies among the Ob-Ugrians Reguly detected are in some cases alive even in the early twenty-first century. But their continuous variability Reguly's data inevitable as a starting point to any further investigation. It is a pity that Reguly did not leave a "complete" description of an Ob-Ugrian shaman's séance. His material still serves as the basis for the later summaries of Ob-Ugrian religion, such as those by Bernát Munkácsi, Géza Róheim, Béla Kálmán, Vilmos Diószegi, Edit Vértes, and Éva Schmidt. Reguly's collections from other Finno-Ugric peoples have a lesser importance for the study of mythology, but they are often the first scholarly collected folklore items of special regions or genres.

SEE ALSO Castrén, Matthias Alexander; Finno-Ugric Religions; Khanty and Mansi Religion; Laestadius, Lars Levi.

BIBLIOGRAPHY

Lázár, Katalin and Enikő Szíj. *Reguly Antal "hangjegyre szedett" finnugor dallamai.* Budapest, 2000. Finno-Ugric folk melodies, collected by Reguly, with musical notes.

Pápay, József. *Reguly Antal emlékezete.* Budapest, 1905. Papers in memoriam of Reguly.

Reguly, Antal. Sciences Research Diary. In the Archives of the Hungarian Academy of Budapest. Unpublished.

Reguly, Antal. *Ethnographisch-geographische Karte des nördlichen Ural Gebietes: Entworfen auf einer Reise in den Jahren 1844 und 1845.* Saint Petersburg, 1846.

Reguly, Antal, Bernát Munkácsi, and Béla Kálmán. *Vogul népköltési gyűjtemény* (Volgul folk poetry). 4 vols. with subvols. Budapest, 1892–1963. Texts, translations, and scholarly notes.

Reguly, Antal, József Pápay, Miklós Zsirai, and Dávid Fokos. *Osztják népköltési gyűjtemény* (Ostiak folk poetry). 3 vols. with subvols. Budapest, 1905–1965. Texts, translations, and scholarly notes.

Róheim, Géza. *Hungarian and Vogul Mythology.* Locust Valley, N.Y., 1954.

Stipa, Günter. *Finnisch-ugrische Sprachforschung.* Helsinki, 1990.

Vértes, Edit. *Szibériai nyelvrokonaink hitvilága.* Budapest, 1990.

Vértes, Edit. *Die Mythologie der Uralier Sibiriens.* Bonn, 2001.

VILMOS VOIGT **(2005)**

REIMARUS, HERMANN SAMUEL

REIMARUS, HERMANN SAMUEL (1694–1768), German theologian and philosopher. Son of a scholar, grandson of a clergyman, student and son-in-law of J. A.

Fabricius (one of the staunchest defenders of orthodoxy of the time), Reimarus was for much of his life a professor of Oriental languages at the Hamburg academic *Gymnasium.* He lived during the period of the German Enlightenment, amidst the evolving discussion of the relation between reason and revelation.

Reimarus's public religious views belong to that stage characterized by the philosophical synthesis of Christian Wolff: (1) revelation may be above reason but not contrary to it, and (2) reason establishes the criteria by which revelation may be judged, namely, necessity and consistency. Publicly, Reimarus argued that the demands of a natural religion of reason only and those of Christianity agree with or complement one another. Natural religion, he contended, lays the ground for Christianity. These public views were set forth most succinctly in his *Abhandlungen von den vornehmsten Wahrheiten der natürlichen Religion* (Essays on the Principal Truths of Natural Religion; 1754). At his death, a colleague would eulogize him as a defender of Christianity.

Reimarus's private views of religion were not known even to his wife. They were part of the rationalism that contended that the criteria of reason judge revelation to be false. Revelation is at odds with reason and must be displaced. Natural religion, he believed, replaces Christianity. Reimarus recorded his private views in a secret manuscript he entitled *Apologie oder Schutzschrift für die vernünftigen Verehrer Gottes* (Apology for or Defense of the Rational Worshiper of God), three copies of which remain. Of the thirty-seven works that he wrote, this one alone has brought him renown. In it he accepts Wolff's contention that the two criteria of necessity and consistency must be satisfied by any alleged revelation before its genuineness can be accepted. He then sets out to show (1) that it is possible to describe the origins of Christianity as entirely natural (not miraculous and therefore not necessary) and (2) that any supposed revelation is filled with contradictions (not logically consistent). Reason thereby undermines the claims of the alleged Christian revelation. Seven fragments of this manuscript were published by G. E. Lessing between 1774 and 1778. Of these the two most influential were the sixth, "On the Resurrection Narratives" (1777), which declares the revelation of the resurrection false on the basis of contradictions, and the seventh, "On the Intentions of Jesus and His Disciples" (1778), which draws a distinction between the message and intention of Jesus and that of the early church.

Reimarus has influenced contemporary thought indirectly through Lessing, David F. Strauss, and Albert Schweitzer. The fragments of the *Apologie* caused Lessing to break with the eighteenth-century assumption that religious truth depended on the historicity of certain alleged events in scripture. Lessing's position, in turn, influenced Kierkegaard, who maintained that Christian truth is established independently of one's estimate of the historical origins of Christianity by God's act in the moment, though history occasions that moment. The fragments also caused Lessing to come to grips with the need for source criticism of the Gospels.

The fragments played a role in Strauss's struggle to establish a mythical view of miracles. Strauss used Reimarus to show that Christianity was not supernatural. As a result, Reimarus confronts the modern reader with the question of the historicity of the miracles.

The fragments also influenced Schweitzer in his work in the area of eschatology. Schweitzer turned to Reimarus to support his view that Jesus' orientation was eschatological, that Jesus expected an imminent end of the world, and that the delay of the Parousia was the main problem of early Christian theology, beginning with Jesus himself.

BIBLIOGRAPHY

Grappin, Pierre. "La théologie naturelle de Reimarus." *Études germaniques* 6 (1951): 169–181.

Lundsteen, A. C. *Hermann Samuel Reimarus und die Anfänge der Leben-Jesu Forschung.* Copenhagen, 1939.

Sieveking, Heinrich. "Hermann Samuel Reimarus, 1694–1768." *Zeitschrift des Vereins für hamburgische Geschichte* 38 (1939): 145–182.

Strauss, David F. *Hermann Samuel Reimarus und seine Schutzschrift für die vernunftigen Verehrer Gottes.* 2d ed. Bonn, 1877.

Talbert, Charles H., ed., *Reimarus: Fragments.* Translated by Ralph S. Fraser. Philadelphia, 1970. Includes my critical introduction (pp. 1–43).

CHARLES H. TALBERT (1987)

REINACH, SALOMON (1858–1932) was a French archaeologist and author of more than seventy books. Reinach is most widely known for his controversial writings in the area of the anthropological-ethnological comparative study of religions. He became conservator of the Musées Nationales in 1893, director of the Musée des Antiquités Nationales in Saint-Germain in 1901, and also served from the following year onward as professor at the École du Louvre in Paris. He was coeditor of the *Revue archéologique,* and from 1896 a member of the Académie des Inscriptions.

Although he branded eighteenth-century rationalism as a "paltry doctrine" seeking "to suppress religion without knowing its essence and without any clear idea of its origin and development" (*Cultes,* vol. 2, p. xviii, my translation), Reinach expressed his admiration for Voltaire, whose ideas about religion he did not share, but whose "incomparable gifts as a narrator" greatly inspired him (*Orpheus,* Eng. ed. of 1930, pp. vi-vii) and in whose spirit he wished to wage a more effective campaign against the church. "The history of humanity is that of a progressive secularisation [*laïcisation*] which is by no means complete as yet" (*Orpheus,* p. 23).

Reinach saw his own role as that of a popularizer of what others—among them Robertson Smith, Frazer, Tylor, Lang, and Jevons—had discovered: "Mine has been a lowlier part—to grasp the ideas of my betters, and to diffuse them as widely as I might" (*Cults*, p. xi). His summary definitions of magic and religion and of totem and taboo are in many ways illustrative of his approach. Reinach described magic as "the strategy of animism," and he based his definition of religion on the Latin word *religio*, calling it "a sum of scruples which impede the free exercise of our faculties" (*Orpheus*, p. 23). On totem and taboo Reinach remarked: "The totem is inconceivable without a taboo, and the logical outcome of a generalised taboo can hardly be anything else than a totem" (*Cults*, p. ix). His admission, made during the Third International Congress for the History of Religions held at Oxford in 1908, that totemism was "an overridden hobby" of which he himself had been "one of the roughriders" was followed by the statement that he "did not yet feel disposed to apologize nor to recant," and this unwillingness seems to hold true for subsequent writings as well. Discussing, for example, the ceremonial killing and eating of a totem, he leaves the possibility open that this idea of "fortifying and sanctifying oneself by assimilation of a divine being" survived in the medieval Christian rite of the Eucharist: "If primitive Christianity, with its theophagistic practices, conquered Europe so rapidly, it was because this idea of the manducation of the god was not new, but simply the presentation of one of the most profound religious instincts of humanity in a more spiritual form" (*Orpheus*, p. 19).

BIBLIOGRAPHY

Reinach wrote extensively in the areas of classical philology, archaeology, and art history. Among his publications in these fields are *Manuel de philologie classique*, 2 vols. (Paris, 1883–1884); *Minerva*, 4th ed. (Paris, 1900); and *Apollo: Histoire générale des arts plastiques* (Paris, 1904), which has been translated by Florence Simmonds as *Apollo: An Illustrated Manual of the History of Art throughout the Ages*, 2d ed. (London, 1907).

Almost one hundred of Reinach's articles, most dealing with the comparative study of religion, were republished in *Cultes, mythes et religions*, 2d ed., 4 vols. (Paris, 1908–1913). Elizabeth Frost selected fourteen of these essays for her translation, *Cults, Myths and Religions* (London, 1912).

Bibliographical sources include E. Pottier's "Salomon Reinach," *Revue archéologique*, 5th series, 36 (1932): 137–154; *Bibliographie de Salomon Reinach, 1874–1922*, with supplement (Saint-Germain, 1922–1927); and *Bibliographie de Salomon Reinach*, with notes by Seymour de Ricci (Paris, 1936). This last volume also includes a biographical sketch of Reinach.

New Sources

Reinach's ideas on the origins and development of religions are summarized in *Orpheus: Histoire générale des religions* (Paris, 1909). This book became extremely popular. It went through thirty editions (30th, Paris, 1921) and was translated into five languages, including Russian during the Soviet era. The English edition, translated by Florence Simmonds as *Orpheus: A General History of Religions* (New York, 1909), went through thirty-eight editions before Reinach's death (the edition quoted in the text is that of 1930).

Every existing publication of *Cults, Myths and Religions* is superseded by a new edition of a broad selection of these articles in French as *Cultes, mythes et religions* (Paris, 1996). This volume is provided with a foreword by Pierre Brunel, a preface, five sectional introductions and complementary notes by Hervé Duchêne. The detailed and well-organized bibliography makes this book an indespensable tool for every research.

Metzger, H. "La Bibliothèque Salomon Reinach." *Bulletin de Liaison de la Société des Amis de la Bibliothèque Salomon Reinach* 2 (1984): 25–27.

Duchêne, Hervé. "Un Athénien: Salomon Reinach." *Bull. Correspondance Hellenique* 120 (1996): 273–284.

Lavagne, Henri. "Lettres inédites de Franz Cumont à Salomon Reinach." *Compre rendus de l'Academie des Inscriptions* 2 (2000): 763–774.

WILLEM A. BIJLEFELD (1987)
Revised Bibliography

REINCARNATION. The doctrine of reincarnation concerns the rebirth of the soul or self in a series of physical or preternatural embodiments, which are customarily human or animal in nature but are in some instances divine, angelic, demonic, vegetative, or astrological (i.e., are associated with the sun, moon, stars, or planets). The concept of rebirth may also be expressed in such terms as *metempsuchōsis* (or more accurately, *metensōmatōsis*, "passage from one body to another") and *palingenesis* (Gr., lit., "to begin again").

The belief in rebirth in one form or another is found in tribal or nonliterate cultures all over the world. The notion is most dramatically evident in the native societies of central Australia and West Africa, where it is intimately associated with the cult of ancestor worship.

It is in ancient India and Greece, however, that the doctrine of rebirth has been most elaborately developed. In India, the precept is linked inextricably with the teachings and practices of Hinduism, Buddhism, Jainism, Sikhism (a hybrid synthesis of Hinduism and Islam founded in the fifteenth century by Gurū Nānak), and Sufism (the mystical branch of Islam); it even figures in the writings of such modern thinkers as Ramakrishna and Aurobindo. In ancient Greece, the idea is identified primarily with the philosophical lineages of Pythagoras, Empedocles, Plato, and Plotinus.

The doctrine of rebirth can also be found in certain ancient Near Eastern religions, for example, the royal cultus of the pharoahs in ancient Egypt and the mystery cult of Orpheus in second-century Greece. It is found in the teachings of Manichaeism, a third-century CE Persian religion founded by the prophet Mani. The concept of reincarnation also figures in such modern schools of thought as the Theosophy of H. P. Blavatsky and Annie Besant and the humanistic psychology of thinkers like C. G. Jung and Fritz Perls; it appears also in the "perennial philosophy" of Aldous Huxley.

ARCHAIC CULTURES. That the belief in reincarnation is of great antiquity in the history of the human species is suggested by the existence of the idea at the core of the belief systems of numerous nonliterate ethnic groups scattered throughout various parts of the world. It is also suggested by the fact that some archaic peoples whose physical culture (domestic architecture, implements of livelihood, etc.) is of an extremely primitive nature (e.g., the Arunta, or Aranda, people who originally inhabited the wastelands of central Australia and who may be classified as a Stone Age society) espouse the ideas of preexistence and reincarnation, which may indicate that this belief arose contemporaneously with the origins of human culture per se.

It is particularly significant that a belief in reincarnation in some form or another is to be found in non-literate cultures all over the world. Other primary cultural areas (besides central Australia) in which this precept is noticeably present are West Africa (among the Ewe, Edo, Igbo, and Yoruba), southern Africa (among the Bantu-speakers and the Zulu), Indonesia, Oceania, New Guinea, and both North and South America (among selected ethnic groups).

In sub-Saharan Africa, for example, reincarnation is not only viewed positively, but failure to be reborn and thereby gain yet another opportunity to improve the world of the living is regarded as an evil (as is the state of childlessness). Weighty emphasis is placed upon fertility rites and the efficacious powers of the shaman to promote the production of offspring (i.e., the rebirth of the ancestral spirits).

Among the Yoruba and Edo peoples, the belief in the rebirth of the departed ancestors remains a strong and vibrant cultural force to the present day. It is their custom to name each boy child "Father Has Returned" and each girl child "Mother Has Returned." The Zulu hold that the spirit of each person undergoes numerous rebirths in the bodies of various beasts, which range in size from tiny insects to huge elephants, until at long last the spirit enters a human body where it is fated to undergo yet another birth. Finally, after reaching the pinnacle of human existence, the soul is united with the supreme spirit from which it originated in the beginning. Here, as in other archaic cultures, the belief in reincarnation is linked directly with the veneration of ancestors, for it is the spirits of deceased ancestors that return in one or another life-form in association with the various totemic groups that form the organizational structure of the society.

For the Australian Aborigines, it is axiomatic that the spirits of human beings are periodically incarnated in animal or plant forms or even in such inanimate entities as water, fire, and wind, or the sun, moon, and stars. This belief is based upon the presupposition that the soul is separable from the body and from any other physical object it may inhabit. By virtue of its capacity to survive independently of a physical abode for at least a brief time, the soul possesses the capacity to travel from body to body and to inhabit a variety of forms ranging from stones and insects to animals and human beings. Because of the centrality of the totemic clan in Aboriginal religion, it was of utmost importance to establish the precise identity of the ancestor being reborn in each instance.

According to Australian Aboriginal religious beliefs, a deceased ancestor, after a sojourn of an unspecified length of time in the land of the dead, returns to the world of the living by entering the body of a mother at the moment of conception. The father is believed to play no direct role in impregnating the mother. Instead, the mother-to-be conceives new life by coming into the proximity of an *oknanikilla*, or local totem center, in which a spirit being (*alcheringa*) or soul of a deceased ancestor is lying in wait to be reborn.

Women who desire children travel to a sacred totem center with the intention of conceiving. The Aborigines also believe that if a woman happens to walk in the revered spots where the *alcheringa* ancestors are located, she will become impregnated without their intending it, even against their will. It is also commonly believed that when a woman conceives a child at a site sacred to a particular clan or totemic group (say, for example, the lizard totem), then that child will belong to the clan identified with the place of conception rather than with the clan of its parents. Thus, clan connections outweigh blood-relationships in cultural significance.

HINDUISM. The whole of the Hindu ethical code laid down in the ancient law books (e.g., *Laws of Manu*) presupposes the survival of the soul after death and assumes that the present life is fundamentally a preparation for the life to come. According to the Hindu conception of transmigration or rebirth (*saṃsāra*, "a course or succession of states of existence"), the circumstances of any given lifetime are automatically determined by the net results of good and evil actions in previous existences. This, in short, is the law of *karman* (action), a universal law of nature that works according to its own inherent necessity. Reward and punishment are thus not decreed by a god or gods nor by any other supernatural personage. It is a person's own actions, in conformity to the moral and cosmic law (*dharma*), that is determinative. The law of *karman* finds synoptic expression in the Upaniṣadic assertion: "By good deeds one becomes good, by evil, evil."

As early as the Upaniṣads human destinies are assigned to two divergent pathways: the pathway of the ancestors (*pitṛs*), which is traversed by those persons who follow worldly pursuits, and the pathway of the gods (*devas*), which is taken by those who meditate with faith and austerity in the forest (*Chāndogya Upaniṣad* 4.15.5, 5.10.1–10). The former path leads to rebirth; the latter, toward brahman and liberation. After the "worldling" has resided in the postmortem realm until the effects of his previous deeds has been consumed, he returns along the same route by which he departed the world to be reborn. By contrast, those who depart by the pathway of the gods reach *brahman*, the Ultimate, and are released from the rule of *saṃsāra* forever. For them, say the scriptures, there is no returning.

The *Bhagavadgītā*, one of the most highly revered texts of Hinduism, asserts that the eternal self (*ātman*) is unaffected even to the slightest degree by the vicissitudes of finite existence. According to this text, the universal soul, or self, in its essential nature neither comes to be nor passes away, for "of the nonexistent there is no coming to be; of the existent, there is no coming not to be" (2.11–25). It is rather the body (*śarīra*) or the embodied form (*jīva*) of the self that is subject to the changing conditions of life: creation and destruction, good and evil, victory and defeat. As the eternal, unchanging, and imperishable spiritual essence of humanity, the self is invincible to alteration of any sort, whether on this side of eternity or beyond.

The succession of finite births has traditionally been regarded by Hindus pessimistically, as an existential misfortune and not as a series of "second chances" to improve one's lot, as it is often viewed in the West. Life is regarded not only as "rough, brutish, and short" but as filled with misery (*duḥkha*). Thus, the multiplication of births within this "vale of tears" merely augments and intensifies the suffering that is the lot of all creatures. Furthermore, this painful existence continues unabated until such time as a person experiences spiritual liberation (*mokṣa*, or *mukti*).

The root cause of this existential bondage to time, ignorance, and suffering is desire (*taṇhā*), or avaricious attachment to objects that at best bring only limited, and often debased, pleasure. Even the life of a deity (*deva*) is governed by the law of death and rebirth. Hence, a person's only hope of escaping the clutches of rebirth is through extinguishing all desires except the desire for perfect unification with the universal self (*brahman*). The empirical self of the liberated person "goes to the *brahman* and becomes the *brahman*." As a result, he is free from the effects of all actions, both good and evil, and from any subsequent participation in existences determined by *karman*. This state of complete union with the universal self is known as *mokṣa* ("release" or "salvation").

Opinions differ among Indian sages as to whether final liberation is attainable while still in an embodied state or only after death. At least from the time of the *Vedānta Sūtra* (second century), the sages believed that salvation could be achieved while still alive. Thus, according to the *Mahābhārata*, the *ātman* is affected by the bonds of finite existence only under the conditions of metaphysical ignorance (*avidyā*), but once a soul is enlightened (*prakāṣita*), the self is freed from the consequences of its good and evil deeds and thereupon becomes indistinguishably identified with the *brahman* (12.267.32–38).

BUDDHISM. Śākyamuni Buddha, like his philosophical and spiritual predecessors, believed that birth and death recur in successive cycles for the person who lives in the grip of ignorance about the true nature of the world. However, he undercut the Vedāntic position by denying that the world of evanescent entities is undergirded and suffused by an eternal and unalterable Self or "soul-stuff" (*ātman*). In place of the doctrine of absolute self, he propagated the precept of "no-self" (*anātman*), namely, that the human person, along with everything else that constitutes the empirical universe, is the offspring (*phala*) of an unbroken, everfluctuating process of creation and destruction and birth and extinction according to the principle of Dependent Co-origination (*pratītya-samutpāda;* Pali, *paṭiccasamuppāda*). The technical formulation of this Law of Causation is as follows: "If this exists [e.g., an acorn], then that comes to be [an oak tree]." The entire universe perishes and is created afresh in every instant; nothing remains the same from one moment to the next, from a single microbe to an entire galaxy.

The human being or personality, therefore, is not to be understood essentially as an integral and enduring mind-body organism but rather as the manifestation of a highly complex succession of psychosomatic moments propelled along the temporal continuum by the force of *karman*. In the Buddhist view, the human person can be broken down into five constitutive elements, or strands (*skandhas*); it is continually changing but is always determined by its previous actions. As such, humans are never the same from moment to moment and therefore are in no sense the projection of a permanent self. Hence, a cardinal teaching of the Buddha is "there is nothing that transmigrates and yet there is rebirth."

If there is no absolute self that survives the death of one body and is reborn in a new one, then how is the doctrine of rebirth to be reconciled with that of "no-self"? The Buddha declares that this question, like other questions pertaining to the fundamental nature of reality, arises out of a misconstruing of the nature of *karman*. *Karman* is not a unified and independently existing entity that moves from life to life, as a traveler might go from place to place. Rightly understood, *karman* is the life process itself, the blending of energy and form that coordinates an unending flow of life moments. That is, the myriad clusters of factors that constitute the universe at any given moment are nothing more than the product of all its pasts. In other words, the sprout is not the temporary projection of some universal "soul-stuff" but rather a permutation of the parent seed. As one Buddhist text declares, "One hundred thousand universes conspire in the creation of the iridescent eye that graces the feather in the peacock's tail." Birth and death, then, are to be construed as nothing more than dramatic interruptions or exceptional innovations in the ongoing life process.

Therefore, neither a single entity (however subtle and rarified) nor a conglomeration of entities passes across from the old life-form to the new, yet the continuity among the phenomena is maintained. That is, all of the constitutive elements of a person's life are present from the moment of conception, just as the sprout preexists in the seed and contains the sum total of all the effects of its antecedent causal elements, at least in a state of potentiality.

According to the doctrine of *karman*, a person may be reborn successively into any one of five classes of living beings: gods, human beings, animals, hungry ghosts, or denizens of hell. Since birth as a human being occurs at the apex of the ladder of existence and is the penultimate stage to full enlightenment, it follows that all humans have undergone a birth in each of the four other orders of existence prior to the current cycle and occupy a privileged position from which to reach the ultimate goal.

While theoretically all human beings possess the capacity to achieve enlightenment and, thence, liberation from rebirth (Zen Buddhists, for example, contend that a person can experience *satori* at any moment simply by dropping off the thinking mind), in practice only those select few who forsake the life of social responsibility in the world and follow the Buddha *dharma* exclusively as monks and nuns have a realistic hope of achieving salvation in this life.

JAINISM. According to the teachings of Mahāvīra (c. 599–527 BCE), the founder of Jainism, the unenlightened soul is bound to follow a course of transmigration that is beginningless and one that will persist for an unimaginable length of time. The soul becomes defiled by involvement in desire-laden actions and thereby attracts increasingly burdensome quantities of karmic matter upon itself. This polluting material, in turn, promotes the further corruption of the soul and causes its inevitable movement through countless incarnations.

The Jains conceive of *karman* as composed of innumerable invisible particles of material substance that pervade all occupied space. Actions of body, mind, and speech project waves of energy that, when combined with the antithetical passions of desire (*rāga*) and hatred (*dveṣa*), attract karmic "dust" to the soul and weigh it down deeper and deeper in the slough of ignorance and rebirth.

Jains also distinguish between the initial awakening to an awareness of one's bondage to ignorance, suffering, death, and rebirth (the most that the layperson can hope to achieve), on the one hand, and the ultimate state of liberation, on the other. This ultimate state of bliss to which aspire all Jains (or at least the adherents of the monastic path) disperses and dissolves the load of karmic matter that encumbers the mind-body ego and transforms the practitioner into an omniscient and totally dispassionate soul.

ANCIENT GREECE. Whether the idea of metempsychosis was imported by the ancient Greeks from the East (more specifically, India) is subject to speculation in face of the absence of conclusive evidence to support one or another view. Be that as it may, the concept of rebirth occupied a central place in Greek thought from the time of Pherecydes of Syros (sixth century BCE), the mentor of Pythagoras (c. 582–507 BCE), and came into full flowering in the writings of Plato (427–347 BCE) and Plotinus (205–270 CE).

Herodotos, the greatest of ancient Greek historians, records that the Egyptians were the first people to embrace the doctrine of reincarnation. According to his sources, the Egyptians believed that the soul is immortal (i.e., subject to rebirth after each death) and that it passes through various species of terrestrial, marine, and aerial creatures before once again becoming embodied in human form, the entire cycle being completed at the end of a period of three thousand years.

Empedocles (490–430 BCE), under the influence of the writings of the mystic-mathematician Pythagoras, asserted that nothing in the cosmos is either created or destroyed. All living things undergo transmutation in accordance with the relationships among the four basic elements (air, fire, water, and earth). The souls of the impure are condemned to transmigrate for thirty thousand years through numerous types of incarnations. In the course of this transition, various lifetimes are affected in diverse ways by each of the four elements. Escape from this dark destiny is achieved through a lengthy purification process, the primary requirement of which is the avoidance of eating the flesh of animals whose souls once may have inhabited human bodies.

Like many other religious and philosophical traditions that hold to a belief in reincarnation, Orphism, an ancient Greek mystery cult that celebrated the life, death, and resurrection of the god Orpheus, is based upon a dualistic conception of humanity. Orphic sages declared that humans are composed of an invisible soul that was originally good and pure but that has become polluted by some kind of primordial sin or error. As a consequence of this ancient transgression, the originally pure soul has become imprisoned within a physical body that is believed to be impure or evil by nature.

The ultimate aim of this mystery was to raise the soul of each devotee to increasingly loftier and purer levels of spiritual existence. The elevation of the soul was promoted by participation in the sacramental practices of the Orphic brotherhoods (*thiasoi*). By performing these sacraments—always in secret places and often in the dead of night—the devotee received the power of the divine life. By continually cultivating this gift through meditation, prayer, and vegetarianism, he eventually gained immortality and thereby achieved release from any future reincarnations.

Orphic eschatology emphasized postmortem rewards and punishments. Because of its essentially spiritual nature, the soul could not achieve its true state of existence until after the last of a lengthy series of lives. Complete and lasting freedom from bondage to the material order could be realized only after undergoing a series of rebirths in a variety of physical forms that were determined by the merits of the previous life or lives. Supposedly it was this mystical teaching that was the heart of the revelation that was given to each novice initiated into the Orphic religion.

Plato drew together and synthesized numerous strands of thought concerning the fate of the individual soul. Under the influence of Empedocles, Pythagoras, the Orphic prophets, and others, he fashioned a theory of the nature and destiny of humanity that is as complex in its philosophical makeup as it is inspiring in its poetical contents. Like the Vedāntins, he believed that the soul (*psuchē*) is immortal. The soul is the governor and indweller of all conscious beings; it descends periodically into the physical realm of existence as a result of metaphysical nescience and bondage to the passions. Like the Vedāntins and the Buddhists, Plato declared that the soul of each human being (except for that of the "true philosopher," who is the one truly enlightened being) is entrapped by the body (and by material reality, generally) because of its attachment to the objects of transitory desire (i.e., objects of pleasure and pain). In a statement in the *Laws* (book 10) that could easily have been lifted directly from the Upaniṣads, he asserts, "Recognize that if you become baser you will go to baser souls, and if higher, to the higher, and in every course of life and death you will do and suffer what like may appropriately suffer at the hands of like."

Even the selection of a new incarnation by each soul at the beginning of a new life cycle is determined by the experiences of the former lifetime. During its journey through a series of births, the soul finds temporary abode not only in a variety of land, air, and water creatures, but, once it has achieved the status of humanity, it may pass through a number of professions of varying degrees of moral quality, ranging from that of a demagogue and tyrant at the nadir of the scale, to a lover, a follower of the Muses, and a seeker after wisdom at the apex (*Phaedrus* 248d–e).

According to Plato's famous myth of Er (*Republic* 10), those souls whose minds are governed by the baser pleasures first travel to the plain of Forgetfulness and take up residence on the banks of the river of Indifference, "where each as he drinks, forgets everything"; they then go to their respective births "like so many shooting stars."

The painful and disorienting wanderings of the soul throughout the various orders of creatures are brought to a halt, and the soul is ushered into a state of eternal and perfectly fulfilling bliss, but only after it has divorced itself completely from the pleasures of the body and the material world, placed all of its appetites and yearnings under the governance of Reason, and attained a pure and undeviating contemplation of the Absolute ("the Good"), thereby obtaining "the veritable knowledge of being that veritably is."

In the end, the liberated soul finds unending sojourn in the "place beyond the heavens" (cf. the *brahman* in Vedānta), where "true being dwells, without color or shape, that cannot be touched; reason alone, man's pilot, can behold it and all true knowledge is knowledge thereof" (*Phaedrus* 247d–e).

CONCLUSION. There is no question but that the twin doctrines of *karman* and reincarnation have done more to shape the whole of Asian thought than any other concept or concepts. It might be difficult to identify an idea or set of ideas that has exercised a comparable influence through the entire scope of Western thought, including the cardinal concepts in the writings of Plato and Aristotle.

Ironically, the notion of reincarnation is beginning to make inroads into contemporary Western thought (particularly in theology, the philosophy of religion, and psychology) by way of a number of circuitous routes. One of the most notable avenues along which the idea is traveling to the West is the number of Asian (primarily Indian) religious traditions that have appeared in Europe and America, along with theosophy, transpersonal psychology, and the academic study of the history of religions and comparative philosophy.

One of the most curious manifestations of the belief in reincarnation in modern times is a new approach to psychotherapy that operates in the United States under the rubric of "rebirthing analysis," which purports to help the client deal with current psychological and spiritual problems by recalling personal experiences during numerous past lifetimes with the aid of meditation, hypnosis, and in some cases, consciousness-altering drugs.

Time alone will tell whether this new imprint on the fabric of Western thought and life will endure to become an integral part of the overall design or will, in time, fade into insignificance and remain only as a vague memory of a short-lived image in Western consciousness.

SEE ALSO Enlightenment; Karman; Mokṣa; Orpheus.

BIBLIOGRAPHY

de Bary, Wm. Theodore, et al., eds. *Sources of Indian Tradition.* New York, 1958.

Ducasse, Curt John. *A Critical Examination of the Belief in the Life after Death.* Springfield, Ill., 1961.

Head, Joseph, and S. L. Cranston, eds. *Reincarnation: The Phoenix Fire Mystery.* New York, 1977.

MacGregor, Geddes. *Reincarnation as a Christian Hope.* London, 1982.

Parrinder, Geoffrey. "Varieties of Belief in Reincarnation." *Hibbert Journal* 55 (April 1957): 260–267.

Radhakrishnan, Sarvepalli, and Charles A. Moore, eds. *A Source Book in Indian Philosophy.* Princeton, 1957.

Stevenson, Ian. *Twenty Cases Suggestive of Reincarnation.* 2d ed. Charlottesville, Va., 1974.

Thomas, N. W., et al. "Transmigration." In *Encyclopaedia of Religion and Ethics,* edited by James Hastings, vol. 12. Edinburgh, 1921.

Tylor, E. B. *Primitive Culture,* vol. 2, *Religion in Primitive Culture* (1871). New York, 1970.

New Sources

Edwards, Paul R. *Reincarnation: A Critical Examination.* Amherst, N.Y., 1996.

Kaplan, Steve. *Concepts of Transmigration: Perspectives on Reincarnation.* Lewiston, N.Y., 1996.

Lewis, James R. *Encyclopedia of Afterlife Beliefs and Phenomena.* Detroit, Mich., 1994.

Mills, Antonia, and Richard Slobodin. *Amerindian Rebirth: Reincarnation Beliefs among North American Indians and Inuit.* Toronto, 1994.

Nawang Gehlek, Rimpoche. *Good Life, Good Death: Tibetan Wisdom on Reincarnation.* New York, 2001.

Obeyesekere, Gananath. *Imagining Karma: Ethical Transformation in Amerindian, Buddhist, and Greek Rebirth.* Berkeley, 2002.

Sanford, John A. *Soul Journey: A Jungian Analyst Looks at Reincarnation.* New York, 1991.

Sharma, Arvind. "On the Distinction between Karma and Rebirth in Hinduism." *Asian Philosophy* 6 (March 1996): 29–36.

J. BRUCE LONG (1987)
Revised Bibliography

REINES, YITSḤAQ YA'AQOV (1839–1915) was one of the founders and first leaders of Mizraḥi, a religious Zionist movement established at the beginning of the twentieth century. Reines was born in Belorussia, studied at the leading *yeshivot* (rabbinic academies), and served as a rabbi in a variety of towns in Lithuania throughout his life. He made a major contribution to rabbinic scholarship, with emphasis on a strictly logical approach to problems in Jewish law. He published a number of important legal works, including *Ḥotam tokhnit* (1880–1881), and a homiletical work, *Nod shel dema'ot* (1891). While serving as rabbi of Sventsyany from 1869 to 1885, Reines established a *yeshivah* that combined traditional studies with secular subjects, but he was forced to close the school after several months as a result of extreme Orthodox opposition. Only in 1905 did he succeed in establishing such a *yeshivah,* in Lida. This new school became the model for religious Zionist education in the Mizraḥi movement and, following World War I, was copied throughout eastern Europe.

In addition to his legal and educational contributions, Reines was active politically. He joined the proto-Zionist movement Ḥibbat Tsiyyon at its inception in the 1880s and proposed religious agricultural settlements in the Land of Israel. Following the creation of the World Zionist Organization in 1897, he became one of Theodor Herzl's most fervent rabbinical supporters in the face of rejection by most other Orthodox authorities. In 1902, Reines published a book defending Zionism entitled *Or ḥadash 'al Tsiyyon* (A new light on Zion).

Despite his support for Herzl, Reines was concerned that the secular leadership of the World Zionist Organization would ignore or even denigrate Jewish religious values in the struggle for a Jewish state. In 1902, he convened a conference of Orthodox Zionists in Vilna that resulted in the establishment of Mizraḥi in 1902. Reines also founded the movement's first journal, *Ha-Mizraḥi.* The movement sought to defend and inculcate traditional Jewish values while supporting the Zionist settlement in the Land of Israel. Mizraḥi established a network of schools in eastern Europe and, later, in Palestine. It became the foundation for the National Religious Party (Mafdal), which plays a critical role in Israeli politics today.

SEE ALSO Zionism.

BIBLIOGRAPHY

In addition to Getzel Kressel's biographical article on Reines in *Encyclopaedia Judaica* (Jerusalem, 1971), appraisals of his life and work can be found in *Sefer ha-Mizraḥi,* edited by Y. L. Maimon (Jerusalem, 1946), pp. 83–101, and in David Vital's *Zionism: The Formative Years* (Oxford, 1982), pp. 215–224.

New Sources

Holzer, Elie. "The Use of Military Force in the Religious Zionist Ideology of Rabbi Yitzhak Ya'akov Reines and His Successors." *Studies in Contemporary Jewry* 18 (2002): 74–94.

DAVID BIALE (1987)
Revised Bibliography

REIYŪKAI KYŌDAN. A Japanese Buddhist lay organization, Reiyūkai Kyōdan was founded between 1919 and 1925 in Tokyo by Kubo Kakutarō (1890–1944) and his sister-in-law Kotani Kimi (1901–1971). As of 1982 it had roughly three million members in Japan, with branches in seventeen foreign countries. Deriving from the tradition of Nichiren, the thirteenth-century religious reformer, Reiyūkai created lay rites of ancestor worship based on daily recitation of an abridgement of the *Lotus Sutra.* Personal salvation is believed to follow upon salvation of one's ancestors, which in turn is brought about through lay rites in the home without priestly mediation. Reiyukai represents a rare example in the history of religions of ancestor worship as the center of a voluntary association that transcends kinship boundaries. In daily life, Reiyūkai emphasizes traditionalist ethics in marriage and the family, linking these ideals to salvation of oneself and one's ancestors.

An employee of the Imperial Household Ministry, Kubo regarded himself as the Nichiren of the Taishō era (1912–1926), and like the medieval saint he set out to alert the world to the catastrophe he believed imminent. In Kubo's day, Japan was undergoing a radical social transformation, even as it had begun to gain place in international politics. Kubo saw in the massive changes about him a threat to traditional values and a need for religious response. He received religious instruction from exponents of Nichirenshugi, a nationalistic political interpretation of Nichiren's thought, but Kubo sought an understanding of contemporary events that would suggest an appropriate course of religious action for the laity. Since he regarded the Buddhist clergy as utterly incapable of providing suitable moral leadership, he set out to found a lay religious society in order to implement his understanding of Nichiren Buddhism.

Kubo believed that the world was beset with war and disaster because modern society had entrusted the rites of ancestor worship to the Buddhist clergy. He believed that social and political upheavals are actually signs of ancestral distress, reflected to the human world to inform the living that their ancestors are in need of ritual care. When descendants fail to worship them directly, ancestors in the spirit world are unable to achieve Buddhahood. Priests claim to be able to transfer merit to them through esoteric ritual, but actually, in Kubo's view, clerics have no karmic bonds with parishioners' ancestors. These are the ties of blood, filiation, and morality, which exist only among persons actually descended from common ancestors, or between spouses. A priest cannot mediate this relationship. Therefore, Kubo concluded, the ancestors' plight will continue to manifest itself as disasters in the human world until lay people perform the rites that will transfer merit effectively and until they implement in their daily lives an ethic that will "satisfy" the ancestors. The terrible earthquake of 1923 increased tremendously Kubo's sense of urgency in propagating this message.

Kubo's ideas might never have gone beyond a small circle of followers had he not been aided by Kotani Kimi. While Kubo elaborated doctrine and refined ritual, it was Kotani who gathered a core of followers. She proselytized in the poor sections of Tokyo, and by sharing the poverty of her converts, nursing them, and performing faith healing, she established herself as a pillar of the organization. Even after her death, Kotani continues to be widely regarded as a "living Buddha." In activities held at the group's mountain training center, Mirokusan, Kotani has been identified with the Buddha of the future, Maitreya.

Among the present membership, 70 percent reside in urban areas and 30 percent in rural areas. Reiyukai is organized into a number of branches formed by the links of proselytization. A person rises in rank by converting others, and conversion forms a pyramid in which all those proselytized by the same person are considered his or her "spiritual children," and the original proselytizer the "spiritual parent." Those at the foot of this pyramid look to an original "parent" as their leader, and that person is placed in charge of a branch headquartered in a certain area. The Eighth Branch, for example, has its headquarters in Osaka, claims roughly six hundred thousand members, and on a daily basis operates independently of the Tokyo headquarters of Reiyūkai.

Reiyūkai ritual consists chiefly of daily recitation morning and evening of the *Blue Sūtra,* an abridgement of the *Lotus Sūtra.* The ritual is structured so as to mobilize the power of the *Lotus Sūtra* for the salvation of the ancestors by simultaneously transferring merit and eliminating negative *karman* through repentence. It is assumed that men and women share equally the responsibilities of ritual, and it is considered most desirable that families unite in these observances. It is also assumed that men and women share equally in the fruits of correct ritual: a happy home, filial descendants, and personal salvation. Adherence to a prescribed ethic in marriage is the counterpart to ritual and is regarded as no less essential to salvation.

In the traditionalist family ethic advocated by Reiyūkai, the ideal of the family follows the prewar form (the *ie*). That is, members idealize a situation in which three generations live together, worship together, and if possible engage in a common economic enterprise. The idea of filial piety is central, as is respect for elders. A hierarchical principle exists between men and women, with men in the dominant position. This idea receives religious formulation in the notion that women have worse *karman* than men and therefore have a greater need for religion. A corollary of this notion holds that if women can overcome their *karman* they can achieve spiritual feats impossible for men, an ideal expressed ritually in shamanistic practices resembling spirit possession, from which men are barred.

Reiyūkai continues to engage in political activity in support of various conservative causes, such as advocating state support for the Yasukuni Shrine, formerly the official shrine of the war dead. It also supports revision of the Constitution, particularly Article 9, which renounces the use of war. It is allied with other right-wing religious groups in this and other causes and supports conservative candidates for election. The extent to which this activity accurately mirrors the sentiments of the general membership is unclear, but it seems certain that this large, well-organized group may, along with other religious groups, wield an important political influence in Japan's future.

See Also New Religious Movements, article on New Religious Movements in Japan.

Bibliography

For a comprehensive introduction to the organization, see my *Lay Buddhism in Contemporary Japan: Reiyūkai Kyōdan* (Princeton, 1984).

Helen Hardacre (1987)

REJUVENATION myths are found all over the world and in varied forms. A concern with being made young and healthy again is found not only in ancient cultures but also in contemporary society. The rejuvenation slogans of the advertising industry have an ancient heritage, as, for example, in the account of beer brewing in the Finnish epic, the *Kalevala,* which says, "The beer of Kalevala strengthens the weak, cheers the sick, and makes the old young again." Myths of rejuvenation are a part of the way humankind has responded to the fear of death and the love of life. To undo the ravages of time, to turn the clock back, has been an age-old longing.

Imitation of Nature. The earliest human cultures were close to nature, experiencing both hardship and joy in the annual change of seasons, lamenting the death of vegetation as it grew old and withered, and rejoicing at the return of spring. The waning of the sun in the west at the close of each day and its rising again to new strength the next day also suggested a rejuvenating power in nature. The Greeks and Celts had stories of a "western paradise" where the aged could obtain youth. Changing Woman, in the Navajo pantheon, transforms herself into a young girl when she becomes old; as wife of the Sun Carrier, her home is in the west. From the idea that the land of the world is surrounded by water, water became associated with the renewal of the sun, as well as with that from which life itself came.

Myths of rejuvenation that focus on the role of sleep reflect an imitation of nature. A myth of the Selk'nam of Tierra del Fuego tells of a culture hero, Kénos, and three of the ancestors who, in old age, tried to fall into a long sleep so as to be rejuvenated. Finally, after several efforts, they went north and there were wrapped in mantles and put in the ground. After a few days they began to stir and whisper, and then, upon rising, they saw that they were young again. They had succeeded in a transformation sleep.

The snake's shedding of its skin has led it to be associated with the power of rejuvenation as well as with healing and transformation. An Icelandic saga describes a man who shed his skin every few centuries and always emerged thirty years old. The *Ṛgveda,* an ancient scripture of India, describes a priest who in old age had been exposed to die but who was rejuvenated by two physician gods who took off his skin as one would a mantle, prolonging his life and making him the "husband of maidens." Depth psychologists report that the association of snakes with the development of a new perspective, one that is presenting itself to consciousness for the first time, is a frequent motif in contemporary dreams.

The Special Elixir. There are many accounts of special fruits, herbs, or waters that rejuvenate or provide everlasting life. Usually these stories are about foods of the gods, or foods in distant lands that, if humans could only obtain them, would assure the desired result. An old Norse story tells of a king grown old who heard of a distant land where there was a special water and a priceless apple that would make one young again. He sent his eldest son in quest of them, but the son was distracted by the pleasures of a strange city. So also with the king's second son. Finally, the third and youngest son, after numerous difficulties, succeeded. However, on his return journey the older brothers took from him his treasures and rejuvenated the king themselves. In a German version it is the "water of life" for which the king sent. In Japanese mythology is the story of Ningyo, the Fisherwoman, a mermaidlike creature who lives in the sea; it is said that women who were fortunate enough to eat of her flesh gained perpetual youth and beauty. In Eddic mythology, the goddess Iðunn guarded the apples that the gods tasted when they began to grow old lest the giants steal them. In Celtic mythology Fraoch went in search of a tree that grew on an island in a lake. Every month it produced sweet fruit that prolonged life for a year and healed sickness. In ancient China it was believed that gold, the metal that never "grows old" (that is, never tarnishes), not only would preserve a dead body from decay but would also, when ingested in the proper way, promote longevity.

E. Washburn Hopkins sought to demonstrate in "The Fountain of Youth" (*Journal of the American Oriental Society* 26, 1905) that all the many European stories of magic springs or fountains of youth were descended originally from a story in the *Mahābhārata,* an Indian epic. In this story an old man who had married a young woman made an agreement with the Aśvins (twin physician gods) that he would make them drinkers of soma, the divine ambrosia, if they would rejuvenate him. They took him to the "youth place," and when he emerged from its water, he had indeed been restored to youthful vigor and appearance. In the European stories the mysterious and miraculous fount is located, usually rather vaguely, in Asia. Hopkins suggested that the Spanish explorer Ponce de León would have been aware of those stories when in the early sixteenth century he set out for India by way of the West Indies, and thus, when he heard stories in Florida of a medicinal and healing spring, he naturally interpreted it as being the famed fountain of youth. Furthermore, Hopkins disagreed with Brinton (*Myths of the New World,* New York, 1896), who contended that the fountain of youth was a universal myth that had emerged from the veneration of water as the female element.

The Reversal of Time. Mircea Eliade described in *Myth and Reality* (New York, 1963) and elsewhere how health and youthfulness are obtained by a "return to the origins," by abolishing the work of time—time "the destroyer," as the Roman poet Ovid called it. The therapies for reversing time usually included a ritual reiteration of the creation of the world, thereby permitting a sick person to be born anew and to recommence existence with the health of earlier years. The ancient Daoist and other Chinese alchemists took up these traditional healing methods and applied them to the cure of the illness that results from the ravages of time, that is, from old age and death. Eliade has pointed out that there is a continuity between the early concern with health and rejuvenation and the alchemical traditions of both the East and the West. All the symbols, rituals, and techniques of these traditions emphasized a basic idea: in order to obtain rejuvenation or long life, it is necessary to return to the origin of life and recommence with the vitality that was then present.

Initiatory rituals often enact a "return to the womb" in which the initiate is placed in isolation for a period and then greeted as a newborn upon his delivery. In ancient China the Daoists had a technique of "embryonic respiration" in which the adept tried to imitate respiration within a closed circuit, in the manner of a fetus. This was believed to drive away old age. Myths concerning a "return to the origin" are on different levels, some more physical, some more spiritual. Eliade has pointed out a similar motif in the psychoanalytic system of Sigmund Freud that involves a "return to the beginning" in its method of healing.

A caution about tampering with time is expressed in the Japanese story of an old woodcutter who, becoming thirsty one day, drank from a stream he had not drunk from before. The water was unusually delicious, flowing clear and swiftly. He went to the pool from which the stream flowed, and as he knelt to drink some more, he saw his reflection in the pool, but his face was that of his youth. Realizing that he had drunk from a fountain of youth, he ran (which he had been unable to do for years) to tell his wife. With difficulty he persuaded her of his identity. She insisted that she must drink of the same water, for he would not want an old wife, and she hurried away. When she did not return, he went in search of her. At the pool he found a baby girl lying on the bank. In her eagerness the old woman had drunk too much from the fountain of youth.

The Realm of the Divine. Many stories of rejuvenation take place in the realm of the divine or involve gifts or rewards from the gods. In a Scandinavian legend the age of Olger the Dane is changed from one hundred years to thirty by means of a ring provided by the fairy Morgana. In Greek mythology, when Zeus heard that Prometheus had stolen fire from him and had given it to humanity, he became indignant and so gave to those who informed him about the theft a drug that was an antidote to old age. And on the return of the Argonauts, the enchantress Medea made Aeson, Jason's father, young again with herbs and incantations.

In a Navajo myth, the two sons of Changing Woman are warned by Old Age not to walk on her path, but, rather, to keep to the left of it. They forgot this counsel, however, and walked on the path. Then they began to feel heavy; they stooped, and their steps became shorter; and finally they could not move, even with the help of canes. Old Age rebuked them and, in a Navajo pattern of creating, sang a song so that in future, she said, everything should reach old age. Then, however, she made them young again and sent them on their way. In some stories continual rejuvenation is the reward for living in an especially holy place or on a blessed island. In Aztec mythology there is a holy mountain, the residence of the great mother of the gods, that one can never entirely climb, for the upper half consists of fine, slippery sand. However, whoever climbs part way, no matter how old, grows young again in proportion to the distance climbed.

Some myths explain why old age and death are inevitable. In Mesopotamian mythology, Gilgamesh is told at the end of a long journey in search of a means of avoiding death that the gods have reserved immortality for themselves. Disappointed, he is told, as a parting gift, of a plant that makes one young again. He dives to the bottom of the sea to get the plant; but on his return journey, when he stops to bathe in a pool, a snake steals the plant, sloughing its skin as it goes—thus obtaining immortality for snakes. In the Hebrew scriptures, eating of the fruit of the Tree of Life, which stood in the midst of the Garden of Eden, enabled one to live forever. After Adam and Eve disobeyed God by eating of the Tree of the Knowledge of Good and Evil they were driven from the garden, and a guard was placed there to protect the path to the tree of life.

Spiritualization of the Quest. Mesopotamian and Egyptian mythologies tended to focus on the quest for immortality or life after death, while in ancient China and Vedic India the quest was much more for rejuvenation and the recovery of youthfulness in this life. In later Indian thought, beginning in the sixth century BCE, for both Hinduism and Buddhism the aim of life was not rejuvenation but liberation from earthly existence. Similarly, beginning in the sixth century BCE, the mystery religions of the Mediterranean world responded to a longing for cleansing and renovating the human spirit and found in nature a model for that renewal; thus their professed aim was to assure eternal life. Christianity then turned the emphasis to an inner, spiritual renewal: "Unless one is born anew, he cannot see the kingdom of God" (*Jn.* 3:3). The water in the baptismal font assured the possibility of life eternal. In one eucharistic liturgy the words of the priest at the moment of delivering the bread and wine indicate their life-giving power: "Preserve thy body and soul to everlasting life."

Implications. The desire for rejuvenation in this life, however, is still present. In the secular culture of the modern world, with its loss to a large extent of any sense of the sacred, there has been a new interest in rejuvenation, not as a gift from the realm of the divine, but as a goal for human endeavor. According to early records, priests and elders in ancient India and China consumed the sexual organs of wild animals in order to resist the effects of old age and restore their youthful vigor; similar attempts at rejuvenation have continued throughout history. In the late nineteenth and early twentieth centuries, a few surgeons in Europe and North America claimed to have achieved rejuvenation by transplanting reproductive glands from animals. The medical community in general rejected the technique and attributed to other factors the apparent results, which were, at best, temporary. Vitamins are now advocated as a means of postponing the consequences of old age.

When the present lacks meaning, discontent expresses itself in a longing for the past. The thirst for rejuvenation may occur precisely at the point in human development when either the culture as a whole or an individual is ready to move on to a new level of understanding but is reluctant to undertake the journey and seeks instead to find meaning in the way life was before. The contemporary developmental understanding of human life as moving from stage to stage, with each stage having its own maturation task to be accomplished or wisdom to be achieved, suggests that the thirst for rejuvenation may stem from a failure to move on to the next level of development. The investigations of the history of religions as well as contemporary psychotherapy demonstrate that humans cannot stand a meaningless life. How this dilemma is to be faced, expressed, and lived out by individuals is the challenge that faces contemporary civilization, with its expanding population of old people.

See Also Death; Elixir; Fountain; Initiation; Quests; Snakes.

Bibliography

Among the numerous anthologies of myths, one that includes numerous myths of rejuvenation is *The Mythology of All Races,* 13 vols., edited by Louis Herbert Gray et al. (Boston, 1916–1932). A short essay by Mircea Eliade, "Rejuvenation and Immortality," in *Patterns in Comparative Religion* (New York, 1958), contrasts and discusses the implications of mythologies that focus on rejuvenation. In the *Forge and the*

Crucible: The Origins and Structures of Alchemy, 2d ed. (Chicago, 1978), Eliade illuminates the attempts of the Chinese and Indian alchemists to accelerate the work of nature and thereby conquer time. A comprehensive collection of legends about the fountain of youth and related stories of rejuvenation is to be found in E. Washburn Hopkins's article titled "The Fountain of Youth," *Journal of the American Oriental Society* 26 (1905): 1–67.

WALLACE B. CLIFT (1987)

RELATIVISM. The term *relativism* is applied to ethical, cultural, and religious views. Relativism contends that such views are to be evaluated relative to the societies or cultures in which they appear and are not to be judged true or false, or good or bad, based on some overall criterion but are to be assessed within the context in which they occur. Thus, what is right or good or true to one person or group may not be considered so by others.

This theory was first presented by certain Greek authors who noted the varieties of religions and moral behavior in the Mediterranean world and suggested that differing mores indicated that there were no absolute standards. Protagoras said, "Man is the measure of all things," and this was interpreted to convey that each person could be his or her own measure. The variations of human, social, political, and ethical behavior were worked into a basic theme of the Greek skeptics. The fact of differences in human behavior is taken to imply that no general standard can possibly apply to all peoples and cultures. Sextus Empiricus even suggested that cannibalism, incest, and other practices considered taboo are just variant kinds of behavior, to be appreciated as acceptable in some cultures and not in others. This reasoning was applied by the Greek skeptics to various religions and their practices. They urged suspension of judgment about right or wrong and undogmatic acceptance of one's own culture.

This relativistic attitude was in sharp contrast to the dogmatic views of the Jews and Christians in the Roman empire, who insisted their revealed information assured them that their religious beliefs and practices were the only correct and acceptable ones. The christianization of the Roman empire and of pagan Europe pushed the relativistic approach aside. There could be some variations in ritual or practice, but in essential beliefs and practices anything different was heretical.

The skeptical-relativist view reappeared in new and forceful ways in the Renaissance, with a rediscovery of the wide variety of beliefs and practices of ancient times, and with the discoveries of radically different cultures all over the world. The rapid development of new kinds of Christian practices resulting from the Reformation also contributed to an emerging view of differences as based on cultural factors. Contrasts with the Ottoman empire made people even more cognizant of the wide range of human beliefs and practices. Montaigne was foremost in presenting the panorama of human beliefs and implying that the fact of difference indicated that each set of beliefs and practices was culturally conditioned. He contended that most people hold their religious views as a result of custom rather than conviction. He also suggested that the religious and moral practices of the "noble savages" were at least as good as those of European Christians.

Montaigne's skepticism and cultural relativism were carried further by the French skeptic Pierre Bayle, who insisted that a society of atheists could be more moral than a society of Christians, since moral behavior results from natural causes such as custom and education and not from religious doctrines. Bayle sought to show that such biblical heroes as David, such leading Christians as Calvin and Luther, and saints and popes throughout the history of Christianity have all acted in the moral sphere because of their own human natures and not because of their religious beliefs.

Bayle's analysis was incorporated into the Enlightenment's quest for a science of humanity that would explain why people acted, behaved, and believed in different ways. This science would deem religious beliefs the effects of different physical and psychological conditions, which might be studied neutrally. Climate, history, customs, education, institutions, and so on would account for the fact that societies differ in their social, cultural, and religious practices. One's personal psychological conditions would account for an individual's strong or weak religious convictions. Hume's *Natural History of Religion* (1757) initiated the study of religion as a manifestation of human behavior in which religious activity is relative to individual and cultural conditions.

This relativistic aspect of religion was identified as a crucial feature of the human condition by the German philosopher J. G. Herder, who contended that every society or culture develops from its own unique idea or character. Ethical and religious norms are part of the expression of these ideas, and no culture is inferior or superior to any other; it is simply different. Thus religion is seen to be relative to the culture in which it appears.

Herder's relativism and the growing interest in comparative studies of language and religion led to the full-blown relativism of Alexander von Humboldt in the nineteenth century, and of many twentieth-century anthropologists. Von Humboldt stated, "There are nations more susceptible of cultivation, more highly civilized, more ennobled by mental cultivation than others—but none in themselves nobler than others. All are in like degree designed for freedom" (*Cosmos,* London, 1888, vol. 1, p. 368).

The relativist position was further reinforced by various theories of the natural causes of beliefs. The theories of Marx and Freud offered ways whereby one could account for the fact that individuals and groups adhere to beliefs without considering whether or not these beliefs are true. Scholars now began to consider instead whether various religious beliefs were beneficial or deleterious, or why a particular belief arose at a certain moment in human history.

The relativist position was forcefully stated by the anthropologist Edward A. Westermarck in his major work *The Origin and Development of Moral Ideas* (1906). Westermarck contended on the basis of historical, sociological, and anthropological evidence that no ethical principles are objectively valid. In *Ethical Relativity* (1932) he further argued his position on philosophic grounds.

Critics of cultural relativism have suggested, first, that evidence of cultural differences does not rule out the possibility that there exist common beliefs and attitudes held by most or all cultures and, second, that factual information about such differences does not eliminate the possibility that one belief system may in fact be better, or more true, than another. Further, philosophers are still arguing about whether causal explanations about people's beliefs evidence the value, truth, or falsity of these beliefs. Yet by the late twentieth century, cultural relativism was a rather common view among many students of ethics and religion.

SEE ALSO Anthropology, Ethnology, and Religion; Apologetics; Freud, Sigmund; Herder, Johann Gottfried; Hume, David; Marx, Karl; Skeptics and Skepticism; Study of Religion, article on Methodological Issues.

BIBLIOGRAPHY

Brandt, Richard B. "Ethical Relativism." In *The Encyclopedia of Philosophy*, edited by Paul Edwards, vol. 3. New York, 1967. A careful presentation and examination of the relativistic theory.

Freud, Sigmund. *Totem and Taboo: Some Points of Agreement between the Mental Lives of Savages and Neurotics.* Authorized translation by James Strachey. New York, 1950. A psychoanalytic interpretation of some features of primitive religion and their present form in ordinary neurotic behavior.

James, William. *The Varieties of Religious Experience: A Study in Human Nature.* New York, 1902. A classical psychological description of the role of religion in human experience.

Jarvie, Ian C. *Rationality and Relativism: In Search of a Philosophy and History of Anthropology.* London, 1984. A critical evaluation of relativism as a proper interpretation of anthropological findings.

Needham, Joseph, ed. *Science, Religion and Reality.* New York, 1925. Contains, among other essays, Bronislaw Malinowski's "Magic, Science and Religion," Charles Singer's "Historical Relations of Religion and Science," and Needham's "Mechanistic Biology and the Religious Consciousness," all pressing a relativistic interpretation of religion.

Westermarck, Edward A. *Ethical Relativity.* New York, 1932. The basic philosophical statement of relativism in the twentieth century.

Yinger, J. Milton. *The Scientific Study of Religion.* New York, 1970. A study of religion in relation to human needs, behavior, and problems. A multidisciplinary approach.

New Sources

Ariel, Yoav, Shlomo Biderman, and Ornan Rotem, eds. *Relativism and Beyond.* New York, 1998.

Devine, Philip. *Relativism, Nihilism, and God.* Notre Dame, Ind., 1989.

Jaki, Stanley. *The Only Chaos and Other Essays.* Lanham, Md., 1990.

Lewis, Charles, ed. *Relativism and Religion.* Blasingstoke, U.K., 1995.

Moody-Adams, Michele. *Fieldwork in Familiar Places: Morality, Culture, and Philosophy.* Cambridge, Mass., 2002.

RICHARD H. POPKIN (1987)
Revised Bibliography

RELICS

RELICS may loosely be defined as the venerated remains of venerable persons. This should be taken to include not only the bodies, bones, or ashes of saints, heroes, martyrs, founders of religious traditions, and other holy men and women but also objects that they once owned and, by extension, things that were once in physical contact with them.

According to the principles of contagious magic, any personal possession or part of a person's body can be thought of as equivalent to his whole self, no matter how minute it may be, or how detached in time and space. Thus a bone, a hair, a tooth, a garment, a footprint can carry the power or saintliness of the person with whom they were once associated and make him or her "present" once again.

Scholars eager to discuss the "origins" of relics have often pointed to the magical use of such objects by "primitive" peoples in rituals of war, healing, rainmaking, or hunting. They have gathered examples from all sorts of ethnographies to show that fetishes and talismans, amulets and medicine bundles were sometimes made of human bones, hair, or organs. They have thereby concluded that the impulse to preserve and use "relics" must be very ancient indeed. They may well be correct, but it is important to try to view such examples within their individual cultural contexts, and not to generalize too quickly from them about the development of relic worship as a whole.

In fact, the veneration of relics is not equally emphasized in the various religions of the world. Highly featured in some traditions (such as Buddhism and Catholicism), it is virtually absent in others (Protestantism, Hinduism, Judaism), and found only incidentally elsewhere (Islam, ancient Greece). This entry, therefore, shall deal primarily with the Roman Catholic and Buddhist traditions. But before doing so, it may be helpful to examine briefly some of the reasons for the other traditions' diversity.

PROTESTANTISM, HINDUISM, AND ISRAELITE RELIGION. The Protestant reformers condemned the veneration of relics partly for theological reasons and partly because it was closely associated in their minds with the sale of indulgences and with other ecclesiastical practices of which they disapproved. From the start, their criticism was thus polemical, and, appealing to reason, it lambasted in particular the fantastic proliferation of relics that had developed in medieval Catholicism. For instance, John Calvin (1509–1564), who wrote a treatise on relics, mockingly commented that in his day the quantity of wood contained in relics of the True Cross was so great that even three hundred men could not have carried it.

In Hinduism, opposition to relic worship occurred for quite different reasons. Though Hindus commonly honor the memories of great saints and teachers and visit sites of pilgrimage associated with them, they do not generally venerate their bodily remains. On the one hand, the doctrine of reincarnation and the belief in the ultimately illusory nature of things of this world simply do not promote relic worship. On the other hand, and probably more importantly, death and things associated with it are, in Hinduism, thought to be highly polluting. For this reason, in fact, Hindu funeral customs stress the total destruction of the body, which is most commonly cremated. The ashes from the pyre and any unburned fragments of bone, though they are treated with respect for a while, are all eventually disposed of, often in a nearby river, ideally in the Ganges.

In ancient Israel, there also existed a concern for purity and for separating the dead from the living. Bodies were not cremated, but they were quickly and carefully buried in the hollowed sides of caves or burial chambers. There it was expected that they would decay, dry up, and disintegrate; thus tombs were commonly reused by family members. Pronounced rites of mourning and lamentation did take place, but, generally speaking, the tomb and the corpse were thought to be unclean, and contact with them was defiling (Lv. 21:1–4, Nm. 19:11–16). Hence, there was little room for any enthusiasm for relics.

It may also be, however, that too great a veneration of the remains of the dead—as in the occasionally mentioned practice of making food offerings in the tombs—was thought of in certain ancient Israelite circles as bordering on idolatry or paganism, and hence to be condemned.

ISLAM. Much the same concern can be found in Islam; certain Qurʾanic scholars periodically denounced the veneration of relics, especially of the bodies of saints, as *shirk* (polytheism), that is, as treating the grave as an idol rather than worshiping God alone. Nevertheless, the cult of relics did manage to grow within the Muslim fold, and it continues to be popular today.

In addition to the various "traces" (*athar*) left by Muḥammad, such as hairs, teeth, autographs, and especially footprints, Muslims have long venerated the remains of saints. This, it should be pointed out, is a cult of bodies rather than of bones, and focuses on the tombs of holy persons that dot the countrysides of those Muslim lands where their worship plays an important role. Though ritual patterns at these tombs may vary, often believers will circumambulate the saint's enshrined coffin, leave votive offerings there, and pray for cures, for help with family problems, or more generally for "blessing" (*barakah*). While some Muslim theologians may claim that such petitions are not technically made to the saint but through the saint to God, it is clear that, in the minds of the faithful, the saint himself is thought to be present in the tomb and able to respond effectively.

In some instances, owing to their great popularity, certain famous saints are reputed to be buried in more than one place. Thus, for example, the body of the great Shīʿī martyr, Ḥusayn ibn ʿAli (d. 680 CE), while usually thought to be enshrined in Karbala, is also reputed to rest in Medina, Damascus, Aleppo, and a number of other places, and his head is said to be in Cairo, where it remains a popular center of piety.

Nonetheless, because of orthodox objections, the cult of relics in Islam seems never to have mushroomed in quite the way it did in Christianity or Buddhism, and it has retained a somewhat ambiguous status. This ambiguity is perhaps best summed up in the recurring legends of mausoleums that were destroyed by the very saints they entombed—the saints themselves thereby posthumously objecting to their own cult (and at the same time showing their even greater glory).

ANCIENT GREECE. In ancient Greece, the veneration of relics was closely connected to the cult of heroes, whose reputed remains—often bones larger than lifesize—were enshrined and honored in towns as a guarantee of their protection and an enhancement of their prestige. Thus Lesbos had the head of Orpheus, Elis the shoulder bone of Pelops (which had been found by a fisherman and identified by an oracle). Tantalos's bones were at Argos, while the remains of Europa were the focus of the great Hellotia festival in Crete. All of these were thought to ward off disease and famine, to encourage fertility and welfare, and sometimes to bring about miraculous cures.

Occasionally the relics of great heroes were the object of searches and, when found, had to be translated to their place of enshrinement. Plutarch, for example, describes in some detail the quest for the bones of Theseus, a hero whose armed ghost many Athenians believed to have helped them achieve their victory at Marathon. Finally, when his remains were discovered on the island of Siphnos, they were transported to Athens with considerable pomp and celebration and enshrined in the center of the city.

In addition to the bones of the heroes, weapons and other objects associated with them were honored. Thus, in a variety of temples, visitors could marvel at Orpheus's lyre, Achilles' spear, Helen's sandal, Agamemnon's scepter, the Argonauts' anchor, the stone swallowed by Kronos, even the tusks of the Erymanthian boar captured by Herakles. Such items were, perhaps, more objects of curiosity than of cults, but they served the important function of drawing pilgrims and of concretizing the myths and glories of a former age.

EARLY CHRISTIANITY. In Christianity one finds an example of the fully developed veneration of relics. Its origins within the Christian tradition are usually traced to the cults that arose around the tombs of the early saints and martyrs. These cults are often compared to the similar hero cults of the Hellenistic world. They stem, however, not only from a desire to venerate the memory of the departed saint, but also from a hope to partake of some of the power and blessing he or she derived from a close and ongoing relationship with God.

It was thought to be beneficial in the early church to be physically close to the saints. Hence, from the start, Christians paid visits to their tombs; there they celebrated the Eucharist on the stone slabs covering their graves. Sometimes, they even decided to settle permanently in the vicinity of these graves. In this way, tombs became altars, and whole cities arose where once had been cemeteries.

Alternatively, the bodies of the saints were sometimes brought to the faithful; they were translated from their graves to existing cities and enshrined in churches there. Thus existing altars also became tombs, and the custom of celebrating mass over the bones of the martyrs was reinforced. In fact, by the fourth century, in the Eastern church, the Eucharist could only be celebrated on an altar covered with an antimension—a cloth into which were sewn fragments of relics. And in the West, the common custom was to enclose relics in a cavity in the altar top itself—a practice that became formalized in 787 when the Second Council of Nicaea declared the presence of such relics to be obligatory for the consecration of a church.

With the toleration of Christianity throughout the Roman empire beginning in the reign of Constantine (272–327), the demand for and veneration of relics grew. Especially in the fourth and fifth centuries, not only were the known remains of martyrs venerated but lost relics of ancient saints started making their appearance. Thus the body of Saint Stephen—the first Christian martyr—was discovered as though it had been waiting for this time and was enshrined in a number of important centers.

At the same time, relics connected with Christ's passion came to be highly esteemed: the crown of thorns, the nails that pierced his hands and feet, and especially the wood of the True Cross on which Christ had died and which, according to legend, had been discovered by Constantine's mother, Helena. The cross was said to have been made of the wood of the Tree of Life, taken belatedly from the Garden of Eden by Adam's son Seth. It was, thus, a powerful symbol of both the death of Christ and the rewards of eternal life. Along with other relics, it was credited with miraculous cures, even resurrections. It was also used as a talisman for magical protection; Gregory of Nyssa's sister Macrina (c. 327–379) always wore around her neck an amulet consisting of a splinter of the True Cross encased in a ring, and she was clearly not the only noblewoman to do so. It comes as no surprise, then, that by the middle of the fourth century, according to one account, wood from the True Cross filled the world (though miraculously the original cross itself still remained whole and undiminished in Jerusalem).

The growth of the cult of relics in the early church, however, was not without controversy and opposition. On the one hand, it was clearly an offense to traditional Roman sensibilities about keeping the dead in their proper place. For example, Julian the Apostate (r. 361–363) denounced the Christians for filling the world with sepulchers and defiling the cities with the bones and skulls of "criminals." On the other hand, even within the Christian community, there were those such as Vigilantius (early fifth century) who were very critical of the worship of relics, claiming that it was grossly superstitious and bordered on idolatry. However, Jerome, in an angry reply to Vigilantius, argued that Christians did not "worship" relics but "honored" them. Doctrinally, then, if not always in practice, a distinction was made that still stands today between the *veneratio* paid to the saints and their relics and the *adoratio* espoused for God and Christ.

Other church leaders, however, were concerned about the veritable traffic in relics that was developing in the fourth and fifth centuries, especially in the East. In 386, therefore, the emperor Theodosius passed legislation restricting the translation of dead bodies and the selling, buying, or dividing of the remains of martyrs. This, however, seems to have had little effect; at the end of the century, Augustine was still complaining of unscrupulous monks who wandered and traded in "members of martyrs if martyrs they be," and over a century later, the emperor Justinian had to issue another decree regulating the exhumation and transfer of saints' bodies.

It is important to realize the many dimensions of these practices and their larger religious and social significance. As Peter Brown has pointed out, the translations of relics that started in the fourth century helped to spread Christianity by making it more mobile and decentralizing it (Brown 1981, p. 88). Because of this, not only local holy men but centrally important saints could be worshiped in places far away from the ancient foci of the faith. It was not necessary to journey to Palestine or Rome to honor the memory of Jesus or of the early martyrs; they could be found—present in various physical objects—more close to home, indeed in any consecrated church. In this, the translation of relics was a perfect complement to the popular practice of pilgrimage; it brought the saints to the people instead of taking the people to the saints. At a somewhat different level, the translation of relics also served to establish an intricate network of "patronage, alliance, and gift giving that linked the lay and clerical elites of East and West," which was crucial in the development of the church (Brown 1981, p. 89). In this, the remains of saints acted as a sort of symbolic exchange commodity.

At the same time, as Brown has also pointed out, the exhumation, dismemberment, and translation of relics has played an important role in divorcing them from too direct an association with death. Precisely because relics are fragments of bones and not whole corpses, precisely because they are in altars or reliquaries and not in coffins, the connotations of death are suppressed, and in the relics the saints can be thought to be "alive."

THE MIDDLE AGES. By the time of the Middle Ages, the veneration of relics had become so widespread, popular, and intense that more than one scholar has called it the true religion of the medieval period. Especially in Europe, churches, monasteries, cathedrals, and other places of pilgrimage seemed to develop an almost insatiable thirst for relics that might add to their sanctity, prestige, and attractiveness to pilgrims. This increasing demand led, in fact, to a renewed search for the bodies of ancient saints in places such as the catacombs in Rome. Quickly, a transalpine trade in bones developed, manned by relic merchants and professional relic thieves, who were eager to supply the needs of Carolingian bishops and abbots and later of Anglo-Saxon kings. Then, with the Crusades, still new sources of relics became accessible—Jerusalem and Constantinople being the most important of these.

Throughout the Middle Ages, relics, in fact, were significant sources of revenue. Offerings made to the shrine of Thomas Becket, for example, accounted for almost half of Canterbury's annual income in the late twelfth century, and this proportion increased when special indulgences were granted to pilgrims there. It is not surprising, then, that persons in power were willing to invest considerably in the acquisition of relics. Louis IX of France (r. 1226–1270), for example, reportedly offered the count of Fondi fifteen thousand florins for the bones of Saint Thomas Aquinas, but, alas, in vain.

When relics were obtained, they were often magnificently enshrined. The reliquaries in which they were encased were some of the most richly adorned products of medieval art; sometimes entire buildings were conceived of as reliquaries, such as the splendid Sainte Chapelle in Paris, which was built to house Christ's crown of thorns.

Given such enthusiasm and piety, it is perhaps not surprising that fraudulent and false relics should also appear. Chaucer, in his *Canterbury Tales*, tells of a relic monger who in his trunk had a pillowcase that he asserted was Our Lady's veil. Other sources mention exhibitions of vials that were said to contain a sneeze of the Holy Spirit, or the sounds of the bells of Solomon's temple, or rays from the star that guided the wise men from the East. One church in Italy even claimed to possess the cross that Constantine saw in his vision.

More generally, however, piety and rival claims led to a bewildering multiplication of the remains of saints. During the Middle Ages, it was rare, in fact, for a saint's body or bones to exist in one place only. At least nineteen churches, for example, claimed to enshrine the jaw of John the Baptist. The body of Saint James was found most famously at Santiago de Compostela in Spain, where, like a magnet, it drew pilgrims from all over Europe along well-established routes; it was also venerated, however, in at least six other places, with additional heads and arms elsewhere. Saint Peter, of course, was honored in Rome, but despite (or because of) his fame there, pilgrims could also venerate significant portions of his body at Arles, Cluny, Constantinople, and Saint-Cloud. While his thumb was to be seen in Toulon, three teeth were in Marseilles, his beard was in Poitiers, and his brain was in Geneva (although John Calvin later claimed it was but a piece of pumice stone).

Relics of more minor saints—six hands of Saint Adrian, various breasts of Saint Agatha—abounded as well. The list is almost endless, and Collin de Plancy easily filled three volumes of a dictionary of relics with references to them.

As for relics of Jesus and the Virgin Mary, they, too, were extremely popular during the Middle Ages, though the doctrine of their bodily ascension to heaven presented some difficulties. In their cases, bones were, for the most part, not legitimately acceptable. Great emphasis, however, could be laid on any object that had once been in contact with their persons.

In the case of the Virgin, these relics tended to emphasize her maternal, nurturing, and domestic characteristics. Thus vials of her breast milk (spilled on various occasions) could be found in countless churches throughout Christendom, later causing Calvin to comment that, had she been a cow all her life, she could not have produced such a quantity. Almost as popular was her tunic (especially that worn at the time of the Annunciation). Threads from it were occasionally worn in protective amulets. Roland, in Spain, for example, fought with a sword in whose hilt was a piece of the Virgin's robe (along with a hair of Saint Denis, a tooth of Saint Peter, and some of Saint Basil's blood). Finally, in Loreto, in central Italy, the whole of the house in which the Virgin had raised the young Jesus in Nazareth could be visited. It was believed to have been miraculously transported there through the air from Palestine in 1296.

In the case of Jesus, the relics were of a more varied character. Some, such as his swaddling clothes and the boards of the manger in which he lay in Bethlehem, brought to mind the figure of the Christ child. Others called up more complex associations, perhaps; no fewer than seven churches claimed to possess his circumcised foreskin, and the one at Coulombs in the diocese of Chartres was venerated by pregnant women hoping for an easy childbirth. Still others simply recalled various episodes recorded in the Gospels: bread crumbs left over from the loaves he had used in feeding the five thousand, one of the pots in which he had turned water into wine, the cloth that had covered the table at the Last Supper, the towel he had used on that occasion to wipe the apostles' feet, the body of the ass on which he had entered Jerusalem.

The greatest veneration and enthusiasm, however, were reserved for relics associated with Christ's passion. Some of these, such as the crown of thorns, the spear that had pierced his side, the nails and wood of the True Cross, had long been popular. But now no detail of Christ's agony escaped attention, and in various churches, pilgrims could also venerate the pillar to which he had been tied, the reeds with which he had been whipped, Veronica's veil on which he had left an image of his face on the way to Calvary, the seamless robe that the soldiers divided, the sponge with which he was offered vinegar, the blood and water that flowed from his side, and, finally, the burial shroud in which he lay in the tomb and on which he left the full imprint of his body. This shroud, now in Turin, was perhaps the last major relic of Christ's passion to come to light. It was first exhibited in the fourteenth century and has, in recent years, become the subject of intensive debate and scientific analysis.

It is sometimes difficult to realize the fervor with which medieval people approached many of these relics. Part of their attraction, of course, lay in their reputed miraculous powers, especially in the form of cures, but there was more to it than this. Relics enabled the pious to relive—to recall experientially—events that were central to their faith. They were visible manifestations of the presence of Christ and of his saints that could, in the words of one bishop, "open the eyes of the heart." They thus provided effective focal points for religious devotion and emotion. Suger, the abbot of Saint-Denis in Paris, has described the scene there in the early twelfth century. The old church, he states, was often filled to overflowing by the faithful, who pressed in closely to implore the help of the saints and strove hard to kiss the nail and crown relics of the Lord. Women found themselves trampled underfoot or squeezed to the point of suffocation, while the brethren themselves, pressed hard by the crowd, periodically had to make their escape with the relics through the windows.

BUDDHISM. Christianity is but one of two major traditions in which relics have played a prominent and popular role. The other—Buddhism—became one of the great propagators of relic worship throughout Asia. Unlike Hinduism, which, as has been seen, had little room for relics, Buddhism was from the start fascinated by, and preoccupied with, death. This does not mean that Buddhists did not share some of the Indian repugnance for dead bodies. They tried, however, to overcome that repugnance, meditating on the impurity and impermanence of the body, dead or alive. The remains of the Buddha and of other enlightened saints, however, were thought not to be impure but worthy of the highest veneration.

The focus in Buddhism has been by and large on the relics of the Buddha himself, even though Buddhists in ancient India did also honor the relics of his disciples, and though still today, in some places, believers will search the ashes of great monks for their *śarīradhātu* (either bits of bone or tiny pieces of what is thought to be metamorphosed bodily substance).

According to tradition, when the Buddha passed away into final *nirvāṇa,* he told his disciples who were monks not to preoccupy themselves with his physical remains but to follow his teaching. After his cremation, therefore, his relics were left to the laity. Almost immediately they became the object of a dispute among various North Indian monarchs, each of whom wanted all the physical remains of the Buddha for his own kingdom. According to the *Mahāparinibbāna Sutta,* this squabble was resolved not by the monks but by a brahman named Drona who divided the Buddha's relics into eight equal shares and distributed them to eight kings, instructing each to build a stupa (a domed funerary mound) over his portion.

The fate of these eight "Drona stupas" (as they were called) is uncertain. According to one legend, however, soon after his conversion to Buddhism, the great Indian emperor Asoka (third century BCE) collected from them the relics, which he then redistributed throughout his empire, this time dividing them into eighty-four thousand shares and building eighty-four thousand stupas to enshrine them. Thus, the Buddha's physical body (his relics), along with his teaching (his Dharma), was spread throughout the Indian subcontinent in a systematic and ordered way. It is clear, however, that Asoka was also using Buddhism and the relics symbolically in order to impose his own authority over the kingdom.

In addition to this legend of the eighty-four thousand stupas, there are a number of other quite different traditions concerning the fate of the Buddha's relics. These focus not so much on his ashes as on the fortune of certain of his bones and teeth. One tooth, for instance, ended up enshrined in Sri Lanka, where today it is an object of veneration by pilgrims who come to the Temple of the Tooth in Kandy to make offerings of flowers and incense. Once a year, in the summer month of Äsa-la, it is paraded in pomp around the city in what remains one of the chief Sri Lankan festivals.

Throughout the precolonial history of Sri Lanka, possession of the Buddha's tooth was seen as an indispensable attribute of kingship. Its cult was the privilege and duty of the legitimate ruler and was thought to ensure social harmony, regular rainfall, bountiful crops, and righteous rule. Its possession meant power. Thus, when the British finally took Kandy in 1815 and captured the tooth, they found to their surprise that resistance to them soon stopped.

The official cult of the tooth relic was and is today carried out by an entire hierarchy of priests. Several times a day, in a series of ceremonies that closely resemble the Hindu pattern of worship of the gods, they ritually entertain the tooth, bathe it, clothe it, and feed it. In this, it is quite clear that the Buddha is thought to be somehow present, despite the doctrine that he has completely transcended the realm of rebirth.

As with the saints in Christianity, this presence of the Buddha in his relics is sometimes emphasized by the occurrence of miracles. For instance, according to the *Mahāvaṃsa* (Great Chronicle) of Sri Lanka, when King Dutthagamani (first century BCE) was about to enshrine some Buddha relics in the great stupa he had built, the casket in which they were kept rose up into the air; it opened of itself, and the relics came out, took on the physical form of the Buddha, and performed all sorts of miracles that had been performed by the Buddha himself during his lifetime. According to some traditions, it might be added, much the same miracle is expected to take place at the end of this present world cycle, when, just prior to the advent of the next Buddha, Maitreya, all of the dispersed relics of the present Buddha will miraculously come together again to form his body one more time, before disappearing forever into the depths of the earth.

Sri Lanka, however, was by no means the only Buddhist nation to enjoy the possession of prestigious Buddha relics. A number of hairs of the Buddha were enshrined in splendor in the great Shwe Dagon pagoda in Rangoon, Burma; and in Lamphun in northern Thailand, several relics of the Buddha became the object of great veneration and elaborate legends. In both of these places, as in many others throughout the Buddhist world, the presence of Buddha relics is closely linked to the first introduction of Buddhism into the country. In other words, the relics were not just objects of veneration for a few but were symbolic of the establishment of the faith in a whole region.

The situation was somewhat different in China, where Buddhism was always in competition with a number of other faiths and ideologies. Nevertheless, in Changan (present-day Sian), the ancient capital of the Tang dynasty, the emperor's periodic reception for the Buddha's finger bone relic (generally kept at a monastery outside the city) was perhaps the greatest religious festival during the ninth century.

As Kenneth Chen put it in his *Buddhism in China*, "Whenever this relic was put on public display, the people . . . would work themselves into such a state of religious frenzy as to belie the statement that the Chinese are rational and practical in their conduct" (Chen 1964, p. 280). Devotees threw themselves on the ground, gave away all their possessions, cut off their hair, burned their scalps, and made fiery offerings of their fingers. It was, in fact, this sort of display that in 819 led the Confucian scholar Han Yü to petition the throne to put an end to such celebrations, pointing out that it was demeaning for the emperor to have anything to do with the bone of a barbarian.

Another famous relic of the Buddha in China was a tooth that was originally brought to Nanking in the fifth century and then taken to Chang'an. Lost for over eight hundred years, it was rediscovered in 1900 and is presently enshrined in a pagoda outside Peking. In the late 1950s and early 1960s, the Chinese government, eager to improve its relations with Buddhist nations of South and Southeast Asia, allowed it to go on a tour to Burma and then Sri Lanka, where it was worshiped by hundreds of thousands of people.

Not all of the Buddha's relics, however, have been bodily remains. In several places in South and Southeast Asia, great stone footprints, reputed to be his, are still venerated today. In northwest India, he is said to have left his shadow or reflected image on the wall of a cave that was a popular pilgrimage site from the fourth to the eighth century. There, given the right amount of devotion and meditation, pilgrims were thought actually to be able to see the Buddha himself in his shadow. Nearby was a rock on which one could discern the pattern of the cloth in the Buddha's robe where he had set it out to dry. Also in the same region was the Buddha's begging bowl, which the Chinese pilgrim Faxian saw during his trip to India (399–414). Faxian recounts a legend concerning the bowl's miraculous migration over the centuries throughout the Buddhist world. According to this, at the end of the present age, it is destined to ascend to the Tusita Heaven, where it will be a sign for the future Buddha Maitreya that the time for him to come down to earth is at hand.

CONCLUSION. In both the Christian and Buddhist traditions, as well as to a lesser extent in Islam and ancient Greece, the examples of relics here considered present a great variety of aspects and have been caught up in a whole gamut of symbolisms. In relics, believers have found the ongoing presence and power of Jesus, of the Buddha, of the saints of different traditions. Everywhere relics have performed miracles of various kinds; they have been used to ward off evil, to effectuate cures, and to ensure the prosperity of individuals, cities, and even nations; they have legitimized the rule of kings and emperors; they have helped spread and popularize religion; they have been bought, stolen, traded, and fought over, and have held social, economic, and political importance.

But for all these many functions, it must be noted that relics remain marked with a certain ambiguity. They are often objects that are normally considered to be impure—dead flesh, bones, and body parts—and yet they are venerated as holy. In this very paradox, however, can be seen some of the ways in which relics work to heighten the holiness and purity of the saints; if even their impurities are venerated, how much purer and more venerable they must be themselves!

Somewhat the same reasoning can be applied to a second and more basic ambiguity found in relics. They are clearly symbols of death and impermanence; they are what is left after the saints and founders of the tradition are no more. Yet, as has been seen repeatedly, they also make manifest the continuing presence and life of these absent beings. In asserting that the saints are "alive in death," or, in the case of Buddhism, that they are paradoxically present despite their final nirvana, relics in both traditions manage to bridge a gap that is one of the great divides of human existence.

SEE ALSO Architecture; Bones; Persecution, article on Christian Experience; Stupa Worship; Tombs.

BIBLIOGRAPHY

For a short introduction to the comparative study of relics, see Gregory Schopen, "Relic," in *Critical Terms for Religious Studies*, edited by Mark C. Taylor (Chicago, 1998), pp. 256–268. For a survey of the field, see James Bentley, *Restless Bones: the Story of Relics* (London, 1985). For the study of relics in early Christianity, Peter Brown's *The Cult of the Saints* (Chicago, 1981) is a good place to begin, while André Grabar's *Martyrium: recherches sur le culte des reliques et l'art chrétien antique* (Paris, 1946) remains a readable classic. More general works on Christian relics extending into Medieval and Modern times are Thomas Head's succinct "Relics" in *Dictionary of the Middle Ages* (New York, 1988), 10: 296–299; Nicole Hermann-Mascard, *Les reliques des saints: formation coutumière d'un droit* (Paris, 1975); and David Sox's more popularly written *Relics and Shrines* (London, 1985). For more specialized studies, see on the True Cross, Anatole Frolow's *La relique de la Vraie Croix: Recherches sur le développement d'un culte* (Paris, 1961); on the medieval traffic in relics in western Europe, Patrick Geary's *Furta Sacra: Thefts of Relics in the Central Middle Ages* (Princeton, N.J., 1978); and on Roman Catholic rules about relics, Eugene A. Dooley, *Church Law on Sacred Relics* (Washington, D.C., 1931). Among the many works to appear on the shroud of Turin, mention might be made of Ian Wilson's *The Shroud of Turin: The Burial Cloth of Jesus Christ?* (Garden City, N.Y., 1978).

For the study of relics in Buddhism, see Kevin Trainor, *Relics, Ritual, and Representation in Buddhism: Rematerializing the Sri Lankan Theravada Tradition* (Cambridge, 1997); Dan Martin, "Pearls from Bones: Relics, Chortens, Tertons and the Signs of Saintly Death in Tibet," *Numen* 41 (1994): 273–324; Bernard Faure, "Relics and Flesh Bodies: The Creation of Ch'an Sites," in *Pilgrims and Sacred Sites in China,* ed. Susan Naquin and Chün-fang Yü (Berkeley, Calif., 1992), pp. 150–189; Brian Ruppert, *Jewel in the Ashes: Buddha Relics and Power in Early Medieval Japan* (Cambridge, 1997); and John S. Strong, *Relics of the Buddha* (Princeton, N.J., 2004). A detailed study of the rituals associated with the Buddha's tooth relic in Sri Lanka can be found in H.L. Seneviratne, *Rituals of the Kandyan State* (Cambridge, 1978). A helpful introduction to the temple of the Buddha's relic in Lamphun, Thailand is Donald K. Swearer's *Wat Haripuñjaya* (Missoula, Mont., 1976). For Buddhist relics in China, see Kenneth Ch'en's *Buddhism in China: A Historical Survey* (Princeton, N.J., 1964).

Finally, two useful works for the study of relics in Islam deserve mention: Ignácz Goldziher's "On the Veneration of the Dead in Paganism and Islam," in volume 1 of *Muslim Studies* (Chicago, 1966), and, on the cult of the saints in Egypt, Jane I. Smith and Yvonne Haddad's *The Islamic Understanding of Death and Resurrection* (Albany, N.Y., 1981), appendix C.

JOHN S. STRONG (1987 AND 2005)

RELIGION [FIRST EDITION]. The very attempt to define *religion,* to find some distinctive or possibly unique essence or set of qualities that distinguish the "religious" from the remainder of human life, is primarily a Western concern. The attempt is a natural consequence of the Western speculative, intellectualistic, and scientific disposition. It is also the product of the dominant Western religious mode, what is called the Judeo-Christian climate or, more accurately, the theistic inheritance from Judaism, Christianity, and Islam. The theistic form of belief in this tradition, even when downgraded culturally, is formative of the dichotomous Western view of religion. That is, the basic structure of theism is essentially a distinction between a transcendent deity and all else, between the creator and his creation, between God and man.

Even Western thinkers who recognize their cultural bias find it hard to escape, because the assumptions of theism permeate the linguistic structures that shape their thought. For example, the term *holy* comes from linguistic roots signifying wholeness, perfection, well-being; the unholy, then, is the fragmentary, the imperfect, the ailing. Sacredness is the quality of being set apart from the usual or ordinary; its antonym, *profane,* literally means "outside the *fane*" (ME, "sacred place"). Thus every sanctuary—synagogue, church, mosque—is a concrete physical embodiment of this separation of the religious from all else. So too, in a more general sense the sacred is what is specifically set apart for holy or religious use; the secular is what is left over, the world outside, the current age and its fashions and concerns. This thoroughgoing separation has been institutionalized in a multitude of forms: sacred rites including sacraments; sacred books and worship paraphernalia; holy days; sacred precincts and buildings; special modes of life and dress; religious fellowships and orders; and so on *ad infinitum.*

Many practical and conceptual difficulties arise when one attempts to apply such a dichotomous pattern across the board to all cultures. In primitive societies, for instance, what the West calls religious is such an integral part of the total ongoing way of life that it is never experienced or thought of as something separable or narrowly distinguishable from the rest of the pattern. Or if the dichotomy is applied to that multifaceted entity called Hinduism, it seems that almost everything can be and is given a religious significance by some sect. Indeed, in a real sense everything that is is divine; existence *per se* appears to be sacred. It is only that the ultimately real manifests itself in a multitude of ways—in the set-apart and the ordinary, in god and so-called devil, in saint and sinner. The real is apprehended at many levels in accordance with the individual's capacity.

The same difficulty arises in another form when considering Daoist, Confucian, and Shintō cultures. These cultures are characterized by what J. J. M. de Groot termed "universism": a holiness, goodness, and perfection of the natural order that has been misunderstood, distorted, and falsified by shallow minds and errant cultural customs. The religious life here is one of harmony with both the natural and human orders, a submersion of individuality in an organic relationship and in an inwardly experienced oneness with them. And Buddhism in all its forms denies the existence of a transcendent creator-deity in favor of an indefinable, nonpersonal, absolute source or dimension that can be experienced as the depth of human inwardness. This, of course, is not to forget the multitudinous godlings, *bodhisattvas,* and spirits who are given ritual reverence in popular adaptations of the high religion to human need.

There is one other important result of the Western concept and practice of religion, here alluded to in passing: the religious community, distinct and more or less set apart from the environing society. This is not absolutely unique to Western religiosity, for in almost every culture there are those individuals believed to have unusual capacities and powers—the soothsayers, shamans, witch doctors, medicine men, and other specialists who are set apart from all others by their powers and who use them in a professional manner. Likewise in most cultures there are those temporary and voluntary groups of initiates into secret or occult fellowships who take upon themselves prescribed special obligations, diets, psychosomatic disciplines, and the like.

But none of these achieves the form or distinctive qualities of the congregations of synagogue, church, or mosque. There is more and other here than the geographical togetherness of worshipers at a Hindu or Buddhist temple or the cultic togetherness of a tribal society. In one sense, a Western-style congregation is a "gathered people," a group of persons who have been divinely called to and have consciously chosen to follow this particular faith rather than other possible faiths or nonfaith. (That geographical, historical, and social factors greatly modify the actuality of the factor of choice is to be understood, but being chosen and choosing remain the ideal model.) Such groups have their chosen leaders, carry on joint worship periodically as well as other corporate activities, and evangelize for their faith among others. Thus, being a member of a body of believers—a term that betrays the Western theistic emphasis upon doctrine—separates individuals to some extent from others in the environing society. And the professional teachers and ritualists—rabbis, ministers, priests, and to some extent mullahs and imams—are by their dress and mode of life even more separated from "the world" than the devout laity are.

Again, this special type of grouping, though produced in part by many other factors as well, is a distinctive product of the Western theistic dichotomous conception of religion as a set of beliefs and practices that are different from surrounding beliefs and practices and that embody a special relation to deity, that transcendent other. The very term *religion* originally indicated a bond of scruple uniting those who shared it closely to each other. Hence *religion* suggests both separation and a separative fellowship. How, then, is religion to be conceptually handled for the purposes of thought and discussion, since the very term itself is so deeply ingrained with specifically Western cultural presuppositions?

DEFINITIONS. So many definitions of religion have been framed in the West over the years that even a partial listing would be impractical. With varying success they have all struggled to avoid, on the one hand, the Scylla of hard, sharp, particularistic definition and, on the other hand, the Charybdis of meaningless generalities. Predictably, Western-derived definitions have tended to emphasize the sharp distinction between the religious and nonreligious dimensions of culture and sometimes have equated religion with beliefs, particularly belief in a supreme being. Obviously such definitions exclude many primitive and Asian religions, if we still wish to use the term.

Such definitional usage has had its critics in the West. As early as the late eighteenth century an attempt was made to shift the emphasis from the conceptual to the intuitive and visceral in defining religion. In a very influential statement, Friedrich Schleiermacher defined religion as "feeling of absolute dependence"—absolute as contrasted to other, relative feelings of dependence. Since that time there have been others who have sought to escape formalistic, doctrinal definitions and to include the experiential, emotive, and intuitive factors, as well as valuational and ethical factors. These factors seemed to be truer to the religious person's sense of what religion is like from the inside, to include what William James called "the enthusiastic temper of espousal." Such definitions appear to be more universally applicable to primitive and Asian religions than belief-oriented ones.

This is surely the case with primitive religion where, as noted, the religious is scarcely distinguishable from the sociocultural, where custom and ritual are abundant while belief structures are scarce, where emotional realities carry more weight than statable ideas. The Asian religious traditions, too, characteristically place their prime emphasis upon the inner states of realization rather than upon the merely instrumental rite or doctrine. Indeed, this is so much the case that in some of the more radical expressions, such as Zen Buddhism and Hindu *bhakti* (devotional faith), creed and tradition are purely secondary or even valueless hindrances. Of course, it should be added that this is not quite the case in actuality. For feeling-based experience never subsists on its own exclusive resources: feeling (and love as in *bhakti*) is always feeling *about* or *toward* some object or other. Experience never happens in a complete ideational vacuum. In all these cases, be they primitive, Buddhist, or Hindu, there is an underlying conceptual context of some sort, and its implicitness or verbal denial does not indicate its total functional absence.

With the rise of the sociological and anthropological disciplines, another factor has been projected into definition making—the social, economic, historical, and cultural contexts in which religion comes to expression. Sociologists and anthropologists rightly argue that religion is never an abstract set of ideas, values, or experiences developed apart from the total cultural matrix and that many religious beliefs, customs, and rituals can only be understood in reference to this matrix. Indeed, some proponents of these disciplines imply or suggest that analysis of religious structures will totally account for religion. Émile Durkheim, a pioneer in this societal interpretation, asserted in *The Elementary Forms of the Religious Life* (New York, 1926) that "a society has all that is necessary to arouse the sensation of the divine in minds, merely by the power that it has over them" (p. 207). Thus the gods are nothing more than society in disguise. Since Durkheim's time, sociologists have refined their methods of analysis, but some still maintain the essential Durkheimian view.

The various forms of psychology come out of the same scientific-humanistic context as the social science disciplines.

The central concerns of psychology are the psychic mechanics and motivational forces that result from human self-consciousness. In some sense, psychological interpretations of religion are more akin to those that stress experiential inwardness than to those that accent intellectual and societal aspects. In the final analysis, however, psychology is more akin to the social sciences in its treatment of religion than to any intrareligious effort at interpretation. It tends, like social studies, to dissolve religion into sets of psychological factors.

It should be observed in passing that the religious person would not be satisfied with such analyses. That person's sense of what is happening in religion seems always to contain some extrasocietal, extrapsychological depth-factor or transcendent dimension, which must be further examined.

Among Western religion scholars there have been attempts to define religion in a manner that avoids the "reductionism" of the various sociological and psychological disciplines that reduce religion to its component factors. A prominent one has been the analysis of religions of varied nature in terms of the presence of an awareness of the sacred or the holy. First proposed by Schleiermacher, this approach found its most notable expression in Rudolf Otto's *The Idea of the Holy* (1917). Analyzing the biblical accounts of the experience of the prophets and saints in their encounters with God, Otto defines the essence of religious awareness as awe, a unique blend of fear and fascination before the divine. Thus Isaiah, upon becoming aware of the presence of the living God (Yahveh) in the temple sanctuary, cried out, "Woe is me, for I am undone!" Isaiah's response expresses both creaturely fear of his creator and his own sense of sinfulness before God's absolute righteousness. Yet he does not flee but remains to worship and to become the bearer of a prophetic message to his people. In Otto's terms, Isaiah and others like him sensed the *mysterium tremendum*, the "wholly otherness" of the divine being. And for Otto this was the prototype of all truly religious experience.

Otto's conception of the essential nature of religious experiences may be acceptable in the context of Western theism, though this type of religious experience seems relatively rare or else is smothered by the religious apparatus that envelops it. But even in Otto's own writings the application of this concept to primitive and Asian religions seems difficult. In primitive religions any sense of the divine in the mode of Isaiah seems missing despite the early attempt of Andrew Lang to find a "high god" tradition in primitive antiquity. Here religion is scarcely distinguishable from magic; rites seem primarily used for the fulfillment of physicial needs; and fear rather than awe predominates. *Sacred* and *profane* are inappropriate terms to apply to this cultural continuum. Of course, it must be said that the powers that are feared, placated, and used, in turn, do have their invisible and esoteric dimensions with which some rites attempt to make contact.

Nor does this definition of religion as the experience of the awe-inspiring wholly other seem to fit Asian religions. To be sure, at the popular level much religion consists of placation and use of spirits and superhuman powers and various rituals reminiscent of theism. But in their own self-definitions Buddhism and Hinduism, for example, seem to have little or no sense of a radically other and ultimate being. In fact, the basic thought and action model here is that of man's oneness with his environing universe. He seeks to live religiously in organic harmony with the ultimate, and the highest level of religious experience tends toward a mystical monism, though with Eastern qualifications. Immanence of the sacred rather than its transcendence is emphasized. Thus Hinduism, Buddhism, and Daoism characteristically find the truly transcendent within the human self itself. The divinized, exteriorized forms given to the holy in theistic religions—and in the popular forms of their own faiths—are viewed as temporary and practically expedient but essentially false means for the final enlightenment of the ignorant.

The most recent and influential formulation of sacredness as the unique and irreducible essence of all religious experience has been that of Mircea Eliade. He has refined and expanded Otto's use of the term extensively. No longer is the sacred to be sought almost exclusively in the God-encounter type of experience; it is abundantly exemplified in the symbolisms and rituals of almost every culture, especially the primitive and Asian cultures. It is embodied as sacred space, for example, in shrines and temples, in taboo areas, even limitedly in the erection of dwellings in accordance with a sense of the *axis mundi*, an orientation to the center of the true (sacred) universe. Indeed, structures often symbolically represent that physically invisible but most real of all universes—the eternally perfect universe to which they seek to relate fruitfully. This sense of sacredness often attaches to trees, stones, mountains, and other like objects in which mysterious power seems to be resident. Many primitive rituals seek to sacramentally repeat the first moment of creation often described in myth when primordial chaos became recognizable order. Sacred time—that is, eternal and unfragmented time—is made vitally present by the reenactment of such myths. In *The Sacred and the Profane* (New York, 1951) Eliade writes, "Every religious festival, every liturgical time, represents the reactualization of a sacred event that took place in a mythical past, in the beginning" (pp. 68–69).

It is a matter of opinion whether Eliade's portraiture of the experience of the sacred, much more elaborate and extended than here stated, escapes the limitations of Otto's view and represents a viable way of defining and describing the religious mode. Sociologists and anthropologists question its verifiability in actual cases as well as Eliade's interpretation of his data. To them sacredness is an ideal construct, not a genuine cultural or experiential entity. Linguists, psychologists, and philosophers also question the identifiability of such a distinctive entity in patterns of language, experience, and thought patterns. For all of these critics the religious experience is a compound of cultural entities and experiences, not a separable thing in and of itself.

Is there no alternative to such reductions of religious experiences and structures into congeries of easily identifiable and nonmysterious psychological, social, political, and economic factors? Conversely, is there no alternative to the definition of the religious as a mystical essence that can be located in every culture by the proper methodology, like the detection of uranium by a geiger counter? The truth in the former views is that a religious awareness, wherever found, occurs in the context of and is given tangible form by cultural, economic, and social factors. Traditionally, these factors condition members of a society to perceive and experience the world in ways given as religious.

On the other hand, it is also true that there is something of a sacred otherness about religious experiences that cannot be easily dissolved or given no weight. Even though an unanalyzable, unqualifiable factor called "the holy" or "the sacred" cannot be isolated from its varied components and contexts, almost every known culture displays elements that, if not wholly other from their context, do show a certain discontinuity with it. When these discontinuous elements are spoken about or related to, there occurs at least a slight shift to another perspective, another realm of discourse, which concerns the more mysterious and indefinable areas of experience and expectation. Or these elements might be discussed in terms of a depth dimension in cultural experiences and customs that hints at the more central, serious, or ultimate concerns and values. Perhaps religions could be seen, then, as the attempt to order individual and societal life in terms of culturally perceived ultimate priorities.

It should be noted, of course, that the form, clarity, and degree of such an ordering of life vary immensely from culture to culture. Thus primitive man adds enhancing rituals and magic incantations to his tool-making and hunting skills, without clearly conceptualizing why he does so. He does not confuse the two means to his end, never substituting religio-magic for good weaponry, or chants for physical skill. Rather, he adds the magic and ritual elements to the humanly possible means in order to ensure their success; the magic and ritual elements are efforts to deal with the powerful and mysterious dimensions of existence that cannot be controlled or affected by ordinary means. This quality of other-than-ordinary also resides in the ritual paraphernalia, in the ritual specialists, and often in the secret content of the rites themselves and certain special localities. Thus even in primitive society there is a vaguely felt and inarticulate awareness of transcendence as strange, more, and different.

In Asian traditions that emphasize immanence rather than transcendence, characterized by continuums rather than discontinuities both of theory and of experience, gradations of both understanding and of experience exist nonetheless. Recognized levels of practice and attainment are buttressed by texts and incorporated into systems of praxis. "Lower" levels of attainment are not considered totally false or wrong but as less than fully true or ultimate. There is, then, a kind of transcendence by degree or stage; the highest is "other" to the lower states, and in some Buddhist and Hindu traditions (i.e., Zen and meditative Advaita) there is a breakthrough experience (*satori* and realization of *brahman*) that experientially is wholly other than or wholly transformative of ordinary awareness.

In summary, it may be said that almost every known culture involves the religious in the above sense of a depth dimension in cultural experiences at all levels—a push, whether ill-defined or conscious, toward some sort of ultimacy and transcendence that will provide norms and power for the rest of life. When more or less distinct patterns of behavior are built around this depth dimension in a culture, this structure constitutes religion in its historically recognizable form. Religion is the organization of life around the depth dimensions of experience—varied in form, completeness, and clarity in accordance with the environing culture.

Distinguishing Characteristics of Religious Experience. If religiousness is a depth-awareness coming to distinctive expression in the forms we call religion, how is religiousness distinguished from various other types of awareness such as the aesthetic and ecstatic—what Abraham Maslow (1964) calls "peak experiences" and Marghanita Laski (1961) terms "non-religious ecstasy"—and the states of "altered consciousness" produced by various psychosomatic techniques or drugs?

Indeed, there are those who would equate all such states with the so-called religious variety. For example, Maslow urges that all peak, that is, highly emotional and ecstatic, experiences should be recognized as equally valid and valuable, whatever the conditions of their occurrence or production. He criticizes religions for preempting the quality of genuineness as proof of the truth of their respective doctrines. Laski likewise fully equates the structured religious experiences of mystics with the "natural" experiences of ecstasy, transcendence, and aesthetic intensity that occur in the presence of some natural wonder, in sexual experience, in childbirth, or by other means. In the case of mystical experiences, she argues, religious "overbeliefs" have gratuitously attached to them and are erroneously considered to be causal.

There have also been many experiments, with and without drugs, in the achievement of a nonindividualized or transpersonalized consciousness. In these experiments the subject is lifted out of the usual narrow, self-oriented awareness into an awareness of the overpowering beauty of ordinary objects, colors, and sounds and of unity with the boundless infinitude of space, time, and being. Some subjects have reported the fusing of all the senses so that color has sound as well as the converse. Others report a sense of oneness with all other beings. Aldous Huxley equated these experiences with those of Christian, Muslim, Daoist, and Hindu mystics. Some practitioners have deliberately fused the use of psychosomatic techniques and drugs with religious practice—Zen, Hindu, American Indian.

However, the true significance of these experiences, misinterpreted in such views, is not found in the likeness of psychosomatic character in all such experiences, whether religious or not. That they can occur in nearly identical forms in a variety of contexts and with varied stimuli (or are they really identical?) indicates at most the similar psychosomatic nature of all human beings. The truly significant element is precisely that ideational and emotional context discarded by Maslow, Laski, and others as dispensable "overbeliefs." Such experiences in and by themselves are anonymous, miscellaneous, and trifling emotional flashes, unless they are connected with some system of ideation that interprets them in terms of meaningful concepts or other like experiences. In short, the ideational system gives the experiences an identity. And by thus having a traditional religious identity, these experiences also have power to affect the whole life—a power denied them as anonymous feeling. Thus the mystical ecstasies of Teresa of Ávila remolded her spirituality and propelled her into a life of strenuous activity in the cause of Roman Catholic Christianity. The same could be said of a Zen *satori* experience, even though it is not expressed in doctrinaire terms. *Satori* dynamically activates the total man because it validates the Zen context of tradition, thought, and values in which it occurs. It is oneness with the absolute Buddha essence; it is an experience of the Buddha mind, of organic harmony with the entire universe, of the felt unity of outer and inner worlds. These experiences are of revolutionary significance to the experiencer because of their contextual religious meaning.

In summary, it may be said that while ecstatic, transic, and intense aesthetic experiences are found both within religious and nonreligious frameworks and have many features in common psychologically, the religious experience is religious precisely because it occurs in a religious context of thought, discipline, and value.

CHARACTERISTICS AND STRUCTURES OF RELIGIOUS LIFE. As previously suggested, religions adopt their tangible historical forms as matrices of cultural and social elements about the depth-centers of culture. Hence the beliefs, patterns of observance, organizational structures, and types of religious experience are as varied as the matrices that give them birth, and that they in turn help form and reform. Even in the midst of this variety, however, we may distinguish certain characteristic elements and categories of structures distinctively religious.

Traditionalism. All attempts to find a primitive religion embodying the primordial form of all subsequent religions have encountered two insurmountable problems. The first is the sheer arbitrariness of seeking the origin of all types of religion in a single form. The second is that wherever religion is recognized—if one uses the above definition of religion as a depth-dimensional structure—one also encounters an existent tradition comprising stylized actions related to the pursuit of cultural goals, however meager or closely geared to survival needs. Present modes of religious activity always seem to look backward for origins, precedents, and standards. As cultures become more complex and literate, these traditions of ancient thought and practice become more elaborate and stylized.

Whatever the degree of elaboration, two things seem to be taken for granted. First, the beginnings—the original creative action, the life and words of an individual founder, even the authorless antiquity of a tradition's scriptures, as in the case of Hinduism—are taken as models of pristine purity and power, fully authoritative for all members of the group or adherents of the faith. Second, no matter how great the actual changes in a particular historical religious tradition—and sometimes this means the entire cultural tradition, more or less—the basic thrust of traditionalism is to maintain itself. Typically, religious reformers speak about a reforming of the religion in terms of its more holy past. Thus Zen seeks to go back directly to the mind of the Buddha, bypassing all historical forms and scripturalism. Revivalist Islam speaks of returning to pure Qur'anic faith and practice. Protestantism sought a return to New Testament Christianity, eliminating all the Roman Catholic "accretions"; and the Roman Catholic church responded that its doctrine and ritual and authority were demonstrably older than anything in Protestantism, going back to Christ himself.

Myth and symbol. Religious traditions are full of myth and replete with symbol. *Myth* in most contemporary use simply means "false"; myths are the fanciful tales of primitives spun out as explanations of beginnings. Hence creation myths are rationalizations of what prescientific cultures cannot understand through other means. Though this explanatory function of myth has been important, an even more basic function has been that of symbolic source. Apparently, even the writers of myths recognized the impossibility of expressing the fundamentally indescribable nature of absolute beginnings and ultimate realities. Hence poetry and symbol were their metier. In this way, religious myths have become modes of action, mankind's way of relating to physical and environmental realities. Thus does religious man seek to grasp the actionable significance of the world and relate to it emotionally. In passing, it should be noted that all disciplines of thought and life have their mythology of guiding images and unproven assumptions.

Symbol is the language of myth. When the crucially important but mysterious nature of ultimate reality—the basic concern of religious man—can only be seen through a glass darkly, how else can one speak of it except in symbolic forms? Ordinary language will not serve for the fullness of either the question or the answer here. Therefore religious language is rich in analogies, metaphors, poetry, stylized actions (ritual), and even silence ("Be still and know that I am God"). For the symbol stands for something other and more than itself; it is only a finger pointing at the moon of reality.

In seeking to deal with man's ultimate concerns, religions are prolific in the production, use, and elaboration of symbolic forms and objects; thus it is not surprising that religions have been the inspiration of an overwhelmingly large and diverse body of art. Indeed, in most cultures of the past, religions have been the central cultural fountainhead. To realize the importance of symbols in religion one need think only of the immense variety of rituals; of the stylized dress, manner, and speech of ritual officiants; of artifacts used in rituals; of paintings and sculptures, of shrines and sanctuaries of all levels and types.

Finally, the tremendous tenacity of symbolic forms and their ritualized vehicles must be emphasized. Many a symbol outlives its parent religion and culture, as the lotus, for example, has lived through centuries of symbolic existence, first in Hinduism and then in Buddhism. Symbols are more lasting than their explanatory doctrinal forms because they speak to the human imagination and to human feelings, not merely to the rational sense. Religious symbols often embody what is felt to be the central religious reality involved; they are its sacramental form, which must be preserved at all costs.

Concepts of salvation. Salvation is but another name for religion. That is, all religions are basically conceived as means of saving men at one level or another. And there are always two aspects to salvation: what men are to be saved *from* and what they are to be saved *to*. It goes without saying that what men are saved from and to varies immensely from culture to culture and from religion to religion.

At the primitive level of religion, salvation both "from" and "to" is achieved mainly in the realm of physical dangers and goods. The primitive seeks by his rituals to save himself from starvation, from death by storm, from disease, from wild animals, and from enemies and to sufficiency of food and shelter, to freedom from danger and disease, and to human fertility. Implicit in this context, and in the realm of mental and emotional malaise, is salvation from mysterious and even malign powers and forces of evil. The achievement of salvation in all these areas is striven for by all possible physical means with the superadded power of ritual, charm, and magic.

Of course, the development of environing cultures implies a change and expansion in the nature of religious salvation. Group values come to play a larger and more conscious role. The group—whether tribal kinship-clan or nation-state—comes to be a sacred entity in its own right, perhaps the preeminent one in some cases. Roman religion, for example, was essentially a state religion whose major purpose was the preservation (salvation) of the state in prosperity and power; a triumphal conquest was a triumph of the Roman deities. In time the emperors themselves were considered incarnate deities, as were the Egyptian pharaohs of an earlier era. Later, inner values, relatively unimportant to primitive and early nationalistic cultures, became matters of prime religious importance. Inner states of mind, the cultivation of ecstasy, and concern about the personal survival of physical death became important, sometimes almost paramount in times of social and political turmoil.

In time, this area of inner development, experiences, and values became the impetus for religious development. The "great" religious traditions of Judaism, Buddhism, Hinduism, Christianity, and Islam are all oriented toward the inner life. Their doctrines, texts, religious disciplines, and even organizations aim to cultivate the inner life of prayer, faith, enlightenment, and purity of character.

Yet the development of the inner life in religion does not completely exclude the lower level of physical-material goods. They remain as the object of perfectly acceptable religious hopes so that prayers are still made for health, safety, rain in times of drought, and sufficiency of food. And in some instances the final higher goods represent only the absolutizing or infinitizing of the physical-material ones. Thus eternal life maximizes the desire for deliverance from death—that primary human desire for survival toward which so much of primitive religion is directed. Indeed, the Greek religion of ancient times seems almost alone in portraying life after death as an unsatisfactory shadow existence. Most pure lands, heavens, and paradises are described as the perpetual enjoyment of life without pain, sorrow, or unhappiness of any sort. Similarly, the indescribable *nibbāna* of Theravāda Buddhism is conceived as the final, absolute end of the emptiness, impermanence, and pain of all embodied existence.

But even given the continuing presence of the lower-level goods sought by religious means in the higher-level religions, it is still true that the inner goals of peace, self-sacrificing love, purity of heart, and awareness of absolute goodness increasingly become central to the religious quest. When they are sought for themselves with no ulterior motives, the possibility of saintliness comes into being.

It is, of course, obvious that religious salvation is as responsive to and expressive of human needs and desires as any secular scheme of salvation. For salvation in religion is a means of fulfilling needs and desires, even when the needs and desires are revealed from "above." Yet the forms fulfillment takes express specially religious values, supplementing and sometimes opposing other, nonreligious values. And it is also evident that the varied cultural contexts of religions each represent a variant perspective on the human situation—its goods and goals, its dangers and evils. These varied perspectives greatly influence the form of religious salvation. Thus the Hindu Advaitin, the African San, the Sunnī Muslim, the Orthodox Jew, the Zen Buddhist, the Protestant, and the Greek Orthodox Christian would define religious needs and goods quite differently.

Is there then any appreciable difference between the ways in which religious and nonreligious modes of need fulfillment proceed? In other words, are there distinguishing characteristics of religious salvation? The first is that religious salvation tends to concentrate on the needs a culture defines as most fundamental, neglecting needs that a culture defines as less important. Religious means of salvation, often indirect and extrahuman, seek to use supersensible forces and powers either in addition to or in place of ordinary tangible means. The second distinguishing characteristic is that religious salvations tend to aim at total, absolute, and sometimes transcendent fulfillment of human needs. As defined by the cultural context, this fulfillment ranges all the way from the fullness of physical satisfactions to the eternal ecstasy of union with the Absolute.

Sacred places and objects. One of the striking features of historically observable religions is the presence of special religious areas and structures set apart from ordinary space by physical, ritual, and psychological barriers. Precincts, churches, mosques, synagogues, and shrines are the highly visible manifestations of religious discontinuity with the surrounding world. Various physical actions are often required of those who enter sacred areas to indicate this separation: ablutions, removal of footwear, prayers and incantations, bowing and kneeling, silence, preparatory fasting, special garb, and preliminary inward acts of contrition.

Further, particularly within the more spacious precincts, there are grades of sacredness that enshrine specially sacred objects or relics in their supremely holy areas. A classic example is the last of the Jewish temples in Jerusalem, in which there was a spatial progression from the outermost court of the Gentiles to the women's court to the men's court to the court of the burnt offering to the priests' enclosure to the Holy of Holies wherein was the Ark of the Covenant and, in some sense, the special presence of Yahveh. In synagogues today the ark containing a copy of the Torah is the most sacred part. In Roman Catholic and Eastern Orthodox churches, the altar supporting the sacramental bread and wine is the focal point of sacredness. Protestant churches display a weaker form of the same principle, centered around the Bible or pulpit. Buddhist shrines in Southeast Asia commonly are pagodas containing sacred relics and/or consecrated Buddha images, which are honored by removing footwear, circumambulating with the central spire to one's right, and presenting floral offerings and obeisances. Japanese Buddhist temples usually contain large Buddha images at the rear of ornately decorated altars. Hindu temples vary somewhat in this respect; some have a holy inner sanctum into which only the ritually pure devotee may enter, while others provide relatively open access to the revered god images. Perhaps the Islamic mosque is the least set apart of religious places. Yet even here ablutions are required before entry, nonbelievers are scarcely welcome, and the semicircular alcove set in the rear wall (*qiblah*) must project toward the Muslim holy of holies, the Kaʿbah in Mecca, so that praying believers always face in that direction.

Quite logically, many of the furnishings and objects used in temples and shrines, particularly in their most sacred rituals, partake of the sacredness of the shrine itself. One thinks here of altar furnishings and utensils, sacrificial paraphernalia, baptismal water, the special garb of temple officiants, special words and gestures, incense, candles and the like. These furnishings and objects are less holy than the shrine and revered relic, which are intrinsically sacred.

But in the final analysis sacred places are sacred because of what has occurred there or may occur there. Their essence is sacramental. Sacred places are cherished and revered because they offer the possibility of directly encountering and partaking of the real in the given tradition. An unusual power has manifested itself in a natural object or taboo place either for good or ill. Or tradition tells that some primordially creative act once took place here and that power still lingers. So in both more and less developed religious traditions, past sanctity and present hope characterize sacred places, The shrine of the Virgin of Guadalupe appears to have been first a center of pagan deity worship before its adoption by the Christian faith; its religious power is centuries old, transfixing past and present devotees. This same quality is found at the Dome of the Rock in Jerusalem, from which Muḥammad reputedly made his ascent into heaven; at the places of the Buddha's birth, enlightenment, first sermon, and death in India; and at the legendary birth and death places of Jesus in Palestine.

Other sacred places and objects (images) particularly emphasize the hope of present and future blessing. The shrine at Lourdes is venerated not simply because a French peasant girl reputedly once saw a vision of the Virgin there but because of the hope of present healing. Similarly, many Buddhists expect to gain merit by praying and making offerings before Buddha images or to reap tangible benefits in the here and now by touching *bodhisattva* images. The Shintō practitioner rings the bell to summon his chosen deity and petition him or her for a specific boon. A Roman Catholic church is made sacred because of its consecrated altar at which the life-giving miracle of bread and wine transformed into the spiritual body of Christ occurs at every mass. The Protestant pulpit is the space where the word of the living God is expounded; at the very least the devout parishioner hopes for some sense of empowerment and renewal for daily living. Every functioning shrine embodies such living and sacred hopes.

Sacred actions (rituals). Just as it is impossible to think of living religions without their sacred places, so is it impossible to conceive of a religion without its rituals, whether simple or elaborate. The forms of ritual are familiar, involving the stylized saying or chanting of certain words, bowing or kneeling, offerings of various kinds including animal sacrifices, dancing and music making.

Several features are prominent in most rituals. One is the element of order. Indeed, an established ritual pattern is the ordered performance of sacred actions under the direction of a leader. This order usually develops early in the history of a given tradition. Initially the sacred actions are more or less informal and spontaneous, then, step by step, become ordered and standardized procedures, and in the end may become elaborate ritual patterns requiring a considerable quantity of equipment and personnel (ritualists, priests). In Christianity we see the beginnings of this in Paul's exhortation to the church in Corinth to conduct their worship "decently and in order" (*1 Cor.* 14:40). He had heard reports of chaotic gatherings at which all participants were under the "inspiration of the Spirit." From this order developed the classical Christian liturgies. However, perhaps the maximal degree of ritualization was achieved in another tradition, for the *Brahmanic* Hindu sacrificial rituals involve an almost unbelievable complexity and rigidity of pattern.

Rigidity of pattern, requiring the utmost care and precision in use of word, action, and material, points to another feature of ritual, maximized in the Hindu sacrifice but more or less present in all fixed rituals: meticulous performance. Analogies may be drawn to magic formulas and scientific experiments, and the resemblance is indeed meaningful. Just as in magic and science, where success depends upon meticulously faithful following of the given formula, so too in religious ritual the desired healing, fertility, safety, prosperity, or inward state will not result if the ritual is improperly performed. Ritual words are words of power. The Hindu sacrificial ritual mentioned above involved priests specifically appointed to cover any lapses (wrong words or incorrect actions) by ritually speaking charms. Of course, cases such as this and some primitive rituals are the extreme manifestation of this quality. In other ritual patterns aesthetic concerns and inner-personal aspirations are important; ritual uniformity also has the practical advantage of giving the worshiper or user a sense of familiarity and ease as well as identity with a given tradition and group.

Yet deep within ritualism there is inherent the concern for accuracy and faithfulness. This is the essentially sacramental nature of ritual that arises from its nature as an ordered symbol system. Thus both symbol and ritual are perceived as intrinsic embodiments of the sacred essence, the supersensible and indescribable ultimacy of a religion. Thus ritual and symbol bring the real presence of the religious depth-dimension into the lives of its experients and in so doing become incredibly precious. This seems to apply across the religious spectrum to magic prayer rituals of the primitive, the Voodoo dance, sacrificial rituals, repetition of the Pure Land Nembutsu, Tibetan mantric *maṇḍala* rituals, and the Roman Catholic Eucharist. The preciousness of myth and symbol explains why religious groups tend to cherish and preserve their rituals more jealously and zealously than any of their doctrinal statements and why ritual patterns often survive longer than their parent traditions.

One final observation is required: ritualism in religion often produces an antiritualistic expression. Many examples could be given. Zen Buddhism was in one sense antiritualistic, as were Hōnen's and Shinran's Pure Land Buddhism. These latter substituted the easy, simple repetition of the name Amida for elaborate and often esoteric rituals. Devotional Hinduism, in which one is saved by love (*bhakti*) wholeheartedly given to a deity, protested against excessive Brahmanic ritualism. And Protestantism, in particular its radical forms, sought freedom from Roman Catholic ritualism. In all cases the motifs were simplicity and ease of access to the sacred.

Sacred writings. In literate societies writings are often of considerable religious importance. (Christianity calls sacred writings scriptures.) Typically sacred writings comprise the reported words of the holy men of the past—prophets, saints, founders of faiths such as Zarathushtra, Moses, the Buddha, Muḥammad, Christ, or Nanak. As such they are of prime importance as statements of the truth and expositions of the right way for believers to live. (Of course, nonliterate societies have their oral traditions that serve the same purpose.) The Hindu Vedas are considered to be without human author or known human channel of transmission.

When scriptures exist, interpreters must also exist. Successive interpretations vary greatly, for interpreters are caught between their desires to be faithful to the original sacred word and to make its exposition relevant and meaningful to their own age. A multitude of sectarian divisions based on variant scriptural interpretation is found in all the major religious traditions. Perhaps the number of writings in the Buddhist and Hindu traditions give interpreters an advantage in this regard, but Christian and Islamic sectarians have been nearly as successful with a smaller scriptural base.

Confucianism, Daoism, and Shintō can scarcely be said to have scriptures in the above sense of a corpus of inspired utterances. Their revered writings—the sayings of Confucius and Mengzi, of Laozi and Zhuangzi, and the *Records of Ancient Matters*—are studied more as the wise counsels of sages than as inerrant statements of truth. (In the latter the apothegms are considered precedent setting.) In general, Buddhist and Hindu scriptures can be interpreted much more flexibly than Western ones because of their greater variety and their emphasis on truth as dependent on the level of the hearer's understanding.

The sacred community. Every religion has some communal sense and structure. Ritual is essentially a group exercise, except for magico-religious rituals geared to personal desires. Hence ritual nearly always involves professional ritualists and a group bound together by its experience. But the communal bonds vary greatly in nature and extent.

Some ritual groupings are quite temporary: one thinks of the occasional, selective, and experience-based spirit groups found among some Native Americans. In other primitive cultures, the religious-ritual grouping is hardly separable from the general clan or tribal social structure and indeed might better be called a social subculture with religious elements centered on certain particular occasions and activities. In many Buddhist and Hindu contexts the religious community is little more than those in the vicinity who attend various religious ceremonies in the local temple and often come on purely personal quests. In such situations the only sacred community seems to be the priests and ritualists at a religious shrine, persons qualified for such functions by character and training.

To be sure, in most of these societies there are special groupings of a secret or semisecret nature open only to initiates. Such are the Native American spirit groups. Late Greek religion developed its "mystery" rites that sought goals and experiences beyond those offered by the ordinary temple and priesthood. Hinduism abounds in such special-interest, special-ritual groups bound together by a particular god, common pilgrimage points, and distinctive rituals; sometimes members live in separate communities built around a leader.

Buddhism and Christianity institutionalized such special-interest groups in their monastic orders. Men and women for a variety of reasons retire from the world to seek a more intensely religious way of life than that possible in ordinary secular pursuits or even as priests having everyday dealings with the laity and major liturgical duties. Some Ṣūfī communities in medieval Islam approximated the monastic life of a community apart from the wider community of believers.

Perhaps it is only in Islam and Christianity, and somewhat limitedly in Judaism, that the concept of a holy fellowship of believers, called a church in Christianity, has been created to express religious faith and practice. The prevailing ethnic qualification in Judaism prevents its description as a purely faith-gathered group. Islam represents a near equivalent to the Christian church, especially as Islamic groups have spread out into other areas than those totally Muslim in nature. Muslims, like Christians, consider themselves members of one sacred group, called out from among others by the faith and practice of their religion, ideally a unity stronger than any other bond. In the early days of Christianity, the apostle Paul could speak glowingly of the Christian community as a universal one in which there was neither Jew nor Greek, neither slave nor freeman, for all were equal in a new Christ-like humanity. Of course, in actuality both Christians and Muslims have divided along lines of race and nation. Both faiths, however, continue to cherish the ideal of the universal fellowship of faith.

It may be observed in passing that such a definition of community comes more naturally and more easily to Islam and Christianity than to most Asian religions. To a large extent this is because of the strong emphasis on doctrinal belief in Islam and Christianity: believers and nonbelievers can be clearly distinguished because religion is seen as a deliberate choice by the individual. In Asian religions, inclusive and naturalistic values predominate: experience rather than doctrine receives emphasis, rendering exclusivist religious formulations almost unknown. It may also be that the underlying Asian patterns of social organization have emphasized the group to such an extent that individual religious decision is nearly impossible.

The sacred experience. The question of whether all depth experiences, experiences of transcendence, or unusual mind-body states should be considered on a par with religious experiences, or are intrinsically religious themselves, has already been discussed. Here are considered only those experiences that occur within a declared religious context and are therefore doubly set apart, both as designatedly religious and as of special clarity and intensity even within that context.

These special experiences represent a continuum from the comparatively mild and frequent experiences to those commonly termed mystical. At the less intense end of the continuum are those instances of a sense of awe in the sacred precincts, a sense of humility before a felt presence, an unusual degree of joy or peace suddenly coming upon one, or the deep conviction of a prayer answered. Then there are those of a much more intense nature such as physical sensations of fire, electric shock, or a strong and sudden conviction of the forgiveness of one's sins such as John Wesley's "warming of the heart" at Aldersgate. Indeed, in some Christian groups special conversion or purification-of-heart experiences are made a matter of explicit emphasis and a condition of church membership. In Pentecostal groups a sudden and unexpected experience of speaking in unknown tongues is considered a sign of the "baptism of the Spirit." There are classical instances of the same phenomenon: Muḥammad hearing the voice of the angel Gabriel commanding him to recite (resulting in the Qurʾān) and Isaiah seeing the Lord high and lifted up with his train filling the temple (resulting in Isaiah's call to prophesy).

At the further end of this experiential continuum are the mystical experiences found in Judaism, Islam, Christianity, Daoism, Hinduism, and Buddhism. Those who have had such experiences (especially in Christian, Hindu, and Muslim contexts) insist that they differ in kind from all other religious experiences, including the less intense ones just discussed. Their distinctive qualities seem to be these: (1) their suddenness and spontaneity (without warning or overt preparation), (2) their irresistibility, (3) their absolute quality of conviction and realistic authority, (4) their quality of clear knowledge, not strong emotion, which is asserted even when the mystically received knowledge is conceptually indescribable. Perhaps the true and basic content of such moments is an assurance of the absolute reality of God, Kṛṣṇa, Brahmā, Dharma, or Buddha nature, that is, the ultimate reality as envisioned by the given faith. Also rather uniformly experienced is the overpowering conviction of knowing directly, climaxing in a felt encounter with the ultimate one or with the basic oneness of the universe.

In any case, these special experiences of prophets, saints, and enlightened persons have played an important role in many religious traditions. Though beyond the reach of ordinary religiosity, they have given a kind of reflected authenticity to faith at all levels, have encouraged the creation of various spiritual methodologies of devotion and meditation, and have vitalized traditions in difficult times. Mystical experiences have kept alive a sense of the reality and availability of religious power and have constantly renewed the whole corpus of ritual, doctrine, and organization.

RELIGION AND MODERNITY. The question whether religion, at least in its traditional forms, will survive the ongoing cultural changes of modern times is often discussed. Certainly many traditional and current formulations, and perhaps entire traditions, will radically change or even disappear. Yet it also seems that as soon as one form of religion disappears, another rises to take its place. Without asserting a religious instinct in mankind, it may perhaps be said that man is incurably religious in one way or another and that the human situation and human nature make it inevitably so. The immense mysteries and uncertainties of the world and man's own inquiring and evaluating self-consciousness make inevitable a reaching out for some sort of ultimate values and realities—which is but another name for the religious quest.

SEE ALSO Architecture; Community; Iconography; Mysticism; Myth; Orthopraxy; Philosophy; Religious Experience; Ritual; Sacred Space; Scripture; Soteriology; Study of Religion; Symbol and Symbolism; Truth.

BIBLIOGRAPHY

Beane, Wendell C., and William G. Doty, eds. *Myths, Rites, Symbols: A Mircea Eliade Reader.* 2 vols. New York, 1975. A well-chosen, substantial anthology of Eliade's writings on various aspects of religion.

Campbell, Joseph. *Masks of God*, vol. 1, *Primitive Mythology*; vol. 2, *Oriental Mythology*; vol. 3, *Occidental Mythology.* New York, 1959–1965. These three volumes present a richly varied portrait, penetrating analysis, and many concrete illustrations of the forms and functions of myth in these three different contexts.

Eliade, Mircea. *Patterns in Comparative Religion.* New York, 1958. The subtitle indicates the nature of this work: *A Study of the Element of the Sacred in the History of Religious Phenomena.*

Huxley, Aldous. *The Doors of Perception.* New York, 1954.

Huxley, Aldous. *Heaven and Hell.* New York, 1956. These two volumes present accounts of Huxley's experiments with psychedelic drugs and his positive interpretations of them.

James, William. *The Varieties of Religious Experience.* New York, 1902. James's Gifford Lectures (1901–1902) are among the early, classic studies of religious experience, offering numerous specific examples and his own interpretations.

King, Winston L. *Introduction to Religion: A Phenomenological Approach.* New York, 1968. A descriptive and analytic study of the various forms and structures of the religious life as expressed in various traditions.

Laski, Marghanita. *Ecstasy: A Study of Some Secular and Religious Experiences.* Westport, Conn., 1961. A thesis of this volume is that transcendent experiences are universally human and not necessarily religious.

Leeuw, Gerardus van der. *Religion in Essence and Manifestation: A Study in Phenomenology* (1938). 2 vols. Gloucester, Mass., 1967. The first major attempt to apply the phenomenological methodology to the field of religion, bracketing normative evaluations of truth and ethical considerations in the interests of describing the religious essence in its essential and characterstic manifestations.

Lessa, William A., and Evon Z. Vogt, eds. *Reader in Comparative Religion: An Anthropological Approach.* 4th ed. New York, 1979. A wide selection of significant readings on the interpretation of religion by various leading anthropologists.

Long, Charles H. *Alpha: The Myths of Creation.* New York, 1963. An anthology of creation myths from the folk tales and religions of the world, organized according to type.

Maslow, Abraham. *Religions, Values, and Peak-Experiences.* Columbus, Ohio, 1964. Maslow calls for religion to make common cause with other areas and disciplines in the constructive use of all peak experiences, whether religious or otherwise.

Masters, R. E. L., and Jean Houston. *The Varieties of Psychedelic Experience.* New York, 1966. An evaluative, critical analysis of psychedelic experiences claiming to be religious.

Noss, John B. *Man's Religions.* 6th ed. New York, 1980. A standard, college-level text describing the major religious traditions of the world.

Otto, Rudolf. *Das Heilige.* Marburg, 1917. Translated by John W. Harvey as *The Idea of the Holy* (1950; Oxford, 1970). The author's own subtitle expresses the thrust of this seminal volume: *An Inquiry into the Non-Rational Factor in the Idea of the Divine and Its Relation to the Rational.*

Pratt, James B. *The Religious Consciousness: A Psychological Study.* New York, 1921. Expressed in psychological terms no longer current but perceptive and suggestive, particularly with respect to mysticism.

Stace, W. T. *Mysticism and Philosophy.* New York, 1960. An acute philosophical analysis of the mystical experience, concluding that "something" objective is there but not quite what the mystic thinks it is.

Tart, Charles T., ed. *Transpersonal Psychologies.* New York, 1975. Analytic discussions from a psychological viewpoint of the qualities, nature, and meaning of a variety of mystical experiences and psychotherapeutic techniques.

Underhill, Evelyn. *Mysticism.* 12th ed. New York, 1961. A longtime classic, Underhill's book is a sympathetic presentation of the mystical life, mainly within the Christian context but including Muslim Ṣūfī materials.

WINSTON L. KING (1987)

RELIGION [FURTHER CONSIDERATIONS] Winston King's entry in the first edition of the *Encyclopedia of Religion* states well one classic position in religious studies: religion results from a particular kind of experience, which King calls "depth-awareness." Even at the time the encyclopedia first appeared, that position was fiercely contested. Indeed, certain characteristic fault lines run through King's account: the difficulty of denoting religious experience in a way that is not obscure ("depth-awareness") or circular ("religious experience is religious precisely because it occurs in a religious context"), for example, and the presence of two different treatments of experience—one in "Definitions" and "Distinguishing Characteristics of Religious Experience," the other in "The Sacred Experience"—separated from one another as far as possible, perhaps in order to hide the repetition.

Alternatives to this position were certainly available at the time. They included Melford Spiro's treatment of religion as "an institution consisting of culturally patterned interaction with culturally postulated superhuman beings" (Spiro 1966, p. 96); Clifford Geertz's account of religion as a system of symbols that integrate worldview and ethos; and Peter Berger's claim that religion is the highest order of legitimation available to human beings in protecting cultural constructs against the perennial threat of anomie. In the past several decades, however, scholarly attention has increasingly turned away from trying to conceptualize religion to reflecting on the act of conceptualization itself. One might say that it has turned away from treating *religion* as a thing to treating it as a word, concept, or category. To help clarify the distinction, this entry will use religion to indicate that the word refers explicitly to religion as a concept. At least three topics deserve consideration in this regard: the history of religion, strategies of definition, and the different discursive purposes that lead humans to conceptualize religion.

HISTORY OF RELIGION. The English word *religion* clearly derives from the Latin word *religio,* as do its cognates in other European languages, but the derivation of the Latin noun is uncertain. It is most commonly linked to one of two Latin verbs, *religare* (to bind or fasten) or *relegere* (to collect again, to go over again [as in reading]). Although the uncertain etymology creates difficulty in writing about the history of the term, it is of little practical consequence, for there is no good reason for etymology to dictate current usage.

In tracing the history of religion from classical antiquity to the present, the German Catholic theologian Ernst Feil discusses three successive meanings of the term. So small a number hardly does justice either to the history of religion or to Feil's (and others') detailed studies of it, but they do serve as a rough initial guide.

According to Feil, the core meaning of *religio* in antiquity was "careful, scrupulous observation, full of awe" (Feil, 2000, p. 18). In other words, religion denoted a set of moral actions or a species of justice—specifically, proper behavior in the matter of actions directed to the gods or God. During the European Middle Ages a more specific version of this definition became important. *Religion* designated not something that everyone had or did but a particular mode of life oriented to the service of God; namely, the life of Christian monks and nuns. This sense is still preserved today when English-speakers use the noun to refer to Catholic priests, monks, and nuns as "religious."

With the appearance in 1799 of Friedrich Schleiermacher's famous *Religion: Speeches to Its Cultured Despisers* and the attempt after the Enlightenment to rescue religion for educated people—or perhaps better, to rescue educated people for the church—religion acquired a very different sense, which Feil identifies as its second meaning.

Genuine religion, Schleiermacher insisted, was neither belief in what educated people usually rejected (the church's claims about miracles and revelation) nor adherence to a restrictive morality. The essence of religion was a feeling, an intuition of the universe as a whole and of oneself as a part of it. In line with this conception, Schleiermacher reformulated central concepts within Christianity, such as miracle, revelation, God, immortality, prophecy, and grace. He also maintained that, although religious intuition was universal, it found its supreme manifestation in Christianity.

Schleiermacher's conception of religion was certainly not the only option available during the next two hundred years. Another important trend arose from Edward Burnett Tylor's notion of religion as a belief in souls and spirits, reformulated by James George Frazer as "a belief in powers higher than man and an attempt to propitiate or please them" (Frazer, 1935, p. 222). But by the second half of the twentieth century, according to Feil, religion in the sense of a distinctive interior experience had become untenable. Feil himself recognized the possibility that a third sense of religion might arise, one suited to the various traditions of meditation that were being imported into Europe and North America from Asia after World War II. But reminiscent of Dietrich Bonhoeffer's "religionless Christianity," he preferred, as a theologian, to follow Wilfred Cantwell Smith and abandon the term *religion* for *faith.*

Other scholars, such as Talal Asad, have explored not the changing meanings of religion but the discursive and political forces that operated upon them, an exploration that Michel Foucault has called genealogy. It is no more possible to explore those forces in detail here than it is to explore religion's changing meanings, but one particularly significant force leading to the formulation of the modern notion of religion, besides the desire to rescue belief and practice from the clutches of rational critique, was dismay at the warfare that beset Europe in the aftermath of the Reformation. Faced with battles that pitted one confession against another, thinkers began to conceive of religion as distinct from the political, and at times as ideally separate from it in practice as well.

They also stressed that the varying claims to particular revelations were of little importance compared with the common core or essence that all confessions shared. One such early thinker, Edward, Lord Herbert of Cherbury, identified what he called "the common notions concerning religion": that God exists, that God should be worshiped, that virtuous deeds are the best way to worship God, that people should repent of their faults, and that virtue will receive its reward and vice its punishment in an afterlife.

During the course of the Enlightenment, the allegedly universal core of religion, innate and so requiring no special revelation, came to be called "natural religion," to distinguish it from the various empirical, or "positive," religions (as they were called then), such as the various forms of Christianity.

Schleiermacher and other Romantic thinkers rejected the idea that natural religion could exist apart from positive religions. In addition, some nineteenth-century thinkers considered religion to have been the primal source from which all cultural, social, and political forms derived. Nevertheless, the idea of religion as a distinct sphere of life having a universal essence remained. In significant respects, then, the modern notion of religion is a European and North American, and particularly a Protestant, attempt to negotiate diversity.

It may, however, be too simple to see religion as merely a European and North American construct. Based on the evidence of interreligious polemics, religious syncretism, and royal edicts regulating religions in places like ancient China and India, Martin Riesebrodt has argued that people in many parts of the globe, not just in Europe and North America, have long recognized different religious traditions as belonging to the same broader class, even if they did not explicitly conceptualize that class as religion. This argument does not address several questions, such as the extent to which the different local classifications are assimilable and whether an overarching assimilation, if desirable, is best conceived of as religion or as, for example, *dharma*. But it does point to significant cognitive issues involved in the history of conceptualizing religion.

Religion is a local category that scholars, along with others, have applied beyond the bounds of its origins. Just as in the centuries following Columbus natural historians in Europe adapted local terms to categorize the new flora and fauna that they encountered, Europeans simultaneously adapted the term *religion* to make sense of unfamiliar thought and behavior that they were encountering in unprecedented richness. Scott Atran has argued that the effort to universally extend classifications in biology was successful because the human mind everywhere employs certain hierarchical strategies in classifying organic life. It is not, however, evident that the mind uses the same conceptual apparatus for human constructs. For example, religion is not one taxon in an exhaustive, hierarchical system with mutually exclusive categories. (A bat is either a bird or a mammal, but if we decide Confucianism is not a religion, what is its taxonomical alternative?) Indeed, religions and other cultural products do not "breed true," and so do not have the stability and distinctness that populations of organisms do. If the above observations are correct—and it is not yet certain that they are—it may not be reasonable to expect the kind of universally acceptable classifications in the study of religions that one finds in a natural science like biology.

In any case, a consideration of history can only raise questions about the adequacy of a category like religion. It cannot answer them. The adequacy of a concept depends upon whether it can be properly formulated and whether it serves the purposes at hand.

Strategies of Definition. During the second half of the twentieth century, scholars repeatedly discussed several issues pertaining to an adequate conceptualization of religion. One of them, introduced by Melford Spiro, was the distinction between functional and substantive definitions.

Some scholars have favored conceptions of religion that are functional; that is, whose *definientes* ("definers," plural of *definiens*) describe what religions do. (Functional *definientes* should not be confused with functionalist explanations.) An example would be describing religion as a set of symbols that, by embodying a society's most important values, evoke collective emotions that create social solidarity. A typical objection to such conceptions concerns the issue of extension: they often encompass phenomena that many scholars have not been prepared to identify as religion. For example, the functional definition just given would include patriotism as a religion.

Scholars like Spiro have responded by demanding that conceptions of religion be substantive, that is, that they contain only *definientes* that refer to properties that make up religion. An example would be Spiro's definition of religion as an institution consisting of culturally postulated interactions with culturally postulated superhuman beings. Once again, a typical objection concerns extension: such conceptions often exclude what are generally seen as instances of religion, such as certain forms of Theravada Buddhism and Confucianism in Spiro's case. Proper extension is certainly an appropriate criterion by which to assess definitions, but isolated from the actual purposes for which a definition is being formulated, limiting conceptions of religion to substantive *definientes* is probably too austere.

Another much discussed issue originates in Wittgenstein's reflections on family resemblances (*Philosophical Investigations*, 1953, pp. 66–67): the possibility of conceiving of religion polythetically rather than monothetically. Although scholars occasionally define religion in terms of a single property (e.g., Stewart Guthrie's "anthropomorphism"; Frederick Streng's "means of ultimate transformation,"), they more often conceive of it in terms of an explicit or implicit conjunction of properties. (They have generally overlooked the possibilities of definition presented by disjunction, as in George Orwell's "Whatever goes on four legs, or has wings, is a friend," from *Animal Farm*.) The traditional approach has been to treat these properties monothetically; that is, to consider all of them as necessary and, when taken together, sufficient to define religion. Polythetic definitions relax these requirements. They see no particular property as necessary to religion and consider the presence of a collection of properties selected from a master set as sufficient to make a specific item a member of the class called *religion*. For example, William Alston suggested that the presence of an unspecified number of any of the following characteristics would make a set of cultural practices a religion:

> (1) Belief in supernatural beings (gods). (2) A distinction between sacred and profane objects. (3) Ritual acts focused on sacred objects. (4) A moral code believed to be sanctioned by the gods. (5) Characteristically religious feelings. (6) Prayer and other forms of communication with gods. (7) A world view, or a general picture of the world as a whole and the place of the individual therein. . . . (8) A more or less total organization of

one's life based on the world view. (9) A social group bound together by the above. (Alston 1967, pp. 141–142)

In principle it is possible to formulate guidelines about what collections of properties are sufficient to make something an instance of religion, but this has not been done. As a result, no polythetic conceptualization of religion proposed to date has been particularly useful, because none yields consistent, intersubjective results.

Benson Saler has tried another approach, one that calls upon the presumed role of prototypes in the formation of categories. People learn what a word means by generalizing from specific instances. For example, upon learning that robins, blue jays, eagles, and other similar species are birds, the human mind formulates an implicit category *bird* that it applies consistently and accurately. The mind also recognizes some members of the class as better representatives than others: robins, blue jays, and eagles are prototypical birds, ostriches and penguins unusual ones. Saler suggests that scholars should approach the category of religion in just this way. For North American and European scholars, religion is a category whose prototypes are Judaism, Christianity, and Islam, perhaps not in that order. Other religions are religions to the extent that they are more or less analogous to these prototypes. This approach can certainly provide an initial expedient, but its utility is limited to a specific geographic or linguistic area. In a globalizing world one can hardly presume that the community of scholars interested in what the European tradition has called religion includes only people whose dominant categories have been shaped by the prototypes of Christianity, Judaism, and Islam.

It is also possible to define religion stipulatively or lexically. That is, scholars may stipulate what a term means (like Isaac Newton defining "derivative" in calculus for the first time) or they may describe how a linguistic community uses a word (like the *Oxford English Dictionary* defining what mathematicians mean by "derivative"). Furthermore, definitions must ordinarily meet several formal criteria. They must have an appropriate extension. They must be clear—for example, they must not use words that are more obscure than the term being defined. They must avoid circularity; that is, they must not include the term to be defined among the *definientes,* either directly or indirectly (like defining sacred as holy, and when pressed for the meaning of holy, defining it as sacred). They must also be appropriate to the purposes for which they are formulated. This last criterion has an impact on the others. For example, a definition does not need to single out every instance of religion; it only needs to single out every instance of religion pertinent to the project at hand. The criterion of suitability deserves more recognition in the study of religions than it has received.

DISCURSIVE PURPOSES. In a widely noted passage, Jonathan Z. Smith has written, "Religion is solely the creation of the scholar's study. It is created for the scholar's analytic purposes by his imaginative acts of comparison and generalization" (J. Z. Smith, 1982, p. xi). Insofar as Smith draws attention to the relationship between conceptualizations of religion and the purposes for which they are formulated, he makes an important point. But his position both assigns too much independent agency to scholars—scholars did not alone create religion—and overlooks significant, nonacademic purposes for which people have used it. Indeed, different discourses make different demands upon religion.

Scholars of religion have frequently argued as if academic purposes required religion to have precise boundaries. For example, during the last half of the twentieth century, some scholars analyzed a long series of unusual institutions as religious, including Marxism (an analysis with political utility), patriotism, psychotherapy, and even sporting events (highly ritualized), shopping malls (sacred spaces in a consumer society), and the stock market (a matter of ultimate concern). Others found the conception of religion in such analyses much too broad and called for demarcating the category precisely. Despite this call, Benson Saler has argued that scholarship requires of its concepts not precision but clarity. (On the difference, consider Samuel Johnson's quip, "The fact that there is such a thing as twilight does not mean that we cannot distinguish between day and night.") A clear concept of religion, even if it has fuzzy edges, allows scholars to explore with insight what institutions like Marxism, patriotism, and even the stock market share with prototypical religions, while still recognizing crucial differences. Such a concept would meet the basic requirements of academic discourse: that one's conceptions be coherent and allow the scholar to say something insightful, whether interpretive or explanatory, about the data.

Religion also plays important roles in discourses outside the academy—in contemporary discourse on law, human rights, and public policy, for example. Many nations guarantee religious freedom—disestablishment is less widely accepted—and so does Article 18 of the Universal Declaration of Human Rights, adopted by the United Nations on December 10, 1948: "Everyone has the right to freedom of thought, conscience and religion; this right includes freedom to change his religion or belief, and freedom, either alone or in community with others and in public or private, to manifest his religion or belief in teaching, practice, worship and observance." Some, however, see this conception of religious freedom as North American and European rather than universal. For example, the Universal Islamic Declaration of Human Rights, adopted September 19, 1981, retains the language of religion (in Articles 10, 12 to 14, and 19) but restates the rights in accordance with Islamic teachings.

Much more than in academic discourse, the adjudication of claims arising within legal discourse about religion presents challenges of precision. Majority communities—Christians in North America and Europe, Hindus in India, Muslims in Muslim-majority states—have at times found it in their own interest to claim that certain practices and convictions were not religious but cultural. Some courts have agreed; for example, in 1966 the Constitution Bench of the Indian Supreme Court found that Hinduism "may broadly be described as a way of life and nothing more," and that the word *Hindu* denoted residence in a certain territory more than religious affiliation. Minority communities such as the Unification Church and the Church of Scientology have argued, at times unsuccessfully, that they were in fact religions, common opinion notwithstanding, and so deserved the protections and privileges that came from that status. In the early 2000s, Europeans who opposed the wearing of head scarves by Muslim women claimed that the very same practice was either religious (in France) or nonreligious (in Germany), because of the different legal status of religion in the two countries.

The extent to which locally variant views of religion are compatible with a universal right remains to be determined, as do the precise boundaries of religion in most systems of law. In practice, such questions also highlight a tension between academic and legal discourse. Those charged with adjudication look to academics for expert advice on religion and cite academic writings to justify their findings. Academics criticize the adequacy of legal and political conceptions, such as the tendency to conceive of new religious movements as cults. Nevertheless, the purposes of academic discourse, which often calls customary boundaries into question in the pursuit of insight, stand in some tension with the needs of legal discourse for precise definitions that enable consistent decisions.

THE FUTURE OF RELIGION. Like Feil, many historians and students of religion—and others, too—have been suspicious of the category. Some have suggested replacing religion with terms like faith (W. C. Smith), worldview (Ninian Smart), social formation, or culture. The anthropologist Talal Asad has been more circumspect. He has argued that "there cannot be a universal definition of religion, not only because its constituent elements and relationships are historically specific, but because that definition is itself the historical product of discursive processes" (Asad, p. 29). What is required, he has claimed, is for scholars to determine what they mean by religion on a case-by-case basis.

Asad's argument leaves him vulnerable to the charge of committing the genetic fallacy (the assumption that an account of the origin and development of a claim can determine its adequacy for present purposes). Still, it is widely thought today that definitions are specific to contexts and purposes, and there is no reason religion should be any different. Specific conceptualizations of religion need to meet certain formal criteria, including the criterion of suitability. Furthermore, the projects for which definitions are formulated are always subject to critique, including moral and political critique. While such critiques will inevitably call specific conceptualizations of religion into question, they do not necessarily require that religion as a concept be abandoned.

BIBLIOGRAPHY

Alston, William P. "Religion." In *Encyclopedia of Philosophy*, vol. 7. New York, 1967. An early attempt to conceive of religion polythetically.

Asad, Talal. *Genealogies of Religion: Discipline and Reasons of Power in Christianity and Islam.* Baltimore, 1993. Its first chapter is a now classic contribution to the genealogy of religion.

Atran, Scott. *Cognitive Foundations of Natural History: Towards an Anthropology of Science.* Cambridge, U.K., 1990. An attempt to examine the cognitive basis of the sciences, focusing on biological classification.

Berger, Peter L. *The Sacred Canopy; Elements of a Sociological Theory of Religion.* Garden City, N.Y., 1967. A classic exposition on religion as legitimation.

Binachi, Ugo, ed. *The Notion of "Religion" in Comparative Research: Selected Proceedings of the sixteenth Congress of the International Association for the History of Religions (Rome, 3rd-8th September, 1990.)* Rome, 1994. Essays from an international range of scholars.

Despland, Michel, and Vallée, Gérard, eds. *La religion dans l'histoire: le mot, l'idée, la réalité* (Religion in history: The word, the idea, the reality). Waterloo, Ontario, 1992.

Dubuisson, Daniel. *The Western Construction of Religion: Myths, Knowledge, and Ideology.* Baltimore, 2003.

Feil, Ernst, ed. *Religio.* 4 vols. Göttingen, Germany, 1986–c. 2004. A detailed examination of the history of religion.

Feil, Ernst, ed. *On the Concept of Religion.* Binghamton, N.Y., 2000. A concise statement of Feil's positions and findings, followed by responses from a variety of German academics and theologians.

Fitzgerald, Timothy. *The Ideology of Religious Studies.* New York, 2000. A critique of religion informed by the author's fieldwork and teaching in India and Japan.

Frazer, James George. *The Golden Bough,* vol. 1, *The Magic Art and the Evolution of Kings.* New York, 1935. Chapter 4 contains Frazer's formulation of the distinction between science and magic.

Geertz, Clifford. "Religion as a Cultural System." In *The Interpretation of Culture: Selected Essays.* New York, 1973. Influential theoretical observations presented as an exposition of a definition of religion.

McCutcheon, Russell T. *Manufacturing Religion: The Discourse on Sui Generis Religion and the Politics of Nostalgia.* New York, 1997. A political critique of the approach to religion represented by Winston King's entry.

Penner, Hans, and Yonan, Edward. "Is a Science of Religion Possible?" *Journal of Religion* 52 (October 1972): 107–133. Important here for observations on definition, especially criteria of definition.

Platvoet, Jan G., and Molendijk, Arie L., eds. *The Pragmatics of Defining Religion: Contexts, Concepts, and Contests.* Leiden, 1999. A wide range of useful essays, revealing the state of discussions among European scholars.

Riesebrodt., Martin. "Überlegungen zur Legitimität eines universalen Religionsbegriffs." In *Religion im kulturellen Diskurs: Festschrift für Hans G. Kippenberg zu seinem 65. Geburtstag*

(Religion in cultural discourse: essays in honor of Hans G. Kippenberg on the occasion of his 65th birthday), edited by Brigitte Luchesi und Kocku von Stuckrad. Berlin and New York, 2004.

Saler, Benson. *Conceptualizing Religion: Immanent Anthropologists, Transcendent Natives, and Unbounded Categories.* New York, 2000. Surveys much previous discussion in developing a prototypical approach to religion.

Smart, Ninian. *Worldviews: Crosscultural Explorations of Human Beliefs.* New York, 1983; reprint, Upper Saddle River, N.J., 2000.

Smith, Jonathan Z. *Imagining Religion: From Babylon to Jonestown.* Chicago, 1982. Set of insightful essays; chapter one is on polythetic definition.

Smith, Jonathan Z. "Religion, Religions, Religious." In *Critical Terms for Religious Studies,* edited by Mark C. Taylor. Chicago, 1998. Contains much interesting material on the history of religion.

Smith, Wilfred Cantwell. *The Meaning and End of Religion: A New Approach to the Religious Traditions of Mankind.* New York, 1963. A classic proposal to replace religion with faith and cumulative tradition.

Southwold, Martin. "Buddhism and the Definition of Religion." *Man* 13 (1978): 362–379. Develops a polythetic approach to religion in a discussion of the peculiar characteristics of Sinhalese Buddhism.

Spiro, Melford. "Religion: Problems of Definition and Explanation." In *Anthropological Approaches to the Study of Religion,* edited by Michael Banton. London, 1966. A major contribution from an anthropologist with a special focus on Buddhism.

Wasserstrom, Steven M. *Religion After Religion: Gershom Scholem, Mircea Eliade, and Henry Corbin at Eranos.* Princeton, N.J., 1999. A critique of the tradition represented by Winston King's entry, combining political, cultural, and religious critiques.

GREGORY D. ALLES (2005)

RELIGIONSGESCHICHTLICHE SCHULE

is the name that was given, beginning in 1903, to a group of German Protestant theologians who consistently applied the history of religions method to the interpretation of the Bible. This school of thought originated at the University of Göttingen, where a number of young theologians became known as the "little Göttingen faculty" because of their common concerns and their critical dissociation from Albrecht Ritschl, who had earlier been their teacher. The group was made up of Hermann Gunkel, Wilhelm Bousset, Johannes Weiss, Ernst Troeltsch, Wilhelm Wrede, Heinrich Hackmann, and Alfred Rahlfs. After 1900, Carl Clemen, Hugo Gressmann, and W. Heitmüller joined the school, while Rudolf Bultmann and Otto Eissfeldt may be reckoned as forming a third generation. All looked upon Albert Eichhorn as the decisive influence on their work.

DEVELOPMENT OF THE SCHOOL. The Religionsgeschichtliche Schule drew theological conclusions from preceding developments in historical science, Orientalism, the history of religions, and ethnology. Many kinds of scholarly endeavors served as godparents for the school: Johann Jakob Wettstein's efforts to produce a complete, annotated edition of the Greek New Testament, including variants (*Hē Kainē Diathēkē: Novum Testamentum Graecum,* 2 vols., 1751–1752) and J. G. Herder's undogmatic and literary approach to the Bible; the discoveries made and the languages deciphered in the Near East; the rise of historical thinking in the works of such scholars as Barthold G. Niebuhr, Leopold von Ranke, and Johann G. Droysen; the discovery and decipherment of new sources from the ancient Near East; the development of literary criticism; the new science of religions as developed by F. Max Müller, C. P. Tiele, P. D. Chantepie de la Saussaye, James G. Frazer, and Nathan Söderblom; the new field of ethnology associated with Adolf Bastian, Friedrich Ratzel, and E. B. Tylor; and the antimetaphysical spirit promoted by Neo-Kantianism in Germany during the second half of the nineteenth century. Even the "Babel and Bible" discussion started by Friedrich Delitzsch, Alfred Jeremias, and Peter Jensen, which to some extent ran parallel to the Religionsgeschichtliche Schule, contributed to the rise of the latter.

Historical criticism in the form of source analysis of biblical documents had already been generally accepted and was causing difficulties for dogmatic theology. The rise of the Religionsgeschichtliche Schule meant the definitive victory of the historical-critical method, but the school supplemented this method with a deeper understanding of the historical process that lay behind the literary sources and with the application of the comparative history of religions to the Bible and Christianity. For this reason the representatives of the approach comprised primarily biblical scholars. Apart from Clemen, only Hackmann opted for the general history of religions. Strictly speaking, this method was a movement within Protestant biblical exegesis, and theologically it was of course in the liberal camp.

Though it was initially a purely academic phenomenon, its representatives attempted, as those of hardly any other theological movement of the past had done, to broadcast their view on a large scale through popular works on the history of religions and through periodicals such as *Theologische Rundschau* (1917–), *Religionsgeschichtliche Volksbücher* (1903–), and *Forschungen zur Religion und Literatur des Alten und Neuen Testaments* (1913–), and collections such as *Die Religion in Geschichte und Gegenwart* (1st ed., Tübingen, 1909–1913), *Die Schriften des Alten Testaments in Auswahl: Übersetzt und für die Gegenwart erklärt,* by Hermann Gunkel (Göttingen, 1910–1915), and *Die Schriften des Neuen Testaments neu übersetzt und für die Gegenwart erklärt,* by Johannes Weiss (Göttingen, 1906). As a result, they were soon in conflict with ecclesiastical authorities, who accused them of destructive, secularizing intentions, an accusation that the school firmly denied.

Historians see the Religionsgeschichtliche Schule as beginning its public activity in 1895, which was the publication year of Gunkel's *Schöpfung und Chaos in Urzeit und Endzeit* (Creation and Chaos in Primordial Time and End Time). But the basic ideas of the school had been clearly at work even earlier in Gunkel's *Die Wirkungen des heiligen Geistes: Nach den populären Anschauungen der apostolisch Zeit* (The Effects of the Holy Spirit according to the Popular Mind of the Apostolic Age; Göttingen, 1888). In this earlier publication Gunkel examined exotic and even irrational features of early Christianity, such as belief in the preternatural, and explained these features as due to the ideas that were popular in the period of "late Judaism." The same approach was soon adopted by Johannes Weiss in his *Die Predigt Jesu vom Reiche Gottes* (Jesus' Preaching of the Kingdom of God; Göttingen, 1892) and by Wilhelm Bousset, who in his *Die Religion des Judentums im neutestamentlichen Zeitalter* (Tübingen, 1903) developed the idea that Judaism in the New Testament era was the real soil from which Jesus and the primitive Christian community sprang. In *Hauptprobleme der Gnosis* (Göttingen, 1907) and *Kyrios Christos* (Göttingen, 1913) Bousset also drew upon the religious history of Hellenism and late antiquity in describing the Christianity of the first and second centuries. By and large, the further work of the school followed the same general lines, though at times the emphasis differed, as in the case of the brilliant but short-lived Wilhelm Wrede, who, in his *Paulus* (Tübingen, 1904), *Das Messiasgeheimnis in den Evangilien* (Göttingen, 1901), and *Vorträge und Studien* (Tübingen, 1907) maintained what were probably the school's most radical views.

In the field of Old Testament studies Gunkel pioneered not only the religio-historical explanation of the Old Testament, especially in his *Genesis* (1901) and *Psalmen* (1926), but also the literary-historical method and, in particular, a reformulated "tradition-historical" approach that ushered in a new age of Old Testament exegesis. Hugo Gressmann followed Gunkel's lead in his *Der Ursprung der israelitisch-jüdischen Eschatologie* (Göttingen, 1905) and *Der Messias* (Göttingen, 1929).

The end of the Religionsgeschichtliche Schule after World War I was due not only to the social changes that the war brought to Germany but also to correlative radical shifts in theology, such as those produced by Karl Barth and dialectical theology, and, surely, to the early deaths of many of the school's leading representatives. Richard Reitzenstein (1861–1931), who wrote *Die Vorgeschichte der christlichen Taufe* (Prehistory of Christian Baptism; Leipzig, 1929) was one of the last champions of the school's ideas, unless one includes Rudolf Bultmann and his school as the third, most recent generation. This third generation reshaped the heritage of the Religionsgeschichtliche Schule and sought to safeguard it, especially in the area of the study of gnosticism, by new methods such as form criticism, redaction history, tradition history, existential interpretation, and demythologization.

CHARACTERISTICS OF THE APPROACH. The mounting criticism, especially after World War II, of the Religionsgeschichtliche Schule and its program cannot gainsay the fact that it brought major progress in the understanding of biblical writings and their history. Questions first raised by the school, such as the role of Canaanite religion, apocalyptic thought, eschatology, pneumatology, gnosis, and Hellenistic Judaism, cultus, and piety in the formation of Christianity, are still vital and have acquired increased relevance due to new discoveries such as those at Ugarit, Khirbat Qumran, and Nag Hammadi. Biblical exegesis, theology, and religious studies cannot retreat to the scholarly situation as it was before the Religionsgeschichtliche Schule was formed. The facts brought to light by the school cannot be dismissed, even if scholars now prefer explanations other than those proposed by the Religionsgeschichtliche Schule.

Plurality of Christianity's origins. The school's members rejected interpreting the New Testament solely in light of the Old Testament. Primitive Christianity, they believed, was not a mere continuation of Old Testament history but had other roots as well.

One of these other roots was Hellenistic Judaism, represented by the thought of Philo Judaeus (d. 45–50 CE), as opposed to rabbinic Judaism, which belongs to a later period. The Hellenistic religious outlook, as expressed in the mystery religions and other Oriental religions of redemption, in gnostic groups, Hermetism, emperor worship, and magic, played an important part in the development of early Christianity. Gunkel, in his *Zum religionsgeschichtlichen Verständnis des Neuen Testaments* (Göttingen, 1903) had already spoken of the "syncretic" character of early Christianity, arguing that, from the historical viewpoint, Christianity had many links with contemporaneous religions. Bousset, though somewhat more cautious on this point, constantly rejected the artificial division between primitive Christianity and its historical environment. He explained the disjunction that appeared between the teachings of Jesus and those of the later church by citing the influence of this early environment. Behind the replacement of "Jesus the itinerant prophet" with "Christ the Lord" was the transition, beginning even before Paul, of primitive Christianity into the Hellenistic-Roman world in the form of a Hellenistic community of Christians at Antioch. The Religionsgeschichtliche Schule was concerned primarily with intellectual links, not with individual derivations or parallels. The same principle held for the Old Testament, whose historical development, the school believed, was to be understood in light of its changing milieu, to which belonged Canaan, Babylon, Egypt, and Iran.

Historical framework. The division between the New Testament and the history of the early church and its dogma, the school believed, is an artificial one. The New Testament canon is a historical product and should be studied only in the framework of a history of early Christian literature. Prominent examples of this approach are found in the works of Eichhorn and Wrede.

Concept of religion. According to the Religionsgeschichtliche Schule, the traditional focus on doctrinal concepts should be replaced by a focus on religion, the religious spirit, and piety. Theology is only one side of religion—the rational, conceptual, and systematic side. The essence of religion, as understood by the Religionsgeschichtliche Schule, is nonrational experience. This concept of religion originated in the works of Friedrich Schleiermacher (1768–1834) and became normative for the theology and philosophy of religion of the subsequent period. The school aimed at writing a history of Christianity as a religion and not simply a history of ideas, dogmas, and doctrines.

Role of religious practice. The Religionsgeschichtliche Schule was part of a current of thought that, in contrast to the overemphasis by some scholars on mythology or ideology, regarded the realm of cult and religious practice as central and as an important expression of piety. The interest in the "theology of the community," that is, the popular religion of the masses (including folk tales and fairy tales, or, in other words, the "seamier side" of religion as contrasted with the "heights" of elitist theology), was already paving the way for a sociological and psychological interpretation of religion. On the other hand, the school also stressed the innovative role of religious individuals and authorities (for example the Old Testament prophets and Jesus), who, according to the school, have a formative influence on the history of religions.

Tradition history. One of the most important but often overlooked discoveries of the school is what is known as "tradition history," which was first proposed by Gunkel. Tradition history is the attempt to get behind the written tradition (i.e., texts) to its prehistory. This approach was considered to be the only way to make texts historically intelligible. The abandonment of classical literary history and criticism for a history of preliterary "form," "genres," or "materials" is a result of the historical approach taken by the Religionsgeschichtliche Schule: a text yields its meaning through its history, its development, and the materials (its "prehistory") used to compose it. This turning of written tradition into something problematic soon became a tool of tradition criticism and made nonsense of many problems regarded as central by literary criticism. The old representatives of literary criticism, such as Wellhausen, rejected Gunkel's works, although they themselves could not avoid raising questions that involved the history of traditions.

This aspect of the school's work is another indication of its concern with "the religion of the community" as a sociopsychological category. The designation "history of traditions" was at times used by members of the school as a synonym for "history of religions." Unfortunately, the Religionsgeschichtliche Schule failed to make a clear distinction here and, more importantly, to introduce a necessary reflection on method, a step that would have spared it a great deal of trouble. Methodological clarification began only with the rise of "form criticism" in the works of Bultmann and Martin Dibelius (1883–1947).

Definition of the field. Consideration of the Bible as a historical religious document that is to be investigated with the same tools as other religious texts soon led to the view that the traditional theological faculties should be replaced by departments of the history of religions. The historical disciplines associated with theology are really no longer theological, Wrede clearly saw; rather, they belong to the history of religions, since they employ the same tools as philology and all other historical sciences.

The school's "leveling down" of Christianity so that it becomes just one more subject of a general or comparative history of religions led to a certain relativism that had an important impact, especially on dogmatic and theological systems. In this situation Troeltsch, who remained faithful to a romantic and ultimately Hegelian concept of development, drew historico-philosophical conclusions that looked to the future development of Christianity in the framework of a universal history of religions. Bousset, too, sought to rescue Christianity from the maelstrom of historical relativization by reverting to the liberal theological emphasis on ethics and morality and to the idea of the irreducible personality of Jesus as a revelation of God. But Christianity cannot be rescued by the tools of historical science; at this point the assertions of faith stand alone against the power of history and critical reflection. To rescue Christianity is the task of theology, not of the history of religions.

The Religionsgeschichtliche Schule began as a movement within theology, but it ended outside theology because its methods and approach were so radical. The attempt to restore the ties connecting the school and Christian theology expresses only the personal piety, or Christian faith, of the school's representatives. Here again the Religionsgeschichtliche Schule created a dilemma, in this case one of the most difficult that the history of religions as such must face: the relation between personal conviction or faith and scientific honesty or objectivity.

See Also Bultmann, Rudolf; Delitzsch, Friedrich; Wellhausen, Julius.

Bibliography

To date there is no successful overall portrait or bibliography of the Religionsgeschichtliche Schule. A number of monographs are available on individual representatives of the school (Gunkel, Bousset, Wrede) or on special topics (gnosis, salvation history, tradition history). More recently, additional materials concerning the beginnings of the school have been published (in particular by Hans Rollman and Friedrich W. Graf). For general orientation, see articles in the first edition of the encyclopedia *Die Religion in Geschichte and Gegenwart,* 5 vols., edited by Friedrich Michael Schiele (Tübingen, 1909–1913), which work as a whole is representative of the school's aims and methods. See also Werner Georg Kümmel's *Das Neue Testament: Geschichte der Erforschung seiner Probleme* (Freiburg, 1958), esp. pp. 259–414; Hans-Joachim Kraus's *Geschichte der historisch-kritischen Erforschung des Alten Testaments von der Reformation bis zur Gegenwart* (Neukirchen, 1956); and Horst Stephan and Martin Schmidt's *Geschichte der evangelischen Theologie in Deutsch-*

land seit dem Idealismus, 3d ed. (Berlin, 1973). The works listed below may also be fruitfully consulted.

Bousset, D. Wilhelm. *Religionsgeschichtliche Studien.* Leiden, 1979.

Clemen, Carl. *Die religionsgeschichtliche Methode in der Theologie.* Giessen, 1904.

Colpe, Carsten. *Die religionsgeschichtliche Schule,* vol. 1. Göttingen, 1961.

Gressmann, Hugo. *Albert Eichhorn und die religionsgeschichtliche Schule.* Göttingen, 1914.

Ittel, Gerhard Wolfgang. *Urchristentum und Fremdreligionen im Urteil der religionsgeschichtlichen Schule.* Erlangen, 1956.

Ittel, Gerhard Wolfgang. "Die Hauptgedanken der 'religionsgeschichtlichen Schule.'" *Zeitschrift fur Religions- und Geistesgeschichte* 10 (1958): 61–78.

Klatt, Werner. *Hermann Gunkel.* Göttingen, 1969.

Morgan, Robert, ed. and trans. *The Nature of New Testament Theology: The Contribution of Wilhelm Wrede and Adolf Schlatter.* Naperville, Ill., 1973. Includes (pp. 68–116) a translation of Wrede's *Über Afgabe und Methode der sogenannten neutestamentlichen Theologie.*

Paulsen, H. "Traditionsgeschichtliche und religionsgeschichtliche Schule." *Zeitschift für Theologie und Kirche* 75 (1958): 22–55.

Reischle, Max. *Theologie und Religionsgeschichte.* Tübingen, 1904.

Renz, Horst, and Friedrich W. Graf, eds. *Troeltsch-Studien,* vol. 1. Gütersloh, 1982. See especially pages 235–290 and 296–305.

Rollman, Hans. "Zwei Briefe Hermann Gunkel an Adolf Jülicher." *Zeitschrift für Theologie und Kirche* 78 (1981): 276–288.

Rollman, Hans. "Duhm, Lagarde, Ritschl und der irrationale Religionsbegriff der Religionsgeschichtlichen Schule." *Zeitschrift für Religions- und Geistesgeschichte* 34 (1982): 276–279.

Rollmann, Hans. "Theologie und Religiongeschichte." *Zeitschrift für Theologie und Kirche* 80 (1983): 69–84.

Sänger, Dieter. "Phänomenologie oder Geschichte? Methodische Anmerkungen zur religionsgeschichtlichen Schule." *Zeitschrift für Religions- und Geistesgeschichte* 32 (1980): 13–27.

Troeltsch, Ernst. "Die 'kleine Göttinger Fakultät' von 1890." *Christliche Welt* 18 (1920): 281–283.

Troeltsch, Ernst. "Die Dogmatik der 'religionsgeschichtlichen Schule.'" In his *Gesammelte Schriften,* 2d ed., vol. 2, pp. 500–524. Aalen, 1962.

Troeltsch, Ernst. "Christentum und Religionsgeschichte." In *Gesammelte Schriften,* 2d ed., vol. 2, pp. 328–363. Aalen, 1962.

Verheule, Anthonie F. *Wilhelm Bousset: Leben und Werk.* Amsterdam, 1973.

New Sources

Berry, Wendell C. "Methodological, Pedagogical, and Philosophical Reflections on Mircea Eliade as Historian of Religions." In *Changing Religious Worlds,* edited by Bryan S. Rennie, pp. 165–189. Albany, N.Y., 2001.

Lehmkühler, Karsten. *Kultus und Theologie: Dogmatic und Exegese in die Religionsgeschichtliche Schule.* Göttingen, 1996.

Lüdeman, Gerd, ed. *Die "Religionsgeschichtliche Schule": Facetten eines theologischen Umrichs.* New York, 1996.

KURT RUDOLPH (1987)
Translated from German by Matthew J. O'Connell
Revised Bibliography

RELIGIONSWISSENSCHAFT SEE COMPARATIVE RELIGION; HISTORY OF RELIGIONS

RELIGIOUS BROADCASTING.

The sophistication, diversification, and influence of religious broadcasting are greatly underappreciated dimensions of the global religious scene at the beginning of the twenty-first century. From India to Europe and from Latin America to the United States, religious broadcasting has become a dominant purveyor of religious teaching and entertainment for vast numbers of the world's population. According to a 2002 report by the respected Barna Research Group, more adults—141 million—experience the Christian faith in a given month in the United States through Christian radio, television, or books than attend Christian churches (132 million). Breaking this finding down, the report discovered that 52 percent of American adults had tuned into a Christian radio program in the previous month, that 38 percent of these listeners tuned in to a teaching, preaching, or talk show program; and that 43 percent of this population had listened to a Christian music station. The survey observed that women and African Americans were overrepresented among these listeners to Christian radio. Forty-three percent of all adults—some 90 million people—were watching Christian television or programming in a given month, about the same number of people who attend Christian churches in any given week. Somewhat surprisingly, more than fifteen million atheists, agnostics, and adult members of non-Christian faiths had some degree of exposure to the Christian faith through various forms of religious broadcasting.

Though precise figures are not available for other regions of the world, the ubiquity of religious programming on satellite broadcasts reaching every continent in the world attests to the fact that religious broadcasting is a phenomenon to be reckoned with by any student of contemporary religion. This influence has been greatly augmented since the 1990s by the growth of religious internet sites and programming. The dominance of religious broadcasting is a tale of entrepreneurism, audacity, competition, zeal, scandal, and triumph. Although this medium has its critics and detractors, both religious and secular, its explosive growth and influence show no signs of diminishing for the foreseeable future.

ORIGINS. The origins of religious broadcasting reach back into the early days of radio in the United States. The first station to receive a radio license from the U.S. Department of Commerce, KDKA Pittsburgh, broadcast the Sunday evening vespers service of the Calvary Episcopal Church choir on January 2, 1921. Although the audience for the program was only in the thousands, the broadcast became a fixture of the station's Sunday evening programming schedule. Soon, the entrepreneurial spirit of America combined with the growing appeal of radio and the missionary zeal of evangelical Christianity to launch dozens of radio ministries.

The evangelist Paul Rader (1879–1938), pastor of the Chicago Gospel Tabernacle, was among the first to recognize the potential of radio to preach the gospel. In the summer of 1922, Rader brought a brass quartet to the roof of city hall and preached a sermon in a makeshift studio on local station WHT. The success of this cameo appearance encouraged Rader to reach an agreement with radio station WBBM to broadcast fourteen hours of religious programming every Sunday. Rader called his once-a-week station WJBT (Where Jesus Blesses Thousands). WJBT's broadcasts included the Sunday evening worship service at Gospel Tabernacle, choral performances, organ concerts, and popular shows such as the *Healing Hour*, the *Back Home Hour*, and the *Bible Drama Hour*. Rader discovered that many of his radio listeners wanted to hear him preach live and that the radio ministry increased attendance at Gospel Tabernacle. Rader's pioneering efforts in creating a diverse programming format and in partnering radio ministries with local churches would have an immense influence on subsequent generations of broadcast evangelists. Rader was aware of the medium's limitations, however, and he warned that radio did not substitute for a community that gathered to worship, sing, pray, and bear mutual joys and sorrows.

Aimee Semple McPherson (1890–1944) was another popular Christian evangelist of the 1920s who saw the potential of radio to spread her message. In 1922 she became the first woman to broadcast a sermon over the radio waves. A year later her Santa Monica–based church, the Angelus Temple, inaugurated the five-hundred-watt station KFSG (Kalling Foursquare Gospel). The station was the first in the nation to be owned and operated by a church. During the 1920s, KFSG broadcast the Angelus Temple's worship services to listeners who crowded into tents set up in nearby suburbs of Los Angeles, such as Venice and Pasadena. In the unregulated early days of radio broadcasting, McPherson and others arbitrarily changed their broadcast frequencies. This practice drew the ire of Secretary of Commerce Herbert Hoover in 1927. In response, the colorful McPherson sent Hoover a telegram stating, "Please order your minions of Satan to leave my station alone. You cannot expect the Almighty to abide by your wavelength nonsense" (Erickson, 1992, p. 127). This salvo was the first in what would become a long-standing battle between federal broadcast communications regulators and the entrepreneurs of religious broadcasting.

Christian evangelicals and fundamentalists were not the only religious ministries to recognize the potential of radio outreach during the 1920s. The Unity School of Christianity, a New Thought–influenced religious organization in Kansas City, Missouri, inaugurated radio broadcasts on station WOQ in 1922 and purchased the station in 1924. In 1927 the Ancient and Mystical Order Rosae Crucis (AMORC), a popular purveyor of Western occultism, purchased radio station WJBB in Tampa and began broadcasting a mixture of drama, choral music, metaphysical discourses, and news. AMORC's imperator, Harvey Spencer Lewis (1883–1939), became a pioneer in short-wave religious broadcasting and aired WJBB's programs throughout North and South America as well as the Caribbean, Africa, and Europe. His station was also the first to sponsor listener call-in programs and morning birthday announcements.

The 1920s and 1930s were a time of acrimony between fundamentalist and modernist Christians in the United States. Both factions sought to control the radio airwaves, and the early winners were the modernists. The U.S. Congress established the Federal Radio Commission (FRC) in 1927, and new regulations issued by the commission for licensed stations effectively closed down over half of the nation's radio ministries, many of them fundamentalist in orientation. Between 1927 and 1934, a movement emerged to reserve certain sections of the radio broadcast spectrum for educational, noncommercial, and religious programming. The Wagner-Hatfield Amendment to the Communications Act of 1934 would have implemented this spectrum allocation. The amendment failed, however, and a compromise plan allowed secular networks such as CBS and NBC to allocate a given amount of free airtime each week to public-interest programming in place of losing entire segments of the radio broadcast spectrum. These allocations were called "sustaining time."

Following passage of the Communications Act of 1934, religious groups across the fundamentalist-modernist spectrum sought a share of the free time allotted by the major networks. When it became apparent that there were more applicants than airtime, the networks and representatives of major national religious bodies such as the Southern Baptist Convention, the Federal Council of Churches, the Jewish Theological Seminary of America, and the National Council of Catholic Men agreed to sort out the competing claims in an equitable manner. The effect of this agreement was to shut out independent evangelicals and fundamentalists who were not represented by national groups. Mainline denominations defended their monopoly of the networks' sustaining-time slots by claiming a national constituency for their programs, in contrast to the regional constituency—the Bible Belt—of fundamentalist programming. Both individual denominations and parachurch groups produced a variety of programming in the sustaining-time slots. This programming ranged from the broadcast of local worship services to instructional documentaries, sermons, and discussions of issues by prominent religious figures.

The sustaining-time monopoly forced independent evangelicals and fundamentalists to purchase commercial time from such networks as the Mutual Broadcasting Network and the American Broadcasting Company (ABC). The most successful of the independent evangelical programs was Charles E. Fuller's (1887–1968) *Old Fashioned Revival Hour.* Fuller began his broadcasting career in the 1920s, teaching Bible classes over the Bible Institute of Los Angeles's privately owned radio station. By 1930, Fuller's Calvary Church Sunday worship service was being broadcast locally, along with a popular phone-in show during which Fuller answered listener questions. In 1933 Fuller decided to concentrate his entire efforts on his radio ministry and its flagship program, *Radio Revival Hour.* Through judicious agreements with regional networks, Fuller's program was soon being heard throughout the western United States. In 1937 the Mutual Broadcasting System purchased the renamed *Old Fashioned Revival Hour* for national broadcast. By 1939 the show had ten million weekly listeners, who were organized into a loose-knit group of financial supporters. The program featured popular gospel songs performed by a professional choir, Fuller's homespun homilies, and a reading of letters from listeners who had been led to God through the broadcast. The ministry's global listenership peaked at twenty million during the 1940s and aired over powerful AM stations in Europe, South America, and Asia in subsequent years. Fuller set the pattern for future independent broadcast ministries that were wholly listener supported and that were focused on personal conversion.

Another consequence of the sustaining-time monopoly was the formation of the National Association of Evangelicals (NAE) in 1942. The association's mission was to protect evangelical radio ministries like that of Fuller and to promote the interests of independent fundamentalists and evangelicals at the national level. The immediate catalyst for NAE's formation was a set of recommendations published by the Institute of Education by Radio, an independent group of academics whose charge was to monitor radio ministries. The large radio networks paid close attention to the Institute's criticism of Charles Fuller's broadcasts and to its recommendation to limit commercial religious programming on their networks. In response to this threat, over 150 conservative radio ministries formed NAE and two years later organized National Religious Broadcasters (NRB) as the official broadcasting arm of NAE. Since then NRB has been instrumental in lobbying Congress and the Federal Communications Commission (which replaced the Federal Radio Commission in 1934) on behalf of its member organizations. Members of NRB adopt a code of ethics that obligates them to maintain the highest technical standards for their programming, to obey governmental regulations, and to adopt high standards of financial accountability. The body's efforts have helped establish numerous independent broadcasting ministries on a solid financial footing and encouraged them to improve their programming quality.

A major change in radio evangelism occurred in the 1970s, when 75 percent of the listening audience shifted to FM stations. This left older, less affluent listeners with AM radio evangelists like those documented by Howard Dorgan in his book, *The Airwaves of Zion: Radio and Religion in Appalachia.* These ministries are run largely by independent Holiness-Pentecostals who have little formal theological training. Their style of preaching is highly emotional, unstructured, and reliant on the inspiration of the moment. They attack everything from lottery sales to roadhouses and from homosexuality to alcohol sales. Some ministries include in their programs recitations of long lists of people in need of prayer. These AM radio preachers can be heard on Sundays and weekdays throughout the United States, but especially in the Southeast. Although these ministries have difficulties attracting advertisers because of their elderly audience profile, they have survived into the twenty-first century on freewill offerings and constitute one of the most durable formats in the history of religious broadcasting in America.

The Rise of Television. With the coming of television in the 1940s, the competition between fundamentalists and modernists became even more intense. Each faction recognized the tremendous cultural influence the medium would have and the promise it held for religious outreach. The National Council of Churches of Christ in the USA (NCC) superseded the old Federal Council of Churches in 1950 and immediately sought to limit television access to those ministries approved of by its member churches. The NCC also requested that the major broadcast networks refuse to sell commercial airtime to religious ministries and that they accept the guidance of the NCC's Broadcast and Film Commission in creating and allotting any sustaining-time programming. These actions succeeded in limiting religious programming on the major networks during the 1950s to the Sunday morning sustaining-time slots and a few other nationally syndicated broadcast ministries.

The three most significant independent television ministries of the 1950s were those of Rex Humbard (b. 1919), Oral Roberts (b. 1918), and Billy Graham (b. 1918). Humbard was an itinerant Pentecostal minister who settled in Akron, Ohio, after a successful revival there in 1952. He began to televise the Sunday worship service of his Calvary Temple on a local Akron station in 1953 with the intention of providing outreach to the sick and elderly. This concern for those unable to attend regular church services would become a common justification for subsequent television ministries nationwide. Humbard also pioneered the religious spectacle genre of programming. He built a five-thousand-seat church in 1958 that featured state-of-the-art camera, lighting, and sound equipment as well as a huge stage that accommodated an orchestra, a choir, and broadcasting personnel. Humbard's *Cathedral of Tomorrow* Sunday broadcasts featured his musical family and his own folksy sermons. The broadcast was essentially a praise and preaching program that highlighted God's love and forgiveness and avoided controversial political or doctrinal debates. By 1971 Humbard's ministry aired on 650 television and 700 radio stations in North America. The ministry would expand to Japan, Australia, Africa, and South America over the next decade. Popular televangelist Robert Schuller (b. 1926) followed in Humbard's footsteps in the late twentieth century with his upbeat and carefully choreographed Crystal Cathedral broadcasts.

Oral Roberts began his career as a Holiness-Pentecostal minister whose healing revivals took him throughout the South and Southwest. With encouragement from Rex Humbard, Roberts gained the financial backing to televise one of his healing crusades in 1955. Within three years, the crusades were being aired on network affiliates to a steadily growing national audience. Roberts was the creator of the live healing-revival format that later became the vehicle by which faith healers Kathryn Kuhlman (1907–1976) and Benny Hinn (b. 1953) rose to prominence. Using high-speed film to compensate for the low lighting inside his tent, Roberts's programs captured the drama and excitement of seemingly miraculous healings by the laying on of hands. Here was religious television that was inspiring, entertaining, and emotionally gripping. Roberts went on to become a successful author, university president, and founder of a broadcast dynasty that is now largely in the hands of his son, Richard Roberts (b. 1948). Oral Roberts also pioneered religious broadcasting's foray into the variety show format. His program, *Oral Roberts and You*, featured upbeat contemporary music, bright-faced young people, the highest technical standards, and a Bible-based sermon. Roberts also broadcast hour-long television specials that featured popular singers such as Minnie Pearl and Mahalia Jackson and was one of the first televangelists to preach the "prosperity gospel," which claimed that God's plan for humanity included both spiritual and material riches.

The popular evangelist Billy Graham came from a more conservative theological background (Presbyterian and Southern Baptist) than either Humbard or Roberts, and his use of television would also be more measured. He gained national fame in 1949 when a planned two-week revival in Los Angeles went on for two months and attracted the attention of the Hearst publishing empire. Beginning in 1950, Graham had his own nationally broadcast radio program, *Hour of Decision*, with an estimated listening audience of twenty million. Following an influential telecast of his crusade in England in 1955, Graham had the clout to arrange the broadcast of his Madison Square Garden Crusade on ABC in 1957. The spectacle of thousands responding to Graham's call for repentance and conversion made these broadcasts riveting television. For the rest of the twentieth century, Graham's crusades became a staple of religious television. They incorporated footage of crowds pouring into athletic stadiums, music and testimonials by popular artists, Graham's powerful sermons, and finally his call for members of the audience to "come forward to Christ." Although Graham never inaugurated a weekly television broadcast, his Billy Graham Evangelistic Association was influential in the formation of the Evangelical Council for Financial Accountability, whose members pledge to abide by strict standards of financial accountability. His own association is a model of financial transparency and makes its yearly audit available to the public. The association's efforts have helped lift the stain of financial scandal that has plagued religious broadcasting ministries since the late 1970s.

While independent televangelists like Humbard, Roberts, and Graham were creating their media empires, mainstream ministries affiliated with the National Council of Churches created more conventional programming for use on Sunday morning sustaining-time slots. The most popular of these mainstream ministries was that of Bishop Fulton J. Sheen (1895–1979). Sheen was already an accomplished Roman Catholic author and speaker when he began *The Catholic Hour* radio program in 1930. This sustaining-time broadcast was aired on NBC radio and attracted millions of listeners. Sheen's first television appearance was on a historic Easter Sunday broadcast in 1940. It was not until the early 1950s, however, that he became a household fixture with his program *Life Is Worth Living*. The broadcast showcased Sheen's personal charisma, flair for the dramatic, and magisterial presence. Unlike the more conversion-focused broadcasts of Graham and Humbard, Sheen made Catholic moral teachings accessible to people from varied religious and secular backgrounds. His show was a success not only with Catholics but also with Protestants. The themes of his talks—sin, guilt, redemption, motherhood, and personal responsibility—were universal in scope and directed to everyman and everywoman. Sheen rejected the trappings of entertainment television and kept to a simple, dignified format. He began his program with a courtly bow and sat in a chair with only a blackboard, a table, and a Bible as props. For dramatic effect, he would sometimes pace the floor, allowing his clerical clothing to fall gracefully from his arms. He would also speak directly into the camera, giving viewers the sense that he was talking personally to them. Sheen's success as a television preacher demonstrated the significance of sheer personal charisma for building and maintaining a religious broadcasting ministry.

THE EMERGENCE OF INDEPENDENT RELIGIOUS NETWORKS. The most significant development in the United States between 1960 and 1990 was the creation of religious broadcasting networks such as Christian Broadcasting Network (CBN), Trinity Broadcasting Network (TBN), Praise the Lord Network (PTL), the Roman Catholic Eternal Word Television Network, LeSea Broadcasting, and Pax TV. These enterprises allowed for the development of diverse programming formats, nonstop religious television and radio coverage, and an expansion around the globe using satellite technology.

The forerunner for these ministries was Pat Robertson's (b. 1930) CBN. The network began with Robertson's purchase in 1959 of a UHF station in Portsmouth, Virginia. During the 1960s, CBN's programming was limited to a daily schedule airing between 7 and 10 P.M. The core program was *The 700 Club*, a talk show during which Robertson invited a host of evangelical authors and musical performers to discuss contemporary social, political, and religious issues. A live call-in segment invited those in need of healing to ask for prayer, exorcism, and words of encouragement from the show's hosts. Robertson began to operate television and FM radio stations throughout the United States in the late 1960s, and by the late 1970s he was sending CBN's programming via the Westar and RCA Satcom satellites to over sixty stations nationwide. The ministry employed a team of volunteer prayer counselors who worked twenty-four hours a day. These workers created a referral system that funneled new converts into local churches. Robertson retooled *The 700 Club* during the 1980s to resemble secular talk show and news magazine formats such as *The Today Show* and *Good Morning America.*

CBN has been a pioneer in the "media blitz," which saturates a given region over a concentrated time period with television programming, radio shows, videotapes, and literature. CBN's Worldreach partners with Christian ministries around the world to spread the gospel using media, discipleship, small-scale church planting, and humanitarian relief efforts. By the late 1990s, CBN International was broadcasting programming in ninety countries and in more than fifty languages. Robertson pioneered religious broadcasting in the Middle East with the launch, in 1982, of CBN's Channel 12/Middle East Television Network. In 1997 the network began broadcasting throughout the Middle East via satellite. Increasingly, other American broadcast ministries, many with millennial hopes, have targeted this biblical region. These include SAT-7, which transmits programming produced in Middle Eastern studios by Middle Eastern Christians in the Arabic language. This network is careful not to attack Islam directly and features culturally sensitive dramas, talk shows, children's programs, and musical programs.

Robertson's enterprises have set the standard for the religious broadcasting empires that have followed in CBN's wake. Robertson himself has been influential in the rise of the religious right as a political force in the United States. He and other broadcasters such as Jerry Falwell (b. 1933) have become respected spokespersons for the evangelical wing of the Republican Party.

Perhaps the most successful of the new broadcasting empires is the Trinity Broadcasting Network. From its humble beginnings in 1973, TBN has grown into a half-billion-dollar television empire that owns and operates over 22 full-power TV stations and over 500 low-power stations nationwide. By the beginning of the new millennium, the network's 3,500 cable affiliates allowed it to reach an audience estimated at thirty million daily. The ministry used twenty-six satellites to broadcast in twenty-four languages on every major continent. Trinity's programming is broadcast twenty-four hours a day and includes the biggest names in televangelism in its lineup. Founders Paul (b. 1934) and Jan Crouch come from Pentecostal backgrounds, and the Pentecostal worship style and theology pervades the network's programming. The network's signature program is the *Praise the Lord* show, which features both variety show and talk show formats. The Crouches cast a wide net and include a cross-section of America's most prominent Christian preachers and musicians on their program. The network has also perfected the biannual telethon, which raises funds for the maintenance and expansion of the ministry. TBN's international outreach has been augmented by its inauguration of TBN Enlace in 2002, which targets the growing Hispanic population of the United States.

Religious Broadcasting Globally. One of the most significant developments in religious broadcasting that has occurred since the mid-1980s is the rapid expansion of networks and programming around the world. Many of the longest-running broadcast ministries in Europe and Asia were radio-based. The earliest of these, HCJB, or the Voice of the Andes, began its short-wave broadcasts blanketing South America in 1931. At the start of the twenty-first century, it was operating three powerful short-wave transmitting stations that send out radio and television programming around the world in a variety of vernacular languages. Vatican Radio also transmitted its inaugural broadcast in 1931. Over the years, this Jesuit-run operation has expanded its programming to include a professional news service, sophisticated musical programs, daily mass, live coverage of papal audiences, and live video streaming of the pope reciting his Sunday Angelus prayers. The broadcasts are offered in thirty-four languages and are sent out on short and medium waves, satellites, and FM. The Far East Broadcasting Company (FEBC) started its radio broadcasts in 1948 on a humble one-thousand-watt transmitter in the Philippines. By the 1950s, FEBC was broadcasting programs in thirty-six languages and dialects to the People's Republic of China and other Asian countries using megawatt transmitters. FEBC airs its Christian programming over thirty stations to Asia, eastern Europe, Australia, and Latin America. Trans World Radio (TWR) managed to break through the prohibitions against evangelical programming that European governments placed on their stations during the 1950s. The station purchased broadcasting rights in the principality of Morocco and began airing its programming throughout Europe on its new 100,000-watt short-wave transmitter in 1960. As the ministry expanded, the station built AM, long-wave, and short-wave transmitters and hired local religious leaders and musicians to produce programming in forty languages. Like FEBC, this station was successful in circumventing the jamming efforts of authorities in Communist countries. Today its broadcasts are global and reach almost 80 percent of the world's population with evangelical Christian programming.

The fall of Communism in eastern Europe (1989–1991) opened a new field for religious broadcasting ministries. By the beginning of the twenty-first century, a number of broadcasters were blanketing the former Soviet Union and its satellites. Among these is Agape Europe, an interdenominational Christian mission organization that distributes Christian television programming throughout eastern and western Europe, and United Christian Broadcasters Europe, which uses digital satellite and cable technology to broadcast preaching, Bible study, music, and world-affairs television programming across the United Kingdom, Ireland, and continental Europe. A major development for Europe occurred in 1990, when the British Parliament passed a law that opened the radio airwaves in Great Britain to independent religious broadcasters. In 1994, Premier Radio was one of the first evangelical ministries to receive an AM license. It now reaches a core audience of committed Christians in Great Britain with programming that expresses Christian values without alienating nonbelievers simply looking for a quality radio option.

Religious broadcasting is booming throughout the world at the dawn of the new millennium. Australia is served by more than 40 Christian radio stations, Latin America by more than 150 Christian TV stations and 1,000 radio stations, and Africa by a growing number of active media outlets. Islamic broadcasters, such as America's Nation of Islam, Egypt's Voice of the Holy Qurʾān, and Libya's Voice of Islam are becoming increasingly sophisticated both in their programming formats and technical expertise. In India all religious groups, including the Jains, Muslims, Sikhs, Christians, and Hindus, have cable television channels that offer nonstop religious programming to their audiences. The range of shows includes everything from the sermons of Islamic clerics to the devotional songs of Hindu musicians and the healing crusades of Benny Hinn. Christian broadcasting still faces enormous challenges in countries such as Sri Lanka, China, Vietnam, and North Korea, where radio frequencies are jammed and broadcast licenses and air time are severely regulated by governmental agencies.

Critiques of Religious Broadcasting. A series of sexual and financial scandals rocked the religious broadcasting industry during the 1980s, and criticisms of television evangelists and their shows have come from across the conservative and liberal spectrum. These criticisms fall out along six principal axes.

First, commentators such as Quentin Schultze offer indictments of televangelism that are theological in focus. These critics allege that televangelism exploits well-intentioned but biblically illiterate believers by delivering a shallow "health and wealth" gospel in return for financial support. This indictment essentially charges that televangelists such as Kenneth Copeland (b. 1937), Robert Tilton (b. 1946), and Robert Schuller are distorters of the traditional gospel values of obedience to God, self-sacrifice, love for the poor, and a rejection of worldly fame and riches. In their growth to affluence, many televangelists have come to the view that material wealth is acceptable and desirable, and that listeners need only ask God for abundance, make a donation to their ministry, and wait for the money to begin rolling in. Gone, these critics charge, is the Protestant ethic that saw wealth as the fruit of diligent labor. Faith and Values Media, which is owned and operated by a coalition of mainstream Catholic, Eastern Orthodox, Jewish, and Protestant churches, has attempted to address these concerns by eschewing the on-air solicitation of funds.

A second line of criticism concerns the dominance of Pentecostal Christianity in religious programming—and this form of Christianity's dualistic, apocalyptic worldview. This critique indicts religious broadcasting for its tendency to view individual and societal moral conflicts within the context of a cosmic war between Satan and God. In this dualistic conception of ultimate good and ultimate evil at war with each other, the ambiguities and subtleties of human moral behavior are left unexplored and absolute moral principles are definitively proclaimed. The tendency of programs such as *Jack Van Impe Presents* and *Hal Lindsey* to read current events through this dualistic lens, critics charge, often results in a jingoistic nationalism that demonizes Russians, Muslims, Palestinians, or Arabs, while blinding viewers to immoral actions by the U.S. government and its allies. The focus of many televangelists on eschatology and prophecy often leads to categorical condemnations of other nations and belief systems and a singular inability to reflect on the collective social injustices that plague American society. The news segments of many televangelistic programs unabashedly blur the distinctions between professional reporting and theologically biased commentary.

A third line of criticism concerns the format and medium of television itself. These criticisms allege that televangelism turns congregations into passive, unreflective audiences and the gospel into another form of popular entertainment. The concern is that the link between the gospel message and people's individual behavior may be lost in the glitz, glamour, and spectacle of many forms of religious programming. This criticism is linked to another line of concern, the possibility that "virtual" communities of believers following televangelist superstars may supersede the vital links of mutual support found in neighborhood church communities. The rise of the internet and of internet religious ministries has added to these fears of individual withdrawal from the close interpersonal interaction that is crucial for emotional health. This criticism acknowledges the demonstrably positive effect of religious broadcasting for shut-ins and handicapped persons unable to participate in local church communities. At the same time, however, it observes that televangelists do not counsel people with marital problems, bury their viewers' dead, visit the sick, or perform baptisms, all staples of a week in the life of a local pastor.

A fourth line of criticism has to do with the increasing influence that radio and television evangelists exercise over America's political process. This criticism voices concerns that the many religious broadcasters who support the Christian right's political and social program are turning the national airwaves into a platform for the Republican Party's political agenda. CBN's Pat Robertson, Jerry Falwell, and *Focus on the Family*'s James Dobson (b. 1936) are just a few examples of religious broadcasters who are using their ministries to create bases of electoral and financial support for conservative political candidates. Constitutional purists see this growing trend as an erosion of the Constitution's separation of church and state and as an unwarranted and illegal intrusion of traditionally nonpartisan (and tax-exempt) religious communities into the nation's political life.

A fifth line of criticism takes aim at the avowed goal of most broadcast ministries—bringing the gospel message to the unconverted. A preponderance of evidence indicates that most regular viewers and listeners already hold evangelical, fundamentalist, or very conservative religious beliefs. What this means is that while religious broadcasting likely reinforces the existing beliefs and behaviors of its viewers, it is not very successful at reaching the unconverted. In the end, religious broadcasting may be mostly an alternative media source for people of religious faith who cannot find other programs that conform to their values and tastes. Put another way, religious broadcasting may answer to a pressing need in society for programming that reflects the conservative, fundamentalist, and evangelical worldviews of a sizeable segment of the American population.

A sixth and final line of criticism pinpoints the anti-intellectualist biases of many religious programs. Broadcast preachers regularly ridicule liberal ministers who tolerate moral ambiguity or who fail to speak plainly and directly. They rarely address the traditional historical concerns of mainstream theologians and instead focus narrowly on personal salvation and the spiritual condition of the world. Religious broadcasters tend to be biblical inerrantists who condemn historical-critical methods of scriptural exegesis and read scripture literally. Critics claim that this anti-intellectual bias dissipates the strength of respected traditions of scholarship as well as the historical experience of Christian communities. It also leaves the religious broadcasting audience bereft of the critical faculties that are necessary to identify the various forms of political, social, and religious propaganda and hucksterism that saturate religious programming.

Religious broadcasting shows no signs of slowing down in the twenty-first century. Radio and television ministries continue to proliferate around the world, and cable television has greatly expanded their outreach to developed and developing countries alike. Religious broadcasting via the World Wide Web also continues to expand, allowing space for even more religious entrepreneurs to attract audiences and build their ministries. As geopolitical developments increasingly take on religious overtones, radio and television channels will become hotly contested sites. The future will likely see partisans of various religious ideologies vying for airtime and political sponsorship. Thus it will be interesting to watch the role of federal and national regulators of the airwaves in the religious battles of the future.

BIBLIOGRAPHY

Bruce, Steve. *Pray TV: Televangelism in America.* New York, 1990. This useful volume employs surveys and other data to explode the myth that religious television is converting millions of people to evangelical Christianity.

Dorgan, Howard. *The Airwaves of Zion: Radio and Religion in Appalachia.* Knoxville, Tenn., 1993. This book is a well documented description and analysis of AM radio evangelism in Appalachia by a professor of communications at Appalachian State University.

Erickson, Hal. *Religious Radio and Television in the United States, 1921–1991: The Programs and Personalities.* Jefferson, N.C., 1992. Erickson's volume is a somewhat uneven encyclopedic treatment of various religious broadcasting personalities and ministries; valuable mainly for its information on less well known ministries.

Fishwick, Marshall, and Ray B. Brown, eds. *The God Pumpers: Religion in the Electronic Age.* Bowling Green, Ohio, 1987. Two critical observers of American popular culture examine the broadcast ministries of Billy Graham, Jimmy Swaggart, Jerry Falwell, Jim and Tammy Bakker, Terry Cole-Whittaker, Marilyn Hickey, Danuto Soderman, and Beverly LaHaye.

Hadden, Jeffrey, and Anson Shupe. *Televangelism: Power and Politics on God's Frontier.* New York, 1988. Two prominent sociologists use social movement theory to examine televangelists and their followers and the cultural revolution in America that they are creating.

Hadden, Jeffrey, and Charles E. Swann. *Prime Time Preachers: The Rising Power of Televangelism.* Reading, Mass., 1981. This book was one of the first in-depth sociological studies of the influence and future of televangelists such as Pat Robertson, Robert Schuller, and Oral Roberts.

Hangen, Tona J. *Redeeming the Dial: Radio, Religion, and Popular Culture in America.* Chapel Hill, N.C., 2002. This excellent historical volume traces how American evangelicals used radio during the mid-twentieth century to build a powerful national coalition and define the parameters of their theology.

Hoover, Stewart M. *Mass Media Religion: The Social Sources of the Electronic Church.* Newbury Park, Calif., 1988. This important sociological and historical study explores how the electronic church affects the way American culture addresses pressing issues such as drug addiction, racism, and militarism.

Matelski, Marilyn J. *Vatican Radio: Propagation by the Airwaves.* Westport, Conn., 1995. The best historical study of HVJ, Vatican Radio, and its role in propagating the religious, social, and political agendas of the Roman Catholic Church.

Melton, J. Gordon, Phillip Charles Lucas, and Jon R. Stone, eds. *Prime-Time Religion: An Encyclopedia of Religious Broadcasting.* Phoenix, Ariz., 1997. The most comprehensive volume available for understanding the personalities and ministries of religious broadcasting both in the United States and throughout the world.

Peck, Janice. *The Gods of Televangelism: The Crisis of Meaning and the Appeal of Religious Television.* Cresskill, N.J., 1993. An insightful examination of Christian Right leadership, separatism, and televangelism in America.

Schultze, Quentin J. *Televangelism and American Culture: The Business of Popular Religion.* Grand Rapids, Mich., 1991. A critical sociological and theological examination of televangelism from the perspective of an insightful Calvinist scholar.

Ward, Mark. *Air of Salvation: The Story of Christian Broadcasting.* Grand Rapids, Mich., 1994. This useful volume by the director of media ministries at Bob Jones University is a triumphalist history of the personalities and ministries that helped establish fundamentalist and evangelical dominance of the American airwaves during the twentieth century.

GREGOR T. GOETHALS (1987)
PHILLIP CHARLES LUCAS (2005)

RELIGIOUS COMMUNITIES

This entry consists of the following articles:

RELIGION, COMMUNITY, AND SOCIETY
CHRISTIAN RELIGIOUS ORDERS

RELIGIOUS COMMUNITIES: RELIGION, COMMUNITY, AND SOCIETY

Religion is both a personal matter and a social reality. In dealing with the latter, one is confronted by a confusion of categories and by terminological difficulties. For example, popular references to "religious community" reflect ambiguities in the current use of the term *community.* From Webster one learns that *community,* derived from the Latin *communitas,* has many meanings, including (1) a body of people having a common organization or interests, or living in the same place under the same laws and regulations, (2) society at large, a commonwealth, a state, (3) joint relationship or ownership, and (4) a common character or commonness.

Students of society have tried to overcome such ambiguities. Under the influence of the later German Enlightenment's notion that society is a product of human will, Ferdinand Julius Tönnies (1855–1936) proposed the famous dichotomy between community (*Gemeinschaft*) and society (*Gesellschaft*). Community embodies natural will (*Wesenwille*) and is maintained by face-to-face interhuman relationships and a sense of solidarity governed by traditional rules. Society, however, is a more complex entity reflecting rational will (*Kürwille*) and characterized by indirect and impersonal interhuman relationships motivated by rational self-interest. Émile Durkheim (1858–1917) also attempted to distinguish between primitive and archaic social groups (roughly analogous to Tönnies's community type) and more complex groups (Tönnies's society type). In Durkheim's model, the former are based on the mechanical solidarity of undifferentiated individuals who live according to the authority of the social group, while the latter are based on the organic solidarity of more differentiated individuals who relate to one another by means of the division of labor. Prior to Tönnies and Durkheim, of course, Karl Marx (1818–1883) had classified various social organizations according to modes of production and the class system, ranging all the way from primitive communism to modern capitalist society. An implicit evolutionary assumption—that the movement from what Tönnies called community to what he called society was irreversible—underlay all these typologies and classifications.

Students of religion generally apply Tönnies's notion of the community type to both archaic and contemporary tribal communities, in which religious and natural bonds coalesce. They also acknowledge that a more stratified society usually develops from community, even though smaller religious or ethnic communities may continue to exist within the framework of a larger society. Beyond this general level, however, students of religion encounter a bewildering variety of religious phenomena that defy simple categorization in terms of community and society. For example, some of the ancient states, from the Hebrew to the Japanese, considered themselves "sacred communities" embracing a number of "religious societies." In the course of time, some of these religious societies themselves developed into religious communities. Other troublesome examples stem from the classical world religions such as Buddhism, Christianity, and Islam. These three considered their fellowships to be "religious communities" or "faith communities" that united different segments with a society or even crossed ethnic, linguistic, cultural, and national lines. Here again, these larger religious communities gave birth to a variety of religious societies that often became *de facto* religious communities, even if they retained the nomenclature of "society," as in the case of the Society of Jesus (the Jesuits).

Thus, for students of religion, the category *religious community* must include at least (1) tribal communities, both natural and religious, archaic and contemporary, (2) sacred national communities, (3) founded religious communities such as the Buddhist, the Christian, and the Islamic, and (4) various religious societies-turned-communities, as for instance orders of monks and nuns. Different though these groups may be, they share what the Dutch scholar Gerardus van der Leeuw (1938) calls the sense of community. This sense "is something not manufactured, but given; it depends not upon sentiment or feeling, but on the Unconscious. It need be founded upon no conviction, because it is self-evident; we do not become members of it, but 'belong to it'" (p. 243).

TRIBAL RELIGIOUS COMMUNITIES. To avoid the misleading adjective *primitive,* many scholars now use expressions—not wholly satisfactory—such as *tribal, nonliterate,* and *folk* to refer to the religious forms of a wide variety of peoples who live in small social groups and who possess a simple material culture and an unwritten language. It is often assumed that there are many similarities between tribal communities in archaic or prehistoric periods and tribal communites of the present. It is indeed possible that archaic and contemporary tribal communities are in some way typologically similar, presumably owing to their simple living conditions. Still, one should not overlook the long span of time that separates them.

Archaeological excavations have unearthed a variety of material remains from the prehistoric period, but very little can be reconstructed of the social system of the peoples or the movements of the so-called tribal migrations, including the prehistoric migration of Native Americans from Eurasia to North and South America. Excavated sites of Neolithic settlements, such as Banpo in Shensi, China, may give glimpses of the physical layouts of archaic tribal communities, but it is difficult to know how prehistoric food-gatherers, hunters, and agriculturalists conducted their personal, communal, or religious affairs. Even so, by piecing together evidence from archaeology, physical anthropology, philology, and other sources, it is conjectured that all activities directed toward subsistence and all cultic and religious activities merged to form a single, unified community. Some scholars even speculate that the archaic tribal community was, so to speak, a "religious universe" in which living itself was a religious act.

The contemporary tribal or folk communities scattered throughout Africa, Asia, Oceania, Australia, and the Americas display a great divergence in complexity of community structure, division of labor, cultic and religious beliefs and practices, and relations with neighboring societies and cultures. Moreover, as E. E. Evans-Pritchard (1951) notes, these communities "have just as long a history as our own, and while they are less developed than our society in some respects they are often more developed in others" (p. 7). Different though they are in many other respects, contemporary tribal communities share one characteristic: They are held together, to quote Robert Redfield (1953), "by common understanding as to the ultimate nature and purpose of life." Each community "exists not so much in the exchange of useful functions as in the common understandings as to the ends given" (p. 12). To these communities, life's ultimate purpose is the creation of a meaningful order through imitation of the celestial model, transmitted by myths and celebrated in rituals.

Unlike their archaic counterparts, contemporary tribal communities have more complex social organizations based on locality, age, sex, and sometimes totemic affiliations. Their nucleus is the kinship system, usually with exogamous clans and local territories. Many tribal communities have secret men's societies, which usually meet in the "men's house," an institution known by different designations in different localities but serving similar purposes—a club house for bachelors, a place for community worship, a residence for young boys during their initiatory seclusion. Such societies are found in Australia, New Guinea, Melanesia, Micronesia, Polynesia, the Philippines, India, Africa, and North, Central, and South America. (For examples, see Hutton Webster's *Primitive Secret Societies,* 1932.)

Today it is becoming increasingly inappropriate to apply the designation *community* to some tribal groups. The term is still applicable to such groups as the hunting and gathering tribes of South America and Australia and to the San of southern Africa, but larger groups like the Navajo Indians, who occupy eighteen million acres in Arizona and New Mexico, and the Inuit (Eskimo), whose habitations stretch from Greenland to the Bering Strait, resemble instead huge conglomerate societies containing a series of smaller communities and subgroups and various kinds of cultic fraternities. In addition, because of the impact of surrounding societies, some tribal groups now live in permanent settlements and so have lost their sense of the traditional tribal-religious community.

SACRED NATIONAL COMMUNITIES. The first great civilization in the history of the world emerged around 3500 BCE on the Mesopotamian plain. It was followed by the rise of other civilizations in Egypt, Crete, India, China, Mexico (Mesoamerica), Peru (Andean), and Palestine. According to the cosmography of these civilizations, the state was more than a political entity: It constituted the sacred national community.

Understandably, different civilizations have understood the meaning of the sacred national community differently. For example, in Mesopotamia the universe as a whole was considered a sovereign state governed by the assembly of the gods. In turn, the national state—made up of many city-states, each owned by its own god and ruled by his human steward—was governed by a king, who was himself guided by the executive officer of the assembly of the gods. Thus, as part of the cosmic commonwealth directed by the united wills of the divine powers, the earthly national community was sacred.

In contrast to the Mesopotamian tradition, the Egyptian national state was considered sacred because the king himself was one of the gods. At the same time, he was the intermediary between the people and the gods, the earthly community's divine representative. He was also the one recognized priest of all the gods, and as such he ruled the nation with the help of deputies, the officials and priests.

A third type of sacred national community, one rarer than the first two, is the Hebrew concept of a community based on a covenant between a god and his people. Despite the fiction of their common ancestry from Abraham, the Israelites were a composite people. As the prophets Hosea and Jeremiah stressed, they understood the sacral character of their commonwealth to depend both on faithful adherence to the covenant and on ethical conduct.

Throughout history, many nations have defined their sacrality in terms of one of these three types—king as deputy, king as god, or covenantal/contractual community—or a combination of them. But with increasing stratification of society and political organization, and the solidification of religious traditions, national communities have eroded. They have been replaced by a variety of relationships between religion and state ranging from theocracy—reminiscent of the sacred national community—to the secular state. But the *idea* of the sacred national community has persisted in various forms into the present century, as in, for example, Japan and Tibet.

FOUNDED RELIGOUS COMMUNITIES. In contrast to the sacred national community, whose *raison d'être* and destiny depend on the corporate life of the sociopolitical entity, the founded religious community, as this author is using the term, refers to a community that derives its initial impetus from the religious experience of the founder of a religion. The better-known classical examples of such founded groups are the Buddhist, Christian, and Islamic communities; lesser known but equally significant are the Jain, Zoroastrian, and Manichaean communities. The founded religious communities of recent origin, such as the Sikh, Baha'i, Mormon, and a number of contemporary new religious communities in Asia, Africa, and the Americas, generally follow a similar pattern.

For convenience of exposition, one can identify three stages in this pattern: (1) the significance of the founder, (2) the process of formation, and (3) the usual, but by no means universal, manner in which such a religious community develops.

For the most part, the actual or legendary accounts of a religious founder (accepted as authentic, of course, by the given religious community) follow—with some notable exceptions—what is often called a law or scenario of sacred biography: the founder's miraculous birth, unusual childhood, ordeal or personal crisis prior to having a decisive religious experience, successful or unsuccessful ministry, and memorable demise, implying death or a new life beyond.

Then, either during or after the founder's lifetime, a circle of disciples becomes the nucleus of an informal brotherhood or fraternity. In the course of time, this brotherhood grows into an egalitarian or hierarchical religious community, with official scriptures, liturgies, and rules of conduct as well as specialists in sacred matters: clergy, scholars, jurists, monastics, bureaucrats, and service personnel. The religious community also develops a channel of authority to coordinate the activities of its scattered branches and faithful.

Finally, the religious community must cope with the surrounding culture, society, and secular political authorities, which view it with varying degrees of positive, negative, or neutral attitudes. Internally, this community often suffers from routinization, clericalization, inertia, spiritual decay, and fossilization. In this process, various kinds of reform and protest movements arise. Whether forward- or backward-looking, they cause change, schism, or secession, or establish small societies of like-minded members within the framework of the larger religious community (*ecclesiola in ecclesia*). The reformers and leaders of schismatic and sectarian groups often become *de facto* founders, and the groups—both inside and outside the larger religious communities—take on the characteristics of religious communities.

Significantly, the idea of the unity of the religious community tends to persist, in spite of schismatic division or the breakup of the community's empirical structure into sects or denominations or possibly both. Thus, all divided Buddhist groups recite the same threefold affirmation of the essential unity of the Buddha, the Dharma (Buddhist doctrine), and the Samgha (the Buddhist community); all traditions of Islam affirm the unity of its community (*ummah*); and all divisions of Christianity accept the Christian community (church) as the one unbroken "body of Christ" that exists beneath its empirical disunity: "Credo in . . . unam sanctam catholicam ecclesiam."

Religious Societies-Turned-Communities. As mentioned earlier, a variety of small religious societies and cultic fraternities tend to emerge within the framework of "sacred national communities" and "founded religious communities." Many such groups, if not formed for limited, temporary, and specific purposes, have the potential to become religious communities. How a religious society, viewed from a sociological perspective, becomes a religious community, may be seen in the initial development of the founded religious community. For example, as E. J. Thomas astutely observes in *The History of Buddhist Thought* (1933), the Buddhist community started "not with a body of doctrine, but with the formation of a society bound by certain rules" (p. 14). But the initiation of a variety of individuals into this society reoriented it toward the corporate soteriological objective and led to a shared experience, so that the society became a religious community.

To take another familiar example, Christianity started as a charismatic society within the fold of the Jewish community. After the Pentecost, it affirmed that those who were initiated into that society, Jews and gentiles alike, became the true Israel by virtue of being grafted onto the stock of Abraham. This in turn transformed them into children of God in the Christian community by being born "not of the will of man, but of God" (*Jn.* 1:13). Similarly, gnostic groups started out as mystery societies or circles at the periphery of the Christian fold but quickly developed into full-fledged religious communities.

The intricate relationship between religious societies and religious communities just illustrated tempts one to count numerous groups of ambiguous character among religious communities. However, this article shall here consider only those societies that were established for specific religious and cultic purposes within larger tribal, sacred national, and founded religious communities, and that were later transformed into more permanent and coherent religious communities possessing such characteristics as rites of initiation, private or corporate religious ceremonies and duties, and independent organizational structures. This article shall give brief typological discussions of (1) secret societies, (2) mystery societies/communities, (3) cult-based communities, (4) religous orders/monastic communities/service societies, and (5) utopian communities.

Secret societies. Secret societies include a wide range of groups that initiate in secret, possess secret symbols or rituals, or transmit esoteric knowledge. In size they range from small societies in tribal religious communities to Freemasonry, whose membership on both sides of the Atlantic numbers 5.9 million. (Freemasonry's satellite groups, among them the Ancient Arabic Order of the Nobles of the Mystic Shrine—popularly known as the Shriners—and the Order of the Eastern Star, are not secret societies. The Ku Klux Klan, on the other hand, is a secret terrorist organization but not a religious society, despite its stress on white Protestant supremacy.)

In part, secret societies overlap with the next two types of society-turned-community—the mystery societies and the cult-based communities. For example, the secret societies of ancient Egypt, Greece, and Rome were in fact mystery societies, with the possible exception of the Pythagorean community, and they will be discussed under that heading. The past ten centuries of Chinese history have been sprinkled with secret societies, some of which—notably the Maitreya Society, the White Lotus Society, the White Cloud Society, and the Triad Society—were inspired by Buddhist-Daoist eclecticism. The last major Chinese secret society was the Society of Shangdi, whose patriarch, Hong Xiuquan, who was influenced in part by Christianity, started the Taiping Rebellion in 1848. Contrary to popular impression, the esoteric schools of Buddhism, which transmit esoteric truth, are not secret societies: Though the transmission of the teaching is secret, membership is open to anyone. In Europe, despite the predominance of Christianity and the threat of the Inquisition, pre-Christian pagan legacies of witchcraft and sorcery were kept alive by secret societies such as the Calsari, while the neo-Manichaean Cathari and other persecuted heretical groups went underground and tried to survive as secret societies.

Among contemporary tribal communities, secret societies are virtually universal phenomena. According to Paul Radin in *The Winnebago* (1923), the Winnebago Indian community has the following four groups: (1) clans or natural groups, which exclude outsiders from their ceremonies, (2) religious societies limited to those who receive the blessings of a special spirit, (3) the medicine group, a mystery society, and (4) associations of warriors and other such groups. As for African secret societies, Wilfrid D. Hambly's *Source-Book for African Anthropology* (1937) depicts the following types: (1) those based on age and sex affinities, (2) those connected with initiation, (3) those concerned with political and legal matters, and (4) those based on economic differentiation. Similar admixtures of religio-cultic, economic, and social factors are found in many other secret societies of contemporary tribal communities in various parts of the world.

Mystery societies/communities. Classical types of mystery societies or communities emerged in the Greco-Roman world and in China, where the mysteries were believed to confer immortality and eternal life. Many mystery cults, such as that of Eleusis, originated with certain families. In the course of time, various Greek mystery cults developed private mystery societies. Under Roman rule, some of these societies became more open cultic communities. Meanwhile, other mystery cults of foreign origin—for instance, the cults of the Great Mother from Asia Minor, of Mithra from Iran, and of Serapis from Egypt—penetrated Greece and Rome. In the Roman world, many joined the cultic groups of Dionysos in search of personal immortality, but the religion of Mithra was probably the most influential mystery cult.

In China, Daoism greatly amplified the belief in immortals (*xian*), which was already very strong. The so-called Huanglao cult (the cult of the legendary Yellow Emperor and Laozi) attracted many immortality-seekers before the beginning of the common era. Vigorously promoted by priest-magicians, this tradition was further developed in the second century CE by Zhang Ling, who inaugurated a magico-religious movement called the Way of the Five Bushels of Rice with Zhang Ling himself as the Heavenly Teacher. Meanwhile, other Daoists combined Daoist philosophy with the Yin-yang school and with alchemy. In the fifith century, Kou Qianji systematized the Daoist community, regulating its theories and cults. Since then Daoism, also called the Religion of Mystery (Xuan Jiao), has exerted great influence not only in China but also in neighboring countries.

Many mystical or semimystical cults, societies, and communities in the Hindu, Buddhist, Islamic, Jewish, and Christian folds exhibit external resemblances to Greco-Roman and Chinese mystery societies and communities. Opinions vary, however, as to how central the "mysteries" are to their communal life.

Cult-based communities. Like the Orgeones, a free cultic association that persisted in Greece at least until the sixth century, certain groups are united primarily by cultic devotion to one or more deities and not by clan, tribal, national, or occupational ties. In other words, their specifically religious interests cut across sectarian and denominational boundaries. Or sometimes different communities participate in common, albeit temporary, cult associations, as do Kwakiutl Indian communities in North America in wartime and during winter dances. The prototype of this category is the *sampradāya* of Hinduism, which may be characterized as a phenomenon halfway between mystery communities and sects or denominations. The members of the *sampradāya,* divided though they are in terms of caste and other affiliations, experience a ritual unity in a communal adherence to particular traditions of teachers, as illustrated by the *sampradāyas* of the deity Viṣṇu, which trace their origin to eminent teachers such as Rāmānuja and Madhva. Similarly, the different groups united in devotion to Śiva trace their origin back to various ascetics. One of the subdivisions of the cult groups of Śiva, the Liṅgāyat, numbers four million members of different backgrounds, who wear the emblem of the phallus as the symbol of their cultic unity.

Similar cult-based communities, by no means as elaborate as the *sampradāya* of Hinduism, are found in many other parts of the world, from ancient Greece to modern Japan. At times, cult seems to be a stronger bond of unity than other features of religious life.

Religious orders/monastic communities/service societies. Important among voluntary groups within larger religious communities are religious orders, which are often, but not always, identified with monastic communities, and sometimes with service societies sponsored by or affiliated with religious bodies. In common English usage, the term *religious* not only connotes "scrupulously faithful" or "devout" but as a noun also refers to those who are bound by monastic vows or devoted to a life of piety and religion, such as monks, friars, and nuns. Similarly, the term *order* signifies a society of persons bound by some common rule, especially an aggregate of separate communities like a monastic brotherhood or community. The term *religious order* could, of course, designate a variety of holy orders that may not practice a monastic form of life. This article, however, shall discuss only those religious orders that come under the category of monastic communities. Similarly, of all the service societies under religious jurisdiction—societies for missionary work, teaching, and philanthropy, and others as well—only those that are organized as communities will be discussed.

Students of religions recognize various kinds of religious brotherhoods, guilds of priests, and monastic communities in different traditions, as for example the Pythagorean brotherhood in ancient Greece, the Bektashī order in Islam, and the Vedanta Society of modern India. Two religious traditions that have developed elaborate systems of monastic communities, Buddhism and Christianity, deserve special attention.

Although the early Buddhist community consisted of four components—monks (*bhikkhu* or *bhukṣu*), nuns (*bhikkhuni* or *bhukṣuṇī*), laymen (*upāsaka*), and laywomen (*upāsikā*)—the most central group was the order of monks. Initially, the monastic order started as an informal assembly of wandering mendicants, but soon it developed into monastic communities in which monks shared a normative discipline (Vinaya). Under the patronage of King Aśoka in the third century BCE, monastic communities played an important role as missionaries propagating Buddhism. In the course of time, great monastic communities became centers of religious and secular education and of cultural activities. Although the Buddhist community divided into Southern (Hīnayāna or Theravāda) and Northern (Mahāyāna) traditions, each with further subdivisions along doctrinal and cultic lines, it was possible for monks of different schools to live in the same monastic communities.

In the main, the Southern tradition follows an elitist model: Monks leave the secular world and enter monasteries for a life of full-time spiritual striving toward their own enlightenment, while the laity receives merit by supporting monastic communities. The most elaborate monastic hierarchy developed in Thailand, where the *sangharāja,* or ruler of the monastic community, was under no other authority except that of the king. In the modern period, the traditionally otherworldly monastic communities in the Southern tradition have become more involved in the affairs of the world. In the Northern tradition, on the other hand, the paths of monastics and laity were always regarded as different but equally important vocations. Mahāyāna monastic communities, inspired as they are by the compassionate bodhisattva ideal, stress active service to all beings.

Monastic communities in the Christian tradition are many and varied. Unlike communities in Western Christendom, Eastern Orthodox communities are not divided into different orders. Having originally developed out of informal fellowships of hermits who lived a life of prayer, they were transformed in the fourth century into monastic communities with three components: those who lead a monastic life without taking vows and two grades of monastics who take permanent vows (monks of "lesser" and "greater" habits). In Western Christendom, the *Rule of Saint Benedict* (c. 540) transformed earlier, loosely organized communities of hermits into disciplined monastic communities. The Rule provided the norm of communal life based on the daily offices, as followed by the Cluniacs and the Cistercians. Meanwhile, more activist orders of friars, such as the Franciscans and the Dominicans, appeared on the European scene. They were followed by the Society of Jesus (the Jesuits), which not only championed the cause of the Counter-Reformation at home but also initiated extensive missionary activities abroad. Both Eastern and Western traditions of Christianity comprise many orders of nuns. Like their male counterparts, some nuns are contemplative while others pursue educational and philanthropic vocations.

Utopian communities. Most religious communities have what might be characterized as utopian features or ideals. Many myths of tribal religious communities reflect their notion of the idealized celestial realm or the paradigmatic activities of gods and heroes at the beginning of time. Many historic religious communities affirm the existence of an ideal state either in their golden past or at the end of history. Philosophers like Confucius and Plato have also attempted to depict the ideal society on earth.

But in a more specific sense, the term *utopia* is derived from Thomas More's *On the Highest State of a Republic and on the New Island of Utopia* (1516). More's idea of an idealized society, realizable on earth, and his critique of the lamentable state of the world, continued to stir literary and religious imagination after his time. From the seventeenth century onward, a number of utopian communities have been established on either side of the Atlantic, including New Harmony in Indiana, Brook Farm in Massachusetts, and Oneida in New York. There have also been such religious utopian communities as the Dutch Mennonite colonies in Delaware, the German Pietist settlements in Indiana and Pennsylvania, and the Bruderhof communities in Germany, England, and North America.

For the most part, utopian elements in the Islamic, Buddhist, and Chinese traditions were absorbed into millenarian and eschatological ideologies, but they did not inspire the establishment of separate communal settlements. In modern Japan, however, a number of utopian communities inspired by Lev Tolstoi and several indigenous messianic cults have emerged. Modern Jewish settlements in Palestine, many of which took the form of *kibbutsim,* exhibit an intricate homology of religious, political, and social utopian features. Most of the "hippie" communes that emerged in America in the 1960s and 1970s can hardly be classified as religious utopian communities, but an increasing number of utopian communities are being generated in North America today by Christians, Theosophists, and new religious groups of diverse origins.

CONCLUSION. Religion, then, is both a personal matter and a social reality. Throughout the history of humankind, from the prehistoric period down to the present day, religion has sought fellowship either by intensifying the existing social fabric—family, clan, tribe, caste, local or national community—or by creating specifically religious communities within, above, or apart from other social and political groupings and institutions. Despite their diversity, these groups all share that unconscious sense that makes them communities to which religious persons belong.

SEE ALSO Community; Monasticism; Mystery Religions; Secret Societies; Utopia.

BIBLIOGRAPHY

Durkheim, Émile. *The Elementary Forms of the Religious Life* (1912). New York, 1965.

Evans-Pritchard, E. E. *Social Anthropology.* Glencoe, Ill., 1951.

Frankfort, Henri, Henriette A. Frankfort, John A. Wilson, Thorkild Jacobsen, and William Irwin. *The Intellectual Adventure of Ancient Man.* Chicago, 1946.

Kitagawa, Joseph M. *Religions of the East.* Enl. ed. Philadelphia, 1968.

Leeuw, Gerardus van der. *Religion in Essence and Manifestation: A Study in Phenomenology* (1933). 2d ed. 2 vols. New York, 1963.

Möller, Christian, and Jacob Katz. "Gemeinde." In *Theologische Realenzyklopädie,* vol. 12, pts. 1–4, edited by Gerhard Krause and Gerhard Müller. Berlin and New York, 1983.

Niebuhr, H. Richard. *The Social Sources of Denominationalism* (1929). New York, 1972.

Popkes, Wiard. "Gemeinschaft." In *Reallexikon für Antike und Christentum,* vol. 9, edited by Theodor Klauser. Stuttgart, 1973–1976.

Redfield, Robert. *The Primitive World and Its Transformations.* Ithaca, N.Y., 1953.

Ringeling, Herman. "Gemeinschaft." In *Theologische Realenzyklopädie,* vol. 12, pts. 1–4, edited by Gerhard Krause and Gerhard Müller. Berlin and New York, 1983.

Thraede, Klaus. "Gesellschaft." In *Reallexikon für Antike und Christentum,* vol. 10, edited by Theodor Klauser. Stuttgart, 1976–1978.

Tönnies, Ferdinand. *Community and Society* (1887). East Lansing, Mich., 1957.

Troeltsch, Ernst. *The Social Teachings of the Christian Churches* (1931). Chicago, 1981.

Turner, Victor. *The Ritual Process: Structure and Anti-Structure* (1969). Ithaca, N. Y., 1977.

Wach, Joachim. *Sociology of Religion* (1944). Chicago, 1962.

Wasziuk, J. H., Carsten Colpe, and Bernhard Kötting. "Genossenschaft." In *Reallexikon für Antike und Christentum,* vol. 10, edited by Theodor Klauser. Stuttgart, 1976–1978.

Weber, Max. *The Sociology of Religion* (1922). Boston, 1963.

Wilson, Bryan R. *Religion in Sociological Perspective.* Oxford, 1982.

Yinger, J. Milton. *Religion, Society and the Individual: An Introduction to the Sociology of Religion.* New York, 1957.

JOSEPH M. KITAGAWA (1987)

RELIGIOUS COMMUNITIES: CHRISTIAN RELIGIOUS ORDERS

Christians have used the term *religious order* in both a narrow, technical sense and a broader, more common one. Popularly, religious orders are thought to include any and all men or women who profess public vows of poverty, chastity, and obedience; follow a common rule of life; engage in a specific kind of work (e.g., teaching, nursing, missionary endeavor); and submit to the directions of superiors who may be either appointed by higher ecclesiastical authority or elected in some manner by the order's members. In this broad sense, virtually all religious communities of Christian men and women may be referred to as orders, but more technically, a religious order is qualified by certain conditions that do not necessarily affect all Christians who choose a life of prayer and service in community with others.

Three qualifications have commonly been attached to this narrower meaning of a religious order: the public profession of "solemn" (as opposed to "simple") vows; an obligation to celebrate publicly each day the Liturgy of the Hours (a pattern of psalms, hymns, scripture readings, and prayers attached to specific times of day and night), and restriction to a cloister or "enclosure" (a defined space, often identified with the physical limits of the monastery or convent, within which members live and from which all outsiders are excluded). In history and practice, however, these qualifications have been neither rigid nor absolute. The Society of Jesus (Jesuits) has been regarded in Western church law as a religious order in the strict sense, even though its members have never been cloistered. Similarly, the exact distinction between solemn and simple vows, unknown before the thirteenth century, has never been entirely clear either to theologians or to experts in church law. In common theory, a solemn vow has been defined as a free, irrevocable promise made to God that binds the individual forever and renders certain actions opposed to the vows (e.g., marriage as opposed to celibacy; the ownership of property as opposed to poverty) not only illicit but null and invalid as well. A simple vow, in contrast, is regarded as having a less absolute character and may thus be made for a limited period of time (e.g., for one year or three years). In practice, however, the distinction blurs, since people may make simple vows in perpetuity, while those who have made irrevocable solemn vows may be released from them through a legal process known as dispensation.

The term *religious order* is more commonly used by Western Christians (e.g., Roman Catholics or members of Protestant communions) than by Eastern Christians (e.g., Greek or Russian Orthodox). Even within the Roman Catholic church, where attention to the precise legal status of religious vows and communities has been examined and evaluated for centuries, ambiguities still exist. Catholic members of religious orders are subject to the definitions and provisions of the Code of Canon Law (1983).

ORIGINS. For centuries, Christian apologists have attempted to find a basis for religious orders in the historical ministry and teaching of Jesus. An early example may be seen in the *Life of Antony* by Athanasius (c. 298–373), which reports Antony of Egypt's (c. 250–355) conversion to a solitary life of prayer and asceticism after hearing Jesus' words in church: "If you would be perfect, go, sell what you possess and give to the poor . . . and come, follow me" (*Mt.* 19:21). This biography helped spread monastic ideals throughout the Roman empire and encouraged the notion that to live alone with God, apart from all human company, is the supreme Christian response to Jesus' message.

There is no clear evidence that Jesus himself observed or promoted the ascetic life, or directly invited or commanded his followers to choose a life of poverty, celibacy, and obedience to human superiors. Central to Jesus' understanding of the relation between God and humankind was the conviction that God's reign (or kingdom) could break in upon the world at any time in any place—and that this reign would guarantee blessing and happiness for those open to receive it. Significant among the traditions associated with Jesus' life and collected in the Gospels are stories that show Jesus enjoying certain events (parties, dinners) and associating with people not ordinarily linked with an ascetic way of living (sinners, prostitutes).

While the remote origins of religious orders cannot be directly assigned to Jesus, possible antecedents to Christian asceticism may be discerned in both Judaism and the Greco-Roman world. Some members of the circle that gathered around John the Baptist probably adhered to a life of strict self-denial and repentance as preparation for God's impending judgment of the world. Most notable among Jewish antecedents were the sectarians of Qumran near the Dead Sea, whose collection of writings, the Dead Sea Scrolls, was discovered in 1947. Many scholars have identified the Qumran sectarians with a Jewish ascetic group known as the Essenes, who are mentioned by Philo of Alexandria (c. 13 BCE–45 to 50 CE), Josephus the Jewish historian (c. 37–100 CE), and Pliny the Elder (23–79 CE). Their descriptions show that the Essenes not only existed during Jesus' time but had developed a highly organized manner of life, which included an arduous three-year novitiate for newcomers, sharing of goods, celibacy, and strict obedience to authorities.

Similar to the Essenes was an Egyptian Jewish group of ascetics called the Therapeutae, whose principal center was a hill just outside Alexandria above Lake Mareotis. Among ancient writers, only Philo describes them. If his report is reliable, the Therapeutae were distinguished from more active groups like the Essenes by their strict seclusion. Each member of the sect seems to have had a separate dwelling, within which a special room was set aside for the daily study of scripture. Weekly, on the Sabbath, members met for common worship, while once every seven weeks a solemn feast, marked by a ritual meal eaten in silence and by the wearing of white clothing, was celebrated. The Therapeutae appear to have been celibate, though persons previously married were permitted to join them. Members were also expected to abjure the use of money, share goods in common, and keep bodily needs to a minimum.

Though the Therapeutae were Jewish, they can hardly have escaped influence from Greek philosophical traditions, especially in the region around Alexandria, the intellectual center of the Hellenistic world in the first century CE. In both the first century BCE and the first century CE, there were non-Jewish ascetic movements inspired by philosophers like Pythagoras (c. 580–500 BCE) and the Neo-Pythagoreans. Pythagoras himself is thought to have established a quasi-religious "club" or school in Croton, Italy, which fostered secret initiation ceremonies, communal sharing of goods, vows, and a vegetarian diet. Neo-Pythagoreans were particularly interested in religious life and theology, and they probably exerted influence upon both Judaism, through Philo of Alexandria, and early Christianity, through Clement of Alexandria (150?–215?).

While the extent of Jewish and Greco-Roman influence on the origins of Christian asceticism is difficult to assess, at least some early Christian congregations are known to have prized celibacy, if freely chosen for religious motives. In the *First Letter to the Corinthians* (c. 57), Paul encourages celibacy as a means of giving undivided attention to the Lord (*1 Cor.* 7:25–35). Because in Christ the final age of salvation has dawned for the world, Paul argues, even married Christians should behave in a manner that leaves them unencumbered by the business and burdens of the world (*1 Cor.* 7:29–31). Similarly, an earlier letter of Paul's to the congregation at Thessalonica (c. 51) had encouraged all Christians to pursue constant prayer and watchfulness (*1 Thes.* 5:1–17), practices later linked to monasticism and the ascetic life.

Before the end of the New Testament period, a distinct body of persons dedicated to prayer, celibacy, and charitable service within the congregation was recognized and regulated by church leaders. The widows described in the *First Letter to Timothy* appear to have been such a body. Widows were expected to be at least sixty years old, to be married only once, to be devoted to hospitality and the care of others, and to attend faithfully regular meetings for prayer and worship. In return, they could expect to receive material support from the congregation. Once admitted to the group, widows were to remain celibate; thus younger women who lost their husbands were advised to remarry (*1 Tm.* 5:11–15).

These examples reveal that the earliest Christians did not think an ascetic way of life should involve separation from the rest of the community. The celibate widows of the *First Letter to Timothy* are organized for the edification and service of the local community; they do not take vows, nor are they set apart through a public ceremony. Neither the widows nor the virgins mentioned by Paul in *1 Corinthians* are seen as having "superiors" distinct from the ordinary local leaders of the congregation. And nowhere in the New Testament are Christians advised to withdraw into solitary isolation.

Historical Development. Despite early Christian de-emphasis on an ascetic way of life separate from the community, the notion that some Christians might be called to a life of extraordinary dedication to God gained ground—and with it the related idea that such a life was more perfect than that of other believers. Both Clement of Alexandria, head of an important Christian school in Alexandria in the late second century, and his pupil Origen (c. 185–c. 254) were enthusiastic for ascetic ideals. Strongly influenced by the philosophy of Middle Platonism, both Clement and Origen spoke rapturously of the "true Christian gnostic" whose knowledge (Gr., *gnōsis*) is perfectly illuminated by faith in Christ, God's Logos (the Greek *logos* meaning both "word" and "reason"). In his commentary on the *Song of Songs,* Origen traced the stages of growth in the Christian's interior life and seemed to suggest that certain degrees of contemplative intimacy with Christ were possible only for the "perfect"—and that such perfect believers were a breed apart from the rest of the community.

Neither Clement nor Origen intended to create sectarian divisions within the church, nor did they want to pit groups of perfect Christians against less perfect ones in a battle for perfection. Still, their discussions of spiritual growth could be interpreted by less subtle thinkers as meaning that the truest Christians are celibate ascetics, while all others are innately inferior. It is not insignificant that Latin Christian writers of this period like Tertullian (c. 160?–225?) and Cyprian of Carthage (third century) also began producing works devoted to the praise of virginity as an ideal state for Christians.

By the fourth century, ascetic ideals were securely entrenched, as was the notion that Christians might legitimately withdraw from society and church in a solitary pursuit of perfection. The example of Antony has already been mentioned. Changes in the relation between church and culture after the emperor Constantine's Edict of Milan (313), which recognized Christianity as a licit religion in the empire, created a new situation. Some Christians felt that acceptance of their religion by the empire posed a serious threat to devout living and perfect union with God. Martyrdom, the oldest form of Christian heroism and a symbol of utmost dedication to God, was displaced by celibate asceticism, a spiritual sacrifice of ultimate value. Numerous ascetic movements began in the fourth century; virgins and monks became the "new martyrs" in an imperialized Christianity.

This notion of protest leads directly to the question of monastic origins. For a long time scholars assumed that Christian monasticism began as an exclusively eremitical phenomenon in Egypt, with people like Antony, and that it spread from there to other parts of the world. Cenobitic monasticism (monks living in community with other monks) was thought to have developed in a similar way, beginning with Pachomius (c. 293?–346) and his cenobitic foundation in the Thebaid near the Nile River (c. 320), but recent scholarship has shown that this hypothesis about monastic origins is untenable. A more likely theory is that monastic life, in both its eremitical and cenobitic forms, developed simultaneously in many different parts of the ancient world—Egypt, Syria, Palestine, Cappadocia, Mesopotamia.

The work of Pachomius was extremely influential because it provided an organized pattern of community life for men and women who wished to devote themselves both to asceticism and to service of others. Pachomian monks met twice daily for prayer and scripture-reading, but they also worked hard, raised their own food, engaged in handicrafts, shipped grain and products down the Nile to Alexandria, cared for orphans and the elderly, and nursed the sick. When Pachomius died in 346, there were eleven cenobitic monasteries, nine for men and two for women.

Elsewhere the development of organized monastic life encountered greater difficulty. In Cappadocia, Basil of Caesarea (c. 329–379) struggled to keep Christian ascetics from both sectarian eccentricity and heretical separation from the church. In that region, the legitimacy of ascetic life had been compromised by the unbalanced views of Eustathius of Sebaste (c. 300–377), who repudiated marriage for Christians, rejected the ministry of married clergy, and encouraged ascetics to hold their own worship services apart from those of the larger church. These views were denounced by the Council of Gangra (c. 345). Through his *Moral Rules* (c. 360) and his *Longer Rules* and *Shorter Rules* (c. 370), Basil tried to root Christian asceticism in texts drawn from the Bible. Rejecting sectarianism of the Eustathian sort, Basil affirmed the necessity of ascetic principles for all Christians and insisted that ascetics should remain close to the life and worship of the local congregation. Eastern Christian monks and nuns still regard Basil's rules as the fundamental charter for their way of life.

In the fourth century in the West, interest in asceticism and monastic life flourished. Jerome (c. 347–420) relates that a disciplined ascetic life, especially for virgins and widows, was well known in Rome and elsewhere in Italy. Bishop Ambrose of Milan (c. 339–397) is known to have consecrated virgins and also to have acted as patron for a monastery of men just outside Milan. Martin of Tours (c. 316–397), traditionally if inaccurately known as "the first monk in the West," promoted monasticism in western France, while in the south, Lérins (actually two islands just off the coast from Cannes) became an influential monastic center after Honoratus, bishop of Arles (d. 429), established a monastery there around the year 410.

In Roman North Africa, too, monasticism was expanding. Augustine of Hippo (354–430) provided advice and structural organization for communities of men and women. His rule (reconstructed from three separate documents) emphasizes such ideals as common ownership of property, communal prayer several times each day, simplicity in food and clothing, manual labor, celibacy, and obedience. At a later period, the Augustinian rule was adopted by groups known as "canons regular" (see below).

The most significant figure in Western monasticism was Benedict of Nursia (c. 480–547). Though almost nothing certain is known of his life, the rule (c. 530) that bears his name became so widely respected that it eventually supplanted most other Western monastic legislation and remains the foundation for the Benedictine order to this day. While it does not reject the eremitical life, the *Rule of Saint Benedict* clearly prefers cenobitic living and proposes a pattern that balances prayer, scripture-reading, rest, and manual labor in almost equal proportion under the government of an abbot responsible to God for the welfare of each individual in the monastery.

Benedictine monasticism, like the other ascetic movements described so far, was primarily "lay" rather than clerical in character. Many early ascetics like Pachomius and Jerome were in fact politely hostile toward the clergy, and while sixth-century documents like Benedict's rule permit ordained people to seek admission to the monastery, they include stern warnings against clerical pride and privilege. After the ninth century especially, it became common to ordain most Benedictine monks to the priesthood, but this practice was a departure from the rule and from earlier tradition.

Like many movements, Christian monasticism periodically needed reform, sometimes to correct abuse, at other times to reinvigorate or redefine ideals. In the West, especially from the time of Charlemagne (r. 768–814) onward, periodic reforms resulted in changes within monasticism and occasionally in the creation of new religious orders. Benedict of Aniane (c. 750–821) helped reorganize monasticism in the Carolingian empire by promoting exclusive allegiance to the Benedictine rule. Toward the end of the eleventh century, the reforming efforts of Gregory VII (r. 1073–1085) had two important effects: the reform of groups known as "canons regular" and the emergence of a new monastic order, the Cistercians. These latter stem from the Monastery of Cîteaux, founded in 1098 by Robert of Molesmes and made most famous by Bernard of Clairvaux, who joined it in 1112. Reacting against the wealth and prestige of Benedictine houses like Cluny (founded in 909), the Cistercians hoped to recall monks to a stricter, more primitive observance of monastic life. The Cistercian order still exists, though it was later reformed by Armand-Jean de Rancé (1626–1700) at the Abbey of La Trappe (hence the name Trappists).

The reform of canons regular, whose way of life had already been organized by Chrodegang of Metz (d. 766) in the eighth century, resulted in adoption of Augustine's rule by groups such as the Augustinian Canons (papal approval in 1059 and 1063) and the Canons of Prémontré (Norbertines, after Norbert, who founded them in 1120). Unlike monks, who were originally laity, canons were from the beginning a body of clergy who lived in common and ministered with the bishop at a diocesan cathedral. As a result of the eleventh-century reforms, canons assumed many features of monastic life (including an abbatial structure of government), much as monks had taken on many characteristics of clerical life.

It was a Spanish canon regular, Dominic (c. 1170–1221), who was largely responsible, along with Francis of Assisi (1181/2–1226), for the emergence of a new type of religious order in the West—the "mendicant friars." Unlike either canons (clergy) or monks (originally lay, but bound to one place by a vow of stability), the mendicants could move about freely to carry on tasks of teaching, preaching, studying, and serving the poor. Dominic's Order of Preachers quickly gained a reputation for scholarship, especially in the thirteenth-century universities. Thomas Aquinas (c. 1225–1274), the great theologian, was an early and brilliant exponent of Dominican ideals, while his contemporary at the University of Paris was Bonaventure (c. 1217–1274), a Franciscan. Like the Augustinian and Norbertine canons, the Dominican and Franciscan friars still exist, with members working in many parts of the world.

In 1215, the Fourth Lateran Council forbade the creation of more religious orders, though in fact new communities have continued to emerge up to the present time. Perhaps the most significant of these newer groups were the "congregations" of religious men and women that appeared after the Council of Trent (1545–1563). Some leaders at Trent appeared to agree with the Protestant reformers and sought to abolish religious orders altogether. But the work of people like Antonio Maria Zaccaria (1502–1539, founder of the Barnabites in 1530), and later of François de Sales (1567–1622) and Jeanne-Françoise de Chantal (1572–1641), founders of the Visitation sisters, helped convince doubters that viable new religious communities were possible. Most of these newer groups stressed active participation in church and society through works like teaching, nursing, care of orphans, and assistance to the needy.

In the nineteenth and twentieth centuries, religious orders also appeared in some Protestant communions, such as the Church of England. A monastic community of men, the Society of Saint John the Evangelist (Cowley Fathers), was founded in 1865 by Richard M. Benson while in 1907, the Sisters of the Love of God were established as a cloistered, contemplative community for women at Fairacres, Oxford. Among Roman Catholics, the Second Vatican Council (1962–1965) caused sweeping changes in religious orders. Old styles of clothing (the religious habit), government (methods of choosing superiors, their terms of office, the practice of obedience), and local customs (rules of fasting, silence, prayer) were modernized or abandoned. For some orders these changes have brought dwindling memberships, while others have continued to grow.

SEE ALSO Asceticism; Benedictines; Cistercians; Dominicans; Eremitism; Essenes; Franciscans; Jesuits; Monastery; Monasticism.

BIBLIOGRAPHY

Annuario Pontificio. Vatican City, 1716–. An annual publication available in most large libraries; includes statistics on Roman Catholic religious orders, together with further information about their founders and origins.

Brown, Peter. "The Rise and Function of the Holy Man in Late Antiquity." *Journal of Roman Studies* 61 (1971): 80–101. A seminal article that studies the complex and changing relations between structures of civil authority in the ancient world and the emerging ascetic heroes and heroines of Christianity.

Brown, Peter. *The World of Late Antiquity, AD 150–750.* New York, 1971. An excellent survey of the people and places that constituted the world within which Christian religious orders first developed, written for the nonspecialist.

Campenhausen, Hans von. "Early Christian Asceticism." In his *Tradition and Life in the Church,* pp. 9–122. Philadelphia, 1968. A penetrating study of the origins of asceticism among Christians by a respected Protestant biblical scholar and church historian.

Chitty, Derwas J. *The Desert a City.* Oxford, 1966. Examines the origins of asceticism and monastic life with special attention to developments in the Christian East.

Gribomont, Jean. "Le monachisme au quatrième siècle en Asie Mineure: De Gangres au Messalianisme." In *Studia Patristica,* vol. 2, pp. 400–415. Berlin, 1957. An important essay that reexamines and repudiates earlier hypotheses about the origins and early evolution of Christian monasticism.

Knowles, David. *The Religious Orders in England.* 3 vols. Cambridge, 1948–1959. An exhaustive study of the history of religious orders in the West, with special attention to their development in the British Isles.

Knowles, David. *Christian Monasticism.* New York, 1969. A brief and lucid exposition of the entire history of Christian monastic life.

The Rule of St. Benedict, RB 1980. Collegeville, Minn., 1980. Latin text of the Benedictine rule with English translation by Timothy Fry and extensive commentaries, notes, and essays on the history of Christian religious life by Imogene Baker, published by American Benedictine monks and nuns on the occasion of Benedict's sesquimillennium.

Southern, Richard W. *Western Society and the Church in the Middle Ages.* Harmondsworth, 1970. See pages 214–299 for a succinct but comprehensive account of the rise of newer religious orders in the medieval West.

Veilleux, Armand. "The Abbatial Office in Cenobitic Life." *Monastic Studies* 6 (1968): 3–45. An important study of government, authority, and obedience in Christian monastic life.

Veilleux, Armand. "Évolution de la vie religieuse dans son contexte historico-spirituel." *Collectanea Cisterciensia* 32 (1970): 129–154. A brilliant and comprehensive survey of all Christian religious orders, with special attention to the social and cultural conditions within which they arose.

New Sources

Brown, Peter. *The Body and Society: Men, Women, and Sexual Renunciation In Early Christianity.* New York, 1988.

Constable, Giles. *Monks, Hermits, and Crusaders in Medieval Europe.* London, 1988.

Hunyadi, Zsolt, and József, eds. *The Crusades and the Military Orders: Expanding Frontiers of Medieval Latin Christianity.* Budapest, 2001.

Kollar, Rene. *A Universal Appeal: Aspects of the Revival of Monasticism in the West in the late 19th and Early 20th Centuries.* San Francisco, 1996.

Lanfranc, Archbishop of Canterbury. *The Monastic Constitutions of Lanfranc.* Rev. ed. Edited and translated by David Knowles and Christopher N. L. Brooke. New York, 2002.

Palmer, Bernard. *Men of Habit: The Franciscan Ideal in Action.* Norwich, U.K., 1994.

Saxby, Trevor Johns. *Pilgrims of a Common Life: Christian Communities of Goods through the Centuries.* Scottsdale, Ariz., 1987.

Sutera, Judith, and Deborah Vess, et al. *The Monastery and the City.* Petersham, Mass., 1988.

Wynne, Edward. *Traditional Catholic Religious Orders: Living in Community.* New Brunswick, N.J., 1988.

NATHAN D. MITCHELL (1987)
Revised Bibliography

RELIGIOUS DIVERSITY.

[*This entry examines the origins and differing patterns of development of the world's major religious traditions, as well as the varying patterns of interaction between these religions and the social, political, and economic frameworks with which they coexist.*]

Religion and religious conceptions, beyond being systems of belief and patterns of worship, constitute a central component, as Max Weber pointed out, in the construction of the basic symbolic and institutional premises of societies and civilizations. This article shall explore systematically the relationship between several crucial aspects of religions and the construction of institutional features of societies and civilizations.

"PAGAN" AND "GREAT" RELIGIONS. This article shall concentrate on the analysis of a basic distinction between two broad types of religions: the so-called pagan religions (without, for reasons of space, going into the many differences between them) and the "great" religions (with some distinctions drawn from within the latter). It will explore some of the major ways in which some of the basic characteristics of these religions, especially of the religious belief systems, have shaped the contours of the respective civilizations in which they were institutionalized.

The societies in which different types of pagan religions were predominant have, of course, been many, and they include all tribal or preliterate societies, as well as many so-called archaic ones such as those of the ancient Near and Middle East, South and Southeast Asia, Japan, Mesoamerica, and many others.

The civilizations shaped by the great religions were denoted by Karl Jaspers in his work *Vom Ursprung und Ziel der Geschichte* (1949), as the "Axial Age" civilizations, including ancient Israel, ancient Greece, the early Christian world, Zoroastrian Iran, early imperial China, the Hindu and Buddhist civilizations, and, though postdating the Axial Age proper, the Islamic world.

The central distinction between these two broad types of religions is focused on the nature of the perception and definition of the relationship between what is mundane, or "given," and what is "transmundane" (otherworldly).

In all human societies, the transmundane order has been perceived as somewhat different, usually higher and stronger, than the mundane one. In pre-Axial Age, pagan civilizations, this higher world was symbolically structured according to principles very similar to those of the mundane or lower one; in other words, there existed a high degree of homology between them. Relatively similar symbolic terms or connotations were used for the definitions of both gods and humans and for both the mundane and transmundane orders, even if there always was a stress on the differences between them. In such societies the transmundane world was usually equated with a concrete setting, "the otherworld," which was the abode of the dead, the world of spirits, not entirely unlike the mundane world in detail.

By contrast, in the Axial Age civilizations, the perception of a sharp disjunction between the mundane and transmundane worlds developed. There was a concomitant stress on the existence of a higher, transcendental moral or metaphysical order that is beyond any given this-worldly or otherworldly reality.

On the symbolic or ideological level the development of these conceptions gives rise to the problem of salvation, to use Weber's terminology. The roots of the quest for salvation are manifest in the consciousness of death and the arbitrariness of human actions and social arrangements. The search for some type of immortality and a way to overcome such arbitrariness are universal to all societies. In societies where the mundane and transmundane worlds are defined in relatively homologous terms, the search for immortality has generally been envisaged in terms of some physical continuity; it is usually seen as conditional to the fulfillment of one's concrete obligation to one's group.

This no longer holds true for civilizations where there is an emphasis on the chasm between the transcendental and the mundane order and a conception of a higher moral or metaphysical order. While the concept of immortality in such civilizations may or may not still be tied to bodily images and to ideas of physical resurrection, the very possibility of some continuity beyond this world is usually seen in terms of the reconstruction of human behavior and personality. This reconstruction tends to be based on the precepts of the higher moral or metaphysical order through which the chasm between the transcendental and mundane orders is bridged; as Gananath Obeyesekere has put it, rebirth eschatology becomes ethicized.

Structure of Axial Age Elites. The conceptions outlined above were developed and articulated by a relatively new social element, a new type of intellectual elite, which became aware of the necessity of actively ordering the world according to some transcendental vision. The best illustrations of such elites are the Jewish prophets and priests, the Greek philosophers and Sophists, the Chinese literati, the Hindu brahmans, the Buddhist *saṃgha,* and the Islamic *'ulamā'*. These new elites, which developed in conjunction with the process of institutionalization of these visions, generally differed from the ritual, magical, and sacral specialists of the pre-Axial Age civilizations. Intellectuals and clerics alike were recruited and legitimized according to distinct criteria, and were organized in autonomous settings, apart from those of their basic ascriptive units. They acquired a society-wide status of their own. They also tended to become independent of other categories of elites and social groups and competed strongly with these others, especially over the articulation and control of symbols and media of communication. Such competition became intensive because a parallel transformation had taken place in the structure of other elites, who also developed claims for an autonomous place in the construction of the cultural and social order. They saw themselves not only as performing specific technical, functional activities, but also as the potential carriers of a distinct cultural and social order related to the transcendental vision prevalent in their respective societies. The nonpolitical cultural elites and the political elites each saw themselves as the autonomous articulators of the new order, with the other type potentially inferior to and accountable to themselves.

Moreover neither of these groups of elites was homogenous. There developed a multiplicity of secondary cultural, political, and educational elites, each of which often carried a different conception of the cultural and social order. These elites were the most active in the restructuring of the world and the institutional creativity that developed in these societies.

Construction of Axial Age Societies. Common to all these elites were several tendencies with respect to the restructuring of the world and the construction of personality, civilization, and social order according to a transcendental vision and the principles of a higher metaphysical, ethical, or sacred order.

The given, mundane order was perceived in these civilizations as incomplete, inferior, and even in need of being reconstructed according to the conception of salvation, or the bridging of the chasm between the transcendental and the mundane orders.

Personal identity was usually taken beyond the definition of humankind in terms of the primordial givens of human existence, beyond the various technical needs of daily activities, to be constructed around the central mode or modes of human action through which the tensions between the transcendental and the mundane order are resolved. Purely personal virtues, such as courage, or interpersonal ones, such as solidarity, mutual help, and the like, have been taken out of their primordial (i.e., given) framework and combined in different, often dialectical, modes with the attributes needed to enact such a resolution. This combination resulted in a new level of tensions in the structure of the personality.

These conceptions also had far-reaching implications for institutions. The most common has been the high degree of symbolic and ideological orientation of the major aspects of institutional structure, manifest in the construction of distinct civilizational frameworks, collectivities, and autonomous centers, as well as the growth of conceptions of the accountability of rulers and new patterns of political struggle.

Civilizational collectivities. Some collectivities and institutional spheres (for instance, political, military, or economic) were singled out as the most appropriate carriers of these attributes that were required for resolution. As a result, new types of collectivities were created, or seemingly natural and "primordial" groups were endowed with special status couched in terms of the perception of the tension between the transcendental and mundane order and its resolution. In this context, the most important innovation was the development of cultural or religious collectivities—as distinct from ethnic or political ones—even if some embryonic elements of this development existed in some of those societies where this tension had not been institutionalized. The membership of these collectivities tended to become imbued with a strong ideological orientation and to become involved in ideological struggle. An aspect of this struggle was the insistence on the exclusiveness and closure of the group, and on the distinction between inner and outer social and cultural space as defined by it. This led to attempts to structure the different cultural, political, and ethnic collectivities in some hierarchical order, which usually became a focus of ideological and political conflict.

Centers and center-periphery relations. Related to the construction of such major collectivities was the tendency toward the development of autonomous organization of the social centers and toward a relatively strong emphasis on the symbolic distinctiveness of the centers in relation to the periphery. Such centers have been conceived as the major loci of the charismatic attributes of the transcendental vision, and hence also of the construction of cultural and societal orders. These attributes of centrality became naturally related to the institutional spheres that show the closest affinity to the focus of the transcendental tension, and the centers most closely related to these spheres became autonomous and distinct from the periphery.

At the same time, the symbolic differentiation of the center gave rise to its tendency to permeate the periphery and to reorganize it according to its own, autonomous criteria. Carriers of the great traditions attempted to pull the little traditions into their orbit, and the latter tried to dissociate themselves from the great traditions, to profane them, and also, paradoxically enough, to generate their own distinct ideology.

In all these civilizations (as distinct from pre-Axial Age civilizations) there also took place a far-reaching reordering of the relationship between the political and the higher, transcendental order. The political order, as the central locus of the mundane order, was usually conceived as lower than the transcendental one; accordingly it had to be restructured according to the precepts of the latter. Above all, the political order had to reflect the perception of the proper mode of overcoming the tension between the transcendental and the mundane order (i.e., "salvation").

At the same time the nature of the rulers became greatly transformed. The king-god, who embodied the cosmic and earthly orders alike, disappeared, and a secular ruler, in principle accountable to some higher order, appeared. Thus there reemerged the conception of the accountability of the rulers and of the community to a higher authority—God, divine law, and the like. Accordingly, the possibility of calling a ruler to judgment emerged.

Autonomous spheres of law and conceptions of human rights also began to develop. These tended to be somewhat distinct from ascriptively bound custom and from purely customary law, and while their scope varied greatly from society to society, all were established according to some distinct and autonomous criteria.

Parallel developments have also taken place in the structuring of social hierarchies and the economy, which became imbued in varying degrees and modes with broader ideological dimensions.

Dynamics of Axial Age civilizations. All these modes of reconstruction of the social and civilizational orders were not, however, static; indeed they were the focus of continuous struggle and change, and cannot be understood except in connection with the tensions inherent in the institutionalization of the tension between the transcendental and the mundane order as well as of the quest to overcome it. Such institutionalization generated an awareness of a great range of possibilities or visions of the very definition of such tensions; of the proper mode of their resolution as well as an awareness of the partiality or incompleteness of any given institutionalization of such vision. Historically, institutionalization was never a simple or peaceful process. It has usually been connected with a continuous struggle among many groups and their respective visions.

Once the conception of a basic tension between the transcendental and the mundane order was fully recognized and institutionalized in a society, or at least within its center, any definition and resolution of this tension became in itself very problematic. It usually contained strong heterogeneous and even contradictory elements, and its elaboration in fully articulated terms generated the possibility of different emphases, directions, and interpretations, all of which have been reinforced by the historical existence of multiple visions carried by different groups. Because of this, no single vision could be taken as given or complete.

This multiplicity of alternative visions gave rise to an awareness of the uncertainty of different roads to salvation, of alternative conceptions of social and cultural order, and of the seeming arbitrariness of any single solution. Such awareness has become a constituent element of the self-consciousness of these civilizations, especially among the carriers of the great traditions. This was closely related to the development of a high degree of "second order" thinking, of a reflexivity turning on the basic premises of the social and cultural orders.

Another element common to all these civilizations emerged from the combination of the conception of possible ways of salvation, alternative cultural and social orders, and the structuring of time. This element is the utopian vision: an alternative cultural and social order beyond any given place or time. Such visions contain many of the millenarian and revivalist elements that can also be found in pagan religions, but they go beyond them by realizing the necessity of constructing the mundane order according to the precepts of the higher one, and of searching for an alternative, "better" order beyond any given time and place.

The full impact of these dynamics can be understood only in connection with the nature of the social groups that were most active in the structuring of these civilizations, the major societal elites that developed within them, and the various autonomous intellectual and political elites mentioned above.

Of crucial importance for my analysis are the following facts: these elites were, as has been indicated above, heterogeneous; they were in constant competition with one another; and they were members not only of the ruling coalition, but also were the most active element in the movements of protest and processes of change that developed in these societies. They were above all involved in the construction of new sects and heterodoxies that upheld various alternative visions and conceptions of the social and cultural order and that became closely connected with the struggle among different elites, indeed often becoming the foci of such struggle. Because of this connection there emerged in these civilizations the possibility of structural and ideological linkages among different movements of protest and foci of political conflict (particularly rebellions, central political struggle, and religious or intellectual heterodoxies), and the possibility that all such movements, as well as sects and heterodoxies, would influence the center or centers of the society.

It is thus that there developed a new type of civilizational dynamics that transformed group conflicts into potential class and ideological conflicts and cult conflicts into struggles between the orthodox and the heterodox. Conflicts between tribes and societies became missionary crusades for the transformation of civilizations. The zeal for reorganization, as shaped by each society's concept of salvation, made the whole world at least potentially subject to cultural-political reconstruction. In all these new developments the different sectarian movements and heterodoxies played a central role.

Differences between Axial Age civilizations. Beyond the characteristics common to all the Axial Age civilizations, far-reaching differences developed among them. These were shaped by many conditions, two of which have been of special importance from the point of view of my analysis. One refers to variations in the basic cultural orientations, in the basic ideas or visions concerning civilizations, and their implications for institutions. The other set of conditions refers to different social arenas in which these institutional tendencies can be played out.

First of all, among the various cultural orientations there are crucial differences in the very definition of the tension between the transcendental and mundane orders and the modes of resolving this tension. There is the distinction between those cases in which the tension was couched in relatively secular terms (as in Confucianism and other classical Chinese belief systems and, in a somewhat different way, in the Greek and Roman worlds), and those cases in which the tension was conceived in terms of a distance between basic religious terms (as in the great monotheistic religions, Hinduism, and Buddhism).

A second distinction within the latter cases is that between the monotheistic religions, in which there was a concept of God standing outside the universe and potentially guiding it, and those systems, like Hinduism and Buddhism, in which the transcendental, cosmic system was conceived in impersonal, almost metaphysical terms, in a state of continuous existential tension with the mundane system.

Another closely related distinction lies in the focus of the resolution of the transcendental tensions, or, again in Weberian terms, salvation. Here the distinction is among purely this-worldly, purely otherworldly, and mixed this-worldly and otherworldly conceptions. It is probably no accident that the secular conception of salvation was connected (as in China and to some degree in the ancient world) with an almost wholly this-worldly approach, while the metaphysical, nondeistic conception of this tension (as in Hinduism and Buddhism), tended toward an otherworldly conception of salvation, and the great monotheistic religions tended to stress combinations of this-worldly and otherworldly conceptions.

These cultural orientations, as articulated by different elites, shaped to a very high degree the symbolic autonomy and characteristics of the new types of elites and ruling coalitions that characterized the post-Axial-Age civilizations. That is, they shaped the relations between them, their place in the ruling coalitions, the modes of control of the major institutional spheres effected by them, and the degree to which different ruling elites, secondary elites, and heterodoxies became involved with processes of societal change and transformation. The differences in the cultural orientations and structure of elites in various Axial Age civilizations had far-reaching impact on their institutions, structure, and dynamics—above all on the structure of centers, of center-periphery relations, and of collectivities—as well as on patterns of societal and civilizational change.

Otherworldly Axial Age civilizations. In most otherworldly civilizations there developed patrimonial regimes, to some degree similar to those that can be found in pre-Axial Age civilizations, yet with some crucial differences.

Such systems were characterized by a relatively low level of economic development, weak internal markets, a stronger orientation toward external markets, and strong extractive policies as well as, on the whole, a low degree of coalescence between the boundaries of the collectivities and the civilizational frameworks. The predominant coalitions within these systems were composed of relatively nonautonomous political and religious elites. The latter were also nonautonomous in most pagan societies, and in the post-Axial Age civilizations they were autonomous in the religious but not the political field.

In a parallel manner, the patrimonial societies were characterized by a relative lack of structural (as compared with ecological and symbolic) distinctiveness of the center from the periphery and usually by an adaptive attitude of the center toward the periphery. Within these patrimonial societies there generally developed a lower degree of society-wide class consciousness and symbolic articulation of the major types of collectivities.

The major distinction between those patrimonial regimes of the great post-Axial Age civilizations (Hindu, Buddhist, Islamic, and Latin American Catholic) and those that belonged to pagan civilizations lay first of all in the fact that the major types of elites (cultural and political alike) in the latter case were embedded in basic ascriptive frameworks, whereas in the former, the religious elites (and the political ones to a smaller degree, as in the Latin American Spanish empire) were autonomous mainly in the religious sphere. The carriers of the cultural and social order were those cultural elites that developed the great traditions and special, broader civilizational frameworks based on a strong perception of the tension between the transcendental and the mundane orders, the likes of which could not be found among the other pagan patrimonial regimes. Concomitantly, those elites created centers that were distinct from their own periphery in the religious sphere, as well as special interlinking networks between these centers and the periphery.

Hence these societies tended to develop more compact and dynamic political regimes (of which one type was the Theravāda Buddhistic gallactic polity as analyzed by Stanley J. Tambiah) while at the same time the national communities became imbued with stronger universal religious symbols. In times of crisis the religious elites also developed some autonomous activities.

Opposed to this development, in Axial Age civilizations in which a this-worldly orientation (as in China), or a mixed this-worldly and otherworldly orientation (as in the Byzantine and Russian empires and, to a smaller degree, the Abbasid and Ottoman empires) was prevalent, imperial systems, or mixed imperial and feudal ones, tended to develop. Western and central Europe are two important examples of such systems, which were characterized by highly coalescent boundaries of the major collectivities, political centralization, relatively developed economic systems, a preponderance of internal markets, and highly autonomous elites.

Most of the elites in the imperial and imperial-feudal societies tended to define themselves in autonomous terms, having their own resource bases and potential access to the center of society, and to each other. This was above all true with respect to the articulators of the cultural and social order (i.e., the cultural and religious elites), the political elite, and, to a lesser degree, the representatives of different collectivities and the economic elite.

Within these societies, moreover, a multiplicity of secondary elites developed, such as various sectarian groups in the religious sphere, or various social and political groups or movements. These elites impinged on those of the center and the periphery, and shaped protest movements and political activities within them. Each of the primary and secondary elites could constitute the starting point of movements of protest or of political struggle possessing a high level of organizational and symbolic articulation.

These elites also generated specific types of center-periphery relations, the major characteristics of which were a high level of symbolic and ecological distinctiveness from their respective centers and the continuous attempts of the centers not only to extract resources from the periphery but also to permeate and reconstruct the periphery according to their own premises. Thus, the political, religious, and cultural centers constituted the foci and loci of the various great traditions that developed in these societies as distinct from the local traditions. The permeation of the periphery by the centers was manifest in the latter's promotion of widespread channels of communication and in the attempts to break through the ascriptive ties of the periphery.

Closely connected to this type of center-periphery relationship in these societies was the development of a high level of articulation of symbols of society-wide social hierarchies, of some political consciousness of the upper strata, and of high ideological symbolization and mutual orientation among the major religious, political, and even ethnic and national collectivities. Although each collectivity tended to develop a relatively high degree of autonomy, they also constituted mutual referents for each other. For example, being a good "Hellene" was identified, in the Byzantine empire, with citizenship, and vice versa. This high degree of symbolic articulation and distinctiveness of the major institutional aspects of these imperial and imperial-feudal societies, was closely related to certain types of cultural orientations which, as has been seen, were articulated by these elites.

The most important difference between imperial and other types of regimes (such as those that were patrimonial or decentralized) was found in the structure of their ruling elites, the cultural orientations they articulated, the modes of control they exercised, and the relative autonomy of the major social strata. Differences existed between the monolithic elites, usually evincing strong this-worldly orientation, and the more heterogeneous ones, usually carrying some combination of this-worldly and otherworldly orientations. The latter patterns could also be distinguished according to the degree to which heterogeneous elites were segregated or interwoven. Both the monolithic and segregated elites tended to exercise relatively restricted modes of control. While the segregated elites were inclined to exert more intensive control than the monolithic ones, the control exercised by the more heterogeneous and closely interwoven elites was more flexible, though often also very intensive. But these possibilities became more fully developed in a political-ecological constellation in certain types of decentralization. This article shall now turn to the analysis of decentralized political-ecological systems.

Religious and social dynamics in Axial Age civilizations. The different Axial Age civilizations were characterized also by patterns of religious and societal dynamics in general and by the impact of religious changes on societal ones in particular. From the point of view of my discussion the most crucial difference is between those civilizations that can legitimately be called heterodoxies and those that are more appropriately labeled sects.

The term *heterodoxy* is, of course, applicable only in cases where one can talk about orthodoxy, and this term in its turn implies certain types of organizational and cognitive doctrinal structures. Organizationally the crucial aspect is, of course, the existence of some type of organized church that attempts to monopolize at least the religious sphere and usually also the relations of this sphere to the political powers. But of no lesser importance is the organization of doctrine, in other words, the very stress on structuring clear cognitive and symbolic boundaries of doctrine.

With respect to both organizational and doctrinal aspects, the major difference among the Axial Age civilizations is that between the monotheistic civilizations (Christianity in particular) and Hinduism and Buddhism. (Confucian China constitutes a sort of in-between type.)

Within Christianity, these organizational and doctrinal aspects of orthodoxy, as well as full-fledged churches that constituted potentially active and autonomous partners of the ruling coalitions, developed in the fullest way. In Judaism and Islam these developments were weaker; there developed rather powerful but not always as fully organized and autonomous organizations of clerics.

Similarly, in Christianity, and to a smaller, but yet not insignificant, degree also in Judaism and Islam, there developed strong tendencies toward the structuring of relatively clear cognitive doctrinal and ritual boundaries.

In comparison, in Hinduism and Buddhism—despite a very strong transcendental and otherworldly orientation—the structuring of cognitive doctrines (as distinct from ritual) did not constitute a central aspect or premise. Hence, though it is not impossible to talk about something akin to church in Buddhism—albeit a much more loosely organized one than in the monotheistic traditions—it is very difficult to talk about heterodoxy. At the same time sectarianism abounds, Buddhism itself being, in a sense, a sect developing out of Hinduism.

The various Hindu sects, and Buddhism itself, did indeed have far-reaching impact on the structuring of the mundane spheres of their respective civilizations. They extended the scope of the different national and political communities and imbued them with new symbolic dimensions. They also changed some of the bases and criteria of participation in the civilizational communities, as was the case in Judaism, in the *bhakti* movement and, above all, in Buddhism when an entirely new civilizational framework was constructed.

Buddhism also introduced new elements into the political scene, above all the special way in which the *saṃgha,* usually a very compliant group politically, could in some cases become a sort of moral conscience of the community, calling the rulers to some accountability.

But this impact was of a different nature from that of the struggles between the ruling orthodoxies and the numerous heterodoxies that developed within the monotheistic civilizations. Of crucial importance has been the fact that, in these latter cases, a central aspect of the struggles was the attempt to reconstruct the political and cultural centers of their respective societies and that, because of this, these struggles became a central part of the histories of these civilizations, shaping the major contours of their development.

The impact of religion on society in China and in the Islamic world was greatly shaped by their prevalent orientations and the structure of their respective elites and heterodoxies, that is, by their respective political-ecological settings; by whether they were small or great societies; by whether they were societies with continuous, compact boundaries, or with cross-cutting, flexible boundaries; by their economic structure; and last by their specific historical experience, especially in terms of encounters with other societies (such as mutual penetration, conquest, or colonization).

The interplay between the different constellations of the cultural orientations analyzed above, their carriers, and their respective visions of restructuring the world (and the concrete arenas and historical conditions in which such visions could be concretized), have shaped the institutional contours and dynamics of different Axial Age civilizations, both in the "historical" periods as well as in the transition to modernity, and in the different modes of modernity, that have developed within them.

SEE ALSO Intellectuals; Modernity.

BIBLIOGRAPHY

Eisenstadt, Shmuel N. *Revolution and the Transformation of Societies.* New York, 1978.

Eisenstadt, Shmuel N. "The Axial Age: The Emergence of Transcendental Visions and the Rise of Clerics." *European Journal of Sociology* 23 (1982): 294–314.

Jaspers, Karl. *Vom Ursprung und Ziel der Geschichte.* Zurich, 1949.

Obeyesekere, Gananath. "The Rebirth Eschatology and Its Transformation: A Contribution to the Sociology of Early Buddhism." In *Karma and Rebirth in Classical Indian Traditions,* edited by Wendy Doniger O'Flaherty, pp. 137–164. Berkeley, Calif., 1980.

Schluchter, Wolfgang. "The Paradox of Rationalisation." In Guenther Roth and Wolfgang Schluchter's *Max Weber's Vision of History: Ethics and Methods,* pp. 11–64. Berkeley, Calif., 1979.

Voegelin, Eric. *Order and History.* 4 vols. Baton Rouge, 1956–1974.

Weber, Max. *The Religion of China: Confucianism and Taoism.* Glencoe, Ill., 1951.

Weber, Max. *Ancient Judaism.* Glencoe, Ill., 1952.

Weber, Max. *The Religion of India: The Sociology of Hindu and Buddhism.* Glencoe, Ill., 1958.

Wisdom, Doubt and Revelation: Perspectives on the First Millennium B. C. Special issue of *Daedalus* 104 (Spring 1975).

New Sources

Arjomand, Said Amir, ed. *The Political Dimension of Religion.* Albany, 1993.

Bloom, Irene, J. Paul Martin, and Wayne Proudfoot, eds. *Religious Diversity and Human Rights.* New York, 1996.

Casanova, José. *Public Religions and the Modern World.* Chicago, 1994.

Chittick, William. *Imaginal Worlds: Ibn Al-ʿArabi and the Problem of Religious Diversity.* Albany, N.Y., 1994.

Griffiths, Paul. *Problems of Religious Diversity.* Malden, Mass., 2001.

McKim, Robert. *Religious Ambiguity and Religious Diversity,* New York, 2001.

Quinn, Philip, and Kevin Meeker, eds. *The Philosophical Challenge of Religious Diversity.* New York, 1999.

SHMUEL N. EISENSTADT (1987)
Revised Bibliography

RELIGIOUS EDUCATION is an issue of considerable controversy and debate in Western societies, for three main reasons. First, there is a conceptual problem, depending on whether it is perceived as a religious activity or an educational activity. In the former case, it may be defined as nurture or faith development; in the latter, it is an activity designed to increase understanding of an important dimension of human existence and to encourage cross-cultural understanding. Second, in terms of actual provision, religious education may mean one of three things: an item on the curriculum of the school; the teaching with which religious groups supplement the public schooling their children receive; or a religious approach to the whole educational process (often found in "faith schools") that rejects contemporary secular values. Third, different religions and denominations have different understandings of religious education, often based on a rich history of provision, and this adds another layer of complexity to the already wide diversity of national policy and established practice in religious education that exists in different countries. The result is that different issues dominate national debates, and international comparisons are difficult. These three issues provide the framework for this entry.

TWO CONCEPTS OF RELIGIOUS EDUCATION. There is an important distinction to be made between education *in* religion and education *about* religion. The former, sometimes called *religious instruction,* is a religious activity designed to nurture young people in a particular faith, and thus to preserve that faith across the generations. The latter is educational in the sense of aiming to develop children's knowledge and understanding of religion while leaving them free to choose their own path in life. Although it is tempting to insist that the former should be called *religious instruction* and only the latter *religious education,* this does not accord with contemporary usage. Both practices are commonly called *religious education,* and one unfortunate outcome is that many people assume that in the United States *all* religious education in public schools is unconstitutional, not just the former kind. For convenience, the former will be called *type A* religious education, the latter *type B.*

Type A religious education may be formal or informal and typically occurs in the home, the family, a place of worship, a religious institution, or with a local community of believers. It also takes place in public schools in countries where the majority of citizens share a single religious faith (including many Muslim and some Roman Catholic countries) and in denominational schools, whether private or state-funded. Sometimes called *catechesis,* or the *confessional* approach, type A religious education involves faith development through the transmission of the teachings of a particular religion or denomination. It is justified in terms of both the interests of the faith group (preserving and perhaps increasing the numbers of adherents and maintaining and developing the faith) and the interests of the child (providing emotional stability and continuity with the beliefs of the child's significant others, and, more importantly, encouraging the child to engage with and be transformed by the truths of the faith). Both globally and historically, the vast majority of religious education is of this kind. However, type A religious education is criticized for paying inadequate attention to such liberal values as critical openness and personal autonomy; for teaching as truth beliefs that are significantly controversial; for defining knowledge in terms of dogma, revelation, and religious authority rather than in terms of rationally justifiable beliefs;

and for failing to prepare children adequately for life in a multicultural, multifaith society.

Type B religious education, on the other hand, involves teaching children about religion—and about a number of different religions—without any expectation that they will necessarily develop their own personal religious commitments. The aim is to produce people who are "religiously educated" or "religiously literate," in the sense of understanding different systems of religious belief and being able to reflect knowledgeably on a range of religious issues. Type B religious education is justified on the grounds that religion is so fundamental to human existence and has had such a profound influence on history, philosophy, art, music, literature, morality, and other domains of knowledge that people can hardly be considered educated if they know nothing of religion. This approach is fully compatible with liberal education in its aims and methods. Teachers are required to adopt a position of neutrality and impartiality in their presentation of a variety of religious and nonreligious worldviews. Teaching children about different religions makes them aware of alternatives and enables them to make informed autonomous choices about their own commitments and ways of life. Learning about the diversity of religions in the world can help to break down religious prejudice and can contribute to the development of a tolerant, harmonious, and respectful multicultural society. This approach to religious education has been promoted strongly in the United States in recent years by scholars such as James W. Fraser, Charles Haynes, Robert Nash, Nel Noddings, and Warren Nord, who make up what is sometimes called the "New Consensus." However, Type B religious education is criticized for reducing what believers call revealed truth to cultural practice, for encouraging relativism, for prioritizing the individual over the community, and for undermining commitment to any particular faith by teaching that all faiths are equally worthy of respect.

At first glance, these two types of religious education are quite incompatible: one cannot both reinforce a religious upbringing and encourage children to adopt a critical stance towards it at the same time. The result would be confusion and uncertainty. However, some scholars have argued that the two approaches can exist in a kind of creative tension. First, though one type involves looking at religion from the inside and the other from the outside, both are examining the same phenomenon. Second, children who feel good about their own identity (which is developed by type A religious education) are in a strong position to be tolerant and respectful towards other faiths and to make a positive contribution to a pluralist society (which are precisely the goals of type B religious education). Third, anxieties about different types of religious education often presuppose an old-fashioned, rigid transmission form of pedagogy; a constructivist approach, on the other hand, suggests that what children take from religious education depends to a large extent on what they bring to it and thus anticipates more open outcomes.

In practical terms, a threefold pattern of provision is likely to emerge in liberal democracies in view of the issues that have been discussed so far: (1) in the public school, students may be introduced to religious beliefs, practices, and issues in a nondogmatic, phenomenological way as part of the school curriculum; (2) in the Sunday school, *madrasah*, synagogue, *gurdwara*, temple, or other place of worship, children will be taught the traditions and practices of their own faith from a believer's perspective; and (3) those parents who are unhappy with the split between secular and religious learning have the option of sending their child to a religious or denominational school, for which they may have to pay fees. Each of these forms of provision is commonly called *religious education.*

PATTERNS OF PROVISION IN RELIGIOUS EDUCATION. In many countries, although not the United States, the term *religious education* commonly refers to an item on the school curriculum; indeed, in England and Wales until 1988, religious education was the only compulsory school subject. In denominational schools, religious education is typically taught from the perspective of a single faith (type A) and in nondenominational schools from the perspective of a diversity of faiths (type B).

In the school curriculum. In England and Wales, the religious education syllabus in nondenominational schools has to be determined by a committee made up of representatives of teachers' unions, local councilors, and representatives from the Church of England and other religious denominations. The justification for teaching religious education as a separate subject is that religion is a distinguishable form of knowledge known at the university level by the titles of theology, religious studies, or divinity, having its own distinctive concepts and truth criteria. Opposition to the separate teaching of religious education comes from two sides: those who believe religion to be a human construct may prefer it to be taught through history, sociology, psychology, anthropology, or its various cultural manifestations (art, literature, music, and so on); while those who believe that all knowledge is religious may prefer religion to be integrated throughout the curriculum.

In nondenominational schools, the subject matter of religious education usually falls into two categories: learning about religion and learning from religion. "Learning about religion" entails learning about the religious beliefs, practices, and values of specific religions, including their festivals, places of worship, ethical codes, sacred texts, prophets and leaders, denominational differences, stories, pilgrimages, rites of passage, symbolism, artifacts, forms of artistic expression, lifestyles, religious experience, language and expression, and forms of prayer, meditation, and worship. There is room for debate about which specific religions should be taught (clearly not all can be taught, since the United States alone is home to more than five hundred different religions, denominations, and sects), but the most common pattern is for up to six major world religions to be taught (typically Hinduism, Judaism, Buddhism, Christianity, Islam, and Sikhism), plus any other religions of particular local significance. Learning about religion should also include learning about religious diversity, natural religion, implicit religion, emotional responses to religion, dialogue between religions, arguments against religious beliefs, and nonreligious worldviews. "Learning from religion" gives space for students to reflect on some of the big questions raised by religion, such as the existence of God, the meaning of death and the possibility of life after death, debates between science and religion or postmodernism and religion, and the problems of evil, suffering, and war. Learning from religion also encourages students to explore such concepts as spirituality, love, right and wrong, and identity and commitment, and to develop sensitivity, tolerance, respect, and understanding towards those whose beliefs differ from their own.

There remain many unresolved questions about religious education as a school subject, particularly relating to the role of the teacher, teaching approaches and strategies, and the sequencing of the subject matter. Do teachers need to have some experience of, or commitment to, religion in order to teach it effectively? Should they share their own beliefs and values with students or keep quiet about them? Should different religions be taught together (for example, through studying a topic such as festivals or sacred books) or is such an approach liable to confuse children? Do young children have a natural spirituality that schools should nurture, or is it the task of religious education, like other school subjects, to develop rational understanding? Most of these are value judgments rather than empirical questions that can be resolved by research, and in any case the amount of research into religious education seems to have declined since Kenneth Hyde's comprehensive review of the topic published in 1990.

In supplementary schooling. In pluralist societies where there is a system of common schools, most faith groups provide some form of supplementary schooling through which their children are nurtured in the faith and taught its basic beliefs and practices. Though few groups would call this *religious education,* preferring a title that identified the specific faith concerned, it is an important part of any overview of the provision of religious teaching. Such teaching may take place in a private house or a place of worship, is usually privately funded by parents or the faith community, and is exclusively type A religious education. There is a close similarity of approach to supplementary schooling among different faiths and countries.

Sunday schools have a long, well-documented history, and they are a major method used by (mainly Protestant) churches to pass on Bible stories and Christian moral teaching to children. Confirmation classes provide a more formal introduction to Christian beliefs and practices, leading to full church membership, while Christian youth clubs, holiday camps, and other activities may be used as a general introduction to Christian values. Bible classes provide continuing adult education. Similarly, many Jews in Western countries send their children for supplementary schooling at the local synagogue, where they learn about Jewish identity, beliefs, values, and practices; study the Torah and perhaps Hebrew; and prepare for the ceremony of bar or bat mitzvah. Though such schools tend to cooperate in large cities, making use of the same teaching materials and organizing joint summer camps and other activities, they are not centrally controlled. Comparatively few children continue with such schooling beyond the age of thirteen. Hindu temples and Sikh *gurdwaras* in the West are beginning to set up evening or Sunday schools to teach children the language of their scriptures and their faith communities and also to supplement the religious education that goes on in the home.

Islamic supplementary education is also well established in most Western countries. Muslim children from the ages of about four to thirteen attend the local *maktab* or *madrasah* (mosque school) for up to two hours daily after regular school to learn Arabic, Qurʾanic recitation, the basic requirements of the *sharīʿah,* and the principal Islamic beliefs. Children who wish to memorize the whole Qurʾān and become a *ḥāfiẓ* may attend in the mornings as well. The language of instruction is commonly Arabic in North America and Australia, Urdu or Punjabi in the United Kingdom, and Turkish in Germany, though the language of the country of residence is increasingly being used. For a variety of reasons, however, many Muslims consider this provision to be educationally unsatisfactory: it makes extra demands on children's time, the premises are often inadequate, the teachers unqualified, and the methods (including rote learning and strict discipline) compare unfavorably with schools in the state system. To solve this problem, while at the same time fostering integration, several European countries (including Belgium, some German provinces, and some British local authorities) have introduced specific Islamic instruction for Muslim students in state schools. This solution also has its problems; in particular, it does nothing to resolve the conflicting values to which Muslim children are exposed. For a growing number of Muslims, the answer is separate Muslim schools.

In faith schools. The third meaning of religious education is full-time schooling that is permeated by religion in a conscious attempt to exclude secular influence. The term *faith school,* which has only recently come into widespread usage, covers all full-time schools with a religious foundation and a religious vision, whether Christian, Muslim, Jewish, or other. Some countries (including Great Britain, Denmark, the Netherlands, and Israel) and some provinces (including Newfoundland in Canada) fund denominational as well as secular state schools, and many other countries (including the United States, France, Belgium, India, Indonesia, and Japan) allow private faith schools. Faith schools typically seek to preserve a religious ethos but vary significantly in terms of the amount of time spent on religious education, their willingness to admit students and employ teachers of other faiths, and their compatibility with liberal democratic values.

In the United States, more than 10 percent of all children attend private religious schools. About half of these attend Catholic schools, while the other half attend fundamentalist Christian schools or schools belonging to a wide range of denominations, sects, and world religions, including Lutheran, Calvinist, Episcopalian, Quaker, Seventh-day Adventist, Orthodox, Mormon, Christian Science, Jewish, Muslim, Buddhist, and Hindu. Proportions are significantly higher in countries where faith schools are state-funded: about two-thirds of all students in the Netherlands and nearly one-quarter of students in Great Britain attend faith schools. Church of England and Roman Catholic schools make up the vast majority of funded faith schools in Great Britain, and Muslim, Hindu, Sikh, and evangelical schools are more numerous in the independent sector.

The reasons for founding faith schools vary widely. Catholic schools were founded because of a perceived Protestant bias in the public schools. Amish schools, on the other hand, seek to reinforce group identity and prepare children to lead a simple, useful, godly life. Muslim schools are typically founded as a result of dissatisfaction with the moral standards in public schools. Jewish schools have been justified as the best way to respond to the danger of absorption into the dominant culture of Western societies. More than anything else, faith schools are an attempt to address an imbalance that many believers find in public schooling, in which secular values take priority over religious ones, religious neutrality silences religious expression in schools, and the message is conveyed that religious belief is either false or unimportant. Faith schools enable parents who are believers to ensure that their children are educated within an appropriate spiritual environment and that their distinctive cultural and religious beliefs are, as far as possible, preserved. Opponents of faith schools, on the other hand, are likely to claim that they are divisive and may encourage intolerance and extremism; that the right of parents to choose their own children's education is trumped by the children's right to an education that does not culturally encapsulate them but liberates them from restrictive backgrounds and develops their personal autonomy; and that parents have no right to expect public funding if they choose a religious education for their children.

Religious Education in the Great Religious Traditions. The nature of the education provided in faith schools depends to a significant extent on the educational theories and practices that have been developed in the religion concerned. Most world faiths have rich traditions of thinking about religious education, often developed over many centuries both by individual scholars and theologians and by the sustained training and research carried out in seminaries and universities.

Within Hinduism, religious education has traditionally been an informal process carried on in the home and local community. Children pick up an understanding of Hindu deities and basic beliefs and practices through participation in daily rituals, such as ablutions and meals, as well as worship at family shrines; through the celebration of festivals, rites of passage, and pilgrimages; and through listening to traditional stories narrated by grandparents, professional storytellers, and temple priests, or (more recently) at the cinema. In classical Hindu teaching, the student stage (*brahmacārin*), centered on the development of spiritual understanding and the relationship between teacher (*gurū*) and disciple, is the first of four stages of life. Since the nineteenth century, a number of educational reformers and leaders (including Rabindranath Tagore, Vivekananda, Mohandas Gandhi, Aurobindo Ghose, Sarvepalli Radhakrishnan, Vinoba Bhave, Jiddu Krishnamurthi, and Sathya Sai Baba) have attempted to develop forms of education in line with Hindu principles. Outside India, Hindus have tended to rely on temple schools to provide children with more structured religious education. There are also some Hindu faith schools in the West, and Hindu University in America, the first Hindu university in the United States, opened in Orlando, Florida, in 2001.

The word *Sikh* means "learner," and this points to the importance of the balanced development of the individual throughout life. At the heart of Sikh education is the development of spiritual and moral values, but Gurū Nānak also displayed a surprisingly modern approach to education in his emphasis on the need for reflection and critical enquiry into traditional ideas. As with Hinduism, the primary responsibility for the religious education of children traditionally lay with the extended family, but outside the Punjab Sikhs have increasingly looked to the *gurdwara* to provide weekend classes in Gurmukhi and the Sikh scriptures for their children. In Great Britain, several full-time Sikh schools have been established as of 2004, including two that are state-funded.

In a sense, the whole of Buddhist teaching is a course of spiritual education, with a strong emphasis on meditation, moral self-discipline, and enlightenment, traditionally passed on by teachers in the monasteries. The Buddha himself made use of many techniques currently favored in contemporary Western religious education, including narrative, analogy, the use of visual aids, and teaching by example, and the qualities expected of teachers in their dealings with pupils are set out in the *Sigālovāda Sutta.* The first full Buddhist universities were established in India and Thailand in the twentieth century, and Soka University of America, the first Buddhist university in the United States, opened in southern California in 2001.

Islam has long-standing traditions of education, and the Qurʾān itself is full of injunctions to pursue knowledge. Of the three Arabic words for education, *tarbīya* implies personal development towards maturity; *taʾdīb* implies moral, social, and cultural refinement; and *taʿlīm* refers to the pursuit of knowledge. The Muslim scholar Abū Ḥāmid al-Ghazālī distinguishes two forms of knowledge: the revealed (which is divine and absolute) and the discovered (which is human and tentative). These should be in harmony and should both lead to God, but the former takes priority.

In the golden age of Islam (750–1150 CE) a large network of educational institutions was established across the Islamic empire, including the *maktab* (writing school), the *ḥalqa* (circle school), the *masjid* (mosque school), and the *madrasah* (school of public instruction), as well as universities in Baghdad, Cairo, and Nishapur. There was an upsurge of Islamic scholarship in all known disciplines at this time, but Islamic education later began to stagnate. European colonizers introduced modern Western systems of education for the elite, leaving traditional Islamic education unchanged for the masses. In the postcolonial period, Islamic states have resolved the inequalities between the two types of education in different ways: some have made Westernized education available to all, others have attempted to Islamize the educational system as thoroughly as possible, and still others have tried to run the two systems side by side as viable alternatives. Muslim immigrants to the West thus arrive with a variety of educational experiences and expectations, though most try to preserve their religious and cultural heritage through supplementary schooling, and a growing number see faith schools as the way to combine the teaching of advanced Western knowledge, especially in science and technology, with a religious ethos that is true to Islamic values and traditions.

Education is a formal requirement of Jewish law, and a system of universal elementary education for Jewish boys seems to have been in place for two thousand years. The traditional school system—the *heder* (or *cheder*) for younger children and the *yeshivah* for older children and adults—taught only the Torah, the Talmud, and other religious writings, but by the late eighteenth century the system diversified as schools came under pressure to include general and vocational studies. At the beginning of the twenty-first century, there is a clear distinction between Jewish education in Israel and Jewish education in the Diaspora. In Israel, except in the religious schools, Jewish identity is developed through Hebrew and the study of Jewish history, literature, and culture, rather than through religious instruction and observances. In the Diaspora, Jewish education is primarily religious and mainly under the control of synagogues, whether Orthodox, Conservative, Reform, or Reconstructionist; like other religious education, it is found in the home, in supplementary schooling for those who attend secular public schools, in full-time faith schools (usually called "day schools" by Jews), in less formal activities (including youth clubs and youth movements), and in the *yeshivah* for higher-level studies.

For many centuries, the history of education in the West was coterminous with the history of Christian education. In the Middle Ages, treatises on education were written by both Augustine and Thomas Aquinas and systems of schooling were developed by teachers like Alcuin. The well-to-do were educated at monastic and cathedral schools, and later at the new universities, while the illiterate were educated mainly through sermons. After the Reformation, greater emphasis was placed on the ability to read the Bible for oneself, and religious education was high on the agenda of Martin Luther and Philipp Melanchthon in Germany, Huldrych Zwingli in Zurich, John Calvin in Geneva, Johannes Amos Comenius in Moravia, and the Anglicans and Puritans or nonconformists in England, the latter including Congregationalists, Baptists, Quakers, and, later, Wesleyans. Each developed their own distinctive forms of religious education and schooling, as well as training colleges for ministers. Meanwhile, new approaches to Catholic education were being developed by the Jesuits and other groups. With the transition to a state system of education in Great Britain in the nineteenth century, the free churches were generally satisfied with the nondenominational religious education provided, which they supplemented with denominational teaching in Sunday schools, and so they abandoned denominational schooling altogether. The Church of England, however, retained its separate schools, and the Catholics built up their own corresponding system of schools. Both systems are state-funded, but whereas the Church of England schools generally see it as their mission to provide an education with a Christian ethos and based on Christian values for the needs of the broader community, the Catholic schools cater primarily to the children of their own faith community.

As of 2004, religious education persists as a compulsory subject in state schools ("community schools") in England and Wales, but now with a world religions focus, and somewhat anachronistically there is still a requirement for a daily act of nondenominational collective worship. In the United States, on the other hand, the clear separation of church and state that is set out in the First Amendment to the U.S. Constitution means that all religious schools must be private establishments and public schools must maintain a position of neutrality between different religions and denominations, and also between religious and nonreligious worldviews. Numerous court cases have clarified precisely where the boundaries lie in terms of the unconstitutional promotion of religion in schools. Elsewhere, liberation theology has had a major impact on the development of education in South America and Africa, and the role of the Orthodox Church in the provision of religious education in Russia has increased dramatically since *perestroika*.

Future Prospects for Religious Education. In countries with adherents from several or all of the above religious traditions—and in some cases many more, for among the 741 accredited colleges and universities in the United States that have a religious affiliation, over seventy different faiths and denominations are represented—the decision to base policy on the liberal values of impartiality, tolerance, and respect for diversity has important consequences for religious education. First, different faith communities should be given opportunities to learn about each other, so that they are more likely to live integrated lives and avoid the fear, prejudice, and intolerance that ignorance breeds. Religious education can play an important role in developing interfaith and cross-cultural understanding. This is in line with the core values of the Religious Education Association of the United States and Canada (founded in 1903), with the approach adopted in British religious education syllabuses since about 1975, and with the views of the New Consensus in the United States, as represented by the writings of Warren Nord, Charles Haynes, and others. It seems likely that, over the first quarter of the twenty-first century, practice in religious education in public schools in different Western pluralist liberal democratic societies will gradually converge. However, this may result in individuals increasingly constructing their own personal religious faith, selecting bits from a smorgasbord of different religions—a phenomenon already being observed among some students exposed to a world faiths approach to religious education. It may also dangerously highlight the split between liberal and fundamentalist approaches to religious education.

Secondly, it is clear that religions and faith groups have the right to nurture their own children in their own faith through religious education, though this does not extend to the right to foreclose children's free choice with respect to religion as they grow older. This means that both supplementary schooling and faith schools will continue to have a place in liberal pluralist societies so long as children are not indoctrinated and so long as they are exposed somewhere within their schooling to other religious and nonreligious worldviews.

Thirdly, it is not the place of a pluralist liberal society to promote one religious worldview over another, or to promote religious belief over nonreligious worldviews. This means that the teaching of an established religion through religious education in a multifaith society is no longer justifiable, and the practice is likely to decline gradually, as is the British requirement of a daily act of collective, nondenominational worship in all British state schools. It also raises questions about the continued funding of faith schools in Western states, although there may be justification for partial funding where faith schools provide a general, as well as a religious, education.

SEE ALSO Initiation, overview article; Scholasticism; Yeshivah.

BIBLIOGRAPHY

Fraser, James W. *Between Church and State: Religion and Public Education in a Multicultural America.* New York, 1999.

Grace, Gerald. *Catholic Schools: Mission, Markets, and Morality.* London, 2002.

Hull, J. M. *Studies in Religious Education.* Lewes, U.K., 1984.

Hyde, Kenneth. *Religion in Childhood and Adolescence: A Comprehensive Review of the Research.* Birmingham, Ala., 1990.

Moran, Gabriel. *Religious Education as a Second Language.* Birmingham, Ala., 1989.

Nash, Robert J. *Faith, Hype, and Clarity: Teaching about Religion in American Schools and Colleges.* New York, 1999.

Nord, Warren A., and Charles C. Haynes *Taking Religion Seriously across the Curriculum.* Alexandria, Va., 1998.

Schreiner, Peter. *Religious Education in Europe.* Münster, Germany, 2000.

Thiessen, Elmer J. *Teaching for Commitment: Liberal Education, Indoctrination, and Christian Nurture.* Montreal, 1993.

Tulasiewicz, Witold, and Cho-Yee To. *World Religions and Educational Practice.* London, 1993.

Journals focusing on religious education include *Religious Education, British Journal of Religious Education, Muslim Education Quarterly,* and *Journal of Beliefs and Values: Studies in Religion and Education.*

J. MARK HALSTEAD (2005)

RELIGIOUS EXPERIENCE.

The term religious experience has been used in three often overlapping senses in the twentieth century: (1) to refer descriptively to the subjective aspect of a tradition or religion in general; (2) to describe the "common core" of religion in general; and (3) to assert a claim with respect to the source of religious knowledge or certainty. In the first instance, it has competed with the terms piety, devotion, and spirituality. In the second and third instances, it has competed with mysticism.

These usages have been associated with key preoccupations of the modern era. In the first case, where the emphasis is on the subjective experience of the individual, experience has been linked with the rise of individualism and the democratization of religious authority. In the second usage, where the emphasis is on the nature of religion, religious experience has been bound up with the problems of commonality and difference in the context of globalization, colonialism, westernization, and the encounter between traditions. In the third usage, where the focus is on how we know (epistemology), religious experience has been associated with the question of truth in the context of Enlightenment critiques of traditional sources of religious knowledge and social scientific explanations of the origins of religion.

This entry provides a history of the use of the concept of religious experience rather than a history of religious experience per se. The use of the term is discussed under the following headings: (1) the concept of experience and its analogues within various traditions; (2) religious experience in relation to religion in general; and (3) critical approaches to religious experience in recent scholarship.

While there are traditional terms within most, if not all, traditions that have experiential overtones to the modern ear, the way and the extent to which these traditional terms have been brought into modern, comparative discourses has varied. The first section provides an overview of the way in which selected traditions have engaged with modern Euro-American experience-related discourses. The second section highlights three key figures—William James (1842–1910), Sarvepalli Radhakrishnan (1888–1975), and Joachim Wach (1889–1955)—each of whom understood religion in general in terms of religious experience, albeit in very different ways.

Disparate theoretical assumptions (philosophical, theological and/or social scientific) led to different understandings of religious experience—both in terms of what counts as religious experience and how it could or should be explained. Depending on the author's underlying theoretical perspective and/or apologetic aims, competing terms, such as enthusiasm, visions, mysticism, spirituality, esotericism, psychical phenomena, and psychopathology, were variously subsumed under, equated with, or distinguished from religious experience. These and other critical issues raised by scholars of religion since the 1970s are discussed in the third section.

EXPERIENCE AND ITS ANALOGUES WITHIN VARIOUS TRADITIONS. Although the use of the Latin term *experientia* in Christian contexts dates back at least to Aquinas, and the use of *experience* in Protestant contexts dates back at least to the seventeenth century, explicit references to religious experience became common in English at the beginning of the nineteenth century and in French *(l'expérience religieuse)* and German *(religiöse Erlebnis, Erfahrung)* toward the end of the nineteenth century. Prior to the late nineteenth century, the use of the term was most common among conversion-oriented Anglo-American Protestants. Over the course of the nineteenth century the English term religious experience was abstracted from its indigenous context within evangelical Protestantism, losing many of its specifically evangelical connotations in the process, and it was recast as a generic term that applied to religion in general. Non-Protestant traditions dealt with this process in various ways. Other terms, such as mysticism and spirituality (indigenous to the Catholic tradition), underwent similar changes during this period and also emerged as comparative terms in the study of religion.

By way of overview, current research suggests the following:

1. Liberal Protestants invested deeply in the concept of experience during the nineteenth century and in the new generic concept of religious experience formalized at the turn of the century by William James. Apart from a few modernists, most of whom were condemned, Catholic theologians dealt with the concepts of experience and religious experience warily if at all in the century and half prior to Vatican II, preferring the indigenous terms mystical and spiritual instead.
2. Universalistic nineteenth-century new religious movements, such as Transcendentalism, Spiritualism, New Thought, and Theosophy utilized experientially related terms (influxes, intuition, revelations, visions, spirits) to understand religion in general, but did not make extensive use of the terms experience or religious experience to refer to these phenomena.
3. Jewish interest in the experiential side of Judaism (Hasidism, Kabbalah) was, for the most part, channeled into discussions of mysticism rather than religious experience. The same seems to hold true for interest in the experiential side of Islam (Sufism).
4. Hindu and Buddhist thinkers more commonly invested in the concept of experience and a few made the concept of religious experience central to their thought.

PRE-REFORMATION CHRISTIANITY AND TRADITIONAL PROTESTANTISM. Within the history of Christianity, church authorities carefully regulated experientially related forms of belief and practice, beginning with the Montanists. In the *Summa Theologia* (1a 2ae q.112 a.5), Thomas Aquinas discussed the experience (experientia) of grace, which he indicated could be known conjecturally by signs of its presence in the believer. However, following Aristotle, he claimed that such knowledge is imperfect, and therefore that the experience of grace could not be known with certainty. This theological understanding undercut individual claims to knowledge based on experience and heightened the authority of the church. Mystical and ascetic theology, as subdisciplines within systematic theology, reflected an orthodox Catholic understanding of experience, while non-orthodox understandings were defined as heretical.

Although Protestant reformers also attempted to regulate experientially related forms of belief and practice, the schismatic tendency inherent in Luther's break with Rome made this more difficult, as Catholic critics did not hesitate to point out. Radical (sectarian) Protestants, especially those who advocated the separation of church and state, often made appeals to experience both in England and the Continent. While Continental Protestants typically made use of related terms, English Puritans made explicit reference to experience and occasionally to spiritual experience by the mid-seventeenth century, generally in reference to claims of direct experiences of inspiration by the Holy Spirit. Proponents of Enlightenment thought, such as John Locke, disputed these claims, redescribed such experiences as enthusiasm, and attempted to account for them in non-religious terms.

From the beginnings of evangelical Protestantism in the transatlantic revivals of the 1730s and 1740s until the present, claims of direct experience of the Holy Spirit or the immediate experience of the presence of God have been asserted by some evangelicals and disputed by others. Jonathan Edwards and John Wesley both defended the idea of a direct experience of the Holy Spirit. Both argued that authentic conversion was accompanied by a "new spiritual sense," which by analogy with the physical senses (cf. John Locke) allowed the believer to apprehend the Spirit directly. References to religious experience were common in the titles of nineteenth century evangelical Protestant memoirs, where the term generally referred to such experiences as conversion, sanctification and/or a call to preach. Methodists typically testified to such experiences in what were known collectively as "experience meetings."

The concept of religious experience underwent a dramatic redefinition within the Anglo-American context over the course of the nineteenth century, largely under the influence of romanticism, the growing interest in other religions, and new universalistic religious movements. Through the early decades of the nineteenth century, Anglo-American

Protestants continued to contrast religious experience, by definition authentic, with enthusiasm and mysticism, both considered false. By the middle decades of the nineteenth century, however, enthusiasm had taken on its more benign modern meaning, while mysticism acquired positive connotations through the writings of the Transcendentalists and widely read Protestant translations of Catholic mystical writers, such as Thomas Upham's *Life of Madame Guyon* (1846).

UNIVERSALISTIC NEW RELIGIOUS MOVEMENTS. Universalistic nineteenth-century new religious movements, such as Transcendentalism, Spiritualism, New Thought, and Theosophy, drew upon experientially related terms (influxes, visions, spirits, intuition) to understand religion in general, but did not make extensive use of the terms experience or religious experience to refer to these phenomena. Ralph Waldo Emerson (1803–1882) contrasted experience, which he understood as the sense experience of materialism, with intuition, ecstasy, and influxes of the Divine into the human soul, which he associated with idealism. Explicitly relying on Immanuel Kant to critique Locke, but also drawing support from Plato, Plotinus, and Emanuel Swedenborg, Emerson argued for the legitimacy of intuition and granted it authority over experience. He viewed enthusiasm and "a tendency toward insanity" as relatively benign concomitants of such divine influxes. Like many romantics with an interest in the perennial wisdom tradition, Emerson viewed all religions as pointing to "a fundamental Unity," which, in his view, reached its highest expression in Hinduism. Reading texts in translation, he linked the religious writings of the East with the thought of Plato, Plotinus, and others in the West (Emerson, pp. 198–199, 392–393, 638).

Later universalistic movements, such as Spiritualism, New Thought, and Theosophy under Helena Blavatsky and Henry Olcott, utilized terms such as spirit communication (Spiritualism) and intuition (New Thought, Theosophy) to describe the means by which individuals might acquire higher non-sense based forms of knowledge. As universalizing movements, they, like the Transcendentalists, maintained that the means in question informed all religions and, thus, religion in general. In contrast to the Transcendentalists, however, these later movements drew extensively on the popular psychology of animal magnetism, arguing that the mental abilities cultivated by mesmerists, such as trance and clairvoyance, provided the psychological substratum upon which their more developed abilities were based.

The Society for Psychical Research, founded in 1882 to assess such claims scientifically, brought together evidence from the Society's investigations of Spiritualist mediums with the latest clinical research on hysteria, the doubling of personality, and hypnosis (the direct descendent of animal magnetism). Frederick Myers, the Society's leading theoretician, linked these phenomena though his theory of the subconscious, which he and William James understood as the means by which non-sense based knowledge might come to consciousness. Whether such knowledge simply surfaced from the recesses of the mind or entered in some other way from beyond it was the focus of much of the Society's research.

LIBERAL PROTESTANT THEOLOGY. Friedrich Schleiermacher (1768–1834), a German Protestant theologian with a Pietist background, is usually credited with initiating the emphasis on the self or subjectivity and, thus, by extension on experience, associated with modern Protestant theology. Through his influence on Rudolf Otto, Schleiermacher also had a major influence on the twentieth-century study of religion. In opposition to Kant's emphasis on religion as morality, Schleiermacher located the essence of religion in the immediate, prereflective intuition and feeling of the infinite *(On Religion).* Later he referred to this essence as "a feeling of absolute dependence" *(Christian Faith).* As Hans-Georg Gadamer noted in *Truth and Method,* Schleiermacher himself did not use the term experience, although his key ideas were transposed into this idiom by later interpreters, such as Wilhelm Dilthey, who used the newly coined term *Erlebnis* in his 1870 biography of Schleiermacher (Gadamer, pp. 60–64).

At the turn of the last century, Schleiermacher's emphasis on immediate intuition and feeling as the basis of religious knowledge—now explicitly framed in terms of experience—enjoyed a revival of interest. The revival was coupled, probably not coincidentally, with a widespread shift in the way scholars understood religion. This shift from the Enlightenment conception of religion as an archaic "survival" to a conception of religion as "power," subjectively understood, implicitly grounded religion in experience. The British anthropologist, R. R. Marett is usually given credit for initiating this shift with his essay on "Pre-Animistic Religion," delivered in 1899. But others, such as William James, were also thinking along similar lines at about the same time.

Protestant theologians with an interest in the comparative study of religion, such as Nathan Söderblom, Friedrich Heiler, and Rudolf Otto, played a major role in this shift. Building on the thought of Schleiermacher, Marett, and Söderblom, Otto argued in *The Idea of the Holy* that a felt experience of a numinous presence logically preceded Schleiermacher's "feeling of dependence." The numinous, he said, evoked feelings of mysterium (wholly otherness), tremendum (dread, awe), and fascination. Otto interpreted mysticism as a subset of the experience of the numinous. He considered religion sui generis, that is, something unique that could not be adequately interpreted or explained in other terms, and located it, following Schleiermacher, in an irreducibly religious domain (Otto, pp. 5-41).

Ernst Troeltsch, Otto's colleague on the theological faculty at the University of Marburg, approached the experiential dimension of Christianity historically and sociologically under the rubric of mysticism. In *Social Teachings of the Christian Churches* (1912; English, 1931), he drew an important distinction between mysticism, in the widest sense of the word, which he understood as "the insistence upon a direct inward and present religious experience" (Troeltsch, II, p. 730), and mysticism as understood more narrowly by the philosophy of religion. His depiction of the latter provides, in effect, a sociological description of the emergence of the "philosophia perennis." While mysticism in the broad sense takes on an "immense variety" of forms within the various traditions, mysticism in the narrower sense may break away from "concrete religion" and "set up a theory of [its] own which takes the place of the concrete religion and of its mythos or doctrine." When this happens, "mysticism realizes that it is an independent religious principle; it sees itself as the real universal heart of all religion, of which the various myth-forms are merely the outer garment. It regards itself as the means of restoring an immediate union with God; it feels independent of all institutional religion" (Troeltsch, II, p. 734).

Catholicism After the Council of Trent. The idea of experience received little development in the Catholic tradition during the post-Reformation period due to its association with Protestantism and movements that were condemned within Catholicism, such as Jansenism, Quietism, and Modernism. The First Vatican Council (1870) reacted to the nineteenth-century emphasis on experience as a source of religious authority, condemning the idea that "men and women ought to be moved to faith only by each one's internal experience or private inspiration" *(De Fide,* Canon 3). In *Pascendi dominici gregis* (1907), Pius X alleged that Catholic modernists wrongly held to the idea that faith and revelation were rooted in religious sentiment or an intuition of the heart. This reliance on "personal experience," the encyclical explained, caused modernists to "fall into the opinion of Protestants and pseudomystics" (para. 14). Moreover, as the encyclical duly noted, an emphasis on experience undercut the Church's exclusivist claims. Given their logic, the encyclical asked, "[W]ith what right will Modernists deny the truth of an experience affirmed by a follower of Islam? With what right can they claim true experience for Catholics alone?" (para. 14) Catholic modernists did embrace the modern turn to the subject and with it a concomitant emphasis on experience, though not in the monolithic way outlined in *Pascendi.*

In the decades prior to the Second Vatican Council (1962–65), twentieth-century Catholic theologians debated whether Thomism could be reconciled with the modern emphasis on subjectivity. The wary appreciation evident in Catholic historian Ronald Knox's *Enthusiasm* (1950) illustrates Catholic ambivalence toward experience prior to the Second Vatican Council. The concept of experience found renewed, though qualified, acceptance at the Second Vatican Council. Among twentieth-century Catholic theologians, Karl Rahner, S. J., and Edward Schillebeeckx, O.P., are particularly known for the emphasis they place on experience.

Judaism and Islam. Scholars of Judaism and Islam, for the most part, discussed experientially related phenomena under the rubric of mysticism, understood to include what in Christian contexts would be distinguished as Gnosticism and esotericism. With the publication of volumes on *Jewish Spirituality* (1988, 1989) and *Islamic Spirituality* (1989, 1991) in the World Spiritualities series, scholars in both traditions adopted spirituality as an encompassing a rubric under which to discuss the subjective aspect of the traditions more broadly.

Two of the most prominent early twentieth-century scholars of Jewish mysticism—Martin Buber (1878–1965) and Gershom Scholem (1897–1982)—were both German Jews who reacted against the Enlightenment rationalism of their era and sought, albeit in different ways, to highlight the non-rational aspects of the Jewish tradition. Buber embraced an ahistorical *Erlebnismystik* early in his career, which Scholem reacted against. Buber's *Ekstatic Confessions* (1909)—a collection of personal accounts from various eastern and western religious traditions—utilized the German distinction between *Erfahrung* (sense experience) and *Erlebnis* (non-sense based experience) to make a case for ecstasy as an undifferentiated experience in which the boundaries between self and other and self and world disappear. This ecstatic experience, he claimed, was common to the Vedas and Upaniṣads, Midrash and Qabbalah, Plato and Jesus. Although Buber grew increasingly uncomfortable with this formulation as his thought matured, the *Ekstatic Confessions* recalled the spirit of Schleiermacher and prefigured Rudolf Otto's *Idea of the Holy.*

In contrast to Buber, who believed that such ecstatic experiences transcended time and thus had no history, Scholem devoted his life to the historical study of Jewish mysticism and in particular to the Qabbalah. He understood the Qabbalah as a suppressed and esoteric tradition that held the key to the continuing vitality of the tradition as a whole. In his hands, myth, symbol, and mysticism rather than religious experience, provided the conceptual categories for surfacing an alternative history of Judaism and, in the process, a different understanding of mysticism. In the late twentieth century, Moshe Idel highlighted the ecstatic side of Qabbalistic mysticism, overlooked by Scholem, and integrated the study of Hasidic mysticism, pioneered by Buber, into the broader history of Jewish mysticism.

Some of the most prominent twentieth-century scholars of Islamic mysticism—Louis Massignon (1883–1962), Henry Corbin (1907–1978), and Annemarie Schimmel (1922–2003)—were non-Muslims who turned to the study of Islamic mysticism in the context of colonialism. During the eighteenth century, scholars associated with the British East India Company discovered the "Sooffees" and soon thereafter coined the term *Sufism.* During the nineteenth century, western intellectuals viewed Sufism positively as a form of mysticism and distinguished it from Islam, which they viewed negatively. By the late nineteenth century, this view had been racialized on the assumption that any mysticism evident in the Semitic religions was actually of Aryan origin. Massignon, through close philological work on the writings of a particular Ṣūfī mystic, al-Ḥallāj, challenged this theory, arguing that Ṣūfī mysticism could be traced directly to the Qur'ān. As a Catholic reconverted to Catholicism through his engagement with the martyred Ṣūfī Massignon was studying, the depiction of al-Ḥallāj as a mystic undoubtedly seemed obvious. He viewed al-Ḥallāj, who died at the hands of the community he was trying to save, as recapitulating the mystical substitution of one life for another that lay at the heart of Massignon's Christocentric Catholic devotional life. The work of Massignon's student, Henry Corbin, also provided an eclectic bridge between traditions. Through a reading of Islam that stressed on-going revelation through Ṣūfī and Shīʿah visionaries—something that he could not find in Christianity—Corbin found a means of critiquing Christianity. Given his interest, Corbin used a broader range of terms—prophetic philosophy, esotericism and the visionary tradition—to depict his approach. Annemarie Schimmel, who taught at Harvard for twenty-five years, emphasized the complexity of the origins of Ṣūfī mysticism. In *The Mystical Dimension of Islam,* she resisted the then still common tendency to explain Sufism as the result of contact with other mystical traditions and, like Massignon, pointed to Ṣūfī-like tendencies present in the Qur'ān.

HINDUISM AND BUDDHISM. The concept of experience played a prominent role in the mediation of Hinduism and Zen Buddhism to the West in the twentieth century. In India and Japan, the heightened emphasis on experience reflected a rethinking of the Hindu and Buddhist traditions amidst the crosscurrents of colonialism, westernization, and nationalist self-assertion. Building on the thought of nineteenth-century Neo-Hindu predecessors, such as Rammohun Roy (1772–1833), Debendranath Tagore (1817–1905), and Vivekananda (1863–1902), the Indian scholar Sarvepalli Radhakrishnan (1888–1975) explicitly embraced the concept of religious experience as central to his understanding of religion in general and Hinduism in particular. In Japan, Daisetz Teitaro (D. T.) Suzuki (1870–1966), influenced by the philosophy of Nishida Kitarō and the "New Buddhism" of the Meiji period (1868–1912), emphasized the "inner experience" of enlightenment (satori) in Zen, the Buddhist tradition, and religion and philosophy in general. As with Christian modernists of the same era, Hindu and Buddhist "modernizers" used the idea of experience to undercut traditional sources of authority and interpret traditional concepts in new ways.

Roy, whose translations of Hindu texts were read by the American Transcendentalists, opened the question of the authority of Hindu scriptures and raised questions regarding the relation of Hindu revelation to the revelation claimed by other traditions. Tagore pursued these questions much more deeply in an attempt to establish how much of the tradition could be accepted as binding. He broke with the Vedānta philosophy of Śankara, replacing Śankara's commentaries with his own. According to Wilhelm Halbfass, Debendranath transferred authority from the texts themselves to "the pure heart, filled with the light of intuitive knowledge," thus placing himself "in the position of a 'seer'" (Halbfass, p. 223). His reinterpretation of authority was simultaneously influenced by Western conceptions of inspiration and intuition and assertively Hindu. According to Halbfass, Debendranath's

> doctrine of intuition and his interpretation of religious texts as documents of inner experience opened up new dimensions of universality and of interaction with other religions, and it paved the way for such exemplary Neo-Hindu views as that of Radhakrishnan, who saw all valid religious documents, both within and without Hinduism, as records of 'experiences,' and thus understood 'intuition' and 'experience' as the basis and the common denominator of all religions (Halbfass, p. 224).

These ideas were promoted in the West in an embodied way through the figure of Ramakrishna—"the most famous representative of 'living Hinduism' and . . . the very symbol of the potential of undogmatic religious experience and ecstasy contained within the Hindu tradition" (Halbfass, p. 227). While, according to Halbfass, Ramakrishna himself cannot be counted as a spokesperson for Neo-Hinduism, "he became the instrument and leading figure of Neo-Hinduism in its encounter with Europe" through the tireless promotional efforts of his student, Vivekananda (Halbfass, p. 230).

D. T. Suzuki's earliest publications reflect the New Buddhist orientation of his teacher, the Rinzai Zen abbot Shaku Sōen, as well as the influence Paul Carus, the western Buddhist advocate with whom Suzuki studied from 1897–1909, but they place little explicit emphasis on the concept of experience. In his *Outlines of Mahayana Buddhism* (1907), Suzuki characterized Nirvana in terms of "the suppression of egoism and the awakening of love." He described the Boddhisattva ideal as one of "all-embracing love" and, like Carus, depicted "this gospel of universal love [as] the consummation of all religious emotions whatever their origin" (Suzuki, pp. 55, 366, 369). Suzuki's turn to experience was apparently prompted by the publication of his friend Nishida Kitarō's *Zen no kenkyū* (An inquiry into the good) in 1911. Kitarō's work, which was influenced by William James, was a rethinking of Japanese philosophy in light of the concept of pure experience (junsui keiken). In "The Zen of Japanese Nationalism," Robert Sharf indicates that the two Japanese words used to translate experience—keiken (for the English experience) and taiken (for the German Erlebnis)—rarely appeared in pre-modern Japanese texts. By the 1920s, Suzuki was interpreting "the doctrine of Enlightenment" as an "inner experience," in which "Enlightenment is grasped immediately without any conceptual medium" *(Essays in Religion,* First Series [1926], p. 73). He used this understanding of enlightenment to argue for the centrality of Zen in the Buddhist tradition and to critique those who tried to "grasp the spirit of Buddhism" through the philosophical study of Buddhist teachings rather than by entering into "the inner essence of Enlightenment [as] experienced by the Buddha" (p. 118).

Enlightenment emerged as Suzuki's primary experiential category. While he was quite open to comparisons, he stressed the difference between the Zen experience and meditation (dhyana) as practiced in India, most theistic forms of Christian mysticism, and "conversion . . . as the term is generally used by Christian converts" (Suzuki, *Essays,* pp. 262–263, 231). At the same time, he viewed "Zen as the ultimate fact of all philosophy and religion." Not only was it "the fountain of Buddhist thought and life," it was "very much alive also in Christianity, Mahommedanism, in Taoism, and even in positivistic Confucianism" (Suzuki, p. 268). With a few exceptions, such as his discussion of Eckhart and Zen in *Mysticism: Christian and Buddhist* (1957), Suzuki stayed with the Japanese concept of satori. While he was willing to translate satori as Enlightenment, interpret it as the "Zen experience," and recognize it in other traditions, he rarely subsumed it under other rubrics, in effect promoting it as a competitor to mysticism and religious experience in the market place of ideas.

USE IN RELATION TO RELIGION IN GENERAL. William James (1842–1910), Sarvepalli Radhakrishnan (1888–1975), and Joachim Wach (1889–1955), each of whom understood religion in general in terms of religious experience, illustrate three different understandings of the concept—empirical (James), perennial (Radhakrishnan), and phenomenological (Wach)—each with its own intellectual antecedents. James's *Varieties of Religious Experience* (1902) marks the transformation of traditional evangelical Protestant understanding of religious experience in the Anglo-American context under the influence of experimental psychology, including psychical research, and new religious movements such as Transcendentalism, Swedenborgianism, Spiritualism, and Theosophy. Radhakrishnan, in writings that date back to the 1920s, highlights the Neo-Hindu transformation of traditional Hindu concepts of *darśana* and *anubhava* in the colonial Indian context under the influence of the East-West exchange, Christian missions, and the rise of Hindu nationalism. Wach represents the explicit codification of the German intellectual tradition represented by Schleiermacher and Otto under the rubric of religious experience within the context of the academic study of religion (the History of Religions) beginning in the 1940s.

WILLIAM JAMES. William James, a philosopher and psychologist who taught at Harvard for over thirty years, is usually given credit for constituting the term religious experience as a technical term in the study of religion. In *Varieties,* religious experience, abstracted from its traditional Protestant meaning, served as an umbrella term that encompassed traditionally Catholic conceptions of sainthood and mysticism as well as the traditionally Protestant idea of conversion. References to other traditions, while not as numerous, appeared throughout the book as well. All were united under the rubric of religious experience, which no longer referred to the understanding of experience that a particular (evangelical Protestant) tradition deemed normative, but to an aspect of religion in general.

James delivered the Gifford Lectures, soon thereafter published as *Varieties,* in Edinburgh in 1901. He defined religion for the purpose of his lectures (that is, heuristically) as "the feelings, acts, and experiences of individual men in their solitude, so far as they apprehend themselves to stand in relation to whatever they may consider divine" (James, p. 34). He stressed that for religious persons "[i]t is as if there were in the human consciousness a sense of reality, a feeling of objective presence, a perception of what we may call 'something there,' more deep and more general than any of the special and particularly 'senses'" (James, p. 55). Utilizing autobiographies and memoirs as data, James focused on what he referred to as first hand experience, that is, on "the original experiences that were the pattern-setters," rather than in the experiences of "ordinary believers." Under the influence of nineteenth-century romanticism, James was particularly interested in "'geniuses' in the religious line." Such persons, he recognized, were frequently subject to extremes of experience; they heard voices, had visions, and fell into trance. James, like Emerson before him, readily conceded that religious geniuses were often depicted as psychopathological in his own day and as "enthusiasts" in earlier times. Nonetheless, James, in contrast to many later psychologists of religion, was convinced that, empirically speaking, the more extreme cases would shed the greatest light on religious experience as a whole.

Although religious experience and mysticism were both viewed positively and much discussed at the turn of the century, the boundary between them was not clearly demarcated. While, according to James, "personal religious experience has its root and centre in mystical states of consciousness," mysticism was not simply a subset of religious experience. There were, in his view, both religious experiences that were not mystical and mystical experiences—such as dreamy states and alcohol and drug induced experiences—that were not religious. At the end of his discussion of mysticism, he conceded that "religious mysticism" actually makes up "only one half of mysticism." The other half, he said, has no traditions other than what "the text-books on insanity supply" (James, p. 337).

Those with a particular interest in mysticism often have read James's chapter on the subject in isolation from the work as a whole, either adopting or critiquing his "four marks" of mysticism—ineffability, noetic quality, transciency, and passivity—and linking him with the tradition descended from Schleiermacher. Recent critics of ahistorical approaches to mysticism, such as Grace Jantzen, have critiqued James on the basis of this sort of reading. While there are resemblances between Schleiermacher, Otto, and James, particularly in terms of their emphasis on emotion, the differences are significant. Troeltsch noted in 1912 that the key difference between James and the European philosophers of religion lay in the latter's commitment to Platonic or Neoplatonic rationalism and the former's commitment to an anti-Platonic radical empiricism. While the Europeans presupposed an "a priori unity of consciousness" upon which they could base a postulated "essence of religion," James did not. James did not consider religion an a priori category and, while he assumed that it had a distinct function that could be identified by means of comparisons with similar phenomena, it was not, in his view, sui generis.

At most points in *Varieties,* James as a result made a clear distinction between the subjective experience of believers (i.e., their phenomenological claims of immediacy), which he recognized, and the truth claims they asserted (i.e., their epistemological claims to immediacy), which were, in his view, open to question. He recognized, for example, that "any object that is infinitely important to us and awakens our devotion feels to us also as if it must be sui generis and unique." Even a crab, he added tongue in cheek, would undoubtedly be filled with "a sense of personal outrage" if it overheard us class it with the crustaceans "and thus dispose of it" (James, p. 17). In contrast to Otto, who made analogies—particularly between religious and aesthetic experience—in order to evoke the "perfectly sui generis" experience of the numinous in his readers, James was an inveterate comparativist who liked nothing better than to construct a graduated series of examples—religious and non-religious—so as to more fully grasp the significance of the phenomena in question.

Also in contrast to Otto, James was interested in mediating between science and religion and did not reject naturalistic explanations of religious claims out of hand. Where Otto seemed to assume the objective reality of the numinous object, James asked whether the seemingly external presence encountered by believers—the "More" as he called it—really existed. James offered the idea of the "subconscious" developed by Frederick Myers, his colleague in the Society for Psychical Research, as a largely naturalistic explanation of such experiences, which nonetheless held open the possibility of influences that originated beyond the self. James himself believed that such influences were possible, as he indicated in his postscript, and he was closely involved with the Society for Psychical Research's attempts to obtain evidence of life after death through their investigations of spiritualist mediums.

SARVEPELLI RADHAKRISHNAN. Radhakrishnan was born near Madras, India, and educated in schools run by Christian missionaries. The missionaries' criticisms of Hinduism led him to examine it for himself and ultimately to take up the Neo-Hindu efforts to modernize the tradition. From 1909 to 1931, he taught philosophy and religion at various colleges and universities in India. Beginning in the mid-1920s, he gave a series of prestigious lectures in England and the United States and, from 1936–39, held the Spalding Chair in Eastern Religions and Ethics at Oxford. Upon his return to India, he assumed a variety of high-ranking administrative and political posts, including from 1962–67, the presidency of India.

Radhakrishnan's perennialist understanding of religious experience blended a distinctly Neo-Hindu form of Vedanta with the philosophical idealism of the West. In a lecture on "Religious Experience" given at Oxford in 1926 (and later published in *A Hindu View of Life* [1927]), he located Hinduism's particular strength in its long history of "welding together heterogeneous elements and enabling them to live together in peace and order." In a world "full of racial, cultural, and religious misunderstandings," he hoped that the Hindu approach to "the problem of religious conflicts" might have lessons for all. Hinduism was able to discover unity amidst diversity because of its grounding in religious experience. Reflecting his debt to Tagore, he wrote that in Hinduism "intellect is subordinated to intuition, dogma to experience, outer expression to inward realization. Religion is not the acceptance of academic abstractions or the celebration of ceremonies, but a kind of life or experience. It is insight into the nature of reality *(darśana),* or experience of reality *(anubhava)*" (Radhakrishnan, p. 15).

As McDermott points out, both Vedanta and idealism share an epistemology (a theory of intuition) and a metaphysics (a theory of the Absolute) in which the case for intuition presupposes the reality of the Absolute and case for the Absolute depends on knowledge supplied by intuition (Radhakrishnan, p. 16). Radhakrishnan equates "religious experience" and intuitive knowledge. In *An Idealist View of Life,* he described religious experience as "a type of experience which is not clearly differentiated into a subject-object state, an integral, undivided consciousness in which not merely this or that side of man's nature but his whole being seems to find itself." (Radhakrishnan, 1932, p. 91). He made use of the idea of the unconscious to explain how the Absolute could be "directly experienced" without making a claim for "pure experience." Thus, he argued:

> immediacy does not mean absence of psychological mediation but only non-mediation by conscious thought. Ideas which seem to come to us with compelling force, without any mediate intellectual process of which we are aware, are generally the results of previous training in traditions imparted to us in our early years. . . . Something is directly experienced, but it is unconsciously interpreted in the terms of the tradition in which the individual is trained (Radhakrishnan, 1932, pp. 98–99).

Thus, as he summed up in *The Hindu View of Life:*

> religious experience is not the pure unvarnished presentment of the real in itself, but is the presentment of the real already influenced by the ideas and prepossessions of the perceiving mind. . . . Each religious genius spells out the mystery of God according to his own endowment, personal, racial, and historical. The variety of the pictures of God is easily intelligible when we realize that religious experience is psychologically mediated (Radhakrishnan, pp. 24–25).

JOACHIM WACH. Wach, a German-born historian of religions, studied with Otto, Heiler, and Troeltsch. He taught at the University of Leipzig until his appointment was terminated in 1935 due to his family's Jewish background. He immigrated to the United States, where he taught at Brown University (1935–45) and the University of Chicago (1946–1955). In his best known work, *The Sociology of Religion,* Wach synthesized the phenomenological method as pioneered by Otto, Max Scheler, and Gerardus van der Leeuw with the sociological approach of Max Weber and Ernst Troeltsch. Relying on Otto, Wach began with religious experience, which he defined as the "experience of the holy." Following the lead of Weber and Troeltsch, Wach focused on the expression of religious experience in the contexts of theory (myth and doctrine), cultus (worship), and, above all, social groups and social relations. By focusing on the interplay between religion and society, Wach hoped to illustrate not only "the cultural significance of religion but also to gain new insight into the relations between the various forms of expression of religious experience and eventually to understand better the various aspects of religious experience itself" (Wach, 1944, p. 5).

In contrast to James who compared religious and nonreligious phenomena and distinguished between such phenomena pragmatically, Wach limited his comparisons to religious experiences, which he held to have an "objective character" that would "ultimately defy any attempt to describe, analyze, and comprehend its meaning scientifically" (Wach, 1944, p. 14). In the wake of the Second World War, perhaps in reaction to Nazism, Wach provided what were, in effect, theological criteria for distinguishing between genuine (i.e., objective) and pseudo-religious experience. While "pseudo religions," such as Marxism, ethnic or racialized religions, and nationalism, in his view, were grounded in finite (i.e., human and subjective) realities, genuine religious experience was, he claimed, grounded in "ultimate reality" (Wach, 1951, pp. 32-33). Wach's stress on the sui generis nature of religion and the objective character of ultimate reality, which he shared with Otto and van der Leeuw, remained characteristic features of the history of religions program at the University of Chicago under Wach's successor, Mircea Eliade (1907–1986).

Eliade, in the eyes of many the dominant figure in the study of religion for the post-war generation, approached the study of religion in light of the distinction between the sacred and the profane rather than religious experience per se. He explicitly linked his understanding of the hierophany, the manifestation of the sacred in the profane, to the Christian ideas of incarnation and sacrament. In *Patterns of Comparative Religion,* he emphasized the idea that "the sacred is always manifested through some thing" (Eliade, p. 26). These things included the natural and built environment (sun, moon, rocks, water; temples); plants, animals, and humans; biological processes (sex and fertility); human activities (agriculture, hunting); and immaterial objects, such as time, symbols, moral laws, and ideas. Indeed, he stressed that there was probably not "anything . . . that has not at some time in human history been somewhere transformed into a hierophany" (Eliade, p. 11). Given his sharp distinction between the sacred and profane, the hierophany represented a "paradoxical coming-together of sacred and profane." Acknowledging the Christian overtones of this formulation, he indicated that "one might even say that all hierophanies are simply prefigurations of the miracle of the Incarnation, that every hierophany is an abortive attempt to reveal the mystery of the coming together of God and man" (Eliade, p. 29).

While anything could potentially manifest the sacred, Eliade also insisted that "a hierophany [nonetheless] implies a choice, a clear-cut separation of this thing which manifests the sacred from everything else around it" (Eliade, p. 13). Sometimes Eliade depicted this act of separation as the result of human choice, and at other times, the result of sacred action. Thus, Eliade acknowledged that humans as historical actors experience, interpret, and revalue the sacred, while, at the same time, insisting that the sacred as suprahistorical agent ultimately reveals, displays, and thus imposes "itself on man from without" (Eliade, p. 369). The conflation of the two perspectives into one "onto-theological system"—to borrow Jonathan Z. Smith's phrase—has been both a source of confusion and the subject of critique in subsequent decades.

Although Eliade did not use the term religious experience in a technical sense, he often used it as a synonym for the experience of the sacred, broadly conceived to include not only hierophanies, but also kratophanies (manifestations of power), totemism, ancestor worship, etc. He stressed that "elementary hierophanies" were always part of a larger religious system made up of "all the religious experiences of the tribe," on the one hand, and "a corpus of traditional theories [e.g. myths] which cannot be reduced to elementary hierophanies," on the other (Eliade, p. 30). In so far as it functioned as an extension of his concept of the sacred, Eliade's understanding of religious experience maintained the sui generis and objective character evident in the lineage from Otto to Wach.

Eliade's colleagues and heirs at the University of Chicago appropriated and critiqued his legacy in various ways. Eliade's seemingly casual subsumption of the sacred under the heading of religious experience was subsequently reinforced by Eliade's colleagues, Charles Long and Joseph Kitagawa, both of whom studied under Joachim Wach and maintained Wach's preference for the term religious experience. Kitagawa, reflecting the influence of Otto on Wach and Eliade, used the term as a catchall for the "unique and irreducible element" of religion (Kitagawa, 1987, p. 28). In essays dating back to the late sixties, Long undercut Eliade's ontological claims by stressing the role of human imagination in the apprehension of the sacred (Long, 1986, pp. 23–25, 27–53, 65–78). Jonathan Z. Smith explicitly criticized Eliade's conflation of the morphological and ontological and argued for the importance of separating the two in order to maintain the integrity of the morphological enterprise in the context of historical analysis (Smith, 2000, p. 346; see also 1978, pp. 88–103, 253–259, 289–310). In *The Symbolism of Evil,* philosopher Paul Ricoeur critiqued Eliade's understanding of symbols, rooting them more deeply in psychological and cultural experience, by arguing, first, that "to manifest the 'sacred' on the 'cosmos' and to manifest it in the 'psyche' are the same thing" and, second, that scholarly engagement with symbols is shaped both by scholars' own situatedness and by the situatedness of the questions they ask (Ricoeur, pp. 12–13, 19–20).

MYSTICISM, THE NUMINOUS, AND RELIGIOUS EXPERIENCE. James understood mysticism and religious experience as overlapping but not coextensive. Radhakrishnan used the term religious experience to refer to what many others would call mysticism. Otto, van der Leeuw, Wach, and Eliade subsumed mysticism under their rubric of choice (the holy, power, religious experience, or the sacred respectively). Wach, Eliade, Kitagawa, and Long, all of whom were interested in the study of religion in general, viewed terms such as religious experience, the sacred, and the holy in relation to a wide range of material and non-material phenomena that were not necessarily associated with the term mysticism. Presumably, they viewed it as a more adequate basis for the study of religion in all its concrete manifestations.

Scholars of mysticism did not demonstrate the same interest in the study of religion in general as did historians of religion. Many were identified primarily as philosophers of religion and brought epistemological concerns to the study of mysticism. During the fifties and sixties, their discussions revolved mostly around matters of definition and boundaries in the study of mysticism. Thus, for example, R. C. Zaehner, who assumed the Spalding Chair in Eastern Religion and Ethics at Oxford upon Radhakrishnan's departure, critiqued both his predecessor's perennialism and that of Aldous Huxley, countering with a more nuanced characterization of mysticism that ruled out psychic and physical phenomena, downplayed the value of drug-induced experiences, and heightened the differences between traditions in a manner congruent with his own Catholic commitments. In *Mysticism and Philosophy,* Walter T. Stace reiterated the consensus view that visions, voices, raptures, trances and "hyperemotionalism" were not part of the "universal core" of mystical experience and sharply differentiated "mystical experience" from "religious experience," arguing that once mystical experience is stripped of "all intellectual interpretation" all that is left is "the undifferentiated unity." What, he asked, "is there that is religious about an undifferentiated unity?" (Stace, p. 23).

The British historian of religions, Ninian Smart (1927–2001), made the most significant attempt to bring discussions of mysticism into the general study of religion during this period. In *Reason and Faiths,* he proposed to move beyond Otto by arguing that the numinous and the mystical represented two different forms of religious experience. He associated the former, with its emphasis on an encounter with the "wholly other," with the monotheistic religions of the West and the latter, with its emphasis on union with the one, with the religions of the East. He used this distinction to structure his influential textbook on world religions, *The Religious Experience of Mankind,* which was reissued in five editions over the succeeding three decades.

THE CRITICS. Because, to paraphrase William James, the use of a concept can be better understood in relation to its near neighbors and closest competitors, this section gives some consideration to critical debates over the concept of mysticism alongside debates over the concept of religious experience. Other competitors, especially "enthusiasm," "the sacred," and "spirituality," could profitably be compared as well. Mysticism, however, was selected for examination because of its prominence as an alternative during most of the period under consideration in this essay. Significant criticism of the underlying assumptions that informed the use of the terms religious experience and mysticism surfaced in the 1970s and gathered momentum over the next two decades. The central question with respect to religious experience (and by extension religion) was whether or not it was sui generis. This question was typically debated in relation to the issue of "reductionism" in the study of religion, that is, the question of whether religion (or religious experience) could be legitimately redescribed in nonreligious terms. The central question with respect to mysticism was whether or not it had a "common core" that united all the disparate forms of mystical experience. This question was typically debated in relation to questions about the nature of experience, specifically the relationship between experience and language.

Both debates were, in a sense, about the autonomy of the experiences in question. The debate over whether or not mysticism had a common core located the question of autonomy in relation to the traditions. Those who argued for a common core, a view typically connected to the philosophia perennis, were in effect arguing for a common esoteric tradition that united the various traditions. The debate over whether or not religious experience was sui generis located the question of autonomy in relation to the academic disciplines. Those who argued for the sui generis nature of religious experience resisted the idea that religion could be adequately understood in nonreligious (i.e. psychological, sociological, historical) terms. The underlying issue was whether or not the phenomenological approach to the study of religion, which made a sharp distinction—loosely following Dilthey and other Continental philosophers—between methods appropriate to the humanities and methods appropriate to the sciences, was adequate for the study of religion or just another way of importing religion itself into the academy.

In its most recent iteration, the debate has turned to the relationship between scholars of religion and what they study. Methodological questions surrounding the selection of data, the nature of comparison, and the influence of the scholar's beliefs and life experiences remain central in a context where some scholars are calling for methods that more effectively distinguish between the voices and agendas of scholars and those of their subjects. The underlying issue has to do with the extent to which scholars construct the object of study and the bearing that role in constructing the object has on the subject.

DEBATES OVER THE NATURE OF RELIGION. The 1970s and early 1980s were a period of rising discontent among scholars interested in the study of religion and the study of mysticism. In both cases discontent focused on critiques of the giants that had dominated these areas of study. In the study of religion, criticism focused above all on Mircea Eliade. Robert Segal's provocative essay "In Defense of Reductionism" directed much of the critical energy. At issue was what Eliade meant by claiming that the "sacred" was "irreducible." Did he mean that the sacred was real for believers and, thus, should not be interpreted in any other terms, or was he claiming that the believers' perspective was in fact epistemologically true? While acknowledging that Eliade's statements were inconsistent in this regard, Segal concluded that Eliade's "willingness to exceed and even violate believers' particular conscious views of the meaning of religion for them suggests that he is concerned with more than its truth for them" (Segal, 101). Segal also made the point, which was shortly thereafter reiterated and generalized by Wayne Proudfoot, that there is no necessary conflict between the humanists' desire to describe the conscious meaning of religion for believers, and the social scientists desire to account for the believer's understanding in terms other than the believer's own.

Building on the different conceptions of interpretation in the hermeneutic and pragmatic traditions, Proudfoot made an important and widely accepted distinction between descriptive and explanatory reduction in Religious Experience. "Descriptive reduction," according to Proudfoot, "is the failure to identify an emotion, practice, or experience under the description by which the subject identifies it." The subject's self-description, he maintained, is normative for describing the experience, but should not prevent scholars from offering their own explanations of the phenomena in question in terms that "are not those of the subject and that might not meet with his approval." This sort of "explanatory reduction," Proudfoot argued, is "perfectly justifiable and is, in fact, normal procedure" (Proudfoot, pp.194–197).

Two volumes edited by Thomas A. Idinopulos and Edward Yonan, *Religion and Reductionism* and *The Sacred and its Scholars* capture much of the flavor of the subsequent debate. Two points are worth emphasizing in relation to the first volume. First, Proudfoot's distinction between descriptive and explanatory reduction was widely accepted. While accepting Proudfoot's distinction, both Segal and Donald Wiebe, another well-known critic of Eliade, emphasized that avoiding descriptive reduction did not mean accepting the tacit explanations of experiences embedded in the descriptive accounts of believers (Idinopulos/Yonan, p. 123). Second, as Ivan Strenski's discussion made clear, reduction involves the redescription of phenomena. "In its home context in the natural sciences and philosophy of science, 'reduction' names a process by which concepts and theories from one domain change by being logically and/or conceptually subsumed by—'reduced to'—those of another. . . . 'Reductionism' is thus the obverse of the view that theories are a priori 'autonomous' and immune to the subsumption by other theories" (Idinopulos/Yonan, p. 97). Although "reduction" is a technical term, it does not refer to a process that is limited to scientists or scholars. As Strenski (Idinopulos/Yonan, p. 102) and Merkur (Idinopulos/Yonan, p. 221) both point out, ordinary believers routinely redescribe the beliefs of those they disagree with.

Several of the essays in *The Sacred and Its Scholars* wrestled with the question of whether Otto, van der Leeuw, Wach, and Eliade were making descriptive claims about the experience of believers or metaphysical claims about religion when they argued that religion is sui generis. Merkur argued that Otto was making a descriptive claim, but that van der Leeuw, Wach, and Eliade were not. Idinopulos disagreed with Merkur, claiming that Otto is hopelessly obscure on precisely this point. In a two-part article commemorating the fiftieth anniversary of the first edition of Eliade's *Patterns in Comparative Religions,* Jonathan Z. Smith advanced this discussion by distinguishing between morphological (i.e., synchronic) and diachronic approaches to history, on the one hand, and ontological claims to transcend history, on the other. Smith argued that *Patterns* reflects Eliade's "persistent attempt to conjoin [a] morphological understanding of history with an ontology that rejects the historical" (Smith, 2000, p. 346). As indicated above, Smith argues for the importance of separating the morphological and ontological in order to uphold the value of synchronic as well as diachronic analyses in the historical enterprise.

DEBATES OVER THE NATURE OF EXPERIENCE. In the study of mysticism, the critical assault began with a symposium organized by Steven T. Katz in the mid-1970s. In *Mysticism and Philosophical Analysis,* Katz set out to advance the discussion and analysis of mysticism "beyond James and Otto, Stace and Zaehner" (Katz, p. 3). Katz framed his symposia and the volumes that emerged from them in relation to the question of experience and interpretation. Katz and most of the contributors to his edited volumes are considered specialists in the history of mysticism within particular traditions. Most followed Katz's lead in arguing that there is no such thing as a pure unmediated experience and, thus, that the idea that all mystical experiences share a "common core" is false. Robert K. C. Forman emerged as Katz's most prominent critic. In *The Problem of Pure Consciousness* and subsequent works, Forman, building on Stace, narrowed the proposed common core to the "Pure Consciousness Event (PCE)," which he defined "as a wakeful though contentless" form of consciousness (Forman, pp. 7–8).

Forman also reframed the debate between himself and Katz, describing Katz as a "constructivist" and himself as a "perennialist" in their approaches to mysticism. The constructivist model, Forman argued, reflected the desire to privilege pluralism and difference over the commonalities highlighted by perennialists. Viewed in this way, the debate between Katz and Forman can be understood as a debate over the autonomy of mystical experience relative to the traditions. Conversely, it is a debate over the legitimacy of the perennialist self-understanding, which, as predicted by Troeltsch, has broken increasingly free of the traditions over the course of the twentieth century. While perennialists may indeed pluck experiences out of their original socio-historical environment, as the historians of mysticism claimed, they do so in order to relocate, that is subsume, them within a perennialist framework. They are engaging, in other words, in a process of redescription that is not always openly acknowledged.

Both the Katz-Forman debate and the debate over reductionism in the study of religion focused on the autonomy of the experiences in question. The debate between Katz and Forman located the question of autonomy in relation to the traditions. Forman, in arguing for a common core, a view that he explicitly linked to perennialism, argued for the academic legitimacy of a perennialist framework undergirding and implicitly linking the various traditions. The debate over whether or not religious experience (religion) was sui generis, in contrast, located the question of autonomy in relation to the academic disciplines. The debate over whether Otto, van der Leeuw, Wach, and Eliade were making descriptive claims about believers or ontological claims about religion in general reflects a parallel uncertainty. Were Otto, van der Leeuw, Wach, and Eliade involved in the empirical study of the religion of their subjects or in creating a generic understanding of religion ontologically grounded in an ostensible experience of the holy or sacred and, thus, tacitly protected from methodological scrutiny? The weight of the scholarship suggests that while they hoped to accomplish the former, they in fact effected the latter, without effectively differentiating between the two aims. Like the perennialists, they too were engaging in an ontologically informed process of redescription that was not overtly acknowledged.

QUESTIONS OF METHOD. The central methodological question for the empirical study of religion is data selection. Douglas Allen clearly articulated the problem when he observed apropos of Eliade that if the historian of religion's "point of departure is the historical data which expresses the religious experiences of mankind[,] . . . how does one know what documents to collect, which phenomena to describe and interpret?" (Allen, pp. 171-172). Proudfoot identified two options: an experience can be designated as religious by the scholar (who must then supply a definition of religion) or by the subject of the experience. In practice, however, matters are not so simple. Many texts that the scholar might intuitively want to consider were written by followers or observers rather than by the ostensible subject of the experience. More crucially, many of those same texts do not explicitly refer to either "religion" or "experience." Moreover, when scholars turn to definitions of religion for assistance, they often find that they employ referents (e.g., ultimate reality, the sacred, the numinous) that are so vague that they offer little assistance in selecting texts. The problem of data selection, thus, leads directly to the underlying question of how (and to what extent) we as scholars constitute our objects of study.

If, as Jonathan Z. Smith has argued, we want to move beyond simply paraphrasing the words of those we are studying, whether on the grounds of their uniqueness or inviolability, we must take responsibility for our role in constructing an object of study. Three options are particularly pertinent with regard to what has traditionally been construed as religious experience, each with its own advantages and disadvantages, depending on the scholar's aims. (1) The scholar can limit him or herself to texts that make explicit use of the term "religious experience" and its near neighbors and competitors, always taking care to note which terms are actually being employed. This is the strategy adopted by Halbfass, Sharf (1995), and this entry. This approach is particularly useful for tracing the use of concepts and the history of ideas. It does not attempt to get at experiences per se. (2) The scholar can decide in advance what he or she will count (i.e. define) as "religious experience" by developing a definition that is sufficiently specific that it can actually be used to select appropriate textual sources for consideration. While this approach allows the scholar to get at experiences, it runs the risk of saying more about the scholar's understanding of religion (substantively or heuristically) than that of his or her subjects. Care, therefore, should be taken to distinguish between the scholar's views and those of his or her sources. (3) The scholar can identify an aspect of experience that is not necessarily co-extensive with what scholars or their subjects take to be religion (e.g., the subjective sense of encountering or being moved by an external power), and analyze the way in which it is understood by persons who stand inside and, if desired, outside one or more traditions. This approach allows scholars to analyze what their subjects understand as authentic experience and to explore the criteria they use for making these judgments. This approach makes controversies over the meaning of a particular type of experience the focus of scholarly analysis. It recognizes (and takes advantage of) the fact that both insiders and outsiders to a tradition regularly describe and redescribe experiences as religious or not religious, authentic or inauthentic. In so doing, this approach allows scholars to recognize and examine boundary issues (e.g. between psychical experience, visions, mysticism, religious experience, spirituality and so on) that may be suppressed by scholarly definitions of religion.

NEW DIRECTIONS. Some of the most interesting new research reflects the interdisciplinary interests of William James and others affiliated with the Society for Psychical Research at the beginning of the twentieth century. Three partially overlapping areas of research look particularly promising: the relationship between religious experience and brain function, between religious experience and psychopathology, and between religious experience and various disciplines or practices. These investigations locate the study of religious experience in relation to cognitive science, clinical psychology, and ritual studies, respectively. Three studies, each of which explores this interdisciplinary terrain in different ways, illustrate three different ways of constructing an object of study.

Etzel Cardeña, Steven Jay Lynn, and Stanley Krippner—all associated with the American Psychological Association's Division 30 (Psychological Hypnosis)—edited *Varieties of Anomalous Experience.* In addition to alluding to James in their title, they view themselves as continuing a tradition of scientific investigation initiated by the Society for Psychical Research and late nineteenth-century clinical researchers. Their object of study is "anomalous experiences," that is, experiences that are either uncommon or are "believed to deviate from ordinary experience or from the usually accepted explanations of reality" (Cardeña/Lynn/Krippner, p. 4). By choosing a term that does not have any necessary associations with either psychopathology or religion, they are free to explore how anomalous experiences relate to either or both in essays on topics such as hallucinatory experiences, synesthesia, lucid dreaming, out-of-body experiences, past-life experiences, and near-death experiences.

Jess Byron Hollenbeck's *Mysticism: Experience, Response, and Empowerment* breaks into the Katz-Forman debate by refusing to exile "visions, locutions, and illuminations from the domain of mysticism," because, he says, in doing so, "we lose sight of a number of fascinating questions that pertain to the psychology of trance." Like James, Hollenbeck takes as his object of study phenomena that fall along a continuum of experience from the more abstract forms of experience typically designated as mystical to "more 'concrete' types of transcendence," such as visions, apparitions, supernormal enhancements of the senses, and experiences of supersensible illumination. These more concrete forms of experience in turn bear some resemblance to everyday sense experience. Reestablishing a continuum of experience allows Hollenbeck to break down the dichotomy between "universal" and "tribal" religions presupposed by the usual definitions of mysticism. He explores the linkages between paranormal experiences, mystical states of consciousness, and practices of recollection (or concentration of the mind)and critiques both the perennialist and contextualist lines of interpretation.

Finally, Ilkka Pyysiäinen's *How Religion Works: Toward a Cognitive Science of Religion* provides a new theory of religious experience based on an object of study that distinguishes between religion and experience and defines religion empirically. Building on the work Pascal Boyer and others, Pyysiäinen hypothesizes that people identify something as "religious" if it involves "counter-intuitive agents," that is, agents that "'violate panhuman intuitive expectations' in a well defined fashion" (Pyysiäinen, p. 23). In contrast to scholars who simply stipulate a definition of religion, Pyysiäian's definition is offered as a hypothesis, which he has tested empirically and which is, thus, potentially open to refutation (Pyysiäinen, p. 225). In discussing the neurological mechanisms associated with what are commonly understood as "religious experiences," he stresses that the mechanisms themselves are "in no way specifically 'religious'" (Pyysiäinen, p. 142). The experiences, in other words, are not necessarily either religious or non-religious; they become religious when they are associated with counter-intuitive representations. By carefully distinguishing between religion and experience, Pyysiäian constructs a theory in which both aspects—the definition of religion and the correlations between experiences and brain processes—are open to experimental testing and potential refutation.

Bibliography

Allen, Douglas. "Mircea Eliade's Phenomenological Analysis of Religious Experience." *Journal of Religion* 52 (1972): 170–186.

Andresen, Jensine. *Religion in Mind: Cognitive Perspectives on Religious Belief, Ritual, and Experience.* Cambridge, U.K., 2001.

Andresen, Jensine, and Robert K. C. Forman. *Cognitive Models and Spiritual Maps: Interdisciplinary Explorations of Religious Experience.* Bowling Green, Ohio, 2000.

Bagger, Matthew C. *Religious Experience, Justification, and History.* Cambridge, U.K., 1999.

Barnard, G. William. "William James and the Origins of Mystical Experience." In *The Innate Capacity: Mysticism, Psychology, and Philosophy*, pp. 161–210. New York, 1998.

Biale, David. *Gershom Scholem: Kabbalah and Counter-History.* Cambridge, Mass., 1979.

Brainard, F. Samuel. "Defining 'Mystica' Experience." *JAAR* 64, no. 2 (1996): 359–393.

Cardeña, Etzel, Steven Jay Lynn, and Stanley Krippner. *Varieties of Anomalous Experience.* Washington, D.C., 2000.

Crouter, Richard. "Introduction." In *On Religion*, edited by Friedrich Schleiermacher, pp. xi–xxxix. Cambridge, U.K., 1996.

Cupitt, Don. *Mysticism after Modernity.* Malden, Mass., 1998.

Dubarle, Dominique. "Modernisme et expérience religieuse." In *Le Modernisme*, edited by P. Colin and others, pp. 181–270. Paris, 1980.

Emerson, Ralph Waldo. *Essays and Lectures.* New York, 1983.

Ernst, Carl W. *The Shambhala Guide to Sufism.* Boston, 1997.

Fitzgerald, Timothy. "Experience." In *The Guide to the Study of Religion*, edited by Willi Braun and Russell T. McCutcheon, 125–139. London, 1997.

Forman, Robert K. C. *The Problem of Pure Consciousness.* New York, 1990.

Fredericks, James L. "A Universal Religious Experience? Comparative Theology as an Alternative to a Theology of Religions." *Horizons* 22, no. 1 (1995): 67–87.

Friedman, Maurice. *Martin Buber's Life and Work: The Early Years 1878–1923.* New York, 1981.

Furse, Margaret Lewis. *Experience and Certainty: William Ernest Hocking and Philosophical Mysticism.* Atlanta, 1988.

Gadamer, Hans-Georg. *Truth and Method.* New York, 1975.

Gude, Mary Louise. *Louis Massignon: The Crucible of Compassion.* Notre Dame, Ind., 1996.

Halbfass, Wilhelm. *India and Europe: An Essay in Understanding.* Albany, N.Y., 1988.

Hanegraaff, Wouter J. "Empirical Method in the Study of Esotericism." *Method and Theory in the Study of Religion* 7 (1995): 99–129.

Hanegraaff, Wouter J. *New Age Religion and Western Culture.* Albany, N.Y., 1998a.

Hanegraaff, Wouter J. "On the Construction of 'Esoteric Traditions'." In *Western Esotericism and the Science of Religion,* edited by Antoine Faivre and Wouter J. Hanegraaff, 11–61. Louvain, 1998b.

Hill, W. J. "Experience, Religious." In *The New Catholic Encyclopedia.* Washington, D.C., 1967.

Hollenback, Jess Byron. *Mysticism: Experience, Response, and Empowerment.* University Park, Pa., 1996.

Hughes, H. Maldwyn. "Experience (Religious)." In *Encyclopedia of Religion and Ethics,* edited by James Hastings. New York, 1912.

Idinopulos, Thomas A., and Edward A. Yonan, eds. *Religion and Reductionism: Essays on Eliade, Segal, and the Challenge of the Social Sciences for the Study of Religion.* Leiden, 1994.

Idinopulos, Thomas A., and Edward A. Yonan, eds. *The Sacred and Its Scholars: Comparative Methodologies for the Study of Primary Religious Data.* Leiden, 1996.

James, William. *The Varieties of Religious Experience* (1902). Cambridge, Mass., 1985.

Jantzen, Grace M. *Power, Gender, and Christian Mysticism.* Cambridge, U.K., 1995.

Katz, Stephen T. *Mysticism and Philosophical Analysis.* New York, 1978.

Kippenberg, Hans G. *Discovering Religious History in the Modern Age.* Princeton, N.J., 2002.

Kitagawa, Joseph M. *The History of Religions: Understanding Human Experience.* Atlanta, 1987.

Kitagawa, Joseph M., ed. *The History of Religions: Retrospect and Prospect.* New York, 1985.

Klein, Lawrence E., and Anthony J. LaVopa, eds. *Enthusiasm and Enlightenment in Europe, 1650–1850.* San Marino, Calif., 1998.

Kripal, Jeffrey J. *Roads of Excess, Palaces of Wisdom: Eroticism and Reflexivity in the Study of Mysticism.* Chicago, 2001.

Lamberth, David. *William James and the Metaphysics of Experience.* Cambridge, U.K., 1999.

Long, Charles. *Significations.* Philadelphia, 1986.

Martin, James Alfred, Jr. "Religious Experience." In *The Encyclopedia of Religion,* edited by Mircea Eliade. New York, 1987.

McCutcheon, Russell T. "The Category 'Religion' in Recent Publications: A Critical Survey." *Numen* 42 (1995): 284–309.

McCutcheon, Russell T. *Manufacturing Religion: The Discourse on Sui Generis Religion and the Politics of Nostalgia.* Oxford, 1997.

McDermott, Robert A., ed. *Radhakrishnan: Selected Writings on Philosophy, Religion, and Culture.* New York, 1970.

Otto, Rudolf. *The Idea of the Holy.* New York, 1923.

Penner, Hans H. "You Don't Read a Myth for Information." In *Radical Interpretation in Religion,* edited by Nancy K. Frankenberry, 153–170. Cambridge, U.K., 2002.

Proudfoot, Wayne. *Religious Experience.* Berkeley, Calif., 1985.

Pyysiäinen, Ilkka. *How Religion Works: Towards a New Cognitive Science of Religion.* Leiden, 2001.

Raphael, Melissa. *Rudolf Otto and the Concept of Holiness.* Oxford, 1997.

Rennie, Bryan, ed. *Changing Religious Worlds: The Meaning and End of Mircea Eliade.* Albany, N.Y., 2001.

Ricoeur, Paul. *The Symbolism of Evil.* Translated by Emerson Buchanan. New York, 1967.

Schmidt, Leigh Eric. "The Making of Modern 'Mysticism.'" *JAAR* 71, no. 2 (2003): 273–303.

Segal, Robert A. "In Defense of Reductionism." *JAAR* 51, no. 1 (1983): 97–124.

Sharf, Robert H. "Buddhist Modernism and the Rhetoric of Meditative Experience." *Numen* 42, no. 3 (1995), 228–283.

Sharf, Robert H. "Experience." In *Critical Terms for Religious Studies,* edited by Mark C. Taylor, 94–116. Chicago, 1998.

Sharf, Robert H. "The Zen of Japanese Nationalism." In *Curators of the Buddha: The Study of Buddhism under Colonialism,* edited by Donald S. Lopez, Jr., pp. 107–160. Chicago, 1995.

Schimmel, Annemarie. *Mystical Dimension of Islam.* Chapel Hill, N.C., 1975.

Sharpe, Eric J. *Comparative Religion.* 2d ed. LaSalle, Ill., 1986.

Smart, Ninian. *Reason and Faiths.* London, 1958.

Smart, Ninian. *The Religious Experience of Mankind.* New York, 1968.

Smith, Jonathan Z. "Acknowledgments: Morphology and History in Mircea Eliade's Patterns in Comparative Religion (1949–1999): Part I & Part II." *History of Religions* 39/4 (2000): 315–351.

Smith, Jonathan Z. *Map Is not Territory: Studies in the History of Religions.* Leiden, 1978.

Smith, Jonathan Z. "A Twice-Told Tale: The History of the History of Religions' History." *Numen* 48/2 (2001): 131–146.

Stace, Walter T. *Mysticism and Philosophy.* Philadelphia, 1960.

Suzuki, D. T. *Outlines of Mahayana Buddhism.* Chicago, 1907.

Taves, Ann. "Detachment and Engagement in the Study of 'Lived Experience.'" *Spiritus* (2003a).

Taves, Ann. *Fits, Trances, and Visions: Experiencing Religion and Explaining Experience from Wesley to James.* Princeton, N.J., 1999.

Taves, Ann. "Religious Experience and the Divisible Self: William James (and Frederick Myers) as Theorist(s) of Religion." *JAAR* 71, no. 2 (2003b): 303–326.

Troeltsch, Ernst. *Social Teachings of the Christian Churches.* Translated by Olive Wyon. New York, 1931.

Twiss, Sumner B. and Walter J. Conser, eds. *The Experience of the Sacred: Readings in the Phenomenology of Religion.* Hanover, N.H., 1992.

Wach, Joachim. *The Comparative Study of Religions.* New York, 1958.

Wach, Joachim. *Types of Religious Experience, Christian and Non-Christian.* Chicago, 1951.

Walter, Peter. *Die Frage der Glaubensbegründung aus Innerer Erfahrung aus dem I.* Vatikanum. Mainz, Germany, 1980.

Wasserstrom, Steven M. *Religion after Religion: Gershom Scholem, Mircea Eliade, and Henry Corbin at Eranos.* Princeton, N.J., 1999.

Welch, Claude. *Protestant Thought in the Nineteenth Century.* 2 vols. New Haven, Conn., 1972, 1985.

Overview. This is the first attempt at an overall history of the use of the term religious experience in the modern period. Previous entries on the topic were written from the perspective of the philosophy and/or theology of religion (see Hughes, Hill, Martin, Smith). Two recent efforts provide critical, albeit largely ahistorical, attempts at deconstruction (Sharf 1998; Fitzgerald). The approach taken here was suggested by Cupitt; Halbfass, "The Concept of Experience in the Encounter between India and the West" in Halbfass; Sharf 1995; and Taves 1999. Hanegraaff 1995 and 1998b, Jantzen, and Kripal provided helpful perspectives on the related histories of Western esotericism and mysticism. Fredericks, Murphy (in Rennie), and Penner provided helpful perspectives on the history of ideas in the modern era.

Pre-Reformation Christianity and Traditional Protestantism. The *Dictionnaire de Spiritualité,* s.v. "Expérience spirituelle," provides a helpful overview of pre-Reformation Christianity. Taves 1999, pp. 13–117, discusses traditional Protestant and early Enlightenment views of experience. For a more detailed discussion of "enthusiasm," see Klein and LaVopa. For a discussion of Protestant's changing view of mysticism, see Schmidt.

Universalistic New Religious Movements. Taken together, Taves 1999, pp.166–260; Taves 2003b; and Hanegraaff, *New Age Religion* (1998), pp. 443–462, provide an overview of these movements and entry into the wider literature.

Liberal Protestant Theology. Welch provides a good overview. Sharpe (pp. 154–69) provides background on Soderblom, Otto, and Heiler. Kippenberg (pp. 125–135), describes the shift from religion as survival to religion as power. Crouter provides a concise overview of the contemporary debate with respect to Schleiermacher and experience in his introduction to On Religion (pp. xxxii–xxxiv). In addition to Merkur and Idinopulos on Otto (in Idinopulos and Yonan 1996), see also Raphael (pp. 60–84, 149–174) for a theologically oriented reassessment of "numinous experience" in the wake of critiques by Smart and Katz. For discussion and critique of recent efforts by Protestant philosophers of religion to defend theism using the concept of religious experience, see Jantzen, pp. 328–339, and Bagger, pp. 109–134, 197–228.

Catholicism after Trent. Hill provides an overview from a Catholic perspective. For further discussion of the Vatican I references to experience, see Walter. For a discussion of Catholic modernism and religious experience, see Dubarle. For an overview of Catholic theology in relation to the modern turn to the subject, Brian J. Shanley, O.P., *The Thomist Tradition* (Boston, 2002), pp. 1–20.

Judaism and Islam. Biale provides an excellent overview of the relationship between Scholem and the early Buber in the context of the study of Judaism in the late nineteenth and twentieth centuries. On Buber's use of Erlebnis, see also Friedman, pp. 76–93, 319–325. Among Moshe Idel's many writings, see *Kabbalah: New Perspectives* (New Haven, 1988) and *Hasidism: Between Ecstasy and Magic* (Albany, 1995). Ernst (1997), pp. 1–17, provides a helpful historical overview of the European discovery and study of Sufism. Gude is the best introduction to Massignon in English. Wasserstrom offers a helpful discussion of Corbin.

Hinduism and Buddhism. Halbfass's essays on "The Concept of Experience" and "Neo-Hinduism" in Halbfass, pp. 378–402, 217–246, provide an excellent overview of the idea of experience in Neo-Hinduism. Sharf's "Buddhist Modernism" and "The Zen of Japanese Nationalism" provide the best overview of the concept of experience in modern Buddhism. On the impact of the World's Parliament of Religions, see "The 1893 World's Parliament of Religions and Its Legacy" in Kitagawa 1987, pp. 353–68, and Judith Snodgrass, *Presenting Japanese Buddhism to the West* (Chapel Hill, 2003).

William James. There is a vast literature on William James. Within religion, most of the recent discussion of *Varieties* has taken place among philosophers of religion and scholars of mysticism (e.g., Proudfoot, Bagger, Barnard, Jantzen, Lamberth). For a good introduction to James in relation to the modern study of mysticism, see Furse, pp. 9–28. Jantzen reads James's chapter on mysticism in relation to Schleiermacher and the Romantic tradition, pp. 304–321, and critiques philosophers of religion for their ahistorical utilization of James's chapter on mysticism, pp. 330–332. Barnard focuses his reading on James's epistemology, utilizing it to support Forman's position in the Katz-Forman debate. Long (pp. 158–172) provides a helpful critical discussion of James and Troeltsch in relation to the study of religion. Taves 2003b, building on Taves 1999: 253–291, treats James from the perspective of comparison in the study of religion.

Sarvepalli Radhakrishnan. For biographical details, see Radhakrishnan's autobiography in McDermott. Radhakrishnan's key writings on religious experience can be found in *The Hindu View of Life* (1927), pp. 11–33, and *An Idealist View of Life* (London, 1932), pp. 84–126. McDermott also provides a helpful philosophically oriented introduction to his thought. *The Philosophy of Sarvepalli Radhakrishnan,* edited by Paul A. Schilpp (New York, 1952), includes numerous tributes to Radhakrishnan, including Wach's somewhat critical contribution, "Radhakrishnan and the Comparative Study of Religion," pp. 443–458.

Joachim Wach and the Chicago Tradition. For a biographical sketch, see Kitagawa 1987: 271–74. Wach's most important writings on religious experience are Sociology of Religion (1944), "Universals in Religion" and "Rudolf Otto and the Idea of the Holy" in Wach, 1951: 30–47, 209–227, and Wach 1958. For Eliade's understanding of the sacred in relation to religious experience, see especially Eliade (1949/58) and J. Z. Smith (2000). For the argument that Eliade might be better positioned in relation to French discourses on the sacred (e.g. Durkheim) than in relation to Protestant phenomenologists such as Otto and van der Leeuw, see William E. Paden in Rennie (pp. 249–259) and in Idinoupolos & Yonan 1994 (pp. 198–210). For a discussion of Otto, Eliade, Kitagawa, and Ricoeur as phenomenologists of religion, see

Twiss & Conser. For histories of the Chicago School under Wach and Eliade by insiders, see Kitagawa, "The History of Religions at Chicago" in Kitagawa 1987: 133–44, and Charles H. Long, "A Look at the Chicago Tradition in the History of Religions," in Kitagawa 1985: 87–104.

Mysticism, the numinous, and religious experience. On Zaehner, see Kripal 2001.

Critics. In addition to Segal (1983), Proudfoot (1985), Idinopulos and Yonan (1994, 1996), see also Long (1986), J. Z. Smith (1978, 2000), McCutcheon 1997 and the essays by McCutcheon, Murphy, and Paden in Rennie. For recent critical discussions of the Katz-Forman debate, see Hollenbeck, 1–25; Jantzen, 322–353; Brainard, and Bagger, 90–108. On method in the study of experience, see Taves 2003a.

New Directions. The essays in Cardeña, Lynn, and Kripner (2000) provide a good point of entry into the literature on religious experience and the clinical disciplines (clinical psychology, transpersonal psychology, and psychiatry). The edited volumes by Andresen (2001) and Pyysiäinen and Anttonen (2002) provide an overview of the most recent work on cognitive science approaches to religion, including several authors that focus on religious experience (see, in addition to Pyysiäian, the articles by McNamara and Barrett in Andresen). The edited volume by Andresen and Forman (2000) draws together a wider range of studies that can be loosely grouped under the heading of conscious studies and religious/spiritual experience. Hollenbeck's interest in supernormal phenomena places him in the tradition of Myers and James and of more recent works, such as Michael Murphy's *The Future of the Body* (Los Angeles, 1992), but raises questions that most scholars of religion have so far avoided.

ANN TAVES (2005)

RENAN, ERNEST (1823–1892) was a French Orientalist and essayist. Joseph Ernest Renan is a fragment of a mirror held up to nineteenth-century France. His life and work reflect especially the appeal of positivist science and its conflict with religion, particularly Roman Catholicism.

Born on February 28, 1823, in Tréguier, Brittany, Renan was raised a Roman Catholic and educated in seminaries until, at the age of twenty-two, he left both the seminary and the church. He wrote to his spiritual director that the church would not allow him the freedom to pursue the kind of scientific study that had increasingly fascinated him. Three years later, in 1848, he wrote *L'avenir de la science* (The Future of Science), a kind of apologia for his conversion to positivist science. In it Renan developed the ideas that would govern virtually all his later work. First, he thought that science would eventually supplant religion in developed societies. "Only science," he wrote, "can resolve eternal human problems." Second, he understood science as an inquiry that exhibits a comparative, skeptical, and nonjudgmental attitude toward its subject, and so distinguishes itself from doctrinaire religion as well as eighteenth-century rationalism.

The Future of Science was not published until 1890, two years before Renan's death; nevertheless, his attitude toward and confidence in science showed clearly in his work on Middle Eastern languages and religion. Renan's interest in the Middle East began during his seminary study in Paris, where he worked under Arthur Le Hir and Étienne Marc Quatremère. In 1848 he won the prestigious Prix Volney for his essay on the history of Semitic languages. In 1852 he was appointed an assistant to the keeper of Eastern manuscripts at the Bibliothèque Nationale in Paris, where he was in charge of Syrian, Sabaean, and Ethiopian manuscripts; this work, he once said, was the most rewarding he had done. During the same period, he published his doctoral thesis on the Arab philosopher Ibn Rushd (Averroës).

As a result of this work Renan had begun to earn a reputation as an Orientalist and so was able to secure a place on a scientific mission to Syria that was organized under the protection of the troops of Napoleon III, who were occupying Beirut. Despite the tragedy of the death of his sister, Henriette, who had always aided and supported his work and who had accompanied him and his wife to Syria, the trip was a milestone for Renan because it cemented his interest in the Middle East and set him to work on what would be the major accomplishment of his professional life, the seven-volume *Histoire des origines du christianisme* (1863–1881) and its five-volume supplement, *Histoire du peuple d'Israël* (1887–1893).

The first volume of *Origines* was the controversial and enormously popular *Vie de Jésus* (Life of Jesus). This little book, which first appeared in 1863, gave educated Frenchmen Renan's idiosyncratic portrait of Jesus. What made the book remarkable in its time, however, was its effort to draw the portrait of Jesus only along the lines roughed out by historical criticism and to project it against the larger background of the Middle Eastern religions. It showed Renan's comparative method at work, and because it failed to make or support the traditional religious claims about the divinity of Jesus or the uniqueness of Christian religion, it was widely condemned by the churches.

Renan returned to the Middle East again in 1864, this time to Egypt, Asia Minor, and Greece. It was on this trip that Renan composed the *Prière sur l'Acropole,* which expressed what he called his religious revelation that the perfection promised by Judaism, Islam, and Christianity actually existed in the Greek civilization that created science, art, and philosophy. Since religion is, in Renan's view, the way people often satisfy their craving for such perfection, he continued to pursue his research into the relationships among Judaism, Christianity, and Islam. His thesis was that Christianity adapted Judaism to the European temperament and Islam adapted it to the Arab.

Renan's historical sense was not always the best, and he clearly preferred to draw his conclusions from what he thought were psychological patterns of the races and religions he studied. He speculated a good deal more freely than scholars are accustomed to do today (for example, he described in detail the physical appearance of Paul of Tarsus), and he was ready to base his judgments on aesthetic principles as much as on historical fact. However, his prose style was provocative and so effective that he often had an impact in excess of the merits of his research. His work earned him appointment as professor of history of religions at the Collège de France in 1862 and again in 1870. In 1878 he was elected to the Académie Française. He died in Paris on October 2, 1892.

Above all, Renan has reserved a place for himself in the religious history of France because he, as much as anyone else, focused public attention on the potential and the consequences of a scientific approach to religious questions. Particularly for the group of French Catholic scholars who followed him, he served as a challenge and a warning to their effort to modernize the church.

BIBLIOGRAPHY

Renan's works have been published in many languages. In French, his *Œuvres complètes,* 10 vols., edited by Henriette Psichari (Paris, 1947–1961), is the basic source. Among his works that have appeared in English editions, translated by various hands, are *The Future of Science, History of the People of Israel, The Life of Jesus,* and *Studies in Religious History.* Renan's two autobiographical pieces are also available under the English title *The Memoirs of Ernest Renan* (London, 1935).

The standard work on Renan in English is Francis Espinasse's *The Life of Ernest Renan* (1895; reprint, Boston, 1980), written only a few years after Renan's death. H. W. Wardman's *Ernest Renan* (London, 1964) is another English-language study. A useful bibliography can be found in Jacques Waardenburg's *Classical Approaches to the Study of Religion,* vol. 2 (The Hague, 1974), pp. 228–241.

New Sources

Yves Marchasson, "Ernest Renan," in *Supplément au Dictionnaire de la Bible,* Vol. 10, Paris, 1985, pp.277–344 provides succinct factual information on Renan's life, works, ideas and legacy. Laudyce Rétat, *Religion et imagination religieuse. Leurs formes et leurs rapports dans l'œuvre d'Ernest Renan,* Paris, 1977, is the most comprehensive monograph in French. David C. J. Lee, *Ernest Renan. In the Shadow of Faith,* London, 1996 explores the conflicts surrounding the process of secularization in the light of Renan's biographical experience. Renan's commmitment to ideologies spread in academic conetemporary milieux (racism, traditionalism) have been scrutinized recently in various works: after the provoking, if somewhat biased, *Orientalism,* by Edward Said (New York, 1978), see Edouard Richard, *Ernest Renan, penseur traditionaliste?* Aix-Marseille, 1996 and Samar Majaes Abdel Nour, *Ernest Renan et l'Orient: ambiguïté d'une relation passionnée,* Lille, 1999.

RICHARD J. RESCH (1987)
Revised Bibliography

REN AND YI

REN AND YI are basic terms in Confucian thought. *Ren* is often translated as "benevolence" or "humaneness," and *yi* as "propriety" or "rightness"; in combination, the expression *ren-yi* refers to the Confucian way of life and is often translated as "morality."

Ren was probably cognate with another term, *ren** (human beings, persons, others), and there are two main scholarly views regarding the early use of *ren.* One theory takes it to refer originally to the desirable attributes making one a distinctive member of certain tribes or aristocratic clans. The other takes it to refer originally to love or the tender part of human feelings, especially the kindness of a ruler toward his subjects. The term is used in the *Analects* of Confucius (sixth to fifth century BCE) more often in a broader sense, but sometimes in a narrower sense. In the broader sense, it refers to an all-encompassing ideal for human beings that includes such desirable attributes as wisdom, courage, filial piety, conscientiousness, trustworthiness, or even caution in speech and the ability to endure adverse circumstances. In the narrower sense, it emphasizes the part of the ethical ideal having to do with affective concern for others, and on one occasion *ren* is explained in terms of love for fellow human beings. This latter use of *ren* is highlighted in the *Mengzi.* Mengzi (also known as Mencius, fourth century BCE) characterizes *ren* in terms of love or concern for others, a concern that involves gradation—one's concern for and obligations to those closer to oneself go beyond one's concern for and obligations to those more distant from oneself. *Ren* also involves a reluctance to cause harm and the capacity to be moved by the suffering of others, where the scope of this concern includes not only human beings but also animals of certain kinds.

Yi was probably a near relative of, if not derived from, *wo* (I, me, myself), and it was used in early texts in relation to distancing oneself from disgrace—someone with *yi* has a proper regard for himself or herself and would not brook an insult or accept disgraceful treatment. By the time of Confucius, *yi* had come to be used more generally in connection with proper conduct, where what is proper is measured against certain ethical standards that go beyond ordinary social honor or disgrace. Both Mengzi and Xunzi (third century BCE) highlight the distinction between what is truly honorable or disgraceful, as measured by certain ethical standards, and what is honorable or disgraceful by ordinary social standards. Unlike Mozi (fifth century BCE), who explains *yi* in terms of *li* (profit, benefit), Mengzi often contrasts *yi* with *li,* emphasizing the priority of *yi* over profit. Mengzi uses *yi* to refer not just to the propriety of conduct but also to a desirable attribute of a person. As such, it involves one's regarding as tainting to oneself what falls below ethical standards, and one's insistence on distancing oneself from such occurrences.

Mengzi contrasts *ren* and *yi* by saying that the former concerns *xin* (heart, mind) of human beings and is that in which one resides, and the latter is the path for human beings and is that which one follows. Also, the former concerns what one cannot bear while the latter concerns what one would not do. Thus, *ren* has to do with affective concern for others, while *yi* has to do with strictness with oneself, a firm commitment to not falling below certain ethical standards.

This contrast between *ren* and *yi* is highlighted by the Han Confucian thinker Dong Zhongshu (179–104 BCE), who points to the link of *ren* to *ren** (others) and of *yi* to *wo* (oneself). According to Dong, *ren* has to do with love for others (rather than oneself) and *yi* with straightening oneself (rather than others). The Tang Confucian thinker Han Yu (768–824) thinks that loving broadly is what is meant by *ren,* while acting in a way that's appropriate is what is meant by *yi.*

The understanding of *ren* and *yi* continued to undergo significant evolvement in later Confucian thought. *Yi* is often related to *dao* (way) and to *li** (pattern, principle) in early texts. The Song Confucian thinker Zhu Xi (1130–1200) distinguishes between these concepts by saying that *dao* emphasizes the proper way of life for human beings in general, while *yi* emphasizes what is proper in relation to specific situations and affairs. *Li** pertains to things and affairs, and is that which accounts for the way things operate and the way they should operate. *Yi,* by contrast, pertains to the actual dealings with affairs by human beings; a person acts with *yi* by following *li** that pertains to the situation. While still often contrasting *yi* with *li* (profit, benefit), Zhu also endorses another early idea that regards *li* as arising from *yi.* While *li** (pattern, principle) is ultimately one, its instantiation in things is differentiated and everything has its own *feng* (allotment, proper place). *Yi* involves following *li** in things, thereby enabling each thing to attain its proper place (*feng*) without interfering with other things; this is what is truly beneficial (*li*) to things.

The early texts *Yijing* (Book of changes) and *Li ji* (Record of rites) refer to *ren* as the *xin* (heart, mind) of heaven and earth, and the Song Confucian thinker Zhang Zai (1020–1077) also speaks of the *ren* of heaven and earth. According to Zhang Zai, *ren* should encompass every thing and affair without omission, and the sage is like heaven in being without regard for himself. Following Zhang Zai, Zhu Xi explicates *ren* in terms of forming one body with ten thousand things; everything is part of oneself, so there is no longer a distinction between self (*wo*) and other things. Following the brothers Cheng Hao (1032–1085) and Cheng Yi (1033–1107), Zhu Xi characterizes *ren* as the *xin* of giving life to and nourishing things, endorsing the Cheng brothers' comparison of *ren* to the life-giving power of a seed of grain. Again drawing from the Cheng brothers, Zhu Xi compares the use of *ren* in an ethical context to its use in a medical context. Everything is part of oneself, just as the four limbs are part of one's body. Just as numbness in a limb is referred to as the lack of *ren* in a medical context, a failure to be sensitive to the wellbeing of other things reflects a lack of *ren* in oneself. This does not mean that one should treat everything equally; just as one might sacrifice one's hand to protect one's head, the wellbeing of those closer to oneself can have priority over the wellbeing of others who are more distant. This is an application of the idea that although *li** (pattern, principle) is one, its instantiation in things is differentiated; differential treatment of things is an appropriate response to the different relations one maintains to different things.

SEE ALSO Confucius; Mengzi.

BIBLIOGRAPHY

Chan, Wing-tsit, trans. and comp. *A Source Book in Chinese Philosophy.* Princeton, 1963.

Graham, A. C. *Disputers of the Tao: Philosophical Argument in Ancient China.* La Salle, Ill., 1989.

Graham, A. C. *Two Chinese Philosophers: The Metaphysics of the Brothers Ch'eng.* La Salle, Ill., 1992.

Nivison, David S. *The Ways of Confucianism: Investigations in Chinese Philosophy.* La Salle, Ill., 1996.

Shun, Kwong-loi. *Mencius and Early Chinese Thought.* Stanford, Calif., 1997.

KWONG-LOI SHUN (2005)

RENNYO

RENNYO (1415–1499), a Japanese Buddhist monk, was the eighth head priest of the Honganji temple of Jōdo Shinshū ("True Pure Land sect"). He was the eldest son of Zonnyo, the sect's seventh head priest. Since Honganji, which was then located in the Higashiyama district of Kyoto, was then affiliated with the Shoren-in belonging to the Tendai sect, it was dominated by Tendai rituals and teachings. At that time, Honganji was nearly deserted, visited by few people.

When Rennyo was six years old, his mother left the temple. At that time, she instructed him to revive the teaching of Shinran (1173–1263), the founder of Jōdo Shinshū. Following his mother's wish, Rennyo, at the age of sixteen, resolved to work for its revival. At seventeen, Rennyo took the tonsure at Shoren-in, and then went to Daijo-in, a subtemple of Kofukuji in Nara, where he studied Buddhist teachings. Rennyo subsequently returned to Honganji and studied Shinran's writings assiduously.

With the death of his father in 1457, Rennyo succeeded to the abbacy of Honganji and began to proselytize Shinran's teachings. He first concentrated his efforts in the province of Omi, which bordered Kyoto to the east. His success provoked the anger of the Tendai sect, which sent armed monks to attack Honganji. The temple was destroyed, and Rennyo barely escaped with his life. This event is called the *Kanshō no Hōnan* (persecution of the Kansho period). Rennyo took refuge in Kanegamori in Omi, where the villagers succeeded in routing the pursuing monks in a pitched battle.

No longer able to work in Omi, which was under the dominance of the Tendai sect, Rennyo moved his base of operation in 1471 to Yoshizaki in Echizen province, a region to the northwest of Kyoto on the Sea of Japan. There he proselytized widely using pastoral letters, called *ofumi* or *gobunshō,* written in colloquial Japanese, and he developed lay religious associations called *ko* to organize his followers. As a result, the number of his adherents increased dramatically. Rennyo's success sparked the jealousy of other local Buddhist groups, including those located at Heisenji and Toyohara-dera. Local warriors also began to show interest in extending their control over Yoshizaki.

In 1473, two years after Rennyo's move, rumors started that these forces were about to attack Yoshizaki. Fearing a battle, Rennyo attempted to leave Yoshizaki, but was persuaded by his adherents residing in Yoshizaki to remain and to protect the town using all necessary means. A resolution adopted at this time states the following: "After mutual discussion, it was decided that (if Yoshizaki is attacked), we must fight to protect the Buddhist dharma, even if we are to die in battle." This resolution became the basis of *ikkō ikki*, which were popular uprisings that sought to protect Buddhist teachings, by force if necessary.

In 1474, followers of the Takada branch of Jōdo Shinshū in the province of Kaga (next to Echizen), in league with the warrior Togashi Yukichio, tried to suppress Rennyo's followers. As a result, the people of Kaga rose up in the so-called Kaga Ikkō Ikki. The Jōdo Shinshū followers of Kaga provided Rennyo with his largest source of economic support. Rennyo justified their action, saying that "they had no choice but to begin their rebellion, since Buddhism was being attacked and *nembutsu* practitioners were being persecuted. Their actions are only natural." However, Rennyo did not desire more fighting. Feeling that the only way to quell the rebellion was for him to vacate Yoshizaki, he left the town in 1475. Nevertheless, the Kaga Ikkō Ikki continued. In 1488, Togashi Masachika, the constable of Kaga, was killed and the *ikkō ikki* took over the province.

After leaving Yoshizaki, Rennyo attempted to restore the Honganji that had been destroyed earlier by Tendai monks. He began a construction project in 1478 in the Yamashina district of Kyoto and completed it after five years. Its many marvelous buildings led people to describe it as being "just like the Buddha's land." A temple town was created around Honganji as believers flocked to settle in the vicinity of the temple. The town quickly became a thriving center of commerce and industry where, it was said, all the people are rich and live in beautiful houses.

While at Yamashina, Rennyo succeeded in unifying the many Jōdo Shinshū branches under his leadership, and his organization spread throughout Japan. Even after he retired and passed on the position of chief abbot to his son, Jitsunyo, in 1489, Rennyo remained an active proselytizer, composing many pastoral letters and constructing a temple in Osaka in Settsu province. Rennyo died in 1499 in Yamashina.

The most important writings by Rennyo are his pastoral letters (Osamu Katata has verified the existence of 252 such letters). In them, Rennyo stressed the importance of faith and argued that the *nembutsu* (the phrase "Namu Amida Butsu" or "I take refuge in Amida Buddha'") should be recited as an expression of gratitude to Amida Buddha, the major object of worship in Jōdo Shinshū, who vowed to save even the most evil person.

Besides his well-known pastoral letters, Rennyo composed the *Shoshinge-chu*, the *Shoshinge tai'i*, and two commentaries on a hymn written by Shinran. The *Shoshinge tai'i*, written in 1457 just after Rennyo became the chief abbot of Honganji, has been the object of much scholarly attention in modern times. Rennyo frequently presented his followers with autographed copies of the so-called "ten character name of Amida Buddha" (the phrase "*kimyo jinjip'po mugeko nyorai*," meaning "I take refuge in the Tathagata of Unhindered Light Illuminating the Ten Quarters") to be used as objects of worship. In the commentary to this work he states the following: "Amida Tathagata is also called Tathagata of Unhindered Light. This is because the saving light of Amida Tathagata cannot be obstructed by human laws" (*Shinshu shogyo zensho,* vol.3, p. 387). *Human laws* here refers to laws of the state and ethical rules, which were often employed as means of oppression. Some people felt liberated by these words and were moved to take part in antiestablishment activities, such as *ikkō ikki.* Perhaps for this reason, Rennyo stopped presenting his followers with the ten character name after he moved to Yoshizaki. Instead he began to present them with the six character name, "Namu Amida Butsu." At the same time, he also repeatedly admonished his followers in his pastoral letters to respect the authorities and to obey social norms and ethical rules. However, Rennyo's adherents found it difficult to forget his earlier teachings.

Rennyo also composed numerous verses in colloquial Japanese on Jōdo Shinshū doctrine. Katata has identified the existence of 316 such verses. Although not works by Rennyo, collections of his sayings and anecdotes about him, such as the *Kuzen kikigaki* and *Jitsugo-ki,* provide insight into Rennyo's character and daily life.

SEE ALSO Jōdo Shinshū; Mappō.

BIBLIOGRAPHY

Rennyo's writings, including his pastoral letters, *Shoshinge-chu*, *Shoshinge tai'i*, and his verses, as well as the *Rennyo shonin goichidai kikigaki*, are found in Osamu Katata, ed., *Shinshū shiryō shūsei* (Collection of Jodō Shinshū documents), vol. 2: *Rennyo to sono kyodan* (Rennyo and his community; Kyoto, 1977). See also *Shinshu shogyo zensho,* 5 vols., Kyoto, 1940-1944. The most recent studies on Rennyo can be found in Jodoshinshu Kyogaku Kenkyujo, ed., *Kōza Rennyo* (Lectures on Rennyo), 6 vols. (Tokyo, 1966–1968), which includes articles on Rennyo's life and thought by leading scholars. For an English study, which includes a translation of Rennyo's pastoral letters, see Minor Rogers and Ann Rogers, *Rennyo: The Second Founder of Shin Buddhism* (Berkeley, 1992).

KENSHI KUSANO (2005)

RENOU, LOUIS (1896–1966) was a French student of the religions of India and a Sanskrit grammarian. Louis Renou gave to the Indological world French translations of the *Ṛgveda* and other studies that have gained central importance in the scholarly understanding of Sanskrit texts as autonomous and internally consistent literatures. His *Études védiques et paninéennes* (1956–1969) and other publications on Sanskrit philology are exacting and precise studies that have elucidated for specialists the often obtuse and difficult, but fundamentally important, literatures of ancient India. His introductory works on the religions of South Asia have helped beginners gain confidence in their understanding of complicated religious systems.

Renou taught himself Sanskrit in his mid-twenties, and by the time he took a course in 1922 with Sylvain Lévi he found that he could read Sanskrit texts with ease. He was frustrated in his initial studies of the language, however, by the paucity of critical or analytical tools, and he became determined to provide such materials for others. He therefore focused his attention in his earlier works on Sanskrit philology, grammar, and literature. From these concerns he then moved into specialized studies and translations of the hymns of the Vedic Samhitās.

Generally taking issue with historical or cultural methods in the critical study of Indian religious systems, and particularly of Vedic canonical texts, Renou insisted throughout his career that the literatures and religious ideas of ancient India should not be understood either in comparison to the religions of other cultures or in their relationship to later developments in the religious systems of India itself. He was particularly assertive in his notion that the verses of the *Ṛgveda* are intentional poems in their own right and are not to be understood as Indian counterparts of Iranian religious literatures or as veiled records of or literary precursors to the Brahmanic ritual. For Renou, data relevant to a text's interpretation lay within the syntax and semantics of the text itself, not in the structures and dynamics of other religious expressions.

Because he maintained that the sacred texts of ancient India should be analyzed in their own terms, Renou's linguistic studies may be characterized as extended critical *explications du text* that eschew sociological, mythological, sacerdotal, developmental, or other contextual concerns. He therefore saw no recourse in commentaries, indigenous or otherwise (even those of the perhaps too widely accepted fourteenth-century Vedic commentator Sāyana), in his pursuit of the meaning of primary texts. His interpretive spirit was thus kindred to that of Panini, a Sanskrit linguist who in the eighth century BCE wrote what many modern scholars hold to be the oldest grammar in the world and whose works Renou studied diligently.

Renou was born in Paris, but through his mother he had a long line of Alsatian ancestors. He was introduced to Indic studies while at the Lycée Janson of Sailly, where he read various articles by Auguste Barth, a family friend. He obtained the *licence ès lettres* in 1921, his studies having been interrupted by his captivity during World War I. During 1921–1922 he taught at the Lycée Corneille in Rouen and was awarded the *docteur ès lettres* in 1925, having written a principal thesis entitled "La valeur du parfait dans les hymns védique" (1925) and a secondary thesis entitled "La géographie de Prolémée: L'Inde (VII 1–4)" (1925), a critical edition and commentary.

Renou was professor of Sanskrit and comparative literature at Lyons from 1925 until 1928, when he moved to a similar positon at the École des Hautes Études in Paris. He was chosen in 1937 to head the department of Indian languages and literatures at the Sorbonne, where he succeeded Alfred Foucher as the director of the Institute de Civilisation Indienne. Renou was elected to the Académie des Inscriptions et Belles Lettres (1946) and to the Académie du Japon (1956) as well as to academic and intellectual societies in India, Denmark, Czechoslovakia, the Netherlands, and other countries. He also was the vice president of the Société Asiatique. Renou gave a series of lectures in India in 1948–1949 and subsequently became active in the Sanskrit Dictionary Project based in Pune (Poona). In 1951 he was invited to give a series of lectures at the University of Louvain and then at the University of London's School of Oriental and African Studies. Renou accepted Franklin Edgerton's invitation to teach at Yale University for the academic year 1952–1953, and from 1954 to 1956 Renou was the director of the Maison Franco-Japonaise in Tokyo, where he developed a course on the *Atharvaveda.*

Despite his concentration on Sanskrit grammar and exegesis, no aspect of Indian culture remained foreign to Renou, and through his writing he contributed much to Indological studies on an international scale.

BIBLIOGRAPHY

From the long list of works written and edited by Renou, he is perhaps best known for the following.

La civilisation de l'Inde ancienne, d'après les textes sanskrits. Paris, 1950. Translated as *The Civilization of Ancient India,* 2d ed. (Calcutta, 1959).

Dictionnaire sanskrit-français. 3 vols. With N. Stchoupak and L. Nitti. Paris, 1931–1932.

Grammaire sanscrite. 2 vols. 2d ed. Paris, 1962.

L'hindouisme. 2d ed. Paris, 1958. Translated as *The Nature of Hinduism* (New York, 1963).

L'Inde classique. With Jean Filliozat et al. 2 vols. Paris, 1947–1953.

Les littératures de l'Inde. 2d ed. Paris, 1966. Translated as *Indian Literature* (New York, 1964).

La poésie religieuse de l'Inde antique. Paris, 1942.

Religions of Ancient India (1953). Reprint, New York, 1968.

New Sources

Balbir, Nalini, and Georges-Jean Pinault Langue, eds. *Langue, style et structure dans le monde indien: centenaire de Louis Renou: actes du Colloque international (Paris, 25–27 janvier 1996).* Paris, 1996.

Pinault, Georges-Jean. *Bibliographie des travaux de Louis Renou, 1896–1966.* Paris, 1997.

Renou, Louis. *Louis Renou: choix d'études indiennes: réunies par Nalini Balbir et Georges-Jean Pinault; préface de Colette Caillat; index par Christine Chojnacki.* Paris, 1997.

MARIE-SIMONE RENOU (1987)
Translated from French by William K. Mahony
Revised Bibliography

RENUNCIATION SEE FASTING; MONASTICISM; NUNS; RETREAT; SAṂ NYĀSA; SLEEP; SPIRITUAL DISCIPLINE

REPENTANCE.

REPENTANCE. The noun *repentance* and the verb *repent* came into modern English via Middle English and Old French from the Latin verb *paenitere,* meaning "to be sorry, to grieve, to regret." As a religious term repentance denotes a change in a person's attitude, will, and behavior, sometimes accompanied by feelings of sorrow and regret for past transgressions and perhaps accompanied also by some form of restitution.

MORPHOLOGY OF REPENTANCE.

Repentance is a phenomenon found in some, but not all, religious traditions. When present it can range along a continuum from informal but socially recognized practices (for example, the repentance preceding conversion in modern Protestant revivalism) to very complex formal institutions (for example, the sacrament of penance in Roman Catholicism). Whether formal or informal, repentance is a ritual procedure; it exists to repair a breach in relations between the gods and an individual (or—since ritual and moral pollution are communicable—between the gods and a group). The establishment and maintenance of good relations with the supernatural order is thus a central preoccupation of religion. The interruption of these relations, when it occurs, is either inferred from the experience of misfortune (frequently thought the result of conscious or unconscious transgressions), or discovered through divination (for example, in the Roman senate, reports of prodigies could be either accepted or rejected; if accepted, some form of divination was used to discover the mode of expiation). Repentance belongs to a constellation of restorative religious techniques (for example, confession of sins, restitution, purification, expiatory sacrifice) that lie at the frontier leading from impurity to purity, from sin to salvation, from the community of the lost to the community of the saved. The primary function of these techniques is to objectify and rectify the cause of the breached relationship. Since many important human activities must be undertaken in a state of ritual and perhaps moral purity (warfare, hunting and fishing, childbirth), taboo violations as well as ritual and moral infractions are often confessed and expiated in preparation for such activities.

Confession of sin and accusation. The confession of sin, nearly always a characteristic of repentance, is the verbalization of wrongs committed and the acceptance of blame for their personal and social consequences. Confession can be made privately (to the gods directly as a penitential prayer, or to a specially credentialed representative of the gods), or it can be made publicly. In many cultures the act of confession is inherently cathartic, the sincerity of the penitent being irrelevant. Confession and accusation are sometimes closely connected, particularly when witchcraft and sorcery are involved; in parts of Africa where the onset of witchcraft is thought involuntary (in contrast to sorcery, which is regarded as a skill to be learned), confessions of witchcraft double as accusations against those who imposed it. Among the Ashanti of Ghana, women often confessed acts of involuntary witchcraft at shrines whose presiding spirits troubled them. The Bete of the Ivory Coast think that confession of witchcraft automatically involves absolution. Among the Iroquois of New York State and Ontario who follow the Good Word religion of Handsome Lake, witchcraft is a serious offense requiring public or private confession. During the Salem, Massachusetts, witchcraft trials of 1692, many publicly accused witches acknowledged their culpability and were publicly forgiven and reintegrated into the community. Confession may be seen as self-accusation: During the revivalist movement known as the Great Awakening, which began in 1734 in New England, many people publicly accused themselves of various moral offenses (thereby avoiding accusation by others) and experienced religious conversion.

Penitential rites. Repentance may take form as a ritual presentation, made by the penitent person to observers, of outward expressions of remorse and sorrow. Penitential sorrow often takes the form of customs associated with mourning for the dead: wearing sackcloth and rags, smearing oneself with ashes or mud, self-inflicted pain, fasting, and sexual abstinence. Confession may be formalized both as a rite with its own efficacy (as among the Indian Shakers of the Pacific Northwest), and as part of a more elaborate expiatory protocol perhaps concluding with a sacrifice (as among the Nuer or the ancient Israelites). Restitution or compensation is often an integral feature of penitential rites, particularly in cases wherein others have been harmed or their property damaged or taken away. Confession is sometimes regarded as the necessary prerequisite for formalized types of expiation, such as public sacrifice or public penitential discipline.

Guilt. Repentance is an institutionally approved means of eliminating excessive guilt stemming from the awareness of having transgressed in thought, word, or deed, and thus its public and ritually prescribed protocol exists for the formal recognition and removal of guilt. In order to understand the ritual removal of guilt, it is useful to bear in mind that an anthropological distinction was formerly made between guilt cultures and shame cultures. This distinction was an attempt to reify the fact that in some (generally small-scale) societies self-control is based primarily on *external* sanctions, namely, fear of shame, ridicule, and punishment, while in other societies (often more complex and stratified) self-control is determined primarily by *internal* sanctions, in particular the desire to avoid painful feelings; this is known also as the inner value-structure of the individual conscience, a phenomenon Freud labeled "the censor."

Conversion. The word *conversion* may be defined as the voluntary entry into a religious movement having exclusive claims that are buttressed by a system of values and norms at variance with the outside world; and for conversion repentance is often a necessary precondition, for it involves abandoning the old in order to embrace the new. Particularly with respect to revitalistic or millenarian movements, repentance is often a necessary step for entry. After the rebellion in 1944 of the Bagasin cult of New Guinea (one of the cargo cults), its members were required to confess all past transgressions—primarily sorcery and quarrels over women—in order to demonstrate their genuine conversion to the new order. Two rebel leaders, Kaum and Dabus, had confessional services each Monday; adherents were told that when God-Kilibob was satisfied with their new intentions he would turn their skins white and send cargo through the spirits of the dead. Another cargo cult, the so-called Vailala Madness of Papua, was characterized by both public accusation and public confession as preparations for reform. (Transgressions included stealing and adultery—the established fine for each was one pig; positive injunctions included Sunday observance and the provision of feasts for ancestors.) The rite of public confession may in this instance have been adapted from Roman Catholicism; whatever its origin, it served to ritualize the embracing of the new morality and abandonment of the old. Again, emphasis on conversion to a new life characterizes the Good Word (Gaiwiio) religion, whose belief system is based on the revelatory visions received from 1799 forward by the Seneca chief Handsome Lake (Ganio ʿDaí Ioʿ), and whose tenets are still maintained by half the fifteen thousand Iroquois in New York State and Ontario. The codification of these visions articulates an ethical and cultural program of accommodation between white person and the Indian. Converts to this religion are required to abstain from drinking, gambling, witchcraft, gossip, vanity, boasting, and pride; in short they are to abandon many aspects of the past. In place of these the precepts of the code are tendered, which require the adoption of the white people's mode of agriculture (including working in the field), the learning of English, and a respect for family life and children.

CLASSICAL GREEK TRADITIONS. Among the ancient Greeks, the causes of illness, injury, or other misfortunes were variously diagnosed as (1) the result of chance, (2) the effect of sorcery, (3) divine revenge for affronting a particular divinity's honor, or (4) a punishment for having committed ritual or moral transgressions. In the event that guilt was incurred—for which the main term was *miasma* (pollution, defilement)—a state of purity might be regained by *katharsis* (ritual purification). Consciousness of sin, that is, guilt, was rarely understood in terms of emotional suffering alone. The views of the Athenian orator Antiphon (fifth century BCE) expressed in *On the Murder of Herodes* 5.93 are a striking exception to this rule; more commonly, guilt looked not inward, but outward in anxious anticipation of the consequences of the deed, that is, physical misfortune. After the fifth century BCE the term *enthumios* ("weighing on the mind") and cognates thereof were often used of religious scruples or anxiety, but used in the sense of anticipating an evil fate to result from evil deeds. Thus Euripides interpreted the Erinyes as hypostatized projections of guilt who pursued Orestes in the form of avenging spirits, symbols of his uneasy conscience over past transgressions (acknowledged in *Orestes* 396).

For the existence of repentance and confession among the Greeks, as for the existence of inwardly directed guilt, only limited evidence can be adduced. For example, Lydian and Phrygian inscriptions of the second and third centuries CE may be cited that were dedicated by persons believing themselves punished with illness for specific transgressions (usually ritual offenses); in their belief, healing was obtained by identifying and confessing the sin. Evidence may be claimed also in Plutarch's description of the superstitious people who confesses numerous transgressions and subjects themselves to various ritual expressions of repentance: wearing sackcloth and rags, rolling in mud, and using various magical means of purification (*On Superstition* 168d). However, these repentance rituals appear to be of Asian origin rather than Greek; Plutarch's example is perhaps borrowed from the cult of Dea Syria, which he is known to have held in general contempt. Again, some might cite the conclusion of the first Hermetic treatise (*Poimandres* 28), a call for repentance very similar to Jewish and Christian appeals. But the phenomenon perhaps closest to the idea of repentance is found in certain rites of purification practiced in the Greek cults, including Orphism and the Samothracian, Eleusinian, and Dionysian mysteries. It must be stressed that ritual, not moral, purity was demanded of initiates; in particular they must be free of blood guilt. Entrance to the mysteries therefore required purification rites, such as smearing oneself with mud lest one wallow in mire in the afterlife. In the mysteries of Samothrace initiates were expected moreover to confess any significant crimes (Plutarch, *Apophthegmata Laconica* 217d, 229d), a requirement involving the expiation of ritual pollution. The phenomenon of conversion existed not in cults but in philosophical schools, which were ideologically exclusivistic and thus made conversion possible. For the idea of conversion Plato uses the word *epistrophē* (*Republic* 518dff.): Cicero calls it *conversio* (*De natura deorum* 1.77). Finally, in the *Pinax* of Cebes (a philosopher of the first century CE), wherein the life of vice and virtue are described, repentance personified as Metanoia provides deliverance from the bad life (chap. 26).

NEAR EASTERN TRADITIONS. Repentance is a particularly important aspect of many ancient Near Eastern religions including Mesopotamian religions, Judaism, Islam, and Christianity. Among these religions illness and misfortune were widely attributed to transgression, whether ritual or moral, deliberate or unconscious. Similarly, Akkadian and Sumerian penitential prayers enumerate ethical as well as ritual transgressions. Ancient Egyptian religion is an apparent exception, if one accepts Henri Frankfort's claim that Egyptians had no real consciousness of sin; certainly they had no conception of original sin. Chapter 125 of the Egyptian *Book of Going Forth by Day* contains a script for recital by the deceased person on entering the hall of judgment, and within this script is the very opposite of a confession of sin, that is, a declaration of innocence, using a stereotyped list of the many kinds of crimes and transgressions *not* committed. Siegfried Morenz, however, correctly insists that this display of innocence is actually funerary magic in which the deceased identifies himself with Osiris to evade judgment. The lengthy protestations of innocence provide indirect evidence of a consciousness of sin; nevertheless the phenomenon of repentance is wholly lacking. (Ceremonial avowals of innocence can be found also in the All Smoking ceremony of the Blackfeet Indians and in the Old Testament (*Dt.* 26:13–14, *Ps.* 26:4–5, *1 Sm.* 12:3).

Judaism. In ancient Israel, as in the rest of the Near East, fear existed concerning the possibility of committing unconscious sin and incurring guilt thereby (*Dt.* 29:28, *1 Sm.* 26:19, *Ps.* 19:13, *Jb.* 1:5). But the Bible deals more extensively with guilt incurred by conscious and deliberate sin, described several ways. Guilt may be a motion of the heart: *1 Samuel* 24:5 and *2 Samuel* 24:10 use the expression "David's heart smote him." Guilt may be physical suffering: In an investigation of the *asham* (guilt) offering, Jacob Milgrom has shown that the verbal root *ʿshm* denotes the pangs and remorse brought on by guilt and that it should be translated as "feel guilty" (cf. *Lv.* 5:24–25, *Nm.* 5:6–7). The Hebrew root *shav* ("turn, turn back") eventually came to denote repentance, that is, a turning back to God. The same root was used to denote sin or apostasy, that is, a turning away from God (*Jos.* 22:16). *Shav* meaning "repent" is emphasized by the eighth-century classical Israelite prophets (*Am.* 4:6–11; *Hos.* 3:5, 5:4; *Is.* 1:27, 6:10), and becomes more popular after the sixth century (variant forms occur twenty-seven times in *Jeremiah,* twenty-three times in *Ezekiel,* and twenty-eight times in the postexilic books). The earlier prophets addressed Israel as a whole and demanded national repentance, but later prophets like Ezekiel emphasized individual repentance (*Ez.* 18:21, 18:27, 33:9, 33:11). The Israelite prophets did not distinguish sharply between ritual and moral transgressions, but called Israel back to an earlier, better relationship to God as defined by the terms of the covenant. For the Deuteronomist historian repentance or conversion is primarily a turning away from cultic sins such as idolatry (*1 Sm.* 7:3, *1 Kgs.* 13:33, *2 Kgs.* 17:7–18).

The repentance demanded by the Israelite prophets is linked to ritual manifestations of repentance, as may be seen in *Joel* 2:12–13: "Return to me [Yahveh] with all your heart, with fasting, with weeping, and with mourning; and rend your hearts and not your garments." These manifestations accord with traditional Near Eastern rites of repentance: fasting, wearing sackcloth or mourning garb, rending one's clothes, strewing earth on one's head, sitting in ashes (*Est.* 4:16, *1 Kgs.* 21:27, *Neh.* 9:1, *Jon.* 3:5–9). These manifestations also include the offering of a sacrifice (*Mi.* 6:6–8, *Is.* 1:10–17; occasionally, as in *Jl.* 2:14, the sacrifice is a gift or blessing rather than an expiation). For the prophets forgiveness of sins is dependent on repentance, by which they mean the shunning of evil (*Is.* 33:15) and the practice of good (*Am.* 5:14–15, *Jer.* 26:13).

For sacrificial expiation to take place, there must first occur confession (*hitvaddut*), restitution of goods to persons, and atonement (*asham*) for offense to God (*Nm.* 5:6–8). In the case of deliberate sin, moreover, remorse must be verbalized (cf. *Dn.* 9:5–20, *Neh.* 1:6–37; sacrificial expiation is not possible for the sinner who does not confess or repent (*Nm.* 15:27–31). In the wisdom literature, confession, a prerequisite for sacrificial expiation, includes admitting having committed a specific sin and accepting the blame for it (*Ps.* 32:5, 38:18; *Prov.* 28:13).

During the Second Temple period (516 BCE-70 CE), the notion of repentance or conversion (Heb., *teshuvah;* Gr., *metanoia*) was of central significance to Judaism. The conception could involve the prophetic notion of restoration as well as the conversion of pagans. The Jewish philosopher Philo Judaeus of Alexandria (d. 45–50 CE) viewed the Jewish tradition of conversion or repentance through the spectacles of Greco-Roman philosophy, whereby a proselyte (*epelus*) underwent a conversion (*metanoia*) from a life of vice to one of virtue (*On the Virtues* 175–186, *On Abraham* 17, *Questions and Answers on Genesis* 1.83.) In every age, the mark of the pious Jew is to turn continually to God. Repentance means a permanent break with sin (*Eccl.* 34:25–26, *Sibylline Oracles* 1.167–170; Philo, *On the Special Law Books* 1.93, 1.240). In rabbinic Judaism repentance (*teshuvah*) and good deeds together describe the ideals of Jewish piety (*Avot* 4.21–4.22). In modern Judaism the Days of Awe (Roʾsh ha-Shanah, followed by a week of repentance, culminating in Yom Kippur), is a period of communal contrition and confession of sins. The ritual blowing of the shofar, or ram's horn, beginning a month before Roʾsh ha-Shanah and ending on the festival day itself, comprises four symbolic sounds: *teqiʿah* (the waking call), *shevarim* (the sobbing of the contrite heart), *teruʿah* (the weeping of a heart aware of guilt), and *teqiʿah* (the awakening sound again). On Yom Kippur sins are confessed through statutory prayers recited privately and in unison publicly.

Islam. The most important theological conception in Islam is that God is compassionate and merciful. Repentance has therefore played a central role throughout the history of Islam. Throughout history messengers from God have tried with little success to call people to return to God, that is, to repent; the Arabic word for repentance, *tawbah,* literally means a "returning" to God. Those who reject the message are unbelievers (Arab., *kuffār,* literally "ungrateful ones"). Nevertheless sinners can always repent, be converted to the truth, and do good deeds (Qurʾān 6:54, 42:25–26). They are cleansed from all sins and restored to their original sinless state. Repentance must be followed by faith and good works (Qurʾān 25:70). *Zakāt* (almsgiving) is a continuing sign of repentance, which must be manifest throughout life (Qurʾān 66:5, 9:112).

Traditional Islam is not as concerned about repentance as the Ṣūfīs and the Muʿtazilah. According to the Ṣūfīs, who are the mystics of Islam, the first station (*maqamāh*) on the mystical path begins with repentance. A spiritual guide (*shaykh*) enrolls the penitent as a disciple (*murīd*) and assigns him a regimen of ascetic practices. Ṣūfīs recognize three degrees of repentance, namely, in ascending order, (1) *tawbah* (turning to God), which is motivated by fear; (2) *inābah* (returning), motivated by the desire for reward; and (3) *awbah* (returning), motivated by the love of obedience. For the Ṣūfī, life is a constant struggle against the *nafs* ("self," i. e., lower nature). The Muʿtazilah, proponents of a liberal theological view within Islam, emphasized three elements in repentance: (1) restitution, (2) the importance of not repeating the offense, and (3) continuing remorse. In most forms of Islam, repentance is a relatively informal institution.

Christianity. The religious reform movements led by John the Baptist and by Jesus of Nazareth were revitalistic or millenarian in character. Both emphasized the necessity for repentance or conversion, and took from Judaism the dual means of restoration and proselytism. Even though the activities of John have been christianized in gospel tradition, it is apparent that John summoned fellow Jews to a repentance that he sealed with a ritual bath reminiscent of the washing of Jewish proselytes (*Mt.* 3:1–12; *Lk.* 3:1–20; *Acts* 13:24, 19:4). Those who underwent this baptism were initiated into an eschatological community preparing for the imminent visitation of divine judgment. Jesus, too, is presented as summoning fellow Jews to repentance (*Mk.* 1:14–15; *Lk.* 13:1–5, 15:7), and the ritual of baptism inherited from John was perpetuated as a rite of initiation into the community of the saved. Thus this emphasis on repentance, which was to characterize many strands of Christianity throughout its history, was inherited primarily from Judaism.

There are two Greek words used in early Christian literature that convey the basic notion of repentance, namely, *metanoia* and *metameleia.* By the time of the Christian era both words had come to convey a change of attitude or purpose as well as a sorrow for past failings, whereas in non-Christian Greek texts the terms are not used in an ethical or religious sense until the late Hellenistic period.

As in Judaism, in early Christianity forms of the term *metanoia* (occurring approximately fifty times in the New Testament) continued to mean conversion to a new faith and abandonment of the old, or restoration within the new faith by confession and rejection of sins. Employing the same word, the *Revelation to John* reports a series of visions in which the risen Jesus demands repentance of Christians in Asia Minor who have made accommodations to paganism (*Rv.* 2:5, 2:16, 2:21, 3:3, 3:19); the ritual protocol involved (if any) is unstated. John uses the same term for the conversion of pagans (*Rv.* 9:20–21, 16:9–11). The ethical rigorism expressed in the *Letter to the Hebrews* (*Heb.* 6:4–6, 10:26–31, 12:14–17) reveals a problem with postbaptismal apostasy.

The ideal of moral purity in the Christian church was contradicted by reality. During the second and third centuries Christianity underwent a penitential crisis. By the second century baptism was thought to confer sinlessness as well as the forgiveness of all previous sins. Since baptism or martyrdom were the only two means of eradicating postbaptismal sin, the practice of adult baptism and deathbed baptism became common. Many reform movements arose. The prophet Elkesai (fl. 100 CE) summoned people to repent and submit to a second baptism to expiate sin. The Marcionites and the Montanists (middle of the second century) proclaimed different forms of ethical rigorism. In a complex document called the *Shepherd of Hermas* (compiled c. 100–150 CE), revelatory visions legitimate the possibility of a second and final repentance. Forms of the word *metanoia* are found therein nearly a hundred times. The prophetic author urges Christians to repent the abuses stemming from the possession of wealth and the conduct of business affairs (*Visions* 3.6.5; *Commandments* 10.1.4; *Similitudes* 9.20.1). Throughout the document there is no explicit connection of the appeal for repentance with a formalized ritual procedure. Tertullian (c. 160–225 CE), before converting to Montanism, wrote *De paenitentia,* in which he dealt both with the repentance required of candidates for baptism (chaps. 4–6) and with a single final opportunity for repentance following baptism (chap. 7), after which the penitent must never again return to sin (chap. 5). The ritual behavior of repentance described by Tertullian includes lying in sackcloth and ashes, severe treatment of the body, restricted food and drink, and weeping (chap. 9). The orthodox tradition developed the practice of auricular ("to the ear") confession to a priest as a surrogate for God. By the third century a system of public penance came to be regarded as a second baptism. Excluded from the Eucharist, the penitent went through a regimen of fasting, prayer, and almsgiving. The Council of Trent (1545–1563) reaffirmed that repentance must involve three elements, namely, contrition, confession, and satisfaction.

TRADITIONS OF SMALL-SCALE SOCIETIES. Among the Nuer of the Sudan, certain acts are regarded as bad because God punishes them. Faults (*dueri*) are against God and he is the one who punishes them. Such faults include incest and adultery as well as offense against certain prohibitions, such as eating with those with whom one's kin have a blood feud and milking one's own cow and drinking the milk. In Nuer belief the person who commits *dueri* places himself in physical danger, for moral faults accumulate and predispose the offender to disaster. Thus faults destroy a person, but they can be "wiped out" (*woc*) by sacrifice. The Nuer have a custom of confessing sin at certain sacrifices, wherein the worshiper must reveal all the resentments and grievances that he or she holds against others if his sacrifice is to be efficacious. (In effect the worshipper confesses the shortcomings of others.) The faults and the feelings of aggrievedness are wiped out by the blood of the sacrificial victim. Such sacrifices are regarded as effective only when accomplished with the will and desire of the sinner.

Among the Indian Shakers of the Pacific Northwest ritual confession was practiced early in the sect's history (late nineteenth and early twentieth centuries), but was later abandoned. The founder, John Slocum, emphasized the necessity of confessing sins and asking for forgiveness in order to attain salvation. Every Friday Slocum would hear the confession of individual penitents privately—though he rang a bell all the while so that he would be unable actually to hear them. Early Shakers believed that the ability to hear confessions was a gift. Louis, a Shaker leader possessing this gift, received penitents who came each carrying a bundle of sticks, a mnemonic device representing their sins. As each sin was confessed (while Louis rang the handbell), a stick was placed on the table, and all were burned at the conclusion of the confession. For the Shakers confession was a catharsis for immediate personal relief and was not connected with spiritual regeneration.

The phenomena of confession and repentance are culture traits indigenous to American Indian cultures quite apart from Christian influences. This conclusion is supported by the early character of the evidence as well as by the fact that tribal confessors are native functionaries. Examples abound. The Aurohuaca Indians of the Columbian Sierra Nevada regard all illness as a punishment for sin. When a shaman is summoned for curing, he will not treat patients until they confess their sins. The Ijca of Columbia abstain from salt and alcohol before confession. In the manner of the Pacific Coast Shakers, when they visit the priest (*mama*) they bring mnemonic devices made of corn shucks and knotted strings to help them remember each sin. Similarly the Huichol of southern Mexico confess sexual transgression on their way north in search of peyote (*híkuri*). Women knot palm-leaf strips for each sin and throw them into the fire after reciting the name of each lover. Among the Maya of Yucatan, women in labor summon native shamans to confess their sins, particularly those of a sexual nature. The Inuit (Eskimo) are anxious lest by conscious or unconscious violation of taboos they offend Sedna, the mistress of animals, who resides at the bottom of the sea and whose displeasure might threaten the food supply. As Weston La Barre has observed, the wages of sin are starvation. If the guilty party confesses, all is well: Seals and caribou are caught. If not, the shaman (*angakkoq*) must ferret out the offender and secure a confession.

SEE ALSO Confession of Sins; Conversion; Merit; Purification.

BIBLIOGRAPHY

The most comprehensive study of the phenomenon of confession, which includes a great deal of information about the related notion of repentance, is Raffaele Pettazzoni's *La confessione dei peccati,* 3 vols. (1929–1936; reprint, Bologna, 1968). However, Pettazzoni's hypothesis proposing an evolutionary development of the notion of confession, from the magical to the theistic, is unconvincing. A more theoretical discussion of the phenomenon of repentance in Albert Esser's *Das Phänomen Reue: Versuch einer Erhellung ihres Selbstverständnisses* (Cologne, 1963). For a shorter discussion from a history of religions perspective, see Geo Widengren's *Religionsphänomenologie* (Berlin, 1969), pp. 258–279). For a critique of the shame-culture or guilt-culture typology, see Gerhart Piers and Milton B. Singer's *Shame and Guilt* (Springfield, Ill., 1953).

For an overview of the notions of confession, repentance, and guilt in antiquity, see Franz Steinleitner's *Die Beicht im Zusammenhänge mit der sakralen Rechtspflege in der Antike* (Leipzig, 1913). For Greco-Roman religions and philosophical systems, see Arthur Darby Nock's *Conversion: The Old and the New in Religion from Alexander the Great to Augustine of Hippo* (Oxford, 1933). An exceptionally complete study of Greek pollution and purity with full bibliography is found in Robert A. Parker's *Miasma: Pollution and Purification in Early Greek Religion* (Oxford, 1983). Still indispensable is Kurt Latte's "Schuld und Sünde in der grieschischen Religion," *Archiv für Religionswissenschaft* 20 (1920–1921): 254–298. For the Roman world, see Anna-Elizabeth Wilhelm-Hooijbergh's *Peccatum: Sin and Guilt in Ancient Rome* (Groningen, 1954).

Henri Frankfort outlines the ancient Egyptian concept of sin and sinlessness in his *Ancient Egyptian Religion* (New York, 1948), pp. 73–80. Frankfort's treatment of the topic has been corrected by Siegfried Morenz's *Egyptian Religion* (Ithaca, N. Y., 1973), pp. 130–133. For the relationship between repentance and sacrificial expiation in ancient Israel, see Jacob Milgrom's *Cult and Conscience: The Asham and the Priestly Doctrine of Repentance* (Leiden, 1976). Also important is William L. Holladay's *The Root Subh in the Old Testament* (Leiden, 1958).

One of the only detailed studies of the Christian concept of repentance within the context of Judaism, Greco-Roman sources, and subsequent patristic evidence is Aloys H. Dirksen's *The New Testament Concept of Metanoia* (Washington, D. C., 1932). A philologically oriented study of Hebrew and early Christian terms and concepts related to repentance, together with a wealth of references to primary sources, is found in the *Theological Dictionary of the New Testament,* edited by Gerhard Kittel and Gerhard Friedrich, vol. 4 (Grand Rapids, Mich., 1967), pp. 975–1008. The most important study of the second- and third-century penitential crisis is Hans Windisch's *Taufe und Sünde im ältesten Christentum bis auf Origenes* (Tübingen, 1908). For a selection of important early Christian texts on repentance in Greek and Latin with German translations, see *Die Busse: Quellen zur Entstehung des altkirchlichen Busswesens* (Zurich, 1969).

On the phenomenon of confession and repentance among small-scale societies, see Weston La Barre's well-documented "Confession as Cathartic Therapy in American Indian Tribes," in *Magic, Faith, and Healing,* edited by Ari Kiev (New York, 1964). Kiev's book contains many relevant essays. Robert I. Levy's *Tahitians: Mind and Experience in the*

Society Islands (Chicago, 1973) is an important study. Bryan R. Wilson's *Magic and the Millennium: A Sociological Study of Movements of Protest among Tribal and Third-World Peoples* (New York, 1973) is an important synthetic study of revitalistic or millenarian movements.

New Sources

Al-Ghazzali, Muhammad. *On Repentance.* Chicago, 2003. Translation of Al-Ghazzali's classic tract on repentance.

Etzioni, Amitai, et alii. *Repentance.* Lanham, Md., 1997.

Hommel, Hildebrecht. "Antike Bussformulare." In *Sebasmata,* vol. 1, pp. 351–370. Tübingen, 1983.

Nave, Guy D. *The Role and Function of Repentance in Luke Acts.* Leiden, 2002.

Ward, Benedicta. *Harlots of the Desert. A Study of Repentance in Early Monastic Sources.* Kalamazoo, Mich., 1987.

Zinniel, Klaus. "Busse." In *Handbuch religionwissenschaftlicher Grundbegriffe,* edited by H. Cancik, B. Gladigow, and M. Laubscher, vol. 2, pp. 188–190. Stuttgart, 1990.

DAVID E. AUNE (1987)
Revised Bibliography

RESHEF

RESHEF is a northwest Semitic god, whose cult is best attested in northern Syria. Its history may be followed for 3,500 years, from the Ebla tablets of the third millennium BCE to the Babylonian Talmud and the *Aggadic Midrash, Exodus Rabbah,* the redaction of which took place, it seems, not earlier than the tenth century CE. By that time, the Reshefs had become birds of prey, after having been viewed as demons dwelling on roofs. This development has a background in the Judeo-Hellenistic interpretation of Reshef in the Septuagint translation of the Bible, which at times assimilates him to a bird of prey, like a vulture or an eagle. Unfortunately, there are no extant myths in which Reshef plays a significant role, except for allusions to the plague he may cause.

EXTENSION OF RESHEF'S CULT. An important and diversified cult of Reshef is attested as early as circa 2300 BCE in cuneiform documents from Ebla, then in various texts from the thirteenth century BCE, found at Ugarit and Ras ibn Hani, and also in compound personal names at Ebla, Mari, Ugarit, and Emar, all from Bronze Age Syria. In the seventeenth century BCE, at Hana/Ana on the Middle Euphrates, Reshef's heteronym *Rushpan* is used as an onomastic element. It does not witness a simple phonetic or dialectal development, but belongs to another nominal pattern, the same as Shulman, a divine name well attested in the area of the Middle Habur. Both names derive from adjectives. Reshef also occurs in the Bible and in many inscriptions from the eighth to the first centuries BCE. In the mid-second millennium BCE worship of Reshef also found its way to Anatolia, where he was called Irshappa, and more importantly to Egypt.

His name was introduced in Anatolia by the Hurrians, whose language does not admit any initial *r*, hence the prosthetic vowel *i-* and the consequent changes in vocalization and stress, leading to the form *Irsháppa.* In Egypt, about fifty stelae and other artifacts have been discovered bearing Reshef's name or image. In hieroglyphic script, the theonym is usually written *Ršpw,* where the *-w* is a vowel sign added in analogy to several Egyptian divine names ending in *-w.* Under Amenhotep II (1453–1419 BCE), the cult of Reshef obtained an official status in Egypt, and this pharaoh even bears the title of "Reshef's beloved" on one of his seals. However, most stelae date from the thirteenth or twelfth centuries BCE and come from Deir el-Medineh, a settlement of Syrian crafters, facing Thebes. Among other attestations of Reshef one can mention the rock shrine of Tushka in Nubia, dating from the eighteenth dynasty (c. 1500–1300 BCE). A procession of five offering bearers approaches three seated deities, identified by hieroglyphic inscriptions as the local Horus, lord of Miam, the deified pharaoh Sesostris III, and Reshef, who brandishes a mace-ax above the head and holds a shield. A stele from el-Simbillawein, from the Ramesside period (c. 1300–1100 BCE), shows Reshef in front of the god Ptah with a scepter and the figure of the Horus falcon above.

ETYMOLOGY AND LOCAL ASSOCIATIONS. Reshef's name is probably a derivative of the same Semitic root as the Akkadian divine epithet *rašbu,* "redoubtable." In fact, interchanges between labials (*b*/*p*) often take place in Semitic languages. Etymologically Reshef is an epithet or a title, and it is often used with a following place name, "Reshef of. . . ," for which many examples can be found at Ebla and Ugarit. It was initially a title used for any tutelary god. Certainly later it became a proper name, but even then it was used for a type of deity, namely a warlike deity, as confirmed by the use of its plural in various texts and by iconography.

Since "inspiring fear" is a notion essential to the nature of the sacred in primitive religion, it is not surprising therefore that the cult of Reshef is recorded already in the third millennium BCE and that several local numina are called in such a way, the plural "Reshefs" being also attested. This is best illustrated in texts from Ebla, where at least eleven different deities named *Rashap* occur with mainly toponymic qualifications. The tablets mention the deity in relation to offers that were brought to Reshef's various sanctuaries, and they specify the number of sheep sacrificed in his honor. There are neither mythological nor ritual and liturgical texts, which could reveal the true nature of the god and show him in action. Nevertheless, an administrative text lists offers made not only to Reshef of Atanni, an important holy place, but also to his emblems, possibly his "quiver," his set of "javelins" or "arrows," and his "mace-ax." If this uncertain interpretation of the logograms is correct, these weapons would appear to be Reshef's attributes. Bow, arrow, and quiver are offered also to the Hurrian god Nubadig, identified with Reshef. Reshef of Gunu, mentioned at Ebla, deserves a special mention, because he is still worshiped one thousand years later at Ugarit.

Local connections of Reshef's worship still appear in some Phoenician inscriptions from the first millennium BCE, possibly at Karatepe, an elevated stronghold on the Ceyhan River in eastern Cilicia (c. 750 BCE). Reshef's name is followed there by *ṣprn* or *ṣprm,* usually explained as "(Reshef) of the goats" or "of the birds." However, his equation with the stag god, which appears in the parallel Hieroglyphic Luwian inscription, does not prove that "goats" are meant. In cuneiform script, the stag god Runt was indicated by the logogram dkal of a protective deity, like Reshef was at Ugarit. Nevertheless, a toponymic connotation was assumed in this case as well, *ṣprm*/*n* being possibly a counterpart of Sepphoris in northern Israel, with the ending *-în/-îm* of place names. On Cyprus, the oldest dedication to Reshef, dating to the seventh century BCE, might refer to "Reshef of Sa[lamis]" (on Cyprus), while later inscriptions from Idalium and Tamassus (Cyprus) identify him with particular types of Apollo, either Cypriot or originally Laconian (Peloponnesus), and call him "Reshef of Amyclae," "Reshef of Helos," and "Reshef of Alashiya," the ancient name of Cyprus or part of it.

There is so far no unequivocal trace of a cult of Reshef in Phoenicia proper, except for two royal cylinder seals from Sidon, dating to around the fourteenth century BCE, and the name of the "Land of Reshefs" given in the fifth century BCE to a city quarter at Sidon. Nor was Reshef worshiped at Carthage or on the island Ibiza. The name Eresh, borne by a West Semitic divine craftsman, was there misread as Reshef, just as the Egyptian god Herishef was confounded by some authors with Reshef, especially at Byblos. Arsūf, a coastal city of Palestine, preserved the name of Reshef. The place name is possibly attested as early as the third millennium BCE at Ebla and is recorded in *1 Chronicles* 7:25 as the name of a son of Ephraim. Its Arabic name, mentioned by Yāqūt (1179–1229 CE) and corrupted by the crusaders into Arsur, bears witness to the Palestinian and Lebanese shift *rašp* > *ršāf,* as in *kafr* > *kfār,* to the phonetic changes *š* > *s* and *ā* > *ō* > *ū,* and to the addition of a prosthetic vowel. Excavations have provided evidence of an early first-millennium BCE occupation at Arsūf, but the settlement of the Bronze Age was probably located at a nearby site. The city was called Apollonia in Hellenistic and Greco-Roman times, depending on Reshef's identification with Apollo. Along with this place name and the biblical references to Reshef, a few Palestinian cylinder seals from the late Bronze Age include a recognizable figure of Reshef.

INDEFINITENESS OF ACTION. Sacred potency, because of the very indefiniteness of action, can heal or strike, be beneficent or unforgiving. Its presence can guarantee peace and security. This is why one of the city gates at Ebla was called "Gate of Reshef" and why personal names witness the recourse to Reshef's patronage, as shown by their meaning: "Servant of Reshef," "Reshef is merciful," "My father is Reshef," "My god is Reshef." On the other hand, Reshef can spread plague and inflict death through his mace-ax, spear, large bow, and arrows. He is not properly a war god, but the god of death inflicted by plague or weapons. It is probable that his arrows, like those of Apollo, killed by spreading the plague. Egyptian stelae show him brandishing his mace-ax over his head, in the same martial stance as the hundreds of bronze statuettes of the so-called Smiting God, found in the Levant and elsewhere. Since these statuettes are not inscribed and the divine characters represented wear various types of crowns, there is no certainty that all these bronzes can be related to Reshef. In particular, no bronze represents the deity with a crown adorned with the typical bent gazelle horns that characterize Reshef on a number of Egyptian stelae. However, these images express the original connotation "redoubtable" attached to his name.

RELATIONSHIP TO OTHER DEITIES. This basic aspect of Reshef's character explains why he could be assimilated to such differing deities as the Mesopotamian god Nergal, the lord of the netherworld; the Hurrian god Nubadig/Nupatik, a tutelary deity known earlier as Lubadaga/Lupatik; the Luwian protective god Runt, represented in hieroglyphic Luwian by a stag; the Egyptian war god Montu; the North-Arabian god Ruḍa, and a major Cypriot deity called Apollo in Greek inscriptions. Even a direct identification of Reshef with Horus is attested in Egypt in the Saite period (c. 663–526 BCE). Reshef's name is engraved in hieroglyphic script on the base of a bronze statuette representing a deity still wearing the "lock of youth," characteristic of "Horus the Child." He wears the red crown of Lower Egypt and his left hand holds a shield, a bow, and an arrow, while a quiver hangs from his shoulder. These are Reshef's typical weapons.

The equation of Reshef with Nergal led some writers to characterize him as a chthonic deity. This equation is already attested in a lexical text from Ebla and thus goes back at least to the twenty-fourth century BCE. At that time, Nergal was still the bull god of Kutha, a city located some twenty-five kilometers north of Kish, which appears to be the oldest Semitic center of power in Babylonia, irradiating as far as Ebla. Nergal's anthropomorphic image in mythology reveals that he was a dying and rising god. Every year, he had to spend six months in the netherworld with Ereshkigal, the queen of the dead. This is stated in a late explanatory text: "on the 18th of Tammuz [July] Nergal goes down to the netherworld, on the 28th of Kislev [December] he comes up." In such a way, he thus appears as a chthonic deity, but essentially he was the "redoubtable" city god, bringing war or peace. In the twenty-first century BCE, his full equipment consisted of a mace, a large bow, arrows, and a dagger, like Reshef's. It is likely that the equation of the two gods was made on this level and it does not justify, in consequence, the characterization of Reshef as a chthonic deity, although he could inflict death like Nergal. The equation of the two deities was so well anchored in the second millennium BCE that logograms of Nergal's name, in particular dmaš.maš and dkal, were used in Ugarit and most likely on Cyprus for Reshef or the Cypriot god identified with him.

The problem of Reshef's spouse would need greater clarification in the sources. The goddess Adamma or Adam appears sometimes as Reshef's consort. Since she is mentioned in a grave inscription from Cyprus in the early ninth century

BCE, she could possess chthonic features, but this is only a remote possibility, since the existence of a relation between her name and the Hebrew noun *ʾădāmāh,* "earth" or "soil," is just a guess based on assonance and analogy with the Greek goddess Gaia or Ge, "earth," resident in the earth and governing it. Egyptian stelae from Deir el-Medineh associate Reshef with Min, an Egyptian god, and with a naked Syrian goddess named Qudšu. However, nothing indicates that she was regarded as his wife. In the year 6 BCE, the priests of the Babylonian goddess Herta at Palmyra dedicated some premises to Herta, to the goddess Nanaya, and to Reshef. Nothing is known about the relationships between these deities.

FIGURATIVE CONNOTATIONS. The name of Reshef does not seem to have ever lost the features of a common noun, since it continued to be used also in the plural. A ritual text from Ugarit alludes to a procession, "when the Reshefs enter the house of the king," and the historical records of Ramses III at Medinet Habu praise the pharaoh's chariot warriors for being "as valiant as Reshefs," while *Psalms* 76:4 refers to "Reshefs with bow, shield, and sword," and a city quarter in Sidon is called "Land of the Reshefs," possibly the garrison. Reshef *ḥṣ* is more likely a "Reshef with arrows" than a "Reshef of the street," corresponding to Apollo Agieus. In fact, "the sons of Reshef" in *Job* 5:7 are his arrows that "fly upwards" (cf. *Psalms* 91:5), while the "Reshefs of fire" in the *Song of Songs* 8:6 are a synecdoche inspired by inflamed arrows shot at besieged cities to set them ablaze. The same synecdoche also occurs in the Hebrew text of *Ben Sira* 43:17, where flying snowflakes are compared to arrows shot by an invisible enemy: "his snow flies like Reshef."

In older biblical texts, such as *Deuteronomy* 32:23–24, *Habakkuk* 3:5, and *Psalms* 78:48, Reshef is a harmful power, bringing plague, as he does in the *Poem of King Keret,* preserved by tablets from Ugarit. In contrast, the Alexandrian translators of the Hebrew Bible regard Reshef as a bird of prey, thus in *Deuteronomy* 32:24, *Job* 5:7, and *Ben Sira* 43:17. They even attribute to him "wings of fire" in the *Song of Songs* 8:6, as if he were the Phoenix, and he is recorded in such a way by the *Greek Apocalypse of Baruch* 6:8. These interpretations probably originated in Egypt, where Reshef was identified also with Horus, often represented as a falcon. The conception of Reshef as a bird seems to have gained wider acceptance, since Reshefs appear in Talmudic literature as "demons dwelling on roofs." There is so far no evidence supporting the view that Reshef was a fertility god, a chthonic deity, or a storm god.

SEE ALSO Apollo; Nergal.

BIBLIOGRAPHY

A comprehensive discussion of the evidence and an annotated bibliography can be found in the studies by Edward Lipiński, *Dieux et déesses de l'univers phénicien et punique* (Louvain, Belgium, 1995), pp. 179–188, and William J. Fulco, *The Canaanite God Rešep* (New Haven, 1976), the latter requiring some updating. For the Egyptian iconographic material, most valuable is Izak Cornelius, *The Iconography of the Canaanite Gods Reshef and Ba'al: Late Bronze and Iron Age I Periods (c. 1500–1000 BCE)* (Fribourg, Switzerland, and Göttingen, Germany, 1994). The bronzes with the "Smiting God" have been studied by, among others, Ora Negbi, *Canaanite Gods in Metal: An Archaeological Study of Ancient Syro-Palestinian Figurines* (Tel Aviv, 1996), and Helga Seeden, *The Standing Armed Figurines in the Levant* (Munich, 1980). The motive of the naked goddess was analyzed by Silvia Schroer, "Die Göttin auf den Stempelsiegeln aus Palästina/Israel," in *Studien zu den Stempelsiegeln aus Palästina/Israel,* vol. 2, edited by Othmar Keel, Hildi Keel-Lev, and Sivia Schroer (Freiburg and Göttingen, Germany, 1989), pp. 89–207. For the cult of Reshef on Cyprus, see Lipiński, "Resheph Amyklos," in *Phoenicia and the East Mediterranean in the First Millennium B.C.* (Louvain, Belgium, 1987), pp. 87–99. Postbiblical Jewish understanding of Reshef was examined by Lipiński, "Rᵉšāfīm: From Gods to Birds of Prey," in *Mythos im Alten Testament und seiner Umwelt: Festschrift für Hans-Peter Müller,* edited by Armin Lange, Hermann Lichtenberger, and Diethard Römheld (Berlin and New York, 1999), pp. 255–259.

EDWARD LIPIŃSKI (2005)

RESH LAQISH SEE SHIMʿON BEN LAQISH

REST SEE SHABBAT; WORK

RESURRECTION. The term *resurrection* is so intricately bound up with Christian ideas that it is extremely difficult to decide when it should be used for similar ideas in other religions. Obviously, the term should not be used to refer to the belief that there is an immortal element in humans (often called "soul" or "spirit") that lives on after the destruction of the body, or to the belief in some kind of continued existence in a shadowy realm of the dead. Also excluded is the idea of reincarnation, which implies that the soul is repeatedly reborn into a new body. If resurrection is defined as the revival of the body, or rather of the person as a whole, after a period of death, one finds phenomena that fit this definition only in Zoroastrianism, Judaism, Christianity, and Islam, with doubtful analogies in Chinese Taoism and ancient Indian and Egyptian religions. Belief in resurrection presupposes either a monistic view of humans, which implies that humanity as a whole disappears in death and is then revived to a new existence; or a dualistic view, according to which the body dies whereas the soul or spirit lives on and is later united with the body into a renewed being. Another phenomenon that should be discussed here is the idea of dying and rising gods, which is found in several religions, some with and some without a belief in resurrection.

DAOISM. In Chinese Daoism there is frequent mention of prolonging life and strengthening the vital force, but there is no uniform doctrine on this subject. The background is the idea that humans, like the universe, consist of several elements, some light, pure, and heavenly, others heavy, impure, and earthly; they are held together by the vital principle, or breath. One early report had it that a certain Bo You managed to strengthen his life to the extent that he actually returned to life after being dead for some time. Most cases, however, told of various practices—meditation, use of alcoholic beverages, magical rites—through which the lower and mortal elements in humans can be replaced by higher and immortal ones and the vital principle can be strengthened so as not to be separated from the body. In this way humans can achieve immortality and ascend to the heavenly world. But this is hardly resurrection in the strict sense of the word.

INDIA. The Vedic religion of ancient India offers a rich variety of beliefs concerning the dead and the life in the hereafter. There is the idea of the dead haunting the living as ghosts; there is the idea of the heavenly world of Yama, the first human, where the ancestors live; and there are hints of a dark world or a kind of hell. The dead were either buried or burned, the latter practice becoming predominant.

The Vedic language possesses several words that have been thought to denote the "soul" as an immortal spiritual substance in humans: *manas* ("thought, thinking"), *asu* ("life"), *ātman* ("breath"), *tanu* ("body, self"). But the equation of any of these words with "soul" is hardly correct. That which appears as a ghost or exists in heaven or hell is not a bodiless spirit but the dead person himself with some kind of body. Any existence without a body is inconceivable. It might seem that the fire in which the corpse is burned would consume it, but in reality the corpse is supposed to be transformed into a heavenly body. In the *Ṛgveda* there are hints that at death the various parts of the body merge with natural phenomena of a similar kind: The flesh goes to the earth, the blood to the water, the breath to the wind, the eye to the sun, the mind (*manas*) to the moon, and so on. These natural phenomena then give the elements of the body back to the deceased as he ascends to heaven in the burning fire. Thus the individual is recreated in the other world as a kind of shadow that looks like his former self but that cannot be touched or embraced. Although this belief differs considerably from the Christian idea of resurrection, it may perhaps be described by this term.

In the Upaniṣads, the term *ātman* ("breath") came to denote the imperishable spiritual element in humans, identical with the "spirit" of the universe, called *brahman.* This correlation opened the way to the idea of mystical union between humanity's spirit and the divine element in the cosmos, and also to the idea that the soul can be reborn into a new body (reincarnation). Thus the idea of resurrection was lost.

EGYPT. The ancient Egyptian ideas of the hereafter are very complicated, partly beause they contain elements of differing origins and belonging to different stages of development. The Egyptian view of humanity presupposes two incorporeal elements, neither corresponding to any modern concept of the soul. The *ba,* usually translated as "soul," is often depicted as a bird; it can mean power or external manifestation, and it represents the ability to "take any form it likes." When a person dies, his or her *ba* leaves the body but hovers near the corpse. The *ka* combines the ideas of vital force, nourishment, double, and genius. The British Egyptologist Alan Gardiner suggests such translations as "personality, soul, individuality, temperament, fortune, or position." *Ba* and *ka* cannot exist without a bodily substrate. Therefore the body is embalmed to secure their existence. In addition, the funerary rites transform the deceased into an *akh,* a "shining" or "transformed" sprit. In this capacity the deceased lives on in the realm of Osiris, the god of the netherworld, who once died but was revived again as the ruler of the dead.

Other beliefs include the judgment in the hall of Osiris of the deeds of the deceased; the latter's taking part in the journey of the sun god, Re, in his bark; the warding off of monsters and other dangers in the netherworld by means of magical formulas; the happy life of the deceased in the Field of Rushes; and so on. One common idea seems to be that of absorption into the great rhythm of the universe. Osiris was, among other things, a symbol of grain; thus, when the dead join Osiris they participate in the renewal of life in the growing grain. Similarly, when the dead join the sun god they partake of the life of the sun that is renewed every morning. It is difficult to decide whether these are beliefs in resurrection or whether they should be given another name.

ZOROASTRIANISM. The earliest documents of Zoroastrian religion do not mention the resurrection of the body but rather the soul's ascent to paradise. But in the later parts of the Avesta there is at least one reference to resurrection: "When the dead rise, the Living Incorruptible One will come and life will be transfigured" (*Yashts* 19.11). The Living One is the savior, Saoshyant (Pahl., Sōshans), who is to come at the end of the present era. Another passage (*Yashts* 13.11), which speaks of joining together bones, hairs, flesh, bowels, feet, and genitals, refers not to resurrection, as has been maintained, but to birth.

In the cosmological treatise the *Bundahishn* (ninth century CE), a doctrine is set forth in detail. Chapter 30 describes what happens at the death of a man. His soul remains near the head of his body for three nights and is then carried away. If the man has been righteous the soul meets a fragrant wind, a sleek cow, and a beautiful young girl and is brought across the Chinvat Bridge to Paradise. If he has been evil the soul meets a foul wind, a gaunt cow, and a hideous girl and is thrown from the bridge into Hell. This description should be read against the background of the ideas set forth in the Avestan fragment *Hadhōkht Nask,* which relates that after the three nights the soul meets its *daēnā,* which, according to his works, appears either as a beautiful girl or as an ugly hag. It becomes apparent that the *daēnā* is the heavenly counterpart or double of the soul, whose character is dependent on the person's deeds in this life. As the two join together, the spritual part of the person is complete and can enter eternal life.

Chapter 33 of the *Bundahishn* describes the course of the world as it evolves in subsequent periods toward the end, when evil is defeated and the world perfected. Chapter 34 deals with resurrection. At the arrival of the third and last savior, Saoshyant, the dead will be roused, first the primeval man, Gaya-maretan, (Pahl., Gayōmard), then the first human pair, Mashyē and Mashyānē, and finally all humankind. Then the great gathering will take place at which everyone's good and evil deeds are revealed. The sinners will be punished and the righteous will enter the bliss of Paradise. A stream of molten metal will spread over the earth, and all people will have to pass through it: The evil will be burned (and purified), the righteous will experience it like lukewarm milk. At the end, all will be saved, and creation will be renewed.

Similar ideas are set forth in chapter 34 of the *Selections of Zatspram* (approximately contemporary with the *Bundahishn*). Here it is asked how creatures who have passed away can receive their bodies back and rise again. The first answer is that it is easier to assemble parts already existing than to create from nothing. If Ahura Mazdā was able to create them, he is also able to assemble the scattered parts again. There are five "storekeepers" that receive the bodily substance of those who have died: The earth keeps flesh and bone; the water, the blood; the plants preserve the head and the hair; the light of the firmament receives the fire; and the wind, the spirit. At the time of the rehabilitation (Frashōkereti; Pahl., Frashkart), Ahura Mazdā will assemble all these elements again then create new human beings. This account is very close to the belief expressed in the Indian *Ṛgveda.* Obviously, these later expositions present a combination of at least two ideas of different origin and character, the idea of the soul joining its counterpart in the other world and the idea of bodily resurrection. Lack of sources prevents scholars from following the process of amalgamation of these ideas.

JUDAISM. The Hebrew scriptures (Old Testament) as a whole have no doctrine of resurrection. When it is said, "I kill and I make alive, I wound and I heal" (*Dt.* 32:39), or "The Lord kills and brings to life, he brings down to She'ol [the realm of death] and raises up" (*1 Sm.* 2:7), the stress is on God as the origin and cause of everything rather than on resurrection. Usually the scriptures assert that "if a man dies, he will not live again" (*Jb.* 14:14) or that "he who goes down to She'ol does not come up" (7:9). In the *Book of Psalms* there is the general conviction that Yahveh is stronger than death and can rescue from She'ol: "You have delivered my soul from death, my eyes from tears. . . . I walk before the Lord in the land of the living" (116:8–9); "I shall not die, but I shall live . . . he has not given me over to death" (118:17–18); "God will ransom my soul from the power of She'ol" (49:15). It is never stated how this deliverance takes place; it is enough for the psalmist to know that God will not give him up to death or She'ol. It is probable that for an explanation of the mechanism of deliverance one must look to the metaphorical language referring to healing of illness or rescue from some deadly danger. Illness or calamity is potential death, and it means being in the grip of She'ol; consequently, rescue from illness or danger is rescue from death. It is interesting to recall that when a Babylonian god is said to be "a reviver of the dead," it clearly means that he cures illness.

Ezekiel 37 reports the prophet's vision of a heap of dry bones in a valley that is revived through "the spirit." At an early stage of Judaism this text was understood as referring to resurrection (e.g., in the paintings of the synagogue at Dura-Europos), but the context indicates that the bones symbolize the Jewish nation, and the message of the vision is that just as it seems impossible for the dead bones to be revived, it also seems impossible for the nation to be restored; however, the impossible is made possible through a divine miracle.

Isaiah 26:19 reads, "Your dead shall live, their bodies shall rise." This passage evidently points back to verse 14, "The dead will not live, the shades will not rise," a reference to the enemies of Israel. It may be, therefore, that verse 19 should be interpreted along the same lines as *Ezekiel* 38: Israel is in a better position than her enemies, therefore Israel shall "live." The next line, however, reads: "Wake up and rejoice, you who sleep in the dust." This may be an early, though vague, reference to the resurrection of the dead. But the chapter belongs to the latest part of the *Book of Isaiah,* the so-called Isaiah apocalypse, and it probably dates from the third century BCE.

The only clear reference to resurrection is found in the *Book of Daniel* (c. 165 BCE). It reads: "Many of those who sleep in the dust will awake, some to eternal life, others to eternal shame" (12:2). There can be no doubt: the dead are described as sleeping, and they are going to wake up from their sleep; consequently they will live again. It is not explicitly said that all the dead shall rise, although "many" (*rabbīm*) often has that connotation. Yet not only the righteous will be resurrected; others will awaken also, but to eternal shame.

It has been suggested that the idea of resurrection in Israel has its roots in Canaanite religion. There, the dying and rising of the god Baal plays a significant part in symbolizing the annual death and renewal of vegetation. But the conclusion that such a resurrection might apply to humanity in general is never drawn, as far as the available evidence goes. It should be noted, however, that *Isaiah* 26:19 combines the revival of the dead with the falling of the dew of light, and that dew plays an important part in Canaanite mythology. It is also very probable that *Hosea* 6:2, "He will revive us after two days, on the third day he will raise us up," goes back to a Canaanite formula quoted by repenting people. The prophet, however, rejects the conversion of the people and does not accept their hope of revival. Thus, there may be Canaanite ideas in the background, but the final development of the idea of resurrection probably did not take place without Zoroastrian influence. The Judaism of the period of the Second Temple develops the idea further, without, however, reaching any consensus regarding the details. Above all, the testimonies differ as to whether resurrection means a reunion of body and soul or a renewal of the person as a totality.

One of the earliest references to resurrection is found in the *Second Book of the Maccabees* (first century BCE). It shows that the idea of resurrection is bound up with belief in just retribution, especially in the case of martyrdom. Seven young brothers are tortured and killed by King Antiochus, and one young man after another confesses his belief in resurrection: "The king of the universe will raise us up to an everlasting renewal of life" (7:9). "We cherish the hope that God gives of being raised again by him, but for you there will be no resurrection to life" (7:14). Finally, their mother addresses her sons: "God will in his mercy give life and breath back to you again" (7:23). The reason for this hope is that the sons are giving their life "for God's laws," and it is repeatedly stated, especially in 7:36, that the king will receive just punishment for his arrogance. No statement is made about the *how* of the resurrection, but the mother, addressing her last son, expresses her hope "to get him back again with his brothers" (7:29), which seems to imply some kind of family life in the other world.

According to Josephus Flavius (37/8–c. 100), the Essenes believed in the immortality of the soul (*Antiquities* 17.18), whereas Hippolytus (*Against Heresies* 9.27) says that they believed in the resurrection of the body. So far no words to this effect have been found in the Qumran writings.

The clearest statements about resurrection appear in documents from the end of the first century CE; they were probably inspired by reaction to the fall of Jerusalem in 70 CE. Though several passages in *1 Enoch* (22, 90:33, 91:10, 92:3) mention the resurrection, it is only in the so-called Similitudes (chapters 37–71, which are absent from the Qumran manuscripts and probably of later origin) that the idea is clearly set forth: "And in those days shall the earth give back that which has been entrusted to it, and She'ol also shall give back that which it has received, and Hell shall give back that which it owes"(*1 En.* 51:1). It is clear from other passages (46:6, 49:9–10) that the sinners do not take part in this resurrection, which is not the joining of body and soul but the renewal of humanity as a whole to live on a new earth (51:5).

Similar statements are found in other documents from approximately the same periods. The passage *4 Ezra* 7:32 reads: "The earth shall give up those who sleep in it, and the dust those who rest there in silence, and the storehouses shall give back the souls entrusted to them." The mention of the souls seems to indicate that death is the separation of body and soul (cf. 7:78) and that resurrection means they are reunited. Similarly, the Syriac *Apocalypse of Baruch* speaks of the opening of the treasuries in which souls are preserved (30:2). The dust is told to give back what is not its own and to let everything arise that it has preserved (42:7); it is said further that the earth shall restore the dead without changing their form (50:2). This last text clearly teaches the resurrection of the body, but the context shows that the righteous will then be transformed into an angelic state. The word *soul* here seems to refer, as in the Old Testament, to humanity as a whole. Finally, the *Liber antiquitatum biblicarum,* falsely ascribed to Philo, says that God will "revive the dead and raise up from the earth those who sleep" (3:10); after that, judgment will be held and everybody will receive according to his work.

These texts use more or less the same formulaic language, but their view of humans is not uniform. Some use *soul* to refer to the human being as a whole, others distinguish between body and soul. Resurrection always implies the restoration of the body and usually its transfiguration. According to Josephus and the New Testament, the Pharisees accepted the resurrection of the righteous, whereas the Sadducees denied it altogether (*Acts* 23:8, *Mt.* 22:23).

The victory of Pharisaism after the fall of Jerusalem led to general acceptance of the belief in resurrection in rabbinic Judaism. Thus in the Mishnah tractate *Sanhedrin,* chapter 10 begins with the statement that the one who denies the resurrection of the dead has no part in the world to come, and the rest of the chapter is devoted to a discussion of who is not going to rise (*qūm*).

Liturgical texts, such as the ʿAmidah, assert that God "makes the dead alive and keeps faith to those who sleep in the dust" (cf. *Dn.* 12:2), and that he "kills and makes alive and causes salvation to sprout forth" (cf. *1 Sm.* 2:6). It is interesting that on some occasions a reference to God as giving wind and rain is inserted into the prayer, which uses the verb "to sprout forth," in its literal sense referring to the growing of plants. This indicates a parallel between the life of nature and the life of humans. The parallel is also suggested by Talmudic comments comparing resurrection with the growing of a grain of wheat (B.T., *San.* 90b; cf., in the New Testament, *1 Cor.* 15:36ff.) and stating that the dead "sprout forth" from the earth (B.T., *Ket.* lllb). Does this language contain a reminiscence of ancient roots in the fertility cult? One rabbinic statement explains resurrection as the reunion of body and soul: "Blessed art thou, who bringest the souls back to the dead bodies" (B.T., *Ber.* 60b). Other passages defend the possibility of resurrection by assuming that a certain part of man, the lowest vertebra or a spoonful of rotten mass, escapes corruption and serves as material for the new body.

CHRISTIANITY. In primitive Christianity the resurrection of Christ was the fundamental fact; belief in it was even regarded as a prerequisite of salvation. The earliest statements, which are found in the letters of Paul, are very simple and state the fact in a credal form: "God raised Jesus from the dead" (*Rom.* 10:9); "Jesus died and rose again" (*1 Thes.* 4:14). Sometimes the significance of Jesus' resurrection is defined: "He was designated the son of God in power by his resurrection from the dead" (*Rom.* 1:4); "He was put to death for our trespasses and raised for our justification" (4:25). The choice of words and the context indicate (1) that he was dead; (2) that it was God who raised him; and (3) that his resurrection was not merely a return to normal life on earth but a transfer into an existence of a higher kind. The question of body and soul is not discussed.

Jesus' death and resurrection are mentioned together also in his predictions of suffering in the Gospels (*Mk.* 8:31, 9:31, 10:34, and parallels), and in the proclamation of the apostles in *Acts of the Apostles* (2:23–24, 10:39–40, 17:3). It is difficult to tell whether the expression "on the third day" derives from an interpretation based on *Hosea* 6:2 (see above) or is based on actual experience.

The Gospels give no detail of the resurrection itself. What they have is the report on the empty tomb (*Mk.* 16:1ff. and parallels), to which Matthew has given an apologetic touch by adding the story of the guard being bribed by the chief priests to report that the disciples stole the body (*Mt.* 28:11–13). There are, however, several reports of appearances of Jesus, some taking place in Jerusalem, others in Galilee. It is a matter of dispute whether these different geographical locations rest on independent traditions and, if not, how they are related. According to Luke the last appearance is connected with Jesus' ascension to heaven; according to Matthew it is associated with his sending the apostles to preach to all nations.

The New Testament seems to have taken over the general idea of resurrection from contemporary Judaism. *Matthew* 12:41 mentions it explicitly ("will arise at the last judgment"), and it is presupposed in many other passages (e.g., *Mt.* 7:22, 8:11, 11:22, 12:41–42). In his answer to the Sadducees, who deny the resurrection, Jesus adopts the idea of an angelic existence of the resurrected (*Mk.* 12:18–27 and parallels).

The first Christians expected the second coming of Christ (the Parousia) to happen in their lifetime. But as several Christians died without having experienced the Parousia, questions arose as to the reliability of the Christian hope. Paul answers such questions in *1 Thessalonians* 4:13–18, asserting that just as Christ died and rose again, the fellowship with him cannot be broken by death: First those who have died in Christ will rise when "the archangel calls and the trumpet sounds," then those who are still alive will be taken away to heaven to Christ. This idea of a two-step process is taken further in the *Book of Revelation,* according to which the righteous will rise at the beginning of the millennium ("the first resurrection," 20:6), the rest at its end (20:12–13). The same idea seems to be present in *1 Corinthians* 15:22–23, where one learns that "all shall be made alive in Christ . . . first at his coming those who belong to Christ; then comes the end," when all evil powers are defeated and everything is laid under his feet. Elsewhere, there is only reference to resurrection in general as one event, which is clearly presupposed in the parable of the Last Judgment in *Matthew* 25.

The question of how the resurrection is going to take place is dealt with by Paul in *1 Corinthians* 15. The body that rises is not the old body but a new one, just as a new plant comes out of a seed. Nothing is said here of an immortal soul. Humanity as a whole is perishable; a human being as a whole is recreated as a "spiritual body." Other New Testament passages seem to imply some kind of existence between death and resurrection, for example, "to be with Christ" (*Phil.* 1:23), "to be in Abraham's bosom" (*Lk.* 16:22), and "to be with Christ in paradise" (23:43). A different approach is represented by the *Gospel of John.* He who believes in Christ receives eternal life here and now (3:36, 5:24). However, other statements in the same gospel, which many exegetes ascribe to a later editor, retain the idea of a resurrection at the end of time (5:28).

Under Greek influence the early church developed the idea of an immortal soul that continues to exist after death and is reunited with the body at the resurrection. This remained the commonly accepted belief of the Christian church into the twentieth century. Modern theology now often tries to view the human being as a unity that is totally dissolved in death, whereas resurrection implies a total recreation of the whole being.

ISLAM. Islam shares with Christianity the belief in a general resurrection followed by a judgment. The stress is rather on the latter. In the Qurʾān the last day is referred to as "the day of resurrection" (*yawm al-qiyāmah*), but also as "the day of judgment" (*yawm ad-dīn*), "the day of reckoning" (*yawm al-hisāb*), or "the day of awakening" (*yawm al-baʿth*). In the Qurʾān there are several very graphic descriptions of the day of resurrection, focusing on the natural phenomena that accompany it and on the outcome of the judgment—the believers entering paradise and the unbelievers being thrown into the fire of hell. It is a day "when the trumpet is blown" (cf. *Mt.* 24:31, *1 Thes.* 4:16) and men "shall come in troops, and heaven is opened and the mountains are set in motion" (surah 78:18–20; cf. 18:99), a day "when heaven is rent asunder . . . when earth is stretched out and casts forth what is in it" (84:1–4; cf. 99:1–2). After these events the dead "shall come forth from their graves unto their Lord; they shall say: Alas for us! Who roused us from our bed?" (36:51–52).

There is no reference in the Qurʾān to an immortal soul, nor is resurrection defined as the reunion of body and soul. *Sūrah* 81:7 states that "the souls shall be coupled"; some Muslim commentators take this to mean that the souls are to be joined to their bodies, whereas others think that they are to be coupled with their equals (good or evil) or that they will be divided into two groups.

When the unbelievers express doubt in the resurrection, the Qurʾān refers to God's omnipotence as the creator: "Does man think we shall not gather his bones? Indeed, we are able to shape again his fingers" (75:3–4); "Man says: Who shall quicken the bones when they are decayed? Say: He shall quicken them who originated them the first time. He knows all creation" (36:78–79; cf. 17:53, 19:68). Again, "O men, if you are in doubt as to the uprising, surely we created you of dust, then of a sperm-drop, then of a blood clot

. . . and we establish in the womb what we wish, till a stated term, then we deliver you as infants. . . . And you see the earth blackened, then we send down water upon it, it quivers and swells and puts forth herbs of every joyous kind. This is because God—he is the Truth—brings the dead to life and is powerful over everything" (22:5–6). Thus God forms the child in the womb, he renews the life of vegetation, so he is also able to raise the dead. Only on one occasion is there a hint that the resurrected body will be different from the present one: "We have decreed among you death . . . that we may exchange the likes of you and make you to grow again in a fashion you do not know" (56:60–61). But the wording is not very specific here.

Later Muslim tradition has developed these ideas in several directions. A great number of signs foretelling the day of resurrection are mentioned; the blast of the trumpet has become three blasts: the blast of consternation, the blast of examination, and the blast of resurrection. There is also the idea that at the resurrection the body will be raised and united to its soul, and that the lower part of the spine is preserved as a basis for the future body (as in the rabbinic idea discussed above). In addition there are speculations about a "punishment in the grave" (*ʿadhāb al-qabr*): immediately after burial the deceased is questioned by the two angels, Munkar and Nakir, and if the deceased is not able to answer the questions concerning God and the Prophet, punishment is inflicted.

Several speculations are based on an interpretation of the obscure word *barzakh* in the Qurʾān (23:100), taken by commentators to denote a bar or obstacle preventing return to the world after death. The word is now defined as the interval or space between this world and the next, or between death and resurrection, a kind of intermediary state. Ibn Qayyim al-Jawzīyah (d. 1350), who wrote a book about the spirit, presents various theories about what happens to the spirit between death and resurrection: The spirits are in or near the grave; the spirits of the believers only are in Paradise, or at the gates of Paradise, or in the sacred well Zamzam, or on the right-hand side of Adam; the unbelievers are in the fire of Hell, or in the well Barhut.

A Possible Precursor. The belief in dying and reviving gods has sometimes been taken as one of the roots of the idea of resurrection. The English anthropologist James G. Frazer (1854–1941) devoted one volume of *The Golden Bough* to "the dying god," interpreting the myth as a symbol of the death and renewal of vegetation. However, the clearest example of a dying god, the Canaanite Aliyan Baal, was not known when the book was written, because the Ugaritic texts were only discovered in 1929. Baal is the god of thunder, rain, and fertility. He is killed by his enemy Mot (whose name means "death" and who represents the dry season), and vegetation withers away. However, Baal's sister Anat defeats Mot, and Baal returns to life, which also implies the renewal of vegetation. The myth probably served as the scenario of a ritual drama, whose aim was to secure the new life of vegetation and promote fertility in general. However, there is no trace of any belief in the resurrection of humans based on the god's return to life.

Another example is the Sumerian god Dumuzi (the Akkadian Tammuz). According to the Sumerian myths, Dumuzi, the god of the flocks and the grain, was killed by demons and had to descend into the netherworld. There are no clear texts referring to his resurrection, but there are hints that it was decided that he spend part of the year in the netherworld and the other part on earth. This would indicate that his death and return to life represent the seasonal cycle. Here too, evidence for a belief in resurrection is lacking.

Elements from these two myths (of Baal and Dumuzi) are clearly recognized in what Greek sources report on the Phoenician-Syrian god Adonis (Phoen., *ʾādōn,* "lord"). He was loved by the goddess Aphrodite and by the lady of the netherworld, Persephone; Zeus finally decided that Adonis should stay one half of the year with Aphrodite and the other half with Persephone. (It is also told that Adonis was killed by a boar and was bitterly mourned by Aphrodite.) In the case of the Egyptian god Osiris, the facts are somewhat more favorable to the theory of belief in resurrection growing out of the myth of the dying god. The myth of Osiris was known in several versions, but their essence is as follows. Osiris was a good king who was killed and dismembered by his brother Seth. His wife, Isis, mourned him, found the body, reassembled its parts, and restored it to life through a magical formula. Isis then was made pregnant and bore a son, Horus, who was recognized as the lawful successor of his father, while Osiris was made ruler of the netherworld. As a god, Osiris had clear connections with the inundation of the Nile and with grain. These connections are manifest in several rites of the Osiris "mysteries," including the burial of an effigy of Osiris made of earth and grain. Growing grain symbolizes the god's return to life. Here, for once, is a clear connection with beliefs concerning human life in the hereafter. Every person who is properly buried becomes an Osiris in the other world and shares the life of the god.

Clearly, there are considerable differences between these dying gods, and it is doubtful whether all of them represent the same specific type of god. Great caution should be exercised in seeking to draw conclusions concerning the role played by these myths in the development of the belief in resurrection.

See Also Dying and Rising Gods.

Bibliography

There is no monograph on resurrection in general. Volume 5 (1965) of the journal *Kairos* has a series of articles on resurrection in different religions, supplemented by two articles on Jewish ideas in volumes 14 (1972) and 15 (1973).

Discussion of Chinese ideas can be found in Henri Maspero's *Mélanges posthumes sur les religions et l'histoire de la Chine,* 3 vols. (Paris, 1950) by consulting the index entries under *immortalité.* Indian ideas are dealt with by Helmuth von Glasenapp in *Unsterblichkeit und Erlösung in den indischen Religionen* (Halle, 1938). For Egyptian ideas, see Alan H. Gardiner's *The Attitude of the Ancient Egyptians to Death and the Dead* (Cambridge, 1935); Herman Kees's *Totenglauben und Jenseitsvorstellungen der alten Ägypter,* 2d ed. (Berlin, 1956), a classic but difficult work; and, for certain aspects, Louis V. Zabkar's *A Study of the Ba Concept in Ancient Egyptian Texts* (Chicago, 1968) and Gertie Englund's *Akh: Une notion religieuse dans l'Egypte pharaonique* (Uppsala, 1978). The only comprehensive study of Iranian conceptions is Nathan Söderblom's *La vie future d'après le Mazdéisme* (Paris 1901). It is now somewhat out of date, but is still useful, as is J. D. C. Pavry's *The Zoroastrian Doctrine of a Future Life* (New York, 1926).

Old Testament ideas have been dealt with by Edmund F. Sutcliffe in *The Old Testament and the Future Life* (Westminster, Md., 1947) and by Robert Martin-Achard in *De la mort à la résurrection . . . dans . . . l'Ancien Testament* (Neuchâtel, 1956). For further discussion, see Harris Birkeland's "The Belief in the Resurrection of the Dead in the Old Testament," *Studia Theologica* 3 (1950): 60–78, and my book *Israelite Religion* (Philadelphia, 1975), pp. 239–247. Among studies dealing with later Jewish and Christian ideas, see R. H. Charles's *A Critical History of the Doctrine of a Future Life in Israel, in Judaism, and in Christianity* (1899; reprint, New York, 1979) and Pierre Grelot's *De la mort à la vie éternelle* (Paris, 1971). For Judaism, see also H. C. C. Cavallin's *Life after Death,* vol. 1, part 1, *An Inquiry into the Jewish Background* (Lund, 1974), a comprehensive study of all relevant texts, and George W. E. Nickelsburg's *Resurrection, Immortality, and Eternal Life in InterTestamental Judaism* (Cambridge, Mass., 1972).

Of the literature on the New Testament only a few books can be mentioned: Murdoch E. Dahl's *The Resurrection of the Body: A Study of 1 Corinthians 15* (London, 1962); *Immortality and Resurrection,* 2d ed., edited by Pierre Benoït and Roland E. Murphy (New York, 1970); Robert C. Tennenhill's *Dying and Rising with Christ* (Berlin, 1967); and Geerhardus Vos's *The Pauline Eschatology* (Grand Rapids, Mich., 1961). Works in German are Oscar Cullman's *Unsterblichkeit der Seele und Auferstehung der Toten* (Stuttgart, 1963), Paul Hoffmann's *Die Toten in Christus: Ein religionsgeschichtliche und exegetische Untersuchung zur paulinischen Eschatologie* (Münster, 1978), and Günter Kegel's *Auferstehung Jesu, Auferstehung der Toten* (Gütersloh, 1970).

On resurrection in Christian theology, see Paul Althaus's *Die letzten Dinge* (1922; Gütersloh, 1956), Walter Künneth's *Theologie der Auferstehung* (1934; Giessen, 1982), and Klaus Kienzler's *Logik der Auferstehung* (Freiburg im Breisgau, 1976), a study of the theologians Rudolf Bultmann, Gerhard Ebeling, and Wolfhart Pannenberg.

For a broad discussion of dying and rising gods, see James G. Frazer's *The Golden Bough,* 3d. ed., rev. & enl., vol. 4, *The Dying God* (1912; London, 1955). On Dumuzi, see Thorkild Jacobsen's *The Treasures of Darkness: A History of Mesopotamian Religion* (New Haven, 1976), pp. 25–73. On Baal, See Arvid S. Kapelrud's *Ba'al in the Ras Shamra Texts* (Copenhagen, 1952); Werner H. Schmidt's "Baals Tod und Auferstehung," *Zeitschrift für Religions- und Geistesgeschichte* 15 (1963): 1–13; and Michael David Coogan's *Stories from Ancient Canaan* (Philadelphia, 1978). On Osiris, E. A. Wallis Budge's *Osiris and the Egyptian Resurrection,* 2 vols. (1911; New York, 1973), and J. Gwyn Griffith's *The Origin of Osiris and His Cult,* 2d ed., rev. & enl. (Leiden, 1980), may be profitably consulted.

New Sources

Bynum, Caroline Walker. *The Resurrection of the Body in Western Christianity, 200–1336.* New York, 1995. A survey of the views of the soul's relationship to the body throughout early and medieval Christianity in a novel perspective.

Casadio, Giovanni. *Vie gnostiche all'immortalità.* Brescia, Italy, 1997. Types of resurrection in Judaism, Zoroastrianism, New Testament and Gnosticism are discussed with attention to the relevant bibliography.

Hornung, Erik and Schabert, Tilo, eds. *Auferstehung und Unsterblichkeit.* Munich, 1993. A volume of the new Eranos series, including cross-cultural studies by historians of religions (Michael von Brück, Giovanni Casadio, Reinhold Merkelbach), philosophers (A. Hilary Armstrong, Rémi Brague), anthropologists (Jean Servier), and psychologists (James Hillman).

Mainville, Odette, and Daniel Marguerat, eds. *Résurrection. L'après mort dans le monde ancien et le Nouveau Testament.* Geneva, 2001. Resurrection in New Testament and ancient world in theological perspective.

HELMER RINGGREN (1987)
Revised Bibliography

RETREAT may be defined as a limited period of isolation during which an individual, either alone or as part of a small group, withdraws from the regular routine of daily life, generally for religious reasons. Retreats are one of the commoner practices in the religious life of nearly all peoples, although they are often restricted to a determinate type or class of persons: those preparing for initiation (e.g., into the adult life of a clan, into a religious group, or into some public office of a religious nature), those undergoing a process of conversion, those in search of a religious vocation, or those seeking a periodic renewal of their spiritual lives. During this period, retreatants interrupt their ordinary routine, break off regular social relationships, and (except for those who already live in monasteries or the like) withdraw into a solitary place or to a special building set apart for such purposes. This isolation, as well as the interruption of social intercourse and ordinary life, is adopted as a condition that enables individual retreatants to enter within themselves in silence, in order to establish contact with the divinity or with the world of the spirits. Hence, retreats often involve the use of various ascetical means, such as fasting, abstinence, prayer, meditation, and techniques aimed at inducing a revelatory dream, trance, or ecstasy.

Various forms of retreat may be distinguished, and participants may engage in retreats with varying frequency. A retreat accompanying a radical conversion of life or the discernment of a vocation may be a rare or even unique event in an individual's life; whereas that aimed at personal spiritual renewal might be repeated periodically. Retreats of initiation may follow quite diverse procedures, depending on the kind of initiation involved. Thus, one may distinguish retreats of tribal initiation; retreats of search for a revelatory dream; retreats of shamanistic or monastic initiaion; and retreats of conversion, discernment, and renewal.

RETREATS OF TRIBAL INITIATION. In generic and somewhat abstract terms (since in reality quite different forms of ritual may be involved), initiation into the life of a tribe entails separating candidates from the social nucleus to which they belong as children, especially from their mother, and isolating them in a well-defined zone, protected by rigid taboos. There they are placed under the direction of elders chosen by the tribe. The neophytes are then subjected to certain strict disciplines (fasting, abstinence, and various taboos), are instructed by the elders in certain traditional truths and beliefs (social and sexual ethics, myths and rituals, techniques of hunting, fishing, or farming), and are forced to undergo certain more or less painful tests. At the end of this period of initiation, after passing through certain liberating rites, the neophytes, having undergone a profound transformation, return to the tribe as adults. The symbolic meaning of this period of isolation seems clear enough. Cultures that practice this kind of initiation regard it as a mutation or deep transformation of the human being: a sort of death and rebirth. Henceforth, all that had previously constituted the life of a child must be suppressed, especially the child's former dependence on its mother. The adolescent through this isolation, enters the world of the sacred, of mythic time, and is often locked in struggle with mysterious force, involving some form of bodily suffering (torture and, above all, circumcision). In this case the retreat is precisely the vehicle that allows this breaking away and entry.

RETREATS OF SEARCH FOR A REVELATORY DREAM. A number of peoples, especially pre-Columbian Indians, submitted their children and adolescents to a period of isolation aimed at enabling them to enter into contact with the spirit who was to guide each of them throughout life. This phenomenon is especially notable among certain Canadian groups, such as the Athapascans, who submitted children as young as five years old to the test. The norm commonly followed involved removing these children or adolescents from their normal world of relationships, abandoning them in a solitary place, and subjecting them to a strict fast until physical weakness induced a state of hallucination. The first image that presented itself to the child or adolescent was the spirit who would accompany and protect him until death, a sort of tutelary *numen* whom he would thence-forward invoke. The Delaware and Algonquin of the Atlantic coast observed much the same procedure with twelve-year-old girls and boys, but introduced the concept of the compassion of the spirits, whom the adolescents were required to invoke while they practiced their total fast. The spirits then put an end to the sufferings of the initiates by revealing themselves to them in a dream. After a certain length of time, the parents visited the adolescents to see whether the revelatory experience had yet occurred. If it had, they brought their offspring back to the tribe, where they were regarded as the depositories of a sacred force (Walter Krickeberg et al., *Die Religionen des Alten Amerika,* Stuttgart, 1961; see also J. Blumensohn, "The Fast among North American Indians," *American Anthropology* 35, 1933, pp. 451–469).

RETREATS OF SHAMANISTIC INITIATION. Mircea Eliade treats shamanism as a religious limit-experience: a form of mysticism originating in a vocation awakened by a crisis that is found in many religions (*Shamanism: Archaic Techniqes of Ecstasy,* rev. and enl. ed., New York, 1964). Here, shamanism is taken in its original, strict sense, as a characteristic and primary expression of the religious life of the peoples of north central Asia. The shaman is an individual who has been suddenly overcome by a spirit and has, by that very fact, received a distinctive gift. The signs whereby this possession becomes known coincide with what the Western mind would call symptoms of epilepsy or, more generally, a form of nervous disorder. Whoever receives such a "dangerous" gift must stay in constant contact with the world of the spirits, and this the shaman does by isolating himself. Frequently, the candidate is instructed by an old shaman, or the whole tribe may take part in the shaman's initiation by contributing to its ritual sacrifices. The future shaman learns the necessary formulas and offertory rites and then retires to the wild in order to learn the techniques of ecstasy by sitting before a fire and repeating certain formulas. At the end of the shaman's retreat, the individual is consecrated in a rite celebrated by the ancient shaman who provided instruction. From this retreat the new shaman emerges endowed with special powers, and can now enter into contact with the world of the spirits, and the new shaman's mediation thus becomes important for the tribe.

RETREATS OF MONASTIC INITIATION. Among the four exemplary stages that Hindu tradition distinguishes in the life of a person—the third, after those of student and father of a family, but before that of wandering holy person—is that of the individual who withdraws in solitude into the forest, where he or she (now called a *vanaptrasthin*) commits to meditation and to certain practices of asceticism. This retreat portends the person's coming to spiritual maturity and eventual irradiation of the surrounding people, by way of the *vanaptrasthin*'s example and teaching. Since a long period of isolation is involved here, this retreat may well be classified as an experience of the eremitical life. Significantly, in the history of Western monasticism, Athanasius, in his *Life of Antony,* describes how his hero, after his conversion, first underwent a stage of basic initiation under the direction of an ascetic, after which he underwent a further stage of isolation in a necropolis, followed by a third and decisive stage of enclosure in a ruined castle, where he remained for twenty years. At the end of this stage, Athanasius relates in terms reminiscent of the mystery cults, that Antony "came forth as from a sanctuary, initiated in the mysteries and filled with the divine spirit" (*Life of Antony* 14). Finally, after receiving the gift of spiritual fecundity, Antony accepted some disciples, although he remained with them in solitude. The parallels to Hindu monasticism are revealing: In both cases there is a retreat into complete solitude, which prepares the individuals for full spiritual maturity and confers on them a certain irradiative power. The Hindu ascetic then embarks upon an itinerant, renunciative life (*saṃnyasa*), returning to society but not forming part of it. The Christian anchorite becomes an elder—a religious father or mother—and accepts disciples, instructing them in the spiritual life.

A similar phenomenon appears in the lives of other Christian saints, who were dedicated not to monastic contemplation but rather to intense activity among people. Ignatius Loyola spent almost an entire year, from March 1522 to February 1523, in Manresa, where he devoted himself to prayer (seven hours daily), fasting, and abstinence. He emerged from this experience transformed and illumined in spirit by revelations of various kinds. Three centuries later, Anthony M. Claret (1807–1870) spent some months at San Andrés del Pruit (Girona, Spain), dedicated to prayer. He went forth from this retreat powerfully consecrated to itinerant preaching. In both cases, the retreat was one of initiation into an intense religious experience, accompanied by an outburst of apostolic irradiation. It would be easy to cite numerous other examples of this type.

A different sort of retreat of monastic initiation is represented by the novitiate, a relatively long period of trial prior to incorporation into a religious community. During the novitiate, candidates are separated from others—even from professed members of the community—and placed under the direction of a master, who instructs them and tests their vocation. The novitiate appears in the Buddhist tradition, where it is called *upasaṃpadā* ("goal, arrival"). Its aim is to prepare the novices for entry upon the way of salvation, and it ends with an anointing ceremony (*abhiṣeka*), which consecrates them. In Christian monasticism, an initial period of instruction and trial originated among the anchorites of the fourth century. It was a rather long period, which ended when the elder in charge adjudged the novice to have reached the required maturity, and invited the novice to withdraw into chosen solitude. In monastic communities, the novitiate was reduced to a period of a year. At present, it lasts from one to two years, according to custom. Originally, the year of novitiate began with investiture of the novice in the habit, while it later came to be terminated with his commitment to the religious life. Besides this investiture, another feature observed in the past was a change of the novice's name, to indicate that a secular individual had died and a religious one had come to birth. The medieval Christian theology of the religious profession as a second baptism referred to this idea of a symbolic death and rebirth.

Retreats of Spiritual Renewal. The practice of withdrawing for a relatively brief period of time in order to revitalize oneself spiritually seems to be evidenced in all religions that attach great importance to the spiritual experience of the individual. The retreat in the woods constitutes one of the stages of the ideal way of the Hindu. Even masters return periodically to the forest solitude, in order to encounter themselves more deeply. But it is above all in Islam and Christianity that this kind of retreat has been most popular.

Islam. The custom of devoting a period of time to prayer and fasting (*khalwah*), while withdrawing from social contacts and ordinary occupations, is amply documented in the Muslim world much earlier than in Christendom. The source of inspiration for this practice is the fact that, according to the Qurʾān, God gave the Law to Moses at the end of a retreat of forty days (*sūrah* 7:142). It is also said that Adam received his life-breath only forty days after he had been formed from the clay. The Prophet himself left an example, by going frequently into retreat. The great Andalusian mystic Muḥammad ibn al-ʿArabī (d. 1240) tells of the revelations he received during a retreat he made as a very young man in Seville (*Al-futūḥāt al-makkīyah,* Cairo, AH 1329/1911 CE, vol. 1, p. 186). Ibn al-ʿArabī also wrote a treatise on the conditions for making a retreat, the *Kitāb al-khalwah.* A century later, the Indian Sharaf al-Dīn Manērī (d. 1381) devoted one of his *Hundred Letters* to explaining the origin and aim of the retreat. An essential element in it is the remembrance of God, that is, the sense of God's presence and the invocation of his name. By reviving the sense of the divine presence, the retreat heals and fortifies the soul, and disposes it to continue in that presence when the retreatant returns to ordinary life.

In Ṣūfī orders, the superior of a house is obliged to go on retreat periodically. The novices, too, must make a retreat, ordinarily for forty days. This forty days' experience must be made in a solitary place or, if one is a member of a community, in a dark cell. Fasting is essential to this kind of retreat: Whoever makes one must reduce their food consumption considerably throughout, and abstain completely from eating during the last three days. The lives of the Ṣūfī mystics contain numerous allusions to this practice (see Javad Nurbakhsh, *Masters of the Path,* New York, 1980, pp. 115, 117). Ibn al-ʿArabī tells of a retreat he made with the master Abū Zakarīyāʾ Yaḥyā ibn Ḥassān (*Sufis of Andalusia,* Berkeley, Calif., 1971, p. 138).

Christianity. In Christianity, especially during the last few centuries, this type of retreat, aimed at the spiritual renewal of the individual through meditation, prayer, and silence, has reached a high level of development. Such a retreat is often made under the direction of a master, who engages in periodic dialogue with the individual retreatant, or else delivers instructions, when the retreat is made by a group.

It is significant that certain popular histories of the retreat begin with the episode narrated by the evangelist Mark (repeated, with amplifications, in the Matthean and Lukan parallels), concerning Jesus' withdrawal into the desert of Judaea after his baptism and the "descent" of the Holy Spirit upon him. The Markan account (*Mk.* 1:12–13) is not only Christological in content, but also exemplary in intention.

Jesus, after his baptism and his anointing by the Spirit, appears as the New Adam, dwelling among the wild beasts and ministered to by angels. During this time (scholars debate whether the passage existed in the tradition prior to Mark), Jesus was tempted by the spirit of evil but, unlike the first Adam, overcame the temptation (see Vincent Taylor, *The Gospel according to Mark,* London, 1955, pp. 162–164). Of itself, the episode did not overtly attribute to Jesus the intention of devoting himself especially to spiritual exercises of prayer. The accounts of Matthew (4:1–11) and Luke (4:1–13) add that Jesus' stay in the desert lasted forty days, and that the temptation came at the end of this period.

The account of Jesus' sojourn in the desert added even richer spiritual implications to the biblical texts on the passage of the Hebrew people through the desert, before their entry into Canaan. The desert now became the symbol of a new spiritual attitude. Origen, in his commentary on *Exodus,* speaks of the need for retreat: One must leave familiar surroundings and go to a place free of worldly preoccupations, a place of silence and interior peace, where one can learn wisdom and come to a deep knowledge of the word of God (*In Exodum Homiliae,* Wilhelm Baehrens, ed., Leipzig, 1920, p. 167).

Drawing their inspiration from the example of Jesus, the Christian churches soon established a period of forty days dedicated to fasting, abstinence, and greater prayer, in order to prepare the faithful for the celebration of the Pascha. Two themes were interwoven in the sermons of the Fathers on Lent: that of participation in Christ's struggles and sufferings during his passion as a preparation for the celebration of the Resurrection, and that of a model projection on it, of the fast and temptations of Jesus in the solitude of the Judean desert. On this fundamental model, they occasionally superimposed the image of the wandering of the Israelites in the desert, with all the trials and temptations to which they were subjected there (see Leo the Great, "Sermons on Lent," *Patrologia Latina,* vol. 54). In addresses to the laity, the latter were not asked to go on retreat (although they are asked to prolong their prayer), but were exhorted to conversion, to charity toward the poor, and to reconciliation with enemies. Traditionally, it was also recommended that they forgo diversions and entertainments.

The anonymous author of the *Rule of the Master* (central Italy, c. 500) introduced three chapters on the observance of Lent by monks, prescribing that they multiply their prayers and perform more acts of fast and abstinence (*Rule of the Master,* chaps. 51–53). Benedict (480–c. 547) reduced the rule for Lent to a single chapter, in which he echoed Leo the Great and the *Rule of the Master.* In it he added a recommendation that monks recite more numerous individual prayers and restrict their dealings with each other (*Rule of Saint Benedict,* chap. 49). Lent thus tended to become a sort of forty-day retreat spent in silence, prayer, fasting, and abstinence. From the Middle Ages on, the monastic orders began to interrupt all contact, even by way of letter, with outsiders, throughout the period of Lent. Thus, the Lenten retreat was fundamentally a retreat of spiritual renewal, in which the individual retreatant relived certain fundamental themes of Christianity, derived primarily from the passion of Christ, but secondarily from his withdrawal and fast in the desert.

It is fitting at this point to inquire into the rise, in Christian churches, of the practice of the retreat proper, that is to say, of that prayerful kind of withdrawal practiced by a person, either alone or as part of a small group, for a certain short period of time. It was precisely the celebration of Lent that suggested the first tentative steps in this direction. Around the end of the fourth century and the beginning of the fifth, Euthymius the Great, a monk of Melitene, adopted the custom of withdrawing during Lent of each year and going to a mountaintop, where he gave himself over to prayer and fasting. Later, he went with a friend each year into the desert of Koutila (see Cyril of Scythopolis, *Life of Euthymius,* edited by E. Schwartz, in *Texte und Untersuchungen,* vol. 49, no. 2, Lipsia, 1939, pp. 3–85). Jesus' stay in the Judean desert thus became a model that was imitated literally. It is quite possible—indeed, probable—that other monks followed the same norm, in an endeavor to practice a stricter eremitical life during Lent.

Yet another historical fact might be considered as a precursor of the modern retreat. Pilgrimages to shrines, which were so frequent during certain periods of the Middle Ages, involved a break with the normal situation of the individual, a going forth from one's city and family, in order to visit some usually distant holy place ("to *ferne* halwes," as Chaucer noted in his prologue to the *Canterbury Tales,* poking fun at English pilgrims who managed to get no farther than Canterbury). Palestine, the tombs of the apostles in Rome, and Compostela were among the most common goals. The deep reason behind these journeys was the desire to visit a sacred place where the presence of the supernatural was more perceptible, thanks to the presence either of the relics of a saint or of some venerable holy image. Sometimes these pilgrimages became the occasion of a process of conversion and separation from the world. It is noteworthy, for example, that the primitive nucleus of twelfth-century hermitages of Our Lady, at Mount Carmel (the future Carmelite order), were constituted by people of western Europe who had established themselves in the Holy Land. In certain cases, the pilgrimage shrine was served by a community of monks who ran a hostelry for those who wished to spend a limited period of prayer and silence nearby. This fact is documented in connection with the shrine and abbey of Einsiedeln, Switzerland, perhaps as early as the twelfth century (Ludwig Raeber, *Our Lady of Hermits,* Einsiedeln, 1961), and, somewhat later, at the shrine and monastery of Montserrat, Spain (Joan Segarra, *Montserrat,* Barcelona, 1961).

But the retreat as commonly known during the past few centuries has its roots, properly speaking, in the spiritual movement called the Devotio Moderna, initiated by Gerhard Groote (1340–1384) in the Low Countries, of which the most widely known representative is Thomas à Kempis (c. 1380–1471). Groote, converted to a fervent life in 1374, withdrew for a time to the charterhouse of Munnikhuizen, near Arnhem on the Rhine. The Brethren of the Common Life and the authors of the Devotio Moderna popularized their form of piety among the secular clergy and the laity, giving it a practical and ascetical interpretation, well suited to the clearly individualistic horizons of the spirituality of the Christian West in their day. Next came the refinement of different methods of meditation, and the compilation of various handbooks of meditations. In the early fourteenth century, the Tuscan Franciscan John de Caulibus published his *Meditations on the Life of Christ;* Gerard of Zutphen (d. 1398), in his *De spiritualibus ascensionibus,* propounded a precise method of meditations and examens, a procedure repeated later by the Dutch canon regular, John Mombaer (d. 1501), the last master of the Devotio Moderna, who used it as an instrument of reform in the monasteries of the clerks regular in France. In 1500, the reforming abbot of Montserrat, Francisco Jiménez de Cisneros, printed his *Ejercitatorio de la vida espiritual,* containing a precise method of meditations, and a plan that structured the various meditations into four successive weeks. The technique developed out of the Devotio Moderna could thus be used in a period set aside especially for prayer and meditation.

This technique culminated in the *Spiritual Exercises* of Ignatius Loyola, the founder of the Society of Jesus. It is a methodical interweaving of meditations, contemplations, and examens, more or less developed, taking place over four weeks and accompanied by a series of counsels and rules. He first sketched out the method during his own retreat at Manresa, and perfected it over the years until the definitive version was approved by Pope Paul III in 1548. Although there are points of contact between Ignatius and some of his predecessors (especially Jiménez de Cisneros, whose method he seems to have known), he is quite original in definitively tying these meditations to a retreat made under the direction of a master, with the basic aim of choosing a proper mode of life for the greater service of God—hence, the rules of discernment that accompany the *Exercises.* Starting with the first companions of the founder, the Jesuits have continued to be trained in the *Exercises* of Ignatius.

In the sixteenth century, retreat exercises according to the Ignatian method had already become popular, although they were practiced only by priests and religious at the time, not by the laity. Retreat houses were established in order to facilitate the arrangement of retreats for those who wished to make them. The first such house was opened in a villa in Siena, Italy, in 1538. This was followed by the retreat houses of Alcala, Spain, in 1553, Cologne, Germany, in 1561, and Louvain, Belgium, in 1569. In the seventeenth century this practice was adopted by the principal representatives of French spirituality. Vincent de Paul (d. 1660) is said to have directed the *Exercises* of more than twenty thousand persons. The *Exercises,* in somewhat modified and shortened form, began to be practiced by the laity in great numbers. An outstanding figure in the history of retreats was the Argentinian María Antonia de San José de la Paz (1730–1799), who organized Ignatian retreats in the course of her life for more than a hundred thousand people. However, the Ignatian retreat was gradually converted into a retreat of spiritual renewal as it came to be repeated periodically by persons who had already chosen a type of Christian life (priestly, religious, or secular) and only sought to be spiritually revitalized through a retreat.

Priests, religious, and seminarians of the Roman Catholic church commonly make eight days of spiritual exercises annually. Many members of the Catholic laity follow the same norm in the present time. Some periodically make even a month's exercises. Hence one may find retreat houses in all countries where the Roman Catholic Church is present. In 1836, the bishop of Viviers, France, approved the Congregation of the Sisters of Our Lady of the Cenacle, founded by Marie Victoire Thérèse Couderc and by Jean-Pierre Étienne Terme. Initially called Dames de la Retraite ("retreat ladies"), the Sisters promoted the practice of retreats among laity. They have retreat houses in England (since 1888), and even more exist in the United States, where they arrived in 1892. A similar end is pursued by the Retreat Sisters of the Sacred Heart, founded in 1678 in Quimper, France, by Claude Thérèse de Kermeno. Other men and women religious are dedicated to the same apostolate. In France, toward the end of the nineteenth century, the Oeuvre des Retraites de Perseverance was founded, and soon the movement spread to Italy. Its aim is to promote yearly retreats and monthly days of recollection among the laity, as a means of renewing Christian life. Besides the month-long and annual eight-day retreat forms, where the dominant influence is Ignatian, there are weekend retreats for laity, which follow many different methods: scriptural, charismatic, healing, and so forth. In the United States, the National Catholic Laymen's Retreat Conference was founded in 1928. A retreat league founded by the Sisters of the Cenacle became, in 1936, the National Laywomen's Retreat Movement.

A particular form of retreat, originally among Catholics, has been propagated by the movement known as Cursillos de Cristiandad, founded by Bishop Hervás in Majorca in 1949, whence it has spread to several other countries. A group of Christians, from almost any walk of life, retreat for a few days dedicated to community reflection, liturgy, dialogue, and private reflection. They examine and share the concrete faith-experience of their ordinary life. The *Cursillos* movement, which has existed for some years in the United States, is organized on national and diocesan levels, and has, to some extent, been practiced by other Christian groups, mainly Lutherans and Episcopalians.

Finally, some mention should be made of the monthly retreat or recollection day. Practiced mainly by religious and priests in the nineteenth century, it became almost obligatory after Pius X recommended it in his exhortation to the Catholic clergy in 1908. The Second Vatican Council, in its Decree on Priests, also recommended the practice of retreats to the clergy (*Presbyterorum Ordinis,* no. 18).

See Also Deserts; Eremitism; Initiation; Monasticism; Quests; Shamanism.

Bibliography

Very little, if anything, of a general nature has been published on the topic of retreat. References to retreats, seclusion, and the like can be found in any general survey on Hindu, Muslim, and Christian mysticism, as well as in works dealing with phenomenology of religion.

Works dealing with specific traditions can, however, be recommended. For a discussion of retreat traditions in tribal societies, see Victor Turner's *The Forest of Symbols* (Ithaca, N.Y., 1969). On the role of seclusion in the Buddhist monastic tradition, see John C. Holt's *Discipline: The Canonical Buddhism of the Vinayapataha* (Delhi, 1981). On retreat in the Christian tradition, the *New Catholic Encyclopedia,* vol. 12 (New York, 1967), includes a valuable article by Thomas E. Dubay. Further discussion of the topic is available in *Historia de la practica de los Ejercicios Espirituales de San Ignacio de Loyola,* 2 vols. (Bilbao, Spain, 1946–1955), by Ignacio Iparraguirre. For the role of retreat in Eastern Orthodox churches, see Catherine de Hueck Doherty's *Sobornost* (Notre Dame, Ind., 1977). For discussion of Muslim retreats, see Muḥammad ibn al-ʿArabī's *Kitāb al-khalwah* (Aya Sofia, 1964) and letters 96 and 22 in Sharafuddin Maneri's *The Hundred Letters,* translated by Paul Jackson (New York, 1980).

Juan Manuel Lozano (1987)

RETRIBUTION

See JUDGMENT OF THE DEAD; REVENGE AND RETRIBUTION

REVEL, BERNARD

REVEL, BERNARD (1885–1940), a rabbinic scholar, was the organizer of American Jewish Orthodoxy. Born in Pren, a suburb of Kaunas (Kovno), Lithuania, where his father was the community rabbi, Revel later studied in the Telz *yeshivah* and was ordained in Kaunas at the age of sixteen. Immigrating to the United States in 1906, Revel received his master of arts degree from New York University in 1909; three years later he completed a Ph.D. at Dropsie College with a thesis entitled "The Karaite Halakhah and Its Relation to Sadducean, Samaritan, and Philonian Halakhah."

Revel first worked in the Oklahoma-based petroleum company of his wife's family, but in 1915 he accepted the presidency of New York's newly merged Yeshivat Etz Chaim and Rabbi Isaac Elchanan Theological Seminary. Under its auspices, Revel then opened the Talmudical Academy, the first such *yeshivah* high school in the United States. He also reorganized the rabbinical school, and in 1928, he continued his expansion program with the opening of Yeshiva College, later Yeshiva University (1945).

Revel guided the schools in the spirit of modern Orthodoxy, attempting to perpetuate the traditional Torah way of life within the context of American society. Yeshiva College, in particular, marked the first effort to provide traditional Talmudic study and liberal arts training under the same auspices. Despite the vigorous opposition of some rabbinical leaders, who feared for the primacy of Torah study in such an institution, Revel forged ahead and in 1937 opened a graduate department in advanced Jewish and cognate studies. In 1941 this school was renamed the Bernard Revel Graduate School in his memory.

Revel was a presidium member of the Union of Orthodox Rabbis of the United States and Canada from 1924 (later honorary president) and vice-president of the Jewish Academy of Arts and Sciences from 1927. He was an associate editor of the *Otsar Yisra'el* encyclopedia (vol. 9, 1913), and his doctoral dissertation was published by Dropsie College (1913). Despite the demands made upon his time by his manifold Yeshiva responsibilities, Revel continued his doctoral research with monographs and studies about deviant *halakhah* systems. He also produced articles of rabbinic scholarship and wrote halakhic *responsa.* His writings were published mainly in the *Jewish Quarterly Review, Yagdil Torah, Ha-Pardes,* and various Yeshiva student publications.

Bibliography

Hoenig, Sidney B. *Rabbinics and Research: The Scholarship of Dr. Bernard Revel.* New York, 1968.

Poupko, Bernard A., ed. *Eidenu: Memorial Publication in Honor of Rabbi Dr. Bernard Revel* (in Hebrew). New York, 1942.

Rakeffet-Rothkoff, Aaron. *Bernard Revel: Builder of American Jewish Orthodoxy.* 2d ed. Jerusalem, 1981.

New Sources

Gurock, Jeffrey S. "An Orthodox Conspiracy Theory: The Travis Family, Bernard Revel, and the Jewish Theological Seminary." *Modern Judaism* 19 (1999): 241–253.

Aaron Rakeffet-Rothkoff (1987)
Revised Bibliography

REVELATION

REVELATION. The concept of revelation is a fundamental one in every religion that in any way traces its origin to God or a divinity. Revelation is a divine communication to human beings. This broad description allows the phenomenologist of religion to include very different manners and degrees of revelation. In fact, the most diverse experiences, ranging from an obscure clue given by a supernatural power to the self-communication of a personal God, are possible from the standpoints of psychology, religious philosophy, and theology.

In general, religious phenomenologists use five different criteria (characteristics or factors) of revelation:

(1) Origin or author: God, spirits, ancestors, power (*mana*), forces. In every case the source of revelation is something supernatural or numinous.

(2) Instrument or means: sacred signs in nature (the stars, animals, sacred places, or sacred times); dreams, visions, ecstasies; finally, words or sacred books.

(3) Content or object: the didactic, helping, or punishing presence, will, being, activity, or commission of the divinity.

(4) Recipients or addressees: medicine men, sorcerers, sacrificing priests, shamans, soothsayers, mediators, prophets with a commission or information intended for individuals or groups, for a people or the entire race.

(5) Effect and consequence for the recipient: personal instruction or persuasion, divine mission, service as oracle—all this through inspiration or, in the supreme case, through incarnation.

It is to be noted that the historians of religion derived the concept of revelation from the Judeo-Christian religion where it received its theological elaboration and then in the course of research into the history of religions was transferred in a broad and analogous sense to other religions. The answer to the question whether one may speak of revelation in the proper sense in animistic, polytheistic, and polydemonistic religions will depend on the understanding of religion maintained by a given Christian scholar. In theologian Karl Barth's view Christianity alone possesses a revelation; historian of religion van der Leeuw, on the other hand, develops a much more inclusive understanding of revelation and therefore a series of types that culminates in the Christian concept of revelation.

It is certain that revelation must be clearly distinguished from magic, since magical practices aim at power over and disposal of the divine, while revelation means in principle a free announcement by the divinity. This announcement even goes beyond hierophanies and epiphanies and involves the manifestation of something holy or the rendering apprehensible of a divine depth, inasmuch as it always clearly includes the distinction between revealing subject and revealed object, between self-revealing God and mystery made known. In any case, this fuller meaning is regularly intended by the Latin *revelatio* and the Greek *apokalupsis.*

Whether gnosis and mysticism are to be regarded as forms of revelation or, on the contrary, as the opposite of revelation depends essentially on the role assigned to divine grace (as help from and self-communication of God) in these manifestations of religious life. Whenever ultimate knowledge and the vision of supreme wisdom are regarded not as the fruit of human effort alone but as a gift from God, then, as in the experience of a profound union with God that cannot be acquired by force or produced by the human being but can only be received as a gift, a self-communication of a personal God comes into play and the concept of revelation is correctly applied.

NATURAL REVELATIONS. It may therefore seem at first sight contradictory to speak of "natural revelation," since the knowledge of God derived from nature seems to involve no personal, here-and-now turning of God to human beings but to result rather from the intellectual efforts of the latter. The objection overlooks the fact that religio-philosophical statements about God can never take the form of knowledge gained by the natural sciences, which turn the object of their investigations into an object of human experience and human categories of thought. God cannot be fully grasped by human thought or defined or adequately described in concepts derived from experience of the spatiotemporal world. This fact is reflected in "negative theology," which regards it as possible to say unreservedly of God only what he is not. Positive statements about him always fall short and are compatible with his absolute transcendence, his wholly-otherness (*totaliter aliter*) and ever-greaterness (*semper maior*), only insofar as they are made with a realization of the analogous structure of human language. In this context "analogy" does not mean mathematical similarity; it refers rather to a fundamental relation of similarity-dissimilarity, due to which every positive assertion of a formal perfection in God (being, goodness, justice, etc.) must immediately be negated. That is, it must be purified of the experienced finiteness that attaches to these concepts in the spatio-temporal world, and then applied to the trancendent God in a nonmaterial sense and in the highest possible degree of perfection. It is clear that in this three-step operation—assertion, negation, and reassertion in the mode of supereminence—negation plays the decisive role.

To make the point more simply: God is a hidden God (*Deus absconditus*). Only if he discloses himself and only to the extent that he makes himself known can he be known by human beings. This is the basic idea behind the concept of "natural revelation," which is proposed at various points in the Western tradition of philosophical theology.

The Bible. In his *Letter to the Romans,* the apostle Paul vividly states the possibility (not the actuality) of a natural knowledge of God: "The wrath of God is revealed from heaven against all ungodliness and wickedness of men who by their wickedness suppress the truth. For what can be known about God is plain to them, because God has shown it to them. Ever since the creation of the world his invisible nature, namely, his eternal power and deity, has been clearly perceived in the things that have been made. So they are without excuse; for although they knew God they did not honor him as God or give thanks to him, but they became futile in their thinking and their senseless minds were darkened" (*Rom.* 1:18–22).

The most important statement here is "God has shown it to them." This clearly brings out the revelational character of the knowledge. The cosmos is not simply *phusis* or nature in the form of an eternally self-subsisting world, such as the Greeks understood it to be; rather, it is *ktisis* or creation, that is, God's handiwork that had a beginning and that as finite nature points to the infinite God as its creator.

Ever since the creation of the world, the invisible being of God has been known by reason. Human beings understand themselves to be creatures and therefore by reason know God's power and deity.

The apostle Paul was evidently referring to a passage in the *Wisdom of Solomon,* which was probably a Jewish composition written in Egypt in the first century BCE. Rejecting Egyptian polytheism, the author says: "All men who were ignorant of God were foolish by nature; and they were unable from the good things that are seen to know him who exists, nor did they recognize the craftsman while paying heed to his works; but they supposed that either fire or wind or swift air, or the circle of the stars, or turbulent water, or the luminaries of heaven were the gods that rule the world. If through delight in the beauty of these things men assumed them to be gods, let them know how much better than these is their Lord, for the author of beauty created them. And if men were amazed at their power and working, let them perceive from them how much more powerful is he who formed them. For from the greatness and beauty of created things comes a corresponding perception of their creator" (*Wis.* 13:1–5).

In this passage myths about the origin of the world and philosophical explanations of the world as emerging from primal matter (water, air, etc.), such as were offered by the Ionian natural philosophers, are being rejected in favor of an understanding in which the beauties of this world are explained as produced by a first cause.

Philosophy of Plato. The very wording of the passage from the *Wisdom of Solomon* betrays the philosophical influence of Plato, who speaks in his dialogue the *Symposium* (178a–c) of the ascent of the soul, via the various degrees of bodily and intellectual beauty, to the primordially beautiful, that is, the idea of Beauty as such. Here as elsewhere in Plato's elaboration of his doctrine of the Ideas, his thinking takes as its point of reference the origin (*arche, proton*) of things. Such is the case in the *Lysis,* where is found the concept of the Primordially Lovable (*philon*), and especially in the *Republic* (505–511), where Plato describes the function of the idea of the Good as such, which is the cause of being and knowledge in everything else that is. In conceiving the world as having its ground in the ideas, Plato provides the philosophical presupposition for understanding everything finite as conditioned and as sustained in being by the idea of God. The world is not intelligible in itself either ontically or noetically, either in its being or in its knowableness. Once this fundamental insight is grasped, it becomes easy to understand the viewpoint of Jewish and Christian thinkers who saw the world as a message conveying God's greatness, beauty, power, and goodness, and therefore as a revelation in the proper sense.

It is for this reason that in the passage from *Romans* Paul says human beings should have advanced from knowledge of God to acknowledgment of him and the payment to him of honor and gratitude. Even natural revelation implies and calls for existential consequences such as reverence and obedience.

Luther for his part interpreted Paul as saying in *Romans* that they are foolish who endeavor to gain a natural knowledge of God from creation as the "work" of God's power and glory. Over and against such a "theology of glory" he set a "theology of the cross" that maintains that "insofar as God's being is made visible and is turned to the world, it is represented there in suffering and the cross" (Heidelberg Disputation of 1518). But, valuable though this emphasis on God's revelation in Christ is, in Paul's view human beings are "foolish" not because they attempt to learn God's eternal power and divinity from creation but because "by their wickedness [they] suppress the truth." In general, evangelical theology still has a negative attitude toward natural theology.

Aristotle and Thomas Aquinas. In the Constitution on Faith of the First Vatican Council (1869–1870), on the other hand, the Catholic church insisted on the possibility and point of natural revelation: "God, the beginning and end of all things, can be known with certainty from the things that were created through the natural light of human reason, for 'ever since the creation of the world His invisible nature has been clearly perceived in the things that have been made' (*Rom.* 1:20)" (Henricus Denzinger and Adolfus Schönmetzer's "Enchiridion symbolorum, no. 3004," *The Christian Faith in the Doctrinal Documents of the Catholic Church,* 36th ed., no. 113, Rome, 1976). The passage goes beyond what is said in *Romans* and speaks of God as not only the ground but also the destination of creation. It is clear from this, as it is from the expression "the natural light of human reason," that the council fathers were here following the teaching of Thomas Aquinas.

In his five "ways" of obtaining knowledge of God (*Summa theologiae* 1.2.3), Thomas was basing his thought on Aristotle rather than Plato. The background of this link in the history of ideas must be briefly sketched. Aristotle had accepted several points made by Plato: the priority of movement proceeding from within over movement initiated by what is outside (*Laws, Phaedrus*); the idea that what is first in the cosmos is an idea, or *eidos* ("spiritual entity"); and, finally, the view that first cause and end are necessarily identical. In the framework of his own theory of potency and act, Aristotle then elaborated his doctrine of God as the First Unmoved Mover (*to proton kinoun akineton auto*), who as self-sufficient intellectual reality (*actus purus*) is not dependent on anything outside of himself, while at the same time all other intellectual and corporeal beings have their ground in him. God is the origin and source of the world and at the same time its ultimate end, since all things strive toward him and he moves them as "that which is loved," that is, as a supreme value that draws them (*Metaphysics* A, 6–9).

All these "movements" of which Aristotle speaks are not to be interpreted in mechanistic terms but intellectually or metaphysically: They are a striving for form or fulfillment in reality or value.

Thomas Aquinas reduces these arguments of Plato and Aristotle to concise systematic form. The first three ways take as their starting point certain facts of experience: that the beings of this world are in movement (in potency); that they do not have their efficient cause in themselves (they are conditioned beings); and that they do not exist necessarily but are finite, temporal, and contingent. These three ways conclude to a First Cause that "moves" everything (in the Aristotelian sense of the word "move"), is the ground of all further causal series, and has the ground of its own being within itself, or, in other words, exists necessarily and eternally.

The inevitability of this conclusion is underscored by the consideration that an infinite regress does not offer an alternative solution and that one must abandon the endless series of causes and conditions (*ab alio*) and accept a First that is of a different kind *(a se)* if anything at all is to be explained. The idea that an infinite regress is impossible bears the clear mark of Platonic thinking, according to which something finite and conditioned is explicable only in terms of something infinite and unconditioned (*anupotheton*). Platonism thus conceived is indispensable for the philosophy of religion.

Thomas's fourth way is likewise based on the gradations of being and value that is found in the doctrine of the ideas. The ground of every goodness is located in the supreme Good as such (in Platonic terms: in the [divine] idea of the Good), which distributes of its goodness and gives a participation in it.

The fifth way concludes from the order found in the world to an orderer who possesses intellectual knowledge and who is all-powerful and so infinitely good that he can bring good even out of evil. The Aristotelian idea of God as end (destination) of the cosmos merges here with the Platonic idea that evil in all its forms is simply a lack of goodness.

If now is added the assertion that these insights (for these are not empirical proofs as this term is used in the natural sciences) are acquired by "the light of reason," the place of this entire body of considerations in the history of ideas becomes clear once again. Just as in the material world the sun gives light and makes things knowable, so the idea of the good gives things being and the power to know (analogy with the sun in the *Republic* 508–509). Augustine therefore says that in every act by which one knows the truth one is illumined by the eternal Truth, and Thomas teaches that human reason participates in "the divine light" (*Summa theologiae* 2.1.91.2).

The circle is now closed. Natural revelation means that it is possible in principle to think about the finitude of the world and one's own existence and come thereby to know something of God's wisdom and creative power, because God himself makes it possible to know him through traces, reflections, and images in his creatures.

In regard to the actual fulfillment of this potentiality Vatican I showed itself rather reserved, noting that "such truths among things divine as of themselves are not beyond human reason can, even in the present condition of mankind, be known by everyone with facility, with firm certitude and with no admixture of error" because God has in fact granted a supernatural revelation (Denzinger-Schönmetzer, no. 3005; Neuner-Dupuis, no. 114). This appraisal of the situation is fully in accord with that of Thomas Aquinas *(Summa theologiae* 1.1.1), for in his view the knowledge made available by natural revelation is indeed possible for the human race in its present condition, but it is by no means easily gained or accessible to all. One is thus brought to a consideration of "supernatural revelation," which will here be called "biblical revelation."

Kant did not join Thomas in this approach. His criticism of the proofs for the existence of God is based on the principle that knowledge is valid only within the realm of sense experience and that there is no correspondence between thought and the truth as it exists in itself.

Old Testament and Judaism. Jewish theology regards it as inconceivable that human beings should know God by their own powers and apart from God making himself known, that is, revealing himself, to them. Like the rest of the Near East, Israel had certain techniques for penetrating the mysteries of God, such as soothsaying, the interpreting of omens and dreams, and the casting of lots. The Old Testament accepted some of these techniques (*Dt.* 33:8, *1 Sm.* 14) and always refused others, for example, astrology. On the other hand, God's action toward Israel in the course of its history is always understood as revelatory in the strict sense. The people experience the nearness of God through external signs and events such as thunderstorms (*Ex.* 19:16), pillars of cloud and pillars of fire (*Ex.* 14:24), and the wind (*1 Kgs.* 19:12). Descriptions of theophanies in human or angelic form (*Gn.* 16:7, 18:2, 48:16) are also found in the early stage of the patriarchal tradition; the "angel of God" *(malakh Yahveh),* in particular, seems obviously to be a device for maintaining the transcendence of God.

As the history of salvation advanced it became increasingly important to interpret God's guidance of Israel. The result was revelation through words, taking the form of auditions and going beyond visions or else interpreting these. God's spirit filled the prophets; his hand was laid on the human beings he chose for this revelation.

Various verbs were used to express the divine act of revelation:

(1) *glh* ("to uncover, unveil"). Yahveh opens the eyes and ears of human beings so that they are able to see and hear (*1 Sm.* 9:15, *Ps.* 119:18); he unveils himself (*Gn.* 35:7, *Is.* 22:14) and his mysteries (*Dt.* 29:29), his glory (*Is.* 40:15), and his justice (*Ps.* 98:2).

(2) *yd'* ("to proclaim, make oneself known"). The essence of revelation according to the Old Testament consists precisely in this self-communication of God to his people as he makes himself known to them (*Ex.* 6:2), speaks to them (*Ex.* 25:22), and, above all, brings them out of Egypt (*Ez.* 20:9) and enters into a covenant with them.

It is for this purpose that he makes known to Israel his name (*Is.* 64:2) and his ways (*Ps.* 25:4), that is, his commandments and his law (the Torah), as well as his wisdom (*Ps.* 119).

(3) *nggd* ("to report, communicate"). This is the most frequent of all the words for revelation and means to manifest something that is hidden: God's name (*Gn.* 32:30), his plan (*Gn.* 41:25), his salvation (*Is.* 42:12), and his hidden wisdom (*Jb.* 11:6). All these contexts have this in common, that God directs his word to human beings. For this reason,

(4) *dvr* can frequently be used for this decisive communication on God's part. God's word to Israel is his most precious gift; in it he communicates himself: "I am the Lord" (*Gn.* 28:13; *Ex.* 6:2, 6:29) and "there is no other" (*Is.* 45:5, *Jl.* 2:27).

The word of God is spoken in a special way to Moses (*Ex.* 20:18). The people perceive only the thunder and lightning, the trumpet blast and the smoke, that accompany the word; they see the "glory" of God but receive the commandments only through a mediator who is therefore regarded as the greatest of the prophets (*Dt.* 18:15). In like manner, all the later prophets are also proclaimers of God's word. He speaks through their mouths, his spirit moves them, his word is given to them; when they speak, "It is I, Yahveh, who speak" (a frequently occurring expression).

The goal and purpose of revelation is the call of Israel to be a covenanted people. This purpose is served by the revelation of God as "the God of Abraham, the God of Isaac, and the God of Jacob" (*Ex.* 3:6), as well as by the announcement of his name, which is at one and the same time a promise of his presence as helper ("I will be there as the One who will be there"; *Ex.* 3:12) and a concealment and withdrawal of God from any control by human beings ("I am who I am"; *Ex.* 3:14). The paradigmatic saving action of God becomes a reality in the deliverance and exodus from Egypt (*Ex.* 14) and, climactically, in the conclusion of the covenant at Sinai (*Ex.* 19–20). The entire religious practice and tradition and the entire liturgical cult of Israel, as well as the attribution of all laws to Moses and the constant warnings of the prophets, all show the fundamental importance of this encounter with God. Not only does the individual Jewish believer live by the light and power of that encounter; the entire social and political life of the people also takes its direction from it.

Since history is the reduction of the covenant to practice it too acquires a theological significance. Successes and catastrophes alike are explained as having their basis in God's plan of salvation, which thus subsumes all the destinies of individuals and all events under a universal saving will that orders everything to the "day of the Lord" (*Am.* 5:18, *Is.* 2:17). That day will bring the definitive fulfillment of God's reign over all of humankind. Revelation thus has a comprehensive meaning; it looks to world history in its entirety, since it sets forth and wins recognition of God's holiness and love. For this reason a special importance is attributed to the end time (eschatology) in Jewish apocalyptic. What is to come and the one who is to come (the Messiah) take on central meaning.

The "revelation of mysteries" (a notion that occurs first in *Daniel* 2:18) becomes a commonplace in the Qumran documents. The devotees at Qumran believe that they possess a special revelation for the end time, a revelation available only to the "wise and initiated."

By contrast, the Judaism of the scribes (beginning with Ezra, fourth century BCE) shows a tendency to regard revelation as closed and to see the prophetic movement as now past. The Jewish tradition generally accepted these positions. Only Jewish mysticism (Qabbalah, Hasidism) regarded not only the once-for-all historical act of divine revelation but also the repeated mystical experience of God as revelatory; the function of the latter is to bring out the implications of the historical revelation and make it intelligible.

New Testament and Christianity. Building on the Old Testament understanding of revelation, the New Testament writers see revelation as the self-communication of God in and through Jesus Christ. This communication is regarded as the supreme, final, irrevocable, and unsurpassable self-disclosure of God in history (*Heb.* 1:1f.). It is unique because, as Christians understand it, in Jesus of Nazareth, agent of revelation and content of revelation (the person, teaching, and redemptive work of Jesus) are identical and make up the sole object of revelation. The theological elaboration of the New Testament concept of revelation is to be found especially in Paul and John.

Paul. To express the idea of revelation, Paul uses above all the words *apokaluptein* ("uncover, remove from concealment") and *phaneroun* ("make apparent, show"). His basic theme is the uncovering of the mystery that has previously been hidden and is now made manifest (*Eph.* 1:9, *Col.* 1:26). Revelation, therefore, means the uncovering or unveiling of the divine plan by which God reconciles the human race to himself in Christ. Revelation is a divine creative activity, an eschatological saving deed, rather than a simple announcing of messages or items of knowledge. God is the really active one in the process of revelation. It is he who from eternity decides that in his Son he will turn in love to the human race. The incarnation of his Son in the womb of a woman (*Gal.* 4:4), this Son's expiatory death on the cross, and the recapitulation or unification of the cosmos under him as head and firstborn from the dead (*Rom.* 3:25, *Col.* 1:18) are the fulfillment of this hidden plan. In this plan Christ himself is what is revealed. The death and resurrection of Christ, and even the church as his body, are elements of this mystery of salvation.

In a derivative application of the term, the apostles also "reveal" the salvific justice of God (*Rom.* 1:17) inasmuch as they proclaim the good news brought by Jesus (*2 Cor.* 2:14). In the fullness of time (*Gal.* 1:16) the gospel is preached to all peoples (*Rom.* 1:16, 16:26), not like an esoteric doctrine of the Hellenistic mystery religions but as a message meant to profit the entire human race, provided men and women are ready to accept the scandal of the cross (*1 Cor.* 1:18–25). For it is of the very essence of revelation that it must be accepted in faith and obedience. It does not supply empirical evidence that forces acceptance; on the other hand, neither may it be accepted or rejected at whim, for it makes a claim upon its hearers and may not be rejected without resultant guilt.

In short, revelation is still incomplete within historical time. Only in its definitive stage of development at the return (Parousia) of Christ will it be complete. At that point, too, the glory promised to the redeemed will be manifested, for it will be clear beyond doubt that the redeemed are risen and that they are the children and heirs of God (*1 Cor.* 1:7; *2 Thes.* 1:7; *Rom.* 8:18–23).

The synoptics. The revelation accomplished in Jesus is extremely important to the early community as well. As a result, the statements made in the synoptic Gospels are in principle the same as those in the preaching of Paul.

There is no doubt that the Old Testament is a vehicle of revelation; nonetheless the fullness of revelation comes only in Christ (*Mt.* 5:17–19). Jesus differs from the other agents of revelation because not only does he claim a complete and direct knowledge of God's saving will (*Mt.* 11:27, *Lk.* 10:22), but his messianic work is also the definitive revelation and calls for an unconditional decision (*Mt.* 4:20, 8:22, 10:37–39; *Mk.* 1:18; and others).

John. The concept of revelation emerges most clearly in John, even though he almost never uses the term *apokaluptein.* He prefers the verb *phaneroun* ("make apparent, show") and likes to use pairs of concepts that were popular in the Hellenistic religious movements of his time, especially gnosticism: light and darkness, truth and falsehood, life and death. The expression "bear witness to the truth" is typical of Johannine theology.

John regards the revelatory event as the center of his message. Not only is Jesus the redeemer by means of his "work"; he is also and above all the proclaimer of God's truth and the life and light of the world (*Jn.* 1:4). God is invisible and unknowable; the Son alone knows the Father, and in him the Father is made visible and understandable (*Jn.* 1:14, *1 Jn.* 1:1). He has brought knowledge of God and borne witness to him (*Jn.* 1:18, 3:11–13); he speaks in plain words of the Father (*Jn.* 8:38). Revelation is therefore given together with the person of the Logos (the Word); it is the manifestation of the life and love of God (*Jn.* 4:7–9). Because Jesus is the only-begotten Son, he reveals the Father in what he says and does. "He who has seen me has seen the Father" (*Jn.* 14:9).

In keeping with the realized eschatology of the gospel according to John, faith, as response to revelation, can even now be described as a "seeing" (*Jn.* 6:40, 12:45, 14:19). What is revealed is already present. Yet, although revelation is essentially completed with the first coming of Jesus, John, like Paul, can speak of the "revelation of Jesus" and of the "glory of the children of God" at the return of Christ (*1 Jn.* 2:28, 3:2).

Revelation. The *Revelation to John* is a New Testament book that focuses its attention on the final age and the return of Christ. It presupposes the proclamation of salvation as achieved through the cross and resurrection of Jesus and, in John's vision on Patmos of the Apocalypse, it interprets the persecutions and sufferings endured by the communities in the light of the hope of their coming fulfillment. The book's images and symbols, taken from Jewish apocalyptic, are intended to urge the reader to perseverance and fidelity. The various hymns of the heavenly liturgy reflect the response of the church to God's judgments, which have for their ultimate purpose the salvation of his creation; this salvation will be achieved despite the terrors that are announced.

ISLAM. Islam's understanding of revelation comes closest to that of the Bible. *Waḥy,* or revelation, comes from God, usually through the agency of the archangel Gabriel. It is concerned with God's decrees, his mysterious will, the announcement of judgment, and his commandments, the divine law (*sharīʿah*). Revelation is given to the prophets and, in its definitive form, to Muḥammad (c. 570–632), who receives it in dreams, visions, and auditions. It is set down in the Qurʾān, the uncreated archetype of which has been taken up to the throne of God in heaven. This uncreated word is not, however, the source of God's self-knowledge (as it is in Christian theology). To this extent, the Muslim conception resembles the Jewish, while at the same time it is distinguished from the latter by the absence of any promise. In the Qurʾān the content of revelation is wisdom and guidance for living and, above all, warnings and the announcement of final judgment. Because it is divine in origin revelation may not be altered.

ZOROASTRIANISM. Zarathushtra (seventh to sixth century BCE) was another nonbiblical prophet. He too saw revelation as having its source in the voluntary action of a unique and personal God. The dualism that is otherwise prevalent in the Iranian world is based on an original revelation to the extent that this last calls for an unqualified ethical decision. Like Ahura Mazda, the Mazdeans opt for the good and against evil. This tension soon hardens, however, into an ontic dualism. The world is divided between good and evil and thus reflects at all cosmic levels the opposition between the virtues and their contraries. History becomes the field of a struggle that is predetermined by God and will end with judgment and transfiguration.

HINDUISM. Even in Hinduism it is possible to speak of revelation as this concept is understood by historians of religion. The Vedas have the status of sacred revelation: *śruti* ("heard," i. e., revealed directly by the gods to seers) is clearly distinguished from *smṛti* ("remembered," i. e., composed by humans). According to Hindu belief, the Vedic literature has existed from eternity, is supernatural in origin, and has been transmitted to human beings by unknown seers of the primordial period.

In the *Ṛgveda,* forces and elements of nature are viewed as divinities. Later on the question arises whether behind the multiplicity of divinities there is hidden an ultimate ground of the world. The Upaniṣads are concerned with the question of the identity of *ātman* and *brahman* (the principles of the individual and the cosmos respectively), and with the transcription of souls and redemption.

Notions of revelation and a consciousness of transcendence are also discernible in other religions, although often only in an obscure and confused form, despite the fact that an especially clear idea of God is evident in archaic forms of religion. Because of this last-named fact many scientists of religion in the past accepted the existence of a primordial revelation in the form of an originally given knowledge of God in the early phase of human history; today, however, this view is generally not accepted.

See Also Divination; Enthusiasm; Hierophany; Inspiration; Oracles; Prophecy.

Bibliography

For basic information concerning the topic, entries in several reference works can be profitably consulted: "Offenbarung," in the *Lexikon für Theologie und Kirche,* 2d ed., vol. 7 (Freiburg, 1962); "Offenbarung," in *Die Religion in Geschichte und Gegenwart,* 3d ed., vol. 4 (Tübingen, 1960); and "Révélation" in the *Dictionnaire de théologie catholique,* vol. 6 (Paris, 1937). Karl Rahner's article "Revelation," in *Sacramentum Mundi: An Encyclopedia of Theology,* vol. 5 (New York, 1969), is especially valuable.

Those aspects of revelation accessible to the phenomenology of religion are summarized in Gerardus van der Leeuw's *Religion in Essence and Manifestation,* 2 vols. (1938; reprint, Gloucester, Mass., 1967), and in Th. P. van Baaren's *Voorstellingen van Openbaring, phaenomenologisch beschouwd* (Utrecht, 1951), which includes an English summary. There is also a very good discussion in Herbert H. Farmer's *Revelation and Religion: Studies in the Theological Interpretation of Religious Types* (New York, 1954). For the history of religions approach, see the standard work of Mircea Eliade, *A History of Religious Ideas,* 3 vols. (Chicago, 1978–1986).

On the treatment of the topic within Islam, see A. J. Arberry's *Revelation and Reason in Islam* (London, 1957). On Hinduism, see K. Satchidananda Murty's *Revelation and Reason in Advaita Vedānta* (1959; reprint, Livingston, N. J., 1974).

For discussions of natural revelation, see Fernand van Steenberghen's *Dieu caché* (Louvain, 1961), translated as *Hidden God: How Do We Know That God Exists?* (Saint Louis, Mo., 1966), and Johannes Hirschberger's *Gottesbeweise: Vergängliches-Unvergängliches in denkender Glaube* (Frankfurt, 1966).

The following works treat the biblical concept of revelation: H. Wheeler Robinson's *Inspiration and Revelation in the Old Testament,* 4th ed. (Oxford, 1956); Erik Voegelin's *Order and History,* vol. 1, *Israel and Revelation* (Baton Rouge, 1956); Ernest Findlay Scott's *The New Testament Idea of Revelation* (New York, 1935); and Frederick C. Grant's *Introduction to New Testament Thought* (New York, 1950). For theological discussions of revelation, see Rudolf Bultmann's "The Concept of Revelation in the New Testament," in *Existence and Faith: Shorter Writings of Rudolf Bultmann,* edited and translated by Schubert M. Ogden (New York, 1960); Romano Guardini's *Die Offenbarung: Ihr Wesen und ihre Formen* (Würzburg, 1940); Karl Barth's *Das christliche Verständnis der Offenbarung* (Munich, 1948); Paul Tillich's *Systematic Theology,* 3 vols. (Chicago, 1951–1963); Karl Rahner's *Hearers of the Word* (New York, 1969); and *Revelation as History* (New York, 1968) by Wolfhart Pannenberg and others.

Johannes Deninger (1987)
Translated from German by Matthew J. O'Connell

REVENGE AND RETRIBUTION.

There are actions by which human beings compensate for something—for a loss by a reimbursement, a gain by a reward, a crime by expiation, an insult by satisfaction, an advantage by a sacrifice, a defeat by a victory. These are all forms of repayment based on an essential connection made between agency and receptivity in action. That connection is tacitly assumed by human beings to be the price paid for every deed; it is an element in the performance of every deed and is the means used to ensure a particular behavior. In it lies the origin of private and public law, which allow for a retribution in which individuals settle scores for themselves, and a retribution in which they become the subject of a settling of scores. They avenge themselves and are penalized.

The instrumental character of retribution finds exemplary expression in the "law of talion," in which the penalty matches the crime, and in the Golden Rule (behave toward others as you wish them to behave toward you). Good deeds bring their reward, and evil deeds their punishment.

Opinions on revenge differ from science to science. Students of the history of law see it as a primitive form of law. From this point of view, it is an unbridled, unreflective, and arbitrary act of retribution, whereas punishment has a purpose and is administered according to laws and on the basis of a judicial sentence. The passage from thinking focused on vengeance to penal law thus represents an ethical advance.

Some ethnologists and structuralist sociologists reject this view and see revenge as moral behavior within the context of the laws of exogamy. It is an act of self-assertion by a group against an outside attacker, "an outward-directed act of solidarity." Revenge is taken exclusively on outsiders. This distinguishes it from punishment, which is imposed by a group on members who violate its order; it is an act of exclusion, "an internal sanction for a lack of solidarity." Punishment is found in primitive legal systems, just as revenge is found in more developed systems. Revenge is a problem connected with the balance between private and public agencies in every system of justice; it resists legal positivism but does not inevitably lead to anarchy.

Many historians of religion and theologians lend support to this nuanced approach. Tribal gods avenge themselves and high gods exercise retribution through rewards and punishments.

The high religions and the world religions set limits on vengefulness and move beyond it. Guilt is compensated for by punishment in a process that is cosmic (as in the Hindu idea of *karman*) or historical (as in the Christian idea of judgment). The dead are no longer agents of retribution (avenging themselves so that they may have peace of soul) but its recipients, as seen in the concepts of the transmigration of souls and the judgment on the dead. Their actions are now significant only for themselves and no longer for their tribe.

Structural differentiation in the ways of making up for guilty acts becomes an existential problem for religion. For revenge can be simultaneously a duty and a crime. Punishment takes different forms in different legal systems; hence "summum ius, summa iniuria" ("strict justice can be the height of injustice"). Greek tragedy presents the myth of unavoidable guilt and the problem of whether or not justice is really done through penal retribution.

A question arises: Is there an unbreakable connection between receptivity and performance in action as such and, therefore, in redemption?

REVENGE AS THE ARCHAIC FORM OF RETRIBUTION. In a system based on vengeance, the reciprocity of sin and expiation is regulated by those directly involved. It entails an exchange of life at all levels of existence. The individual and the group are mutually accountable. Vengeance places authority, prestige, and material possessions on the same level of value. Those who avenge themselves gain prestige; they take part in the social life of the group and become respected. They represent the honor of their clan.

Retribution exercised by individuals is a problem in the anthropology and theology of religion.

Regulation of vengeance in archaic societies. Groups in which revenge is an institution are of a kinship or totemic type. They are made up of families and clans (or subclans). In them, personal existence and collective existence are regarded as interchangeable. The group is the vital sphere for the individual, and the individual is a quantity in the vital capital of the group. For individuals to be avenged means, therefore, that the group stands up for them. The group is the vehicle of individuals' right to life. It establishes an identification between what they are in themselves (their existence as persons) and what they stand for in the group (their prestige). Murder and homocide are, therefore, offenses to the family, as are rape and theft. A slander can be regarded as a crime deserving of death, and theft can be regarded as murder. Blood vengeance, substitutional vengeance, and symbolic vengeance each represent a different aspect of the identification of individual and societal life, namely, the power of blood, the property of the family, and the honor of the clan.

An example of such interchangeableness is the Australian Aborigines' custom of obtaining blood vengeance by the wounding, not the killing, of a culprit. Magical rites also provide an illustration; Lucien Lévy-Bruhl (1927) speaks of a "mystical compensation." Another example is the identification of bride-price and blood-price, because in each case there is a question not of purchasing a life but of presenting gifts that symbolize life, and, therefore, of an exchange of life. In this sense the blood-price is equivalent to life itself, just as the bride-price replaces the bride who is exchanged for it.

This explains why many languages use the same word for bride-price and blood-price. Among the Maengue of New Britain, the word *kuru* (literally, "head") means "both the human life demanded in revenge and treasures given to a bride's family at her marriage" (Verdier, 1980, p. 28). The bride herself may be a blood-price. Among the bedouin, the daughter of the nearest relative of a murderer is the price paid. She belongs to the son, brother, or father of the slain man as a substitute for the loss suffered, until she bears a son; she regains her freedom only when this child has grown up and can bear arms. "Among the Mundang of Africa the king can compensate the brother of a victim with a woman instead of cattle; when she brings a son into the world, the reparation is complete; the husband must then in turn pay a price to his parents-in-law" (ibid., p. 29). Revenge may therefore take a bloodless form and contribute to peace; the person who exercises vengeance now breathes freely and is satisfied. His act asserts the right to life and honor: "The righteous will rejoice when he sees the vengeance; he will bathe his feet in the blood of the wicked" (*Ps.* 58:11). To avenge a murder is thus to avenge honor and wipe out a disgrace. In many societies this is the decisive motive at work in revenge. "A man reviled is like a weakling. He cannot regain his honor without shedding blood" (ibid., p. 19). Among the Moussey of Cameroon, a man is judged by the enemies he has killed. When he marries, he must answer his father-in-law's ritual question: "Whom have you killed in order to win my daughter's hand?" Vengeance rests on a complex involving feelings of honor and disgrace.

The reciprocity of individual and collective existence is the source of linguistic peculiarities and helps in the understanding of various legal provisions. The German expression that means "to pay someone back" is understood as "to take revenge on him." Among the Beti of Africa, the equivalent expression can mean "to return evil" or "to recompense someone" or "to take advantage of him"; among the two Maengue groups, "to pay a price" or "to set a price"; among the Kikuyu, "to remove someone's guilt"; among the Hausa, "to cancel his debt"; among the Kabyle, "to pay the price of a corpse," which indicates payment for a death. The wiping out of guilt for a crime and the wiping out of debts (in a business matter) are forms of making up for a loss that a possessor has suffered in each case.

These forms of wiping out are ruled by the principle of harm done, not of culpability; that is, it is the act itself, and not the responsibility for it, that evokes revenge. Moreover, the principle of collective liability, not individual liability, is operative: The group, and not the culprit, is liable; in addition, the rank of the person harmed is taken into account in the compensation. Only those acknowledged by law as persons, and not slaves, are capable of revenge.

The principle of representation also comes into play. The person harmed and his avenger, on the one hand, and the culprit, on the other, are members of different groups. Each represents the right and duties of his group and acts in its name. The duty of revenge depends on the degree of kinship with the person harmed, the order being son, brother, uncle, nephew; there can also, however, be hired representatives. The principle of representation accounts for the phenomenon of sequential vengeance, inasmuch as the representative, too, is subject to the principle of the collective liability of his kindred. The result is feuds and wars.

Revenge is taken on outsiders, not on fellow members of the same group. That is, the principle of exogamy comes into play. As a result, different persons are affected, depending on whether the society is matriarchal or patriarchal.

The rules governing vengeance also include provisions meant to prevent escalation into cycles of revenge. Among these provisions are the exclusion of damages that do not justify revenge (homicide as distinct from murder), the determination of places and times to which revenge is limited (the criminal caught in the act), an expanded range of compensations and substitutions that can replace vengeance (*wergeld*), and the provision of sanctuaries or places where revenge is utterly forbidden (sanctuary cities, palaces, temples, churches).

The religious basis of vengeance. Guilt binds the guilty party to the debtor by means of the conscience, which accuses him, and a curse that pursues him. Guilt thus takes on an aspect of revenge, for conscience and the curse exercise retribution and are nevertheless agencies in the overall order of life. They are vengeance exercised by the gods. They represent the vital force of the gods and their power to prevail, the necessity directing the gods to restore their own honor and to fulfill the responsibility they have on earth. Consequently, the symbolism associated with vengeance is very closely linked to ancestor worship, the cult of the dead, belief in the soul, the ownership of land, and magical rituals.

In primitive religion, the souls of the dead themselves commit acts of retribution because they have lost life and now demand it back. The living fear the vengeance of the dead because it can be undirected and therefore strike anyone at all. It is told of the Negritos of northern Luzon in the Philippines that "one who has trodden on the grave of a stranger is slain with arrows from safe ambush by the relatives of the dead person who keep watch at the grave" (S. R. Steinmetz, 1928, vol. 1, p. 337). The Manobos of Mindanao, also in the Philippines, are said to go into the forests at the death of a family member "in order to make reparation for the death, which they do by killing the first person that comes along" (ibid., p. 338). In New Zealand it used to be the custom "after a murder for friends of the slain person to go out sometimes and kill the first person, friend or foe, who came along" (ibid., p. 223). The Maori would kill someone at random after a murder. Among the inhabitants of Daghstan someone would be slain at random after a death from unknown causes, and custom demanded that the parents of a murdered man appear in front of the mosque and declare someone guilty at random. For guilt and expiation are part of life as such, and therefore revenge is taken in the name of life.

> On the one hand, fear of the souls of the dead and specifically a fear of revenge the dead may take on those who violate the social order, and, on the other hand, the hope of protection and support for those who behave in an orderly way—or, in short, belief in the retributive role played by the souls of the dead—are the basis of the ancestor worship that was so widespread among early human beings. (Kelsen, 1941, p. 12)

This fear and hope are the basis of tradition and one reason for belief in retribution generally. For one may not "overlook the fact that the concept of the soul arose out of the concept of the souls of the dead, and that the original function of the soul, its first effect as it were, is revenge" (ibid., p. 238).

Vengeance is religious in character and can be applied to everything that has life or is regarded as living. Thus animals and plants, and also mountains and rocks, the soil, and indeed the earth in its totality can be seats of the living soul and can exercise vengeance. The existence of the dead and the retribution they exercise thus go together. An unexpiated death is like a life without honor, life as a mere shadow. Revenge, on the other hand, restores honor, wipes away disgrace, and gives the soul power. "A Bedouin seeks to wipe out his disgrace through blood vengeance or even, in the spirit of the pre-Islamic Arabs, to satisfy thereby the soul of the slain person, for after a violent death the soul is transformed into an owl that seeks unwearyingly to drink the blood of its enemy" (Joseph Chelhod, in Verdier, 1980, p. 125).

Blood is the symbol of the soul, of a family's life, and of honor itself. When blood is shed, dangerous forces are unloosed; it cries out for revenge. It has been dishonored, and the lack of peace that afflicts it stains the earth. The spirits of blood call for compensation, for they possess the earth, and the latter cannot exist apart from the integrity of the soul that these spirits embody.

The land is a clan's living space and, therefore, the root of its being. "The ancestral land is 'therefore' often regarded as the source and refuge of life and on this score embodies a spiritual quality. Every attack on the life of a group is consequently an attack on the land" that the group inhabits and on the spirits that possess the land and are its real owners. Every conflict will be avenged on it (ibid., p. 22).

Among the Mundang of Chad, it is therefore customary to give the land on which someone has been killed to the clan to which the dead man belonged. This exchange reflects the view that the land is the possession of the blood and that the blood is the soul of a tribe. The tribe accepts possession of this land by virtue of the soul that is embodied in its blood. For among the Mundang the blood is "the root of one of the souls (*masen-byane:* God of my birth) which constitute the person; but it is also the root of a less differentiated power which may be described as a life-force and which the Mundang call *ma-zwe-su* (spirit or genius of the body)" (Alfred Adler, in Verdier, p. 83). One who sheds blood and thereby releases the interior and the exterior soul inflames the land and excites the spirits that possess it. One who effects a reconciliation creates a new existence. This process takes place in the offering of gifts. For one who gives something of his own can take something for himself. By means of the sacrifice one makes a space for himself in the area of another's life. In that area he is restored to himself. "A blood-price . . . like a bride-price consists therefore not in a transfer of wealth but in sacrificial blood by means of which the two parties recover their integrity" (ibid., p. 84). The blood is the offering and acceptance of their common will to be reconciled.

Chthonic divinities are spirits that wreak vengeance. The Greeks and Romans called them Erinyes or Furies respectively. They were "the embodiment, as it were, of the spilt blood, which, because it had turned against itself, resulted in madness. . . . For there is not yet any such thing as punishment in the modern sense: it is the power of the outraged blood itself that reacts against the murderer" (van der Leeuw, vol. 1, 1933, p. 248). Vengeful gods are demonic in many myths. They are therefore warded off and exorcised by magic.

RETRIBUTION AS PUNISHMENT. Guilt is not only avenged but is also punished, for there are on the one hand offenses against life itself and on the other hand offenses against the rules that protect life and are instituted to defend life. These latter offenses are made up by punishment, which is directed not against the clan but against the offender. The principles at work here are not those of representation but of culpability (the responsible agent is punished); individual liability; personal responsibility; as well as the principle of endogamous sanction (that is, the sanction applies only to subjects of the group's own juridical order, not to subjects of an outside juridical order). What is reflected here is the passage from particularity to universality in the concept of religion.

The "law of talion." Retribution through punishment is regulated by bodies of law whose sets of rules describe cases, define responsibilities, and determine the kind and extent of payment. The guilty party is looked upon as a member of a juridical community and, depending on the harm he has done to this community, he suffers harm in turn and is thereby excluded from the community.

The "law of talion" is one of the oldest forms of payment for crime. The term comes from the Latin *lex talionis* ("law of retaliation") and is first documented in the law of the Twelve Tables (451–450 BCE): "If someone breaks another's limb and does not come to an agreement on it, he shall suffer the same and equal punishment." *Talio* refers to a codified numerical equality in every punishment (for example, one eye for one eye, one hand for one hand, and so on). For a correct understanding of *talio,* one should omit the element of vengeance implied by the English term *retaliation.*

The provisions are as follows: The case in question is the destruction of a bodily member, and the injured party has a right to retribution, member for member. "If the talion exceeded the measure provided in the law, the person justified in taking talion was himself now subject to a new talion. If the injured party was unable personally to take talion, his nearest male relative was appointed to take it" (Jüngling, 1984, p. 3).

Roman law provided for talion-like punishments or analogous talion: "mirror punishments," as they were called. Under this heading came the death penalty for homicide and murder, "but especially punishments in which the culprit was punished by the instrument used in the commission of his crime (death by fire for an arsonist) or was punished in the bodily member used in the crime (by cutting off a thief's hand or cutting out a perjurer's tongue)" (ibid., p. 4). These punishments were imposed by courts. They were quite different from talion in the proper sense, and for this reason some scholars urge that they not be called talion at all.

The legal principle embodied here is found in many non-Roman legal systems as well. Among these are cuneiform law, Mosaic law, and Islamic law.

The Code of Hammurabi (c. 1795–1750 BCE) is characteristic of this principle: a slave for a slave, an eye for an eye, a broken bone for a broken bone, a tooth for a tooth. The code treats citizens differently from slaves, men differently from women. The agents who carry out the sentence are those affected by the misdeed: the plaintiff and his relatives.

In the Hebrew scriptures (Old Testament), the administration of talion is, unlike that found in Roman and Babylonian law, still a tribal matter (see *Dt.* 19:21, *Lv.* 24:20, *Ex.* 21:23–25). Talion here is a juridical principle that operates in the framework of basic legal responsibility and is not to be defined independently of the principle of just exchange and its life-enhancing character. It is a formula for giving and taking within the sphere of authority over the clan. It is located in a personal framework: "If any harm follows, then you shall give life for life, eye for eye, tooth for tooth, hand for hand, foot for foot, burn for burn, wound for wound, stripe for stripe" (*Ex.* 21:23–25).

Islam has two sources for retributive law: blood vengeance and judicial punishments. The clan has the right to kill the murderer of one of its members, provided the murderer acted on his own responsibility and deliberately. But Muḥammad limits the application even further: The right can be exercised only on the legally and morally responsible individual.

Legal punishments are imposed for offenses against religion and public order. But talion for these offenses is limited to cases in which there can be complete equality, for example, "the loss of a hand, a foot, or a tooth, etc. If the guilty party has cut off the same hand of two persons, his punishment is to lose that same hand; for the second hand he must pay a blood-price" (Schacht, 1964, p.185).

In Christianity the law of talion is inverted. It requires that evil be repaid not with evil but with good, so that the evil may be turned to good. "You have heard that it was said, 'An eye for an eye and a tooth for a tooth.' But I say to you, Do not resist one who is evil. But if any one strikes you on the right cheek, turn to him the other also. . . . Give to him who begs from you, and do not refuse him who would borrow from you" (*Mt.* 5:38–42). In this new principle retribution continues to be retribution, but it is put on a new level: The guilt of the guilty party becomes a means of conversion (see *Rom.* 12:20).

The Myth of Guilt and Retribution through Punishment. In the transition from archaic retribution through revenge to official retribution through punishment, retribution itself became problematic. A person is obliged to exercise it, yet it is forbidden; it is a right, but it also creates injustice; it is both destiny and sacrifice. This contradiction and the impossibility of avoiding it become a central theme in both Greek tragedy and the Bible. It is a basic motif in biblical myth and theology.

In Greek thought, retribution is justice in the form of punishment. It is the context in which Greek thought comes to grips with justice as regulative of revenge:

> The word *dikē* occurs in such phrases as *dikēn didonai, dikēn tinein,* literally to give, to pay, justice, which signify "to be punished." The word *tisis* means "payment," "compensation," but also "revenge," for justice and revenge are not very different, indeed they coincide when vengeance is taken for wrongdoing. A product of this kind of justice is the *ius talionis* which was usual in early times and finds pregnant expression in the saying "an eye for an eye and a tooth for a tooth." This is to be traced among the Greeks also; for them, justice is retributive justice. . . . This view was so deep-rooted that it comes out now and then in the older philosophers when they are describing the course of nature. Anaximandros of Miletos said: "The boundless is the origin of all that is. It is the law of necessity that things should perish and go back to their origin. For they give satisfaction and pay the penalty (*didonai dikēn kai tisin*) to one another for their injustice *(adikia)* according to the ordinance of Time." (Nilsson, 1948, pp. 35–36)

An order of justice that includes both patriarchal and matriarchal rights is unthinkable in the system ruled by the Erinyes. Aeschylus tackles this problem in the *Oresteia,* where the Erinyes do not pursue Clytemnestra, who has murdered her husband, but do pursue Orestes, who has murdered his mother. The regime under which the clan lives has confronted Orestes with an insoluble conflict: The patriarchal code demands that he avenge his father, but the matriarchal code prohibits his attacking his mother. Whichever course he chooses, he contravenes archaic law. He is trapped in the myth of guilt:

> The Erinyes who pursue Orestes because he has killed his mother appear here as divinities of an earlier time and representatives of the blood vengeance that is connected with the kinship group. They are sharply contrasted with the younger gods, Apollo and Pallas Athene, who represent the higher principle of the law of Zeus and the right of the state to pass judgment and are therefore unwilling to hand Orestes over to the vengeance of the Erinyes. (Kelsen, 1941, p. 220)

In Homer and the tragedians, the Erinyes are an agency of justice that belongs to an earlier time. Aeschylus has them say in *The Eumenides,* "That is the way of the younger gods: they alter things by violence and laugh all justice to scorn" (165). And again: "Novelty is breaking in and overturning all that is old, if guilt and the horror of matricide are victorious at the judgment seat" (466). They plead with Apollo: "You are destroying the power of the ancient divinities" (697).

The chthonic goddesses that embodied a matriarchal order were related in several ways to the Olympian gods. The shrine of Zeus at Olympia, the sanctuary of Apollo at Delphi, and Athens, the city of Athena, were all places where the chthonic goddesses were originally venerated. Daughters of Gaia, the supreme agency of justice on earth, these goddesses included Demeter (one of whose titles was Erinys) and Themis, goddess of communities and rights of assembly. Among them were also many other divinities of later derivation whose myths point to the irreconcilability of earthly justice and heavenly retribution, of divine law and earthly destiny. Nemesis, goddess of retribution, and the Moirai, goddesses of destiny, were daughters of Night (the goddess Nux). They punished hubris and took revenge on those who achieved happiness, for injustice was punished by injustice, and happiness unaccompanied by unhappiness aroused the envy of the gods.

The symbols of the court—the wolf, the serpent, and the lightning bolt—are part of the myth of guilt and punishment. They are also symbols of the soul that seeks revenge, and of the Olympian gods who represent the rights of such individuals. Apollo is defender of the rights of blood but also god of purification from blood guilt. He contracts this guilt but also purifies himself from it. He grants oracles concerning the future. He establishes norms by subjecting himself to them: "The god who forbids and punishes murder, must himself murder and be punished for it; this identification of the addressee of norms with the authority behind the norms, of the god who punishes with man who is punished, is a very ancient motif in the establishment of the efficacious norms" (Kelsen, 1941, p. 364).

There is a cycle of guilt, and there is deliverance from guilt, a pattern that constantly repeats itself. The transmigration of souls represents this mystery of life in the Orphic and Eleusinian religions.

Retribution nonetheless involves not only vengeance and punishment but also promise. But those who open themselves to a new hope must achieve deliverance from old guilt. This notion is the basis for the discussion of the concept of retribution in the Bible, and has therefore an archaic as well as an eschatological meaning. The biblical concept is one of God's acting as God. Both aspects are fundamental for the biblical concept of retribution. He who does something undergoes a fate, and he who undergoes a fate has to do something as well. Many biblical expressions contain this reciprocity: To do evil is identical with suffering misfortune, to do good is to incur blessing. The evildoer is he who finds himself in misfortune. To make oneself guilty is like declaring someone guilty; fidelity like steadiness; badness like downfall; reward like work; path of life like way of life. This reciprocity of action and result is guaranteed by Yahveh himself, the tribal God of Israel. It is he who unfolds this reciprocity fully.

The Bible is thus able to include God in the framework of retribution, because he himself exercises vengeance. When in *Genesis* 4:10 the voice of spilled blood cries out to him from the ground, he punishes the murderer by expelling him; he avenges himself sevenfold, however, on anyone who then avenges the murderer. God's clan is the entire human race, and he himself acts on behalf of the race and is its source of strength. He punishes those who attack the race and set themselves against him, and punishes any transgression, taking vengeance on those who avenge the transgression: Thus he restores his own honor. Retribution, therefore, is not only a response to action but surpasses it.

SEE ALSO Ancestors; Blood; Conscience; Judgment of the Dead; Soul.

BIBLIOGRAPHY

Bowers, Fredson. *Elizabethan Revenge Tragedy, 1587–1642.* Princeton, N.J., 1966.

Coppet, Daniel de. "Cycles de meurtes et cycles funéraires: Esquisse de deux structures d'échanges." In *Échanges et communications,* edited by Jean Pouillon and Pierre Maranda, vol. 2, pp. 759–781. The Hague, 1970.

Girard, René. *Violence and the Sacred.* Translated by Patrick Gregory. Baltimore, 1977.

Hermesdorf, Bernardus H. D. *Poena talionis.* Utrecht and Nijmegen, 1965.

Jüngling, Hans-Winfried. "'Auge für Auge, Zahn für Zahn': Bemerkungen zu Sinn und Geltung der altestamentlichen Talionsformeln." *Theologie und Philosophie* 59 (1984): 1–38.

Kelsen, Hans. *Vergeltung und Kausalität: Eine soziologische Untersuchung.* The Hague, 1941. Translated as *Society and Nature: A Sociological Inquiry* (Chicago, 1943).

Koch, Klaus, ed. *Um das Prinzip der Vergeltung in Religion und Recht des Alten Testaments.* Wege der Forschung, no. 125. Darmstadt, 1972.

Kohler, Josef. *Zur Lehre der Blutrache.* Würzburg, 1885.

Kohler, Josef. *Shakespeare vor dem Forum der Jurisprudenz.* Berlin, 1919.

Leeuw, Gerardus van der. *Phänomenologie der Religion.* Tübingen, 1933. Translated as *Religion in Essence and Manifestation* (1938; 2d ed., 2 vols., New York, 1963).

Lévy-Bruhl, Lucien. *L'âme primitive.* Paris, 1927. Translated as *The "Soul" of the Primitive* (New York, 1928).

Malinowski, Bronislaw. *Crime and Custom in Savage Society.* London, 1926.

Mauss, Marcel. "La religion et les origines du droit pénal d'après un livre récent." In his *Œuvres,* vol. 2, pp. 65–698. Paris, 1969.

Nilsson, Martin P. *Grekisk religiositetet.* Stockholm, 1946. Translated as *Greek Piety* (Oxford, 1948).

Onuf, Nicholas G. *Reprisals: Rituals, Rules, Rationales.* Princeton, N.J., 1974.

Pigliaru, Antonio. *Il banditismo in Sardegna.* 2d ed. Milan, 1975.

Schacht, Joseph. *An Introduction to Islamic Law.* Oxford, 1964.

Steinmetz, Sebald Rudolf. *Ethnologische Studien zur ersten Entwicklung der Strafe nebst einer psychologischen Abhandlung über Grausamkeit und Rachsucht.* 2 vols. Groningen, 1928.

Thurnwald, Richard. "Blutrache." In *Reallexikon der Vorgeschichte,* edited by Max Ebert, vol. 2, pp. 30–41. Berlin, 1925.

Thurnwald, Richard. "Vergeltung." In *Reallexikon der Vorgeschichte,* edited by Max Ebert, vol. 14, pp. 130–131. Berlin, 1929.

Tobien, E. S. *Die Blutrache nach altem Russischem Recht, verglichen mit der Blutrache der Israeliten und Araber, der Griechen und Römer und der Germanen.* Dorpat, 1840.

Verdier, Raymond, ed. *La vengeance: Études d'ethnologie, d'histoire et de philosophie,* vol. 1, *Vengeance et pouvoir dans quel-ques sociétés extra-occidentales.* Paris, 1980.

Weidkuhn, Peter. *Aggressivität, Ritus, Säkularisierung: Biologische Grundformen religiöser Prozesse.* Basel, 1965.

ELMAR KLINGER (1987)
Translated from German by Matthew J. O'Connell

REVIVAL AND RENEWAL. The phenomena of revival and renewal have been classified and described by various terms reflecting a wide range of analytical frameworks based on such criteria as overt purposes, main emphases or characteristics, historical period, and location. The catalog of relevant terms thus bears examination.

The terms *accommodative, acculturative, adaptive, adjustive,* and *syncretic* are largely interpretive, indicating that revival and renewal activities took place in, and as a response to, a situation in which two or more different sociocultural orders were in contact and were more or less in opposition or conflict, as, for example, in the colonial situation. The terms *denunciatory, militant,* and *nativistic* speak mainly to what seem to have been the main emphases or characteristics of revival, as, for instance, the vehement reactions to the dominant culture in the colonial process. The terms *dynamic, revitalization,* and *vitalistic* interpret revival activities as more positively creative rather than merely responsive. *Devotional* and *pious* are usually used to describe movements of renewal that occur squarely within an established religious tradition. In these cases the objective is a deeper understanding of, and closer conformity with, the perceived truths of the tradition. But since revival and renewal activities may become heterodox and refractory with the discovery of new truths, the terms belong in the general lexicon. In activities described as *reformative* and *revivalist* new truths, heterodoxy, and criticisms of the given tradition are explicit.

Utopian, more familiarly descriptive of literary works, proposals, and indirect suggestions for a better world, is often used to describe revival and renewal activities because they appear to have as their purpose an impractical state of perfection or bliss. The word *cargo* has been reserved for revival activities occurring in Oceania, particularly in the islands of Melanesia, where the overt purpose is to gain access to European manufactured goods, called in Pidgin *kago* ("cargo").

The terms *enthusiastic* and *enthusiasms* refer specifically to movements within the Christian tradition during the seventeenth, eighteenth, and nineteenth centuries. But because the activities were heterodox, antinomian, and anticlerical, and because they sought new truths in a direct relation with the godhead without the intervention of clergy and envisaged a state of comparative bliss, the terms have come into a more general usage. *Millenarian* is gaining ground as a general portmanteau term, but it specifically refers to those activities in the European medieval period whose overt purposes and emphases were grounded in an expectation of the second coming of Christ. *Adventism* carries much the same connotations as *millenarian* but is usually used to describe more recent Christian movements and sects. Although *messianic* refers particularly to the Judeo-Christian tradition, it is also used more widely for any activities hinging on the advent of a leader-redeemer. Hence the term *prophet movements* is also used. Finally, while *charismatic,* like so many other words of specific Christian reference, is now used more loosely and generally, as in "charismatic leader," within the Christian tradition it refers more precisely to a form of worship centered on the "gift of tongues," glossalalia, a supposed charism of the Holy Spirit.

The above list of labels is not exhaustive. But since the bulk of those remaining are differing forms of, or are derived from, the terms provided, it will suffice. Whether the number of terms—so many of which are synonyms of each other—indicate significant phenomenological differences or are distinctions without a difference is a moot question. Still, for the most part the labels refer to activities that are heterodox, refractory, or rebellious in relation to a given tradition and appear to anticipate the discovery of new truths and new moralities, looking forward to a more certain redemption and better or even blissful times. Hence it is perhaps permissible to consider them as millenarian-type activities and their leaders, charismatic or otherwise, as prophets.

MORPHOLOGY. Briefly and generally, what happens in millenarian-type activities is that an individual, usually a man but sometimes a woman, the prophet, articulates to a given community a seemingly imperative program of action. When the program falls on deaf ears, the prophet is regarded as more or less insane or deranged. If, on the other hand, members of the community take up and pursue the program, something significant is beginning to happen even though nonparticipants may regard the collective action as insane, ill-considered, or foolish. Behind the articulation, bizarre and odd though the program may sometimes seem, has lain a period of hard thought and imaginative wrestlings, which culminate in a vivid and compelling inspirational experience. This, revelatory in nature, usually occurs in a dream, vision, or trancelike state but also in that more controlled mode in which a number of apparently intractable problems, mulled over in the mind, suddenly cohere into a resolution to act. In any case, the prophet usually disclaims personal authority except insofar as he or she is the agent of some transcendent source: God, Christ, the Holy Spirit, the Virgin Mary, the Great Spirit, an angel, an ancestor or ancestors, a figure or passage from mythology, a particularly powerful spirit or ghost in human or animal form, or passages from the sacred scriptures. There are many such sources. It suffices that the program for action has a divine warrant, usually also sanctioned by threats of imminent disaster—a destructive flood, storm, tidal wave, earthquake, volcanic eruption, holocaust, or, more simply, eternal damnation. Sometimes the disaster is muted into a life of continuing misery and helplessness. The point is that while participants will be saved or redeemed or will enjoy happiness, nonparticipants will deserve the fate reserved for them.

The general framework of revival and renewal activities may be described in terms of two phases between a prologue and an epilogue, with the caution that during the course of the action the parts of one phase may well overlap those of the other.

The prologue consists of the development of an ambience of general dissatisfaction with the way things are. People talk and gossip about their present difficulties, hark back to a time when, supposedly, all was well with them, and cast forward to a misty future when all might be well again, the heart's desires capable of being satisfied, the good life possible, and an earthly as well as a heavenly or spiritual redemption obtainable. The present appears as a kind of limbo, a transitional time of disappointment and dysphoria sandwiched between two kinds of well-being. In literate societies there is recourse to the sacred scriptures. Reinterpretations are bandied about, talked over, rethought. In nonliterate societies new meanings are pulled out of old myths; the new meanings then interact with present circumstances to form, in effect, new myths. In either case the following are the implicit questions: What is the truth of things? How may the good and moral life be lived in accordance with the truth? How is redemption to be obtained? In both cases it is thought that somewhere along the way something has gone wrong and that if it could be put right, a new age—envisaged as a new set of moral relationships in which each person will be able to satisfy his or her desires through others—will dawn. One or two in the community may already have attempted, publicly, to articulate a program to resolve present problems. Others have heard them but have rejected them as false prophets. Nevertheless, the early speakers have brought some things together and have created an expectation that someone sometime will get it right.

The development of the prologue seems essential to the effectiveness of a prophet. A particular connection—whose constituents are not easily unraveled—between prologue and revelation creates an authenticity in the prophet, sparks the revival and renewal activities, makes explicit what has been incipient and implicit in the prologue. The issues are, generally, the creation of new moralities, the construction of a new and relevant semantic environment of meaning, the transformation of a state of misery and helplessness into one of happiness, control, and the promise of redemption.

The first phase, assuming the form of a classic rite of transition, consists of a symbolic—and actual—return to first beginnings. Essentially, participants strip themselves of extant statuses, roles, and moralities to become, in effect, a noncommunity of mere selves. This is done most commonly by dancing a new dance to exhaustion; by dramatized orgies of sexual promiscuity; by the use of drugs; by the destruction of crops, animals, and property; or, in a more modern idiom, by the organization of encounter groups or mutual confessional sessions. There are other techniques. Glossalalia often occurs, for example. But whatever the mode employed, it is vital that an extant self be at least temporarily deprived of or released from its social and moral supports, that it understand itself and relate to other selves as well as to the divine outside of a sociocultural matrix that has become, by definition, intolerable. In short, to paraphrase a Christian idiom, participants are invited to die to themselves in order to put on the new person.

The second phase is the reverse or obverse of the first: a definition of the new social self both internally among the participants and externally by reference to outsiders. Special badges may be worn; exclusive modes of greeting, address, and apparel may be adopted. Gatherings of the faithful assume a distinctive, ritualized form; set procedures are carefully followed, especially when directed toward releasing the self from social constraints. Even in specifically secular movements, ritualized social observances (brushing or flossing one's teeth, practicing drills, performing the daily round of activities in prescribed ways) strengthen internal solidarities and emphasize the distinction between insiders and outsiders, the elect and the lost, the saved and the damned. The use of money—to which prophets often advert in their revelations—is strictly controlled, and narrow, rigorous moralities govern community interrelationships. Finding fault in others, at first a necessary adjunct to maintaining the new ways and moralities, becomes a major concern. Where the prologue and first phase had been informed by sentiments of love and egalitarianism and by the transcending of status barriers and competing interests, now hierarchy and close definitions of status and relative worth begin to seem more important. Although new recruits may be welcomed, they are closely examined. Backsliders are denounced and made to atone or are expelled from the community in disgrace.

The epilogue is by no means always a sad ending to hopeful beginnings. Many Christian sects and denominations—indeed, Christianity itself—have started in a variety of modulations of the way outlined and have survived. And there are many other communities which, whether regarded as part of or distinct from and independent of a larger fold, have survived in quietist and particularist modes. On the other hand, what more often occurs is that government forces intervene, either to bring an end to the activities of the first phase, because they appear to disturb the peace and seem contrary to good order, or to extirpate the movement because the new moralities are seen to have political overtones that challenge government authority. Alternatively, the activities of the prologue and the first phase may never actually cohere into a definable movement and simply evaporate as the collective will to continue dissipates in uncertainty.

Whether the prologue develops into a pious movement of renewal within an established church, the foundation of a religious order, the formation of an independent sect or denomination, or into a position wholly independent of its parents, the new community and its moralities cannot be other than syncretic, evoking the first group of terms mentioned at the outset of this article. Ideas from a variety of sources are brought together and reformulated as the prologue develops. The freshness of the new moralities lies not so much in the rituals (although these may seem peculiar enough to an outsider) as in the wider appreciations and deeper understandings brought to a novel hierarchical arrangement of what had existed before. What had once seemed intractable and intolerable is transformed into a semantic environment of relevance, an environment of meanings that guarantee the truth of things, indicate the good and worthwhile life, and assure members of the community that at the end of a good life lies redemption.

The force of the prophet's revelatory experience lies in the fact that it seems to make entirely possible the realization of what had been before in large part a kind of wish-dream. While the duration of a prologue varies greatly, and while there must always be a "first time," it is unusual for an effective prophet not to have had precursors. This indicates that the prologue may take some time to develop. Furthermore, interventions by governments aside, for a movement to be viable, the initial revelation perforce has to be developed and modified. And for this, political skills are required. Sometimes the prophet possesses such skills. More often, however, the survival of the movement depends on the managerial and political abilities of participants other than the prophet, who is shunted more usefully into an honorary, advisory position.

In principle, millenarian-type activities represent a general human proclivity realizable in any culture. Instances have occurred within Islam, Hinduism, and Buddhism. Oral traditions suggest that instances also have occurred in nonliterate societies of all types. Indeed, in an evolutionary context renewal and revival activities enable groups or communities to survive by creating more meaningful semantic environments, whereas otherwise they might have perished.

However, the incidence of recorded instances of revival and renewal shows that the vast bulk have occurred within a Christian ambience. This is not simply a function of colonialism or the European passion for recording. The nature and history of Christianity reveal it as peculiarly susceptible to millenarian-type activities. The history of Christianity in Europe is replete with instances, and as Europeans and Christian missionaries have moved into other lands, the instances have multiplied. If it seems odd to think that Christianity, variegated though it is in its denominational manifestations, yet contains within itself such a recreative evolutionary property, it is at least a possibility not to be lightly dismissed.

The idea of an alternative sociocultural order or semantic environment informed by perfected moralities, as well as attempts to realize such orders, comprise an integral part of Christianity. From first beginnings under the coercive aegis of the Roman hegemony, Christianity developed in a variety of differing cultural milieus. Given the Christian affirmation of the world as well as of things divine, its promise of new earths as well as new heavens, two contrasting models of community became dominant. Although both spoke to the greater perfection of morality, the first model of community was egalitarian, characterized by the mutual sharing of property and goods and held together by a set of transcendent beliefs, particularly in the guidance of the Holy Spirit. The second model, derived from Plato's ideal society, was hierarchical with supposedly mathematically harmonious structures and was grounded, at least initially, in measures of physical coercion. The permutation and combination of the contraries contained in the two models continually generate possible alternative sociocultural orders. And this process, sociologically speaking, would seem to have been largely responsible not only for the multiplicity of Christian sects and denominations but also for utopian writings, the formation of secular movements intent on an ambience of more perfect moralities, and the founding of experimental and ideal secular as well as religious communities. The history of Euro-Christian, or Western, civilization teems with examples.

This is not to say that an idea of the alternative sociocultural order has been absent from traditional societies and communities outside or beyond the Christian ambience and influence. But manifestations have been only sporadic. On the other hand, as Christian-derived Western ideas have spread, so have notions of the alternative moral community; and the incidence of attempts to realize such alternatives has been increasing, particularly in Japan since the end of World War II. Traditionally, however, in spite of historical change, whatever existed in any one lifetime has had to be taken as given: The good life has had to be managed either within its terms; in spite of them, through techniques of gaining an inner spiritual peace; or by renunciation.

Interpretive Theories. Description inevitably involves interpretation, and with millenarian-type activities there are further difficulties. The evidence for what has actually occurred is rarely obtained firsthand and usually becomes accessible only through the reports of those who were unsympathetic if not actively hostile. Because it is almost impossible for a competent observer to be in the right place at the right time, only a fraction of the data that might have been available ever comes to light. Questions as to whether the prophet and participants mean what they say in a literal or a symbolic sense and how these senses relate to each other and to the activities are difficult to disentangle and form into a relatively unimpeachable statement of what is really happening. Social scientists and professional ethnographers began to investigate millenarian-type movements only in the second decade of this century, and it was not until the late forties that the activities began to be investigated more or less systematically. Even then the large bulk of the work has concentrated on activities in the colonial situation, virtually ignoring the specifically Christian inheritance and contribution. Finally, although the force of the transcendent is clearly of great significance, social scientists, whatever their personal views, must either ignore the transcendent or reduce or translate it into sociocultural factors.

In such circumstances, accounting for or having a theory about millenarian-type activities presents problems. Moreover, an adequate theory should consist of a set of integrated statements about a phenomenon that, in accounting for the positive instance, also should account for the negative. For example, the disaster theory holds that millenarian-type activities follow upon what is perceived as a disaster, the last conceived broadly and including sociocultural as well as physical circumstances. In cases where an outsider identifies such a disaster but where no revival or renewal activities occur, it is likely that the insiders have not perceived the disaster as such. That is, the identification of a disaster is dependent on the activities, and the problem becomes one of specificity about the kinds of disaster involved. At present, such specifics are lacking.

In another example, a significant difference between what are thought of as legitimate expectations or aspirations and social realities has given rise to the "relative deprivation" hypothesis. That is, where social realities hinder legitimate expectations, revival and renewal activities occur. But since legitimate expectations may be economic ("we ought to have as much wealth as . . .") or political ("we ought to deploy as much power as . . .") or religious ("we ought to have the same opportunities for spiritual redemption as . . ."), and since there are few groups that do not consider themselves "deprived" in one or another sense in relation to another group, the negative instances are legion and unexplained. While the activities define the cause, the latter fails in its effects much more often than it succeeds.

One of the first professional social scientists to consider the problem, A. C. Haddon, described the parameters neatly enough:

> An awakening of religious activity is a frequent characteristic of periods of social unrest. The weakening or disruption of the old social order may stimulate new and often bizarre ideals, and these may give rise to religious movements that strive to sanction social and political aspirations. Communities that feel themselves oppressed anticipate the emergence of a hero who will restore their prosperity and prestige. And when the people are imbued with religious fervour the expected hero will be regarded as a Messiah. Phenomena of this kind are well known in history, and are not unknown at the present day among peoples in all stages of civilization. (Haddon, 1917, p. 455)

However, with the intervention of World War I, the implications of Haddon's statement were lost for a generation and more. While Ronald Knox's (1950) study of "enthusiasims" did not go wholly unoticed, when social scientists again addressed the problem, they turned to psychology rather than sociology and history.

Psychological interpretations were, and to a great extent still are, centered around the notions of "cognitive dissonance" or "collective flights from reality," where proper cognitions and reality were and are taken as givens. Although from this point of view, one might suppose forms of schizophrenia, Norman R. C. Cohn (1970) identified collective paranoia as the leitmotif of medieval millenarism. Thus arises the question of whether in the light of social unrest, oppression, disasters, and relative deprivation, the paranoia reflected reality or represented an avoidance of reality—like the rabbits of Richard Adams's *Watership Down* (New York, 1972) who escaped the destruction meted out to their fellows through just such a "collective flight from reality" and after many adventures eventually realized a comparative state of earthly bliss.

If the participants in millenarian-type activities feel that something is wrong with their world that they want to put right, psychological interpretations generally move toward the view that something is wrong with or lacking in the participants. (Anthony F. C. Wallace's 1956 article on revitalization is the notable exception.) The same is true of biological interpretations, which cite brain lesions or the complexities of the interconnections and relations between the right and left hemispheres of the brain. Thus it has been suggested that leaders who are followed despite their apparently irrational demands are wont to have brain lesions. Yet, as history informs us, true leaders cannot be other than extraordinary people. Perhaps such lesions are necessary to leadership with a vision of the future. And since left-hemisphere dominance is thought to give rise to logical thought and science, whereas right-hemisphere dominance is typical of the intuitive and nonrational approach of charismatics, it is likely that prophets will be right-hemisphere-dominant. Suggestive, but waiting on a great deal of further research, biological interpretations raise questions about whether they will provide further information about what one needs or wants to know or, more pertinently, whether they will reveal what questions remain to be asked.

Biological and psychological interpretations must tend toward the identification of a lesion—something wrong or abnormal. Moving from the opposite premise, that there may be something reasonable and expectable rather than something amiss or lacking in millenarian-type activities, many scholars working in sociological or anthropological modes have attempted explication rather than explanation. That is, accepting that some kinds of explanation must be inherent in an explication, these scholars have not sought causes like disaster and deprivation theories but have sought to tease out and define the relevances of the phenomenon. Some examples follow.

Breaking out of the anthropological functionalism that often inhibited studies of millenarian-type activities by insisting on equilibrium, synchronic analyses, and virtual denial of historical relevances, Peter Lawrence's detailed explication of a cargo movement in Papua New Guinea (Lawrence, 1964) demonstrates in historical depth, and with particular reference to the influence of Christian missionaries, how historic events and political and economic circumstances interacted with traditional mythologies and cohered into a movement. Lawrence is particularly illuminating on the nature of the prophet involved, Yali: not mad or insane or given to wild imaginings but experienced, traveled, and particularly affected by the differences in lifestyle, power, and economic resources obtaining between black and white peoples. In a similar study (Burridge, 1960), I have done much the same as Lawrence in an adjacent area, but, lacking the detailed historical data, my study accents traditional and symbolic elements in relation to social, political, economic, and cognitive features inherent in the colonial process and missionary activity. In later and more general works I consider a variety of features, including money and interpretive modes (Burridge, 1969) and the relevances of identity, individuality, Christianity, and contrasting models of community (Burridge, 1979).

Johannes Fabian's 1971 study of the Jamaa movement, which started as a pious movement within the Roman Catholic church and whose prophet was a Roman Catholic missionary priest, emphasizes semantic and organizational changes largely through detailed analyses of what was said and done. Although the prophet's maxim was "organization kills the movement," participants began to feel the necessity to organize once church authorities had removed the prophet. Fabian shows how organization was achieved not so much purposively and directly as through what was inherent and implicit in the discussions and activities of the participants. He also shows how the process of becoming organized in itself began to move the participants into an independent position, no longer a pious movement within the church.

Peter Worsley's classic study of Melanesian cargo activities (Worsley, 1957) is both historical and developmental, framed within an analysis of the politico-economic features of the colonial process. Worsley shows how millenarian-type activities are the only way in which a generally nonliterate and subject people can, lacking other means, signal their objections to the way things are. Not only are nonrational means adopted because no rational means exist, but the people themselves, in their traditional lives, habitually make use of transcendent sources or nonrational means when what is called rationality in the European view seems to fail them. Stephen Fuchs (1965) emphasizes themes of economic disadvantage, political disfranchisement, oppression, and consequent rebellion. Vittorio Lanternari (1963) does much the same. Bryan R. Wilson (1973) has pursued the problem of the rational and the irrational, concluding that thaumaturgical desires—command of transcendent or divine forces as well as of politico-economic and social features—are the basis for millenarian-type activities, and are thus inappropriate in or to rational and industrialized society.

Whether the interpretation be biological, psychological, cultural, or sociological, studies of millenarian-type activities have converged and reached a point at which, traditional methodologies having been more or less exhausted, a phase of consolidation and rethinking has started. Over a period of fifty years or so, systematic studies have moved from virtually dismissing the activities as forms of insanity or madness to considerations of different kinds of reality, their construction and interrelations, and the implications of terms such as *rational, nonrational,* and *irrational.* Ideologies, symbolic constructs, and notions of the transcendent are coming to be viewed as not simply epiphenomenal, products of the realities of politico-economic relations and modes of production, but as themselves kinds of reality that react back on other arrangements in ways not yet wholly understood. While the painting on a cave wall depicting a buffalo transfixed by a spear may be thought of as a magical and irrational way of attaining an end, it is also a means by which the hunter makes explicit to himself and fixes in symbolic terms an image of what he desires to accomplish. Similarly, the making of airplanes, radio stations, ships, and storage sheds from palm leaves and rattan (as well as many other apparently odd activities so frequently encountered in cargo movements) is now appreciated not simply as magical or irrational fantasy but as the forming of symbolic constructs of desired ends.

Studies of historical depth have made it abundantly clear that millenarian-type activities and their modulations are likely to occur in situations characterized by contradictory juxtapositions of affective and impersonal relations, particularly where differences of culture or subculture, lifestyle, modes of production, economic opportunity, and kinds of access to political control are involved—industrialized society notwithstanding. Why the problems that arise from these juxtapositions should cohere in a religious idiom, and why this should be thought irrational, are perhaps the main issues. For even in secular activities it is possible to discern a vital and essentially religious element. Too little is known about the nature of reality and about the transcendent and its relations to forms of redemption. The symbolic resonances of money—in particular its effects on moral affective and impersonal relationships—require much closer attention. Examination of the relevances of literacy—the quantum leap in symbolic and logical competence, the different kinds of effects wrought by the written and spoken word, the release from thralldom to a learned and literate clergy and secular elite—will surely provide further insights.

Finally, beyond their intrinsic human interest millenarian-type activities remain a crucial challenge to social scientists. They invite the statement through which particular actions and rationalizations, presently confined to specific situations, may aspire to a more general ontological validity. Absurd or irrational though they may seem, millenarian-type activities reveal human beings in the crisis of deciding how to be true to themselves and their future.

SEE ALSO African Religions; Australian Indigenous Religions, article on New Religious Movements; Enthusiasm; Millenarianism; North American Indian Religions; Reform; Syncretism; Utopia.

BIBLIOGRAPHY

A. C. Haddon's early remarks appear in "Five New Religious Cults in British New Guinea," by E. W. P. Chinnery and A. C. Haddon, *Hibbert Journal* 15 (1917): 448–463. The article is worth reading in its entirety. There are many excellent accounts of revival and renewal based on fieldwork: *The Peyote Religion among the Navaho* (New York, 1966) by David F. Aberle; my own work, *Mambu: A Melanesian Millennium* (London, 1960); *Jamaa: A Charismatic Movement in Katanga* (Evanston, Ill., 1971) by Johannes Fabian; *Rebellious Prophets* (New York, 1965) by Stephen Fuchs; and *Road Belong Cargo: A Study of the Cargo Movement in the Southern Madang District, New Guinea* (Manchester, 1964) by Peter Lawrence. *Enthusiasm: A Chapter in the History of Religion, with Special Reference to the Seventeenth and Eighteenth Centuries* (Oxford, 1950) by Ronald Knox is a brilliant study of enthusiastic movements in socio-theological perspective. Norman R. C. Cohn's *Pursuit of the Millennium,* 3d ed. (New York, 1970), and Anthony F. C. Wallace's "Revitalization Movements," *American Anthropologist* 58 (April 1956): 264–281, provide the most notable sociopsychological studies. Of the more general works, Michael Barkun presents a good analysis of disaster theory in *Disaster and the Millennium* (New Haven, 1974). A short but comprehensive survey can be found in my book, *New Heaven, New Earth* (New York, 1969), and a discussion of the implications on a wider level is provided in my later work, *Someone, No One: An Essay on Individuality* (Princeton, N.J., 1979). *The Religions of the Oppressed: A Study of Modern Messianic Cults* (New York, 1963) by Vittorio Lanternari is an excellent portrait of the political and economic aspects of the subject. Bryan R. Wilson relates thaumaturgies and religious change in his full yet compendious survey of *Magic and the Millennium: A Sociological Study of Religious Movements of Protest among Tribal and Third-World Peoples* (New York, 1973). A landmark study of colonial problems and politico-economic relations is provided by Peter Worsley's *The Trumpet Shall Sound: A Study of "Cargo" Cults in Melanesia* (1957; New York, 1968). In some ways the fullest and most rounded account, in which the actors are rabbits, is *Watership Down* (New York, 1972) by Richard Adams.

New Sources

Cairns, Earle Edwin. *An Endless Line of Splendor: Revivals and Their Leaders from the Great Awakening to the Present.* Wheaton, Ill., 1986.

Cox, Harvey. *Fire from Heaven: The Rise of Pentecostalism Spirituality and the Reshaping of Religion in the Twenty-first Century.* Reading, Mass., 1995.

Duin, Julia. "Catholics on the Pentecostal Trail." *Christianity Today* 36/7 (1992): 24–27.

Freston, Paul. "Pentecostalism in Latin America: Characteristics and Controversies." *Social Compass* 45/3 (1998): 335–358.

Kramer, Martin S. *Arab Awakening and Islamic Revival: The Politics of Ideas in the Middle East.* New Brunswick, N.J., 1996.

Misztal, B., and Anson Shupe, eds. *Religion and Politics in Comparitive Perspective: Revival of Religious Fundamentalism in East and West.* Westport, Conn., 1992.

Stark, Rodney. *Religious Movements: Genesis, Exodus, and Numbers.* New York, 1985.

Stark, Rodney and William Bainbridge. *The Future of Religion: Secularization, Revival and Cult Formation.* Berkeley, Calif. 1985.

KENELM BURRIDGE (1987)
Revised Bibliography

REVIVALISM

SEE EVANGELICAL AND FUNDAMENTAL CHRISTIANITY; PENTECOSTAL AND CHARISMATIC CHRISTIANITY; REFORM; REVIVAL AND RENEWAL

REVOLUTION.

Throughout the course of history, religion has functioned as a source of social solidarity, and this fact is undoubtedly related to the very essence of religion, which provides a set of basic values for the regulation of human life on earth and guidance in the search for meaning and salvation. Since in all traditional societies both nature and society were regarded as part of the same cosmic universe controlled by gods or spirits, a religious legitimation of the social order developed as a matter of course.

The integrative role of religion has been known for a very long time. The eighteenth-century rationalist Voltaire assured his noble pupil, Frederick the Great, that a "wise and courageous prince, with money, troops, and laws, can perfectly well govern men without the aid of religion," but most rulers of humankind and the sages counseling them have preferred not to take any chances on the firmness and sway of political authority. In his *Discourses* (1517) Machiavelli called religion "the most necessary and assured support of any civil society," and he exhorted princes and heads of republics "to uphold the foundations of the religion of their countries, for then it is easy to keep their people religious, and consequently well conducted and united." The duration of empires, argued the French conservative Joseph de Maistre, writing after the French Revolution, "has always been proportionate to the influence that the religious principle has acquired in the political system." The emphasis on the importance to society of a sense of shared values endeared de Maistre to his fellow countryman, the sociologist Émile Durkheim, probably the best-known modern spokesman for the view that the primary function of religion is the preservation of social unity.

But religion has often also functioned as an agent of revolutionary mobilization. Religion involves transcendent moral standards that define an ideal against which human performance can be measured. Hence those who are dissatisfied—politically, economically, socially, or spiritually—may find in religion strong support for their attack upon the status quo. Religion can be a powerful agent pushing the thoughts of leaders beyond tradition; it may become the spiritual dynamic of revolution that Georges Sorel called the "social myth." As the judicious Richard Hooker observed in the sixteenth century, during a period of great religious and social upheaval, when the minds of leaders are once "persuaded that it is the will of God to have those things done which they fancy, their opinions are as thorns in their sides, never suffering them to take rest till they have brought their speculations into practice." Religion can provide individual with the zeal of true believers who know that they are right and who act with fortitude since they carry out God's will and count on God's helping hand.

While some religious ideas, such as the conception of sacred kingship to be found in many premodern societies, have reinforced a pattern of political subservience and quietism, most religious views of rulership have not had such unequivocal political consequences. The ancient Chinese doctrine of the mandate of Heaven, for example, legitimized the rule of the emperor, the Son of Heaven, who traced his title to deified ancestors upon whom Heaven, the supreme deity, had conferred the right to rule. And yet, the mandate of Heaven was not seen as granted in perpetuity or unconditionally. Heaven demanded righteousness and good government and deposed rulers who abused their exalted office. Hence, just as the concept had apparently come into being to justify the seizure of power by the Zhou dynasty (around 1028 BCE), which claimed a divine mandate for overthrowing the Shang, so the mandate of Heaven could later be invoked by new aspirants to the supreme rulership. Indeed, in Chinese a revolution is called *ge ming*—"breaking of the mandate."

The Christian ideas of divine providence and of the divine origin and sanction of rulership also have had diverse results: They have helped shore up and sanctify political authority, but they also have been used to justify rebellion. In the deterministic worldview of Augustine of Hippo, nothing could exist without divine approval. Divine providence has arranged things in such a way that every evil in the world is directed to some good. God appoints rulers according to the merits of the people, and in view of his omnipotence and justice tyrants must be considered God's retribution for the perversity of the people. Both just kings and cruel tyrants reign by God's providence; none may be resisted.

This gospel of submissiveness, a justification for a theologian desirous of obtaining secular support for the suppression of heresy or for a Martin Luther in need of assistance from the princes of the Holy Roman Empire, was a burdensome handicap for Christians eager to fight the pretensions of absolute temporal power. Hence, in the later sixteenth century, in particular, the doctrine of divine providence was reinterpreted so as to make possible certain political actions. Theodore Beza, a disciple of Calvin, conceded that nothing can exist without divine approval and that God uses the evil deeds of sinners to punish other sinners. But, he asked, why could it not be God's will that tyrants be punished by the people rather than people by tyrants? During the Puritan Revolution (English Civil War) the Christian humanist John Milton rejected the suggestion that God had put the English nation in slavery to Charles Stuart and that only God, therefore, could be relied upon to release it. If God can be said to give a people into slavery whenever a tyrant prevails over a people, he asked, why ought God not as well be said to set them free whenever people prevail over a tyrant?

But this kind of politically useful theological reasoning did not originate with either Beza or Milton. Around 1110, Hugh of Fleury had taught in his *De regia potestate* that God punishes bad princes by the insubordination of their people, and the same idea is found in Eastern Christendom. The Kievan chronicler considered a revolt of the citizens against their prince an act of God's will, punishing the prince for his misconduct. More recently a pastoral letter issued in 1967 by "Sixteen Bishops of the Third World" declared that "Christians and their pastors should know how to recognize the hand of the Almighty in those events that from time to time put down the mighty from their thrones and raise up the humble." Needless to say, the impressment of God for the cause of rebellion is today no monopoly of the political left. After the military coup of 1964 in Brazil, a group of Brazilian archbishops and bishops thanked God for having listened to their prayers for deliverance from the communist peril. Divine providence, they said, had made itself felt in a tangible manner.

Other contradictory consequences of the doctrine of divine providence must be noted. The acceptance of the omnipotent role of the deity can lead to fatalism and inaction, but it can also spur people to mighty effort because of the conviction that God is on their side. Thus the early Jewish apocalyptic writers counseled complete reliance upon God's direct intervention, which would redeem Israel, whereas the later Zealots, engaged in eschatological war against Rome, believed that God would usher in the new age of freedom and justice only if pious Jewish warriors actively participated in the realization of the divine plan. Here strong faith in the certainty of divine assistance acted to inspire superior exertion and fortitude and gave the struggle against Rome the character of a holy war. Revolutionary action merged with messianic utopianism and led to an utter disregard of Rome's overwhelming might, a realistic appraisal of which would have discouraged any hope of success.

The fact that most religious doctrines are protean in character and are open to different readings does not mean that the doctrinal content of a religion is entirely irrelevant to politics. Though all religions have both quietistic and revolutionary potentials, the relative proportions of these differing political implications vary. Considering the phenomenon of revolutionary millenarianism, for example, we see that certain religious traditions are more conducive to expectations of a coming age of bliss than others. The cyclical view of history in Hinduism and Buddhism, providing as it does for perpetual flux and endless repetition of the cosmic drama, appears to discourage millenarian ideas, just as the linear theory of history and the expectation of a final salvation of humanity in Judaism, Christianity, and Islam provide inspiration for the millenarian dream of eternal terrestrial redemption.

The leadership of religious organizations or movements is often of considerable importance in determining that group's political posture. A charismatic leader of a millenarian movement is a potent agent of radical change. As the bearer of chiliastic prophecy, he is not just a champion of felt needs or a catalyst but also a cause of the movement he is heading. The millenarian prophet's ambitious and challenging vision of what the world ought to be increases expectations and dissatisfactions, which can lead to a revolutionary situation. The limited success of *conscientização,* the attempted "raising of the consciousness" of the subservient peasant population of South America by various radical groups, shows that this enterprise encounters serious difficulties when entrusted to persons of ordinary and secular cast.

In sum, religion can be both a prop for the established institutions of society and a revolutionary force, since it includes elements for integration as well as for radical change. Religion can defuse social conflict by devaluing earthly concerns and emphasizing happiness in the world beyond, but its promise of divine intervention in human affairs can also strengthen the hope that a better life is possible here on earth. Hence many times different groups within one religion will line up on opposite sides of the barricades. God's will, when seen through the lenses of human desires and interests, can be, and in fact usually is, read in several different ways.

Whether religion discourages or promotes revolution depends on variables such as the relationship of the religious institution to the state or the presence or absence of a forceful leader. All religions known to us can assume both roles, though the intellectual and organizational traditions they hold will incline some more in one direction than in the other. Situational factors, such as the relative chances for success of a revolt, will also be important. In all there are four ways in which religion can assume a revolutionary posture:

(1) *Millenarian revolts* occur (a) when situations of distress or disorientation develop, and the causes are not clearly perceived or appear insoluble by ordinary and available remedies; (b) when a society or group is deeply attached to religious ways of thinking about the world and when the religion of that society attaches importance to millenarian ideas; and (c) when an individual or group of individuals obsessed with salvationist fantasies succeeds in establishing charismatic leadership over a social movement.

(2) *Militant religious nationalism* arises among colonized people in situations of awakening national consciousness. Religion supplies a sense of national identity; it becomes a symbol of self-assertion against the colonial regime, which is usually indifferent, if not hostile, to the native creed.

(3) *The leaders of religious bodies with a developed ecclesiastical organization support a revolutionary upheaval* because they are sympathetic to the aims of this revolution, or because they are protecting the interests of the religious institution. These interests can be temporal or spiritual or both. They can involve the defense of worldly possessions or the protection of the mission of the religious institution as the channel of divine grace to humanity.

(4) *Individual theologians or laymen support a revolutionary movement* to give a concrete social and political meaning to the transcendent elements of their faith, as in the Christian "theology of revolution." Such religious revolutionaries often work in concert with secular revolutionary movements and many lose their identity in them.

Just as in earlier times religion was often used to support the status quo, religion has, in many parts of the world today, become the handmaiden of revolution. The cross of Christianity, the crescent of Islam, and even the peaceful prayer wheel of Buddhism have been enlisted to shore up revolutionary movements and regimes, which are often identified with liberation, modernization, and progress, although, as especially in the case of Islamic revolutionary movements, the radical and far-reaching change instigated by revolution can entail fighting modernization and restoring the old ways. Whether this new positive relationship of religion and revolution will indeed promote human liberty and happiness is, of course, a question nobody can as yet answer. Religion has its part in this celebration of heroic ruthlessness and violence. It continues to inspire killing in Northern Ireland as much as on the Indian subcontinent and in the Philippines, demonstrating once again that religious zeal can be a powerful force for love but also an important force for hatred and cruelty. The various theologies of revolution make people slight the cruelties and the hatreds that commonly accompany revolutionary upheavals. What the theologizing of revolution cannot do is to establish the progressive character of such revolts. That judgment is reserved to future generations, who will have the opportunity to live with the consequences.

Bibliography

The classic study of the integrative role of religion remains Émile Durkheim's *The Elementary Forms of the Religious Life* (New York, 1915). On the phenomenon of revolutionary millenarianism, see *Magic and the Millennium* (New York, 1973) by Bryan R. Wilson and *Millennial Dreams in Action*, edited by Sylvia L. Thrupp (1962; reprint, New York, 1970), especially the essay by Norman Cohn, "Medieval Millenarianism: Its Bearing on the Study of Millenarian Movements." For the political manifestations of Christianity, consult Ernst Troeltsch's *The Social Teachings of the Christian Churches*, 2 vols. (1911; reprint, London, 1931), and for the important sixteenth century, see John William Allen's *A History of Political Thought in the Sixteenth Century*, 3d ed. (London, 1951). For a fuller treatment of the subject of this essay and further bibliography, see my own work, *Religion and Revolution* (Oxford, 1974).

New Sources

Elbaum, Max. *Revolution in the Air: Sixties Radicals Turn to Lenin, Mao, and Che.* New York, 2002.

Ellul, Jacques. *Anarchy and Christianity.* Translated by Geoffrey Bromiley. Grand Rapids, Mich., 1991.

Holloway, John. *Change the World without Taking Power: The Meaning of Revolution Today.* London, 2002.

Olsen, Gerald Wayne, ed. *Religion and Revolution in Early-Industrial England: The Halévy Crisis and Its Critics.* Lanham, Md., 1990.

Vaage, Lief, ed. *Subversive Scriptures: Revolutionary Christian Readings of the Bible in Latin America.* Harrisburg, Pa., 1997.

Guenter Lewy (1987)
Revised Bibliography

RICCI, MATTEO (1552–1610), Jesuit missionary. Born at Macerata, in the Papal States, Ricci studied law at Rome and entered the Jesuit novitiate in 1571. He volunteered for the missions and was sent to Portugal (1577) and then to Goa (1578). He finished his theological studies in Goa and in 1580 was ordained at Cochin, on the Malabar coast. In 1582 he went to Macao to study Chinese language and culture. The next year, with unprecedented permission from Chinese authorities, Ricci and Michele Ruggier (1543–1607) traveled to Zhaoqing, China. Beardless, with shaven heads, they assumed garb similar to that worn by Buddhist monks. They sought to spread Christian doctrine unobtrusively, attracting educated visitors with their world map, Western clocks, and prisms. Ricci's use of the term *tianzhu* (lord of Heaven) to refer to God dates from that period. In 1588 Ricci, known in Chinese as Li Madou, took charge of the mission. Ordered by local authorities to leave (1589), the missionaries went to Shaozhou (modern-day Guangdong). There they were advised by Qu Rukui, an early convert who had initially been attracted by rumors of the foreigners' expertise in alchemy. It was probably he who counseled the Jesuits to present themselves as scholars rather than as monks. At Shaozhou Ricci appears to have completed a Latin translation (now lost) of the Confucian Four Books.

After a brief visit to Nanjing (1595), the Jesuits settled in Nanzhang (modern-day Jiangxi), appearing with hair and beards and wearing Confucian robes. At Nanzhang Ricci wrote, in Chinese, *Jiaoyou lun* (On friendship), dedicated to an imperial prince he had met, and also completed his catechism *(Tianzhu shiyi).* In 1598 the Jesuits went to Beijing, but they stayed only two months, as people feared to associate with them at the time of the Chinese involvement in Japan's invasion of Korea. They settled in Nanjing (1599), where the atmosphere had improved; there Ricci met many scholars, including Li Zhi and Jiao Hong, and published a revised edition of his world map (1600). That same year the Jesuits left once more for Beijing, reinforced with presents for the emperor, including clocks, clavichords, statues, and crucifixes. At Tianjin a eunuch confiscated some articles and held the party for nearly six months.

When the Jesuits finally reached Beijing in January 1601, their gifts so pleased the emperor that he allowed them to stay on and even granted them a monthly stipend. Ricci associated there with scholar-officials including grand secretary Shen Yiguan, minister of rites Feng Qi, and minister of personnel Li Dai, with whom Ricci discussed science and religion. Feng Yingjing, editor of an encyclopedia, was prevented from receiving baptism by his untimely death. Another convert, Li Zhizao, helped Ricci publish his world map, his catechism, and his treatise on friendship. By 1604 Ricci had also published a short treatise, *Ershiwu yan* (Twenty-five sayings), and became sole superior of the China mission, now independent of Macao. In 1608 he also published a work on ethics, *Qiren shipian* (Ten dialogues of a nonconformist). With Xu Guangqi, another collaborator baptized at Nanjing, who would rise to the position of grand secretary, Ricci translated the first six chapters of Euclid's *Elements* (1607) and other texts on astronomy, trigonometry, geometry, and arithmetic. He prepared a special copy of the world map for the emperor, as well as various polemics directed against Buddhism, especially the *Bianxue yidu.* By this time the Jesuits had bought a compound inside the Xuanwu Gate, later known as Nantang (South Church). There they met Ai Tian, a Chinese Jew from Kaifeng, who told them about the Nestorian presence in China. By then also, their suspicion that China was identical with the legendary land of Cathay had been confirmed. Ricci died of illness at age fifty-seven. He was buried outside the western city-gate of Beijing, in Zhala'er. His grave, destroyed by the Boxers in 1900, was desecrated again in 1966 but was subsequently repaired; it has been open to the public since 1980.

Ricci's gentle personality, his expertise in Western science and philosophy, and his knowledge of Chinese culture made him one of the great cultural mediators of all time. He was venerated posthumously by Chinese clockmakers as their patron. His method of cultural accommodation in the China mission left its legacy of controversy. Whether Chinese converts to Christianity should still be permitted to participate in Chinese rites was a question long debated in China and Europe by missionaries and philosophers, Chinese emperors, and papal legates. Such participation was condemned as intrinsically evil by popes Clement XI (1704) and Benedict XIV (1742). Even a later papal decision in 1939 to allow a measure of "Chinese rites" did not fully rehabilitate Ricci's institutional position. His ideas were ahead of his time, although his exclusive preferences for early Confucian morals as an ally of Christianity and his opposition to neo-Confucian philosophy and to Buddhism is not entirely acceptable to even more ecumenically minded modern missionaries.

BIBLIOGRAPHY

No satisfactory book-length biography of Ricci is available in English. Vincent Cronin's *The Wise Man from the West* (New York, 1955) is a popular work. Wolfgang Franke's scholarly entry in *Dictionary of Ming Biography, 1369–1644,* vol. 2 (New York, 1976), is short but full. R. P. Bernard's *Le Père Matthieu Ricci et la société chinoise de son temps,* 2 vols. (Tianjin, 1937), is still useful. Ricci's diary has been translated into English by Louis Gallagher as *China in the Sixteenth Century: The Journals of Matteo Ricci, 1583–1610* (New York, 1953).

Serious scholars must still consult *Opere storiche del P. Matteo Ricci,* 2 vols., edited by Pietro Tacchi Venturi (Macerata, 1911–1913); *Fonti Ricciane,* 3 vols., edited by Pasquale Maria d'Elia (Rome, 1942–1949); and the Jesuit Archives in Rome. There are two chronological biographies available in Chinese, by Li'ou and by Fang Hao, collected in *Li Madou yanjiu lunji,* edited by Zhou Kangxie (n.p., 1971).

JULIA CHING (1987)

RICHARDSON, CYRIL C.

RICHARDSON, CYRIL C. (1909–1976) was an American church historian. Born in London, England, Cyril Charles Richardson emigrated to Canada in 1927 and was educated at the University of Saskatchewan (B.A., 1930) and Emmanuel College, Saskatoon (Lic. Theol., 1931). He pursued graduate study at Union Theological Seminary, New York City (Th.D., 1934) and, in Europe, at the universities of Göttingen, Dijon, and Basel. He was ordained to the priesthood of the Protestant Episcopal church in 1934 and became a naturalized American citizen in 1940. From 1934 until his death he taught at Union Theological Seminary, New York, becoming the seminary's fifth Washburn Professor of Church History in 1949 and its dean of graduate studies in 1954.

A brilliant lecturer and prolific writer, Richardson specialized in early Christian literature, patristic theology, and the history of Christian worship and spirituality. He also wrote extensively on the relationship of Christian faith to mental health, spiritual healing, and parapsychology—interests engendered by his hospitalization and successful treatment for tuberculosis from 1943 to 1945. His churchmanship, at once practical and innovative, showed itself in his lifelong concern for Christian unity and in his advocacy, already in the early 1950s, of the ordination of women to the priesthood.

Richardson viewed church history as a specifically theological discipline, whose chief aim is not to study "Christianity," understood as a phenomenon in the general history of religions, but to recount the story of the "holy community" called into being by God's saving acts. Thus church history is "the tale of redemption" and "the medium of revelation," which requires not only a critical sifting of the historical evidence but, above all, the use of symbolic language, or what Richardson referred to as "myth," to convey the ultimate meanings of events.

He is the author of five monographs: *The Christianity of Ignatius of Antioch* (1935); *The Church through the Centuries* (1938); *The Sacrament of Reunion* (1940), a historical examination of the ministry, apostolic succession, and the Eucharist as bases for Christian unity; *Zwingli and Cranmer on the Eucharist* (1949), showing Archbishop Thomas Cranmer's indebtedness to the sacramental theology of the Swiss reformer Ulrich Zwingli; and *The Doctrine of the Trinity* (1958), wherein he argues that the church's classical trinitarian dogma is an "artifical construct" that fails to resolve the profound theological problems it addresses. This pathbreaking book, which generated intense controversy in academic and church circles, typifies Richardson's scholarship, combining mastery of historical detail with acute philosophical criticism and deep religious faith.

He also edited two highly regarded volumes in the Library of Christian Classics series: *Early Christian Fathers* (1953) and, with Edward R. Hardy, *Christology of the Later Fathers* (1954). He collaborated on eleven books, including the second, revised edition of Williston Walker's widely used textbook, *A History of the Christian Church* (1959). He contributed over one hundred articles and a like number of book reviews to theological and historical journals.

Richardson's eminent abilities as a director of doctoral students and his many publications, remarkable for their chronological scope and weight of learning, earned him international repute as one of the leading church historians of the mid-twentieth century.

Bibliography

To date there has been no biographical study of Richardson or full-scale appraisal of his scholarship. His understanding of the discipline of church history is summarized in his inaugural lecture, "Church History Past and Present," *Union Seminary Quarterly Review* 5 (November 1949): 1–11. He discussed the doctrine of the Trinity in numerous publications (besides his controversial book *The Doctrine of the Trinity*), including "The Enigma of the Trinity," in *A Companion to the Study of St. Augustine,* edited by Roy W. Battenhouse (New York, 1955); "A Preface to Christology," *Religion in Life* 27 (Autumn 1958): 504–514; and "The Trinity and the Enhypostasia," *Canadian Journal of Theology* 5 (April 1959): 73–78. The journal *Religion in Life* 29 (Winter 1959–1960) featured assays on the Trinity by Richardson and Claude Welch, followed by a sharp exchange of views between these two scholars ("The Doctrine of the Trinity," pp. 7–31). Richardon's liturgical scholarship is best represented by his essays, "The Foundations of Christian Symbolism," in *Religious Symbolism,* edited by F. Ernest Johnson (New York, 1962); "Worship in New Testament Times, Christian," in *The Interpreter's Dictionary of the Bible,* edited by George A. Buttrick, vol. 4 (New York, 1962); and "Word and Sacrament in Protestant Worship," in *Ecumenical Dialogue at Harvard: The Roman Catholic-Protestant Colloquium,* edited by Samuel H. Miller and G. Ernest Wright (Cambridge, Mass., 1964).

David W. Lotz (1987)

RIDDLES See PARADOX AND RIDDLES

RIGHT AND LEFT See LEFT AND RIGHT

RISSHŌ KŌSEIKAI

RISSHŌ KŌSEIKAI (Society Establishing Righteousness and Harmony) is one of the new religions of postwar Japan. It was founded in 1938 by Niwano Nikkyō (1906–1999), at that time a minor leader of Reiyūkai, and his disciple and assistant Naganuma Myōkō (1889–1957), a woman with shamanic attributes. The school regards the *Lotus Sutra* as the ultimate source of their teachings.

Niwano Nikkyō was born into a farming household in a mountain village in Niigata Prefecture, went to Tokyo in 1923, and eventually became a shopkeeper. In his early twenties he studied systems of fortune-telling based on people's names and on rules governing auspicious and inauspicious dates (*rokuyō*) and directions (*shichishin*) derived from ancient Chinese forms. In 1934, when his daughter became seriously ill, he turned to Arai Sukenobu, a chapter leader in the Reiyūkai organization and a renowned scholar of the *Lotus Sutra,* for advice. Convinced that the *Lotus Sutra* provided answers to the problems of suffering, Niwano became active in the Reiyūkai movement. However, by 1938 his increasing doubts about Reiyūkai, especially its insistence that lectures on the *Lotus Sutra* were unnecessary, led him to form a new organization, Risshō Kōsekai.

Early in its development, Kōseikai taught that adverse karmic causes and effects caused by bad deeds in a previous existence or by the bad deeds of one's ancestors could be overcome by means of ancestor veneration in which the *Lotus Sutra* was chanted, by religious training for the improvement of one's personality, and by guiding others to the faith. This teaching, which stemmed primarily from Reiyūkai doctrine and practice, was complemented by Niwano's use of fortune-telling techniques in order to attract converts to the movement. Niwano also instituted mutual counseling sessions, known as *hōza,* designed to improve the mental outlook of practitioners.

In keeping with the doctrinal roots of the movement, the original iconographic focus of Kōseikai devotion was the Daimoku ("Hail to the *Lotus Sutra*") *maṇḍala* transmitted in the Nichiren tradition. But as Niwano became increasingly disillusioned with the Nichiren sect and the possibility of carrying on joint missionary work with it, he began his own study of the *Lotus Sutra.* In 1958, as a result of his study of the text, he declared the focus of Kōseikai devotion to be the Eternal Buddha of the *Lotus,* and an image of this Buddha was installed in the movement's headquarters in 1964. From around this time a change took place in the composition of the Kōseikai members, as an increasing number of them sought a more meaningful life rather than mere respite from worldly problems. This reflects perhaps the rising standard of living in the Japan of the 1960s. With the changing concern of its followers, and also with the emergence of second-generation members, the core of the Kōseikai doctrine shifted from the attainment of happiness by the elimination of negative karmic effects to the perfection of the personality and the realization of peace on earth.

The basic unit of membership in Risshō Kōsekai is the household rather than the individual. Kōseikai claimed a membership of about a thousand households in 1945. Since then, its membership has increased dramatically: 50,000 in 1950, 399,000 in 1960, 973,000 in 1970, and 1,640,000 in 1980. Members are not requested to end all former religious affiliations. While no clergy-laity distinction exists, the formal status of "teacher" is institutionalized; in 1980, 173,000 people had this qualification. Originally, new members were installed in the same branch as the senior member who brought them to Kōseikai (a system called *oya-ko,* literally, "parent-child"). There were nine such branches in 1945. In 1959, there was a reform in branch organization, and the *oya-ko* system was replaced by one based on propinquity, whereby a branch was made up of members living near one another irrespective of *oya-ko* relations; 138 new branches were set up by this system. A further reform instituted in 1969 defined the boundaries of a branch as coincident with those of municipalities. In 1982 there were 224 branches in Japan, with additional ones in Korea, Brazil, and the United States. These reforms promoted local Kōseikai activities, including campaign work for local and national elections and dissemination of its teachings to nonmembers. Around 1970, Kōseikai launched the Brighter Society Movement (a public-spirited movement bringing together secular, religious, and governmental organizations to create a better society) and an international movement for the attainment of world peace through interreligious cooperation. The headquarters of Kōseikai have been located in Wada, Suginami-ku, Tokyo, since its foundation. Full-time workers at the headquarters and its affiliates numbered a little more than five hundred in 1980. No position is hereditary, with the exception of the presidency, which is held by lineal descendants of Niwano.

Kōseikai, the second largest new religion in contemporary Japan, is unique in a number of ways. Although it may be said to stem in part from Nichiren Buddhism, today it stresses basic *bodhisattva* practices as well as faith in the Eternal Buddha. While Kōseikai emphasizes traditional values such as reverence of ancestors, modesty, and harmony, it is neither nativistic nor nationalistic, as demonstrated by its peace movement. It is not meditation-oriented; rather it is practice- or action-oriented on the basis of inner reflection. Its organization is unlike that of other new religions in that the municipality-based local branches are linked to the highly developed bureaucracy at the headquarters.

See Also New Religious Movements, article on New Religious Movements in Japan.

Bibliography

Dale, Kenneth J., and Akahoshi Susumu. *Circle of Harmony: A Case Study in Popular Japanese Buddhism with Implications for Christian Mission.* Tokyo, 1975. A valuable study of *hōza,* the small mutual discussion and counseling group that is the center of Kōseikai's teaching and training activities.

Kyōdanshi Hensan Iinkai, ed. *Risshō Kōsekai shi.* 5 vols. Tokyo, 1984. A history of Risshō Kōsekai written by nonmember specialists.

Niwano Nikkyō. *A Buddhist Approach to Peace.* Tokyo and Rutland, Vt., 1977. Translated and compiled by Masuo Nezu. Based mainly on the author's *Heiwa e no michi* (Tokyo, 1972).

Niwano Nikkyō. *Lifetime Beginner: An Autobiography.* Tokyo and Rutland, Vt., 1978. Translated by Richard L. Gage. An autobiography of the founder of Risshō Kōsekai based on Niwano's two books, *Shoshin issho* (Tokyo, 1975) and *Niwano Nikkyo jiden* (Tokyo, 1976).

Risshō Kōsekai, ed. *Niwano Nikkyo howa senshu.* 7 vols. Tokyo, 1978–1982. A comprehensive collection of Niwano's sermons, speeches, and essays. Very detailed biographical notes are appended to volume one.

New Sources

Guthrie, Stewart. *A Japanese New Religion: Rissho Kosei-kai in a Mountain Hamlet.* Ann Arbor, 1988.

Morioka Kiyomi (1987)
Revised Bibliography

RITES OF PASSAGE

This entry consists of the following articles:

RITES OF PASSAGE: AN OVERVIEW [FIRST EDITION]

Rites of passage are a category of rituals that mark the passage of a person through the life cycle, from one stage to another over time, from one role or social position to another, integrating the human and cultural experiences with biological destiny: birth, reproduction, and death. These ceremonies make the basic distinctions, observed in all groups, between young and old, male and female, living and dead. The interplay of biology and culture is at the heart of all rites of passage, and the struggle between these two spheres asserts the essential paradox of humanity's mortal heritage. Humans dwell in an equivocal world, for they belong to both nature and culture, as Claude Lévi-Strauss has pointed out. It is through rites of passage that people are able to contemplate, to formulate and reformulate, their ambivalent condition of animal and human. Biology dictates the fundamentals of human experience—birth, reproduction, and death—yet the ways in which individuals manipulate and modify these imperatives through cultural means are endless.

Tribal Societies. That certain physiological "facts" are as much cultural or social as biological is brought home time and time again if one searches the vast, intricate descriptions of rites of passage in tribal societies. And the message is clear: men and women are not simply born, nor do they merely procreate and die; they are made what they are through ceremonies. An act of procreation alone cannot make a bride; a wedding must be performed. And brides who can neither copulate nor procreate can be made from infants; many years may separate betrothal from puberty. Sometimes, a female must be initiated into fertility by her society before she is allowed to mate; a girl's social definition as "woman" is provided by ceremony, whether she has begun to menstruate or not. Similarly, males frequently must satisfy certain social conditions before they are allowed to mate; for a boy, a successful hunt or the cutting of his foreskin may be required for passport into adulthood.

In rites of passage one is reminded, too, that the ages of a life are not ordained by laws of nature; most of the ages universally acknowledged are socially or culturally created. As Philippe Ariès has demonstrated in *Centuries of Childhood: A Social History of Family Life* (New York, 1962), "childhood" is an invention of post-Renaissance Europe, not a distinctive, universally recognized condition. Prior to modern history, a child was treated, dressed, and regarded as a miniature adult, without special needs or privileges. In like manner, adolescence represents a recently invented, rather than a biologically ineluctable, phase of the human life cycle; G. Stanley Hall established the concept with his book *Adolescence* in 1904. Since then, all manner of social agencies, commercial enterprises, psychologists, physicians, legislators, and educators have arisen to articulate and serve the needs of teenagers. And, as Margaret Mead in *Coming of Age in Samoa* (New York, 1928) has pointed out, the menstrual cramps and discomforts that American women regard as inevitable were unknown among Samoan adolescent girls, attesting that biology is not always destiny and that physiological symptoms may result from social or cultural conditions. To be sure, it is often quite forgotten how complex and how numerous are the cultural templates individuals lay over their biological essence.

Celebration of paradox. Rites of passage embody paradox, the inevitable legacy of one's humanity, vividly calling attention to, and allowing one to announce and renounce, the most profound enigma of all: that humans live out their lives suspended between the borders of nature and culture. This is the essential paradox, but other paradoxes are played out as well. Because rites of passage mark distinctions in an otherwise continuous life course, they celebrate and facilitate change or disruption of standard social categories, while at the same time they preserve them. A third paradox represented reveals the conflict between one's aspirations and strivings for individual ventures, and yearnings for assurance and sustenance from one's social group. In actual physiological fact, each person is born and dies quite alone, unique and separate, but also does so as members of a group, a group that seeks to preserve the continuity of its values and understandings, a group that therefore defines birth, aging, and death and that reassures one that life is meaningful.

Hence, during the performance of these life-crisis rituals, societies may inscribe their designs both literally and figuratively upon the initiate, and in doing so, life's paradoxes are proclaimed, contemplated, and dramatized. The struggle between nature and culture is evidenced in Bali, where before a young man or woman may marry, he or she undergoes a tooth-filing ceremony, in which the canine tooth, the mark of the beast, is smoothed so that the smile is less reminiscent of an animal's snarl. The theme of disruption and continuity is enacted in certain African societies, where, as Victor Turner has described, an initiate undergoing male puberty ceremonies ingests a powder ground from the burned foreskins of previous initiates, thereby incorporating into his body the vitality and power of his forebears. And James Fernandez has called attention to the interdependence of the individual and the collectivity in "Reflections on Looking into Mirrors" (*Semiotica,* 1980) by describing an initiation ceremony in which a neophyte stares into a looking glass until the face of an ancestor appears and merges with his own.

In the extreme expression of the interdependence between the individual and his or her social group, the initiate is construed as a microcosm of society, and what is enacted by or upon the individual is thought to transform the collectivity. Rites of transition performed for divine royalty—

birth, marriage, procreation, and death—are rites performed for the perpetuity of the kingdom as a whole, and in certain cultures a king has been killed annually in order to rejuvenate and ensure the fertility of the land. Moreover, certain rites of passage, such as healing rituals, may serve to resolve social problems and to perpetuate the social order directly as well as indirectly because they treat not only the sick or diseased person but also the entire society.

For all that societies use rites of passage to instill their values and configurations in the individual, they also take advantage of these ceremonies to foster the arousal of self-conscious questioning, for rites of passage are also times of what Victor Turner terms "reflexivity." Individuals (as well as the society itself) may be moved to the edge of profound self-investigation and exploration: social categories are played with, inverted, suspended; social borders are liquidated, crossed, blurred; identity symbols are stripped away and affixed anew. Such play is facilitated through the use of mirrors, masks, costumes, and other kinds of novelty. Free reign of reflexive awareness is permitted, even expedited—but only within the formal constraints of the ritual itself.

Paradox, then, lies at the heart of rites of passage. The paradoxes and conflicts in people's lives as humans may produce great anxiety because they defy their desire to live in a logically consistent and comprehensible world. Ritual exposes these paradoxes and accentuates them; tension is heightened and resolution is eagerly sought. But precisely because these paradoxes are cognitively or logically irresolvable, no actual resolution can be gained. But the familiar bounds and safety that ritual provides allow individuals to experience their truth, and thereby to discover the intractable parameters of their fate as humans. In this way, rites of passage not only accentuate anxiety but also alleviate it.

History of study. The structure of rites of passage was clearly articulated early on in the discipline of anthropology by Arnold van Gennep, who in 1907 discerned a fundamental tripartite form inherent in all rites of passage: separation, transition, and incorporation. Van Gennep noted that a person had to be separated from one role or status before he or she could be incorporated into a new one. He thus identified not only those phases of separation and incorporation but a transitional, or liminal, one as well. Consequently, for van Gennep ritual truly represented a process, and he thus stood apart from mainstream Victorian anthropology, which emphasized evolutionary phases and the tracking down of the origins of customs. In this way, van Gennep laid much of the groundwork for the modern interest in symbolic and ritual studies.

Building on van Gennep's work, Victor Turner has generated exceptionally rich and fruitful theories for the study of ritual processes; his works articulating the concept of liminality are especially generative and far-ranging. Through Turner's work, *liminality* has been extended far beyond its original sense of an intermediate or marginal ritual phase and has taken on new meaning as an autonomous and sometimes enduring category of people who are "betwixt and between." All manner of those who inhabit and cross the edges of social boundaries and codes—tricksters, clowns, poets, shamans, court jesters, monks, "dharma bums," and holy mendicants—represent liminal beings. Not only people but also social movements, such as millenarian cults, and social principles, such as matrilaterality in patrilineal systems, may be viewed as liminal. These ideas are developed in *The Ritual Process* (Chicago, 1969) and *Dramas, Fields, and Metaphors: Symbolic Action in Human Society* (Ithaca, N.Y., 1974).

What do these persons or principles have in common with neophytes in a liminal phase of ritual transition? The point is made in many ways: the symbols used for them are similar, emphasizing innocence, rebirth, vulnerability, fertility, change, emotion, paradox, disorder, anomaly, opposition, and the like. Such people, because they dwell on and between the borders of categories, as Mary Douglas affirms in *Purity and Danger* (London, 1966), are designated taboo or polluted simply because they are out of place. Like ritual neophytes they are neither here nor there, and like ritual neophytes they threaten one's orderly conceptualizations. Yet, because they are out of place, they are mysterious and powerful; and liminal beings or phases can also be, as Turner shows, the sources of renewal, innovation, and creativity.

The liminal phase also contains another universal and critical element. Turner observes that among the neophytes living outside the norms and fixed categories of the social system a feeling of solidarity and unity emerges, and this oneness, or *communitas,* also has a structure, although its purpose is antistructural. Equality, undifferentiated humanness, androgyny, and humility characterize this condition, and neophytes are symbolically represented as a kind of *tabula rasa,* pure, undetermined possibility—the converse of social structure, which emphasizes differentiation, hierarchy, and separation. Even historical periods may be liminal, transitional times, when the past has lost its grip and the future has not yet taken definite shape. At those times, the "subjunctive" mood of the culture prevails, and play, imagination, and paradox are encouraged, all as part of a self-conscious quest for the basic truths of the human condition.

Another structuralist interpretation of initiation rites is advanced by Mary Douglas in *Purity and Danger,* in which she seeks to explain the sex and role reversals so common to these ceremonies. Douglas sees them as a reflection of the usual social symmetry. That is, the impersonation of women by boys is a statement of symmetry that echoes a fundamental social structural principle in societies in which wife exchange between two groups must articulate the symmetry and equality between the two groups.

Mircea Eliade in *Rites and Symbols of Initiation* (New York, 1958) contends that the dynamics in rites of passage provide a means through which participants may achieve religious perfection. The concepts of male and female provide a fundamental structural complementarity in the usual social order, but complementarity also fosters envy between men and women. Each is fascinated with the special attributes of the other. Because rites of passage abound with sexual symbolism, particularly evident in cross-dressing and role-play reversal between the sexes, they allow the neophyte the chance to experience the usually repressed other half. Accordingly, the neophyte can then become the incarnation of totality, can then reach perfection, and can then transcend irreducible quotidian complementarity.

Some scholars hold that rites of passage function to underscore the social importance of the group or sex that is the focus of the celebration. This stance is illustrated by Alice Schlegel and Herbert Barry in "The Evolutionary Significance of Adolescent Initiation Ceremonies" (*American Ethnologist,* 1980), in which they show that puberty ceremonies for girls predominate in those societies where female participation in food production exceeds or is more important than male contribution. They also add an evolutionary scheme by contending that as societies grow more complex, gender as a classificatory principle recedes in importance, and fewer initiation ceremonies are found altogether. A further twist on the evolutionary scheme is put forth by Martha and Morton Fried in *Transitions: Four Rituals in Eight Cultures* (New York, 1980). The Frieds examine four critical transitions (birth, puberty, marriage, death) and find that they are not crucially linked to the success of social cohesion or of social operation. They also conclude that ritual may not be a critical element in the success of social groups, for they note that ritual seems to have appeared rather late on the human scene. The evidence available for this is the flower-strewn remains of Neanderthal humans, which date from only about 40,000 BCE.

Learning and experience through ritual. Whether or not rites of passage, or any ritual activity, is *necessary* to human existence is a debatable matter, yet rites of passage do provide for and fulfill at least one crucial task: that of inculcating a society's rules and values to those who are to become its full-fledged members. Because rites of passage occur at great moments of anxiety (life crises) and because they even provoke anxiety by vividly calling attention to irresolvable human paradoxes, they provide an atmosphere in which the neophyte is rendered most susceptible to learning. Initiates are almost always separated from society; their previous habits of acting, thinking, and feeling are stripped away. Thus cut off from their usual ways of apprehending the world—their routines and their customary ways of communicating—they are placed in a highly suggestible state for learning. But how does this learning take place? How does learning permeate the various levels of consciousness and unconsciousness so that the person is filled with motivation and desire to become what he or she must become in addition to absorbing knowledge?

One way the communication of society's arcane knowledge is achieved is through direct instruction. Sometimes secret names of deities or ancestors are revealed; sometimes the mythical history of the society is recounted in full; sometimes special incantations or creeds are taught. All of these do much to transmit the store of esoteric principles to the initiates, and they are often encouraged, if not forced, to reflect upon this knowledge.

Yet certainly this is not the only kind of teaching and learning that transpires during rites of passage. What is to be made of the masks and images that incorporate grotesque combinations and weird juxtapositions of animal and human parts; what of the bold body decorations or scarifications; what of the driving, incessant beat of the music that accompanies ritual? Symbolic experience—whether in drama, poetry, myth, the arts, or trance—holds forth its particular kind of information, eluding words but nonetheless significant and real. On other deeper, less verbal, less cognitive levels, people are moved to understand something of their lives and their places within the cosmos when they enact ritual. Because rites of passage are *performed*—that is, carried out physically and mentally—*experience*—affective and subjective as well as cognitive—may well represent the crux of ritual. Unfortunately, for the most part, anthropologists have failed to deal with the experiences of ritual participants—private, subjective, psychological, conscious, and unconscious—in their endeavors to explain ritual, and this represents an enormous barrier to an understanding of the subject.

There are notable exceptions to this truism, however. There are some who have pioneered an examination of emotion and learning in ritual. In the classic study *Religion: An Anthropological View* (New York, 1966), Anthony Wallace presents the concept of a "ritual learning process," which essentially works through what he calls the "law of dissociation." That is, because the neophyte has been placed in a stage in which he or she is radically dissociated from past knowledge before being presented with much new information, cognitive and affective restructuring is facilitated. Wallace outlines the various phases of this kind of learning: prelearning or anticipation; separation (through sensory deprivation, monotonous stimuli, extreme physical stress, and the like); suggestion (high suggestibility associated with trance or dissociation, sometimes thought of as conversion or possession); execution (achievement of a new cognitive structure); and maintenance (through repetition or reinforcement), occasionally involving a resynthesis.

Jerome Frank uses a similar paradigm in *Persuasion and Healing: A Comprehensive Study of Psychotherapy* (Baltimore, 1961). However, Wallace's and Frank's work do not seem to have been utilized, at least not systematically, in subsequent studies of ritual, and it is clear that a complete comprehension of the manner in which learning takes place in ritual calls for psychologically informed theories and hypotheses.

One that stands out is cognitive dissonance theory. Leon Festinger asserts in the seminal *A Theory of Cognitive Dissonance* (Evanston, Ill., 1957) that there is a direct relationship between the degree to which persons suffer for an experience and the value that they attach to the experience. The higher the psychological price paid, the more likely are subjects to pronounce it worthwhile. It is noteworthy that rites of passage, especially rites of puberty, may be acutely painful, involving as they often do tattooing, circumcision, scarification, cicatrization, and other forms of mutilation. Yet, the application of this theory has not been systematically applied to initiation rites.

Psychologists, for their part, have not availed themselves of the opportunity to test learning theories against the vast and rich ethnographic literature on rites of passage. True enough, there has been enormous interest generated for puberty rites among psychologists, but this attention has been limited generally to the use of psychoanalytical theory in explanation. Freudians, particularly, have focused on the dramatic aspects of puberty rites, seeing in them support for the ideas that Sigmund Freud advanced in *Totem und Tabu* (1913). In his "Oedipus theory" Freud proposed that the beginning of civilization occurred when an ancestral patriarch was slain by his jealous sons because of his monopolization of the females in the group. The patriarchs in turn punished their sons for their incestuous yearnings toward their mothers and for the sons' desire to overthrow the authority of their elders. In this view, puberty rites celebrate this moment in human history by recreating these episodes, especially through circumcision or other forms of genital mutilation.

The diverse and plentiful symbols of procreation and birth in adolescent initiation rites led Bruno Bettelheim to expound another interpretation of these rituals in *Symbolic Wounds* (New York, 1954). Noting that circumcision and subincision of the penis cause bleeding and that often puberty rites stipulate that boys must move through the legs of older men (symbolizing rebirth), Bettelheim concludes that male initiation ceremonies are thus forums for the expression of envy of the procreative powers of women. Circumcision is seen as imitative of menstruation, giving birth to new life, and extreme cases of subincision are viewed as making male genitals superficially similar to those of women. Envy and emulation are thus the key messages and purposes of male puberty rites.

Another psychological view holds that male initiation rites serve to expedite the resolution of Oedipal conflicts and to establish masculine identity. This perspective, represented in Frank Young's *Initiation Ceremonies: A Cross-cultural Study of Status Dramatization* (New York, 1965), further contends that in societies where the mother-son bond is particularly strong, elaborate and painful ceremonies are needed to vigorously and decisively break a male child's identification with his mother (and hence with other women) and to install him in the psychological and social company of his father's group.

Most psychological treatments of initiation ceremonies have investigated those of male puberty; discussions of female initiation rites are scarce. In *The Drums of Affliction* (London, 1968), Victor Turner describes the girls' initiation rites observed and analyzed by him and Edith Turner while among the Ndembu of Zambia. The rites express woman's ultimate structural dominance in a matrilineal system. The central symbol, a "milk" tree, with white sap, is not merely an emblem of womanhood, it also represents the value set on matriliny as the hub around which the whole society revolves. The rites oppose women to men as a sex before they reunite them with men as joint producers of children. The great aim of initiation is to convert a girl into a fruitful married woman. Other writings on girls' initiation have emphasized the bonding between females that occurs at these times; however, they describe rites whose main function is to communicate female inferiority and the suppression of female sexuality.

As has been made clear in the foregoing paragraphs, the literature on rites of passage is profuse and much research attention has been devoted to the subject. These rituals of transition and initiation have yielded forth many distinct lines of explanation: structural, functional, religious, symbolic, and psychoanalytical, each articulating an aspect of what these ceremonial activities *tell* the participants and onlookers. Many of these interpretations have gone a long way toward analyzing the multilayered meanings contained in rites of passage. Unfortunately, however, anthropologists and other scholars have paid disappointingly little heed to what these rites *do* to people. It is necessary to know how, in fact, culture is transmitted—not merely as a codified system of principles and messages, but as an intrinsic learning process, embracing experience so that, as Victor Turner puts it, one's duty becomes one's desire. Anthropology cannot possibly reach an understanding of the transmission of culture, of the maintenance of values, without expanding its conceptions of learning theory and symbolic processes, unconscious and conscious.

Modern, Industrial Society. In persuing the literature on rites of passage, one finds, in addition to scholarly interpretations, descriptions (and often photographs) of fantastic, elaborate masks, costumes, or other body decoration, and while these certainly may be intriguing, Westerners may be quite thankful that they do not have to endure tooth filing, circumcision, subincision, cicatrization, tattooing, and the like. Still, the impression one is frequently left with is that rites of passage are elaborate affairs occurring in small-scale societies in which every member of the community takes part. What meaning, if any, do rites of passage hold for the modern, industrial world? Have people lost sight of their need to move people clearly and safely from one life stage to another? Is the safety and assurance that ritual provides no longer possible, or even applicable for those in complex societies?

Early twenty-first century society may be characterized as fragmented, confusing, complex, and disorderly. People put a premium on their individuality; they pay dearly, though, for the individuality so cherished. The cost of freedom is often adjustment to life's transitions quite alone, and with private, not public, symbols. Contemporary society is so multifarious and diffuse that individuals must entrust their lives into the hands of experts and anonymous agencies or individuals who care for only a small part of their human needs. People are born, for the most part, in hospitals, and usually die there. Birth and death, the irreducible entrance and exit, become merely secular affairs, matters of the most profound emotional significance that are left publicly uncelebrated.

There may well be dire consequences for this lack of public ritual. Long ago, Émile Durkheim made evident in his classic work *Suicide* (1897) that the lack of social connection, the unacknowledged existence, and the feeling of anomie may be expressed by the individual in the form of suicide. More recently, Solon Kimball remarks in the introduction to a reprint of van Gennep's *Rites of Passage* (Chicago, 1960) that one result of the strain of undergoing individualistic ritual may be mental illness.

Some scholars argue that genuine rites of passage are not possible in modern societies because of the limited, specialized, or attenuated social relations experienced in them. For example, Max Gluckman asserts in *Essays on the Ritual of Social Relations* (Manchester, 1962) that rites of passage are "sacred" and thus can exist only in societies where the social is also religious, where social relations serve multiple purposes and are charged with moral valuations.

But ritual is not synonymous with religion, and it may well be that religion operates more through conscious cognitive faculties than does ritual. The differences are informative. One of ritual's distinguishing features is that it is *performed.* One must engage more than merely cognitive processes in order to *carry out* ritualistic activity, for ritual absorbs and employs all the senses, and indeed it probably involves different centers in the brain from those of cognition. As Mircea Eliade puts it so well, one may become what one performs; hence, critical thinking may not be so essential an element here as it may be in religious belief. Rituals also incorporate paradox and conflict; problems of codification and consistency, therefore, may not be so relevant as they are in religious belief. Rituals are indeed "transformative" experiences, as Victor Turner affirms; and as Sherry Ortner observes in *Sherpas through Their Rituals* (Cambridge, 1978), individuals approach ritual with a cultural problem, stated or unstated, and then work various operations upon it, arriving at "solutions"—reorganizations and reinterpretations of the elements that produce a newly meaningful whole. Achieving the appropriate shift in consciousness is the work of ritual.

It is important to note that rituals are *constructed*—fabricated, built, created—for that indicates that individuals may then be able to create and provide them for themselves if they are not already bestowed by society. Studies of crises in the adult life cycle in Western society (e.g., Roger Gould's *Transformation: Growth in Adult Life,* Louisville, Ky., 1978, and Gail Sheehy's *Passages: Predictable Crises of Adult Life,* New York, 1974) have highlighted the creation of various life phases and the various cultural and psychological problems that result from them. These works, however, have not considered the relation and importance of ritual to these junctures in individual lives.

People in modern Western society indeed experience numerous forms of crises and transitions: menopause, surgery, "empty nests," divorce, retirement. They are traumatic and anxiety-provoking, and yet they regularly occur uncelebrated. People do make attempts to enact rituals at several crossroads in their lives, although they usually do so alone and secluded. Burning an unfaithful lover's photograph, returning gifts from one no longer cherished, changing a hairstyle, and cleaning house are all ways to announce that one phase of life has ended and a new one is beginning.

Dwellers in Western society do not live in the same kind of world as do those in tribal or traditional societies, yet they surely experience the same anxiety and uncertainty at life's crisis points. And they surely share the same conceptual quandaries about life: that they are natural yet cultural beings; that their lives are marked both by disruption and by continuity; and that humans are individual yet collective. These are the fundamental paradoxes that everyone everywhere experiences, and that rites of passage announce, instruct, and help individuals to transcend.

See Also Birth; Funeral Rites; Initiation; Marriage; Ordination; Sacrament, overview article.

Bibliography

Eliade, Mircea. *Rites and Symbols of Initiation: The Mysteries of Birth and Rebirth.* New York, 1958. A classic work on initiation in its religious aspect. Eliade deals with the transcendence of sexual opposition in initiation.

Gennep, Arnold van. *Les rites de passage.* Paris, 1909. Translated by Monika B. Vizedom and Gabrielle L. Caffee as *The Rites of Passage* (Chicago, 1960). The essential handbook on rites of passage. Van Gennep, the pioneer in this study, laid out the three stages: separation, the transitional or liminal stage, and reincorporation.

Gluckman, Max. "Les Rites de Passage." In *Essays on the Ritual of Social Relations,* edited by Max Gluckman, pp. 1–52. Manchester, 1962. A useful commentary on van Gennep's *Les rites de passage.* Gluckman, a social anthropologist, discusses the social roles and processes involved in such rites.

Mahdi, Louise, Steven Foster, and Meredith Little, eds. *Betwixt and Between: Patterns of Masculine and Feminine Initiation.* La Salle, Ill., 1987. Studies of human ritual from childhood to death at the times of threshold, liminality, and change.

Mahdi, Louise, Nancy Christopher, and Michael Meade, eds. *Crossroads: The Quest for Contemporary Rites of Passage.* Chicago, 1996. Studies of the practice of rites of passage for young people in the modern era.

Mead, Margaret. *Coming of Age in Samoa.* New York, 1928. The controversial study of the life of girls in a Polynesian culture.

Turner, Victor. "Mukanda: The Rite of Circumcision." In his *The Forest of Symbols: Aspects of Ndembu Ritual,* chap. 7. Ithaca, N.Y., 1967. A detailed account and anthropological analysis of boys' initiation among the Ndembu.

Turner, Victor. "Nkang'a." In his *The Drums of Affliction: A Study of Religious Processes among the Ndembu of Zambia,* chaps. 7 and 8. London, 1968. A detailed account and anthropological analysis of girls' initiation among the Ndembu.

Turner, Victor. *The Ritual Process: Structure and Anti-Structure.* Chicago, 1969. Turner goes beyond van Gennep in exploring the liminal domain found in rites of passage, where that domain exists in a number of different cultures and periods of history.

BARBARA G. MYERHOFF (1987)
LINDA A. CAMINO (1987)
EDITH TURNER (1987 AND 2005)

RITES OF PASSAGE: AN OVERVIEW [FURTHER CONSIDERATIONS]

The publication of Mircea Eliade's *Rites and Symbols of Initiation* in 1958, the appearance in 1960 of an English translation of Arnold van Gennep's *Les rites de passage,* and Victor Turner's influential and widely read *The Ritual Process: Structure and Anti-Structure,* published in 1969, are the three pillars on which classical rites of passage theory was constructed. The generation of scholars following these three men has done the work of developing, adding to, applying, and critiquing their contributions. The work of Eliade, van Gennep, and Turner informed a surge of popular interest in North America and Europe—beginning in earnest in the 1980s—in passage rites. Their thinking on rites of passage has been disseminated to a wide audience through secondary texts, programs, institutes, and weekend workshops, and has helped cultivate an ethos of ritual experimentation around the "canonical" big four: rites of birth, initiation, weddings, and funerals, as well as a host of other events in the life cycles of men and women in the modern West: divorce, graduation, serious illness, abortion, leaving home, mid-life, retirement, same-sex marriage, and menopause.

In the 1980s, as cultural theory, analysis, and criticism became dominant in the academy, theorizing rites of passage gave way to the critical analysis of both ritual theory and ritual practice. The new direction was marked by Ronald Grimes's 1990 work *Ritual Criticism,* which called for a hard-nosed examination of the political and normative nature of rites and ritual theory, but also, following Victor Turner, called for awareness of the critical dimensions of ritual—ritual itself as a way of doing criticism, encouraging reflexivity, and creatively responding to social and individual needs and concerns. One outcome of cultural theory has been to validate the study of popular culture and spirituality; in two subsequent works, Grimes applied his notion of "ritual criticism" to the rising phenomenon of ritualizing passage rites and the appeal to classical rites of passage theorists for justification. Criticism of theory and criticism of practice coalesced, since so much of the creative ritualizing was being driven by a dominant theoretical paradigm derived from a fusion of van Gennep's, Eliade's, and Turner's work.

INITIATION AS PARADIGM. One limitation of classical rites of passage theory is that it uses rites of initiation, and, moreover, male initiation, as the paradigm for all passage. Van Gennep's 1909 text is predominately concerned with initiation. The paradigmatic tripartite pattern, derived from ethnographic accounts of rites in indigenous cultures, is that of a group of boys separated from domestic space and their mothers, taken to a sequestered, liminal zone where they endure ordeals and trials that generate their transition to adulthood, and then are returned and incorporated into the village as full-fledged men. Eliade viewed such initiation rites as the fundamental means by which people become human and the cosmos made sacred, believing initiation to be a "metacultural" and "transhistorical" phenomenon. Turner used van Gennep's schema to study the internal dynamics of social change associated with rites that evoke liminality and *communitas,* and initiation rites (along with pilgrimage and festival) were the focus of his attention.

But whereas the male initiation rites of many cultures may be said to exhibit a three-phased structure, it is not clear that all passage rites do; actual descriptions of rites, as Grimes has shown in *Deeply Into the Bone,* reveal far more than simply three phases—detailed phenomenological descriptions of rites reveal the limits of abstract, universalized summaries, or models. Bruce Lincoln, in *Emerging From the Chrysalis,* a study of women's initiation rites in five cultures, does develop a three-phased model, but it is not the classic pattern of separation, transition, and incorporation that defines the rites he studied, but instead one of enclosure, metamorphosis, and emergence. Initiation, not to mention the diverse practices that are grouped under the phrase "rites of passage," is a complex phenomenon; van Gennep's tripartite schema has been shaped by male initiation rites, overextended in its application to other passage rites, and also bears traces of Hegelian dialectics and Trinitarian theology, implicitly drawing on a conceptual paradigm that has long influenced the Western intellectual tradition. In theorizing passage rites greater attention needs to be given to birth rites, weddings, and funerals and to female passage rites in general.

LIMINALITY. Essential to classical rites of passage theory is the notion of transformation. Society is composed of a set of recognized status positions, and the work of passage rites is to move individuals through these (often age-related) social positions by transforming them from one state to another, from adolescence to adulthood, from being single to being married. The emphasis on transformation in theory has meant an emphasis on liminality, since it is the liminal (or transitional) phase of a rite of passage that does the work of transforming the individual. For Turner, all authentic ritual is transformative, and therefore requires liminality. In Eliade's language, in passage rites one ritually "dies" to an old state, enters the womb of renewal and transformation, and returns to the world reborn and remade; implicitly, liminality is where the sacred is found, and is therefore more important than separation or incorporation. But such claims may be universalizing aspects of male initiation rites, male experience, and the role of ritual in effecting passage into social positions traditionally occupied by males.

In her study of women's experiences in the late Middle Ages, Carolyn Walker Bynum argues that women's stories and symbols, though often dramatic, do not entail the processual movement found in men's stories. Transformation requires movement to some social position or state of status, and whereas male biographers shaped women's lives into a narrative of "situation, rupture, resolution," women's dramas were in actuality, argues Bynum, fragmented and incomplete (p. 112). Women's stories were sources of liminality for men, but do not reflect liminal, transformative, status-changing processes in women's lives. Bruce Lincoln offers a similar critique of the gender bias inherent in the notion of liminality and the way it can misrepresent the trajectory of women's experience. Liminality may, as the authors of the previous entry write, situate one "betwixt and between" the edges of social boundaries and codes, "tricksters, clowns, poets, shamans, court jesters, monks, 'dharma bums,' and holy mendicants" may "represent liminal beings," but these vocations have been traditionally occupied by males (p. 382).The tendency to implicitly or explicitly equate liminality with the sacred and transformative power is to privilege male access to and control of the sacred. The description and classification of rites on the basis of a particular characteristic or function can serve to reinforce a particular theoretical orientation. Some passage rites may involve liminal processes but making liminality the heart of all passage rites is to closely associate them with rites of inversion, leading to a distended typology of rites, and implicitly grants greater moral and religious worth to rites emphasizing liminality and anti-structure, rather than status system and structure.

RITUALIZING. Eliade opened his classic 1958 text on initiation by framing the plight of "modern man" as that of living in a "desacralized cosmos," and linked this state to the "disappearance of meaningful rites of passage" (p. ix). Since Eliade, it is commonly claimed that in industrial, modern, secular society, passage rites have either disappeared entirely or are no longer effective, and a connection is typically made between a (supposed) pervasive spiritual and social anomie in Western culture and a lack of rites of passage to serve as markers to guide and move individuals through the various phases and crises of the life cycle. This assumption has generated a good deal of ritualizing, a term introduced by Grimes to distinguish formal and traditionally accepted rites from the practice of deliberately cultivating new rites.

It was van Gennep who first associated rites of passage with individual life crises, but this needs to be seen as a partly interpretive move; passage rites do not necessarily coincide with life crisis events, and to label any life crisis a "rite of passage," as is commonly done, is to so stretch the term that it threatens to become meaningless. There remains, however, a close conceptual and typological tie between life crisis and passage rites, a fact evidenced by the widespread study of ritual and ritualizing of passage rites in pastoral care, family therapy and social work, by child and youth care workers, drug addiction counselors, and hospice culture. Anxiety over potentially troublesome life stages and passage drives interest in ritual experimentation, but weddings, funerals and initiation are also driven by the forces of market capitalism, advertising, an ethos of spiritual questing and the promise of personal transformation or healing that has come to be closely associated with rites of passage in the West.

In Western cultures, the call for recovery of rites of passage has been strongly directed at initiation, and in particular male initiation. In the absence of passage rites it is not uncommon that major transitions or stages in the life cycle become ritualized; in the case of adolescent males, as Ray Raphael demonstrated in his 1988 work *From Men to Boys*, unsupervised, spontaneous, unconscious and often violent ritualized initiation practices commonly occur. Classical rites of passage theory has been a prominent source for ritualizing coming of age ceremonies for young men and women. The ritualized practices and theoretical framework in the popular and influential *Crossroads: The Quest for Contemporary Rites of Passage*, published in 1996, and *Betwxit and Between: Patterns of Masculine and Feminine Intitiation*, published in 1987, both edited by Louis Carus Mahdi, draw heavily on classical rites of passage theory, and are representative of the widespread ritualizing of passage in Eurocentric culture. But such practices are not without problems.

As Grimes notes in *Deeply into the Bone*, much contemporary ritualizing has cobbled together the work of van Gennep, Eliade, and Turner with the archetypal psychology of Carl Gustav Jung and Joseph Campbell's narrative of the hero's journey with the result that "*invented* patterns, treated as if they were *discovered*, came to be *prescribed* as if they were laws determining how rites should be structured" (1990, p. 107). Many self-constructed rites thereby unwittingly incorporate the gender (male) and cultural (Christian and Western) biases that have been shown to exist in this body of theory. When the ritual imagination becomes trapped in producing rites derived from uncritical acceptance and application of theory, ritual cannot perform the self-reflexive, critical and socially constructive work that Victor Turner ascribes to it.

Second, invented initiation rites rely on a good deal of ritual borrowing. The assumption that the ritual practices of "traditional" societies are fecund tools for the revitalization of modern, industrial society idealizes those practices and creates a hunger for them, encouraging ritual appropriation. Many North Americans of European descent have turned to Native religion for their spiritual goods: sweat lodges, vision quests, sacred pipes, rattles, and spirit catchers make up the bill of fare of many workshops and retreats. Steven Foster and Meredith Little, cofounders of the School of Lost Borders and Rites of Passage Inc., are among those to have developed initiation practices based on vision questing or *Hanblecheyapi*, a traditional coming-of-age rite in Plains culture. But for many Native people, non-Native fascination with Native religious, symbolic, and ritual systems represents the ongoing colonization of Native North Americans. The appropriation debate first focused on issues of land claims and the return of artifacts and human remains, but has widened to include ritual practices.

A third problem with invented male initiation rites is that they potentially reinforce a heroic, individualistic style of masculinity. Ray Raphael argues that the use of the vision quest model for initiation practice in Eurocentric culture is an isolationist model, a "perfect model for a rite of passage in an individualistic culture"; it represents "the privatization of our initiations [and] fails to provide any structural support to help us with our personal struggles, and so it does little to help ensure success in our difficult time of transition" (1988, p. 198). The connections in North American culture between spiritual questing, heroic individualism, and colonial expansion need further study.

POWER, PARADOX, AND DOUBLE BINDS. Classical rites of passage theory draws attention to the interplay of biology and culture. With the rise of cultural theory, attention turned to the dynamic and often contentious process by which meaning and power are produced, maintained, and negotiated, and work on passage rites during the 1990s gave considerable attention to the intersection of the human body and structures of power. Elaine Combs-Schilling, in her study of Moroccan marriage rites, and Robbie Davis-Floyd, in her analysis of the ritualization of hospital birth, argue that societies use life cycle passages to literally inscribe their most fundamental values and assumptions into the body. Passage rites involve more than a struggle between nature and culture that proclaims fundamental paradoxes of human being—they may be highly politicized sites through which power is wielded and maintained. "Culture," writes Combs-Schilling, "can make its elaborations appear true by embedding them within the body's most biological truths. The physical groundings—sexual intercourse, bloodspilling and birth—independently and panhumanly exist, while the cultural elaborations do not (they are culture-specific). Once fused, they are hard to pull apart" (1991, p. 678). Combs-Schilling suggests that by timing rites of passage with periods in the life cycle in which the body is potentially weakened or exposed, those rites can embed social values and power structure deep into the body. She offers an analysis of the Moroccan rite of *hinna'* associated with marriage practices and conjugal intercourse in terms of its power to "etch" both male and female bodies with patriarchal values and subservience to monarchical rule. Similarly, Davis-Floyd treats the medical procedures of Western hospital birth as ritual, arguing that the extreme openness of women during birth is the prime occasion for Western society to imprint fundamental values on the bodies and minds of its members; these values are principally those of technocracy, efficiency, and distrust of instincts and the body.

Ronald Grimes and Eric Schieffelin have considerably advanced understanding of ritual action through the notion of "ritual failure." Rites may not always work, they may be exploitive, and they may not always do what practitioners or even ritual theorists say they do. Passage rites may be imbued with the deep paradox of having one foot planted in nature and the other in culture, yet they may fail to unify these two domains. A rite may be deeply disjunctive, detached from its physiological roots, out of time with bodily rhythms; when they are, they can place ritual participants in severe double binds. Grimes offers several examples of ritual failure and disjunction between ritual, biological, and cultural scenarios in his *Deeply into the Bone*. Passage rites may aim to weave together body and culture, but the result can be far from seamless.

SEE ALSO Initiation, overview article and articles on Men's Initiation and Women's Initiation; Liminality; Ritual.

BIBLIOGRAPHY

Bynum, Caroline Walker. "Women's Stories, Women's Symbols: A Critique of Victor Turner's Theory of Liminality." In *Anthropology and the Study of Religion*, edited by Robert L. Moore and Frank E. Reynolds, pp. 105–125. Chicago, 1984. Turner's theory of liminality has had widespread influence. Bynum argues that it is implicitly a male model that fails to understand or take into account women's experience.

Combs-Schilling, Elaine. "Etching Patriarchal Rule: Ritual Dye, Erotic Potency, and the Moroccan Monarchy." *Journal of the History of Sexuality* 1, no. 4 (1991): 658–681. A study of how wedding rites are implicated in the maintenance of patriarchal values and rule in Morocco.

Davis-Floyd, Robbie. *Birth as an American Rite of Passage*. Berkeley, 1992. Davis-Floyd takes critical aim at the interplay of biology and culture in her treatment of hospital birth as a rite of passage.

Foster, Steven and Meredith Little. "The Vision Quest: Passing from Childhood to Adulthood." In *Betwixt and Between: Patterns of Masculine and Feminine Initiation*, edited by Louise Carus Mahdi et al., pp. 79–110. La Salle, Ill., 1987. An account of efforts to create initiation rites based on the model of the vision quest.

Grimes, Ronald L. *Ritual Criticism: Case Studies in Its Practice, Essays on Its Theory*. Columbia, S.C., 1990. The first and final chapters develop a theory of ritual criticism that can be readily applied to the study of rites of passage.

Grimes, Ronald L. *Marrying and Burying: Rites of Passage in a Man's Life*. Boulder, Colo., 1995. In this autobiographical work, Grimes uses his own experience of life passages and his work as a scholar of religion and ritual to critically reflect on the place and practice of rites of passage in contemporary North America.

Grimes, Ronald L. *Deeply into the Bone: Reinventing Rites of Passage*. Berkeley, Calif., 2000. This work integrates detailed narrative accounts with critical questioning and theoretical reflection on such topics as the invention of passage rites, the practice of ritual borrowing, the marketing and consumption of rites of passage. Includes a comprehensive bibliography.

Hill, Paul, Jr. *The Journey (Adolescent Rites of Passage): Organizational Manual*. Cleveland, 1998. This volume, produced by the National Rites of Passage Institute, is representative of the effort in African American communities to use passage rites with social and urban issues, cultural solidarity and celebration, and the formation of identity.

Holm, Jean, and John Bowker, eds. *Rites of Passage.* New York, 1994. A survey work of the rites of passage in Judaism, Christianity, Islam, Buddhism and Hinduism.

Jocks, Christopher Ronwaniènte. "Spirituality for Sale." *American Indian Quarterly* 20, no. 3 (1996): 415–432. A stinging critique of non-Native use and selling of Native spirituality, including Native ceremonies and rites.

Klassen, Pamela. *Blessed Events: Religion and Home Birth in America.* Princeton, 2001. Utilizing a narrative approach, Klassen explores the religious and ritualized dimensions of home birth. The book is a welcome compliment to sociological based studies.

LaFleur, William. *Liquid Life: Abortion and Buddhism in Japan.* Princeton, 1992. One of LaFleur's aims is to understand how it is that abortion debates in Japan have not reached the same level of divisiveness in North America, and he suggests that the development of abortion rites serve to contain, meditate and resolve personal and social tensions and anxieties around the act of abortion.

Lincoln, Bruce. *Emerging from the Chrysalis: Studies in Rituals of Women's Initiation.* Cambridge, U.K., 1991. An expanded edition of the original study first published in 1981, dealing with women's initiation practices in five cultures. The book explores the social construction of gender, the role of ritual in society and the politics of ritual.

Mahdi, Louis Carus, et al. *Crossroads: The Quest for Contemporary Rites of Passage.* Chicago, 1996. This collection of essays focuses on the creation of passage rites to avert what is described as a "youth crisis" in contemporary, Western culture. It is an influential example of the kinds of ritualizing being done with adolescents, and the theoretical frameworks and assumptions informing the practice.

Raphael, Ray. *The Men from the Boys: Rites of Passage in Male America.* Lincoln, Neb., 1988. A plethora of books emerged in the 1990s dealing with male initiation. Raphael's work was one of the first of the genre.

Stephenson, Barry. "Ritual Criticism of a Contemporary Rite of Passage." *Journal of Ritual Studies* 17, no. 1 (2003): 32–41. A critique of the "vision quest" initiation rite designed by Steven Foster and Meredith Little.

BARRY STEPHENSON (2005)

RITES OF PASSAGE: AFRICAN RITES

Rituals in Africa, just as in other parts of the world, utilize symbols to express and convey meanings, verbally and nonverbally. In traditional African societies, a firm stress is placed on the performance of rituals as customary, standardized, and symbolic social communication that is repeatable according to fixed patterns. All African societies have different age-linked rituals, and mark the passage from one to another, but not all have the same rituals, either in number or in kind. The following are typical: (1) prenatal rituals (e.g., rituals to confirm pregnancy, for fetal growth, and for safe delivery); (2) naming rituals; (3) pre-pubertal and pubertal initiation rituals for the entrance into adulthood; (4) betrothal and marriage; (5) initiation into prestige-bestowing adult associations; (6) rituals elevating individuals to high office or to priestly functions; and (7) funeral (Turner, 1985).

African rituals thus can be analyzed helpfully under the category "life cycle rituals," or what have been called "rites of passage" since the publication of the book of the same title in 1908 by Arnold van Gennep and expanded later by the British anthropologist Victor Turner. Van Gennep identified three phases in such rituals: rites of separation, which provide a socially accepted way to move away from a prior status; rites of transition, which safeguard participants during the dangerous liminal, or "in-between," period; and rites of incorporation, which ensure that the participants have been reinstated properly into society and legitimated by the community in their new roles. Turner argued that the entire ritual process, from separation through transition to incorporation, can be understood as liminal because each phase occurs in a time between times and in a space that is set apart from other places.

Because Africa consists of vast regions and multiple traditional societies, examples of selected groups from different parts of the continent illustrate the way various rites of passage are understood and practiced.

NDEBELE BIRTH RITUAL. A typical birth ritual among the Ndebele-speaking people of Zimbabwe begins with the woman leaving her husband during her ninth month of pregnancy to go to her own parents' home. This constitutes the separation phase, which involves women preparing the room by polishing the floor with cow dung. After the room is cleaned thoroughly, no one is allowed into it until the mother is nearing the time for the delivery. When the time approaches for the birth, the liminal phase of the ritual begins. The pregnant woman is accompanied into the room by her mother and grandmother and any other women assisting in the childbirth. It is forbidden for any man to enter the room when a woman is giving birth, even her own husband. Before touching the pregnant woman, the woman acting as midwife, usually the grandmother, washes her hands in water that contains herbs prescribed by a traditional healer. When the baby comes out of the mother's womb, the midwife is the first to touch the baby by cleaning the blood off with the medicated water. The umbilical cord of the baby is then cut, but some of it is left hanging to its navel and tied with a string. The midwife then washes the baby again in the medicated water. While the baby is sleeping, but before the baby is allowed to feed from its mother, a fire is prepared in the room. Specially selected herbs are put onto the fire, which is allowed to reduce to burning coals. The baby is then awakened and its head placed in the smoke from the fire containing the herbs. The baby may be held over the fire for over an hour before being allowed to suck from the mother. The next day, the same process of putting the baby in the smoke from the medicated fire is repeated, and is continued until the umbilical cord falls off, which may take up to a week. After the umbilical cord falls off, the liminal phase ends when the baby is recognized as a person and given a name. As a sign that the mother and baby have been incorporated into the community, people outside the room are called in to celebrate the birth by bringing gifts; only after this is the father of the baby allowed to see his child. To complete the ritual, the father is given the piece of umbilical cord, which he takes to a place near the homestead and buries, offering thanks to the ancestors and asking them to protect the new baby. After these events, the father, mother, and baby return to the father's home, fully reincorporated into society in their new status as parents with a child (Cox, 1998).

Agikuyu Initiation Rites. The Agikuyu of Kenya are organized around the age-set system (*marika*), and thus male and female initiation rites (*irua*) play a central social role. These involve prolonged and intensive puberty rituals that culminate with male and female circumcision. Although boys and girls are taken to separate locations for the rituals, those circumcised at the same time are considered age-mates, and those circumcised during the same season are regarded as age-sets. The process of separation begins with the slaughtering of a goat that is eaten while members of the extended family, under the direction of the chief elder, consider if any of them might have broken any social rules that would result in harm coming to the initiates during the rite of passage to adulthood. If some breach of the social code is discovered, the initiates are not allowed to take part in the ritual until a purification ritual is performed for the family. If no rules have been broken, the next stage of preparation takes place with the slaughtering of another goat, which is dedicated to the ancestors. Those to be initiated then leave their own families to go other, "adopted" families for the actual ritual. This signals that they are separating from their biological families and becoming part of the larger Agikuyu community. The initiates sing and dance all night at the homesteads of their adopted families. The following morning, ceremonial elders anoint them with a white soil that is considered to be sacred. Further rituals then occur, including more dancing and singing, competitive games between initiates, and additional purification ceremonies. When the actual circumcisions are performed, each initiate receives a sponsor, experienced women for the girls and senior men for the boys, who in the former cases nurse the wounds caused by the cutting of the genitalia. After the circumcisions are completed, both boys and girls remain in seclusion until their wounds heal, during which time they are instructed fully by their sponsors in the social and moral norms of Agikuyu society, including sex education. They then return from the period of seclusion to be recognized by members of the community as "emerging" adults. They are allowed to remain still in a kind liminal phase for a few weeks, as if on a holiday, with no responsibilities. Finally, they are incorporated into the community as adults through a ritual called *menjo*, which involves shaving their heads, symbolizing that they have been transformed into different people during the rituals; they were separated from their biological families as children and have returned, reborn as it were, as adults (Hinga, 1998).

Marriage in Tswana Culture. In most African societies, kinship relations are closely connected to economic security that is ensured through childbearing. Because marriage rituals solidify alliances between kinship groups, they formalize the material conditions on which the alliances have been forged and on which the continuation of the lineage depends. Within traditional Tswana society in Botswana, for example, the separation phase in a marriage ritual is marked by an agreement between the families of the boy and the girl that a formal kinship alliance will be made. This can occur even when the boy and girl are children, or in some cases, even before they are born. The next stage of separating a woman from her own family involves a payment (*bogadi*—sometimes translated as "bride price") from the husband's family to the wife's family (Amanze, 1998). Although today compensation is often made in cash, typically the bride price is satisfied by offering cattle to the girl's family, usually between four and ten head, with the number decided entirely by the boy's family. Once the payment is made, the girl is regarded as entering into a liminal phase that transfers her labor and her childbearing properties to her husband's family. In some parts of Tswana society, particularly in sections where longstanding traditional patterns persist, this stage is extended by the boy cohabiting with the girl at her parents' home for up to a year, during which time the girl might become pregnant as a sign that she is fertile. If for any reason she is not able to bear children, the contract between the families can be abrogated. In this sense, the liminal phase becomes potentially dangerous, because the couple have not yet been incorporated into society, which only occurs when the couple returns to set up a household at the boy's parental home. Although this system of marriage is based on strictly defined kinship relations that in some senses are quite specific to Tswana culture and to subgroups within it, from the point of view of ritual activity, it conforms to the general pattern throughout Africa that marriage never occurs between two people, but is based on a contractual agreement between two extended families (Schapera, 1950).

Sacred Kingship amongst the Edo. Although initiation into sacred kingship amongst the Edo (Benin) people of Nigeria begins with a series of funeral rituals for the deceased king, it is best classified as a rite of passage into a high office. The death rituals for the king of Benin (*oba*) correspond to the annual cycles of nature because he is believed to represent in his person a variety of nature spirits that are essential for ensuring the well-being of the people. For this reason, he is regarded as qualitatively different from other humans, and becomes an object of worship in himself. He is thought not to eat or drink as other humans do. Elaborate measures are taken to safeguard him against becoming sick, but if he does fall ill, no direct references are made to this among the people. Rather, the *oba* is said to be sleeping, as expressed in the proverb, "the leopard is resting." Because the *oba* symbolizes the whole of the Edo people in his person, when he dies, his eldest son (the crown prince, or *edaiken*) acts out on behalf of the whole nation quasi-historical legends that relate great deeds performed by the royal ancestors. This dramatization is reinforced graphically and concretely by effigies of past *obas* that have been cast in bronze and placed on ancestral altars around the palace compound. After the burial of his father, the *edaiken* begins a year-long process of separating from his role as a prince, enters the liminal stage, and finally is incorporated into Edo society in his new role as the divine earthly ruler, the *oba* of Benin. During the hazardous liminal phase, the *edaiken's* life cycles are reinacted ritually by recounting first his passage from childhood to youth, then his period as a novice-in-training learning princely responsibilities, and finally his rise to full maturity as the *oba*. The ceremonies are concluded when the crown prince is installed as the *oba*, one who in the eyes of the people has been transformed from being a human to one who is sacred (Kaplan, 2000).

LIMBA FUNERAL RITUALS. Amongst the Limba of Sierra Leone, the belief in the ability of ancestor spirits to affect the living is demonstrated by the care with which funerary rituals are performed. Burial ceremonies are thought to be the first steps in the transformation of the deceased into an ancestor. In the separation phase, the corpse must be cleaned, wrapped, and prepared ritually for burial, only after which can the social roles that have been left vacant by the deceased be filled and the property distributed to the next of kin. From the time of the burial until a ritual called *aboreh* is performed, a period of between forty days and one year elapses, during which time the spirit of the deceased is in a state of liminality, neither in the world of the living nor in the company of the family ancestors. The *aboreh* ritual, which lasts for one week, must be conducted to effect a transition that removes the spirit of the deceased from a condition of roaming about the bush dangerously to one who assumes ancestral duties, such as protecting the family from misfortune, illness, and witchcraft attacks. If the deceased had been a member of a secret society (*Gbangbani* for men; *Bondo* for women), during the first few days of the *aboreh* ritual, members of the secret society perform special rites which nonmembers are prohibited from attending. When the ritual becomes public later in the week, the whole community is involved. Of particular importance in the public ritual are singers who praise the ancestors of the deceased, rehearse the names and deeds of the ancestors, and appeal for the ancestors to accept the one who has died as one of them. On the last day of the ritual, at dawn, a white fowl is carried to the grave of the deceased by some of the elders. Rice is placed on the grave while the chief elder, who holds the fowl in his hand, praises the ancestors and implores them once again to receive the deceased among them. When the elder completes his speech, the fowl jumps from his hand and eats the rice on the grave to indicate that the spirit of the deceased has now been accepted as an ancestor. The fowl is then killed and its blood poured on the grave. After the sacrifice is completed, a stone known as *betiyeh* is taken from the grave of the deceased and kept in a special container at the homestead, symbolizing that the deceased has now become an ancestor and can protect the family from misfortune (John, 1999).

CONCLUSION. Additional cases could have been multiplied both in types of rituals and from different societies to illustrate the many ways rites of passage are practiced and understood in Africa. Nevertheless, these instances, which follow closely the transitional stages outlined by van Gennep and Turner, demonstrate that for practitioners of African indigenous religions, life crises are overcome successfully by performing ritual acts precisely and meticulously. In this way, African societies make sense of major social transitions and, at the same time, ensure that traditional authority is maintained.

SEE ALSO Liminality.

BIBLIOGRAPHY

Amanze, James N. *African Christianity in Botswana.* Gweru, Zimbabwe, 1998. Focuses on African Independent Churches, but begins with a helpful description of traditional Tswana religion.

Cox, James L. *Rational Ancestors. Scientific Rationality and African Indigenous Religions.* Cardiff, Wales, 1998. Contains numerous descriptions of Ndebele and Shona calendrical, life-cycle, and crisis rituals.

Hinga, Teresia M. "Christianity and Female Puberty Rites in Africa: The Agikuyu Case." In *Rites of Passage in Contemporary Africa,* edited by James L. Cox, pp. 168–179. Cardiff, U.K., 1998. Included among several articles analyzing the changing nature of African rites of passage, particularly under the influence of Christianity.

John, Irene. "The Changing Face of *Kabudu*: An Examination of Community and Community Relationships in Sierra Leone since 1960, with Specific Reference to the Rise of the Evangelical Christian Groups in Freetown." Unpublished Ph.D. thesis, University of Edinburgh, 1999. Contains recent fieldwork material from members of the Limba people who fled to Freetown to escape war in rural areas.

Kaplan, Flora Edouwaye S. "Some Thoughts on Ideology, Beliefs, and Sacred Kingship among the Edo (Benin) People of Nigeria." In *African Spirituality. Forms, Meanings, and Expressions,* edited by Jacob K. Olupona, pp. 114–153. New York, 2000. A thorough outline of field-based studies of sacred kingship within the Kingdom of Benin (Nigeria).

Schapera, I. "Kinship and Marriage Among the Tswana." In *African Systems of Kinship and Marriage,* edited by A.R. Radcliffe-Brown and Daryll Forde, pp. 140–165. Oxford, U.K., 1950. A dated, but detailed anthropological study of kinship and marriage among the Tswana as it was practiced during the first half of the twentieth century.

Turner, Victor W. "Liminality, Kabbalah, and the Media." *Religion* 15 (1985): 205–217. One of Turner's last contributions to his theory of liminality.

Van Gennep, Arnold. *Rites of Passage.* Chicago, 1960 [1909].

JAMES L. COX (2005)

RITES OF PASSAGE: OCEANIC RITES

Arnold van Gennep published the classic French text *Rites de passage* in 1908. Basing his study on ethnological reports, including some from Australia and parts of Melanesia and Polynesia, he noted how people change their social status throughout their lives. The break between these social spaces is like a pivot upon which one's life trajectory alters direction. These pivots, or liminal periods, are critical moments, and ritual is the principal means of safely navigating through to the next stage.

One may question whether van Gennep's theory tends to impose a threefold pattern of separation, transition and incorporation onto complex rites. Nevertheless, Oceanic cultures generally accept that people are "made," not born; that is, they are formed by social recognition as much as biological gestation. Rites of passage, common throughout Oceania, accompany transitions in people's lives: childless people into parents, children into adults, living people into ancestors.

BIRTH AND PARENTHOOD. Most Oceanic cultures have traditionally provided ways of recognizing parenthood and acknowledging the presence of new life in the community. In Aotearoa, New Zealand, the Maori would perform a *tohi* rite in which a newborn child was dedicated to a particular god while immersing it in water or sprinkling it with water from a branch dipped in a stream or the sea. Severing of the umbilical cord at this time was symbolic of separating the child from the world of darkness and its incorporation into the world of light. The umbilical cord was buried with stones placed on top—one for every night the mother had experienced the trials of childbirth. The rite was usually performed only for male children, though in a few cases a first-born female might be honored in this way.

Throughout Oceania, naming ceremonies might occur months or even years after the birth of the child. In the past, infant mortality was so high that it wasn't until after a year had passed that the family could be reasonably confident that the child was out of danger. In Tahiti, the infant was known as "milk eater" until the time it began to crawl, after which it was referred to as a child and addressed by its given name.

Birth order can affect ritual. Gilbert Herdt describes how, for the Sambia people of Papua New Guinea, the birth of a first child is elaborately celebrated. The next birth, however, is observed in a more truncated fashion, and birth ceremonies are suspended after the fourth child. Rites welcoming new life also serve to recognize parents in their new status in the community. Once parenthood is established there is less need to acknowledge it further.

In modern times in Palau, in Micronesia, particularly if a woman is a mother for the first time, she goes into seclusion and spends time in an enclosure to be bathed with hot water steeped with aromatic herbs. This procedure, called *omesurech,* is meant to cleanse her and to promote healing. However it is also a rite of social recognition. The number of days of bathing and steaming depends on the social rank of the woman. After the proper number of days has elapsed, the new mother is decorated and emerges from the steam chamber. Later, in a more private setting, kin exchange gifts. These gifts used to be beads and crescent-shaped objects that women wore as neck ornaments; nowadays, U.S. dollars are given.

In rites such as these, Oceanic cultures acknowledge biological events in social ways, leading to the recognition of personhood and identity, and ultimately to what it means to be human.

TRANSITION TO ADULTHOOD. Initiation rites received special treatment in van Gennep's *Rites de Passage.* However, there has been much discussion in academic circles as to what constitutes initiation rites, and whether, or in what ways, they differ from puberty rites. Is the circumcision of a seven-year-old boy a late birth rite or an early initiation rite? Is the seclusion of a girl when she experiences her first menstruation a puberty rite that is essentially different from the group initiation rites of her brothers? With only the gradual appearance of male features such as facial hair, becoming a "man" can be a long and complex process.

Biology is not the sole marker of social identity. Culture intervenes in ritual forms, and often there may be a series of initiation rites spanning many years, all contributing to the achievement of full adulthood. In *The Voice of the Tambaran,* Donald Tuzin gives an account of the Arapesh *tambaran* cult in Papua New Guinea, describing how the Arapesh male goes through five grades of the cult, from the naiveties of early childhood to the wisdom and authority of old age.

Initiation rites in Oceania include combinations of various elements: being instructed by mentors; acquiring sacred, sexual, or cultural knowledge; displaying subservience; being acquainted with sacred objects; overcoming pain and fear; observing food, sexual, and other taboos; regressing to child-like states; preparing to assume new responsibilities; dreaming; receiving a new name; and body marking, such as genital operations, extracting a tooth, or receiving tattoos.

Female initiation is not practiced as widely as male initiation and where it does occur, it is usually associated with a girl's first menstruation. In the Sepik region of Papua New Guinea, after a time of special dietary restrictions and instruction in the ways of women, a girl is ceremonially bathed, as if after birth, and then reintroduced to the community amid much celebration. In some societies, full initiation into womanhood is complete only after the birth of her first child.

Tattooing. In much of the Pacific, receiving a tattoo was once both a spiritual process and a cultural requirement for those wishing to hold various positions within society. Tattooing does more than alter the appearance of the body: it transforms the wearers' sense of self. For men in Samoa, the traditional tattoo, called *pe'a,* runs from just above the waist to just below the knees. In the past, most boys would begin the tattoo process between the ages of fourteen and eighteen. Completion of the *pe'a* signaled the boy's transition to manhood. Today the *pe'a* is performed on fewer men as they reevaluate the pain, cost, and social worth of wearing one.

The traditional tattoo of Samoan women, called *malu,* was performed on young women somewhere between the ages of fourteen and twenty-five. The *malu* is placed primarily on the thighs and knees, but it can also be found on the lower abdomen, wrists, and hands. *Malu* means "to protect," and while women's tattoos may have had protective significance in the past, in contemporary culture they are discussed in terms of family status and cultural commitment.

As a display of cultural pride, many Polynesians, both male and female, now wear forms of tattoo that draw upon both traditional Polynesian and contemporary Western motifs. Modern-day tattoos may differ from traditional tattoos in placement and design. One sees tattoos on wrists, arms, and lower legs, and some modern armbands are called *Tatau Pisikoa* (Peace Corps tattoos). Moreover, tattoos may now be on only one arm or leg, thus breaking with the bilateral body symmetry of traditional *tatau*. One even sees tattooed words, such at *Talofa* (greeting).

Genital operations. Operations on the penis are widely practiced in Oceania. Often they involve superincision, whereby the foreskin is cut at the top but not completely removed. In parts of Papua New Guinea, particularly among Austronesian speaking groups, superincision is still practiced. The ritual is documented in the film *Napalunga* (Katim Skin), by Bike Johnstone and Ignatius Talania.

Among the Kabana of the West New Britain district of Papua New Guinea, a boy is "superincised" while lying on top of his father's or mother's younger sister. The woman gets on her hands and knees and the boy lies on her back. The man chosen to cut the child inserts a small piece of bamboo under the foreskin, says a spell on the razor, spits a fine spray of ginger juice on the boy's penis to anesthetize it, and with a smooth stroke cuts the top of the foreskin. After the incision the boy's penis is wrapped in a leaf, and a burning ember is placed on the ground between his feet to heat the wound and facilitate the drying process.

Circumcision and allied genital operations have been interpreted in various ways: as a mark of subjection, a test of endurance, a hygienic precaution, a sanctification of procreation, a badge of incorporation into the tribal community, a symbolic castration by a dominating father figure, and an expression of male envy of women's menstruation. On Wogeo Island off the north coast of Papua New Guinea people actually refer to penile incision as men's menstruation.

Genital operations in themselves are often only part of a rite of passage. Robert Levy is of the opinion that for the Tahitians, "supercision" [sic] was part of becoming an adult but the operation was never conceived as the point of transition. Raymond Firth has noted how, on Tikopia in the Solomon Islands, the "kindling of the ovens" of youth involving superincision for young males was accompanied by exchanges of food and other goods. While it was part of a wider ritual process, it did give the boys a new status, allowing them to participate in adult assemblies. Throughout the Pacific, genital operations are generally limited to young males, though in the past among some aboriginal Australian groups, female initiation might include ritual defloration or laceration of the vulva.

DEATH. People in the Pacific treat death with more solemnity than any other event in a person's existence. Customs vary in ways of treating the corpse, mourning, and preservation of the remains. Death rites differ according to the status of the deceased, beliefs about veneration of the ancestors, and whether it was a "good" or "bad" death. A transition period is marked primarily by the mourning period around the body of the dead person. However, in most societies there are commemorations by the family after certain periods of time. The commemoration reminds the living that the deceased family member has finally passed into the place of the ancestors.

In New Zealand, particularly among the Maori population, people may gather to hear the last wishes of the dying person. At the time of death the *tuku karakia* is chanted, with the intention of releasing the person's spirit from the body so as to commence the journey to the underworld. Later, during the funeral *(tangi)*, songs and chants are addressed to the dead person. A year later there is an unveiling of the headstone for the grave. This replaces the traditional *hahunga* ceremony, when the bones of the deceased would be disinterred and placed in a receptacle for placement in a sacred location reserved for the bones of the ancestors.

In Australia, a dead person's close relatives will sing and invoke the sacred names of the dead person's water hole and country, with its mythological associations. In Papua New Guinea, rites for the dead and dying involve many layers of meaning. There are fears and concerns over the possible malicious intent of the ghost of the deceased, financial obligations, and consequences of accusations of poison or sorcery. The family member has been transformed into one of the living dead, often leaving the family in a state of anxiety and fear.

Death is not necessarily an event, but rather a condition that may last for years. It is the state between life and afterlife, but may also include the sick and very old. In recent times in Papua New Guinea, some elderly people are officiating at their own funerals while still alive and relatively healthy. They take the opportunity to say farewell to friends and family, seek to reconcile sour relationships, bequeath their valuables to family and friends, and conduct a feast. This growing practice demonstrates creativity and initiative by the principal actor in the transition from elder to ancestor.

PERSONAL SIGNIFICANCE. How do individuals cope with rites of passage, particularly initiation experiences in their personal lives? Papua New Guinean Celine Yakasere, now a Catholic sister, has written about her initiation experience. "I felt that I was isolated from the rest of the village people, especially my friends. When the hair is shaved off, you feel shy to walk in public, or afraid of your school mates who will make fun of you. . . . Finally, when a girl has gone through this process she feels proud that she is now a woman and not a girl anymore" (Yakasere, 1991, p. 4).

Many rites are concerned with defining proper male and female roles. Marilyn Strathern claims that among certain groups in Melanesia, initiations dismantle identities that were originally androgynous in order to create single-sex people capable of reproducing in relationships with each other. Often, concepts of male and female emphasize the differences between the sexes, yet they are seen as complementary rather than oppositional, and both are viewed as essential to the continuity of the social whole.

Some rites of passage divide a person's life into "before" and "after." One is never the same again. Other rites occur in stages and effect a more gradual transition. Some, such as the Tikopian superincision rites, confront the young man with some of his basic social ties, reaffirming them and thus making him well aware of the time when he will have to adopt them in earnest.

Social Significance. Rites of passage, particularly those associated with initiation, nearly always involve a social withdrawal, signified by movement away from the group or camp, and a return to that life as an active participant but with a different status. The change in social status is represented by symbolic actions such as ritual bathing, a public reception, or physical changes like scarring of the body.

Scholars differ in their interpretations of the social significance of such actions. Functionalists see sociopolitical solidarity in the support given to participants as they make a social transition in their lives. Structuralists tend to focus on sex and role reversals during the rites, while those basing their analysis on psychological theories detect in men an envy and desire to emulate the procreative powers of women. In the late twentieth century, studies have focused on the cultural construction of masculinity.

Despite differing theoretical approaches, most will agree that rites of passage are social events. Male initiation tends to be more public. The number of people involved in female initiation is normally more restricted, yet female rites celebrate both a woman's role within the domestic realm and her political and economic role within the public realm. Rites of passage usually have socioeconomic significance as well, with gifts and services offered both at the time of the rite and for the future.

Cosmic Significance. Rites of passage are cultural means of defining birth, maturity, aging, and death, and the means of making the transitions between these social spaces. The elaborate cosmologies typical of Pacific peoples are rich in their ability to give sacred meaning to these life crises. Death is seen as a transition through which a person passes to another life not entirely unlike the one he or she has left. The transition is foreshadowed in the symbolic death and rebirth that is the central focus of much initiation ritual.

The many Oceanic cultures vary in their ways of expressing the underlying dynamics of birth and death. Circumcision is not only a ritual killing, but the boy who has lost his foreskin is sometimes said to have emerged from his mother. Many rituals symbolize regeneration in return to a primordial event that took place at the beginning of time. Through initiation the novice establishes a relationship with the sacred history of the community.

Oceanic rites often involve secret and sacred objects that have symbolic significance and mythical associations. People continue to learn about sacred ritual and myth throughout their lives. Thus, rites of passage open up new possibilities for entering into this metacultural and trans-historical realm.

Rites in the Modern World. People in Oceania continue to move from one stage of life to another. Yet with the demise of many traditional rites of passage, transitions can become ritualized in various ways, such as adolescents initiating adolescents, sometimes violently. Evidence of this is seen in an upsurge in membership in occult movements in Papua New Guinea secondary schools. For example, members of a "generation name" group or "family" use secret words or signs to greet one another when they meet. They are also expected to monitor each other's behavior for adherence to the generation-name "character." For example, a certain generation name may have a promiscuous character, and all students bearing that generation name from year to year are expected to display promiscuous sexual behavior in accordance with the character of the name. Other generation-name characters include hating teachers, being a fire bug, and satan worship. Generation names are passed on at initiation ceremonies of an abusive type known as bastardization rituals, often involving alcohol, drugs and physical assault.

Forms of circumcision and superincision continue to be practiced today in the Pacific. Uncircumcised males in Tonga, Samoa, and among ethnic Fijians would find themselves the object of jokes and derision. To be called "uncut" is an insult. In Vanuatu, the Bislama term *dip-skin* ("deep skin," i.e., uncircumcised) is used as a generalized swear word. In some circles, traditional genital operations are replaced by inserting ball bearings under the skin of the penis—a procedure supposed to increase one's sexual prowess.

The initiate of the older generation is being replaced by the graduate of the younger generation. With most young people attending school, leaving little time for or interest in traditional initiation rites, they are left to experiment with novel ways to gain prestige and social standing. For some, reaching drinking age or gaining a driver's license opens the door to a new status, as does secondary school or university graduation.

In many parts of Oceania, ceremonies are now often blessed by church ministers or accompanied by prayer. In places like Samoa, weddings, funerals, and the conferring of titles involve a mixture of Christian rites and neotraditional exchanges. The vow ceremonies of indigenous members of Catholic religious orders often demonstrate unique combinations of Catholic worship and traditional rites of passage. In the East Sepik Province of Papua New Guinea, Sister Theresia Nakankwien of Yangoru, wearing traditional attire, had to bend over to make her way through the tunnel formed by the linked arms of her uncles. Having performed this gesture of humble submission, she stood erect to face the community as a woman to be respected. She then changed from her traditional attire and turned toward the altar to pronounce her vows as a Sister of Mercy. Ten years after the event she says, "I still feel that new identity, both within me and within my community."

BIBLIOGRAPHY

Allen, Michael R. *Male Cults and Secret Initiations in Melanesia.* Melbourne, 1967.

Berndt, Ronald M., and Catherine H. Berndt. *The World of the First Australians: Aboriginal Traditional Life: Past and Present.* Canberra, 1988.

Best, Elsdon. *The Whare Kohanga and Its Lore.* 1929; reprint, Wellington, New Zealand, 1975.

Eliade, Mircea. *Australian Religions: An Introduction.* Ithaca, N.Y., 1973.

Firth, Raymond. *We, the Tikopia.* 2d ed. Boston, 1957.

Herdt, Gilbert H., ed. *Rituals of Manhood: Male Initiation in Papua New Guinea.* Berkeley, 1982.

Hezel, Francis Z. *The New Shape of Old Island Cultures: A Half Century of Social Change in Micronesia.* Honolulu, 2001.

Hogbin, Ian. *The Island of Menstruating Men: Religion in Wogeo, New Guinea.* Scranton, Pa., 1970.

Irwin, James. *An Introduction to Maori Religion: Its Character Before European Contact and Its Survival in Contemporary Maori.* Bedford Park, S. Australia, 1984.

Johnstone, Bike, and Ignatius Talania. *Napalunga (Katim Skin): A Circumcision Ceremony.* Video. National Film Institute, Papua New Guinea.

Levy, Robert I. *Tahitians: Mind and Experience in the Society Islands.* Chicago, 1973.

Lutkehaus, Nancy C., and Paul B. Roscoe, eds. *Gender Rituals: Female Initiation in Melanesia.* New York, 1995.

McPherson, Naomi. *Primogeniture and Primogenitor: Firstborn Child and Mortuary Ceremonies Among the Kabana (Bariai), West New Britain, Papua New Guinea.* Ph.D. diss., McMaster University, 1985.

Schoeffel, Penelope. "Samoan Exchange and 'Fine Mats': An Historical Reconsideration." *Journal of the Polynesian Society* 108, no. 2 (1999): 117–148.

Strathern, Marilyn. *Reproducing the Future: Anthropology, Kinship, and the New Reproductive Technologies.* New York, 1992.

Te Rangi, Hiroa. "Mangaian Society." *Bishop Museum Bulletin* 122 (1934).

Tuzin, Donald F. *The Voice of the Tambaran.* Berkeley, 1980.

Van Gennep, Arnold. *The Rites of Passage* (1908). Translated by Monika B. Vizedom and Gabrielle L. Caffee. Chicago, 1960.

Yakasere, Celine. "The Initiation of Young Girls in Sassoya." *Grassroots Bulletin* 1, no. 2 (1991): 2–4.

PHILIP GIBBS (2005)

RITES OF PASSAGE: MESOAMERICAN RITES

In Mesoamerica, the most human of all religious rituals, rites of passage, mark people's changing relationships with their fellow human and nonhuman beings. Points in the life cycle most stressed include birth, marriage, and death. Rites, however, mark many other transitions, including children's and adolescents' development, the transition from illness to health, and initiation into new careers. Communities small and large also celebrate rites that move human corporate bodies from one status to another. Finally, because both the cosmos itself and those things that inhabit it are also considered living beings analogous to humans, even cosmic entities such as the sun move through transitory moments celebrated as rites of passage.

HISTORICAL DOCUMENTATION. Mesoamerica's long history dates back to approximately twenty-three thousand years ago. Fairly secure archaeological dating techniques have been able to place humans in the region at that point, although some suggest an even earlier occupation. After a very long and slow period of development, four cultures in particular have played formative roles: the Olmec (c. 2250–300 BCE); the Oaxaca (c. 1400 BCE–present); the Mexican highlands people (c. 1200 BCE–present); and the Maya (c. 400 BCE–present). The Spanish Conquest in 1521 produced a cataclysmic change in the region, destroying almost all indigenous pictorial documents and wreaking havoc on architectural, sculptural, and other material remains. The conquerors sought radical cultural and religious change as well, working hard to turn indigenous Mesoamericans into Spanish-like Catholics. However, this venture was not as successful, so the cultural and spiritual conquests of New Spain proved less complete than the political and material ones.

Historical records in the modern sense for anything prior to the Spanish Conquest are largely lacking. This does not mean indigenous history was not recorded. Mesoamericans kept records not in script but in pictorial, partly hieroglyphic, partly phonetic forms of writing, sometimes inscribed on stone stelae (stone slabs), buildings that were used ritually, and often in screen-folded books, the last of which the Spanish mostly destroyed. Hence, what scholars know about cultural practices before the Conquest relies almost exclusively on material remains, and what they know after it relies heavily on documents influenced, collected, or written by the Spanish.

Although written records prove both scarce and difficult, because the cultural and spiritual conquests were never complete, in the early twenty-first century one often can find strong continuity among historical and contemporary versions of various indigenous religious traditions, especially in those areas removed from the centers of Conquest. This means that what scholars now know about Mesoamerican rites of passage depends on four broad sources of information: material remains from before and after the Conquest, accounts commissioned and sometimes written by the Spanish conquerors, historical documents and travelers' accounts produced in the years since the Conquest, and ethnographic and indigenous reports of living traditions. Thorough investigations of both historical and living traditions rely on all four, for none alone can either account for the disruption of the Conquest or present a picture with any depth.

Besides marking birth, marriage, and death as the key points in a person's life, all rites tend to take a very long view of these and other transitions. Rites of passage mark human life stages, among other events. The Mexica (Aztecs) said that life was divided into four broad periods: childhood; puberty; maturity; and old age, a sequence echoed by many other Mesoamerican groups. However, Alfredo López Austin (1988) reports that, within these four, the Mexica used many words that made much finer distinctions, such as a baby in the uterus; a nursing infant; a person under or over six years of age; a youthful, then nubile male or female; early and advances middle age; early and advanced old age; and more. Clearly, one's particular life stage was noted with precision. Moreover, the words seem to say that life continuously changes and is far more complicated than simply getting born, growing up, becoming old, and dying.

Life's continuous changes are similarly expressed in the structure of Mesoamerican rites of passage. These rituals say that change never stops, and moreover, major change takes a particularly long time; in fact, it takes one's whole life span and more. Mesoamerican rites reflect the ongoing nature of all transitions in a way that extends considerably the classic three-stage model advanced by Arnold van Gennep in 1909. Van Gennep proposed that life changes are marked by rituals that: (1) separate the individual in transition; (2) restructure that individual to effect the change; (3) end by reintegrating him or her back into the community transformed by his or her new status. One must understand van Gennep, however, in the most expansive manner possible when considering Mesoamerican rites. These are not simple discrete rituals that move through just three stages (no matter how complex those stages might be) and end at the third with the reintegration of the individual into his or her community in his or her new status; rites of passage in Mesoamerica never quite end.

Each ritual of status change and reintegration is also an anticipation of the next transformation and therefore must be seen as multiple sets of van Gennep's three ritual steps strung together, each set of three moving to another set of three on the ritual's "string," none ever quite ending. In this way, the person moves through and toward his or her life changes, recognizing life's innate transitory character. In Mesoamerican rites, one may gain a new status, but that status is always temporary, to be enhanced or replaced by the next new status. Sixteenth-century Mexica birth rituals, for example, did not simply mark the new status of a baby in a community and then end. They began with early pregnancy; marked pregnancy's later stages; structured birth itself, including the possibility of death; and if successful, named the baby. But even then, the naming ceremony didn't just celebrate the birth and introduce the child to the family; it also explicitly anticipated future rites tying the child to its community, such as schooling, marriage, parenthood, and death. These birth rites recognized one's whole life and beyond by symbolically referencing future rites. Moreover, when their times came, those future rites referred back to the previous ones. It becomes difficult to separate one of these moments from the rest, for ultimately all are connected, even if some major changes like birth, marriage, or death are particularly noted.

An ancient 260-day divinitory calendar, dating back at least to the seventh-century BCE, determined everything from naming a child, determining her or his occupation, and deciding when he or she would marry to deciding the time for installing rulers and for making good trips, successful business deals, and victorious wars. All Mesoamerican rites of passage were, and many still are, set by this calendar, and most share a similar ongoing, transitory character. Nevertheless, rites can vary considerably in their details regionally and throughout history.

Examples of Mesoamerican Rites of Passage. Mexica noble birth rituals are among some of the most extensive and poignant appearing in the sixteenth-century resources. Their sympathetic Spanish reporter, Fray Bernardino de Sahagún, took particular interest in the numerous and lengthy formal speeches made throughout by the family members, the young mother, and the midwife. This series of formal rituals began with the first knowledge of pregnancy. Gathered for a meal and speeches, the relatives noted that the Lord of the Near and Nigh had placed a "precious necklace, a precious feather" within the young woman. They wondered if this impending birth worried their dead ancestors, those who had gone to "the water," "the cave," "the land of the dead," those who had departed but nevertheless might yet be present. Since the godly creator couple, Ometecutli and Omecihuatl, had instructed that a child be born, the speakers now must warn the young woman to not lift heavy objects and advise the young parents about sexual matters. They reminded them that they now had become protectors like the "silk cotton wood and cypress trees" that shield people. With pregnancy, the couple took from their ancestors the carrying frame, the burden of mother and fatherhood. The new mother thanked her parents for all the suffering that she had put them through, noting that now it was her turn. So began the long difficult road to bringing forth and fostering a new life.

In the seventh or eighth month, similar rites were performed with a midwife who introduced the young woman to the sweat bath. There, the midwife called on various godly powers, including those of healing, motherhood in general, mothers who had died in childbirth, and the night, and she massaged the young woman vigorously. She also advised her at length on what she should and should not do to assure a safe birth. During birth—the most dangerous moment in the whole ongoing ritualized event—godly powers that would help the girl were enlisted as well as those that would help should death occur. Birth was a battle with the young women warriors in pursuit of their children. The goddess Cihuacoatl, who assisted the second in command of all the Mexica, also assisted the midwife with her war strategy. Male warriors sacrificed in state rituals became gods who captured the sun from the land of the dead at daybreak, carrying it to the sky's roof; women who died in childbirth's sacrificial battles became goddesses who captured the sun from the male warriors at noon, carrying it back to the western house at dusk. But if a birth was successful, the midwife gave war whoops to celebrate the victory.

A baby girl's umbilical cord was given to Ometecutli and Omecihuatl and buried in the corner of the house, for she would become the hearth, the cook, the spinner, and the weaver. A baby boy's was given to the Lord and Lady of the Healing Night (the sweat bath), the Earth Lord, and the Sun and was buried in a battlefield by seasoned warriors, for that was his destiny. The family named the child within a week or two on a day propitious for its future character, and before it crawled, they promised it to one of the schools for religious training—which taught boys and girls in separate institutions—or to one that trained boys for warfare. A babe thus was brought into an extended family, which included living and deceased generations, and dedicated to the community, society, and cosmos in which it lived. Its past, present, and future combined to assist the production of a healthy child and future family member and citizen. In a similar fashion, the child would be sent off to school, into marriage, and eventual ancestorhood.

Other Mesoamerican groups celebrated and continue to celebrate similar, yet different, birth rites. The sixteenth-century Maya placed the goddess Ix Chel's image under women's beds to induce pregnancy and, as did the Mexica, named their babies on propitious days. Seventeenth-century Zapotec families in Oaxaca fortified their newborns by fasting for three days and abstaining from sex for twenty. When forty days had passed, the family took the child, along with its godparents, to be baptized in the church. As the Mexica baby was dedicated to its future school, so too the Zapotec child was dedicated to the church in which it would be trained. And in the early twenty-first century in Guatemala, the Quiché Maya say that the divinatory calendar that has determined all rites of passage for centuries marks passage of the same amount of time that it takes for the gestation of a baby.

Mesoamericans also mark children's developmental stages. In the sixteenth century, Yucatec Maya dedicated their children when they were old enough to be carried on the hip: three months for girls, probably because the hearth fire had three stones, and four for boys, because a cornfield had four corners. Godparents were ceremonially introduced to the child, taking up the task of helping with its development. Every four years, the Mexica dedicated their very young children along with honorary aunts and uncles, who later would introduce them to school. The children were symbolically singed or cooked over the fire and stretched so that they would grow tall. At the celebration, the new aunts and uncles carried the children on their backs or, if the children were old enough, danced with them.

Clothes and hair often marked childhood stages. Yucatec children ran naked until they were about five years old, when little boys began wearing a cloth like their fathers and little girls a skirt like their mothers. A boy received a small white bead to wear in his hair, and a girl received a string with a red shell, which was tied around her waist. They wore these until puberty. A little Otomí girl wore her hair very short, then shoulder-length with bangs when older, and bound it on her head after she herself had become a mother. A little Mexica boy sported a shorn head, but at age ten he was allowed to grow a tuft until he had captured his first warrior at about age fifteen, when his hair was cut to hang long over the right ear. His grandfather warned him to quickly capture another or else he would continue to wear his hair like a girl. Scarification on one breast and hip marked a young Mexica girl ready for school, and a lip plug marked a young boy. Each was ceremonially advised on proper behavior and the expectations of their large families before embarking on their formal education. Mexica youths remained guarded in the schools until marriage moved them from childhood to adulthood. Yucatec youths could not marry until their childhood adornments were formally removed from them in a ceremony. These ceremonies, however, were not necessarily performed at puberty but at an older stage of childhood just before puberty. And they were not performed individually but in a community of children close in age. They married only when their parents deemed it appropriate.

Marriage, not puberty, often officially moved youth into adulthood and almost always allied the two families. After ceremonially informing his schoolmaster, a Mexica boy's family carefully chose his mate, and a matchmaker ritually negotiated the union. On a calendrically propitious day, a matron of her own family carried the bride on her back to her new family home. Surrounding her on this sad, scary trip of leave-taking were all her female relatives with whom she had lived. The mothers each dressed their respective new child-in-law, and then an elderly day keeper (diviner) literally tied the knot by tying their capes together. After the elderly matchmakers put the couple in their wedding bed, they guarded their door through the night, all the while getting drunk. Yucatec Maya, however, could betroth their children when they were young, becoming honorary in-laws until the two actually married. The groom lived with and worked for the bride's family for five to six years.

Contemporary Nahua men, ancestors of the ancient Mexica, also use matchmakers to negotiate a marriage. The groom must pay for the entire process and so sometimes must postpone marriage. The marriage alliance is negotiated over much food and alcohol, and a generous gift of more food and drink seals the deal. During the twenty-four-hour ceremony, they stage mock displays of anger, which are smoothed over, indicating the two families' peaceful union to come. A sacred web of incense woven around the couple and their godparents finalizes the alliance, and the godparents dance with dough images of their future children.

The elderly play many key roles in these ceremonies, and death marks their transition to ancestorhood, beginning a continuous flow of sacred powers between the dead and the living. According to David Friedel and Linda Schele, the sarcophagus lid of the seventh-century Maya Lord Pacal of Palenque, Mexico, shows the dead ruler sliding down the Milky Way into the underworld's skeletal jaws. At each winter solstice's sunset, a flash of light illuminated a frieze depicting the deceased Pacal handing on the leadership to his son Chan Balum. After traveling through the underworld, Pacal will emerge at dawn as the new ancestral sun warming the earth. Some Mexica dead were sent to the underworld "place where no smoke escapes, the place of no chimney" in rites that extended over as much as five years. Repeated cremations moved these dead to beyond the "wide waters" in the Land of the Dead, carried there by a small yellow dog. In the case of a ruler, elaborate rituals reestablished the state's relations with both their alliances and enemies. In the 1930s the Panajachel Maya dead traveled through the underworld to emerge as stars, and before birth, their babies lived as stars following the sun. The twenty-first-century Maya of Yalcoba say that their deserving deceased relatives appear at dawn and dusk as pink clouds floating in the still skies.

Both cosmic and human rites marked the transitional nature of all existence. The Mexica ritual that gave birth to a new sun every 52 solar years—just when 73 rounds of the 260-day calendar had ended—acted as a cosmic transformative rite of passage. The sun was birthed in a series of steps that never quite ended, thereby anticipating its continuing life and eventual death. Even suns in the Mexica world were born, lived, and died according to the ongoing calendrical patterns governing all transitions. Similarly, Quiché day keepers—those who count the sun's days—receive their calling and are trained and initiated in an extended series of rituals closely following the same calendar. Moreover, the initial rite is not necessarily their last. Even as they perform rites of passage for others, they can train further, going through more rites of their own. And so human life continues as the cosmos continues, transiting from one stage to another and on.

BIBLIOGRAPHY

The highly readable *Rites of Passage* by Arnold van Gennep and translated by Monika B. Vizedom and Gabrielle Caffee (London, 1909) is probably the seminal work on the nature of rites of passage. Expanding on van Gennep's idea of liminality, Victor Turner explores rites of passage as a social drama of Hidalgo men and as examples of *communitas* in Mexican and other pilgrimages in *Dramas, Fields, and Metaphors* (Ithaca, N.Y., 1974).

An extraordinarily rich source of information on the Mexica (Aztecs) was compiled by a sixteenth-century Franciscan father, Bernardino de Sahagún, in his *Historia general de las cosas de la Nueva España*, translated by Arthur J. O. Anderson and Charles E. Dibble as *Florentine Codex: A General History of the Things of New Spain*, 13 vols. (Santa Fe, N.Mex., 1950–1982). Although information pertaining to rites of passage is spread throughout almost all the volumes, Book 6 contains particularly extensive material on pregnancy, childbirth, and childhood. *Representing Aztec Ritual: Performance, Text, and Image in the Work of Sahagún*, edited by Eloise Quiñones Keber (Boulder, Colo., 2002), pp. 143–174, offers a number of useful individual articles on Nahua ritual found in the corpus of Sahagún. Alfredo López Austin presents a detailed picture of Aztec or Nahua cosmic, religious, and physiological ideas, including a complete list of life-stage terms, in *The Human Body and Ideology: Concepts of the Ancient Nahuas*, translated by Thelma Ortiz de Montellano and Bernard Ortiz de Montellano, 2 vols. (Salt Lake City, Utah, 1988). Kay Read's *Time and Sacrifice in the Aztec Cosmos* (Bloomington, Ind., 1998) offers a comprehensive discussion of the transitional nature of Aztec cosmology and a description of the solar rite of passage. Equally useful is Davíd Carrasco's retrospective *City of Sacrifice: The Aztec Empire and the Role of Violence in Civilization* (Boston, 1999), which gathers articles spanning over fifteen years and exploring topics ranging from cosmology to ritual. In 1566 Fray Diego de Landa described a number of rites, primarily of the Yucatec Maya, in his *Yucatan before and after the Conquest*, translated by William Gates in 1937 (New York, 1978). One of the few sources on religion in Oaxaca, including information on rites of passage, is José Alcina Franch's *Calendario y religión entre los Zapotecos* (Mexico City, 1993), which explores religion and calendrics among the seventeenth-century Zapotec.

James Taggart's *Nahuat Myth and Social Structure* (Austin, Tex., 1983) presents limited descriptions of contemporary Nahuat marriage ceremonies. *Maya Cosmos: Three Thousand Years on the Shaman's Path* by David Freidel, Linda Schele, and Joy Parker (New York, 1993) offers a comprehensive picture of Maya cosmology with information on death and the afterlife sprinkled throughout. Barbara Tedlock's *Time and the Highland Maya* (Albuquerque, N. Mex., 1992) gives ample examples of initiation rites of Quiché Maya ritual specialists, includes information on some other rites, and explains the 260-day ritual calendar. *Rituals of Sacrifice: Walking the Face of the Earth on the Sacred Path of the Sun: A Journey through the Tz'utujil Maya World of Santiago Atitlán* by Vincent James Stanzione (Albuquerque, N. Mex., 2003) is an excellent book on the rituals of the Tz'utujil, another contemporary Maya group.

KAY A. READ (2005)

RITES OF PASSAGE: HINDU RITES

India is a land of many ethnic, tribal, and linguistic groups, and of numerous castes and sects, each with its distinctive customs and practices. This article does not presume to be an exhaustive survey of the rites of passage practiced by all these groups. Its scope is limited to those rites handed down in the mainstream Brahmanic tradition and described in its normative texts.

Rites of passage are defined as the rites that accompany a change of state, whether it be age or social position. This study will focus on three classifications formulated within the Hindu tradition that partly overlap and together indicate what are called rites of passage as well as the states that they initiate: *saṃskāra, dīkṣā,* and *āśrama.* This discussion also includes rites performed at various junctures of an individual's life even though there is no change of state; the Hindu category of *saṃskāra* includes these life-cycle rites, as well as strict rites of passage.

SAṂSKĀRA. Hindu theologians define *saṃskāra* as a rite that prepares a person or thing for a function by imparting new qualities and/or by removing taints. It consecrates and purifies. The term, therefore, covers a broad group of preparatory rites, including sacrifices and the consecration of sacrificial utensils. The texts on Hindu domestic rites (Gṛhyasūtras) and the law books *(Dharmaśāstras)* apply the term more specifically to rites associated with the human life cycle. "Sacrament," the customary translation of *saṃskāra,* captures only a part of its significance and is liable to cause misunderstanding.

Sources do not agree on the number or the procedures of the *saṃskāras*. Some list as many as forty, using the term broadly to cover numerous domestic rites, while others give just twelve. The medieval handbooks enumerate sixteen. The descriptions of these rites also show marked discrepancies. The texts themselves acknowledge the existence of local and caste differences and often ask the reader to consult women, the custodians of folk customs. Our account, therefore, offers only a partial glimpse of these rites as they were performed at various times and places.

Marriage. It is customary for modern accounts of *saṃskāras* to begin with the prenatal rites. The Gṛhyasūtras, however, begin with marriage, and for good reason. It is the central Hindu institution: only a married man accompanied by his wife is the complete *persona religiosa* entitled to perform the principal religious acts of sacrifice and procreation. The Vedic texts declare that a man becomes complete after securing a wife and begetting a son. Other *saṃskāras* either lead up to marriage or flow from it.

Sources contain detailed instructions regarding the selection of a partner, the marriageable age of a boy and a girl, the auspicious times for marriage, and the like. The betrothal takes place some time before the marriage: the father of the groom asks for the bride's hand and her father formally gives his consent.

The rite of marriage, more than any other *saṃskāra,* is subject to local variations. Four rites, however, form the core of the ceremony:

1. Several oblations are made into the sacred fire.
2. The bridegroom takes the bride's hand, saying: "I take your hand for happiness."
3. He guides her three times around the fire. After each circumambulation he makes her step on a stone, saying: "Tread on this stone. Be firm like a stone. Overcome the enemies. Trample down the foes."
4. He makes her take seven steps toward the northeast, saying: "Take one step for sap, two for juice, three for prospering in wealth, four for comfort, five for cattle, six for the seasons. Be my friend with your seventh step! May you be devoted to me. Let us have many sons. May they reach old age." Most authorities consider these seven steps as the essential rite of matrimony; if the bridegroom dies before this rite is performed, the bride is not considered a widow.

Prenatal *saṃskāras.* There are three principal rites performed before birth to promote conception and to ensure the safety of the mother and the fetus. Garbhādhāna, the conception rite, is performed between the fourth and the sixteenth day after the beginning of the wife's monthly period. Puṃsavana, which literally means "quickening of a male child," is performed in the third or fourth month of pregnancy to ensure a male progeny, and also contains ritual and medicinal safeguards against miscarriage. Sīmantonnayana, ceremonial parting of the mother's hair, is performed between the fourth and the eighth month of pregnancy to protect the fetus from evil spirits.

It is very likely that the prenatal *saṃskāras* once formed a part of the marriage ceremony to promote the fertility of the bride. Their transfer to a later time may have resulted from the progressive lowering of the marriageable age of girls. When prepubertal marriage became the custom, rites associated with intercourse and conception would have seemed inappropriate within the marriage ceremony. Some features of these *saṃskāras*, moreover, recall their original context. For example, invocations of many sons and prayers for fertility abound. Further, the conception rite, the parting of the hair, and, according to some, even the quickening of a male child are performed only for the first pregnancy. Accordingly, these rites are viewed by many Hindu theologians as directed at the purification of the mother rather than of the fetus.

Childhood *saṃskāras.* The largest number of *saṃskāras* belong to the period between birth and adolescence, the most precarious time of life in premodern societies. Sources differ widely regarding the number, the names, and the procedures of these rites. The most significant of them are: Jātakarman (birth rites), one of the oldest of the *saṃskāras* and performed immediately after birth; Nāmakaraṇa (naming ceremony) on the tenth or the twelfth day after birth; Niṣkramaṇa (exit from the birthing room) between the twelfth day and the fourth month from birth; Annaprāśana (first eating of solid food) in the sixth month; Karṇavedha (ear piercing) performed between the twelfth day and the fifth year; Cūḍākaraṇa or Caula (first haircutting) in the third year.

***Saṃskāras* of adolescence.** While the childhood *saṃskāras* are aimed at protecting and nurturing the child, those of adolescence have a markedly social significance. They prepare the youth to assume the social and religious responsibilities of the adult world. They are, therefore, associated with education, and the teacher plays a central role in them.

The main *saṃskāra* of adolescence is Vedic initiation (Upanayana). It is regarded as the second birth of the initiate. The teacher who performs the initiation and who imparts the Veda is said to bear the pupil within him like an embryo and to cause him to be born again in the Veda. Thus the *brāhmaṇas*, *kṣatriyas*, and *vaiśyas*, who form the first three social classes (*varṇa*), are called "twice-born" because they undergo initiation, whereas the *śūdras*, who are not qualified for initiation, are said to have only a single birth—the physical birth from the parents. Before initiation a child of the upper classes is not subject to the norms that minutely regulate the lives of adult Hindus, and, therefore, he is likened to a *śūdra*.

The standard age for initiation is eight years for *brāhmaṇas*, eleven for *kṣatriyas*, and twelve for *vaiśyas*, although all are permitted to undergo initiation at a younger or an older age. Men of the three upper classes who remain uninitiated after the ages of sixteen, twenty-two, and twenty-four respectively are considered sinners. Social intercourse with them is forbidden.

Before the rite the boy takes his final meal in the company of his mother. Then his head is shaved and he is bathed. He is given a girdle, a deerskin, a staff, and a sacred thread. The sacred thread consists of three cords, and each cord is made by twisting three strands. It is normally worn over the left shoulder and hangs under the right arm. Though the sacred thread is not mentioned in the earliest sources, it has come to be regarded as the central element of initiation and as the symbol of a person's second birth. Today the rite is often called the "thread ceremony." At first the thread was probably a substitute for the upper garment worn during ritual activities.

The teacher performs several symbolic acts that establish an intimate relationship between him and his new pupil. The initiatory rite reaches its climax when the teacher reaches over the pupil's right shoulder, places his hand over the pupil's heart, and says: "Into my will I take thy heart. Thy mind shall follow my mind. In my word thou shalt rejoice with all thy heart. May Bṛhaspati join thee to me." The teacher then imparts the sacred Sāvitrī formula: "That excellent glory of Savitṛ [Sun], the god, we meditate, that he may stimulate our prayers" (*Ṛgveda* 3.62.10). The centrality of these rites is pointed out by an ancient Vedic text, the *Śatapatha Brāhmaṇa* (11.5.4.12): "By laying his right hand on the pupil the teacher becomes pregnant with him. In the third night he is born a *brāhmaṇa* with the Sāvitri." The initiate, who is called a *brahmacārin,* then puts wood into the sacred fire. This is his first encounter with the sacrifice, the central religious act of the Vedic religion.

The pupil remains for many years at the teacher's house, away from his home and family. This is a liminal period. The number of years is not determined; twelve, the number most often given, probably has a symbolic value, signifying completeness. The pupil is reduced to the level of a servant, without status, rank, or property; he obtains even his food by begging from house to house. Humility, obedience, and chastity are his main virtues.

Samāvartana is the *saṃskāra* that concludes the period of studentship. Initiation separates the boy from the social community, while Samāvartana reincorporates the youth into the adult world. The term literally means the return of the scholar to his parents' home after graduation. The central feature of the ceremony is a ritual bath. The rite, therefore, is often termed *snāna* (bath), and the young graduate is called a *snātaka* (the bathed). This feature, present also in the rite that ends the period of seclusion following the consecration (*dīkṣā*) for a Vedic sacrifice, indicates that it is the concluding act of the initiatory ritual, rather than a separate *saṃskāra.* After the bath the youth discards the student's attire and puts on ornaments and fine clothes; he assumes his new status in society. The young adult is now ready to get married and establish a household, and a search for a suitable bride will soon begin.

Funeral. The funeral is the last *saṃskāra.* It prepares a person for existence after death. From the earliest period of Indian history human remains were normally cremated. With the growth of sacrificial speculation in the late Vedic period, cremation came to be regarded as one's last sacrifice (Antyeṣṭi), in which one's own body is offered in the fire. From this sacrifice the deceased person is born again into a new existence in the company of his or her ancestors. Vedic texts call it a person's third birth. The funeral, therefore, is a rite of passage from the earthly existence to the world of the fathers.

Cremation, however, does not conclude the funeral; it is believed that newly deceased people pass through a liminal period lasting twelve days or one year, during which they live as ghosts (*pretas*). The dead are then dangerous, and their relatives are impure. During this time special offerings of food and water are made for the newly deceased (Ekoddiṣṭa-śrāddha). On the twelfth day, which is the current practice, or after one year, the newly deceased person is ritually united with his or her dead ancestors through a rite called Sapiṇḍīkaraṇa or Sapiṇḍāṇa. Four rice balls are prepared, three for the three preceding generations of ancestors and one for the newly dead person. The latter is cut into three parts, which are then mixed with the three balls intended for the ancestors. The union of rice balls symbolizes the union of the deceased with his or her ancestors. It is the final act of the funeral. Henceforth, the dead person will participate in all the normal offerings that his or her relatives will make to their ancestors.

The Upaniṣads contain information on a rite performed by a father when he feels that his death is imminent. In it he transfers his duties and powers—his ritual persona—to his son. This rite of transmission (Saṃpratti or Saṃpradāna) by which a son succeeds his father was later assimilated into the rite of renunciation, which also results in the ritual death of the father.

A remarkable feature of the funeral as well as the other *saṃskāras* is that they do not refer at all to the common Indian beliefs of rebirth (*saṃsāra*) and liberation (*mokṣa*). These Hindu rituals are founded on a different worldview that celebrates life and fertility, shrinks from pollution and death, and, when death comes, ritually transports the dead to the world of the fathers.

DĪKṢĀ. Like *saṃskāra, dīkṣā* is a preparatory rite. It is, however, more closely associated with the assumption of a new state. While *saṃskāras* are obligatory for all, most *dīkṣās* are undertaken voluntarily. It is, however, impossible to define either term precisely because they are often used as synonyms, and *dīkṣā* frequently refers to a wide variety of purificatory and other rites.

The most famous *dīkṣā* is the consecration of a man for a Vedic sacrifice. It prepares the sacrificer for the solemn act by purifying him and by transferring him to a new but temporary state similar to that of the gods. In *dīkṣā* the sacrificer is ritually transformed into an embryo and is born again with a new and more perfect body. Many elements of the rite symbolize the birthing process. The consecrated man (*dīkṣita*) is surrounded by taboos. He is sacred and dangerous: others are not allowed to touch him or to pronounce his name. At the conclusion of the sacrifice the consecratory period ends with a ritual bath, after which the sacrificer returns to his normal state.

The royal consecration is also called *dīkṣā*. It shares many common features with the sacrificial *dīkṣā*. Like the sacrificer, the new king is ritually reborn at his consecration. His period of *dīkṣā* lasts a year, during which time he is deprived of his royal prerogatives.

In the post-Vedic religions of India the most common forms of *dīkṣā* are associated with the entry into voluntary religious groups. The earliest such *dīkṣā* was probably that of ascetics. Buddhist and Jain sources indicate that at a very early period these sects developed rites of entry into their respective monastic orders. Brahmanical sources contain information on the *dīkṣā* of renouncers (*saṃnyāsins*) and forest hermits. These rites symbolically enact the death of the novice and his rebirth into the new ascetic life. Some rites include ordeals, such as pulling the hair by the roots and branding. At the conclusion of the rite the ascetic assumes a new name and the insignia of the new state: ascetic garb, tonsure, staff, begging bowl, and so forth. Initiatory rites of ascetics often assume an educational dimension in imitation of the Vedic initiation. The teacher plays an important role in them and imparts a secret formula (*mantra*) to the novice. The ascetic *dīkṣā* begins a long period of training for the novice.

Medieval Hindu sects, where admission is not limited to ascetics, devised *dīkṣās* for admitting lay members. They are patterned after the Vedic initiation and are regarded as constituting a new birth of the initiate. In some sects, such as the Virasaiva, the voluntary nature of *dīkṣā* is eliminated and a child is initiated at birth. Admission to each higher level or rank within a sect also entails special *dīkṣās*.

Dīkṣā introduces a new state, either temporary like the sacrificer's or permanent like the ascetic's. The term, therefore, is used as a synonym of *vrata* (vow) that often indicates a special mode of life. This meaning of *dīkṣā* is very close to that of *āśrama.*

ĀŚRAMA. By the sixth century BCE new religious ideas advocating a life of renunciation, celibacy, and poverty were sweeping the Ganges River valley. New religions, such as Buddhism and Jainism, broke with the Vedic tradition. Considering human beings as bound to an endless cycle of births and deaths, they questioned the value of central Vedic institutions such as sacrifice and marriage, and even of society as such.

There were brahman thinkers at this time who also advocated these new ideals but were unwilling to break completely with the Vedic tradition. They attempted to find theological formulas that would give scriptural legitimacy to renunciation while maintaining the religious significance of marriage and other Vedic institutions. One such formula was the system of the *āśramas*. Historically it was the most significant.

The term *āśrama* in all probability referred originally to "places of austerity" or hermitages. Its meaning was then extended to include lifestyles devoted to religious exertion. The term has the latter meaning when used within the context of the *āśrama* system. Its earliest formulation, which one may call the preclassical, is found in the ancient law books, the Dharmasūtras, the earliest of which were composed around the fourth century BCE. The preclassical system considers the four *āśramas*—Vedic student, householder, forest hermit, and renouncer—not as temporary stages but as permanent vocations. A young adult, after completing the period of study following Vedic initiation, is allowed to choose one of these *āśramas*. It is clear, therefore, that in the preclassical system the first *āśrama* was that of a permanent student, who remained with the teacher until death. The temporary period of study following initiation, on the other hand, was not regarded as an *āśrama* but as a period of preparation for all *āśramas*.

Āśrama represents a theological understanding and evaluation of several social institutions; it cannot be equated with the institutions themselves. They existed prior to the invention of the *āśrama* system, and even afterwards continue to exist independently of that system both within and outside the Hindu tradition. Certain forms of Hindu marriage and the renunciation of women and *śūdras*, for example, fall outside the *āśrama* system. The system gives the institutions religious legitimacy. The *āśramas* are proposed as a new fourfold division of *dharma*, paralleling its older division into the four social classes (*varṇa*), and as four alternative paths leading to the heavenly world. These institutions are thus made integral parts of *dharma* and, therefore, of the Vedic tradition.

Although it represented an important theological breakthrough for Brahmanism, the preclassical system had several drawbacks. It allowed choice in a matter of *dharma.* Choice or option was never encouraged by Brahmanic hermeneutics; even in minor matters of ritual it was used as a last resort in interpreting conflicting injunctions. Choice with regard to how one will spend one's adult life, moreover, gave rise to debates on the relative superiority of the *āśrama*s and in particular eliminated the obligatory nature of marriage. Some used the Vedic theory of the three debts of man—study, procreation, and sacrifice—as an argument against the *āśrama* system: if one does not marry, one is not able to repay the debts of procreation and sacrifice. Others even suggested that the Veda authorized only one *āśrama,* namely that of the householder.

Toward the beginning of the common era a new formulation of the *āśrama* system, which one may call the classical, gained wide acceptance. It is given in the authoritative *Laws of Manu,* composed around the beginning of the common era. The preclassical system all but disappeared from the later Hindu tradition, and even modern scholars are often ignorant of its very existence.

The classical system conceived of the *āśrama*s not as permanent vocations but as temporary stages of life through which an individual passes as he grows old. The *āśrama* system thus came to parallel the *saṃskāra* system, and the two central *saṃskāra*s—initiation and marriage—became the rites of entry into the first two *āśrama*s. The first *āśrama* is no longer the permanent studentship but the temporary period of study following initiation. Thus, according to Manu, a person should undergo initiation and live the first part of his life in the student's *āśrama.* After graduation (Samāvartana) he should marry and enter the householder's *āśrama.* When he is a grandfather and when, as Manu says, he sees his hair turning gray and his skin wrinkled, he should retire to the forest as a hermit. After spending some time there, he should enter the fourth *āśrama,* renunciation.

These, then, are the states that recur in the life of each individual. They are viewed as four rungs in the ladder leading up to liberation. The ladder image replaces the path image of the preclassical system. The rites of passage from one *āśrama* to the next are called *saṃskāra* and *dīkṣā* indiscriminately. The passage, however, takes place only in one direction; one is not permitted to return to an *āśrama* one has left. A person who does so—for example, a renouncer who reverts to the household life—is considered an outcaste.

The classical system eliminates choice and reaffirms the centrality of the householder. The ascetic orders are relegated to old age and retirement. The Vedic doctrine of three debts, once used as an argument against the preclassical system, is now seen as a scriptural basis for the *āśrama*s. Payment of the debts is carried out by passing through at least the first two *āśrama*s.

The third *āśrama* (forest hermit) had already become obsolete by the early centuries of the common era. Passage through the other three *āśrama*s is today, as it probably was even during the time of Manu, an ideal rather than a reality in the lives of most Hindus. Yet the theological understanding of these four central socioreligious institutions as hierarchical stages of life that one enters and leaves through rites of passage became a cornerstone of Hindu doctrine and practice. It is this theology that has given *āśrama* a place alongside *varṇa* as the two pillars of Hinduism and made the compound term *varṇāśramadharma* the closest Sanskrit approximation to the foreign term *Hinduism.*

WOMEN AND RITES OF PASSAGE. Hinduism has always been a patriarchal religion. Women play a decidedly secondary role in it. This is especially so with regard to ritual activity. It is generally accepted that the prenatal and childhood *saṃskāra*s, and of course the funeral, are performed also for women belonging to the twice-born *varṇa*s. The Vedic formulas normally recited at these rites, however, are omitted, since women are forbidden to study the Veda. However, there is some evidence to suggest that in ancient times girls were allowed to be initiated and to study the Veda. By the time of Manu's lawbook this practice had been discontinued. Marriage, it was claimed, constituted initiation for women.

The position of women in Hindu sects varies considerably. The major sects follow the Brahmanic prohibition against female initiation. Many fringe and anti-structural sects, such as the Vīraśaiva, however, admit women to initiation and full membership.

Women are also excluded from direct participation in the *āśrama* system. In marriage and, according to some, also in the hermit's *āśrama,* a woman participates in the *āśrama* of her husband. Female renouncers are found in Buddhism, Jainism, and in many medieval Hindu sects, and even mainstream Brahmanism acknowledges their existence. A woman's life in these institutions, however, is not theologically interpreted as constituting an *āśrama.*

ŚŪDRAS AND RITES OF PASSAGE. *Śūdra*s, by which is meant all the groups that do not belong to the twice-born *varna*s, are excluded from reciting or even hearing the Veda. Thus they cannot be admitted to Vedic initiation. It is quite likely, however, that these groups did possess their own initiatory rites, although no information on them has come down to us. Regarding the other *saṃskāra*s, however, there is a conflict of opinion. Some hold that no *saṃskāra* should be performed for a *śūdra,* while others allow them the prenatal and childhood *saṃskāra*s, as well as marriage and funeral rites, but without Vedic formulas.

*Śūdra*s are similarly excluded from the *āśrama* system, though some authorities recognize their marriage as an *āśrama.* Many medieval sects permit a type of *dīkṣā* for *śūdra*s and admit them to membership.

CONCLUSION. Hinduism has no single dogma or doctrine. Its cohesion is found in its rites and observances. The central rites of Hinduism, whether it be mainstream Brahmanism or sectarian cults, have traditionally been the rites of passage.

The situation in modern India, however, is very different. The only *saṃskāras* regularly practiced in the early twenty-first century are marriage and funeral. Vedic initiation, where it is still practiced, has become the prerogative of brahmans to such a degree that the sacred thread has become the hallmark of a brahman.

The practice has changed, but the theology has remained the same: the modern Hindu villager as well as the modern Hindu theologian will, if asked, define Hinduism as *varṇāṣramadharma.*

SEE ALSO Domestic Observances, article on Hindu Practices; Saṃnyāsa; Śāstra Literature; Sūtra Literature.

BIBLIOGRAPHY

Bhattacharyya, N. N. *Indian Puberty Rites.* Calcutta, 1968. A comprehensive survey of male and female initiation rites using textual and ethnographic data.

Gonda, Jan. "The Sīmantonnayana as Described in the Gṛhyasūtras." *East and West* 7 (1956): 12–31. A detailed analysis of a prenatal rite with significant methodological implications for the study of other *saṃskāras*.

Gonda, Jan. *Change and Continuity in Indian Religion.* The Hague, 1965. An extensive and penetrating study of initiatory rites (pp. 315–462), pupilage (pp. 284–314), and the role of the teacher (pp. 229–283).

Kane, P. V. *History of Dharmaśāstra,* vol. 2. 2d ed., rev. & enl. Poona, 1974. The most detailed and comprehensive account available of *varṇa* (pp. 19–187), *saṃskāra* (pp. 188–415, 426–636), and *āśrama* (pp. 416–426).

Mookerji, Radhakumud. *Ancient Indian Education, Brahmanical and Buddhist.* 2d ed. London, 1951. An extensive survey of the educational institutions and practices of ancient India, including initiatory rites preceding education.

Olivelle, Patrick. "Renouncer and Renunciation in the Dharmaśāstras." In *Studies in Dharmaśāstra,* edited by Richard W. Lariviere, pp. 81–152. Calcutta, 1984. A historical account of renunciation and of the *āśrama* system.

Olivelle, Patrick. *The Āśrama System: The History and Hermeneutics of a Religious Institution.* New York, 1993.

Pandey, Raj Bali. *Hindu Saṃskāras: A Socio-Religious Study of the Hindu Sacraments.* 2d rev. ed. Delhi, 1969. A useful description of all Hindu *saṃskāras* without much historical analysis.

Sprockhoff, J. F. "Die Alten im alten Indien: Ein Versuch nach brahmanischen Quellen." *Saeculum* 30 (1979): 374–433. An extensive analysis of customs and institutions relating to old age in ancient India.

Stevenson, Margaret S. *The Rites of the Twice-Born* (1920). Reprint, New Delhi, 1971. A dated but still useful description of the rites of passage practiced by modern brahmans based on the author's personal observations.

PATRICK OLIVELLE (1987 AND 2005)

RITES OF PASSAGE: JEWISH RITES

Jewish rites of passage are diverse in their historical development and reflect the dynamic relation between social conditions, local customs, and the continued reinterpretation of classic texts. Only one rite, that of circumcision, derives explicitly from a commandment, or *mitzvah* (pl. *mitzvot*), in the Hebrew Bible, but images from the Bible linked to marriage and death have been mobilized in the evolution of weddings and funerals. Bar mitzvah is not mentioned in the Bible, Mishnah, or Talmud, and the Bible has no ritual of conversion. In some circumstances rites of passages have been linked to other biblical-based celebrations such as festivals and pilgrimages. Jews' involvement in the wider society has shaped rites of passage from antiquity through the Middle Ages under Christianity and Islam and continuing into the contemporary world. A modern development is the explicit attention to life-passage rituals for women, and the greater place of women in ritual life in general. The notion of "life cycle" was not traditionally an explicit principle organizing rabbinic discussions of *halakhah,* or law concerning rituals: bar mitzvah appeared in discussions of the daily prayer routine, while weddings appeared in considerations of laws of marriage and divorce. An awareness of the life cycle appears in the early modern period in Europe and grew within both the orthodox and liberal streams of Judaism that evolved in the nineteenth century. With the personalization of religion that has characterized Western culture, much attention is now paid to the different ways life milestones may be linked to Jewish tradition.

CIRCUMCISION, NAMING, AND REDEMPTION OF THE FIRSTBORN. The commandment that Israelite males be circumcised is presented in *Genesis* 17 as part of God's evolving relationship with Abraham and his descendants. The set date of eight days is unusual in the world's cultures, where ritual operations on male genitals usually takes place closer to puberty. This very low age, coupled with the story of the great age of Abraham and Sarah when Isaac was born, emphasizes that fertility is not dependent on circumcision but on Divine will. The biblical text builds upon existing cultural associations, mobilizing them for its purposes. It turns circumcision into a sign of a covenant between God and the Abrahamid line. The notion of covenant (*brit*) also emerges from the context of mundane kin relations and protective alliances, stressing that Abraham is ultimately dependent on God rather than on human patronage. The narrative assumes that the procedure of circumcision is known and stresses its Israelite meaning.

Some neighboring groups in the biblical world may have practiced circumcision, while the Philistines were marked as those who did not. In the Hellenistic period, the ritual came to symbolize Jewish particularity, and this meaning was later reinforced by Christianity. Literature from the Mishnah and Talmudic periods describes the procedure as consisting of three stages: (1) *milah,* the removal of the foreskin; (2) *peri'ah,* the tearing off and folding back of the mucous membrane to expose the glans; (3) and *metsitsah,* the suction of the blood from the wound. The latter step probably was accepted surgical procedure of the day. A passage from *Luke* (1:59) indicates that circumcision was also the occasion of naming a boy.

The standard form of the circumcision ceremony took shape in the Middle Ages. Tradition views the father as being obligated to circumcise his son, but it allows him to appoint a specialist, the *mohel*. In the Middle Ages the synagogue became the preferred site for the occasion, typically at the end of morning prayer. Both these developments extended communal authority into family celebrations and restricted the participation of women. Auxiliary roles emerged, such as the *sandaq*, typically a grandfather to the child, who held the baby on his lap during the procedure. Other roles, entailing both women and men, ceremoniously brought the infant from his mother and the circle of women into the main ritual arena. A series of texts were made standard, such as the formula for praying for the health of the mother and naming the boy. Some practices lacked ancient authority, such as drinking and reciting the blessing for wine on the occasion. In medieval Europe the blood drawn in circumcision took on meanings that competed with understandings of sacramental blood in Christianity. In general, circumcisions were occasions in which popular notions coexisted with or strained against halakhic norms. During the eighth century an idea appeared—that Elijah the Biblical prophet, viewed as the protector of children, is present at every circumcision, and the practice emerged of setting aside an honorary chair for him. Later, there is evidence of an elaborate celebration or vigil taking place throughout the night preceding a circumcision, in which the presence of many people guarded the child. At first these were raucous occasions, but rabbinic influence subdued them and inserted readings from sacred texts, like the Zohar. This basic configuration was common both in European communities, where circumcision was a mark of being Jewish, and in Middle Eastern settings, where Muslims circumcised as well, but at a different age and with different theological claims.

The modern era and emancipation created new perceptions of circumcision. As Jews became citizens of European nation-states, they became subject to laws regulating the recording of births and deaths, and to laws regarding health. New concepts of disease raised the question of whether *metsitsah*, normally carried out by the *mohel* directly sucking blood from the wound, had to be maintained as part of the ceremony, but it was defended by the nineteenth-century movement of Orthodoxy. Some spokesmen for Reform, which developed at the same period, claimed that circumcision was no longer required, but the majority of Jews maintained the custom even as new hygienic procedures for carrying it out became common and new theories as to the health-based rationale of the operation became popular. These ideas became widespread among Gentiles in the United States, in comparison to Europe, and in the course of the twentieth century it became common for the training of a *mohel* to include both ritual and medical preparation.

Feminism, which rose in the mid-twentieth century, both critiqued the male-oriented connotations of the rituals and suggested practices whereby baby girls could "enter the covenant" and be named publicly. There had been various ways of naming girls in the past. In European (Ashkenazi) tradition, the father would be called to recite the blessings over the public reading of the Torah on a Sabbath soon after the birth. On that occasion, a prayer for the mother's convalescence was read and the baby was given a name, even if the mother were not present. An alternative or complementary practice, *holekreish*, took place at home after the mother was strong. The baby was raised in its cradle while surrounded by people and given a name. Girls often had Yiddish names rather than Hebrew ones, and the same ceremony might give boys a Yiddish name to complement the Hebrew one from his circumcision. *Holekreish* appears to stem from a local custom warding off a monster that threatened babies. A similar tradition may have existed in Spain, where rabbis established a home naming-ceremony for girls, including a liturgical component in Hebrew called *zeved ha-bat*, the gift of a daughter. From Spain it has spread to other areas of the Spanish-Jewish (Sephardi) world and now constitutes one model for contemporary girl-naming ceremonies.

Innovations for naming girls have appeared in all streams of Judaism. Orthodox Jews have introduced changes within the framework of *halakhah*, while a Hebrew neologism, *britah*, suggesting the feminine of *brit*, has emerged among secular Israelis. The timing of the ceremony has been derived from different spheres of practice, such as the Sabbath or the New Moon, which traditionally was important to women. Liturgical content has been taken from such diverse sources as circumcision or marriage. Some have introduced a physical gesture in girls' ceremonies to parallel circumcision: an example is "washing the feet," based on Abraham and Sarah welcoming harbingers of her giving birth (*Gn.* 18). Innovations regarding girls have influenced the way circumcisions are treated. The Reform movement now trains women to be a *mohel*, and discussions arise as to whether modern anesthesia should be used in circumcisions. Both contemporary circumcision and baby girl-naming reflect the contemporary diversity of Jewish life.

Another infancy rite, based on *Exodus* 13:12–13, is the redemption of the firstborn male. The term redemption, *padoh* in Hebrew, refers to an exchange that moves a person or thing from one category to another, and firstborn is here defined as a male who has "opened the womb" of his mother. This definition highlights the holiness attributed to "firstness" in the Bible, because if a male baby is born after his mother has given birth to a girl, or after she has miscarried, the redemption commandment does not apply to him. A father does not apply to fetuses who are not carried to term but are lost in a miscarriage, highlighting the holiness attributed to "firstness" in the Biblical view. The father redeems his firstborn son by transferring a sum of money, "five *sheqalim*," to a person from the priestly Aaronid line (a *kohen*), and in exchange the son is removed from the category of being holy. Rabbinic Judaism gave shape to the biblical injunction by adding texts and a formal blessing. In the Geonic period (c. seventh–eleventh centuries), a blessing for the mother to recite was composed but did not gain wide acceptance and disappeared from tradition. In some versions of the rite today, a mother is asked to testify that this baby is the first to "escape" her womb. Because it applies only to a fraction of children, the ceremony continues today, but it has attracted less general attention than has circumcision. Some strictly orthodox Jews seek opportunities of carrying out the redemption of firstlings of domestic animals.

BAR AND BAT MITZVAH AND RITUALS OF EDUCATION. The obligation to both obey and love God's words was expressed in *Deuteronomy* 6:4–9, where there also is a demand to write and recite them. The Deuteronomic text may represent a stage in which involvement with divine instructions and teachings, which with time collectively came to be called Torah, was being expanded beyond the priesthood and directed to all Israelites. The textual world of Torah and its evolving interpretations became a hallmark of Jewish life, and entrance into that world by male children constituted a significant passage. There are hints in the Bible, as in the beginning of *1 Samuel,* that weaning was viewed as a significant transition that could thrust a youngster into a setting of education. There is no clear evidence of rituals accompanying the entrance into the realm of Torah within Talmudic literature, but such rituals are known from France and the Rhineland (Ashkenaz) in the Middle Ages. They involved:

1. Carrying the child from his home to the synagogue;
2. The synagogue teacher's exposing the child to Hebrew letters that he in some form ingests as sweets;
3. Engaging in incantations intended to ward off forgetfulness;
4. Walking to the river from the synagogue.

A difference between the French and German sources is that in France the ceremony took place whenever a child reached the appropriate age, while in the Rhineland it was prescribed for the festival of Shavuʿot, the date to which tradition assigned the revelation at Sinai. Both in textual references mobilized within the ceremony and in one illuminated manuscript depicting it, the child's entrance into the realm of instruction is portrayed as analogous to the Israelites receiving the Torah at Sinai and then traveling to the next stage on the banks of the Jordan River. Some of the illuminated material shows the child on the knee of a teacher in a manner parallel to the way the infant Jesus sits on Mary's lap in contemporary art, suggesting that there was polemic content to the ceremony as well. In the medieval European setting, the ritual was important to the whole community, for which it recapitulated its sacred history and reinforced its identity. Aspects of the ceremony, such as associating the text of the Pentateuch with sweetness, survive in customs today, but toward the end of the Middle Ages this custom declined in centrality in comparison to the growing importance of bar mitzvah.

The age of thirteen appears in some classic sources; for example, males from that age must fast on the Day of Atonement, while females fast from the age of twelve. In the late Middle Ages in Europe, with the growing sense of the individual and the cultural recognition of stages of life, this was systematized into a general rule as to when a young person was obligated to observe the *mitsvot.* For a male, the salient expression of reaching this stage was the donning of phylacteries, or *tefillin* (containing the Deuteronomic passage discussed above, and related verses), during morning prayer and being counted in a prayer quorum. In the late sixteenth century the personal and communal elements now associated with bar mitzvah coalesced into a pattern. The year before a boy's thirteenth birthday was devoted to instruction in synagogue skills, and teachers exhorted him about his new moral and religious duties. The obligation to observe all the commandments was made public in his donning *tefillin* and being called to recite the blessings over the reading of the Torah. Families began to celebrate the event, and rabbis considered whether the occasion was appropriate for an official *mitzvah* feast like those accompanying a circumcision or wedding. The practice spread throughout Europe and beyond it.

In many Sephardi regions the practice was accepted, but the details differed. The name given the occasion varied; often it included the term *tefillin.* In some settings the celebration had two phases: the first of donning the *tefillin* on a weekday, and the second on the following Sabbath, when an extensive reading of the Torah and the Prophets in the synagogue gave the initiate more opportunity to demonstrate his skills. In North Africa the idea and the celebration were accepted, but into the twentieth century it was common to stage the occasion as soon as a youngster had the ability to go through the ceremony successfully, even if this preceded his thirteenth birthday. A bar mitzvah ritual never evolved among the Jews in Yemen.

A religious majority celebration for girls, now referred to by the feminine form bat mitzvah, first arose in the nineteenth century. It is linked to the creation of the confirmation ceremony first appearing in Central Europe early in that century as a complement to bar mitzvah. This stemmed from the critique that boys went through bar mitzvah ceremonies on a rote basis without adequate knowledge or personal commitment. Confirmation was to reflect further study and took place later in the teenage years in a public setting. Youths in the synagogue were quizzed on their knowledge and beliefs in a manner parallel to catechism, after which their joining the adult community was "confirmed." Classes preparing for this event began to include girls as well as boys. Most Orthodox leaders opposed the innovation, which initially was shaped on a Christian model, but with time some accepted it as it was embellished with traditional symbolism, such as taking place on the festival of Shavuʿot. The inclusion of girls in public rituals also evolved into various and occasional forms of celebrating bat mitzvah, reported in the nineteenth century and the early twentieth century both in Europe and the Middle East. Both confirmation and bat mitzvah became regularized in Reform and Conservative synagogues in North America in the twentieth century. In Conservative synagogues, bat mitzvah celebrations were different from bar mitzhah, taking place on Friday nights rather than Saturday mornings. They featured elements traditionally associated with women, such as lighting the Sabbath candles, but also included reading from the Prophets, as with boys. Feminism influenced all streams of Judaism to expand the education of women, and bar and bat mitzvah ceremonies were identical by the start of the twenty-first century in liberal branches of Judaism. This trend also led to the training of women cantors and rabbis in non-Orthodox rabbinic seminaries. In these matters, religious leadership responded to expectations that had become accepted among contemporary Jews.

A development in the late twentieth century was organized travel among young people to supplement Jewish education. Travel to Israel is a central destination, but the purpose typically is to reinforce Jewish identity among those in the Diaspora. Travel to sites of the European Holocaust by Israeli high school students has become a standard practice in the Jewish state for reinforcing national culture. Identity-bolstering travel also is utilized for people in later stages of life.

Another ritual connected to study is the convening of a *siyyum,* a celebration of conclusion, when an individual or group finishes studying a sacred book, traditionally a tractate of the Talmud. An ancient theme in Jewish symbolism likens a Torah scroll or a sacred book to a person. Thus, when a sacred book is no longer usable, it is not treated as refuse but should be buried in a manner parallel to burying human beings. Different practices evolved in relation to this norm. One was to bury worn-out books on the occasion of the burial of a sage, and another took place on a set date in the year, linked to one of the festivals. The overall notion links the individual to sacred texts throughout life and even in death.

MARRIAGE. As in many societies, marriage was the occasion of the most elaborate life-cycle rituals among Jews. The biblical blessing to humankind to "be fruitful and multiply" (*Gn.* 1:28) was a value taken for granted, and rabbinic writings assumed that marriage was the normal state for adults. In premodern times, weddings and the accompanying celebrations were the first occasion on which a woman was central in a public celebration. In various locales, the onset of menarche was recognized by traditional gestures within the family, but these were never linked to textual traditions. By contrast, the Bible and especially rabbinic law pay close attention to menstruation with regard to married women and their husbands' access to them. In the latter, a strict set of procedures evolved in which a woman terminates menstrual impurity after two weeks with immersion in a ritual bath, or *miqveh.*

The Bible and rabbinic law also portray men as the active partner in initiating and terminating marriage. Feminist literature debates how to interpret these texts and the historic developments behind them. The "patriarchal period" portrayed in *Genesis* features men in the public sphere, but the "matriarchs" are not passive actors, even though institutions like polygamy are taken for granted.

Talmudic literature provided detailed principles regulating marriage and divorce. These are based on the notion that a man acquires rights with regard to a woman, while she agrees to his acquisition of those rights. Contemporary weddings consist of two phases that were separated in time during antiquity. The first is called *kiddushin,* or *erusin,* and the second is *nisu'in. Nisu'in* is normally translated as "marriage," while *kiddushin* means "engagement" in modern Hebrew. In the context of formal marriage procedures, however, *kiddushin* establishes a ritual and legal relationship between a woman and man who perform the act. Related to the Hebrew term *kadosh,* or holy, the Talmud interprets *kiddushin* as a woman being "set aside" for a single sacred purpose; after that, no other man may have sexual access to her. *Kiddushin* takes place when a man gives a women an object of defined minimum value (now typically a ring) while he declares his intention to "consecrate" her and she agrees. Once this occurs, a permanent relationship is established, and if there is a decision not to continue with the marriage, a *get,* or bill of divorce, must be written. In antiquity, months or more passed between *kiddushin* and *nisu'in,* after which a woman could permanently co-reside with her husband. In eleventh-century France it became the practice to combine both phases of the ceremony, and this was widely adopted in Europe and later became common elsewhere. In several Middle Eastern communities, the separation of the phases continued until much more recent times.

The *ketubba,* or marriage contract, is also a post-biblical institution. It states the economic obligations of a man to a woman if the marriage relationship terminates. Its contents have varied over time and place. It might specify the dowry brought into the marriage by a woman or contain specific conditions. For example, within Sephardi tradition, where polygamy remained a theoretical option, it might stipulate that a man may take a second wife only with the permission of the first. Traditionally a *ketubba* is written in Aramaic and signed by two witnesses. Often, parts of it are read or explained at wedding ceremonies between the *kiddushin* and *nisu'in* phases, but this is not required to make it binding. At various times, artistic traditions of *ketubba* illumination developed. Today, in liberal branches of Judaism, opportunities are offered to a couple to formulate their own mutual commitments in written form, and they may choose to place an elaborately decorated *ketubba* on a wall in their new home. These practices both hold on to and reinterpret aspects of an ancient *halakhic* pattern.

The *nisu'in* phase in antiquity entailed a woman moving permanently into her husband's home. The wedding canopy, or *ḥuppa,* which became common in the Ashkenazi Middle Ages, is seen as symbolizing this stage. Another pattern, still common in some Sephardi traditions, is for the groom to spread his prayer shawl over the head of the bride. Liturgically, *nisu'in* is marked by the recital of seven blessings from Talmudic literature. They may be summarized as follows:

1. A blessing over wine;
2. Three blessings citing God's fashioning humankind with the power of procreation;
3. A blessing over the ingathering of Jews to Jerusalem;
4. Two blessings citing the joy of the bride and groom.

This order moves from the most inclusive category of humanity through Jewish peoplehood and then highlights the single couple. The fifth and the last blessings mention, respectively, Zion and Jerusalem, with the latter expressing the hope that the joy of weddings will soon be heard again in that city. This theme is also associated with the well-known feature of Jewish weddings of breaking a glass, which now typically concludes the ceremony. Formally, it is only a custom, but for many it marks the high point of Jewish weddings. It carries many general meanings, such as breaking the hymen, severance from the natal family, and the irreversibility of passage, which energize the now standard rabbinic gloss that it reminds people of the destroyed ancient Temple in Jerusalem. This illustrates how rabbinic rules and interpretations interlace with popular practices and understandings that traditionally featured festivities taking place during the days preceding and following the wedding itself.

At the turn of the twenty-first century, a major factor embellishing basic marriage ritual is the expectation of equality between the partners, and in liberal branches of Judaism rabbis may encourage couples to suggest their own innovations. Orthodox rabbis open to this trend have also found ways to express equality, such as including women friends among the those who hold up the *ḥuppa* or having the bride give the groom a ring in addition to the formal *kiddushin.* A personally formulated *ketubba*, viewed either as the essential marriage contract in liberal ceremonies or as a supplementary document in some Orthodox instances, is another feature that is spreading.

Divorce, while discouraged in Jewish tradition, has always been a possibility and is explicitly mentioned in *Deuteronomy* 24:1. There is symmetry between divorce and marriage in rabbinic law; they are both actions taken by the man to which a woman acquiesces (or refuses). The necessity of having a woman agree to accept a bill of divorce was instituted by authorities in medieval Ashkenaz. A *get* is a short document, addressed to a woman from her husband, which releases her from her commitment to him and makes her "permissible to any man." In contrast to a *ketubba,* it cannot be a standard form in which the names and date are filled in, but must be prepared expressly for the divorce in question. After it is written, a *get* must be delivered to a woman, and it must be clear that she received and accepted it. If there are mistakes in a *get*, or a lack of clarity, it may be claimed that a woman is not formally divorced. If she then enters into a relationship with another man, she is committing adultery. Rabbis have always been concerned with the exactitude of the *get* procedure, not only with regard to the "morality" of women but with reference to potential illegitimate children (*mamzerim*) issuing from an adulterous union, who themselves would be severely restricted as to whom they could marry.

This has given rise to the problem of the *aguna*, an "anchored" women who is no longer in an active marriage but has not received a *get*, making it impossible for her to remarry within a Jewish framework. Classically, this concerns women whose husbands have disappeared without proof of death. In modern times this problem has become acute in places where Jews live under civil law within a nation-state while their marital status is also subject to rabbinic law either because they are Jewish citizens of Israel or because they choose to follow *halakhah*. Cases exist of husbands who effectively have separated from their wives but refuse to give them a *get* out of indifference or hostility. This critical life-cycle issue is now discussed within organizations and networks that span the Jewish world, in the attempt to find both *halakhic* and practical solutions for women in the status of *aguna.*

Death, Mourning, and Memory. The Hebrew Bible contains only a few explicit rules concerning death and mourning, but many practices and attitudes are reflected throughout it that became models for customs and regulations that were systematized later. These include repugnance over delay in burying corpses, the rending of garments by a mourner, eulogies, a meal initiating the process of reconciliation with loss, and the expectation that friends visit and console a mourner. Part of the rabbinic liturgy during burial is a quote from the *Book of Job* (1:21): "The Lord gave, and the Lord hath taken away: blessed be the name of the Lord." Several rules separate the realms of sacrificial sanctity and of a *kohen* from death: a priest should not have contact with the dead except with regard to his immediate family (*Lv.* 21:1–3). A tendency in Pentateuchal law is to encourage ordinary Israelites to adopt priestlike standards, as in the prohibition against gashing one's skin when hearing news of death (*Dt.* 14:1–2). This practice, violating the prohibition, still took place in the twentieth century among women from some communities in the Middle East.

Rabbinic laws were systematized in an extra-Talmudic compilation that acquired the euphemistic name *Semaḥot*, or rejoicings. It opens by asserting that a person who is dying is to be considered alive in every respect: nothing should be done to hasten death. It also defines periods of mourning: the first intense week (*shivʿah*), thirty days, and a year. During *shivʿah,* one should stay at home and refrain from washing, anointing oneself, wearing shoes, and sexual intercourse. Friends are obligated to visit and console a mourner during this period. The Bible and early rabbinic writings did not provide elaborate images of life after death. Some claim that such notions grew subsequent to the devastation that followed the second-century CE revolt against Roman power.

Much later, beginning in the late eleventh century, the suffering associated with the Crusades in Western Europe were the context for a liturgical development that has become central in Jewish mourning and commemoration: the *kaddish* prayer.

Communities in Ashkenaz compiled memory books with the names of people murdered during the Crusades, including the names of women, and created ritual occasions (*yizkor*), upon which these names were read aloud. This created a nexus between personal and communal memorialization. The notion also developed, based on Talmudic and extra-Talmudic sources, that a person could assist the soul of a deceased parent by bringing the community to declare, in Aramaic, "May the name of God be blessed forever and ever" (*Dn.* 2:20). This is the kernel of the *kaddish* that exists in various versions and came to fulfill various liturgical functions, but which is saliently associated with memorialization. It is recited by a mourner in daily prayer during the first year after death, on the anniversary of death, and on *yizkor* occasions. Some Sephardi scholars resisted the notion of an impact upon the soul of the deceased, but the idea spread throughout the Jewish world. Traditionally, it was associated with males only, but in liberal streams of Judaism women also recite *kaddish.*

Late medieval Ashkenaz was also the site of the evolution of the *ḥevra kaddisha,* the burial society charged with dealing with sick people on their death bed and making funeral arrangements. It emerged at a time when traditional communal authority was weakening and concerned itself with many matters like collecting and distributing charity or providing funds for the dowries and weddings of orphans. Its power derived from vivid images of the afterlife of the soul that were developing with the diffusion of qabbalistic notions through wide social circles, with the *ḥevra kaddisha* becoming the gatekeeper for the correct ritual transition from this world to the next. At this point, specialized manuals dealing with the soul, death, and burial began to appear and may reflect a step in the explicit recognition of "the" life cycle. Similar developments occurred elsewhere, and a professional *ḥevra kaddisha* is still the main framework for dealing with death. In smaller communities in North America where there is no *ḥevra kaddisha,* many funeral homes send morticians to train someone so that proper last rites are provided for local Jews. A late-twentieth-century development in such communities is that "ordinary" Jews have banded together to form a *ḥevra kaddisha* on a voluntary basis.

Modern science and emancipation created some clashes between rabbinic norms regarding burial and the nation-states of which they became citizens. The traditional expectation was that a person would be buried as soon after death as possible. Late in the eighteenth century there was growing concern over the possibility of "false death"—that a person would appear to be dead and mistakenly be buried alive. Rabbinic criteria of establishing death had to be coordinated with prevailing secular concepts and laws. Issues of difference and possible coordination continue to exist over matters such as "brain death," organ transplants, and mercy killing. Another example concerns the death of infants under thirty days old. Traditional *halakhah* does not provide for any burial ceremony, while pregnancies assisted by modern prenatal examinations often imbue an unborn fetus with individual characteristics resulting in a personal sense of loss even in the case of a prefers miscarriage. In all these areas contemporary rabbis within both liberal and orthodox streams of Judaism have forged a variety of approaches to abandoning some burial and mourning practices, maintaining and reinterpreting others, and in some cases shaping new ones.

Practices of memorialization have also accommodated to modern circumstances. The anonymous death of millions in the Nazi Holocaust meant that the date of death of close relatives often was not known. Israel's chief rabbinate selected the tenth of the Hebrew month of Tevet, a fast day marking the siege of Jerusalem in the sixth century BCE, as a date appropriate for the recital of *kaddish* on behalf of these Holocaust victims. Individual mourning thus continues to be linked to collective definitions. Within the United States, suburban synagogues built in the second half of the twentieth century often incorporated within them memorial boards, carrying the names of deceased individuals, that had been removed from defunct synagogues in areas where Jews no longer lived. One example concerns Jews in South Africa, from which there is continued out-migration. Cremation is not permitted by *halakhah,* but some Jews there have requested to be cremated in order to make their remains transportable, because they realize that there will be no children nearby to visit their graves. Here is an example of one traditional pattern clashing with another in changed circumstances.

CONVERSION. While not an inevitable phase of the life cycle, conversion ritual can be viewed as a rite of passage: the Talmud states that a proselyte is like a newborn child. The Bible envisions the possibility of foreigners joining the Israelites and participating in rituals but does not provide a single marker of that process. *Exodus* (12:48) insists that foreigners among the Israelites be circumcised in order to partake of the Passover sacrifice, and *Deutoronomy* (21:10–14) specifies how a woman captured in war may become a legitimate wife. The Mishnah does not contain a tractate dealing with proselytes, or *gerim,* but Talmudic literature includes debates over which conversion rituals are the most critical ones: circumcision, immersion in amiqveh, or both together. One source states that a proselyte must be informed about some of the weightier *mitzvot,* along with some less central ones, but there is little stress on understanding the motivations of the individual proselyte. None of the sources emphasizes conversion as a personal religious transformation, but they do stress the affiliation with a new collectivity and its norms. The notion of examining the motives of a potential convert began to emerge only in the Middle Ages. For much of the medieval period, the actual likelihood of Christians or Muslims converting to Judaism was minimal, so the rabbinic legal tradition in this area was not tested by the crucible of historical experience. With emancipation in Europe, issues of intermarriage and potential conversion arose with a new poignancy.

As with other ritual issues, diverse approaches developed toward conversion. Orthodox rabbis have been hesitant to accept converts on the grounds that their motives may be extraneous, and do so only when convinced that the proselyte will lead an orthodox life. The liberal streams have been more open, but Conservative Judaism demands preparatory study, circumcision, and immersion, while Reform Judaism does not insist upon the ritual requirements. In the wake of widespread intermarriage in the United States in the late twentieth century, Reform Judaism also decided that a person can claim Jewish status through descent either from a father or a mother, while traditional *halakhah* sees only the mother as determinative. The small Reform movement in Israel did not encourage this innovation because the situation in that country, where the state privileges Orthodoxy, raises questions of whether ritual matters that effect personal status might create permanent splits within the Jewish population. Given the links between Israel and Jews all over the world, life-cycle events can become global political issues. On the background of growing choice in all cultural realms, questions of community and of religious authority at the beginning of the twenty-first century often appear as aspects of individual life cycles.

SEE ALSO Conservative Judaism; Orthodox Judaism; Reconstructionist Judaism; Reform Judaism.

BIBLIOGRAPHY

Boyarin, Daniel. *Carnal Israel: Reading Sex in Talmudic Culture.* Berkeley, Calif., 1993.

Goldberg, Harvey E. *Jewish Passages: Cycles of Jewish Life.* Berkeley, Calif., 2003.

Goldberg, Sylvie-Anne. *Crossing the Jabbok: Illness and Death in Ashkenazi Judaism in Sixteenth-through-Nineteenth-Century Prague.* Translated by Carol Cosman. Berkeley, Calif., 1996.

Hoffman, Lawrence A. *Covenant of Blood: Circumcision and Gender in Rabbinic Judaism.* Chicago, 1996.

Horowitz, Elliot. "The Eve of Circumcision: A Chapter in the History of Jewish Nightlife." *Journal of Social History* 23 (1989): 45–69.

Klein, Isaac. *A Guide to Jewish Religious Practice.* New York, 1979.

Lamm, Maurice. *The Jewish Way in Death and Mourning.* New York, 1969.

Marcus, Ivan. *Rituals of Childhood: Jewish Acculturation in Medieval Europe.* New Haven, Conn., 1996.

Orenstein, Debra, ed. *Lifecycles: Jewish Women on Life Passages and Personal Milestones.* Woodstock, Vt., 1994.

Rubin, Nisan. *The Beginning of Life: Rites of Birth, Circumcision and Redemption of the First-Born in the Talmud and Midrash.* Tel Aviv, Israel, 1995. In Hebrew.

Wasserfall, Rahel R., ed. *Women and Water: Menstruation in Jewish Life and Law.* Hanover, N.H., 1999.

Weissler, Chava. *Voices of the Matriarchs: Listening to the Prayers of Early Modern Jewish Women.* Boston, 1998.

HARVEY E. GOLDBERG (2005)

RITES OF PASSAGE: MUSLIM RITES

While Muslims throughout the world emphasize the unity of Islam, they also recognize the impressive diversity of cultural and historical contexts in which Islamic civilization has been elaborated and expressed. Because of this diversity, rites of passage in the Islamic world draw equally upon ritual forms and metaphors specific to local cultural contexts and upon the more universal elements of the Islamic tradition. Some of these ritual and expressive forms existed prior to the advent of Islam in the seventh century CE and were incorporated with appropriate shifts in context and meaning into the Islamic tradition. Others developed concurrently with the Islamic tradition.

Some transitions marked by rites of passage, including birth, naming, circumcision, social puberty, betrothal, marriage, pregnancy, motherhood, fatherhood, death, and mourning, are not specific to the Islamic world. These rites show an especially wide diversity of form and content because they incorporate major elements of local belief and practice. Marriage, for instance, is a secular contract in Islam. Muslim jurisprudence specifies certain legal requirements but not the form taken by marriage ceremonies. Provided that preexisting rites of passage are not directly contrary to the more universalistic aspects of the Islamic tradition, they remain a part of accepted local practice. Likewise, socially recognized transitions considered significant in some Islamic societies may be given much less emphasis in others. Some transitions, including the completion of Qurʾanic schooling and the pilgrimage (*ḥājj*) to Mecca, are specifically Islamic, yet how these occasions are ritually marked varies considerably with location.

Because of this diversity, rites of passage considered to be inherent components of the Islamic tradition in some parts of the Islamic world or by some social groups are not always accepted as having anything to do with Islam by Muslims elsewhere. For example, before departing for the pilgrimage to Mecca, many North African Muslims first circumambulate their town or village, visiting its principal shrines in the company of friends and relatives. Flags or banners associated with these shrines are carried in the procession. On their return from Mecca, the pilgrims participate in a similar procession and visit local shrines before crossing the thresholds of their homes. Modernist Muslims claim that these "local" ceremonies have nothing to do with Islam or the pilgrimage proper, but for many North Africans these practices remain an integral part of Islam as they practice and understand their faith. Modernist sentiments are even more intense against the annual festivals (*mūsims*) of some ethnic groups in North Africa, especially Morocco, in which ethnic collectivities renew their "covenant" (*ʿahd*) with particular saints and their living descendants through the offering of a sacrifice. Many such festivals occur annually just before the planting season and the moving of herds from summer to winter pastures. Similarly, the Alevi (Arab., ʿAlawī) Muslims of eastern Turkey, Syria, and northern Iraq fast only twelve days per year, in honor of the twelve imams (leaders of the Islamic community) whom they recognize, instead of for an entire lunar month. Alevis also consider that the true *ḥājj* is carried out in one's heart, not in travel to Mecca. Their interpretation of Islamic obligations and practice is not recognized as valid by neighboring Muslims of other sects.

Although some rites of passage resemble one another in general form throughout the Muslim world, a thorough knowledge of how they are locally elaborated is essential to understanding their contextual meaning. Most of these rites derive in part from formal Islamic doctrine but are equally shaped by, and in turn shape, diverse underlying local conceptions of society. In Marrakesh, for example, the ceremonies marking birth, circumcision, marriage, and pilgrimage resemble one another because they share an underlying conception of social boundaries and social space. These conceptions are not derived from Islamic doctrine, but neither are they opposed to it. After a woman gives birth, she and her child are confined for seven days to the room in which the birth took place. Ceremonies involving only close relatives are then performed, but until the fortieth day after birth, the mother and her child refrain from crossing the threshold of the house. At the end of this period, they visit one of the principal shrines of Marrakesh. After a child is circumcised, he and his mother are likewise confined to one room of the house for the first week then to the entire house for another interval; finally, all restrictions on movement end after a visit to one of the major local shrines. For marriage, newly wed couples remain seven days in the nuptial chamber, followed by a few days in the house itself and finally a visit to one of the principal shrines. Returning pilgrims, once they have entered their houses, follow a similar progression to regain the full use of social space and to reincorporate themselves into ordinary society. Even with the widespread expansion of mass education in recent years, which has the effect in many parts of the world of modifying or eliminating local ritual practices, those of Marrakesh remain largely intact.

In Islamic societies, as in others, the social and cultural significance accorded to specific rites of passage becomes clear only when the rites are considered in their full social context. In some parts of the Muslim world—in Silwa, a village in Egypt's Aswan province, for example—weddings are an important marker of transition, especially for women. Upon marriage a woman leaves the residence of her own parents and becomes part of her husband's domestic group. However, the significance of marriage elsewhere—as in Atjeh, in northern Sumatra, for example—is overshadowed by a woman's first live birth. In Atjeh, when a woman becomes a mother, she also becomes an adult and takes legal possession of her house. The ceremonies associated with her becoming a mother and the naming of her child are locally regarded as much more significant than marriage itself: Women claim that they are girls until they have children.

In the interior of Oman, a country in the southeastern corner of the Arabian Peninsula, marriages generally occur within the extended family and often involve a move of no more than several hundred feet for the bride, from the house of her father to that of a nearby relative. She continues to spend the better part of the day in the house of her own mother, although elsewhere in the Muslim world it is common to have a period of avoidance between a new wife and her family of birth. Marriage ceremonies in the Omani interior are such subdued, private occasions that non-family members often learn that they have taken place only after the event. In contrast, once a woman gives birth, the naming ceremony for her child is elaborate. It occasions visits from every household in the community and results in the mother's achieving full social status as a woman. The mother, not the child, is the center of attention at naming ceremonies.

Since the interpretation of rites of passage is dependent upon local cultural contexts, principal Moroccan practices are described here to illustrate a complete set of major social transitions. Examples are also provided from elsewhere in the Islamic world to indicate the range of major variation.

Birth and Naming. In Morocco, if a woman wishes to induce pregnancy or fears a difficult one, she visits the sanctuaries of marabouts (*walīs*) reputed for their efficacy in dealing with such difficulties. She will often leave a strip of cloth from her own dress as a promise that, if her childbirth occurs, she will return and sacrifice a sheep or goat, distributing its meat either to descendants of the *walī* or to the poor. Once a woman knows she is pregnant, she begins to eat special foods and to receive visits from female neighbors and relatives, practices that are common elsewhere in the Islamic world.

After she has given birth, a woman is confined to her house for a period that varies from a week to forty days. During this period she is regarded as ritually unclean and is unable to pray and fast, an indication of her marginal status. At the end of her confinement she is taken by female friends and relatives to the public bath, resumes normal activities, and is able once again to leave her house. The child is kept in its swaddling clothes during this period and is constantly guarded for fear that he or she might be exchanged for a malevolent spirit *(jinnī)*. Most women unaffected by modernist Islamic belief and practice perform a series of rituals designed to propitiate any such spirits that might be nearby.

The most important event in the child's life is the naming ceremony (*subūʿ*), which ideally occurs a week after the birth of a child of either sex. On this day the child is named, usually by its father but in agreement with the mother and other relatives. The mother is bathed, dressed in new clothes, and painted with henna, often by the midwife who has delivered the child. The child also has henna applied to its face, hands, and feet, both because henna is thought to be pleasing to the eye and because it is thought to protect the child's spirit from harm. The mother receives visits from female relatives and neighbors on this occasion.

There is no fixed set of relatives involved in the naming of a child in Morocco. The choice is primarily a personal one and may also involve consultation with patrons or close friends. Likewise, the selection of names reflects a variety of influences and personal choices. Some persons prefer distinctly religious names such as Muḥammad (Mḥā in Berber-speaking regions) or ʿAbd Allāh ("servant of God") for men, and Fāṭimah, the name of the Prophet's daughter, for women. Other children are named after a religious feast day, such as Mulūdī for a man born on or near the Prophet's birthday (colloquially, ʿĪd al-Mulūd). Other names reflect a commitment to nationalism, as in using the name ʿAllāl, after the Moroccan nationalist leader ʿAllāl al-Fāsī. The name chosen may honor a recently deceased relative; it is a bad omen to name a child after a living relative. In non-Arabic-speaking countries, such as Indonesia and Bangladesh, the growing use of Arabic names instead of non-Islamic ones or names in local languages is a direct result of a growing commitment to reform Islam.

For boys in Morocco, the naming ceremony is always accompanied by the sacrifice of a sheep or goat, although a blood sacrifice is often omitted in the case of girls. This sacrifice is known as the *ʿaqīqah* ceremony. The male relatives and friends of the father are invited to a midday feast, the child's hair is cut for the first time, and alms are distributed to the poor. A separate feast is held for female relatives in the evening. This rite of passage is so significant that in wealthy families it is not unusual for hundreds of guests from throughout the country to attend. In many villages, each part of the sacrificed animal has a special significance and is designated for particular persons. The liver is eaten only by members of the household, and the heart and stomach fat are eaten by the mother alone. Other parts of the animal, usually including the skin and entrails, are destined for the midwife.

Moroccans consider the sacrifice for the naming ceremony to be an Islamic obligation, although of the four legal schools of Sunnī Islam only the Ḥanbali school regards it as compulsory. The other schools merely allow the practice, although Islamic tradition ascribes the sacrifice, which has pre-Islamic antecedents, to the prophet Muḥammad (d. 632). The sacrifice, like the haircutting, is thought to avert evil from the child by offering a substitute sacrifice. At the same time, with the acquisition of a name, the child becomes a full social person.

Circumcision. Circumcision is the next major rite of passage for boys. It usually occurs between the ages of two and seven. There is no equivalent ceremony in Morocco for girls. The day before the circumcision, the boy is bathed, and his head is shaved. His mother paints henna on his hands and feet to ward off the evil eye. A sacrifice is made, and a feast is prepared for friends, neighbors, and relatives, to which the guests bring small gifts. Many households wait until ʿĪd al-Aḍḥā or a marriage in the family or arrange with other households to have their children circumcised together. On the day after the circumcision feast, the boy, dressed in fine clothes and accompanied by musicians, is led around town on a mule. In the past in some areas, his clothes would have resembled those of a bride. Elements of the circumcision ceremonies are exactly parallel to those of marriage. The boy's mother and sisters wear their hair loose, as they would for a wedding. Just before the circumcision itself, usually performed by an itinerant specialist but increasingly by medical personnel, the boy is dressed in a new, white shift, often similar to that worn by pilgrims to Mecca. The garment is another indication of the purificatory intent of the ritual.

In classical Arabic, circumcision is known as *khitān,* although in Morocco and elsewhere in the Arab world it is usually known as *ṭahārah* ("purification"), and in Turkey as *sünnet,* or the practice of the Prophet. Although not mentioned in the Qurʾān, circumcision is attributed to the Prophet and recognized as a pre-Islamic Arabian tradition; it appears to have been performed at puberty and as a preliminary to marriage. There is a modern tendency among educated Moroccans to have their children circumcised at an earlier age, sometimes even at birth, although for most families circumcision still takes place when a child, toward the age of six or seven, prepares to assume the responsibilities of an adult Muslim, including the daily prayers and the Ramaḍān fast.

In Morocco, as elsewhere in the Muslim world, the possession of reason *(ʿaql)* informed by accepted Islamic practice implies the ability of Muslims to subordinate their "natural" passions or personal inclinations (*hawa nafs*) to God's will. The concepts of *ʿaql* and *hawa nafs* occur in almost all Islamic societies. Children are said to be "ignorant" *(jāhil)* because they lack knowledge of the Islamic code of conduct and the capacity to abide by it. Thus, when circumcision occurs at the traditionally preferred age of six or seven, it marks the beginning of full participation in the Islamic community. Memorization of the Qurʾān, for those children who accomplish this feat, also sets a child apart from ordinary society through the mnemonic possession of the word of God. Like circumcision, the event is marked by a public procession and announcement of the child's new status.

Marriage. After discreet private negotiations between the families involved, a date for the wedding and the size of the marriage payment (*ṣadāq*) are set. This payment, relative to the value placed on the girl and her family, is used to buy domestic furnishings that remain the bride's property. By Islamic law, payment must be made in order for the marriage to be valid. The contract is usually signed in the presence of notaries or valid witnesses just after a ceremonial dinner at the girl's home at which her father or guardian is formally asked for her hand. Later, an engagement party is held. This is primarily a woman's party, with dancing and singing, the closing of the marriage contract, and payment of the bridewealth.

A day or two before the actual wedding, the bride's family delivers to the bridegroom's home the furnishings purchased with the *ṣadāq* money. These are publicly displayed, often on the back of a truck, and accompanied by drummers and musicians. There is often a small celebration at the woman's house before she is taken to that of her future husband. In rural areas, the groom's party may bring an animal to be sacrificed at her house. Several days later they return to carry the bride away to the groom's house, where the major ceremony is held. As the groom's party, often accompanied by the blowing of horns and drumming, approaches the woman's house, there is a mock battle between the bride's family and the groom's, at the end of which the girl is allowed to be taken away. She has been prepared by purification with water and henna.

The day before the wedding, the groom also undergoes purification. He goes to the bath, accompanied by his friends, and is treated as if he were a sultan with his court. He is often painted with henna and entertained by musicians. In the past in some regions, the groom was himself dressed like a bride for a brief period, a custom that emphasized all the more the imminent transformation of his status. Afterward, he is washed, shaved, and dressed in new clothes.

Upon arrival at the groom's house, the bride is ceremonially dressed in heavy layers of fine brocades and jewels, often rented for the occasion. After a long evening of music and feasting, the groom leaves his guests, enters the bridal chamber, lifts the bride's veil, and ceremonially offers her milk and dates. Depending upon the region of Morocco and the social class, close relatives may visit the couple briefly at this stage. Wedding gifts are publicly announced and displayed at this time. Religious specialists are invited to the wedding feast, where they recite the Qurʾān and invoke blessings upon the couple but do not play a central role. Celebrations continue until proof of the bride's virginity is brought to the guests, although Moroccans are rapidly abandoning this practice. For a week thereafter, the wife remains confined to her husband's house, receiving visits only from close female friends. So that the bride may become accustomed to new patterns of domestic authority, she is forbidden to see her father, brothers, and other male relatives for at least three months. The public nature of parts of the ceremony, the bride's change of residence, and the restrictions on her conduct formally denote the couple's change of marital status.

DEATH. Deaths and funeral ceremonies show the most consistency in essential features throughout the Muslim world. More so than the other rites of passage, those for death and mourning are largely common to all Muslims. If the death is expected, the Qurʾān is recited continuously in the presence of the ailing person. At the point of death, the eyes and mouth of the person are closed, and the arms are straightened alongside the body. The deceased is placed with his or her face turned toward Mecca. For the duration of mourning, regular social life is suspended for those affected. A person of the same sex who knows the prescribed ritual washing and preparation of the dead is called in. The women of the family are expected to cry and lose their composure, but men's expressions of grief are expected to be much more restrained. The deceased is wrapped in a white seamless cloth similar to that worn for the pilgrimage; in the case of those who have actually made the *ḥājj*, the seamless white garments worn while in Mecca are used. The Qurʾān is recited. Burial occurs quickly, on the same day if death occurs in the morning or early afternoon; if death occurs late in the day, burial is postponed until the next morning. Friends and relatives accompany the procession to the cemetery, where a prayer for the dead is recited by a religious specialist. On returning from the cemetery, participants in the procession are provided with a meal at the house of the deceased. In some rural areas, food is also placed over the grave for the first three days after death.

Mourning continues for three days, the period thought to be sanctioned by the Qurʾān, and consolations are received by the relatives of the deceased. Since death is ordained by God, proper conduct for a Muslim after the initial shock of grief is to accept the will of God. The lack of forbearance and composure (*ʿazaʾ*) implies a lack of reason, in this context the capacity to adjust to an expression of God's will. A widow remains in seclusion for four months and ten days, a period prescribed by the Qurʾān and the minimum legal waiting period (*ʿiddah*) before she is allowed to remarry. In Morocco, it is not unusual for elaborate stone markers or enclosures to be erected around the grave, a sharp contrast with, for example, the custom of the Ibāḍīyah of Oman, who indicate the equality of all Muslims after death by marking graves with simple stones, none of which carry inscriptions.

MAJOR VARIATIONS. If there are numerous points of resemblance among rites of passage in the Islamic world, divergences are just as pronounced. In Egyptian villages along the Nile, women visit shrines and cross the river to encourage conception; the latter practice is directly related to a wish to induce a change in the woman's status. In these practices, the parallels with Morocco are almost exact, yet divergences also become clear when overall patterns are considered. In Atjeh, for instance, an elaborate series of visits takes place between the mothers of the wife and the husband, both before and after births, accompanied by complex food restrictions. Some of these restrictions occur only for odd-numbered pregnancies. In Java, the various rituals associated with birth are timed by the Javanese calendar, in which each month has thirty-five days. Many of the rituals involve a rich mixture of Islamic, Hindu-Buddhist, and indigenous spirits, and each food and gesture associated with these rituals has a specific implication. Thus, in the small feast for household members only, which occurs just before birth, a dish of rice is served with a peeled banana in the middle, to symbolize an easy birth. The precision with which events are timed and the punctilious concern with ritual detail are alien to other parts of the Islamic world. After childbirth in Atjeh, a woman may not leave her house for forty-four days. For much of this time, she lies on a platform over hot bricks with her legs extended and her ankles together. The idea behind this "roasting" is to become as dry as possible in order to expel the aftereffects of childbirth, again a set of notions without direct correspondences elsewhere.

The obligations incurred by guests at life-crisis ceremonies and the comportment appropriate to them also show considerable range. Egyptian villagers keep punctilious written accounts of the gifts they give to other members of the community and the value of those they receive in return. By contrast, the notion of strict, explicit equality of value is lacking in the Arabian Peninsula and is there considered to be against the spirit of Islam. In Java, certain foods such as wafer-thin disks of rice are served at major life-crisis feasts. Sharing them is meant to symbolize that all guests are internally composed and free from strong emotions such as envy, hate, and jealousy, a concern not equally emphasized elsewhere.

Circumcision shows two major patterns of variation throughout the Islamic world. Although all males are circumcised, women are circumcised only in certain areas, notably in Upper Egypt, the Sudan, Somalia, Ethiopia, West Africa, and Atjeh. Circumcision for women, which occurs between the ages of six or seven (Egypt) and twelve (Atjeh), occasions a minimum of ceremony. It does not result in any significant change of status for a girl, although the operation is considered a necessary prerequisite to marriage. Unlike boys undergoing circumcision, girls are allowed and even encouraged to cry out in pain. The Islamic jurist al-Shāfiʿī (767–820 CE) argues that circumcision is obligatory for both sexes. Other jurists argue that it is merely "honorable" for women. The more extreme forms of circumcision, including infibulation, have been declared illegal in recent years by many governments, although enforcement is highly variable.

The age at which male circumcision occurs varies according to its significance in a particular cultural context. In northern Yemen, for example, circumcision until recently took place between the ages of twelve and fifteen and, despite official government bans, continues in some areas. The youth is surrounded by men and women of his village. A knife is held to his foreskin as he recites three times, "There is no god but God and Muḥammad is his Prophet." The foreskin is then cut and thrown into the crowd. The youth retrieves it and is carried on his mother's shoulders while he continues to display it proudly, leading a procession of dancers and brandishing his dagger. He is humiliated for life if he shows any sign of pain. In this context, circumcision is more a test of virility and a marker of young adult status than a point of entry into participation in the religious community, which is the case when circumcision occurs at the age of six or seven, as in Morocco. In Java, it traditionally occurred after a youth had completed religious studies, between the ages of ten and fourteen; two transitions that are kept separate elsewhere in the Islamic world were thus fused. Circumcision is also seen as a prelude to marriage, which is not the case when it occurs at a much younger age.

The vitality of the Islamic tradition is indicated in its capacity for self-renewal and transformation. The rites of passage described here for the Islamic world are inseparable from basic notions of social and cultural identity. As notions of identity shift, so do the forms of many of these rituals, even in the face of traditions previously accepted and taken for granted in specific contexts. Since the late nineteenth century, modernist and reform movements in Islam have given impetus to a reappraisal of the links between Islam and personal identity. Likewise, the abandonment or modification of practices not considered authentically Islamic, even if locally tolerated, signifies that notions of self and community are in a process of change, a process that is ongoing throughout the Islamic world.

BIBLIOGRAPHY

The relevant entries in the old edition of *The Encyclopaedia of Islam,* 4 vols. and supplement (Leiden, 1913–1938), and the new edition in progress (Leiden, 1960–) are strongest in summarizing Islamic legal thought and classical writing on rites of passage and include extensive bibliographies for these fields. W. Robertson Smith's *Kinship and Marriage in Early Arabia,* edited by Stanley A. Cook (1903; new ed., Oosterhout, Netherlands, 1966), and *Lectures on the Religion of the Semites,* 2d ed. (1894; reprint, New York, 1956), remain valuable for comparing early Islamic rites of passage with earlier Semitic practice. Christiaan Snouck Hurgronje's *Mekka in the Latter Part of the Nineteenth Century* (1888–1889), translated by J. H. Monahan (1931; reprint, Leiden, 1970), provides extensive ethnographic description. For Morocco, Edward A. Westermarck's *Marriage Ceremonies in Morocco* (1914; reprint, London, 1972) and *Ritual and Belief in Morocco,* vol. 2 (1926; reprint, New Hyde Park, N. Y., 1968), provides meticulous ethnographic detail useful to contrast with descriptions contained in studies of more recent practice.

Among modern studies, see my *Moroccan Islam: Tradition and Society in a Pilgrimage Center* (Austin, Tex, 1976). For a psychoanalytic perspective on a single ritual, see Vincent Crapanzano's "Rite of Return: Circumcision in Morocco," in volume 9 of *The Psychoanalytic Study of Society,* edited by Warner Muensterberger and L. Bryce Boyer (New York, 1981), pp. 15–36. Excellent discussions of rites of passage in other countries are included in Hamed Ammar's *Growing Up in an Egyptian Village* (1954; reprint, London, 1956); James T. Siegel's *The Rope of God* (Berkeley, 1969), for Atjeh; Clifford Geertz's *The Religion of Java* (New York, 1964); and John R. Bowen's "Death and the History of Islam in Highland Aceh," *Indonesia* 38 (October 1984): 21–38. For an excellent study of historical change in naming practices, see Richard W. Bulliet's "First Names and Political Change in Modern Turkey," *International Journal of Middle East Studies* 9 (November 1978): 489–495.

DALE F. EICKELMAN (1987)

RITES OF PASSAGE: NEOPAGAN RITES

Rites of passage, like most forms of Neopagan ritual, take place within a sacred circle. The basic ritual form of the circle casting illustrates the ways in which deity is in the world, not outside it. While different variations on circle casting exist, most circles are oriented with the four cardinal directions, and the four directions are typically associated with forces of nature: fire, air, water, and earth. Some Neopagans address the "powers" of a particular direction, while others address the "winds." Depending on the ritual, specific gods and goddesses are invoked and invited to be present in the circle or embodied by participants. During the ritual, participants are often led on an "astral journey" in which they visualize another realm of existence, the spirit world, or astral reality. The presence of deities, journeys through other worlds, and shifts of consciousness all contribute to participants' experience of the rite. Because it is designated as a safe and sacred space, the circle facilitates initiations, the passing from one phase of life to another, and the shifting from one type of consciousness to another.

Rites of passage include personal initiations within specific Neopagan traditions. Witchcraft covens and Neopagan ritual groups include initiation rites to mark the passage of members from one stage of learning and skill to another. For instance, Gardnerian Witchcraft, named for Gerald Gardner (1883–1964), includes different degrees that participants can attain through training and study within a coven led by a priest and priestess who offer the initiation when they believe their students are ready. Traditional Witchcraft of this type and other forms of Neopaganism are mystery religions in which secret knowledge is passed through a series of initiations, and the individuals who undergo these initiations are expected to be transformed by them.

Seasonal Rituals. Wiccans, or Witches, are the largest Neopagan tradition, and their Wheel of the Year provides a model for other Neopagan celebrations of seasonal festivals. The Wheel is based on the ever-changing relationship of a goddess and a god as they move through the cycle of the seasons. The goddess has varied meanings for Wiccans and among Neopagans in general. She may be seen as a great goddess who encompasses all of life or as the partner of a god. She is also sometimes seen as having three aspects: maiden, mother, and crone (old woman). The maiden aspect of the goddess is celebrated in the spring, the mother in summer, and the crone in winter. The god plays different roles in different seasons as well. He may be referred to as any of the following: Lord of the Greenwood, Sun King, Corn King, Lord of Life and Death, or Leader of the Wild Hunt. The Wheel that the goddess and god move through includes eight sabbats: Yule or Winter Solstice on December 21, Brigid's Day or Candlemas on February 2, Eostar or Spring Equinox on March 21, Beltane on May 1, Litha or Summer Solstice on June 21, Lammas or Lughnasad on August 1, Mabon or Fall Equinox on September 21, and Samhain or Halloween on November 1.

Rituals for these sabbats are designed to celebrate seasonal changes and at the same time to lead participants through personal changes appropriate to the seasons. Beltane, or May Day, for instance, is a celebration of fertility. Neopagan rituals at this time of year might involve selecting a May queen and king who would be symbolically married. Neopagan marriages, called *handfastings*, might be performed on Beltane. Such unions are ritualized in a variety of ways for both homosexual and heterosexual lovers. Some are long-term commitments, while others are for "a year and a day," to be renewed at a later time if the participants are willing.

Rituals designed for Samhain, the festival of the dead, might include a ritualized journey through the land of the dead and remembrances of dead loved ones. Many Samhain rituals refer to some version of the "Descent of the Goddess" in which the goddess descends to the land of the dead to restore the god, who has become the lord of death, to a new life. She sleeps with him and creates him anew so that he will be reborn on the Winter Solstice. In Samhain rites, participants may symbolically undergo this passage from life into the land of death. They may also express their grief for dead ones within a collective ritual process. These seasonal rituals affirm Neopaganism's identity as an earth religion and help people align the changes in their lives with the cycles of the natural world.

Rituals to Mark Life Changes. The Wheel of the Year is also paralleled by the life passages of men and women in the community. Creating new rites of passage is at the heart of Neopagan religion, and these rites are a common feature of Neopagan festivals and other gatherings. Rites of passage are an important way that Neopagans celebrate embodied life changes and create religious community. The goal of these rites is not simply to help a person celebrate significant life changes but also to bind the community together. Starhawk, a famous Neopagan writer and activist, discusses rites of passage in her book *Truth or Dare* (1987), observing that, "Ritual affirms the common patterns, the values, the shared joys, risks, sorrows, and changes that bind a community together. . . . A living community develops its own rituals to celebrate life passages and ease times of transition, to connect us with the round of the changing seasons and the moon's flux, to anchor us in time" (p. 296). Neopagans have created new rituals and reinvented old ones to draw in their community members around pregnancy and birth, marriage, puberty, and death.

Neopagans design rituals to celebrate life experiences from birth to death. For instance, some Neopagans borrow the Navajo "blessingway" tradition to bless a new baby and welcome him or her into the community. Others call their welcoming rite a *wiccaning* or *saining*, which is designed to initiate a child into the community. This ritual may include introducing the child to the deities, giving the community a chance to meet the child and to give gifts and offerings to the child, perhaps even the gift of a personal quality or character trait. But most Neopagans do not see this initiation as determining their child's religious identity, and they are adamant that the child will eventually make his or her own choices. Rituals that mark the end of life and facilitate mourning are similarly diverse and also involve offerings. Sometimes Neopagans set up shrines for the dead in their homes or at nature sanctuaries.

Rites of passage among Neopagans are also directed toward women's and men's specific life changes. The impact of the feminist movement, especially in the United States, has shaped a wide range of women's ritualizing in Witchcraft and other forms of Neopaganism. According to some feminist Neopagans, pregnancy, labor, delivery, and breastfeeding are ways that women embody the goddess in the biological events of their lives. Some feminist Neopagans label their rites of passage "women's mysteries"; the mysteries are seen as physical, emotional, spiritual, and psychic rites of passage that women experience by having been born into a female body. Women's mysteries celebrate the earth's seasonal cycles of birth, death, and regeneration, as well as women's cyclical nature, and they include birth, menstruation, childbirth and lactation, menopause, and death. These women imagine that a society made over by goddess-worshipping Neopagans would sanctify birth and menses. They seek to transform what they see as destructive and disempowering images of body and self by identifying women with goddesses and ancient myths. In this way, female bodies are made sacred, and bodily experience becomes an important aspect of moving from one stage of life to another.

One ritual that some Neopagans have reclaimed is the so-called sacred marriage between a goddess and a god. The sacred marriage that takes place among other kinds of fertility rites on the Neopagan holiday Beltane (May 1) is both marriage and initiation for the man and woman who take part in it by becoming goddess and god. The practice of contemporary "sex magic" includes the sacred marriage, or Great Rite—ritualized intercourse, often between priest and priestess. The Great Rite can take two forms: *actual*, involving intercourse, or *symbolic*, in which the union of the male and female principles is symbolized by putting the athame (ritual knife) into the chalice to bless the wine on the ritual altar. The idea behind the Great Rite is that through ritual a woman becomes the goddess and a man becomes the god. Journalist Margot Adler explains this process in her study of Neopaganism, *Drawing Down the Moon* (1986): "Two people who have drawn down into themselves these archetypal forces, or, if you will, have allowed these forces within them to surface—can have a spiritual and physical union that is truly divine" (p. 110). The actual ritual is sometimes used in traditional Witchcraft initiations and in some handfastings. Because sexuality is seen as a source of spiritual power, Neopagans often include it, both actually and symbolically, in their ritual lives.

Sexual freedom is important to many Neopagans because they believe that sexuality is both natural and sacred, but freedom is translated to mean the right to choose a homosexual relationship, to have multiple lovers, to be celibate, or to commit to a monogamous heterosexual relationship. Some rituals focus on healing or changing aspects of the self that are related to gender and sexuality. Healing from rape and unhealthy sexual relationships is a common focus of ritual work, as are rituals and guided meditations that explore gendered aspects of the self (e.g., men exploring their "feminine side"). Neopagans create theatrical rituals with ancient deities and encourage participants to act out sexual abuse or try on different gender identities. Men wear skirts and gowns for some Neopagan rituals and festivals. All of these rituals are intentionally designed to replace outdated rites and to address the absence of rites of passage and initiatory experiences that Neopagans believe characterizes Western cultures.

Some Neopagans, and especially Neopagan women, have created initiation rites for adolescents. They believe that negative views of the body and sexuality are taught to young children, and particularly to adolescents, and that the way to change this is to celebrate the physical changes that mark the onset of adolescence, such as a girl's first menses. For instance, Starhawk tells the story of how her coven created a ritual to celebrate the first menstruation of a coven member's daughter. It involved a ritual symbolizing the daughter's separation from her mother and ended with each of the women giving the girl a special and personal gift. Starhawk's description of the first menses ritual provides a model for other communities looking for alternative rites of passage for their adolescents.

In Neopaganism, old women, mothers, and adolescent women are each celebrated in unique ways. Many Witches and other Neopagans believe in the "Triple Goddess" of maiden, mother, and crone that originated with the first Neopagans in mid-twentieth-century England. For Neopagans, the Goddess is expansive and encompasses all women's roles. The idea of the Triple Goddess has its origins in the studies of classical Greek and Roman mythology by British scholars Jane Ellen Harrison (1850–1928) and Sir James Frazer (1854–1941), whose works were consulted by the earliest Neopagans. Through the Triple Goddess, women at all stages of life can identify with a sacred feminine ideal. The revaluing of women's bodies at all stages of life and the identification of the feminine as divine has made possible many of the new rites of passage Neopagans have created. Neopagans redefine the archetypes of maiden, mother, and crone (wise old woman), leaving them open to personal interpretation by the women who look to them for guidance. *Cronings*, for instance, honor women who have become elders in their communities. During croning rituals, the lifelong achievements of older women are honored, and they are given gifts to symbolize the new stage of life they have entered.

MEN'S RITES. Rites for women are much more common than rites for men, in part because of the tremendous popularity of images and stories of goddesses and the disproportionate influence of the feminist movement on Neopagan communities. Many Neopagans share the desire to affirm and make positive those aspects of gendered behavior that they believe have been repressed or are seen as evil, such as homosexual relationships, women celebrating their sexuality outside of marriage, and men choosing more traditionally feminine roles. But Neopagans also include men's rituals at their gatherings.

Robert Bly's discussion of gender roles in *Iron John* (1990) and Sam Keen's men's movement classic, *Fire in the Belly: On Being a Man* (1991), inspired the men's movement of the 1990s and encouraged Neopagans to explore masculinity and celebrate the variety of male gods that men can look to as models. The approaches of Bly and Keen have resulted in many men's events and have also influenced Neopagan gatherings, so that workshops and rituals on men's issues and for men only now coexist with women-centered activities. Pantheacon, a Neopagan convention held in the San Francisco Bay Area in 2003, included sessions on "Mystery and the Masculine: Connecting to the Male Divine" and "Liturgy for Chiron the Centaur as Sage." New Age and Neopagan men have followed feminist strategies in borrowing images of deities from ancient cultures that they believe offer more diverse models for masculinity and allow men to explore their human potential without being subject to rigid male ideals such as the emotionless warrior. Feminists and men's movement leaders both argue that previous patterns of socialization have been oppressive and limiting. All men and women, they say, need to heal old wounds and change certain ways of doing things before they will be free to explore their full potential as human beings. It is through ritual work that these changes take place.

Men's rites have been more slowly accepted than women's rites, and they sometimes receive mixed reactions when they occur at large Neopagan festivals. Sometimes these rites are called "male mysteries" and explore images of the warrior and hunter. Some Neopagan communities design initiations and workshops for men that might include, for example, flint-napping, making coal from plants, fire-starting, and beer-making. In men-only and women-only spaces, Neopagans say they feel free to explore aspects of femininity and masculinity that have been shaped by biology and culture. The ritual work that Neopagans do with gender and sexuality involves mending and strengthening the spiritual aspects of relationships.

CONCLUSION. Neopagans focus on cyclical changes in nature and in the lives of individuals, but they also see spiritual practice itself as a series of initiatory experiences. Neopagan rituals often involve initiatory journeys of self-exploration to bring about personal growth, healing, and empowerment. They may facilitate healing by externalizing suffering and loss and helping individuals to process painful aspects of their lives within a supportive group setting. Neopagan festivals often include rituals and workshops geared toward inner transformation, such as "Pagan Meditation: The Inner Work of the Old Ways," "Guided Shamanic Journey," and "Metamorphosis: An Approach to Addressing Prenatal Patterns and Means of Change." In some sense, almost all Neopagan rituals are rites of passage in that they involve moving from one phase of life to another. Personal initiation, life passages, and seasonal celebrations share this emphasis. Rites for healing the damage done to sexuality and gender identity and rites that honor and celebrate love relationships, sexual expression, life passages, and bodily experience are all ways that Neopagans incorporate rituals into their lives.

BIBLIOGRAPHY

Adler, Margot. *Drawing Down the Moon: Witches, Druids, Goddess-Worshippers, and Other Pagans in America Today.* New York, 1979. Rev. ed., Boston, 1986.

Berger, Helen A. *A Community of Witches: Contemporary Neo-Paganism and Witchcraft in the United States.* Columbia, S.C., 1999.

Bly, Robert. *Iron John: A Book about Men.* Reading, Mass., 1990.

Griffin, Wendy, ed. *Daughters of the Goddess: Studies of Healing, Identity, and Empowerment.* Walnut Creek, Calif., 2000.

Harvey, Graham. *Contemporary Paganism: Listening People, Speaking Earth.* New York, 1997.

Keen, Sam. *Fire in the Belly: On Being a Man.* New York, 1991.

Pike, Sarah M. *Earthly Bodies, Magical Selves: Contemporary Pagans and the Search for Community.* Berkeley and Los Angeles, 2001.

Salomonsen, Jone. *Enchanted Feminism: Ritual, Gender and Divinity among the Reclaiming Witches of San Francisco.* London and New York, 2002.

Starhawk. *Truth or Dare: Encounters with Power, Authority, and Mystery.* San Francisco, 1987.

Starhawk and M. Macha Nightmare. *The Pagan Book of Living and Dying: Practical Rituals, Prayers, Blessings, and Meditations on Crossing Over.* San Francisco, 1997.

SARAH PIKE (2005)

RITSCHL, ALBRECHT (1822–1889) was a German Protestant theologian. Born in Berlin, the son of a pastor and bishop of the Evangelical church, he was reared in Stettin (present-day Szczecin, Poland), in the Prussian province of Pomerania. From 1839 to 1846 he studied at the universities of Bonn, Halle (Ph. D., 1843), Heidelberg, and Tübingen (where he learned the church historian's craft from Ferdinand Christian Baur). From 1846 to 1864 he taught at Bonn, and from 1864 until his death he was professor of dogmatics (systematic theology) at Göttingen.

Ritschl's teaching and writing at first concentrated on the New Testament and early church history. The views of Baur and his "Tübingen school"—which regarded late second-century Christianity ("old Catholicism") as the outcome and reconciliation of struggles between Jewish Christians ("Petrinists") and gentile Christians ("Paulinists")—informed Ritschl's first two books: *Das Evangelium Marcions und das kanonische Evangelium des Lukas* (The Gospel of Marcion and the Canonical Gospel of Luke; 1846) and *Die Entstehung der altkatholischen Kirche* (The Rise of the Old

Catholic Church; 1851). The second edition of the latter book (1857) marked a dramatic personal and academic break with Baur, whose "conflict model" of early church history Ritschl now repudiated as too speculative or "Hegelian." He insisted, rather, that all the apostles proclaimed a fundamentally similar message, interpreting the ministry of Jesus in the light of its Old Testament presuppositions; that the differences between Jewish and gentile Christians were relative, not substantive, with only a few groups of Judaistic Christians opposing Paul; and that early Catholicism, far from being a Jewish-gentile "synthesis," was wholly a gentile phenomenon, the result of a gradual "de-judaization" of Christianity.

During the 1850s Ritschl's interests turned increasingly to dogmatic theology. While at Göttingen he published two monumental works, each occupying three volumes: *Die christliche Lehre von der Rechtfertigung und Versöhnung* (The Christian Doctrine of Justification and Reconciliation; 1870–1874) and *Geschichte des Pietismus* (History of Pietism; 1880–1886). These works, in tandem with numerous essays and several short monographs—notably *Unterricht in der christlichen Religion* (Instruction in the Christian Religion; 1875)—established Ritschl's international reputation as the foremost Protestant systematic theologian of his time. His disciples occupied the leading chairs in theology at the German universities well into the twentieth century. The most prominent Ritschlians were Adolf von Harnack, Wilhelm Herrmann, and (at an early stage of his career) Ernst Troeltsch.

Ritschl's paramount aim during his Göttingen years was to fashion a comprehensive interpretation of the Christian religion based on the doctrine of justification and reconciliation, as set forth by the New Testament (chiefly the letters of Paul) and by the Protestant reformers (chiefly Martin Luther in his writings of 1515–1520). In Ritschl's judgment, however, the reformers, while recovering essential components of New Testament Christianity and turning them to church-reforming effect, had failed to order their religious insights in a holistic theological system. They had neglected, not least, to correlate their fundamental teaching on justification by faith alone with the biblical teaching on the kingdom of God. Thus they left the impression that Christianity is primarily a religion of personal redemption from sin, and not equally one of corporate ethical activity directed to the moral reconstruction of society. Viewed in respect of its formal theological productions, therefore, the Protestant Reformation was unfinished.

Ritschl contended, moreover, that post-Reformation Protestantism had continued and heightened the "theological atrophy" of the Reformation era, leading to serious "deformations" of authentic biblical-Reformation Christianity—as evidenced, for example, in the intellectualism (neoscholasticism) of Protestant orthodoxy, in the emergence within the Lutheran and Reformed churches of a "half-Catholic" mysticism, in the sectarianism and "otherworldliness" of Pietism, in the rationalism ("natural religion") and eudaemonism ("self-justification") of Enlightenment theology, and in the flight from the historical Christian revelation in Hegelian speculation. To be sure, Immanuel Kant and Friedrich Schleiermacher had given significant impulses for the reconstruction of Protestant theology on the basis of Reformation religion, but their gains had soon been surrendered by their epigones.

Ritschl took it as his own vocational task, therefore, to effect a true reformation of Protestant theology by recovering the reformers' religious root ideas through critical-historical scholarship and by articulating these ideas, with the aid of constructs supplied by Kant and Schleiermacher, in a "homogeneous" theological system. Thereby, he believed, the unfinished Reformation would be brought to theological completion; classical Protestant Christianity would be vindicated before its cultured despisers and its newly resurgent Roman Catholic foes; and the Reformation's epoch-making significance, including its immediate relevance for the modern world, would be displayed, all with the result that a debilitated Protestantism would at last be purged of "alien growths" and so would attain "maturity."

The main themes of Ritschl's doctrinal system are presented in the third volume of *Justification and Reconciliation.* God, for the sake of Christ, freely pardons sinful humanity ("justification"), thereby overcoming the sinner's fear, mistrust, alienation, and enervating consciousness of guilt, and thus making possible the individual's entrance into a new, confident relationship to God as Father ("reconciliation"). This relationship is verified, first, in the religious virtues of trust in God's providential guidance of the world, patience, humility, and prayer (whereby the believer attains "spiritual lordship over the world" and the vindication of the unique worth of spirit, or the "order of persons," vis-à-vis nature, or the "order of things"); and, second, in the moral virtues of fidelity in one's secular vocation and active love for the neighbor (whereby the kingdom of God, or "moral society of nations," is ultimately to be realized). Ritschl claimed that this doctrine was faithful to the biblical-Reformation heritage because it centered entirely on God's self-revelation as loving Father in Jesus Christ ("history")—a revelation mediated to individuals solely by and within the community of believers ("church"), and appropriated solely through lively personal trust ("faith"). This doctrine, therefore, entailed the explicit repudiation of all "disinterested" knowledge of God, metaphysical speculation, "natural theology," ahistorical mysticism, monastic-ascetic piety ("flight from the world"), ethical quietism, and unchurchly individualism.

From about 1920 to 1960 Ritschl's theology suffered an almost total eclipse. The leading representatives of the then-dominant Protestant neoorthodoxy, Karl Barth and Emil Brunner, charged Ritschl (and Ritschlianism) with egregious departures from classical Christianity, including religious subjectivism, moralism, capitulation to the cultural *Zeitgeist,* and, in sum, a return to the anthropocentrism of Enlightenment religion in its "chastened" (antimetaphysical) Kantian form. Since the 1960s, however, there has been a noteworthy Ritschl renaissance, which has defended Ritschl before his neoorthodox detractors by eschewing "criticism by catchwords," by relating his total theological program to its immediate historical context, and by taking seriously his claim to have constructed his system on biblical and Reformation foundations.

BIBLIOGRAPHY

The only biography of Ritschl is that by his son, Otto, *Albrecht Ritschls Leben,* 2 vols. (Freiburg im Breisgau, 1892–1896). Otto Ritschl also edited his father's *Gesammelte Aufsätze,* 2 vols. (Freiburg im Breisgau, 1893–1896). There are English translations of volumes 1 and 3 of Ritschl's magnum opus: *A Critical History of the Christian Doctrine of Justification and Reconciliation,* translated from the first edition by John S. Black (Edinburgh, 1872), and *The Christian Doctrine of Justification and Reconciliation: The Positive Development of the Doctrine,* translated from the third edition by H. R. Mackintosh and A. B. Macaulay (1900; reprint, Clifton, N. J., 1966). Ritschl's "Prolegomena" to *The History of Pietism, Theology and Metaphysics,* and *Instruction in the Christian Religion* have been translated by Philip J. Hefner in *Albrecht Ritschl: Three Essays* (Philadelphia, 1972)—the best place to begin for the first-time reader of Ritschl. Valuable older studies are A. E. Garvie's *The Ritschlian Theology, Critical and Constructive,* 2d ed. (Edinburgh, 1902), and Gösta Hök's *Die elliptische Theologie Albrecht Ritschls: Nach Ursprung und innerem Zusammenhang* (Uppsala, 1942). The fullest expositions of Ritschl's relationship to Reformation thought are my *Ritschl and Luther: A Fresh Perspective on Albrecht Ritschl's Theology in the Light of His Luther Study* (Nashville, 1974), which includes a translation of Ritschl's important "Festival Address on the Four Hundredth Anniversary of the Birth of Martin Luther" (1883); and "Albrecht Ritschl and the Unfinished Reformation," *Harvard Theological Review* 73 (1980): 337–372. Four pathbreaking studies of Ritschl's theological system, offered as "correctives" to neoorthodox criticisms, are Philip J. Hefner's *Faith and the Vitalities of History: A Theological Study Based on the Work of Albrecht Ritschl* (New York, 1966), Rolf Schäfer's *Ritschl: Grundlinien eines fast verschollenen dogmatischen Systems* (Tübingen, 1968), David L. Mueller's *An Introduction to the Theology of Albrecht Ritschl* (Philadelphia, 1969), and James Richmond's *Ritschl: A Reappraisal* (London, 1978).

DAVID W. LOTZ (1987)

RITUAL [FIRST EDITION]. Although it would seem to be a simple matter to define *ritual,* few terms in the study of religion have been explained and applied in more confusing ways. For example, Edmund Leach, a contemporary cultural anthropologist, after noting the general disagreement among anthropological theorists, suggested that the term *ritual* should be applied to all "culturally defined sets of behavior," that is, to the symbolical dimension of human behavior as such, regardless of its explicit religious, social, or other content (Leach, 1968, p. 524). Thus one could presumably discuss the ritual significance of scientific experimental procedures, for example. For Leach, such behavior should be regarded as a form of social communication or a code of information and analyzed in terms of its "grammar." Ritual is treated as a cognitive category.

Only slightly less vast a definition, but one that covers a very different set of phenomena, is implied by the common use of the term *ritual* to label religion as such, as in "the ritual view of life" or "ritual man in Africa," the title of an article by Robert Horton (reprinted in Lessa and Vogt, 1979). Many modern theories of religion are in fact primarily theories of ritual, and study of the literature on either topic would provide an introduction to the other.

Another very broad but commonly encountered usage is the one favored by, for example, psychoanalytic theory, in which notably nonrational or formalized symbolic behavior of any kind is distinguished as "ritual," as distinct from pragmatic, clearly ends-directed behavior that is rationally linked to empirical goals. Here "ritual" is often contrasted to "science" and even to common sense. Without much further ado, religious rituals can even be equated with neurotic compulsions, and its symbols to psychological complexes or genetically linked archetypes. Sociologists and anthropologists who favor such a contrast between ritualistic and rational behavior are usually interested in ritual's sociocultural functions, in which religious values shrink to social affirmations. (Some social anthropologists distinguish between "ritual"—stylized repetitious behavior that is explicitly religious—and "ceremony," which is merely social even in explicit meaning.) According to these theorists, the manifest religious content of ritual masks its more basic, "latent" social goals. However, there are anthropologists, such as Clifford Geertz and Victor Turner, who are interested in the explicit religious meaning of ritual symbolisms and who point out that ritual acts do endow culturally important cosmological conceptions and values with persuasive emotive force, thus unifying individual participants into a genuine community. Here ritual is viewed sociologically, to be sure, but in terms of its existential import and explicit meanings rather than its purely cognitive grammar, its psychological dynamics, or its merely social reference.

Such an approach comes closest to that adopted by most scholars in the history and phenomenology of religions. According to Rudolf Otto and Mircea Eliade, for example, ritual arises from and celebrates the encounter with the "numinous," or "sacred," the mysterious reality that is always manifested as of a wholly different order from ordinary or "natural" realities. Religious persons seek to live in continual contact with those realities and to flee or to transform the inconsequential banality of ordinary life, thus giving rise to the repetitions and "archetypal nostalgias" of ritual. In this approach, there is the attempt to define ritual by its actual intention or focus. This intentionality molds the formal symbolisms and repetitions of ritual at their origins, so that when the rituals are repeated, the experience of holiness can be more or less fully reappropriated by new participants.

For the purposes of this article, "ritual" shall be understood as those conscious and voluntary, repetitious and stylized symbolic bodily actions that are centered on cosmic structures and/or sacred presences. (Verbal behavior such as chant, song, and prayer are of course included in the category of bodily actions.) The conscious and voluntary aspects of ritual rule out the inclusion of personal habits or neurotic compulsions in this definition, as does the stress on a transcendent focus (as Freud has shown, neurotic obsessions refer back to infantile traumas and represent contorted efforts of the self to communicate with itself: the focus of neurotic compulsion is the self).

Even more fundamentally, ritual is intentional bodily engagement in the paradigmatic forms and relationships of reality. As such, ritual brings not only the body but also that body's social and cultural identity to the encounter with the transcendental realm. By conforming to models or paradigms that refer to the primordial past and that can be shared by many people, ritual also enables each person to transcend the individual self, and thus it can link many people together into enduring and true forms of community. As a result, ritual draws into itself every aspect of human life, and almost every discipline of the social sciences and humanities has something to say about it. This article shall begin this analysis of ritual, however, with an attempt to articulate its manifest religious orientation and how this gives rise to repetitious behaviors. After that it shall turn to other approaches that highlight the latent factors in ritual, such as its personal or social value. By its conclusion this article will have reviewed the major theoretical approaches to ritual

THE RELIGIOUS MEANING OF RITUAL. Ritual appears in all religions and societies, even those that are nominally antiritualistic. Although it is common to contrast "ritualism" with "deeper spirituality" and mysticism, ritual is especially stressed in mystical groups (Zen monasteries, Ṣūfī orders, Jewish mystical communities, Hindu yogic ashrams, etc.); in such groups ritual often expands to fill every moment of daily life. The body is evidently more important in religious experience than is often thought.

Ritual centers on the body, and to understand ritual one shall have to take the body seriously as a vehicle for religious experience. It is evident that without a body one would have no awareness of a world at all. The infant builds up an understanding of the world out of sensory-motor experience, and as Jean Piaget and Sigmund Freud, among others, have shown, this understanding underlies and sustains the adult experience of space, time, number, and personal identity. The self is first of all a bodily self. As a result, physical experiences and actions engage consciousness more immediately and irresistibly, and bestow a much stronger sense of reality, than any merely mental philosophy or affirmation of faith. Much ritual symbolism draws on the simplest and most intense sensory experiences, such as eating, sexuality, and pain. Such experiences have been repeated so often or so intimately by the body that they have become primary forms of bodily awareness. In ritual, they are transformed into symbolic experiences of the divine, and even into the form of the cosmic drama itself. One may therefore speak of a "prestige of the body" in ritual. In the bodily gesture, the chant, dance, and stride of participants, primordial presences are made actual again, time is renewed, and the universe is regenerated.

Ritual is more than merely symbolic action, it is hieratic. Almost all human activity is symbolic, even the most "rationally" pragmatic. People would never trouble to fix cars if cars had no cultural value; even scientific experiments would be meaningless without a tacit reference to a specific kind of world and society that validates such activities. However, ritual underlines and makes emphatic its symbolic intention. Hence the stylized manner of ritual: the special clothes, the altered manner of speech, the distinctive places and times. But above all, behavior is repetitive and consciously follows a model. Repetition, after all, is a natural way for the body to proclaim, enact, and experience the choice of true as opposed to false things and ways, and to dwell self-consciously in determinative model realities, in the "holy."

The use of model roles and identities is crucial to ritual. As Mircea Eliade has shown, ritual is shaped by archetypes, by the "first gestures" and dramas from the beginning of time, which must be represented again in the ritual and reexperienced by the participants. It is easy to stress the imaginative and mythic aspect of these dramas, and to ignore their significance specifically as bodily enactments. In ritual, people voluntarily submit to their bodily existence and assume very specific roles with highly patterned rules—rules and roles that conform the self to all others who have embodied these "typical" roles in the past. To contact reality, in short, the conscious self must sacrifice its individual autonomy, its freedom in fantasy to "be" anything.

The self is not utterly unique and self-generated, and it cannot control life as it wishes. This is no doubt one of the deepest reasons for the common resentment of ritual: it locates and imprisons individuals in a particular reality whose consequences can no longer be avoided. The power of ritual is wryly indicated by stories about the bride left abandoned at the altar: in the specificity of the wedding ritual and its implications, the singular and immortal youth who exulted in the eternity of romantic dreams must become merely one of many mortals who have passed this way before. The autonomous and infinitely free self is transformed ritually into "groom" (remorselessly implying the series "father," "grandfather," and dead "ancestor"). The ritual makes him take his place in the cycle of the generations. Thus it signifies human limitation, and even death. He becomes what he had always undeniably been, a bodily, mortal being. Through ritual, the self is discovered as a public, external reality, which can be known only through perspectives mediated by others and especially by transcendent others: the self is something already determined and presented, which can be understood above all and most truly in the ritual act itself. In these actions and encounters the primal beings provide the model and the source of life. The ritual participants must submit to those deeper realities. They must will their own bodies into identities and movements that stem from the ancestral past. They must be humble.

This essential preliminary movement of the self may be called "recentering": there is in a kind of standing outside of oneself, a taking up of the position of the divine "other" and acting on its behalf that is expressed explicitly as a personal submission to it and that is experienced directly as a submersion of the personal will in the divine will. The ritual comes from the ancients and was a gift from the divine; to repeat it means to receive their stamp upon the self and to make their world one's own.

In a wide-ranging study of native religions, Adolf E. Jensen (1963) has defended the thesis that the various epochs of human history have been characterized by distinctive visions of the universe. Although the details and applications of these visions vary enormously from society to society and era to era, the basic visions themselves are not numerous. Early agriculture, for example, was made culturally possible by a certain way of seeing the world and understanding life, death, and humanity, a way that transformed the "burial" of the root or seed, its "rebirth" (or "resurrection") as a plant, and its "murderous" harvesting as food into a kind of mystery, a compelling and salvific vision. The first seer to whom the divine revealed itself in this way must have had a shattering experience. Here, according to Jensen, is the fundamental origin of the rituals of the early agriculturalists: these rituals arose to induct neophytes into the mystery and to enable full initiates to reexperience the shattering revelations of the primal reality. The participants remember the creative acts that made them what they are, and thus they are able to dwell in a world that has meaning. Farming itself becomes not only possible, but necessary.

Eliade (1959) terms these primal, constitutive encounters with the sacred *hierophanies* (self-disclosures of the holy) and *kratophanies* (revelations of overwhelming power). It is the underlying purpose of rituals to recall and renew such experiences of reality. These powerful visions—which are usually devoted to the mythic origins of the universe or to those aspects of the creation that hold special consequence for mankind, but which are preserved within the sacred field of ritual enactment—provide a focus and framework for living in the "profane" world of everyday activity. They even sanctify this activity, and so rescue it from the terror of inconsequentiality and meaninglessness. However, ordinary life, with its egoisms, pressures, and attractions, constantly threatens to erode a wider sense of reality. Crises arise that make the challenge acute. The regular enactment of rituals renews the experiential focus on the sacred. In the recentering process, the overall meaning of life and the reality of transcendental powers are again made paramount over merely egoistic or social concerns. The ordering that ritual effects can even be directly healing, inasmuch as many physical ailments have a significant psychosomatic component, and social crises are above all crises in accommodating individuals or groups to each other and to cultural norms.

There is a tendency among phenomenologists of religion concerned with ritual to emphasize the personal encounter with divine beings as the focus of ritual experience. Rudolf Otto, in his influential *The Idea of the Holy* (first published in 1917), was explicitly guided by Christian (and specifically Lutheran) assumptions when he described the holy, or "numinous," this way. However, there are many religions in which the focus of ritual is mostly or entirely impersonal, or in which there are no prayers or sacrifices made to divine beings. Rather, ritual action consists in repeating the primal deeds of beings not now actively present. It is the deeds, not the persons, that are important. Most Australian Aboriginal ritual fits in this category; a striking parallel can be found in the teachings of the ritual texts of late Vedic Hinduism. The *Śatapatha Brāhmaṇa,* for example, states repeatedly that the priests are to perform the sacrifices because this is what the gods themselves did to create the world; in fact, it is by performing these rites that the gods became gods and immortal. Therefore the priests recreate the world when they repeat certain actions, and all who participate in the sacrifice become gods and immortal as well.

In this view, the dynamic of reality is sacrificial; it is renewed only through sacrifice and attained only by those who sacrifice. Through sacrifice one becomes equal to the gods, or even their master, since they too depend on sacrifice. In later Hinduism, there developed a philosophy of ritual, the Pūrva Mīmāṃsā (also called the Karma Mīmāṃsā), which in some versions was explicitly atheistic: The process underlying the universe was a ritual process repeated in and sustained by Brahmanic ritual performances alone. However, the enactment of the duties (*dharma*) appropriate to one's caste, sex, and age is also a form of this ritual world maintenance, especially if done with the fully conscious intention of sustaining the impersonal ritual order of the universe. This may be called a structural rather than a personal focus to ritual action. The aim of such ritual is to enact and perhaps even regenerate the structure of reality, the deep structure that consists of a certain pattern of relationships and their dynamic regeneration. It can even be argued that this structural focus is the real or deeper one in most rituals directed to personal beings, for commonly those personal beings are addressed in ritual in order to assure the proper changing of the seasons, the fertility of the fields, the restoration of health, prosperity in business and everyday affairs, or perhaps more profoundly the general preservation of social tranquillity and universal harmony.

One need not expect to find that ritual emerges first as the result of a personal experience of encounter with a divinity, although traditional cultures often explain their rituals in this fashion. Rituals are also found to be taking shape in conformity with a general sense of what is right and fitting to do in the context of a given situation. This structural sense of what is "right and fitting" may well lack much precision, at least on the conscious level, but despite this a preconscious (or "unconscious") awareness of the nature of the world and the way in which it relates to the ritual situation may operate to determine ritual details with great exactitude. Monographs on particular ritual systems often illustrate this vividly.

As Bruce Kapferer (1983) has shown for exorcism rituals in Sri Lanka, the details of cult can only be understood in terms of the general sense of life, and the overall existential environment, of ritual participants, although they may not be able to explain these details and simply accept them as "traditional." In fact, participants insensibly adapt rituals to specific situations, personal experiences, and training. James W. Fernandez (1982) has provided an astonishingly rich analysis of the symbolic coherence of an African religious movement that shows how conscious thought and prereflective experience interact to produce ritual behavior. At times, the conscious component may be very high: Stanley J. Tambiah's (1970) description of spirit cults in Thailand necessarily involves a discussion of Buddhist metaphysics at certain points, but even here most of the structure of the ritual conforms to unspoken but vividly present folk realities.

One of the most telling instances of the influence of a general sense of the "right and fitting" on ritual behavior, however, is described in W. Lloyd Warner's classic study of Memorial Day and other rituals in a New England community, *The Living and the Dead: A Study of the Symbolic Life of Americans* (1959). Warner describes how the celebration of the holiday was planned and carried out one spring. Many people were involved; in fact almost all groups in the community were represented. Many random factors and issues intervened, but the result can be regarded as a crystallization of the American ethos as it existed at that time and place. There is here neither the calculated imposition of ritualized ideology on underclasses by an authoritarian, hypocritical elite nor solitary ecstatic encounters with sacred beings used as models for community cult (two current theories of the origin of ritual). Instead, one finds the voluntary community enactment of a felt reality, which in turn makes the common dream an actuality, at least in the festival itself. The felt reality is also a dream, an ideal, for it consists of those experienced values that at the deepest level guide members of the community, and in terms of which they understand and, on occasion, even criticize each other and themselves.

Shame and death in ritual. This phenomenon of criticism, and especially of self-criticism, is an essential part of ritual. It is part of the "recentering" that has already been mentioned, a self-transformation that is necessary if there is to be any hope of escaping personal fantasies and encountering authentic realities outside the self. For reality, which the self longs for as a secure grounding, at the same time must include other things and beings, which in turn must condition and limit the self. Encounters with these other presences will be chaotic and destructive, however, unless some harmonious and stable mode of interaction is discovered. In ritual, the bodily self enacts the true and enduring forms of relationships within a cosmic order that has a constructive place for the self. But this enactment must begin with an acceptance of personal limitation. So it is commonly found that ritual sequences may begin with explicit declarations of personal flaw, shame, or guilt existing in the participants or in their world that it will be the task of the ritual to assuage or nullify. The "flaw" need not be narrowly moral, of course: it may only be, for example, that a youngster is growing into an adult without yet knowing or assuming adult responsibilities and roles. If this willful autonomy were to continue, or to become common, the sanctified social order would cease; therefore, initiation is necessary to rectify the disharmony introduced by the child-adult.

Rituals cluster especially around those primary realities (such as sexuality, death, strife, and failure) that force individuals to face their personal limits and their merely relative existence. In many Indo-European and Semitic languages the very word for "shame" felt before the opposite sex (especially in regard to their sexual organs) is the same as that for "respect" before the elderly, the rulers, the dead, and the gods; it is also the word for "ritual awe." This deeply felt "shame-awe" provides people with the proper stance and poise to accept their mere relativity and their limits, and thereby to restore harmony to the world. Beginning with a shamed sense of flaw and submission, one comes in the course of the ritual to perceive the self from the perspective of the holy. From this perspective and this transcendental center, one wills the ritual actions until the identification of wills results in making the ritual one's voluntary, autonomous, and bodily enactment of truth. Although ritual commonly begins in duty or submission, it generally ends in voluntary and even joyful affirmation. In this way, the dread and the enchantment that R. R. Marett and Rudolf Otto found to be two aspects of the experience of the sacred articulate also the actual structure of most ritual sequences, which begin in disequilibrium and end in harmony after confession, submission, purification sacrifice, or other ritual strategies.

Connected with this is what might be called the ritual barter of immortalities. In ritual, one inevitably and implicitly wills one's own death, since one takes on a merely partial identity as "man" or "woman," "elder" or "youth," the identity of an actual finite self existing within boundaries and under obligations, defined through relationships with others and destined to die. It is therefore both as a kind of palliative and as a necessary consequence of the search for reality that rituals of initiation, the New Year, and so on place such stress on immortality and mythic eternity. The consolation for accepting one's death is the awareness that through this one attains to another kind of eternity, as part of a larger cosmic reality. The seeming eternity of one's immediate desires and wishes are given up for an eternity mediated through the divine order, which certainly endures beyond all individuals and embodies the "otherness" that limits us.

There should be nothing surprising in this intimate mixture of personal need and ruthless objectivity, for ritual as such is constituted by the longing to place the self in enduring contact with absolute or source realities. This necessarily requires a relationship compounded of both self and other, of heteronomy and autonomy. (It would therefore be incorrect to identify ritual action with heteronomy, as Kant, Friedrich Schleiermacher, and others have done.) W. Brede Kristensen, the Dutch phenomenologist of religions, refers to this connection of self and other as the fundamental "compact," "agreement," or "covenant," "man's Law of life" that underlies all rituals, for in them humanity and the divine bind themselves together to sustain a unified and stable order of the universe.

Space and time in ritual. Through ritual, then, the self is inducted into the necessary forms of space and time, and these forms are disclosed as harmonious with the body. The space and time of ritual are organic experiences. Time, for example, waxes and wanes; like organisms it can grow and decay, and must be regenerated. Time has neither static eternity nor monotonous regularity but the rhythms of the body, even if it embraces the universe. Yearly festivals mark the moments in the "life" of the year, from birth through fertility to death. The rites of passage, including birth, initiation, marriage, and death, translate the patterns of time into the individual life cycle, giving the chief transitions of every life the authentic resonance of the sacred. Even the minor moments of ritual, ignored by participants, render an architecture in time in which the girders are ceremonial gestures, the rhythms of chant, the turn, and the stride.

Space, as well, is drawn into the ritual field of correspondences and boundaries and is given a shape that hospitably welcomes the body. The cosmos is revealed as a house and a temple, and, reflexively, the personal and physical house and temple are disclosed as the cosmos made immanent. The mountain is the "throne" of the gods, the heavens their "chamber"; the shaman's drum is his "horse," by which he ecstatically mounts through the "roof" of heaven. The Brahmanic altar is shaped in the form of a woman in order to tempt the gods to approach the sacrificial place. And if the center of the universe is brought symbolically into one's midst, so too is the beginning of creation, which can then ritually be repeated in one's central shrines. Ritual makes all of this immediately and bodily present. The universe itself may be embodied in the participants, so that the marriage of king and queen may at once simulate and stimulate the marriage of heaven and earth, and the slaying of slaves may accomplish the overthrow of chaos. The elementary sensory-motor experiences of up and down, in and out, and left and right, rudimentary though one may think them, are utilized in ritual, often in astonishingly systematic fashion, showing to what degree ritual is a meditation on the final and basic experiences of the body, an attempt to discover deeper meanings in them. Left and right symbolisms, for example, are everywhere in the world correlated through ritual equivalences and oppositions between male and female, day and night, order and disorder, the sun and moon, and other basic elements in experience. Robert Hertz, who first noted that rituals worldwide share these left and right symbolisms, suggested that they were rooted in the general human experience of skill and mastery in the right hand and relative weakness and clumsiness in the left, which then served to characterize and give order to a wide range of other experiences and perceptions (see essays in Needham, 1973). Ernst Cassirer (1955, pp. 83ff.) has shown how specific bodily organizations of experience of other sorts, especially of space, time, number, and self, are ritually integrated into cosmological enactments.

Certainly ritual definitively breaks up the homogeneity of space and establishes places in it for humanity. The body itself is a common model for the universe. Puranic descriptions of the universe develop this idea in astonishing detail, in schemes that are often reproduced in Hindu temples and iconography. The Hindu temple has a waist, trunk, and head. In Nepal, Buddhist stupas often have two eyes painted on the dome and are topped with a small parasol, just as the Buddha himself used to have. Such ritual symbolisms make such actions as moving through the temple a journey through the various heavens and lend shape to meditation as well. The yogin may practice visualizing his body as the temple-universe, finding within it all the gods and heavens. It is common even in folk religions to find ritual identification of the cardinal points with the four limbs, and the center of the world identified as an omphalos, or umbilicus, which may be located at the center of one's village or enshrined as the goal of religious pilgrimage. In every example, the religious motivation is to establish necessary links between the body and the world, to make these links "natural" in the very fabric of things, to make secure continuities that give the self access to transcendent and sacred life.

A major strategy employed by ritual to achieve this goal is simply to reenact with the participants' own bodies the primeval or constitutive acts by which the cosmos came into being. Mircea Eliade, who has devoted many studies to this almost universal trait in ritual, has called it "the myth of the eternal return." To exist truly is to remember, and even more to reenact, the foundational events; to forget is to dissolve the world in chaos. By repeating the primordial deeds of the gods, human beings become as the gods, posturing out their will and establishing their divine world. Precisely as bodily beings, and through the body, they enter eternity and "become" the transcendent others who control their lives. The personal distancing of the self from the self mentioned earlier permits this ritual ecstasy, which perhaps achieves its most extreme form in trances of possession or mystical union, when the sense of self is entirely blotted out. However, the ritual dialectic of self and other much more usually seeks to retain the full consciousness of both in reciprocal harmony. New Year's festivals, initiations, funerals, and coronations all show this passion for the abiding dynamic process, the eternal form of the universe.

When, in the Finnish epic *Kalevala,* Väinämöinen, the shaman hero, wishes to heal himself of a wound caused by an iron weapon, he ritually chants the myth of the first creation of iron and so is able to reverse and negate the impure and wrong unfolding of time (*Kalevala,* rune 9). The first act of Columbus when he set foot on the soil of the New World was to hold a religious service, praying to God and drawing this new and alien territory into the same universe of dedication that contained God, sovereign rulers, and Spain. The terra incognita thus became a domesticated Spanish territory.

These two instances show the prayerfulness of "magic," and the magic of prayer. Väinämöinen's chant was also prayerful, for it was grounded in submission to foundational realities and mysteries. The very need for comprehensive accuracy in the wording of the myth recital obviously signifies the necessity of complete obedience to a sacred and powerful reality that is formal in nature. Of course, faith in this chant is also faith in those divinities named in it, who made iron and who, by transmitting the chant, created it. And, for his part, Columbus followed archetypal forms in his petition to the sacred beings who made the entire world and this new land as well, and he even transformed the entire service into a kind of legal statement of territorial appropriation, so that personal prayer followed the logic of a deeper impersonal and "magical" transubstantiation of the land. Like Väinämöinen, he overcame anomaly through a cosmological recitation. Such reflections show the emptiness of distinctions between religious and magical rituals and, even more importantly, provides an awareness of the two basic modes of the sacred, impersonal archetypal form and personal sacred presence. Archetypal form consists of cosmological structures that shape a divine order and may be renewed through ritual reenactments. Sacred beings must be ritually invoked and acknowledged. As the instances of Väinämöinen and Columbus show, the two modes of the sacred often occur together in the same rite and can inspire the same sense of awe and personal submission.

The symbolic integrations of ritual. Religious ritual is evidently not a simple or infantile manifestation but is based on a kind of final summing-up of, acknowledgement of, and submission to reality. Ritual engages all levels of experience and weaves them together. It has often been noted, for example, that ritual symbolisms often center on such elementary acts as eating and sex. From this strong emphasis, in fact, Freudian psychoanalysis was able to draw evidence for its hypothesis that religion consists of sublimated or projected sexual hungers and symbols. Other theorists (in the modern period, most notably those emphasizing totemism and the Myth and Ritual school) deduced from the importance of food and eating in ritual that rituals were economic in origin and concerned with magical or proto-scientific control of the food supply. However, not only in the areas of sexuality and eating (two of the most rudimentary of bodily experiences), but also elsewhere, ritual makes use of activities that are familiar and deeply intimate, that when engaged in involve the body very strongly, or that have been repeated so often that they take on a habitual, automatic nature. The power that ritual has to make these acts conscious and, simultaneously, to bring them into relationship with central religious realities is a major part of its attraction and fascination. In effect, ritual sacramentalizes the sensory-motor sphere by lifting it into the sphere of the ultimate, while the energy of elemental awareness is reshaped and drawn into the support of the structures of clear consciousness and ultimate concerns. The secular is transformed by the sacred.

The process can be observed in terms of particular ritual symbols. Each symbol is multivalent: it refers to many things, which may not be clearly present to consciousness but that exist in a kind of preconscious halo around it. Victor Turner, in a number of richly detailed studies, has emphasized a bipolar structure to this multivalency of ritual symbols: they are often drawn from sensory experience and passion (the "orectic" pole) and are made to represent social ideals (the "ideological" pole). So, as he shows, initiation rituals among the Ndembu of Zambia are structured around ideologically defined natural symbols (colors, plant species, etc.), which in the course of traumatic ordeals work deeply into the consciousness of candidates, reshaping their self-conception and view of the world and society. In the same way, Ndembu "cults of affliction" turn painfully destructive impulses and social tension, and even mental and physical illness, into affirmative communal experiences. This analysis can be elaborated further: A single symbol can draw on orectic sensual urges; can implicitly relate to a larger cognitive and *dispositional* structure that organizes all sensory experience into a coherent perception of the natural world; can be part of a ritual used by a participant to advance his or her own *ego-centered* utilitarian aims; can embody the social values of the actual group and perhaps even indicate the group identity; can be seen to point to wider *sociocultural* and *ideological* issues; and, finally, can be directed to *transcendental* spiritual beings or cosmological structures. This sixfold layering of symbolic meaning may be generally characterized as relating to the body's organic world, the social world, and the cosmological or transcendental realm. The ego's concerns connect the first and second, while ideological and broadly ecological issues connect the second and third, producing five levels of general symbolic significance that are unified in ritual enactments.

A Multidisciplinary Approach to Ritual. The various levels of symbolic reference in ritual assist in understanding of the applicability of many disciplines and theories to ritual. These can be seen as applying to one or another aspect or level of ritual action, although obviously this applicability also suggests that any one theory or discipline in itself cannot claim sole truth and must be supplemented and corrected by other approaches. For example, Freudian theory has helped researchers to see the relevance of organic processes in the development of personality, from infancy to the organization of behavior in adults. Freud was the first to show in detail just how, through sublimation, repression, projection, and other transformations, bodily symbolisms can be expanded in dreams, art, language, and ritual into entire cosmological dramas. Freud also showed how each organic symbolism organizes increasingly wider ranges of experience within it. This expansive tendency of each symbol, which may be called its imperialistic tendency to organize all experience around itself, brings it into competition with other symbols and even with conscious thought. However, as Volney Gay has shown, Freud's own restriction of meaningfulness to this organic level alone, and even solely to sexual complexes, and his general antipathy to religion, led him to suggest that religion and ritual are infantile and to equate the latter with regressive neurotic compulsions.

The operations by which bodily symbols are organized into coherent general dispositional structures of perception have been illuminated by the work of such psychologists as Jean Piaget, Heinz Werner and Bernard Kaplan, and C. G. Jung, each in his own way enlarging their understanding. Ernst Cassirer's philosophically sophisticated analysis of how cognition comes to organize space, time, and identity, enacting paradigms of these in ritual, may almost be taken as a philosophical phenomenology supplementing Mircea Eliade's researches and detailed demonstrations. Such studies enhance but also correct the often highly speculative approach of Jungian psychology to ritual symbolism. Of great importance is the work of structuralist anthropology, a field founded by Claude Lévi-Strauss and dedicated to the analysis of cognitive organization in cultural creations. According to this theory, rituals, myths, and other aspects of culture are structured cognitively by processes resembling binary computer operations. These mental operations lie finally outside of all meaning and simply reflect an autonomous cognitive drive toward order. Lévi-Strauss suggests in some of his works that each culture works out a tight and utterly consistent logic in its rituals and myths; elsewhere that coherence can only be found on a regional and even a global scale, particular cultures exemplifying only partial and unconscious cognitive unifications. It must be added that Lévi-Strauss (1979) finds ritual far more incoherent than myth, due largely to ritual's explicitly religious and emotive focus. However, other structural anthropologists have shown astonishingly coherent organizations of symbols in even the slightest details of ritual; action becomes a coded text or hidden language conveying information about the social and cultural universe of the performers. The actual meaning of the ritual to the actors may be considered irrelevant.

Critics of this approach have suggested that ritual may not be concerned after all with the cognitive classification of things but may instead relate to others of the six levels that have been distinguished in ritual symbolic reference. Fredrick Barth points out that, as the media of social interaction, relatively unsystematic and incoherent symbolic networks may be sufficient or even especially desirable. He describes a Melanesian culture in which ritual symbols have only loose chains of analogical associations, varying from individual to individual and only imperfectly worked together. Since these metaphors and symbols by their very looseness underlie at some point or another every participant's experience, they can be variously meaningful to all and serve to bring them together. More generally, a purely cognitive approach ignores the possibility that ritual may be concerned above all with the cultivation of a basic stance on life, involving the recentering that I have earlier discussed. As Gilbert Lewis has suggested, rituals may even emphasize precisely the illogic and incoherence of symbols in an effort to capture the paradox, mystery, and transcendental reality of the sacred. Even more basically, if possible, the multivalence of symbols necessarily insures their ultimate formal incoherence, since the relational meanings often accrete to a symbol by experienced conjunction, not logic, and the "imperialism" of symbols makes each incompatible at some points with others. Particular rituals may achieve a unified meaning by making one symbolism dominant, using the rich though submerged associations of subordinate symbols simply to contribute to the sense of depth and authenticity of the rite.

The value of ritual to the ego world of rational calculation and social manipulation and interaction has been emphasized by a number of theorists. Some cultures and religions make such an approach easier than others; for example, as Emily Ahern has emphasized, in Chinese religions the heavenly spirits and gods are ranked in a bureaucratic hierarchy that is a transcendental continuation of earthly Chinese society and government. Prayers, offerings, and modes of address can therefore be interpreted in an almost wholly social and manipulative mode, if one is so inclined. Much of the debate about the "rationality" of ritual among anthropologists, referred to earlier, applies to this level of ritual meaning as well. These discussions have revived the viewpoints of E. B. Tylor, James G. Frazer, and others from the end of the nineteenth and beginning of the twentieth century that ritual was in its origins a pragmatic attempt to control nature, a rational even if scientifically ill-founded activity. Such theorists as Adolf Jensen and Robin Horton go on to make a distinction between "expressive" and "instrumental," or manipulative, aspects of ritual; the former relates to faith and is authentically religious, while the latter is said to be materialistic, pragmatic, and inauthentic. But such viewpoints not only ignore the recentering process underlying even the most utilitarian ritual; they have difficulty accounting for the fact that in many religions it is precisely the pragmatic application of cult that directly expresses the faith that the springs of reality flow forth in the actualities of human existence and that reality is benevolently concerned with human needs. There is no separation of spirit and flesh in such religions, and the aim of religion is to sanctify life. Still, in the multileveled significance of ritual symbolisms, rational ego-oriented calculations have a role.

So do social and political calculations, conscious or otherwise, for these act as a necessary check on a population of competing egos and permit a community to exist. The recentering that ritual forces on the ego, as in initiations, provides an intersubjective, social confirmation of reality necessary even for the individual ego, if it is to participate in a world it cannot wholly control. Inner structures of awareness are thus shared with others, and a community is created that has legitimacy to the degree that it is anchored in transcendental cosmological realities. Thus one finds that in all religions ritual has enormous social value. Society can enhance itself by fusing transcendental symbolisms with its own norms, and ritual can be quite functional in overcoming tensions and divisions in the community (in this way sublimating violence).

This was quite powerfully brought out by the French sociologist Émile Durkheim in *The Elementary Forms of the Religious Life* (1912). Societies image themselves in their ritual symbols, he maintained; the "sacred" is the essential social idea. Religion is not for Durkheim (as it was for Otto) about abnormal personal states, but about normal social and natural life: the rainfall, the crops, good hunting, good health, children, and social continuity. Even relationships to particular spiritual beings are cast in terms of this deeper, more normative, structural and cosmological orientation. In effect, Durkheim brought to the attention of researchers a mode of the sacred they had ignored until then, the structural and cosmological mode. But he saw it chiefly in terms of social groupings and values; even individual spiritual beings symbolized the group or its relations with other groups. The community is recreated at times of initiation and festival.

Such ideas were developed into "functionalist" anthropology in the Anglo-Saxon countries under the leadership of A. R. Radcliffe-Brown and Bronislaw Malinowski. The organic interconnections between social values and rituals were demonstrated by this approach in many striking studies. Taboos, for example, do not so much arise from individual fears or longings as they do from the social purpose of identifying to participants the proper sentiments to feel in particular situations. Groups are identified by the rites they practice, roles within the group are differentiated (a special necessity in small-scale societies, in which roles overlap and daily interaction may be filled with personal antipathies and preferences), and tensions resolved by the community feeling engendered by the rites. The functionalists taught their contemporaries that even the most bizarre or apparently harmful practices (e.g., witchcraft and sorcery, painful initiatory ordeals, ritual head-hunting) might be socially constructive. But the genuinely needed tolerance that characterizes their work has recently been criticized as static, ahistorical, a priori, and Panglossian.

That ritual symbolisms may correspond to a society's economic and political forces and relate to historical changes in these forces as well has been a theme of recent Marxist anthropology. Whereas functionalists tended to limit their concern to the ideological structures elaborated by particular societies and often more or less consciously recognized by participants, Marxist analysis locates itself at a more comparative and materialistic level: the more extreme theorists, for example, argue in the vein of Enlightenment critics of religion that ritual consists of systematic falsehoods designed by ruling circles to justify their exploitation of the underprivileged (e.g., see Bloch, 1977). In any case, ritual is about political power or economic forces.

Some studies have extended insight into the integrative power of ritual to include a culture's relationship to its larger natural environment. One of the most striking demonstrations of this ecological function of ritual, in which ritual acts as a central control on a wide range of forces, is Roy A. Rappaport's description of the pig festival of the Tsembaga of Papua New Guinea (Rappaport, in Lessa and Vogt, 1979). Warfare, human fertility rates, land-occupation densities, protein supply during crises, wild pig marauders, and many other factors are kept in balance by this festival, truly bringing the Tsembaga into harmony with the ecological forces affecting their lives and even their survival. Once again, and from an unexpected perspective, one finds a multiform unity between self and other, expressive and instrumental elements in ritual.

THE TYPES OF RITUAL. Two basic approaches to the classification of ritual may be found in the literature on the subject, which may be called the functional-enumerative and the structural-analytical. The first has the attraction of seeming inductive, empirically firm, and precise: one simply notes down each kind of ritual behavior as one finds it, defining it by its function or explicit use. The result is usually a long and imposing list. Each item on the list is a special case to be explained separately. It is usually not noticed that rituals of different levels of generality are mixed together. For example, Crawford Howell Toy, in his *Introduction to the History of Religion* (1913), in an admittedly "not exhaustive list," presents the principal forms of early ceremonies as follows: emotional and dramatic (religious dances and plays, processions, circumambulations); decorative and curative; economic (hunting and farming rites, dietary rules, rainmaking); apotropaic (averting or expelling evil spirits or influences); puberty and initiation; marriage, birth, burial, purification and consecration; and periodic and seasonal. In a separate chapter he considers "totemism" (a supposed cult belonging to a specific cultural-historical epoch) and taboo (a universal ritual type), and in a third chapter "magic" (a general way of using rites) and divination (a specific kind of ritual). Toy's approach is often informative, but haphazard.

More systematic is the functional classification offered by Anthony F. C. Wallace (1966). He distinguishes between technological rituals aimed at the control of nonhuman nature (divination, "intensification" rites to increase food supply, protective rites to avert misfortune); therapy and antitherapy rituals affecting humans (curing rites and rites with injurious ends, like witchcraft and sorcery); ideology rituals directed to the control of social groups and values (passage rites of the life cycle and territorial movement, "social intensification" rites to renew group solidarity, like Sunday services, arbitrary ceremonial obligations, like taboos, and rebellion rites, which allow catharsis); salvation rituals enabling individuals to cope with personal difficulties (possession rites, shamanic rites, mystic rites, and expiation rites); and, finally, revitalization rituals designed to cure societal difficulties and identity crises, such as millenarian movements.

This classification system is clearly much more useful. However, its functional precision is not entirely adequate, since a single ritual may in actual performance belong to several or even all of these classes: For instance, Easter in a medieval Polish village was a technological ritual (as a spring festival and as a protective rite); offered therapy to ill believers and antitherapy to nonparticipants, such as Jews; was an ideology ritual that renewed group solidarity and included arbitrary ceremonial obligations; and was a salvation and, on occasion, even a revitalization ritual.

Such overlap is almost impossible to avoid in classifications of ritual, due to the integrative thrust and multileveled nature of ritual. The main criterion in distinguishing rituals should perhaps be the overall intention or emphasis of the performers: thus one can say that Easter has in a general way moved historically from a revitalization ritual to a salvation ritual in the early church, and thereafter to a technological and therapy ritual in the Middle Ages, and finally to an ideology ritual at the present time. But if that is so, the external forms of the ritual do not necessarily help to classify it, nor do they always correspond to a specific function. To put the matter a little differently, function is at base a structural matter and depends on context.

Wallace's classification, then, may be supplemented with a structural one. Two of the founding classics of the modern study of religion suggest a starting point. Émile Durkheim, in his study of religion mentioned above, divided all rites into positive and negative kinds. By negative rituals he meant taboos, whose purpose, he said, was to separate the sacred from the profane, preserving the transcendence of the former and the everyday normality of the latter. Positive rituals chiefly included sacrificial rites, in the course of which the sacred and profane realms were brought together and the ordinary life of performers was infused with the ideal and the normative. The cultic life of religion moves continually between these two phases, maintaining and regenerating the stable universal order.

Sigmund Freud also distinguished similar basic types of ritual in his *Totem and Taboo* (1913). By "totem" Freud referred to the totemic sacrifice that, according to him, reenacted the primordial parricide.

Generalizing from these two classics, one may say that all rituals may be divided into those whose purpose is to maintain distinctions within a divine order and those whose purpose is to bridge divisions and effect transformations, renewing that order when it is threatened by internal or external change. These two traits, of structure maintenance and transformation, must exist in any system if it is to endure in a stable fashion, integrating change into itself without altering its basic form. Although both Durkheim and Freud saw structure maintenance in a negative light and in terms of taboos, it is evident that positive injunctions are also important and, indeed, that negative prohibitions often have a very positive intention. This article, therefore, shall call rituals of this kind "confirmatory rituals," for in them the basic boundaries and internal spaces of the divine order are confirmed without change, while rituals that bridge divisions and regenerate the structure shall be called "transformatory rituals."

Confirmatory rituals. Both confirmatory and transformatory rituals act by centering the will in transcendental sources, that is, they anchor the immediate order in a realm that transcends it. As shall be seen, these orders may nest hierarchically within each other: reverence to clan ancestors helps to establish the clan within the cosmos, but larger human groupings may need to center themselves in more inclusive realities. This suggests that the order that is being affirmed is to a certain degree situational and relative, and that it therefore may contain a certain amount of overlap, incoherence, and contradiction. These are existential realities, not logical postulates, as has been determined, although certain religions do indeed work out their inner structures with remarkable clarity.

Confirmatory rituals do not include only taboos, although this is the category that has been most thoroughly discussed. Positive injunctions are merely the other side of taboos, so that in some cases stress on one or the other aspect is merely a matter of temperament. Greetings of a religious nature, blessings, prayers of affirmation, and rituals of meditation that stress the sustained perception of transcendental meanings present in ordinary experience are further instances of confirmatory rituals. For example, observant Jews have traditionally been accustomed to recite blessings focused on God on every occasion of everyday life, from the time of rising in the morning to going to bed at night, on meeting strangers, friends, wise persons or individuals remarkable in any way, witnessing or hearing of strange occurrences, encountering good news or bad, seeing a beautiful tree or tasting a new fruit, and so forth. As religious Jews come to see all of life as an opportunity to dwell in God's presence, so do Buddhist monks discover the void within all events, analyzing every perception, thought, and event in terms of yogic categories and *śūnyatā*. Such practices ritualize consciousness, and are especially important for mystical groups of almost all world religions.

Such practices express a more general attribute of ritual: it acts as a frame to awareness. Recognizing within the fluid continuum of ordinary occurrences a specific way of directing one's behavior immediately removes one from a complete immersion in mere activity. It creates self-conscious choice of behavior, so that one chooses this way, not that; actions referring to a larger meaning or presence, not actions merely referring to self. As George Albert Coe remarked in

The Psychology of Religion (Chicago, 1917), prayer "is a way of getting one's self together, of mobilizing and concentrating one's dispersed capacities, of begetting the confidence that tends toward victory over difficulties. It produces in a distracted mind the repose that is power. It freshens a mind deadened by routine. It reveals new truth, because the mind is made more elastic and more capable of sustained attention" (pp. 312–313). This power of confirmatory rituals is shared with transformatory rituals. However, confirmatory rituals tend to be more abbreviated, because their aim is to direct the performer into the world in a certain way and not simply to transform the performer. If such rites were drawn out and emphasized in themselves, they would have a contrary effect: the symbolic references within the rituals themselves would become the subject of concentration, replacing the focus on the ordinary field of activity. The internal nesting of symbols would displace banal realities, isolate the performers, and reveal a world of transcendental truths outside of common experience. This is what transformatory rituals do. Thus such rituals as taboo and sacrifice are closely related to each other, varying modes of the experience of liminality.

The framing power of ritual acts to shape consciousness itself and in confirmatory rituals sustains that modified consciousness as an enduring thing, producing the specific kind of self-consciousness and worldview aimed at by the particular religion. This power of ritual over consciousness creates cultural realities and so even from an empirical viewpoint actually produces changes in the environment. Godfrey Lienhardt (1961) has shown how such processes operate in detail among the Dinka of the southern Sudan: when a tardy herdsman, hurrying home before the sun falls, stops to tie a knot in a tuft of grass, he not only concentrates his mind but he actually modifies his reality, and this action as a whole has objective results. No Dinka supposes that commonsense efforts are actually replaced by such acts; such efforts are still needed, but a "slant" or framework of reality has been generated that facilitates activity. As Clifford Geertz has put it, ritual is both a "model of" and a "model for" reality (Geertz, in Lessa and Vogt, 1979), or, to use Martin Heidegger's term, ritual defines a "project," a way of entering into existence and bodily seizing it. Sherry Ortner (1978) has shown how key symbols operate ritually in this way among the Buddhist Sherpas of Nepal, sustaining pervasive moods or dispositional orientations to life and generating characteristic choices of behavior among the performers.

Striking advances have been made in recent years in the understanding of taboos. Decades ago it was common to regard taboos as superstitious, even infantile fear responses designed to ward off the sacred or perhaps lacking even that semirational goal. As recently as 1958, Jean Cazeneuve argued at length that taboos and purifications are intended to reject the sacred and to create an autonomous human sphere in which transcendence is an"impurity." With this view, Cazeneuve was building on Durkheim's important insight that taboos act to distinguish and thus to preserve both the sacred and the profane. However, more recent studies lead one to question whether there is any really profane sphere bereft of sacred quality and significance in most premodern religious systems. As Steiner showed, the profane was not to be understood as the "secular" in those systems, but simply as the common and everyday, as distinguished from the special quality of specifically transcendental things. Thus the profane could have sacred value. It is striking that the word *qadosh* ("holy") and its derivatives, such as *lehitqadesh* ("to make holy, to sanctify"), are used much more often in the Pentateuch about activities and things in this world and even the human sphere than they are about God. The first use of the root in the Bible is in regard to God making the Sabbath day holy (*Gn.* 2:3). The taboos of biblical Judaism describe ways of dwelling with God and not of keeping away from him: "You shall be holy, for I the Lord your God am holy" (*Lv.* 19:2). In effect, the taboos permit the sacred to be diffused in a controlled way through the entire world, building up a divine order rather than destroying it, as would occur if the shattering holiness of God were totally unveiled. (This important meaning of *qadosh* was entirely overlooked by Rudolf Otto in his *The Idea of the Holy,* leading to an unfortunate disregard for the cosmological and structural aspect of the sacred and a considerable distortion of the spirituality of the religions he described.)

Taboos not only surround sacred persons, places, and times, so as to preserve the intensity and specialness of these against the encroaching banality of ordinary life, but they also delineate the shifting frameworks of holiness that follow a person through life, at one time defining the sacred path for one to walk as a youth, at another time the path of the newly initiated, the married person, the elder, and so on. Different things are "sacred" to a person as he or she passes through the stages of life, and different things are "profane." Arnold van Gennep (1960) called this the "pivoting of the sacred" and concluded from it that the sacred is not an absolute quality, but a relative one. Taboos mark out these stages and confine the individual in them. For example, among the Aborigines of the northern Flinders Range in southern Australia, women and uninitiated males are not permitted to approach the areas set aside for men's initiations. These areas, the author of this article was told, were sacred and therefore taboo to women and young boys. But as novices the boys are led to those grounds, and henceforth they are allowed to go there: The taboo is lifted.

Taboos also define the enduring gradations in a continuum of sacrality. Among the Adnjamathanha people just mentioned, for example, anyone could go to the burial grounds, but certain things had to be done before entering them, and the only time that people could visit was in the late afternoon. As was mentioned, the men's sacred grounds were more taboo, with women and uninitiated men forbidden at all times; however, these grounds were divided into two parts, one near to the ordinary camp (which women could approach) and another in a remote part of the bush that was tabooed even to initiated men, except at times of special ceremonies. Taboos on food, noise, and even the things one carried differed according to which place one wished to visit. Taboos therefore can distinguish the more sacred from the less sacred. A striking account of the social impact of such taboos for Hindu society and caste was made by Edward B. Harper (1964): caste hierarchies are preserved by strict taboos governing personal relations, eating habits, marriage, and much else. These taboos are phrased in terms of purity and pollution. A brahman priest, after careful purifications, may serve the divinity in the temple, washing the divine image, changing its clothes, and offering food and flowers. The priest may thus "take the dirt" of the divinity, eating the offered food, carrying off the "dirty" clothes, and so on. Other castes are renewed by "taking the dirt" of the priest, and the process continues down to the outcastes who sweep, launder, and do other "impure" tasks for everyone. In this way the divine energy flows through the entire caste system, sustaining all of its gradations. The specific taboos thus have as their basic aim the preservation of the entire divine order, which is tacitly present at each observance. By keeping ten paces from the priest, one sustains the world.

Taboos also distinguish different species of the sacred from each other. Among the Adnjamathanha, as among most Australian Aboriginal peoples, the entire society was divided into totemic clans and divisions. Each clan had certain taboos to observe in regard to their own totem, which were not obligatory for other totems. For example, a clan would not hunt their own totem even though there was no taboo on eating it as there was among some other tribes. The entire society was symbolically divided in half, and each moiety had its own totems and its own special taboos. These taboos also controlled relationships between the two moieties, that is, they were not only directed to the natural world but structured the social world as well.

Finally, taboos act to distinguish fundamentally different modes of the sacred from each other, such as male sacrality and female sacrality, each gender having its own food prohibitions, its own tabooed activities, its special ceremonial centers tabooed to the other, and so on. The "pure" and the "impure" is another such pair of opposing modes. The "impure" often has the dangerous quality of being formless or anomalous and therefore threatening to the structures of the divine order. Death, for example, is often considered "impure" for this reason, even though it is also a form of the sacred, and so will be surrounded by taboos. What may be called positive and negative sacrality (e.g., "good" and "evil") are also distinguished by taboo. Positive liminality builds up the divine order, while negative liminality destroys it.

To summarize, confirmatory rituals such as taboos serve as framing devices that (1) bring the transcendental and ordinary realms into relationship while preserving each, (2) define and create, through the pivoting of the taboos and other rites, the transitory grades, stages, and roles of life, (3) fix the enduring gradations and divisions of social space (as in the caste system) and physical space (as in the various grounds and areas of the Adnjamathanha region), (4) distinguish the various species of the sacred from each other (as in Australian Aboriginal totemism), and (5) contrast the polar modes of the sacred (male-female, pure-impure, positive-negative).

Transformatory rituals. If confirmatory rituals sanctify the distinctions and boundaries that structure the cosmos (and therefore cluster especially around liminal points to preserve and define differences), transformatory rituals serve to bridge the various departments and divisions thus established, regenerating the cosmos in whole or in part when it is threatened by change. These rituals arise in response to anomaly, fault, disequilibrium, and decay, and they have as their aim the restoration of harmony and ideal patterns. Recentering is their essential dynamic. They all accomplish this in basically the same way, in accordance with a sacrificial logic: (1) the disturbing element is disconnected from its surroundings, by literal spatial dislocation, if possible; (2) it is brought directly into contact with the transcendental source or master in the sacred, which dissolves it and reforms it—this is the time of flux, outside of ordinary structures; and (3) the reshaped element is relocated in the divine order. These rites often separate out from the disturbing element or situation those positive potentially integrative factors that can be reshaped into a constructive part of the divine order and the negative disintegrative factors that must be located in some peripheral and bounded part of the cosmos, where they belong.

One may further loosely distinguish between transitional rituals, which place the disturbing element in a new location in the divine order (e.g., through initiation, the child enters the adult sphere; in funerals the living person is acknowledged as fully dead, perhaps as an ancestor, etc.), and restorative rituals, which return the regenerated element to its previous place in the whole. Examples of transitional rituals include "rites of passage" (birth, initiation, marriage, mortuary rites), calendrical rites (seasonal and other regularly enacted rites, sometimes called rites of intensification), consecration rituals (founding a new village, accepting a stranger into the community, sanctifying a house, etc.), and conversionary rituals (penitential practices, rituals inducing radical personal change or ecstasy, and conversions as such). Restorative rituals include purifications, healing rites (which generally attempt to reintegrate the ailing organ or patient into a state of harmony with the body or community), divination, and crisis rites. Millenarian or revitalization movements exhibit both restorative and transitional features in different proportions in different movements, often combining themes from life cycle, calendrical, and conversionary rituals, and from all forms of restorative rituals as well. This is not surprising, since in these movements the struggle for a divine order becomes all-embracing and desperate. Depending on the emphasis, then, the rites common to these movements may be put in either the restorative or the transitional categories, as intensified forms of conversionary rites, or as vaster crisis rites.

In any case, one can only speak of general emphasis rather than sharp distinctions between the two sub-categories of transformative rites. In most religions, for example, when New Year or harvest ceremonies are celebrated they both renew the annual cycle and restore the primordial form of things. Theodor H. Gaster (1961) has suggested that the seasonal rites of ancient Near Eastern religions sustained a "topocosm," the world as an organic whole. Reviving the world when it decayed, these renewals reenacted the ideal forms of the creation myths, so that their transitions were essentially restorative.

The liminal phase. Arnold van Gennep (1960), in his classic study of "rites of passage" (even the terms are his), emphasized that the crucial phase of these rites is the middle, liminal, or threshold phase, during which one is outside of ordinary life and exposed more directly to the sacred. The transcendental and transformative power of the liminal is indicated ritually in many characteristic symbolisms. Often one finds "rituals of reversal," in which ordinary behavior is turned upside down: people might don the clothes of the other sex or indulge obligatorily in orgiastic or "mad" behavior (although ordinary life may be very restrained—thus the Carnival in several Mediterranean societies); the powerful may be humiliated and the weak may purge resentments. (The king of the Swazi was ritually slapped and the people acted out rebellious behavior during their harvest festivals; ordinarily modest and retiring Hindu women douse men with ochred water during the riotous Holi festival; children in the guise of monster beings threaten adults and extort sweets from them during American celebrations of Halloween). There is a certain sense of *communitas,* as Victor Turner (1969) puts it: the participants feel joined together in a unity that lies outside of ordinary social structures and that expresses the prior flux and even formlessness out of which those structures have emerged. Yet the exaggerated reversal of roles and behaviors serves to emphasize the goodness of social structures, which are returned to with a sense of refreshment after the liminal period; in the liminal rites themselves, as many anthropological studies have stressed, one may find the ideal roles of a society and the ideal patterns of the universe enacted with particular emphasis and clarity, although these patterns and roles may have become obscured by the personal interactions, forgetfulness, and above all the confusion of overlapping roles that occur in small-scale communities. However, in sectarian movements or otherworldly religions in more complex civilizations, this *communitas* and its contrast to ordinary life can be understood as access to an antithetical realm of the spirit denied to those in general society. In any case, the liminal period is "betwixt and between" and is appropriately the time for the triumph of monstrous and anomalous things, for inverted and extreme behaviors, for ecstasies, paradoxes, and the abnormal. The increased closeness to the primordial flux may be represented in masked dances, initiative rituals centering on devouring monsters, and the entry of transcendental beings and forces into the sacred area. The ritual follows the archetypal patterns laid down when these things were first done in the beginning by the ancestors and gods, or it obeys the teachings then given by the divine beings. For all is not formless and utter flux: there is a sacred form that *communitas* takes, which is that of the pristine dynamic that defines and sustains reality. Participants are unified by this common form, even if they each have different roles within its hierarchies.

The triumph of liminality is also demonstrated by distortions of ordinary sensory things. The body image is altered, for example: decorations cover the body, scarifications are made, distinctive clothes are worn, movement is severely restricted or is contorted, parts of the body are removed, or things are stuck into the flesh in painful ordeals. Distinctive treatment of the hair is a common indication of liminal status. Operations are also performed on nonhuman things (animals, plants, newly consecrated houses, sacred rocks, etc.) to indicate the dominance in them of spiritual meaning over perceptual or physical facticity. The self-sustaining integrity of merely perceptual experience is shattered, to be transformed by the authentic realities of the "ideal." The ability of the self to define reality on its own terms is thereby shaken, and it is forced to submit to the central and defining force of the transcendental other. Even the self is defined by the other, sustained by it, and required to acknowledge it. This is the essential point of sacrifice as such, the enactment of which takes so many forms in transformatory rituals.

Sacrifice. A great deal has been written about sacrifice, and often there has been an attempt to explain all forms of it in terms of one application or use of it (gifts given to a deity so as to obligate him to the giver, communion, etc.). Long lists of types of sacrifice based on their uses have been compiled. However, almost every actual instance can be shown to involve many of these functions. E. E. Evans-Pritchard (1956), in a celebrated analysis of sacrifice among the Nuer of the southern Sudan, was able to list no less than fourteen different ideas simultaneously present in those rites: communion, gift, apotropaic rite, bargain, exchange, ransom, elimination, expulsion, purification, expiation, propitiation, substitution, abnegation, and homage. He asserted, nevertheless, that the central meaning was substitution: all that is oneself already belongs to the transcendental presences and powers, which is explicitly acknowledged in the sacrifice by giving back to the divine some part of what defines the self or symbolizes it. Phenomenological studies of religion agree with this anthropological analysis or extend it further, stating that one offers back to the divine what is thus acknowledged as already belonging to it, including the entire world one uses and dwells in. All of these views confirm that sacrifice consists above all in actively recentering the self and its entire world and renouncing personal autonomy. One is experientially and cognitively placed in a divine order, in which the merely physical or perceptual sensual connections of phenomena are broken and the transcendentally centered meaning is made to dominate.

The French sociologists Henri Hubert and Marcel Mauss showed that sacrifice served to bring into a mediated relationship a human group and the sacred powers that affected it, via manipulation of a victim who through consecration or general usage symbolically embodied or substituted for the group or some aspect of it (e.g., the scapegoat above all embodies the sins or flaws of the group, which are then expelled with him). By the conclusion of the rites, the victim might be taken up entirely into the sacred realm, or returned to the human group and shared among them. The first option, removal of the mediatory victim, desacralizes the community, expelling a surplus of perhaps baleful sacred power from the group and in any case preserving the separation of sacred and profane, while the second option, return of the now-transformed victim to the group, exemplifies the tendency to sacralize the community and establishes a mediated continuity with the divine. Luc de Heusch has called these the "conjunctive" and "disjunctive" powers of sacrifice.

However, as Kristensen (1961) has shown, the victim often symbolizes the god who receives it rather than the group that offers it. Water was sacrificed to Osiris, who was the Nile; wild animals were offered to Artemis, Mistress of the Wild; dogs were given to Hekate, for both were of the underworld. And even enemies of the divinity may be sacrificed to the god, demonstrating his power over everything. Everything is made to center on the sacred pivot of life.

J. H. M. Beattie (1980) notes that some theories of sacrifice emphasize the power and divinity of the recipient of sacrificial offerings (as in the gift theory of E. B. Tylor), while others emphasize the dynamic interchange of energies involved and even underline impersonal structures (as in the approach of James G. Frazer). Beattie classifies all sacrifices into four basic types, derived from the aim or focus of the participants: (1) sacrifice to maintain or gain close contact with spiritual beings, (2) sacrifice to separate the sacrificers from those beings, (3) sacrifice to gain access to or control of dynamic impersonal modes of liminality, and (4) sacrifice to separate such forces from the sacrificer or the person for whom the sacrifice is enacted. Such a schema can be applied only very loosely, however: impersonal and personal elements usually coexist, as, for example, in the Roman Catholic Mass, where personal prayers are part of the essential sacramental transformations that are effective regardless of personal intentions. Similarly, conjunctive and disjunctive motifs usually occur together. For example, in Hebrew sacrifice certain parts of the victim's body, including its blood, were removed and given to God before the flesh could be shared among the communicants and eaten. It would not be correct to assume from this that the blood was a form of negative liminality, to be expelled from the community in a purgative rite; quite simply, the essence of everything, in this case the blood or "life," belongs to God. Kristensen again provides assistance in distinguishing predominantly positive sacrificial rites of sanctification from sacrifices with the predominantly negative aim of causing a misfortune to cease.

Sacrifice is often literally present in transformatory rituals, but it need not be. It may be symbolically enacted in other ways. W. E. H. Stanner (1966) has shown in a detailed structural analysis of the initiation rites of the Murinbata Aborigines of northern Australia that the treatment of the novice precisely follows the dynamic of sacrifice—although this community, like almost all Australian Aboriginal societies, has no explicitly sacrificial rituals. Similar parallels to sacrifice have been noted in the treatment of the death and replacement of divine kings in Africa. Some religions do without literal sacrifice altogether, having sublimated the notion into the entire ritual system. Thus the rabbis consoled themselves after the fall of the Temple in 70 CE that prayer, charity, and good deeds would fully replace the sacrifices offered there; so too Protestant Christianity has generally abandoned sacrifices.

In any case, the essential dynamic of sacrifice is symbolical and spiritual. It operates within a world in which everything is a metaphor for the divine life. As a result, even religions with a great stress on sacrifice need not make use of bloody immolations (with which sacrifices seem to be associated in the common mind). The favored offerings in Hinduism are clarified butter and flowers. The Nuer are quite content to symbolize cattle with cucumbers in their sacrifices.

Cross-cultural and Historical Variations. Religions can clearly differ significantly in their reliance on ritual, the kinds of ritual preferred, and the purposes of ritual in general. The major variations are still being vigorously debated. Maurice Bloch (1977), arguing from a Marxist anthropological perspective, claims that the more institutionalized hierarchies a society has, the more ritual there is, especially of the "eternal return" type, which repeats past events. This is because rituals are highly limited codes of information that can be easily manipulated by the holders of power to falsify the sense of reality of the exploited classes; therefore ritual legitimates social inequality and must be greatest in those societies that are the most politically differentiated. However, American society, for example, is highly differentiated politically but tends to be anti-ritualistic and has little ritualism, whereas the Australian Aborigines devote a great deal of their time to ritual reenactments of events in the ancestral Dreaming. Max Gluckman (1965), on the other hand, has suggested that rituals are necessary in relatively undifferentiated societies to distinguish roles that tend to blur and overlap in everyday life, while in more complex societies role specialization is so advanced that ritual definitions of social structure are no longer needed. Ritual is therefore reduced to temple and priestly cult, while the rest of society is increasingly secularized.

A more ambitious and detailed historical schema is offered by Robert Bellah, an American sociologist (see his essay in Lessa and Vogt, 1972). He distinguishes a "primitive" stage of religion (erroneously identified with the Australian Aborigines) in which ritual is the continual reenactment of ancestral deeds, with all things supposedly so fused that no external or self-conscious perspective is possible; an "archaic" stage (found among most native cultures) in which worship, prayer, and sacrifice first appear, the result of a widening gap between humanity and divinity; a "historic" stage in which for the first time the gap between the sacred and profane is so great and society so complex that rituals stress salvation from the world rather than inclusion in it, and in which a religious elite emerges separate from the political elite to administer the otherworldly rites and specialize in or embody religious ideals; and finally, "early modern" and "modern" stages of religion (identified with Western culture) in which salvation is democratized and ritual is extended into the whole of life, made subjective, and finally dissolved in secularism (cf. Bellah's article, reprinted in Lessa and Vogt, 1972). Although instructive, such vast generalizations suggest that due caution is required.

Mary Douglas (1970) has tried to characterize the variations that can be found within religions at almost any level of complexity, without essaying sweeping historical syntheses. Cosmologies vary according to whether they tend to stress clear-cut rules and principles underlying the universe and society or the absence of such rules; they also vary in the identification of true being as located in a group or in the individual person apart from the group. These two polarities combine to produce four basic cosmologies. (1) Groups with a strong sense of rules ("grid") and of group identity tend to be highly ritualized, with fairly elaborate rites to demarcate the various sectors of the cosmology and with rich and dense symbolisms that thus define sin and sacramental salvation. These religions see the material and spiritual worlds as interfused. (2) Groups with very weak "grid" and weak sense of group identity, on the other hand, tend to have quite abstract ritual symbols, and indeed little use for ritual as such; here, what ritual exists is oriented toward personal states of ecstasy or aesthetic display. An instance might be contemporary counterculture communities. (3) Societies with weak "grid" but strong group identity tend to see salvation as obtained by belonging to the group; ritual stresses "we-them" polarities, which, because not rationalized in any coherent structure of principles or rules, tend toward strongly emotive fear of the "them" as evil persons or groups outside of any comprehensible order. Ritual is often used for self-purgation or for counter-witchcraft, and within the group ritual is used to stress ecstatic subjective states of *communitas* and to reenact the formation of the group. There may be an otherwordly, salvation-oriented type of cult, as in early Christianity. Sectarian movements are not uncommonly of this type. (4) Cultures or individuals with a strong sense of "grid" but weak on group identity characteristically produce ritual that services personal goals. In many Melanesian societies of this sort, ritual is used mainly to increase personal powers and to defeat personal enemies, to make one's own fields prosper, and so on. If the "grid" is understood in a moral sense, one may have a stoic outlook—cool, impersonal, and indifferent to society, but at the same time personally demanding. Variations of these four basic types can be found on every level of cultural complexity, and this is not a historical scheme as is Bellah's.

The use of ritual in modern cultures varies considerably. However, a number of paradoxical assertions can be made. First, antiritualism is quite strong in many circles, due to a number of factors. Ritual is oriented toward equilibrium and stability, but the modern period is a time of rapid change even in religious institutions. Ritual draws upon shared bodily experiences, which it uses to delineate a common cosmos; however, life experiences are highly varied today, and there is little agreement on the larger cosmos either. Religious institutions as such "do" very little in a scientistic, secularized world. Subjective and private experience is considered the realm of the spiritual, but it is often asserted that the sacred has never been so remote from actual human life. Yet the search for authentic realities continues, and when these are found, rituals reassert themselves. Industrialized Western societies spontaneously generate ritual and so do militantly antiritualistic communist societies.

Much of the current debate about the impact of secularism on religion is really about the forms, intensity, and purpose of ritual in modern life. The literature on secularism cannot be reviewed here, but it may be said that this literature has shown that the extent of ritual practice in Western and communist societies is much greater and more diverse than statistics on church attendance might suggest. Especially when one takes into account the structural or cosmological focus of much religious ritual, it becomes evident that many community and national festivities are genuinely religious in nature.

W. Lloyd Warner's study of community ritual in "Yankee City," mentioned earlier, bears this out. In recent decades much has been written about "civil religion" in the United States and elsewhere. Robert Bocock, in a study of ritual in modern England (1973), has suggested that another form of ritualism in modern life can be termed "aesthetic" ritual. It is found in dance halls, art galleries, and sports stadiums, and its purpose is to orchestrate sensual and aesthetic experience of a personal nature. However, more obviously religious are ritual practices derived from new religious movements and personal cults, which offer the individual spiritual enhancement or attunement to the world: meditational practices, theosophical study groups, even many of the personal therapy groups that have assumed cultic form.

See Also Archetypes; Ceremony; Ecstasy; Hierophany; Rites of Passage; Sacrament; Sacred Space; Sacred Time; Sacrifice; Seasonal Ceremonies; Secularization; Taboo; Worship and Devotional Life.

Bibliography

References

Ahern, Emily M. *Chinese Ritual and Politics.* Cambridge, 1981.

Barth, Fredrick. *Ritual and Knowledge among the Baktaman of New Guinea.* New Haven, Conn., 1975.

Beattie, J. H. M. "On Understanding Sacrifice." In *Sacrifice,* edited by M. F. C. Bourdillon and Meyer Fortes. New York, 1980.

Binns, Christopher A. P. "The Changing Face of Power: Revolution and Accommodation in the Development of the Soviet Ceremonial System." *Man,* n.s. 14 (December 1979): 585–606; n.s. 15 (March 1980): 170–187.

Bloch, Maurice. "The Past and Present in the Present." *Man,* n.s. 12 (August 1977): 278–292.

Bocock, Robert. *Ritual in Industrial Society: A Sociological Analysis of Ritualism in Modern England.* London, 1973.

Cassirer, Ernst. *The Philosophy of Symbolic Forms,* vol. 2, *Mythical Thought.* New Haven, Conn., 1955.

Cazeneuve, Jean. *Les rites et la condition humaine.* Paris, 1958.

Douglas, Mary. *Purity and Danger.* New York, 1966.

Douglas, Mary. *Natural Symbols.* New York, 1970.

Durkheim, Émile. *The Elementary Forms of the Religious Life* (1915). New York, 1965.

Eliade, Mircea. *Cosmos and History: The Myth of the Eternal Return.* New York, 1954.

Eliade, Mircea. *The Sacred and the Profane.* New York, 1959.

Evans-Pritchard, E. E. *Nuer Religion.* Oxford, 1956.

Fernandez, James W. *Bwiti: An Ethnography of the Religious Imagination in Africa.* Princeton, N. J., 1982.

Freud, Sigmund. *Totem and Taboo.* New York, 1918.

Gaster, Theodor H. *Thespis.* New York, 1950.

Gay, Volney Patrick. *Freud on Ritual.* Missoula, Mont., 1979.

Gennep, Arnold van. *The Rites of Passage.* Chicago, 1960.

Girard, René. *Violence and the Sacred.* Baltimore, 1977.

Gluckman, Max. "Les rites de passage." In *Essays on the Ritual of Social Relations,* edited by Max Gluckman, pp. 1–52. Manchester, 1962.

Gluckman, Max. *Politics, Law and Ritual in Tribal Society.* Chicago, 1965.

Harper, Edward B. "Ritual Pollution as an Integrator of Caste and Religion." In *Religion in South Asia,* edited by Edward B. Harper. Seattle, 1964.

Horton, Robin. "A Definition of Religion, and Its Uses." *Journal of the Royal Anthropological Institute* 90 (1960): 201–226.

Horton, Robin. "African Traditional Thought and Western Science." In *Rationality,* edited by Bryan Wilson. Oxford, 1970.

Hubert, Henri, and Marcel Mauss. *Sacrifice: Its Nature and Function.* Chicago, 1964.

Jenson, Adolf E. *Myth and Cult among Primitive Peoples.* Chicago, 1963.

Kapferer, Bruce. *A Celebration of Demons.* Bloomington, Ind., 1983.

Kristensen, W. Brede. *The Meaning of Religion.* The Hague, 1960.

Lane, Christel. *The Rites of Rulers: Ritual in Industrial Society: The Soviet Case.* Cambridge, 1981.

Leach, Edmund R. "Ritual." In *International Encyclopaedia of the Social Sciences,* edited by David L. Sills, vol. 13. New York, 1968.

Leeuw, Gerardus van der. *Religion in Essence and Manifestation.* London, 1938.

Leinhardt, Godfrey. *Divinity and Experience: The Religion of the Dinka.* Oxford, 1961.

Lessa, William A., and Evon Z. Vogt, eds. *Reader in Comparative Religion.* 4 eds. to date. New York, 1958, 1965, 1972, 1979.

Lévi-Strauss, Claude. *The Savage Mind.* London, 1966.

Lévi-Strauss, Claude. *The Origin of Table Manners.* New York, 1979.

Lewis, Gilbert. *Day of Shining Red: An Essay on Understanding Ritual.* Cambridge, 1980.

Lifton, Robert Jay. *Revolutionary Immortality.* New York, 1968.

Needham, Rodney, ed. *Right and Left: Essays on Dual Symbolic Classification.* Chicago, 1973.

Ortner, Sherry. *Sherpas through Their Rituals.* Cambridge, 1978.

Otto, Rudolf. *The Idea of the Holy.* Baltimore, 1959.

Stanner, W. E. H. *On Aboriginal Religion.* Sydney, 1964.

Steiner, Franz. *Taboo.* New York, 1956.

Tambiah, Stanley J. *Buddhism and the Spirit Cults in Northeast Thailand.* Cambridge, 1970.

Toy, Crawford Howell. *Introduction to the History of Religions.* Boston, 1913.

Turner, Victor. *The Forest of Symbols.* Ithaca, 1967.

Turner, Victor. *The Drums of Affliction.* London, 1968.

Turner, Victor. *The Ritual Process.* Ithaca, 1969.

Turner, Victor. *Dramas, Fields and Metaphors.* Ithaca, 1974.

Wallace, Anthony F. C. *Religion: An Anthropological View.* New York, 1966.

Warner, W. Lloyd. *The Living and the Dead; A Study of the Symbolic Life of Americans.* New Haven, Conn., 1959.

Zuesse, Evan M. "Meditation on Ritual." *Journal of the American Academy of Religion* 43 (September 1975): 517–530.

Zuesse, Evan M. Ritual Cosmos. Athens, Ohio, 1979.

General Works

Most good introductions to cultural anthropology have one or more chapters devoted to ritual and religion. An excellent one-hundred page overview unusual in that it draws upon both anthropological and religious studies is by W. Richard Comstock in a volume edited by him, *Religion and Man: An Introduction* (New York, 1971). The overview is separately printed as *The Study of Religion and Primitive Religions* (New York, 1972); the bibliography is very useful. The various editions of *Reader in Comparative Religion,* edited by William A. Lessa and Evon Z. Vogt (see "References" above) provide a continuously updated anthology and survey of anthropological research on ritual. The bibliographies are especially full, and one of them offers an annotated listing of the best monographs on the religions of particular native cultures. Also very useful are the three volumes edited by John Middleton anthologizing anthropological articles: *Gods and Rituals* (Garden City, N. Y., 1967), *Myth and Cosmos* (Garden City, N. Y., 1967), and finally *Magic, Witchcraft and Curing* (Garden City, N. Y., 1967).

For a historical survey of theories about religion and ritual since classical antiquity, especially strong on the nineteenth century and European schools, see Jan de Vries's *The Study of Religion: A Historical Approach* (New York, 1967). Robert Lowie's *The History of Ethnological Theory* (New York, 1937) and E. E. Evans-Pritchard's *Theories of Primitive Religion* (Oxford, 1965) are among the more penetrating anthropological accounts.

I have emphasized anthropology thus far. A good instance of how Freudian psychology can treat ritual structures in an illuminating way is Géza Róheim's *The Eternal Ones of the Dream* (New York, 1945). The work deals with central Australian Aboriginal rituals. Erik Erikson's psychoanalytic *Childhood and Society* (New York, 1950) shows the connection between ritual and games. Jean Piaget has reflected on the role and meaning of games in the psychological development of children in numerous books, such as his *Plays, Dreams, and Imitation in Childhood* (New York, 1961); many of his observations have a bearing on ritual. However, the classic study of this fascinating topic is Johann Huizinga's *Homo Ludens* (London, 1949), written not from a psychological but a humanistic perspective.

A synthetic, multidisciplinary approach to ritual, making use of the contributions of specialists in a variety of natural and social sciences within the context of a single theory of human development, is *The Spectrum of Ritual: A Bio-Genetic Structural Analysis,* edited by Eugene G. d'Aquili (New York, 1979).

The study of ritual in terms of its explicitly religious significance remains the province of scholars in the history and phenomenology of religions, for example, Mircea Eliade, Theodor H. Gaster, W. Brede Kristensen, and Gerardus van der Leeuw (see "References").

Major contributions to the general understanding of ritual are to be found in studies from within specific religious traditions, or in works devoted to their classic sources on ritual. As examples, I should mention from the Jewish tradition Gersion Appel's *A Philosophy of Mizvot* (New York, 1975) and Max Kadushin's *The Rabbinic Mind,* 2d ed. (New York, 1965); from the Catholic tradition Louis Bouyer's *Rite and Man* (Notre Dame, Ind., 1963) and Roger Grainger's *The Language of the Rite* (London, 1974); and from the Confucian tradition the classic *Li Ji* (The Book of Rites), translated by James Legge and edited by Chu Zhai and Winberg Zhai (New York, 1967)—the James Legge translation first appeared in "Sacred Books of the East," vols. 27 and 28 (London, 1885)—and the philosophic commentary by Herbert Fingarette, *Confucius: The Secular as Sacred* (New York, 1972). Reference has been made in the essay to some classic works on Hindu ritual; these are available in English translation. Arthur Berriedale Keith's *Karma-Mimamsa* (Calcutta, 1921) gives a general introduction to this school of philosophy, while Raj Bali Pandey's *Hindu Samskaras,* 2d ed. (Delhi, 1969), gives a good insight into the traditional understanding of personal rituals.

Ritual provides a way of dealing not only with the positive sides of the human condition but also its negative sides. One study has approached even the cultural phenomenon of the "feud" in terms of ritual theory: Jacob Black-Michaud's *Cohesive Force: Feud in the Mediterranean and the Middle East* (New York, 1975). One of the major ways of controlling violence is through the ritualization of it; a penetrating examination of the implications of this is René Girard's *Violence and the Sacred,* listed in the "References" above. Also see Ernest Becker's *Escape from Evil* (New York, 1975) and Eli Sagan's *Cannibalism: Human Aggression and Cultural Form* (New York, 1974), although both of these works tend to generalize overhastily—for example, some research casts doubt on almost every European report of "savage cannibalism."

An overall bibliographic survey of study on ritual is available by Ronald L. Grimes, entitled "Sources for the Study of Ritual," *Religious Studies Review* 10 (April 1984): 134–145.

EVAN M. ZUESSE (1987)

RITUAL [FURTHER CONSIDERATIONS].

The term *ritual* remains difficult to define, which is hardly surprising, since central activities and concepts are always the ones probed most restlessly. The difficulties attending the definition of *ritual* testify to the fundamental role it is given in religion and social life, as well as to its attractiveness as a focus for current theorizing about religion in general. The definitional difficulties may also suggest the variety of input into the discussion. For these reasons, ritual has been identified in many unexpected places; rarely does an analysis decide something is not ritual. Nevertheless, the study of ritual in numerous settings is driving theory in several disciplines to work through, and past, the symbol-culture model of the 1970s and 1980s—in some cases to engage the contributions and ramifications of postmodernism, in other cases to forge a new science to depict the importance of ritual. The results, a matter of highly visible differences with more subtle areas of consensus, are the context for much of the contemporary study of religion.

Many current theories of ritual use the term *ritualization,* which goes back at least as far as the work of Max Gluckman (1962) and Julian Huxley (1966), in order to foreground the dynamics by which people actually do rites, perform rituals, or act ritually. The term challenges a number of positions, starting with the assumptions that rites are the unchanging elements of a religious tradition, and that they all have some underlying, universal structure. Even when rituals proclaim their faithful adherence to ancient models, they always involve choices and changes; the degree to which change is denied, minimized, or embraced is important for any interpretation. The more deeply rooted longing to articulate a universal structure for ritual—a scheme that does not change when other features do (i.e., that which makes a rite a rite)—has taken on a special significance due either to a semi-theological concern for absolutes or, more likely, a pragmatic instinct to ground "religion" itself. In a prosaic but remedial manner, ritualization also announces that it is the activity itself, not texts or doctrines or pantheons, that will be taken as important and as the place to start analysis. Ritualization also signals an understanding that any activity can be ritualized; that is, made into a ritual or a ritual-like performance, usually by invoking features such as formality, repetition, and the use of more traditional models. Naturally, then, the term appreciates that there are degrees of ritualization and the example of one rite might not be the best example for all rites. While not all of these points are embraced by every theorist, there is a consensus that the activities themselves should be the main focus, and theorists seek the best theoretical model for doing that.

Using the terms *ritual, ritualization,* or *performance,* attention to ritual is frequent in the major disciplines—anthropology, sociology, history, communication, and even philosophy. Collections such as *A Reader in the Anthropology of Religion* by Michael Lambek (2002) and *Handbook of the Sociology of Religion* by Michele Dillon (2003) feature sections on ritual that attempt, in their different disciplinary ways, to organize this fast-paced area of research so as to suggest a coherent direction. Within the collection of methods that make up the field of religious studies, these terms are also used with a new self-consciousness in biblical studies, church history, psychology of religion, and, naturally, liturgical studies. The most comprehensive bibliography of ritual covering all these areas since Ronald Grimes's *Research in Ritual Studies* (1985) is the extensively annotated and thematic catalog appended to *Theorizing Rituals: Classical Topics, Theoretical Approaches, Analytical Concepts, Annotated Bibliography,* edited by Jens Kreinath, Jans Snoek, and Michael Stausberg (2005).

Just as *ritual* remains hard to define, the ability of ritual to pull together scholars of different subjects, approaches, and disciplines—witnessed in the many conference panels and subsequently published collections—remains remarkable. Interdisciplinary projects will often involve the widest mix of cultures and historical periods, and some even go out of their way to use particularly unconventional notions of ritual, such as the scratching of medieval graffiti on the walls of a small church in Italy (Rollo-Koster, 2002, p. 127). These projects testify to a lingering desire to identify something common in all the examples identified as ritual, even when careful historical contextualizing makes each set of activities stand out in their uniqueness. Still, these collections vividly illustrate something else as well: that attention to so-called ritual activities in multiple contexts can bring into focus forms of behavior relevant to the study of religion and society that would have fallen under the radar of other analytical terms.

CURRENT THEORIES: A ROUGH GUIDE. There are two theoretical points of departure dominating the study of ritual at the beginning of the twenty-first century, each with distinct but not mutually exclusive positions on ritualization, religion, and the role of theories about them. While these "camps" read each other, they do not often refer to each other clearly. Hence, a guide of sorts may help clarify the main lines of argument. Of course, any general rubric for organizing approaches, such as distinguishing those theories that emphasize ritual as a form of communication from those that emphasize it as a form of action, can be precise only at a certain level of generality. In regard to ritual and the whole ragtag set of issues that have defined the study of religion in modern times, it sometimes seems that the most telling distinctions among theories are not found in the introductory assumptions—where one starts, so to speak—but in where one ends up. As a "rough guide" to the current scene, a first-order distinction can be made between theories that remain heavily rooted in cultural explanation and those that are recreating naturalistic (or scientific) models of explanation. Yet even within these two general positions, no two theories are alike. In addition, several popular theories resist categorization even within a sorting this broad; they might be said to take a more or less psychoanalytic view of the role of ritual in human history—a view that often seems distinctly literary, romantic, and even mythic, even as it alludes to the science of the psychoanalytic enterprise.

Ritual theory through the 1980s often took it for granted that ritual is primarily a form of communication, although such communication involves much more than the simple conveyance of information. Earlier theories of this sort emphasized the symbolic nature of ritual action, with later ones showing a preference for focusing on the expressive or performative aspects of ritual communication. Pushing at the margins of the influence wielded by Victor Turner and Clifford Geertz throughout the 1970s and 1980s. Mary Douglas and Barbara Myerhoff were prominent in portraying the complexity of ritual's symbolic communication in generating meaningful interpretations of the social and cultural order. For these theorists, the encoded symbols and performance sequences understood as ritual are flexible forms of symbolic activity that reaffirm cultural values and a sense of order—both social and cosmic. In other words, rituals are frameworks for mobilizing meaning. But resistance to this approach has been building widely in anthropology, with Talal Asad's challenge to Geertz's notion of a symbol often cited as something of a turning point (Asad, 1993).

COMMUNICATION AND A NEW NATURALISM. During the 1990s, several projects were launched that explore ritual's essentially communicative functions in ways that differ from the Geertzian symbol-culture-meaning approach. This new approach foregrounds communication in the doing or performing of ritual, but stresses the relative unimportance of any "meaning" for participants, as well as for theorists (contrast Rothbuhler, 1998). This note was first sounded by Frits Staal in 1975, and its later rearticulation can be understood perhaps as reluctance to objectify religion and culture as required by most theories of ritual as communication. In one project, the anthropologist Roy Rappaport consolidated thirty years of theories from a number of disciplines into a massive study entitled *Ritual and Religion in the Making of Humanity* (1999), which expands the insights of his earlier work, notably *Ecology, Meaning, and Religion* (1979). In another echo of Staal, Rappaport declares ritual to be "the social act basic to humanity" (1979, p. 198; 1999, p. 31) because ritual involves adaptive features as important to the evolution of human beings as language itself. As an essentially performative mode of communication, with more emphasis on the communication aspect, ritual does more than merely *convey* religious ideas. Rather, Rappaport attempts to show how ritual *creates* religious ideas and experiences. In his early work he argued that ritual communicates both indexical (self-referential) messages and canonical (pertaining to cultural tradition) information. The later analysis expands this to include how ritual activities generate, ratify, and normalize "the Holy" in a set of "Ultimate Sacred Postulates" (1979, pp. 210–211; 1999, pp. 263–290). Ritual communicates, Rappaport argues, but it communicates an informationless and unquestionable order of things in which the performer and the performed are indistinguishable from the certainties expressed and, inevitably, accepted.

For Rappaport, ritual performs two explicit and socially indispensable communicative functions: in its creation and communication of the Ultimate Sacred Postulates, ritual does not lie and it does not sanction alternatives to itself. Drawing these terms from Martin Buber's analysis of the stages of evil (1952), the lie and the possibility of choice (and indecision), Rapport uses them to describe the forces that constantly threaten to unravel the social fabric. Ritual denies the possibility of both by asserting a true and unchallengeable order of things. It creates (and communicates) a discourse of sacrality, defined as "the quality of unquestionableness" that participants intellectually attribute to things that cannot be proven (Rappaport, 1999, p. 281). Simultaneously, ritual affords participants an affective experience of the numinous, which Rappaport defines as an emotional consciousness of transcendence comparable to the discussions of *das heilige* (the holy) by Rudolf Otto (1869–1937) and others at the turn of the twentieth century. Indeed, within Rappaport's rubric, the conjunction of the sacred and the numinous creates the holy. The "meaninglessness" of a rite is an essential quality of the holy, which is generated by the rite. Meaninglessness is the product of both a ritual's "canonical invariance," as Rappaport puts it, and the basic emptiness of the sacred postulates endorsed by ritual. Not only is meaning not needed, it would impede what a ritual is doing. Instead of meaning, the critical factor is the social ratification invoked in and demanded by ritual, not the diffusion of meaning in the fashion suggested by Geertz among others (Rappaport, 1979, p. 263). Ritual is the language-like communication of what is socially indispensable; it is what sets the human species apart—but it is not a provider of meaning. Eventually locating his argument more fully in the biological language of human evolution, Rappaport contends that ritual is the indispensable evolutionary adaptation that established social conventions and mandated their acceptance (Rappaport, 1999, p. 124). He concludes with the same amused finale that closed his earlier work: ritual is the means by which "the unfalsifiable supported by the undeniable yields the unquestionable which transforms the dubious, the arbitrary, and the conventional into the correct, the necessary, and the natural" (1979, p. 217; 1999, p. 405).

Rappaport's study is subtle, repetitive, and synthetically indebted to many. Still, in both its 1979 and 1999 articulations, he contributes one of the most complete descriptions of how "the religious" may be constituted. The role of ritual is central in this process, perhaps well beyond what anyone but a ritual studies scholar could possibly appreciate. In his major step beyond Émile Durkheim (1859–1917) and Geertz, Rappaport describes ritual as doing more than simply supplying the "effervescence" that enables individuals and society to create social identities (Durkheim) or mechanistically restoring the fit between the mental orientation of a worldview and the emotional tendencies of a cultural ethos (Geertz). Yet he follows the same structural style of argument basic to the analyses and conclusions of Durkheim and Geertz; that is, he also casts ritual as the means for reuniting the terms of a previously drawn analytical distinction— an essentially circular argument. In his case, ritual creates the holy by conjoining the sacred and the numinous, defined in intellectual and emotional language, respectively. This seductive pattern of theorizing about ritual—to distinguish two properties (thought and action, individual and society, spiritual and material, etc.) and then work one's way toward a definition and analysis in which ritual is the means for reuniting them—is thoroughly critiqued in Catherine Bell's *Ritual Theory, Ritual Practice* (1992). Still, while evoking Geertz's categories in particular, Rappaport does what Geertz never; he ventures to describe *how* the sacred and the numinous each come into being and then come together in an experience of the holy. This is a provocative phenomenological exercise, although Rapport does not see this as phenomenology. It took him many years to determine how best to cast his arguments, and he chose evolutionary biology; the meta-argument of his later book maintains that the mental requirements for ritual activity, defined as the construction of the holy, functioned as the adaptive evolutionary prerequisites for a fully human consciousness.

Rappaport is not the first scholar to return to the role of ritual and religion in evolution. This was a major topic of eighteenth- and nineteenth-century anthropology, when Giovanni Battista Vico, David Hume, Auguste Comte, and Edward Burnett Tylor all presented new "sciences" of religion that cast religiosity as a stage somewhere between early emotional attempts to placate unknown powers and the dispassionate pursuit of science seen in the Enlightenment. After Tylor, Julian Huxley and Konrad Lorenz in the 1930s also proposed their ethological examinations of ritual practices among animals and humans. With E. O. Wilson's widely discussed theories of sociobiology in the 1970s and 1980s, there began to be analyses of the adaptive benefits of altruism and other aspects of religion. In the 1980s Eugene d'Aquili and his colleagues were writing about how the cognitive dimensions of ritual activity might have been important to, or made possible by, the evolution of specific neurological systems in the brain (d'Aquili, 1979; 1985). The renowned classicist Walter Burkert took up the evolution of the broad and questionable patterns he saw in ritual among both human beings and animals in *Creation of the Sacred: Tracks of Biology in Early Religions* (1996). In the most general biological-evolutionary explanations of morality and religion, such as Frans de Waal's *Good Natured: The Origins of Right and Wrong in Humans and Other Animals* (1996) and David Wilson's *Darwin's Cathedral: Evolution, Religion, and the Nature of Society* (2002), ritual is an important component for explaining the evolutionary or biological significance of religion, although in many of these studies ritual is characterized primarily by emotionalism, strict repetition, and illiterate cultural settings. For all of these works, religion is still an "other" to be explained with the proven analytical frameworks of science, or at least something that looks like science.

Rappaport's concluding, nearly apocalyptic, appeal to the role of ritual in the past and future of humankind is, therefore, part of a fairly constant interplay between cultural explanations and natural/scientific ones. During the 1990s the tendency for a popular shift every few years in the winning focus found greater substance in the emergence of "cognitive" theories of religion—and ritual. Cognitive studies are not actually new. A standard textbook on psychology and religion (Wulff, 1997) has three extensive chapters on biological, behavioral, and laboratory-based natural theories of belief and ritual going back a full century. Still, a study of ritual by E. Thomas Lawson and Robert N. McCauley, *Rethinking Religion: Connecting Cognition and Culture* (1990), claimed to be launching a "science of religion" due to the sense of fresh developments in evolutionary psychology and neurobiology. Lawson and McCauley's argument for the existence of certain rules in the performance of ritual generated fresh enthusiasm for explanations as empirical hypotheses that could be tested by others, a scientific process new to religious studies. In *Bringing Ritual to Mind: Psychological Foundations of Cultural Forms* (2002), they were even bolder, using the tools of an action-representation system to address another specific aspect of ritual, the link between the frequency of a ritual and the degree to which it is marked by elaborate and varied modes of expression. Their science of religion has been accompanied by a provocative line-up of studies espousing a wide array of theses (Andresen, 2001; Atran, 2002; Boyer, 2001; Pyysiäinen, 2001; and Whitehouse, 2000, 2004, among others). While some of these works propose very reductive theories of religion ("apparently pointless behaviors," and "snares for thought" [Boyer, 2001, pp. 262–263]), others are more moderate and nuanced. Cognitive approaches are also attempting to address issues in theology and the psychology of religion by explaining the constraints and the formative impulses in how and why people believe what they believe, or remember what they remember—still ritual is a common and often central concern.

McCauley and Lawson are careful with the language of reductionism. They are apt to speak of an "intuitive knowledge" of a system of ritual that is not dependent on socialization or instruction, suggesting that a type of ritual grammar exists in human beings, much like the innate generative grammar for language proposed by Noam Chomsky in *Syntactic Structures* (1957). As a grammar, a language, or some analogous scheme, a ritual system is seen as a rule-governed expression of an evolutionary adaptive basic competence. For McCauley and Lawson, theirs contributes another model of ritual as communication, but one that builds on the work of cognitive psychology, in contrast to the evolutionary anthropology of Rappaport, where the rules are less amendable to empirical testing. In their first book, Lawson and McCauley specifically looked at the way in which ritual structures are linked to types of beliefs about the supernatural. They proposed two universal principles: the principle of *superhuman agency* and the principle of *superhuman immediacy.* The first finds that the most central rites are those in which a superhuman being is the active agent, compared to those more peripheral rites in which the god is inactive or passive. The principle of superhuman immediacy argues that the more central rites are less complex, that is, they include fewer "enabling" activities and superhuman agents. These two principles, say Lawson and McCauley, will explain the basic competence of people to produce fitting rituals in their cultural setting and suggest the adaptive function of religion.

Their second book is concerned with the relation between ritual form (the structures generated by their first analysis) and ritual frequency (how seldom or often a ritual is performed). Since rituals motivate participants to recall and re-enact performances, Lawson and McCauley generate a "ritual form hypothesis" to explain the low levels of emotionalism attending frequent rites compared to the high levels of stimulation found in rites that are less often performed. In their analyses, the psychological processes that Lawson and McCauley attempt to uncover do not derive from social or cultural contexts but from cognitive structures, forms, or abilities within the human brain, with the assumption that scholars can imagine precultural forms of cognition. While it is assumed that ritual knowledge confers adaptive social benefits, ritual—as ritual—is not seen as a fundamentally social phenomenon. Among those who turn away from cultural-symbolic explanations of meaning, the Lawson-McCauley theory of cognition attempts to go the furthest in delineating "very general features of religious ritual form [that] are independent of both semantic and cultural contents" (2002, p. 10). Their acultural analysis addresses "religious ritual" tightly defined as the same universal form everywhere (secular rites are never discussed as "ritual"). Whatever cultural content and context might contribute, what makes a set of actions a ritual lies beyond culture: thus, the rules uncovered among the Baktaman of New Guinea, for example, should be valid for religious rituals of the eighteenth-century Chinese court. In effect, and unlike Rappaport, McCauley and Lawson are not drawing on the history of the study of ritual; they are operating among the literature and issues defining the branch of competence theory in the field of neuropsychology. Their ability to contribute to a broader study of ritual cannot be discounted, nor can that of the other cognitive approaches being developed. Yet the primary assumptions, as well as the terminology and style, are difficult for people in religious studies and cultural anthropology. While addressed at some length here, these two works are not the best introduction to the cognitive approach. Jensine Andresen's "Introduction: Towards a Cognitive Science of Religion" (2001) and Ilkka Pyysiäinen's *How Religion Works* (2001) are clearer in tracing the origins of the cognitive model and its relationship to older models of religion.

Practice and Performance. The other general approach to ritual works within the assumptions of a fully cultural perspective—namely, that the social and cultural life of a community is responsible for the emergence and style of ritualization, and the category of "ritual" is a historical one as much as it is an analytical one. From a sociocultural perspective, the origin of ritual has not been much addressed since Durkheim led a general abandonment of "origins" arguments. But a naturalistic explanation of the evolutionary origins of ritual could be welcomed by those who avow to be nonscientists—as long as the formidable role of culture is not left out of any aspect of ritualization, even its evolutionary roles or neurological rules. Recent cultural theories have tended to regard ritualization as a fundamentally performative action or practice, rejecting the stress on communication, although Rappaport and others considered ritual as performative communication. Among the many discussions of performance, the notion of practice exerts great influence. Rooted in the work of Pierre Bourdieu, Maurice Bloch, and Sherry Ortner, practice approaches to ritual are used in the work of Jean Comaroff and Talal Asad, with the most developed theoretical presentation in Bell's *Ritual Theory, Ritual Practice.* The starting point for Bell is the notion that ritual might be more accurately approached if it is not classified as some structurally distinct and primal cultural activity; that is, unlike all other ways of acting. Rather, ritual activity should be returned to the context of cultural action in general, as action among actions. Only in the context of many ways of acting—a functional semiological system—can one approach the construction, meaning, and efficacy of ritualized practices. The term *practice,* historically indebted to Karl Marx's notion of *praxis,* simply refers to culturally shaped and shaping activities.

For many of the great theoreticians of religion, there was no question that ritual possessed a distinctive identifying structure. The dominant models of ritual in the twentieth century, such as those of Arnold van Gennep, Durkheim, Mircea Eliade, Turner, and Geertz, understood ritual as a fundamentally different sort of social event. Just as Durkheim described the distinction between the sacred and profane as starkly clear, these models assume that ritual—as a symbolic (non-instrumental) mode of acting, directed toward what is sacred—by definition must differ completely from profane modes of acting. In making this argument theorists needed to name the something extra or different that is found in rituals, such as traffic with supernatural beings, awe of the *mysterium tremendum,* or a specific structuring of social symbols and symbolic stages of experience. For example, Turner saw ritual in terms of a distinctive pattern of "structure" and "*communitas,*" while Geertz saw a characteristic harmonization of the symbolic references that make up a social arrangement (ethos) and a sacred cosmology (worldview). The many adoptions and adaptations of the Turner and Geertz models to interpret an ever elastic set of activities have shown how impossible it may be to define ritual as a clear category. Some theorists have been logically drawn into the enterprise of constructing typologies in order to deal with those rites that had a "fuzzier" nature; they wrestle with taxonomies to distinguish liturgy from rite from ceremony from ceremonial, and, naturally, religious ritual from secular and civic ritual. The impulse to see ritual as a very distinct form of action is, according to Bell (1992), a position that replicates a fundamental dichotomy between thought and action, and eventuates in an overly structured discourse that strongly defines scholars as those who are not ritual actors, the observed and the analyzed.

Bell's approach builds on (1) the notion of practice, (2) the dynamics of the so-called ritual body, and (3) ultimately, the arrangements of power that make ritualization the culturally effective thing to do. Drawing in part on Bourdieu (1977), Bell suggests four basic features of cultural practice or activity in general. First, practice is situational, with a contingency that eludes any attempt to grasp its objective meaning, thus evoking Edward Said's description of the "endless deferral of meaning." Second, practices are strategic (i.e., exploitative or expedient), with an instrumental logic that remains as implicit and improvisational as possible. Third, practices misrecognize their own dynamics; generally focusing only on their goal, they do not see how their activity towards it shifts the nature of the goal and the whole landscape of action to attain it. Finally, practices are guided by the need to act as much as possible within an interpretation of domination and subordination that provides all involved with a measure of empowerment, however modest or even illusionary—a concept dubbed "redemptive hegemony" (Bell, 1992, pp. 81–85). As cultural practice, ritual activity will be all these things; it will share these features with other activities, such as cooking a meal, though some features will be more stressed than others. Ritual is not an intrinsically special way of acting, but it is a distinct orchestration of activities: the commonality of ritualization with other actions allows a better focus on what is distinctive about the choices involved in it. In terms of this commonality, ritualization should be analyzed in context of its situational strategies and misrecognitions, which create a form of redemptive hegemony able to exercise some dominance over other activities in the world.

According to Bell, the distinctive significance of ritualization starts in the type of contrast it generates with other actions. Acting ritually appears to establish, in the very manner in which the activity is performed, a "privileged distinction" between it and other implicated actions: "acting ritually is first and foremost a matter of nuanced contrasts and the evocation of strategic, value-laden distinctions" (1992, p. 90). Bell's suggestion that ritualization seeks to establish a privileged differentiation means that a Sunday service is not a ritual by virtue of an intrinsic structure it alone possesses, but by virtue of the way its activities stress contrasts with other activities that make the ritualized acts special (people dress up for Sunday service, gather in a large room according to a what is understood as a tradition, sing an order of songs, address God in prayer through a minister's leadership—in contrast to their daily dress-down routines, infrequent gatherings, individual prayer, and self-determination, etc.). Through an action's creation of this type of privileged distinction, "ritual is always contingent, provisional, and defined by difference" (1992, p. 91). Therefore, formalism or repetition or traditionalism are not intrinsic qualities of ritual practices, but common strategies for producing acts that can dominate their context in important and useful ways. On this basis, a universal characterization of ritualization may be impossible; it may be describable only in general terms since even the most widespread strategies could mean different things in different cultural contexts. Bell's "theory" of ritual, therefore, is an experiment in backing away from all the universal qualities usually assigned to ritual to make it an a priori event structured similarly in Madras and Manhattan.

Yet the privileged opposition at the base of ritualized practices is only part of what goes on in ritualizing. Another distinct feature for Bell is the way in which ritual strategies of action are rooted in the individual, socialized body: "the interaction of the social body with a symbolically constituted spatial and temporal environment" is a circular process by which the body shapes the space that shapes the body. The socialized body misrecognizes this shaping: it does not see itself shaping its environment so much as reacting to an order or pre-existing arrangement of forces. Nonetheless, as bodies (with minds and voices, not just limbs and gestures, etc.) absorb the logic of spaces and temporal events, they then project these structural schemes, reproducing liturgical arrangements out of their own "sense" of the fitness of things. This process of embodiment and projection produces, and is indicative of a "ritualized body," a body that can naturally produce ritualized schemes. Even outside the ritual arena, the ritualized body will exercise quiet ways of reinterpreting (thereby dominating) social circumstances based on the dense, flexible logic of schemes learned in the rite. This theory of the "ritual mastery" of the socialized body draws upon Marcel Mauss's analysis of the "*technique de la corps*" (1935), as well as to Bourdieu's innovative re-description of Mauss's notion of "habitus" (Bourdieu, 1977). For Bell, the goal of ritualizing activity is always the production of a ritualized and ritualizing agent who acts beyond the rite, while the situation in which this particular set of circular misrecognitions is played out is one in which the participants are seeking a particular organization of domination and power, that is as emanating more or less directly from sources deemed beyond the human community but still subject to some channeling or control or intercession.

The contextualization of ritual as cultural practice opens up new dimensions of analysis. For example, the theorist can ask why ritual is chosen as the most efficacious way of acting in a situation? What types of power are defined for all involved? What is the difference for a community between ad hoc ritualizing and a "tradition" of ritual forms controlled by whom? The choice to use ritualized practices to act on the world can lend a peculiar efficacy to action, an efficacy that has everything to do with ritual's own qualities of misrecognition and its redemptive sense of empowerment. It might also lend a particular retreat to a situation by defining the problem and solution in terms that leave the dispensation of power outside of the community. This practice theory of ritual has proven to be usefully elastic for a number of fields and disciplines, especially the interpretation of so-called secular rituals and the emergence of new ritualizing, neither addressed by preceding theories.

The anthropologists Caroline Humphrey and James Laidlaw propose a different theory of ritual as action. They see ritualization as the distinctive way in which any action may be performed, but they suggest that ritualized activities will always differ clearly from routine actions for a cultural community. First, ritualization is "a qualitative departure from the normal intentional character" mobilized for any action (1994, p. 89). Second, ritual actions are always stipulated in advance, already formed, ready to do, or prescribed. Hence, the intentions of the actor make no difference to what the actions are or how they are done. This is, in part, a way of dealing with the ritual tradition as something that is given yet also freshly exercised. These ritual precedents, which Humphrey and Laidlaw call "archetypal," have no intrinsic meaning for the ritual actors or the participants. People are free to assign meanings and argue about the rites in broad or detailed terms, which they certainly do. A third and crucial point for Humphrey and Laidlaw is that these rites are perceived as external, elemental, or object-like entities. As such they appear to exact a type of fundamental acquiescence to the facticity of one's social world. In their extended analysis, liturgies or "liturgy-centered rites" can be seen as characteristically ritualized, while more performance-centered rites are only weakly ritualized, leaving more to the actors to determine.

Humphrey and Laidlaw's theory of ritualizing action is particularly concerned with challenging the assumption in anthropology that ritual is a paradigmatic form of cultural communication with discursive meaning for all involved. Bell rejects any suggestion that ritual is universal, and she is hesitant even to grant universality to any particular strategy of ritualization, such as formalism. Similarly, Humphrey and Laidlaw argue that since cultural attitudes toward ritualization are inseparable from it, ritual can never be the same across cultures, but ritualization as they define it remains a universally available form of action. This contrasts strongly with Bell's move away from universalism and power of tradition.

Performance theory invokes the emphases on communication and performance that have characterized so much theorizing about ritual, while identifying a spectrum of ritualized gestures and acts (Bell, 1998). At one end of a spectrum, some theorists emphasize the performative aspects of ritualization, in contrast to theorists in theater studies, for example, who explore the ritualized dimensions of performance.

Some analyze performance as communication, while others approach performance theory as liberation from communication models. Pushing out from all of these positions, the focus on performance has opened up many avenues of inquiry. For example, it highlights ritual as a multisensory experience of sights, sounds, flavors, and smells, as well as a physical language of gestures and embodiment (Sullivan, 1986; Schechner, 1985). Performance approaches also generate analysis of the ways in which ritual is a matter of "frames" and what framing accomplishes interactively between actor and audience (Bateson, 1955; Goffman, 1974; Handelman, 1990). While some scholars point to an underlying notion of "illusion" in the language of performance, this is challenged by those who articulate both ritual and performance as central to the social construction of reality (Schieffelin, 1985). As evidence of its synthetic tendencies, a view of ritual as performance will foreground the limits on, and yet necessity for, inventive spontaneity suited to the moment, in addition to time-honored classical models that provide a larger sense of context and identity (Hughes-Freeland, 1998). A number of anthropological studies of performance attempt to chart the social and cultural ramifications of transitions from a local traditional rite to a more tourist-oriented performance, certainly a very common development in the last century. Finally, performance theorists have been particularly alert to the importance of a culture's own approach to performing, letting cultural specificity dominate theoretical categories (Laderman and Roseman, 1996). Still, the implied question of universal aspects to ritual and performance, even when answered in the negative, often underlies the issues brought to the study of "ritual performance."

The popular theories of Georges Bataille (1973) and René Girard (1986) forge distinctive routes through the issues of culture, nature, communication, and practice to express themes that have been consistent threads throughout the twentieth-century's study of religion. Bataille and Girard are regularly cited for their distinctive analyses of sacrifice, with both using approaches that are vaguely psychoanalytic in a Freudian way and loosely ahistorical in a Eliadian way, focusing on primal emotional conflicts that endure, they argue, in ritual today. For both theorists, sacrifice is the origin of religion (and much else) and the preeminent form of ritual in general. For Bataille, ritual is born of desire and destruction; for Girard, ritual is mimetic desire (envious imitation) and violence. Within an encompassing theory of religion, Bataille argues that the sacrificial destruction of an animal transforms it from an external object in the world of things into something more intimate and immanent to human beings: a part of the divine world. The sacrificer negates the profane order of reality for the priority of the mythical or sacred order, yet, paradoxically, each order exists in order to neutralize the other (as Bataille acknowledges). Sacrificial killing is an act of destructive consumption (in contrast to the productivity of profane reality) in which the transformation of the separate, objective life of the animal is, mysteriously, the transformation of the separate identity and reality of the individuals involved in the act. In the death and consumption of the animal, human beings experience a transgression of the bounds of life and death. While Girard laments the heavy moral demands of sacrifice, Bataille argues that the cruelty and anguish of sacrificial killing are essential in opening the only route to transcendence.

Bemoaning the failure of religious anthropology to solve "the mystery of ritual," Girard lays out a theory that roots all ritual forms in primitive, or primal, sacrifice. Convinced that primitive societies are "obsessed" with mimetic rivalry, in which one person desires that which another has, Girard casts ritual as a "theatrical reenactment" of the social crisis that results from such rivalry, a destructive paroxysm in which the group can purify itself by killing a victim, a scapegoat. The purpose of ritual, therefore, is collective reconciliation and reordering—a Frazerian process of regeneration (Girard, 1996, pp. 10–14)—via the shared act of violence. It is not so hard to understand why Bataille is regularly cited, although not usually in formal studies of ritual, since his explanation is so close to Christian theology despite his insistence on outsider status. It is more curious that Girard's bleak reductionism has been found so provocative to many, although its attractions are undoubtedly a version of the theological as well— if only the atheology of Sigmund Freud himself, who tried to account for religion by collapsing history into the psyche, with religion as the necessary illusion that keeps us more or less content in a civilization constructed on the sacrificial killing of the father.

NEW DIRECTIONS. In the words of one theorist, the interaction of the concepts of ritual, practice, and performance has generated a "rapidly changing intellectual geography" (Hughes-Freeland, 1998, p. 2); certainly none of the preceding approaches will keep their current shape for long. The study of ritual practices will undoubtedly continue to pursue several directions of inquiry, perhaps with lopsided influences on each other. Cultural-practice theories are proving amenable to further refinement and wide application. The various arguments of cognitive science may not be unraveling that many ritual milieus, but so far they have generated suggestive ideas and drawn much attention in a post-postmodern milieu. The assumption that cognitive universals underlie the panoply of culture reintroduces an old position, of course, but with fresh enthusiasm for scientific forms of evidence and the mysteries of adaptive evolution (Pyysiäinen, 2001). For decades the study of religion was mapped in terms of the poles of *eklaren* (explanation) and *verstehen* (interpretation); and again we hear the cry for a truly scientific explanation and a rejection of vague cultural interpretation. Yet for students and readers of Eliade, it is hard to read the introductory chapters to this new scientific literature without thinking of the grand comparative-religion project of the twentieth century. With a sentence that could have come from Eliade's *Patterns in Comparative Religion* (1958), one proponent of the new cognitive science writes that "there are quite obviously recurrent patterns of religious phenomena across cultures, and it is these patterns that form the object of the study of religion" (Pyysiäinen,, 2001). Eliade's morphology of the forms of religious symbolism, with its semi-scientific intentions of collection and analysis, capped a century of what was understood to be the scientific study of religion. Eliade eventually reached out to be more than scientific, in part because science was having such a hard time actually comprehending religion. As in the anthropological and psychological sciences, interpretation became a rich and complex method, as well as an object of study itself.

In a summary of recent studies of ritual, the sociologist Robert Bellah asserts that ritual is the basic social event and "the most fundamental category for the understanding of social action" (Bellah, 2003, p. 32). He then traces the evidence for its emergence in this role and its evolutionary contributions in the transition from primates to humans, raising interesting questions about ritual's relationship with language and music. Bellah is strongly committed to maintaining "general terms in the social sciences"—although they warrant a "healthy skepticism" since they are "of recent and Western origin." Still he argues, there is no need to doubt that they "refer to real features of the real world" (p. 44). Bellah is specifically responding to Bell's suggested doubt that the category of ritual refers to a real, universally distinct phenomenon. Thus, even as culturally oriented a sociologist as Bellah finds it impossible to adopt a perspective that he undoubtedly sees as the continued nihilism of postmodernism. He also turns to various discussions of the evolutionary roots of ritual with their promises of real evidence.

Cognitive approaches to ritual might be most valuable if they were to find a clear, realistic place for cultural analysis. Practice theories of ritual, for their part, need to continue to demonstrate greater ethnographic utility, not merely in the broad outlines. Surely the nature versus nurture debate is foolishly conceived, and we will inevitably find that these two extreme categories refer to realities that are harder to differentiate. In the end it is not surprising that ritual studies is the site of such different approaches; it has always been a area for cross-disciplinary exchange, and it undoubtedly will continue to be that.

Future theories of ritual may address some of the evidence for how people are actually ritualizing today. Around the globe, several major changes in ritual practices are occurring. First of all, the loss of undisturbed tribal cultures is certainly complete, so the rites of tribal peoples today must be understood to represent incredibly complex cultural interactions, dominations, and inversions. Second, the twentieth century saw the conversion of many peoples of the world to Islam and Christianity, both of which invite forms of nationalism and transnationalism not possible among earlier cultural differences. Third, the evangelical movement in the United States, perhaps another great awakening, may be again emptying the mainstream churches and filling up the so-called mega-churches with their distinctive style of worship and their openness to immigrant populations. Fourth, the sense of a personal spirituality that does not require affiliation or clear doctrines, or more than minimal ad hoc rituals, cannot continue to be dismissed as New Age-ism; while people of this persuasion have been active consumers of books and paraphernalia on how to ritualize the main events of their lives, the language of an unaffiliated spirituality is now quite pervasive (Grimes, 2000). Together, all of these developments do not predict any greater coherence and unity in ritual studies than we have seen up to this point. Following the words of the cognitive theorist Ilkka Pyysiäinen, perhaps a theory of ritual is unreasonable, but we can have theories about ritual (2001, p. viii). For religious studies in general, the mid-century move from Biblical sources about ritual, with their particular focus on sacrifice, to more anthropological ones, makes religious studies a player alongside the other social disciplines. So, within the field of religion, ritual studies inevitably struggles to identify its peculiar contribution, which is less likely to be a special position or method as a stubborn refusal to reduce—in analysis or in significance—so-called religious phenomenon into fully other (that is, non-religious, un-holy) components or conclusions.

SEE ALSO Ritual Studies.

BIBLIOGRAPHY

Andresen, Jensine, ed. *Religion in Mind: Cognitive Perspectives on Religious Belief, Ritual, and Experience.* Cambridge, U.K., 2001.

Asad, Talal. *Genealogies of Religion: Discipline and Reasons of Power in Christianity and Islam.* Baltimore, 1993.

Atran, Scott. *In Gods We Trust: The Evolutionary Landscape of Religion.* Oxford, 2002.

Bataille, Georges. *Theory of Religion* (1973). Translated by Robert Hurley. New York, 1989.

Bateson, Gregory. *Steps to an Ecology of Mind.* 1955; reprint, New York, 1978.

Bell, Catherine. *Ritual Theory, Ritual Practice.* New York and Oxford, 1992.

Bell, Catherine. *Ritual: Perspectives and Dimensions.* New York and Oxford, 1997.

Bell, Catherine. "Performance." In *Critical Terms for Religious Studies*, edited by Charles C. Taylor, pp. 205-224. Chicago, 1998.

Bellah, Robert. "The Ritual Roots of Society and Culture." In *Handbook of the Sociology of Religion*, edited by Michele Dillon. Cambridge, pp. 31-44. U.K., 2003.

Bial, Henry, ed. *The Performance Studies Reader.* New York, 2004.

Bourdieu, Pierre. *Outline of a Theory of Practice.* Translated by Richard Nice. Cambridge, U.K., 1977.

Boyer, Pascal. *The Naturalness of Religious Ideas: A Cognitive Theory of Religion.* Berkeley, 1994.

Boyer, Pascal. *Religion Explained: The Evolutionary Origins of Religious Thought.* New York, 2001.

Buber, Max. *Good and Evil: Two Interpretations.* New York, 1952.

Burkert, Walter. *Creation of the Sacred: Tracks of Biology in Early Religions.* Cambridge, Mass., 1996.

Chomsky, Noam. *Syntactic Structures.* The Hague, 1957.

Comaroff, Jean. *Body of Power, Spirit of Resistance: The Culture and History of a South African People.* Chicago, 1985.

d'Aquili, Eugene G., Charles D. Laughlin, and John McManus, eds. *The Spectrum of Ritual: A Biogenetic Structural Analysis.* New York, 1979.

de Waal, Frans. *Good Natured: The Origins of Right and Wrong in Humans and Other Animals.* Cambridge, Mass., 1996.

Dillon, Michele. *Handbook of the Sociology of Religion.* Cambridge, UK, 2003.

Eliade, Mircea. *Patterns in Comparative Religion.* Translated by Rosemary Sheed. New York, 1958.

Girard, René. *The Scapegoat.* Translated by Yvonne Freccero. Baltimore, 1986.

Girard, René. *The Girard Reader,* edited by James G. Williams. New York, 1996.

Gluckman, Max. *Essays on the Ritual of Social Relations.* Manchester, 1962.

Goffman, Erving. *Frame Analysis: An Essay on the Organization of Experience.* New York, 1974.

Grimes, Ronald A. *Research in Ritual Studies: A Programmatic Essay and Bibliography.* Chicago and Metuchen, N.J., 1985.

Grimes, Ronald A. *Deeply into the Bone: Re-Inventing Rites of Passage.* Berkeley, 2000.

Handelman, Don. *Models and Mirrors: Towards an Anthropology of Public Events.* Cambridge, U.K., 1990.

Hughes-Freeland, Felicia, ed. *Ritual, Performance, Media.* London, 1998.

Humphrey, Caroline, and James Laidlaw. *The Archetypal Actions of Ritual: A Theory of Ritual Illustrated by Jain Rite of Worship.* Oxford, 1994.

Huxley, Julian, ed. *A Discussion on Ritualization of Behavior in Animals and Man.* London, 1966.

Kreinath, Jens, Jans Snoek, and Michael Stausberg, eds. *Theorizing Rituals: Classical Topics, Theoretical Approaches, Analytical Concepts, Annotated Bibliography.* Leiden, 2005.

Laderman, Carol, and Marina Roseman, eds. *The Performance of Healing.* London, 1996.

Lambek, Michael, ed. *A Reader in the Anthropology of Religion.* Maldon, Mass., 2002.

Lawson, E. Thomas, and Robert N. McCauley. *Rethinking Religion: Connecting Cognition and Culture.* Cambridge, U.K., 1990.

Lorenz, Konrad Z. "Evolution of Ritualization in the Biological and Cultural Spheres." In *A Discussion on Ritualization of Behavior in Animals and Man,* edited by Julian Huxley, pp. 273–284. London, 1966.

Mauss, Marcel. *Techniques of the Body.* 1935. Translated by Ben Brewster in *Economy and Society* 2, no. 1 (February 1973): 70–88.

McCauley, Robert N., and E. Thomas Lawson. *Bringing Ritual to Mind: Psychological Foundations of Cultural Forms.* Cambridge, U.K., 2002.

Myerhoff, Barbara. "A Death in Due Time." In *Rite, Drama, Festival, Spectacle: Rehearsals Toward a Theory of Cultural Performance,* edited by John J. McAloon, pp. 149–178. Philadelphia, 1984.

Pyysiäinen, Ilkka. *How Religion Works: Towards a New Cognitive Science of Religion.* Leiden, 2001.

Rappaport, Roy A. *Ecology, Meaning, and Religion.* Richmond, Calif., 1979.

Rappaport, Roy A. *Ritual and Religion in the Making of Humanity.* Cambridge, U.K., 1999.

Rollo-Koster, Joëlle, ed. *Medieval and Early Modern Ritual: Formalized Behavior in Europe, China, and Japan.* Leiden, 2002.

Rothenbuhler, Eric W. *Ritual Communication: From Everyday Conversation to Mediated Ceremony.* Thousand Oaks, Calif.: 1998.

Schechner, Richard. *Between Theater and Anthropology.* Philadelphia, 1985.

Schieffelin, E. L. "Performance and the Cultural Construction of Reality." *American Ethnologist* 12, no. 4 (1985): 707–724.

Staal, Fritz. *Rules without Meaning: Ritual, Mantras, and the Human Sciences.* New York, 1989.

Sullivan, Lawrence E. "Sound and Senses: Toward a Hermeneutics of Performance." *History of Religions* 26, no. 1 (1986): 1–33.

Whitehouse, Harvey. *Arguments and Icons: Divergent Modes of Religiosity.* Oxford, 2000.

Whitehouse, Harvey, and James Laidlaw, eds. *Ritual and Memory: Toward a Comparative Anthropology of Religion.* Altamira, 2004.

Wilson, David Sloan. *Darwin's Cathedral: Evolution, Religion, and the Nature of Society.* Chicago, 2002.

Wilson, Edward O. *Sociobiology: The New Synthesis.* Cambridge, Mass., 1975.

Wulff, David M. *Psychology of Religion: Classic and Contemporary.* 2d ed. New York, 1997.

For an overview of theoretical interpretations, the many types of rituals identified, and the roles ritual plays in social life, see Bell's *Ritual: Perspectives and Dimensions.* It is usefully supplemented by Humphrey and Laidlaw, *The Archetypical Actions of Ritual,* which develops an extensive example in Jain ritual. McCauley and Lawson's *Bringing Ritual to Mind,* from two major scholars, is not the easiest introduction to cognitive analysis of ritual per se, but it is the most complete. One could also start with the articles by McCauley and Lawson in Andresen's *Religion in Mind.* Rappaport's *Ritual and Religion in the Making of Humanity,* the other major work since the mid-1980s, is also not a simple study, but Lambek's *Reader in the Anthropology of Religion* excerpts a credible selection. Bial's *The Performance Studies Reader* assembles a thorough collection of the major theoretical sources for a performance perspective on ritual.

CATHERINE M. BELL (2005)

RITUAL STUDIES as a field of inquiry began with a research group established in 1977 by the American Academy of Religion (AAR), the international society of religious studies scholars. A decade later Ronald L. Grimes and Fred W. Clothey cofounded the *Journal of Ritual Studies.* Ritual studies is a distinct academic field that gives special attention to the performance aspect of the rites themselves (gesture, aesthetics, space, choreography, praxis, meaning) and not just to a rite's social function or cultural context.

Although the term *ritual studies* is often misapplied as a catchall category for widely divergent research, the field of ritual studies aspires to more than simply cultivating conversation and exchange among scholars from different disciplines. Ritual studies requires a research approach that is truly interdisciplinary. This field of study represents a movement away from more traditional text-oriented conceptions of ritual, and like anthropology and sociology, ritual studies endorses participatory fieldwork when possible. Yet ritual studies differs from the social sciences in its interest in both experiential meaning (phenomenology) and textual interpretation (hermeneutics) and in its concern with studying ritual's relationship to language, narrative, and myth. An excellent example that strikes the ritual studies ideal of balance in simultaneously studying text, action, and context is Sam Gill's *Native American Religious Action* (1998). Gill combines fieldwork data from Navajo culture with a careful exposition of the semantic content of prayer texts to show that the most culturally responsible way to study Navajo prayer is to consider it as a performative, pragmatic, and poetic ritual medium. Gill notes that the referential meaning of the prayer's words ought not be privileged apart from the prayer's actual performance or cultural context. In Gill's study prayer as a rite is not severed from its proper place in the history of Navajo oral tradition nor from its current position in the larger healing ceremony of which it is part.

Because many of the field's leading scholars work in religious studies departments, ritual studies has adopted the cardinal premise of the academic study of religion: that no single ritual tradition or practice ought to be used as a normative standard for analysis or classification. Any type of theoretical interpretation performed in ritual studies is understood as a comparative judgment, not as a value judgment. This does not mean that ritual studies eschews theology or liturgics. Once only the purview of Christianity, *liturgics* increasingly refers to the study of worship ritual in a variety of religious traditions. Whereas the global study of religious rites past and present is an expected province of ritual studies, it is not presumed that religious ritual is the highest form or most fully developed type of ritual. Ritual studies follows the lead of Sally F. Moore and Barbara Myerhoff's *Secular Ritual* (1977) in pursuing the study of secular ceremony and ritual as well.

A good reading list of texts on ritual is in Ronald L. Grimes's anthology, *Readings in Ritual Studies* (1996). Grimes's succinct introductions to each entry highlight many of the scholars and debates pertinent to the study of ritual. Reading these in conjunction with Catherine Bell's *Ritual Theory, Ritual Practice* (1992) will provide a thorough introduction to the academic discourse on ritual. As Bell notes, many classic theories are marked by the use of binary oppositions and the Western philosophical split between thought and action, observer and observed. Because ritual is often viewed as simultaneously representing and fusing these polarities, Bell invites a more thorough integration of practice theory into ritual studies to resolve this seeming paradox. The concerns and sensibilities of ritual studies as a field are best articulated in Grimes's first monograph for classroom use, *Beginnings in Ritual Studies* (1982). Grimes also produced the first bibliography of ritual, *Research in Ritual Studies* (1985), that covers 1960 to 1983. This resource paired with Madeline Duntley's updated bibliographic essay "Ritual in the United States" (1997) organizes the diverse range and types of modern writings on ritual available to scholars in both the academic and popular press.

Since 1977 ritual studies has made significant strides in interdisciplinary research in three key areas: (1) mind-body and language; (2) popular culture and ritual; and (3) theoretical analysis and construction.

MIND-BODY AND LANGUAGE. Ritual studies provides a variety of ways to study ritual in the wider context of human behavior. One option is performance studies. Richard Schechner defines *performance* as ritualized behavior both conditioned and permeated by play. Building upon Victor Turner's pioneering work, *From Ritual to Theatre: The Human Seriousness of Play* (1982), Schechner measures "play acts" using six templates: structure, process, experience, function, ideology, and frame. In *The Future of Ritual* (1993) Schechner claims that players, spectators, and observers each may be independently analyzed in terms of these six templates, which in turn helps to break down the dichotomy of observer and observed (Schechner, 1993, pp. 25–26). Performance studies has ties to kinesics (the study of the communicative role of bodily movements and facial expressions). Because ritual action often takes the form of carefully framed gestures, methods such as kinesic-style film study and dance-annotation analysis of ritual hold great potential for the study of ritual. But to date the theory of gesture remains rooted in conceptual categories of interaction ritual first established by Erving Goffman in *The Presentation of Self in Everyday Life* (1959).

Biogenetic structuralism is an approach in ritual studies exploring the connection between ritual and myth from a neurological and evolutionary point of view. It tempers the humanistic orientation in ritual theory by suggesting that ritual mediates between genetic codes and ecological adaptation. In *The Mystical Mind* (1999) the psychiatrists Eugene G. d'Aquili and Andrew B. Newberg map responses to ritual action in various areas of the brain. For example, the site of emotional discharges associated with different types of religious experiences can be located using brain imaging experiments on Tibetan Buddhist meditators. D'Aquili also collaborated with Charles Laughlin and John McManus in *The Spectrum of Ritual* (1979), a collection of essays on the genetic foundations of ritual, and in *Brain, Symbol, and Experience* (1990).

Studies of ritual and violence often begin with the findings of ethologists such as Julian Huxley in the article "A Discussion on Ritualized Behavior in Animals and Man" (1966). Ethologists see many connections between animal and human ritualized behavior, especially in human imitation of animal behavior in certain totemic rites in aboriginal societies. Human aggression and gender display, like those of animals, are hedged with stylization, symbolization, and repetitiveness. This is a topic addressed by Walter Burkert, René Girard, and Jonathan Z. Smith in *Violent Origins* (1987). The three authors' diverging viewpoints on violence and ritual are typical of academic debates over the role of violence in the origins of religion itself. Whereas this book deals with the universal tendency of ritual to take violent form in sacrifice and scapegoating, other scholars prefer an evolutionary perspective to locate the origins of ritual as engendering less-negative contributions to human society and community. For instance, Roy A. Rappaport's *Ritual and Religion in the Making of Humanity* (1999) treats ritual in a positive way—as humanity's "basic social act." Rappaport combines evolutionary biology with ecology, semiotics, philosophy, and communications theory to argue that ritual both communicates and creates morality, obligation, and convention. Ritual, in short, makes society possible.

Interest in psychology within ritual studies begins with Volney Patrick Gay's *Freud on Ritual* (1979), where Gay challenges the commonly held interpretation of Sigmund Freud's negative view of ritual as repressive and as a collective version of personal neurosis. Ritual studies recognizes the existence of nonpathological, private ritualizing and explores the therapeutic uses of ritual. A major part of *Religious and Social Ritual* (1996), edited by Michael B. Aune and Valerie DeMarinis, is devoted to the effective use of ritual in clinical settings and of the similarities and differences between ritual and psychotherapy.

The collaborative work of Robert N. McCauley and E. Thomas Lawson represents the best examples of the cognitive science of ritual. McCauley and Lawson examine the cognitive machinery essential to a participant's ritual competence. In *Bringing Ritual to Mind* (2002) McCauley and Lawson utilize experimental research in cognitive psychology. They look at ritual transmission and those factors that determine the survival of ritual systems and what motivates participants to perpetuate them over time. McCauley also presents research on what he calls "sensory pageantry" in "Ritual, Memory, and Emotion: Comparing Two Cognitive Hypotheses" (2001). McCauley explores how ritual meaning and experience are contingent upon environment and how ritual frequency and infrequency contribute to a rite's meaning and efficacy.

McCauley and Lawson also forge important links between semantics and ritual in *Rethinking Religion* (1990). Here they argue that linguistic theories offer strategic insights for the study of religious rituals, especially for examining the internal structure of ritual. Another volume examining the interconnection between ritual and language is *Ritual and Semiotics* (1997), edited by J. Ralph Lindgren and Jay Knaak. Of particular interest is Lindgren's work on magic, where he argues that a semiotic (the study of signs and symbols) investigation of ritual reveals the process of social beliefs in flux and in turn allows one to see ritual as an open-ended, flexible sign system.

Ancient Magic and Ritual Power (1995), edited by Marvin Meyer and Paul Mirecki, offers several linguistic analyses of ritual and magic. Magic presents a taxonomic (categorical) challenge to the study of ritual that these authors resolve in part by substituting the term *ritual power* for *magic*. Magic is thus liberated from its negative connotations by revisioning it as empowerment by ritual means. Another treatment of ritual and language is Richard K. Fenn's *Liturgies and Trials* (1982), a study of performative utterance and the ritual efficacy of language used in court proceedings. Grimes's *Ritual Criticism* (1990) also utilizes J. L. Austin's speech-act theory for use in determining and assessing the many ways a rite can fail. Grimes presents nineteen categories of ritual failure, some of which are: gloss (covers up problems), breach (failure to follow through), opacity (act unrecognizable or unintelligible), misframe (genre misconstrued), contagion (act leaps beyond proper boundaries), flop (failure to evoke proper mood), and violation (act effective but demeaning).

POPULAR CULTURE AND RITUAL. One of ritual studies' most important contributions is its ability to bridge academic and public interest in ritual. *Liberating Rites* (1998) by Tom Driver and *Mighty Stories, Dangerous Rituals* (1998) by Herbert Anderson and Edward Foley are books by theologians who target both popular and academic audiences. Anderson and Foley offer guides for creating new rites for nontraditional life transitions (divorce, retirement, miscarriage), and Driver provides theoretical guidelines and maxims for improving existing rituals. Driver also distinguishes between two central types or modes of ritual action: confessional (effecting revelatory self-disclosure) and ethical (effecting social change through action). Yet Driver also notes how these two modes overlap. First, the two modes serve in tandem to enhance ritual's potential to inspire liberation and justice. Second, the ethical and confessional modes work together to impede ritual's destructive tendencies.

Anderson and Foley offer new perspectives on the interconnection between ritual and narrative. Narrative is not simply the particular mythic story a rite imparts but is the actual storytelling occurring before, during, and after the rite that in part imbues ritual action with meaning. Narrative is emotionally charged because it augments and frames ritual action in life transition ceremonies of birth, marriage, and death. Far from taking the creation or refinement of new rituals flippantly, Anderson and Foley are aware of the profound danger and risk involved in the task of ritual revitalization and innovation. Ritual may be used intentionally and unwittingly to embarrass, destroy, or disturb as well as to unify, satisfy, and heal. Their discussion of the categories "mythic" (a rite that intentionally glosses over contradictions and enacts the ideal) and "parabolic" (a rite that intentionally addresses and resolves contradictions and problems) is applicable beyond the Christian context and helps interpret secular and non-Christian rites as well.

Ritual studies research in popular culture helps locate new ritual practices and media on the ritual spectrum. Gregor Goethals's *The TV Ritual* (1981) shows ways in which television viewing, especially of such sporting events as the Super Bowl, share many of the dynamics and characteristics typically associated with ritual. Bobby C. Alexander, in *Televangelism Reconsidered* (1994), argues that televangelism is itself a ritual practice. Television viewing becomes a ritual site of the celebration of community and legitimacy of conservative subcultures rather than merely a reflection of such ritual activity occurring elsewhere.

Studies of life passages experienced by women offer new critiques of old theoretical paradigms. In *Birth as an American Rite of Passage* (1992) Robbie E. Davis-Floyd presents hospital obstetrical procedures as ritual. For mothers, the social convention of in-hospital birth becomes a status quo–enforcing rite of passage. In this so-called technocratic birth rite, the mother is made subservient to and accepting of her obligation both to patriarchal institutions and to society's cultural control over natural processes such as birth and death. Other fieldwork studies of modern women use feminist theory to refocus attention upon the role of the body in rites of passage. Jone Salomonsen's *Enchanted Feminism* (2001) suggests how ritual in a coven is perceived as a reclamation of divine immanence. Thus self-healing and transformation are dependent upon actualizing eco-magico interdependence through ritual. Nikki Bado-Fralick's article "A Turning on the Wheel of Life: Wiccan Rites of Death" (1998) also uses field research on Wiccans to claim that ritual transformation is more than a spontaneous mental attitude or reorientation that results from a ritual event. Instead, transformation is itself a somatic process that is learned by the body over time. This requires a much longer time frame to take effect than implied by theories such as the instantaneous participatory unity that Turner calls "communitas." Here ritual studies provides gender-specific case studies that build upon the concept of "ritual knowledge"—the idea that ritual meaning is acquired primarily through somatic or bodily performance first articulated by Theodore W. Jennings Jr. in "On Ritual Knowledge" (1982).

Theoretical Analysis and Construction. Because scholars of ritual studies recognize the importance of studying contemporary ritual, many of the field's most notable contributions to theory are in the areas of ritual change and ritual criticism. Elizabeth H. Pleck's *Celebrating the Family* (2000) assigns ethnic identity an important role in the alteration of family celebrations over time. She also links many drastic changes in holidays and rites of passage directly to commercialization and emphasizes the often ignored market dimension of rituals as a product. Several of Pleck's examples highlight the latent ethnocentricity in many interpretive strategies concerning life transition rituals. For example, in the Hispanic *quinceañera* (coming of age or debutante birthday ball for fifteen-year-old girls) scholars may focus on the event as a secular occasion with sexist conservative gender and restrictive status implications. Yet the participant herself may see the event as a mystical religious rite of blessing and consecration that directly results in status elevation. Grimes's *Ritual Criticism* (1990) introduces an interdisciplinary method called ritual criticism to resolve this dilemma of how to include scholar and participant views in one interpretive framework. Ritual criticism is "the interpretation of a rite or ritual system with a view to implicating (involving) its practice" (Grimes, 1990, p. 16). Ritual criticism uses evaluative judgments only insofar as they are necessary to take into account the contexts and circumstances in which ritual knowledge is produced.

Yet another way to discover ritual's "core" is to use the typologies offered by Bell in *Ritual* (1997). Ritual attributes of formalism, traditionalism, disciplined invariance, rule-governance, sacral symbolism, and performance help interpret and organize a wide range of contemporary examples of "ritual-like" activities that often fall outside other interpretive and classificatory models. Bell also broadens the concept of ritual change, which is usually defined as ritual alteration and innovation, to include ritual immutability by showing how changelessness is an important way ritual is actively responsive to rapidly changing social contexts.

In *Deeply into the Bone* (2000) Grimes shows the theoretical implications of realizing that rites of passage paradigms are theoretical hybrids constructed from the work of Arnold van Gennep, Turner, and Mircea Eliade. Grimes demonstrates that the widely accepted tripartite model of separation, transition, and reincorporation so often used as the template for all rites of passage is far from universal in scope. In fact rites of passage theory is rooted in data gleaned specifically from aboriginal male initiation rites. Yet in the twentieth century this three-part rites of passage model came to be used as the theoretical lens for viewing virtually all types of ritual activity, ancient and modern, aboriginal and postindustrial. Current research in ritual studies demonstrates that theories originally based on aboriginal male initiation are less useful in interpreting contemporary life transition rites and women's rituals. If rites of passage theory is not the reflection of universal human ritual experience that it was once commonly believed to be, then both practitioner and scholar must avoid the temptation to conform ritual experience and interpretation to fit the expectations and parameters supplied by these classic rites of passage templates. Grimes provides more flexible theoretical guidelines for interpreting contemporary rites of passage; these guidelines respond to situational variety and offer an alternative to the fixed typologies proposed by Bell in *Ritual.*

Once dominated by North American researchers, ritual studies is gaining international exposure both in research groups and in degree-granting programs. *Ritualtheorien: En einführendes Handbuch* (1998) is the premier handbook for European use. The Institut für Religionswissenschaft at Germany's University of Heidelberg hosts the *Heidelberger e-Journal für Ritualwissenschaft.* This institute's theoretical contributions include introducing new methods called inter-rituality and ritualistics—the comparative study of complexes of structurally interlinked rituals. In the Netherlands, Thomas Quartier leads a ritual group at the University of Nijmegen, and the Netherlands School for Advanced Studies in Theology and Religion (NOSTER) sponsors research on liturgics, ritual praxis, and community. Helen Phelan of the University of Limerick in Ireland directs a master of arts degree program in chant and ritual song. One of the insights of Phelan's edited collection *Anáil Dé, the Breath of God: Music, Ritual, and Spirituality* (2001) is how the study of ritual music demonstrates the viability of the practice-performance model as a research method for ritual studies (Phelan, 2001, p. 56).

Europeans are also engaged in developing definitional and conceptual alternatives to the term *ritual.* Jan A. M. Snoek challenges the North American tendency to use *rite* and *ritual* as synonyms, in contrast to non-American scholars, who use rite to refer to the building blocks of ceremonies. The international standardization of ritual studies terminology remains a challenge for the field, especially regarding key concepts such as *ritualization* or *ritualizing*—variously employed as synonyms for ritual action, for emergent rites-in-the-making, or in reference to habitual, repetitive gestures that parallel, but do not qualify as, rites.

SEE ALSO Anthropology, Ethnology, and Religion; Ceremony; Liturgy; Performance and Ritual; Rites of Passage, overview article; Ritual.

BIBLIOGRAPHY

Alexander, Bobby C. *Televangelism Reconsidered: Ritual in the Search for Human Community.* Atlanta, 1994.

Anderson, Herbert, and Edward Foley. *Mighty Stories, Dangerous Rituals: Weaving Together the Human and the Divine.* San Francisco, 1998.

Andresen, Jensine, ed. *Religion in Mind: Cognitive Perspective on Religious Belief, Ritual, and Experience.* Cambridge, U.K., 2001.

Aune, Michael B., and Valerie DeMarinis, eds. *Religious and Social Ritual: Interdisciplinary Explorations.* Albany, N.Y., 1996.

Bado-Fralick, Nikki. "A Turning on the Wheel of Life: Wiccan Rites of Death." *Folklore Forum* 29, no. 1 (1998): 3–22.

Bell, Catherine. *Ritual Theory, Ritual Practice.* Oxford, U.K., 1992.

Bell, Catherine. *Ritual: Perspectives and Dimensions.* Oxford, U.K., 1997.

Bellinger, Andrea, and David J. Krieger, eds. *Ritualtheorien: En einführendes Handbuch.* Opladen and Weisbaden, Germany, 1998.

d'Aquili, Eugene G., and Andrew B. Newberg. *The Mystical Mind: Probing the Biology of Religious Experience.* Minneapolis, 1999.

d'Aquili, Eugene G., Charles Laughlin, and John McManus. *The Spectrum of Ritual: A Biogenetic Structural Analysis.* New York, 1979.

d'Aquili, Eugene G., Charles Laughlin, and John McManus. *Brain, Symbol, and Experience: Toward a Neurophenomenology of Human Consciousness.* Boston, 1990.

Davis-Floyd, Robbie E. *Birth as an American Rite of Passage.* Berkeley, Calif., 1992.

Driver, Tom F. *Liberating Rites: Understanding the Transformative Power of Ritual.* Boulder, Colo., 1998. Originally published as *The Magic of Ritual.* San Francisco, 1991.

Duntley, Madeline. "Ritual in the United States." In *Anthropology of Religion: A Handbook,* edited by Stephen D. Glazier, pp. 257–275. Westport, Conn., 1997.

Fenn, Richard K. *Liturgies and Trials: The Secularization of Religious Language.* New York, 1982.

Gay, Volney Patrick. *Freud on Ritual: Reconstruction and Critique.* Missoula, Mont., 1979.

Gill, Sam. *Native American Religious Action: A Performance Approach to Religion.* Columbia, S.C., 1987.

Goethals, Gregor. *The TV Ritual: Worship at the Video Altar.* Boston, 1981.

Goffman, Erving. *The Presentation of Self in Everyday Life.* Garden City, N.Y., 1959.

Grimes, Ronald L. *Beginnings in Ritual Studies.* Columbia, S.C., 1982; rev. ed., 1995.

Grimes, Ronald L. *Research in Ritual Studies: A Programmatic Essay and Bibliography.* Metuchen, N.J., 1985.

Grimes, Ronald L. *Ritual Criticism: Case Studies in Its Practice, Essays on Its Theory.* Columbia, S.C., 1990.

Grimes, Ronald L. *Deeply into the Bone: Re-Inventing Rites of Passage.* Berkeley, Calif., 2000.

Grimes, Ronald L., ed. *Readings in Ritual Studies.* Upper Saddle River, N.J., 1996.

Hamerton-Kelly, Robert G., ed. *Violent Origins: Walter Burkert, René Girard, and Jonathan Z. Smith on Ritual Killing and Cultural Formation.* Stanford, Calif., 1987.

Huxley, Julian. "A Discussion on Ritualized Behavior in Animals and Man." *Philosophical Transactions of the Royal Society of London,* ser. B, 251, no. 772 (1966): 274–524.

Jennings, Theodore W., Jr. "On Ritual Knowledge." *Journal of Religion* 62 (1982): 111–127.

Lindgren, J. Ralph, and Jay Knaak, eds. *Ritual and Semiotics.* New York, 1997.

McCauley, Robert N. "Ritual, Memory, and Emotion: Comparing Two Cognitive Hypotheses." In *Religion in Mind: Cognitive Perspective on Religious Belief, Ritual, and Experience,* edited by Jensine Andresen, pp. 115–140. Cambridge, U.K., 2001.

McCauley, Robert N., and E. Thomas Lawson. *Rethinking Religion: Connecting Cognition and Culture.* Cambridge, U.K., 1990.

McCauley, Robert N., and E. Thomas Lawson. *Bringing Ritual to Mind: Psychological Foundations of Cultural Forms.* Cambridge, U.K., 2002.

Meyer, Marvin, and Paul Mirecki, eds. *Ancient Magic and Ritual Power.* Leiden, Netherlands, 1995.

Moore, Sally F., and Barbara G. Myerhoff, eds. *Secular Ritual: Symbol and Politics in Communal Ideology.* Assen, Netherlands, 1977.

Phelan, Helen, ed. *Anáil Dé, the Breath of God: Music, Ritual, and Spirituality.* Dublin, 2001.

Pleck, Elizabeth H. *Celebrating the Family: Ethnicity, Consumer Culture, and Family Rituals.* Cambridge, Mass., 2000.

Rappaport, Roy A. *Ritual and Religion in the Making of Humanity.* Cambridge, U.K., 1999.

Salomonsen, Jone. *Enchanted Feminism: Ritual Construction of Gender, Agency, and Divinity among the Reclaiming Witches of San Francisco.* New York, 2001.

Schechner, Richard. *The Future of Ritual: Writings on Culture and Performance.* New York, 1993.

Turner, Victor. *From Ritual to Theatre: The Human Seriousness of Play.* New York, 1982.

MADELINE DUNTLEY (2005)

RIVERS. Among the Native American Yurok people, who live along the Yurok River in northern California, orientation in the world was not provided by the four cardinal directions, but by the river itself: upstream and downstream. To these salmon fishermen, dependent upon the river for livelihood, the river alone was the primary axis of orientation.

In ancient times too, there were great civilizations whose life was so oriented toward one major river that they have come to be called river civilizations: Mesopotamia along the Tigris and Euphrates, Egypt along the Nile, the Indus Valley civilization along the Indus. In all these it is not surprising that the river itself should function as a fundamental means of world orientation and become associated with yearly inundation, fertility, and with life in its fullest sense.

Ancient Mesopotamian civilization made a distinction between Tiamat, the great mother of the salt waters of chaos and creation, and Apsu, the lord who ruled the "sweet waters" under the earth that fill the rivers and the springs. Ea was a descendent of Apsu, and Ea's offspring included Marduk, who was "born within the holy Apsu," associated with rivers, and called in one hymn the creator of the Tigris and Euphrates. Among his other creative tasks, Marduk "has opened the fountains [and] has apportioned waters in abundance" (Heidel, 1942, p. 56). Tammuz, too, is called a "son of the deep" and is the corn spirit who comes to life each year with the fertilizing waters of the rivers.

Ancient Egyptian civilization also saw fresh waters as springing from the abyss beneath the earth. There were said to be two rivers called the Nile, however, one that flowed on earth and one that flowed across the sky in heaven. This vision of the heavenly river, identified with the Milky Way, is also part of the mythology of the river Ganges in India. In ancient Egypt the Nile was so central that many of the great gods and goddesses are associated with the river in some way. The river itself is often depicted as the male god Hapi, with two full breasts, from which the northern and southern branches of the Nile spring; he holds two vases, which represent in another fashion the northern and southern Nile. The goddesses Anuket and Isis are both identified with the Nile as she inundates the land and fertilizes the fields. Khnemu (Khnum), the water deity with four rams' heads, is seen to represent the four sources of the Nile. Osiris, the dying and rising god, is also identified with the Nile as it sinks and rises again.

Although there is no systematic mythology available from the Indus Valley civilization to clarify how the inhabitants regarded the river itself, there is surely evidence in the large bathing pool of Mohenjo-Daro and in the elaborate drainage systems of both Harappa and Mohenjo-Daro that the inhabitants cared greatly for the cleansing properties of running water. Later Indian civilization, preserving this emphasis on running water and purification, has developed a full range of mythological and ritual traditions concerning sacred rivers.

During the Vedic period, sacred rivers are mentioned, often numbering seven: the five rivers of the Punjab, plus the Indus and the mysterious Sarasvati. Later on, with the movement of the center of Aryan civilization into the Ganges Valley, the river Ganges (Skt., Gaṅgā) becomes preeminent among rivers. As a female divinity in the form of a heavenly river, Gaṅgā agreed in her mercy to flow upon the earth, falling first upon the head of Śiva, who broke the force of her cascade from heaven. It is said in the Hindu epics and Purāṇas, which tell the tale of Gaṅgā's descent and which contain descriptions of the world's mythic geography, that Gaṅgā actually split into four streams when she fell. From Mount Meru, the cosmic mountain in the form of a lotus flower at the center of the world, Gaṅgā flowed north, south, east, and west—watering the whole world with the waters of life. The southern branch became the Ganges of India.

The importance of the Ganges as the paradigmatic river—holy, cleansing, and life-giving—is further seen in its widespread duplication in other rivers. Today, India counts seven sacred rivers, often called the Seven Gaṅgās, that are thought to supply the whole of India with sacred waters. In addition to the Ganges, there are the Indus, also called Sindhu; the Sarasvatī, said to have disappeared from earth and to flow underground; the Yamuna, which flows from the Himalayas, through North India, past Kṛṣṇa's birthplace at Mathura, and on to its confluence with the Ganges at Prayāga, the modern Allahabad; the Narmadā, which flows west across central India from its source in Amarakaṇṭaka to the Arabian Sea; the Godāvārī, which flows eastward from its sacred source above the temple of Tryambaka in Maharashtra; and the Kāverī, which flows eastward across southern India from its source at Talai Kāverī in Coorg country.

The ritual treatment of such rivers in India confirms their sanctity. The Narmadā, for instance, is circumambulated in a long pilgrimage that takes several years to complete. The confluence of rivers, like that at Prayāga where the Ganges, Yamunā, and Sarasvatī are said to meet, is an especially holy place and often becomes the site of special pilgrimage observances like the great Kumbha Melā held every twelve years. Along the banks of the Ganges, or at the source of the Narmadā or Kāverī, one may see the tall multiwicked lamps of the evening *āratī,* a ritual prayer performed for the very waters of the river itself.

RIVER GODS AND DEITIES. For Hindus, the Ganges is not only a sacred river but a liquid form of the divine. She is called "liquid *śakti,*" or female energy, and is said to be Śakti, the female counterpart of the great lord Śiva, in the form of a river. Gaṅgā as a goddess is depicted as utterly auspicious, holding a lotus and a water pot while riding a crocodile. She is often addressed as Gaṅgā Mātā, Mother Ganges; the other seven rivers are similarly depicted as goddesses and addressed as "Mother."

Among many African peoples, rivers and streams are considered the homes of water spirits. The feminine names of rivers often signify a direct connection between flowing waters, fecundity, and the female. Some rivers are themselves seen as goddesses. The goddess Yemọja of the Yoruba, for instance, is said to have turned into the river Ogun and is symbolized by river-worn stones through which offerings are made to Yemọja. Yemọja's son was Ṣango, whose many wives were rivers. The most important among them was the faithful Ọya, who became the river Niger.

The personification of rivers and their identification with spirits was also prominent in ancient Syria, where the *baalim* had seats on the banks of streams and springs, as well as in ancient Greece, where Homer speaks of altars built upon river banks and of bulls sacrificed to the river. Native Americans have also identified rivers as spirits. In the Southwest, the Colorado River was traditionally thought of as female, and the San Juan River as male. The confluence of the two near Navajo Mountain in Utah was traditionally called the "nuptial bed," where numerous "water children" of springs, clouds, and rains were born.

LIVING WATERS. It has been noted that Hindu cosmology views the heavenly river Gaṅgā as flowing in four, or sometimes seven, streams into the four quarters of the earth. The waters of the Ganges, identified with the milk of mother cows, are truly life-giving waters, and are called "mother" as they are sipped by devout Hindus. The vision of Eden presented briefly in *Genesis* 2 also evokes a river issuing forth from the garden and splitting into four streams. Of the four, the Tigris and Euphrates are named and well known, but concerning the Pishon and the Gihon there is disagreement, although some speculation identified the Pishon with the Indus and the Gihon with the Nile. Josephus Flavius in the first century CE, Eusebius in the third century, and others after them identified the Pishon with the sacred Ganges, which by that time had become well known in the ancient world. The notion that such divine waters issue forth from Paradise is also present in the Sumerian myth of the land of Dilmun, where the living waters are associated with Tammuz. The Egyptian Nile, with its four sources, has also been identified with Osiris and Isis, both of whom are associated with the notion of the river as "living waters."

In one of the prophet Ezekiel's visions (*Ez.* 47), he sees a stream of water issuing from beneath the main door of the Temple in Jerusalem, flowing from the Holy of Holies itself. At first it is ankle-deep. Gradually it becomes a great river, deep enough to swim in. Its waters are the waters of life; even the salt waters become sweet and living waters once this sacred river flows into them. Along the banks of the river, on both sides, are trees of all kinds, bearing fresh fruit and healing leaves.

This vision is repeated in the *Revelation to John* in the New Testament (*Rv.* 22). An angel shows John the heavenly Jerusalem: There is no temple, but the Christ, the Light, the Lord alone, sits enthroned at the center. From "the throne of God and of the Lamb" flows the river of the waters of life. "Bright as crystal," it flows through the city and produces on either side the tree of life, bearing twelve kinds of fruits and yielding leaves for "the healing of the nations."

PURIFICATION AND REBIRTH. Living waters are purifying waters. The running water of rivers is often used ritually for purification, or where it is not available, the pouring of water may accomplish the same aim. The Hindu ritual tradition makes it clear that water used in purification must not be standing water, but flowing, living water. Lustrations with such water prepare one ritually for worship, or for eating, and remove the impurity associated with childbirth or with death. Bathing in the Ganges is said to purify not only the sins of this birth but also those of many previous births.

Such use of running water, which is homologized to river water, is common elsewhere as well. Greek ritual prescribed bathing in a river or spring after an expiatory sacrifice. As recorded by Fray Bernardino de Sahagún, the Aztec prayer over a newborn child asks, "May this water purify and whiten thy heart: may it wash away all that is evil." Similar rites of baptism, in the Isis tradition as well as in the Christian tradition, use the symbolic power of living water to wash away the sins of the past.

Rites of healing are a form of rites of purification. The rivers of biblical Syria, Abana, and Pharpar were famous for healing. So it was with indignation that Naaman, the commander of the army of the king of Syria, received word from the prophet Elisha that he should bathe in the river Jordan seven times in order to be cleansed of his leprosy (*2 Kgs.* 5). To the present day the Jordan retains its reputation for healing, but especially so among Christians. The source of the Euphrates River was also famous for healing, and a bath there in the springtime was said to keep one free of disease all year long. The healing properties of the river Ganges are also well known, and pilgrims bring small sealed bottles of Ganges water home for medicinal use. Among the Hindus of Bali, the springs of Tampak Siring are filled with healing waters.

RIVERS OF DEATH. Crossing the river at the time of death, as part of the journey to another world, is a common part of the symbolic passage that people have seen as part of one's journey after death. In the *Epic of Gilgamesh,* the hero encounters a boatman who ferries him across the waters of death as he seeks the secret of immortality. The river Styx of Greek mythology is well known as the chief river of Hades, said to flow nine times around its borders. Styx is married to the Titan Pallas and according to Hesiod counts as her children Rivalry, Victory, Power, and Force. The power of the Styx is evidenced in the fact that Achilles gained his invulnerability by being dipped in the river as a baby held by his heel, the only part of his body thereafter vulnerable to mortal wounds. In addition, the most inviolable oath of the gods is sworn with a jug of water from the Styx, poured out while the oath is being uttered.

In Hindu mythology, the river Vaitaraṇī marks the boundary between the living and the dead; in the Aztec journey, the river Mictlan must be crossed on the way to the underworld; in Japan, rivers are part of certain landscapes designated as realms of the dead in both the Shintō and Buddhist traditions. The Sanzunokawa, for example, is said to divide the realms of the living and the dead. The dry riverbed of Sainokawara is said to be the destination of dead children.

The far shore of the river of life and death, or birth and death, thus becomes an important symbol for the destination of one's spiritual journey in many religious traditions. In the Buddhist tradition, *nirvāṇa* is referred to as the "far shore." In the Hindu tradition, holy places are called *tīrtha*s ("fords") because they enable one to make that crossing safely. Riverbank *tīrtha*s, such as Banaras and Prayaga, are thought to be especially good places to die. In the Christian tradition, crossing over the Jordan has come to have a similar symbolism. On the far shore is not only the promised land, but the spiritual promised land of heaven. Home is on the far shore. As the African American spiritual puts it:

> I look'd over Jordan and what did I see?
> Comin' for to carry me home.
> A band of angels comin' after me.
> Comin' for to carry me home.

SEE ALSO Baptism; Boats; Ganges River; Water.

BIBLIOGRAPHY

Darian, Steven G. *The Ganges in Myth and History.* Honolulu, 1978. A study of mythology, symbolism, sculpture, and history of the Ganges River.

Eck, Diana. "Gaṅgā: The Goddess in Hindu Sacred Geography." In *The Divine Consort: Rādhā and the Goddesses of India,* edited by John Stratton Hawley and Donna M. Wulff. Berkeley, 1982. A study of the mythology, ritual, and theology associated with the river Gaṅgā in the Hindu tradition.

Eliade, Mircea. *Patterns in Comparative Religion.* New York, 1958. An investigation of the nature of religion through the classification of hierophanies. See especially chapter 5, "The Waters and Water Symbolism."

Glueck, Nelson. *The River Jordan.* New York, 1968. An exploration of the geography, the archaeology, and the history of the valley of the Jordan.

Heidel, Alexander. *The Babylonian Genesis.* Chicago, 1942. A translation of the published cuneiform tablets of various Babylonian creation myths.

Hopkins, E. Washburn. "The Sacred Rivers of India." In *Studies in the History of Religions Presented to Crawford Howell Toy,* edited by D. G. Lyon and George Foot Moore, pp. 213–229. New York, 1912. An overview in short compass of India's sacred rivers.

Zahan, Dominique. *The Religion, Spirituality, and Thought of Traditional Africa.* Translated by Kate Ezra Martin and Lawrence M. Martin. Chicago, 1979. See especially the chapter "The Elementary 'Cathedrals,' Worship and Sacrifice," which discusses natural manifestations of divinity in Africa, including the places associated with water.

New Sources

Feldhaus, Anne. *Water and Womanhood.* New York, 1995.

Fineman, Mark. "A Scheme to Harness India's Sacred Waters Brings Tempers to a Boil." *Smithsonian* 21(1990): 118 ff.

Lai, Whalen W. "Looking for Mr Ho Po: Unmasking the River God of Ancient China." *History of Religions* 29 (May 1990): 335–350.

Mason, John. *Olóòkun: Owner of Rivers and Seas.* Brooklyn, N.Y., 1996.

Sauer, James A. "The River Runs Dry: Creation Story Preserves Historical Memory." *Biblical Archaeology Review* 22 (July–August 1996): 52–57, 64.

Sinclair, Bryan T. "Merging Streams: The Importance of the River in the Slaves' Religious World." *Journal of Religious Thought* nos. 53–54 (Winter–Fall 1997): 1–19.

Wrigley, Christopher. "The River-God and the Historians: Myth in the Shire Valley and Elsewhere." *Journal of African History* 29, no. 3 (1988): 367–383.

DIANA L. ECK (1987)
Revised Bibliography

ISBN 0-02-865980-5
90000
9 780028 659800